Bankruptcy Code, Rules and Forms

2009 Edition

Featuring:

Bankruptcy Code and Related Statutes

Bankruptcy Rules and Official Forms

Highlights of Recent Bankruptcy Developments

Federal Regulations Relating to Bankruptcy Trustees

Including:

Federal Rules of Civil Procedure and Federal Rules of Evidence

Mat #40589425

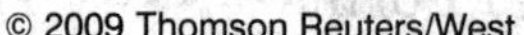

This publication was created to provide you with accurate and authoritative information concerning the subject matter covered; however, this publication was not necessarily prepared by persons licensed to practice law in a particular jurisdiction. The publisher is not engaged in rendering legal or other professional advice and this publication is not a substitute for the advice of an attorney. If you require legal or other expert advice, you should seek the services of a competent attorney or other professional.

ISBN: 978-0–314–97526–3
ISSN: 1079–381X

WEST'S BANKRUPTCY LIBRARY

CD–ROMS

Bankruptcy Library CD–ROM Premise
West's Norton/Bankruptcy Service Plus

TREATISES

2005 Bankruptcy Reform Legislation with Analysis 2d
Bankruptcy and Domestic Relations Manual
Bankruptcy and Secured Lending in Cyberspace
Bankruptcy Code Manual
Bankruptcy Desk Guide
Bankruptcy Forms Guide
Bankruptcy Evidence Manual
Bankruptcy Exemption Manual
Bankruptcy Law Fundamentals
Bankruptcy Law Manual 5th
Bankruptcy Procedure Manual
Bankruptcy Litigation 2d
Bankruptcy Practice for the General Practitioner 3d
Bankruptcy Practice Handbook 2d
Bankruptcy Service Lawyers Ed.
Business Workouts Manual 2d
Chapter 11 Reorganizations 2d
Chapter 13: Practice & Procedure
Commercial Bankruptcy Litigation
Consumer Bankruptcy Manual 2d
Creditors' Rights in Bankruptcy 2d
Electronic Case Management and Filing in Bankruptcy Court
Environmental Obligations in Bankruptcy
Fraudulent Transfers: Applications and Implications
Guide to Effective Bankruptcy Litigation
Herzog's Bankruptcy Forms and Practice
Norton Annual Review of International Insolvency
Norton Annual Survey of Bankruptcy Law
Norton Bankruptcy Law and Practice 3d
Norton Creditors' Rights Handbook
Norton Handbook for Bankruptcy Trustees, Debtors in Possession and Committees
Practice Systems Library: Bankruptcy
Strategic Alternatives for Distressed Businesses
Tax Aspects of Bankruptcy Law and Practice 3d
The Law of Debtors and Creditors: Bankruptcy, Security Interests, Collection, rev. ed.
The Law of Fraudulent Transactions

CASE REPORTERS

West's Bankruptcy Reporter (includes West's Bankruptcy Digest)

DIGESTS

Bankruptcy Law Digest 2d
West's Bankruptcy Digest

CODE AND RULES PAMPHLETS

West's Bankruptcy Code, Rules and Forms
Bankruptcy Code and Rules-Compact Edition
Bankruptcy Code, Rules & Official Forms
Norton Bankruptcy Law and Practice 3d Code and Rules pamphlets
Norton Quick-Reference pamphlet

PERIODICALS

Bankruptcy Law Letter
Bankruptcy Litigation Reporter
Bankruptcy Service Current Awareness Alert
Norton Bankruptcy Law Adviser
Norton Journal of Bankruptcy Law and Practice

*

PREFACE

This publication contains the current Bankruptcy Code (11 U.S.C.) and related provisions of United States Code Title 18 and 28, as amended through Pub.L. 110–448, approved October 22, 2008.

The current bankruptcy court fee schedule, including changes effective in 2008, appears following 28 U.S.C. § 1930.

Judge William H. Brown, Lawrence R. Ahern, III and Nancy Fraas Maclean prepared the "Bankruptcy Highlights" feature, in which they discuss recent bankruptcy law developments, including 2008 amendments to the Federal Rules of Bankruptcy Procedure, recent Supreme Court and lower court decisions relevant to bankruptcy practitioners, and significant legislation from the 110th Congress.

Amendments to the Federal Rules of Bankruptcy Procedure became effective December 1, 2008. Those amendments supersede the Interim Bankruptcy Rules previously adopted by local federal bankruptcy courts. Most courts, however, have retained Interim Bankruptcy Rule 5012 (Communication and Cooperation with Foreign Courts and Foreign Representatives). Rule 5012 has not yet been adopted as a national rule.

The Federal Rules of Civil Procedure and Federal Rules of Evidence have been included to provide the practitioner with a "single source" reference for current bankruptcy laws, rules and forms. The Federal Rules of Civil Procedure govern adversary proceedings under Part VII and contested matters under Part IX of the Federal Rules of Bankruptcy Procedure. Bankruptcy Rule 9017 provides that the Federal Rules of Evidence govern evidentiary matters in bankruptcy proceedings.

The Department of Justice regulations relating to the United States Trustees—including United States Trustee Guidelines for Compensation and Reimbursement of Expenses Filed Under 11 U.S.C. § 330—are included, as well.

For comprehensive coverage of all aspects of bankruptcy law, see *Norton Bankruptcy Law and Practice*. The *Bankruptcy Code Manual* by Michael J. Holleran, Donna Larsen Holleran, John D. McMickle, and John B. Corr contains a section-by-section explanation of Title 11. The *Bankruptcy Procedure Manual* by Lawrence R. Ahern, III and Nancy Fraas MacLean provides comprehensive commentary and practical advice relating to the Federal Rules of Bankruptcy proceedings are treated in the *Bankruptcy Evidence Manual* by Judge Barry Russell. The *Bankruptcy Exemption Manual* by Judge William H. Brown, Lawrence R. Ahern, III and Nancy Fraas MacLean discusses the use of state and federal exemptions to shelter assets in bankruptcy, and contains a detailed comparison of each state's exemption. The *Financial Handbook for Bankruptcy Professionals* by Jay Alix, Robert J. Rock, and Ted Stenger gives a full treatment of the legal concepts and business and financial issues that impact a company in trouble. Additional bankruptcy forms and commentary are provided in Volumes 6 and 6A of *West's Federal Forms* (by Hon. William Houston Brown, Lawrence R. Ahern, III and Nancy Fraas MacLean) and in volumes 9 and 9A of *West's Legal Forms* (by Judge William H. Brown, Lawrence R. Ahern III and Nancy Fraas MacLean).

For researching bankruptcy cases, see West's Bankruptcy Reporter and West's Bankruptcy Digest. Cross-references to the West Key Number System are provided throughout this 2009 Edition.

RELATED PRODUCTS IN FEDERAL LAW FROM WEST

FEDERAL PRACTICE

COURTROOM HANDBOOK ON FEDERAL EVIDENCE
Steven Goode and Olin Guy Wellborn III

FEDERAL CIVIL RULES HANDBOOK
Steven Baicker–McKee, William Janssen and John B. Corr

FEDERAL CRIMINAL RULES HANDBOOK
Laurie L. Levenson

MODERN SCIENTIFIC EVIDENCE
David L. Faigman, David H. Kaye, Michael J. Saks, Joseph Sanders, and Edward K. Cheng

FEDERAL JURY PRACTICE AND INSTRUCTIONS
Kevin F. O'Malley, Jay E. Grenig and William C. Lee
[Also available in CD–ROM]

FEDERAL PRACTICE AND PROCEDURE
Charles Alan Wright, Arthur R. Miller, Mary Kay Kane, Edward H. Cooper, Richard L. Marcus, Kenneth W. Graham, Victor James Gold, Richard D. Freer, Vikram David Amar, Joan E. Steinman, Andrew D. Leipold, Peter J. Henning, Sarah H. Welling, Nancy J. King, Susan R. Klein, Charles H. Koch, Jr., Catherine T. Struve, and Michael H. Graham
[Also available in CD–ROM]

WEST'S FEDERAL ADMINISTRATIVE PRACTICE
Authored by Federal Practice Experts

WEST'S FEDERAL FORMS
Authored by Federal Practice Experts
[Also available in CD–ROM]

FEDERAL COURT OF APPEALS MANUAL
David G. Knibb

FEDERAL PRACTICE AND PROCEDURE—FEDERAL PRACTICE DESKBOOK
Charles Alan Wright and Mary Kay Kane

HANDBOOK OF FEDERAL EVIDENCE
Michael H. Graham

TREATISE ON CONSTITUTIONAL LAW
Ronald D. Rotunda and John E. Nowak

THE JUDGE'S EVIDENCE BENCHBOOK
Leo H. Whinery, Theodore P. Roberts, and Robert B. Smith

ADMINISTRATIVE LAW AND PRACTICE
Charles H. Koch, Jr.

FEDERAL TRIAL OBJECTIONS
Charles B. Gibbons

BUSINESS AND COMMERCIAL LITIGATION IN FEDERAL COURTS
Robert L. Haig, Editor–In–Chief

RELATED PRODUCTS

NEWBERG ON CLASS ACTIONS, 3rd
Herbert Newberg and Alba Conte

HANDBOOK OF FEDERAL CIVIL DISCOVERY AND DISCLOSURE
Jay E. Grenig and Jeffrey S. Kinsler
[Includes forms on Disk]

ANNOTATED MANUAL FOR COMPLEX LITIGATION
David F. Herr

MULTIDISTRICT LITIGATION MANUAL
David F. Herr

FEDERAL STANDARDS OF REVIEW
Hon. Harry T. Edwards and Linda A. Elliott

United States Code Annotated
West's Federal Practice Digest 4th
United States Code Congressional and Administrative News

CRIMINAL PRACTICE

SEARCH AND SEIZURE
Wayne R. LaFave

SUBSTANTIVE CRIMINAL LAW
Wayne R. LaFave

CRIMINAL LAW DEFENSES
Paul H. Robinson

CRIMINAL PROCEDURE
Wayne R. LaFave, Jerold H. Israel, and Nancy J. King

FEDERAL SENTENCING LAW AND PRACTICE
Thomas W. Hutchison, Peter B. Hoffman, Deborah Young, and Sigmund G. Popko

FEDERAL SENTENCING GUIDELINES HANDBOOK
Roger W. Haines, Jr., Frank O. Bowman III, and Jennifer C. Woll

---

Corpus Juris Secundum
West's Federal Case News
Federal Civil Judicial Procedure and Rules
Federal Criminal Code and Rules
Federal Environmental Laws
Federal Immigration Laws and Regulations
Federal Labor Laws
Federal Sentencing Guidelines
Federal Social Security Laws, Selected Statutes and Regulations
Federal Intellectual Property Laws and Regulations
Federal Litigator

RELATED PRODUCTS

Reference Manual on Scientific Evidence, Second
Manual for Complex Litigation, Fourth

TAX PUBLICATIONS

Federal Tax Regulations
Internal Revenue Code
Internal Revenue Acts

Westlaw®

WestCheck.com™

West CD–ROM Libraries™

To order any of these Federal practice tools, call your West Representative or **1–800–328–9352**.

NEED RESEARCH HELP?

You can get quality research results with free help—call the West Reference Attorneys when you have questions concerning Westlaw or West Publications at **1–800–REF–ATTY (1–800–733–2889)**.

INTERNET ACCESS

Contact the West Editorial Department directly with your questions and suggestions by e-mail at west.editor@thomson.com. Visit West's home page at west.thomson.com.

*

WESTLAW ELECTRONIC RESEARCH GUIDE

Westlaw—Expanding the Reach of Your Library

Westlaw is West's online legal research service. With Westlaw, you experience the same quality and integrity that you have come to expect from West books, plus quick, easy access to West's vast collection of statutes, case law materials, public records, and other legal resources, in addition to current news articles and business information. For the most current and comprehensive legal research, combine the strengths of West books and Westlaw.

When you research with westlaw.com you get the convenience of the Internet combined with comprehensive and accurate Westlaw content, including exclusive editorial enhancements, plus features found only in westlaw.com such as ResultsPlus™ or StatutesPlus.™

Accessing Databases Using the Westlaw Directory

The Westlaw Directory lists all databases on Westlaw and contains links to detailed information relating to the content of each database. Click **Directory** on the westlaw.com toolbar. There are several ways to access a database even when you don't know the database identifier. Browse a directory view. Scan the directory. Type all or part of a database name in the Search these Databases box. The Find a Database Wizard can help you select relevant databases for your search. You can access up to ten databases at one time for user-defined multibase searching.

Retrieving a Specific Document

To retrieve a specific document by citation or title on westlaw.com click **Find&Print** on the toolbar to display the Find a Document page. If you are unsure of the correct citation format, type the publication abbreviation, e.g., **xx st** (where xx is a state's two-letter postal abbreviation), in the Find this document by citation box and click **Go** to display a fill-in-the-blank template. To retrieve a specific case when you know one or more parties' names, click **Find a Case by Party Name**.

KeyCite®

KeyCite, the citation research service on Westlaw, makes it easy to trace the history of your case, statute, administrative decision or regulation to determine if there are recent updates, and to find other documents that cite your document. KeyCite will also find pending legislation relating to federal or state statutes. Access the powerful features of KeyCite from the westlaw.com toolbar, the **Links** tab, or KeyCite flags in a document display. KeyCite's red and yellow warning flags tell you at a glance whether your document has negative history. Depth-of-treatment stars help you focus on the most important citing references. KeyCite Alert allows you to monitor the status of your case, statute or rule, and automatically sends you updates at the frequency you specify.

ResultsPlus™

ResultsPlus is a Westlaw technology that automatically suggests additional information related to your search. The suggested materials are accessible by a set of links that appear to the right of your westlaw.com search results:

- Go directly to relevant ALR® articles and Am Jur® annotations.
- Find on-point resources by key number.
- See information from related treatises and law reviews.

StatutesPlus™

When you access a statutes database in westlaw.com you are brought to a powerful Search Center which collects, on one toolbar, the tools that are most useful for fast, efficient retrieval of statutes documents:

- Have a few key terms? Click **Statutes Index**.
- Know the common name? Click **Popular Name Table**.
- Familiar with the subject matter? Click **Table of Contents**.
- Have a citation or section number? Click **Find by Citation**.
- Interested in topical surveys providing citations across multiple state statutes? Click **50 State Surveys**.
- Or, simply search with **Natural Language** or **Terms and Connectors.**

When you access a statutes section, click on the **Links** tab for all relevant links for the current document that will also include a KeyCite section with a description of the KeyCite status flag. Depending on your document, links may also include administrative, bill text, and other sources that were previously only available by accessing and searching other databases.

Additional Information

Westlaw is available on the Web at westlaw.com.

For search assistance, call the West Reference Attorneys at 1–800–REF–ATTY (1–800–733–2889).

For technical assistance, call West Customer Technical Support at 1–800–WESTLAW (1–800–937–8529).

TABLE OF CONTENTS

TABLE OF CONTENTS

BANKRUPTCY HIGHLIGHTS

By

William Houston Brown

United States Bankruptcy Judge, 1987–2006

Western District of Tennessee

Lawrence R. Ahern III

Burr & Forman LLP

Nashville, Tennessee

Nancy Fraas MacLean

of the Tennessee Bar

I. Amendments to the Federal Rules of Bankruptcy Procedure

The Bankruptcy Abuse Prevention and Consumer Protection Act of 2005, Pub. L. No. 109–08, 119 Stat. 23 ("BAPCPA") made significant changes to the Bankruptcy Code and affected many aspects of bankruptcy practice. Because the procedure for promulgating rules requires up to two years for final adoption, "Interim Bankruptcy Rules" were established in order to implement the new provisions of BAPCPA. The Interim rules were then adopted locally by the bankruptcy courts.

The 2008 amendments to the Federal Rules of Bankruptcy Procedure were based substantially on the Interim Rules. Effective December 1, 2008, Bankruptcy Rules 1005, 1006, 1007, 1009, 1010, 1011, 1015, 1017, 1019, 1020, 2002, 2003, 2007.1, 2015, 3002, 3003, 3016, 3017.1, 3019, 4002, 4003, 4004, 4006, 4007, 4008, 5001, 5003, 6004, 7012, 7022, 7023.1, 8001, 8003, 9006, 9009, and 9024 were amended, and new Rules 1021, 2007.2, 2015.1, 2015.2, 2015.3, 5008, and 6011 were added. The highlights of these amendments, as noted by the Advisory Committee on Bankruptcy Rules, are set forth below.

Bankruptcy Rule 1005 (Caption of Petition) was amended to require disclosure of all names used by the debtor in the past eight years (instead of six years) and disclosure of the last four digits of the debtor's taxpayer identification number.

BANKRUPTCY HIGHLIGHTS

Bankruptcy Rule 1006 (Filing Fee) was amended to allow the court to waive payment of the filing fee or to allow the debtor to pay in installments. It is no longer a condition of permission to pay by installment that the debtor has not paid any money to the attorney in the case. The debtor is instructed to use the Official Form.

Bankruptcy Rule 1007 (Lists, Schedules, Statements, and other Documents; Time Limits) was amended: (1) to require the debtor to file additional documents mandated under the Act including a certificate of compliance with the credit counseling requirement and completion of a personal financial management course, (2) to limit extensions of time for small business debtors to file schedules and statements, and (3) to require the chapter 15 debtor to include a list of entities with whom the chapter 15 debtor is engaged in litigation.

Bankruptcy Rule 1009 (Amendments of Voluntary Petitions, Lists, Schedules, and Statements) was amended to correct a cross reference.

Bankruptcy Rule 1010 (Service of Involuntary Petition and Summons; Petition For Recognition of a Foreign Nonmain Proceeding) was amended to require the service of a summons and petition on a debtor and other entity against whom the representative is seeking provisional relief in a pending foreign nonmain proceeding.

Bankruptcy Rule 1011 (Responsive Pleading or Motion in Involuntary and Cross–Border Cases) was amended to require that a corporation involved in a cross-border insolvency file a corporate disclosure ownership statement.

Bankruptcy Rule 1015 (Consolidation or Joint Administration of Cases Pending in Same Court) was amended to correct cross references.

Bankruptcy Rule 1017 (Dismissal or Conversion of Case; Suspension) was amended to permit a party (as well as the court or U.S. trustee) to move to dismiss a chapter 7 consumer-debtor case for abuse. A showing of *substantial* abuse is no longer required.

Bankruptcy Rule 1019 (Conversion of a Chapter 11 Reorganization Case, Chapter 12 Family Farmer's Debt Adjustment Case, or Chapter 13 Individual's Debt Adjustment Case to a Chapter 7 Liquidation Case) was amended to preserve a creditor's right to bring a motion to dismiss under Code § 707 upon conversion of a case from another chapter to a case under chapter 7.

Bankruptcy Rule 1020 (Small Business Chapter 11 Reorganization Case) was amended to provide procedures to determine whether a debtor is a small business and to set a deadline for objections to the designation.

Bankruptcy Rule 1021 (Health Care Business Case) was added to provide procedures for designating a debtor as a health-care business and procedures for objecting to the designation.

Bankruptcy Rule 2002 (Notices to Creditors, Equity Security Holders, Administrators in Foreign Proceedings, Persons Against Whom Provisional Relief is Sought in Ancillary and Other Cross–Border Cases, United States, and United States Trustee) was amended to require the court to promptly provide all creditors with a statement by the trustee as to whether the debtor's case is presumed abusive.

Bankruptcy Rule 2003 (Meeting of Creditors or Equity Security Holders) was amended to authorize the court to order that a meeting of creditors not be convened if the debtor has solicited acceptances of a plan prior to the commencement of a case.

Bankruptcy Rule 2007.1 (Appointment of Trustee or Examiner in a Chapter 11 Reorganization Case) was amended to require the elected trustee to file an affidavit with information on that person's connection with creditors and others with an interest in the case.

BANKRUPTCY HIGHLIGHTS

Bankruptcy Rule 2007.2 (Appointment of Patient Care Ombudsman in a Health Care Business Case) was added to require the appointment of a health care ombudsman in the first 30 days of all health care business cases unless the court finds it unnecessary and provides for parties in interest to object to the appointment.

Bankruptcy Rule 2015 (Duty to Keep Records, Make Reports, and Give Notice of Case or Change of Status) was amended to require a small-business chapter 11 debtor to file periodic financial and operating reports. Also it requires foreign representatives to report to court and sets the time for filing reports.

Bankruptcy Rule 2015.1 (Patient Care Ombudsman) was added to govern reports issued by a health-care ombudsman and to protect a patient's privacy when an ombudsman requests access to patient records.

Bankruptcy Rule 2015.2 (Transfer of Patient in Health Care Business Case) was added to require the trustee to issue notice when relocating patients from a health-care business debtor's facility that is closing.

Bankruptcy Rule 2015.3 (Reports of Financial Information on Entities in Which a Chapter 11 Estate Holds a Controlling or Substantial Interest) was added to require a debtor to file periodic reports regarding the value and profitability of any entity in which the debtor has a substantial or controlling interest.

Bankruptcy Rule 3002 (Filing Proof of Claim or Interest) was amended to conform the time period for filing proofs of government claims under Code § 1308 to time periods under Code § 502. The amendment gives the court discretion to extend the time for a foreign creditor to file a proof of claim.

Bankruptcy Rule 3003 (Filing Proof of Claim or Equity Security Interest in Chapter 9 Municipality or Chapter 11 Reorganization Cases) was amended to require the court to grant additional time to a creditor with a foreign address to file a proof of claim in a chapter 9 or chapter 11 case.

Bankruptcy Rule 3016 (Filing of Plan and Disclosure Statement in a Chapter 9 Municipality or Chapter 11 Reorganization Case) was amended to relieve a small-business debtor from the requirement of filing a disclosure statement in a chapter 9 or 11 case if the plan itself includes adequate information and the court finds that a separate disclosure statement is unnecessary.

Bankruptcy Rule 3017.1 (Court Consideration of Disclosure Statement in a Small Business Case) was amended to authorize the court in a small-business chapter 11 case to conditionally approve a plan if adequate information is provided.

Bankruptcy Rule 3019 (Modification of Accepted Plan Before or After Confirmation in a Chapter 9 Municipality or Chapter 11 Reorganization Case) was amended to establish procedures for filing and objecting to a proposed modification of a confirmed plan.

Bankruptcy Rule 4002 (Duties of Debtor) was amended to require a debtor to provide additional evidence of personal identity, current income, recent federal income tax returns or tax transcripts, and financial account information existing at the commencement of the case.

Bankruptcy Rule 4003 (Exemptions) was amended to extend the deadline for filing objections to exemptions from 30 days to 60 days and allows the trustee to object to an exemption up to one year after the case is closed if the exemption was fraudulent.

Bankruptcy Rule 4004 (Grant or Denial of Discharge) was amended to require the debtor to complete a financial management program before the court enters discharge, and allows the court to postpone discharge to determine whether the debtor committed a felony or owes money arising from certain causes of action.

Bankruptcy Rule 4006 (Notice of No Discharge) was amended to require the clerk to notify parties in interest, including the debtor, that no discharge was entered if the debtor failed to complete financial management course.

Bankruptcy Rule 4007 (Determination of Dischargeability of a Debt) was amended to expand the exceptions to discharge upon completion of a chapter 13 plan.

Bankruptcy Rule 4008 (Filing of Reaffirmation Agreement; Statement in Support of Reaffirmation Agreement) was amended to establish a deadline for filing a reaffirmation agreement. The amendment requires the debtor to file a signed statement showing total income and expenses from schedules and an explanation of any discrepancies so that the court can evaluate the reaffirmation for undue hardship.

Bankruptcy Rule 5001 (Courts and Clerks' Offices) was amended to permit the bankruptcy judge in an emergency situation to hold a hearing outside of the district in which the case is pending.

Bankruptcy Rule 5003 (Records Kept By the Clerk) was amended to allow the taxing authorities to designate addresses to use for the service of a request under Code § 505(b)(1).

Bankruptcy Rule 5008 (Notice Regarding Presumption of Abuse in Chapter 7 Cases of Individual Debtors) was added to require the clerk to give written notice to all creditors not later than 10 days after the filing of a petition that a presumption of abuse has arisen.

Bankruptcy Rule 6004 (Use, Sale, or Lease of Property) was amended to require the appointment of a consumer privacy ombudsman in certain circumstances when a debtor proposes to sell personally identifiable information.

Bankruptcy Rule 6011 (Disposal of Patient Records in Health Care Business Case) was added to require the trustee to notify patients before destroying their medical records.

Bankruptcy Rule 7012 was amended to include the application of F.R.Civ.P. 12(i) in adversary proceedings.

Bankruptcy Rule 7022 was amended to conform to the stylistic amendment of F.R.Civ.P. Rule 22.

Bankruptcy Rule 7023.1 was amended to conform its title to the amendment of F.R.Civ.P. Rule 23.1.

Bankruptcy Rule 8001 (Manner of Taking Appeal; Voluntary Dismissal; Certification to Court of Appeals) was amended to authorize an appeal directly to the courts of appeals upon certification either by the bankruptcy or district court or the bankruptcy appellate panel. Permission to appeal to the court of appeals requires a timely notice of appeal.

Bankruptcy Rule 8003 (Leave to Appeal) was amended to implement the direct appeal provisions that of the Act. A certification by the lower court or the allowance of leave to appeal by the court of appeals satisfies the requirement for leave to appeal regardless of whether a motion for leave to appeal has been filed.

Bankruptcy Rule 9006 (Time) was amended to limit extensions of time for filing schedules and a statement of financial affairs by a small business debtor to the time set in the Code. The amendment also limits the enlargement and reduction of time for filing a reaffirmation agreement.

Bankruptcy Rule 9009 (Forms) was amended to permit a plan proponent in a small business chapter 11 case to use either an Official Form of a plan of reorganization and disclosure statement or a form adopted locally.

Bankruptcy Rule 9024 was amended to conform to the stylistic amendment of F.R.Civ.P. Rule 60.

II. Amendments to the Federal Rules of Civil Procedure

Effective December 1, 2008, Supplemental Rule C(6)(a)(i) of the Supplemental Rules for Admiralty or Maritime Claims and Asset Forfeiture Actions was amended to correct a technical omission. There was no substantive change and there were no other amendments to the Federal Rules of Civil Procedure.

III. Amendments to Official Bankruptcy Forms

Because of changes to procedure that were required by enactment of BAPCA, the Official Bankruptcy Forms have undergone numerous changes as practice under BAPCPA has developed. The Official Forms that have been amended since publication of the 2008 edition of Highlights, are as follows:

Official Forms revised effective December 1, 2007:

Official Form 3A (Application to Pay Filing Fee in Installments) was amended to state that, until the filing fee is paid in full, the debtor will not make any additional payment or transfer any additional property for services in connection with the case.

Official Form 3B (Application for Waiver of the Chapter 7 Filing Fee for Individuals Who Cannot Pay the Filing Fee in Full or in Installments) was amended to permit courts to waive the filing fee or permit the debtor to pay in installments in a case under Chapter 7.

Official Form 4 (List of Creditors Holding 20 Largest Unsecured Claims) was amended to provide more information concerning notification to a guardian or other adult when a minor child is a creditor in a bankruptcy case.

Official Form 5 (Involuntary Petition) was amended to facilitate collection in an involuntary case the same statistical information as in a voluntary case.

Official Form 6 (Schedules) was amended to facilitate statistical reporting requirements and other conforming amendments.

Official Form 7 (Statement of Financial Affairs) was amended to conform to Bankruptcy Rule 9037.

Official Forms 9 (Notice of Commencement of Case, Meeting of Creditors and Deadlines) were amended, with Forms 9G and 9H adding family fisherman as a category of debtor eligible for bankruptcy relief under Chapter 12 of the Bankruptcy Code. The amended Chapter 13 Form 9I will permit Internal Revenue Service to assert a claim in a Chapter 13 case based on a debtor's income tax return filed during the three to five years the case is pending.

Official Form 10 (Proof of Claim) was amended to conform with the changed priority scheme in the Code. It also provides more accurate addresses for transmittal of payments and notices and updates the Instructions and Definitions portions of the form.

Official Form 16A (Caption (Full)) and *Official Form 18* (Discharge of Debtor in a Chapter 7 Case) were amended to require disclosure of all names used by the debtor in the past eight years and last four digits of debtor's taxpayer-identification number. They also reflect changes to the Bankruptcy Code governing nondischargeability of certain obligations.

Official Form 19A (Declaration and Signature of Non–Attorney Bankruptcy Petition Preparer) was amended to change the former certification to declaration and contains additional language mandated by the 2005 Act.

Official Form 19B (Notice to Debtor by Non–Attorney Bankruptcy Petition Preparer) was amended to contain the notice that a non-attorney bankruptcy petition preparer is required to give a debtor.

Official Form 21 (Statement of Social–Security Number) was amended to require taxpayers that do not have a social-security number to provide a taxpayer-identification number on form.

Official Form 23 (Debtor's Certification of Completion of Instructional Course Concerning Personal Financial Management) was amended to require the debtor to provide the number of the certificate of completion received from the course, requires debtor to indicate any applicable exception to the requirement to complete the course, and states deadlines for filing the certification in a Chapter 7 case and a Chapter 13 case.

Official Form 24 (Certification to Court of Appeals by All Parties) will be used to file any certification of an appeal, bankruptcy court judgment, order, or decree directly to the United States Court of Appeals by all the appellants and appellees acting jointly.

Official Forms revised effective January 1, 2008:

Official Form 1 (Voluntary Petition) was amended to revise requests for information about the debtor and to add the statutory definition of consumer debt. *Exhibit D to Official Form 1* (Individual Debtor's Statement of Compliance with Credit Counseling Requirement) alerts debtors to the prepetition credit counseling requirement.

Official Form 22A (Chapter 7 Statement of Current Monthly Income and Means–Test Calculation) was amended to delete the phrase in default in recognition that a debtor may be required to make additional payments to a creditor even if the loan is not in default.

Official Form 22B (Chapter 11 Statement of Current Monthly Income) was amended to allow calculation of disposable income under judicially-determined standards, rather than pursuant to the means-test deductions specified for higher-income Chapter 13 debtors.

Official Form 22C (Chapter 13 Statement of Current Monthly Income and Calculation of Commitment Period and Disposable Income) was amended to require all Chapter 13 debtors, including those whose income is below the applicable median, to complete Part III of the form.

Official Forms revised and pending to be effective December 1, 2008:

The revised forms scheduled to be effective December 1, 2008, are set forth below:

Official Form 1 (Voluntary Petition) *Exhibit D to Official Form 1* (Individual Debtor's Statement of Compliance with Credit Counseling Requirement) is to be further amended for debtors' compliance with the prepetition credit counseling requirement.

Official Form 8 (Chapter 7 Individual Debtor's Statement of Intention) will be further amended concerning surrender or other compliance with retention of secured property.

Official Form 9F (Notice of Chapter 11 Bankruptcy Case, Meeting of Creditors and Deadlines) will be amended to delete the debtor's phone number in conformity with other versions of Official Form 9.

Official Form 10 (Proof of Claim) will be further amended to conform with the changed priority scheme in the Code. It also will provide more accurate addresses for transmittal of payments and notices and updates the Instructions and Definitions portions of the form.

Official Form 23 (Debtor's Certification of Completion of Instructional Course Concerning Personal Financial Management) will be amended to include a reference to § 1141(d)(5)(B) in the paragraph describing filing deadlines at the bottom of the form.

New Official Forms scheduled to be effective December 1, 2008:

Official Form 25A (Plan of Reorganization in Small Business Case Under Chapter 11) will be a new form regarding the reorganization plan to be used in small business cases under Chapter 11.

Official Form 25B (Disclosure Statement in Small Business Case) will be a new form regarding the disclosure statement to be used in small business cases under Chapter 11.

Official Form 25C (Small Business Monthly Operating Report) will be a new form to assist small business debtors in Chapter 11 cases to fulfill their financial reporting responsibilities.

Official Form 26 (Periodic Report Regarding Value, Operations and Profitability of Entities in Which the Debtor's Estate Holds a Substantial or Controlling Interest) will be a new form to be used when required by new Bankruptcy Rule 2015.3 to file periodic reports on the profitability of any entities in which a Chapter 11 debtor holds a substantial or controlling interest.

Other future proposed amendments to Official Forms:

The Judicial Conference Advisory Committee on Bankruptcy Rules has begun a Bankruptcy Forms Modernization Project, with the completion expected to require five to seven years. The mission statement of the Project is to obtain input and collaboration of judges, bankruptcy clerks, lawyers, trustees, and information technology experts, among others, to review and revise the Official Bankruptcy Forms. The modernized Official Forms will, consistent with Judicial Conference policies, simplify and improve the collection of necessary information and, through integration with evolving technologies, provide improved analytical resources to the judiciary and parties in interest for the administration of bankruptcy cases and the resolution of contested matters and adversary proceedings. Comments concerning improvements of the Official Forms may be emailed to AO_Forms_Modernization_Project@ao.uscourts.gov.

IV. Recent Supreme Court Decisions of Interest to Bankruptcy Practitioners

A. *An assignee of a legal claim for money has standing to sue regardless of whether or not the assignee has promised to pass all litigation proceeds back to the assignor. Sprint Communications Co., L.P. v. APCC Services, Inc., 128 S.Ct. 2605 (2008).*

When long-distance carriers failed to compensate payphone operators, the payphone operators assigned their claims to collection firms. For a fee, the collection firms promised to remit all proceeds to the payphone operators. The long-distance carriers complained that the collection firms lacked standing to sue because they had no personal stake in the outcome—they had not suffered an injury and they were not ultimately to be the recipients of any damages to be awarded. The United States Supreme Court rejected that argument, citing the long history and tradition of permitting an assignee standing to sue as long as there was an injury suffered by the assignor, caused by the defendant, and redressed by a favorable decision. The fact that the damages would be remitted to the assignor did not impact the assignee's standing.

Dissenting, Chief Justice Roberts, joined by Justices Scalia, Thomas, and Alito, argued that, because the collection firms had nothing to gain by their suit, there was no case or controversy and the case should have been dismissed.

B. *The stamp tax exemption of the Bankruptcy Code applies only to a transfer made pursuant to a confirmed chapter 11 plan, not to a transfer made before confirmation. Florida Dept. of Revenue v. Piccadilly Cafeterias, Inc., 128 S.Ct. 2326 (2008).*

The Bankruptcy Code provides that the transfer of an asset under a plan confirmed . . . may not be taxed under any law imposing a stamp tax or similar tax. 11 U.S.C. § 1146(a). The Florida Department of Revenue imposed a tax on transfers made prior to the confirmation of the chapter 11 plan. The Bankruptcy Court, District Court and Eleventh Circuit Court of Appeals all held that the stamp tax exemption applied because the transfers were made pursuant to a plan which was confirmed. They held that the statute applied to transfers made pursuant to a plan, regardless of whether it was confirmed before or after the transfers were made. The United States Supreme Court agreed with Florida's literal reading of the statute and held that the statute did not exempt from a stamp tax any transfer made prior to the confirmation of a chapter 11 plan, even if the transfer were made pursuant to a plan which was subsequently confirmed.

Justice Breyer dissented, joined by Justice Stevens. Citing the ambiguity of the Code section, the practical realities of reorganization, and legislative intent, the dissent argues for the application of the stamp tax exemption to transfers made under a chapter 11 plan that is yet to be confirmed.

V. Circuit Court Decisions Interpreting the Bankruptcy Abuse Prevention and Consumer Protection Act of 2005

The monthly Norton Bankruptcy Law Adviser, available from Thomson West in print or on Westlaw, publishes summaries of circuit court decisions affecting bankruptcy. Selected from the Adviser, the following circuit court decisions over the past year interpret Bankruptcy Code sections that were added or amended by the Bankruptcy Abuse Prevention and Consumer Protection Act of 2005 (BAPCPA).

First Circuit

Larson v. Howell (In re Larson), 513 F.3d 325 (1st Cir. 2008). The state crime of negligent vehicular homicide qualifies as a criminal act that would cap a debtor's homestead exemption at $125,000 under § 522(q)(1)(B)(iv). Debtor was found criminally liable for negligent vehicular homicide. The court found that § 522(q)(1)(B)(iv) applied to a criminal act, even if based in negligence rather than intentional, willful or reckless conduct.

Third Circuit

Perlin v. Hitachi Capital Am. Corp., 497 F.3d 364 (3d Cir. 2007). BAPCPA's amendment of § 707(b) creating a presumption of abuse against debtors who have primarily consumer debts and have sufficient income to repay their debts did not prohibit a bankruptcy court from considering a debtor's income and expenses in ruling on a motion to dismiss under § 707(a). In deciding a motion to dismiss under § 707(a), a bankruptcy court may consider a debtor's substantial earnings and lavish lifestyle together with any other facts and circumstances surrounding the debtor's Chapter 7 filing. However, dismissal may not be premised exclusively or primarily on a debtor's substantial financial means. Otherwise, dismissal would essentially be based upon a debtor's mere ability to repay, which is prohibited. In this case, the bankruptcy court did not err in denying creditor's motion to dismiss. Although debtors' annual income was approximately $370,000, debtors spent considerable amounts on luxury items, such as two Lexus automobiles and private school tuition of $5,000 per month. Also, debtors had saved more than $430,000 for retirement. There was no evidence that debtors schemed to conceal or misrepresent income, inflated expenses to hide income, filed misleading statements or schedules to defraud creditors, unduly interfered with the judicial process, or engaged in other misconduct.

Fourth Circuit

Tidewater Fin. Co. v. Kenney, 531 F.3d 312 (4th Cir. 2008). Hanging paragraph at end of § 1325(a) does not deprive undersecured 910 creditor of its deficiency claim. Although the hanging paragraph eliminates a creditor's access to a federal remedy under § 506(a), the parties remain bound to their contractual rights and obligations under state law.

Branigan v. Bateman (In re Bateman), 515 F.3d 272 (4th Cir. 2008). (1) Two-year prohibition under § 1328(f) on discharge in consecutive Chapter 13 cases runs from filing date of first Chapter 13 petition to filing date of second Chapter 13 petition. (2) Even if a debtor is prohibited from receiving a discharge under § 1328(f), the debtor may still obtain confirmation of a Chapter 13 plan that pays all allowed claims in full. Section 1328(f) is a limitation on discharge, not filing, and Chapter 13 debtors may file a petition for reasons other than to obtain discharge. The unavailability of discharge to the debtor does not mean the petition was filed in bad faith in violation of § 1325(a)(7). The availability of discharge is only one factor relevant in considering whether a plan was proposed in bad faith, and that factor standing alone is insufficient to support a finding of bad faith.

Fifth Circuit

Drive Fin. Servs., L.P. v. Jordan, 521 F.3d 343 (5th Cir. 2008). Chapter 13 plan may modify the interest rate on a 910–day PMSI car claim from the contract rate to a lower prime-plus rate under § 1325(a)(5) when the debtor does not surrender the vehicle securing the claim. The Supreme Court previously addressed the issue and rejected the presumptive contract rate approach as too generous to creditors in *Till v. SCS Credit Corp.*, 541 U.S. 465, 124 S. Ct. 1951, 158 L. Ed. 2d 787 (2004).

Wallace v. Rogers (In re Rogers), 513 F.3d 212 (5th Cir. 2008). Homestead exemption cap, § 522(p)(1), does not apply to homestead interest established less than 1,215 days prepetition if debtor acquired title to property more than 1,215 days prepetition. Debtor acquired property more than 10 years before filing bankruptcy, but debtor lived elsewhere. Less than two years prepetition, debtor moved to property and claimed it as her homestead. Section 522(p)(1) only applies to a claim of exemption in property acquired during 1,215 days preceding petition.

Ad Hoc Group of Timber Noteholders v. Pacific Lumber Co. (In re Scotia Pacific Co., LLC), 508 F.3d 214 (5th Cir. 2007). (1) Even though case was still pending in the bankruptcy court when the district court certified the appeal to the circuit court pursuant to 28 U.S.C. § 158(d)(2), the circuit court still had jurisdiction over the appeal. Interim Rule 8001(f) requires that the bankruptcy court make the certification while the matter is pending in the bankruptcy court. The bankruptcy court apparently believed it no longer had jurisdiction because an appeal had been taken. However, the appeal had not been docketed, so the case was still pending in the bankruptcy court, which recommended that the district court certify the appeal. Where both courts wish to certify the case for appeal, the error is technical in nature and the error does not affect substantial rights, the court may exercise its discretion to decide the appeal on the merits. (2) Debtor was not a single asset real estate debtor under § 101(51B) because substantial business other than the operation of the real estate occurred on the property. The debtor had more than 60 employees in its timber operation. Sophisticated operations took place, such as planning, growing, and maintaining the timber as well as building and maintenance of roads on the property.

Sixth Circuit

Phar-Mor, Inc. v. McKesson Corp., 534 F.3d 502 (6th Cir. 2008). Reclaiming creditor's administrative expense priority claim was not extinguished when the goods subject to reclamation were sold and proceeds used to satisfy a secured creditor's superior claim. Under § 546(c)(2), a request for reclamation may be denied only if the claimant is granted an administrative expense claim. Debtor's argument that the right of reclamation was subject to the secured claim under UCC 2–207(3) failed because a secured creditor is not the type of good faith purchaser addressed in UCC 2–207(3).

Schultz v. United States, 529 F.3d 343 (6th Cir. 2008). BAPCPA means test for determining abuse of Chapter 7 and applicable commitment period in Chapter 13 does not violate uniformity clause in Article I, section 8, clause 4 of the Constitution. Debtors argued that the means test, based on the median income in the state and county of the debtor's residence, produces nonuniform results. The uniformity requirement, however, does not deny Congress the power to take into account regional differences so long as the law applies equally to all creditors and debtors and operates uniformly upon a given class of creditors and debtors.

Americredit Fin. Servs., Inc. v. Long (In re Long), 519 F.3d 288 (6th Cir. 2008). The hanging paragraph at the end of § 1325(a) does not eliminate an undersecured creditor's deficiency claim when Chapter 13 plan surrenders a car purchased less than 910 days prepetition. Although the majority position is to disallow the deficiency claim, completely eliminating a deficiency judgment upon surrender under § 1325(a)(5)(C) would be in conflict with congressional intent and give debtors the power to wipe out a legitimately incurred debt entirely. Courts applying state law to preserve deficiency claims are in error, as such dependence undermines the intended uniformity of the Bankruptcy Code. Until Congress corrects its mistake and fills the gap in the statute, the hanging paragraph should be filled by prior law allowing collection of the deficiency claim.

In re Davis, 512 F.3d 856 (6th Cir. 2008). Decision whether to allow direct appeal under 28 U.S.C. § 158(d)(2) from the bankruptcy court is committed to discretion of circuit court. After Chapter 13 plan was confirmed, trustee appealed, questioning whether vehicle ownership expense is allowable when debtor has no loan or lease payment. Direct appeal may be justified when decision would materially advance the litigation. Here, allowing the case to percolate through the district court would likely facilitate a wise and well-informed decision.

Seventh Circuit

In re Wright, 492 F.3d 829 (7th Cir. 2007). A creditor holding a purchase money security interest in a Chapter 13 debtor's automobile acquired for personal use within 910 days before the petition has a deficiency claim after surrender of the car. Section 1325(a)'s hanging paragraph, added by BAPCPA, provides that § 506 does not apply to a 910–day PMSI car claim. By knocking out § 506, the hanging paragraph leaves the parties to their state law and contractual entitlements. Since the debtor's agreement with the creditor allowed the creditor to seek a deficiency judgment after liquidating the collateral, the bankruptcy court properly refused to confirm debtor's plan that would surrender the car and pay nothing on account of the deficiency.

Eighth Circuit

Addison v. Seaver (In re Addison),___ F.3d ___, Nos. 07–2064 & 07–2727, 2008 WL 3077066 (8th Cir. Aug. 7, 2008). Debtor's day-of-filing mortgage payment was not done with the intent to hinder, delay or defraud a creditor under § 522(*o*). A debtor's conversion of non-exempt property to exempt property on the eve of bankruptcy for the express purpose of placing that property beyond the reach of creditors, without more, will not deprive the debtor of the exemption. For fraudulent intent to be found there must be some facts extrinsic to the conversion indicative of fraud. The debtor merely took funds out of an account and paid $11,500 toward his mortgage. Examples of indicia of fraud include borrowing money to place into exempt assets, obtaining goods on credit and selling them to raise money for an exempt account or concealing the transfers in bankruptcy filings. Debtor's Roth IRA transfer was allowed for the same reasons. However, two § 529 tuition savings accounts the debtor had opened for the benefit of his children were nonexempt property of the bankruptcy estate under pre-BAPCPA law.

Capital One Auto Finance v. Osborn, 515 F.3d 817 (8th Cir. 2008), and *AmeriCredit Fin. Servs., Inc. v. Moore*, 517 F.3d 987 (8th Cir. 2008). The hanging paragraph in § 1325(a) does not eliminate an undersecured creditor's deficiency claim when the debtor's Chapter 13 plan proposes to surrender a car purchased less than 910 days prepetition. Although the majority position is to disallow the deficiency claim, the trend is toward allowing the claim. The hanging paragraph makes § 506(a) inapplicable to 910–car claims; however, the court concluded that the claim may still be bifurcated under state law and the applicable security agreement. To hold otherwise would essentially turn a recourse loan into a nonrecourse loan. Unlike the retention option in § 1325(a)(5)(B), the surrender option in § 1325(a)(5)(C) does not speak to satisfaction of the claim.

Ninth Circuit

Maney v. Kagenveama (In re Kagenveama), ___ F.3d ___, No. 06–17083, 2008 WL 2485570 (9th Cir. June 23, 2008) (as amended). Chapter 13 debtor's projected disposable income is calculated by multiplying disposable income by the applicable commitment period; applicable commitment period is inapplicable when debtor has no projected disposable income. Debtor's projected disposable income was negative, but debtor voluntarily proposed to pay $1,000 per month for three years. Chapter 13 trustee argued that projected disposable income should be a flexible concept and take into account potential future increases in income. The court disagreed, based on the plain language of 1325(b) and the fact that a plan may be modified under 1329.

Tenth Circuit

Wachovia Dealer Servs .. v. Jones (In re Jones), 530 F.3d 1284 (10th Cir. 2008). (1) A Chapter 13 plan that pays no postpetition interest on a claim secured by an automobile may not be confirmed over the creditor's objection. A creditor whose claim is secured by a 910 vehicle is entitled to the present value of the claim under § 1325(a)(5)(B). (2) The provisions of § 1325(a) are mandatory requirements for confirmation of a Chapter 13 plan but even the right to interest on a secured claim can be waived by silence.

DaimlerChrysler Fin. Servs. Ams. LLC v. Ballard (In re Ballard), 526 F.3d 634 (10th Cir. 2008). The hanging paragraph at the end of § 1325(a) does not prevent a creditor secured by an automobile purchased within 910 days prepetition from pursuing a deficiency claim. By choosing to surrender, debtor satisfies requirements for plan confirmation under § 1325(a)(5) with respect to claim secured by the vehicle. However, creditor may have state law right to collect any deficiency after the vehicle is liquidated, and this right may exist independent of § 506.

Eleventh Circuit

Graupner v. Nuvell Credit Corp. (In re Graupner), ___ F.3d ___, No. 07–13657, 2008 WL 2993570 (11th Cir. Aug. 6, 2008). A purchase money security interest, for purposes of the hanging paragraph at the end of § 1325(a), includes negative equity from debtor's trade-in of previous vehicle. In a prepetition transaction, debtor owed more on his trade-in than the vehicle was worth. Lender financed the purchase price of debtor's new vehicle and the negative equity from the debtor's trade in. The negative equity on the trade-in was purchase money debt because it was for the money required to make the purchase of the new vehicle and inextricably intertwined with the sales transaction and the financing of the purchase. The bankruptcy court, thus, properly sustained lender's objection to a Chapter 13 plan that proposed to bifurcate and cram down the lender's claim.

VI. Government Accountability Office Cost Report on Bankruptcy Abuse Prevention and Consumer Protection Act of 2005

At the request of Congress, the Government Accountability Office (GAO) issued on June 27, 2008, its report, GAO–08–697, on the Dollar Costs Associated with the Bankruptcy Abuse Prevention and Consumer Protection Act of 2005. The complete report, GAO–08–697, is available at www.gao.gov, but the introductory statement and summary of the report provide:

> Congress enacted major bankruptcy reform legislation with the Bankruptcy Abuse Prevention and Consumer Protection Act of 2005 (Bankruptcy Reform Act), most of the provisions of which became effective in October 2005. The act made many significant changes to the administration of consumer bankruptcy relief and has resulted in certain new responsibilities for the various entities involved in the bankruptcy process. Within the judicial branch (or federal judiciary), these entities include the 90 bankruptcy courts; the Administrative Office of the United States Courts, which provides the courts with central support functions; and the bankruptcy administrators in the six judicial districts in Alabama and North Carolina. Within the executive branch, the Department of Justice's U.S. Trustee Program (Trustee Program) oversees bankruptcy case administration in most federal judicial districts and litigates to enforce the bankruptcy laws. The Bankruptcy Reform Act also has affected the roles and responsibilities of the approximately 1,400 private trustees. These trustees are private individuals who are appointed and supervised by the Trustee Program or bankruptcy administrators and are responsible for administering bankruptcy estates and distributing assets as appropriate to creditors.
>
> Among other things, the Bankruptcy Reform Act established a means test for determining whether a consumer is eligible for bankruptcy relief under Chapter 7 (in which assets are liquidated and debts discharged) or must file under Chapter 13 (which involves a court-approved plan for repayment of debts) or under Chapter 11. The act required procedures be established for audits of consumer bankruptcy cases by a certified public or licensed accountant. Further, the act required the federal judiciary to collect and publish certain annual statistics on bankruptcy cases. In addition, consumers must receive approved credit counseling before filing a petition in bankruptcy court and take an approved debtor education course before having debts discharged. The act also increased bankruptcy filing fees, and is widely believed to have affected the fees bankruptcy attorneys charge consumers for these cases. The number of new consumer bankruptcy filings declined after implementation of the Bankruptcy Reform Act—about 600,000 people filed for bankruptcy in 2006 as compared with an average of 1.5 million people annually from 2001 through 2004.
>
> In light of these changes, you asked us to report on new costs resulting from the Bankruptcy Reform Act. The specific objectives of this report are to examine (1) new costs incurred as a result of the Bankruptcy Reform Act by the Department of Justice and the federal judiciary, (2) new costs incurred as a result of the act by consumers filing for bankruptcy, and (3) the impact of the act on private trustees. Our review focused on the impact of the act with regard to consumer (that is, personal) bankruptcies and not business bankruptcies. Further, the scope of the first two objectives is limited to the monetary (dollar) costs incurred by federal entities and consumers and not on other ways the Bankruptcy Reform Act may have affected them. The scope of this report also is limited to costs directly related to the process of filing for bankruptcy, and not on the overall financial impact the act may be having on consumers. Finally, this report did not seek to assess the benefits of the Bankruptcy Reform Act and is therefore not an evaluation of the merits of the act.
>
> To address the objectives, we obtained documentation from, and interviewed representatives of, the Trustee Program; the federal judiciary, including the Administrative Office of the

United States Courts (AOUSC) and selected individual bankruptcy courts; Congressional Budget Office; and organizations representing consumers, bankruptcy attorneys, the financial services industry, and Chapter 7 and Chapter 13 trustees. For the first objective, we reviewed available data on the budgets of the Trustee Program and the federal judiciary for fiscal years 2003 to 2009. We asked the Trustee Program and the judiciary to provide estimates of their spending, including staff time, dedicated to implementing the Bankruptcy Reform Act. We did not verify these estimates, although we reviewed and analyzed them and we interviewed the staff who provided the estimates to understand how they were created. We determined that the estimates were sufficiently reliable for our purposes. For the second objective, to determine changes in attorney fees for Chapter 7 bankruptcy cases, we selected two random and projectable samples of cases (from before and after the act) and collected information on the attorney compensation, if any, from the disclosure statements regarding compensation that are required to be filed by debtors' attorneys. To determine changes in attorney fees for Chapter 13 cases, we collected data on the standard fees set by 48 judicial districts or divisions (a sublevel below that of judicial district). These fees represent the amount most attorneys charge consumers to handle a Chapter 13 case in those divisions or districts. To determine costs associated with credit counseling and debtor education courses, we obtained data from the Trustee Program and a credit counseling trade organization and reviewed information we collected previously for a report on that topic. To determine changes in filing fees, we reviewed changes in fees made by the Bankruptcy Reform Act and subsequent budget legislation. For the third objective, we reviewed provisions of the Bankruptcy Reform Act that affect private trustees' roles and responsibilities and the Trustee Program's policy and procedure manuals for private trustees. We also interviewed professional associations representing private trustees and conducted individual and group interviews of, collectively, 21 Chapter 7 and Chapter 13 private trustees, who were chosen because they served in districts that represented a range of sizes and geographic regions. A more extensive discussion of our scope and methodology appears in appendix I.

We conducted this performance audit from June 2007 through June 2008 in accordance with generally accepted government auditing standards. Those standards require that we plan and perform the audit to obtain sufficient, appropriate evidence to provide a reasonable basis for our findings and conclusions based on our audit objectives. We believe that the evidence obtained provides a reasonable basis for our findings and conclusions based on our audit objectives.

Results in Brief:

The Trustee Program and the federal judiciary have both incurred new costs—mostly in staff resources—as a result of the Bankruptcy Reform Act, but these costs are difficult to measure since it is not always possible to isolate the amount of staff time devoted specifically to implementing the act's requirements. At our request, the Trustee Program estimated that for fiscal years 2005 through 2007, its costs related to carrying out responsibilities resulting from the Bankruptcy Reform Act were approximately $72.4 million, mostly for personnel. The costs included $42.5 million to implement the means test, $6.1 million related to credit counseling and debtor education requirements, and $3.0 million to supervise and conduct debtor audits. Additional funds were spent for studies, reporting requirements, and information technology needs related to the act. The federal judiciary could not isolate costs specifically resulting from the Bankruptcy Reform Act since the act had a broad effect on nearly all bankruptcy court staff and operations. However, the judiciary did estimate that $48.4 million was incurred in costs for specific start-up activities associated with the initial implementation of the act's requirements. The largest of these costs was for staff time dedicated to revisions of the Bankruptcy Rules, official forms, court operating procedures, and the courts' electronic filing, docketing, and case management system. Other major expenses were for training, statistical and reporting requirements, and new responsibilities for the bankruptcy administrators who oversee cases in certain districts. The cost estimates for the Trustee Program and the judiciary do not incorporate the effect of the decline in bankruptcy filings since the act, which presumably has helped reduce their overall costs to some extent. As a result of the decline in bankruptcy filings since the passage of the act, revenues from bankruptcy-related filing and other fees declined between fiscal year 2005 and fiscal year 2007—from $74 million to $52 million for the Trustee Program and from $237 million to $135 million for the federal judiciary.

Since the implementation of the Bankruptcy Reform Act, there have been increased costs to individual consumers filing for bankruptcy resulting from higher attorney fees and filing fees, as well as new fees to meet credit counseling and debtor education requirements. Based on a review of legal fee disclosure forms in our random sample of Chapter 7 personal bankruptcy filings, we estimate that the average attorney fee for a Chapter 7 case increased from $712 in February–March 2005 to $1,078 in February–March 2007. The proportion of Chapter 7 debtors filing without an attorney (pro se) was about 11 percent in February–March 2005, according to our sample estimate, as compared to 5.9 percent in calendar year 2007, according to AOUSC data. We did not find a statistically significant difference in the proportion of Chapter 7 debtors receiving free legal assistance between the 2 years. For Chapter 13 cases, our review found the standard attorney fee approved by courts (and which, in practice, is the fee Chapter 13 attorneys typically charge their clients) rose in nearly all the districts and divisions with such fees. In more than half of these cases, the increase was 55 percent or more. The act raised Chapter 7 filing fees by $65 and reduced Chapter 13 filing fees by $5. However, as a result of further changes to filing fees made by the Deficit Reduction Act of 2005, total bankruptcy filing fees since 2005 have risen from $209 to $299 for Chapter 7 filers and from $194 to $274 for Chapter 13 filers. The act included a new provision allowing these filing fees to be waived for qualified Chapter 7 debtors, and these fees were waived in 2.1 percent of Chapter 7 personal bankruptcy cases filed in fiscal year 2007. The Bankruptcy Reform Act also included a new requirement that consumers receive credit counseling from an approved provider before filing for bankruptcy and complete a debtor education course before debts can be discharged. Most consumers pay about $100 to fulfill these requirements since credit counseling and debtor education providers typically charge about $50 per session, according to data from the Trustee Program and other sources. The act requires that these services be provided without regard to a client's ability to pay, but providers vary significantly in their policies for waiving or reducing fees. To address this variation, the Trustee Program issued a proposed rule in February 2008 stating that a client's inability to pay for credit counseling shall be presumed if the client's household income is less than 150 percent of the poverty line.

The Bankruptcy Reform Act has affected the responsibilities and caseloads of Chapter 7 and Chapter 13 private trustees. As a result of new provisions in the act, trustees must collect, track, store, and safeguard additional documents such as tax returns; notify appropriate parties of domestic support obligations; check calculations and review the accuracy of information in forms associated with the means test; and, once finalized, will be required to comply with new requirements for uniform final reports. Private trustees told us that these new responsibilities have significantly increased the time and resources required to administer a bankruptcy case. The $60 fee Chapter 7 trustees collect for each case they administer remained unchanged with the passage of the Bankruptcy Reform Act. The caseload of private trustees has declined since the act in concert with the decline in filings. From fiscal years 2004 through 2007, Chapter 7 filings—personal and business—declined from 1.2 million to 484,000, and Chapter 13 filings declined from 454,412 to 310,802. However, the one-time surge in filings that occurred just prior to the act helped offset these declines in caseload since Chapter 7 trustees receive a portion of assets liquidated and Chapter 13 trustees receive a portion of payments to creditors, both of which can take several years to complete. Our analysis of data provided by the Trustee Program showed that Chapter 7 trustees collectively received an estimated $192 million in total compensation in fiscal year 2005 and an estimated $212 million in fiscal year 2007, while Chapter 13 trustees received about $31 million in fiscal year 2005 and about $32 million in fiscal year 2007. Attrition among private trustees has not changed significantly since the implementation of the Bankruptcy Reform Act, according to our analysis of Trustee Program data, although the program is moving more slowly to fill trustee vacancies given the reduced number of bankruptcy filings.

For a discussion of this GAO report, see Robert M. Lawless & Heather A. Miller, *GAO Report Finds Increased Costs from BAPCPA*, Norton Bankruptcy Law Adviser (October 2008).

VII. U.S. Department of Justice, Executive Office for United States Trustee Report to Congress: Evaluation of Instructional Classes in Personal Financial Management for Consumer Bankruptcy Debtors

In May, 2008, the Executive Office for United States Trustee (EOUST) issued its report to Congress, as required by section 105 of the Bankruptcy Abuse Prevention and Consumer Protection Act of 2005, concerning the EOUST's evaluation of instructional classes in personal financial management for consumer bankruptcy debtors. Section 105 required the EOUST to develop a financial management training curriculum and materials to educate individuals filing for bankruptcy relief on how to manage their finances, to test and evaluate the effectiveness of the curriculum and materials, and to report to Congress findings about the effectiveness. The complete report is available at www.usdoj/ust, but the introductory summary of the report states that three curricula were tested in six judicial districts, with the findings of effectiveness concluding:

> Almost all of the consumer bankruptcy debtors (97 percent) in the pilot study who took the course utilizing the financial management training curriculum and materials developed for the EOUST expressed a high level of satisfaction with the curriculum. Further, almost half of the consumer bankruptcy debtors in the pilot study reported their intention to change at least one financial practice. The pilot study did not, however, find substantial improvement in knowledge and financial practices, likely due to pre-existing knowledge regarding the topics measured.

VIII. 110th Congress House and Senate Legislation

Significant legislation enacted during the 110th Congress that has an impact on bankruptcy included:

The Mortgage Forgiveness Debt Relief Act of 2007, Public Law No. 110–142.

This Act was signed into law on December 20, 2007, amending the Internal Revenue Code to exclude from gross income discharges of indebtedness on qualified principal residences that result from restructuring of the debt or foreclosure.

The Housing and Economic Recovery Act of 2008, Public Law No. 110–289

President Bush signed into law this Act on July 30, 2008, with the goal announced by the Bill's sponsor of assisting 400,000 homeowners facing foreclosure, by permitting refinancing of current mortgages through a Federal Housing Administration loan. Under the portion of the Act called the Hope of Homeowners' Program, up to $300 billion in mortgages may be subject to refinancing as thirty-year government-backed loans, subject to limitations within the Act. The Act also increases government-backed loan limits, with conforming loan limits increased permanently to $625,000. The portion of the Act called the Mortgage Disclosure Improvement Act increases mortgage disclosure requirements concerning adjustable rate mortgages for consumers. Additional provisions of the Act include: creation of the National Affordable Housing Trust Fund; increases in mortgage revenue bonds to encourage refinancing of subprime mortgages; establishment of minimum standards for mortgage originators; establishment of the Federal Housing Finance Agency to oversee Fannie Mae, Freddie Mac and the Federal Home Loan Banks (a role expanded to ownership direction now that the government has taken control of Fannie Mae and Freddie Mac); temporarily increases maximum loan amount for certain VA loans and provides mortgage counseling for servicemembers returning from service abroad; provides $4 billion in emergency assistance to states and cities to redevelop abandoned and foreclosed homes; and establishes a first-time buyers tax credit, with a maximum of $7,500, that is required to be repaid interest free over fifteen years.

Bankruptcy Code, Rules and Forms

*

UNITED STATES CODE ANNOTATED

TITLE 11

BANKRUPTCY

[1] So in original. Does not conform to chapter heading.

TABLE I

This Table lists the sections of former Title 11, Bankruptcy, and indicates the sections of Title 11, as revised by Pub.L. 95–598 which cover similar and related subject matter.

Title 11 Former Sections	*Title 11 New Sections*
1(1)–(3)	Rep.
1(4)	101(12)
1(5)–(7)	Rep.
1(8)	101(8)
1(9), (10)	Rep.
1(11)	101(9)
1(12), (13)	Rep.
1(14)	101(11)
1(15), (16)	Rep.
1(17)	101(17), (18)
1(18)	Rep.
1(19)	101(26)
1(20)–(22)	Rep.
1(23)	101(30)
1(24)	101(31)
1(25), (26)	Rep.
1(27)	101(34)
1(28), (29)	Rep.
1(29a)	101(38)
1(30)	101(40)
1(31)	Rep.
1(32)	101(24)
1(33), (34)	Rep.
1(35)	102(7)
11(a)(1)	109(a)
11(a)(2)	502(j)
11(a)(2A)	505(a), (b)
11(a)(3), (4)	Rep.
11(a)(5)	721
11(a)(6)	Rep.
11(a)(7)	363
11(a)(8)	350
11(a)(9)–(14)	Rep.
11(a)(15)	105
11(a)(16)	Rep.
11(a)(17)	324
11(a)(18)	303(i)
11(a)(19), (20)	Rep.
11(a)(21)	543(b), (c)
11(a)(22)	305(a)(2)
11(b)	Rep.
21	303(h)
22	109(b)
22(a)	301
22(b)	303(a)
23(a)	Rep.
23(b)	303(b)
23(c)–(f)	Rep.
23(g)	723
23(h)–(k)	Rep.
24	522
25(a)(1)	343, 521(4)
25(a)(2)	Rep.
25(a)(3)	521(2)
25(a)(4)	521(3)
25(a)(5)	521(3)
25(a)(6)	521(2)
25(a)(7)	521(2)
25(a)(8), (9)	521(1)
25(a)(10)	343, 344
25(a)(11)	521(3)
25(b)	Rep.
26	541(a)
27, 28	Rep.
29(a)	362
29(b)–(d)	Rep.
29(e)	108(a), (b)
29(f)	108(c)
30, 31	(See former 501–1103)
32(a)	727(a)(10), 1141(d)(4)
32(b)	727(c)
32(c)(1)	727(a)(2), (4)

Title 11 Former Sections	Title 11 New Sections
32(c)(2)	727(a)(3)
32(c)(3)	727(a)(4)
32(c)(4)	727(a)(2)
32(c)(5)	727(a)(8), (9)
32(c)(6)	727(a)(6)
32(c)(7)	727(a)(5)
32(c)(8)	Rep.
32(d), (e)	Rep.
32(f)	524(a)
32(g), (h)	Rep.
33	727(d), (e), 1328(e)
34	524(e)
35(a)(1)	523(a)(1)
35(a)(2)	523(a)(2)
35(a)(3)	523(a)(3)
35(a)(4)	523(a)(4)
35(a)(5), (6)	Rep.
35(a)(7)	523(a)(5)
35(a)(8)	523(a)(6)
35(b)	523(b), 349(a)
35(c)	523(c)
35(c)(4)	362
41(a)	Rep.
41(b)	303(d)
41(c)–(e)	Rep.
41(f)	301
42	Omitted
43	Rep.
44(a)	343
44(b)–(f)	Rep.
44(g)	549(c)
44(h)–(*l*)	Rep.
45–51	Rep.
52, 53	Rep.
54	Rep.
55	Omitted
61–71	Rep.
72(a)	702
72(b)	705
72(c)	327(c)
73	321
74	325, 703(a)
75(a)(1)	704(1)
75(a)(2)	345
75(a)(3)	704(2)
75(a)(4)	Rep.
75(a)(5)	704(2)
75(a)(6)	Rep.
75(a)(7)	704(3)
75(a)(8)	704(4)
75(a)(9)	704(5)
75(a)(10)	704(6)
75(a)(11), (12)	Rep.
75(a)(13)	704(8)
75(a)(14)	Rep.
75(b), (c)	Rep.
76(a), (b)	Rep.
76(c)	326(a), 330
76(d)	Rep.
76(e)	326(d)
76(f), (g)	Rep.
76a	330
77	107
78(a)	Rep.
78(b)	322(a)
78(c)	322(b)(1)
78(d)	322(b)(2)
78(e)	Rep.
78(f), (g)	322(b)(2)
78(h)	Rep.
78(i)	322(c)
78(j)–(*l*)	Rep.
78(m)	322(d)
78(n)	Rep.
79–82	Rep.
91, 92	341
93(a)–(c)	Rep.
93(d)	502(a), (c)
93(e)	Rep.
93(f)	502(b)
93(g)	502(d)
93(h)	506(a), (b)
93(i)	501(b), 509
93(j)	724(a)
93(k)	502(j)
93(*l*), (m)	Rep.
93(n)	501(a), 726(a)(3)
93a	Rep.
94	342
95(a)	301
95(b)	303(b)
95(c), (d)	Rep.
95(e)	303(b)
95(f)	303(c)
95(g)	303(j), 707
95(h)	Rep.
96	547
96(a)(4)	547(e)(1)(B)
96(b)	550, 551
96(c)	547(c)(4), 553
96(d)	329
96(e)(1)	741
96(e)(2)	745, 751, 752
96(e)(3)	753
96(e)(5)	749
101	345
101a	Rep.
102(a)(1)	503(b)(2)
102(a)(2)–(4)	Rep.
102(b)	Rep.
102(c)	504
102(d)	Rep.
103	101(4)
103(a)(9)	502(b)(7)
103(c)	365
103a	Rep.
104(a)	507
104(a)(1)	503(b)
104(a)(2)	507(a)(3)
104(a)(4)	502(b)(4), 505(a), (b)
104(b)	Rep.
105(a)–(c)	Rep.
105(d)	508
105(e)	Rep.

Title 11 Former Sections	*Title 11 New Sections*
106(a)	347(a)
106(b)	Rep.
107(a)	349(b), 547(b), (d), 551
107(b), (c)	545
107(c)(1)(A)	545(1)
107(c)(1)(B)	545(2), 546(b)
107(c)(1)(C)	545(3), (4)
107(c)(2)	551
107(c)(3)	724(b)
107(d)(1)(a)–(c)	Rep.
107(d)(1)(d)	101(26)
107(d)(1)(e)	Rep.
107(d)(2)	548(a)
107(d)(3)	550
107(d)(4)	548(b)
107(d)(5)	548(d)(1)
107(d)(6)	548(c), 550, 551
107(d)(7)	Rep.
107(e), (f)	Rep.
108	502(b)(3), 553
109(a)	303(e)
109(b)	303(i)
109(c)	Rep.
109(d)	303(g), 543(b), (c)
110(a)	541(a)
110(a)(3)	541(b)
110(a)(5)	522(d)(7), (8)
110(b)	365
110(c)	541(e), 544(a)
110(d)(1)	549(a)
110(d)(2), (3)	542(c)
110(d)(4), (5)	Rep.
110(e)	544(b)
110(f)	363
110(g)–(i)	Rep.
111, 112	Rep.
201, 202	(See former 501–1103)
202a–204	Rep.
205(a)	Rep.
205(b)	1171(b), 1172
205(c)(1)	1163
205(c)(2)	1166
205(c)(3)–(5)	Rep.
205(c)(6)	1169
205(c)(7)–(13)	Rep.
205(d)	Rep.
205(e)	1173
205(f)–(i)	Rep.
205(j)	1168
205(k), (*l*)	Rep.
205(m)	101(33)
205(n)	1167, 1171(a)
205(*o*)	1170
205(p)–(s)	Rep.
205a	Rep.
206, 207	(See former 501–1103)
208	Rep.
301–303	Rep.
401(1)	101(4)
401(2)	Rep.
401(3)	101(9)
401(4)	Rep.
401(5)	101(11)
401(6)	101(28)
401(7)	101(30)
401(8)	101(12)
401(9)	Rep.
401(10)	902(2)
401(11)	903(3)
402(a)	Rep.
402(b)(1), (2)	901
402(b)(3)	Rep.
402(c)	904
402(d)	921(b)
403	903
404	101(29), 109(c)
405(a)	921(a), (c)–(f)
405(b)	901, 924
405(c)	Rep.
405(d)	923
405(e)	901
405(e)(1)	922(a)
405(f), (g)	Rep.
405(h)	901, 926
406, 407	Rep.
408(a)	925
408(b)	901
408(c)	Rep.
409	901
410(a)	941, 942
410(b)	942
411, 412	901
413	901, 943(a)
414(a)	901
414(b)(1)	943(b)(5), (6)
414(b)(2)	943(b)(2)
414(b)(3)	Rep.
414(b)(4)	943(b)(3)
414(b)(5)	Rep.
414(b)(6)	943(b)(4)
415(a)	944(a)
415(b)(1)	944(b)
415(b)(2)	944(c)
416(a)	Rep.
416(b)	901
416(c)	Rep.
416(d)	347(b), 901
416(e)	945(a)
416(f)	Rep.
417	946
418	927
501, 502	Rep.
506(1)	101(4)
506(2), (3)	Rep.
506(4)	101(9)
506(5)	101(12)
506(6)	101(11)
506(7)	Rep.
506(8)	101(23)
506(9)	101(31)
506(10)	Rep.
506(11)	101(35)
506(12), (13)	Rep.
507	1124

Title 11 Former Sections	*Title 11 New Sections*
511, 512	Rep.
513	362
514, 515	Rep.
516(1)	365
516(2)	364
516(3)	363
516(4)	362
516(5), (6)	1110
517–521	Rep.
526	303(b)
527	Rep.
528	Omitted
529–533	Rep.
536, 537	303(d)
541–549	Rep.
556	1104(a)
557	327
558	101(13)
559	1105
560	324, 1104(c)
561, 562	Rep.
563	1107(a)
564	1106(a)(2)
565	Rep.
566	107
567(1)	1106(a)(3)
567(2)	Rep.
567(3)	1106(a)(4)(A)
567(4)	Rep.
567(5)	1106(a)(4)
567(6)	Rep.
568	1104(b), 1106(b)
569	1106(a)(5)
570	1121
571–574	Rep.
575	1125(d)
576	1125(b)
577, 578	Rep.
579	1126, 1128(a)
580	1128(b)
586	541(a)
587	1106
588	1107(a)
589	1108
590	Rep.
591	327
596	501(a), 1111
597	1122
598	501(a)
599	1126(a)
600, 601	Rep.
602	502(b)(7)
603	1126(e)
604	1143
605	347(b)
606	1109(b)
607	1109
608	1109(a)
609–613	Rep.
616(1)	1123(b)(1)
616(2)	1123(a)(5), (b)(4)
616(3)	Rep.
616(4)	1123(b)(2)
616(5)	1123(a)(3)
616(6)	1123(a)(2)
616(7)–(9)	Rep.
616(10)	1123(a)(5)
616(11)	1123(a)(7)
616(12)(a)	1123(a)(6)
616(12)(b)	Rep.
616(13)	1123(b)(3)
616(14)	1123(b)(5)
621(1)	1129(a)(1)
621(2)	1129(a)(7), (11)
621(3)	1129(a)(3)
621(4)	1129(a)(4)
621(5)	1129(a)(5)
622	1127
623	1127(d)
624(1)	1141(a)
624(2)	1129(a)(6), 1142(a)
624(3), (4)	Rep.
625	Rep.
626	1141(c)
627	1142(b)
628(1)	1141(d)(1)–(3)
628(2)–(4)	Rep.
629(a)	1101(2)
629(b)	Rep.
629(c)	1127(b)
636	1112(b)
637	Rep.
638	348
641(1), (2)	Rep.
641(3), (4)	330
641(5)	503(b)(4)
642(1)	503(b)(3), (5)
642(2)	Rep.
642(3)	503(b)(4)
643	503(b)(3), (4)
644(1)	330
644(2)	503(b)(4)
644(3)	330
644(4)	503(b)(3), (4)
645–650	Rep.
656–659	Rep.
661	108(c)
662	Rep.
663	362
664(a)	1145(a)
664(b)	1145(b)
665, 666	Rep.
667	1146(c)
668	346(j)(1)
669	1129(d)
670	346(j)(5)
671, 672	Rep.
676	Rep.
701, 702	Rep.
706(1), (2)	Rep.
706(3)	101(12), 109(d)
706(4)	Rep.
706(5)	101(31)
707(1)	101(9)

Title 11 Former Sections	Title 11 New Sections
707(2)	101(4), (11)
708	1124
711, 712	Rep.
713(1)	365
713(2)	363
713(3)	Rep.
714	362
715, 716	Rep.
721–728	Rep.
731–733	Rep.
734	341
735	341
735(3)	1128(a)
736	341
736(2)	501(a)
736(3)	343
737(1)	Rep.
737(2)	1129(a)(9)
737(3)	1128(a)
738	1102
739(1)(a)	1103(c)(2)
739(1)(b)–(e)	1103(c)(3)
739(1)(f)	1104(c)(5)
739(2)	503(b)(4), 1103(a)
741	Rep.
742	1107(a)
743	1108
744	364
751	1122
752	Rep.
753	502(b)(7)
754, 755	Rep.
755a	501(a)
756	Rep.
757(1)	Rep.
757(2)	1123(b)(2)
757(3)–(7)	Rep.
757(8)	1123(b)(5)
761	1129(a)(3)
762	Rep.
763	1127
764	1127(d)
765	1127(c)
766(1)	1129(a)(1)
766(2)	1129(a)(7), (11)
766(3)	1129(a)(2)
766(4)	1129(a)(3)
767(1)	1141(a)
767(2)–(4)	Rep.
768–770	Rep.
771	1141(d)(1)–(3)
772	Rep.
776, 777	1112(b)
778	348
779–781	Rep.
786	1144
787(1)	1127(b)
787(2)	1127(c)
787(3)	1127(d)
787(4)	Rep.
791	108(c)
792	Rep.
793(a)	1145(a)
793(b)	1145(b)
794	Rep.
795	346(j)(1)
796	346(j)(5)
797	Rep.
799	Rep.
801, 802	Rep.
806(1)	Rep.
806(2)	101(4)
806(3), (4)	Rep.
806(5)	101(9)
806(6)	101(12), 109(d)
806(7)	101(11)
806(8)	101(23)
806(9)	101(31)
807	1124
811, 812	Rep.
813(1)	365
813(2)	363
813(3)	Rep.
814	362
815, 816	Rep.
821–827	Rep.
828	362
831	Rep.
832	1104(a)
833	Rep.
834	341
835	341, 1128(a)
836	341
836(2)	501(a)
836(3)	343
837(1)	1104(a)
837(2)	Rep.
837(3)	1128(a)
841	Rep.
842	1106
843	348
844	1107(a)
845	1108
846	364
851	501(a), 1111
852	1122
853	Rep.
854	501(a)
855–857	Rep.
858	502(b)(7)
859	Rep.
861(1)–(3)	Rep.
861(4)	1123(b)(2)
861(5), (6)	Rep.
861(7)	1123(b)(4)
861(8)	Rep.
861(9)	1123(a)(3)
861(10)	1123(a)(2)
861(11)	Rep.
861(12)	1123(a)(5)
861(13)	1123(b)(5)
866	Rep.
867	1129(a)(3)
868	Rep.

Title 11 Former Sections	Title 11 New Sections
869	1127(a), (b)
870	1127(d)
871	1127(c)
872(1)	1129(a)(1)
872(2)	1129(a)(7), (11)
872(3)	1129(a)(2)
872(4)	1129(a)(3)
872(5)	1129(a)(4)
873(1)	1141(a)
873(2)	1142(a)
873(3)	Rep.
874	1141(c)
875	1142(b)
876	1141(d)(1)–(3)
877	Rep.
881, 882	1112(b)
883	348
884–886	Rep.
891(1)	Rep.
891(2), (3)	330
892(1)	503(b)(3)
892(2)	Rep.
892(3)	503(b)(4)
893(1)	Rep.
893(2)	503(b)(4)
893(3)	330
893(4)	503(b)(4)
894–898	Rep.
906–909	Rep.
911	1144
916	108(c)
917	362
918(a)	1145(a)
918(b)	1145(b)
919	Rep.
920	346(j)(1)
921	1129(d)
922	346(j)(5)
923	Rep.
926	Rep.
1001, 1002	Rep.
1006(1)	101(4)
1006(2)	101(9)
1006(3)	101(12), 109(e)
1006(4)	101(11)
1006(5)	Rep.
1006(6)	101(31)
1006(7)	Rep.
1006(8)	101(24), 109(e)
1007	Rep.
1011, 1012	Rep.
1013(1)	365
1013(2)	Rep.
1014	362
1015, 1016	Rep.
1021–1026	Rep.
1031	Rep.
1032, 1033	341
1033(1)	343, 501(a)
1033(2)	1321
1033(5)	1324
1036	1303
1037	Rep.
1041–1044	Rep.
1046(1)	1322(b)(1)
1046(2)	1322(b)(2)
1046(3)	1322(a)(2)
1046(4)	1322(a)(1)
1046(5)	1329(a)
1046(6)	1322(b)(7)
1046(7)	1322(b)(10)
1051	1325(a)(3)
1052	Rep.
1053	1323(a)
1054	1323(c)
1055	Rep.
1056(a)(1)	1325(a)(1)
1056(a)(2)	1325(a)(6)
1056(a)(3)	Rep.
1056(a)(4)	1325(a)(3)
1056(b)	502(b)
1057	1327(a)
1058	Rep.
1059	1326(a)
1060	1328(a), (c), (d)
1061	1328(b)
1062	Rep.
1066	348, 1307
1067	348
1068, 1069	Rep.
1071	1330
1076	108(c)
1077–1079	Rep.
1080	1305(a)(1)
1086	Rep.
1101–1103	Rep.
1200–1255	Rep.

TABLE II

This Table lists the sections of revised Title 11, Bankruptcy, and indicates the sections of former Title 11, which covered similar and related subject matter.

Title 11 New Sections	Title 11 Former Sections
101(1)–(3)	
101(4)	103, 401(1), 506(1), 707(2), 806(2), 1006(1)
101(5)–(7)	
101(8)	1(8)
101(9)	1(11), 401(3), 506(4), 707(1), 806(5), 1062(2)
101(10)	
101(11)	1(14), 401(5), 506(6), 707(2), 806(7), 1006(4)
101(12)	1(4), 401(8), 506(5), 706(3), 806(6), 1006(3)
101(13)	553
101(14)–(16)	
101(17), (18)	1(17)
101(19)–(21)	
101(22)	T. 15 § 77ccc(7)

Title 11 New Sections	Title 11 Former Sections
101(23)	506(8), 806(8)
101(24)	1(32), 1006(8)
101(25)	
101(26)	1(19), 107(d)(1)(d)
101(27)	
101(28)	401(6)
101(29)	404
101(30)	1(23), 401(7)
101(31)	1(24), 506(9), 706(5), 806(9), 1006(6)
101(32)	
101(33)	205(m)
101(34)	1(27)
101(35)	506(11)
101(36), (37)	
101(38)	1(29a)
101(39)	T. 15 § 78c(a)(4), (5)
101(40)	1(30)
102(1)–(6)	
102(7)	1(35)
102(8)	
103, 104	
105	11(a)(15)
106	
107	77, 566
108(a), (b)	29(e)
108(c)	29(f), 661, 791, 1076
109(a)	11(a)(1)
109(b)	22
109(c)	404
109(d)	706(3), 806(6)
109(e)	1006(3), (8)
301	22(a), 41(f), 95(a)
302	
303(a)	22(b)
303(b)	23(b), 95(b), (e), 526
303(c)	95(f)
303(d)	41(b), 536, 537
303(e)	109(a)
303(f)	
303(g)	109(d)
303(h)	21
303(i)	11(a)(18), 19(b)
303(j)	95(g)
303(k)	
304	
305(a)(1)	
305(a)(2)	11(a)(22)
305(b), (c)	
306	
321	73
322(a)	78(b)
322(b)(1)	78(c)
322(b)(2)	78(d), (f), (g)
322(c)	78(i)
322(d)	78(m)
323	
324	11(a)(17), 560
325	74
326(a)	76(c)
326(b), (c)	
326(d)	76(e)

Title 11 New Sections	Title 11 Former Sections
327	557, 591
327(c)	72(c)
328	
329	96(d)
330	76(c), 76a, 641(3), (4), 644(1), (3), 891(2), (3), 893(3)
331	
341	91, 92, 734–736, 834–836, 1032, 1033
342	94
343	44(a), 25(a)(1), (10), 736(3), 836(3), 1033(1)
344	25(a)(10)
345	101, 75(a)(2)
346(a)–(i)	
346(j)(1)	668, 795, 920
346(j)(2)–(4)	
346(j)(5)	670, 796, 922
346(j)(6), (7)	
347(a)	106(a)
347(b)	416(d), 605
348	638, 778, 843, 1066, 1067
349(a)	35(b)
349(b)	107(a)
350	11(a)(8)
361	
362	29(a), 35(c)(4), 513, 516(4), 663, 714, 814, 828, 917, 1014
363	11(a)(7), 110(f), 516(3), 713(2), 813(2)
364	516(2), 744, 846
365	103(c), 110(b), 516(1), 713(1), 813(1), 1013(1)
366	
501(a)	93(n), 596, 598, 736(2), 755a, 836(2), 851, 854, 1033(1)
501(b)	93(i)
501(c), (d)	
502(a)	93(d)
502(b)	93(f), 1056(b)
502(b)(3)	108
502(b)(4)	104(a)(4)
502(b)(7)	103(a)(9), 602, 753, 858
502(c)	93(d)
502(d)	93(g)
502(e)–(i)	
502(j)	93(k), 11(a)(2)
503(a)	
503(b)	104(a)(1)
503(b)(2)	102(a)(1)
503(b)(3)	642(1), 643, 644(4), 892(1)
503(b)(4)	641(5), 642(3), 643, 644(2), (4), 739(2), 892(3), 893(2), (4)
503(b)(5)	642(1)
504	102(c)
505(a), (b)	11(a)(2A), 104(a)(4)
505(c)	
506(a), (b)	93(h)
506(c), (d)	
507	104(a)
507(a)(3)	104(a)(2)
508	105(d)

Title 11 New Sections	Title 11 Former Sections
509	93(i)
510	
521(1)	25(a)(8), (9)
521(2)	25(a)(3), (6), (7)
521(3)	25(a)(4), (5), (11)
521(4)	25(a)(1)
522	24
523(a)(1)	35(a)(1)
523(a)(2)	35(a)(2)
523(a)(3)	35(a)(3)
523(a)(4)	35(a)(4)
523(a)(5)	35(a)(7)
523(a)(6)	35(a)(8)
523(a)(7)–(9)	
523(b)	35(b)
523(c)	35(c)
523(d)	
524(a)	32(f)
524(b)–(d)	
524(e)	34
525	
541(a)	26, 110(a), 586
541(b)	110(a)(3)
541(c), (d)	
541(e)	110(c)
542(a), (b)	
542(c)	110(d)(2), (3)
542(d), (e)	
543(a)	
543(b), (c)	11(a)(21), 109(d)
543(d)	
544(a)	110(c)
544(b)	110(e)
545	107(b), (c)
545(1)	107(c)(1)(A)
545(2)	107(c)(1)(B)
545(3), (4)	107(c)(1)(C)
546(a)	
546(b)	107(c)(1)(B)
546(c)	
547	96
547(b)	107(a)
547(c)(4)	96(c)
547(d)	107(a)
547(e)(1)(B)	96(a)(4)
548(a)	107(d)(2)
548(b)	107(d)(4)
548(c)	107(d)(6)
548(d)(1)	107(d)(5)
548(d)(2)	
549(a)	110(d)(1)
549(b)	
549(c)	44(g)
549(d)	
550	96(b), 107(d)(3), (6)
551	96(b), 107(a)(3), (c)(2), (d)(6), 110(e)(2)
552	
553	96(c), 108
554	
701	
702	72(a)
703(a)	74
703(b), (c)	
704(1)	75(a)(1)
704(2)	75(a)(3), (5)
704(3)	75(a)(7)
704(4)	75(a)(8)
704(5)	75(a)(9)
704(6)	75(a)(10)
704(7)	
704(8)	75(a)(13)
705	72(b)
706	
707	95(g)
721	11(a)(5)
722	
723	23(g)
724(a)	93(j)
724(b)	107(c)(3)
724(c), (d)	
725	
726(a)(1), (2)	
726(a)(3)	93(n)
726(a)(4)–(6), (b), (c)	
727(a)(1)	
727(a)(2)	32(c)(1), (4)
727(a)(3)	32(c)(2)
727(a)(4)	32(c)(1), (3)
727(a)(5)	32(c)(7)
727(a)(6)	32(c)(6)
727(a)(7)	
727(a)(8), (9)	32(c)(5)
727(a)(10)	32(a)
727(b)	
727(c)	32(b)
727(d), (e)	33
728	
741	96(e)(1)
742–744	
745	96(e)(2)
746–748	
749	96(e)(5)
750	
751	96(e)(2)
752	96(e)(2), (3)
761–766	
901	402(b)(1), (2), 405(b), (e), (h), 408(b), 409, 411, 412, 413, 414(a), 416(b), (d)
902(1)	
902(2)	401(10)
902(3)	401(11)
902(4)	
903	403
904	402(c)
921(a)	405(a)
921(b)	402(d)
921(c)–(f)	405(a)
922(a)	405(e)(1)
922(b)	
923	405(d)
924	405(b)
925	408(a)

Title 11 New Sections	Title 11 Former Sections
926	405(h)
927	418
941	410(a)
942	410(a), (b)
943(a)	413
943(b)(1)	
943(b)(2)	414(b)(2)
943(b)(3)	414(b)(4)
943(b)(4)	414(b)(6)
943(b)(5), (6)	414(b)(1)
944(a)	415(a)
944(b)	415(b)(1)
944(c)	415(b)(2)
945(a)	416(e)
945(b)	
946	417
1101(1)	
1101(2)	629(a)
1102	738
1103(a)	739(2)
1103(b), (c)(1)	
1103(c)(2)	739(1)(a)
1103(c)(3)	739(1)(b)–(e)
1103(c)(4)	
1103(c)(5)	739(1)(f)
1103(d)	
1104(a)	556, 832, 837(1)
1104(b)	568
1104(c)	560
1105	559
1106	587, 842
1106(a)(2)	564
1106(a)(3)	567(1)
1106(a)(4)	567(5)
1106(a)(4)(A)	567(3)
1106(a)(5)	569
1106(b)	568
1107(a)	563, 588, 742, 844
1107(b)	
1108	589, 743, 845
1109	607
1109(a)	608
1109(b)	606
1110	516(5), (6)
1111	596, 851
1112(a)	
1112(b)	636, 776, 777, 881, 882
1112(c)–(e)	
1121	570
1122	597, 751, 852
1123(a)(1)	
1123(a)(2)	616(6), 861(10)
1123(a)(3)	616(5), 861(9)
1123(a)(4)	
1123(a)(5)	616(2), (10), 861(12)
1123(a)(6)	616(12)(a)
1123(a)(7)	616(11)
1123(b)(1)	616(1)
1123(b)(2)	616(4), 757(2), 861(4)
1123(b)(3)	616(13)
1123(b)(4)	616(2), 861(7)
1123(b)(5)	616(14), 757(8), 861(13)

Title 11 New Sections	Title 11 Former Sections
1123(c)	
1124	507, 708, 807
1125(a)	
1125(b)	576
1125(c)	
1125(d)	575
1125(e)	
1126	579
1126(a)	599
1126(e)	603
1127	622, 763
1127(a)	869
1127(b)	629(c), 787(1), 869
1127(c)	765, 787(2), (3), 871
1127(d)	623, 764, 870
1128(a)	579, 735(3), 737(3), 835, 837(3)
1128(b)	580
1129(a)(1)	621(1), 766(1), 872(1)
1129(a)(2)	766(3), 872(3)
1129(a)(3)	621(3), 761, 766(4), 867, 872(4)
1129(a)(4)	621(4), 872(5)
1129(a)(5)	621(5)
1129(a)(6)	624(2)
1129(a)(7)	621(2), 766(2), 872(2)
1129(a)(8)	
1129(a)(9)	737(2)
1129(a)(10)	
1129(a)(11)	621(2), 766(2), 872(2)
1129(b), (c)	
1129(d)	669, 921
1141(a)	624(1), 767(1), 873(1)
1141(b)	
1141(c)	626, 874
1141(d)(1)–(3)	628(1), 771, 876
1141(d)(4)	32(a)
1142(a)	624(2), 873(2)
1142(b)	627, 875
1143	604
1144	786, 911
1145(a)	664(a), 793(a), 918(a)
1145(b)	664(b), 793(b), 918(b)
1145(c), (d)	
1146(a), (b)	
1146(c)	667
1146(d)	
1161, 1162	
1163	205(c)(1)
1164, 1165	
1166	205(c)(2)
1167	205(n)
1168	205(j)
1169	205(c)(6)
1170	205(*o*)
1171(a)	205(n)
1171(b)	205(b)
1172	205(b)
1173	205(e)
1174	
1301, 1302	
1303	1036
1304	
1305(a)(1)	1080

Title 11 New Sections	*Title 11 Former Sections*
1305(a)(2), (b), (c)	
1306	
1307	1066
1321	1033(2)
1322(a)(1)	1046(4)
1322(a)(2)	1046(3)
1322(a)(3)	
1322(b)(1)	1046(1)
1322(b)(2)	1046(2)
1322(b)(3)–(6)	
1322(b)(7)	1046(6)
1322(b)(8), (9)	
1322(b)(10)	1046(7)
1322(c)	
1323(a)	1053
1323(b)	
1323(c)	1054
1324	1033(5)
1325(a)(1)	1056(a)(1)
1325(a)(2)	
1325(a)(3)	1051, 1056(a)(4)
1325(a)(4), (5)	
1325(a)(6)	1056(a)(2)
1325(b)	
1326(a)	1059
1326(b)	
1327(a)	1057
1327(b), (c)	
1328(a)	1060
1328(b)	1061
1328(c), (d)	1060
1328(e)	33
1329(a)	1046(5)
1329(b), (c)	
1330	1071
1501–151326	

HISTORICAL AND STATUTORY NOTES

Enacting Clause

Pub.L. 95–598, Title I, § 101, Nov. 6, 1978, 92 Stat. 2549, provided in part: "The law relating to bankruptcy is codified and enacted as title 11 of the United States Code, entitled 'Bankruptcy', and may be cited as 11 U.S.C. § ___."

Effective and Applicability Provisions

2005 Acts. Amendments by Pub.L. 109–8 effective, except as otherwise provided, 180 days after April 20, 2005, and inapplicable with respect to cases commenced under Title 11 before the effective date, see Pub.L. 109–8, § 1501, set out as a note under 11 U.S.C.A. § 101.

1994 Acts. Amendment by Pub.L. 103–394 effective on Oct. 22, 1994, and not to apply with respect to cases commenced under Title 11 of the United States Code before Oct. 22, 1994, see section 702 of Pub.L. 103–394, set out as a note under section 101 of this title.

1978 Acts. Pub.L. 95–598, Title IV, § 402, Nov. 6, 1978, 92 Stat. 2682, as amended by Pub.L. 98–249, § 1(a), Mar. 31, 1984, 98 Stat. 116; Pub.L. 98–271, § 1(a), Apr. 30, 1984, 98 Stat. 163; Pub.L. 98–299, § 1(a), May 25, 1984, 98 Stat. 214; Pub.L. 98–325, § 1(a), June 20, 1984, 98 Stat. 268; Pub.L. 98–353, Title I, §§ 113, 121(a), July 10, 1984, 98 Stat. 343, 345; Pub.L. 98–454, Title X, § 1001, Oct. 5, 1984, 98 Stat. 1745, provided that:

"**(a)** Except as otherwise provided in this title [sections 401 to 411 of Pub.L. 95–598, this Act [see Tables for classification] shall take effect on October 1, 1979.

"**(b)** Except as provided in subsections (c) and (d) of this section, the amendments made by title II of this Act [sections 201 to 252 of Pub.L. 95–598] shall not be effective.

"**(c)** The amendments made by sections 210, 214, 219, 220, 222, 224, 225, 228, 229, 235, 244, 245, 246, 249, and 251 of this Act shall take effect on October 1, 1979.

"**(d)** The amendments made by sections 217, 218, 230, 247, 302, 314(j), 317, 327, 328, 338, and 411 of this Act shall take effect on the date of enactment of this Act [Nov. 6, 1978]."

[**(e)** Repealed. Pub.L. 98–454, Title X, § 1001, Oct. 5, 1984, 98 Stat. 1745.]

[Section 121(a) of Pub.L. 98–353 purported to amend section 402(b) of Pub.L. 95–598 by substituting "the date of enactment of the Bankruptcy Amendments and Federal Judgeship Act of 1984 [i.e. July 10, 1984]" for "June 28, 1984". This amendment was not executed as the probable intent of Congress in view of the prior amendment to section 402(b) of Pub.L. 95–598 by section 113 of Pub.L. 98–353.]

[Amendment of section 402(b) of Pub.L. 95–598 by section 113 of Pub.L. 98–353 effective June 27, 1984, see section 122(c) of Pub.L. 98–353, set out as an Effective Date note under section 151 of Title 28, Judiciary and Judicial Procedure.]

Repeals

Pub.L. 95–598, Title IV, § 401(a), Nov. 6, 1978, 92 Stat. 2682, provided that: "The Bankruptcy Act [Act July 1, 1898, c. 541, 30 Stat. 544, as amended] is repealed."

Savings Provisions

Pub.L. 95–598, Title IV, § 403, Nov. 6, 1978, 92 Stat. 2683, as amended by Pub.L. 98–353, Title III, § 382, July 10, 1984, 98 Stat. 364, provided that:

"**(a)** A case commenced under the Bankruptcy Act [Act July 1, 1898, c. 541, 30 Stat. 544, as amended], and all matters and proceedings in or relating to any such case, shall be conducted and determined under such Act as if this Act had not been enacted, and the substantive rights of parties in connection with any such bankruptcy case, matter, or proceeding shall continue to be governed by the law applicable to such case, matter, or proceeding as if the [this] Act had not been enacted.

"**(b)** Notwithstanding subsection (a) of this section, sections 1165, 1167, 1168, 1169, and 1171 of title 11 of the United States Code, as enacted by section 101 of this Act, apply to cases pending under section 77 of the Bankruptcy Act ([former] 11 U.S.C. 205) on the date of enactment of this Act [Nov. 6, 1978] in which the trustee has not filed a plan of reorganization.

"**(c)** The repeal made by section 401(a) of this Act [repealing the Bankruptcy Act does not affect any right of a referee in bankruptcy, United States bankruptcy judge, or survivor of a referee in bankruptcy or United States bankruptcy judge to receive any annuity or other payment under the civil service retirement laws.

"**(d)** The amendments made by section 314 of this Act [see Tables] do not affect the application of chapter 9, chapter 96, section 2516, section 3057, or section 3284 of title 18 of the United States Code to any act of any person—

"(1) committed before October 1, 1979; or

"(2) committed after October 1, 1979, in connection with a case commenced before such date.

"(e) Notwithstanding subsection (a) of this section—

"(1) a fee may not be charged under section 40c(2)(a) of the Bankruptcy Act [former 11 U.S.C.A. § 68(c)(2)(a)] in a case pending under such Act after September 30, 1979, to the extent that such fee exceeds $200,000;

"(2) a fee may not be charged under section 40c(2)(b) of the Bankruptcy Act in a case in which the plan is confirmed after September 30, 1978, or in which the final determination as to the amount of such fee is made after September 30, 1979, notwithstanding an earlier confirmation date, to the extent that such fee exceeds $100,000;

"(3) after September 30, 1979, all moneys collected for payment into the referees' salary and expense fund in cases filed under the Bankruptcy Act shall be collected and paid into the general fund of the Treasury; and

"(4) any balance in the referees' salary and expense fund in the Treasury on October 1, 1979, shall be transferred to the general fund of the Treasury and the referees' salary and expense fund account shall be closed."

Pub.L. 98–353, Title III, § 381, July 10, 1984, 98 Stat. 364, provided that: "This subtitle [§§ 381, 382 of Pub.L. 98–353], [amending subsec. (e) of this note] may be cited as the 'Referees Salary and Expense Fund Act of 1984'."

Separability of Provisions

If any provision of or amendment made by Pub.L. 103–394 or the application of such provision or amendment to any person or circumstance is held to be unconstitutional, the remaining provisions of and amendments made by Pub.L. 103–394 and the application of such provisions and amendments to any person or circumstance shall not be affected thereby, see section 701 of Pub.L. 103–394, set out as a note under section 101 of this title.

Commission on the Bankruptcy Laws of the United States

Pub.L. 91–354, §§ 1–6, July 24, 1970, 84 Stat. 468, as amended by Pub.L. 92–251, Mar. 17, 1972, 86 Stat. 63; Pub.L. 93–56, § 1, July 1, 1973, 87 Stat. 140, established the Commission on the Bankruptcy Laws of the United States, to study and recommend changes to this title, which ceased to exist 30 days after the date of submission of its final report which was required prior to July 31, 1973.

History of Bankruptcy Acts

The bankruptcy laws were revised generally and enacted as Title 11, Bankruptcy, by Pub.L. 96–598, Nov. 6, 1978, 92 Stat. 2549.

Earlier bankruptcy laws included the following Acts:

Apr. 4, 1800, c. 19, 2 Stat. 19, repealed Dec. 19, 1803, ch. 6, 2 Stat. 248.

Aug. 19, 1841, c. 9, 5 Stat. 440, repealed Mar. 3, 1843, ch. 82, 5 Stat. 614.

Mar. 2, 1867, c. 176, 14 Stat. 517, the provisions of which were incorporated in Rev.Stat.Title LXI, §§ 4972 to 5132, were materially amended June 22, 1874, c. 390, 18 Stat. 178, and were repealed June 7, 1878, c. 160, 20 Stat. 99.

The Bankruptcy Act of July 1, 1898, c. 541, 30 Stat. 544, as amended, sometimes called the Nelson Act, repealed by Pub.L. 95–598.

The Chandler Act of July 22, 1938, c. 575, 52 Stat. 883, which revised the Bankruptcy Act generally and materially amended the provisions covering corporate reorganizations, repealed by Pub.L. 95–598.

National Bankruptcy Review Commission

Pub.L. 103–394, Title VI, Oct. 22, 1994, 108 Stat. 4147, provided that:

"Sec. 601. Short title.

"This title [this note] may be cited as the 'National Bankruptcy Review Commission Act'.

"Sec. 602. Establishment.

"There is established the National Bankruptcy Review Commission (referred to as the 'Commission').

"Sec. 603. Duties of the Commission.

"The duties of the Commission are—

"(1) to investigate and study issues and problems relating to title 11, United States Code (commonly known as the 'Bankruptcy Code');

"(2) to evaluate the advisability of proposals and current arrangements with respect to such issues and problems;

"(3) to prepare and submit to the Congress, the Chief Justice, and the President a report in accordance with section 608; and

"(4) to solicit divergent views of all parties concerned with the operation of the bankruptcy system.

"Sec. 604. Membership.

"(a) **Number and appointment.**—The Commission shall be composed of 9 members as follows:

"(1) Three members appointed by the President, 1 of whom shall be designated as chairman by the President.

"(2) One member shall be appointed by the President pro tempore of the Senate.

"(3) One member shall be appointed by the Minority Leader of the Senate.

"(4) One member shall be appointed by the Speaker of the House of Representatives.

"(5) One member shall be appointed by the Minority Leader of the House of Representatives.

"(6) Two members appointed by the Chief Justice.

Members of Congress, and officers and employees of the executive branch, shall be ineligible for appointment to the Commission.

"(b) **Term.**—Members of the Commission shall be appointed for the life of the Commission.

"(c) **Quorum.**—Five members of the Commission shall constitute a quorum, but a lesser number may conduct meetings.

"(d) **Appointment deadline.**—The first appointments made under subsection (a) shall be made within 60 days after the date of enactment of this Act [Oct. 22, 1994].

"(e) **First meeting.**—The first meeting of the Commission shall be called by the chairman and shall be held within 210 days after the date of enactment of this Act [Oct. 22, 1994].

"(f) **Vacancy.**—A vacancy on the Commission resulting from the death or resignation of a member shall not affect its powers and shall be filled in the same manner in which the original appointment was made.

"(g) **Continuation of membership.**—If any member of the Commission who was appointed to the Commission as an officer or employee of a government leaves that office, or if any member of the Commission who was not appointed in such a capacity becomes an officer or employee of a government, the member may continue as a member of the Commission for not longer than the 90–day period beginning on the date the member leaves that office or becomes such an officer or employee, as the case may be.

"(h) **Consultation prior to appointment.**—Prior to the appointment of members of the Commission, the President, the President pro tempore of the Senate, the Speaker of the House of Representatives, and the Chief Justice shall consult with each other to ensure fair and equitable representation of various points of view in the Commission and its staff.

"Sec. 605. Compensation of the Commission.

"(a) **Pay.**—

"(1) **Nongovernment employees.**—Each member of the Commission who is not otherwise employed by the United States Government shall be entitled to receive the daily equivalent of the annual rate of basic pay payable for level IV of the Executive Schedule under section 5315 of title 5, United States Code [section 5315 of Title 5, Government Organization and Employees], for each day (including travel time) during which he or she is engaged in the actual performance of duties as a member of the Commission.

"(2) **Government employees.**—A member of the Commission who is an officer or employee of the United States Government shall serve without additional compensation.

"(b) **Travel.**—Members of the Commission shall be reimbursed for travel, subsistence, and other necessary expenses incurred by them in the performance of their duties.

"Sec. 606. Staff of Commission; experts and consultants.

"(a) **Staff.**—

"(1) **Appointment.**—The chairman of the Commission may, without regard to the civil service laws and regulations, appoint, and terminate an executive director and such other personnel as are necessary to enable the Commission to perform its duties. The employment of an executive director shall be subject to confirmation by the Commission.

"(2) **Compensation.**—The chairman of the Commission may fix the compensation of the executive director and other personnel without regard to the provisions of chapter 51 and subchapter II of chapter 53 of title 5, United States Code [sections 5101 et seq. and 5311 et seq. of Title 5], relating to classification of positions and General Schedule pay rates, except that the rate of pay for the executive director and other personnel may not exceed the rate payable for level V of the Executive Schedule under section 5316 of that title [section 5316 of Title 5].

"(b) **Experts and consultants.**—The Commission may procure temporary and intermittent services of experts and consultants under section 3109(b) of title 5, United States Code [section 3109(b) of Title 5].

"Sec. 607. Powers of the Commission.

"(a) **Hearings and meetings.**—The Commission or, on authorization of the Commission, a member of the Commission, may hold such hearings, sit and act at such time and places, take such testimony, and receive such evidence, as the Commission considers appropriate. The Commission or a member of the Commission may administer oaths or affirmations to witnesses appearing before it.

"(b) **Official data.**—The Commission may secure directly from any Federal department, agency, or court information necessary to enable it to carry out this title [this note]. Upon request of the chairman of the Commission, the head of a Federal department or agency or chief judge of a Federal court shall furnish such information, consistent with law, to the Commission.

"(c) **Facilities and support services.**—The Administrator of General Services shall provide to the Commission on a reimbursable basis such facilities and support services as the Commission may request. Upon request of the Commission, the head of a Federal department or agency may make any of the facilities or services of the agency available to the Commission to assist the Commission in carrying out its duties under this title [this note].

"(d) **Expenditures and contracts.**—The Commission or, on authorization of the Commission, a member of the Commission may make expenditures and enter into contracts for the procurement of such supplies, services, and property as the Commission or member considers appropriate for the purposes of carrying out the duties of the Commission. Such expenditures and contracts may be made only to such extent or in such amounts as are provided in appropriation Acts.

"(e) **Mails.**—The Commission may use the United States mails in the same manner and under the same conditions as other Federal departments and agencies of the United States.

"(f) **Gifts.**—The Commission may accept, use, and dispose of gifts or donations of services or property.

"Sec. 608. Report.

"The Commission shall submit to the Congress, the Chief Justice, and the President a report not later than 2 years after the date of its first meeting. The report shall contain a detailed statement of the findings and conclusions of the Commission, together with its recommendations for such legislative or administrative action as it considers appropriate.

"Sec. 609. Termination.

"The Commission shall cease to exist on the date that is 30 days after the date on which it submits its report under section 608.

"Sec. 610. Authorization of appropriations.

"There is authorized to be appropriated $1,500,000 to carry out this title [this note]."

CROSS REFERENCES

Additional information on bankruptcy filings required, see 15 USCA § 1681c.

Amount of unfunded vested benefits allocable to employer withdrawn from pension plan as including uncollectible amounts for reasons arising out of cases or proceedings under this title, see 29 USCA § 1391.

Applicability of provisions of Securities Act of 1933 to certain classes of securities exchanged in cases under this title, see 15 USCA § 77c.

Applicability of rules to bankruptcy proceedings—

Federal Rules of Civil Procedure, see Fed.Rules Civ. Proc. Rule 81, 28 USCA.

Federal Rules of Evidence, see Fed.Rules Evid. Rule 1101, 28 USCA.

Applicability of this title to district court of—

Guam, see 48 USCA § 1424–4.

Northern Mariana Islands, see 48 USCA § 1821.

Virgin Islands, see 48 USCA § 1614.

Applicability to case under this title of provisions relating to special pay to selected reserve health care professionals in critically short wartime specialties, see 37 USCA § 302g.

Approval by Federal Trade Commission of fees, expenses, and remuneration paid in connection with case brought under this title involving public utility holding company, see 15 USCA § 79k.

Assertion of claim against guarantor providing evidence of financial responsibility in cases where owner or operator is in bankruptcy under this title for corrective action relating to—

Hazardous waste treatment, storage and disposal facilities, see 42 USCA § 6924.

Release of hazardous substances from facilities, see 42 USCA § 9608.

Underground storage tanks, see 42 USCA §§ 6991b and 6991c.

Authority of Attorney General to investigate official acts, records and accounts of trustees in cases under this title, see 28 USCA § 526.

Automatic protection of lands conveyed pursuant to Alaska Native Claims Settlement Act provided such lands are not sold to third parties from judgments resulting from claims arising under this title, see 43 USCA § 1636.

"Bankruptcy Act" defined as this title for purposes of Trust Indenture Act of 1939, see 15 USCA § 77ccc.

Benefit accrual requirements and prohibition on increases where plan sponsor is in bankruptcy, see 29 USCA § 1054.

"Bridge owner" as including bridge in possession or under control of trustee in case under this title for purposes of alteration of bridges over navigable waters, see 33 USCA § 511.

Change of venue in cases or proceedings under this title, see 28 USCA § 1412.

"Company" defined as including trustee in case under this title for purposes of—

Subchapter I of Investment Advisers Act of 1940, see 15 USCA § 80a–2.

Subchapter II of Investment Advisers Act of 1940, see 15 USCA § 80b–2.

Compromise, adjustment or cancellation of farm loans upon discharge of indebtedness in proceeding under this title, see 12 USCA § 1150.

Concealment of assets, false oaths or claims, and bribery in cases under this title, see 18 USCA § 152.

Congressional finding of railroad insolvency and reorganization under this title for purposes of enacting Regional Rail Reorganization Act of 1973, see 45 USCA § 701.

Congressional power to establish uniform bankruptcy laws throughout United States, see USCA Const. Art. I § 8, cl. 4.

Coordination of Internal Revenue Code provisions with cases under this title, see 26 USCA § 6658.

Court procedures for cases under this title, see 28 USCA § 157.

Credits against unemployment tax, see 26 USCA § 3302.

"Debtor" defined under this title as having same meaning for purposes of crimes in bankruptcy, see 18 USCA § 151.

Disclosure of confidential tax returns and return information to trustee in cases under this title, see 26 USCA § 6103.

Duties of United States trustees and supervision by Attorney General, see 28 USCA § 586.

Effect of discharge in bankruptcy under this title on discharge of debt arising from—

Advanced educational assistance loan, see 10 USCA § 2005.

Aviation service agreement, see 37 USCA § 301b.

Child support obligation assigned to State, see 42 USCA § 656.

Critical acquisition positions service agreement, see 37 USCA § 317.

Engineering and scientific career service agreement, see 37 USCA § 315.

Enlistment in elements of Ready Reserve, see 37 USCA § 308g.

Health professionals educational assistance, see 38 USCA § 7635.

Indian Health Scholarship, see 25 USCA § 1613a.

Indian health service loan, see 25 USCA § 1616a.

Multiyear retention bonus for medical officers of armed forces, see 37 USCA § 301d.

Nurse officer agreement, see 10 USCA § 2130a.

Prior service enlistment bonus, see 37 USCA § 308i.

Reenlistment, enlistment, or voluntary extension of enlistment in elements of Ready Reserve, see 37 USCA § 308h.

Reserve affiliation agreement, see 37 USCA § 308e.

Special pay for dental officers of armed forces, see 37 USCA §§ 302b, 302h.

Special pay for medical officers of armed forces, see 37 USCA § 302.

Special pay for nurse anesthetists, see 37 USCA § 302e.

Special pay for registered nurses, see 37 USCA § 302d.

Effect of Federal debt collection procedure on this title, see 28 USCA § 3003.

Employee protection benefits available under this title deemed waived upon receipt of assistance by employee under—

Milwaukee Railroad Restructuring Act, see 45 USCA § 912.

Rock Island Railroad Transition and Employee Assistance Act, see 45 USCA § 1007.

Employer Retirement Income new reportable events, see 29 USCA § 1343.

Extension of time for paying tax claims in cases under this title, see 26 USCA § 6161.

Fee agreements in cases under this title, see 18 USCA § 155.

"Filing date" as meaning date on which petition filed under this title for purposes of Securities Investor Protection Act of 1970, see 15 USCA § 78*lll*.

Fraud and consumer issues under this chapter, see 18 USCA § 157.

Immediate assessment for tax deficiencies with respect to certain cases under this title, see 26 USCA § 6871.

Inapplicability of § 421(a) of Title 26 to transfers of stock acquired pursuant to exercise of incentive stock option by debtor in proceeding under this title, see 26 USCA § 422.

Inapplicability to case under this title of provision relating to—

Limitation on net operating loss carry forwards following ownership change for tax purposes, see 26 USCA § 382.

Limitation on pension plan withdrawal liability to employers undergoing reorganization, see 29 USCA § 1405.

Postponement of certain time periods in determining tax liability by reason of service in combat zone, see 26 USCA § 7508.

Priority of government claims, see 31 USCA § 3713.

Transfers to corporation controlled by transferor, see 26 USCA § 351.

Inappropriate transfers included in determining net worth of employer, see 29 USCA § 1362.

Income tax rules relating to individuals' cases under this title, see 26 USCA § 1398.

Inferiority of rights of trustee and other parties under this title to rights of—

Federal Deposit Insurance Corporation as conservator or liquidating agent in connection with avoidance of fraudulent transfers, see 12 USCA § 1821.

National Credit Union Administration Board as conservator or liquidating agent in connection with avoidance of fraudulent transfers, see 12 USCA § 1787.

Insolvency and liquidation of holding companies by trustee pursuant to provisions of this title, see 12 USCA § 1467a.

Interception of wires or oral communications involving fraud under this title, see 18 USCA § 2516.

Intervention by trustee of debtor's estate in case under this title in proceeding before Tax Court to which debtor is party, see 26 USCA § 7464.

Jurisdiction and power of court over Securities Investor Protection Act decrees same as under this title, see 15 USCA § 78eee.

Jurisdiction of district courts in cases under this title, see 28 USCA § 1334.

Jury trials, see 28 USCA § 1411.

Lien of Black Lung Disability Trust Fund treated in same manner as lien for taxes due United States for purposes of this title, see 30 USCA § 934.

Limitations period for concealment of assets of debtor in case under this title begins to run upon final discharge or denial of discharge, see 18 USCA § 3284.

Liquidation proceedings under Securities Investor Protection Act conducted in accordance with chapters 1, 3, and 5 and subchapters I and II of chapter 7 of this title, see 15 USCA § 78fff.

No separate taxable entity resulting from commencement of case under this title, see 26 USCA § 1399.

Nonenforcement of guarantee of legal custody and financial ability for certain aliens when sponsor adjudicated bankrupt under this title, see 8 USCA § 1154.

Notice to creditors of commencement of liquidation proceeding for purposes of Securities Investor Protection Act of 1970 given in manner prescribed by this title, see 15 USCA § 78fff–2.

Notice to Secretary of Treasury of qualification as trustee in case under this title for purposes of Internal Revenue Code, see 26 USCA § 6036.

Original and exclusive jurisdiction of courts under this title over civil actions for adjudication of direct payment procedure for purposes of Securities Investor Protection Act of 1970, see 15 USCA § 78fff–4.

Ownership of copyright, see 17 USCA § 201.

Partition of multiemployer pension plan if reduction in amount of aggregate contributions will result from case or proceeding under this title, see 29 USCA § 1413.

"Person" defined as including trustees in cases under this title for purposes of—

Equal Employment Opportunity Act of 1972, see 42 USCA § 2000e.

Fair housing, see 42 USCA § 3602.

HIV health care services program, see 42 USCA § 300ff–76.

Labor–Management Reporting and Disclosure Act of 1959, see 29 USCA § 402.

National Labor Relations Act, see 29 USCA § 152.

Walsh–Healey provisions, see 41 USCA § 41.

"Personal holding company" for income tax purposes defined as excluding corporation subject to jurisdiction of court in cases under this title, see 26 USCA § 542.

Powers and duties of trustee same as under this title for purposes of Securities Investor Protection Act of 1970, see 15 USCA § 78fff–1.

Priority of—

Claims of United States arising out of any contract authorized by Boulder Canyon Project Act, see 43 USCA § 617p.

Liens for pension plan contribution of employer in cases under this title, see 29 USCA § 1368.

Procedure on default of housing and small business loans, see 38 USCA § 3732.

Prohibition on benefit increases while sponsor is in bankruptcy, see 26 USCA § 401.

Public disclosure of data in connection with bankruptcy proceedings for purposes of Commodity Exchange Act, see 7 USCA § 12.

"Qualifying event" as including proceeding in case under this title for purposes of—

Determination of excise taxes for failure to satisfy continuation coverage requirements of group health plans, see 26 USCA § 4980B.

Providing group health plan continuation coverage under Employee Retirement Income Security Act of 1974, see 29 USCA § 1163.

"Racketeering activity" for purposes of RICO as including any offense involving fraud connected with case under this title, see 18 USCA § 1961.

Reduction in basis of property held by taxpayer by portion of discharge of indebtedness under this title, see 26 USCA § 1017.

Regulations respecting commodity broker debtors notwithstanding provisions of this title, see 7 USCA § 24.

Reimbursements to multiemployer pension plans for payments due from employers uncollectible as result of employer involvement in cases under this title, see 29 USCA § 1402.

Relationship of Regional Rail Reorganization Act of 1973 to this title, see 45 USCA § 791.

"Reorganization" defined as certain transfers by corporation of all or part of its assets to another corporation in case under this title for purposes of income tax provisions relating to corporate organizations and reorganizations, see 26 USCA § 368.

Rules of bankruptcy, power of Supreme Court to prescribe, see 28 USCA § 2075.

Settlement common stock of Alaska native regional corporation not treated as asset under this title, see 43 USCA § 1606.

Suspension of limitations period for assessment and collection of tax, see 26 USCA § 6503.

Suspension of period on tax assessment in cases under this title where notice of qualification of fiduciary required to be given Secretary of Treasury, see 26 USCA § 6872.

Time for filing petition with Tax Court for redetermination of deficiency, see 26 USCA § 6213.

Treatment of income from discharge of indebtedness under this title for purposes of Internal Revenue Code, see 26 USCA § 108.

Trustee in case under this title deemed importer of record of merchandise consigned to insolvent for purposes of customs duties declaration, see 19 USCA § 1485.

Utilization by courts of facilities or services which pertain to parties in cases filed under this title, see 28 USCA § 156.

Venue of—

Cases under this title, see 28 USCA § 1408.

Proceedings arising in or related to cases under this title, see 28 USCA § 1409.

CHAPTER 1—GENERAL PROVISIONS

HISTORICAL AND STATUTORY NOTES

Effective and Applicability Provisions

2005 Acts. Amendments by Pub.L. 109–8 effective, except as otherwise provided, 180 days after April 20, 2005, and inapplicable with respect to cases commenced under Title 11 before the effective date, see Pub.L. 109–8, § 1501, set out as a note under 11 U.S.C.A. § 101.

§ 101. Definitions

In this title the following definitions shall apply:

(1) The term "accountant" means accountant authorized under applicable law to practice public accounting, and includes professional accounting association, corporation, or partnership, if so authorized.

(2) The term "affiliate" means—

(A) entity that directly or indirectly owns, controls, or holds with power to vote, 20 percent or more of the outstanding voting securities of the debtor, other than an entity that holds such securities—

(i) in a fiduciary or agency capacity without sole discretionary power to vote such securities; or

(ii) solely to secure a debt, if such entity has not in fact exercised such power to vote;

(B) corporation 20 percent or more of whose outstanding voting securities are directly or indirectly owned, controlled, or held with power to vote, by the debtor, or by an entity that directly or indirectly owns, controls, or holds with power to vote, 20 percent or more of the outstanding voting securities of the debtor, other than an entity that holds such securities—

(i) in a fiduciary or agency capacity without sole discretionary power to vote such securities; or

(ii) solely to secure a debt, if such entity has not in fact exercised such power to vote;

(C) person whose business is operated under a lease or operating agreement by a debtor, or person substantially all of whose property is operated under an operating agreement with the debtor; or

(D) entity that operates the business or substantially all of the property of the debtor under a lease or operating agreement.

(3) The term "assisted person" means any person whose debts consist primarily of consumer debts and the value of whose nonexempt property is less than $164,250 [1].

(4) The term "attorney" means attorney, professional law association, corporation, or partnership, authorized under applicable law to practice law.

(4A) The term "bankruptcy assistance" means any goods or services sold or otherwise provided to an assisted person with the express or implied purpose of providing information, advice, counsel, document preparation, or filing, or attendance at a creditors' meeting or appearing in a case or proceeding on behalf of another or providing legal representation with respect to a case or proceeding under this title.

(5) The term "claim" means—

(A) right to payment, whether or not such right is reduced to judgment, liquidated, unliquidated, fixed, contingent, matured, unmatured, disputed, undisputed, legal, equitable, secured, or unsecured; or

(B) right to an equitable remedy for breach of performance if such breach gives rise to a right to payment, whether or not such right to an equitable remedy is reduced to judgment, fixed, contingent, matured, unmatured, disputed, undisputed, secured, or unsecured.

(6) The term "commodity broker" means futures commission merchant, foreign futures commission merchant, clearing organization, leverage transaction merchant, or commodity options dealer, as defined in section 761 of this title, with respect to which there is a customer, as defined in section 761 of this title.

(7) The term "community claim" means claim that arose before the commencement of the case concerning the debtor for which property of the kind specified in section 541(a)(2) of this title is liable, whether or not there is any such property at the time of the commencement of the case.

(7A) The term "commercial fishing operation" means—

(A) the catching or harvesting of fish, shrimp, lobsters, urchins, seaweed, shellfish, or other aquatic species or products of such species; or

(B) for purposes of section 109 and chapter 12, aquaculture activities consisting of raising for market any species or product described in subparagraph (A).

(7B) The term "commercial fishing vessel" means a vessel used by a family fisherman to carry out a commercial fishing operation.

(8) The term "consumer debt" means debt incurred by an individual primarily for a personal, family, or household purpose.

(9) The term "corporation"—

(A) includes—

(i) association having a power or privilege that a private corporation, but not an individual or a partnership, possesses;

(ii) partnership association organized under a law that makes only the capital subscribed responsible for the debts of such association;

(iii) joint-stock company;

(iv) unincorporated company or association; or

(v) business trust; but

(B) does not include limited partnership.

(10) The term "creditor" means—

(A) entity that has a claim against the debtor that arose at the time of or before the order for relief concerning the debtor;

(B) entity that has a claim against the estate of a kind specified in section 348(d), 502(f), 502(g), 502(h) or 502(i) of this title; or

(C) entity that has a community claim.

(10A) The term "current monthly income"—

(A) means the average monthly income from all sources that the debtor receives (or in a joint case the debtor and the debtor's spouse receive) without regard to whether such income is taxable income, derived during the 6-month period ending on—

(i) the last day of the calendar month immediately preceding the date of the commencement of the case if the debtor files the schedule of current income required by section 521(a)(1)(B)(ii); or

(ii) the date on which current income is determined by the court for purposes of this title if the debtor does not file the schedule of current income required by section 521(a)(1)(B)(ii); and

(B) includes any amount paid by any entity other than the debtor (or in a joint case the debtor and the debtor's spouse), on a regular basis for the household expenses of the debtor or the debtor's dependents (and in a joint case the debtor's spouse if not otherwise a dependent), but excludes benefits received under the Social Security Act, payments to victims of war crimes or crimes against humanity on account of their status as victims of such crimes, and payments to victims of international terrorism (as defined in section 2331 of title 18) or domestic terrorism (as defined in section 2331 of title 18) on account of their status as victims of such terrorism.

(11) The term "custodian" means—

(A) receiver or trustee of any of the property of the debtor, appointed in a case or proceeding not under this title;

(B) assignee under a general assignment for the benefit of the debtor's creditors; or

(C) trustee, receiver, or agent under applicable law, or under a contract, that is appointed or authorized to take charge of property of the debtor for the purpose of enforcing a lien against such property, or for the purpose of general administration of such property for the benefit of the debtor's creditors.

(12) The term "debt" means liability on a claim.

(12A) The term "debt relief agency" means any person who provides any bankruptcy assistance to an assisted person in return for the payment of money or other valuable consideration, or who is a bankruptcy petition preparer under section 110, but does not include—

(A) any person who is an officer, director, employee, or agent of a person who provides such assistance or of the bankruptcy petition preparer;

(B) a nonprofit organization that is exempt from taxation under section 501(c)(3) of the Internal Revenue Code of 1986;

(C) a creditor of such assisted person, to the extent that the creditor is assisting such assisted person to restructure any debt owed by such assisted person to the creditor;

(D) a depository institution (as defined in section 3 of the Federal Deposit Insurance Act) or any Federal credit union or State credit union (as those terms are defined in section 101 of the Federal Credit Union Act), or any affiliate or subsidiary of such depository institution or credit union; or

(E) an author, publisher, distributor, or seller of works subject to copyright protection under title 17, when acting in such capacity.

(13) The term "debtor" means person or municipality concerning which a case under this title has been commenced.

(13A) The term "debtor's principal residence"—

(A) means a residential structure, including incidental property, without regard to whether that structure is attached to real property; and

(B) includes an individual condominium or cooperative unit, a mobile or manufactured home, or trailer.

(14) The term "disinterested person" means a person that—

(A) is not a creditor, an equity security holder, or an insider;

(B) is not and was not, within 2 years before the date of the filing of the petition, a director, officer, or employee of the debtor; and

(C) does not have an interest materially adverse to the interest of the estate or of any class of creditors or equity security holders, by reason of any direct or indirect relationship to, connection with, or interest in, the debtor, or for any other reason.

(14A) The term "domestic support obligation" means a debt that accrues before, on, or after the date of the order for relief in a case under this title, including interest that accrues on that debt as provided under applicable nonbankruptcy law notwithstanding any other provision of this title, that is—

(A) owed to or recoverable by—

(i) a spouse, former spouse, or child of the debtor or such child's parent, legal guardian, or responsible relative; or

(ii) a governmental unit;

(B) in the nature of alimony, maintenance, or support (including assistance provided by a governmental unit) of such spouse, former spouse, or child of the debtor or such child's parent, without regard to whether such debt is expressly so designated;

(C) established or subject to establishment before, on, or after the date of the order for relief in a case under this title, by reason of applicable provisions of—

(i) a separation agreement, divorce decree, or property settlement agreement;

(ii) an order of a court of record; or

(iii) a determination made in accordance with applicable nonbankruptcy law by a governmental unit; and

(D) not assigned to a nongovernmental entity, unless that obligation is assigned voluntarily by the spouse, former spouse, child of the debtor, or such child's parent, legal guardian, or responsible relative for the purpose of collecting the debt.

(15) The term "entity" includes person, estate, trust, governmental unit, and United States trustee.

(16) The term "equity security" means—

(A) share in a corporation, whether or not transferable or denominated "stock", or similar security;

(B) interest of a limited partner in a limited partnership; or

(C) warrant or right, other than a right to convert, to purchase, sell, or subscribe to a share, security, or interest of a kind specified in subparagraph (A) or (B) of this paragraph.

(17) The term "equity security holder" means holder of an equity security of the debtor.

(18) The term "family farmer" means—

(A) individual or individual and spouse engaged in a farming operation whose aggregate debts do not exceed $3,544,525 [1] and not less than 50 percent of whose aggregate noncontingent, liquidated debts (excluding a debt for the principal residence of such individual or such individual and spouse unless such debt arises out of a farming operation), on the date the case is filed, arise out of a farming operation owned or operated by such individual or such individual and spouse, and such individual or such individual and spouse receive from such farming operation more than 50 percent of such individual's or such individual and spouse's gross income for—

(i) the taxable year preceding; or

(ii) each of the 2d and 3d taxable years preceding;

the taxable year in which the case concerning such individual or such individual and spouse was filed; or

(B) corporation or partnership in which more than 50 percent of the outstanding stock or equity is held by one family, or by one family and the relatives of the members of such family, and such family or such relatives conduct the farming operation, and

(i) more than 80 percent of the value of its assets consists of assets related to the farming operation;

(ii) its aggregate debts do not exceed $3,544,525 [1] and not less than 50 percent of its aggregate noncontingent, liquidated debts (excluding a debt for one dwelling which is owned by such corporation or partnership and which a shareholder or partner maintains as a principal residence, unless such debt arises out of a farming operation), on the date the case is filed, arise out of the farming operation owned or operated by such corporation or such partnership; and

(iii) if such corporation issues stock, such stock is not publicly traded.

(19) The term "family farmer with regular annual income" means family farmer whose annual income is sufficiently stable and regular to enable such family farmer to make payments under a plan under chapter 12 of this title.

(19A) The term "family fisherman" means—

(A) an individual or individual and spouse engaged in a commercial fishing operation—

(i) whose aggregate debts do not exceed $1,642,500 [1] and not less than 80 percent of whose aggregate noncontingent, liquidated debts (excluding a debt for the principal residence of such individual or such individual and spouse, unless such debt arises out of a commercial fishing operation), on the date the case is filed, arise out of a commercial fishing operation owned or operated by such individual or such individual and spouse; and

(ii) who receive from such commercial fishing operation more than 50 percent of such individual's or such individual's and spouse's gross income for the taxable year preceding the taxable year in which the case concerning such individual or such individual and spouse was filed; or

(B) a corporation or partnership—

(i) in which more than 50 percent of the outstanding stock or equity is held by—

(I) 1 family that conducts the commercial fishing operation; or

(II) 1 family and the relatives of the members of such family, and such family or such relatives conduct the commercial fishing operation; and

(ii)(I) more than 80 percent of the value of its assets consists of assets related to the commercial fishing operation;

(II) its aggregate debts do not exceed $1,642,500 [1] and not less than 80 percent of its aggregate noncontingent, liquidated debts (excluding a debt for 1 dwelling which is owned by such corporation or partnership and which a shareholder or partner maintains as a principal residence, unless such debt arises out of a commercial fishing operation), on the date the case is filed, arise out of a commercial fishing operation owned or operated by such corporation or such partnership; and

(III) if such corporation issues stock, such stock is not publicly traded.

(19B) The term "family fisherman with regular annual income" means a family fisherman whose annual income is sufficiently stable and regular to enable such family fisherman to make payments under a plan under chapter 12 of this title.

(20) The term "farmer" means (except when such term appears in the term "family farmer") person that received more than 80 percent of such person's gross income during the taxable year of such person immediately preceding the taxable year of such person during which the case under this title concerning such person was commenced from a farming operation owned or operated by such person.

(21) The term "farming operation" includes farming, tillage of the soil, dairy farming, ranching, production or raising of crops, poultry, or livestock, and production of poultry or livestock products in an unmanufactured state.

(21A) The term "farmout agreement" means a written agreement in which—

(A) the owner of a right to drill, produce, or operate liquid or gaseous hydrocarbons on property agrees or has agreed to transfer or assign all or a part of such right to another entity; and

(B) such other entity (either directly or through its agents or its assigns), as consideration, agrees to perform drilling, reworking, recompleting, testing, or similar or related operations, to develop or produce liquid or gaseous hydrocarbons on the property.

(21B) The term "Federal depository institutions regulatory agency" means—

(A) with respect to an insured depository institution (as defined in section 3(c)(2) of the Federal Deposit Insurance Act) for which no conservator or receiver has been appointed, the appropriate Federal banking agency (as defined in section 3(q) of such Act);

(B) with respect to an insured credit union (including an insured credit union for which the National Credit Union Administration has been appointed conservator or liquidating agent), the National Credit Union Administration;

(C) with respect to any insured depository institution for which the Resolution Trust Corporation has been appointed conservator or receiver, the Resolution Trust Corporation; and

(D) with respect to any insured depository institution for which the Federal Deposit Insurance Corporation has been appointed conservator or receiver, the Federal Deposit Insurance Corporation.

(22) The term "financial institution" means—

(A) a Federal reserve bank, or an entity that is a commercial or savings bank, industrial savings bank, savings and loan association, trust company, federally-insured credit union, or receiver, liquidating agent, or conservator for such entity and, when any such Federal reserve bank, receiver, liquidating agent, conservator or entity is acting as agent or custodian for a customer (whether or not a "customer", as defined in section 741) in connection with a securities contract (as defined in section 741) such customer; or

(B) in connection with a securities contract (as defined in section 741) an investment company registered under the Investment Company Act of 1940.

(22A) The term "financial participant" means—

(A) an entity that, at the time it enters into a securities contract, commodity contract, swap agreement, repurchase agreement, or forward contract, or at the time of the date of the filing of the petition, has one or more agreements or transactions described in paragraph (1), (2), (3), (4), (5), or (6) of section 561(a) with the debtor or any other entity (other than an affiliate) of a total gross dollar value of not less than $1,000,000,000 in notional or actual principal amount outstanding (aggregated across counterparties) at such time or on any day during the 15–month period preceding the date of the filing of the petition, or has gross mark-to-market positions of not less than $100,000,000 (aggregated across counterparties) in one or more such agreements or transactions with the debtor or any other entity (other than an affiliate) at such time or on any day during the 15–month period preceding the date of the filing of the petition; or

(B) a clearing organization (as defined in section 402 of the Federal Deposit Insurance Corporation Improvement Act of 1991).

(23) The term "foreign proceeding" means a collective judicial or administrative proceeding in a foreign country, including an interim proceeding, under a law relating to insolvency or adjustment of debt in which proceeding the assets and affairs of the debtor are subject to control or supervision by a foreign court, for the purpose of reorganization or liquidation.

(24) The term "foreign representative" means a person or body, including a person or body appointed on an interim basis, authorized in a foreign proceeding to administer the reorganization or the liquidation of the debtor's assets or affairs or to act as a representative of such foreign proceeding.

(25) The term "forward contract" means—

(A) a contract (other than a commodity contract, as defined in section 761) for the purchase, sale, or transfer of a commodity, as defined in section 761(8) of this title, or any similar good, article, service, right, or interest which is presently or in the future becomes the subject of dealing in the forward contract trade, or product or byproduct thereof, with a maturity date more than two days after the date the contract is entered into, including, but not limited to, a repurchase or reverse repurchase transaction (whether or not such repurchase or reverse repurchase transaction is a "repurchase agreement", as defined in this section)[2] consignment, lease, swap, hedge transaction, deposit, loan, option, allocated transaction, unallocated transaction, or any other similar agreement;

(B) any combination of agreements or transactions referred to in subparagraphs (A) and (C);

(C) any option to enter into an agreement or transaction referred to in subparagraph (A) or (B);

(D) a master agreement that provides for an agreement or transaction referred to in subparagraph (A), (B), or (C), together with all supplements to any such master agreement, without regard to whether such master agreement provides for an agreement or transaction that is not a forward contract under this paragraph, except that such master agreement shall be considered to be a forward contract under this paragraph only with respect to each agreement or transaction under such master agreement that is referred to in subparagraph (A), (B), or (C); or

(E) any security agreement or arrangement, or other credit enhancement related to any agreement or transaction referred to in subparagraph (A), (B), (C), or (D), including any guarantee or reimbursement obligation by or to a forward contract merchant or financial participant in connection with any agreement or transaction referred to in any such subparagraph, but not to exceed the damages in connection with any such agreement or transaction, measured in accordance with section 562.

(26) The term "forward contract merchant" means a Federal reserve bank, or an entity the business of which consists in whole or in part of entering into forward contracts as or with merchants in a commodity (as defined in section 761) or any similar good, article, service, right, or interest which is presently or in the future becomes the subject of dealing in the forward contract trade.

(27) The term "governmental unit" means United States; State; Commonwealth; District; Territory; municipality; foreign state; department, agency, or instrumentality of the United States (but not a United States trustee while serving as a trustee in a case under this title), a State, a Commonwealth, a District, a Territory, a municipality, or a foreign state; or other foreign or domestic government.

(27A) The term "health care business"—

(A) means any public or private entity (without regard to whether that entity is organized for profit or not for profit) that is primarily engaged in offering to the general public facilities and services for—

(i) the diagnosis or treatment of injury, deformity, or disease; and

(ii) surgical, drug treatment, psychiatric, or obstetric care; and

(B) includes—

(i) any—

(I) general or specialized hospital;

(II) ancillary ambulatory, emergency, or surgical treatment facility;

(III) hospice;

(IV) home health agency; and

(V) other health care institution that is similar to an entity referred to in subclause (I), (II), (III), or (IV); and

(ii) any long-term care facility, including any—

(I) skilled nursing facility;

(II) intermediate care facility;

(III) assisted living facility;

(IV) home for the aged;

(V) domiciliary care facility; and

(VI) health care institution that is related to a facility referred to in subclause (I), (II), (III), (IV), or (V), if that institution is primarily engaged in offering room, board, laundry, or personal assistance with activities of daily living and incidentals to activities of daily living.

(27B) The term "incidental property" means, with respect to a debtor's principal residence—

(A) property commonly conveyed with a principal residence in the area where the real property is located;

(B) all easements, rights, appurtenances, fixtures, rents, royalties, mineral rights, oil or gas rights or profits, water rights, escrow funds, or insurance proceeds; and

(C) all replacements or additions.

(28) The term "indenture" means mortgage, deed of trust, or indenture, under which there is outstanding a security, other than a voting-trust certificate, constituting a claim against the debtor, a claim secured by a lien on any of the debtor's property, or an equity security of the debtor.

(29) The term "indenture trustee" means trustee under an indenture.

(30) The term "individual with regular income" means individual whose income is sufficiently stable and regular to enable such individual to make payments under a plan under chapter 13 of this title, other than a stockbroker or a commodity broker.

(31) The term "insider" includes—

(A) if the debtor is an individual—

(i) relative of the debtor or of a general partner of the debtor;

(ii) partnership in which the debtor is a general partner;

(iii) general partner of the debtor; or

(iv) corporation of which the debtor is a director, officer, or person in control;

(B) if the debtor is a corporation—

(i) director of the debtor;

(ii) officer of the debtor;

(iii) person in control of the debtor;

(iv) partnership in which the debtor is a general partner;

(v) general partner of the debtor; or

(vi) relative of a general partner, director, officer, or person in control of the debtor;

(C) if the debtor is a partnership—

(i) general partner in the debtor;

(ii) relative of a general partner in, general partner of, or person in control of the debtor;

(iii) partnership in which the debtor is a general partner;

(iv) general partner of the debtor; or

(v) person in control of the debtor;

(D) if the debtor is a municipality, elected official of the debtor or relative of an elected official of the debtor;

(E) affiliate, or insider of an affiliate as if such affiliate were the debtor; and

(F) managing agent of the debtor.

(32) The term "insolvent" means—

(A) with reference to an entity other than a partnership and a municipality, financial condition such that the sum of such entity's debts is greater than all of such entity's property, at a fair valuation, exclusive of—

(i) property transferred, concealed, or removed with intent to hinder, delay, or defraud such entity's creditors; and

(ii) property that may be exempted from property of the estate under section 522 of this title;

(B) with reference to a partnership, financial condition such that the sum of such partnership's debts is greater than the aggregate of, at a fair valuation—

(i) all of such partnership's property, exclusive of property of the kind specified in subparagraph (A)(i) of this paragraph; and

(ii) the sum of the excess of the value of each general partner's nonpartnership property, exclusive of property of the kind specified in subparagraph (A) of this paragraph, over such partner's nonpartnership debts; and

(C) with reference to a municipality, financial condition such that the municipality is—

(i) generally not paying its debts as they become due unless such debts are the subject of a bona fide dispute; or

(ii) unable to pay its debts as they become due.

(33) The term "institution-affiliated party"—

(A) with respect to an insured depository institution (as defined in section 3(c)(2) of the Federal

Deposit Insurance Act), has the meaning given it in section 3(u) of the Federal Deposit Insurance Act; and

(B) with respect to an insured credit union, has the meaning given it in section 206(r) of the Federal Credit Union Act.

(34) The term "insured credit union" has the meaning given it in section 101(7) of the Federal Credit Union Act.

(35) The term "insured depository institution"—

(A) has the meaning given it in section 3(c)(2) of the Federal Deposit Insurance Act; and

(B) includes an insured credit union (except in the case of paragraphs (23) and (35) of this subsection).

(35A) The term "intellectual property" means—

(A) trade secret;

(B) invention, process, design, or plant protected under title 35;

(C) patent application;

(D) plant variety;

(E) work of authorship protected under title 17; or

(F) mask work protected under chapter 9 of title 17;

to the extent protected by applicable nonbankruptcy law.

(36) The term "judicial lien" means lien obtained by judgment, levy, sequestration, or other legal or equitable process or proceeding.

(37) The term "lien" means charge against or interest in property to secure payment of a debt or performance of an obligation.

(38) The term "margin payment" means, for purposes of the forward contract provisions of this title, payment or deposit of cash, a security or other property, that is commonly known in the forward contract trade as original margin, initial margin, maintenance margin, or variation margin, including mark-to-market payments, or variation payments.

(38A) The term "master netting agreement"—

(A) means an agreement providing for the exercise of rights, including rights of netting, setoff, liquidation, termination, acceleration, or close out, under or in connection with one or more contracts that are described in any one or more of paragraphs (1) through (5) of section 561(a), or any security agreement or arrangement or other credit enhancement related to one or more of the foregoing, including any guarantee or reimbursement obligation related to 1 or more of the foregoing; and

(B) if the agreement contains provisions relating to agreements or transactions that are not contracts described in paragraphs (1) through (5) of section 561(a), shall be deemed to be a master netting agreement only with respect to those agreements or transactions that are described in any one or more of paragraphs (1) through (5) of section 561(a).

(38B) The term "master netting agreement participant" means an entity that, at any time before the date of the filing of the petition, is a party to an outstanding master netting agreement with the debtor.

(39) The term "mask work" has the meaning given it in section 901(a)(2) of title 17.

(39A) The term "median family income" means for any year—

(A) the median family income both calculated and reported by the Bureau of the Census in the then most recent year; and

(B) if not so calculated and reported in the then current year, adjusted annually after such most recent year until the next year in which median family income is both calculated and reported by the Bureau of the Census, to reflect the percentage change in the Consumer Price Index for All Urban Consumers during the period of years occurring after such most recent year and before such current year.

(40) The term "municipality" means political subdivision or public agency or instrumentality of a State.

(40A) The term "patient" means any individual who obtains or receives services from a health care business.

(40B) The term "patient records" means any written document relating to a patient or a record recorded in a magnetic, optical, or other form of electronic medium.

(41) The term "person" includes individual, partnership, and corporation, but does not include governmental unit, except that a governmental unit that—

(A) acquires an asset from a person—

(i) as a result of the operation of a loan guarantee agreement; or

(ii) as receiver or liquidating agent of a person;

(B) is a guarantor of a pension benefit payable by or on behalf of the debtor or an affiliate of the debtor; or

(C) is the legal or beneficial owner of an asset of—

(i) an employee pension benefit plan that is a governmental plan, as defined in section 414(d) of the Internal Revenue Code of 1986; or

(ii) an eligible deferred compensation plan, as defined in section 457(b) of the Internal Revenue Code of 1986;

shall be considered, for purposes of section 1102 of this title, to be a person with respect to such asset or such benefit.

(41A) The term "personally identifiable information" means—

(A) if provided by an individual to the debtor in connection with obtaining a product or a service from the debtor primarily for personal, family, or household purposes—

(i) the first name (or initial) and last name of such individual, whether given at birth or time of adoption, or resulting from a lawful change of name;

(ii) the geographical address of a physical place of residence of such individual;

(iii) an electronic address (including an e-mail address) of such individual;

(iv) a telephone number dedicated to contacting such individual at such physical place of residence;

(v) a social security account number issued to such individual; or

(vi) the account number of a credit card issued to such individual; or

(B) if identified in connection with 1 or more of the items of information specified in subparagraph (A)—

(i) a birth date, the number of a certificate of birth or adoption, or a place of birth; or

(ii) any other information concerning an identified individual that, if disclosed, will result in contacting or identifying such individual physically or electronically.

(42) The term "petition" means petition filed under section 301, 302, 303, or 304 of this title, as the case may be, commencing a case under this title.

(42A) The term "production payment" means a term overriding royalty satisfiable in cash or in kind—

(A) contingent on the production of a liquid or gaseous hydrocarbon from particular real property; and

(B) from a specified volume, or a specified value, from the liquid or gaseous hydrocarbon produced from such property, and determined without regard to production costs.

(43) The term "purchaser" means transferee of a voluntary transfer, and includes immediate or mediate transferee of such a transferee.

(44) The term "railroad" means common carrier by railroad engaged in the transportation of individuals or property or owner of trackage facilities leased by such a common carrier.

(45) The term "relative" means individual related by affinity or consanguinity within the third degree as determined by the common law, or individual in a step or adoptive relationship within such third degree.

(46) The term "repo participant" means an entity that, at any time before the filing of the petition, has an outstanding repurchase agreement with the debtor.

(47) The term "repurchase agreement" (which definition also applies to a reverse repurchase agreement)—

(A) means—

(i) an agreement, including related terms, which provides for the transfer of one or more certificates of deposit, mortgage related securities (as defined in section 3 of the Securities Exchange Act of 1934), mortgage loans, interests in mortgage related securities or mortgage loans, eligible bankers' acceptances, qualified foreign government securities (defined as a security that is a direct obligation of, or that is fully guaranteed by, the central government of a member of the Organization for Economic Cooperation and Development), or securities that are direct obligations of, or that are fully guaranteed by, the United States or any agency of the United States against the transfer of funds by the transferee of such certificates of deposit, eligible bankers' acceptances, securities, mortgage loans, or interests, with a simultaneous agreement by such transferee to transfer to the transferor thereof certificates of deposit, eligible bankers' acceptance, securities, mortgage loans, or interests of the kind described in this clause, at a date certain not later than 1 year after such transfer or on demand, against the transfer of funds;

(ii) any combination of agreements or transactions referred to in clauses (i) and (iii);

(iii) an option to enter into an agreement or transaction referred to in clause (i) or (ii);

(iv) a master agreement that provides for an agreement or transaction referred to in clause (i), (ii), or (iii), together with all supplements to any such master agreement, without regard to whether such master agreement provides for an agreement or transaction that is not a repurchase agreement under this paragraph, except that such master agreement shall be considered to be a repurchase agreement under this paragraph only with respect to each agreement or transaction under the master agreement that is referred to in clause (i), (ii), or (iii); or

(v) any security agreement or arrangement or other credit enhancement related to any agreement or transaction referred to in clause (i), (ii), (iii), or (iv), including any guarantee or reimbursement obligation by or to a repo participant or financial participant in connection with any agreement or transaction referred to in any such clause, but not to exceed the damages in connection with any such agreement or transaction, measured in accordance with section 562 of this title; and

(B) does not include a repurchase obligation under a participation in a commercial mortgage loan.

(48) The term "securities clearing agency" means person that is registered as a clearing agency under section 17A of the Securities Exchange Act of 1934, or exempt from such registration under such section pursuant to an order of the Securities and Exchange Commission, or whose business is confined to the performance of functions of a clearing agency with respect to exempted securities, as defined in section 3(a)(12) of such Act for the purposes of such section 17A.

(48A) The term "securities self regulatory organization" means either a securities association registered with the Securities and Exchange Commission under section 15A of the Securities Exchange Act of 1934 or a national securities exchange registered with the Securities and Exchange Commission under section 6 of the Securities Exchange Act of 1934.

(49) The term "security"—

(A) includes—

(i) note;

(ii) stock;

(iii) treasury stock;

(iv) bond;

(v) debenture;

(vi) collateral trust certificate;

(vii) pre-organization certificate or subscription;

(viii) transferable share;

(ix) voting-trust certificate;

(x) certificate of deposit;

(xi) certificate of deposit for security;

(xii) investment contract or certificate of interest or participation in a profit-sharing agreement or in an oil, gas, or mineral royalty or lease, if such contract or interest is required to be the subject of a registration statement filed with the Securities and Exchange Commission under the provisions of the Securities Act of 1933, or is exempt under section 3(b) of such Act from the requirement to file such a statement;

(xiii) interest of a limited partner in a limited partnership;

(xiv) other claim or interest commonly known as "security"; and

(xv) certificate of interest or participation in, temporary or interim certificate for, receipt for, or warrant or right to subscribe to or purchase or sell, a security; but

(B) does not include—

(i) currency, check, draft, bill of exchange, or bank letter of credit;

(ii) leverage transaction, as defined in section 761 of this title;

(iii) commodity futures contract or forward contract;

(iv) option, warrant, or right to subscribe to or purchase or sell a commodity futures contract;

(v) option to purchase or sell a commodity;

(vi) contract or certificate of a kind specified in subparagraph (A)(xii) of this paragraph that is not required to be the subject of a registration statement filed with the Securities and Exchange Commission and is not exempt under section 3(b) of the Securities Act of 1933 from the requirement to file such a statement; or

(vii) debt or evidence of indebtedness for goods sold and delivered or services rendered.

(50) The term "security agreement" means agreement that creates or provides for a security interest.

(51) The term "security interest" means lien created by an agreement.

(51A) The term "settlement payment" means, for purposes of the forward contract provisions of this title, a preliminary settlement payment, a partial settlement payment, an interim settlement payment, a settlement payment on account, a final settlement payment, a net settlement payment, or any other similar payment commonly used in the forward contract trade.

(51B) The term "single asset real estate" means real property constituting a single property or project, other than residential real property with fewer than 4 residential units, which generates substantially all of the gross income of a debtor who is not a family farmer and on which no substantial business is being conducted by a debtor other than the business of operating the real property and activities incidental.

(51C) The term "small business case" means a case filed under chapter 11 of this title in which the debtor is a small business debtor.

(51D) The term "small business debtor"—

(A) subject to subparagraph (B), means a person engaged in commercial or business activities (including any affiliate of such person that is also a debtor under this title and excluding a person whose primary activity is the business of owning or operating real property or activities incidental thereto) that has aggregate noncontingent liquidated secured and unsecured debts as of the date of the petition or the date of the order for relief in an amount not more than $2,190,000 [1] (excluding debts owed to 1 or more affiliates or insiders) for a case in which the United States trustee has not appointed under section 1102(a)(1) a committee of unsecured creditors or where the court has determined that the committee of unsecured creditors is not sufficiently active and representative to provide effective oversight of the debtor; and

(B) does not include any member of a group of affiliated debtors that has aggregate noncontingent liquidated secured and unsecured debts in an amount greater than $2,190,000 [1] (excluding debt owed to 1 or more affiliates or insiders).

(52) The term "State" includes the District of Columbia and Puerto Rico, except for the purpose of defining who may be a debtor under chapter 9 of this title.

(53) The term "statutory lien" means lien arising solely by force of a statute on specified circumstances or conditions, or lien of distress for rent, whether or not statutory, but does not include security interest or judicial lien, whether or not such interest or lien is provided by or is dependent on a statute and whether or not such interest or lien is made fully effective by statute.

(53A) The term "stockbroker" means person—

(A) with respect to which there is a customer, as defined in section 741 of this title; and

(B) that is engaged in the business of effecting transactions in securities—

(i) for the account of others; or

(ii) with members of the general public, from or for such person's own account.

(53B) The term "swap agreement"—

(A) means—

(i) any agreement, including the terms and conditions incorporated by reference in such agreement, which is—

(I) an interest rate swap, option, future, or forward agreement, including a rate floor, rate cap, rate collar, cross-currency rate swap, and basis swap;

(II) a spot, same day-tomorrow, tomorrow-next, forward, or other foreign exchange, precious metals, or other commodity agreement;

(III) a currency swap, option, future, or forward agreement;

(IV) an equity index or equity swap, option, future, or forward agreement;

(V) a debt index or debt swap, option, future, or forward agreement;

(VI) a total return, credit spread or credit swap, option, future, or forward agreement;

(VII) a commodity index or a commodity swap, option, future, or forward agreement;

(VIII) a weather swap, option, future, or forward agreement;

(IX) an emissions swap, option, future, or forward agreement; or

(X) an inflation swap, option, future, or forward agreement;

(ii) any agreement or transaction that is similar to any other agreement or transaction referred to in this paragraph and that—

(I) is of a type that has been, is presently, or in the future becomes, the subject of recurrent dealings in the swap or other derivatives markets (including terms and conditions incorporated by reference therein); and

(II) is a forward, swap, future, option, or spot transaction on one or more rates, currencies, commodities, equity securities, or other equity instruments, debt securities or other debt instruments, quantitative measures associated with an occurrence, extent of an occurrence, or contingency associated with a financial, commercial, or economic consequence, or economic or financial indices or measures of economic or financial risk or value;

(iii) any combination of agreements or transactions referred to in this subparagraph;

(iv) any option to enter into an agreement or transaction referred to in this subparagraph;

(v) a master agreement that provides for an agreement or transaction referred to in clause (i), (ii), (iii), or (iv), together with all supplements to any such master agreement, and without regard to whether the master agreement contains an agreement or transaction that is not a swap agreement under this paragraph, except that the master agreement shall be considered to be a swap agreement under this paragraph only with respect to each agreement or transaction under the master agreement that is referred to in clause (i), (ii), (iii), or (iv); or

(vi) any security agreement or arrangement or other credit enhancement related to any agreements or transactions referred to in clause (i) through (v), including any guarantee or reimbursement obligation by or to a swap participant or financial participant in connection with any agreement or transaction referred to in any such clause, but not to exceed the damages in connection with any such agreement or transaction, measured in accordance with section 562; and

(B) is applicable for purposes of this title only, and shall not be construed or applied so as to challenge or affect the characterization, definition, or treatment of any swap agreement under any other statute, regulation, or rule, including the Gramm–Leach–Bliley Act, the Legal Certainty for Bank Products Act of 2000, the securities laws (as such term is defined in section 3(a)(47) of the Securities Exchange Act of 1934) and the Commodity Exchange Act.

(53C) The term "swap participant" means an entity that, at any time before the filing of the petition, has an outstanding swap agreement with the debtor.

(56A) [3] The term "term overriding royalty" means an interest in liquid or gaseous hydrocarbons in place or to be produced from particular real property that entitles the owner thereof to a share of production, or the value thereof, for a term limited by time, quantity, or value realized.

(53D) The term "timeshare plan" means and shall include that interest purchased in any arrangement, plan, scheme, or similar device, but not including exchange programs, whether by membership, agreement, tenancy in common, sale, lease, deed, rental agreement, license, right to use agreement, or by any other means, whereby a purchaser, in exchange for consideration, receives a right to use accommodations, facilities, or recreational sites, whether improved or unimproved, for a specific period of time less than a full year during any given year, but not necessarily for consecutive years, and which extends for a period of more than three years. A "timeshare interest" is that interest purchased in a timeshare plan which grants the purchaser the right to use and occupy accommodations, facilities, or recreational sites, whether improved or unimproved, pursuant to a timeshare plan.

(54) The term "transfer" means—

(A) the creation of a lien;

(B) the retention of title as a security interest;

(C) the foreclosure of a debtor's equity of redemption; or

(D) each mode, direct or indirect, absolute or conditional, voluntary or involuntary, of disposing of or parting with—

(i) property; or

(ii) an interest in property.

(54A) The term "uninsured State member bank" means a State member bank (as defined in section 3 of the Federal Deposit Insurance Act) the deposits of which are not insured by the Federal Deposit Insurance Corporation.

(55) The term "United States", when used in a geographical sense, includes all locations where the judicial jurisdiction of the United States extends, including territories and possessions of the United States.

(Pub.L. 95–598, Nov. 6, 1978, 92 Stat. 2549; Pub.L. 97–222, § 1, July 27, 1982, 96 Stat. 235; Pub.L. 98–353, Title III, §§ 391, 401, 421, July 10, 1984, 98 Stat. 364, 366, 367; Pub.L. 99–554, Title II, §§ 201, 251, 283(a), Oct. 27, 1986, 100 Stat. 3097, 3104, 3116; Pub.L. 100–506, § 1(a), Oct. 18, 1988, 102 Stat. 2538; Pub.L. 100–597, § 1, Nov. 3, 1988, 102 Stat. 3028; Pub.L. 101–311, Title I, § 101, Title II, § 201, June 25, 1990, 104 Stat. 267, 268; Pub.L. 101–647, Title XXV, § 2522(e), Nov. 29, 1990, 104 Stat. 4867; Pub.L. 102–486, Title XXX, § 3017(a), Oct. 24, 1992, 106 Stat. 3130; Pub.L. 103–394, Title I, § 106, Title II, §§ 208(a), 215, 217(a), 218(a), Title III, § 304(a), Title V, § 501(a), (b)(1), (d)(1), Oct. 22, 1994, 108 Stat. 4111, 4124, 4126–4128, 4132, 4141–4143; Pub.L. 106–554, § 1(a)(5) [Title I, § 112(c)(3), (4)], Dec. 21, 2000, 114 Stat. 2763, 2763A–393; Pub.L. 109–8, Title I, § 102(b), (k), Title II, §§ 211, 226(a), 231(b), Title III, § 306(c), Title IV, §§ 401(a), 414, 432(a), Title VIII, § 802(b), Title IX, § 907(a)(1), (b), (c), Title X, §§ 1004, 1005, 1007(a), Title XI, § 1101(a), (b), Title XII, § 1201, Apr. 20, 2005, 119 Stat. 32, 35, 50, 66, 73, 80, 104, 107, 110, 145, 170, 175, 186, 187, 189, 192; Pub.L. 109–390, § 5(a)(1), Dec. 12, 2006, 120 Stat. 2695.)

[1] Dollar amount as adjusted by the Judicial Conference of the United States. See Adjustment of Dollar Amounts notes set out under this section and 11 U.S.C.A. § 104.

[2] So in original. A comma should probably appear.

[3] So in original. Par. (56A) was inserted between pars. (53C) and (53D).

HISTORICAL AND STATUTORY NOTES

Revision Notes and Legislative Reports

1978 Acts. Section 101 of title 11 contains 40 definitions:

Paragraph (1) defines "accountant" as an accountant authorized under applicable law to practice accounting. The term includes a professional accounting association, corporation, or partnership if applicable law authorizes such a unit to practice accounting.

Paragraph (2) defines "affiliate." An affiliate is an entity with a close relationship to the debtor. It includes a 20 percent parent or subsidiary of the debtor, whether a corporate, partnership, individual, or estate parent.

The use of "directly or indirectly" in subparagraphs (A) and (B) is intended to cover situations in which there is an opportunity to control, and where the existence of that opportunity operates as indirect control.

"Affiliate" is defined primarily for use in the definition of insider, infra, and for use in the chapter 11 reorganization cases. The definition of "affiliate" does not include an entity acting in a fiduciary or agency capacity if the entity does not have the sole discretionary power to vote 20 percent of the voting securities but hold them solely as security and have not exercised the power to vote. This restriction applies to a corporate affiliate under subparagraph (B) of paragraph (2).

Subsections (C) and (D) of paragraph (2) define affiliate also as those persons and entities whose business or substantially all of whose property is operated under a lease or operating agreement by a debtor and whose business or property is more than 50 percent under the control of the debtor.

The definition of "attorney" in paragraph (3) is similar to the definition of accountant.

Paragraph (4) defines "claim." The effect of the definition is a significant departure from present law. Under present law, "claim" is not defined in straight bankruptcy. Instead it is simply used, along with the concept of provability in section 63 of the Bankruptcy Act [section 103 of former Title 11], to limit the kinds of obligations that are payable in a bankruptcy case. The term is defined in the debtor rehabilitation chapters of present law far more broadly. The definition in paragraph (4) adopts an even broader definition of claim than is found in the present debtor rehabilitation chapters. The definition is any right to payment, whether or not reduced to judgment, liquidated, unliquidated, fixed, contingent, matured, unmatured, disputed, undisputed, legal, equitable, secured, or unsecured. The definition also includes as a claim an equitable right to performance that does not give rise to a right to payment. By this broadest possible definition and by the use of the term throughout the title 11, especially in subchapter I of chapter 5, the bill contemplates that all legal obligations of the debtor, no matter how remote or contingent, will be able to be dealt with in the bankruptcy case. It permits the broadest possible relief in the bankruptcy court.

Paragraph (5) defines "commodity broker" by reference to various terms used and defined in subchapter IV of chapter 7, Commodity Broker Liquidation. The terms are described in connection with section 761, infra.

Paragraph (6) defines "community claim" for those eight States that have community property laws. The definition is keyed to the liability of the debtor's property for a claim against either the debtor or the debtor's spouse. If the debtor's property is liable for a claim against either, that claim is a community claim.

Paragraph (7) defines "consumer debt". The definition is adapted from the definition used in various consumer protection laws. It encompasses only a debt incurred by an individual primarily for a personal, family, or household purpose.

The definition of "corporation" in paragraph (8) is similar to the definition in current law, section 1(8) [section 1(8) of former Title 11]. The term encompasses any association having the power or privilege that a private corporation, but not an individual or partnership, has; partnership associations organized under a law that makes only the capital subscribed responsible for the debts of the partnership; joint-stock company; unincorporated company or association; and business trust. "Unincorporated association" is intended specifically to include a labor union, as well as other bodies that come under that phrase as used under current law. The exclusion of limited partnerships is explicit, and not left to the case law.

Paragraph (9) defines "court" as the bankruptcy judge in the district in which the case is pending except in municipal adjustment and railroad reorganization cases, where "court" means the Federal district judge.

Paragraph (10) defines "creditor" to include holders of prepetition claims against the debtor. However, it also encompasses certain holders of claims that are deemed to arise before the date of the filing of the petition, such as those injured by the rejection of an executory contract or unexpired lease, certain investment tax credit recapture claim holders, "involuntary gap" creditors, and certain holders of the right of setoff. The term also includes the holder of a prepetition community claim. A guarantor of or surety for a claim against the debtor is also a creditor, because he holds a contingent claim against the debtor that becomes fixed when he pays the creditor whose claim he has guaranteed or insured.

Paragraph (11) defines "custodian." There is no similar definition in current law. It is defined to facilitate drafting, and means a prepetition liquidator of the debtor's property, such as an assignee for the benefit of creditors, a receiver of the debtor's property, or administrator of the debtor's property. The definition of custodian to include a receiver or trustee is descriptive, and not meant to be limited to court officers with those titles. The definition is intended to include other officers of the court if their functions are substantially similar to those of a receiver or trustee.

"Debt" is defined in paragraph (12) as a liability on a claim. The terms "debt" and "claim" are coextensive: a creditor has a "claim" against the debtor; the debtor owes a "debt" to the creditor. This definition of "debt" and the definition of "claim" on which it is based, proposed 11 U.S.C. 101(4), does not include a transaction such as a policy loan on an insurance policy. Under that kind of transaction, the debtor is not liable to the insurance company for repayment; the amount owed is merely available to the company for setoff against any benefits that become payable under the policy. As such, the loan is not a claim (it is not a right to payment) that the company can assert against the estate; nor is the debtor's obligation a debt (a liability on a claim) that will be discharged under proposed 11 U.S.C. 523 or 524.

Paragraph (13) defines "debtor." Debtor means person or municipality concerning which a case under title II [probably means 11] has been commenced. This is a change in terminology from present law, which identifies the person by or against whom a petition is filed in a straight bankruptcy liquidation case as the "bankrupt", and a person or municipality that is proceeding under a debtor rehabilitation chapter (chapters VIII through XIII of the Bankruptcy Act) [chapters 8 through 13 of former Title 11] as a "debtor." The term "debtor" is used for both kinds of cases in this bill, for ease of reference in chapters 1, 3, and 5 (which apply to straight bankruptcy and reorganization cases).

Paragraph (14) defines "disinterested person." The definition is adapted from section 158 of chapter X of current law [section 558 of former Title 11], though it is expanded and modified in some respects. A person is a disinterested person if the person is not a creditor, equity security holder, or insider; is not and was not an investment banker of the debtor for any outstanding security of the debtor (the change from underwriter in current law to investment banker is to make the term more descriptive and to avoid conflict with the definition of underwriter in section 2(11) of the Securities Act of 1933 (15 U.S.C. 77b(11)) [15 U.S.C.A. § 77(b)(11)]; has not been an investment banker for a security of the debtor within 3 years before the date of the filing of the petition (the change from five years to three years here conforms the definition with the statute of limitations in the Securities Act of 1933) [15 U.S.C.A. § 77n], or an attorney for such an investment banker; is not an insider of the debtor or of such an investment banker; and does not have an interest materially adverse to the estate.

"Entity" is defined, for convenience, in paragraph (15), to include person, estate, trust, and governmental unit. It is the most inclusive of the various defined terms relating to bodies or units.

Paragraph (16) defines "equity security." The term includes a share or stock in a corporation, a limited partner's interest in a limited partnership, and a warrant or right to subscribe to an equity security. The term does not include a security, such as a convertible debenture, that is convertible into equity security, but has not been converted.

Paragraph (17) defines "equity security holder" for convenience as the holder of an equity securing of the debtor.

Paragraph (18) defines "farmer". It encompasses only those persons for whom farming operations contribute 75 percent or more of their total income.

Paragraphs (19) and (20) define "foreign proceeding" and "foreign representative". A foreign proceeding is a proceeding in another country in which the debtor has some substantial connection for the purpose of liquidating the estate of the debtor or the purpose of financial rehabilitation of the debtor. A foreign representative is the representative of the estate in a foreign proceeding, such as a trustee or administrator.

Paragraph (21) defines "governmental unit" in the broadest sense. The definition encompasses the United States, a State, Commonwealth, District, Territory, municipality, or foreign state, and a department, agency, or instrumentality of any of those entities. "Department, agency, or instrumentality" does not include an entity that owes its existence to State action, such as the granting of a charter or a license but that has no other connection with a State or local government or the Federal Government. The relationship must be an active one in which the department, agency, or instrumentality is actually carrying out some governmental function.

Paragraph (22) defines "indenture." It is similar to the definition of indenture in the Trust Indenture Act of 1939 [15 U.S.C.A. § 77ccc(7)]. An indenture is the instrument under which securities, either debt or equity, of the debtor are outstanding.

Paragraph (23) defines "indenture trustee" as the trustee under an indenture.

Paragraph (24) defines "individual with regular income." The effect of this definition, and of its use in section 109(e), is to expand substantially the kinds of individuals that are eligible for relief under chapter 13, Adjustment of Debts of an Individual with Regular Income. Chapter XIII [chapter 13 of former Title 11] is now available only for wage earners. The definition encompasses all individuals with incomes that are sufficiently stable and regular to enable them to make payments under a chapter 13 plan. Thus, individuals on welfare, social security, fixed pension incomes, or who live on investment incomes, will be able to work out repayment plans with their creditors rather than being forced into straight bankruptcy. Also, self-employed individuals will be eligible to use chapter 13 if they have regular incomes.

However, the definition excludes certain stockbrokers and commodity brokers, in order to prohibit them from proceeding under chapter 13 and avoiding the customer protection provisions of chapter 7.

"Insider", defined in paragraph (25), is a new term. An insider is one who has a sufficiently close relationship with the debtor that his conduct is made subject to closer scrutiny than those dealing at arms length with the debtor. If the debtor is an individual, then a relative of the debtor, a partnership in which the debtor is a general partner, a general partner of the debtor, and a corporation controlled by the debtor are all insiders. If the debtor is a corporation, then a controlling person, a relative of a controlling person, a partnership in which the debtor is a general partner, and a general partner of the debtor are all insiders. If the debtor is a partnership, then a general partner of or in the debtor, a relative of a general partner in the debtor, and a person in control are all insiders. If the debtor is a municipality, then an elected official of the debtor is an insider. In addition, affiliates of the debtor and managing agents are insiders.

The definition of "insolvent" in paragraph (26) is adopted from section 1(19) of current law [section 1(19) of former Title 11]. An entity is insolvent if its debts are greater than its assets, at a fair valuation, exclusive of property exempted or fraudulently transferred. It is the traditional bankruptcy balance sheet test of insolvency. For a partnership, the definition is modified to account for the liability of a general partner for the partnership's debts. The difference in this definition from that in current law is in the exclusion of exempt property for all purposes in the definition of insolvent.

Paragraph (27) defines "judicial lien." It is one of three kinds of liens defined in this section. A judicial lien is a lien obtained by judgment, levy, sequestration, or other legal or equitable process or proceeding.

Paragraph (28) defines "lien." The definition is new and is very broad. A lien is defined as a charge against or interest in property to secure payment of a debt or performance of an obligation. It includes inchoate liens. In general, the concept of lien is divided into three kinds of liens: judicial liens, security interests, and statutory liens. Those three categories are mutually exclusive and are exhaustive except for certain common law liens.

Paragraph (29) defines "municipality." The definition is adapted from the terms used in the chapter IX (municipal bankruptcy) [chapter 9 of former Title 11] amendment to the Bankruptcy Act enacted in 1976 (Pub.L. 94–260). That amendment spoke in terms of "political subdivision or public agency or instrumentality of a State". Bankruptcy Act sec. 84 [section 404 of former Title 11]. The term municipality is defined by those three terms for convenience. It does not include the District of Columbia or any territories of the United States.

"Person" is defined in paragraph (30). The definition is a change in wording, but not in substance, from the definition in section 1(23) of the Bankruptcy Act [section 1(23) of former Title 11]. The definition is also similar to the one contained in 1 U.S.C. sec. 1, but is repeated here for convenience and ease of reference. Person includes individual partnership, and corporation. The exclusion of governmental units is made explicit in order to avoid any confusion that may arise if, for example, a municipality is incorporated and thus is legally a corporation as well as governmental unit. The definition does not include an estate or a trust, which are included only in the definition of "entity" in proposed 11 U.S.C. 101(14).

"Petition" is defined for convenience in paragraph (31). Petition is a petition under section 301, 302, 303, or 304 of the bankruptcy code—that is, a petition that commences a case under title 11.

Paragraph (32) defines purchaser as a transferee of a voluntary transfer, such as a sale or gift, and includes an immediate or mediate transferee of a purchaser.

The definition of "railroad" in paragraph (33) is derived from section 77 of the Bankruptcy Act [section 205 of former Title 11]. A railroad is a common carrier by railroad engaged in the transportation of individuals or property, or an owner of trackage facilities leased by such a common carrier. The effect of the definition and the use of the term in section 109(d) is to eliminate the limitation now found in section 77 of the Bankruptcy Act that only railroads engaged in interstate commerce may proceed under the railroad reorganization provisions. The limitation may have been inserted because of a doubt that the commerce power could not reach intrastate railroads. Be that as it may, this bill is enacted under the bankruptcy power.

Paragraph (34) defines "relative" as an individual related by affinity or consanguinity within the third degree as determined by the common law, and includes individuals in a step or adoptive relationship. The definition is similar to current law, but adds the latter phrase. This definition should be applied as of the time when the transaction that it concerns took place. Thus, a former spouse is not a relative, but if, for example, for purposes of the preference section, proposed 11 U.S.C. 547(b)(4)(B), the transferee was a spouse of the debtor at the time of the transfer sought to be avoided, then the transferee would be relative and subject to the insider rules, even if the transferee was no longer married to the debtor at the time of the commencement of the case or at the time of the commencement of the preference recovery proceeding.

Paragraph (35) defines "security." The definition is new and is modeled on the most recent draft of the American Law Institute's proposed securities code, with some exceptions. The interest of a limited partner in a limited partnership is included in order to make sure that everything that is defined as an equity security is also a "security." The definition, as with the definition of "entity", "insider", and "person", is open-ended because the term is not susceptible of precise specification. Thus the courts will be able to use the characterization provided in this definition to treat with new kinds of documents on a flexible basis.

Paragraphs (36) and (37) defined "security agreement" and "security interest." A security interest is one of the kinds of liens. It is a lien created by an agreement. Security agreement is defined as the agreement creating the security interest. Though these terms are similar to the same terms in the Uniform Commercial Code, article IX, they are broader. For example, the U.C.C. does not cover real property mortgages. Under this definition, such a mortgage is included, as are all other liens created by agreement, even though not covered by the U.C.C. All U.C.C. security interests and security agreements are, however, security interests and security agreements under this definition. Whether a consignment or a lease constitutes a security interest under the bankruptcy code will depend on whether it constitutes a security interest under applicable State or local law.

Paragraph (38) defines another kind of lien, "statutory lien." The definition, derived from current law, states that a statutory lien is a lien arising solely by force of statute on specified circumstances or conditions and includes a lien of distress for rent (whether statutory, common law, or otherwise). The definition excludes judicial liens and security interests, whether or not they are provided for or are dependent on a statute, and whether or not they are made fully effective by statute. A statutory lien is only one that arises automatically, and is not based on an agreement to give a lien or on judicial action. Mechanics', materialmen's, and warehousemen's liens are examples. Tax liens are also included in the definition of statutory lien.

"Stockbroker" is defined in paragraph (39) as a person engaged in the business of effecting transactions in securities for the account of others or with members of the general public from or for such person's own account, if the person has a customer, as defined. Thus, the definition, derived from a combination of the definitions of "broker" and "dealer" in the Securities Exchange Act of 1934 [15 U.S.C.A. § 78c], encompasses both brokers and dealers. The definition is used in section 109 and in subchapter III of chapter 7, Stockholder Liquidation. The term does not encompass an employee who acts for a principal that "effects" transaction or deals with the public, because such an employee will not have a "customer".

Paragraph (40) defines "transfer." It is derived and adapted, with stylistic changes, from section 1(30) of the Bankruptcy Act [section 1(30) of former Title 11]. A transfer is a disposition of an interest in property. The definition of transfer is as broad as possible. Many of the potentially limiting words in current law are deleted, and the language is simplified. Under this definition, any transfer of an interest in property is a transfer, including a transfer of possession, custody, or control even if there is no transfer of title, because possession, custody, and control are interests in property. A deposit in a bank account or similar account is a transfer. Senate Report No. 95–989.

1982 Acts. House Report No. 97–420, see 1982 U.S. Code Cong. and Adm. News, p. 583.

1984 Acts. Statements by Legislative Leaders, see 1984 U.S. Code Cong. and Adm. News, p. 576.

1986 Acts. House Report No. 99–764 and House Conference Report No. 99–958, see 1986 U.S. Code Cong. and Adm. News, p. 5227.

1988 Acts. Senate Report No. 100–505, see 1988 U.S. Code Cong. and Adm. News, p. 3200.

House Report No. 100–1011, see 1988 U.S. Code Cong. and Adm. News, p. 4115.

1990 Acts. House Report No. 101–484, see 1990 U.S. Code Cong. and Adm. News, p. 223.

House Report No. 101–681(Part I), see 1990 U.S. Code Cong. and Adm. News, p. 6472.

1994 Acts. House Report No. 103–835, see 1994 U.S. Code Cong. and Adm. News, p. 3340.

2000 Acts. House Report No. 106–645 and Statement by President, see 2000 U.S. Code Cong. and Adm. News, p. 2459.

2005 Acts. House Report No. 109–31(Part I), see 2005 U.S. Code Cong. and Adm. News, p. 88.

Legislative Statements

Section 101(2) defines "affiliate." The House amendment contains a provision that is a compromise between the definition in the House-passed version of H.R. 8200 and the Senate amendment in the nature of a substitute to H.R. 8200. Subparagraphs (A) and (B) are derived from the Senate amendment and subparagraph (D) is taken from the House bill, while subparagraph (C) represents a compromise, taking the House position with respect to a person whose business is operated under a lease or an operating agreement by the debtor and with respect to a person substantially all of whose property is operated under an operating agreement by the debtor and with respect to a person substantially all of whose property is operated under an operating agreement by the debtor and the Senate position on leased property. Thus, the definition of "affiliate" excludes persons substantially all of whose property is operated under a lease agreement by a debtor, such as a small company which owns equipment all of which is leased to a larger nonrelated company.

Section 101(4)(B) represents a modification of the House-passed bill to include the definition of "claim" a right to an equitable remedy for breach of performance if such breach gives rise to a right to payment. This is intended to cause the liquidation or estimation of contingent rights of payment for which there may be an alternative equitable remedy with the result that the equitable remedy will be susceptible to being discharged in bankruptcy. For example, in some States, a judgment for specific performance may be satisfied by an alternative right to payment, in the event performance is refused; in that event, the creditor entitled to specific performance would have a "claim" for purposes of a proceeding under title 11.

On the other hand, rights to an equitable remedy for a breach of performance with respect to which such breach does not give rise to a right to payment are not "claims" and would therefore not be susceptible to discharge in bankruptcy.

In a case under chapter 9 to title 11, "claim" does not include a right to payment under an industrial development bond issued by a municipality as a matter of convenience for a third party.

Municipalities are authorized, under section 103(c) of the Internal Revenue Code of 1954, as amended [section 103(c) of Title 26, Internal Revenue Code], to issue tax-exempt industrial development revenue bonds to provide for the financing of certain projects for privately owned companies. The bonds are sold on the basis of the credit of the company on whose behalf they are issued, and the principal, interest, and premium, if any, are payable solely from payments made by the company to the trustee under the bond indenture and do not constitute claims on the tax revenues or other funds of the issuing municipalities. The municipality merely acts as the vehicle to enable the bonds to be issued on a tax-exempt basis. Claims that arise by virtue of these bonds are not among the claims defined by this paragraph and amounts owed by private companies to the holders of industrial development revenue bonds are not to be included among the assets of the municipality that would be affected by the plan.

Section 101(6) defines "community claim" as provided by the Senate amendment in order to indicate that a community claim exists whether or not there is community property in the estate as of the commencement of the case.

Section 101(7) of the House amendment contains a definition of consumer debt identical to the definition in the House bill and Senate amendment. A consumer debt does not include a debt to any extent the debt is secured by real property.

Section 101(9) of the Senate amendment contained a definition of "court." The House amendment deletes the provision as unnecessary in light of the pervasive jurisdiction of a bankruptcy court under all chapters of title 11 as indicated in title II of the House amendment to H.R. 8200.

Section 101(11) defines "debt" to mean liability on a claim, as was contained in the House-passed version of H.R. 8200. The Senate amendment contained language indicating that "debt" does not include a policy loan made by a life insurance company to the debtor. That language is deleted in the House amendment as unnecessary since a life insurance company clearly has no right to have a policy loan repaid by the debtor, although such company does have a right of offset with respect to such policy loan. Clearly, then, a "debt" does not include a policy loan made by a life insurance company. Inclusion of the language contained in the Senate amendment would have required elaboration of other legal relationships not arising by a liability on a claim. Further the language would have required clarification that interest on a policy loan made by a life insurance company is a debt, and that the insurance company does have right to payment to that interest.

Section 101(14) adopts the definition of "entity" contained in the Senate-passed version of H.R. 8200. Since the Senate amendment to H.R. 8200 deleted the U.S. trustee, a corresponding definitional change is made in chapter 15 of the House amendment for U.S. trustees under the pilot program. Adoption by the House amendment of a pilot program for U.S. trustees under chapter 15 requires insertion of "United States trustee" in many sections. Several provisions in chapter 15 of the House amendment that relate to the U.S. trustee were not contained in the Senate amendment in the nature of a substitute.

Section 101(17) defines "farmer," as in the Senate amendment with an income limitation percentage of 80 percent instead of 75 percent.

Section 101(18) contains a new definition of "farming operation" derived from present law and the definition of "farmer" in the Senate amendment. This definition gives a broad construction to the term "farming operation".

Section 101(20) contains a definition of "foreign representative". It clarifies the House bill and Senate amendment by indicating that a foreign representative must be duly selected in a foreign proceeding.

Section 101(35) defines "security" as contained in the Senate amendment. H.R. 8200 as adopted by the House excluded certain commercial notes from the definition of "security", and that exclusion is deleted.

Section 101(40) defines "transfer" as in the Senate amendment. The definition contained in H.R. 8200 as passed by the House included "setoff" in the definition of "transfer". Inclusion of "setoff" is deleted. The effect is that a "setoff" is not subject to being set aside as a preferential "transfer" but will be subject to special rules.

2006 Acts. House Report No. 109–648(Part I), see 2006 U.S. Code Cong. and Adm. News, p. 1585.

References in Text

Chapter 12, referred to in pars. (7A)(B) and (19B), is chapter 12 of this title, which is classified to 11 U.S.C.A. § 1201 et seq.

The Social Security Act, referred to in par. (10A)(B), is Act Aug. 14, 1935, c. 531, 49 Stat. 620, as amended, which is classified generally to chapter 7 of Title 42, 42 U.S.C.A. § 301 et seq.

Section 501(c)(3) of the Internal Revenue Code of 1986, referred to in par. (12A)(B), is classified to 26 U.S.C.A. § 501(c)(3).

Section 3 of the Federal Deposit Insurance Act, referred to in pars. (12A)(D), (21B)(A), (33)(A), (35)(A), and (54A) is Act Sept. 21, 1950, c. 967, § 2 [3], 64 Stat. 873, which is classified to 12 U.S.C.A. § 1813.

Section 101 of the Federal Credit Union Act, referred to in pars. (12A)(D), (34), is Act June 26, 1934, c. 750, Title I, § 101, formerly § 2, 48 Stat. 1216, as amended, which is classified to 12 U.S.C.A. § 1752.

The Investment Company Act of 1940, referred to in par. (22)(B), is Act Aug. 22, 1940, c. 686, Title I, 54 Stat. 789, as amended, which is classified principally to subchapter 1 of chapter 2D of title 15, 15 U.S.C.A. § 80a–1 et seq. For complete classification, see Short Title set out as 15 U.S.C.A. § 80a–51 and Tables.

Section 402 of the Federal Deposit Insurance Corporation Improvement Act of 1991, referred to in par. (22A)(B), is Pub.L. 102–242, Title IV, § 402, Dec. 19, 1991, 105 Stat. 2372, which is classified to 12 U.S.C.A. § 4402.

Section 206 of the Federal Credit Union Act, referred to in par. (33)(B), is section 206 of Act June 26, 1934, c. 750, Title II, as added Oct. 19, 1970, Pub.L. 91–468, § 1(3), 84 Stat. 1003, which is classified to section 1786 of Title 12.

Sections 414(d) and 457(b) of the Internal Revenue Code of 1986, referred to in par. (41)(C), are sections 414(d) and 457(b), respectively, of Title 26, Internal Revenue Code.

Section 304 of this title, referred to in par. (42), was repealed by Pub.L. 109–8, Title VIII, § 802(d)(3), Apr. 20, 2005, 119 Stat. 146.

Section 3 of the Securities and Exchange Act of 1934, referred to in par. (47), is Act June 6, 1934, c. 404, Title I, § 3, 48 Stat. 882, which is classified to 15 U.S.C.A. § 78c.

Section 17A of the Securities and Exchange Act of 1934, referred to in par. (48), is section 17A of Act June 6, 1934, c. 404, Title I, as added June 4, 1975, Pub.L. 94–29, § 15, 89 Stat. 141, which is classified to section 78q–1 of Title 15, Commerce and Trade.

Section 3(a)(12) of such Act, referred to in par. (48), is Section 3 of the Securities and Exchange Act of 1934, Act June 6, 1934, c. 404, Title I, 48 Stat. 882, which is classified to 15 U.S.C.A. § 78c(a)(12).

Section 15A of the Securities Exchange Act of 1934, referred to in par. (48A), is June 6, 1934, c. 404, Title I, § 15A, as added June 25, 1938, c. 677, § 1, 52 Stat. 1070, and amended which is classified to 15 U.S.C.A. § 78*o*–3.

Section 6 of the Securities Exchange Act of 1934, referred to in par. (48A), is June 6, 1934, c. 404, Title I, § 6, 48 Stat. 885, as amended, which is classified to 15 U.S.C.A. § 78c.

The Securities Act of 1933, referred to in par. (49)(A)(xii), is Act May 27, 1933, c. 38, Title I, 48 Stat. 74, as amended, which is classified generally to subchapter I (section 77a et seq.) of chapter 2A of Title 15, Commerce and Trade. For complete classification of this Act to the Code, see section 77a of Title 15 and Tables.

Section 3 of the Securities Act of 1933, referred to in pars. (49)(A)(xii) and (B)(vi), is section 3 of Act May 27, 1933, c. 38, Title I, 48 Stat. 75, which is classified to section 77c of Title 15.

Chapter 11 of this title, referred to in par. (51C), is 11 U.S.C.A. § 1101 et seq.

The Securities Exchange Act of 1934, referred to in par. (53B)(B), is Act June 6, 1934, c. 404, 48 Stat. 881, as amended, which is classified principally to chapter 2B of Title 15, 15 U.S.C.A. § 78a et seq. Section 3(a)(47) of the Act, as amended, is classified to 15 U.S.C.A. § 78c(a)(47). For complete classification, see Short Title set out as 15 U.S.C.A. § 78a and Tables.

The Commodity Exchange Act, referred to in par. (53B), is Act Sept. 21, 1922, c. 369, 42 Stat. 998, as amended, which is classified principally to chapter 1 of Title 7, 7 U.S.C.A. § 1 et seq. For complete classification, see Short Title set out as 7 U.S.C.A. § 1 and Tables.

The Gramm-Leach-Bliley Act, referred to in par. (53B), is Pub.L. 106–102, Nov. 12, 1999, 113 Stat. 1338, also known as the Financial Services Modernization Act of 1999, which principally enacted chapters 93, 94 and 95 of Title 15, 15 U.S.C.A. § 6701 et seq., 15 U.S.C.A. § 6801 et seq., and 15 U.S.C.A. § 6901 et seq., respectively, and amended chapters 16 and 17 of Title 12, 12 U.S.C.A. § 1811 et seq., and 12 U.S.C.A. § 1841 et seq. For complete classification, see Tables.

The Legal Certainty for Bank Products Act of 2000, referred to in par. (53B), is Pub.L. 106–554, § 1(a)(5) [Title IV, §§ 401 to 408], Dec. 21, 2000, 114 Stat. 2763, 2763A–457, which enacted 7 U.S.C.A. §§ 27 and 27a to 27f. For complete classification, see Short Title set out as a note under 7 U.S.C.A. § 1 and Tables.

Effective and Applicability Provisions

2007 Acts. Increase of dollar amounts by Judicial Conference of the United States by notice published Feb. 14, 2007, 72 F.R. 7082 effective April 1, 2007, and increase not applicable to cases commenced before the effective date of the adjustments, i.e., April 1, 2007. See Adjustment of Dollar Amounts notes under 11 U.S.C.A. § 104 and this section.

2005 Acts. Pub.L. 109–8, Title XV, § 1501, Apr. 20, 2005, 119 Stat. 216, provided that:

"(a) Effective date.—Except as otherwise provided in this Act, this Act and the amendments made by this Act [see Tables for classification] shall take effect 180 days after the date of enactment of this Act [Apr. 20, 2005].

"(b) Application of amendments.—

"(1) In general.—Except as otherwise provided in this Act and paragraph (2), the amendments made by this Act [see Tables for classification] shall not apply with respect to cases commenced under title 11, United States Code, before the effective date of this Act.

"(2) Certain limitations applicable to debtors.—The amendments made by sections 308 [amending 11 § 522], 322 [amending 11 U.S.C.A. §§ 104 and 522], and 330 [amending 11 U.S.C.A. §§ 727, 1141, 1228, and 1328] shall apply with respect to cases commenced under title 11,

United States Code, on or after the date of the enactment of this Act [Apr. 20, 2005]."

1994 Acts. Section 702 of Pub.L. 103–394 provided that:

"**(a) Effective date.**—Except as provided in subsection (b), this Act [see Short Title of 1994 Amendments set out under this section] shall take effect on the date of the enactment of this Act [Oct. 22, 1994].

"**(b) Application of amendments.—(1)** Except as provided in paragraph (2), the amendments made by this Act shall not apply with respect to cases commenced under title 11 of the United States Code before the date of the enactment of this Act [Oct. 22, 1994].

"**(2)(A)** Paragraph (1) shall not apply with respect to the amendment made by section 111 [enacting subsecs. (g) and (h) of section 524 of this title and a provision set out as a note under 11 U.S.C.A. § 524].

"**(B)** The amendments made by sections 113 and 117 [amending 11 U.S.C.A. §§ 106 and 330, respectively] shall apply with respect to cases commenced under title 11 of the United States Code before, on, and after the date of the enactment of this Act [Oct. 22, 1994].

"**(C)** Section 1110 of title 11, United States Code, as amended by section 201 of this Act [11 U.S.C.A. § 1110], shall apply with respect to any lease, as defined in such section 1110(c) as so amended, entered into in connection with a settlement of any proceeding in any case pending under title 11 of the United States Code on the date of the enactment of this Act [Oct. 22, 1994].

"**(D)** The amendments made by section 305 [amending 11 U.S.C.A. §§ 1123, 1222, 1322] shall apply only to agreements entered into after the date of enactment of this Act [Oct. 22, 1994]."

1992 Acts. Section 3017(c) of Pub.L. 102–486 provided that:

"**(1)** Except as provided in paragraph (2), the amendments made by this section [amending this section and 11 U.S.C.A. § 541] shall take effect on the date of the enactment of this Act [Oct. 24, 1992].

"**(2)** The amendments made by this section [amending this section and 11 U.S.C.A. § 541] shall not apply with respect to cases commenced under title 11 of the United States Code [this title] before the date of the enactment of this Act [Oct. 24, 1992]."

1988 Acts. Section 12 of Pub.L. 100–597 provided that:

"**(a) Effective date.**—Except as provided in subsection (b), this Act and the amendments made by this Act [enacting 11 U.S.C.A. §§ 927 to 929, amending 11 U.S.C.A. §§ 101, 109, 901, 902, 922, 926, 943, and renumbering former section 927 as 930 of this title] shall take effect on the date of the enactment of this Act [Nov. 3, 1988].

"**(b) Application of amendments.**—The amendments made by this Act shall not apply with respect to cases commenced under title 11 of the United States Code before the date of the enactment of this Act [Nov. 3, 1988]."

Section 2 of Pub.L. 100–506 provided that:

"**(a) Effective date.**—Except as provided in subsection (b), this Act and the amendments made by this Act [amending 11 U.S.C.A. §§ 101 and 365] shall take effect on the date of the enactment of this Act [Oct. 18, 1988].

"**(b) Application of amendments.**—The amendments made by this Act shall not apply with respect to any case commenced under title 11 of the United States Code before the date of the enactment of this Act [Oct. 18, 1988]."

1986 Acts. Amendment by Pub.L. 99–554 effective 30 days after Oct. 27, 1986, except as otherwise provided for, see section 302(a) of Pub.L. 99–554, set out as a note under 28 U.S.C.A. § 581.

Amendment by Pub.L. 99–554, § 201, not to become effective in or with respect to certain specified judicial districts until, or apply to cases while pending in such district before, the expiration of the 270–day period beginning 30 days after Oct. 27, 1986, or of the 30–day period beginning on the date the Attorney General certifies under section 303 of Pub.L. 99–554 the region specified in a paragraph of section 581(a) of Title 28, as amended by section 111(a) of Pub.L. 99–554, that includes such district, whichever occurs first, see section 302(d)(1) of Pub.L. 99–554, set out as a note under 28 U.S.C.A. § 581.

Amendment by Pub.L. 99–554, § 201, not to become effective in or with respect to certain specified judicial districts until, or apply to cases while pending in such district before, the expiration of the 2–year period beginning 30 days after Oct. 27, 1986, or of the 30–day period beginning on the date the Attorney General certifies under section 303 of Pub.L. 99–554 the region specified in a paragraph of section 581(a) of Title 28, as amended by section 111(a) of Pub.L. 99–554, that includes such district, whichever occurs first, see section 302(d)(2) of Pub.L. 99–554, set out as a note under 28 U.S.C.A. § 581.

Amendment by Pub.L. 99–554, § 201, not to become effective in or with respect to judicial districts established for the States of Alabama and North Carolina until, or apply to cases while pending in such district before, such district elects to be included in a bankruptcy region established in section 581(a) of Title 28, as amended by section 111(a) of Pub.L. 99–554, or Oct. 1, 2002, whichever occurs first, and, except as otherwise provided for, with respect to cases under chapters 7, 11, 12, and 13 of Title 11 commenced before 30 days after Oct. 27, 1986, and pending in a judicial district in the States of Alabama or North Carolina before any election made under section 302(d)(3)(A) of Pub.L. 99–554 by such district becomes effective or Oct. 1, 2002, whichever occurs first, amendments, by Pub.L. 99–554 not to apply until Oct. 1, 2003, or the expiration of the 1–year period beginning on the date such election becomes effective, whichever occurs first, and further, in any judicial district in Alabama or North Carolina not making the election described in section 302(d)(3)(A) of Pub.L. 99–554, any person appointed under regulations issued by the Judicial Conference to administer estates in cases under Title 11 authorized to establish, etc., a panel of private trustees, and to supervise cases and trustees in cases under chapters 7, 11, 12, and 13 of Title 11, until amendments by sections 201 to 231 of Pub.L. 99–554 effective in such district, see section 302(d)(3)(A) to (F), (H), (I) of Pub.L. 99–554, set out as a note under 28 U.S.C.A. § 581.

Amendment by Pub.L. 99–554, § 201, except as otherwise provided, with respect to cases under chapters 7, 11, 12, and 13 of Title 11 commenced before 30 days after Oct. 27, 1986, and pending in a judicial district referred to in section 581(a) of Title 28, as amended by section 111(a) of Pub.L. 99–554, for which a United States trustee is not authorized before 30 days after Oct. 27, 1986 to be appointed, not applicable until the expiration of the 3-year period beginning on Oct. 27, 1986, or of the 1-year period beginning on the date the Attorney General certifies section 303 of Pub.L. 99–554 the region specified in a paragraph of such section 581(a) that includes, such district, whichever occurs first, see section 302(e)(1), (2) of Pub.L. 99–554, set out as a note under 28 U.S.C.A. § 581.

Amendments by Pub.L. 99–554, § 251, effective 30 days after Oct. 27, 1986, but not to apply with respect to cases commenced under this title before that date, see section 302(a), (c)(1) of Pub.L. 99–554, set out as a note under 28 U.S.C.A. § 581.

Amendment by Pub.L. 99–554, § 283, effective 30 days after Oct. 27, 1986, see section 302(a) of Pub.L. 99–554, set out as a note under 28 U.S.C.A. § 581.

1984 Acts. Section 552, formerly section 553 of Title III (§§ 301 to 553) of Pub.L. 98–353, as redesignated by Pub.L. 98–531, §§ 1(2), Oct. 19, 1984, 98 Stat. 2704, eff. July 10, 1984, provided that:

"**(a)** Except as otherwise provided in this section the amendments made by this title [see Tables for classification] shall become effective to [sic] cases filed 90 days after the date of enactment of this Act [July 10, 1984].

"**(b)** The amendments made by section 426(b) [amending 11 U.S.C.A. § 303] shall become effective upon the date of enactment of this Act [July 10, 1984].

"**(c)** The amendments made by subtitle J [enacting 11 U.S.C.A. § 1113], shall become effective as provided in section 541(c) [set out as a note under 11 U.S.C.A. § 1113]."

Separability of Provisions

Section 701 of Pub.L. 103–394 provided that: "If any provision of this Act or amendment made by this Act [see Short Title of 1994 Amendments note set out under this section] or the application of such provision or amendment to any person or circumstance is held to be unconstitutional, the remaining provisions of and amendments made by this Act and the application of such other provisions and amendments to any person or circumstance shall not be affected thereby."

Section 551 of Title III (§§ 301 to 553) of Pub.L. 98–353 provided that: "If any provision of this title or any amendment made by this title [see Tables for classification], or the application thereof to any person or circumstance is held invalid, the provisions of every other part, and their application shall not be affected thereby."

Savings Provisions

Pub.L. 109–8, Title IX, § 912, as added by Pub.L. 109–390, § 5(d), Dec. 12, 2006, 120 Stat. 2698, provided that: "The meanings of terms used in this title [Title IX of the Bankruptcy Abuse Prevention and Consumer Protection Act of 2005, Pub.L. 109–8, Title IX (§§ 901 to 912), Apr. 20, 2005, 119 Stat. 146; see Tables for complete classification] are applicable for the purposes of this title only, and shall not be construed or applied so as to challenge or affect the characterization, definition, or treatment of any similar terms under any other statute, regulation, or rule, including the Gramm–Leach–Bliley Act [Pub.L. 106–102, Nov. 12, 1999, 113 Stat. 1338; see Tables for complete classification], the Legal Certainty for Bank Products Act of 2000 [Pub.L. 106–554, § 1(a)(5) (Title IV, §§ 401 to 408), Dec. 21, 2000, 114 Stat. 2763, 2763A–457, which enacted 7 U.S.C.A. §§ 27 and 27a to 27f; for complete classification, see Short Title note set out under 7 U.S.C.A. § 1 and Tables], the securities laws (as such term is defined in section 3(a)(47) of the Securities Exchange Act of 1934) [15 U.S.C.A. § 78c(a)(47)], and the Commodity Exchange Act [Act Sept. 21, 1922, c. 369, 42 Stat. 998, as amended, which is classified principally to chapter 1 of Title 7, 7 U.S.C.A. § 1 et seq.; for complete classification, see Short Title set out as 7 U.S.C.A. § 1 and Tables]."

Short Title

2008 Amendments. Pub.L. 110–438, § 1, Oct. 20, 2008, 122 Stat. 5000, provided that: "This Act [amending 11 U.S.C.A. § 707, and enacting provisions set out as a note under 11 U.S.C.A. § 707] may be cited as the 'National Guard and Reservists Debt Relief Act of 2008'."

2006 Amendments. Pub.L. 109–439, § 1, Dec. 20, 2006, 120 Stat. 3285, provided that: "This Act [amending 11 U.S.C.A. § 1325] may be cited as the 'Religious Liberty and Charitable Donation Clarification Act of 2006'."

Pub.L. 109–390, § 1, Dec. 12, 2006, 120 Stat. 2692, provided that: "This Act [amending this section, 11 U.S.C.A. §§ 362, 546, and 741, 12 U.S.C.A. §§ 1787, 1821, 4403, and 4404, and 15 U.S.C.A. § 78eee, and enacting provisions set out as notes under this section] may be cited as the 'Financial Netting Improvements Act of 2006'."

2005 Amendments. Pub.L. 109–8, § 1(a), Apr. 20, 2005, 119 Stat. 23, provided that: "This Act [see Tables for complete classification] may be cited as the 'Bankruptcy Abuse Prevention and Consumer Protection Act of 2005'." This Act is also commonly known as the BAPCPA.

Pub.L. 109–8, Title III, § 332(a), Apr. 20, 2005, 119 Stat. 103, provided that: "This section [amending 11 U.S.C.A. § 303 and 18 U.S.C.A. § 157] may be cited as the 'Involuntary Bankruptcy Improvement Act of 2005'."

2004 Amendments. Pub.L. 108–369, § 1, Oct. 25, 2004, 118 Stat. 1749, provided that: "This Act [enacting provisions set out as a note under 11 U.S.C.A. § 1201 and amending 11 U.S.C.A. §§ 1201 to 1208, 1221 to 1231, and provisions set out as a note under 11 U.S.C.A. § 1201] may be cited as the 'Family Farmer Bankruptcy Relief Act of 2004'."

2003 Amendments. Pub.L. 108–73, § 1, Aug. 15, 2003, 117 Stat. 891, provided that: "This Act [enacting provisions set out as a note under 11 U.S.C.A. § 1201 and amending 11 U.S.C.A. §§ 1201 to 1208, 1221 to 1231, and provisions set out as a note under 11 U.S.C.A. § 1201] may be cited as the 'Family Farmer Bankruptcy Relief Act of 2003'."

2002 Amendments. Pub.L. 107–377, § 1, Dec. 19, 2002, 116 Stat. 3115, provided that: "This Act [amending 11 U.S.C.A. §§ 1201 to 1208, 1221 to 1231, enacting provisions set out as notes under 11 U.S.C.A. § 1201, and amending provisions set out as notes under 11 U.S.C.A. § 1201] may be cited as the 'Protection of Family Farmers Act of 2002'."

1998 Amendments. Pub.L. 105–183, § 1, June 19, 1998, 112 Stat. 517, provided that: "This Act [amending 11 U.S.C.A. §§ 544, 546, 548, 707, and 1325 and enacting provisions set out as a note under 11 U.S.C.A. § 544] may be cited as the 'Religious Liberty and Charitable Donation Protection Act of 1998'."

1994 Amendments. Section 1(a) of Pub.L. 103–394 provided that: "This Act [enacting 11 U.S.C.A. § 110 and 18 U.S.C.A. §§ 156, 157, amending 11 U.S.C.A. §§ 101, 104, 105, 106, 109, 303, 322, 326, 330, 341, 342, 345, 346, 348, 349, 362, 363, 364, 365, 502, 503, 507, 522, 523, 524, 525, 541, 542, 543,

546, 547, 548, 549, 550, 552, 553, 555, 556, 559, 706, 723, 724, 726, 741, 742, 743, 745, 761, 1102, 1104, 1106, 1110, 1112, 1121, 1123, 1124, 1125, 1129, 1145, 1166, 1167, 1168, 1222, 1226, 1302, 1322, 1326, and 1328, rule 7004 of the Federal Rules of Bankruptcy Procedure, 12 U.S.C.A. §§ 1787, 1821, 18 U.S.C.A. §§ 152, 153, 154, 1961, and 28 U.S.C.A. §§ 157, 158, 586, 1334, 2073, 2075, and enacting provisions section out as notes preceding 11 U.S.C.A. § 101 and 11 U.S.C.A. §§ 101, 341, 501, 524] may be cited as the 'Bankruptcy Reform Act of 1994'."

1990 Amendments. Pub.L. 101–647, Title XXXI, § 3101, Nov. 29, 1990, 104 Stat. 4916, provided that: "This title [amending 11 U.S.C.A. §§ 523, 1328 and enacting provisions set out as a note under 11 U.S.C.A. § 523] may be cited as the 'Criminal Victims Protection Act of 1990'."

Pub.L. 101–581, § 1, Nov. 15, 1990, 104 Stat. 2865, provided that: "This Act [amending 11 U.S.C.A. §§ 523, 1328 and enacting provisions set out as notes under 11 U.S.C.A. § 523] may be cited as the 'Criminal Victims Protection Act of 1990'."

1988 Amendments. Pub.L. 100–334, § 1, June 16, 1988, 102 Stat. 610, provided that: "This Act [enacting 11 U.S.C.A. § 1114, amending 11 U.S.C.A. § 1129, enacting provisions set out as a note under 11 U.S.C.A. § 1114, and amending and repealing provisions set out as notes under 11 U.S.C.A. § 1106] may be cited as the 'Retiree Benefits Bankruptcy Protection Act of 1988'."

1986 Amendments. Pub.L. 99–554, § 1, Oct. 27, 1986, 100 Stat. 3088, provided that said Act [enacting 11 U.S.C.A. §§ 307, 1201 to 1231 and 28 U.S.C.A. § 589a, amending 11 U.S.C.A. §§ 101 to 103, 105, 108, 109, 303, 321, 322, 324, 326, 327, 329, 330, 341, 343, 345 to 348, 362 to 365, 502, 503, 521 to 524, 546 to 549, 554, 557, 701, 703 to 707, 724, 726 to 728, 743, 1102, 1104 to 1106, 1112, 1121, 1129, 1163, 1202, 1302, 1306, 1307, 1324 to 1326, Bankruptcy Form No. 1, set out in the Appendix to Title 11, 28 U.S.C.A. §§ 49, 96, 152, 156, 157, 526, 581, 582, 584 to 587, 604, 1334, 1930, repealing 11 U.S.C.A. §§ 1201 to 1231, 1501 to 151326, enacting provisions set out as notes under 28 U.S.C.A. §§ 581, 589, amending provisions set out as a note under 28 U.S.C.A. § 152, and repealing provisions set out as a note preceding 28 U.S.C.A. § 581] may be cited as the "Bankruptcy Judges, United States Trustees, and Family Farmer Bankruptcy Act of 1986". See note set out under 28 U.S.C.A. § 581.

1984 Amendments. Section 361 of Subtitle C (§§ 361 to 363) of Title III of Pub.L. 98–353 provided that: "This subtitle [amending this section and 11 U.S.C.A. §§ 362, 365, 541] may be cited as the 'Leasehold Management Bankruptcy Amendments Act of 1983'."

Adjustment of Dollar Amounts

For adjustment of dollar amounts specified in pars. (3), (18), (19A), (51D) of this section by the Judicial Conference of the United States, effective Apr. 1, 2007, see note set out under 11 U.S.C.A. § 104 of this title.

By notice dated Feb. 14, 2007, 72 F.R. 7082, the Judicial Conference of the United States adjusted the dollar amounts in provisions specified in pars. (3), (18), (19A), (51D) of this section, effective Apr. 1, 2007, as follows:

In par. (3) adjusted $150,000 to $164,250.

In par. (18) adjusted $3,237,000 (each time it appears) to $3,544,525 (each time it appears).

In par. (19A) adjusted $1,500,000 (each time it appears) to $1,642,500 (each time it appears).

In par. (51D) adjusted $2,000,000 (each time it appears) to $2,190,000 (each time it appears).

Scope of Application

Pub.L. 109–390, § 7, Dec. 12, 2006, 120 Stat. 2700, provided that: "The amendments made by this Act [amending this section, 11 U.S.C.A. §§ 362, 546, and 741, 12 U.S.C.A. §§ 1787, 1821, 4403, and 4404, and 15 U.S.C.A. § 78eee, and enacting provisions set out as notes under this section] shall not apply to any cases commenced under title 11, United States Code, or appointments made under any Federal or State law, before the date of the enactment of this Act [Dec. 12, 2006]."

Nonlimitation of Information

Pub.L. 109–8, Title I, § 102(e), Apr. 20, 2005, 119 Stat. 33, provided that: "Nothing in this title [see Tables for classification] shall limit the ability of a creditor to provide information to a judge (except for information communicated ex parte, unless otherwise permitted by applicable law), United States trustee (or bankruptcy administrator, if any), or trustee."

[Except as otherwise provided, this note effective 180 days after April 20, 2005, and inapplicable with respect to cases commenced under Title 11 before the effective date, see Pub.L. 109–8, Title XV, § 1501, Apr. 20, 2005, 119 Stat. 216, set out as a note under this section.]

Rule of Construction

Pub.L. 109–8, Title X, § 1007(e), Apr. 20, 2005, 119 Stat. 188, provided that: "**Applicability.**—Nothing in this section [amending this section and 11 U.S.C.A. §§ 109, 1203, 1206, and the chapter heading and table of contents for Chapter 12 of Title 11] shall change, affect, or amend the Fishery Conservation and Management Act of 1976 [officially titled the Magnuson-Stevens Fishery Conservation and Management Act, which is Pub.L. 94–265, Apr. 13, 1976, 90 Stat. 331, as amended, and which is principally classified to chapter 38 of Title 16] (16 U.S.C. § 1801 et seq.)."

Pub.L. 109–8, Title XI, § 1101(c), Apr. 20, 2005, 119 Stat. 189, provided that: "The amendments made by subsection (a) of this section [amending this section by redesignating par. (27A) as par. (27B) and inserting a new par. (27A) and pars. (40A) and (40B)] shall not affect the interpretation of section 109(b) of title 11, United States Code."

[Except as otherwise provided, this note effective 180 days after April 20, 2005, and inapplicable with respect to cases commenced under Title 11 before the effective date, see Pub.L. 109–8, Title XV, § 1501, Apr. 20, 2005, 119 Stat. 216, set out as a note under this section.]

Judicial Education

Pub.L. 109–8, Title XII, § 1226, Apr. 20, 2005, 119 Stat. 199, provided that: "The Director of the Federal Judicial Center, in consultation with the Director of the Executive Office for United States Trustees, shall develop materials and conduct such training as may be useful to courts in implementing this Act [see Short Title 2005 Amendments note set out under this section] and the amendments made by this Act, including the requirements relating to the means test under section 707(b), and reaffirmation agreements under section 524, of title 11 of the United States Code, as amended by this Act."

[Except as otherwise provided, this note effective 180 days after April 20, 2005, and inapplicable with respect to cases commenced under Title 11 before the effective date, see Pub.L. 109–8, Title XV, § 1501, Apr. 20, 2005, 119 Stat. 216, set out as a note under this section.]

CROSS REFERENCES

"Commodity broker", as defined under this section, determining powers and duties of Securities Investor Protection Act trustees, see 15 USCA § 78fff–1.

Crime victims' rights, rights afforded and best efforts to accord rights, procedures to promote compliance, see 18 USCA § 3771.

"Forward contract", "repurchase agreement," and "transfer" defined under this section as having same meaning for purposes of—

Federal credit union insurance, see 12 USCA § 1787.

Federal deposit insurance, see 12 USCA § 1821.

"Insolvent" defined under this section as having same meaning for purposes of Securities Investor Protection Act decrees, see 15 USCA § 78eee.

List of creditors, unsecured claims, see Official Bankr. Form 4, 11 USCA.

"Margin payment" and "settlement payment" as defined under this section determining exclusion of certain setoffs from automatic stay, see 11 USCA § 362.

"Railroad," as defined under this section, determining bankruptcy fees, see 28 USCA § 1930.

Statement of financial affairs, see Official Bankr. Form 7, 11 USCA.

§ 102. Rules of construction

In this title—

(1) "after notice and a hearing", or a similar phrase—

(A) means after such notice as is appropriate in the particular circumstances, and such opportunity for a hearing as is appropriate in the particular circumstances; but

(B) authorizes an act without an actual hearing if such notice is given properly and if—

(i) such a hearing is not requested timely by a party in interest; or

(ii) there is insufficient time for a hearing to be commenced before such act must be done, and the court authorizes such act;

(2) "claim against the debtor" includes claim against property of the debtor;

(3) "includes" and "including" are not limiting;

(4) "may not" is prohibitive, and not permissive;

(5) "or" is not exclusive;

(6) "order for relief" means entry of an order for relief;

(7) the singular includes the plural;

(8) a definition, contained in a section of this title that refers to another section of this title, does not, for the purpose of such reference, affect the meaning of a term used in such other section; and

(9) "United States trustee" includes a designee of the United States trustee.

(Pub.L. 95–598, Nov. 6, 1978, 92 Stat. 2554; Pub.L. 98–353, Title III, § 422, July 10, 1984, 98 Stat. 369; Pub.L. 99–554, Title II, § 202, Oct. 27, 1986, 100 Stat. 3097.)

HISTORICAL AND STATUTORY NOTES

Revision Notes and Legislative Reports

1978 Acts. Section 102 provides seven rules of construction. Some are derived from current law; others are derived from 1 U.S.C. 1; a few are new. They apply generally throughout proposed title 11. These are terms that are not appropriate for definition, but that require an explanation.

Paragraph (1) defines the concept of "after notice and a hearing." The concept is central to the bill and to the separation of the administrative and judicial functions of bankruptcy judges. The phrase means after such notice as is appropriate in the particular circumstances (to be prescribed by either the Rules of Bankruptcy Procedure or by the court in individual circumstances that the Rules do not cover. In many cases, the Rules will provide for combined notice of several proceedings), and such opportunity for a hearing as is appropriate in the particular circumstances. Thus, a hearing will not be necessary in every instance. If there is no objection to the proposed action, the action may go ahead without court action. This is a significant change from present law, which requires the affirmative approval of the bankruptcy judge for almost every action. The change will permit the bankruptcy judge to stay removed from the administration of the bankruptcy or reorganization case, and to become involved only when there is a dispute about a proposed action, that is, only when there is an objection. The phrase "such opportunity for a hearing as is appropriate in the particular circumstances" is designed to permit the Rules and the courts to expedite or dispense with hearings when speed is essential. The language "or similar phrase" is intended to cover the few instances in the bill where "after notice and a hearing" is interrupted by another phrase, such as "after notice to the debtor and a hearing."

Paragraph (2) specifies that "claim against the debtor" includes claim against property of the debtor. This paragraph is intended to cover nonrecourse loan agreements where the creditor's only rights are against property of the debtor, and not against the debtor personally. Thus, such an agreement would give rise to a claim that would be treated as a claim against the debtor personally, for the purposes of the bankruptcy code.

Paragraph (3) is a codification of *American Surety Co. v. Marotta*, 287 U.S. 513 (1933) [53 S.Ct. 260, 77 L.Ed. 466]. It specifies that "includes" and "including" are not limiting.

Paragraph (4) specifies that "may not" is prohibitive and not permissive (such as in "might not").

Paragraph (5) specifies that "or" is not exclusive. Thus, if a party "may do (a) or (b)", then the party may do either or both. The party is not limited to a mutually exclusive choice between the two alternatives.

Paragraph (6) makes clear that "order for relief" means entry of an order for relief. If the court orally orders relief, but the order is not entered until a later time, then any time measurements in the bill are from entry, not from the oral order. In a voluntary case, the entry of the order for relief is the filing of the petition commencing the voluntary case.

Paragraph (7) specifies that the singular includes the plural. The plural, however, generally does not include the singular. The bill uses only the singular, even when the item in question most often is found in plural quantities, in order to avoid the confusion possible if both rules of construction applied. When an item is specified in the plural, the plural is intended. Senate Report No. 95–989.

1984 Acts. Statements by Legislative Leaders, see 1984 U.S.Code Cong. and Adm.News, p. 576.

1986 Acts. House Report No. 99–764 and House Conference Report No. 99–958, see 1986 U.S.Code Cong. and Adm.News, p. 5227.

Legislative Statements

Section 102 specifies various rules of construction but is not exclusive. Other rules of construction that are not set out in title 11 are nevertheless intended to be followed in construing the bankruptcy code. For example, the phrase "on request of a party in interest" or a similar phrase, is used in connection with an action that the court may take in various sections of the Code. The phrase is intended to restrict the court from acting sua sponte. Rules of bankruptcy procedure or court decisions will determine who is a party in interest for the particular purposes of the provision in question, but the court will not be permitted to act on its own.

Although "property" is not construed in this section, it is used consistently throughout the code in its broadest sense, including cash, all interests in property, such as liens, and every kind of consideration including promises to act or forbear to act as in section 548(d).

Section 102(1) expands on a rule of construction contained in H.R. 8200 as passed by the House and in the Senate amendment. The phrase "after notice and a hearing", or a similar phrase, is intended to be construed according to the particular proceeding to mean after such notice as is appropriate in the particular circumstances, and such opportunity, if any, for a hearing as is appropriate in the particular circumstances. If a provision of title 11 authorizes an act to be taken "after notice and a hearing" this means that if appropriate notice is given and no party to whom such notice is sent timely requests a hearing, then the act sought to be taken may be taken without an actual hearing.

In very limited emergency circumstances, there will be insufficient time for a hearing to be commenced before an action must be taken. The action sought to be taken may be taken if authorized by the court at an ex parte hearing of which a record is made in open court. A full hearing after the fact will be available in such an instance.

In some circumstances, such as under section 1128, the bill requires a hearing and the court may act only after a hearing is held. In those circumstances the judge will receive evidence before ruling. In other circumstances, the court may take action "after notice and a hearing," if no party in interest requests a hearing. In that event a court order authorizing the action to be taken is not necessary as the ultimate action taken by the court implies such an authorization.

Section 102(8) is new. It contains a rule of construction indicating that a definition contained in a section in title 11 that refers to another section of title 11 does not, for the purposes of such reference, take the meaning of a term used in the other section. For example, section 522(a)(2) defines "value" for the purposes of section 522. Section 548(d)(2) defines "value" for purposes of section 548. When section 548 is incorporated by reference in section 522, this rule of construction makes clear that the definition of "value" in section 548 governs its meaning in section 522 notwithstanding a different definition of "value" in section 522(a)(2).

Effective and Applicability Provisions

1986 Acts. Amendment by Pub.L. 99–554 effective 30 days after Oct. 27, 1986, except as otherwise provided for, see section 302(a) of Pub.L. 99–554, set out as a note under section 581 of Title 28, Judiciary and Judicial Procedure.

Amendment by Pub.L. 99–554, § 202, not to become effective in or with respect to certain specified judicial districts until, or apply to cases while pending in such district before, the expiration of the 270-day period beginning 30 days after Oct. 27, 1986, or of the 30-day period beginning on the date the Attorney General certifies under section 303 of Pub.L. 99–554 the region specified in a paragraph of section 581(a) of Title 28, as amended by section 111(a) of Pub.L. 99–554, that includes such district, whichever occurs first, see section 302(d)(1) of Pub.L. 99–554, set out as a note under section 581 of Title 28.

Amendment by Pub.L. 99–554, § 202, not to become effective in or with respect to certain specified judicial districts until, or apply to cases while pending in such district before, the expiration of the 2-year period beginning 30 days after Oct. 27, 1986, or of the 30-day period beginning on the date the Attorney General certifies under section 303 of Pub.L. 99–554 the region specified in a paragraph of section 581(a) of Title 28, as amended by section 111(a) of Pub.L. 99–554, that includes such district, whichever occurs first, see section 302(d)(2) of Pub.L. 99–554, set out as a note under section 581 of Title 28.

Amendment by Pub.L. 99–554, § 202, not to become effective in or with respect to judicial districts established for the States of Alabama and North Carolina until, or apply to cases while pending in such district before, such district elects to be included in a bankruptcy region established in section 581(a) of Title 28, as amended by section 111(a) of Pub.L. 99–554, or Oct. 1, 2002, whichever occurs first, and, except as otherwise provided, with respect to cases under chapters 7, 11, 12 and 13 of Title 11 commenced before 30 days after Oct. 27, 1986, and pending in a judicial district in the States of Alabama or North Carolina before any election made under section 302(d)(3)(A) of Pub.L. 99–554 by such district becomes effective or Oct. 1, 2002, whichever occurs first, amendments by Pub.L. 99–554 not to apply until Oct. 1, 2003, or the expiration of the 1-year period beginning on the date such election becomes effective, whichever occurs first, and further, in any judicial district in Alabama or North Carolina not making the election described in section 302(d)(3)(A) of Pub.L. 99–554, any person appointed under regulations issued by the Judicial Conference to administer estates in cases under Title 11 authorized to establish, etc., a panel of private trustees, and to supervise cases and trustees in cases under chapters 7, 11, 12, and 13 of Title 11, until amendments by sections 201 to 231 of Pub.L. 99–554 effective in such district, see section 302(d)(3)(A) to (F), (H), (I) of Pub.L. 99–554, set out as a note under section 581 of Title 28.

Amendment by Pub.L. 99–554, § 202, except as otherwise provided, with respect to cases under chapters 7, 11, 12, and 13 of Title 11 commenced before 30 days after Oct. 27, 1986, and pending in a judicial district referred to in section 581(a) of Title 28, as amended by section 111(a) of Pub.L. 99–554, for which a United States trustee is not authorized before 30 days after Oct. 27, 1986 to be appointed, not applicable until the expiration of the 3-year period beginning on Oct. 27, 1986, or of the 1-year period beginning on the date the Attorney General certifies under section 303 of Pub.L. 99–554 the region specified in a paragraph of such section 581(a) that includes such district, whichever occurs first, see section 302(e)(1), (2) of Pub.L. 99–554, set out as a note under section 581 of Title 28.

1984 Acts. Amendment by Pub.L. 98–353 effective with respect to cases filed 90 days after July 10, 1984, see section 552(a), formerly 553(a) of Pub.L. 98–353, set out as a note under section 101 of this title.

§ 103. Applicability of chapters

(a) Except as provided in section 1161 of this title, chapters 1, 3, and 5 of this title apply in a case under chapter 7, 11, 12, or 13 of this title, and this chapter, sections 307, 362(n), 555 through 557, and 559 through 562 apply in a case under chapter 15.

(b) Subchapters I and II of chapter 7 of this title apply only in a case under such chapter.

(c) Subchapter III of chapter 7 of this title applies only in a case under such chapter concerning a stockbroker.

(d) Subchapter IV of chapter 7 of this title applies only in a case under such chapter concerning a commodity broker.

(e) Scope of application.—Subchapter V of chapter 7 of this title shall apply only in a case under such chapter concerning the liquidation of an uninsured State member bank, or a corporation organized under section 25A of the Federal Reserve Act, which operates, or operates as, a multilateral clearing organization pursuant to section 409 of the Federal Deposit Insurance Corporation Improvement Act of 1991.

(f) Except as provided in section 901 of this title, only chapters 1 and 9 of this title apply in a case under such chapter 9.

(g) Except as provided in section 901 of this title, subchapters I, II, and III of chapter 11 of this title apply only in a case under such chapter.

(h) Subchapter IV of chapter 11 of this title applies only in a case under such chapter concerning a railroad.

(i) Chapter 13 of this title applies only in a case under such chapter.

(j) Chapter 12 of this title applies only in a case under such chapter.

(k) Chapter 15 applies only in a case under such chapter, except that—

(1) sections 1505, 1513, and 1514 apply in all cases under this title; and

(2) section 1509 applies whether or not a case under this title is pending.

(Pub.L. 95–598, Nov. 6, 1978, 92 Stat. 2555; Pub.L. 97–222, § 2, July 27, 1982, 96 Stat. 235; Pub.L. 98–353, Title III, § 423, July 10, 1984, 98 Stat. 369; Pub.L. 99–554, Title II, § 252, Oct. 27, 1986, 100 Stat. 3104; Pub.L. 106–554, § 1(a)(5) [Title I, § 112(c)(5)(A)], Dec. 21, 2000, 114 Stat. 2763, 2763A–394; Pub.L. 109–8, Title VIII, § 802(a), Apr. 20, 2005, 119 Stat. 145.)

HISTORICAL AND STATUTORY NOTES

Revision Notes and Legislative Reports

1978 Acts. Section 103 prescribes which chapters of the proposed bankruptcy code apply in various cases. All cases, other than cases ancillary to foreign proceedings, are filed under chapter 7, 9, 11, or 13, the operative chapters of the proposed bankruptcy code. The general provisions that apply no matter which chapter a case is filed under are found in chapters 1, 3, and 5. Subsection (a) makes this explicit, with an exception for chapter 9. The other provisions, which are self-explanatory, provide the special rules for Stockbroker Liquidations, Commodity Broker Liquidations, Municipal Debt Adjustments, and Railroad Reorganizations. Senate Report No. 95–989.

1982 Acts. House Report No. 97–420, see 1982 U.S.Code Cong. and Adm.News, p. 583.

1984 Acts. Statements by Legislative Leaders, see 1984 U.S.Code Cong. and Adm.News, p. 576.

1986 Acts. House Report No. 99–764 and House Conference Report No. 99–958, see 1986 U.S.Code Cong. and Adm.News, p. 5227.

2000 Acts. House Report No. 106–645 and Statement by President, see 2000 U.S. Code Cong. and Adm. News, p. 2459.

2005 Acts. House Report No. 109–31(Part I), see 2005 U.S. Code Cong. and Adm. News, p. 88.

References in Text

Chapters 1, 3, and 5 of this title, referred to in subsec. (a), are 11 U.S.C.A. §§ 101 et seq., 301 et seq., and 501 et seq.

Chapter 7, 11, 12, or 13 of this title, referred to in subsec. (a), is 11 U.S.C.A. § 701 et seq., 11 U.S.C.A. § 1101 et seq., 11 U.S.C.A. § 1201 et seq., or 11 U.S.C.A. § 1301 et seq., respectively.

Chapter 15, referred to in subsecs. (a) and (k), is chapter 15 of this title, which is classified to 11 U.S.C.A. § 1501 et seq.

Subchapters I and II of chapter 7 of this title, referred to in subsec. (b), are 11 U.S.C.A. §§ 701 et seq. and 721 et seq., respectively.

Subchapter III of chapter 7 of this title, referred to in subsec. (c), is 11 U.S.C.A. § 741 et seq.

Subchapter IV of chapter 7 of this title, referred to in subsecs. (d) and (h), is 11 U.S.C.A. § 761 et seq.

Subchapter V of chapter 7 of this title, referred to in subsec. (e), is 11 U.S.C.A. § 781 et seq.

Section 25A of the Federal Reserve Act, referred to in subsec. (e), is Dec. 23, 1913, c. 6, § 25A, formerly § 25(a), as added Dec. 24, 1919, c. 18, 41 Stat. 378, as amended, which is classified to subchapter II of chapter 6 of Title 12, 12 U.S.C.A. § 611 et seq.

Section 409 of the Federal Deposit Insurance Corporation Improvement Act of 1991, referred to in subsec. (e), is Pub.L. 102–242, Title IV, § 409, as added by Pub.L. 106–554, § 1(a)(5) [Title I, § 112(a)(3)], Dec. 21, 2000, 114 Stat. 2763, 2763A–394, which is classified as 12 U.S.C.A. § 4422.

Chapter 13 of this title, referred to in subsec. (i), is 11 U.S.C.A. § 1301 et seq.

Chapter 12 of this title, referred to in subsec. (j), is 11 U.S.C.A. § 1201 et seq.

Effective and Applicability Provisions

2005 Acts. Amendments by Pub.L. 109–8 effective, except as otherwise provided, 180 days after April 20, 2005, and inapplicable with respect to cases commenced under Title 11 before the effective date, see Pub.L. 109–8, § 1501, set out as a note under 11 U.S.C.A. § 101.

1986 Acts. Amendment by Pub.L. 99–554 effective 30 days after Oct. 27, 1986, but not applicable to cases commenced under this title before that date, see section 302(a), (c)(1) of Pub.L. 99–554, set out as a note under section 581 of Title 28, Judiciary and Judicial Procedure.

1984 Acts. Amendment by Pub.L. 98–353 effective with respect to cases filed 90 days after July 10, 1984, see section 552(a), formerly 553(a), of Pub.L. 98–353, set out as a note under section 101 of this title.

CROSS REFERENCES

Confirmation of Chapter 9 plan complying with provisions of this title made applicable by this section, see 11 USCA § 943.

Terms as defined in this title made applicable to Chapter 9 by this section, see 11 USCA § 901.

Terms "property of the estate" and "trustee" made applicable to Chapter 9 by this section, defined for purposes of such chapter, see 11 USCA § 902.

§ 104. Adjustment of dollar amounts

(a) On April 1, 1998, and at each 3–year interval ending on April 1 thereafter, each dollar amount in effect under sections 101(3), 101(18), 101(19A), 101(51D), 109(e), 303(b), 507(a), 522(d), 522(f)(3) and 522(f)(4), 522(n), 522(p), 522(q), 523(a)(2)(C), 541(b), 547(c)(9), 707(b), 1322(d), 1325(b), and 1326(b)(3) of this title and section 1409(b) of title 28 immediately before such April 1 shall be adjusted—

(1) to reflect the change in the Consumer Price Index for All UrbanConsumers, published by the Department of Labor, for the most recent 3–year period ending immediately before January 1 preceding such April 1, and

(2) to round to the nearest $25 the dollar amount that represents such change.

(b) Not later than March 1, 1998, and at each 3–year interval ending on March 1 thereafter, the Judicial Conference of the United States shall publish in the Federal Register the dollar amounts that will become effective on such April 1 under sections 101(3), 101(18), 101(19A), 101(51D), 109(e), 303(b), 507(a), 522(d), 522(f)(3) and 522(f)(4), 522(n), 522(p), 522(q), 523(a)(2)(C), 541(b), 547(c)(9), 707(b), 1322(d), 1325(b), and 1326(b)(3) of this title and section 1409(b) of title 28.

(c) Adjustments made in accordance with subsection (a) shall not apply with respect to cases commenced before the date of such adjustments.

(Pub.L. 95–598, Nov. 6, 1978, 92 Stat. 2555; Pub.L. 103–394, Title I, § 108(e), Oct. 22, 1994, 108 Stat. 4112; Pub.L. 109–8, Title I, § 102(j), Title II, §§ 224(e)(2), 226(b), Title III, § 322(b), Title IV, § 432(c), Title X, § 1002, Title XII, § 1202, Apr. 20, 2005, 119 Stat. 35, 65, 67, 97, 110, 186, 193; Pub.L. 110–406, § 7, Oct. 13, 2008, 122 Stat. 4293.)

HISTORICAL AND STATUTORY NOTES

Revision Notes and Legislative Reports

1978 Acts. This section requires that the Director of the Administrative Office of the U. S. Courts report to Congress and the President before Oct. 1, 1985, and before May 1 every 6 years thereafter a recommendation for adjustment in dollar amounts found in this title. The Committee feels that regular adjustment of the dollar amounts by the Director will conserve congressional time and yet assure that the relative dollar amounts used in the bill are maintained. Changes in the cost of living should be a significant, but not necessarily the only, factor considered by the Director. The fact that there has been an increase in the cost of living does not necessarily mean that an adjustment of dollar amounts would be needed or warranted. Senate Report No. 95–989.

This section requires the Judicial Conference to report to the Congress every four years after the effective date of the bankruptcy code any changes that have occurred in the cost of living during the preceding four years, and the appropriate adjustments to the dollar amounts in the bill. The dollar amounts are found primarily in the exemption section (11 U.S.C. 522), the wage priority (11 U.S.C. 507), and the eligibility for chapter 13 (11 U.S.C. 109). This section requires that the Conference recommend uniform percentage changes in these amounts based solely on cost of living changes. The dollar amounts in the bill would not change on that recommendation, absent Congressional veto. Instead, Congress is required to take affirmative action, by passing a law amending the appropriate section, if it wishes to accomplish the change.

If the Judicial Conference has policy recommendations concerning the appropriate dollar amounts in the bankruptcy code based other than on cost of living considerations there are adequate channels through which it may communicate its views. This section is solely for the housekeeping function of maintaining the dollar amounts in the code at fairly constant real dollar levels. House Report No. 95–595.

1994 Acts. House Report No. 103–835, see 1994 U.S. Code Cong. and Adm. News, p. 3340.

2005 Acts. House Report No. 109–31(Part I), see 2005 U.S. Code Cong. and Adm. News, p. 88.

Legislative Statements

Section 104 represents a compromise between the House bill and the Senate amendment with respect to the adjustment of dollar amounts in title 11. The House amendment authorizes the Judicial Conference of the United States to transmit a recommendation for the uniform percentage of adjustment for each dollar amount in title 11 and in 28 U.S.C. 1930 to the Congress and to the President before May 1, 1985, and before May 1 of every sixth year thereafter. The requirement in the House bill that each such recommendation be based only on any change in the cost-of-living increase during the period immediately preceding the recommendation is deleted.

Effective and Applicability Provisions

2005 Acts. Amendments by Pub.L. 109–8, § 322, effective, except as otherwise provided, 180 days after April 20, 2005, and applicable with respect to cases commenced under Title 11 on or after April 20, 2005, see Pub.L. 109–8, § 1501, set out as a note under 11 U.S.C.A. § 101.

Amendments by Pub.L. 109–8 effective, except as otherwise provided, 180 days after April 20, 2005, and inapplicable with respect to cases commenced under Title 11 before the effective date, see Pub.L. 109–8, § 1501, set out as a note under 11 U.S.C.A. § 101.

1994 Acts. Amendment by Pub.L. 103–394 effective on Oct. 22, 1994, and not to apply with respect to cases commenced under Title 11 of the United States Code before Oct. 22, 1994, see section 702 of Pub.L. 103–394, set out as a note under section 101 of this title.

Termination of Reporting Requirements

For termination, effective May 15, 2000, of provisions of law requiring submittal to Congress of any annual, semiannual, or other regular periodic report listed in House Document No. 103–7 (in which a report required under subsec. (a) of this section is listed in the 15th item on page 12, which references a note but probably means this section), see section 3003 of Pub. L. 104–66, as amended, set out as a note under 31 U.S.C.A. § 1113.

Separability of Provisions

If any provision of or amendment made by Pub.L. 103–394 or the application of such provision or amendment to any person or circumstance is held to be unconstitutional, the remaining provisions of and amendments made by Pub.L. 103–394 and the application of such provisions and amendments to any person or circumstance shall not be affected thereby, see section 701 of Pub.L. 103–394, set out as a note under section 101 of this title.

Adjustment of Dollar Amounts

By notice published Feb. 14, 2007, 72 F.R. 7082, the Judicial Conference of the United States increased the dollar amounts in provisions specified in subsec. (b) of this section, effective Apr. 1, 2007, and provided also that these increases do not apply to cases commenced before the effective date of the adjustments, i.e., April 1, 2007. The dollar amounts are adjusted as set out in the following chart.

	Dollar amount to be adjusted	New (adjusted) dollar amount
28 U.S.C.:		
1409(b)—a trustee may commence a proceeding arising in or related to a case to recover:		
(1)—money judgment of or property worth less than	$1,000	$1,100
(2)—a consumer debt less than	$15,000	$16,425
(3)—a non consumer debt against a non insider less than	$10,000	$10,950
11 U.S.C.:		
Section 101(3)—definition of assisted person	$150,000	$164,250
Section 101(18)—definition of family farmer	$3,237,000 (each time it appears)	$3,544,525 (each time it appears)
101(19A)—definition of family fisherman	$1,500,000 (each time it appears)	$1,642,500 (each time it appears)
101(51D)—definition of small business debtor	$2,000,000 (each time it appears)	$2,190,000 (each time it appears)
Section 109(e)—allowable debt limits for individual filing bankruptcy under chapter 13	$307,675 (each time it appears)	$336,900 (each time it appears)

	Dollar amount to be adjusted	New (adjusted) dollar amount
	$922,975 (each time it appears)	$1,010,650 (each time it appears)
Section 303(b)—minimum aggregate claims needed for the commencement of involuntary chapter 7 or chapter 11 bankruptcy:		
(1)—in paragraph (1)	$12,300	$13,475
(2)—in paragraph (2)	$12,300	$13,475
Section 507(a)—priority expenses and claims		
(1)—in paragraph (4)	$10,000	$10,950
(2)—in paragraph (5)	$10,000	$10,950
(3)—in paragraph (6)	$4,925	$5,400
(4)—in paragraph (7)	$2,225	$2,425
Section 522(d)—value of property exemptions allowed to the debtor		
(1)—in paragraph (1)	$18,450	$20,200
(2)—in paragraph (2)	$2,950	$3,225
(3)—in paragraph (3)	$475	$525
	$9,850	$10,775
(4)—in paragraph (4)	$1,225	$1,350
(5)—in paragraph (5)	$975	$1,075
	$9,250	$10,125
(6)—in paragraph (6)	$1,850	$2,025
(7)—in paragraph (8)	$9,850	$10,775
(8)—in paragraph (11)(D)	$18,450	$20,200
522(f)(3)—exception to lien avoidance under certain state laws	$5,000	$5,475
522(f)(4)—items excluded from definition of household goods for lien avoidance purposes	$500 (each time it appears)	$550 (each time it appears)
522(n)—maximum aggregate value of assets in individual retirement accounts exempted	$1,000,000	$1,095,000
522(p)—qualified homestead exemption	$125,000	$136,875
522(q)—state homestead exemption	$125,000	$136,875
523(a)(2)(C)—exceptions to discharge:		
in subclause (i)(I)—consumer debts, incurred ≤ 90 days before filing owed to a single creditor in the aggregate	$500	$550
in subclause (i)(II)—cash advances incurred ≤ 70 days before filing in the aggregate	$750	$825
541(b)—property of the estate exclusions:		
(1)—in paragraph (5)(C)—education IRA funds in the aggregate	$5,000	$5,475
(2)—in paragraph (6)(C)—prepurchased tuition credits in the aggregate	$5,000	$5,475
547(c)(9)—preferences, trustee may not avoid a transfer if, in a case filed by a debtor whose debts are		

	Dollar amount to be adjusted	New (adjusted) dollar amount
not primarily consumer debts, the aggregate value of property is less than	$5,000	$5,475
707(b)—dismissal of a case or conversion to a case under chapter 11 or 13 (means test):		
(1)—in paragraph (2)(A)(i)(I)	$6,000	$6,575
(2)—in paragraph (2)(A)(i)(II)	$10,000	$10,950
(3)—in paragraph (2)(A)(ii)(IV)	$1,500	$1,650
(4)—in paragraph (5)(B)	$1,000	$1,100
(5)—in paragraph 6(C)	$525	$575
(6)—in paragraph 7(A)	$525	$575
1322(d)—contents of chapter 13 plan, monthly income	$525 (each time it appears)	$575 (each time it appears)
1325(b)—chapter 13 confirmation of plan, disposable income	$525 (each time it appears)	$575 (each time it appears)
1326(b)(3)—payments to former chapter 7 trustee	$25	$25

Previous adjustments of the dollar amounts in provisions specified in subsec. (b) of this section were contained in the following:

Notice published Feb. 18, 2004, 69 F.R. 8482, effective Apr. 1, 2004.

Notice published Feb. 20, 2001, 66 F.R. 10910, effective Apr. 1, 2001.

Notice published Feb. 3, 1998, 63 F.R. 7179, effective Apr. 1, 1998.

§ 105. Power of court

(a) The court may issue any order, process, or judgment that is necessary or appropriate to carry out the provisions of this title. No provision of this title providing for the raising of an issue by a party in interest shall be construed to preclude the court from, sua sponte, taking any action or making any determination necessary or appropriate to enforce or implement court orders or rules, or to prevent an abuse of process.

(b) Notwithstanding subsection (a) of this section, a court may not appoint a receiver in a case under this title.

(c) The ability of any district judge or other officer or employee of a district court to exercise any of the authority or responsibilities conferred upon the court under this title shall be determined by reference to the provisions relating to such judge, officer, or employee set forth in title 28. This subsection shall not be interpreted to exclude bankruptcy judges and other officers or employees appointed pursuant to chapter 6 of title 28 from its operation.

(d) The court, on its own motion or on the request of a party in interest—

(1) shall hold such status conferences as are necessary to further the expeditious and economical resolution of the case; and

(2) unless inconsistent with another provision of this title or with applicable Federal Rules of Bankruptcy Procedure, issue an order at any such conference prescribing such limitations and conditions as the court deems appropriate to ensure that the case is handled expeditiously and economically, including an order that—

(A) sets the date by which the trustee must assume or reject an executory contract or unexpired lease; or

(B) in a case under chapter 11 of this title—

(i) sets a date by which the debtor, or trustee if one has been appointed, shall file a disclosure statement and plan;

(ii) sets a date by which the debtor, or trustee if one has been appointed, shall solicit acceptances of a plan;

(iii) sets the date by which a party in interest other than a debtor may file a plan;

(iv) sets a date by which a proponent of a plan, other than the debtor, shall solicit acceptances of such plan;

(v) fixes the scope and format of the notice to be provided regarding the hearing on approval of the disclosure statement; or

(vi) provides that the hearing on approval of the disclosure statement may be combined with the hearing on confirmation of the plan.

(Pub.L. 95–598, Nov. 6, 1978, 92 Stat. 2555; Pub.L. 98–353, Title I, § 118, July 10, 1984, 98 Stat. 344; Pub.L. 99–554, Title II, § 203, Oct. 27, 1986, 100 Stat. 3097; Pub.L. 103–394,

Title I, § 104(a), Oct. 22, 1994, 108 Stat. 4108; Pub.L. 109–8, Title IV, § 440, Apr. 20, 2005, 119 Stat. 114.)

HISTORICAL AND STATUTORY NOTES

Revision Notes and Legislative Reports

1978 Acts. Section 105 is derived from section 2a(15) of present law [section 11(a)(15) of former Title 11], with two changes. First, the limitation on the power of a bankruptcy judge (the power to enjoin a court being reserved to the district judge) is removed as inconsistent with the increased powers and jurisdiction of the new bankruptcy court. Second, the bankruptcy judge is prohibited from appointing a receiver in a case under title 11 under any circumstances. The bankruptcy code has ample provision for the appointment of a trustee when needed. Appointment of a receiver would simply circumvent the established procedures.

This section is also an authorization, as required under 28 U.S.C. 2283, for a court of the United States to stay the action of a State court. As such, *Toucey v. New York Life Insurance Company,* 314 U.S. 118 (1941) [62 S.Ct. 139, 86 L.Ed. 100, 137 A.L.R. 967], is overruled. Senate Report No. 95–989.

1984 Acts. Statements by Legislative Leaders, see 1984 U.S.Code Cong. and Adm.News, p. 576.

1986 Acts. House Report No. 99–764 and House Conference Report No. 99–958, see 1986 U.S.Code Cong. and Adm.News, p. 5227.

1994 Acts. House Report No. 103–835, see 1994 U.S. Code Cong. and Adm. News, p. 3340.

2005 Acts. House Report No. 109–31(Part I), see 2005 U.S. Code Cong. and Adm. News, p. 88.

References in Text

The Federal Rules of Bankruptcy Procedure, referred to in subsec. (d)(2), are set out in this title.

Effective and Applicability Provisions

2005 Acts. Amendments by Pub.L. 109–8 effective, except as otherwise provided, 180 days after April 20, 2005, and inapplicable with respect to cases commenced under Title 11 before the effective date, see Pub.L. 109–8, § 1501, set out as a note under 11 U.S.C.A. § 101.

1994 Acts. Amendment by Pub.L. 103–394 effective on Oct. 22, 1994, and not to apply with respect to cases commenced under Title 11 of the United States Code before Oct. 22, 1994, see section 702 of Pub.L. 103–394, set out as a note under section 101 of this title.

1986 Acts. Amendment by Pub.L. 99–554 effective 30 days after Oct. 27, 1986, except as otherwise provided for, see section 302(a) of Pub.L. 99–554, set out as a note under section 581 of Title 28, Judiciary and Judicial Procedure.

Amendment by Pub.L. 99–554, § 203, not to become effective in or with respect to certain specified judicial districts until, or apply to cases while pending in such district before, the expiration of the 270-day period beginning 30 days after Oct. 27, 1986, or of the 30-day period beginning on the date the Attorney General certifies under section 303 of Pub.L. 99–554 the region specified in a paragraph of section 581(a) of Title 28, as amended by section 111(a) of Pub.L. 99–554, that includes such district, whichever occurs first, see section 302(d)(1) of Pub.L. 99–554, set out as a note under section 581 of Title 28.

Amendment by Pub.L. 99–554, § 203, not to become effective in or with respect to certain specified judicial districts until, or apply to cases while pending in such district before, the expiration of the 2-year period beginning 30 days after Oct. 27, 1986, or of the 30-day period beginning on the date the Attorney General certifies under section 303 of Pub.L. 99–554 the region specified in a paragraph of section 581(a) of Title 28, as amended by section 111(a) of Pub.L. 99–554, that includes such district, whichever occurs first, see section 302(d)(2) of Pub.L. 99–554, set out as a note under section 581 of Title 28.

Amendment by Pub.L. 99–554, § 203, not to become effective in or with respect to judicial districts established for the States of Alabama and North Carolina until, or apply to cases while pending in such district before, such district elects to be included in a bankruptcy region established in section 581(a) of Title 28, as amended by section 111(a) of Pub.L. 99–554, or Oct. 1, 2002, whichever occurs first, except that the amendment to subsec. (a) of this section shall become effective as of Dec. 1, 1990, and, except as otherwise provided, with respect to cases under chapters 7, 11, 12, and 13 of Title 11 commenced before 30 days after Oct. 27, 1986, and pending in a judicial district in the States of Alabama or North Carolina before any election made under section 302(d)(3)(A) of Pub.L. 99–554 by such district becomes effective or Oct. 1, 2002, whichever occurs first, amendments by Pub.L. 99–554 not to apply until Oct. 1, 2003, or the expiration of the 1-year period beginning on the date such election becomes effective, whichever occurs first, and further, in any judicial district in Alabama or North Carolina not making the election described in section 302(d)(3)(A) of Pub.L. 99–554, any person appointed under regulations issued by the Judicial Conference to administer estates in cases under Title 11 authorized to establish, etc., a panel of private trustees, and to supervise cases and trustees in cases under chapters 7, 11, 12, and 13 of Title 11, until amendments by sections 201 to 231 of Pub.L. 99–554 effective in such district, see section 302(d)(3)(A) to (F), (H), and (I) of Pub.L. 99–554, set out as a note under section 581 of Title 28.

Amendment by Pub.L. 99–554, § 203, except as otherwise provided, with respect to cases under chapters 7, 11, 12, and 13 of Title 11 commenced before 30 days after Oct. 27, 1986, and pending in a judicial district referred to in section 581(a) of Title 28, as amended by section 111(a) of Pub.L. 99–554, for which a United States trustee is not authorized before 30 days after Oct. 27, 1986 to be appointed, not applicable until the expiration of the 3-year period beginning on Oct. 27, 1986, or of the 1-year period beginning on the date the Attorney General certifies under section 303 of Pub.L. 99–554 the region specified in a paragraph of such section 581(a) that includes such district, whichever occurs first, see section 302(e)(1), (2) of Pub.L. 99–554, set out as a note under section 581 of Title 28.

1984 Acts. Amendment by Pub.L. 98–353 effective July 10, 1984, see section 122(a) of Pub.L. 98–353, set out as a note under section 151 of Title 28, Judiciary and Judicial Procedure.

Separability of Provisions

If any provision of or amendment made by Pub.L. 103–394 or the application of such provision or amendment to any person or circumstance is held to be unconstitutional, the remaining provisions of and amendments made by Pub.L.

103–394 and the application of such provisions and amendments to any person or circumstance shall not be affected thereby, see section 701 of Pub.L. 103–394, set out as a note under section 101 of this title.

CROSS REFERENCES

Bankruptcy investigations, see 18 USCA § 3057.

§ 106. Waiver of sovereign immunity

(a) Notwithstanding an assertion of sovereign immunity, sovereign immunity is abrogated as to a governmental unit to the extent set forth in this section with respect to the following:

(1) Sections 105, 106, 107, 108, 303, 346, 362, 363, 364, 365, 366, 502, 503, 505, 506, 510, 522, 523, 524, 525, 542, 543, 544, 545, 546, 547, 548, 549, 550, 551, 552, 553, 722, 724, 726, 728, 744, 749, 764, 901, 922, 926, 928, 929, 944, 1107, 1141, 1142, 1143, 1146, 1201, 1203, 1205, 1206, 1227, 1231, 1301, 1303, 1305, and 1327 of this title.

(2) The court may hear and determine any issue arising with respect to the application of such sections to governmental units.

(3) The court may issue against a governmental unit an order, process, or judgment under such sections or the Federal Rules of Bankruptcy Procedure, including an order or judgment awarding a money recovery, but not including an award of punitive damages. Such order or judgment for costs or fees under this title or the Federal Rules of Bankruptcy Procedure against any governmental unit shall be consistent with the provisions and limitations of section 2412(d)(2)(A) of title 28.

(4) The enforcement of any such order, process, or judgment against any governmental unit shall be consistent with appropriate nonbankruptcy law applicable to such governmental unit and, in the case of a money judgment against the United States, shall be paid as if it is a judgment rendered by a district court of the United States.

(5) Nothing in this section shall create any substantive claim for relief or cause of action not otherwise existing under this title, the Federal Rules of Bankruptcy Procedure, or nonbankruptcy law.

(b) A governmental unit that has filed a proof of claim in the case is deemed to have waived sovereign immunity with respect to a claim against such governmental unit that is property of the estate and that arose out of the same transaction or occurrence out of which the claim of such governmental unit arose.

(c) Notwithstanding any assertion of sovereign immunity by a governmental unit, there shall be offset against a claim or interest of a governmental unit any claim against such governmental unit that is property of the estate.

(Pub.L. 95–598, Nov. 6, 1978, 92 Stat. 2555; Pub.L. 103–394, Title I, § 113, Oct. 22, 1994, 108 Stat. 4117.)

HISTORICAL AND STATUTORY NOTES

Revision Notes and Legislative Reports

1978 Acts. Section 106 provides for a limited waiver of sovereign immunity in bankruptcy cases. Though Congress has the power to waive sovereign immunity for the Federal government completely in bankruptcy cases, the policy followed here is designed to achieve approximately the same result that would prevail outside of bankruptcy. Congress does not, however, have the power to waive sovereign immunity completely with respect to claims of a bankrupt estate against a State, though it may exercise its bankruptcy power through the supremacy clause to prevent or prohibit State action that is contrary to bankruptcy policy.

There is, however, a limited change from the result that would prevail in the absence of bankruptcy; the change is two-fold and is within Congress' power vis-a-vis both the Federal Government and the States. First, the filing of a proof of claim against the estate by a governmental unit is a waiver by that governmental unit of sovereign immunity with respect to compulsory counterclaims, as defined in the Federal Rules of Civil Procedure [set out in Title 28, Judiciary and Judicial Procedure], that is, counterclaims arising out of the same transaction or occurrence. The governmental unit cannot receive a distribution from the estate without subjecting itself to any liability it has to the estate within the confines of a compulsory counterclaim rule. Any other result would be one-sided. The counterclaim by the estate against the governmental unit is without limit.

Second, the estate may offset against the allowed claim of a governmental unit, up to the amount of the governmental unit's claim, any claim that the debtor, and thus the estate, has against the governmental unit, without regard to whether the estate's claim arose out of the same transaction or occurrence as the government's claim. Under this provision, the setoff permitted is only to the extent of the governmental unit's claim. No affirmative recovery is permitted. Subsection (a) governs affirmative recovery.

Though this subsection creates a partial waiver of immunity when the governmental unit files a proof of claim, it does not waive immunity if the debtor or trustee, and not the governmental unit, files proof of a governmental unit's claim under proposed 11 U.S.C. 501(c).

This section does not confer sovereign immunity on any governmental unit that does not already have immunity. It simply recognizes any immunity that exists and prescribes the proper treatment of claims by and against that sovereign. Senate Report No. 92–989.

1994 Acts. House Report No. 103–835, see 1994 U.S. Code Cong. and Adm. News, p. 3340.

Legislative Statements

Section 106(c) relating to sovereign immunity is new. The provision indicates that the use of the term "creditor," "entity," or "governmental unit" in title 11 applies to governmental units notwithstanding any assertion of sovereign immunity and that an order of the court binds governmental units. The provision is included to comply with the requirement in case law that an express waiver of sovereign immunity is required in order to be effective. Section 106(c) codifies *In re Gwilliam*, 519 F.2d 407 (9th Cir., 1975), and *In re Dolard*,

519 F.2d 282 (9th Cir., 1975), permitting the bankruptcy court to determine the amount and dischargeability of tax liabilities owing by the debtor or the estate prior to or during a bankruptcy case whether or not the governmental unit to which such taxes are owed files a proof of claim. Except as provided in sections 106(a) and (b) subsection (c) is not limited to those issues, but permits the bankruptcy court to bind governmental units on other matters as well. For example, section 106(c) permits a trustee or debtor in possession to assert avoiding powers under title 11 against a governmental unit; contrary language in the House report to H.R. 8200 is thereby overruled.

References in Text

Section 728 of this title, referred to in subsec. (a)(1), was repealed by Pub.L. 109–8, Title VII, § 719(b)(1), Apr. 20, 2005, 119 Stat. 133.

The Federal Rules of Bankruptcy Procedure, referred to in subsec. (a)(3) and (5), are set out in this title.

Effective and Applicability Provisions

1994 Acts. Amendment by section 113 of Pub.L. 103–394 effective on Oct. 22, 1994, and applicable with respect to cases commenced under Title 11 of the United States Code before, on, and after Oct. 22, 1994, see section 702 of Pub.L. 103–394, set out as a note under section 101 of this title.

Separability of Provisions

If any provision of or amendment made by Pub.L. 103–394 or the application of such provision or amendment to any person or circumstance is held to be unconstitutional, the remaining provisions of and amendments made by Pub.L. 103–394 and the application of such provisions and amendments to any person or circumstance shall not be affected thereby, see section 701 of Pub.L. 103–394, set out as a note under section 101 of this title.

§ 107. Public access to papers

(a) Except as provided in subsections (b) and (c) of this section and subject to section 112, a paper filed in a case under this title and the dockets of a bankruptcy court are public records and open to examination by an entity at reasonable times without charge.

(b) On request of a party in interest, the bankruptcy court shall, and on the bankruptcy court's own motion, the bankruptcy court may—

(1) protect an entity with respect to a trade secret or confidential research, development, or commercial information; or

(2) protect a person with respect to scandalous or defamatory matter contained in a paper filed in a case under this title.

(c)(1) The bankruptcy court, for cause, may protect an individual, with respect to the following types of information to the extent the court finds that disclosure of such information would create undue risk of identity theft or other unlawful injury to the individual or the individual's property:

(A) Any means of identification (as defined in section 1028(d) of title 18) contained in a paper filed, or to be filed, in a case under this title.

(B) Other information contained in a paper described in subparagraph (A).

(2) Upon ex parte application demonstrating cause, the court shall provide access to information protected pursuant to paragraph (1) to an entity acting pursuant to the police or regulatory power of a domestic governmental unit.

(3) The United States trustee, bankruptcy administrator, trustee, and any auditor serving under section 586(f) of title 28—

(A) shall have full access to all information contained in any paper filed or submitted in a case under this title; and

(B) shall not disclose information specifically protected by the court under this title.

(Pub.L. 95–598, Nov. 6, 1978, 92 Stat. 2556; Pub.L. 109–8, Title II, §§ 233(c), 234(a), (c), Apr. 20, 2005, 119 Stat. 74, 75.)

HISTORICAL AND STATUTORY NOTES

Revision Notes and Legislative Reports

1978 Acts. Subsection (a) of this section makes all papers filed in a bankruptcy case and the dockets of the bankruptcy court public and open to examination at reasonable times without charge. "Docket" includes the claims docket, the proceedings docket, and all papers filed in a case.

Subsection (b) permits the court, on its own motion, and requires the court, on the request of a party in interest, to protect trade secrets, confidential research, development, or commercial information, and to protect persons against scandalous or defamatory matter. Senate Report No. 95–989.

2005 Acts. House Report No. 109–31(Part I), see 2005 U.S. Code Cong. and Adm. News, p. 88.

Codifications

Pub.L. 109–8, §§ 233(c) and 234(c), which directed that subsec. (a) is amended by inserting "and subject to section 112" after "section", and by striking "subsection (b)," and inserting "subsections (b) and (c),", respectively, was executed by striking "subsection (b) of this section," and inserting "subsections (b) and (c) of this section and subject to section 112," as the probable intent of Congress.

Effective and Applicability Provisions

2005 Acts. Amendments by Pub.L. 109–8 effective, except as otherwise provided, 180 days after April 20, 2005, and inapplicable with respect to cases commenced under Title 11 before the effective date, see Pub.L. 109–8, § 1501, set out as a note under 11 U.S.C.A. § 101.

CROSS REFERENCES

Application for search of records, see Fed.Rules Bankr. Proc. Form B 132, 11 USCA.

Documents relating to adverse interest and conduct of officers of estate, see 18 USCA § 154.

Reporting of obsolete information prohibited, see 15 USCA § 1681c.

§ 108. Extension of time

(a) If applicable nonbankruptcy law, an order entered in a nonbankruptcy proceeding, or an agreement fixes a period within which the debtor may commence an action, and such period has not expired before the date of the filing of the petition, the trustee may commence such action only before the later of—

(1) the end of such period, including any suspension of such period occurring on or after the commencement of the case; or

(2) two years after the order for relief.

(b) Except as provided in subsection (a) of this section, if applicable nonbankruptcy law, an order entered in a nonbankruptcy proceeding, or an agreement fixes a period within which the debtor or an individual protected under section 1201 or 1301 of this title may file any pleading, demand, notice, or proof of claim or loss, cure a default, or perform any other similar act, and such period has not expired before the date of the filing of the petition, the trustee may only file, cure, or perform, as the case may be, before the later of—

(1) the end of such period, including any suspension of such period occurring on or after the commencement of the case; or

(2) 60 days after the order for relief.

(c) Except as provided in section 524 of this title, if applicable nonbankruptcy law, an order entered in a nonbankruptcy proceeding, or an agreement fixes a period for commencing or continuing a civil action in a court other than a bankruptcy court on a claim against the debtor, or against an individual with respect to which such individual is protected under section 1201 or 1301 of this title, and such period has not expired before the date of the filing of the petition, then such period does not expire until the later of—

(1) the end of such period, including any suspension of such period occurring on or after the commencement of the case; or

(2) 30 days after notice of the termination or expiration of the stay under section 362, 922, 1201, or 1301 of this title, as the case may be, with respect to such claim.

(Pub.L. 95–598, Nov. 6, 1978, 92 Stat. 2556; Pub.L. 98–353, Title III, § 424, July 10, 1984, 98 Stat. 369; Pub.L. 99–554, Title II, § 257(b), Oct. 27, 1986, 100 Stat. 3114; Pub.L. 109–8, Title XII, § 1203, Apr. 20, 2005, 119 Stat. 193.)

HISTORICAL AND STATUTORY NOTES

Revision Notes and Legislative Reports

1978 Acts. Subsections (a) and (b), derived from Bankruptcy Act section 11 [section 29 of former Title 11], permit the trustee, when he steps into the shoes of the debtor, an extension of time for filing an action or doing some other act that is required to preserve the debtor's rights. Subsection (a) extends any statute of limitation for commencing or continuing an action by the debtor for two years after the date of the order for relief, unless it would expire later. Subsection (b) gives the trustee 60 days to take other actions not covered under subsection (a), such as filing a pleading, demand, notice, or proof of claim or loss (such as an insurance claim), unless the period for doing the relevant act expires later than 60 days after the date of the order for relief.

Subsection (c) extends the statute of limitations for creditors. Thus, if a creditor is stayed from commencing or continuing an action against the debtor because of the bankruptcy case, then the creditor is permitted an additional 30 days after notice of the event by which the stay is terminated, whether that event be relief from the automatic stay under proposed 11 U.S.C. 362 or 1301, the closing of the bankruptcy case (which terminates the stay), or the exception from discharge of the debts on which the creditor claims.

In the case of Federal tax liabilities, the Internal Revenue Code [Title 26] suspends the statute of limitations on a tax liability of a taxpayer from running while his assets are in the control or custody of a court and for 6 months thereafter (sec. 6503(b) of the Code) [Title 26]. The amendment applies this rule in a title 11 proceeding. Accordingly, the statute of limitations on collection of a nondischargeable Federal tax liability of a debtor will resume running after 6 months following the end of the period during which the debtor's assets are in the control or custody of the bankruptcy court. This rule will provide the Internal Revenue Service adequate time to collect nondischargeable taxes following the end of the title 11 proceedings. Senate Report No. 95–989.

1984 Acts. Statements by Legislative Leaders, see 1984 U.S.Code Cong. and Adm.News, p. 576.

1986 Acts. House Report No. 99–764 and House Conference Report No. 99–958, see 1986 U.S.Code Cong. and Adm.News, p. 5227.

2005 Acts. House Report No. 109–31(Part I), see 2005 U.S. Code Cong. and Adm. News, p. 88.

Legislative Statements

Extension of time: The House amendment adopts section 108(c)(1) of the Senate amendment which expressly includes any special suspensions of statutes of limitation periods on collection outside bankruptcy when assets are under the authority of a court. For example, section 6503(b) of the Internal Revenue Code [Title 26] suspends collection of tax liabilities while the debtor's assets are in the control or custody of a court, and for 6 months thereafter. By adopting the language of the Senate amendment, the House amendment insures not only that the period for collection of the taxes outside bankruptcy will not expire during the title 11 proceedings, but also that such period will not expire until at least 6 months thereafter, which is the minimum suspension period provided by the Internal Revenue Code [Title 26].

Codifications

Amendment by Pub.L. 99–554, § 257(b)(2)(B), which directed amendment of subsec. (c)(2) by inserting "1201," after "722," was incapable of execution.

Effective and Applicability Provisions

2005 Acts. Amendments by Pub.L. 109–8 effective, except as otherwise provided, 180 days after April 20, 2005, and inapplicable with respect to cases commenced under Title 11

before the effective date, see Pub.L. 109–8, § 1501, set out as a note under 11 U.S.C.A. § 101.

1986 Acts. Amendment by Pub.L. 99–554 effective 30 days after Oct. 27, 1986, but not applicable to cases commenced under this title before that date, see section 302(a), (c)(1) of Pub.L. 99–554, set out as a note under section 581 of Title 28, Judiciary and Judicial Procedure.

1984 Acts. Amendment by Pub.L. 98–353 effective with respect to cases filed 90 days after July 10, 1984, see section 552(a), formerly 553(a) of Pub.L. 98–353, set out as a note under section 101 of this title.

§ 109. Who may be a debtor

(a) Notwithstanding any other provision of this section, only a person that resides or has a domicile, a place of business, or property in the United States, or a municipality, may be a debtor under this title.

(b) A person may be a debtor under chapter 7 of this title only if such person is not—

(1) a railroad;

(2) a domestic insurance company, bank, savings bank, cooperative bank, savings and loan association, building and loan association, homestead association, a New Markets Venture Capital company as defined in section 351 of the Small Business Investment Act of 1958, a small business investment company licensed by the Small Business Administration under section 301 of the Small Business Investment Act of 1958, credit union, or industrial bank or similar institution which is an insured bank as defined in section 3(h) of the Federal Deposit Insurance Act, except that an uninsured State member bank, or a corporation organized under section 25A of the Federal Reserve Act, which operates, or operates as, a multilateral clearing organization pursuant to section 409 of the Federal Deposit Insurance Corporation Improvement Act of 1991 may be a debtor if a petition is filed at the direction of the Board of Governors of the Federal Reserve System; or

(3)(A) a foreign insurance company, engaged in such business in the United States; or

(B) a foreign bank, savings bank, cooperative bank, savings and loan association, building and loan association, or credit union, that has a branch or agency (as defined in section 1(b) of the International Banking Act of 1978 [1] in the United States.

(c) An entity may be a debtor under chapter 9 of this title if and only if such entity—

(1) is a municipality;

(2) is specifically authorized, in its capacity as a municipality or by name, to be a debtor under such chapter by State law, or by a governmental officer or organization empowered by State law to authorize such entity to be a debtor under such chapter;

(3) is insolvent;

(4) desires to effect a plan to adjust such debts; and

(5)(A) has obtained the agreement of creditors holding at least a majority in amount of the claims of each class that such entity intends to impair under a plan in a case under such chapter;

(B) has negotiated in good faith with creditors and has failed to obtain the agreement of creditors holding at least a majority in amount of the claims of each class that such entity intends to impair under a plan in a case under such chapter;

(C) is unable to negotiate with creditors because such negotiation is impracticable; or

(D) reasonably believes that a creditor may attempt to obtain a transfer that is avoidable under section 547 of this title.

(d) Only a railroad, a person that may be a debtor under chapter 7 of this title (except a stockbroker or a commodity broker), and an uninsured State member bank, or a corporation organized under section 25A of the Federal Reserve Act, which operates, or operates as, a multilateral clearing organization pursuant to section 409 of the Federal Deposit Insurance Corporation Improvement Act of 1991 may be a debtor under chapter 11 of this title.

(e) Only an individual with regular income that owes, on the date of the filing of the petition, noncontingent, liquidated, unsecured debts of less than $336,900 [2] and noncontingent, liquidated, secured debts of less than $1,010,650 [2], or an individual with regular income and such individual's spouse, except a stockbroker or a commodity broker, that owe, on the date of the filing of the petition, noncontingent, liquidated, unsecured debts that aggregate less than $336,900 [2] and noncontingent, liquidated, secured debts of less than $1,010,650 [2] may be a debtor under chapter 13 of this title.

(f) Only a family farmer or family fisherman with regular annual income may be a debtor under chapter 12 of this title.

(g) Notwithstanding any other provision of this section, no individual or family farmer may be a debtor under this title who has been a debtor in a case pending under this title at any time in the preceding 180 days if—

(1) the case was dismissed by the court for willful failure of the debtor to abide by orders of the court, or to appear before the court in proper prosecution of the case; or

(2) the debtor requested and obtained the voluntary dismissal of the case following the filing of a request for relief from the automatic stay provided by section 362 of this title.

(h)(1) Subject to paragraphs (2) and (3), and notwithstanding any other provision of this section, an individual may not be a debtor under this title unless such individual has, during the 180–day period preceding the date of filing of the petition by such individual, received from an approved nonprofit budget and credit counseling agency described in section 111(a) an individual or group briefing (including a briefing conducted by telephone or on the Internet) that outlined the opportunities for available credit counseling and assisted such individual in performing a related budget analysis.

(2)(A) Paragraph (1) shall not apply with respect to a debtor who resides in a district for which the United States trustee (or the bankruptcy administrator, if any) determines that the approved nonprofit budget and credit counseling agencies for such district are not reasonably able to provide adequate services to the additional individuals who would otherwise seek credit counseling from such agencies by reason of the requirements of paragraph (1).

(B) The United States trustee (or the bankruptcy administrator, if any) who makes a determination described in subparagraph (A) shall review such determination not later than 1 year after the date of such determination, and not less frequently than annually thereafter. Notwithstanding the preceding sentence, a nonprofit budget and credit counseling agency may be disapproved by the United States trustee (or the bankruptcy administrator, if any) at any time.

(3)(A) Subject to subparagraph (B), the requirements of paragraph (1) shall not apply with respect to a debtor who submits to the court a certification that—

(i) describes exigent circumstances that merit a waiver of the requirements of paragraph (1);

(ii) states that the debtor requested credit counseling services from an approved nonprofit budget and credit counseling agency, but was unable to obtain the services referred to in paragraph (1) during the 5–day period beginning on the date on which the debtor made that request; and

(iii) is satisfactory to the court.

(B) With respect to a debtor, an exemption under subparagraph (A) shall cease to apply to that debtor on the date on which the debtor meets the requirements of paragraph (1), but in no case may the exemption apply to that debtor after the date that is 30 days after the debtor files a petition, except that the court, for cause, may order an additional 15 days.

(4) The requirements of paragraph (1) shall not apply with respect to a debtor whom the court determines, after notice and hearing, is unable to complete those requirements because of incapacity, disability, or active military duty in a military combat zone. For the purposes of this paragraph, incapacity means that the debtor is impaired by reason of mental illness or mental deficiency so that he is incapable of realizing and making rational decisions with respect to his financial responsibilities; and "disability" means that the debtor is so physically impaired as to be unable, after reasonable effort, to participate in an in person, telephone, or Internet briefing required under paragraph (1).

(Pub.L. 95–598, Nov. 6, 1978, 92 Stat. 2557; Pub.L. 97–320, Title VII, § 703(d), Oct. 15, 1982, 96 Stat. 1539; Pub.L. 98–353, Title III, §§ 301, 425, July 10, 1984, 98 Stat. 352, 369; Pub.L. 99–554, Title II, § 253, Oct. 27, 1986, 100 Stat. 3105; Pub.L. 100–597, § 2, Nov. 3, 1988, 102 Stat. 3028; Pub.L. 103–394, Title I, § 108(a), Title II, § 220, Title IV, § 402, Title V, § 501(d)(2), Oct. 22, 1994, 108 Stat. 4111, 4129, 4141, 4143; Pub.L. 106–554, § 1(a)(5) [Title I, § 112(c)(1), (2)], (8) [§ 1(e)], Dec. 21, 2000, 114 Stat. 2763, 2763A–393, 2763A–665; Pub.L. 109–8, Title I, § 106(a), Title VIII, § 802(d)(1), Title X, § 1007(b), Title XII, § 1204(1), Apr. 20, 2005, 119 Stat. 37, 146, 188, 193.)

1 So in original. Probably should be followed by a closing parenthesis.

2 Dollar amount as adjusted by the Judicial Conference of the United States. See Adjustment of Dollar Amounts notes set out under this section and 11 U.S.C.A. § 104.

HISTORICAL AND STATUTORY NOTES

Revision Notes and Legislative Reports

1978 Acts. This section specifies eligibility to be a debtor under the bankruptcy laws. The first criterion, found in the current Bankruptcy Act section 2a(1) [section 11(a)(1) of former Title 11] requires that the debtor reside or have a domicile, a place of business, or property in the United States.

Subsection (b) defines eligibility for liquidation under chapter 7. All persons are eligible except insurance companies, and certain banking institutions. These exclusions are contained in current law. However, the banking institution exception is expanded in light of changes in various banking laws since the current law was last amended on this point. A change is also made to clarify that the bankruptcy laws cover foreign banks and insurance companies not engaged in the banking or insurance business in the United States but having assets in the United States. Banking institutions and insurance companies engaged in business in this country are excluded from liquidation under the bankruptcy laws because they are bodies for which alternate provision is made for their liquidation under various State or Federal regulatory laws. Conversely, when a foreign bank or insurance company is not engaged in the banking or insurance business in the United States, then those regulatory laws do not apply, and the bankruptcy laws are the only ones available for administration of any assets found in United States.

The first clause of subsection (b) provides that a railroad is not a debtor except where the requirements of section 1174 are met.

Subsection (c) provides that only a person who may be a debtor under chapter 7 and a railroad may also be a debtor under chapter 11, but a stockbroker or commodity broker is eligible for relief only under chapter 7. Subsection (d) establishes dollar limitations on the amount of indebtedness that an individual with regular income can incur and yet file under chapter 13. Senate Report No. 95–989.

Subsection (c) defines eligibility for chapter 9. Only a municipality that is unable to pay its debts as they mature, and that is not prohibited by State law from proceeding under chapter 9, is permitted to be a chapter 9 debtor. The subsection is derived from Bankruptcy Act section 84 [section 404 of former Title 11], with two changes. First, section 84 requires that the municipality be "generally authorized to file a petition under this chapter by the legislature, or by a governmental officer or organization empowered by State law to authorize the filing of a petition." The "generally authorized" language is unclear, and has generated a problem for a Colorado Metropolitan District that attempted to use chapter IX [chapter 9 of former Title 11] in 1976. The "not prohibited" language provides flexibility for both the States and the municipalities involved, while protecting State sovereignty as required by *Ashton v. Cameron County Water District No. 1,* 298 U.S. 513 (1936) [56 S.Ct. 892, 80 L.Ed. 1309, 31 Am.Bankr.Rep.N.S. 96, rehearing denied 57 S.Ct. 5, 299 U.S. 619, 81 L.Ed. 457] and *Bekins v. United States,* 304 U.S. 27 (1938) [58 S.Ct. 811, 82 L.Ed. 1137, 36 Am.Bankr. Rep.N.S. 187, rehearing denied 58 S.Ct. 1043, 1044, 304 U.S. 589, 82 L.Ed. 1549].

The second change deletes the four prerequisites to filing found in section 84 [section 404 of former Title 11]. The prerequisites require the municipality to have worked out a plan in advance, to have attempted to work out a plan without success, to fear that a creditor will attempt to obtain a preference, or to allege that prior negotiation is impracticable. The loopholes in those prerequisites are larger than the requirement itself. It was a compromise from pre-1976 chapter IX [chapter 9 of former Title 11] under which a municipality could file only if it had worked out an adjustment plan in advance. In the meantime, chapter IX protection was unavailable. There was some controversy at the time of the enactment of current chapter IX concerning deletion of the pre-negotiation requirement. It was argued that deletion would lead to a rash of municipal bankruptcies. The prerequisites now contained in section 84 were inserted to assuage that fear. They are largely cosmetic and precatory, however, and do not offer any significant deterrent to use of chapter IX. Instead, other factors, such as a general reluctance on the part of any debtor, especially a municipality, to use the bankruptcy laws, operates as a much more effective deterrent against capricious use.

Subsection (d) permits a person that may proceed under chapter 7 to be a debtor under chapter 11, Reorganization, with two exceptions. Railroads, which are excluded from chapter 7, are permitted to proceed under chapter 11. Stockbrokers and commodity brokers, which are permitted to be debtors under chapter 7, are excluded from chapter 11. The special rules for treatment of customer accounts that are the essence of stockbroker and commodity broker liquidations are available only in chapter 7. Customers would be unprotected under chapter 11. The special protective rules are unavailable in chapter 11 because their complexity would make reorganization very difficult at best, and unintelligible at worst. The variety of options available in reorganization cases make it extremely difficult to reorganize and continue to provide the special customer protection necessary in these cases.

Subsection (e) specifies eligibility for chapter 13, Adjustment of Debts of an Individual with Regular Income. An individual with regular income, or an individual with regular income and the individual's spouse, may proceed under chapter 13. As noted in connection with the definition of the term "individual with regular income", this represents a significant departure from current law. The change might have been too great, however, without some limitation. Thus, the debtor (or the debtor and spouse) must have unsecured debts that aggregate less than $100,000, and secured debts that aggregate less than $500,000. These figures will permit the small sole proprietor, for whom a chapter 11 reorganization is too cumbersome a procedure, to proceed under chapter 13. It does not create a presumption that any sole proprietor within that range is better off in chapter 13 than chapter 11. The conversion rules found in section 1307 will govern the appropriateness of the two chapters for any particular individual. The figures merely set maximum limits.

Whether a small business operated by a husband and wife, the so-called "mom and pop grocery store," will be a partnership and thus excluded from chapter 13, or a business owned by an individual, will have to be determined on the facts of each case. Even if partnership papers have not been filed, for example, the issue will be whether the assets of the grocery store are for the benefit of all creditors of the debtor or only for business creditors, and whether such assets may be the subject of a chapter 13 proceeding. The intent of the section is to follow current law that a partnership by estoppel may be adjudicated in bankruptcy and therefore would not prevent a chapter 13 debtor from subjecting assets in such a partnership to the reach of all creditors in a chapter 13 case. However, if the partnership is found to be a partnership by agreement, even informal agreement, then a separate entity exists and the assets of that entity would be exempt from a case under chapter 13. House Report No. 95–595.

1982 Acts. Senate Report No. 97–536 and Senate Conference Report No. 97–641, see 1982 U.S. Code Cong. and Adm. News, p. 3054.

1984 Acts. Statements by Legislative Leaders, see 1984 U.S. Code Cong. and Adm. News, p. 576.

1986 Acts. House Report No. 99–764 and House Conference Report No. 99–958, see U.S. Code Cong. and Adm. News, p. 5227.

1988 Acts. House Report No. 100–1011, see 1988 U.S. Code Cong. and Adm. News, p. 4115.

1994 Acts. House Report No. 103–835, see 1994 U.S. Code Cong. and Adm. News, p. 3340.

2000 Acts. House Report No. 106–645 and Statement by President, see 2000 U.S. Code Cong. and Adm. News, p. 2459.

2005 Acts. House Report No. 109–31(Part I), see 2005 U.S. Code Cong. and Adm. News, p. 88.

Legislative Statements

Section 109(b) of the House amendment adopts a provision contained in H.R. 8200 as passed by the House. Railroad liquidations will occur under chapter 11, not chapter 7.

Section 109(c) contains a provision which tracks the Senate amendment as to when a municipality may be a debtor under chapter 11 of title 11. As under the Bankruptcy Act [former

Title 11], State law authorization and prepetition negotiation efforts are required.

Section 109(e) represents a compromise between H.R. 8200 as passed by the House and the Senate amendment relating to the dollar amounts restricting eligibility to be a debtor under chapter 13 of title 11. The House amendment adheres to the limit of $100,000 placed on unsecured debts in H.R. 8200 as passed by the House. It adopts a midpoint of $350,000 as a limit on secured claims, a compromise between the level of $500,000 in H.R. 8200 as passed by the House and $200,000 as contained in the Senate amendment.

References in Text

Section 351 of the Small Business Investment Act of 1958, referred to in subsec. (b)(2), is section 351 of Pub.L. 85–699, which is classified to 15 U.S.C.A. § 689.

Subsection (c) or (d) of section 301 of the Small Business Investment Act of 1958, referred to in subsec. (b)(2), is subsection (c) or (d) of section 301 of Pub.L. 85–699, Title III, Aug. 21, 1958, which is classified to 15 U.S.C.A. § 681(c) or (d). Subsection (d) of section 301 was repealed by Pub.L. 104–208, Div. D, Title II, § 208(b)(3)(A), Sept. 30, 1996, 110 Stat. 3009–742.

Section 3 of the Federal Deposit Insurance Act, referred to in subsec. (b)(2), is section 2[3] of Act Sept. 21, 1950, c. 967, 64 Stat. 873, which is classified to 12 U.S.C.A. § 1813.

Section 25A of the Federal Reserve Act, referred to in subsecs. (b)(2) and (d), is Dec. 23, 1913, c. 6, § 25A, formerly § 25(a), as added Dec. 24, 1919, c. 18, 41 Stat. 378, as amended, which is classified to subchapter II of chapter 6 of Title 12 (12 U.S.C.A. § 611 et seq.).

Section 409 of the Federal Deposit Insurance Corporation Improvement Act of 1991, referred to in subsecs. (b)(2) and (d), is Pub.L. 102–242, Title IV, § 409, as added by Pub.L. 106–554, § 1(a)(5) [Title I, § 112(a)(3)], Dec. 21, 2000, 114 Stat. 2763, 2763A–391, which is classified as 12 U.S.C.A. § 4422.

Section 1(b) of the International Banking Act of 1978, referred to in subsec. (b)(3)(B), is Pub.L. 95–369, § 1(b), Sept. 17, 1978, 92 Stat. 607, as amended, which is classified to 12 U.S.C.A. § 3101.

Chapter 7 of this title, referred to in subsec. (d), is 11 U.S.C.A. § 701 et seq.

Chapter 11 of this title, referred to in subsec. (d), is 11 U.S.C.A. § 1101 et seq.

Effective and Applicability Provisions

2007 Acts. Increase of dollar amounts by Judicial Conference of the United States by notice published Feb. 14, 2007, 72 F.R. 7082 effective April 1, 2007, and increase not applicable to cases commenced before the effective date of the adjustments, i.e., April 1, 2007. See Adjustment of Dollar Amounts notes under 11 U.S.C.A. § 104 and this section.

2005 Acts. Amendments by Pub.L. 109–8 effective, except as otherwise provided, 180 days after April 20, 2005, and inapplicable with respect to cases commenced under Title 11 before the effective date, see Pub.L. 109–8, § 1501, set out as a note under 11 U.S.C.A. § 101.

2004 Acts. Adjustment of dollar amounts by Judicial Conference of the United States by notice dated Feb. 18, 2004, 69 F.R. 8482 effective April 1, 2004, and adjustment not applicable to cases commenced before the effective date of the adjustments, i.e., April 1, 2004. See Adjustment of Dollar Amounts notes under 11 U.S.C.A. § 104 and this section.

2001 Acts. Adjustment of dollar amounts by Judicial Conference of the United States by notice dated Feb. 20, 2001, 66 F.R. 10910 effective April 1, 2001, and adjustment not applicable to cases commenced before the effective date of the adjustments, i.e., April 1, 2001. See Adjustment of Dollar Amounts notes under 11 U.S.C.A. § 104 and this section.

1998 Acts. Adjustment of dollar amounts by Judicial Conference of the United States by notice dated Feb. 3, 1998, 63 F.R. 7179 effective April 1, 1998, and adjustment not applicable to cases commenced before the effective date of the adjustments, i.e., April 1, 1998. See Adjustment of Dollar Amounts notes under 11 U.S.C.A. § 104 and this section.

1994 Acts. Amendments by Pub.L. 103–394 effective on Oct. 22, 1994, and not to apply with respect to cases commenced under Title 11 of the United States Code before Oct. 22, 1994, see section 702 of Pub.L. 103–394, set out as a note under section 101 of this title.

1988 Acts. Amendment by Pub.L. 100–597 effective Nov. 3, 1988, but not applicable to any case commenced under this title before that date, see section 12 of Pub.L. 100–597, set out as a note under section 101 of this title.

1986 Acts. Amendment by Pub.L. 99–554 effective 30 days after Oct. 27, 1986, but not applicable to cases commended under this title before that date, see section 302(a), (c)(1) of Pub.L. 99–554, set out as a note under section 581 of Title 28, Judiciary and Judicial Procedure.

1984 Acts. Amendment by Pub.L. 98–353 effective with respect to cases filed 90 days after July 10, 1984, see section 552(a), formerly 553(a), of Pub.L. 98–353, set out as a note under section 101 of this title.

Separability of Provisions

If any provision of or amendment made by Pub.L. 103–394 or the application of such provision or amendment to any person or circumstance is held to be unconstitutional, the remaining provisions of and amendments made by Pub.L. 103–394 and the application of such provisions and amendments to any person or circumstance shall not be affected thereby, see section 701 of Pub.L. 103–394, set out as a note under section 101 of this title.

Adjustment of Dollar Amounts

For adjustment of dollar amounts specified in subsec. (e) of this section by the Judicial Conference of the United States, effective Apr. 1, 2007, see note set out under 11 U.S.C.A. § 104.

By notice published Feb. 14, 2007, 72 F.R. 7082, the Judicial Conference of the United States adjusted the dollar amounts in provisions specified in subsec. (e) of this section, effective Apr. 1, 2007, as follows:

Adjusted $307,675 (each time it appears) to $336,900 (each time it appears).

Adjusted $922,975 (each time it appears) to $1,010,650 (each time it appears).

By notice dated Feb. 18, 2004, 69 F.R. 8482, the Judicial Conference of the United States adjusted the dollar amounts in provisions specified in subsec. (e) of this section, effective Apr. 1, 2004, as follows:

Adjusted $290,525 (each time it appears) to $307,675 (each time it appears).

Adjusted $871,550 to $922,975.

By notice dated Feb. 20, 2001, 66 F.R. 10910, the Judicial Conference of the United States adjusted the dollar amounts in provisions specified in subsec. (e) of this section, effective Apr. 1, 2001, as follows:

Adjusted $269,250 (each time it appears) to $290,525 (each time it appears).

Adjusted $807,750 (each time it appears) to $871,550 (each time it appears).

By notice dated Feb. 3, 1998, 63 F.R. 7179, the Judicial Conference of the United States adjusted the dollar amounts in provisions specified in subsec. (e) of this section, effective Apr. 1, 1998, as follows:

Adjusted $250,000 (each time it appears) to $269,250 (each time it appears).

Adjusted $750,000 (each time it appears) to $807,750 (each time it appears).

CROSS REFERENCES

Filing of Chapter 9 petition by certain unincorporated tax or special assessment districts notwithstanding provisions under this section, see 11 USCA § 921.

Nonprejudicial dismissal, except as provided by this section, see 11 USCA § 349.

§ 110. Penalty for persons who negligently or fraudulently prepare bankruptcy petitions

(a) In this section—

(1) "bankruptcy petition preparer" means a person, other than an attorney for the debtor or an employee of such attorney under the direct supervision of such attorney, who prepares for compensation a document for filing; and

(2) "document for filing" means a petition or any other document prepared for filing by a debtor in a United States bankruptcy court or a United States district court in connection with a case under this title.

(b)(1) A bankruptcy petition preparer who prepares a document for filing shall sign the document and print on the document the preparer's name and address. If a bankruptcy petition preparer is not an individual, then an officer, principal, responsible person, or partner of the bankruptcy petition preparer shall be required to—

(A) sign the document for filing; and

(B) print on the document the name and address of that officer, principal, responsible person, or partner.

(2)(A) Before preparing any document for filing or accepting any fees from a debtor, the bankruptcy petition preparer shall provide to the debtor a written notice which shall be on an official form prescribed by the Judicial Conference of the United States in accordance with rule 9009 of the Federal Rules of Bankruptcy Procedure.

(B) The notice under subparagraph (A)—

(i) shall inform the debtor in simple language that a bankruptcy petition preparer is not an attorney and may not practice law or give legal advice;

(ii) may contain a description of examples of legal advice that a bankruptcy petition preparer is not authorized to give, in addition to any advice that the preparer may not give by reason of subsection (e)(2); and

(iii) shall—

(I) be signed by the debtor and, under penalty of perjury, by the bankruptcy petition preparer; and

(II) be filed with any document for filing.

(c)(1) A bankruptcy petition preparer who prepares a document for filing shall place on the document, after the preparer's signature, an identifying number that identifies individuals who prepared the document.

(2)(A) Subject to subparagraph (B), for purposes of this section, the identifying number of a bankruptcy petition preparer shall be the Social Security account number of each individual who prepared the document or assisted in its preparation.

(B) If a bankruptcy petition preparer is not an individual, the identifying number of the bankruptcy petition preparer shall be the Social Security account number of the officer, principal, responsible person, or partner of the bankruptcy petition preparer.

(3) [Repealed. Pub.L. 109–8, Title II, § 221(3)(B), Apr. 20, 2005, 119 Stat. 60]

(d) A bankruptcy petition preparer shall, not later than the time at which a document for filing is presented for the debtor's signature, furnish to the debtor a copy of the document.

(e)(1) A bankruptcy petition preparer shall not execute any document on behalf of a debtor.

(2)(A) A bankruptcy petition preparer may not offer a potential bankruptcy debtor any legal advice, including any legal advice described in subparagraph (B).

(B) The legal advice referred to in subparagraph (A) includes advising the debtor—

(i) whether—

(I) to file a petition under this title; or

(II) commencing a case under chapter 7, 11, 12, or 13 is appropriate;

(ii) whether the debtor's debts will be discharged in a case under this title;

(iii) whether the debtor will be able to retain the debtor's home, car, or other property after commencing a case under this title;

(iv) concerning—

(I) the tax consequences of a case brought under this title; or

(II) the dischargeability of tax claims;

(v) whether the debtor may or should promise to repay debts to a creditor or enter into a reaffirmation agreement with a creditor to reaffirm a debt;

(vi) concerning how to characterize the nature of the debtor's interests in property or the debtor's debts; or

(vii) concerning bankruptcy procedures and rights.

(f) A bankruptcy petition preparer shall not use the word "legal" or any similar term in any advertisements, or advertise under any category that includes the word "legal" or any similar term.

(g) A bankruptcy petition preparer shall not collect or receive any payment from the debtor or on behalf of the debtor for the court fees in connection with filing the petition.

(h)(1) The Supreme Court may promulgate rules under section 2075 of title 28, or the Judicial Conference of the United States may prescribe guidelines, for setting a maximum allowable fee chargeable by a bankruptcy petition preparer. A bankruptcy petition preparer shall notify the debtor of any such maximum amount before preparing any document for filing for a debtor or accepting any fee from the debtor.

(2) A declaration under penalty of perjury by the bankruptcy petition preparer shall be filed together with the petition, disclosing any fee received from or on behalf of the debtor within 12 months immediately prior to the filing of the case, and any unpaid fee charged to the debtor. If rules or guidelines setting a maximum fee for services have been promulgated or prescribed under paragraph (1), the declaration under this paragraph shall include a certification that the bankruptcy petition preparer complied with the notification requirement under paragraph (1).

(3)(A) The court shall disallow and order the immediate turnover to the bankruptcy trustee any fee referred to in paragraph (2) found to be in excess of the value of any services—

(i) rendered by the bankruptcy petition preparer during the 12–month period immediately preceding the date of the filing of the petition; or

(ii) found to be in violation of any rule or guideline promulgated or prescribed under paragraph (1).

(B) All fees charged by a bankruptcy petition preparer may be forfeited in any case in which the bankruptcy petition preparer fails to comply with this subsection or subsection (b), (c), (d), (e), (f), or (g).

(C) An individual may exempt any funds recovered under this paragraph under section 522(b).

(4) The debtor, the trustee, a creditor, the United States trustee (or the bankruptcy administrator, if any) or the court, on the initiative of the court, may file a motion for an order under paragraph (2).

(5) A bankruptcy petition preparer shall be fined not more than $500 for each failure to comply with a court order to turn over funds within 30 days of service of such order.

(i)(1) If a bankruptcy petition preparer violates this section or commits any act that the court finds to be fraudulent, unfair, or deceptive, on the motion of the debtor, trustee, United States trustee (or the bankruptcy administrator, if any), and after notice and a hearing, the court shall order the bankruptcy petition preparer to pay to the debtor—

(A) the debtor's actual damages;

(B) the greater of—

(i) $2,000; or

(ii) twice the amount paid by the debtor to the bankruptcy petition preparer for the preparer's services; and

(C) reasonable attorneys' fees and costs in moving for damages under this subsection.

(2) If the trustee or creditor moves for damages on behalf of the debtor under this subsection, the bankruptcy petition preparer shall be ordered to pay the movant the additional amount of $1,000 plus reasonable attorneys' fees and costs incurred.

(j)(1) A debtor for whom a bankruptcy petition preparer has prepared a document for filing, the trustee, a creditor, or the United States trustee in the district in which the bankruptcy petition preparer resides, has conducted business, or the United States trustee in any other district in which the debtor resides may bring a civil action to enjoin a bankruptcy petition preparer from engaging in any conduct in violation of this section or from further acting as a bankruptcy petition preparer.

(2)(A) In an action under paragraph (1), if the court finds that—

(i) a bankruptcy petition preparer has—

(I) engaged in conduct in violation of this section or of any provision of this title;

(II) misrepresented the preparer's experience or education as a bankruptcy petition preparer; or

(III) engaged in any other fraudulent, unfair, or deceptive conduct; and

(ii) injunctive relief is appropriate to prevent the recurrence of such conduct,

the court may enjoin the bankruptcy petition preparer from engaging in such conduct.

(B) If the court finds that a bankruptcy petition preparer has continually engaged in conduct described in subclause (I), (II), or (III) of clause (i) and that an injunction prohibiting such conduct would not be sufficient to prevent such person's interference with the proper administration of this title, has not paid a penalty imposed under this section, or failed to disgorge all fees ordered by the court the court may enjoin the person from acting as a bankruptcy petition preparer.

(3) The court, as part of its contempt power, may enjoin a bankruptcy petition preparer that has failed to comply with a previous order issued under this section. The injunction under this paragraph may be issued on the motion of the court, the trustee, or the United States trustee (or the bankruptcy administrator, if any).

(4) The court shall award to a debtor, trustee, or creditor that brings a successful action under this subsection reasonable attorneys' fees and costs of the action, to be paid by the bankruptcy petition preparer.

(k) Nothing in this section shall be construed to permit activities that are otherwise prohibited by law, including rules and laws that prohibit the unauthorized practice of law.

(*l*)(1) A bankruptcy petition preparer who fails to comply with any provision of subsection (b), (c), (d), (e), (f), (g), or (h) may be fined not more than $500 for each such failure.

(2) The court shall triple the amount of a fine assessed under paragraph (1) in any case in which the court finds that a bankruptcy petition preparer—

(A) advised the debtor to exclude assets or income that should have been included on applicable schedules;

(B) advised the debtor to use a false Social Security account number;

(C) failed to inform the debtor that the debtor was filing for relief under this title; or

(D) prepared a document for filing in a manner that failed to disclose the identity of the bankruptcy petition preparer.

(3) A debtor, trustee, creditor, or United States trustee (or the bankruptcy administrator, if any) may file a motion for an order imposing a fine on the bankruptcy petition preparer for any violation of this section.

(4)(A) Fines imposed under this subsection in judicial districts served by United States trustees shall be paid to the United States trustees, who shall deposit an amount equal to such fines in the United States Trustee Fund.

(B) Fines imposed under this subsection in judicial districts served by bankruptcy administrators shall be deposited as offsetting receipts to the fund established under section 1931 of title 28, and shall remain available until expended to reimburse any appropriation for the amount paid out of such appropriation for expenses of the operation and maintenance of the courts of the United States.

(Added Pub.L. 103–394, Title III, § 308(a), Oct. 22, 1994, 108 Stat. 4135, and amended Pub.L. 109–8, Title II, § 221, Title XII, § 1205, Apr. 20, 2005, 119 Stat. 59, 194; Pub.L. 110–161, Div. B, Title II, § 212(b), Dec. 26, 2007, 121 Stat. 1914.)

HISTORICAL AND STATUTORY NOTES

Revision Notes and Legislative Reports

1994 Acts. House Report No. 103–835, see 1994 U.S. Code Cong. and Adm. News, p. 3340.

2005 Acts. House Report No. 109–31(Part I), see 2005 U.S. Code Cong. and Adm. News, p. 88.

2007 Acts. House Report No. 110–197, see 2007 U.S. Code Cong. and Adm. News, p. 661.

Statement by President, see 2007 U.S. Code Cong. and Adm. News, p. S34.

References in Text

The Federal Rules of Bankruptcy Procedure, referred to in subsec. (b)(2)(A), are set out in the Appendix to this title.

Chapter 7, 11, 12, or 13, referred to in subsec. (e)(2)(B)(i)(II), is chapter 7, 11, 12, or 13 of this title, 11 U.S.C.A. § 701 et seq., 11 U.S.C.A. § 1101 et seq., 11 U.S.C.A. § 1201 et seq., or 11 U.S.C.A. § 1301 et seq., respectively.

Paragraph (2), referred to in subsec. (h)(4), was redesignated as par. (3) and repealed and a new par. (3) was added by Pub.L. 109–8, Title II, § 221(8)(A), (D), Apr. 20, 2005, 119 Stat. 59. The new par. (3) provides for court orders similar to those provided for in former par. (2).

Effective and Applicability Provisions

2005 Acts. Amendments by Pub.L. 109–8 effective, except as otherwise provided, 180 days after April 20, 2005, and inapplicable with respect to cases commenced under Title 11 before the effective date, see Pub.L. 109–8, § 1501, set out as a note under 11 U.S.C.A. § 101.

1994 Acts. Section effective on Oct. 22, 1994, and not to apply with respect to cases commenced under Title 11 of the United States Code before Oct. 22, 1994, see section 702 of Pub.L. 103–394, set out as a note under section 101 of this title.

Separability of Provisions

If any provision of or amendment made by Pub.L. 103–394 or the application of such provision or amendment to any person or circumstance is held to be unconstitutional, the remaining provisions of and amendments made by Pub.L. 103–394 and the application of such provisions and amendments to any person or circumstance shall not be affected thereby, see section 701 of Pub.L. 103–394, set out as a note under section 101 of this title.

§ 111. Nonprofit budget and credit counseling agencies; financial management instructional courses

(a) The clerk shall maintain a publicly available list of—

(1) nonprofit budget and credit counseling agencies that provide 1 or more services described in section 109(h) currently approved by the United States trustee (or the bankruptcy administrator, if any); and

(2) instructional courses concerning personal financial management currently approved by the United States trustee (or the bankruptcy administrator, if any), as applicable.

(b) The United States trustee (or bankruptcy administrator, if any) shall only approve a nonprofit budget and credit counseling agency or an instructional course concerning personal financial management as follows:

(1) The United States trustee (or bankruptcy administrator, if any) shall have thoroughly reviewed the qualifications of the nonprofit budget and credit counseling agency or of the provider of the instructional course under the standards set forth in this section, and the services or instructional courses that will be offered by such agency or such provider, and may require such agency or such provider that has sought approval to provide information with respect to such review.

(2) The United States trustee (or bankruptcy administrator, if any) shall have determined that such agency or such instructional course fully satisfies the applicable standards set forth in this section.

(3) If a nonprofit budget and credit counseling agency or instructional course did not appear on the approved list for the district under subsection (a) immediately before approval under this section, approval under this subsection of such agency or such instructional course shall be for a probationary period not to exceed 6 months.

(4) At the conclusion of the applicable probationary period under paragraph (3), the United States trustee (or bankruptcy administrator, if any) may only approve for an additional 1-year period, and for successive 1-year periods thereafter, an agency or instructional course that has demonstrated during the probationary or applicable subsequent period of approval that such agency or instructional course—

(A) has met the standards set forth under this section during such period; and

(B) can satisfy such standards in the future.

(5) Not later than 30 days after any final decision under paragraph (4), an interested person may seek judicial review of such decision in the appropriate district court of the United States.

(c)(1) The United States trustee (or the bankruptcy administrator, if any) shall only approve a nonprofit budget and credit counseling agency that demonstrates that it will provide qualified counselors, maintain adequate provision for safekeeping and payment of client funds, provide adequate counseling with respect to client credit problems, and deal responsibly and effectively with other matters relating to the quality, effectiveness, and financial security of the services it provides.

(2) To be approved by the United States trustee (or the bankruptcy administrator, if any), a nonprofit budget and credit counseling agency shall, at a minimum—

(A) have a board of directors the majority of which—

(i) are not employed by such agency; and

(ii) will not directly or indirectly benefit financially from the outcome of the counseling services provided by such agency;

(B) if a fee is charged for counseling services, charge a reasonable fee, and provide services without regard to ability to pay the fee;

(C) provide for safekeeping and payment of client funds, including an annual audit of the trust accounts and appropriate employee bonding;

(D) provide full disclosures to a client, including funding sources, counselor qualifications, possible impact on credit reports, and any costs of such program that will be paid by such client and how such costs will be paid;

(E) provide adequate counseling with respect to a client's credit problems that includes an analysis of such client's current financial condition, factors that caused such financial condition, and how such client can develop a plan to respond to the problems without incurring negative amortization of debt;

(F) provide trained counselors who receive no commissions or bonuses based on the outcome of the counseling services provided by such agency, and who have adequate experience, and have been adequately trained to provide counseling services to individuals in financial difficulty, including the matters described in subparagraph (E);

(G) demonstrate adequate experience and background in providing credit counseling; and

(H) have adequate financial resources to provide continuing support services for budgeting plans over the life of any repayment plan.

(d) The United States trustee (or the bankruptcy administrator, if any) shall only approve an instructional course concerning personal financial management—

(1) for an initial probationary period under subsection (b)(3) if the course will provide at a minimum—

(A) trained personnel with adequate experience and training in providing effective instruction and services;

(B) learning materials and teaching methodologies designed to assist debtors in understanding personal financial management and that are consistent with stated objectives directly related to the goals of such instructional course;

(C) adequate facilities situated in reasonably convenient locations at which such instructional course is offered, except that such facilities may include the provision of such instructional course by telephone or through the Internet, if such instructional course is effective;

(D) the preparation and retention of reasonable records (which shall include the debtor's bankruptcy case number) to permit evaluation of the effectiveness of such instructional course, including any evaluation of satisfaction of instructional course requirements for each debtor attending such instructional course, which shall be available for inspection and evaluation by the Executive Office for United States Trustees, the United States trustee (or the bankruptcy administrator, if any), or the chief bankruptcy judge for the district in which such instructional course is offered; and

(E) if a fee is charged for the instructional course, charge a reasonable fee, and provide services without regard to ability to pay the fee.

(2) for any 1-year period if the provider thereof has demonstrated that the course meets the standards of paragraph (1) and, in addition—

(A) has been effective in assisting a substantial number of debtors to understand personal financial management; and

(B) is otherwise likely to increase substantially the debtor's understanding of personal financial management.

(e) The district court may, at any time, investigate the qualifications of a nonprofit budget and credit counseling agency referred to in subsection (a), and request production of documents to ensure the integrity and effectiveness of such agency. The district court may, at any time, remove from the approved list under subsection (a) a nonprofit budget and credit counseling agency upon finding such agency does not meet the qualifications of subsection (b).

(f) The United States trustee (or the bankruptcy administrator, if any) shall notify the clerk that a nonprofit budget and credit counseling agency or an instructional course is no longer approved, in which case the clerk shall remove it from the list maintained under subsection (a).

(g)(1) No nonprofit budget and credit counseling agency may provide to a credit reporting agency information concerning whether a debtor has received or sought instruction concerning personal financial management from such agency.

(2) A nonprofit budget and credit counseling agency that willfully or negligently fails to comply with any requirement under this title with respect to a debtor shall be liable for damages in an amount equal to the sum of—

(A) any actual damages sustained by the debtor as a result of the violation; and

(B) any court costs or reasonable attorneys' fees (as determined by the court) incurred in an action to recover those damages.

(Added Pub.L. 109-8, Title I, § 106(e)(1), Apr. 20, 2005, 119 Stat. 39.)

HISTORICAL AND STATUTORY NOTES

Revision Notes and Legislative Reports

2005 Acts. House Report No. 109-31(Part I), see 2005 U.S. Code Cong. and Adm. News, p. 88.

Effective and Applicability Provisions

2005 Acts. Amendments by Pub.L. 109-8 effective, except as otherwise provided, 180 days after April 20, 2005, and inapplicable with respect to cases commenced under Title 11 before the effective date, see Pub.L. 109-8, § 1501, set out as a note under 11 U.S.C.A. § 101.

Debtor Financial Management Training Test Program

Pub.L. 109-8, Title I, § 105, Apr. 20, 2005, 119 Stat. 36, provided that:

"**(a) Development of financial management and training curriculum and materials.**—The Director of the Executive Office for United States Trustees (in this section referred to as the 'Director') shall consult with a wide range of individuals who are experts in the field of debtor education, including trustees who serve in cases under chapter 13 of title 11, United States Code [11 U.S.C.A. § 1301 et seq.], and who operate financial management education programs for debtors, and shall develop a financial management training curriculum and materials that can be used to educate debtors who are individuals on how to better manage their finances.

"**(b) Test.**—

"**(1) Selection of districts.**—The Director shall select 6 judicial districts of the United States in which to test the effectiveness of the financial management training curriculum and materials developed under subsection (a) [of this note].

"**(2) Use.**—For an 18-month period beginning not later than 270 days after the date of the enactment of this Act [April 20, 2005], such curriculum and materials shall be, for the 6 judicial districts selected under paragraph (1), used as the instructional course concerning personal financial management for purposes of section 111 of title 11, United States Code.

"**(c) Evaluation.**—

"**(1) In general.**—During the 18-month period referred to in subsection (b) [of this note], the Director shall evaluate the effectiveness of—

"(A) the financial management training curriculum and materials developed under subsection (a) [of this note]; and

"(B) a sample of existing consumer education programs such as those described in the Report of the National Bankruptcy Review Commission (October 20, 1997) that are representative of consumer education programs carried out by the credit industry, by trustees serving under chapter 13 of title 11, United States Code [11 U.S.C.A. § 1301 et seq.], and by consumer counseling groups.

"(2) **Report.**—Not later than 3 months after concluding such evaluation, the Director shall submit a report to the Speaker of the House of Representatives and the President pro tempore of the Senate, for referral to the appropriate committees of the Congress, containing the findings of the Director regarding the effectiveness of such curriculum, such materials, and such programs and their costs."

[Amendments by Pub.L. 109–8 effective, except as otherwise provided, 180 days after April 20, 2005, and inapplicable with respect to cases commenced under Title 11 before the effective date, see Pub.L. 109–8, § 1501, set out as a note under 11 U.S.C.A. § 101.]

§ 112. Prohibition on disclosure of name of minor children

The debtor may be required to provide information regarding a minor child involved in matters under this title but may not be required to disclose in the public records in the case the name of such minor child. The debtor may be required to disclose the name of such minor child in a nonpublic record that is maintained by the court and made available by the court for examination by the United States trustee, the trustee, and the auditor (if any) serving under section 586(f) of title 28, in the case. The court, the United States trustee, the trustee, and such auditor shall not disclose the name of such minor child maintained in such nonpublic record.

(Added Pub.L. 109–8, Title II, § 233(a), Apr. 20, 2005, 119 Stat. 74.)

HISTORICAL AND STATUTORY NOTES

Revision Notes and Legislative Reports

2005 Acts. House Report No. 109–31(Part I), see 2005 U.S. Code Cong. and Adm. News, p. 88.

Effective and Applicability Provisions

2005 Acts. Amendments by Pub.L. 109–8 effective, except as otherwise provided, 180 days after April 20, 2005, and inapplicable with respect to cases commenced under Title 11 before the effective date, see Pub.L. 109–8, § 1501, set out as a note under 11 U.S.C.A. § 101.

§§ 113 to 300. Reserved for future legislation

CHAPTER 3—CASE ADMINISTRATION

[1] So in original. Does not conform to section catchline.

HISTORICAL AND STATUTORY NOTES

Effective and Applicability Provisions

2005 Acts. Amendments by Pub.L. 109–8, § 434, effective, 60 days after the date on which rules are prescribed under 28 U.S.C.A. § 2075, to establish forms to be used to comply with 11 U.S.C.A. § 308, see Pub.L. 109–8, § 434(b), set out as a note under 11 U.S.C.A. § 308.

Amendments by Pub.L. 109–8 effective, except as otherwise provided, 180 days after April 20, 2005, and inapplicable with respect to cases commenced under Title 11 before the effective date, see Pub.L. 109–8, § 1501, set out as a note under 11 U.S.C.A. § 101.

CROSS REFERENCES

Applicability of this chapter to—

Cases under Chapters 7, 11, 12, or 13 of this title, see 11 USCA § 103.

Investor protection liquidation proceedings, see 15 USCA § 78fff.

SUBCHAPTER I—COMMENCEMENT OF A CASE

§ 301. Voluntary cases

(a) A voluntary case under a chapter of this title is commenced by the filing with the bankruptcy court of a petition under such chapter by an entity that may be a debtor under such chapter.

(b) The commencement of a voluntary case under a chapter of this title constitutes an order for relief under such chapter.

(Pub.L. 95–598, Nov. 6, 1978, 92 Stat. 2558; Pub.L. 109–8, Title V, § 501(b), Apr. 20, 2005, 119 Stat. 118.)

HISTORICAL AND STATUTORY NOTES

Revision Notes and Legislative Reports

1978 Acts. Section 301 specifies the manner in which a voluntary bankruptcy case is commenced. The debtor files a petition under this section under the particular operative chapter of the bankruptcy code under which he wishes to proceed. The filing of the petition constitutes an order for relief in the case under that chapter. The section contains no change from current law, except for the use of the phrase "order for relief" instead of "adjudication." The term adjudication is replaced by a less pejorative phrase in light of the clear power of Congress to permit voluntary bankruptcy without the necessity for an adjudication, as under the 1898 act [former Title 11], which was adopted when voluntary bankruptcy was a concept not thoroughly tested. Senate Report No. 95–989.

2005 Acts. House Report No. 109–31(Part I), see 2005 U.S. Code Cong. and Adm. News, p. 88.

Legislative Statements

Sections 301, 302, 303, and 304, are all modified in the House amendment to adopt an idea contained in sections 301 and 303 of the Senate amendment requiring a petition commencing a case to be filed with the bankruptcy court. The exception contained in section 301 of the Senate bill relating to cases filed under chapter 9 is deleted. Chapter 9 cases will be handled by a bankruptcy court as are other title 11 cases.

Effective and Applicability Provisions

2005 Acts. Amendments by Pub.L. 109–8 effective, except as otherwise provided, 180 days after April 20, 2005, and inapplicable with respect to cases commenced under Title 11 before the effective date, see Pub.L. 109–8, § 1501, set out as a note under 11 U.S.C.A. § 101.

CROSS REFERENCES

Applicability of this section in Chapter 9 cases, see 11 USCA § 901.

Automatic stay, see 11 USCA § 362.

Commencement of Chapter 9 cases concerning certain unincorporated tax or special assessment districts, see 11 USCA § 921.

Exemptions elected in estates administered jointly, see 11 USCA § 522.

Fees, see 28 USCA § 1930.

"Petition" defined, see 11 USCA § 101.

Property of estate, see 11 USCA § 541.

§ 302. Joint cases

(a) A joint case under a chapter of this title is commenced by the filing with the bankruptcy court of a single petition under such chapter by an individual that may be a debtor under such chapter and such individual's spouse. The commencement of a joint case under a chapter of this title constitutes an order for relief under such chapter.

(b) After the commencement of a joint case, the court shall determine the extent, if any, to which the debtors' estates shall be consolidated.

(Pub.L. 95–598, Nov. 6, 1978, 92 Stat. 2558.)

HISTORICAL AND STATUTORY NOTES

Revision Notes and Legislative Reports

1978 Acts. A joint case is a voluntary bankruptcy case concerning a wife and husband. Under current law, there is no explicit provision for joint cases. Very often, however, in the consumer debtor context, a husband and wife are jointly liable on their debts, and jointly hold most of their property. A joint case will facilitate consolidation of their estates, to the benefit of both the debtors and their creditors, because the cost of administration will be reduced, and there will be only one filing fee.

Section 302 specifies that a joint case is commenced by the filing of a petition under an appropriate chapter by an individual and that individual's spouse. Thus, one spouse cannot take the other into bankruptcy without the other's knowledge or consent. The filing of the petition constitutes an order for relief under the chapter selected.

Subsection (b) requires the court to determine the extent, if any, to which the estates of the two debtors will be consolidated; that is, assets and liabilities combined in a single pool to pay creditors. Factors that will be relevant in the court's determination include the extent of jointly held property and the amount of jointly-owned debts. The section, of course, is not license to consolidate in order to avoid other provisions of the title to the detriment of either the debtors or their creditors. It is designed mainly for ease of administration. Senate Report No. 95–989.

CROSS REFERENCES

Automatic stay, see 11 USCA § 362.

Exempt property, see 11 USCA § 522.

Fees, see 28 USCA § 1930.

"Petition" defined, see 11 USCA § 101.

Property of estate, see 11 USCA § 541.

§ 303. Involuntary cases

(a) An involuntary case may be commenced only under chapter 7 or 11 of this title, and only against a person, except a farmer, family farmer, or a corporation that is not a moneyed, business, or commercial corporation, that may be a debtor under the chapter under which such case is commenced.

(b) An involuntary case against a person is commenced by the filing with the bankruptcy court of a petition under chapter 7 or 11 of this title—

(1) by three or more entities, each of which is either a holder of a claim against such person that is not contingent as to liability or the subject of a bona fide dispute as to liability or amount, or an indenture trustee representing such a holder, if such noncontingent, undisputed claims aggregate at least $13,475 [1] more than the value of any lien on property of the debtor securing such claims held by the holders of such claims;

(2) if there are fewer than 12 such holders, excluding any employee or insider of such person and any transferee of a transfer that is voidable under section 544, 545, 547, 548, 549, or 724(a) of this title, by one or more of such holders that hold in the aggregate at least $13,475 [1] of such claims;

(3) if such person is a partnership—

(A) by fewer than all of the general partners in such partnership; or

(B) if relief has been ordered under this title with respect to all of the general partners in such partnership, by a general partner in such partnership, the trustee of such a general partner, or a holder of a claim against such partnership; or

(4) by a foreign representative of the estate in a foreign proceeding concerning such person.

(c) After the filing of a petition under this section but before the case is dismissed or relief is ordered, a creditor holding an unsecured claim that is not contingent, other than a creditor filing under subsection (b) of this section, may join in the petition with the same effect as if such joining creditor were a petitioning creditor under subsection (b) of this section.

(d) The debtor, or a general partner in a partnership debtor that did not join in the petition, may file an answer to a petition under this section.

(e) After notice and a hearing, and for cause, the court may require the petitioners under this section to file a bond to indemnify the debtor for such amounts as the court may later allow under subsection (i) of this section.

(f) Notwithstanding section 363 of this title, except to the extent that the court orders otherwise, and until an order for relief in the case, any business of the debtor may continue to operate, and the debtor may continue to use, acquire, or dispose of property as if an involuntary case concerning the debtor had not been commenced.

(g) At any time after the commencement of an involuntary case under chapter 7 of this title but before an order for relief in the case, the court, on request of a party in interest, after notice to the debtor and a hearing, and if necessary to preserve the property of the estate or to prevent loss to the estate, may order the United States trustee to appoint an interim trustee under section 701 of this title to take possession of the property of the estate and to operate any business of the debtor. Before an order for relief, the debtor may regain possession of property in the possession of a trustee ordered appointed under this subsection if the debtor files such bond as the court requires, conditioned on the debtor's accounting for and delivering to the trustee, if there is an order for relief in the case, such property, or the value, as of the date the debtor regains possession, of such property.

(h) If the petition is not timely controverted, the court shall order relief against the debtor in an involuntary case under the chapter under which the petition was filed. Otherwise, after trial, the court shall order relief against the debtor in an involuntary case under the chapter under which the petition was filed, only if—

(1) the debtor is generally not paying such debtor's debts as such debts become due unless such debts are the subject of a bona fide dispute as to liability or amount; or

(2) within 120 days before the date of the filing of the petition, a custodian, other than a trustee, receiver, or agent appointed or authorized to take charge of less than substantially all of the property of the debtor for the purpose of enforcing a lien against such property, was appointed or took possession.

(i) If the court dismisses a petition under this section other than on consent of all petitioners and the debtor, and if the debtor does not waive the right to judgment under this subsection, the court may grant judgment—

(1) against the petitioners and in favor of the debtor for—

(A) costs; or

(B) a reasonable attorney's fee; or

(2) against any petitioner that filed the petition in bad faith, for—

(A) any damages proximately caused by such filing; or

(B) punitive damages.

(j) Only after notice to all creditors and a hearing may the court dismiss a petition filed under this section—

(1) on the motion of a petitioner;

(2) on consent of all petitioners and the debtor; or

(3) for want of prosecution.

(k) [Repealed. Pub.L. 109–8, Title VIII, § 802(d)(2), Apr. 20, 2005, 119 Stat. 146]

(*l*)(1) If—

(A) the petition under this section is false or contains any materially false, fictitious, or fraudulent statement;

(B) the debtor is an individual; and

(C) the court dismisses such petition,

the court, upon the motion of the debtor, shall seal all the records of the court relating to such petition, and all references to such petition.

(2) If the debtor is an individual and the court dismisses a petition under this section, the court may enter an order prohibiting all consumer reporting agencies (as defined in section 603(f) of the Fair Credit Reporting Act (15 U.S.C. 1681a(f))) from making any consumer report (as defined in section 603(d) of that Act) that contains any information relating to such petition or to the case commenced by the filing of such petition.

(3) Upon the expiration of the statute of limitations described in section 3282 of title 18, for a violation of section 152 or 157 of such title, the court, upon the motion of the debtor and for good cause, may expunge any records relating to a petition filed under this section.

(Pub.L. 95–598, Nov. 6, 1978, 92 Stat. 2559; Pub. L. 98–353, Title III, §§ 426, 427, July 10, 1984, 98 Stat. 369; Pub.L. 99–554, Title II, §§ 204, 254, 283(b), Oct. 27, 1986, 100 Stat. 3097, 3105, 3116; Pub.L. 103–394, Title I, § 108(b), Oct. 22, 1994, 108 Stat. 4112; Pub.L. 109–8, Title III, § 332(b), Title VIII, § 802(d)(2), Title XII, § 1234(a), Apr. 20, 2005, 119 Stat. 103, 146, 204.)

1 Dollar amount as adjusted by the Judicial Conference of the United States. See Adjustment of Dollar Amounts notes set out under this section and 11 U.S.C.A. § 104.

HISTORICAL AND STATUTORY NOTES

Revision Notes and Legislative Reports

1978 Acts. Section 303 governs the commencement of involuntary cases under title 11. An involuntary case may be commenced only under chapter 7, Liquidation, or chapter 11, Reorganization. Involuntary cases are not permitted for municipalities, because to do so may constitute an invasion of State sovereignty contrary to the 10th amendment, and would constitute bad policy, by permitting the fate of a municipality, governed by officials elected by the people of the municipality, to be determined by a small number of creditors of the municipality. Involuntary chapter 13 cases are not permitted either. To do so would constitute bad policy, because chapter 13 only works when there is a willing debtor that wants to repay his creditors. Short of involuntary servitude, it is difficult to keep a debtor working for his creditors when he does not want to pay them back. See chapter 3, supra.

The exceptions contained in current law that prohibit involuntary cases against farmers, ranchers and eleemosynary institutions are continued. Farmers and ranchers are excepted because of the cyclical nature of their business. One drought year or one year of low prices, as a result of which a farmer is temporarily unable to pay his creditors, should not subject him to involuntary bankruptcy. Eleemosynary institutions, such as churches, schools, and charitable organizations and foundations, likewise are exempt from involuntary bankruptcy.

The provisions for involuntary chapter 11 cases is a slight change from present law, based on the proposed consolidation of the reorganization chapters. Currently, involuntary cases are permitted under chapters X and XII [chapters 10 and 12 of former Title 11] but not under chapter XI [chapter 11 of former Title 11]. The consolidation requires a single rule for all kinds of reorganization proceedings. Because the assets of an insolvent debtor belong equitably to his creditors, the bill permits involuntary cases in order that creditors may realize on their assets through reorganization as well as through liquidation.

Subsection (b) of the section specifies who may file an involuntary petition. As under current law, if the debtor has more than 12 creditors, three creditors must join in the involuntary petition. The dollar amount limitation is changed from current law to $5,000. The new amount applies both to liquidation and reorganization cases in order that there not be an artificial difference between the two chapters that would provide an incentive for one or the other. Subsection (b)(1) makes explicit the right of an indenture trustee to be one of the three petitioning creditors on behalf of the creditors the trustee represents under the indenture. If all of the general partners in a partnership are in bankruptcy, then the trustee of a single general partner may file an involuntary petition against the partnership. Finally, a foreign representative may file an involuntary case concerning the debtor in the foreign proceeding, in order to administer assets in this country. This subsection is not intended to overrule Bankruptcy Rule 104(d), which places certain restrictions on the transfer of claims for the purpose of commencing an involuntary case. That Rule will be continued under section 405(d) of this bill.

Subsection (c) permits creditors other than the original petitioning creditors to join in the petition with the same effect as if the joining creditor had been one of the original petitioning creditors. Thus, if the claim of one of the original petitioning creditors is disallowed, the case will not be dismissed for want of three creditors or want of $5,000 in petitioning claims if the joining creditor suffices to fulfill the statutory requirements.

Subsection (d) permits the debtor to file an answer to an involuntary petition. The subsection also permits a general partner in a partnership debtor to answer an involuntary petition against the partnership if he did not join in the petition. Thus, a partnership petition by less than all of the general partners is treated as an involuntary, not a voluntary, petition.

The court may, under subsection (e), require the petitioners to file a bond to indemnify the debtor for such amounts as the court may later allow under subsection (i). Subsection (i) provides for costs, attorneys fees, and damages in certain circumstances. The bonding requirement will discourage frivolous petitions as well as spiteful petitions based on a desire to embarrass the debtor (who may be a competitor of a petitioning creditor) or to put the debtor out of business without good cause. An involuntary petition may put a debtor out of business even if it is without foundation and is later dismissed.

Subsection (f) is both a clarification and a change from existing law. It permits the debtor to continue to operate any business of the debtor and to dispose of property as if the case had not been commenced. The court is permitted, however, to control the debtor's powers under this subsection by appropriate orders, such as where there is a fear that the debtor may attempt to abscond with assets, dispose of them at less than their fair value, or dismantle his business, all to the detriment of the debtor's creditors.

The court may also, under subsection (g), appoint an interim trustee to take possession of the debtor's property and to operate any business of the debtor, pending trial on the involuntary petition. The court may make such an order only on the request of a party in interest, and after notice to the debtor and a hearing. There must be a showing that a trustee is necessary to preserve the property of the estate or to prevent loss to the estate. The debtor may regain possession by posting a sufficient bond.

Subsection (h) provides the standard for an order for relief on an involuntary petition. If the petition is not timely controverted (the Rules of Bankruptcy Procedure will fix time limits), the court orders relief after a trial, only if the debtor is generally unable to pay its debts as they mature, or if the debtor has failed to pay a major portion of his debts as they become due, or if a custodian was appointed during the 90-day period preceding the filing of the petition. The first two tests are variations of the equity insolvency test. They represent the most significant departure from present law concerning the grounds for involuntary bankruptcy, which requires an act of bankruptcy. Proof of the commission of an act of bankruptcy has frequently required a showing that the debtor was insolvent on a "balance-sheet" test when the act was committed. This bill abolishes the concept of acts of bankruptcy.

The equity insolvency test has been in equity jurisprudence for hundreds of years, and though it is new in the bankruptcy context (except in chapter X [former chapter 10 of former Title 11 (former section 501 et seq. of former Title 11)]), the bankruptcy courts should have no difficulty in applying it. The third test, appointment of a custodian within ninety days before the petition, is provided for simplicity. It is not a partial re-enactment of acts of bankruptcy. If a custodian of all or substantially all of the property of the debtor has been appointed, this paragraph creates an irrebuttable presumption that the debtor is unable to pay its debts as they mature. Moreover, once a proceeding to liquidate assets has been commenced, the debtor's creditors have an absolute right to have the liquidation (or reorganization) proceed in the bankruptcy court and under the bankruptcy laws with all of the appropriate creditor and debtor protections that those laws provide. Ninety days gives creditors ample time in which to seek bankruptcy liquidation after the appointment of a custodian. If they wait beyond the ninety day period, they are not precluded from filing an involuntary petition. They are simply required to prove equity insolvency rather than the more easily provable custodian test.

Subsection (i) permits the court to award costs, reasonable attorney's fees, or damages if an involuntary petition is dismissed other than by consent of all petitioning creditors and the debtor. The damages that the court may award are those that may be caused by the taking of possession of the debtor's property under subsection (g) or section 1104 of the bankruptcy code. In addition, if a petitioning creditor filed the petition in bad faith, the court may award the debtor any damages proximately caused by the filing of the petition. These damages may include such items as loss of business during and after the pendency of the case, and so on. "Or" is not exclusive in this paragraph. The court may grant any or all of the damages provided for under the provision. Dismissal in the best interests of credits under section 305(a)(1) would not give rise to a damages claim.

Under subsection (j), the court may dismiss the petition by consent only after giving notice to all creditors. The purpose of the subsection is to prevent collusive settlements among the debtor and the petitioning creditors while other creditors, that wish to see relief ordered with respect to the debtor but that did not participate in the case, are left without sufficient protection.

Subsection (k) governs involuntary cases against foreign banks that are not engaged in business in the United States but that have assets located here. The subsection prevents a foreign bank from being placed into bankruptcy in this country unless a foreign proceeding against the bank is pending. The special protection afforded by this section is needed to prevent creditors from effectively closing down a foreign bank by the commencement of an involuntary bankruptcy case in this country unless that bank is involved in a proceeding under foreign law. An involuntary case commenced under this subsection gives the foreign representative and alternative to commencing a case ancillary to a foreign proceeding under section 304. Senate Report No. 95–989.

1984 Acts. Statements by Legislative Leaders, see 1984 U.S. Code Cong. and Adm. News, p. 576.

1986 Acts. House Report No. 99–764 and House Conference Report No. 99–958, see 1986 U.S. Code Cong. and Adm. News, p. 5227.

1994 Acts. House Report No. 103–835, see 1994 U.S. Code Cong. and Adm. News, p. 3340.

2005 Acts. House Report No. 109–31(Part I), see 2005 U.S. Code Cong. and Adm. News, p. 88.

Legislative Statements

Section 303(b)(1) is modified to make clear that unsecured claims against the debtor must be determined by taking into account liens securing property held by third parties.

Section 303(b)(3) adopts a provision contained in the Senate amendment indicating that an involuntary petition may be commenced against a partnership by fewer than all of the general partners in such partnership. Such action may be taken by fewer than all of the general partners notwithstanding a contrary agreement between the partners or State or local law.

Section 303(h)(1) in the House amendment is a compromise of standards found in H.R. 8200 as passed by the House and the Senate amendment pertaining to the standards that must be met in order to obtain an order for relief in an involuntary case under title 11. The language specifies that the court will order such relief only if the debtor is generally not paying debtor's debts as they become due.

Section 303(h)(2) reflects a compromise pertaining to section 543 of title 11 relating to turnover of property by a custodian. It provides an alternative test to support an order for relief in an involuntary case. If a custodian, other than a trustee, receiver, or agent appointed or authorized to take charge of less than substantially all of the property of the debtor for the purpose of enforcing a lien against such property, was appointed or took possession within 120 days before the date of the filing of the petition, then the court may order relief in the involuntary case. The test under section 303(h)(2) differs from section 3a(5) of the Bankruptcy Act [section 21(a)(5) of former Title 11], which requires an involuntary case to be commenced before the earlier of time such custodian was appointed or took possession. The test in section 303(h)(2) authorizes an order for relief to be entered in an involuntary case from the later date on which the custodian was appointed or took possession.

References in Text

Section 603 of the Fair Credit Reporting Act, referred to in subsec. (*l*)(2), is Pub.L. 90–321, Title VI, § 603, as added Pub.L. 91–508, Title IV, § 601, Oct. 26, 1970, 84 Stat. 1128, and amended, which is classified to 15 U.S.C.A. § 1681a.

Effective and Applicability Provisions

2007 Acts. Increase of dollar amounts by Judicial Conference of the United States by notice published Feb. 14, 2007, 72 F.R. 7082 effective April 1, 2007, and increase not applicable to cases commenced before the effective date of the adjustments, i.e., April 1, 2007. See Adjustment of Dollar Amounts notes under 11 U.S.C.A. § 104 and this section.

2005 Acts. Pub.L. 109–8, Title XII, § 1234(b), Apr. 20, 2005, 119 Stat. 204, provided that: "This section and the amendments made by this section [amending this section] shall take effect on the date of the enactment of this Act [Apr. 20, 2005] and shall apply with respect to cases commenced under title 11 of the United States Code before, on, and after such date."

Amendments by sections 332(b) and 802(d)(2) of Pub.L. 109–8 effective, except as otherwise provided, 180 days after April 20, 2005, and inapplicable with respect to cases commenced under Title 11 before the effective date, see Pub.L. 109–8, § 1501, set out as a note under 11 U.S.C.A. § 101.

2004 Acts. Adjustment of dollar amounts by Judicial Conference of the United States by notice dated Feb. 18, 2004, 69

F.R. 8482 effective April 1, 2004, and adjustment not applicable to cases commenced before the effective date of the adjustments, i.e., April 1, 2004. See Adjustment of Dollar Amounts notes under 11 U.S.C.A. § 104 and this section.

2001 Acts. Adjustment of dollar amounts by Judicial Conference of the United States by notice dated Feb. 20, 2001, 66 F.R. 10910 effective April 1, 2001, and adjustment not applicable to cases commenced before the effective date of the adjustments, i.e., April 1, 2001. See Adjustment of Dollar Amounts notes under 11 U.S.C.A. § 104 and this section.

1998 Acts. Adjustment of dollar amounts by Judicial Conference of the United States by notice dated Feb. 3, 1998, 63 F.R. 7179 effective April 1, 1998, and adjustment not applicable to cases commenced before the effective date of the adjustments, i.e., April 1, 1998. See Adjustment of Dollar Amounts notes under 11 U.S.C.A. § 104 and this section.

1994 Acts. Amendment by Pub.L. 103–394 effective on Oct. 22, 1994, and not to apply with respect to cases commenced under Title 11 of the United States Code before Oct. 22, 1994, see section 702 of Pub.L. 103–394, set out as a note under section 101 of this title.

1986 Acts. Amendment by Pub.L. 99–554 effective 30 days after Oct. 27, 1986, except as otherwise provided for, see section 302(a) of Pub.L. 99–554, set out as a note under section 581 of Title 28, Judiciary and Judicial Procedure.

Amendment by Pub.L. 99–554, § 204, not to become effective in or with respect to certain specified judicial districts until, or apply to cases while pending in such district before, the expiration of the 270-day period beginning 30 days after Oct. 27, 1986, or of the 30-day period beginning on the date the Attorney General certifies under section 303 of Pub.L. 99–554 the region specified in a paragraph of section 581(a) of Title 28, as amended by section 111(a) of Pub.L. 99–554, that includes such district, whichever occurs first, see section 302(d)(1) of Pub.L. 99–554, set out as a note under section 581 of Title 28.

Amendment by Pub.L. 99–554, § 204, not to become effective in or with respect to certain specified judicial districts until, or apply to cases while pending in such districts before, the expiration of the 2-year period beginning 30 days after Oct. 27, 1986, or of the 30-day period beginning on the date the Attorney General certifies under section 303 of Pub.L. 99–554 the region specified in a paragraph of section 581(a) of Title 28, as amended by section 111(a) of Pub.L. 99–554, that includes such district, whichever occurs first, see section 302(d)(2) of Pub.L. 99–554, set out as a note under section 581 of Title 28.

Amendment by Pub.L. 99–554, § 204, not to become effective in or with respect to judicial districts established for the States of Alabama and North Carolina until, or apply to cases while pending in such district before, such district elects to be included in a bankruptcy region established in section 581(a) of Title 28, as amended by section 111(a) of Pub.L. 99–554, or Oct. 1, 2002, whichever occurs first, and, except as otherwise provided, with respect to cases under chapters 7, 11, 12, and 13 of Title 11 commenced before 30 days after Oct. 27, 1986, and pending in a judicial district in the States of Alabama or North Carolina before any election made under section 302(d)(3)(A) of Pub.L. 99–554 by such district becomes effective or Oct. 1, 2002, whichever occurs first, amendments by Pub.L. 99–554 not to apply until Oct. 1, 2003, or the expiration of the 1-year period beginning on the date such election becomes effective, whichever occurs first, and further, in any judicial district in Alabama or North Carolina not making the election described in section 302(d)(3)(A) of Pub.L. 99–554, any person appointed under regulations issued by the Judicial Conference to administer estates in cases under Title 11 authorized to establish, etc., a panel of private trustees, and to supervise cases and trustees in cases under chapters 7, 11, 12, and 13 of Title 11, until amendments by sections 201 to 231 of Pub.L. 99–554 effective in such district, see section 302(d)(3)(A) to (F), (H), and (I) of Pub.L. 99–554, set out as a note under section 581 of Title 28.

Amendment by Pub.L. 99–554, § 204, except as otherwise provided, with respect to cases under chapters 7, 11, 12, and 13 of Title 11 commenced before 30 days after Oct. 27, 1986, and pending in a judicial district referred to in section 581(a) of Title 28, as amended by section 111(a) of Pub.L. 99–554, for which a United States trustee is not authorized before 30 days after Oct. 27, 1986 to be appointed, not applicable until the expiration of the 3-year period beginning on Oct. 27, 1986, or of the 1-year period beginning on the date the Attorney General certifies under section 303 of Pub.L. 99–554 the region specified in a paragraph of such section 581(a) that includes, such district, whichever occurs first, see section 302(e)(1), (2) of Pub.L. 99–554, set out as a note under section 581 of Title 28.

Amendment by Pub.L. 99–554, § 254, effective 30 days after Oct. 27, 1986, but not applicable to cases commenced under this title before that date, see section 302(a), (c)(1) of Pub.L. 99–554, set out as a note under section 581 of Title 28.

Amendment by Pub.L. 99–554, § 283, effective 30 days after Oct. 27, 1986, see section 302(a) of Pub.L. 99–554, set out as a note under section 581 of Title 28.

1984 Acts. Amendment by sections 426(a) and 427 of Pub.L. 98–353 effective with respect to cases filed 90 days after July 10, 1984, and amendment by section 426(b) of Pub.L. 98–353 effective July 10, 1984, see section 552(a), (b) of Pub.L. 98–353, set out as a note under section 101 of this title.

Separability of Provisions

If any provision of or amendment made by Pub.L. 103–394 or the application of such provision or amendment to any person or circumstance is held to be unconstitutional, the remaining provisions of and amendments made by Pub.L. 103–394 and the application of such provisions and amendments to any person or circumstance shall not be affected thereby, see section 701 of Pub.L. 103–394, set out as a note under section 101 of this title.

Adjustment of Dollar Amounts

For adjustment of dollar amounts specified in subsec. (b)(1), (2) of this section by the Judicial Conference of the United States, effective Apr. 1, 2007, see note set out under 11 U.S.C.A. § 104.

By notice published Feb. 14, 2007, 72 F.R. 7082, the Judicial Conference of the United States adjusted the dollar amounts in provisions specified in subsec. (b)(1), (2) of this section, effective Apr. 1, 2007, as follows:

In subsec. (b)(1) adjusted $12,300 to $13,475.

In subsec. (b)(2) adjusted $12,300 to $13,475.

By notice dated Feb. 18, 2004, 69 F.R. 8482, the Judicial Conference of the United States adjusted the dollar amounts in provisions specified in subsec. (b)(1), (2) of this section, effective Apr. 1, 2004, as follows:

In subsec. (b)(1) adjusted $11,625 to $12,300.

In subsec. (b)(2) adjusted $11,625 to $12,300.

By notice dated Feb. 20, 2001, 66 F.R. 10910, the Judicial Conference of the United States adjusted the dollar amounts in provisions specified in subsec. (b)(1), (2) of this section, effective Apr. 1, 2001, as follows:

In subsec. (b)(1) adjusted $10,775 to $11,625.

In subsec. (b)(2) adjusted $10,775 to $11,625.

By notice dated Feb. 3, 1998, 63 F.R. 7179, the Judicial Conference of the United States adjusted the dollar amounts in provisions specified in subsec. (b)(1), (2) of this section, effective Apr. 1, 1998, as follows:

In subsec. (b)(1) adjusted $10,000 to $10,775.

In subsec. (b)(2) adjusted $10,000 to $10,775.

CROSS REFERENCES

Allowance of administrative expenses incurred by creditor filing petition, see 11 USCA § 503.

Automatic stay, see 11 USCA § 362.

Exempt property, see 11 USCA § 522.

Fees, see 28 USCA § 1930.

Involuntary case—

Future adjustments, see 11 USCA § 104.

Jury trials, see 28 USCA § 1411.

Lists, schedules, statements and fees, see Fed.Rules Bankr.Proc. Form B 200, 11 USCA.

"Petition" defined, see 11 USCA § 101.

Postpetition transactions, see 11 USCA § 549.

Property of estate, see 11 USCA § 541.

Sharing of compensation between attorneys, see 11 USCA § 504.

[§ 304. Repealed. Pub.L. 109–8, Title VIII, § 802(d)(3), Apr. 20, 2005, 119 Stat. 146]

HISTORICAL AND STATUTORY NOTES

Section, Pub.L. 95–598, Nov. 6, 1978, 92 Stat. 2560, related to cases ancillary to foreign proceedings.

See, now, 11 U.S.C.A. § 1501 et seq. and 28 U.S.C.A. § 1410.

Effective Date of Repeal

Repeal effective, except as otherwise provided, 180 days after April 20, 2005, and inapplicable with respect to cases commenced under Title 11 before the effective date, see Pub.L. 109–8, § 1501, set out as a note under 11 U.S.C.A. § 101.

§ 305. Abstention

(a) The court, after notice and a hearing, may dismiss a case under this title, or may suspend all proceedings in a case under this title, at any time if—

(1) the interests of creditors and the debtor would be better served by such dismissal or suspension; or

(2)(A) a petition under section 1515 for recognition of a foreign proceeding has been granted; and

(B) the purposes of chapter 15 of this title would be best served by such dismissal or suspension.

(b) A foreign representative may seek dismissal or suspension under subsection (a)(2) of this section.

(c) An order under subsection (a) of this section dismissing a case or suspending all proceedings in a case, or a decision not so to dismiss or suspend, is not reviewable by appeal or otherwise by the court of appeals under section 158(d), 1291, or 1292 of title 28 or by the Supreme Court of the United States under section 1254 of title 28.

(Pub.L. 95–598, Nov. 6, 1978, 92 Stat. 2561; Pub.L. 101–650, Title III, § 309(a), Dec. 1, 1990, 104 Stat. 5113; Pub.L. 102–198, § 5, Dec. 9, 1991, 105 Stat. 1623; Pub.L. 109–8, Title VIII, § 802(d)(6), Apr. 20, 2005, 119 Stat. 146.)

HISTORICAL AND STATUTORY NOTES

Revision Notes and Legislative Reports

1978 Acts. A principle of the common law requires a court with jurisdiction over a particular matter to take jurisdiction. This section recognizes that there are cases in which it would be appropriate for the court to decline jurisdiction. Abstention under this section, however, is of jurisdiction over the entire case. Abstention from jurisdiction over a particular proceeding in a case is governed by proposed 28 U.S.C. 1471(c). Thus, the court is permitted, if the interests of creditors and the debtor would be better served by dismissal of the case or suspension of all proceedings in the case, to so order. The court may dismiss or suspend under the first paragraph, for example, if an arrangement is being worked out by creditors and the debtor out of court, there is no prejudice to the results of creditors in that arrangement, and an involuntary case has been commenced by a few recalcitrant creditors to provide a basis for future threats to extract full payment. The less expensive out-of-court workout may better serve the interests in the case. Likewise, if there is pending a foreign proceeding concerning the debtor and the factors specified in proposed 11 U.S.C. 304(c) warrant dismissal or suspension, the court may so act.

Subsection (b) gives a foreign representative authority to appear in the bankruptcy court to request dismissal or suspension. Subsection (c) makes the dismissal or suspension order nonreviewable by appeal or otherwise. The bankruptcy court, based on its experience and discretion is vested with the power of decision. Senate Report No. 95–989.

1990 Acts. Senate Report No. 101–416, see 1990 U.S.Code Cong. and Adm.News, p. 6802.

1991 Acts. House Report No. 102–322, see 1991 U.S.Code Cong. and Adm.News, p. 1303.

2005 Acts. House Report No. 109–31(Part I), see 2005 U.S. Code Cong. and Adm. News, p. 88.

References in Text

Chapter 15 of this title, referred to in subsec. (a)(2)(B), is classified to 11 U.S.C.A. § 1501 et seq.

Effective and Applicability Provisions

2005 Acts. Amendments by Pub.L. 109–8 effective, except as otherwise provided, 180 days after April 20, 2005, and inapplicable with respect to cases commenced under Title 11 before the effective date, see Pub.L. 109–8, § 1501, set out as a note under 11 U.S.C.A. § 101.

§ 306. Limited appearance

An appearance in a bankruptcy court by a foreign representative in connection with a petition or request under section 303 or 305 of this title does not submit such foreign representative to the jurisdiction of any court in the United States for any other purpose, but the bankruptcy court may condition any order under section 303 or 305 of this title on compliance by such foreign representative with the orders of such bankruptcy court.

(Pub.L. 95–598, Nov. 6, 1978, 92 Stat. 2561; Pub.L. 109–8, Title VIII, § 802(d)(5), Apr. 20, 2005, 119 Stat. 146.)

HISTORICAL AND STATUTORY NOTES

Revision Notes and Legislative Reports

1978 Acts. Section 306 permits a foreign representative that is seeking dismissal or suspension under section 305 of an ancillary case or that is appearing in connection with a petition under section 303 or 304 to appear without subjecting himself to the jurisdiction of any other court in the United States, including State courts. The protection is necessary to allow the foreign representative to present his case and the case of the foreign estate, without waiving the normal jurisdictional rules of the foreign country. That is, creditors in this country will still have to seek redress against the foreign estate according to the host country's jurisdictional rules. Any other result would permit local creditors to obtain unfair advantage by filing an involuntary case, thus requiring the foreign representative to appear, and then obtaining local jurisdiction over the representative in connection with his appearance in this country. That kind of bankruptcy law would legalize an ambush technique that has frequently been rejected by the common law in other contexts.

However, the bankruptcy court is permitted under section 306 to condition any relief under section 303, 304, or 305 on the compliance by the foreign representative with the orders of the bankruptcy court. The last provision is not carte blanche to the bankruptcy court to require the foreign representative to submit to jurisdiction in other courts contrary to the general policy of the section. It is designed to enable the bankruptcy court to enforce its own orders that are necessary to the appropriate relief granted under section 303, 304, or 305. Senate Report No. 95–989.

2005 Acts. House Report No. 109–31(Part I), see 2005 U.S. Code Cong. and Adm. News, p. 88.

Effective and Applicability Provisions

2005 Acts. Amendments by Pub.L. 109–8 effective, except as otherwise provided, 180 days after April 20, 2005, and inapplicable with respect to cases commenced under Title 11 before the effective date, see Pub.L. 109–8, § 1501, set out as a note under 11 U.S.C.A. § 101.

§ 307. United States trustee

The United States trustee may raise and may appear and be heard on any issue in any case or proceeding under this title but may not file a plan pursuant to section 1121(c) of this title.

(Added Pub.L. 99–554, Title II, § 205(a), Oct. 27, 1986, 100 Stat. 3098.)

HISTORICAL AND STATUTORY NOTES

Revision Notes and Legislative Reports

1986 Acts. House Report No. 99–764 and House Conference Report No. 99–958, see 1986 U.S.Code Cong. and Adm.News, p. 5227.

Effective and Applicability Provisions

1986 Acts. Enactment by Pub.L. 99–554, effective 30 days after Oct. 27, 1986, except as otherwise provided for, see section 302(a) of Pub.L. 99–554, set out as a note under section 581 of Title 28, Judiciary and Judicial Procedure.

Enactment by Pub.L. 99–554, § 205(a), not to become effective in or with respect to certain specified judicial districts until, or apply to cases while pending in such district before, the expiration of the 270-day period beginning 30 days after Oct. 27, 1986, or of the 30-day period beginning on the date the Attorney General certifies under section 303 of Pub.L. 99–554 the region specified in a paragraph of section 581(a) of Title 28, as amended by section 111(a) of Pub.L. 99–554, that includes such district, whichever occurs first, see section 302(d)(1) of Pub.L. 99–554, set out as a note under section 581 of Title 28.

Enactment by Pub.L. 99–554, § 205(a), not to become effective in or with respect to certain specified judicial districts until, or apply to cases while pending in such district before, the expiration of the 2-year period beginning 30 days after Oct. 27, 1986, or of the 30-day period beginning on the date the Attorney General certifies under section 303 of Pub.L. 99–554 the region specified in a paragraph of section 581(a) of Title 28, as amended by section 111(a) of Pub.L. 99–554, that includes such district, whichever occurs first, see section 302(d)(2) of Pub.L. 99–554, set out as a note under section 581 of Title 28.

Enactment by Pub.L. 99–554, § 205(a), not to become effective in or with respect to judicial districts established for the States of Alabama and North Carolina until, or apply to cases while pending in such district before, such district elects to be included in a bankruptcy region established in section 581(a) of Title 28, as amended by section 111(a) of Pub.L. 99–554, or Oct. 1, 2002, whichever occurs first, and, except as otherwise provided for, with respect to cases under chapters 7, 11, 12, and 13 of Title 11 commenced before 30 days after Oct. 27, 1986, and pending in a judicial district in the States of Alabama or North Carolina before an election made under section 302(d)(3)(A) of Pub.L. 99–554 by such district becomes effective or Oct. 1, 2002, whichever occurs first, amendments by Pub.L. 99–554 not to apply until Oct. 1, 2003, or the expiration of the 1-year period beginning on the date such election becomes effective, whichever occurs first, and further, in any judicial district in Alabama or North Carolina not making the election described in section 302(d)(3)(A) of Pub.L. 99–554, any person appointed under regulations issued by the Judicial Conference to administer estates in cases under Title 11 authorized to establish, etc., a panel of private trustees, and to supervise cases and trustees in cases under chapters 7, 11, 12, and 13 of Title 11, until amendments by sections 201 to 231 of Pub.L. 99–554 effective in such district, see section 302(d)(3)(A) to (F), (H), and (I), of Pub.L. 99–554, set out as a note under section 581 of Title 28.

Standing and Authority of Bankruptcy Administrator

Pub.L. 101–650, Title III, § 317(b), Dec. 1, 1990, 104 Stat. 5115, provided that: "A bankruptcy administrator may raise and may appear and be heard on any issue in any case under title 11, United States Code, but may not file a plan pursuant to section 1121(c) of such title."

§ 308. Debtor reporting requirements

(a) For purposes of this section, the term "profitability" means, with respect to a debtor, the amount of money that the debtor has earned or lost during current and recent fiscal periods.

(b) A small business debtor shall file periodic financial and other reports containing information including—

(1) the debtor's profitability;

(2) reasonable approximations of the debtor's projected cash receipts and cash disbursements over a reasonable period;

(3) comparisons of actual cash receipts and disbursements with projections in prior reports;

(4)(A) whether the debtor is—

(i) in compliance in all material respects with postpetition requirements imposed by this title and the Federal Rules of Bankruptcy Procedure; and

(ii) timely filing tax returns and other required government filings and paying taxes and other administrative expenses when due;

(B) if the debtor is not in compliance with the requirements referred to in subparagraph (A)(i) or filing tax returns and other required government filings and making the payments referred to in subparagraph (A)(ii), what the failures are and how, at what cost, and when the debtor intends to remedy such failures; and

(C) such other matters as are in the best interests of the debtor and creditors, and in the public interest in fair and efficient procedures under chapter 11 of this title.

(Added Pub.L. 109–8, Title IV, § 434(a)(1), Apr. 20, 2005, 119 Stat. 111.)

HISTORICAL AND STATUTORY NOTES

Revision Notes and Legislative Reports

2005 Acts. House Report No. 109–31(Part I), see 2005 U.S. Code Cong. and Adm. News, p. 88.

References in Text

The Federal Rules of Bankruptcy Procedure, referred to in subsec. (b)(4)(A)(i), are set out in the Appendix to this title.

Chapter 11 of this title, referred to in subsec. (b)(4)(C), is 11 U.S.C.A. § 1101 et seq.

Effective and Applicability Provisions

2005 Acts. Pub.L. 109–8, Title IV, § 434(b), Apr. 20, 2005, 119 Stat. 111, provided that: "The amendments made by subsection (a) [enacting this section] shall take effect 60 days after the date on which rules are prescribed under section 2075 of title 28, United States Code, to establish forms to be used to comply with section 308 of title 11, United States Code, as added by subsection (a) [enacting this section]."

Amendments by Pub.L. 109–8 effective, except as otherwise provided, 180 days after April 20, 2005, and inapplicable with respect to cases commenced under Title 11 before the effective date, see Pub.L. 109–8, § 1501, set out as a note under 11 U.S.C.A. § 101.

SUBCHAPTER II—OFFICERS

§ 321. Eligibility to serve as trustee

(a) A person may serve as trustee in a case under this title only if such person is—

(1) an individual that is competent to perform the duties of trustee and, in a case under chapter 7, 12, or 13 of this title, resides or has an office in the judicial district within which the case is pending, or in any judicial district adjacent to such district; or

(2) a corporation authorized by such corporation's charter or bylaws to act as trustee, and, in a case under chapter 7, 12, or 13 of this title, having an office in at least one of such districts.

(b) A person that has served as an examiner in the case may not serve as trustee in the case.

(c) The United States trustee for the judicial district in which the case is pending is eligible to serve as trustee in the case if necessary.

(Pub.L. 95–598, Nov. 6, 1978, 92 Stat. 2561; Pub. L. 98–353, Title III, § 428, July 10, 1984, 98 Stat. 369; Pub.L. 99–554, Title II, §§ 206, 257(c), Oct. 27, 1986, 100 Stat. 3098, 3114.)

HISTORICAL AND STATUTORY NOTES

Revision Notes and Legislative Reports

1978 Acts. Section 321 is adapted from current Bankruptcy Act section 45 [section 73 of former Title 11] and Bankruptcy Rule 209. Subsection (a) specifies that an individual may serve as trustee in a bankruptcy case only if he is competent to perform the duties of trustee and resides or has an office in the judicial district within which the case is pending, or in an adjacent judicial district. A corporation must be authorized by its charter or bylaws to act as trustee, and, for chapter 7 or 13 cases, must have an office in any of the above mentioned judicial districts. Senate Report No. 95–989.

1984 Acts. Statements by Legislative Leaders, see 1984 U.S.Code Cong. and Adm.News, p. 576.

1986 Acts. House Report No. 99–764 and House Conference Report No. 99–958, see 1986 U.S.Code Cong. and Adm.News, p. 5227.

Legislative Statements

Section 321 indicates that an examiner may not serve as a trustee in the case.

Effective and Applicability Provisions

1986 Acts. Amendment by Pub.L. 99–554 effective 30 days after Oct. 27, 1986, except as otherwise provided for, see section 302(a) of Pub.L. 99–554, set out as a note under section 581 of Title 28, Judiciary and Judicial Procedure.

Amendment by Pub.L. 99–554, § 206, not to become effective in or with respect to certain specified judicial districts until, or apply to cases while pending in such district before, the expiration of the 270-day period beginning 30 days after Oct. 27, 1986, or of the 30-day period beginning on the date the Attorney General certifies under section 303 of Pub.L. 99–554 the region specified in a paragraph of section 581(a) of Title 28, as amended by section 111(a) of Pub.L. 99–554, that includes such district, whichever occurs first, see section 302(d)(1) of Pub.L. 99–554, set out as a note under section 581 of Title 28.

Amendment by Pub.L. 99–554, § 206, not to become effective in or with respect to certain specified judicial districts until, or apply to cases while pending in such district before, the expiration of the 2-year period beginning 30 days after Oct. 27, 1986, or of the 30-day period beginning on the date the Attorney General certifies under section 303 of Pub.L. 99–554 the region specified in a paragraph of section 581(a) of Title 28, as amended by section 111(a) of Pub.L. 99–554, that includes such district, whichever occurs first, see section 302(d)(2) of Pub.L. 99–554, set out as a note under section 581 of Title 28.

Amendment by Pub.L. 99–554, § 206, not to become effective in or with respect to judicial districts established for the States of Alabama and North Carolina until, or apply to cases while pending in such district before, such district elects to be included in a bankruptcy region established in section 581(a) of Title 28, as amended by section 111(a) of Pub.L. 99–554, or Oct. 1, 2002, whichever occurs first, and, except as otherwise provided for, with respect to cases under chapters 7, 11, 12, and 13 of Title 11 commenced before 30 days after Oct. 27, 1986, and pending in a judicial district in the States of Alabama or North Carolina before any election made under section 302(d)(3)(A) of Pub.L. 99–554 by such district becomes effective or Oct. 1, 2002, whichever occurs first, amendments by Pub.L. 99–554 not to apply until Oct. 1, 2003, or the expiration of the 1-year period beginning on the date such election becomes effective whichever occurs first, and further, in any judicial district in Alabama or North Carolina not making the election described in section 302(d)(3)(A) of Pub.L. 99–554, any person appointed under regulations issued by the Judicial Conference to administer estates in cases under Title 11 authorized to establish, etc., a panel of private trustees, and to supervise cases and trustees in cases under chapters 7, 11, 12, and 13 of Title 11, until amendments by sections 201 to 231 of Pub.L. 99–554 effective in such district, see section 302(d)(3)(A) to (F), (H), and (I) of Pub.L. 99–554, set out as a note under section 581 of Title 28.

Amendment by Pub.L. 99–554, § 206, except as otherwise provided, with respect to cases under chapters, 7, 11, 12, and 13 of Title 11 commenced before 30 days after Oct. 27, 1986, and pending in a judicial district referred to in section 581(a) of Title 28, as amended by section 111(a) of Pub.L. 99–554, for which a United States trustee is not authorized before 30 days after Oct. 27, 1986 to be appointed, not applicable until the expiration of the 3-year period beginning on Oct. 27, 1986, or of the 1-year period beginning on the date the Attorney General certifies under section 303 of Pub.L. 99–554 the region specified in a paragraph of such section 581(a) that includes, such district, whichever occurs first, see section 302(e)(1), (2) of Pub.L. 99–554, set out as a note under section 581 of Title 28.

Amendment by Pub.L. 99–554, § 257(c) effective 30 days after Oct. 27, 1986, but not applicable with respect to cases commenced under this title before that date, see section 302(a), (c)(1) of Pub.L. 99–554, set out as a note under section 581 of Title 28.

1984 Acts. Amendment by Pub.L. 98–353 effective with respect to cases filed 90 days after July 10, 1984, see section 552(a), formerly 553(a), of Pub.L. 98–353, set out as a note under section 101 of this title.

§ 322. Qualification of trustee

(a) Except as provided in subsection (b)(1), a person selected under section 701, 702, 703, 1104, 1163, 1202, or 1302 of this title to serve as trustee in a case under this title qualifies if before five days after such selection, and before beginning official duties, such person has filed with the court a bond in favor of the United States conditioned on the faithful performance of such official duties.

(b)(1) The United States trustee qualifies wherever such trustee serves as trustee in a case under this title.

(2) The United States trustee shall determine—

(A) the amount of a bond required to be filed under subsection (a) of this section; and

(B) the sufficiency of the surety on such bond.

(c) A trustee is not liable personally or on such trustee's bond in favor of the United States for any penalty or forfeiture incurred by the debtor.

(d) A proceeding on a trustee's bond may not be commenced after two years after the date on which such trustee was discharged.

(Pub.L. 95–598, Nov. 6, 1978, 92 Stat. 2562; Pub. L. 98–353, Title III, § 429, July 10, 1984, 98 Stat. 369; Pub.L. 99–554, Title II, §§ 207, 257(d), Oct. 27, 1986, 100 Stat. 3098, 3114; Pub.L. 103–394, Title V, § 501(d)(3), Oct. 22, 1994, 108 Stat. 4143.)

HISTORICAL AND STATUTORY NOTES

Revision Notes and Legislative Reports

1978 Acts. A trustee qualifies in a case by filing, within five days after selection, a bond in favor of the United States, conditioned on the faithful performance of his official duties. This section is derived from the Bankruptcy Act section 50b [section 78(b) of former Title 11]. The court is required to determine the amount of the bond and the sufficiency of the surety on the bond. Subsection (c), derived from Bankruptcy Act section 50i [section 78(i) of former Title 11], relieves the trustee from personal liability and from liability on his bond for any penalty or forfeiture incurred by the debtor. Subsection (d), derived from section 50m [section 78(m) of former Title 11], fixes a two-year statute of limitations on any action on a trustee's bond. Finally, subsection (e) dispenses with the bonding requirement for the United States trustee. Senate Report No. 95-989.

1984 Acts. Statements by Legislative Leaders, see 1984 U.S.Code Cong. and Adm.News, p. 576.

1986 Acts. House Report No. 99–764 and House Conference Report No. 99–958, see 1986 U.S.Code Cong. and Adm.News, p. 5227.

1994 Acts. House Report No. 103–835, see 1994 U.S. Code Cong. and Adm. News, p. 3340.

Legislative Statements

Section 322(a) is modified to include a trustee serving in a railroad reorganization under subchapter IV of chapter 11.

Effective and Applicability Provisions

1994 Acts. Amendment by Pub.L. 103–394 effective on Oct. 22, 1994, and not to apply with respect to cases commenced under Title 11 of the United States Code before Oct. 22, 1994, see section 702 of Pub.L. 103–394, set out as a note under section 101 of this title.

1986 Acts. Amendment by Pub.L. 99–554 effective 30 days after Oct. 27, 1986, except as otherwise provided for, see section 302(a) of Pub.L. 99–554, set out as a note under section 581 of Title 28, Judiciary and Judicial Procedure.

Amendment by Pub.L. 99–554, § 207, not to become effective in or with respect to certain specified judicial districts until, or apply to cases while pending in such district before, the expiration of the 270-day period beginning 30 days after Oct. 27, 1986, or of the 30-day period beginning on the date the Attorney General certifies under section 303 of Pub.L. 99–554 the region specified in a paragraph of section 581(a) of Title 28, as amended by section 111(a) of Pub.L. 99–554, that includes such district, whichever occurs first, see section 302(d)(1) of Pub.L. 99–554, set out as a note under section 581 of Title 28.

Amendment by Pub.L. 99–554, § 207, not to become effective in or with respect to certain specified judicial districts until, or apply to cases while pending in such district before, the expiration of the 2-year period beginning 30 days after Oct. 27, 1986, or of the 30-day period beginning on the date the Attorney General certifies under section 303 of Pub.L. 99–554 the region specified in a paragraph of section 581(a) of Title 28, as amended by section 111(a) of Pub.L. 99–554, that includes such district, whichever occurs first, see section 302(d)(2) of Pub.L. 99–554, set out as a note under section 581 of Title 28.

Amendment by Pub.L. 99–554, § 207, not to become effective in or with respect to judicial districts established for the States of Alabama and North Carolina until, or apply to cases while pending in such district before, such district elects to be included in a bankruptcy region established in section 581(a) of Title 28, as amended by section 111(a) of Pub.L. 99–554, or Oct. 1, 2002, whichever occurs first, and, except as otherwise provided for, with respect to cases under chapters 7, 11, 12, and 13 of Title 11 commenced before 30 days after Oct. 27, 1986, and pending in a judicial district in the States of Alabama or North Carolina before any election made under section 302(d)(3)(A) of Pub.L. 99–554 by such district becomes effective or Oct. 1, 2002, whichever occurs first, amendments by Pub.L. 99–554 not to apply until Oct. 1, 2003, or the expiration of the 1-year period beginning on the date such election becomes effective, whichever occurs first, and further, in any judicial district in Alabama or North Carolina not making the election described in section 302(d)(3)(A) of Pub.L. 99–554, any person appointed under regulations issued by the Judicial Conference to administer estates in cases under Title 11 authorized to establish, etc., a panel of private trustees, and to supervise cases and trustees in cases under chapters 7, 11, 12, and 13 of Title 11, until amendments by sections 201 to 231 of Pub.L. 99–554 effective in such district, see section 302(d)(3)(A) to (F), (H), and (I) of Pub.L. 99–554, set out as a note under section 581 of Title 28.

Amendment by Pub.L. 99–554, § 207, except as otherwise provided, with respect to cases under chapters 7, 11, 12, and 13 of Title 11 commenced before 30 days after Oct. 27, 1986, and pending in a judicial district referred to in section 581(a) of Title 28, as amended by section 111(a) of Pub.L. 99–554, for which a United States trustee is not authorized before 30 days after Oct. 27, 1986 to be appointed, not applicable until the expiration of the 3-year period beginning on Oct. 27, 1986, or of the 1-year period beginning on the date the Attorney General certifies under section 303 of Pub.L. 99–554 the region specified in a paragraph of such section 581(a) that includes, such district, whichever occurs first, see section 302(e)(1), (2) of Pub.L. 99–554, set out as a note under section 581 of Title 28.

Amendment by Pub.L. 99–554, § 257(d), effective 30 days after Oct. 27, 1986, but not applicable with respect to cases commenced under this title before that date, see section 302(a), (c)(1) of Pub.L. 99–554, set out as a note under section 581 of Title 28.

1984 Acts. Amendment by Pub.L. 98–353 effective with respect to cases filed 90 days after July 10, 1984, see section 552(a), formerly 553(a), of Pub.L. 98–353, set out as a note under section 101 of this title.

Separability of Provisions

If any provision of or amendment made by Pub.L. 103–394 or the application of such provision or amendment to any person or circumstance is held to be unconstitutional, the remaining provisions of and amendments made by Pub.L. 103–394 and the application of such provisions and amendments to any person or circumstance shall not be affected thereby, see section 701 of Pub.L. 103–394, set out as a note under section 101 of this title.

CROSS REFERENCES

Appointment of trustee or examiner upon failure to qualify, see 11 USCA § 1104.

Certain customer transactions affected before qualification of trustee, see 11 USCA § 746.

"Debtor in possession" defined as debtor except when qualified person is serving as trustee under this section, see 11 USCA § 1101.

Interim trustee, see 11 USCA § 701.

Qualification of trustee and attorney in investor protection liquidation proceedings, see 15 USCA § 78eee.

Standing trustee—

Chapter 12 cases, see 11 USCA § 1202.

Chapter 13 cases, see 11 USCA § 1302.

Successor trustee, see 11 USCA § 703.

§ 323. Role and capacity of trustee

(a) The trustee in a case under this title is the representative of the estate.

(b) The trustee in a case under this title has capacity to sue and be sued.

(Pub.L. 95–598, Nov. 6, 1978, 92 Stat. 2562.)

HISTORICAL AND STATUTORY NOTES

Revision Notes and Legislative Reports

1978 Acts. Subsection (a) of this section makes the trustee the representative of the estate. Subsection (b) grants the trustee the capacity to sue and to be sued. If the debtor remains in possession in a chapter 11 case, section 1107 gives the debtor in possession these rights of the trustee: the debtor in possession becomes the representative of the estate, and may sue and be sued. The same applies in a chapter 13 case. Senate Report No. 95–989.

§ 324. Removal of trustee or examiner

(a) The court, after notice and a hearing, may remove a trustee, other than the United States trustee, or an examiner, for cause.

(b) Whenever the court removes a trustee or examiner under subsection (a) in a case under this title, such trustee or examiner shall thereby be removed in all other cases under this title in which such trustee or examiner is then serving unless the court orders otherwise.

(Pub.L. 95–598, Nov. 6, 1978, 92 Stat. 2562; Pub.L. 99–554, Title II, § 208, Oct. 27, 1986, 100 Stat. 3098.)

HISTORICAL AND STATUTORY NOTES

Revision Notes and Legislative Reports

1978 Acts. This section permits the court, after notice and a hearing, to remove a trustee for cause. Senate Report No. 95–989.

1986 Acts. House Report No. 99–764 and House Conference Report No. 99–958, see 1986 U.S.Code Cong. and Adm.News, p. 5227.

Effective and Applicability Provisions

1986 Acts. Amendment by Pub.L. 99–554 effective 30 days after Oct. 27, 1986, except as otherwise provided for, see section 302(a) of Pub.L. 99–554, set out as a note under section 581 of Title 28, Judiciary and Judicial Procedure.

Amendment by Pub.L. 99–554, § 208 not to become effective in or with respect to certain specified judicial districts until, or apply to cases while pending in such district before, the expiration of the 270-day period beginning 30 days after Oct. 27, 1986, or of the 30-day period beginning on the date the Attorney General certifies under section 303 of Pub.L. 99–554 the region specified in a paragraph of section 581(a) of Title 28, as amended by section 111(a) of Pub.L. 99–554, that includes such district, whichever occurs first, see section 302(d)(1) of Pub.L. 99–554, set out as a note under section 581 of Title 28.

Amendment by Pub.L. 99–554, § 208, not to become effective in or with respect to certain specified judicial districts until, or apply to cases while pending in such district before, the expiration of the 2-year period beginning 30 days after Oct. 27, 1986, or of the 30-day period beginning on the date the Attorney General certifies under section 303 of Pub.L. 99–554 the region specified in a paragraph of section 581(a) of Title 28, as amended by section 111(a) of Pub.L. 99–554, that includes such district, whichever occurs first, see section 302(d)(2) of Pub.L. 99–554, set out as a note under section 581 of Title 28.

Amendment by Pub.L. 99–554, § 208, not to become effective in or with respect to judicial districts established for the States of Alabama and North Carolina until, or apply to cases while pending in such district before, such district elects to be included in a bankruptcy region established in section 581(a) of Title 28, as amended by section 111(a) of Pub.L. 99–554, or Oct. 1, 2002, whichever occurs first, and, except as otherwise provided for, with respect to cases under chapters 7, 11, 12, and 13 of Title 11 commenced before 30 days after Oct. 27, 1986, and pending in a judicial district in the States of Alabama or North Carolina before any election made under section 302(d)(3)(A) of Pub.L. 99–554 by such district becomes effective or Oct. 1, 2002, whichever occurs first, amendments by Pub.L. 99–554 not to apply until Oct. 1, 2003, or the expiration of the 1-year period beginning on the date such election becomes effective, whichever occurs first, and further, in any judicial district in Alabama or North Carolina not making the election described in section 302(d)(3)(A) of Pub.L. 99–554, any person appointed under regulations issued by the Judicial Conference to administer estates in cases under Title 11 authorized to establish, etc., a panel of private trustees, and to supervise cases and trustees in cases under chapters 7, 11, 12, and 13 of Title 11, until amendments by sections 201 to 231 of Pub.L. 99–554 effective in such district, see section 302(d)(3)(A) to (F), (H), and (I) of Pub.L. 99–554, set out as a note under section 581 of Title 28.

Amendment by Pub.L. 99–554, § 208, except as otherwise provided, with respect to cases under chapters 7, 11, 12, and 13 of Title 11 commenced before 30 days after Oct. 27, 1986, and pending in a judicial district referred to in section 581(a) of Title 28, as amended by section 111(a) of Pub.L. 99–554, for which a United States trustee is not authorized before 30 days after Oct. 27, 1986 to be appointed, not applicable until the expiration of the 3-year period beginning on Oct. 27, 1986, or of the 1-year period beginning on the date the Attorney General certifies under section 303 of Pub.L. 99–554 the region specified in a paragraph of such section 581(a) that includes, such district, whichever occurs first, see section 302(e)(1), (2) of Pub.L. 99–554, set out as a note under section 581 of Title 28.

CROSS REFERENCES

Adverse interest and conduct of officers of estate, see 18 USCA § 154.

Appointment of trustee or examiner upon removal, see 11 USCA § 1104.

Authority of Attorney General to investigate trustees, see 28 USCA § 526.

Embezzlement by trustee, see 18 USCA § 153.

Successor trustee, see 11 USCA § 703.

§ 325. Effect of vacancy

A vacancy in the office of trustee during a case does not abate any pending action or proceeding, and the successor trustee shall be substituted as a party in such action or proceeding.

(Pub.L. 95–598, Nov. 6, 1978, 92 Stat. 2562.)

HISTORICAL AND STATUTORY NOTES

Revision Notes and Legislative Reports

1978 Acts. Section 325, derived from Bankruptcy Act section 46 [section 74 of former Title 11] and Bankruptcy Rule 221(b), specifies that a vacancy in the office of trustee during a case does not abate any pending action or proceeding. The successor trustee, when selected and qualified, is substituted as a party in any pending action or proceeding. Senate Report No. 95–989.

§ 326. Limitation on compensation of trustee

(a) In a case under chapter 7 or 11, the court may allow reasonable compensation under section 330 of this title of the trustee for the trustee's services, payable after the trustee renders such services, not to exceed 25 percent on the first $5,000 or less, 10 percent on any amount in excess of $5,000 but not in excess of $50,000, 5 percent on any amount in excess of $50,000 but not in excess of $1,000,000, and reasonable compensation not to exceed 3 percent of such moneys in excess of $1,000,000, upon all moneys disbursed or turned over in the case by the trustee to parties in interest, excluding the debtor, but including holders of secured claims.

(b) In a case under chapter 12 or 13 of this title, the court may not allow compensation for services or reimbursement of expenses of the United States trustee or of a standing trustee appointed under section 586(b) of title 28, but may allow reasonable compensation under section 330 of this title of a trustee appointed under section 1202(a) or 1302(a) of this title for the trustee's services, payable after the trustee renders such services, not to exceed five percent upon all payments under the plan.

(c) If more than one person serves as trustee in the case, the aggregate compensation of such persons for such service may not exceed the maximum compensation prescribed for a single trustee by subsection (a) or (b) of this section, as the case may be.

(d) The court may deny allowance of compensation for services or reimbursement of expenses of the trustee if the trustee failed to make diligent inquiry into facts that would permit denial of allowance under section 328(c) of this title or, with knowledge of such facts, employed a professional person under section 327 of this title.

(Pub.L. 95–598, Nov. 6, 1978, 92 Stat. 2562; Pub. L. 98–353, Title III, § 430(a), (b), July 10, 1984, 98 Stat. 369; Pub.L. 99–554, Title II, § 209, Oct. 27, 1986, 100 Stat. 3098; Pub.L. 103–394, Title I, § 107, Oct. 22, 1994, 108 Stat. 4111.)

HISTORICAL AND STATUTORY NOTES

Revision Notes and Legislative Reports

1978 Acts. This section is derived in part from section 48c of the Bankruptcy Act [section 76(c) of former Title 11]. It must be emphasized that this section does not authorize compensation of trustees. This section simply fixes the maximum compensation of a trustee. Proposed 11 U.S.C. section 330 authorizes and fixes the standard of compensation. Under section 48c of current law, the maximum limits have tended to become minimums in many cases. This section is not intended to be so interpreted. The limits in this section, together with the limitations found in section 330, are to be applied as outer limits and not as grants or entitlements to the maximum fees specified.

The maximum fee schedule is derived from section 48c(1) of the present act [section 76(c)(1) of former Title 11], but with a change relating to the bases on which the percentage maxima are computed. The maximum fee schedule is based on decreasing percentages of increasing amounts. The amounts are the amounts of money distributed by the trustee to parties in interest, excluding the debtor, but including secured creditors. These amounts were last amended in 1952. Since then, the cost of living has approximately doubled. Thus, the bases were doubled.

It should be noted that the bases on which the maximum fee is computed includes moneys turned over to secured creditors, to cover the situation where the trustee liquidates property subject to a lien and distributes the proceeds. It does not cover cases in which the trustee simply turns over the property to the secured creditor, nor where the trustee abandons the property and the secured creditor is permitted to foreclose. The provision is also subject to the rights of the secured creditor generally under proposed section 506, especially section 506(c). The $150 discretionary fee provision of current law is retained.

Subsection (b) of this section entitles an operating trustee to a reasonable fee, without any limitation based on the maximum provided for a liquidating trustee as in current law, Bankruptcy Act section 48c(2) [section 76(c)(2) of former Title 11].

Subsection (c) permits a maximum fee of five percent on all payments to creditors under a chapter 13 plan to the trustee appointed in the case.

Subsection (d) provides a limitation not found in current law. Even if more than one trustee serves in the case, the maximum fee payable to all trustees does not change. For example, if an interim trustee is appointed and an elected trustee replaces him, the combined total of the fees payable to the interim trustee and the permanent trustee may not exceed the amount specified in this section. Under current law, very often a receiver receives a full fee and a subsequent trustee also receives a full fee. The resultant "double-dipping", especially in cases in which the receiver and the trustee are the same individual, is detrimental to the interests of creditors, by needlessly increasing the cost of administering bankruptcy estates.

Subsection (e) permits the court to deny compensation to a trustee if the trustee has been derelict in his duty by employing counsel, who is not disinterested. Senate Report No. 95–989.

1984 Acts. Statements by Legislative Leaders, see 1984 U.S.Code Cong. and Adm.News, p. 576.

1986 Acts. House Report No. 99–764 and House Conference Report No. 99–958, see 1986 U.S.Code Cong. and Adm.News, p. 5227.

1994 Acts. House Report No. 103–835, see 1994 U.S. Code Cong. and Adm. News, p. 3340.

Legislative Statements

Section 326(a) of the House amendment modifies a provision as contained in H.R. 8200 as passed by the House. The percentage limitation on the fees of a trustee contained in the House bill is retained, but no additional percentage is specified for cases in which a trustee operates the business of the debtor. Section 326(b) of the Senate amendment, is deleted as an unnecessary restatement of the limitation contained in section 326(a) as modified. The provision contained in section 326(a) of the Senate amendment authorizing a trustee to receive a maximum fee of $150 regardless of the availability of assets in the estate is deleted. It will not be necessary in view of the increase in section 326(a) and the doubling of the minimum fee as provided in section 330(b).

Section 326(b) of the House amendment derives from section 326(c) of H.R. 8200 as passed by the House. It is a conforming amendment to indicate a change with respect to the selection of a trustee in a chapter 13 case under section 1302(a) of Title 11.

Effective and Applicability Provisions

1994 Acts. Amendment by Pub.L. 103–394 effective on Oct. 22, 1994, and not to apply with respect to cases commenced under Title 11 of the United States Code before Oct. 22, 1994, see section 702 of Pub.L. 103–394, set out as a note under section 101 of this title.

1986 Acts. Amendment by Pub.L. 99–554 effective 30 days after Oct. 27, 1986, except as otherwise provided for, see section 302(a) of Pub.L. 99–554, set out as a note under section 581 of Title 28, Judiciary and Judicial Procedure.

Until amendments made by section 209 of Pub.L. 99–554 become effective in a district and apply to a case, for purposes of such case any references in subsec. (b) of this section to chapter 13 of this title, to section 1302(d) of this title, or to section 1302(a) of this title deemed references to other provisions of the Code, see section 302(c)(3)(A)(i) to (iii) of Pub.L. 99–554, set out as a note under section 581 of Title 28.

Amendment by Pub.L. 99–554, § 209, not to become effective in or with respect to certain specified judicial districts until, or apply to cases while pending in such district before, the expiration of the 270-day period beginning 30 days after Oct. 27, 1986, or of the 30-day period beginning on the date the Attorney General certifies under section 303 of Pub.L. 99–554 the region specified in a paragraph of section 581(a) of Title 28, as amended by section 111(a) of Pub.L. 99–554, that includes such district, whichever occurs first, see section 302(d)(1) of Pub.L. 99–554, set out as a note under section 581 of Title 28.

Amendment by Pub.L. 99–554, § 209, not to become effective in or with respect to certain specified judicial districts until, or apply to cases while pending in such district before, the expiration of the 2-year period beginning 30 days after Oct. 27, 1986, or of the 30-day period beginning on the date the Attorney General certifies under section 303 of Pub.L. 99–554 the region specified in a paragraph of section 581(a) of Title 28, as amended by section 111(a) of Pub.L. 99–554, that includes such district, whichever occurs first, see section 302(d)(2) of Pub.L. 99–554, set out as a note under section 581 of Title 28.

Amendment by Pub.L. 99–554, § 209, not to become effective in or with respect to judicial districts established for the States of Alabama and North Carolina until, or apply to cases while pending in such district before, such district elects to be included in a bankruptcy region established in section 581(a) of Title 28, as amended by section 111(a) of Pub.L. 99–554, or Oct. 1, 2002, whichever occurs first, and, except as otherwise provided for, with respect to cases under chapters 7, 11, 12, and 13 of Title 11 commenced before 30 days after Oct. 27, 1986, and pending in a judicial district in the States of Alabama or North Carolina before any election made under section 302(d)(3)(A) of Pub.L. 99–554 by such district becomes effective or Oct. 1, 2002, whichever occurs first, amendments by Pub.L. 99–554 not to apply until Oct. 1, 2003, or the expiration of the 1-year period beginning on the date such election becomes effective, whichever occurs first, and further, in any judicial district in Alabama or North Carolina not making the election described in section 302(d)(3)(A) of Pub.L. 99–554, any person appointed under regulations issued by the Judicial Conference to administer estates in cases under Title 11 authorized to establish, etc., a panel of private trustees, and to supervise cases and trustees in cases under chapters 7, 11, 12, and 13 of Title 11, until amendments by sections 201 to 231 of Pub.L. 99–554 effective in such district, see section 302(d)(3)(A) to (F), (H), and (I) of Pub.L. 99–554, set out as a note under section 581 of Title 28.

Amendment by Pub.L. 99–554, § 209, except as otherwise provided, with respect to cases under chapters 7, 11, 12, and 13 of Title 11 commenced before 30 days after Oct. 27, 1986, and pending in a judicial district referred to in section 581(a) of Title 28, as amended by section 111(a) of Pub.L. 99–554, for which a United States trustee is not authorized before 30 days after Oct. 27, 1986 to be appointed, not applicable until the expiration of the 3-year period beginning on Oct. 27, 1986, or of the 1-year period beginning on the date the Attorney General certifies under section 303 of Pub.L. 99–554 the region specified in a paragraph of such section 581(a) that includes, such district, whichever occurs first, see section 302(e)(1), (2) of Pub.L. 99–554, set out as a note under section 581 of Title 28.

1984 Acts. Amendment by Pub.L. 98–353 effective with respect to cases filed 90 days after July 10, 1984, see section 552(a), formerly 553(a), of Pub.L. 98–353, set out as a note under section 101 of this title.

Separability of Provisions

If any provision of or amendment made by Pub.L. 103–394 or the application of such provision or amendment to any person or circumstance is held to be unconstitutional, the remaining provisions of and amendments made by Pub.L. 103–394 and the application of such provisions and amendments to any person or circumstance shall not be affected thereby, see section 701 of Pub.L. 103–394, set out as a note under section 101 of this title.

CROSS REFERENCES

Grain storage facility bankruptcies, expedited determinations, see 11 USCA § 557.

§ 327. Employment of professional persons

(a) Except as otherwise provided in this section, the trustee, with the court's approval, may employ one or more attorneys, accountants, appraisers, auctioneers, or other professional persons, that do not hold or represent an interest adverse to the estate, and that are disinterested persons, to represent or assist the trustee in carrying out the trustee's duties under this title.

(b) If the trustee is authorized to operate the business of the debtor under section 721, 1202, or 1108 of this title, and if the debtor has regularly employed attorneys, accountants, or other professional persons on salary, the trustee may retain or replace such professional persons if necessary in the operation of such business.

(c) In a case under chapter 7, 12, or 11 of this title, a person is not disqualified for employment under this section solely because of such person's employment by or representation of a creditor, unless there is objection by another creditor or the United States trustee, in which case the court shall disapprove such employment if there is an actual conflict of interest.

(d) The court may authorize the trustee to act as attorney or accountant for the estate if such authorization is in the best interest of the estate.

(e) The trustee, with the court's approval, may employ, for a specified special purpose, other than to represent the trustee in conducting the case, an attorney that has represented the debtor, if in the best interest of the estate, and if such attorney does not represent or hold any interest adverse to the debtor or to the estate with respect to the matter on which such attorney is to be employed.

(f) The trustee may not employ a person that has served as an examiner in the case.

(Pub.L. 95–598, Nov. 6, 1978, 92 Stat. 2563; Pub. L. 98–353, Title III, § 430(c), July 10, 1984, 98 Stat. 370; Pub.L. 99–554, Title II, §§ 210, 257(e), Oct. 27, 1986, 100 Stat. 3099, 3114.)

HISTORICAL AND STATUTORY NOTES

Revision Notes and Legislative Reports

1978 Acts. This section authorizes the trustee, subject to the court's approval, to employ professional persons, such as attorneys, accountants, appraisers, and auctioneers, to represent or perform services for the estate. The trustee may employ only disinterested persons that do not hold or represent an interest adverse to the estate.

Subsection (b) is an exception, and authorizes the trustee to retain or replace professional persons that the debtor has employed if necessary in the operation of the debtor's business.

Subsection (c) provides a professional person is not disqualified for employment solely because of the person's prior employment by or representation of a secured or unsecured creditor.

Subsection (d) permits the court to authorize the trustee, if qualified to act as his own counsel or accountant.

Subsection (e) permits the trustee, subject to the court's approval, to employ for a specified special purpose an attorney that has represented the debtor, if such employment is in the best interest of the estate and if the attorney does not hold or represent an interest adverse to the debtor of the estate with respect to the matter on which he is to be employed. This subsection does not authorize the employment of the debtor's attorney to represent the estate generally or to represent the trustee in the conduct of the bankruptcy case. The subsection will most likely be used when the debtor is involved in complex litigation, and changing attorneys in the middle of the case after the bankruptcy case has commenced would be detrimental to the progress of that other litigation. Senate Report No. 95–989.

Subsection (c) is an additional exception. The trustee may employ as his counsel a nondisinterested person if the only reason that the attorney is not disinterested is because of his representation of an unsecured creditor. House Report No. 95–595.

1984 Acts. Statements by Legislative Leaders, see 1984 U.S.Code Cong. and Adm.News, p. 576.

1986 Acts. House Report No. 99–764 and House Conference Report No. 99–958, see 1986 U.S.Code Cong. and Adm.News, p. 5227.

Legislative Statements

Section 327(a) of the House amendment contains a technical amendment indicating that attorneys, and perhaps other officers enumerated therein, represent, rather than assist, the trustee in carrying out the trustee's duties.

Section 327(c) represents a compromise between H.R. 8200 as passed by the House and the Senate amendment. The provision states that former representation of a creditor, whether secured or unsecured, will not automatically disqualify a person from being employed by a trustee, but if such person is employed by the trustee, the person may no longer represent the creditor in connection with the case.

Section 327(f) prevents an examiner from being employed by the trustee.

Codifications

Amendment by Pub.L. 99–554, § 257(e)(1), has been executed to text following "section 721" as the probable intent of Congress, notwithstanding directory language which required amendment to be executed following "section 721,".

Amendment by Pub.L. 99–554, § 257(e)(2), has been executed to text following "chapter 7" as the probable intent of Congress, notwithstanding directory language which required amendment to be executed following "section 7".

Effective and Applicability Provisions

1986 Acts. Amendment by Pub.L. 99–554 effective 30 days after Oct. 27, 1986, except as otherwise provided for, see section 302(a) of Pub.L. 99–554, set out as a note under section 581 of Title 28, Judiciary and Judicial Procedure.

Amendment by Pub.L. 99–554, § 210, not to become effective in or with respect to certain specified judicial districts until, or apply to cases while pending in such district before, the expiration of the 270-day period beginning 30 days after Oct. 27, 1986, or of the 30-day period beginning on the date the Attorney General certifies under section 303 of Pub.L. 99–554 the region specified in a paragraph of section 581(a) of Title 28, as amended by section 111(a) of Pub.L. 99–554, that includes such district, whichever occurs first, see section 302(d)(1) of Pub.L. 99–554, set out as a note under section 581 of Title 28.

Amendment by Pub.L. 99–554, § 210, not to become effective in or with respect to certain specified judicial districts until, or apply to cases while pending in such district before, the expiration of the 2-year period beginning 30 days after Oct. 27, 1986, or of the 30-day period beginning on the date the Attorney General certifies under section 303 of Pub.L. 99–554 the region specified in a paragraph of section 581(a) of Title 28, as amended by section 111(a) of Pub.L. 99–554, that includes such district, whichever occurs first, see section 302(d)(2) of Pub.L. 99–554, set out as a note under section 581 of Title 28.

Amendment by Pub.L. 99–554, § 210, not to become effective in or with respect to judicial districts established for the States of Alabama and North Carolina until, or apply to cases while pending in such district before, such district elects to be included in a bankruptcy region established in section 581(a) of Title 28, as amended by section 111(a) of Pub.L. 99–554, or Oct. 1, 2002, whichever occurs first, and, except as otherwise provided for, with respect to cases under chapters 7, 11, 12, and 13 of Title 11 commenced before 30 days after Oct. 27, 1986, and pending in a judicial district in the States of Alabama or North Carolina before any election made under section 302(d)(3)(A) of Pub.L. 99–554 by such district becomes effective or Oct. 1, 2002, whichever occurs first, amendments by Pub.L. 99–554 not to apply until Oct. 1, 2003, or the expiration of the 1-year period beginning on the date such election becomes effective, whichever occurs first, and further, in any judicial district in Alabama or North Carolina not making the election described in section 302(d)(3)(A) of Pub.L. 99–554, any person appointed under regulations issued by the Judicial Conference to administer estates in cases under Title 11 authorized to establish, etc., a panel of private trustees, and to supervise cases and trustees in cases under chapters 7, 11, 12, and 13 of Title 11, until amendments by sections 201 to 231 of Pub.L. 99–554 effective in such district, see section 302(d)(3)(A) to (F), (H), and (I) of Pub.L. 99–554, set out as a note under section 581 of Title 28.

Amendment by Pub.L. 99–554, § 210, except as otherwise provided, with respect to cases under chapters 7, 11, 12, and 13 of Title 11 commenced before 30 days after Oct. 27, 1986, and pending in a judicial district referred to in section 581(a) of Title 28, as amended by section 111(a) of Pub.L. 99–554, for which a United States trustee is not authorized before 30 days after Oct. 27, 1986 to be appointed, not applicable until the expiration of the 3-year period beginning on Oct. 27, 1986, or of the 1-year period beginning on the date the Attorney General certifies under section 303 of Pub.L. 99–554 the region specified in a paragraph of such section 581(a) that includes, such district, whichever occurs first, see section 302(e)(1), (2) of Pub.L. 99–554, set out as a note under section 581 of Title 28.

Amendment by Pub.L. 99–554, § 257(e), effective 30 days after Oct. 27, 1986, but not applicable to cases commenced under this title before that date, see section 302(a), (c)(1) of Pub.L. 99–554, set out as a note under section 581 of Title 28.

1984 Acts. Amendment by Pub.L. 98–353 effective with respect to cases filed 90 days after July 10, 1984, see section 552(a), formerly 553(a), of Pub.L. 98–353, set out as a note under section 101 of this title.

CROSS REFERENCES

Duty of United States trustee to monitor applications, see 28 USCA § 586.

Qualification for employment by debtor in possession despite prior employment or representation, see 11 USCA § 1107.

§ 328. Limitation on compensation of professional persons

(a) The trustee, or a committee appointed under section 1102 of this title, with the court's approval, may employ or authorize the employment of a professional person under section 327 or 1103 of this title, as the case may be, on any reasonable terms and conditions of employment, including on a retainer, on an hourly basis, on a fixed or percentage fee basis, or on a contingent fee basis. Notwithstanding such terms and conditions, the court may allow compensation different from the compensation provided under such terms and conditions after the conclusion of such employment, if such terms and conditions prove to have been improvident in light of developments not capable of being anticipated at the time of the fixing of such terms and conditions.

(b) If the court has authorized a trustee to serve as an attorney or accountant for the estate under section 327(d) of this title, the court may allow compensation for the trustee's services as such attorney or accountant only to the extent that the trustee performed services as attorney or accountant for the estate and not for performance of any of the trustee's duties that are generally performed by a trustee without the assistance of an attorney or accountant for the estate.

(c) Except as provided in section 327(c), 327(e), or 1107(b) of this title, the court may deny allowance of compensation for services and reimbursement of expenses of a professional person employed under section 327 or 1103 of this title if, at any time during such professional person's employment under section 327 or 1103 of this title, such professional person is not a disinterested person, or represents or holds an interest adverse to the interest of the estate with respect to the matter on which such professional person is employed.

(Pub.L. 95–598, Nov. 6, 1978, 92 Stat. 2563; amended Pub. L. 98–353, Title III, § 431, July 10, 1984, 98 Stat. 370; Pub.L. 109–8, Title XII, § 1206, Apr. 20, 2005, 119 Stat. 194.)

HISTORICAL AND STATUTORY NOTES

Revision Notes and Legislative Reports

1978 Acts. This section, which is parallel to § 326, fixes the maximum compensation allowable to a professional person employed under section 327. It authorizes the trustee, with the court's approval, to employ professional persons on any reasonable terms, including on a retainer, on an hourly or on a contingent fee basis. Subsection (a) further permits the court to allow compensation different from the compensation provided under the trustee's agreement if the prior agreement proves to have been improvident in light of development unanticipatable at the time of the agreement. The court's power includes the power to increase as well as decrease the agreed upon compensation. This provision is permissive, not mandatory, and should not be used by the court if to do so would violate the code of ethics of the professional involved.

Subsection (b) limits a trustee that has been authorized to serve as his own counsel to only one fee for each service. The purpose of permitting the trustee to serve as his own counsel is to reduce costs. It is not included to provide the trustee with a bonus by permitting him to receive two fees for the same service or to avoid the maxima fixed in section 326. Thus, this subsection requires the court to differentiate between the trustee's services as trustee, and his services as trustee's counsel, and to fix compensation accordingly. Services that a trustee normally performs for an estate without assistance of counsel are to be compensated under the limits fixed in section 326. Only services that he performs that are normally performed by trustee's counsel may be compensated under the maxima imposed by this section.

Subsection (c) permits the court to deny compensation for services and reimbursement of expenses if the professional person is not disinterested or if he represents or holds an interest adverse to the estate on the matter on which he is employed. The subsection provides a penalty for conflicts of interest. Senate Report No. 95–989.

1984 Acts. Statements by Legislative Leaders, see 1984 U.S.Code Cong. and Adm.News, p. 576.

2005 Acts. House Report No. 109–31(Part I), see 2005 U.S. Code Cong. and Adm. News, p. 88.

Legislative Statements

Section 328(c) adopts a technical amendment contained in the Senate amendment indicating that an attorney for the debtor in possession is not disqualified for compensation for services and reimbursement of expenses simply because of prior representation of the debtor.

Effective and Applicability Provisions

2005 Acts. Amendments by Pub.L. 109–8 effective, except as otherwise provided, 180 days after April 20, 2005, and inapplicable with respect to cases commenced under Title 11 before the effective date, see Pub.L. 109–8, § 1501, set out as a note under 11 U.S.C.A. § 101.

1984 Acts. Amendment by Pub.L. 98–353 effective with respect to cases filed 90 days after July 10, 1984, see section 552(a), formerly 553 of Pub.L. 98–353, set out as a note under section 101 of this title.

§ 329. Debtor's transactions with attorneys

(a) Any attorney representing a debtor in a case under this title, or in connection with such a case, whether or not such attorney applies for compensation under this title, shall file with the court a statement of the compensation paid or agreed to be paid, if such payment or agreement was made after one year before the date of the filing of the petition, for services rendered or to be rendered in contemplation of or in connection with the case by such attorney, and the source of such compensation.

(b) If such compensation exceeds the reasonable value of any such services, the court may cancel any such agreement, or order the return of any such payment, to the extent excessive, to—

(1) the estate, if the property transferred—

(A) would have been property of the estate; or

(B) was to be paid by or on behalf of the debtor under a plan under chapter 11, 12, or 13 of this title; or

(2) the entity that made such payment.

(Pub.L. 95–598, Nov. 6, 1978, 92 Stat. 2564; Pub. L. 98–353, Title III, § 432, July 10, 1984, 98 Stat. 370; Pub.L. 99–554, Title II, § 257(c), Oct. 27, 1986, 100 Stat. 3114.)

HISTORICAL AND STATUTORY NOTES

Revision Notes and Legislative Reports

1978 Acts. This section, derived in large part from current Bankruptcy Act section 60d [section 96(d) of former Title 11], requires the debtor's attorney to file with the court a statement of the compensation paid or agreed to be paid to the attorney for services in contemplation of and in connection with the case, and the source of the compensation. Payments to a debtor's attorney provide serious potential for evasion of creditor protection provisions of the bankruptcy laws, and serious potential for overreaching by the debtor's attorney, and should be subject to careful scrutiny.

Subsection (b) permits the court to deny compensation to the attorney, to cancel an agreement to pay compensation, or to order the return of compensation paid, if the compensation exceeds the reasonable value of the services provided. The return of payments already made are generally to the trustee for the benefit of the estate. However, if the property would not have come into the estate in any event, the court will order it returned to the entity that made the payment.

The Bankruptcy Commission recommended a provision similar to this that would have also permitted an examination of the debtor's transactions with insiders. S. 236, 94th Cong., 1st sess., sec. 4–311(b) (1975). Its exclusion here is to permit it to be dealt with by the Rules of Bankruptcy Procedure. It is not intended that the provision be deleted entirely, only that the flexibility of the rules is more appropriate for such evidentiary matters. Senate Report No. 95–989.

1984 Acts. Statements by Legislative Leaders, see 1984 U.S.Code Cong. and Adm.News, p. 576.

1986 Acts. House Report No. 99–764 and House Conference Report No. 99–958, see 1986 U.S.Code Cong. and Adm.News, p. 5227.

Effective and Applicability Provisions

1986 Acts. Amendment by Pub.L. 99–554 effective 30 days after Oct. 27, 1986, but not applicable to cases commenced under this title before that date, see section 302(a), (c)(1) of Pub.L. 99–554, set out as a note under section 581 of Title 28, Judiciary and Judicial Procedure.

1984 Acts. Amendment by Pub.L. 98–353 effective with respect to cases filed 90 days after July 10, 1984, see section 552(a), formerly 553(a), of Pub.L. 98–353, set out as a note under section 101 of this title.

CROSS REFERENCES

Disclosure of compensation, debtor's attorney, see Fed. Rules Bankr.Proc. Form B 203, 11 USCA.

Fee agreements, see 18 USCA § 155.

Lists, schedules, statements and fees, see Fed.Rules Bankr.Proc. Form B 200, 11 USCA.

Property of estate, see 11 USCA § 541.

§ 330. Compensation of officers

(a)(1) After notice to the parties in interest and the United States Trustee and a hearing, and subject to sections 326, 328, and 329, the court may award to a trustee, a consumer privacy ombudsman appointed under section 332, an examiner, an ombudsman appointed under section 333, or a professional person employed under section 327 or 1103—

(A) reasonable compensation for actual, necessary services rendered by the trustee, examiner, ombudsman, professional person, or attorney and by any paraprofessional person employed by any such person; and

(B) reimbursement for actual, necessary expenses.

(2) The court may, on its own motion or on the motion of the United States Trustee, the United States Trustee for the District or Region, the trustee for the estate, or any other party in interest, award compensation that is less than the amount of compensation that is requested.

(3) In determining the amount of reasonable compensation to be awarded to an examiner, trustee under chapter 11, or professional person, the court shall consider the nature, the extent, and the value of such services, taking into account all relevant factors, including—

(A) the time spent on such services;

(B) the rates charged for such services;

(C) whether the services were necessary to the administration of, or beneficial at the time at which the service was rendered toward the completion of, a case under this title;

(D) whether the services were performed within a reasonable amount of time commensurate with the complexity, importance, and nature of the problem, issue, or task addressed;

(E) with respect to a professional person, whether the person is board certified or otherwise has demonstrated skill and experience in the bankruptcy field; and

(F) whether the compensation is reasonable based on the customary compensation charged by comparably skilled practitioners in cases other than cases under this title.

(4)(A) Except as provided in subparagraph (B), the court shall not allow compensation for—

(i) unnecessary duplication of services; or

(ii) services that were not—

(I) reasonably likely to benefit the debtor's estate; or

(II) necessary to the administration of the case.

(B) In a chapter 12 or chapter 13 case in which the debtor is an individual, the court may allow reasonable compensation to the debtor's attorney for representing the interests of the debtor in connection with the bankruptcy case based on a consideration of the benefit and necessity of such services to the debtor and the other factors set forth in this section.

(5) The court shall reduce the amount of compensation awarded under this section by the amount of any interim compensation awarded under section 331, and, if the amount of such interim compensation exceeds the amount of compensation awarded under this section, may order the return of the excess to the estate.

(6) Any compensation awarded for the preparation of a fee application shall be based on the level and skill reasonably required to prepare the application.

(7) In determining the amount of reasonable compensation to be awarded to a trustee, the court shall treat such compensation as a commission, based on section 326.

(b)(1) There shall be paid from the filing fee in a case under chapter 7 of this title $45 to the trustee serving in such case, after such trustee's services are rendered.

(2) The Judicial Conference of the United States—

(A) shall prescribe additional fees of the same kind as prescribed under section 1914(b) of title 28; and

(B) may prescribe notice of appearance fees and fees charged against distributions in cases under this title;

to pay $15 to trustees serving in cases after such trustees' services are rendered. Beginning 1 year after the date of the enactment of the Bankruptcy

Reform Act of 1994, such $15 shall be paid in addition to the amount paid under paragraph (1).

(c) Unless the court orders otherwise, in a case under chapter 12 or 13 of this title the compensation paid to the trustee serving in the case shall not be less than $5 per month from any distribution under the plan during the administration of the plan.

(d) In a case in which the United States trustee serves as trustee, the compensation of the trustee under this section shall be paid to the clerk of the bankruptcy court and deposited by the clerk into the United States Trustee System Fund established by section 589a of title 28.

(Pub.L. 95–598, Nov. 6, 1978, 92 Stat. 2564; Pub.L. 98–353, Title III, §§ 433, 434, July 10, 1984, 98 Stat. 370; Pub.L. 99–554, Title II, §§ 211, 257(f), Oct. 27, 1986, 100 Stat. 3099, 3114; Pub.L. 103–394, Title I, § 117, Title II, § 224(b), Oct. 22, 1994, 108 Stat. 4119, 4130; Pub.L. 109–8, Title II, § 232(b), Title IV, §§ 407, 415, Title XI, 1104(b), Apr. 20, 2005, 119 Stat. 74, 106, 107, 192.)

HISTORICAL AND STATUTORY NOTES

Revision Notes and Legislative Reports

1978 Acts. Section 330 authorizes the court to award compensation for services and reimbursement of expenses of officers of the estate, and other professionals. The compensation is to be reasonable, for economy in administration is the basic objective. Compensation is to be for actual necessary services, based on the time spent, the nature, the extent and the value of the services rendered, and the cost of comparable services in nonbankruptcy cases. There are the criteria that have been applied by the courts as analytic aids in defining "reasonable" compensation.

The reference to "the cost of comparable services" in a nonbankruptcy case is not intended as a change of existing law. In a bankruptcy cases fees are not a matter for private agreement. There is inherent a "public interest" that "must be considered in awarding fees," *Massachusetts Mutual Life Insurance Co. v. Brock*, 405 F.2d 429, 432 (C.A.5, 1968), cert. denied, 395 U.S. 906 (1969) [89 S.Ct. 1748, 23 L.Ed.2d 220]. An allowance is the result of a balance struck between moderation in the interest of the estate and its security holders and the need to be "generous enough to encourage" lawyers and others to render the necessary and exacting services that bankruptcy cases often require. *In re Yale Express System, Inc.*, 366 F.Supp. 1376, 1381 (S.D.N.Y.1973). The rates for similar kinds of services in private employment is one element, among others, in that balance. Compensation in private employment noted in subsection (a) is a point of reference, not a controlling determinant of what shall be allowed in bankruptcy cases.

One of the major reforms in 1938, especially for reorganization cases, was centralized control over fees in the bankruptcy courts. See *Brown v. Gerdes*, 321 U.S. 178, 182–184 (1944) [64 S.Ct. 487, 88 L.Ed. 659]; *Leiman v. Guttman*, 336 U.S. 1, 4–9, (1949) [69 S.Ct. 371, 93 L.Ed. 453]. It was intended to guard against a recurrence of "the many sordid chapters" in "the history of fees in corporate reorganizations." *Dickinson Industrial Site, Inc. v. Cowan*, 309 U.S. 382, 388 (1940) [60 S.Ct. 595, 84 L.Ed. 819, rehearing denied 60 S.Ct. 806, 309 U.S. 698, 84 L.Ed. 1037]. In the years since then the bankruptcy bar has flourished and prospered, and persons of merit and quality have not eschewed public service in bankruptcy cases merely because bankruptcy courts, in the interest of economy in administration, have not allowed them compensation that may be earned in the private economy of business or the professions. There is no reason to believe that, in generations to come, their successors will be less persuaded by the need to serve in the public interest because of stronger allures of private gain elsewhere.

Subsection (a) provides for compensation of paraprofessional in order to reduce the cost of administering bankruptcy cases. Paraprofessionals can be employed to perform duties which do not require the full range of skills of a qualified professional. Some courts have not hesitated to recognize paraprofessional services as compensable under existing law. An explicit provision to that effect is useful and constructive.

The last sentence of subsection (a) provides that in the case of a public company—defined in section 1101(3)—the court shall refer, after a hearing, all applications to the Securities and Exchange Commission for a report, which shall be advisory only. In Chapter X cases in which the Commission has appeared, it generally filed reports on fee applications. Usually, courts have accorded the SEC's views substantial weight, as representing the opinion of a disinterested agency skilled and experienced in reorganization affairs. The last sentence intends for the advisory assistance of the Commission to be sought only in case of a public company in reorganization under chapter 11.

Subsection (b) reenacts section 249 of Chapter X of the Bankruptcy Act ([former] 11 U.S.C. 649). It is a codification of equitable principles designed to prevent fiduciaries in the case from engaging in the specified transactions since they are in a position to gain inside information or to shape or influence the course of the reorganization. *Wolf v. Weinstein*, 372 U.S. 633 (1963) [83 S.Ct. 969, 10 L.Ed.2d 33, rehearing denied 83 S.Ct. 1522, 373 U.S. 928, 10 L.Ed.2d 427]. The statutory bar of compensation and reimbursement is based on the principle that such transactions involve conflicts of interest. Private gain undoubtedly prompts the purchase or sale of claims or stock interests, while the fiduciary's obligation is to render loyal and disinterested service which his position of trust has imposed upon him. Subsection (b) extends to a trustee, his attorney, committees and their attorneys, or any other persons "acting in the case in a representative or fiduciary capacity." It bars compensation to any of the foregoing, who after assuming to act in such capacity has purchased or sold, directly or indirectly, claims against, or stock in the debtor. The bar is absolute. It makes no difference whether the transaction brought a gain or loss, or neither, and the court is not authorized to approve a purchase or sale, before or after the transaction. The exception is for an acquisition or transfer "otherwise" than by a voluntary purchase or sale, such as an acquisition by bequest. See *Otis & Co. v. Insurance Bldg. Corp.*, 110 F.2d 333, 335 (C.A.1, 1940).

Subsection (c) is intended for no asset liquidation cases where minimal compensation for trustees is needed. The sum of $20 will be allowed in each case, which is double the amount provided under current law. Senate Report No. 95–989.

Section 330 authorizes compensation for services and reimbursement of expenses of officers of the estate. It also prescribes the standards on which the amount of compensation is to be determined. As noted above, the compensation allowable under this section is subject to the maxima set out in sections 326, 328, and 329. The compensation is to be reasonable, for actual necessary services rendered, based on the time, the nature, the extent, and the value of the services rendered, and on the cost of comparable services other than in a case under the bankruptcy code. The effect of the last provision is to overrule *In re Beverly Crest Convalescent Hospital, Inc.*, 548 F.2d 817 (9th Cir.1976, as amended 1977), which set an arbitrary limit on fees payable, based on the amount of a district judge's salary, and other, similar cases that require fees to be determined based on notions of conservation of the estate and economy of administration. If that case were allowed to stand, attorneys that could earn much higher incomes in other fields would leave the bankruptcy arena. Bankruptcy specialists, who enable the system to operate smoothly, efficiently, and expeditiously, would be driven elsewhere, and the bankruptcy field would be occupied by those who could not find other work and those who practice bankruptcy law only occasionally almost as a public service. Bankruptcy fees that are lower than fees in other areas of the legal profession may operate properly when the attorneys appearing in bankruptcy cases do so intermittently, because a low fee in a small segment of a practice can be absorbed by other work. Bankruptcy specialists, however, if required to accept fees in all of their cases that are consistently lower than fees they could receive elsewhere, will not remain in the bankruptcy field.

This subsection provides for reimbursement of actual, necessary expenses. It further provides for compensation of paraprofessionals employed by professional persons employed by the estate of the debtor. The provision is included to reduce the cost of administering bankruptcy cases. In nonbankruptcy areas, attorneys are able to charge for a paraprofessional's time on an hourly basis, and not include it in overhead. If a similar practice does not pertain in bankruptcy cases then the attorney will be less inclined to use paraprofessionals even where the work involved could easily be handled by an attorney's assistant, at much lower cost to the estate. This provision is designed to encourage attorneys to use paraprofessional assistance where possible, and to insure that the estate, not the attorney, will bear the cost, to the benefit of both the estate and the attorneys involved. House Report No. 95–595.

1984 Acts. Statements by Legislative Leaders, see 1984 U.S.Code Cong. and Adm.News, p. 576.

1986 Acts. House Report No. 99–764 and House Conference Report No. 99–958, see 1986 U.S.Code Cong. and Adm.News, p. 5227.

1994 Acts. House Report No. 103–835, see 1994 U.S. Code Cong. and Adm. News, p. 3340.

2005 Acts. House Report No. 109–31(Part I), see 2005 U.S. Code Cong. and Adm. News, p. 88.

Legislative Statements

Section 330(a) contains the standard of compensation adopted in H.R. 8200 as passed by the House rather than the contrary standard contained in the Senate amendment. Attorneys' fees in bankruptcy cases can be quite large and should be closely examined by the court. However bankruptcy legal services are entitled to command the same competency of counsel as other cases. In that light, the policy of this section is to compensate attorneys and other professionals serving in a case under title 11 at the same rate as the attorney or other professional would be compensated for performing comparable services other than in a case under title 11. Contrary language in the Senate report accompanying S. 2266 is rejected, and *Massachusetts Mutual Life Insurance Company v. Brock*, 405 F.2d 429, 432 (5th Cir.1968) is overruled. Notions of economy of the estate in fixing fees are outdated and have no place in a bankruptcy code.

Section 330(a)(2) of the Senate amendment is deleted although the Securities and Exchange Commission retains a right to file an advisory report under section 1109.

Section 330(b) of the Senate amendment is deleted as unnecessary, as the limitations contained therein are covered by section 328(c) of H.R. 8200 as passed by the House and contained in the House amendment.

Section 330(c) of the Senate amendment providing for a trustee to receive a fee of $20 for each estate from the filing fee paid to the clerk is retained as section 330(b) of the House amendment. The section will encourage private trustees to serve in cases under title 11 and in pilot districts will place less of a burden on the U.S. trustee to serve in no-asset cases.

Section 330(b) of H.R. 8200 as passed by the House is retained by the House amendment as section 330(c) [section 15330].

Effective and Applicability Provisions

2005 Acts. Amendments by Pub.L. 109–8 effective, except as otherwise provided, 180 days after April 20, 2005, and inapplicable with respect to cases commenced under Title 11 before the effective date, see Pub.L. 109–8, § 1501, set out as a note under 11 U.S.C.A. § 101.

1994 Acts. Amendment by section 117 of Pub.L. 103–394 effective on Oct. 22, 1994, and applicable with respect to cases commenced under Title 11 of the United States Code before, on, and after Oct. 22, 1994, see section 702(a), (b)(2)(B) of Pub.L. 103–394, set out as a note under section 101 of this title.

Amendment by section 224(b) of Pub.L. 103–394 effective Oct. 22, 1994, and shall not apply with respect to cases commenced under this title before Oct. 22, 1994, see section 702(a), (b)(1) of Pub.L. 103–394, set out as a note under section 101 of this title.

1986 Acts. Amendment by Pub.L. 99–554 effective 30 days after Oct. 27, 1986, except as otherwise provided for, see section 302(a) of Pub.L. 99–554, set out as a note under section 581 of Title 28, Judiciary and Judicial Procedure.

Amendment by Pub.L. 99–554, § 211, not to become effective in or with respect to certain specified judicial districts until, or apply to cases while pending in such district before, the expiration of the 270-day period beginning 30 days after Oct. 27, 1986, or of the 30-day period beginning on the date the Attorney General certifies under section 303 of Pub.L. 99–554 the region specified in a paragraph of section 581(a) of Title 28, as amended by section 111(a) of Pub.L. 99–554, that includes such district, whichever occurs first, see section 302(d)(1) of Pub.L. 99–554, set out as a note under section 581 of Title 28.

Amendment by Pub.L. 99–554, § 211, not to become effective in or with respect to certain specified judicial districts until, or apply to cases while pending in such district before, the expiration of the 2-year period beginning 30 days after Oct. 27, 1986, or of the 30-day period beginning on the date the Attorney General certifies under section 303 of Pub.L. 99–554 the region specified in a paragraph of section 581(a) of Title 28, as amended by section 111(a) of Pub.L. 99–554, that includes such district, whichever occurs first, see section 302(d)(2) of Pub.L. 99–554, set out as a note under section 581 of Title 28.

Amendment by Pub.L. 99–554, § 211, not to become effective in or with respect to judicial districts established for the States of Alabama and North Carolina until, or apply to cases while pending in such district before, such district elects to be included in a bankruptcy region established in section 581(a) of Title 28, as amended by section 111(a) of Pub.L. 99–554, or Oct. 1, 2002, whichever occurs first, and, except as otherwise provided for, with respect to cases under chapters 7, 11, 12, and 13 of Title 11 commenced before 30 days after Oct. 27, 1986, and pending in a judicial district in the States of Alabama or North Carolina before any election made under section 302(d)(3)(A) of Pub.L. 99–554 by such district becomes effective or Oct. 1, 2002, whichever occurs first, amendments by Pub.L. 99–554 not to apply until Oct. 1, 2003, or the expiration of the 1-year period beginning on the date such election becomes effective, whichever occurs first, and further, in any judicial district in Alabama or North Carolina not making the election described in section 302(d)(3)(A) of Pub.L. 99–554, any person appointed under regulations issued by the Judicial Conference to administer estates in cases under Title 11 authorized to establish, etc., a panel of private trustees, and to supervise cases and trustees in cases under chapters 7, 11, 12, and 13 of Title 11, until amendments by sections 201 to 231 of Pub.L. 99–554 effective in such district, see section 302(d)(3)(A) to (F), (H), and (I) of Pub.L. 99–554, set out as a note under section 581 of Title 28.

Amendment by Pub.L. 99–554, § 211, except as otherwise provided, with respect to cases under chapters 7, 11, 12, and 13 of Title 11 commenced before 30 days after Oct. 27, 1986, and pending in a judicial district referred to in section 581(a) of Title 28, as amended by section 111(a) of Pub.L. 99–554, for which a United States trustee is not authorized before 30 days after Oct. 27, 1986 to be appointed, not applicable until the expiration of the 3-year period beginning on Oct. 27, 1986, or of the 1-year period beginning on the date the Attorney General certifies under section 303 of Pub.L. 99–554 the region specified in a paragraph of such section 581(a) that includes, such district, whichever occurs first, see section 302(e)(1), (2) of Pub.L. 99–554, set out as a note under section 581 of Title 28.

Amendment by Pub.L. 99–554, § 257(f), effective 30 days after Oct. 27, 1986, but not applicable to cases commenced under this title before that date, see section 302(a), (c)(1) of Pub.L. 99–554, set out as a note under section 581 of Title 28.

1984 Acts. Amendment by Pub.L. 98–353 effective with respect to cases filed 90 days after July 10, 1984, see section 552(a), formerly 553(a), of Pub.L. 98–353, set out as a note under section 101 of this title.

Separability of Provisions

If any provision of or amendment made by Pub.L. 103–394 or the application of such provision or amendment to any person or circumstance is held to be unconstitutional, the remaining provisions of and amendments made by Pub.L. 103–394 and the application of such provisions and amendments to any person or circumstance shall not be affected thereby, see section 701 of Pub.L. 103–394, set out as a note under section 101 of this title.

CROSS REFERENCES

Adverse interest and conduct of officers of estate, see 18 USCA § 154.

Allowances to trustee and trustee's attorney in investor protection liquidation proceedings, see 15 USCA § 78eee.

Approval of Securities and Exchange Commission for payment of fees, expenses and remuneration in cases involving holding companies under this title, see 15 USCA § 79k.

Debtor in possession's right of compensation—

Chapter 11 cases, see 11 USCA § 1107.

Chapter 12 cases, see 11 USCA § 1203.

Guidelines for reviewing applications for compensation and reimbursement of expenses, see Fed.Rules Bankr.Proc. Rule 2016, 11 USCA.

Officers' compensation as administrative expense, see 11 USCA § 503.

Supervision by Attorney General, see 28 USCA § 586.

United States Trustee System Fund establishment and purpose, see 28 USCA § 589a.

§ 331. Interim compensation

A trustee, an examiner, a debtor's attorney, or any professional person employed under section 327 or 1103 of this title may apply to the court not more than once every 120 days after an order for relief in a case under this title, or more often if the court permits, for such compensation for services rendered before the date of such an application or reimbursement for expenses incurred before such date as is provided under section 330 of this title. After notice and a hearing, the court may allow and disburse to such applicant such compensation or reimbursement.

(Pub.L. 95–598, Nov. 6, 1978, 92 Stat. 2564.)

HISTORICAL AND STATUTORY NOTES

Revision Notes and Legislative Reports

1978 Acts. Section 331 permits trustees and professional persons to apply to the court not more than once every 120 days for interim compensation and reimbursement payments. The court may permit more frequent applications if the circumstances warrant, such as in very large cases where the legal work is extensive and merits more frequent payments. The court is authorized to allow and order disbursement to the applicant of compensation and reimbursement that is otherwise allowable under section 330. The only effect of this section is to remove any doubt that officers of the estate may apply for, and the court may approve, compensation and reimbursement during the case, instead of being required to wait until the end of the case, which in some instances, may be years. The practice of interim compensation is followed in some courts today, but has been subject to some question. This section explicitly authorizes it.

This section will apply to professionals such as auctioneers and appraisers only if they are not paid on a per job basis. Senate Report No. 95–989.

§ 332. Consumer privacy ombudsman

(a) If a hearing is required under section 363(b)(1)(B), the court shall order the United States trustee to appoint, not later than 5 days before the commencement of the hearing, 1 disinterested person (other than the United States trustee) to serve as the consumer privacy ombudsman in the case and shall require that notice of such hearing be timely given to such ombudsman.

(b) The consumer privacy ombudsman may appear and be heard at such hearing and shall provide to the court information to assist the court in its consideration of the facts, circumstances, and conditions of the proposed sale or lease of personally identifiable information under section 363(b)(1)(B). Such information may include presentation of—

(1) the debtor's privacy policy;

(2) the potential losses or gains of privacy to consumers if such sale or such lease is approved by the court;

(3) the potential costs or benefits to consumers if such sale or such lease is approved by the court; and

(4) the potential alternatives that would mitigate potential privacy losses or potential costs to consumers.

(c) A consumer privacy ombudsman shall not disclose any personally identifiable information obtained by the ombudsman under this title.

(Added Pub.L. 109–8, Title II, § 232(a), Apr. 20, 2005, 119 Stat. 73.)

HISTORICAL AND STATUTORY NOTES

Revision Notes and Legislative Reports

2005 Acts. House Report No. 109–31(Part I), see 2005 U.S. Code Cong. and Adm. News, p. 88.

Effective and Applicability Provisions

2005 Acts. Amendments by Pub.L. 109–8 effective, except as otherwise provided, 180 days after April 20, 2005, and inapplicable with respect to cases commenced under Title 11 before the effective date, see Pub.L. 109–8, § 1501, set out as a note under 11 U.S.C.A. § 101.

§ 333. Appointment of patient care ombudsman

(a)(1) If the debtor in a case under chapter 7, 9, or 11 is a health care business, the court shall order, not later than 30 days after the commencement of the case, the appointment of an ombudsman to monitor the quality of patient care and to represent the interests of the patients of the health care business unless the court finds that the appointment of such ombudsman is not necessary for the protection of patients under the specific facts of the case.

(2)(A) If the court orders the appointment of an ombudsman under paragraph (1), the United States trustee shall appoint 1 disinterested person (other than the United States trustee) to serve as such ombudsman.

(B) If the debtor is a health care business that provides long-term care, then the United States trustee may appoint the State Long–Term Care Ombudsman appointed under the Older Americans Act of 1965 for the State in which the case is pending to serve as the ombudsman required by paragraph (1).

(C) If the United States trustee does not appoint a State Long–Term Care Ombudsman under subparagraph (B), the court shall notify the State Long–Term Care Ombudsman appointed under the Older Americans Act of 1965 for the State in which the case is pending, of the name and address of the person who is appointed under subparagraph (A).

(b) An ombudsman appointed under subsection (a) shall—

(1) monitor the quality of patient care provided to patients of the debtor, to the extent necessary under the circumstances, including interviewing patients and physicians;

(2) not later than 60 days after the date of appointment, and not less frequently than at 60–day intervals thereafter, report to the court after notice to the parties in interest, at a hearing or in writing, regarding the quality of patient care provided to patients of the debtor; and

(3) if such ombudsman determines that the quality of patient care provided to patients of the debtor is declining significantly or is otherwise being materially compromised, file with the court a motion or a written report, with notice to the parties in interest immediately upon making such determination.

(c)(1) An ombudsman appointed under subsection (a) shall maintain any information obtained by such ombudsman under this section that relates to patients (including information relating to patient records) as confidential information. Such ombudsman may not review confidential patient records unless the court approves such review in advance and imposes restrictions on such ombudsman to protect the confidentiality of such records.

(2) An ombudsman appointed under subsection (a)(2)(B) shall have access to patient records consistent with authority of such ombudsman under the Older Americans Act of 1965 and under non-Federal laws governing the State Long–Term Care Ombudsman program.

(Added Pub.L. 109–8, Title XI, § 1104(a)(1), Apr. 20, 2005, 119 Stat. 191.)

HISTORICAL AND STATUTORY NOTES

Revision Notes and Legislative Reports

2005 Acts. House Report No. 109–31(Part I), see 2005 U.S. Code Cong. and Adm. News, p. 88.

References in Text

Chapter 7, 9, or 11, referred to in subsec. (a)(1), means chapter 7, 9, or 11 of this title, 11 U.S.C.A. § 701 et seq., 11 U.S.C.A. § 901 et seq., or 11 U.S.C.A. § 1101 et seq., respectively.

The Older Americans Act of 1965, referred to in subsecs. (a)(2)(B), (C) and (c)(2), is Pub.L. 89–73, July 14, 1965, 79 Stat. 218, as amended, which is classified principally to chapter 35 of Title 42, 42 U.S.C.A. § 3001 et seq. For complete classification, see Short Title note set out under 42 U.S.C.A. § 3001 and Tables.

Effective and Applicability Provisions

2005 Acts. Enactment of this section by Pub.L. 109–8 effective, except as otherwise provided, 180 days after April 20, 2005, and inapplicable with respect to cases commenced under Title 11 before the effective date, see Pub.L. 109–8, § 1501, set out as a note under 11 U.S.C.A. § 101.

Corpus Juris Secundum

CJS Bankruptcy § 764, Consumer Privacy and Patient Care Ombudsmen.

§§ 334 to 340. Reserved for future legislation

SUBCHAPTER III—ADMINISTRATION

§ 341. Meetings of creditors and equity security holders

(a) Within a reasonable time after the order for relief in a case under this title, the United States trustee shall convene and preside at a meeting of creditors.

(b) The United States trustee may convene a meeting of any equity security holders.

(c) The court may not preside at, and may not attend, any meeting under this section including any final meeting of creditors. Notwithstanding any local court rule, provision of a State constitution, any otherwise applicable nonbankruptcy law, or any other requirement that representation at the meeting of creditors under subsection (a) be by an attorney, a creditor holding a consumer debt or any representative of the creditor (which may include an entity or an employee of an entity and may be a representative for more than 1 creditor) shall be permitted to appear at and participate in the meeting of creditors in a case under chapter 7 or 13, either alone or in conjunction with an attorney for the creditor. Nothing in this subsection shall be construed to require any creditor to be represented by an attorney at any meeting of creditors.

(d) Prior to the conclusion of the meeting of creditors or equity security holders, the trustee shall orally examine the debtor to ensure that the debtor in a case under chapter 7 of this title is aware of—

(1) the potential consequences of seeking a discharge in bankruptcy, including the effects on credit history;

(2) the debtor's ability to file a petition under a different chapter of this title;

(3) the effect of receiving a discharge of debts under this title; and

(4) the effect of reaffirming a debt, including the debtor's knowledge of the provisions of section 524(d) of this title.

(e) Notwithstanding subsections (a) and (b), the court, on the request of a party in interest and after notice and a hearing, for cause may order that the United States trustee not convene a meeting of creditors or equity security holders if the debtor has filed a plan as to which the debtor solicited acceptances prior to the commencement of the case.

(Pub.L. 95–598, Nov. 6, 1978, 92 Stat. 2564; Pub.L. 99–554, Title II, § 212, Oct. 27, 1986, 100 Stat. 3099; Pub.L. 103–394, Title I, § 115, Oct. 22, 1994, 108 Stat. 4118; Pub.L. 109–8, Title IV, §§ 402, 413, Apr. 20, 2005, 119 Stat. 104, 107.)

HISTORICAL AND STATUTORY NOTES

Revision Notes and Legislative Reports

1978 Acts. Section [subsection] (a) of this section requires that there be a meeting of creditors within a reasonable time after the order for relief in the case. The Bankruptcy Act [former Title 11] and the current Rules of Bankruptcy Procedure provide for a meeting of creditors, and specify the time and manner of the meeting, and the business to be conducted. This bill leaves those matters to the rules. Under section 405(d) of the bill, the present rules will continue to govern until new rules are promulgated. Thus, pending the adoption of different rules, the present procedure for the meeting will continue.

Subsection (b) authorizes the court to order a meeting of equity security holders in cases where such a meeting would be beneficial or useful, for example, in a chapter 11 reorganization case where it may be necessary for the equity security holders to organize in order to be able to participate in the negotiation of a plan of reorganization.

Subsection (c) makes clear that the bankruptcy judge is to preside at the meeting of creditors. Senate Report No. 95–989.

1986 Acts. House Report No. 99–764 and House Conference Report No. 99–958, see 1986 U.S.Code Cong. and Adm.News, p. 5227.

1994 Acts. House Report No. 103–835, see 1994 U.S. Code Cong. and Adm. News, p. 3340.

2005 Acts. House Report No. 109–31(Part I), see 2005 U.S. Code Cong. and Adm. News, p. 88.

Legislative Statements

Section 341(c) of the Senate amendment is deleted and a contrary provision is added indicating that the bankruptcy judge will not preside at or attend the first meeting of creditors or equity security holders but a discharge hearing for all individuals will be held at which the judge will preside.

References in Text

Chapter 7, referred to in subsecs. (c) and (d), is chapter 7 of this title, 11 U.S.C.A. § 701 et seq.

Chapter 13, referred to in subsec. (c), is chapter 13 of this title, 11 U.S.C.A. § 1301 et seq.

Effective and Applicability Provisions

2005 Acts. Amendments by Pub.L. 109–8 effective, except as otherwise provided, 180 days after April 20, 2005, and inapplicable with respect to cases commenced under Title 11 before the effective date, see Pub.L. 109–8, § 1501, set out as a note under 11 U.S.C.A. § 101.

1994 Acts. Amendment by Pub.L. 103–394 effective on Oct. 22, 1994, and not to apply with respect to cases commenced under Title 11 of the United States Code before Oct. 22, 1994, see section 702 of Pub.L. 103–394, set out as a note under section 101 of this title.

1986 Acts. Amendment by Pub.L. 99–554 effective 30 days after Oct. 27, 1986, except as otherwise provided for, see section 302(a) of Pub.L. 99–554, set out as a note under section 581 of Title 28, Judiciary and Judicial Procedure.

Amendment by Pub.L. 99–554, § 212, not to become effective in or with respect to certain specified judicial districts until, or apply to cases while pending in such district before, the expiration of the 270-day period beginning 30 days after Oct. 27, 1986, or of the 30-day period beginning on the date the Attorney General certifies under section 303 of Pub.L. 99–554 the region specified in a paragraph of section 581(a) of Title 28, as amended by section 111(a) of Pub.L. 99–554, that includes such district, whichever occurs first, see section 302(d)(1) of Pub.L. 99–554, set out as a note under section 581 of Title 28.

Amendment by Pub.L. 99–554, § 212, not to become effective in or with respect to certain specified judicial districts until, or apply to cases while pending in such district before, the expiration of the 2-year period beginning 30 days after Oct. 27, 1986, or of the 30-day period beginning on the date the Attorney General certifies under section 303 of Pub.L. 99–554 the region specified in a paragraph of section 581(a) of Title 28, as amended by section 111(a) of Pub.L. 99–554, that includes such district, whichever occurs first, see section 302(d)(2) of Pub.L. 99–554, set out as a note under section 581 of Title 28.

Amendment by Pub.L. 99–554, § 212, not to become effective in or with respect to judicial districts established for the States of Alabama and North Carolina until, or apply to cases while pending in such district before, such district elects to be included in a bankruptcy region established in section 581(a) of Title 28, as amended by section 111(a) of Pub.L. 99–554, or Oct. 1, 2002, whichever occurs first, and, except as otherwise provided, with respect to cases under chapters 7, 11, 12, and 13 of Title 11 commenced before 30 days after Oct. 27, 1986, and pending in a judicial district in the States of Alabama or North Carolina before any election made under section 302(d)(3)(A) of Pub.L. 99–554 by such district becomes effective or Oct. 1, 2003, whichever occurs first, amendments by Pub.L. 99–554 not to apply until Oct. 1, 1992, or the expiration of the 1-year period beginning on the date such election becomes effective whichever occurs first, and further, in any judicial district in Alabama or North Carolina not making the election described in section 302(d)(3)(A) of Pub.L. 99–554, any person appointed under regulations issued by the Judicial Conference to administer estates in cases under Title 11 authorized to establish, etc., a panel of private trustees, and to supervise cases and trustees in cases under chapters 7, 11, 12, and 13 of Title 11, until amendments by sections 201 to 231 of Pub.L. 99–554 effective in such district, see section 302(d)(3)(A) to (F), (H), and (I) of Pub.L. 99–554, set out as a note under section 581 of Title 28.

Amendment by Pub.L. 99–554, § 212, except as otherwise provided, with respect to cases under chapters 7, 11, 12 and 13 of Title 11 commenced before 30 days after Oct. 27, 1986, and pending in a judicial district referred to in section 581(a) of Title 28, as amended by section 111(a) of Pub.L. 99–554, for which a United States trustee is not authorized before 30 days after Oct. 27, 1986 to be appointed, not applicable until the expiration of the 3-year period beginning on Oct. 27, 1986, or of the 1-year period beginning on the date the Attorney General certifies under section 303 of Pub.L. 99–554 the region specified in a paragraph of such section 581(a) that includes, such district, whichever occurs first, see section 302(e)(1), (2) of Pub.L. 99–554, set out as a note under section 581 of Title 28.

Separability of Provisions

If any provision of or amendment made by Pub.L. 103–394 or the application of such provision or amendment to any person or circumstance is held to be unconstitutional, the remaining provisions of and amendments made by Pub.L. 103–394 and the application of such provisions and amendments to any person or circumstance shall not be affected thereby, see section 701 of Pub.L. 103–394, set out as a note under section 101 of this title.

Participation by Bankruptcy Administrator at Meetings of Creditors and Equity Security Holders

Section 105 of Pub.L. 103–394 provided that:

"(a) Presiding officer.—A bankruptcy administrator appointed under section 302(d)(3)(I) of the Bankruptcy Judges, United States Trustees, and Family Farmer Bankruptcy Act of 1986 (28 U.S.C. 581 note; Public Law 99–554; 100 Stat. 3123), as amended by section 317(a) of the Federal Courts Study Committee Implementation Act of 1990 (Public Law 101–650; 104 Stat. 5115), or the bankruptcy administrator's designee may preside at the meeting of creditors convened under section 341(a) of title 11, United States Code [subsec. (a) of this section]. The bankruptcy administrator or the bankruptcy administrator's designee may preside at any meeting of equity security holders convened under section 341(b) of title 11, United States Code [subsec. (b) of this section].

"(b) Examination of the debtor.—The bankruptcy administrator or the bankruptcy administrator's designee may examine the debtor at the meeting of creditors and may administer the oath required under section 343 of title 11, United States Code [section 343 of this title]."

CROSS REFERENCES

Election of—

Creditors' committee, see 11 USCA § 705.

Trustee, see 11 USCA § 702.

Inapplicability of this section in railroad reorganization cases, see 11 USCA § 1161.

§ 342. Notice

(a) There shall be given such notice as is appropriate, including notice to any holder of a community claim, of an order for relief in a case under this title.

(b) Before the commencement of a case under this title by an individual whose debts are primarily consumer debts, the clerk shall give to such individual written notice containing—

(1) a brief description of—

(A) chapters 7, 11, 12, and 13 and the general purpose, benefits, and costs of proceeding under each of those chapters; and

(B) the types of services available from credit counseling agencies; and

(2) statements specifying that—

(A) a person who knowingly and fraudulently conceals assets or makes a false oath or statement under penalty of perjury in connection with a case under this title shall be subject to fine, imprisonment, or both; and

(B) all information supplied by a debtor in connection with a case under this title is subject to examination by the Attorney General.

(c)(1) If notice is required to be given by the debtor to a creditor under this title, any rule, any applicable law, or any order of the court, such notice shall contain the name, address, and last 4 digits of the taxpayer identification number of the debtor. If the notice concerns an amendment that adds a creditor to the schedules of assets and liabilities, the debtor shall include the full taxpayer identification number in the notice sent to that creditor, but the debtor shall include only the last 4 digits of the taxpayer identification number in the copy of the notice filed with the court.

(2)(A) If, within the 90 days before the commencement of a voluntary case, a creditor supplies the debtor in at least 2 communications sent to the debtor with the current account number of the debtor and the address at which such creditor requests to receive correspondence, then any notice required by this title to be sent by the debtor to such creditor shall be sent to such address and shall include such account number.

(B) If a creditor would be in violation of applicable nonbankruptcy law by sending any such communication within such 90–day period and if such creditor supplies the debtor in the last 2 communications with the current account number of the debtor and the address at which such creditor requests to receive correspondence, then any notice required by this title to be sent by the debtor to such creditor shall be sent to such address and shall include such account number.

(d) In a case under chapter 7 of this title in which the debtor is an individual and in which the presumption of abuse arises under section 707(b), the clerk shall give written notice to all creditors not later than 10 days after the date of the filing of the petition that the presumption of abuse has arisen.

(e)(1) In a case under chapter 7 or 13 of this title of a debtor who is an individual, a creditor at any time may both file with the court and serve on the debtor a notice of address to be used to provide notice in such case to such creditor.

(2) Any notice in such case required to be provided to such creditor by the debtor or the court later than 5 days after the court and the debtor receive such creditor's notice of address, shall be provided to such address.

(f)(1) An entity may file with any bankruptcy court a notice of address to be used by all the bankruptcy courts or by particular bankruptcy courts, as so specified by such entity at the time such notice is filed, to provide notice to such entity in all cases under chapters 7 and 13 pending in the courts with respect to which such notice is filed, in which such entity is a creditor.

(2) In any case filed under chapter 7 or 13, any notice required to be provided by a court with respect to which a notice is filed under paragraph (1), to such entity later than 30 days after the filing of such notice under paragraph (1) shall be provided to such address unless with respect to a particular case a different address is specified in a notice filed and served in accordance with subsection (e).

(3) A notice filed under paragraph (1) may be withdrawn by such entity.

(g)(1) Notice provided to a creditor by the debtor or the court other than in accordance with this section (excluding this subsection) shall not be effective notice until such notice is brought to the attention of such creditor. If such creditor designates a person or an organizational subdivision of such creditor to be responsible for receiving notices under this title and establishes reasonable procedures so that such notices receivable by such creditor are to be delivered to such person or such subdivision, then a notice provided to such creditor other than in accordance with this section (excluding this subsection) shall not be considered to have been brought to the attention of such creditor until such notice is received by such person or such subdivision.

(2) A monetary penalty may not be imposed on a creditor for a violation of a stay in effect under section 362(a) (including a monetary penalty imposed under section 362(k)) or for failure to comply with section 542 or 543 unless the conduct that is the basis of such violation or of such failure occurs after such creditor receives notice effective under this section of the order for relief.

(Pub.L. 95–598, Nov. 6, 1978, 92 Stat. 2565; Pub.L. 98–353, Title III, §§ 302, 435, July 10, 1984, 98 Stat. 352, 370; Pub.L. 103–394, Title II, § 225, Oct. 22, 1994, 108 Stat. 4131; Pub.L. 109–8, Title I, §§ 102(d), 104, Title II, § 234(b), Title III, § 315(a), Apr. 20, 2005, 119 Stat. 33, 35, 75, 88.)

HISTORICAL AND STATUTORY NOTES

Revision Notes and Legislative Reports

1978 Acts. Subsection (a) of section 342 requires the clerk of the bankruptcy court to give notice of the order for relief. The rules will prescribe to whom the notice should be sent and in what manner notice will be given. The rules already prescribe such things, and they will continue to govern unless changed as provided in section 404(a) of the bill. Due process will certainly require notice to all creditors and equity security holders. State and Federal governmental representatives responsible for collecting taxes will also receive notice. In cases where the debtor is subject to regulation, the regulatory agency with jurisdiction will receive notice. In order to insure maximum notice to all parties in interest, the Rules will include notice by publication in appropriate cases and for appropriate issues. Other notices will be given as appropriate.

Subsections (b) and (c) are derived from section 21g of the Bankruptcy Act [section 44(g) of former Title 11]. They specify that the trustee may file notice of the commencement of the case in land recording offices in order to give notice of the pendency of the case to potential transferees of the debtor's real property. Such filing is unnecessary in the county in which the bankruptcy case is commenced. If notice is properly filed, a subsequent purchaser of the property will not be a bona fide purchaser. Otherwise, a purchaser, including a purchaser at a judicial sale, that has no knowledge of the case, is not prevented from obtaining the status of a bona fide purchaser by the mere commencement of the case. "County" is defined in title 1 of the United States Code [1 U.S.C.A. § 2] to include other political subdivisions where counties are not used. Senate Report No. 95–989.

1984 Acts. Statements by Legislative Leaders, see 1984 U.S.Code Cong. and Adm.News, p. 576.

1994 Acts. House Report No. 103–835, see 1994 U.S. Code Cong. and Adm. News, p. 3340.

2005 Acts. House Report No. 109–31(Part I), see 2005 U.S. Code Cong. and Adm. News, p. 88.

Legislative Statements

Section 342(b) and (c) of the Senate amendment are adopted in principle but moved to section 549(c), in lieu of section 342(b) of H.R. 8200 as passed by the House.

Section 342(c) of H.R. 8200 as passed by the House is deleted as a matter to be left to the Rules of Bankruptcy Procedure.

References in Text

Chapters 7, 11, 12, and 13, referred to in subsec. (b)(1), are chapters 7, 11, 12, and 13 of this title, 11 U.S.C.A. § 701 et seq., 11 U.S.C.A. § 1101 et seq., 11 U.S.C.A. § 1201 et seq., and 11 U.S.C.A. § 1301 et seq., respectively.

Chapter 7 of this title, referred to in subsec. (d), is 11 U.S.C.A. § 701 et seq.

Chapter 7 or 13, referred to in subsecs. (e)(1), (f)(1), (2), is chapter 7 or 13 of this title, 11 U.S.C.A. § 701 et seq. or 11 U.S.C.A. § 1301 et seq., respectively.

Effective and Applicability Provisions

2005 Acts. Amendments by Pub.L. 109–8 effective, except as otherwise provided, 180 days after April 20, 2005, and inapplicable with respect to cases commenced under Title 11 before the effective date, see Pub.L. 109–8, § 1501, set out as a note under 11 U.S.C.A. § 101.

1994 Acts. Amendment by Pub.L. 103–394 effective on Oct. 22, 1994, and not to apply with respect to cases commenced under Title 11 of the United States Code before Oct. 22, 1994, see section 702 of Pub.L. 103–394, set out as a note under section 101 of this title.

1984 Acts. Amendment by Pub.L. 98–353 effective with respect to cases filed 90 days after July 10, 1984, see section 552(a), formerly 553(a), of Pub.L. 98–353, set out as a note under section 101 of this title.

Separability of Provisions

If any provision of or amendment made by Pub.L. 103–394 or the application of such provision or amendment to any person or circumstance is held to be unconstitutional, the remaining provisions of and amendments made by Pub.L. 103–394 and the application of such provisions and amendments to any person or circumstance shall not be affected thereby, see section 701 of Pub.L. 103–394, set out as a note under section 101 of this title.

CROSS REFERENCES

Instructions in notice to customers, see 11 USCA § 765.

"Net equity" defined in relation to payments made by customers to trustee within 60 days after notice, see 11 USCA § 741.

Notice in—

Commodity broker liquidation cases, see 11 USCA § 762.

Investor protection liquidation proceedings, see 15 USCA § 78fff–2.

Stockbroker liquidation cases, see 11 USCA § 743.

§ 343. Examination of the debtor

The debtor shall appear and submit to examination under oath at the meeting of creditors under section 341(a) of this title. Creditors, any indenture trustee, any trustee or examiner in the case, or the United States trustee may examine the debtor. The United States trustee may administer the oath required under this section.

(Pub.L. 95–598, Nov. 6, 1978, 92 Stat. 2565; Pub.L. 98–353, Title III, § 436, July 10, 1984, 98 Stat. 370; Pub.L. 99–554, Title II, § 213, Oct. 27, 1986, 100 Stat. 3099.)

HISTORICAL AND STATUTORY NOTES

Revision Notes and Legislative Reports

1978 Acts. This section, derived from section 21a of the Bankruptcy Act [section 44(a) of former Title 11], requires the debtor to appear at the meeting of creditors and submit to examination under oath. The purpose of the examination is to enable creditors and the trustee to determine if assets have improperly been disposed of or concealed or if there are grounds for objection to discharge. The scope of the examination under this section will be governed by the Rules of Bankruptcy Procedure, as it is today. See rules 205(d), 10–213(c), and 11–26. It is expected that the scope prescribed by these rules for liquidation cases, that is, "only the debtor's acts, conduct, or property, or any matter that may affect the administration of the estate, or the debtor's right to discharge" will remain substantially unchanged. In reorganization cases, the examination would be broader, including inquiry into the liabilities and financial condition of the debtor, the operation of his business, and the desirability of the continuance thereof, and other matters relevant to the case and to the formulation of the plan. Examination of other persons in connection with the bankruptcy case is left completely to the rules, just as examination of witnesses in civil cases is governed by the Federal Rules of Civil Procedure. Senate Report No. 95–989.

1984 Acts. Statements by Legislative Leaders, see 1984 U.S.Code Cong. and Adm.News, p. 576.

1986 Acts. House Report No. 99–764 and House Conference Report No. 99–958, see 1986 U.S.Code Cong. and Adm.News, p. 5227.

Effective and Applicability Provisions

1986 Acts. Amendment by Pub.L. 99–554 effective 30 days after Oct. 27, 1986, except as otherwise provided for, see section 302(a) of Pub.L. 99–554, set out as a note under section 581 of Title 28, Judiciary and Judicial Procedure.

Amendment by Pub.L. 99–554, § 213, not to become effective in or with respect to certain specified judicial districts until, or apply to cases while pending in such district before, the expiration of the 270-day period beginning 30 days after Oct. 27, 1986, or of the 30-day period beginning on the date the Attorney General certifies under section 303 of Pub.L. 99–554 the region specified in a paragraph of section 581(a) of Title 28, as amended by section 111(a) of Pub.L. 99–554, that includes such district, whichever occurs first, see section 302(d)(1) of Pub.L. 99–554, set out as a note under section 581 of Title 28.

Amendment by Pub.L. 99–554, § 213, not to become effective in or with respect to certain specified judicial districts until, or apply to cases while pending in such district before, the expiration of the 2-year period beginning 30 days after Oct. 27, 1986, or of the 30-day period beginning on the date the Attorney General certifies under section 303 of Pub.L. 99–554 the region specified in a paragraph of section 581(a) of Title 28, as amended by section 111(a) of Pub.L. 99–554, that includes such district, whichever occurs first, see section 302(d)(2) of Pub.L. 99–554, set out as a note under section 581 of Title 28.

Amendment by Pub.L. 99–554, § 213, not to become effective in or with respect to judicial districts established for the States of Alabama and North Carolina until, or apply to cases while pending in such district before, such district elects to be included in a bankruptcy region established in section 581(a) of Title 28, as amended by section 111(a) of Pub.L. 99–554, or Oct. 1, 2002, whichever occurs first, and, except as otherwise provided for, with respect to cases under chapters 7, 11, 12, and 13 of Title 11 commenced before 30 days after Oct. 27, 1986, and pending in a judicial district in the States of Alabama or North Carolina before any election made under section 302(d)(3)(A) of Pub.L. 99–554 by such district becomes effective or Oct. 1, 2002, whichever occurs first, amendments by Pub.L. 99–554 not to apply until Oct. 1, 2003, or the expiration of the 1-year period beginning on the date such election becomes effective, whichever occurs first, and further, in any judicial district in Alabama or North Carolina not making the election described in section 302(d)(3)(A) of Pub.L. 99–554, any person appointed under regulations issued by the Judicial Conference to administer estates in cases under Title 11 authorized to establish, etc., a panel of private trustees, and to supervise cases and trustees in cases under chapters 7, 11, 12, and 13 of Title 11, until amendments by sections 201 to 231 of Pub.L. 99–554 effective in such district, see section 302(d)(3)(A) to (F), (H), and (I) of Pub.L. 99–554, set out as a note under section 581 of Title 28.

Amendment by Pub.L. 99–554, § 213, except as otherwise provided, with respect to cases under chapters 7, 11, 12, and 13 of Title 11 commenced before 30 days after Oct. 27, 1986, and pending in a judicial district referred to in section 581(a) of Title 28, as amended by section 111(a) of Pub.L. 99–554, for which a United States trustee is not authorized before 30 days after Oct. 27, 1986 to be appointed, not applicable until the expiration of the 3-year period beginning on Oct. 27, 1986, or of the 1-year period beginning on the date the Attorney General certifies under section 303 of Pub.L. 99–554 the region specified in a paragraph of such section 581(a) that includes, such district, whichever occurs first, see section 302(e)(1), (2) of Pub.L. 99–554, set out as a note under section 581 of Title 28.

1984 Acts. Amendment by Pub.L. 98–353 effective with respect to cases filed 90 days after July 10, 1984, see section 552(a), formerly 553(a), of Pub.L. 98–353, set out as a note under section 101 of this title.

Participation by Bankruptcy Administrator at Meetings of Creditors and Equity Security Holders

The bankruptcy administrator or the bankruptcy's designee may examine the debtor at the meeting of the creditors and may administer the oath required by this section, see section 105 of Pub.L. 103–394, set out as a note under section 341 of this title.

CROSS REFERENCES

Concealment of assets deemed continuing offense, see 18 USCA § 3284.

Concealment of assets; false oaths and claims, see 18 USCA § 152.

Inapplicability of this section in railroad reorganization cases, see 11 USCA § 1161.

§ 344. Self-incrimination; immunity

Immunity for persons required to submit to examination, to testify, or to provide information in a case under this title may be granted under part V of title 18.

(Pub.L. 95–598, Nov. 6, 1978, 92 Stat. 2565.)

HISTORICAL AND STATUTORY NOTES

Revision Notes and Legislative Reports

1978 Acts. Part V of title 18 of the United States Code [18 U.S.C.A. § 6001 et seq.] governs the granting of immunity to witnesses before Federal tribunals. The immunity provided under part V is only use immunity, not transactional immunity. Part V applies to all proceedings before Federal courts, before Federal grand juries, before administrative agencies, and before Congressional committees. It requires the Attorney General or the U.S. attorney to request or to approve any grant of immunity, whether before a court, grand jury, agency, or congressional committee.

This section carries part V over into bankruptcy cases. Thus, for a witness to be ordered to testify before a bankruptcy court in spite of a claim of privilege, the U.S. attorney for the district in which the court sits would have to request from the district court for that district the immunity order. The rule would apply to both debtors, creditors, and any other witnesses in a bankruptcy case. If the immunity were granted, the witness would be required to testify. If not, he could claim the privilege against self-incrimination.

Part V [section 6001 et seq. of Title 18, Crimes and Criminal Procedure] is a significant departure from current law. Under section 7a(10) of the Bankruptcy Act [section 25(a)(10) of former Title 11] a debtor is required to testify in all circumstances, but any testimony he gives may not be used against him in any criminal proceeding, except testimony given in any hearing on objections to discharge. With that exception, section 7a(10) amounts to a blanket grant of use immunity to all debtors. Immunity for other witnesses in bankruptcy courts today is governed by part V of title 18.

The consequences of a claim of privileges by a debtor under proposed law and under current law differ as well. Under section 14c(6) of current law [section 32(c)(6) of former Title 11], any refusal to answer a material question approved by the court will result in the denial of a discharge, even if the refusal is based on the privilege against self incrimination. Thus, the debtor is confronted with the choice between losing his discharge and opening himself up to possible criminal prosecution.

Under section 727(a)(6) of the proposed title 11, a debtor is only denied a discharge if he refuses to testify after having been granted immunity. If the debtor claims the privilege and the U.S. attorney does not request immunity from the district courts, then the debtor may refuse to testify and still retain his right to a discharge. It removes the Scylla and Charibdis choice for debtors that exists under the Bankruptcy Act [former Title 11]. Senate Report No. 95–989.

CROSS REFERENCES

Applicability of this section in chapter 9 cases, see 11 USCA § 901.

Debtor's duty to surrender records despite grant of immunity under this section, see 11 USCA § 521.

§ 345. Money of estates

(a) A trustee in a case under this title may make such deposit or investment of the money of the estate for which such trustee serves as will yield the maximum reasonable net return on such money, taking into account the safety of such deposit or investment.

(b) Except with respect to a deposit or investment that is insured or guaranteed by the United States or by a department, agency, or instrumentality of the United States or backed by the full faith and credit of the United States, the trustee shall require from an entity with which such money is deposited or invested—

(1) a bond—

(A) in favor of the United States;

(B) secured by the undertaking of a corporate surety approved by the United States trustee for the district in which the case is pending; and

(C) conditioned on—

(i) a proper accounting for all money so deposited or invested and for any return on such money;

(ii) prompt repayment of such money and return; and

(iii) faithful performance of duties as a depository; or

(2) the deposit of securities of the kind specified in section 9303 of title 31;

unless the court for cause orders otherwise.

(c) An entity with which such moneys are deposited or invested is authorized to deposit or invest such moneys as may be required under this section.

(Pub.L. 95–598, Nov. 6, 1978, 92 Stat. 2565; Pub.L. 97–258, § 3(c), Sept. 13, 1982, 96 Stat. 1064; Pub.L. 98–353, Title III, § 437, July 10, 1984, 98 Stat. 370; Pub.L. 99–554, Title II, § 214, Oct. 27, 1986, 100 Stat. 3099; Pub.L. 103–394, Title II, § 210, Oct. 22, 1994, 108 Stat. 4125.)

HISTORICAL AND STATUTORY NOTES

Revision Notes and Legislative Reports

1978 Acts. This section is a significant departure from section 61 of the Bankruptcy Act [section 101 of former Title 11]. It permits a trustee in a bankruptcy case to make such deposit of investment of the money of the estate for which he serves as will yield the maximum reasonable net return on the money, taking into account the safety of such deposit or investment. Under current law, the trustee is permitted to deposit money only with banking institutions. Thus, the trustee is generally unable to secure a high rate of return on money of estates pending distribution, to the detriment of creditors. Under this section, the trustee may make deposits in savings and loans, may purchase government bonds, or make such other deposit or investment as is appropriate. Under proposed 11 U.S.C. 541(a)(6), and except as provided in subsection (c) of this section, any interest or gain realized on the deposit or investment of funds under this section with become property of the estate, and will thus enhance the recovery of creditors.

In order to protect the creditors, subsection (b) requires certain precautions against loss of the money so deposited or invested. The trustee must require from a person with which he deposits or invests money of an estate a bond in favor of the United States secured by approved corporate surety and conditioned on a proper accounting for all money deposited or invested and for any return on such money.

Alternately, the trustee may require the deposit of securities of the kind specified in section 15 of title 6 of the United States Code [31 U.S.C.A. § 9303], which governs the posting of security by banks that receive public moneys on deposit. These bonding requirements do not apply to deposits or investments that are insured or guaranteed the United States or a department, agency, or instrumentality of the United States, or that are backed by the full faith and credit of the United States.

These provisions do not address the question of aggregation of funds by a private chapter 13 trustee and are not to be construed as excluding such possibility. The Rules of Bankruptcy Procedure may provide for aggregation under appropriate circumstances and adequate safeguards in cases where there is a significant need, such as in districts in which there is a standing chapter 13 trustee. In such case, the interest or return on the funds would help defray the cost of administering the cases in which the standing trustee serves. Senate Report No. 95–989.

1982 Acts. House Report No. 97–651, see 1982 U.S.Code Cong. and Adm.News, p. 1895.

1984 Acts. Statements by Legislative Leaders, see 1984 U.S.Code Cong. and Adm.News, p. 576.

1986 Acts. House Report No. 99–764 and House Conference Report No. 99–958, see 1986 U.S.Code Cong. and Adm.News, p. 5227.

1994 Acts. House Report No. 103–835, see 1994 U.S. Code Cong. and Adm. News, p. 3340.

Legislative Statements

The House amendment moves section 345(c) of the House bill to chapter 15 as part of the pilot program for the U.S. trustees. The bond required by section 345(b) may be a blanket bond posted by the financial depository sufficient to cover deposits by trustees in several cases, as is done under current law.

Effective and Applicability Provisions

1994 Acts. Amendment by Pub.L. 103–394 effective on Oct. 22, 1994, and not to apply with respect to cases commenced under Title 11 of the United States Code before Oct. 22, 1994, see section 702 of Pub.L. 103–394, set out as a note under section 101 of this title.

1986 Acts. Amendment by Pub.L. 99–554 effective 30 days after Oct. 27, 1986, except as otherwise provided for, see section 302(a) of Pub.L. 99–554, set out as a note under section 581 of Title 28, Judiciary and Judicial Procedure.

Amendment by Pub.L. 99–554, § 214, not to become effective in or with respect to certain specified judicial districts until, or apply to cases while pending in such district before, the expiration of the 270-day period beginning 30 days after Oct. 27, 1986, or of the 30-day period beginning on the date the Attorney General certifies under section 303 of Pub.L. 99–554 the region specified in a paragraph of section 581(a) of Title 28, as amended by section 111(a) of Pub.L. 99–554, that includes such district, whichever occurs first, see section 302(d)(1) of Pub.L. 99–554, set out as a note under section 581 of Title 28.

Amendment by Pub.L. 99–554, § 214, not to become effective in or with respect to certain specified judicial districts until, or apply to cases while pending in such district before, the expiration of the 2-year period beginning 30 days after Oct. 27, 1986, or of the 30-day period beginning on the date the Attorney General certifies under section 303 of Pub.L. 99–554 the region specified in a paragraph of section 581(a) of Title 28, as amended by section 111(a) of Pub.L. 99–554, that includes such district, whichever occurs first, see section 302(d)(2) of Pub.L. 99–554, set out as a note under section 581 of Title 28.

Amendment by Pub.L. 99–554, § 214, not to become effective in or with respect to judicial districts established for the States of Alabama and North Carolina until, or apply to cases while pending in such district before, such district elects to be included in a bankruptcy region established in section 581(a) of Title 28, as amended by section 111(a) of Pub.L. 99–554, or Oct. 1, 2002, whichever occurs first, and except as otherwise provided, with respect to cases under chapters 7, 11, 12, and 13 of Title 11 commenced before 30 days after Oct. 27, 1986, and pending in a judicial district in the States of Alabama or North Carolina before any election made under section 302(d)(3)(A) of Pub.L. 99–554 by such district becomes effective or Oct. 1, 2002, whichever occurs first, amendments by Pub.L. 99–554 not to apply until Oct. 1, 2003, or the expiration of the 1-year period beginning on the date such election becomes effective, whichever occurs first, and further, in any judicial district in Alabama or North Carolina not making the election described in section 302(d)(3)(A) of Pub.L. 99–554, any person appointed under regulations issued by the Judicial Conference to administer estates in cases under Title 11 authorized to establish, etc., a panel of private trustees, and to supervise cases and trustees in cases under chapters 7, 11, 12, and 13 of Title 11, until amendments by sections 201 to 231 of Pub.L. 99–554 effective in such district, see section 302(d)(3)(A) to (F), (H), and (I) of Pub.L. 99–554, set out as a note under section 581 of Title 28.

Amendment by Pub.L. 99–554, § 214, except as otherwise provided, with respect to cases under chapters 7, 11, 12, and 13 of Title 11 commenced before 30 days after Oct. 27, 1986, and pending in a judicial district referred to in section 581(a) of Title 28, as amended by section 111(a) of Pub.L. 99–554, for which a United States trustee is not authorized before 30 days after Oct. 27, 1986, to be appointed, not applicable until the expiration of the 3-year period beginning on Oct. 27, 1986, or of the 1-year period beginning on the date the Attorney General certifies under section 303 of Pub.L. 99–554 the region specified in a paragraph of such section 581(a) that includes, such district, whichever occurs first, see section 302(e)(1), (2) of Pub.L. 99–554, set out as a note under section 581 of Title 28.

1984 Acts. Amendment by Pub.L. 98–353 effective with respect to cases filed 90 days after July 10, 1984, see section 552(a), formerly 553(a), of Pub.L. 98–353, set out as a note under section 101 of this title.

Separability of Provisions

If any provision of or amendment made by Pub.L. 103–394 or the application of such provision or amendment to any person or circumstance is held to be unconstitutional, the remaining provisions of and amendments made by Pub.L. 103–394 and the application of such provisions and amendments to any person or circumstance shall not be affected thereby, see section 701 of Pub.L. 103–394, set out as a note under section 101 of this title.

CROSS REFERENCES

Adverse interest and conduct of officers of estate, see 18 USCA § 154.

Duty of United States trustee to deposit or invest money, see 28 USCA § 586.

Embezzlement by trustee, see 18 USCA § 153.

§ 346. Special provisions related to the treatment of State and local taxes

(a) Whenever the Internal Revenue Code of 1986 provides that a separate taxable estate or entity is created in a case concerning a debtor under this title, and the income, gain, loss, deductions, and credits of such estate shall be taxed to or claimed by the estate, a separate taxable estate is also created for purposes of any State and local law imposing a tax on or measured by income and such income, gain, loss, deductions, and credits shall be taxed to or claimed by the estate and may not be taxed to or claimed by the debtor. The preceding sentence shall not apply if the case is dismissed. The trustee shall make tax returns of income required under any such State or local law.

(b) Whenever the Internal Revenue Code of 1986 provides that no separate taxable estate shall be created in a case concerning a debtor under this title, and the income, gain, loss, deductions, and credits of an estate shall be taxed to or claimed by the debtor, such income, gain, loss, deductions, and credits shall be taxed to or claimed by the debtor under a State or local law imposing a tax on or measured by income and may not be taxed to or claimed by the estate. The trustee shall make such tax returns of income of corporations and of partnerships as are required under any State or local law, but with respect to partnerships, shall make such returns only to the extent such returns are also required to be made under such Code. The estate shall be liable for any tax imposed on such corporation or partnership, but not for any tax imposed on partners or members.

(c) With respect to a partnership or any entity treated as a partnership under a State or local law imposing a tax on or measured by income that is a debtor in a case under this title, any gain or loss resulting from a distribution of property from such partnership, or any distributive share of any income, gain, loss, deduction, or credit of a partner or member that is distributed, or considered distributed, from such partnership, after the commencement of the case, is gain, loss, income, deduction, or credit, as the case may be, of the partner or member, and if such partner or member is a debtor in a case under this title, shall be subject to tax in accordance with subsection (a) or (b).

(d) For purposes of any State or local law imposing a tax on or measured by income, the taxable period of a debtor in a case under this title shall terminate only if and to the extent that the taxable period of such debtor terminates under the Internal Revenue Code of 1986.

(e) The estate in any case described in subsection (a) shall use the same accounting method as the debtor used immediately before the commencement of the case, if such method of accounting complies with applicable nonbankruptcy tax law.

(f) For purposes of any State or local law imposing a tax on or measured by income, a transfer of property from the debtor to the estate or from the estate to the debtor shall not be treated as a disposition for purposes of any provision assigning tax consequences to a disposition, except to the extent that such transfer is treated as a disposition under the Internal Revenue Code of 1986.

(g) Whenever a tax is imposed pursuant to a State or local law imposing a tax on or measured by income pursuant to subsection (a) or (b), such tax shall be imposed at rates generally applicable to the same types of entities under such State or local law.

(h) The trustee shall withhold from any payment of claims for wages, salaries, commissions, dividends, interest, or other payments, or collect, any amount required to be withheld or collected under applicable State or local tax law, and shall pay such withheld or collected amount to the appropriate governmental unit at the time and in the manner required by such tax law, and with the same priority as the claim from which such amount was withheld or collected was paid.

(i)(1) To the extent that any State or local law imposing a tax on or measured by income provides for the carryover of any tax attribute from one taxable period to a subsequent taxable period, the estate shall succeed to such tax attribute in any case in which such estate is subject to tax under subsection (a).

(2) After such a case is closed or dismissed, the debtor shall succeed to any tax attribute to which the estate succeeded under paragraph (1) to the extent consistent with the Internal Revenue Code of 1986.

(3) The estate may carry back any loss or tax attribute to a taxable period of the debtor that ended before the date of the order for relief under this title to the extent that—

(A) applicable State or local tax law provides for a carryback in the case of the debtor; and

(B) the same or a similar tax attribute may be carried back by the estate to such a taxable period of the debtor under the Internal Revenue Code of 1986.

(j)(1) For purposes of any State or local law imposing a tax on or measured by income, income is not realized by the estate, the debtor, or a successor to the debtor by reason of discharge of indebtedness in a case under this title, except to the extent, if any, that such income is subject to tax under the Internal Revenue Code of 1986.

(2) Whenever the Internal Revenue Code of 1986 provides that the amount excluded from gross income in respect of the discharge of indebtedness in a case under this title shall be applied to reduce the tax attributes of the debtor or the estate, a similar reduction shall be made under any State or local law imposing a tax on or measured by income to the extent such State or local law recognizes such attributes. Such State or local law may also provide for the reduction of other attributes to the extent that the full amount of income from the discharge of indebtedness has not been applied.

(k)(1) Except as provided in this section and section 505, the time and manner of filing tax returns and the items of income, gain, loss, deduction, and credit of any taxpayer shall be determined under applicable nonbankruptcy law.

(2) For Federal tax purposes, the provisions of this section are subject to the Internal Revenue Code of 1986 and other applicable Federal nonbankruptcy law.

(Pub.L. 95–598, Nov. 6, 1978, 92 Stat. 2565; Pub.L. 98–353, Title III, § 438, July 10, 1984, 98 Stat. 370; Pub.L. 99–514, § 2, Oct. 22, 1986, 100 Stat. 2095; Pub.L. 99–554, Title II, §§ 257(g), 283(c), Oct. 27, 1986, 100 Stat. 3114, 3116; Pub.L. 103–394, Title V, § 501(d)(4), Oct. 22, 1994, 108 Stat. 4143; Pub.L. 109–8, Title VII, § 719(a)(1), Apr. 20, 2005, 119 Stat. 131.)

HISTORICAL AND STATUTORY NOTES

Revision Notes and Legislative Reports

1978 Acts. Subsection (a) indicates that subsections (b), (c), (d), (e), (g), (h), (i), and (j) apply notwithstanding any State or local tax law, but are subject to Federal tax law.

Subsection (b)(1) provides that in a case concerning an individual under chapter 7 or 11 of title 11, income of the estate is taxable only to the estate and not to the debtor. The second sentence of the paragraph provides that if such individual is a partner, the tax attributes of the partnership are distributable to the partner's estate rather than to the partner, except to the extent that section 728 of title 11 provides otherwise.

Subsection (b)(2) states a general rule that the estate of an individual is to be taxed as an estate. The paragraph is made subject to the remainder of section 346 and section 728 of title 11.

Subsection (b)(3) requires the accounting method, but not necessarily the accounting period, of the estate to be the same as the method used by the individual debtor.

Subsection (c)(1) states a general rule that the estate of a partnership or a corporated debtor is not a separate entity for tax purposes. The income of the debtor is to be taxed as if the case were not commenced, except as provided in the remainder of section 346 and section 728.

Subsection (c)(2) requires the trustee, except as provided in section 728 of title 11, to file all tax returns on behalf of the partnership or corporation during the case.

Subsection (d) indicates that the estate in a chapter 13 case is not a separate taxable entity and that all income of the estate is to be taxed to the debtor.

Subsection (e) establishes a business deduction consisting of allowed expenses of administration except for tax or capital expenses that are not otherwise deductible. The deduction may be used by the estate when it is a separate taxable entity or by the entity to which the income of the estate is taxed when it is not.

Subsection (f) imposes a duty on the trustee to comply with any Federal, State, or local tax law requiring withholding or collection of taxes from any payment of wages, salaries, commissions, dividends, interest, or other payments. Any amount withheld is to be paid to the taxing authority at the same time and with the same priority as the claim from which such amount withheld was paid.

Subsection (g)(1)(A) indicates that neither gain nor loss is recognized on the transfer by law of property from the debtor or a creditor to the estate. Subparagraph (B) provides a similar policy if the property of the estate is returned from the estate to the debtor other than by a sale of property to debtor. Subparagraph (C) also provides for nonrecognition of gain or loss in a case under chapter 11 if a corporate debtor transfers property to a successor corporation or to an affiliate under a joint plan. An exception is made to enable a taxing authority to cause recognition of gain or loss to the extent provided in IRC section 371 (as amended by section 109 of this bill) [section 371 of Title 26, Internal Revenue Code].

Subsection (g)(2) provides that any of the three kinds of transferees specified in paragraph (1) take the property with the same character, holding period, and basis in the hands of the transferor at the time of such transfer. The transferor's basis may be adjusted under section 346(j)(5) even if the discharge of indebtedness occurs after the transfer of property. Of course, no adjustment will occur if the transfer is from the debtor to the estate or if the transfer is from an entity that is not discharged.

Subsection (h) provides that the creation of the estate of an individual under chapter 7 or 11 of title 11 as a separate taxable entity does not affect the number of taxable years for purposes of computing loss carryovers or carrybacks. The section applies with respect to carryovers or carrybacks of the debtor transferred into the estate under section 346(i)(1) of title 11 or back to the debtor under section 346(i)(2) of title 11.

Subsection (i)(1) states a general rule that an estate that is a separate taxable entity nevertheless succeeds to all tax attributes of the debtor. The six enumerated attributes are illustrative and not exhaustive.

Subsection (i)(2) indicates that attributes passing from the debtor into an estate that is a separate taxable entity will return to the debtor if unused by the estate. The debtor is permitted to use any such attribute as though the case had not been commenced.

Subsection (i)(3) permits an estate that is a separate taxable entity to carryback losses of the estate to a taxable period of the debtor that ended before the case was filed. The estate is treated as if it were the debtor with respect to time limitations and other restrictions. The section makes clear that the debtor may not carryback any loss of his own from a tax year during the pendency of the case to such a period until the case is closed. No tolling of any period of limitation is provided with respect to carrybacks by the debtor of post-petition losses.

Subsection (j) sets forth seven special rules treating with the tax effects of forgiveness or discharge of indebtedness. The terms "forgiveness" and "discharge" are redundant, but are used to clarify that "discharge" in the context of a special tax provision in title 11 includes forgiveness of indebtedness whether or not such indebtedness is "discharged" in the bankruptcy sense.

Paragraph (1) states the general rule that forgiveness of indebtedness is not taxable except as otherwise provided in paragraphs (2)–(7). The paragraph is patterned after sections 268, 395, and 520 of the Bankruptcy Act [sections 668, 795 and 920 of former Title 11].

Paragraph (2) disallows deductions for liabilities of a deductible nature in any year during or after the year of cancellation of such liabilities. For the purposes of this paragraph, "a deduction with respect to a liability" includes a capital loss incurred on the disposition of a capital asset with respect to a liability that was incurred in connection with the acquisition of such asset.

Paragraph (3) causes any net operating loss of a debtor that is an individual or corporation to be reduced by any discharge of indebtedness except as provided in paragraphs (2) or (4). If a deduction is disallowed under paragraph (2), then no double counting occurs. Thus, paragraph (3) will reflect the reduction of losses by liabilities that have been forgiven, including deductible liabilities or nondeductible liabilities such as repayment of principal on borrowed funds.

Paragraph (4) specifically excludes two kinds of indebtedness from reduction of net operating losses under paragraph (3) or from reduction of basis under paragraph (5). Subparagraph (A) excludes items of a deductible nature that were not deducted or that could not be deducted such as gambling losses or liabilities for interest owed to a relative of the debtor. Subparagraph (B) excludes indebtedness of a debtor that is an individual or corporation that resulted in deductions which did not offset income and that did not contribute to an unexpired net operating loss or loss carryover. In these situations, the debtor has derived no tax benefit so there is no need to incur an offsetting reduction.

Paragraph (5) provides a two-point test for reduction of basis. The paragraph replaces sections 270, 396, and 522 of the Bankruptcy Act [sections 670, 796, and 922 of former Title 11]. Subparagraph (A) sets out the maximum amount by which basis may be reduced—the total indebtedness forgiven less adjustments made under paragraphs (2) and (3). This avoids double counting. If a deduction is disallowed under paragraph (2) or a carryover is reduced under paragraph (3) then the tax benefit is neutralized, and there is no need to reduce basis. Subparagraph (B) reduces basis to the extent the debtor's total basis of assets before the discharge exceeds total preexisting liabilities still remaining after discharge of indebtedness. This is a "basis solvency" limitation which differs from the usual test of solvency because it measures against the remaining liabilities the benefit aspect of assets, their basis, rather than their value. Paragraph (5) applies so that any transferee of the debtor's property who is required to use the debtor's basis takes the debtor's basis reduced by the lesser of (A) and (B). Thus, basis will be reduced, but never below a level equal to undischarged liabilities.

Paragraph (6) specifies that basis need not be reduced under paragraph (5) to the extent the debtor treats discharged indebtedness as taxable income. This permits the debtor to elect whether to recognize income, which may be advantageous if the debtor anticipates subsequent net operating losses, rather than to reduce basis.

Paragraph (7) establishes two rules excluding from the category of discharged indebtedness certain indebtedness that is exchanged for an equity security issued under a plan or that is forgiven as a contribution to capital by an equity security holder. Subparagraph (A) creates the first exclusion to the extent indebtedness consisting of items not of a deductible nature is exchanged for an equity security, other than the interests of a limited partner in a limited partnership, issued by the debtor or is forgiven as a contribution to capital by an equity security holder. Subparagraph (B) excludes indebtedness consisting of items of a deductible nature, if the exchange of stock for debts has the same effect as a cash payment equal to the value of the equity security, in the amount of the fair market value of the equity security or, if less, the extent to which such exchange has such effect. The two provisions treat the debtor as if it had originally issued stock instead of debt. Subparagraph (B) rectifies the inequity under current law between a cash basis and accrual basis debtor concerning the issuance of stock in exchange for previous services rendered that were of a greater value than the stock. Subparagraph (B) also changes current law by taxing forgiveness of indebtedness to the extent that stock is exchanged for the accrued interest component of a security, because the recipient of such stock would not be regarded as having received money under the *Carman* doctrine. Senate Report No. 95-989.

1984 Acts. Statements by Legislative Leaders, see 1984 U.S.Code Cong. and Adm.News, p. 576.

1986 Acts. House Report No. 99-764 and House Conference Report No. 99-958, see 1986 U.S.Code Cong. and Adm.News, p. 5227.

1994 Acts. House Report No. 103-835, see 1994 U.S. Code Cong. and Adm. News, p. 3340.

2005 Acts. House Report No. 109-31(Part I), see 2005 U.S. Code Cong. and Adm. News, p. 88.

Legislative Statements

Section 346 of the House amendment, together with sections 728 and 1146, represent special tax provisions applicable in bankruptcy. The policy contained in those sections reflects the policy that should he applied in Federal, State, and local taxes in the view of the House Committee on the Judiciary. The House Ways and Means Committee and the Senate Finance Committee did not have time to process a bankruptcy tax bill during the 95th Congress. It is anticipated that early in the 96th Congress, and before the effective date of the bankruptcy code [Oct. 1, 1979], the tax committees of Congress will have an opportunity to consider action with respect to amendments to the Internal Revenue Code [Title 26] and the special tax provisions in title 11. Since the special tax provisions are likely to be amended during the first part of the 96th Congress, it is anticipated that the bench and bar will also study and comment on these special tax provisions prior to their revision.

Special tax provisions: State and local rules. This section provides special tax provisions dealing with the treatment, under State or local, but not Federal, tax law, of the method of taxing bankruptcy estates of individuals, partnerships, and corporations; survival and allocation of tax attributes between the bankrupt and the estate; return filing requirements; and the tax treatment of income from discharge of indebtedness. The Senate bill removed these rules pending adoption of Federal rules on these issues in the next Congress. The House amendment returns the State and local tax rules to section 346 so that they may be studied by the bankruptcy and tax bars who may wish to submit comments to Congress.

Withholding rules: Both the House bill and Senate amendment provide that the trustee is required to comply with the normal withholding rules applicable to the payment of wages and other payments. The House amendment retains this rule for State and local taxes only. The treatment of withholding of Federal taxes will be considered in the next Congress.

Section 726 of the Senate amendment provides that the rule requiring pro rata payment of all expenses within a priority category does not apply to the payment of amounts withheld by a bankruptcy trustee. The purpose of this rule was to insure that the trustee pay the full amount of the withheld taxes to the appropriate governmental tax authority. The House amendment deletes this rule as unnecessary because the existing practice conforms essentially to that rule. If the trustee fails to pay over in full amounts that he withheld, it is a violation of his trustee's duties which would permit the taxing authority to sue the trustee on his bond.

When taxes considered "incurred": The Senate amendment contained rules of general application dealing with when a tax is "incurred" for purposes of the various tax collection rules affecting the debtor and the estate. The House amendment adopts the substance of these rules and transfers them to section 507 of title 11.

Penalty for failure to pay tax: The Senate amendment contains a rule which relieves the debtor and the trustee from certain tax penalties for failure to make timely payment of a tax to the extent that the bankruptcy rules prevent the trustee or the debtor from paying the tax on time. Since most of these penalties relate to Federal taxes, the House amendment deletes these rules pending consideration of Federal tax rules affecting bankruptcy in the next Congress.

References in Text

The Internal Revenue Code of 1986, referred to in text, is classified to Title 26 of the Code.

Codifications

Amendment of subsecs. (a) and (g)(1)(C) by section 501(d)(4) of Pub.L. 103–394, which directed the substitution of "Internal Revenue Code of 1986" for "Internal Revenue Code of 1954 (26 U.S.C. 1 et seq.)" and "Internal Revenue Code of 1986" for "Internal Revenue Code of 1954 (26 U.S.C. 371)" was executed by deleting the parenthetical references only, as the probable intent of Congress. Prior substitution of "Internal Revenue Code of 1986" for "Internal Revenue Code of 1954" was executed pursuant to section 2 of Pub.L. 99–514.

Effective and Applicability Provisions

2005 Acts. Amendments by Pub.L. 109–8 effective, except as otherwise provided, 180 days after April 20, 2005, and inapplicable with respect to cases commenced under Title 11 before the effective date, see Pub.L. 109–8, § 1501, set out as a note under 11 U.S.C.A. § 101.

1994 Acts. Amendment by of Pub.L. 103–394 effective on Oct. 22, 1994, and not to apply with respect to cases commenced under Title 11 of the United States Code before Oct. 22, 1994, see section 702 of Pub.L. 103–394, set out as a note under section 101 of this title.

1986 Acts. Amendment by Pub.L. 99–554, § 257(g), effective 30 days after Oct. 27, 1986, but not applicable with respect to cases commenced under this title before that date, see section 302(a), (c)(1) of Pub.L. 99–554, set out as a note under section 581 of Title 28, Judiciary and Judicial Procedure.

Amendment by Pub.L. 99–554, § 283(c), effective 30 days after Oct. 27, 1986, see section 302(a) of Pub.L. 99–554, set out as a note under section 581 of Title 28.

1984 Acts. Amendment by Pub.L. 98–353 effective with respect to cases filed 90 days after July 10, 1984, see section 552(a), formerly 553(a), of Pub.L. 98–353, set out as a note under section 101 of this title.

Separability of Provisions

If any provision of or amendment made by Pub.L. 103–394 or the application of such provision or amendment to any person or circumstance is held to be unconstitutional, the remaining provisions of and amendments made by Pub.L. 103–394 and the application of such provisions and amendments to any person or circumstance shall not be affected thereby, see section 701 of Pub.L. 103–394, set out as a note under section 101 of this title.

CROSS REFERENCES

Request for determination of tax effects of—

Chapter 12 plan, see 11 USCA § 1231.

Reorganization plan, see 11 USCA § 1146.

§ 347. Unclaimed property

(a) Ninety days after the final distribution under section 726, 1226, or 1326 of this title in a case under chapter 7, 12, or 13 of this title, as the case may be, the trustee shall stop payment on any check remaining unpaid, and any remaining property of the estate shall be paid into the court and disposed of under chapter 129 of title 28.

(b) Any security, money, or other property remaining unclaimed at the expiration of the time allowed in a case under chapter 9, 11, or 12 of this title for the presentation of a security or the performance of any other act as a condition to participation in the distribution under any plan confirmed under section 943(b), 1129, 1173, or 1225 of this title, as the case may be, becomes the property of the debtor or of the entity acquiring the assets of the debtor under the plan, as the case may be.

(Pub.L. 95–598, Nov. 6, 1978, 92 Stat. 2568; Pub.L. 99–554, Title II, § 257(h), Oct. 27, 1986, 100 Stat. 3114.)

HISTORICAL AND STATUTORY NOTES

Revision Notes and Legislative Reports

1978 Acts. Section 347 is derived from Bankruptcy Act § 66 [section 106 of former Title 11]. Subsection (a) requires the trustee to stop payment on any distribution check that is unpaid 90 days after the final distribution in a case under chapter 7 or 13. The unclaimed funds, and any other property of the estate are paid into the court and disposed of under chapter 129 of title 28 [section 2041 et seq. of Title 28, Judiciary and Judicial Procedure], which requires the clerk of court to hold the funds for their owner for 5 years, after which they escheat to the Treasury.

Subsection (b) specifies that any property remaining unclaimed at the expiration of the time allowed in a chapter 9 or 11 case for presentation (exchange) of securities or the performance of any other act as a condition to participation in the plan reverts to the debtor or the entity acquiring the assets of the debtor under the plan. Conditions to participation under a plan include such acts as cashing a check, surrendering securities for cancellation, and so on. Similar provisions are found in sections 96(d) and 205 [sections 416(d) and 605 of former Title 11] of current law. Senate Report No. 95–989.

1986 Acts. House Report No. 99–764 and House Conference Report No. 99–958, see 1986 U.S.Code Cong. and Adm.News, p. 5227.

Legislative Statements

Section 347(a) of the House amendment adopts a comparable provision contained in the Senate amendment instructing the trustee to stop payment on any check remaining unpaid more than 90 days after the final distribution in a case under Chapter 7 or 13. Technical changes are made in section 347(b) to cover distributions in a railroad reorganization.

Effective and Applicability Provisions

1986 Acts. Amendment by Pub.L. 99–554, § 257(h), effective 30 days after Oct. 27, 1986, but not applicable with respect to cases commenced under this title before that date, see section 302(a), (c)(1) of Pub.L. 99–554, set out as a note under section 581 of Title 28, Judiciary and Judicial Procedure.

CROSS REFERENCES

Applicability of subsec. (b) of this section in Chapter 9 cases, see 11 USCA § 901.

Applicability of this section in Chapter 9 cases, see 11 USCA § 901.

"Creditor" defined, see 11 USCA § 101.

§ 348. Effect of conversion

(a) Conversion of a case from a case under one chapter of this title to a case under another chapter of this title constitutes an order for relief under the chapter to which the case is converted, but, except as provided in subsections (b) and (c) of this section, does not effect a change in the date of the filing of the petition, the commencement of the case, or the order for relief.

(b) Unless the court for cause orders otherwise, in sections 701(a), 727(a)(10), 727(b), 728(a), 728(b), 1102(a), 1110(a)(1), 1121(b), 1121(c), 1141(d)(4), 1146(a), 1146(b), 1201(a), 1221, 1228(a), 1301(a), and 1305(a) of this title, "the order for relief under this chapter" in a chapter to which a case has been converted under section 706, 1112, 1208, or 1307 of this title means the conversion of such case to such chapter.

(c) Sections 342 and 365(d) of this title apply in a case that has been converted under section 706, 1112, 1208, or 1307 of this title, as if the conversion order were the order for relief.

(d) A claim against the estate or the debtor that arises after the order for relief but before conversion in a case that is converted under section 1112, 1208, or 1307 of this title, other than a claim specified in section 503(b) of this title, shall be treated for all purposes as if such claim had arisen immediately before the date of the filing of the petition.

(e) Conversion of a case under section 706, 1112, 1208, or 1307 of this title terminates the service of any trustee or examiner that is serving in the case before such conversion.

(f)(1) Except as provided in paragraph (2), when a case under chapter 13 of this title is converted to a case under another chapter under this title—

(A) property of the estate in the converted case shall consist of property of the estate, as of the date of filing of the petition, that remains in the possession of or is under the control of the debtor on the date of conversion;

(B) valuations of property and of allowed secured claims in the chapter 13 case shall apply only in a case converted to a case under chapter 11 or 12, but not in a case converted to a case under chapter 7, with allowed secured claims in cases under chapters 11 and 12 reduced to the extent that they have been paid in accordance with the chapter 13 plan; and

(C) with respect to cases converted from chapter 13—

(i) the claim of any creditor holding security as of the date of the petition shall continue to be secured by that security unless the full amount of such claim determined under applicable nonbankruptcy law has been paid in full as of the date of conversion, notwithstanding any valuation or determination of the amount of an allowed secured claim made for the purposes of the case under chapter 13; and

(ii) unless a prebankruptcy default has been fully cured under the plan at the time of conversion, in any proceeding under this title or otherwise, the default shall have the effect given under applicable nonbankruptcy law.

(2) If the debtor converts a case under chapter 13 of this title to a case under another chapter under this

title in bad faith, the property of the estate in the converted case shall consist of the property of the estate as of the date of conversion.

(Pub.L. 95–598, Nov. 6, 1978, 92 Stat. 2568; Pub.L. 99–554, Title II, § 257(i), Oct. 27, 1986, 100 Stat. 3115; Pub.L. 103–394, Title III, § 311, Title V, § 501(d)(5), Oct. 22, 1994, 108 Stat. 4138, 4144; Pub.L. 109–8, Title III, § 309(a), Title XII, § 1207, Apr. 20, 2005, 119 Stat. 82, 194.)

HISTORICAL AND STATUTORY NOTES

Revision Notes and Legislative Reports

1978 Acts. This section governs the effect of the conversion of a case from one chapter of the bankruptcy code to another chapter. Subsection (a) specifies that the date of the filing of the petition, the commencement of the case, or the order for relief are unaffected by conversion, with some exceptions specified in subsections (b) and (c).

Subsection (b) lists certain sections in the operative chapters of the bankruptcy code in which there is a reference to "the order for relief under this chapter." In those sections, the reference is to be read as a reference to the conversion order if the case has been converted into the particular chapter. Subsection (c) specifies that notice is to be given of the conversion order the same as notice was given of the order for relief, and that the time the trustee (or debtor in possession) has for assuming or rejecting executory contracts recommences, thus giving an opportunity for a newly appointed trustee to familiarize himself with the case.

Subsection (d) provides for special treatment of claims that arise during chapter 11 or 13 cases before the case is converted to a liquidation case. With the exception of claims specified in proposed 11 U.S.C. 503(b) (administrative expenses), preconversion claims are treated the same as prepetition claims.

Subsection (e) provides that conversion of a case terminates the service of any trustee serving in the case prior to conversion. Senate Report No. 95–989.

1986 Acts. House Report No. 99–764 and House Conference Report No. 99–958, see 1986 U.S.Code Cong. and Adm.News, p. 5227.

1994 Acts. House Report No. 103–835, see 1994 U.S. Code Cong. and Adm. News, p. 3340.

2005 Acts. House Report No. 109–31(Part I), see 2005 U.S. Code Cong. and Adm. News, p. 88.

Legislative Statements

The House amendment adopts section 348(b) of the Senate amendment with slight modifications, as more accurately reflecting sections to which this particular effect of conversion should apply.

Section 348(e) of the House amendment is a stylistic revision of similar provisions contained in H.R. 8200 as passed by the House and in the Senate amendment. Termination of services is expanded to cover any examiner serving in the case before conversion, as done in H.R. 8200 as passed by the House.

References in Text

1146(a), (b) of this title, referred to in subsec. (b), was repealed by Pub.L. 109–8, Title VII, § 719(b)(3), Apr. 20, 2005, 119 Stat. 133, which also redesignated former subsecs. (c) and (d) of 11 U.S.C.A. § 1146 as subsecs. (a) and (b) of 11 U.S.C.A. § 1146.

Section 728 of this title, referred to in subsec. (b), was repealed by Pub.L. 109–8, Title VII, § 719(b)(1), Apr. 20, 2005, 119 Stat. 133.

Chapter 7, 11, 12, or 13, referred to in subsec. (f)(1), is chapter 7, 11, 12, or 13 of this title, 11 U.S.C.A. § 701 et seq., 11 U.S.C.A. § 1101 et seq., 11 U.S.C.A. § 1201 et seq., or 11 U.S.C.A. § 1301 et seq., respectively.

Effective and Applicability Provisions

2005 Acts. Amendments by Pub.L. 109–8 effective, except as otherwise provided, 180 days after April 20, 2005, and inapplicable with respect to cases commenced under Title 11 before the effective date, see Pub.L. 109–8, § 1501, set out as a note under 11 U.S.C.A. § 101.

1994 Acts. Amendments by Pub.L. 103–394 effective on Oct. 22, 1994, and not to apply with respect to cases commenced under Title 11 of the United States Code before Oct. 22, 1994, see section 702 of Pub.L. 103–394, set out as a note under section 101 of this title.

1986 Acts. Amendment by Pub.L. 99–554, effective 30 days after Oct. 27, 1986, but not applicable with respect to cases commenced under this title before that date see section 302(a), (c)(1) of Pub.L. 99–554, set out as a note under section 581 of Title 28, Judiciary and Judicial Procedure.

Separability of Provisions

If any provision of or amendment made by Pub.L. 103–394 or the application of such provision or amendment to any person or circumstance is held to be unconstitutional, the remaining provisions of and amendments made by Pub.L. 103–394 and the application of such provisions and amendments to any person or circumstance shall not be affected thereby, see section 701 of Pub.L. 103–394, set out as a note under section 101 of this title.

§ 349. Effect of dismissal

(a) Unless the court, for cause, orders otherwise, the dismissal of a case under this title does not bar the discharge, in a later case under this title, of debts that were dischargeable in the case dismissed; nor does the dismissal of a case under this title prejudice the debtor with regard to the filing of a subsequent petition under this title, except as provided in section 109(g) of this title.

(b) Unless the court, for cause, orders otherwise, a dismissal of a case other than under section 742 of this title—

(1) reinstates—

(A) any proceeding or custodianship superseded under section 543 of this title;

(B) any transfer avoided under section 522, 544, 545, 547, 548, 549, or 724(a) of this title, or preserved under section 510(c)(2), 522(i)(2), or 551 of this title; and

(C) any lien voided under section 506(d) of this title;

(2) vacates any order, judgment, or transfer ordered, under section 522(i)(1), 542, 550, or 553 of this title; and

(3) revests the property of the estate in the entity in which such property was vested immediately before the commencement of the case under this title.

(Pub.L. 95–598, Nov. 6, 1978, 92 Stat. 2569; Pub.L. 98–353, Title III, § 303, July 10, 1984, 98 Stat. 352; Pub.L. 103–394, Title V, § 501(d)(6), Oct. 22, 1994, 108 Stat. 4144.)

HISTORICAL AND STATUTORY NOTES

Revision Notes and Legislative Reports

1978 Acts. Subsection (a) specifies that unless the court for cause orders otherwise, the dismissal of a case is without prejudice. The debtor is not barred from receiving a discharge in a later case of debts that were dischargeable in the case dismissed. Of course, this subsection refers only to pre-discharge dismissals. If the debtor has already received a discharge and it is not revoked, then the debtor would be barred under section 727(a) from receiving a discharge in a subsequent liquidation case for six years. Dismissal of an involuntary [sic] on the merits will generally not give rise to adequate cause so as to bar the debtor from further relief.

Subsection (b) specifies that the dismissal reinstates proceedings or custodianships that were superseded by the bankruptcy case, reinstates avoided transfers, reinstates voided liens, vacates any order, judgment, or transfer ordered as a result of the avoidance of a transfer, and revests the property of the estate in the entity in which the property was vested at the commencement of the case. The court is permitted to order a different result for cause. The basic purpose of the subsection is to undo the bankruptcy case, as far as practicable, and to restore all property rights to the position in which they were found at the commencement of the case. This does not necessarily encompass undoing sales of property from the estate to a good faith purchaser. Where there is a question over the scope of the subsection, the court will make the appropriate orders to protect rights acquired in reliance on the bankruptcy case. Senate Report No. 95–989.

1984 Acts. Statements by Legislative Leaders, see 1984 U.S.Code Cong. and Adm.News, p. 576.

1994 Acts. House Report No. 103–835, see 1994 U.S. Code Cong. and Adm. News, p. 3340.

Legislative Statements

Section 349(b)(2) of the House amendment adds a cross reference to section 553 to reflect the new right of recovery of setoffs created under that section. Corresponding changes are made throughout the House amendment.

Effective and Applicability Provisions

1994 Acts. Amendment by Pub.L. 103–394 effective on Oct. 22, 1994, and not to apply with respect to cases commenced under Title 11 of the United States Code before Oct. 22, 1994, see section 702 of Pub.L. 103–394, set out as a note under section 101 of this title.

1984 Acts. Amendment by Pub.L. 98–353 effective with respect to cases filed 90 days after July 10, 1984, see section 552(a), formerly 553(a), of Pub.L. 98–353, set out as a note under section 101 of this title.

Separability of Provisions

If any provision of or amendment made by Pub.L. 103–394 or the application of such provision or amendment to any person or circumstance is held to be unconstitutional, the remaining provisions of and amendments made by Pub.L. 103–394 and the application of such provisions and amendments to any person or circumstance shall not be affected thereby, see section 701 of Pub.L. 103–394, set out as a note under section 101 of this title.

§ 350. Closing and reopening cases

(a) After an estate is fully administered and the court has discharged the trustee, the court shall close the case.

(b) A case may be reopened in the court in which such case was closed to administer assets, to accord relief to the debtor, or for other cause.

(Pub.L. 95–598, Nov. 6, 1978, 92 Stat. 2569; Pub.L. 98–353, Title III, § 439, July 10, 1984, 98 Stat. 370.)

HISTORICAL AND STATUTORY NOTES

Revision Notes and Legislative Reports

1978 Acts. Subsection (a) requires the court to close a bankruptcy case after the estate is fully administered and the trustee discharged. The Rules of Bankruptcy Procedure will provide the procedure for case closing. Subsection (b) permits reopening of the case to administer assets, to accord relief to the debtor, or for other cause. Though the court may permit reopening of a case so that the trustee may exercise an avoiding power, laches may constitute a bar to an action that has been delayed too long. The case may be reopened in the court in which it was closed. The rules will prescribe the procedure by which a case is reopened and how it will be conducted after reopening. Senate Report No. 95–989.

1984 Acts. Statements by Legislative Leaders, see 1984 U.S.Code Cong. and Adm.News, p. 576.

Effective and Applicability Provisions

1984 Acts. Amendment by Pub.L. 98–353 effective with respect to cases filed 90 days after July 10, 1984, see section 552(a), formerly 553(a), of Pub.L. 98–353, set out as a note under section 101 of this title.

CROSS REFERENCES

Applicability of subsec. (b) of this section in Chapter 9 cases, see 11 USCA § 901.

Scheduled property deemed abandoned, see 11 USCA § 554.

Successor trustee, see 11 USCA § 703.

§ 351. Disposal of patient records

If a health care business commences a case under chapter 7, 9, or 11, and the trustee does not have a sufficient amount of funds to pay for the storage of patient records in the manner required under applicable Federal or State law, the following requirements shall apply:

(1) The trustee shall—

(A) promptly publish notice, in 1 or more appropriate newspapers, that if patient records are not claimed by the patient or an insurance provider (if applicable law permits the insurance provider to make that claim) by the date that is 365 days after the date of that notification, the trustee will destroy the patient records; and

(B) during the first 180 days of the 365–day period described in subparagraph (A), promptly attempt to notify directly each patient that is the subject of the patient records and appropriate insurance carrier concerning the patient records by mailing to the most recent known address of that patient, or a family member or contact person for that patient, and to the appropriate insurance carrier an appropriate notice regarding the claiming or disposing of patient records.

(2) If, after providing the notification under paragraph (1), patient records are not claimed during the 365–day period described under that paragraph, the trustee shall mail, by certified mail, at the end of such 365–day period a written request to each appropriate Federal agency to request permission from that agency to deposit the patient records with that agency, except that no Federal agency is required to accept patient records under this paragraph.

(3) If, following the 365–day period described in paragraph (2) and after providing the notification under paragraph (1), patient records are not claimed by a patient or insurance provider, or request is not granted by a Federal agency to deposit such records with that agency, the trustee shall destroy those records by—

(A) if the records are written, shredding or burning the records; or

(B) if the records are magnetic, optical, or other electronic records, by otherwise destroying those records so that those records cannot be retrieved.

(Added Pub.L. 109–8, Title XI, § 1102(a), Apr. 20, 2005, 119 Stat. 189.)

HISTORICAL AND STATUTORY NOTES

Revision Notes and Legislative Reports

2005 Acts. House Report No. 109–31(Part I), see 2005 U.S. Code Cong. and Adm. News, p. 88.

References in Text

Chapter 7, 9, or 11, referred to in the introductory paragraph, means chapter 7, 9, or 11 of this title, 11 U.S.C.A. § 701 et seq., 11 U.S.C.A. § 901 et seq., or 11 U.S.C.A. § 1101 et seq., respectively.

Effective and Applicability Provisions

2005 Acts. Enactment of this section by Pub.L. 109–8 effective, except as otherwise provided, 180 days after April 20, 2005, and inapplicable with respect to cases commenced under Title 11 before the effective date, see Pub.L. 109–8, § 1501, set out as a note under 11 U.S.C.A. § 101.

SUBCHAPTER IV—ADMINISTRATIVE POWERS

§ 361. Adequate protection

When adequate protection is required under section 362, 363, or 364 of this title of an interest of an entity in property, such adequate protection may be provided by—

(1) requiring the trustee to make a cash payment or periodic cash payments to such entity, to the extent that the stay under section 362 of this title, use, sale, or lease under section 363 of this title, or any grant of a lien under section 364 of this title results in a decrease in the value of such entity's interest in such property;

(2) providing to such entity an additional or replacement lien to the extent that such stay, use, sale, lease, or grant results in a decrease in the value of such entity's interest in such property; or

(3) granting such other relief, other than entitling such entity to compensation allowable under section 503(b)(1) of this title as an administrative expense, as will result in the realization by such entity of the indubitable equivalent of such entity's interest in such property.

(Pub.L. 95–598, Nov. 6, 1978, 92 Stat. 2569; Pub.L. 98–353, Title III, § 440, July 10, 1984, 98 Stat. 370.)

HISTORICAL AND STATUTORY NOTES

Revision Notes and Legislative Reports

1978 Acts. Sections 362, 363, and 364 require, in certain circumstances, that the court determine in noticed hearings whether the interest of a secured creditor or co-owner of property with the debtor is adequately protected in connection with the sale or use of property. The interests of which the court may provide protection in the ways described in this section include equitable as well as legal interests. For example, a right to enforce a pledge and a right to recover property delivered to a debtor under a consignment agreement or an agreement of sale or return are interests that may be entitled to protection. This section specifies means by which adequate protection may be provided but, to avoid placing the court in an administrative role, does not require the court to provide it. Instead, the trustee or debtor in possession or the creditor will provide or propose a protection method. If the party that is affected by the proposed action objects, the court will determine whether the protection provided is adequate. The purpose of this section is to illustrate means by which it may be provided and to define the limits of the concept.

The concept of adequate protection is derived from the fifth amendment protection of property interests as enunciated by the Supreme Court. See *Wright v. Union Central Life Ins. Co.*, 311 U.S. 273 (1940) [61 S.Ct. 196, 85 L.Ed. 184, rehearing denied 61 S.Ct. 445, 312 U.S. 711, 85 L.Ed. 1142]; *Louisville Joint Stock Land Bank v. Radford*, 295 U.S. 555 (1935) [55 S.Ct. 854, 79 L.Ed. 1593].

The automatic stay also provides creditor protection. Without it, certain creditors would be able to pursue their own remedies against the debtor's property. Those who acted first would obtain payment of the claims in preference to and to the detriment of other creditors. Bankruptcy is designed to provide an orderly liquidation procedure under which all creditors are treated equally. A race of diligence by creditors for the debtor's assets prevents that.

Subsection (a) defines the scope of the automatic stay, by listing the acts that are stayed by the commencement of the case. The commencement or continuation, including the issuance of process, of a judicial, administrative or other proceeding against the debtor that was or could have been commenced before the commencement of the bankruptcy case is stayed under paragraph (1). The scope of this paragraph is broad. All proceedings are stayed, including arbitration, administrative, and judicial proceedings. Proceeding in this sense encompasses civil actions and all proceedings even if they are not before governmental tribunals.

The stay is not permanent. There is adequate provision for relief from the stay elsewhere in the section. However, it is important that the trustee have an opportunity to inventory the debtor's position before proceeding with the administration of the case. Undoubtedly the court will lift the stay for proceedings before specialized or nongovernmental tribunals to allow those proceedings to come to a conclusion. Any party desiring to enforce an order in such a proceeding would thereafter have to come before the bankruptcy court to collect assets. Nevertheless, it will often be more appropriate to permit proceedings to continue in their place of origin, when no great prejudice to the bankruptcy estate would result, in order to leave the parties to their chosen forum and to relieve the bankruptcy court from many duties that may be handled elsewhere.

Paragraph (2) stays the enforcement, against the debtor or against property of the estate, of a judgment obtained before the commencement of the bankruptcy case. Thus, execution and levy against the debtors' prepetition property are stayed, and attempts to collect a judgment from the debtor personally are stayed.

Paragraph (3) stays any act to obtain possession of property of the estate (that is, property of the debtor as of the date of the filing of the petition) or property from the estate (property over which the estate has control or possession). The purpose of this provision is to prevent dismemberment of the estate. Liquidation must proceed in an orderly fashion. Any distribution of property must be by the trustee after he has had an opportunity to familiarize himself with the various rights and interests involved and with the property available for distribution.

Paragraph (4) stays lien creation against property of the estate. Thus, taking possession to perfect a lien or obtaining court process is prohibited. To permit lien creation after bankruptcy would give certain creditors preferential treatment by making them secured instead of unsecured.

Paragraph (5) stays any act to create or enforce a lien against property of the debtor, that is, most property that is acquired after the date of the filing of the petition, property that is exempted, or property that does not pass to the estate, to the extent that the lien secures a prepetition claim. Again, to permit postbankruptcy lien creation or enforcement would permit certain creditors to receive preferential treatment. It may also circumvent the debtors' discharge.

Paragraph (6) prevents creditors from attempting in any way to collect a prepetition debt. Creditors in consumer cases occasionally telephone debtors to encourage repayment in spite of bankruptcy. Inexperienced, frightened, or ill-counseled debtors may succumb to suggestions to repay notwithstanding their bankruptcy. This provision prevents evasion of the purpose of the bankruptcy laws by sophisticated creditors.

Paragraph (7) stays setoffs of mutual debts and credits between the debtor and creditors. As with all other paragraphs of subsection (a), this paragraph does not affect the right of creditors. It simply stays its enforcement pending an orderly examination of the debtor's and creditors' rights.

Subsection (b) lists seven exceptions to the automatic stay. The effect of an exception is not to make the action immune from injunction.

The court has ample other powers to stay actions not covered by the automatic stay. Section 105, of proposed title 11, derived from Bankruptcy Act, § 2a(15), [section 11(a)(15) of former Title 11], grants the power to issue orders necessary or appropriate to carry out the provisions of title 11. The district court and the bankruptcy court as its adjunct have all the traditional injunctive powers of a court of equity, 28 U.S.C. §§ 151 and 164 as proposed in S. 2266, § 201, and 28 U.S.C. § 1334, as proposed in S. 2266, § 216. Stays or injunctions issued under these other sections will not be automatic upon the commencement of the case, but will be granted or issued under the usual rules for the issuance of injunctions. By excepting an act or action from the automatic stay, the bill simply requires that the trustee move the court into action, rather than requiring the stayed party to request relief from the stay. There are some actions, enumerated in the exceptions, that generally should not be stayed automatically upon the commencement of the case, for reasons of either policy or practicality. Thus, the court will have to determine on a case-by-case basis whether a particular action which may be harming the estate should be stayed.

With respect to stays issued under other powers, or the application of the automatic stay, to governmental actions, this section and the other sections mentioned are intended to be an express waiver of sovereign immunity of the Federal Government, and an assertion of the bankruptcy power over State governments under the supremacy clause notwithstanding a State's sovereign immunity.

The first exception is of criminal proceedings against the debtor. The bankruptcy laws are not a haven for criminal offenders, but are designed to give relief from financial overextension. Thus, criminal actions and proceedings may proceed in spite of bankruptcy.

Paragraph (2) excepts from the stay the collection of alimony, maintenance or support from property that is not property of the estate. This will include property acquired after the commencement of the case, exempted property, and property that does not pass to the estate. The automatic stay is one means of protecting the debtor's discharge. Alimony, maintenance and support obligations are excepted from discharge. Staying collection of them, when not to the detriment of other creditors (because the collection effort is against property that is not property of the estate) does not further that goal. Moreover, it could lead to hardship on the part of the protected spouse or children.

Paragraph (3) excepts any act to perfect an interest in property to the extent that the trustee's rights and powers are limited under section 546(a) of the bankruptcy code. That section permits postpetition perfection of certain liens to be effective against the trustee. If the act of perfection, such as filing, were stayed, the section would be nullified.

Paragraph (4) excepts commencement or continuation of actions and proceedings by governmental units to enforce police or regulatory powers. Thus, where a governmental unit is suing a debtor to prevent or stop violation of fraud, environmental protection, consumer protection, safety, or similar police or regulatory laws, or attempting to fix damages for violation of such a law, the action or proceeding is not stayed under the automatic stay.

Paragraph (5) makes clear that the exception extends to permit an injunction and enforcement of an injunction, and to permit the entry of a money judgment, but does not extend to permit enforcement of a money judgment. Since the assets of the debtor are in the possession and control of the bankruptcy court, and since they constitute a fund out of which all creditors are entitled to share, enforcement by a governmental unit of a money judgment would give it preferential treatment to the detriment of all other creditors.

Paragraph (6) excepts the setoff of any mutual debt and claim for commodity transactions.

Paragraph (7) excepts actions by the Secretary of Housing and Urban Development to foreclose or take possession in a case of a loan insured under the National Housing Act [12 U.S.C.A. § 1701 et seq.]. A general exception for such loans is found in current sections 263 and 517 [sections 663 and 917 of former Title 11], the exception allowed by this paragraph is much more limited.

Subsection (c) of section 362 specifies the duration of the automatic stay. Paragraph (1) terminates a stay of an act against property of the estate when the property ceases to be property of the estate, such as by sale, abandonment, or exemption. It does not terminate the stay against property of the debtor if the property leaves the estate and goes to the debtor. Paragraph (2) terminates the stay of any other act on the earliest of the time the case is closed, the time the case is dismissed, or the time a discharge is granted or denied (unless the debtor is a corporation or partnership in a chapter 7 case).

Subsection (c) governs automatic termination of the stay. Subsections (d) through (g) govern termination of the stay by the court on the request of a party in interest.

Subsection (d) requires the court, upon motion of a party in interest, to grant relief from the stay for cause, such as by terminating, annulling, modifying, or conditioning the stay. The lack of adequate protection of an interest in property is one cause for relief, but is not the only cause. Other causes might include the lack of any connection with or interference with the pending bankruptcy case. Generally, proceedings in which the debtor is a fiduciary or involving postpetition activities of the debtor, need not be stayed because they bear no relationship to the purpose of the automatic stay, which is protection of the debtor and his estate from his creditors.

Upon the court's finding that the debtor has no equity in the property subject to the stay and that the property is not necessary to an effective reorganization of the debtor, the subsection requires the court grant relief from the stay. To aid in this determination, guidelines are established where the property subject to the stay is real property. An exception to "the necessary to an effective reorganization" requirement is made for real property on which no business is being conducted other than operating the real property and activities incident thereto. The intent of this exception is to reach the single-asset apartment type cases which involve primarily tax-shelter investments and for which the bankruptcy laws have provided a too facile method to relay conditions, but not the operating shopping center and hotel cases where attempts at reorganization should be permitted. Property in which the debtor has equity but which is not necessary to an effective reorganization of the debtor should be sold under section 363. Hearings under this subsection are given calendar priority to ensure that court congestion will not unduly prejudice the rights of creditors who may be obviously entitled to relief from the operation of the automatic stay.

Subsection (e) provides protection that is not always available under present law. The subsection sets a time certain within which the bankruptcy court must rule on the adequacy of protection provided for the secured creditor's interest. If the court does not rule within 30 days from a request by motion for relief from the stay, the stay is automatically terminated with respect to the property in question. To accommodate more complex cases, the subsection permits the court to make a preliminary ruling after a preliminary hearing. After a preliminary hearing, the court may continue the stay only if there is a reasonable likelihood that the party opposing relief from the stay will prevail at the final hearing. Because the stay is essentially an injunction, the three stages of the stay may be analogized to the three stages of an injunction. The filing of the petition which gives rise to the automatic stay is similar to a temporary restraining order. The preliminary hearing is similar to the hearing on a preliminary injunction, and the final hearing and order are similar to the hearing and issuance or denial of a permanent injunction. The main difference lies in which party must bring the issue before the court. While in the injunction setting, the party seeking the injunction must prosecute the action, in proceeding for relief from the automatic stay, the enjoined party must move. The difference does not, however, shift the burden of proof. Subsection (g) leaves that burden on the party opposing relief from the stay (that is, on the party seeking continuance of the injunction) on the issue of adequate protection and existence of an equity. It is not, however, intended to be confined strictly to the constitutional requirement. This section and the concept of adequate protection are based as much on policy grounds as on constitutional grounds. Secured creditors should not be deprived of the benefit of their bargain. There may be situations in bankruptcy where giving a secured creditor an absolute right to his bargain may be impossible or seriously detrimental to the policy of the bankruptcy laws. Thus, this section recognizes the availability of alternate means of protecting a secured creditor's interest where such steps are a necessary part of the rehabilitative process. Though the creditor might not be able to retain his lien upon the specific collateral held at the time of filing, the purpose of the section is to insure that the secured creditor receives the value for which he bargained.

The section specifies two exclusive means of providing adequate protection, both of which may require an approximate determination of the value of the protected entity's interest in the property involved. The section does not specify how value is to be determined, nor does it specify

Complete Annotation Materials, see Title 11, U.S.C.A.

when it is to be determined. These matters are left to case-by-case interpretation and development. In light of the restrictive approach of the section to the availability of means of providing adequate protection, this flexibility is important to permit the courts to adapt to varying circumstances and changing modes of financing.

Neither is it expected that the courts will construe the term value to mean, in every case, forced sale liquidation value or full going concern value. There is wide latitude between those two extremes although forced sale liquidation value will be a minimum.

In any particular case, especially a reorganization case, the determination of which entity should be entitled to the difference between the going concern value and the liquidation value must be based on equitable considerations arising from the facts of the case. Finally, the determination of value is binding only for the purposes of the specific hearing and is not to have a res judicata effect.

The first method of adequate protection outlined is the making of cash payments to compensate for the expected decrease in value of the opposing entity's interest. This provision is derived from *In re Bermec Corporation,* 445 F.2d 367 (2d Cir. 1971), though in that case it is not clear whether the payments offered were adequate to compensate the secured creditors for their loss. The use of periodic payments may be appropriate where, for example, the property in question is depreciating at a relatively fixed rate. The periodic payments would be to compensate for the depreciation and might, but need not necessarily, be in the same amount as payments due on the secured obligation.

The second method is the fixing of an additional or replacement lien on other property of the debtor to the extent of the decrease in value or actual consumption of the property involved. The purpose of this method is to provide the protected entity with an alternative means of realizing the value of the original property, if it should decline during the case, by granting an interest in additional property from whose value the entity may realize its loss. This is consistent with the view expressed in *Wright v. Union Central Life Ins. Co.,* 311 U.S. 273 (1940) [61 S.Ct. 196, 85 L.Ed. 184, rehearing denied 61 S.Ct. 445, 312 U.S. 711, 85 L.Ed. 1142], where the Court suggested that it was the value of the secured creditor's collateral, and not necessarily his rights in specific collateral, that was entitled to protection.

The section makes no provision for the granting of an administrative priority as a method of providing adequate protection to an entity as was suggested in *In re Yale Express System, Inc.,* 384 F.2d 990 (2d Cir. 1967), because such protection is too uncertain to be meaningful. Senate Report No. 95–989.

The section specifies four means of providing adequate protection. They are neither exclusive nor exhaustive. They all rely, however, on the value of the protected entity's interest in the property involved. The section does not specify how value is to be determined, nor does it specify when it is to be determined. These matters are left to case-by-case interpretation and development. It is expected that the courts will apply the concept in light of facts of each case and general equitable principles. It is not intended that the courts will develop a hard and fast rule that will apply in every case. The time and method of valuation is not specified precisely, in order to avoid that result. There are an infinite number of variations possible in dealings between debtors and creditors, the law is continually developing, and new ideas are continually being implemented in this field. The flexibility is important to permit the courts to adapt to varying circumstances and changing modes of financing.

Neither is it expected that the courts will construe the term value to mean, in every case, forced sale liquidation value or full going concern value. There is wide latitude between those two extremes. In any particular case, especially a reorganization case, the determination of which entity should be entitled to the difference between the going concern value and the liquidation value must be based on equitable considerations based on the facts of the case. It will frequently be based on negotiation between the parties. Only if they cannot agree will the court become involved.

The first method of adequate protection specified is periodic cash payments by the estate, to the extent of a decrease in value of the opposing entity's interest in the property involved. This provision is derived from *In re Yale Express, Inc.,* 384 F.2d 990 (2d Cir. 1967) (though in that case it is not clear whether the payments required were adequate to compensate the secured creditors for their loss). The use of periodic payments may be appropriate, where for example, the property in question is depreciating at a relatively fixed rate. The periodic payments would be to compensate for the depreciation.

The second method is the provision of an additional or replacement lien on other property to the extent of the decrease in value of the property involved. The purpose of this method is to provide the protected entity with a means of realizing the value of the original property, if it should decline during the case, by granting an interest in additional property from whose value the entity may realize its loss.

The third method is the granting of an administrative expense priority to the protected entity to the extent of his loss. This method, more than the others, requires a prediction as to whether the unencumbered assets that will remain if the case if converted from reorganization to liquidation will be sufficient to pay the protected entity in full. It is clearly the most risky, from the entity's perspective, and should be used only when there is relative certainty that administrative expenses will be able to be paid in full in the event of liquidation.

The fourth method gives the parties and the courts flexibility by allowing such other relief as will result in the realization by the protected entity of the value of its interest in the property involved. Under this provision, the courts will be able to adapt to new methods of financing and to formulate protection that is appropriate to the circumstances of the case if none of the other methods would accomplish the desired result. For example, another form of adequate protection might be the guarantee by a third party outside the judicial process of compensation for any loss incurred in the case. Adequate protection might also, in some circumstances, be provided by permitting a secured creditor to bid in his claim at the sale of the property and to offset the claim against the price bid in.

The paragraph also defines, more clearly than the others, the general concept of adequate protection, by requiring such relief as will result in the realization of value. It is the general category, and as such, is defined by the concept involved rather than any particular method of adequate protection. House Report No. 95–595.

1984 Acts. Statements by Legislative Leaders, see 1984 U.S.Code Cong. and Adm.News, p. 576.

Legislative Statements

Section 361 of the House amendment represents a compromise between H.R. 8200 as passed by the House and the Senate amendment regarding the issue of "adequate protection" of a secured party. The House amendment deletes the provision found in section 361(3) of H.R. 8200 as passed by the House. It would have permitted adequate protection to be provided by giving the secured party an administrative expense regarding any decrease in the value of such party's collateral. In every case there is the uncertainty that the estate will have sufficient property to pay administrative expenses in full.

Section 361(4) of H.R. 8200 as passed by the House is modified in section 361(3) of the House amendment to indicate that the court may grant other forms of adequate protection, other than an administrative expense, which will result in the realization by the secured creditor of the indubitable equivalent of the creditor's interest in property. In the special instance where there is a reserve fund maintained under the security agreement, such as in the typical bondholder case, indubitable equivalent means that the bondholders would be entitled to be protected as to the reserve fund, in addition to the regular payments needed to service the debt. Adequate protection of an interest of an entity in property is intended to protect a creditor's allowed secured claim. To the extent the protection proves to be inadequate after the fact, the creditor is entitled to a first priority administrative expense under section 503(b).

In the special case of a creditor who has elected application of creditor making an election under section 1111(b)(2), that creditor is entitled to adequate protection of the creditor's interest in property to the extent of the value of the collateral not to the extent of the creditor's allowed secured claim, which is inflated to cover a deficiency as a result of such election.

Effective and Applicability Provisions

1984 Acts. Amendment by Pub.L. 98–353 effective with respect to cases filed 90 days after July 10, 1984, see section 552(a), formerly 553(a), of Pub.L. 98–353, set out as a note under section 101 of this title.

CROSS REFERENCES

Applicability of this section in Chapter 9 cases, see 11 USCA § 901.

Inapplicability of this section in Chapter 12 cases, see 11 USCA § 1205.

§ 362. Automatic stay

(a) Except as provided in subsection (b) of this section, a petition filed under section 301, 302, or 303 of this title, or an application filed under section 5(a)(3) of the Securities Investor Protection Act of 1970, operates as a stay, applicable to all entities, of—

(1) the commencement or continuation, including the issuance or employment of process, of a judicial, administrative, or other action or proceeding against the debtor that was or could have been commenced before the commencement of the case under this title, or to recover a claim against the debtor that arose before the commencement of the case under this title;

(2) the enforcement, against the debtor or against property of the estate, of a judgment obtained before the commencement of the case under this title;

(3) any act to obtain possession of property of the estate or of property from the estate or to exercise control over property of the estate;

(4) any act to create, perfect, or enforce any lien against property of the estate;

(5) any act to create, perfect, or enforce against property of the debtor any lien to the extent that such lien secures a claim that arose before the commencement of the case under this title;

(6) any act to collect, assess, or recover a claim against the debtor that arose before the commencement of the case under this title;

(7) the setoff of any debt owing to the debtor that arose before the commencement of the case under this title against any claim against the debtor; and

(8) the commencement or continuation of a proceeding before the United States Tax Court concerning a corporate debtor's tax liability for a taxable period the bankruptcy court may determine or concerning the tax liability of a debtor who is an individual for a taxable period ending before the date of the order for relief under this title.

(b) The filing of a petition under section 301, 302, or 303 of this title, or of an application under section 5(a)(3) of the Securities Investor Protection Act of 1970, does not operate as a stay—

(1) under subsection (a) of this section, of the commencement or continuation of a criminal action or proceeding against the debtor;

(2) under subsection (a)—

(A) of the commencement or continuation of a civil action or proceeding—

(i) for the establishment of paternity;

(ii) for the establishment or modification of an order for domestic support obligations;

(iii) concerning child custody or visitation;

(iv) for the dissolution of a marriage, except to the extent that such proceeding seeks to determine the division of property that is property of the estate; or

(v) regarding domestic violence;

(B) of the collection of a domestic support obligation from property that is not property of the estate;

(C) with respect to the withholding of income that is property of the estate or property of the debtor for payment of a domestic support obligation under a judicial or administrative order or a statute;

(D) of the withholding, suspension, or restriction of a driver's license, a professional or occupational license, or a recreational license, under State law, as specified in section 466(a)(16) of the Social Security Act;

(E) of the reporting of overdue support owed by a parent to any consumer reporting agency as specified in section 466(a)(7) of the Social Security Act;

(F) of the interception of a tax refund, as specified in sections 464 and 466(a)(3) of the Social Security Act or under an analogous State law; or

(G) of the enforcement of a medical obligation, as specified under title IV of the Social Security Act;

(3) under subsection (a) of this section, of any act to perfect, or to maintain or continue the perfection of, an interest in property to the extent that the trustee's rights and powers are subject to such perfection under section 546(b) of this title or to the extent that such act is accomplished within the period provided under section 547(e)(2)(A) of this title;

(4) under paragraph (1), (2), (3), or (6) of subsection (a) of this section, of the commencement or continuation of an action or proceeding by a governmental unit or any organization exercising authority under the Convention on the Prohibition of the Development, Production, Stockpiling and Use of Chemical Weapons and on Their Destruction, opened for signature on January 13, 1993, to enforce such governmental unit's or organization's police and regulatory power, including the enforcement of a judgment other than a money judgment, obtained in an action or proceeding by the governmental unit to enforce such governmental unit's or organization's police or regulatory power;

[(5) **Repealed.** Pub.L. 105–277, Div. I, Title VI, § 603(1), Oct. 21, 1998, 112 Stat. 2681–886]

(6) under subsection (a) of this section, of the exercise by a commodity broker, forward contract merchant, stockbroker, financial institution, financial participant, or securities clearing agency of any contractual right (as defined in section 555 or 556) under any security agreement or arrangement or other credit enhancement forming a part of or related to any commodity contract, forward contract or securities contract, or of any contractual right (as defined in section 555 or 556) to offset or net out any termination value, payment amount, or other transfer obligation arising under or in connection with 1 or more such contracts, including any master agreement for such contracts;

(7) under subsection (a) of this section, of the exercise by a repo participant or financial participant of any contractual right (as defined in section 559) under any security agreement or arrangement or other credit enhancement forming a part of or related to any repurchase agreement, or of any contractual right (as defined in section 559) to offset or net out any termination value, payment amount, or other transfer obligation arising under or in connection with 1 or more such agreements, including any master agreement for such agreements;

(8) under subsection (a) of this section, of the commencement of any action by the Secretary of Housing and Urban Development to foreclose a mortgage or deed of trust in any case in which the mortgage or deed of trust held by the Secretary is insured or was formerly insured under the National Housing Act and covers property, or combinations of property, consisting of five or more living units;

(9) under subsection (a), of—

(A) an audit by a governmental unit to determine tax liability;

(B) the issuance to the debtor by a governmental unit of a notice of tax deficiency;

(C) a demand for tax returns; or

(D) the making of an assessment for any tax and issuance of a notice and demand for payment of such an assessment (but any tax lien that would otherwise attach to property of the estate by reason of such an assessment shall not take effect unless such tax is a debt of the debtor that will not be discharged in the case and such property or its proceeds are transferred out of the estate to, or otherwise revested in, the debtor).

(10) under subsection (a) of this section, of any act by a lessor to the debtor under a lease of nonresidential real property that has terminated by the expiration of the stated term of the lease before the commencement of or during a case under this title to obtain possession of such property;

(11) under subsection (a) of this section, of the presentment of a negotiable instrument and the giving of notice of and protesting dishonor of such an instrument;

(12) under subsection (a) of this section, after the date which is 90 days after the filing of such petition, of the commencement or continuation, and conclusion to the entry of final judgment, of an action which involves a debtor subject to reorganization pursuant to chapter 11 of this title and which was brought by the Secretary of Transportation under section 31325 of title 46 (including distribution of any proceeds of sale) to foreclose a preferred ship or fleet mortgage, or a security interest in or relating to a vessel or vessel under construction, held by the Secretary of Transportation under chapter 537 of title 46 or section 109(h) of title 49, or under applicable State law;

(13) under subsection (a) of this section, after the date which is 90 days after the filing of such petition, of the commencement or continuation, and conclusion to the entry of final judgment, of an action which involves a debtor subject to reorganization pursuant to chapter 11 of this title and which was brought by the Secretary of Commerce under section 31325 of title 46 (including distribution of any proceeds of sale) to foreclose a preferred ship or fleet mortgage in a vessel or a mortgage, deed of trust, or other security interest in a fishing facility held by the Secretary of Commerce under chapter 537 of title 46;

(14) under subsection (a) of this section, of any action by an accrediting agency regarding the accreditation status of the debtor as an educational institution;

(15) under subsection (a) of this section, of any action by a State licensing body regarding the licensure of the debtor as an educational institution;

(16) under subsection (a) of this section, of any action by a guaranty agency, as defined in section 435(j) of the Higher Education Act of 1965 or the Secretary of Education regarding the eligibility of the debtor to participate in programs authorized under such Act;

(17) under subsection (a) of this section, of the exercise by a swap participant or financial participant of any contractual right (as defined in section 560) under any security agreement or arrangement or other credit enhancement forming a part of or related to any swap agreement, or of any contractual right (as defined in section 560) to offset or net out any termination value, payment amount, or other transfer obligation arising under or in connection with 1 or more such agreements, including any master agreement for such agreements;

(18) under subsection (a) of the creation or perfection of a statutory lien for an ad valorem property tax, or a special tax or special assessment on real property whether or not ad valorem, imposed by a governmental unit, if such tax or assessment comes due after the date of the filing of the petition;

(19) under subsection (a), of withholding of income from a debtor's wages and collection of amounts withheld, under the debtor's agreement authorizing that withholding and collection for the benefit of a pension, profit-sharing, stock bonus, or other plan established under section 401, 403, 408, 408A, 414, 457, or 501(c) of the Internal Revenue Code of 1986, that is sponsored by the employer of the debtor, or an affiliate, successor, or predecessor of such employer—

(A) to the extent that the amounts withheld and collected are used solely for payments relating to a loan from a plan under section 408(b)(1) of the Employee Retirement Income Security Act of 1974 or is subject to section 72(p) of the Internal Revenue Code of 1986; or

(B) a loan from a thrift savings plan permitted under subchapter III of chapter 84 of title 5, that satisfies the requirements of section 8433(g) of such title;

but nothing in this paragraph may be construed to provide that any loan made under a governmental plan under section 414(d), or a contract or account under section 403(b), of the Internal Revenue Code of 1986 constitutes a claim or a debt under this title;

(20) under subsection (a), of any act to enforce any lien against or security interest in real property following entry of the order under subsection (d)(4) as to such real property in any prior case under this title, for a period of 2 years after the date of the entry of such an order, except that the debtor, in a subsequent case under this title, may move for relief from such order based upon changed circumstances or for other good cause shown, after notice and a hearing;

(21) under subsection (a), of any act to enforce any lien against or security interest in real property—

(A) if the debtor is ineligible under section 109(g) to be a debtor in a case under this title; or

(B) if the case under this title was filed in violation of a bankruptcy court order in a prior case under this title prohibiting the debtor from being a debtor in another case under this title;

(22) subject to subsection (*l*), under subsection (a)(3), of the continuation of any eviction, unlawful detainer action, or similar proceeding by a lessor against a debtor involving residential property in which the debtor resides as a tenant under a lease or rental agreement and with respect to which the lessor has obtained before the date of the filing of the bankruptcy petition, a judgment for possession of such property against the debtor;

(23) subject to subsection (m), under subsection (a)(3), of an eviction action that seeks possession of the residential property in which the debtor resides as a tenant under a lease or rental agreement based on endangerment of such property or the illegal use of controlled substances on such property, but only if the lessor files with the court, and serves upon the debtor, a certification under penalty of perjury that such an eviction action has been filed, or that the debtor, during the 30–day period preceding the date of the filing of the certification, has endangered property or illegally used or allowed to be used a controlled substance on the property;

(24) under subsection (a), of any transfer that is not avoidable under section 544 and that is not avoidable under section 549;

(25) under subsection (a), of—

(A) the commencement or continuation of an investigation or action by a securities self regulatory organization to enforce such organization's regulatory power;

(B) the enforcement of an order or decision, other than for monetary sanctions, obtained in an action by such securities self regulatory organization to enforce such organization's regulatory power; or

(C) any act taken by such securities self regulatory organization to delist, delete, or refuse to permit quotation of any stock that does not meet applicable regulatory requirements;

(26) under subsection (a), of the setoff under applicable nonbankruptcy law of an income tax refund, by a governmental unit, with respect to a taxable period that ended before the date of the order for relief against an income tax liability for a taxable period that also ended before the date of the order for relief, except that in any case in which the setoff of an income tax refund is not permitted under applicable nonbankruptcy law because of a pending action to determine the amount or legality of a tax liability, the governmental unit may hold the refund pending the resolution of the action, unless the court, on the motion of the trustee and after notice and a hearing, grants the taxing authority adequate protection (within the meaning of section 361) for the secured claim of such authority in the setoff under section 506(a);

(27) under subsection (a) of this section, of the exercise by a master netting agreement participant of any contractual right (as defined in section 555, 556, 559, or 560) under any security agreement or arrangement or other credit enhancement forming a part of or related to any master netting agreement, or of any contractual right (as defined in section 555, 556, 559, or 560) to offset or net out any termination value, payment amount, or other transfer obligation arising under or in connection with 1 or more such master netting agreements to the extent that such participant is eligible to exercise such rights under paragraph (6), (7), or (17) for each individual contract covered by the master netting agreement in issue; and

(28) under subsection (a), of the exclusion by the Secretary of Health and Human Services of the debtor from participation in the medicare program or any other Federal health care program (as defined in section 1128B(f) of the Social Security Act pursuant to title XI or XVIII of such Act).

The provisions of paragraphs (12) and (13) of this subsection shall apply with respect to any such petition filed on or before December 31, 1989.

(c) Except as provided in subsections (d), (e), (f), and (h) of this section—

(1) the stay of an act against property of the estate under subsection (a) of this section continues until such property is no longer property of the estate;

(2) the stay of any other act under subsection (a) of this section continues until the earliest of—

(A) the time the case is closed;

(B) the time the case is dismissed; or

(C) if the case is a case under chapter 7 of this title concerning an individual or a case under chapter 9, 11, 12, or 13 of this title, the time a discharge is granted or denied;

(3) if a single or joint case is filed by or against debtor who is an individual in a case under chapter 7, 11, or 13, and if a single or joint case of the debtor was pending within the preceding 1-year period but was dismissed, other than a case refiled under a chapter other than chapter 7 after dismissal under section 707(b)—

(A) the stay under subsection (a) with respect to any action taken with respect to a debt or property securing such debt or with respect to any lease shall terminate with respect to the debtor on the 30th day after the filing of the later case;

(B) on the motion of a party in interest for continuation of the automatic stay and upon notice and a hearing, the court may extend the stay in particular cases as to any or all creditors (subject to such conditions or limitations as the court may then impose) after notice and a hearing completed before the expiration of the 30-day period only if the party in interest demonstrates that the filing of the later case is in good faith as to the creditors to be stayed; and

(C) for purposes of subparagraph (B), a case is presumptively filed not in good faith (but such presumption may be rebutted by clear and convincing evidence to the contrary)—

(i) as to all creditors, if—

(I) more than 1 previous case under any of chapters 7, 11, and 13 in which the individual was a debtor was pending within the preceding 1-year period;

(II) a previous case under any of chapters 7, 11, and 13 in which the individual was a debtor was dismissed within such 1-year period, after the debtor failed to—

(aa) file or amend the petition or other documents as required by this title or the court without substantial excuse (but mere inadvertence or negligence shall not be a substantial excuse unless the dismissal was caused by the negligence of the debtor's attorney);

(bb) provide adequate protection as ordered by the court; or

(cc) perform the terms of a plan confirmed by the court; or

(III) there has not been a substantial change in the financial or personal affairs of the debtor since the dismissal of the next most previous case under chapter 7, 11, or 13 or any other reason to conclude that the later case will be concluded—

(aa) if a case under chapter 7, with a discharge; or

(bb) if a case under chapter 11 or 13, with a confirmed plan that will be fully performed; and

(ii) as to any creditor that commenced an action under subsection (d) in a previous case in which the individual was a debtor if, as of the date of dismissal of such case, that action was still pending or had been resolved by terminating, conditioning, or limiting the stay as to actions of such creditor; and

(4)(A)(i) if a single or joint case is filed by or against a debtor who is an individual under this title, and if 2 or more single or joint cases of the debtor were pending within the previous year but were dismissed, other than a case refiled under section 707(b), the stay under subsection (a) shall not go into effect upon the filing of the later case; and

(ii) on request of a party in interest, the court shall promptly enter an order confirming that no stay is in effect;

(B) if, within 30 days after the filing of the later case, a party in interest requests the court may order the stay to take effect in the case as to any or all creditors (subject to such conditions or limitations as the court may impose), after notice and a hearing, only if the party in interest demonstrates that the filing of the later case is in good faith as to the creditors to be stayed;

(C) a stay imposed under subparagraph (B) shall be effective on the date of the entry of the order allowing the stay to go into effect; and

(D) for purposes of subparagraph (B), a case is presumptively filed not in good faith (but such presumption may be rebutted by clear and convincing evidence to the contrary)—

(i) as to all creditors if—

(I) 2 or more previous cases under this title in which the individual was a debtor were pending within the 1-year period;

(II) a previous case under this title in which the individual was a debtor was dismissed within the time period stated in this paragraph after the debtor failed to file or amend the petition or other documents as required by this title or the court without substantial excuse (but mere inadvertence or negligence shall not be substantial excuse unless the dismissal was caused by the negligence of the debtor's attorney), failed to provide adequate protection as ordered by the court, or failed to perform the terms of a plan confirmed by the court; or

(III) there has not been a substantial change in the financial or personal affairs of the debtor since the dismissal of the next most previous case under this title, or any other reason to conclude that the later case will not be concluded, if a case under chapter 7, with a discharge, and if a case under chapter 11 or 13, with a confirmed plan that will be fully performed; or

(ii) as to any creditor that commenced an action under subsection (d) in a previous case in which the individual was a debtor if, as of the date of dismissal of such case, such action was still pending or had been resolved by terminating, conditioning, or limiting the stay as to such action of such creditor.

(d) On request of a party in interest and after notice and a hearing, the court shall grant relief from the stay provided under subsection (a) of this section, such as by terminating, annulling, modifying, or conditioning such stay—

(1) for cause, including the lack of adequate protection of an interest in property of such party in interest;

(2) with respect to a stay of an act against property under subsection (a) of this section, if—

(A) the debtor does not have an equity in such property; and

(B) such property is not necessary to an effective reorganization;

(3) with respect to a stay of an act against single asset real estate under subsection (a), by a creditor whose claim is secured by an interest in such real estate, unless, not later than the date that is 90 days after the entry of the order for relief (or such later date as the court may determine for cause by order entered within that 90-day period) or 30 days after the court determines that the debtor is subject to this paragraph, whichever is later—

(A) the debtor has filed a plan of reorganization that has a reasonable possibility of being confirmed within a reasonable time; or

(B) the debtor has commenced monthly payments that—

(i) may, in the debtor's sole discretion, notwithstanding section 363(c)(2), be made from rents or other income generated before, on, or after the date of the commencement of the case by or from the property to each creditor whose claim is secured by such real estate (other than a claim secured by a judgment lien or by an unmatured statutory lien); and

(ii) are in an amount equal to interest at the then applicable nondefault contract rate of interest on the value of the creditor's interest in the real estate; or

(4) with respect to a stay of an act against real property under subsection (a), by a creditor whose claim is secured by an interest in such real property, if the court finds that the filing of the petition was part of a scheme to delay, hinder, and defraud creditors that involved either—

(A) transfer of all or part ownership of, or other interest in, such real property without the consent of the secured creditor or court approval; or

(B) multiple bankruptcy filings affecting such real property.

If recorded in compliance with applicable State laws governing notices of interests or liens in real property, an order entered under paragraph (4) shall be binding in any other case under this title purporting to affect such real property filed not later than 2 years after the date of the entry of such order by the court, except that a debtor in a subsequent case under this title may move for relief from such order based upon changed circumstances or for good cause shown, after notice and a hearing. Any Federal, State, or local governmental unit that accepts notices of interests or liens in real property shall accept any certified copy of an order described in this subsection for indexing and recording.

(e)(1) Thirty days after a request under subsection (d) of this section for relief from the stay of any act against property of the estate under subsection (a) of this section, such stay is terminated with respect to the party in interest making such request, unless the court, after notice and a hearing, orders such stay continued in effect pending the conclusion of, or as a result of, a final hearing and determination under subsection (d) of this section. A hearing under this subsection may be a preliminary hearing, or may be consolidated with the final hearing under subsection (d) of this section. The court shall order such stay continued in effect pending the conclusion of the final hearing under subsection (d) of this section if there is a reasonable likelihood that the party opposing relief from such stay will prevail at the conclusion of such final hearing. If the hearing under this subsection is a preliminary hearing, then such final hearing shall be concluded not later than thirty days after the conclusion of such preliminary hearing, unless the 30-day period is extended with the consent of the parties in interest or for a specific time which the court finds is required by compelling circumstances.

(2) Notwithstanding paragraph (1), in a case under chapter 7, 11, or 13 in which the debtor is an individual, the stay under subsection (a) shall terminate on the date that is 60 days after a request is made by a party in interest under subsection (d), unless—

(A) a final decision is rendered by the court during the 60-day period beginning on the date of the request; or

(B) such 60-day period is extended—

(i) by agreement of all parties in interest; or

(ii) by the court for such specific period of time as the court finds is required for good cause, as described in findings made by the court.

(f) Upon request of a party in interest, the court, with or without a hearing, shall grant such relief from the stay provided under subsection (a) of this section as is necessary to prevent irreparable damage to the interest of an entity in property, if such interest will suffer such damage before there is an opportunity for notice and a hearing under subsection (d) or (e) of this section.

(g) In any hearing under subsection (d) or (e) of this section concerning relief from the stay of any act under subsection (a) of this section—

(1) the party requesting such relief has the burden of proof on the issue of the debtor's equity in property; and

(2) the party opposing such relief has the burden of proof on all other issues.

(h)(1) In a case in which the debtor is an individual, the stay provided by subsection (a) is terminated with respect to personal property of the estate or of the debtor securing in whole or in part a claim, or subject to an unexpired lease, and such personal property shall no longer be property of the estate if the debtor fails within the applicable time set by section 521(a)(2)—

(A) to file timely any statement of intention required under section 521(a)(2) with respect to such personal property or to indicate in such statement that the debtor will either surrender such personal property or retain it and, if retaining such personal property, either redeem such personal property pursuant to section 722, enter into an agreement of the kind specified in section 524(c) applicable to the debt secured by such personal property, or assume such unexpired lease pursuant to section 365(p) if the trustee does not do so, as applicable; and

(B) to take timely the action specified in such statement, as it may be amended before expiration of the period for taking action, unless such statement specifies the debtor's intention to reaffirm such debt on the original contract terms and the creditor refuses to agree to the reaffirmation on such terms.

(2) Paragraph (1) does not apply if the court determines, on the motion of the trustee filed before the expiration of the applicable time set by section 521(a)(2), after notice and a hearing, that such personal property is of consequential value or benefit to the estate, and orders appropriate adequate protection of the creditor's interest, and orders the debtor to deliver any collateral in the debtor's possession to the trustee. If the court does not so determine, the stay provided by subsection (a) shall terminate upon the conclusion of the hearing on the motion.

(i) If a case commenced under chapter 7, 11, or 13 is dismissed due to the creation of a debt repayment plan, for purposes of subsection (c)(3), any subsequent case commenced by the debtor under any such chapter shall not be presumed to be filed not in good faith.

(j) On request of a party in interest, the court shall issue an order under subsection (c) confirming that the automatic stay has been terminated.

(k)(1) Except as provided in paragraph (2), an individual injured by any willful violation of a stay provided by this section shall recover actual damages, including costs and attorneys' fees, and, in appropriate circumstances, may recover punitive damages.

(2) If such violation is based on an action taken by an entity in the good faith belief that subsection (h) applies to the debtor, the recovery under paragraph (1) of this subsection against such entity shall be limited to actual damages.

(*l*)(1) Except as otherwise provided in this subsection, subsection (b) (22) shall apply on the date that is 30 days after the date on which the bankruptcy petition is filed, if the debtor files with the petition and serves upon the lessor a certification under penalty of perjury that—

(A) under nonbankruptcy law applicable in the jurisdiction, there are circumstances under which the debtor would be permitted to cure the entire monetary default that gave rise to the judgment for possession, after that judgment for possession was entered; and

(B) the debtor (or an adult dependent of the debtor) has deposited with the clerk of the court, any rent that would become due during the 30–day period after the filing of the bankruptcy petition.

(2) If, within the 30–day period after the filing of the bankruptcy petition, the debtor (or an adult dependent of the debtor) complies with paragraph (1) and files with the court and serves upon the lessor a further certification under penalty of perjury that the debtor (or an adult dependent of the debtor) has cured, under nonbankrupcty[1] law applicable in the jurisdiction, the entire monetary default that gave rise to the judgment under which possession is sought by the lessor, subsection (b)(22) shall not apply, unless ordered to apply by the court under paragraph (3).

(3)(A) If the lessor files an objection to any certification filed by the debtor under paragraph (1) or (2), and serves such objection upon the debtor, the court shall hold a hearing within 10 days after the filing and service of such objection to determine if the certification filed by the debtor under paragraph (1) or (2) is true.

(B) If the court upholds the objection of the lessor filed under subparagraph (A)—

(i) subsection (b)(22) shall apply immediately and relief from the stay provided under subsection (a)(3) shall not be required to enable the lessor to complete the process to recover full possession of the property; and

(ii) the clerk of the court shall immediately serve upon the lessor and the debtor a certified copy of the court's order upholding the lessor's objection.

(4) If a debtor, in accordance with paragraph (5), indicates on the petition that there was a judgment for possession of the residential rental property in which the debtor resides and does not file a certification under paragraph (1) or (2)—

(A) subsection (b)(22) shall apply immediately upon failure to file such certification, and relief from the stay provided under subsection (a)(3) shall not be required to enable the lessor to complete the process to recover full possession of the property; and

(B) the clerk of the court shall immediately serve upon the lessor and the debtor a certified copy of the docket indicating the absence of a filed certification and the applicability of the exception to the stay under subsection (b)(22).

(5)(A) Where a judgment for possession of residential property in which the debtor resides as a tenant under a lease or rental agreement has been obtained by the lessor, the debtor shall so indicate on the bankruptcy petition and shall provide the name and address of the lessor that obtained that pre-petition judgment on the petition and on any certification filed under this subsection.

(B) The form of certification filed with the petition, as specified in this subsection, shall provide for the debtor to certify, and the debtor shall certify—

(i) whether a judgment for possession of residential rental housing in which the debtor resides has been obtained against the debtor before the date of the filing of the petition; and

(ii) whether the debtor is claiming under paragraph (1) that under nonbankruptcy law applicable in the jurisdiction, there are circumstances under which the debtor would be permitted to cure the entire monetary default that gave rise to the judgment for possession, after that judgment of possession was entered, and has made the appropriate deposit with the court.

(C) The standard forms (electronic and otherwise) used in a bankruptcy proceeding shall be amended to reflect the requirements of this subsection.

(D) The clerk of the court shall arrange for the prompt transmittal of the rent deposited in accordance with paragraph (1)(B) to the lessor.

(m)(1) Except as otherwise provided in this subsection, subsection (b) (23) shall apply on the date that is 15 days after the date on which the lessor files and serves a certification described in subsection (b)(23).

(2)(A) If the debtor files with the court an objection to the truth or legal sufficiency of the certification described in subsection (b)(23) and serves such objection upon the lessor, subsection (b)(23) shall not apply, unless ordered to apply by the court under this subsection.

(B) If the debtor files and serves the objection under subparagraph (A), the court shall hold a hearing within 10 days after the filing and service of such objection to determine if the situation giving rise to the lessor's certification under paragraph (1) existed or has been remedied.

(C) If the debtor can demonstrate to the satisfaction of the court that the situation giving rise to the lessor's certification under paragraph (1) did not exist or has been remedied, the stay provided under subsection (a)(3) shall remain in effect until the termination of the stay under this section.

(D) If the debtor cannot demonstrate to the satisfaction of the court that the situation giving rise to the lessor's certification under paragraph (1) did not exist or has been remedied—

(i) relief from the stay provided under subsection (a)(3) shall not be required to enable the lessor to proceed with the eviction; and

(ii) the clerk of the court shall immediately serve upon the lessor and the debtor a certified copy of the court's order upholding the lessor's certification.

(3) If the debtor fails to file, within 15 days, an objection under paragraph (2)(A)—

(A) subsection (b)(23) shall apply immediately upon such failure and relief from the stay provided under subsection (a)(3) shall not be required to enable the lessor to complete the process to recover full possession of the property; and

(B) the clerk of the court shall immediately serve upon the lessor and the debtor a certified copy of the docket indicating such failure.

(n)(1) Except as provided in paragraph (2), subsection (a) does not apply in a case in which the debtor—

(A) is a debtor in a small business case pending at the time the petition is filed;

(B) was a debtor in a small business case that was dismissed for any reason by an order that became final in the 2-year period ending on the date of the order for relief entered with respect to the petition;

(C) was a debtor in a small business case in which a plan was confirmed in the 2-year period ending on the date of the order for relief entered with respect to the petition; or

(D) is an entity that has acquired substantially all of the assets or business of a small business debtor described in subparagraph (A), (B), or (C), unless such entity establishes by a preponderance of the evidence that such entity acquired substantially all of the assets or business of such small business debtor in good faith and not for the purpose of evading this paragraph.

(2) Paragraph (1) does not apply—

(A) to an involuntary case involving no collusion by the debtor with creditors; or

(B) to the filing of a petition if—

(i) the debtor proves by a preponderance of the evidence that the filing of the petition resulted from circumstances beyond the control of the debtor not foreseeable at the time the case then pending was filed; and

(ii) it is more likely than not that the court will confirm a feasible plan, but not a liquidating plan, within a reasonable period of time.

(*o*) The exercise of rights not subject to the stay arising under subsection (a) pursuant to paragraph (6), (7), (17), or (27) of subsection (b) shall not be stayed by any order of a court or administrative agency in any proceeding under this title.

(Pub.L. 95–598, Nov. 6, 1978, 92 Stat. 2570; Pub.L. 97–222, § 3, July 27, 1982, 96 Stat. 235; Pub.L. 98–353, Title III, §§ 304, 363(b), 392, 441, July 10, 1984, 98 Stat. 352, 363, 365, 371; Pub.L. 99–509, Title V, § 5001(a), Oct. 21, 1986, 100 Stat. 1911; Pub.L. 99–554, Title II, §§ 257(j), 283(d), Oct. 27, 1986, 100 Stat. 3115, 3116; Pub.L. 101–311, Title I, § 102, Title II, § 202, June 25, 1990, 104 Stat. 267, 269; Pub.L. 101–508, Title III, § 3007(a)(1), Nov. 5, 1990, 104 Stat. 1388–28; Pub.L. 103–394, Title I, §§ 101, 116, Title II, §§ 204(a), 218(b), Title III, § 304(b), Title IV, § 401, Title V, § 501(b)(2), (d)(7), Oct. 22, 1994, 108 Stat. 4107, 4119, 4122, 4128, 4132, 4141, 4142, 4144; Pub.L. 105–277, Div. I, Title VI, § 603, Oct. 21, 1998, 112 Stat. 2681–886; Pub.L. 109–8, Title I, § 106(f), Title II, §§ 214, 224(b), Title III, §§ 302, 303, 305(1), 311, 320, Title IV, §§ 401(b), 441, 444, Title VII,

§§ 709, 718, Title IX, § 907(d), (*o*)(1), (2), Title XI, § 1106, Title XII, § 1225, Apr. 20, 2005, 119 Stat. 41, 54, 64, 75, 77, 79, 84, 94, 104, 114, 117, 127, 131, 176, 181, 182, 192, 199; Pub.L. 109–304, § 17(b)(1), Oct. 6, 2006, 120 Stat. 1706; Pub.L. 109–390, § 5(a)(2), Dec. 12, 2006, 120 Stat. 2696.)

[1] So in original. Probably should be "nonbankruptcy".

HISTORICAL AND STATUTORY NOTES

Revision Notes and Legislative Reports

1978 Acts. The automatic stay is one of the fundamental debtor protections provided by the bankruptcy laws. It gives the debtor a breathing spell from his creditors. It stops all collection efforts, all harassment, and all foreclosure actions. It permits the debtor to attempt a repayment or reorganization plan, or simply to be relieved of the financial pressures that drove him into bankruptcy.

The action commenced by the party seeking relief from the stay is referred to as a motion to make it clear that at the expedited hearing under subsection (e), and at hearings on relief from the stay, the only issue will be the lack of adequate protection, the debtor's equity in the property, and the necessity of the property to an effective reorganization of the debtor, or the existence of other cause for relief from the stay. This hearing will not be the appropriate time at which to bring in other issues, such as counterclaims against the creditor, which, although relevant to the question of the amount of the debt, concern largely collateral or unrelated matters. This approach is consistent with that taken in cases such as *In re Essex Properties, Ltd.*, 430 F.Supp. 1112 (N.D.Cal.1977), that an action seeking relief from the stay is not the assertion of a claim which would give rise to the right or obligation to assert counterclaims. Those counterclaims are not to be handled in the summary fashion that the preliminary hearing under this provision will be. Rather, they will be the subject of more complete proceedings by the trustee to recover property of the estate or to object to the allowance of a claim. However, this would not preclude the party seeking continuance of the stay from presenting evidence on the existence of claims which the court may consider in exercising its discretion. What is precluded is a determination of such collateral claims on the merits at the hearing. Senate Report No. 95–989.

[For additional discussion, see Revision Notes and Legislative Reports, Senate Report No. 95–989, set out under section 361 of this title.]

Paragraph (7) [of subsec. (a)] stays setoffs of mutual debts and credits between the debtor and creditors. As with all other paragraphs of subsection (a), this paragraph does not affect the right of creditors. It simply stays its enforcement pending an orderly examination of the debtor's and creditors' rights.

Subsection (c) governs automatic termination of the stay. Subsections (d) through (g) govern termination of the stay by the court on the request of a party in interest. Subsection (d) requires the court, on request of a party in interest, to grant relief from the stay, such as by terminating, annulling, modifying, or conditioning the stay, for cause. The lack of adequate protection of an interest in property of the party requesting relief from the stay is one cause for relief, but is not the only cause. As noted above, a desire to permit an action to proceed to completion in another tribunal may provide another cause. Other causes might include the lack of any connection with or interference with the pending bankruptcy case. For example, a divorce or child custody proceeding involving the debtor may bear no relation to the bankruptcy case. In that case, it should not be stayed. A probate proceeding in which the debtor is the executor or administrator of another's estate usually will not be related to the bankruptcy case, and should not be stayed. Generally, proceedings in which the debtor is a fiduciary, or involving postpetition activities of the debtor, need not be stayed because they bear no relationship to the purpose of the automatic stay, which is debtor protection from his creditors. The facts of each request will determine whether relief is appropriate under the circumstances.

Subsection (e) provides a protection for secured creditors that is not available under present law. The subsection sets a time certain within which the bankruptcy court must rule on the adequacy of protection provided of the secured creditor's interest. If the court does not rule within 30 days from a request for relief from the stay, the stay is automatically terminated with respect to the property in question. In order to accommodate more complex cases, the subsection permits the court to make a preliminary ruling after a preliminary hearing. After a preliminary hearing, the court may continue the stay only if there is a reasonable likelihood that the party opposing relief from the stay will prevail at the final hearing. Because the stay is essentially an injunction, the three stages of the stay may be analogized to the three stages of an injunction. The filing of the petition which gives rise to the automatic stay is similar to a temporary restraining order. The preliminary hearing is similar to the hearing on a preliminary injunction, and the final hearing and order is similar to a permanent injunction. The main difference lies in which party must bring the issue before the court. While in the injunction setting, the party seeking the injunction must prosecute the action, in proceedings for relief from the automatic stay, the enjoined party must move. The difference does not, however, shift the burden of proof. Subsection (g) leaves that burden on the party opposing relief from the stay (that is, on the party seeking continuance of the injunction) on the issue of adequate protection.

At the expedited hearing under subsection (e), and at all hearings on relief from the stay, the only issue will be the claim of the creditor and the lack of adequate protection or existence of other cause for relief from the stay. This hearing will not be the appropriate time at which to bring in other issues, such as counterclaims against the creditor on largely unrelated matters. Those counterclaims are not to be handled in the summary fashion that the preliminary hearing under this provision will be. Rather, they will be the subject of more complete proceedings by the trustees to recover property of the estate or to object to the allowance of a claim. House Report No. 95–595.

1982 Acts. House Report No. 97–420, see 1982 U.S. Code Cong. and Adm. News, p. 583.

1984 Acts. Statements by Legislative Leaders, see 1984 U.S. Code Cong. and Adm. News, p. 576.

1986 Acts. House Report No. 99–727, House Conference Report No. 99–1012, and Statement by President, see 1986 U.S. Code Cong. and Adm. News, p. 3607.

House Report No. 99–764 and House Conference Report No. 99–958, see 1986 U.S. Code Cong. and Adm. News, p. 5227.

1990 Acts. House Report No. 101–484, see 1990 U.S. Code Cong. and Adm. News, p. 223.

House Report No. 101–881, House Conference Report No. 101–964, and Statement by President, see 1990 U.S. Code Cong. and Adm. News, p. 2017.

1994 Acts. House Report No. 103–835, see 1994 U.S. Code Cong. and Adm. News, p. 3340.

1998 Acts. Statement by President, see 1998 U.S. Code Cong. and Adm. News, p. 576.

2005 Acts. House Report No. 109–31(Part I), see 2005 U.S. Code Cong. and Adm. News, p. 88.

2006 Acts. House Report No. 109–170, see 2006 U.S. Code Cong. and Adm. News, p. 972.

House Report No. 109–648(Part I), see 2006 U.S. Code Cong. and Adm. News, p. 1585.

Legislative Statements

Section 362(a)(1) of the House amendment adopts the provision contained in the Senate amendment enjoining the commencement or continuation of a judicial, administrative, or other proceeding to recover a claim against the debtor that arose before the commencement of the case. The provision is beneficial and interacts with section 362(a)(6), which also covers assessment, to prevent harassment of the debtor with respect to pre-petition claims.

Section 362(a)(7) contains a provision contained in H.R. 8200 as passed by the House. The differing provision in the Senate amendment was rejected. It is not possible that a debt owing to the debtor may be offset against an interest in the debtor.

Section 362(a)(8) is new. The provision stays the commencement or continuation of any proceeding concerning the debtor before the U.S. Tax Court.

Section 362(b)(4) indicates that the stay under section 362(a)(1) does not apply to affect the commencement or continuation of an action or proceeding by a governmental unit to enforce the governmental unit's police or regulatory power. This section is intended to be given a narrow construction in order to permit governmental units to pursue actions to protect the public health and safety and not to apply to actions by a governmental unit to protect a pecuniary interest in property of the debtor or property of the estate.

Section 362(b)(6) of the House amendment adopts a provision contained in the Senate amendment restricting the exception to the automatic stay with respect to setoffs to permit only the setoff of mutual debts and claims. Traditionally, the right of setoff has been limited to mutual debts and claims and the lack of the clarifying term "mutual" in H.R. 8200 as passed by the House created an unintentional ambiguity. Section 362(b)(7) of the House amendment permits the issuance of a notice of tax deficiency. The House amendment rejects section 362(b)(7) in the Senate amendment. It would have permitted a particular governmental unit to obtain a pecuniary advantage without a hearing on the merits contrary to the exceptions contained in sections 362(b)(4) and (5).

Section 362(d) of the House amendment represents a compromise between comparable provisions in the House bill and Senate amendment. Under section 362(d)(1) of the House amendment, the court may terminate, annul, modify, or condition the automatic stay for cause, including lack of adequate protection of an interest in property of a secured party. It is anticipated that the Rules of Bankruptcy Procedure will provide that those hearings will receive priority on the calendar. Under section 362(d)(2) the court may alternatively terminate, annul, modify, or condition the automatic stay for cause including inadequate protection for the creditor. The court shall grant relief from the stay if there is no equity and it is not necessary to an effective reorganization of the debtor.

The latter requirement is contained in section 362(d)(2). This section is intended to solve the problem of real property mortgage foreclosures of property where the bankruptcy petition is filed on the eve of foreclosure. The section is not intended to apply if the business of the debtor is managing or leasing real property, such as a hotel operation, even though the debtor has no equity if the property is necessary to an effective reorganization of the debtor. Similarly, if the debtor does have an equity in the property, there is no requirement that the property be sold under section 363 of title 11 as would have been required by the Senate amendment.

Section 362(e) of the House amendment represents a modification of provisions in H.R. 8200 as passed by the House and the Senate amendment to make clear that a final hearing must be commenced within 30 days after a preliminary hearing is held to determine whether a creditor will be entitled to relief from the automatic stay. In order to insure that those hearings will in fact occur within such 30–day period, it is anticipated that the rules of bankruptcy procedure provide that such final hearings receive priority on the court calendar.

Section 362(g) places the burden of proof on the issue of the debtor's equity in collateral on the party requesting relief from the automatic stay and the burden on other issues on the debtor.

An amendment has been made to section 362(b) to permit the Secretary of the Department of Housing and Urban Development to commence an action to foreclose a mortgage or deed of trust. The commencement of such an action is necessary for tax purposes. The section is not intended to permit the continuation of such an action after it is commenced nor is the section to be construed to entitle the Secretary to take possession in lieu of foreclosure.

Automatic stay: Sections 362(b)(8) and (9) contained in the Senate amendment are largely deleted in the House amendment. Those provisions add to the list of actions not stayed (a) jeopardy assessments, (b) other assessments, and (c) the issuance of deficiency notices. In the House amendment, jeopardy assessments against property which ceases to be property of the estate is already authorized by section 362(c)(1). Other assessments are specifically stayed under section 362(a)(6), while the issuance of a deficiency notice is specifically permitted. Stay of the assessment and the permission to issue a statutory notice of a tax deficiency will permit the debtor to take his personal tax case to the Tax Court, if the bankruptcy judge authorizes him to do so (as explained more fully in the discussion of section 505.)

References in Text

Chapter 7, 11, or 13, referred to in text, is chapter 7, 11, or 13 of this title, 11 U.S.C.A. § 701 et seq., 11 U.S.C.A. § 1101 et seq., or 11 U.S.C.A. § 1301 et seq., respectively.

Section 5(a)(3) of the Securities Investor Protection Act of 1970, referred to in subsecs. (a) and (b), is section 5(a)(3) of

Pub.L. 91–598, Dec. 30, 1970, 84 Stat. 1644, which is classified to section 78eee of Title 15, Commerce and Trade.

Section 466 of the Social Security Act, referred to in subsec. (b)(2)(D) to (F), is Act Aug. 14, 1935, c. 531, Title IV, § 466, as added Aug. 16, 1984, Pub.L. 98–378, § 3(b), 98 Stat. 1306, and amended, which is classified to 42 U.S.C.A. § 666.

Section 464 of the Social Security Act, referred to in subsec. (b)(2)(F), is Act Aug. 14, 1935, c. 531, Title IV, § 464, as added Aug. 13, 1981, Pub.L. 97–35, Title XXIII, § 2331(a), 95 Stat. 860, and amended, which is classified to 42 U.S.C.A. § 664.

Title IV of the Social Security Act, referred to in subsec. (b)(2)(G), is Act Aug. 14, 1935, c. 531, Title IV, § 401 et seq., as added Aug. 22, 1996, Pub.L. 104–193, Title I, § 103(a)(1), 110 Stat. 2113, and amended, which is classified principally to subchapter IV of chapter 7 of Title 42, 42 U.S.C.A. § 601 et seq. For complete classification, see Tables.

The National Housing Act, referred to in subsec. (b)(8), is Act June 27, 1934, c. 847, 48 Stat. 1246, as amended, which is classified principally to chapter 13 (section 1701 et seq.) of Title 12, Banks and Banking. For complete classification of this Act to the Code, see section 1701 of Title 12 and Tables.

Chapter 537 of title 46, referred to in subsecs. (b)(12) and (13), is Loans and Guarantees, 46 U.S.C.A. § 53701 et seq.

The Higher Education Act of 1965, including such Act, referred to in subsec. (b)(16), is Pub.L. 89–329, Nov. 8, 1965, 79 Stat. 1219, as amended, which is classified principally to chapter 28 (§ 1001 et seq.) of Title 20, Education. Section 435(j) of the Act is classified to section 1085(j) of Title 20. For complete classification of this Act to the Code, see Short Title note set out under section 1001 of Title 20 and Tables.

Section 401, 403, 408, 408A, 414, 457, or 501(c) of the Internal Revenue Code of 1986, referred to in subsec. (b)(19), is classified to 26 U.S.C.A. § 401, 403, 408, 408A, 414, 457, or 501(c).

Section 414(d) or section 403(b) of the Internal Revenue Code, referred to in subsec. (b)(19), is classified to 26 U.S.C.A. § 414(d) or 26 U.S.C.A. § 403(b).

Section 408(b)(1) of the Employee Retirement Income Security Act of 1974, referred to in subsec. (b)(19)(A), is Pub.L. 93–406, Title I, § 408(b)(1), Sept. 2, 1974, 88 Stat. 883, as amended, which is classified to 29 U.S.C.A. § 1108(b)(1).

Section 72(p) of the Internal Revenue Code of 1986, referred to in subsec. (b)(19)(A), is classified to 26 U.S.C.A. § 72(p).

Subchapter III of chapter 84 of title 5, referred to in subsec. (b)(19)(B), is 5 U.S.C.A. § 8431 et seq.

Section 1128B(f) of the Social Security Act, referred to in subsec. (b)(28), is Act Aug. 14, 1935, c. 531, Title XI, § 1128B, formerly Title XVIII, § 1877(d), and Title XIX, § 1909, as added and amended Oct. 30, 1972, Pub.L. 92–603, Title II, §§ 242(c), 278(b)(9), 86 Stat. 1419, 1454, which is classified to 42 U.S.C.A. § 1320a–7b(f).

Title XI of such Act, referred to in subsec. (b)(28), means title XI of the Social Security Act, Act Aug. 14, 1935, c. 531, Title XI, § 1101 et seq., 49 Stat. 647, as amended, which is classified principally to subchapter XI of chapter 7 of Title 42, 42 U.S.C.A. § 1301 et seq.

Title XVIII of such Act, referred to in subsec. (b)(28), means title XVIII of the Social Security Act, Act Aug. 14, 1935, c. 531, Title XVIII, § 1801 et seq., as added July 30, 1965, Pub.L. 89–97, Title I, § 102(a), 79 Stat. 291, and amended, which is classified principally to subchapter XVIII of chapter 7 of Title 42, 42 U.S.C.A. § 1395 et seq.

Chapter 7, 9, 11, 12, or 13 of this title, referred to in subsec. (c)(2)(C), is 11 U.S.C.A. § 701 et seq., 11 U.S.C.A. § 901 et seq., 11 U.S.C.A. § 1101 et seq., 11 U.S.C.A. § 1201 et seq., or 11 U.S.C.A. § 1301 et seq., respectively.

Codifications

Renumbering and conforming amendments by Pub.L. 101–508 failed to take into consideration prior renumbering and conforming amendments by Pub.L. 101–311, thereby resulting in two pars. numbered "(14)". To accommodate such duplication, the renumbering reflects changes by Pub.L. 101–311 set out first, and by Pub.L. 101–508 set out second, but does not reflect the minor conforming amendments.

Effective and Applicability Provisions

2005 Acts. Amendments by Pub.L. 109–8 effective, except as otherwise provided, 180 days after April 20, 2005, and inapplicable with respect to cases commenced under Title 11 before the effective date, see Pub.L. 109–8, § 1501, set out as a note under 11 U.S.C.A. § 101.

1994 Acts. Amendments by Pub.L. 103–394 effective on Oct. 22, 1994, and not to apply with respect to cases commenced under this title before Oct. 22, 1994, see section 702 of Pub.L. 103–394, set out as a note under section 101 of this title.

1990 Acts. Section 3007(a)(3) of Pub.L. 101–508 provided that: "The amendments made by this subsection [amending this section and section 541 this title] shall be effective upon date of enactment of this Act [Nov. 5, 1990]."

Section 3008 of Pub.L. 101–508, which provided that the amendments made by this subtitle [subtitle A (§§ 3001–3008) of Title III of Pub.L. 101–508, amending this section, sections 541 and 1328 of this title, and sections 1078, 1078–1, 1078–7, 1085, 1088, and 1091 of Title 20, Education, and provisions set out as a note under section 1078–1 of Title 20, and enacting provisions set out as notes under this section, and section 1328 of this title, and sections 1001, 1078–1, 1078–7, 1085, and 1088 of Title 20] were to cease to be effective on October 1, 1996, was repealed by Pub.L. 102–325, Title XV, § 1558, July 23, 1992, 106 Stat. 841.

1986 Acts. Amendment by Pub.L. 99–554, § 257(j), effective 30 days after Oct. 27, 1986, but not applicable with respect to cases commenced under this title before that date, see section 302(a), (a)(1) of Pub.L. 99–554, set out as a note under section 581 of Title 28, Judiciary and Judicial Procedure.

Amendment by Pub.L. 99–554, § 283(d), effective 30 days after Oct. 27, 1986, see section 302(a) of Pub.L. 99–554, set out as a note under section 581 of Title 28.

Section 5001(b) of Pub.L. 99–509 provided that: "The amendments made by subsection (a) of this section [amending this section and enacting a provision set out as a note under this section] shall apply only to petitions filed under section 362 of title 11, United States Code, which are made after August 1, 1986."

1984 Acts. Amendment by Pub.L. 98–353 effective with respect to cases filed 90 days after July 10, 1984, see section 552(a), formerly 553 of Pub.L. 98–353, set out as a note under section 101 of this title.

Separability of Provisions

If any provision of or amendment made by Pub.L. 103–394 or the application of such provision or amendment to any person or circumstance is held to be unconstitutional, the remaining provisions of and amendments made by Pub.L. 103–394 and the application of such provisions and amendments to any person or circumstance shall not be affected thereby, see section 701 of Pub.L. 103–394, set out as a note under section 101 of this title.

CROSS REFERENCES

Abstention of district court from hearing a proceeding based upon State law as cause of action, provision as not limiting applicability of stay under this section, see 28 USCA § 1334.

Adequate protection in Chapter 12 cases, method of obtaining, see 11 USCA § 1205.

Applicability of this section in Chapter 9 cases, see 11 USCA § 901.

Assessment of taxes against estate, see 11 USCA § 505.

Denial of debtor status to debtor who obtained voluntary dismissal following filing of relief from provisions of this section, see 11 USCA § 109.

Effect of this section on subchapter III of Chapter 7, see 11 USCA § 742.

Enforcement of claims against debtor in Chapter 9 cases, automatic stay of, see 11 USCA § 922.

Extension of time, see 11 USCA § 108.

Grain storage facility bankruptcies, expedited determinations, see 11 USCA § 557.

Priorities, see 11 USCA § 507.

Right of possession of party with security interest in—

Aircraft equipment and vessel, see 11 USCA § 1110.

Rolling stock equipment, see 11 USCA § 1168.

Secretary of Commerce or Transportation as mortgagee, see 46 USCA § 31308.

Setoff, see 11 USCA § 553.

Turnover of property to estate, see 11 USCA § 542.

§ 363. Use, sale, or lease of property

(a) In this section, "cash collateral" means cash, negotiable instruments, documents of title, securities, deposit accounts, or other cash equivalents whenever acquired in which the estate and an entity other than the estate have an interest and includes the proceeds, products, offspring, rents, or profits of property and the fees, charges, accounts or other payments for the use or occupancy of rooms and other public facilities in hotels, motels, or other lodging properties subject to a security interest as provided in section 552(b) of this title, whether existing before or after the commencement of a case under this title.

(b)(1) The trustee, after notice and a hearing, may use, sell, or lease, other than in the ordinary course of business, property of the estate, except that if the debtor in connection with offering a product or a service discloses to an individual a policy prohibiting the transfer of personally identifiable information about individuals to persons that are not affiliated with the debtor and if such policy is in effect on the date of the commencement of the case, then the trustee may not sell or lease personally identifiable information to any person unless—

(A) such sale or such lease is consistent with such policy; or

(B) after appointment of a consumer privacy ombudsman in accordance with section 332, and after notice and a hearing, the court approves such sale or such lease—

(i) giving due consideration to the facts, circumstances, and conditions of such sale or such lease; and

(ii) finding that no showing was made that such sale or such lease would violate applicable nonbankruptcy law.

(2) If notification is required under subsection (a) of section 7A of the Clayton Act in the case of a transaction under this subsection, then—

(A) notwithstanding subsection (a) of such section, the notification required by such subsection to be given by the debtor shall be given by the trustee; and

(B) notwithstanding subsection (b) of such section, the required waiting period shall end on the 15th day after the date of the receipt, by the Federal Trade Commission and the Assistant Attorney General in charge of the Antitrust Division of the Department of Justice, of the notification required under such subsection (a), unless such waiting period is extended—

(i) pursuant to subsection (e)(2) of such section, in the same manner as such subsection (e)(2) applies to a cash tender offer;

(ii) pursuant to subsection (g)(2) of such section; or

(iii) by the court after notice and a hearing.

(c)(1) If the business of the debtor is authorized to be operated under section 721, 1108, 1203, 1204, or 1304 of this title and unless the court orders otherwise, the trustee may enter into transactions, including the sale or lease of property of the estate, in the ordinary course of business, without notice or a hearing, and may use property of the estate in the ordinary course of business without notice or a hearing.

(2) The trustee may not use, sell, or lease cash collateral under paragraph (1) of this subsection unless—

(A) each entity that has an interest in such cash collateral consents; or

(B) the court, after notice and a hearing, authorizes such use, sale, or lease in accordance with the provisions of this section.

(3) Any hearing under paragraph (2)(B) of this subsection may be a preliminary hearing or may be consolidated with a hearing under subsection (e) of this section, but shall be scheduled in accordance with the needs of the debtor. If the hearing under paragraph (2)(B) of this subsection is a preliminary hearing, the court may authorize such use, sale, or lease only if there is a reasonable likelihood that the trustee will prevail at the final hearing under subsection (e) of this section. The court shall act promptly on any request for authorization under paragraph (2)(B) of this subsection.

(4) Except as provided in paragraph (2) of this subsection, the trustee shall segregate and account for any cash collateral in the trustee's possession, custody, or control.

(d) The trustee may use, sell, or lease property under subsection (b) or (c) of this section only—

(1) in accordance with applicable nonbankruptcy law that governs the transfer of property by a corporation or trust that is not a moneyed, business, or commercial corporation or trust; and

(2) to the extent not inconsistent with any relief granted under subsection (c), (d), (e), or (f) of section 362.

(e) Notwithstanding any other provision of this section, at any time, on request of an entity that has an interest in property used, sold, or leased, or proposed to be used, sold, or leased, by the trustee, the court, with or without a hearing, shall prohibit or condition such use, sale, or lease as is necessary to provide adequate protection of such interest. This subsection also applies to property that is subject to any unexpired lease of personal property (to the exclusion of such property being subject to an order to grant relief from the stay under section 362).

(f) The trustee may sell property under subsection (b) or (c) of this section free and clear of any interest in such property of an entity other than the estate, only if—

(1) applicable nonbankruptcy law permits sale of such property free and clear of such interest;

(2) such entity consents;

(3) such interest is a lien and the price at which such property is to be sold is greater than the aggregate value of all liens on such property;

(4) such interest is in bona fide dispute; or

(5) such entity could be compelled, in a legal or equitable proceeding, to accept a money satisfaction of such interest.

(g) Notwithstanding subsection (f) of this section, the trustee may sell property under subsection (b) or (c) of this section free and clear of any vested or contingent right in the nature of dower or curtesy.

(h) Notwithstanding subsection (f) of this section, the trustee may sell both the estate's interest, under subsection (b) or (c) of this section, and the interest of any co-owner in property in which the debtor had, at the time of the commencement of the case, an undivided interest as a tenant in common, joint tenant, or tenant by the entirety, only if—

(1) partition in kind of such property among the estate and such co-owners is impracticable;

(2) sale of the estate's undivided interest in such property would realize significantly less for the estate than sale of such property free of the interests of such co-owners;

(3) the benefit to the estate of a sale of such property free of the interests of co-owners outweighs the detriment, if any, to such co-owners; and

(4) such property is not used in the production, transmission, or distribution, for sale, of electric energy or of natural or synthetic gas for heat, light, or power.

(i) Before the consummation of a sale of property to which subsection (g) or (h) of this section applies, or of property of the estate that was community property of the debtor and the debtor's spouse immediately before the commencement of the case, the debtor's spouse, or a co-owner of such property, as the case may be, may purchase such property at the price at which such sale is to be consummated.

(j) After a sale of property to which subsection (g) or (h) of this section applies, the trustee shall distribute to the debtor's spouse or the co-owners of such property, as the case may be, and to the estate, the proceeds of such sale, less the costs and expenses, not including any compensation of the trustee, of such sale, according to the interests of such spouse or co-owners, and of the estate.

(k) At a sale under subsection (b) of this section of property that is subject to a lien that secures an allowed claim, unless the court for cause orders otherwise the holder of such claim may bid at such sale, and, if the holder of such claim purchases such property, such holder may offset such claim against the purchase price of such property.

(*l*) Subject to the provisions of section 365, the trustee may use, sell, or lease property under subsection (b) or (c) of this section, or a plan under chapter 11, 12, or 13 of this title may provide for the use, sale, or lease of property, notwithstanding any provision in a contract, a lease, or applicable law that is conditioned on the insolvency or financial condition of the debtor, on the commencement of a case under this title concerning the debtor, or on the appointment of or the taking possession by a trustee in a case under this title or a custodian, and that effects, or gives an option to effect, a forfeiture, modification, or termination of the debtor's interest in such property.

(m) The reversal or modification on appeal of an authorization under subsection (b) or (c) of this section of a sale or lease of property does not affect the validity of a sale or lease under such authorization to an entity that purchased or leased such property in good faith, whether or not such entity knew of the pendency of the appeal, unless such authorization and such sale or lease were stayed pending appeal.

(n) The trustee may avoid a sale under this section if the sale price was controlled by an agreement among potential bidders at such sale, or may recover from a party to such agreement any amount by which the value of the property sold exceeds the price at which such sale was consummated, and may recover any costs, attorneys' fees, or expenses incurred in avoiding such sale or recovering such amount. In addition to any recovery under the preceding sentence, the court may grant judgment for punitive damages in favor of the estate and against any such party that entered into such an agreement in willful disregard of this subsection.

(*o*) Notwithstanding subsection (f), if a person purchases any interest in a consumer credit transaction that is subject to the Truth in Lending Act or any interest in a consumer credit contract (as defined in section 433.1 of title 16 of the Code of Federal Regulations (January 1, 2004), as amended from time to time), and if such interest is purchased through a sale under this section, then such person shall remain subject to all claims and defenses that are related to such consumer credit transaction or such consumer credit contract, to the same extent as such person would be subject to such claims and defenses of the consumer had such interest been purchased at a sale not under this section.

(p) In any hearing under this section—

(1) the trustee has the burden of proof on the issue of adequate protection; and

(2) the entity asserting an interest in property has the burden of proof on the issue of the validity, priority, or extent of such interest.

(Pub.L. 95–598, Nov. 6, 1978, 92 Stat. 2572; Pub.L. 98–353, Title III, § 442, July 10, 1984, 98 Stat. 371; Pub.L. 99–554, Title II, § 257(k), Oct. 27, 1986, 100 Stat. 3115; Pub.L. 103–394, Title I, § 109, Title II, §§ 214(b), 219(c), Title V, § 501(d)(8), Oct. 22, 1994, 108 Stat. 4113, 4126, 4129, 4144; Pub.L. 109–8, Title II, §§ 204, 231(a), Title XII, § 1221(a), Apr. 20, 2005, 119 Stat. 49, 72, 195.)

HISTORICAL AND STATUTORY NOTES

Revision Notes and Legislative Reports

1978 Acts. This section defines the right and powers of the trustee with respect to the use, sale or lease of property and the rights of other parties that have interests in the property involved. It applies in both liquidation and reorganization cases.

Subsection (a) defines "cash collateral" as cash, negotiable instruments, documents of title, securities, deposit accounts, or other cash equivalents in which the estate and an entity other than the estate have an interest, such as a lien or a co-ownership interest. The definition is not restricted to property of the estate that is cash collateral on the date of the filing of the petition. Thus, if "non-cash" collateral is disposed of and the proceeds come within the definition of "cash collateral" as set forth in this subsection, the proceeds would be cash collateral as long as they remain subject to the original lien on the "non-cash" collateral under section 52(b). To illustrate, rents received from real property before or after the commencement of the case would be cash collateral to the extent that they are subject to a lien.

Subsection (b) permits the trustees to use, sell, or lease, other than in the ordinary course of business, property of the estate upon notice and opportunity for objections and hearing thereon.

Subsection (c) governs use, sale, or lease in the ordinary course of business. If the business of the debtor is authorized to be operated under section 721, 1108, or 1304 of the bankruptcy code, then the trustee may use, sell, or lease property in the ordinary course of business or enter into ordinary course transactions without need for notice and hearing. This power is subject to several limitations. First, the court may restrict the trustee's powers in the order authorizing operation of the business. Second, with respect to cash collateral, the trustee may not use, sell, or lease cash collateral except upon court authorization after notice and a hearing, or with the consent of each entity that has an interest in such cash collateral. The same preliminary hearing procedure in the automatic stay section applies to a hearing under this subsection. In addition, the trustee is required to segregate and account for any cash collateral in the trustee's possession, custody, or control.

Under subsections (d) and (e), the use, sale, or lease of property is further limited by the concept of adequate protection. Sale, use, or lease of property in which an entity other than the estate has an interest may be effected only to the extent not inconsistent with any relief from the stay granted to that interest's holder. Moreover, the court may prohibit or condition the use, sale, or lease as is necessary to provide adequate protection of that interest. Again, the trustee has the burden of proof on the issue of adequate protection. Subsection (e) also provides that where a sale of the property is proposed, an entity that has an interest in such property may bid at the sale thereof and set off against the purchase price up to the amount of such entity's claim. No prior valuation under section 506(a) would limit this bidding right, since the bid at the sale would be determinative of value.

Subsection (f) permits sale of property free and clear of any interest in the property of an entity other than the estate. The trustee may sell free and clear if applicable nonbankruptcy law permits it, if the other entity consents, if the interest is a lien and the sale price of the property is greater than the amount secured by the lien, if the interest is in bona fide dispute, or if the other entity could be compelled to accept a money satisfaction of the interest in a legal or equitable proceeding. Sale under this subsection is subject to the adequate protection requirement. Most often, adequate protection in connection with a sale free and clear of other interests will be to have those interests attach to the proceeds of the sale.

At a sale free and clear of other interests, any holder of any interest in the property being sold will be permitted to bid. If that holder is the high bidder, he will be permitted to offset the value of his interest against the purchase price of the property. Thus, in the most common situation, a holder of a lien on property being sold may bid at the sale and, if successful, may offset the amount owed to him that is secured by the lien on the property (but may not offset other amounts owed to him) against the purchase price, and be liable to the trustee for the balance of the sale price, if any.

Subsection (g) permits the trustee to sell free and clear of any vested or contingent right in the nature of dower or curtesy.

Subsection (h) permits sale of a co-owner's interest in property in which the debtor had an undivided ownership interest such as a joint tenancy, a tenancy in common, or a tenancy by the entirety. Such a sale is permissible only if partition is impracticable, if sale of the estate's interest would realize significantly less for the estate than sale of the property free of the interests of the co-owners, and if the benefit to the estate of such a sale outweighs any detriment to the co-owners. This subsection does not apply to a co-owner's interest in a public utility when a disruption of the utilities services could result.

Subsection (i) provides protections for co-owners and spouses with dower, curtesy, or community property rights. It gives a right of first refusal to the co-owner or spouse at the price at which the sale is to be consummated.

Subsection (j) requires the trustee to distribute to the spouse or co-owner the appropriate portion of the proceeds of the sale, less certain administrative expenses.

Subsection (k) permits the trustee to use, sell, or lease property notwithstanding certain bankruptcy or ipso facto clauses that terminate the debtor's interest in the property or that work a forfeiture or modification of that interest. This subsection is not as broad as the anti-ipso facto provision in proposed 11 U.S.C. 541(c)(1).

Subsection (*l*) protects good faith purchasers of property sold under this section from a reversal on appeal of the sale authorization, unless the authorization for the sale and the sale itself were stayed pending appeal. The purchaser's knowledge of the appeal is irrelevant to the issue of good faith.

Subsection (m) is directed at collusive bidding on property sold under this section. It permits the trustee to void a sale if the price of the sale was controlled by an agreement among potential bidders. The trustees may also recover the excess of the value of the property over the purchase price, and may recover any costs, attorney's fees, or expenses incurred in voiding the sale or recovering the difference. In addition, the court is authorized to grant judgment in favor of the estate and against the collusive bidder if the agreement controlling the sale price was entered into in willful disregard of this subsection. The subsection does not specify the precise measure of damages, but simply provides for punitive damages, to be fixed in light of the circumstances. Senate Report No. 95–989.

1984 Acts. Statements by Legislative Leaders, see 1984 U.S.Code Cong. and Adm.News, p. 576.

1986 Acts. House Report No. 99–764 and House Conference Report No. 99–958, see 1986 U.S.Code Cong. and Adm.News, p. 5227.

1994 Acts. House Report No. 103–835, see 1994 U.S. Code Cong. and Adm. News, p. 3340.

2005 Acts. House Report No. 109–31(Part I), see 2005 U.S. Code Cong. and Adm. News, p. 88.

Legislative Statements

Section 363(a) of the House amendment defines "cash collateral" as defined in the Senate amendment. The broader definition of "soft collateral" contained in H.R. 8200 as passed by the House is deleted to remove limitations that were placed on the use, lease, or sale of inventory, accounts, contract rights, general intangibles, and chattel paper by the trustee or debtor in possession.

Section 363(c)(2) of the House amendment is derived from the Senate amendment. Similarly, sections 363(c)(3) and (4) are derived from comparable provisions in the Senate amendment in lieu of the contrary procedure contained in section 363(c) as passed by the House. The policy of the House amendment will generally require the court to schedule a preliminary hearing in accordance with the needs of the debtor to authorize the trustee or debtor in possession to use, sell, or lease cash collateral. The trustee or debtor in possession may use, sell, or lease cash collateral in the ordinary course of business only "after notice and a hearing."

Section 363(f) of the House amendment adopts an identical provision contained in the House bill, as opposed to an alternative provision contained in the Senate amendment.

Section 363(h) of the House amendment adopts a new paragraph (4) representing a compromise between the House bill and Senate amendment. The provision adds a limitation indicating that a trustee or debtor in possession sell jointly owned property only if the property is not used in the production, transmission, or distribution for sale, of electric energy or of natural or synthetic gas for heat, light, or power. This limitation is intended to protect public utilities from being deprived of power sources because of the bankruptcy of a joint owner.

Section 363(k) of the House amendment is derived from the third sentence of section 363(e) of the Senate amendment. The provision indicates that a secured creditor may bid in the full amount of the creditor's allowed claim, including the secured portion and any unsecured portion thereof in the event the creditor is undersecured, with respect to property that is subject to a lien that secures the allowed claim of the sale of the property.

References in Text

Section 7A of the Clayton Act, referred to in subsec. (b)(2), is section 7A of Act Oct. 15, 1914, c. 323, as added Sept. 30, 1976, Pub.L. 94–435, Title II, § 201, 90 Stat. 1390, which is classified to section 18a of Title 15, Commerce and Trade.

The Truth in Lending Act, referred to in subsec. (*o*), is Title I of Pub.L. 90–321, May 29, 1968, 82 Stat. 146, as amended, also known as TILA, which is classified principally to subchapter I of chapter 41 of Title 15, 15 U.S.C.A. § 1601 et seq. For complete classification, see Short Title note set out under 15 U.S.C.A. § 1601 and Tables.

Effective and Applicability Provisions

2005 Acts. Amendments by Pub.L. 109–8 effective, except as otherwise provided, 180 days after April 20, 2005, and inapplicable with respect to cases commenced under Title 11 before the effective date, see Pub.L. 109–8, § 1501, set out as a note under 11 U.S.C.A. § 101.

Pub.L. 109–8, Title XII, § 1221(d), Apr. 20, 2005, 119 Stat. 196, provided that: "The amendments made by this section [amending this section and 11 U.S.C.A. §§ 541 and 1129, and enacting provisions set out as a note under this section] shall apply to a case pending under title 11, United States Code [11 U.S.C.A. § 101 et seq.], on the date of enactment of this Act [Apr. 20, 2005], or filed under that title on or after that date of enactment, except that the court shall not confirm a plan under chapter 11 of title 11, United States Code [11 U.S.C.A. § 1101 et seq.], without considering whether this section would substantially affect the rights of a party in interest who first acquired rights with respect to the debtor after the date of the filing of the petition. The parties who may appear and be heard in a proceeding under this section include the attorney general of the State in which the debtor is incorporated, was formed, or does business."

1994 Acts. Amendments by Pub.L. 103–394 effective on Oct. 22, 1994, and not to apply with respect to cases commenced under this title before Oct. 22, 1994, see section 702 of Pub.L. 103–394, set out as a note under section 101 of this title.

1986 Acts. Amendment by Pub.L. 99–554 effective 30 days after Oct. 27, 1986, but not applicable with respect to cases commenced under this title before that date, see section 302(a), (c)(1) of Pub.L. 99–554, set out as a note under section 581 of Title 28, Judiciary and Judicial Procedure.

1984 Acts. Amendment by Pub.L. 98–353 effective with respect to cases filed 90 days after July 10, 1984, see section 552(a), formerly 553(a) of Pub.L. 98–353, set out as a note under section 101 of this title.

Separability of Provisions

If any provision of or amendment made by Pub.L. 103–394 or the application of such provision or amendment to any person or circumstance is held to be unconstitutional, the remaining provisions of and amendments made by Pub.L. 103–394 and the application of such provisions and amendments to any person or circumstance shall not be affected thereby, see section 701 of Pub.L. 103–394, set out as a note under section 101 of this title.

Rule of Construction

Pub.L. 109–8, Title XII, § 1221(e), Apr. 20, 2005, 119 Stat. 196, provided that: "Nothing in this section [amending this section and 11 U.S.C.A. §§ 541 and 1129, and enacting provisions set out as a note under this section] shall apply to a case pending under title 11, United States Code [11 U.S.C.A. § 101 et seq.] shall be construed to require the court in which a case under chapter 11 of title 11, United States Code [11 U.S.C.A. § 1101 et seq.], is pending to remand or refer any proceeding, issue, or controversy to any other court or to require the approval of any other court for the transfer of property."

CROSS REFERENCES

Adequate protection in chapter 12 cases, method of obtaining, see 11 USCA § 1205.

Adverse interest and conduct of officers of estate, see 18 USCA § 154.

Confirmation of plan, see 11 USCA § 1129.

Continuity of business operation and use, acquisition or disposition of property by debtor, see 11 USCA § 303.

Grain storage facility bankruptcies, expedited determinations, see 11 USCA § 557.

Identical rights and powers of debtor in Chapter 13 cases, see 11 USCA § 1303.

Postpetition effect of security interest, see 11 USCA § 552.

Priorities, see 11 USCA § 507.

Property of estate, see 11 USCA § 541.

Right of possession of party with security interest in—

Aircraft equipment and vessels, see 11 USCA § 1110.

Rolling stock equipment, see 11 USCA § 1168.

Rights and powers of debtor engaged in business, see 11 USCA § 1304.

Sale of property as affecting allowance of claim secured by lien on property of estate, see 11 USCA § 1111.

Sales free of interests, see 11 USCA § 1206.

Setoff, see 11 USCA § 553.

Turnover of property to estate, see 11 USCA § 542.

§ 364. Obtaining credit

(a) If the trustee is authorized to operate the business of the debtor under section 721, 1108, 1203, 1204, or 1304 of this title, unless the court orders otherwise, the trustee may obtain unsecured credit and incur unsecured debt in the ordinary course of business allowable under section 503(b)(1) of this title as an administrative expense.

(b) The court, after notice and a hearing, may authorize the trustee to obtain unsecured credit or to incur unsecured debt other than under subsection (a) of this section, allowable under section 503(b)(1) of this title as an administrative expense.

(c) If the trustee is unable to obtain unsecured credit allowable under section 503(b)(1) of this title as an administrative expense, the court, after notice and a hearing, may authorize the obtaining of credit or the incurring of debt—

(1) with priority over any or all administrative expenses of the kind specified in section 503(b) or 507(b) of this title;

(2) secured by a lien on property of the estate that is not otherwise subject to a lien; or

(3) secured by a junior lien on property of the estate that is subject to a lien.

(d)(1) The court, after notice and a hearing, may authorize the obtaining of credit or the incurring of debt secured by a senior or equal lien on property of the estate that is subject to a lien only if—

(A) the trustee is unable to obtain such credit otherwise; and

(B) there is adequate protection of the interest of the holder of the lien on the property of the estate on which such senior or equal lien is proposed to be granted.

(2) In any hearing under this subsection, the trustee has the burden of proof on the issue of adequate protection.

(e) The reversal or modification on appeal of an authorization under this section to obtain credit or incur debt, or of a grant under this section of a priority or a lien, does not affect the validity of any debt so incurred, or any priority or lien so granted, to an entity that extended such credit in good faith, whether or not such entity knew of the pendency of the appeal, unless such authorization and the incurring of such debt, or the granting of such priority or lien, were stayed pending appeal.

(f) Except with respect to an entity that is an underwriter as defined in section 1145(b) of this title, section 5 of the Securities Act of 1933, the Trust Indenture Act of 1939, and any State or local law requiring registration for offer or sale of a security or registration or licensing of an issuer of, underwriter of, or broker or dealer in, a security does not apply to the offer or sale under this section of a security that is not an equity security.

(Pub.L. 95–598, Nov. 6, 1978, 92 Stat. 2574; Pub.L. 99–554, Title II, § 257(*l*), Oct. 27, 1986, 100 Stat. 3115; Pub.L. 103–394, Title V, § 501(d)(9), Oct. 22, 1994, 108 Stat. 4144.)

HISTORICAL AND STATUTORY NOTES

Revision Notes and Legislative Reports

1978 Acts. This section is derived from provisions in current law governing certificates of indebtedness, but is much broader. It governs all obtaining of credit and incurring of debt by the estate.

Subsection (a) authorizes the obtaining of unsecured credit and the incurring of unsecured debt in the ordinary course of business if the business of the debtor is authorized to be operated under section 721, 1108, or 1304. The debts so incurred are allowable as administrative expenses under section 503(b)(1). The court may limit the estate's ability to incur debt under this subsection.

Subsection (b) permits the court to authorize the trustee to obtain unsecured credit and incur unsecured debts other than in the ordinary course of business, such as in order to wind up a liquidation case, or to obtain a substantial loan in an operating case. Debt incurred under this subsection is allowable as an administrative expense under section 503(b)(1).

Subsection (c) is closer to the concept of certificates of indebtedness in current law. It authorizes the obtaining of credit and the incurring of debt with some special priority, if the trustee is unable to obtain unsecured credit under subsection (a) or (b). The various priorities are (1) with priority over any or all administrative expenses; (2) secured by a lien on unencumbered property of the estate; or (3) secured by a junior lien on encumbered property. The priorities granted under this subsection do not interfere with existing property rights.

Subsection (d) grants the court the authority to authorize the obtaining of credit and the incurring of debt with a superiority [sic], that is a lien on encumbered property that is senior or equal to the existing lien on the property. The court may authorize such a super-priority [sic] only if the trustee is otherwise unable to obtain credit, and if there is adequate protection of the original lien holder's interest. Again, the trustee has the burden of proof on the issue of adequate protection.

Subsection (e) provides the same protection for credit extenders pending an appeal of an authorization to incur debt as is provided under section 363(*l*) for purchasers: the credit is not affected on appeal by reversal of the authorization and the incurring of the debt were stayed pending appeal. The protection runs to a good faith lender, whether or not he knew of the pendency of the appeal.

A claim arising as a result of lending or borrowing under this section will be a priority claim, as defined in proposed section 507(a)(1), even if the claim is granted a super-priority over administrative expenses and is to be paid in advance of other first priority claims. Senate Report No. 95–989.

1986 Acts. House Report No. 99–764 and House Conference Report No. 99–958, see 1986 U.S.Code Cong. and Adm.News, p. 5227.

1994 Acts. House Report No. 103–835, see 1994 U.S. Code Cong. and Adm. News, p. 3340.

Legislative Statements

Section 364(f) of the House amendment is new. This provision continues the exemption found in section 3(a)(7) of the Securities Act of 1933 [15 U.S.C.A. § 77c(a)(7)] for certificates of indebtedness issued by a trustee in bankruptcy. The exemption applies to any debt security issued under section 364 of title 11. The section does not intend to change present law which exempts such securities from the Trust Indenture Act, 15 U.S.C. 77aaa, et seq. (1976).

References in Text

Section 5 of the Securities Act of 1933, referred to in subsec. (f), is section 5 of Act May 27, 1933, c. 38, Title I, 48 Stat. 77, which is classified to section 77e of Title 15, Commerce and Trade.

The Trust Indenture Act of 1939, referred to in subsec. (f), is Title III of Act May 27, 1933, c. 38, as added Aug. 3, 1939, c. 411, 53 Stat. 1149, as amended, which is classified generally to subchapter III (§ 77aaa et seq.) of chapter 2A of Title 15, Commerce and Trade. For complete classification of this Act to the Code, see section 77aaa of Title 15 and Tables.

Effective and Applicability Provisions

1994 Acts. Amendment by Pub.L. 103–394 effective on Oct. 22, 1994, and not to apply with respect to cases commenced under this title before Oct. 22, 1994, see section 702 of Pub.L. 103–394, set out as a note under section 101 of this title.

1986 Acts. Amendment by Pub.L. 99–554 effective 30 days after Oct. 27, 1986, but not applicable with respect to cases commenced under this title before that date, see section 302(a), (c)(1) of Pub.L. 99–554, set out as a note under section 581 of Title 28, Judiciary and Judicial Procedure.

Separability of Provisions

If any provision of or amendment made by Pub.L. 103–394 or the application of such provision or amendment to any person or circumstance is held to be unconstitutional, the remaining provisions of and amendments made by Pub.L. 103–394 and the application of such provisions and amendments to any person or circumstance shall not be affected thereby, see section 701 of Pub.L. 103–394, set out as a note under section 101 of this title.

CROSS REFERENCES

Adequate protection in Chapter 12 cases, method of obtaining, see 11 USCA § 1205.

Applicability of subsecs. (c) to (f) of this section in Chapter 9 cases, see 11 USCA § 901.

Enforcement of claims against debtor in Chapter 9 cases, automatic stay of, see 11 USCA § 922.

Priorities, see 11 USCA § 507.

Reversal on appeal of finding of jurisdiction as affecting validity of debt incurred, see 11 USCA § 921.

Rights and powers of debtor engaged in business, see 11 USCA § 1304.

§ 365. Executory contracts and unexpired leases

(a) Except as provided in sections 765 and 766 of this title and in subsections (b), (c), and (d) of this section, the trustee, subject to the court's approval, may assume or reject any executory contract or unexpired lease of the debtor.

(b)(1) If there has been a default in an executory contract or unexpired lease of the debtor, the trustee may not assume such contract or lease unless, at the time of assumption of such contract or lease, the trustee—

(A) cures, or provides adequate assurance that the trustee will promptly cure, such default other than a default that is a breach of a provision relating to the satisfaction of any provision (other than a penalty rate or penalty provision) relating to a default arising from any failure to perform nonmonetary obligations under an unexpired lease of real property, if it is impossible for the trustee to cure such default by performing nonmonetary acts at and after the time of assumption, except that if such default arises from a failure to operate in accordance with a nonresidential real property lease, then such default shall be cured by performance at and after the time of assumption in accordance with such lease, and pecuniary losses resulting from such default shall be compensated in accordance with the provisions of this paragraph;

(B) compensates, or provides adequate assurance that the trustee will promptly compensate, a party other than the debtor to such contract or lease, for any actual pecuniary loss to such party resulting from such default; and

(C) provides adequate assurance of future performance under such contract or lease.

(2) Paragraph (1) of this subsection does not apply to a default that is a breach of a provision relating to—

(A) the insolvency or financial condition of the debtor at any time before the closing of the case;

(B) the commencement of a case under this title;

(C) the appointment of or taking possession by a trustee in a case under this title or a custodian before such commencement; or

(D) the satisfaction of any penalty rate or penalty provision relating to a default arising from any failure by the debtor to perform nonmonetary obligations under the executory contract or unexpired lease.

(3) For the purposes of paragraph (1) of this subsection and paragraph (2)(B) of subsection (f), adequate assurance of future performance of a lease of real property in a shopping center includes adequate assurance—

(A) of the source of rent and other consideration due under such lease, and in the case of an assignment, that the financial condition and operating performance of the proposed assignee and its guarantors, if any, shall be similar to the financial condition and operating performance of the debtor and its guarantors, if any, as of the time the debtor became the lessee under the lease;

(B) that any percentage rent due under such lease will not decline substantially;

(C) that assumption or assignment of such lease is subject to all the provisions thereof, including (but not limited to) provisions such as a radius, location, use, or exclusivity provision, and will not breach any such provision contained in any other lease, financing agreement, or master agreement relating to such shopping center; and

(D) that assumption or assignment of such lease will not disrupt any tenant mix or balance in such shopping center.

(4) Notwithstanding any other provision of this section, if there has been a default in an unexpired lease of the debtor, other than a default of a kind specified in paragraph (2) of this subsection, the trustee may not require a lessor to provide services or supplies incidental to such lease before assumption of such lease unless the lessor is compensated under the terms of such lease for any services and supplies provided under such lease before assumption of such lease.

(c) The trustee may not assume or assign any executory contract or unexpired lease of the debtor, whether or not such contract or lease prohibits or restricts assignment of rights or delegation of duties, if—

(1)(A) applicable law excuses a party, other than the debtor, to such contract or lease from accepting performance from or rendering performance to an entity other than the debtor or the debtor in possession, whether or not such contract or lease prohibits or restricts assignment of rights or delegation of duties; and

(B) such party does not consent to such assumption or assignment; or

(2) such contract is a contract to make a loan, or extend other debt financing or financial accommodations, to or for the benefit of the debtor, or to issue a security of the debtor; or

(3) such lease is of nonresidential real property and has been terminated under applicable nonbankruptcy law prior to the order for relief.

[**(4)** Repealed. Pub.L. 109–8, Title III, § 328(a)(2)(C), Apr. 20, 2005, 119 Stat. 100]

(d)(1) In a case under chapter 7 of this title, if the trustee does not assume or reject an executory contract or unexpired lease of residential real property or of personal property of the debtor within 60 days after the order for relief, or within such additional time as the court, for cause, within such 60-day period, fixes, then such contract or lease is deemed rejected.

(2) In a case under chapter 9, 11, 12, or 13 of this title, the trustee may assume or reject an executory contract or unexpired lease of residential real property or of personal property of the debtor at any time before the confirmation of a plan but the court, on the request of any party to such contract or lease, may order the trustee to determine within a specified period of time whether to assume or reject such contract or lease.

(3) The trustee shall timely perform all the obligations of the debtor, except those specified in section 365(b)(2), arising from and after the order for relief under any unexpired lease of nonresidential real property, until such lease is assumed or rejected, notwithstanding section 503(b)(1) of this title. The court may extend, for cause, the time for performance of any such obligation that arises within 60 days after the date of the order for relief, but the time for performance shall not be extended beyond such 60-day period. This subsection shall not be deemed to affect the trustee's obligations under the provisions of subsection (b) or (f) of this section. Acceptance of any such performance does not constitute waiver or relinquishment of the lessor's rights under such lease or under this title.

(4)(A) Subject to subparagraph (B), an unexpired lease of nonresidential real property under which the debtor is the lessee shall be deemed rejected, and the trustee shall immediately surrender that nonresidential real property to the lessor, if the trustee does not assume or reject the unexpired lease by the earlier of—

(i) the date that is 120 days after the date of the order for relief; or

(ii) the date of the entry of an order confirming a plan.

(B)(i) The court may extend the period determined under subparagraph (A), prior to the expiration of the 120–day period, for 90 days on the motion of the trustee or lessor for cause.

(ii) If the court grants an extension under clause (i), the court may grant a subsequent extension only upon prior written consent of the lessor in each instance.

(5) The trustee shall timely perform all of the obligations of the debtor, except those specified in section 365(b)(2), first arising from or after 60 days after the order for relief in a case under chapter 11 of this title under an unexpired lease of personal property (other than personal property leased to an individual primarily for personal, family, or household purposes), until such lease is assumed or rejected notwithstanding section 503(b)(1) of this title, unless the court, after notice and a hearing and based on the equities of the case, orders otherwise with respect to the obligations or timely performance thereof. This subsection shall not be deemed to affect the trustee's obligations under the provisions of subsection (b) or (f). Acceptance of any such performance does not constitute waiver or relinquishment of the lessor's rights under such lease or under this title.

[**(6) to (9)** Repealed. Pub.L. 109–8, Title III, § 328(a)(3)(A), Apr. 20, 2005, 119 Stat. 100]

[**(10)** Redesignated (5)]

(e)(1) Notwithstanding a provision in an executory contract or unexpired lease, or in applicable law, an executory contract or unexpired lease of the debtor may not be terminated or modified, and any right or obligation under such contract or lease may not be terminated or modified, at any time after the commencement of the case solely because of a provision in such contract or lease that is conditioned on—

(A) the insolvency or financial condition of the debtor at any time before the closing of the case;

(B) the commencement of a case under this title; or

(C) the appointment of or taking possession by a trustee in a case under this title or a custodian before such commencement.

(2) Paragraph (1) of this subsection does not apply to an executory contract or unexpired lease of the debtor, whether or not such contract or lease prohibits or restricts assignment of rights or delegation of duties, if—

(A)(i) applicable law excuses a party, other than the debtor, to such contract or lease from accepting performance from or rendering performance to the trustee or to an assignee of such contract or lease, whether or not such contract or lease prohibits or restricts assignment of rights or delegation of duties; and

(ii) such party does not consent to such assumption or assignment; or

(B) such contract is a contract to make a loan, or extend other debt financing or financial accommodations, to or for the benefit of the debtor, or to issue a security of the debtor.

(f)(1) Except as provided in subsections (b) and (c) of this section, notwithstanding a provision in an executory contract or unexpired lease of the debtor, or in applicable law, that prohibits, restricts, or conditions the assignment of such contract or lease, the trustee may assign such contract or lease under paragraph (2) of this subsection.

(2) The trustee may assign an executory contract or unexpired lease of the debtor only if—

(A) the trustee assumes such contract or lease in accordance with the provisions of this section; and

(B) adequate assurance of future performance by the assignee of such contract or lease is provided, whether or not there has been a default in such contract or lease.

(3) Notwithstanding a provision in an executory contract or unexpired lease of the debtor, or in applicable law that terminates or modifies, or permits a party other than the debtor to terminate or modify, such contract or lease or a right or obligation under such contract or lease on account of an assignment of such contract or lease, such contract, lease, right, or obligation may not be terminated or modified under such provision because of the assumption or assignment of such contract or lease by the trustee.

(g) Except as provided in subsections (h)(2) and (i)(2) of this section, the rejection of an executory contract or unexpired lease of the debtor constitutes a breach of such contract or lease—

(1) if such contract or lease has not been assumed under this section or under a plan confirmed under chapter 9, 11, 12, or 13 of this title, immediately before the date of the filing of the petition; or

(2) if such contract or lease has been assumed under this section or under a plan confirmed under chapter 9, 11, 12, or 13 of this title—

(A) if before such rejection the case has not been converted under section 1112, 1208, or 1307 of this title, at the time of such rejection; or

(B) if before such rejection the case has been converted under section 1112, 1208, or 1307 of this title—

(i) immediately before the date of such conversion, if such contract or lease was assumed before such conversion; or

(ii) at the time of such rejection, if such contract or lease was assumed after such conversion.

(h)(1)(A) If the trustee rejects an unexpired lease of real property under which the debtor is the lessor and—

(i) if the rejection by the trustee amounts to such a breach as would entitle the lessee to treat such lease as terminated by virtue of its terms, applicable nonbankruptcy law, or any agreement made by the lessee, then the lessee under such lease may treat such lease as terminated by the rejection; or

(ii) if the term of such lease has commenced, the lessee may retain its rights under such lease (including rights such as those relating to the amount and timing of payment of rent and other amounts payable by the lessee and any right of use, possession, quiet enjoyment, subletting, assignment, or hypothecation) that are in or appurtenant to the real property for the balance of the term of such lease and for any renewal or extension of such rights to the extent that such rights are enforceable under applicable nonbankruptcy law.

(B) If the lessee retains its rights under subparagraph (A)(ii), the lessee may offset against the rent reserved under such lease for the balance of the term after the date of the rejection of such lease and for the term of any renewal or extension of such lease, the value of any damage caused by the nonperformance after the date of such rejection, of any obligation of the debtor under such lease, but the lessee shall not have any other right against the estate or the debtor on account of any damage occurring after such date caused by such nonperformance.

(C) The rejection of a lease of real property in a shopping center with respect to which the lessee elects to retain its rights under subparagraph (A)(ii) does not affect the enforceability under applicable nonbankruptcy law of any provision in the lease pertaining to radius, location, use, exclusivity, or tenant mix or balance.

(D) In this paragraph, "lessee" includes any successor, assign, or mortgagee permitted under the terms of such lease.

(2)(A) If the trustee rejects a timeshare interest under a timeshare plan under which the debtor is the timeshare interest seller and—

(i) if the rejection amounts to such a breach as would entitle the timeshare interest purchaser to treat the timeshare plan as terminated under its terms, applicable nonbankruptcy law, or any agreement made by timeshare interest purchaser, the timeshare interest purchaser under the timeshare plan may treat the timeshare plan as terminated by such rejection; or

(ii) if the term of such timeshare interest has commenced, then the timeshare interest purchaser may retain its rights in such timeshare interest for the balance of such term and for any term of renewal or extension of such timeshare interest to the extent that such rights are enforceable under applicable nonbankruptcy law.

(B) If the timeshare interest purchaser retains its rights under subparagraph (A), such timeshare interest purchaser may offset against the moneys due for such timeshare interest for the balance of the term after the date of the rejection of such timeshare interest, and the term of any renewal or extension of such timeshare interest, the value of any damage caused by the nonperformance after the date of such rejection, of any obligation of the debtor under such timeshare plan, but the timeshare interest purchaser shall not have any right against the estate or the debtor on account of any damage occurring after such date caused by such nonperformance.

(i)(1) If the trustee rejects an executory contract of the debtor for the sale of real property or for the sale of a timeshare interest under a timeshare plan, under which the purchaser is in possession, such purchaser may treat such contract as terminated, or, in the alternative, may remain in possession of such real property or timeshare interest.

(2) If such purchaser remains in possession—

(A) such purchaser shall continue to make all payments due under such contract, but may,[1] offset against such payments any damages occurring after the date of the rejection of such contract caused by the nonperformance of any obligation of the debtor after such date, but such purchaser does not have any rights against the estate on account of any damages arising after such date from such rejection, other than such offset; and

(B) the trustee shall deliver title to such purchaser in accordance with the provisions of such contract, but is relieved of all other obligations to perform under such contract.

(j) A purchaser that treats an executory contract as terminated under subsection (i) of this section, or a party whose executory contract to purchase real property from the debtor is rejected and under which such party is not in possession, has a lien on the interest of the debtor in such property for the recovery of any portion of the purchase price that such purchaser or party has paid.

(k) Assignment by the trustee to an entity of a contract or lease assumed under this section relieves the trustee and the estate from any liability for any breach of such contract or lease occurring after such assignment.

(*l*) If an unexpired lease under which the debtor is the lessee is assigned pursuant to this section, the lessor of the property may require a deposit or other security for the performance of the debtor's obligations under the lease substantially the same as would have been required by the landlord upon the initial leasing to a similar tenant.

(m) For purposes of this section 365 and sections 541(b)(2) and 362(b)(10), leases of real property shall include any rental agreement to use real property.

(n)(1) If the trustee rejects an executory contract under which the debtor is a licensor of a right to intellectual property, the licensee under such contract may elect—

(A) to treat such contract as terminated by such rejection if such rejection by the trustee amounts to such a breach as would entitle the licensee to treat such contract as terminated by virtue of its own terms, applicable nonbankruptcy law, or an agreement made by the licensee with another entity; or

(B) to retain its rights (including a right to enforce any exclusivity provision of such contract, but excluding any other right under applicable nonbankruptcy law to specific performance of such contract) under such contract and under any agreement supplementary to such contract, to such intellectual property (including any embodiment of such intellectual property to the extent protected by applicable nonbankruptcy law), as such rights existed immediately before the case commenced, for—

(i) the duration of such contract; and

(ii) any period for which such contract may be extended by the licensee as of right under applicable nonbankruptcy law.

(2) If the licensee elects to retain its rights, as described in paragraph (1)(B) of this subsection, under such contract—

(A) the trustee shall allow the licensee to exercise such rights;

(B) the licensee shall make all royalty payments due under such contract for the duration of such contract and for any period described in paragraph (1)(B) of this subsection for which the licensee extends such contract; and

(C) the licensee shall be deemed to waive—

(i) any right of setoff it may have with respect to such contract under this title or applicable nonbankruptcy law; and

(ii) any claim allowable under section 503(b) of this title arising from the performance of such contract.

(3) If the licensee elects to retain its rights, as described in paragraph (1)(B) of this subsection, then on the written request of the licensee the trustee shall—

(A) to the extent provided in such contract, or any agreement supplementary to such contract, provide to the licensee any intellectual property (including such embodiment) held by the trustee; and

(B) not interfere with the rights of the licensee as provided in such contract, or any agreement supplementary to such contract, to such intellectual property (including such embodiment) including any right to obtain such intellectual property (or such embodiment) from another entity.

(4) Unless and until the trustee rejects such contract, on the written request of the licensee the trustee shall—

(A) to the extent provided in such contract or any agreement supplementary to such contract—

(i) perform such contract; or

(ii) provide to the licensee such intellectual property (including any embodiment of such intellectual property to the extent protected by applicable nonbankruptcy law) held by the trustee; and

(B) not interfere with the rights of the licensee as provided in such contract, or any agreement supplementary to such contract, to such intellectual property (including such embodiment), including any right to obtain such intellectual property (or such embodiment) from another entity.

(*o*) In a case under chapter 11 of this title, the trustee shall be deemed to have assumed (consistent with the debtor's other obligations under section 507), and shall immediately cure any deficit under, any commitment by the debtor to a Federal depository institutions regulatory agency (or predecessor to such agency) to maintain the capital of an insured depository institution, and any claim for a subsequent breach of the obligations thereunder shall be entitled to priority under section 507. This subsection shall not extend any commitment that would otherwise be terminated by any act of such an agency.

(p)(1) If a lease of personal property is rejected or not timely assumed by the trustee under subsection (d), the leased property is no longer property of the estate and the stay under section 362(a) is automatically terminated.

(2)(A) If the debtor in a case under chapter 7 is an individual, the debtor may notify the creditor in writing that the debtor desires to assume the lease. Upon being so notified, the creditor may, at its option, notify the debtor that it is willing to have the lease assumed by the debtor and may condition such assumption on cure of any outstanding default on terms set by the contract.

(B) If, not later than 30 days after notice is provided under subparagraph (A), the debtor notifies the lessor in writing that the lease is assumed, the liability under the lease will be assumed by the debtor and not by the estate.

(C) The stay under section 362 and the injunction under section 524(a) (2) shall not be violated by notification of the debtor and negotiation of cure under this subsection.

(3) In a case under chapter 11 in which the debtor is an individual and in a case under chapter 13, if the debtor is the lessee with respect to personal property and the lease is not assumed in the plan confirmed by the court, the lease is deemed rejected as of the conclusion of the hearing on confirmation. If the lease is rejected, the stay under section 362 and any stay under section 1301 is automatically terminated with respect to the property subject to the lease.

(Pub.L. 95–598, Nov. 6, 1978, 92 Stat. 2574; Pub.L. 98–353, Title III, §§ 362, 402–404, July 10, 1984, 98 Stat. 361, 367; Pub.L. 99–554, Title II, §§ 257(j), (m), 283(e), Oct. 27, 1986, 100 Stat. 3115, 3117; Pub.L. 100–506, § 1(b), Oct. 18, 1988, 102 Stat. 2538; Pub.L. 101–647, Title XXV, § 2522(c), Nov. 29, 1990, 104 Stat. 4866; Pub.L. 102–365, § 19(b)–(e), Sept. 3, 1992, 106 Stat. 982–984; Pub.L. 103–394, Title II, §§ 205(a), 219(a), (b), Title V, § 501(d)(10), Oct. 22, 1994, 108 Stat. 4122, 4128, 4145; Pub.L. 103–429, § 1, Oct. 31, 1994, 108 Stat. 4377; Pub.L. 109–8, Title III, §§ 309(b), 328(a), Title IV, § 404, Apr. 20, 2005, 119 Stat. 82, 100, 104.)

1 So in original. The comma probably should not appear.

HISTORICAL AND STATUTORY NOTES

Revision Notes and Legislative Reports

1978 Acts. Subsection (a) of this section authorizes the trustee, subject to the court's approval, to assume or reject an executory contract or unexpired lease. Though there is no precise definition of what contracts are executory, it generally includes contracts on which performance remains due to some extent on both sides. A note is not usually an executory contract if the only performance that remains is repayment. Performance on one side of the contract would have been completed and the contract is no longer executory.

Because of the volatile nature of the commodities markets and the special provisions governing commodity broker liquidations in subchapter IV of chapter 7, the provisions governing distribution in section 765(a) will govern if any conflict between those provisions and the provisions of this section arise.

Subsections (b), (c), and (d) provide limitations on the trustee's powers. Subsection (b) requires the trustee to cure any default in the contract or lease and to provide adequate assurance of future performance if there has been a default, before he may assume. This provision does not apply to defaults under ipso facto or bankruptcy clauses, which is a significant departure from present law.

Subsection (b)(3) permits termination of leases entered into prior to the effective date of this title in liquidation cases if certain other conditions are met.

Subsection (b)(4) prohibits the trustee's assumption of an executory contract requiring the other party to make a loan or deliver equipment to or to issue a security of the debtor. The purpose of this subsection is to make it clear that a party to a transaction which is based upon the financial strength of a debtor should not be required to extend new credit to the debtor whether in the form of loans, lease financing, or the purchase or discount of notes.

Subsection (b)(5) provides that in lease situations common to shopping centers, protections must be provided for the lessor if the trustee assumes the lease, including protection against decline in percentage rents, breach of agreements with other tenants, and preservation of the tenant mix. Protection for tenant mix will not be required in the office building situation.

Subsection (c) prohibits the trustee from assuming or assigning a contract or lease if applicable nonbankruptcy law excuses the other party from performance to someone other than the debtor, unless the other party consents. This prohibition applies only in the situation in which applicable law excuses the other party from performance independent of any restrictive language in the contract or lease itself.

Subsection (d) places time limits on assumption and rejection. In a liquidation case, the trustee must assume within 60 days (or within an additional 60 days, if the court, for cause, extends the time). If not assumed, the contract or lease is deemed rejected. In a rehabilitation case, the time limit is not fixed in the bill. However, if the other party to the contract or lease requests the court to fix a time, the court may specify a time within which the trustee must act. This provision will prevent parties in contractual or lease relationships with the debtor from being left in doubt concerning their status vis-a-vis the estate.

Subsection (e) invalidates ipso facto or bankruptcy clauses. These clauses, protected under present law, automatically terminate the contract or lease, or permit the other contracting party to terminate the contract or lease, in the event of bankruptcy. This frequently hampers rehabilitation efforts. If the trustee may assume or assign the contract under the limitations imposed by the remainder of the section, the contract or lease may be utilized to assist in the debtor's rehabilitation or liquidation.

The unenforceability of ipso facto or bankruptcy clauses proposed under this section will require the courts to be sensitive to the rights of the nondebtor party to executory contracts and unexpired leases. If the trustee is to assume a contract or lease, the court will have to insure that the trustee's performance under the contract or lease gives the other contracting party the full benefit of his bargain.

This subsection does not limit the application of an ipso facto or bankruptcy clause if a new insolvency or receivership occurs after the bankruptcy case is closed. That is, the clause is not invalidated in toto, but merely made inapplicable during the case for the purposes of disposition of the executory contract or unexpired lease.

Subsection (f) partially invalidates restrictions on assignment of contracts or leases by the trustee to a third party. The subsection imposes two restrictions on the trustee: he must first assume the contract or lease, subject to all the restrictions on assumption found in the section, and adequate assurance of future performance must be provided to the other contracting party. Paragraph (3) of the subsection invalidates contractual provisions that permit termination or modification in the event of an assignment, as contrary to the policy of this subsection.

Subsection (g) defines the time as of which a rejection of an executory contract or unexpired lease constitutes a breach of the contract or lease. Generally, the breach is as of the date immediately preceding the date of the petition. The purpose is to treat rejection claims as prepetition claims. The remainder of the subsection specifies different times for cases that are converted from one chapter to another. The provisions of this subsection are not a substantive authorization to breach or reject an assumed contract. Rather, they prescribe the rules for the allowance of claims in case an assumed contract is breached, or if a case under chapter 11 in which a contract has been assumed is converted to a case under chapter 7 in which the contract is rejected.

Subsection (h) protects real property lessees of the debtor if the trustee rejects an unexpired lease under which the debtor is the lessor (or sublessor). The subsection permits the lessee to remain in possession of the leased property or to treat the lease as terminated by the rejection. The balance of the term of the lease referred to in paragraph (1) will include any renewal terms that are enforceable by the tenant, but not renewal terms if the landlord had an option to terminate. Thus, the tenant will not be deprived of his estate for the term for which he bargained. If the lessee remains in possession, he may offset the rent reserved under the lease against damages caused by the rejection, but does not have any affirmative rights against the estate for any damages after the rejection that result from the rejection.

Subsection (i) gives a purchaser of real property under a land installment sales contract similar protection. The purchaser, if the contract is rejected, may remain in possession or may treat the contract as terminated. If the purchaser remains in possession, he is required to continue to make the payments due, but may offset damages that occur after rejection. The trustee is required to deliver title, but is relieved of all other obligations to perform.

A purchaser that treats the contract as terminated is granted a lien on the property to the extent of the purchase price paid. A party with a contract to purchase land from the debtor has a lien on the property to secure the price already paid, if the contract is rejected and the purchaser is not yet in possession.

Subsection (k) relieves the trustee and the estate of liability for a breach of an assigned contract or lease that occurs after the assignment. Senate Report No. 95–989.

Subsection (c) prohibits the trustee from assuming or assigning a contract or lease if applicable nonbankruptcy law excuses the other party from performance to someone other than the debtor, unless the other party consents. This prohibition applies only in the situation in which applicable law excuses the other party from performance independent of any restrictive language in the contract or lease itself. The purpose of this subsection, at least in part, is to prevent the trustee from requiring new advances of money or other property. The section permits the trustee to continue to use and pay for property already advanced, but is not designed to permit the trustee to demand new loans or additional transfers of property under lease commitments.

Thus, under this provision, contracts such as loan commitments and letters of credit are nonassignable, and may not be assumed by the trustee.

Subsection (e) invalidates ipso facto or bankruptcy clauses. These clauses, protected under present law, automatically terminate the contract or lease, or permit the other contracting party to terminate the contract or lease, in the event of bankruptcy. This frequently hampers rehabilitation efforts. If the trustee may assume or assign the contract under the limitations imposed by the remainder of the section, then the contract or lease may be utilized to assist in the debtor's rehabilitation or liquidation.

The unenforceability of ipso facto or bankruptcy clauses proposed under this section will require the courts to be sensitive to the rights of the nondebtor party to executory contracts and unexpired leases. If the trustee is to assume a contract or lease, the courts will have to insure that the trustee's performance under the contract or lease gives the other contracting party the full benefit of his bargain. An example of the complexity that may arise in these situations and the need for a determination of all aspects of a particular executory contract or unexpired lease is the shopping center lease under which the debtor is a tenant in a shopping center.

A shopping center is often a carefully planned enterprise, and though it consists of numerous individual tenants, the center is planned as a single unit, often subject to a master lease or financing agreement. Under these agreements, the tenant mix in a shopping center may be as important to the lessor as the actual promised rental payments, because certain mixes will attract higher patronage of the stores in the center, and thus a higher rental for the landlord from those stores that are subject to a percentage of gross receipts rental agreement. Thus, in order to assure a landlord of his bargained for exchange, the court would have to consider such factors as the nature of the business to be conducted by the trustee or his assignee, whether that business complies with the requirements of any master agreement, whether the kind of business proposed will generate gross sales in an amount such that the percentage rent specified in the lease is substantially the same as what would have been provided by the debtor, and whether the business proposed to be conducted would result in a breach of other clauses in master agreements relating, for example, to tenant mix and location.

This subsection does not limit the application of an ipso facto or bankruptcy clause to a new insolvency or receivership after the bankruptcy case is closed. That is, the clause is not invalidated in toto, but merely made inapplicable during the case for the purpose of disposition of the executory contract or unexpired lease. House Report No. 95–595.

1984 Acts. Statements by Legislative Leaders, see 1984 U.S.Code Cong. and Adm.News, p. 576.

1986 Acts. House Report No. 99–764 and House Conference Report No. 99–958, see 1986 U.S.Code Cong. and Adm.News, p. 5227.

1988 Acts. Senate Report No. 100–505, see 1988 U.S.Code Cong. and Adm.News, p. 3200.

1990 Acts. House Report No. 101–681(I), see 1990 U.S.Code Cong. and Adm.News, p. 6472.

1992 Acts. House Report No. 102–205, see U.S.Code Cong. and Adm.News, p. 866.

1994 Acts. House Report No. 103–835, see 1994 U.S. Code Cong. and Adm. News, p. 3340.

House Report No. 103–831, see 1994 U.S. Code Cong. and Adm. News, p. 3579.

2005 Acts. House Report No. 109–31(Part I), see 2005 U.S. Code Cong. and Adm. News, p. 88.

Legislative Statements

Section 365(b)(3) represents a compromise between H.R. 8200 as passed by the House and the Senate amendment. The provision adopts standards contained in section 365(b)(5) of the Senate amendment to define adequate assurance of future performance of a lease of real property in a shopping center.

Section 365(b)(4) of the House amendment indicates that after default the trustee may not require a lessor to supply services or materials without assumption unless the lessor is compensated as provided in the lease.

Section 365(c)(2) and (3) likewise represent a compromise between H.R. 8200 as passed by the House and the Senate amendment. Section 365(c)(2) is derived from section 365(b)(4) of the Senate amendment but does not apply to a contract to deliver equipment as provided in the Senate amendment. As contained in the House amendment, the provision prohibits a trustee or debtor in possession from assuming or assigning an executory contract of the debtor to make a loan, or extend other debt financing or financial accommodations, to or for the benefit of the debtor, or the issuance of a security of the debtor.

Section 365(e) is a refinement of comparable provisions contained in the House bill and Senate amendment. Sections 365(e)(1) and (2)(A) restate section 365(e) of H.R. 8200 as passed by the House. Sections 365(e)(2)(B) expands the section to permit termination of an executory contract or unexpired lease of the debtor if such contract is a contract to make a loan, or extend other debt financing or financial accommodations, to or for the benefit of the debtor, or for the issuance of a security of the debtor.

Characterization of contracts to make a loan, or extend other debt financing or financial accommodations, is limited to the extension of cash or a line of credit and is not intended to embrace ordinary leases or contracts to provide goods or services with payments to be made over time.

Section 365(f) is derived from H.R. 8200 as passed by the House. Deletion of language in section 365(f)(3) of the Senate amendment is done as a matter of style. Restrictions with respect to assignment of an executory contract or unexpired lease are superfluous since the debtor may assign an executory contract or unexpired lease of the debtor only if such contract is first assumed under section 364(f)(2)(A) of the House amendment.

Section 363(h) of the House amendment represents a modification of section 365(h) of the Senate amendment. The House amendment makes clear that in the case of a bankrupt lessor, a lessee may remain in possession for the balance of the term of a lease and any renewal or extension of the term only to the extent that such renewal or extension may be obtained by the lessee without the permission of the landlord or some third party under applicable non-bankruptcy law.

References in Text

Chapter 7, referred to in subsec. (p)(1), is chapter 7 of this title, 11 U.S.C.A. § 701 et seq.

Chapter 11 or 13, referred to in subsec. (p)(3), is chapter 11 or 13 of this title, 11 U.S.C.A. § 1101 et seq. or 11 U.S.C.A. § 1301 et seq., respectively.

Codifications

Amendment to subsec. (c)(1)(A) by Pub.L. 99–554, § 283(e)(1)(1), struck out "or an assignee of such contract or lease" as the probable intent of Congress, notwithstanding directory language requiring "or and assignee of such contract or lease" be struck out.

Amendment by section 501(d)(10)(A) of Pub.L. 103–394, purporting to amend subsec. (d)(6)(C) of this section by substituting "section 40102 of title 49" for "the Federal Aviation Act of 1958 (49 U.S.C. 1301)", could not be executed, as the latter phrase did not appear in text.

Amendment by section 1(2) of Pub.L. 103–429, purporting to amend subsec. (p) of this section by substituting "section 40102(a) of title 49" for "section 101(3) of the Federal Aviation Act of 1958", could not be executed, as subsec. (p) had already been stricken out pursuant to section 510(d)(10)(E) of Pub.L. 103–394.

Effective and Applicability Provisions

2005 Acts. Amendments by Pub.L. 109–8 effective, except as otherwise provided, 180 days after April 20, 2005, and inapplicable with respect to cases commenced under Title 11 before the effective date, see Pub.L. 109–8, § 1501, set out as a note under 11 U.S.C.A. § 101.

1994 Acts. Amendments by Pub.L. 103–394 effective on Oct. 22, 1994, and not to apply with respect to cases commenced under this title before Oct. 22, 1994, see section 702 of Pub.L. 103–394, set out as a note under section 101 of this title.

1992 Acts. Section 19(f) of Pub.L. 102–365 provided that:

"The amendments made by this section [amending this section and enacting provisions set out as a note under this section] shall be in effect for the 12–month period that begins on the date of enactment of this Act [Sept. 3, 1992] and shall apply in all proceedings involving an affected air carrier (as defined in section 365(p) of title 11, United States Code, as amended by this section [subsec. (p) of this section]) that are pending during such 12–month period. Not later than 9 months after the date of enactment [Sept. 3, 1992], the Administrator of the Federal Aviation Administration shall report to the Committee on Commerce, Science, and Transportation and Committee on the Judiciary of the Senate and the Committee on the Judiciary and Committee on Public Works and Transportation of the House of Representatives on whether this section shall apply to proceedings that are commenced after such 12–month period."

[Any reference in any provision of law enacted before Jan. 4, 1995, to the Committee on Public Works and Transportation of the House of Representatives treated as referring to the Committee on Transportation and Infrastructure of the House of Representatives, see section 1(a)(9) of Pub.L. 104–14, set out as a note preceding section 21 of Title 2, The Congress.]

1988 Acts. Amendment by Pub.L. 100–506 effective on Oct. 18, 1988, except with respect to any case commenced under this title before such date, see section 2 of Pub.L. 100–506, set out as a note under section 101 of this title.

1986 Acts. Amendment by Pub.L. 99–554, § 257, effective 30 days after Oct. 27, 1986, but not applicable with respect to cases commenced under this title before that date, see section 302(a), (c)(1) of Pub.L. 99–554, set out as a note under section 581 of Title 28, Judiciary and Judicial Procedure.

Amendment by Pub.L. 99–554, § 283, effective 30 days after Oct. 27, 1986, except as otherwise provided for, see section 302(a) of Pub.L. 99–554, set out as a note under section 581 of Title 28.

1984 Acts. Amendment by Pub.L. 98–353 effective with respect to cases filed 90 days after July 10, 1984, see section 552(a), formerly 553(a), of Pub.L. 98–353, set out as a note under section 101 of this title.

Separability of Provisions

If any provision of or amendment made by Pub.L. 103–394 or the application of such provision or amendment to any person or circumstance is held to be unconstitutional, the remaining provisions of and amendments made by Pub.L. 103–394 and the application of such provisions and amendments to any person or circumstance shall not be affected thereby, see section 701 of Pub.L. 103–394, set out as a note under section 101 of this title.

Congressional Findings Concerning Airport Gate Leases

Section 19(a) of Pub.L. 102–365 provided that:

"Congress finds that—

"**(1)** there are major airports served by an air carrier that has leased a substantial majority of the airport's gates;

"**(2)** the commerce in the region served by such a major airport can be disrupted if the air carrier that leases most of its gates enters bankruptcy and either discontinues or materially reduces service; and

"**(3)** it is important that such airports be empowered to continue service in the event of such a disruption."

CROSS REFERENCES

Allowance of claims, see 11 USCA § 502.

Applicability of this section in Chapter 9 cases, see 11 USCA § 901.

Assumption or rejection of certain executory contracts within reasonable time after order for relief, see 11 USCA § 744.

Collective bargaining agreements, see 11 USCA § 1167.

Contents of plan, see 11 USCA § 1222.

Contractual right to liquidate—

Commodities contract or forward contract, see 11 USCA § 556.

Repurchase agreement, see 11 USCA § 559.

Securities contract, see 11 USCA § 555.

Contractual right to terminate a swap agreement, see 11 USCA § 560.

Effect of—

Conversion, see 11 USCA § 348.

Rejection of lease of railroad line, see 11 USCA § 1169.

Grain storage facility bankruptcies, expedited determinations, see 11 USCA § 557.

Impairment of claims or interests by plans which cure certain defaults, see 11 USCA § 1124.

Municipal leases, see 11 USCA § 929.

Provisions in plan for assumption or rejection of certain executory contracts or unexpired leases, see 11 USCA §§ 1123 and 1322.

Right of possession of party with security interest as affected by default—

Aircraft equipment and vessels, see 11 USCA § 1110.

Rolling stock equipment, see 11 USCA § 1168.

Setoff, see 11 USCA § 553.

§ 366. Utility service

(a) Except as provided in subsections (b) and (c) of this section, a utility may not alter, refuse, or discontinue service to, or discriminate against, the trustee or the debtor solely on the basis of the commencement of a case under this title or that a debt owed by the debtor to such utility for service rendered before the order for relief was not paid when due.

(b) Such utility may alter, refuse, or discontinue service if neither the trustee nor the debtor, within 20 days after the date of the order for relief, furnishes adequate assurance of payment, in the form of a deposit or other security, for service after such date. On request of a party in interest and after notice and a hearing, the court may order reasonable modification of the amount of the deposit or other security necessary to provide adequate assurance of payment.

(c)(1)(A) For purposes of this subsection, the term "assurance of payment" means—

(i) a cash deposit;

(ii) a letter of credit;

(iii) a certificate of deposit;

(iv) a surety bond;

(v) a prepayment of utility consumption; or

(vi) another form of security that is mutually agreed on between the utility and the debtor or the trustee.

(B) For purposes of this subsection an administrative expense priority shall not constitute an assurance of payment.

(2) Subject to paragraphs (3) and (4), with respect to a case filed under chapter 11, a utility referred to in subsection (a) may alter, refuse, or discontinue utility service, if during the 30-day period beginning on the date of the filing of the petition, the utility does not receive from the debtor or the trustee adequate assurance of payment for utility service that is satisfactory to the utility.

(3)(A) On request of a party in interest and after notice and a hearing, the court may order modification of the amount of an assurance of payment under paragraph (2).

(B) In making a determination under this paragraph whether an assurance of payment is adequate, the court may not consider—

(i) the absence of security before the date of the filing of the petition;

(ii) the payment by the debtor of charges for utility service in a timely manner before the date of the filing of the petition; or

(iii) the availability of an administrative expense priority.

(4) Notwithstanding any other provision of law, with respect to a case subject to this subsection, a utility may recover or set off against a security deposit provided to the utility by the debtor before the date of the filing of the petition without notice or order of the court.

(Pub.L. 95–598, Nov. 6, 1978, 92 Stat. 2578; Pub.L. 98–353, Title III, § 443, July 10, 1984, 98 Stat. 373; Pub.L. 109–8, Title IV, § 417, Apr. 20, 2005, 119 Stat. 108.)

HISTORICAL AND STATUTORY NOTES

Revision Notes and Legislative Reports

1978 Acts. This section gives debtors protection from a cut-off of service by a utility because of the filing of a bankruptcy case. This section is intended to cover utilities that have some special position with respect to the debtor, such as an electric company, gas supplier, or telephone company that is a monopoly in the area so that the debtor cannot easily obtain comparable service from another utility. The utility may not alter, refuse, or discontinue service because of the nonpayment of a bill that would be discharged in the bankruptcy case. Subsection (b) protects the utility company by requiring the trustee or the debtor to provide, within ten days, adequate assurance of payment for service provided after the date of the petition. Senate Report No. 95–989.

1984 Acts. Statements by Legislative Leaders, see 1984 U.S.Code Cong. and Adm.News, p. 576.

2005 Acts. House Report No. 109–31(Part I), see 2005 U.S. Code Cong. and Adm. News, p. 88.

Legislative Statements

Section 366 of the House amendment represents a compromise between comparable provisions contained in H.R. 8200 as passed by the House and the Senate amendment. Subsection (a) is modified so that the applicable date is the date of the order for relief rather than the date of the filing of the petition. Subsection (b) contains a similar change but is otherwise derived from section 366(b) of the Senate amendment, with the exception that a time period for continued service of 20 days rather than 10 days is adopted.

References in Text

Chapter 11, referred to in subsec. (c)(2), is chapter 11 of this title, 11 U.S.C.A. § 1101 et seq.

Effective and Applicability Provisions

2005 Acts. Amendments by Pub.L. 109–8 effective, except as otherwise provided, 180 days after April 20, 2005, and inapplicable with respect to cases commenced under Title 11

before the effective date, see Pub.L. 109–8, § 1501, set out as a note under 11 U.S.C.A. § 101.

1984 Acts. Amendment by Pub.L. 98–353 effective with respect to cases filed 90 days after July 10, 1984, see section 552(a), formerly 553(a) of Pub.L. 98–353, set out as a note under section 101 of this title.

CROSS REFERENCES

Applicability of this section in Chapter 9 cases, see 11 USCA § 901.

§§ 367 to 500. Reserved for future legislation

CHAPTER 5—CREDITORS, THE DEBTOR, AND THE ESTATE

[1] So in original. Does not conform to section catchline.

HISTORICAL AND STATUTORY NOTES

Effective and Applicability Provisions

2005 Acts. Amendments by Pub.L. 109–8 effective, except as otherwise provided, 180 days after April 20, 2005, and inapplicable with respect to cases commenced under Title 11 before the effective date, see Pub.L. 109–8, § 1501, set out as a note under 11 U.S.C.A. § 101.

CROSS REFERENCES

Applicability of this chapter to—

Cases under Chapter 7, 11, 12, or 13 of this title, see 11 USCA § 103.

Investor protection liquidation proceedings, see 15 USCA § 78fff.

SUBCHAPTER I—CREDITORS AND CLAIMS

§ 501. Filing of proofs of claims or interests

(a) A creditor or an indenture trustee may file a proof of claim. An equity security holder may file a proof of interest.

(b) If a creditor does not timely file a proof of such creditor's claim, an entity that is liable to such creditor with the debtor, or that has secured such creditor, may file a proof of such claim.

(c) If a creditor does not timely file a proof of such creditor's claim, the debtor or the trustee may file a proof of such claim.

(d) A claim of a kind specified in section 502(e)(2), 502(f), 502(g), 502(h) or 502(i) of this title may be filed under subsection (a), (b), or (c) of this section the same as if such claim were a claim against the debtor and had arisen before the date of the filing of the petition.

(e) A claim arising from the liability of a debtor for fuel use tax assessed consistent with the requirements of section 31705 of title 49 may be filed by the base jurisdiction designated pursuant to the International Fuel Tax Agreement (as defined in section 31701 of title 49) and, if so filed, shall be allowed as a single claim.

(Pub.L. 95–598, Nov. 6, 1978, 92 Stat. 2578; Pub.L. 98–353, Title III, § 444, July 10, 1984, 98 Stat. 373; Pub.L. 109–8, Title VII, § 702, Apr. 20, 2005, 119 Stat. 125.)

HISTORICAL AND STATUTORY NOTES

Revision Notes and Legislative Reports

1978 Acts. This section governs the means by which creditors and equity security holders present their claims or interests to the court. Subsection (a) permits a creditor to file a proof of claim or interest. An indenture trustee representing creditors may file a proof of claim on behalf of the creditors he represents.

This subsection is permissive only, and does not require filing of a proof of claim by any creditor. It permits filing where some purpose would be served, such as where a claim that appears on a list filed under proposed 11 U.S.C. 924 or 1111 was incorrectly stated or listed as disputed, contingent, or unliquidated, where a creditor with a lien is undersecured and asserts a claim for the balance of the debt owed him (his unsecured claim, as determined under proposed 11 U.S.C. 506(a)), or in a liquidation case where there will be a distribution of assets to the holders of allowed claims. In other instances, such as in no-asset liquidation cases, in situations where a secured creditor does not assert any claim against the estate and a determination of his claim is not made under proposed 11 U.S.C. 506, or in situations where the claim asserted would be subordinated and the creditor would not recover from the estate in any event, filing of a proof of claim may simply not be necessary. The Rules of Bankruptcy Procedure and practice under the law will guide creditors as to when filing is necessary and when it may be dispensed with. In general, however, unless a claim is listed in a chapter 9 or chapter 11 case and allowed as a result of the list, a proof of claim will be a prerequisite to allowance for unsecured claims, including priority claims and the unsecured portion of a claim asserted by the holder of a lien.

The Rules of Bankruptcy Procedure will set the time limits, the form, and the procedure for filing, which will determine whether claims are timely or tardily filed. The rules governing time limits for filing proofs of claims will continue to apply under section 405(d) of the bill. These provide a 6-month-bar date for the filing of tax claims.

Subsection (b) permits a codebtor, surety, or guarantor to file a proof of claim on behalf of the creditor to which he is liable if the creditor does not timely file a proof of claim.

In liquidation and individual repayment plan cases, the trustee or the debtor may file a proof of claim under subsection (c) if the creditor does not timely file. The purpose of this subsection is mainly to protect the debtor if the creditor's claim is nondischargeable. If the creditor does not file, there would be no distribution on the claim, and the debtor would have a greater debt to repay after the case is closed than if the claim were paid in part or in full in the case or under the plan.

Subsection (d) governs the filing of claims of the kind specified in subsections (f), (g), (h), (i), or (j) of proposed 11 U.S.C. 502. The separation of this provision from the other claim-filing provisions in this section is intended to indicate that claims of the kind specified, which do not become fixed or do not arise until after the commencement of the case, must be treated differently for filing purposes such as the bar date for filing claims. The rules will provide for later filing of claims of these kinds.

Subsection (e) gives governmental units (including tax authorities) at least six months following the date for the first meeting of creditors in a chapter 7 or chapter 13 case within which to file proof of claims. Senate Report No. 95–989.

1984 Acts. Statements by Legislative Leaders, see 1984 U.S.Code Cong. and Adm.News, p. 576.

2005 Acts. House Report No. 109–31(Part I), see 2005 U.S. Code Cong. and Adm. News, p. 88.

Legislative Statements

The House amendment adopts section 501(b) of the Senate amendment leaving the Rules of Bankruptcy Procedure free to determine where a proof of claim must be filed.

Section 501(c) expands language contained in section 501(c) of the House bill and Senate amendment to permit the debtor to file a proof of claim if a creditor does not timely file a proof of the creditor's claim in a case under title 11.

The House amendment deletes section 501(e) of the Senate amendment as a matter to be left to the rules of bankruptcy procedure. It is anticipated that the rules will enable governmental units, like other creditors, to have a reasonable time to file proofs of claim in bankruptcy cases.

For purposes of section 501, a proof of "interest" includes the interest of a general or limited partner in a partnership, the interest of a proprietor in a sole proprietorship, or the interest of a common or preferred stockholder in a corporation.

Effective and Applicability Provisions

2005 Acts. Amendments by Pub.L. 109–8 effective, except as otherwise provided, 180 days after April 20, 2005, and inapplicable with respect to cases commenced under Title 11 before the effective date, see Pub.L. 109–8, § 1501, set out as a note under 11 U.S.C.A. § 101.

1984 Acts. Amendment by Pub.L. 98–353 effective with respect to cases filed 90 days after July 10, 1984, see section 552(a), formerly 553 of Pub.L. 98–353, set out as a note under section 101 of this title.

Child Support Creditors or Their Representatives; Appearance Before Court

Pub.L. 103–394, Title IV, § 304(g), Oct. 22, 1994, 108 Stat. 4134, provided that: "Child support creditors or their representatives shall be permitted to appear and intervene without charge, and without meeting any special local court rule requirement for attorney appearances, in any bankruptcy case or proceeding in any bankruptcy court or district court of the United States if such creditors or representatives file a form in such court that contains information detailing the child support debt, its status, and other characteristics."

CROSS REFERENCES

Applicability of this section in Chapter 9 cases, see 11 USCA § 901.

Binding effect of confirmation whether or not claim is filed or deemed filed, see 11 USCA § 944.

Discharge of—

Debtor after confirmation of plan, see 11 USCA § 1141.

Liabilities on claims whether or not filed, see 11 USCA § 727.

Distribution of property of estate, see 11 USCA § 726.

False oaths and claims, see 18 USCA § 152.

Proof of claim deemed filed in—

Chapter 11 cases, see 11 USCA § 1111.

Chapter 9 cases, see 11 USCA § 925.

§ 502. Allowance of claims or interests

(a) A claim or interest, proof of which is filed under section 501 of this title, is deemed allowed, unless a party in interest, including a creditor of a general partner in a partnership that is a debtor in a case under chapter 7 of this title, objects.

(b) Except as provided in subsections (e)(2), (f), (g), (h) and (i) of this section, if such objection to a claim is made, the court, after notice and a hearing, shall determine the amount of such claim in lawful currency of the United States as of the date of the filing of the petition, and shall allow such claim in such amount, except to the extent that—

(1) such claim is unenforceable against the debtor and property of the debtor, under any agreement or applicable law for a reason other than because such claim is contingent or unmatured;

(2) such claim is for unmatured interest;

(3) if such claim is for a tax assessed against property of the estate, such claim exceeds the value of the interest of the estate in such property;

(4) if such claim is for services of an insider or attorney of the debtor, such claim exceeds the reasonable value of such services;

(5) such claim is for a debt that is unmatured on the date of the filing of the petition and that is excepted from discharge under section 523(a)(5) of this title;

(6) if such claim is the claim of a lessor for damages resulting from the termination of a lease of real property, such claim exceeds—

(A) the rent reserved by such lease, without acceleration, for the greater of one year, or 15 percent, not to exceed three years, of the remaining term of such lease, following the earlier of—

(i) the date of the filing of the petition; and

(ii) the date on which such lessor repossessed, or the lessee surrendered, the leased property; plus

(B) any unpaid rent due under such lease, without acceleration, on the earlier of such dates;

(7) if such claim is the claim of an employee for damages resulting from the termination of an employment contract, such claim exceeds—

(A) the compensation provided by such contract, without acceleration, for one year following the earlier of—

(i) the date of the filing of the petition; or

(ii) the date on which the employer directed the employee to terminate, or such employee terminated, performance under such contract; plus

(B) any unpaid compensation due under such contract, without acceleration, on the earlier of such dates;

(8) such claim results from a reduction, due to late payment, in the amount of an otherwise applicable credit available to the debtor in connection with an employment tax on wages, salaries, or commissions earned from the debtor; or

(9) proof of such claim is not timely filed, except to the extent tardily filed as permitted under paragraph (1), (2), or (3) of section 726(a) of this title or under the Federal Rules of Bankruptcy Procedure, except that a claim of a governmental unit shall be timely filed if it is filed before 180 days after the date of the order for relief or such later time as the Federal Rules of Bankruptcy Procedure may provide, and except that in a case under chapter 13, a claim of a governmental unit for a tax with respect to a return filed under section 1308 shall be timely if the claim is filed on or before the date that is 60 days after the date on which such return was filed as required.

(c) There shall be estimated for purpose of allowance under this section—

(1) any contingent or unliquidated claim, the fixing or liquidation of which, as the case may be, would unduly delay the administration of the case; or

(2) any right to payment arising from a right to an equitable remedy for breach of performance.

(d) Notwithstanding subsections (a) and (b) of this section, the court shall disallow any claim of any entity from which property is recoverable under section 542, 543, 550, or 553 of this title or that is a transferee of a transfer avoidable under section 522(f), 522(h), 544, 545, 547, 548, 549, or 724(a) of this title, unless such entity or transferee has paid the amount, or turned over any such property, for which such entity or transferee is liable under section 522(i), 542, 543, 550, or 553 of this title.

(e)(1) Notwithstanding subsections (a), (b), and (c) of this section and paragraph (2) of this subsection, the court shall disallow any claim for reimbursement or contribution of an entity that is liable with the debtor on or has secured the claim of a creditor, to the extent that—

(A) such creditor's claim against the estate is disallowed;

(B) such claim for reimbursement or contribution is contingent as of the time of allowance or disallowance of such claim for reimbursement or contribution; or

(C) such entity asserts a right of subrogation to the rights of such creditor under section 509 of this title.

(2) A claim for reimbursement or contribution of such an entity that becomes fixed after the commencement of the case shall be determined, and shall be allowed under subsection (a), (b), or (c) of this section, or disallowed under subsection (d) of this section, the same as if such claim had become fixed before the date of the filing of the petition.

(f) In an involuntary case, a claim arising in the ordinary course of the debtor's business or financial affairs after the commencement of the case but before the earlier of the appointment of a trustee and the order for relief shall be determined as of the date such claim arises, and shall be allowed under subsection (a), (b), or (c) of this section or disallowed under subsection (d) or (e) of this section, the same as if such claim had arisen before the date of the filing of the petition.

(g)(1) A claim arising from the rejection, under section 365 of this title or under a plan under chapter 9, 11, 12, or 13 of this title, of an executory contract or unexpired lease of the debtor that has not been assumed shall be determined, and shall be allowed under subsection (a), (b), or (c) of this section or disallowed under subsection (d) or (e) of this section, the same as if such claim had arisen before the date of the filing of the petition.

(2) A claim for damages calculated in accordance with section 562 shall be allowed under subsection (a), (b), or (c), or disallowed under subsection (d) or (e), as if such claim had arisen before the date of the filing of the petition.

(h) A claim arising from the recovery of property under section 522, 550, or 553 of this title shall be determined, and shall be allowed under subsection (a), (b), or (c) of this section, or disallowed under subsection (d) or (e) of this section, the same as if such claim had arisen before the date of the filing of the petition.

(i) A claim that does not arise until after the commencement of the case for a tax entitled to priority under section 507(a)(8) of this title shall be determined, and shall be allowed under subsection (a), (b), or (c) of this section, or disallowed under subsection (d) or (e) of this section, the same as if such claim had arisen before the date of the filing of the petition.

(j) A claim that has been allowed or disallowed may be reconsidered for cause. A reconsidered claim may be allowed or disallowed according to the equities of the case. Reconsideration of a claim under this subsection does not affect the validity of any payment or transfer from the estate made to a holder of an allowed claim on account of such allowed claim that is not reconsidered, but if a reconsidered claim is allowed and is of the same class as such holder's claim, such holder may not receive any additional payment or transfer from the estate on account of such holder's allowed claim until the holder of such reconsidered and allowed claim receives payment on account of such claim proportionate in value to that already received by such other holder. This subsection does not alter or modify the trustee's right to recover from a creditor any excess payment or transfer made to such creditor.

(k)(1) The court, on the motion of the debtor and after a hearing, may reduce a claim filed under this section based in whole on an unsecured consumer debt by not more than 20 percent of the claim, if—

(A) the claim was filed by a creditor who unreasonably refused to negotiate a reasonable alternative repayment schedule proposed on behalf of the debtor by an approved nonprofit budget and credit counseling agency described in section 111;

(B) the offer of the debtor under subparagraph (A)—

(i) was made at least 60 days before the date of the filing of the petition; and

(ii) provided for payment of at least 60 percent of the amount of the debt over a period not to exceed the repayment period of the loan, or a reasonable extension thereof; and

(C) no part of the debt under the alternative repayment schedule is nondischargeable.

(2) The debtor shall have the burden of proving, by clear and convincing evidence, that—

(A) the creditor unreasonably refused to consider the debtor's proposal; and

(B) the proposed alternative repayment schedule was made prior to expiration of the 60–day period specified in paragraph (1)(B)(i).

(Pub.L. 95–598, Nov. 6, 1978, 92 Stat. 2579; Pub.L. 98–353, Title III, § 445, July 10, 1984, 98 Stat. 373; Pub.L. 99–554, Title II, §§ 257(j), 283(f), Oct. 27, 1986, 100 Stat. 3115, 3117; Pub.L. 103–394, Title II, § 213(a), Title III, § 304(h)(1), Oct. 22, 1994, 108 Stat. 4125, 4134; Pub.L. 109–8, Title II, § 201(a), Title VII, § 716(d), Title IX, § 910(b), Apr. 20, 2005, 119 Stat. 42, 130. 184.)

HISTORICAL AND STATUTORY NOTES

Revision Notes and Legislative Reports

1978 Acts. A proof of claim or interest is prima facie evidence of the claim or interest. Thus, it is allowed under subsection (a) unless a party in interest objects. The rules and case law will determine who is a party in interest for purposes of objection to allowance. The case law is well developed on this subject today. As a result of the change in the liability of a general partner's estate for the debts of this partnership, see proposed 11 U.S.C. 723, the category of persons that are parties in interest in the partnership case will be expanded to include a creditor of a partner against whose estate the trustee of the partnership estate may proceed under proposed 11 U.S.C. 723(c).

Subsection (b) prescribes the grounds on which a claim may be disallowed. The court will apply these standards if there is an objection to a proof of claim. The burden of proof on the issue of allowance is left to the Rules of Bankruptcy Procedure. Under the current chapter XIII [section 1001 et seq. of former Title 11] rules, a creditor is required to prove that his claim is free from usury, rule 13–301. It is expected that the rules will make similar provision for both liquidation and individual repayment plan cases. See Bankruptcy Act § 656(b) [section 1056(b) of former Title 11]; H.R. 31, 94th Cong., 1st sess., sec. 6–104(a) (1975).

Paragraph (1) requires disallowance if the claim is unenforceable against the debtor for any reason (such as usury, unconscionability, or failure of consideration) other than because it is contingent or unmatured. All such contingent or unmatured claims are to be liquidated by the bankruptcy court in order to afford the debtor complete bankruptcy relief; these claims are generally not provable under present law.

Paragraph (2) requires disallowance to the extent that the claim is for unmatured interest as of the date of the petition. Whether interest is matured or unmatured on the date of bankruptcy is to be determined without reference to any ipso facto or bankruptcy clause in the agreement creating the claim. Interest disallowed under this paragraph includes postpetition interest that is not yet due and payable, and any portion of prepaid interest that represents an original discounting of the claim, yet that would not have been earned on the date of bankruptcy. For example, a claim on a $1,000 note issued the day before bankruptcy would only be allowed to the extent of the cash actually advanced. If the original discount was 10 percent so that the cash advanced was only $900, then notwithstanding the face amount of note, only $900 would be allowed. If $900 was advanced under the note some time before bankruptcy, the interest component of the note would have to be prorated and disallowed to the extent it was for interest after the commencement of the case.

Section 502(b) thus contains two principles of present law. First, interest stops accruing at the date of the filing of the petition, because any claim for unmatured interest is disallowed under this paragraph. Second, bankruptcy operates as the acceleration of the principal amount of all claims against the debtor. One unarticulated reason for this is that the discounting factor for claims after the commencement of the case is equivalent to contractual interest rate on the claim. Thus, this paragraph does not cause disallowance of claims that have not been discounted to a present value because of the irrebuttable presumption that the discounting rate and the contractual interest rate (even a zero interest rate) are equivalent.

Paragraph (3) requires disallowance of a claim to the extent that the creditor may offset the claim against a debt owing to the debtor. This will prevent double recovery, and permit the claim to be filed only for the balance due. This follows section 68 of the Bankruptcy Act [section 108 of former Title 11].

Paragraph (4) requires disallowance of a property tax claim to the extent that the tax due exceeds the value of the property. This too follows current law to the extent the property tax is ad valorem.

Paragraph (5) prevents overreaching by the debtor's attorneys and concealing of assets by debtors. It permits the court to examine the claim of a debtor's attorney independently of any other provision of this subsection, and to disallow it to the extent that it exceeds the reasonable value of the attorneys' services.

Postpetition alimony, maintenance or support claims are disallowed under paragraph (6). They are to be paid from the debtor's postpetition property, because the claims are nondischargeable.

Paragraph (7), derived from current law, limits the damages allowable to a landlord of the debtor. The history of this provision is set out at length in *Oldden v. Tonto Realty Co.*, 143 F.2d 916 (2d Cir. 1944). It is designed to compensate the landlord for his loss while not permitting a claim so large (based on a long-term lease) as to prevent other general unsecured creditors from recovering a dividend from the estate. The damages a landlord may assert from termination of a lease are limited to the rent reserved for the greater of one year or ten percent of the remaining lease term, not to exceed three years, after the earlier of the date of the filing of the petition and the date of surrender or repossession in a chapter 7 case and 3 years lease payments in a chapter 9, 11, or 13 case. The sliding scale formula for chapter 7 cases is new and designed to protect the long-term lessor. This subsection does not apply to limit administrative expense claims for use of the leased premises to which the landlord is otherwise entitled.

This paragraph will not overrule *Oldden*, or the proposition for which it has been read to stand: To the extent that a landlord has a security deposit in excess of the amount of his claim allowed under this paragraph, the excess comes into the estate. Moreover, his allowed claim is for his total damages, as limited by this paragraph. By virtue of proposed 11 U.S.C. 506(a) and 506(d), the claim will be divided into a secured portion and an unsecured portion in those cases in which the deposit that the landlord holds is less than his damages. As under *Oldden*, he will not be permitted to offset his actual damages against his security deposit and then claim for the balance under this paragraph. Rather, his security deposit will be applied in satisfaction of the claim that is allowed under this paragraph.

As used in section 502(b)(7), the phrase "lease of real property" applies only to a "true" or "bona fide" lease and does not apply to financing leases of real property or interests therein, or to leases of such property which are intended as security.

Historically, the limitation on allowable claims of lessors of real property was based on two considerations. First, the amount of the lessor's damages on breach of a real estate lease was considered contingent and difficult to prove. Partly for this reason, claims of a lessor of real estate were not provable prior to the 1934 amendments to the Bankruptcy Act [former Title 11]. Second, in a true lease of real property, the lessor retains all risk and benefits as to the value of the real estate at the termination of the lease. Historically, it was, therefore, considered equitable to limit the claims of a real estate lessor.

However, these considerations are not present in "lease financing" transactions where, in substance, the "lease" involves a sale of the real estate and the rental payments are in substance the payment of principal and interest on a secured loan or sale. In a financing lease the lessor is essentially a secured or unsecured creditor (depending upon whether his interest is perfected or not) of the debtor, and the lessor's claim should not be subject to the 502(b)(7) limitation. Financing "leases" are in substance installment sales or loans. The "lessors" are essentially sellers or lenders and should be treated as such for purposes of the bankruptcy law.

Whether a "lease" is true or bona fide lease or, in the alternative, a financing "lease" or a lease intended as security, depends upon the circumstances of each case. The distinction between a true lease and a financing transaction is based upon the economic substance of the transaction and not, for example, upon the locus of title, the form of the transaction or the fact that the transaction is denominated as a "lease". The fact that the lessee, upon compliance with the terms of the lease, becomes or has the option to become the owner of the leased property for no additional consideration or for nominal consideration indicates that the transaction is a financing lease or lease intended as security. In such cases, the lessor has no substantial interest in the leased property at the expiration of the lease term. In addition, the fact that the lessee assumes and discharges substantially all the risks and obligations ordinarily attributed to the outright ownership of the property is more indicative of a financing transaction than of a true lease. The rental payments in such cases are in substance payments of principal and interest either on a loan secured by the leased real property or on the purchase of the leased real property. See, e.g., Financial Accounting Standards Board Statement No. 13 and SEC Reg. S–X, 17 C.F.R. sec. 210.3–16(q) (1977); cf. *First National Bank of Chicago v. Irving Trust Co.*, 74 F.2d 263 (2nd Cir. 1934); and Albenda and Lief, "Net Lease Financing Transactions Under the Proposed Bankruptcy Act of 1973," 30 Business Lawyer, 713 (1975).

Paragraph (8) is new. It tracks the landlord limitation on damages provision in paragraph (7) for damages resulting from the breach by the debtor of an employment contract, but limits the recovery to the compensation reserved under an employment contract for the year following the earlier of the date of the petition and the termination of employment.

Subsection (c) requires the estimation of any claim liquidation of which would unduly delay the closing of the estate, such as a contingent claim, or any claim for which applicable law provides only an equitable remedy, such as specific performance. This subsection requires that all claims against the debtor be converted into dollar amounts.

Subsection (d) is derived from present law. It requires disallowance of a claim of a transferee of a voidable transfer in toto if the transferee has not paid the amount or turned over the property received as required under the sections under which the transferee's liability arises.

Subsection (e), also derived from present law, requires disallowance of the claim for reimbursement or contribution of a codebtor, surety or guarantor of an obligation of the debtor, unless the claim of the creditor on such obligation has been paid in full. The provision prevents competition between a creditor and his guarantor for the limited proceeds in the estate.

Subsection (f) specifies that "involuntary gap" creditors receive the same treatment as prepetition creditors. Under the allowance provisions of this subsection, knowledge of the commencement of the case will be irrelevant. The claim is to be allowed "the same as if such claim had arisen before the date of the filing of the petition." Under voluntary petition, proposed 11 U.S.C. 303(f), creditors must be permitted to deal with the debtor and be assured that their claims will be paid. For purposes of this subsection, "creditors" include governmental units holding claims for tax liabilities incurred during the period after the petition is filed and before the earlier of the order for relief or appointment of a trustee.

Subsection (g) gives entities injured by the rejection of an executory contract or unexpired lease, either under section 365 or under a plan or reorganization, a prepetition claim for any resulting damages, and requires that the injured entity be treated as a prepetition creditor with respect to that claim.

Subsection (h) gives a transferee of a setoff that is recovered by one trustee a prepetition claim for the amount recovered.

Subsection (i) answers the nonrecourse loan problem and gives the creditor an unsecured claim for the difference between the value of the collateral and the debt in response to the decision in *Great National Life Ins. Co. v. Pine Gate Associates, Ltd.*, Bankruptcy Case No. B75–4345A (N.D.Ga. Sept. 16, 1977).

The bill, as reported, deletes a provision in the bill as originally introduced (former sec. 502(i)) requiring a tax authority to file a proof of claim for recapture of an investment credit where, during title 11 proceedings, the trustee sells or otherwise disposes of property before the title 11 case began. The tax authority should not be required to submit a formal claim for a taxable event (a sale or other disposition of the asset) of whose occurrence the trustee necessarily knows better than the taxing authority. For procedural purposes, the recapture of investment credit is to be treated as an administrative expense, as to which only a request for payment is required. Senate Report No. 95–989.

Paragraph (9) [of subsec. (b)] requires disallowance of certain employment tax claims. These relate to a Federal tax credit for State unemployment insurance taxes which is disallowed if the State tax is paid late. This paragraph disallows the Federal claim for the tax the same as if the credit had been allowed in full on the Federal return. House Report No. 95–595.

1984 Acts. Statements by Legislative Leaders, see 1984 U.S. Code Cong. and Adm. News, p. 576.

1986 Acts. House Report No. 99–764 and House Conference Report No. 99–958, see 1986 U.S. Code Cong. and Adm. News, p. 5227.

1994 Acts. House Report No. 103–835, see 1994 U.S. Code Cong. and Adm. News, p. 3340.

2005 Acts. House Report No. 109–31(Part I), see 2005 U.S. Code Cong. and Adm. News, p. 88.

Legislative Statements

The House amendment adopts a compromise position in section 502(a) between H.R. 8200, as passed by the House, and the Senate amendment. Section 502(a) has been modified to make clear that a party in interest includes a creditor of a partner in a partnership that is a debtor under chapter 7. Since the trustee of the partnership is given an absolute claim against the estate of each general partner under section 723(c), creditors of the partner must have standing to object to claims against the partnership at the partnership level because no opportunity will be afforded at the partner's level for such objection.

The House amendment contains a provision in section 502(b)(1) that requires disallowance of a claim to the extent that such claim is unenforceable against the debtor and unenforceable against property of the debtor. This is intended to result in the disallowance of any claim for deficiency by an undersecured creditor on a non-recourse loan or under a State antideficiency law, special provision for which is made in section 1111, since neither the debtor personally, nor the property of the debtor is liable for such a deficiency. Similarly claims for usurious interest or which could be barred by an agreement between the creditor and the debtor would be disallowed.

Section 502(b)(7)(A) represents a compromise between the House bill and the Senate amendment. The House amendment takes the provision in H.R. 8200 as passed by the House of Representatives but increases the percentage from 10 to 15 percent.

As used in section 502(b)(7), the phrase "lease of real property" applies only to a "true" or "bona fide" lease and does not apply to financing leases of real property or interests therein, or to leases of such property which are intended as security.

Historically, the limitation on allowable claims of lessors of real property was based on two considerations. First, the amount of the lessor's damages on breach of a real estate lease was considered contingent and difficult to prove. Partly for this reason, claims of a lessor of real estate were not provable prior to the 1934 amendments, to the Bankruptcy Act. Second, in a true lease of real property, the lessor retains all risks and benefits as to the value of the real estate at the termination of the lease. Historically, it was, therefore, considered equitable to limit the claims of real estate lessor.

However, these considerations are not present in "lease financing" transactions where, in substance, the "lease" involves a sale of the real estate and the rental payments are in substance the payment of principal and interest on a secured loan or sale. In a financing lease the lessor is essentially a secured or unsecured creditor (depending upon whether his interest is perfected or not) of the debtor, and the lessor's claim should not be subject to the 502(b)(7) limitation. Financing "leases" are in substance installment sales or loans. The "lessors" are essentially sellers or lenders and should be treated as such for purposes of the bankruptcy law.

Whether a "lease" is true or bona fide lease or, in the alternative a financing "lease" or a lease intended as security, depends upon the circumstances of each case. The distinction between a true lease and a financing transaction is based upon the economic substance of the transaction and not, for example, upon the locus of title, the form of the transaction or the fact that the transaction is denominated as a "lease." The fact that the lessee, upon compliance with the terms of the lease, becomes or has the option to become the owner of the leased property for no additional consideration or for nominal consideration indicates that the transaction is a financing lease or lease intended as security. In such cases, the lessor has no substantial interest in the leased property at the expiration of the lease term. In addition, the fact that the lessee assumes and discharges substantially all the risks and obligations ordinarily attributed to the outright ownership of the property is more indicative of a financing transaction than of a true lease. The rental payments in such cases are in substance payments of principal and interest either on a loan secured by the leased real property or on the purchase of the leased real property. See, e.g., Financial Accounting Standards Board Statement No. 13 and SEC Reg. S–X, 17 C.F.R. sec. 210.3–16(q) (1977); cf. First National Bank of Chicago v. Irving Trust Co., 74 F.2d 263 (2nd Cir.1934); and Albenda and Lief, "Net Lease Financing Transactions Under the Proposed Bankruptcy Act of 1973," 30 Business Lawyer, 713 (1975).

Section 502(c) of the House amendment presents a compromise between similar provisions contained in the House bill and the Senate amendment. The compromise language is consistent with an amendment to the definition of "claim" in section 104(4)(B) of the House amendment and requires estimation of any right to an equitable remedy for breach of performance if such breach gives rise to a right to payment. To the extent language in the House and Senate reports indicate otherwise, such language is expressly overruled.

Section 502(e) of the House amendment contains language modifying a similar section in the House bill and Senate amendment. Section 502(e)(1) states the general rule requiring the court to disallow any claim for reimbursement or contribution of an entity that is liable with the debtor on, or that has secured, the claim of a creditor to any extent that the creditor's claim against the estate is disallowed. This adopts a policy that a surety's claim for reimbursement or contribution is entitled to no better status than the claim of the creditor assured by such surety. Section 502(e)(1)(B) alternatively disallows any claim for reimbursement or contribution by a surety to the extent such claim is contingent as of the time of allowance. Section 502(e)(2) is clear that to the extent a claim for reimbursement or contribution becomes fixed after the commencement of the case that it is to be considered a prepetition claim for purposes of allowance. The combined effect of sections 502(e)(1)(B) and 502(e)(2) is that a surety or codebtor is generally permitted a claim for reimbursement or contribution to the extent the surety or codebtor has paid the assured party at the time of allowance. Section 502(e)(1)(C) alternatively indicates that a claim for reimbursement or contribution of a surety or codebtor is disallowed to the extent the surety or codebtor requests subrogation under section 509 with respect to the rights of the assured party. Thus, the surety or codebtor has a choice; to the extent a claim for contribution or reimbursement would be advantageous, such as in the case where such a claim is secured, a surety or codebtor may opt for reimbursement or contribution under section 502(e). On the other hand, to the extent the claim for such surety or codebtor by way of subrogation is more advantageous, such as where such claim is secured, the surety may elect subrogation under section 509.

The section changes current law by making the election identical in all other respects. To the extent a creditor's claim is satisfied by a surety or codebtor, other creditors should not benefit by the surety's inability to file a claim against the estate merely because such surety or codebtor has failed to pay such creditor's claim in full. On the other hand, to the extent the creditor's claim against the estate is otherwise disallowed, the surety or codebtor should not be entitled to increased rights by way of reimbursement or contribution, to the detriment of competing claims of other unsecured creditors, than would be realized by way of subrogation.

While the foregoing scheme is equitable with respect to other unsecured creditors of the debtor, it is desirable to preserve present law to the extent that a surety or codebtor is not permitted to compete with the creditor he has assured until the assured party's claim has paid in full [sic]. Accordingly, section 509(c) of the House amendment subordinates both a claim by way of subrogation or a claim for reimbursement or contribution of a surety or codebtor to the claim of the assured party until the assured party's claim is paid in full.

Section 502(h) of the House amendment expands similar provisions contained in the House bill and the Senate amendment to indicate that any claim arising from the recovery of property under section 522(i), 550, or 553 shall be determined as though it were a prepetition claim.

Section 502(i) of the House amendment adopts a provision contained in section 502(j) of H.R. 8200 as passed by the House but that was not contained in the Senate amendment.

Section 502(i) of H.R. 8200 as passed by the House, but was not included in the Senate amendment, is deleted as a matter to be left to the bankruptcy tax bill next year.

The House amendment deletes section 502(i) of the Senate bill but adopts the policy of that section to a limited extent for confirmation of a plan of reorganization in section 1111(b) of the House amendment.

Section 502(j) of the House amendment is new. The provision codifies section 57k of the Bankruptcy Act [section 93(k) of former Title 11].

Allowance of Claims or Interest: The House amendment adopts section 502(b)(9) of the House bill which disallows any tax claim resulting from a reduction of the Federal Unemployment Tax Act (FUTA) credit (sec. 3302 of the Internal Revenue Code [26 U.S.C.A. § 3302]) on account of a tardy contribution to a State unemployment fund if the contribution is attributable to ways or other compensation paid by the debtor before bankruptcy. The Senate amendment allowed this reduction, but would have subordinated it to other claims in the distribution of the estate's assets by treating it as a punitive (nonpecuniary loss) penalty. The House amendment would also not bar reduction of the FUTA credit on account of a trustee's late payment of a contribution to a State unemployment fund if the contribution was attributable to a trustee's payment of compensation earned from the estate.

Section 511 of the Senate amendment is deleted. Its substance is adopted in section 502(b)(9) of the House amendment which reflects an identical provision contained in H.R. 8200 as passed by the House.

References in Text

Chapter 7 of this title, referred to in subsec. (a), is 11 U.S.C.A. § 701 et seq.

The Federal Rules of Bankruptcy Procedure, referred to in subsec. (b)(9), are set out in this title.

Chapter 13, referred to in subsec. (b)(9), is chapter 13 of this title, 11 U.S.C.A. § 1301.

Chapter 9, 11, 12, or 13 of this title, referred to in subsec. (g), is 11 U.S.C.A. § 901 et seq., 11 U.S.C.A. § 1101 et seq., 11 U.S.C.A. § 1201 et seq., or 11 U.S.C.A. § 1301 et seq., respectively.

Effective and Applicability Provisions

2005 Acts. Amendments by Pub.L. 109–8 effective, except as otherwise provided, 180 days after April 20, 2005, and inapplicable with respect to cases commenced under Title 11 before the effective date, see Pub.L. 109–8, § 1501, set out as a note under 11 U.S.C.A. § 101.

1994 Acts. Amendments by Pub.L. 103–394 effective on Oct. 22, 1994, and not to apply with respect to cases commenced under Title 11 of the United States Code before Oct. 22, 1994, see section 702 of Pub.L. 103–394, set out as a note under section 101 of this title.

1986 Acts. Amendments by Pub.L. 99–554, § 257(j) effective 30 days after Oct. 27, 1986, but not to apply with respect to cases commenced under this title before that date, see section 302(a)(c)(1) of Pub.L. 99–554, set out as a note under section 581 of Title 28, Judiciary and Judicial Procedure.

Amendment by Pub.L. 99–554, § 283, effective 30 days after Oct. 27, 1986, except as otherwise provided for, see section 302(a) of Pub.L. 99–554, set out as a note under section 581 of Title 28.

1984 Acts. Amendment by Pub.L. 98–353 effective with respect to cases filed 90 days after July 10, 1984, see section 552(a), formerly 553(a) of Pub.L. 98–353, set out as a note under section 101 of this title.

Separability of Provisions

If any provision of or amendment made by Pub.L. 103–394 or the application of such provision or amendment to any person or circumstance is held to be unconstitutional, the remaining provisions of and amendments made by Pub.L. 103–394 and the application of such provisions and amendments to any person or circumstance shall not be affected thereby, see section 701 of Pub.L. 103–394, set out as a note under section 101 of this title.

CROSS REFERENCES

Acceptance of plan by holders of claims or interests, see 11 USCA § 1126.

Applicability of this section in Chapter 9 cases, see 11 USCA § 901.

Certain claims for which partner and partnership are liable, see 11 USCA § 723.

Claims secured by lien on property of estate, see 11 USCA § 1111.

Creditor as meaning entity having certain claims specified in this section, see 11 USCA § 101.

Deductibility of allowed claim, see 11 USCA § 346.

Discharge of liabilities on claims in—

Chapter 7 cases, see 11 USCA § 727.

Chapter 13 cases, see 11 USCA § 1328.

Chapter 12 cases, see 11 USCA § 1228.

Effect of confirmation in—

Chapter 11 cases, see 11 USCA § 1141.

Chapter 9 cases, see 11 USCA § 944.

Filing and allowance of postpetition claims, see 11 USCA § 1305.

Liability of exempted property for debtor's debt, see 11 USCA § 522.

Municipal leases, see 11 USCA § 929.

Payment of insurance benefits to retired employees, see 11 USCA § 1114.

Setoff, see 11 USCA § 553.

Trustee as lien creditor and as successor to certain creditors and purchasers, see 11 USCA § 544.

§ 503. Allowance of administrative expenses

(a) An entity may timely file a request for payment of an administrative expense, or may tardily file such request if permitted by the court for cause.

(b) After notice and a hearing, there shall be allowed administrative expenses, other than claims allowed under section 502(f) of this title, including—

(1)(A) the actual, necessary costs and expenses of preserving the estate including—

(i) wages, salaries, and commissions for services rendered after the commencement of the case; and

(ii) wages and benefits awarded pursuant to a judicial proceeding or a proceeding of the National Labor Relations Board as back pay attributable to any period of time occurring after commencement of the case under this title, as a result of a violation of Federal or State law by the debtor, without regard to the time of the occurrence of unlawful conduct on which such award is based or to whether any services were rendered, if the court determines that payment of wages and benefits by reason of the operation of this clause will not substantially increase the probability of layoff or termination of current employees, or of nonpayment of domestic support obligations, during the case under this title;

(B) any tax—

(i) incurred by the estate, whether secured or unsecured, including property taxes for which liability is in rem, in personam, or both, except a tax of a kind specified in section 507(a)(8) of this title; or

(ii) attributable to an excessive allowance of a tentative carryback adjustment that the estate received, whether the taxable year to which such adjustment relates ended before or after the commencement of the case;

(C) any fine, penalty, or reduction in credit relating to a tax of a kind specified in subparagraph (B) of this paragraph; and

(D) notwithstanding the requirements of subsection (a), a governmental unit shall not be required to file a request for the payment of an expense described in subparagraph (B) or (C), as a condition of its being an allowed administrative expense;

(2) compensation and reimbursement awarded under section 330(a) of this title;

(3) the actual, necessary expenses, other than compensation and reimbursement specified in paragraph (4) of this subsection, incurred by—

(A) a creditor that files a petition under section 303 of this title;

(B) a creditor that recovers, after the court's approval, for the benefit of the estate any property transferred or concealed by the debtor;

(C) a creditor in connection with the prosecution of a criminal offense relating to the case or to the business or property of the debtor;

(D) a creditor, an indenture trustee, an equity security holder, or a committee representing creditors or equity security holders other than a committee appointed under section 1102 of this title, in making a substantial contribution in a case under chapter 9 or 11 of this title;

(E) a custodian superseded under section 543 of this title, and compensation for the services of such custodian; or

(F) a member of a committee appointed under section 1102 of this title, if such expenses are incurred in the performance of the duties of such committee;

(4) reasonable compensation for professional services rendered by an attorney or an accountant of an entity whose expense is allowable under subparagraph (A), (B), (C), (D), or (E) of paragraph (3) of this subsection, based on the time, the nature, the extent, and the value of such services, and the cost of comparable services other than in a case under this title, and reimbursement for actual, necessary expenses incurred by such attorney or accountant;

(5) reasonable compensation for services rendered by an indenture trustee in making a substantial contribution in a case under chapter 9 or 11 of this title, based on the time, the nature, the extent, and the value of such services, and the cost of comparable services other than in a case under this title;

(6) the fees and mileage payable under chapter 119 of title 28;

(7) with respect to a nonresidential real property lease previously assumed under section 365, and subsequently rejected, a sum equal to all monetary obligations due, excluding those arising from or relating to a failure to operate or a penalty provision, for the period of 2 years following the later of the rejection date or the date of actual turnover of the premises, without reduction or setoff for any reason whatsoever except for sums actually received or to be received from an entity other than the debtor, and the claim for remaining sums due for the balance of the term of the lease shall be a claim under section 502(b)(6);

(8) the actual, necessary costs and expenses of closing a health care business incurred by a trustee or by a Federal agency (as defined in section 551(1) of title 5) or a department or agency of a State or political subdivision thereof, including any cost or expense incurred—

(A) in disposing of patient records in accordance with section 351; or

(B) in connection with transferring patients from the health care business that is in the process of being closed to another health care business; and

(9) the value of any goods received by the debtor within 20 days before the date of commencement of a case under this title in which the goods have been sold to the debtor in the ordinary course of such debtor's business.

(c) Notwithstanding subsection (b), there shall neither be allowed, nor paid—

(1) a transfer made to, or an obligation incurred for the benefit of, an insider of the debtor for the purpose of inducing such person to remain with the debtor's business, absent a finding by the court based on evidence in the record that—

(A) the transfer or obligation is essential to retention of the person because the individual has a bona fide job offer from another business at the same or greater rate of compensation;

(B) the services provided by the person are essential to the survival of the business; and

(C) either—

(i) the amount of the transfer made to, or obligation incurred for the benefit of, the person is not greater than an amount equal to 10 times the amount of the mean transfer or obligation of a similar kind given to nonmanagement employees for any purpose during the calendar year in which the transfer is made or the obligation is incurred; or

(ii) if no such similar transfers were made to, or obligations were incurred for the benefit of, such nonmanagement employees during such calendar year, the amount of the transfer or obligation is not greater than an amount equal to 25 percent of the amount of any similar transfer or obligation made to or incurred for the benefit of such insider for any purpose during the calendar year before the year in which such transfer is made or obligation is incurred;

(2) a severance payment to an insider of the debtor, unless—

(A) the payment is part of a program that is generally applicable to all full-time employees; and

(B) the amount of the payment is not greater than 10 times the amount of the mean severance pay given to nonmanagement employees during the calendar year in which the payment is made; or

(3) other transfers or obligations that are outside the ordinary course of business and not justified by the facts and circumstances of the case, including transfers made to, or obligations incurred for the benefit of, officers, managers, or consultants hired after the date of the filing of the petition.

(Pub.L. 95–598, Nov. 6, 1978, 92 Stat. 2581; Pub.L. 98–353, Title III, § 446, July 10, 1984, 98 Stat. 374; Pub.L. 99–554, Title II, § 283(g), Oct. 27, 1986, 100 Stat. 3117; Pub.L. 103–394, Title I, § 110, Title II, § 213(c), Title III, § 304(h)(2), Oct. 22, 1994, 108 Stat. 4113, 4126, 4134; Pub.L. 109–8, Title III, §§ 329, 331, Title IV, § 445, Title VII, § 712(b), (c), Title XI, § 1103, Title XII, §§ 1208, 1227(b), Apr. 20, 2005, 119 Stat. 101, 102, 117, 128, 190, 194, 200.)

HISTORICAL AND STATUTORY NOTES

Revision Notes and Legislative Reports

1978 Acts. Subsection (a) of this section permits administrative expense claimants to file with the court a request for payment of an administrative expense. The Rules of Bankruptcy Procedure will specify the time, the form, and the method of such a filing.

Subsection (b) specifies the kinds of administrative expenses that are allowable in a case under the bankruptcy code. The subsection is derived mainly from section 64a(1) of the Bankruptcy Act [section 104(a)(1) of former Title 11], with some changes. The actual, necessary costs and expenses of preserving the estate, including wages, salaries, or commissions for services rendered after the order for relief, and any taxes on, measured by, or withheld from such wages, salaries, or commissions, are allowable as administrative expenses.

In general, administrative expenses include taxes which the trustee incurs in administering the debtor's estate, including taxes on capital gains from sales of property by the trustee and taxes on income earned by the estate during the case. Interest on tax liabilities and certain tax penalties incurred by the trustee are also included in this first priority.

Taxes which the Internal Revenue Service may find due after giving the trustee a so-called "quickie" tax refund and later doing an audit of the refund are also payable as administrative expenses. The tax code [Title 26, Internal Revenue Code] permits the trustee of an estate which suffers a net operating loss to carry back the loss against an earlier profit year of the estate or of the debtor and to obtain a tentative refund for the earlier year, subject, however, to a later full audit of the loss which led to the refund. The bill, in effect, requires the Internal Revenue Service to issue a tentative refund to the trustee (whether the refund was applied for by the debtor or by the trustee), but if the refund later proves to have been erroneous in amount, the Service can request that the tax attributable to the erroneous refund be payable by the estate as an administrative expense.

Postpetition payments to an individual debtor for services rendered to the estate are administrative expenses, and are not property of the estate when received by the debtor. This situation would most likely arise when the individual was a sole proprietor and was employed by the estate to run the business after the commencement of the case. An individual debtor in possession would be so employed, for example. See *Local Loan v. Hunt,* 292 U.S. 234, 243 (1933) [54 S.Ct. 695, 78 L.Ed. 1230].

Compensation and reimbursement awarded officers of the estate under section 330 are allowable as administrative expenses. Actual, necessary expenses, other than compensation of a professional person, incurred by a creditor that files an involuntary petition, by a creditor that recovers property for the benefit of the estate, by a creditor that acts in connection with the prosecution of a criminal offense relating to the case, by a creditor, indenture, trustee, equity security holder, or committee of creditors or equity security holders (other than official committees) that makes a substantial contribution to a reorganization or municipal debt adjustment case, or by a superseded custodian, are all allowable administrative expenses. The phrase "substantial contribution in the case" is derived from Bankruptcy Act §§ 242 and 243 [sections 642 and 643 of former Title 11]. It does not require a contribution that leads to confirmation of a plan, for in many cases, it will be a substantial contribution if the person involved uncovers facts that would lead to a denial of confirmation, such as fraud in connection with the case.

Paragraph (4) permits reasonable compensation for professional services rendered by an attorney or an accountant of an equity whose expense is compensable under the previous paragraph. Paragraph (5) permits reasonable compensation for an indenture trustee in making a substantial contribution in a reorganization or municipal debt adjustment case. Finally, paragraph (6) permits witness fees and mileage as prescribed under chapter 119 of title 28 [section 1821 et seq. of Title 28, Judiciary and Judicial Procedure]. Senate Report No. 95–989.

1984 Acts. Statements by Legislative Leaders, see 1984 U.S. Code Cong. and Adm. News, p. 576.

1986 Acts. House Report No. 99–764 and House Conference Report No. 99–958, see 1986 U.S. Code Cong. and Adm. News, p. 5227.

1994 Acts. House Report No. 103–835, see 1994 U.S. Code Cong. and Adm. News, p. 3340.

2005 Acts. House Report No. 109–31(Part I), see 2005 U.S. Code Cong. and Adm. News, p. 88.

Legislative Statements

Section 503(a) of the House amendment represents a compromise between similar provisions in the House bill and the Senate amendment by leaving to the Rules of Bankruptcy Procedure the determination of the location at which a request for payment of an administrative expense may be filed. The preamble to section 503(b) of the House bill makes a similar change with respect to the allowance of administrative expenses.

Section 503(b)(1) adopts the approach taken in the House bill as modified by some provisions contained in the Senate amendment. The preamble to section 503(b) makes clear that none of the paragraphs of section 503(b) apply to claims or expenses of the kind specified in section 502(f) that arise in the ordinary course of the debtor's business or financial affairs and that arise during the gap between the commencement of an involuntary case and the appointment of a trustee or the order for relief, whichever first occurs. The remainder of section 503(b) represents a compromise between H.R. 8200 as passed by the House and the Senate amendments. Section 503(b)(3)(E) codifies present law in cases such as *Randolph v. Scruggs,* 190 U.S. 533, which accords administrative expense status to services rendered by a prepetition custodian or other party to the extent such services actually benefit the estate. Section 503(b)(4) of the House amendment conforms to the provision contained in H.R. 8200 as passed by the House and deletes language contained in the Senate amendment providing a different standard of compensation under section 330 of that amendment.

Effective and Applicability Provisions

2005 Acts. Amendments by Pub.L. 109–8 effective, except as otherwise provided, 180 days after April 20, 2005, and inapplicable with respect to cases commenced under Title 11 before the effective date, see Pub.L. 109–8, § 1501, set out as a note under 11 U.S.C.A. § 101.

1994 Acts. Amendments by Pub.L. 103–394 effective on Oct. 22, 1994, and not to apply with respect to cases commenced under Title 11 of the United States Code before Oct. 22, 1994, see section 702 of Pub.L. 103–394, set out as a note under section 101 of this title.

1986 Acts. Amendment by Pub.L. 99–554 effective 30 days after Oct. 27, 1986, except as otherwise provided for, see section 302(a) of Pub.L. 99–554, set out as a note under section 581 of Title 28, Judiciary and Judicial Procedure.

1984 Acts. Amendment by Pub.L. 98–353 effective with respect to cases filed 90 days after July 10, 1984, see section 552(a), formerly 553(a), of Pub.L. 98–353, set out as a note under section 101 of this title.

Separability of Provisions

If any provision of or amendment made by Pub.L. 103–394 or the application of such provision or amendment to any person or circumstance is held to be unconstitutional, the remaining provisions of and amendments made by Pub.L. 103–394 and the application of such provisions and amendments to any person or circumstance shall not be affected thereby, see section 701 of Pub.L. 103–394, set out as a note under section 101 of this title.

CROSS REFERENCES

Adequate protection, other than granting certain administrative expenses, see 11 USCA § 361.

Applicability of this section in Chapter 9 cases, see 11 USCA § 901.

Claims arising from automatic stay, see 11 USCA § 922.

Discharge of liabilities on claims in Chapter 12 cases, see 11 USCA § 1228.

Deductibility of allowed claim, see 11 USCA § 346.

Deduction of administrative expenses for income tax purposes, see 26 USCA § 1398.

Deduction of administrative expenses from payments received by trustee if plan not confirmed in—

Chapter 13 cases, see 11 USCA § 1326.

Chapter 12 cases, see 11 USCA § 1226.

Distribution of property of estate, see 11 USCA § 726.

Effect of conversion, see 11 USCA § 348.

Grain storage facility bankruptcies, expedited determinations, see 11 USCA § 557.

Method of obtaining adequate protection in Chapter 12 case, see 11 USCA § 1205.

Payment of insurance benefits to retired employees, see 11 USCA § 1114.

Performance of obligations under executory contracts and unexpired leases notwithstanding subsec. (b)(1) of this section, see 11 USCA § 365.

Proof of claim, see Official Bankr. Form 10, 11 USCA.

Unsecured debt as administrative expense or having priority over certain administrative expenses, see 11 USCA § 364.

§ 504. Sharing of compensation

(a) Except as provided in subsection (b) of this section, a person receiving compensation or reimbursement under section 503(b)(2) or 503(b)(4) of this title may not share or agree to share—

(1) any such compensation or reimbursement with another person; or

(2) any compensation or reimbursement received by another person under such sections.

(b)(1) A member, partner, or regular associate in a professional association, corporation, or partnership may share compensation or reimbursement received under section 503(b)(2) or 503(b)(4) of this title with another member, partner, or regular associate in such association, corporation, or partnership, and may share in any compensation or reimbursement received under such sections by another member, partner, or regular associate in such association, corporation, or partnership.

(2) An attorney for a creditor that files a petition under section 303 of this title may share compensation and reimbursement received under section 503(b)(4) of this title with any other attorney contributing to the services rendered or expenses incurred by such creditor's attorney.

(c) This section shall not apply with respect to sharing, or agreeing to share, compensation with a bona fide public service attorney referral program that operates in accordance with non-Federal law regulating attorney referral services and with rules of professional responsibility applicable to attorney acceptance of referrals.

(Pub.L. 95–598, Nov. 6, 1978, 92 Stat. 2582; Pub.L. 109–8, Title III, § 326, Apr. 20, 2005, 119 Stat. 99.)

HISTORICAL AND STATUTORY NOTES

Revision Notes and Legislative Reports

1978 Acts. Section 504 prohibits the sharing of compensation, or fee splitting, among attorneys, other professionals, or trustees. The section provides only two exceptions: partners or associates in the same professional association, partnership, or corporation may share compensation inter se; and attorneys for petitioning creditors that join in a petition commencing an involuntary case may share compensation. Senate Report No. 95–989.

2005 Acts. House Report No. 109–31(Part I), see 2005 U.S. Code Cong. and Adm. News, p. 88.

Effective and Applicability Provisions

2005 Acts. Amendments by Pub.L. 109–8 effective, except as otherwise provided, 180 days after April 20, 2005, and inapplicable with respect to cases commenced under Title 11 before the effective date, see Pub.L. 109–8, § 1501, set out as a note under 11 U.S.C.A. § 101.

CROSS REFERENCES

Applicability of restrictions on sharing of compensation to allowances in investor protection liquidation proceedings, see 15 USCA § 78eee.

Applicability of this section in Chapter 9 cases, see 11 USCA § 901.

§ 505. Determination of tax liability

(a)(1) Except as provided in paragraph (2) of this subsection, the court may determine the amount or legality of any tax, any fine or penalty relating to a tax, or any addition to tax, whether or not previously assessed, whether or not paid, and whether or not contested before and adjudicated by a judicial or administrative tribunal of competent jurisdiction.

(2) The court may not so determine—

(A) the amount or legality of a tax, fine, penalty, or addition to tax if such amount or legality was contested before and adjudicated by a judicial or administrative tribunal of competent jurisdiction before the commencement of the case under this title;

(B) any right of the estate to a tax refund, before the earlier of—

(i) 120 days after the trustee properly requests such refund from the governmental unit from which such refund is claimed; or

(ii) a determination by such governmental unit of such request; or

(C) the amount or legality of any amount arising in connection with an ad valorem tax on real or personal property of the estate, if the applicable period for contesting or redetermining that amount under any law (other than a bankruptcy law) has expired.

(b)(1)(A) The clerk shall maintain a list under which a Federal, State, or local governmental unit responsible for the collection of taxes within the district may—

(i) designate an address for service of requests under this subsection; and

(ii) describe where further information concerning additional requirements for filing such requests may be found.

(B) If such governmental unit does not designate an address and provide such address to the clerk under subparagraph (A), any request made under this subsection may be served at the address for the filing of a tax return or protest with the appropriate taxing authority of such governmental unit.

(2) A trustee may request a determination of any unpaid liability of the estate for any tax incurred during the administration of the case by submitting a tax return for such tax and a request for such a determination to the governmental unit charged with responsibility for collection or determination of such tax at the address and in the manner designated in paragraph (1). Unless such return is fraudulent, or contains a material misrepresentation, the estate, the trustee, the debtor, and any successor to the debtor are discharged from any liability for such tax—

(A) upon payment of the tax shown on such return, if—

(i) such governmental unit does not notify the trustee, within 60 days after such request, that such return has been selected for examination; or

(ii) such governmental unit does not complete such an examination and notify the trustee of any tax due, within 180 days after such request or within such additional time as the court, for cause, permits;

(B) upon payment of the tax determined by the court, after notice and a hearing, after completion by such governmental unit of such examination; or

(C) upon payment of the tax determined by such governmental unit to be due.

(c) Notwithstanding section 362 of this title, after determination by the court of a tax under this section, the governmental unit charged with responsibility for collection of such tax may assess such tax against the estate, the debtor, or a successor to the debtor, as the case may be, subject to any otherwise applicable law.

(Pub.L. 95–598, Nov. 6, 1978, 92 Stat. 2582; Pub.L. 98–353, Title III, § 447, July 10, 1984, 98 Stat. 374; Pub.L. 109–8, Title VII, §§ 701(b), 703, 715, Apr. 20, 2005, 119 Stat. 124, 125, 129.)

HISTORICAL AND STATUTORY NOTES

Revision Notes and Legislative Reports

1978 Acts. Subsections (a) and (b) are derived, with only stylistic changes, from section 2a(2A) of the Bankruptcy Act [section 11(a)(2A) of former Title 11]. They permit determination by the bankruptcy court of any unpaid tax liability of the debtor that has not been contested before or adjudicated by a judicial or administrative tribunal of competent jurisdiction before the bankruptcy case, and the prosecution by the trustee of an appeal from an order of such a body if the time for review or appeal has not expired before the commencement of the bankruptcy case. As under current Bankruptcy Act section 2a(2A), *Arkansas Corporation Commissioner v. Thompson*, 313 U.S. 132 (1941) [61 S.Ct. 888, 85 L.Ed. 1244], remains good law to permit abstention where uniformity of assessment is of significant importance.

Section (c) [sic] deals with procedures for obtaining a prompt audit of tax returns filed by the trustee in a liquidation or reorganization case. Under the bill as originally introduced, a trustee who is "in doubt" concerning tax liabilities of the estate incurred during a title 11 proceeding could obtain a discharge from personal liability for himself and the debtor (but not for the debtor or the debtor's successor in a reorganization), provided that certain administrative procedures were followed. The trustee could request a prompt tax audit by the local, State, or Federal governmental unit. The taxing authority would have to notify the trustee and the court within sixty days whether it accepted the return or desired to audit the returns more fully. If an audit were conducted, the tax office would have to notify the trustee of any tax deficiency within 4 months (subject to an extension of time if the court approved). These procedures would apply only to tax years completed on or before the case was closed and for which the trustee had filed a tax return.

The committee bill eliminates the "in doubt" rule and makes mandatory (rather than optional) the trustee's request for a prompt audit of the estate's tax returns. In many cases, the trustee could not be certain that his returns raised no doubt about possible tax issues. In addition, it is desirable not to create a situation where the taxing authority asserts a tax liability against the debtor (as transferee of surplus assets, if any, return to him) after the case is over; in any such situation, the debtor would be called on to defend a tax return which he did not prepare. Under the amendment, all disputes concerning these returns are to be resolved by the bankruptcy court, and both the trustee and the debtor himself do not then face potential post-bankruptcy tax liabilities based on these returns. This result would occur as to the debtor, however, only in a liquidation case.

In a reorganization in which the debtor or a successor to the debtor continues in existence, the trustee could obtain a discharge from personal liability through the prompt audit procedure, but the Treasury could still claim a deficiency against the debtor (or his successor) for additional taxes due on returns filed during the title 11 proceedings. Senate Report No. 95–989.

Subsection (c) is new. It codifies in part the referee's decision in *In re Statmaster Corp.*, 465 F.2d 987 (5th Cir. 1972). Its purpose is to protect the trustee from personal liability for a tax falling on the estate that is not assessed until after the case is closed. If necessary to permit expeditious closing of the case, the court, on request of the trustee, must order the governmental unit charged with the responsibility for collection or determination of the tax to audit the trustee's return or be barred from attempting later collection. The court will be required to permit sufficient time to perform an audit, if the taxing authority requests it. The final order of the court and the payment of the tax determined in that order discharges the trustee, the debtor, and any successor to the debtor from any further liability for the tax. See Plumb, The Tax Recommendations of the Commission on the Bankruptcy Laws: Tax Procedures, 88 Harv. L.Rev. 1360, 1423–42 (1975). House Report No. 95–595.

1984 Acts. Statements by Legislative Leaders, see 1984 U.S.Code Cong. and Adm.News, p. 576.

2005 Acts. House Report No. 109–31(Part I), see 2005 U.S. Code Cong. and Adm. News, p. 88.

Legislative Statements

Section 505 of the House amendment adopts a compromise position with respect to the determination of tax liability from the position taken in H.R. 8200 as passed by the House and in the Senate amendment.

Determinations of tax liability: Authority of bankruptcy court to rule on merits of tax claims.—The House amendment authorizes the bankruptcy court to rule on the merits of any tax claim involving an unpaid tax, fine, or penalty relating to a tax, or any addition to a tax, of the debtor or the estate. This authority applies, in general, whether or not the tax, penalty, fine, or addition to tax had been previously assessed or paid. However, the bankruptcy court will not have jurisdiction to rule on the merits of any tax claim which has been previously adjudicated, in a contested proceeding, before a court of competent jurisdiction. For this purpose, a proceeding in the U.S. Tax Court is to be considered "contested" if the debtor filed a petition in the Tax Court by the commencement of the case and the Internal Revenue Service had filed an answer to the petition. Therefore, if a petition and answer were filed in the Tax Court before the title II petition was filed, and if the debtor later defaults in the Tax Court, then, under res judicata principles, the bankruptcy court could not then rule on the debtor's or the estate's liability for the same taxes.

The House amendment adopts the rule of the Senate bill that the bankruptcy court can, under certain conditions, determine the amount of tax refund claim by the trustee. Under the House amendment, if the refund results from an offset or counterclaim to a claim or request for payment by the Internal Revenue Service, or other tax authority, the trustee would not first have to file an administrative claim for refund with the tax authority.

However, if the trustee requests a refund in other situations, he would first have to submit an administrative claim for the refund. Under the House amendment, if the Internal Revenue Service, or other tax authority does not rule on the refund claim within 120 days, then the bankruptcy court may rule on the merits of the refund claim.

Under the Internal Revenue Code [Title 26, Internal Revenue Code], a suit for refund of Federal taxes cannot be filed until 6 months after a claim for refund is filed with the Internal Revenue Service (sec. 6532(a) [26 U.S.C.A. § 6532(a)]). Because of the bankruptcy aim to close the estate as expeditiously as possible, the House amendment shortens to 120 days the period for the Internal Revenue Service to decide the refund claim.

The House amendment also adopts the substance of the Senate bill rule permitting the bankruptcy court to determine the amount of any penalty, whether punitive or pecuniary in nature, relating to taxes over which it has jurisdiction.

Jurisdiction of the tax court in bankruptcy cases: The Senate amendment provided a detailed series of rules concerning the jurisdiction of the U.S. Tax Court, or similar State or local administrative tribunal to determine personal tax liabilities of an individual debtor. The House amendment deletes these specific rules and relies on procedures to be derived from broad general powers of the bankruptcy court.

Under the House amendment, as under present law, a corporation seeking reorganization under chapter 11 is considered to be personally before the bankruptcy court for purposes of giving that court jurisdiction over the debtor's personal liability for a nondischargeable tax.

The rules are more complex where the debtor is an individual under chapter 7, 11, or 13. An individual debtor or the tax authority can, as under section 17c of the present Bankruptcy Act [section 35(c) of former Title 11], file a request that the bankruptcy court determine the debtor's personal liability for the balance of any nondischargeable tax not satisfied from assets of the estate. The House amendment intends to retain these procedures and also adds a rule staying commencement or continuation of any proceeding in the Tax Court after the bankruptcy petition is filed, unless and until that stay is lifted by the bankruptcy judge under section 362(a)(8). The House amendment also stays assessment as well as collection of a prepetition claim against the debtor (sec. 362(a)(6)). A tax authority would not, however, be stayed from issuing a deficiency notice during the bankruptcy case (sec. (b)(7)). The Senate amendment repealed the existing authority of the Internal Revenue Service to make an immediate assessment of taxes upon bankruptcy (sec. 6871(a) of the code [26 U.S.C.A. § 6871(a)]). See section of the Senate bill. As indicated, the substance of that provision, also affecting State and local taxes, is contained in section 362(a)(6) of the House amendment. The statute of limitations is tolled under the House amendment while the bankruptcy case is pending.

Where no proceeding in the Tax Court is pending at the commencement of the bankruptcy case, the tax authority can, under the House amendment, file a claim against the estate for a prepetition tax liability and may also file a request that the bankruptcy court hear arguments and decide the merits of an individual debtor's personal liability for the balance of any nondischargeable tax liability not satisfied from assets of the estate. Bankruptcy terminology refers to the latter type of request as a creditor's complaint to determine the dischargeability of a debt. Where such a complaint is filed, the bankruptcy court will have personal jurisdiction over an individual debtor, and the debtor himself would have no access to the Tax Court, or to any other court, to determine his personal liability for nondischargeable taxes.

If a tax authority decides not to file a claim for taxes which would typically occur where there are few, if any, assets in the estate, normally the tax authority would also not request the bankruptcy court to rule on the debtor's personal liability for a nondischargeable tax. Under the House amendment, the tax authority would then have to follow normal procedures in order to collect a nondischargeable tax. For example, in the case of nondischargeable Federal income taxes, the Internal Revenue Service would be required to issue a deficiency notice to an individual debtor, and the debtor could then file a petition in the Tax Court—or a refund suit in a district court—as the forum in which to litigate his personal liability for a nondischargeable tax.

Under the House amendment, as under present law, an individual debtor can also file a complaint to determine dischargeability. Consequently, where the tax authority does not file a claim or a request that the bankruptcy court determine dischargeability of a specific tax liability, the debtor could file such a request on his own behalf, so that the bankruptcy court would then determine both the validity of the claim against assets in the estate and also the personal liability of the debtor for any nondischargeable tax.

Where a proceeding is pending in the Tax Court at the commencement of the bankruptcy case, the commencement of the bankruptcy case automatically stays further action in the Tax Court case unless and until the stay is lifted by the bankruptcy court. The Senate amendment repealed a provision of the Internal Revenue case barring a debtor from filing a petition in the Tax Court after commencement of a bankruptcy case (sec. 6871(b) of the code) [26 U.S.C.A. § 6871(b)]. See section 321 of the Senate bill. As indicated earlier, the equivalent of the code amendment is embodied in section 362(a)(8) of the House amendment, which automatically stays commencement or continuation of any proceeding in the Tax Court until the stay is lifted or the case is terminated. The stay will permit sufficient time for the bankruptcy trustee to determine if he desires to join the Tax Court proceeding on behalf of the estate. Where the trustee chooses to join the Tax Court proceeding, it is expected that he will seek permission to intervene in the Tax Court case and then request that the stay on the Tax Court proceeding be lifted. In such a case, the merits of the tax liability will be determined by the Tax Court, and its decision will bind both the individual debtor as to any taxes which are nondischargeable and the trustee as to the tax claim against the estate.

Where the trustee does not want to intervene in the Tax Court, but an individual debtor wants to have the Tax Court determine the amount of his personal liability for nondischargeable taxes, the debtor can request the bankruptcy court to lift the automatic stay on existing Tax Court proceedings. If the stay is lifted and the Tax Court reaches its decision before the bankruptcy court's decision on the tax claim against the estate, the decision of the Tax Court would bind the bankruptcy court under principles of res judicata because the decision of the Tax Court affected the personal liability of the debtor. If the trustee does not wish to subject the estate to the decision of the Tax Court if the latter court decides the issues before the bankruptcy court rules, the trustee could resist the lifting of the stay on the existing Tax Court proceeding. If the Internal Revenue Service had issued a deficiency notice to the debtor before the bankruptcy case began, but as of the filing of the bankruptcy petition the 90-day period for filing in the Tax Court was still running, the debtor would be automatically stayed from filing a petition in the Tax Court. If either the debtor or the Internal Revenue Service then files a complaint to determine dischargeability in the bankruptcy court, the decision of the bankruptcy court would bind both the debtor and the Internal Revenue Service.

The bankruptcy judge could, however, lift the stay on the debtor to allow him to petition the Tax Court, while reserving the right to rule on the tax authority's claim against assets of the estate. The bankruptcy court could also, upon request by the trustee, authorize the trustee to intervene in the Tax Court for purposes of having the estate also governed by the decision of the Tax Court.

In essence, under the House amendment, the bankruptcy judge will have authority to determine which court will determine the merits of the tax claim both as to claims against the estate and claims against the debtor concerning his personal liability for nondischargeable taxes. Thus, if the Internal Revenue Service, or a State or local tax authority, files a petition to determine dischargeability, the bankruptcy judge can either rule on the merits of the claim and continue the stay on any pending Tax Court proceeding or lift the stay on the Tax Court and hold the dischargeability complaint in abeyance. If he rules on the merits of the complaint before the decision of the Tax Court is reached, the bankruptcy court's decision would bind the debtor as to nondischargeable taxes and the Tax Court would be governed by that decision under principles of res judicata. If the bankruptcy judge does not rule on the merits of the complaint before the decision of the Tax Court is reached, the bankruptcy court will be bound by the decision of the Tax Court as it affects the amount of any claim against the debtor's estate.

If the Internal Revenue Service does not file a complaint to determine dischargeability and the automatic stay on a pending Tax Court proceeding is not lifted, the bankruptcy court could determine the merits of any tax claim against the estate. That decision will not bind the debtor personally because he would not have been personally before the bankruptcy court unless the debtor himself asks the bankruptcy court to rule on his personal liability. In any such situation where no party filed a dischargeability petition, the debtor would have access to the Tax Court to determine his personal liability for a nondischargeable tax debt. While the Tax Court in such a situation could take into account the ruling of the bankruptcy court on claims against the estate in deciding the debtor's personal liability, the bankruptcy court's ruling would not bind the Tax Court under principles of res judicata, because the debtor, in that situation, would not have been personally before the bankruptcy court.

If neither the debtor nor the Internal Revenue Service files a claim against the estate or a request to rule on the debtor's personal liability, any pending tax court proceeding would be stayed until the closing of the bankruptcy case, at which time the stay on the tax court would cease and the tax court case could continue for purposes of deciding the merits of the debtor's personal liability for nondischargeable taxes.

Audit of trustee's returns: Under both bills, the bankruptcy court could determine the amount of any administrative period taxes. The Senate amendment, however, provided for an expedited audit procedure, which was mandatory in some cases. The House amendment (sec. 505(b)), adopts the provision of the House bill allowing the trustee discretion in all cases whether to ask the Internal Revenue Service, or State or local tax authority for a prompt audit of his returns on behalf of the estate. The House amendment, however, adopts the provision of the Senate bill permitting a prompt audit only on the basis of tax returns filed by the trustee for completed taxable periods. Procedures for a prompt audit set forth in the Senate bill are also adopted in modified form.

Under the procedure, before the case can be closed, the trustee may request a tax audit by the local, State or Federal tax authority of all tax returns filed by the trustee. The taxing authority would have to notify the trustee and the bankruptcy court within 60 days whether it accepts returns or desires to audit the returns more fully. If an audit is conducted, the taxing authority would have to notify the trustee of tax deficiency within 180 days after the original request, subject to extensions of time if the bankruptcy court approves. If the trustee does not agree with the results of the audit, the trustee could ask the bankruptcy court to resolve the dispute. Once the trustee's tax liability for administration period taxes has thus been determined, the legal effect in a case under chapter 7 or 11 would be to discharge the trustee and any predecessor of the trustee, and also the debtor, from any further liability for these taxes.

The prompt audit procedure would not be available with respect to any tax liability as to which any return required to be filed on behalf of the estate is not filed with the proper tax authority. The House amendment also specifies that a discharge of the trustee or the debtor which would otherwise occur will not be granted, or will be void if the return filed on behalf of the estate reflects fraud or material misrepresentation of facts.

For purposes of the above prompt audit procedures, it is intended that the tax authority with which the request for audit is to be filed is, as to Federal taxes, the office of the District Director in the district where the bankruptcy case is pending.

Under the House amendment, if the trustee does not request a prompt audit, the debtor would not be discharged from possible transferee liability if any assets are returned to the debtor.

Assessment after decision: As indicated above, the commencement of a bankruptcy case automatically stays assessment of any tax (sec. 362(a)(6)). However, the House amendment provides (sec. 505(c)) that if the bankruptcy court renders a final judgment with regard to any tax (under the rules discussed above), the tax authority may then make an assessment (if permitted to do so under otherwise applicable tax law) without waiting for termination of the case or confirmation of a reorganization plan.

Trustee's authority to appeal tax cases: The equivalent provision in the House bill (sec. 505(b)) and in the Senate bill (sec. 362(h)) authorizing the trustee to prosecute an appeal or review of a tax case are deleted as unnecessary. Section 541(a) of the House amendment provides that property of the estate is to include all legal or equitable interests of the debtor. These interests include the debtor's causes of action, so that the specific provisions of the House and Senate bills are not needed.

Effective and Applicability Provisions

2005 Acts. Amendments by Pub.L. 109–8 effective, except as otherwise provided, 180 days after April 20, 2005, and inapplicable with respect to cases commenced under Title 11 before the effective date, see Pub.L. 109–8, § 1501, set out as a note under 11 U.S.C.A. § 101.

1984 Acts. Amendment by Pub.L. 98–353 effective with respect to cases filed 90 days after July 10, 1984, see section 552(a), formerly 553(a), of Pub.L. 98–353, set out as a note under section 101 of this title.

CROSS REFERENCES

Declaratory judgments, see 28 USCA § 2201.

§ 506. Determination of secured status

(a)(1) An allowed claim of a creditor secured by a lien on property in which the estate has an interest, or that is subject to setoff under section 553 of this title, is a secured claim to the extent of the value of such creditor's interest in the estate's interest in such property, or to the extent of the amount subject to setoff, as the case may be, and is an unsecured claim to the extent that the value of such creditor's interest or the amount so subject to setoff is less than the amount of such allowed claim. Such value shall be determined in light of the purpose of the valuation and of the proposed disposition or use of such property, and in conjunction with any hearing on such disposition or use or on a plan affecting such creditor's interest.

(2) If the debtor is an individual in a case under chapter 7 or 13, such value with respect to personal property securing an allowed claim shall be determined based on the replacement value of such property as of the date of the filing of the petition without deduction for costs of sale or marketing. With respect to property acquired for personal, family, or household purposes, replacement value shall mean the price a retail merchant would charge for property of that kind considering the age and condition of the property at the time value is determined.

(b) To the extent that an allowed secured claim is secured by property the value of which, after any recovery under subsection (c) of this section, is greater than the amount of such claim, there shall be allowed to the holder of such claim, interest on such claim, and any reasonable fees, costs, or charges provided for under the agreement or State statute under which such claim arose.

(c) The trustee may recover from property securing an allowed secured claim the reasonable, necessary costs and expenses of preserving, or disposing of, such property to the extent of any benefit to the holder of such claim, including the payment of all ad valorem property taxes with respect to the property.

(d) To the extent that a lien secures a claim against the debtor that is not an allowed secured claim, such lien is void, unless—

(1) such claim was disallowed only under section 502(b)(5) or 502(e) of this title; or

(2) such claim is not an allowed secured claim due only to the failure of any entity to file a proof of such claim under section 501 of this title.

(Pub.L. 95–598, Nov. 6, 1978, 92 Stat. 2583; Pub.L. 98–353, Title III, § 448, July 10, 1984, 98 Stat. 374; Pub.L. 109–8, Title III, § 327, Title VII, § 712(d), Apr. 20, 2005, 119 Stat. 99, 128.)

HISTORICAL AND STATUTORY NOTES

Revision Notes and Legislative Reports

1978 Acts. Subsection (a) of this section separates an undersecured creditor's claim into two parts: He has a secured claim to the extent of the value of his collateral; and he has an unsecured claim for the balance of his claim. The subsection also provides for the valuation of claims which involve setoffs under section 553. While courts will have to determine value on a case-by-case basis, the subsection makes it clear that valuation is to be determined in light of the purpose of the valuation and the proposed disposition or use of the subject property. This determination shall be made in conjunction with any hearing on such disposition or use of property or on a plan affecting the creditor's interest. To illustrate, a valuation early in the case in a proceeding under sections 361–363 would not be binding upon the debtor or creditor at the time of confirmation of the plan. Throughout the bill, references to secured claims are only to the claim determined to be secured under this subsection, and not to the full amount of the creditor's claim. This provision abolishes the use of the terms "secured creditor" and "unsecured creditor" and substitutes in their places the terms "secured claim" and "unsecured claim."

Subsection (b) codifies current law by entitling a creditor with an oversecured claim to any reasonable fees (including attorney's fees), costs, or charges provided under the agreement under which the claim arose. These fees, costs, and charges are secured claims to the extent that the value of the collateral exceeds the amount of the underlying claim.

Subsection (c) also codifies current law by permitting the trustee to recover from property the value of which is greater than the sum of the claims secured by a lien on that property the reasonable, necessary costs and expenses of preserving, or disposing of, the property. The recovery is limited to the extent of any benefit to the holder of such claim.

Subsection (d) provides that to the extent a secured claim is not allowed, its lien is void unless the holder had neither actual notice nor knowledge of the case, the lien was not listed by the debtor in a chapter 9 or 11 case or such claim was disallowed only under section 502(e). Senate Report No. 95–989.

Subsection (d) permits liens to pass through the bankruptcy case unaffected. However, if a party in interest requests the court to determine and allow or disallow the claim secured by the lien under section 502 and the claim is not allowed, then the lien is void to the extent that the claim is not allowed. The voiding provision does not apply to claims disallowed only under section 502(e), which requires disallowance of certain claims against the debtor by a codebtor, surety, or guarantor for contribution or reimbursement. House Report No. 95–595.

1984 Acts. Statements by Legislative Leaders, see 1984 U.S.Code Cong. and Adm.News, p. 576.

2005 Acts. House Report No. 109–31(Part I), see 2005 U.S. Code Cong. and Adm. News, p. 88.

Legislative Statements

Section 506(a) of the House amendment adopts the provision contained in the Senate amendment and rejects a contrary provision as contained in H.R. 8200 as passed by the House. The provision contained in the Senate amendment and adopted by the House amendment recognizes that an amount subject to set-off is sufficient to recognize a secured status in the holder of such right. Additionally a determination of what portion of an allowed claim is secured and what portion is unsecured is binding only for the purpose for which the determination is made. Thus determinations for purposes of adequate protection is not binding for purposes of "cram down" on confirmation in a case under chapter 11.

Section 506(b) of the House amendment adopts language contained in the Senate amendment and rejects language contained in H.R. 8200 as passed by the House. If the security agreement between the parties provides for attorneys' fees, it will be enforceable under title 11, notwithstanding contrary law, and is recoverable from the collateral after any recovery under section 506(c).

Section 506(c) of the House amendment was contained in H.R. 8200 as passed by the House and adopted, verbatim, in the Senate amendment. Any time the trustee or debtor in possession expends money to provide for the reasonable and necessary cost and expenses of preserving or disposing of a secured creditor's collateral, the trustee or debtor in possession is entitled to recover such expenses from the secured party or from the property securing an allowed secured claim held by such party.

Section 506(d) of the House amendment is derived from H.R. 8200 as passed by the House and is adopted in lieu of the alternative test provided in section 506(d) of the Senate amendment. For purposes of section 506(d) of the House amendment, the debtor is a party in interest.

Determination of Secured Status: The House amendment deletes section 506(d)(3) of the Senate amendment, which insures that a tax lien securing a nondischargeable tax claim is not voided because a tax authority with notice or knowledge of the bankruptcy case fails to file a claim for the liability (as it may elect not to do, if it is clear there are insufficient assets to pay the liability). Since the House amendment retains section 506(d) of the House bill that a lien is not voided unless a party in interest has requested that the court determine and allow or disallow the claim, provision of the Senate amendment is not necessary.

References in Text

Chapter 7 or 13, referred to in subsec. (a)(2), is chapter 7 or 13 of this title, 11 U.S.C.A. § 701 et seq. or 11 U.S.C.A. § 1301 et seq.

Effective and Applicability Provisions

2005 Acts. Amendments by Pub.L. 109–8 effective, except as otherwise provided, 180 days after April 20, 2005, and inapplicable with respect to cases commenced under Title 11 before the effective date, see Pub.L. 109–8, § 1501, set out as a note under 11 U.S.C.A. § 101.

1984 Acts. Amendment by Pub.L. 98–353 effective with respect to cases filed 90 days after July 10, 1984, see section 552(a), formerly 553(a), of Pub.L. 98–353, set out as a note under section 101 of this title.

CROSS REFERENCES

Applicability of this section in Chapter 9 cases, see 11 USCA § 901.

Automatic preservation of avoided transfer, see 11 USCA § 551.

Claims secured by lien on property of estate, see 11 USCA § 1111.

Contents of plan and interest on interest, see 11 USCA §§ 1123, 1222 and 1322.

Effect of dismissal, see 11 USCA § 349.

Liability of exempted property for debtor's debt, see 11 USCA § 522.

Postpetition effect of security interest, see 11 USCA § 552.

§ 507. Priorities

(a) The following expenses and claims have priority in the following order:

(1) First:

(A) Allowed unsecured claims for domestic support obligations that, as of the date of the filing of the petition in a case under this title, are owed to or recoverable by a spouse, former spouse, or child of the debtor, or such child's parent, legal guardian, or responsible relative, without regard to whether the claim is filed by such person or is filed by a governmental unit on behalf of such person, on the condition that funds received under this paragraph by a governmental unit under this title after the date of the filing of the petition shall be applied and distributed in accordance with applicable nonbankruptcy law.

(B) Subject to claims under subparagraph (A), allowed unsecured claims for domestic support obligations that, as of the date of the filing of the petition, are assigned by a spouse, former spouse, child of the debtor, or such child's parent, legal guardian, or responsible relative to a governmental unit (unless such obligation is assigned voluntarily by the spouse, former spouse, child, parent, legal guardian, or responsible relative of the child for the purpose of collecting the debt) or are owed directly to or recoverable by a governmental unit under applicable nonbankruptcy law, on the condition that funds received under this paragraph by a governmental unit under this title after the date of the filing of the petition be applied and distributed in accordance with applicable nonbankruptcy law.

(C) If a trustee is appointed or elected under section 701, 702, 703, 1104, 1202, or 1302, the administrative expenses of the trustee allowed under paragraphs (1)(A), (2), and (6) of section 503(b) shall be paid before payment of claims under subparagraphs (A) and (B), to the extent that the trustee administers assets that are otherwise available for the payment of such claims.

(2) Second, administrative expenses allowed under section 503(b) of this title, and any fees and charges assessed against the estate under chapter 123 of title 28.

(3) Third, unsecured claims allowed under section 502(f) of this title.

(4) Fourth, allowed unsecured claims, but only to the extent of $10,950 [1] for each individual or corporation, as the case may be, earned within 180 days before the date of the filing of the petition or the date of the cessation of the debtor's business, whichever occurs first, for—

(A) wages, salaries, or commissions, including vacation, severance, and sick leave pay earned by an individual; or

(B) sales commissions earned by an individual or by a corporation with only 1 employee, acting as an independent contractor in the sale of goods or services for the debtor in the ordinary course of the debtor's business if, and only if, during the 12 months preceding that date, at least 75 percent of the amount that the individual or corporation earned by acting as an independent contractor in the sale of goods or services was earned from the debtor.

(5) Fifth, allowed unsecured claims for contributions to an employee benefit plan—

(A) arising from services rendered within 180 days before the date of the filing of the petition or the date of the cessation of the debtor's business, whichever occurs first; but only

(B) for each such plan, to the extent of—

(i) the number of employees covered by each such plan multiplied by $10,950 [1]; less

(ii) the aggregate amount paid to such employees under paragraph (4) of this subsection, plus the aggregate amount paid by the estate on behalf of such employees to any other employee benefit plan.

(6) Sixth, allowed unsecured claims of persons—

(A) engaged in the production or raising of grain, as defined in section 557(b) of this title, against a debtor who owns or operates a grain storage facility, as defined in section 557(b) of this title, for grain or the proceeds of grain, or

(B) engaged as a United States fisherman against a debtor who has acquired fish or fish produce from a fisherman through a sale or conversion, and who is engaged in operating a fish produce storage or processing facility—

but only to the extent of $5,400 [1] for each such individual.

(7) Seventh, allowed unsecured claims of individuals, to the extent of $2,425 [1] for each such individual, arising from the deposit, before the commencement of the case, of money in connection with the purchase, lease, or rental of property, or the purchase of services, for the personal, family, or household use of such individuals, that were not delivered or provided.

(8) Eighth, allowed unsecured claims of governmental units, only to the extent that such claims are for—

(A) a tax on or measured by income or gross receipts for a taxable year ending on or before the date of the filing of the petition—

(i) for which a return, if required, is last due, including extensions, after three years before the date of the filing of the petition;

(ii) assessed within 240 days before the date of the filing of the petition, exclusive of—

(I) any time during which an offer in compromise with respect to that tax was pending or in effect during that 240-day period, plus 30 days; and

(II) any time during which a stay of proceedings against collections was in effect in a prior case under this title during that 240-day period, plus 90 days.

(iii) other than a tax of a kind specified in section 523(a)(1)(B) or 523(a)(1)(C) of this title, not assessed before, but assessable, under applicable law or by agreement, after, the commencement of the case;

(B) a property tax incurred before the commencement of the case and last payable without penalty after one year before the date of the filing of the petition;

(C) a tax required to be collected or withheld and for which the debtor is liable in whatever capacity;

(D) an employment tax on a wage, salary, or commission of a kind specified in paragraph (4) of this subsection earned from the debtor before the date of the filing of the petition, whether or not actually paid before such date, for which a return is last due, under applicable law or under any extension, after three years before the date of the filing of the petition;

(E) an excise tax on—

(i) a transaction occurring before the date of the filing of the petition for which a return, if required, is last due, under applicable law or under any extension, after three years before the date of the filing of the petition; or

(ii) if a return is not required, a transaction occurring during the three years immediately preceding the date of the filing of the petition;

(F) a customs duty arising out of the importation of merchandise—

(i) entered for consumption within one year before the date of the filing of the petition;

(ii) covered by an entry liquidated or reliquidated within one year before the date of the filing of the petition; or

(iii) entered for consumption within four years before the date of the filing of the petition but unliquidated on such date, if the Secretary of the Treasury certifies that failure to liquidate such entry was due to an investigation pending on such date into assessment of antidumping or countervailing duties or fraud, or if information needed for the proper appraisement or classification of such merchandise was not available to the appropriate customs officer before such date; or

(G) a penalty related to a claim of a kind specified in this paragraph and in compensation for actual pecuniary loss.

An otherwise applicable time period specified in this paragraph shall be suspended for any period during which a governmental unit is prohibited under applicable nonbankruptcy law from collecting a tax as a result of a request by the debtor for a hearing and an appeal of any collection action taken or proposed against the debtor, plus 90 days; plus any time during which the stay of proceedings was in effect in a prior case under this title or during which collection was precluded by the existence of 1 or more confirmed plans under this title, plus 90 days.

(9) Ninth, allowed unsecured claims based upon any commitment by the debtor to a Federal depository institutions regulatory agency (or predecessor to such agency) to maintain the capital of an insured depository institution.

(10) Tenth, allowed claims for death or personal injury resulting from the operation of a motor vehicle or vessel if such operation was unlawful because the debtor was intoxicated from using alcohol, a drug, or another substance.

(b) If the trustee, under section 362, 363, or 364 of this title, provides adequate protection of the interest of a holder of a claim secured by a lien on property of the debtor and if, notwithstanding such protection, such creditor has a claim allowable under subsection (a)(2) of this section arising from the stay of action against such property under section 362 of this title, from the use, sale, or lease of such property under section 363 of this title, or from the granting of a lien under section 364(d) of this title, then such creditor's claim under such subsection shall have priority over every other claim allowable under such subsection.

(c) For the purpose of subsection (a) of this section, a claim of a governmental unit arising from an erroneous refund or credit of a tax has the same priority as a claim for the tax to which such refund or credit relates.

(d) An entity that is subrogated to the rights of a holder of a claim of a kind specified in subsection (a)(1), (a)(4), (a)(5), (a)(6), (a)(7), (a)(8), or (a)(9) of this section is not subrogated to the right of the holder of such claim to priority under such subsection.

(Pub.L. 95–598, Nov. 6, 1978, 92 Stat. 2583; Pub.L. 98–353, Title III, §§ 350, 449, July 10, 1984, 98 Stat. 358, 374; Pub.L. 101–647, Title XXV, § 2522(d), Nov. 29, 1990, 104 Stat. 4867; Pub.L. 103–394, Title I, § 108(c), Title II, § 207, Title III, § 304(c), Title V, § 501(b)(3), (d)(11), Oct. 22, 1994, 108 Stat. 4112, 4123, 4132, 4142, 4145; Pub.L. 109–8, Title II, §§ 212, 223, Title VII, §§ 705, 706, Title XIV, § 1401, Title XV, § 1502(a)(1), Apr. 20, 2005, 119 Stat. 51, 62, 126, 214, 216.)

[1] Dollar amount as adjusted by the Judicial Conference of the United States. See Adjustment of Dollar Amounts notes set out under this section and 11 U.S.C.A. § 104.

HISTORICAL AND STATUTORY NOTES

Revision Notes and Legislative Reports

1978 Acts. Section 507 specifies the kinds of claims that are entitled to priority in distribution, and the order of their priority. Paragraph (1) grants first priority to allowed administrative expenses and to fees and charges assessed against the estate under chapter 123 of title 28 [section 1911 et seq. of Title 28, Judiciary and Judicial Procedure]. Taxes included as administrative expenses under section 503(b)(1) of the bill generally receive the first priority, but the bill makes certain qualifications: Examples of these specially treated claims are the estate's liability for recapture of an investment tax credit claimed by the debtor before the title 11 case (this liability receives sixth priority) and the estate's employment tax liabilities on wages earned before, but paid after, the petition was filed (this liability generally receives the same priority as the wages).

"Involuntary gap" creditors, granted first priority under current law, are granted second priority by paragraph (2). This priority, covering claims arising in the ordinary course of the debtor's business or financial affairs after a title 11 case has begun but before a trustee is appointed or before the order for relief, includes taxes incurred during the conduct of such activities.

Paragraph (3) expands and increases the wage priority found in current section 64a(2) [section 104(a)(2) of former Title 11]. The amount entitled to priority is raised from $600 to $1800. The former figure was last adjusted in 1926. Inflation has made it nearly meaningless, and the bill brings it more than up to date. The three month limit of current law is retained, but is modified to run from the earlier of the date of the filing of the petition or the date of the cessation of the debtor's business. The priority is expanded to cover vacation, severance, and sick leave pay. The bill adds to the third priority so-called "trust fund" taxes, that is, withheld income taxes and the employees' share of the social security or railroad retirement taxes, but only to the extent that the wages on which taxes are imposed are themselves entitled to third priority.

The employer's share, the employment tax and the employer's share of the social security or railroad retirement tax on third priority compensation, is also included in the third priority category, but only if, and to the extent that the wages and related trust fund taxes have first been paid in full. Because of the claimants urgent need for their wages in the typical cases, the employer's taxes should not be paid before the wage claims entitled to priority, as well as the related trust fund taxes, are fully paid.

Paragraph (4) overrules *United States v. Embassy Restaurant*, 359 U.S. 29 (1958) [79 S.Ct. 554, 3 L.Ed.2d 601], which held that fringe benefits were not entitled to wage priority status. The bill recognizes the realities of labor contract negotiations, where fringe benefits may be substituted for wage demands. The priority granted is limited to claims for contributions to employee benefit plans such as pension plans, health or life insurance plans, and others, arising from services rendered within 120 days before the commencement of the case or the date of cessation of the debtor's business, whichever occurs first. The dollar limit placed on the total of all contributions payable under this paragraph is equal to the difference between the maximum allowable priority under paragraph (3), $1,800, times the number of employees covered by the plan less the actual distributions under paragraph (3) with respect to these employees.

Paragraph (5) is a new priority for consumer creditors—those who have deposited money in connection with the purchase, lease, or rental of property, or the purchase of services, for their personal, family, or household use, that were not delivered or provided. The priority amount is not to exceed $600. In order to reach only those persons most deserving of this special priority, it is limited to individuals whose adjustable gross income from all sources derived does not exceed $20,000. See Senate Hearings, testimony of Prof. Vern Countryman, at pp. 848–849. The income of the husband and wife should be aggregated for the purposes of the $20,000 limit if either or both spouses assert such a priority claim.

The sixth priority is for certain taxes. Priority is given to income taxes for a taxable year that ended on or before the date of the filing of the petition, if the last due date of the return for such year occurred not more than 3 years immediately before the date on which the petition was filed (§ 507(a)(6)(A)(i)). For the purposes of this rule, the last due date of the return is the last date under any extension of time to file the return which the taxing authority may have granted the debtor.

Employment taxes and transfer taxes (including gift, estate, sales, use and other excise taxes) are also given sixth priority if the transaction or event which gave rise to the tax occurred before the petition date, provided that the required return or report of such tax liabilities was last due within 3 years before the petition was filed or was last due after the petition date (§ 507(a)(6)(A)(ii).) The employment taxes covered under this rule are the employer's share of the social security and railroad retirement taxes and required employer payments toward unemployment insurance.

Priority is given to income taxes and other taxes of a kind described in section 507(a)(6)(A)(i) and (ii) which the Federal, State, or local tax authority had assessed within 3 years after the last due date of the return, that is, including any extension of time to file the return, if the debtor filed in title 11 within 240 days after the assessment was made (§ 507(a)(6)(B)(i)). This rule may bring into the sixth priority the debtor's tax liability for some taxable years which would not qualify for priority under the general three-year rule of section 507(a)(6)(A).

The sixth priority category also includes taxes which the tax authority was barred by law from assessing or collecting at any time during the 300 days before the petition under title 11 was filed (§ 507(a)(6)(B)(ii)). In the case of certain Federal taxes, this preserves a priority for tax liabilities for years more than three years before the filing of the petition where the debtor and the Internal Revenue Service were negotiating over an audit of the debtor's returns or were engaged in litigation in the Tax Court. In such situations, the tax law prohibits the service's right to assess a tax deficiency until ninety days after the service sends the taxpayer a deficiency letter or, if the taxpayer files a petition in the Tax Court during that 90-day period, until the outcome of the litigation. A similar priority exists in present law, except that the taxing authority is allowed no time to assess and collect the taxes after the restrictions on assessment (discussed above) are lifted. Some taxpayers have exploited this loophole by filing in bankruptcy immediately after the end of the 90-day period or immediately after the close of Tax Court proceedings. The bill remedies this defect by preserving a priority for taxes the assessment of which was barred by law by giving the tax authority 300 days within which to make the assessment after the lifting of the bar and then to collect or file public notice of its tax lien. Thus, if a taxpayer files a title 11 petition at any time during that 300-day period, the tax deficiency will be entitled to priority. If the petition is filed more than 300 days after the restriction on assessment was lifted, the taxing authority will not have priority for the tax deficiency.

Taxes for which an offer in compromise was withdrawn by the debtor, or rejected by a governmental unit, within 240 days before the petition date (§ 507(a)(6)(B)(iii)) will also receive sixth priority. This rule closes a loophole under present law under which, following an assessment of tax, some taxpayers have submitted a formal offer in compromise, dragged out negotiations with the taxing authority until the tax liability would lose priority under the three-year priority period of present law, and then filed in bankruptcy before the governmental unit could take collection steps.

Also included are certain taxes for which no return or report is required by law (§ 507(a)(6)(C)), if the taxable transaction occurred within three years before the petition was filed.

Taxes (not covered by the third priority) which the debtor was required by law to withhold or collect from others and for which he is liable in any capacity, regardless of the age of the tax claims (§ 507(a)(6)(D)) are included. This category covers the so-called "trust fund" taxes, that is, income taxes which an employer is required to withhold from the pay of his employees, the employees' shares of social security and railroad retirement taxes, and also Federal unemployment insurance. This category also includes excise taxes which a seller of goods or services is required to collect from a buyer and pay over to a taxing authority.

This category also covers the liability of a responsible corporate officer under the Internal Revenue Code [Title 26] for income taxes or for the employees' share of employment taxes which, under the tax law, the employer was required to withhold from the wages of employees. This priority will operate where a person found to be a responsible officer has himself filed a petition under title 11, and the priority covers the debtor's liability as an officer under the Internal Revenue Code [Title 26], regardless of the age of the tax year to which the tax relates.

The priority rules under the bill governing employment taxes can be summarized as follows: In the case of wages earned and actually paid before the petition under title 11 was filed, the liability for the employees' share of the employment taxes, regardless of the prepetition year in which the wages were earned and paid. The employer's share of the employment taxes on all wages earned and paid before the petition receive sixth priority; generally, these taxes will be those for which a return was due within three years before the petition. With respect to wages earned by employees before the petition but actually paid by the trustee after the title 11 case commenced, taxes required to be withheld receives the same priority as the wages themselves. Thus, the employees' share of taxes on third priority wages also receives third priority. Taxes on the balance of such wages receive no priority and are collectible only as general claims because the wages themselves are payable only as general claims and liability for the taxes arises only to the extent the wages are actually paid. The employer's share of employment taxes on third priority wages earned before the petition but paid after the petition was filed receives third priority, but only if the wages in this category have first been paid in full. Assuming there are sufficient funds to pay third priority wages and the related employer taxes in full, the employer's share of taxes on the balance of wage payments becomes a general claim (because the wages themselves are payable as general claims). Both the employees' and the employer's share of employment taxes on wages earned and paid after the petition was filed receive first priority as administrative expenses.

Also covered by this sixth priority are property taxes required to be assessed within 3 years before the filing of the petition (§ 507(a)(6)(E)).

Taxes attributable to a tentative carryback adjustment received by the debtor before the petition was filed, such as a "quickie refund" received under section 6411 of the Internal Revenue Code [section 6411 of Title 26, Internal Revenue Code] (§ 507(a)(6)(F)) are included. However, the tax claim against the debtor will rein a prepetition loss year for which the tax return was last due, including extensions, within 3 years before the petition was filed.

Taxes resulting from a recapture, occasioned by a transfer during bankruptcy, of a tax credit or deduction taken during an earlier tax year (§ 507(a)(6)(G)) are included. A typical example occurs when there is a sale by the trustee of depreciable property during the case and depreciation deductions taken in prepetition years are subject to recapture under section 1250 of the Code [section 1250 of Title 26, Internal Revenue Code].

Taxes owed by the debtor as a transferee of assets from another person who is liable for a tax, if the tax claim against the transferor would have received priority in a chapter 11 case commenced by the transferor within 1 year before the date of the petition filed by the transferee (§ 507(a)(6)(H)), are included.

Also included are certain tax payments required to have been made during the 1 year immediately before the petition was filed, where the debtor had previously entered into a deferred payment agreement (including an offer in compromise) to pay an agreed liability in periodic installments but had become delinquent in one or more installments before the petition was filed (§ 507(a)(6)(I)). This priority covers all types of deferred or part payment agreements. The priority covers only installments which first became due during the 1 year before the petition but which remained unpaid at the date of the petition. The priority does not come into play, however, if before the case began or during the case, the debtor and the taxing authority agree to a further extension of time to pay the delinquent amounts.

Certain tax-related liabilities which are not true taxes or which are not collected by regular assessment procedures (§ 507(a)(6)(J)) are included. One type of liability covered in this category is the liability under section 3505 of the Internal Revenue Code [section 3505 of Title 26, Internal Revenue Code] of a lender who pays wages directly to employees of another employer or who supplies funds to an employer for the payment of wages. Another is the liability under section 6332 of the Internal Revenue Code [section 6332 of Title 26, Internal Revenue Code], of a person who fails to turn over money or property of the taxpayer in response to a levy. Since the taxing authority must collect such a liability from the third party by suit rather than normal assessment procedures, an extra year is added to the normal 3-year priority periods. If a suit was commenced by the taxing authority within the four-year period and before the petition was filed, the priority is also preserved, provided that the suit had not terminated more than 1 year before the date of the filing of the petition.

Also included are certain unpaid customs duties which have not grown unreasonably "stale" (§ 507(a)(6)(K)). These include duties on imports entered for consumption with 3 years before the filing of the petition if the duties are still unliquidated on the petition date. If an import entry has been liquidated (in general, liquidation is in an administrative determination of the value and tariff rate of the item) or reliquidated, within two years of the filing of the petition the customs liability is given priority. If the Secretary of the Treasury certifies that customs duties were not liquidated because of an investigation into possible assessment of antidumping or countervailing duties, or because of fraud penalties, duties not liquidated for this reason during the five years before the importer filed under title 11 also will receive priority.

Subsection (a) of this section also provides specifically that interest on sixth priority tax claims accrued before the filing of the petition is also entitled to sixth priority.

Subsection (b) of this section provides that any fine or penalty which represents compensation for actual pecuniary loss of a governmental unit, and which involves a tax liability entitled to sixth priority, is to receive the same priority.

Subsection (b) also provides that a claim arising from an erroneous refund or credit of tax is to be given the same priority as the tax to which the refund or credit relates. Senate Report No. 95–989.

1984 Acts. Statements by Legislative Leaders, see 1984 U.S. Code Cong. and Adm. News, p. 576.

1990 Acts. House Report No. 101–681(I), see 1990 U.S. Code Cong. and Adm. News, p. 6472.

1994 Acts. House Report No. 103–835, see 1994 U.S. Code Cong. and Adm. News, p. 3340.

2005 Acts. House Report No. 109–31(Part I), see 2005 U.S. Code Cong. and Adm. News, p. 88.

Legislative Statements

Section 507(a)(3) of the House amendment represents a compromise dollar amount and date for the priority between similar provisions contained in H.R. 8200 as passed by the House and the Senate amendments. A similar compromise is contained in section 507(a)(4).

Section 507(a)(5) represents a compromise on amount between the priority as contained in H.R. 8200 as passed by the House and the Senate amendment. The Senate provision for limiting the priority to consumers having less than a fixed gross income is deleted.

Section 507(a)(6) of the House amendment represents a compromise between similar provisions contained in H.R. 8200 as passed by the House and the Senate amendment.

Section 507(b) of the House amendment is new and is derived from the compromise contained in the House amendment with respect to adequate protection under section 361. Subsection (b) provides that to the extent adequate protection of the interest of a holder of a claim proves to be inadequate, then the creditor's claim is given priority over every other allowable claim entitled to distribution under section 507(a). Section 507(b) of the Senate amendment is deleted.

Section 507(c) of the House amendment is new. Section 507(d) of the House amendment prevents subrogation with respect to priority for certain priority claims. Subrogation with respect to priority is intended to be permitted for administrative claims and claims arising during the gap period.

Priorities: Under the House amendment, taxes receive priority as follows:

First. Administration expenses: The amendment generally follows the Senate amendment in providing expressly that taxes incurred during the administration of the estate share the first priority given to administrative expenses generally. Among the taxes which receives first priority, as defined in section 503, are the employees' and the employer's shares of employment taxes on wages earned and paid after the petition is filed. Section 503(b)(1) also includes in administration expenses a tax liability arising from an excessive allowance by a tax authority of a "quickie refund" to the estate. (In the case of Federal taxes, such refunds are allowed under special rules based on net operating loss carrybacks (section 6411 of the Internal Revenue Code) [section 6411 of Title 26, Internal Revenue Code]).

An exception is made to first priority treatment for taxes incurred by the estate with regard to the employer's share of employment taxes on wages earned from the debtor before the petition but paid from the estate after the petition has been filed. In this situation, the employer's tax receives either sixth priority or general claim treatment.

The House amendment also adopts the provisions of the Senate amendment which include in the definition of administrative expenses under section 503 any fine, penalty (including "additions to tax" under applicable tax laws) or reduction in credit imposed on the estate.

Second. "Involuntary gap" claims: "Involuntary gap" creditors are granted second priority by paragraph (2) of section 507(a). This priority includes tax claims arising in the ordinary course of the debtor's business or financial affairs after he has been placed involuntarily in bankruptcy but before a trustee is appointed or before the order for relief.

Third. Certain taxes on prepetition wages: Wage claims entitled to third priority are for compensation which does not exceed $2,000 and was earned during the 90 days before the filing of the bankruptcy petition or the cessation of the debtor's business. Certain employment taxes receive third priority in payment from the estate along with the payment of wages to which the taxes relate. In the case of wages earned before the filing of the petition, but paid by the trustee (rather than by the debtor) after the filing of the petition, claims or the employees' share of the employment taxes (withheld income taxes and the employees' share of the social security or railroad retirement tax) receive third priority to the extent the wage claims themselves are entitled to this priority.

In the case of wages earned from and paid by the debtor before the filing of the petition, the employer's share of the employment taxes on these wages paid by the debtor receives sixth priority or, if not entitled to that priority, are treated only as general claims. Under the House amendment, the employer's share of employment taxes on wages earned by employees of the debtor, but paid by the trustee after the filing of the bankruptcy petition, will also receive sixth priority to the extent that claims for the wages receive third priority. To the extent the claims for wages do not receive third priority, but instead are treated only as general claims, claims for the employer's share of the employment taxes attributable to those wages will also be treated as general claims. In calculating the amounts payable as general wage claims, the trustee must pay the employer's share of employment taxes on such wages.

Sixth priority. The House amendment modifies the provisions of both the House bill and Senate amendment in the case of sixth priority taxes. Under the amendment, the following Federal, State and local taxes are included in the sixth priority:

First. Income and gross receipts taxes incurred before the date of the petition for which the last due date of the return, including all extensions of time granted to file the return, occurred within 3 years before the date on which the petition was filed, or after the petition date. Under this rule, the due date of the return, rather than the date on which the taxes were assessed, determines the priority.

Second. Income and gross receipts taxes assessed at any time within 240 days before the petition date. Under this rule, the date on which the governmental unit assesses the tax, rather than the due date of the return, determines the priority.

If, following assessment of a tax, the debtor submits an offer in compromise to the governmental unit, the House amendment provides that the 240-day period is to be suspended for the duration of the offer and will resume running after the offer is withdrawn or rejected by the governmental unit, but the tax liability will receive priority if the title 11 petition is filed during the balance of the 240-day period or during a minimum of 30 days after the offer is withdrawn or rejected. This rule modifies a provision of the Senate amendment dealing specifically with offers in compromise. Under the modified rule, if, after the assessment, an offer in compromise is submitted by the debtor and is still pending (without having been accepted or rejected) at the date on which a title 11 petition is filed, the underlying liability will receive sixth priority. However, if an assessment of a tax liability is made but the tax is not collected within 240 days, the tax will not receive priority under section 507(a)(6)(A)(i) and the debtor cannot revive a priority for that tax by submitting an offer in compromise.

Third. Income and gross receipts taxes not assessed before the petition date but still permitted, under otherwise applicable tax laws, to be assessed. Thus, for example, a prepetition tax liability is to receive sixth priority under this rule if, under the applicable statute of limitations, the tax liability can still be assessed by the tax authority. This rule also covers situations referred to in section 507(a)(6)(B)(ii) of the Senate amendment where the assessment or collection of a tax was prohibited before the petition pending exhaustion of judicial or administrative remedies, except that the House amendment eliminates the 300-day limitation of the Senate bill. So, for example, if before the petition a debtor was engaged in litigation in the Tax Court, during which the Internal Revenue Code [Title 26] bars the Internal Revenue Service from assessing or collecting the tax, and if the tax court decision is made in favor of the Service before the petition under title 11 is filed, thereby lifting the restrictions on assessment and collection, the tax liability will receive sixth priority even if the tax authority does not make an assessment within 300 days before the petition (provided, of course, that the statute of limitations on assessment has not expired by the petition date).

In light of the above categories of the sixth priority, and tax liability of the debtor (under the Internal Revenue Code [Title 26] or State or local law) as a transferee of property from another person will receive sixth priority without the limitations contained in the Senate amendment so long as the transferee liability had not been assessed by the tax authority by the petition date but could still have been assessed by that date under the applicable tax statute of limitations or, if the transferee liability had been assessed before the petition, the assessment was made no more than 240 days before the petition date.

Also in light of the above categories, the treatment of prepetition tax liabilities arising from an excessive allowance to the debtor of a tentative carryback adjustment, such as a "quickie refund" under section 6411 of the Internal Revenue Code [section 6411 of Title 26, Internal Revenue Code], is revised as follows: If the tax authority has assessed the additional tax before the petition, the tax liability will receive priority if the date of assessment was within 240 days before the petition date. If the tax authority had not assessed the additional tax by the petition, the tax liability will still receive priority so long as, on the petition date, assessment of the liability is not barred by the statute of limitations.

Fourth. Any property tax assessed before the commencement of the case and last payable without penalty within 1 year before the petition, or thereafter.

Fifth. Taxes which the debtor was required by law to withhold or collect from others and for which he is liable in any capacity, regardless of the age of the tax claims. This category covers the so-called "trust fund" taxes, that is, income taxes which an employer is required to withhold from the pay of his employees, and the employees' share of social security taxes.

In addition, this category includes the liability of a responsible officer under the Internal Revenue Code (Sec. 6672 [section 6672 of Title 26, Internal Revenue Code]) for income taxes or for the employees' share of social security taxes which that officer was responsible for withholding from the wages of employees and paying to the Treasury, although he was not himself the employer. This priority will operate when a person found to be a responsible officer has himself filed in title 11, and the priority will cover the debtor's responsible officer liability regardless of the age of the tax year to which the tax relates. The U.S. Supreme Court has interpreted present law to require the same result as will be reached under this rule. *U.S. v. Sotelo,* 436 U.S. 268 (1978) [98 S.Ct. 1795, 56 L.Ed.2d 275, rehearing denied 98 S.Ct. 3126, 438 U.S. 907, 57 L.Ed.2d 1150].

This category also includes the liability under section 3505 of the Internal Revenue Code [section 3505 of Title 26, Internal Revenue Code] of a taxpayer who loans money for the payment of wages or other compensation.

Sixth. The employer's share of employment taxes on wages paid before the petition and on third-priority wages paid postpetition by the estate. The priority rules under the House amendment governing employment taxes can thus be summarized as follows: Claims for the employees' shares of employment taxes attributable to wages both earned and paid before the filing of the petition are to receive sixth priority. In the case of employee wages earned, but not paid, before the filing of the bankruptcy petition, claims for the employees' share of employment taxes receive third priority to the extent the wages themselves receive third priority. Claims which relate to wages earned before the petition, but not paid before the petition (and which are not entitled to the third priority under the rule set out above), will be paid as general claims. Since the related wages will receive no priority, the related employment taxes would also be paid as nonpriority general claims.

The employer's share of the employment taxes on wages earned and paid before the bankruptcy petition will receive sixth priority to the extent the return for these taxes was last due (including extensions of time) within 3 years before the filing of the petition, or was due after the petition was filed. Older tax claims of this nature will be payable as general claims. In the case of wages earned by employees before the petition, but actually paid by the trustee (as claims against the estate) after the title 11 case commenced, the employer's share of the employment taxes on third priority wages will be payable as sixth priority claims and the employer's taxes on prepetition wages which are treated only as general claims will be payable only as general claims. In calculating the amounts payable as general wage claims, the trustee must pay the employer's share of employment taxes on such wages. The House amendment thus deletes the provision of the Senate amendment that certain employer taxes receive third priority and are to be paid immediately after payment of third priority wages and the employees' shares of employment taxes on those wages.

In the case of employment taxes relating to wages earned and paid after the petition, both the employees' shares and the employer's share will receive first priority as administration expenses of the estate.

Seventh. Excise taxes on transactions for which a return, if required, is last due, under otherwise applicable law or under any extension of time to file the return, within 3 years before the petition was filed, or thereafter. If a return is not required with regard to a particular excise tax, priority is given if the transaction or event itself occurred within 3 years before the date on which the title 11 petition was filed. All Federal, State or local taxes generally considered or expressly treated as excises are covered by this category, including sales taxes, estate and gift taxes, gasoline and special fuel taxes, and wagering and truck taxes.

Eighth. Certain unpaid customs duties. The House amendment covers in this category duties on imports entered for consumption within 1 year before the filing of the petition, but which are still unliquidated on the petition date; duties covered by an entry liquidated or reliquidated within 1 year before the petition date; and any duty on merchandise entered for consumption within 4 years before the petition but not liquidated on the petition date, if the Secretary of the Treasury or his delegate certifies that duties were not liquidated because of possible assessment of antidumping or countervailing duties or fraud penalties.

For purposes of the above priority rules, the House amendment adopts the provision of the Senate bill that any tax liability which, under otherwise applicable tax law, is collectible in the form of a "penalty," is to be treated in the same manner as a tax liability. In bankruptcy terminology, such tax liabilities are referred to as pecuniary loss penalties. Thus, any tax liability which under the Internal Revenue Code [Title 26] or State or local tax law is payable as a "penalty," in addition to the liability of a responsible person under section 6672 of the Internal Revenue Code [section 6672 of Title 26, Internal Revenue Code] will be entitled to the priority which the liability would receive if it were expressly labeled as a "tax" under the applicable tax law. However, a tax penalty which is punitive in nature is given subordinated treatment under section 726(a)(4).

The House amendment also adopts the provision of the Senate amendment that a claim arising from an erroneous refund or credit of tax, other than a "quickie refund," is to receive the same priority as the tax to which the refund or credit relates.

The House amendment deletes the express provision of the Senate amendment that a tax liability is to receive sixth priority if it satisfies any one of the subparagraphs of section 507(a)(6) even if the liability fails to satisfy the terms of one or more other subparagraphs. No change of substance is intended by the deletion, however, in light of section 102(5) of the House amendment, providing a rule of construction that the word "or" is not intended to be exclusive.

The House amendment deletes from the express priority categories of the Senate amendment the priority for a debtor's liability as a third party for failing to surrender property or to pay an obligation in response to a levy for taxes of another, and the priority for amounts provided for under deferred payment agreements between a debtor and the tax authority.

The House amendment also adopts the substance of the definition in section 346(a) the Senate amendment of when taxes are to be considered "incurred" except that the House amendment applies these definitions solely for purposes of determining which category of section 507 tests the priority of a particular tax liability. Thus, for example, the House amendment contains a special rule for the treatment of taxes under the 45-day exception to the preference rules under section 547 and the definitions of when a tax is incurred for priority purposes are not to apply to such preference rules. Under the House amendment, for purposes of the priority rules, a tax on income for a particular period is to be considered "incurred" on the last day of the period. A tax on or measured by some event, such as the payment of wages or a transfer by reason of death or gift, or an excise tax on a sale or other transaction, is to be considered "incurred" on the date of the transaction or event.

Codifications

Amendments by Pub.L. 109–8, § 1401, to pars. (4) and (5) of subsec. (a) of this section, as amended by section 212 of Pub.L. 109–8, were made to pars. (3) and (4) of subsec. (a) of this section, as the probable intent of Congress. The redesignation of pars. (3) and (4) as pars. (4) and (5) by section 212 of Pub.L. 109–8 does not take effect until 180 days after April 20, 2005.

Effective and Applicability Provisions

2007 Acts. Increase of dollar amounts by Judicial Conference of the United States by notice published Feb. 14, 2007, 72 F.R. 7082 effective April 1, 2007, and increase not applicable to cases commenced before the effective date of the adjustments, i.e., April 1, 2007. See Adjustment of Dollar Amounts notes under 11 U.S.C.A. § 104 and this section.

2005 Acts. Pub.L. 109–8, Title XIV, § 1406, Apr. 20, 2005, 119 Stat. 215, provided that:

"**(a) Effective date.**—Except as provided in subsection (b) [of this note], this title and the amendments made by this title [amending this section and 11 U.S.C.A. §§ 523, 548, 1104, 1114, and enacting provisions set out as a note under 11 U.S.C.A. § 523] shall take effect on the date of the enactment of this Act [Apr. 20, 2005].

"**(b) Application of amendments.**—

"(1) **In general.**—[Ex]cept as provided in paragraph (2), the amendments made by this title [amending this section and 11 U.S.C.A. §§ 523, 548, 1104, 1114, and enacting provisions set out as a note under 11 U.S.C.A. § 523] shall apply only with respect to cases commenced under title 11 of the United States Code [11 U.S.C.A. § 101 et seq.] on or after the date of the enactment of this Act [Apr. 20, 2005].

"(2) **Avoidance period.**—The amendment made by section 1402(1) [amending 11 U.S.C.A. § 548] shall apply only with respect to cases commenced under title 11 of the United States Code more than 1 year after the date of the enactment of this Act [Apr. 20, 2005]."

Amendments by Pub.L. 109–8 effective, except as otherwise provided, 180 days after April 20, 2005, and inapplicable with respect to cases commenced under Title 11 before the effective date, see Pub.L. 109–8, § 1501, set out as a note under 11 U.S.C.A. § 101.

2004 Acts. Adjustment of dollar amounts by Judicial Conference of the United States by notice dated Feb. 18, 2004, 69 F.R. 8482 effective April 1, 2004, and adjustment not applicable to cases commenced before the effective date of the adjustments, i.e., April 1, 2004. See Adjustment of Dollar Amounts notes under 11 U.S.C.A. § 104 and this section.

2001 Acts. Adjustment of dollar amounts by Judicial Conference of the United States by notice dated Feb. 20, 2001, 66 F.R. 10910 effective April 1, 2001, and adjustment not applicable to cases commenced before the effective date of the adjustments, i.e., April 1, 2001. See Adjustment of Dollar Amounts notes under 11 U.S.C.A. § 104 and this section.

1998 Acts. Adjustment of dollar amounts by Judicial Conference of the United States by notice dated Feb. 3, 1998, 63 F.R. 7179 effective April 1, 1998, and adjustment not applicable to cases commenced before the effective date of the adjustments, i.e., April 1, 1998. See Adjustment of Dollar Amounts notes under 11 U.S.C.A. § 104 and this section.

1994 Acts. Amendments by Pub.L. 103–394 effective on Oct. 22, 1994, and not to apply with respect to cases commenced under Title 11 of the United States Code before Oct. 22, 1994, see section 702 of Pub.L. 103–394, set out as a note under section 101 of this title.

1984 Acts. Amendment by Pub.L. 98–353 effective with respect to cases filed 90 days after July 10, 1984, see section 552(a), formerly 553(a) of Pub.L. 98–353, set out as a note under section 101 of this title.

Separability of Provisions

If any provision of or amendment made by Pub.L. 103–394 or the application of such provision or amendment to any person or circumstance is held to be unconstitutional, the remaining provisions of and amendments made by Pub.L. 103–394 and the application of such provisions and amendments to any person or circumstance shall not be affected thereby, see section 701 of Pub.L. 103–394, set out as a note under section 101 of this title.

Adjustment of Dollar Amounts

For adjustment of dollar amounts specified in subsec. (a)(4), (5), (6), (7) of this section by the Judicial Conference of the United States, effective Apr. 1, 2007, see note set out under 11 U.S.C.A. § 104.

By notice dated Feb. 14, 2007, 72 F.R. 7082, the Judicial Conference of the United States adjusted the dollar amounts in provisions specified in subsec. (a)(4), (5), (6), (7) of this section, effective Apr. 1, 2007, as follows:

In subsec. (a)(4) adjusted $10,000 to $10,950.

In subsec. (a)(5) adjusted $10,000 to $10,950.

In subsec. (a)(6) adjusted $4,925 to $5,400.

In subsec. (a)(7) adjusted $2,225 to $2,425.

By notice dated Feb. 18, 2004, 69 F.R. 8482, the Judicial Conference of the United States adjusted the dollar amounts in provisions specified in subsec. (a)(3), (4)(B)(i), (5), (6) of this section, effective Apr. 1, 2004, as follows:

In subsec. (a)(3) adjusted $4,650 to $4,925.

In subsec. (a)(4)(B)(i) adjusted $4,650 to $4,925.

In subsec. (a)(5) adjusted $4,650 to $4,925.

In subsec. (a)(6) adjusted $2,100 to $2,225.

By notice dated Feb. 20, 2001, 66 F.R. 10910, the Judicial Conference of the United States adjusted the dollar amounts in provisions specified in subsec. (a)(3), (4)(B)(i), (5), (6) of this section, effective Apr. 1, 2001, as follows:

In subsec. (a)(3) adjusted $4,300 to $4,650.

In subsec. (a)(4)(B)(i) adjusted $4,300 to $4,650.

In subsec. (a)(5) adjusted $4,300 to $4,650.

In subsec. (a)(6) adjusted $1,950 to $2,100.

By notice dated Feb. 3, 1998, 63 F.R. 7179, the Judicial Conference of the United States adjusted the dollar amounts in provisions specified in subsec. (a)(3), (4)(B)(i), (5), (6) of this section, effective Apr. 1, 1998, as follows:

In subsec. (a)(3) adjusted $4,000 to $4,300.

In subsec. (a)(4)(B)(i) adjusted $4,000 to $4,300.

In subsec. (a)(5) adjusted $4,000 to $4,300.

In subsec. (a)(6) adjusted $1,800 to $1,950.

CROSS REFERENCES

Applicability of subsec. (a)(1) of this section in Chapter 9 cases, see 11 USCA § 901.

Confirmation upon payment of administrative expenses, fees, and charges, see 11 USCA § 943.

Contents of plan in—

Chapter 13 cases, see 11 USCA § 1322.

Chapter 12 cases, see 11 USCA § 1222.

Designation by plan of classes of claims, see 11 USCA § 1123.

Distribution of—

Certain estate property subject to liens, see 11 USCA § 724.

Customer property in commodity broker liquidation cases, see 11 USCA § 766.

Customer property in stockbroker liquidation cases, see 11 USCA § 752.

Property of estate, see 11 USCA § 726.

Executory contracts and unexpired leases, see 11 USCA § 365.

Involuntary cases future adjustments, see 11 USCA § 104.

Proof of claim, see Official Bankr. Form 10, 11 USCA.

Recoupment of funds advanced by Securities Investor Protection Corporation as priority administrative expense, see 15 USCA § 78fff.

Tax or customs duty excepted from discharge, see 11 USCA § 523.

Time of payment of administrative expenses, fees and charges in—

Chapter 13 cases, see 11 USCA § 1326.

Chapter 12 cases, see 11 USCA § 1226.

Treatment of certain claims as affecting confirmation of plan, see 11 USCA § 1129.

Unsecured debt having priority over certain administrative expenses, see 11 USCA § 364.

Unsecured priority claims, see Official Bankr. Form 6, 11 USCA.

§ 508. Effect of distribution other than under this title

If a creditor of a partnership debtor receives, from a general partner that is not a debtor in a case under chapter 7 of this title, payment of, or a transfer of property on account of, a claim that is allowed under this title and that is not secured by a lien on property of such partner, such creditor may not receive any payment under this title on account of such claim until each of the other holders of claims on account of which such holders are entitled to share equally with such creditor under this title has received payment under this title equal in value to the consideration received by such creditor from such general partner.

(Pub.L. 95–598, Nov. 6, 1978, 92 Stat. 2585; Pub.L. 109–8, Title VIII, § 802(d)(7), Apr. 20, 2005, 119 Stat. 146.)

HISTORICAL AND STATUTORY NOTES

Revision Notes and Legislative Reports

1978 Acts. This section prohibits a creditor from receiving any distribution in the bankruptcy case if he has received payment of a portion of his claim in a foreign proceeding, until the other creditors in the bankruptcy case in this country that are entitled to share equally with that creditor have received as much as he has in the foreign proceeding. Senate Report No. 95–989.

2005 Acts. House Report No. 109–31(Part I), see 2005 U.S. Code Cong. and Adm. News, p. 88.

Legislative Statements

Section 508(b) of the House amendment is new and provides an identical rule with respect to a creditor of a partnership who receives payment from a partner, to that of a creditor of a debtor who receives a payment in a foreign proceeding involving the debtor.

Effective and Applicability Provisions

2005 Acts. Amendments by Pub.L. 109–8 effective, except as otherwise provided, 180 days after April 20, 2005, and inapplicable with respect to cases commenced under Title 11 before the effective date, see Pub.L. 109–8, § 1501, set out as a note under 11 U.S.C.A. § 101.

§ 509. Claims of codebtors

(a) Except as provided in subsection (b) or (c) of this section, an entity that is liable with the debtor on, or that has secured, a claim of a creditor against the debtor, and that pays such claim, is subrogated to the rights of such creditor to the extent of such payment.

(b) Such entity is not subrogated to the rights of such creditor to the extent that—

(1) a claim of such entity for reimbursement or contribution on account of such payment of such creditor's claim is—

(A) allowed under section 502 of this title;

(B) disallowed other than under section 502(e) of this title; or

(C) subordinated under section 510 of this title; or

(2) as between the debtor and such entity, such entity received the consideration for the claim held by such creditor.

(c) The court shall subordinate to the claim of a creditor and for the benefit of such creditor an allowed claim, by way of subrogation under this section, or for reimbursement or contribution, of an entity that is liable with the debtor on, or that has secured, such creditor's claim, until such creditor's claim is paid in full, either through payments under this title or otherwise.

(Pub.L. 95–598, Nov. 6, 1978, 92 Stat. 2585; Pub.L. 98–353, Title III, § 450, July 10, 1984, 98 Stat. 375.)

HISTORICAL AND STATUTORY NOTES

Revision Notes and Legislative Reports

1978 Acts. Section 509 deals with codebtors generally, and is in addition to the disallowance provision in section 502(e). This section is based on the notion that the only rights available to a surety, guarantor, or comaker are contribution, reimbursement, and subrogation. The right that applies in a particular situation will depend on the agreement between the debtor and the codebtor, and on whether and how payment was made by the codebtor to the creditor. The claim of a surety or codebtor for contribution or reimbursement is discharged even if the claim is never filed, as is any claim for subrogation even if the surety or codebtor chooses to file a claim for contribution or reimbursement instead.

Subsection (a) subrogates the codebtor (whether as a codebtor, surety, or guarantor) to the rights of the creditor, to the extent of any payment made by the codebtor to the creditor. Whether the creditor's claim was filed under section 501(a) or 501(b) is irrelevant. The right of subrogation will exist even if the primary creditor's claim is allowed by virtue of being listed under proposed 11 U.S.C. 924 or 1111, and not by reason of a proof of claim.

Subsection (b) permits a subrogated codebtor to receive payments in the bankruptcy case only if the creditor has been paid in full, either through payments under the bankruptcy code or otherwise. Senate Report No. 95–989.

1984 Acts. Statements by Legislative Leaders, see 1984 U.S.Code Cong. and Adm.News, p. 576.

Legislative Statements

Section 509 of the House amendment represents a substantial revision of provisions contained in H.R. 8200 as passed by the House and in the Senate amendment. Section 509(a) states a general rule that a surety or co-debtor is subrogated to the rights of a creditor assured by the surety or codebtor to the extent the surety or codebtor pays such creditor. Section 509(b) states a general exception indicating that subrogation is not granted to the extent that a claim of a surety or co-debtor for reimbursement or contribution is allowed under section 502 or disallowed other than under section 502(e). Additionally, section 509(b)(1)(C) provides that such claims for subrogation are subordinated to the extent that a claim of the surety or co-debtor for reimbursement or contribution is subordinated under section 510(a)(1) or 510(b). Section 509(b)(2) reiterates the well-known rule that prevents a debtor that is ultimately liable on the debt from recovering from a surety or a co-debtor. Although the language in section 509(b)(2) focuses in terms of receipt of consideration, legislative history appearing elsewhere indicates that an agreement to share liabilities should prevail over an agreement to share profits throughout title 11. This is particularly important in the context of codebtors who are partners. Section 509(c) subordinates the claim of a surety or co-debtor to the claim of an assured creditor until the creditor's claim is paid in full.

Effective and Applicability Provisions

1984 Acts. Amendment by Pub.L. 98–353 effective with respect to cases filed 90 days after July 10, 1984, see section 552(a), formerly 553(a) of Pub.L. 98–353, set out as a note under section 101 of this title.

CROSS REFERENCES

Applicability of this section in Chapter 9 cases, see 11 USCA § 901.

§ 510. Subordination

(a) A subordination agreement is enforceable in a case under this title to the same extent that such agreement is enforceable under applicable nonbankruptcy law.

(b) For the purpose of distribution under this title, a claim arising from rescission of a purchase or sale of a security of the debtor or of an affiliate of the debtor, for damages arising from the purchase or sale of such a security, or for reimbursement or contribution allowed under section 502 on account of such a claim, shall be subordinated to all claims or interests that are senior to or equal the claim or interest represented by such security, except that if such security is common stock, such claim has the same priority as common stock.

(c) Notwithstanding subsections (a) and (b) of this section, after notice and a hearing, the court may—

(1) under principles of equitable subordination, subordinate for purposes of distribution all or part of an allowed claim to all or part of another allowed claim or all or part of an allowed interest to all or part of another allowed interest; or

(2) order that any lien securing such a subordinated claim be transferred to the estate.

(Pub.L. 95–598, Nov. 6, 1978, 92 Stat. 2586; Pub.L. 98–353, Title III, § 451, July 10, 1984, 98 Stat. 375.)

HISTORICAL AND STATUTORY NOTES

Revision Notes and Legislative Reports

1978 Acts. Subsection (a) requires the court to enforce subordination agreements. A subordination agreement will not be enforced, however, in a reorganization case in which the class that is the beneficiary of the agreement has accepted, as specified in proposed 11 U.S.C. 1126, a plan that waives their rights under the agreement. Otherwise, the agreement would prevent just what chapter 11 contemplates: that seniors may give up rights to juniors in the interest of confirmation of a plan and rehabilitation of the debtor. The subsection also requires the court to subordinate in payment any claim for rescission of a purchase or sale of a security of the debtor or of an affiliate, or for damages arising from the purchase or sale of such a security, to all claims and interests that are senior to the claim or interest represented by the security. Thus, the later subordination varies with the claim or interest involved. If the security is a debt instrument, the damages or rescission claim will be granted the status of a general unsecured claim. If the security is an equity security, the damages or rescission claim is subordinated to all creditors and treated the same as the equity security itself.

Subsection (b) authorizes the bankruptcy court, in ordering distribution of assets, to subordinate all or any part of any claim to all or any part of another claim, regardless of the priority ranking of either claim. In addition, any lien securing such a subordinated claim may be transferred to the estate. The bill provides, however, that any subordination ordered under this provision must be based on principles of equitable subordination. These principles are defined by case law, and have generally indicated that a claim may normally be subordinated only if its holder is guilty of misconduct. As originally introduced, the bill provided specifically that a tax claim may not be subordinated on equitable grounds. The bill deletes this express exception, but the effect under the amendment should be much the same in most situations since, under the judicial doctrine of equitable subordination, a tax claim would rarely be subordinated. Senate Report No. 95–989.

1984 Acts. Statements by Legislative Leaders, see 1984 U.S.Code Cong. and Adm.News, p. 576.

Legislative Statements

Section 510(c)(1) of the House amendment represents a compromise between similar provisions in the House bill and Senate amendment. After notice and a hearing, the court may, under principles of equitable subordination, subordinate for purposes of distribution all or part of an allowed claim to all or part of another allowed claim or all or part of an allowed interest to all or part of another allowed interest. As a matter of equity, it is reasonable that a court subordinate claims to claims and interests to interests. It is intended that the term "principles of equitable subordination" follow existing case law and leave to the courts development of this principle. To date, under existing law, a claim is generally subordinated only if holder of such claim is guilty of inequitable conduct, or the claim itself is of a status susceptible to subordination, such as a penalty or a claim for damages arising from the purchase or sale of a security of the debtor. The fact that such a claim may be secured is of no consequence to the issue of subordination. However, it is inconceivable that the status of a claim as a secured claim could ever be grounds for justifying equitable subordination.

Subordination: Since the House amendment authorizes subordination of claims only under principles of equitable subordination, and thus incorporates principles of existing case law, a tax claim would rarely be subordinated under this provision of the bill.

Section 511 of the Senate amendment is deleted. Its substance is adopted in section 502(b)(9) of the House amendment which reflects an identical provision contained in H.R. 8200 as passed by the House.

Effective and Applicability Provisions

1984 Acts. Amendment by Pub.L. 98–353 effective with respect to cases filed 90 days after July 10, 1984, see section 552(a), formerly 553(a) of Pub.L. 98–353, set out as a note under section 101 of this title.

CROSS REFERENCES

Applicability of this section in Chapter 9 cases, see 11 USCA § 901.

Certain customer claims in stockbroker liquidation proceedings, see 11 USCA § 747.

Confirmation of plan, see 11 USCA § 1129.

Distribution of—

Customer property, see 11 USCA § 752.

Property of estate, see 11 USCA § 726.

Effect of dismissal, see 11 USCA § 349.

Property of estate, see 11 USCA § 541.

Property recoverable by trustee as exempt, see 11 USCA § 522.

Unpaid portion of certain claims as entitled to distribution, see 11 USCA § 766.

§ 511. Rate of interest on tax claims

(a) If any provision of this title requires the payment of interest on a tax claim or on an administrative expense tax, or the payment of interest to enable a creditor to receive the present value of the allowed amount of a tax claim, the rate of interest shall be the rate determined under applicable nonbankruptcy law.

(b) In the case of taxes paid under a confirmed plan under this title, the rate of interest shall be determined as of the calendar month in which the plan is confirmed.

(Added Pub.L. 109–8, Title VII, § 704(a), Apr. 20, 2005, 119 Stat. 125.)

HISTORICAL AND STATUTORY NOTES

Revision Notes and Legislative Reports

2005 Acts. House Report No. 109–31(Part I), see 2005 U.S. Code Cong. and Adm. News, p. 88.

Effective and Applicability Provisions

2005 Acts. Section effective, except as otherwise provided, 180 days after April 20, 2005, and inapplicable with respect to cases commenced under Title 11 before the effective date, see Pub.L. 109–8, § 1501, set out as a note under 11 U.S.C.A. § 101.

§§ 512 to 520. Reserved for future legislation

SUBCHAPTER II—DEBTOR'S DUTIES AND BENEFITS

§ 521. Debtor's duties

(a) The debtor shall—

(1) file—

(A) a list of creditors; and

(B) unless the court orders otherwise—

(i) a schedule of assets and liabilities;

(ii) a schedule of current income and current expenditures;

(iii) a statement of the debtor's financial affairs and, if section 342(b) applies, a certificate—

(I) of an attorney whose name is indicated on the petition as the attorney for the debtor, or a bankruptcy petition preparer signing the petition under section 110(b)(1), indicating that such attorney or the bankruptcy petition preparer delivered to the debtor the notice required by section 342(b); or

(II) if no attorney is so indicated, and no bankruptcy petition preparer signed the petition, of the debtor that such notice was received and read by the debtor;

(iv) copies of all payment advices or other evidence of payment received within 60 days before the date of the filing of the petition, by the debtor from any employer of the debtor;

(v) a statement of the amount of monthly net income, itemized to show how the amount is calculated; and

(vi) a statement disclosing any reasonably anticipated increase in income or expenditures over the 12–month period following the date of the filing of the petition;

(2) if an individual debtor's schedule of assets and liabilities includes debts which are secured by property of the estate—

(A) within thirty days after the date of the filing of a petition under chapter 7 of this title or on or before the date of the meeting of creditors, whichever is earlier, or within such additional time as the court, for cause, within such period fixes, the debtor shall file with the clerk a statement of his intention with respect to the retention or surrender of such property and, if applicable, specifying that such property is claimed as exempt, that the debtor intends to redeem such property, or that the debtor intends to reaffirm debts secured by such property;

(B) within 30 days after the first date set for the meeting of creditors under section 341(a), or within such additional time as the court, for cause, within such 30–day period fixes, the debtor shall perform his intention with respect to such property, as specified by subparagraph (A) of this paragraph; and

(C) nothing in subparagraphs (A) and (B) of this paragraph shall alter the debtor's or the trustee's rights with regard to such property under this title, except as provided in section 362(h);

(3) if a trustee is serving in the case or an auditor serving under section 586(f) of title 28, cooperate with the trustee as necessary to enable the trustee to perform the trustee's duties under this title;

(4) if a trustee is serving in the case or an auditor serving under section 586(f) of title 28, surrender to the trustee all property of the estate and any recorded information, including books, documents, records, and papers, relating to property of the estate, whether or not immunity is granted under section 344 of this title;

(5) appear at the hearing required under section 524(d) of this title;

(6) in a case under chapter 7 of this title in which the debtor is an individual, not retain possession of personal property as to which a creditor has an allowed claim for the purchase price secured in whole or in part by an interest in such personal property unless the debtor, not later than 45 days after the first meeting of creditors under section 341(a), either—

(A) enters into an agreement with the creditor pursuant to section 524(c) with respect to the claim secured by such property; or

(B) redeems such property from the security interest pursuant to section 722; and

(7) unless a trustee is serving in the case, continue to perform the obligations required of the administrator (as defined in section 3 of the Employee Retirement Income Security Act of 1974) of an employee benefit plan if at the time of the commencement of the case the debtor (or any entity designated by the debtor) served as such administrator.

If the debtor fails to so act within the 45–day period referred to in paragraph (6), the stay under section 362(a) is terminated with respect to the personal property of the estate or of the debtor which is affected, such property shall no longer be property of the estate, and the creditor may take whatever action as to such property as is permitted by applicable nonbankruptcy law, unless the court determines on the motion of the trustee filed before the expiration of such 45–day period, and after notice and a hearing, that such property is of consequential value or benefit to the estate, orders appropriate adequate protection of the creditor's interest, and orders the debtor to deliver any collateral in the debtor's possession to the trustee.

(b) In addition to the requirements under subsection (a), a debtor who is an individual shall file with the court—

(1) a certificate from the approved nonprofit budget and credit counseling agency that provided the debtor services under section 109(h) describing the services provided to the debtor; and

(2) a copy of the debt repayment plan, if any, developed under section 109(h) through the approved nonprofit budget and credit counseling agency referred to in paragraph (1).

(c) In addition to meeting the requirements under subsection (a), a debtor shall file with the court a record of any interest that a debtor has in an education individual retirement account (as defined in section 530(b)(1) of the Internal Revenue Code of 1986) or under a qualified State tuition program (as defined in section 529(b)(1) of such Code).

(d) If the debtor fails timely to take the action specified in subsection (a)(6) of this section, or in paragraphs (1) and (2) of section 362(h), with respect to property which a lessor or bailor owns and has leased, rented, or bailed to the debtor or as to which a creditor holds a security interest not otherwise voidable under section 522(f), 544, 545, 547, 548, or 549, nothing in this title shall prevent or limit the operation of a provision in the underlying lease or agreement that has the effect of placing the debtor in default under such lease or agreement by reason of the occurrence, pendency, or existence of a proceeding under this title or the insolvency of the debtor. Nothing in this subsection shall be deemed to justify limiting such a provision in any other circumstance.

(e)(1) If the debtor in a case under chapter 7 or 13 is an individual and if a creditor files with the court at any time a request to receive a copy of the petition, schedules, and statement of financial affairs filed by the debtor, then the court shall make such petition, such schedules, and such statement available to such creditor.

(2)(A) The debtor shall provide—

(i) not later than 7 days before the date first set for the first meeting of creditors, to the trustee a copy of the Federal income tax return required under applicable law (or at the election of the debtor, a transcript of such return) for the most recent tax year ending immediately before the commencement of the case and for which a Federal income tax return was filed; and

(ii) at the same time the debtor complies with clause (i), a copy of such return (or if elected under clause (i), such transcript) to any creditor that timely requests such copy.

(B) If the debtor fails to comply with clause (i) or (ii) of subparagraph (A), the court shall dismiss the case unless the debtor demonstrates that the failure to so comply is due to circumstances beyond the control of the debtor.

(C) If a creditor requests a copy of such tax return or such transcript and if the debtor fails to provide a copy of such tax return or such transcript to such creditor at the time the debtor provides such tax return or such transcript to the trustee, then the court shall dismiss the case unless the debtor demonstrates that the failure to provide a copy of such tax return or such transcript is due to circumstances beyond the control of the debtor.

(3) If a creditor in a case under chapter 13 files with the court at any time a request to receive a copy of the plan filed by the debtor, then the court shall make available to such creditor a copy of the plan—

(A) at a reasonable cost; and

(B) not later than 5 days after such request is filed.

(f) At the request of the court, the United States trustee, or any party in interest in a case under chapter 7, 11, or 13, a debtor who is an individual shall file with the court—

(1) at the same time filed with the taxing authority, a copy of each Federal income tax return required under applicable law (or at the election of the debtor, a transcript of such tax return) with respect to each tax year of the debtor ending while the case is pending under such chapter;

(2) at the same time filed with the taxing authority, each Federal income tax return required under applicable law (or at the election of the debtor, a transcript of such tax return) that had not been filed with such authority as of the date of the commencement of the case and that was subsequently filed for any tax year of the debtor ending in the 3–year period ending on the date of the commencement of the case;

(3) a copy of each amendment to any Federal income tax return or transcript filed with the court under paragraph (1) or (2); and

(4) in a case under chapter 13—

(A) on the date that is either 90 days after the end of such tax year or 1 year after the date of the commencement of the case, whichever is later, if a plan is not confirmed before such later date; and

(B) annually after the plan is confirmed and until the case is closed, not later than the date that is 45 days before the anniversary of the confirmation of the plan;

a statement, under penalty of perjury, of the income and expenditures of the debtor during the tax year of the debtor most recently concluded before such statement is filed under this paragraph, and of the monthly income of the debtor, that shows how income, expenditures, and monthly income are calculated.

(g)(1) A statement referred to in subsection (f)(4) shall disclose—

(A) the amount and sources of the income of the debtor;

(B) the identity of any person responsible with the debtor for the support of any dependent of the debtor; and

(C) the identity of any person who contributed, and the amount contributed, to the household in which the debtor resides.

(2) The tax returns, amendments, and statement of income and expenditures described in subsections (e)(2)(A) and (f) shall be available to the United States trustee (or the bankruptcy administrator, if any), the trustee, and any party in interest for inspection and copying, subject to the requirements of section 315(c) of the Bankruptcy Abuse Prevention and Consumer Protection Act of 2005.

(h) If requested by the United States trustee or by the trustee, the debtor shall provide—

(1) a document that establishes the identity of the debtor, including a driver's license, passport, or other document that contains a photograph of the debtor; or

(2) such other personal identifying information relating to the debtor that establishes the identity of the debtor.

(i)(1) Subject to paragraphs (2) and (4) and notwithstanding section 707(a), if an individual debtor in a voluntary case under chapter 7 or 13 fails to file all of the information required under subsection (a)(1) within 45 days after the date of the filing of the petition, the case shall be automatically dismissed effective on the 46th day after the date of the filing of the petition.

(2) Subject to paragraph (4) and with respect to a case described in paragraph (1), any party in interest may request the court to enter an order dismissing the case. If requested, the court shall enter an order of dismissal not later than 5 days after such request.

(3) Subject to paragraph (4) and upon request of the debtor made within 45 days after the date of the filing of the petition described in paragraph (1), the court may allow the debtor an additional period of not to exceed 45 days to file the information required under subsection (a)(1) if the court finds justification for extending the period for the filing.

(4) Notwithstanding any other provision of this subsection, on the motion of the trustee filed before the expiration of the applicable period of time specified in paragraph (1), (2), or (3), and after notice and a hearing, the court may decline to dismiss the case if the court finds that the debtor attempted in good faith to file all the information required by subsection (a)(1)(B)(iv) and that the best interests of creditors would be served by administration of the case.

(j)(1) Notwithstanding any other provision of this title, if the debtor fails to file a tax return that becomes due after the commencement of the case or to properly obtain an extension of the due date for filing such return, the taxing authority may request that the court enter an order converting or dismissing the case.

(2) If the debtor does not file the required return or obtain the extension referred to in paragraph (1) within 90 days after a request is filed by the taxing authority under that paragraph, the court shall convert or dismiss the case, whichever is in the best interests of creditors and the estate.

(Pub.L. 95–598, Nov. 6, 1978, 92 Stat. 2586; Pub.L. 98–353, Title III, §§ 305, 452, July 10, 1984, 98 Stat. 352, 375; Pub.L. 99–554, Title II, § 283(h), Oct. 27, 1986, 100 Stat. 3117; Pub.L. 109–8, Title I, § 106(d), Title II, § 225(b), Title III, §§ 304(1), 305(2), 315(b), 316, Title IV, § 446(a), Title VI, § 603(c), Title VII, § 720, Apr. 20, 2005, 119 Stat. 38, 66, 78, 80, 89, 90, 92, 118, 123, 133.)

HISTORICAL AND STATUTORY NOTES

Revision Notes and Legislative Reports

1978 Acts. This section lists three duties of the debtor in a bankruptcy case. The Rules of Bankruptcy Procedure will specify the means of carrying out these duties. The first duty is to file with the court a list of creditors and, unless the court orders otherwise, a schedule of assets and liabilities and a statement of his financial affairs. Second, the debtor is required to cooperate with the trustee as necessary to enable the trustee to perform the trustee's duties. Finally, the debtor must surrender to the trustee all property of the estate, and any recorded information, including books, documents, records, and papers, relating to property of the estate. This phrase "recorded information, including books, documents, records, and papers," has been used here and throughout the bill as a more general term, and includes such other forms of recorded information as date in computer storage or in other machine readable forms.

The list in this section is not exhaustive of the debtor's duties. Others are listed elsewhere in proposed title 11, such as in section 343, which requires the debtor to submit to examination, or in the Rules of Bankruptcy Procedure, as continued by § 404(a) of S. 2266, such as the duty to attend any hearing on discharge, Rule 402(2). Senate Reports 95–989.

1984 Acts. Statements by Legislative Leaders, see 1984 U.S.Code Cong. and Adm.News, p. 576.

1986 Acts. House Report No. 99–764 and House Conference Report No. 99–958, see 1986 U.S.Code Cong. and Adm.News, p. 5227.

2005 Acts. House Report No. 109–31(Part I), see 2005 U.S. Code Cong. and Adm. News, p. 88.

Legislative Statements

Section 521 of the House amendment modifies a comparable provision contained in the House bill and Senate amendment. The Rules of Bankruptcy Procedure should provide where the list of creditors is to be filed. In addition, the debtor is required to attend the hearing on discharge under section 524(d).

References in Text

Chapter 7, referred to in text, is chapter 7 of this title, 11 U.S.C.A. § 701 et seq.

Chapter 13, referred to in text, is chapter 13 of this title, 11 U.S.C.A. § 1301 et seq.

Section 3 of the Employee Retirement Income Security Act of 1974, referred to in subsec. (a)(7), is Pub.L. 93–406, Title I, § 3, Sept. 2, 1974, 88 Stat. 833, which is classified to 29 U.S.C.A. § 1002.

Section 530(b)(1) of the Internal Revenue Code of 1986, referred to in subsec. (c), is classified to 26 U.S.C.A. § 530(b)(1).

Section 529(b)(1) of such Code, referred to in subsec. (c), is classified to 26 U.S.C.A. § 529(b)(1).

Chapter 11, referred to in subsec. (f), is chapter 11 of this title, 11 U.S.C.A. § 1101 et seq.

Section 315(c) of the Bankruptcy Abuse Prevention and Consumer Protection Act of 2005, referred to in subsec. (g)(2), is Pub.L. 109–8, Title III, § 315(c), Apr. 20, 2005, 119 Stat. 91, which is set out as a note under this section.

Effective and Applicability Provisions

2005 Acts. Pub.L. 109–8, Title VI, § 603(e), Apr. 20, 2005, 119 Stat. 123, provided that: "The amendments made by this section [amending this section and 11 U.S.C.A. § 727, and 28 U.S.C.A. § 586, and enacting provisions set out as a note under 28 U.S.C.A. § 586] shall take effect 18 months after the date of enactment of this Act [Apr. 20, 2005]."

Amendments by Pub.L. 109–8 effective, except as otherwise provided, 180 days after April 20, 2005, and inapplicable with respect to cases commenced under Title 11 before the effective date, see Pub.L. 109–8, § 1501, set out as a note under 11 U.S.C.A. § 101.

1986 Acts. Amendment by Pub.L. 99–554 effective 30 days after Oct. 27, 1986, except as otherwise provided for, see section 302(a) of Pub.L. 99–554, set out as a note under section 581 of Title 28, Judiciary and Judicial Procedure.

1984 Acts. Amendment by Pub.L. 98–353 effective with respect to cases filed 90 days after July 10, 1984, see section 552(a), formerly 553(a), of Pub.L. 98–353, set out as a note under section 101 of this title.

Confidentiality of Tax Information

Pub.L. 109–8, Title III, § 315(c), Apr. 20, 2005, 119 Stat. 91, provided that:

"(1) Not later than 180 days after the date of the enactment of this Act [Apr. 20, 2005], the Director of the Administrative Office of the United States Courts shall establish procedures for safeguarding the confidentiality of any tax information required to be provided under this section.

"(2) The procedures under paragraph (1) shall include restrictions on creditor access to tax information that is required to be provided under this section.

"(3) Not later than 540 days after the date of enactment of this Act [Apr. 20, 2005], the director of the administrative office of the United States courts shall prepare and submit to the President pro tempore of the Senate and the speaker of the House of Representatives a report that—

"(A) assesses the effectiveness of the procedures established under paragraph (1); and

"(B) If appropriate, includes proposed legislation to—

"(i) further protect the confidentiality of tax information; and

"(ii) provide penalties for the improper use by any person of the tax information required to be provided under this section."

[Amendments by Pub.L. 109–8 effective, except as otherwise provided, 180 days after April 20, 2005, and inapplicable with respect to cases commenced under Title 11 before the effective date, see Pub.L. 109–8, § 1501, set out as a note under 11 U.S.C.A. § 101.]

Providing Requested Tax Documents to the Court.

Pub.L. 109–8, Title XII, § 1228, Apr. 20, 2005, 119 Stat. 200, provided that:

"(a) **Chapter 7 cases.**—The court shall not grant a discharge in the case of an individual who is a debtor in a case under chapter 7 of title 11, United States Code [11 U.S.C.A. § 701 et seq.], unless requested tax documents have been provided to the court.

"(b) **Chapter 11 and chapter 13 cases.**—The court shall not confirm a plan of reorganization in the case of an individual under chapter 11 or 13 of title 11, United States Code [11 U.S.C.A. § 1101 et seq. or 1301 et seq.], unless requested tax documents have been filed with the court.

"(c) **Document retention.**—The court shall destroy documents submitted in support of a bankruptcy claim not sooner than 3 years after the date of the conclusion of a case filed by an individual under chapter 7, 11, or 13 of title 11, United States Code [11 U.S.C.A. § 701 et seq. or 1101 et seq., or 1301 et seq.]. In the event of a pending audit or enforcement action, the court may extend the time for destruction of such requested tax documents."

[Amendments by Pub.L. 109–8 effective, except as otherwise provided, 180 days after April 20, 2005, and inapplicable with respect to cases commenced under Title 11 before the effective date, see Pub.L. 109–8, § 1501, set out as a note under 11 U.S.C.A. § 101.]

CROSS REFERENCES

Conversion or dismissal of—

Chapter 11 case, see 11 USCA § 1112.

Chapter 13 case, see 11 USCA § 1307.

Debtor's statement of intention, see Official Bankr. Form 8, 11 USCA.

Dismissal of Chapter 7 case, see 11 USCA § 707.

Filing of list, schedule and statement by trustee, see 11 USCA § 1106.

Lists, schedules, statements and fees, see Fed.Rules Bankr.Proc. Form B 200, 11 USCA.

Order converting case, see Fed.Rules Bankr.Proc. Form B 221A et seq., 11 USCA.

Penalty for persons who negligently or fraudulently prepare bankruptcy petitions or failure to file bankruptcy papers, see 11 USCA § 110.

Proof of claim or interest deemed filed if scheduled, see 11 USCA § 1111.

Property scheduled but unadministered before close of case deemed abandoned, see 11 USCA § 554.

Trustee's duty to ensure performance of debtor's intention as specified in subsec. (2)(B) of this section, see 11 USCA § 704.

§ 522. Exemptions

(a) In this section—

(1) "dependent" includes spouse, whether or not actually dependent; and

(2) "value" means fair market value as of the date of the filing of the petition or, with respect to property that becomes property of the estate after such date, as of the date such property becomes property of the estate.

(b)(1) Notwithstanding section 541 of this title, an individual debtor may exempt from property of the estate the property listed in either paragraph (2) or, in the alternative, paragraph (3) of this subsection. In joint cases filed under section 302 of this title and individual cases filed under section 301 or 303 of this title by or against debtors who are husband and wife, and whose estates are ordered to be jointly administered under Rule 1015(b) of the Federal Rules of Bankruptcy Procedure, one debtor may not elect to exempt property listed in paragraph (2) and the other debtor elect to exempt property listed in paragraph (3) of this subsection. If the parties cannot agree on the alternative to be elected, they shall be deemed to elect paragraph (2), where such election is permitted under the law of the jurisdiction where the case is filed.

(2) Property listed in this paragraph is property that is specified under subsection (d), unless the State law that is applicable to the debtor under paragraph (3)(A) specifically does not so authorize.

(3) Property listed in this paragraph is—

(A) subject to subsections (*o*) and (p), any property that is exempt under Federal law, other than subsection (d) of this section, or State or local law that is applicable on the date of the filing of the petition at the place in which the debtor's domicile has been located for the 730 days immediately preceding the date of the filing of the petition or if the debtor's domicile has not been located at a single State for such 730–day period, the place in which the debtor's domicile was located for 180 days immediately preceding the 730–day period or for a longer portion of such 180–day period than in any other place;

(B) any interest in property in which the debtor had, immediately before the commencement of the case, an interest as a tenant by the entirety or joint tenant to the extent that such interest as a tenant by the entirety or joint tenant is exempt from process under applicable nonbankruptcy law; and

(C) retirement funds to the extent that those funds are in a fund or account that is exempt from taxation under section 401, 403, 408, 408A, 414, 457, or 501(a) of the Internal Revenue Code of 1986.

If the effect of the domiciliary requirement under subparagraph (A) is to render the debtor ineligible for any exemption, the debtor may elect to exempt property that is specified under subsection (d).

(4) For purposes of paragraph (3)(C) and subsection (d)(12), the following shall apply:

(A) If the retirement funds are in a retirement fund that has received a favorable determination under section 7805 of the Internal Revenue Code of 1986, and that determination is in effect as of the date of the filing of the petition in a case under this title, those funds shall be presumed to be exempt from the estate.

(B) If the retirement funds are in a retirement fund that has not received a favorable determination under such section 7805, those funds are exempt from the estate if the debtor demonstrates that—

(i) no prior determination to the contrary has been made by a court or the Internal Revenue Service; and

(ii)(I) the retirement fund is in substantial compliance with the applicable requirements of the Internal Revenue Code of 1986; or

(II) the retirement fund fails to be in substantial compliance with the applicable requirements of the Internal Revenue Code of 1986 and the debtor is not materially responsible for that failure.

(C) A direct transfer of retirement funds from 1 fund or account that is exempt from taxation under section 401, 403, 408, 408A, 414, 457, or 501(a) of the Internal Revenue Code of 1986, under section 401(a)(31) of the Internal Revenue Code of 1986, or otherwise, shall not cease to qualify for exemption under paragraph (3)(C) or subsection (d)(12) by reason of such direct transfer.

(D)(i) Any distribution that qualifies as an eligible rollover distribution within the meaning of section 402(c) of the Internal Revenue Code of 1986 or that is described in clause (ii) shall not cease to qualify for exemption under paragraph (3)(C) or subsection (d)(12) by reason of such distribution.

(ii) A distribution described in this clause is an amount that—

(I) has been distributed from a fund or account that is exempt from taxation under section 401, 403, 408, 408A, 414, 457, or 501(a) of the Internal Revenue Code of 1986; and

(II) to the extent allowed by law, is deposited in such a fund or account not later than 60 days after the distribution of such amount.

(c) Unless the case is dismissed, property exempted under this section is not liable during or after the case for any debt of the debtor that arose, or that is determined under section 502 of this title as if such debt had arisen, before the commencement of the case, except—

(1) a debt of a kind specified in paragraph (1) or (5) of section 523(a) (in which case, notwithstanding any provision of applicable nonbankruptcy law to the contrary, such property shall be liable for a debt of a kind specified in section 523(a)(5));

(2) a debt secured by a lien that is—

(A)(i) not avoided under subsection (f) or (g) of this section or under section 544, 545, 547, 548, 549, or 724(a) of this title; and

(ii) not void under section 506(d) of this title; or

(B) a tax lien, notice of which is properly filed;

(3) a debt of a kind specified in section 523(a)(4) or 523(a)(6) of this title owed by an institution-affiliated party of an insured depository institution to a Federal depository institutions regulatory agency acting in its capacity as conservator, receiver, or liquidating agent for such institution; or

(4) a debt in connection with fraud in the obtaining or providing of any scholarship, grant, loan, tuition, discount, award, or other financial assistance for purposes of financing an education at an institution of higher education (as that term is defined in section 101 of the Higher Education Act of 1965 (20 U.S.C. 1001)).

(d) The following property may be exempted under subsection (b)(2) of this section:

(1) The debtor's aggregate interest, not to exceed $20,200 [1] in value, in real property or personal property that the debtor or a dependent of the debtor uses as a residence, in a cooperative that owns property that the debtor or a dependent of the debtor uses as a residence, or in a burial plot for the debtor or a dependent of the debtor.

(2) The debtor's interest, not to exceed $3,225 [1] in value, in one motor vehicle.

(3) The debtor's interest, not to exceed $525 [1] in value in any particular item or $10,775 [1] in aggregate value, in household furnishings, household goods, wearing apparel, appliances, books, animals, crops, or musical instruments, that are held primarily for the personal, family, or household use of the debtor or a dependent of the debtor.

(4) The debtor's aggregate interest, not to exceed $1,350 [1] in value, in jewelry held primarily for the personal, family, or household use of the debtor or a dependent of the debtor.

(5) The debtor's aggregate interest in any property, not to exceed in value $1,075 [1] plus up to $10,125 [1] of any unused amount of the exemption provided under paragraph (1) of this subsection.

(6) The debtor's aggregate interest, not to exceed $2,025 [1] in value, in any implements, professional books, or tools, of the trade of the debtor or the trade of a dependent of the debtor.

(7) Any unmatured life insurance contract owned by the debtor, other than a credit life insurance contract.

(8) The debtor's aggregate interest, not to exceed in value $10,775 [1] less any amount of property of the estate transferred in the manner specified in section 542(d) of this title, in any accrued dividend or interest under, or loan value of, any unmatured life insurance contract owned by the debtor under which the insured is the debtor or an individual of whom the debtor is a dependent.

(9) Professionally prescribed health aids for the debtor or a dependent of the debtor.

(10) The debtor's right to receive—

(A) a social security benefit, unemployment compensation, or a local public assistance benefit;

(B) a veterans' benefit;

(C) a disability, illness, or unemployment benefit;

(D) alimony, support, or separate maintenance, to the extent reasonably necessary for the support of the debtor and any dependent of the debtor;

(E) a payment under a stock bonus, pension, profitsharing, annuity, or similar plan or contract on account of illness, disability, death, age, or length of service, to the extent reasonably necessary for the support of the debtor and any dependent of the debtor, unless—

(i) such plan or contract was established by or under the auspices of an insider that employed the debtor at the time the debtor's rights under such plan or contract arose;

(ii) such payment is on account of age or length of service; and

(iii) such plan or contract does not qualify under section 401(a), 403(a), 403(b), or 408 of the Internal Revenue Code of 1986.

(11) The debtor's right to receive, or property that is traceable to—

(A) an award under a crime victim's reparation law;

(B) a payment on account of the wrongful death of an individual of whom the debtor was a dependent, to the extent reasonably necessary for the support of the debtor and any dependent of the debtor;

(C) a payment under a life insurance contract that insured the life of an individual of whom the debtor was a dependent on the date of such individual's death, to the extent reasonably necessary for the support of the debtor and any dependent of the debtor;

(D) a payment, not to exceed $20,200,[1] on account of personal bodily injury, not including pain and suffering or compensation for actual pecuniary loss, of the debtor or an individual of whom the debtor is a dependent; or

(E) a payment in compensation of loss of future earnings of the debtor or an individual of whom the debtor is or was a dependent, to the extent reasonably necessary for the support of the debtor and any dependent of the debtor.

(12) Retirement funds to the extent that those funds are in a fund or account that is exempt from taxation under section 401, 403, 408, 408A, 414, 457, or 501(a) of the Internal Revenue Code of 1986.

(e) A waiver of an exemption executed in favor of a creditor that holds an unsecured claim against the debtor is unenforceable in a case under this title with respect to such claim against property that the debtor may exempt under subsection (b) of this section. A waiver by the debtor of a power under subsection (f) or (h) of this section to avoid a transfer, under subsection (g) or (i) of this section to exempt property, or under subsection (i) of this section to recover property or to preserve a transfer, is unenforceable in a case under this title.

(f)(1) Notwithstanding any waiver of exemptions but subject to paragraph (3), the debtor may avoid the fixing of a lien on an interest of the debtor in property to the extent that such lien impairs an exemption to which the debtor would have been entitled under subsection (b) of this section, if such lien is—

(A) a judicial lien, other than a judicial lien that secures a debt of a kind that is specified in section 523(a)(5); or

(B) a nonpossessory, nonpurchase-money security interest in any—

(i) household furnishings, household goods, wearing apparel, appliances, books, animals, crops, musical instruments, or jewelry that are held primarily for the personal, family, or household use of the debtor or a dependent of the debtor;

(ii) implements, professional books, or tools, of the trade of the debtor or the trade of a dependent of the debtor; or

(iii) professionally prescribed health aids for the debtor or a dependent of the debtor.

(2)(A) For the purposes of this subsection, a lien shall be considered to impair an exemption to the extent that the sum of—

(i) the lien;

(ii) all other liens on the property; and

(iii) the amount of the exemption that the debtor could claim if there were no liens on the property;

exceeds the value that the debtor's interest in the property would have in the absence of any liens.

(B) In the case of a property subject to more than 1 lien, a lien that has been avoided shall not be considered in making the calculation under subparagraph (A) with respect to other liens.

(C) This paragraph shall not apply with respect to a judgment arising out of a mortgage foreclosure.

(3) In a case in which State law that is applicable to the debtor—

(A) permits a person to voluntarily waive a right to claim exemptions under subsection (d) or prohibits a debtor from claiming exemptions under subsection (d); and

(B) either permits the debtor to claim exemptions under State law without limitation in amount, except to the extent that the debtor has permitted the fixing of a consensual lien on any property or prohibits avoidance of a consensual lien on property otherwise eligible to be claimed as exempt property;

the debtor may not avoid the fixing of a lien on an interest of the debtor or a dependent of the debtor in property if the lien is a nonpossessory, nonpurchase-money security interest in implements, professional books, or tools of the trade of the debtor or a dependent of the debtor or farm animals or crops of the debtor or a dependent of the debtor to the extent the value of such implements, professional books, tools of the trade, animals, and crops exceeds $5,475 [1].

(4)(A) Subject to subparagraph (B), for purposes of paragraph (1)(B), the term "household goods" means—

(i) clothing;

(ii) furniture;

(iii) appliances;

(iv) 1 radio;

(v) 1 television;

(vi) 1 VCR;

(vii) linens;

(viii) china;

(ix) crockery;

(x) kitchenware;

(xi) educational materials and educational equipment primarily for the use of minor dependent children of the debtor;

(xii) medical equipment and supplies;

(xiii) furniture exclusively for the use of minor children, or elderly or disabled dependents of the debtor;

(xiv) personal effects (including the toys and hobby equipment of minor dependent children and wedding rings) of the debtor and the dependents of the debtor; and

(xv) 1 personal computer and related equipment.

(B) The term "household goods" does not include—

(i) works of art (unless by or of the debtor, or any relative of the debtor);

(ii) electronic entertainment equipment with a fair market value of more than $550 [1] in the aggregate (except 1 television, 1 radio, and 1 VCR);

(iii) items acquired as antiques with a fair market value of more than $550 [1] in the aggregate;

(iv) jewelry with a fair market value of more than $550 [1] in the aggregate (except wedding rings); and

(v) a computer (except as otherwise provided for in this section), motor vehicle (including a tractor or lawn tractor), boat, or a motorized recreational device, conveyance, vehicle, watercraft, or aircraft.

(g) Notwithstanding sections 550 and 551 of this title, the debtor may exempt under subsection (b) of this section property that the trustee recovers under section 510(c)(2), 542, 543, 550, 551, or 553 of this title, to the extent that the debtor could have exempted such property under subsection (b) of this section if such property had not been transferred, if—

(1)(A) such transfer was not a voluntary transfer of such property by the debtor; and

(B) the debtor did not conceal such property; or

(2) the debtor could have avoided such transfer under subsection (f)(1)(B) of this section.

(h) The debtor may avoid a transfer of property of the debtor or recover a setoff to the extent that the debtor could have exempted such property under subsection (g)(1) of this section if the trustee had avoided such transfer, if—

(1) such transfer is avoidable by the trustee under section 544, 545, 547, 548, 549, or 724(a) of this title or recoverable by the trustee under section 553 of this title; and

(2) the trustee does not attempt to avoid such transfer.

(i)(1) If the debtor avoids a transfer or recovers a setoff under subsection (f) or (h) of this section, the debtor may recover in the manner prescribed by, and subject to the limitations of, section 550 of this title, the same as if the trustee had avoided such transfer, and may exempt any property so recovered under subsection (b) of this section.

(2) Notwithstanding section 551 of this title, a transfer avoided under section 544, 545, 547, 548, 549, or 724(a) of this title, under subsection (f) or (h) of this section, or property recovered under section 553 of this title, may be preserved for the benefit of the debtor to the extent that the debtor may exempt such property under subsection (g) of this section or paragraph (1) of this subsection.

(j) Notwithstanding subsections (g) and (i) of this section, the debtor may exempt a particular kind of property under subsections (g) and (i) of this section only to the extent that the debtor has exempted less property in value of such kind than that to which the debtor is entitled under subsection (b) of this section.

(k) Property that the debtor exempts under this section is not liable for payment of any administrative expense except—

(1) the aliquot share of the costs and expenses of avoiding a transfer of property that the debtor exempts under subsection (g) of this section, or of recovery of such property, that is attributable to the value of the portion of such property exempted in relation to the value of the property recovered; and

(2) any costs and expenses of avoiding a transfer under subsection (f) or (h) of this section, or of recovery of property under subsection (i)(1) of this section, that the debtor has not paid.

(*l*) The debtor shall file a list of property that the debtor claims as exempt under subsection (b) of this section. If the debtor does not file such a list, a dependent of the debtor may file such a list, or may claim property as exempt from property of the estate on behalf of the debtor. Unless a party in interest objects, the property claimed as exempt on such list is exempt.

(m) Subject to the limitation in subsection (b), this section shall apply separately with respect to each debtor in a joint case.

(n) For assets in individual retirement accounts described in section 408 or 408A of the Internal Revenue Code of 1986, other than a simplified employee pension under section 408(k) of such Code or a simple retirement account under section 408(p) of such Code, the aggregate value of such assets exempted under this section, without regard to amounts attributable to rollover contributions under section 402(c), 402(e)(6), 403(a)(4), 403(a) (5), and 403(b)(8) of the Internal Revenue Code of 1986, and earnings thereon, shall not exceed $1,095,000 [1] in a case filed by a debtor who is an individual, except that such amount may be increased if the interests of justice so require.

(*o*) For purposes of subsection (b)(3)(A), and notwithstanding subsection (a), the value of an interest in—

(1) real or personal property that the debtor or a dependent of the debtor uses as a residence;

(2) a cooperative that owns property that the debtor or a dependent of the debtor uses as a residence;

(3) a burial plot for the debtor or a dependent of the debtor; or

(4) real or personal property that the debtor or a dependent of the debtor claims as a homestead;

shall be reduced to the extent that such value is attributable to any portion of any property that the debtor disposed of in the 10–year period ending on the date of the filing of the petition with the intent to hinder, delay, or defraud a creditor and that the debtor could not exempt, or that portion that the debtor could not exempt, under subsection (b), if on such date the debtor had held the property so disposed of.

(p)(1) Except as provided in paragraph (2) of this subsection and sections 544 and 548, as a result of electing under subsection (b)(3)(A) to exempt property under State or local law, a debtor may not exempt any amount of interest that was acquired by the debtor during the 1215–day period preceding the date of the filing of the petition that exceeds in the aggregate $136,875 [1] in value in—

(A) real or personal property that the debtor or a dependent of the debtor uses as a residence;

(B) a cooperative that owns property that the debtor or a dependent of the debtor uses as a residence;

(C) a burial plot for the debtor or a dependent of the debtor; or

(D) real or personal property that the debtor or dependent of the debtor claims as a homestead.

(2)(A) The limitation under paragraph (1) shall not apply to an exemption claimed under subsection (b)(3)(A) by a family farmer for the principal residence of such farmer.

(B) For purposes of paragraph (1), any amount of such interest does not include any interest transferred from a debtor's previous principal residence (which was acquired prior to the beginning of such 1215–day period) into the debtor's current principal residence, if the debtor's previous and current residences are located in the same State.

(q)(1) As a result of electing under subsection (b)(3)(A) to exempt property under State or local law, a debtor may not exempt any amount of an interest in property described in subparagraphs (A), (B), (C), and (D) of subsection (p)(1) which exceeds in the aggregate $136,875 [1] if—

(A) the court determines, after notice and a hearing, that the debtor has been convicted of a felony (as defined in section 3156 of title 18), which under the circumstances, demonstrates that the filing of the case was an abuse of the provisions of this title; or

(B) the debtor owes a debt arising from—

(i) any violation of the Federal securities laws (as defined in section 3(a)(47) of the Securities Exchange Act of 1934), any State securities laws, or any regulation or order issued under Federal securities laws or State securities laws;

(ii) fraud, deceit, or manipulation in a fiduciary capacity or in connection with the purchase or sale of any security registered under section 12 or 15(d) of the Securities Exchange Act of 1934 or under section 6 of the Securities Act of 1933;

(iii) any civil remedy under section 1964 of title 18; or

(iv) any criminal act, intentional tort, or willful or reckless misconduct that caused serious physical injury or death to another individual in the preceding 5 years.

(2) Paragraph (1) shall not apply to the extent the amount of an interest in property described in subparagraphs (A), (B), (C), and (D) of subsection (p)(1) is reasonably necessary for the support of the debtor and any dependent of the debtor.

(Pub.L. 95–598, Nov. 6, 1978, 92 Stat. 2586; Pub.L. 98–353, Title III, §§ 306, 453, July 10, 1984, 98 Stat. 353, 375; Pub.L. 99–514, § 2, Oct. 22, 1986, 100 Stat. 2095; Pub.L. 99–554, Title II, § 283(i), Oct. 27, 1986, 100 Stat. 3117; Pub.L. 101–647, Title XXV, § 2522(b), Nov. 29, 1990, 104 Stat. 4866; Pub.L. 103–394, Title I, § 108(d), Title III, §§ 303, 304(d), 310, Title V, § 501(d)(12), Oct. 22, 1994, 108 Stat. 4112, 4132, 4133, 4137, 4145; Pub.L. 106–420, § 4, Nov. 1, 2000, 114 Stat. 1868; Pub.L. 109–8, Title II, §§ 216, 224(a), (e)(1), Title III, §§ 307, 308, 313(a), 322(a), Apr. 20, 2005, 119 Stat. 55, 62, 65, 81, 87, 96.)

[1] Dollar amount as adjusted by the Judicial Conference of the United States. See Adjustment of Dollar Amounts notes set out under this section and 11 U.S.C.A. § 104.

HISTORICAL AND STATUTORY NOTES

Revision Notes and Legislative Reports

1978 Acts. Subsection (a) of this section defines two terms: "dependent" includes the debtor's spouse, whether or not actually dependent; and "value" means fair market value as of the date of the filing of the petition.

Subsection (b) tracks current law. It permits a debtor the exemptions to which he is entitled under other Federal law and the law of the State of his domicile. Some of the items that may be exempted under Federal laws other than title 11 include:

Foreign Service Retirement and Disability payments, 22 U.S.C. 1104 [1] [section 1104 of Title 22, Foreign Relations and Intercourse];

Social security payments, 42 U.S.C. 407 [section 407 of Title 42, The Public Health and Welfare];

Injury or death compensation payments from war risk hazards, 42 U.S.C. 1717 [section 1717 of Title 42];

Wages of fishermen, seamen, and apprentices, 46 U.S.C. 601 [2] [section 601 of Title 46, Shipping];

Civil service retirement benefits, 5 U.S.C. 729, 2265 [3] [sections 729 and 2265 of Title 5, Government Organization and Employees];

Longshoremen's and Harbor Workers' Compensation Act death and disability benefits, 33 U.S.C. 916 [section 916 of Title 33, Navigation and Navigable Waters];

Railroad Retirement Act annuities and pensions, 45 U.S.C. 228(L) [4] [former section 2281 of Title 45, Railroads];

Veterans benefits, 45 U.S.C. 352(E) [5] [section 352(e) of Title 45];

Special pensions paid to winners of the Congressional Medal of Honor, 38 U.S.C. 3101 [6] [section 3101 of Title 38, Veterans' Benefits]; and

Federal homestead lands on debts contracted before issuance of the patent, 43 U.S.C. 175 [section 175 of Title 43, Public Lands].

He may also exempt an interest in property in which the debtor had an interest as a tenant by the entirety or joint tenant to the extent that interest would have been exempt from process under applicable nonbankruptcy law.

Under proposed section 541, all property of the debtor becomes property of the estate, but the debtor is permitted to exempt certain property from property of the estate under this section. Property may be exempted even if it is subject to a lien, but only the unencumbered portion of the property is to be counted in computing the "value" of the property for the purposes of exemption.

As under current law, the debtor will be permitted to convert nonexempt property into exempt property before filing a bankruptcy petition. The practice is not fraudulent as to creditors, and permits the debtor to make full use of the exemptions to which he is entitled under the law. [Ed. Note: cf. Mickelson v. Anderson, Bkrtcy.Minn.1982, 31 B.R. 635.]

Subsection (c) insulates exempt property from prepetition claims other than tax claims (whether or not dischargeable), and other than alimony, maintenance, or support claims that are excepted from discharge. The bankruptcy discharge does not prevent enforcement of valid liens. The rule of *Long v. Bullard*, 117 U.S. 617 (1886) [6 S.Ct. 917, 29 L.Ed. 1004], is accepted with respect to the enforcement of valid liens on nonexempt property as well as on exempt property. Cf. *Louisville Joint Stock Land Bank v. Radford*, 295 U.S. 555, 583 (1935) [55 S.Ct. 854].

Subsection (c)(3) permits the collection of dischargeable taxes from exempt assets. Only assets exempted from levy under section 6334 of the Internal Revenue Code [section 6334 of Title 26, Internal Revenue Code] or under applicable state or local tax law cannot be applied to satisfy these tax claims. This rule applies to prepetition tax claims against the debtor regardless of whether the claims do or do not receive priority and whether they are dischargeable or nondischargeable. Thus, even if a tax is dischargeable vis-a-vis the debtor's after-acquired assets, it may nevertheless be collectible from exempt property held by the estate. (Taxes incurred by the debtor's estate which are collectible as first priority administrative expenses are not collectible from the debtor's estate which are collectible as first priority administrative expenses are not collectible from the debtor's exempt assets.)

Subsection (d) protects the debtor's exemptions, either Federal or State, by making unenforceable in a bankruptcy case a waiver of exemptions or a waiver of the debtor's avoiding powers under the following subsections.

Subsection (e) protects the debtor's exemptions, his discharge, and thus his fresh start by permitting him to avoid certain liens on exempt property. The debtor may avoid a judicial lien on any property to the extent that the property could have been exempted in the absence of the lien, and may similarly avoid a nonpurchase-money security interest in certain household and personal goods. The avoiding power is independent of any waiver of exemptions.

Subsection (f) gives the debtor the ability to exempt property that the trustee recovers under one of the trustee's avoiding powers if the property was involuntarily transferred away from the debtor (such as by the fixing of a judicial lien) and if the debtor did not conceal the property. The debtor is also permitted to exempt property that the trustee recovers as the result of the avoiding of the fixing of certain security interests to the extent that the debtor could otherwise have exempted the property.

Subsection (g) provides that if the trustee does not exercise an avoiding power to recover a transfer of property that would be exempt, the debtor may exercise it and exempt the property, if the transfer was involuntary and the debtor did not conceal the property. If the debtor wishes to preserve his right to pursue any action under this provision, then he must intervene in any action brought by the trustee based on the same cause of action. It is not intended that the debtor be given an additional opportunity to avoid a transfer or that the transferee should have to defend the same action twice. Rather, the section is primarily designed to give the debtor the rights the trustee could have, but has not, pursued. The debtor is given no greater rights under this provision than the trustee, and thus, the debtor's avoiding powers under proposed sections 544, 545, 547, and 548, are subject to proposed 546, as are the trustee's powers.

These subsections are cumulative. The debtor is not required to choose which he will use to gain an exemption. Instead, he may use more than one in any particular instance, just as the trustee's avoiding powers are cumulative.

Subsection (h) permits recovery by the debtor of property transferred by an avoided transfer from either the initial or subsequent transferees. It also permits preserving a transfer for the benefit of the debtor. In either event, the debtor may exempt the property recovered or preserved.

Subsection (i) makes clear that the debtor may exempt property under the avoiding subsections (f) and (h) only to the extent he has exempted less property than allowed under subsection (b).

Subsection (j) makes clear that the liability of the debtor's exempt property is limited to the debtor's aliquot share of the costs and expenses recovery of property that the trustee recovers and the debtor later exempts, and any costs and expenses of avoiding a transfer by the debtor that the debtor has not already paid.

Subsection (k) requires the debtor to file a list of property that he claims as exempt from property of the estate. Absent an objection to the list, the property is exempted. A dependent of the debtor may file it and thus be protected if the debtor fails to file the list.

Subsection (*l*) provides the rule for a joint case. Senate Report No. 95–989.

1 Replaced by 22 USCA § 4060(c).

2 Replaced by 46 USCA §§ 11108, 11109.

3 Replaced by 5 USCA § 8346.

4 Replaced by 45 USCA § 231m.

5 Railroad unemployment benefits are covered by 45 USCA § 352(e).

6 Veterans benefits generally are covered by 38 USCA § 5301.

Subsection (a) of this section defines two terms: "dependent" includes the debtor's spouse, whether or not actually dependent; and "value" means fair market value as of the date of the filing of the petition.

Subsection (b), the operative subsection of this section, is a significant departure from present law. It permits an individual debtor in a bankruptcy case a choice between exemption systems. The debtor may choose the Federal exemptions prescribed in subsection (d), or he may choose the exemptions to which he is entitled under other Federal law and the law of the State of his domicile. If the debtor chooses the latter, some of the items that may be exempted under other Federal laws include:

—Foreign Service Retirement and Disability payments, 22 U.S.C. 1104 [1] [section 1104 of Title 22, Foreign Relations and Intercourse];

—Social security payments, 42 U.S.C. 407 [section 407 of Title 42, The Public Health and Welfare];

—Injury or death compensation payments from war risk hazards, 42 U.S.C. 1717 [section 1717 of Title 42];

—Wages of fishermen, seamen, and apprentices, 46 U.S.C. 601 [section 601 of Title 46, Shipping];

—Civil service retirement benefits, 5 U.S.C. 729, 2265 [2] [sections 729, 2265 of Title 5, Government Organization and Employees];

—Longshoremen's and Harbor Workers' Compensation Act death and disability benefits, 33 U.S.C. 916 [section 916 of Title 33, Navigation and Navigable Waters];

—Railroad Retirement Act annuities and pensions, 45 U.S.C. 228(*l*) [3]; [former section 228l of Title 45, Railroads];

—Veterans benefits, 45 U.S.C. 352(E) [4] [section 352(e) of Title 45];

—Special pensions paid to winners of the Congressional Medal of Honor, 38 U.S.C. 3101 [section 3101 of Title 38, Veterans' Benefits]; [5] and

—Federal homestead lands on debts contracted before issuance of the patent, 43 U.S.C. 175 [section 175 of Title 43, Public Lands].

He may also exempt an interest in property in which the debtor had an interest as a tenant by the entirety or joint tenant to the extent that interest would have been exempt from process under applicable nonbankruptcy law. The Rules will provide for the situation where the debtor's choice of exemption, Federal or State, was improvident and should be changed, for example, where the court has ruled against the debtor with respect to a major exemption.

Under proposed 11 U.S.C. 541, all property of the debtor becomes property of the estate, but the debtor is permitted to exempt certain property from property of the estate under this section. Property may be exempted even if it is subject to a lien, but only the unencumbered portion of the property is to be counted in computing the "value" of the property for the purposes of exemption. Thus, for example, a residence worth $30,000 with a mortgage of $25,000 will be exemptable to the extent of $5,000. This follows current law. The remaining value of the property will be dealt with in the bankruptcy case as is any interest in property that is subject to a lien.

As under current law, the debtor will be permitted to convert nonexempt property into exempt property before filing a bankruptcy petition. See Hearings, pt. 3, at 1355–58. The practice is not fraudulent as to creditors and permits the debtor to make full use of the exemptions to which he is entitled under the law.

Subsection (c) insulates exempt property from prepetition claims, except tax and alimony, maintenance, or support claims that are excepted from discharge. The bankruptcy discharge will not prevent enforcement of valid liens. The rule of *Long v. Bullard,* 117 U.S. 617 (1886) [6 S.Ct. 917, 29 L.Ed. 1004], is accepted with respect to the enforcement of valid liens on nonexempt property as well as on exempt property. Cf. *Louisville Joint Stock Land Bank v. Radford,* 295 U.S. 555, 583 (1935) [55 S.Ct. 854].

Subsection (d) specifies the Federal exemptions to which the debtor is entitled. They are derived in large part from the Uniform Exemptions Act, promulgated by the Commissioners of Uniform State Laws in August, 1976. Eleven categories of property are exempted. First is a homestead to the extent of $10,000, which may be claimed in real or personal property that the debtor or a dependent of the debtor uses as a residence. Second, the debtor may exempt a motor vehicle to the extent of $1500. Third, the debtor may exempt household goods, furnishings, clothing, and similar household items, held primarily for the personal, family, or household use of the debtor or a dependent of the debtor. "Animals" includes all animals, such as pets, livestock, poultry, and fish, if they are held primarily for personal, family or household use. The limitation for third category items is $300 on any particular item. The debtor may also exempt up to $750 of personal jewelry.

Paragraph (5) permits the exemption of $500, plus any unused amount of the homestead exemption, in any property, in order not to discriminate against the nonhomeowner. Paragraph (6) grants the debtor up to $1000 in implements, professional books, or tools, of the trade of the debtor a dependent. Paragraph (7) exempts a life insurance contract, other than a credit life insurance contract, owned by the debtor. This paragraph refers to the life insurance contract itself. It does not encompass any other rights under the contract, such as the right to borrow out the loan value. Because of this provision, the trustee may not surrender a life insurance contract, which remains property of the debtor if he chooses the Federal exemptions. Paragraph (8) permits the debtor to exempt up to $5000 in loan value in a life insurance policy owned by the debtor under which the debtor or an individual of whom the debtor is a dependent is the insured. The exemption provided by this paragraph and paragraph (7) will also include the debtor's rights in a group insurance certificate under which the insured is an individual of whom the debtor is a dependent (assuming the debtor has rights in the policy that could be exempted) or the debtor. A trustee is authorized to collect the entire loan value on every life insurance policy owned by the debtor as property of the estate. First, however, the debtor will choose which policy or policies under which the loan value will be exempted. The $5000 figure is reduced by the amount of any automatic premium loan authorized after the date of the filing of the petition under section 542(d). Paragraph (9) exempts professionally prescribed health aids.

Paragraph (10) exempts certain benefits that are akin to future earnings of the debtor. These include social security, unemployment compensation, or public assistance benefits, veteran's benefits, disability, illness, or unemployment benefits, alimony, support, or separate maintenance (but only to the extent reasonably necessary for the support of the debtor and any dependents of the debtor), and benefits under a certain stock bonus, pension, profitsharing, annuity or similar plan based on illness, disability, death, age or length of service. Paragraph (11) allows the debtor to exempt certain compensation for losses. These include crime victim's reparation benefits, wrongful death benefits (with a reasonably necessary for support limitation), life insurance proceeds (same limitation), compensation for bodily injury, not including pain and suffering ($10,000 limitation), and loss of future earnings payments (support limitation). This provision in subparagraph (D)(11) is designed to cover payments in compensation of actual bodily injury, such as the loss of a limb, and is not intended to include the attendant costs that accompany such a loss, such as medical payments, pain and suffering, or loss of earnings. Those items are handled separately by the bill.

Subsection (e) protects the debtor's exemptions, either Federal or State, by making unenforceable in a bankruptcy case a waiver of exemptions or a waiver of the debtor's avoiding powers under the following subsections.

Subsection (f) protects the debtor's exemptions, his discharge, and thus his fresh start by permitting him to avoid certain liens on exempt property. The debtor may avoid a judicial lien on any property to the extent that the property could have been exempted in the absence of the lien, and may similarly avoid a nonpurchase-money security interest in certain household and personal goods. The avoiding power is independent of any waiver of exemptions.

Subsection (g) gives the debtor the ability to exempt property that the trustee recovers under one of the trustee's avoiding powers if the property was involuntarily transferred away from the debtor (such as by the fixing of a judicial lien) and if the debtor did not conceal the property. The debtor is also permitted to exempt property that the trustee recovers as the result of the avoiding of the fixing of certain security interests to the extent that the debtor could otherwise have exempted the property.

If the trustee does not pursue an avoiding power to recover a transfer of property that would be exempt, the debtor may pursue it and exempt the property, if the transfer was involuntary and the debtor did not conceal the property. If the debtor wishes to preserve his right to pursue an action under this provision, then he must intervene in any action brought by the trustee based on the same cause of action. It is not intended that the debtor be given an additional opportunity to avoid a transfer or that the transferee have to defend the same action twice. Rather, the section is primarily designed to give the debtor the rights the trustee could have pursued if the trustee chooses not to pursue them. The debtor is given no greater rights under this provision than the trustee, and thus the debtor's avoiding powers under proposed 11 U.S.C. 544, 545, 547, and 548, are subject to proposed 11 U.S.C. 546, as are the trustee's powers.

These subsections are cumulative. The debtor is not required to choose which he will use to gain an exemption. Instead, he may use more than one in any particular instance, just as the trustee's avoiding powers are cumulative.

Subsection (i) permits recovery by the debtor of property transferred in an avoided transfer from either the initial or subsequent transferees. It also permits preserving a transfer for the benefit of the debtor. Under either case the debtor may exempt the property recovered or preserved.

Subsection (k) makes clear that the debtor's aliquot share of the costs and expenses [for] recovery of property that the trustee recovers and the debtor later exempts, and any costs and expenses of avoiding a transfer by the debtor that the debtor has not already paid.

Subsection (*l*) requires the debtor to file a list of property that he claims as exempt from property of the estate. Absent an objection to the list, the property is exempted. A dependent of the debtor may file it and thus be protected if the debtor fails to file the list.

Subsection (m) requires the clerk of the bankruptcy court to give notice of any exemptions claimed under subsection (*l*), in order that parties in interest may have an opportunity to object to the claim.

Subsection (n) provides the rule for a joint case: each debtor is entitled to the Federal exemptions provided under this section or to the State exemptions, whichever the debtor chooses. House Report 95–595.

1 Replaced by 22 USCA § 4060(c).

2 Replaced by 5 USCA § 8346.

3 Replaced by 45 USCA § 231m.

4 Railroad unemployment benefits are covered by 45 USCA § 352(e).

5 Veteran benefits generally are covered by 38 USCA § 5301.

1984 Acts. Statements by Legislative Leaders, see 1984 U.S. Code Cong. and Adm. News, p. 576.

1986 Acts. House Report No. 99–764 and House Conference Report No. 99–958, see 1986 U.S. Code Cong. and Adm. News, p. 5227.

House Conference Report No. 99–841 and Statement by President, see 1986 U.S. Code Cong. and Adm. News, p. 4075.

1990 Acts. House Report No. 101–681(I), see 1990 U.S. Code Cong. and Adm. News, p. 6472.

1994 Acts. House Report No. 103–835, see 1994 U.S. Code Cong. and Adm. News, p. 3340.

2005 Acts. House Report No. 109–31(Part I), see 2005 U.S. Code Cong. and Adm. News, p. 88.

Legislative Statements

Section 522 of the House amendment represents a compromise on the issue of exemptions between the position taken in the House bill, and that taken in the Senate amendment. Dollar amounts specified in section 522(d) of the House bill have been reduced from amounts as contained in H.R. 8200 as passed by the House. The States may, by passing a law, determine whether the Federal exemptions will apply as an alternative to State exemptions in bankruptcy cases.

Section 522(c)(1) tracks the House bill and provides that dischargeable tax claims may not be collected out of exempt property.

Section 522(f)(2) is derived from the Senate amendment restricting the debtor to avoidance of nonpossessory, nonpurchase money security interests.

Exemptions: Section 522(c)(1) of the House amendment adopts a provision contained in the House bill that dischargeable taxes cannot be collected from exempt assets. This changes present law, which allows collection of dischargeable taxes from exempt property, a rule followed in the Senate amendment. Nondischargeable taxes, however, will continue to the [be] collectable [sic] out of exempt property. It is anticipated that in the next session Congress will review the exemptions from levy currently contained in the Internal Revenue Code [Title 26] with a view to increasing the exemptions to more realistic levels.

References in Text

The Federal Rules of Bankruptcy Procedure, referred to in subsec. (b), are set out in the Appendix to this title.

Section 401, 403, 408, 408A, 414, 457, or 501(a) of the Internal Revenue Code of 1986, referred to in subsecs. (b)(2)(C), (4)(C), (D)(ii)(I), (d)(12), is classified to 26 U.S.C.A. § 401, 403, 408, 408A, 414, 457, or 501(a).

Section 7805 of the Internal Revenue Code of 1986, referred to in subsec. (b)(4)(A), (B), is 26 U.S.C.A. § 7805.

The Internal Revenue Code of 1986, referred to in subsec. (b)(4)(B)(ii)(I), (II), is classified to Title 26 of the Code.

Section 402(c) of the Internal Revenue Code of 1986, referred to in subsec. (b)(4)(D)(i), is 26 U.S.C.A. § 402(c).

Section 401(a), 403(a), 403(b), or 408, of the Internal Revenue Code of 1986, referred to in subsec. (d)(10)(E)(iii), is classified to 26 U.S.C.A. § 401(a), 403(a), 403(b), or 408.

Section 408 or 408A of the Internal Revenue Code of 1986, referred to in subsec. (n), is classified to 26 U.S.C.A. § 408 or 408A.

Section 402(c), 402(e)(6), 403(a)(4), 403(a)(5), and 403(b)(8) of the Internal Revenue Code of 1986, referred to in subsec. (n), are classified to 26 U.S.C.A. §§ 402(c), 402(e)(6), 403(a)(4), 403(a)(5), and 403(b)(8).

Section 3(a)(47) of the Securities Exchange Act of 1934, referred to in subsec. (q)(1)(B)(i), is June 6, 1934, c. 404, Title I, § 3(a)(47), 48 Stat. 882, as amended, which is classified to 15 U.S.C.A. § 78c(a)(47).

Section 12 or 15(d) of the Securities Exchange Act of 1934, referred to in subsec. (q)(1)(B)(ii), is June 6, 1934, c. 404, Title I, § 12 or 15, 48 Stat. 892 or 895, as amended, which is classified to 15 U.S.C.A. § 78*l* or 15 U.S.C.A. § 78*o*.

Section 6 of the Securities Act of 1933, referred to in subsec. (q)(1)(B)(ii), is Act May 27, 1933, c. 38, Title I, § 6, 48 Stat. 78, which is classified to 15 U.S.C.A. § 77f.

Codifications

Section 501(d)(12)(B)(ii) of Pub.L. 103–394, which directed the amendment of subsec. (d)(10)(E)(iii) of this section by substituting "Internal Revenue Code of 1986" for "Internal Revenue Code of 1954 (26 U.S.C. 401(a), 403(a), 403(b), 408, or 409)", was executed by substituting "Internal Revenue Code of 1986" for "Internal Revenue Code of 1986 (26 U.S.C. 401(a), 403(a), 403(b), 408, or 409)", as the probable intent of Congress.

Effective and Applicability Provisions

2007 Acts. Increase of dollar amounts by Judicial Conference of the United States by notice published Feb. 14, 2007, 72 F.R. 7082 effective April 1, 2007, and increase not applicable to cases commenced before the effective date of the adjustments, i.e., April 1, 2007. See Adjustment of Dollar Amounts notes under 11 U.S.C.A. § 104 and this section.

2005 Acts. Amendments by Pub.L. 109–8 effective 180 days after Apr. 20, 2005, with amendments by sections 216, 224(a), (e)(1), 307, and 313(a) of Pub.L. 109–8 not applicable with respect to cases commenced under this title before such effective date, except as otherwise provided, and amendments by sections 308 and 322(a) of Pub.L. 109–8 applicable with respect to cases commenced under this title on or after Apr. 20, 2005, see Pub.L. 109–8, § 1501, set out as a note under 11 U.S.C.A. § 101.

2004 Acts. Adjustment of dollar amounts by Judicial Conference of the United States by notice dated Feb. 18, 2004, 69 F.R. 8482 effective April 1, 2004, and adjustment not applicable to cases commenced before the effective date of the adjustments, i.e., April 1, 2004. See Adjustment of Dollar Amounts notes under 11 U.S.C.A. § 104 and this section.

2001 Acts. Adjustment of dollar amounts by Judicial Conference of the United States by notice dated Feb. 20, 2001, 66 F.R. 10910 effective April 1, 2001, and adjustment not applicable to cases commenced before the effective date of the adjustments, i.e., April 1, 2001. See Adjustment of Dollar Amounts notes under 11 U.S.C.A. § 104 and this section.

1998 Acts. Adjustment of dollar amounts by Judicial Conference of the United States by notice dated Feb. 3, 1998, 63 F.R. 7179 effective April 1, 1998, and adjustment not applicable to cases commenced before the effective date of the adjustments, i.e., April 1, 1998. See Adjustment of Dollar Amounts notes under 11 U.S.C.A. § 104 and this section.

1994 Acts. Amendments by Pub.L. 103–394 effective on Oct. 22, 1994, and not to apply with respect to cases commenced under Title 11 of the United States Code before Oct. 22, 1994, see section 702 of Pub.L. 103–394, set out as a note under section 101 of this title.

1986 Acts. Amendment by Pub.L. 99–554 effective 30 days after Oct. 27, 1986, except as otherwise provided for, see section 302(a) of Pub.L. 99–554, set out as a note under section 581 of Title 28, Judiciary and Judicial Procedure.

1984 Acts. Amendment by Pub.L. 98–353 effective with respect to cases filed 90 days after July 10, 1984, see section 552(a), formerly 553(a) of Pub.L. 98–353, set out as a note under section 101 of this title.

Separability of Provisions

If any provision of or amendment made by Pub.L. 103–394 or the application of such provision or amendment to any person or circumstance is held to be unconstitutional, the remaining provisions of and amendments made by Pub.L. 103–394 and the application of such provisions and amendments to any person or circumstance shall not be affected thereby, see section 701 of Pub.L. 103–394, set out as a note under section 101 of this title.

Adjustment of Dollar Amounts

For adjustment of dollar amounts specified in subsecs. (d)(1) to (6), (8), (11)(D), (f)(3), (4), (n), (p), (q) of this section by the Judicial Conference of the United States, effective Apr. 1, 2007, see note set out under 11 U.S.C.A. § 104 of this title.

By notice dated Feb. 14, 2007, 72 F.R. 7082, the Judicial Conference of the United States adjusted the dollar amounts in provisions specified in subsecs. (d)(1) to (6), (8), (11)(D), (f)(3), (4), (n), (p), (q) of this section, effective Apr. 1, 2007, as follows:

In subsec. (d)(1) adjusted $18,450 to $20,200.

In subsec. (d)(2) adjusted $2,950 to $3,225.

In subsec. (d)(3) adjusted $475 to $525 and $9,850 to $10,775.

In subsec. (d)(4) adjusted $1,225 to $1,350.

In subsec. (d)(5) adjusted $975 to $1,075, and $9,250 to $10,125.

In subsec. (d)(6) adjusted $1,850 to $2,025.

In subsec. (d)(8) adjusted $9,850 to $10,775.

In subsec. (d)(11)(D) adjusted $18,450 to $20,200.

In subsec. (f)(3) adjusted $5,000 to $5,475.

In subsec. (f)(4) adjusted $500 (each time it appears) to $550 (each time it appears).

In subsec. (n) adjusted $1,000,000 to $1,095,000.

In subsec. (p) adjusted $125,000 to $136,875.

In subsec. (q) adjusted $125,000 to $136,875.

By notice dated Feb. 18, 2004, 69 F.R. 8482, the Judicial Conference of the United States adjusted the dollar amounts in provisions specified in subsec. (d)(1) to (6), (8), (11)(D) of this section, effective Apr. 1, 2004, as follows:

In subsec. (d)(1) adjusted $17,425 to $18,450.

In subsec. (d)(2) adjusted $2,775 to $2,950.

In subsec. (d)(3) adjusted $450 to $475 and $9,300 to $9,850.

In subsec. (d)(4) adjusted $1,150 to $1,225.

In subsec. (d)(5) adjusted $925 to $975, and $8,725 to $9,250.

In subsec. (d)(6) adjusted $1,750 to $1,850.

In subsec. (d)(8) adjusted $9,300 to $9,850.

In subsec. (d)(11)(D) adjusted $17,425 to $18,450.

By notice dated Feb. 20, 2001, 66 F.R. 10910, the Judicial Conference of the United States adjusted the dollar amounts in provisions specified in subsec. (d)(1) to (6), (8), (11)(D) of this section, effective Apr. 1, 2001, as follows:

In subsec. (d)(1) adjusted $16,150 to $17,425.

In subsec. (d)(2) adjusted $2,575 to $2,775.

In subsec. (d)(3) adjusted $425 to $450 and $8,625 to $9,300.

In subsec. (d)(4) adjusted $1,075 to $1,150.

In subsec. (d)(5) adjusted $850 to $925, and $8,075 to $8,725.

In subsec. (d)(6) adjusted $1,625 to $1,750.

In subsec. (d)(8) adjusted $8,625 to $9,300.

In subsec. (d)(11)(D) adjusted $16,150 to $17,425.

By notice dated Feb. 3, 1998, 63 F.R. 7179, the Judicial Conference of the United States adjusted the dollar amounts in provisions specified in subsec. (d)(1) to (6), (8), (11)(D) of this section, effective Apr. 1, 1998, as follows:

In subsec. (d)(1) adjusted $15,000 to $16,150.

In subsec. (d)(2) adjusted $2,400 to $2,575.

In subsec. (d)(3) adjusted $400 to $425 and $8,000 to $8,625.

In subsec. (d)(4) adjusted $1,000 to $1,075.

In subsec. (d)(5) adjusted $800 to $850 and $7,500 to $8,075.

In subsec. (d)(6) adjusted $1,500 to $1,625.

In subsec. (d)(8) adjusted $8,000 to $8,625.

In subsec. (d)(11)(D) adjusted $15,000 to $16,150.

CROSS REFERENCES

Allowance of claims or interests, see 11 USCA § 502.

Automatic preservation of avoided transfer, see 11 USCA § 551.

Effect of dismissal, see 11 USCA § 349.

Election to terminate debtor's taxable year for purposes of Internal Revenue Code not available to debtor with no assets other than property treated as exempt under this section, see 26 USCA § 1398.

Exempt property as including property treated as exempt under this section for purposes of Federal Debt Collection Act, see 28 USCA § 3014.

Insolvent as meaning financial condition wherein entity's debts are greater than entity's property exclusive of property that may be exempted under this section, see 11 USCA § 101.

Involuntary cases and future adjustments, see 11 USCA § 104.

Penalty for persons who negligently or fraudulently prepare bankruptcy petitions and exempt funds, see 11 USCA § 110.

Postpetition effect of security interest, see 11 USCA § 552.

Property claimed as exempt, see Official Bankr. Form 6, 11 USCA.

Property exempt under this section not subject to enforcement of withdrawal liability for purposes of Employee Retirement Income Security Act Program, see 29 USCA § 1405.

Provisions in plan for use, sale or lease of exempt property, see 11 USCA § 1123.

Redemption, see 11 USCA § 722.

Reduction in basis not allowed for property exempt under this section for purposes of Internal Revenue Code, see 26 USCA § 1017.

Turnover of property to estate, see 11 USCA § 542.

§ 523. Exceptions to discharge

(a) A discharge under section 727, 1141, 1228(a), 1228(b), or 1328(b) of this title does not discharge an individual debtor from any debt—

(1) for a tax or a customs duty—

(A) of the kind and for the periods specified in section 507(a)(3) or 507(a)(8) of this title, whether or not a claim for such tax was filed or allowed;

(B) with respect to which a return, or equivalent report or notice, if required—

(i) was not filed or given; or

(ii) was filed or given after the date on which such return, report, or notice was last due, under applicable law or under any extension, and after two years before the date of the filing of the petition; or

(C) with respect to which the debtor made a fraudulent return or willfully attempted in any manner to evade or defeat such tax;

(2) for money, property, services, or an extension, renewal, or refinancing of credit, to the extent obtained by—

(A) false pretenses, a false representation, or actual fraud, other than a statement respecting the debtor's or an insider's financial condition;

(B) use of a statement in writing—

(i) that is materially false;

(ii) respecting the debtor's or an insider's financial condition;

(iii) on which the creditor to whom the debtor is liable for such money, property, services, or credit reasonably relied; and

(iv) that the debtor caused to be made or published with intent to deceive; or

(C)(i) for purposes of subparagraph (A)—

(I) consumer debts owed to a single creditor and aggregating more than $550 [1] for luxury goods or services incurred by an individual debtor on or within 90 days before the order for relief under this title are presumed to be nondischargeable; and

(II) cash advances aggregating more than $825 [1] that are extensions of consumer credit under an open end credit plan obtained by an individual debtor on or within 70 days before the order for relief under this title, are presumed to be nondischargeable; and

(ii) for purposes of this subparagraph—

(I) the terms "consumer", "credit", and "open end credit plan" have the same meanings as in section 103 of the Truth in Lending Act; and

(II) the term "luxury goods or services" does not include goods or services reasonably necessary for the support or maintenance of the debtor or a dependent of the debtor.

(3) neither listed nor scheduled under section 521(1) of this title, with the name, if known to the debtor, of the creditor to whom such debt is owed, in time to permit—

(A) if such debt is not of a kind specified in paragraph (2), (4), or (6) of this subsection, timely filing of a proof of claim, unless such creditor had notice or actual knowledge of the case in time for such timely filing; or

(B) if such debt is of a kind specified in paragraph (2), (4), or (6) of this subsection, timely filing of a proof of claim and timely request for a determination of dischargeability of such debt under one of such paragraphs, unless such creditor had notice or actual knowledge of the case in time for such timely filing and request;

(4) for fraud or defalcation while acting in a fiduciary capacity, embezzlement, or larceny;

(5) for a domestic support obligation;

(6) for willful and malicious injury by the debtor to another entity or to the property of another entity;

(7) to the extent such debt is for a fine, penalty, or forfeiture payable to and for the benefit of a governmental unit, and is not compensation for actual pecuniary loss, other than a tax penalty—

(A) relating to a tax of a kind not specified in paragraph (1) of this subsection; or

(B) imposed with respect to a transaction or event that occurred before three years before the date of the filing of the petition;

(8) unless excepting such debt from discharge under this paragraph would impose an undue hardship on the debtor and the debtor's dependents, for—

(A)(i) an educational benefit overpayment or loan made, insured, or guaranteed by a governmental unit, or made under any program funded in whole or in part by a governmental unit or nonprofit institution; or

(ii) an obligation to repay funds received as an educational benefit, scholarship, or stipend; or

(B) any other educational loan that is a qualified education loan, as defined in section 221(d)(1) of the Internal Revenue Code of 1986, incurred by a debtor who is an individual;

(9) for death or personal injury caused by the debtor's operation of a motor vehicle, vessel, or aircraft if such operation was unlawful because the debtor was intoxicated from using alcohol, a drug, or another substance;

(10) that was or could have been listed or scheduled by the debtor in a prior case concerning the debtor under this title or under the Bankruptcy Act in which the debtor waived discharge, or was denied a discharge under section 727(a)(2), (3), (4), (5), (6), or (7) of this title, or under section 14c(1), (2), (3), (4), (6), or (7) of such Act;

(11) provided in any final judgment, unreviewable order, or consent order or decree entered in any court of the United States or of any State, issued by a Federal depository institutions regulatory agency, or contained in any settlement agreement entered into by the debtor, arising from any act of fraud or defalcation while acting in a fiduciary capacity committed with respect to any depository institution or insured credit union;

(12) for malicious or reckless failure to fulfill any commitment by the debtor to a Federal depository institutions regulatory agency to maintain the capital of an insured depository institution, except that this paragraph shall not extend any such commitment which would otherwise be terminated due to any act of such agency; or

(13) for any payment of an order of restitution issued under title 18, United States Code;

(14) incurred to pay a tax to the United States that would be nondischargeable pursuant to paragraph (1);

(14A) incurred to pay a tax to a governmental unit, other than the United States, that would be nondischargeable under paragraph (1);

(14B) incurred to pay fines or penalties imposed under Federal election law;

(15) to a spouse, former spouse, or child of the debtor and not of the kind described in paragraph (5) that is incurred by the debtor in the course of a divorce or separation or in connection with a separation agreement, divorce decree or other order of a court of record, or a determination made in accordance with State or territorial law by a governmental unit;

(16) for a fee or assessment that becomes due and payable after the order for relief to a membership association with respect to the debtor's interest in a unit that has condominium ownership, in a share of a cooperative corporation, or a lot in a homeowners association, for as long as the debtor or the trustee has a legal, equitable, or possessory ownership interest in such unit, such corporation, or such lot, but nothing in this paragraph shall except from discharge the debt of a debtor for a membership association fee or assessment for a period arising before entry of the order for relief in a pending or subsequent bankruptcy case;

(17) for a fee imposed on a prisoner by any court for the filing of a case, motion, complaint, or appeal, or for other costs and expenses assessed with respect to such filing, regardless of an assertion of poverty by the debtor under subsection (b) or (f)(2) of section 1915 of title 28 (or a similar non–Federal law), or the debtor's status as a prisoner, as defined in section 1915(h) of title 28 (or a similar non–Federal law);

(18) owed to a pension, profit-sharing, stock bonus, or other plan established under section 401,

403, 408, 408A, 414, 457, or 501(c) of the Internal Revenue Code of 1986, under—

(A) a loan permitted under section 408(b)(1) of the Employee Retirement Income Security Act of 1974, or subject to section 72(p) of the Internal Revenue Code of 1986; or

(B) a loan from a thrift savings plan permitted under subchapter III of chapter 84 of title 5, that satisfies the requirements of section 8433(g) of such title;

but nothing in this paragraph may be construed to provide that any loan made under a governmental plan under section 414(d), or a contract or account under section 403(b), of the Internal Revenue Code of 1986 constitutes a claim or a debt under this title; or

(19) that—

(A) is for—

(i) the violation of any of the Federal securities laws (as that term is defined in section 3(a)(47) of the Securities Exchange Act of 1934), any of the State securities laws, or any regulation or order issued under such Federal or State securities laws; or

(ii) common law fraud, deceit, or manipulation in connection with the purchase or sale of any security; and

(B) results, before, on, or after the date on which the petition was filed, from—

(i) any judgment, order, consent order, or decree entered in any Federal or State judicial or administrative proceeding;

(ii) any settlement agreement entered into by the debtor; or

(iii) any court or administrative order for any damages, fine, penalty, citation, restitutionary payment, disgorgement payment, attorney fee, cost, or other payment owed by the debtor.

For purposes of this subsection, the term "return" means a return that satisfies the requirements of applicable nonbankruptcy law (including applicable filing requirements). Such term includes a return prepared pursuant to section 6020(a) of the Internal Revenue Code of 1986, or similar State or local law, or a written stipulation to a judgment or a final order entered by a nonbankruptcy tribunal, but does not include a return made pursuant to section 6020(b) of the Internal Revenue Code of 1986, or a similar State or local law.

(b) Notwithstanding subsection (a) of this section, a debt that was excepted from discharge under subsection (a)(1), (a)(3), or (a)(8) of this section, under section 17a(1), 17a(3), or 17a(5) of the Bankruptcy Act, under section 439A of the Higher Education Act of 1965, or under section 733(g) of the Public Health Service Act in a prior case concerning the debtor under this title, or under the Bankruptcy Act, is dischargeable in a case under this title unless, by the terms of subsection (a) of this section, such debt is not dischargeable in the case under this title.

(c)(1) Except as provided in subsection (a)(3)(B) of this section, the debtor shall be discharged from a debt of a kind specified in paragraph (2), (4), or (6) of subsection (a) of this section, unless, on request of the creditor to whom such debt is owed, and after notice and a hearing, the court determines such debt to be excepted from discharge under paragraph (2), (4), or (6), as the case may be, of subsection (a) of this section.

(2) Paragraph (1) shall not apply in the case of a Federal depository institutions regulatory agency seeking, in its capacity as conservator, receiver, or liquidating agent for an insured depository institution, to recover a debt described in subsection (a)(2), (a)(4), (a)(6), or (a)(11) owed to such institution by an institution-affiliated party unless the receiver, conservator, or liquidating agent was appointed in time to reasonably comply, or for a Federal depository institutions regulatory agency acting in its corporate capacity as a successor to such receiver, conservator, or liquidating agent to reasonably comply, with subsection (a)(3)(B) as a creditor of such institution-affiliated party with respect to such debt.

(d) If a creditor requests a determination of dischargeability of a consumer debt under subsection (a)(2) of this section, and such debt is discharged, the court shall grant judgment in favor of the debtor for the costs of, and a reasonable attorney's fee for, the proceeding if the court finds that the position of the creditor was not substantially justified, except that the court shall not award such costs and fees if special circumstances would make the award unjust.

(e) Any institution-affiliated party of an insured depository institution shall be considered to be acting in a fiduciary capacity with respect to the purposes of subsection (a)(4) or (11).

(Pub.L. 95–598, Nov. 6, 1978, 92 Stat. 2590; Pub.L. 96–56, § 3, Aug. 14, 1979, 93 Stat. 387; Pub.L. 97–35, Title XXIII, § 2334(b), Aug. 13, 1981, 95 Stat. 863; Pub.L. 98–353, Title III, §§ 307, 371, 454, July 10, 1984, 98 Stat. 353, 364, 375; Pub.L. 99–554, Title II, §§ 257(n), 281, 283(j), Oct. 27, 1986, 100 Stat. 3115 to 3117; Pub.L. 101–581, § 2(a), Nov. 15, 1990, 104 Stat. 2865; Pub.L. 101–647, Title XXV, § 2522(a), Title XXXI, § 3102(a), Title XXXVI, § 3621, Nov. 29, 1990, 104 Stat. 4865, 4916, 4964; Pub.L. 103–322, Title XXXII, § 320934, Sept. 13, 1994, 108 Stat. 2135; Pub.L. 103–394, Title II, § 221, Title III, §§ 304(e), (h)(3), 306, 309, Title V, § 501(d)(13), Oct. 22, 1994, 108 Stat. 4129, 4133 to 4135, 4137, 4145; Pub.L. 104–134, Title I, § 101[(a)][Title VIII, § 804(b)], Apr. 26, 1996, 110 Stat. 1321–74; renumbered Title I Pub.L. 104–140, § 1(a), May 2, 1996, 110 Stat. 1327, and amended Pub.L. 104–193, Title III, § 374(a), Aug. 22, 1996, 110 Stat. 2255; Pub.L. 105–244, Title IX, § 971(a), Oct. 7, 1998, 112 Stat. 1837; Pub.L. 107–204, Title VIII, § 803, July 30, 2002, 116 Stat. 801; Pub.L. 109–8, Title II, §§ 215, 220,

224(c), Title III, §§ 301, 310, 314(a), Title IV, § 412, Title VII, § 714, Title XII, §§ 1209, 1235, Title XIV, § 1404(a), Title XV, § 1502(a)(2), Apr. 20, 2005, 119 Stat. 54, 59, 64, 75, 84, 88, 107, 128, 194, 204, 215, 216.)

1 Dollar amount as adjusted by the Judicial Conference of the United States. See Adjustment of Dollar Amounts notes set out under this section and 11 U.S.C.A. § 104.

HISTORICAL AND STATUTORY NOTES

Revision Notes and Legislative Reports

1978 Acts. This section specifies which of the debtor's debts are not discharged in a bankruptcy case, and certain procedures for effectuating the section. The provision in Bankruptcy Act § 17c [section § 35(c) of former Title 11] granting the bankruptcy courts jurisdiction to determine dischargeability is deleted as unnecessary, in view of the comprehensive grant of jurisdiction prescribed in proposed 28 U.S.C. 1334(b), which is adequate to cover the full jurisdiction that the bankruptcy courts have today over dischargeability and related issues under Bankruptcy Act § 17c [section 35(c) of former Title 11]. The Rules of Bankruptcy Procedure will specify, as they do today, who may request determinations of dischargeability, subject, of course, to proposed 11 U.S.C. 523(c), and when such a request may be made. Proposed 11 U.S.C. 350, providing for reopening of cases, provides one possible procedure for a determination of dischargeability and related issues after a case is closed.

Subsection (a) lists nine kinds of debts excepted from discharge. Taxes that are excepted from discharge are set forth in paragraph (1). These include claims against the debtor which receive priority in the second, third and sixth categories (§ 507(a)(3)(B) and (C) and (6)). These categories include taxes for which the tax authority failed to file a claim against the estate or filed its claim late. Whether or not the taxing authority's claim is secured will also not affect the claim's nondischargeability if the tax liability in question is otherwise entitled to priority.

Also included in the nondischargeable debts are taxes for which the debtor had not filed a required return as of the petition date, or for which a return had been filed beyond its last permitted due date (§ 523(a)(1)(B)). For this purpose, the date of the tax year to which the return relates is immaterial. The late return rule applies, however, only to the late returns filed within three years before the petition was filed, and to late returns filed after the petition in title 11 was filed. For this purpose, the taxable year in question need not be one or more of the three years immediately preceding the filing of the petition.

Tax claims with respect to which the debtor filed a fraudulent return, entry or invoice, or fraudulently attempted to evade or defeat any tax (§ 523(a)(1)(C)) are included. The date of the taxable year with regard to which the fraud occurred is immaterial.

Also included are tax payments due under an agreement for deferred payment of taxes, which a debtor had entered into with the Internal Revenue Service (or State or local tax authority) before the filing of the petition and which relate to a prepetition tax liability (§ 523(a)(1)(D)) are also nondischargeable. This classification applies only to tax claims which would have received priority under section 507(a) if the taxpayer had filed a title 11 petition on the date on which the deferred payment agreement was entered into. This rule also applies only to installment payments which become due during and after the commencement of the title 11 case. Payments which had become due within one year before the filing of the petition receive sixth priority, and will be nondischargeable under the general rule of section 523(a)(1)(A).

The above categories of nondischargeability apply to customs duties as well as to taxes.

Paragraph (2) provides that as under Bankruptcy Act § 17a(2) [section 35(a)(2) of former Title 11], a debt for obtaining money, property, services, or a refinancing extension or renewal of credit by false pretenses, a false representation, or actual fraud, or by use of a statement in writing respecting the debtor's financial condition that is materially false, on which the creditor reasonably relied, and which the debtor made or published with intent to deceive, is excepted from discharge. This provision is modified only slightly from current section 17a(2) [section 35(a)(2) of former Title 11]. First, "actual fraud" is added as a ground for exception from discharge. Second, the creditor must not only have relied on a false statement in writing, but the reliance must have been reasonable. This codifies case law construing present section 17a(2) [section 35(a)(2) of former Title 11]. Third, the phrase "in any manner whatsoever" that appears in current law after "made or published" is deleted as unnecessary, the word "published" is used in the same sense that it is used in defamation cases.

Unscheduled debts are excepted from discharge under paragraph (3). The provision, derived from section 17a(3) [section 35(a)(3) of former Title 11], follows current law, but clarifies some uncertainties generated by the case law construing 17a(3) [section 35(a)(3) of former Title 11]. The debt is excepted from discharge if it was not scheduled in time to permit timely action by the creditor to protect his rights, unless the creditor had notice or actual knowledge of the case.

Paragraph (4) excepts debts for fraud incurred by the debtor while acting in a fiduciary capacity or for defalcation, embezzlement, or misappropriation.

Paragraph (5) provides that debts for willful and malicious conversion or injury by the debtor to another entity or the property of another entity are nondischargeable. Under this paragraph "willful" means deliberate or intentional. To the extent that *Tinker v. Colwell,* 139 U.S. 473 (1902) [24 S.Ct. 505, 48 L.Ed. 754, 11 Am.Bankr.Rep. 568], held that a less strict standard is intended, and to the extent that other cases have relied on *Tinker* to apply a "reckless disregard" standard, they are overruled.

Paragraph (6) excepts from discharge debts to a spouse, former spouse, or child of the debtor for alimony to, maintenance for, or support of the spouse or child. This language, in combination with the repeal of section 456(b) of the Social Security Act (42 U.S.C. 656(b)) [section 656(b) of Title 42, The Public Health and Welfare] by section 326 of the bill, will apply to make nondischargeable only alimony, maintenance, or support owed directly to a spouse or dependent. What constitutes alimony, maintenance, or support, will be determined under the bankruptcy law, not State law. Thus, cases such as *In re Waller,* 494 F.2d 447 (6th Cir. 1974), are overruled, and the result in cases such as *Fife v. Fife,* 1 Utah 2d 281, 265 P.2d 642 (1952) is followed. The proviso, however, makes nondischargeable any debts resulting from an agreement by the debtor to hold the debtor's spouse harmless on joint debts, to the extent that the agreement is in payment of alimony, maintenance, or support of the spouse, as determined under bankruptcy law considerations as to whether a particular agreement to pay money to a spouse is actually alimony or a property settlement.

Paragraph (7) makes nondischargeable certain liabilities for penalties including tax penalties if the underlying tax with respect to which the penalty was imposed is also nondischargeable (sec. 523(a)(7)). These latter liabilities cover those which, but are penal in nature, as distinct from so-called "pecuniary loss" penalties which, in the case of taxes, involve basically the collection of a tax under the label of a "penalty." This provision differs from the bill as introduced, which did not link the nondischarge of a tax penalty with the treatment of the underlying tax. The amended provision reflects the existing position of the Internal Revenue Service as to tax penalties imposed by the Internal Revenue Code [Title 26] (Rev.Rul. 68–574, 1968–2 C.B. 595).

Paragraph (8) follows generally current law and excerpts [sic] from discharge student loans until such loans have been due and owing for five years. Such loans include direct student loans as well as insured and guaranteed loans. This provision is intended to be self-executing and the lender or institution is not required to file a complaint to determine the nondischargeability of any student loan.

Paragraph (9) excepts from discharge debts that the debtor owed before a previous bankruptcy case concerning the debtor in which the debtor was denied a discharge other than on the basis of the six-year bar.

Subsection (b) of this section permits discharge in a bankruptcy case of an unscheduled debt from a prior case. This provision is carried over from Bankruptcy Act § 17b [section 35(b) of former Title 11]. The result dictated by the subsection would probably not be different if the subsection were not included. It is included nevertheless for clarity.

Subsection (c) requires a creditor who is owed a debt that may be excepted from discharge under paragraph (2), (4), or (5), (false statements, defalcation or larceny misappropriation, or willful and malicious injury) to initiate proceedings in the bankruptcy court for an exception to discharge. If the creditor does not act, the debt is discharged. This provision does not change current law.

Subsection (d) is new. It provides protection to a consumer debtor that dealt honestly with a creditor who sought to have a debt excepted from discharge on the ground of falsity in the incurring of the debt. The debtor may be awarded costs and a reasonable attorney's fee for the proceeding to determine the dischargeability of a debt under subsection (a)(2), if the court finds that the proceeding was frivolous or not brought by its creditor in good faith.

The purpose of the provision is to discourage creditors from initiating proceedings to obtaining a false financial statement exception to discharge in the hope of obtaining a settlement from an honest debtor anxious to save attorney's fees. Such practices impair the debtor's fresh start and are contrary to the spirit of the bankruptcy laws. Senate Report 95–989.

Subsection (a) lists eight kinds of debts excepted from discharge. Taxes that are entitled to priority are excepted from discharge under paragraph (1). In addition, taxes with respect to which the debtor made a fraudulent return or willfully attempted to evade or defeat, or with respect to which a return (if required) was not filed or was not filed after the due date and after one year before the bankruptcy case are excepted from discharge. If the taxing authority's claim has been disallowed, then it would be barred by the more modern rules of collateral estoppel from reasserting that claim against the debtor after the case was closed. See Plumb, The Tax Recommendations of the Commission on the Bankruptcy Laws: Tax Procedures, 88 Harv.L.Rev. 1360, 1388 (1975).

As under Bankruptcy Act § 17a(2) [section 35(a)(2) of former Title 11], a debt for obtaining money, property, services, or an extension or renewal of credit by false pretenses, a false representation, or actual fraud, or by use of a statement in writing respecting the debtor's financial condition that is materially false, on which the creditor reasonably relied, and that the debtor made or published with intent to deceive, is excepted from discharge. This provision is modified only slightly from current section 17a(2). First, "actual fraud" is added as a grounds for exception from discharge. Second, the creditor must not only have relied on a false statement in writing, the reliance must have been reasonable. This codifies case law construing this provision. Third, the phrase "in any manner whatsoever" that appears in current law after "made or published" is deleted as unnecessary. The word "published" is used in the same sense that it is used in slander actions.

Unscheduled debts are excepted from discharge under paragraph (3). The provision, derived from section 17a(3) [section 35(a)(3) of former Title 11], follows current law, but clarifies some uncertainties generated by the case law construing 17a(3). The debt is excepted from discharge if it was not scheduled in time to permit timely action by the creditor to protect his rights, unless the creditor had notice or actual knowledge of the case.

Paragraph (4) excepts debts for embezzlement or larceny. The deletion of willful and malicious conversion from § 17a(2) [section 35(a)(2) of former Title 11] of the Bankruptcy Act is not intended to effect a substantive change. The intent is to include in the category of non-dischargeable debts a conversion under which the debtor willfully and maliciously intends to borrow property for a short period of time with no intent to inflict injury but on which injury is in fact inflicted.

Paragraph (5) excepts from discharge debts to a spouse, former spouse, or child of the debtor for alimony to, maintenance for, or support of, the spouse or child. This language, in combination with the repeal of section 456(b) of the Social Security Act (42 U.S.C. 656(b)) [former section 656(b) of Title 42, The Public Health and Welfare] by section 327 of the bill, will apply to make nondischargeable only alimony, maintenance, or support owed directly to a spouse or dependent. See Hearings, pt. 2, at 942. What constitutes alimony, maintenance, or support, will be determined under the bankruptcy laws, not State law. Thus, cases such as *In re Waller,* 494 F.2d 447 (6th Cir. 1974); Hearings, pt. 3, at 1308–10, are overruled, and the result in cases such as *Fife v. Fife,* 1 Utah 2d 281, 265 P.2d 642 (1952) is followed. This provision will, however, make nondischargeable any debts resulting from an agreement by the debtor to hold the debtor's spouse harmless on joint debts, to the extent that the agreement is in payment of alimony, maintenance, or support of the spouse, as determined under bankruptcy law considerations that are similar to considerations of whether a particular agreement to pay money to a spouse is actually alimony or a property settlement. See Hearings, pt. 3, at 1287–1290.

Paragraph (6) excepts debts for willful and malicious injury by the debtor to another person or to the property of another person. Under this paragraph, "willful" means deliberate or intentional. To the extent that *Tinker v. Colwell,* 193 U.S. 473 (1902) [24 S.Ct. 505, 48 L.Ed. 754, 11 Am.Bankr. Rep. 568], held that a looser standard is intended, and to the extent that other cases have relied on *Tinker* to apply a "reckless disregard" standard, they are overruled.

Paragraph (7) excepts from discharge a debt for a fine, penalty, or forfeiture payable to and for the benefit of a governmental unit, that is not compensation for actual pecuniary loss.

Paragraph (8) [now (9)] excepts from discharge debts that the debtor owed before a previous bankruptcy case concerning the debtor in which the debtor was denied a discharge other than on the basis of the six-year bar.

Subsection (b) of this section permits discharge in a bankruptcy case of an unscheduled debt from a prior case. This provision is carried over from Bankruptcy Act § 17b [section 35(b) of former Title 11]. The result dictated by the subsection would probably not be different if the subsection were not included. It is included nevertheless for clarity.

Subsection (c) requires a creditor who is owed a debt that may be expected from discharge under paragraph (2), (4), or (6) (false statements, embezzlement or larceny, or willful and malicious injury) to initiate proceedings in the bankruptcy court for an exception to discharge. If the creditor does not act, the debt is discharged. This provision does not change current law.

Subsection (d) is new. It provides protection to a consumer debtor that dealt honestly with a creditor who sought to have a debt excepted from discharge on grounds of falsity in the incurring of the debt. The debtor is entitled to costs of and a reasonable attorney's fee for the proceeding to determine the dischargeability of a debt under subsection (a)(2), if the creditor initiated the proceeding and the debt was determined to be dischargeable. The court is permitted to award any actual pecuniary loss that the debtor may have suffered as a result of the proceeding (such as loss of a day's pay). The purpose of the provision is to discourage creditors from initiating false financial statement exception to discharge actions in the hopes of obtaining a settlement from an honest debtor anxious to save attorney's fees. Such practices impair the debtor's fresh start. House Report No. 95–595.

1979 Acts. Senate Report No. 96–230, see 1979 U.S. Code Cong. and Adm. News, p. 936.

1981 Acts. Senate Report No. 97–139 and House Conference Report No. 97–208, see 1981 U.S. Code Cong. and Adm. News, p. 396.

1984 Acts. Statements by Legislative Leaders, see 1984 U.S. Code Cong. and Adm. News, p. 576.

1986 Acts. House Report No. 99–764 and House Conference Report No. 99–958, see 1986 U.S. Code Cong. and Adm. News, p. 5227.

1990 Acts. House Report No. 101–681(Part I), see 1990 U.S. Code Cong. and Adm. News, p. 6472.

Senate Report No. 101–434, see 1990 U.S. Code Cong. and Adm. News, p. 4065.

1994 Acts. House Report Nos. 103–324 and 103–489, and House Conference Report No. 103–711, see 1994 U.S. Code Cong. and Adm. News, p. 1801.

House Report No. 103–835, see 1994 U.S. Code Cong. and Adm. News, p. 3340.

1996 Acts. House Report No. 104–651 and House Conference Report No. 104–725, see 1996 U.S. Code Cong. and Adm. News, p. 2183.

1998 Acts. House Conference Report No. 105–750, see 1998 U.S. Code Cong. and Adm. News, p. 417.

2002 Acts. House Conference Report No. 107–610 and Statement by President, see 2002 U.S. Code Cong. and Adm. News, p. 542.

2005 Acts. House Report No. 109–31(Part I), see 2005 U.S. Code Cong. and Adm. News, p. 88.

Legislative Statements

Section 523(a)(1) represents a compromise between the position taken in the House bill and the Senate amendment. Section 523(a)(2) likewise represents a compromise between the position taken in the House bill and the Senate amendment with respect to the false financial statement exception to discharge. In order to clarify that a "renewal of credit" includes a "refinancing of credit", explicit reference to a refinancing of credit is made in the preamble to section 523(a)(2). A renewal of credit or refinancing of credit that was obtained by a false financial statement within the terms of section 523(a)(2) is nondischargeable. However, each of the provisions of section 523(a)(2) must be proved. Thus, under section 523(a)(2)(A) a creditor must prove that the debt was obtained by false pretenses, a false representation, or actual fraud, other than a statement respecting the debtor's or an insider's financial condition. Subparagraph (A) is intended to codify current case law e.g., *Neal v. Clark,* 95 U.S. 704 (1887) [24 L.Ed. 586], which interprets "fraud" to mean actual or positive fraud rather than fraud implied in law. Subparagraph (A) is mutually exclusive from subparagraph (B). Subparagraph (B) pertains to the so-called false financial statement. In order for the debt to be nondischargeable, the creditor must prove that the debt was obtained by the use of a statement in writing (i) that is materially false; (ii) respecting the debtor's or an insider's financial condition; (iii) on which the creditor to whom the debtor is liable for obtaining money, property, services, or credit reasonably relied; (iv) that the debtor caused to be made or published with intent to deceive. Section 523(a)(2)(B)(iv) is not intended to change from present law since the statement that the debtor causes to be made or published with the intent to deceive automatically includes a statement that the debtor actually makes or publishes with an intent to deceive. Section 523(a)(2)(B) is explained in the House report. Under section 523(a)(2)(B)(i) a discharge is barred only as to that portion of a loan with respect to which a false financial statement is materially false.

In many cases, a creditor is required by state law to refinance existing credit on which there has been no default. If the creditor does not forfeit remedies or otherwise rely to his detriment on a false financial statement with respect to existing credit, then an extension, renewal, or refinancing of such credit is nondischargeable only to the extent of the new money advanced; on the other hand, if an existing loan is in default or the creditor otherwise reasonably relies to his detriment on a false financial statement with regard to an existing loan, then the entire debt is nondischargeable under section 523(a)(2)(B). This codifies the reasoning expressed by the second circuit in *In re Danns*, 558 F.2d 114 (2d Cir. 1977).

Section 523(a)(3) of the House amendment is derived from the Senate amendment. The provision is intended to overrule *Birkett v. Columbia Bank*, 195 U.S. 345 (1904) [25 S.Ct. 38, 49 L.Ed. 231, 12 Am.Bankr.Rep. 691].

Section 523(a)(4) of the House amendment represents a compromise between the House bill and the Senate amendment.

Section 523(a)(5) is a compromise between the House bill and the Senate amendment. The provision excepts from discharge a debt owed to a spouse, former spouse or child of the debtor, in connection with a separation agreement, divorce decree, or property settlement agreement, for alimony to, maintenance for, or support of such spouse or child but not to the extent that the debt is assigned to another entity. If the debtor has assumed an obligation of the debtor's spouse to a third party in connection with a separation agreement, property settlement agreement, or divorce proceeding, such debt is dischargeable to the extent that payment of the debt by the debtor is not actually in the nature of alimony, maintenance, or support of debtor's spouse, former spouse, or child.

Section 523(a)(6) adopts the position taken in the House bill and rejects the alternative suggested in the Senate amendment. The phrase "willful and malicious injury" covers a willful and malicious conversion.

Section 523(a)(7) of the House amendment adopts the position taken in the Senate amendment and rejects the position taken in the House bill. A penalty relating to a tax cannot be nondischargeable unless the tax itself is nondischargeable.

Section 523(a)(8) represents a compromise between the House bill and the Senate amendment regarding educational loans. This provision is broader than current law which is limited to federally insured loans. Only educational loans owing to a governmental unit or a nonprofit institution of higher education are made nondischargeable under this paragraph.

Section 523(b) is new. The section represents a modification of similar provisions contained in the House bill and the Senate amendment.

Section 523(c) of the House amendment adopts the position taken in the Senate amendment.

Section 523(d) represents a compromise between the position taken in the House bill and the Senate amendment on the issue of attorneys' fees in false financial statement complaints to determine dischargeability. The provision contained in the House bill permitting the court to award damages is eliminated. The court must grant the debtor judgment or a reasonable attorneys' fee unless the granting of judgment would be clearly inequitable.

Nondischargeable debts: The House amendment retains the basic categories of nondischargeable tax liabilities contained in both bills, but restricts the time limits on certain nondischargeable taxes. Under the amendment, nondischargeable taxes cover taxes entitled to priority under section 507(a)(6) of title 11 and, in the case of individual debtors under chapters 7, 11, or 13, tax liabilities with respect to which no required return had been filed or as to which a late return had been filed if the return became last due, including extensions, within 2 years before the date of the petition or became due after the petition or as to which the debtor made a fraudulent return, entry or invoice or fraudulently attempted to evade or defeat the tax.

In the case of individuals in liquidation under chapter 7 or in reorganization under chapter 11 of title 11, section 1141(d)(2) incorporates by reference the exceptions to discharge continued in section 523. Different rules concerning the discharge of taxes where a partnership or corporation reorganizes under chapter 11, apply under section 1141.

The House amendment also deletes the reduction rule contained in section 523(e) of the Senate amendment. Under that rule, the amount of an otherwise nondischargeable tax liability would be reduced by the amount which a governmental tax authority could have collected from the debtor's estate if it had filed a timely claim against the estate but which it did not collect because no such claim was filed. This provision is deleted in order not to effectively compel a tax authority to file claim against the estate in "no asset" cases, along with a dischargeability petition. In no-asset cases, therefore, if the tax authority is not potentially penalized by failing to file a claim, the debtor in such cases will have a better opportunity to choose the prepayment forum, bankruptcy court or the Tax Court, in which to litigate his personal liability for a nondischargeable tax.

The House amendment also adopts the Senate amendment provision limiting the nondischargeability of punitive tax penalties, that is, penalties other than those which represent collection of a principal amount of tax liability through the form of a "penalty." Under the House amendment, tax penalties which are basically punitive in nature are to be nondischargeable only if the penalty is computed by reference to a related tax liability which is nondischargeable or, if the amount of the penalty is not computed by reference to a tax liability, the transaction or event giving rise to the penalty occurred during the 3-year period ending on the date of the petition.

References in Text

Section 6020(a) of the Internal Revenue Code of 1986, referred to in subsec. (a), is classified to 26 U.S.C.A. § 6020(a).

Section 6020(b) of the Internal Revenue Code of 1986, referred to in subsec. (a), is classified to 26 U.S.C.A. § 6020(b).

The Consumer Credit Protection Act, referred to in subsec. (a)(2)(C), is Pub.L. 90–321, May 29, 1968, 82 Stat. 146, as amended, which is classified principally to chapter 41 (section 1601 et seq.) of Title 15, Commerce and Trade. For complete classification of this Act to the Code, see Short Title note set out under section 1601 of Title 15 and Tables.

Section 103 of the Truth in Lending Act, referred to in subsec. (a)(2)(C)(ii)(I), is Pub.L. 90–321, Title I, § 103, May 29, 1968, 82 Stat. 147, as amended, which is classified to 15 U.S.C.A. § 1602.

The Social Security Act, referred to in subsec. (a)(5)(A), (18)(B), is Act Aug. 14, 1935, c. 531, 49 Stat. 620, as amended. Section 408(a)(3) of that Act is classified to section 608(a)(3) of Title 42, The Public Health and Welfare. Part D of Title IV of such Act is classified generally to part D (section 651 et seq.) of subchapter IV of chapter 7 of Title 42. For complete classification of this Act to the Code, see section 1305 of Title 42 and Tables.

Section 221(d)(1) of the Internal Revenue Code of 1986, referred to in subsec. (a)(8)(B), is classified to 26 U.S.C.A. § 221(d)(1).

The Bankruptcy Act, referred to in subsecs. (a)(10) and (b), is Act July 1, 1898, c. 541, 30 Stat. 544, as amended, which was classified generally to former Title 11. Sections 14c and 17a of the Bankruptcy Act were classified to sections 32(c) and 35(a) of former Title 11.

Section 401, 403, 408, 408A, 414, 457, or 501(c) of the Internal Revenue Code of 1986, referred to in subsec. (a)(18), is classified to 26 U.S.C.A. § 401, 403, 408, 408A, 414, 457, or 501(c).

Section 408(b)(1) of the Employee Retirement Income Security Act of 1974, referred to in subsec. (a)(18)(A), is Pub.L. 93–406, Title I, § 408(b)(1), Sept. 2, 1974, 88 Stat. 883, as amended, which is classified to 29 U.S.C.A. § 1108(b)(1).

Section 72(p) of the Internal Revenue Code of 1986, referred to in subsec. (a)(18)(A), is classified to 26 U.S.C.A. § 72(p).

Subchapter III of chapter 84 of title 5, referred to in subsec. (a)(18)(B), is 5 U.S.C.A. § 8431 et seq.

Section 414(d) or section 403(b) of the Internal Revenue Code, referred to in the undesignated paragraph following subsec. (a)(18), is classified to 26 U.S.C.A. § 414(d) or 26 U.S.C.A. § 403(b).

Section 3(a)(47) of the Securities Exchange Act of 1934, referred to in subsec. (a)(19)(A)(i), is section 3(a)(47) of Act June 6, 1934, c. 404, Title I, 48 Stat. 882, as amended, which is classified to 15 U.S.C.A. § 78c(a)(47).

Section 439A of the Higher Education Act of 1965, referred to in subsec. (b), is section 439A of Pub.L. 89–329, Title IV, as added Pub.L. 94–482, Title I, § 127(a), Oct. 12, 1976, 90 Stat. 2141, which was classified to section 1087–3 of Title 20, Education, and was repealed by Pub.L. 95–598, Title III, § 317, Nov. 6, 1978, 92 Stat. 2678.

Section 733 of the Public Health Service Act, referred to in subsec. (b), is section 733 of Act July 1, 1944, c. 373, Title VII as added Oct. 12, 1976, Pub.L. 94–484, Title IV, § 401(b)(3), 90 Stat. 2262, which was classified to section 294f of Title 42, The Public Health and Welfare, and which was repealed by Pub.L. 95–598, Title III, § 327, Nov. 6, 1978, 92 Stat. 2679. A subsec. (g), containing similar provisions, was added to section 733 by Pub.L. 97–35, Title XXVII, § 2730, Aug. 13, 1981, 95 Stat. 919. Section 733 was subsequently omitted in the general revision of subchapter V of chapter 6A of Title 42 by Pub.L. 102–408, Title I, § 102, Oct. 13, 1992, 106 Stat. 1992.

Codifications

Amendment by section 215(3) of Pub.L. 109–8, directing the amendment of par. (15) as added by Public Law 103–394, was executed by amending par. (15) of subsec. (a), as the probable intent of Congress.

Amendment by section 304(e) of Pub.L. 103–394, directing the addition of par. (15), was executed by adding par. (15) to subsec. (a), as the probable intent of Congress.

Pub.L. 101–581 and Pub.L. 101–647, § 3102(a), made identical amendments to subsec. (a)(9) of this section. See 1990 Amendments note set out under this section.

Amendment by section 283(j)(1) of Pub.L. 99–554, which redesignated the second par. (9) of subsec. (a) as (10), has been executed by redesignating as (10), par. (9) as enacted by Pub.L. 95–598 as the probable intent of Congress in view of amendment by section 371(2) of Pub.L. 98–353, which directed the addition of par. (9), as presently set out, to follow par. (8).

Effective and Applicability Provisions

2007 Acts. Increase of dollar amounts by Judicial Conference of the United States by notice published Feb. 14, 2007, 72 F.R. 7082 effective April 1, 2007, and increase not applicable to cases commenced before the effective date of the adjustments, i.e., April 1, 2007. See Adjustment of Dollar Amounts notes under 11 U.S.C.A. § 104 and this section.

2005 Acts. Pub.L. 109–8, Title XIV, § 1404(b), Apr. 20, 2005, 119 Stat. 215, provided that: "**Effective date upon enactment of Sarbanes–Oxley Act.**—The amendment made by subsection (a) [amending subsec. (a)(19)(B) of this section] is effective beginning July 30, 2002."

Amendments by Pub.L. 109–8, Title XIV, effective, except as otherwise provided, on Apr. 20, 2005, and applicable only with respect to cases commenced under Title 11 on or after Apr. 20, 2005, see Pub.L. 109–8, § 1406, set out as a note under 11 U.S.C.A. § 507.

Amendments by Pub.L. 109–8 effective, except as otherwise provided, 180 days after April 20, 2005, and inapplicable with respect to cases commenced under Title 11 before the effective date, see Pub.L. 109–8, § 1501, set out as a note under 11 U.S.C.A. § 101.

2004 Acts. Adjustment of dollar amounts by Judicial Conference of the United States by notice dated Feb. 18, 2004, 69 F.R. 8482 effective April 1, 2004, and adjustment not applicable to cases commenced before the effective date of the adjustments, i.e., April 1, 2004. See Adjustment of Dollar Amounts notes under 11 U.S.C.A. § 104 and this section.

2001 Acts. Adjustment of dollar amounts by Judicial Conference of the United States by notice dated Feb. 20, 2001, 66 F.R. 10910 effective April 1, 2001, and adjustment not applicable to cases commenced before the effective date of the adjustments, i.e., April 1, 2001. See Adjustment of Dollar Amounts notes under 11 U.S.C.A. § 104 and this section.

1998 Acts. Amendment by Pub.L. 105–244 effective Oct. 1, 1998, except as otherwise provided, see section 3 of Pub.L. 105–244, set out as a note under section 1001 of Title 20.

Pub.L. 105–244, Title IX, § 971(b), Oct. 7, 1998, 112 Stat. 1837, provided that: "The amendment made by subsection (a) [amending subsec. (a)(8) of this section] shall apply only with respect to cases commenced under title 11, United States Code, after the date of enactment of this Act [Oct. 7, 1998]."

Adjustment of dollar amounts by Judicial Conference of the United States by notice dated Feb. 3, 1998, 63 F.R. 7179 effective April 1, 1998, and adjustment not applicable to cases commenced before the effective date of the adjustments, i.e., April 1, 1998. See Adjustment of Dollar Amounts notes under 11 U.S.C.A. § 104 and this section.

1996 Acts. For effective date of Title III of Pub.L. 104–193, see section 395(a) to (c) of Pub.L. 104–193, set out as a note under section 654 of Title 42, The Public Health and Welfare.

Section 374(c) of Pub.L. 104–193 provided that: "The amendments made by this section [amending this section and section 656 of Title 42, The Public Health and Welfare] shall apply only with respect to cases commenced under title 11 of the United States Code [this title] after the date of the enactment of this Act [Aug. 22, 1996]."

1994 Acts. Amendments by Pub.L. 103–394 effective on Oct. 22, 1994, and not to apply with respect to cases commenced under Title 11 of the United States Code before Oct. 22, 1994, see section 702 of Pub.L. 103–394, set out as a note under section 101 of this title.

1990 Acts. Section 3104 of Title XXXI of Pub.L. 101–647 provided that:

"(a) Effective date.—This title and the amendments made by this title [amending this section and section 1328 of this title and enacting provisions set out as a note under section 101 of this title] shall take effect on the date of the enactment of this Act [Nov. 29, 1990].

"(b) Application of amendments.—The amendments made by this title [amending this section and section 1328 of this title] shall not apply with respect to cases commenced under title 11 of the United States Code before the date of the enactment of this Act."

Amendment by section 3621 of Pub.L. 101–647 effective 180 days after Nov. 29, 1990, see section 3631 of Pub.L. 101–647, set out as a note under section 3001 of Title 28, Judiciary and Judicial Procedure.

Section 4 of Pub.L. 101–581 provided that:

"(a) Effective date.—This Act and the amendments made by this Act [amending this section and section 1328 of this title and enacting provisions set out as a note under section 101 of this title] shall take effect on the date of the enactment of this Act [Nov. 15, 1990.]"

"(b) Application of amendments.—The amendments made by this Act [amending this section and section 1328 of this title] shall not apply with respect to cases commenced under title 11 of the United States Code [this title] before the date of the enactment of this Act [Nov. 5, 1990.]"

1986 Acts. Amendment by sections 281 and 283 of Pub.L. 99–554 effective 30 days after Oct. 27, 1986, except as otherwise provided for, see section 302(a) of Pub.L. 99–554, set out as a note under section 581 of Title 28, Judiciary and Judicial Procedure.

Amendment by section 257 of Pub.L. 99–554 effective 30 days after Oct. 27, 1986, but not applicable to cases commenced under this title before that date, see section 302(a), (c)(1) of Pub.L. 99–554, set out as a note under section 581 of Title 28.

1984 Acts. Amendment by Pub.L. 98–353 effective with respect to cases filed 90 days after July 10, 1984, see section 552(a), formerly 553 of Pub.L. 98–353, set out as a note under section 101 of this title.

1981 Acts. Amendment by Pub.L. 97–35 effective on Aug. 13, 1981, see section 2334(c) of Pub.L. 97–35, set out as a note under section 656 of Title 42, The Public Health and Welfare.

Separability of Provisions

If any provision of section 101[a] [Title VIII] of Pub.L. 104–134, an amendment made by such Title, or the application of such provision or amendment to any person or circumstance is held to be unconstitutional, the remainder of such Title, the amendments made by such Title, and the application of the provisions of such Title to any person or circumstance not affected thereby, see section 101[a] [Title VIII, § 810] of Pub.L. 104–134, set out as a note under section 3626 of Title 18, Crimes and Criminal Procedure.

If any provision of or amendment made by Pub.L. 103–394 or the application of such provision or amendment to any person or circumstance is held to be unconstitutional, the remaining provisions of and amendments made by Pub.L. 103–394 and the application of such provisions and amendments to any person or circumstance shall not be affected thereby, see section 701 of Pub.L. 103–394, set out as a note under section 101 of this title.

Adjustment of Dollar Amounts

For adjustment of dollar amounts specified in subsec. (a)(2)(C)(i)(I), (II) of this section by the Judicial Conference of the United States, effective Apr. 1, 2007, see note set out under 11 U.S.C.A. § 104.

By notice published Feb. 14, 2007, 72 F.R. 7082, the Judicial Conference of the United States adjusted the dollar amounts in provisions specified in subsec. (a)(2)(C)(i)(I), (II) of this section, effective Apr. 1, 2007, as follows:

In subsec. (a)(2)(C)(i)(I) adjusted $500 to $550.

In subsec. (a)(2)(C)(i)(II) adjusted $750 to $825.

By notice dated Feb. 18, 2004, 69 F.R. 8482, the Judicial Conference of the United States adjusted the dollar amounts in provisions specified in subsec. (a)(2)(C) of this section, effective Apr. 1, 2004, as follows:

Adjusted $1,150 (each time it appears) to $1,225 (each time it appears).

By notice dated Feb. 20, 2001, 66 F.R. 10910, the Judicial Conference of the United States adjusted the dollar amounts in provisions specified in subsec. (a)(2)(C) of this section, effective Apr. 1, 2001, as follows:

Adjusted $1,075 (each time it appears) to $1,150 (each time it appears).

By notice dated Feb. 3, 1998, 63 F.R. 7179, the Judicial Conference of the United States adjusted the dollar amounts in provisions specified in subsec. (a)(2)(C) of this section, effective Apr. 1, 1998, as follows:

Adjusted $1,000 (each time it appears) to $1,075 (each time it appears).

CROSS REFERENCES

Disallowance of claim to extent claim is for unmatured debt and excepted from discharge as debt for alimony, maintenance or support, see 11 USCA § 502.

Discharge of debtor—

Generally, see Official Bankr. Form 18, 11 USCA.

Chapter 7 cases, see 11 USCA § 727.

Chapter 12 cases, see 11 USCA § 1228.

Chapter 13 cases, see 11 USCA § 1328.

Effect of confirmation, see 11 USCA § 1141.

Extent of priorities for unsecured claims of governmental units, see 11 USCA § 507.

Involuntary cases and future adjustments, see 11 USCA § 104.

Notice of filing, creditors and dates, see Official Bankr. Form 9, 11 USCA.

§ 524. Effect of discharge

(a) A discharge in a case under this title—

(1) voids any judgment at any time obtained, to the extent that such judgment is a determination of the personal liability of the debtor with respect to any debt discharged under section 727, 944, 1141, 1228, or 1328 of this title, whether or not discharge of such debt is waived;

(2) operates as an injunction against the commencement or continuation of an action, the employment of process, or an act, to collect, recover or offset any such debt as a personal liability of the debtor, whether or not discharge of such debt is waived; and

(3) operates as an injunction against the commencement or continuation of an action, the employment of process, or an act, to collect or recover from, or offset against, property of the debtor of the kind specified in section 541(a)(2) of this title that is acquired after the commencement of the case, on account of any allowable community claim, except a community claim that is excepted from discharge under section 523, 1228(a)(1), or 1328(a)(1), or that would be so excepted, determined in accordance with the provisions of sections 523(c) and 523(d) of this title, in a case concerning the debtor's spouse commenced on the date of the filing of the petition in the case concerning the debtor, whether or not discharge of the debt based on such community claim is waived.

(b) Subsection (a)(3) of this section does not apply if—

(1)(A) the debtor's spouse is a debtor in a case under this title, or a bankrupt or a debtor in a case under the Bankruptcy Act, commenced within six years of the date of the filing of the petition in the case concerning the debtor; and

(B) the court does not grant the debtor's spouse a discharge in such case concerning the debtor's spouse; or

(2)(A) the court would not grant the debtor's spouse a discharge in a case under chapter 7 of this title concerning such spouse commenced on the date of the filing of the petition in the case concerning the debtor; and

(B) a determination that the court would not so grant such discharge is made by the bankruptcy court within the time and in the manner provided for a determination under section 727 of this title of whether a debtor is granted a discharge.

(c) An agreement between a holder of a claim and the debtor, the consideration for which, in whole or in part, is based on a debt that is dischargeable in a case under this title is enforceable only to any extent enforceable under applicable nonbankruptcy law, whether or not discharge of such debt is waived, only if—

(1) such agreement was made before the granting of the discharge under section 727, 1141, 1228, or 1328 of this title;

(2) the debtor received the disclosures described in subsection (k) at or before the time at which the debtor signed the agreement;

(3) such agreement has been filed with the court and, if applicable, accompanied by a declaration or an affidavit of the attorney that represented the debtor during the course of negotiating an agreement under this subsection, which states that—

(A) such agreement represents a fully informed and voluntary agreement by the debtor;

(B) such agreement does not impose an undue hardship on the debtor or a dependent of the debtor; and

(C) the attorney fully advised the debtor of the legal effect and consequences of—

(i) an agreement of the kind specified in this subsection; and

(ii) any default under such an agreement;

(4) the debtor has not rescinded such agreement at any time prior to discharge or within sixty days after such agreement is filed with the court, whichever occurs later, by giving notice of rescission to the holder of such claim;

(5) the provisions of subsection (d) of this section have been complied with; and

(6)(A) in a case concerning an individual who was not represented by an attorney during the course of negotiating an agreement under this subsection, the court approves such agreement as—

(i) not imposing an undue hardship on the debtor or a dependent of the debtor; and

(ii) in the best interest of the debtor.

(B) Subparagraph (A) shall not apply to the extent that such debt is a consumer debt secured by real property.

(d) In a case concerning an individual, when the court has determined whether to grant or not to grant a discharge under section 727, 1141, 1228, or 1328 of this title, the court may hold a hearing at which the debtor shall appear in person. At any such hearing, the court shall inform the debtor that a discharge has been granted or the reason why a discharge has not been granted. If a discharge has been granted and if the debtor desires to make an agreement of the kind specified in subsection (c) of this section and was not represented by an attorney during the course of negotiating such agreement, then the court shall hold a hearing at which the debtor shall appear in person and at such hearing the court shall—

(1) inform the debtor—

(A) that such an agreement is not required under this title, under nonbankruptcy law, or under any agreement not made in accordance with the provisions of subsection (c) of this section; and

(B) of the legal effect and consequences of—

(i) an agreement of the kind specified in subsection (c) of this section; and

(ii) a default under such an agreement; and

(2) determine whether the agreement that the debtor desires to make complies with the requirements of subsection (c)(6) of this section, if the consideration for such agreement is based in whole or in part on a consumer debt that is not secured by real property of the debtor.

(e) Except as provided in subsection (a)(3) of this section, discharge of a debt of the debtor does not affect the liability of any other entity on, or the property of any other entity for, such debt.

(f) Nothing contained in subsection (c) or (d) of this section prevents a debtor from voluntarily repaying any debt.

(g)(1)(A) After notice and hearing, a court that enters an order confirming a plan of reorganization under chapter 11 may issue, in connection with such order, an injunction in accordance with this subsection to supplement the injunctive effect of a discharge under this section.

(B) An injunction may be issued under subparagraph (A) to enjoin entities from taking legal action for the purpose of directly or indirectly collecting, recovering, or receiving payment or recovery with respect to any claim or demand that, under a plan of reorganization, is to be paid in whole or in part by a trust described in paragraph (2)(B)(i), except such legal actions as are expressly allowed by the injunction, the confirmation order, or the plan of reorganization.

(2)(A) Subject to subsection (h), if the requirements of subparagraph (B) are met at the time an injunction described in paragraph (1) is entered, then after entry of such injunction, any proceeding that involves the validity, application, construction, or modification of such injunction, or of this subsection with respect to such injunction, may be commenced only in the district court in which such injunction was entered, and such court shall have exclusive jurisdiction over any such proceeding without regard to the amount in controversy.

(B) The requirements of this subparagraph are that—

(i) the injunction is to be implemented in connection with a trust that, pursuant to the plan of reorganization—

(I) is to assume the liabilities of a debtor which at the time of entry of the order for relief has been named as a defendant in personal injury, wrongful death, or property-damage actions seeking recovery for damages allegedly caused by the presence of, or exposure to, asbestos or asbestos-containing products;

(II) is to be funded in whole or in part by the securities of 1 or more debtors involved in such plan and by the obligation of such debtor or debtors to make future payments, including dividends;

(III) is to own, or by the exercise of rights granted under such plan would be entitled to own if specified contingencies occur, a majority of the voting shares of—

(aa) each such debtor;

(bb) the parent corporation of each such debtor; or

(cc) a subsidiary of each such debtor that is also a debtor; and

(IV) is to use its assets or income to pay claims and demands; and

(ii) subject to subsection (h), the court determines that—

(I) the debtor is likely to be subject to substantial future demands for payment arising out of the same or similar conduct or events that gave rise to the claims that are addressed by the injunction;

(II) the actual amounts, numbers, and timing of such future demands cannot be determined;

(III) pursuit of such demands outside the procedures prescribed by such plan is likely to threaten the plan's purpose to deal equitably with claims and future demands;

(IV) as part of the process of seeking confirmation of such plan—

(aa) the terms of the injunction proposed to be issued under paragraph (1)(A), including any provisions barring actions against third parties pursuant to paragraph (4)(A), are set out in such plan and in any disclosure statement supporting the plan; and

(bb) a separate class or classes of the claimants whose claims are to be addressed by a trust described in clause (i) is established and votes, by at least 75 percent of those voting, in favor of the plan; and

(V) subject to subsection (h), pursuant to court orders or otherwise, the trust will operate through mechanisms such as structured, periodic, or supplemental payments, pro rata distributions, matrices, or periodic review of estimates of the numbers and values of present claims and future demands, or other comparable mechanisms, that provide reasonable assurance that the trust will value, and be in a financial position to pay, present claims and future demands that involve similar claims in substantially the same manner.

(3)(A) If the requirements of paragraph (2)(B) are met and the order confirming the plan of reorganization was issued or affirmed by the district court that has jurisdiction over the reorganization case, then after the time for appeal of the order that issues or affirms the plan—

(i) the injunction shall be valid and enforceable and may not be revoked or modified by any court except through appeal in accordance with paragraph (6);

(ii) no entity that pursuant to such plan or thereafter becomes a direct or indirect transferee of, or successor to any assets of, a debtor or trust that is the subject of the injunction shall be liable with respect to any claim or demand made against such entity by reason of its becoming such a transferee or successor; and

(iii) no entity that pursuant to such plan or thereafter makes a loan to such a debtor or trust or to such a successor or transferee shall, by reason of making the loan, be liable with respect to any claim or demand made against such entity, nor shall any pledge of assets made in connection with such a loan be upset or impaired for that reason;

(B) Subparagraph (A) shall not be construed to—

(i) imply that an entity described in subparagraph (A)(ii) or (iii) would, if this paragraph were not applicable, necessarily be liable to any entity by reason of any of the acts described in subparagraph (A);

(ii) relieve any such entity of the duty to comply with, or of liability under, any Federal or State law regarding the making of a fraudulent conveyance in a transaction described in subparagraph (A)(ii) or (iii); or

(iii) relieve a debtor of the debtor's obligation to comply with the terms of the plan of reorganization, or affect the power of the court to exercise its authority under sections 1141 and 1142 to compel the debtor to do so.

(4)(A)(i) Subject to subparagraph (B), an injunction described in paragraph (1) shall be valid and enforceable against all entities that it addresses.

(ii) Notwithstanding the provisions of section 524(e), such an injunction may bar any action directed against a third party who is identifiable from the terms of such injunction (by name or as part of an identifiable group) and is alleged to be directly or indirectly liable for the conduct of, claims against, or demands on the debtor to the extent such alleged liability of such third party arises by reason of—

(I) the third party's ownership of a financial interest in the debtor, a past or present affiliate of the debtor, or a predecessor in interest of the debtor;

(II) the third party's involvement in the management of the debtor or a predecessor in interest of the debtor, or service as an officer, director or employee of the debtor or a related party;

(III) the third party's provision of insurance to the debtor or a related party; or

(IV) the third party's involvement in a transaction changing the corporate structure, or in a loan or other financial transaction affecting the financial condition, of the debtor or a related party, including but not limited to—

(aa) involvement in providing financing (debt or equity), or advice to an entity involved in such a transaction; or

(bb) acquiring or selling a financial interest in an entity as part of such a transaction.

(iii) As used in this subparagraph, the term "related party" means—

(I) a past or present affiliate of the debtor;

(II) a predecessor in interest of the debtor; or

(III) any entity that owned a financial interest in—

(aa) the debtor;

(bb) a past or present affiliate of the debtor; or

(cc) a predecessor in interest of the debtor.

(B) Subject to subsection (h), if, under a plan of reorganization, a kind of demand described in such plan is to be paid in whole or in part by a trust described in paragraph (2)(B)(i) in connection with which an injunction described in paragraph (1) is to be implemented, then such injunction shall be valid and enforceable with respect to a demand of such kind made, after such plan is confirmed, against the debtor or debtors involved, or against a third party described in subparagraph (A)(ii), if—

(i) as part of the proceedings leading to issuance of such injunction, the court appoints a legal representative for the purpose of protecting the rights of persons that might subsequently assert demands of such kind, and

(ii) the court determines, before entering the order confirming such plan, that identifying such debtor or debtors, or such third party (by name or as part of an identifiable group), in such injunction with respect to such demands for purposes of this subparagraph is fair and equitable with respect to the persons that might subsequently assert such demands, in light of the benefits provided, or to be provided, to such trust on behalf of such debtor or debtors or such third party.

(5) In this subsection, the term "demand" means a demand for payment, present or future, that—

(A) was not a claim during the proceedings leading to the confirmation of a plan of reorganization;

(B) arises out of the same or similar conduct or events that gave rise to the claims addressed by the injunction issued under paragraph (1); and

(C) pursuant to the plan, is to be paid by a trust described in paragraph (2)(B)(i).

(6) Paragraph (3)(A)(i) does not bar an action taken by or at the direction of an appellate court on appeal of an injunction issued under paragraph (1) or of the order of confirmation that relates to the injunction.

(7) This subsection does not affect the operation of section 1144 or the power of the district court to refer a proceeding under section 157 of title 28 or any reference of a proceeding made prior to the date of the enactment of this subsection.

(h) Application to existing injunctions.—For purposes of subsection (g)—

(1) subject to paragraph (2), if an injunction of the kind described in subsection (g)(1)(B) was issued before the date of the enactment of this Act, as part of a plan of reorganization confirmed by an order entered before such date, then the injunction shall be considered to meet the requirements of subsection (g)(2)(B) for purposes of subsection (g)(2)(A), and to satisfy subsection (g)(4)(A)(ii), if—

(A) the court determined at the time the plan was confirmed that the plan was fair and equitable in accordance with the requirements of section 1129(b);

(B) as part of the proceedings leading to issuance of such injunction and confirmation of such plan, the court had appointed a legal representative for the purpose of protecting the rights of persons that might subsequently assert demands described in subsection (g)(4)(B) with respect to such plan; and

(C) such legal representative did not object to confirmation of such plan or issuance of such injunction; and

(2) for purposes of paragraph (1), if a trust described in subsection (g)(2)(B)(i) is subject to a court order on the date of the enactment of this Act staying such trust from settling or paying further claims—

(A) the requirements of subsection (g)(2)(B)(ii)(V) shall not apply with respect to such trust until such stay is lifted or dissolved; and

(B) if such trust meets such requirements on the date such stay is lifted or dissolved, such trust shall be considered to have met such requirements continuously from the date of the enactment of this Act.

(i) The willful failure of a creditor to credit payments received under a plan confirmed under this title, unless the order confirming the plan is revoked, the plan is in default, or the creditor has not received payments required to be made under the plan in the manner required by the plan (including crediting the amounts required under the plan), shall constitute a violation of an injunction under subsection (a)(2) if the act of the creditor to collect and failure to credit payments in the manner required by the plan caused material injury to the debtor.

(j) Subsection (a)(2) does not operate as an injunction against an act by a creditor that is the holder of a secured claim, if—

(1) such creditor retains a security interest in real property that is the principal residence of the debtor;

(2) such act is in the ordinary course of business between the creditor and the debtor; and

(3) such act is limited to seeking or obtaining periodic payments associated with a valid security interest in lieu of pursuit of in rem relief to enforce the lien.

(k)(1) The disclosures required under subsection (c)(2) shall consist of the disclosure statement described in paragraph (3), completed as required in that paragraph, together with the agreement specified in subsection (c), statement, declaration, motion and order described, respectively, in paragraphs (4) through (8), and shall be the only disclosures required in connection with entering into such agreement.

(2) Disclosures made under paragraph (1) shall be made clearly and conspicuously and in writing. The terms "Amount Reaffirmed" and "Annual Percentage Rate" shall be disclosed more conspicuously than other terms, data or information provided in connection with this disclosure, except that the phrases "Before agreeing to reaffirm a debt, review these important disclosures" and "Summary of Reaffirmation Agreement" may be equally conspicuous. Disclosures may be made in a different order and may use terminology different from that set forth in paragraphs (2) through (8), except that the terms "Amount Reaffirmed" and "Annual Percentage Rate" must be used where indicated.

(3) The disclosure statement required under this paragraph shall consist of the following:

(A) The statement: "Part A: Before agreeing to reaffirm a debt, review these important disclosures:";

(B) Under the heading "Summary of Reaffirmation Agreement", the statement: "This Summary is made pursuant to the requirements of the Bankruptcy Code";

(C) The "Amount Reaffirmed", using that term, which shall be—

(i) the total amount of debt that the debtor agrees to reaffirm by entering into an agreement of the kind specified in subsection (c), and

(ii) the total of any fees and costs accrued as of the date of the disclosure statement, related to such total amount.

(D) In conjunction with the disclosure of the "Amount Reaffirmed", the statements—

(i) "The amount of debt you have agreed to reaffirm"; and

(ii) "Your credit agreement may obligate you to pay additional amounts which may come due after the date of this disclosure. Consult your credit agreement."

(E) The "Annual Percentage Rate", using that term, which shall be disclosed as—

(i) if, at the time the petition is filed, the debt is an extension of credit under an open end credit plan, as the terms "credit" and "open end credit plan" are defined in section 103 of the Truth in Lending Act, then—

(I) the annual percentage rate determined under paragraphs (5) and (6) of section 127(b) of the Truth in Lending Act, as applicable, as disclosed to the debtor in the most recent periodic statement prior to entering into an agreement of the kind specified in subsection (c) or, if no such periodic statement has been given to the debtor during the prior 6 months, the annual percentage rate as it would have been so disclosed at the time the disclosure statement is given to the debtor, or to the extent this annual percentage rate is not readily available or not applicable, then

(II) the simple interest rate applicable to the amount reaffirmed as of the date the disclosure statement is given to the debtor, or if different simple interest rates apply to different balances, the simple interest rate applicable to each such balance, identifying the amount of each such balance included in the amount reaffirmed, or

(III) if the entity making the disclosure elects, to disclose the annual percentage rate under subclause (I) and the simple interest rate under subclause (II); or

(ii) if, at the time the petition is filed, the debt is an extension of credit other than under an open end credit plan, as the terms "credit" and "open end credit plan" are defined in section 103 of the Truth in Lending Act, then—

(I) the annual percentage rate under section 128(a)(4) of the Truth in Lending Act, as disclosed to the debtor in the most recent disclosure statement given to the debtor prior to the entering into an agreement of the kind specified in subsection (c) with respect to the debt, or, if no such disclosure statement was given to the debtor, the annual percentage rate as it would have been so disclosed at the time the disclosure statement is given to the debtor, or to the extent this annual percentage rate is not readily available or not applicable, then

(II) the simple interest rate applicable to the amount reaffirmed as of the date the disclosure statement is given to the debtor, or if different simple interest rates apply to different balances, the simple interest rate applicable to each such balance, identifying the amount of such balance included in the amount reaffirmed, or

(III) if the entity making the disclosure elects, to disclose the annual percentage rate under (I) and the simple interest rate under (II).

(F) If the underlying debt transaction was disclosed as a variable rate transaction on the most recent disclosure given under the Truth in Lending Act, by stating "The interest rate on your loan may be a variable interest rate which changes from time to time, so that the annual percentage rate disclosed here may be higher or lower."

(G) If the debt is secured by a security interest which has not been waived in whole or in part or determined to be void by a final order of the court at the time of the disclosure, by disclosing that a security interest or lien in goods or property is asserted over some or all of the debts the debtor is reaffirming and listing the items and their original purchase price that are subject to the asserted security interest, or if not a purchase-money security interest then listing by items or types and the original amount of the loan.

(H) At the election of the creditor, a statement of the repayment schedule using 1 or a combination of the following—

(i) by making the statement: "Your first payment in the amount of $___ is due on ___ but the future payment amount may be different. Consult your reaffirmation agreement or credit agreement, as applicable.", and stating the amount of the first payment and the due date of that payment in the places provided;

(ii) by making the statement: "Your payment schedule will be:", and describing the repayment schedule with the number, amount, and due dates or period of payments scheduled to repay the debts reaffirmed to the extent then known by the disclosing party; or

(iii) by describing the debtor's repayment obligations with reasonable specificity to the extent then known by the disclosing party.

(I) The following statement: "Note: When this disclosure refers to what a creditor 'may' do, it does not use the word 'may' to give the creditor specific permission. The word 'may' is used to tell you what might occur if the law permits the creditor to take the action. If you have questions about your reaffirming a debt or what the law requires, consult with the attorney who helped you negotiate this agreement reaffirming a debt. If you don't have an attorney helping you, the judge will explain the effect of your reaffirming a debt when the hearing on the reaffirmation agreement is held."

(J)(i) The following additional statements:

"Reaffirming a debt is a serious financial decision. The law requires you to take certain steps to make sure the decision is in your best interest. If these steps are not completed, the reaffirmation agreement is not effective, even though you have signed it.

"1. Read the disclosures in this Part A carefully. Consider the decision to reaffirm carefully. Then, if you want to reaffirm, sign the reaffirmation agreement in Part B (or you may use a separate agreement you and your creditor agree on).

"2. Complete and sign Part D and be sure you can afford to make the payments you are agreeing to make and have received a copy of the disclosure statement and a completed and signed reaffirmation agreement.

"3. If you were represented by an attorney during the negotiation of your reaffirmation agreement, the attorney must have signed the certification in Part C.

"4. If you were not represented by an attorney during the negotiation of your reaffirmation agreement, you must have completed and signed Part E.

"5. The original of this disclosure must be filed with the court by you or your creditor. If a separate reaffirmation agreement (other than the one in Part B) has been signed, it must be attached.

"6. If you were represented by an attorney during the negotiation of your reaffirmation agreement, your reaffirmation agreement becomes effective upon filing with the court unless the reaffirmation is presumed to be an undue hardship as explained in Part D.

"7. If you were not represented by an attorney during the negotiation of your reaffirmation agreement, it will not be effective unless the court approves it. The court will notify you of the hearing on your reaffirmation agreement. You must attend this hearing in bankruptcy court where the judge will review your reaffirmation agreement. The bankruptcy court must approve your reaffirmation agreement as consistent with your best interests, except that no court approval is required if your reaffirmation agreement is for a consumer debt secured by a mortgage, deed of trust, security deed, or other lien on your real property, like your home.

"Your right to rescind (cancel) your reaffirmation agreement. You may rescind (cancel) your reaffirmation agreement at any time before the bankruptcy court enters a discharge order, or before the expiration of the 60–day period that begins on the date your reaffirmation agreement is filed with the court, whichever occurs later. To rescind (cancel) your reaffirmation agreement, you must notify the creditor that your reaffirmation agreement is rescinded (or canceled).

"What are your obligations if you reaffirm the debt? A reaffirmed debt remains your personal legal obligation. It is not discharged in your bankruptcy case. That means that if you default on your reaffirmed debt after your bankruptcy case is over, your creditor may be able to take your property or your wages. Otherwise, your obligations will be determined by the reaffirmation agreement which may have changed the terms of the original agreement. For example, if you are reaffirming an open end credit agreement, the creditor may be permitted by that agreement or applicable law to change the terms of that agreement in the future under certain conditions.

"Are you required to enter into a reaffirmation agreement by any law? No, you are not required to reaffirm a debt by any law. Only agree to reaffirm a debt if it is in your best interest. Be sure you can afford the payments you agree to make.

"What if your creditor has a security interest or lien? Your bankruptcy discharge does not eliminate any lien on your property. A 'lien' is often referred to as a security interest, deed of trust, mortgage or security deed. Even if you do not reaffirm and your personal liability on the debt is discharged, because of the lien your creditor may still have the right to take the security property if you do not pay the debt or default on it. If the lien is on an item of personal property that is exempt under your State's law or that the trustee has abandoned, you may be able to redeem the item rather than reaffirm the debt. To redeem, you make a single payment to the creditor equal to the current value of the security property, as agreed by the parties or determined by the court."

(ii) In the case of a reaffirmation under subsection (m)(2), numbered paragraph 6 in the disclosures required by clause (i) of this subparagraph shall read as follows:

"6. If you were represented by an attorney during the negotiation of your reaffirmation agreement, your reaffirmation agreement becomes effective upon filing with the court."

(4) The form of such agreement required under this paragraph shall consist of the following:

"Part B: Reaffirmation Agreement. I (we) agree to reaffirm the debts arising under the credit agreement described below.

"Brief description of credit agreement:

"Description of any changes to the credit agreement made as part of this reaffirmation agreement:

"Signature: Date:

"Borrower:

"Co-borrower, if also reaffirming these debts:

"Accepted by creditor:

"Date of creditor acceptance:".

(5) The declaration shall consist of the following:

(A) The following certification:

"Part C: Certification by Debtor's Attorney (If Any).

"I hereby certify that (1) this agreement represents a fully informed and voluntary agreement by the debtor; (2) this agreement does not impose an undue hardship on the debtor or any dependent of the debtor; and (3) I have fully advised the debtor of the legal effect and consequences of this agreement and any default under this agreement.

"Signature of Debtor's Attorney: Date:".

(B) If a presumption of undue hardship has been established with respect to such agreement, such certification shall state that in the opinion of the attorney, the debtor is able to make the payment.

(C) In the case of a reaffirmation agreement under subsection (m)(2), subparagraph (B) is not applicable.

(6)(A) The statement in support of such agreement, which the debtor shall sign and date prior to filing with the court, shall consist of the following:

"Part D: Debtor's Statement in Support of Reaffirmation Agreement.

"1. I believe this reaffirmation agreement will not impose an undue hardship on my dependents or me. I can afford to make the payments on the reaffirmed debt because my monthly income (take home pay plus any other income received) is $___, and my actual current monthly expenses including monthly payments on post-bankruptcy debt and other reaffirmation agreements total $___, leaving $___ to make the required payments on this reaffirmed debt. I understand that if my income less my monthly expenses does not leave enough to make the payments, this reaffirmation agreement is presumed to be an undue hardship on me and must be reviewed by the court. However, this presumption may be overcome if I explain to the satisfaction of the court how I can afford to make the payments here: ___.

"2. I received a copy of the Reaffirmation Disclosure Statement in Part A and a completed and signed reaffirmation agreement."

(B) Where the debtor is represented by an attorney and is reaffirming a debt owed to a creditor defined in section 19(b)(1)(A)(iv) of the Federal Reserve Act, the statement of support of the reaffirmation agreement, which the debtor shall sign and date prior to filing with the court, shall consist of the following:

"I believe this reaffirmation agreement is in my financial interest. I can afford to make the payments on the reaffirmed debt. I received a copy of the Reaffirmation Disclosure Statement in Part A and a completed and signed reaffirmation agreement."

(7) The motion that may be used if approval of such agreement by the court is required in order for it to be effective, shall be signed and dated by the movant and shall consist of the following:

"Part E: Motion for Court Approval (To be completed only if the debtor is not represented by an attorney.). I (we), the debtor(s), affirm the following to be true and correct:

"I am not represented by an attorney in connection with this reaffirmation agreement.

"I believe this reaffirmation agreement is in my best interest based on the income and expenses I have disclosed in my Statement in Support of this reaffirmation agreement, and because (provide any additional relevant reasons the court should consider):

"Therefore, I ask the court for an order approving this reaffirmation agreement."

(8) The court order, which may be used to approve such agreement, shall consist of the following:

"Court Order: The court grants the debtor's motion and approves the reaffirmation agreement described above."

(*l*) Notwithstanding any other provision of this title the following shall apply:

(1) A creditor may accept payments from a debtor before and after the filing of an agreement of the kind specified in subsection (c) with the court.

(2) A creditor may accept payments from a debtor under such agreement that the creditor believes in good faith to be effective.

(3) The requirements of subsections (c)(2) and (k) shall be satisfied if disclosures required under those subsections are given in good faith.

(m)(1) Until 60 days after an agreement of the kind specified in subsection (c) is filed with the court (or such additional period as the court, after notice and a hearing and for cause, orders before the expiration of such period), it shall be presumed that such agreement is an undue hardship on the debtor if the debtor's monthly income less the debtor's monthly expenses as shown on the debtor's completed and signed statement in support of such agreement required under subsection (k)(6)(A) is less than the scheduled payments on the reaffirmed debt. This presumption shall be reviewed by the court. The presumption may be rebutted in writing by the debtor if the statement includes an explanation that identifies additional sources of funds to make the payments as agreed upon under the terms of such agreement. If the presumption is not rebutted to the satisfaction of the court, the court may disapprove such agreement. No agreement shall be disapproved without notice and a hearing to the debtor and creditor, and such hearing shall be concluded before the entry of the debtor's discharge.

(2) This subsection does not apply to reaffirmation agreements where the creditor is a credit union, as defined in section 19(b)(1)(A)(iv) of the Federal Reserve Act.

(Pub.L. 95–598, Nov. 6, 1978, 92 Stat. 2592; Pub.L. 98–353, Title III, §§ 308, 455, July 10, 1984, 98 Stat. 354, 376; Pub.L. 99–554, Title II, §§ 257(*o*), 282, 283(k), Oct. 27, 1986, 100 Stat. 3115–3117; Pub.L. 103–394, Title I, §§ 103, 111(a), Title V, § 501(d)(14), Oct. 22, 1994, 108 Stat. 4108, 4113, 4145; Pub.L. 109–8, Title II, §§ 202, 203(a), Title XII, § 1210, Apr. 20, 2005, 119 Stat. 43, 194.)

HISTORICAL AND STATUTORY NOTES

Revision Notes and Legislative Reports

1978 Acts. Subsection (a) specifies that a discharge in a bankruptcy case voids any judgment to the extent that it is a determination of the personal liability of the debtor with respect to a prepetition debt, and operates as an injunction against the commencement or continuation of an action, the employment of process, or any act, including telephone calls, letters, and personal contacts, to collect, recover, or offset any discharged debt as a personal liability of the debtor, or from property of the debtor, whether or not the debtor has waived discharge of the debt involved. The injunction is to give complete effect to the discharge and to eliminate any doubt concerning the effect of the discharge as a total prohibition on debt collection efforts. This paragraph has been expanded over a comparable provision in Bankruptcy Act § 14f [section 32(f) of former Title 11] to cover any act to collect, such as dunning by telephone or letter, or indirectly through friends, relatives, or employers, harassment, threats of repossession, and the like. The change is consonant with the new policy forbidding binding reaffirmation agreements under proposed 11 U.S.C. 524(b), and is intended to insure that once a debt is discharged, the debtor will not be pressured in any way to repay it. In effect, the discharge extinguishes the debt, and creditors may not attempt to avoid that. The language "whether or not discharge of such debt is waived" is intended to prevent waiver of discharge of a particular debt from defeating the purposes of this section. It is directed at waiver of discharge of a particular debt, not waiver of discharge in toto as permitted under section 727(a)(9).

Subsection (a) also codifies the split discharge for debtors in community property states. If community property was in the estate and community claims were discharged, the discharge is effective against community creditors of the nondebtor spouse as well as of the debtor spouse.

Subsection (b) gives further effect to the discharge. It prohibits reaffirmation agreements after the commencement of the case with respect to any dischargeable debt. The prohibition extends to agreements the consideration for which in whole or in part is based on a dischargeable debt, and it applies whether or not discharge of the debt involved in the agreement has been waived. Thus, the prohibition on reaffirmation agreements extends to debts that are based on discharged debts. Thus, "second generation" debts, which included all or a part of a discharged debt could not be included in any new agreement for new money. This subsection will not have any effect on reaffirmations of debts discharged under the Bankruptcy Act [former Title 11]. It will only apply to discharges granted if commenced under the new title 11 bankruptcy code.

Subsection (c) grants an exception to the anti-reaffirmation provision. It permits reaffirmation in connection with the settlement of a proceeding to determine the dischargeability of the debt being reaffirmed, or in connection with a redemption agreement permitted under section 722. In either case, the reaffirmation agreement must be entered into in good faith and must be approved by the court.

Subsection (d) provides the discharge of the debtor does not affect co-debtors or guarantors. Senate Report No. 95–989.

1984 Acts. Statements by Legislative Leaders, see 1984 U.S. Code Cong. and Adm. News, p. 576.

1986 Acts. House Report No. 99–764 and House Conference Report No. 99–958, see 1986 U.S. Code Cong. and Adm. News, p. 5227.

1994 Acts. House Report No. 103–835, see 1994 U.S. Code Cong. and Adm. News, p. 3340.

2005 Acts. House Report No. 109–31(Part I), see 2005 U.S. Code Cong. and Adm. News, p. 88.

Legislative Statements

Section 524(a) of the House amendment represents a compromise between the House bill and the Senate amendment. Section 524(b) of the House amendment is new, and represents standards clarifying the operation of section 524(a)(3) with respect to community property.

Sections 524(c) and (d) represent a compromise between the House bill and Senate amendment on the issue of reaffirmation of a debt discharged in bankruptcy. Every reaffirmation to be enforceable must be approved by the court, and any debtor may rescind a reaffirmation for 30 days from the time the reaffirmation becomes enforceable. If the debtor is an individual the court must advise the debtor of various effects of reaffirmation at a hearing. In addition, to any extent the debt is a consumer debt that is not secured by real property of the debtor reaffirmation is permitted only if the court approves the reaffirmation agreement, before granting a discharge under section 727, 1141, or 1328, as not imposing a hardship on the debtor or a dependent of the debtor and in the best interest of the debtor; alternatively, the court may approve an agreement entered into in good faith that is in settlement of litigation of a complaint to determine dischargeability or that is entered into in connection with redemption under section 722. The hearing on discharge under section 524(d) will be held whether or not the debtor desires to reaffirm any debts.

References in Text

The Bankruptcy Act, referred to in subsec. (b)(1), is Act July 1, 1898, c. 541, 30 Stat. 544, as amended, which was classified generally to former Title 11.

The date of enactment of this subsection, referred to in subsec. (g), is the date of enactment of section 111(a) of Pub.L. 103–394, which enacted subsec. (g) of this section and which was approved Oct. 22, 1994.

The date of enactment of this Act, referred to in subsec. (h), probably means the date of enactment of Pub.L. 103–394, known as the Bankruptcy Reform Act of 1994, which was approved Oct. 22, 1994.

Section 103 of the Truth in Lending Act, referred to in subsec. (k)(3)(E)(i), (ii), is Pub.L. 90–321, Title I, § 103, May 29, 1968, 82 Stat. 147, as amended, which is classified to 15 U.S.C.A. § 1602.

Section 127(b) of the Truth in Lending Act, referred to in subsec. (k)(3)(E)(i)(I), is Pub.L. 90–321, Title I, § 127(b), May 29, 1968, 82 Stat. 153, as amended, which is classified to 15 U.S.C.A. § 1637(b).

Section 128(a)(4) of the Truth in Lending Act, referred to in subsec. (k)(3)(E)(ii)(I), is Pub.L. 90–321, Title I, § 128(a)(4), May 29, 1968, 82 Stat. 155, as amended, which is classified to 15 U.S.C.A. § 1638(a)(4).

The Truth in Lending Act, referred to in subsec. (k)(3)(F), is Title I of Pub.L. 90–321, May 29, 1968, 82 Stat. 146, as amended, also known as TILA, which is classified principally to subchapter I of chapter 41 of Title 15, 15 U.S.C.A. § 1601 et seq. For complete classification, see Short Title note set out under 15 U.S.C.A. § 1601 and Tables.

Section 19(b)(1)(A)(iv) of the Federal Reserve Act, referred to in subsecs. (k)(6)(B), (m)(2), is Act Dec. 23, 1913, c. 6, § 19(b)(1)(A)(iv), 38 Stat. 270, as amended, which is classified to 12 U.S.C.A. § 461(b)(1)(A)(iv).

Effective and Applicability Provisions

2005 Acts. Amendments by Pub.L. 109–8 effective, except as otherwise provided, 180 days after April 20, 2005, and inapplicable with respect to cases commenced under Title 11 before the effective date, see Pub.L. 109–8, § 1501, set out as a note under 11 U.S.C.A. § 101.

1994 Acts. Amendments by sections 103 and 501(d)(14) of Pub.L. 103–394 effective on Oct. 22, 1994, and not to apply with respect to cases commenced under Title 11 of the United States Code before Oct. 22, 1994, see section 702 of Pub.L. 103–394, set out as a note under section 101 of this title.

Amendment by section 111 of Pub.L. 103–394 [enacting subsecs. (g) and (h) of this section and a provision set out as a note under this section] effective Oct. 22, 1994, see section 702 of Pub.L. 103–394, set out as a note under section 101 of this title.

1986 Acts. Amendment by sections 282 and 283 of Pub.L. 99–554 effective 30 days after Oct. 27, 1986, see section 302(a) of Pub.L. 99–554, set out as a note under section 581 of Title 28, Judiciary and Judicial Procedure.

Amendment by section 257 of Pub.L. 99–554 effective 30 days after Oct. 27, 1986, but not applicable to cases commenced under this title before that date, see section 302(a), (c)(1) of Pub.L. 99–554, set out as a note under Section 581 of Title 28.

1984 Acts. Amendment by Pub.L. 98–353 effective with respect to cases filed 90 days after July 10, 1984, see section 552(a), formerly 553(a) of Pub.L. 98–353, set out as a note under section 101 of this title.

Separability of Provisions

If any provision of or amendment made by Pub.L. 103–394 or the application of such provision or amendment to any person or circumstance is held to be unconstitutional, the remaining provisions of and amendments made by Pub.L. 103–394 and the application of such provisions and amendments to any person or circumstance shall not be affected thereby, see section 701 of Pub.L. 103–394, set out as a note under section 101 of this title.

Rule of Construction

Section 111(b) of Pub.L. 103–394 provided that: "Nothing in subsection (a), or in the amendments made by subsection (a) [enacting subsecs. (g) and (h) of this section], shall be construed to modify, impair, or supersede any other authority the court has to issue injunctions in connection with an order confirming a plan of reorganization."

CROSS REFERENCES

Applicability of subsec. (a)(1), (2) of this section in Chapter 9 cases, see 11 USCA § 901.

Cancellation of indebtedness from discharged farm loans, see 12 USCA § 1150.

Extension of time generally, see 11 USCA § 108.

Meetings of creditors and equity security holders reaffirming a debt, see 11 USCA § 341.

§ 525. Protection against discriminatory treatment

(a) Except as provided in the Perishable Agricultural Commodities Act, 1930, the Packers and Stockyards Act, 1921, and section 1 of the Act entitled "An Act making appropriations for the Department of Agriculture for the fiscal year ending June 30, 1944, and for other purposes," approved July 12, 1943, a governmental unit may not deny, revoke, suspend, or refuse to renew a license, permit, charter, franchise, or other similar grant to, condition such a grant to, discriminate with respect to such a grant against, deny employment to, terminate the employment of, or discriminate with respect to employment against, a person that is or has been a debtor under this title or a bankrupt or a debtor under the Bankruptcy Act, or another person with whom such bankrupt or debtor has been associated, solely because such bankrupt or debtor is or has been a debtor under this title or a bankrupt or debtor under the Bankruptcy Act, has been insolvent before the commencement of the case under this title, or during the case but before the debtor is granted or denied a discharge, or has not paid a debt that is dischargeable in the case under this title or that was discharged under the Bankruptcy Act.

(b) No private employer may terminate the employment of, or discriminate with respect to employment against, an individual who is or has been a debtor under this title, a debtor or bankrupt under the Bankruptcy Act, or an individual associated with such debtor or bankrupt, solely because such debtor or bankrupt—

(1) is or has been a debtor under this title or a debtor or bankrupt under the Bankruptcy Act;

(2) has been insolvent before the commencement of a case under this title or during the case but before the grant or denial of a discharge; or

(3) has not paid a debt that is dischargeable in a case under this title or that was discharged under the Bankruptcy Act.

(c)(1) A governmental unit that operates a student grant or loan program and a person engaged in a business that includes the making of loans guaranteed or insured under a student loan program may not deny a student grant, loan, loan guarantee, or loan insurance to a person that is or has been a debtor under this title or a bankrupt or debtor under the Bankruptcy Act, or another person with whom the debtor or bankrupt has been associated, because the debtor or bankrupt is or has been a debtor under this title or a bankrupt or debtor under the Bankruptcy Act, has been insolvent before the commencement of a case under this title or during the pendency of the case but before the debtor is granted or denied a discharge, or has not paid a debt that is dischargeable in the case under this title or that was discharged under the Bankruptcy Act.

(2) In this section, "student loan program" means any program operated under title IV of the Higher Education Act of 1965 or a similar program operated under State or local law.

(Pub.L. 95–598, Nov. 6, 1978, 92 Stat. 2593; Pub.L. 98–353, Title III, § 309, July 10, 1984, 98 Stat. 354; Pub.L. 103–394, Title III, § 313, Title V, § 501(d)(15), Oct. 22, 1994, 108 Stat. 4140, 4145; Pub.L. 109–8, Title XII, § 1211, Apr. 20, 2005, 119 Stat. 194.)

HISTORICAL AND STATUTORY NOTES

Revision Notes and Legislative Reports

1978 Acts. This section is additional debtor protection. It codifies the result of *Perez v. Campbell*, 402 U.S. 637 (1971) [91 S.Ct. 1704, 29 L.Ed.2d 233], which held that a State would frustrate the Congressional policy of a fresh start for a debtor if it were permitted to refuse to renew a drivers license because a tort judgment resulting from an automobile accident had been unpaid as a result of a discharge in bankruptcy.

Notwithstanding any other laws, section 525 prohibits a governmental unit from denying, revoking, suspending, or refusing to renew a license, permit, charter, franchise, or other similar grant to, from conditioning such a grant to, from discrimination with respect to such a grant against, deny employment to, terminate the employment of, or discriminate with respect to employment against, a person that is or has been a debtor or that is or has been associated with a debtor. The prohibition extends only to discrimination or other action based solely on the basis of the bankruptcy, on the basis of insolvency before or during bankruptcy prior to a determination of discharge, or on the basis of nonpayment of a debt discharged in the bankruptcy case (the *Perez* situation). It does not prohibit consideration of other factors, such as future financial responsibility or ability, and does not prohibit imposition of requirements such as net capital rules, if applied nondiscriminatorily.

In addition, the section is not exhaustive. The enumeration of various forms of discrimination against former bankrupts is not intended to permit other forms of discrimination. The courts have been developing the *Perez* rule. This section permits further development to prohibit actions by governmental or quasi-governmental organizations that perform licensing functions, such as a State bar association or a medical society, or by other organizations that can seriously affect the debtors' livelihood or fresh start, such as exclusion from a union on the basis of discharge of a debt to the union's credit union.

The effect of the section, and of further interpretations of the *Perez* rule, is to strengthen the anti-reaffirmation policy found in section 524(b). Discrimination based solely on nonpayment could encourage reaffirmations, contrary to the expressed policy.

The section is not so broad as a comparable section proposed by the Bankruptcy Commission, S. 236, 94th Cong., 1st Sess. § 4–508 (1975), which would have extended the prohibition to any discrimination, even by private parties. Nevertheless, it is not limiting either, as noted. The courts will continue to mark the contours of the anti-discrimination provision in pursuit of sound bankruptcy policy. Senate Report No. 95–989.

1984 Acts. Statements by Legislative Leaders, see 1984 U.S. Code Cong. and Adm. News, p. 576.

1994 Acts. House Report No. 103–835, see 1994 U.S. Code Cong. and Adm. News, p. 3340.

2005 Acts. House Report No. 109–31(Part I), see 2005 U.S. Code Cong. and Adm. News, p. 88.

References in Text

The Perishable Agricultural Commodities Act, 1930, referred to in subsec. (a), is Act June 10, 1930, c. 436, 46 Stat. 531, as amended, which is classified principally to chapter 20A (section 499a et seq.) of Title 7, Agriculture. For complete classification of this Act to the Code, see section 499a of Title 7 and Tables.

The Packers and Stockyards Act, 1921, referred to in subsec. (a), is Act Aug. 15, 1921, c. 64, 42 Stat. 159, which is classified principally to chapter 9 (section 181 et seq.) of Title 7, Agriculture. For complete classification of this Act to the Code, see section 181 of Title 7 and Tables.

Section 1 of an Act entitled "An Act making appropriations for the Department of Agriculture for the fiscal year ending

June 30, 1944, and for other purposes," approved July 12, 1943, referred to in subsec. (a), is section 1 of Act July 12, 1943, c. 215, 57 Stat. 422, which is classified to section 204 of Title 7, Agriculture.

The Bankruptcy Act, referred to in subsecs. (a), (b), and (c)(1), is Act July 1, 1898, c. 541, 30 Stat. 544, as amended, which was classified generally to former Title 11.

The Higher Education Act of 1965, referred to in subsec. (c)(2), is Pub.L. 89–329, Nov. 8, 1965, 79 Stat. 1219, as amended. Title IV of the Act is classified generally to subchapter IV of chapter 28 of Title 20, 20 U.S.C.A. § 1070 et seq., and part C of subchapter I of chapter 34 of Title 42, 42 U.S.C.A. § 2751 et seq. For complete classification, see Short Title note set out under 20 U.S.C.A. § 1001 and Tables.

Effective and Applicability Provisions

2005 Acts. Amendments by Pub.L. 109–8 effective, except as otherwise provided, 180 days after April 20, 2005, and inapplicable with respect to cases commenced under Title 11 before the effective date, see Pub.L. 109–8, § 1501, set out as a note under 11 U.S.C.A. § 101.

1994 Acts. Amendments by Pub.L. 103–394 effective on Oct. 22, 1994, and not to apply with respect to cases commenced under Title 11 of the United States Code before Oct. 22, 1994, see section 702 of Pub.L. 103–394, set out as a note under section 101 of this title.

1984 Acts. Amendment by Pub.L. 98–353 effective with respect to cases filed 90 days after July 10, 1984, see section 552(a), formerly 553(a) of Pub.L. 98–353, set out as a note under section 101 of this title.

Separability of Provisions

If any provision of or amendment made by Pub.L. 103–394 or the application of such provision or amendment to any person or circumstance is held to be unconstitutional, the remaining provisions of and amendments made by Pub.L. 103–394 and the application of such provisions and amendments to any person or circumstance shall not be affected thereby, see section 701 of Pub.L. 103–394, set out as a note under section 101 of this title.

CROSS REFERENCES

Reporting of obsolete information prohibited, see 15 USCA § 1681c.

§ 526. Restrictions on debt relief agencies

(a) A debt relief agency shall not—

(1) fail to perform any service that such agency informed an assisted person or prospective assisted person it would provide in connection with a case or proceeding under this title;

(2) make any statement, or counsel or advise any assisted person or prospective assisted person to make a statement in a document filed in a case or proceeding under this title, that is untrue and misleading, or that upon the exercise of reasonable care, should have been known by such agency to be untrue or misleading;

(3) misrepresent to any assisted person or prospective assisted person, directly or indirectly, affirmatively or by material omission, with respect to—

(A) the services that such agency will provide to such person; or

(B) the benefits and risks that may result if such person becomes a debtor in a case under this title; or

(4) advise an assisted person or prospective assisted person to incur more debt in contemplation of such person filing a case under this title or to pay an attorney or bankruptcy petition preparer fee or charge for services performed as part of preparing for or representing a debtor in a case under this title.

(b) Any waiver by any assisted person of any protection or right provided under this section shall not be enforceable against the debtor by any Federal or State court or any other person, but may be enforced against a debt relief agency.

(c)(1) Any contract for bankruptcy assistance between a debt relief agency and an assisted person that does not comply with the material requirements of this section, section 527, or section 528 shall be void and may not be enforced by any Federal or State court or by any other person, other than such assisted person.

(2) Any debt relief agency shall be liable to an assisted person in the amount of any fees or charges in connection with providing bankruptcy assistance to such person that such debt relief agency has received, for actual damages, and for reasonable attorneys' fees and costs if such agency is found, after notice and a hearing, to have—

(A) intentionally or negligently failed to comply with any provision of this section, section 527, or section 528 with respect to a case or proceeding under this title for such assisted person;

(B) provided bankruptcy assistance to an assisted person in a case or proceeding under this title that is dismissed or converted to a case under another chapter of this title because of such agency's intentional or negligent failure to file any required document including those specified in section 521; or

(C) intentionally or negligently disregarded the material requirements of this title or the Federal Rules of Bankruptcy Procedure applicable to such agency.

(3) In addition to such other remedies as are provided under State law, whenever the chief law enforcement officer of a State, or an official or agency designated by a State, has reason to believe that any person has violated or is violating this section, the State—

(A) may bring an action to enjoin such violation;

(B) may bring an action on behalf of its residents to recover the actual damages of assisted persons arising from such violation, including any liability under paragraph (2); and

(C) in the case of any successful action under subparagraph (A) or (B), shall be awarded the costs of the action and reasonable attorneys' fees as determined by the court.

(4) The district courts of the United States for districts located in the State shall have concurrent jurisdiction of any action under subparagraph (A) or (B) of paragraph (3).

(5) Notwithstanding any other provision of Federal law and in addition to any other remedy provided under Federal or State law, if the court, on its own motion or on the motion of the United States trustee or the debtor, finds that a person intentionally violated this section, or engaged in a clear and consistent pattern or practice of violating this section, the court may—

(A) enjoin the violation of such section; or

(B) impose an appropriate civil penalty against such person.

(d) No provision of this section, section 527, or section 528 shall—

(1) annul, alter, affect, or exempt any person subject to such sections from complying with any law of any State except to the extent that such law is inconsistent with those sections, and then only to the extent of the inconsistency; or

(2) be deemed to limit or curtail the authority or ability—

(A) of a State or subdivision or instrumentality thereof, to determine and enforce qualifications for the practice of law under the laws of that State; or

(B) of a Federal court to determine and enforce the qualifications for the practice of law before that court.

(Added Pub.L. 109–8, Title II, § 227(a), Apr. 20, 2005, 119 Stat. 67.)

HISTORICAL AND STATUTORY NOTES

Revision Notes and Legislative Reports

2005 Acts. House Report No. 109–31(Part I), see 2005 U.S. Code Cong. and Adm. News, p. 88.

References is Text

The Federal Rules of Bankruptcy Procedure, referred to in subsec. (c)(2)(C), are set out in the Appendix to this title.

Effective and Applicability Provisions

2005 Acts. Amendments by Pub.L. 109–8 effective, except as otherwise provided, 180 days after April 20, 2005, and inapplicable with respect to cases commenced under Title 11 before the effective date, see Pub.L. 109–8, § 1501, set out as a note under 11 U.S.C.A. § 101.

Corpus Juris Secundum

CJS Bankruptcy § 18, Debt-Relief Agencies.

§ 527. Disclosures

(a) A debt relief agency providing bankruptcy assistance to an assisted person shall provide—

(1) the written notice required under section 342(b)(1); and

(2) to the extent not covered in the written notice described in paragraph (1), and not later than 3 business days after the first date on which a debt relief agency first offers to provide any bankruptcy assistance services to an assisted person, a clear and conspicuous written notice advising assisted persons that—

(A) all information that the assisted person is required to provide with a petition and thereafter during a case under this title is required to be complete, accurate, and truthful;

(B) all assets and all liabilities are required to be completely and accurately disclosed in the documents filed to commence the case, and the replacement value of each asset as defined in section 506 must be stated in those documents where requested after reasonable inquiry to establish such value;

(C) current monthly income, the amounts specified in section 707(b)(2), and, in a case under chapter 13 of this title, disposable income (determined in accordance with section 707(b)(2)), are required to be stated after reasonable inquiry; and

(D) information that an assisted person provides during their case may be audited pursuant to this title, and that failure to provide such information may result in dismissal of the case under this title or other sanction, including a criminal sanction.

(b) A debt relief agency providing bankruptcy assistance to an assisted person shall provide each assisted person at the same time as the notices required under subsection (a)(1) the following statement, to the extent applicable, or one substantially similar. The statement shall be clear and conspicuous and shall be in a single document separate from other documents or notices provided to the assisted person:

"IMPORTANT INFORMATION ABOUT BANKRUPTCY ASSISTANCE SERVICES FROM AN ATTORNEY OR BANKRUPTCY PETITION PREPARER.

"If you decide to seek bankruptcy relief, you can represent yourself, you can hire an attorney to represent you, or you can get help in some localities from a bankruptcy petition preparer who is not an attorney.

THE LAW REQUIRES AN ATTORNEY OR BANKRUPTCY PETITION PREPARER TO GIVE YOU A WRITTEN CONTRACT SPECIFYING WHAT THE ATTORNEY OR BANKRUPTCY PETITION PREPARER WILL DO FOR YOU AND HOW MUCH IT WILL COST. Ask to see the contract before you hire anyone.

"The following information helps you understand what must be done in a routine bankruptcy case to help you evaluate how much service you need. Although bankruptcy can be complex, many cases are routine.

"Before filing a bankruptcy case, either you or your attorney should analyze your eligibility for different forms of debt relief available under the Bankruptcy Code and which form of relief is most likely to be beneficial for you. Be sure you understand the relief you can obtain and its limitations. To file a bankruptcy case, documents called a Petition, Schedules and Statement of Financial Affairs, as well as in some cases a Statement of Intention need to be prepared correctly and filed with the bankruptcy court. You will have to pay a filing fee to the bankruptcy court. Once your case starts, you will have to attend the required first meeting of creditors where you may be questioned by a court official called a 'trustee' and by creditors.

"If you choose to file a chapter 7 case, you may be asked by a creditor to reaffirm a debt. You may want help deciding whether to do so. A creditor is not permitted to coerce you into reaffirming your debts.

"If you choose to file a chapter 13 case in which you repay your creditors what you can afford over 3 to 5 years, you may also want help with preparing your chapter 13 plan and with the confirmation hearing on your plan which will be before a bankruptcy judge.

"If you select another type of relief under the Bankruptcy Code other than chapter 7 or chapter 13, you will want to find out what should be done from someone familiar with that type of relief.

"Your bankruptcy case may also involve litigation. You are generally permitted to represent yourself in litigation in bankruptcy court, but only attorneys, not bankruptcy petition preparers, can give you legal advice.".

(c) Except to the extent the debt relief agency provides the required information itself after reasonably diligent inquiry of the assisted person or others so as to obtain such information reasonably accurately for inclusion on the petition, schedules or statement of financial affairs, a debt relief agency providing bankruptcy assistance to an assisted person, to the extent permitted by nonbankruptcy law, shall provide each assisted person at the time required for the notice required under subsection (a)(1) reasonably sufficient information (which shall be provided in a clear and conspicuous writing) to the assisted person on how to provide all the information the assisted person is required to provide under this title pursuant to section 521, including—

(1) how to value assets at replacement value, determine current monthly income, the amounts specified in section 707(b)(2) and, in a chapter 13 case, how to determine disposable income in accordance with section 707(b)(2) and related calculations;

(2) how to complete the list of creditors, including how to determine what amount is owed and what address for the creditor should be shown; and

(3) how to determine what property is exempt and how to value exempt property at replacement value as defined in section 506.

(d) A debt relief agency shall maintain a copy of the notices required under subsection (a) of this section for 2 years after the date on which the notice is given the assisted person.

(Added Pub.L. 109–8, Title II, § 228(a), Apr. 20, 2005, 119 Stat. 69.)

HISTORICAL AND STATUTORY NOTES

Revision Notes and Legislative Reports

2005 Acts. House Report No. 109–31(Part I), see 2005 U.S. Code Cong. and Adm. News, p. 88.

References in Text

Chapter 13, referred to in text, is chapter 13 of this title, 11 U.S.C.A. § 1301 et seq.

Chapter 7, referred to in text, is chapter 7 of this title, 11 U.S.C.A. § 701 et seq.

Effective and Applicability Provisions

2005 Acts. Amendments by Pub.L. 109–8 effective, except as otherwise provided, 180 days after April 20, 2005, and inapplicable with respect to cases commenced under Title 11 before the effective date, see Pub.L. 109–8, § 1501, set out as a note under 11 U.S.C.A. § 101.

§ 528. Requirements for debt relief agencies

(a) A debt relief agency shall—

(1) not later than 5 business days after the first date on which such agency provides any bankruptcy assistance services to an assisted person, but prior to such assisted person's petition under this title being filed, execute a written contract with such assisted person that explains clearly and conspicuously—

(A) the services such agency will provide to such assisted person; and

(B) the fees or charges for such services, and the terms of payment;

(2) provide the assisted person with a copy of the fully executed and completed contract;

(3) clearly and conspicuously disclose in any advertisement of bankruptcy assistance services or of the benefits of bankruptcy directed to the general public (whether in general media, seminars or specific mailings, telephonic or electronic messages, or otherwise) that the services or benefits are with respect to bankruptcy relief under this title; and

(4) clearly and conspicuously use the following statement in such advertisement: "We are a debt relief agency. We help people file for bankruptcy relief under the Bankruptcy Code." or a substantially similar statement.

(b)(1) An advertisement of bankruptcy assistance services or of the benefits of bankruptcy directed to the general public includes—

(A) descriptions of bankruptcy assistance in connection with a chapter 13 plan whether or not chapter 13 is specifically mentioned in such advertisement; and

(B) statements such as "federally supervised repayment plan" or "Federal debt restructuring help" or other similar statements that could lead a reasonable consumer to believe that debt counseling was being offered when in fact the services were directed to providing bankruptcy assistance with a chapter 13 plan or other form of bankruptcy relief under this title.

(2) An advertisement, directed to the general public, indicating that the debt relief agency provides assistance with respect to credit defaults, mortgage foreclosures, eviction proceedings, excessive debt, debt collection pressure, or inability to pay any consumer debt shall—

(A) disclose clearly and conspicuously in such advertisement that the assistance may involve bankruptcy relief under this title; and

(B) include the following statement: "We are a debt relief agency. We help people file for bankruptcy relief under the Bankruptcy Code." or a substantially similar statement.

(Added Pub.L. 109–8, Title II, § 229(a), Apr. 20, 2005, 119 Stat. 71.)

HISTORICAL AND STATUTORY NOTES

Revision Notes and Legislative Reports

2005 Acts. House Report No. 109–31(Part I), see 2005 U.S. Code Cong. and Adm. News, p. 88.

References in Text

Chapter 13, referred to in subsec. (b)(1)(A), (B), is chapter 13 of this title, 11 U.S.C.A. § 1301 et seq.

Effective and Applicability Provisions

2005 Acts. Amendments by Pub.L. 109–8 effective, except as otherwise provided, 180 days after April 20, 2005, and inapplicable with respect to cases commenced under Title 11 before the effective date, see Pub.L. 109–8, § 1501, set out as a note under 11 U.S.C.A. § 101.

§§ 529 to 540. Reserved for future legislation

SUBCHAPTER III—THE ESTATE

§ 541. Property of the estate

(a) The commencement of a case under section 301, 302, or 303 of this title creates an estate. Such estate is comprised of all the following property, wherever located and by whomever held:

(1) Except as provided in subsections (b) and (c)(2) of this section, all legal or equitable interests of the debtor in property as of the commencement of the case.

(2) All interests of the debtor and the debtor's spouse in community property as of the commencement of the case that is—

(A) under the sole, equal, or joint management and control of the debtor; or

(B) liable for an allowable claim against the debtor, or for both an allowable claim against the debtor and an allowable claim against the debtor's spouse, to the extent that such interest is so liable.

(3) Any interest in property that the trustee recovers under section 329(b), 363(n), 543, 550, 553, or 723 of this title.

(4) Any interest in property preserved for the benefit of or ordered transferred to the estate under section 510(c) or 551 of this title.

(5) Any interest in property that would have been property of the estate if such interest had been an interest of the debtor on the date of the filing of the petition, and that the debtor acquires or becomes entitled to acquire within 180 days after such date—

(A) by bequest, devise, or inheritance;

(B) as a result of a property settlement agreement with the debtor's spouse, or of an interlocutory or final divorce decree; or

(C) as a beneficiary of a life insurance policy or of a death benefit plan.

(6) Proceeds, product, offspring, rents, or profits of or from property of the estate, except such as are earnings from services performed by an individual debtor after the commencement of the case.

(7) Any interest in property that the estate acquires after the commencement of the case.

(b) Property of the estate does not include—

(1) any power that the debtor may exercise solely for the benefit of an entity other than the debtor;

(2) any interest of the debtor as a lessee under a lease of nonresidential real property that has termi-

nated at the expiration of the stated term of such lease before the commencement of the case under this title, and ceases to include any interest of the debtor as a lessee under a lease of nonresidential real property that has terminated at the expiration of the stated term of such lease during the case;

(3) any eligibility of the debtor to participate in programs authorized under the Higher Education Act of 1965 (20 U.S.C. 1001 et seq.; 42 U.S.C. 2751 et seq.), or any accreditation status or State licensure of the debtor as an educational institution;

(4) any interest of the debtor in liquid or gaseous hydrocarbons to the extent that—

(A)(i) the debtor has transferred or has agreed to transfer such interest pursuant to a farmout agreement or any written agreement directly related to a farmout agreement; and

(ii) but for the operation of this paragraph, the estate could include the interest referred to in clause (i) only by virtue of section 365 or 544(a)(3) of this title; or

(B)(i) the debtor has transferred such interest pursuant to a written conveyance of a production payment to an entity that does not participate in the operation of the property from which such production payment is transferred; and

(ii) but for the operation of this paragraph, the estate could include the interest referred to in clause (i) only by virtue of section 365 or 542 of this title;

(5) funds placed in an education individual retirement account (as defined in section 530(b)(1) of the Internal Revenue Code of 1986) not later than 365 days before the date of the filing of the petition in a case under this title, but—

(A) only if the designated beneficiary of such account was a child, stepchild, grandchild, or stepgrandchild of the debtor for the taxable year for which funds were placed in such account;

(B) only to the extent that such funds—

(i) are not pledged or promised to any entity in connection with any extension of credit; and

(ii) are not excess contributions (as described in section 4973(e) of the Internal Revenue Code of 1986); and

(C) in the case of funds placed in all such accounts having the same designated beneficiary not earlier than 720 days nor later than 365 days before such date, only so much of such funds as does not exceed $5,475 [1];

(6) funds used to purchase a tuition credit or certificate or contributed to an account in accordance with section 529(b)(1)(A) of the Internal Revenue Code of 1986 under a qualified State tuition program (as defined in section 529(b)(1) of such Code) not later than 365 days before the date of the filing of the petition in a case under this title, but—

(A) only if the designated beneficiary of the amounts paid or contributed to such tuition program was a child, stepchild, grandchild, or stepgrandchild of the debtor for the taxable year for which funds were paid or contributed;

(B) with respect to the aggregate amount paid or contributed to such program having the same designated beneficiary, only so much of such amount as does not exceed the total contributions permitted under section 529(b)(7) of such Code with respect to such beneficiary, as adjusted beginning on the date of the filing of the petition in a case under this title by the annual increase or decrease (rounded to the nearest tenth of 1 percent) in the education expenditure category of the Consumer Price Index prepared by the Department of Labor; and

(C) in the case of funds paid or contributed to such program having the same designated beneficiary not earlier than 720 days nor later than 365 days before such date, only so much of such funds as does not exceed $5,475 [1];

(7) any amount—

(A) withheld by an employer from the wages of employees for payment as contributions—

(i) to—

(I) an employee benefit plan that is subject to title I of the Employee Retirement Income Security Act of 1974 or under an employee benefit plan which is a governmental plan under section 414(d) of the Internal Revenue Code of 1986;

(II) a deferred compensation plan under section 457 of the Internal Revenue Code of 1986; or

(III) a tax-deferred annuity under section 403(b) of the Internal Revenue Code of 1986;

except that such amount under this subparagraph shall not constitute disposable income as defined in section 1325(b)(2); or

(ii) to a health insurance plan regulated by State law whether or not subject to such title; or

(B) received by an employer from employees for payment as contributions—

(i) to—

(I) an employee benefit plan that is subject to title I of the Employee Retirement Income Security Act of 1974 or under an employee benefit plan which is a governmental plan under section 414(d) of the Internal Revenue Code of 1986;

(II) a deferred compensation plan under section 457 of the Internal Revenue Code of 1986; or

(III) a tax-deferred annuity under section 403(b) of the Internal Revenue Code of 1986;

except that such amount under this subparagraph shall not constitute disposable income, as defined in section 1325(b)(2); or

(ii) to a health insurance plan regulated by State law whether or not subject to such title;

(8) subject to subchapter III of chapter 5, any interest of the debtor in property where the debtor pledged or sold tangible personal property (other than securities or written or printed evidences of indebtedness or title) as collateral for a loan or advance of money given by a person licensed under law to make such loans or advances, where—

(A) the tangible personal property is in the possession of the pledgee or transferee;

(B) the debtor has no obligation to repay the money, redeem the collateral, or buy back the property at a stipulated price; and

(C) neither the debtor nor the trustee have exercised any right to redeem provided under the contract or State law, in a timely manner as provided under State law and section 108(b); or

(9) any interest in cash or cash equivalents that constitute proceeds of a sale by the debtor of a money order that is made—

(A) on or after the date that is 14 days prior to the date on which the petition is filed; and

(B) under an agreement with a money order issuer that prohibits the commingling of such proceeds with property of the debtor (notwithstanding that, contrary to the agreement, the proceeds may have been commingled with property of the debtor),

unless the money order issuer had not taken action, prior to the filing of the petition, to require compliance with the prohibition.

Paragraph (4) shall not be construed to exclude from the estate any consideration the debtor retains, receives, or is entitled to receive for transferring an interest in liquid or gaseous hydrocarbons pursuant to a farmout agreement.

(c)(1) Except as provided in paragraph (2) of this subsection, an interest of the debtor in property becomes property of the estate under subsection (a)(1), (a)(2), or (a)(5) of this section notwithstanding any provision in an agreement, transfer instrument, or applicable nonbankruptcy law—

(A) that restricts or conditions transfer of such interest by the debtor; or

(B) that is conditioned on the insolvency or financial condition of the debtor, on the commencement of a case under this title, or on the appointment of or taking possession by a trustee in a case under this title or a custodian before such commencement, and that effects or gives an option to effect a forfeiture, modification, or termination of the debtor's interest in property.

(2) A restriction on the transfer of a beneficial interest of the debtor in a trust that is enforceable under applicable nonbankruptcy law is enforceable in a case under this title.

(d) Property in which the debtor holds, as of the commencement of the case, only legal title and not an equitable interest, such as a mortgage secured by real property, or an interest in such a mortgage, sold by the debtor but as to which the debtor retains legal title to service or supervise the servicing of such mortgage or interest, becomes property of the estate under subsection (a)(1) or (2) of this section only to the extent of the debtor's legal title to such property, but not to the extent of any equitable interest in such property that the debtor does not hold.

(e) In determining whether any of the relationships specified in paragraph (5)(A) or (6)(A) of subsection (b) exists, a legally adopted child of an individual (and a child who is a member of an individual's household, if placed with such individual by an authorized placement agency for legal adoption by such individual), or a foster child of an individual (if such child has as the child's principal place of abode the home of the debtor and is a member of the debtor's household) shall be treated as a child of such individual by blood.

(f) Notwithstanding any other provision of this title, property that is held by a debtor that is a corporation described in section 501(c)(3) of the Internal Revenue Code of 1986 and exempt from tax under section 501(a) of such Code may be transferred to an entity that is not such a corporation, but only under the same conditions as would apply if the debtor had not filed a case under this title.

(Pub.L. 95–598, Nov. 6, 1978, 92 Stat. 2594; Pub.L. 98–353, Title III, §§ 363(a), 456, July 10, 1984, 98 Stat. 363, 376; Pub.L. 101–508, Title III, § 3007(a)(2), Nov. 5, 1990, 104 Stat. 1388–28; Pub.L. 102–486, Title XXX, § 3017(b), Oct. 24, 1992, 106 Stat. 3130; Pub.L. 103–394, Title II, §§ 208(b), 223, Oct. 22, 1994, 108 Stat. 4124, 4129; Pub.L. 109–8, Title II, § 225(a), Title III, § 323, Title XII, §§ 1212, 1221(c), 1230, Apr. 20, 2005, 119 Stat. 65, 66, 97, 194, 196, 201.)

1 Dollar amount as adjusted by the Judicial Conference of the United States. See Adjustment of Dollar Amounts notes set out under this section and 11 U.S.C.A. § 104.

HISTORICAL AND STATUTORY NOTES

Revision Notes and Legislative Reports

1978 Acts. This section defines property of the estate, and specifies what property becomes property of the estate. The commencement of a bankruptcy case creates an estate. Under paragraph (1) of subsection (a), the estate is comprised of all legal or equitable interest of the debtor in property, wherever located, as of the commencement of the case. The scope of this paragraph is broad. It includes all kinds of property, including tangible or intangible property, causes of action (see Bankruptcy Act § 70a(6) [section 110(a)(6) of former Title 11]), and all other forms of property currently specified in section 70a of the Bankruptcy Act § 70a [sic] [section 110(a) of former Title 11], as well as property recovered by the trustee under section 542 of proposed title 11, if the property recovered was merely out of the possession of the debtor, yet remained "property of the debtor." The debtor's interest in property also includes "title" to property, which is an interest, just as are a possessory interest, or leasehold interest, for example. The result of *Segal v. Rochelle,* 382 U.S. 375 (1966) [86 S.Ct. 511, 15 L.Ed.2d 428], is followed, and the right to a refund is property of the estate.

Though this paragraph will include choses in action and claims by the debtor against others, it is not intended to expand the debtor's rights against others more than they exist at the commencement of the case. For example, if the debtor has a claim that is barred at the time of the commencement of the case by the statute of limitations, then the trustee would not be able to pursue that claim, because he too would be barred. He could take no greater rights than the debtor himself had. But see proposed 11 U.S.C. 108, which would permit the trustee a tolling of the statute of limitations if it had not run before the date of the filing of the petition.

Paragraph (1) has the effect of overruling *Lockwood v. Exchange Bank,* 190 U.S. 294 (1903) [23 S.Ct. 751, 47 L.Ed. 1061, 10 Am.Bankr.Rep. 107], because it includes as property of the estate all property of the debtor, even that needed for a fresh start. After the property comes into the estate, then the debtor is permitted to exempt it under proposed 11 U.S.C. 522, and the court will have jurisdiction to determine what property may be exempted and what remains as property of the estate. The broad jurisdictional grant in proposed 28 U.S.C. 1334 would have the effect of overruling *Lockwood* independently of the change made by this provision.

Paragraph (1) also has the effect of overruling *Lines v. Frederick,* 400 U.S. 18 (1970) [91 S.Ct. 113, 27 L.Ed.2d 124].

Situations occasionally arise where property ostensibly belonging to the debtor will actually not be property of the debtor, but will be held in trust for another. For example, if the debtor has incurred medical bills that were covered by insurance, and the insurance company had sent the payment of the bills to the debtor before the debtor had paid the bill for which the payment was reimbursement, the payment would actually be held in a constructive trust for the person to whom the bill was owed. This section and proposed 11 U.S.C. 545 also will not affect various statutory provisions that give a creditor of the debtor a lien that is valid outside as well as inside bankruptcy, or that creates a trust fund for the benefit of a creditor of the debtor. See Packers and Stockyards Act § 206, 7 U.S.C. 196 [7 U.S.C.A. § 196].

Bankruptcy Act § 8 [section 26 of former Title 11] has been deleted as unnecessary. Once the estate is created, no interests in property of the estate remain in the debtor. Consequently, if the debtor dies during the case, only property exempted from property of the estate or acquired by the debtor after the commencement of the case and not included as property of the estate will be available to the representative of the debtor's probate estate. The bankruptcy proceeding will continue in rem with respect to property of the state [sic], and the discharge will apply in personam to relieve the debtor, and thus his probate representative, of liability for dischargeable debts.

The estate also includes the interests of the debtor and the debtor's spouse in community property, subject to certain limitations; property that the trustee recovers under the avoiding powers; property that the debtor acquires by bequest, devise, inheritance, a property settlement agreement with the debtor's spouse, or as the beneficiary of a life insurance policy within 180 days after the petition; and proceeds, product, offspring, rents, and profits of or from property of the estate, except such as are earning from services performed by an individual debtor after the commencement of the case. Proceeds here is not used in a confining sense, as defined in the Uniform Commercial Code, but is intended to be a broad term to encompass all proceeds of property of the estate. The conversion in form of property of the estate does not change its character as property of the estate.

Subsection (b) excludes from property of the estate any power, such as a power of appointment, that the debtor may exercise solely for the benefit of an entity other than the debtor. This changes present law which excludes powers solely benefiting other persons but not other entities.

Subsection (c) invalidates restrictions on the transfer of property of the debtor, in order that all of the interests of the debtor in property will become property of the estate. The provisions invalidated are those that restrict or condition transfer of the debtor's interest, and those that are conditioned on the insolvency or financial condition of the debtor, on the commencement of a bankruptcy case, or on the appointment of a custodian of the debtor's property. Paragraph (2) of subsection (c), however, preserves restrictions on a transfer of a spendthrift trust that the restriction is enforceable nonbankruptcy law to the extent of the income reasonably necessary for the support of a debtor and his dependents.

Subsection (d), derived from section 70c of the Bankruptcy Act [section 110(c) of former Title 11], gives the estate the benefit of all defenses available to the debtor as against an entity other than the estate, including such defenses as statutes of limitations, statutes of frauds, usury, and other personal defenses, and makes waiver by the debtor after the commencement of the case ineffective to bind the estate.

Section 541(e) confirms the current status under the Bankruptcy Act [former Title 11] of bona fide secondary mortgage market transactions as the purchase and sale of assets. Mortgages or interests in mortgages sold in the secondary market should not be considered as part of the debtor's estate. To permit the efficient servicing of mortgages or interests in mortgages the seller often retains the original mortgage notes and related documents, and the purchaser records under State recording statutes the purchaser's ownership of the mortgages or interests in mortgages purchased. Section 541(e) makes clear that the seller's retention of the mortgage documents and the purchaser's decision not to record do not impair the asset sale character of secondary mortgage market transactions. The committee notes that in secondary mortgage market transactions the parties may characterize their relationship as one of trust, agency, or independent contractor. The characterization adopted by the parties should not affect the statutes in bankruptcy on bona fide secondary mortgage market purchases and sales. Senate Report No. 95–989.

1984 Acts. Statements by Legislative Leaders, see 1984 U.S. Code Cong. and Adm. News, p. 576.

1990 Acts. House Report No. 101–881, House Conference Report No. 101–964, and President's Signing Statement, see 1990 U.S. Code Cong. and Adm. News, p. 2017.

1994 Acts. House Report No. 103–835, see 1994 U.S. Code Cong. and Adm. News, p. 3340.

2005 Acts. House Report No. 109–31(Part I), see 2005 U.S. Code Cong. and Adm. News, p. 88.

Legislative Statements

Section 541(a)(7) is new. The provision clarifies that any interest in property that the estate acquires after the commencement of the case is property of the estate; for example, if the estate enters into a contract, after the commencement of the case, such a contract would be property of the estate. The addition of this provision by the House amendment merely clarifies that section 541(a) is an all-embracing definition which includes charges on property, such as liens held by the debtor on property of a third party, or beneficial rights and interests that the debtor may have in property of another. However, only the debtor's interest in such property becomes property of the estate. If the debtor holds bare legal title or holds property in trust for another, only those rights which the debtor would have otherwise had emanating from such interest pass to the estate under section 541. Neither this section nor section 545 will affect various statutory provisions that give a creditor a lien that is valid both inside and outside bankruptcy against a bona fide purchaser of property from the debtor, or that creates a trust fund for the benefit of creditors meeting similar criteria. See Packers and Stockyards Act § 206, 7 U.S.C. 196 (1976) [7 U.S.C.A. § 196].

Section 541(c)(2) follows the position taken in the House bill and rejects the position taken in the Senate amendment with respect to income limitations on a spend-thrift trust.

Section 541(d) of the House amendment is derived from section 541(e) of the Senate amendment and reiterates the general principle that where the debtor holds bare legal title without any equitable interest, that the estate acquires bare legal title without any equitable interest in the property. The purpose of section 541(d) as applied to the secondary mortgage market is identical to the purpose of section 541(e) of the Senate amendment and section 541(d) will accomplish the same result as would have been accomplished by section 541(e). Even if a mortgage seller retains for purposes of servicing legal title to mortgages or interests in mortgages sold in the secondary mortgage market, the trustee would be required by section 541(d) to turn over the mortgages or interests in mortgages to the purchaser of those mortgages.

The seller of mortgages in the secondary mortgage market will often retain the original mortgage notes and related documents and the seller will not endorse the notes to reflect the sale to the purchaser. Similarly, the purchaser will often not record the purchaser's ownership of the mortgages or interests in mortgages under State recording statutes. These facts are irrelevant and the seller's retention of the mortgage documents and the purchaser's decision not to record do not change the trustee's obligation to turn the mortgages or interests in mortgages over to the purchaser. The application of section 541(d) to secondary mortgage market transactions will not be affected by the terms of the servicing agreement between the mortgage servicer and the purchaser of the mortgages. Under section 541(d), the trustee is required to recognize the purchaser's title to the mortgages or interests in mortgages and to turn this property over to the purchaser. It makes no difference whether the servicer and the purchaser characterize their relationship as one of trust, agency, or independent contractor.

The purpose of section 541(d) as applied to the secondary mortgage market is therefore to make certain that secondary mortgage market sales as they are currently structured are not subject to challenge by bankruptcy trustees and that purchasers of mortgages will be able to obtain the mortgages or interests in mortgages which they have purchased from trustees without the trustees asserting that a sale of mortgages is a loan from the purchaser to the seller.

Thus, as section 541(a)(1) clearly states, the estate is comprised of all legal or equitable interests of the debtor in property as of the commencement of the case. To the extent such an interest is limited in the hands of the debtor, it is equally limited in the hands of the estate except to the extent that defenses which are personal against the debtor are not effective against the estate.

Property of the estate: The Senate amendment provided that property of the estate does not include amounts held by the debtor as trustee and any taxes withheld or collected from others before the commencement of the case. The House amendment removes these two provisions. As to property held by the debtor as a trustee, the House amendment provides that property of the estate will include whatever interest the debtor held in the property at the commencement of the case. Thus, where the debtor held only legal title to the property and the beneficial interest in that property belongs to another, such as exists in the case of property held in trust, the property of the estate includes the legal title, but not the beneficial interest in the property.

As to withheld taxes, the House amendment deletes the rule in the Senate bill as unnecessary since property of the estate does not include the beneficial interest in property held by the debtor as a trustee. Under the Internal Revenue Code of 1954 (section 7501 [26 U.S.C.A. § 7501]), the amounts of withheld taxes are held to be a special fund in trust for the United States. Where the Internal Revenue Service can demonstrate that the amounts of taxes withheld are still in the possession of the debtor at the commencement of the case, then if a trust is created, those amounts are not property of the estate. Compare *In re Shakesteers Coffee Shops,* 546 F.2d 821 (9th Cir. 1976) with *In re Glynn Wholesale Building Materials, Inc.* (S.D.Ga.1978) and *In re Progress Tech Colleges, Inc.,* 42 Aftr 2d 78–5573 (S.D.Ohio 1977).

Where it is not possible for the Internal Revenue Service to demonstrate that the amounts of taxes withheld are still in the possession of the debtor at the commencement of the case, present law generally includes amounts of withheld taxes as property of the estate. See, e.g., *United States v. Randall,* 401 U.S. 513 (1973) [91 S.Ct. 991, 28 L.Ed.2d 273] and *In re Tamasha Town and Country Club,* 483 F.2d 1377 (9th Cir. 1973). Nonetheless, a serious problem exists where "trust fund taxes" withheld from others are held to be property of the estate where the withheld amounts are commingled with other assets of the debtor. The courts should permit the use of reasonable assumptions under which the Internal Revenue Service, and other tax authorities, can demonstrate that amounts of withheld taxes are still in the possession of the debtor at the commencement of the case. For example, where the debtor had commingled that amount of withheld taxes in his general checking account, it might be reasonable to assume that any remaining amounts in that account on the commencement of the case are the withheld taxes. In addition, Congress may consider future amendments to the Internal Revenue Code making clear that amounts of withheld taxes are held by the debtor in a trust relationship and, consequently, that such amounts are not property of the estate.

References in Text

The Higher Education Act of 1965, referred to in subsec. (b)(3), is Pub.L. 89–329, Nov. 8, 1965, 79 Stat. 1219, as amended, which is classified principally to chapter 28 (§ 1001 et seq.) of Title 20, Education. For complete classification of this Act to the Code, see Short Title note set out under section 1001 of Title 20 and Tables.

Section 530(b)(1) of the Internal Revenue Code of 1986, referred to in subsec. (b)(5), is classified to 26 U.S.C.A. § 530(b)(1).

Section 4973(e) of the Internal Revenue Code of 1986, referred to in subsec. (b)(5)(B)(ii), is classified to 26 U.S.C.A. § 4973(e).

Section 529(b)(1), (7) of the Internal Revenue Code of 1986, referred to in subsec. (b)(6), is classified to 26 U.S.C.A. § 529(b)(1), (7).

Title I of the Employee Retirement Income Security Act of 1974, referred to in subsec. (b)(7)(A)(i)(I), (B)(i)(I), means Pub.L. 93–406, Title I, Sept. 2, 1974, 88 Stat. 829, which principally enacted subchapter I of chapter 18 of Title 29, 29 U.S.C.A. § 1001 et seq.; see Tables for complete classification.

Section 414(d) of the Internal Revenue Code of 1986, referred to in subsec. (b)(7)(A)(i)(I), (B)(i)(I), is 26 U.S.C.A. § 414(d).

Section 457 of the Internal Revenue Code of 1986, referred to in subsec. (b)(7)(A)(i)(II), (B)(i)(II), is 26 U.S.C.A. § 457.

Section 403(b) of the Internal Revenue Code of 1986, referred to in subsec. (b)(7)(A)(i)(III), (B)(i)(III), is 26 U.S.C.A. § 403(b).

Codifications

Section 223(2) of Pub.L. 103–394, directing that subsec. (b)(4) of this section be amended by striking out the period at the end and inserting "; or", was executed by inserting "or" following the semicolon at the end of subsec. (b)(4)(B)(ii) of this section, as added by section 208(b)(3) of Pub.L. 103–394, as the probable intent of Congress.

Effective and Applicability Provisions

2007 Acts. Increase of dollar amounts by Judicial Conference of the United States by notice published Feb. 14, 2007, 72 F.R. 7082 effective April 1, 2007, and increase not applicable to cases commenced before the effective date of the adjustments, i.e., April 1, 2007. See Adjustment of Dollar Amounts notes under 11 U.S.C.A. § 104 and this section.

2005 Acts. Amendments to this section by Pub.L. 109–8, § 1221, applicable to case pending under this title on April 20, 2005, or filed under this title on or after that date, except that the court shall not confirm a plan under chapter 11 of this title without considering whether this section would substantially affect the rights of a party in interest who first acquired rights with respect to the debtor after the date of the filing of the petition, see Pub.L. 109–8, § 1221(d), set out as a note under 11 U.S.C.A. § 363.

Amendments by Pub.L. 109–8 effective, except as otherwise provided, 180 days after April 20, 2005, and inapplicable with respect to cases commenced under Title 11 before the effective date, see Pub.L. 109–8, § 1501, set out as a note under 11 U.S.C.A. § 101.

1994 Acts. Amendment by Pub.L. 103–394 effective on Oct. 22, 1994, and not to apply with respect to cases commenced under Title 11 of the United States Code before Oct. 22, 1994, see section 702 of Pub.L. 103–394, set out as a note under section 101 of this title.

1992 Acts. Enactment of subsec. (b)(4) by Pub.L. 102–486 effective Oct. 24, 1992, see section 3017(c) of Pub.L. 102–486, set out as a note under section 101 of this title.

1990 Acts. Section 3008 of Pub.L. 101–508, which had provided that the amendment to this section by Pub.L. 101–508 was to cease to be effective on Oct. 1, 1996, was repealed by Pub.L. 102–325, Title XV, § 1558, July 23, 1992, 106 Stat. 841.

1984 Acts. Amendment by Pub.L. 98–353 effective with respect to cases filed 90 days after July 10, 1984, see section 552(a), formerly 553(a) of Pub.L. 98–353, set out as a note under section 101 of this title.

Separability of Provisions

If any provision of or amendment made by Pub.L. 103–394 or the application of such provision or amendment to any person or circumstance is held to be unconstitutional, the remaining provisions of and amendments made by Pub.L. 103–394 and the application of such provisions and amendments to any person or circumstance shall not be affected thereby, see section 701 of Pub.L. 103–394, set out as a note under section 101 of this title.

Adjustment of Dollar Amounts

For adjustment of dollar amounts specified in subsec. (b)(5)(C), (6)(C) of this section by the Judicial Conference of the United States, effective Apr. 1, 2007, see note set out under 11 U.S.C.A. § 104.

By notice published Feb. 14, 2007, 72 F.R. 7082, the Judicial Conference of the United States adjusted the dollar amounts in provisions specified in subsec. (b)(5)(C), (6)(C) of this section, effective Apr. 1, 2007, as follows:

In subsec. (b)(5)(C) adjusted $5,000 to $5,475.

In subsec. (b)(6)(C) adjusted $5,000 to $5,475.

CROSS REFERENCES

Community claim defined, see 11 USCA § 101.

Distribution of property of estate, see 11 USCA § 726.

Effect of discharge, see 11 USCA § 524.

Executory contracts and unexpired leases, see 11 USCA § 365.

Exemptions, see 11 USCA § 522.

Ownership of copyright, see 17 USCA § 201.

Property of estate in—

Chapter 13 cases, see 11 USCA § 1306.

Chapter 12 cases, see 11 USCA § 1207.

Special tax provisions concerning estates of partners and partnerships, see 11 USCA § 728.

Trustee considered consignee of merchandise consigned to deceased or insolvent persons, see 19 USCA § 1485.

Venue of action brought under this title by trustee as statutory successor under this section to debtor, see 28 USCA § 1409.

§ 542. Turnover of property to the estate

(a) Except as provided in subsection (c) or (d) of this section, an entity, other than a custodian, in possession, custody, or control, during the case, of property that the trustee may use, sell, or lease under section 363 of this title, or that the debtor may exempt under section 522 of this title, shall deliver to the trustee, and account for, such property or the value of such property, unless such property is of inconsequential value or benefit to the estate.

(b) Except as provided in subsection (c) or (d) of this section, an entity that owes a debt that is property of the estate and that is matured, payable on demand, or payable on order, shall pay such debt to, or on the order of, the trustee, except to the extent that such debt may be offset under section 553 of this title against a claim against the debtor.

(c) Except as provided in section 362(a)(7) of this title, an entity that has neither actual notice nor actual knowledge of the commencement of the case concerning the debtor may transfer property of the estate, or pay a debt owing to the debtor, in good faith and other than in the manner specified in subsection (d) of this section, to an entity other than the trustee, with the same effect as to the entity making such transfer or payment as if the case under this title concerning the debtor had not been commenced.

(d) A life insurance company may transfer property of the estate or property of the debtor to such company in good faith, with the same effect with respect to such company as if the case under this title concerning the debtor had not been commenced, if such transfer is to pay a premium or to carry out a nonforfeiture insurance option, and is required to be made automatically, under a life insurance contract with such company that was entered into before the date of the filing of the petition and that is property of the estate.

(e) Subject to any applicable privilege, after notice and a hearing, the court may order an attorney, accountant, or other person that holds recorded information, including books, documents, records, and papers, relating to the debtor's property or financial affairs, to turn over or disclose such recorded information to the trustee.

(Pub.L. 95–598, Nov. 6, 1978, 92 Stat. 2595; Pub.L. 98–353, Title III, § 457, July 10, 1984, 98 Stat. 376; Pub.L. 103–394, Title V, § 501(d)(16), Oct. 22, 1994, 108 Stat. 4146.)

HISTORICAL AND STATUTORY NOTES

Revision Notes and Legislative Reports

1978 Acts. Subsection (a) of this section requires anyone holding property of the estate on the date of the filing of the petition, or property that the trustee may use, sell, or lease under section 363, to deliver it to the trustee. The subsection also requires an accounting. The holder of property of the estate is excused from the turnover requirement of this subsection if the property held is of inconsequential value to the estate. However, this provision must be read in conjunction with the remainder of the subsection, so that if the property is of inconsequential monetary value, yet has a significant use value for the estate, the holder of the property would not be excused from turnover.

Subsection (b) requires an entity that owes money to the debtor as of the date of the petition, or that holds money payable on demand or payable on order, to pay the money to the order of the trustee. An exception is made to the extent that the entity has a valid right of setoff, as recognized by section 553.

Subsection (c) provides an exception to subsections (a) and (b). It protects an entity that has neither actual notice nor actual knowledge of the case and that transfers, in good faith, property that is deliverable or payable to the trustee to someone other than to the estate or on order of the estate. This subsection codifies the result of *Bank of Marin v. England,* 385 U.S. 99 (1966) [87 S.Ct. 274, 17 L.Ed.2d 197], but does not go so far as to permit bank setoff in violation of the automatic stay, proposed 11 U.S.C. 362(a)(7), even if the bank offsetting the debtor's balance has no knowledge of the case.

Subsection (d) protects life insurance companies that are required by contract to make automatic premium loans from property that might otherwise be property of the estate.

Subsection (e) requires an attorney, accountant, or other professional that holds recorded information relating to the debtor's property or financial affairs, to surrender it to the trustee. This duty is subject to any applicable claim of privilege, such as attorney-client privilege. It is a new provision that deprives accountants and attorneys of the leverage that they have today, under State law lien provisions, to receive payment in full ahead of other creditors when the information they hold is necessary to the administration of the estate. Senate Report No. 95–989.

1984 Acts. Statements by Legislative Leaders, see 1984 U.S. Code Cong. and Adm. News, p. 576.

1994 Acts. House Report No. 103–835, see 1994 U.S. Code Cong. and Adm. News, p. 3340.

Legislative Statements

Section 542(a) of the House amendment modifies similar provisions contained in the House bill and the Senate amendment treating with turnover of property to the estate. The section makes clear that any entity, other than a custodian, is required to deliver property of the estate to the trustee or debtor in possession whenever such property is acquired by the entity during the case, if the trustee or debtor in possession may use, sell, or lease the property under section 363, or if the debtor may exempt the property under section 522, unless the property is of inconsequential value or benefit to the estate. This section is not intended to require an entity to deliver property to the trustee if such entity has obtained an order of the court authorizing the entity to retain possession, custody or control of the property.

The House amendment adopts section 542(c) of the House bill in preference to a similar provision contained in section 542(c) of the Senate amendment. Protection afforded by section 542(c) applies only to the transferor or payor and not to a transferee or payee receiving a transfer or payment, as the case may be. Such transferee or payee is treated under section 549 and section 550 of title 11.

The extent to which the attorney client privilege is valid against the trustee is unclear under current law and is left to be determined by the courts on a case by case basis.

Effective and Applicability Provisions

1994 Acts. Amendment by Pub.L. 103–394 effective on Oct. 22, 1994, and not to apply with respect to cases commenced under Title 11 of the United States Code before Oct. 22, 1994, see section 702 of Pub.L. 103–394, set out as a note under section 101 of this title.

1984 Acts. Amendment by Pub.L. 98–353 effective with respect to cases filed 90 days after July 10, 1984, see section 552(a), formerly 553 of Pub.L. 98–353, set out as a note under section 101 of this title.

Separability of Provisions

If any provision of or amendment made by Pub.L. 103–394 or the application of such provision or amendment to any person or circumstance is held to be unconstitutional, the remaining provisions of and amendments made by Pub.L. 103–394 and the application of such provisions and amendments to any person or circumstance shall not be affected thereby, see section 701 of Pub.L. 103–394, set out as a note under section 101 of this title.

CROSS REFERENCES

Assignability or accrual to third persons of farm loan agreements respecting credits or principal and interest, see 42 USCA § 1473.

Concealment of assets, see 18 USCA § 152.

Disallowance of claims of entity from which property is recoverable, see 11 USCA § 502.

Effect of dismissal, see 11 USCA § 349.

Exemptions, see 11 USCA § 522.

§ 543. Turnover of property by a custodian

(a) A custodian with knowledge of the commencement of a case under this title concerning the debtor may not make any disbursement from, or take any action in the administration of, property of the debtor, proceeds, product, offspring, rents, or profits of such property, or property of the estate, in the possession, custody, or control of such custodian, except such action as is necessary to preserve such property.

(b) A custodian shall—

(1) deliver to the trustee any property of the debtor held by or transferred to such custodian, or proceeds, product, offspring, rents, or profits of such property, that is in such custodian's possession, custody, or control on the date that such custodian acquires knowledge of the commencement of the case; and

(2) file an accounting of any property of the debtor, or proceeds, product, offspring, rents, or profits of such property, that, at any time, came into the possession, custody, or control of such custodian.

(c) The court, after notice and a hearing, shall—

(1) protect all entities to which a custodian has become obligated with respect to such property or proceeds, product, offspring, rents, or profits of such property;

(2) provide for the payment of reasonable compensation for services rendered and costs and expenses incurred by such custodian; and

(3) surcharge such custodian, other than an assignee for the benefit of the debtor's creditors that was appointed or took possession more than 120 days before the date of the filing of the petition, for any improper or excessive disbursement, other than a disbursement that has been made in accordance with applicable law or that has been approved, after notice and a hearing, by a court of competent jurisdiction before the commencement of the case under this title.

(d) After notice and hearing, the bankruptcy court—

(1) may excuse compliance with subsection (a), (b), or (c) of this section if the interests of creditors and, if the debtor is not insolvent, of equity security holders would be better served by permitting a custodian to continue in possession, custody, or control of such property, and

(2) shall excuse compliance with subsections (a) and (b)(1) of this section if the custodian is an assignee for the benefit of the debtor's creditors that was appointed or took possession more than 120 days before the date of the filing of the petition, unless compliance with such subsections is necessary to prevent fraud or injustice.

(Pub.L. 95–598, Nov. 6, 1978, 92 Stat. 2595; Pub.L. 98–353, Title III, § 458, July 10, 1984, 98 Stat. 376; Pub.L. 103–394, Title V, § 501(d)(17), Oct. 22, 1994, 108 Stat. 4146.)

HISTORICAL AND STATUTORY NOTES

Revision Notes and Legislative Reports

1978 Acts. This section requires a custodian appointed before the bankruptcy case to deliver to the trustee and to account for property that has come into his possession, custody, or control as a custodian. "Property of the debtor" in section (a) [sic] includes property that was property of the debtor at the time the custodian took the property, but the title to which passed to the custodian. The section requires the court to protect any obligations incurred by the custodian, provide for the payment of reasonable compensation for services rendered and costs and expenses incurred by the custodian, and to surcharge the custodian for any improper or excessive disbursement, unless it has been approved by a court of competent jurisdiction. Subsection (d) reinforces the general abstention policy in § 305 by permitting the bankruptcy court to authorize the custodianship to proceed notwithstanding this section. Senate Report No. 95–989.

1984 Acts. Statements by Legislative Leaders, see 1984 U.S. Code Cong. and Adm. News, p. 576.

1994 Acts. House Report No. 103–835, see 1994 U.S. Code Cong. and Adm. News, p. 3340.

Legislative Statements

Section 543(a) is a modification of similar provisions contained in the House bill and the Senate amendment. The provision clarifies that a custodian may always act as is necessary to preserve property of the debtor. Section 543(c)(3) excepts from surcharge a custodian that is an assignee for the benefit of creditors, who was appointed or took possession before 120 days before the date of the filing of the petition, whichever is later. The provision also prevents a custodian from being surcharged in connection with payments made in accordance with applicable law.

Effective and Applicability Provisions

1994 Acts. Amendment by Pub.L. 103–394 effective on Oct. 22, 1994, and not to apply with respect to cases commenced under Title 11 of the United States Code before Oct. 22, 1994, see section 702 of Pub.L. 103–394, set out as a note under section 101 of this title.

1984 Acts. Amendment by Pub.L. 98–353 effective with respect to cases filed 90 days after July 10, 1984, see section 552(a)(7), formerly 553 of Pub.L. 98–353, set out as a note under section 101 of this title.

Separability of Provisions

If any provision of or amendment made by Pub.L. 103–394 or the application of such provision or amendment to any person or circumstance is held to be unconstitutional, the remaining provisions of and amendments made by Pub.L. 103–394 and the application of such provisions and amendments to any person or circumstance shall not be affected thereby, see section 701 of Pub.L. 103–394, set out as a note under section 101 of this title.

CROSS REFERENCES

Administrative expenses of superseded custodians, see 11 USCA § 503.

Concealment of assets, see 18 USCA § 152.

Disallowance of claim of entity from which property is recoverable, see 11 USCA § 502.

Effect of dismissal, see 11 USCA § 349.

Order of payment on claims for expenses of superseded custodians, see 11 USCA § 726.

Property recoverable by trustee as exempt, see 11 USCA § 522.

§ 544. Trustee as lien creditor and as successor to certain creditors and purchasers

(a) The trustee shall have, as of the commencement of the case, and without regard to any knowledge of the trustee or of any creditor, the rights and powers of, or may avoid any transfer of property of the debtor or any obligation incurred by the debtor that is voidable by—

(1) a creditor that extends credit to the debtor at the time of the commencement of the case, and that obtains, at such time and with respect to such credit, a judicial lien on all property on which a creditor on a simple contract could have obtained such a judicial lien, whether or not such a creditor exists;

(2) a creditor that extends credit to the debtor at the time of the commencement of the case, and obtains, at such time and with respect to such credit, an execution against the debtor that is returned unsatisfied at such time, whether or not such a creditor exists; or

(3) a bona fide purchaser of real property, other than fixtures, from the debtor, against whom applicable law permits such transfer to be perfected, that obtains the status of a bona fide purchaser and has perfected such transfer at the time of the commencement of the case, whether or not such a purchaser exists.

(b)(1) Except as provided in paragraph (2), the trustee may avoid any transfer of an interest of the debtor in property or any obligation incurred by the debtor that is voidable under applicable law by a creditor holding an unsecured claim that is allowable under section 502 of this title or that is not allowable only under section 502(e) of this title.

(2) Paragraph (1) shall not apply to a transfer of a charitable contribution (as that term is defined in section 548(d)(3)) that is not covered under section 548(a)(1)(B), by reason of section 548(a)(2). Any claim by any person to recover a transferred contribution described in the preceding sentence under Federal or State law in a Federal or State court shall be preempted by the commencement of the case.

(Pub.L. 95–598, Nov. 6, 1978, 92 Stat. 2596; Pub.L. 98–353, Title III, § 459, July 10, 1984, 98 Stat. 377; Pub.L. 105–183, §§ 3(b), June 19, 1998, 112 Stat. 518.)

HISTORICAL AND STATUTORY NOTES

Revision Notes and Legislative Reports

1978 Acts. Subsection (a) is the "strong arm clause" of current law, now found in Bankruptcy Act § 70c [section 110(c) of former Title 11]. It gives the trustee the rights of a creditor on a simple contract with a judicial lien on the property of the debtor as of the date of the petition; of a creditor with a writ of execution against the property of the debtor unsatisfied as of the date of the petition; and a bona fide purchaser of the real property of the debtor as of the date of the petition. "Simple contract" as used here is derived from Bankruptcy Act § 60a(4) [section 96(a)(4) of former title 11]. The third status, that of a bona fide purchaser of real property, is new.

Subsection (b) is derived from current section 70e [former § 110(e) of former Title 11]. It gives the trustee the rights of actual unsecured creditors under applicable law to void transfers. It follows *Moore v. Bay,* 284 U.S. 4 (1931) [52 S.Ct. 3, 76 L.Ed. 133, 18 Am.Bankr.Rep.N.S. 675.], and overrules those cases that hold section 70e [section 110(e) of former Title 11] gives the trustee the rights of secured creditors. Senate Report No. 95–989.

1984 Acts. Statements by Legislative Leaders, see 1984 U.S.Code Cong. and Adm.News, p. 576.

1998 Acts. Statement by President, see 1998 U.S. Code Cong. and Adm. News, p. 230.

Legislative Statements

Section 544(a)(3) modifies similar provisions contained in the House bill and Senate amendment so as not to require a creditor to perform the impossible in order to perfect his interest. Both the lien creditor test in section 544(a)(1), and the bona fide purchaser test in section 544(a)(3) should not require a transferee to perfect a transfer against an entity with respect to which applicable law does not permit perfection. The avoiding powers under section 544(a)(1), (2), and (3) are new. In particular, section 544(a)(1) overrules *Pacific Finance Corp. v. Edwards,* 309 F.2d 224 (9th Cir. 1962), and *In re Federals, Inc.,* 553 F.2d 509 (6th Cir. 1977), insofar as those cases held that the trustee did not have the status of a creditor who extended credit immediately prior to the commencement of the case.

The House amendment deletes section 544(c) of the House bill.

Effective and Applicability Provisions

1984 Acts. Amendment by Pub.L. 98–353 effective with respect to cases filed 90 days after July 10, 1984, see section 552(a), formerly 553 of Pub.L. 98–353, set out as a note under section 101 of this title.

Applicability

Pub.L. 105–183, § 5, June 19, 1998, 112 Stat. 518, provided that: "This Act and the amendments made by this Act [amending this section and sections 546, 548, 707, and 1325 of this title and enacting this note and provisions set out as notes under this section and section 101 of this title] shall apply to any case brought under an applicable provision of title 11, United States Code, [this title] that is pending or commenced on or after the date of enactment of this Act [June 19, 1998]."

Rule of Construction

Pub.L. 105–183, § 6, June 19, 1998, 112 Stat. 519, provided that: "Nothing in the amendments made by this Act [amending this section and sections 546, 548, 707, and 1325 of this title and enacting this note and provisions set out as notes under this section and section 101 of this title] is intended to limit the applicability of the Religious Freedom Restoration Act of 1993 (42 U.S.C. 2002bb et seq.)."

CROSS REFERENCES

Applicability of this section in Chapter nine cases, see 11 USCA § 901.

Appointment of trustee upon debtor's refusal to pursue cause of action under this section, see 11 USCA § 926.

Commencement of involuntary cases by transferees of voidable transfer, see 11 USCA § 303.

Disallowance of claims of entity that is transferee of avoidable transfer, see 11 USCA § 502.

Effect of dismissal, see 11 USCA § 349.

Exemptions, see 11 USCA § 522.

Recovery of voidable transfers in investor protection liquidation proceedings, see 15 USCA § 78fff–2.

Venue of action brought under this title by trustee as statutory successor under this section to creditors, see 28 USCA § 1409.

Voidable transfers in—

Commodity broker liquidation cases, see 11 USCA § 764.

Stockbroker liquidation proceedings, see 11 USCA § 749.

§ 545. Statutory liens

The trustee may avoid the fixing of a statutory lien on property of the debtor to the extent that such lien—

(1) first becomes effective against the debtor—

(A) when a case under this title concerning the debtor is commenced;

(B) when an insolvency proceeding other than under this title concerning the debtor is commenced;

(C) when a custodian is appointed or authorized to take or takes possession;

(D) when the debtor becomes insolvent;

(E) when the debtor's financial condition fails to meet a specified standard; or

(F) at the time of an execution against property of the debtor levied at the instance of an entity other than the holder of such statutory lien;

(2) is not perfected or enforceable at the time of the commencement of the case against a bona fide purchaser that purchases such property at the time of the commencement of the case, whether or not such a purchaser exists, except in any case in which a purchaser is a purchaser described in section 6323 of the Internal Revenue Code of 1986, or in any other similar provision of State or local law;

(3) is for rent; or

(4) is a lien of distress for rent.

(Pub.L. 95–598, Nov. 6, 1978, 92 Stat. 2597; Pub.L. 98–353, Title III, § 460, July 10, 1984, 98 Stat. 377; Pub.L. 109–8, Title VII, § 711, Apr. 20, 2005, 119 Stat. 127.)

HISTORICAL AND STATUTORY NOTES

Revision Notes and Legislative Reports

1978 Acts. This section permits the trustee to avoid the fixing of certain statutory liens. It is derived from subsections 67b and 67c of present law [sections 107(b) and (c) former Title 11]. Liens that first become effective on the bankruptcy or insolvency of the debtor are voidable by the trustee. Liens that are not perfected or enforceable on the date of the petition against a bona fide purchaser are voidable. If a transferee is able to perfect under section 546(a) and that perfection relates back to an earlier date, then in spite of the filing of the bankruptcy petition, the trustee would not be able to defeat the lien, because the lien would be perfected and enforceable against a bona fide purchaser that purchased the property on the date of the filing of the petition. Finally, a lien for rent or of distress for rent is voidable, whether the lien is a statutory lien or a common law lien of distress for rent. See proposed 11 U.S.C. 101(37); Bankruptcy Act § 67(c)(1)(C) [section 107(c)(1)(C) of former Title 11]. The trustee may avoid a lien under this section even if the lien has been enforced by sale before the commencement of the case. To that extent, Bankruptcy Act section 67c(5) [section 107(c)(5) of former Title 11] is not followed.

Subsection (b) limits the trustee's power to avoid tax liens under Federal, state, or local law. For example, under section 6323 of the Internal Revenue Code [Title 26]. Once public notice of a tax lien has been filed, the Government is generally entitled to priority over subsequent lienholders. However, certain purchasers who acquire an interest in certain specific kinds of personal property will take free of an existing filed tax lien attaching to such property. Among the specific kinds of personal property which a purchaser can acquire free of an existing tax lien (unless the buyer knows of the existence of the lien) are stocks and securities, motor vehicles, inventory, and certain household goods. Under the present Bankruptcy Act (section 67(c)(1) [section 107(c)(1) of former Title 11]), the trustee may be viewed as a bona fide purchaser, so that he can take over any such designated items free of tax liens even if the tax authority has perfected its lien. However, the reasons for enabling a bona fide purchaser to take these kinds of assets free of an unfiled tax lien, that is, to encourage free movement of these assets in general commerce, do not apply to a trustee in a title 11 case, who is not in the same position as an ordinary bona fide purchaser as to such property. The bill accordingly adds a new subsection (b) to sec. 545 providing, in effect, that a trustee in bankruptcy does not have the right under this section to take otherwise specially treated items of personal property free of a tax lien filed before the filing of the petition. Senate Report No. 95–989.

1984 Acts. Statements by Legislative Leaders, see 1984 U.S.Code Cong. and Adm.News, p. 576.

2005 Acts. House Report No. 109–31(Part I), see 2005 U.S. Code Cong. and Adm. News, p. 88.

Legislative Statements

Section 545 of the House amendment modifies similar provisions contained in the House bill and Senate amendment to make clear that a statutory lien may be avoided under section 545 only to the extent the lien violates the perfection standards of section 545. Thus a Federal tax lien is invalid under section 545(2) with respect to property specified in sections 6323(b) and (c) of the Internal Revenue Code of 1954 [sections 6323(b) and (c) of Title 26, Internal Revenue Code]. As a result of this modification, section 545(b) of the Senate amendment is deleted as unnecessary.

Statutory liens: The House amendment retains the provision of section 545(2) of the House bill giving the trustee in a bankruptcy case the same power which a bona fide purchaser has to take over certain kinds of personal property despite the existence of a tax lien covering that property. The amendment thus retains present law, and deletes section 545(b) of the Senate amendment which would have no longer allowed the trustee to step into the shoes of a bona fide purchaser for this purpose.

References in Text

Section 6323 of the Internal Revenue Code of 1986, referred to in par. (2), is classified to 26 U.S.C.A. § 6323.

Effective and Applicability Provisions

2005 Acts. Amendments by Pub.L. 109–8 effective, except as otherwise provided, 180 days after April 20, 2005, and inapplicable with respect to cases commenced under Title 11 before the effective date, see Pub.L. 109–8, § 1501, set out as a note under 11 U.S.C.A. § 101.

1984 Acts. Amendment by Pub.L. 98–353 effective with respect to cases filed 90 days after July 10, 1984, see section 552(a), formerly 553(a) of Pub.L. 98–353, set out as a note under section 101 of this title.

CROSS REFERENCES

Applicability of this section in Chapter nine cases, see 11 USCA § 901.

Appointment of trustee upon debtor's refusal to pursue cause of action under this section, see 11 USCA § 926.

Commencement of involuntary cases by transferees of voidable transfers, see 11 USCA § 303.

Disallowance of claims of entity that is a transferee of an avoidable transfer, see 11 USCA § 502.

Effect of dismissal, see 11 USCA § 349.

Exemptions, see 11 USCA § 522.

Recovery of voidable transfers in investor protection liquidation proceedings, see 15 USCA § 78fff–2.

Voidable transfers in—

Commodity broker liquidation cases, see 11 USCA § 764.

Stockbroker liquidation cases, see 11 USCA § 749.

§ 546. Limitations on avoiding powers

(a) An action or proceeding under section 544, 545, 547, 548, or 553 of this title may not be commenced after the earlier of—

(1) the later of—

(A) 2 years after the entry of the order for relief; or

(B) 1 year after the appointment or election of the first trustee under section 702, 1104, 1163, 1202, or 1302 of this title if such appointment or such election occurs before the expiration of the period specified in subparagraph (A); or

(2) the time the case is closed or dismissed.

(b)(1) The rights and powers of a trustee under sections 544, 545, and 549 of this title are subject to any generally applicable law that—

(A) permits perfection of an interest in property to be effective against an entity that acquires rights in such property before the date of perfection; or

(B) provides for the maintenance or continuation of perfection of an interest in property to be effective against an entity that acquires rights in such property before the date on which action is taken to effect such maintenance or continuation.

(2) If—

(A) a law described in paragraph (1) requires seizure of such property or commencement of an action to accomplish such perfection, or maintenance or continuation of perfection of an interest in property; and

(B) such property has not been seized or such an action has not been commenced before the date of the filing of the petition;

such interest in such property shall be perfected, or perfection of such interest shall be maintained or continued, by giving notice within the time fixed by such law for such seizure or such commencement.

(c)(1) Except as provided in subsection (d) of this section and in section 507(c), and subject to the prior rights of a holder of a security interest in such goods or the proceeds thereof, the rights and powers of the trustee under sections 544(a), 545, 547, and 549 are subject to the right of a seller of goods that has sold goods to the debtor, in the ordinary course of such seller's business, to reclaim such goods if the debtor has received such goods while insolvent, within 45 days before the date of the commencement of a case under this title, but such seller may not reclaim such goods unless such seller demands in writing reclamation of such goods—

(A) not later than 45 days after the date of receipt of such goods by the debtor; or

(B) not later than 20 days after the date of commencement of the case, if the 45-day period expires after the commencement of the case.

(2) If a seller of goods fails to provide notice in the manner described in paragraph (1), the seller still may assert the rights contained in section 503(b)(9).

(d) In the case of a seller who is a producer of grain sold to a grain storage facility, owned or operated by the debtor, in the ordinary course of such seller's business (as such terms are defined in section 557 of this title) or in the case of a United States fisherman who has caught fish sold to a fish processing facility owned or operated by the debtor in the ordinary course of such fisherman's business, the rights and powers of the trustee under sections 544(a), 545, 547, and 549 of this title are subject to any statutory or common law right of such producer or fisherman to reclaim such grain or fish if the debtor has received such grain or fish while insolvent, but—

(1) such producer or fisherman may not reclaim any grain or fish unless such producer or fisherman demands, in writing, reclamation of such grain or fish before ten days after receipt thereof by the debtor; and

(2) the court may deny reclamation to such a producer or fisherman with a right of reclamation that has made such a demand only if the court secures such claim by a lien.

(e) Notwithstanding sections 544, 545, 547, 548(a)(1)(B), and 548(b) of this title, the trustee may not avoid a transfer that is a margin payment, as defined in section 101, 741, or 761 of this title, or settlement payment, as defined in section 101 or 741 of this title, made by or to (or for the benefit of) a commodity broker, forward contract merchant, stockbroker, financial institution, financial participant, or securities clearing agency, or that is a transfer made by or to (or for the benefit of) a commodity broker, forward contract merchant, stockbroker, financial institution, financial participant, or securities clearing agency, in connection with a securities contract, as defined in section 741(7), commodity contract, as defined in section 761(4), or forward contract, that is made before the commencement of the case, except under section 548(a)(1)(A) of this title.

(f) Notwithstanding sections 544, 545, 547, 548(a)(1)(B), and 548(b) of this title, the trustee may not avoid a transfer made by or to (or for the benefit of) a repo participant or financial participant, in connection with a repurchase agreement and that is made before the commencement of the case, except under section 548(a)(1)(A) of this title.

(g) Notwithstanding sections 544, 545, 547, 548(a)(1)(B) and 548(b) of this title, the trustee may not avoid a transfer, made by or to (or for the benefit of) a swap participant or financial participant, under or in connection with any swap agreement and that is made before the commencement of the case, except under section 548(a)(1)(A) of this title.

(h) Notwithstanding the rights and powers of a trustee under sections 544(a), 545, 547, 549, and 553, if the court determines on a motion by the trustee made not later than 120 days after the date of the order for relief in a case under chapter 11 of this title and after notice and a hearing, that a return is in the best interests of the estate, the debtor, with the consent of a creditor and subject to the prior rights of holders of security interests in such goods or the proceeds of such goods, may return goods shipped to the debtor by the creditor before the commencement of the case, and the creditor may offset the purchase price of such goods against any claim of the creditor against the debtor that arose before the commencement of the case.

(i)(1) Notwithstanding paragraphs (2) and (3) of section 545, the trustee may not avoid a warehouseman's lien for storage, transportation, or other costs incidental to the storage and handling of goods.

(2) The prohibition under paragraph (1) shall be applied in a manner consistent with any State statute applicable to such lien that is similar to section 7–209 of the Uniform Commercial Code, as in effect on the date of enactment of the Bankruptcy Abuse Prevention and Consumer Protection Act of 2005, or any successor to such section 7–209.

(j) Notwithstanding sections 544, 545, 547, 548(a)(1)(B), and 548(b) the trustee may not avoid a transfer made by or to (or for the benefit of) a master netting agreement participant under or in connection with any master netting agreement or any individual contract covered thereby that is made before the commencement of the case, except under section 548(a)(1)(A) and except to the extent that the trustee could otherwise avoid such a transfer made under an individual contract covered by such master netting agreement.

(Pub.L. 95–598, Nov. 6, 1978, 92 Stat. 2597; Pub.L. 97–222, § 4, July 27, 1982, 96 Stat. 236; Pub.L. 98–353, Title III, §§ 351, 393, 461, July 10, 1984, 98 Stat. 358, 365, 377; Pub.L. 99–554, Title II, §§ 257(d), 283*(l)*, Oct. 27, 1986, 100 Stat. 3114, 3117; Pub.L. 101–311, Title I, § 103, Title II, § 203, June 25, 1990, 104 Stat. 268, 269; Pub.L. 103–394, Title II, §§ 204(b), 209, 216, 222(a), Title V, § 501(b)(4), Oct. 22, 1994, 108 Stat. 4122, 4125, 4126, 4129, 4142; Pub.L. 105–183, § 3(c), June 19, 1998, 112 Stat. 518; Pub.L. 109–8, Title IV, § 406, Title IX, §§ 907(e), 907*(o)*(2), (3), Title XII, § 1227(a), Apr. 20, 2005, 119 Stat. 105, 177, 182, 199; Pub.L. 109–390, § 5(b), Dec. 12, 2006, 120 Stat. 2697.)

HISTORICAL AND STATUTORY NOTES

Revision Notes and Legislative Reports

1978 Acts. The trustee's rights and powers under certain of the avoiding powers are limited by section 546. First, if an interest holder against whom the trustee would have rights still has, under applicable nonbankruptcy law, and as of the date of the petition, the opportunity to perfect his lien against an intervening interest holder, then he may perfect his interest against the trustee. If applicable law requires seizure for perfection, then perfection is by notice to the trustee instead. The rights granted to a creditor under this subsection prevail over the trustee only if the transferee has perfected the transfer in accordance with applicable law, and that perfection relates back to a date that is before the commencement of the case.

The phrase "generally applicable law" relates to those provisions of applicable law that apply both in bankruptcy cases and outside of bankruptcy cases. For example, many State laws, under the Uniform Commercial Code, permit perfection of a purchase-money security interest to relate back to defeat an earlier levy by another creditor if the former was perfected within ten days of delivery of the property. U.C.C. § 9–301(2). Such perfection would then be able to defeat an intervening hypothetical judicial lien creditor on the date of the filing of the petition. The purpose of the subsection is to protect, in spite of the surprise intervention of a bankruptcy petition, those whom State law protects by allowing them to perfect their liens or interests as of an effective date that is earlier than the date of perfection. It is not designed to give the States an opportunity to enact disguised priorities in the form of liens that apply only in bankruptcy cases.

Subsection (b) specifies that the trustee's rights and powers under the strong arm clause, the successor to creditors provision, the preference section, and the postpetition transaction section are all subject to any statutory or common-law right of a seller, in the ordinary course of business, of goods to the debtor to reclaim the goods if the debtor received the goods on credit while insolvent. The seller must demand reclamation within ten days after receipt of the goods by the debtor. As under nonbankruptcy law, the right is subject to any superior rights of secured creditors. The purpose of the provision is to recognize, in part, the validity of section 2–702 of the Uniform Commercial Code, which has generated much litigation, confusion, and divergent decisions in different circuits. The right is subject, however, to the power of the court to deny reclamation and protect the seller by granting him a priority as an administrative expense for his claim arising out of the sale of the goods.

Subsection (c) adds a statute of limitations to the use by the trustee of the avoiding powers. The limitation is two years after his appointment, or the time the case is closed or dismissed, whichever occurs later. Senate Report No. 95–989.

1982 Acts. House Report No. 97–420, see 1982 U.S. Code Cong. and Adm. News, p. 583.

1984 Acts. Statements by Legislative Leaders, see 1984 U.S. Code Cong. and Adm. News, p. 576.

1986 Acts. House Report No. 99–764 and House Conference Report No. 99–958, see 1986 U.S. Code Cong. and Adm. News, p. 5227.

1990 Acts. House Report No. 101–484, see 1990 U.S. Code Cong. and Adm. News, p. 223.

1994 Acts. House Report No. 103–835, see 1994 U.S. Code Cong. and Adm. News, p. 3340.

1998 Acts. Statement by President, see 1998 U.S. Code Cong. and Adm. News, p. 230.

2005 Acts. House Report No. 109–31(Part I), see 2005 U.S. Code Cong. and Adm. News, p. 88.

2006 Acts. House Report No. 109–648(Part I), see 2006 U.S. Code Cong. and Adm. News, p. 1585.

Legislative Statements

Section 546(a) of the House amendment is derived from section 546(c) of the Senate amendment. Section 546(c) of the House amendment is derived from section 546(b) of the Senate amendment. It applies to receipt of goods on credit as well as by cash sales. The section clarifies that a demand for reclamation must be made in writing anytime before 10 days after receipt of the goods by the debtor. The section also permits the court to grant the reclaiming creditor a lien or an administrative expense in lieu of turning over the property.

References in Text

The date of enactment of the Bankruptcy Abuse Prevention and Consumer Protection Act of 2005, referred to in subsec. (i)(2), is April 20, 2005, the approval date of Pub.L. 109–8, 119 Stat. 23.

Codifications

The amendment by Pub.L. 105–183, § 3(c)(3), to subsec. (g) of this section was executed to the first subsec. (g) of this section as the probable intent of Congress since the phrases being amended, "section 548(a)(1)" and "548(a)(2)", appeared only in the first subsec. (g).

Effective and Applicability Provisions

2005 Acts. Amendments by Pub.L. 109–8 effective, except as otherwise provided, 180 days after April 20, 2005, and inapplicable with respect to cases commenced under Title 11 before the effective date, see Pub.L. 109–8, § 1501, set out as a note under 11 U.S.C.A. § 101.

1994 Acts. Amendments by Pub.L. 103–394 effective on Oct. 22, 1994, and not to apply with respect to cases commenced under Title 11 of the United States Code before Oct. 22, 1994, see section 702 of Pub.L. 103–394, set out as a note under section 101 of this title.

1986 Acts. Amendments by Pub.L. 99–554, § 257(d), effective 30 days after Oct. 27, 1986, but not to apply with respect to cases commenced under this title before that date, see section 302(a), (c)(1) of Pub.L. 99–554, set out as a note under section 581 of Title 28, Judiciary and Judicial Procedure.

Amendment by Pub.L. 99–554, § 283, effective 30 days after Oct. 27, 1986, except as otherwise provided for, see section 302(a) of Pub.L. 99–554, set out as a note under section 581 of Title 28.

1984 Acts. Amendment by Pub.L. 98–353 effective with respect to cases filed 90 days after July 10, 1984, see section 552(a), formerly 553 of Pub.L. 98–353, set out as a note under section 101 of this title.

Separability of Provisions

If any provision of or amendment made by Pub.L. 103–394 or the application of such provision or amendment to any person or circumstance is held to be unconstitutional, the remaining provisions of and amendments made by Pub.L. 103–394 and the application of such provisions and amendments to any person or circumstance shall not be affected thereby, see section 701 of Pub.L. 103–394, set out as a note under section 101 of this title.

Applicability

Applicability of amendments made by Pub.L. 105–183 to any case brought under an applicable provision of this title that is pending or commenced on or after June 19, 1998, see Pub.L. 105–183, § 5, June 19, 1998, 112 Stat. 518, set out as a note under section 544 of this title.

Rule of Construction

Amendments made by Pub.L. 105–183 not intended to limit the applicability of the Religious Freedom Restoration Act of 1993 (42 U.S.C. 2002bb et seq.), see Pub.L. 105–183, § 6, June 19, 1998, 112 Stat. 519, set out as a note under section 544 of this title.

CROSS REFERENCES

Applicability of this section in Chapter nine cases, see 11 USCA § 901.

Automatic stay, see 11 USCA § 362.

Concealment of debtor's assets deemed continuing offense, see 18 USCA § 3284.

§ 547. Preferences

(a) In this section—

(1) "inventory" means personal property leased or furnished, held for sale or lease, or to be furnished under a contract for service, raw materials, work in process, or materials used or consumed in a business, including farm products such as crops or livestock, held for sale or lease;

(2) "new value" means money or money's worth in goods, services, or new credit, or release by a transferee of property previously transferred to such transferee in a transaction that is neither void nor voidable by the debtor or the trustee under any applicable law, including proceeds of such property, but does not include an obligation substituted for an existing obligation;

(3) "receivable" means right to payment, whether or not such right has been earned by performance; and

(4) a debt for a tax is incurred on the day when such tax is last payable without penalty, including any extension.

(b) Except as provided in subsections (c) and (i) of this section, the trustee may avoid any transfer of an interest of the debtor in property—

(1) to or for the benefit of a creditor;

(2) for or on account of an antecedent debt owed by the debtor before such transfer was made;

(3) made while the debtor was insolvent;

(4) made—

(A) on or within 90 days before the date of the filing of the petition; or

(B) between ninety days and one year before the date of the filing of the petition, if such creditor at the time of such transfer was an insider; and

(5) that enables such creditor to receive more than such creditor would receive if—

(A) the case were a case under chapter 7 of this title;

(B) the transfer had not been made; and

(C) such creditor received payment of such debt to the extent provided by the provisions of this title.

(c) The trustee may not avoid under this section a transfer—

(1) to the extent that such transfer was—

(A) intended by the debtor and the creditor to or for whose benefit such transfer was made to be a contemporaneous exchange for new value given to the debtor; and

(B) in fact a substantially contemporaneous exchange;

(2) to the extent that such transfer was in payment of a debt incurred by the debtor in the ordinary course of business or financial affairs of the debtor and the transferee, and such transfer was—

(A) made in the ordinary course of business or financial affairs of the debtor and the transferee; or

(B) made according to ordinary business terms;

(3) that creates a security interest in property acquired by the debtor—

(A) to the extent such security interest secures new value that was—

(i) given at or after the signing of a security agreement that contains a description of such property as collateral;

(ii) given by or on behalf of the secured party under such agreement;

(iii) given to enable the debtor to acquire such property; and

(iv) in fact used by the debtor to acquire such property; and

(B) that is perfected on or before 30 days after the debtor receives possession of such property;

(4) to or for the benefit of a creditor, to the extent that, after such transfer, such creditor gave new value to or for the benefit of the debtor—

(A) not secured by an otherwise unavoidable security interest; and

(B) on account of which new value the debtor did not make an otherwise unavoidable transfer to or for the benefit of such creditor;

(5) that creates a perfected security interest in inventory or a receivable or the proceeds of either, except to the extent that the aggregate of all such transfers to the transferee caused a reduction, as of the date of the filing of the petition and to the prejudice of other creditors holding unsecured claims, of any amount by which the debt secured by such security interest exceeded the value of all security interests for such debt on the later of—

(A)(i) with respect to a transfer to which subsection (b)(4)(A) of this section applies, 90 days before the date of the filing of the petition; or

(ii) with respect to a transfer to which subsection (b)(4)(B) of this section applies, one year before the date of the filing of the petition; or

(B) the date on which new value was first given under the security agreement creating such security interest;

(6) that is the fixing of a statutory lien that is not avoidable under section 545 of this title;

(7) to the extent such transfer was a bona fide payment of a debt for a domestic support obligation;

(8) if, in a case filed by an individual debtor whose debts are primarily consumer debts, the aggregate value of all property that constitutes or is affected by such transfer is less than $600; or

(9) if, in a case filed by a debtor whose debts are not primarily consumer debts, the aggregate value of all property that constitutes or is affected by such transfer is less than $5,475 [1].

(d) The trustee may avoid a transfer of an interest in property of the debtor transferred to or for the benefit of a surety to secure reimbursement of such a surety that furnished a bond or other obligation to dissolve a judicial lien that would have been avoidable by the trustee under subsection (b) of this section. The liability of such surety under such bond or obligation shall be discharged to the extent of the value of such property recovered by the trustee or the amount paid to the trustee.

(e)(1) For the purposes of this section—

(A) a transfer of real property other than fixtures, but including the interest of a seller or purchaser under a contract for the sale of real property, is perfected when a bona fide purchaser of such property from the debtor against whom applicable law permits such transfer to be perfected cannot acquire an interest that is superior to the interest of the transferee; and

(B) a transfer of a fixture or property other than real property is perfected when a creditor on a simple contract cannot acquire a judicial lien that is superior to the interest of the transferee.

(2) For the purposes of this section, except as provided in paragraph (3) of this subsection, a transfer is made—

(A) at the time such transfer takes effect between the transferor and the transferee, if such transfer is perfected at, or within 30 days after, such time, except as provided in subsection (c)(3)(B);

(B) at the time such transfer is perfected, if such transfer is perfected after such 30 days; or

(C) immediately before the date of the filing of the petition, if such transfer is not perfected at the later of—

(i) the commencement of the case; or

(ii) 30 days after such transfer takes effect between the transferor and the transferee.

(3) For the purposes of this section, a transfer is not made until the debtor has acquired rights in the property transferred.

(f) For the purposes of this section, the debtor is presumed to have been insolvent on and during the 90 days immediately preceding the date of the filing of the petition.

(g) For the purposes of this section, the trustee has the burden of proving the avoidability of a transfer under subsection (b) of this section, and the creditor or party in interest against whom recovery or avoidance is sought has the burden of proving the nonavoidability of a transfer under subsection (c) of this section.

(h) The trustee may not avoid a transfer if such transfer was made as a part of an alternative repayment schedule between the debtor and any creditor of the debtor created by an approved nonprofit budget and credit counseling agency.

(i) If the trustee avoids under subsection (b) a transfer made between 90 days and 1 year before the date of the filing of the petition, by the debtor to an entity that is not an insider for the benefit of a creditor that is an insider, such transfer shall be considered to be avoided under this section only with respect to the creditor that is an insider.

(Pub.L. 95–598, Nov. 6, 1978, 92 Stat. 2597; Pub.L. 98–353, Title III, §§ 310, 462, July 10, 1984, 98 Stat. 355, 377; Pub.L. 99–554, Title II, § 283(m), Oct. 27, 1986, 100 Stat. 3117; Pub.L. 103–394, Title II, § 203, Title III, § 304(f), Oct. 22, 1994, 108 Stat. 4121, 4133; Pub.L. 109–8, Title II, §§ 201(b), 217, Title IV, §§ 403, 409, Title XII, § 1213(a), 1222, Apr. 20, 2005, 119 Stat. 42, 55, 104, 106, 194, 196.)

1 Dollar amount as adjusted by the Judicial Conference of the United States. See Adjustment of Dollar Amounts notes set out under this section and 11 U.S.C.A. § 104.

HISTORICAL AND STATUTORY NOTES

Revision Notes and Legislative Reports

1978 Acts. This section is a substantial modification of present law. It modernizes the preference provisions and brings them more into conformity with commercial practice and the Uniform Commercial Code.

Subsection (a) contains three definitions. Inventory, new value, and receivable are defined in their ordinary senses, but are defined to avoid any confusion or uncertainty surrounding the terms.

Subsection (b) is the operative provision of the section. It authorizes the trustee to avoid a transfer if five conditions are met. These are the five elements of a preference action. First, the transfer must be to or for the benefit of a creditor. Second, the transfer must be for or on account of an antecedent debt owed by the debtor before the transfer was made. Third, the transfer must have been made when the debtor was insolvent. Fourth, the transfer must have been made during the 90 days immediately preceding the commencement of the case. If the transfer was to an insider, the trustee may avoid the transfer if it was made during the period that begins one year before the filing of the petition and ends 90 days before the filing, if the insider to whom the transfer was made had reasonable cause to believe the debtor was insolvent at the time the transfer was made.

Finally, the transfer must enable the creditor to whom or for whose benefit it was made to receive a greater percentage of his claim than he would receive under the distributive provisions of the bankruptcy code. Specifically, the creditor must receive more than he would if the case were a liquidation case, if the transfer had not been made, and if the creditor received payment of the debt to the extent provided by the provisions of the code.

The phrasing of the final element changes the application of the greater percentage test from that employed under current law. Under this language, the court must focus on the relative distribution between classes as well as the amount that will be received by the members of the class of which the creditor is a member. The language also requires the court to focus on the allowability of the claim for which the preference was made. If the claim would have been entirely disallowed, for example, then the test of paragraph (5) will be met, because the creditor would have received nothing under the distributive provisions of the bankruptcy code.

The trustee may avoid a transfer of a lien under this section even if the lien has been enforced by sale before the commencement of the case.

Subsection (b)(2) of this section in effect exempts from the preference rules payments by the debtor of tax liabilities, regardless of their priority status.

Subsection (c) contains exceptions to the trustee's avoiding power. If a creditor can qualify under any one of the exceptions, then he is protected to that extent. If he can qualify under several, he is protected by each to the extent that he can qualify under each.

The first exception is for a transfer that was intended by all parties to be a contemporaneous exchange for new value, and was in fact substantially contemporaneous. Normally, a check is a credit transaction. However, for the purposes of this paragraph, a transfer involving a check is considered to be "intended to be contemporaneous", and if the check is presented for payment in the normal course of affairs, which the Uniform Commercial Code specifies as 30 days, U.C.C. § 3–503(2)(a), that will amount to a transfer that is "in fact substantially contemporaneous."

The second exception protects transfers in the ordinary course of business (or of financial affairs, where a business is not involved) transfers. For the case of a consumer, the paragraph uses the phrase "financial affairs" to include such nonbusiness activities as payment of monthly utility bills. If the debt on account of which the transfer was made was incurred in the ordinary course of both the debtor and the transferee, if the transfer was made not later than 45 days after the debt was incurred, if the transfer itself was made in the ordinary course of both the debtor and the transferee, and if the transfer was made according to ordinary business terms, then the transfer is protected. The purpose of this exception is to leave undisturbed normal financial relations, because it does not detract from the general policy of the preference section to discourage unusual action by either the debtor or his creditors during the debtor's slide into bankruptcy.

The third exception is for enabling loans in connection with which the debtor acquires the property that the loan enabled him to purchase after the loan is actually made.

The fourth exception codifies the net result rule in section 60c of current law [section 96(c) of former Title 11]. If the creditor and the debtor have more than one exchange during the 90-day period, the exchanges are netted out according to the formula in paragraph (4). Any new value that the creditor advances must be unsecured in order for it to qualify under this exception.

Paragraph (5) codifies the improvement in position test, and thereby overrules such cases as *DuBay v. Williams,* 417 F.2d 1277 (C.A.9, 1966), and *Grain Merchants of Indiana, Inc. v. Union Bank and Savings Co.,* 408 F.2d 209 (C.A.7, 1969). A creditor with a security interest in a floating mass, such as inventory or accounts receivable, is subject to preference attack to the extent he improves his position during the 90-day period before bankruptcy. The test is a two-point test, and requires determination of the secured creditor's position 90 days before the petition and on the date of the petition. If new value was first given after 90 days before the case, the date on which it was first given substitutes for the 90-day point.

Paragraph (6) excepts statutory liens validated under section 545 from preference attack. It also protects transfers in satisfaction of such liens, and the fixing of a lien under section 365(j), which protects a vendee whose contract to purchase real property from the debtor is rejected.

Subsection (d), derived from section 67a of the Bankruptcy Act [section 107(a) of former Title 11], permits the trustee to avoid a transfer to reimburse a surety that posts a bond to dissolve a judicial lien that would have been avoidable under this section. The second sentence protects the surety from double liability.

Subsection (e) determines when a transfer is made for the purposes of the preference section. Paragraph (1) defines when a transfer is perfected. For real property, a transfer is perfected when it is valid against a bona fide purchaser. For personal property and fixtures, a transfer is perfected when it is valid against a creditor on a simple contract that obtains a judicial lien after the transfer is perfected. "Simple contract" as used here is derived from Bankruptcy Act § 60a(4) [section 96(a)(4) of former Title 11]. Paragraph (2) specifies that a transfer is made when it takes effect between the transferor and the transferee if it is perfected at or within 10 days after that time. Otherwise, it is made when the transfer is perfected. If it is not perfected before the commencement of the case, it is made immediately before the commencement of the case. Paragraph (3) specifies that a transfer is not made until the debtor has acquired rights in the property transferred. This provision, more than any other in the section, overrules *DuBay and Grain Merchants,* and in combination with subsection (b)(2), overrules *In re King-Porter Co.,* 446 F.2d 722 (5th Cir. 1971).

Subsection (e) is designed to reach the different results under the 1962 version of Article 9 of the U.C.C. and under the 1972 version because different actions are required under each version in order to make a security agreement affective between the parties.

Subsection (f) creates a presumption of insolvency for the 90 days preceding the bankruptcy case. The presumption is as defined in Rule 301 of the Federal Rules of Evidence [Title 28, Judiciary and Judicial Procedure], made applicable in bankruptcy cases by sections 224 and 225 of the bill. The presumption requires the party against whom the presumption exists to come forward with some evidence to rebut the presumption, but the burden of proof remains on the party in whose favor the presumption exists. Senate Report No. 95–989.

1984 Acts. Statements by Legislative Leaders, see 1984 U.S. Code Cong. and Adm. News, p. 576.

1986 Acts. House Report No. 99–764 and House Conference Report No. 99–958, see 1986 U.S. Code Cong. and Adm. News, p. 5227.

1994 Acts. House Report No. 103–835, see 1994 U.S. Code Cong. and Adm. News, p. 3340.

2005 Acts. House Report No. 109–31(Part I), see 2005 U.S. Code Cong. and Adm. News, p. 88.

Legislative Statements

No limitation is provided for payments to commodity brokers as in section 766 of the Senate amendment other than the amendment to section 548 of title 11. Section 547(c)(2) protects most payments.

Section 547(b)(2) of the House amendment adopts a provision contained in the House bill and rejects an alternative contained in the Senate amendment relating to the avoidance of a preferential transfer that is payment of a tax claim owing to a governmental unit. As provided, section 106(c) of the House amendment overrules contrary language in the House report with the result that the Government is subject to avoidance of preferential transfers.

Contrary to language contained in the House report, payment of a debt by means of a check is equivalent to a cash payment, unless the check is dishonored. Payment is considered to be made when the check is delivered for purposes of sections 547(c)(1) and (2).

Section 547(c)(6) of the House bill is deleted and is treated in a different fashion in section 553 of the House amendment.

Section 547(c)(6) represents a modification of a similar provision contained in the House bill and Senate amendment. The exception relating to satisfaction of a statutory lien is deleted. The exception for a lien created under title 11 is deleted since such a lien is a statutory lien that will not be avoidable in a subsequent bankruptcy.

Section 547(e)(1)(B) is adopted from the House bill and Senate amendment without change. It is intended that the simple contract test used in this section will be applied as under section 544(a)(1) not to require a creditor to perfect against a creditor on a simple contract in the event applicable law makes such perfection impossible. For example, a purchaser from a debtor at an improperly noticed bulk sale may take subject to the rights of a creditor on a simple contract of the debtor for 1 year after the bulk sale. Since the purchaser cannot perfect against such a creditor on a simple contract, he should not be held responsible for failing to do the impossible. In the event the debtor goes into bankruptcy within a short time after the bulk sale, the trustee should not be able to use the avoiding powers under section 544(a)(1) or 547 merely because State law has made some transfers of personal property subject to the rights of a creditor on a simple contract to acquire a judicial lien with no opportunity to perfect against such a creditor.

Preferences: The House amendment deletes from the category of transfers on account of antecedent debts which may be avoided under the preference rules, section 547(b)(2), the exception in the Senate amendment for taxes owed to governmental authorities. However, for purposes of the "ordinary course" exception to the preference rules contained in section 547(c)(2), the House amendment specifies that the 45-day period referred to in section 547(c)(2)(B) is to begin running, in the case of taxes from the last due date, including extensions, of the return with respect to which the tax payment was made.

Effective and Applicability Provisions

2007 Acts. Increase of dollar amounts by Judicial Conference of the United States by notice published Feb. 14, 2007, 72 F.R. 7082 effective April 1, 2007, and increase not applicable to cases commenced before the effective date of the adjustments, i.e., April 1, 2007. See Adjustment of Dollar Amounts notes under 11 U.S.C.A. § 104 and this section.

2005 Acts. Pub.L. 109–8, Title XII, § 1213(b), Apr. 20, 2005, 119 Stat. 195, provided that: "The amendments made by this section [amending this section] shall apply to any case that is pending or commenced on or after the date of enactment of this Act [Apr. 20, 2005]."

Amendments by Pub.L. 109–8 effective, except as otherwise provided, 180 days after April 20, 2005, and inapplicable with respect to cases commenced under Title 11 before the effective date, see Pub.L. 109–8, § 1501, set out as a note under 11 U.S.C.A. § 101.

1994 Acts. Amendments by Pub.L. 103–394 effective on Oct. 22, 1994, and not to apply with respect to cases commenced under Title 11 of the United States Code before Oct. 22, 1994, see section 702 of Pub.L. 103–394, set out as a note under section 101 of this title.

1986 Acts. Amendment by Pub.L. 99–554 effective 30 days after Oct. 27, 1986, except as otherwise provided for, see section 302(a) of Pub.L. 99–554, set out as a note under section 581 of Title 28, Judiciary and Judicial Procedure.

1984 Acts. Amendment by Pub.L. 98–353 effective with respect to cases filed 90 days after July 10, 1984, see section 552(a), formerly 553(a), of Pub.L. 98–353, set out as a note under section 101 of this title.

Separability of Provisions

If any provision of or amendment made by Pub.L. 103–394 or the application of such provision or amendment to any person or circumstance is held to be unconstitutional, the remaining provisions of and amendments made by Pub.L. 103–394 and the application of such provisions and amendments to any person or circumstance shall not be affected thereby, see section 701 of Pub.L. 103–394, set out as a note under section 101 of this title.

Adjustment of Dollar Amounts

For adjustment of dollar amounts specified in subsec. (c)(9) of this section by the Judicial Conference of the United States, effective Apr. 1, 2007, see note set out under 11 U.S.C.A. § 104.

By notice published Feb. 14, 2007, 72 F.R. 7082, the Judicial Conference of the United States adjusted the dollar amounts in provisions specified in subsec. (c)(9) of this section, effective Apr. 1, 2007, as follows:

Adjusted $5,000 to $5,475.

CROSS REFERENCES

Applicability of this section in Chapter nine cases, see 11 USCA § 901.

Appointment of trustee upon debtor's refusal to pursue cause of action under this section, see 11 USCA § 926.

Automatic stay, see 11 USCA § 362.

Commencement of involuntary cases by transferees of voidable transfers, see 11 USCA § 303.

Disallowance of claims of entity that is transferee of avoidable transfer, see 11 USCA § 502.

Effect of dismissal, see 11 USCA § 349.

Exemptions, see 11 USCA § 522.

Persons who may be debtors in Chapter nine case, see 11 USCA § 109.

Recovery of voidable transfers in investor protection liquidation proceedings, see 15 USCA § 78fff–2.

Transfers to defeat cases under this title, see 18 USCA § 152.

Voidable transfers in—

Commodity broker liquidation cases, see 11 USCA § 764.

Stockbroker liquidation cases, see 11 USCA § 749.

§ 548. Fraudulent transfers and obligations

(a)(1) The trustee may avoid any transfer (including any transfer to or for the benefit of an insider under an employment contract) of an interest of the debtor in property, or any obligation (including any obligation to or for the benefit of an insider under an employment contract) incurred by the debtor, that was made or incurred on or within 2 years before the date of the filing of the petition, if the debtor voluntarily or involuntarily—

(A) made such transfer or incurred such obligation with actual intent to hinder, delay, or defraud any entity to which the debtor was or became, on or after the date that such transfer was made or such obligation was incurred, indebted; or

(B)(i) received less than a reasonably equivalent value in exchange for such transfer or obligation; and

(ii)(I) was insolvent on the date that such transfer was made or such obligation was incurred, or became insolvent as a result of such transfer or obligation;

(II) was engaged in business or a transaction, or was about to engage in business or a transaction, for which any property remaining with the debtor was an unreasonably small capital;

(III) intended to incur, or believed that the debtor would incur, debts that would be beyond the debtor's ability to pay as such debts matured; or

(IV) made such transfer to or for the benefit of an insider, or incurred such obligation to or for the benefit of an insider, under an employment contract and not in the ordinary course of business.

(2) A transfer of a charitable contribution to a qualified religious or charitable entity or organization shall not be considered to be a transfer covered under paragraph (1)(B) in any case in which.—

(A) the amount of that contribution does not exceed 15 percent of the gross annual income of the debtor for the year in which the transfer of the contribution is made; or

(B) the contribution made by a debtor exceeded the percentage amount of gross annual income specified in subparagraph (A), if the transfer was consistent with the practices of the debtor in making charitable contributions.

(b) The trustee of a partnership debtor may avoid any transfer of an interest of the debtor in property, or any obligation incurred by the debtor, that was made or incurred on or within 2 years before the date of the filing of the petition, to a general partner in the debtor, if the debtor was insolvent on the date such transfer was made or such obligation was incurred, or became insolvent as a result of such transfer or obligation.

(c) Except to the extent that a transfer or obligation voidable under this section is voidable under section 544, 545, or 547 of this title, a transferee or obligee of such a transfer or obligation that takes for value and in good faith has a lien on or may retain any interest transferred or may enforce any obligation incurred, as the case may be, to the extent that such transferee or obligee gave value to the debtor in exchange for such transfer or obligation.

(d)(1) For the purposes of this section, a transfer is made when such transfer is so perfected that a bona fide purchaser from the debtor against whom applicable law permits such transfer to be perfected cannot acquire an interest in the property transferred that is superior to the interest in such property of the transferee, but if such transfer is not so perfected before the commencement of the case, such transfer is made immediately before the date of the filing of the petition.

(2) In this section—

(A) "value" means property, or satisfaction or securing of a present or antecedent debt of the debtor, but does not include an unperformed promise to furnish support to the debtor or to a relative of the debtor;

(B) a commodity broker, forward contract merchant, stockbroker, financial institution, financial participant, or securities clearing agency that receives a margin payment, as defined in section 101, 741, or 761 of this title, or settlement payment, as defined in section 101 or 741 of this title, takes for value to the extent of such payment;

(C) a repo participant or financial participant that receives a margin payment, as defined in section 741 or 761 of this title, or settlement payment, as defined in section 741 of this title, in connection with a repurchase agreement, takes for value to the extent of such payment;

(D) a swap participant or financial participant that receives a transfer in connection with a swap agreement takes for value to the extent of such transfer; and

(E) a master netting agreement participant that receives a transfer in connection with a master netting agreement or any individual contract covered thereby takes for value to the extent of such transfer, except that, with respect to a transfer under any individual contract covered thereby, to the extent that such master netting agreement participant otherwise did not take (or is otherwise not deemed to have taken) such transfer for value.

(3) In this section, the term "charitable contribution" means a charitable contribution, as that term is defined in section 170(c) of the Internal Revenue Code of 1986, if that contribution—

(A) is made by a natural person; and

(B) consists of.—

(i) a financial instrument (as that term is defined in section 731(c)(2)(C) of the Internal Revenue Code of 1986); or

(ii) cash.

(4) In this section, the term "qualified religious or charitable entity or organization" means—

(A) an entity described in section 170(c)(1) of the Internal Revenue Code of 1986; or

(B) an entity or organization described in section 170(c)(2) of the Internal Revenue Code of 1986.

(e)(1) In addition to any transfer that the trustee may otherwise avoid, the trustee may avoid any transfer of an interest of the debtor in property that was made on or within 10 years before the date of the filing of the petition, if—

(A) such transfer was made to a self-settled trust or similar device;

(B) such transfer was by the debtor;

(C) the debtor is a beneficiary of such trust or similar device; and

(D) the debtor made such transfer with actual intent to hinder, delay, or defraud any entity to which the debtor was or became, on or after the date that such transfer was made, indebted.

(2) For the purposes of this subsection, a transfer includes a transfer made in anticipation of any money judgment, settlement, civil penalty, equitable order, or criminal fine incurred by, or which the debtor believed would be incurred by—

(A) any violation of the securities laws (as defined in section 3(a)(47) of the Securities Exchange Act of 1934 (15 U.S.C. 78c(a)(47))), any State securities laws, or any regulation or order issued under Federal securities laws or State securities laws; or

(B) fraud, deceit, or manipulation in a fiduciary capacity or in connection with the purchase or sale of any security registered under section 12 or 15(d) of the Securities Exchange Act of 1934 (15 U.S.C. 78l and 78o(d)) or under section 6 of the Securities Act of 1933 (15 U.S.C. 77f).

(Pub.L. 95–598, Nov. 6, 1978, 92 Stat. 2600; Pub.L. 97–222, § 5, July 27, 1982, 96 Stat. 236; Pub.L. 98–353, Title III, §§ 394, 463, July 10, 1984, 98 Stat. 365, 378; Pub.L. 99–554, Title II, § 283(n), Oct. 27, 1986, 100 Stat. 3117; Pub.L. 101–311, Title I, § 104, Title II, § 204, June 25, 1990, 104 Stat. 268, 269; Pub.L. 103–394, Title V, § 501(b)(5), Oct. 22, 1994, 108 Stat. 4142; Pub.L. 105–183, §§ 2, 3(a), June 19, 1998, 112 Stat. 517; Pub.L. 109–8, Title IX, § 907(f), (*o*)(4) to (6), Title XIV, § 1402, Apr. 20, 2005, 119 Stat. 177, 182, 214.)

HISTORICAL AND STATUTORY NOTES

Revision Notes and Legislative Reports

1978 Acts. This section is derived in large part from section 67d of the Bankruptcy Act [section 107(d) of former Title 11]. It permits the trustee to avoid transfers by the debtor in fraud of his creditors. Its history dates from the statute of 13 Eliz. c. 5 (1570).

The trustee may avoid fraudulent transfers or obligations if made with actual intent to hinder, delay, or defraud a past or future creditor. Transfers made for less than a reasonably equivalent consideration are also vulnerable if the debtor was or thereby becomes insolvent, was engaged in business with an unreasonably small capital, or intended to incur debts that would be beyond his ability to repay.

The trustee of a partnership debtor may avoid any transfer of partnership property to a partner in the debtor if the debtor was or thereby became insolvent.

If a transferee's only liability to the trustee is under this section, and if he takes for value and in good faith, then subsection (c) grants him a lien on the property transferred, or other similar protection.

Subsection (d) specifies that for the purposes of fraudulent transfer section, a transfer is made when it is valid against a subsequent bona fide purchaser. If not made before the commencement of the case, it is considered made immediately before then. Subsection (d) also defines "value" to mean property, or the satisfaction or securing of a present or antecedent debt, but does not include an unperformed promise to furnish support to the debtor or a relative of the debtor. Senate Report No. 95–989.

1982 Acts. House Report No. 97–420, see 1982 U.S. Code Cong. and Adm. News, p. 583.

1984 Acts. Statements by Legislative Leaders, see 1984 U.S. Code Cong. and Adm. News, p. 576.

1986 Acts. House Report No. 99–764 and House Conference Report No. 99–958, see 1986 U.S. Code Cong. and Adm. News, p. 5227.

1990 Acts. House Report No. 101–484, see 1990 U.S. Code Cong. and Adm. News, p. 223.

1994 Acts. House Report No. 103–835, see 1994 U.S. Code Cong. and Adm. News, p. 3340.

1998 Acts. Statement by President, see 1998 U.S. Code Cong. and Adm. News, p. 230.

2005 Acts. House Report No. 109–31(Part I), see 2005 U.S. Code Cong. and Adm. News, p. 88.

Legislative Statements

Section 548(d)(2) is modified to reflect general application of a provision contained in section 766 of the Senate amendment with respect to commodity brokers. In particular, section 548(d)(2)(B) of the House amendment makes clear that a commodity broker who receives a margin payment is considered to receive the margin payment in return for "value" for purposes of section 548.

References in Text

The Internal Revenue Code of 1986, referred to in subsec. (d)(3) and (4), is classified generally to Title 26.

Section 3(a)(47) of the Securities Exchange Act of 1934, referred to in subsec. (e)(2)(A), is June 6, 1934, c. 404, Title I, § 3(a)(47), 48 Stat. 882, as amended, which is classified to 15 U.S.C.A. § 78c(a)(47).

Section 12 of the Securities Exchange Act of 1934, referred to in subsec. (e)(2)(B), is June 6, 1934, c. 404, Title I, § 12, 48 Stat. 892, as amended, which is classified to 15 U.S.C.A. § 78*l*.

Section 15(d) of the Securities Exchange Act of 1934, referred to in subsec. (e)(2)(B), is June 6, 1934, c. 404, Title I, § 15(d), 48 Stat. 895, as amended, which is classified to 15 U.S.C.A. § 78*o*.

Section 6 of the Securities Act of 1933, referred to in subsec. (e)(2)(B), is Act May 27, 1933, c. 38, Title I, § 6, 48 Stat. 78, as amended, which is classified to 15 U.S.C.A. § 77f.

Effective and Applicability Provisions

2005 Acts. Amendments by Pub.L. 109–8, Title XIV, effective, except as otherwise provided, on Apr. 20, 2005, and applicable only with respect to cases commenced under Title 11 on or after Apr. 20, 2005. Amendments by Pub.L. 109–8, § 1402(1), to subsecs. (a) and (b) of this section applicable only with respect to cases commenced under Title 11 more than 1 year after April 20, 2005; see Pub.L. 109–8, § 1406, set out as a note under 11 U.S.C.A. § 507.

Amendments by Pub.L. 109–8 effective, except as otherwise provided, 180 days after April 20, 2005, and inapplicable with respect to cases commenced under Title 11 before the effective date, see Pub.L. 109–8, § 1501, set out as a note under 11 U.S.C.A. § 101.

1994 Acts. Amendment by Pub.L. 103–394 effective on Oct. 22, 1994, and not to apply with respect to cases commenced under Title 11 of the United States Code before Oct. 22, 1994, see section 702 of Pub.L. 103–394, set out as a note under section 101 of this title.

1986 Acts. Amendment by Pub.L. 99–554, effective 30 days after Oct. 27, 1986, except as otherwise provided for, see section 302(a) of Pub.L. 99–554, set out as a note under section 581 of Title 28, Judiciary and Judicial Procedure.

1984 Acts. Amendment by Pub.L. 98–353 effective with respect to cases filed 90 days after July 10, 1984, see section 552(a), formerly 553(a), of Pub.L. 98–353, set out as a note under section 101 of this title.

Separability of Provisions

If any provision of or amendment made by Pub.L. 103–394 or the application of such provision or amendment to any person or circumstance is held to be unconstitutional, the remaining provisions of and amendments made by Pub.L. 103–394 and the application of such provisions and amendments to any person or circumstance shall not be affected thereby, see section 701 of Pub.L. 103–394, set out as a note under section 101 of this title.

Applicability

Applicability of amendments made by Pub.L. 105–183 to any case brought under an applicable provision of this title that is pending or commenced on or after June 19, 1998, see Pub.L. 105–183, § 5, June 19, 1998, 112 Stat. 518, set out as a note under section 544 of this title.

Rule of Construction

Amendments made by Pub.L. 105–183 not intended to limit the applicability of the Religious Freedom Restoration Act of 1993 (42 U.S.C. 2002bb et seq.), see Pub.L. 105–183, § 6, June 19, 1998, 112 Stat. 519, set out as a note under section 544 of this title.

CROSS REFERENCES

Applicability of this section in Chapter nine cases, see 11 USCA § 901.

Appointment of trustee upon debtor's refusal to pursue cause of action under this section, see 11 USCA § 926.

Commencement of involuntary cases by transferees of voidable transfers, see 11 USCA § 303.

Disallowance of claims of entity that is transferee of avoidable transfer, see 11 USCA § 502.

Effect of dismissal, see 11 USCA § 349.

Exemptions, see 11 USCA § 522.

Inappropriate transfers included in determining net worth of employer, see 29 USCA § 1362.

Recovery of voidable transfers in investor protection liquidation proceedings, see 15 USCA § 78fff–2.

Transfers to defeat cases under this title, see 18 USCA § 152.

Voidable transfers in—

Commodity broker liquidation cases, see 11 USCA § 764.

Stockbroker liquidation cases, see 11 USCA § 749.

§ 549. Postpetition transactions

(a) Except as provided in subsection (b) or (c) of this section, the trustee may avoid a transfer of property of the estate—

(1) that occurs after the commencement of the case; and

(2)(A) that is authorized only under section 303(f) or 542(c) of this title; or

(B) that is not authorized under this title or by the court.

(b) In an involuntary case, the trustee may not avoid under subsection (a) of this section a transfer made after the commencement of such case but before the order for relief to the extent any value, including services, but not including satisfaction or securing of a debt that arose before the commencement of the case, is given after the commencement of the case in exchange for such transfer, notwithstanding any notice or knowledge of the case that the transferee has.

(c) The trustee may not avoid under subsection (a) of this section a transfer of an interest in real property to a good faith purchaser without knowledge of the commencement of the case and for present fair equivalent value unless a copy or notice of the petition was filed, where a transfer of an interest in such real property may be recorded to perfect such transfer, before such transfer is so perfected that a bona fide purchaser of such real property, against whom applicable law permits such transfer to be perfected, could not acquire an interest that is superior to such interest of such good faith purchaser. A good faith purchaser without knowledge of the commencement of the case and for less than present fair equivalent value has a lien on the property transferred to the extent of any present value given, unless a copy or notice of the petition was so filed before such transfer was so perfected.

(d) An action or proceeding under this section may not be commenced after the earlier of—

(1) two years after the date of the transfer sought to be avoided; or

(2) the time the case is closed or dismissed.

(Pub.L. 95–598, Nov. 6, 1978, 92 Stat. 2601; Pub.L. 98–353, Title III, § 464, July 10, 1984, 98 Stat. 379; Pub.L. 99–554, Title II, § 283(*o*), Oct. 27, 1986, 100 Stat. 3117; Pub.L. 103–394, Title V, § 501(d)(18), Oct. 22, 1994, 108 Stat. 4146; Pub.L. 109–8, Title XII, § 1214, 119 Stat. 195.)

HISTORICAL AND STATUTORY NOTES

Revision Notes and Legislative Reports

1978 Acts. This section modifies section 70d of current law [section 110(d) of former Title 11]. It permits the trustee to avoid transfers of property that occur after the commencement of the case. The transfer must either have been unauthorized, or authorized under a section that protects only the transferor. Subsection (b) protects "involuntary gap" transferees to the extent of any value (including services, but not including satisfaction of a debt that arose before the commencement of the case), given after commencement in exchange for the transfer. Notice or knowledge of the transferee is irrelevant in determining whether he is protected under this provision. Senate Report No. 95–989.

1984 Acts. Statements by Legislative Leaders, see 1984 U.S. Code Cong. and Adm. News, p. 576.

1986 Acts. House Report No. 99–764 and House Conference Report No. 99–958, see 1986 U.S. Code Cong. and Adm. News, p. 5227.

1994 Acts. House Report No. 103–835, see 1994 U.S. Code Cong. and Adm. News, p. 3340.

2005 Acts. House Report No. 109–31(Part I), see 2005 U.S. Code Cong. and Adm. News, p. 88.

Legislative Statements

Section 549 of the House amendment has been redrafted in order to incorporate section 342(b) and (c) of the Senate amendment. Those sections have been consolidated and redrafted in section 549(c) of the House amendment. Section 549(d) of the House amendment adopts a provision contained in section 549(c) of the Senate amendment.

Effective and Applicability Provisions

2005 Acts. Amendments by Pub.L. 109–8 effective, except as otherwise provided, 180 days after April 20, 2005, and inapplicable with respect to cases commenced under Title 11 before the effective date, see Pub.L. 109–8, § 1501, set out as a note under 11 U.S.C.A. § 101.

1994 Acts. Amendment by Pub.L. 103–394 effective on Oct. 22, 1994, and not to apply with respect to cases commenced under Title 11 of the United States Code before Oct. 22, 1994, see section 702 of Pub.L. 103–394, set out as a note under section 101 of this title.

1986 Acts. Amendment by Pub.L. 99–554 effective 30 days after Oct. 27, 1986, except as otherwise provided for, see section 302(a) of Pub.L. 99–554, set out as a note under section 581 of Title 28, Judiciary and Judicial Procedure.

1984 Acts. Amendment by Pub.L. 98–353 effective with respect to cases filed 90 days after July 10, 1984, see section 552(a), formerly 553(a), of Pub.L. 98–353, set out as a note under section 101 of this title.

Separability of Provisions

If any provision of or amendment made by Pub.L. 103–394 or the application of such provision or amendment to any person or circumstance is held to be unconstitutional, the remaining provisions of and amendments made by Pub.L. 103–394 and the application of such provisions and amendments to any person or circumstance shall not be affected thereby, see section 701 of Pub.L. 103–394, set out as a note under section 101 of this title.

CROSS REFERENCES

Applicability of subsecs. (a), (c) and (d) of this section in Chapter 9 cases, see 11 USCA § 901.

Appointment of trustee upon debtor's refusal to pursue cause of action under this section, see 11 USCA § 926.

Commencement of involuntary cases by transferees of voidable transfers, see 11 USCA § 303.

Disallowance of claims of entity that is transferee of avoidable transfer, see 11 USCA § 502.

Effect of dismissal, see 11 USCA § 349.

Exemptions, see 11 USCA § 522.

Inappropriate transfers included in determining net worth of employer, see 29 USCA § 1362.

Recovery of voidable transfers in investor liquidation proceedings, see 15 USCA § 78fff–2.

Voidable transfers in—

Commodity broker liquidation cases, see 11 USCA § 764.

Stockbroker liquidation cases, see 11 USCA § 749.

§ 550. Liability of transferee of avoided transfer

(a) Except as otherwise provided in this section, to the extent that a transfer is avoided under section 544, 545, 547, 548, 549, 553(b), or 724(a) of this title, the trustee may recover, for the benefit of the estate, the property transferred, or, if the court so orders, the value of such property, from—

(1) the initial transferee of such transfer or the entity for whose benefit such transfer was made; or

(2) any immediate or mediate transferee of such initial transferee.

(b) The trustee may not recover under section[1] (a)(2) of this section from—

(1) a transferee that takes for value, including satisfaction or securing of a present or antecedent debt, in good faith, and without knowledge of the voidability of the transfer avoided; or

(2) any immediate or mediate good faith transferee of such transferee.

(c) If a transfer made between 90 days and one year before the filing of the petition—

(1) is avoided under section 547(b) of this title; and

(2) was made for the benefit of a creditor that at the time of such transfer was an insider;

the trustee may not recover under subsection (a) from a transferee that is not an insider.

(d) The trustee is entitled to only a single satisfaction under subsection (a) of this section.

(e)(1) A good faith transferee from whom the trustee may recover under subsection (a) of this section has a lien on the property recovered to secure the lesser of—

(A) the cost, to such transferee, of any improvement made after the transfer, less the amount of any profit realized by or accruing to such transferee from such property; and

(B) any increase in the value of such property as a result of such improvement, of the property transferred.

(2) In this subsection, "improvement" includes—

(A) physical additions or changes to the property transferred;

(B) repairs to such property;

(C) payment of any tax on such property;

(D) payment of any debt secured by a lien on such property that is superior or equal to the rights of the trustee; and

(E) preservation of such property.

(f) An action or proceeding under this section may not be commenced after the earlier of—

(1) one year after the avoidance of the transfer on account of which recovery under this section is sought; or

(2) the time the case is closed or dismissed.

(Pub.L. 95–598, Nov. 6, 1978, 92 Stat. 2601; Pub.L. 98–353, Title III, § 465, July 10, 1984, 98 Stat. 379; Pub.L. 103–394, Title II, § 202, Oct. 22, 1994, 108 Stat. 4121.)

[1] So in original. Probably should be "subsection".

HISTORICAL AND STATUTORY NOTES

Revision Notes and Legislative Reports

1978 Acts. Section 550 prescribes the liability of a transferee of an avoided transfer, and enunciates the separation between the concepts of avoiding a transfer and recovering from the transferee. Subsection (a) permits the trustee to recover from the initial transferee of an avoided transfer or from any immediate or mediate transferee of the initial transferee. The words "to the extent that" in the lead in to this subsection are designed to incorporate the protection of transferees found in proposed 11 U.S.C. 549(b) and 548(c). Subsection (b) limits the liability of an immediate or mediate transferee of the initial transferee if such secondary transferee takes for value, in good faith and without knowledge of the voidability of the transfer. An immediate or mediate good faith transferee of a protected secondary transferee is also shielded from liability. This subsection is limited to the trustee's right to recover from subsequent transferees under subsection (a)(2). It does not limit the trustee's rights against the initial transferee under subsection (a)(1). The phrase "good faith" in this paragraph is intended to prevent a transferee from whom the trustee could recover from transferring the recoverable property to an innocent transferee, and receiving a retransfer from him, that is, "washing" the transaction through an innocent third party. In order for the transferee to be excepted from liability under this paragraph, he himself must be a good faith transferee. Subsection (c) is a further limitation on recovery. It specifies that the trustee is entitled to only one satisfactory, under subsection (a), even if more than one transferee is liable.

Subsection (d) protects good faith transferees, either initial or subsequent, to the extent of the lesser of the cost of any improvement the transferee makes in the transferred property and the increase in value of the property as a result of the improvement. Paragraph (2) of the subsection defines improvement to include physical additions or changes to the property, repairs, payment of taxes on the property, payment of a debt secured by a lien on the property, discharge of a lien on the property, and preservation of the property.

Subsection (e) establishes a statute of limitations on avoidance by the Trustee. The limitation is one year after the avoidance of the transfer or the time the case is closed or dismissed, whichever is earlier. Senate Report No. 95–989.

1984 Acts. Statements by Legislative Leaders, see 1984 U.S. Code Cong. and Adm. News, p. 576.

1994 Acts. House Report No. 103–835, see 1994 U.S. Code Cong. and Adm. News, p. 3340.

Legislative Statements

Section 550(a)(1) of the House amendment has been modified in order to permit recovery from an entity for whose benefit an avoided transfer is made in addition to a recovery from the initial transferee of the transfer. Section 550(c) would still apply, and the trustee is entitled only to a single satisfaction. The liability of a transferee under section 550(a) applies only "to the extent that a transfer is avoided". This means that liability is not imposed on a transferee to the extent that a transferee is protected under a provision such as section 548(c) which grants a good faith transferee for value of a transfer that is avoided only as a fraudulent transfer, a lien on the property transferred to the extent of value given.

Section 550(b) of the House amendment is modified to indicate that value includes satisfaction or securing of a present antecedent debt. This means that the trustee may not recover under subsection (a)(2) from a subsequent transferee that takes for "value", provided the subsequent transferee also takes in good faith and without knowledge of the transfer avoided.

Section 550(e) of the House amendment is derived from section 550(e) of the Senate amendment.

Effective and Applicability Provisions

1994 Acts. Amendment by Pub.L. 103–394 effective on Oct. 22, 1994, and not to apply with respect to cases commenced under Title 11 of the United States Code before Oct. 22, 1994, see section 702 of Pub.L. 103–394, set out as a note under section 101 of this title.

1984 Acts. Amendment by Pub.L. 98–353 effective with respect to cases filed 90 days after July 10, 1984, see section 552(a), formerly 553(a), of Pub.L. 98–353, set out as a note under section 101 of this title.

Separability of Provisions

If any provision of or amendment made by Pub.L. 103–394 or the application of such provision or amendment to any person or circumstance is held to be unconstitutional, the remaining provisions of and amendments made by Pub.L. 103–394 and the application of such provisions and amendments to any person or circumstance shall not be affected thereby, see section 701 of Pub.L. 103–394, set out as a note under section 101 of this title.

CROSS REFERENCES

Allowance of claims or interests, see 11 USCA § 502.

Applicability of this section in Chapter 9 cases, see 11 USCA § 901.

Appointment of trustee upon debtor's refusal to pursue cause of action under this section, see 11 USCA § 926.

Effect of dismissal, see 11 USCA § 349.

Exemptions, see 11 USCA § 522.

§ 551. Automatic preservation of avoided transfer

Any transfer avoided under section 522, 544, 545, 547, 548, 549, or 724(a) of this title, or any lien void under section 506(d) of this title, is preserved for the benefit of the estate but only with respect to property of the estate.

(Pub.L. 95–598, Nov. 6, 1978, 92 Stat. 2602.)

HISTORICAL AND STATUTORY NOTES

Revision Notes and Legislative Reports

1978 Acts. This section is a change from present law. It specifies that any avoided transfer is automatically preserved for the benefit of the estate. Under current law, the court must determine whether or not the transfer should be preserved. The operation of the section is automatic, unlike current law, even though preservation may not benefit the estate in every instance. A preserved lien may be abandoned by the trustee under proposed 11 U.S.C. 554 if the preservation does not benefit the estate. The section as a whole prevents junior lienors from improving their position at the expense of the estate when a senior lien is avoided. Senate Report No. 95–989.

1984 Acts. Statements by Legislative Leaders, see 1984 U.S.Code Cong. and Adm.News, p. 576.

Legislative Statements

Section 551 is adopted from the House bill and the alternative in the Senate amendment is rejected. The section is clarified to indicate that a transfer avoided or a lien that is void is preserved for the benefit of the estate, but only with respect to property of the estate. This prevents the trustee from asserting an avoided tax lien against after acquired property of the debtor.

CROSS REFERENCES

Applicability of this section in Chapter 9 cases, see 11 USCA § 901.

Effect of dismissal, see 11 USCA § 349.

Exemptions, see 11 USCA § 522.

§ 552. Postpetition effect of security interest

(a) Except as provided in subsection (b) of this section, property acquired by the estate or by the debtor after the commencement of the case is not subject to any lien resulting from any security agreement entered into by the debtor before the commencement of the case.

(b)(1) Except as provided in sections 363, 506(c), 522, 544, 545, 547, and 548 of this title, if the debtor and an entity entered into a security agreement before the commencement of the case and if the security interest created by such security agreement extends to property of the debtor acquired before the commencement of the case and to proceeds, products, offspring, or profits of such property, then such security interest extends to such proceeds, products, offspring, or profits acquired by the estate after the commencement of the case to the extent provided by such security agreement and by applicable nonbankruptcy law, except to any extent that the court, after notice and a hearing and based on the equities of the case, orders otherwise.

(2) Except as provided in sections 363, 506(c), 522, 544, 545, 547, and 548 of this title, and notwithstanding section 546(b) of this title, if the debtor and an entity entered into a security agreement before the commencement of the case and if the security interest created by such security agreement extends to property of the debtor acquired before the commencement of the case and to amounts paid as rents of such property or the fees, charges, accounts, or other payments for the use or occupancy of rooms and other public facilities in hotels, motels, or other lodging properties, then such security interest extends to such rents and such fees, charges, accounts, or other payments acquired by the estate after the commencement of the case to the extent provided in such security agreement, except to any extent that the court, after notice and a hearing and based on the equities of the case, orders otherwise.

(Pub.L. 95–598, Nov. 6, 1978, 92 Stat. 2602; Pub.L. 98–353, Title III, § 466, July 10, 1984, 98 Stat. 380; Pub.L. 103–394, Title II, § 214(a), Oct. 22, 1994, 108 Stat. 4126; Pub.L. 109–8, Title XII, § 1204(2), Apr. 20, 2005, 119 Stat. 194.)

HISTORICAL AND STATUTORY NOTES

Revision Notes and Legislative Reports

1978 Acts. Under the Uniform Commercial Code, article 9, creditors may take security interests in after-acquired property. Section 552 governs the effect of such a prepetition security interest in postpetition property. It applies to all security interests as defined in section 101(37) of the bankruptcy code, not only to U.C.C. security interests.

As a general rule, if a security agreement is entered into before the commencement of the case, then property that the estate acquires is not subject to the security interest created by a provision in the security agreement extending the security interest to after-acquired property. Subsection (b) provides an important exception consistent with the Uniform Commercial Code. If the security agreement extends to proceeds, product, offspring, rents, or profits of the property in question, then the proceeds would continue to be subject to the security interest pursuant to the terms of the security agreement and provisions of applicable law, except to the extent that where the estate acquires the proceeds at the expense of other creditors holding unsecured claims, the expenditure resulted in an improvement in the position of the secured party.

The exception covers the situation where raw materials, for example, are converted into inventory, or inventory into accounts, at some expense to the estate, thus depleting the fund available for general unsecured creditors, but is limited to the benefit inuring to the secured party thereby. Situations in which the estate incurs expense in simply protecting collateral are governed by 11 U.S.C. 506(c). In ordinary circumstances, the risk of loss in continued operations will remain with the estate. Senate Report No. 95–989.

Under the Uniform Commercial Code, Article 9, creditors may take security interests in after-acquired property. This section governs the effect of such a prepetition security interest in postpetition property. It applies to all security interests as defined in section 101 of the bankruptcy code, not only to U.C.C. security interests.

As a general rule, if a security agreement is entered into before the case, then property that the estate acquires is not subject to the security interest created by the security agreement. Subsection (b) provides the only exception. If the security agreement extends to proceeds, product, offspring, rents, or profits of property that the debtor had before the commencement of the case, then the proceeds, etc., continue to be subject to the security interest, except to the extent that the estate acquired the proceeds to the prejudice of other creditors holding unsecured claims. "Extends to" as used here would include an automatically arising security interest in proceeds, as permitted under the 1972 version of the Uniform Commercial Code, as well as an interest in proceeds specifically designated, as required under the 1962 Code or similar statutes covering property not covered by the Code. "Prejudice" is not intended to be a broad term here, but is designed to cover the situation where the estate expends funds that result in an increase in the value of collateral. The exception is to cover the situation where raw materials, for example, are converted into inventory, or inventory into accounts, at some expense to the estate, thus depleting the fund available for general unsecured creditors. The term "proceeds" is not limited to the technical definition of that term in the U.C.C., but covers any property into which property subject to the security interest is converted. House Report No. 95–595.

1984 Acts. Statements by Legislative Leaders, see 1984 U.S. Code Cong. and Adm. News, p. 576.

1994 Acts. House Report No, 103–835, see 1994 U.S. Code Cong. and Adm. News, p. 3340.

2005 Acts. House Report No. 109–31(Part I), see 2005 U.S. Code Cong. and Adm. News, p. 88.

Legislative Statements

Section 552(a) is derived from the House bill and the alternative provision in the Senate amendment is rejected. Section 552(b) represents a compromise between the House bill and the Senate amendment. Proceeds coverage, but not after acquired property clauses, are valid under title 11. The provision allows the court to consider the equities in each case. In the course of such consideration the court may evaluate any expenditures by the estate relating to proceeds and any related improvement in position of the secured party. Although this section grants a secured party a security interest in proceeds, product, offspring, rents, or profits, the section is explicitly subject to other sections of title 11. For example, the trustee or debtor in possession may use, sell, or lease proceeds, product, offspring, rents or profits under section 363.

Effective and Applicability Provisions

2005 Acts. Amendments by Pub.L. 109–8 effective, except as otherwise provided, 180 days after April 20, 2005, and inapplicable with respect to cases commenced under Title 11 before the effective date, see Pub.L. 109–8, § 1501, set out as a note under 11 U.S.C.A. § 101.

1994 Acts. Amendment by Pub.L. 103–394 effective on Oct. 22, 1994, and not to apply with respect to cases commenced under Title 11 of the United States Code before Oct. 22, 1994, see section 702 of Pub.L. 103–394, set out as a note under section 101 of this title.

1984 Acts. Amendment by Pub.L. 98–353 effective with respect to cases filed 90 days after July 10, 1984, see section 552, formerly 553, of Pub.L. 98–353, set out as a note under section 101 of this title.

Separability of Provisions

If any provision of or amendment made by Pub.L. 103–394 or the application of such provision or amendment to any person or circumstance is held to be unconstitutional, the remaining provisions of and amendments made by Pub.L. 103–394 and the application of such provisions and amendments to any person or circumstance shall not be affected thereby, see section 701 of Pub.L. 103–394, set out as a note under section 101 of this title.

CROSS REFERENCES

Applicability of this section in Chapter 9 cases, see 11 USCA § 901.

"Cash collateral" as including proceeds, products, offspring, rents or profits of property subject to security interest as provided in this section, see 11 USCA § 363.

Special revenues acquired by debtor after commencement of Chapter 9 case subject to security interest, see 11 USCA § 928.

§ 553. Setoff

(a) Except as otherwise provided in this section and in sections 362 and 363 of this title, this title does not affect any right of a creditor to offset a mutual debt owing by such creditor to the debtor that arose before the commencement of the case under this title against a claim of such creditor against the debtor that arose before the commencement of the case, except to the extent that—

(1) the claim of such creditor against the debtor is disallowed;

(2) such claim was transferred, by an entity other than the debtor, to such creditor—

(A) after the commencement of the case; or

(B)(i) after 90 days before the date of the filing of the petition; and

(ii) while the debtor was insolvent (except for a setoff of a kind described in section 362(b)(6), 362(b)(7), 362(b)(17), 362(b)(27), 555, 556, 559, 560, or 561); or

(3) the debt owed to the debtor by such creditor was incurred by such creditor—

(A) after 90 days before the date of the filing of the petition;

(B) while the debtor was insolvent; and

(C) for the purpose of obtaining a right of setoff against the debtor (except for a setoff of a kind described in section 362(b)(6), 362(b)(7), 362(b)(17), 362(b)(27), 555, 556, 559, 560, or 561).

(b)(1) Except with respect to a setoff of a kind described in section 362(b)(6), 362(b)(7), 362(b)(17), 362(b)(27), 555, 556, 559, 560, 561, 365(h), 546(h), or 365(i)(2) of this title, if a creditor offsets a mutual debt owing to the debtor against a claim against the debtor on or within 90 days before the date of the filing of the petition, then the trustee may recover from such creditor the amount so offset to the extent that any insufficiency on the date of such setoff is less than the insufficiency on the later of—

(A) 90 days before the date of the filing of the petition; and

(B) the first date during the 90 days immediately preceding the date of the filing of the petition on which there is an insufficiency.

(2) In this subsection, "insufficiency" means amount, if any, by which a claim against the debtor exceeds a mutual debt owing to the debtor by the holder of such claim.

(c) For the purposes of this section, the debtor is presumed to have been insolvent on and during the 90 days immediately preceding the date of the filing of the petition.

(Pub.L. 95–598, Nov. 6, 1978, 92 Stat. 2602; Pub.L. 98–353, Title III, §§ 395, 467, July 10, 1984, 98 Stat. 365, 380; Pub.L. 101–311, Title I, § 105, June 25, 1990, 104 Stat. 268; Pub.L. 103–394, Title II, §§ 205(b), 222(b), Title V, § 501(d)(19), Oct. 22, 1994, 108 Stat. 4123, 4129, 4146; Pub.L. 109–8, Title IX, § 907(n), Apr. 20, 2005, 119 Stat. 181.)

HISTORICAL AND STATUTORY NOTES

Revision Notes and Legislative Reports

1978 Acts. This section preserves, with some changes, the right of setoff in bankruptcy cases now found in section 68 of the Bankruptcy Act [section 108 of former Title 11]. One exception to the right is the automatic stay, discussed in connection with proposed 11 U.S.C. 362. Another is the right of the trustee to use property under section 363 that is subject to a right of setoff.

The section states that the right of setoff is unaffected by the bankruptcy code except to the extent that the creditor's claim is disallowed, the creditor acquired (other than from the debtor) the claim during the 90 days preceding the case while the debtor was insolvent, the debt being offset was incurred for the purpose of obtaining a right of setoff, while the debtor was insolvent and during the 90-day prebankruptcy period, or the creditor improved his position in the 90-day period (similar to the improvement in position test found in the preference section 547(c)(5)). Only the last exception is an addition to current law.

As under section 547(f), the debtor is presumed to have been insolvent during the 90 days before the case. Senate Report No. 95–989.

1984 Acts. Statements by Legislative Leaders, see 1984 U.S. Code Cong. and Adm. News, p. 576.

1990 Acts. House Report No. 101–484, see 1990 U.S. Code Cong. and Adm. News, p. 223.

1994 Acts. House Report No. 103–835, see 1994 U.S. Code Cong. and Adm. News, p. 3340.

2005 Acts. House Report No. 109–31(Part I), see 2005 U.S. Code Cong. and Adm. News, p. 88.

Legislative Statements

Section 553 of the House amendment is derived from a similar provision contained in the Senate amendment, but is modified to clarify application of a two-point test with respect to setoffs.

Effective and Applicability Provisions

2005 Acts. Amendments by Pub.L. 109–8 effective, except as otherwise provided, 180 days after April 20, 2005, and inapplicable with respect to cases commenced under Title 11 before the effective date, see Pub.L. 109–8, § 1501, set out as a note under 11 U.S.C.A. § 101.

1994 Acts. Amendments by Pub.L. 103–394 effective on Oct. 22, 1994, and not to apply with respect to cases commenced under Title 11 of the United States Code before Oct. 22, 1994, see section 702 of Pub.L. 103–394, set out as a note under section 101 of this title.

1984 Acts. Amendment by Pub.L. 98–353 effective with respect to cases filed 90 days after July 10, 1984, see section 552(a), formerly 553(a), of Pub.L. 98–353, set out as a note under section 101 of this title.

Separability of Provisions

If any provision of or amendment made by Pub.L. 103–394 or the application of such provision or amendment to any person or circumstance is held to be unconstitutional, the remaining provisions of and amendments made by Pub.L. 103–394 and the application of such provisions and amendments to any person or circumstance shall not be affected thereby, see section 701 of Pub.L. 103–394, set out as a note under section 101 of this title.

CROSS REFERENCES

Allowance of claims or interests, see 11 USCA § 502.

Applicability of this section in Chapter 9 cases, see 11 USCA § 901.

Determination of secured status, see 11 USCA § 506.

Effect of dismissal, see 11 USCA § 349.

Recovered property as exempt, see 11 USCA § 522.

Stay of pending actions in investor protection liquidation proceedings, see 15 USCA § 78eee.

§ 554. Abandonment of property of the estate

(a) After notice and a hearing, the trustee may abandon any property of the estate that is burdensome to the estate or that is of inconsequential value and benefit to the estate.

(b) On request of a party in interest and after notice and a hearing, the court may order the trustee to abandon any property of the estate that is burdensome to the estate or that is of inconsequential value and benefit to the estate.

(c) Unless the court orders otherwise, any property scheduled under section 521(1) of this title not otherwise administered at the time of the closing of a case is abandoned to the debtor and administered for purposes of section 350 of this title.

(d) Unless the court orders otherwise, property of the estate that is not abandoned under this section and that is not administered in the case remains property of the estate.

(Pub.L. 95–598, Nov. 6, 1978, 92 Stat. 2603; Pub.L. 98–353, Title III, § 468, July 10, 1984, 98 Stat. 380; Pub.L. 99–554, Title II, § 283(p), Oct. 27, 1986, 100 Stat. 3118.)

HISTORICAL AND STATUTORY NOTES

Revision Notes and Legislative Reports

1978 Acts. Under this section the court may authorize the trustee to abandon any property of the estate that is burdensome to the estate or that is of inconsequential value to the estate. Abandonment may be to any party with a possessory interest in the property abandoned. In order to aid administration of the case, subsection (b) deems the court to have authorized abandonment of any property that is scheduled under section 521(1) and that is not administered before the case is closed. That property is deemed abandoned to the debtor. Subsection (c) specifies that if property is neither abandoned nor administered it remains property of the estate. Senate Report No. 95–989.

1984 Acts. Statements by Legislative Leaders, see 1984 U.S.Code Cong. and Adm.News, p. 576.

1986 Acts. House Report No. 99–764 and House Conference Report No. 99–958, see 1986 U.S.Code Cong. and Adm.News, p. 5227.

Legislative Statements

Section 554(b) is new and permits a party in interest to request the court to order the trustee to abandon property of the estate that is burdensome to the estate or that is of inconsequential value to the estate.

Effective and Applicability Provisions

1986 Acts. Amendment by Pub.L. 99–554 effective 30 days after Oct. 27, 1986, except as otherwise provided, see section 302(a) of Pub.L. 99–554, set out as a note under section 581 of Title 28, Judiciary and Judicial Procedure.

1984 Acts. Amendment by Pub.L. 98–353 effective with respect to cases filed 90 days after July 10, 1984, see section 552(a), formerly 553(a) of Pub.L. 98–353, set out as a note under section 101 of this title.

CROSS REFERENCES

Grain storage facility bankruptcies, expedited determinations, see 11 USCA § 557.

Redemption, see 11 USCA § 722.

§ 555. Contractual right to liquidate, terminate, or accelerate a securities contract

The exercise of a contractual right of a stockbroker, financial institution, financial participant, or securities clearing agency to cause the liquidation, termination, or acceleration of a securities contract, as defined in section 741 of this title, because of a condition of the kind specified in section 365(e)(1) of this title shall not be stayed, avoided, or otherwise limited by operation of any provision of this title or by order of a court or administrative agency in any proceeding under this title unless such order is authorized under the provisions of the Securities Investor Protection Act of 1970 or any statute administered by the Securities and Exchange Commission. As used in this section, the term "contractual right" includes a right set forth in a rule or bylaw of a derivatives clearing organization (as defined in the Commodity Exchange Act), a multilateral clearing organization (as defined in the Federal Deposit Insurance Corporation Improvement Act of 1991), a national securities exchange, a national securities association, a securities clearing agency, a contract market designated under the Commodity Exchange Act, a derivatives transaction execution facility registered under the Commodity Exchange Act, or a board of trade (as defined in the Commodity Exchange Act), or in a resolution of the governing board thereof, and a right, whether or not in writing, arising under common law, under law merchant, or by reason of normal business practice.

(Added Pub.L. 97–222, § 6(a), July 27, 1982, 96 Stat. 236, and amended Pub.L. 98–353, Title III, § 469, July 10, 1984, 98 Stat. 380; Pub.L. 103–394, Title V, § 501(b)(6), (d)(20), Oct. 22, 1994, 108 Stat. 4143, 4146; Pub.L. 109–8, Title IX, § 907(g), (*o*)(7), Apr. 20, 2005, 119 Stat. 177, 182.)

HISTORICAL AND STATUTORY NOTES

Revision Notes and Legislative Reports

1982 Acts. House Report No. 97–420, see 1982 U.S. Code Cong. and Adm. News, p. 583.

1984 Acts. Statements by Legislative Leaders, see 1984 U.S. Code Cong. and Adm. News, p. 576.

1994 Acts. House Report No. 103–835, see 1994 U.S. Code Cong. and Adm. News, p. 3340.

2005 Acts. House Report No. 109–31(Part I), see 2005 U.S. Code Cong. and Adm. News, p. 88.

References in Text

The Securities Investor Protection Act of 1970, referred to in text, is Pub.L. 91–598, Dec. 30, 1970, 84 Stat. 1636, as amended, which is classified generally to chapter 2B–1 (section 78aaa et seq.) of Title 15, Commerce and Trade. For complete classification of this Act to the Code, see section 78aaa of Title 15 and Tables.

The Commodity Exchange Act, referred to in text, is Act Sept. 21, 1922, c. 369, 42 Stat. 998, as amended, which is classified principally to chapter 1 of Title 7, 7 U.S.C.A. § 1 et seq. For complete classification, see Short Title set out as 7 U.S.C.A. § 1 and Tables.

The Federal Deposit Insurance Corporation Improvement Act of 1991, referred to in text, is Pub.L. 102–242, Dec. 19, 1991, 105 Stat. 2236. See Tables for classification.

Effective and Applicability Provisions

2005 Acts. Amendments by Pub.L. 109–8 effective, except as otherwise provided, 180 days after April 20, 2005, and inapplicable with respect to cases commenced under Title 11 before the effective date, see Pub.L. 109–8, § 1501, set out as a note under 11 U.S.C.A. § 101.

1994 Acts. Amendments by Pub.L. 103–394 effective on Oct. 22, 1994, and not to apply with respect to cases commenced under Title 11 of the United States Code before Oct. 22, 1994, see section 702 of Pub.L. 103–394, set out as a note under section 101 of this title.

1984 Acts. Amendment by Pub.L. 98–353 effective with respect to cases filed 90 days after July 10, 1984, see section 552(a), formerly 553(a) of Pub.L. 98–353, set out as a note under section 101 of this title.

Separability of Provisions

If any provision of or amendment made by Pub.L. 103–394 or the application of such provision or amendment to any person or circumstance is held to be unconstitutional, the remaining provisions of and amendments made by Pub.L. 103–394 and the application of such provisions and amendments to any person or circumstance shall not be affected thereby, see section 701 of Pub.L. 103–394, set out as a note under section 101 of this title.

§ 556. Contractual right to liquidate, terminate, or accelerate a commodities contract or forward contract

The contractual right of a commodity broker, financial participant, or forward contract merchant to cause the liquidation, termination, or acceleration of a commodity contract, as defined in section 761 of this title, or forward contract because of a condition of the kind specified in section 365(e)(1) of this title, and the right to a variation or maintenance margin payment received from a trustee with respect to open commodity contracts or forward contracts, shall not be stayed, avoided, or otherwise limited by operation of any provision of this title or by the order of a court in any proceeding under this title. As used in this section, the term "contractual right" includes a right set forth in a rule or bylaw of a derivatives clearing organization (as defined in the Commodity Exchange Act), a multilateral clearing organization (as defined in the Federal Deposit Insurance Corporation Improvement Act of 1991), a national securities exchange, a national securities association, a securities clearing agency, a contract market designated under the Commodity Exchange Act, a derivatives transaction execution facility registered under the Commodity Exchange Act, or a board of trade (as defined in the Commodity Exchange Act) or in a resolution of the governing board thereof and a right, whether or not evidenced in writing, arising under common law, under law merchant or by reason of normal business practice.

(Added Pub.L. 97–222, § 6(a), July 27, 1982, 96 Stat. 236, and amended Pub.L. 101–311, Title II, § 205, June 25, 1990, 104 Stat. 270; Pub.L. 103–394, Title V, § 501(b)(7), Oct. 22, 1994, 108 Stat. 4143; Pub.L. 109–8, Title IX, § 907(h), (*o*)(8), Apr. 20, 2005, 119 Stat. 178, 182.)

HISTORICAL AND STATUTORY NOTES

Revision Notes and Legislative Reports

1982 Acts. House Report No. 97–420, see 1982 U.S. Code Cong. and Adm. News, p. 583.

1990 Acts. House Report No. 101–484, see 1990 U.S. Code Cong. and Adm. News, p. 223.

1994 Acts. House Report No. 103–835, see 1994 U.S. Code Cong. and Adm. News, p. 3340.

2005 Acts. House Report No. 109–31(Part I), see 2005 U.S. Code Cong. and Adm. News, p. 88.

References in Text

The Commodity Exchange Act, referred to in text, is Act Sept. 21, 1922, c. 369, 42 Stat. 998, as amended, which is classified principally to chapter 1 of Title 7, 7 U.S.C.A. § 1. For complete classification, see Short Title set out as 7 U.S.C.A. § 1 and Tables.

The Federal Deposit Insurance Corporation Improvement Act of 1991, referred to in text, is Pub.L. 102–242, Dec. 19, 1991, 105 Stat. 2236. See Tables for classification.

Effective and Applicability Provisions

2005 Acts. Amendments by Pub.L. 109–8 effective, except as otherwise provided, 180 days after April 20, 2005, and inapplicable with respect to cases commenced under Title 11 before the effective date, see Pub.L. 109–8, § 1501, set out as a note under 11 U.S.C.A. § 101.

1994 Acts. Amendment by Pub.L. 103–394 effective on Oct. 22, 1994, and not to apply with respect to cases commenced under Title 11 of the United States Code before Oct. 22, 1994, see section 702 of Pub.L. 103–394, set out as a note under section 101 of this title.

Separability of Provisions

If any provision of or amendment made by Pub.L. 103–394 or the application of such provision or amendment to any person or circumstance is held to be unconstitutional, the remaining provisions of and amendments made by Pub.L. 103–394 and the application of such provisions and amendments to any person or circumstance shall not be affected thereby, see section 701 of Pub.L. 103–394, set out as a note under section 101 of this title.

§ 557. Expedited determination of interests in, and abandonment or other disposition of grain assets

(a) This section applies only in a case concerning a debtor that owns or operates a grain storage facility and only with respect to grain and the proceeds of grain. This section does not affect the application of any other section of this title to property other than grain and proceeds of grain.

(b) In this section—

(1) "grain" means wheat, corn, flaxseed, grain sorghum, barley, oats, rye, soybeans, other dry edible beans, or rice;

(2) "grain storage facility" means a site or physical structure regularly used to store grain for producers, or to store grain acquired from producers for resale; and

(3) "producer" means an entity which engages in the growing of grain.

(c)(1) Notwithstanding sections 362, 363, 365, and 554 of this title, on the court's own motion the court may, and on the request of the trustee or an entity that claims an interest in grain or the proceeds of grain the court shall, expedite the procedures for the determination of interests in and the disposition of grain and the proceeds of grain, by shortening to the greatest extent feasible such time periods as are otherwise applicable for such procedures and by establishing, by order, a timetable having a duration of not to exceed 120 days for the completion of the applicable procedure specified in subsection (d) of this section. Such time periods and such timetable may be modified by the court, for cause, in accordance with subsection (f) of this section.

(2) The court shall determine the extent to which such time periods shall be shortened, based upon—

(A) any need of an entity claiming an interest in such grain or the proceeds of grain for a prompt determination of such interest;

(B) any need of such entity for a prompt disposition of such grain;

(C) the market for such grain;

(D) the conditions under which such grain is stored;

(E) the costs of continued storage or disposition of such grain;

(F) the orderly administration of the estate;

(G) the appropriate opportunity for an entity to assert an interest in such grain; and

(H) such other considerations as are relevant to the need to expedite such procedures in the case.

(d) The procedures that may be expedited under subsection (c) of this section include—

(1) the filing of and response to—

(A) a claim of ownership;

(B) a proof of claim;

(C) a request for abandonment;

(D) a request for relief from the stay of action against property under section 362(a) of this title;

(E) a request for determination of secured status;

(F) a request for determination of whether such grain or the proceeds of grain—

(i) is property of the estate;

(ii) must be turned over to the estate; or

(iii) may be used, sold, or leased; and

(G) any other request for determination of an interest in such grain or the proceeds of grain;

(2) the disposition of such grain or the proceeds of grain, before or after determination of interests in such grain or the proceeds of grain, by way of—

(A) sale of such grain;

(B) abandonment;

(C) distribution; or

(D) such other method as is equitable in the case;

(3) subject to sections 701, 702, 703, 1104, 1202, and 1302 of this title, the appointment of a trustee or examiner and the retention and compensation of any professional person required to assist with respect to matters relevant to the determination of interests in or disposition of such grain or the proceeds of grain; and

(4) the determination of any dispute concerning a matter specified in paragraph (1), (2), or (3) of this subsection.

(e)(1) Any governmental unit that has regulatory jurisdiction over the operation or liquidation of the debtor or the debtor's business shall be given notice of any request made or order entered under subsection (c) of this section.

(2) Any such governmental unit may raise, and may appear and be heard on, any issue relating to grain or the proceeds of grain in a case in which a request is made, or an order is entered, under subsection (c) of this section.

(3) The trustee shall consult with such governmental unit before taking any action relating to the disposition of grain in the possession, custody, or control of the debtor or the estate.

(f) The court may extend the period for final disposition of grain or the proceeds of grain under this section beyond 120 days if the court finds that—

(1) the interests of justice so require in light of the complexity of the case; and

(2) the interests of those claimants entitled to distribution of grain or the proceeds of grain will not be materially injured by such additional delay.

(g) Unless an order establishing an expedited procedure under subsection (c) of this section, or determining any interest in or approving any disposition of grain or the proceeds of grain, is stayed pending appeal—

(1) the reversal or modification of such order on appeal does not affect the validity of any procedure, determination, or disposition that occurs before such reversal or modification, whether or not any entity knew of the pendency of the appeal; and

(2) neither the court nor the trustee may delay, due to the appeal of such order, any proceeding in the case in which such order is issued.

(h)(1) The trustee may recover from grain and the proceeds of grain the reasonable and necessary costs and expenses allowable under section 503(b) of this title attributable to preserving or disposing of grain or the proceeds of grain, but may not recover from such grain or the proceeds of grain any other costs or expenses.

(2) Notwithstanding section 326(a) of this title, the dollar amounts of money specified in such section include the value, as of the date of disposition, of any grain that the trustee distributes in kind.

(i) In all cases where the quantity of a specific type of grain held by a debtor operating a grain storage facility exceeds ten thousand bushels, such grain shall be sold by the trustee and the assets thereof distributed in accordance with the provisions of this section.

(Added Pub.L. 98–353, Title III, § 352(a), July 10, 1984, 98 Stat. 359, and amended Pub.L. 99–554, Title II, § 257(p), Oct. 27, 1986, 100 Stat. 3115.)

HISTORICAL AND STATUTORY NOTES

Revision Notes and Legislative Reports

1984 Acts. Statements by Legislative Leaders, see 1984 U.S. Code Cong. and Adm.News, p. 576.

1986 Acts. House Report No. 99–764 and House Conference Report No. 99–958, see 1986 U.S.Code Cong. and Adm.News, p. 5227.

Effective and Applicability Provisions

1986 Acts. Amendment by Pub.L. 99–554 effective 30 days after Oct. 27, 1986, but not applicable to cases commenced under this title before that date, see section 302(a)(c)(1) of Pub.L. 99–554, set out as a note under section 581 of Title 28, Judiciary and Judicial Procedure.

1984 Acts. Section effective with respect to cases filed 90 days after July 10, 1984, see section 552(a), formerly 553(a), of Pub.L. 98–353, set out as a note under section 101 of this title.

CROSS REFERENCES

Applicability of this section in Chapter nine cases, see 11 USCA § 901.

Priorities, see 11 USCA § 507.

Rights and powers of trustee subject to right of seller who is "producer" of "grain" sold to "grain storage facility" owned or operated by debtor, as such terms are defined under this section, see 11 USCA § 546.

§ 558. Defenses of the estate

The estate shall have the benefit of any defense available to the debtor as against any entity other than the estate, including statutes of limitation, statutes of frauds, usury, and other personal defenses. A waiver of any such defense by the debtor after the commencement of the case does not bind the estate.

(Added Pub.L. 98–353, Title III, § 470(a), July 10, 1984, 98 Stat. 380.)

HISTORICAL AND STATUTORY NOTES

Revision Notes and Legislative Reports

1984 Acts. Statements by Legislative Leaders, see 1984 U.S.Code Cong. and Adm.News, p. 576.

Effective and Applicability Provisions

1984 Acts. Section effective with respect to cases filed 90 days after July 10, 1984, see section 552(a), formerly 553(a), of Pub.L. 98–353, set out as a note under section 101 of this title.

§ 559. Contractual right to liquidate, terminate, or accelerate a repurchase agreement

The exercise of a contractual right of a repo participant or financial participant to cause the liquidation, termination, or acceleration of a repurchase agreement because of a condition of the kind specified in section 365(e)(1) of this title shall not be stayed, avoided, or otherwise limited by operation of any provision of this title or by order of a court or administrative agency in any proceeding under this title, unless, where the debtor is a stockbroker or securities clearing agency, such order is authorized under the provisions of the Securities Investor Protection Act of 1970 or any statute administered by the Securities and Exchange Commission. In the event that a repo participant or financial participant liquidates one or more repurchase agreements with a debtor and under the terms of one or more such agreements has agreed to deliver assets subject to repurchase agreements to the debtor, any excess of the market prices received on liquidation of such assets (or if any such assets are not disposed of on the date of liquidation of such repurchase agreements, at the prices available at the time of liquidation of such repurchase agreements from a generally recognized source or the most recent closing bid quotation from such a source) over the sum of the stated repurchase prices and all expenses in connection with the liquidation of such repurchase agreements shall be deemed property of the estate, subject to the available rights of setoff. As used in this section, the term "contractual right" includes a right set forth in a rule or bylaw of a derivatives clearing organization (as defined in the Commodity Exchange Act), a multilateral clearing organization (as defined in the Federal Deposit Insurance Corporation Improvement Act of 1991), a national securities exchange, a national securities association, a securities clearing agency, a contract market designated under the Commodity Exchange Act, a derivatives transaction execution facility registered under the Commodity Exchange Act, or a board of trade (as defined in the Commodity Exchange Act) or in a resolution of the governing board thereof and a right, whether or not evidenced in writing, arising under common law, under law merchant or by reason of normal business practice.

(Added Pub.L. 98–353, Title III, § 396(a), July 10, 1984, 98 Stat. 366, and amended Pub.L. 103–394, Title V, § 501(d)(21), Oct. 22, 1994, 108 Stat. 4146; Pub.L. 109–8, Title IX, § 907(i), (*o*)(9), Apr. 20, 2005, 119 Stat. 178, 182.)

HISTORICAL AND STATUTORY NOTES

Revision Notes and Legislative Reports

1984 Acts. Statements by Legislative Leaders, see 1984 U.S. Code Cong. and Adm. News, p. 576.

1994 Acts. House Report No. 103–835, see 1994 U.S. Code Cong. and Adm. News, p. 3340.

2005 Acts. House Report No. 109–31(Part I), see 2005 U.S. Code Cong. and Adm. News, p. 88.

References in Text

The Securities Investor Protection Act of 1970, referred to in text, is Pub. L. 91–598, Dec. 30, 1970, 84 Stat. 1636, as amended, which is classified generally to chapter 2B–1 (section 78aaa et seq.) of Title 15, Commerce and Trade. For complete classification of this Act to the Code, see section 78aaa of Title 15 and Tables.

The Commodity Exchange Act, referred to in text, is Act Sept. 21, 1922, c. 369, 42 Stat. 998, as amended, which is classified principally to chapter 1 of Title 7, 7 U.S.C.A. § 1. For complete classification, see Short Title set out as 7 U.S.C.A. § 1 and Tables.

The Federal Deposit Insurance Corporation Improvement Act of 1991, referred to in text, is Pub.L. 102–242, Dec. 19, 1991, 105 Stat. 2236. See Tables for classification.

Effective and Applicability Provisions

2005 Acts. Amendments by Pub.L. 109–8 effective, except as otherwise provided, 180 days after April 20, 2005, and inapplicable with respect to cases commenced under Title 11 before the effective date, see Pub.L. 109–8, § 1501, set out as a note under 11 U.S.C.A. § 101.

1994 Acts. Amendment by Pub.L. 103–394 effective on Oct. 22, 1994, and not to apply with respect to cases commenced under Title 11 of the United States Code before Oct. 22, 1994, see section 702 of Pub.L. 103–394, set out as a note under section 101 of this title.

1984 Acts. Section effective with respect to cases filed 90 days after July 10, 1984, see section 552(a), formerly 553(a), of Pub.L. 98–353, set out as a note under section 101 of this title.

Separability of Provisions

If any provision of or amendment made by Pub.L. 103–394 or the application of such provision or amendment to any person or circumstance is held to be unconstitutional, the remaining provisions of and amendments made by Pub.L. 103–394 and the application of such provisions and amendments to any person or circumstance shall not be affected thereby, see section 701 of Pub.L. 103–394, set out as a note under section 101 of this title.

§ 560. Contractual right to liquidate, terminate, or accelerate a swap agreement

The exercise of any contractual right of any swap participant or financial participant to cause the liquidation, termination, or acceleration of one or more swap agreements because of a condition of the kind specified in section 365(e)(1) of this title or to offset or net out any termination values or payment amounts arising under or in connection with the termination, liquidation, or acceleration of one or more swap agreements shall not be stayed, avoided, or otherwise limited by operation of any provision of this title or by order of a court or administrative agency in any proceeding under this title. As used in this section, the term "contractual right" includes a right set forth in a rule or bylaw of a derivatives clearing organization (as defined in the Commodity Exchange Act), a multilateral clearing organization (as defined in the Federal Deposit Insurance Corporation Improvement Act of 1991), a national securities exchange, a national securities association, a securities clearing agency, a contract market designated under the Commodity Exchange Act, a derivatives transaction execution facility registered under the Commodity Exchange Act, or a board of trade (as defined in the Commodity Exchange Act) or in a resolution of the governing board thereof and a right, whether or not evidenced in writing, arising under common law, under law merchant, or by reason of normal business practice.

(Added Pub.L. 101–311, Title I, § 106(a), June 25, 1990, 104 Stat. 268, and amended Pub.L. 109–8, Title IX, § 907(j), (*o*)(10), Apr. 20, 2005, 119 Stat. 178, 182.)

HISTORICAL AND STATUTORY NOTES

Revision Notes and Legislative Reports

1990 Acts. House Report No. 101–484, see 1990 U.S.Code Cong. and Adm.News, p. 223.

2005 Acts. House Report No. 109–31(Part I), see 2005 U.S. Code Cong. and Adm. News, p. 88.

References in Text

The Commodity Exchange Act, referred to in text, is Act Sept. 21, 1922, c. 369, 42 Stat. 998, as amended, which is classified principally to chapter 1 of Title 7, 7 U.S.C.A. § 1. For complete classification, see Short Title set out as 7 U.S.C.A. § 1 and Tables.

The Federal Deposit Insurance Corporation Improvement Act of 1991, referred to in text, is Pub.L. 102–242, Dec. 19, 1991, 105 Stat. 2236. See Tables for classification.

Effective and Applicability Provisions

2005 Acts. Amendments by Pub.L. 109–8 effective, except as otherwise provided, 180 days after April 20, 2005, and inapplicable with respect to cases commenced under Title 11 before the effective date, see Pub.L. 109–8, § 1501, set out as a note under 11 U.S.C.A. § 101.

§ 561. Contractual right to terminate, liquidate, accelerate, or offset under a master netting agreement and across contracts; proceedings under chapter 15

(a) Subject to subsection (b), the exercise of any contractual right, because of a condition of the kind specified in section 365(e)(1), to cause the termination, liquidation, or acceleration of or to offset or net termination values, payment amounts, or other transfer obligations arising under or in connection with one or more (or the termination, liquidation, or acceleration of one or more)—

(1) securities contracts, as defined in section 741(7);

(2) commodity contracts, as defined in section 761(4);

(3) forward contracts;

(4) repurchase agreements;

(5) swap agreements; or

(6) master netting agreements,

shall not be stayed, avoided, or otherwise limited by operation of any provision of this title or by any order of a court or administrative agency in any proceeding under this title.

(b)(1) A party may exercise a contractual right described in subsection (a) to terminate, liquidate, or accelerate only to the extent that such party could exercise such a right under section 555, 556, 559, or 560 for each individual contract covered by the master netting agreement in issue.

(2) If a debtor is a commodity broker subject to subchapter IV of chapter 7—

(A) a party may not net or offset an obligation to the debtor arising under, or in connection with, a commodity contract traded on or subject to the rules of a contract market designated under the Commodity Exchange Act or a derivatives transaction execution facility registered under the Commodity Exchange Act against any claim arising under, or in connection with, other instruments, contracts, or agreements listed in subsection (a) except to the extent that the party has positive net equity in the commodity accounts at the debtor, as calculated under such subchapter; and

(B) another commodity broker may not net or offset an obligation to the debtor arising under, or in connection with, a commodity contract entered into or held on behalf of a customer of the debtor and traded on or subject to the rules of a contract market designated under the Commodity Exchange Act or a derivatives transaction execution facility registered under the Commodity Exchange Act against any claim arising under, or in connection with, other instruments, contracts, or agreements listed in subsection (a).

(3) No provision of subparagraph (A) or (B) of paragraph (2) shall prohibit the offset of claims and obligations that arise under—

(A) a cross-margining agreement or similar arrangement that has been approved by the Commodity Futures Trading Commission or submitted to the Commodity Futures Trading Commission under paragraph (1) or (2) of section 5c(c) of the Commodity Exchange Act and has not been abrogated or rendered ineffective by the Commodity Futures Trading Commission; or

(B) any other netting agreement between a clearing organization (as defined in section 761) and another entity that has been approved by the Commodity Futures Trading Commission.

(c) As used in this section, the term "contractual right" includes a right set forth in a rule or bylaw of a derivatives clearing organization (as defined in the Commodity Exchange Act), a multilateral clearing organization (as defined in the Federal Deposit Insurance Corporation Improvement Act of 1991), a national securities exchange, a national securities association, a securities clearing agency, a contract market designated under the Commodity Exchange Act, a derivatives transaction execution facility registered under the Commodity Exchange Act, or a board of trade (as defined in the Commodity Exchange Act) or in a resolution of the governing board thereof, and a right, whether or not evidenced in writing, arising under common law, under law merchant, or by reason of normal business practice.

(d) Any provisions of this title relating to securities contracts, commodity contracts, forward contracts, repurchase agreements, swap agreements, or master netting agreements shall apply in a case under chapter 15, so that enforcement of contractual provisions of such contracts and agreements in accordance with their terms will not be stayed or otherwise limited by operation of any provision of this title or by order of a court in any case under this title, and to limit avoidance powers to the same extent as in a proceeding under chapter 7 or 11 of this title (such enforcement not to be limited based on the presence or absence of assets of the debtor in the United States).

(Added Pub.L. 109–8, Title IX, § 907(k)(1), Apr. 20, 2005, 119 Stat. 179.)

HISTORICAL AND STATUTORY NOTES

Revision Notes and Legislative Reports

2005 Acts. House Report No. 109–31(Part I), see 2005 U.S. Code Cong. and Adm. News, p. 88.

References in Text

Subchapter IV of chapter 7, referred to in subsec. (b)(2), is subchapter IV of chapter 7 of this title, 11 U.S.C.A. § 761 et seq.

The Commodity Exchange Act, referred to in subsecs. (b)(2)(A) and (c), is Act Sept. 21, 1922, c. 369, 42 Stat. 998, as amended, which is classified principally to chapter 1 of Title 7, 7 U.S.C.A. § 1 et seq. For complete classification, see Short Title set out as 7 U.S.C.A. § 1 and Tables.

Section 5c(c) of the Commodity Exchange Act, referred to in subsec. (b)(2)(A), is Act Sept. 21, 1922, c. 369, § 5c, as added and amended Dec. 21, 2000, Pub.L. 106–554, § 1(a)(5) [Title I, § 113, Title II, § 251(h)], 114 Stat. 2763, 2763A-399, 2763a–444, which is classified to 7 U.S.C.A. § 7a–2.

The Federal Deposit Insurance Corporation Improvement Act of 1991, referred to in subsec. (c), is Pub.L. 102–242, Dec. 19, 1991, 105 Stat. 2236. See Tables for classification.

Chapter 15, referred to in subsec. (d), is chapter 15 of this title, 11 U.S.C.A. § 1501 et seq.

Chapter 7 or 11 of this title, referred to in subsec. (d), is 11 U.S.C.A. § 701 et seq., or 11 U.S.C.A. 1101 et seq., respectively.

Effective and Applicability Provisions

2005 Acts. Amendments by Pub.L. 109–8 effective, except as otherwise provided, 180 days after April 20, 2005, and inapplicable with respect to cases commenced under Title 11

before the effective date, see Pub.L. 109–8, § 1501, set out as a note under 11 U.S.C.A. § 101.

§ 562. Timing of damage measurement in connection with swap agreements, securities contracts, forward contracts, commodity contracts, repurchase agreements, and master netting agreements

(a) If the trustee rejects a swap agreement, securities contract (as defined in section 741), forward contract, commodity contract (as defined in section 761), repurchase agreement, or master netting agreement pursuant to section 365(a), or if a forward contract merchant, stockbroker, financial institution, securities clearing agency, repo participant, financial participant, master netting agreement participant, or swap participant liquidates, terminates, or accelerates such contract or agreement, damages shall be measured as of the earlier of—

(1) the date of such rejection; or

(2) the date or dates of such liquidation, termination, or acceleration.

(b) If there are not any commercially reasonable determinants of value as of any date referred to in paragraph (1) or (2) of subsection (a), damages shall be measured as of the earliest subsequent date or dates on which there are commercially reasonable determinants of value.

(c) For the purposes of subsection (b), if damages are not measured as of the date or dates of rejection, liquidation, termination, or acceleration, and the forward contract merchant, stockbroker, financial institution, securities clearing agency, repo participant, financial participant, master netting agreement participant, or swap participant or the trustee objects to the timing of the measurement of damages—

(1) the trustee, in the case of an objection by a forward contract merchant, stockbroker, financial institution, securities clearing agency, repo participant, financial participant, master netting agreement participant, or swap participant; or

(2) the forward contract merchant, stockbroker, financial institution, securities clearing agency, repo participant, financial participant, master netting agreement participant, or swap participant, in the case of an objection by the trustee,

has the burden of proving that there were no commercially reasonable determinants of value as of such date or dates.

(Added Pub.L. 109–8, Title IX, § 910(a)(1), Apr. 20, 2005, 119 Stat. 184.)

HISTORICAL AND STATUTORY NOTES

Revision Notes and Legislative Reports

2005 Acts. House Report No. 109–31(Part I), see 2005 U.S. Code Cong. and Adm. News, p. 88.

Effective and Applicability Provisions

2005 Acts. Amendments by Pub.L. 109–8 effective, except as otherwise provided, 180 days after April 20, 2005, and inapplicable with respect to cases commenced under Title 11 before the effective date, see Pub.L. 109–8, § 1501, set out as a note under 11 U.S.C.A. § 101.

§§ 563 to 700. Reserved for future legislation.

CHAPTER 7—LIQUIDATION

HISTORICAL AND STATUTORY NOTES

Effective and Applicability Provisions

2005 Acts. Amendments by Pub.L. 109–8 effective, except as otherwise provided, 180 days after April 20, 2005, and inapplicable with respect to cases commenced under Title 11 before the effective date, see Pub.L. 109–8, § 1501, set out as a note under 11 U.S.C.A. § 101.

CROSS REFERENCES

Amount received for claim through liquidation under this chapter as standard for confirmation requirement in—

Chapter eleven cases, see 11 USCA § 1129.

Chapter thirteen cases, see 11 USCA § 1325.

Chapter twelve cases, see 11 USCA § 1225.

Amount received for claim through liquidation under this chapter as standard for discharge requirement in—

Chapter thirteen cases, see 11 USCA § 1328.

Chapter twelve cases, see 11 USCA § 1228.

Applicability of income tax provisions to cases under this chapter, see 26 USCA § 1398.

Certain provisions respecting commodity brokers under this chapter, see 7 USCA § 24.

Chapters 1, 3 and 5 of this title applicable in case under this chapter, see 11 USCA § 103.

Commencement of involuntary cases, see 11 USCA § 303.

Conversion to this chapter from—

Chapter eleven, see 11 USCA § 1112.

Chapter thirteen, see 11 USCA § 1307.

Chapter twelve, see 11 USCA § 1208.

Debtor's duty under this chapter to file statement of intentions with respect to schedule of assets and liabilities, see 11 USCA § 521.

Denial of discharge under this chapter as affecting operation of injunction, see 11 USCA § 524.

Determination of net worth of person subject to liability for termination of single-employer plans includes improper transfers of assets in cases under this chapter, see 29 USCA § 1362.

Distribution of certain proceeds and property under this chapter as requirement for confirmation of plan, see 11 USCA § 1173.

Duration of automatic stay in case concerning an individual under this chapter, see 11 USCA § 362.

Duties of trustee in investor protection liquidation proceedings same as under this chapter, see 15 USCA § 78fff–1.

Duties of United States trustees, see 28 USCA § 586.

Effect of confirmation, see 11 USCA § 1141.

Effect of distribution other than under this title, see 11 USCA § 508.

Eligibility to serve as trustee, see 11 USCA § 321.

Employment of professional persons, see 11 USCA § 327.

Executory contracts and unexpired leases, see 11 USCA § 365.

Filing fees, see 28 USCA § 1930.

Limitation on compensation of trustee, see 11 USCA § 326.

Liquidation in railroad reorganization case as if under this chapter, see 11 USCA § 1174.

Meetings of creditors and equity security holders and oral examination of debtor, see 11 USCA § 341.

Objection to allowance of claims by creditor of partner in partnership that is debtor under this chapter, see 11 USCA § 502.

Payment of trustee from filing fee, see 11 USCA § 330.

Persons required to make returns of income under this chapter, see 26 USCA § 6012.

Persons who may be debtors under this chapter, see 11 USCA § 109.

Property of estate in cases converted to this chapter from—

Chapter thirteen, see 11 USCA § 1306.

Chapter twelve, see 11 USCA § 1207.

Recommendation by trustee of conversion from chapter 11 to this chapter, see 11 USCA § 1106.

Special tax provisions, see 11 USCA § 346.

Stay of action against codebtor in cases converted to this chapter from—

Chapter thirteen, see 11 USCA § 1301.

Chapter twelve, see 11 USCA § 1201.

Transfers enabling creditor to receive more than under this chapter, see 11 USCA § 547.

Treatment of debtor's estate in cases under this chapter as taxpayer for certain income tax purposes, see 26 USCA § 108.

Unclaimed property, see 11 USCA § 347.

SUBCHAPTER I—OFFICERS AND ADMINISTRATION

CROSS REFERENCES

Applicability of this subchapter in investor protection liquidation proceedings, see 15 USCA § 78fff.

Subchapter applicable only in case under this chapter, see 11 USCA § 103.

§ 701. Interim trustee

(a)(1) Promptly after the order for relief under this chapter, the United States trustee shall appoint one disinterested person that is a member of the panel of private trustees established under section 586(a)(1) of title 28 or that is serving as trustee in the case immediately before the order for relief under this chapter to serve as interim trustee in the case.

(2) If none of the members of such panel is willing to serve as interim trustee in the case, then the United States trustee may serve as interim trustee in the case.

(b) The service of an interim trustee under this section terminates when a trustee elected or designated under section 702 of this title to serve as trustee in the case qualifies under section 322 of this title.

(c) An interim trustee serving under this section is a trustee in a case under this title.

(Pub.L. 95–598, Nov. 6, 1978, 92 Stat. 2604; Pub.L. 99–554, Title II, § 215, Oct. 27, 1986, 100 Stat. 3100.)

HISTORICAL AND STATUTORY NOTES

Revision Notes and Legislative Reports

1978 Acts. This section requires the court to appoint an interim trustee. The appointment must be made from the panel of private trustees established and maintained by the Director of the Administrative Office under proposed 28 U.S.C. 604(e).

Subsection (a) requires the appointment of an interim trustee to be made promptly after the order for relief, unless a trustee is already serving in the case, such as before a conversion from a reorganization to a liquidation case.

Subsection (b) specifies that the appointment of an interim trustee expires when the permanent trustee is elected or designated under section 702.

Subsection (c) makes clear that an interim trustee is a trustee in a case under the bankruptcy code.

Subsection (d) provides that in a commodity broker case where speed is essential the interim trustee must be appointed by noon of the business day immediately following the order for relief. Senate Report No. 95–989.

1986 Acts. House Report No. 99–764 and House Conference Report No. 99–958, see 1986 U.S.Code Cong. and Adm.News, p. 5227.

Legislative Statements

The House amendment deletes section 701(d) of the Senate amendment. It is anticipated that the Rules of Bankruptcy Procedure will require the appointment of an interim trustee at the earliest practical moment in commodity broker bankruptcies, but no later than noon of the day after the date of the filing of the petition, due to the volatility of such cases.

Effective and Applicability Provisions

1986 Acts. Amendment by Pub.L. 99–554 effective 30 days after Oct. 27, 1986, except as otherwise provided for, see section 302(a) of Pub.L. 99–554, set out as a note under section 581 of Title 28, Judiciary and Judicial Procedure.

Amendment by Pub.L. 99–554, § 215, not to become effective in or with respect to certain specified judicial districts until, or apply to cases while pending in such district before, the expiration of the 270-day period beginning 30 days after Oct. 27, 1986, or of the 30-day period beginning on the date the Attorney General certifies under section 303 of Pub.L. 99–554 the region specified in a paragraph of section 581(a) of Title 28, as amended by section 111(a) of Pub.L. 99–554, that includes such district, whichever occurs first, see section 302(d)(1) of Pub.L. 99–554, set out as a note under section 581 of Title 28.

Amendment by Pub.L. 99–554, § 215, not to become effective in or with respect to certain specified judicial districts until, or apply to cases while pending in such district before, the expiration of the 2-year period beginning 30 days after Oct. 27, 1986, or of the 30-day period beginning on the date the Attorney General certifies under section 303 of Pub.L. 99–554 the region specified in a paragraph of section 581(a) of Title 28, as amended by section 111(a) of Pub.L. 99–554, that includes such district, whichever occurs first, see section 302(d)(2) of Pub.L. 99–554, set out as a note under section 581 of Title 28.

Amendment by Pub.L. 99–554, § 215, not to become effective in or with respect to judicial districts established for the States of Alabama and North Carolina until, or apply to cases while pending in such district before, such district elects to be included in a bankruptcy region established in section 581(a) of Title 28, as amended by section 111(a) of Pub.L. 99–554, or Oct. 1, 2002, whichever occurs first, and, except as otherwise provided, with respect to cases under chapters 7, 11, 12, and 13 of Title 11 commenced before 30 days after Oct. 27, 1986, and pending in a judicial district in the States of Alabama or North Carolina before any election made under section 302(d)(3)(A) of Pub.L. 99–554 by such district becomes effective or Oct. 1, 2002, whichever occurs first, amendments by Pub.L. 99–554 not to apply until Oct. 1, 2003, or the expiration of the 1-year period beginning on the date such election becomes effective, whichever occurs first, and further, in any judicial district in Alabama or North Carolina not making the election described in section 302(d)(3)(A) of Pub.L. 99–554, any person appointed under regulations issued by the Judicial Conference to administer estates in cases under Title 11 authorized to establish, etc., a panel of private trustees, and to supervise cases and trustees in cases under chapters 7, 11, 12 and 13 of Title 11, until amendments by sections 201 to 231 of Pub.L. 99–554 effective in such district, see section 302(d)(3)(A) to (F), (H), and (I) of Pub.L. 99–554, set out as a note under section 581 of Title 28.

Amendment by Pub.L. 99–554, § 215, except as otherwise provided, with respect to cases under chapters 7, 11, 12, and 13 of Title 11 commenced before 30 days after Oct. 27, 1986, and pending in a judicial district referred to in section 581(a) of Title 28, as amended by section 111(a) of Pub.L. 99–554, for which a United States trustee is not authorized before 30 days after Oct. 27, 1986 to be appointed, not applicable until the expiration of the 3-year period beginning on Oct. 27, 1986 or of the 1-year period beginning on the date the Attorney General certifies under section 303 of Pub.L. 99–554 the region specified in a paragraph of such section 581(a) that includes, such district, whichever occurs first, see section 302(e)(1)(2) of Pub.L. 99–554, set out as a note under section 581 of Title 28.

CROSS REFERENCES

Appointment of interim trustee after commencement of involuntary case, see 11 USCA § 303.

Effect of conversion, see 11 USCA § 348.

Grain storage facility bankruptcies, expedited appointment of trustee, see 11 USCA § 557.

Qualification of trustee, see 11 USCA § 322.

§ 702. Election of trustee

(a) A creditor may vote for a candidate for trustee only if such creditor—

(1) holds an allowable, undisputed, fixed, liquidated, unsecured claim of a kind entitled to distribution under section 726(a)(2), 726(a)(3), 726(a)(4), 752(a), 766(h), or 766(i) of this title;

(2) does not have an interest materially adverse, other than an equity interest that is not substantial in relation to such creditor's interest as a creditor, to the interest of creditors entitled to such distribution; and

(3) is not an insider.

(b) At the meeting of creditors held under section 341 of this title, creditors may elect one person to serve as trustee in the case if election of a trustee is requested by creditors that may vote under subsection (a) of this section, and that hold at least 20 percent in amount of the claims specified in subsection (a)(1) of this section that are held by creditors that may vote under subsection (a) of this section.

(c) A candidate for trustee is elected trustee if—

(1) creditors holding at least 20 percent in amount of the claims of a kind specified in subsection (a)(1) of this section that are held by creditors that may vote under subsection (a) of this section vote; and

(2) such candidate receives the votes of creditors holding a majority in amount of claims specified in subsection (a)(1) of this section that are held by creditors that vote for a trustee.

(d) If a trustee is not elected under this section, then the interim trustee shall serve as trustee in the case.

(Pub.L. 95–598, Nov. 6, 1978, 92 Stat. 2604; Pub.L. 97–222, § 7, July 27, 1982, 96 Stat. 237; Pub.L. 98–353, Title III, § 472, July 10, 1984, 98 Stat. 380.)

HISTORICAL AND STATUTORY NOTES

Revision Notes and Legislative Reports

1978 Acts. Subsection (a) of this section specifies which creditors may vote for a trustee. Only a creditor that holds an allowable, undisputed, fixed, liquidated, unsecured claim that is not entitled to priority, that does not have an interest materially adverse to the interest of general unsecured creditors, and that is not an insider may vote for a trustee. The phrase "materially adverse" is currently used in the Rules of Bankruptcy Procedure, rule 207(d). The application of the standard requires a balancing of various factors, such as the nature of the adversity. A creditor with a very small equity position would not be excluded from voting solely because he holds a small equity in the debtor. The Rules of Bankruptcy Procedure also currently provide for temporary allowance of claims, and will continue to do so for the purposes of determining who is eligible to vote under this provision.

Subsection (b) permits creditors at the meeting of creditors to elect one person to serve as trustee in the case.

Creditors holding at least 20 percent in amount of the claims specified in the preceding paragraph must request election before creditors may elect a trustee. Subsection (c) specifies that a candidate for trustee is elected trustee if creditors holding at least 20 percent in amount of those claims actually vote, and if the candidate receives a majority in amount of votes actually cast.

Subsection (d) specifies that if a trustee is not elected, then the interim trustee becomes the permanent trustee and serves in the case permanently. Senate Report No. 95–989.

1982 Acts. House Report No. 97–420, see 1982 U.S.Code Cong. and Adm.News, p. 583.

1984 Acts. Statements by Legislative Leaders, see 1984 U.S.Code Cong. and Adm.News, p. 576.

Legislative Statements

The House amendment adopts section 702(a)(2) of the Senate amendment. An insubstantial equity interest does not disqualify a creditor from voting for a candidate for trustee.

Effective and Applicability Provisions

1984 Acts. Amendment by Pub.L. 98–353 effective with respect to cases filed 90 days after July 10, 1984, see section 552(a), formerly 553(a), of Pub.L. 98–353, set out as a note under section 101 of this title.

CROSS REFERENCES

Grain storage facility bankruptcies, expedited appointment of trustee, see 11 USCA § 557.

Qualification of trustee, see 11 USCA § 322.

Time for bringing action, see 11 USCA § 546.

§ 703. Successor trustee

(a) If a trustee dies or resigns during a case, fails to qualify under section 322 of this title, or is removed under section 324 of this title, creditors may elect, in the manner specified in section 702 of this title, a person to fill the vacancy in the office of trustee.

(b) Pending election of a trustee under subsection (a) of this section, if necessary to preserve or prevent loss to the estate, the United States trustee may appoint an interim trustee in the manner specified in section 701(a).

(c) If creditors do not elect a successor trustee under subsection (a) of this section or if a trustee is needed in a case reopened under section 350 of this title, then the United States trustee—

(1) shall appoint one disinterested person that is a member of the panel of private trustees established under section 586(a)(1) of title 28 to serve as trustee in the case; or

(2) may, if none of the disinterested members of such panel is willing to serve as trustee, serve as trustee in the case.

(Pub.L. 95–598, Nov. 6, 1978, 92 Stat. 2605; Pub.L. 98–353, Title III, § 473, July 10, 1984, 98 Stat. 381; Pub.L. 99–554, Title II, § 216, Oct. 27, 1986, 100 Stat. 3100.)

HISTORICAL AND STATUTORY NOTES

Revision Notes and Legislative Reports

1978 Acts. If the office of trustee becomes vacant during the case, this section makes provision for the selection of a successor trustee. The office might become vacant through death, resignation, removal, failure to qualify under section 322 by posting bond, or the reopening of a case. If it does, creditors may elect a successor in the same manner as they may elect a trustee under the previous section. Pending the election of a successor, the court may appoint an interim trustee in the usual manner if necessary to preserve or prevent loss to the estate. If creditors do not elect a successor, or if a trustee is needed in a reopened case, then the court appoints a disinterested member of the panel of private trustees to serve. Senate Report No. 95–989.

1984 Acts. Statements by Legislative Leaders, see 1984 U.S.Code Cong. and Adm.News, p. 576.

1986 Acts. House Report No. 99–764 and House Conference Report No. 99–958, see 1986 U.S.Code Cong. and Adm.News, p. 5227.

Effective and Applicability Provisions

1986 Acts. Amendment by Pub.L. 99–554 effective 30 days after Oct. 27, 1986, except as otherwise provided for, see section 302(a) of Pub.L. 99–554, set out as a note under section 581 of Title 28, Judiciary and Judicial Procedure.

Amendment by Pub.L. 99–554, § 216, not to become effective in or with respect to certain specified judicial districts until, or apply to cases while pending in such district before, the expiration of the 270-day period beginning 30 days after Oct. 27, 1986, or of the 30-day period beginning on the date the Attorney General certifies under section 303 of Pub.L. 99–554 the region specified in a paragraph of section 581(a) of Title 28, as amended by section 111(a) of Pub.L. 99–554, that includes such district, whichever occurs first, see section 302(d)(1) of Pub.L. 99–554, set out as a note under section 581 of Title 28.

Amendment by Pub.L. 99–554, § 216, not to become effective in or with respect to certain specified judicial districts until, or apply to cases while pending in such district before, the expiration of the 2-year period beginning 30 days after Oct. 27, 1986, or of the 30-day period beginning on the date the Attorney General certifies under section 303 of Pub.L. 99–554 the region specified in a paragraph of section 581(a) of Title 28, as amended by section 111(a) of Pub.L. 99–554, that includes such district, whichever occurs first, see section 302(d)(2) of Pub.L. 99–554, set out as a note under section 581 of Title 28.

Amendment by Pub.L. 99–554, § 216, not to become effective in or with respect to judicial districts established for the States of Alabama and North Carolina until, or apply to cases while pending in such district before, such district elects to be included in a bankruptcy region established in section 581(a) of Title 28, as amended by section 111(a) of Pub.L. 99–554, or Oct. 1, 2002, whichever occurs first, and, except as otherwise provided, with respect to cases under chapters 7, 11, 12, and 13 of Title 11 commenced before 30 days after Oct. 27, 1986, and pending in a judicial district in the States of Alabama or North Carolina before any election made under section 302(d)(3)(A) of Pub.L. 99–554 by such district becomes effective or Oct. 1, 2002, whichever occurs first, amendments by Pub.L. 99–554 not to apply until Oct. 1,

2003, or the expiration of the 1-year period beginning on the date such election becomes effective, whichever occurs first, and further, in any judicial district in Alabama or North Carolina not making the election described in section 302(d)(3)(A) of Pub.L. 99–554, any person appointed under regulations issued by the Judicial Conference to administer estates in cases under Title 11 authorized to establish, etc., a panel of private trustees, and to supervise cases and trustees in cases under chapters 7, 11, 12, and 13 of Title 11, until amendments by sections 201 to 231 of Pub.L. 99–554 effective in such district, see section 302(d)(3)(A) to (F), (H), and (I) of Pub.L. 99–554, set out as a note under section 581 of Title 28.

Amendment by Pub.L. 99–554, § 216, except as otherwise provided, with respect to cases under chapters 7, 11, 12, and 13 of Title 11 commenced before 30 days after Oct. 27, 1986, and pending in a judicial district referred to in section 581(a) of Title 28, as amended by section 111(a) of Pub.L. 99–554, for which a United States trustee is not authorized before 30 days after Oct. 27, 1986 to be appointed, not applicable until the expiration of the 3-year period beginning on Oct. 27, 1986, or of the 1-year period beginning on the date the Attorney General certifies under section 303 of Pub.L. 99–554 the region specified in a paragraph of such section 581(a) that includes, such district, whichever occurs first, see section 302(e)(1), (2) of Pub.L. 99–554, set out as a note under section 581 of Title 28.

1984 Acts. Amendment by Pub.L. 98–353 effective with respect to cases filed 90 days after July 10, 1984, see section 552(a), formerly 553(a), of Pub.L. 98–353, set out as a note under section 101 of this title.

CROSS REFERENCES

Effect of vacancy in office of trustee, see 11 USCA § 325.

Grain storage facility bankruptcies, expedited appointment of trustee, see 11 USCA § 557.

Qualification of trustee, see 11 USCA § 322.

§ 704. Duties of trustee

(a) The trustee shall—

(1) collect and reduce to money the property of the estate for which such trustee serves, and close such estate as expeditiously as is compatible with the best interests of parties in interest;

(2) be accountable for all property received;

(3) ensure that the debtor shall perform his intention as specified in section 521(2)(B) of this title;

(4) investigate the financial affairs of the debtor;

(5) if a purpose would be served, examine proofs of claims and object to the allowance of any claim that is improper;

(6) if advisable, oppose the discharge of the debtor;

(7) unless the court orders otherwise, furnish such information concerning the estate and the estate's administration as is requested by a party in interest;

(8) if the business of the debtor is authorized to be operated, file with the court, with the United States trustee, and with any governmental unit charged with responsibility for collection or determination of any tax arising out of such operation, periodic reports and summaries of the operation of such business, including a statement of receipts and disbursements, and such other information as the United States trustee or the court requires;

(9) make a final report and file a final account of the administration of the estate with the court and with the United States trustee;

(10) if with respect to the debtor there is a claim for a domestic support obligation, provide the applicable notice specified in subsection (c);

(11) if, at the time of the commencement of the case, the debtor (or any entity designated by the debtor) served as the administrator (as defined in section 3 of the Employee Retirement Income Security Act of 1974) of an employee benefit plan, continue to perform the obligations required of the administrator; and

(12) use all reasonable and best efforts to transfer patients from a health care business that is in the process of being closed to an appropriate health care business that—

(A) is in the vicinity of the health care business that is closing;

(B) provides the patient with services that are substantially similar to those provided by the health care business that is in the process of being closed; and

(C) maintains a reasonable quality of care.

(b)(1) With respect to a debtor who is an individual in a case under this chapter—

(A) the United States trustee (or the bankruptcy administrator, if any) shall review all materials filed by the debtor and, not later than 10 days after the date of the first meeting of creditors, file with the court a statement as to whether the debtor's case would be presumed to be an abuse under section 707(b); and

(B) not later than 5 days after receiving a statement under subparagraph (A), the court shall provide a copy of the statement to all creditors.

(2) The United States trustee (or bankruptcy administrator, if any) shall, not later than 30 days after the date of filing a statement under paragraph (1), either file a motion to dismiss or convert under section 707(b) or file a statement setting forth the reasons the United States trustee (or the bankruptcy administrator, if any) does not consider such a motion to be appropriate, if the United States trustee (or the bankruptcy administrator, if any) determines that the debtor's case should be presumed to be an abuse under

section 707(b) and the product of the debtor's current monthly income, multiplied by 12 is not less than—

(A) in the case of a debtor in a household of 1 person, the median family income of the applicable State for 1 earner; or

(B) in the case of a debtor in a household of 2 or more individuals, the highest median family income of the applicable State for a family of the same number or fewer individuals.

(c)(1) In a case described in subsection (a)(10) to which subsection (a)(10) applies, the trustee shall—

(A)(i) provide written notice to the holder of the claim described in subsection (a)(10) of such claim and of the right of such holder to use the services of the State child support enforcement agency established under sections 464 and 466 of the Social Security Act for the State in which such holder resides, for assistance in collecting child support during and after the case under this title;

(ii) include in the notice provided under clause (i) the address and telephone number of such State child support enforcement agency; and

(iii) include in the notice provided under clause (i) an explanation of the rights of such holder to payment of such claim under this chapter;

(B)(i) provide written notice to such State child support enforcement agency of such claim; and

(ii) include in the notice provided under clause (i) the name, address, and telephone number of such holder; and

(C) at such time as the debtor is granted a discharge under section 727, provide written notice to such holder and to such State child support enforcement agency of—

(i) the granting of the discharge;

(ii) the last recent known address of the debtor;

(iii) the last recent known name and address of the debtor's employer; and

(iv) the name of each creditor that holds a claim that—

(I) is not discharged under paragraph (2), (4), or (14A) of section 523(a); or

(II) was reaffirmed by the debtor under section 524(c).

(2)(A) The holder of a claim described in subsection (a)(10) or the State child support enforcement agency of the State in which such holder resides may request from a creditor described in paragraph (1)(C)(iv) the last known address of the debtor.

(B) Notwithstanding any other provision of law, a creditor that makes a disclosure of a last known address of a debtor in connection with a request made under subparagraph (A) shall not be liable by reason of making such disclosure.

(Pub.L. 95–598, Nov. 6, 1978, 92 Stat. 2605; Pub.L. 98–353, Title III, §§ 311(a), 474, July 10, 1984, 98 Stat. 355, 381; Pub.L. 99–554, Title II, § 217, Oct. 27, 1986, 100 Stat. 3100; Pub.L. 109–8, Title I, § 102(c), Title II, § 219(a), Title IV, § 446(b), Title XI, § 1105(a), Apr. 20, 2005, 119 Stat. 32, 55, 118, 192.)

HISTORICAL AND STATUTORY NOTES

Revision Notes and Legislative Reports

1978 Acts. The essential duties of the trustee are enumerated in this section. Others, or elaborations on these, may be prescribed by the Rules of Bankruptcy Procedure to the extent not inconsistent with those prescribed by this section. The duties are derived from section 47a of the Bankruptcy Act [section 75(a) of former Title 11].

The trustee's principal duty is to collect and reduce to money the property of the estate for which he serves, and to close up the estate as expeditiously as is compatible with the best interests of parties in interest. He must be accountable for all property received, and must investigate the financial affairs of the debtor. If a purpose would be served (such as if there are assets that will be distributed), the trustee is required to examine proofs of claims and object to the allowance of any claim that is improper. If advisable, the trustee must oppose the discharge of the debtor, which is for the benefit of general unsecured creditors whom the trustee represents.

The trustee is responsible to furnish such information concerning the estate and its administration as is requested by a party in interest. If the business of the debtor is authorized to be operated, then the trustee is required to file with governmental units charged with the responsibility for collection or determination of any tax arising out of the operation of the business periodic reports and summaries of the operation, including a statement of receipts and disbursements, and such other information as the court requires. He is required to give constructive notice of the commencement of the case in the manner specified under section 342(b). Senate Report No. 95–989.

1984 Acts. Statements by Legislative Leaders, see 1984 U.S.Code Cong. and Adm.News, p. 576.

1986 Acts. House Report No. 99–764 and House Conference Report No. 99–958, see 1986 U.S.Code Cong. and Adm.News, p. 5227.

2005 Acts. House Report No. 109–31(Part I), see 2005 U.S. Code Cong. and Adm. News, p. 88.

Legislative Statements

Section 704(8) of the Senate amendment is deleted in the House amendment. Trustees should give constructive notice of the commencement of the case in the manner specified under section 549(c) of title 11.

References in Text

Section 3 of the Employee Retirement Income Security Act of 1974, referred to in subsec. (a)(11), is Pub.L. 93–406, Title I, § 3, Sept. 2, 1974, 88 Stat. 833, which is classified to 29 U.S.C.A. § 1002.

Section 464 of the Social Security Act, referred to in subsec. (c)(1)(A)(i), is Act Aug. 14, 1935, c. 531, Title IV,

§ 464, as added Aug. 13, 1981, Pub.L. 97–35, Title XXIII, § 2331(a), 95 Stat. 860, and amended, which is classified to 42 U.S.C.A. § 664.

Section 466 of the Social Security Act, referred to in subsec. (c)(1)(A)(i), is Act Aug. 14, 1935, c. 531, Title IV, § 466, as added Aug. 16, 1984, Pub.L. 98–378, § 3(b), 98 Stat. 1306, and amended, which is classified to 42 U.S.C.A. § 666.

Effective and Applicability Provisions

2005 Acts. Amendments by Pub.L. 109–8 effective, except as otherwise provided, 180 days after April 20, 2005, and inapplicable with respect to cases commenced under Title 11 before the effective date, see Pub.L. 109–8, § 1501, set out as a note under 11 U.S.C.A. § 101.

1986 Acts. Amendment by Pub.L. 99–554 effective 30 days after Oct. 27, 1986, except as otherwise provided for, see section 302(a) of Pub.L. 99–554, set out as a note under section 581 of Title 28, Judiciary and Judicial Procedure.

Amendment by Pub.L. 99–554, § 217, not to become effective in or with respect to certain specified judicial districts until, or apply to cases while pending in such district before, the expiration of the 270-day period beginning 30 days after Oct. 27, 1986, or of the 30-day period beginning on the date the Attorney General certifies under section 303 of Pub.L. 99–554 the region specified in a paragraph of section 581(a) of Title 28, as amended by section 111(a) of Pub.L. 99–554, that includes such district, whichever occurs first, see section 302(d)(1) of Pub.L. 99–554, set out as a note under section 581 of Title 28.

Amendment by Pub.L. 99–554, § 217, not to become effective in or with respect to certain specified judicial districts until, or apply to cases while pending in such district before, the expiration of the 2-year period beginning 30 days after Oct. 27, 1986, or of the 30-day period beginning on the date the Attorney General certifies under section 303 of Pub.L. 99–554 the region specified in a paragraph of section 581(a) of Title 28, as amended by section 111(a) of Pub.L. 99–554, that includes such district, whichever occurs first, see section 302(d)(2) of Pub.L. 99–554, set out as a note under section 581 of Title 28.

Amendment by Pub.L. 99–554, § 217, not to become effective in or with respect to judicial districts established for the States of Alabama and North Carolina until, or apply to cases while pending in such district before, such district elects to be included in a bankruptcy region established in section 581(a) of Title 28, as amended by section 111(a) of Pub.L. 99–554, or Oct. 1, 2002, whichever occurs first, and, except as otherwise provided for, with respect to cases under chapters 7, 11, 12 and 13 of Title 11 commenced before 30 days after Oct. 27, 1986, and pending in a judicial district in the States of Alabama or North Carolina before any election made under section 302(d)(3)(A) of Pub.L. 99–554 by such district becomes effective or Oct. 1, 2002, whichever occurs first, amendments by Pub.L. 99–554 not to apply until Oct. 1, 2003, or the expiration of the 1-year period beginning on the date such election becomes effective, whichever occurs first, and further, in any judicial district in Alabama or North Carolina not making the election described in section 302(d)(3)(A) of Pub.L. 99–554, any person appointed under regulations issued by the Judicial Conference to administer estates in cases under Title 11 authorized to establish, etc., a panel of private trustees, and to supervise cases and trustees in cases under chapters 7, 11, 12 and 13 of Title 11, until amendments by sections 201 to 231 of Pub.L. 99–554 effective in such district, see section 302(d)(3)(A) to (F), (H), and (I) of Pub.L. 99–554, set out as a note under section 581 of Title 28.

Amendment by Pub.L. 99–554, § 217, except as otherwise provided, with respect to cases under chapters 7, 11, 12, and 13 of Title 11 commenced before 30 days after Oct. 27, 1986, and pending in a judicial district referred to in section 581(a) of Title 28, as amended by section 111(a) of Pub.L. 99–554, for which a United States trustee is not authorized before 30 days after Oct. 27, 1986 to be appointed, not applicable until the expiration of the 3-year period beginning on Oct. 27, 1986, or of the 1-year period beginning on the date the Attorney General certifies under section 303 of Pub.L. 99–554 the region specified in a paragraph of such section 581(a) that includes, such district, whichever occurs first, see section 302(e)(1), (2) of Pub.L. 99–554, set out as a note under section 581 of Title 28.

1984 Acts. Amendment by Pub.L. 98–353 effective with respect to cases filed 90 days after July 10, 1984, see section 552(a), formerly 553(a), of Pub.L. 98–353, set out as a note under section 101 of this title.

CROSS REFERENCES

Duties of trustee in—

- Chapter eleven cases, see 11 USCA § 1106.
- Chapter thirteen cases, see 11 USCA § 1302.
- Chapter twelve cases, see 11 USCA § 1202.
- Multiemployer plan termination proceedings, see 29 USCA § 1342.

Filing of reports and summaries by debtor engaged in business, see 11 USCA § 1304.

Powers and duties of trustee in investor protection liquidation proceedings, see 15 USCA § 78fff–1.

§ 705. Creditors' committee

(a) At the meeting under section 341(a) of this title, creditors that may vote for a trustee under section 702(a) of this title may elect a committee of not fewer than three, and not more than eleven, creditors, each of whom holds an allowable unsecured claim of a kind entitled to distribution under section 726(a)(2) of this title.

(b) A committee elected under subsection (a) of this section may consult with the trustee or the United States trustee in connection with the administration of the estate, make recommendations to the trustee or the United States trustee respecting the performance of the trustee's duties, and submit to the court or the United States trustee any question affecting the administration of the estate.

(Pub.L. 95–598, Nov. 6, 1978, 92 Stat. 2605; Pub.L. 99–554, Title II, § 218, Oct. 27, 1986, 100 Stat. 3100.)

HISTORICAL AND STATUTORY NOTES

Revision Notes and Legislative Reports

1978 Acts. This section is derived from section 44b of the Bankruptcy Act [section 72(b) of former Title 11] without substantial change. It permits election by general unsecured creditors of a committee of not fewer than 3 members and not more than 11 members to consult with the trustee in connection with the administration of the estate, to make recommendations to the trustee respecting the performance of his duties, and to submit to the court any question affecting the administration of the estate. There is no provision for compensation or reimbursement of its counsel. Senate Report No. 95–989.

1986 Acts. House Report No. 99–764 and House Conference Report No. 99–958, see 1986 U.S.Code Cong. and Adm.News, p. 5227.

Legislative Statements

Section 705(a) of the House amendment adopts a provision contained in the Senate amendment that limits a committee of creditors to not more than 11; the House bill contained no maximum limitation.

Effective and Applicability Provisions

1986 Acts. Amendment by Pub.L. 99–554 effective 30 days after Oct. 27, 1986, except as otherwise provided for, see section 302(a) of Pub.L. 99–554, set out as a note under section 581 of Title 28, Judiciary and Judicial Procedure.

Amendment by Pub.L. 99–554, § 218, not to become effective in or with respect to certain specified judicial districts until, or apply to cases while pending in such district before, the expiration of the 270-day period beginning 30 days after Oct. 27, 1986, or of the 30-day period beginning on the date the Attorney General certifies under section 303 of Pub.L. 99–554 the region specified in a paragraph of section 581(a) of Title 28, as amended by section 111(a) of Pub.L. 99–554, that includes such district, whichever occurs first, see section 302(d)(1) of Pub.L. 99–554, set out as a note under section 581 of Title 28.

Amendment by Pub.L. 99–554, § 218, not to become effective in or with respect to certain specified judicial districts until, or apply to cases while pending in such district before, the expiration of the 2-year period beginning 30 days after Oct. 27, 1986, or of the 30-day period beginning on the date the Attorney General certifies under section 303 of Pub.L. 99–554 the region specified in a paragraph of section 581(a) of Title 28, as amended by section 111(a) of Pub.L. 99–554, that includes such district, whichever occurs first, see section 302(d)(2) of Pub.L. 99–554, set out as a note under section 581 of Title 28.

Amendment by Pub.L. 99–554, § 218, not to become effective in or with respect to judicial districts established for the States of Alabama and North Carolina until, or apply to cases while pending in such district before, such district elects to be included in a bankruptcy region established in section 581(a) of Title 28, as amended by section 111(a) of Pub.L. 99–554, or Oct. 1, 2002, whichever occurs first, and, except as otherwise provided, with respect to cases under chapters 7, 11, 12, and 13 of Title 11 commenced before 30 days after Oct. 27, 1986, and pending in a judicial district in the States of Alabama or North Carolina before any election made under section 302(d)(3)(A) of Pub.L. 99–554 by such district becomes effective or Oct. 1, 2002, whichever occurs first, amendments by Pub.L. 99–554 not to apply until Oct. 1, 2003, or the expiration of the 1-year period beginning on the date such election becomes effective, whichever occurs first, and further, in any judicial district in Alabama or North Carolina not making the election described in section 302(d)(3)(A) of Pub.L. 99–554, any person appointed under regulations issued by the Judicial Conference to administer estates in cases under Title 11 authorized to establish, etc., a panel of private trustees, and to supervise cases and trustees in cases under chapters 7, 11, 12, and 13 of Title 11, until amendments by sections 201 to 231 of Pub.L. 99–554 effective in such district, see section 302(d)(3)(A) to (F), (H), and (I) of Pub.L. 9–554, set out as a note under section 581 of Title 28.

Amendment by Pub.L. 99–554, § 218, except as otherwise provided, with respect to cases under chapters 7, 11, 12, and 13 of Title 11 commenced before 30 days after Oct. 27, 1986, and pending in a judicial district referred to in section 581(a) of Title 28, as amended by section 111(a) of Pub.L. 99–554, for which a United States trustee is not authorized before 30 days after Oct. 27, 1986 to be appointed, not applicable until the expiration of the 3-year period beginning on Oct. 27, 1986, or of the 1-year period beginning on the date the Attorney General certifies under section 303 of Pub.L. 99–554 the region specified in a paragraph of such section 581(a) that includes, such district, whichever occurs first, see section 302(e)(1), (2) of Pub.L. 99–554, set out as a note under section 581 of Title 28.

CROSS REFERENCES

Appointment of creditors' and equity security holders' committees in chapter 11 cases, see 11 USCA § 1102.

Powers and duties of committees in chapter 11 cases, see 11 USCA § 1103.

§ 706. Conversion

(a) The debtor may convert a case under this chapter to a case under chapter 11, 12, or 13 of this title at any time, if the case has not been converted under section 1112, 1208, or 1307 of this title. Any waiver of the right to convert a case under this subsection is unenforceable.

(b) On request of a party in interest and after notice and a hearing, the court may convert a case under this chapter to a case under chapter 11 of this title at any time.

(c) The court may not convert a case under this chapter to a case under chapter 12 or 13 of this title unless the debtor requests or consents to such conversion.

(d) Notwithstanding any other provision of this section, a case may not be converted to a case under another chapter of this title unless the debtor may be a debtor under such chapter.

(Pub.L. 95–598, Nov. 6, 1978, 92 Stat. 2606; Pub.L. 99–554, Title II, § 257(q), Oct. 27, 1986, 100 Stat. 3115; Pub.L. 103–394, Title V, § 501(d)(22), Oct. 22, 1994, 108 Stat. 4146; Pub.L. 109–8, Title I, § 101, Apr. 20, 2005, 119 Stat. 27.)

HISTORICAL AND STATUTORY NOTES

Revision Notes and Legislative Reports

1978 Acts. Subsection (a) of this section gives the debtor the one-time absolute right of conversion of a liquidation case to a reorganization or individual repayment plan case. If the case has already once been converted from chapter 11 or 13 to chapter 7, then the debtor does not have that right. The policy of the provision is that the debtor should always be given the opportunity to repay his debts, and a waiver of the right to convert a case is unenforceable.

Subsection (b) permits the court, on request of a party in interest and after notice and a hearing, to convert the case to chapter 11 at any time. The decision whether to convert is left in the sound discretion of the court, based on what will most inure to the benefit of all parties in interest.

Subsection (c) is part of the prohibition against involuntary chapter 13 cases, and prohibits the court from converting a case to chapter 13 without the debtor's consent.

Subsection (d) reinforces section 109 by prohibiting conversion to a chapter unless the debtor is eligible to be a debtor under that chapter. Senate Report No. 95–989.

1986 Acts. House Report No. 99–764 and House Conference Report No. 99–958, see 1986 U.S.Code Cong. and Adm.News, p. 5227.

1994 Acts. House Report No. 103–835, see 1994 U.S. Code Cong. and Adm. News, p. 3340.

2005 Acts. House Report No. 109–31(Part I), see 2005 U.S. Code Cong. and Adm. News, p. 88.

Legislative Statements

Section 706(a) of the House amendment adopts a provision contained in the Senate amendment indicating that a waiver of the right to convert a case under section 706(a) is unenforceable. The explicit reference in title 11 forbidding the waiver of certain rights is not intended to imply that other rights, such as the right to file a voluntary bankruptcy case under section 301, may be waived.

Section 706 of the House amendment adopts a similar provision contained in H.R. 8200 as passed by the House. Competing proposals contained in section 706(c) and section 706(d) of the Senate amendment are rejected.

Effective and Applicability Provisions

2005 Acts. Amendments by Pub.L. 109–8 effective, except as otherwise provided, 180 days after April 20, 2005, and inapplicable with respect to cases commenced under Title 11 before the effective date, see Pub.L. 109–8, § 1501, set out as a note under 11 U.S.C.A. § 101.

1994 Acts. Amendment by Pub.L. 103–394 effective on Oct. 22, 1994, and not to apply with respect to cases commenced under Title 11 of the United States Code before Oct. 22, 1994, see section 702 of Pub.L. 103–394, set out as a note under section 101 of this title.

1986 Acts. Amendment by Pub.L. 99–554 effective 30 days after Oct. 27, 1986, but not applicable to cases commenced under this title before that date, see section 302(a), (c)(1) of Pub.L. 99–554, set out as a note under section 581 of Title 28, Judiciary and Judicial Procedure.

Separability of Provisions

If any provision of or amendment made by Pub.L. 103–394 or the application of such provision or amendment to any person or circumstance is held to be unconstitutional, the remaining provisions of and amendments made by Pub.L. 103–394 and the application of such provisions and amendments to any person or circumstance shall not be affected thereby, see section 701 of Pub.L. 103–394, set out as a note under section 101 of this title.

CROSS REFERENCES

Conversion or dismissal of—
  Chapter eleven cases, see 11 USCA § 1112.
  Chapter thirteen cases, see 11 USCA § 1307.
  Chapter twelve cases, see 11 USCA § 1208.
Effect of conversion, see 11 USCA § 348.
Termination of debtor's taxable period in—
  Chapter eleven cases, see 11 USCA § 1146.
  Chapter twelve cases, see 11 USCA § 1231.

§ 707. Dismissal of a case or conversion to a case under chapter 11 or 13

(a) The court may dismiss a case under this chapter only after notice and a hearing and only for cause, including—

(1) unreasonable delay by the debtor that is prejudicial to creditors;

(2) nonpayment of any fees or charges required under chapter 123 of title 28; and

(3) failure of the debtor in a voluntary case to file, within fifteen days or such additional time as the court may allow after the filing of the petition commencing such case, the information required by paragraph (1) of section 521, but only on a motion by the United States trustee.

(b)(1) After notice and a hearing, the court, on its own motion or on a motion by the United States trustee, trustee (or bankruptcy administrator, if any), or any party in interest, may dismiss a case filed by an individual debtor under this chapter whose debts are primarily consumer debts, or, with the debtor's consent, convert such a case to a case under chapter 11 or 13 of this title, if it finds that the granting of relief would be an abuse of the provisions of this chapter. In making a determination whether to dismiss a case under this section, the court may not take into consideration whether a debtor has made, or continues to make, charitable contributions (that meet the definition of "charitable contribution" under section 548(d)(3)) to any qualified religious or charitable entity or organization (as that term is defined in section 548(d)(4)).

(2)(A)(i) In considering under paragraph (1) whether the granting of relief would be an abuse of the provisions of this chapter, the court shall presume abuse exists if the debtor's current monthly income reduced by the amounts determined under clauses (ii), (iii), and (iv), and multiplied by 60 is not less than the lesser of—

(I) 25 percent of the debtor's nonpriority unsecured claims in the case, or $6,575 [1], whichever is greater; or

(II) $10,950 [1].

(ii)(I) The debtor's monthly expenses shall be the debtor's applicable monthly expense amounts specified under the National Standards and Local Standards, and the debtor's actual monthly expenses for the categories specified as Other Necessary Expenses issued by the Internal Revenue Service for the area in which the debtor resides, as in effect on the date of the order for relief, for the debtor, the dependents of the debtor, and the spouse of the debtor in a joint case, if the spouse is not otherwise a dependent. Such expenses shall include reasonably necessary health insurance, disability insurance, and health savings account expenses for the debtor, the spouse of the debtor, or the dependents of the debtor. Notwithstanding any other provision of this clause, the monthly expenses of the debtor shall not include any payments for debts. In addition, the debtor's monthly expenses shall include the debtor's reasonably necessary expenses incurred to maintain the safety of the debtor and the family of the debtor from family violence as identified under section 309 of the Family Violence Prevention and Services Act, or other applicable Federal law. The expenses included in the debtor's monthly expenses described in the preceding sentence shall be kept confidential by the court. In addition, if it is demonstrated that it is reasonable and necessary, the debtor's monthly expenses may also include an additional allowance for food and clothing of up to 5 percent of the food and clothing categories as specified by the National Standards issued by the Internal Revenue Service.

(II) In addition, the debtor's monthly expenses may include, if applicable, the continuation of actual expenses paid by the debtor that are reasonable and necessary for care and support of an elderly, chronically ill, or disabled household member or member of the debtor's immediate family (including parents, grandparents, siblings, children, and grandchildren of the debtor, the dependents of the debtor, and the spouse of the debtor in a joint case who is not a dependent) and who is unable to pay for such reasonable and necessary expenses.

(III) In addition, for a debtor eligible for chapter 13, the debtor's monthly expenses may include the actual administrative expenses of administering a chapter 13 plan for the district in which the debtor resides, up to an amount of 10 percent of the projected plan payments, as determined under schedules issued by the Executive Office for United States Trustees.

(IV) In addition, the debtor's monthly expenses may include the actual expenses for each dependent child less than 18 years of age, not to exceed $1,650 [1] per year per child, to attend a private or public elementary or secondary school if the debtor provides documentation of such expenses and a detailed explanation of why such expenses are reasonable and necessary, and why such expenses are not already accounted for in the National Standards, Local Standards, or Other Necessary Expenses referred to in subclause (I).

(V) In addition, the debtor's monthly expenses may include an allowance for housing and utilities, in excess of the allowance specified by the Local Standards for housing and utilities issued by the Internal Revenue Service, based on the actual expenses for home energy costs if the debtor provides documentation of such actual expenses and demonstrates that such actual expenses are reasonable and necessary.

(iii) The debtor's average monthly payments on account of secured debts shall be calculated as the sum of—

(I) the total of all amounts scheduled as contractually due to secured creditors in each month of the 60 months following the date of the petition; and

(II) any additional payments to secured creditors necessary for the debtor, in filing a plan under chapter 13 of this title, to maintain possession of the debtor's primary residence, motor vehicle, or other property necessary for the support of the debtor and the debtor's dependents, that serves as collateral for secured debts;

divided by 60.

(iv) The debtor's expenses for payment of all priority claims (including priority child support and alimony claims) shall be calculated as the total amount of debts entitled to priority, divided by 60.

(B)(i) In any proceeding brought under this subsection, the presumption of abuse may only be rebutted by demonstrating special circumstances, such as a serious medical condition or a call or order to active duty in the Armed Forces, to the extent such special circumstances that justify additional expenses or adjustments of current monthly income for which there is no reasonable alternative.

(ii) In order to establish special circumstances, the debtor shall be required to itemize each additional expense or adjustment of income and to provide—

(I) documentation for such expense or adjustment to income; and

(II) a detailed explanation of the special circumstances that make such expenses or adjustment to income necessary and reasonable.

(iii) The debtor shall attest under oath to the accuracy of any information provided to demonstrate that additional expenses or adjustments to income are required.

(iv) The presumption of abuse may only be rebutted if the additional expenses or adjustments to income referred to in clause (i) cause the product of the debtor's current monthly income reduced by the amounts determined under clauses (ii), (iii), and (iv) of subparagraph (A) when multiplied by 60 to be less than the lesser of—

(I) 25 percent of the debtor's nonpriority unsecured claims, or $6,000, whichever is greater; or

(II) $10,000.

(C) As part of the schedule of current income and expenditures required under section 521, the debtor shall include a statement of the debtor's current monthly income, and the calculations that determine whether a presumption arises under subparagraph (A)(i), that show how each such amount is calculated.

(D) Subparagraphs (A) through (C) shall not apply, and the court may not dismiss or convert a case based on any form of means testing, if the debtor is a disabled veteran (as defined in section 3741(1) of title 38), and the indebtedness occurred primarily during a period during which he or she was—

(i) on active duty (as defined in section 101(d)(1) of title 10); or

(ii) performing a homeland defense activity (as defined in section 901(1) of title 32).

(3) In considering under paragraph (1) whether the granting of relief would be an abuse of the provisions of this chapter in a case in which the presumption in subparagraph (A)(i) of such paragraph does not arise or is rebutted, the court shall consider—

(A) whether the debtor filed the petition in bad faith; or

(B) the totality of the circumstances (including whether the debtor seeks to reject a personal services contract and the financial need for such rejection as sought by the debtor) of the debtor's financial situation demonstrates abuse.

(4)(A) The court, on its own initiative or on the motion of a party in interest, in accordance with the procedures described in rule 9011 of the Federal Rules of Bankruptcy Procedure, may order the attorney for the debtor to reimburse the trustee for all reasonable costs in prosecuting a motion filed under section 707(b), including reasonable attorneys' fees, if—

(i) a trustee files a motion for dismissal or conversion under this subsection; and

(ii) the court—

(I) grants such motion; and

(II) finds that the action of the attorney for the debtor in filing a case under this chapter violated rule 9011 of the Federal Rules of Bankruptcy Procedure.

(B) If the court finds that the attorney for the debtor violated rule 9011 of the Federal Rules of Bankruptcy Procedure, the court, on its own initiative or on the motion of a party in interest, in accordance with such procedures, may order—

(i) the assessment of an appropriate civil penalty against the attorney for the debtor; and

(ii) the payment of such civil penalty to the trustee, the United States trustee (or the bankruptcy administrator, if any).

(C) The signature of an attorney on a petition, pleading, or written motion shall constitute a certification that the attorney has—

(i) performed a reasonable investigation into the circumstances that gave rise to the petition, pleading, or written motion; and

(ii) determined that the petition, pleading, or written motion—

(I) is well grounded in fact; and

(II) is warranted by existing law or a good faith argument for the extension, modification, or reversal of existing law and does not constitute an abuse under paragraph (1).

(D) The signature of an attorney on the petition shall constitute a certification that the attorney has no knowledge after an inquiry that the information in the schedules filed with such petition is incorrect.

(5)(A) Except as provided in subparagraph (B) and subject to paragraph (6), the court, on its own initiative or on the motion of a party in interest, in accordance with the procedures described in rule 9011 of the Federal Rules of Bankruptcy Procedure, may award a debtor all reasonable costs (including reasonable attorneys' fees) in contesting a motion filed by a party in interest (other than a trustee or United States trustee (or bankruptcy administrator, if any)) under this subsection if—

(i) the court does not grant the motion; and

(ii) the court finds that—

(I) the position of the party that filed the motion violated rule 9011 of the Federal Rules of Bankruptcy Procedure; or

(II) the attorney (if any) who filed the motion did not comply with the requirements of clauses (i) and (ii) of paragraph (4)(C), and the motion was made solely for the purpose of coercing a debtor into waiving a right guaranteed to the debtor under this title.

(B) A small business that has a claim of an aggregate amount less than $1,100 [1] shall not be subject to subparagraph (A)(ii)(I).

(C) For purposes of this paragraph—

(i) the term "small business" means an unincorporated business, partnership, corporation, association, or organization that—

(I) has fewer than 25 full-time employees as determined on the date on which the motion is filed; and

(II) is engaged in commercial or business activity; and

(ii) the number of employees of a wholly owned subsidiary of a corporation includes the employees of—

(I) a parent corporation; and

(II) any other subsidiary corporation of the parent corporation.

(6) Only the judge or United States trustee (or bankruptcy administrator, if any) may file a motion under section 707(b), if the current monthly income of the debtor, or in a joint case, the debtor and the debtor's spouse, as of the date of the order for relief, when multiplied by 12, is equal to or less than—

(A) in the case of a debtor in a household of 1 person, the median family income of the applicable State for 1 earner;

(B) in the case of a debtor in a household of 2, 3, or 4 individuals, the highest median family income of the applicable State for a family of the same number or fewer individuals; or

(C) in the case of a debtor in a household exceeding 4 individuals, the highest median family income of the applicable State for a family of 4 or fewer individuals, plus $575 [1] per month for each individual in excess of 4.

(7)(A) No judge, United States trustee (or bankruptcy administrator, if any), trustee, or other party in interest may file a motion under paragraph (2) if the current monthly income of the debtor, including a veteran (as that term is defined in section 101 of title 38), and the debtor's spouse combined, as of the date of the order for relief when multiplied by 12, is equal to or less than—

(i) in the case of a debtor in a household of 1 person, the median family income of the applicable State for 1 earner;

(ii) in the case of a debtor in a household of 2, 3, or 4 individuals, the highest median family income of the applicable State for a family of the same number or fewer individuals; or

(iii) in the case of a debtor in a household exceeding 4 individuals, the highest median family income of the applicable State for a family of 4 or fewer individuals, plus $575 [1] per month for each individual in excess of 4.

(B) In a case that is not a joint case, current monthly income of the debtor's spouse shall not be considered for purposes of subparagraph (A) if—

(i)(I) the debtor and the debtor's spouse are separated under applicable nonbankruptcy law; or

(II) the debtor and the debtor's spouse are living separate and apart, other than for the purpose of evading subparagraph (A); and

(ii) the debtor files a statement under penalty of perjury—

(I) specifying that the debtor meets the requirement of subclause (I) or (II) of clause (i); and

(II) disclosing the aggregate, or best estimate of the aggregate, amount of any cash or money payments received from the debtor's spouse attributed to the debtor's current monthly income.

(c)(1) In this subsection—

(A) the term "crime of violence" has the meaning given such term in section 16 of title 18; and

(B) the term "drug trafficking crime" has the meaning given such term in section 924(c)(2) of title 18.

(2) Except as provided in paragraph (3), after notice and a hearing, the court, on a motion by the victim of a crime of violence or a drug trafficking crime, may when it is in the best interest of the victim dismiss a voluntary case filed under this chapter by a debtor who is an individual if such individual was convicted of such crime.

(3) The court may not dismiss a case under paragraph (2) if the debtor establishes by a preponderance of the evidence that the filing of a case under this chapter is necessary to satisfy a claim for a domestic support obligation.

(Pub.L. 95–598, Nov. 6, 1978, 92 Stat. 2606; Pub.L. 98–353, Title III, §§ 312, 475, July 10, 1984, 98 Stat. 355, 381; Pub.L. 99–554, Title II, § 219, Oct. 27, 1986, 100 Stat. 3100; Pub.L. 105–183, § 4(b), June 19, 1998, 112 Stat. 518; Pub.L. 109–8, Title I, § 102(a), (f), Apr. 20, 2005, 119 Stat. 27, 33.)

[1] Dollar amount as adjusted by the Judicial Conference of the United States. See Adjustment of Dollar Amounts notes set out under this section and 11 U.S.C.A. § 104.

Amendment of subsec. (b)(2)(D)

Pub.L. 110–438, §§ 2, 4, Oct. 20, 2008, 122 Stat. 5000, 5002, provided that, effective 60 days after Oct. 20, 2008, but applicable only with respect to cases commenced under Title 11 in the 3–year period beginning on the effective date of this Act, subsection (b)(2)(D) is amended—

(1) in clauses (i) and (ii)—

(A) by indenting the left margin of such clauses 2 ems to the right, and

(B) by redesignating such clauses as subclauses (I) and (II), respectively,

(2) by striking "testing, if the debtor is a disabled veteran" and inserting the following:

testing—

(i) if the debtor is a disabled veteran

(3) by striking the period at the end and inserting "; or", and

(4) by adding at the end the following:

(ii) with respect to the debtor, while the debtor is—

(I) on, and during the 540–day period beginning immediately after the debtor is released from, a period of active duty (as defined in section 101(d)(1) of title 10) of not less than 90 days; or

(II) performing, and during the 540–day period beginning immediately after the debtor is no longer performing, a homeland defense activity (as defined in section 901(1) of title 32) performed for a period of not less than 90 days;

if after September 11, 2001, the debtor while a member of a reserve component of the Armed Forces or a member of the National Guard, was called to such active duty or performed such homeland defense activity.

HISTORICAL AND STATUTORY NOTES

Revision Notes and Legislative Reports

1978 Acts. This section authorizes the court to dismiss a liquidation case only for cause, such as unreasonable delay by the debtor that is prejudicial to creditors or nonpayment of any fees and charges required under chapter 123 of title 28 [section 1911 et seq. of Title 28, Judiciary and Judicial Procedure]. These causes are not exhaustive, but merely illustrative. The section does not contemplate, however, that the ability of the debtor to repay his debts in whole or in part constitutes adequate cause for dismissal. To permit dismissal on that ground would be to enact a non-uniform mandatory chapter 13, in lieu of the remedy of bankruptcy. Senate Report No. 95–989.

1984 Acts. Statements by Legislative Leaders, see 1984 U.S.Code Cong. and Adm.News, p. 576.

1986 Acts. House Report No. 99–764 and House Conference Report No. 99–958, see 1986 U.S.Code Cong. and Adm.News, p. 5227.

1998 Acts. Statement by President, see 1998 U.S. Code Cong. and Adm. News, p. 230.

2005 Acts. House Report No. 109–31(Part I), see 2005 U.S. Code Cong. and Adm. News, p. 88.

Legislative Statements

Section 707 of the House amendment indicates that the court may dismiss a case only after notice and a hearing.

References in Text

Chapter 11 of this title, referred to in subsec. (b)(1), is 11 U.S.C.A. § 1101 et seq.

Chapter 13 of this title, referred to in subsec. (b)(1), (2)(A)(ii)(III), (iii)(II), is 11 U.S.C.A. § 1301 et seq.

Section 309 of the Family Violence Prevention and Services Act, referred to in subsec. (b)(2)(A)(ii)(I), was redesignated section 320 of the Act by Pub.L. 108–36, Title IV, § 415(5), June 25, 2003, 117 Stat. 830, and is classified to 42 U.S.C.A. § 10421.

The Federal Rules of Bankruptcy Procedure, referred to in subsec. (b)(4)(A), (B), (5)(A), are set out in the Appendix to this title.

Effective and Applicability Provisions

2008 Acts. Pub.L. 110–438, § 4, Oct. 20, 2008, 122 Stat. 5002, provided that:

"(a) Effective date.—Except as provided in subsection (b), this Act and the amendments made by this Act [amending this section and enacting provisions set out as a note under 11 U.S.C.A. § 101] shall take effect 60 days after the date of enactment of this Act [Oct. 20, 2008].

"(b) Application of amendments.—The amendments made by this Act [amending this section] shall apply only with respect to cases commenced under title 11 of the United States Code [11 U.S.C.A. § 101 et seq.] in the 3-year period beginning on the effective date of this Act [set out in this note]."

2007 Acts. Increase of dollar amounts by Judicial Conference of the United States by notice published Feb. 14, 2007, 72 F.R. 7082 effective April 1, 2007, and increase not applicable to cases commenced before the effective date of the adjustments, i.e., April 1, 2007. See Adjustment of Dollar Amounts notes under 11 U.S.C.A. § 104 and this section.

2005 Acts. Amendments by Pub.L. 109–8 effective, except as otherwise provided, 180 days after April 20, 2005, and inapplicable with respect to cases commenced under Title 11 before the effective date, see Pub.L. 109–8, § 1501, set out as a note under 11 U.S.C.A. § 101.

1986 Acts. Amendment by Pub.L. 99–554 effective 30 days after Oct. 27, 1986, except as otherwise provided for, see section 302(a) of Pub.L. 99–554, set out as a note under section 581 of Title 28, Judiciary and Judicial Procedure.

Amendment by Pub.L. 99–554, § 219, not to become effective in or with respect to certain specified judicial districts until, or apply to cases while pending in such district before, the expiration of the 270-day period beginning 30 days after Oct. 27, 1986, or of the 30-day period beginning on the date the Attorney General certifies under section 303 of Pub.L. 99–554 the region specified in a paragraph of section 581(a) of Title 28, as amended by section 111(a) of Pub.L. 99–554, that includes such district, whichever occurs first, see section 302(d)(1) of Pub.L. 99–554, set out as a note under section 581 of Title 28.

Amendment by Pub.L. 99–554, § 219, not to become effective in or with respect to certain specified judicial districts until, or apply to cases while pending in such district before, the expiration of the 2-year period beginning 30 days after Oct. 27, 1986, or of the 30-day period beginning on the date the Attorney General certifies under section 303 of Pub.L. 99–554 the region specified in a paragraph of section 581(a) of Title 28, as amended by section 111(a) of Pub.L. 99–554, that includes such district, whichever occurs first, see section 302(d)(2) of Pub.L. 99–554, set out as a note under section 581 of Title 28.

Amendment by Pub.L. 99–554, § 219, not to become effective in or with respect to judicial districts established for the States of Alabama and North Carolina until, or apply to cases while pending in such district before, such district elects to be included in a bankruptcy region established in section 581(a) of Title 28, as amended by section 111(a) of Pub.L. 99–554, or Oct. 1, 2002, whichever occurs first, and, except as otherwise provided, with respect to cases under chapters 7, 11, 12, and 13 of Title 11 commenced before 30 days after Oct. 27, 1986, and pending in a judicial district in the States of Alabama or North Carolina before any election made under section 302(d)(3)(A) of Pub.L. 99–554 by such district becomes effective or Oct. 1, 2002, whichever occurs first, amendments by Pub.L. 99–554 not to apply until Oct. 1, 2003, or the expiration of the 1-year period beginning on the date such election becomes effective, whichever occurs first, and further, in any judicial district in Alabama or North Carolina not making the election described in section 302(d)(3)(A) of Pub.L. 99–554, any person appointed under regulations issued by the Judicial Conference to administer estates in cases under Title 11 authorized to establish, etc., a panel of private trustees, and to supervise cases and trustees in cases under chapters 7, 11, 12, and 13 of Title 11, until amendments by sections 201 to 231 of Pub.L. 99–554 effective in such district, see section 302(d)(3)(A) to (F), (H), and (I) of Pub.L. 99–554, set out as a note under section 581 of Title 28.

Amendment by Pub.L. 99–554, § 219, except as otherwise provided, with respect to cases under chapters 7, 11, 12, and 13 of Title 11 commenced before 30 days after Oct. 27, 1986, and pending in a judicial district referred to in section 581(a) of Title 28, as amended by section 111(a) of Pub.L. 99–554, for which a United States trustee is not authorized before 30 days after Oct. 27, 1986 to be appointed, not applicable until the expiration of the 3-year period beginning on Oct. 27, 1986, or of the 1-year period beginning on the date the Attorney General certifies under section 303 of Pub.L. 99–554 the region specified in a paragraph of such section 581(a) that includes, such district, whichever occurs first, see section 302(e)(1), (2) of Pub.L. 99–554, set out as a note under section 581 of Title 28.

1984 Acts. Amendment by Pub.L. 98–353 effective with respect to cases filed 90 days after July 10, 1984, see section 552(a), formerly 553(a), of Pub.L. 98–353, set out as a note under section 101 of this title.

Applicability

Applicability of amendments made by Pub.L. 105–183 to any case brought under an applicable provision of this title that is pending or commenced on or after June 19, 1998, see Pub.L. 105–153, § 5, June 19, 1998, 112 Stat. 518, set out as a note under section 544 of this title.

Adjustment of Dollar Amounts

For adjustment of dollar amounts specified in subsec. (b)(2)(A)(i)(I), (II), (ii)(IV), (5)(B), (6)(C), (7)(A) of this section by the Judicial Conference of the United States, effective Apr. 1, 2007, see note set out under 11 U.S.C.A. § 104 of this title.

By notice dated Feb. 14, 2007, 72 F.R. 7082, the Judicial Conference of the United States adjusted the dollar amounts in provisions specified in subsec. (b)(2)(A)(i)(I), (II), (ii)(IV), (5)(B), (6)(C), (7)(A) of this section, effective Apr. 1, 2007, as follows:

In subsec. (b)(2)(A)(i)(I) adjusted $6,000 to $6,575.

In subsec. (b)(2)(A)(i)(II) adjusted $10,000 to $10,950.

In subsec. (b)(2)(A)(ii)(IV) adjusted $1,500 to $1,650.

In subsec. (b)(5)(B) adjusted $1,000 to $1,100.

In subsec. (b)(6)(C) adjusted $525 to $575.

In subsec. (b)(7)(A) adjusted $525 to $575.

Schedules of Reasonable and Necessary Expenses

Pub.L. 109–8, Title I, § 107, Apr. 20, 2005, 119 Stat. 42, provided that: "For purposes of section 707(b) of title 11, United States Code [subsec. (b) of this section], as amended by this Act [Bankruptcy Abuse Prevention and Consumer Protection Act of 2005, Pub.L. 109–8, April 20, 2005, 119 Stat. 23, see Tables for classification], the Director of the Executive Office for United States Trustees shall, not later than 180 days after the date of enactment of this Act [April 20, 2005], issue schedules of reasonable and necessary administrative expenses of administering a chapter 13 plan [chapter 13 of this title is 11 U.S.C.A. § 1301 et seq.] for each judicial district of the United States."

Rule of Construction

Amendments made by Pub.L. 105–183 not intended to limit the applicability of the Religious Freedom Restoration Act of 1993 (42 U.S.C. 2002bb et seq.), see Pub.L. 105–183, § 6, June 19, 1998, 112 Stat. 519, set out as a note under section 544 of this title.

Rules Promulgated by Supreme Court

United States Supreme Court to prescribe general rules implementing the practice and procedure to be followed under subsec. (b) of this section, with section 2075 of Title 28, Judiciary and Judicial Procedure, to apply with respect to such general rules, see section 320 of Pub.L. 98–353, set out as a note under section 2075 of Title 28.

CROSS REFERENCES

Conversion or dismissal of—

Chapter eleven cases, see 11 USCA § 1112.

Chapter thirteen cases, see 11 USCA § 1307.

Crime victims' rights, rights afforded and best efforts to accord rights, procedures to promote compliance, see 18 USCA § 3771.

Dismissal of Chapter nine cases, see 11 USCA § 930.

Effect of dismissal, see 11 USCA § 349.

SUBCHAPTER II—COLLECTION, LIQUIDATION, AND DISTRIBUTION OF THE ESTATE

CROSS REFERENCES

Applicability of this subchapter in investor protection liquidation proceedings, see 15 USCA § 78fff.

Subchapter applicable only in case under this chapter, see 11 USCA § 103.

§ 721. Authorization to operate business

The court may authorize the trustee to operate the business of the debtor for a limited period, if such operation is in the best interest of the estate and consistent with the orderly liquidation of the estate.

(Pub.L. 95–598, Nov. 6, 1978, 92 Stat. 2606.)

HISTORICAL AND STATUTORY NOTES

Revision Notes and Legislative Reports

1978 Acts. This section is derived from section 2a(5) of the Bankruptcy Act [section 11(a)(5) of former Title 11]. It permits the court to authorize the operation of any business of the debtor for a limited period, if the operation is in the best interest of the estate and consistent with orderly liquidation of the estate. An example is the operation of a watch company to convert watch movements and cases into completed watches which will bring much higher prices than the component parts would have brought. Senate Report No. 95–989.

CROSS REFERENCES

Authorization to operate business in Chapter eleven cases, see 11 USCA § 1108.

Debtor engaged in business in Chapter thirteen cases, see 11 USCA § 1304.

Executory contracts and unexpired leases, see 11 USCA § 365.

Executory contracts in stockbroker liquidation cases, see 11 USCA § 744.

Obtaining credit, see 11 USCA § 364.

Retention or replacement of professional persons, see 11 USCA § 327.

Treatment of accounts in—

Commodity broker liquidation cases, see 11 USCA § 763.

Stockbroker liquidation cases, see 11 USCA § 745.

Use, sale or lease of property, see 11 USCA § 363.

Utility service, see 11 USCA § 366.

§ 722. Redemption

An individual debtor may, whether or not the debtor has waived the right to redeem under this section, redeem tangible personal property intended primarily for personal, family, or household use, from a lien securing a dischargeable consumer debt, if such property is exempted under section 522 of this title or has been abandoned under section 554 of this title, by paying the holder of such lien the amount of the allowed secured claim of such holder that is secured by such lien in full at the time of redemption.

(Pub.L. 95–598, Nov. 6, 1978, 92 Stat. 2606; Pub.L. 109–8, Title III, § 304(2), Apr. 20, 2005, 119 Stat. 79.)

HISTORICAL AND STATUTORY NOTES

Revision Notes and Legislative Reports

1978 Acts. This section is new and is broader than rights of redemption under the Uniform Commercial Code. It authorizes an individual debtor to redeem tangible personal property intended primarily for personal, family, or household use, from a lien securing a nonpurchase money dischargeable consumer debt. It applies only if the debtor's interest in the property is exempt or has been abandoned.

This right to redeem is a very substantial change from current law. To prevent abuses such as may occur when the debtor deliberately allows the property to depreciate in value, the debtor will be required to pay the fair market value of the goods or the amount of the claim if the claim is less. The right is personal to the debtor and not assignable. Senate Report No. 95–989.

This section is new and is broader than rights of redemption under the Uniform Commercial Code. It authorizes an individual debtor to redeem tangible personal property intended primarily for personal, family, or household use, from a lien securing a dischargeable consumer debt. It applies only if the debtor's interest in the property is exempt or has been abandoned.

The right to redeem extends to the whole of the property, not just the debtor's exempt interest in it. Thus, for example, if a debtor owned a $2,000 car, subject to a $1,200 lien, the debtor could exempt his $800 interest in the car. The debtor is permitted a $1,500 exemption in a car, proposed 11 U.S.C. 522(d)(2). This section permits him to pay the holder of the lien $1,200 and redeem the entire car, not just the remaining $700 of his exemption. The redemption is accomplished by paying the holder of the lien the amount of the allowed claim secured by the lien. The provision amounts to a right of first refusal for the debtor in consumer goods that might otherwise be repossessed. The right of redemption under this section is not waivable. House Report No. 95–595.

2005 Acts. House Report No. 109–31(Part I), see 2005 U.S. Code Cong. and Adm. News, p. 88.

Legislative Statements

Section 722 of the House amendment adopts the position taken in H.R. 8200 as passed by the House and rejects the alternative contained in section 722 of the Senate amendment.

Effective and Applicability Provisions

2005 Acts. Amendments by Pub.L. 109–8 effective, except as otherwise provided, 180 days after April 20, 2005, and inapplicable with respect to cases commenced under Title 11 before the effective date, see Pub.L. 109–8, § 1501, set out as a note under 11 U.S.C.A. § 101.

§ 723. Rights of partnership trustee against general partners

(a) If there is a deficiency of property of the estate to pay in full all claims which are allowed in a case under this chapter concerning a partnership and with respect to which a general partner of the partnership is personally liable, the trustee shall have a claim against such general partner to the extent that under applicable nonbankruptcy law such general partner is personally liable for such deficiency.

(b) To the extent practicable, the trustee shall first seek recovery of such deficiency from any general partner in such partnership that is not a debtor in a case under this title. Pending determination of such deficiency, the court may order any such partner to provide the estate with indemnity for, or assurance of payment of, any deficiency recoverable from such partner, or not to dispose of property.

(c) Notwithstanding section 728(c) of this title, the trustee has a claim against the estate of each general partner in such partnership that is a debtor in a case under this title for the full amount of all claims of creditors allowed in the case concerning such partnership. Notwithstanding section 502 of this title, there shall not be allowed in such partner's case a claim against such partner on which both such partner and such partnership are liable, except to any extent that such claim is secured only by property of such partner and not by property of such partnership. The claim of the trustee under this subsection is entitled to distribution in such partner's case under section 726(a) of this title the same as any other claim of a kind specified in such section.

(d) If the aggregate that the trustee recovers from the estates of general partners under subsection (c) of this section is greater than any deficiency not recovered under subsection (b) of this section, the court, after notice and a hearing, shall determine an equitable distribution of the surplus so recovered, and the trustee shall distribute such surplus to the estates of the general partners in such partnership according to such determination.

(Pub.L. 95–598, Nov. 6, 1978, 92 Stat. 2606; Pub.L. 98–353, Title III, § 476, July 10, 1984, 98 Stat. 381; Pub.L. 103–394, Title II, § 212, Oct. 22, 1994, 108 Stat. 4125.)

HISTORICAL AND STATUTORY NOTES

Revision Notes and Legislative Reports

1978 Acts. This section is a significant departure from present law. It repeals the jingle rule, which, for ease of administration, denied partnership creditors their rights against general partners by permitting general partners' individual creditors to share in their estates first to the exclusion of partnership creditors. The result under this section more closely tracks generally applicable partnership law, without a significant administrative burden.

Subsection (a) specifies that each general partner in a partnership debtor is liable to the partnership's trustee for any deficiency of partnership property to pay in full all administrative expenses and all claims against the partnership.

Subsection (b) requires the trustee to seek recovery of the deficiency from any general partner that is not a debtor in a bankruptcy case. The court is empowered to order that partner to indemnify the estate or not to dispose of property pending a determination of the deficiency. The language of the subsection is directed to cases under the bankruptcy code. However, if, during the early stages of the transition period, a partner in a partnership is proceeding under the Bankruptcy Act [former Title 11] while the partnership is proceeding under the bankruptcy code, the trustee should not first seek recovery against the Bankruptcy Act partner. Rather, the Bankruptcy Act partner should be deemed for the purposes of this section and the rights of the trustee to be proceeding under title 11.

Subsection (c) requires the partnership trustee to seek recovery of the full amount of the deficiency from the estate of each general partner that is a debtor in a bankruptcy case. The trustee will share equally with the partners' individual creditors in the assets of the partners' estates. Claims of partnership creditors who may have filed against the partner will be disallowed to avoid double counting.

Subsection (d) provides for the case where the total recovery from all of the bankrupt general partners is greater than the deficiency of which the trustee sought recovery. This case would most likely occur for a partnership with a large number of general partners. If the situation arises, the court is required to determine an equitable redistribution of the surplus to the estate of the general partners. The determination will be based on factors such as the relative liability of each of the general partners under the partnership agreement and the relative rights of each of the general partners in the profits of the enterprise under the partnership agreement. Senate Report No. 95–989.

1984 Acts. Statements by Legislative Leaders, see 1984 U.S.Code Cong. and Adm.News, p. 576.

1994 Acts. House Report No. 103–835, see 1994 U.S. Code Cong. and Adm. News, p. 3340.

Legislative Statements

Section 723(c) of the House amendment is a compromise between similar provisions contained in the House bill and Senate amendment. The section makes clear that the trustee of a partnership has a claim against each general partner for the full amount of all claims of creditors allowed in the case concerning the partnership. By restricting the trustee's rights to claims of "creditors," the trustee of the partnership will not have a claim against the general partners for administrative expenses or claims allowed in the case concerning the partnership. As under present law, sections of the Bankruptcy Act [former title 11] applying to codebtors and sureties apply to the relationship of a partner with respect to a partnership debtor. See sections 501(b), 502(e), 506(d)(2), 509, 524(d), and 1301 of title 11.

References in Text

Section 728(a), (b) of this title, referred to in subsec. (b), is subsecs. (a) and (b) of 11 U.S.C.A. § 728, which was repealed by Pub.L. 109–8, Title VII, § 719(b)(1), Apr. 20, 2005, 119 Stat. 133.

Effective and Applicability Provisions

1994 Acts. Amendment by Pub.L. 103–394 effective on Oct. 22, 1994, and not to apply with respect to cases commenced under Title 11 of the United States Code before Oct. 22, 1994, see section 702 of Pub.L. 103–394, set out as a note under section 101 of this title.

1984 Acts. Amendment by Pub.L. 98–353 effective with respect to cases filed 90 days after July 10, 1984, see section 552(a), formerly 553(a), of Pub.L. 98–353, set out as a note under section 101 of this title.

Separability of Provisions

If any provision of or amendment made by Pub.L. 103–394 or the application of such provision or amendment to any person or circumstance is held to be unconstitutional, the remaining provisions of and amendments made by Pub.L. 103–394 and the application of such provisions and amendments to any person or circumstance shall not be affected thereby, see section 701 of Pub.L. 103–394, set out as a note under section 101 of this title.

CROSS REFERENCES

Property of estate, see 11 USCA § 541.

§ 724. Treatment of certain liens

(a) The trustee may avoid a lien that secures a claim of a kind specified in section 726(a)(4) of this title.

(b) Property in which the estate has an interest and that is subject to a lien that is not avoidable under this title (other than to the extent that there is a properly perfected unavoidable tax lien arising in connection with an ad valorem tax on real or personal property of the estate) and that secures an allowed claim for a tax, or proceeds of such property, shall be distributed—

(1) first, to any holder of an allowed claim secured by a lien on such property that is not avoidable under this title and that is senior to such tax lien;

(2) second, to any holder of a claim of a kind specified in section 507(a)(1) (except that such expenses, other than claims for wages, salaries, or commissions that arise after the date of the filing of the petition, shall be limited to expenses incurred under chapter 7 of this title and shall not include expenses incurred under chapter 11 of this title), 507(a)(2), 507(a)(3), 507(a)(4), 507(a)(5), 507(a)(6), or 507(a)(7) of this title, to the extent of the amount of such allowed tax claim that is secured by such tax lien;

(3) third, to the holder of such tax lien, to any extent that such holder's allowed tax claim that is secured by such tax lien exceeds any amount distributed under paragraph (2) of this subsection;

(4) fourth, to any holder of an allowed claim secured by a lien on such property that is not avoidable under this title and that is junior to such tax lien;

(5) fifth, to the holder of such tax lien, to the extent that such holder's allowed claim secured by such tax lien is not paid under paragraph (3) of this subsection; and

(6) sixth, to the estate.

(c) If more than one holder of a claim is entitled to distribution under a particular paragraph of subsection (b) of this section, distribution to such holders under such paragraph shall be in the same order as distribution to such holders would have been other than under this section.

(d) A statutory lien the priority of which is determined in the same manner as the priority of a tax lien under section 6323 of the Internal Revenue Code of 1986 shall be treated under subsection (b) of this section the same as if such lien were a tax lien.

(e) Before subordinating a tax lien on real or personal property of the estate, the trustee shall—

(1) exhaust the unencumbered assets of the estate; and

(2) in a manner consistent with section 506(c), recover from property securing an allowed secured claim the reasonable, necessary costs and expenses of preserving or disposing of such property.

(f) Notwithstanding the exclusion of ad valorem tax liens under this section and subject to the requirements of subsection (e), the following may be paid from property of the estate which secures a tax lien, or the proceeds of such property:

(1) Claims for wages, salaries, and commissions that are entitled to priority under section 507(a)(4).

(2) Claims for contributions to an employee benefit plan entitled to priority under section 507(a)(5).

(Pub.L. 95–598, Nov. 6, 1978, 92 Stat. 2607; Pub.L. 98–353, Title III, § 477, July 10, 1984, 98 Stat. 381; Pub.L. 99–514, § 2, Oct. 22, 1986, 100 Stat. 2095; Pub.L. 99–554, Title II, § 283(r), Oct. 27, 1986, 100 Stat. 3118; Pub.L. 103–394, Title III, § 304(h)(4), Title V, § 501(d)(23), Oct. 22, 1994, 108 Stat. 4134, 4146; Pub.L. 109–8, Title VII, § 701(a), Apr. 20, 2005, 119 Stat. 124.)

HISTORICAL AND STATUTORY NOTES

Revision Notes and Legislative Reports

1978 Acts. Subsection (a) of section 724 permits the trustee to avoid a lien that secures a fine, penalty, forfeiture, or multiple, punitive, or exemplary damages claim to the extent that the claim is not compensation for actual pecuniary loss. The subsection follows the policy found in section 57j of the Bankruptcy Act [section 93(j) of former Title 11] of protecting unsecured creditors from the debtor's wrongdoing, but expands the protection afforded. The lien is made voidable rather than void in chapter 7, in order to permit the lien to be revived if the case is converted to chapter 11 under which penalty liens are not voidable. To make the lien void would be to permit the filing of a chapter 7, the voiding of the lien, and the conversion to a chapter 11, simply to avoid a penalty lien, which should be valid in a reorganization case.

Subsection (b) governs tax liens. This provision retains the rule of present bankruptcy law (section 67(C)(3) of the Bankruptcy Act [section 107(c)(3) of former Title 11]) that a tax lien on personal property, if not avoidable by the trustee, is subordinated in payment to unsecured claims having a higher priority than unsecured tax claims. Those other claims may be satisfied from the amount that would otherwise have been applied to the tax lien, and any excess of the amount of the lien is then applied to the tax. Any personal property (or sale proceeds) remaining is to be used to satisfy claims secured by liens which are junior to the tax lien. Any proceeds remaining are next applied to pay any unpaid balance of the tax lien.

Subsection (d) specifies that any statutory lien whose priority is determined in the same manner as a tax lien is to be treated as a tax lien under this section, even if the lien does not secure a claim for taxes. An example is the ERISA [29 U.S.C.A. § 1001 et seq.] lien. Senate Report No. 95–989.

Subsection (b) governs tax liens. It is derived from section 67c(3) of the Bankruptcy Act [section 107(c)(3) of former Title 11], without substantial modification in result. It subordinates tax liens to administrative expense and wage claims, and solves certain circuity of liens problems that arise in connection with the subordination. The order of distribution of property subject to a tax lien is as follows: First, to holders of liens senior to the tax lien; second, to administrative expenses, wage claims, and consumer creditors that are granted priority, but only to the extent of the amount of the allowed tax claim secured by the lien. In other words, the priority claimants step into the shoes of the tax collector. Third, to the tax claimant, to the extent that priority claimants did not use up his entire claim. Fourth, to junior lien holders. Fifth, to the tax collector to the extent that he was not paid under paragraph (3). Finally, any remaining property goes to the estate. The result of these provisions are to leave senior and junior lienors and holders of unsecured claims undisturbed. If there are any liens that are equal in status to the tax lien, they share pari passu with the tax lien under the distribution provisions of this subsection. House Report No. 95–595.

1984 Acts. Statements by Legislative Leaders, see 1984 U.S.Code Cong. and Adm.News, p. 576.

1986 Acts. House Report No. 99–764 and House Conference Report No. 99–958, see 1986 U.S.Code Cong. and Adm.News, p. 5227.

House Conference Report No. 99–841 and Statement by President, see 1986 U.S.Code Cong. and Adm.News, p. 4075.

1994 Acts. House Report No. 103–835, see 1994 U.S. Code Cong. and Adm. News, p. 3340.

2005 Acts. House Report No. 109–31(Part I), see 2005 U.S. Code Cong. and Adm. News, p. 88.

Legislative Statements

Section 724 of the House amendment adopts the provision taken in the House bill and rejects the provision taken in the Senate amendment. In effect, a tax claim secured by a lien is treated as a claim between the fifth and sixth priority in a case under chapter 7 rather than as a secured claim.

Treatment of certain liens: The House amendment modifies present law by requiring the subordination of tax liens on both real and personal property to the payment of claims having a priority. This means that assets are to be distributed from the debtor's estate to pay higher priority claims before the tax claims are paid, even though the tax claims are properly secured. Under present law and the Senate amendment only tax liens on personal property, but not on real property, are subordinated to the payment of claims having a priority above the priority for tax claims.

References in Text

Chapter 7, referred to in subsec. (b)(2), is chapter 7 of this title, 11 U.S.C.A. § 701 et seq.

Chapter 11 of this title, referred to in subsec. (b)(2), is 11 U.S.C.A. § 1101 et seq.

Section 6323 of the Internal Revenue Code of 1986, referred to in subsec. (d), is classified to section 6323 of Title 26, Internal Revenue Code.

Codifications

Amendment to subsec. (d) by section 501(d)(23) of Pub.L. 103–394, which directed that "Internal Revenue Code of 1986" be substituted for "Internal Revenue Code of 1954 (26 U.S.C. 6323)", was executed by striking out "(26 U.S.C. 6323)" after "Internal Revenue Code of 1986", as the probable intent of Congress.

Effective and Applicability Provisions

2005 Acts. Amendments by Pub.L. 109–8 effective, except as otherwise provided, 180 days after April 20, 2005, and inapplicable with respect to cases commenced under Title 11 before the effective date, see Pub.L. 109–8, § 1501, set out as a note under 11 U.S.C.A. § 101.

1994 Acts. Amendments by Pub.L. 103–394 effective on Oct. 22, 1994, and not to apply with respect to cases commenced under Title 11 of the United States Code before Oct. 22, 1994, see section 702 of Pub.L. 103–394, set out as a note under section 101 of this title.

1986 Acts. Amendment by Pub.L. 99–554 effective 30 days after Oct. 27, 1986, except as otherwise provided, see section 302(a) of Pub.L. 99–554, set out as a note under section 581 of Title 28, Judiciary and Judicial Procedure.

1984 Acts. Amendment by Pub.L. 98–353 effective with respect to cases filed 90 days after July 10, 1984, see section 552(a), formerly 553(a), of Pub.L. 98–353, set out as a note under section 101 of this title.

Separability of Provisions

If any provision of or amendment made by Pub.L. 103–394 or the application of such provision or amendment to any person or circumstance is held to be unconstitutional, the remaining provisions of and amendments made by Pub.L. 103–394 and the application of such provisions and amendments to any person or circumstance shall not be affected thereby, see section 701 of Pub.L. 103–394, set out as a note under section 101 of this title.

CROSS REFERENCES

Automatic preservation of avoided transfer, see 11 USCA § 551.

Commencement of involuntary cases by transferees of voidable transfers, see 11 USCA § 303.

Disallowance of claims of entity that is transferee of avoidable transfer, see 11 USCA § 502.

Effect of dismissal, see 11 USCA § 349.

Exemptions, see 11 USCA § 522.

Liability of transferee of avoided transfer, see 11 USCA § 550.

Recovery of voidable transfers in investor protection liquidation proceedings, see 15 USCA § 78fff–2.

Voidable transfers in commodity broker liquidation cases, see 11 USCA § 764.

§ 725. Disposition of certain property

After the commencement of a case under this chapter, but before final distribution of property of the estate under section 726 of this title, the trustee, after notice and a hearing, shall dispose of any property in which an entity other than the estate has an interest, such as a lien, and that has not been disposed of under another section of this title.

(Pub.L. 95–598, Nov. 6, 1978, 92 Stat. 2607; Pub.L. 98–353, Title III, § 478, July 10, 1984, 98 Stat. 381.)

HISTORICAL AND STATUTORY NOTES

Revision Notes and Legislative Reports

1978 Acts. This section requires the court to determine the appropriate disposition of property in which the estate and an entity other than the estate have an interest. It would apply, for example, to property subject to a lien or property co-owned by the estate and another entity. The court must make the determination with respect to property that is not disposed of under another section of the bankruptcy code, such as by abandonment under section 554, by sale or distribution under 363, or by allowing foreclosure by a secured creditor by lifting the stay under section 362. The purpose of the section is to give the court appropriate authority to ensure that collateral or its proceeds is returned to the proper secured creditor, that consigned or bailed goods are returned to the consignor or bailor and so on. Current law is curiously silent on this point, though case law has grown to fill the void. The section is in lieu of a section that would direct a certain distribution to secured creditors. It gives the court greater flexibility to meet the circumstances, and it is broader, permitting disposition of property subject to a co-ownership interest. Senate Report No. 95–989.

1984 Acts. Statements by Legislative Leaders, see 1984 U.S.Code Cong. and Adm.News, p. 576.

Legislative Statements

Section 725 of the House amendment adopts the substance contained in both the House bill and Senate amendment but transfers an administrative function to the trustee in accordance with the general thrust of this legislation to separate the administrative and the judicial functions where appropriate.

Effective and Applicability Provisions

1984 Acts. Amendment by Pub.L. 98–353 effective with respect to cases filed 90 days after July 10, 1984, see section 552(a), formerly 553(a), of Pub.L. 98–353, set out as a note under section 101 of this title.

§ 726. Distribution of property of the estate

(a) Except as provided in section 510 of this title, property of the estate shall be distributed—

(1) first, in payment of claims of the kind specified in, and in the order specified in, section 507 of this title, proof of which is timely filed under section 501 of this title or tardily filed on or before the earlier of—

(A) the date that is 10 days after the mailing to creditors of the summary of the trustee's final report; or

(B) the date on which the trustee commences final distribution under this section;

(2) second, in payment of any allowed unsecured claim, other than a claim of a kind specified in paragraph (1), (3), or (4) of this subsection, proof of which is—

(A) timely filed under section 501(a) of this title;

(B) timely filed under section 501(b) or 501(c) of this title; or

(C) tardily filed under section 501(a) of this title, if—

(i) the creditor that holds such claim did not have notice or actual knowledge of the case in time for timely filing of a proof of such claim under section 501(a) of this title; and

(ii) proof of such claim is filed in time to permit payment of such claim;

(3) third, in payment of any allowed unsecured claim proof of which is tardily filed under section 501(a) of this title, other than a claim of the kind specified in paragraph (2)(C) of this subsection;

(4) fourth, in payment of any allowed claim, whether secured or unsecured, for any fine, penalty, or forfeiture, or for multiple, exemplary, or punitive damages, arising before the earlier of the order for relief or the appointment of a trustee, to the extent that such fine, penalty, forfeiture, or damages are not compensation for actual pecuniary loss suffered by the holder of such claim;

(5) fifth, in payment of interest at the legal rate from the date of the filing of the petition, on any claim paid under paragraph (1), (2), (3), or (4) of this subsection; and

(6) sixth, to the debtor.

(b) Payment on claims of a kind specified in paragraph (1), (2), (3), (4), (5), (6), (7), or (8) of section 507(a) of this title, or in paragraph (2), (3), (4), or (5) of subsection (a) of this section, shall be made pro rata among claims of the kind specified in each such particular paragraph, except that in a case that has been converted to this chapter under section 1112, 1208, or 1307 of this title, a claim allowed under section 503(b) of this title incurred under this chapter after such conversion has priority over a claim allowed under section 503(b) of this title incurred under any other chapter of this title or under this chapter before such conversion and over any expenses of a custodian superseded under section 543 of this title.

(c) Notwithstanding subsections (a) and (b) of this section, if there is property of the kind specified in section 541(a)(2) of this title, or proceeds of such property, in the estate, such property or proceeds shall be segregated from other property of the estate, and such property or proceeds and other property of the estate shall be distributed as follows:

(1) Claims allowed under section 503 of this title shall be paid either from property of the kind specified in section 541(a)(2) of this title, or from other property of the estate, as the interest of justice requires.

(2) Allowed claims, other than claims allowed under section 503 of this title, shall be paid in the order specified in subsection (a) of this section, and, with respect to claims of a kind specified in a particular paragraph of section 507 of this title or subsection (a) of this section, in the following order and manner:

(A) First, community claims against the debtor or the debtor's spouse shall be paid from property of the kind specified in section 541(a)(2) of this title, except to the extent that such property is solely liable for debts of the debtor.

(B) Second, to the extent that community claims against the debtor are not paid under subparagraph (A) of this paragraph, such community claims shall be paid from property of the kind specified in section 541(a)(2) of this title that is solely liable for debts of the debtor.

(C) Third, to the extent that all claims against the debtor including community claims against the debtor are not paid under subparagraph (A) or (B) of this paragraph such claims shall be paid from property of the estate other than property of the kind specified in section 541(a)(2) of this title.

(D) Fourth, to the extent that community claims against the debtor or the debtor's spouse are not paid under subparagraph (A), (B), or (C) of this paragraph, such claims shall be paid from all remaining property of the estate.

(Pub.L. 95–598, Nov. 6, 1978, 92 Stat. 2608; Pub.L. 98–353, Title III, § 479, July 10, 1984, 98 Stat. 381; Pub.L. 99–554, Title II, §§ 257(r), 283(s), Oct. 27, 1986, 100 Stat. 3115, 3118; Pub.L. 103–394, Title II, § 213(b), Title III, § 304(h)(5), Title V, § 501(d)(24), Oct. 22, 1994, 108 Stat. 4126, 4134, 4146; Pub.L. 109–8, Title VII, § 713, Title XII, § 1215, Apr. 20, 2005, 119 Stat. 128, 195.)

HISTORICAL AND STATUTORY NOTES

Revision Notes and Legislative Reports

1978 Acts. This section is the general distribution section for liquidation cases. It dictates the order in which distribution of property of the estate, which has usually been reduced to money by the trustee under the requirements of section 704(1).

First, property is distributed among priority claimants, as determined by section 507, and in the order prescribed by section 507. Second, distribution is to general unsecured creditors. This class excludes priority creditors and the two classes of subordinated creditors specified below. The provision is written to permit distribution to creditors that tardily file claims if their tardiness was due to lack of notice or knowledge of the case. Though it is in the interest of the estate to encourage timely filing, when tardy filing is not the result of a failure to act by the creditor, the normal subordination penalty should not apply. Third distribution is to general unsecured creditors who tardily file. Fourth distribution is to holders of fine, penalty, forfeiture, or multiple, punitive, or exemplary damage claims. More of these claims are disallowed entirely under present law. They are simply subordinated here.

Paragraph (4) provides that punitive penalties, including prepetition tax penalties, are subordinated to the payment of all other classes of claims, except claims for interest accruing during the case. In effect, these penalties are payable out of the estate's assets only if and to the extent that a surplus of assets would otherwise remain at the close of the case for distribution back to the debtor.

Paragraph (5) provides that postpetition interest on prepetition claims is also to be paid to the creditor in a subordinated position. Like prepetition penalties, such interest will be paid from the estate only if and to the extent that a surplus of assets would otherwise remain for return to the debtor at the close of the case.

This section also specifies that interest accrued on all claims (including priority and nonpriority tax claims) which accrued before the date of the filing of the title 11 petition is to be paid in the same order of distribution of the estate's assets as the principal amount of the related claims.

Any surplus is paid to the debtor under paragraph (6).

Subsection (b) follows current law. It specifies that claims within a particular class are to be paid pro rata. This provision will apply, of course, only when there are inadequate funds to pay the holders of claims of a particular class in full. The exception found in the section, which also follows current law, specifies that liquidation administrative expenses are to be paid ahead of reorganization administrative expenses if the case has been converted from a reorganization case to a liquidation case, or from an individual repayment plan case to a liquidation case.

Subsection (c) governs distributions in cases in which there is community property and other property of the estate. The section requires the two kinds of property to be segregated. The distribution is as follows: First, administrative expenses are to be paid, as the court determines on any reasonable equitable basis, from both kinds of property. The court will divide administrative expenses according to such factors as the amount of each kind of property in the estate, the cost of preservation and liquidation of each kind of property, and whether any particular administrative expenses are attributable to one kind of property or the other. Second, claims are to be paid as provided under subsection (a) (the normal liquidation case distribution rules) in the following order and manner: First, community claims against the debtor or the debtor's spouse are paid from community property, except such as is liable solely for the debts of the debtor.

Second, community claims against the debtor, to the extent not paid under the first provision, are paid from community property that is solely liable for the debts of the debtor. Third, community claims, to the extent they remain unpaid, and all other claims against the debtor, are paid from noncommunity property. Fourth, if any community claims against the debtor or the debtor's spouse remain unpaid, they are paid from whatever property remains in the estate. This would occur if community claims against the debtor's spouse are large in amount and most of the estate's property is property solely liable, under nonbankruptcy law, for debts of the debtor.

The marshalling rules in this section apply only to property of the estate. However, they will provide a guide to the courts in the interpretation of proposed 11 U.S.C. 725, relating to distribution of collateral, in cases in which there is community property. If a secured creditor has a lien on both community and non-community property, the marshalling rules here—by analogy would dictate that the creditor be satisfied first out of community property, and then out of separate property. Senate Report No. 95–989.

1984 Acts. Statements by Legislative Leaders, see 1984 U.S.Code Cong. and Adm.News, p. 576.

1986 Acts. House Report No. 99–764 and House Conference Report No. 99–958, see 1986 U.S.Code Cong. and Adm.News, p. 5227.

1994 Acts. House Report No. 103–835, see 1994 U.S. Code Cong. and Adm. News, p. 3340.

2005 Acts. House Report No. 109–31(Part I), see 2005 U.S. Code Cong. and Adm. News, p. 88.

Legislative Statements

Section 726(a)(4) adopts a provision contained in the Senate amendment subordinating prepetition penalties and penalties arising in the involuntary gap period to the extent the penalties are not compensation for actual pecuniary laws.

The House amendment deletes a provision following section 726(a)(6) of the Senate amendment providing that the term "claim" includes interest due owed before the date of the filing of the petition as unnecessary since a right to payment for interest due is a right to payment which is within the definition of "claim" in section 101(4) of the House amendment.

Effective and Applicability Provisions

2005 Acts. Amendments by Pub.L. 109–8 effective, except as otherwise provided, 180 days after April 20, 2005, and inapplicable with respect to cases commenced under Title 11 before the effective date, see Pub.L. 109–8, § 1501, set out as a note under 11 U.S.C.A. § 101.

1994 Acts. Amendments by Pub.L. 103–394 effective on Oct. 22, 1994, and not to apply with respect to cases commenced under Title 11 of the United States Code before Oct. 22, 1994, see section 702 of Pub.L. 103–394, set out as a note under section 101 of this title.

1986 Acts. Amendments by Pub.L. 99–554, § 257(r), effective 30 days after Oct. 27, 1986, but not to apply with respect to cases commenced under this title before that date, see section 302(a), (c)(1) of Pub.L. 99–554, set out as a note under section 581 of Title 28, Judiciary and Judicial Procedure.

Amendment by Pub.L. 99–554, § 283, effective 30 days after Oct. 27, 1986, see section 302(a) of Pub.L. 99–554, set out as a note under section 581 of Title 28.

1984 Acts. Amendment by Pub.L. 98–353 effective with respect to cases filed 90 days after July 10, 1984, see section 552(a), formerly 553(a), of Pub.L. 98–353, set out as a note under section 101 of this title.

Separability of Provisions

If any provision of or amendment made by Pub.L. 103–394 or the application of such provision or amendment to any person or circumstance is held to be unconstitutional, the remaining provisions of and amendments made by Pub.L. 103–394 and the application of such provisions and amendments to any person or circumstance shall not be affected thereby, see section 701 of Pub.L. 103–394, set out as a note under section 101 of this title.

CROSS REFERENCES

Customer property, distribution in—

Commodity broker liquidation cases, see 11 USCA § 766.

Stockbroker liquidation cases, see 11 USCA § 752.

Distribution in Chapter eleven cases, see 11 USCA § 1143.

Distribution of securities in stockbroker liquidation cases, see 11 USCA § 750.

Election of creditors holding certain claims entitled to distribution to creditors' committee, see 11 USCA § 705.

Election of trustee by creditors holding claims entitled to distribution, see 11 USCA § 702.

Impairment of claims and interests and objection to claims filed untimely, see 11 USCA § 502.

Ownership of copyright, see 17 USCA § 201.

Payment stopped on checks remaining unpaid 90 days after final distribution, see 11 USCA § 347.

Priorities of distribution in investor liquidation proceedings, see 15 USCA § 78fff.

Student Loan Marketing Association of the Robert T. Stafford Student Loan Program deemed person within meaning of this title for purposes of distribution of its property pursuant to this section, see 20 USCA § 1087–2.

§ 727. Discharge

(a) The court shall grant the debtor a discharge, unless—

(1) the debtor is not an individual;

(2) the debtor, with intent to hinder, delay, or defraud a creditor or an officer of the estate charged with custody of property under this title, has transferred, removed, destroyed, mutilated, or concealed, or has permitted to be transferred, removed, destroyed, mutilated, or concealed—

(A) property of the debtor, within one year before the date of the filing of the petition; or

(B) property of the estate, after the date of the filing of the petition;

(3) the debtor has concealed, destroyed, mutilated, falsified, or failed to keep or preserve any recorded information, including books, documents, records, and papers, from which the debtor's financial condition or business transactions might be ascertained, unless such act or failure to act was justified under all of the circumstances of the case;

(4) the debtor knowingly and fraudulently, in or in connection with the case—

(A) made a false oath or account;

(B) presented or used a false claim;

(C) gave, offered, received, or attempted to obtain money, property, or advantage, or a promise of money, property, or advantage, for acting or forbearing to act; or

(D) withheld from an officer of the estate entitled to possession under this title, any recorded information, including books, documents, records, and papers, relating to the debtor's property or financial affairs;

(5) the debtor has failed to explain satisfactorily, before determination of denial of discharge under this paragraph, any loss of assets or deficiency of assets to meet the debtor's liabilities;

(6) the debtor has refused, in the case—

(A) to obey any lawful order of the court, other than an order to respond to a material question or to testify;

(B) on the ground of privilege against self-incrimination, to respond to a material question approved by the court or to testify, after the debtor has been granted immunity with respect to the matter concerning which such privilege was invoked; or

(C) on a ground other than the properly invoked privilege against self-incrimination, to respond to a material question approved by the court or to testify;

(7) the debtor has committed any act specified in paragraph (2), (3), (4), (5), or (6) of this subsection, on or within one year before the date of the filing of the petition, or during the case, in connection with another case, under this title or under the Bankruptcy Act, concerning an insider;

(8) the debtor has been granted a discharge under this section, under section 1141 of this title, or under section 14, 371, or 476 of the Bankruptcy Act, in a case commenced within 8 years before the date of the filing of the petition;

(9) the debtor has been granted a discharge under section 1228 or 1328 of this title, or under section 660 or 661 of the Bankruptcy Act, in a case commenced within six years before the date of the filing of the petition, unless payments under the plan in such case totaled at least—

(A) 100 percent of the allowed unsecured claims in such case; or

(B)(i) 70 percent of such claims; and

(ii) the plan was proposed by the debtor in good faith, and was the debtor's best effort;

(10) the court approves a written waiver of discharge executed by the debtor after the order for relief under this chapter;

(11) after filing the petition, the debtor failed to complete an instructional course concerning personal financial management described in section 111, except that this paragraph shall not apply with respect to a debtor who is a person described in section 109(h)(4) or who resides in a district for which the United States trustee (or the bankruptcy administrator, if any) determines that the approved instructional courses are not adequate to service the additional individuals who would otherwise be required to complete such instructional courses under this section (The United States trustee (or the bankruptcy administrator, if any) who makes a determination described in this paragraph shall review such determination not later than 1 year after the date of such determination, and not less frequently than annually thereafter.); or

(12) the court after notice and a hearing held not more than 10 days before the date of the entry of the order granting the discharge finds that there is reasonable cause to believe that—

(A) section 522(q)(1) may be applicable to the debtor; and

(B) there is pending any proceeding in which the debtor may be found guilty of a felony of the kind described in section 522(q)(1)(A) or liable for a debt of the kind described in section 522(q)(1)(B).

(b) Except as provided in section 523 of this title, a discharge under subsection (a) of this section discharges the debtor from all debts that arose before the date of the order for relief under this chapter, and any liability on a claim that is determined under section 502 of this title as if such claim had arisen before the commencement of the case, whether or not a proof of claim based on any such debt or liability is filed under section 501 of this title, and whether or not a claim based on any such debt or liability is allowed under section 502 of this title.

(c)(1) The trustee, a creditor, or the United States trustee may object to the granting of a discharge under subsection (a) of this section.

(2) On request of a party in interest, the court may order the trustee to examine the acts and conduct of the debtor to determine whether a ground exists for denial of discharge.

(d) On request of the trustee, a creditor, or the United States trustee, and after notice and a hearing, the court shall revoke a discharge granted under subsection (a) of this section if—

(1) such discharge was obtained through the fraud of the debtor, and the requesting party did not know of such fraud until after the granting of such discharge;

(2) the debtor acquired property that is property of the estate, or became entitled to acquire property that would be property of the estate, and knowingly and fraudulently failed to report the acquisition of or entitlement to such property, or to deliver or surrender such property to the trustee;

(3) the debtor committed an act specified in subsection (a)(6) of this section; or

(4) the debtor has failed to explain satisfactorily—

(A) a material misstatement in an audit referred to in section 586(f) of title 28; or

(B) a failure to make available for inspection all necessary accounts, papers, documents, financial records, files, and all other papers, things, or property belonging to the debtor that are requested for an audit referred to in section 586(f) of title 28.

(e) The trustee, a creditor, or the United States trustee may request a revocation of a discharge—

(1) under subsection (d)(1) of this section within one year after such discharge is granted; or

(2) under subsection (d)(2) or (d)(3) of this section before the later of—

(A) one year after the granting of such discharge; and

(B) the date the case is closed.

(Pub.L. 95–598, Nov. 6, 1978, 92 Stat. 2609; Pub.L. 98–353, Title III, § 480, July 10, 1984, 98 Stat. 382; Pub.L. 99–554, Title II, §§ 220, 257(s), Oct. 27, 1986, 100 Stat. 3101, 3116; Pub.L. 109–8, Title I, § 106(b), Title III, §§ 312(1), 330(a), Title VI, § 603(d), Apr. 20, 2005, 119 Stat. 38, 86, 101, 123.)

HISTORICAL AND STATUTORY NOTES

Revision Notes and Legislative Reports

1978 Acts. This section is the heart of the fresh start provisions of the bankruptcy law. Subsection (a) requires the court to grant a debtor a discharge unless one of nine conditions is met. The first condition is that the debtor is not an individual. This is a change from present law, under which corporations and partnerships may be discharged in liquidation cases, though they rarely are. The change in policy will avoid trafficking in corporate shells and in bankrupt partnerships. "Individual" includes a deceased individual, so that if the debtor dies during the bankruptcy case, he will nevertheless be released from his debts, and his estate will not be liable for them. Creditors will be entitled to only one satisfaction—from the bankruptcy estate and not from the probate estate.

The next three grounds for denial of discharge center on the debtor's wrongdoing in or in connection with the bankruptcy case. They are derived from Bankruptcy Act § 14c [section 32(c) of former Title 11]. If the debtor, with intent to hinder, delay, or defraud his creditors or an officer of the estate, has transferred, removed, destroyed, mutilated, or concealed, or has permitted any such action with respect to, property of the debtor within the year preceding the case, or property of the estate after the commencement of the case, then the debtor is denied discharge. The debtor is also denied discharge if he has concealed, destroyed, mutilated, falsified, or failed to keep or preserve any books and records from which his financial condition might be ascertained, unless the act or failure to act was justified under all the circumstances of the case. The fourth ground for denial of discharge is the commission of a bankruptcy crime, although the standard of proof is preponderance of the evidence rather than proof beyond a reasonable doubt. These crimes include the making of a false oath or account, the use or presentation of a false claim, the giving or receiving of money for acting or forbearing to act, and the withholding from an officer of the estate entitled to possession of books and records relating to the debtor's financial affairs.

The fifth ground for denial of discharge is the failure of the debtor to explain satisfactorily any loss of assets or deficiency of assets to meet the debtor's liabilities. The sixth ground concerns refusal to testify. It is a change from present law, under which the debtor may be denied discharge for legitimately exercising his right against self-incrimination. Under this provision, the debtor may be denied discharge if he refuses to obey any lawful order of the court, or if he refuses to testify after having been granted immunity or after improperly invoking the constitutional privilege against self-incrimination.

The seventh ground for denial of discharge is the commission of an act specified in grounds two through six during the year before the debtor's case in connection with another bankruptcy case concerning an insider.

The eighth ground for denial of discharge is derived from § 14c(5) of the Bankruptcy Act [section 32(c)(5) of former Title 11]. If the debtor has been granted a discharge in a case commenced within 6 years preceding the present bankruptcy case, he is denied discharge. This provision, which is no change from current law with respect to straight bankruptcy, is the 6-year bar to discharge. Discharge under chapter 11 will bar a discharge for 6 years. As under current law, confirmation of a composition wage earner plan under chapter 13 is a basis for invoking the 6-year bar.

The ninth ground is approval by the court of a waiver of discharge.

Subsection (b) specifies that the discharge granted under this section discharges the debtor from all debts that arose before the date of the order for relief. It is irrelevant whether or not a proof of claim was filed with respect to the debt, and whether or not the claim based on the debt was allowed.

Subsection (c) permits the trustee, or a creditor, to object to discharge. It also permits the court, on request of a party in interest, to order the trustee to examine the acts and conduct of the debtor to determine whether a ground for denial of discharge exists.

Subsection (d) requires the court to revoke a discharge already granted in certain circumstances. If the debtor obtained the discharge through fraud, if he acquired and concealed property of the estate, or if he refused to obey a court order or to testify, the discharge is to be revoked.

Subsection (e) permits the trustee or a creditor to request revocation of a discharge within 1 year after the discharge is granted, on the grounds of fraud, and within one year of discharge or the date of the closing of the case, whichever is later, on other grounds. Senate Report No. 95–989.

1984 Acts. Statements by Legislative Leaders, see 1984 U.S.Code Cong. and Adm.News, p. 576.

1986 Acts. House Report No. 99–764 and House Conference Report No. 99–958, see 1986 U.S.Code Cong. and Adm.News, p. 5227.

2005 Acts. House Report No. 109–31(Part I), see 2005 U.S. Code Cong. and Adm. News, p. 88.

Legislative Statements

Sections 727(a)(8) and (9) of the House amendment represent a compromise between provisions contained in section 727(a)(8) of the House bill and Senate amendment. Section 727(a)(8) of the House amendment adopts section 727(a)(8) of the House bill. However, section 727(a)(9) of the House amendment contains a compromise based on section 727(a)(8) of the Senate amendment with respect to the circumstances under which a plan by way of composition under Chapter XIII of the Bankruptcy Act [chapter 13 of former Title 11 (section 1001 et seq.)] should be a bar to discharge in a subsequent proceeding under Title 11. The paragraph provides that a discharge under section 660 or 661 of the Bankruptcy Act [sections 1060 or 1061 of former Title 11] or section 1328 of Title 11 in a case commenced within 6 years before the date of the filing of the petition in a subsequent case, operates as a bar to discharge unless, first, payments under the plan totaled at least 100 percent of the allowed unsecured claims in the case; or second, payments under the plan totaled at least 70 percent of the allowed unsecured claims in the case and the plan was proposed by the debtor in good faith and was the debtor's best effort.

It is expected that the Rules of Bankruptcy Procedure will contain a provision permitting the debtor to request a determination of whether a plan is the debtor's "best effort" prior to confirmation of a plan in a case under chapter 13 of title 11. In determining whether a plan is the debtor's "best effort" the court will evaluate several factors. Different facts and circumstances in cases under chapter 13 operate to make any rule of thumb of limited usefulness. The court should balance the debtor's assets, including family income, health insurance, retirement benefits, and other wealth, a sum which is generally determinable, against the foreseeable necessary living expenses of the debtor and the debtor's dependents, which unfortunately is rarely quantifiable. In determining the expenses of the debtor and the debtor's dependents, the court should consider the stability of the debtor's employment, if any, the age of the debtor, the number of the debtor's dependents and their ages, the condition of equipment and tools necessary to the debtor's employment or to the operation of his business, and other foreseeable expenses that the debtor will be required to pay during the period of the plan, other than payments to be made to creditors under the plan.

Section 727(a)(10) of the House amendment clarifies a provision contained in section 727(a)(9) of the House bill and Senate amendment indicating that a discharge may be barred if the court approves a waiver of discharge executed in writing by the debtor after the order for relief under chapter 7.

Section 727(b) of the House amendment adopts a similar provision contained in the Senate amendment modifying the effect of discharge. The provision makes clear that the debtor is discharged from all debts that arose before the date of the order for relief under chapter 7 in addition to any debt which is determined under section 502 as if it were a prepetition claim. Thus, if a case is converted from chapter 11 or chapter 13 to a case under chapter 7, all debts prior to the time of conversion are discharged, in addition to debts determined after the date of conversion of a kind specified in section 502, that are to be determined as prepetition claims. This modification is particularly important with respect to an individual debtor who files a petition under chapter 11 or chapter 13 of title 11 if the case is converted to chapter 7. The logical result of the House amendment is to equate the result that obtains whether the case is converted from another chapter to chapter 7, or whether the other chapter proceeding is dismissed and a new case is commenced by filing a petition under chapter 7.

References in Text

The Bankruptcy Act, referred to in subsec. (a)(7), is Act July 1, 1898, c. 541, 30 Stat. 544, as amended, which was classified generally to former Title 11, prior to repeal of such Act by Pub.L. 95–598, Title IV, § 401(a), Nov. 6, 1978, 92 Stat. 2692.

Sections 14, 371, and 476 of the Bankruptcy Act, referred to in subsec. (a)(8), are section 14 of Act July 1, 1898, c. 541, 30 Stat. 550, and sections 371 and 476 of Act July 1, 1898, c. 541, as added June 22, 1938, c. 575, § 1, 52 Stat. 912, 924, which were classified to sections 32, 771, and 876 of former Title 11, respectively.

Sections 660 and 661 of the Bankruptcy Act, referred to in subsec. (a)(9), are sections 660 and 661 of Act July 1, 1898, c. 541, as added June 22, 1938, c. 575, § 1, 52 Stat. 935, 936, which were classified, respectively, to sections 1060 and 1061 of former Title 11.

Effective and Applicability Provisions

2005 Acts. Amendments by sections 106(b), 312(1), and 330(a) of Pub.L. 109–8 effective 180 days after Apr. 20, 2005, with amendments by sections 106(b) and 312(1) of Pub.L. 109–8 not applicable with respect to cases commenced under this title before such effective date, except as otherwise provided, and amendment by section 330(a) of Pub.L. 109–8 applicable with respect to cases commenced under this title on or after Apr. 20, 2005, see Pub.L. 109–8, § 1501, set out as a note under 11 U.S.C.A. § 101.

Amendments by Pub.L. 109–8, § 603, effective 18 months after Apr. 20, 2005, see Pub.L. 109–8, § 603(e), set out as a note under 11 U.S.C.A. § 521.

1986 Acts. Amendment by section 257 Pub.L. 99–554 effective 30 days after Oct. 27, 1986, except as otherwise provided for, see section 302(a) of Pub.L. 99–554, set out as a note under section 581 of Title 28, Judiciary and Judicial Procedure.

Amendment by Pub.L. 99–554, § 220 not to become effective in or with respect to certain specified judicial districts until, or apply to cases while pending in such district before, the expiration of the 270-day period beginning 30 days after Oct. 27, 1986, or of the 30-day period beginning on the date the Attorney General certifies under section 303 of Pub.L. 99–554 the region specified in a paragraph of section 581(a) of Title 28, as amended by section 111(a) of Pub.L. 99–554, that includes such district, whichever occurs first, see section 302(d)(1) of Pub.L. 99–554, set out as a note under section 581 of Title 28.

Amendment by Pub.L. 99–554, § 220, not to become effective in or with respect to certain specified judicial districts until, or apply to cases while pending in such district before, the expiration of the 2-year period beginning 30 days after Oct. 27, 1986, or of the 30-day period beginning on the date the Attorney General certifies under section 303 of Pub.L. 99–554 the region specified in a paragraph of section 581(a) of Title 28, as amended by section 111(a) of Pub.L. 99–554, that includes such district, whichever occurs first, see section

302(d)(2) of Pub.L. 99–554, set out as a note under section 581 of Title 28.

Amendment by Pub.L. 99–554, § 220, not to become effective in or with respect to judicial districts established for the States of Alabama and North Carolina until, or apply to cases while pending in such district before, such district elects to be included in a bankruptcy region established in section 581(a) of Title 28, as amended by section 111(a) of Pub.L. 99–554, or Oct. 1, 2002, whichever occurs first, and, except as otherwise provided, with respect to cases under chapters 7, 11, 12, and 13 of Title 11 commenced before 30 days after Oct. 27, 1986, and pending in a judicial district in the States of Alabama or North Carolina before any election made under section 302(d)(3)(A) of Pub.L. 99–554 by such district becomes effective or Oct. 1, 2002, whichever occurs first, amendments by Pub.L. 99–554 not to apply until Oct. 1, 2003, or the expiration of the 1-year period beginning on the date such election becomes effective, whichever occurs first, and further, in any judicial district in Alabama or North Carolina not making the election described in section 302(d)(3)(A) of Pub.L. 99–554, any person appointed under regulations issued by the Judicial Conference to administer estates in cases under Title 11 authorized to establish, etc., a panel of private trustees, and to supervise cases and trustees in cases under chapters 7, 11, 12, and 13 of Title 11, until amendments by sections 201 to 231 of Pub.L. 99–554 effective in such district, see section 302(d)(3)(A) to (F), (H), and (I) of Pub.L. 99–554, set out as a note under section 581 of Title 28.

Amendment by Pub.L. 99–554, § 220, except as otherwise provided, with respect to cases under chapters 7, 11, 12, and 13 of Title 11 commenced before 30 days after Oct. 27, 1986, and pending in a judicial district referred to in section 581(a) of Title 28, as amended by section 111(a) of Pub.L. 99–554, for which a United States trustee is not authorized before 30 days after Oct. 27, 1986 to be appointed, not applicable until the expiration of the 3-year period beginning on Oct. 27, 1986, or of the 1-year period beginning on the date the Attorney General certifies under section 303 of Pub.L. 99–554 the region specified in a paragraph of such section 581(a) that includes, such district, whichever occurs first, see section 302(e)(1), (2) of Pub.L. 99–554, as amended, set out as a note under section 581 of Title 28.

Amendment by Pub.L. 99–554, § 257(s), effective 30 days after Oct. 27, 1986, but not applicable to cases commenced under this title before that date, see section 302(a), (c)(1) of Pub.L. 99–554, set out as a note under section 581 of Title 28.

1984 Acts. Amendment by Pub.L. 98–353 effective with respect to cases filed 90 days after July 10, 1984, see section 552(a), formerly 553(a), of Pub.L. 98–353, set out as a note under section 101 of this title.

CROSS REFERENCES

Cancellation of indebtedness from discharged farm loans, see 12 USCA § 1150.

Concealment of assets; false oaths and claims, see 18 USCA § 152.

Confirmation of plan as affecting discharge in—

Chapter eleven cases, see 11 USCA § 1141.

Chapter nine cases, see 11 USCA § 944.

Discharge in Chapter thirteen cases, see 11 USCA § 1328.

Duty of trustee to oppose discharge, see 11 USCA § 704.

Effect of—

Conversion, see 11 USCA § 348.

Discharge, see 11 USCA § 524.

Exceptions to discharge, see 11 USCA § 523.

Nondischargeability of capital improvement loans for multifamily housing projects in proceedings under this section, see 12 USCA § 1715z–1a.

[§ 728. Repealed. Pub.L. 109–8, Title VII, § 719(b)(1), Apr. 20, 2005, 119 Stat. 133]

HISTORICAL AND STATUTORY NOTES

Section, Pub.L. 95–598, Nov. 6, 1978, 92 Stat. 2611; Pub.L. 98–353, Title III, § 481, July 10, 1984, 98 Stat. 382; Pub.L. 99–554, Title II, § 257(t), Oct. 27, 1986, 100 Stat. 3116, related to special tax provisions applying to state and local taxation.

See, now, 11 U.S.C.A. § 346.

Effective Date of Repeal

Amendments by Pub.L. 109–8 effective, except as otherwise provided, 180 days after April 20, 2005, and inapplicable with respect to cases commenced under Title 11 before the effective date, see Pub.L. 109–8, § 1501, set out as a note under 11 U.S.C.A. § 101.

SUBCHAPTER III—STOCKBROKER LIQUIDATION

CROSS REFERENCES

Subchapter applicable only in case under chapter concerning stockholder, see 11 USCA § 103.

§ 741. Definitions for this subchapter

In this subchapter—

(1) "Commission" means Securities and Exchange Commission;

(2) "customer" includes—

(A) entity with whom a person deals as principal or agent and that has a claim against such person on account of a security received, acquired, or held by such person in the ordinary course of such person's business as a stockbroker, from or for the securities account or accounts of such entity—

(i) for safekeeping;

(ii) with a view to sale;

(iii) to cover a consummated sale;

(iv) pursuant to a purchase;

(v) as collateral under a security agreement; or

(vi) for the purpose of effecting registration of transfer; and

(B) entity that has a claim against a person arising out of—

(i) a sale or conversion of a security received, acquired, or held as specified in subparagraph (A) of this paragraph; or

(ii) a deposit of cash, a security, or other property with such person for the purpose of purchasing or selling a security;

(3) "customer name security" means security—

(A) held for the account of a customer on the date of the filing of the petition by or on behalf of the debtor;

(B) registered in such customer's name on such date or in the process of being so registered under instructions from the debtor; and

(C) not in a form transferable by delivery on such date;

(4) "customer property" means cash, security, or other property, and proceeds of such cash, security, or property, received, acquired, or held by or for the account of the debtor, from or for the securities account of a customer—

(A) including—

(i) property that was unlawfully converted from and that is the lawful property of the estate;

(ii) a security held as property of the debtor to the extent such security is necessary to meet a net equity claim of a customer based on a security of the same class and series of an issuer;

(iii) resources provided through the use or realization of a customer's debit cash balance or a debit item includible in the Formula for Determination of Reserve Requirement for Brokers and Dealers as promulgated by the Commission under the Securities Exchange Act of 1934; and

(iv) other property of the debtor that any applicable law, rule, or regulation requires to be set aside or held for the benefit of a customer, unless including such property as customer property would not significantly increase customer property; but

(B) not including—

(i) a customer name security delivered to or reclaimed by a customer under section 751 of this title; or

(ii) property to the extent that a customer does not have a claim against the debtor based on such property;

(5) "margin payment" means payment or deposit of cash, a security, or other property, that is commonly known to the securities trade as original margin, initial margin, maintenance margin, or variation margin, or as a mark-to-market payment, or that secures an obligation of a participant in a securities clearing agency;

(6) "net equity" means, with respect to all accounts of a customer that such customer has in the same capacity—

(A)(i) aggregate dollar balance that would remain in such accounts after the liquidation, by sale or purchase, at the time of the filing of the petition, of all securities positions in all such accounts, except any customer name securities of such customer; minus

(ii) any claim of the debtor against such customer in such capacity that would have been owing immediately after such liquidation; plus

(B) any payment by such customer to the trustee, within 60 days after notice under section 342 of this title, of any business related claim of the debtor against such customer in such capacity;

(7) "securities contract"—

(A) means—

(i) a contract for the purchase, sale, or loan of a security, a certificate of deposit, a mortgage loan, any interest in a mortgage loan, a group or index of securities, certificates of deposit, or mortgage loans or interests therein (including an interest therein or based on the value thereof), or option on any of the foregoing, including an option to purchase or sell any such security, certificate of deposit, mortgage loan, interest, group or index, or option, and including any repurchase or reverse repurchase transaction on any such security, certificate of deposit, mortgage loan, interest, group or index, or option (whether or not such repurchase or reverse repurchase transaction is a "repurchase agreement", as defined in section 101);

(ii) any option entered into on a national securities exchange relating to foreign currencies;

(iii) the guarantee (including by novation) by or to any securities clearing agency of a settlement of cash, securities, certificates of deposit, mortgage loans or interests therein, group or index of securities, or mortgage loans or interests therein (including any interest therein or based on the value thereof), or option on any of the foregoing, including an option to purchase or sell any such security, certificate of deposit, mortgage loan, interest, group or index, or option (whether or not such settlement is in connection with any agreement or transaction referred to in clauses (i) through (xi));

(iv) any margin loan;

(v) any extension of credit for the clearance or settlement of securities transactions;

(vi) any loan transaction coupled with a securities collar transaction, any prepaid forward securities transaction, or any total return swap transaction coupled with a securities sale transaction;

(vii) any other agreement or transaction that is similar to an agreement or transaction referred to in this subparagraph;

(viii) any combination of the agreements or transactions referred to in this subparagraph;

(ix) any option to enter into any agreement or transaction referred to in this subparagraph;

(x) a master agreement that provides for an agreement or transaction referred to in clause (i), (ii), (iii), (iv), (v), (vi), (vii), (viii), or (ix), together with all supplements to any such master agreement, without regard to whether the master agreement provides for an agreement or transaction that is not a securities contract under this subparagraph, except that such master agreement shall be considered to be a securities contract under this subparagraph only with respect to each agreement or transaction under such master agreement that is referred to in clause (i), (ii), (iii), (iv), (v), (vi), (vii), (viii), or (ix); or

(xi) any security agreement or arrangement or other credit enhancement related to any agreement or transaction referred to in this subparagraph, including any guarantee or reimbursement obligation by or to a stockbroker, securities clearing agency, financial institution, or financial participant in connection with any agreement or transaction referred to in this subparagraph, but not to exceed the damages in connection with any such agreement or transaction, measured in accordance with section 562; and

(B) does not include any purchase, sale, or repurchase obligation under a participation in a commercial mortgage loan;

(8) "settlement payment" means a preliminary settlement payment, a partial settlement payment, an interim settlement payment, a settlement payment on account, a final settlement payment, or any other similar payment commonly used in the securities trade; and

(9) "SIPC" means Securities Investor Protection Corporation.

(Pub.L. 95–598, Nov. 6, 1978, 92 Stat. 2611; Pub.L. 97–222, § 8, July 27, 1982, 96 Stat. 237; Pub.L. 98–353, Title III, § 482, July 10, 1984, 98 Stat. 382; Pub.L. 103–394, Title V, § 501(d)(25), Oct. 22, 1994, 108 Stat. 4146; Pub.L. 109–8, Title IX, § 907(a)(2), Apr. 20, 2005, 119 Stat. 173; Pub.L. 109–390, § 5(a)(3), Dec. 12, 2006, 120 Stat. 2697)

HISTORICAL AND STATUTORY NOTES

Revision Notes and Legislative Reports

1978 Acts. Section 741 sets forth definitions for subchapter III of chapter 7.

Paragraph (1) defines "Commission" to mean the Securities and Exchange Commission.

Paragraph (2) defines "customer" to include anybody that interacts with the debtor in a capacity that concerns securities transactions. The term embraces cash or margin customers of a broker or dealer in the broadest sense.

Paragraph (3) defines "customer name security" in a restrictive fashion to include only non-transferrable securities that are registered, or in the process of being registered in a customer's own name. The securities must not be endorsed by the customer and the stockbroker must not be able to legally transfer the securities by delivery, by a power of attorney, or otherwise.

Paragraph (4) defines "customer property" to include all property of the debtor that has been segregated for customers or property that should have been segregated but was unlawfully converted. Clause (i) refers to customer property not properly segregated by the debtor or customer property converted and then recovered so as to become property of the estate. Unlawfully converted property that has been transferred to a third party is excluded until it is recovered as property of the estate by virtue of the avoiding powers. The concept excludes customer name securities that have been delivered to or reclaimed by a customer and any property properly belonging to the stockholder, such as money deposited by a customer to pay for securities that the stockholder has distributed to such customer.

Paragraph (5) defines "net equity" to establish the extent to which a customer will be entitled to share in the single and separate fund. Accounts of a customer are aggregated and offset only to the extent the accounts are held by the customer in the same capacity. Thus, a personal account is separate from an account held as trustee. In a community property state an account held for the community is distinct from an account held as separate property.

The net equity is computed by liquidating all securities positions in the accounts and crediting the account with any amount due to the customer. Regardless of the actual dates, if any, of liquidation, the customer is only entitled to the liquidation value at the time of the filing of the petition. To avoid double counting, the liquidation value of customer name securities belonging to a customer is excluded from net equity. Thus, clause (ii) includes claims against a customer resulting from the liquidation of a security under clause (i). The value of a security on which trading has been suspended at the time of the filing of the petition will be estimated. Once the net liquidation value is computed, any amount that the customer owes to the stockbroker is subtracted including any amount that would be owing after the hypothetical liquidation, such as brokerage fees. Debts owed by the customer to the debtor, other than in a securities related transaction, will not reduce the net equity of the customer. Finally, net equity is increased by any payment by the customer to the debtor actually paid within 60 days after notice. The principal reason a customer would make such a payment is to reclaim customer name securities under § 751.

Paragraph (6) defines "1934 Act" to mean the Securities Exchange Act of 1934 [15 U.S.C.A. § 78a et seq.].

Paragraph (7) defines "SIPC" to mean the Securities Investor Protection Corporation. Senate Report No. 95–989.

1982 Acts. House Report No. 97–420, see 1982 U.S.Code Cong. and Adm.News, p. 583.

1984 Acts. Statements by Legislative Leaders, see 1984 U.S.Code Cong. and Adm.News, p. 576.

1994 Acts. House Report No. 103–835, see 1994 U.S. Code Cong. and Adm. News, p. 3340.

2005 Acts. House Report No. 109–31(Part I), see 2005 U.S. Code Cong. and Adm. News, p. 88.

2006 Acts. House Report No. 109–648(Part I), see 2006 U.S. Code Cong. and Adm. News, p. 1585.

Legislative Statements

Section 741(6) of the House bill and Senate amendment is deleted by the House amendment since the defined term is used only in section 741(4)(A)(iii). A corresponding change is made in that section.

References in Text

The Securities Exchange Act of 1934, referred to in par. (4)(A)(iii), is Act June 6, 1934, c. 404, 48 Stat. 881, as amended, which is classified principally to chapter 2B (section 78a et seq.) of Title 15, Commerce and Trade. For complete classification of this Act to the Code, see section 781 of Title 15 and Tables.

Effective and Applicability Provisions

2005 Acts. Amendments by Pub.L. 109–8 effective, except as otherwise provided, 180 days after April 20, 2005, and inapplicable with respect to cases commenced under Title 11 before the effective date, see Pub.L. 109–8, § 1501, set out as a note under 11 U.S.C.A. § 101.

1994 Acts. Amendment by Pub.L. 103–394 effective on Oct. 22, 1994, and not to apply with respect to cases commenced under Title 11 of the United States Code before Oct. 22, 1994, see section 702 of Pub.L. 103–394, set out as a note under section 101 of this title.

1984 Acts. Amendment by Pub.L. 98–353 effective with respect to cases filed 90 days after July 10, 1984, see section 552(a), formerly 553(a), of Pub.L. 98–353, set out as a note under section 101 of this title.

Separability of Provisions

If any provision of or amendment made by Pub.L. 103–394 or the application of such provision or amendment to any person or circumstance is held to be unconstitutional, the remaining provisions of and amendments made by Pub.L. 103–394 and the application of such provisions and amendments to any person or circumstance shall not be affected thereby, see section 701 of Pub.L. 103–394, set out as a note under section 101 of this title.

CROSS REFERENCES

Certain persons acting as agent or custodian for customer in connection with "securities contract" as defined under this section considered a financial institution for purposes of this title, see 11 USCA § 101.

Contractual right to liquidate "securities contract" as defined under this section not stayed, avoided or limited by operation of any provision of this title, see 11 USCA § 555.

"Customer" defined under this section as determining who is a stockbroker for purposes of this title, see 11 USCA § 101.

Definitions applicable in—

Chapter eleven cases, see 11 USCA § 1101.

Chapter nine cases, see 11 USCA § 902.

Commodity broker liquidation cases, see 11 USCA § 761.

Railroad reorganization cases, see 11 USCA § 1162.

Limitation on power of trustee to avoid transfer of "margin payment" and "settlement payment" as defined under this section, see 11 USCA § 546.

Receipt of "margin payment" or "settlement payment" as defined under this section is taking for value for purposes of avoidance of fraudulent transfers and obligations, see 11 USCA § 548.

"Securities contract" as defined under this section as having same meaning for purposes of—

Federal credit union insurance, see 12 USCA § 1787.

Federal deposit insurance corporation, see 12 USCA § 1821.

Setoff of mutual debt in connection with "securities contract", "margin payment" or "settlement payment", not stayed by filing of petitions for voluntary cases, joint cases or involuntary cases or protective decrees in investor protection liquidation proceedings, see 11 USCA § 362.

§ 742. Effect of section 362 of this title in this subchapter

Notwithstanding section 362 of this title, SIPC may file an application for a protective decree under the Securities Investor Protection Act of 1970. The filing of such application stays all proceedings in the case under this title unless and until such application is dismissed. If SIPC completes the liquidation of the debtor, then the court shall dismiss the case.

(Pub.L. 95–598, Nov. 6, 1978, 92 Stat. 2613; Pub.L. 97–222, § 9, July 27, 1982, 96 Stat. 237; Pub.L. 103–394, Title V, § 501(d)(26), Oct. 22, 1994, 108 Stat. 4146.)

HISTORICAL AND STATUTORY NOTES

Revision Notes and Legislative Reports

1978 Acts. Section 742 indicates that the automatic stay does not prevent SIPC from filing an application for a protective decree under SIPA. If SIPA does file such an application, then all bankruptcy proceedings are suspended until the SIPC action is completed. If SIPC completes liquidation of the stockbroker then the bankruptcy case is dismissed. Senate Report No. 95–989.

1982 Acts. House Report No. 97–420, see 1982 U.S.Code Cong. and Adm.News, p. 583.

1994 Acts. House Report No. 103–835, see 1994 U.S. Code Cong. and Adm. News, p. 3340.

Legislative Statements

Section 742 of the House amendment deletes a sentence contained in the Senate amendment requiring the trustee in an interstate stock-brokerage liquidation to comply with the provisions of subchapter IV of chapter 7 if the debtor is also a commodity broker. The House amendment expands the requirement to require the SIPC trustee to perform such duties, if the debtor is a commodity broker, under section 7(b) of the Securities Investor Protection Act [15 U.S.C. 78ggg(b)]. The requirement is deleted from section 742 since the trustee of an intrastate stockbroker will be bound by the provisions of subchapter IV of chapter 7 if the debtor is also a commodity broker by reason of section 103 of title 11.

References in Text

The Securities Investor Protection Act of 1970, referred to in text, is Pub.L. 91–598, Dec. 30, 1970, 84 Stat. 1636, as amended, which is classified generally to chapter 2B–1 (section 78aaa et seq.) of Title 15, Commerce and Trade. For complete classification of this Act to the Code, see section 78aaa of Title 15 and Tables.

Effective and Applicability Provisions

1994 Acts. Amendment by Pub.L. 103–394 effective on Oct. 22, 1994, and not to apply with respect to cases commenced under Title 11 of the United States Code before Oct. 22, 1994, see section 702 of Pub.L. 103–394, set out as a note under section 101 of this title.

Separability of Provisions

If any provision of or amendment made by Pub.L. 103–394 or the application of such provision or amendment to any person or circumstance is held to be unconstitutional, the remaining provisions of and amendments made by Pub.L. 103–394 and the application of such provisions and amendments to any person or circumstance shall not be affected thereby, see section 701 of Pub.L. 103–394, set out as a note under section 101 of this title.

CROSS REFERENCES

Automatic stay of enforcement of claims against debtor in Chapter 9 cases, see 11 USCA § 922.

Effect of dismissal, see 11 USCA § 349.

Stay of action against codebtor in Chapter 13 cases, see 11 USCA § 1301.

§ 743. Notice

The clerk shall give the notice required by section 342 of this title to SIPC and to the Commission.

(Pub.L. 95–598, Nov. 6, 1978, 92 Stat. 2613; Pub.L. 99–554, Title II, § 283(t), Oct. 27, 1986, 100 Stat. 3118); Pub.L. 103–394, Title V, § 501(d)(27), Oct. 22, 1994, 108 Stat. 4146.)

HISTORICAL AND STATUTORY NOTES

Revision Notes and Legislative Reports

1978 Acts. Section 743 requires that notice of the order for relief be given to SIPC and to the SEC in every stockbroker case. Senate Report No. 95–989.

1986 Acts. House Report No. 99–764 and House Conference Report No. 99–958, see 1986 U.S.Code Cong. and Adm.News, p. 5227.

1994 Acts. House Report No. 103–835, see 1994 U.S. Code Cong. and Adm. News, p. 3340.

Codifications

Pub.L. 99–554, Title II, § 283(t), Oct. 27, 1986, 100 Stat. 3118, provided that this section be amended by striking out "(d)", which amendment was incapable of execution in view of present language of text.

Effective and Applicability Provisions

1994 Acts. Amendment by Pub.L. 103–394 effective on Oct. 22, 1994, and not to apply with respect to cases commenced under Title 11 of the United States Code before Oct. 22, 1994, see section 702 of Pub.L. 103–394, set out as a note under section 101 of this title.

Separability of Provisions

If any provision of or amendment made by Pub.L. 103–394 or the application of such provision or amendment to any person or circumstance is held to be unconstitutional, the remaining provisions of and amendments made by Pub.L. 103–394 and the application of such provisions and amendments to any person or circumstance shall not be affected thereby, see section 701 of Pub.L. 103–394, set out as a note under section 101 of this title.

CROSS REFERENCES

Notice in Chapter nine cases, see 11 USCA § 923.

Notice to the Commodity Futures Trading Commission, see 11 USCA § 762.

§ 744. Executory contracts

Notwithstanding section 365(d) (1) of this title, the trustee shall assume or reject, under section 365 of this title, any executory contract of the debtor for the purchase or sale of a security in the ordinary course of the debtor's business, within a reasonable time after the date of the order for relief, but not to exceed 30 days. If the trustee does not assume such a contract within such time, such contract is rejected.

(Pub.L. 95–598, Nov. 6, 1978, 92 Stat. 2613; Pub.L. 97–222, § 10, July 27, 1982, 96 Stat. 238.)

HISTORICAL AND STATUTORY NOTES

Revision Notes and Legislative Reports

1978 Acts. Section 744 instructs the court to give the trustee a reasonable time, not to exceed 30 days, to assume or reject any executory contract of the stockbroker to buy or sell securities. Any contract not assumed within the time fixed by the court is considered to be rejected. Senate Report No. 95–989.

1982 Acts. House Report No. 97–420, see 1982 U.S.Code Cong. and Adm.News, p. 583.

CROSS REFERENCES

Effect of rejection of lease of railroad line, see 11 USCA § 1169.

§ 745. Treatment of accounts

(a) Accounts held by the debtor for a particular customer in separate capacities shall be treated as accounts of separate customers.

(b) If a stockbroker or a bank holds a customer net equity claim against the debtor that arose out of a transaction for a customer of such stockbroker or bank, each such customer of such stockbroker or bank shall be treated as a separate customer of the debtor.

(c) Each trustee's account specified as such on the debtor's books, and supported by a trust deed filed with, and qualified as such by, the Internal Revenue Service, and under the Internal Revenue Code of 1986, shall be treated as a separate customer account for each beneficiary under such trustee account.

(Pub.L. 95–598, Nov. 6, 1978, 92 Stat. 2613; Pub.L. 97–222, § 11, July 27, 1982, 96 Stat. 238; Pub.L. 98–353, Title III, § 483, July 10, 1984, 98 Stat. 383; Pub.L. 99–514, § 2, Oct. 22, 1986, 100 Stat. 2095; Pub.L. 103–394, Title V, § 501(d)(28), Oct. 22, 1994, 108 Stat. 4146.)

HISTORICAL AND STATUTORY NOTES

Revision Notes and Legislative Reports

1978 Acts. Section 745(a) indicates that each account held by a customer in a separate capacity is to be considered a separate account. This prevents the offset of accounts held in different capacities.

Subsection (b) indicates that a bank or another stockbroker that is a customer of a debtor is considered to hold its customers accounts in separate capacities. Thus a bank or other stockbroker is not treated as a mutual fund for purposes of bulk investment. This protects unrelated customers of a bank or other stockholder [sic] from having their accounts offset.

Subsection (c) effects the same result with respect to a trust so that each beneficiary is treated as the customer of the debtor rather than the trust itself. This eliminates any doubt whether a trustee holds a personal account in a separate capacity from his trustee's account. Senate Report No. 95–989.

1982 Acts. House Report No. 97–420, see 1982 U.S.Code Cong. and Adm.News, p. 583.

1986 Acts. House Conference Report No. 99–841 and Statement by President, see 1986 U.S.Code Cong. and Adm. News, p. 4075.

1994 Acts. House Report No. 103–835, see 1994 U.S. Code Cong. and Adm. News, p. 3340.

References in Text

The Internal Revenue Code of 1986, referred to in subsec. (c), is classified to Title 26, Internal Revenue Code.

Codifications

Amendment of subsec. (c) by section 501(d)(28) of Pub.L. 103–394, which directed that "Internal Revenue Code of 1986" be substituted for "Internal Revenue Code of 1954 (26 U.S.C. 1 et seq.)", was executed by striking out "(26 U.S.C. 1 et seq.)" after "Internal Revenue Code of 1986", as the probable intent of Congress.

Effective and Applicability Provisions

1994 Acts. Amendment by Pub.L. 103–394 effective on Oct. 22, 1994, and not to apply with respect to cases commenced under Title 11 of the United States Code before Oct. 22, 1994, see section 702 of Pub.L. 103–394, set out as a note under section 101 of this title.

1984 Acts. Amendment by Pub.L. 98–353 effective with respect to cases filed 90 days after July 10, 1984, see section 552(a), formerly 553(a), of Pub.L. 98–353, set out as a note under section 101 of this title.

Separability of Provisions

If any provision of or amendment made by Pub.L. 103–394 or the application of such provision or amendment to any person or circumstance is held to be unconstitutional, the remaining provisions of and amendments made by Pub.L. 103–394 and the application of such provisions and amendments to any person or circumstance shall not be affected thereby, see section 701 of Pub.L. 103–394, set out as a note under section 101 of this title.

CROSS REFERENCES

Stockbroker defined, see 11 USCA § 101.

Treatment of accounts in commodity broker liquidation cases, see 11 USCA § 763.

§ 746. Extent of customer claims

(a) If, after the date of the filing of the petition, an entity enters into a transaction with the debtor, in a manner that would have made such entity a customer had such transaction occurred before the date of the filing of the petition, and such transaction was entered into by such entity in good faith and before the qualification under section 322 of this title of a trustee, such entity shall be deemed a customer, and the date of such transaction shall be deemed to be the date of the filing of the petition for the purpose of determining such entity's net equity.

(b) An entity does not have a claim as a customer to the extent that such entity transferred to the debtor cash or a security that, by contract, agreement, understanding, or operation of law, is—

(1) part of the capital of the debtor; or

(2) subordinated to the claims of any or all creditors.

(Pub.L. 95–598, Nov. 6, 1978, 92 Stat. 2613; Pub.L. 97–222, § 12, July 27, 1982, 96 Stat. 238.)

HISTORICAL AND STATUTORY NOTES

Revision Notes and Legislative Reports

1978 Acts. Section 746(a) protects entities who deal in good faith with the debtor after the filing of the petition and before a trustee is appointed by deeming such entities to be customers. The principal application of this section will be in an involuntary case before the order for relief, because § 701(b) requires prompt appointment of an interim trustee after the order for relief.

Subsection (b) indicates that an entity who holds securities that are either part of the capital of the debtor or that are subordinated to the claims of any creditor of the debtor is not a customer with respect to those securities. This subsection will apply when the stockbroker has sold securities in itself to the customer or when the customer has otherwise placed such securities in an account with the stockbroker. Senate Report No. 95–989.

1982 Acts. House Report No. 97–420, see 1982 U.S.Code Cong. and Adm.News, p. 583.

CROSS REFERENCES

Allowance of claims or interests, see 11 USCA § 502.

§ 747. Subordination of certain customer claims

Except as provided in section 510 of this title, unless all other customer net equity claims have been paid in full, the trustee may not pay in full or pay in part, directly or indirectly, any net equity claim of a customer that was, on the date the transaction giving rise to such claim occurred—

(1) an insider;

(2) a beneficial owner of at least five percent of any class of equity securities of the debtor, other than—

(A) nonconvertible stock having fixed preferential dividend and liquidation rights; or

(B) interests of limited partners in a limited partnership;

(3) a limited partner with a participation of at least five percent in the net assets or net profits of the debtor; or

(4) an entity that, directly or indirectly, through agreement or otherwise, exercised or had the power to exercise control over the management or policies of the debtor.

(Pub.L. 95–598, Nov. 6, 1978, 92 Stat. 2613; Pub.L. 97–222, § 13, July 27, 1982, 96 Stat. 238.)

HISTORICAL AND STATUTORY NOTES

Revision Notes and Legislative Reports

1978 Acts. Section 747 subordinates to other customer claims, all claims of a customer who is an insider, a five percent owner of the debtor, or otherwise in control of the debtor. Senate Report No. 95–989.

1982 Acts. House Report No. 97–420, see 1982 U.S.Code Cong. and Adm.News, p. 583.

CROSS REFERENCES

Insider defined, see 11 USCA § 101.

§ 748. Reduction of securities to money

As soon as practicable after the date of the order for relief, the trustee shall reduce to money, consistent with good market practice, all securities held as property of the estate, except for customer name securities delivered or reclaimed under section 751 of this title.

(Pub.L. 95–598, Nov. 6, 1978, 92 Stat. 2614.)

HISTORICAL AND STATUTORY NOTES

Revision Notes and Legislative Reports

1978 Acts. Section 748 requires the trustee to liquidate all securities, except for customer name securities, of the estate in a manner consistent with good market practice. The trustee should refrain from flooding a thin market with a large percentage of shares in any one issue. If the trustee holds restricted securities or securities in which trading has been suspended, then the trustee must arrange to liquidate such securities in accordance with the securities laws. A private placement may be the only exemption available with the customer of the debtor the best prospect for such a placement. The subsection does not permit such a customer to bid in his net equity as part of the purchase price; a contrary result would permit a customer to receive a greater percentage on his net equity claim than other customers. Senate Report No. 95–989.

CROSS REFERENCES

Reduction of certain securities and property to money in commodity broker liquidation cases, see 11 USCA § 766.

§ 749. Voidable transfers

(a) Except as otherwise provided in this section, any transfer of property that, but for such transfer, would have been customer property, may be avoided by the trustee, and such property shall be treated as customer property, if and to the extent that the trustee avoids such transfer under section 544, 545, 547, 548, or 549 of this title. For the purpose of such sections, the property so transferred shall be deemed to have been property of the debtor and, if such transfer was made to a customer or for a customer's benefit, such customer shall be deemed, for the purposes of this section, to have been a creditor.

(b) Notwithstanding sections 544, 545, 547, 548, and 549 of this title, the trustee may not avoid a transfer made before five days after the order for relief if such transfer is approved by the Commission by rule or order, either before or after such transfer, and if such transfer is—

(1) a transfer of a securities contract entered into or carried by or through the debtor on behalf of a customer, and of any cash, security, or other property margining or securing such securities contract; or

(2) the liquidation of a securities contract entered into or carried by or through the debtor on behalf of a customer.

(Pub.L. 95–598, Nov. 6, 1978, 92 Stat. 2614; Pub.L. 97–222, § 14, July 27, 1982, 96 Stat. 238.)

HISTORICAL AND STATUTORY NOTES

Revision Notes and Legislative Reports

1978 Acts. Section 749 indicates that if the trustee avoids a transfer, property recovered is customer property to any extent it would have been customer property but for the transfer. The section clarifies that a customer who receives a transfer of property of the debtor is a creditor and that property in a customer's account is property of a creditor for purposes of the avoiding powers. Senate Report No. 95–989.

1982 Acts. House Report No. 97–420, see 1982 U.S.Code Cong. and Adm.News, p. 583.

CROSS REFERENCES

Voidable transfers in commodity broker liquidation cases, see 11 USCA § 764.

§ 750. Distribution of securities

The trustee may not distribute a security except under section 751 of this title.

(Pub.L. 95–598, Nov. 6, 1978, 92 Stat. 2614.)

HISTORICAL AND STATUTORY NOTES

Revision Notes and Legislative Reports

1978 Acts. Section 750 forbids the trustee from distributing a security other than a customer name security. The term "distribution" refers to a distribution to customers in satisfaction of net equity claims and is not intended to preclude the trustee from liquidating securities under proposed 11 U.S.C. 748. Senate Report No. 95–989.

CROSS REFERENCES

Distribution in Chapter eleven cases, see 11 USCA § 1143.

Distribution of property of estate, see 11 USCA § 726.

§ 751. Customer name securities

The trustee shall deliver any customer name security to or on behalf of the customer entitled to such security, unless such customer has a negative net equity. With the approval of the trustee, a customer may reclaim a customer name security after payment to the trustee, within such period as the trustee allows, of any claim of the debtor against such customer to the extent that such customer will not have a negative net equity after such payment.

(Pub.L. 95–598, Nov. 6, 1978, 92 Stat. 2614.)

HISTORICAL AND STATUTORY NOTES

Revision Notes and Legislative Reports

1978 Acts. Section 751 requires the trustee to deliver a customer name security to the customer entitled to such security unless the customer has a negative net equity. The customer's net equity will be negative when the amount owed by the customer to the stockbroker exceeds the liquidation value of the non-customer name securities in the customer's account. If the customer is a net debtor of the stockbroker, then the trustee may permit the customer to repay debts to the stockbroker so that the customer will no longer be in debt to the stockbroker. If the customer refuses to pay such amount, then the court may order the customer to endorse the security in order that the trustee may liquidate such property. Senate Report No. 95–989.

§ 752. Customer property

(a) The trustee shall distribute customer property ratably to customers on the basis and to the extent of such customers' allowed net equity claims and in priority to all other claims, except claims of the kind specified in section 507(a)(2) of this title that are attributable to the administration of such customer property.

(b)(1) The trustee shall distribute customer property in excess of that distributed under subsection (a) of this section in accordance with section 726 of this title.

(2) Except as provided in section 510 of this title, if a customer is not paid the full amount of such customer's allowed net equity claim from customer property, the unpaid portion of such claim is a claim entitled to distribution under section 726 of this title.

(c) Any cash or security remaining after the liquidation of a security interest created under a security agreement made by the debtor, excluding property excluded under section 741(4)(B) of this title, shall be apportioned between the general estate and customer property in the same proportion as the general estate of the debtor and customer property were subject to such security interest.

(Pub.L. 95–598, Nov. 6, 1978, 92 Stat. 2614; Pub.L. 97–222, § 15, July 27, 1982, 96 Stat. 238; Pub.L. 98–353, Title III, § 484, July 10, 1984, 98 Stat. 383; Pub.L. 109–8, Title XV, § 1502(a)(3), Apr. 20, 2005, 119 Stat. 216.)

HISTORICAL AND STATUTORY NOTES

Revision Notes and Legislative Reports

1978 Acts. Section 752(a) requires the trustee to distribute customer property to customers based on the amount of their net equity claims. Customer property is to be distributed in priority to all claims except expenses of administration entitled to priority under § 507(1). It is anticipated that the court will apportion such administrative claims on an equitable basis between the general estate and the customer property of the debtor.

Subsection (b)(1) indicates that in the event customer property exceeds customers net equity claims and administrative expenses, the excess pours over into the general estate. This event would occur if the value of securities increased dramatically after the order for relief but before liquidation by the trustee. Subsection (b)(2) indicates that the unpaid portion of a customer's net equity claim is entitled to share in the general estate as an unsecured claim unless subordinated by the court under proposed 11 U.S.C. 501. A net equity claim of a customer that is subordinated under section 747 is entitled to share in distribution under section 726(a)(2) unless subordinated under section 510 independently of the subordination under section 747.

Subsection (c) provides for apportionment between customer property and the general estate of any equity of the debtor in property remaining after a secured creditor liquidates a security interest. This might occur if a stockbroker hypothecates securities of his own and of his customers if the value of the hypothecated securities exceeds the debt owed to the secured party. The apportionment is to be made according to the ratio of customer property and general property of the debtor that comprised the collateral. The subsection refers to cash and securities of customers to include any customer property unlawfully converted by the stockbroker in the course of such a transaction. The apportionment is made subject to section 741(4)(B) to insure that property in a customer's account that is owed to the stockbroker will not be considered customer property. This recognizes the right of the stockbroker to withdraw money that has been erroneously placed in a customer's account or that is otherwise owing to the stockbroker. Senate Report No. 95–989.

1982 Acts. House Report No. 97–420, see 1982 U.S.Code Cong. and Adm.News, p. 583.

1984 Acts. Statements by Legislative Leaders, see 1984 U.S.Code Cong. and Adm.News, p. 576.

2005 Acts. House Report No. 109–31(Part I), see 2005 U.S. Code Cong. and Adm. News, p. 88.

Codifications

Amendment by section 484(a)(3) of Pub.L. 98–353, directing that subsec. (a) of this section be amended by inserting "such" before "customer property", has been executed by inserting "such" before "customer property" following "the administration of" as the probable intent of Congress.

Effective and Applicability Provisions

2005 Acts. Amendments by Pub.L. 109–8 effective, except as otherwise provided, 180 days after April 20, 2005, and inapplicable with respect to cases commenced under Title 11 before the effective date, see Pub.L. 109–8, § 1501, set out as a note under 11 U.S.C.A. § 101.

1984 Acts. Amendment by Pub.L. 98–353 effective with respect to cases filed 90 days after July 10, 1984, see section 552(a), formerly 553(a), of Pub.L. 98–353, set out as a note under section 101 of this title.

CROSS REFERENCES

Distribution in Chapter eleven cases, see 11 USCA § 1143.

Distribution of—

Customer property in commodity broker liquidation cases, see 11 USCA § 766.

Property of the estate, see 11 USCA § 726.

Election of trustee by creditors holding claims entitled to distribution, see 11 USCA § 702.

Priorities, see 11 USCA § 507.

§ 753. Stockbroker liquidation and forward contract merchants, commodity brokers, stockbrokers, financial institutions, financial participants, securities clearing agencies, swap participants, repo participants, and master netting agreement participants

Notwithstanding any other provision of this title, the exercise of rights by a forward contract merchant, commodity broker, stockbroker, financial institution, financial participant, securities clearing agency, swap participant, repo participant, or master netting agreement participant under this title shall not affect the priority of any unsecured claim it may have after the exercise of such rights.

(Added Pub.L. 109–8, Title IX, § 907(m), Apr. 20, 2005, 119 Stat. 181.)

HISTORICAL AND STATUTORY NOTES

Revision Notes and Legislative Reports

2005 Acts. House Report No. 109–31(Part I), see 2005 U.S. Code Cong. and Adm. News, p. 88.

Effective and Applicability Provisions

2005 Acts. Amendments by Pub.L. 109–8 effective, except as otherwise provided, 180 days after April 20, 2005, and inapplicable with respect to cases commenced under Title 11 before the effective date, see Pub.L. 109–8, § 1501, set out as a note under 11 U.S.C.A. § 101.

SUBCHAPTER IV—COMMODITY BROKER LIQUIDATION

CROSS REFERENCES

Certain terms defined under this section as having same meaning for purposes of Commodity Exchange Act, see 7 USCA § 24.

Powers and duties of trustee in investor liquidation proceedings, see 15 USCA § 78fff–1.

Subchapter generally applicable only in case under chapter concerning commodity broker, see 11 USCA § 103.

§ 761. Definitions for this subchapter

In this subchapter—

(1) "Act" means Commodity Exchange Act;

(2) "clearing organization" means a derivatives clearing organization registered under the Act;

(3) "Commission" means Commodity Futures Trading Commission;

(4) "commodity contract" means—

(A) with respect to a futures commission merchant, contract for the purchase or sale of a commodity for future delivery on, or subject to the rules of, a contract market or board of trade;

(B) with respect to a foreign futures commission merchant, foreign future;

(C) with respect to a leverage transaction merchant, leverage transaction;

(D) with respect to a clearing organization, contract for the purchase or sale of a commodity for future delivery on, or subject to the rules of, a contract market or board of trade that is cleared by such clearing organization, or commodity option traded on, or subject to the rules of, a contract market or board of trade that is cleared by such clearing organization;

(E) with respect to a commodity options dealer, commodity option;

(F) any other agreement or transaction that is similar to an agreement or transaction referred to in this paragraph;

(G) any combination of the agreements or transactions referred to in this paragraph;

(H) any option to enter into an agreement or transaction referred to in this paragraph;

(I) a master agreement that provides for an agreement or transaction referred to in subparagraph (A), (B), (C), (D), (E), (F), (G), or (H), together with all supplements to such master agreement, without regard to whether the master agreement provides for an agreement or transaction that is not a commodity contract under this paragraph, except that the master agreement shall be considered to be a commodity contract under this paragraph only with respect to each agreement or transaction under the master agreement that is referred to in subparagraph (A), (B), (C), (D), (E), (F), (G), or (H); or

(J) any security agreement or arrangement or other credit enhancement related to any agreement or transaction referred to in this paragraph, including any guarantee or reimbursement obligation by or to a commodity broker or financial participant in connection with any agreement or transaction referred to in this paragraph, but not to exceed the damages in connection with any such agreement or transaction, measured in accordance with section 562;

(5) "commodity option" means agreement or transaction subject to regulation under section 4c(b) of the Act;

(6) "commodity options dealer" means person that extends credit to, or that accepts cash, a security, or other property from, a customer of such person for the purchase or sale of an interest in a commodity option;

(7) "contract market" means a registered entity;

(8) "contract of sale", "commodity", "derivatives clearing organization" , "future delivery", "board of trade", "registered entity", and "futures commission merchant" have the meanings assigned to those terms in the Act;

(9) "customer" means—

(A) with respect to a futures commission merchant—

(i) entity for or with whom such futures commission merchant deals and that holds a claim against such futures commission merchant on account of a commodity contract made, received, acquired, or held by or through such futures commission merchant in the ordinary course of such futures commission merchant's business as a futures commission merchant from or for the commodity futures account of such entity; or

(ii) entity that holds a claim against such futures commission merchant arising out of—

(I) the making, liquidation, or change in the value of a commodity contract of a kind specified in clause (i) of this subparagraph;

(II) a deposit or payment of cash, a security, or other property with such futures commission merchant for the purpose of making or margining such a commodity contract; or

(III) the making or taking of delivery on such a commodity contract;

(B) with respect to a foreign futures commission merchant—

(i) entity for or with whom such foreign futures commission merchant deals and that holds a claim against such foreign futures commission merchant on account of a commodity contract made, received, acquired, or held by or through such foreign futures commission merchant in the ordinary course of such foreign futures commission merchant's business as a foreign futures commission merchant from or for the foreign futures account of such entity; or

(ii) entity that holds a claim against such foreign futures commission merchant arising out of—

(I) the making, liquidation, or change in value of a commodity contract of a kind specified in clause (i) of this subparagraph;

(II) a deposit or payment of cash, a security, or other property with such foreign futures commission merchant for the purpose of making or margining such a commodity contract; or

(III) the making or taking of delivery on such a commodity contract;

(C) with respect to a leverage transaction merchant—

(i) entity for or with whom such leverage transaction merchant deals and that holds a claim against such leverage transaction merchant on account of a commodity contract engaged in by or with such leverage transaction merchant in the ordinary course of such leverage transaction merchant's business as a leverage transaction merchant from or for the leverage account of such entity; or

(ii) entity that holds a claim against such leverage transaction merchant arising out of—

(I) the making, liquidation, or change in value of a commodity contract of a kind specified in clause (i) of this subparagraph;

(II) a deposit or payment of cash, a security, or other property with such leverage transaction merchant for the purpose of entering into or margining such a commodity contract; or

(III) the making or taking of delivery on such a commodity contract;

(D) with respect to a clearing organization, clearing member of such clearing organization with whom such clearing organization deals and that holds a claim against such clearing organization on account of cash, a security, or other property received by such clearing organization to margin, guarantee, or secure a commodity contract in such clearing member's proprietary account or customers' account; or

(E) with respect to a commodity options dealer—

(i) entity for or with whom such commodity options dealer deals and that holds a claim on account of a commodity contract made, received, acquired, or held by or through such commodity options dealer in the ordinary course of such commodity options dealer's business as a commodity options dealer from or for the commodity options account of such entity; or

(ii) entity that holds a claim against such commodity options dealer arising out of—

(I) the making of, liquidation of, exercise of, or a change in value of, a commodity contract of a kind specified in clause (i) of this subparagraph; or

(II) a deposit or payment of cash, a security, or other property with such commodity options dealer for the purpose of making, exercising, or margining such a commodity contract;

(10) "customer property" means cash, a security, or other property, or proceeds of such cash, security, or property, received, acquired, or held by or for the account of the debtor, from or for the account of a customer—

(A) including—

(i) property received, acquired, or held to margin, guarantee, secure, purchase, or sell a commodity contract;

(ii) profits or contractual or other rights accruing to a customer as a result of a commodity contract;

(iii) an open commodity contract;

(iv) specifically identifiable customer property;

(v) warehouse receipt or other document held by the debtor evidencing ownership of or title to property to be delivered to fulfill a commodity contract from or for the account of a customer;

(vi) cash, a security, or other property received by the debtor as payment for a commodity to be delivered to fulfill a commodity contract from or for the account of a customer;

(vii) a security held as property of the debtor to the extent such security is necessary to meet a net equity claim based on a security of the same class and series of an issuer;

(viii) property that was unlawfully converted from and that is the lawful property of the estate; and

(ix) other property of the debtor that any applicable law, rule, or regulation requires to be set aside or held for the benefit of a customer, unless including such property as customer property would not significantly increase customer property; but

(B) not including property to the extent that a customer does not have a claim against the debtor based on such property;

(11) "foreign future" means contract for the purchase or sale of a commodity for future delivery on, or subject to the rules of, a board of trade outside the United States;

(12) "foreign futures commission merchant" means entity engaged in soliciting or accepting orders for the purchase or sale of a foreign future or that, in connection with such a solicitation or acceptance, accepts cash, a security, or other property, or extends credit to margin, guarantee, or secure any trade or contract that results from such a solicitation or acceptance;

(13) "leverage transaction" means agreement that is subject to regulation under section 19 of the Commodity Exchange Act, and that is commonly known to the commodities trade as a margin account, margin contract, leverage account, or leverage contract;

(14) "leverage transaction merchant" means person in the business of engaging in leverage transactions;

(15) "margin payment" means payment or deposit of cash, a security, or other property, that is commonly known to the commodities trade as original margin, initial margin, maintenance margin, or variation margin, including mark-to-market payments, settlement payments, variation payments, daily settlement payments, and final settlement payments made as adjustments to settlement prices;

(16) "member property" means customer property received, acquired, or held by or for the account of a debtor that is a clearing organization, from or for the proprietary account of a customer that is a clearing member of the debtor; and

(17) "net equity" means, subject to such rules and regulations as the Commission promulgates under the Act, with respect to the aggregate of all of a customer's accounts that such customer has in the same capacity—

(A) the balance remaining in such customer's accounts immediately after—

(i) all commodity contracts of such customer have been transferred, liquidated, or become identified for delivery; and

(ii) all obligations of such customer in such capacity to the debtor have been offset; plus

(B) the value, as of the date of return under section 766 of this title, of any specifically identifiable customer property actually returned to such customer before the date specified in subparagraph (A) of this paragraph; plus

(C) the value, as of the date of transfer, of—

(i) any commodity contract to which such customer is entitled that is transferred to another person under section 766 of this title; and

(ii) any cash, security, or other property of such customer transferred to such other person under section 766 of this title to margin or secure such transferred commodity contract.

(Pub.L. 95–598, Nov. 6, 1978, 92 Stat. 2615; Pub.L. 97–222, § 16, July 27, 1982, 96 Stat. 238; Pub.L. 98–353, Title III, § 485, July 10, 1984, 98 Stat. 383; Pub.L. 103–394, Title V, § 501(d)(29), Oct. 22, 1994, 108 Stat. 4146; Pub.L. 106–554, § 1(a)(5) [Title I, § 112(c)(6)], Dec. 21, 2000, 114 Stat. 2763, 2763A–395; Pub.L. 109–8, Title IX, § 907(a)(3), Apr. 20, 2005, 119 Stat. 174.)

HISTORICAL AND STATUTORY NOTES

Revision Notes and Legislative Reports

1978 Acts. Paragraph (1) defines "Act" to mean the Commodity Exchange Act [7 U.S.C.A. § 1 et seq.].

Paragraph (2) defines "clearing organization" to mean an organization that clears (i.e., matches purchases and sales) commodity futures contracts made on or subject to the rules of a contract market or commodity options transactions made on or subject to the rules of a commodity option exchange. Although commodity option trading on exchanges is currently prohibited, it is anticipated that CFTC may permit such trading in the future.

Paragraphs (3) and (4) define terms "Commission" and "commodity futures contract".

Paragraph (5) defines "commodity contract" to mean a commodity futures contract (§ 761(4)), a commodity option (§ 761(6)), or a leverage contract (§ 761(15)).

Paragraph (b) [probably should be "(6)" defines "commodity option" by reference to section 4c(b) of the Commodity Exchange Act [7 U.S.C.A. § 6c(b)].

Paragraphs (7), (8), and (9), define "commodity options dealer," "contract market," "contract of sale," "commodity," "future delivery," "board of trade," and "futures commission merchant."

Paragraph (10) defines the term "customer" to mean with respect to a futures commission merchant or a foreign futures commission merchant, the entity for whom the debtor carries a commodity futures contract or foreign future, or with whom such a contract is carried (such as another commodity broker), or from whom the debtor has received, acquired, or holds cash, securities, or other property arising out of or connected with specified transactions involving commodity futures contracts or foreign futures. This section also defines "customer" in the context of leverage transaction merchants, clearing organizations, and commodity options dealers. Persons associated with a commodity broker, such as its employees, officers, or partners, may be customers under this definition.

The definition of "customer" serves to isolate that class of persons entitled to the protection subchapter IV provides to customers. In addition, section 101(5) defines "commodity broker" to mean a futures commission merchant, foreign futures commission merchant, clearing organization, leverage transaction merchant, or commodity options dealer, with respect to which there is a customer. Accordingly, the definition of customer also serves to designate those entities which must utilize chapter 7 and are precluded from reorganizing under chapter 11.

Paragraph (11) defines "customer property" to mean virtually all property or proceeds thereof, received, acquired, or held by or for the account of the debtor for a customer arising out of or in connection with a transaction involving a commodity contract.

Paragraph (12) defines "distribution share" to mean the amount to which a customer is entitled under section 765(a).

Paragraphs (13), (14), (15), and (16), define "foreign future," "foreign futures commission merchant," "leverage transaction," and "leverage transaction merchant."

Paragraph (17) defines "margin payment" to mean a payment or deposit commonly known to the commodities trade as original margin, initial margin, or variation margin.

Paragraph (18) defines "member property."

Paragraph (19) defines "net equity" to be the sum of (A) the value of all customer property remaining in a customer's account immediately after all commodity contracts of such customer have been transferred, liquidated, or become identified for delivery and all obligations of such customer to the debtor have been offset (such as margin payments, whether or not called, and brokerage commissions) plus (B) the value of specifically identifiable customer property previously returned to the customer by the trustee, plus (C) if the trustee has transferred any commodity contract to which the customer is entitled or any margin or security for such contract, the value of such contract and margin or security. Net equity, therefore, will be the total amount of customer property to which a customer is entitled as of the date of the filing of the bankruptcy petition, although valued at subsequent dates. The Commission is given authority to promulgate rules and regulations to further refine this definition. Senate Report No. 95–989.

Paragraph (8) is a dynamic definition of "contractual commitment". The definition will vary depending on the character of the debtor in each case. If the debtor is a futures commission merchant or a clearing organization, then subparagraphs (A) and (D) indicate that the definition means a contract of sale of a commodity for future delivery on a contract market. If the debtor is a foreign futures commission merchant, a leverage transaction merchant, or a commodity options dealer, then subparagraphs (B), (C), and (E) indicate that the definition means foreign future, leverage transaction, or commodity option, respectively.

Paragraph (9) defines "customer" in a similar style. It is anticipated that a debtor with multifaceted characteristics will have separate estates for each different kind of customer. Thus, a debtor that is a leverage transaction merchant and a commodity options dealer would have separate estates for the leverage transaction customers and for the options customers, and a general estate for other creditors. Customers for each kind of commodity broker, except the clearing organization, arise from either of two relationships. In subparagraphs (A), (B), (C), and (E), clause (i) treats with customers to the extent of contractual commitments with the debtor in either a broker or a dealer relationship. Clause (ii) treats with customers to the extent of proceeds from contractual commitments or deposits for the purpose of making contractual commitments. The customer of the clearing organization is a member with a proprietary or customers' account.

Paragraph (10) defines "customer property" to include all property in customer accounts and property that should have been in those accounts but was diverted through conversion or mistake. Clause (i) refers to customer property not properly segregated by the debtor or customer property converted and then recovered so as to become property of the estate. Clause (vii) is intended to exclude property that would cost more to recover from a third party than the value of the property itself. Subparagraph (B) excludes property in a customer's account that belongs to the commodity broker, such as a contract placed in the account by error, or cash due the broker for a margin payment that the broker has made.

Paragraph (15) defines "net equity" to include the value of all contractual commitments at the time of liquidation or transfer less any obligations owed by the customer to the debtor, such as brokerage fees. In addition, the term includes the value of any specifically identifiable property as of the date of return to the customer and the value of any customer property transferred to another commodity broker as of the date of transfer. This definition places the risk of market fluctuations on the customer until commitments leave the estate. House Report No. 95–595.

1982 Acts. House Report No. 97–420, see 1982 U.S.Code Cong. and Adm.News, p. 583.

1984 Acts. Statements by Legislative Leaders, see 1984 U.S.Code Cong. and Adm.News, p. 576.

1994 Acts. House Report No. 103–835, see 1994 U.S. Code Cong. and Adm. News, p. 3340.

2000 Acts. House Report No. 106–645 and Statement by President, see 2000 U.S. Code Cong. and Adm. News, p. 2459.

2005 Acts. House Report No. 109–31(Part I), see 2005 U.S. Code Cong. and Adm. News, p. 88.

Legislative Statements

Subchapter IV of chapter 7 represents a compromise between similar chapters in the House bill and Senate amendment. Section 761(2) of the House amendment defines "clearing organization" to cover an organization that clears commodity contracts on a contract market or a board of trade; the expansion of the definition is intended to include clearing organizations that clear commodity options. Section 761(4) of the House amendment adopts the term "commodity contract" as used in section 761(5) of the Senate amendment but with the more precise substantive definitions contained in section 761(8) of the House bill. The definition is modified to insert "board of trade" to cover commodity options. Section 761(5) of the House amendment adopts the definition contained in section 761(6) of the Senate amendment in preference to the definition contained in section 761(4) of the House bill which erroneously included onions. Section 761(9) of the House amendment represents a compromise between similar provisions contained in section 761(10) of the Senate amendment and section 761(9) of the House bill. The compromise adopts the substance contained in the House bill and adopts the terminology of "commodity contract" in lieu of "contractual commitment" as suggested in the Senate amendment. Section 761(10) of the House amendment represents a compromise between similar sections in the House bill and Senate amendment regarding the definition of "customer property." The definition of "distribution share" contained in section 761(12) of the Senate amendment is deleted as unnecessary. Section 761(12) of the House amendment adopts a definition of "foreign futures commission merchant" similar to the definition contained in section 761(14) of the Senate amendment. The definition is modified to cover either an entity engaged in soliciting orders or the purchase or sale of a foreign future, or an entity that accepts cash, a security, or other property for credit in connection with such a solicitation or acceptance. Section 761(13) of the House amendment adopts a definition of "leverage transaction" identical to the definition contained in section 761(15) of the Senate amendment. Section 761(15) of the House amendment adopts the definition of "margin payment" contained in section 761(17) of the Senate amendment. Section 761(17) of the House amendment adopts a definition of "net equity" derived from section 761(15) of the House bill.

References in Text

The Commodity Exchange Act or the Act, referred to in pars. (1), (8), and (17), is Act Sept. 21, 1922, c. 369, 42 Stat. 998, as amended, which is classified generally to chapter 1 (section 1 et seq.) of Title 7, Agriculture. For complete classification of this Act to the Code, see section 1 of Title 7 and Tables.

Section 4c of the Commodity Exchange Act, referred to in par. (5), is section 4c of Act Sept. 21, 1922, c. 369, as added June 15, 1936, c. 545, § 5, 49 Stat. 1494, which is classified to section 6c of Title 7, Agriculture.

Section 19 of the Commodity Exchange Act, referred to in par. (13), is section 19 of Act Sept. 21, 1922, c. 369, as added Sept. 30, 1978, Pub.L. 95–405, § 23, 92 Stat. 876, which is classified to section 23 of Title 7.

Effective and Applicability Provisions

2005 Acts. Amendments by Pub.L. 109–8 effective, except as otherwise provided, 180 days after April 20, 2005, and inapplicable with respect to cases commenced under Title 11 before the effective date, see Pub.L. 109–8, § 1501, set out as a note under 11 U.S.C.A. § 101.

1994 Acts. Amendment by Pub.L. 103–394 effective on Oct. 22, 1994, and not to apply with respect to cases commenced under Title 11 of the United States Code before Oct. 22, 1994, see section 702 of Pub.L. 103–394, set out as a note under section 101 of this title.

1984 Acts. Amendment by Pub.L. 98–353 effective with respect to cases filed 90 days after July 10, 1984, see section 552(a), formerly 553(a), of Pub.L. 98–353, set out as a note under section 101 of this title.

Separability of Provisions

If any provision of or amendment made by Pub.L. 103–394 or the application of such provision or amendment to any person or circumstance is held to be unconstitutional, the remaining provisions of and amendments made by Pub.L. 103–394 and the application of such provisions and amendments to any person or circumstance shall not be affected thereby, see section 701 of Pub.L. 103–394, set out as a note under section 101 of this title.

CROSS REFERENCES

Certain terms having same meanings as under this section, see 7 USCA § 24.

Commodity broker defined, see 11 USCA § 101.

"Commodity contract" defined under this section as having same meaning for purposes of Federal deposit insurance corporation, see 12 USCA § 1821.

Contractual right to liquidate "commodity contract" as defined under this section not stayed, avoided or limited by operation of any provision of this title, see 11 USCA § 556.

Definitions applicable in—

Chapter eleven cases, see 11 USCA § 1101.

Chapter nine cases, see 11 USCA § 902.

Railroad reorganization cases, see 11 USCA § 1162.

Stockbroker liquidation cases, see 11 USCA § 741.

Limitation on power of trustee to avoid transfer of "margin payment" as defined in this section, see 11 USCA § 546.

Reception of margin payments by commodity brokers or forward contract merchants as taking for value, see 11 USCA § 548.

Setoff of mutual debt in connection with "commodity contracts" or "margin payment" not stayed by filing of petitions for voluntary cases, joint cases or involuntary cases or protective decrees in investor protection liquidation proceedings, see 11 USCA § 362.

§ 762. Notice to the Commission and right to be heard

(a) The clerk shall give the notice required by section 342 of this title to the Commission.

(b) The Commission may raise and may appear and be heard on any issue in a case under this chapter.

(Pub.L. 95–598, Nov. 6, 1978, 92 Stat. 2618.)

HISTORICAL AND STATUTORY NOTES

Revision Notes and Legislative Reports

1978 Acts. Section 762 provides that the Commission shall be given such notice as is appropriate of an order for relief in a bankruptcy case and that the Commission may raise and may appear and may be heard on any issue in case involving a commodity broker liquidation. Senate Report No. 95–989.

CROSS REFERENCES

Notice in—

Chapter nine cases, see 11 USCA § 923.

Stockbroker liquidation proceedings, see 11 USCA § 743.

§ 763. Treatment of accounts

(a) Accounts held by the debtor for a particular customer in separate capacities shall be treated as accounts of separate customers.

(b) A member of a clearing organization shall be deemed to hold such member's proprietary account in a separate capacity from such member's customers' account.

(c) The net equity in a customer's account may not be offset against the net equity in the account of any other customer.

(Pub.L. 95–598, Nov. 6, 1978, 92 Stat. 2618; Pub.L. 98–353, Title III, § 486, July 10, 1984, 98 Stat. 383.)

HISTORICAL AND STATUTORY NOTES

Revision Notes and Legislative Reports

1978 Acts. Section 763 provides for separate treatment of accounts held in separate capacities. A deficit in one account held for a customer may not be offset against the net equity in another account held by the same customer in a separate capacity or held by another customer. Senate Report No. 95–989.

1984 Acts. Statements by Legislative Leaders, see 1984 U.S.Code Cong. and Adm.News, p. 576.

Effective and Applicability Provisions

1984 Acts. Amendment by Pub.L. 98–353 effective with respect to cases filed 90 days after July 10, 1984, see section 552(a), formerly 553(a), of Pub.L. 98–353, set out as a note under section 101 of this title.

CROSS REFERENCES

Treatment of accounts in stockbroker liquidation cases, see 11 USCA § 745.

§ 764. Voidable transfers

(a) Except as otherwise provided in this section, any transfer by the debtor of property that, but for such transfer, would have been customer property, may be avoided by the trustee, and such property shall be treated as customer property, if and to the extent that the trustee avoids such transfer under section 544, 545, 547, 548, 549, or 724(a) of this title. For the purpose of such sections, the property so transferred shall be deemed to have been property of the debtor, and, if such transfer was made to a customer or for a customer's benefit, such customer shall be deemed, for the purposes of this section, to have been a creditor.

(b) Notwithstanding sections 544, 545, 547, 548, 549, and 724(a) of this title, the trustee may not avoid a transfer made before five days after the order for relief, if such transfer is approved by the Commission by rule or order, either before or after such transfer, and if such transfer is—

(1) a transfer of a commodity contract entered into or carried by or through the debtor on behalf of

a customer, and of any cash, securities, or other property margining or securing such commodity contract; or

(2) the liquidation of a commodity contract entered into or carried by or through the debtor on behalf of a customer.

(Pub.L. 95–598, Nov. 6, 1978, 92 Stat. 2618; Pub.L. 97–222, § 17, July 27, 1982, 96 Stat. 240; Pub.L. 98–353, Title III, § 487, July 10, 1984, 98 Stat. 383.)

HISTORICAL AND STATUTORY NOTES

Revision Notes and Legislative Reports

1978 Acts. Section 764 permits the trustee to void any transfer of property that, except for such transfer, would have been customer property, to the extent permitted under section 544, 545, 547, 548, 549, or 724(a). Senate Report No. 95–989.

Section 764 indicates the extent to which the avoiding powers may be used by the trustee under subchapter IV of chapter 7. If property recovered would have been customer property if never transferred, then subsection (a) indicates that it will be so treated when recovered.

Subsection (b) prohibits avoiding any transaction that occurs before or within five days after the petition if the transaction is approved by the Commission and concerns an open contractual commitment. This enables the Commission to exercise its discretion to protect the integrity of the market by insuring that transactions cleared with other brokers will not be undone on a preference or a fraudulent transfer theory.

Subsection (c) insulates variation margin payments and other deposits from the avoiding powers except to the extent of actual fraud under section 548(a)(1). This facilitates prepetition transfers and protects the ordinary course of business in the market. House Report No. 95–595.

1982 Acts. House Report No. 97–420, see 1982 U.S.Code Cong. and Adm.News, p. 583.

1984 Acts. Statements by Legislative Leaders, see 1984 U.S.Code Cong. and Adm.News, p. 576.

Legislative Statements

Section 764 of the House amendment is derived from the House bill.

Effective and Applicability Provisions

1984 Acts. Amendment by Pub.L. 98–353 effective with respect to cases filed 90 days after July 10, 1984, see section 552(a), formerly 553(a), of Pub.L. 98–353, set out as a note under section 101 of this title.

CROSS REFERENCES

Voidable transfers in stockbroker liquidation cases, see 11 USCA § 749.

§ 765. Customer instructions

(a) The notice required by section 342 of this title to customers shall instruct each customer—

(1) to file a proof of such customer's claim promptly, and to specify in such claim any specifically identifiable security, property, or commodity contract; and

(2) to instruct the trustee of such customer's desired disposition, including transfer under section 766 of this title or liquidation, of any commodity contract specifically identified to such customer.

(b) The trustee shall comply, to the extent practicable, with any instruction received from a customer regarding such customer's desired disposition of any commodity contract specifically identified to such customer. If the trustee has transferred, under section 766 of this title, such a commodity contract, the trustee shall transmit any such instruction to the commodity broker to whom such commodity contract was so transferred.

(Pub.L. 95–598, Nov. 6, 1978, 92 Stat. 2619; Pub.L. 97–222, § 18, July 27, 1982, 96 Stat. 240; Pub.L. 98–353, Title III, § 488, July 10, 1984, 98 Stat. 383.)

HISTORICAL AND STATUTORY NOTES

Revision Notes and Legislative Reports

1978 Acts. For Revision Notes and Legislative Reports for this section, see Revision Notes and Legislative Reports set out under section 766 of this title.

1982 Acts. House Report No. 97–420, see 1982 U.S.Code Cong. and Adm.News, p. 583.

1984 Acts. Statements by Legislative Leaders, see 1984 U.S.Code Cong. and Adm.News, p. 576.

Effective and Applicability Provisions

1984 Acts. Amendment by Pub.L. 98–353 effective with respect to cases filed 90 days after July 10, 1984, see section 552(a), formerly 553(a), of Pub.L. 98–353, set out as a note under section 101 of this title.

CROSS REFERENCES

Executory contracts and unexpired leases, see 11 USCA § 365.

§ 766. Treatment of customer property

(a) The trustee shall answer all margin calls with respect to a specifically identifiable commodity contract of a customer until such time as the trustee returns or transfers such commodity contract, but the trustee may not make a margin payment that has the effect of a distribution to such customer of more than that to which such customer is entitled under subsection (h) or (i) of this section.

(b) The trustee shall prevent any open commodity contract from remaining open after the last day of trading in such commodity contract, or into the first day on which notice of intent to deliver on such commodity contract may be tendered, whichever occurs first. With respect to any commodity contract that has remained open after the last day of trading in such commodity contract or with respect to which delivery must be made or accepted under the rules of the contract market on which such commodity contract was made, the trustee may operate the business of the debtor for the purpose of—

(1) accepting or making tender of notice of intent to deliver the physical commodity underlying such commodity contract;

(2) facilitating delivery of such commodity; or

(3) disposing of such commodity if a party to such commodity contract defaults.

(c) The trustee shall return promptly to a customer any specifically identifiable security, property, or commodity contract to which such customer is entitled, or shall transfer, on such customer's behalf, such security, property, or commodity contract to a commodity broker that is not a debtor under this title, subject to such rules or regulations as the Commission may prescribe, to the extent that the value of such security, property, or commodity contract does not exceed the amount to which such customer would be entitled under subsection (h) or (i) of this section if such security, property, or commodity contract were not returned or transferred under this subsection.

(d) If the value of a specifically identifiable security, property, or commodity contract exceeds the amount to which the customer of the debtor is entitled under subsection (h) or (i) of this section, then such customer to whom such security, property, or commodity contract is specifically identified may deposit cash with the trustee equal to the difference between the value of such security, property, or commodity contract and such amount, and the trustee then shall—

(1) return promptly such security, property, or commodity contract to such customer; or

(2) transfer, on such customer's behalf, such security, property, or commodity contract to a commodity broker that is not a debtor under this title, subject to such rules or regulations as the Commission may prescribe.

(e) Subject to subsection (b) of this section, the trustee shall liquidate any commodity contract that—

(1) is identified to a particular customer and with respect to which such customer has not timely instructed the trustee as to the desired disposition of such commodity contract;

(2) cannot be transferred under subsection (c) of this section; or

(3) cannot be identified to a particular customer.

(f) As soon as practicable after the commencement of the case, the trustee shall reduce to money, consistent with good market practice, all securities and other property, other than commodity contracts, held as property of the estate, except for specifically identifiable securities or property distributable under subsection (h) or (i) of this section.

(g) The trustee may not distribute a security or other property except under subsection (h) or (i) of this section.

(h) Except as provided in subsection (b) of this section, the trustee shall distribute customer property ratably to customers on the basis and to the extent of such customers' allowed net equity claims, and in priority to all other claims, except claims of a kind specified in section 507(a)(2) of this title that are attributable to the administration of customer property. Such distribution shall be in the form of—

(1) cash;

(2) the return or transfer, under subsection (c) or (d) of this section, of specifically identifiable customer securities, property, or commodity contracts; or

(3) payment of margin calls under subsection (a) of this section.

Notwithstanding any other provision of this subsection, a customer net equity claim based on a proprietary account, as defined by Commission rule, regulation, or order, may not be paid either in whole or in part, directly or indirectly, out of customer property unless all other customer net equity claims have been paid in full.

(i) If the debtor is a clearing organization, the trustee shall distribute—

(1) customer property, other than member property, ratably to customers on the basis and to the extent of such customers' allowed net equity claims based on such customers' accounts other than proprietary accounts, and in priority to all other claims, except claims of a kind specified in section 507(a)(2) of this title that are attributable to the administration of such customer property; and

(2) member property ratably to customers on the basis and to the extent of such customers' allowed net equity claims based on such customers' proprietary accounts, and in priority to all other claims, except claims of a kind specified in section 507(a)(2) of this title that are attributable to the administration of member property or customer property.

(j)(1) The trustee shall distribute customer property in excess of that distributed under subsection (h) or (i) of this section in accordance with section 726 of this title.

(2) Except as provided in section 510 of this title, if a customer is not paid the full amount of such customer's allowed net equity claim from customer property, the unpaid portion of such claim is a claim entitled to distribution under section 726 of this title.

(Pub.L. 95–598, Nov. 6, 1978, 92 Stat. 2619; Pub.L. 97–222, § 19, July 27, 1982, 96 Stat. 240; Pub.L. 98–353, Title III, § 489, July 10, 1984, 98 Stat. 383; Pub.L. 109–8, Title XV, § 1502(a)(4), Apr. 20, 2005, 119 Stat. 216.)

HISTORICAL AND STATUTORY NOTES

Revision Notes and Legislative Reports

1978 Acts. [Section 765] Subsection (a) of this section [now section 766(h)] provides that with respect to liquidation of commodity brokers which are not clearing organizations, the trustee shall distribute customer property to customers on the basis and to the extent of such customers' allowed net equity claims, and in priority to all other claims. This section grants customers' claims first priority in the distribution of the estate. Subsection (b) [now section 766(i)] grants the same priority to member property and other customer property in the liquidation of a clearing organization. A fundamental purpose of these provisions is to ensure that the property entrusted by customers to their brokers will not be subject to the risks of the broker's business and will be available for disbursement to customers if the broker becomes bankrupt.

As a result of section 765, a customer need not trace any funds in order to avoid treatment as a general creditor as was required by the Seventh Circuit in *In re Rosenbaum Grain Corporation.*

Section 766 lists certain transfers which are not voidable by the trustee of a commodity broker. Subsection (a) exempts transfers approved by the Commission by rule or order, either before or after the transfer. It is expected that the Commission will use this power sparingly and only when necessary to effectuate the remedial purposes of this legislation, bearing in mind that the immediate transfer of customer accounts from bankrupt commodity brokers to solvent commodity brokers is one of the primary goals of this subchapter. The committee considered and rejected a provision in subsection (b) that would have exempted payments made to a commodity broker. The Commission may not by rule exempt such transfers. The Commission's prompt attention to the promulgation of such rules and regulations is expected.

Subsection (b) [now section 764(c)] provides for the nonavoidability of margin payments made by a commodity broker, other than a clearing organization. If such payments are made by or to a clearing organization, they are nonavoidable pursuant to subsection (c). All other margin payments made by a commodity broker, other than a clearing organization, are nonavoidable if they meet the conditions set forth in subsection (b). Subsections (b)(1) and (b)(2) parallel the requirements for avoidance of fraudulent transfers and obligations under section 548. Subsection (b)(3) adds a requirement that there be collusion between the transferee and transferor in order for such payments to be voidable. It would be unfair to permit recovery from an innocent commodity broker since such brokers are, for the most part, simply conduits for margin payments and do not retain margin for use in their operations. Subsection (b)(4) would permit recovery of a subsequent transferee only if it had actual knowledge at the time of that subsequent transfer of the scheme to defraud. Again it should be noted that if the transfer is a margin payment and the subsequent transferee is a clearing organization, the transfer is nonavoidable under section 766(c).

Subsection (c) [now section 548(d)(2)] overrules *Seligson v. New York Produce Exchange*, and provides as a matter of law that margin payments made by or to a clearing organization are not voidable.

Section 767 sets forth the procedures to be followed by the trustee. It should be emphasized that many of the duties imposed on the trustee are required to be discharged by the trustee immediately upon his appointment. The earlier these duties are discharged the less potential market disruption can result.

The initial duty of the trustee is to endeavor to transfer to another commodity broker or brokers all identified customer accounts together with the customer property margining such accounts, to the extent the trustee deems appropriate. Although it is preferable for all such accounts to be transferred, exigencies may dictate a partial transfer. The requirement that the value of the accounts and property transferred not exceed the customer's distribution share may necessitate a slight delay until the trustee can submit to the court, for its disapproval, an estimate of each customer's distribution share pursuant to section 768.

Subsection (c) [now section 766(e)] provides that contemporaneously with the estimate of the distribution share and the transfer of identified customer accounts and property, subsection (c) provides that the trustee should make arrangements for the liquidation of all commodity contracts maintained by the debtor that are not identifiable to specific customers. These contracts would, of course, include all such contracts held in the debtor's proprietary account.

At approximately the same time, the trustee should notify each customer of the debtor's bankruptcy and instruct each customer immediately to submit a claim including any claim to a specifically identifiable security or other property, and advise the trustee as to the desired disposition of commodity contracts carried by the debtor for the customer.

This requirement is placed upon the trustee to insure that producers who have hedged their production in the commodities market are allowed the opportunity to preserve their positions. The theory of the commodity market is that it exists for producers and buyers of commodities and not for the benefit of the speculators whose transactions now comprise the overwhelming majority of trades. Maintenance of positions by hedges may require them to put up additional margin payments in the hours and days following the commodity broker bankruptcy, which they may be unable or unwilling to do. In such cases, their positions will be quickly liquidated by the trustee, but they must have the opportunity to make those margin payments before they are summarily liquidated out of the market to the detriment of their growing crop. The failure of the customer to advise the trustee as to disposition of the customer's commodity contract will not delay a transfer of a contract pursuant to subsection (b) so long as the contract can otherwise be identified to the customer. Nor will the failure of the customer to submit a claim prevent the customer from recovering the net equity in that customer's account, absent a claim the customer cannot participate in the determination of the net equity in the account.

If the customer submits instructions pursuant to subsection (a) after the customer's commodity contracts are transferred to another commodity broker, the trustee must transmit the instruction to the transferee. If the customer's commodity contracts are not transferred before the customer's instructions are received, the trustee must attempt to comply with the instruction, subject to the provisions of section 767(d).

Under subsection (d) [now section 766(e)], the trustee has discretion to liquidate any commodity contract carried by the debtor at any time. This discretion must be exercised with restraint in such cases, consistent with the purposes of this subchapter and good business practices. The committee intends that hedged accounts will be given special consideration before liquidation as discussed in connection with subsection (c).

Subsection (e) [now section 766(c)] instructs the trustee as to the disposition of any security or other property, not disposed of pursuant to subsection (b) or (d), that is specifically identifiable to a customer and to which the customer is entitled. Such security or other property must be returned to the customer or promptly transferred to another commodity broker for the benefit of the customer. If the value of the security or other property retained or transferred, together with any other distribution made by the trustee to or on behalf of the customer, exceeds the customer's distribution share the customer must deposit cash with the trustee equal to that difference before the return or transfer of the security or other property.

Subsection (f) [now section 766(a)] requires the trustee to answer margin calls on specifically identifiable customer commodity contracts, but only to the extent that the margin payment, together with any other distribution made by the trustee to or on behalf of the customer, does not exceed the customer's distribution share.

Subsection (g) [now section 766(b)] requires the trustee to liquidate all commodity futures contracts prior to the close of trading in that contract, or the first day on which notice of intent to deliver on that contract may be tendered, whichever occurs first. If the customer desires that the contract be kept open for delivery, the contract should be transferred to another commodity broker pursuant to subsection (b).

If for some reason the trustee is unable to transfer a contract on which delivery must be made or accepted and is unable to close out such contract, the trustee is authorized to operate the business of the debtor for the purpose of accepting or making tender of notice of intent to deliver the physical commodity underlying the contract, facilitating delivery of the physical commodity or disposing of the physical commodity in the event of a default. Any property received, not previously held, by the trustee in connection with its operation of the business of the debtor for these purposes, is not by the terms of this subchapter specifically included in the definition of customer property.

Finally, subsection (h) [now section 766(f)] requires the trustee to liquidate the debtor's estate as soon as practicable and consistent with good market practice, except for specifically identifiable securities or other property distributable under subsection (e).

Section 768 is an integral part of the commodity broker liquidation procedures outlined in section 767. Prompt action by the trustee to transfer or liquidate customer commodity contracts is necessary to protect customers, the debtor's estate, and the marketplace generally. However, transfers of customer accounts and property valued in excess of the customer's distribution share are prohibited. Since a determination of the customer's distribution share requires a determination of the customer's net equity and the total dollar value of customer property held by or for the account of the debtor, it is possible that the customer's distribution share will not be determined, and thus the customer's contracts and property will not be transferred, on a timely basis. To avoid this problem, and to expedite transfers of customer property, section 768 permits the trustee to make distributions to customers in accordance with a preliminary estimate of the debtor's customer property and each customer's distribution share.

It is acknowledged that the necessity for prompt action may not allow the trustee to assemble all relevant facts before such an estimate is made. However, the trustee is expected to develop as accurate an estimate as possible based on the available facts. Further, in order to permit expeditious action, section 768 does not require that notice be given to customers or other creditors before the court approves or disapproves the estimate. Nor does section 768 require that customer claims be received pursuant to section 767(a) before the trustee may act upon and in accordance with the estimate. If the estimate is inaccurate, the trustee is absolved of liability for a distribution share so long as the distribution did not exceed the customer's estimated distribution share. However, a trustee may have a claim back against a customer who received more than its actual distribution share. Senate Report No. 95–989.

Section 765(a) indicates that a customer must file a proof of claim, including any claim to specifically identifiable property, within such time as the court fixes.

Subsection (c) [subsec. (c) of section 765 of H. Bill] sets forth the general rule requiring the trustee to liquidate contractual commitments that are either not specifically identifiable or with respect to which a customer has not instructed the trustee during the time fixed by the court. Subsection (d) [subsec. (d) of section 765 of H. Bill] indicates an exception to the time limits in the rule by requiring the trustee to liquidate any open contractual commitment before the last day of trading or the first day during which delivery may be demanded, whichever first occurs, if transfer cannot be effectuated.

Section 766(a) indicates that the trustee may distribute securities or other property only under section 768. This does not preclude a distribution of cash under section 767(a) or distribution of any excess customer property under section 767(c) to the general estate.

Subsection (b) indicates that the trustee shall liquidate all securities and other property that is not specifically identifiable property as soon as practicable after the commencement of the case and in accordance with good market practice. If securities are restricted or trading has been suspended, the trustee will have to make an exempt sale or file a registration statement. In the event of a private placement, a customer is not entitled to "bid in" his net equity claim. To do so would enable him to receive a greater percentage recovery than other customers.

Section 767(a) provides for the trustee to distribute customer property pro rata according to customers' net equity claims. The court will determine an equitable portion of customer property to pay administrative expenses. Paragraphs (2) and (3) indicate that the return of specifically identifiable property constitutes a distribution of net equity.

Subsection (b) indicates that if the debtor is a clearing organization, customer property is to be segregated into customers' accounts and proprietary accounts and distributed accordingly without offset. This protects a member's customers from having their claims offset against the member's proprietary account. Subsection (c)(1) indicates that any excess customer property will pour over into the general estate. This unlikely event would occur only if customers fail to file proofs of claim. Subsection (c)(2) indicates that to the extent customers are not paid in full, they are entitled to share in the general estate as unsecured creditors, unless subordinated by the court under proposed 11 U.S.C. 510.

Section 768(a) requires the trustee to return specifically identifiable property to the extent that such distribution will not exceed a customer's net equity claim. Thus, if the customer owes money to a commodity broker, this will be offset under section 761(15)(A)(ii). If the value of the specifically identifiable property exceeds the net equity claim, then the customer may deposit cash with the trustee to make up the difference after which the trustee may return or transfer the customer's property.

Subsection (c) permits the trustee to answer all margin calls, to the extent of the customer's net equity claim, with respect to any specifically identifiable open contractual commitment. It should be noted that any payment under subsections (a) or (c) will be considered a reduction of the net equity claim under section 767(a). Thus the customer's net equity claim is a dynamic amount that varies with distributions of specifically identifiable property or margin payments on such property. This approach differs from the priority given to specifically identifiable property under subchapter III of chapter 7 by limiting the priority effect to a right to receive specific property as part of, rather than in addition to, a ratable share of customer property. This policy is designed to protect the small customer who is unlikely to have property in specifically identifiable form as compared with the professional trader. The CFTC is authorized to make rules defining specifically identifiable property under section 302 of the bill, in title III. House Report No. 95–595.

1982 Acts. House Report No. 97–420, see 1982 U.S.Code Cong. and Adm.News, p. 583.

1984 Acts. Statements by Legislative Leaders, see 1984 U.S.Code Cong. and Adm.News, p. 576.

2005 Acts. House Report No. 109–31(Part I), see 2005 U.S. Code Cong. and Adm. News, p. 88.

Legislative Statements

Sections 765 and 766 of the House amendment represent a consolidation and redraft of sections 765, 766, 767, and 768 of the House bill and sections 765, 766, 767, and 768 of the Senate amendment. In particular, section 765(a) of the House amendment is derived from section 765(a) of the House bill and section 767(a) of the Senate amendment. Under section 765(a) of the House amendment customers are notified of the opportunity to immediately file proofs of claim and to identify specifically identifiable securities, property, or commodity contracts. The customer is also afforded an opportunity to instruct the trustee regarding the customer's desires concerning disposition of the customer's commodity contracts. Section 767(b) [probably should be 765(b)] makes clear that the trustee must comply with instructions received to the extent practicable, but in the event the trustee has transferred commodity contracts to a commodity broker, such instructions shall be forwarded to the broker.

Section 766(a) of the House amendment is derived from section 768(c) of the House bill and section 767(f) of the Senate amendment. Section 766(b) of the House amendment is derived from section 765(d) of the House bill, and section 767(g) of the Senate amendment. Section 766(c) of the House amendment is derived from section 768(a) of the House bill and section 767(e) of the Senate amendment. Section 766(d) of the House amendment is derived from section 768(b) of the House bill and the second sentence of section 767(e) of the Senate amendment.

Section 766(e) of the House amendment is derived from section 765(c) of the House bill and sections 767(c) and (d) of the Senate amendment. The provision clarifies that the trustee may liquidate a commodity contract only if the commodity contract cannot be transferred to a commodity broker under section 766(c), cannot be identified to a particular customer, or has been identified with respect to a particular customer, but with respect to which the customer's instructions have not been received.

Section 766(f) of the House amendment is derived from section 766(b) of the House bill and section 767(h) of the Senate amendment. The term "all securities and other property" is not intended to include a commodity contract. Section 766(g) of the House amendment is derived from section 766(a) of the House bill. Section 766(h) of the House amendment is derived from section 767(a) of the House bill and section 765(a) of the Senate amendment. In order to induce private trustees to undertake the difficult and risky job of liquidating a commodity broker, the House amendment contains a provision insuring that a pro rata share of administrative claims will be paid. The provision represents a compromise between the position taken in the House bill, subordinating customer property to all expenses of administration, and the position taken in the Senate amendment requiring the distribution of customer property in advance of any expenses of administration. The position in the Senate amendment is rejected since customers, in any event, would have to pay a brokerage commission or fee in the ordinary course of business. The compromise provision requires customers to pay only those administrative expenses that are attributable to the administration of customer property.

Section 766(i) of the House amendment is derived from section 767(b) of the House bill and contains a similar compromise with respect to expenses of administration as the compromise detailed in connection with section 766(h) of the House amendment. Section 766(j) of the House amendment is derived from section 767(c) of the House bill. No counterpart is contained in the Senate amendment. The provision takes account of the rare case where the estate has customer property in excess of customer claims and administrative expenses attributable to those claims. The section also specifies that to the extent a customer is not paid in full out of customer property, that the unpaid claim will be treated the same as any other general unsecured creditor.

Section 768 of the Senate amendment was deleted from the House amendment as unwise. The provision in the Senate amendment would have permitted the trustee to distribute customer property based upon an estimate of value of the customer's account, with no provision for recapture of excessive disbursements. Moreover, the section would have exonerated the trustee from any liability for such an excessive disbursement. Furthermore, the section is unclear with respect to the customer's rights in the event the trustee makes a distribution less than the share to which the customer is entitled. The provision is deleted in the House amendment so that this difficult problem may be handled on a case-by-case basis by the courts as the facts and circumstances of each case require.

Section 769 of the Senate amendment is deleted in the House amendment as unnecessary. The provision was intended to codify *Board of Trade v. Johnson,* 264 U.S. 1 (1924) [Ill.1924, 44 S.Ct. 232]. *Board of Trade against Johnson* is codified in section 363(f) of the House amendment which indicates the only five circumstances in which property may be sold free and clear of an interest in such property of an entity other than the estate.

Section 770 of the Senate amendment is deleted in the House amendment as unnecessary. That section would have permitted commodity brokers to liquidate commodity contracts, notwithstanding any contrary order of the court. It would require an extraordinary circumstance, such as a threat to the national security, to enjoin a commodity broker from liquidating a commodity contract. However, in those circumstances, an injunction must prevail. Failure of the House amendment to incorporate section 770 of the Senate amendment does not imply that the automatic stay prevents liquidation of commodity contracts by commodity brokers. To the contrary, whenever by contract, or otherwise, a commodity broker is entitled to liquidate a position as a result of a condition specified in a contract, other than a condition or default of the kind specified in section 365(b)(2) of title 11, the commodity broker may engage in such liquidation. To this extent, the commodity broker's contract with his customer is treated no differently than any other contract under section 365 of Title 11.

Effective and Applicability Provisions

2005 Acts. Amendments by Pub.L. 109–8 effective, except as otherwise provided, 180 days after April 20, 2005, and inapplicable with respect to cases commenced under Title 11 before the effective date, see Pub.L. 109–8, § 1501, set out as a note under 11 U.S.C.A. § 101.

1984 Acts. Amendment by Pub.L. 98–353 effective with respect to cases filed 90 days after July 10, 1984, see section 552(a), formerly 553(a), of Pub.L. 98–353, set out as a note under section 101 of this title.

CROSS REFERENCES

Distribution in Chapter eleven cases, see 11 USCA § 1143.

Distribution of—

Customer property in stockbroker liquidation cases, see 11 USCA § 752.

Property of estate, see 11 USCA § 726.

Election of trustee by creditors holding claims entitled to distribution, see 11 USCA § 702.

Executory contracts and unexpired leases, see 11 USCA § 365.

Provisions relating to transferability of customer property and commodity contracts, see 7 USCA § 24.

§ 767. Commodity broker liquidation and forward contract merchants, commodity brokers, stockbrokers, financial institutions, financial participants, securities clearing agencies, swap participants, repo participants, and master netting agreement participants

Notwithstanding any other provision of this title, the exercise of rights by a forward contract merchant, commodity broker, stockbroker, financial institution, financial participant, securities clearing agency, swap participant, repo participant, or master netting agreement participant under this title shall not affect the priority of any unsecured claim it may have after the exercise of such rights.

(Added Pub.L. 109–8, Title IX, § 907(*l*), Apr. 20, 2005, 119 Stat. 181.)

HISTORICAL AND STATUTORY NOTES

Revision Notes and Legislative Reports

2005 Acts. House Report No. 109–31(Part I), see 2005 U.S. Code Cong. and Adm. News, p. 88.

Effective and Applicability Provisions

2005 Acts. Amendments by Pub.L. 109–8 effective, except as otherwise provided, 180 days after April 20, 2005, and inapplicable with respect to cases commenced under Title 11 before the effective date, see Pub.L. 109–8, § 1501, set out as a note under 11 U.S.C.A. § 101.

SUBCHAPTER V—CLEARING BANK LIQUIDATION

§ 781. Definitions

For purposes of this subchapter, the following definitions shall apply:

(1) Board.—The term "Board" means the Board of Governors of the Federal Reserve System.

(2) Depository institution.—The term "depository institution" has the same meaning as in section 3 of the Federal Deposit Insurance Act.

(3) Clearing bank.—The term "clearing bank" means an uninsured State member bank, or a corporation organized under section 25A of the Federal Reserve Act, which operates, or operates as, a multilateral clearing organization pursuant to section 409 of the Federal Deposit Insurance Corporation Improvement Act of 1991.

(Added Pub.L. 106–554, § 1(a)(5) [Title I, § 112(c)(5)(B)], Dec. 21, 2000, 114 Stat. 2763, 2763A–394.)

HISTORICAL AND STATUTORY NOTES

Revision Notes and Legislative Reports

2000 Acts. House Report No. 106–645 and Statement by President, see 2000 U.S. Code Cong. and Adm. News, p. 2459.

References in Text

Section 3 of the Federal Deposit Insurance Act, referred to in par. (2), is Act Sept. 21, 1950, c. 967, § 2[3], 64 Stat. 873, which is classified to 12 U.S.C.A. § 1813.

Section 25A of the Federal Reserve Act, referred to in par. (3), is Dec. 23, 1913, c. 6, § 25A, formerly § 25(a), as added Dec. 24, 1919, c. 18, 41 Stat. 378, as amended, which is classified to subchapter II of chapter 6 of Title 12, 12 U.S.C.A. § 611 et seq.

Section 409 of the Federal Deposit Insurance Corporation Improvement Act of 1991, referred to in par. (3), is Pub.L.

102–242, Title IV, § 409, as added by Pub.L. 106–554, § 1(a)(5) [Title I, § 112(a)(3)], Dec. 21, 2000, 114 Stat. 2763, 2763A–392, which is classified as 12 U.S.C.A. § 4422.

§ 782. Selection of trustee

(a) In general.—

(1) Appointment.—Notwithstanding any other provision of this title, the conservator or receiver who files the petition shall be the trustee under this chapter, unless the Board designates an alternative trustee.

(2) Successor.—The Board may designate a successor trustee if required.

(b) Authority of trustee.—Whenever the Board appoints or designates a trustee, chapter 3 and sections 704 and 705 of this title shall apply to the Board in the same way and to the same extent that they apply to a United States trustee.

(Added Pub.L. 106–554, § 1(a)(5) [Title I, § 112(c)(5)(B)], Dec. 21, 2000, 114 Stat. 2763, 2763A–394.)

HISTORICAL AND STATUTORY NOTES

Revision Notes and Legislative Reports

2000 Acts. House Report No. 106–645 and Statement by President, see 2000 U.S. Code Cong. and Adm. News, p. 2459.

References in Text

Chapter 3, referred to in subsec. (b), is classified to 11 U.S.C.A. § 301 et seq.

§ 783. Additional powers of trustee

(a) Distribution of property not of the estate.—The trustee under this subchapter has power to distribute property not of the estate, including distributions to customers that are mandated by subchapters III and IV of this chapter.

(b) Disposition of institution.—The trustee under this subchapter may, after notice and a hearing—

(1) sell the clearing bank to a depository institution or consortium of depository institutions (which consortium may agree on the allocation of the clearing bank among the consortium);

(2) merge the clearing bank with a depository institution;

(3) transfer contracts to the same extent as could a receiver for a depository institution under paragraphs (9) and (10) of section 11(e) of the Federal Deposit Insurance Act;

(4) transfer assets or liabilities to a depository institution; and

(5) transfer assets and liabilities to a bridge depository institution as provided in paragraphs (1), (3)(A), (5), and (6) of section 11(n) of the Federal Deposit Insurance Act, paragraphs (9) through (13) of such section, and subparagraphs (A) through (H) and subparagraph (K) of paragraph (4) of such section 11(n), except that—

(A) the bridge depository institution to which such assets or liabilities are transferred shall be treated as a clearing bank for the purpose of this subsection; and

(B) any references in any such provision of law to the Federal Deposit Insurance Corporation shall be construed to be references to the appointing agency and that references to deposit insurance shall be omitted.

(c) Certain transfers included.—Any reference in this section to transfers of liabilities includes a ratable transfer of liabilities within a priority class.

(Added Pub.L. 106–554, § 1(a)(5) [Title I, § 112(c)(5)(B)], Dec. 21, 2000, 114 Stat. 2763, 2763A–395, and amended Pub.L. 110–289, Div. A, Title VI, § 1604(b)(3), July 30, 2008, 122 Stat. 2826.)

HISTORICAL AND STATUTORY NOTES

Revision Notes and Legislative Reports

2000 Acts. House Report No. 106–645 and Statement by President, see 2000 U.S. Code Cong. and Adm. News, p. 2459.

References in Text

Subchapters III and IV of this chapter, referred to in subsec. (a), are 11 U.S.C.A. §§ 741 et seq. and 761 et seq.

Paragraphs (9) and (10) of section 11(e) of the Federal Deposit Insurance Act, referred to in subsec. (b)(3), are classified to 12 U.S.C.A. § 1821(e)(9), (10).

Paragraphs (1), (3)(A), (5), and (6) of section 11(n) of the Federal Deposit Insurance Act, paragraphs (9) through (13) of such section, and subparagraphs (A) through (H) and subparagraph (K) of paragraph (4) of such section 11(n), referred to in subsec. (b)(5), are classified to 12 U.S.C.A. § 1821(n)(1), (3)(A), (5), (6), and (4)(A) to (K).

Codifications

Amendment by Pub.L. 110–289, § 1604(b)(3), which directed striking out "bridge bank" and inserting "bridge depository institution", was executed to both locations where the term appeared in subsec. (b)(5), as the probable intent of Congress. See 2008 Amendments note set out under this section.

§ 784. Right to be heard

The Board or a Federal reserve bank (in the case of a clearing bank that is a member of that bank) may raise and may appear and be heard on any issue in a case under this subchapter.

(Added Pub.L. 106–554, § 1(a)(5) [Title I, § 112(c)(5)(B)], Dec. 21, 2000, 114 Stat. 2763, 2763A–395.)

HISTORICAL AND STATUTORY NOTES

Revision Notes and Legislative Reports

2000 Acts. House Report No. 106–645 and Statement by President, see 2000 U.S. Code Cong. and Adm. News, p. 2459.

§§ 785 to 900. Reserved for future legislation

CHAPTER 9—ADJUSTMENT OF DEBTS OF A MUNICIPALITY

SUBCHAPTER I—GENERAL PROVISIONS

CROSS REFERENCES

Allowance of administrative expenses of substantial contributors in cases under this chapter, see 11 USCA § 503.

Chapter one of this title and this chapter solely applicable in cases under this chapter except as provided in § 901 of this title, see 11 USCA § 103.

Claims arising from rejection of executory contracts or unexpired leases under this chapter's plans, see 11 USCA § 502.

Definitions applicable in this title, see 11 USCA § 101.

Duration of automatic stay, see 11 USCA § 362.

Entities which may be debtors under this chapter, see 11 USCA § 109.

Executory contracts and unexpired leases, see 11 USCA § 365.

Filing fees, see 28 USCA § 1930.

Unclaimed property, see 11 USCA § 347.

§ 901. Applicability of other sections of this title

(a) Sections 301, 344, 347(b), 349, 350(b), 361, 362, 364(c), 364(d), 364(e), 364(f), 365, 366, 501, 502, 503, 504, 506, 507(a)(2), 509, 510, 524(a)(1), 524(a)(2), 544, 545, 546, 547, 548, 549(a), 549(c), 549(d), 550, 551, 552, 553, 555, 556, 557, 559, 560, 561, 562, 1102, 1103, 1109, 1111(b), 1122, 1123(a)(1), 1123(a)(2), 1123(a)(3), 1123(a)(4), 1123(a)(5), 1123(b), 1123(d), 1124, 1125, 1126(a), 1126(b), 1126(c), 1126(e), 1126(f), 1126(g), 1127(d), 1128, 1129(a)(2), 1129(a)(3), 1129(a)(6), 1129(a)(8), 1129(a)(10), 1129(b)(1), 1129(b)(2)(A), 1129(b)(2)(B), 1142(b), 1143, 1144, and 1145 of this title apply in a case under this chapter.

(b) A term used in a section of this title made applicable in a case under this chapter by subsection (a) of this section or section 103(e) of this title has the meaning defined for such term for the purpose of such applicable section, unless such term is otherwise defined in section 902 of this title.

(c) A section made applicable in a case under this chapter by subsection (a) of this section that is operative if the business of the debtor is authorized to be operated is operative in a case under this chapter. (Pub.L. 95–598, Nov. 6, 1978, 92 Stat. 2621; Pub.L. 98–353, Title III, §§ 353, 490, July 10, 1984, 98 Stat. 361, 383; Pub.L. 100–597, § 3, Nov. 3, 1988, 102 Stat. 3028; Pub.L. 109–8, Title V, § 502, Title XII, § 1216, Title XV, § 1502(a)(5), Apr. 20, 2005, 119 Stat. 118, 195, 216.)

HISTORICAL AND STATUTORY NOTES

Revision Notes and Legislative Reports

1978 Acts. Section 901 makes applicable appropriate provisions of other chapters of proposed title 11. The general rule set out in section 103(e) is that only the provisions of chapters 1 and 9 apply in a chapter 9 case. Section 901 is the exception, and specifies other provisions that do apply. They are as follows:

§ 301. Voluntary cases. Application of this section makes clear, as under current chapter IX [former chapter 9 (section 401 et seq.) of former Title 11], that a municipal case can be commenced only by the municipality itself. There are no involuntary chapter 9 cases.

§ 344. Self-incrimination; immunity. Application of this section is of no substantive effect for the administration of the case, but merely provides that the general rules in part V of title 18 [section 6001 et seq. of Title 18, Crimes and Criminal Procedure] govern immunity.

§ 347(b). Unclaimed property. This provision currently appears in section 96(d) of chapter IX [section 416(d) of this former Title 11].

§ 349. Effect of dismissal. This section governs the effect of a dismissal of a chapter 9 case. It provides in substance that rights that existed before the case that were disturbed by the commencement of the case are reinstated. This section does not concern grounds for dismissal, which are found in § 926.

§ 361. Adequate protection. Section 361 provides the general standard for the protection of secured creditors whose property is used in a case under title 11. Its importance lies in its application to sections 362 and 364.

§ 362. **Automatic stay.** The automatic stay provisions of the general portions of the title are incorporated into chapter 9. There is an automatic stay provided in current Bankruptcy Act section 85(e) [section 405(e) of former title 11]. The thrust of section 362 is the same as that of section 85(e), but, of course, its application in chapter 9 is modernized and drafted to conform with the stay generally applicable under the bankruptcy code. An additional part of the automatic stay applicable only to municipal cases is included in section 922.

§§ **364(c), 364(d), 364(e). Obtaining credit.** This section governs the borrowing of money by a municipality in reorganization. It is narrower than a comparable provision in current law, section 82(b)(2) [section 402(b)(2) of former title 11]. The difference lies mainly in the removal under the bill of the authority of the court to supervise borrowing by the municipality in instances in which none of the special bankruptcy powers are involved. That is, if a municipality could borrow money outside of the bankruptcy court, then it should have the same authority in bankruptcy court, under the doctrine of *Ashton v. Cameron Water District No. 1,* 298 U.S. 513 (1936) [Tex.1936, 56 S.Ct. 892, 80 L.Ed. 1309, 31 Am.Bankr.Rep.N.S. 96, rehearing denied 57 S.Ct. 5, 299 U.S. 619, 81 L.Ed. 457] and *National League of Cities v. Usery,* 426 U.S. 833 (1976) [Dist.Col.1976, 96 S.Ct. 2465, 49 L.Ed.2d 245, on remand 429 F.Supp. 703]. Only when the municipality needs special authority, such as subordination of existing liens, or special priority for the borrowed funds, will the court become involved in the authorization.

§ 365. **Executory contracts and unexpired leases.** The applicability of section 365 incorporates the general power of a bankruptcy court to authorize the assumption or rejection of executory contracts or unexpired leases found in other chapters of the title. This section is comparable to section 82(b)(1) [section 402(b)(1) of former Title 11] of current law.

§ 366. **Utility service.** This section gives a municipality the same authority as any other debtor with respect to continuation of utility service during the proceeding, provided adequate assurance of future payment is provided. No comparable explicit provision is found in current law, although the case law seems to support the same result.

§ 501. **Filing of proofs of claims.** This section permits filing of proofs of claims in a chapter 9 case. Note, however, that section 924 permits listing of creditors' claims, as under chapter 11 and under section 85(b) of chapter IX [section 405(b) of former Title 11].

§ 502. **Allowance of claims.** This section applies the general allowance rules to chapter 9 cases. This is no change from current law.

§ 503. **Administrative expenses.** Administrative expenses as defined in section 503 will be paid in a chapter 9 case, as provided under section 89(1) of current law [section 409(1) of former Title 11].

§ 504. **Sharing of compensation.** There is no comparable provision in current law. However, this provision applies generally throughout the proposed law, and will not affect the progress of the case, only the interrelations between attorneys and other professionals that participate in the case.

§ 506. **Determination of secured status.** Section 506 specifies that claims secured by a lien should be separated, to the extent provided, into secured and unsecured claims. It applies generally. Current law follows this result, though there is no explicit provision.

§ 507(1). **Priorities.** Paragraph (1) of section 507 requires that administrative expenses be paid first. This rule will apply in chapter 9 cases. It is presently found in section 89(1) [section 409(1) of former Title 11]. The two other priorities presently found in section 89 have been deleted. The second, for claims arising within 3 months before the case is commenced, is deleted from the statute, but may be within the court's equitable power to award, under the case of *Fosdick v. Schall,* 99 U.S. 235 (1878). Leaving the provision to the courts permits greater flexibility, as under railroad cases, than an absolute three-month rule. The third priority under current law, for claims which are entitled to priority under the laws of the United States, is deleted because of the proposed amendment to section 3466 of the Revised Statutes [former 31 U.S.C.A. § 191, see 31 U.S.C.A. § 3713(a)] contained in section 321(a) of title III of the bill, which previously has given the United States an absolute first priority in Chapter X [former Chapter 10 (section 501 et seq.) of former Title 11] and section 77 [section 205 of former Title 1] cases. Because the priority rules are regularized and brought together in the bankruptcy laws by this bill, the need for incorporation of priorities elsewhere specified is eliminated.

§ 509. **Claims of codebtors.** This section provides for the treatment of sureties, guarantors, and codebtors. The general rule of postponement found in the other chapters will apply in chapter 9. This section adopts current law.

§ 510. **Subordination of claims.** This section permits the court to subordinate, on equitable grounds, any claim, and requires enforcement of contractual subordination agreements, and subordination of securities rescission claims. The section recognizes the inherent equitable power of the court under current law, and the practice followed with respect to contractual provisions.

§ 547. **Preferences.** Incorporation of section 547 will permit the debtor to recover preferences. This power will be used primarily when those who gave the preferences have been replaced by new municipal officers or when creditors coerced preferential payments. Unlike Bankruptcy Act § 85(h) [section 405(h) of former Title 11], the section does not permit the appointment of a trustee for the purpose of pursuing preferences. Moreover, this bill does not incorporate the other avoiding powers of a trustee for chapter 9, found in current section 85(h).

§ 550. **Liability of transfers.** Incorporation of this section is made necessary by the incorporation of the preference section, and permits recovery by the debtor from a transferee of an avoided preference.

§ 551. **Automatic preservation of avoided transfer.** Application of section 551 requires preservation of any avoided preference for the benefit of the estate.

§ 552. **Postpetition effect of security interest.** This section will govern the applicability after the commencement of the case of security interests granted by the debtor before the commencement of the case.

§ 553. **Setoff.** Under current law, certain setoff is stayed. Application of this section preserves that result, though the setoffs that are permitted under section 553 are better defined than under present law. Application of this section is necessary to stay the setoff and to provide the offsetting creditor with the protection to which he is entitled under present law.

§ 1122. **Classification of claims.** This section is derived from current section 88(b) [section 408(b) of former Title 11], and is substantially similar.

§ 1123(a)(1)–(4), (b). **Contents of plan.** The general provisions governing contents of a chapter 11 plan are made applicable here, with two exceptions relating to the rights of stockholders, which are not applicable in chapter 9 cases. This section expands current law by specifying the contents of a plan in some detail. Section 91 of current law [section 411 of former Title 11] speaks only in general terms. The substance of the two sections is substantially the same, however.

§ 1124. **Impairment of claims.** The confirmation standards adopted in chapter 9 are the same as those of chapter 11. This changes current chapter IX [former chapter 9 (section 401 et seq.) of former Title 11], which requires compliance with the fair and equitable rule. The greater flexibility of proposed chapter 11 is carried over into chapter 9, for there appears to be no reason why the confirmation standards for the two chapters should be different, or why the elimination of the fair and equitable rule from corporate reorganizations should not be followed in municipal debt adjustments. The current chapter IX rule is based on the confirmation rules of current chapter X [chapter 10 of former Title 11]. The change in the latter suggests a corresponding change in the former. Section 1124 is one part of the new confirmation standard. It defines impairment, for use in section 1129.

§ 1125. **Postpetition disclosure and solicitation.** The change in the confirmation standard necessitates a corresponding change in the disclosure requirements for solicitation of acceptances of a plan. Under current chapter IX [former chapter 9 (section 401 et seq.) of former Title 11] there is no disclosure requirement. Incorporation of section 1125 will insure that creditors receive adequate information before they are required to vote on a plan.

§ 1126(a), (b), (c), (e), (f), (g). **Acceptance of plan.** Section 1126 incorporates the current chapter IX [former chapter 9 (section 401 et seq.) of former Title 11] acceptance requirement: two-thirds in amount and a majority in number, Bankruptcy Act § 92 [section 412 of former Title 11]. Section 1125 permits exclusion of certain acceptances from the computation if the acceptances were obtained in bad faith or, unlike current law, if there is a conflict of interest motivating the acceptance.

§ 1127(d). **Modification of plan.** This section governs the change of a creditor's vote on the plan after a modification is proposed. It is derived from current section 92(e) [section 412(e) of former Title 11].

§ 1128. **Hearing on confirmation.** This section requires a hearing on the confirmation of the plan, and permits parties in interest to object. It is the same as Bankruptcy Act §§ 93 and 94(a) [section 413 and section 414(a) of former Title 11], though the provision, comparable to section 206 of current chapter X [section 606 of former Title 11], permitting a labor organization to appear and be heard on the economic soundness of the plan, has been deleted as more appropriate for the Rules.

§ 1129(a)(2), (3), (8), (b)(1), (2). **Confirmation of plan.** This section provides the boiler-plate language that the plan be proposed in good faith and that it comply with the provisions of the chapter, and also provides the financial standard for confirmation, which replaces the fair and equitable rule. See § 1124, supra.

§ 1142(b). **Execution of plan.** Derived from Bankruptcy Act § 96(b) [section 416(b) of former Title 11], this section permits the court to order execution and delivery of instruments in order to execute the plan.

§ 1143. **Distribution.** This section is the same in substance as section 96(d) [section 416(d) of former Title 11], which requires presentment or delivery of securities within five years, and bars creditors that do not act within that time.

§ 1144. **Revocation of order of confirmation.** This section permits the court to revoke the order of confirmation and the discharge if the confirmation of the plan was procured by fraud. There is no comparable provision in current chapter IX [former chapter 9 (section 401 et seq.) of former Title 11]. House Report No. 95–595.

1984 Acts. Statements by Legislative Leaders, see 1984 U.S.Code Cong. and Adm.News, p. 576.

1988 Acts. House Report No. 100–1011, see 1988 U.S.Code Cong. and Adm.News, p. 4115.

2005 Acts. House Report No. 109–31(Part I), see 2005 U.S. Code Cong. and Adm. News, p. 88.

Legislative Statements

Chapter 9 of the House amendment represents a compromise between chapter 9 of the House bill and 9 of the Senate amendment. In most respects this chapter follows current law with respect to the adjustment of debts of a municipality. Stylistic changes and minor substantive revisions have been made in order to conform this chapter with other new chapters of the bankruptcy code [this title]. There are few major differences between the House bill and the Senate amendment on this issue. Section 901 indicates the applicability of other sections of title 11 in cases under chapter 9. Included are sections providing for creditors' committees under sections 1102 and 1103.

References in Text

Section 103(e) of this title, referred to in subsec. (b), was redesignated subsec. (f) and a new subsec. (e) was added by Pub.L. 106–554, § 1(a)(5) [Title I, § 112(c)(5)(A)], Dec. 21, 2000, 114 Stat. 2763, 2763A–394.

Effective and Applicability Provisions

2005 Acts. Amendments by Pub.L. 109–8 effective, except as otherwise provided, 180 days after April 20, 2005, and inapplicable with respect to cases commenced under Title 11 before the effective date, see Pub.L. 109–8, § 1501, set out as a note under 11 U.S.C.A. § 101.

1988 Acts. Amendment by Pub.L. 100–597 effective Nov. 3, 1988, but not applicable to any case commenced under this title before that date, see section 12 of Pub.L. 100–597, set out as a note under section 101 of this title.

1984 Acts. Amendment by Pub.L. 98–353 effective with respect to cases filed 90 days after July 10, 1984, see section 552(a), formerly 553(a), of Pub.L. 98–353, set out as a note under section 101 of this title.

CROSS REFERENCES

Chapters one and nine of this title solely applicable in cases under Chapter nine except as provided in this section, see 11 USCA § 103.

Confirmation in Chapter nine cases upon compliance with provisions of this title made applicable by this section, see 11 USCA § 943.

§ 902. Definitions for this chapter

In this chapter—

(1) "property of the estate", when used in a section that is made applicable in a case under this chapter by section 103(e) or 901 of this title, means property of the debtor;

(2) "special revenues" means—

(A) receipts derived from the ownership, operation, or disposition of projects or systems of the debtor that are primarily used or intended to be used primarily to provide transportation, utility, or other services, including the proceeds of borrowings to finance the projects or systems;

(B) special excise taxes imposed on particular activities or transactions;

(C) incremental tax receipts from the benefited area in the case of tax-increment financing;

(D) other revenues or receipts derived from particular functions of the debtor, whether or not the debtor has other functions; or

(E) taxes specifically levied to finance one or more projects or systems, excluding receipts from general property, sales, or income taxes (other than tax-increment financing) levied to finance the general purposes of the debtor;

(3) "special tax payer" means record owner or holder of legal or equitable title to real property against which a special assessment or special tax has been levied the proceeds of which are the sole source of payment of an obligation issued by the debtor to defray the cost of an improvement relating to such real property;

(4) "special tax payer affected by the plan" means special tax payer with respect to whose real property the plan proposes to increase the proportion of special assessments or special taxes referred to in paragraph (2) of this section assessed against such real property; and

(5) "trustee", when used in a section that is made applicable in a case under this chapter by section 103(e) or 901 of this title, means debtor, except as provided in section 926 of this title.

(Pub.L. 95–598, Nov. 6, 1978, 92 Stat. 2622; Pub.L. 98–353, Title III, § 491, July 10, 1984, 98 Stat. 383; Pub.L. 100–597, § 4, Nov. 3, 1988, 102 Stat. 3028.)

HISTORICAL AND STATUTORY NOTES

Revision Notes and Legislative Reports

1978 Acts. There are six definitions for use in chapter 9. Paragraph (1) defines what claims are included in a chapter 9 case and adopts the definition now found in section 81(1) [section 401(1) of former Title 11]. All claims against the petitioner generally will be included, with one significant exception. Municipalities are authorized, under section 103(c) of the Internal Revenue Code of 1954 [section 103(c) of Title 26, Internal Revenue Code], as amended, to issue tax-exempt industrial development revenue bonds to provide for the financing of certain projects for privately owned companies. The bonds are sold on the basis of the credit of the company on whose behalf they are issued, and the principal, interest, and premium, if any, are payable solely from payments made by the company to the trustee under the bond indenture and do not constitute claims on the tax revenues or other funds of the issuing municipalities. The municipality merely acts as the vehicle to enable the bonds to be issued on a tax-exempt basis. Claims that arise by virtue of these bonds are not among the claims defined by this paragraph and amounts owed by private companies to the holders of industrial development revenue bonds are not to be included among the assets of the municipality that would be affected by the plan. See Cong. Record, 94th Cong., 1st Sess. H.R. 12073 (statement by Mr. Don Edwards, floor manager of the bill in the House). Paragraph (2) defines the court which means the federal district court or federal district judge before which the case is pending. Paragraph (3) specifies that when the term "property of the estate" is used in a section in another chapter made applicable in chapter 9 cases, the term means "property of the debtor". Paragraphs (4) and (5) adopt the definition of "special taxpayer affected by the plan" that appears in current sections 81(10) and 81(11) [section 401(10) and (11) of former Title 11] of the Bankruptcy Act. Paragraph (6) provides that "trustee" means "debtor" when used in conjunction with chapter 9. Senate Report No. 95–989.

There are only four definitions for use only in chapter 9. The first specifies that when the term "property of the estate" is used in a section in another chapter made applicable in chapter 9 cases, the term will mean "property of the debtor". Paragraphs (2) and (3) adopt the definition of "special taxpayer affected by the plan" that appears in current section 81(10) and 81(11) [section 401(10) and (11) of former Title 11]. Paragraphs [sic] (4) provides for "trustee" the same treatment as provided for "property of the estate", specifying that it means "debtor" when used in conjunction with chapter 9. House Report No. 95–595.

1984 Acts. Statements by Legislative Leaders, see 1984 U.S.Code Cong. and Adm.News, p. 576.

1988 Acts. House Report No. 100–1011, see 1988 U.S.Code Cong. and Adm.News, p. 4115.

Legislative Statements

Section 902(2) of the Senate amendment is deleted since the bankruptcy court will have jurisdiction over all cases under chapter 9. The concept of a claim being materially and adversely affected reflected in section 902(1) of the Senate amendment has been deleted and replaced with the new concept of "impairment" set forth in section 1124 of the House amendment and incorporated by reference into chapter 9.

References in Text

Section 103(e) of this title, referred to in pars. (1) and (5), was redesignated section 103(f) and a new section 103(e) was added by Pub.L. 106–554, § 1(a)(5) [Title I, § 112(c)(5)(A)], Dec. 21, 2000, 114 Stat. 2763, 2763A–394.

Effective and Applicability Provisions

1988 Acts. Amendment by Pub.L. 100–597 effective Nov. 3, 1988, but not applicable to any case commenced under this title before that date, see section 12 of Pub.L. 100–597, set out as a note under section 101 of this title.

1984 Acts. Amendment by Pub.L. 98–353 effective with respect to cases filed 90 days after July 10, 1984, see section 552(a), formerly 553(a), of Pub.L. 98–353, set out as a note under section 101 of this title.

CROSS REFERENCES

Definitions applicable in—

Cases under this title, see 11 USCA § 101.

Chapter eleven cases, see 11 USCA § 1101.

Commodity broker liquidation cases, see 11 USCA § 761.

Railroad reorganization cases, see 11 USCA § 1162.

Stockbroker liquidation cases, see 11 USCA § 741.

§ 903. Reservation of State power to control municipalities

This chapter does not limit or impair the power of a State to control, by legislation or otherwise, a municipality of or in such State in the exercise of the political or governmental powers of such municipality, including expenditures for such exercise, but—

(1) a State law prescribing a method of composition of indebtedness of such municipality may not bind any creditor that does not consent to such composition; and

(2) a judgment entered under such a law may not bind a creditor that does not consent to such composition.

(Pub.L. 95–598, Nov. 6, 1978, 92 Stat. 2622; Pub.L. 98–353, Title III, § 492, July 10, 1984, 98 Stat. 383.)

HISTORICAL AND STATUTORY NOTES

Revision Notes and Legislative Reports

1978 Acts. Section 903 is derived, with stylistic changes, from section 83 of current Chapter IX [section 403 of former Title 11]. It sets forth the primary authority of a State, through its constitution, laws, and other powers, over its municipalities. The proviso in section 83, prohibiting State composition procedures for municipalities, is retained. Deletion of the provision would "permit all States to enact their own versions of Chapter IX [former chapter 9 (section 401 et seq.) of former Title 11]", Municipal Insolvency, 50 Am. Bankr.L.J. 55, 65, which would frustrate the constitutional mandate of uniform bankruptcy laws. Constitution of the United States, Art. I, Sec. 8.

This section provides that the municipality can consent to the court's orders in regard to use of its income or property. It is contemplated that such consent will be required by the court for the issuance of certificates of indebtedness under section 364(c). Such consent could extend to enforcement of the conditions attached to the certificates or the municipal services to be provided during the proceedings. Senate Report No. 95–989.

1984 Acts. Statements by Legislative Leaders, see 1984 U.S.Code Cong. and Adm.News, p. 576.

Legislative Statements

Section 903 of the House amendment represents a stylistic revision of section 903 of the Senate amendment. To the extent section 903 of the House bill would have changed present law, such section is rejected.

Effective and Applicability Provisions

1984 Acts. Amendment by Pub.L. 98–353 effective with respect to cases filed 90 days after July 10, 1984, see section 552(a), formerly 553(a), of Pub.L. 98–353, set out as a note under section 101 of this title.

CROSS REFERENCES

Authorization by state to be debtor under this chapter, see 11 USCA § 109.

§ 904. Limitation on jurisdiction and powers of court

Notwithstanding any power of the court, unless the debtor consents or the plan so provides, the court may not, by any stay, order, or decree, in the case or otherwise, interfere with—

(1) any of the political or governmental powers of the debtor;

(2) any of the property or revenues of the debtor; or

(3) the debtor's use or enjoyment of any income-producing property.

(Pub.L. 95–598, Nov. 6, 1978, 92 Stat. 2622.)

HISTORICAL AND STATUTORY NOTES

Revision Notes and Legislative Reports

1978 Acts. This section adopts the policy of section 82(c) of current law [section 402(c) of former Title 11]. The only change in this section from section 82(c) is to conform the section to the style and cross-references of S. 2266. Senate Report No. 95–989.

This section adopts the policy of section 82(c) of current law [section 402(c) of former Title 11]. The *Usery* case underlines the need for this limitation on the court's powers. The only change in this section from section 82(c) is to conform the section to the style and cross-references of H.R. 8200. This section makes clear that the court may not interfere with the choices a municipality makes as to what services and benefits it will provide to its inhabitants. House Report No. 95–595.

CROSS REFERENCES

Power of court, see 11 USCA § 105.

SUBCHAPTER II—ADMINISTRATION

§ 921. Petition and proceedings relating to petition

(a) Notwithstanding sections 109(d) and 301 of this title, a case under this chapter concerning an unincorporated tax or special assessment district that does not have such district's own officials is commenced by the filing under section 301 of this title of a petition under this chapter by such district's governing authority or the board or body having authority to levy taxes or assessments to meet the obligations of such district.

(b) The chief judge of the court of appeals for the circuit embracing the district in which the case is commenced shall designate the bankruptcy judge to conduct the case.

(c) After any objection to the petition, the court, after notice and a hearing, may dismiss the petition if the debtor did not file the petition in good faith or if the petition does not meet the requirements of this title.

(d) If the petition is not dismissed under subsection (c) of this section, the court shall order relief under this chapter notwithstanding section 301(b).

(e) The court may not, on account of an appeal from an order for relief, delay any proceeding under this chapter in the case in which the appeal is being taken; nor shall any court order a stay of such proceeding pending such appeal. The reversal on appeal of a finding of jurisdiction does not affect the validity of any debt incurred that is authorized by the court under section 364(c) or 364(d) of this title.

(Pub.L. 95–598, Nov. 6, 1978, 92 Stat. 2622; Pub.L. 98–353, Title III, § 494, July 10, 1984, 98 Stat. 383; Pub.L. 109–8, Title V, § 501(a), Apr. 20, 2005, 119 Stat. 118.)

HISTORICAL AND STATUTORY NOTES

Revision Notes and Legislative Reports

1978 Acts. Section 905 adopts the procedures for selection of the judge for the chapter 9 case as found in current section 82(d) [section 402(d) of former Title 11]. It is expected that the large chapter 9 case might take up almost all the judicial time of the presiding judge and involve very complex legal questions. Selection should not be left to chance or the luck of the draw. This provision will insure that calendar demands and levels of experience can be considered in the selection of the judge in a chapter 9 case. Senate Report No. 95–989.

Subsection (a) is derived from section 85(a) [section 405(a) of former Title 11], second sentence, of current law. There is no substantive change in the law. The subsection permits a municipality that does not have its own officers to be moved into chapter 9 by the action of the body or board that has authority to levy taxes for the municipality.

Subsection (b) permits a party in interest to object to the filing of the petition not later than 15 days after notice. This provision tracks the third sentence of section 85(a) [section 405(a) of former Title 11], except that the provision for publication in section 85(a) is left to the Rules (See Rule 9–14 [Rules of Bankruptcy Procedure, this title]), and therefore the determinative date is left less definite.

Subsection (c) permits the court to dismiss a petition not filed in good faith or not filed in compliance with the requirements of the chapter. This provision is the fourth sentence of section 85(a) [section 405(a) of former Title 11].

Subsection (d) directs the court to order relief on the petition if it does not dismiss the case under subsection (c).

Subsection (e) contains the fifth and sixth sentences of section 85(a) [section 405(a) of former Title 11]. House Report No. 95–595.

1984 Acts. Statements by Legislative Leaders, see 1984 U.S.Code Cong. and Adm.News, p. 576.

2005 Acts. House Report No. 109–31(Part I), see 2005 U.S. Code Cong. and Adm. News, p. 88.

Legislative Statements

Section 905 of the Senate amendment is incorporated as section 921(b) of the House amendment with the difference that the chief judge of the circuit embracing the district in which the case is commenced designates a bankruptcy judge to conduct the case in lieu of a district judge as under present law. It is intended that a municipality may commence a case in any district in which the municipality is located, as under present law. Section 906 of the Senate amendment has been adopted in substance in section 109(c) of the House amendment.

Effective and Applicability Provisions

2005 Acts. Amendments by Pub.L. 109–8 effective, except as otherwise provided, 180 days after April 20, 2005, and inapplicable with respect to cases commenced under Title 11 before the effective date, see Pub.L. 109–8, § 1501, set out as a note under 11 U.S.C.A. § 101.

1984 Acts. Amendment by Pub.L. 98–353 effective with respect to cases filed 90 days after July 10, 1984, see section 552(a), formerly 553(a), of Pub.L. 98–353, set out as a note under section 101 of this title.

§ 922. Automatic stay of enforcement of claims against the debtor

(a) A petition filed under this chapter operates as a stay, in addition to the stay provided by section 362 of this title, applicable to all entities, of—

(1) the commencement or continuation, including the issuance or employment of process, of a judicial, administrative, or other action or proceeding against an officer or inhabitant of the debtor that seeks to enforce a claim against the debtor; and

(2) the enforcement of a lien on or arising out of taxes or assessments owed to the debtor.

(b) Subsections (c), (d), (e), (f), and (g) of section 362 of this title apply to a stay under subsection (a) of this section the same as such subsections apply to a stay under section 362(a) of this title.

(c) If the debtor provides, under section 362, 364, or 922 of this title, adequate protection of the interest of the holder of a claim secured by a lien on property of the debtor and if, notwithstanding such protection such creditor has a claim arising from the stay of action against such property under section 362 or 922 of this title or from the granting of a lien under section 364(d) of this title, then such claim shall be allowable as an administrative expense under section 503(b) of this title.

(d) Notwithstanding section 362 of this title and subsection (a) of this section, a petition filed under this chapter does not operate as a stay of application of pledged special revenues in a manner consistent with section 927 of this title to payment of indebtedness secured by such revenues.

(Pub.L. 95–598, Nov. 6, 1978, 92 Stat. 2623; Pub.L. 98–353, Title III, § 495, July 10, 1984, 98 Stat. 384; Pub.L. 100–597, § 5, Nov. 3, 1988, 102 Stat. 3029.)

HISTORICAL AND STATUTORY NOTES

Revision Notes and Legislative Reports

1978 Acts. The automatic stay provided under section 362 of title 11 is incomplete for a municipality, because there is the possibility of action by a creditor against an officer or inhabitant of the municipality to collect taxes due the municipality. Section 85(e)(1) of current chapter IX [section 405(e)(1) of former Title 11] stays such actions. Section 922 carries over that protection into the proposed chapter 9. Subsection (b) applies the provisions for relief from the stay that apply generally in section 362 to the stay under section 922. House Report No. 95–595.

1984 Acts. Statements by Legislative Leaders, see 1984 U.S.Code Cong. and Adm.News, p. 576.

1988 Acts. House Report No. 100–1011, see 1988 U.S.Code Cong. and Adm.News, p. 4115.

Effective and Applicability Provisions

1988 Acts. Amendment by Pub.L. 100–597 effective Nov. 3, 1988, but not applicable to any case commenced under this title before that date, see section 12 of Pub.L. 100–597, set out as a note under section 101 of this title.

1984 Acts. Amendment by Pub.L. 98–353 effective with respect to cases filed 90 days after July 10, 1984, see section 552(a), formerly 553(a), of Pub.L. 98–353, set out as a note under section 101 of this title.

CROSS REFERENCES

Effect of § 362 of this title in stockbroker liquidation cases, see 11 USCA § 742.

Extension of time generally, see 11 USCA § 108.

Stay of action against codebtor in—

Chapter thirteen cases, see 11 USCA § 1301.

Chapter twelve cases, see 11 USCA § 1201.

§ 923. Notice

There shall be given notice of the commencement of a case under this chapter, notice of an order for relief under this chapter, and notice of the dismissal of a case under this chapter. Such notice shall also be published at least once a week for three successive weeks in at least one newspaper of general circulation published within the district in which the case is commenced, and in such other newspaper having a general circulation among bond dealers and bondholders as the court designates.

(Pub.L. 95–598, Nov. 6, 1978, 92 Stat. 2623.)

HISTORICAL AND STATUTORY NOTES

Revision Notes and Legislative Reports

1978 Acts. The notice provisions in section 923 are significantly more sparse than those provided under section 85(d) of chapter IX [section § 405(d) of former Title 11]. The exact contours of the notice to be given under chapter 9 are left to the Rules [Rules of Bankruptcy Procedure, this title]. Because the Rules deal with notice in a municipal case (Rule 9–14), and because section 405(d) of title IV of the bill continues those Rules in effect to the extent not inconsistent with the bill, the notice provisions of current law and Rules would continue to apply. House Report No. 95–595.

Legislative Statements

Section 923 of the House amendment represents a compromise with respect to the notice provisions contained in comparable provisions of the House bill and Senate amendment. As a general matter, title 11 leaves most procedural issues to be determined by the Rules of Bankruptcy Procedure. Section 923 of the House amendment contains certain important aspects of procedure that have been retained from present law. It is anticipated that the Rules of Bankruptcy Procedure will adopt rules similar to the present rules for chapter IX of the Bankruptcy Act [former chapter 9 (section 401 et seq.) of former Title 11].

CROSS REFERENCES

Notice in—

Commodity broker liquidation cases, see 11 USCA § 762.

Stockbroker liquidation cases, see 11 USCA § 743.

Notice of order for relief, see 11 USCA § 342.

§ 924. List of creditors

The debtor shall file a list of creditors.

(Pub.L. 95–598, Nov. 6, 1978, 92 Stat. 2623.)

HISTORICAL AND STATUTORY NOTES

Revision Notes and Legislative Reports

1978 Acts. This section adopts the provision presently contained in section 85(b) of Chapter IX [section 405(b) of former Title 11]. A list of creditors, as complete and accurate as practicable, must be filed with the court. Senate Report No. 95–989.

This section directs the debtor to file a list of creditors with the court. A comparable provision is presently contained in section 85(b) of chapter IX [section 405(b) of former Title 11]. The Rules, [Rules of Bankruptcy Procedure, this title], in Rule 9–7, copy the provisions of section 85(b), with additional matter. As noted above, section 405(d) of title IV will continue those Rules in effect. Because the form, time of filing, and nature of the list, are procedural matters that may call for some flexibility, those details have been left to the Rules. House Report No. 95–595.

Legislative Statements

Section 924 of the House amendment is derived from section 924 of the House bill with the location of the filing of the list of creditors to be determined by the rules of bankruptcy procedure. The detailed requirements of section 724 [924] of the Senate bill are anticipated to be incorporated in the rules of bankruptcy procedure.

CROSS REFERENCES

Duty of—

Debtor to file list of creditors, see 11 USCA § 521.

Trustee to file list of creditors in Chapter 11 cases, see 11 USCA § 1106.

§ 925. Effect of list of claims

A proof of claim is deemed filed under section 501 of this title for any claim that appears in the list filed under section 924 of this title, except a claim that is listed as disputed, contingent, or unliquidated.

(Pub.L. 95–598, Nov. 6, 1978, 92 Stat. 2623.)

HISTORICAL AND STATUTORY NOTES

Revision Notes and Legislative Reports

1978 Acts. Section 926 [now section 925] follows the policy contained in section 88(a) of the present Act [section 408(a) of former Title 11], though certain details are left to the Rules. The language of section 926 is the same as that of proposed 11 U.S.C. 1111, which applies in chapter 11 cases. The list of creditors filed under section 924 is given weight as prima facie evidence of the claims listed (except claims that are listed as disputed, contingent, or unliquidated), which are deemed filed under section 501, obviating the need for listed creditors to file proofs of claim. Senate Report No. 95–989.

Legislative Statements

Section 925 of the Senate amendment regarding venue and fees has been deleted.

§ 926. Avoiding powers

(a) If the debtor refuses to pursue a cause of action under section 544, 545, 547, 548, 549(a), or 550 of this title, then on request of a creditor, the court may appoint a trustee to pursue such cause of action.

(b) A transfer of property of the debtor to or for the benefit of any holder of a bond or note, on account of such bond or note, may not be avoided under section 547 of this title.

(Pub.L. 95–598, Nov. 6, 1978, 92 Stat. 2623; Pub.L. 100–597, § 6, Nov. 3, 1988, 102 Stat. 3029.)

HISTORICAL AND STATUTORY NOTES

Revision Notes and Legislative Reports

1978 Acts. This section [928 (now section 926)] adopts current section 85(h) [section 405(h) of former Title 11] which provides for a trustee to be appointed for the purpose of pursuing an action under an avoiding power, if the debtor refuses to do so. This section is necessary because a municipality might, by reason of political pressure or desire for future good relations with a particular creditor or class of creditors, make payments to such creditors in the days preceding the petition to the detriment of all other creditors. No change in the elected officials of such a city would automatically occur upon filing of the petition, and it might be very awkward for those same officials to turn around and demand the return of the payments following the filing of the petition. Hence, the need for a trustee for such purpose.

The general avoiding powers are incorporated by reference in section 901 and are broader than under current law. Preferences, fraudulent conveyances, and other kinds of transfers will thus be voidable.

Incorporated by reference also is the power to accept or reject executory contracts and leases (section 365). Within the definition of executory contracts are collective bargaining agreements between the city and its employees. Such contracts may be rejected despite contrary State laws. Courts should readily allow the rejection of such contracts where they are burdensome, the rejection will aid in the municipality's reorganization and in consideration of the equities of each case. On the last point, "[e]quities in favor of the city in chapter 9 will be far more compelling than the equities in favor of the employer in chapter 11. Onerous employment obligations may prevent a city from balancing its budget for some time. The prospect of an unbalanced budget may preclude judicial confirmation of the plan. Unless a city can reject its labor contracts, lack of funds may force cutbacks in police, fire, sanitation, and welfare services, imposing hardships on many citizens. In addition, because cities in the past have often seemed immune to the constraint of "profitability" faced by private businesses, their wage contracts may be relatively more onerous than those in the private sector." Executory Contracts and Municipal Bankruptcy, 85 Yale L.J. 957, 965 (1976) (footnote omitted). Rejection of the contracts may require the municipalities to renegotiate such contracts by state collective bargaining laws. It is intended that the power to reject collective bargaining agreements will preempt state termination provisions, but not state collective bargaining laws. Thus, a city would not be required to maintain existing employment terms during the renegotiation period. Senate Report No. 95–989.

1988 Acts. House Report No. 100–1011, see 1988 U.S.Code Cong. and Adm.News, p. 4115.

Legislative Statements

Section 926 of the House amendment is derived from section 928 of the Senate bill. The provision enables creditors to request the court to appoint a trustee to pursue avoiding powers if the debtor refuses to exercise those powers. Section 901 of the House amendment makes a corresponding change to incorporate avoiding powers included in the Senate amendment, but excluded from the House bill.

Effective and Applicability Provisions

1988 Acts. Amendment by Pub.L. 100–597 effective Nov. 3, 1988, but not applicable to any case commenced under this title before that date, see section 12 of Pub.L. 100–597, set out as a note under section 101 of this title.

CROSS REFERENCES

Appointment of trustee in—

Chapter eleven cases, see 11 USCA § 1104.

Chapter thirteen cases, see 11 USCA § 1302.

Railroad reorganization cases, see 11 USCA § 1163.

Trustee defined when used in sections made applicable to cases under this chapter, see 11 USCA § 902.

§ 927. Limitation on recourse

The holder of a claim payable solely from special revenues of the debtor under applicable nonbankruptcy law shall not be treated as having recourse against the debtor on account of such claim pursuant to section 1111(b) of this title.

(Added Pub.L. 100–597, § 7(2), Nov. 3, 1988, 102 Stat. 3029.)

HISTORICAL AND STATUTORY NOTES

Revision Notes and Legislative Reports

1988 Acts. House Report No. 100–1011, see 1988 U.S.Code Cong. and Adm.News, p. 4115.

Effective and Applicability Provisions

1988 Acts. Section effective Nov. 3, 1988, but not applicable to any case commenced under this title before that date, see section 12 of Pub.L. 100–597, set out as an Effective Date of 1988 Amendment note under section 101 of this title.

§ 928. Post petition effect of security interest

(a) Notwithstanding section 552(a) of this title and subject to subsection (b) of this section, special revenues acquired by the debtor after the commencement of the case shall remain subject to any lien resulting from any security agreement entered into by the debtor before the commencement of the case.

(b) Any such lien on special revenues, other than municipal betterment assessments, derived from a project or system shall be subject to the necessary operating expenses of such project or system, as the case may be.

(Added Pub.L. 100–597, § 8, Nov. 3, 1988, 102 Stat. 3029.)

HISTORICAL AND STATUTORY NOTES

Revision Notes and Legislative Reports

1988 Acts. House Report No. 100–1011, see 1988 U.S.Code Cong. and Adm.News, p. 4115.

Effective and Applicability Provisions

1988 Acts. Section effective Nov. 3. 1988, but not applicable to any case commenced under this title before that date, see section 12 of Pub.L. 100–597, set out as an Effective Date of 1988 Amendment note under section 101 of this title.

§ 929. Municipal leases

A lease to a municipality shall not be treated as an executory contract or unexpired lease for the purposes of section 365 or 502(b)(6) of this title solely by reason of its being subject to termination in the event the debtor fails to appropriate rent.

(Added Pub.L. 100–597, § 9, Nov. 3, 1988, 102 Stat. 3030.)

HISTORICAL AND STATUTORY NOTES

Revision Notes and Legislative Reports

1988 Acts. House Report No. 100–1011, see 1988 U.S.Code Cong. and Adm.News, p. 4115.

Effective and Applicability Provisions

1988 Acts. Section effective Nov. 3, 1988, but not applicable to any case commenced under this title before that date, see section 12 of Pub.L. 100–597, set out as an Effective Date of 1988 Amendment note under section 101 of this title.

§ 930. Dismissal

(a) After notice and a hearing, the court may dismiss a case under this chapter for cause, including—

(1) want of prosecution;

(2) unreasonable delay by the debtor that is prejudicial to creditors;

(3) failure to propose a plan within the time fixed under section 941 of this title;

(4) if a plan is not accepted within any time fixed by the court;

(5) denial of confirmation of a plan under section 943(b) of this title and denial of additional time for filing another plan or a modification of a plan; or

(6) if the court has retained jurisdiction after confirmation of a plan—

(A) material default by the debtor with respect to a term of such plan; or

(B) termination of such plan by reason of the occurrence of a condition specified in such plan.

(b) The court shall dismiss a case under this chapter if confirmation of a plan under this chapter is refused.

(Pub.L. 95–598, Nov. 6, 1978, 92 Stat. 2623, § 927; Pub.L. 98–353, Title III, § 496, July 10, 1984, 98 Stat. 384; renumbered § 930, Pub.L. 100–597, § 7(1), Nov. 3, 1988, 102 Stat. 3029.)

HISTORICAL AND STATUTORY NOTES

Revision Notes and Legislative Reports

1978 Acts. Section 927 conforms to section 98 [section 418 of former Title 11] of current law. The Section [sic] permits dismissal by the court for unreasonable delay by the debtor, failure to propose a plan, failure of acceptance of a plan, or default by the debtor under a conformed plan. Mandatory dismissal is required if confirmation is refused. Senate Report No. 95–989.

Section 926 [now 927] generally conforms to section 98(a) [section 418(a) of former title 11] of current law. Stylistic changes have been made to conform the language with that used in chapter 11, section 1112. The section permits dismissal by the court for unreasonable delay by the debtor that is prejudicial to creditors, failure to propose a plan, failure of confirmation of a plan, or material default by the debtor under a confirmed plan. The only significant change from current law lies in the second ground. Currently, section 98(a)(2) provides for dismissal if a proposed plan is not accepted, and section 98(b) *requires* dismissal if an accepted plan is not confirmed. In order to provide greater flexibility to the court, the debtor, and creditors, the bill allows the court to permit the debtor to propose another plan if the first plan is not confirmed. In that event the debtor need not, as under current law, commence the case all over again. This could provide savings in time and administrative expenses if a plan is denied confirmation. House Report No. 95–595.

1984 Acts. Statements by Legislative Leaders, see 1984 U.S.Code Cong. and Adm.News, p. 576.

1988 Acts. House Report No. 100–1011, see 1988 U.S.Code Cong. and Adm.News, p. 4115.

Legislative Statements

Section 927(b) of the House amendment is derived from section 927(b) of the Senate bill. The provision requires mandatory dismissal if confirmation of a plan is refused.

The House amendment deletes section 929 of the Senate amendment as unnecessary since the bankruptcy court has original exclusive jurisdiction of all cases under chapter 9.

The House amendment deletes section 930 of the Senate amendment and incorporates section 507(a)(1) by reference.

Effective and Applicability Provisions

1984 Acts. Amendment by Pub.L. 98–353 effective with respect to cases filed 90 days after July 10, 1984, see section 552(a), formerly 553(a), of Pub.L. 98–353, set out as a note under section 101 of this title.

CROSS REFERENCES

Conversion or dismissal of—

Chapter eleven cases, see 11 USCA § 1112.

Chapter thirteen cases, see 11 USCA § 1307.

Dismissal of Chapter seven cases, see 11 USCA § 707.

Effect of dismissal, see 11 USCA § 349.

SUBCHAPTER III—THE PLAN

§ 941. Filing of plan

The debtor shall file a plan for the adjustment of the debtor's debts. If such a plan is not filed with the petition, the debtor shall file such a plan at such later time as the court fixes.

(Pub.L. 95–598, Nov. 6, 1978, 92 Stat. 2624.)

HISTORICAL AND STATUTORY NOTES

Revision Notes and Legislative Reports

1978 Acts. Section 941 gives the debtor the exclusive right to propose a plan, and directs that the debtor propose one either with the petition or within such time as the court directs. The section follows section 90(a) of current law [section 410(a) of former Title 11]. Senate Report No. 95–989.

1984 Acts. Statements by Legislative Leaders, see 1984 U.S.Code Cong. and Adm.News, p. 576.

CROSS REFERENCES

Dismissal for failure to timely propose plan, see 11 USCA § 930.

Filing of plan in Chapter thirteen cases, see 11 USCA § 1321.

Who may file a plan in Chapter eleven cases, see 11 USCA § 1121.

§ 942. Modification of plan

The debtor may modify the plan at any time before confirmation, but may not modify the plan so that the plan as modified fails to meet the requirements of this chapter. After the debtor files a modification, the plan as modified becomes the plan.

(Pub.L. 95–598, Nov. 6, 1978, 92 Stat. 2624.)

HISTORICAL AND STATUTORY NOTES

Revision Notes and Legislative Reports

1978 Acts. Section 942 permits the debtor to modify the plan at any time before confirmation, as does section 90(a) of current law [section 410(a) of former Title 11]. Senate Report No.95–989.

Legislative Statements

The House amendment deletes section 942 of the Senate amendment in favor of incorporating section 1125 by cross-reference. Similarly, the House amendment does not incorporate section 944 or 945 of the Senate amendment since incorporation of several sections in chapter 11 in section 901 is sufficient.

CROSS REFERENCES

Modification of plan after confirmation in—

Chapter thirteen cases, see 11 USCA § 1329.

Chapter twelve cases, see 11 USCA § 1229.

Modification of plan before confirmation in—

Chapter thirteen cases, see 11 USCA § 1323.

Chapter twelve cases, see 11 USCA § 1223.

Modification of plan in Chapter eleven cases, see 11 USCA § 1127.

§ 943. Confirmation

(a) A special tax payer may object to confirmation of a plan.

(b) The court shall confirm the plan if—

(1) the plan complies with the provisions of this title made applicable by sections 103(e) and 901 of this title;

(2) the plan complies with the provisions of this chapter;

(3) all amounts to be paid by the debtor or by any person for services or expenses in the case or incident to the plan have been fully disclosed and are reasonable;

(4) the debtor is not prohibited by law from taking any action necessary to carry out the plan;

(5) except to the extent that the holder of a particular claim has agreed to a different treatment of such claim, the plan provides that on the effective date of the plan each holder of a claim of a kind specified in section 507(a)(2) of this title will receive on account of such claim cash equal to the allowed amount of such claim;

(6) any regulatory or electoral approval necessary under applicable nonbankruptcy law in order to carry out any provision of the plan has been obtained, or such provision is expressly conditioned on such approval; and

(7) the plan is in the best interests of creditors and is feasible.

(Pub.L. 95–598, Nov. 6, 1978, 92 Stat. 2624; Pub.L. 98–353, Title III, § 497, July 10, 1984, 98 Stat. 384; Pub.L. 100–597, § 10, Nov. 3, 1988, 102 Stat. 3030; Pub.L. 109–8, Title XV, § 1502(a)(6), Apr. 20, 2005, 119 Stat. 216.)

HISTORICAL AND STATUTORY NOTES

Revision Notes and Legislative Reports

1978 Acts. Section 946 [now this section] is adopted from current section 94 [section 414 of former Title 11]. The test for confirmation is whether or not the plan is fair and equitable and feasible. The fair and equitable test tracts current chapter X [former chapter 10 (section 501 et seq.) of this title] and is known as the strict priority rule. Creditors must be provided, under the plan, the going concern value of their claims. The going concern value contemplates a "comparison of revenues and expenditures taking into account the taxing power and the extent to which tax increases are both necessary and feasible" Municipal Insolvency, supra, at p. 64, and is intended to provide more of a return to creditors than the liquidation value if the city's assets could be liquidated like those of a private corporation. Senate Report No. 95–989.

In addition to the confirmation requirements incorporated from section 1129 by section 901, this section specifies additional requirements. Paragraph (1) requires compliance with the provisions of the title made applicable in chapter 9 cases. This provision follows section 94(b)(2) [section 414(b)(2) of former Title 11]. Paragraph (2) requires compliance with the provisions of chapter 9, as does section 94(b)(2) [section 414(b)(2) of former Title 11]. Paragraph (3) adopts section 94(b)(4) [section 414(b)(4) of former Title 11], requiring disclosure and reasonableness of all payments to be made in connection with the plan or the case. Paragraph (4), copied from section 92(b)(6) [probably should be "94(b)(6)", which was section 414(b)(6) of former Title 11], requires that the debtor not be prohibited by law from taking any action necessary to carry out the plan. Paragraph (5) departs from current law by requiring that administrative expenses be paid in full, but not necessarily in cash. Finally, paragraph (6) requires that the plan be in the best interest of creditors and feasible. The best interest test was deleted in section 94(b)(1) of current chapter IX [section 414(b)(1) of former Title 11] from previous chapter IX [former chapter 9 (section 401 et seq.) of former Title 11], because it was redundant with the fair and equitable rule. However, this bill proposes a new confirmation standard generally for reorganization, one element of which is the best interest of creditors test; see section 1129(a)(7). In that section, the test is phrased in terms of liquidation of the debtor. Because that is not possible in a municipal case, the test here is phrased in its more traditional form, using the words of art "best interest of creditors." The best interest of creditors test here is in addition to the financial standards imposed on the plan by section 1129(a)(8) and 1129(b), just as those provisions are in addition to the comparable best interest test in chapter 11, 11 U.S.C. 1129(a)(7). The feasibility requirement, added in the revision of chapter IX [former chapter 9 (section 401 et seq.) of former Title 11] last year, is retained. House Report No. 95–595.

1984 Acts. Statements by Legislative Leaders, see 1984 U.S.Code Cong. and Adm.News, p. 576.

1988 Acts. House Report No. 100–1011, see 1988 U.S.Code Cong. and Adm.News, p. 4115.

2005 Acts. House Report No. 109–31(Part I), see 2005 U.S. Code Cong. and Adm. News, p. 88.

Legislative Statements

Section 943(a) of the House amendment makes clear that a special taxpayer may object to confirmation of a plan. Section 943(b) of the House amendment is derived from section 943 of the House bill respecting confirmation of a plan under chapter 9. It must be emphasized that these standards of confirmation are in addition to standards in section 1129 that are made applicable to chapter 9 by section 901 of the House amendment. In particular, if the requirements of section 1129(a)(8) are not complied with, then the proponent may request application of section 1129(b). The court will then be required to confirm the plan if it complies with the "fair and equitable" test and is in the best interests of creditors. The best interests of creditors test does not mean liquidation value as under chapter XI of the Bankruptcy Act [former chapter 11 (section 701 et seq.) of former Title 11]. In making such a determination, it is expected that the court will be guided by standards set forth in *Kelley v. Everglades Drainage District,* 319 U.S. 415 (1943) [Fla.1943, 63 S.Ct. 1141, 87 L.Ed. 1485, rehearing denied 63 S.Ct. 1444, 320 U.S. 214, 87 L.Ed. 1851, motion denied 64 S.Ct. 783, 321 U.S. 754, 88 L.Ed. 1054] and *Fano v. Newport Heights Irrigation Dist.,* 114 F.2d 563 (9th Cir. 1940), as under present law, the bankruptcy court should make findings as detailed as possible to support a conclusion that this test has been met. However, it must be emphasized that unlike current law, the fair and equitable test under section 1129(b) will not apply if section 1129(a)(8) has been satisfied in addition to the other confirmation standards specified in section 943 and incorporated by reference in section 901 of the House amendment. To the extent that *American United Mutual Life Insurance Co. v. City of Avon Park,* 311 U.S. 138 (1940) [Fla.1940, 61 S.Ct. 157, 85 L.Ed. 91, 136 A.L.R. 860, rehearing denied 61 S.Ct. 395, 311 U.S. 730, 85 L.Ed. 475] and other cases are to the contrary, such cases are overruled to that extent.

References in Text

Section 103(e) of this title, referred to in subsec. (b), was redesignated subsec. (f) and a new subsec. (e) was added by Pub.L. 106–554, § 1(a)(5) [Title I, § 112(c)(5)(A)], Dec. 21, 2000, 114 Stat. 2763, 2763A–394.

Effective and Applicability Provisions

2005 Acts. Amendments by Pub.L. 109–8 effective, except as otherwise provided, 180 days after April 20, 2005, and inapplicable with respect to cases commenced under Title 11 before the effective date, see Pub.L. 109–8, § 1501, set out as a note under 11 U.S.C.A. § 101.

1988 Acts. Amendment by Pub.L. 100–597 effective Nov. 3, 1988, but not applicable to any case commenced under this title before that date, see section 12 of Pub.L. 100–597, set out as a note under section 101 of this title.

1984 Acts. Amendment by Pub.L. 98–353 effective with respect to cases filed 90 days after July 10, 1984, see section 552(a), formerly 553(a), of Pub.L. 98–353, set out as a note under section 101 of this title.

CROSS REFERENCES

Confirmation hearing in—

Chapter eleven cases, see 11 USCA § 1128.

Chapter thirteen cases, see 11 USCA § 1324.

Chapter twelve cases, see 11 USCA § 1224.

Confirmation of plan in—

Chapter eleven cases, see 11 USCA § 1129.

Chapter thirteen cases, see 11 USCA § 1325.

Chapter twelve cases, see 11 USCA § 1225.

Railroad reorganization cases, see 11 USCA § 1173.

Dismissal for denial of confirmation of plan, see 11 USCA § 930.

Unclaimed property, see 11 USCA § 347.

§ 944. Effect of confirmation

(a) The provisions of a confirmed plan bind the debtor and any creditor, whether or not—

(1) a proof of such creditor's claim is filed or deemed filed under section 501 of this title;

(2) such claim is allowed under section 502 of this title; or

(3) such creditor has accepted the plan.

(b) Except as provided in subsection (c) of this section, the debtor is discharged from all debts as of the time when—

(1) the plan is confirmed;

(2) the debtor deposits any consideration to be distributed under the plan with a disbursing agent appointed by the court; and

(3) the court has determined—

(A) that any security so deposited will constitute, after distribution, a valid legal obligation of the debtor; and

(B) that any provision made to pay or secure payment of such obligation is valid.

(c) The debtor is not discharged under subsection (b) of this section from any debt—

(1) excepted from discharge by the plan or order confirming the plan; or

(2) owed to an entity that, before confirmation of the plan, had neither notice nor actual knowledge of the case.

(Pub.L. 95–598, Nov. 6, 1978, 92 Stat. 2624.)

HISTORICAL AND STATUTORY NOTES

Revision Notes and Legislative Reports

1978 Acts. [Section 947] Subsection (a) [now section 944(a)] makes the provisions of a confirmed plan binding on the debtor and creditors. It is derived from section 95(a) of chapter 9 [section 415(a) of former Title 11].

Subsections (b) and (c) [now section 944(b) and (c)] provide for the discharge of a municipality. The discharge is essentially the same as that granted under section 95(b) of the Bankruptcy Act [section 415(b) of former Title 11]. Senate Report No. 95–989.

CROSS REFERENCES

Discharge in—

Chapter seven cases, see 11 USCA § 727.

Chapter thirteen cases, see 11 USCA § 1328.

Chapter twelve cases, see 11 USCA § 1228.

Effect of confirmation in—

Chapter eleven cases, see 11 USCA § 1141.

Chapter thirteen cases, see 11 USCA § 1327.

Chapter twelve cases, see 11 USCA § 1227.

Effect of discharge, see 11 USCA § 524.

Exceptions to discharge, see 11 USCA § 523.

§ 945. Continuing jurisdiction and closing of the case

(a) The court may retain jurisdiction over the case for such period of time as is necessary for the successful implementation of the plan.

(b) Except as provided in subsection (a) of this section, the court shall close the case when administration of the case has been completed.

(Pub.L. 95–598, Nov. 6, 1978, 92 Stat. 2625; Pub.L. 98–353, Title III, § 498, July 10, 1984, 98 Stat. 384.)

HISTORICAL AND STATUTORY NOTES

Revision Notes and Legislative Reports

1978 Acts. Section 948 [now this section] permits the court to retain jurisdiction over the case to ensure successful execution of the plan. The provision is the same as that found in section 96(e) of Chapter 9 of the present Act [former section 416(e) of former Title 11]. Senate Report No. 95–989.

1984 Acts. Statements by Legislative Leaders, see 1984 U.S.Code Cong. and Adm.News, p. 576.

Effective and Applicability Provisions

1984 Acts. Amendment by Pub.L. 98–353 effective with respect to cases filed 90 days after July 10, 1984, see section 552(a), formerly 553(a), of Pub.L. 98–353, set out as a note under section 101 of this title.

CROSS REFERENCES

Closing and reopening cases, see 11 USCA § 350.

§ 946. Effect of exchange of securities before the date of the filing of the petition

The exchange of a new security under the plan for a claim covered by the plan, whether such exchange occurred before or after the date of the filing of the petition, does not limit or impair the effectiveness of the plan or of any provision of this chapter. The amount and number specified in section 1126(c) of this title include the amount and number of claims formerly held by a creditor that has participated in any such exchange.

(Pub.L. 95–598, Nov. 6, 1978, 92 Stat. 2625.)

HISTORICAL AND STATUTORY NOTES

Revision Notes and Legislative Reports

1978 Acts. [Section 949] This section [now section 946], which follows section 97 of current law [section 417 of former Title 11], permits an exchange of a security before the case is filed to constitute an acceptance of the plan if the exchange was under a proposal that later becomes the plan. Section Report No. 95–989.

Legislative Statements

The House amendment deletes section 950 of the Senate amendment as unnecessary. The constitutionality of chapter 9 of the House amendment is beyond doubt.

CHAPTER 11—REORGANIZATION

CROSS REFERENCES

Allowance of administrative expenses of substantial contributors to cases under this chapter, see 11 USCA § 503.

Applicability of income tax provisions to cases under this chapter, see 26 USCA § 1398.

Chapters one, three, and five of this title applicable in cases under this chapter except as provided in § 1161 of this title, see 11 USCA § 103.

Claims arising from rejection under chapter plans of executory contracts or unexpired leases, see 11 USCA § 502.

Commencement of involuntary cases, see 11 USCA § 303.

Conversion to this chapter from—

Chapter seven, see 11 USCA § 706.

Chapter thirteen, see 11 USCA § 1307.

Core proceedings, see 28 USCA § 157.

Distress termination of single-employer plans in cases under this chapter, see 29 USCA § 1341.

Duration of automatic stay, see 11 USCA § 362.

Duties of United States trustees, see 28 USCA § 586.

Employment of professional persons, see 11 USCA § 327.

Establishment, operation and termination of Bankruptcy Appellate Panel Service and undue delay or increased costs, see 28 USCA § 158.

Executory contracts and unexpired leases, see 11 USCA § 365.

Filing fees, see 28 USCA § 1930.

Jurisdiction of courts in termination proceedings of employer plans brought by Pension Benefit Guaranty Corporation same as jurisdiction of courts in cases under this chapter, see 29 USCA § 1342.

Limitation on compensation of trustee, see 11 USCA § 326.

Persons required to make returns of income under this chapter, see 26 USCA § 6012.

Persons who may be debtors under this chapter, see 11 USCA § 109.

Powers of Courts to set date to file disclosure, see 11 USCA § 105.

Property of estate in cases converted from Chapter 13, see 11 USCA § 1306.

Provisions concerning reorganization plan of investment companies not to affect or derogate from powers of courts with reference to reorganizations under this title, see 15 USCA § 80a–25.

Return of excessive attorney compensation if transferred property was to be paid by debtor under plan under this chapter, see 11 USCA § 329.

Rights and powers of debtor in Chapter twelve case not encompassing certain duties of trustee serving in case under this chapter, see 11 USCA § 1203.

Special tax provisions, see 11 USCA § 346.

Stay of action against Chapter thirteen codebtor in cases converted to this chapter, see 11 USCA § 1301.

Supplemental injunctions and notice and hearings, see 11 USCA § 524.

Treatment of debtor's estate in cases under this chapter as taxpayer for certain income tax purposes, see 26 USCA § 108.

Unclaimed property, see 11 USCA § 347.

Use, sale or lease of property under plan under this chapter, see 11 USCA § 363.

SUBCHAPTER I—OFFICERS AND ADMINISTRATION

CROSS REFERENCES

Subchapter applicable only in case under this chapter except as provided in § 901 of this title, see 11 USCA § 103.

§ 1101. Definitions for this chapter

In this chapter—

(1) "debtor in possession" means debtor except when a person that has qualified under section 322 of this title is serving as trustee in the case;

(2) "substantial consummation" means—

(A) transfer of all or substantially all of the property proposed by the plan to be transferred;

(B) assumption by the debtor or by the successor to the debtor under the plan of the business or of the management of all or substantially all of the property dealt with by the plan; and

(C) commencement of distribution under the plan.

(Pub.L. 95–598, Nov. 6, 1978, 92 Stat. 2626.)

HISTORICAL AND STATUTORY NOTES

Revision Notes and Legislative Reports

1978 Acts. This section contains definitions of three terms that are used in chapter 11. Paragraph (1) defines debtor in possession to mean the debtor, except when a trustee who has qualified is serving in the case.

Paragraph (2), derived from section 229a of current law [section 629(a) of former Title 11], defines substantial consummation. Substantial consummation of a plan occurs when transfer of all or substantially all of the property proposed by the plan to be transferred is actually transferred; when the debtor (or its successor) has assumed the business of the debtor or the management of all or substantially all of the property dealt with by the plan; and when distribution under the plan has commenced.

Paragraph (3) defines for purposes of Chapter 11 a public company to mean "a debtor who, within 12 months prior to the filing of a petition for relief under this chapter, had outstanding liabilities of $5 million or more, exclusive of liabilities for goods, services, or taxes and not less than 1,000 security holders." There are, as noted, special safeguards for public investors related to the reorganization of a public company, as so defined.

Both requirements must be met: liabilities, excluding tax obligations and trade liabilities, must be $5 million or more; and (2) the number of holders of securities, debt or equity, or both, must be not less than 1,000. The amount and number are to be determined as of any time within 12 months prior to the filing of the petition for reorganization. Senate Report No. 95–989.

CROSS REFERENCES

Definitions applicable in—

Cases under this title, see 11 USCA § 101.

Chapter nine cases, see 11 USCA § 902.

Commodity broker liquidation cases, see 11 USCA § 761.

Railroad reorganization cases, see 11 USCA § 1162.

Stockbroker liquidation cases, see 11 USCA § 741.

§ 1102. Creditors' and equity security holders' committees

(a)(1) Except as provided in paragraph (3), as soon as practicable after the order for relief under chapter 11 of this title, the United States trustee shall appoint a committee of creditors holding unsecured claims and may appoint additional committees of creditors or of equity security holders as the United States trustee deems appropriate.

(2) On request of a party in interest, the court may order the appointment of additional committees of creditors or of equity security holders if necessary to assure adequate representation of creditors or of equity security holders. The United States trustee shall appoint any such committee.

(3) On request of a party in interest in a case in which the debtor is a small business debtor and for cause, the court may order that a committee of creditors not be appointed.

(4) On request of a party in interest and after notice and a hearing, the court may order the United States trustee to change the membership of a committee appointed under this subsection, if the court determines that the change is necessary to ensure adequate representation of creditors or equity security holders. The court may order the United States trustee to increase the number of members of a committee to include a creditor that is a small business concern (as described in section 3(a)(1) of the Small Business Act), if the court determines that the creditor holds claims (of the kind represented by the committee) the aggregate amount of which, in comparison to the annual gross revenue of that creditor, is disproportionately large.

(b)(1) A committee of creditors appointed under subsection (a) of this section shall ordinarily consist of the persons, willing to serve, that hold the seven largest claims against the debtor of the kinds represented on such committee, or of the members of a committee organized by creditors before the commencement of the case under this chapter, if such committee was fairly chosen and is representative of the different kinds of claims to be represented.

(2) A committee of equity security holders appointed under subsection (a)(2) of this section shall ordinarily consist of the persons, willing to serve, that hold the seven largest amounts of equity securities of the debtor of the kinds represented on such committee.

(3) A committee appointed under subsection (a) shall—

(A) provide access to information for creditors who—

(i) hold claims of the kind represented by that committee; and

(ii) are not appointed to the committee;

(B) solicit and receive comments from the creditors described in subparagraph (A); and

(C) be subject to a court order that compels any additional report or disclosure to be made to the creditors described in subparagraph (A).

(Pub.L. 95–598, Nov. 6, 1978, 92 Stat. 2626; Pub.L. 98–353, Title III, § 499, July 10, 1984, 98 Stat. 384; Pub.L. 99–554, Title II, § 221, Oct. 27, 1986, 100 Stat. 3101; Pub.L. 103–394, Title II, § 217(b), Oct. 22, 1994, 108 Stat. 4127; Pub.L. 109–8, Title IV, §§ 405, 432(b), Apr. 20, 2005, 119 Stat. 105, 110.)

HISTORICAL AND STATUTORY NOTES

Revision Notes and Legislative Reports

1978 Acts. This section provides for the election and appointment of committees. Subsection (c) provides that this section does not apply in case of a public company, as to which a trustee, appointed under section 1104(a) will have responsibility to administer the estate and to formulate a plan as provided in section 1106(a).

There is no need for the election or appointment of committees for which the appointment of a trustee is mandatory. In the case of a public company there are likely to be several committees, each representing a different class of security holders and seeking authority to retain accountants, lawyers, and other experts, who will expect to be paid. If in the case of a public company creditors or stockholders wish to organize committees, they may do so, as authorized under section 1109(a). Compensation and reimbursement will be allowed for contributions to the reorganization pursuant to section 503(b)(3) and (4). Senate Report No. 95–989.

This section provides for the appointment of creditors' and equity security holders' committees, which will be the primary negotiating bodies for the formulation of the plan of reorganization. They will represent the various classes of creditors and equity security holders from which they are selected. They will also provide supervision of the debtor in possession and of the trustee, and will protect their constituents' interests.

Subsection (a) requires the court to appoint at least one committee. That committee is to be composed of creditors holding unsecured claims. The court is authorized to appoint such additional committees as are necessary to assure adequate representation of creditors and equity security holders. The provision will be relied upon in cases in which the debtor proposes to affect several classes of debt or equity holders under the plan, and in which they need representation.

Subsection (b) contains precatory language directing the court to appoint the persons holding the seven largest claims against the debtor of the kinds represented on a creditors' committee, or the members of a prepetition committee organized by creditors before the order for relief under chapter 11. The court may continue prepetition committee members only if the committee was fairly chosen and is representative of the different kinds of claims to be represented. The court is restricted to the appointment of persons in order to exclude governmental holders of claims or interests.

Paragraph (2) of subsection (b) requires similar treatment for equity security holders' committees. The seven largest holders are normally to be appointed, but the language is only precatory.

Subsection (c) authorizes the court, on request of a party in interest, to change the size or the membership of a creditors' or equity security holders' committee if the membership of the committee is not representative of the different kinds of claims or interests to be represented. This subsection is intended, along with the nonbinding nature of subsection (b), to afford the court latitude in appointing a committee that is manageable and representative in light of the circumstances of the case. House Report No. 95–595.

1984 Acts. Statements by Legislative Leaders, see 1984 U.S.Code Cong. and Adm.News, p. 576.

1986 Acts. House Report No. 99–764 and House Conference Report No. 99–958, see 1986 U.S.Code Cong. and Adm.News, p. 5227.

1994 Acts. House Report No. 103–835, see 1994 U.S. Code Cong. and Adm. News, p. 3340.

2005 Acts. House Report No. 109–31(Part I), see 2005 U.S. Code Cong. and Adm. News, p. 88.

Legislative Statements

Section 1102(a) of the House amendment adopts a compromise between the House bill and Senate amendment requiring appointment of a committee of creditors holding unsecured claims by the court; the alternative of creditor committee election is rejected.

Section 1102(b) of the House amendment represents a compromise between the House bill and the Senate amendment by preventing the appointment of creditors who are unwilling to serve on a creditors committee.

References in Text

Section 3(a)(1) of the Small Business Act, referred to in subsec. (a)(4), is section 3(a)(1) of Pub.L. 85–536 § 2[3], July 18, 1958, 72 Stat. 384, as amended, which is classified to 15 U.S.C.A. § 632(a)(1). For complete classification, see Short Title note under 15 U.S.C.A. § 631 and Tables.

Effective and Applicability Provisions

2005 Acts. Amendments by Pub.L. 109–8 effective, except as otherwise provided, 180 days after April 20, 2005, and inapplicable with respect to cases commenced under Title 11 before the effective date, see Pub.L. 109–8, § 1501, set out as a note under 11 U.S.C.A. § 101.

1994 Acts. Amendment by Pub.L. 103–394 effective on Oct. 22, 1994, and not to apply with respect to cases commenced under Title 11 of the United States Code before Oct. 22, 1994, see section 702 of Pub.L. 103–394, set out as a note under section 101 of this title.

1986 Acts. Amendment by Pub.L. 99–554 effective 30 days after Oct. 27, 1986, except as otherwise provided for, see section 302(a) of Pub.L. 99–554, set out as a note under section 581 of Title 28, Judiciary and Judicial Procedure.

Amendment by Pub.L. 99–554, § 221, not to become effective in or with respect to certain specified judicial districts until, or apply to cases while pending in such district before, the expiration of the 270–day period beginning 30 days after Oct. 27, 1986, or of the 30–day period beginning on the date the Attorney General certifies under section 303 of Pub.L. 99–554 the region specified in a paragraph of section 581(a) of Title 28, as amended by section 111(a) of Pub.L. 99–554, that includes such district, whichever occurs first, see section 302(d)(1) of Pub.L. 99–554, set out as a note under section 581 of Title 28.

Amendment by Pub.L. 99–554, § 221, not to become effective in or with respect to certain specified judicial districts until, or apply to cases while pending in such district before, the expiration of the 2–year period beginning 30 days after Oct. 27, 1986, or of the 30–day period beginning on the date the Attorney General certifies under section 303 of Pub.L. 99–554 the region specified in a paragraph of section 581(a) of Title 28, as amended by section 111(a) of Pub.L. 99–554, that includes such district, whichever occurs first, see section 302(d)(2) of Pub.L. 99–554, set out as a note under section 581 of Title 28.

Amendment by Pub.L. 99–554, § 221, not to become effective in or with respect to judicial districts established for the States of Alabama and North Carolina until, or apply to cases while pending in such district before, such district elects to be included in a bankruptcy region established in section 581(a) of Title 28, as amended by section 111(a) of Pub.L. 99–554, or Oct. 1, 2002, whichever occurs first, and, except as otherwise provided for, with respect to cases under chapters 7, 11, 12, and 13 of Title 11 commenced before 30 days after Oct. 27, 1986, and pending in a judicial district in the States of Alabama or North Carolina before any election made under section 302(d)(3)(A) of Pub.L. 99–554 by such district becomes effective or Oct. 1, 2002, whichever occurs first, amendments by Pub.L. 99–554 not to apply until Oct. 1, 2003, or the expiration of the 1–year period beginning on the date such election becomes effective, whichever occurs first, and further, in any judicial district in Alabama or North Carolina not making the election described in section 302(d)(3)(A) of Pub.L. 99–554, any person appointed under regulations issued by the Judicial Conference to administer estates in cases under Title 11 authorized to establish, etc., a panel of private trustees, and to supervise cases and trustees in cases under chapters 7, 11, 12 and 13 of Title 11, until amendments by sections 201 to 231 of Pub.L. 99–554 effective in such district, see section 302(d)(3)(A) to (F), (H), (I), of Pub.L. 99–554, set out as a note under section 581 of Title 28.

Amendment by Pub.L. 99–554, § 221, except as otherwise provided, with respect to cases under chapters 7, 11, 12 and 13 of Title 11 commenced before 30 days after Oct. 27, 1986, and pending in a judicial district referred to in section 581(a) of Title 28, as amended by section 111(a) of Pub.L. 99–554, for which a United States trustee is not authorized before 30 days after Oct. 27, 1986 to be appointed, not applicable until the expiration of the 3–year period beginning on Oct. 27, 1986, or of the 1–year period beginning on the date the Attorney General certifies under section 303 of Pub.L. 99–554 the region specified in a paragraph of such section 581(a) that includes, such district, whichever occurs first, see section 302(e)(1), (2) of Pub.L. 99–554, set out as a note under section 581 of Title 28.

1984 Acts. Amendment by Pub.L. 98–353 effective with respect to cases filed 90 days after July 10, 1984, see section 552(a), formerly 553(a), of Pub.L. 98–353, set out as a note under section 101 of this title.

Separability of Provisions

If any provision of or amendment made by Pub.L. 103–394 or the application of such provision or amendment to any person or circumstance is held to be unconstitutional, the remaining provisions of and amendments made by Pub.L. 103–394 and the application of such provisions and amendments to any person or circumstance shall not be affected thereby, see section 701 of Pub.L. 103–394, set out as a note under section 101 of this title.

CROSS REFERENCES

Allowance of creditor committee expenses, see 11 USCA § 503.

Applicability of this section in Chapter nine cases, see 11 USCA § 901.

Creditors' committees in Chapter seven cases, see 11 USCA § 705.

Disallowance of administrative expenses for creditors' and equity security holders' committees, see 11 USCA § 503.

Effect of conversion, see 11 USCA § 348.

Inapplicability of subsec. (a)(1) of this section to railroad reorganization cases, see 11 USCA § 1161.

Limitation on compensation of professional persons, see 11 USCA § 328.

"Person" defined for purposes of this section, see 11 USCA § 101.

§ 1103. Powers and duties of committees

(a) At a scheduled meeting of a committee appointed under section 1102 of this title, at which a majority of the members of such committee are present, and with the court's approval, such committee may select and authorize the employment by such committee of one or more attorneys, accountants, or other agents, to represent or perform services for such committee.

(b) An attorney or accountant employed to represent a committee appointed under section 1102 of this title may not, while employed by such committee, represent any other entity having an adverse interest in connection with the case. Representation of one or more creditors of the same class as represented by the committee shall not per se constitute the representation of an adverse interest.

(c) A committee appointed under section 1102 of this title may—

(1) consult with the trustee or debtor in possession concerning the administration of the case;

(2) investigate the acts, conduct, assets, liabilities, and financial condition of the debtor, the operation of the debtor's business and the desirability of the continuance of such business, and any other matter relevant to the case or to the formulation of a plan;

(3) participate in the formulation of a plan, advise those represented by such committee of such committee's determinations as to any plan formulated, and collect and file with the court acceptances or rejections of a plan;

(4) request the appointment of a trustee or examiner under section 1104 of this title; and

(5) perform such other services as are in the interest of those represented.

(d) As soon as practicable after the appointment of a committee under section 1102 of this title, the trustee shall meet with such committee to transact such business as may be necessary and proper.

(Pub.L. 95–598, Nov. 6, 1978, 92 Stat. 2627; Pub.L. 98–353, Title III, §§ 324, 500, July 10, 1984, 98 Stat. 358, 384.)

HISTORICAL AND STATUTORY NOTES

Revision Notes and Legislative Reports

1978 Acts. This section defines the powers and duties of a committee elected or appointed under section 1102.

Under subsection (a) the committee may, if authorized by the court, employ one or more attorneys, accountants, or other agents to represent or perform services for the committee. Normally one attorney should suffice; more than one may be authorized for good cause. The same considerations apply to the services of others, if the need for any at all is demonstrated.

Under subsections (c) and (d) the committee, like any party in interest, may confer with the trustee or debtor regarding the administration of the estate; may advise the court on the need for a trustee under section 1104(b). The committee may investigate matters specified in paragraph (2) of subsection (c), but only if authorized by the court and if no trustee or examiner is appointed. Senate Report No. 95–989.

Subsection (a) of this section authorizes a committee appointed under section 1102 to select and authorize the employment of counsel, accountants, or other agents, to represent or perform services for the committee. The committee's selection and authorization is subject to the court's approval, and may only be done at a meeting of the committee at which a majority of its members are present. The subsection provides for the employment of more than one attorney. However, this will be the exception, and not the rule; cause must be shown to depart from the normal standard.

Subsection (b) requires a committee's counsel to cease representation of any other entity in connection with the case after he begins to represent the committee. This will prevent the potential of severe conflicts of interest.

Subsection (c) lists a committee's functions in a chapter 11 case. The committee may consult with the trustee or debtor in possession concerning the administration of the case, may investigate the acts, conduct, assets, liabilities and financial condition of the debtor, the operation of the debtor's business, and the desirability of the continuance of the business, and any other matter relevant to the case or to the formulation of a plan. The committee may participate in the formulation of a plan, advise those it represents of the committee's recommendation with respect to any plan formulated, and collect and file acceptances. These will be its most important functions. The committee may also determine the need for the appointment of a trustee, if one has not previously been appointed, and perform such other services as are in the interest of those represented.

Subsection (d) requires the trustee and each committee to meet as soon as practicable after their appointments to transact such business as may be necessary and proper. House Report No. 95–595.

1984 Acts. Statements by Legislative Leaders, see 1984 U.S.Code Cong. and Adm.News, p. 576.

Effective and Applicability Provisions

1984 Acts. Amendment by Pub.L. 98–353 effective with respect to cases filed 90 days after July 10, 1984, see section 552(a), formerly 553(a), of Pub.L. 98–353, set out as a note under section 101 of this title.

CROSS REFERENCES

Applicability of this section in Chapter nine cases, see 11 USCA § 901.

Compensation of officers, see 11 USCA § 330.

Creditors' committees in Chapter seven cases, see 11 USCA § 705.

Interim compensation for professional persons, see 11 USCA § 331.

Limitation on compensation of professional persons, see 11 USCA § 328.

§ 1104. Appointment of trustee or examiner

(a) At any time after the commencement of the case but before confirmation of a plan, on request of a party in interest or the United States trustee, and after notice and a hearing, the court shall order the appointment of a trustee—

(1) for cause, including fraud, dishonesty, incompetence, or gross mismanagement of the affairs of the debtor by current management, either before or after the commencement of the case, or similar cause, but not including the number of holders of securities of the debtor or the amount of assets or liabilities of the debtor;

(2) if such appointment is in the interests of creditors, any equity security holders, and other interests of the estate, without regard to the number of holders of securities of the debtor or the amount of assets or liabilities of the debtor; or

(3) if grounds exist to convert or dismiss the case under section 1112, but the court determines that the appointment of a trustee or an examiner is in the best interests of creditors and the estate.

(b)(1) Except as provided in section 1163 of this title, on the request of a party in interest made not later than 30 days after the court orders the appointment of a trustee under subsection (a), the United

States trustee shall convene a meeting of creditors for the purpose of electing one disinterested person to serve as trustee in the case. The election of a trustee shall be conducted in the manner provided in subsections (a), (b), and (c) of section 702 of this title.

(2)(A) If an eligible, disinterested trustee is elected at a meeting of creditors under paragraph (1), the United States trustee shall file a report certifying that election.

(B) Upon the filing of a report under subparagraph (A)—

(i) the trustee elected under paragraph (1) shall be considered to have been selected and appointed for purposes of this section; and

(ii) the service of any trustee appointed under subsection (d) shall terminate.

(C) The court shall resolve any dispute arising out of an election described in subparagraph (A).

(c) If the court does not order the appointment of a trustee under this section, then at any time before the confirmation of a plan, on request of a party in interest or the United States trustee, and after notice and a hearing, the court shall order the appointment of an examiner to conduct such an investigation of the debtor as is appropriate, including an investigation of any allegations of fraud, dishonesty, incompetence, misconduct, mismanagement, or irregularity in the management of the affairs of the debtor of or by current or former management of the debtor, if—

(1) such appointment is in the interests of creditors, any equity security holders, and other interests of the estate; or

(2) the debtor's fixed, liquidated, unsecured debts, other than debts for goods, services, or taxes, or owing to an insider, exceed $5,000,000.

(d) If the court orders the appointment of a trustee or an examiner, if a trustee or an examiner dies or resigns during the case or is removed under section 324 of this title, or if a trustee fails to qualify under section 322 of this title, then the United States trustee, after consultation with parties in interest, shall appoint, subject to the court's approval, one disinterested person other than the United States trustee to serve as trustee or examiner, as the case may be, in the case.

(e) The United States trustee shall move for the appointment of a trustee under subsection (a) if there are reasonable grounds to suspect that current members of the governing body of the debtor, the debtor's chief executive or chief financial officer, or members of the governing body who selected the debtor's chief executive or chief financial officer, participated in actual fraud, dishonesty, or criminal conduct in the management of the debtor or the debtor's public financial reporting.

(Pub.L. 95–598, Nov. 6, 1978, 92 Stat. 2627; Pub.L. 99–554, Title II, § 222, Oct. 27, 1986, 100 Stat. 3102; Pub.L. 103–394, Title II, § 211(a), Title V, § 501(d)(30), Oct. 22, 1994, 108 Stat. 4125, 4146; Pub.L. 109–8, Title IV, §§ 416, 442(b), Title XIV, § 1405, Apr. 20, 2005, 119 Stat. 107, 116, 215.)

HISTORICAL AND STATUTORY NOTES

Revision Notes and Legislative Reports

1978 Acts. Subsection (a) provides for the mandatory appointment of a disinterested trustee in the case of a public company, as defined in section 1101(3), within 10 days of the order for relief, or of a successor, in the event of a vacancy, as soon as practicable.

Section 156 of chapter X [section 516 (556) of former Title 11] requires the appointment of a disinterested trustee if the debtor's liabilities are $250,000 or over. Section 1104(a) marks a substantial change. The appointment of a trustee is mandatory only for a public company, which under section 1101(3), has $5 million in liabilities, excluding tax and trade obligations, and 1,000 security holders. In view of past experience, cases involving public companies will under normal circumstances probably be relatively few in number but of vast importance in terms of public investor interest.

In case of a nonpublic company, the appointment or election of a trustee is discretionary if the interests of the estate and its security holders would be served thereby. A test based on probable costs and benefits of a trusteeship is not practical. The appointment may be made at any time prior to confirmation of the plan.

In case of a nonpublic company, if no trustee is appointed, the court may under subsection (c) appoint an examiner, if the appointment would serve the interests of the estate and security holders. The purpose of his appointment is specified in section 1106(b). Senate Report No. 95–989.

Subsection (a) of this section governs the appointment of trustees in reorganization cases. The court is permitted to order the appointment of one trustee at any time after the commencement of the case if a party in interest so requests. The court may order appointment only if the protection afforded by a trustee is needed and the costs and expenses of a trustee would not be disproportionately higher than the value of the protection afforded.

The protection afforded by a trustee would be needed, for example, in cases where the current management of the debtor has been fraudulent or dishonest, or has grossly mismanaged the company, or where the debtor's management has abandoned the business. A trustee would not necessarily be needed to investigate misconduct of former management of the debtor, because an examiner appointed under this section might well be able to serve that function adequately without displacing the current management. Generally, a trustee would not be needed in any case where the protection afforded by a trustee could equally be afforded by an examiner. Though the device of examiner appears in current chapter X [chapter 10 (section 501 et seq.) of former Title 11], it is rarely used because of the nearly absolute presumption in favor of the appointment of a trustee. Its use here will give the courts, debtors, creditors, and equity security holders greater flexibility in handling the affairs of an insolvent debtor, permitting the court to tailor the remedy to the case.

The second test, relating to the costs and expenses of a trustee, is not intended to be a strict cost/benefit analysis. It is included to require the court to have due regard for any additional costs or expenses that the appointment of a trustee would impose on the estate.

Subsection (b) permits the court, at any time after the commencement of the case and on request of a party in interest, to order the appointment of an examiner, if the court has not ordered the appointment of a trustee. The examiner would be appointed to conduct such an investigation of the debtor as is appropriate under the particular circumstances of the case, including an investigation of any allegations of fraud, dishonesty, or gross mismanagement of the debtor of or by current or former management of the debtor. The standards for the appointment of an examiner are the same as those for the appointment of a trustee: the protection must be needed, and the costs and expenses must not be disproportionately high.

By virtue of proposed 11 U.S.C. 1109, an indenture trustee and the Securities and Exchange Commission will be parties in interest for the purpose of requesting the appointment of a trustee or examiner.

Subsection (c) directs that the United States trustee actually select and appoint the trustee or examiner ordered appointed under this section. The United States trustee is required to consult with various parties in interest before selecting and appointing a trustee. He is not bound to select one of the members of the panel of private trustees established under proposed 28 U.S.C. 586(a)(1) which exists only for the purpose of providing trustees for chapter 7 cases. Neither is he precluded from selecting a panel member if the member is qualified to serve as chapter 11 trustee. Appointment by the United States trustee will remove the court from the often criticized practice of appointing an officer that will appear in litigation before the court against an adverse party. House Report No. 95–595.

1986 Acts. House Report No. 99–764 and House Conference Report No. 99–958, see 1986 U.S.Code Cong. and Adm.News, p. 5227.

1994 Acts. House Report No. 103–835, see 1994 U.S. Code Cong. and Adm. News, p. 3340.

2005 Acts. House Report No. 109–31(Part I), see 2005 U.S. Code Cong. and Adm. News, p. 88.

Legislative Statements

Section 1104 of the House amendment represents a compromise between the House bill and the Senate amendment concerning the appointment of a trustee or examiner. The method of appointment rather than election, is derived from the House bill; the two alternative standards of appointment are derived with modifications from the Senate amendment, instead of the standard stated in the House bill. For example, if the current management of the debtor gambled away rental income before the filing of the petition, a trustee should be appointed after the petition, whether or not post-petition mismanagement can be shown. However, under no circumstances will cause include the number of security holders of the debtor or the amount of assets or liabilities of the debtor. The standard also applies to the appointment of an examiner in those circumstances in which mandatory appointment, as previously detailed, is not required.

Effective and Applicability Provisions

2005 Acts. Amendments by Pub.L. 109–8, Title XIV, effective, except as otherwise provided, on Apr. 20, 2005, and applicable only with respect to cases commenced under Title 11 on or after Apr. 20, 2005, see Pub.L. 109–8, § 1406, set out as a note under 11 U.S.C.A. § 507.

Amendments by Pub.L. 109–8 effective, except as otherwise provided, 180 days after April 20, 2005, and inapplicable with respect to cases commenced under Title 11 before the effective date, see Pub.L. 109–8, § 1501, set out as a note under 11 U.S.C.A. § 101.

1994 Acts. Amendments by Pub.L. 103–394 effective on Oct. 22, 1994, and not to apply with respect to cases commenced under Title 11 of the United States Code before Oct. 22, 1994, see section 702 of Pub.L. 103–394, set out as a note under section 101 of this title.

1986 Acts. Amendment by Pub.L. 99–554 effective 30 days after Oct. 27, 1986, except as otherwise provided for, see section 302(a) of Pub.L. 99–554, set out as a note under section 581 of Title 28, Judiciary and Judicial Procedure.

Amendment by Pub.L. 99–554, § 222, not to become effective in or with respect to certain specified judicial districts until, or apply to cases while pending in such district before, the expiration of the 270–day period beginning 30 days after Oct. 27, 1986, or of the 30–day period beginning on the date the Attorney General certifies under section 303 of Pub.L. 99–554 the region specified in a paragraph of section 581(a) of Title 28, as amended by section 111(a) of Pub.L. 99–554, that includes such district, whichever occurs first, see section 302(d)(1) of Pub.L. 99–554, set out as a note under section 581 of Title 28.

Amendment by Pub.L. 99–554, § 222, not to become effective in or with respect to certain specified judicial districts until, or apply to cases while pending in such district before, the expiration of the 2–year period beginning 30 days after Oct. 27, 1986, or of the 30–day period beginning on the date the Attorney General certifies under section 303 of Pub.L. 99–554 the region specified in a paragraph of section 581(a) of Title 28, as amended by section 111(a) of Pub.L. 99–554, that includes such district, whichever occurs first, see section 302(d)(2) of Pub.L. 99–554, set out as a note under section 581 of Title 28.

Amendment by Pub.L. 99–554, § 222, not to become effective in or with respect to judicial districts established for the States of Alabama and North Carolina until, or apply to cases while pending in such district before, such district elects to be included in a bankruptcy region established in section 581(a) of Title 28, as amended by section 111(a) of Pub.L. 99–554, or Oct. 1, 2002, whichever occurs first, and, except as otherwise provided for, with respect to cases under chapters 7, 11, 12, and 13 of Title 11 commenced before 30 days after Oct. 27, 1986, and pending in a judicial district in the States of Alabama or North Carolina before any election made under section 302(d)(3)(A) of Pub.L. 99–554 by such district becomes effective or Oct. 1, 2992, whichever occurs first, amendments by Pub.L. 99–554 not to apply until Oct. 1, 2003, or the expiration of the 1–year period beginning on the date such election becomes effective, whichever occurs first, and further, in any judicial district in Alabama or North Carolina not making the election described in section 302(d)(3)(A) of Pub.L. 99–554, any person appointed under regulations issued by the Judicial Conference to administer estates in cases under Title 11 authorized to establish, etc., a panel of private trustees, and to supervise cases and trustees in cases under chapters 7, 11, 12, and 13 of Title 11, until amendments by sections 201 to 231 of Pub.L. 99–554 effective in such district, see section 302(d)(3)(A) to (F), (H), (I), of Pub.L. 99–554, set out as a note under section 581 of Title 28.

Amendment by Pub.L. 99–554, § 222, except as otherwise provided, with respect to cases under chapters 7, 11, 12, and 13 of Title 11 commenced before 30 days after Oct. 27, 1986, and pending in a judicial district referred to in section 581(a) of Title 28, as amended by section 111(a) of Pub.L. 99–554, for which a United States trustee is not authorized before 30 days after Oct. 27, 1986 to be appointed, not applicable until the expiration of the 3–year period beginning on Oct. 27, 1986, or of the 1–year period beginning on the date the Attorney General certifies under section 303 of Pub.L. 99–554 the region specified in a paragraph of such section 581(a) that includes, such district, whichever occurs first, see section 302(e)(1), (2) of Pub.L. 99–554 set out as a note under section 581 of Title 28.

Separability of Provisions

If any provision of or amendment made by Pub.L. 103–394 or the application of such provision or amendment to any person or circumstance is held to be unconstitutional, the remaining provisions of and amendments made by Pub.L. 103–394 and the application of such provisions and amendments to any person or circumstance shall not be affected thereby, see section 701 of Pub.L. 103–394, set out as a note under section 101 of this title.

CROSS REFERENCES

Appointment of Secretary of Transportation as sole trustee, see 46 USCA § 50305.

Appointment of trustee in—

Chapter thirteen cases, see 11 USCA § 1302.

Chapter twelve cases, see 11 USCA § 1202.

Railroad reorganization cases, see 11 USCA § 1163.

Election of trustee in Chapter seven cases, see 11 USCA § 702.

Grain storage facility bankruptcies, expedited appointment of trustee or examiner, see 11 USCA § 557.

Inapplicability of this section to railroad reorganization cases, see 11 USCA § 1161.

Qualification of trustee, see 11 USCA § 322.

Time for bringing action, see 11 USCA § 546.

§ 1105. Termination of trustee's appointment

At any time before confirmation of a plan, on request of a party in interest or the United States trustee, and after notice and a hearing, the court may terminate the trustee's appointment and restore the debtor to possession and management of the property of the estate and of the operation of the debtor's business.

(Pub.L. 95–598, Nov. 6, 1978, 92 Stat. 2628; Pub.L. 98–353, Title III, § 501, July 10, 1984, 98 Stat. 384; Pub.L. 99–554, Title II, § 223, Oct. 27, 1986, 100 Stat. 3102.)

HISTORICAL AND STATUTORY NOTES

Revision Notes and Legislative Reports

1978 Acts. This section authorizes the court to terminate the trustee's appointment and to restore the debtor to possession and management of the property of the estate and to operation of the debtor's business. Section 1104(a) provides that this section does not apply in the case of a public company, for which the appointment of a trustee is mandatory. Senate Report No. 95–989.

This section authorizes the court to terminate the trustee's appointment and to restore the debtor to possession and management of the property of the estate, and to operation of the debtor's business. This section would permit the court to reverse its decision to order the appointment of a trustee in light of new evidence. House Report No. 95–595.

1984 Acts. Statements by Legislative Leaders, see 1984 U.S.Code Cong. and Adm.News, p. 576.

1986 Acts. House Report No. 99–764 and House Conference Report No. 99–958, see 1986 U.S.Code Cong. and Adm.News, p. 5227.

Effective and Applicability Provisions

1986 Acts. Amendment by Pub.L. 99–554 effective 30 days after Oct. 27, 1986, except as otherwise provided for, see section 302(a) of Pub.L. 99–554, set out as a note under section 581 of Title 28, Judiciary and Judicial Procedure.

Amendment by Pub.L. 99–554, § 223, not to become effective in or with respect to certain specified judicial districts until, or apply to cases while pending in such district before, the expiration of the 270–day period beginning 30 days after Oct. 27, 1986, or of the 30–day period beginning on the date the Attorney General certifies under section 303 of Pub.L. 99–554 the region specified in a paragraph of section 581(a) of Title 28, as amended by section 111(a) of Pub.L. 99–554, that includes such district, whichever occurs first, see section 302(d)(1) of Pub.L. 99–554, set out as a note under section 581 of Title 28.

Amendment by Pub.L. 99–554, § 223, not to become effective in or with respect to certain specified judicial districts until, or apply to cases while pending in such district before, the expiration of the 2–year period beginning 30 days after Oct. 27, 1986, or of the 30–day period beginning on the date the Attorney General certifies under section 303 of Pub.L. 99–554 the region specified in a paragraph of section 581(a) of Title 28, as amended by section 111(a) of Pub.L. 99–554, that includes such district, whichever occurs first, see section 302(d)(2) of Pub.L. 99–554, set out as a note under section 581 of Title 28.

Amendment by Pub.L. 99–554, § 223, not to become effective in or with respect to judicial districts established for the States of Alabama and North Carolina until, or apply to cases while pending in such district before, such district elects to be included in a bankruptcy region established in section 581(a) of Title 28, as amended by section 111(a) of Pub.L. 99–554, or Oct. 1, 2002, whichever occurs first, and, except as otherwise provided for, with respect to cases under chapters 7, 11, 12, and 13 of Title 11 commenced before 30 days after Oct. 27, 1986, and pending in a judicial district in the States of Alabama or North Carolina before any election made under section 302(d)(3)(A) of Pub.L. 99–554 by such district becomes effective or Oct. 1, 2002, whichever occurs first, amendments by Pub.L. 99–554 not to apply until Oct. 1,

2003, or the expiration of the 1–year period beginning on the date such election becomes effective, whichever occurs first, and further, in any judicial district in Alabama or North Carolina not making the election described in section 302(d)(3)(A) of Pub.L. 99–554, any person appointed under regulations issued by the Judicial Conference to administer estates in cases under Title 11 authorized to establish, etc., a panel of private trustees, and to supervise cases and trustees in cases under chapters 7, 11, 12, and 13 of Title 11, until amendments by sections 201 to 231 of Pub.L. 99–554 effective in such district, see section 302(d)(3)(A) to (F), (H), (I) of Pub.L. 99–554, set out as a note under section 581 of Title 28.

Amendment by Pub.L. 99–554, § 223, except as otherwise provided, with respect to cases under chapters 7, 11, 12, and 13 of Title 11 commenced before 30 days after Oct. 27, 1986, and pending in a judicial district referred to in section 581(a) of Title 28, as amended by section 111(a) of Pub.L. 99–554, for which a United States trustee is not authorized before 30 days after Oct. 27, 1986 to be appointed, not applicable until the expiration of the 3–year period beginning on Oct. 27, 1986, or of the 1–year period beginning on the date the Attorney General certifies under section 303 of Pub.L. 99–554, the region specified in a paragraph of such section 581(a) that includes, such district, whichever occurs first, see section 302(e)(1), (2) of Pub.L. 99–554, set out as a note under section 581 of Title 28.

1984 Acts. Amendment by Pub.L. 98–353 effective with respect to cases filed 90 days after July 10, 1984, see section 552(a), formerly 553(a), of Pub.L. 98–353, set out as a note under section 101 of this title.

CROSS REFERENCES

Effect of vacancy in office of trustee, see 11 USCA § 325.

Inapplicability of this section to railroad reorganization cases, see 11 USCA § 1161.

Removal of trustee, see 11 USCA § 324.

§ 1106. Duties of trustee and examiner

(a) A trustee shall—

(1) perform the duties of the trustee, as specified in paragraphs (2), (5), (7), (8), (9), (10), (11), and (12) of section 704;

(2) if the debtor has not done so, file the list, schedule, and statement required under section 521(1) of this title;

(3) except to the extent that the court orders otherwise, investigate the acts, conduct, assets, liabilities, and financial condition of the debtor, the operation of the debtor's business and the desirability of the continuance of such business, and any other matter relevant to the case or to the formulation of a plan;

(4) as soon as practicable—

(A) file a statement of any investigation conducted under paragraph (3) of this subsection, including any fact ascertained pertaining to fraud, dishonesty, incompetence, misconduct, mismanagement, or irregularity in the management of the affairs of the debtor, or to a cause of action available to the estate; and

(B) transmit a copy or a summary of any such statement to any creditors' committee or equity security holders' committee, to any indenture trustee, and to such other entity as the court designates;

(5) as soon as practicable, file a plan under section 1121 of this title, file a report of why the trustee will not file a plan, or recommend conversion of the case to a case under chapter 7, 12, or 13 of this title or dismissal of the case;

(6) for any year for which the debtor has not filed a tax return required by law, furnish, without personal liability, such information as may be required by the governmental unit with which such tax return was to be filed, in light of the condition of the debtor's books and records and the availability of such information;

(7) after confirmation of a plan, file such reports as are necessary or as the court orders; and

(8) if with respect to the debtor there is a claim for a domestic support obligation, provide the applicable notice specified in subsection (c).

(b) An examiner appointed under section 1104(d) of this title shall perform the duties specified in paragraphs (3) and (4) of subsection (a) of this section, and, except to the extent that the court orders otherwise, any other duties of the trustee that the court orders the debtor in possession not to perform.

(c)(1) In a case described in subsection (a)(8) to which subsection (a)(8) applies, the trustee shall—

(A)(i) provide written notice to the holder of the claim described in subsection (a)(8) of such claim and of the right of such holder to use the services of the State child support enforcement agency established under sections 464 and 466 of the Social Security Act for the State in which such holder resides, for assistance in collecting child support during and after the case under this title; and

(ii) include in the notice required by clause (i) the address and telephone number of such State child support enforcement agency;

(B)(i) provide written notice to such State child support enforcement agency of such claim; and

(ii) include in the notice required by clause (i) the name, address, and telephone number of such holder; and

(C) at such time as the debtor is granted a discharge under section 1141, provide written notice to such holder and to such State child support enforcement agency of—

(i) the granting of the discharge;

(ii) the last recent known address of the debtor;

(iii) the last recent known name and address of the debtor's employer; and

(iv) the name of each creditor that holds a claim that—

(I) is not discharged under paragraph (2), (4), or (14A) of section 523(a); or

(II) was reaffirmed by the debtor under section 524(c).

(2)(A) The holder of a claim described in subsection (a)(8) or the State child enforcement support agency of the State in which such holder resides may request from a creditor described in paragraph (1)(C)(iv) the last known address of the debtor.

(B) Notwithstanding any other provision of law, a creditor that makes a disclosure of a last known address of a debtor in connection with a request made under subparagraph (A) shall not be liable by reason of making such disclosure.

(Pub.L. 95–598, Nov. 6, 1978, 92 Stat. 2628; Pub.L. 98–353, Title III, §§ 311(b)(1), 502, July 10, 1984, 98 Stat. 355, 384; Pub.L. 99–554, Title II, § 257(c), Oct. 27, 1986, 100 Stat. 3114; Pub.L. 103–394, Title II, § 211(b), Oct. 22, 1994, 108 Stat. 4125; Pub.L. 109–8, Title II, § 219(b), Title IV, § 446(c), Title XI, § 1105(b), Apr. 20, 2005, 119 Stat. 56, 118, 192.)

HISTORICAL AND STATUTORY NOTES

Revision Notes and Legislative Reports

1978 Acts. Subsection (a) of this section prescribes the trustee's duties. He is required to perform the duties of a trustee in a liquidation case specified in section 704(2), (4), (6), (7), (8), and (9). These include reporting and informational duties, and accountability for all property received. Paragraph (2) of this subsection requires the trustee to file with the court, if the debtor has not done so, the list of creditors, schedule of assets and liabilities, and statement of affairs required under section 521(1).

Paragraph (3) of S. 1106 requires the trustee to investigate the acts, conduct, assets, liabilities, and financial condition of the debtor, the operation of the debtor's business, and the desirability of the continuance of the business, and any other matter relevant to the case or to the formulation of a plan. Paragraph (4) requires the trustee to report the results of his investigation to the court and to creditors' committees, equity security holders' committees, indenture trustees and any other entity the court designates.

Paragraph (5) requires the trustee to file a plan or to report why a plan cannot be formulated, or to recommend conversion to liquidation or to an individual repayment plan case, or dismissal. It is anticipated that the trustee will consult with creditors and other parties in interest in the formulation of a plan, just as the debtor in possession would.

Paragraph (6) [now (7)] requires final reports by the trustee, as the court orders.

Subsection (b) gives the trustee's investigative duties to an examiner, if one is appointed. The court is authorized to give the examiner additional duties as the circumstances warrant.

Paragraphs (3), (4), and (5) of subsection (a) are derived from sections 165 and 169 of chapter X (11 U.S.C. 565, 569) [former sections 565 and 569 of former Title 11, respectively]. Senate Report No. 95–989.

1984 Acts. Statements by Legislative Leaders, see 1984 U.S.Code Cong. and Adm.News, p. 576.

1986 Acts. House Report No. 99–764 and House Conference Report No. 99–958, see 1986 U.S.Code Cong. and Adm.News, p. 5227.

1994 Acts. House Report No. 103–835, see 1994 U.S. Code Cong. and Adm. News, p. 3340.

2005 Acts. House Report No. 109–31(Part I), see 2005 U.S. Code Cong. and Adm. News, p. 88.

References in Text

Section 464 of the Social Security Act, referred to in subsec. (c)(1)(A)(i), is Act Aug. 14, 1935, c. 531, Title IV, § 464, as added Aug. 13, 1981, Pub.L. 97–35, Title XXIII, § 2331(a), 95 Stat. 860, and amended, which is classified to 42 U.S.C.A. § 664.

Section 466 of the Social Security Act, referred to in subsec. (c)(1)(A)(i), is Act Aug. 14, 1935, c. 531, Title IV, § 466, as added Aug. 16, 1984, Pub.L. 98–378, § 3(b), 98 Stat. 1306, and amended, which is classified to 42 U.S.C.A. § 666.

Effective and Applicability Provisions

2005 Acts. Amendments by Pub.L. 109–8 effective, except as otherwise provided, 180 days after April 20, 2005, and inapplicable with respect to cases commenced under Title 11 before the effective date, see Pub.L. 109–8, § 1501, set out as a note under 11 U.S.C.A. § 101.

1994 Acts. Amendment by Pub.L. 103–394 effective on Oct. 22, 1994, and not to apply with respect to cases commenced under Title 11 of the United States Code before Oct. 22, 1994, see section 702 of Pub.L. 103–394, set out as a note under section 101 of this title.

1986 Acts. Amendment by Pub.L. 99–554 effective 30 days after Oct. 27, 1986, but not applicable to cases commenced under this title before that date, see section 302(a), (c)(1), of Pub.L. 99–554, set out as a note under section 581 of Title 28, Judiciary and Judicial Procedure.

1984 Acts. Amendment by Pub.L. 98–353 effective with respect to cases filed 90 days after July 10, 1984, see section 552(a), formerly 553(a), of Pub.L. 98–353, set out as a note under section 101 of this title.

Separability of Provisions

If any provision of or amendment made by Pub.L. 103–394 or the application of such provision or amendment to any person or circumstance is held to be unconstitutional, the remaining provisions of and amendments made by Pub.L. 103–394 and the application of such provisions and amendments to any person or circumstance shall not be affected thereby, see section 701 of Pub.L. 103–394, set out as a note under section 101 of this title.

Payment of Certain Benefits to Retired Former Employees

Pub.L. 99–500, § 101(b) [Title VI, § 608], Oct. 18, 1986, 100 Stat. 1783–39, 1783–74, and Pub.L. 99–591, § 101(b) [Title VI, § 608], Oct. 30, 1986, 100 Stat. 3341–74, as amended by Pub.L. 100–41, May 15, 1987, 101 Stat. 309; Pub.L.

100–99, Aug. 18, 1987, 101 Stat. 716; Pub.L. 100–334, § 3(a), June 16, 1988, 102 Stat. 613, provided that:

"**(a)(1)** Subject to paragraphs (2), (3), (4), and (5), and notwithstanding title 11 of the United States Code [this title], the trustee shall pay benefits to retired former employees under a plan, fund, or program maintained or established by the debtor prior to filing a petition (through the purchase of insurance or otherwise) for the purpose of providing medical, surgical, or hospital care benefits, or benefits in the event of sickness, accident, disability, or death.

"(2) The level of benefits required to be paid by this subsection may be modified prior to confirmation of a plan under section 1129 of such title [section 1129 of this title] if—

"**(A)** the trustee and an authorized representative of the former employees with respect to whom such benefits are payable agree to the modification of such benefit payments; or

"**(B)** the court finds that a modification proposed by the trustee meets the standards of section 1113(b)(1)(A) of such title [section 1113(b)(1)(A) of this title] and the balance of the equities clearly favors the modification.

If such benefits are covered by a collective bargaining agreement, the authorized representative shall be the labor organization that is signatory to such collective bargaining agreement unless there is a conflict of interest.

"(3) The trustee shall pay benefits in accordance with this subsection until—

"**(A)** the dismissal of the case involved; or

"**(B)** the effective date of a plan confirmed under section 1129 of such title which provides for the continued payment after confirmation of the plan of all such benefits at the level established under paragraph (2) of this subsection, at any time prior to the confirmation of the plan, for the duration of the period the debtor (as defined in such title) has obligated itself to provide such benefits.

"(4) No such benefits paid between the filing of a petition in a case covered by this section and the time a plan confirmed under section 1129 of such title with respect to such case becomes effective shall be deducted or offset from the amount allowed as claims for any benefits which remain unpaid, or from the amount to be paid under the plan with respect to such claims for unpaid benefits, whether such claims for unpaid benefits are based upon or arise from a right to future benefits or from any benefit not paid as a result of modifications allowed pursuant to this section.

"(5) No claim for benefits covered by this section shall be limited by section 502(b)(7) of such title [section 502(b)(7) of this title].

"**(b)(1)** Notwithstanding any provision of title 11 of the United States Code [this title], the trustee shall pay an allowable claim of any person for a benefit paid—

"**(A)** before the filing of the petition under title 11 of the United States Code; and

"**(B)** directly or indirectly to a retired former employee under a plan, fund, or program described in subsection (a)(1);

if, as determined by the court, such person is entitled to recover from such employee, or any provider of health care to such employee, directly or indirectly, the amount of such benefit for which such person receives no payment from the debtor.

"(2) For purposes of paragraph (1), the term 'provider of health care' means a person who—

"**(A)** is the direct provider of health care (including a physician, dentist, nurse, podiatrist, optometrist, physician assistant, or ancillary personnel employed under the supervision of a physician); or

"**(B)** administers a facility or institution (including a hospital, alcohol and drug abuse treatment facility, outpatient facility, or health maintenance organization) in which health care is provided.

"**(c)** This section is effective with respect to cases commenced under chapter 11, of title 11, United States Code [this chapter], in which a plan for reorganization has not been confirmed by the court and in which any such benefit is still being paid on October 2, 1986, and in cases that become subject to chapter 11, title 11, United States Code, after October 2, 1986 and before the date of the enactment of the Retiree Benefits Bankruptcy Protection Act of 1988 [June 16, 1988].

"**(d)** This section shall not apply during any period in which a case is subject to chapter 7, title 11, United States Code [11 U.S.C.A. § 701 et seq.]."

Similar provisions were contained in Pub.L. 99–656, § 2, Nov. 14, 1986, 100 Stat. 3668, as amended by Pub.L. 100–41, May 15, 1987, 101 Stat. 309; Pub.L. 100–99, Aug. 18, 1987, 101 Stat. 716, and were repealed by Pub.L. 100–334, § 3(b), June 16, 1988, 102 Stat. 614.

CROSS REFERENCES

Duties of trustees in—

Chapter thirteen cases, see 11 USCA § 1302.

Chapter twelve cases, see 11 USCA § 1202.

Powers and duties of trustee in investor protection liquidation proceedings, see 15 USCA § 78fff–1.

Rights and powers of debtor in Chapter twelve case not encompassing duties specified in subsec. (a)(3) and (4) of this section, see 11 USCA § 1203.

§ 1107. Rights, powers, and duties of debtor in possession

(a) Subject to any limitations on a trustee serving in a case under this chapter, and to such limitations or conditions as the court prescribes, a debtor in possession shall have all the rights, other than the right to compensation under section 330 of this title, and powers, and shall perform all the functions and duties, except the duties specified in sections 1106(a)(2), (3), and (4) of this title, of a trustee serving in a case under this chapter.

(b) Notwithstanding section 327(a) of this title, a person is not disqualified for employment under section 327 of this title by a debtor in possession solely because of such person's employment by or representation of the debtor before the commencement of the case.

(Pub.L. 95–598, Nov. 6, 1978, 92 Stat. 2628; Pub.L. 98–353, Title III, § 503, July 10, 1984, 98 Stat. 384.)

HISTORICAL AND STATUTORY NOTES

Revision Notes and Legislative Reports

1978 Acts. This section places a debtor in possession in the shoes of a trustee in every way. The debtor is given the rights and powers of a chapter 11 trustee. He is required to perform the functions and duties of a chapter 11 trustee (except the investigative duties). He is also subject to any limitations on a chapter 11 trustee, and to such other limitations and conditions as the court prescribes cf. *Wolf v. Weinstein*, 372 U.S. 633, 649–650 (1963). Senate Report No. 95–989.

1984 Acts. Statements by Legislative Leaders, see 1984 U.S.Code Cong. and Adm.News, p. 576.

Legislative Statements

The House amendment adopts section 1107(b) of the Senate amendment which clarifies a point not covered by the House bill.

Effective and Applicability Provisions

1984 Acts. Amendment by Pub.L. 98–353 effective with respect to cases filed 90 days after July 10, 1984, see section 552(a), formerly 553(a), of Pub.L. 98–353, set out as a note under section 101 of this title.

CROSS REFERENCES

Debtor engaged in business in Chapter thirteen cases, see 11 USCA § 1304.

Debtor's duties, see 11 USCA § 521.

Inapplicability of this section in railroad reorganization cases, see 11 USCA § 1161.

Limitation on compensation of professional persons, see 11 USCA § 328.

Rights and powers of debtor in—

Chapter thirteen cases, see 11 USCA § 1303.

Chapter twelve cases, see 11 USCA § 1203.

§ 1108. Authorization to operate business

Unless the court, on request of a party in interest and after notice and a hearing, orders otherwise, the trustee may operate the debtor's business.

(Pub.L. 95–598, Nov. 6, 1978, 92 Stat. 2629; Pub.L. 98–353, Title III, § 504, July 10, 1984, 98 Stat. 384.)

HISTORICAL AND STATUTORY NOTES

Revision Notes and Legislative Reports

1978 Acts. This section permits the debtor's business to continue to be operated, unless the court orders otherwise. Thus, in a reorganization case, operation of the business will be the rule, and it will not be necessary to go to the court to obtain an order authorizing operation. Senate Report No. 95–989.

This section does not presume that a trustee will be appointed to operate the business of the debtor. Rather, the power granted to trustee under this section is one of the powers that a debtor in possession acquires by virtue of proposed 11 U.S.C. 1107. House Report No. 95–595.

1984 Acts. Statements by Legislative Leaders, see 1984 U.S.Code Cong. and Adm.News, p. 576.

Legislative Statements

The House amendment adopts section 1108 of the House bill in preference to the style of an identical substantive provision contained in the Senate amendment. Throughout title 11 references [sic] to a "trustee" is read to include other parties under various sections of the bill. For example, section 1107 applies to give the debtor in possession all the rights and powers of a trustee in a case under chapter 11; this includes the power of the trustee to operate the debtor's business under section 1108.

Effective and Applicability Provisions

1984 Acts. Amendment by Pub.L. 98–353 effective with respect to cases filed 90 days after July 10, 1984, see section 552(a), formerly 553(a), of Pub.L. 98–353, set out as a note under section 101 of this title.

CROSS REFERENCES

Authorization to operate business in Chapter seven cases, see 11 USCA § 721.

Executory contracts and unexpired leases, see 11 USCA § 365.

Executory contracts in stockbroker liquidation cases, see 11 USCA § 744.

Obtaining credit, see 11 USCA § 364.

Retention or replacement of professional persons, see 11 USCA § 327.

Treatment of accounts in—

Commodity broker liquidation cases, see 11 USCA § 763.

Stockbroker liquidation cases, see 11 USCA § 745.

Use, sale or lease of property, see 11 USCA § 363.

Utility service, see 11 USCA § 366.

§ 1109. Right to be heard

(a) The Securities and Exchange Commission may raise and may appear and be heard on any issue in a case under this chapter, but the Securities and Exchange Commission may not appeal from any judgment, order, or decree entered in the case.

(b) A party in interest, including the debtor, the trustee, a creditors' committee, an equity security holders' committee, a creditor, an equity security holder, or any indenture trustee, may raise and may appear and be heard on any issue in a case under this chapter.

(Pub.L. 95–598, Nov. 6, 1978, 92 Stat. 2629.)

HISTORICAL AND STATUTORY NOTES

Revision Notes and Legislative Reports

1978 Acts. Subsection (a) provides, in unqualified terms, that any creditor, equity security holder, or an indenture trustee shall have the right to be heard as a party in interest under this chapter in person, by an attorney, or by a committee. It is derived from section 206 of chapter X (11 U.S.C. 606) [section 606 of former Title 11].

Subsection (b) provides that the Securities and Exchange Commission may appear by filing an appearance in a case of a public company and may appear in other cases if authorized or requested by the court. As a party in interest in either case, the Commission may raise and be heard on any issue. The Commission may not appeal from a judgment, order, or decree in a case, but may participate in any appeal by any other party in interest. This is the present law under section 208 of chapter X (11 U.S.C. 608) [section 608 of former Title 11]. Senate Report No. 95–989.

Section 1109 authorizes the Securities and Exchange Commission and any indenture trustee to intervene in the case at any time on any issue. They may raise an issue or may appear and be heard on an issue that is raised by someone else. The section, following current law, denies the right of appeal to the Securities and Exchange Commission. It does not, however, prevent the Commission from joining or participating in an appeal taken by a true party in interest. The Commission is merely prevented from initiating the appeal in any capacity. House Report No. 95–595.

Legislative Statements

Section 1109 of the House amendment represents a compromise between comparable provisions in the House bill and Senate amendment. As previously discussed the section gives the Securities and Exchange Commission the right to appear and be heard and to raise any issue in a case under chapter 11; however, the Securities and Exchange Commission is not a party in interest and the Commission may not appeal from any judgment, order, or decree entered in the case. Under section 1109(b) a party in interest, including the debtor, the trustee, creditors committee, equity securities holders committee, a creditor, an equity security holder, or an indentured trustee, may raise and may appear and be heard on any issue in a case under chapter 11. Section 1109(c) of the Senate amendment has been moved to subchapter IV pertaining to Railroad Reorganizations.

CROSS REFERENCES

Applicability of this section in Chapter 9 cases, see 11 USCA § 901.

Right of Commodity Futures Trading Commission to be heard in commodity broker liquidation cases, see 11 USCA § 762.

Right of Interstate Commerce Commission, Department of Transportation, and State or local regulatory commission to be heard in railroad reorganization, see 11 USCA § 1164.

§ 1110. Aircraft equipment and vessels

(a)(1) Except as provided in paragraph (2) and subject to subsection (b), the right of a secured party with a security interest in equipment described in paragraph (3), or of a lessor or conditional vendor of such equipment, to take possession of such equipment in compliance with a security agreement, lease, or conditional sale contract, and to enforce any of its other rights or remedies, under such security agreement, lease, or conditional sale contract, to sell, lease, or otherwise retain or dispose of such equipment, is not limited or otherwise affected by any other provision of this title or by any power of the court.

(2) The right to take possession and to enforce the other rights and remedies described in paragraph (1) shall be subject to section 362 if—

(A) before the date that is 60 days after the date of the order for relief under this chapter, the trustee, subject to the approval of the court, agrees to perform all obligations of the debtor under such security agreement, lease, or conditional sale contract; and

(B) any default, other than a default of a kind specified in section 365(b)(2), under such security agreement, lease, or conditional sale contract—

(i) that occurs before the date of the order is cured before the expiration of such 60–day period;

(ii) that occurs after the date of the order and before the expiration of such 60–day period is cured before the later of—

(I) the date that is 30 days after the date of the default; or

(II) the expiration of such 60–day period; and

(iii) that occurs on or after the expiration of such 60–day period is cured in compliance with the terms of such security agreement, lease, or conditional sale contract, if a cure is permitted under that agreement, lease, or contract.

(3) The equipment described in this paragraph—

(A) is—

(i) an aircraft, aircraft engine, propeller, appliance, or spare part (as defined in section 40102 of title 49) that is subject to a security interest granted by, leased to, or conditionally sold to a debtor that, at the time such transaction is entered into, holds an air carrier operating certificate issued pursuant to chapter 447 of title 49 for aircraft capable of carrying 10 or more individuals or 6,000 pounds or more of cargo; or

(ii) a vessel documented under chapter 121 of title 46 that is subject to a security interest granted by, leased to, or conditionally sold to a debtor that is a water carrier that, at the time such transaction is entered into, holds a certificate of public convenience and necessity or permit issued by the Department of Transportation; and

(B) includes all records and documents relating to such equipment that are required, under the terms of the security agreement, lease, or conditional sale contract, to be surrendered or returned by the debtor in connection with the surrender or return of such equipment.

(4) Paragraph (1) applies to a secured party, lessor, or conditional vendor acting in its own behalf or acting as trustee or otherwise in behalf of another party.

(b) The trustee and the secured party, lessor, or conditional vendor whose right to take possession is protected under subsection (a) may agree, subject to the approval of the court, to extend the 60–day period specified in subsection (a)(1).

(c)(1) In any case under this chapter, the trustee shall immediately surrender and return to a secured party, lessor, or conditional vendor, described in subsection (a)(1), equipment described in subsection (a)(3), if at any time after the date of the order for relief under this chapter such secured party, lessor, or conditional vendor is entitled pursuant to subsection (a)(1) to take possession of such equipment and makes a written demand for such possession to the trustee.

(2) At such time as the trustee is required under paragraph (1) to surrender and return equipment described in subsection (a)(3), any lease of such equipment, and any security agreement or conditional sale contract relating to such equipment, if such security agreement or conditional sale contract is an executory contract, shall be deemed rejected.

(d) With respect to equipment first placed in service on or before October 22, 1994, for purposes of this section—

(1) the term 'lease' includes any written agreement with respect to which the lessor and the debtor, as lessee, have expressed in the agreement or in a substantially contemporaneous writing that the agreement is to be treated as a lease for Federal income tax purposes; and

(2) the term "security interest" means a purchase- money equipment security interest.

(Pub.L. 95–598, Nov. 6, 1978, 92 Stat. 2629; Pub.L. 103–272, § 5(c), July 5, 1994, 108 Stat. 1373; Pub.L. 103–394, Title II, § 201(a), Oct. 22, 1994, 108 Stat. 4119; Pub.L. 106–181, Title VII, § 744(b), Apr. 5, 2000, 114 Stat. 177; Pub.L. 109–304, § 17(b)(2), Oct. 6, 2006, 120 Stat. 1707.)

HISTORICAL AND STATUTORY NOTES

Revision Notes and Legislative Reports

1978 Acts. This section, to a large degree, preserves the protection given lessors and conditional vendors of aircraft to a certificated air carrier or of vessels to a certificated water carrier under sections 116(5) and 116(6) of present Chapter X [sections 516(5) and 516(6) of former Title 11]. It is modified to conform with the consolidation of Chapters X [former chapter 10, section 501 et seq.] and XI [former chapter 11 (section 701 et seq.) of former Title 11] and with the new chapter 11 generally. It is also modified to give the trustee in a reorganization case an opportunity to continue in possession of the equipment in question by curing defaults and by making the required lease or purchase payments. This removes the absolute veto power over a reorganization that lessors and conditional vendors have under present law, while entitling them to protection of their investment.

The section overrides the automatic stay or any power of the court to enjoin taking of possession of certain leased, conditionally sold, or liened equipment, unless, [sic] the trustee agrees to perform the debtor's obligations and cures all prior defaults (other than defaults under ipso facto or bankruptcy clauses) within 60 days after the order for relief. The trustee and the equipment financer are permitted to extend the 60-day period by agreement. During the first 60 days, the automatic stay will apply to prevent foreclosure unless the creditor gets relief from the stay.

The effect of this section will be the same if the debtor has granted the security interest to the financer or if the debtor is leasing equipment from a financer that has leveraged the lease and leased the equipment subject to a security interest of a third party. Senate Report No. 95–989.

1994 Acts. House Report No. 103–180, see 1994 U.S. Code Cong. and Adm. News, p. 818.

House Report No. 103–835, see 1994 U.S. Code Cong. and Adm. News, p. 3340.

2000 Acts. House Conference Report No. 106–513 and Statement by President, see 2000 U.S. Code Cong. and Adm. News, p. 80.

Revision Notes and Legislative Reports

2006 Acts. House Report No. 109–170, see 2006 U.S. Code Cong. and Adm. News, p. 972.

Legislative Statements

Section 1110 of the House amendment adopts an identical provision contained in the House bill without modifications contained in the Senate amendment. This section protects a limited class of financiers of aircraft and vessels and is intended to be narrowly construed to prevent secured parties or lessors from gaining the protection of the section unless the interest of such lessor or secured party is explicitly enumerated therein. It should be emphasized that under section 1110(a) a debtor in possession or trustee is given 60 days after the order for relief in a case under chapter 11, to have an opportunity to comply with the provisions of section 1110(a).

During this time the automatic stay will apply and may not be lifted prior to the expiration of the 60-day period. Under section 1110(b), the debtor and secured party or lessor are given an opportunity to extend the 60-day period, but no right to reduce the period is intended. It should additionally be noted that under section 1110(a) the trustee or debtor in possession is not required to assume the executory contract or unexpired lease under section 1110; rather, if the trustee or debtor in possession complies with the requirements of section 1110(a), the trustee or debtor in possession is entitled to retain the aircraft or vessels subject to the normal requirements of section 365. The discussion regarding aircraft and vessels likewise applies with respect to railroad rolling stock in a railroad reorganization under section 1168.

References in Text

Chapter 447 of Title 49, referred to in subsec. (a)(3)(A)(i), is classified to 49 U.S.C.A. § 44701 et seq.

Chapter 121 of this title, referred to in subsec. (a)(3)(A)(ii), is Documentation of Vessels, 46 U.S.C.A. § 12101 et seq.

Effective and Applicability Provisions

2000 Acts. Amendment by Pub.L. 106–181 applicable only to fiscal years beginning after September 30, 1999, see section 3 of Pub.L. 106–181, set out as a note under section 106 of this title.

1994 Acts. Amendment by Pub.L. 103–394 effective on Oct. 22, 1994, with this section as amended by section 201 of Pub.L. 103–394 applicable with respect to any lease, as defined by subsec. (c) of this section as so amended, entered into in connection with a settlement of any proceeding in any case pending under Title 11 of the United States Code on Oct. 22, 1994, see section 702 of Pub.L. 103–394, set out as a note under section 101 of this title.

Separability of Provisions

If any provision of or amendment made by Pub.L. 103–394 or the application of such provision or amendment to any person or circumstance is held to be unconstitutional, the remaining provisions of and amendments made by Pub.L. 103–394 and the application of such provisions and amendments to any person or circumstance shall not be affected thereby, see section 701 of Pub.L. 103–394, set out as a note under section 101 of this title.

Abolition of Interstate Commerce Commission and Transfer of Functions

Interstate Commerce Commission abolished and functions of Commission transferred, except as otherwise provided in Pub.L. 104–88, to Surface Transportation Board effective Jan. 1, 1996, by section 702 of Title 49, Transportation, and section 101 of Pub.L. 104–88, set out as a note under section 701 of Title 49. References to Interstate Commerce Commission deemed to refer to Surface Transportation Board, a member or employee of the Board, or Secretary of Transportation, as appropriate, see section 205 of Pub.L. 104–88, set out as a note under section 701 of Title 49.

Aircraft Equipment Settlement Leases Act of 1993

Pub.L. 103–7, Mar. 17, 1993, 107 Stat. 36, provided:

"Section 1. Short Title.

"This Act [this note] may be cited as the 'Aircraft Equipment Settlement Leases Act of 1993'.

"Sec. 2. Treatment of Aircraft Equipment Settlement Leases with the Pension Benefit Guaranty Corporation.

"In the case of any settlement of liability under title IV of the Employee Retirement Income Security Act of 1974 [29 U.S.C.A. § 1301 et seq.], entered into by the Pension Benefit Guaranty Corporation and one or more other parties, if—

"(1) such settlement was entered into before, on, or after the date of the enactment of this Act [Mar. 17, 1993],

"(2) at least one party to such settlement was a debtor under title 11 of the United States Code [this title], and

"(3) an agreement that is entered into as part of such settlement provides that such agreement is to be treated as a lease,

then such agreement shall be treated as a lease for purposes of section 1110 of such title 11 [this section]."

Termination of Civil Aeronautics Board and Transfer of Certain Functions

All functions, powers, and duties of the Civil Aeronautics Board were terminated or transferred by section 1551 of Title 49, Appendix, Transportation, effective in part on Dec. 31, 1981, in part on Jan. 1, 1983, and in part on Jan. 1, 1985.

CROSS REFERENCES

Effect of conversion, see 11 USCA § 348.

Rights of certain secured parties in rolling stock equipment, see 11 USCA § 1168.

§ 1111. Claims and interests

(a) A proof of claim or interest is deemed filed under section 501 of this title for any claim or interest that appears in the schedules filed under section 521(1) or 1106(a)(2) of this title, except a claim or interest that is scheduled as disputed, contingent, or unliquidated.

(b)(1)(A) A claim secured by a lien on property of the estate shall be allowed or disallowed under section 502 of this title the same as if the holder of such claim had recourse against the debtor on account of such claim, whether or not such holder has such recourse, unless—

(i) the class of which such claim is a part elects, by at least two-thirds in amount and more than half in number of allowed claims of such class, application of paragraph (2) of this subsection; or

(ii) such holder does not have such recourse and such property is sold under section 363 of this title or is to be sold under the plan.

(B) A class of claims may not elect application of paragraph (2) of this subsection if—

(i) the interest on account of such claims of the holders of such claims in such property is of inconsequential value; or

(ii) the holder of a claim of such class has recourse against the debtor on account of such claim and such property is sold under section 363 of this title or is to be sold under the plan.

(2) If such an election is made, then notwithstanding section 506(a) of this title, such claim is a secured claim to the extent that such claim is allowed.

(Pub.L. 95–598, Nov. 6, 1978, 92 Stat. 2630.)

HISTORICAL AND STATUTORY NOTES

Revision Notes and Legislative Reports

1978 Acts. Senate Report No. 95–989 and House Report No. 95–595, see 1978 U.S.Code Cong. and Adm.News, p. 5787.

This section dispenses with the need for every creditor and equity security holder to file a proof of claim or interest in a reorganization case. Usually the debtor's schedules are accurate enough that they will suffice to determine the claims or interests allowable in the case. Thus, the section specifies that any claim or interest included on the debtor's schedules is deemed filed under section 501. This does not apply to claims or interests that are scheduled as disputed, contingent, or unliquidated. Senate Report No. 95–989.

Legislative Statements

A discussion of section 1111(b) of the House amendment is best considered in the context of confirmation and will therefore, [sic] be discussed in connection with section 1129.

CROSS REFERENCES

Applicability of subsec. (b) of this section in Chapter nine cases, see 11 USCA § 901.

Effect of list of claims in Chapter nine cases, see 11 USCA § 925.

Election as affecting confirmation of plan, see 11 USCA § 1129.

Filing and allowance of postpetition claims in Chapter thirteen cases, see 11 USCA § 1305.

Limitation on recourse of claim payable solely from special revenues of debtor, see 11 USCA § 927.

§ 1112. Conversion or dismissal

(a) The debtor may convert a case under this chapter to a case under chapter 7 of this title unless—

(1) the debtor is not a debtor in possession;

(2) the case originally was commenced as an involuntary case under this chapter; or

(3) the case was converted to a case under this chapter other than on the debtor's request.

(b)(1) Except as provided in paragraph (2) of this subsection, subsection (c) of this section, and section 1104(a)(3), on request of a party in interest, and after notice and a hearing, absent unusual circumstances specifically identified by the court that establish that the requested conversion or dismissal is not in the best interests of creditors and the estate, the court shall convert a case under this chapter to a case under chapter 7 or dismiss a case under this chapter, whichever is in the best interests of creditors and the estate, if the movant establishes cause.

(2) The relief provided in paragraph (1) shall not be granted absent unusual circumstances specifically identified by the court that establish that such relief is not in the best interests of creditors and the estate, if the debtor or another party in interest objects and establishes that—

(A) there is a reasonable likelihood that a plan will be confirmed within the timeframes established in sections 1121(e) and 1129(e) of this title, or if such sections do not apply, within a reasonable period of time; and

(B) the grounds for granting such relief include an act or omission of the debtor other than under paragraph (4)(A)—

(i) for which there exists a reasonable justification for the act or omission; and

(ii) that will be cured within a reasonable period of time fixed by the court.

(3) The court shall commence the hearing on a motion under this subsection not later than 30 days after filing of the motion, and shall decide the motion not later than 15 days after commencement of such hearing, unless the movant expressly consents to a continuance for a specific period of time or compelling circumstances prevent the court from meeting the time limits established by this paragraph.

(4) For purposes of this subsection, the term 'cause' includes—

(A) substantial or continuing loss to or diminution of the estate and the absence of a reasonable likelihood of rehabilitation;

(B) gross mismanagement of the estate;

(C) failure to maintain appropriate insurance that poses a risk to the estate or to the public;

(D) unauthorized use of cash collateral substantially harmful to 1 or more creditors;

(E) failure to comply with an order of the court;

(F) unexcused failure to satisfy timely any filing or reporting requirement established by this title or by any rule applicable to a case under this chapter;

(G) failure to attend the meeting of creditors convened under section 341(a) or an examination ordered under rule 2004 of the Federal Rules of Bankruptcy Procedure without good cause shown by the debtor;

(H) failure timely to provide information or attend meetings reasonably requested by the United States trustee (or the bankruptcy administrator, if any);

(I) failure timely to pay taxes owed after the date of the order for relief or to file tax returns due after the date of the order for relief;

(J) failure to file a disclosure statement, or to file or confirm a plan, within the time fixed by this title or by order of the court;

(K) failure to pay any fees or charges required under chapter 123 of title 28;

(L) revocation of an order of confirmation under section 1144;

(M) inability to effectuate substantial consummation of a confirmed plan;

(N) material default by the debtor with respect to a confirmed plan;

(O) termination of a confirmed plan by reason of the occurrence of a condition specified in the plan; and

(P) failure of the debtor to pay any domestic support obligation that first becomes payable after the date of the filing of the petition.

(c) The court may not convert a case under this chapter to a case under chapter 7 of this title if the debtor is a farmer or a corporation that is not a moneyed, business, or commercial corporation, unless the debtor requests such conversion.

(d) The court may convert a case under this chapter to a case under chapter 12 or 13 of this title only if—

(1) the debtor requests such conversion;

(2) the debtor has not been discharged under section 1141(d) of this title; and

(3) if the debtor requests conversion to chapter 12 of this title, such conversion is equitable.

(e) Except as provided in subsections (c) and (f), the court, on request of the United States trustee, may convert a case under this chapter to a case under chapter 7 of this title or may dismiss a case under this chapter, whichever is in the best interest of creditors and the estate if the debtor in a voluntary case fails to file, within fifteen days after the filing of the petition commencing such case or such additional time as the court may allow, the information required by paragraph (1) of section 521, including a list containing the names and addresses of the holders of the twenty largest unsecured claims (or of all unsecured claims if there are fewer than twenty unsecured claims), and the approximate dollar amounts of each of such claims.

(f) Notwithstanding any other provision of this section, a case may not be converted to a case under another chapter of this title unless the debtor may be a debtor under such chapter.

(Pub.L. 95–598, Nov. 6, 1978, 92 Stat. 2630; Pub.L. 98–353, Title III, § 505, July 10, 1984, 98 Stat. 384; Pub.L. 99–554, Title II, §§ 224, 256, Oct. 27, 1986, 100 Stat. 3102, 3114; Pub.L. 103–394, Title II, § 217(c), Oct. 22, 1994, 108 Stat. 4127; Pub.L. 109–8, Title IV, § 442(a), Apr. 20, 2005, 119 Stat. 115.)

HISTORICAL AND STATUTORY NOTES

Revision Notes and Legislative Reports

1978 Acts. This section brings together all of the conversion and dismissal rules for chapter 11 cases. Subsection (a) gives the debtor an absolute right to convert a voluntarily commenced chapter 11 case in which the debtor remains in possession to a liquidation case.

Subsection (b) gives wide discretion to the court to make an appropriate disposition of the case sua sponte or upon motion of a party in interest, or the court is permitted to convert a reorganization case to a liquidation case or to dismiss the case, whichever is in the best interest of creditors and the estate, but only for cause. Cause may include the continuing loss to or diminution of the estate of an insolvent debtor, the absence of a reasonable likelihood of rehabilitation, the inability to effectuate a plan, unreasonable delay by the debtor that is prejudicial to creditors, failure to file a plan within the appropriate time limits, denial of confirmation and any opportunity to modify or propose a new plan, revocation of confirmation and denial of confirmation of a modified plan, inability to effectuate substantial consummation of a confirmed plan, material default by the debtor under the plan, and termination of the plan by reason of the occurrence of a condition specified in the plan. This list is not exhaustive. The court will be able to consider other factors as they arise, and to use its equitable powers to reach an appropriate result in individual cases. The power of the court to act sua sponte should be used sparingly and only in emergency situations.

Subsection (c) prohibits the court from converting a case concerning a farmer or an eleemosynary institution to a liquidation case unless the debtor consents.

Subsection (d) prohibits conversion of a reorganization case to a chapter 13 case unless the debtor requests conversion and his discharge had not been granted or has been revoked.

Subsection (e) reinforces section 109 by prohibiting conversion of a chapter 11 case to a case under another chapter proceedings under which the debtor is not permitted to proceed. Senate Report No. 95–989.

1984 Acts. Statements by Legislative Leaders, see 1984 U.S.Code Cong. and Adm.News, p. 576.

1986 Acts.. House Report No. 99–764 and House Conference Report No. 99–958, see 1986 U.S.Code Cong. and Adm.News, p. 5227.

1994 Acts. House Report No. 103–835, see 1994 U.S. Code Cong. and Adm. News, p. 3340.

2005 Acts. House Report No. 109–31(Part I), see 2005 U.S. Code Cong. and Adm. News, p. 88.

Legislative Statements

Section 1112 of the House amendment represents a compromise between the House bill and Senate amendment with respect to the factors constituting cause for conversion of a case to chapter 7 or dismissal. The House amendment combines two separate factors contained in section 1112(b)(1) and section 1112(b)(2) of the Senate amendment. Section 1112(b)(1) of the House amendment permits the court to convert a case to a case under chapter 7 or to dismiss the case if there is both a continuing loss to or diminution of the estate and the absence of a reasonable likelihood of rehabilitation; requiring both factors to be present simultaneously represents a compromise from the House bill which eliminated both factors from the list of causes enumerated.

Sections 1112(c) and 1112(d) of the House amendment is derived from the House bill which differs from the Senate amendment only as a matter of style.

References in Text

Chapter 7 of this title, referred to in text, is 11 U.S.C.A. § 701 et seq.

The Federal Rules of Bankruptcy Procedure, referred to in subsec. (b)(4)(G), are set out in the Appendix to this title.

Chapter 123 of title 28, referred to in subsec. (b)(4)(K), is 28 U.S.C.A. § 1911 et seq.

Chapter 12 or 13 of this title, referred to in subsec. (d), is 11 U.S.C.A. § 1201 et seq. or 11 U.S.C.A. § 1301 et seq., respectively.

Effective and Applicability Provisions

2005 Acts. Amendments by Pub.L. 109–8 effective, except as otherwise provided, 180 days after April 20, 2005, and inapplicable with respect to cases commenced under Title 11 before the effective date, see Pub.L. 109–8, § 1501, set out as a note under 11 U.S.C.A. § 101.

1994 Acts. Amendment by Pub.L. 103–394 effective on Oct. 22, 1994, and not to apply with respect to cases commenced under Title 11 of the United States Code before Oct. 22, 1994, see section 702 of Pub.L. 103–394, set out as a note under section 101 of this title.

1986 Acts. Amendment by Pub.L. 99–554 effective 30 days after Oct. 27, 1986, except as otherwise provided for, see section 302(a) of Pub.L. 99–554, set out as a note under section 581 of Title 28, Judiciary and Judicial Procedure.

Amendment by Pub.L. 99–554, § 224, not to become effective in or with respect to certain specified judicial districts until, or apply to cases while pending in such district before, the expiration of the 270–day period beginning 30 days after Oct. 27, 1986, or of the 30–day period beginning on the date the Attorney General certifies under section 303 of Pub.L. 99–554 the region specified in a paragraph of section 581(a) of Title 28, as amended by section 111(a) of Pub.L. 99–554, that includes such district, whichever occurs first, see section 302(d)(1) of Pub.L. 99–554, set out as a note under section 581 of Title 28.

Amendment by Pub.L. 99–554, § 224, not to become effective in or with respect to certain specified judicial districts until, or apply to cases while pending in such district before, the expiration of the 2–year period beginning 30 days after Oct. 27, 1986, or of the 30–day period beginning on the date the Attorney General certifies under section 303 of Pub.L. 99–554 the region specified in a paragraph of section 581(a) of Title 28, as amended by section 111(a) of Pub.L. 99–554, that includes such district, whichever occurs first, see section 302(d)(2) of Pub.L. 99–554, set out as a note under section 581 of Title 28.

Amendment by Pub.L. 99–554, § 224, not to become effective in or with respect to judicial districts established for the States of Alabama and North Carolina until, or apply to cases while pending in such district before, such district elects to be included in a bankruptcy region established in section 581(a) of Title 28, as amended by section 111(a) of Pub.L. 99–554, or Oct. 1, 2002, whichever occurs first, and, except as otherwise provided for, with respect to cases under chapters 7, 11, 12, and 13 of Title 11 commenced before 30 days after Oct. 27, 1986, and pending in a judicial district in the States of Alabama or North Carolina before any election made under section 302(d)(3)(A) of Pub.L. 99–554 by such district becomes effective or Oct. 1, 2002, whichever occurs first, amendments by Pub.L. 99–554 not to apply until Oct. 1, 2003, or the expiration of the 1–year period beginning on the date such election becomes effective, whichever occurs first, and further, in any judicial district in Alabama or North Carolina not making the election described in section 302(d)(3)(A) of Pub.L. 99–554, any person appointed under regulations issued by the Judicial Conference to administer estates in cases under Title 11 authorized to establish, etc., a panel of private trustees, and to supervise cases and trustees in cases under chapters 7, 11, 12, and 13 of Title 11, until amendments by sections 201 to 231 of Pub.L. 99–554 effective in such district, see section 302(d)(3)(A) to (F), (H), (I) of Pub.L. 99–554, set out as a note under section 581 of Title 28.

Amendment by Pub.L. 99–554, § 224, except as otherwise provided, with respect to cases under chapters 7, 11, 12, and 13 of Title 11 commenced before 30 days after Oct. 27, 1986, and pending in a judicial district referred to in section 581(a) of Title 28, as amended by section 111(a) of Pub.L. 99–554, for which a United States trustee is not authorized before 30 days after Oct. 27, 1986 to be appointed, not applicable until the expiration of the 3–year period beginning on Oct. 27, 1986, or of the 1–year period beginning on the date the Attorney General certifies under section 303 of Pub.L. 99–554 the region specified in a paragraph of such section 581(a) that includes, such district, whichever occurs first, see section 302(e)(1), (2) of Pub.L. 99–554, set out as a note under section 581 of Title 28.

Amendments by Pub.L. 99–554, § 256, not to apply with respect to cases commenced under Title 11, Bankruptcy, before 30 days after Oct. 27, 1986, see section 302(c)(1) of Pub.L. 99–554, set out as a note under section 581 of Title 28.

1984 Acts. Amendment by Pub.L. 98–353 effective with respect to cases filed 90 days after July 10, 1984, see section 552(a), formerly 553(a), of Pub.L. 98–353, set out as a note under section 101 of this title.

Separability of Provisions

If any provision of or amendment made by Pub.L. 103–394 or the application of such provision or amendment to any person or circumstance is held to be unconstitutional, the remaining provisions of and amendments made by Pub.L. 103–394 and the application of such provisions and amendments to any person or circumstance shall not be affected thereby, see section 701 of Pub.L. 103–394, set out as a note under section 101 of this title.

CROSS REFERENCES

Conversion of—

Chapter seven cases, see 11 USCA § 706.

Chapter thirteen cases, see 11 USCA § 1307.

Chapter twelve cases, see 11 USCA § 1208.

Dismissal of—

Chapter nine cases, see 11 USCA § 930.

Chapter seven cases, see 11 USCA § 707.

Distribution of property of estate converted to Chapter seven, see 11 USCA § 726.

Effect of conversion, see 11 USCA § 348.

Effect of dismissal, see 11 USCA § 349.

Executory contracts and unexpired leases, see 11 USCA § 365.

Liquidation of estate in railroad reorganization cases, see 11 USCA § 1174.

Termination of debtor's taxable period for cases converted to Chapter seven, see 11 USCA § 728.

§ 1113. Rejection of collective bargaining agreements

(a) The debtor in possession, or the trustee if one has been appointed under the provisions of this chapter, other than a trustee in a case covered by subchapter IV of this chapter and by title I of the Railway Labor Act, may assume or reject a collective bargaining agreement only in accordance with the provisions of this section.

(b)(1) Subsequent to filing a petition and prior to filing an application seeking rejection of a collective bargaining agreement, the debtor in possession or trustee (hereinafter in this section "trustee" shall include a debtor in possession), shall—

(A) make a proposal to the authorized representative of the employees covered by such agreement, based on the most complete and reliable information available at the time of such proposal, which provides for those necessary modifications in the employees benefits and protections that are necessary to permit the reorganization of the debtor and assures that all creditors, the debtor and all of the affected parties are treated fairly and equitably; and

(B) provide, subject to subsection (d)(3), the representative of the employees with such relevant information as is necessary to evaluate the proposal.

(2) During the period beginning on the date of the making of a proposal provided for in paragraph (1) and ending on the date of the hearing provided for in subsection (d)(1), the trustee shall meet, at reasonable times, with the authorized representative to confer in good faith in attempting to reach mutually satisfactory modifications of such agreement.

(c) The court shall approve an application for rejection of a collective bargaining agreement only if the court finds that—

(1) the trustee has, prior to the hearing, made a proposal that fulfills the requirements of subsection (b)(1);

(2) the authorized representative of the employees has refused to accept such proposal without good cause; and

(3) the balance of the equities clearly favors rejection of such agreement.

(d)(1) Upon the filing of an application for rejection the court shall schedule a hearing to be held not later than fourteen days after the date of the filing of such application. All interested parties may appear and be heard at such hearing. Adequate notice shall be provided to such parties at least ten days before the date of such hearing. The court may extend the time for the commencement of such hearing for a period not exceeding seven days where the circumstances of the case, and the interests of justice require such extension, or for additional periods of time to which the trustee and representative agree.

(2) The court shall rule on such application for rejection within thirty days after the date of the commencement of the hearing. In the interests of justice, the court may extend such time for ruling for such additional period as the trustee and the employees' representative may agree to. If the court does not rule on such application within thirty days after the date of the commencement of the hearing, or within such additional time as the trustee and the employees' representative may agree to, the trustee may terminate or alter any provisions of the collective bargaining agreement pending the ruling of the court on such application.

(3) The court may enter such protective orders, consistent with the need of the authorized representative of the employee to evaluate the trustee's proposal and the application for rejection, as may be necessary to prevent disclosure of information provided to such representative where such disclosure could compromise the position of the debtor with respect to its competitors in the industry in which it is engaged.

(e) If during a period when the collective bargaining agreement continues in effect, and if essential to the continuation of the debtor's business, or in order to avoid irreparable damage to the estate, the court, after notice and a hearing, may authorize the trustee to implement interim changes in the terms, conditions, wages, benefits, or work rules provided by a collective bargaining agreement. Any hearing under this paragraph shall be scheduled in accordance with the needs of the trustee. The implementation of such interim changes shall not render the application for rejection moot.

(f) No provision of this title shall be construed to permit a trustee to unilaterally terminate or alter any provisions of a collective bargaining agreement prior to compliance with the provisions of this section.

(Added Pub.L. 98–353, Title III, § 541(a), July 10, 1984, 98 Stat. 390.)

HISTORICAL AND STATUTORY NOTES

Revision Notes and Legislative Reports

1984 Acts. Statements by Legislative Leaders, see 1984 U.S.Code Cong. and Adm.News, p. 576.

References in Text

The Railway Labor Act, referred to in subsec. (a), is Act May 20, 1926, c. 347, 44 Stat. 577, as amended. Title I of the Railway Labor Act is classified principally to subchapter I (section 151 et seq.) of chapter 8 of Title 45, Railroads. For complete classification of this Act to the Code, see section 151 of Title 45 and Tables.

Effective and Applicability Provisions

1984 Acts. Section 541(c) of Pub.L. 98–353 provided that: "The amendments made by this section [enacting this section] shall become effective upon the date of enactment of this Act [July 10, 1984]; provided that this section shall not apply to cases filed under title 11 of the United States Code [this title] which were commenced prior to the date of enactment of this section [July 10, 1984]."

§ 1114. Payment of insurance benefits to retired employees

(a) For purposes of this section, the term "retiree benefits" means payments to any entity or person for the purpose of providing or reimbursing payments for retired employees and their spouses and dependents, for medical, surgical, or hospital care benefits, or benefits in the event of sickness, accident, disability, or death under any plan, fund, or program (through the purchase of insurance or otherwise) maintained or established in whole or in part by the debtor prior to filing a petition commencing a case under this title.

(b)(1) For purposes of this section, the term "authorized representative" means the authorized representative designated pursuant to subsection (c) for persons receiving any retiree benefits covered by a collective bargaining agreement or subsection (d) in the case of persons receiving retiree benefits not covered by such an agreement.

(2) Committees of retired employees appointed by the court pursuant to this section shall have the same rights, powers, and duties as committees appointed under sections 1102 and 1103 of this title for the purpose of carrying out the purposes of sections 1114 and 1129(a)(13) and, as permitted by the court, shall have the power to enforce the rights of persons under this title as they relate to retiree benefits.

(c)(1) A labor organization shall be, for purposes of this section, the authorized representative of those persons receiving any retiree benefits covered by any collective bargaining agreement to which that labor organization is signatory, unless (A) such labor organization elects not to serve as the authorized representative of such persons, or (B) the court, upon a motion by any party in interest, after notice and hearing, determines that different representation of such persons is appropriate.

(2) In cases where the labor organization referred to in paragraph (1) elects not to serve as the authorized representative of those persons receiving any retiree benefits covered by any collective bargaining agreement to which that labor organization is signatory, or in cases where the court, pursuant to paragraph (1) finds different representation of such persons appropriate, the court, upon a motion by any party in interest, and after notice and a hearing, shall appoint a committee of retired employees if the debtor seeks to modify or not pay the retiree benefits or if the court otherwise determines that it is appropriate, from among such persons, to serve as the authorized representative of such persons under this section.

(d) The court, upon a motion by any party in interest, and after notice and a hearing, shall order the appointment of a committee of retired employees if the debtor seeks to modify or not pay the retiree benefits or if the court otherwise determines that it is appropriate, to serve as the authorized representative, under this section, of those persons receiving any retiree benefits not covered by a collective bargaining agreement. The United States trustee shall appoint any such committee.

(e)(1) Notwithstanding any other provision of this title, the debtor in possession, or the trustee if one has been appointed under the provisions of this chapter (hereinafter in this section "trustee" shall include a debtor in possession), shall timely pay and shall not modify any retiree benefits, except that—

(A) the court, on motion of the trustee or authorized representative, and after notice and a hearing, may order modification of such payments, pursuant to the provisions of subsections (g) and (h) of this section, or

(B) the trustee and the authorized representative of the recipients of those benefits may agree to modification of such payments,

after which such benefits as modified shall continue to be paid by the trustee.

(2) Any payment for retiree benefits required to be made before a plan confirmed under section 1129 of this title is effective has the status of an allowed administrative expense as provided in section 503 of this title.

(f)(1) Subsequent to filing a petition and prior to filing an application seeking modification of the retiree benefits, the trustee shall—

(A) make a proposal to the authorized representative of the retirees, based on the most complete and reliable information available at the time of such proposal, which provides for those necessary modifications in the retiree benefits that are necessary to permit the reorganization of the debtor and assures that all creditors, the debtor and all of the affected parties are treated fairly and equitably; and

(B) provide, subject to subsection (k)(3), the representative of the retirees with such relevant information as is necessary to evaluate the proposal.

(2) During the period beginning on the date of the making of a proposal provided for in paragraph (1), and ending on the date of the hearing provided for in subsection (k)(1), the trustee shall meet, at reasonable times, with the authorized representative to confer in good faith in attempting to reach mutually satisfactory modifications of such retiree benefits.

(g) The court shall enter an order providing for modification in the payment of retiree benefits if the court finds that—

(1) the trustee has, prior to the hearing, made a proposal that fulfills the requirements of subsection (f);

(2) the authorized representative of the retirees has refused to accept such proposal without good cause; and

(3) such modification is necessary to permit the reorganization of the debtor and assures that all creditors, the debtor, and all of the affected parties are treated fairly and equitably, and is clearly favored by the balance of the equities;

except that in no case shall the court enter an order providing for such modification which provides for a modification to a level lower than that proposed by the trustee in the proposal found by the court to have complied with the requirements of this subsection and subsection (f): *Provided, however,* That at any time after an order is entered providing for modification in the payment of retiree benefits, or at any time after an agreement modifying such benefits is made between the trustee and the authorized representative of the recipients of such benefits, the authorized representative may apply to the court for an order increasing those benefits which order shall be granted if the increase in retiree benefits sought is consistent with the standard set forth in paragraph (3): *Provided further,* That neither the trustee nor the authorized representative is precluded from making more than one motion for a modification order governed by this subsection.

(h)(1) Prior to a court issuing a final order under subsection (g) of this section, if essential to the continuation of the debtor's business, or in order to avoid irreparable damage to the estate, the court, after notice and a hearing, may authorize the trustee to implement interim modifications in retiree benefits.

(2) Any hearing under this subsection shall be scheduled in accordance with the needs of the trustee.

(3) The implementation of such interim changes does not render the motion for modification moot.

(i) No retiree benefits paid between the filing of the petition and the time a plan confirmed under section 1129 of this title becomes effective shall be deducted or offset from the amounts allowed as claims for any benefits which remain unpaid, or from the amounts to be paid under the plan with respect to such claims for unpaid benefits, whether such claims for unpaid benefits are based upon or arise from a right to future unpaid benefits or from any benefits not paid as a result of modifications allowed pursuant to this section.

(j) No claim for retiree benefits shall be limited by section 502(b)(7) of this title.

(k)(1) Upon the filing of an application for modifying retiree benefits, the court shall schedule a hearing to be held not later than fourteen days after the date of the filing of such application. All interested parties may appear and be heard at such hearing. Adequate notice shall be provided to such parties at least ten days before the date of such hearing. The court may extend the time for the commencement of such hearing for a period not exceeding seven days where the circumstances of the case, and the interests of justice require such extension, or for additional periods of time to which the trustee and the authorized representative agree.

(2) The court shall rule on such application for modification within ninety days after the date of the commencement of the hearing. In the interests of justice, the court may extend such time for ruling for such additional period as the trustee and the authorized representative may agree to. If the court does not rule on such application within ninety days after the date of the commencement of the hearing, or within such additional time as the trustee and the authorized representative may agree to, the trustee may implement the proposed modifications pending the ruling of the court on such application.

(3) The court may enter such protective orders, consistent with the need of the authorized representative of the retirees to evaluate the trustee's proposal and the application for modification, as may be necessary to prevent disclosure of information provided to such representative where such disclosure could compromise the position of the debtor with respect to its competitors in the industry in which it is engaged.

(*l*) If the debtor, during the 180-day period ending on the date of the filing of the petition—

(1) modified retiree benefits; and

(2) was insolvent on the date such benefits were modified;

the court, on motion of a party in interest, and after notice and a hearing, shall issue an order reinstating as of the date the modification was made, such benefits as in effect immediately before such date unless the court finds that the balance of the equities clearly favors such modification.

(m) This section shall not apply to any retiree, or the spouse or dependents of such retiree, if such retiree's gross income for the twelve months preceding the filing of the bankruptcy petition equals or exceeds $250,000, unless such retiree can demonstrate to the satisfaction of the court that he is unable to obtain health, medical, life, and disability coverage for himself, his spouse, and his dependents who would otherwise be covered by the employer's insurance plan, comparable to the coverage provided by the employer on the day before the filing of a petition under this title.

(Added Pub.L. 100–334, § 2(a), June 16, 1988, 102 Stat. 610, and amended Pub.L. 109–8, Title IV, § 447, Title XIV, § 1403, Apr. 20, 2005, 119 Stat. 118, 215.)

HISTORICAL AND STATUTORY NOTES

Revision Notes and Legislative Reports

1988 Acts. Senate Report No. 100–119, see 1988 U.S.Code Cong. and Adm.News, p. 683.

2005 Acts. House Report No. 109–31(Part I), see 2005 U.S. Code Cong. and Adm. News, p. 88.

Effective and Applicability Provisions

2005 Acts. Amendments by Pub.L. 109–8 effective, except as otherwise provided, 180 days after April 20, 2005, and inapplicable with respect to cases commenced under Title 11 before the effective date, see Pub.L. 109–8, § 1501, set out as a note under 11 U.S.C.A. § 101.

Amendments by Pub.L. 109–8, Title XIV, effective, except as otherwise provided, on Apr. 20, 2005, and applicable only with respect to cases commenced under Title 11 on or after Apr. 20, 2005, see Pub.L. 109–8, § 1406, set out as a note under 11 U.S.C.A. § 507.

1988 Acts. Section 4 of Pub.L. 100–334 provided that:

"(a) **General Effective Date.**—Except as provided in subsection (b), this Act and the amendments made by this Act [enacting this section, amending section 1129 of this title, enacting provisions set out as a note under section 101 of this title, and amending and repealing provisions set out as notes under section 1106 of this title] shall take effect on the date of the enactment of this Act [June 16, 1988].

"(b) **Application of Amendments.**—The amendments made by section 2 [enacting this section and amending section 1129 of this title] shall not apply with respect to cases commenced under title 11 of the United States Code [this title] before the date of the enactment of this Act [June 16, 1988]."

Payment of Certain Benefits to Retired Former Employees

For payment of benefits by bankruptcy trustee to retired employees in enumerated circumstances with respect to cases commenced under this chapter in which a plan for reorganization had not been confirmed by the court and in which any such benefit was still being paid on October 2, 1986, and in cases that became subject to this chapter after October 2, 1986, and before June 16, 1988, see section 101(b) [title VI, § 608] of Pub.L. 99–500, and Pub.L. 99–591, as amended, set out as a note under section 1106 of this title.

CROSS REFERENCES

Confirmation of plan if plan provides for continuation of "retiree benefits" as defined under this section, see 11 USCA § 1129.

§ 1115. Property of the estate

(a) In a case in which the debtor is an individual, property of the estate includes, in addition to the property specified in section 541—

(1) all property of the kind specified in section 541 that the debtor acquires after the commencement of the case but before the case is closed, dismissed, or converted to a case under chapter 7, 12, or 13, whichever occurs first; and

(2) earnings from services performed by the debtor after the commencement of the case but before the case is closed, dismissed, or converted to a case under chapter 7, 12, or 13, whichever occurs first.

(b) Except as provided in section 1104 or a confirmed plan or order confirming a plan, the debtor shall remain in possession of all property of the estate.

(Added Pub.L. 109–8, Title III, § 321(a)(1), Apr. 20, 2005, 119 Stat. 94.)

HISTORICAL AND STATUTORY NOTES

Revision Notes and Legislative Reports

2005 Acts. House Report No. 109–31(Part I), see 2005 U.S. Code Cong. and Adm. News, p. 88.

References in Text

Chapter 7, 12, or 13, referred to in subsec. (a)(1), (2), is chapter 7, 12, or 13 of this title, 11 U.S.C.A. § 701 et seq., 11 U.S.C.A. § 1201 et seq., or 11 U.S.C.A. § 1301 et seq., respectively.

Effective and Applicability Provisions

2005 Acts. Amendments by Pub.L. 109–8 effective, except as otherwise provided, 180 days after April 20, 2005, and inapplicable with respect to cases commenced under Title 11 before the effective date, see Pub.L. 109–8, § 1501, set out as a note under 11 U.S.C.A. § 101.

§ 1116. Duties of trustee or debtor in possession in small business cases

In a small business case, a trustee or the debtor in possession, in addition to the duties provided in this title and as otherwise required by law, shall—

(1) append to the voluntary petition or, in an involuntary case, file not later than 7 days after the date of the order for relief—

(A) its most recent balance sheet, statement of operations, cash-flow statement, and Federal income tax return; or

(B) a statement made under penalty of perjury that no balance sheet, statement of operations, or cash-flow statement has been prepared and no Federal tax return has been filed;

(2) attend, through its senior management personnel and counsel, meetings scheduled by the court or the United States trustee, including initial debtor interviews, scheduling conferences, and meetings of creditors convened under section 341 unless the court, after notice and a hearing, waives that requirement upon a finding of extraordinary and compelling circumstances;

(3) timely file all schedules and statements of financial affairs, unless the court, after notice and a hearing, grants an extension, which shall not extend such time period to a date later than 30 days after the date of the order for relief, absent extraordinary and compelling circumstances;

(4) file all postpetition financial and other reports required by the Federal Rules of Bankruptcy Procedure or by local rule of the district court;

(5) subject to section 363(c)(2), maintain insurance customary and appropriate to the industry;

(6)(A) timely file tax returns and other required government filings; and

(B) subject to section 363(c)(2), timely pay all taxes entitled to administrative expense priority except those being contested by appropriate proceedings being diligently prosecuted; and

(7) allow the United States trustee, or a designated representative of the United States trustee, to inspect the debtor's business premises, books, and records at reasonable times, after reasonable prior written notice, unless notice is waived by the debtor.

(Added Pub.L. 109–8, Title IV, § 436(a), Apr. 20, 2005, 119 Stat. 112.)

HISTORICAL AND STATUTORY NOTES

Revision Notes and Legislative Reports

2005 Acts. House Report No. 109–31(Part I), see 2005 U.S. Code Cong. and Adm. News, p. 88.

References in Text

The Federal Rules of Bankruptcy Procedure, referred to in par. (4), are set out in the Appendix to this title.

Effective and Applicability Provisions

2005 Acts. Amendments by Pub.L. 109–8 effective, except as otherwise provided, 180 days after April 20, 2005, and inapplicable with respect to cases commenced under Title 11 before the effective date, see Pub.L. 109–8, § 1501, set out as a note under 11 U.S.C.A. § 101.

SUBCHAPTER II—THE PLAN

CROSS REFERENCES

Subchapter applicable only in case under this chapter except as provided in § 901 of this title, see 11 USCA § 103.

§ 1121. Who may file a plan

(a) The debtor may file a plan with a petition commencing a voluntary case, or at any time in a voluntary case or an involuntary case.

(b) Except as otherwise provided in this section, only the debtor may file a plan until after 120 days after the date of the order for relief under this chapter.

(c) Any party in interest, including the debtor, the trustee, a creditors' committee, an equity security holders' committee, a creditor, an equity security holder, or any indenture trustee, may file a plan if and only if—

(1) a trustee has been appointed under this chapter;

(2) the debtor has not filed a plan before 120 days after the date of the order for relief under this chapter; or

(3) the debtor has not filed a plan that has been accepted, before 180 days after the date of the order for relief under this chapter, by each class of claims or interests that is impaired under the plan.

(d)(1) Subject to paragraph (2), on request of a party in interest made within the respective periods specified in subsections (b) and (c) of this section and after notice and a hearing, the court may for cause reduce or increase the 120-day period or the 180-day period referred to in this section.

(2)(A) The 120–day period specified in paragraph (1) may not be extended beyond a date that is 18 months after the date of the order for relief under this chapter.

(B) The 180–day period specified in paragraph (1) may not be extended beyond a date that is 20 months after the date of the order for relief under this chapter.

(e) In a small business case—

(1) only the debtor may file a plan until after 180 days after the date of the order for relief, unless that period is—

(A) extended as provided by this subsection, after notice and a hearing; or

(B) the court, for cause, orders otherwise;

(2) the plan and a disclosure statement (if any) shall be filed not later than 300 days after the date of the order for relief; and

(3) the time periods specified in paragraphs (1) and (2), and the time fixed in section 1129(e) within which the plan shall be confirmed, may be extended only if—

(A) the debtor, after providing notice to parties in interest (including the United States trustee), demonstrates by a preponderance of the evidence that it is more likely than not that the court will confirm a plan within a reasonable period of time;

(B) a new deadline is imposed at the time the extension is granted; and

(C) the order extending time is signed before the existing deadline has expired.

(Pub.L. 95–598, Nov. 6, 1978, 92 Stat. 2631; Pub.L. 98–353, Title III, § 506, July 10, 1984, 98 Stat. 385; Pub.L. 99–554, Title II, § 283(u), Oct. 27, 1986, 100 Stat. 3118; Pub.L. 103–394, Title II, § 217(d), Oct. 22, 1994, 108 Stat. 4127; Pub.L. 109–8, Title IV, §§ 411, 437, Apr. 20, 2005, 119 Stat. 106, 113.)

HISTORICAL AND STATUTORY NOTES

Revision Notes and Legislative Reports

1978 Acts. Subsection (a) permits the debtor to file a reorganization plan with a petition commencing a voluntary case or at any time during a voluntary or involuntary case.

Subsection (b) gives the debtor the exclusive right to file a plan during the first 120 days of the case. There are exceptions, however, enumerated in subsection (c). If a trustee has been appointed, if the debtor does not meet the 120-day deadline, or if the debtor fails to obtain the required consent within 180 days after the filing of the petition, any party in interest may propose a plan. This includes the debtor, the trustee, a creditors' committee, an equity security holders' committee, a creditor, an equity security holder, and an indenture trustee. The list is not exhaustive. In the case of a public company, a trustee is appointed within 10 days of the petition. In such a case, for all practical purposes, any party in interest may file a plan.

Subsection (d) permits the court, for cause, to increase or reduce the 120-day and 180-day periods specified. Since, [sic] the debtor has an exclusive privilege for 6 months during which others may not file a plan, the granted extension should be based on a showing of some promise of probable success. An extension should not be employed as a tactical device to put pressure on parties in interest to yield to a plan they consider unsatisfactory. Senate Report No. 95–989.

1984 Acts. Statements by Legislative Leaders, see 1984 U.S.Code Cong. and Adm.News, p. 576.

1986 Acts. House Report No. 99–764 and House Conference Report No. 99–958, see 1986 U.S.Code Cong. and Adm.News, p. 5227.

1994 Acts. House Report No. 103–835, see 1994 U.S. Code Cong. and Adm. News, p. 3340.

2005 Acts. House Report No. 109–31(Part I), see 2005 U.S. Code Cong. and Adm. News, p. 88.

Legislative Statements

Section 1121 of the House amendment is derived from section 1121 of the House bill; section 1121(c)(1) will be satisfied automatically in a case under subchapter IV of title 11.

Effective and Applicability Provisions

2005 Acts. Amendments by Pub.L. 109–8 effective, except as otherwise provided, 180 days after April 20, 2005, and inapplicable with respect to cases commenced under Title 11 before the effective date, see Pub.L. 109–8, § 1501, set out as a note under 11 U.S.C.A. § 101.

1994 Acts. Amendment by Pub.L. 103–394 effective on Oct. 22, 1994, and not to apply with respect to cases commenced under Title 11 of the United States Code before Oct. 22, 1994, see section 702 of Pub.L. 103–394, set out as a note under section 101 of this title.

1986 Acts. Amendment by Pub.L. 99–554 effective 30 days after Oct. 27, 1986, except as otherwise provided for, see section 302(a) of Pub.L. 99–554, set out as a note under section 581 of Title 28, Judiciary and Judicial Procedure.

1984 Acts. Amendment by Pub.L. 98–353 effective with respect to cases filed 90 days after July 10, 1984, see section 552(a), formerly 553(a), of Pub.L. 98–353, set out as a note under section 101 of this title.

Separability of Provisions

If any provision of or amendment made by Pub.L. 103–394 or the application of such provision or amendment to any person or circumstance is held to be unconstitutional, the remaining provisions of and amendments made by Pub.L. 103–394 and the application of such provisions and amendments to any person or circumstance shall not be affected thereby, see section 701 of Pub.L. 103–394, set out as a note under section 101 of this title.

CROSS REFERENCES

Effect of conversion, see 11 USCA § 348.

Failure to propose plan as cause for conversion or dismissal, see 11 USCA § 1112.

Filing of plan by trustee, see 11 USCA § 1106.

Filing of plan in—

Chapter nine cases, see 11 USCA § 941.

Chapter thirteen cases, see 11 USCA § 1321.

Chapter twelve cases, see 11 USCA § 1221.

United States trustee not permitted to file plan, see 11 USCA § 307.

§ 1122. Classification of claims or interests

(a) Except as provided in subsection (b) of this section, a plan may place a claim or an interest in a particular class only if such claim or interest is substantially similar to the other claims or interests of such class.

(b) A plan may designate a separate class of claims consisting only of every unsecured claim that is less than or reduced to an amount that the court approves as reasonable and necessary for administrative convenience.

(Pub.L. 95–598, Nov. 6, 1978, 92 Stat. 2631.)

HISTORICAL AND STATUTORY NOTES

Revision Notes and Legislative Reports

1978 Acts. This section codifies current case law surrounding the classification of claims and equity securities. It requires classification based on the nature of the claims or interests classified, and permits inclusion of claims or interests in a particular class only if the claim or interest being included is substantially similar to the other claims or interests of the class.

Subsection (b), also a codification of existing practice, contains an exception. The plan may designate a separate class of claims consisting only of every unsecured claim that is less than or reduced to an amount that the court approves as reasonable and necessary for administrative convenience. Senate Report No. 95–989.

CROSS REFERENCES

Applicability of this section in Chapter 9 cases, see 11 USCA § 901.

Contents of plan filed in—

Chapter thirteen cases, see 11 USCA § 1322.

Chapter twelve cases, see 11 USCA § 1222.

Filing and allowance of postpetition claims in Chapter 13 cases, see 11 USCA § 1305.

Filing of proofs of claims or interests, see 11 USCA § 501.

§ 1123. Contents of plan

(a) Notwithstanding any otherwise applicable nonbankruptcy law, a plan shall—

(1) designate, subject to section 1122 of this title, classes of claims, other than claims of a kind specified in section 507(a)(2), 507(a)(3), or 507(a)(8) of this title, and classes of interests;

(2) specify any class of claims or interests that is not impaired under the plan;

(3) specify the treatment of any class of claims or interests that is impaired under the plan;

(4) provide the same treatment for each claim or interest of a particular class, unless the holder of a particular claim or interest agrees to a less favorable treatment of such particular claim or interest;

(5) provide adequate means for the plan's implementation, such as—

(A) retention by the debtor of all or any part of the property of the estate;

(B) transfer of all or any part of the property of the estate to one or more entities, whether organized before or after the confirmation of such plan;

(C) merger or consolidation of the debtor with one or more persons;

(D) sale of all or any part of the property of the estate, either subject to or free of any lien, or the distribution of all or any part of the property of the estate among those having an interest in such property of the estate;

(E) satisfaction or modification of any lien;

(F) cancellation or modification of any indenture or similar instrument;

(G) curing or waiving of any default;

(H) extension of a maturity date or a change in an interest rate or other term of outstanding securities;

(I) amendment of the debtor's charter; or

(J) issuance of securities of the debtor, or of any entity referred to in subparagraph (B) or (C) of this paragraph, for cash, for property, for existing securities, or in exchange for claims or interests, or for any other appropriate purpose;

(6) provide for the inclusion in the charter of the debtor, if the debtor is a corporation, or of any corporation referred to in paragraph (5)(B) or (5)(C) of this subsection, of a provision prohibiting the issuance of nonvoting equity securities, and providing, as to the several classes of securities possessing voting power, an appropriate distribution of such power among such classes, including, in the case of any class of equity securities having a preference over another class of equity securities with respect to dividends, adequate provisions for the election of directors representing such preferred class in the event of default in the payment of such dividends;

(7) contain only provisions that are consistent with the interests of creditors and equity security holders and with public policy with respect to the manner of selection of any officer, director, or trustee under the plan and any successor to such officer, director, or trustee; and

(8) in a case in which the debtor is an individual, provide for the payment to creditors under the plan of all or such portion of earnings from personal services performed by the debtor after the commencement of the case or other future income of the debtor as is necessary for the execution of the plan.

(b) Subject to subsection (a) of this section, a plan may—

(1) impair or leave unimpaired any class of claims, secured or unsecured, or of interests;

(2) subject to section 365 of this title, provide for the assumption, rejection, or assignment of any executory contract or unexpired lease of the debtor not previously rejected under such section;

(3) provide for—

(A) the settlement or adjustment of any claim or interest belonging to the debtor or to the estate; or

(B) the retention and enforcement by the debtor, by the trustee, or by a representative of the estate appointed for such purpose, of any such claim or interest;

(4) provide for the sale of all or substantially all of the property of the estate, and the distribution of the proceeds of such sale among holders of claims or interests;

(5) modify the rights of holders of secured claims, other than a claim secured only by a security interest in real property that is the debtor's principal residence, or of holders of unsecured claims, or leave unaffected the rights of holders of any class of claims; and

(6) include any other appropriate provision not inconsistent with the applicable provisions of this title.

(c) In a case concerning an individual, a plan proposed by an entity other than the debtor may not provide for the use, sale, or lease of property exempted under section 522 of this title, unless the debtor consents to such use, sale, or lease.

(d) Notwithstanding subsection (a) of this section and sections 506(b), 1129(a)(7), and 1129(b) of this title, if it is proposed in a plan to cure a default the amount necessary to cure the default shall be determined in accordance with the underlying agreement and applicable nonbankruptcy law.

(Pub.L. 95–598, Nov. 6, 1978, 92 Stat. 2631; Pub.L. 98–353, Title III, § 507, July 10, 1984, 98 Stat. 385; Pub.L. 103–394, Title II, § 206, Title III, §§ 304(h)(6), 305(a), Title V, § 501(d)(31), Oct. 22, 1994, 108 Stat. 4123, 4134, 4146; Pub.L. 109–8, Title III, § 321(b), Title XV, § 1502(a)(7), Apr. 20, 2005, 119 Stat. 95, 216.)

HISTORICAL AND STATUTORY NOTES

Revision Notes and Legislative Reports

1978 Acts. Subsection (a) specifies what a plan of reorganization must contain. The plan must designate classes of claims and interests, and specify, by class, the claims or interests that are unimpaired under the plan. Priority claims are not required to be classified because they may not have arisen when the plan is filed. The plan must provide the same treatment for each claim or interest of a particular class, unless the holder of a particular claim or interest agrees to a different, but not better, treatment of his claim or interest.

Paragraph (3) applies to claims, not creditors. Thus, if a creditor is undersecured, and thus has a secured claim and an unsecured claim, this paragraph will be applied independently to each of his claims.

Paragraph (4) of subsection (a) is derived from section 216 of chapter X [section 616 of former Title 11] with some modifications. It requires the plan to provide adequate means for the plans [sic] execution. These means may include retention by the debtor of all or any part of the property of the estate, transfer of all or any part of the property of the estate to one or more entities, whether organized pre- or postconfirmation, merger or consolidation of the debtor with one or more persons, sale and distribution of all or any part of the property of the estate, satisfaction or modification of any lien, cancellation or modification of any indenture or similar instrument, curing or waiving of any default, extension of maturity dates or change in interest rates of securities, amendment of the debtor's charter, and issuance of securities.

Subparagraph (C), as it applies in railroad cases, has the effect of overruling *St. Joe Paper Co. v. Atlantic Coast Line R.R.*, 347 U.S. 298 (1954). [Fla.1954, 74 S.Ct. 574, 98 L.Ed. 710, rehearing denied 74 S.Ct. 734, 347 U.S. 980, 98 L.Ed. 1118]. It will allow the trustee or creditors to propose a plan of merger with another railroad without the consent of the debtor, and the debtor will be bound under proposed 11 U.S.C. 1141(a). See Hearings, pt. 3, at 1616. "Similar instrument" referred to in subparagraph (F) might include a deposit with an agent for distribution, other than an indenture trustee, such as an agent under an agreement in a railroad conditional sale or lease financing agreement.

Paragraphs (5) and (6) and subsection (b) are derived substantially from section 216 of Chapter X (11 U.S.C. 616) [section 616 of former Title 11]. Paragraph (5) requires the plan to prohibit the issuance of nonvoting equity securities, and to provide for an appropriate distribution of voting power among the various classes of equity securities. Paragraph (6) requires that the plan contain only provisions that are consistent with the interests of creditors and equity security holders, and with public policy with respect to the selection of officers, directors, and trustees, and their successors.

Subsection (b) specifies the matters that the plan may propose. The plan may impair or leave unimpaired any claim or interest. The plan may provide for the assumption or rejection of executory contracts or unexpired leases not previously rejected under section 365. The plan may also provide for the treatment of claims by the debtor against other entities that are not settled before the confirmation of the plan. The plan may propose settlement or adjustment of any claim or equity security belonging to the estate, or may propose retention and enforcement of such claim or interest by the debtor or by an agent appointed for that purpose.

The plan may also propose the sale of all or substantially all of the property of the estate, and the distribution of the proceeds of the sale among creditors and equity security holders. This would be a liquidating plan. The subsection permits the plan to include any other appropriate provision not inconsistent with the applicable provisions of the bankruptcy code.

Subsection (c) protects an individual debtor's exempt property by prohibiting its use, sale, or lease under a plan proposed by someone other than the debtor, unless the debtor consents. Senate Report No. 95–989.

1984 Acts. Statements by Legislative Leaders, see 1984 U.S.Code Cong. and Adm.News, p. 576.

1994 Acts. House Report No. 103–835, see 1994 U.S. Code Cong. and Adm. News, p. 3340.

2005 Acts. House Report No. 109–31(Part I), see 2005 U.S. Code Cong. and Adm. News, p. 88.

Legislative Statements

Section 1123 of the House amendment represents a compromise between similar provisions in the House bill and Senate amendment. The section has been clarified to clearly indicate that both secured and unsecured claims, or either of them, may be impaired in a case under title 11. In addition assumption or rejection of an executory contract under a plan must comply with section 365 of title 11. Moreover, section 1123(a)(1) has been substantively modified to permit classification of certain kinds of priority claims. This is important for purposes of confirmation under section 1129(a)(9).

Section 1123(a)(5) of the House amendment is derived from a similar provision in the House bill and Senate amendment but deletes the language pertaining to "fair upset price" as an unnecessary restriction. Section 1123 is also intended to indicate that a plan may provide for any action specified in section 1123 in the case of a corporation without a resolution of the board of directors. If the plan is confirmed, then any action proposed in the plan may be taken notwithstanding any otherwise applicable nonbankruptcy law in accordance with section 1142(a) of title 11.

Effective and Applicability Provisions

2005 Acts. Amendments by Pub.L. 109–8 effective, except as otherwise provided, 180 days after April 20, 2005, and inapplicable with respect to cases commenced under Title 11 before the effective date, see Pub.L. 109–8, § 1501, set out as a note under 11 U.S.C.A. § 101.

1994 Acts. Amendments by sections 206, 304(h)(6), and 501(d)(31) of Pub.L. 103–394 effective on Oct. 22, 1994, and not to apply with respect to cases commenced under Title 11 of the United States Code before Oct. 22, 1994, see section 702 of Pub.L. 103–394, set out as a note under section 101 of this title.

Amendment by section 305(a) of Pub.L. 103–394 effective Oct. 22, 1994, and applicable only to agreements entered into after Oct. 22, 1994, see section 702 of Pub.L.103–394, set out as a note under section 101 of this title.

1984 Acts. Amendment by Pub.L. 98–353 effective with respect to cases filed 90 days after July 10, 1984, see section

552(a), formerly 553(a), of Pub.L. 98–353, set out as a note under section 101 of this title.

Separability of Provisions

If any provision of or amendment made by Pub.L. 103–394 or the application of such provision or amendment to any person or circumstance is held to be unconstitutional, the remaining provisions of and amendments made by Pub.L. 103–394 and the application of such provisions and amendments to any person or circumstance shall not be affected thereby, see section 701 of Pub.L. 103–394, set out as a note under section 101 of this title.

CROSS REFERENCES

Applicability of subsecs. (a)(1) to (5) and (b) of this section in Chapter 9 cases, see 11 USCA § 901.

Contents of plan filed in—

Chapter thirteen cases, see 11 USCA § 1322.

Chapter twelve cases, see 11 USCA § 1222.

Railroad reorganization cases, see 11 USCA § 1172.

§ 1124. Impairment of claims or interests

Except as provided in section 1123(a)(4) of this title, a class of claims or interests is impaired under a plan unless, with respect to each claim or interest of such class, the plan—

(1) leaves unaltered the legal, equitable, and contractual rights to which such claim or interest entitles the holder of such claim or interest; or

(2) notwithstanding any contractual provision or applicable law that entitles the holder of such claim or interest to demand or receive accelerated payment of such claim or interest after the occurrence of a default—

(A) cures any such default that occurred before or after the commencement of the case under this title, other than a default of a kind specified in section 365(b)(2) of this title or of a kind that section 365(b)(2) expressly does not require to be cured;

(B) reinstates the maturity of such claim or interest as such maturity existed before such default;

(C) compensates the holder of such claim or interest for any damages incurred as a result of any reasonable reliance by such holder on such contractual provision or such applicable law;

(D) if such claim or such interest arises from any failure to perform a nonmonetary obligation, other than a default arising from failure to operate a nonresidential real property lease subject to section 365(b)(1)(A), compensates the holder of such claim or such interest (other than the debtor or an insider) for any actual pecuniary loss incurred by such holder as a result of such failure; and

(E) does not otherwise alter the legal, equitable, or contractual rights to which such claim or interest entitles the holder of such claim or interest.

(Pub.L. 95–598, Nov. 6, 1978, 92 Stat. 2633; Pub.L. 98–353, Title III, § 508, July 10, 1984, 98 Stat. 385; Pub.L. 103–394, Title II, § 213(d), Oct. 22, 1994, 108 Stat. 4126; Pub.L. 109–8, Title III, § 328(b), Apr. 20, 2005, 119 Stat. 100.)

HISTORICAL AND STATUTORY NOTES

Revision Notes and Legislative Reports

1978 Acts. The basic concept underlying this section is not new. It rests essentially on Section [sic] 107 of Chapter X (11 U.S.C. 507) [section 507 of former Title 11], which states that creditors or stockholders or any class thereof "shall be deemed to be 'affected' by a plan only if their or its interest shall be materially and adversely affected thereby."

This section is designed to indicate when contractual rights of creditors or interest holders are not materially affected. It specifies three ways in which the plan may leave a claim or interest unimpaired.

First, the plan may propose not to alter the legal, equitable, or contractual rights to which the claim or interest entitled its holder.

Second, a claim or interest is unimpaired by curing the effect of a default and reinstating the original terms of an obligation when maturity was brought on or accelerated by the default. The intervention of bankruptcy and the defaults represent a temporary crisis which the plan of reorganization is intended to clear away. The holder of a claim or interest who under the plan is restored to his original position, when others receive less or get nothing at all, is fortunate indeed and has no cause to complain. Curing of the default and the assumption of the debt in accordance with its terms is an important reorganization technique for dealing with a particular class of claims, especially secured claims.

Third, a claim or interest is unimpaired if the plan provides for their payment in cash. In the case of a debt liability, the cash payment is for the allowed amount of the claim, which does not include a redemption premium. If it is an equity security with a fixed liquidation preference, such as a preferred stock, the allowed amount is such liquidation preference, with no redemption premium. With respect to any other equity security, such as a common stock, cash payment must be equal to the "value of such holder's interest in the debtor."

Section 1124 does not include payment "in property" other than cash. Except for a rare case, claims or interests are not by their terms payable in property, but a plan may so provide and those affected thereby may accept or reject the proposed plan. They may not be forced to accept a plan declaring the holders' claims or interests to be "unimpaired." Senate Report No. 95–989.

This section is new. It is designed to indicate when contractual rights of creditors or interest holders are not materially affected. The section specifies three ways in which the plan may leave a claim or interest unimpaired.

First, the plan may propose not to alter the legal, equitable, or contractual rights to which the claim or interest entitled its holder.

Second, the plan is permitted to reinstate a claim or interest and thus leave it unimpaired. Reinstatement consists of curing any default (other than a default under an ipso facto or bankruptcy clause) and reinstatement of the maturity of the claim or interest. Further, the plan may not otherwise alter any legal, equitable, or contractual right to which the claim or interest entitles its holder.

Third, the plan may leave a claim or interest unimpaired by paying its amount in full other than in securities of the debtor, an affiliate of the debtor participating in a joint plan, or a successor to the debtor. These securities are excluded because determination of their value would require a valuation of the business being reorganized. Use of them to pay a creditor or equity security holder without his consent may be done only under section 1129(b) and only after a valuation of the debtor. Under this paragraph, the plan must pay the allowed amount of the claim in full, in cash or other property, or, in the case of an equity security, must pay the greatest of any fixed liquidation preference to which the terms of the equity security entitle its holder, any fixed price at which the debtor, under the terms of the equity security may redeem such equity security, and the value, as of the effective date of the plan, of the holder's interest in the debtor. The value of the holder's interest need not be determined precisely by valuing the debtor's business if such value of clearly below redemption or liquidation preference values. If such value would require a full-scale valuation of the business, then such interest should be treated as impaired. But, if the debtor corporation is clearly insolvent, then the value of the common stock holder's interest in the debtor is zero, and offering them nothing under the plan of reorganization will not impair their rights.

"Value, as of the effective date of the plan," as used in paragraph (3) and in proposed 11 U.S.C. 1179(a)(7)(B), 1129(a)(9), 1129(b), 1172(2), 1325(a)(4), 1325(a)(5)(B), and 1328(b), indicates that the promised payment under the plan must be discounted to present value as of the effective date of the plan. The discounting should be based only on the unpaid balance of the amount due under the plan, until that amount, including interest, is paid in full. House Report No. 95–595.

1984 Acts. Statements by Legislative Leaders, see 1984 U.S.Code Cong. and Adm.News, p. 576.

1994 Acts. House Report No. 103–835, see 1994 U.S. Code Cong. and Adm. News, p. 3340.

2005 Acts. House Report No. 109–31(Part I), see 2005 U.S. Code Cong. and Adm. News, p. 88.

Legislative Statements

Section 1124 of the House amendment is derived from a similar provision in the House bill and Senate amendment. The section defines the new concept of "impairment" of claims or interests; the concept differs significantly from the concept of "materially and adversely affected" under the Bankruptcy Act [former Title 11]. Section 1124(3) of the House amendment provides that a holder of a claim or interest is not impaired, if the plan provides that the holder will receive the allowed amount of the holder's claim, or in the case of an interest with a fixed liquidation preference or redemption price, the greater of such price. This adopts the position contained in the House bill and rejects the contrary standard contained in the Senate amendment.

Section 1124(3) of the House amendment rejects a provision contained in section 1124(3)(B)(iii) of the House bill which would have considered a class of interest not to be impaired by virtue of the fact that the plan provided cash or property for the value of the holder's interest in the debtor.

The effect of the House amendment is to permit an interest not to be impaired only if the interest has a fixed liquidation preference or redemption price. Therefore, a class of interests such as common stock, must either accept a plan under section 1129(a)(8), or the plan must satisfy the requirements of section 1129(b)(2)(C) in order for a plan to be confirmed.

A compromise reflected in section 1124(2)(C) of the House amendment indicates that a class of claims is not impaired under the circumstances of section 1124(2) if damages are paid to rectify reasonable reliance engaged in by the holder of a claim or interest arising from the prepetition breach of a contractual provision, such as an ipso facto or bankruptcy clause, or law. Where the rights of third parties are concerned, such as in the case of lease premises which have been rerented to a third party, it is not intended that there will be adequate damages to compensate the third party.

Effective and Applicability Provisions

2005 Acts. Amendments by Pub.L. 109–8 effective, except as otherwise provided, 180 days after April 20, 2005, and inapplicable with respect to cases commenced under Title 11 before the effective date, see Pub.L. 109–8, § 1501, set out as a note under 11 U.S.C.A. § 101.

1994 Acts. Amendment by Pub.L. 103–394 effective on Oct. 22, 1994, and not to apply with respect to cases commenced under Title 11 of the United States Code before Oct. 22, 1994, see section 702 of Pub.L. 103–394, set out as a note under section 101 of this title.

1984 Acts. Amendment by Pub.L. 98–353 effective with respect to cases filed 90 days after July 10, 1984, see section 552(a), formerly 553(a), of Pub.L. 98–353, set out as a note under section 101 of this title.

Separability of Provisions

If any provision of or amendment made by Pub.L. 103–394 or the application of such provision or amendment to any person or circumstance is held to be unconstitutional, the remaining provisions of and amendments made by Pub.L. 103–394 and the application of such provisions and amendments to any person or circumstance shall not be affected thereby, see section 701 of Pub.L. 103–394, set out as a note under section 101 of this title.

CROSS REFERENCES

Allowance of claims or interests, see 11 USCA § 502.

Applicability of this section in Chapter nine cases, see 11 USCA § 901.

Claims and interests generally, see 11 USCA § 1111.

Filing of proofs of claims or interests, see 11 USCA § 501.

§ 1125. Postpetition disclosure and solicitation

(a) In this section—

(1) "adequate information" means information of a kind, and in sufficient detail, as far as is reasonably practicable in light of the nature and history of the debtor and the condition of the debtor's books and records, including a discussion of the potential material Federal tax consequences of the plan to

the debtor, any successor to the debtor, and a hypothetical investor typical of the holders of claims or interests in the case, that would enable such a hypothetical investor of the relevant class to make an informed judgment about the plan, but adequate information need not include such information about any other possible or proposed plan and in determining whether a disclosure statement provides adequate information, the court shall consider the complexity of the case, the benefit of additional information to creditors and other parties in interest, and the cost of providing additional information; and

(2) "investor typical of holders of claims or interests of the relevant class" means investor having—

(A) a claim or interest of the relevant class;

(B) such a relationship with the debtor as the holders of other claims or interests of such class generally have; and

(C) such ability to obtain such information from sources other than the disclosure required by this section as holders of claims or interests in such class generally have.

(b) An acceptance or rejection of a plan may not be solicited after the commencement of the case under this title from a holder of a claim or interest with respect to such claim or interest, unless, at the time of or before such solicitation, there is transmitted to such holder the plan or a summary of the plan, and a written disclosure statement approved, after notice and a hearing, by the court as containing adequate information. The court may approve a disclosure statement without a valuation of the debtor or an appraisal of the debtor's assets.

(c) The same disclosure statement shall be transmitted to each holder of a claim or interest of a particular class, but there may be transmitted different disclosure statements, differing in amount, detail, or kind of information, as between classes.

(d) Whether a disclosure statement required under subsection (b) of this section contains adequate information is not governed by any otherwise applicable nonbankruptcy law, rule, or regulation, but an agency or official whose duty is to administer or enforce such a law, rule, or regulation may be heard on the issue of whether a disclosure statement contains adequate information. Such an agency or official may not appeal from, or otherwise seek review of, an order approving a disclosure statement.

(e) A person that solicits acceptance or rejection of a plan, in good faith and in compliance with the applicable provisions of this title, or that participates, in good faith and in compliance with the applicable provisions of this title, in the offer, issuance, sale, or purchase of a security, offered or sold under the plan, of the debtor, of an affiliate participating in a joint plan with the debtor, or of a newly organized successor to the debtor under the plan, is not liable, on account of such solicitation or participation, for violation of any applicable law, rule, or regulation governing solicitation of acceptance or rejection of a plan or the offer, issuance, sale, or purchase of securities.

(f) Notwithstanding subsection (b), in a small business case—

(1) the court may determine that the plan itself provides adequate information and that a separate disclosure statement is not necessary;

(2) the court may approve a disclosure statement submitted on standard forms approved by the court or adopted under section 2075 of title 28; and

(3)(A) the court may conditionally approve a disclosure statement subject to final approval after notice and a hearing;

(B) acceptances and rejections of a plan may be solicited based on a conditionally approved disclosure statement if the debtor provides adequate information to each holder of a claim or interest that is solicited, but a conditionally approved disclosure statement shall be mailed not later than 25 days before the date of the hearing on confirmation of the plan; and

(C) the hearing on the disclosure statement may be combined with the hearing on confirmation of a plan.

(g) Notwithstanding subsection (b), an acceptance or rejection of the plan may be solicited from a holder of a claim or interest if such solicitation complies with applicable nonbankruptcy law and if such holder was solicited before the commencement of the case in a manner complying with applicable nonbankruptcy law.

(Pub.L. 95–598, Nov. 6, 1978, 92 Stat. 2633; Pub.L. 98–353, Title III, § 509, July 10, 1984, 98 Stat. 385; Pub.L. 103–394, Title II, § 217(e), Oct. 22, 1994, 108 Stat. 4127; Pub.L. 109–8, Title IV, §§ 408, 431, Title VII, § 717, Apr. 20, 2005, 119 Stat. 106, 109, 110, 131.)

HISTORICAL AND STATUTORY NOTES

Revision Notes and Legislative Reports

1978 Acts. This section extends disclosure requirements in connection with solicitations to all cases under chapter 11. Heretofore this subject was dealt with by the Bankruptcy Act [former Title 11] mainly in the special contexts of railroad reorganizations and chapter X [former Chapter 10 (section 501 et seq.) of former Title 11 cases.

Subsection (a) defines (1) the subject matter of disclosure as "adequate information" and relates the standard of adequacy to an (2) "investor typical of holders or claims or interests of the relevant class." "Investor" is used broadly here, for it will almost always include a trade creditor or other creditors who originally had no investment intent or interest. It refers to the investment-type decision by those called upon to accept a plan to modify their claims or interests, which typically will involve acceptance of new securities or of a cash payment in lieu thereof.

Both the kind and form of information are left essentially to the judicial discretion of the court, guided by the specification in subparagraph (a)(1) that it be of a kind and in sufficient detail that a reasonable and typical investor can make an informed judgment about the plan. The information required will necessarily be governed by the circumstances of the case.

Reporting and audit standards devised for solvent and continuing businesses do not necessarily fit a debtor in reorganization. Subsection (a)(1) expressly incorporates consideration of the nature and history of the debtor and the condition of its books and records into the determination of what is reasonably practicable to supply. These factors are particularly pertinent to historical data and to discontinued operations of no future relevance.

A plan is necessarily predicated on knowledge of the assets and liabilities being dealt with and on factually supported expectations as to the future course of the business sufficient to meet the feasibility standard in section 1130(a)(11) [now section 1129(a)(11)] of this title. It may thus be necessary to provide estimates or judgments for that purpose. Yet it remains practicable to describe, in such detail as may be relevant and needed, the basis for the plan and the data on which supporters of the plan rely.

Subsection (b) establishes the jurisdiction of the court over this subject by prohibiting solicitation of acceptance or rejection of a plan after the commencement of the case, unless the person solicited receives, before or at the time of the solicitation, a written disclosure statement approved by the court, after notice and hearing, as containing adequate information. As under present law, determinations of value, by appraisal or otherwise, are not required if not needed to accomplish the purpose specified in subsection (a)(1).

Subsection (c) requires that the same disclosure statement be transmitted to each member of a class. It recognizes that the information needed for an informed judgment about the plan may differ among classes. A class whose rights under the plan center on a particular fund or asset would have no use for an extensive description of other matters that could not affect them.

Subsection (d) relieves the court of the need to follow any otherwise applicable Federal or state law in determining the adequacy of the information contained in the disclosure statement submitted for its approval. It authorizes an agency or official, Federal or state, charged with administering cognate laws so preempted to advise the court on the adequacy of proposed disclosure statement. But they are not authorized to appeal the court's decision.

Solicitations with respect to a plan do not involve just mere requests for opinions. Acceptance of the plan vitally affects creditors and shareholders, and most frequently the solicitation involves an offering of securities in exchange for claims or interests. The present bankruptcy statute [former Title 11] has exempted such offerings under each of its chapters from the registration and disclosure requirements of the Securities Act of 1933 [section 77a et seq. of Title 15, Commerce and Trade], an exemption also continued by section 1145(a)(2) of this title. The extension of the disclosure requirements to all chapter 11 cases justifies the coordinate extension of these exemptions. By the same token, no valid purpose is served not to exempt from the requirements of similar state laws in a matter under the exclusive jurisdiction of the Federal bankruptcy laws.

Subsection (e) exonerates any person who, in good faith and in compliance with this title, solicits or participates in the offer, issuance, sale or purchase, under the plan, of a security from any liability, on account of such solicitation or participation, for violation of any law, rule, or regulation governing the offer, issuance, sale, or purchase of securities. This exoneration is coordinate with the exemption from Federal or State registration or licensing requirements provided by section 1145 of this title.

In the nonpublic case, the court, when approving the disclosure statement, has before it the texts of the plan, a proposed disclosure document, and such other information the plan proponents and other interested parties may present at the hearing. In the final analysis the exoneration which subsection (e) grants must depend on the good faith of the plan proponents and of those who participate in the preparation of the disclosure statement and in the solicitation. Subsection (e) does not affect civil or criminal liability for defects and inadequacies that are beyond the limits of the exoneration that good faith provides.

Section 1125 applies to public companies as well, subject to the qualifications of subsection (f). In case of a public company no solicitations of acceptance is permitted unless authorized by the court upon or after approval of the plan pursuant to section 1128(c). In addition to the documents specified in subsection (b), subsection (f) requires transmission of the opinion and order of the court approving the plan and, if filed, the advisory report of the Securities and Exchange Commission or a summary thereof prepared by the Commission. Senate Report No. 95–989.

This section is new. It is the heart of the consolidation of the various reorganization chapters found in current law. It requires disclosure before solicitation of acceptances of a plan or reorganization.

Subsection (a) contains two definitions. First, "adequate information" is defined to mean information of a kind, and insufficient [sic] detail, as far as is reasonably practical in light of the nature and history of the debtor and the condition of the debtor's books and records, that would enable a hypothetical reasonable investor typical of holders of claims or interests of the relevant class to make an informed judgment about the plan. Second, "investor typical of holders of claims or interests of the relevant class" is defined to mean an investor having a claim or interest of the relevant class, having such a relationship with the debtor as the holders of other claims or interests of the relevant class have, and having such ability to obtain information from sources other than the disclosure statement as holders of claims or interests of the relevant class have, and having such ability to obtain information from sources other than the disclosure statement as holders of claims or interests of the relevant class have. That is, the hypothetical investor against which the disclosure is measured must not be an insider if other members of the class are not insiders, and so on. In other words, the adequacy of disclosure is measured against the typical investor, not an extraordinary one.

The Supreme Court's rulemaking power will not extend to rulemaking that will prescribe what constitutes adequate information. That standard is a substantive standard. Precisely what constitutes adequate information in any particular instance will develop on a case-by-case basis. Courts will take a practical approach as to what is necessary under the circumstances of each case, such as the cost of preparation of the statements, the need for relative speed in solicitation and confirmation, and, of course, the need for investor protection. There will be a balancing of interests in each case. In reorganization cases, there is frequently great uncertainty. Therefore the need for flexibility is greatest.

Subsection (b) is the operative subsection. It prohibits solicitation of acceptances or rejections of a plan after the commencement of the case unless, at the time of the solicitation or before, there is transmitted to the solicitee the plan or a summary of the plan, and a written disclosure statement approved by the court as containing adequate information. The subsection permits approval of the statement without the necessity of a valuation of the debtor or an appraisal of the debtor's assets. However, in some cases, a valuation or appraisal will be necessary to develop adequate information. The court will be able to determine what is necessary in light of the facts and circumstances of each particular case.

Subsection (c) requires that the same disclosure statement go to all members of a particular class, but permits different disclosure to different classes.

Subsection (d) excepts the disclosure statements from the requirements of the securities laws (such as section 14 of the 1934 Act [section 78n of Title 15, Commerce and Trade] and section 5 of the 1933 Act [section 77e of Title 15]), and from similar State securities laws (blue sky laws, for example). The subsection permits an agency or official whose duty is to administer or enforce such laws (such as the Securities and Exchange Commission or State Corporation Commissioners) to appear and be heard on the issue of whether a disclosure statement contains adequate information, but the agencies and officials are not granted the right of appeal from an adverse determination in any capacity. They may join in an appeal by a true party in interest, however.

Subsection (e) is a safe harbor provision, and is necessary to make the exemption provided by subsection (d) effective. Without it, a creditor that solicited an acceptance or rejection in reliance on the court's approval of a disclosure statement would be potentially liable under antifraud sections designed to enforce the very sections of the securities laws from which subsection (d) excuses compliance. The subsection protects only persons that solicit in good faith and in compliance with the applicable provisions of the reorganization chapter. It provides protection from legal liability as well as from equitable liability based on an injunctive action by the SEC [Securities and Exchange Commission] or other agency or official. House Report No. 95–595.

1984 Acts. Statements by Legislative Leaders, see 1984 U.S.Code Cong. and Adm.News, p. 576.

1994 Acts. House Report No. 103–835, see 1994 U.S. Code Cong. and Adm. News, p. 3340.

2005 Acts. House Report No. 109–31(Part I), see 2005 U.S. Code Cong. and Adm. News, p. 88.

Legislative Statements

Section 1125 of the House amendment is derived from section 1125 of the House bill and Senate amendment except with respect to section 1125(f) of the Senate amendment. It will not be necessary for the court to consider the report of the examiner prior to approval of a disclosure statement. The investigation of the examiner is to proceed on an independent basis from the procedure of the reorganization under chapter 11. In order to ensure that the examiner's report will be expeditious and fair, the examiner is precluded from serving as a trustee in the case or from representing a trustee if a trustee is appointed, whether the case remains in chapter 11 or is converted to chapter 7 or 13.

Effective and Applicability Provisions

2005 Acts. Amendments by Pub.L. 109–8 effective, except as otherwise provided, 180 days after April 20, 2005, and inapplicable with respect to cases commenced under Title 11 before the effective date, see Pub.L. 109–8, § 1501, set out as a note under 11 U.S.C.A. § 101.

1994 Acts. Amendment by Pub.L. 103–394 effective on Oct. 22, 1994, and not to apply with respect to cases commenced under Title 11 of the United States Code before Oct. 22, 1994, see section 702 of Pub.L. 103–394, set out as a note under section 101 of this title.

1984 Acts. Amendment by Pub.L. 98–353 effective with respect to cases filed 90 days after July 10, 1984, see section 552(a), formerly 553(a), of Pub.L. 98–353, set out as a note under section 101 of this title.

Separability of Provisions

If any provision of or amendment made by Pub.L. 103–394 or the application of such provision or amendment to any person or circumstance is held to be unconstitutional, the remaining provisions of and amendments made by Pub.L. 103–394 and the application of such provisions and amendments to any person or circumstance shall not be affected thereby, see section 701 of Pub.L. 103–394, set out as a note under section 101 of this title.

CROSS REFERENCES

Applicability of this section in Chapter nine cases, see 11 USCA § 901.

Duty of United States trustee to file comments with respect to plans and disclosure statements filed in connection with hearings under this section, see 28 USCA § 586.

Exemption from securities laws of certain transactions in which disclosure statements are provided, see 11 USCA § 1145.

§ 1126. Acceptance of plan

(a) The holder of a claim or interest allowed under section 502 of this title may accept or reject a plan. If the United States is a creditor or equity security holder, the Secretary of the Treasury may accept or reject the plan on behalf of the United States.

(b) For the purposes of subsections (c) and (d) of this section, a holder of a claim or interest that has accepted or rejected the plan before the commencement of the case under this title is deemed to have accepted or rejected such plan, as the case may be, if—

(1) the solicitation of such acceptance or rejection was in compliance with any applicable nonbankruptcy law, rule, or regulation governing the adequacy of disclosure in connection with such solicitation; or

(2) if there is not any such law, rule, or regulation, such acceptance or rejection was solicited after disclosure to such holder of adequate information, as defined in section 1125(a) of this title.

(c) A class of claims has accepted a plan if such plan has been accepted by creditors, other than any entity designated under subsection (e) of this section, that hold at least two-thirds in amount and more than one-half in number of the allowed claims of such class held by creditors, other than any entity designated under subsection (e) of this section, that have accepted or rejected such plan.

(d) A class of interests has accepted a plan if such plan has been accepted by holders of such interests, other than any entity designated under subsection (e) of this section, that hold at least two-thirds in amount of the allowed interests of such class held by holders of such interests, other than any entity designated under subsection (e) of this section, that have accepted or rejected such plan.

(e) On request of a party in interest, and after notice and a hearing, the court may designate any entity whose acceptance or rejection of such plan was not in good faith, or was not solicited or procured in good faith or in accordance with the provisions of this title.

(f) Notwithstanding any other provision of this section, a class that is not impaired under a plan, and each holder of a claim or interest of such class, are conclusively presumed to have accepted the plan, and solicitation of acceptances with respect to such class from the holders of claims or interests of such class is not required.

(g) Notwithstanding any other provision of this section, a class is deemed not to have accepted a plan if such plan provides that the claims or interests of such class do not entitle the holders of such claims or interests to receive or retain any property under the plan on account of such claims or interests.

(Pub.L. 95–598, Nov. 6, 1978, 92 Stat. 2634; Pub.L. 98–353, Title III, § 510, July 10, 1984, 98 Stat. 386.)

HISTORICAL AND STATUTORY NOTES

Revision Notes and Legislative Reports

1978 Acts. Subsection (a) of this section permits the holder of a claim or interest allowed under section 502 to accept or reject a proposed plan of reorganization. The subsection also incorporates a provision now found in section 199 of chapter X [section 599 of former Title 11] that authorizes the Secretary of the Treasury to accept or reject a plan on behalf of the United States when the United States is a creditor or equity security holder.

Subsection (b) governs acceptances and rejections of plans obtained before commencement of a reorganization for a nonpublic company. Paragraph (3) expressly states that subsection (b) does not apply to a public company.

Prepetition solicitation is a common practice under chapter XI [former chapter 11 (section 701 et seq.) of former Title 11] today, and chapter IX [former chapter 9 (section 401 et seq.) of former Title 11] current makes explicit provision for it. Section 1126(b) counts a prepetition acceptance or rejection toward the required amounts and number of acceptances only if the solicitation of the acceptance or rejection was in compliance with any applicable nonbankruptcy law, rule, or regulation governing the adequacy of disclosure in connection with such solicitation. If there is not any such applicable law, rule, or regulation, then the acceptance or rejection is counted only if it was solicited after disclosure of adequate information, to the holder, as defined in section 1125(a)(1). This permits the court to ensure that the requirements of section 1125 are not avoided by prepetition solicitation.

Subsection (c) specifies the required amount and number of acceptances for a class of creditors. A class of creditors has accepted a plan if at least two-thirds in amount and more than one-half in number of the allowed claims of the class that are voted are cast in favor of the plan. The amount and number are computed on the basis of claims actually voted for or against the plan, not as under chapter X [former chapter 10 (section 501 et seq.) of former Title 11] on the basis of the allowed claims in the class. Subsection (f) excludes from all these calculations claims not voted in good faith, and claims procured or solicited not in good faith or not in accordance with the provisions of this title.

Subsection (c) requires that the same disclosure statement be transmitted to each member of a class. It recognizes that the information needed for an informed judgment about the plan may differ among classes. A class whose rights under the plan center on a particular fund or asset would have no use for an extensive description of other matters that could not affect them.

Subsection (d) relieves the court of the need to follow any otherwise applicable Federal or state law in determining the adequacy of the information contained in the disclosure statement submitted for its approval. It authorizes an agency or official, Federal or state, charged with administering cognate laws so pre-empted to advise the court on the adequacy of proposed disclosure statement. But they are not authorized to appeal the court's decision.

Solicitations with respect to a plan do not involve just mere requests for opinions. Acceptance of the plan vitally affects creditors and shareholders, and most frequently the solicitation involves an offering of securities in exchange for claims or interests. The present Bankruptcy Act [former Title 11] has exempted such offerings under each of its chapters from the registration and disclosure requirements of the Securities Act of 1933 [section 77a of Title 15, Commerce and Trade], et seq., an exemption also continued by section 1145 of this title. The extension of the disclosure requirements to all chapter 11 cases is justified by the integration of the separate chapters into the single chapter 11. By the same token, no valid purpose is served by failing to provide exemption from the requirements of similar state laws in a matter under the exclusive jurisdiction of the Federal bankruptcy laws.

Under subsection (d), with respect to a class of equity securities, it is sufficient for acceptance of the plan if the amount of securities voting for the plan is at least two-thirds of the total actually voted.

Subsection (e) provides that no acceptances are required from any class whose claims or interests are unimpaired under the plan or in the order confirming the plan.

Subsection (g) provides that any class denied participation under the plan is conclusively deemed to have rejected the plan. There is obviously no need to submit a plan for a vote by a class that is to receive nothing. But under subsection (g) the excluded class is like a class that has not accepted, and is a dissenting class for purposes of confirmation under section 1130. Senate Report No. 95–989.

1984 Acts. Statements by Legislative Leaders, see 1984 U.S.Code Cong. and Adm.News, p. 576.

Legislative Statements

Section 1126 of the House amendment deletes section 1126(e) as contained in the House bill. Section 105 of the bill constitutes sufficient power in the court to designate exclusion of a creditor's claim on the basis of a conflict of interest. Section 1126(f) of the House amendment adopts a provision contained in section 1127(f) of the Senate bill indicating that a class that is not impaired under a plan is deemed to have accepted a plan and solicitation of acceptances from such class is not required.

Effective and Applicability Provisions

1984 Acts. Amendment by Pub.L. 98–353 effective with respect to cases filed 90 days after July 10, 1984, see section 552(a), formerly 553(a), of Pub.L. 98–353, set out as a note under section 101 of this title.

CROSS REFERENCES

Amount and number of claims within class as including claims formerly held by certain creditors, see 11 USCA § 946.

Applicability of subsecs. (a) to (c) and (e) to (g) of this section in Chapter nine cases, see 11 USCA § 901.

§ 1127. Modification of plan

(a) The proponent of a plan may modify such plan at any time before confirmation, but may not modify such plan so that such plan as modified fails to meet the requirements of sections 1122 and 1123 of this title. After the proponent of a plan files a modification of such plan with the court, the plan as modified becomes the plan.

(b) The proponent of a plan or the reorganized debtor may modify such plan at any time after confirmation of such plan and before substantial consummation of such plan, but may not modify such plan so that such plan as modified fails to meet the requirements of sections 1122 and 1123 of this title. Such plan as modified under this subsection becomes the plan only if circumstances warrant such modification and the court, after notice and a hearing, confirms such plan as modified, under section 1129 of this title.

(c) The proponent of a modification shall comply with section 1125 of this title with respect to the plan as modified.

(d) Any holder of a claim or interest that has accepted or rejected a plan is deemed to have accepted or rejected, as the case may be, such plan as modified, unless, within the time fixed by the court, such holder changes such holder's previous acceptance or rejection.

(e) If the debtor is an individual, the plan may be modified at any time after confirmation of the plan but before the completion of payments under the plan, whether or not the plan has been substantially consummated, upon request of the debtor, the trustee, the United States trustee, or the holder of an allowed unsecured claim, to—

(1) increase or reduce the amount of payments on claims of a particular class provided for by the plan;

(2) extend or reduce the time period for such payments; or

(3) alter the amount of the distribution to a creditor whose claim is provided for by the plan to the extent necessary to take account of any payment of such claim made other than under the plan.

(f)(1) Sections 1121 through 1128 and the requirements of section 1129 apply to any modification under subsection (a).

(2) The plan, as modified, shall become the plan only after there has been disclosure under section 1125 as the court may direct, notice and a hearing, and such modification is approved.

(Pub.L. 95–598, Nov. 6, 1978, 92 Stat. 2635; Pub.L. 98–353, Title III, § 511, July 10, 1984, 98 Stat. 386; Pub.L. 109–8, Title III, § 321(e), Apr. 20, 2005, 119 Stat. 96.)

HISTORICAL AND STATUTORY NOTES

Revision Notes and Legislative Reports

1978 Acts. Under subsection (a) the proponent may file a proposal to modify a plan prior to confirmation. In the case of a public company the modifying proposal may be filed prior to approval.

Subsection (b) provides that a party in interest eligible to file a plan may file instead of a plan a proposal to modify a plan filed by another. Under subsection (c) a party in interest objecting to some feature of a plan may submit a proposal to modify the plan to meet the objection.

After a plan has been confirmed, but before its substantial consummation, a plan may be modified by leave of court, which subsection (d) provides shall be granted for good cause. Subsection (e) provides that a proposal to modify a plan is subject to the disclosure requirements of section 1125 and as provided in subsection (f). It provides that a creditor or stockholder who voted for or against a plan is deemed to have accepted or rejected the modifying proposal. But if the modification materially and adversely affects any of their interests, they must be afforded an opportunity to change their vote in accordance with the disclosure and solicitation requirements of section 1125.

Under subsection (g) a plan, if modified prior to confirmation, shall be confirmed if it meets the requirements of section 1130. Senate Report No. 95–989.

Subsection (a) permits the proponent of a plan to modify it at any time before confirmation, subject, of course, to the requirements of sections 1122 and 1123, governing classification and contents of a plan. After the proponent of a plan files a modification with the court, the plan as modified becomes the plan, and is to be treated the same as an original plan.

Subsection (b) permits modification of a plan after confirmation under certain circumstances. The modification must be proposed before substantial consummation of the plan. The requirements of sections 1122 and 1123 continue to apply. The plan as modified under this subsection becomes the plan only if the court confirms the plan as modified under section 1129 and the circumstances warrant the modification.

Subsection (c) requires the proponent of a modification to comply with the disclosure provisions of section 1125. Of course, if the modification were sufficiently minor, the court might determine that additional disclosure was not required under the circumstances.

Subsection (d) simplifies modification procedure by deeming any creditor or equity security holder that has already accepted or rejected the plan to have accepted or rejected the modification, unless, within the time fixed by the court, the creditor or equity security holder changes this previous acceptance or rejection. House Report No. 95–595.

1984 Acts. Statements by Legislative Leaders, see 1984 U.S. Code Cong. and Adm. News, p. 576.

2005 Acts. House Report No. 109–31(Part I), see 2005 U.S. Code Cong. and Adm. News, p. 88.

Legislative Statements

Section 1127(a) of the House amendment adopts a provision contained in the House bill permitting only the proponent of a plan to modify the plan and rejection the alternative of open modification contained in the Senate amendment.

Effective and Applicability Provisions

2005 Acts. Amendments by Pub.L. 109–8 effective, except as otherwise provided, 180 days after April 20, 2005, and inapplicable with respect to cases commenced under Title 11 before the effective date, see Pub.L. 109–8, § 1501, set out as a note under 11 U.S.C.A. § 101.

1984 Acts. Amendment by Pub.L. 98–353 effective with respect to cases filed 90 days after July 10, 1984, see section 552(a), formerly 553(a), of Pub.L. 98–353, set out as a note under section 101 of this title.

CROSS REFERENCES

Applicability of subsec. (d) of this section in Chapter nine cases, see 11 USCA § 901.

Modification of plan after confirmation in—

Chapter thirteen cases, see 11 USCA § 1329.

Chapter twelve cases, see 11 USCA § 1229.

Modification of plan before confirmation in—

Chapter thirteen cases, see 11 USCA § 1323.

Chapter twelve cases, see 11 USCA § 1223.

Modification of plan in Chapter nine cases, see 11 USCA § 942.

§ 1128. Confirmation hearing

(a) After notice, the court shall hold a hearing on confirmation of a plan.

(b) A party in interest may object to confirmation of a plan.

(Pub.L. 95–598, Nov. 6, 1978, 92 Stat. 2635.)

HISTORICAL AND STATUTORY NOTES

Revision Notes and Legislative Reports

1978 Acts. [Section 1129 (now section 1128)] Subsection (a) requires that there be a hearing in every case on the confirmation of the plan. Notice is required.

Subsection (b) permits any party in interest to object to the confirmation of the plan. The Securities and Exchange Commission and indenture trustees, as parties in interest under section 1109, may object to confirmation of the plan. Senate Report No. 95–989.

CROSS REFERENCES

Applicability of this section in Chapter nine cases, see 11 USCA § 901.

Confirmation hearing in—

Chapter thirteen cases, see 11 USCA § 1324.

Chapter twelve cases, see 11 USCA § 1224.

Duty of United States trustee to file comments with respect to plans and disclosure statements filed in connection with hearings under this section, see 28 USCA § 586.

Right to be heard in cases under this chapter, see 11 USCA § 1109.

§ 1129. Confirmation of plan

(a) The court shall confirm a plan only if all of the following requirements are met:

(1) The plan complies with the applicable provisions of this title.

(2) The proponent of the plan complies with the applicable provisions of this title.

(3) The plan has been proposed in good faith and not by any means forbidden by law.

(4) Any payment made or to be made by the proponent, by the debtor, or by a person issuing securities or acquiring property under the plan, for services or for costs and expenses in or in connection with the case, or in connection with the plan and incident to the case, has been approved by, or is subject to the approval of, the court as reasonable.

(5)(A)(i) The proponent of the plan has disclosed the identity and affiliations of any individual proposed to serve, after confirmation of the plan, as a director, officer, or voting trustee of the debtor, an affiliate of the debtor participating in a joint plan with the debtor, or a successor to the debtor under the plan; and

(ii) the appointment to, or continuance in, such office of such individual, is consistent with the interests of creditors and equity security holders and with public policy; and

(B) the proponent of the plan has disclosed the identity of any insider that will be employed or retained by the reorganized debtor, and the nature of any compensation for such insider.

(6) Any governmental regulatory commission with jurisdiction, after confirmation of the plan, over the rates of the debtor has approved any rate change provided for in the plan, or such rate change is expressly conditioned on such approval.

(7) With respect to each impaired class of claims or interests—

(A) each holder of a claim or interest of such class—

(i) has accepted the plan; or

(ii) will receive or retain under the plan on account of such claim or interest property of a value, as of the effective date of the plan, that is not less than the amount that such holder would so receive or retain if the debtor were liquidated under chapter 7 of this title on such date; or

(B) if section 1111(b)(2) of this title applies to the claims of such class, each holder of a claim of such class will receive or retain under the plan on account of such claim property of a value, as of the effective date of the plan, that is not less than the value of such holder's interest in the estate's interest in the property that secures such claims.

(8) With respect to each class of claims or interests—

(A) such class has accepted the plan; or

(B) such class is not impaired under the plan.

(9) Except to the extent that the holder of a particular claim has agreed to a different treatment of such claim, the plan provides that—

(A) with respect to a claim of a kind specified in section 507(a)(2) or 507(a)(3) of this title, on the effective date of the plan, the holder of such claim will receive on account of such claim cash equal to the allowed amount of such claim;

(B) with respect to a class of claims of a kind specified in section 507(a)(1), 507(a)(4), 507(a)(5), 507(a)(6), or 507(a)(7) of this title, each holder of a claim of such class will receive—

(i) if such class has accepted the plan, deferred cash payments of a value, as of the effective date of the plan, equal to the allowed amount of such claim; or

(ii) if such class has not accepted the plan, cash on the effective date of the plan equal to the allowed amount of such claim;

(C) with respect to a claim of a kind specified in section 507(a)(8) of this title, the holder of such claim will receive on account of such claim regular installment payments in cash—

(i) of a total value, as of the effective date of the plan, equal to the allowed amount of such claim;

(ii) over a period ending not later than 5 years after the date of the order for relief under section 301, 302, or 303; and

(iii) in a manner not less favorable than the most favored nonpriority unsecured claim provided for by the plan (other than cash payments made to a class of creditors under section 1122(b)); and

(D) with respect to a secured claim which would otherwise meet the description of an unsecured claim of a governmental unit under section 507(a)(8), but for the secured status of that claim, the holder of that claim will receive on account of that claim, cash payments, in the same manner and over the same period, as prescribed in subparagraph (C).

(10) If a class of claims is impaired under the plan, at least one class of claims that is impaired under the plan has accepted the plan, determined without including any acceptance of the plan by any insider.

(11) Confirmation of the plan is not likely to be followed by the liquidation, or the need for further financial reorganization, of the debtor or any successor to the debtor under the plan, unless such liquidation or reorganization is proposed in the plan.

(12) All fees payable under section 1930 of title 28, as determined by the court at the hearing on confirmation of the plan, have been paid or the plan provides for the payment of all such fees on the effective date of the plan.

(13) The plan provides for the continuation after its effective date of payment of all retiree benefits, as that term is defined in section 1114 of this title, at the level established pursuant to subsection (e)(1)(B) or (g) of section 1114 of this title, at any time prior to confirmation of the plan, for the duration of the period the debtor has obligated itself to provide such benefits.

(14) If the debtor is required by a judicial or administrative order, or by statute, to pay a domestic support obligation, the debtor has paid all amounts payable under such order or such statute for such obligation that first become payable after the date of the filing of the petition.

(15) In a case in which the debtor is an individual and in which the holder of an allowed unsecured claim objects to the confirmation of the plan—

(A) the value, as of the effective date of the plan, of the property to be distributed under the plan on account of such claim is not less than the amount of such claim; or

(B) the value of the property to be distributed under the plan is not less than the projected disposable income of the debtor (as defined in section 1325(b)(2)) to be received during the 5-year period beginning on the date that the first payment is due under the plan, or during the period for which the plan provides payments, whichever is longer.

(16) All transfers of property of the plan shall be made in accordance with any applicable provisions of nonbankruptcy law that govern the transfer of property by a corporation or trust that is not a moneyed, business, or commercial corporation or trust.

(b)(1) Notwithstanding section 510(a) of this title, if all of the applicable requirements of subsection (a) of this section other than paragraph (8) are met with respect to a plan, the court, on request of the proponent of the plan, shall confirm the plan notwithstanding the requirements of such paragraph if the plan does not discriminate unfairly, and is fair and equitable, with respect to each class of claims or interests that is impaired under, and has not accepted, the plan.

(2) For the purpose of this subsection, the condition that a plan be fair and equitable with respect to a class includes the following requirements:

(A) With respect to a class of secured claims, the plan provides—

(i)(I) that the holders of such claims retain the liens securing such claims, whether the property subject to such liens is retained by the debtor or transferred to another entity, to the extent of the allowed amount of such claims; and

(II) that each holder of a claim of such class receive on account of such claim deferred cash payments totaling at least the allowed amount of such claim, of a value, as of the effective date of the plan, of at least the value of such holder's interest in the estate's interest in such property;

(ii) for the sale, subject to section 363(k) of this title, of any property that is subject to the liens securing such claims, free and clear of such liens, with such liens to attach to the proceeds of such sale, and the treatment of such liens on proceeds under clause (i) or (iii) of this subparagraph; or

(iii) for the realization by such holders of the indubitable equivalent of such claims.

(B) With respect to a class of unsecured claims—

(i) the plan provides that each holder of a claim of such class receive or retain on account of such claim property of a value, as of the effective date of the plan, equal to the allowed amount of such claim; or

(ii) the holder of any claim or interest that is junior to the claims of such class will not receive or retain under the plan on account of such junior claim or interest any property, except that in a case in which the debtor is an individual, the debtor may retain property included in the estate under section 1115, subject to the requirements of subsection (a)(14) of this section.

(C) With respect to a class of interests—

(i) the plan provides that each holder of an interest of such class receive or retain on account of such interest property of a value, as of the effective date of the plan, equal to the greatest of the allowed amount of any fixed liquidation preference to which such holder is entitled, any fixed redemption price to which such holder is entitled, or the value of such interest; or

(ii) the holder of any interest that is junior to the interests of such class will not receive or retain under the plan on account of such junior interest any property.

(c) Notwithstanding subsections (a) and (b) of this section and except as provided in section 1127(b) of this title, the court may confirm only one plan, unless the order of confirmation in the case has been revoked under section 1144 of this title. If the requirements of subsections (a) and (b) of this section are met with respect to more than one plan, the court shall consider the preferences of creditors and equity security holders in determining which plan to confirm.

(d) Notwithstanding any other provision of this section, on request of a party in interest that is a governmental unit, the court may not confirm a plan if the principal purpose of the plan is the avoidance of taxes or the avoidance of the application of section 5 of the Securities Act of 1933. In any hearing under this subsection, the governmental unit has the burden of proof on the issue of avoidance.

(e) In a small business case, the court shall confirm a plan that complies with the applicable provisions of this title and that is filed in accordance with section 1121(e) not later than 45 days after the plan is filed unless the time for confirmation is extended in accordance with section 1121(e)(3).

(Pub.L. 95–598, Nov. 6, 1978, 92 Stat. 2635; Pub.L. 98–353, Title III, § 512, July 10, 1984, 98 Stat. 386; Pub.L. 99–554, Title II, §§ 225, 283(v), Oct. 27, 1986, 100 Stat. 3102, 3118; Pub.L. 100–334, § 2(b), June 16, 1988, 102 Stat. 613; Pub.L. 103–394, Title III, § 304(h)(7), Title V, § 501(d)(32), Oct. 22, 1994, 108 Stat. 4134, 4146; Pub.L. 109–8, Title II, § 213(1), Title III, § 321(c), Title IV, § 438, Title VII, § 710, Title XII, § 1221(b), Title XV, § 1502(a)(8), Apr. 20, 2005, 119 Stat. 52, 95, 113, 127, 196, 216.)

HISTORICAL AND STATUTORY NOTES

Revision Notes and Legislative Reports

1978 Acts. [Section 1130 (now section 1129)] Subsection (a) enumerates the requirement governing confirmation of a plan. The court is required to confirm a plan if and only if all of the requirements are met.

Paragraph (1) requires that the plan comply with the applicable provisions of chapter 11, such as sections 1122 and 1123, governing classification and contents of plan.

Paragraph (2) requires that the proponent of the plan comply with the applicable provisions of chapter 11, such as section 1125 regarding disclosure.

Paragraph (3) requires that the plan have been proposed in good faith, and not by any means forbidden by law.

Paragraph (4) is derived from section 221 of chapter X [section 621 of former Title 11]. It requires that any payment made or promised by the proponent, the debtor, or person issuing securities or acquiring property under the plan, for services or for costs and expenses in, or in connection with the case, or in connection with the plan and incident to the case, be disclosed to the court. In addition, any payment made before confirmation must have been reasonable, and any payment to be fixed after confirmation must be subject to the approval of the court as reasonable.

Paragraph (5) is also derived from section 221 of chapter X [section 621 of former Title 11]. It requires the plan to disclose the identity and affiliations of any individual proposed to serve, after confirmation, as a director, officer, or voting trustee of the reorganized debtor. The appointment to or continuance in one of these offices by the individual must be consistent with the interests of creditors and equity security holders and with public policy. The plan must also disclose the identity of any insider that will be employed or retained by the reorganized debtor, and the nature of any compensation to be paid to the insider.

Paragraph (6) permits confirmation only if any regulatory commission that will have jurisdiction over the debtor after confirmation of the plan has approved any rate change provided for in the plan. As an alternative, the rate change may be conditioned on such approval.

Paragraph (7) provides that in the case of a public company the court shall confirm the plan if it finds the plan to be fair and equitable and the plan either (1) has been accepted by classes of claims or interests as provided in section 1126, or (2), if not so accepted, satisfies the requirements of subsection (b) of this section.

Paragraphs (8) and (9) apply only in nonpublic cases. Paragraph (8) does not apply the fair and equitable standards in two situations. The first occurs if there is unanimous consent of all affected holders of claims and interests. It is also sufficient for purposes of confirmation if each holder of a claim or interest receives or retains consideration of a value, as of the effective date of the plan, that is not less than each would have or receive if the debtor were liquidated under chapter 7 of this title. This standard adapts the test of "best interest of creditors" as interpreted by the courts under chapter XI [former chapter 11 (section 701 et seq.) of former Title 11]. It is given broader application in chapter 11 of this title since a plan under chapter 11 may affect not only unsecured claims but secured claims and stock as well.

Under paragraph (9)(A), if a class of claims or interests has not accepted the plan, the court will confirm the plan if, for the dissenting class and any class of equal rank, the negotiated plan provides in value no less than under a plan that is fair and equitable. Such review and determination are not required for any other classes that accepted the plan.

Paragraph 9(A) would permit a senior creditor to adjust his participation for the benefit of stockholders. In such a case, junior creditors, who have not been satisfied in full, may not object if, absent the "give-up", they are receiving all that a fair and equitable plan would give them. To illustrate, suppose the estate is valued at $1.5 million and claims and stock are:

	Claims and stock (millions)	**Equity (millions)**
(1) Senior debt	$1.2	$1.2
(2) Junior debt	.5	.3
(3) Stock	(1)	—
Total	1.7	1.5

Under the plan, the senior creditor gives up $100,000 in value for the benefit of stockholders as follows:

	Millions
(1) Senior debt	$1.1
(2) Junior debt	.3
(3) Stock	.1
Total	1.5

1 No value.

If the junior creditors dissent, the court may nevertheless confirm the plan since under the fair and equitable standard they had an equity of only $300,000 and the allocation to equity security holders did not affect them.

Paragraph 9(A)[(9)(A)] provides a special alternative with respect to secured claims. A plan may be confirmed against a dissenting class of secured claims if the plan or order of confirmation provides for the realization of their security (1) by the retention of the property subject to such security; (2) by a sale of the property and transfer of the claim to the proceeds of sale if the secured creditors were permitted to bid at the sale and set off against the purchase price up to the allowed amount of their claims; or (3) by such other method that will assure them the realization of the indubitable equivalent of the allowed amount of their secured claims. The indubitable equivalent language is intended to follow the strict approach taken by Judge Learned Hand in *In Re Murel Holding Corp.*, 7 5 [75] F.2d 941 (2nd Cir. 1935).

Paragraph (9)(B) provides that, if a class of claims or interests is excluded from participation under the plan, the court may nevertheless confirm the plan if it determines that no class on a parity with or junior to such participates under the plan. In the previous illustration, no confirmation would be permitted if the negotiated plan would grant a participation to stockholders but nothing for junior creditors. As noted elsewhere, by reason of section 1126(g), an excluded class is a dissenting class under section 1130.

Paragraph (10) states that, to be confirmed, the plan must provide that each holder of a claim under section 507 will receive property, as therein noted, of a value equal to the allowed amount of the claim. There are two exceptions: (A) The holder thereof may agree to a different settlement in part or in whole; (B) where a debtor's business is reorganized under chapter 11, this provision requires that taxes entitled to priority (including administrative claims or taxes) must be paid in cash not later than 120 days after the plan is confirmed, unless the Secretary of the Treasury agrees to other terms or kinds of payment. The bill, as introduced, required full payment in cash within 60 days after the plan is confirmed.

Paragraph (11) requires a determination regarding feasibility of the plan. It is a slight elaboration of the law that has developed in the application of the word "feasible" in Chapter X of the present Act [former chapter 10 (section 501 et seq.) of former Title 11].

Paragraph (12) requires that at least one class must accept the plan, but any claims or interests held by insiders are not to be included for purposes of determining the number and amount of acceptances.

Subsection (b) provides that if, in the case of a public company, the plan meets the requirements of subsection (a) (except paragraphs (8) and (9) which do not apply to such a company), the court is to confirm the plan if the plan or the order of confirmation provides adequate protection for the realization of the value of the claims or interests of each class not accepting the plan. The intent is to incorporate inclusively, as a guide to the meaning of subsection (a) the provisions of section 216(7) (11 U.S.C. 616(7)) [section 616(7) of former Title 11] with respect to claims and section 216(8) (11 U.S.C. 616(8)) [section 616(8) of former Title 11] with respect to equity security interests.

Under subsection (c) the court may confirm only one plan, unless the order of confirmation has been revoked under section 1144. If the requirements for confirmation are met with respect to more than one plan, the court shall consider the preferences of creditors and stockholders in deciding which plan to confirm.

Subsection (d) provides that the bankruptcy court may not confirm a plan of reorganization if its principal purpose is the avoidance of taxes or the avoidance of section 5 of the Securities Act of 1933 (15 U.S.C. 77e) [section 77e of Title 15, Commerce and Trade]. This rule modifies a similar provision of present law (section 269 of the Bankruptcy Act) [section 669 of former title 11]. Senate Report No. 95–989.

Paragraph (7) [of subsec. (a)] incorporates the former "best interest of creditors" test found in chapter 11, but spells out precisely what is intended. With respect to each class, the holders of the claims or interests of that class must receive or retain under the plan on account of those claims or interest property of a value, as of the effective date of the plan, that is not less than the amount that they would so receive or retain if the debtor were liquidated under chapter 7 on the effective date of the plan.

In order to determine the hypothetical distribution in a liquidation, the court will have to consider the various subordination provisions of proposed 11 U.S.C. 510, 726(a)(3), 726(a)(4), and the postponement provisions of proposed 11 U.S.C. 724. Also applicable in appropriate cases will be the rules governing partnership distributions under proposed 11 U.S.C. 723, and distributions of community property under proposed 11 U.S.C. 726(c). Under subparagraph (A), a particular holder is permitted to accept less than liquidation value, but his acceptance does not bind the class.

Property under subparagraph (B) may include securities of the debtor. Thus, the provision will apply in cases in which the plan in confirmed under proposed 11 U.S.C. 1129(b).

Paragraph (8) is central to the confirmation standards. It requires that each class either have accepted the plan or be unimpaired.

Paragraph (9) augments the requirements of paragraph (8) by requiring payment of each priority claim in full. It permits payments over time and payment other than in cash, but payment in securities is not intended to be permitted without consent of the priority claimant even if the class has consented. It also permits a particular claimant to accept less than full payment.

Subsection (b) permits the court to confirm a plan notwithstanding failure of compliance with paragraph (8) of subsection (a). The plan must comply with all other paragraphs of subsection (a), including paragraph (9). This subsection contains the so-called cramdown. It requires simply that the plan meet certain standards of fairness to dissenting creditors or equity security holders. The general principle of the subsection permits confirmation notwithstanding nonacceptance by an impaired class if that class and all below it in priority are treated according to the absolute priority rule. The dissenting class must be paid in full before any junior class may share under the plan. If it is paid in full, then junior classes may share. Treatment of classes of secured creditors is slightly different because they do not fall in the priority ladder, but the principle is the same.

Specifically, the court may confirm a plan over the objection of a class of secured claims if the members of that class are unimpaired or if they are to receive under the plan property of a value equal to the allowed amount of their secured claims, as determined under proposed 11 U.S.C. 506(a). The property is to be valued as of the effective date of the plan, thus recognizing the time-value of money. As used throughout this subsection, "property" includes both tangible and intangible property, such as a security of the debtor or a successor to the debtor under a reorganization plan.

The court may confirm over the dissent of a class of unsecured claims, including priority claims, only if the members of the class are unimpaired, if they will receive under the plan property of a value equal to the allowed amount of their unsecured claims, or if no class junior will share under the plan. That is, if the class is impaired, then they must be paid in full or, if paid less than in full, then no class junior may receive anything under the plan. This codifies the absolute priority rule from the dissenting class on down.

With respect to classes of equity, the court may confirm over a dissent if the members of the class are unimpaired, if they receive their liquidation preference or redemption rights, if any, or if no class junior shares under the plan. This, too, is a codification of the absolute priority rule with respect to equity. If a partnership agreement subordinates limited partners to general partners to any degree, then the general principles of paragraph (3) of this subsection would apply to prevent the general partners from being squeezed out.

One requirement applies generally to all classes before the court may confirm under this subsection. No class may be paid more than in full.

The partial codification of the absolute priority rule here is not intended to deprive senior creditor [sic] of compensation for being required to take securities in the reorganized debtor that are of an equal priority with the securities offered to a junior class. Under current law, seniors are entitled to compensation for their loss of priority, and the increased risk put upon them by being required to give up their priority will be reflected in a lower value of the securities given to them than the value of comparable securities given to juniors that have not lost a priority position.

Finally, the proponent must request use of this subsection. The court may not confirm notwithstanding nonacceptance unless the proponent requests and the court may then confirm only if subsection (b) is complied with. The court may not rewrite the plan.

A more detailed explanation follows:

The test to be applied by the court is set forth in the various paragraphs of section 1129(b). The elements of the test are new [,] departing from both the absolute priority rule and the best interests of creditors tests found under the Bankruptcy Act [former Title 11]. The court is not permitted to alter the terms of the plan. It must merely decide whether the plan complies with the requirements of section 1129(b). If so, the plan is confirmed, if not the plan is denied confirmation.

The procedure followed is simple. The court examines each class of claims or interests designated under section 1123(a)(1) to see if the requirements of section 1129(b) are met. If the class is a class of secured claims, then paragraph (1) contains two tests that must be complied with in order for confirmation to occur. First, under subparagraph (A), the court must be able to find that the consideration given under the plan on account of the secured claim does not exceed the allowed amount of the claim. This condition is not prescribed as a matter of law under section 1129(a), because if the secured claim is compensated in securities of the debtor, a valuation of the business would be necessary to determine the value of the consideration. While section 1129(a) does not contemplate a valuation of the debtor's business, such a valuation will almost always be required under section 1129(b) in order to determine the value of the consideration to be distributed under the plan. Once the valuation is performed, it becomes a simple matter to impose the criterion that no claim will be paid more than in full.

Application of the test under subparagraph (A) also requires a valuation of the consideration "as of the effective date of the plan". This contemplates a present value analysis that will discount value to be received in the future; of course, if the interest rate paid is equivalent to the discount rate used, the present value and face future value will be identical. On the other hand, if no interest is proposed to be paid, the present value will be less than the face future value. For example, consider an allowed secured claim of $1,000 in a class by itself. One plan could propose to pay $1,000 on account of this claim as of the effective date of the plan. Another plan could propose to give a note with a $1,000 face amount due five years after the effective date of the plan on account of this claim. A third plan could propose to give a note in a face amount of $1,000 due five years from the effective date of the plan plus six percent annual interest commencing on the effective date of the plan on account of this claim. The first plan clearly meets the requirements of subparagraph (A) because the amount received on account of the second claim has an equivalent present value as of the effective date of the plan equal to the allowed amount of such claim.

The second plan also meets the requirements of subparagraph (A) because the present value of the five years note as of the effective date of the plan will never exceed the allowed amount of the secured claim; the higher the discount rate, the less present value the note will have. Whether the third plan complies with subparagraph (A) depends on whether the discount rate is less than six percent. Normally, the interest rate used in the plan will be prima facie evidence of the discount rate because the interest rate will reflect an arms length determination of the risk of the security involved and feasibility considerations will tend to understate interest payments. If the court found the discount rate to be greater than or equal to the interest rate used in the plan, then subparagraph (A) would be complied with because the value of the note as of the effective date of the plan would not exceed the allowed amount of the second claim. If, however, the court found the discount rate to be less than the interest rate proposed under the plan, then the present value of the note would exceed $1,000 and the plan would fail of confirmation. On the other hand, it is important to recognize that the future principal amount of a note in excess of the allowed amount of a secured claim may have a present value less than such allowed amount, if the interest rate under the plan is correspondingly less than the discount rate.

Even if the requirements of subparagraph (A) are complied with, the class of secured claims must satisfy one of the three clauses in paragraph (B) in order to pass muster. It is sufficient for confirmation if the class has accepted the plan, or if the claims of the class are unimpaired, or if each holder of a secured claim in the class will receive property of a value as of the effective date of the plan equal to the allowed amount of such claim (unless he has agreed to accept less). It is important to note that under section 506(a), the allowed amount of the secured claim will not include any extent to which the amount of such claim exceeds the value of the property securing such claim. Thus, instead of focusing on secured creditors or unsecured creditors, the statute focuses on secured claims and unsecured claims.

After the court has applied paragraph (1) to each class of secured claims, it then applies paragraph (2) to each class of unsecured claims. Again two separate components must be tested. Subparagraph (A) is identical with the test under section 1129(b)(1)(A) insofar as the holder of an unsecured claim is not permitted to receive property of a value as of the effective date of the plan on account of such claim that is greater than the allowed amount of such claim. In addition, subparagraph (B) requires compliance with one of four conditions. The conditions in clauses (i)–(iii) mirror the conditions of acceptance unimpairment, or full value found in connection with secured claims in section 1129(b)(1)(B).

The condition contained in section 1129(b)(2)(B)(iv) provides another basis for confirming the plan with respect to a class of unsecured claims. It will be of greatest use when an impaired class that has not accepted the plan is to receive less than full value under the plan. The plan may be confirmed under clause (iv) in those circumstances if the class is not unfairly discriminated against with respect to equal classes and if junior classes will receive nothing under the plan. The second criterion is the easier to understand. It is designed to prevent a senior class from giving up consideration to a junior class unless every intermediate class consents, is paid in full, or is unimpaired. This gives intermediate creditors a great deal of leverage in negotiating with senior or secured creditors who wish to have a plan that gives value to equity. One aspect of this test that is not obvious is that whether one class is senior, equal, or junior to another class is relative and not absolute. Thus from the perspective of trade creditors holding unsecured claims,

claims of senior and subordinated debentures may be entitled to share on an equal basis with the trade claims. However, from the perspective of the senior unsecured debt, the subordinated debentures are junior.

This point illustrates the lack of precision in the first criterion which demands that a class not be unfairly discriminated against with respect to equal classes. From the perspective of unsecured trade claims, there is no unfair discrimination as long as the total consideration given all other classes of equal rank does not exceed the amount that would result from an exact aliquot distribution. Thus if trade creditors, senior debt, and subordinate debt are each owed $100 and the plan proposes to pay the trade debt $15, the senior debt $30, and the junior debt $0, the plan would not unfairly discriminate against the trade debt nor would any other allocation of consideration under the plan between the senior and junior debt be unfair as to the trade debt as long as the aggregate consideration is less than $30. The senior debt could take $25 and give up $5 to the junior debt and the trade debt would have no cause to complain because as far as it is concerned the junior debt is an equal class.

However, in this latter case the senior debt would have been unfairly discriminated against because the trade debt was being unfairly over-compensated; of course the plan would also fail unless the senior debt was unimpaired, received full value, or accepted the plan, because from its perspective a junior class received property under the plan. Application of the test from the perspective of senior debt is best illustrated by the plan that proposes to pay trade debt $15, senior debt $25, and junior debt $0. Here the senior debt is being unfairly discriminated against with respect to the equal trade debt even though the trade debt receives less than the senior debt. The discrimination arises from the fact that the senior debt is entitled to the rights of the junior debt which in this example entitle the senior debt to share on a 2:1 basis with the trade debt.

Finally, it is necessary to interpret the first criterion from the perspective of subordinated debt. The junior debt is subrogated to the rights of senior debt once the senior debt is paid in full. Thus, while the plan that pays trade debt $15, senior debt $25, and junior debt $0 is not unfairly discriminatory against the junior debt, a plan that proposes to pay trade debt $55, senior debt $100, and junior debt $1, would be unfairly discriminatory. In order to avoid discriminatory treatment against the junior debt, at least $10 would have to be received by such debt under those facts.

The criterion of unfair discrimination is not derived from the fair and equitable rule or from the best interests of creditors test. Rather it preserves just treatment of a dissenting class from the class's own perspective.

If each class of secured claims satisfies the requirements of section 1129(b)(1) and each class of unsecured claims satisfies the requirements of section 1129(b)(2), then the court must still see if each class of interests satisfies section 1129(b)(3) before the plan may be confirmed. Again, two separate criteria must be met. Under subparagraph (A) if the interest entitles the holder thereof to a fixed liquidation preference or if such interest may be redeemed at a fixed price, then the holder of such interest must not receive under the plan on account of such interest property of a value as of the effective date of the plan greater than the greater of these two values of the interest. Preferred stock would be an example of an interest likely to have liquidation preference or redemption price.

If an interest such as most common stock or the interest of a general partnership has neither a fixed liquidation preference nor a fixed redemption price, then the criterion in subparagraph (A) is automatically fulfilled. In addition subparagraph (B) contains five clauses that impose alternative conditions of which at least one must be satisfied in order to warrant confirmation. The first two clauses contain requirements of acceptance or unimpairment similar to the first two clauses in paragraphs (1)(B) and (2)(B). Clause (iii) is similar to the unimpairment test contained in section 1124(3)(B), except that it will apply to cover the issuance securities of the debtor of a value as of the effective date of the plan equal to the greater of any fixed liquidation preference or redemption price. The fourth clause allows confirmation if junior interests are not compensated under the plan and the fifth clause allows confirmation if there are no junior interests. These clauses recognized that as long as senior classes receive no more than full payment, the objection of a junior class will not defeat confirmation unless a class junior to it is receiving value under the plan and the objecting class is impaired. While a determination of impairment may be made under section 1124(3)(B)(iii) without a precise valuation of the business when common stock is clearly under water, once section 1129(b) is used, a more detailed valuation is a necessary byproduct. Thus, if no property is given to a holder of an interest under the plan, the interest should be clearly worthless in order to find unimpairment under section 1124(3)(B)(iii) and section 1129(a)(8); otherwise, since a class of interests receiving no property is deemed to object under section 1126(g), the more precise valuation of section 1129(b) should be used.

If all of the requirements of section 1129(b) are complied with, then the court may confirm the plan subject to other limitations such as those found in section 1129(a) and (d).

Subsection (c) of section 1129 governs confirmation when more than one plan meets the requirements of the section. The court must consider the preferences of creditors and equity security holders in determining which plan to confirm.

Subsection (d) requires the court to deny confirmation if the principal purpose of the plan is the avoidance of taxes (through use of sections 346 and 1146, and applicable provisions of State law or the Internal Revenue Code [Title 26] governing bankruptcy reorganizations) or the avoidance of section 5 of the Securities Act of 1933 [section 77e of Title 15, Commerce and Trade] (through use of section 1145). House Report No. 95–595.

1984 Acts. Statements by Legislative Leaders, see 1984 U.S.Code Cong. and Adm.News, p. 576.

1986 Acts. House Report No. 99–764 and House Conference Report No. 99–958, see 1986 U.S.Code Cong. and Adm.News, p. 5227.

1988 Acts. Senate Report No. 100–119, see 1988 U.S.Code Cong. and Adm.News, p. 683.

1994 Acts. House Report No. 103–835, see 1994 U.S. Code Cong. and Adm. News, p. 3340.

2005 Acts. House Report No. 109–31(Part I), see 2005 U.S. Code Cong. and Adm. News, p. 88.

Legislative Statements

Section 1129 of the House amendment relates to confirmation of a plan in a case under chapter 11. Section 1129(a)(3) of the House amendment adopts the position taken in the Senate amendment and section 1129(a)(5) takes the position adopted in the House bill. Section 1129(a)(7) adopts the position taken in the House bill in order to insure that the dissenting members of an accepting class will receive at least what they would otherwise receive under the best interest of creditors test; it also requires that even the members of a class that has rejected the plan be protected by the best interest of creditors test for those rare cramdown cases where a class of creditors would receive more on liquidation than under reorganization of the debtor. Section 1129(a)(7)(C) is discussed in connection with section 1129(b) and section 1111(b). Section 1129(a)(8) of the House amendment adopts the provision taken in the House bill which permits confirmation of a plan as to a particular class without resort to the fair and equitable test if the class has accepted a plan or is unimpaired under the plan.

Section 1129(a)(9) represents a compromise between a similar provision contained in the House bill and the Senate amendment. Under subparagraph (A) claims entitled to priority under section 507(a)(1) or (2) are entitled to receive cash on the effective date of the plan equal to the amount of the claim. Under subparagraph (B) claims entitled to priority under section 507(a)(3), (4), or (5), are entitled to receive deferred cash payments of a present value as of the effective date of the plan equal to the amount of the claims if the class has accepted the plan or cash payments on the effective date of the plan otherwise. Tax claims entitled to priority under section 507(a)(6) of different governmental units may not be contained in one class although all claims of one such unit may be combined and such unit may be required to take deferred cash payments over a period not to exceed 6 years after the date of assessment of the tax with the present value equal to the amount of the claim.

Section 1129(a)(10) is derived from section 1130(a)(12) of the Senate amendment.

Section 1129(b) is new. Together with section 1111(b) and section 1129(a)(7)(C), this section provides when a plan may be confirmed, notwithstanding the failure of an impaired class to accept the plan under section 1129(a)(8). Before discussing section 1129(b) an understanding of section 1111(b) is necessary. Section 1111(b)(1), the general rule that a secured claim is to be treated as a recourse claim in chapter 11 whether or not the claim is nonrecourse by agreement or applicable law. This preferred status for a nonrecourse loan terminates if the property securing the loan is sold under section 363 or is to be sold under the plan.

The preferred status also terminates if the class of which the secured claim is a part elects application of section 1111(b)(2). Section 1111(b)(2) provides that an allowed claim is a secured claim to the full extent the claim is allowed rather than to the extent of the collateral as under section 506(a). A class may elect application of paragraph (2) only if the security is not of inconsequential value and, if the creditor is a recourse creditor, the collateral is not sold under section 363 or to be sold under the plan. Sale of property under section 363 or under the plan is excluded from treatment under section 1111(b) because of the secured party's right to bid in the full amount of his allowed claim at any sale of collateral under section 363(k) of the House amendment.

As previously noted, section 1129(b) sets forth a standard by which a plan may be confirmed notwithstanding the failure of an impaired class to accept the plan.

Paragraph (1) makes clear that this alternative confirmation standard, referred to as "cram down," will be called into play only on the request of the proponent of the plan. Under this cramdown test, the court must confirm the plan if the plan does not discriminate unfairly, and is "fair and equitable," with respect to each class of claims or interests that is impaired under, and has not accepted, the plan. The requirement of the House bill that a plan not "discriminate unfairly" with respect to a class is included for clarity; the language in the House report interpreting that requirement, in the context of subordinated debentures, applies equally under the requirements of section 1129(b)(1) of the House amendment.

Although many of the factors interpreting "fair and equitable" are specified in paragraph (2), others, which were explicated in the description of section 1129(b) in the House report, were omitted from the House amendment to avoid statutory complexity and because they would undoubtedly be found by a court to be fundamental to "fair and equitable" treatment of a dissenting class. For example, a dissenting class should be assured that no senior class receives more than 100 percent of the amount of its claims. While that requirement was explicitly included in the House bill, the deletion is intended to be one of style and not one of substance.

Paragraph (2) provides guidelines for a court to determine whether a plan is fair and equitable with respect to a dissenting class. It must be emphasized that the fair and equitable requirement applies only with respect to dissenting classes. Therefore, unlike the fair and equitable rule contained in chapter X [former chapter 10 (section 501 et seq.) of former Title 11] and section 77 of the Bankruptcy Act [section 205 of former Title 11] under section 1129(b)(2), senior accepting classes are permitted to give up value to junior classes as long as no dissenting intervening class receives less than the amount of its claims in full. If there is no dissenting intervening class and the only dissent is from a class junior to the class to which value have [sic] been given up, then the plan may still be fair and equitable with respect to the dissenting class, as long as no class senior to the dissenting class has received more than 100 percent of the amount of its claims.

Paragraph (2) contains three subparagraphs, each of which applies to a particular kind of class of claims or interests that is impaired and has not accepted the plan. Subparagraph (A) applies when a class of secured claims is impaired and has not accepted the plan. The provision applies whether or not section 1111(b) applies. The plan may be crammed down notwithstanding the dissent of a secured class only if the plan complies with clause (i), (ii), or (iii).

Clause (i) permits cramdown if the dissenting class of secured claims will retain its lien on the property whether the property is retained by the debtor or transferred. It should be noted that the lien secures the allowed secured claim held by such holder. The meaning of "allowed secured claim" will vary depending on whether section 1111(b)(2) applies to such class.

If section 1111(b)(2) applies then the "electing" class is entitled to have the entire allowed amount of the debt related to such property secured by a lien even if the value of the collateral is less than the amount of the debt. In addition, the plan must provide for the holder to receive, on account of the allowed secured claims, payments, either present or deferred, of a principal face amount equal to the amount of the debt and of a present value equal to the value of the collateral.

For example, if a creditor loaned $15,000,000 to a debtor secured by real property worth $18,000,000 and the value of the real property had dropped to $12,000,000 by the date when the debtor commenced a proceeding under chapter 11, the plan could be confirmed notwithstanding the dissent of the creditor as long as the lien remains on the collateral to secure a $15,000,000 debt, the face amount of present or extended payments to be made to the creditor under the plan is at least $15,000,000, and the present value of the present or deferred payments is not less than $12,000,000. The House report accompanying the House bill described what is meant by "present value".

Clause (ii) is self explanatory. Clause (iii) requires the court to confirm the plan notwithstanding the dissent of the electing secured class if the plan provides for the realization by the secured class of the indubitable equivalents of the secured claims. The standard of "indubitable equivalents" is taken from *In re Murel Holding Corp.*, 75 F.2d 941 (2d Cir. 1935) (Learned Hand, Jr.).

Abandonment of the collateral to the creditor would clearly satisfy indubitable equivalence, as would a lien on similar collateral. However, present cash payments less than the secured claim would not satisfy the standard because the creditor is deprived of an opportunity to gain from a future increase in value of the collateral. Unsecured notes as to the secured claim or equity securities of the debtor would not be the indubitable equivalent. With respect to an oversecured creditor, the secured claim will never exceed the allowed claim.

Although the same language applies, a different result pertains with respect to a class of secured claims to which section 1111(b)(2) does not apply. This will apply to all claims secured by a right of setoff. The court must confirm the plan notwithstanding the dissent of such a class of secured claims if any of three alternative requirements is met. Under clause (i) the plan may be confirmed if the class retains a right of setoff or a lien securing the allowed secured claims of the class and the holders will receive payments of a present value equal to the allowed amount of their secured claims. Contrary to electing classes of secured creditors who retain a lien under subparagraph (A)(i)(I) to the extent of the entire claims secured by such lien, nonelecting creditors retain a lien on collateral only to the extent of their allowed secured claims and not to the extent of any deficiency, and such secured creditors must receive present or deferred payments with a present value equal to the allowed secured claim, which in turn is only the equivalent of the value of the collateral under section 506(a).

Any deficiency claim of a nonelecting class of secured claims is treated as an unsecured claim and is not provided for under subparagraph (A). The plan may be confirmed under clause (ii) if the plan proposes to sell the property free and clear of the secured party's lien as long as the lien will attach to the proceeds and will receive treatment under clause (i) or (iii). Clause (iii) permits confirmation if the plan provides for the realization by the dissenting nonelecting class of secured claims of the indubitable equivalent of the secured claims of such class.

Contrary to an "electing" class to which section 1111(b)(2) applies, the nonelecting class need not be protected with respect to any future appreciation in value of the collateral since the secured claim of such a class is never undersecured by reason of section 506(a). Thus the lien secures only the value of interest of such creditor in the collateral. To the extent deferred payments exceed that amount, they represent interest. In the event of a subsequent default, the portion of the face amount of deferred payments representing unaccrued interest will not be secured by the lien.

Subparagraph (B) applies to a dissenting class of unsecured claims. The court must confirm the plan notwithstanding the dissent of a class of impaired unsecured claims if the plan provides for such claims to receive property with a present value equal to the allowed amount of the claims. Unsecured claims may receive any kind of "property," which is used in its broadest sense, as long as the present value of the property given to the holders of unsecured claims is equal to the allowed amount of the claims. Some kinds of property, such as securities, may require difficult valuations by the court; in such circumstances the court need only determine that there is a reasonable likelihood that the property given the dissenting class of impaired unsecured claims equals the present value of such allowed claims.

Alternatively, under clause (ii), the court must confirm the plan if the plan provides that holders of any claims or interests junior to the interests of the dissenting class of impaired unsecured claims will not receive any property under the plan on account of such junior claims or interests. As long as senior creditors have not been paid more than in full, and classes of equal claims are being treated so that the dissenting class of impaired unsecured claims is not being discriminated against unfairly, the plan may be confirmed if the impaired class of unsecured claims receives less than 100 cents on the dollar (or nothing at all) as long as no class junior to the dissenting class receives anything at all. Such an impaired dissenting class may not prevent confirmation of a plan by objection merely because a senior class has elected to give up value to a junior class that is higher in priority than the impaired dissenting class of unsecured claims as long as the above safeguards are met.

Subparagraph (C) applies to a dissenting class of impaired interests. Such interests may include the interests of general or limited partners in a partnership, the interests of a sole proprietor in a proprietorship, or the interest of common or preferred stockholders in a corporation. If the holders of such interests are entitled to a fixed liquidation preference or fixed redemption price on account of such interests then the plan may be confirmed notwithstanding the dissent of such class of interests as long as it provides the holders property of a present value equal to the greatest of the fixed redemption price, or the value of such interests. In the event there is no fixed liquidation preference or redemption price, then the plan may be confirmed as long as it provides the holders of such interests property of a present value equal to the value of such interests. If the interests are "under water" then they will be valueless and the plan may be confirmed notwithstanding the dissent of that class of interests even if the plan provides that the holders of such interests will not receive any property on account of such interests.

Alternatively, under clause (ii), the court must confirm the plan notwithstanding the dissent of a class of interests if the plan provides that holders of any interests junior to the dissenting class of interests will not receive or retain any property on account of such junior interests. Clearly, if there are no junior interests junior to the class of dissenting interests, then the condition of clause (ii) is satisfied. The safeguards that no claim or interest receive more than 100 percent of the allowed amount of such claim or interest and that no class be discriminated against unfairly will insure that the plan is fair and equitable with respect to the dissenting class of interests.

Except to the extent of the treatment of secured claims under subparagraph (A) of this statement, the House report remains an accurate description of confirmation of section 1129(b). Contrary to the example contained in the Senate report, a senior class will not be able to give up value to a junior class over the dissent of an intervening class unless the intervening class receives the full amount, as opposed to value, of its claims or interests.

One last point deserves explanation with respect to the admittedly complex subject of confirmation. Section 1129(a)(7)(C) in effect exempts secured creditors making an election under section 1111(b)(2) from application of the best interest of creditors test. In the absence of an election the amount such creditors receive in a plan of liquidation would be the value of their collateral plus any amount recovered on the deficiency in the case of a recourse loan. However, under section 1111(b)(2), the creditors are given an allowed secured claim to the full extent the claim is allowed and have no unsecured deficiency. Since section 1129(b)(2)(A) makes clear that an electing class need receive payments of a present value only equal to the value of the collateral, it is conceivable that under such a "cram down" the electing creditors would receive nothing with respect to their deficiency. The advantage to the electing creditors is that they have a lien securing the full amount of the allowed claim so that if the value of the collateral increases after the case is closed, the deferred payments will be secured claims. Thus it is both reasonable and necessary to exempt such electing class from application of section 1129(a)(7) as a logical consequence of permitting election under section 1111(b)(2).

Section 1131 of the Senate amendment is deleted as unnecessary in light of the protection given a secured creditor under section 1129(b) of the House amendment.

Payment of taxes in reorganizations: Under the provisions of section 1141 as revised by the House amendment, an individual in reorganization under chapter 11 will not be discharged from any debt, including prepetition tax liabilities, which are nondischargeable under section 523. Thus, an individual debtor whose plan of reorganization is confirmed under chapter 11 will remain liable for prepetition priority taxes, as defined in section 507, and for tax liabilities which receive no priority but are nondischargeable under section 523, including no return, late return, and fraud liabilities.

In the case of a partnership or a corporation in reorganization under chapter 11 of title 11, section 1141(d)(1) of the House amendment adopts a provision limiting the taxes that must be provided for in a plan before a plan can be confirmed to taxes which receive priority under section 507. In addition, the House amendment makes dischargeable, in effect, tax liabilities attributable to no return, late return, or fraud situations. The amendment thus does not adopt a shareholder continuity test such as was contained in section 1141(d)(2)(A)(iii) of the Senate amendment. However, the House amendment amends section 1106, relating to duties of the trustee, to require the trustee to furnish, on request of a tax authority and without personal liability, information available to the trustee concerning potential prepetition tax liabilities for unfiled returns of the debtor. Depending on the condition of the debtor's books and records, this information may include schedules and files available to the business. The House amendment also does not prohibit a tax authority from disallowing any tax benefit claimed after the reorganization if the item originated in a deduction, credit, or other item improperly reported before the reorganization occurred. It may also be appropriate for the Congress to consider in the future imposing civil or criminal liability on corporate officers for preparing a false or fraudulent tax return. The House amendment also contemplates that the Internal Revenue Service will monitor the relief from liabilities under this provision and advise the Congress if, and to the extent, any significant tax abuse may be resulting from the provision.

Medium of payment of taxes: Federal, State, and local taxes incurred during the administration period of the estate, and during the "gap" period in an involuntary case, are to be paid solely in cash. Taxes relating to third priority wages are to be paid, under the general rules, in cash on the effective date of the plan, if the class has not accepted the plan, in an amount equal to the allowed amount of the claim. If the class has accepted the plan, the taxes must be paid in cash but the payments must be made at the time the wages are paid which may be paid in deferred periodic installments having a value, on the effective date of the plan, equal to the allowed amount of the tax claims. Prepetition taxes entitled to sixth priority under section 507(a)(6) also must be paid in cash, but the plan may also permit the debtor whether a corporation, partnership, or an individual, to pay the allowed taxes in installments over a period not to exceed 6 years following the date on which the tax authority assesses the tax liability, provided the value of the deferred payments representing principal and interest, as of the effective date of the plan, equals the allowed amount of the tax claim.

The House amendment also modifies the provisions of both bills dealing with the time when tax liabilities of a debtor in reorganization may be assessed by the tax authority. The House amendment follows the Senate amendment in deleting the limitation in present law under which a priority tax assessed after a reorganization plan is confirmed must be assessed within 1 year after the date of the filing of the petition. The House amendment specifies broadly that after the bankruptcy court determines the liability of the estate for a prepetition tax or for an administration period tax, the governmental unit may thereafter assess the tax against the estate, debtor, or successor to the debtor. The party to be assessed will, of course, depend on whether the case is under chapter 7, 11, or 13, whether the debtor is an individual, partnership, or a corporation, and whether the court is determining an individual debtor's personal liability for a nondischargeable tax. Assessment of the tax may only be made, however, within the limits of otherwise applicable law, such as the statute of limitations under the tax law.

Tax avoidance purpose: The House bill provided that no reorganization plan may be approved if the principal purpose of the plan is the avoidance of taxes. The Senate amendment modified the rule so that the bankruptcy court need make a determination of tax avoidance purpose only if it is asked to do so by the appropriate tax authority. Under the Senate amendment, if the tax authority does not request the bankruptcy court to rule on the purpose of the plan, the tax authority would not be barred from later asserting a tax avoidance motive with respect to allowance of a deduction or other tax benefit claimed after the reorganization. The House amendment adopts the substance of the Senate amendment, but does not provide a basis by which a tax authority may collaterally attack confirmation of a plan of reorganization other than under section 1144.

References in Text

Section 5 of the Securities Act of 1933, referred to in subsec. (d), is section 5 of Act May 27, 1933, c. 38, Title I, 48 Stat. 77, which is classified to section 77e of Title 15, Commerce and Trade.

Effective and Applicability Provisions

2005 Acts. Amendments to this section by Pub.L. 109–8, § 1221, applicable to case pending under this title on Apr. 20, 2005, or filed under this title on or after that date, except that the court shall not confirm a plan under chapter 11 of this title without considering whether this section would substantially affect the rights of a party in interest who first acquired rights with respect to the debtor after the date of the filing of the petition, see Pub.L. 109–8, § 1221(d), set out as a note under 11 U.S.C.A. § 363.

Amendments by Pub.L. 109–8 effective, except as otherwise provided, 180 days after April 20, 2005, and inapplicable with respect to cases commenced under Title 11 before the effective date, see Pub.L. 109–8, § 1501, set out as a note under 11 U.S.C.A. § 101.

1994 Acts. Amendments by Pub.L. 103–394 effective on Oct. 22, 1994, and not to apply with respect to cases commenced under Title 11 of the United States Code before Oct. 22, 1994, see section 702 of Pub.L. 103–394, set out as a note under section 101 of this title.

1988 Acts. Amendment by Pub.L. 100–334 effective on June 16, 1988, but not applicable to cases commenced under this title before that date, see section 4 of Pub.L. 100–334, set out as an Effective Date note under section 1114 of this title.

1986 Acts. Amendment by Pub.L. 99–554 effective 30 days after Oct. 27, 1986, except as otherwise provided for, see section 302(a) of Pub.L. 99–554, set out as a note under section 581 of Title 28, Judiciary and Judicial Procedure.

Amendment by Pub.L. 99–554, § 225, not to become effective in or with respect to certain specified judicial districts until, or apply to cases while pending in such district before, the expiration of the 270–day period beginning 30 days after Oct. 27, 1986, or of the 30–day period beginning on the date the Attorney General certifies under section 303 of Pub.L. 99–554 the region specified in a paragraph of section 581(a) of Title 28, as amended by section 111(a) of Pub.L. 99–554, that includes such district, whichever occurs first, see section 302(d)(1) of Pub.L. 99–554, set out as a note under section 581 of Title 28.

Amendment by Pub.L. 99–554, § 225, not to become effective in or with respect to certain specified judicial districts until, or apply to cases while pending in such district before, the expiration of the 2–year period beginning 30 days after Oct. 27, 1986, or of the 30–day period beginning on the date the Attorney General certifies under section 303 of Pub.L. 99–554 the region specified in a paragraph of section 581(a) of Title 28, as amended by section 111(a) of Pub.L. 99–554, that includes such district, whichever occurs first, see section 302(d)(2) of Pub.L. 99–554, set out as a note under section 581 of Title 28.

Amendment by Pub.L. 99–554, § 225, not to become effective in or with respect to judicial districts established for the States of Alabama and North Carolina until, or apply to cases while pending in such district before, such district elects to be included in a bankruptcy region established in section 581(a) of Title 28, as amended by section 111(a) of Pub.L. 99–554, or Oct. 1, 2002, whichever occurs first, and, except as otherwise provided for, with respect to cases under chapters 7, 11, 12, and 13 of Title 11 commenced before 30 days after Oct. 27, 1986, and pending in a judicial district in the States of Alabama or North Carolina before any election made under section 302(d)(3)(A) of Pub.L. 99–554 by such district becomes effective or Oct. 1, 2002, whichever occurs first, amendments by Pub.L. 99–554 not to apply until Oct. 1, 2003, or the expiration of the 1–year period beginning on the date such election becomes effective, whichever occurs first, and further, in any judicial district in Alabama or North Carolina not making the election described in section 302(d)(3)(A) of Pub.L. 99–554, any person appointed under regulations issued by the Judicial Conference to administer estates in cases under Title 11 authorized to establish, etc., a panel of private trustees, and to supervise cases and trustees in cases under chapters 7, 11, 12, and 13 of Title 11, until amendments by sections 201 to 231 of Pub.L. 99–554 effective in such district, see section 302(d)(3)(A) to (F), (H), (I) of Pub.L. 99–554, set out as a note under section 581 of Title 28.

Amendment by Pub.L. 99–554, § 225, except as otherwise provided, with respect to cases under chapters 7, 11, 12, and 13 of Title 11 commenced before 30 days after Oct. 27, 1986, and pending in a judicial district referred to in section 581(a) of Title 28, as amended by section 111(a) of Pub.L. 99–554, for which a United States trustee is not authorized before 30 days after Oct. 27, 1986 to be appointed, not applicable until the expiration of the 3–year period beginning on Oct. 27, 1986, or of the 1–year period beginning on the date the Attorney General certifies under section 303 of Pub.L. 99–554 the region specified in a paragraph of such section 581(a) that includes, such district, whichever occurs first, see section 302(e)(1), (2) of Pub.L. 99–554, set out as a note under section 581 of Title 28.

1984 Acts. Amendment by Pub.L. 98–353 effective with respect to cases filed 90 days after July 10, 1984, see section 552(a), formerly 553(a), of Pub.L. 98–353, set out as a note under section 101 of this title.

Separability of Provisions

If any provision of or amendment made by Pub.L. 103–394 or the application of such provision or amendment to any person or circumstance is held to be unconstitutional, the remaining provisions of and amendments made by Pub.L. 103–394 and the application of such provisions and amendments to any person or circumstance shall not be affected thereby, see section 701 of Pub.L. 103–394, set out as a note under section 101 of this title.

CROSS REFERENCES

Applicability of subsecs. (a)(2), (3), (6), (8), (10) and (b)(1), (2)(A), (2)(B) of this section in Chapter nine cases, see 11 USCA § 901.

Confirmation of plan in—

Chapter nine cases, see 11 USCA § 943.

Chapter thirteen cases, see 11 USCA § 1325.

Chapter twelve cases, see 11 USCA § 1225.

Railroad reorganization cases, see 11 USCA § 1173.

Denial of confirmation of plan as cause for conversion or dismissal, see 11 USCA § 1112.

Effect of confirmation in cases under this chapter, see 11 USCA § 1141.

Inapplicability of subsecs. (a)(7) and (c) of this section in railroad reorganization cases, see 11 USCA § 1161.

Payment of insurance benefits to retired employees, see 11 USCA § 1114.

Revocation of order of confirmation in cases under this chapter, see 11 USCA § 1144.

Special tax provisions for certain dispositions of securities or instruments under confirmed plan, see 11 USCA § 1146.

Supplemental injunctions and plan fair and equitable, see 11 USCA § 524.

Unclaimed property, see 11 USCA § 347.

SUBCHAPTER III—POSTCONFIRMATION MATTERS

CROSS REFERENCES

Subchapter applicable only in case under this chapter except as provided in § 901 of this title, see 11 USCA § 103.

§ 1141. Effect of confirmation

(a) Except as provided in subsections (d)(2) and (d)(3) of this section, the provisions of a confirmed plan bind the debtor, any entity issuing securities under the plan, any entity acquiring property under the plan, and any creditor, equity security holder, or general partner in the debtor, whether or not the claim or interest of such creditor, equity security holder, or general partner is impaired under the plan and whether or not such creditor, equity security holder, or general partner has accepted the plan.

(b) Except as otherwise provided in the plan or the order confirming the plan, the confirmation of a plan vests all of the property of the estate in the debtor.

(c) Except as provided in subsections (d)(2) and (d)(3) of this section and except as otherwise provided in the plan or in the order confirming the plan, after confirmation of a plan, the property dealt with by the plan is free and clear of all claims and interests of creditors, equity security holders, and of general partners in the debtor.

(d)(1) Except as otherwise provided in this subsection, in the plan, or in the order confirming the plan, the confirmation of a plan—

(A) discharges the debtor from any debt that arose before the date of such confirmation, and any debt of a kind specified in section 502(g), 502(h), or 502(i) of this title, whether or not—

(i) a proof of the claim based on such debt is filed or deemed filed under section 501 of this title;

(ii) such claim is allowed under section 502 of this title; or

(iii) the holder of such claim has accepted the plan; and

(B) terminates all rights and interests of equity security holders and general partners provided for by the plan.

(2) A discharge under this chapter does not discharge a debtor who is an individual from any debt excepted from discharge under section 523 of this title.

(3) The confirmation of a plan does not discharge a debtor if—

(A) the plan provides for the liquidation of all or substantially all of the property of the estate;

(B) the debtor does not engage in business after consummation of the plan; and

(C) the debtor would be denied a discharge under section 727(a) of this title if the case were a case under chapter 7 of this title.

(4) The court may approve a written waiver of discharge executed by the debtor after the order for relief under this chapter.

(5) In a case in which the debtor is an individual—

(A) unless after notice and a hearing the court orders otherwise for cause, confirmation of the plan does not discharge any debt provided for in the plan until the court grants a discharge on completion of all payments under the plan;

(B) at any time after the confirmation of the plan, and after notice and a hearing, the court may grant a discharge to the debtor who has not completed payments under the plan if—

(i) the value, as of the effective date of the plan, of property actually distributed under the plan on account of each allowed unsecured claim is not less than the amount that would have been paid on such claim if the estate of the debtor had been liquidated under chapter 7 on such date; and

(ii) modification of the plan under section 1127 is not practicable; and

(C) unless after notice and a hearing held not more than 10 days before the date of the entry of the order granting the discharge, the court finds that there is no reasonable cause to believe that—

(i) section 522(q)(1) may be applicable to the debtor; and

(ii) there is pending any proceeding in which the debtor may be found guilty of a felony of the kind described in section 522(q)(1)(A) or liable for a debt of the kind described in section 522(q)(1)(B).

(6) Notwithstanding paragraph (1), the confirmation of a plan does not discharge a debtor that is a corporation from any debt—

(A) of a kind specified in paragraph (2)(A) or (2)(B) of section 523(a) that is owed to a domestic governmental unit, or owed to a person as the result of an action filed under subchapter III of chapter 37 of title 31 or any similar State statute; or

(B) for a tax or customs duty with respect to which the debtor—

(i) made a fraudulent return; or

(ii) willfully attempted in any manner to evade or to defeat such tax or such customs duty.

(Pub.L. 95–598, Nov. 6, 1978, 92 Stat. 2638; Pub.L. 98–353, Title III, § 513, July 10, 1984, 98 Stat. 387; Pub.L. 109–8, Title III, §§ 321(d), 330(b), Title VII, § 708, Apr. 20, 2005, 119 Stat. 95, 101, 126.)

HISTORICAL AND STATUTORY NOTES

Revision Notes and Legislative Reports

1978 Acts. Subsection (a) of this section makes the provisions of a confirmed plan binding on the debtor, any entity issuing securities under the plan, any entity acquiring property under the plan, and any creditor, equity security holder, or general partner in the debtor, whether or not the claim or interest of the creditor, equity security holder, or partner is impaired under the plan and whether or not he has accepted the plan. There are two exceptions, enumerated in paragraph (2) and (3) of subsection (d).

Unless the plan or the order confirming the plan provides otherwise, the confirmation of a plan vests all of the property of the estate in the debtor and releases it from all claims and interests of creditors, equity security holders and general partners.

Subsection (d) contains the discharge for a reorganized debtor. Paragraph (1) specifies that the confirmation of a plan discharges the debtor from any debt that arose before the date of the order for relief unless the plan or the order confirming the plan provides otherwise. The discharge is effective against those claims whether or not proof of the claim is filed (or deemed filed), and whether or not the claim is allowed. The discharge also terminates all rights and interests of equity security holders and general partners provided for by the plan. The paragraph permits the plan or the order confirming the plan to provide otherwise, and excepts certain debts from the discharge as provided in paragraphs (2) and (3).

Paragraph (2) of subsection (d) makes clear what taxes remain nondischargeable in the case of a corporate debtor emerging from a reorganization under chapter 11. Nondischargeable taxes in such a reorganization are the priority taxes (under section 507) and tax payments which come due during and after the proceeding under a deferred or part-payment agreement which the debtor had entered into with the tax authority before the bankruptcy proceedings began. On the other hand, a corporation which is taken over by its creditors through a plan of reorganization will not continue to be liable for nonpriority taxes arising from the corporation's prepetition fraud, failure to file a return, or failure to file a timely return, since the creditors who take over the reorganized company should not bear the burden of acts for which the creditors were not at fault.

Paragraph (3) specifies that the debtor is not discharged by the confirmation of a plan if the plan is a liquidating plan and if the debtor would be denied discharge in a liquidation case under section 727. Specifically, if all or substantially all of the distribution under the plan is of all or substantially all of the property of the estate or the proceeds of it, if the business, if any, of the debtor does not continue, and if the debtor would be denied a discharge under section 727 (such as if the debtor were not an individual or if he had committed an act that would lead to a denial of discharge), the chapter 11 discharge is not granted.

Paragraph (4) authorizes the court to approve a waiver of discharge by the debtor. Senate Report No. 95–989.

Paragraph (2) [of subsec. (d)] makes applicable to an individual debtor the general exceptions to discharge that are enumerated in section 523(a) of the bankruptcy code [this title]. House Report No. 95–595.

1984 Acts. Statements by Legislative Leaders, see 1984 U.S.Code Cong. and Adm.News, p. 576.

2005 Acts. House Report No. 109–31(Part I), see 2005 U.S. Code Cong. and Adm. News, p. 88.

Legislative Statements

Section 1141(d) of the House amendment is derived from a comparable provision contained in the Senate amendment. However, section 1141(d)(2) of the House amendment is derived from the House bill as preferable to the Senate amendment. It is necessary for a corporation or partnership undergoing reorganization to be able to present its creditors with a fixed list of liabilities upon which the creditors or third parties can make intelligent decisions. Retaining an exception for discharge with respect to nondischargeable taxes would leave an undesirable uncertainty surrounding reorganizations that is unacceptable. Section 1141(d)(3) is derived from the Senate amendment. Section 1141(d)(4) is likewise derived from the Senate amendment.

References in Text

Chapter 7, referred to in subsec. (d)(5)(B)(i), is chapter 7 of this title, 11 U.S.C.A. § 701 et seq.

Subchapter III of chapter 37 of title 31, referred to in subsec. (d)(6)(A), is 31 U.S.C.A. § 3721 et seq.

Codifications

Amendment by Pub.L. 109–8, § 330(b), adding a new subparagraph (C) "at the end" of subsection (d) "as amended by section 321 [of Pub.L. 109–8, which added a new paragraph (5) to subsection (d) of this section]" was executed by adding the new subparagraph to the end of paragraph (5) of subsection (d), as the probable intent of Congress.

Effective and Applicability Provisions

2005 Acts. Amendments by Pub.L. 109–8 effective 180 days after Apr. 20, 2005, with amendments by sections 321(d) and 708 of Pub.L. 109–8 not applicable with respect to cases commenced under this title before such effective date, except as otherwise provided, and amendment by section 330(b) of Pub.L. 109–8 applicable with respect to cases commenced under this title on or after Apr. 20, 2005, see Pub.L. 109–8, § 1501, set out as a note under 11 U.S.C.A. § 101.

1984 Acts. Amendment by Pub.L. 98–353 effective with respect to cases filed 90 days after July 10, 1984, see section 552(a), formerly 553(a), of Pub.L. 98–353, set out as a note under section 101 of this title.

CROSS REFERENCES

Confirmation of plan filed under this chapter, see 11 USCA § 1129.

Discharge under Chapter seven, see 11 USCA § 727.

Effect of confirmation of plans filed in—

Chapter nine cases, see 11 USCA § 944.

Chapter thirteen cases, see 11 USCA § 1327.

Chapter twelve cases, see 11 USCA § 1227.

Effect of conversion, see 11 USCA § 348.

Effect of discharge, see 11 USCA § 524.

Exceptions to discharge, see 11 USCA § 523.

Failure of discharge as cause for conversion, see 11 USCA § 1112.

Nondischargeability of capital improvement loans for multifamily housing projects in proceedings under this section, see 12 USCA § 1715z–1a.

Supplemental injunctions, debtor and plan of reorganization, see 11 USCA § 524.

§ 1142. Implementation of plan

(a) Notwithstanding any otherwise applicable nonbankruptcy law, rule, or regulation relating to financial condition, the debtor and any entity organized or to be organized for the purpose of carrying out the plan shall carry out the plan and shall comply with any orders of the court.

(b) The court may direct the debtor and any other necessary party to execute or deliver or to join in the execution or delivery of any instrument required to effect a transfer of property dealt with by a confirmed plan, and to perform any other act, including the satisfaction of any lien, that is necessary for the consummation of the plan.

(Pub.L. 95–598, Nov. 6, 1978, 92 Stat. 2639; Pub.L. 98–353, Title III, § 514(a), (c), (d), July 10, 1984, 98 Stat. 387.)

HISTORICAL AND STATUTORY NOTES

Revision Notes and Legislative Reports

1978 Acts. Senate Report No. 95–989 and House Report No. 95–595, see 1978 U.S.Code Cong. and Adm.News, p. 5787.

1984 Acts. Statements by Legislative Leaders, see 1984 U.S.Code Cong. and Adm.News, p. 576.

Effective and Applicability Provisions

1984 Acts. Amendment by Pub.L. 98–353 effective with respect to cases filed 90 days after July 10, 1984, see section 552(a), formerly 553 of Pub.L. 98–353, set out as a note under section 101 of this title.

CROSS REFERENCES

Applicability of subsec. (b) of this section in Chapter nine cases, see 11 USCA § 901.

Supplemental injunctions, debtor and plan of reorganization, see 11 USCA § 524.

§ 1143. Distribution

If a plan requires presentment or surrender of a security or the performance of any other act as a condition to participation in distribution under the plan, such action shall be taken not later than five years after the date of the entry of the order of confirmation. Any entity that has not within such time presented or surrendered such entity's security or taken any such other action that the plan requires may not participate in distribution under the plan.

(Pub.L. 95–598, Nov. 6, 1978, 92 Stat. 2639.)

HISTORICAL AND STATUTORY NOTES

Revision Notes and Legislative Reports

1978 Acts. Section 1143 fixes a 5-year limitation on presentment or surrender of securities or the performance of any other act that is a condition to participation in distribution under the plan. The 5 years runs from the date of the entry of the order of confirmation. Any entity that does not take the appropriate action with the 5-year period is barred from participation in the distribution under the plan. Senate Report No. 95–989.

CROSS REFERENCES

Applicability of this section in Chapter nine cases, see 11 USCA § 901.

Distribution of property of estate in Chapter seven cases, see 11 USCA § 726.

Distribution of securities in stockbroker liquidation cases, see 11 USCA § 750.

Ownership of copyright, see 17 USCA § 201.

§ 1144. Revocation of an order of confirmation

On request of a party in interest at any time before 180 days after the date of the entry of the order of confirmation, and after notice and a hearing, the court may revoke such order if and only if such order was procured by fraud. An order under this section revoking an order of confirmation shall—

(1) contain such provisions as are necessary to protect any entity acquiring rights in good faith reliance on the order of confirmation; and

(2) revoke the discharge of the debtor.

(Pub.L. 95–598, Nov. 6, 1978, 92 Stat. 2639; Pub.L. 98–353, Title III, § 515, July 10, 1984, 98 Stat. 387.)

HISTORICAL AND STATUTORY NOTES

Revision Notes and Legislative Reports

1978 Acts. If an order of confirmation was procured by fraud, then the court may revoke the order on request of a party in interest if the request is made before 180 days after the date of the entry of the order of confirmation. The order revoking the order of confirmation must revoke the discharge of the debtor, and contain such provisions as are necessary to protect any entity acquiring rights in good faith reliance on the order of confirmation. Senate Report No. 95–989.

1984 Acts. Statements by Legislative Leaders, see 1984 U.S.Code Cong. and Adm.News, p. 576.

Effective and Applicability Provisions

1984 Acts. Amendment by Pub.L. 98–353 effective with respect to cases filed 90 days after July 10, 1984, see section 552(a), formerly 553(a), of Pub.L. 98–353, set out as a note under section 101 of this title.

CROSS REFERENCES

Applicability of this section in Chapter nine cases, see 11 USCA § 901.

Confirmation of one plan as affected by revocation, see 11 USCA § 1129.

Revocation of confirmation order as cause for conversion or dismissal, see 11 USCA § 1112.

Revocation of order of confirmation in—

Chapter thirteen cases, see 11 USCA § 1330.

Chapter twelve cases, see 11 USCA § 1230.

Supplemental injunctions, see 11 USCA § 524.

§ 1145. Exemption from securities laws

(a) Except with respect to an entity that is an underwriter as defined in subsection (b) of this section, section 5 of the Securities Act of 1933 and any State or local law requiring registration for offer or sale of a security or registration or licensing of an issuer of, underwriter of, or broker or dealer in, a security do not apply to—

(1) the offer or sale under a plan of a security of the debtor, of an affiliate participating in a joint plan with the debtor, or of a successor to the debtor under the plan—

(A) in exchange for a claim against, an interest in, or a claim for an administrative expense in the case concerning, the debtor or such affiliate; or

(B) principally in such exchange and partly for cash or property;

(2) the offer of a security through any warrant, option, right to subscribe, or conversion privilege that was sold in the manner specified in paragraph (1) of this subsection, or the sale of a security upon the exercise of such a warrant, option, right, or privilege;

(3) the offer or sale, other than under a plan, of a security of an issuer other than the debtor or an affiliate, if—

(A) such security was owned by the debtor on the date of the filing of the petition;

(B) the issuer of such security is—

(i) required to file reports under section 13 or 15(d) of the Securities Exchange Act of 1934; and

(ii) in compliance with the disclosure and reporting provision of such applicable section; and

(C) such offer or sale is of securities that do not exceed—

(i) during the two-year period immediately following the date of the filing of the petition, four percent of the securities of such class outstanding on such date; and

(ii) during any 180-day period following such two-year period, one percent of the securities outstanding at the beginning of such 180-day period; or

(4) a transaction by a stockbroker in a security that is executed after a transaction of a kind specified in paragraph (1) or (2) of this subsection in such security and before the expiration of 40 days after the first date on which such security was bona fide offered to the public by the issuer or by or through an underwriter, if such stockbroker provides, at the time of or before such transaction by such stockbroker, a disclosure statement approved under section 1125 of this title, and, if the court orders, information supplementing such disclosure statement.

(b)(1) Except as provided in paragraph (2) of this subsection and except with respect to ordinary trading transactions of an entity that is not an issuer, an entity is an underwriter under section 2(11) of the Securities Act of 1933, if such entity—

(A) purchases a claim against, interest in, or claim for an administrative expense in the case concerning, the debtor, if such purchase is with a view to distribution of any security received or to be received in exchange for such a claim or interest;

(B) offers to sell securities offered or sold under the plan for the holders of such securities;

(C) offers to buy securities offered or sold under the plan from the holders of such securities, if such offer to buy is—

(i) with a view to distribution of such securities; and

(ii) under an agreement made in connection with the plan, with the consummation of the plan, or with the offer or sale of securities under the plan; or

(D) is an issuer, as used in such section 2(11), with respect to such securities.

(2) An entity is not an underwriter under section 2(11) of the Securities Act of 1933 or under paragraph (1) of this subsection with respect to an agreement that provides only for—

(A)(i) the matching or combining of fractional interests in securities offered or sold under the plan into whole interests; or

(ii) the purchase or sale of such fractional interests from or to entities receiving such fractional interests under the plan; or

(B) the purchase or sale for such entities of such fractional or whole interests as are necessary to adjust for any remaining fractional interests after such matching.

(3) An entity other than an entity of the kind specified in paragraph (1) of this subsection is not an underwriter under section 2(11) of the Securities Act of 1933 with respect to any securities offered or sold to such entity in the manner specified in subsection (a)(1) of this section.

(c) An offer or sale of securities of the kind and in the manner specified under subsection (a)(1) of this section is deemed to be a public offering.

(d) The Trust Indenture Act of 1939 does not apply to a note issued under the plan that matures not later than one year after the effective date of the plan.

(Pub.L. 95–598, Nov. 6, 1978, 92 Stat. 2639; Pub.L. 98–353, Title III, § 516, July 10, 1984, 98 Stat. 387; Pub.L. 103–394, Title V, § 501(d)(33), Oct. 22, 1994, 108 Stat. 4146.)

HISTORICAL AND STATUTORY NOTES

Revision Notes and Legislative Reports

1978 Acts. This section, derived from similar provisions found in sections 264, 393, and 518 of the Bankruptcy Act [sections 664, 793, and 918 of former title 11], provides a limited exemption from the securities laws for securities issued under a plan of reorganization and for certain other securities. Subsection (a) exempts from the requirements of section 5 of the Securities Act of 1933 [section 77e of Title 15, Commerce and Trade] and from any State or local law requiring registration or licensing of an issuer of, underwriter of, or broker or dealer in, a security, the offer or sale of certain securities.

Paragraph (1) of subsection (a) exempts the offer or sale under section 364 of any security that is not an equity security or convertible into an equity security. This paragraph is designed to facilitate the issuance of certificates of indebtedness, and should be read in light of the amendment made in section 306 of title III to section 3(a)(7) of the 1933 act [section 77c(a)(7) of Title 15, Commerce and Trade].

Paragraph (2) of subsection (a) exempts the offer or sale of any security of the debtor, a successor to the debtor, or an affiliate in a joint plan, distributed under a plan if such security is exchanged in principal part for securities of the debtor or for allowed claims or administrative expenses. This exemption is carried over from present law, except as to administrative claims, but is limited to prevent distribution of securities to other than claim holders or equity security holders of the debtor or the estate.

Paragraph (3) of subsection (a) exempts the offer or sale of any security that arises from the exercise of a subscription right or from the exercise of a conversion privilege when such subscription right or conversion privilege was issued under a plan. This exemption is necessary in order to enhance the marketability of subscription rights or conversion privileges, including warrants, offered or sold under a plan. This is present law.

Paragraph (4) of subsection (a) exempts sales of portfolio securities, excluding securities of the debtor or its affiliate, owned by the debtor on the date of the filing of the petition. The purpose of this exemption is to allow the debtor or trustee to sell or distribute, without allowing manipulation schemes, restricted portfolio securities held or acquired by the debtor. Subparagraph (B) of section 1145(a)(4) limits the exemption to securities of a company that is required to file reports under section 13 of the Securities Act [section 78m of Title 15, Commerce and Trade] and that is in compliance with all requirements for the continuance of trading those securities. This limitation effectively prevents selling into the market "cats and dogs" of a nonreporting company. Subparagraph (C) places a limitation on the amount of restricted securities that may be distributed. During the case, the trustee may sell up to 4 percent of each class of restricted securities at any time during the first 2 years and 1 percent during any 180-day period thereafter. This relaxation of the resale rules for debtors in holding restricted securities is similar to but less extensive than the relaxation in SEC [Securities and Exchange Commission] Rule 114(c)(3)(v) for the estates of deceased holders of securities.

Paragraph (5) contains an exemption for brokers and dealers (stockbrokers, as defined in title 11) akin to the exemption provided by section 4(3)(A) of the Securities Act of 1933 [section 77d(3)(A) of Title 15, Commerce and Trade]. Instead of being required to supply a prospectus, however, the stockbroker is required to supply the approved disclosure statement, and if the court orders, information supplementing the disclosure statement. Under present law, the stockholders is not required to supply anything.

Subsection (b) is new. The subsection should be read in light of the amendment in section 306 of Title III to the 1933 act [section 77c(a)(7), (9), (10) of Title 15, Commerce and Trade]. It specifies the standards under which a creditor, equity security holder, or other entity acquiring securities under the plan may resell them. The Securities Act places limitations on sales by underwriters. This subsection defines who is an underwriter, and thus restricted, and who is free to resell. Paragraph (1) enumerates real underwriters that participate in a classical underwriting. A person is an underwriter if he purchases a claim against, interest in, or claim for an administrative expense in the case concerning, the debtor, with a view to distribution or interest. This provision covers the purchase of a certificate of indebtedness issued under proposed 11 U.S.C. 364 and purchased from the debtor, if the purchase of the certificate was with a view to distribution.

A person is also an underwriter if he offers to sell securities offered or sold under the plan for the holders of such securities, or offers to buy securities offered or sold under the plan from the holders of such securities, if the offer to buy is with a view to distribution of the securities and under an agreement made in connection with the plan, with the consummation of the plan or with the offer or sale of securities under the plan. Finally, a person is an underwriter if he is an issuer, as used in section 2(11) of the Securities Act of 1933 [section 77b(11) of Title 15, Commerce and Trade].

Paragraph (2) of subsection (b) exempts from the definition of underwriter any entity to the extent that any agreement that would bring the entity under the definition in paragraph (1) provides only for the matching combination of fractional interests in the covered securities or the purchase or sale of fractional interests. This paragraph and paragraph (1) are modeled after former rule 133 of the Securities and Exchange Commission.

Paragraph (3) specifies that if an entity is not an underwriter under the provisions of paragraph (1), as limited by paragraph (2), then the entity is not an underwriter for the purposes of the Securities Act of 1933 [section 77a et seq. of Title 15, Commerce and Trade] with respect to the covered securities, that is, those offered or sold in an exempt transaction specified in subsection (a)(2). This makes clear that the current definition of underwriter in section 2(11) of the Securities Act of 1933 [section 77b(11) of Title 15] does not apply to such a creditor. The definition in that section technically applies to any person that purchases securities with "a view to distribution." If literally applied, it would prevent any creditor in a bankruptcy case from selling securities received without filing a registration statement or finding another exemption.

Subsection (b) is a first run transaction exemption and does not exempt a creditor that, for example, some years later becomes an underwriter by reacquiring securities originally issued under a plan.

Subsection (c) makes an offer or sale of securities under the plan in an exempt transaction (as specified in subsection (a)(2)) a public offering, in order to prevent characterization of the distribution as a "private placement" which would result in restrictions, under rule 144 of the SEC [Securities and Exchange Commission] on the resale of the securities. Senate Report No. 95–989.

1984 Acts. Statements by Legislative Leaders, see 1984 U.S. Code Cong. and Adm. News, p. 576.

1994 Acts. House Report No. 103–835, see 1994 U.S. Code Cong. and Adm. News, p. 3340.

Legislative Statements

Section 1145 of the House amendment deletes a provision contained in section 1145(a)(1) of the House bill in favor of a more adequate provision contained in section 364(f) of the House amendment. In addition, section 1145(d) has been added to indicate that the Trust Indenture Act [section 77aaa et seq. of Title 15, Commerce and Trade] does not apply to a commercial note issued under a plan, if the note matures not later than 1 year after the effective date of the plan. Some commercial notes receive such an exemption under 304(a)(4) of the Trust Indenture Act of 1939 (15 U.S.C. § 77ddd(a)(4)) [section 77ddd(a)(4) of Title 15] and others may receive protection by incorporation by reference into the Trust Indenture Act of securities exempt under section 3a(3), (7), (9), or (10) of the Securities Act of 1933 [section 77c(a)(3), (7), (9) and (10) of Title 15, respectively].

In light of the amendments made to the Securities Act of 1933 [section 77a et seq. of Title 15, Commerce and Trade] in title III of the House amendment to H.R. 8200, a specific exemption from the Trust Indenture Act [section 77aaa et seq. of Title 15, Commerce and Trade] is required in order to create certainty regarding plans of reorganization. Section 1145(d) is not intended to imply that commercial notes issued under a plan that matures more than 1 year after the effective date of the plan are automatically covered by the Trust Indenture Act of 1939 since such notes may fall within another exemption thereto.

One other point with respect to Section [sic] 1145 deserves comment. Section 1145(a)(3) grants a debtor in possession or trustee in chapter 11 an extremely narrow portfolio security exemption from section 5 of the Securities Act of 1933 [section 77e of Title 15, Commerce and Trade] or any comparable State law. The provision was considered by Congress and adopted after much study. The exemption is reasonable and is more restrictive than comparable provisions under the Securities Act [section 77a et seq. of Title 15, Commerce and Trade] relating to the estates of decedents. Subsequent to passage of H.R. 8200 by the House of Representatives, the Securities and Exchange Commission promulgated Rule 148 to treat with this problem under existing law. Members of Congress received opinions from attorneys indicating dissatisfaction with the Commission's rule although the rule has been amended, the ultimate limitation of 1 percent promulgated by the Commission is wholly unacceptable.

The Commission rule would permit a trustee or debtor in possession to distribute securities at the rate of 1 percent every 6 months. Section 1145(a)(3) permits the trustee to distribute 4 percent of the securities during the 2-year period immediately following the date of the filing of the petition. In addition, the security must be of a reporting company under section 13 of the Securities and Exchange Act of 1934 [section 78m of Title 15, Commerce and Trade], and must be in compliance with all applicable requirements for the continuing of trading in the security on the date that the trustee offers or sells the security.

With these safeguards the trustee or debtor in possession should be able to distribute 4 percent of the securities of a class at any time during the 2-year period immediately following the date of the filing of the petition in the interests of expediting bankruptcy administration. The same rationale that applies in expeditiously terminating decedents' estates applies no less to an estate under title 11.

References in Text

Section 5 of the Securities Act of 1933, referred to in subsec. (a), is section 5 of Act May 27, 1933, c. 38, Title I, 48 Stat. 77, which is classified to section 77e of Title 15, Commerce and Trade.

Section 13 or 15 of the Securities Exchange Act of 1934, referred to in subsec. (a)(3)(B)(i), are section 13 and 15 of Act June 6, 1934, c. 404, Title I, 48 Stat. 894, 895, which are classified to sections 78m and 78*o*, respectively, of Title 15.

Section 2(11) of the Securities Act of 1933, referred to in subsec. (b), was redesignated section 2(a)(11) of the Act by Pub.L. 104–290, title I, § 106(a)(1), Oct. 11, 1996, 110 Stat. 3424, and is classified to section 77b(a)(11) of Title 15, Commerce and Trade.

The Trust Indenture Act of 1939, referred to in subsec. (d), is Title III of Act May 27, 1933, ch. 38, as added Aug. 3, 1939, ch. 411, 53 Stat. 1149, as amended, which is classified generally to subchapter III (section 77aaa et seq.) of chapter 2A of Title 15. For complete classification of this Act to the Code, see section 77aaa of Title 15 and Tables.

Effective and Applicability Provisions

1994 Acts. Amendment by Pub.L. 103–394 effective on Oct. 22, 1994, and not to apply with respect to cases commenced under Title 11 of the United States Code before Oct. 22, 1994, see section 702 of Pub.L. 103–394, set out as a note under section 101 of this title.

1984 Acts. Amendment by Pub.L. 98–353 effective with respect to cases filed 90 days after July 10, 1984, see section 552(a), formerly 553(a), of Pub.L. 98–353, set out as a note under section 101 of this title.

Separability of Provisions

If any provision of or amendment made by Pub.L. 103–394 or the application of such provision or amendment to any person or circumstance is held to be unconstitutional, the remaining provisions of and amendments made by Pub.L. 103–394 and the application of such provisions and amendments to any person or circumstance shall not be affected thereby, see section 701 of Pub.L. 103–394, set out as a note under section 101 of this title.

CROSS REFERENCES

Applicability of term "security" to offers or sales under § 364 of this title to underwriters, see 11 USCA § 364.

Applicability of this section in Chapter nine cases, see 11 USCA § 901.

Protection of securities customers, see 15 USCA § 78eee.

Racketeering activity defined as offense involving fraud in sale of securities in case under this title, see 18 USCA § 1961.

Securities exempted from Securities Act of 1933, see 15 USCA § 77c.

§ 1146. Special tax provisions

(a) The issuance, transfer, or exchange of a security, or the making or delivery of an instrument of transfer under a plan confirmed under section 1129 of this title, may not be taxed under any law imposing a stamp tax or similar tax.

(b) The court may authorize the proponent of a plan to request a determination, limited to questions of law, by a State or local governmental unit charged with responsibility for collection or determination of a tax on or measured by income, of the tax effects, under section 346 of this title and under the law imposing such tax, of the plan. In the event of an actual controversy, the court may declare such effects after the earlier of—

(1) the date on which such governmental unit responds to the request under this subsection; or

(2) 270 days after such request.

[**(c)** Redesignated (a)]

[**(d)** Redesignated (b)]

(Pub.L. 95–598, Nov. 6, 1978, 92 Stat. 2641; Pub.L. 98–353, Title III, § 517, July 10, 1984, 98 Stat. 388; Pub.L. 109–8, Title VII, § 719(b)(3), Apr. 20, 2005, 119 Stat. 133.)

HISTORICAL AND STATUTORY NOTES

Revision Notes and Legislative Reports

1978 Acts. Section 1146 provides special tax rules applicable to Title 11 reorganizations. Subsection (a) provides that the taxable period of an individual debtor terminates on the date of the order for relief, unless the case has been converted into a reorganization from a liquidation proceeding.

Subsection (b) requires the trustee of the estate of an individual debtor in a reorganization to file a tax return for each taxable period while the case is pending after the order for relief. For corporations in chapter 11, the trustee is required to file the tax returns due while the case is pending (section 346(c)(2)).

Subsection (c) exempts from Federal, State, or local stamp taxes the issuance, transfer, or exchange of a security, or the making or delivery of an instrument of transfer under a plan. This subsection is derived from section 267 of the present Bankruptcy Act [section 667 of former Title 11].

Subsection (d) permits the court to authorize the proponent of a reorganization plan to request from the Internal Revenue Service (or State or local tax authority) an advance ruling on the tax effects of the proposed plan. If a ruling is not obtained within 270 days after the request was made, or if a ruling is obtained but the proponent of the plan disagrees with the ruling, the bankruptcy court may resolve the dispute and determine the tax effects of the proposed plan.

Subsection (e) provides that prepetition taxes which are nondischargeable in a reorganization, and all taxes arising during the administration period of the case, may be assessed and collected from the debtor or the debtor's successor in a reorganization (see sec. 505(c) of the bill). Senate Report No. 95–989.

Section 1146 of title 11 specifies five subsections which embody special tax provisions that apply in a case under chapter 11 of title 11. Subsection (a) indicates that the tax year of an individual debtor terminates on the date of the order for relief under chapter 11. Termination of the taxable year of the debtor commences the tax period of the estate. If the case was converted from chapter 7 of title 11 then the estate is created as a separate taxable entity dating from the order for relief under chapter 7. If multiple conversion of the case occurs, then the estate is treated as a separate taxable entity on the date of the order for relief under the first chapter under which the estate is a separate taxable entity.

Subsection (d) permits the court to authorize the proponent of a plan to request a taxing authority to declare the tax effects of such plan. In the event of an actual controversy, the court may declare the tax effects of the plan of reorganization at any time after the earlier of action by such taxing authority or 270 days after the request. Such a declaration, unless appealed, becomes a final judgment and binds any tax authority that was requested by the proponent to determine the tax effects of the plan. House Report No. 95–595.

1984 Acts. Statements by Legislative Leaders, see 1984 U.S.Code Cong. and Adm.News, p. 576.

2005 Acts. House Report No. 109–31(Part I), see 2005 U.S. Code Cong. and Adm. News, p. 88.

Legislative Statements

Section 1146 of the House amendment represents a compromise between the House bill and Senate amendment.

Special tax provisions: reorganization: The House bill provided rules on the effect of bankruptcy on the taxable year of the debtor and on tax return filing requirements for State and local taxes only. The House bill also exempted from State or local stamp taxes the issuance, transfer, or exchange of a security, or the making or delivery of an instrument of transfer under a plan. The House bill also authorized the bankruptcy court to declare the tax effects of a reorganization plan after the proponent of the plan had requested a ruling from State or local tax authority and either had received an unfavorable ruling or the tax authority had not issued a ruling within 270 days.

The Senate amendment deleted the rules concerning the taxable years of the debtor and tax return filing requirements since the Federal rules were to be considered in the next Congress. It broadened the rule exempting transfers of securities to include Federal stamp or similar taxes, if any. In addition, the Senate amendment deleted the provision which permitted the bankruptcy court to determine the tax effects of a plan.

The House amendment retains the State and local rules in the House bill with one modification. Under the House amendment, the power of the bankruptcy court to declare the tax effects of the plan is limited to issues of law and not to questions of fact such as the allowance of specific deductions. Thus, the bankruptcy court could declare whether the reorganization qualified for taxfree status under State or local tax rules, but it could not declare the dollar amount of any tax attributes that survive the reorganization.

Effective and Applicability Provisions

2005 Acts. Amendments by Pub.L. 109–8 effective, except as otherwise provided, 180 days after April 20, 2005, and inapplicable with respect to cases commenced under Title 11 before the effective date, see Pub.L. 109–8, § 1501, set out as a note under 11 U.S.C.A. § 101.

1984 Acts. Amendment by Pub.L. 98–353 effective with respect to cases filed 90 days after July 10, 1984, see section 552(a), formerly 553(a), of Pub.L. 98–353, set out as a note under section 101 of this title.

CROSS REFERENCES

Declaratory judgments, see 28 USCA § 2201.

Determination of—

Number of taxable periods during which debtor may use loss carryover or carryback, see 11 USCA § 346.

Tax liability, see 11 USCA § 505.

Effect of conversion, see 11 USCA § 348.

Special tax provisions in Chapter 7 cases, see 11 USCA § 728.

SUBCHAPTER IV—RAILROAD REORGANIZATION

CROSS REFERENCES

"Carrier subject to liquidation" as meaning carrier subject to proceeding under this subchapter, see 45 USCA § 915.

Collective bargaining agreement, manner of assumption or rejection by trustee other than a trustee in a case covered by this subchapter, see 11 USCA § 1113.

Subchapter applicable only in cases under this chapter concerning railroad, see 11 USCA § 103.

Temporary operating approval granted to carrier subject to this subchapter as of January 14, 1983, see 45 USCA § 1017.

§ 1161. Inapplicability of other sections

Sections 341, 343, 1102(a)(1), 1104, 1105, 1107, 1129(a)(7), and 1129(c) of this title do not apply in a case concerning a railroad.

(Pub.L. 95–598, Nov. 6, 1978, 92 Stat. 2641.)

HISTORICAL AND STATUTORY NOTES

Revision Notes and Legislative Reports

1978 Acts. This section makes inapplicable sections of the bill which are either inappropriate in railroad reorganizations, or relate to matters which are otherwise dealt with in subchapter IV. Senate Report No. 95–989.

CROSS REFERENCES

Applicability of Chapters 1, 3, and 5 of this title to cases under Chapters 7, 11, or 13 of this title except as provided in this section, see 11 USCA § 103.

§ 1162. Definition

In this subchapter, "Board" means the "Surface Transportation Board".

(Added Pub.L. 104–88, Title III, § 302(1), Dec. 29, 1995, 109 Stat. 943.)

HISTORICAL AND STATUTORY NOTES

Revision Notes and Legislative Reports

1995 Acts. House Report No. 104–311 and House Conference Report No. 104–422, see 1995 U.S. Code Cong. and Adm. News, p. 793.

Effective and Applicability Provisions

1995 Acts. Section effective Jan. 1, 1996, see section 2 of Pub.L. 104–88, set out as a note under section 701 of Title 49, Transportation.

§ 1163. Appointment of trustee

As soon as practicable after the order for relief the Secretary of Transportation shall submit a list of five disinterested persons that are qualified and willing to serve as trustees in the case. The United States trustee shall appoint one of such persons to serve as trustee in the case.

(Pub.L. 95–598, Nov. 6, 1978, 92 Stat. 2641; Pub.L. 99–554, Title II, § 226, Oct. 27, 1986, 100 Stat. 3102.)

HISTORICAL AND STATUTORY NOTES

Revision Notes and Legislative Reports

1978 Acts. [Section 1166 (now section 1163)] Requires the court to appoint a trustee in every case. Since the trustee may employ whatever help he needs, multiple trusteeships are unnecessary and add to the cost of administration. The present requirement of section 77(c)(1) [section 205(c)(1) of former Title 11] that the trustee be approved by the Interstate Commerce Commission is unnecessary, since the trustee will be selected either from the panel established under section 606(f) of title 28 [section 606(f) of Title 28, Judiciary and Judicial Procedure], or someone certified by the Director of the Administrative Office of the United States Courts as qualified to become a member of that panel. Senate Report No. 95–989.

[Section 1162] This section [now section 1163] requires the appointment of an independent trustee in a railroad reorganization case. The court may appoint one or more disinterested persons to serve as trustee in the case. House Report No. 95–595.

1986 Acts. House Report No. 99–764 and House Conference Report No. 99–958, see 1986 U.S.Code Cong. and Adm.News, p. 5227.

Legislative Statements

Section 1163 of the House amendment represents a compromise between the House bill and Senate amendment with respect to the appointment of a trustee in a railroad reorganization. As soon as practicable after the order for relief, the Secretary of Transportation is required to submit a list of five disinterested persons who are qualified to serve as trustee and the court will then appoint one trustee from the list to serve as trustee in the case.

The House amendment deletes section 1163 of the Senate amendment in order to cover intrastate railroads in a case under subchapter IV of chapter 11. The bill does not confer jurisdiction on the Interstate Commerce Commission with respect to intrastate railroads.

Effective and Applicability Provisions

1986 Acts. Amendment by Pub.L. 99–554 effective 30 days after Oct. 27, 1986, except as otherwise provided for, see section 302(a) of Pub.L. 99–554, set out as a note under section 581 of Title 28, Judiciary and Judicial Procedure.

Amendment by Pub.L. 99–554, § 226, not to become effective in or with respect to certain specified judicial districts until, or apply to cases while pending in such district before, the expiration of the 270–day period beginning 30 days after Oct. 27, 1986, or of the 30–day period beginning on the date the Attorney General certifies under section 303 of Pub.L. 99–554 the region specified in a paragraph of section 581(a) of Title 28, as amended by section 111(a) of Pub.L. 99–554, that includes such district, whichever occurs first, see section 302(d)(1) of Pub.L. 99–554, set out as a note under section 581 of Title 28.

Amendment by Pub.L. 99–554, § 226, not to become effective in or with respect to certain specified judicial districts until, or apply to cases while pending in such district before, the expiration of the 2–year period beginning 30 days after Oct. 27, 1986, or of the 30–day period beginning on the date the Attorney General certifies under section 303 of Pub.L. 99–554 the region specified in a paragraph of section 581(a) of Title 28, as amended by section 111(a) of Pub.L. 99–554, that includes such district, whichever occurs first, see section 302(d)(2) of Pub.L. 99–554, set out as a note under section 581 of Title 28.

Amendment by Pub.L. 99–554, § 226, not to become effective in or with respect to judicial districts established for the States of Alabama and North Carolina until, or apply to cases while pending in such district before, such district elects to be included in a bankruptcy region established in section 581(a) of Title 28, as amended by section 111(a) of Pub.L. 99–554, or Oct. 1, 2002, whichever occurs first, and, except as otherwise provided for, with respect to cases under chapters 7, 11, 12, and 13 of Title 11 commenced before 30 days after Oct. 27, 1986, and pending in a judicial district in the States of Alabama or North Carolina before any election made under section 302(d)(3)(A) of Pub.L. 99–554 by such district becomes effective or Oct. 1, 2002, whichever occurs first, amendments by Pub.L. 99–554 not to apply until Oct. 1, 2003, or the expiration of the 1–year period beginning on the date such election becomes effective, whichever occurs first, and further, in any judicial district in Alabama or North Carolina not making the election described in section 302(d)(3)(A) of Pub.L. 99–554, any person appointed under regulations issued by the Judicial Conference to administer estates in cases under Title 11 authorized to establish, etc., a panel of private trustees, and to supervise cases and trustees in cases under chapters 7, 11, 12, and 13 of Title 11, until amendments by sections 201 to 231 of Pub.L. 99–554 effective in such district, see section 302(d)(3)(A) to (F), (H), (I) of Pub.L. 99–554, set out as a note under section 581 of Title 28.

Amendment by Pub.L. 99–554, § 226, except as otherwise provided, with respect to cases under chapters 7, 11, 12, and 13 of Title 11 commenced before 30 days after Oct. 27, 1986, and pending in a judicial district referred to in section 581(a) of Title 28, as amended by section 111(a) of Pub.L. 99–554, for which a United States trustee is not authorized before 30 days after Oct. 27, 1986 to be appointed, not applicable until the expiration of the 3–year period beginning on Oct. 27, 1986, or of the 1–year period beginning on the date the Attorney General certifies under section 303 of Pub.L. 99–554 the region specified in a paragraph of such section 581(a) that includes, such district, whichever occurs first, see section 302(e)(1), (2) of Pub.L. 99–554, set out as a note under section 581 of Title 28.

CROSS REFERENCES

Appointment of trustee in—

Cases under this chapter, see 11 USCA § 1104.

Chapter thirteen cases, see 11 USCA § 1302.

Chapter twelve cases, see 11 USCA § 1202.

Collective bargaining agreement, manner of assumption or rejection by trustee other than a trustee in a case covered by this subchapter, see 11 USCA § 1113.

Election of trustee in Chapter seven cases, see 11 USCA § 702.

Guarantees of certificates, see 45 USCA § 662.

Qualification of trustee, see 11 USCA § 322.

Time for bringing action, see 11 USCA § 546.

§ 1164. Right to be heard

The Board, the Department of Transportation, and any State or local commission having regulatory jurisdiction over the debtor may raise and may appear and be heard on any issue in a case under this chapter, but may not appeal from any judgment, order, or decree entered in the case.

(Pub.L. 95–598, Nov. 6, 1978, 92 Stat. 2641; Pub.L. 104–88, Title III, § 302(2), Dec. 29, 1995, 109 Stat. 943.)

HISTORICAL AND STATUTORY NOTES

Revision Notes and Legislative Reports

1978 Acts. [Section 1163] This section [now section 1164] gives the same right to raise, and appear and be heard on, any issue in a railroad reorganization case to the Interstate Commerce Commission, the Department of Transportation, and any State or local commission having regulatory jurisdiction over the debtor as is given to the SEC [Securities and Exchange Commission] and indenture trustees under section 1109 in ordinary reorganization cases. The right of appeal is denied the ICC [Interstate Commerce Commission], the Department of Transportation, and State and local regulatory agencies, the same as it is denied the SEC. House Report No. 95–595.

1995 Acts. House Report No. 104–311 and House Conference Report No. 104–422, see 1995 U.S. Code Cong. and Adm. News, p. 793.

Legislative Statements

Section 1164 of the Senate amendment is deleted as a matter to be left to the Rules of Bankruptcy Procedure. It is anticipated that the rules will require a petition in a railroad reorganization to be filed with the Interstate Commerce Commission and the Secretary of Transportation in a case concerning an interstate railroad.

Section 1164 of the House amendment is derived from section 1163 of the House bill. The section makes clear that the Interstate Commerce Commission, the Department of Transportation, and any State or local commission having regulatory jurisdiction over the debtor may raise and appear and be heard on any issue in a case under subchapter IV of chapter 11, but may not appeal from any judgment, order, or decree in the case. As under section 1109 of title 11, such intervening parties are not parties in interest.

Effective and Applicability Provisions

1995 Acts. Amendment by Pub.L. 104–88 effective Jan. 1, 1996, see section 2 of Pub.L. 104–88, set out as a note under section 701 of Title 49, Transportation.

CROSS REFERENCES

Right of Commodity Futures Trading Commission to be heard, see 11 USCA § 762.

Right of Securities and Exchange Commission and party in interest to be heard in case under this chapter, see 11 USCA § 1109.

§ 1165. Protection of the public interest

In applying sections 1166, 1167, 1169, 1170, 1171, 1172, 1173, and 1174 of this title, the court and the trustee shall consider the public interest in addition to the interests of the debtor, creditors, and equity security holders.

(Pub.L. 95–598, Nov. 6, 1978, 92 Stat. 2641.)

HISTORICAL AND STATUTORY NOTES

Revision Notes and Legislative Reports

1978 Acts. Section 1165 requires the court, in consideration of the relief to be granted upon the filing of an involuntary petition, to take into account the "public interest" in the preservation of the debtor's rail service. This is an important factor in railroad reorganization, which distinguishes them from other business reorganizations. Hence, this section modifies the provisions in sections 303 and 305 that govern generally when the business of a debtor may continue to operate, when relief under the Act sought should be granted, and when the petition should be dismissed.

Section 1167 [now section 1165] imposes on the trustee the obligations, in addition to his other duties and responsibilities, to take into account the "public interest" in the preservation of the debtor's rail service. Senate Report No. 95–989.

Legislative Statements

Section 1165 of the House amendment represents a modification of sections 1165 and 1167 of the Senate amendment requiring the court and the trustee to consider the broad, general public interest in addition to the interests of the debtor, creditors, and equity security holders in applying specific sections of the subchapter.

Savings Provisions

Section to apply to cases pending under section 77 of the Bankruptcy Act [section 205 of former Title 11] on Nov. 6, 1978, in which the trustee had not filed a plan of reorganization, see section 403(b) of Pub. L. 95–598, set out as a note preceding section 101 of this title.

§ 1166. Effect of subtitle IV of title 49 and of Federal, State, or local regulations

Except with respect to abandonment under section 1170 of this title, or merger, modification of the financial structure of the debtor, or issuance or sale of securities under a plan, the trustee and the debtor are subject to the provisions of subtitle IV of title 49 that are applicable to railroads, and the trustee is subject to orders of any Federal, State, or local regulatory body to the same extent as the debtor would be if a petition commencing the case under this chapter had not been filed, but—

(1) any such order that would require the expenditure, or the incurring of an obligation for the expenditure, of money from the estate is not effective unless approved by the court; and

(2) the provisions of this chapter are subject to section 601(b) of the Regional Rail Reorganization Act of 1973.

(Pub.L. 95–598, Nov. 6, 1978, 92 Stat. 2642; Pub.L. 97–449, § 5(a)(2), Jan. 12, 1983, 96 Stat. 2442; Pub.L. 98–353, Title III, § 518, July 10, 1984, 98 Stat. 388; Pub.L. 103–394, Title V, § 501(d)(34), Oct. 22, 1994, 108 Stat. 4146.)

HISTORICAL AND STATUTORY NOTES

Revision Notes and Legislative Reports

1978 Acts. Section 1168 [now this section] makes the trustee subject to the Interstate Commerce Act [section 10101 et seq. of Title 49, Transportation] and to lawful orders of the Interstate Commerce Commission, the U.S. Department of Transportation, and State and regulatory bodies. The approval of the court is required, however, if the order requires the expenditure of money or the incurring of an expenditure other than the payment of certain interline accounts. The limitation of "lawful orders" of State commissions to those involving "safety, location of tracks, and terminal facilities," which is contained in present section 77(c)(2) [section 205(c)(2) of former Title 11], is eliminated.

Subsection (1) further provides that the debtor must pay in cash all amounts owed other carriers for current balances owed for interline freight, passenger and per diem, including incentive per diem, for periods both prior and subsequent to the filing of the petition, without the necessity of court approval.

Subsection (2) makes the provisions of the chapter subject to section 601(b) of the Regional Rail Reorganization Act [section 791(b) of Title 45, Railroads], which excludes the Interstate Commerce Commission from any participation in the reorganization of certain northeast railroads that have transferred their rail properties to Consolidated Rail Corporation (Conrail). Senate Report No. 95–989.

Section 1164 [now 1166] makes the debtor railroad subject to the provisions of the Interstate Commerce Act [section 10101 et seq. of Title 49, Transportation] that are applicable to railroads, and the trustee subject to the orders of the Interstate Commerce Commission to the same extent as the debtor would have been if the case had not been commenced. There are several exceptions. The section does not apply with respect to abandonment of rail lines, which is provided for under section 1169, or with respect to merger under a plan, modification of the financial structure of the debtor by reason of the plan, or the issuance or sale of securities under a plan. Further, the orders of the ICC [Interstate Commerce Commission] are not effective if the order would require the expenditure or the incurring of an obligation for the expenditure of money from the estate, unless approved by the court, and the provisions of this chapter are subject to section 601(b) of the Regional Rail Reorganization Act of 1973 [section 791(b) of Title 45, Railroads].

[Section 1165 (now section 1166)] The same rules apply with respect to Federal, State, or local regulations. The trustee is subject to the orders of a Federal, State, or local regulatory body to the same extent as the debtor would be if the case had not been commenced. However, any order that would require the expenditure, or the incurring of an obligation for the expenditure, of money is not effective under [until] approved by the court. House Report No. 95–595.

1983 Acts. Detailed Explanation prepared by the Office of the Law Revision Counsel, see 1982 U.S.Code Cong. and Adm.News, p. 4220.

1984 Acts. Statements by Legislative Leaders, see 1984 U.S.Code Cong. and Adm.News, p. 576.

1994 Acts. House Report No. 103–835, see 1994 U.S. Code Cong. and Adm. News, p. 3340.

Legislative Statements

Section 1166 of the House amendment is derived from sections 1164 and 1165 of the House bill. An alternative proposal contained in section 1168(1) of the Senate bill is rejected as violative of the principle or [sic] equal treatment of all creditors under title 11.

References in Text

Section 601(b) of Regional Rail Reorganization Act of 1973, referred to in par. (2), is section 601(b) of Pub.L. 93–236, Title VI, Jan. 2, 1974, 87 Stat. 1021, which is classified to section 791(b) of Title 45, Railroads.

Codifications

Pub.L. 98–353, Title III, § 518, July 10, 1984, 98 Stat. 388, substituted "subtitle IV of title 49" for "the Interstate Commerce Act (49 U.S.C. 1 et seq.)", which amendment was previously made by Pub.L. 97–449, thereby requiring no further change in text.

Effective and Applicability Provisions

1994 Acts. Amendment by Pub.L. 103–394 effective on Oct. 22, 1994, and not to apply with respect to cases commenced under Title 11 of the United States Code before Oct. 22, 1994, see section 702 of Pub.L. 103–394, set out as a note under section 101 of this title.

1984 Acts. Amendment by Pub.L. 98–353 effective with respect to cases filed 90 days after July 10, 1984, see section 552(a), formerly 553(a), of Pub.L. 98–353, set out as a note under section 101 of this title.

Separability of Provisions

If any provision of or amendment made by Pub.L. 103–394 or the application of such provision or amendment to any person or circumstance is held to be unconstitutional, the remaining provisions of and amendments made by Pub.L. 103–394 and the application of such provisions and amendments to any person or circumstance shall not be affected thereby, see section 701 of Pub.L. 103–394, set out as a note under section 101 of this title.

CROSS REFERENCES

Management and operation of property according to state law, see 28 USCA § 959.

§ 1167. Collective bargaining agreements

Notwithstanding section 365 of this title, neither the court nor the trustee may change the wages or working conditions of employees of the debtor established by a collective bargaining agreement that is subject to the Railway Labor Act except in accordance with section 6 of such Act.

(Pub.L. 95–598, Nov. 6, 1978, 92 Stat. 2642; Pub.L. 103–394, Title V, § 501(d)(35), Oct. 22, 1994, 108 Stat. 4146.)

HISTORICAL AND STATUTORY NOTES

Revision Notes and Legislative Reports

1978 Acts. Section 1176 [now this section] is derived from present section 77(n) [section 205(n) of former Title 11]. It provides that notwithstanding the general section governing the rejection of executory contracts (section 365), neither the court nor the trustee may change the wages or working conditions of employees of the debtor established by a collective bargaining agreement that is subject to the Railway Labor Act [section 151 et seq. of Title 45, Railroads], except in accordance with section 6 of that Act [section 156 of Title 45]. As reported by the subcommittee this section provided that wages and salaries of rail employees could not be affected by the trustee, but that work rules could be rejected by the trustee. The reorganization court was given the authority to review the trustee's decisions and to settle any disputes arising from the rejection. This provision was withdrawn by the full committee, and hearings will be conducted next year by the Human Resources Committee in the area of rail labor contracts and the trustee's ability to reject them in a bankruptcy situation. Senate Report No. 95–989.

Section 1167 is derived from present section 77(n) [section 205(n) of former title 11]. It provides that notwithstanding the general section governing the rejection of executory contracts (section 365), neither the court nor the trustee may change the wages or working conditions of employees of the debtor established by a collective bargaining agreement that is subject to the Railway Labor Act [section 151 et seq. of Title 45, Railroads], except in accordance with section 6 of that Act [section 156 of Title 45]. The subject of railway labor is too delicate and has too long a history for this code to upset established relationships. The balance has been struck over the years. This provision continues that balance unchanged. House Report No. 95–595.

1994 Acts. House Report No. 103–835, see 1994 U.S. Code Cong. and Adm. News, p. 3340.

References in Text

The Railway Labor Act, referred to in text, is Act May 20, 1926, c. 347, 44 Stat. 577, as amended, which is classified principally to chapter 8 (section 151 et seq.) of Title 45, Railroads. Section 6 of such Act is classified to section 156 of Title 15. For complete classification of this Act to the Code, see section 151 of Title 45 and Tables.

Effective and Applicability Provisions

1994 Acts. Amendment by Pub.L. 103–394 effective on Oct. 22, 1994, and not to apply with respect to cases commenced under Title 11 of the United States Code before Oct. 22, 1994, see section 702 of Pub.L. 103–394, set out as a note under section 101 of this title.

Savings Provisions

Section to apply to cases pending under section 77 of the Bankruptcy Act [section 205 of former Title 11] on Nov. 6, 1978, in which the trustee had not filed a plan of reorganization, see section 403(b) of Pub. L. 95–598, set out as a note preceding section 101 of this title.

Separability of Provisions

If any provision of or amendment made by Pub.L. 103–394 or the application of such provision or amendment to any person or circumstance is held to be unconstitutional, the remaining provisions of and amendments made by Pub.L. 103–394 and the application of such provisions and amendments to any person or circumstance shall not be affected thereby, see section 701 of Pub.L. 103–394, set out as a note under section 101 of this title.

CROSS REFERENCES

Authorization of trustee to operate business, see 11 USCA § 1108.

§ 1168. Rolling stock equipment

(a)(1) The right of a secured party with a security interest in or of a lessor or conditional vendor of equipment described in paragraph (2) to take possession of such equipment in compliance with an equipment security agreement, lease, or conditional sale contract, and to enforce any of its other rights or remedies under such security agreement, lease, or conditional sale contract, to sell, lease, or otherwise retain or dispose of such equipment, is not limited or otherwise affected by any other provision of this title or by any power of the court, except that right to take possession and enforce those other rights and remedies shall be subject to section 362, if—

(A) before the date that is 60 days after the date of commencement of a case under this chapter, the trustee, subject to the court's approval, agrees to perform all obligations of the debtor under such security agreement, lease, or conditional sale contract; and

(B) any default, other than a default of a kind described in section 365(b)(2), under such security agreement, lease, or conditional sale contract—

(i) that occurs before the date of commencement of the case and is an event of default therewith is cured before the expiration of such 60–day period;

(ii) that occurs or becomes an event of default after the date of commencement of the case and before the expiration of such 60–day period is cured before the later of—

(I) the date that is 30 days after the date of the default or event of the default; or

(II) the expiration of such 60–day period; and

(iii) that occurs on or after the expiration of such 60–day period is cured in accordance with the terms of such security agreement, lease, or conditional sale contract, if cure is permitted under that agreement, lease, or conditional sale contract.

(2) The equipment described in this paragraph—

(A) is rolling stock equipment or accessories used on rolling stock equipment, including superstructures or racks, that is subject to a security interest granted by, leased to, or conditionally sold to a debtor; and

(B) includes all records and documents relating to such equipment that are required, under the terms of the security agreement, lease, or conditional sale contract, that is to be surrendered or returned by the debtor in connection with the surrender or return of such equipment.

(3) Paragraph (1) applies to a secured party, lessor, or conditional vendor acting in its own behalf or acting as trustee or otherwise in behalf of another party.

(b) The trustee and the secured party, lessor, or conditional vendor whose right to take possession is protected under subsection (a) may agree, subject to the court's approval, to extend the 60–day period specified in subsection (a)(1).

(c)(1) In any case under this chapter, the trustee shall immediately surrender and return to a secured party, lessor, or conditional vendor, described in subsection (a)(1), equipment described in subsection (a)(2), if at any time after the date of commencement of the case under this chapter such secured party, lessor, or conditional vendor is entitled pursuant to subsection (a)(1) to take possession of such equipment and makes a written demand for such possession of the trustee.

(2) At such time as the trustee is required under paragraph (1) to surrender and return equipment described in subsection (a)(2), any lease of such equipment, and any security agreement or conditional sale contract relating to such equipment, if such security agreement or conditional sale contract is an executory contract, shall be deemed rejected.

(d) With respect to equipment first placed in service on or prior to October 22, 1994, for purposes of this section—

(1) the term "lease" includes any written agreement with respect to which the lessor and the debtor, as lessee, have expressed in the agreement or in a substantially contemporaneous writing that the agreement is to be treated as a lease for Federal income tax purposes; and

(2) the term "security interest" means a purchase- money equipment security interest.

(e) With respect to equipment first placed in service after October 22, 1994, for purposes of this section, the term "rolling stock equipment" includes rolling stock equipment that is substantially rebuilt and accessories used on such equipment.

(Pub.L. 95–598, Nov. 6, 1978, 92 Stat. 2642; Pub.L. 98–353, Title III, § 519, July 10, 1984, 98 Stat. 388; Pub.L. 103–394, Title II, § 201(b), Oct. 22, 1994, 108 Stat. 4120; Pub.L. 106–181, Title VII, § 744(a), Apr. 5, 2000, 114 Stat. 175.)

HISTORICAL AND STATUTORY NOTES

Revision Notes and Legislative Reports

1978 Acts. Section 1175 [now this section] continues the protection accorded in present section 77(j) [section 205(j) of former Title 11] to the rights of holders of purchase-money equipment security, and of lessors or conditional vendors of railroad rolling stock, but accords to the trustee a limited period within which to assume the debtor's obligation and to cure any defaults. The rights of such lenders are not affected by the automatic stay and related provisions of sections 362 and 363, or by any power of the court, unless (1) within 60 days after the commencement of the case (or such longer period as may be agreed to by the secured party, lessor or conditional vendor) the trustees, with the approval of the court, agrees [sic] to perform all of the debtor's obligations under the security agreement, lease or conditional sale contract, and (2) all defaults are cured within the 60-day period. Defaults described in section 365(b)(2)—defaults which are breaches of provisions relating to the insolvency or financial condition of the debtor, or the commencement of a case under this title, or the appointment of a trustee—are for obvious reasons, excepted. Senate Report No. 95–989.

[Section 1166] This section, [now section 1168] derived with changes from the last sentence of present section 77(j) [section 205(j) of former Title 11], protects the interests of rolling stock equipment financers, while providing the trustee with some opportunity to cure defaults, agree to make payments, and retain and use the equipment. The provision is parallel to section 1110, concerning aircraft equipment and vessels. House Report No. 95–595.

1984 Acts. Statements by Legislative Leaders, see 1984 U.S.Code Cong. and Adm.News, p. 576.

1994 Acts. House Report No. 103–835, see 1994 U.S. Code Cong. and Adm. News, p. 3340.

2000 Acts. House Conference Report No. 106–513 and Statement by President, see 2000 U.S. Code Cong. and Adm. News, p. 80.

Legislative Statements

Section 1168 of the House amendment incorporates a provision contained in section 1166 of the House bill instead of the provision contained in section 1175 of the Senate amendment for the reasons stated in connection with the discussion of section 1110 of the House amendment.

Effective and Applicability Provisions

2000 Acts. Amendment by Pub.L. 106–181 applicable only to fiscal years beginning after September 30, 1999, see section 3 of Pub.L. 106–181, set out as a note under section 106 of this title.

1994 Acts. Amendment by Pub.L. 103–394 effective on Oct. 22, 1994, and not to apply with respect to cases commenced under Title 11 of the United States Code before Oct. 22, 1994, see section 702 of Pub.L. 103–394, set out as a note under section 101 of this title.

1984 Acts. Amendment by Pub.L. 98–353 effective with respect to cases filed 90 days after July 10, 1984, see section 552(a), formerly 553(a), of Pub.L. 98–353, set out as a note under section 101 of this title.

Savings Provisions

Section to apply to cases pending under section 77 of the Bankruptcy Act [section 205 of former Title 11] on Nov. 6, 1978, in which the trustee had not filed a plan of reorganization, see section 403(b) of Pub. L. 95–598, set out as a note preceding section 101 of this title.

Separability of Provisions

If any provision of or amendment made by Pub.L. 103–394 or the application of such provision or amendment to any person or circumstance is held to be unconstitutional, the remaining provisions of and amendments made by Pub.L. 103–394 and the application of such provisions and amendments to any person or circumstance shall not be affected thereby, see section 701 of Pub.L. 103–394, set out as a note under section 101 of this title.

CROSS REFERENCES

Rights of certain secured parties in aircraft equipment and vessels, see 11 USCA § 1110.

§ 1169. Effect of rejection of lease of railroad line

(a) Except as provided in subsection (b) of this section, if a lease of a line of railroad under which the debtor is the lessee is rejected under section 365 of this title, and if the trustee, within such time as the court fixes, and with the court's approval, elects not to operate the leased line, the lessor under such lease, after such approval, shall operate the line.

(b) If operation of such line by such lessor is impracticable or contrary to the public interest, the court, on request of such lessor, and after notice and a hearing, shall order the trustee to continue operation of such line for the account of such lessor until abandonment is ordered under section 1170 of this title, or until such operation is otherwise lawfully terminated, whichever occurs first.

(c) During any such operation, such lessor is deemed a carrier subject to the provisions of subtitle IV of title 49 that are applicable to railroads.

(Pub.L. 95–598, Nov. 6, 1978, 92 Stat. 2643; Pub.L. 97–449, § 5(a)(3), Jan. 12, 1983, 96 Stat. 2442; Pub.L. 98–353, Title III, § 520, July 10, 1984, 98 Stat. 388.)

HISTORICAL AND STATUTORY NOTES

Revision Notes and Legislative Reports

1978 Acts. Section 1177 [now this section] continues, essentially without change, the provisions relating to the rejection by the trustee of a lease of a line of railroad now contained in section 77(c)(6) [section 205(c)(6) of former Title 11]. Subsection (a) requires the lessor of a line of railroad to operate it if the lease is rejected by the trustee and the trustee, with the approval of the court, elects not to operate the leased line. Subsection (b), however, further provides that if operation by the lessor is impractical or contrary to the public interest, the court shall require the trustee to operate the line for the account of the lessor until the operation is lawfully terminated. Subsection (c) provides that during such operation, the lessor is a carrier subject to the Interstate Commerce Act [section 10101 et seq. of Title 49, Transportation]. Senate Report No. 95–989.

[Section 1168] This section [now section 1169] governs the effect of the rejection by the trustee of an unexpired lease of railroad line under which the debtor is the lessee. If the trustee rejects such a lease, and if the trustee, within such time as the court allows, and with the approval of the court, elects not to operate the leased line, then the lessor under the lease must operate the line.

Subsection (b) excuses the lessor from the requirement to operate the line under certain circumstances. If operation of the line by the lessor is impracticable or contrary to the public interest, the court, on request of the lessor, must order the trustee to continue operation of the line for the account of the lessor until abandonment is ordered under section 1169, governing abandonments generally, or until the operation is otherwise lawfully terminated, such as by an order of the ICC.

Subsection (c) deems the lessor a carrier subject to the provisions of the Interstate Commerce Act [section 10101 et seq. of Title 49, Transportation] during the operation of the line before abandonment. House Report No. 95–595.

1983 Acts. Detailed Explanation prepared by the Office of the Law Revision Counsel, see 1982 U.S.Code Cong. and Adm.News, p. 4220.

1984 Acts. Statements by Legislative Leaders, see 1984 U.S.Code Cong. and Adm.News, p. 576.

Legislative Statements

Section 1169 of the Senate amendment is deleted from the House amendment as unnecessary since 28 U.S.C. 1407 [section 1407 of Title 28, Judiciary and Judicial Procedure] treating with the judicial panel on multi-district litigation will apply by its terms to cases under title 11.

Codifications

Pub.L. 98–353, Title III, § 520, July 10, 1984, 98 Stat. 388, substituted "subtitle IV of title 49" for "the Interstate Commerce Act (49 U.S.C. 1 et seq.)", which amendment was previously made by Pub.L. 97–449, thereby requiring no further change in text.

Effective and Applicability Provisions

1984 Acts. Amendment by Pub.L. 98–353 effective with respect to cases filed 90 days after July 10, 1984, see section 552(a), formerly 553(a), of Pub.L. 98–353, set out as a note under section 101 of this title.

Savings Provisions

Section to apply to cases pending under section 77 of the Bankruptcy Act [section 205 of former Title 11] on Nov. 6, 1978, in which the trustee had not filed a plan of reorganization, see section 403(b) of Pub. L. 95–598, set out as a note preceding section 101 of this title.

CROSS REFERENCES

Executory contracts in stockbroker liquidation cases, see 11 USCA § 744.

§ 1170. Abandonment of railroad line

(a) The court, after notice and a hearing, may authorize the abandonment of all or a portion of a railroad line if such abandonment is—

(1)(A) in the best interest of the estate; or

(B) essential to the formulation of a plan; and

(2) consistent with the public interest.

(b) If, except for the pendency of the case under this chapter, such abandonment would require approval by the Board under a law of the United States, the trustee shall initiate an appropriate application for such abandonment with the Board. The court may fix a time within which the Board shall report to the court on such application.

(c) After the court receives the report of the Board, or the expiration of the time fixed under subsection (b) of this section, whichever occurs first, the court may authorize such abandonment, after notice to the Board, the Secretary of Transportation, the trustee, any party in interest that has requested notice, any affected shipper or community, and any other entity prescribed by the court, and a hearing.

(d)(1) Enforcement of an order authorizing such abandonment shall be stayed until the time for taking an appeal has expired, or, if an appeal is timely taken, until such order has become final.

(2) If an order authorizing such abandonment is appealed, the court, on request of a party in interest, may authorize suspension of service on a line or a portion of a line pending the determination of such appeal, after notice to the Board, the Secretary of Transportation, the trustee, any party in interest that has requested notice, any affected shipper or community, and any other entity prescribed by the court, and a hearing. An appellant may not obtain a stay of the enforcement of an order authorizing such suspension by the giving of a supersedeas bond or otherwise, during the pendency of such appeal.

(e)(1) In authorizing any abandonment of a railroad line under this section, the court shall require the rail carrier to provide a fair arrangement at least as protective of the interests of employees as that established under section 11326(a) of title 49.

(2) Nothing in this subsection shall be deemed to affect the priorities or timing of payment of employee protection which might have existed in the absence of this subsection.

(Pub.L. 95–598, Nov. 6, 1978, 92 Stat. 2643; Pub.L. 96–448, Title II, § 227(a), Oct. 14, 1980, 94 Stat. 1931; Pub.L. 98–353, Title III, § 521, July 10, 1984, 98 Stat. 388; Pub.L. 104–88, Title III, § 302(2), Dec. 29, 1995, 109 Stat. 943; Pub.L. 109–8, Title XII, § 1217, Apr. 20, 2005, 119 Stat. 195.)

HISTORICAL AND STATUTORY NOTES

Revision Notes and Legislative Reports

1978 Acts. Subsection (a) of section 1178 [now this section] permits the court to authorize the abandonment of a railroad line if the abandonment is consistent with the public interest and either in the best interest of the estate or essential to the formulation of a plan. This avoids the normal abandonment requirements of generally applicable railroad regulatory law.

Subsection (b) permits some participation by the Interstate Commerce Commission in the abandonment process. The Commission's role, however, is only advisory. The Commission will represent the public interest, while the trustee and various creditors and equity security holders will represent the interests of those who have invested money in the enterprise. The court will balance the various interests and make an appropriate decision. The subsection specifies that if, except for the pendency of the railroad reorganization case, the proposed abandonment would require Commission approval, then the trustee, with the approval of the court, must initiate an application for the abandonment with the Commission. The court may then fix a time within which the Commission must report to the court on the application.

Subsection (c) permits the court to act after it has received the report of the Commission or the time fixed under subsection (b) has expired, whichever occurs first. The court may then authorize the abandonment after notice and a hearing. The notice must go to the Commission, the Secretary of Transportation, the trustee, and party in interest that has requested notice, any affected shipper or community, and any other entity that the court specifies.

Subsection (d) stays the enforcement of an abandonment until the time for taking an appeal has expired, or if an appeal has been taken, until the order has become final. However, the court may, and after notice and a hearing, on request of a party in interest authorize termination of service on the line or a portion of the line pending the determination of the appeal. The notice required is the same as that required under subsection (c). If the court authorizes termination of service pending determination of the appeal, an appellant may not obtain a stay of the enforcement of the order authorizing termination, either by the giving of a supersedeas bond or otherwise, during the pendency of the appeal. Senate Report No. 95–989.

1980 Acts. House Report No. 96–1035 and House Conference Report No. 96–1430, see 1980 U.S.Code Cong. and Adm.News, p. 3978.

1984 Acts. Statements by Legislative Leaders, see 1984 U.S.Code Cong. and Adm.News, p. 576.

1995 Acts. House Report No. 104–311 and House Conference Report No. 104–422, see 1995 U.S. Code Cong. and Adm. News, p. 793.

2005 Acts. House Report No. 109–31(Part I), see 2005 U.S. Code Cong. and Adm. News, p. 88.

Effective and Applicability Provisions

2005 Acts. Amendments by Pub.L. 109–8 effective, except as otherwise provided, 180 days after April 20, 2005, and inapplicable with respect to cases commenced under Title 11 before the effective date, see Pub.L. 109–8, § 1501, set out as a note under 11 U.S.C.A. § 101.

1995 Acts. Amendment by Pub.L. 104–88 effective Jan. 1, 1996, see section 2 of Pub.L. 104–88, set out as a note under section 701 of Title 49, Transportation.

1984 Acts. Amendment by Pub.L. 98–353 effective with respect to cases filed 90 days after July 10, 1984, see section 552(a), formerly 553(a), of Pub.L. 98–353, set out as a note under section 101 of this title.

1980 Acts. Section 710 of Pub.L. 96–448 provided that:

"**(a)** Except as provided in subsections (b), (c), and (d) of this section, the provisions of this Act and the amendments made by this Act shall take effect on October 1, 1980.

"**(b)** Section 206 of this Act [enacting former section 10712 of Title 49, Transportation], shall take effect on January 1, 1981.

"**(c)** Section 218(b) of this Act [amending former section 10705 of Title 49] shall take effect on October 1, 1983.

"**(d)** Section 701 of this Act [enacting section 1018 of Title 45, Railroads and amending sections 231, 825, 906, 913, 914, 1002, 1005, 1007, and 1008 of Title 45] shall take effect on the date of enactment of this Act [Oct. 14, 1980]."

CROSS REFERENCES

Abandonment of lines of Milwaukee Railroad in cases pending under § 77 of Bankruptcy Act on November 4, 1979, see 45 USCA § 915.

Abandonment of lines of Milwaukee Railroad under this section, see 45 USCA § 904.

Abandonment of property of estate, see 11 USCA § 554.

§ 1171. Priority claims

(a) There shall be paid as an administrative expense any claim of an individual or of the personal representative of a deceased individual against the debtor or the estate, for personal injury to or death of such individual arising out of the operation of the debtor or the estate, whether such claim arose before or after the commencement of the case.

(b) Any unsecured claim against the debtor that would have been entitled to priority if a receiver in equity of the property of the debtor had been appointed by a Federal court on the date of the order for relief under this title shall be entitled to the same priority in the case under this chapter.

(Pub.L. 95–598, Nov. 6, 1978, 92 Stat. 2643; Pub.L. 98–353, Title III, § 522, July 10, 1984, 98 Stat. 388.)

HISTORICAL AND STATUTORY NOTES

Revision Notes and Legislative Reports

1978 Acts. [Section 1170] This section [now section 1171] is derived from current law. Subsection (a) grants an administrative expense priority to the claim of any individual (or of the personal representative of a deceased individual) against the debtor or the estate for personal injury to or death of the individual arising out of the operation of the debtor railroad or the estate, whether the claim arose before or after commencement of the case. The priority under current law, found in section 77(n) [section 205(n) of former Title 11], applies only to employees of the debtor. This subsection expands the protection provided.

Subsection (b) follows present section 77(b) of the Bankruptcy Act [section 205(b) of former Title] by giving priority to any unsecured claims that would be entitled to priority if a receiver in equity of the property of the debtor had been appointed by a Federal court on the date of the order for relief under the bankruptcy laws. As under current law, the courts will determine the precise contours of the priority recognized by this subsection in each case. House Report No. 95–595.

1984 Acts. Statements by Legislative Leaders, see 1984 U.S.Code Cong. and Adm.News, p. 576.

Legislative Statements

Section 1171 of the House amendment is derived from section 1170 of the House bill in lieu of section 1173(a)(9) of the Senate amendment.

Effective and Applicability Provisions

1984 Acts. Amendment by Pub.L. 98–353 effective with respect to cases filed 90 days after July 10, 1984, see section 552(a), formerly 553(a), of Pub.L. 98–353, set out as a note under section 101 of this title.

Savings Provisions

Section to apply to cases pending under section 77 of the Bankruptcy Act [section 205 of former Title 11] on Nov. 6, 1978, in which the trustee had not filed a plan of reorganization, see section 403(b) of Pub. L. 95–598, set out as a note preceding section 101 of this title.

CROSS REFERENCES

Allowance of administrative expenses, see 11 USCA § 503.

Priorities, see 11 USCA § 507.

§ 1172. Contents of plan

(a) In addition to the provisions required or permitted under section 1123 of this title, a plan—

(1) shall specify the extent to and the means by which the debtor's rail service is proposed to be continued, and the extent to which any of the debtor's rail service is proposed to be terminated; and

(2) may include a provision for—

(A) the transfer of any or all of the operating railroad lines of the debtor to another operating railroad; or

(B) abandonment of any railroad line in accordance with section 1170 of this title.

(b) If, except for the pendency of the case under this chapter, transfer of, or operation of or over, any of the debtor's rail lines by an entity other than the debtor or a successor to the debtor under the plan would require approval by the Board under a law of the United States, then a plan may not propose such a transfer or such operation unless the proponent of the plan initiates an appropriate application for such a transfer or such operation with the Board and, within such time as the court may fix, not exceeding 180 days, the Board, with or without a hearing, as the Board may determine, and with or without modification or condition, approves such application, or does not act on such application. Any action or order of the Board approving, modifying, conditioning, or disapproving such application is subject to review by the court only under sections 706(2)(A), 706(2)(B), 706(2)(C), and 706(2)(D) of title 5.

(c)(1) In approving an application under subsection (b) of this section, the Board shall require the rail carrier to provide a fair arrangement at least as protective of the interests of employees as that established under section 11326(a) of title 49.

(2) Nothing in this subsection shall be deemed to affect the priorities or timing of payment of employee protection which might have existed in the absence of this subsection.

(Pub.L. 95–598, Nov. 6, 1978, 92 Stat. 2644; Pub.L. 96–448, Title II, § 227(b), Oct. 14, 1980, 94 Stat. 1931; Pub.L. 104–88, Title III, § 302(2), Dec. 29, 1995, 109 Stat. 943; Pub.L. 109–8, Title XII, § 1218, Apr. 20, 2005, 119 Stat. 195.)

HISTORICAL AND STATUTORY NOTES

Revision Notes and Legislative Reports

1978 Acts. Section 1170 [now this section] adds to the general provisions required or permitted in reorganization plans by section 1123. Subsection (1) requires that a reorganization plan under the railroad subchapter specify the means by which the value of the claims of creditors and the interests of equity holders which are materially and adversely affected by the plan are to be realized. Subsection (2) permits a plan to include provisions for the issuance of warrants. Subsection (3) requires that the plan provide for fixed charges by probable earnings for their payment. Subsection (4) requires that the plan specify the means by which, and the extent to which, the debtor's rail service is to be continued, and shall identify any rail service to be terminated. Subsection (5) permits other appropriate provisions not inconsistent with the chapter. With the exception of subsection (4), the requirements are comparable to those of present section 77(b) [section 205(b) of former Title 11]; subsection (4) emphasizes the public interest in the preservation of rail transportation.

Section 1171 imposes on the court, rather than the Interstate Commerce Commission, as in present section 77 [section 205 of former title 11], the responsibility for the plan of reorganization. The Commission is empowered to make final decisions subject only to review by the court under the standards of the Administrative Procedure Act [sections 551 et seq. and 701 et seq. of Title 5, Government Organization and Employees] as to any part of the plan which deals with transportation matters, such as the grant of operating rights of or over, or transfer of, the debtor's rail lines to other carriers.

Subsection (a) requires the trustee to file a plan of reorganization within 18 months after the petition is filed, and permits the court, for good cause shown, to extend such time limit. Subsection (b) permits a plan to be proposed by any interested person, and permits the trustee to revise his plan at any time before it is approved by the court.

Subsections (c), (d) and (e) require the court, when a plan is submitted by the trustee or, if the court deems it worthy of consideration, a plan submitted is proposed by any other person proposes the transfer of, or operation of or over, any of the debtor's lines by other carriers, to refer to such provisions of the plan to the Interstate Commerce Commission. The Commission, within 240 days, and after a hearing if the Commission so determines, is to report to the court the effects of such provisions of the plan in the light of national transportation policy and sections 5(3)(f)(A), (B), and (D), (F)–(I) of the Interstate Commerce Act [section 11350(b)(1), (2), (4), (6)–(9) of Title 49, Transportation]. The report of the Commission is conclusive in all further hearings on the plan by the court, subject only to review pursuant to 5 U.S.C. 706(2)(A)–(D). Senate Report no. 95–989.

[Section 1171 (now section 1172)] A plan in a railroad reorganization case may include provisions in addition to those required and permitted under an ordinary reorganization plan. It may provide for the transfer of any or all of the operating railroad lines of the debtor to another operating railroad.

Paragraph (1) contemplates a liquidating plan for the debtor's rail lines, much as occurred in the Penn Central case by transfer of operating lines to ConRail. Such a liquidating plan is not per se contrary to the public interest, and the court will have to determine on a case-by-case basis, with the guidance of the Interstate Commerce Commission and of other parties in interest, whether the particular plan proposed is in the public interest, as required under proposed 11 U.S.C. 1172(3).

The plan may also provide for abandonment in accordance with section 1169, governing abandonment generally. Neither of these provisions in a plan, transfer or abandonment of lines, requires ICC approval. Confirmation of the plan by the court authorizes the debtor to comply with the plan in accordance with section 1142(a) notwithstanding any bankruptcy law to the contrary. House Report No. 95–595.

1980 Acts. House Report No. 96–1035 and House Conference Report No. 96–1430, see 1980 U.S.Code Cong. and Adm.News, p. 3978.

1995 Acts. House Report No. 104–311 and House Conference Report No. 104–422, see 1995 U.S. Code Cong. and Adm. News, p. 793.

2005 Acts. House Report No. 109–31(Part I), see 2005 U.S. Code Cong. and Adm. News, p. 88.

Legislative Statements

Section 1172 of the House amendment is derived from section 1171 of the House bill in preference to section 1170 of the Senate amendment with the exception that section 1170(4) of the Senate amendment is incorporated into section 1172(a)(1) of the House amendment.

Section 1172(b) of the House amendment is derived from section 1171(c) of the Senate amendment. The section gives the Interstate Commerce Commission the exclusive power to approve or disapprove the transfer of, or operation of or over, any of the debtor's rail lines over which the Commission has jurisdiction, subject to review under the Administrative Procedures Act [sections 551 et seq. and 701 et seq. of Title 5, Government Organization and Employees]. The section does not apply to a transfer of railroad lines to a successor of the debtor under a plan of reorganization by merger or otherwise.

The House amendment deletes section 1171(a) of the Senate amendment as a matter to be determined by the Rules of Bankruptcy Procedure. It is anticipated that the rules will specify the period of time, such as 18 months, within which a trustee must file with the court a proposed plan of reorganization for the debtor or a report why a plan cannot be formulated. Incorporation by reference of section 1121 in section 1161 of title 11 means that a party in interest will also have a right to file a plan of reorganization. This differs from the position taken in the Senate amendment which would have permitted the Interstate Commerce Commission to file a plan of reorganization.

Effective and Applicability Provisions

2005 Acts. Amendments by Pub.L. 109–8 effective, except as otherwise provided, 180 days after April 20, 2005, and inapplicable with respect to cases commenced under Title 11 before the effective date, see Pub.L. 109–8, § 1501, set out as a note under 11 U.S.C.A. § 101.

1995 Acts. Amendment by Pub.L. 104–88 effective Jan. 1, 1996, see section 2 of Pub.L. 104–88, set out as a note under section 701 of Title 49, Transportation.

1980 Acts. Amendment by Pub.L. 96–448 effective Oct. 1, 1980, see section 710(a) of Pub.L. 96–448, set out as a note under section 1170 of Title 11, Bankruptcy.

CROSS REFERENCES

Contents of plan filed in—

Chapter thirteen cases, see 11 USCA § 1322.

Chapter twelve cases, see 11 USCA § 1222.

§ 1173. Confirmation of plan

(a) The court shall confirm a plan if—

(1) the applicable requirements of section 1129 of this title have been met;

(2) each creditor or equity security holder will receive or retain under the plan property of a value, as of the effective date of the plan, that is not less than the value of property that each such creditor or equity security holder would so receive or retain if all of the operating railroad lines of the debtor were sold, and the proceeds of such sale, and the other property of the estate, were distributed under chapter 7 of this title on such date;

(3) in light of the debtor's past earnings and the probable prospective earnings of the reorganized debtor, there will be adequate coverage by such prospective earnings of any fixed charges, such as interest on debt, amortization of funded debt, and rent for leased railroads, provided for by the plan; and

(4) the plan is consistent with the public interest.

(b) If the requirements of subsection (a) of this section are met with respect to more than one plan, the court shall confirm the plan that is most likely to maintain adequate rail service in the public interest.

(Pub.L. 95–598, Nov. 6, 1978, 92 Stat. 2644; Pub.L. 98–353, Title III, § 523, July 10, 1984, 98 Stat. 388.)

HISTORICAL AND STATUTORY NOTES

Revision Notes and Legislative Reports

1978 Acts. Section 1173 adapts the provisions dealing with reorganization plans generally contained in section 1130 to the particular requirements of railroad reorganization plans, as set out in present section 77(e) [section 205(e) of former Title 11]. Subsection (a) specifies the findings which the court must make before approving a plan: (1) The plan complies with the applicable provisions of the chapter; (2) the proponent of the plan complies with the applicable provisions of the chapter; (3) the plan has been proposed in good faith; (4) any payments for services or for costs or expenses in connection with the case or the plan are disclosed to the court and are reasonable, or, if to be paid later, are subject to the approval of the court as reasonable; (5) the proponent of the plan has disclosed the identity and affiliations of the individuals who will serve as directors, officers, or voting trustees, such appointments or continuations in office are consistent with the interests of creditors, equity security holders, and the proponent the public, and has disclosed the identity and compensation of any insider who will be employed or retained under the plan; (6) that rate changes proposed in the plan have been approved by the appropriate regulatory commission, or that the plan is contingent on such approval; (7) that confirmation of the plan is not likely to be followed by further reorganization or liquidation, unless it is contemplated by the plan; (8) that the plan, if there is more than one, is the one most likely to maintain adequate rail service and (9) that the plan provides the priority traditionally accorded by section 77(b) [section 205(b) of former Title 11] to claims by rail creditors for necessary services rendered during the 6 months preceding the filing of the petition in bankruptcy.

Subsection (b) continues the present power of the court in section 77(e) [section 205(e) of former Title 11] to confirm a plan over the objections of creditors or equity security holders who are materially and adversely affected. The subsection also confirms the authority of the court to approve a transfer of all or part of a debtor's property or its merger over the objections of equity security holders if it finds (1) that the "public interest" in continued rail transportation outweighs any adverse effect on creditors and equity security holders, and (2) that the plan is fair and equitable, affords due recognition to the rights of each class, and does not discriminate unfairly against any class.

Subsection (c) permits modification of a plan confirmed by a final order only for fraud. Senate Report No. 95–989.

[Section 1172] This section [now section 1173] requires the court to confirm a plan if the applicable requirements of section 1129 (relating to confirmation of reorganization plans generally) are met, if the best interest test is met, and if the plan is compatible with the public interest.

The test in this paragraph is similar to the test prescribed for ordinary corporate reorganizations. However, since a railroad cannot liquidate its assets and sell them for scrap to satisfy its creditors, the test focuses on the value of the railroad as a going concern. That is, the test is based on what the assets, sold as operating rail lines, would bring.

The public interest requirement, found in current law, will now be decided by the court, with the ICC [Interstate Commerce Commission] representing the public interest before the court, rather than in the first instance by the ICC. Liquidation of the debtor is not, per se, contrary to the public interest. House Report No. 95–595.

1984 Acts. Statements by Legislative Leaders, see 1984 U.S.Code Cong. and Adm.News, p. 576.

Legislative Statements

Section 1173 of the House amendment concerns confirmation of a plan of railroad reorganization and is derived from section 1172 of the House bill as modified. In particular, section 1173(a)(3) of the House amendment is derived from section 1170(3) of the Senate amendment. Section 1173(b) is derived from section 1173(a)(8) of the Senate amendment.

Effective and Applicability Provisions

1984 Acts. Amendment by Pub.L. 98–353 effective with respect to cases filed 90 days after July 10, 1984, see section 552(a), formerly 553(a), of Pub.L. 98–353, set out as a note under section 101 of this title.

CROSS REFERENCES

Confirmation of plan in—

Chapter nine cases, see 11 USCA § 943.

Chapter thirteen cases, see 11 USCA § 1325.

Chapter twelve cases, see 11 USCA § 1225.

Effect of confirmation in cases under this chapter, see 11 USCA § 1141.

Nonrecognition of gain or loss for income tax purposes of exchanges of stock and securities in reorganizations confirmed under this section, see 26 USCA § 354.

Revocation of order of confirmation in cases under this chapter, see 11 USCA § 1144.

Unclaimed property, see 11 USCA § 347.

§ 1174. Liquidation

On request of a party in interest and after notice and a hearing, the court may, or, if a plan has not been confirmed under section 1173 of this title before five years after the date of the order for relief, the court shall, order the trustee to cease the debtor's operation and to collect and reduce to money all of the property of the estate in the same manner as if the case were a case under chapter 7 of this title.

(Pub.L. 95–598, Nov. 6, 1978, 92 Stat. 2644.)

HISTORICAL AND STATUTORY NOTES

Revision Notes and Legislative Reports

1978 Acts. Section 1174 permits the court to convert the case to a liquidation under chapter 7 if the court finds that the debtor cannot be reorganized, or if various time limits specified in the subchapter are not met. Section 77 [section 205 of former Title 11] does not authorize a liquidation of a railroad under the Bankruptcy Act [former Title 11]. If the railroad is not reorganizable, the only action open to the court is to dismiss the petition, which would in all likelihood be followed by a State court receivership, with all of its attendant disadvantages. If reorganization is impossible, the debtor should be liquidated under the Bankruptcy Act. Senate Report No. 95–989.

Legislative Statements

Section 1174 of the House amendment represents a compromise between the House bill and Senate amendment on the issue of liquidation of a railroad. The provision permits a party in interest at any time to request liquidation. In addition, if a plan has not been confirmed under section 1173 of the House amendment before 5 years after the date of order for relief, the court must order the trustee to cease the debtor's operation and to collect and reduce to money all of the property of the estate in the same manner as if the case were a case under chapter 7 of title 11. The approach differs from the conversion to chapter 7 under section 1174 of the Senate bill in order to make special provisions contained in subchapter IV of chapter 11 applicable to liquidation. However, maintaining liquidation in the context of chapter 11 is not intended to delay liquidation of the railroad to a different extent than if the case were converted to chapter 7.

Although the House amendment does not adopt provisions contained in section 1170(1), (2), (3), or (5), of the Senate amendment such provisions are contained explicitly or implicitly in section 1123 of the House amendment.

CROSS REFERENCES

Conversion of—

Chapter eleven cases, see 11 USCA § 1112.

Chapter seven cases, see 11 USCA § 706.

Chapter thirteen cases, see 11 USCA § 1307.

Chapter twelve cases, see 11 USCA § 1208.

Dismissal of—

Chapter nine cases, see 11 USCA § 930.

Chapter seven cases, see 11 USCA § 707.

CHAPTER 12—ADJUSTMENT OF DEBTS OF A FAMILY FARMER OR FISHERMAN WITH REGULAR ANNUAL INCOME

SUBCHAPTER I—OFFICERS, ADMINISTRATION, AND THE ESTATE

SUBCHAPTER II—THE PLAN

HISTORICAL AND STATUTORY NOTES

Effective and Applicability Provisions

2005 Acts. Amendments by Pub.L. 109–8 effective, except as otherwise provided, 180 days after April 20, 2005, and inapplicable with respect to cases commenced under Title 11 before the effective date, see Pub.L. 109–8, § 1501, set out as a note under 11 U.S.C.A. § 101.

Reenactment of Chapter

This chapter as in effect on June 30, 2005, reenacted effective July 1, 2005, see Pub.L. 109–8, § 1001(a), set out as a note under 11 U.S.C.A. § 1201.

Repeal of chapter; extension of provisions

Pub.L. 99–554, Title III, § 302(f), Oct. 27, 1986, 100 Stat. 3124, as amended Pub.L. 103–65, § 1, Aug. 6, 1993, 107 Stat. 311, which provided that, effective Oct. 1, 1998, this chapter is repealed, but that all cases commenced or pending under this chapter, and all matters and proceedings in or relating to such cases, shall be conducted and determined under this chapter as if such chapter had not been repealed, and that the substantive rights of parties in connection with such cases, matters, and proceedings shall continue to be governed under the laws applicable to such cases, matters, and proceedings as if such chapter had not been repealed, was superceded by the reenactment of this chapter by Pub.L. 109–8, Title X, § 1001(a), Apr. 20, 2005, 119 Stat. 185, set out as a note under 11 U.S.C.A. § 1201.

Pub.L. 105–277, Div. C, Title I, § 149, Oct. 21, 1998, 112 Stat. 2681–610, as amended Pub.L. 106–5, §§ 1, 2, Mar. 30, 1999, 113 Stat. 9; Pub.L. 106–70, §§ 1, 2, Oct. 9, 1999, 113 Stat. 1031; Pub.L. 107–8, §§ 1, 2, May 11, 2001, 115 Stat. 10; Pub.L. 107–17, §§ 1, 2, June 26, 2001, 115 Stat. 151; Pub.L. 107–170, §§ 1, 2, May 7, 2002, 116 Stat. 133; Pub.L. 107–171, Title X, § 10814, May 13, 2002, 116 St. 532; Pub.L. 107–377, § 2, Dec. 19, 2002, 116 Stat. 3115; Pub.L. 108–73, § 2(a), Aug. 15, 2003, 117 Stat. 891; Pub.L. 108–369, § 2(a), Oct. 25, 2004, 118 Stat. 1749, provided that, to take effect on January 1, 2004, chapter 12 of Title 11 [this chapter; 11 U.S.C.A. § 1201 et seq.], as in effect on December 31, 2003, is reenacted for the period beginning on January 1, 2004, and ending on July 1, 2005, but that all cases commenced or pending under this chapter 12, as reenacted under section 149(a) of Pub.L. 105–277, and all matters and proceedings in or relating to such cases, shall be conducted and determined under such chapter as if such chapter were continued in effect after July 1, 2005, and that the substantive rights of parties in connection with such cases, matters, and proceedings shall continue to be governed under the law applicable to such cases, matters, and proceedings as if such chapter were continued in effect after July 1, 2005, was superceded by the reenactment of this chapter by Pub.L. 109–8, Title X, § 1001(a), Apr. 20, 2005, 119 Stat. 185, set out as a note under 11 U.S.C.A. § 1201.

SUBCHAPTER I—OFFICERS, ADMINISTRATION, AND THE ESTATE

§ 1201. Stay of action against codebtor

(a) Except as provided in subsections (b) and (c) of this section, after the order for relief under this chapter, a creditor may not act, or commence or continue any civil action, to collect all or any part of a consumer debt of the debtor from any individual that is liable on such debt with the debtor, or that secured such debt, unless—

(1) such individual became liable on or secured such debt in the ordinary course of such individual's business; or

(2) the case is closed, dismissed, or converted to a case under chapter 7 of this title.

(b) A creditor may present a negotiable instrument, and may give notice of dishonor of such an instrument.

(c) On request of a party in interest and after notice and a hearing, the court shall grant relief from the stay provided by subsection (a) of this section with respect to a creditor, to the extent that—

(1) as between the debtor and the individual protected under subsection (a) of this section, such individual received the consideration for the claim held by such creditor;

(2) the plan filed by the debtor proposes not to pay such claim; or

(3) such creditor's interest would be irreparably harmed by continuation of such stay.

(d) Twenty days after the filing of a request under subsection (c)(2) of this section for relief from the stay provided by subsection (a) of this section, such stay is terminated with respect to the party in interest making such request, unless the debtor or any individual that is liable on such debt with the debtor files and serves upon such party in interest a written objection to the taking of the proposed action.

(Added and amended Pub.L. 99–554, Title II, § 255, Title III, § 302(f), Oct. 27, 1986, 100 Stat. 3105, 3124; Pub.L. 103–65, § 1, Aug. 6, 1993, 107 Stat. 311; Pub.L. 105–277, Div. C, Title I, § 149(a), Oct. 21, 1998, 112 Stat. 2681–610; Pub.L. 106–5, § 1(1),(2), Mar. 30, 1999, 113 Stat. 9; Pub.L. 106–70, § 1, Oct. 9, 1999, 113 Stat. 1031; Pub.L. 107–8, § 1, May 11, 2001, 115 Stat. 10; Pub.L. 107–17, § 1, June 26, 2001, 115 Stat. 151; Pub.L. 107–170, § 1, May 7, 2002, 116 Stat. 133; Pub.L. 107–171, Title X, § 10814(a), May 13, 2002, 116 Stat. 532; Pub.L. 107–377, § 2(a), Dec. 19, 2002, 116 Stat. 3115; Pub.L. 108–73, § 2(a), Aug. 15, 2003, 117 Stat. 891; Pub.L. 108–369, § 2(a), Oct. 25, 2004, 118 Stat. 1749; Pub.L. 109–8, Title X, § 1001(a)(1), Apr. 20, 2005, 119 Stat. 185.)

HISTORICAL AND STATUTORY NOTES

Revision Notes and Legislative Reports

1986 Acts. House Report No. 99–764 and House Conference Report No. 99–958, see 1986 U.S. Code Cong. and Adm. News, p. 5227.

1993 Acts. House Report No. 103–32, see 1993 U.S. Code Cong. and Adm. News, p. 373.

1998 Acts. Statement by President, see 1998 U.S. Code Cong. and Adm. News, p. 582.

1999 Acts. Statement by President, see 1999 U.S. Code Cong. and Adm. News, p. 4.

Statement by President, see 1999 U.S. Code Cong. and Adm. News, p. 102.

2001 Acts. House Report No. 107–2, see 2001 U.S. Code Cong. and Adm. News, p. 6.

2005 Acts. House Report No. 109–31(Part I), see 2005 U.S. Code Cong. and Adm. News, p. 88.

Effective and Applicability Provisions

2005 Acts. Amendments by Pub.L. 109–8 effective, except as otherwise provided, 180 days after April 20, 2005, and inapplicable with respect to cases commenced under Title 11 before the effective date, see Pub.L. 109–8, § 1501, set out as a note under 11 U.S.C.A. § 101.

2004 Acts. Pub.L. 108–369, § 2(b), Oct. 25, 2004, 118 Stat. 1749, provided that: "The amendments made by subsection (a) [amending this section, 11 U.S.C.A. §§ 1202 to 1208, 1221 to 1231, and provisions set out as a note under this section] are deemed to have taken effect on January 1, 2004."

2003 Acts. Pub.L. 108–73, § 2(b), Aug. 15, 2003, 117 Stat. 891, provided that: "The amendments made by subsection (a) [amending this section, 11 U.S.C.A. §§ 1202 to 1208, 1221 to 1231, and provisions set out as a note under this section] take effect on July 1, 2003."

2002 Acts. Pub.L. 107–377, § 2(b), Dec. 19, 2002, 116 Stat. 3115, provided that: "The amendments made by subsection (a) [amending this section and 11 U.S.C.A. §§ 1202 to 1208, 1221 to 1231] shall take effect on January 1, 2003."

Pub.L. 107–171, Title X, § 10814(b), May 13, 2002, 116 Stat. 532, provided that: "The amendments made by subsection (a) [amending this section, 11 U.S.C.A. §§ 1202 to 1208, 1221 to 1231, and provisions set out as a note under this section] shall take effect on June 1, 2002."

Pub.L. 107–170, § 2, May 7, 2002, 116 Stat. 133, provided that: "The amendments made by section 1 [amending this section, 11 U.S.C.A. §§ 1202 to 1208, 1221 to 1231, and provisions set out as a note under this section] shall take effect on October 1, 2001."

2001 Acts. Pub.L. 107–17, § 2, June 26, 2001, 115 Stat. 151, provided that: "The amendments made by section 1 [amending this section, 11 U.S.C.A. §§ 1202 to 1208, 1221 to 1231, and provisions set out as a note under this section] shall take effect on June 1, 2001."

Pub.L. 107–8, § 2, May 11, 2001, 115 Stat. 10, provided that: "The amendments made by section 1 [amending this section, 11 U.S.C.A. §§ 1202 to 1208, 1221 to 1231, and provisions set out as a note under this section] shall take effect on July 1, 2000."

1999 Acts. Section 2 of Pub.L. 106–70 provided that: "The amendments made by section 1 [amending this section, 11 U.S.C.A. §§ 1202 to 1208, 1221 to 1231, and provisions set out as a note under this section] shall take effect on October 1, 1999."

Section 2 of Pub.L. 106–5 provided that: "The amendments made by section 1 [amending this section and 11 U.S.C.A. §§ 1202 to 1208, 1221 to 1231, and provisions set out as a note under this section] shall take effect on April 1, 1999."

1998 Acts. Section 149 of Pub.L. 105–277, as amended Pub.L. 106–5, § 1, Mar. 30, 1999, 113 Stat. 9; Pub.L. 106–70, § 1, Oct. 9, 1999, 113 Stat. 1031; Pub.L. 107–8, § 1, May 11, 2001, 115 Stat. 10; Pub.L. 107–17, § 1, June 26, 2001, 115 Stat. 151; Pub.L. 107–170, § 1, May 7, 2002, 116 Stat. 133; Pub.L.107–171, Title X, § 10814(a), May 13, 2002, 116 Stat. 532; Pub.L. 107–377, § 2(a), Dec. 19, 2002, 116 Stat. 3115; Pub.L. 108–73, § 2(a), Aug. 15, 2003, 117 Stat. 891; Pub.L. 108–369, § 2(a), Oct. 25, 2004, 118 Stat. 1749, provided that:

"(a) Chapter 12 of title 11 of the United States Code [this chapter; 11 U.S.C.A. § 1201 et seq.], as in effect on December 31, 2003, is hereby reenacted for the period beginning on January 1, 2004, and ending on July 1, 2005.

"(b) All cases commenced or pending under chapter 12 of title 11, United States Code [this chapter; 11 U.S.C.A. § 1201 et seq.], as reenacted under subsection (a) [of this note], and all matters and proceedings in or relating to such cases, shall be conducted and determined under such chapter as if such chapter were continued in effect after July 1, 2004. The substantive rights of parties in connection with such cases, matters, and proceedings shall continue to be governed under the law applicable to such cases, matters, and proceedings as if such chapter were continued in effect after July 1, 2005.

"(c) [Repealed. Pub.L. 106–5, § 1(3), March 30, 1999, 113 Stat. 9.]"

1993 Acts. Amendment by Pub.L. 103–65, extending to Oct. 1, 1998 the date of repeal of this chapter, to take effect Aug. 6, 1993, see section 3 of Pub.L. 103–65, set out as a note under 11 U.S.C.A. § 1221.

1986 Acts. Section repealed effective Oct. 1, 1998, see section 302(f) of Pub.L. 99–554, as amended, set out in a note under section 581 of Title 28. However, for extension of provisions, see section 149 of Pub.L. 105–277, set out as a note under this section.

Section effective 30 days after Oct. 27, 1986, but not applicable to cases commenced under this title before that date, see section 302(a), (c)(1) of Pub.L. 99–554, set out as a note under 28 U.S.C.A. § 581.

Reenactment of Chapter 12

Pub.L. 109–8, Title X, § 1001(a), (b), Apr. 20, 2005, 119 Stat. 185, 186, provided that:

"(a) **Reenactment.**—

"(1) **In general.**—Chapter 12 of title 11, United States Code [this chapter], as reenacted by section 149 of division C of the Omnibus Consolidated and Emergency Supplemental Appropriations Act, 1999 (Public Law 105–277) [Pub.L. 105–277, Div. C, Title I, § 149, Oct. 21, 1998, 112 Stat. 2681–610, as amended, set out as a note under this section], and as in effect on June 30, 2005, is hereby reenacted.

"(2) **Effective date of reenactment.**—Paragraph (1) shall take effect on July 1, 2005.

"(b) **Amendments.**—Chapter 12 of title 11, United States Code, as reenacted by subsection (a) [of this note], is amended by this Act [Pub.L. 109–8, Apr. 20, 2005, 119 Stat. 23; see Tables for classifications]."

Repeal of Chapter; Extension of Provisions

Pub.L. 99–554, Title III, § 302(f), Oct. 27, 1986, 100 Stat. 3124, as amended Pub.L. 103–65, § 1, Aug. 6, 1993, 107 Stat. 311, which provided that, effective Oct. 1, 1998, this chapter is repealed, but that all cases commenced or pending under this chapter, and all matters and proceedings in or relating to such cases, shall be conducted and determined under this chapter as if such chapter had not been repealed, and that the substantive rights of parties in connection with such cases, matters, and proceedings shall continue to be governed under the laws applicable to such cases, matters, and proceedings as if such chapter had not been repealed, was superceded by the reenactment of this chapter by Pub.L. 109–8, Title X, § 1001(a), Apr. 20, 2005, 119 Stat. 185, set out as a note under this section.

Pub.L. 105–277, Div. C, Title I, § 149, Oct. 21, 1998, 112 Stat. 2681–610, as amended Pub.L. 106–5, §§ 1, 2, Mar. 30, 1999, 113 Stat. 9; Pub.L. 106–70, §§ 1, 2, Oct. 9, 1999, 113 Stat. 1031; Pub.L. 107–8, §§ 1, 2, May 11, 2001, 115 Stat. 10; Pub.L. 107–17, §§ 1, 2, June 26, 2001, 115 Stat. 151; Pub.L. 107–170, §§ 1, 2, May 7, 2002, 116 Stat. 133; Pub.L. 107–171, Title X, § 10814, May 13, 2002, 116 St. 532; Pub.L. 107–377, § 2, Dec. 19, 2002, 116 Stat. 3115; Pub.L. 108–73, § 2(a), Aug. 15, 2003, 117 Stat. 891; Pub.L. 108–369, § 2(a), Oct. 25, 2004, 118 Stat. 1749, which provided that, to take effect on January 1, 2004, chapter 12 of Title 11 [this chapter; 11 U.S.C.A. § 1201 et seq.], as in effect on December 31, 2003, is reenacted for the period beginning on January 1, 2004, and ending on July 1, 2005, but that all cases commenced or pending under this chapter 12, as reenacted under section 149(a) of Pub.L. 105–277, and all matters and proceedings in or relating to such cases, shall be conducted and determined under such chapter as if such chapter were continued in effect after July 1, 2005, and that the substantive rights of parties in connection with such cases, matters, and proceedings shall continue to be governed under the law applicable to such cases, matters, and proceedings as if such chapter were continued in effect after July 1, 2005, was superceded by the reenactment of this chapter by Pub.L. 109–8, Title X, § 1001(a), Apr. 20, 2005, 119 Stat. 185, set out as a note under this section.

CROSS REFERENCES

Automatic stay, see 11 USCA § 362.

Automatic stay of enforcement of claims against debtor in Chapter nine cases, see 11 USCA § 922.

Claims of codebtors, see 11 USCA § 509.

Effect of conversion, see 11 USCA § 348.

Effect of § 362 of this title in stockbroker liquidation cases, see 11 USCA § 742.

Extension of time generally, see 11 USCA § 108.

§ 1202. Trustee

(a) If the United States trustee has appointed an individual under section 586(b) of title 28 to serve as standing trustee in cases under this chapter and if such individual qualifies as a trustee under section 322 of this title, then such individual shall serve as trustee in any case filed under this chapter. Otherwise, the United States trustee shall appoint one disinterested person to serve as trustee in the case or the United States trustee may serve as trustee in the case if necessary.

(b) The trustee shall—

(1) perform the duties specified in sections 704(2), 704(3), 704(5), 704(6), 704(7), and 704(9) of this title;

(2) perform the duties specified in section 1106(a)(3) and 1106(a)(4) of this title if the court, for cause and on request of a party in interest, the trustee, or the United States trustee, so orders;

(3) appear and be heard at any hearing that concerns—

(A) the value of property subject to a lien;

(B) confirmation of a plan;

(C) modification of the plan after confirmation; or

(D) the sale of property of the estate;

(4) ensure that the debtor commences making timely payments required by a confirmed plan;

(5) if the debtor ceases to be a debtor in possession, perform the duties specified in sections 704(8), 1106(a)(1), 1106(a)(2), 1106(a)(6), 1106(a)(7), and 1203; and

(6) if with respect to the debtor there is a claim for a domestic support obligation, provide the applicable notice specified in subsection (c).

(c)(1) In a case described in subsection (b)(6) to which subsection (b)(6) applies, the trustee shall—

(A)(i) provide written notice to the holder of the claim described in subsection (b)(6) of such claim and of the right of such holder to use the services of the State child support enforcement agency established under sections 464 and 466 of the Social Security Act for the State in which such holder resides, for assistance in collecting child support during and after the case under this title; and

(ii) include in the notice provided under clause (i) the address and telephone number of such State child support enforcement agency;

(B)(i) provide written notice to such State child support enforcement agency of such claim; and

(ii) include in the notice provided under clause (i) the name, address, and telephone number of such holder; and

(C) at such time as the debtor is granted a discharge under section 1228, provide written notice to such holder and to such State child support enforcement agency of—

(i) the granting of the discharge;

(ii) the last recent known address of the debtor;

(iii) the last recent known name and address of the debtor's employer; and

(iv) the name of each creditor that holds a claim that—

(I) is not discharged under paragraph (2), (4), or (14A) of section 523(a); or

(II) was reaffirmed by the debtor under section 524(c).

(2)(A) The holder of a claim described in subsection (b)(6) or the State child support enforcement agency of the State in which such holder resides may request from a creditor described in paragraph (1)(C)(iv) the last known address of the debtor.

(B) Notwithstanding any other provision of law, a creditor that makes a disclosure of a last known address of a debtor in connection with a request made under subparagraph (A) shall not be liable by reason of making that disclosure.

(Added and amended Pub.L. 99–554, Title II, §§ 227, 255, Title III, § 302(f), Oct. 27, 1986, 100 Stat. 3103, 3106, 3124; Pub.L. 103–65, § 1, Aug. 6, 1993, 107 Stat. 311; Pub.L. 105–277, Div. C, Title I, § 149(a), Oct. 21, 1998, 112 Stat. 2681–610; Pub.L. 106–5, §§ 1(1), (2), Mar. 30, 1999, 113 Stat. 9; Pub.L. 106–70, § 1, Oct. 9, 1999, 113 Stat. 1031; Pub.L. 107–8, § 1, May 11, 2001, 115 Stat. 10; Pub.L. 107–17, § 1, June 26, 2001, 115 Stat. 151; Pub.L. 107–170, § 1, May 7, 2002, 116 Stat. 133; Pub.L. 107–171, Title X, § 10814(a), May 13, 2002, 116 Stat. 532; Pub.L. 107–377, § 2(a), Dec. 19, 2002, 116 Stat. 3115; Pub.L. 108–73, § 2(a), Aug. 15, 2003, 117 Stat. 891; Pub.L. 108–369, § 2(a), Oct. 25, 2004, 118 Stat. 1749; Pub.L. 109–8, Title II, § 219(c), Title X, § 1001(a)(1), Apr. 20, 2005, 119 Stat. 57, 185.)

HISTORICAL AND STATUTORY NOTES

Revision Notes and Legislative Reports

1986 Acts. House Report No. 99–764 and House Conference Report No. 99–958, see 1986 U.S. Code Cong. and Adm. News, p. 5227.

1993 Acts. House Report No. 103–32, see 1993 U.S. Code Cong. and Adm. News, p. 373.

1998 Acts. Statement by President, see 1998 U.S. Code Cong. and Adm. News, p. 582.

1999 Acts. Statement by President, see 1999 U.S. Code Cong. and Adm. News, p. 4.

Statement by President, see 1999 U.S. Code Cong. and Adm. News, p. 102.

2001 Acts. House Report No. 107–2, see 2001 U.S. Code Cong. and Adm. News, p. 6.

2005 Acts. House Report No. 109–31(Part I), see 2005 U.S. Code Cong. and Adm. News, p. 88.

References in Text

Section 464 of the Social Security Act, referred to in subsec. (c)(1)(A)(i), is Act Aug. 14, 1935, c. 531, Title IV, § 464, as added Aug. 13, 1981, Pub.L. 97–35, Title XXIII, § 2331(a), 95 Stat. 860, and amended, which is classified to 42 U.S.C.A. § 664.

Section 466 of the Social Security Act, referred to in subsec. (c)(1)(A)(i), is Act Aug. 14, 1935, c. 531, Title IV, § 466, as added Aug. 16, 1984, Pub.L. 98–378, § 3(b), 98 Stat. 1306, and amended, which is classified to 42 U.S.C.A. § 666.

Effective and Applicability Provisions

2005 Acts. Amendments by Pub.L. 109–8 effective, except as otherwise provided, 180 days after April 20, 2005, and inapplicable with respect to cases commenced under Title 11 before the effective date, see Pub.L. 109–8, § 1501, set out as a note under 11 U.S.C.A. § 101.

2004 Acts. Amendment by Pub.L. 108–369, § 2(a), extending to July 1, 2005, the date of repeal of this chapter, to take effect Jan. 1, 2004, see Pub.L. 108–369, § 2(b), set out as a note under 11 U.S.C.A. § 1201.

2003 Acts. Amendment by Pub.L. 108–73, § 2(a), extending to Jan. 1, 2004, the date of repeal of this chapter, to take effect July 1, 2003, see Pub.L. 108–73, § 2(b), set out as a note under 11 U.S.C.A. § 1201.

2002 Acts. Amendment by Pub.L. 107–377, § 2(a), extending to July 1, 2003, the date of repeal of this chapter, to take effect Jan. 1, 2003, see Pub.L. 107–377, § 2(b), set out as a note under 11 U.S.C.A. § 1201.

Amendment by Pub.L. 107–171, extending to Jan. 1, 2003, the date of repeal of this chapter, to take effect June 1, 2002, see section 10814(b) of Pub.L. 107–171, set out as a note under 11 U.S.C.A. § 1201.

Amendment by Pub.L. 107–170, extending to June 1, 2002, the date of repeal of this chapter, to take effect October 1, 2001, see section 2 of Pub.L. 107–170, set out as a note under 11 U.S.C.A. § 1201.

2001 Acts. Amendment by Pub.L. 107–17, extending to October 1, 2001, the date of repeal of this chapter, to take effect June 1, 2001, see section 2 of Pub.L. 107–17, set out as a note under 11 U.S.C.A. § 1201.

Amendment by Pub.L. 107–8, extending to June 1, 2001, the date of repeal of this chapter, to take effect July 1, 2000, see section 2 of Pub.L. 107–8, set out as a note under 11 U.S.C.A. § 1201.

1999 Acts. Amendment by Pub.L. 106–70, extending to July 1, 2000, the date of repeal of this chapter, to take effect Oct. 1, 1999, see section 2 of Pub.L. 106–70, set out as a note under section 1201 of this title.

Amendment by Pub.L. 106–5, extending to Oct. 1, 1999 the date of repeal of this chapter, to take effect Apr. 1, 1999, see section 2 of Pub.L. 106–5, set out as a note under section 1201 of this title.

1998 Acts. Section reenacted, eff. Oct. 1, 1998, for the period beginning on Oct. 1, 1998, and ending on Apr. 1, 1999, but all cases commenced or pending under this chapter 12, as reenacted under section 149(a) of Pub.L. 105–277, and all matters and proceedings in or relating to such cases, to be conducted and determined under such chapter as if such chapter were continued in effect after Apr. 1, 1999, and the substantive rights of parties in connection with such cases, matters, and proceedings to continue to be governed under the law applicable to such cases, matters, and proceedings as if such chapter were continued in effect after Apr. 1, 1999, see section 149 of Pub.L. 105–277, set out as a note under section 1201 of this title.

1993 Acts. Amendment by Pub.L. 103–65, extending to Oct. 1, 1998 the date of repeal of this chapter, to take effect Aug. 6, 1993, see section 3 of Pub.L. 103–65, set out as a note under section 1221 of this title.

1986 Acts. Section repealed effective Oct. 1, 1998, see section 302(f) of Pub.L. 99–554, as amended, set out in a note under section 581 of Title 28. However, for extension of provisions, see section 149 of Pub.L. 105–277, set out as a note under section 1201 of this title.

Enactment by Pub.L. 99–554 effective 30 days after Oct. 27, 1986, except as otherwise provided for, see section 302(a) of Pub.L. 99–554, set out as a note under section 581 of Title 28, Judiciary and Judicial Procedure.

Enactment by Pub.L. 99–554, § 255, not to apply with respect to cases commenced under Title 11, Bankruptcy, before 30 days after Oct. 27, 1986, see section 302(c)(1) of Pub.L. 99–554, set out as a note under section 581 of Title 28.

Enactment by section 255 of Pub.L. 99–554 to take effect 30 days after Oct. 27, 1986, and before amendment made by section 227 of Pub.L. 99–554, striking out subsecs. (c) and (d) of this section, see section 302(c)(2) of Pub.L. 99–554, set out as a note under section 581 of Title 28.

Amendment by Pub.L. 99–554, § 227, not to become effective in or with respect to certain specified judicial districts until, or apply to cases while pending in such district before, the expiration of the 270–day period beginning 30 days after Oct. 27, 1986, or of the 30–day period beginning on the date the Attorney General certifies under section 303 of Pub.L. 99–554 the region specified in a paragraph of section 581(a) of Title 28, as amended by section 111(a) of Pub.L. 99–554, that includes such district, whichever occurs first, see section 302(d)(1) of Pub.L. 99–554, set out as a note under section 581 of Title 28.

Amendment by Pub.L. 99–554, § 227, not to become effective in or with respect to certain specified judicial districts until, or apply to cases while pending in such district before, the expiration of the 2–year period beginning 30 days after Oct. 27, 1986, or of the 30–day period beginning on the date the Attorney General certifies under section 303 of Pub.L. 99–554 the region specified in a paragraph of section 581(a) of Title 28, as amended by section 111(a) of Pub.L. 99–554, that includes such district, whichever occurs first, see section 302(d)(2) of Pub.L. 99–554, set out as a note under section 581 of Title 28.

Amendment by Pub.L. 99–554, § 227, not to become effective in or with respect to judicial districts established for the States of Alabama and North Carolina until, or apply to cases while pending in such district before, such district elects to be included in a bankruptcy region established in section 581(a) of Title 28, as amended by section 111(a) of Pub.L. 99–554, or Oct. 1, 2002, whichever occurs first, and except as otherwise provided for, with respect to cases under chapters 7, 11, 12, and 13 of Title 11 commenced before 30 days after Oct. 27, 1986, and pending in a judicial district in the States of Alabama or North Carolina before any election made under section 302(d)(3)(A) of Pub.L. 99–554 by such district becomes effective or Oct. 1, 2002, whichever occurs first, amendments by Pub.L. 99–554 not to apply until Oct. 1, 2003, or the expiration of the 1–year period beginning on the date such election becomes effective, whichever occurs first, and further, in any judicial district in Alabama or North Carolina not making the election described in section 302(d)(3)(A) of Pub.L. 99–554, any person appointed under regulations issued by the Judicial Conference to administer estates in cases under Title 11 authorized to establish, etc., a panel of private trustees, and to supervise cases and trustees in cases under chapters 7, 11, 12, and 13 of Title 11, until amendments by section 201 to 231 of Pub.L. 99–554 becomes effective in such district, see section 302(d)(3)(A) to (F), (H), (I) of Pub.L. 99–554, set out as a note under section 581 of Title 28.

Amendment by Pub.L. 99–554, § 227, except as otherwise provided, with respect to cases under chapters 7, 11, 12, and 13 of Title 11 commenced before 30 days after Oct. 27, 1986, and pending in a judicial district referred to in section 581(a) of Title 28, as amended by section 111(a) of Pub.L. 99–554, for which a United States trustee is not authorized before 30 days after Oct. 27, 1986 to be appointed, not applicable until the expiration of the 3–year period beginning on Oct. 27, 1986, or of the 1–year period beginning on the date the Attorney General certifies under section 303 of Pub.L. 99–554 the region specified in a paragraph of such section 581(a) that includes, such district, whichever occurs first, see section 302(e)(1), (2) of Pub.L. 99–554, set out as a note under section 581 of Title 28.

Reenactment of Chapter

This section as in effect on June 30, 2005, reenacted effective July 1, 2005, see Pub.L. 109–8, § 1001(a), set out as a note under 11 U.S.C.A. § 1201.

Repeal of Chapter; Extension of Provisions

Pub.L. 99–554, Title III, § 302(f), Oct. 27, 1986, 100 Stat. 3124, as amended Pub.L. 103–65, § 1, Aug. 6, 1993, 107 Stat. 311, which provided that, effective Oct. 1, 1998, this chapter is repealed, but that all cases commenced or pending under this chapter, and all matters and proceedings in or relating to such cases, shall be conducted and determined under this chapter as if such chapter had not been repealed, and that the substantive rights of parties in connection with such cases, matters, and proceedings shall continue to be governed under the laws applicable to such cases, matters, and proceedings as if such chapter had not been repealed, was superceded by the reenactment of this chapter by Pub.L. 109–8, Title X, § 1001(a), Apr. 20, 2005, 119 Stat. 185, set out as a note under 11 U.S.C.A. § 1201.

Pub.L. 105–277, Div. C, Title I, § 149, Oct. 21, 1998, 112 Stat. 2681–610, as amended Pub.L. 106–5, §§ 1, 2, Mar. 30, 1999, 113 Stat. 9; Pub.L. 106–70, §§ 1, 2, Oct. 9, 1999, 113 Stat. 1031; Pub.L. 107–8, §§ 1, 2, May 11, 2001, 115 Stat. 10; Pub.L. 107–17, §§ 1, 2, June 26, 2001, 115 Stat. 151; Pub.L. 107–170, §§ 1, 2, May 7, 2002, 116 Stat. 133; Pub.L. 107–171, Title X, § 10814, May 13, 2002, 116 St. 532; Pub.L. 107–377, § 2, Dec. 19, 2002, 116 Stat. 3115; Pub.L. 108–73, § 2(a), Aug. 15, 2003, 117 Stat. 891; Pub.L. 108–369, § 2(a), Oct. 25, 2004, 118 Stat. 1749, provided that, to take effect on January 1, 2004, chapter 12 of Title 11 [this chapter; 11 U.S.C.A. § 1201 et seq.], as in effect on December 31, 2003, is reenacted for the period beginning on January 1, 2004, and ending on July 1, 2005, but that all cases commenced or pending under this chapter 12, as reenacted under section 149(a) of Pub.L. 105–277, and all matters and proceedings in or relating to such cases, shall be conducted and determined under such chapter as if such chapter were continued in effect after July 1, 2005, and that the substantive rights of parties in connection with such cases, matters, and proceedings shall continue to be governed under the law applicable to such cases, matters, and proceedings as if such chapter were continued in effect after July 1, 2005, was superceded by the reenactment of this chapter by Pub.L. 109–8, Title X, § 1001(a), Apr. 20, 2005, 119 Stat. 185, set out as a note under 11 U.S.C.A. § 1201.

References in Subsection (a) Temporarily Deemed to be References to Other Provisions

Until the amendments made by subtitle A (sections 201 to 231) of Title II of Pub.L. 99–554 become effective in a district and apply to a case, in subsec. (a) of this section—

(1) the first two references to the United States trustee are deemed to be references to the court, and

(2) any reference to section 586(b) of Title 28, Judiciary and Judicial Procedure, is deemed to be a reference to subsec. (c) of this section,

see section 302(c)(3)(B), (d), (e) of Pub.L. 99–554, set out as an Effective Date note under section 581 of Title 28.

CROSS REFERENCES

Appointment of trustee in—

Chapter eleven cases, see 11 USCA § 1104.

Chapter thirteen cases, see 11 USCA § 1302.

Railroad reorganization cases, see 11 USCA § 1163.

Compensation of officers, see 11 USCA § 330.

Election of trustee in Chapter seven case, see 11 USCA § 702.

Eligibility to serve as trustee, see 11 USCA § 321.

Grain storage facility bankruptcies, expedited appointment of trustee or examiner, see 11 USCA § 557.

Limitation on compensation of trustee, see 11 USCA § 326.

Qualification of trustee, see 11 USCA § 322.

Removal of trustee, see 11 USCA § 324.

Retention or replacement of professional persons, see 11 USCA § 327.

Role and capacity of trustee, see 11 USCA § 323.

Time of bringing action, see 11 USCA § 546.

Time of payment of percentage fee fixed for standing trustee, see 11 USCA § 1226.

§ 1203. Rights and powers of debtor

Subject to such limitations as the court may prescribe, a debtor in possession shall have all the rights, other than the right to compensation under section 330, and powers, and shall perform all the functions and duties, except the duties specified in paragraphs (3) and (4) of section 1106(a), of a trustee serving in a case under chapter 11, including operating the debtor's farm or commercial fishing operation.

(Added and amended Pub.L. 99–554, Title II, § 255, Title III, § 302(f), Oct. 27, 1986, 100 Stat. 3107, 3124; Pub.L. 103–65, § 1, Aug. 6, 1993, 107 Stat. 311; Pub.L. 105–277, Div. C, Title I, § 149(a), Oct. 21, 1998, 112 Stat. 2681–610; Pub.L. 106–5, § 1(1), (2), Mar. 30, 1999, 113 Stat. 9; Pub.L. 106–70, § 1, Oct. 9, 1999, 113 Stat. 1031; Pub.L. 107–8, § 1, May 11, 2001, 115 Stat. 10; Pub.L. 107–17, § 1, June 26, 2001, 115 Stat. 151; Pub.L. 107–170, § 1, May 7, 2002, 116 Stat. 133; Pub.L. 107–171, Title X, § 10814(a), May 13, 2002, 116 Stat. 532; Pub.L. 107–377, § 2(a), Dec. 19, 2002, 116 Stat. 3115; Pub.L. 108–73, § 2(a), Aug. 15, 2003, 117 Stat. 891; Pub.L. 108–369, § 2(a), Oct. 25, 2004, 118 Stat. 1749; Pub.L. 109–8, Title X, §§ 1001(a)(1), 1007(c)(2), Apr. 20, 2005, 119 Stat. 185, 188.)

HISTORICAL AND STATUTORY NOTES

Revision Notes and Legislative Reports

1986 Acts. House Report No. 99–764 and House Conference Report No. 99–958, see 1986 U.S. Code Cong. and Adm. News, p. 5227.

1993 Acts. House Report No. 103–32, see 1993 U.S. Code Cong. and Adm. News, p. 373.

1998 Acts. Statement by President, see 1998 U.S. Code Cong. and Adm. News, p. 582.

1999 Acts. Statement by President, see 1999 U.S. Code Cong. and Adm. News, p. 4.

Statement by President, see 1999 U.S. Code Cong. and Adm. News, p. 102.

2001 Acts. House Report No. 107–2, see 2001 U.S. Code Cong. and Adm. News, p. 6.

2005 Acts. House Report No. 109–31(Part I), see 2005 U.S. Code Cong. and Adm. News, p. 88.

Effective and Applicability Provisions

2005 Acts. Amendments by Pub.L. 109–8 effective, except as otherwise provided, 180 days after April 20, 2005, and inapplicable with respect to cases commenced under Title 11 before the effective date, see Pub.L. 109–8, § 1501, set out as a note under 11 U.S.C.A. § 101.

2004 Acts. Amendment by Pub.L. 108–369, § 2(a), extending to July 1, 2005, the date of repeal of this chapter, to take effect Jan. 1, 2004, see Pub.L. 108–369, § 2(b), set out as a note under 11 U.S.C.A. § 1201.

2003 Acts. Amendment by Pub.L. 108–73, § 2(a), extending to Jan. 1, 2004, the date of repeal of this chapter, to take effect July 1, 2003, see Pub.L. 108–73, § 2(b), set out as a note under 11 U.S.C.A. § 1201.

2002 Acts. Amendment by Pub.L. 107–377, § 2(a), extending to July 1, 2003, the date of repeal of this chapter, to take effect Jan. 1, 2003, see Pub.L. 107–377, § 2(b), set out as a note under 11 U.S.C.A. § 1201.

Amendment by Pub.L. 107–171, extending to Jan. 1, 2003, the date of repeal of this chapter, to take effect June 1, 2002, see section 10814(b) of Pub.L. 107–171, set out as a note under 11 U.S.C.A. § 1201.

Amendment by Pub.L. 107–170, extending to June 1, 2002, the date of repeal of this chapter, to take effect October 1, 2001, see section 2 of Pub.L. 107–170, set out as a note under 11 U.S.C.A. § 1201.

2001 Acts. Amendment by Pub.L. 107–17, extending to October 1, 2001, the date of repeal of this chapter, to take effect June 1, 2001, see section 2 of Pub.L. 107–17, set out as a note under 11 U.S.C.A. § 1201.

Amendment by Pub.L. 107–8, extending to June 1, 2001, the date of repeal of this chapter, to take effect July 1, 2000, see section 2 of Pub.L. 107–8, set out as a note under 11 U.S.C.A. § 1201.

1999 Acts. Amendment by Pub.L. 106–70, extending to July 1, 2000, the date of repeal of this chapter, to take effect Oct. 1, 1999, see section 2 of Pub.L. 106–70, set out as a note under section 1201 of this title.

Amendment by Pub.L. 106–5, extending to Oct. 1, 1999 the date of repeal of this chapter, to take effect Apr. 1, 1999, see section 2 of Pub.L. 106–5, set out as a note under section 1201 of this title.

1998 Acts. Section reenacted, eff. Oct. 1, 1998, for the period beginning on Oct. 1, 1998, and ending on Apr. 1, 1999, but all cases commenced or pending under this chapter 12, as reenacted under section 149(a) of Pub.L. 105–277, and all matters and proceedings in or relating to such cases, to be conducted and determined under such chapter as if such chapter were continued in effect after Apr. 1, 1999, and the substantive rights of parties in connection with such cases, matters, and proceedings to continue to be governed under the law applicable to such cases, matters, and proceedings as if such chapter were continued in effect after Apr. 1, 1999, see section 149 of Pub.L. 105–277, set out as a note under section 1201 of this title.

1993 Acts. Amendment by Pub.L. 103–65, extending to Oct. 1, 1998 the date of repeal of this chapter, to take effect Aug. 6, 1993, see section 3 of Pub.L. 103–65, set out as a note under section 1221 of this title.

1986 Acts. Section repealed effective Oct. 1, 1998, see section 302(f) of Pub.L. 99–554, as amended, set out in a note under section 581 of Title 28. However, for extension of provisions, see section 149 of Pub.L. 105–277, set out as a note under section 1201 of this title.

Section effective 30 days after Oct. 27, 1986, but not applicable to cases commenced under this title before that date, see section 302(a), (c)(1) of Pub.L. 99–554, set out as a note under section 581 of Title 28, Judiciary and Judicial Procedure.

Reenactment of Chapter

This section as in effect on June 30, 2005, reenacted effective July 1, 2005, see Pub.L. 109–8, § 1001(a), set out as a note under 11 U.S.C.A. § 1201.

Repeal of Chapter; Extension of Provisions

Pub.L. 99–554, Title III, § 302(f), Oct. 27, 1986, 100 Stat. 3124, as amended Pub.L. 103–65, § 1, Aug. 6, 1993, 107 Stat. 311, which provided that, effective Oct. 1, 1998, this chapter is repealed, but that all cases commenced or pending under this chapter, and all matters and proceedings in or relating to such cases, shall be conducted and determined under this chapter as if such chapter had not been repealed, and that the substantive rights of parties in connection with such cases, matters, and proceedings shall continue to be governed under the laws applicable to such cases, matters, and proceedings as if such chapter had not been repealed, was superceded by the reenactment of this chapter by Pub.L. 109–8, Title X, § 1001(a), Apr. 20, 2005, 119 Stat. 185, set out as a note under 11 U.S.C.A. § 1201.

Pub.L. 105–277, Div. C, Title I, § 149, Oct. 21, 1998, 112 Stat. 2681–610, as amended Pub.L. 106–5, §§ 1, 2, Mar. 30, 1999, 113 Stat. 9; Pub.L. 106–70, §§ 1, 2, Oct. 9, 1999, 113 Stat. 1031; Pub.L. 107–8, §§ 1, 2, May 11, 2001, 115 Stat. 10; Pub.L. 107–17, §§ 1, 2, June 26, 2001, 115 Stat. 151; Pub.L. 107–170, §§ 1, 2, May 7, 2002, 116 Stat. 133; Pub.L. 107–171, Title X, § 10814, May 13, 2002, 116 St. 532; Pub.L. 107–377, § 2, Dec. 19, 2002, 116 Stat. 3115; Pub.L. 108–73, § 2(a), Aug. 15, 2003, 117 Stat. 891; Pub.L. 108–369, § 2(a), Oct. 25, 2004, 118 Stat. 1749, provided that, to take effect on January 1, 2004, chapter 12 of Title 11 [this chapter; 11 U.S.C.A. § 1201 et seq.], as in effect on December 31, 2003, is reenacted for the period beginning on January 1, 2004, and ending on July 1, 2005, but that all cases commenced or pending under this chapter 12, as reenacted under section 149(a) of Pub.L. 105–277, and all matters and proceedings in or relating to such cases, shall be conducted and determined under such chapter as if such chapter were continued in effect after July 1, 2005, and that the substantive rights of parties in connection with such cases, matters, and proceedings shall continue to be governed under the law applicable to such cases, matters, and proceedings as if such chapter were continued in effect after July 1, 2005, was superceded by the reenactment of this chapter by Pub.L. 109–8, Title X, § 1001(a), Apr. 20, 2005, 119 Stat. 185, set out as a note under 11 U.S.C.A. § 1201.

CROSS REFERENCES

Obtaining credit, see 11 USCA § 364.

Rights and powers of debtor in—

Chapter eleven cases, see 11 USCA § 1107.

Chapter thirteen cases, see 11 USCA § 1303.

Use, sale or lease of property, see 11 USCA § 363.

§ 1204. Removal of debtor as debtor in possession

(a) On request of a party in interest, and after notice and a hearing, the court shall order that the debtor shall not be a debtor in possession for cause, including fraud, dishonesty, incompetence, or gross mismanagement of the affairs of the debtor, either before or after the commencement of the case.

(b) On request of a party in interest, and after notice and a hearing, the court may reinstate the debtor in possession.

(Added and amended Pub.L. 99–554, Title II, § 255, Title III, § 302(f), Oct. 27, 1986, 100 Stat. 3107, 3124; Pub.L. 103–65, § 1, Aug. 6, 1993, 107 Stat. 311; Pub.L. 105–277, Div. C, Title I, § 149(a), Oct. 21, 1998, 112 Stat. 2681–610; Pub.L. 106–5, § 1(1), (2), Mar. 30, 1999, 113 Stat. 9; Pub.L. 106–70, § 1, Oct. 9, 1999, 113 Stat. 1031; Pub.L. 107–8, § 1, May 11, 2001, 115 Stat. 10; Pub.L. 107–17, § 1, June 26, 2001, 115 Stat. 151; Pub.L. 107–170, § 1, May 7, 2002, 116 Stat. 133; Pub.L. 107–171, Title X, § 10814(a), May 13, 2002, 116 Stat. 532; Pub.L. 107–377, § 2(a), Dec. 19, 2002, 116 Stat. 3115; Pub.L. 108–73, § 2(a), Aug. 15, 2003, 117 Stat. 891; Pub.L. 108–369, § 2(a), Oct. 25, 2004, 118 Stat. 1749; Pub.L. 109–8, Title X, § 1001(a)(1), Apr. 20, 2005, 119 Stat. 185.)

HISTORICAL AND STATUTORY NOTES

Revision Notes and Legislative Reports

1986 Acts. House Report No. 99–764 and House Conference Report No. 99–958, see 1986 U.S. Code Cong. and Adm. News, p. 5227.

1993 Acts. House Report No. 103–32, see 1993 U.S. Code Cong. and Adm. News, p. 373.

1998 Acts. Statement by President, see 1998 U.S. Code Cong. and Adm. News, p. 582.

1999 Acts. Statement by President, see 1999 U.S. Code Cong. and Adm. News, p. 4.

Statement by President, see 1999 U.S. Code Cong. and Adm. News, p. 102.

2001 Acts. House Report No. 107–2, see 2001 U.S. Code Cong. and Adm. News, p. 6.

2005 Acts. House Report No. 109–31(Part I), see 2005 U.S. Code Cong. and Adm. News, p. 88.

Effective and Applicability Provisions

2005 Acts. Amendments by Pub.L. 109–8 effective, except as otherwise provided, 180 days after April 20, 2005, and inapplicable with respect to cases commenced under Title 11 before the effective date, see Pub.L. 109–8, § 1501, set out as a note under 11 U.S.C.A. § 101.

2004 Acts. Amendment by Pub.L. 108–369, § 2(a), extending to July 1, 2005, the date of repeal of this chapter, to take effect Jan. 1, 2004, see Pub.L. 108–369, § 2(b), set out as a note under 11 U.S.C.A. § 1201.

2003 Acts. Amendment by Pub.L. 108–73, § 2(a), extending to Jan. 1, 2004, the date of repeal of this chapter, to take effect July 1, 2003, see Pub.L. 108–73, § 2(b), set out as a note under 11 U.S.C.A. § 1201.

2002 Acts. Amendment by Pub.L. 107–377, § 2(a), extending to July 1, 2003, the date of repeal of this chapter, to take effect Jan. 1, 2003, see Pub.L. 107–377, § 2(b), set out as a note under 11 U.S.C.A. § 1201.

Amendment by Pub.L. 107–171, extending to Jan. 1, 2003, the date of repeal of this chapter, to take effect June 1, 2002, see section 10814(b) of Pub.L. 107–171, set out as a note under 11 U.S.C.A. § 1201.

Amendment by Pub.L. 107–170, extending to June 1, 2002, the date of repeal of this chapter, to take effect October 1, 2001, see section 2 of Pub.L. 107–170, set out as a note under 11 U.S.C.A. § 1201.

2001 Acts. Amendment by Pub.L. 107–17, extending to October 1, 2001, the date of repeal of this chapter, to take effect June 1, 2001, see section 2 of Pub.L. 107–17, set out as a note under 11 U.S.C.A. § 1201.

Amendment by Pub.L. 107–8, extending to June 1, 2001, the date of repeal of this chapter, to take effect July 1, 2000, see section 2 of Pub.L. 107–8, set out as a note under 11 U.S.C.A. § 1201.

1999 Acts. Amendment by Pub.L. 106–70, extending to July 1, 2000, the date of repeal of this chapter, to take effect Oct. 1, 1999, see section 2 of Pub.L. 106–70, set out as a note under section 1201 of this title.

Amendment by Pub.L. 106–5, extending to Oct. 1, 1999 the date of repeal of this chapter, to take effect Apr. 1, 1999, see section 2 of Pub.L. 106–5, set out as a note under section 1201 of this title.

1998 Acts. Section reenacted, eff. Oct. 1, 1998, for the period beginning on Oct. 1, 1998, and ending on Apr. 1, 1999, but all cases commenced or pending under this chapter 12, as reenacted under section 149(a) of Pub.L. 105–277, and all matters and proceedings in or relating to such cases, to be conducted and determined under such chapter as if such chapter were continued in effect after Apr. 1, 1999, and the substantive rights of parties in connection with such cases, matters, and proceedings to continue to be governed under the law applicable to such cases, matters, and proceedings as if such chapter were continued in effect after Apr. 1, 1999, see section 149 of Pub.L. 105–277, set out as a note under section 1201 of this title.

1993 Acts. Amendment by Pub.L. 103–65, extending to Oct. 1, 1998 the date of repeal of this chapter, to take effect Aug. 6, 1993, see section 3 of Pub.L. 103–65, set out as a note under section 1221 of this title.

1986 Acts. Section repealed effective Oct. 1, 1998, see section 302(f) of Pub.L. 99–554, as amended, set out in a note under section 581 of Title 28. However, for extension of provisions, see section 149 of Pub.L. 105–277, set out as a note under section 1201 of this title.

Section effective 30 days after Oct. 27, 1986, but not applicable to cases commenced under this title before that date, see section 302(a), (c)(1) of Pub.L. 99–554, set out as a note under section 581 of Title 28, Judiciary and Judicial Procedure.

Reenactment of Chapter

This section as in effect on June 30, 2005, reenacted effective July 1, 2005, see Pub.L. 109–8, § 1001(a), set out as a note under 11 U.S.C.A. § 1201.

Repeal of Chapter; Extension of Provisions

Pub.L. 99–554, Title III, § 302(f), Oct. 27, 1986, 100 Stat. 3124, as amended Pub.L. 103–65, § 1, Aug. 6, 1993, 107 Stat. 311, which provided that, effective Oct. 1, 1998, this chapter is repealed, but that all cases commenced or pending under this chapter, and all matters and proceedings in or relating to such cases, shall be conducted and determined under this chapter as if such chapter had not been repealed, and that the substantive rights of parties in connection with such cases, matters, and proceedings shall continue to be governed under the laws applicable to such cases, matters, and proceedings as if such chapter had not been repealed, was superceded by the reenactment of this chapter by Pub.L. 109–8, Title X, § 1001(a), Apr. 20, 2005, 119 Stat. 185, set out as a note under 11 U.S.C.A. § 1201.

Pub.L. 105–277, Div. C, Title I, § 149, Oct. 21, 1998, 112 Stat. 2681–610, as amended Pub.L. 106–5, §§ 1, 2, Mar. 30, 1999, 113 Stat. 9; Pub.L. 106–70, §§ 1, 2, Oct. 9, 1999, 113 Stat. 1031; Pub.L. 107–8, §§ 1, 2, May 11, 2001, 115 Stat. 10; Pub.L. 107–17, §§ 1, 2, June 26, 2001, 115 Stat. 151; Pub.L. 107–170, §§ 1, 2, May 7, 2002, 116 Stat. 133; Pub.L. 107–171, Title X, § 10814, May 13, 2002, 116 St. 532; Pub.L. 107–377, § 2, Dec. 19, 2002, 116 Stat. 3115; Pub.L. 108–73, § 2(a), Aug. 15, 2003, 117 Stat. 891; Pub.L. 108–369, § 2(a), Oct. 25, 2004, 118 Stat. 1749, provided that, to take effect on January 1, 2004, chapter 12 of Title 11 [this chapter; 11 U.S.C.A. § 1201 et seq.], as in effect on December 31, 2003, is reenacted for the period beginning on January 1, 2004, and ending on July 1, 2005, but that all cases commenced or pending under this chapter 12, as reenacted under section 149(a) of Pub.L. 105–277, and all matters and proceedings in or relating to such cases, shall be conducted and determined under such chapter as if such chapter were continued in effect after July 1, 2005, and that the substantive rights of parties in connection with such cases, matters, and proceedings shall continue to be governed under the law applicable to such cases, matters, and proceedings as if such chapter were continued in effect after July 1, 2005, was superceded by the reenactment of this chapter by Pub.L. 109–8, Title X, § 1001(a), Apr. 20, 2005, 119 Stat. 185, set out as a note under 11 U.S.C.A. § 1201.

CROSS REFERENCES

Obtaining credit, see 11 USCA § 364.

Revocation of an order of confirmation, see 11 USCA § 1230.

Use, sale or lease of property, see 11 USCA § 363.

§ 1205. Adequate protection

(a) Section 361 does not apply in a case under this chapter.

(b) In a case under this chapter, when adequate protection is required under section 362, 363, or 364 of this title of an interest of an entity in property, such adequate protection may be provided by—

(1) requiring the trustee to make a cash payment or periodic cash payments to such entity, to the extent that the stay under section 362 of this title, use, sale, or lease under section 363 of this title, or any grant of a lien under section 364 of this title results in a decrease in the value of property securing a claim or of an entity's ownership interest in property;

(2) providing to such entity an additional or replacement lien to the extent that such stay, use, sale, lease, or grant results in a decrease in the value of property securing a claim or of an entity's ownership interest in property;

(3) paying to such entity for the use of farmland the reasonable rent customary in the community where the property is located, based upon the rental value, net income, and earning capacity of the property; or

(4) granting such other relief, other than entitling such entity to compensation allowable under section 503(b)(1) of this title as an administrative expense, as will adequately protect the value of property securing a claim or of such entity's ownership interest in property.

(Added and amended Pub.L. 99–554, Title II, § 255, Title III, § 302(f), Oct. 27, 1986, 100 Stat. 3107, 3124; Pub.L. 103–65, § 1, Aug. 6, 1993, 107 Stat. 311; Pub.L. 105–277, Div. C, Title I, § 149(a), Oct. 21, 1998, 112 Stat. 2681–610; Pub.L. 106–5, § 1(1), (2), Mar. 30, 1999, 113 Stat. 9; Pub.L. 106–70, § 1, Oct. 9, 1999, 113 Stat. 1031; Pub.L. 107–8, § 1, May 11, 2001, 115 Stat. 10; Pub.L. 107–17, § 1, June 26, 2001, 115 Stat. 151; Pub.L. 107–170, § 1, May 7, 2002, 116 Stat. 133; Pub.L. 107–171, Title X, § 10814(a), May 13, 2002, 116 Stat. 532; Pub.L. 107–377, § 2(a), Dec. 19, 2002, 116 Stat. 3115; Pub.L. 108–73, § 2(a), Aug. 15, 2003, 117 Stat. 891; Pub.L. 108–369, § 2(a), Oct. 25, 2004, 118 Stat. 1749; Pub.L. 109–8, Title X, § 1001(a)(1), Apr. 20, 2005, 119 Stat. 185.)

HISTORICAL AND STATUTORY NOTES

Revision Notes and Legislative Reports

1986 Acts. House Report No. 99–764 and House Conference Report No. 99–958, see 1986 U.S. Code Cong. and Adm. News, p. 5227.

1993 Acts. House Report No. 103–32, see 1993 U.S. Code Cong. and Adm. News, p. 373.

1998 Acts. Statement by President, see 1998 U.S. Code Cong. and Adm. News, p. 582.

1999 Acts. Statement by President, see 1999 U.S. Code Cong. and Adm. News, p. 4.

Statement by President, see 1999 U.S. Code Cong. and Adm. News, p. 102.

2001 Acts. House Report No. 107–2, see 2001 U.S. Code Cong. and Adm. News, p. 6.

2005 Acts. House Report No. 109–31(Part I), see 2005 U.S. Code Cong. and Adm. News, p. 88.

Effective and Applicability Provisions

2005 Acts. Amendments by Pub.L. 109–8 effective, except as otherwise provided, 180 days after April 20, 2005, and inapplicable with respect to cases commenced under Title 11 before the effective date, see Pub.L. 109–8, § 1501, set out as a note under 11 U.S.C.A. § 101.

2004 Acts. Amendment by Pub.L. 108–369, § 2(a), extending to July 1, 2005, the date of repeal of this chapter, to take effect Jan. 1, 2004, see Pub.L. 108–369, § 2(b), set out as a note under 11 U.S.C.A. § 1201.

2003 Acts. Amendment by Pub.L. 108–73, § 2(a), extending to Jan. 1, 2004, the date of repeal of this chapter, to take effect July 1, 2003, see Pub.L. 108–73, § 2(b), set out as a note under 11 U.S.C.A. § 1201.

2002 Acts. Amendment by Pub.L. 107–377, § 2(a), extending to July 1, 2003, the date of repeal of this chapter, to take effect Jan. 1, 2003, see Pub.L. 107–377, § 2(b), set out as a note under 11 U.S.C.A. § 1201.

Amendment by Pub.L. 107–171, extending to Jan. 1, 2003, the date of repeal of this chapter, to take effect June 1, 2002, see section 10814(b) of Pub.L. 107–171, set out as a note under 11 U.S.C.A. § 1201.

Amendment by Pub.L. 107–170, extending to June 1, 2002, the date of repeal of this chapter, to take effect October 1, 2001, see section 2 of Pub.L. 107–170, set out as a note under 11 U.S.C.A. § 1201.

2001 Acts. Amendment by Pub.L. 107–17, extending to October 1, 2001, the date of repeal of this chapter, to take effect June 1, 2001, see section 2 of Pub.L. 107–17, set out as a note under 11 U.S.C.A. § 1201.

Amendment by Pub.L. 107–8, extending to June 1, 2001, the date of repeal of this chapter, to take effect July 1, 2000, see section 2 of Pub.L. 107–8, set out as a note under 11 U.S.C.A. § 1201.

1999 Acts. Amendment by Pub.L. 106–70, extending to July 1, 2000, the date of repeal of this chapter, to take effect Oct. 1, 1999, see section 2 of Pub.L. 106–70, set out as a note under section 1201 of this title.

Amendment by Pub.L. 106–5, extending to Oct. 1, 1999 the date of repeal of this chapter, to take effect Apr. 1, 1999, see section 2 of Pub.L. 106–5, set out as a note under section 1201 of this title.

1998 Acts. Section reenacted, eff. Oct. 1, 1998, for the period beginning on Oct. 1, 1998, and ending on Apr. 1, 1999, but all cases commenced or pending under this chapter 12, as reenacted under section 149(a) of Pub.L. 105–277, and all matters and proceedings in or relating to such cases, to be conducted and determined under such chapter as if such chapter were continued in effect after Apr. 1, 1999, and the substantive rights of parties in connection with such cases, matters, and proceedings to continue to be governed under the law applicable to such cases, matters, and proceedings as if such chapter were continued in effect after Apr. 1, 1999, see section 149 of Pub.L. 105–277, set out as a note under section 1201 of this title.

1993 Acts. Amendment by Pub.L. 103–65, extending to Oct. 1, 1998 the date of repeal of this chapter, to take effect Aug. 6, 1993, see section 3 of Pub.L. 103–65, set out as a note under section 1221 of this title.

1986 Acts. Section repealed effective Oct. 1, 1998, see section 302(f) of Pub.L. 99–554, as amended, set out in a note under section 581 of Title 28. However, for extension of provisions, see section 149 of Pub.L. 105–277, set out as a note under section 1201 of this title.

Section effective 30 days after Oct. 27, 1986, but not applicable to cases commenced under this title before that date, see section 302(a), (c)(1) of Pub.L. 99–554, set out as a note under section 581 of Title 28, Judiciary and Judicial Procedure.

Reenactment of Chapter

This section as in effect on June 30, 2005, reenacted effective July 1, 2005, see Pub.L. 109–8, § 1001(a), set out as a note under 11 U.S.C.A. § 1201.

Repeal of Chapter; Extension of Provisions

Pub.L. 99–554, Title III, § 302(f), Oct. 27, 1986, 100 Stat. 3124, as amended Pub.L. 103–65, § 1, Aug. 6, 1993, 107 Stat. 311, which provided that, effective Oct. 1, 1998, this chapter is repealed, but that all cases commenced or pending under this chapter, and all matters and proceedings in or relating to such cases, shall be conducted and determined under this chapter as if such chapter had not been repealed, and that the substantive rights of parties in connection with such cases, matters, and proceedings shall continue to be governed under the laws applicable to such cases, matters, and proceedings as if such chapter had not been repealed, was superceded by the reenactment of this chapter by Pub.L. 109–8, Title X, § 1001(a), Apr. 20, 2005, 119 Stat. 185, set out as a note under 11 U.S.C.A. § 1201.

Pub.L. 105–277, Div. C, Title I, § 149, Oct. 21, 1998, 112 Stat. 2681–610, as amended Pub.L. 106–5, §§ 1, 2, Mar. 30, 1999, 113 Stat. 9; Pub.L. 106–70, §§ 1, 2, Oct. 9, 1999, 113 Stat. 1031; Pub.L. 107–8, §§ 1, 2, May 11, 2001, 115 Stat. 10; Pub.L. 107–17, §§ 1, 2, June 26, 2001, 115 Stat. 151; Pub.L. 107–170, §§ 1, 2, May 7, 2002, 116 Stat. 133; Pub.L. 107–171, Title X, § 10814, May 13, 2002, 116 St. 532; Pub.L. 107–377, § 2, Dec. 19, 2002, 116 Stat. 3115; Pub.L. 108–73, § 2(a), Aug. 15, 2003, 117 Stat. 891; Pub.L. 108–369, § 2(a), Oct. 25, 2004, 118 Stat. 1749, provided that, to take effect on January 1, 2004, chapter 12 of Title 11 [this chapter; 11 U.S.C.A. § 1201 et seq.], as in effect on December 31, 2003, is reenacted for the period beginning on January 1, 2004, and ending on July 1, 2005, but that all cases commenced or pending under this chapter 12, as reenacted under section 149(a) of Pub.L. 105–277, and all matters and proceedings in or relating to such cases, shall be conducted and determined under such chapter as if such chapter were continued in effect after July 1, 2005, and that the substantive rights of parties in connection with such cases, matters, and proceedings shall continue to be governed under the law applicable to such cases, matters, and proceedings as if such chapter were continued in effect after July 1, 2005, was superceded by the reenactment of this chapter by Pub.L. 109–8, Title X, § 1001(a), Apr. 20, 2005, 119 Stat. 185, set out as a note under 11 U.S.C.A. § 1201.

§ 1206. Sales free of interests

After notice and a hearing, in addition to the authorization contained in section 363(f), the trustee in a case under this chapter may sell property under section 363(b) and (c) free and clear of any interest in such property of an entity other than the estate if the property is farmland, farm equipment, or property used to carry out a commercial fishing operation (including a commercial fishing vessel), except that the proceeds of such sale shall be subject to such interest.

(Added and amended Pub.L. 99–554, Title II, § 255, Title III, § 302(f), Oct. 27, 1986, 100 Stat. 3108, 3124; Pub.L. 103–65, § 1, Aug. 6, 1993, 107 Stat. 311; Pub.L. 105–277, Div. C, Title I, § 149(a), Oct. 21, 1998, 112 Stat. 2681–610; Pub.L. 106–5, § 1(1), (2), Mar. 30, 1999, 113 Stat. 9; Pub.L. 106–70, § 1, Oct. 9, 1999, 113 Stat. 1031; Pub.L. 107–8, § 1, May 11, 2001, 115 Stat. 10; Pub.L. 107–17, § 1, June 26, 2001, 115 Stat. 151; Pub.L. 107–170, § 1, May 7, 2002, 116 Stat. 133; Pub.L. 107–171, Title X, § 10814(a), May 13, 2002, 116 Stat. 532; Pub.L. 107–377, § 2(a), Dec. 19, 2002, 116 Stat. 3115; Pub.L. 108–73, § 2(a), Aug. 15, 2003, 117 Stat. 891; Pub.L. 108–369, § 2(a), Oct. 25, 2004, 118 Stat. 1749; Pub.L. 109–8, Title X, §§ 1001(a)(1), 1007(c)(3), Apr. 20, 2005, 119 Stat. 185, 188.)

HISTORICAL AND STATUTORY NOTES

Revision Notes and Legislative Reports

1986 Acts. House Report No. 99–764 and House Conference Report No. 99–958, see 1986 U.S. Code Cong. and Adm. News, p. 5227.

1993 Acts. House Report No. 103–32, see 1993 U.S. Code Cong. and Adm. News, p. 373.

1998 Acts. Statement by President, see 1998 U.S. Code Cong. and Adm. News, p. 582.

1999 Acts. Statement by President, see 1999 U.S. Code Cong. and Adm. News, p. 4.

Statement by President, see 1999 U.S. Code Cong. and Adm. News, p. 102.

2001 Acts. House Report No. 107–2, see 2001 U.S. Code Cong. and Adm. News, p. 6.

2005 Acts. House Report No. 109–31(Part I), see 2005 U.S. Code Cong. and Adm. News, p. 88.

Effective and Applicability Provisions

2005 Acts. Amendments by Pub.L. 109–8 effective, except as otherwise provided, 180 days after April 20, 2005, and inapplicable with respect to cases commenced under Title 11 before the effective date, see Pub.L. 109–8, § 1501, set out as a note under 11 U.S.C.A. § 101.

2004 Acts. Amendment by Pub.L. 108–369, § 2(a), extending to July 1, 2005, the date of repeal of this chapter, to take effect Jan. 1, 2004, see Pub.L. 108–369, § 2(b), set out as a note under 11 U.S.C.A. § 1201.

2003 Acts. Amendment by Pub.L. 108–73, § 2(a), extending to Jan. 1, 2004, the date of repeal of this chapter, to take effect July 1, 2003, see Pub.L. 108–73, § 2(b), set out as a note under 11 U.S.C.A. § 1201.

2002 Acts. Amendment by Pub.L. 107–377, § 2(a), extending to July 1, 2003, the date of repeal of this chapter, to take effect Jan. 1, 2003, see Pub.L. 107–377, § 2(b), set out as a note under 11 U.S.C.A. § 1201.

Amendment by Pub.L. 107–171, extending to Jan. 1, 2003, the date of repeal of this chapter, to take effect June 1, 2002, see section 10814(b) of Pub.L. 107–171, set out as a note under 11 U.S.C.A. § 1201.

Amendment by Pub.L. 107–170, extending to June 1, 2002, the date of repeal of this chapter, to take effect October 1, 2001, see section 2 of Pub.L. 107–170, set out as a note under 11 U.S.C.A. § 1201.

2001 Acts. Amendment by Pub.L. 107–17, extending to October 1, 2001, the date of repeal of this chapter, to take effect June 1, 2001, see section 2 of Pub.L. 107–17, set out as a note under 11 U.S.C.A. § 1201.

Amendment by Pub.L. 107–8, extending to June 1, 2001, the date of repeal of this chapter, to take effect July 1, 2000, see section 2 of Pub.L. 107–8, set out as a note under 11 U.S.C.A. § 1201.

1999 Acts. Amendment by Pub.L. 106–70, extending to July 1, 2000, the date of repeal of this chapter, to take effect Oct. 1, 1999, see section 2 of Pub.L. 106–70, set out as a note under section 1201 of this title.

Amendment by Pub.L. 106–5, extending to Oct. 1, 1999 the date of repeal of this chapter, to take effect Apr. 1, 1999, see section 2 of Pub.L. 106–5, set out as a note under section 1201 of this title.

1998 Acts. Section reenacted, eff. Oct. 1, 1998, for the period beginning on Oct. 1, 1998, and ending on Apr. 1, 1999, but all cases commenced or pending under this chapter 12, as reenacted under section 149(a) of Pub.L. 105–277, and all matters and proceedings in or relating to such cases, to be conducted and determined under such chapter as if such chapter were continued in effect after Apr. 1, 1999, and the substantive rights of parties in connection with such cases, matters, and proceedings to continue to be governed under the law applicable to such cases, matters, and proceedings as if such chapter were continued in effect after Apr. 1, 1999, see section 149 of Pub.L. 105–277, set out as a note under section 1201 of this title.

1993 Acts. Amendment by Pub.L. 103–65, extending to Oct. 1, 1998 the date of repeal of this chapter, to take effect Aug. 6, 1993, see section 3 of Pub.L. 103–65, set out as a note under section 1221 of this title.

1986 Acts. Section repealed effective Oct. 1, 1998, see section 302(f) of Pub.L. 99–554, as amended, set out in a note under section 581 of Title 28. However, for extension of provisions, see section 149 of Pub.L. 105–277, set out as a note under section 1201 of this title.

Section effective 30 days after Oct. 27, 1986, but not applicable to cases commenced under this title before that date, see section 302(a), (c)(1) of Pub.L. 99–554, set out as a note under section 581 of Title 28, Judiciary and Judicial Procedure.

Reenactment of Chapter

This section as in effect on June 30, 2005, reenacted effective July 1, 2005, see Pub.L. 109–8, § 1001(a), set out as a note under 11 U.S.C.A. § 1201.

Repeal of Chapter; Extension of Provisions

Pub.L. 99–554, Title III, § 302(f), Oct. 27, 1986, 100 Stat. 3124, as amended Pub.L. 103–65, § 1, Aug. 6, 1993, 107 Stat. 311, which provided that, effective Oct. 1, 1998, this chapter is repealed, but that all cases commenced or pending under this chapter, and all matters and proceedings in or relating to such cases, shall be conducted and determined under this chapter as if such chapter had not been repealed, and that the substantive rights of parties in connection with such cases, matters, and proceedings shall continue to be governed under the laws applicable to such cases, matters, and proceedings as if such chapter had not been repealed, was superceded by the reenactment of this chapter by Pub.L. 109–8, Title X, § 1001(a), Apr. 20, 2005, 119 Stat. 185, set out as a note under 11 U.S.C.A. § 1201.

Pub.L. 105–277, Div. C, Title I, § 149, Oct. 21, 1998, 112 Stat. 2681–610, as amended Pub.L. 106–5, §§ 1, 2, Mar. 30, 1999, 113 Stat. 9; Pub.L. 106–70, §§ 1, 2, Oct. 9, 1999, 113 Stat. 1031; Pub.L. 107–8, §§ 1, 2, May 11, 2001, 115 Stat. 10; Pub.L. 107–17, §§ 1, 2, June 26, 2001, 115 Stat. 151; Pub.L. 107–170, §§ 1, 2, May 7, 2002, 116 Stat. 133; Pub.L. 107–171, Title X, § 10814, May 13, 2002, 116 St. 532; Pub.L. 107–377, § 2, Dec. 19, 2002, 116 Stat. 3115; Pub.L. 108–73, § 2(a), Aug. 15, 2003, 117 Stat. 891; Pub.L. 108–369, § 2(a), Oct. 25, 2004, 118 Stat. 1749, provided that, to take effect on January 1, 2004, chapter 12 of Title 11 [this chapter; 11 U.S.C.A. § 1201 et seq.], as in effect on December 31, 2003, is reenacted for the period beginning on January 1, 2004, and ending on July 1, 2005, but that all cases commenced or pending under this chapter 12, as reenacted under section 149(a) of Pub.L. 105–277, and all matters and proceedings in or relating to such cases, shall be conducted and determined under such chapter as if such chapter were continued in effect after July 1, 2005, and that the substantive rights of parties in connection with such cases, matters, and proceedings shall continue to be governed under the law applicable to such cases, matters, and proceedings as if such chapter were continued in effect after July 1, 2005, was superceded by the reenactment of this chapter by Pub.L. 109–8, Title X, § 1001(a), Apr. 20, 2005, 119 Stat. 185, set out as a note under 11 U.S.C.A. § 1201.

§ 1207. Property of the estate

(a) Property of the estate includes, in addition to the property specified in section 541 of this title—

(1) all property of the kind specified in such section that the debtor acquires after the commencement of the case but before the case is closed, dismissed, or converted to a case under chapter 7 of this title, whichever occurs first; and

(2) earnings from services performed by the debtor after the commencement of the case but before the case is closed, dismissed, or converted to a case under chapter 7 of this title, whichever occurs first.

(b) Except as provided in section 1204, a confirmed plan, or an order confirming a plan, the debtor shall remain in possession of all property of the estate. (Added and amended Pub.L. 99–554, Title II, § 255, Title III, § 302(f), Oct. 27, 1986, 100 Stat. 3108, 3124; Pub.L. 103–65, § 1, Aug. 6, 1993, 107 Stat. 311; Pub.L. 105–277, Div. C, Title I, § 149(a), Oct. 21, 1998, 112 Stat. 2681–610; Pub.L. 106–5, § 1(1), (2), Mar. 30, 1999, 113 Stat. 9; Pub.L. 106–70, § 1, Oct. 9, 1999, 113 Stat. 1031; Pub.L. 107–8, § 1, May 11, 2001, 115 Stat. 10; Pub.L. 107–17, § 1, June 26, 2001, 115 Stat. 151; Pub.L. 107–170, § 1, May 7, 2002, 116 Stat. 133; Pub.L. 107–171, Title X, § 10814(a), May 13, 2002, 116 Stat. 532; Pub.L. 107–377, § 2(a), Dec. 19, 2002, 116 Stat. 3115; Pub.L. 108–73, § 2(a), Aug. 15, 2003, 117 Stat. 891; Pub.L. 108–369, § 2(a), Oct. 25, 2004, 118 Stat. 1749; Pub.L. 109–8, Title X, § 1001(a)(1), Apr. 20, 2005, 119 Stat. 185.)

HISTORICAL AND STATUTORY NOTES

Revision Notes and Legislative Reports

1986 Acts. House Report No. 99–764 and House Conference Report No. 99–958, see 1986 U.S. Code Cong. and Adm. News, p. 5227.

1993 Acts. House Report No. 103–32, see 1993 U.S. Code Cong. and Adm. News, p. 373.

1998 Acts. Statement by President, see 1998 U.S. Code Cong. and Adm. News, p. 582.

1999 Acts. Statement by President, see 1999 U.S. Code Cong. and Adm. News, p. 4.

Statement by President, see 1999 U.S. Code Cong. and Adm. News, p. 102.

2001 Acts. House Report No. 107–2, see 2001 U.S. Code Cong. and Adm. News, p. 6.

2005 Acts. House Report No. 109–31(Part I), see 2005 U.S. Code Cong. and Adm. News, p. 88.

Effective and Applicability Provisions

2005 Acts. Amendments by Pub.L. 109–8 effective, except as otherwise provided, 180 days after April 20, 2005, and inapplicable with respect to cases commenced under Title 11 before the effective date, see Pub.L. 109–8, § 1501, set out as a note under 11 U.S.C.A. § 101.

2004 Acts. Amendment by Pub.L. 108–369, § 2(a), extending to July 1, 2005, the date of repeal of this chapter, to take effect Jan. 1, 2004, see Pub.L. 108–369, § 2(b), set out as a note under 11 U.S.C.A. § 1201.

2003 Acts. Amendment by Pub.L. 108–73, § 2(a), extending to Jan. 1, 2004, the date of repeal of this chapter, to take effect July 1, 2003, see Pub.L. 108–73, § 2(b), set out as a note under 11 U.S.C.A. § 1201.

2002 Acts. Amendment by Pub.L. 107–377, § 2(a), extending to July 1, 2003, the date of repeal of this chapter, to take effect Jan. 1, 2003, see Pub.L. 107–377, § 2(b), set out as a note under 11 U.S.C.A. § 1201.

Amendment by Pub.L. 107–171, extending to Jan. 1, 2003, the date of repeal of this chapter, to take effect June 1, 2002, see section 10814(b) of Pub.L. 107–171, set out as a note under 11 U.S.C.A. § 1201.

Amendment by Pub.L. 107–170, extending to June 1, 2002, the date of repeal of this chapter, to take effect October 1, 2001, see section 2 of Pub.L. 107–170, set out as a note under 11 U.S.C.A. § 1201.

2001 Acts. Amendment by Pub.L. 107–17, extending to October 1, 2001, the date of repeal of this chapter, to take effect June 1, 2001, see section 2 of Pub.L. 107–17, set out as a note under 11 U.S.C.A. § 1201.

Amendment by Pub.L. 107–8, extending to June 1, 2001, the date of repeal of this chapter, to take effect July 1, 2000, see section 2 of Pub.L. 107–8, set out as a note under 11 U.S.C.A. § 1201.

1999 Acts. Amendment by Pub.L. 106–70, extending to July 1, 2000, the date of repeal of this chapter, to take effect Oct. 1, 1999, see section 2 of Pub.L. 106–70, set out as a note under section 1201 of this title.

Amendment by Pub.L. 106–5, extending to Oct. 1, 1999 the date of repeal of this chapter, to take effect Apr. 1, 1999, see section 2 of Pub.L. 106–5, set out as a note under section 1201 of this title.

1998 Acts. Section reenacted, eff. Oct. 1, 1998, for the period beginning on Oct. 1, 1998, and ending on Apr. 1, 1999, but all cases commenced or pending under this chapter 12, as reenacted under section 149(a) of Pub.L. 105–277, and all matters and proceedings in or relating to such cases, to be conducted and determined under such chapter as if such chapter were continued in effect after Apr. 1, 1999, and the substantive rights of parties in connection with such cases, matters, and proceedings to continue to be governed under the law applicable to such cases, matters, and proceedings as if such chapter were continued in effect after Apr. 1, 1999, see section 149 of Pub.L. 105–277, set out as a note under section 1201 of this title.

1993 Acts. Amendment by Pub.L. 103–65, extending to Oct. 1, 1998 the date of repeal of this chapter, to take effect Aug. 6, 1993, see section 3 of Pub.L. 103–65, set out as a note under section 1221 of this title.

1986 Acts. Section repealed effective Oct. 1, 1998, see section 302(f) of Pub.L. 99–554, as amended, set out in a note under section 581 of Title 28. However, for extension of provisions, see section 149 of Pub.L. 105–277, set out as a note under section 1201 of this title.

Section effective 30 days after Oct. 27, 1986, but not applicable to cases commenced under this title before that date, see section 302(a), (c)(1) of Pub.L. 99–554, set out as a note under section 581 of Title 28, Judiciary and Judicial Procedure.

Reenactment of Chapter

This section as in effect on June 30, 2005, reenacted effective July 1, 2005, see Pub.L. 109–8, § 1001(a), set out as a note under 11 U.S.C.A. § 1201.

Repeal of Chapter; Extension of Provisions

Pub.L. 99–554, Title III, § 302(f), Oct. 27, 1986, 100 Stat. 3124, as amended Pub.L. 103–65, § 1, Aug. 6, 1993, 107 Stat. 311, which provided that, effective Oct. 1, 1998, this chapter is repealed, but that all cases commenced or pending under this chapter, and all matters and proceedings in or relating to such cases, shall be conducted and determined under this chapter as if such chapter had not been repealed, and that the substantive rights of parties in connection with such cases, matters, and proceedings shall continue to be governed under the laws applicable to such cases, matters, and proceedings as if such chapter had not been repealed, was superceded by the reenactment of this chapter by Pub.L. 109–8, Title X, § 1001(a), Apr. 20, 2005, 119 Stat. 185, set out as a note under 11 U.S.C.A. § 1201.

Pub.L. 105–277, Div. C, Title I, § 149, Oct. 21, 1998, 112 Stat. 2681–610, as amended Pub.L. 106–5, §§ 1, 2, Mar. 30, 1999, 113 Stat. 9; Pub.L. 106–70, §§ 1, 2, Oct. 9, 1999, 113 Stat. 1031; Pub.L. 107–8, §§ 1, 2, May 11, 2001, 115 Stat. 10; Pub.L. 107–17, §§ 1, 2, June 26, 2001, 115 Stat. 151; Pub.L. 107–170, §§ 1, 2, May 7, 2002, 116 Stat. 133; Pub.L. 107–171, Title X, § 10814, May 13, 2002, 116 St. 532; Pub.L. 107–377, § 2, Dec. 19, 2002, 116 Stat. 3115; Pub.L. 108–73, § 2(a), Aug. 15, 2003, 117 Stat. 891; Pub.L. 108–369, § 2(a), Oct. 25, 2004, 118 Stat. 1749, provided that, to take effect on January 1, 2004, chapter 12 of Title 11 [this chapter; 11 U.S.C.A. § 1201 et seq.], as in effect on December 31, 2003, is reenacted for the period beginning on January 1, 2004, and ending on July 1, 2005, but that all cases commenced or pending under this chapter 12, as reenacted under section 149(a) of Pub.L. 105–277, and all matters and proceedings in or relating to such cases, shall be conducted and determined under such chapter as if such chapter were continued in effect after July 1, 2005, and that the substantive rights of parties in connection with such cases, matters, and proceedings shall continue to be governed under the law applicable to such cases, matters, and proceedings as if such chapter were continued in effect after July 1, 2005, was superceded by the reenactment of this chapter by Pub.L. 109–8, Title X, § 1001(a), Apr. 20, 2005, 119 Stat. 185, set out as a note under 11 U.S.C.A. § 1201.

§ 1208. Conversion or dismissal

(a) The debtor may convert a case under this chapter to a case under chapter 7 of this title at any time. Any waiver of the right to convert under this subsection is unenforceable.

(b) On request of the debtor at any time, if the case has not been converted under section 706 or 1112 of this title, the court shall dismiss a case under this chapter. Any waiver of the right to dismiss under this subsection is unenforceable.

(c) On request of a party in interest, and after notice and a hearing, the court may dismiss a case under this chapter for cause, including—

(1) unreasonable delay, or gross mismanagement, by the debtor that is prejudicial to creditors;

(2) nonpayment of any fees and charges required under chapter 123 of title 28;

(3) failure to file a plan timely under section 1221 of this title;

(4) failure to commence making timely payments required by a confirmed plan;

(5) denial of confirmation of a plan under section 1225 of this title and denial of a request made for additional time for filing another plan or a modification of a plan;

(6) material default by the debtor with respect to a term of a confirmed plan;

(7) revocation of the order of confirmation under section 1230 of this title, and denial of confirmation of a modified plan under section 1229 of this title;

(8) termination of a confirmed plan by reason of the occurrence of a condition specified in the plan;

(9) continuing loss to or diminution of the estate and absence of a reasonable likelihood of rehabilitation; and

(10) failure of the debtor to pay any domestic support obligation that first becomes payable after the date of the filing of the petition.

(d) On request of a party in interest, and after notice and a hearing, the court may dismiss a case under this chapter or convert a case under this chapter to a case under chapter 7 of this title upon a showing that the debtor has committed fraud in connection with the case.

(e) Notwithstanding any other provision of this section, a case may not be converted to a case under another chapter of this title unless the debtor may be a debtor under such chapter.

(Added and amended Pub.L. 99–554, Title II, § 255, Title III, § 302(f), Oct. 27, 1986, 100 Stat. 3108, 3124; Pub.L. 103–65, § 1, Aug. 6, 1993, 107 Stat. 311; Pub.L. 105–277, Div. C, Title I, § 149(a), Oct. 21, 1998, 112 Stat. 2681–610; Pub.L. 106–5, § 1(1), (2), Mar. 30, 1999, 113 Stat. 9; Pub.L. 106–70, § 1, Oct. 9, 1999, 113 Stat. 1031; Pub.L. 107–8, § 1, May 11, 2001, 115 Stat. 10; Pub.L. 107–17, § 1, June 26, 2001, 115 Stat. 151; Pub.L. 107–170, § 1, May 7, 2002, 116 Stat. 133; Pub.L. 107–171, Title X, § 10814(a), May 13, 2002, 116 Stat. 532; Pub.L. 107–377, § 2(a), Dec. 19, 2002, 116 Stat. 3115; Pub.L. 108–73, § 2(a), Aug. 15, 2003, 117 Stat. 891; Pub.L. 108–369, § 2(a), Oct. 25, 2004, 118 Stat. 1749; Pub.L. 109–8, Title II, § 213(2), Title X, § 1001(a)(1), Apr. 20, 2005, 119 Stat. 52, 185.)

HISTORICAL AND STATUTORY NOTES

Revision Notes and Legislative Reports

1986 Acts. House Report No. 99–764 and House Conference Report No. 99–958, see 1986 U.S. Code Cong. and Adm. News, p. 5227.

1993 Acts. House Report No. 103–32, see 1993 U.S. Code Cong. and Adm. News, p. 373.

1998 Acts. Statement by President, see 1998 U.S. Code Cong. and Adm. News, p. 582.

1999 Acts. Statement by President, see 1999 U.S. Code Cong. and Adm. News, p. 4.

Statement by President, see 1999 U.S. Code Cong. and Adm. News, p. 102.

2001 Acts. House Report No. 107–2, see 2001 U.S. Code Cong. and Adm. News, p. 6.

2005 Acts. House Report No. 109–31(Part I), see 2005 U.S. Code Cong. and Adm. News, p. 88.

Effective and Applicability Provisions

2005 Acts. Amendments by Pub.L. 109–8 effective, except as otherwise provided, 180 days after April 20, 2005, and inapplicable with respect to cases commenced under Title 11 before the effective date, see Pub.L. 109–8, § 1501, set out as a note under 11 U.S.C.A. § 101.

2004 Acts. Amendment by Pub.L. 108–369, § 2(a), extending to July 1, 2005, the date of repeal of this chapter, to take effect Jan. 1, 2004, see Pub.L. 108–369, § 2(b), set out as a note under 11 U.S.C.A. § 1201.

2003 Acts. Amendment by Pub.L. 108–73, § 2(a), extending to Jan. 1, 2004, the date of repeal of this chapter, to take effect July 1, 2003, see Pub.L. 108–73, § 2(b), set out as a note under 11 U.S.C.A. § 1201.

2002 Acts. Amendment by Pub.L. 107–377, § 2(a), extending to July 1, 2003, the date of repeal of this chapter, to take effect Jan. 1, 2003, see Pub.L. 107–377, § 2(b), set out as a note under 11 U.S.C.A. § 1201.

Amendment by Pub.L. 107–171, extending to Jan. 1, 2003, the date of repeal of this chapter, to take effect June 1, 2002, see section 10814(b) of Pub.L. 107–171, set out as a note under 11 U.S.C.A. § 1201.

Amendment by Pub.L. 107–170, extending to June 1, 2002, the date of repeal of this chapter, to take effect Oct. 1, 2001, see section 2 of Pub.L. 107–170, set out as a note under 11 U.S.C.A. § 1201.

2001 Acts. Amendment by Pub.L. 107–17, extending to Oct. 1, 2001, the date of repeal of this chapter, to take effect June 1, 2001, see section 2 of Pub.L. 107–17, set out as a note under 11 U.S.C.A. § 1201.

Amendment by Pub.L. 107–8, extending to June 1, 2001, the date of repeal of this chapter, to take effect July 1, 2000, see section 2 of Pub.L. 107–8, set out as a note under 11 U.S.C.A. § 1201.

1999 Acts. Amendment by Pub.L. 106–70, extending to July 1, 2000, the date of repeal of this chapter, to take effect Oct. 1, 1999, see section 2 of Pub.L. 106–70, set out as a note under section 1201 of this title.

Amendment by Pub.L. 106–5, extending to Oct. 1, 1999, the date of repeal of this chapter, to take effect Apr. 1, 1999, see section 2 of Pub.L. 106–5, set out as a note under section 1201 of this title.

1998 Acts. Section reenacted, eff. Oct. 1, 1998, for the period beginning on Oct. 1, 1998, and ending on Apr. 1, 1999, but all cases commenced or pending under this chapter 12, as reenacted under section 149(a) of Pub.L. 105–277, and all matters and proceedings in or relating to such cases, to be conducted and determined under such chapter as if such chapter were continued in effect after Apr. 1, 1999, and the substantive rights of parties in connection with such cases, matters, and proceedings to continue to be governed under the law applicable to such cases, matters, and proceedings as if such chapter were continued in effect after Apr. 1, 1999, see section 149 of Pub.L. 105–277, set out as a note under section 1201 of this title.

1993 Acts. Amendment by Pub.L. 103–65, extending to Oct. 1, 1998 the date of repeal of this chapter, to take effect Aug. 6, 1993, see section 3 of Pub.L. 103–65, set out as a note under section 1221 of this title.

1986 Acts. Section repealed effective Oct. 1, 1998, see section 302(f) of Pub.L. 99–554, as amended, set out in a note under section 581 of Title 28. However, for extension of provisions, see section 149 of Pub.L. 105–277, set out as a note under section 1201 of this title.

Section effective 30 days after Oct. 27, 1986, but not applicable to cases commenced under this title before that date, see section 302(a), (c)(1) of Pub.L. 99–554, set out as a note under section 581 of Title 28, Judiciary and Judicial Procedure.

Reenactment of Chapter

This section as in effect on June 30, 2005, reenacted effective July 1, 2005, see Pub.L. 109–8, § 1001(a), set out as a note under 11 U.S.C.A. § 1201.

Repeal of Chapter; Extension of Provisions

Pub.L. 99–554, Title III, § 302(f), Oct. 27, 1986, 100 Stat. 3124, as amended Pub.L. 103–65, § 1, Aug. 6, 1993, 107 Stat. 311, which provided that, effective Oct. 1, 1998, this chapter is repealed, but that all cases commenced or pending under this chapter, and all matters and proceedings in or relating to such cases, shall be conducted and determined under this chapter as if such chapter had not been repealed, and that the substantive rights of parties in connection with such cases, matters, and proceedings shall continue to be governed under the laws applicable to such cases, matters, and proceedings as if such chapter had not been repealed, was superceded by the reenactment of this chapter by Pub.L. 109–8, Title X, § 1001(a), Apr. 20, 2005, 119 Stat. 185, set out as a note under 11 U.S.C.A. § 1201.

Pub.L. 105–277, Div. C, Title I, § 149, Oct. 21, 1998, 112 Stat. 2681–610, as amended Pub.L. 106–5, §§ 1, 2, Mar. 30, 1999, 113 Stat. 9; Pub.L. 106–70, §§ 1, 2, Oct. 9, 1999, 113 Stat. 1031; Pub.L. 107–8, §§ 1, 2, May 11, 2001, 115 Stat. 10; Pub.L. 107–17, §§ 1, 2, June 26, 2001, 115 Stat. 151; Pub.L. 107–170, §§ 1, 2, May 7, 2002, 116 Stat. 133; Pub.L. 107–171, Title X, § 10814, May 13, 2002, 116 St. 532; Pub.L. 107–377, § 2, Dec. 19, 2002, 116 Stat. 3115; Pub.L. 108–73, § 2(a), Aug. 15, 2003, 117 Stat. 891; Pub.L. 108–369, § 2(a), Oct. 25, 2004, 118 Stat. 1749, provided that, to take effect on January 1, 2004, chapter 12 of Title 11 [this chapter; 11 U.S.C.A. § 1201 et seq.], as in effect on December 31, 2003, is reenacted for the period beginning on January 1, 2004, and ending on July 1, 2005, but that all cases commenced or pending under this chapter 12, as reenacted under section 149(a) of Pub.L.

105–277, and all matters and proceedings in or relating to such cases, shall be conducted and determined under such chapter as if such chapter were continued in effect after July 1, 2005, and that the substantive rights of parties in connection with such cases, matters, and proceedings shall continue to be governed under the law applicable to such cases, matters, and proceedings as if such chapter were continued in effect after July 1, 2005, was superceded by the reenactment of this chapter by Pub.L. 109–8, Title X, § 1001(a), Apr. 20, 2005, 119 Stat. 185, set out as a note under 11 U.S.C.A. § 1201.

CROSS REFERENCES

Conversion from Chapter seven, see 11 USCA § 706.

Dismissal of Chapter thirteen cases where not converted under this section, see 11 USCA § 1307.

Distribution of property of estate converted to Chapter seven, see 11 USCA § 726.

Effect of—

Conversion, see 11 USCA § 348.

Dismissal, see 11 USCA § 349.

Executory contracts and unexpired leases, see 11 USCA § 365.

Liquidation of estate in railroad reorganization cases, see 11 USCA § 1174.

Termination of debtor's taxable period for cases converted to Chapter 7, see 11 USCA § 728.

SUBCHAPTER II—THE PLAN

§ 1221. Filing of plan

The debtor shall file a plan not later than 90 days after the order for relief under this chapter, except that the court may extend such period if the need for an extension is attributable to circumstances for which the debtor should not justly be held accountable. (Added and amended Pub.L. 99–554, Title II, § 255, Title III, § 302(f), Oct. 27, 1986, 100 Stat. 3109, 3124; Pub.L. 103–65, §§ 1, 2, Aug. 6, 1993, 107 Stat. 311; Pub.L. 105–277, Div. C, Title I, § 149(a), Oct. 21, 1998, 112 Stat. 2681–610; Pub.L. 106–5, § 1(1), (2), Mar. 30, 1999, 113 Stat. 9; Pub.L. 106–70, § 1, Oct. 9, 1999, 113 Stat. 1031; Pub.L. 107–8, § 1, May 11, 2001, 115 Stat. 10; Pub.L. 107–17, § 1, June 26, 2001, 115 Stat. 151; Pub.L. 107–170, § 1, May 7, 2002, 116 Stat. 133; Pub.L. 107–171, Title X, § 10814(a), May 13, 2002, 116 Stat. 532; Pub.L. 107–377, § 2(a), Dec. 19, 2002, 116 Stat. 3115; Pub.L. 108–73, § 2(a), Aug. 15, 2003, 117 Stat. 891; Pub.L. 108–369, § 2(a), Oct. 25, 2004, 118 Stat. 1749; Pub.L. 109–8, Title X, § 1001(a)(1), Apr. 20, 2005, 119 Stat. 185.)

HISTORICAL AND STATUTORY NOTES

Revision Notes and Legislative Reports

1986 Acts. House Report No. 99–764 and House Conference Report No. 99–958, see 1986 U.S. Code Cong. and Adm. News, p. 5227.

1993 Acts. House Report No. 103–32, see 1993 U.S. Code Cong. and Adm. News, p. 373.

1998 Acts. Statement by President, see 1998 U.S. Code Cong. and Adm. News, p. 582.

1999 Acts. Statement by President, see 1999 U.S. Code Cong. and Adm. News, p. 4.

Statement by President, see 1999 U.S. Code Cong. and Adm. News, p. 102.

2001 Acts. House Report No. 107–2, see 2001 U.S. Code Cong. and Adm. News, p. 6.

2005 Acts. House Report No. 109–31(Part I), see 2005 U.S. Code Cong. and Adm. News, p. 88.

Effective and Applicability Provisions

2005 Acts. Amendments by Pub.L. 109–8 effective, except as otherwise provided, 180 days after April 20, 2005, and inapplicable with respect to cases commenced under Title 11 before the effective date, see Pub.L. 109–8, § 1501, set out as a note under 11 U.S.C.A. § 101.

2004 Acts. Amendment by Pub.L. 108–369, § 2(a), extending to July 1, 2005, the date of repeal of this chapter, to take effect Jan. 1, 2004, see Pub.L. 108–369, § 2(b), set out as a note under 11 U.S.C.A. § 1201.

2003 Acts. Amendment by Pub.L. 108–73, § 2(a), extending to Jan. 1, 2004, the date of repeal of this chapter, to take effect July 1, 2003, see Pub.L. 108–73, § 2(b), set out as a note under 11 U.S.C.A. § 1201.

2002 Acts. Amendment by Pub.L. 107–377, § 2(a), extending to July 1, 2003, the date of repeal of this chapter, to take effect Jan. 1, 2003, see Pub.L. 107–377, § 2(b), set out as a note under 11 U.S.C.A. § 1201.

Amendment by Pub.L. 107–171, extending to Jan. 1, 2003, the date of repeal of this chapter, to take effect June 1, 2002, see section 10814(b) of Pub.L. 107–171, set out as a note under 11 U.S.C.A. § 1201.

Amendment by Pub.L. 107–170, extending to June 1, 2002, the date of repeal of this chapter, to take effect October 1, 2001, see section 2 of Pub.L. 107–170, set out as a note under 11 U.S.C.A. § 1201.

2001 Acts. Amendment by Pub.L. 107–17, extending to October 1, 2001, the date of repeal of this chapter, to take effect June 1, 2001, see section 2 of Pub.L. 107–17, set out as a note under 11 U.S.C.A. § 1201.

Amendment by Pub.L. 107–8, extending to June 1, 2001, the date of repeal of this chapter, to take effect July 1, 2000, see section 2 of Pub.L. 107–8, set out as a note under 11 U.S.C.A. § 1201.

1999 Acts. Amendment by Pub.L. 106–70, extending to July 1, 2000, the date of repeal of this chapter, to take effect Oct. 1, 1999, see section 2 of Pub.L. 106–70, set out as a note under section 1201 of this title.

Amendment by Pub.L. 106–5, extending to Oct. 1, 1999 the date of repeal of this chapter, to take effect Apr. 1, 1999, see section 2 of Pub.L. 106–5, set out as a note under section 1201 of this title.

1998 Acts. Section reenacted, eff. Oct. 1, 1998, for the period beginning on Oct. 1, 1998, and ending on Apr. 1, 1999, but all cases commenced or pending under this chapter 12, as reenacted under section 149(a) of Pub.L. 105–277, and all matters and proceedings in or relating to such cases, to be conducted and determined under such chapter as if such chapter were continued in effect after Apr. 1, 1999, and the substantive rights of parties in connection with such cases, matters, and proceedings to continue to be governed under the law applicable to such cases, matters, and proceedings as if such chapter were continued in effect after Apr. 1, 1999, see section 149 of Pub.L. 105–277, set out as a note under 11 U.S.C.A. § 1201.

1993 Acts. Section 3 of Pub.L. 103–65 provided that:

"**(a) Effective date.**—Except as provided in subsection (b), this Act and the amendments made by this Act [amending this section and provisions set out as a note under 28 U.S.C.A. § 581, and extending the date of repeal of this chapter to Oct. 1, 1998] shall take effect on the date of the enactment of this Act [Aug. 6, 1993].

"**(b) Application of amendment made by section 2.**—The amendment made by section 2 [amending this section] shall not apply with respect to cases commenced under title 11 of the United States Code [this title] before the date of the enactment of this Act [Aug. 6, 1993]."

1986 Acts. Section repealed effective Oct. 1, 1998, see section 302(f) of Pub.L. 99–554, as amended, set out as a note under 28 U.S.C.A. § 581. However, for extension of provisions, see section 149 of Pub.L. 105–277, set out as a note under 11 U.S.C.A. § 1201.

Section effective 30 days after Oct. 27, 1986, but not applicable to cases commenced under this title before that date, see section 302(a), (c)(1) of Pub.L. 99–554, set out as a note under 28 U.S.C.A. § 581.

Reenactment of Chapter

This section as in effect on June 30, 2005, reenacted effective July 1, 2005, see Pub.L. 109–8, § 1001(a), set out as a note under 11 U.S.C.A. § 1201.

Repeal of Chapter; Extension of Provisions

Pub.L. 99–554, Title III, § 302(f), Oct. 27, 1986, 100 Stat. 3124, as amended Pub.L. 103–65, § 1, Aug. 6, 1993, 107 Stat. 311, which provided that, effective Oct. 1, 1998, this chapter is repealed, but that all cases commenced or pending under this chapter, and all matters and proceedings in or relating to such cases, shall be conducted and determined under this chapter as if such chapter had not been repealed, and that the substantive rights of parties in connection with such cases, matters, and proceedings shall continue to be governed under the laws applicable to such cases, matters, and proceedings as if such chapter had not been repealed, was superceded by the reenactment of this chapter by Pub.L. 109–8, Title X, § 1001(a), Apr. 20, 2005, 119 Stat. 185, set out as a note under 11 U.S.C.A. § 1201.

Pub.L. 105–277, Div. C, Title I, § 149, Oct. 21, 1998, 112 Stat. 2681–610, as amended Pub.L. 106–5, §§ 1, 2, Mar. 30, 1999, 113 Stat. 9; Pub.L. 106–70, §§ 1, 2, Oct. 9, 1999, 113 Stat. 1031; Pub.L. 107–8, §§ 1, 2, May 11, 2001, 115 Stat. 10; Pub.L. 107–17, §§ 1, 2, June 26, 2001, 115 Stat. 151; Pub.L. 107–170, §§ 1, 2, May 7, 2002, 116 Stat. 133; Pub.L. 107–171, Title X, § 10814, May 13, 2002, 116 St. 532; Pub.L. 107–377, § 2, Dec. 19, 2002, 116 Stat. 3115; Pub.L. 108–73, § 2(a), Aug. 15, 2003, 117 Stat. 891; Pub.L. 108–369, § 2(a), Oct. 25, 2004, 118 Stat. 1749, provided that, to take effect on January 1, 2004, chapter 12 of Title 11 [this chapter; 11 U.S.C.A. § 1201 et seq.], as in effect on December 31, 2003, is reenacted for the period beginning on January 1, 2004, and ending on July 1, 2005, but that all cases commenced or pending under this chapter 12, as reenacted under section 149(a) of Pub.L. 105–277, and all matters and proceedings in or relating to such cases, shall be conducted and determined under such chapter as if such chapter were continued in effect after July 1, 2005, and that the substantive rights of parties in connection with such cases, matters, and proceedings shall continue to be governed under the law applicable to such cases, matters, and proceedings as if such chapter were continued in effect after July 1, 2005, was superceded by the reenactment of this chapter by Pub.L. 109–8, Title X, § 1001(a), Apr. 20, 2005, 119 Stat. 185, set out as a note under 11 U.S.C.A. § 1201.

CROSS REFERENCES

Conversion or dismissal for failure to timely file plan, see 11 USCA § 1208.

Effect of conversion, see 11 USCA § 348.

Filing of plan in—

Chapter nine cases, see 11 USCA § 941.

Chapter thirteen cases, see 11 USCA § 1321.

Who may file plan in Chapter eleven cases, see 11 USCA § 1121.

§ 1222. Contents of plan

(a) The plan shall—

(1) provide for the submission of all or such portion of future earnings or other future income of the debtor to the supervision and control of the trustee as is necessary for the execution of the plan;

(2) provide for the full payment, in deferred cash payments, of all claims entitled to priority under section 507, unless—

(A) the claim is a claim owed to a governmental unit that arises as a result of the sale, transfer, exchange, or other disposition of any farm asset used in the debtor's farming operation, in which case the claim shall be treated as an unsecured claim that is not entitled to priority under section 507, but the debt shall be treated in such manner only if the debtor receives a discharge; or

(B) the holder of a particular claim agrees to a different treatment of that claim;

(3) if the plan classifies claims and interests, provide the same treatment for each claim or interest within a particular class unless the holder of a particular claim or interest agrees to less favorable treatment; and

(4) notwithstanding any other provision of this section, a plan may provide for less than full payment of all amounts owed for a claim entitled to priority under section 507(a)(1)(B) only if the plan provides that all of the debtor's projected disposable income for a 5-year period beginning on the date that the first payment is due under the plan will be applied to make payments under the plan.

(b) Subject to subsections (a) and (c) of this section, the plan may—

(1) designate a class or classes of unsecured claims, as provided in section 1122 of this title, but may not discriminate unfairly against any class so designated; however, such plan may treat claims for a consumer debt of the debtor if an individual is liable on such consumer debt with the debtor differently than other unsecured claims;

(2) modify the rights of holders of secured claims, or of holders of unsecured claims, or leave unaffected the rights of holders of any class of claims;

(3) provide for the curing or waiving of any default;

(4) provide for payments on any unsecured claim to be made concurrently with payments on any secured claim or any other unsecured claim;

(5) provide for the curing of any default within a reasonable time and maintenance of payments while the case is pending on any unsecured claim or secured claim on which the last payment is due after the date on which the final payment under the plan is due;

(6) subject to section 365 of this title, provide for the assumption, rejection, or assignment of any executory contract or unexpired lease of the debtor not previously rejected under such section;

(7) provide for the payment of all or part of a claim against the debtor from property of the estate or property of the debtor;

(8) provide for the sale of all or any part of the property of the estate or the distribution of all or any part of the property of the estate among those having an interest in such property;

(9) provide for payment of allowed secured claims consistent with section 1225(a)(5) of this title, over a period exceeding the period permitted under section 1222(c);

(10) provide for the vesting of property of the estate, on confirmation of the plan or at a later time, in the debtor or in any other entity;

(11) provide for the payment of interest accruing after the date of the filing of the petition on unsecured claims that are nondischargeable under section 1228(a), except that such interest may be paid only to the extent that the debtor has disposable income available to pay such interest after making provision for full payment of all allowed claims; and

(12) include any other appropriate provision not inconsistent with this title.

(c) Except as provided in subsections (b)(5) and (b)(9), the plan may not provide for payments over a period that is longer than three years unless the court for cause approves a longer period, but the court may not approve a period that is longer than five years.

(d) Notwithstanding subsection (b)(2) of this section and sections 506(b) and 1225(a)(5) of this title, if it is proposed in a plan to cure a default, the amount necessary to cure the default, shall be determined in accordance with the underlying agreement and applicable nonbankruptcy law.

(Added and amended Pub.L. 99–554, Title II, § 255, Title III, § 302(f), Oct. 27, 1986, 100 Stat. 3109, 3124; Pub.L. 103–65, § 1, Aug. 6, 1993, 107 Stat. 311; Pub.L. 103–394, Title III, § 305(b), Oct. 22, 1994, 108 Stat. 4134; Pub.L. 105–277, Div. C, Title I, § 149(a), Oct. 21, 1998, 112 Stat. 2681–610; Pub.L. 106–5, § 1(1), (2), Mar. 30, 1999, 113 Stat. 9; Pub.L. 106–70, § 1, Oct. 9, 1999, 113 Stat. 1031; Pub.L. 107–8, § 1, May 11, 2001, 115 Stat. 10; Pub.L. 107–17, § 1, June 26, 2001, 115 Stat. 151; Pub.L. 107–170, § 1, May 7, 2002, 116 Stat. 133; Pub.L. 107–171, Title X, § 10814(a), May 13, 2002 116 Stat. 532; Pub.L. 107–377, § 2(a), Dec. 19, 2002, 116 Stat. 3115; Pub.L. 108–73, § 2(a), Aug. 15, 2003, 117 Stat. 891; Pub.L. 108–369, § 2(a), Oct. 25, 2004, 118 Stat. 1749; Pub.L. 109–8, Title II, § 213(3), (4) Title X, §§ 1001(a)(1), 1003(a), Apr. 20, 2005, 119 Stat. 52, 185, 186.)

HISTORICAL AND STATUTORY NOTES

Revision Notes and Legislative Reports

1986 Acts. House Report No. 99–764 and House Conference Report No. 99–958, see 1986 U.S. Code Cong. and Adm. News, p. 5227.

1993 Acts. House Report No. 103–32, see 1993 U.S. Code Cong. and Adm. News, p. 373.

1994 Acts. House Report No. 103–835, see 1994 U.S. Code Cong. and Adm. News, p. 3340.

1998 Acts. Statement by President, see 1998 U.S. Code Cong. and Adm. News, p. 582.

1999 Acts. Statement by President, see 1999 U.S. Code Cong. and Adm. News, p. 4.

Statement by President, see 1999 U.S. Code Cong. and Adm. News, p. 102.

2001 Acts. House Report No. 107–2, see 2001 U.S. Code Cong. and Adm. News, p. 6.

2005 Acts. House Report No. 109–31(Part I), see 2005 U.S. Code Cong. and Adm. News, p. 88.

Effective and Applicability Provisions

2005 Acts. Pub.L. 109–8, Title X, § 1003(c), Apr. 20, 2005, 119 Stat. 186, provided that: "This section and the amendments made by this section [amending subsec. (a)(2) of this section and 11 U.S.C.A. § 1231(b)] shall take effect on the date of the enactment of this Act [Apr. 20, 2005] and shall not apply with respect to cases commenced under title 11 of the United States Code before such date."

Amendment by section 213(3), (4), Pub.L. 109–8 effective, except as otherwise provided, 180 days after April 20, 2005, and inapplicable with respect to cases commenced under Title 11 before the effective date, see Pub.L. 109–8, § 1501, set out as a note under 11 U.S.C.A. § 101.

2004 Acts. Amendment by Pub.L. 108–369, § 2(a), extending to July 1, 2005, the date of repeal of this chapter, to take effect Jan. 1, 2004, see Pub.L. 108–369, § 2(b), set out as a note under 11 U.S.C.A. § 1201.

2003 Acts. Amendment by Pub.L. 108–73, § 2(a), extending to Jan. 1, 2004, the date of repeal of this chapter, to take effect July 1, 2003, see Pub.L. 108–73, § 2(b), set out as a note under 11 U.S.C.A. § 1201.

2002 Acts. Amendment by Pub.L. 107–377, § 2(a), extending to July 1, 2003, the date of repeal of this chapter, to take effect Jan. 1, 2003, see Pub.L. 107–377, § 2(b), set out as a note under 11 U.S.C.A. § 1201.

Amendment by Pub.L. 107–171, extending to Jan. 1, 2003, the date of repeal of this chapter, to take effect June 1, 2002, see section 10814(b) of Pub.L. 107–171, set out as a note under 11 U.S.C.A. § 1201.

Amendment by Pub.L. 107–170, extending to June 1, 2002, the date of repeal of this chapter, to take effect October 1, 2001, see section 2 of Pub.L. 107–170, set out as a note under 11 U.S.C.A. § 1201.

2001 Acts. Amendment by Pub.L. 107–17, extending to October 1, 2001, the date of repeal of this chapter, to take effect June 1, 2001, see section 2 of Pub.L. 107–17, set out as a note under 11 U.S.C.A. § 1201.

Amendment by Pub.L. 107–8, extending to June 1, 2001, the date of repeal of this chapter, to take effect July 1, 2000, see section 2 of Pub.L. 107–8, set out as a note under 11 U.S.C.A. § 1201.

1999 Acts. Amendment by Pub.L. 106–70, extending to July 1, 2000, the date of repeal of this chapter, to take effect Oct. 1, 1999, see section 2 of Pub.L. 106–70, set out as a note under section 1201 of this title.

Amendment by Pub.L. 106–5, extending to Oct. 1, 1999 the date of repeal of this chapter, to take effect Apr. 1, 1999, see section 2 of Pub.L. 106–5, set out as a note under section 1201 of this title.

1998 Acts. Section reenacted, eff. Oct. 1, 1998, for the period beginning on Oct. 1, 1998, and ending on Apr. 1, 1999, but all cases commenced or pending under this chapter 12, as reenacted under section 149(a) of Pub.L. 105–277, and all matters and proceedings in or relating to such cases, to be conducted and determined under such chapter as if such chapter were continued in effect after Apr. 1, 1999, and the substantive rights of parties in connection with such cases, matters, and proceedings to continue to be governed under the law applicable to such cases, matters, and proceedings as if such chapter were continued in effect after Apr. 1, 1999, see section 149 of Pub.L. 105–277, set out as a note under 11 U.S.C.A. § 1201.

1994 Acts. Amendment by Pub.L. 103–394 effective on Oct. 22, 1994, and applicable only to agreements entered into after Oct. 22, 1994, see section 702 of Pub.L. 103–394, set out as a note under 11 U.S.C.A. § 101.

1993 Acts. Amendment by Pub.L. 103–65, extending to Oct. 1, 1998 the date of repeal of this chapter, to take effect Aug. 6, 1993, see section 3 of Pub.L. 103–65, set out as a note under 11 U.S.C.A. § 1221.

1986 Acts. Section repealed effective Oct. 1, 1998, see section 302(f) of Pub.L. 99–554, as amended, set out in a note under 28 U.S.C.A. § 581. However, for extension of provisions, see section 149 of Pub.L. 105–277, set out as a note under 11 U.S.C.A. § 1201.

Section effective 30 days after Oct. 27, 1986, but not applicable to cases commenced under this title before that date, see section 302(a), (c)(1) of Pub.L. 99–554, set out as a note under section 581 of Title 28, Judiciary and Judicial Procedure.

Separability of Provisions

If any provision of or amendment made by Pub.L. 103–394 or the application of such provision or amendment to any person or circumstance is held to be unconstitutional, the remaining provisions of and amendments made by Pub.L. 103–394 and the application of such provisions and amendments to any person or circumstance shall not be affected thereby, see section 701 of Pub.L. 103–394, set out as a note under section 101 of this title.

Reenactment of Chapter

This section as in effect on June 30, 2005, reenacted effective July 1, 2005, see Pub.L. 109–8, § 1001(a), set out as a note under 11 U.S.C.A. § 1201.

Repeal of Chapter; Extension of Provisions

Pub.L. 99–554, Title III, § 302(f), Oct. 27, 1986, 100 Stat. 3124, as amended Pub.L. 103–65, § 1, Aug. 6, 1993, 107 Stat. 311, which provided that, effective Oct. 1, 1998, this chapter is repealed, but that all cases commenced or pending under this chapter, and all matters and proceedings in or relating to such cases, shall be conducted and determined under this chapter as if such chapter had not been repealed, and that the substantive rights of parties in connection with such cases, matters, and proceedings shall continue to be governed under the laws applicable to such cases, matters, and proceedings as if such chapter had not been repealed, was superceded by the reenactment of this chapter by Pub.L. 109–8, Title X, § 1001(a), Apr. 20, 2005, 119 Stat. 185, set out as a note under 11 U.S.C.A. § 1201.

Pub.L. 105–277, Div. C, Title I, § 149, Oct. 21, 1998, 112 Stat. 2681–610, as amended Pub.L. 106–5, §§ 1, 2, Mar. 30, 1999, 113 Stat. 9; Pub.L. 106–70, §§ 1, 2, Oct. 9, 1999, 113 Stat. 1031; Pub.L. 107–8, §§ 1, 2, May 11, 2001, 115 Stat. 10; Pub.L. 107–17, §§ 1, 2, June 26, 2001, 115 Stat. 151; Pub.L. 107–170, §§ 1, 2, May 7, 2002, 116 Stat. 133; Pub.L. 107–171, Title X, § 10814, May 13, 2002, 116 St. 532; Pub.L. 107–377, § 2, Dec. 19, 2002, 116 Stat. 3115; Pub.L. 108–73, § 2(a), Aug. 15, 2003, 117 Stat. 891; Pub.L. 108–369, § 2(a), Oct. 25, 2004, 118 Stat. 1749, provided that, to take effect on January 1, 2004, chapter 12 of Title 11 [this chapter; 11 U.S.C.A. § 1201 et seq.], as in effect on December 31, 2003, is reenacted for the period beginning on January 1, 2004, and ending on July 1, 2005, but that all cases commenced or pending under this chapter 12, as reenacted under section 149(a) of Pub.L. 105–277, and all matters and proceedings in or relating to such cases, shall be conducted and determined under such chapter as if such chapter were continued in effect after July 1, 2005, and that the substantive rights of parties in connection with such cases, matters, and proceedings shall continue to be governed under the law applicable to such cases, matters, and proceedings as if such chapter were continued in effect after July 1, 2005, was superceded by the reenactment of this chapter by Pub.L. 109–8, Title X, § 1001(a), Apr. 20, 2005, 119 Stat. 185, set out as a note under 11 U.S.C.A. § 1201.

CROSS REFERENCES

Contents of plan filed in—

Chapter eleven cases, see 11 USCA § 1123.

Chapter thirteen cases, see 11 USCA § 1322.

Railroad reorganization cases, see 11 USCA § 1172.

§ 1223. Modification of plan before confirmation

(a) The debtor may modify the plan at any time before confirmation, but may not modify the plan so that the plan as modified fails to meet the requirements of section 1222 of this title.

(b) After the debtor files a modification under this section, the plan as modified becomes the plan.

(c) Any holder of a secured claim that has accepted or rejected the plan is deemed to have accepted or rejected, as the case may be, the plan as modified, unless the modification provides for a change in the rights of such holder from what such rights were under the plan before modification, and such holder changes such holder's previous acceptance or rejection.

(Added and amended Pub.L. 99–554, Title II, § 255, Title III, § 302(f), Oct. 27, 1986, 100 Stat. 3110, 3124; Pub.L. 103–65, § 1, Aug. 6, 1993, 107 Stat. 311; Pub.L. 105–277, Div. C, Title I, § 149(a), Oct. 21, 1998, 112 Stat. 2681–610; Pub.L. 106–5, § 1(1), (2), Mar. 30, 1999, 113 Stat. 9; Pub.L. 106–70, § 1, Oct. 9, 1999, 113 Stat. 1031; Pub.L. 107–8, § 1, May 11, 2001, 115 Stat. 10; Pub.L. 107–17, § 1, June 26, 2001, 115 Stat. 151; Pub.L. 107–170, § 1, May 7, 2002, 116 Stat. 133; Pub.L. 107–171, Title X, § 10814(a), May 13, 2002, 116 Stat. 532; Pub.L. 107–377, § 2(a), Dec. 19, 2002, 116 Stat. 3115; Pub.L. 108–73, § 2(a), Aug. 15, 2003, 117 Stat. 891; Pub.L. 108–369, § 2(a), Oct. 25, 2004, 118 Stat. 1749; Pub.L. 109–8, Title X, § 1001(a)(1), Apr. 20, 2005, 119 Stat. 185.)

HISTORICAL AND STATUTORY NOTES

Revision Notes and Legislative Reports

1986 Acts. House Report No. 99–764 and House Conference Report No. 99–958, see 1986 U.S. Code Cong. and Adm. News, p. 5227.

1993 Acts. House Report No. 103–32, see 1993 U.S. Code Cong. and Adm. News, p. 373.

1998 Acts. Statement by President, see 1998 U.S. Code Cong. and Adm. News, p. 582.

1999 Acts. Statement by President, see 1999 U.S. Code Cong. and Adm. News, p. 4.

Statement by President, see 1999 U.S. Code Cong. and Adm. News, p. 102.

2001 Acts. House Report No. 107–2, see 2001 U.S. Code Cong. and Adm. News, p. 6.

2005 Acts. House Report No. 109–31(Part I), see 2005 U.S. Code Cong. and Adm. News, p. 88.

Effective and Applicability Provisions

2005 Acts. Amendments by Pub.L. 109–8 effective, except as otherwise provided, 180 days after April 20, 2005, and inapplicable with respect to cases commenced under Title 11 before the effective date, see Pub.L. 109–8, § 1501, set out as a note under 11 U.S.C.A. § 101.

2004 Acts. Amendment by Pub.L. 108–369, § 2(a), extending to July 1, 2005, the date of repeal of this chapter, to take effect Jan. 1, 2004, see Pub.L. 108–369, § 2(b), set out as a note under 11 U.S.C.A. § 1201.

2003 Acts. Amendment by Pub.L. 108–73, § 2(a), extending to Jan. 1, 2004, the date of repeal of this chapter, to take effect July 1, 2003, see Pub.L. 108–73, § 2(b), set out as a note under 11 U.S.C.A. § 1201.

2002 Acts. Amendment by Pub.L. 107–377, § 2(a), extending to July 1, 2003, the date of repeal of this chapter, to take effect Jan. 1, 2003, see Pub.L. 107–377, § 2(b), set out as a note under 11 U.S.C.A. § 1201.

Amendment by Pub.L. 107–171, extending to Jan. 1, 2003, the date of repeal of this chapter, to take effect June 1, 2002, see section 10814(b) of Pub.L. 107–171, set out as a note under 11 U.S.C.A. § 1201.

Amendment by Pub.L. 107–170, extending to June 1, 2002, the date of repeal of this chapter, to take effect October 1, 2001, see section 2 of Pub.L. 107–170, set out as a note under 11 U.S.C.A. § 1201.

2001 Acts. Amendment by Pub.L. 107–17, extending to October 1, 2001, the date of repeal of this chapter, to take effect June 1, 2001, see section 2 of Pub.L. 107–17, set out as a note under 11 U.S.C.A. § 1201.

Amendment by Pub.L. 107–8, extending to June 1, 2001, the date of repeal of this chapter, to take effect July 1, 2000, see section 2 of Pub.L. 107–8, set out as a note under 11 U.S.C.A. § 1201.

1999 Acts. Amendment by Pub.L. 106–70, extending to July 1, 2000, the date of repeal of this chapter, to take effect Oct. 1, 1999, see section 2 of Pub.L. 106–70, set out as a note under 11 U.S.C.A. § 1201.

Amendment by Pub.L. 106–5, extending to Oct. 1, 1999 the date of repeal of this chapter, to take effect Apr. 1, 1999, see section 2 of Pub.L. 106–5, set out as a note under 11 U.S.C.A. § 1201.

1998 Acts. Section reenacted, eff. Oct. 1, 1998, for the period beginning on Oct. 1, 1998, and ending on Apr. 1, 1999, but all cases commenced or pending under this chapter 12, as reenacted under section 149(a) of Pub.L. 105–277, and all matters and proceedings in or relating to such cases, to be conducted and determined under such chapter as if such chapter were continued in effect after Apr. 1, 1999, and the substantive rights of parties in connection with such cases, matters, and proceedings to continue to be governed under the law applicable to such cases, matters, and proceedings as if such chapter were continued in effect after Apr. 1, 1999, see section 149 of Pub.L. 105–277, set out as a note under 11 U.S.C.A. § 1201.

1993 Acts. Amendment by Pub.L. 103–65, extending to Oct. 1, 1998 the date of repeal of this chapter, to take effect Aug. 6, 1993, see section 3 of Pub.L. 103–65, set out as a note under 11 U.S.C.A. § 1221.

1986 Acts. Section repealed effective Oct. 1, 1998, see section 302(f) of Pub.L. 99–554, as amended, set out in a note under 28 U.S.C.A. § 581. However, for extension of provisions, see section 149 of Pub.L. 105–277, set out as a note under 11 U.S.C.A. § 1201.

Section effective 30 days after Oct. 27, 1986, but not applicable to cases commenced under this title before that date, see section 302(a), (c)(1) of Pub.L. 99–554, set out as a note under 28 U.S.C.A. § 581.

Reenactment of Chapter

This section as in effect on June 30, 2005, reenacted effective July 1, 2005, see Pub.L. 109–8, § 1001(a), set out as a note under 11 U.S.C.A. § 1201.

Repeal of Chapter; Extension of Provisions

Pub.L. 99–554, Title III, § 302(f), Oct. 27, 1986, 100 Stat. 3124, as amended Pub.L. 103–65, § 1, Aug. 6, 1993, 107 Stat. 311, which provided that, effective Oct. 1, 1998, this chapter is repealed, but that all cases commenced or pending under this chapter, and all matters and proceedings in or relating to such cases, shall be conducted and determined under this chapter as if such chapter had not been repealed, and that the substantive rights of parties in connection with such cases, matters, and proceedings shall continue to be governed under the laws applicable to such cases, matters, and proceedings as if such chapter had not been repealed, was superceded by the reenactment of this chapter by Pub.L. 109–8, Title X, § 1001(a), Apr. 20, 2005, 119 Stat. 185, set out as a note under 11 U.S.C.A. § 1201.

Pub.L. 105–277, Div. C, Title I, § 149, Oct. 21, 1998, 112 Stat. 2681–610, as amended Pub.L. 106–5, §§ 1, 2, Mar. 30, 1999, 113 Stat. 9; Pub.L. 106–70, §§ 1, 2, Oct. 9, 1999, 113 Stat. 1031; Pub.L. 107–8, §§ 1, 2, May 11, 2001, 115 Stat. 10; Pub.L. 107–17, §§ 1, 2, June 26, 2001, 115 Stat. 151; Pub.L. 107–170, §§ 1, 2, May 7, 2002, 116 Stat. 133; Pub.L. 107–171, Title X, § 10814, May 13, 2002, 116 St. 532; Pub.L. 107–377, § 2, Dec. 19, 2002, 116 Stat. 3115; Pub.L. 108–73, § 2(a), Aug. 15, 2003, 117 Stat. 891; Pub.L. 108–369, § 2(a), Oct. 25, 2004, 118 Stat. 1749, provided that, to take effect on January 1, 2004, chapter 12 of Title 11 [this chapter; 11 U.S.C.A. § 1201 et seq.], as in effect on December 31, 2003, is reenacted for the period beginning on January 1, 2004, and ending on July 1, 2005, but that all cases commenced or pending under this chapter 12, as reenacted under section 149(a) of Pub.L. 105–277, and all matters and proceedings in or relating to such cases, shall be conducted and determined under such chapter as if such chapter were continued in effect after July 1, 2005, and that the substantive rights of parties in connection with such cases, matters, and proceedings shall continue to be governed under the law applicable to such cases, matters, and proceedings as if such chapter were continued in effect after July 1, 2005, was superceded by the reenactment of this chapter by Pub.L. 109–8, Title X, § 1001(a), Apr. 20, 2005, 119 Stat. 185, set out as a note under 11 U.S.C.A. § 1201.

CROSS REFERENCES

Modification of plan filed in—

Chapter eleven cases, see 11 USCA § 1127.

Chapter nine cases, see 11 USCA § 942.

Chapter thirteen cases, see 11 USCA § 1323.

§ 1224. Confirmation hearing

After expedited notice, the court shall hold a hearing on confirmation of the plan. A party in interest, the trustee, or the United States trustee may object to the confirmation of the plan. Except for cause, the hearing shall be concluded not later than 45 days after the filing of the plan.

(Added and amended Pub.L. 99–554, Title II, § 255, Title III, § 302(f), Oct. 27, 1986, 100 Stat. 3110, 3124; Pub.L. 103–65, § 1, Aug. 6, 1993, 107 Stat. 311; Pub.L. 105–277, Div. C, Title I, § 149(a), Oct. 21, 1998, 112 Stat. 2681–610; Pub.L. 106–5, § 1(1), (2), Mar. 30, 1999, 113 Stat. 9; Pub.L. 106–70, § 1, Oct. 9, 1999, 113 Stat. 1031; Pub.L. 107–8, § 1, May 11, 2001, 115 Stat. 10; Pub.L. 107–17, § 1, June 26, 2001, 115 Stat. 151; Pub.L. 107–170, § 1, May 7, 2002, 116 Stat. 133; Pub.L. 107–171, Title X, § 10814(a), May 13, 2002, 116 Stat. 532; Pub.L. 107–377, § 2(a), Dec. 19, 2002, 16 Stat. 3115; Pub.L. 108–73, § 2(a), Aug. 15, 2003, 117 Stat. 891; Pub.L. 108–369, § 2(a), Oct. 25, 2004, 118 Stat. 1749; Pub.L. 109–8, Title X, § 1001(a)(1), Apr. 20, 2005, 119 Stat. 185.)

HISTORICAL AND STATUTORY NOTES

Revision Notes and Legislative Reports

1986 Acts. House Report No. 99–764 and House Conference Report No. 99–958, see 1986 U.S. Code Cong. and Adm. News, p. 5227.

1993 Acts. House Report No. 103–32, see 1993 U.S. Code Cong. and Adm. News, p. 373.

1998 Acts. Statement by President, see 1998 U.S. Code Cong. and Adm. News, p. 582.

1999 Acts. Statement by President, see 1999 U.S. Code Cong. and Adm. News, p. 4.

Statement by President, see 1999 U.S. Code Cong. and Adm. News, p. 102.

2001 Acts. House Report No. 107–2, see 2001 U.S. Code Cong. and Adm. News, p. 6.

2005 Acts. House Report No. 109–31(Part I), see 2005 U.S. Code Cong. and Adm. News, p. 88.

Effective and Applicability Provisions

2005 Acts. Amendments by Pub.L. 109–8 effective, except as otherwise provided, 180 days after April 20, 2005, and inapplicable with respect to cases commenced under Title 11 before the effective date, see Pub.L. 109–8, § 1501, set out as a note under 11 U.S.C.A. § 101.

2004 Acts. Amendment by Pub.L. 108–369, § 2(a), extending to July 1, 2005, the date of repeal of this chapter, to take effect Jan. 1, 2004, see Pub.L. 108–369, § 2(b), set out as a note under 11 U.S.C.A. § 1201.

2003 Acts. Amendment by Pub.L. 108–73, § 2(a), extending to Jan. 1, 2004, the date of repeal of this chapter, to take effect July 1, 2003, see Pub.L. 108–73, § 2(b), set out as a note under 11 U.S.C.A. § 1201.

2002 Acts. Amendment by Pub.L. 107–377, § 2(a), extending to July 1, 2003, the date of repeal of this chapter, to take effect Jan. 1, 2003, see Pub.L. 107–377, § 2(b), set out as a note under 11 U.S.C.A. § 1201.

Amendment by Pub.L. 107–171, extending to Jan. 1, 2003, the date of repeal of this chapter, to take effect June 1, 2002, see section 10814(b) of Pub.L. 107–171, set out as a note under 11 U.S.C.A. § 1201.

Amendment by Pub.L. 107–170, extending to June 1, 2002, the date of repeal of this chapter, to take effect October 1, 2001, see section 2 of Pub.L. 107–170, set out as a note under 11 U.S.C.A. § 1201.

2001 Acts. Amendment by Pub.L. 107–17, extending to October 1, 2001, the date of repeal of this chapter, to take effect June 1, 2001, see section 2 of Pub.L. 107–17, set out as a note under 11 U.S.C.A. § 1201.

Amendment by Pub.L. 107–8, extending to June 1, 2001, the date of repeal of this chapter, to take effect July 1, 2000, see section 2 of Pub.L. 107–8, set out as a note under 11 U.S.C.A. § 1201.

1999 Acts. Amendment by Pub.L. 106–70, extending to July 1, 2000, the date of repeal of this chapter, to take effect Oct. 1, 1999, see section 2 of Pub.L. 106–70, set out as a note under 11 U.S.C.A. § 1201.

Amendment by Pub.L. 106–5, extending to Oct. 1, 1999 the date of repeal of this chapter, to take effect Apr. 1, 1999, see section 2 of Pub.L. 106–5, set out as a note under 11 U.S.C.A. § 1201.

1998 Acts. Section reenacted, eff. Oct. 1, 1998, for the period beginning on Oct. 1, 1998, and ending on Apr. 1, 1999, but all cases commenced or pending under this chapter 12, as reenacted under section 149(a) of Pub.L. 105–277, and all matters and proceedings in or relating to such cases, to be conducted and determined under such chapter as if such chapter were continued in effect after Apr. 1, 1999, and the substantive rights of parties in connection with such cases, matters, and proceedings to continue to be governed under the law applicable to such cases, matters, and proceedings as if such chapter were continued in effect after Apr. 1, 1999, see section 149 of Pub.L. 105–277, set out as a note under 11 U.S.C.A. § 1201.

1993 Acts. Amendment by Pub.L. 103–65, extending to Oct. 1, 1998 the date of repeal of this chapter, to take effect Aug. 6, 1993, see section 3 of Pub.L. 103–65, set out as a note under 11 U.S.C.A. § 1221.

1986 Acts. Section repealed effective Oct. 1, 1998, see section 302(f) of Pub.L. 99–554, as amended, set out in a note under 28 U.S.C.A. § 581. However, for extension of provisions, see section 149 of Pub.L. 105–277, set out as a note under 11 U.S.C.A. § 1201.

Section effective 30 days after Oct. 27, 1986, but not applicable to cases commenced under this title before that date, see section 302(a), (c)(1) of Pub.L. 99–554, set out as a note under 28 U.S.C.A. § 581.

Reenactment of Chapter

This section as in effect on June 30, 2005, reenacted effective July 1, 2005, see Pub.L. 109–8, § 1001(a), set out as a note under 11 U.S.C.A. § 1201.

Repeal of Chapter; Extension of Provisions

Pub.L. 99–554, Title III, § 302(f), Oct. 27, 1986, 100 Stat. 3124, as amended Pub.L. 103–65, § 1, Aug. 6, 1993, 107 Stat. 311, which provided that, effective Oct. 1, 1998, this chapter is repealed, but that all cases commenced or pending under this chapter, and all matters and proceedings in or relating to such cases, shall be conducted and determined under this chapter as if such chapter had not been repealed, and that the substantive rights of parties in connection with such cases, matters, and proceedings shall continue to be governed under the laws applicable to such cases, matters, and proceedings as if such chapter had not been repealed, was superceded by the reenactment of this chapter by Pub.L. 109–8, Title X, § 1001(a), Apr. 20, 2005, 119 Stat. 185, set out as a note under 11 U.S.C.A. § 1201.

Pub.L. 105–277, Div. C, Title I, § 149, Oct. 21, 1998, 112 Stat. 2681–610, as amended Pub.L. 106–5, §§ 1, 2, Mar. 30, 1999, 113 Stat. 9; Pub.L. 106–70, §§ 1, 2, Oct. 9, 1999, 113 Stat. 1031; Pub.L. 107–8, §§ 1, 2, May 11, 2001, 115 Stat. 10; Pub.L. 107–17, §§ 1, 2, June 26, 2001, 115 Stat. 151; Pub.L. 107–170, §§ 1, 2, May 7, 2002, 116 Stat. 133; Pub.L. 107–171, Title X, § 10814, May 13, 2002, 116 St. 532; Pub.L. 107–377, § 2, Dec. 19, 2002, 116 Stat. 3115; Pub.L. 108–73, § 2(a), Aug. 15, 2003, 117 Stat. 891; Pub.L. 108–369, § 2(a), Oct. 25, 2004, 118 Stat. 1749, provided that, to take effect on January 1, 2004, chapter 12 of Title 11 [this chapter; 11 U.S.C.A. § 1201 et seq.], as in effect on December 31, 2003, is reenacted for the period beginning on January 1, 2004, and ending on July 1, 2005, but that all cases commenced or pending under this chapter 12, as reenacted under section 149(a) of Pub.L. 105–277, and all matters and proceedings in or relating to such cases, shall be conducted and determined under such chapter as if such chapter were continued in effect after July 1, 2005, and that the substantive rights of parties in connection with such cases, matters, and proceedings shall continue to be governed under the law applicable to such cases, matters, and proceedings as if such chapter were continued in effect after July 1, 2005, was superceded by the reenactment of this chapter by Pub.L. 109–8, Title X, § 1001(a), Apr. 20, 2005, 119 Stat. 185, set out as a note under 11 U.S.C.A. § 1201.

CROSS REFERENCES

Confirmation hearing in—

Chapter eleven cases, see 11 USCA § 1128.

Chapter thirteen cases, see 11 USCA § 1324.

Duties of United States trustee, see 28 USCA § 586.

§ 1225. Confirmation of plan

(a) Except as provided in subsection (b), the court shall confirm a plan if—

(1) the plan complies with the provisions of this chapter and with the other applicable provisions of this title;

(2) any fee, charge, or amount required under chapter 123 of title 28, or by the plan, to be paid before confirmation, has been paid;

(3) the plan has been proposed in good faith and not by any means forbidden by law;

(4) the value, as of the effective date of the plan, of property to be distributed under the plan on account of each allowed unsecured claim is not less than the amount that would be paid on such claim if the estate of the debtor were liquidated under chapter 7 of this title on such date;

(5) with respect to each allowed secured claim provided for by the plan—

(A) the holder of such claim has accepted the plan;

(B)(i) the plan provides that the holder of such claim retain the lien securing such claim; and

(ii) the value, as of the effective date of the plan, of property to be distributed by the trustee or the debtor under the plan on account of such claim is not less than the allowed amount of such claim; or

(C) the debtor surrenders the property securing such claim to such holder;

(6) the debtor will be able to make all payments under the plan and to comply with the plan; and

(7) the debtor has paid all amounts that are required to be paid under a domestic support obligation and that first become payable after the date of the filing of the petition if the debtor is required by a judicial or administrative order, or by statute, to pay such domestic support obligation.

(b)(1) If the trustee or the holder of an allowed unsecured claim objects to the confirmation of the plan, then the court may not approve the plan unless, as of the effective date of the plan—

(A) the value of the property to be distributed under the plan on account of such claim is not less than the amount of such claim;

(B) the plan provides that all of the debtor's projected disposable income to be received in the three-year period, or such longer period as the court may approve under section 1222(c), beginning on the date that the first payment is due under the plan will be applied to make payments under the plan; or

(C) the value of the property to be distributed under the plan in the 3–year period, or such longer period as the court may approve under section 1222(c), beginning on the date that the first distribution is due under the plan is not less than the debtor's projected disposable income for such period.

(2) For purposes of this subsection, "disposable income" means income which is received by the debtor and which is not reasonably necessary to be expended—

(A) for the maintenance or support of the debtor or a dependent of the debtor or for a domestic support obligation that first becomes payable after the date of the filing of the petition; or

(B) for the payment of expenditures necessary for the continuation, preservation, and operation of the debtor's business.

(c) After confirmation of a plan, the court may order any entity from whom the debtor receives income to pay all or any part of such income to the trustee.

(Added and amended Pub.L. 99–554, Title II, § 255, Title III, § 302(f), Oct. 27, 1986, 100 Stat. 3110, 3124; Pub.L. 103–65, § 1, Aug. 6, 1993, 107 Stat. 311; Pub.L. 105–277, Div. C, Title I, § 149(a), Oct. 21, 1998, 112 Stat. 2681–610; Pub.L. 106–5, § 1(1), (2), Mar. 30, 1999, 113 Stat. 9; Pub.L. 106–70, § 1, Oct. 9, 1999, 113 Stat. 1031; Pub.L. 107–8, § 1, May 11, 2001, 115 Stat. 10; Pub.L. 107–17, § 1, June 26, 2001, 115 Stat. 151; Pub.L. 107–170, § 1, May 7, 2002, 116 Stat. 133; Pub.L. 107–171, Title X, § 10814(a), May 13, 2002, 116 Stat. 532; Pub.L. 107–377, § 2(a), Dec. 19, 2002, 116 Stat. 3115; Pub.L. 108–73, § 2(a), Aug. 15, 2003, 117 Stat. 891; Pub.L. 108–369, § 2(a), Oct. 25, 2004, 118 Stat. 1749; Pub.L. 109–8, Title II, §§ 213(5), 218, Title X, §§ 1001(a)(1), 1006(a), Apr. 20, 2005, 119 Stat. 52, 55, 185, 187.)

HISTORICAL AND STATUTORY NOTES

Revision Notes and Legislative Reports

1986 Acts. House Report No. 99–764 and House Conference Report No. 99–958, see 1986 U.S. Code Cong. and Adm. News, p. 5227.

1993 Acts. House Report No. 103–32, see 1993 U.S. Code Cong. and Adm. News, p. 373.

1998 Acts. Statement by President, see 1998 U.S. Code Cong. and Adm. News, p. 582.

1999 Acts. Statement by President, see 1999 U.S. Code Cong. and Adm. News, p. 4.

Statement by President, see 1999 U.S. Code Cong. and Adm. News, p. 102.

2001 Acts. House Report No. 107–2, see 2001 U.S. Code Cong. and Adm. News, p. 6.

2005 Acts. House Report No. 109–31(Part I), see 2005 U.S. Code Cong. and Adm. News, p. 88.

Effective and Applicability Provisions

2005 Acts. Amendments by Pub.L. 109–8 effective, except as otherwise provided, 180 days after April 20, 2005, and inapplicable with respect to cases commenced under Title 11 before the effective date, see Pub.L. 109–8, § 1501, set out as a note under 11 U.S.C.A. § 101.

2004 Acts. Amendment by Pub.L. 108–369, § 2(a), extending to July 1, 2005, the date of repeal of this chapter, to take effect Jan. 1, 2004, see Pub.L. 108–369, § 2(b), set out as a note under 11 U.S.C.A. § 1201.

2003 Acts. Amendment by Pub.L. 108–73, § 2(a), extending to Jan. 1, 2004, the date of repeal of this chapter, to take effect July 1, 2003, see Pub.L. 108–73, § 2(b), set out as a note under 11 U.S.C.A. § 1201.

2002 Acts. Amendment by Pub.L. 107–377, § 2(a), extending to July 1, 2003, the date of repeal of this chapter, to take effect Jan. 1, 2003, see Pub.L. 107–377, § 2(b), set out as a note under 11 U.S.C.A. § 1201.

Amendment by Pub.L. 107–171, extending to Jan. 1, 2003, the date of repeal of this chapter, to take effect June 1, 2002, see section 10814(b) of Pub.L. 107–171, set out as a note under 11 U.S.C.A. § 1201.

Amendment by Pub.L. 107–170, extending to June 1, 2002, the date of repeal of this chapter, to take effect October 1, 2001, see section 2 of Pub.L. 107–170, set out as a note under 11 U.S.C.A. § 1201.

2001 Acts. Amendment by Pub.L. 107–17, extending to October 1, 2001, the date of repeal of this chapter, to take effect June 1, 2001, see section 2 of Pub.L. 107–17, set out as a note under 11 U.S.C.A. § 1201.

Amendment by Pub.L. 107–8, extending to June 1, 2001, the date of repeal of this chapter, to take effect July 1, 2000, see section 2 of Pub.L. 107–8, set out as a note under 11 U.S.C.A. § 1201.

1999 Acts. Amendment by Pub.L. 106–70, extending to July 1, 2000, the date of repeal of this chapter, to take effect Oct. 1, 1999, see section 2 of Pub.L. 106–70, set out as a note under 11 U.S.C.A. § 1201.

Amendment by Pub.L. 106–5, extending to Oct. 1, 1999 the date of repeal of this chapter, to take effect Apr. 1, 1999, see section 2 of Pub.L. 106–5, set out as a note under 11 U.S.C.A. § 1201.

1998 Acts. Section reenacted, eff. Oct. 1, 1998, for the period beginning on Oct. 1, 1998, and ending on Apr. 1, 1999, but all cases commenced or pending under this chapter 12, as reenacted under section 149(a) of Pub.L. 105–277, and all matters and proceedings in or relating to such cases, to be conducted and determined under such chapter as if such chapter were continued in effect after Apr. 1, 1999, and the substantive rights of parties in connection with such cases, matters, and proceedings to continue to be governed under the law applicable to such cases, matters, and proceedings as if such chapter were continued in effect after Apr. 1, 1999, see section 149 of Pub.L. 105–277, set out as a note under 11 U.S.C.A. § 1201.

1993 Acts. Amendment by Pub.L. 103–65, extending to Oct. 1, 1998 the date of repeal of this chapter, to take effect Aug. 6, 1993, see section 3 of Pub.L. 103–65, set out as a note under 11 U.S.C.A. § 1221.

1986 Acts. Section repealed effective Oct. 1, 1998, see section 302(f) of Pub.L. 99–554, as amended, set out in a note under 28 U.S.C.A. § 581. However, for extension of provisions, see section 149 of Pub.L. 105–277, set out as a note under 28 U.S.C.A. § 1201.

Section effective 30 days after Oct. 27, 1986, but not applicable to cases commenced under this title before that date, see section 302(a), (c)(1) of Pub.L. 99–554, set out as a note under 28 U.S.C.A. § 581.

Reenactment of Chapter

This section as in effect on June 30, 2005, reenacted effective July 1, 2005, see Pub.L. 109–8, § 1001(a), set out as a note under 11 U.S.C.A. § 1201.

Repeal of Chapter; Extension of Provisions

Pub.L. 99–554, Title III, § 302(f), Oct. 27, 1986, 100 Stat. 3124, as amended Pub.L. 103–65, § 1, Aug. 6, 1993, 107 Stat. 311, which provided that, effective Oct. 1, 1998, this chapter is repealed, but that all cases commenced or pending under this chapter, and all matters and proceedings in or relating to such cases, shall be conducted and determined under this chapter as if such chapter had not been repealed, and that the substantive rights of parties in connection with such cases, matters, and proceedings shall continue to be governed under the laws applicable to such cases, matters, and proceedings as if such chapter had not been repealed, was superceded by the reenactment of this chapter by Pub.L. 109–8, Title X, § 1001(a), Apr. 20, 2005, 119 Stat. 185, set out as a note under 11 U.S.C.A. § 1201.

Pub.L. 105–277, Div. C, Title I, § 149, Oct. 21, 1998, 112 Stat. 2681–610, as amended Pub.L. 106–5, §§ 1, 2, Mar. 30, 1999, 113 Stat. 9; Pub.L. 106–70, §§ 1, 2, Oct. 9, 1999, 113 Stat. 1031; Pub.L. 107–8, §§ 1, 2, May 11, 2001, 115 Stat. 10; Pub.L. 107–17, §§ 1, 2, June 26, 2001, 115 Stat. 151; Pub.L. 107–170, §§ 1, 2, May 7, 2002, 116 Stat. 133; Pub.L. 107–171, Title X, § 10814, May 13, 2002, 116 St. 532; Pub.L. 107–377, § 2, Dec. 19, 2002, 116 Stat. 3115; Pub.L. 108–73, § 2(a), Aug. 15, 2003, 117 Stat. 891; Pub.L. 108–369, § 2(a), Oct. 25, 2004, 118 Stat. 1749, provided that, to take effect on January 1, 2004, chapter 12 of Title 11 [this chapter; 11 U.S.C.A. § 1201 et seq.], as in effect on December 31, 2003, is reenacted for the period beginning on January 1, 2004, and ending on July 1, 2005, but that all cases commenced or pending under this chapter 12, as reenacted under section 149(a) of Pub.L. 105–277, and all matters and proceedings in or relating to such cases, shall be conducted and determined under such chapter as if such chapter were continued in effect after July 1, 2005, and that the substantive rights of parties in connection with such cases, matters, and proceedings shall continue to be governed under the law applicable to such cases, matters, and proceedings as if such chapter were continued in effect after July 1, 2005, was superceded by the reenactment of this chapter by Pub.L. 109–8, Title X, § 1001(a), Apr. 20, 2005, 119 Stat. 185, set out as a note under 11 U.S.C.A. § 1201.

CROSS REFERENCES

Confirmation of plan in—

Chapter eleven cases, see 11 USCA § 1129.

Chapter nine cases, see 11 USCA § 943.

Chapter thirteen cases, see 11 USCA § 1325.

Railroad reorganization cases, see 11 USCA § 1173.

Conversion or dismissal, see 11 USCA § 1208.

Unclaimed property, see 11 USCA § 347.

§ 1226. Payments

(a) Payments and funds received by the trustee shall be retained by the trustee until confirmation or denial of confirmation of a plan. If a plan is confirmed, the trustee shall distribute any such payment in accordance with the plan. If a plan is not confirmed, the trustee shall return any such payments to the debtor, after deducting—

(1) any unpaid claim allowed under section 503(b) of this title; and

(2) if a standing trustee is serving in the case, the percentage fee fixed for such standing trustee.

(b) Before or at the time of each payment to creditors under the plan, there shall be paid—

(1) any unpaid claim of the kind specified in section 507(a)(2) of this title; and

(2) if a standing trustee appointed under section 1202(c) of this title is serving in the case, the percentage fee fixed for such standing trustee under section 1202(d) of this title.

(c) Except as otherwise provided in the plan or in the order confirming the plan, the trustee shall make payments to creditors under the plan.

(Added and amended Pub.L. 99–554, Title II, § 255, Title III, § 302(f), Oct. 27, 1986, 100 Stat. 3111, 3124; Pub.L. 103–65, § 1, Aug. 6, 1993, 107 Stat. 311; Pub.L. 103–394, Title V, § 501(d)(36), Oct. 22, 1994, 108 Stat. 4147; Pub.L. 105–277, Div. C, Title I, § 149(a), Oct. 21, 1998, 112 Stat. 2681–610; Pub.L. 106–5, § 1(1), (2), Mar. 30, 1999, 113 Stat.

9; Pub.L. 106–70, § 1, Oct. 9, 1999, 113 Stat. 1031; Pub.L. 107–8, § 1, May 11, 2001, 115 Stat. 10; Pub.L. 107–17, § 1, June 26, 2001, 115 Stat. 151; Pub.L. 107–170, § 1, May 7, 2002, 116 Stat. 133; Pub.L. 107–171, Title X, § 10814(a), May 13, 2002, 116 Stat. 532; Pub.L. 107–377, § 2(a), Dec. 19, 2002, 116 Stat. 3115; Pub.L. 108–73, § 2(a), Aug. 15, 2003, 117 Stat. 891; Pub.L. 108–369, § 2(a), Oct. 25, 2004, 118 Stat. 1749; Pub.L. 109–8, Title X, § 1001(a)(1), Title XV, § 1502(a)(9), Apr. 20, 2005, 119 Stat. 185, 217.)

HISTORICAL AND STATUTORY NOTES

Revision Notes and Legislative Reports

1986 Acts. House Report No. 99–764 and House Conference Report No. 99–958, see 1986 U.S. Code Cong. and Adm. News, p. 5227.

1993 Acts. House Report No. 103–32, see 1993 U.S. Code Cong. and Adm. News, p. 373.

1994 Acts. House Report No. 103–835, see 1994 U.S. Code Cong. and Adm. News, p. 3340.

1998 Acts. Statement by President, see 1998 U.S. Code Cong. and Adm. News, p. 582.

1999 Acts. Statement by President, see 1999 U.S. Code Cong. and Adm. News, p. 4.

Statement by President, see 1999 U.S. Code Cong. and Adm. News, p. 102.

2001 Acts. House Report No. 107–2, see 2001 U.S. Code Cong. and Adm. News, p. 6.

2005 Acts. House Report No. 109–31(Part I), see 2005 U.S. Code Cong. and Adm. News, p. 88.

References in Text

Section 1202(c) and (d) of this title, referred to in subsec. (b)(2), were repealed by section 227 of Pub.L. 99–554, and provisions relating to appointment of and fixing percentage fees for standing trustees are contained in section 586(b) and (e) of Title 28, Judiciary and Judicial Procedure, as amended by section 113(b) and (c) of Pub.L. 99–554.

Effective and Applicability Provisions

2005 Acts. Amendments by Pub.L. 109–8 effective, except as otherwise provided, 180 days after April 20, 2005, and inapplicable with respect to cases commenced under Title 11 before the effective date, see Pub.L. 109–8, § 1501, set out as a note under 11 U.S.C.A. § 101.

2004 Acts. Amendment by Pub.L. 108–369, § 2(a), extending to July 1, 2005, the date of repeal of this chapter, to take effect Jan. 1, 2004, see Pub.L. 108–369, § 2(b), set out as a note under 11 U.S.C.A. § 1201.

2003 Acts. Amendment by Pub.L. 108–73, § 2(a), extending to Jan. 1, 2004, the date of repeal of this chapter, to take effect July 1, 2003, see Pub.L. 108–73, § 2(b), set out as a note under 11 U.S.C.A. § 1201.

2002 Acts. Amendment by Pub.L. 107–377, § 2(a), extending to July 1, 2003, the date of repeal of this chapter, to take effect Jan. 1, 2003, see Pub.L. 107–377, § 2(b), set out as a note under 11 U.S.C.A. § 1201.

Amendment by Pub.L. 107–171, extending to Jan. 1, 2003, the date of repeal of this chapter, to take effect June 1, 2002, see section 10814(b) of Pub.L. 107–171, set out as a note under 11 U.S.C.A. § 1201.

Amendment by Pub.L. 107–170, extending to June 1, 2002, the date of repeal of this chapter, to take effect October 1, 2001, see section 2 of Pub.L. 107–170, set out as a note under 11 U.S.C.A. § 1201.

2001 Acts. Amendment by Pub.L. 107–17, extending to October 1, 2001, the date of repeal of this chapter, to take effect June 1, 2001, see section 2 of Pub.L. 107–17, set out as a note under 11 U.S.C.A. § 1201.

Amendment by Pub.L. 107–8, extending to June 1, 2001, the date of repeal of this chapter, to take effect July 1, 2000, see section 2 of Pub.L. 107–8, set out as a note under 11 U.S.C.A. § 1201.

1999 Acts. Amendment by Pub.L. 106–70, extending to July 1, 2000, the date of repeal of this chapter, to take effect Oct. 1, 1999, see section 2 of Pub.L. 106–70, set out as a note under 11 U.S.C.A. § 1201.

Amendment by Pub.L. 106–5, extending to Oct. 1, 1999 the date of repeal of this chapter, to take effect Apr. 1, 1999, see section 2 of Pub.L. 106–5, set out as a note under 11 U.S.C.A. § 1201.

1998 Acts. Section reenacted, eff. Oct. 1, 1998, for the period beginning on Oct. 1, 1998, and ending on Apr. 1, 1999, but all cases commenced or pending under this chapter 12, as reenacted under section 149(a) of Pub.L. 105–277, and all matters and proceedings in or relating to such cases, to be conducted and determined under such chapter as if such chapter were continued in effect after Apr. 1, 1999, and the substantive rights of parties in connection with such cases, matters, and proceedings to continue to be governed under the law applicable to such cases, matters, and proceedings as if such chapter were continued in effect after Apr. 1, 1999, see section 149 of Pub.L. 105–277, set out as a note under 11 U.S.C.A. § 1201.

1994 Acts. Amendment by Pub.L. 103–394 effective on Oct. 22, 1994, and not to apply with respect to cases commenced under Title 11 of the United States Code before Oct. 22, 1994, see section 702 of Pub.L. 103–394, set out as a note under 11 U.S.C.A. § 101.

1993 Acts. Amendment by Pub.L. 103–65, extending to Oct. 1, 1998 the date of repeal of this chapter, to take effect Aug. 6, 1993, see section 3 of Pub.L. 103–65, set out as a note under 11 U.S.C.A. § 1221.

1986 Acts. Section repealed effective Oct. 1, 1998, see section 302(f) of Pub.L. 99–554, as amended, set out in a note under 28 U.S.C.A. § 581. However, for extension of provisions, see section 149 of Pub.L. 105–277, set out as a note under 11 U.S.C.A. § 1201.

Section effective 30 days after Oct. 27, 1986, but not applicable to cases commenced under this title before that date, see section 302(a), (c)(1) of Pub.L. 99–554, set out as a note under 28 U.S.C.A. § 581.

Separability of Provisions

If any provision of or amendment made by Pub.L. 103–394 or the application of such provision or amendment to any person or circumstance is held to be unconstitutional, the remaining provisions of and amendments made by Pub.L. 103–394 and the application of such provisions and amendments to any person or circumstance shall not be affected thereby, see section 701 of Pub.L. 103–394, set out as a note under 11 U.S.C.A. § 101.

Reenactment of Chapter

This section as in effect on June 30, 2005, reenacted effective July 1, 2005, see Pub.L. 109–8, § 1001(a), set out as a note under 11 U.S.C.A. § 1201.

Repeal of Chapter; Extension of Provisions

Pub.L. 99–554, Title III, § 302(f), Oct. 27, 1986, 100 Stat. 3124, as amended Pub.L. 103–65, § 1, Aug. 6, 1993, 107 Stat. 311, which provided that, effective Oct. 1, 1998, this chapter is repealed, but that all cases commenced or pending under this chapter, and all matters and proceedings in or relating to such cases, shall be conducted and determined under this chapter as if such chapter had not been repealed, and that the substantive rights of parties in connection with such cases, matters, and proceedings shall continue to be governed under the laws applicable to such cases, matters, and proceedings as if such chapter had not been repealed, was superceded by the reenactment of this chapter by Pub.L. 109–8, Title X, § 1001(a), Apr. 20, 2005, 119 Stat. 185, set out as a note under 11 U.S.C.A. § 1201.

Pub.L. 105–277, Div. C, Title I, § 149, Oct. 21, 1998, 112 Stat. 2681–610, as amended Pub.L. 106–5, §§ 1, 2, Mar. 30, 1999, 113 Stat. 9; Pub.L. 106–70, §§ 1, 2, Oct. 9, 1999, 113 Stat. 1031; Pub.L. 107–8, §§ 1, 2, May 11, 2001, 115 Stat. 10; Pub.L. 107–17, §§ 1, 2, June 26, 2001, 115 Stat. 151; Pub.L. 107–170, §§ 1, 2, May 7, 2002, 116 Stat. 133; Pub.L. 107–171, Title X, § 10814, May 13, 2002, 116 St. 532; Pub.L. 107–377, § 2, Dec. 19, 2002, 116 Stat. 3115; Pub.L. 108–73, § 2(a), Aug. 15, 2003, 117 Stat. 891; Pub.L. 108–369, § 2(a), Oct. 25, 2004, 118 Stat. 1749, provided that, to take effect on January 1, 2004, chapter 12 of Title 11 [this chapter; 11 U.S.C.A. § 1201 et seq.], as in effect on December 31, 2003, is reenacted for the period beginning on January 1, 2004, and ending on July 1, 2005, but that all cases commenced or pending under this chapter 12, as reenacted under section 149(a) of Pub.L. 105–277, and all matters and proceedings in or relating to such cases, shall be conducted and determined under such chapter as if such chapter were continued in effect after July 1, 2005, and that the substantive rights of parties in connection with such cases, matters, and proceedings shall continue to be governed under the law applicable to such cases, matters, and proceedings as if such chapter were continued in effect after July 1, 2005, was superceded by the reenactment of this chapter by Pub.L. 109–8, Title X, § 1001(a), Apr. 20, 2005, 119 Stat. 185, set out as a note under 11 U.S.C.A. § 1201.

CROSS REFERENCES

Payment stopped on checks remaining unpaid 90 days after final distribution, see 11 USCA § 347.

Payments in Chapter thirteen cases, see 11 USCA § 1326.

§ 1227. Effect of confirmation

(a) Except as provided in section 1228(a) of this title, the provisions of a confirmed plan bind the debtor, each creditor, each equity security holder, and each general partner in the debtor, whether or not the claim of such creditor, such equity security holder, or such general partner in the debtor is provided for by the plan, and whether or not such creditor, such equity security holder, or such general partner in the debtor has objected to, has accepted, or has rejected the plan.

(b) Except as otherwise provided in the plan or the order confirming the plan, the confirmation of a plan vests all of the property of the estate in the debtor.

(c) Except as provided in section 1228(a) of this title and except as otherwise provided in the plan or in the order confirming the plan, the property vesting in the debtor under subsection (b) of this section is free and clear of any claim or interest of any creditor provided for by the plan.

(Added and amended Pub.L. 99–554, Title II, § 255, Title III, § 302(f), Oct. 27, 1986, 100 Stat. 3112, 3124; Pub.L. 103–65, § 1, Aug. 6, 1993, 107 Stat. 311; Pub.L. 105–277, Div. C, Title I, § 149(a), Oct. 21, 1998, 112 Stat. 2681–610; Pub.L. 106–5, § 1(1), (2), Mar. 30, 1999, 113 Stat. 9; Pub.L. 106–70, § 1, Oct. 9, 1999, 113 Stat. 1031; Pub.L. 107–8, § 1, May 11, 2001, 115 Stat. 10; Pub.L. 107–17, § 1, June 26, 2001, 115 Stat. 151; Pub.L. 107–170, § 1, May 7, 2002, 116 Stat. 133; Pub.L. 107–171, Title X, § 10814(a), May 13, 2002, 116 Stat. 532; Pub.L. 107–377, § 2(a), Dec. 19, 2002, 116 Stat. 3115; Pub.L. 108–73, § 2(a), Aug. 15, 2003, 117 Stat. 891; Pub.L. 108–369, § 2(a), Oct. 25, 2004, 118 Stat. 1749; Pub.L. 109–8, Title X, § 1001(a)(1), Apr. 20, 2005, 119 Stat. 185.)

HISTORICAL AND STATUTORY NOTES

Revision Notes and Legislative Reports

1986 Acts. House Report No. 99–764 and House Conference Report No. 99–958, see 1986 U.S. Code Cong. and Adm. News, p. 5227.

1993 Acts. House Report No. 103–32, see 1993 U.S. Code Cong. and Adm. News, p. 373.

1998 Acts. Statement by President, see 1998 U.S. Code Cong. and Adm. News, p. 582.

1999 Acts. Statement by President, see 1999 U.S. Code Cong. and Adm. News, p. 4.

Statement by President, see 1999 U.S. Code Cong. and Adm. News, p. 102.

2001 Acts. House Report No. 107–2, see 2001 U.S. Code Cong. and Adm. News, p. 6.

2005 Acts. House Report No. 109–31(Part I), see 2005 U.S. Code Cong. and Adm. News, p. 88.

Effective and Applicability Provisions

2005 Acts. Amendments by Pub.L. 109–8 effective, except as otherwise provided, 180 days after April 20, 2005, and inapplicable with respect to cases commenced under Title 11 before the effective date, see Pub.L. 109–8, § 1501, set out as a note under 11 U.S.C.A. § 101.

2004 Acts. Amendment by Pub.L. 108–369, § 2(a), extending to July 1, 2005, the date of repeal of this chapter, to take effect Jan. 1, 2004, see Pub.L. 108–369, § 2(b), set out as a note under 11 U.S.C.A. § 1201.

2003 Acts. Amendment by Pub.L. 108–73, § 2(a), extending to Jan. 1, 2004, the date of repeal of this chapter, to take effect July 1, 2003, see Pub.L. 108–73, § 2(b), set out as a note under 11 U.S.C.A. § 1201.

2002 Acts. Amendment by Pub.L. 107–377, § 2(a), extending to July 1, 2003, the date of repeal of this chapter, to take effect Jan. 1, 2003, see Pub.L. 107–377, § 2(b), set out as a note under 11 U.S.C.A. § 1201.

Amendment by Pub.L. 107–171, extending to Jan. 1, 2003, the date of repeal of this chapter, to take effect June 1, 2002, see section 10814(b) of Pub.L. 107–171, set out as a note under 11 U.S.C.A. § 1201.

Amendment by Pub.L. 107–170, extending to June 1, 2002, the date of repeal of this chapter, to take effect October 1, 2001, see section 2 of Pub.L. 107–170, set out as a note under 11 U.S.C.A. § 1201.

2001 Acts. Amendment by Pub.L. 107–17, extending to October 1, 2001, the date of repeal of this chapter, to take effect June 1, 2001, see section 2 of Pub.L. 107–17, set out as a note under 11 U.S.C.A. § 1201.

Amendment by Pub.L. 107–8, extending to June 1, 2001, the date of repeal of this chapter, to take effect July 1, 2000, see section 2 of Pub.L. 107–8, set out as a note under 11 U.S.C.A. § 1201.

1999 Acts. Amendment by Pub.L. 106–70, extending to July 1, 2000, the date of repeal of this chapter, to take effect Oct. 1, 1999, see section 2 of Pub.L. 106–70, set out as a note under 11 U.S.C.A. § 1201.

Amendment by Pub.L. 106–5, extending to Oct. 1, 1999 the date of repeal of this chapter, to take effect Apr. 1, 1999, see section 2 of Pub.L. 106–5, set out as a note under 11 U.S.C.A. § 1201.

1998 Acts. Section reenacted, eff. Oct. 1, 1998, for the period beginning on Oct. 1, 1998, and ending on Apr. 1, 1999, but all cases commenced or pending under this chapter 12, as reenacted under section 149(a) of Pub.L. 105–277, and all matters and proceedings in or relating to such cases, to be conducted and determined under such chapter as if such chapter were continued in effect after Apr. 1, 1999, and the substantive rights of parties in connection with such cases, matters, and proceedings to continue to be governed under the law applicable to such cases, matters, and proceedings as if such chapter were continued in effect after Apr. 1, 1999, see section 149 of Pub.L. 105–277, set out as a note under 11 U.S.C.A. § 1201.

1993 Acts. Amendment by Pub.L. 103–65, extending to Oct. 1, 1998 the date of repeal of this chapter, to take effect Aug. 6, 1993, see section 3 of Pub.L. 103–65, set out as a note under 11 U.S.C.A. § 1221.

1986 Acts. Section repealed effective Oct. 1, 1998, see section 302(f) of Pub.L. 99–554, as amended, set out in a note under 28 U.S.C.A. § 581. However, for extension of provisions, see section 149 of Pub.L. 105–277, set out as a note under 11 U.S.C.A. § 1201.

Section effective 30 days after Oct. 27, 1986, but not applicable to cases commenced under this title before that date, see section 302(a), (c)(1) of Pub.L. 99–554, set out as a note under 28 U.S.C.A. § 581.

Reenactment of Chapter

This section as in effect on June 30, 2005, reenacted effective July 1, 2005, see Pub.L. 109–8, § 1001(a), set out as a note under 11 U.S.C.A. § 1201.

Repeal of Chapter; Extension of Provisions

Pub.L. 99–554, Title III, § 302(f), Oct. 27, 1986, 100 Stat. 3124, as amended Pub.L. 103–65, § 1, Aug. 6, 1993, 107 Stat. 311, which provided that, effective Oct. 1, 1998, this chapter is repealed, but that all cases commenced or pending under this chapter, and all matters and proceedings in or relating to such cases, shall be conducted and determined under this chapter as if such chapter had not been repealed, and that the substantive rights of parties in connection with such cases, matters, and proceedings shall continue to be governed under the laws applicable to such cases, matters, and proceedings as if such chapter had not been repealed, was superceded by the reenactment of this chapter by Pub.L. 109–8, Title X, § 1001(a), Apr. 20, 2005, 119 Stat. 185, set out as a note under 11 U.S.C.A. § 1201.

Pub.L. 105–277, Div. C, Title I, § 149, Oct. 21, 1998, 112 Stat. 2681–610, as amended Pub.L. 106–5, §§ 1, 2, Mar. 30, 1999, 113 Stat. 9; Pub.L. 106–70, §§ 1, 2, Oct. 9, 1999, 113 Stat. 1031; Pub.L. 107–8, §§ 1, 2, May 11, 2001, 115 Stat. 10; Pub.L. 107–17, §§ 1, 2, June 26, 2001, 115 Stat. 151; Pub.L. 107–170, §§ 1, 2, May 7, 2002, 116 Stat. 133; Pub.L. 107–171, Title X, § 10814, May 13, 2002, 116 St. 532; Pub.L. 107–377, § 2, Dec. 19, 2002, 116 Stat. 3115; Pub.L. 108–73, § 2(a), Aug. 15, 2003, 117 Stat. 891; Pub.L. 108–369, § 2(a), Oct. 25, 2004, 118 Stat. 1749, provided that, to take effect on January 1, 2004, chapter 12 of Title 11 [this chapter; 11 U.S.C.A. § 1201 et seq.], as in effect on December 31, 2003, is reenacted for the period beginning on January 1, 2004, and ending on July 1, 2005, but that all cases commenced or pending under this chapter 12, as reenacted under section 149(a) of Pub.L. 105–277, and all matters and proceedings in or relating to such cases, shall be conducted and determined under such chapter as if such chapter were continued in effect after July 1, 2005, and that the substantive rights of parties in connection with such cases, matters, and proceedings shall continue to be governed under the law applicable to such cases, matters, and proceedings as if such chapter were continued in effect after July 1, 2005, was superceded by the reenactment of this chapter by Pub.L. 109–8, Title X, § 1001(a), Apr. 20, 2005, 119 Stat. 185, set out as a note under 11 U.S.C.A. § 1201.

CROSS REFERENCES

Effect of confirmation in—

Chapter eleven cases, see 11 USCA § 1141.

Chapter nine cases, see 11 USCA § 944.

Chapter thirteen cases, see 11 USCA § 1327.

§ 1228. Discharge

(a) Subject to subsection (d), as soon as practicable after completion by the debtor of all payments under the plan, and in the case of a debtor who is required by a judicial or administrative order, or by statute, to pay a domestic support obligation, after such debtor certifies that all amounts payable under such order or such statute that are due on or before the date of the certification (including amounts due before the petition was filed, but only to the extent provided for by the plan) have been paid, other than payments to holders of allowed claims provided for under section 1222(b)(5) or 1222(b)(9) of this title, unless the court approves a written waiver of discharge executed by the debtor after the order for relief under this chapter, the court shall grant the debtor a discharge of all debts provided for by the plan allowed under section

503 of this title or disallowed under section 502 of this title, except any debt—

(1) provided for under section 1222(b)(5) or 1222(b)(9) of this title; or

(2) of the kind specified in section 523(a) of this title.

(b) Subject to subsection (d), at any time after the confirmation of the plan and after notice and a hearing, the court may grant a discharge to a debtor that has not completed payments under the plan only if—

(1) the debtor's failure to complete such payments is due to circumstances for which the debtor should not justly be held accountable;

(2) the value, as of the effective date of the plan, of property actually distributed under the plan on account of each allowed unsecured claim is not less than the amount that would have been paid on such claim if the estate of the debtor had been liquidated under chapter 7 of this title on such date; and

(3) modification of the plan under section 1229 of this title is not practicable.

(c) A discharge granted under subsection (b) of this section discharges the debtor from all unsecured debts provided for by the plan or disallowed under section 502 of this title, except any debt—

(1) provided for under section 1222(b)(5) or 1222(b)(9) of this title; or

(2) of a kind specified in section 523(a) of this title.

(d) On request of a party in interest before one year after a discharge under this section is granted, and after notice and a hearing, the court may revoke such discharge only if—

(1) such discharge was obtained by the debtor through fraud; and

(2) the requesting party did not know of such fraud until after such discharge was granted.

(e) After the debtor is granted a discharge, the court shall terminate the services of any trustee serving in the case.

(f) The court may not grant a discharge under this chapter unless the court after notice and a hearing held not more than 10 days before the date of the entry of the order granting the discharge finds that there is no reasonable cause to believe that—

(1) section 522(q)(1) may be applicable to the debtor; and

(2) there is pending any proceeding in which the debtor may be found guilty of a felony of the kind described in section 522(q)(1)(A) or liable for a debt of the kind described in section 522(q)(1)(B).

(Added and amended Pub.L. 99–554, Title II, § 255, Title III, § 302(f), Oct. 27, 1986, 100 Stat. 3112, 3124; Pub.L. 103–65, § 1, Aug. 6, 1993, 107 Stat. 311; Pub.L. 105–277, Div. C, Title I, § 149(a), Oct. 21, 1998, 112 Stat. 2681–610; Pub.L. 106–5, § 1(1), (2), Mar. 30, 1999, 113 Stat. 9; Pub.L. 106–70, § 1, Oct. 9, 1999, 113 Stat. 1031; Pub.L. 106–518, Title II, § 208, Nov. 13, 2000, 114 Stat. 2415; Pub.L. 107–8, § 1, May 11, 2001, 115 Stat. 10; Pub.L. 107–17, § 1, June 26, 2001, 115 Stat. 151; Pub.L. 107–170, § 1, May 7, 2002, 116 Stat. 133; Pub.L. 107–171, Title X, § 10814(a), May 13, 2002, 116 Stat. 532; Pub.L. 107–377, § 2(a), Dec. 19, 2002, 116 Stat. 3115; Pub.L. 108–73, § 2(a), Aug. 15, 2003, 117 Stat. 891; Pub.L. 108–369, § 2(a), Oct. 25, 2004, 118 Stat. 1749; Pub.L. 109–8, Title II, § 213(6), Title III, § 330(c), Title X, § 1001(a)(1), Apr. 20, 2005, 119 Stat. 53, 101, 102, 185.)

HISTORICAL AND STATUTORY NOTES

Revision Notes and Legislative Reports

1986 Acts. House Report No. 99–764 and House Conference Report No. 99–958, see 1986 U.S. Code Cong. and Adm. News, p. 5227.

1993 Acts. House Report No. 103–32, see 1993 U.S. Code Cong. and Adm. News, p. 373.

1998 Acts. Statement by President, see 1998 U.S. Code Cong. and Adm. News, p. 582.

1999 Acts. Statement by President, see 1999 U.S. Code Cong. and Adm. News, p. 4.

Statement by President, see 1999 U.S. Code Cong. and Adm. News, p. 102.

2001 Acts. House Report No. 107–2, see 2001 U.S. Code Cong. and Adm. News, p. 6.

2005 Acts. House Report No. 109–31(Part I), see 2005 U.S. Code Cong. and Adm. News, p. 88.

Effective and Applicability Provisions

2005 Acts. Amendments by sections 213(6) and 330(c) of Pub.L. 109–8 effective 180 days after Apr. 20, 2005, with amendments by section 213(6) of Pub.L. 109–8 not applicable with respect to cases commenced under this title before such effective date, except as otherwise provided, and amendment by section 330(c) of Pub.L. 109–8 applicable with respect to cases commenced under this title on or after Apr. 20, 2005, see Pub.L. 109–8, § 1501, set out as a note under 11 U.S.C.A. § 101.

2004 Acts. Amendment by Pub.L. 108–369, § 2(a), extending to July 1, 2005, the date of repeal of this chapter, to take effect Jan. 1, 2004, see Pub.L. 108–369, § 2(b), set out as a note under 11 U.S.C.A. § 1201.

2003 Acts. Amendment by Pub.L. 108–73, § 2(a), extending to Jan. 1, 2004, the date of repeal of this chapter, to take effect July 1, 2003, see Pub.L. 108–73, § 2(b), set out as a note under 11 U.S.C.A. § 1201.

2002 Acts. Amendment by Pub.L. 107–377, § 2(a), extending to July 1, 2003, the date of repeal of this chapter, to take effect Jan. 1, 2003, see Pub.L. 107–377, § 2(b), set out as a note under 11 U.S.C.A. § 1201.

Amendment by Pub.L. 107–171, extending to Jan. 1, 2003, the date of repeal of this chapter, to take effect June 1, 2002, see section 10814(b) of Pub.L. 107–171, set out as a note under 11 U.S.C.A. § 1201.

Amendment by Pub.L. 107–170, extending to June 1, 2002, the date of repeal of this chapter, to take effect October 1,

2001, see section 2 of Pub.L. 107–170, set out as a note under 11 U.S.C.A. § 1201.

2001 Acts. Amendment by Pub.L. 107–17, extending to October 1, 2001, the date of repeal of this chapter, to take effect June 1, 2001, see section 2 of Pub.L. 107–17, set out as a note under 11 U.S.C.A. § 1201.

Amendment by Pub.L. 107–8, extending to June 1, 2001, the date of repeal of this chapter, to take effect July 1, 2000, see section 2 of Pub.L. 107–8, set out as a note under 11 U.S.C.A. § 1201.

1999 Acts. Amendment by Pub.L. 106–70, extending to July 1, 2000, the date of repeal of this chapter, to take effect Oct. 1, 1999, see section 2 of Pub.L. 106–70, set out as a note under 11 U.S.C.A. § 1201.

Amendment by Pub.L. 106–5, extending to Oct. 1, 1999 the date of repeal of this chapter, to take effect Apr. 1, 1999, see section 2 of Pub.L. 106–5, set out as a note under 11 U.S.C.A. § 1201.

1998 Acts. Section reenacted, eff. Oct. 1, 1998, for the period beginning on Oct. 1, 1998, and ending on Apr. 1, 1999, but all cases commenced or pending under this chapter 12, as reenacted under section 149(a) of Pub.L. 105–277, and all matters and proceedings in or relating to such cases, to be conducted and determined under such chapter as if such chapter were continued in effect after Apr. 1, 1999, and the substantive rights of parties in connection with such cases, matters, and proceedings to continue to be governed under the law applicable to such cases, matters, and proceedings as if such chapter were continued in effect after Apr. 1, 1999, see section 149 of Pub.L. 105–277, set out as a note under 11 U.S.C.A. § 1201.

1993 Acts. Amendment by Pub.L. 103–65, extending to Oct. 1, 1998 the date of repeal of this chapter, to take effect Aug. 6, 1993, see section 3 of Pub.L. 103–65, set out as a note under 11 U.S.C.A. § 1221.

1986 Acts. Section repealed effective Oct. 1, 1998, see section 302(f) of Pub.L. 99–554, as amended, set out in a note under 28 U.S.C.A. § 581. However, for extension of provisions, see section 149 of Pub.L. 105–277, set out as a note under 11 U.S.C.A. § 1201.

Section effective 30 days after Oct. 27, 1986, but not applicable to cases commenced under this title before that date, see section 302(a), (c)(1) of Pub.L. 99–554, set out as a note under 28 U.S.C.A. § 581.

Reenactment of Chapter

This section as in effect on June 30, 2005, reenacted effective July 1, 2005, see Pub.L. 109–8, § 1001(a), set out as a note under 11 U.S.C.A. § 1201.

Repeal of Chapter; Extension of Provisions

Pub.L. 99–554, Title III, § 302(f), Oct. 27, 1986, 100 Stat. 3124, as amended Pub.L. 103–65, § 1, Aug. 6, 1993, 107 Stat. 311, which provided that, effective Oct. 1, 1998, this chapter is repealed, but that all cases commenced or pending under this chapter, and all matters and proceedings in or relating to such cases, shall be conducted and determined under this chapter as if such chapter had not been repealed, and that the substantive rights of parties in connection with such cases, matters, and proceedings shall continue to be governed under the laws applicable to such cases, matters, and proceedings as if such chapter had not been repealed, was superceded by the reenactment of this chapter by Pub.L. 109–8, Title X, § 1001(a), Apr. 20, 2005, 119 Stat. 185, set out as a note under 11 U.S.C.A. § 1201.

Pub.L. 105–277, Div. C, Title I, § 149, Oct. 21, 1998, 112 Stat. 2681–610, as amended Pub.L. 106–5, §§ 1, 2, Mar. 30, 1999, 113 Stat. 9; Pub.L. 106–70, §§ 1, 2, Oct. 9, 1999, 113 Stat. 1031; Pub.L. 107–8, §§ 1, 2, May 11, 2001, 115 Stat. 10; Pub.L. 107–17, §§ 1, 2, June 26, 2001, 115 Stat. 151; Pub.L. 107–170, §§ 1, 2, May 7, 2002, 116 Stat. 133; Pub.L. 107–171, Title X, § 10814, May 13, 2002, 116 St. 532; Pub.L. 107–377, § 2, Dec. 19, 2002, 116 Stat. 3115; Pub.L. 108–73, § 2(a), Aug. 15, 2003, 117 Stat. 891; Pub.L. 108–369, § 2(a), Oct. 25, 2004, 118 Stat. 1749, provided that, to take effect on January 1, 2004, chapter 12 of Title 11 [this chapter; 11 U.S.C.A. § 1201 et seq.], as in effect on December 31, 2003, is reenacted for the period beginning on January 1, 2004, and ending on July 1, 2005, but that all cases commenced or pending under this chapter 12, as reenacted under section 149(a) of Pub.L. 105–277, and all matters and proceedings in or relating to such cases, shall be conducted and determined under such chapter as if such chapter were continued in effect after July 1, 2005, and that the substantive rights of parties in connection with such cases, matters, and proceedings shall continue to be governed under the law applicable to such cases, matters, and proceedings as if such chapter were continued in effect after July 1, 2005, was superceded by the reenactment of this chapter by Pub.L. 109–8, Title X, § 1001(a), Apr. 20, 2005, 119 Stat. 185, set out as a note under 11 U.S.C.A. § 1201.

CROSS REFERENCES

Cancellation of indebtedness from discharged farm loans, see 12 USCA § 1150.

Discharge in—

Chapter seven cases, see 11 USCA § 727.

Chapter thirteen cases, see 11 USCA § 1328.

Effect of—

Conversion, see 11 USCA § 348.

Discharge, see 11 USCA § 524.

Exceptions to discharge, see 11 USCA § 523.

§ 1229. Modification of plan after confirmation

(a) At any time after confirmation of the plan but before the completion of payments under such plan, the plan may be modified, on request of the debtor, the trustee, or the holder of an allowed unsecured claim, to—

(1) increase or reduce the amount of payments on claims of a particular class provided for by the plan;

(2) extend or reduce the time for such payments; or

(3) alter the amount of the distribution to a creditor whose claim is provided for by the plan to the extent necessary to take account of any payment of such claim other than under the plan.

(b)(1) Sections 1222(a), 1222(b), and 1223(c) of this title and the requirements of section 1225(a) of this title apply to any modification under subsection (a) of this section.

(2) The plan as modified becomes the plan unless, after notice and a hearing, such modification is disapproved.

(c) A plan modified under this section may not provide for payments over a period that expires after three years after the time that the first payment under the original confirmed plan was due, unless the court, for cause, approves a longer period, but the court may not approve a period that expires after five years after such time.

(d) A plan may not be modified under this section—

(1) to increase the amount of any payment due before the plan as modified becomes the plan;

(2) by anyone except the debtor, based on an increase in the debtor's disposable income, to increase the amount of payments to unsecured creditors required for a particular month so that the aggregate of such payments exceeds the debtor's disposable income for such month; or

(3) in the last year of the plan by anyone except the debtor, to require payments that would leave the debtor with insufficient funds to carry on the farming operation after the plan is completed.

(Added and amended Pub.L. 99–554, Title II, § 255, Title III, § 302(f), Oct. 27, 1986, 100 Stat. 3113, 3124; Pub.L. 103–65, § 1, Aug. 6, 1993, 107 Stat. 311; Pub.L. 105–277, Div. C, Title I, § 149(a), Oct. 21, 1998, 112 Stat. 2681–610; Pub.L. 106–5, § 1(1), (2), Mar. 30, 1999, 113 Stat. 9; Pub.L. 106–70, § 1, Oct. 9, 1999, 113 Stat. 1031; Pub.L. 107–8, § 1, May 11, 2001, 115 Stat. 10; Pub.L. 107–17, § 1, June 26, 2001, 115 Stat. 151; Pub.L. 107–170, § 1, May 7, 2002, 116 Stat. 133; Pub.L. 107–171, Title X, § 10814(a), May 13, 2002, 116 Stat. 532; Pub.L. 107–377, § 2(a), Dec. 19, 2002, 116 Stat. 3115; Pub.L. 108–73, § 2(a), Aug. 15, 2003, 117 Stat. 891; Pub.L. 108–369, § 2(a), Oct. 25, 2004, 118 Stat. 1749; Pub.L. 109–8, Title X, §§ 1001(a)(1), 1006(b), Apr. 20, 2005, 199 Stat. 185, 187.)

HISTORICAL AND STATUTORY NOTES

Revision Notes and Legislative Reports

1986 Acts. House Report No. 99–764 and House Conference Report No. 99–958, see 1986 U.S. Code Cong. and Adm. News, p. 5227.

1993 Acts. House Report No. 103–32, see 1993 U.S. Code Cong. and Adm. News, p. 373.

1998 Acts. Statement by President, see 1998 U.S. Code Cong. and Adm. News, p. 582.

1999 Acts. Statement by President, see 1999 U.S. Code Cong. and Adm. News, p. 4.

Statement by President, see 1999 U.S. Code Cong. and Adm. News, p. 102.

2001 Acts. House Report No. 107–2, see 2001 U.S. Code Cong. and Adm. News, p. 6.

2005 Acts. House Report No. 109–31(Part I), see 2005 U.S. Code Cong. and Adm. News, p. 88.

Effective and Applicability Provisions

2005 Acts. Amendments by Pub.L. 109–8 effective, except as otherwise provided, 180 days after April 20, 2005, and inapplicable with respect to cases commenced under Title 11 before the effective date, see Pub.L. 109–8, § 1501, set out as a note under 11 U.S.C.A. § 101.

2004 Acts. Amendment by Pub.L. 108–369, § 2(a), extending to July 1, 2005, the date of repeal of this chapter, to take effect Jan. 1, 2004, see Pub.L. 108–369, § 2(b), set out as a note under 11 U.S.C.A. § 1201.

2003 Acts. Amendment by Pub.L. 108–73, § 2(a), extending to Jan. 1, 2004, the date of repeal of this chapter, to take effect July 1, 2003, see Pub.L. 108–73, § 2(b), set out as a note under 11 U.S.C.A. § 1201.

2002 Acts. Amendment by Pub.L. 107–377, § 2(a), extending to July 1, 2003, the date of repeal of this chapter, to take effect Jan. 1, 2003, see Pub.L. 107–377, § 2(b), set out as a note under 11 U.S.C.A. § 1201.

Amendment by Pub.L. 107–171, extending to Jan. 1, 2003, the date of repeal of this chapter, to take effect June 1, 2002, see section 10814(b) of Pub.L. 107–171, set out as a note under 11 U.S.C.A. § 1201.

Amendment by Pub.L. 107–170, extending to June 1, 2002, the date of repeal of this chapter, to take effect October 1, 2001, see section 2 of Pub.L. 107–170, set out as a note under 11 U.S.C.A. § 1201.

2001 Acts. Amendment by Pub.L. 107–17, extending to October 1, 2001, the date of repeal of this chapter, to take effect June 1, 2001, see section 2 of Pub.L. 107–17, set out as a note under 11 U.S.C.A. § 1201.

Amendment by Pub.L. 107–8, extending to June 1, 2001, the date of repeal of this chapter, to take effect July 1, 2000, see section 2 of Pub.L. 107–8, set out as a note under 11 U.S.C.A. § 1201.

1999 Acts. Amendment by Pub.L. 106–70, extending to July 1, 2000, the date of repeal of this chapter, to take effect Oct. 1, 1999, see section 2 of Pub.L. 106–70, set out as a note under 11 U.S.C.A. § 1201.

Amendment by Pub.L. 106–5, extending to Oct. 1, 1999, the date of repeal of this chapter, to take effect Apr. 1, 1999, see section 2 of Pub.L. 106–5, set out as a note under 11 U.S.C.A. § 1201.

1998 Acts. Section reenacted, eff. Oct. 1, 1998, for the period beginning on Oct. 1, 1998, and ending on Apr. 1, 1999, but all cases commenced or pending under this chapter 12, as reenacted under section 149(a) of Pub.L. 105–277, and all matters and proceedings in or relating to such cases, to be conducted and determined under such chapter as if such chapter were continued in effect after Apr. 1, 1999, and the substantive rights of parties in connection with such cases, matters, and proceedings to continue to be governed under the law applicable to such cases, matters, and proceedings as if such chapter were continued in effect after Apr. 1, 1999, see section 149 of Pub.L. 105–277, set out as a note under 11 U.S.C.A. § 1201.

1993 Acts. Amendment by Pub.L. 103–65, extending to Oct. 1, 1998, the date of repeal of this chapter, to take effect Aug. 6, 1993, see section 3 of Pub.L. 103–65, set out as a note under 11 U.S.C.A. § 1221.

1986 Acts. Section repealed effective Oct. 1, 1998, see section 302(f) of Pub.L. 99–554, as amended, set out in a note under 28 U.S.C.A. § 581. However, for extension of provisions, see section 149 of Pub.L. 105–277, set out as a note under 11 U.S.C.A. § 1201.

Section effective 30 days after Oct. 27, 1986, but not applicable to cases commenced under this title before that date, see section 302(a), (c)(1) of Pub.L. 99–554, set out as a note under 28 U.S.C.A. § 581.

Reenactment of Chapter

This section as in effect on June 30, 2005, reenacted effective July 1, 2005, see Pub.L. 109–8, § 1001(a), set out as a note under 11 U.S.C.A. § 1201.

Repeal of Chapter; Extension of Provisions

Pub.L. 99–554, Title III, § 302(f), Oct. 27, 1986, 100 Stat. 3124, as amended Pub.L. 103–65, § 1, Aug. 6, 1993, 107 Stat. 311, which provided that, effective Oct. 1, 1998, this chapter is repealed, but that all cases commenced or pending under this chapter, and all matters and proceedings in or relating to such cases, shall be conducted and determined under this chapter as if such chapter had not been repealed, and that the substantive rights of parties in connection with such cases, matters, and proceedings shall continue to be governed under the laws applicable to such cases, matters, and proceedings as if such chapter had not been repealed, was superceded by the reenactment of this chapter by Pub.L. 109–8, Title X, § 1001(a), Apr. 20, 2005, 119 Stat. 185, set out as a note under 11 U.S.C.A. § 1201.

Pub.L. 105–277, Div. C, Title I, § 149, Oct. 21, 1998, 112 Stat. 2681–610, as amended Pub.L. 106–5, §§ 1, 2, Mar. 30, 1999, 113 Stat. 9; Pub.L. 106–70, §§ 1, 2, Oct. 9, 1999, 113 Stat. 1031; Pub.L. 107–8, §§ 1, 2, May 11, 2001, 115 Stat. 10; Pub.L. 107–17, §§ 1, 2, June 26, 2001, 115 Stat. 151; Pub.L. 107–170, §§ 1, 2, May 7, 2002, 116 Stat. 133; Pub.L. 107–171, Title X, § 10814, May 13, 2002, 116 St. 532; Pub.L. 107–377, § 2, Dec. 19, 2002, 116 Stat. 3115; Pub.L. 108–73, § 2(a), Aug. 15, 2003, 117 Stat. 891; Pub.L. 108–369, § 2(a), Oct. 25, 2004, 118 Stat. 1749, provided that, to take effect on January 1, 2004, chapter 12 of Title 11 [this chapter; 11 U.S.C.A. § 1201 et seq.], as in effect on December 31, 2003, is reenacted for the period beginning on January 1, 2004, and ending on July 1, 2005, but that all cases commenced or pending under this chapter 12, as reenacted under section 149(a) of Pub.L. 105–277, and all matters and proceedings in or relating to such cases, shall be conducted and determined under such chapter as if such chapter were continued in effect after July 1, 2005, and that the substantive rights of parties in connection with such cases, matters, and proceedings shall continue to be governed under the law applicable to such cases, matters, and proceedings as if such chapter were continued in effect after July 1, 2005, was superceded by the reenactment of this chapter by Pub.L. 109–8, Title X, § 1001(a), Apr. 20, 2005, 119 Stat. 185, set out as a note under 11 U.S.C.A. § 1201.

CROSS REFERENCES

Conversion or dismissal upon denial of confirmation of modified plan, see 11 USCA § 1208.

Duties of United States trustee, see 28 USCA § 586.

Modification of plan in—

Chapter eleven cases, see 11 USCA § 1127.

Chapter nine cases, see 11 USCA § 942.

Chapter thirteen cases, see 11 USCA § 1329.

§ 1230. Revocation of an order of confirmation

(a) On request of a party in interest at any time within 180 days after the date of the entry of an order of confirmation under section 1225 of this title, and after notice and a hearing, the court may revoke such order if such order was procured by fraud.

(b) If the court revokes an order of confirmation under subsection (a) of this section, the court shall dispose of the case under section 1207 of this title, unless, within the time fixed by the court, the debtor proposes and the court confirms a modification of the plan under section 1229 of this title.

(Added and amended Pub.L. 99–554, Title II, § 255, Title III, § 302(f), Oct. 27, 1986, 100 Stat. 3113, 3124; Pub.L. 103–65, § 1, Aug. 6, 1993, 107 Stat. 311; Pub.L. 105–277, Div. C, Title I, § 149(a), Oct. 21, 1998, 112 Stat. 2681–610; Pub.L. 106–5, § 1(1), (2), Mar. 30, 1999, 113 Stat. 9; Pub.L. 106–70, § 1, Oct. 9, 1999, 113 Stat. 1031; Pub.L. 107–8, § 1, May 11, 2001, 115 Stat. 10; Pub.L. 107–17, § 1, June 26, 2001, 115 Stat. 151; Pub.L. 107–170, § 1, May 7, 2002, 116 Stat. 133; Pub.L. 107–171, Title X, § 10814(a), May 13, 2002, 116 Stat. 532; Pub.L. 107–377, § 2(a), Dec. 19, 2002, 116 Stat. 3115; Pub.L. 108–73, § 2(a), Aug. 15, 2003, 117 Stat. 891; Pub.L. 108–369, § 2(a), Oct. 25, 2004, 118 Stat. 1749; Pub.L. 109–8, Title X, § 1001(a)(1), Apr. 20, 2005, 119 Stat. 185.)

HISTORICAL AND STATUTORY NOTES

Revision Notes and Legislative Reports

1986 Acts. House Report No. 99–764 and House Conference Report No. 99–958, see 1986 U.S. Code Cong. and Adm. News, p. 5227.

1993 Acts. House Report No. 103–32, see 1993 U.S. Code Cong. and Adm. News, p. 373.

1998 Acts. Statement by President, see 1998 U.S. Code Cong. and Adm. News, p. 582.

1999 Acts. Statement by President, see 1999 U.S. Code Cong. and Adm. News, p. 4.

Statement by President, see 1999 U.S. Code Cong. and Adm. News, p. 102.

2001 Acts. House Report No. 107–2, see 2001 U.S. Code Cong. and Adm. News, p. 6.

2005 Acts. House Report No. 109–31(Part I), see 2005 U.S. Code Cong. and Adm. News, p. 88.

Effective and Applicability Provisions

2005 Acts. Amendments by Pub.L. 109–8 effective, except as otherwise provided, 180 days after April 20, 2005, and inapplicable with respect to cases commenced under Title 11 before the effective date, see Pub.L. 109–8, § 1501, set out as a note under 11 U.S.C.A. § 101.

2004 Acts. Amendment by Pub.L. 108–369, § 2(a), extending to July 1, 2005, the date of repeal of this chapter, to take effect Jan. 1, 2004, see Pub.L. 108–369, § 2(b), set out as a note under 11 U.S.C.A. § 1201.

2003 Acts. Amendment by Pub.L. 108–73, § 2(a), extending to Jan. 1, 2004, the date of repeal of this chapter, to take effect July 1, 2003, see Pub.L. 108–73, § 2(b), set out as a note under 11 U.S.C.A. § 1201.

2002 Acts. Amendment by Pub.L. 107–377, § 2(a), extending to July 1, 2003, the date of repeal of this chapter, to take effect Jan. 1, 2003, see Pub.L. 107–377, § 2(b), set out as a note under 11 U.S.C.A. § 1201.

Amendment by Pub.L. 107–171, extending to Jan. 1, 2003, the date of repeal of this chapter, to take effect June 1, 2002, see section 10814(b) of Pub.L. 107–171, set out as a note under 11 U.S.C.A. § 1201.

Amendment by Pub.L. 107–170, extending to June 1, 2002, the date of repeal of this chapter, to take effect October 1, 2001, see section 2 of Pub.L. 107–170, set out as a note under 11 U.S.C.A. § 1201.

2001 Acts. Amendment by Pub.L. 107–17, extending to October 1, 2001, the date of repeal of this chapter, to take effect June 1, 2001, see section 2 of Pub.L. 107–17, set out as a note under 11 U.S.C.A. § 1201.

Amendment by Pub.L. 107–8, extending to June 1, 2001, the date of repeal of this chapter, to take effect July 1, 2000, see section 2 of Pub.L. 107–8, set out as a note under 11 U.S.C.A. § 1201.

1999 Acts. Amendment by Pub.L. 106–70, extending to July 1, 2000, the date of repeal of this chapter, to take effect Oct. 1, 1999, see section 2 of Pub.L. 106–70, set out as a note under 11 U.S.C.A. § 1201.

Amendment by Pub.L. 106–5, extending to Oct. 1, 1999, the date of repeal of this chapter, to take effect Apr. 1, 1999, see section 2 of Pub.L. 106–5, set out as a note under 11 U.S.C.A. § 1201.

1998 Acts. Section reenacted, eff. Oct. 1, 1998, for the period beginning on Oct. 1, 1998, and ending on Apr. 1, 1999, but all cases commenced or pending under this chapter 12, as reenacted under section 149(a) of Pub.L. 105–277, and all matters and proceedings in or relating to such cases, to be conducted and determined under such chapter as if such chapter were continued in effect after Apr. 1, 1999, and the substantive rights of parties in connection with such cases, matters, and proceedings to continue to be governed under the law applicable to such cases, matters, and proceedings as if such chapter were continued in effect after Apr. 1, 1999, see section 149 of Pub.L. 105–277, set out as a note under 11 U.S.C.A. § 1201.

1993 Acts. Amendment by Pub.L. 103–65, extending to Oct. 1, 1998, the date of repeal of this chapter, to take effect Aug. 6, 1993, see section 3 of Pub.L. 103–65, set out as a note under 11 U.S.C.A. § 1221.

1986 Acts. Section repealed effective Oct. 1, 1998, see section 302(f) of Pub.L. 99–554, as amended, set out in a note under 28 U.S.C.A. § 581. However, for extension of provisions, see section 149 of Pub.L. 105–277, set out as a note under 11 U.S.C.A. § 1201.

Section effective 30 days after Oct. 27, 1986, but not applicable to cases commenced under this title before that date, see section 302(a), (c)(1) of Pub.L. 99–554, set out as a note under 28 U.S.C.A. § 581.

Reenactment of Chapter

This section as in effect on June 30, 2005, reenacted effective July 1, 2005, see Pub.L. 109–8, § 1001(a), set out as a note under 11 U.S.C.A. § 1201.

Repeal of Chapter; Extension of Provisions

Pub.L. 99–554, Title III, § 302(f), Oct. 27, 1986, 100 Stat. 3124, as amended Pub.L. 103–65, § 1, Aug. 6, 1993, 107 Stat. 311, which provided that, effective Oct. 1, 1998, this chapter is repealed, but that all cases commenced or pending under this chapter, and all matters and proceedings in or relating to such cases, shall be conducted and determined under this chapter as if such chapter had not been repealed, and that the substantive rights of parties in connection with such cases, matters, and proceedings shall continue to be governed under the laws applicable to such cases, matters, and proceedings as if such chapter had not been repealed, was superceded by the reenactment of this chapter by Pub.L. 109–8, Title X, § 1001(a), Apr. 20, 2005, 119 Stat. 185, set out as a note under 11 U.S.C.A. § 1201.

Pub.L. 105–277, Div. C, Title I, § 149, Oct. 21, 1998, 112 Stat. 2681–610, as amended Pub.L. 106–5, §§ 1, 2, Mar. 30, 1999, 113 Stat. 9; Pub.L. 106–70, §§ 1, 2, Oct. 9, 1999, 113 Stat. 1031; Pub.L. 107–8, §§ 1, 2, May 11, 2001, 115 Stat. 10; Pub.L. 107–17, §§ 1, 2, June 26, 2001, 115 Stat. 151; Pub.L. 107–170, §§ 1, 2, May 7, 2002, 116 Stat. 133; Pub.L. 107–171, Title X, § 10814, May 13, 2002, 116 St. 532; Pub.L. 107–377, § 2, Dec. 19, 2002, 116 Stat. 3115; Pub.L. 108–73, § 2(a), Aug. 15, 2003, 117 Stat. 891; Pub.L. 108–369, § 2(a), Oct. 25, 2004, 118 Stat. 1749, provided that, to take effect on January 1, 2004, chapter 12 of Title 11 [this chapter; 11 U.S.C.A. § 1201 et seq.], as in effect on December 31, 2003, is reenacted for the period beginning on January 1, 2004, and ending on July 1, 2005, but that all cases commenced or pending under this chapter 12, as reenacted under section 149(a) of Pub.L. 105–277, and all matters and proceedings in or relating to such cases, shall be conducted and determined under such chapter as if such chapter were continued in effect after July 1, 2005, and that the substantive rights of parties in connection with such cases, matters, and proceedings shall continue to be governed under the law applicable to such cases, matters, and proceedings as if such chapter were continued in effect after July 1, 2005, was superceded by the reenactment of this chapter by Pub.L. 109–8, Title X, § 1001(a), Apr. 20, 2005, 119 Stat. 185, set out as a note under 11 U.S.C.A. § 1201.

CROSS REFERENCES

Conversion or dismissal upon denial of confirmation of modified plan, see 11 USCA § 1208.

Revocation of order of confirmation in—

Chapter eleven cases, see 11 USCA § 1144.

Chapter thirteen cases, see 11 USCA § 1330.

§ 1231. Special tax provisions

(a) The issuance, transfer, or exchange of a security, or the making or delivery of an instrument of transfer under a plan confirmed under section 1225 of this title, may not be taxed under any law imposing a stamp tax or similar tax.

(b) The court may authorize the proponent of a plan to request a determination, limited to questions of law, by any governmental unit charged with responsibility for collection or determination of a tax on or measured by income, of the tax effects, under section 346 of this title and under the law imposing such tax, of the plan. In the event of an actual controversy, the court may declare such effects after the earlier of—

(1) the date on which such governmental unit responds to the request under this subsection; or

(2) 270 days after such request.

(c), (d) Redesignated (a), (b)

(Added and amended Pub.L. 99–554, Title II, § 255, Title III, § 302(f), Oct. 27, 1986, 100 Stat. 3113, 3124; Pub.L. 103–65, § 1, Aug. 6, 1993, 107 Stat. 311; Pub.L. 105–277, Div. C, Title I, § 149(a), Oct. 21, 1998, 112 Stat. 2681–610; Pub.L. 106–5, § 1(1), (2), Mar. 30, 1999, 113 Stat. 9; Pub.L. 106–70, § 1, Oct. 9, 1999, 113 Stat. 1031; Pub.L. 107–8, § 1, May 11, 2001, 115 Stat. 10; Pub.L. 107–17, § 1, June 26, 2001, 115 Stat. 151; Pub.L. 107–170, § 1, May 7, 2002, 116 Stat. 133; Pub.L. 107–171, Title X, § 10814(a), May 13, 2002, 116 Stat. 532; Pub.L. 107–377, § 2(a), Dec. 19, 2002, 116 Stat. 3115; Pub.L. 108–73, § 2(a), Aug. 15, 2003, 117 Stat. 891; Pub.L. 108–369, § 2(a), Oct. 25, 2004, 118 Stat. 1749; Pub.L. 109–8, Title VII, § 719(b)(4), Title X, §§ 1001(a)(1), 1003(b), Apr. 20, 2005, 119 Stat. 133, 185, 186.)

HISTORICAL AND STATUTORY NOTES

Revision Notes and Legislative Reports

1986 Acts. House Report No. 99–764 and House Conference Report No. 99–958, see 1986 U.S. Code Cong. and Adm. News, p. 5227.

1993 Acts. House Report No. 103–32, see 1993 U.S. Code Cong. and Adm. News, p. 373.

1998 Acts. Statement by President, see 1998 U.S. Code Cong. and Adm. News, p. 582.

1999 Acts. Statement by President, see 1999 U.S. Code Cong. and Adm. News, p. 4.

Statement by President, see 1999 U.S. Code Cong. and Adm. News, p. 102.

2001 Acts. House Report No. 107–2, see 2001 U.S. Code Cong. and Adm. News, p. 6.

2005 Acts. House Report No. 109–31(Part I), see 2005 U.S. Code Cong. and Adm. News, p. 88.

Effective and Applicability Provisions

2005 Acts. Amendment to subsec. (b) of this section, which was formerly designated as subsec. (d) of this section, effective Apr. 20, 2005, and not applicable with respect to cases commenced under this title before that date, see Pub.L. 109–8, § 1003(c), set out as a note under 11 U.S.C.A. § 1222.

Amendments by Pub.L. 109–8 effective, except as otherwise provided, 180 days after April 20, 2005, and inapplicable with respect to cases commenced under Title 11 before the effective date, see Pub.L. 109–8, § 1501, set out as a note under 11 U.S.C.A. § 101.

2004 Acts. Amendment by Pub.L. 108–369, § 2(a), extending to July 1, 2005, the date of repeal of this chapter, to take effect Jan. 1, 2004, see Pub.L. 108–369, § 2(b), set out as a note under 11 U.S.C.A. § 1201.

2003 Acts. Amendment by Pub.L. 108–73, § 2(a), extending to Jan. 1, 2004, the date of repeal of this chapter, to take effect July 1, 2003, see Pub.L. 108–73, § 2(b), set out as a note under 11 U.S.C.A. § 1201.

2002 Acts. Amendment by Pub.L. 107–377, § 2(a), extending to July 1, 2003, the date of repeal of this chapter, to take effect Jan. 1, 2003, see Pub.L. 107–377, § 2(b), set out as a note under 11 U.S.C.A. § 1201.

Amendment by Pub.L. 107–171, extending to Jan. 1, 2003, the date of repeal of this chapter, to take effect June 1, 2002, see section 10814(b) of Pub.L. 107–171, set out as a note under 11 U.S.C.A. § 1201.

Amendment by Pub.L. 107–170, extending to June 1, 2002, the date of repeal of this chapter, to take effect October 1, 2001, see section 2 of Pub.L. 107–170, set out as a note under 11 U.S.C.A. § 1201.

2001 Acts. Amendment by Pub.L. 107–17, extending to October 1, 2001, the date of repeal of this chapter, to take effect June 1, 2001, see section 2 of Pub.L. 107–17, set out as a note under 11 U.S.C.A. § 1201.

Amendment by Pub.L. 107–8, extending to June 1, 2001, the date of repeal of this chapter, to take effect July 1, 2000, see section 2 of Pub.L. 107–8, set out as a note under 11 U.S.C.A. § 1201.

1999 Acts. Amendment by Pub.L. 106–70, extending to July 1, 2000, the date of repeal of this chapter, to take effect Oct. 1, 1999, see section 2 of Pub.L. 106–70, set out as a note under 11 U.S.C.A. § 1201.

Amendment by Pub.L. 106–5, extending to Oct. 1, 1999, the date of repeal of this chapter, to take effect Apr. 1, 1999, see section 2 of Pub.L. 106–5, set out as a note under 11 U.S.C.A. § 1201.

1998 Acts. Section reenacted, eff. Oct. 1, 1998, for the period beginning on Oct. 1, 1998, and ending on Apr. 1, 1999, but all cases commenced or pending under this chapter 12, as reenacted under section 149(a) of Pub.L. 105–277, and all matters and proceedings in or relating to such cases, to be conducted and determined under such chapter as if such chapter were continued in effect after Apr. 1, 1999, and the substantive rights of parties in connection with such cases, matters, and proceedings to continue to be governed under the law applicable to such cases, matters, and proceedings as if such chapter were continued in effect after Apr. 1, 1999, see section 149 of Pub.L. 105–277, set out as a note under 11 U.S.C.A. § 1201.

1993 Acts. Amendment by Pub.L. 103–65, extending to Oct. 1, 1998, the date of repeal of this chapter, to take effect Aug. 6, 1993, see section 3 of Pub.L. 103–65, set out as a note under 11 U.S.C.A. § 1221.

1986 Acts. Section repealed effective Oct. 1, 1998, see section 302(f) of Pub.L. 99–554, as amended, set out in a note under 28 U.S.C.A. § 581. However, for extension of provisions, see section 149 of Pub.L. 105–277, set out as a note under 11 U.S.C.A. § 1201.

Section effective 30 days after Oct. 27, 1986, but not applicable to cases commenced under this title before that date, see section 302(a), (c)(1) of Pub.L. 99–554, set out as a note under 28 U.S.C.A. § 581.

Reenactment of Chapter

This section as in effect on June 30, 2005, reenacted effective July 1, 2005, see Pub.L. 109–8, § 1001(a), set out as a note under 11 U.S.C.A. § 1201.

Repeal of Chapter; Extension of Provisions

Pub.L. 99–554, Title III, § 302(f), Oct. 27, 1986, 100 Stat. 3124, as amended Pub.L. 103–65, § 1, Aug. 6, 1993, 107 Stat. 311, which provided that, effective Oct. 1, 1998, this chapter is repealed, but that all cases commenced or pending under this chapter, and all matters and proceedings in or relating to such cases, shall be conducted and determined under this chapter as if such chapter had not been repealed, and that the substantive rights of parties in connection with such cases, matters, and proceedings shall continue to be governed under the laws applicable to such cases, matters, and proceedings as if such chapter had not been repealed, was superceded by the reenactment of this chapter by Pub.L. 109–8, Title X, § 1001(a), Apr. 20, 2005, 119 Stat. 185, set out as a note under 11 U.S.C.A. § 1201.

Pub.L. 105–277, Div. C, Title I, § 149, Oct. 21, 1998, 112 Stat. 2681–610, as amended Pub.L. 106–5, §§ 1, 2, Mar. 30, 1999, 113 Stat. 9; Pub.L. 106–70, §§ 1, 2, Oct. 9, 1999, 113 Stat. 1031; Pub.L. 107–8, §§ 1, 2, May 11, 2001, 115 Stat. 10; Pub.L. 107–17, §§ 1, 2, June 26, 2001, 115 Stat. 151; Pub.L. 107–170, §§ 1, 2, May 7, 2002, 116 Stat. 133; Pub.L. 107–171, Title X, § 10814, May 13, 2002, 116 St. 532; Pub.L. 107–377, § 2, Dec. 19, 2002, 116 Stat. 3115; Pub.L. 108–73, § 2(a), Aug. 15, 2003, 117 Stat. 891; Pub.L. 108–369, § 2(a), Oct. 25, 2004, 118 Stat. 1749, provided that, to take effect on January 1, 2004, chapter 12 of Title 11 [this chapter; 11 U.S.C.A. § 1201 et seq.], as in effect on December 31, 2003, is reenacted for the period beginning on January 1, 2004, and ending on July 1, 2005, but that all cases commenced or pending under this chapter 12, as reenacted under section 149(a) of Pub.L. 105–277, and all matters and proceedings in or relating to such cases, shall be conducted and determined under such chapter as if such chapter were continued in effect after July 1, 2005, and that the substantive rights of parties in connection with such cases, matters, and proceedings shall continue to be governed under the law applicable to such cases, matters, and proceedings as if such chapter were continued in effect after July 1, 2005, was superceded by the reenactment of this chapter by Pub.L. 109–8, Title X, § 1001(a), Apr. 20, 2005, 119 Stat. 185, set out as a note under 11 U.S.C.A. § 1201.

CHAPTER 13—ADJUSTMENT OF DEBTS OF AN INDIVIDUAL WITH REGULAR INCOME

SUBCHAPTER I—OFFICERS, ADMINISTRATION, AND THE ESTATE

HISTORICAL AND STATUTORY NOTES

Effective and Applicability Provisions

2005 Acts. Amendments by Pub.L. 109–8 effective, except as otherwise provided, 180 days after April 20, 2005, and inapplicable with respect to cases commenced under Title 11 before the effective date, see Pub.L. 109–8, § 1501, set out as a note under 11 U.S.C.A. § 101.

CROSS REFERENCES

Chapters 1, 3 and 5 of this title applicable in cases under this chapter, see 11 USCA § 103.

Claims arising from rejection of executory contracts or unexpired leases by plans under this chapter, see 11 USCA § 502.

Compensation of trustee, see 11 USCA § 330.

Conversion from—

Chapter eleven, see 11 USCA § 1112.

Chapter seven, see 11 USCA § 706.

Chapter thirteen, see 11 USCA § 348.

Core proceedings, see 28 USCA § 157.

Duration of automatic stay, see 11 USCA § 362.

Eligibility to serve as trustee, see 11 USCA § 321.

Executory contracts and unexpired leases, see 11 USCA § 365.

Filing fees, see 28 USCA § 1930.

Inapplicability of restrictions on garnishment to orders of bankruptcy courts under this chapter, see 15 USCA § 1673.

"Individual with regular income" defined, see 11 USCA § 101.

Individuals who may be debtors under this chapter, see 11 USCA § 109.

Limitation on compensation of trustee, see 11 USCA § 326.

Recommendation by trustee of conversion from Chapter eleven to this chapter, see 11 USCA § 1106.

Return of excessive attorney compensation if transferred property was to be paid by debtor under plan under this chapter, see 11 USCA § 329.

Special tax provisions, see 11 USCA § 346.

Supervision of United States trustees' duties by Attorney General, see 28 USCA § 586.

Unclaimed property, see 11 USCA § 347.

Use, sale or lease of property under plan under this chapter, see 11 USCA § 363.

SUBCHAPTER I—OFFICERS, ADMINISTRATION, AND THE ESTATE

§ 1301. Stay of action against codebtor

(a) Except as provided in subsections (b) and (c) of this section, after the order for relief under this chapter, a creditor may not act, or commence or continue any civil action, to collect all or any part of a consumer debt of the debtor from any individual that is liable on such debt with the debtor, or that secured such debt, unless—

(1) such individual became liable on or secured such debt in the ordinary course of such individual's business; or

(2) the case is closed, dismissed, or converted to a case under chapter 7 or 11 of this title.

(b) A creditor may present a negotiable instrument, and may give notice of dishonor of such an instrument.

(c) On request of a party in interest and after notice and a hearing, the court shall grant relief from the stay provided by subsection (a) of this section with respect to a creditor, to the extent that—

(1) as between the debtor and the individual protected under subsection (a) of this section, such individual received the consideration for the claim held by such creditor;

(2) the plan filed by the debtor proposes not to pay such claim; or

(3) such creditor's interest would be irreparably harmed by continuation of such stay.

(d) Twenty days after the filing of a request under subsection (c)(2) of this section for relief from the stay provided by subsection (a) of this section, such stay is terminated with respect to the party in interest making such request, unless the debtor or any individual that is liable on such debt with the debtor files and serves upon such party in interest a written objection to the taking of the proposed action.

(Pub.L. 95–598, Nov. 6, 1978, 92 Stat. 2645; Pub.L. 98–353, Title III, §§ 313, 524, July 10, 1984, 98 Stat. 355, 388.)

HISTORICAL AND STATUTORY NOTES

Revision Notes and Legislative Reports

1978 Acts. Subsection (a) automatically stays the holder of a claim based on a consumer debt of the chapter 13 debtor from acting or proceeding in any way, except as authorized pursuant to subsections (b) and (c), against an individual or the property of an individual liable with the chapter 13 debtor, unless such codebtor became liable in the ordinary course of his business, or unless the case is closed, dismissed, or converted to another chapter.

Under the terms of the agreement with the codebtor who is not in bankruptcy, the creditor has a right to collect all payments to the extent they are not made by the debtor at the time they are due. To the extent to which a chapter 13 plan does not propose to pay a creditor his claims, the creditor may obtain relief from the court from the automatic stay and collect such claims from the codebtor. Conversely, a codebtor obtains the benefit of any payments made to the creditor under the plan. If a debtor defaults on scheduled payments under the plan, then the codebtor would be liable for the remaining deficiency; otherwise, payments not made under the plan may never be made by the codebtor. The obligation of the codebtor to make the creditor whole at the time payments are due remains.

The automatic stay under this section pertains only to the collection of a consumer debt, defined by section 101(7) of this title to mean a debt incurred by an individual primarily for a personal, family, or household purpose. Therefore, not all debts owed by a chapter 13 debtor will be subject to the stay of the codebtor, particularly those business debts incurred by an individual with regular income, as defined by section 101(24) of this title, engaged in business, that is permitted by virtue of section 109(b) and section 1304 to obtain chapter 13 relief.

Subsection (b) excepts the giving of notice of dishonor of a negotiable instrument from the reach of the codebtor stay.

Under subsection (c), if the codebtor has property out of which the creditor's claim can be satisfied, the court can grant relief from the stay absent the transfer of a security interest in that property by the codebtor to the creditor. Correspondingly, if there is reasonable cause to believe that property is about to be disposed of by the codebtor which could be used to satisfy his obligation to the creditor, the court should lift the stay to allow the creditor to perfect his rights against such property. Likewise, if property is subject to rapid depreciation or decrease in value the stay should be lifted to allow the creditor to protect his rights to reach such property. Otherwise, the creditor's interest would be irreparably harmed by such stay. Property which could be used to satisfy the claim could be disposed of or encumbered and placed beyond the reach of the creditor. The creditor should be allowed to protect his rights to reach property which could satisfy his claim and prevent its erosion in value, disposal, or encumbrance. Senate Report No. 95–989.

This section is new. It is designed to protect a debtor operating under a chapter 13 individual repayment plan case by insulating him from indirect pressures from his creditors exerted through friends or relatives that may have cosigned an obligation of the debtor. The protection is limited, however, to ensure that the creditor involved does not lose the benefit of the bargain he made for a cosigner. He is entitled to full compensation, including any interest, fees, and costs provided for by the agreement under which the debtor obtained his loan. The creditor is simply required to share with other creditors to the extent that the debtor will repay him under the chapter 13 plan. The creditor is delayed, but his substantive rights are not affected.

Subsection (a) is the operative subsection. It stays action by a creditor after an order for relief under chapter 13. The creditor may not act, or commence or continue any civil action, to collect all or any part of a consumer debt of the debtor from any individual that is liable on such debt with the debtor, or that has secured the debt, unless the individual became liable or secured the debt in the ordinary course of his business, or the case is closed, dismissed, or converted to chapter 7 or 11.

Subsection (b) permits the creditor, notwithstanding the stay, to present a negotiable instrument and to give notice of dishonor of the instrument, in order to preserve his substantive rights against the codebtor as required by applicable nonbankruptcy law.

Subsection (c) requires the court to grant relief from the stay in certain circumstances. The court must grant relief to the extent that the debtor does not propose to pay, under the plan, the amount owed to the creditor. The court must also grant relief to the extent that the debtor was really the codebtor in the transaction, that is, to the extent that the nondebtor party actually received the consideration for the claim held by the creditor. Finally, the court must grant relief to the extent that the creditor's interest would be irreparably harmed by the stay, for example, where the codebtor filed bankruptcy himself, or threatened to leave the locale, or lost his job. House Report No. 95–595.

1984 Acts. Statements by Legislative Leaders, see 1984 U.S.Code Cong. and Adm.News, p. 576.

Legislative Statements

Section 1301 of the House amendment is identical with the provision contained in section 1301 of the House bill and adopted by the Senate amendment. Section 1301(c)(1) indicates that a basis for lifting the stay is that the debtor did not receive consideration for the claim by the creditor, or in other words, the debtor is really the "codebtor." As with other sections in title 11, the standard of receiving consideration is a general rule, but where two co-debtors have agreed to share liabilities in a different manner than profits it is the individual who does not ultimately bear the liability that is protected by the stay under section 1301.

Effective and Applicability Provisions

1984 Acts. Amendment by Pub.L. 98–353 effective with respect to cases filed 90 days after July 10, 1984, see section 552(a), formerly 553(a), of Pub.L. 98–353, set out as a note under 11 U.S.C.A. § 101.

CROSS REFERENCES

Automatic stay, see 11 USCA § 362.

Automatic stay of enforcement of claims against debtor in Chapter nine cases, see 11 USCA § 922.

Claims of codebtors, see 11 USCA § 509.

Effect of conversion, see 11 USCA § 348.

Effect of § 362 of this title in stockbroker liquidation cases, see 11 USCA § 742.

Extension of time generally, see 11 USCA § 108.

§ 1302. Trustee

(a) If the United States trustee appoints an individual under section 586(b) of title 28 to serve as standing trustee in cases under this chapter and if such individual qualifies under section 322 of this title, then such individual shall serve as trustee in the case. Otherwise, the United States trustee shall appoint one disinterested person to serve as trustee in the case or the United States trustee may serve as a trustee in the case.

(b) The trustee shall—

(1) perform the duties specified in sections 704(2), 704(3), 704(4), 704(5), 704(6), 704(7), and 704(9) of this title;

(2) appear and be heard at any hearing that concerns—

(A) the value of property subject to a lien;

(B) confirmation of a plan; or

(C) modification of the plan after confirmation;

(3) dispose of, under regulations issued by the Director of the Administrative Office of the United States Courts, moneys received or to be received in a case under chapter XIII of the Bankruptcy Act;

(4) advise, other than on legal matters, and assist the debtor in performance under the plan;

(5) ensure that the debtor commences making timely payments under section 1326 of this title; and

(6) if with respect to the debtor there is a claim for a domestic support obligation, provide the applicable notice specified in subsection (d).

(c) If the debtor is engaged in business, then in addition to the duties specified in subsection (b) of this section, the trustee shall perform the duties specified in sections 1106(a)(3) and 1106(a)(4) of this title.

(d)(1) In a case described in subsection (b)(6) to which subsection (b)(6) applies, the trustee shall—

(A)(i) provide written notice to the holder of the claim described in subsection (b)(6) of such claim and of the right of such holder to use the services of the State child support enforcement agency established under sections 464 and 466 of the Social Security Act for the State in which such holder resides, for assistance in collecting child support during and after the case under this title; and

(ii) include in the notice provided under clause (i) the address and telephone number of such State child support enforcement agency;

(B)(i) provide written notice to such State child support enforcement agency of such claim; and

(ii) include in the notice provided under clause (i) the name, address, and telephone number of such holder; and

(C) at such time as the debtor is granted a discharge under section 1328, provide written notice to such holder and to such State child support enforcement agency of—

(i) the granting of the discharge;

(ii) the last recent known address of the debtor;

(iii) the last recent known name and address of the debtor's employer; and

(iv) the name of each creditor that holds a claim that—

(I) is not discharged under paragraph (2) or (4) of section 523(a); or

(II) was reaffirmed by the debtor under section 524(c).

(2)(A) The holder of a claim described in subsection (b)(6) or the State child support enforcement agency of the State in which such holder resides may request from a creditor described in paragraph (1)(C)(iv) the last known address of the debtor.

(B) Notwithstanding any other provision of law, a creditor that makes a disclosure of a last known address of a debtor in connection with a request made under subparagraph (A) shall not be liable by reason of making that disclosure.

(Pub.L. 95–598, Nov. 6, 1978, 92 Stat. 2645; Pub.L. 98–353, Title III, §§ 314, 525, July 10, 1984, 98 Stat. 356, 388; Pub.L. 99–554, Title II, §§ 228, 283(w), Oct. 27, 1986, 100 Stat. 3103, 3118; Pub.L. 103–394, Title V, § 501(d)(37), Oct. 22, 1994, 108 Stat. 4147; Pub.L. 109–8, Title II, § 219(d), Apr. 20, 2005, 119 Stat. 58.)

HISTORICAL AND STATUTORY NOTES

Revision Notes and Legislative Reports

1978 Acts. The principal administrator in a chapter 13 case is the chapter 13 trustee. Experience under chapter XIII of the Bankruptcy Act [former chapter 13 (section 1001 et seq.) of former Title 11] has shown that the more efficient and effective wage earner programs have been conducted by standing chapter XIII trustees who exercise a broad range of responsibilities in both the design and the effectuation of debtor plans.

Subsection (a) provides administrative flexibility by permitting the bankruptcy judge to appoint an individual from the panel of trustees established pursuant to 28 U.S.C. § 604(f) and qualified under section 322 of title 11, either to serve as a standing trustee in all chapter 13 cases filed in the district or a portion thereof, or to serve in a single case.

Subsection (b)(1) makes it clear that the chapter 13 trustee is no mere disbursing agent of the monies paid to him by the debtor under the plan [section 1322(a)(1)], by imposing upon him certain relevant duties of a liquidation trustee prescribed by section 704 of this title.

Subsection (b)(2) requires the chapter 13 trustee to appear before and be heard by the bankruptcy court whenever the value of property secured by a lien or the confirmation or modification of a plan after confirmation as provided by sections 1323–1325 is considered by the court.

Subsection (b)(3) requires the chapter 13 trustee to advise and counsel the debtor while under chapter 13, except on matters more appropriately left to the attorney for the debtor. The chapter 13 trustee must also assist the debtor in performance under the plan by attempting to tailor the requirements of the plan to the changing needs and circumstances of the debtor during the extension period.

Subsection (c) imposes on the trustee in a chapter 13 case filed by a debtor engaged in business the investigative and reporting duties normally required of a chapter 11 debtor or trustee as prescribed by section 1106(a)(3) and (4). Notes of Committee on the Judiciary, Senate Report No. 95–989.

Subsection (d) gives the trustee an additional duty if the debtor is engaged in business, as defined in section 1304. The trustee must perform the duties specified in sections 1106(a)(3) and 1106(a)(4), relating to investigation of the debtor. House Report No. 95–595.

1984 Acts. Statements by Legislative Leaders, see 1984 U.S.Code Cong. and Adm.News, p. 576.

1986 Acts. House Report No. 99–764 and House Conference Report No. 99–958, see 1986 U.S.Code Cong. and Adm.News, p. 5227.

1994 Acts. House Report No. 103–835, see 1994 U.S. Code Cong. and Adm. News, p. 3340.

2005 Acts. House Report No. 109–31(Part I), see 2005 U.S. Code Cong. and Adm. News, p. 88.

Legislative Statements

Section 1302 of the House amendment adopts a provision contained in the Senate amendment instead of the position taken in the House bill. Sections 1302(d) and (e) are modeled on the standing trustee system contained in the House bill with the court assuming supervisory functions in districts not under the pilot program.

References in Text

Chapter XIII of the Bankruptcy Act, referred to in subsec. (b)(3), is chapter XIII of Act July 1, 1898, c. 541, as added June 22, 1938, c. 575, § 1, 52 Stat. 930, which was classified to chapter 13 (section 1001 et seq.) of former Title 11.

Section 464 of the Social Security Act, referred to in subsec. (d)(1)(A)(i), is Act Aug. 14, 1935, c. 531, Title IV, § 464, as added Aug. 13, 1981, Pub.L. 97–35, Title XXIII, § 2331(a), 95 Stat. 860, and amended, which is classified to 42 U.S.C.A. § 664.

Section 466 of the Social Security Act, referred to in subsec. (d)(1)(A)(i), is Act Aug. 14, 1935, c. 531, Title IV, § 466, as added Aug. 16, 1984, Pub.L. 98–378, § 3(b), 98 Stat. 1306, and amended, which is classified to 42 U.S.C.A. § 666.

Effective and Applicability Provisions

2005 Acts. Amendments by Pub.L. 109–8 effective, except as otherwise provided, 180 days after April 20, 2005, and inapplicable with respect to cases commenced under Title 11 before the effective date, see Pub.L. 109–8, § 1501, set out as a note under 11 U.S.C.A. § 101.

1994 Acts. Amendment by Pub.L. 103–394 effective on Oct. 22, 1994, and not to apply with respect to cases commenced under Title 11 of the United States Code before Oct. 22, 1994, see section 702 of Pub.L. 103–394, set out as a note under section 101 of this title.

1986 Acts. Amendment by section 283 of Pub.L. 99–554 effective 30 days after Oct. 27, 1986, except as otherwise provided for, see section 302(a) of Pub.L. 99–554, set out as a note under section 581 of Title 28, Judiciary and Judicial Procedure.

Amendment by Pub.L. 99–554, § 228, not to become effective in or with respect to certain specified judicial districts until, or apply to cases while pending in such district before, the expiration of the 270–day period beginning 30 days after Oct. 27, 1986, or of the 30–day period beginning on the date the Attorney General certifies under section 303 of Pub.L. 99–554 the region specified in a paragraph of section 581(a) of Title 28, as amended by section 111(a) of Pub.L. 99–554, that includes such district, whichever occurs first, see section 302(d)(1) of Pub.L. 99–554, set out as a note under section 581 of Title 28.

Amendment by Pub.L. 99–554, § 228, not to become effective in or with respect to certain specified judicial districts until, or apply to cases while pending in such district before, the expiration of the 2–year period beginning 30 days after Oct. 27, 1986, or of the 30–day period beginning on the date the Attorney General certifies under section 303 of Pub.L. 99–554 the region specified in a paragraph of section 581(a) of Title 28, as amended by section 111(a) of Pub.L. 99–554, that includes such district, whichever occurs first, see section 302(d)(2) of Pub.L. 99–554, set out as a note under section 581 of Title 28.

Amendment by Pub.L. 99–554, § 228, not to become effective in or with respect to judicial districts established for the States of Alabama and North Carolina until, or apply to cases while pending in such district before, such district elects to be included in a bankruptcy region established in section 581(a) of Title 28, as amended by section 111(a) of Pub.L. 99–554, or Oct. 1, 2002, whichever occurs first, and, except as otherwise provided for, with respect to cases under chapters 7, 11, 12, and 13 of Title 11 commenced before 30 days after Oct. 27, 1986, and pending in a judicial district in the States of Alabama or North Carolina before any election made under section 302(d)(3)(A) of Pub.L. 99–554 by such district becomes effective or Oct. 1, 2002, whichever occurs first, amendments by Pub.L. 99–554 not to apply until Oct. 1, 2003, or the expiration of the 1–year period beginning on the date such election becomes effective, whichever occurs first, and further, in any judicial district in Alabama or North Carolina not making the election described in section 302(d)(3)(A) of Pub.L. 99–554, any person appointed under regulations issued by the Judicial Conference to administer estates in cases under Title 11 authorized to establish, etc., a panel of private trustees, and to supervise cases and trustees in cases under chapters 7, 11, 12, and 13 of Title 11, until amendments by sections 201 to 231 of Pub.L. 99–554 effective in such district, see section 302(d)(3)(A) to (F), (H), (I) of Pub.L. 99–554, set out as a note under section 581 of Title 28.

Amendment by Pub.L. 99–554, § 228, except as otherwise provided, with respect to cases under chapters 7, 11, 12, and 13 of Title 11 commenced before 30 days after Oct. 27, 1986, and pending in a judicial district referred to in section 581(a) of Title 28, as amended by section 111(a) of Pub.L. 99–554, for which a United States trustee is not authorized before 30 days after Oct. 27, 1986 to be appointed, not applicable until the expiration of the 3–year period beginning on Oct. 27, 1986, or of the 1–year period beginning on the date the Attorney General certifies under section 303 of Pub.L. 99–554 the region specified in a paragraph of such section 581(a) that includes, such district, whichever occurs first, see section 302(e)(1), (2) of Pub.L. 99–554, set out as a note under section 581 of Title 28.

1984 Acts. Amendment by Pub.L. 98–353 effective with respect to cases filed 90 days after July 10, 1984, see section 552(a), formerly 553(a), of Pub.L. 98–353, set out as a note under section 101 of this title.

Separability of Provisions

If any provision of or amendment made by Pub.L. 103–394 or the application of such provision or amendment to any person or circumstance is held to be unconstitutional, the remaining provisions of and amendments made by Pub.L. 103–394 and the application of such provisions and amendments to any person or circumstance shall not be affected thereby, see section 701 of Pub.L. 103–394, set out as a note under section 101 of this title.

CROSS REFERENCES

Appointment of trustee in—

Chapter eleven cases, see 11 USCA § 1104.

Chapter twelve cases, see 11 USCA § 1202.

Railroad reorganization cases, see 11 USCA § 1163.

Compensation of officers, see 11 USCA § 330.

Election of trustee, see 11 USCA § 702.

Eligibility to serve as trustee, see 11 USCA § 321.

Grain storage facility bankruptcies, expedited appointment of trustee or examiner, see 11 USCA § 557.

Limitation on compensation of trustee, see 11 USCA § 326.

Qualification of trustee, see 11 USCA § 322.

Removal of trustee, see 11 USCA § 324.

Role and capacity of trustee, see 11 USCA § 323.

Time of bringing action, see 11 USCA § 546.

§ 1303. Rights and powers of debtor

Subject to any limitations on a trustee under this chapter, the debtor shall have, exclusive of the trustee, the rights and powers of a trustee under sections 363(b), 363(d), 363(e), 363(f), and 363(*l*), of this title.

(Pub.L. 95–598, Nov. 6, 1978, 92 Stat. 2646.)

HISTORICAL AND STATUTORY NOTES

Revision Notes and Legislative Reports

1978 Acts. A chapter 13 debtor is vested with the identical rights and powers, and is subject to the same limitations in regard to their exercise, as those given a liquidation trustee by virtue of section 363(b), (d), (e), (f), and (h) of title 11, relating to the sale, use or lease of property. Notes of Committee on the Judiciary, Senate Report No. 95–989.

Legislative Statements

Section 1303 of the House amendment specifies rights and powers that the debtor has exclusive of the trustees. The section does not imply that the debtor does not also possess other powers concurrently with the trustee. For example, although section 1323 is not specified in section 1303, certainly it is intended that the debtor has the power to sue and be sued.

CROSS REFERENCES

Rights and powers of debtor in—

Chapter eleven cases, see 11 USCA § 1107.

Chapter twelve cases, see 11 USCA § 1203.

§ 1304. Debtor engaged in business

(a) A debtor that is self-employed and incurs trade credit in the production of income from such employment is engaged in business.

(b) Unless the court orders otherwise, a debtor engaged in business may operate the business of the debtor and, subject to any limitations on a trustee under sections 363(c) and 364 of this title and to such limitations or conditions as the court prescribes, shall have, exclusive of the trustee, the rights and powers of the trustee under such sections.

(c) A debtor engaged in business shall perform the duties of the trustee specified in section 704(8) of this title.

(Pub.L. 95–598, Nov. 6, 1978, 92 Stat. 2646; Pub.L. 98–353, Title III, §§ 311(b)(2), 526, July 10, 1984, 98 Stat. 355, 389.)

HISTORICAL AND STATUTORY NOTES

Revision Notes and Legislative Reports

1978 Acts. Increased access to the simpler, speedier, and less expensive debtor relief provisions of chapter 13 is accomplished by permitting debtors engaged in business to proceed under chapter 13, provided their income is sufficiently stable and regular to permit compliance with a chapter 13 plan [section 101(24)] and that the debtor (or the debtor and spouse) do not owe liquidated, noncontingent unsecured debts of $50,000, or liquidated, noncontingent secured debts of $200,000 (§ 109(d)).

Section 1304(a) states that a self-employed individual who incurs trade credit in the production of income is a debtor engaged in business.

Subsection (b) empowers a chapter 13 debtor engaged in business to operate his business, subject to the rights, powers and limitations that pertain to a trustee under sections 363(c) and 364 of title 11, and subject to such further limitations and conditions as the court may prescribe.

Subsection (c) requires a chapter 13 debtor engaged in business to file with the court certain financial statements relating to the operation of the business. Notes of Committee on the Judiciary, Senate Report No. 95–989.

Legislative Statements

Section 1304(b) of the House amendment adopts the approach taken in the comparable section of the Senate amendment as preferable to the position taken in the House bill.

1984 Acts. Statements by Legislative Leaders, see 1984 U.S.Code Cong. and Adm.News, p. 576.

Effective and Applicability Provisions

1984 Acts. Amendment by Pub.L. 98–353 effective with respect to cases filed 90 days after July 10, 1984, see section 552(a), formerly 553(a), of Pub.L. 98–353, set out as a note under section 101 of this title.

CROSS REFERENCES

Authorization of trustee to operate business in—

Chapter eleven cases, see 11 USCA § 1108.

Chapter seven cases, see 11 USCA § 721.

Obtaining credit, see 11 USCA § 364.

Rights, powers and duties of debtor in possession in Chapter 11 cases, see 11 USCA § 1107.

Use, sale or lease of property, see 11 USCA § 363.

§ 1305. Filing and allowance of postpetition claims

(a) A proof of claim may be filed by any entity that holds a claim against the debtor—

(1) for taxes that become payable to a governmental unit while the case is pending; or

(2) that is a consumer debt, that arises after the date of the order for relief under this chapter, and that is for property or services necessary for the debtor's performance under the plan.

(b) Except as provided in subsection (c) of this section, a claim filed under subsection (a) of this section shall be allowed or disallowed under section 502 of this title, but shall be determined as of the date such claim arises, and shall be allowed under section 502(a), 502(b), or 502(c) of this title, or disallowed under section 502(d) or 502(e) of this title, the same as if such claim had arisen before the date of the filing of the petition.

(c) A claim filed under subsection (a)(2) of this section shall be disallowed if the holder of such claim knew or should have known that prior approval by the trustee of the debtor's incurring the obligation was practicable and was not obtained.

(Pub.L. 95–598, Nov. 6, 1978, 92 Stat. 2647.)

HISTORICAL AND STATUTORY NOTES

Revision Notes and Legislative Reports

1978 Acts. Section 1305, exclusively applicable in chapter 13 cases, supplements the provisions of sections 501–511 of title 11, dealing with the filing and allowance of claims. Sections 501–511 apply in chapter 13 cases by virtue of section 103(a) of this title. Section 1305(a) provides for the filing of a proof of claim for taxes and other obligations incurred after the filing of the chapter 13 case. Subsection (b) prescribes that section 502 of title 11 governs the allowance of section 1305(a) claims, except that its standards shall be applied as of the date of allowance of the claim, rather than the date of filing of the petition. Subsection (c) requires the disallowance of a postpetition claim for property or services necessary for the debtor's performance under the plan, if the holder of the claim knew or should have known that prior approval by the trustee of the debtor's incurring of the obligation was practicable and was not obtained. Senate Report No. 95–989.

Subsection (a) permits the filing of a proof of a claim against the debtor that is for taxes that become payable to a governmental unit while the case is pending, or that arises after the date of the filing of the petition for property or services that are necessary for the debtor's performance under the plan, such as auto repairs in order that the debtor will be able to get to work, or medical bills. The effect of the latter provision, in paragraph (2), is to treat postpetition credit extended to a chapter 13 debtor the same as a prepetition claim for purposes of allowance, distribution, and so on. House Report No. 95–595.

Legislative Statements

Section 1305(a)(2) of the House amendment modifies similar provisions contained in the House and Senate bills by restricting application of the paragraph to a consumer debt. Debts of the debtor that are not consumer debts should not be subjected to section 1305(c) or section 1328(d) of the House amendment.

Section 1305(b) of the House amendment represents a technical modification of similar provisions contained in the House bill and Senate amendment.

The House amendment deletes section 1305(d) of the Senate amendment as unnecessary. Section 502(b)(1) is sufficient to disallow any claim to the extent the claim represents the usurious interest or any other charge forbidden by applicable law. It is anticipated that the Rules of Bankruptcy Procedure may require a creditor filing a proof of claim in a case under chapter 13 to include an affirmative statement as contemplated by section 1305(d) of the Senate amendment.

CROSS REFERENCES

Allowance and filing of claims and interests in Chapter 11 cases, see 11 USCA § 1111.

Discharge of certain consumer debts, see 11 USCA § 1328.

Effect of conversion, see 11 USCA § 348.

Filing of proofs of claims or interests, see 11 USCA § 501.

Provisions in plans for payment of claims, see 11 USCA § 1322.

§ 1306. Property of the estate

(a) Property of the estate includes, in addition to the property specified in section 541 of this title—

(1) all property of the kind specified in such section that the debtor acquires after the commencement of the case but before the case is closed, dismissed, or converted to a case under chapter 7, 11, or 12 of this title, whichever occurs first; and

(2) earnings from services performed by the debtor after the commencement of the case but before the case is closed, dismissed, or converted to a case under chapter 7, 11, or 12 of this title, whichever occurs first.

(b) Except as provided in a confirmed plan or order confirming a plan, the debtor shall remain in possession of all property of the estate.

(Pub.L. 95–598, Nov. 6, 1978, 92 Stat. 2647; Pub.L. 99–554, Title II, § 257(u), Oct. 27, 1986, 100 Stat. 3116.)

HISTORICAL AND STATUTORY NOTES

Revision Notes and Legislative Reports

1978 Acts. Section 541 is expressly made applicable to chapter 13 cases by section 103(a). Section 1306 broadens the definition of property of the estate for chapter 13 purposes to include all property acquired and all earnings from services performed by the debtor after the commencement of the case.

Subsection (b) nullifies the effect of section 521(3), otherwise applicable, by providing that a chapter 13 debtor need not surrender possession of property of the estate, unless required by the plan or order of confirmation. Notes of Committee on the Judiciary, Senate Report No. 95–989.

1986 Acts. House Report No. 99–764 and House Conference Report No. 99–958, see 1986 U.S.Code Cong. and Adm.News, p. 5227.

Legislative Statements

Section 1306(a)(2) adopts a provision contained in the Senate amendment in preference to a similar provision contained in the House bill.

Effective and Applicability Provisions

1986 Acts. Amendment by Pub.L. 99–554 effective 30 days after Oct. 27, 1986, but not applicable to cases commenced under this title before that date, see section 302(a), (c)(1) of Pub.L. 99–554, set out as a note under section 581 of Title 28, Judiciary and Judicial Procedure.

CROSS REFERENCES

Ownership of copyright, see 17 USCA § 201.

§ 1307. Conversion or dismissal

(a) The debtor may convert a case under this chapter to a case under chapter 7 of this title at any time. Any waiver of the right to convert under this subsection is unenforceable.

(b) On request of the debtor at any time, if the case has not been converted under section 706, 1112, or 1208 of this title, the court shall dismiss a case under this chapter. Any waiver of the right to dismiss under this subsection is unenforceable.

(c) Except as provided in subsection (e) of this section, on request of a party in interest or the United States trustee and after notice and a hearing, the court may convert a case under this chapter to a case under chapter 7 of this title, or may dismiss a case under this chapter, whichever is in the best interests of creditors and the estate, for cause, including—

(1) unreasonable delay by the debtor that is prejudicial to creditors;

(2) nonpayment of any fees and charges required under chapter 123 of title 28;

(3) failure to file a plan timely under section 1321 of this title;

(4) failure to commence making timely payments under section 1326 of this title;

(5) denial of confirmation of a plan under section 1325 of this title and denial of a request made for additional time for filing another plan or a modification of a plan;

(6) material default by the debtor with respect to a term of a confirmed plan;

(7) revocation of the order of confirmation under section 1330 of this title, and denial of confirmation of a modified plan under section 1329 of this title;

(8) termination of a confirmed plan by reason of the occurrence of a condition specified in the plan other than completion of payments under the plan;

(9) only on request of the United States trustee, failure of the debtor to file, within fifteen days, or such additional time as the court may allow, after the filing of the petition commencing such case, the information required by paragraph (1) of section 521;

(10) only on request of the United States trustee, failure to timely file the information required by paragraph (2) of section 521; or

(11) failure of the debtor to pay any domestic support obligation that first becomes payable after the date of the filing of the petition.

(d) Except as provided in subsection (e) of this section, at any time before the confirmation of a plan under section 1325 of this title, on request of a party in interest or the United States trustee and after notice and a hearing, the court may convert a case under this chapter to a case under chapter 11 or 12 of this title.

(e) Upon the failure of the debtor to file a tax return under section 1308, on request of a party in interest or the United States trustee and after notice and a hearing, the court shall dismiss a case or convert a case under this chapter to a case under chapter 7 of this title, whichever is in the best interest of the creditors and the estate.

(f) The court may not convert a case under this chapter to a case under chapter 7, 11, or 12 of this title if the debtor is a farmer, unless the debtor requests such conversion.

(g) Notwithstanding any other provision of this section, a case may not be converted to a case under another chapter of this title unless the debtor may be a debtor under such chapter.

(Pub.L. 95–598, Nov. 6, 1978, 92 Stat. 2647; Pub.L. 98–353, Title III, §§ 315, 527, July 10, 1984, 98 Stat. 356, 389; Pub.L. 99–554, Title II, §§ 229, 257(v), Oct. 27, 1986, 100 Stat. 3103,

3116; Pub.L. 109–8, Title II, § 213(7), Title VII, § 716(c), Apr. 20, 2005, 119 Stat. 53, 130.)

HISTORICAL AND STATUTORY NOTES

Revision Notes and Legislative Reports

1978 Acts. Subsections (a) and (b) confirm, without qualification, the rights of a chapter 13 debtor to convert the case to a liquidating bankruptcy case under chapter 7 of title 11, at any time, or to have the chapter 13 case dismissed. Waiver of any such right is unenforceable. Subsection (c) specifies various conditions for the exercise of the power of the court to convert a chapter 13 case to one under chapter 7 or to dismiss the case. Subsection (d) deals with the conversion of a chapter 13 case to one under chapter 11. Subsection (e) prohibits conversion of the chapter 13 case filed by a farmer to chapter 7 or 11 except at the request of the debtor. No case is to be converted from chapter 13 to any other chapter, unless the debtor is an eligible debtor under the new chapter. Senate Report No. 95–989.

Subsection (f) reinforces section 109 by prohibiting conversion to a chapter under which the debtor is not eligible to proceed. House Report No. 95–595.

1984 Acts. Statements by Legislative Leaders, see 1984 U.S.Code Cong. and Adm.News, p. 576.

1986 Acts. House Report No. 99–764 and House Conference Report No. 99–958, see 1986 U.S.Code Cong. and Adm.News, p. 5227.

2005 Acts. House Report No. 109–31(Part I), see 2005 U.S. Code Cong. and Adm. News, p. 88.

Legislative Statements

Section 1307(a) is derived from the Senate amendment in preference to a comparable provision contained in the House bill.

References in Text

Chapter 7 of this title, referred to in text, is 11 U.S.C.A. § 701 et seq.

Subsection (e) of this section, referred to in subsec. (c), was redesignated as subsec. (d) of this section, and a new subsec. (e) was added, by Pub.L. 109–8, Title VII, § 716(c), Apr. 20, 2005, 119 Stat. 130.

Effective and Applicability Provisions

2005 Acts. Amendments by Pub.L. 109–8 effective, except as otherwise provided, 180 days after April 20, 2005, and inapplicable with respect to cases commenced under Title 11 before the effective date, see Pub.L. 109–8, § 1501, set out as a note under 11 U.S.C.A. § 101.

1986 Acts. Amendment by Pub.L. 99–554 effective 30 days after Oct. 27, 1986, except as otherwise provided for, see section 302(a) of Pub.L. 99–554, set out as a note under section 581 of Title 28, Judiciary and Judicial Procedure.

Amendment by Pub.L. 99–554, § 229, not to become effective in or with respect to certain specified judicial districts until, or apply to cases while pending in such district before, the expiration of the 270–day period beginning 30 days after Oct. 27, 1986, or of the 30–day period beginning on the date the Attorney General certifies under section 303 of Pub.L. 99–554 the region specified in a paragraph of section 581(a) of Title 28, as amended by section 111(a) of Pub.L. 99–554, that includes such district, whichever occurs first, see section 302(d)(1) of Pub.L. 99–554, set out as a note under section 581 of Title 28.

Amendment by Pub.L. 99–554, § 229, not to become effective in or with respect to certain specified judicial districts until, or apply to cases while pending in such district before, the expiration of the 2–year period beginning 30 days after Oct. 27, 1986, or of the 30–day period beginning on the date the Attorney General certifies under section 303 of Pub.L. 99–554 the region specified in a paragraph of section 581(a) of Title 28, as amended by section 111(a) of Pub.L. 99–554, that includes such district, whichever occurs first, see section 302(d)(2) of Pub.L. 99–554, set out as a note under section 581 of Title 28.

Amendment by Pub.L. 99–554, § 229, not to become effective in or with respect to judicial districts established for the States of Alabama and North Carolina until, or apply to cases while pending in such district before, such district elects to be included in a bankruptcy region established in section 581(a) of Title 28, as amended by section 111(a) of Pub.L. 99–554, or Oct. 1, 2002, whichever occurs first, and, except as otherwise provided for, with respect to cases under chapters 7, 11, 12, and 13 of Title 11 commenced before 30 days after Oct. 27, 1986, and pending in a judicial district in the States of Alabama or North Carolina before any election made under section 302(d)(3)(A) of Pub.L. 99–554 by such district becomes effective or Oct. 1, 2002, whichever occurs first, amendments by Pub.L. 99–554 not to apply, until Oct. 1, 2003, or the expiration of the 1–year period beginning on the date such election becomes effective, whichever occurs first, and further, in any judicial district in Alabama or North Carolina not making the election described in section 302(d)(3)(A) of Pub.L. 99–554, any person appointed under regulations issued by the Judicial Conference to administer estates in cases under Title 11 authorized to establish, etc., a panel of private trustees, and to supervise cases and trustees in cases under chapters 7, 11, 12, and 13 of Title 11, until amendments by sections 201 to 231 of Pub.L. 99–554 effective in such district, see section 302(d)(3)(A) to (F), (H), (I) of Pub.L. 99–554, set out as a note under section 581 of Title 28.

Amendments by Pub.L. 99–554, § 257(v), not to apply with respect to cases commenced under Title 11, Bankruptcy, before 30 days after Oct. 27 1986, see section 302(c)(1) of Pub.L. 99–554, set out as a note under section 581 of Title 28.

Amendment by Pub.L. 99–554, § 229 except as otherwise provided, with respect to cases under chapters 7, 11, 12, and 13 of Title 11 commenced before 30 days after Oct. 27, 1986, and pending in a judicial district referred to in section 581(a) of Title 28, as amended by section 111(a) of Pub.L. 99–554, for which a United States trustee is not authorized before 30 days after Oct. 27, 1986 to be appointed, not applicable until the expiration of the 3–year period beginning on Oct. 27, 1986, or of the 1–year period beginning on the date the Attorney General certifies under section 303 of Pub.L. 99–554 the region specified in a paragraph of such section 581(a) that includes, such district, whichever occurs first, see section 302(e)(1), (2) of Pub.L. 99–554, set out as a note under section 581 of Title 28.

1984 Acts. Amendment by Pub.L. 98–353 effective as to cases filed 90 days after July 10, 1984, see section 552(a), formerly 553(a), of Pub.L. 98–353, set out as a note under section 101 of this title.

CROSS REFERENCES

Conversion from Chapter seven, see 11 USCA § 706.

Conversion or dismissal upon revocation of order of confirmation, see 11 USCA § 1330.

Dismissal of—

Chapter nine cases, see 11 USCA § 930.

Chapter seven case, see 11 USCA § 707.

Distribution of property of estate converted to Chapter seven, see 11 USCA § 726.

Effect of—

Conversion, see 11 USCA § 348.

Dismissal, see 11 USCA § 349.

Executory contracts and unexpired leases, see 11 USCA § 365.

Liquidation of estate in railroad reorganization case, see 11 USCA § 1174.

§ 1308. Filing of prepetition tax returns

(a) Not later than the day before the date on which the meeting of the creditors is first scheduled to be held under section 341(a), if the debtor was required to file a tax return under applicable nonbankruptcy law, the debtor shall file with appropriate tax authorities all tax returns for all taxable periods ending during the 4–year period ending on the date of the filing of the petition.

(b)(1) Subject to paragraph (2), if the tax returns required by subsection (a) have not been filed by the date on which the meeting of creditors is first scheduled to be held under section 341(a), the trustee may hold open that meeting for a reasonable period of time to allow the debtor an additional period of time to file any unfiled returns, but such additional period of time shall not extend beyond—

(A) for any return that is past due as of the date of the filing of the petition, the date that is 120 days after the date of that meeting; or

(B) for any return that is not past due as of the date of the filing of the petition, the later of—

(i) the date that is 120 days after the date of that meeting; or

(ii) the date on which the return is due under the last automatic extension of time for filing that return to which the debtor is entitled, and for which request is timely made, in accordance with applicable nonbankruptcy law.

(2) After notice and a hearing, and order entered before the tolling of any applicable filing period determined under this subsection, if the debtor demonstrates by a preponderance of the evidence that the failure to file a return as required under this subsection is attributable to circumstances beyond the control of the debtor, the court may extend the filing period established by the trustee under this subsection for—

(A) a period of not more than 30 days for returns described in paragraph (1); and

(B) a period not to extend after the applicable extended due date for a return described in paragraph (2) [1].

(c) For purposes of this section, the term "return" includes a return prepared pursuant to subsection (a) or (b) of section 6020 of the Internal Revenue Code of 1986, or a similar State or local law, or a written stipulation to a judgment or a final order entered by a nonbankruptcy tribunal.

(Added Pub.L. 109–8, Title VII, § 716(b)(1), Apr. 20, 2005, 119 Stat. 129.)

[1] So in original.

HISTORICAL AND STATUTORY NOTES

Revision Notes and Legislative Reports

2005 Acts. House Report No. 109–31(Part I), see 2005 U.S. Code Cong. and Adm. News, p. 88.

References in Text

Subsection (a) or (b) of section 6020 of the Internal Revenue Code of 1986, referred to in subsec. (c), is classified to 26 U.S.C.A. § 6020(a) or (b).

Effective and Applicability Provisions

2005 Acts. Amendments by Pub.L. 109–8 effective, except as otherwise provided, 180 days after April 20, 2005, and inapplicable with respect to cases commenced under Title 11 before the effective date, see Pub.L. 109–8, § 1501, set out as a note under 11 U.S.C.A. § 101.

§§ 1309 to 1320. Reserved for future legislation

SUBCHAPTER II—THE PLAN

§ 1321. Filing of plan

The debtor shall file a plan.

(Pub.L. 95–598, Nov. 6, 1978, 92 Stat. 2648.)

HISTORICAL AND STATUTORY NOTES

Revision Notes and Legislative Reports

1978 Acts. Chapter 13 contemplates the filing of a plan only by the debtor. Senate Report No. 95–989.

CROSS REFERENCES

Conversion or dismissal for failure to timely file plan, see 11 USCA § 1307.

Filing of plan in—

Chapter nine cases, see 11 USCA § 941.

Chapter twelve cases, see 11 USCA § 1221.

Who may file plan in Chapter eleven cases, see 11 USCA § 1121.

§ 1322. Contents of plan

(a) The plan shall—

(1) provide for the submission of all or such portion of future earnings or other future income of the debtor to the supervision and control of the trustee as is necessary for the execution of the plan;

(2) provide for the full payment, in deferred cash payments, of all claims entitled to priority under section 507 of this title, unless the holder of a particular claim agrees to a different treatment of such claim;

(3) if the plan classifies claims, provide the same treatment for each claim within a particular class; and.

(4) notwithstanding any other provision of this section, a plan may provide for less than full payment of all amounts owed for a claim entitled to priority under section 507(a)(1)(B) only if the plan provides that all of the debtor's projected disposable income for a 5–year period beginning on the date that the first payment is due under the plan will be applied to make payments under the plan.

(b) Subject to subsections (a) and (c) of this section, the plan may—

(1) designate a class or classes of unsecured claims, as provided in section 1122 of this title, but may not discriminate unfairly against any class so designated; however, such plan may treat claims for a consumer debt of the debtor if an individual is liable on such consumer debt with the debtor differently than other unsecured claims;

(2) modify the rights of holders of secured claims, other than a claim secured only by a security interest in real property that is the debtor's principal residence, or of holders of unsecured claims, or leave unaffected the rights of holders of any class of claims;

(3) provide for the curing or waiving of any default;

(4) provide for payments on any unsecured claim to be made concurrently with payments on any secured claim or any other unsecured claim;

(5) notwithstanding paragraph (2) of this subsection, provide for the curing of any default within a reasonable time and maintenance of payments while the case is pending on any unsecured claim or secured claim on which the last payment is due after the date on which the final payment under the plan is due;

(6) provide for the payment of all or any part of any claim allowed under section 1305 of this title;

(7) subject to section 365 of this title, provide for the assumption, rejection, or assignment of any executory contract or unexpired lease of the debtor not previously rejected under such section;

(8) provide for the payment of all or part of a claim against the debtor from property of the estate or property of the debtor;

(9) provide for the vesting of property of the estate, on confirmation of the plan or at a later time, in the debtor or in any other entity;

(10) provide for the payment of interest accruing after the date of the filing of the petition on unsecured claims that are nondischargeable under section 1328(a), except that such interest may be paid only to the extent that the debtor has disposable income available to pay such interest after making provision for full payment of all allowed claims; and

(11) include any other appropriate provision not inconsistent with this title.

(c) Notwithstanding subsection (b)(2) and applicable nonbankruptcy law—

(1) a default with respect to, or that gave rise to, a lien on the debtor's principal residence may be cured under paragraph (3) or (5) of subsection (b) until such residence is sold at a foreclosure sale that is conducted in accordance with applicable nonbankruptcy law; and

(2) in a case in which the last payment on the original payment schedule for a claim secured only by a security interest in real property that is the debtor's principal residence is due before the date on which the final payment under the plan is due, the plan may provide for the payment of the claim as modified pursuant to section 1325(a)(5) of this title.

(d)(1) If the current monthly income of the debtor and the debtor's spouse combined, when multiplied by 12, is not less than—

(A) in the case of a debtor in a household of 1 person, the median family income of the applicable State for 1 earner;

(B) in the case of a debtor in a household of 2, 3, or 4 individuals, the highest median family income of the applicable State for a family of the same number or fewer individuals; or

(C) in the case of a debtor in a household exceeding 4 individuals, the highest median family income of the applicable State for a family of 4 or fewer individuals, plus $575 [1] per month for each individual in excess of 4,

the plan may not provide for payments over a period that is longer than 5 years.

(2) If the current monthly income of the debtor and the debtor's spouse combined, when multiplied by 12, is less than—

(A) in the case of a debtor in a household of 1 person, the median family income of the applicable State for 1 earner;

(B) in the case of a debtor in a household of 2, 3, or 4 individuals, the highest median family income of the applicable State for a family of the same number or fewer individuals; or

(C) in the case of a debtor in a household exceeding 4 individuals, the highest median family income of the applicable State for a family of 4 or fewer individuals, plus $575 [1] per month for each individual in excess of 4,

the plan may not provide for payments over a period that is longer than 3 years, unless the court, for cause, approves a longer period, but the court may not approve a period that is longer than 5 years.

(e) Notwithstanding subsection (b)(2) of this section and sections 506(b) and 1325(a)(5) of this title, if it is proposed in a plan to cure a default, the amount necessary to cure the default, shall be determined in accordance with the underlying agreement and applicable nonbankruptcy law.

(f) A plan may not materially alter the terms of a loan described in section 362(b)(19) and any amounts required to repay such loan shall not constitute "disposable income" under section 1325.

(Pub.L. 95–598, Nov. 6, 1978, 92 Stat. 2648; Pub.L. 98–353, Title III, §§ 316, 528, July 10, 1984, 98 Stat. 356, 389; Pub.L. 103–394, Title III, §§ 301, 305(c), Oct. 22, 1994, 108 Stat. 4131, 4134; Pub.L. 109–8, Title II, §§ 213(8), (9), 224(d), Title III, § 318(1), Apr. 20, 2005, 119 Stat. 53, 65, 93.)

[1] Dollar amount as adjusted by the Judicial Conference of the United States. See Adjustment of Dollar Amounts notes set out under this section and 11 U.S.C.A. § 104.

HISTORICAL AND STATUTORY NOTES

Revision Notes and Legislative Reports

1978 Acts. Chapter 13 is designed to serve as a flexible vehicle for the repayment of part or all of the allowed claims of the debtor. Section 1322 emphasizes that purpose by fixing a minimum of mandatory plan provisions.

Subsection (a) requires that the plan submit whatever portion of the future income of the debtor is necessary to implement the plan to the control of the trustee, mandates payment in full of all section 507 priority claims, and requires identical treatment for all claims of a particular class.

Subsection (b) permits a chapter 13 plan to (1) divide unsecured claims not entitled to priority under section 507 into classes in the manner authorized for chapter 11 claims; (2) modify the rights of holders of secured and unsecured claims, except claims wholly secured by real estate mortgages; (3) cure or waive any default; (4) propose payments on unsecured claims concurrently with payments on any secured claim or any other class of unsecured claims; (5) provide for curing any default on any secured or unsecured claim on which the final payment is due after the proposed final payment under the plan; (6) provide for payment of any allowed postpetition claim; (7) assume or reject any previously unrejected executory contract or unexpired lease of the debtor; (8) propose the payment of all or any part of any claim from property of the estate or of the debtor; (9) provide for the vesting of property of the estate; and (10) include any other provision not inconsistent with other provisions of title 11.

Subsection (c) limits the payment period under the plan to 3 years, except that a 4-year payment period may be permitted by the court. Senate Report No. 95–989.

1984 Acts. Statements by Legislative Leaders, see 1984 U.S.Code Cong. and Adm.News, p. 576.

1994 Acts. House Report No. 103–835, see 1994 U.S. Code Cong. and Adm. News, p. 3340.

2005 Acts. House Report No. 109–31(Part I), see 2005 U.S. Code Cong. and Adm. News, p. 88.

Legislative Statements

Section 1322(b)(2) of the House amendment represents a compromise agreement between similar provisions in the House bill and Senate amendment. Under the House amendment, the plan may modify the rights of holders of secured claims other than a claim secured by a security interest in real property that is the debtor's principal residence. It is intended that a claim secured by the debtor's principal residence may be treated with under section 1322(b)(5) of the House amendment.

Section 1322(c) adopts a 5-year period derived from the House bill in preference to a 4-year period contained in the Senate amendment. A conforming change is made in section 1329(c) adopting the provision in the House bill in preference to a comparable provision in the Senate amendment.

Tax payments in wage earner plans: The House bill provided that a wage earner plan had to provide that all priority claims would be paid in full. The Senate amendment contained a special rule in section 1325(c) requiring that Federal tax claims must be paid in cash, but that such tax claims can be paid in deferred cash installments under the general rules applicable to the payment of debts in a wage earner plan, unless the Internal Revenue Service negotiates with the debtor for some different medium or time for payment of the tax liability.

The House bill adopts the substance of the Senate amendment rule under section 1322(a)(2) of the House amendment. A wage earner plan must provide for full payment in deferred cash payments, of all priority claims, unless the holder of a particular claim agrees with a different treatment of such claim.

Effective and Applicability Provisions

2007 Acts. Increase of dollar amounts by Judicial Conference of the United States by notice published Feb. 14, 2007, 72 F.R. 7082 effective April 1, 2007, and increase not applicable to cases commenced before the effective date of the adjustments, i.e., April 1, 2007. See Adjustment of Dollar Amounts notes under 11 U.S.C.A. § 104 and this section.

2005 Acts. Amendments by Pub.L. 109–8 effective, except as otherwise provided, 180 days after April 20, 2005, and inapplicable with respect to cases commenced under Title 11 before the effective date, see Pub.L. 109–8, § 1501, set out as a note under 11 U.S.C.A. § 101.

1994 Acts. Amendment by section 301 of Pub.L. 103–394 [enacting subsec. (c) of this section and redesignating former subsec. (c) as (d)] effective on Oct. 22, 1994, and not to apply with respect to cases commenced under Title 11 of the United States Code before Oct. 22, 1994, see section 702 of

Pub.L. 103–394, set out as a note under section 101 of this title.

Amendment by section 305(c) of Pub.L. 103–394 [enacting subsec. (e) of this section] effective Oct. 22, 1994, and applicable only to agreements entered into after Oct. 22, 1994, see section 702 of Pub.L. 103–394, set out as a note under section 101 of this title.

1984 Acts. Amendment by Pub. L. 98–353 effective as to cases filed 90 days after July 10, 1984, see section 552(a), formerly 553(a), of Pub. L. 98–353, set out as a note under section 101 of this title.

Separability of Provisions

If any provision of or amendment made by Pub.L. 103–394 or the application of such provision or amendment to any person or circumstance is held to be unconstitutional, the remaining provisions of and amendments made by Pub.L. 103–394 and the application of such provisions and amendments to any person or circumstance shall not be affected thereby, see section 701 of Pub.L. 103–394, set out as a note under section 101 of this title.

Adjustment of Dollar Amounts

For adjustment of dollar amounts specified in subsec. (d) of this section by the Judicial Conference of the United States, effective Apr. 1, 2007, see note set out under 11 U.S.C.A. § 104.

By notice published Feb. 14, 2007, 72 F.R. 7082, the Judicial Conference of the United States adjusted the dollar amounts in provisions specified in subsec. (d) of this section, effective Apr. 1, 2007, as follows:

Adjusted $525 (each time it appears) to $575 (each time it appears).

CROSS REFERENCES

Contents of plan filed in—

Chapter eleven cases, see 11 USCA § 1123.

Chapter twelve cases, see 11 USCA § 1222.

Railroad reorganization cases, see 11 USCA § 1172.

§ 1323. Modification of plan before confirmation

(a) The debtor may modify the plan at any time before confirmation, but may not modify the plan so that the plan as modified fails to meet the requirements of section 1322 of this title.

(b) After the debtor files a modification under this section, the plan as modified becomes the plan.

(c) Any holder of a secured claim that has accepted or rejected the plan is deemed to have accepted or rejected, as the case may be, the plan as modified, unless the modification provides for a change in the rights of such holder from what such rights were under the plan before modification, and such holder changes such holder's previous acceptance or rejection.

(Pub.L. 95–598, Nov. 6, 1978, 92 Stat. 2649.)

HISTORICAL AND STATUTORY NOTES

Revision Notes and Legislative Reports

1978 Acts. The debtor is permitted to modify the plan before confirmation without court approval so long as the modified plan, which becomes the plan on filing, complies with the requirements of section 1322.

The original acceptance or rejection of a plan by the holder of a secured claim remains binding unless the modified plan changes the rights of the holder and the holder withdraws or alters its earlier acceptance or rejection. Senate Report No. 95–989.

CROSS REFERENCES

Modification of plan filed in—

Chapter eleven cases, see 11 USCA § 1127.

Chapter nine cases, see 11 USCA § 942.

Chapter twelve cases, see 11 USCA § 1223.

§ 1324. Confirmation hearing

(a) Except as provided in subsection (b) and after notice, the court shall hold a hearing on confirmation of the plan. A party in interest may object to confirmation of the plan.

(b) The hearing on confirmation of the plan may be held not earlier than 20 days and not later than 45 days after the date of the meeting of creditors under section 341(a), unless the court determines that it would be in the best interests of the creditors and the estate to hold such hearing at an earlier date and there is no objection to such earlier date.

(Pub.L. 95–598, Nov. 6, 1978, 92 Stat. 2649; Pub.L. 98–353, Title III, § 529, July 10, 1984, 98 Stat. 389; Pub.L. 99–554, Title II, § 283(x), Oct. 27, 1986, 100 Stat. 3118; Pub.L. 109–8, Title III, § 317, Apr. 20, 2005, 119 Stat. 92.)

HISTORICAL AND STATUTORY NOTES

Revision Notes and Legislative Reports

1978 Acts. Any party in interest may object to the confirmation of a plan, as distinguished from merely rejecting a plan. An objection to confirmation is predicated on failure of the plan or the procedures employed prior to confirmation to conform with the requirements of chapter 13. The bankruptcy judge is required to provide notice and an opportunity for hearing any such objection to confirmation. Senate Report No. 95–989.

1984 Acts. Statements by Legislative Leaders, see 1984 U.S.Code Cong. and Adm.News, p. 576.

1986 Acts. House Report No. 99–764 and House Conference Report No. 99–958, see 1986 U.S.Code Cong. and Adm.News, p. 5227.

2005 Acts. House Report No. 109–31(Part I), see 2005 U.S. Code Cong. and Adm. News, p. 88.

Effective and Applicability Provisions

2005 Acts. Amendments by Pub.L. 109–8 effective, except as otherwise provided, 180 days after April 20, 2005, and inapplicable with respect to cases commenced under Title 11 before the effective date, see Pub.L. 109–8, § 1501, set out as a note under 11 U.S.C.A. § 101.

1986 Acts. Amendment by Pub.L. 99–554 effective 30 days after Oct. 27, 1986, see section 302(a) of Pub.L. 99–554, set out as a note under section 581 of Title 28, Judiciary and Judicial Procedure.

1984 Acts. Amendment by Pub.L. 98–353 effective with respect to cases filed 90 days after July 10, 1984, see section 552(a), formerly 553(a), of Pub.L. 98–353, set out as a note under section 101 of this title.

CROSS REFERENCES

Confirmation hearing in—

Chapter eleven cases, see 11 USCA § 1128.

Chapter twelve cases, see 11 USCA § 1224.

Duties of United States trustee, see 28 USCA § 586.

§ 1325. Confirmation of plan

(a) Except as provided in subsection (b), the court shall confirm a plan if—

(1) the plan complies with the provisions of this chapter and with the other applicable provisions of this title;

(2) any fee, charge, or amount required under chapter 123 of title 28, or by the plan, to be paid before confirmation, has been paid;

(3) the plan has been proposed in good faith and not by any means forbidden by law;

(4) the value, as of the effective date of the plan, of property to be distributed under the plan on account of each allowed unsecured claim is not less than the amount that would be paid on such claim if the estate of the debtor were liquidated under chapter 7 of this title on such date;

(5) with respect to each allowed secured claim provided for by the plan—

(A) the holder of such claim has accepted the plan;

(B)(i) the plan provides that—

(I) the holder of such claim retain the lien securing such claim until the earlier of—

(aa) the payment of the underlying debt determined under nonbankruptcy law; or

(bb) discharge under section 1328; and

(II) if the case under this chapter is dismissed or converted without completion of the plan, such lien shall also be retained by such holder to the extent recognized by applicable nonbankruptcy law;

(ii) the value, as of the effective date of the plan, of property to be distributed under the plan on account of such claim is not less than the allowed amount of such claim; and

(iii) if—

(I) property to be distributed pursuant to this subsection is in the form of periodic payments, such payments shall be in equal monthly amounts; and

(II) the holder of the claim is secured by personal property, the amount of such payments shall not be less than an amount sufficient to provide to the holder of such claim adequate protection during the period of the plan; or

(C) the debtor surrenders the property securing such claim to such holder;

(6) the debtor will be able to make all payments under the plan and to comply with the plan;

(7) the action of the debtor in filing the petition was in good faith;

(8) the debtor has paid all amounts that are required to be paid under a domestic support obligation and that first become payable after the date of the filing of the petition if the debtor is required by a judicial or administrative order, or by statute, to pay such domestic support obligation; and

(9) the debtor has filed all applicable Federal, State, and local tax returns as required by section 1308.

For purposes of paragraph (5), section 506 shall not apply to a claim described in that paragraph if the creditor has a purchase money security interest securing the debt that is the subject of the claim, the debt was incurred within the 910–day preceding the date of the filing of the petition, and the collateral for that debt consists of a motor vehicle (as defined in section 30102 of title 49) acquired for the personal use of the debtor, or if collateral for that debt consists of any other thing of value, if the debt was incurred during the 1–year period preceding that filing.

(b)(1) If the trustee or the holder of an allowed unsecured claim objects to the confirmation of the plan, then the court may not approve the plan unless, as of the effective date of the plan—

(A) the value of the property to be distributed under the plan on account of such claim is not less than the amount of such claim; or

(B) the plan provides that all of the debtor's projected disposable income to be received in the applicable commitment period beginning on the date that the first payment is due under the plan will be applied to make payments to unsecured creditors under the plan.

(2) For purposes of this subsection, the term "disposable income" means current monthly income received by the debtor (other than child support payments, foster care payments, or disability payments for a dependent child made in accordance with applicable nonbankruptcy law to the extent reasonably necessary to be expended for such child) less amounts reasonably necessary to be expended—

(A)(i) for the maintenance or support of the debtor or a dependent of the debtor, or for a domestic support obligation, that first becomes payable after the date the petition is filed; and

(ii) for charitable contributions (that meet the definition of "charitable contribution" under section 548(d)(3) [1] to a qualified religious or charitable entity or organization (as defined in section 548(d)(4)) in an amount not to exceed 15 percent of gross income of the debtor for the year in which the contributions are made; and

(B) if the debtor is engaged in business, for the payment of expenditures necessary for the continuation, preservation, and operation of such business.

(3) Amounts reasonably necessary to be expended under paragraph (2), other than subparagraph (A)(ii) of paragraph (2), shall be determined in accordance with subparagraphs (A) and (B) of section 707(b)(2), if the debtor has current monthly income, when multiplied by 12, greater than—

(A) in the case of a debtor in a household of 1 person, the median family income of the applicable State for 1 earner;

(B) in the case of a debtor in a household of 2, 3, or 4 individuals, the highest median family income of the applicable State for a family of the same number or fewer individuals; or

(C) in the case of a debtor in a household exceeding 4 individuals, the highest median family income of the applicable State for a family of 4 or fewer individuals, plus $575 [2] per month for each individual in excess of 4.

(4) For purposes of this subsection, the "applicable commitment period"—

(A) subject to subparagraph (B), shall be—

(i) 3 years; or

(ii) not less than 5 years, if the current monthly income of the debtor and the debtor's spouse combined, when multiplied by 12, is not less than—

(I) in the case of a debtor in a household of 1 person, the median family income of the applicable State for 1 earner;

(II) in the case of a debtor in a household of 2, 3, or 4 individuals, the highest median family income of the applicable State for a family of the same number or fewer individuals; or

(III) in the case of a debtor in a household exceeding 4 individuals, the highest median family income of the applicable State for a family of 4 or fewer individuals, plus $575 [2] per month for each individual in excess of 4; and

(B) may be less than 3 or 5 years, whichever is applicable under subparagraph (A), but only if the plan provides for payment in full of all allowed unsecured claims over a shorter period.

(c) After confirmation of a plan, the court may order any entity from whom the debtor receives income to pay all or any part of such income to the trustee.

(Pub.L. 95–598, Nov. 6, 1978, 92 Stat. 2649; Pub.L. 98–353, Title III, §§ 317, 530, July 10, 1984, 98 Stat. 356, 389; Pub.L. 99–554, Title II, § 283(y), Oct. 27, 1986, 100 Stat. 3118; Pub.L. 105–183, § 4(a), June 19, 1998, 112 Stat. 518; Pub.L. 109–8, Title I, § 102(g), (h), Title II, § 213(10), Title III, §§ 306(a), (b), 309(c)(1), 318(2), (3), Title VII, § 716(a), Apr. 20, 2005, 119 Stat. 33, 53, 80, 83, 93 129; Pub.L. 109–439, § 2, Dec. 20, 2006, 120 Stat. 3285.)

[1] So in original. Probably should be "548(d)(3))".

[2] Dollar amount as adjusted by the Judicial Conference of the United States. See Adjustment of Dollar Amounts notes set out under this section and 11 U.S.C.A. § 104.

HISTORICAL AND STATUTORY NOTES

Revision Notes and Legislative Reports

1978 Acts. The bankruptcy court must confirm a plan if (1) the plan satisfies the provisions of chapter 13 and other applicable provisions of title 11; (2) it is proposed in good faith; (3) it is in the best interests of creditors, and defined by subsection (a)(4) of Section 1325; (4) it has been accepted by the holder of each allowed secured claim provided for the plan or where the holder of any such secured claim is to receive value under the plan not less than the amount of the allowed secured claim, or where the debtor surrenders to the holder the collateral securing any such allowed secured claim; (5) the plan is feasible; and (6) the requisite fees and charges have been paid.

Subsection (b) authorizes the court to order an entity, as defined by section 101(15), to pay any income of the debtor to the trustee. Any governmental unit is an entity subject to such an order. Senate Report No. 95–989.

1984 Acts. Statements by Legislative Leaders, see 1984 U.S.Code Cong. and Adm.News, p. 576.

1986 Acts. House Report No. 99–764 and House Conference Report No. 99–958, see 1986 U.S.Code Cong. and Adm.News, p. 5227.

1998 Acts. Statement by President, see 1998 U.S. Code Cong. and Adm. News, p. 230.

2005 Acts. House Report No. 109–31(Part I), see 2005 U.S. Code Cong. and Adm. News, p. 88.

Legislative Statements

Section 1325(a)(5)(B) of the House amendment modifies the House bill and Senate amendment to significantly protect secured creditors in chapter 13. Unless the secured creditor accepts the plan, the plan must provide that the secured creditor retain the lien securing the creditor's allowed secured claim in addition to receiving value, as of the effective date of the plan of property to be distributed under the plan on account of the claim not less than the allowed amount of the claim. To this extent, a secured creditor in a case under chapter 13 is treated identically with a recourse creditor under section 1111(b)(1) of the House amendment except that the secured creditor in a case under chapter 13 may receive any property of a value as of the effective date of the plan equal to the allowed amount of the creditor's secured claim rather than being restricted to receiving deferred cash payments. Of course, the secured creditors' lien only secures the value of the collateral and to the extent property is distributed of a present value equal to the allowed amount of the creditor's secured claim the creditor's lien will have been satisfied in full. Thus the lien created under section 1325(a)(5)(B)(i) is effective only to secure deferred payments to the extent of the amount of the allowed secured claim. To the extent the deferred payments exceed the value of the allowed amount of the secured claim and the debtor subsequently defaults, the lien will not secure unaccrued interest represented in such deferred payments.

Effective and Applicability Provisions

2007 Acts. Increase of dollar amounts by Judicial Conference of the United States by notice published Feb. 14, 2007, 72 F.R. 7082 effective April 1, 2007, and increase not applicable to cases commenced before the effective date of the adjustments, i.e., April 1, 2007. See Adjustment of Dollar Amounts notes under 11 U.S.C.A. § 104 and this section.

2005 Acts. Amendments by Pub.L. 109–8 effective, except as otherwise provided, 180 days after April 20, 2005, and inapplicable with respect to cases commenced under Title 11 before the effective date, see Pub.L. 109–8, § 1501, set out as a note under 11 U.S.C.A. § 101.

1986 Acts. Amendment by Pub.L. 99–554 effective 30 days after Oct. 27, 1986, see section 302(a) of Pub.L. 99–554, set out as a note under section 581 of Title 28, Judiciary and Judicial Procedure.

1984 Acts. Amendment by Pub.L. 98–353 effective with respect to cases filed 90 days after July 10, 1984, see section 552(a), formerly 553(a), of Pub.L. 98–353, set out as a note under section 101 of this title.

Adjustment of Dollar Amounts

For adjustment of dollar amounts specified in subsec. (b) of this section by the Judicial Conference of the United States, effective Apr. 1, 2007, see note set out under 11 U.S.C.A. § 104.

By notice published Feb. 14, 2007, 72 F.R. 7082, the Judicial Conference of the United States adjusted the dollar amounts in provisions specified in subsec. (b) of this section, effective Apr. 1, 2007, as follows:

Adjusted $525 (each time it appears) to $575 (each time it appears).

Applicability

Applicability of amendments made by Pub.L. 105–183 to any case brought under an applicable provision of this title that is pending or commenced on or after June 19, 1998, see Pub.L. 105–183, § 5, June 19, 1998, 112 Stat. 518, set out as a note under section 544 of this title.

Rule of Construction

Amendments made by Pub.L. 105–183 not intended to limit the applicability of the Religious Freedom Restoration Act of 1993 (42 U.S.C. 2002bb et seq.), see Pub.L. 105–183, § 6, June 19, 1998, 112 Stat. 519, set out as a note under section 544 of this title.

CROSS REFERENCES

Confirmation of plan in—

Chapter eleven cases, see 11 USCA § 1129.

Chapter nine cases, see 11 USCA § 943.

Chapter twelve cases, see 11 USCA § 1225.

Railroad reorganization cases, see 11 USCA § 1173.

Conversion or dismissal, see 11 USCA § 1307.

§ 1326. Payments

(a)(1) Unless the court orders otherwise, the debtor shall commence making payments not later than 30 days after the date of the filing of the plan or the order for relief, whichever is earlier, in the amount—

(A) proposed by the plan to the trustee;

(B) scheduled in a lease of personal property directly to the lessor for that portion of the obligation that becomes due after the order for relief, reducing the payments under subparagraph (A) by the amount so paid and providing the trustee with evidence of such payment, including the amount and date of payment; and

(C) that provides adequate protection directly to a creditor holding an allowed claim secured by personal property to the extent the claim is attributable to the purchase of such property by the debtor for that portion of the obligation that becomes due after the order for relief, reducing the payments under subparagraph (A) by the amount so paid and providing the trustee with evidence of such payment, including the amount and date of payment.

(2) A payment made under paragraph (1)(A) shall be retained by the trustee until confirmation or denial of confirmation. If a plan is confirmed, the trustee shall distribute any such payment in accordance with the plan as soon as is practicable. If a plan is not confirmed, the trustee shall return any such payments not previously paid and not yet due and owing to creditors pursuant to paragraph (3) to the debtor, after deducting any unpaid claim allowed under section 503(b).

(3) Subject to section 363, the court may, upon notice and a hearing, modify, increase, or reduce the payments required under this subsection pending confirmation of a plan.

(4) Not later than 60 days after the date of filing of a case under this chapter, a debtor retaining possession of personal property subject to a lease or securing a claim attributable in whole or in part to the purchase price of such property shall provide the lessor or secured creditor reasonable evidence of the maintenance of any required insurance coverage with respect to the use or ownership of such property and continue to do so for so long as the debtor retains possession of such property.

(b) Before or at the time of each payment to creditors under the plan, there shall be paid—

(1) any unpaid claim of the kind specified in section 507(a)(2) of this title;

(2) if a standing trustee appointed under section 586(b) of title 28 is serving in the case, the percentage fee fixed for such standing trustee under section 586(e)(1)(B) of title 28; and

(3) if a chapter 7 trustee has been allowed compensation due to the conversion or dismissal of the debtor's prior case pursuant to section 707(b), and some portion of that compensation remains unpaid in a case converted to this chapter or in the case dismissed under section 707(b) and refiled under this chapter, the amount of any such unpaid compensation, which shall be paid monthly—

(A) by prorating such amount over the remaining duration of the plan; and

(B) by monthly payments not to exceed the greater of—

(i) $25 [1]; or

(ii) the amount payable to unsecured nonpriority creditors, as provided by the plan, multiplied by 5 percent, and the result divided by the number of months in the plan.

(c) Except as otherwise provided in the plan or in the order confirming the plan, the trustee shall make payments to creditors under the plan.

(d) Notwithstanding any other provision of this title—

(1) compensation referred to in subsection (b)(3) is payable and may be collected by the trustee under that paragraph, even if such amount has been discharged in a prior case under this title; and

(2) such compensation is payable in a case under this chapter only to the extent permitted by subsection (b)(3).

(Pub.L. 95–598, Nov. 6, 1978, 92 Stat. 2650; Pub.L. 98–353, Title III, §§ 318(a), 531, July 10, 1984, 98 Stat. 357, 389; Pub.L. 99–554, Title II, §§ 230, 283(z), Oct. 27, 1986, 100 Stat. 3103, 3118; Pub.L. 103–394, Title III, § 307, Oct. 22, 1994, 108 Stat. 4135; Pub.L. 109–8, Title III, § 309(c)(2), Title XII, § 1224, Title XV, § 1502(a)(10), Apr. 20, 2005, 119 Stat. 83, 199, 217.)

1 Dollar amount as adjusted by the Judicial Conference of the United States. See Adjustment of Dollar Amounts notes set out under this section and 11 U.S.C.A. § 104.

HISTORICAL AND STATUTORY NOTES

Revision Notes and Legislative Reports

1978 Acts. Section 1326 supplements the priorities provisions of section 507. Subsection (a) requires accrued costs of administration and filing fees, as well as fees due the chapter 13 trustee, to be disbursed before payments to creditors under the plan. Subsection (b) makes it clear that the chapter 13 trustee is normally to make distribution to creditors of the payments made under the plan by the debtor. Senate Report No. 95–989.

Subsection (a) requires that before or at the time of each payment any outstanding administrative expenses [and] any percentage fee due for a private standing chapter 13 trustee be paid in full. House Report No. 95–595.

1984 Acts. Statements by Legislative Leaders, see 1984 U.S.Code Cong. and Adm.News, p. 576.

1986 Acts. House Report No. 99–764 and House Conference Report No. 99–958, see 1986 U.S.Code Cong. and Adm.News, p. 5227.

1994 Acts. House Report No. 103–835, see 1994 U.S. Code Cong. and Adm. News, p. 3340.

2005 Acts. House Report No. 109–31(Part I), see 2005 U.S. Code Cong. and Adm. News, p. 88.

Legislative Statements

Section 1326(a)(2) of the House amendment adopts a comparable provision contained in the House bill providing for standing trustees.

Effective and Applicability Provisions

2007 Acts. Increase of dollar amounts by Judicial Conference of the United States by notice published Feb. 14, 2007, 72 F.R. 7082 effective April 1, 2007, and increase not applicable to cases commenced before the effective date of the adjustments, i.e., April 1, 2007. See Adjustment of Dollar Amounts notes under 11 U.S.C.A. § 104 and this section.

2005 Acts. Amendments by Pub.L. 109–8 effective, except as otherwise provided, 180 days after April 20, 2005, and inapplicable with respect to cases commenced under Title 11 before the effective date, see Pub.L. 109–8, § 1501, set out as a note under 11 U.S.C.A. § 101.

1994 Acts. Amendment by Pub.L. 103–394 effective on Oct. 22, 1994, and not to apply with respect to cases commenced under Title 11 of the United States Code before Oct. 22, 1994, see section 702 of Pub.L. 103–394, set out as a note under section 101 of this title.

1986 Acts. Amendment by section 283 of Pub.L. 99–554 effective 30 days after Oct. 27, 1986, except as otherwise provided for, see section 302(a) of Pub.L. 99–554, set out as a note under section 581 of Title 28, Judiciary and Judicial Procedure.

Amendment by Pub.L. 99–554, § 230, not to become effective in or with respect to certain specified judicial districts until, or apply to cases while pending in such district before, the expiration of the 270–day period beginning 30 days after Oct. 27, 1986, or of the 30–day period beginning on the date the Attorney General certifies under section 303 of Pub.L. 99–554 the region specified in a paragraph of section 581(a) of Title 28, as amended by section 111(a) of Pub.L. 99–554, that includes such district, whichever occurs first, see section 302(d)(1) of Pub.L. 99–554, set out as a note under section 581 of Title 28.

Amendment by Pub.L. 99–554, § 230, not to become effective in or with respect to certain specified judicial districts until, or apply to cases while pending in such district before, the expiration of the 2–year period beginning 30 days after Oct. 27, 1986, or of the 30–day period beginning on the date the Attorney General certifies under section 303 of Pub.L. 99–554 the region specified in a paragraph of section 581(a) of Title 28, as amended by section 111(a) of Pub.L. 99–554, that includes such district, whichever occurs first, see section

302(d)(2) of Pub.L. 99–554, set out as a note under section 581 of Title 28.

Amendment by Pub.L. 99–554, § 230, not to become effective in or with respect to judicial districts established for the States of Alabama and North Carolina until, or apply to cases while pending in such district before, such district elects to be included in a bankruptcy region established in section 581(a) of Title 28, as amended by section 111(a) of Pub.L. 99–554, or Oct. 1, 2002, whichever occurs first, and, except as otherwise provided for, with respect to cases under chapters 7, 11, 12, and 13 of Title 11 commenced before 30 days after Oct. 27, 1986, and pending in a judicial district in the States of Alabama or North Carolina before any election made under section 302(d)(3)(A) of Pub.L. 99–554 by such district becomes effective or Oct. 1, 2002, whichever occurs first, amendments by Pub.L. 99–554 not to apply until Oct. 1, 2003, or the expiration of the 1–year period beginning on the date such election becomes effective, whichever occurs first, and further, in any judicial district in Alabama or North Carolina not making the election described in section 302(d)(3)(A) of Pub.L. 99–554, any person appointed under regulations issued by the Judicial Conference to administer estates in cases under Title 11 authorized to establish, etc., a panel of private trustees, and to supervise cases and trustees in cases under chapters 7, 11, 12, and 13 of Title 11, until amendments by sections 201 to 231 of Pub.L. 99–554 effective in such district, see section 302(d)(3)(A) to (F), (H), (I) of Pub.L. 99–554, set out as a note under section 581 of Title 28.

Amendment by Pub.L. 99–554, § 230, except as otherwise provided, with respect to cases under chapters 7, 11, 12, and 13 of Title 11 commenced before 30 days after Oct. 27, 1986, and pending in a judicial district referred to in section 581(a) of Title 28, as amended by section 111(a) of Pub.L. 99–554, for which a United States trustee is not authorized before 30 days after Oct. 27, 1986 to be appointed, not applicable until the expiration of the 3–year period beginning on Oct. 27, 1986, or of the 1–year period beginning on the date the Attorney General certifies under section 303 of Pub.L. 99–554 the region specified in a paragraph of such section 581(a) that includes, such district, whichever occurs first, see section 302(e)(1), (2) of Pub.L. 99–554, set out as a note under section 581 of Title 28.

1984 Acts. Amendment by Pub.L. 98–353 effective with respect to cases filed 90 days after July 10, 1984, see section 552(a), formerly 553(a), of Pub.L. 98–353, set out as a note under section 101 of this title.

Separability of Provisions

If any provision of or amendment made by Pub.L. 103–394 or the application of such provision or amendment to any person or circumstance is held to be unconstitutional, the remaining provisions of and amendments made by Pub.L. 103–394 and the application of such provisions and amendments to any person or circumstance shall not be affected thereby, see section 701 of Pub.L. 103–394, set out as a note under section 101 of this title.

Adjustment of Dollar Amounts

For adjustment of dollar amounts specified in subsec. (b)(3) of this section by the Judicial Conference of the United States, effective Apr. 1, 2007, see note set out under 11 U.S.C.A. § 104.

By notice published Feb. 14, 2007, 72 F.R. 7082, the Judicial Conference of the United States purported to adjust the dollar amounts in provisions specified in subsec. (b)(3) of this section, effective Apr. 1, 2007, as follows:

Adjusted $25 to $25 [resulting in no change in text].

CROSS REFERENCES

Conversion or dismissal for failure to commence making timely payments under this section, see 11 USCA § 1307.

Duty of trustee to ensure that debtor commences making timely payments under this section, see 11 USCA § 1302.

Payment stopped on checks remaining unpaid 90 days after final distribution, see 11 USCA § 347.

§ 1327. Effect of confirmation

(a) The provisions of a confirmed plan bind the debtor and each creditor, whether or not the claim of such creditor is provided for by the plan, and whether or not such creditor has objected to, has accepted, or has rejected the plan.

(b) Except as otherwise provided in the plan or the order confirming the plan, the confirmation of a plan vests all of the property of the estate in the debtor.

(c) Except as otherwise provided in the plan or in the order confirming the plan, the property vesting in the debtor under subsection (b) of this section is free and clear of any claim or interest of any creditor provided for by the plan.

(Pub.L. 95–598, Nov. 6, 1978, 92 Stat. 2650.)

HISTORICAL AND STATUTORY NOTES

Revision Notes and Legislative Reports

1978 Acts. Subsection (a) binds the debtor and each creditor to the provisions of a confirmed plan, whether or not the claim of the creditor is provided for by the plan and whether or not the creditor has accepted, rejected, or objected to the plan. Unless the plan itself or the order confirming the plan otherwise provides, confirmation is deemed to vest all property of the estate in the debtor, free and clear of any claim or interest of any creditor provided for by the plan. Senate Report No. 95–989.

CROSS REFERENCES

Effect of confirmation in—

Chapter eleven cases, see 11 USCA § 1141.

Chapter nine cases, see 11 USCA § 944.

Chapter twelve cases, see 11 USCA § 1227.

§ 1328. Discharge

(a) Subject to subsection (d), as soon as practicable after completion by the debtor of all payments under the plan, and in the case of a debtor who is required by a judicial or administrative order, or by statute, to pay a domestic support obligation, after such debtor certifies that all amounts payable under such order or such statute that are due on or before the date of the certification (including amounts due before the petition was filed, but only to the extent provided for by the plan) have been paid, unless the court approves a written waiver of discharge executed by the debtor after the order for relief under this chapter, the court shall grant the debtor a discharge of all debts provided for by the plan or disallowed under section 502 of this title, except any debt—

(1) provided for under section 1322(b)(5);

(2) of the kind specified in section 507(a)(8)(C) or in paragraph (1)(B), (1)(C), (2), (3), (4), (5), (8), or (9) of section 523(a);

(3) for restitution, or a criminal fine, included in a sentence on the debtor's conviction of a crime; or

(4) for restitution, or damages, awarded in a civil action against the debtor as a result of willful or malicious injury by the debtor that caused personal injury to an individual or the death of an individual.

(b) Subject to subsection (d), at any time after the confirmation of the plan and after notice and a hearing, the court may grant a discharge to a debtor that has not completed payments under the plan only if—

(1) the debtor's failure to complete such payments is due to circumstances for which the debtor should not justly be held accountable;

(2) the value, as of the effective date of the plan, of property actually distributed under the plan on account of each allowed unsecured claim is not less than the amount that would have been paid on such claim if the estate of the debtor had been liquidated under chapter 7 of this title on such date; and

(3) modification of the plan under section 1329 of this title is not practicable.

(c) A discharge granted under subsection (b) of this section discharges the debtor from all unsecured debts provided for by the plan or disallowed under section 502 of this title, except any debt—

(1) provided for under section 1322(b)(5) of this title; or

(2) of a kind specified in section 523(a) of this title.

(d) Notwithstanding any other provision of this section, a discharge granted under this section does not discharge the debtor from any debt based on an allowed claim filed under section 1305(a)(2) of this title if prior approval by the trustee of the debtor's incurring such debt was practicable and was not obtained.

(e) On request of a party in interest before one year after a discharge under this section is granted, and after notice and a hearing, the court may revoke such discharge only if—

(1) such discharge was obtained by the debtor through fraud; and

(2) the requesting party did not know of such fraud until after such discharge was granted.

(f) Notwithstanding subsections (a) and (b), the court shall not grant a discharge of all debts provided for in the plan or disallowed under section 502, if the debtor has received a discharge—

(1) in a case filed under chapter 7, 11, or 12 of this title during the 4-year period preceding the date of the order for relief under this chapter, or

(2) in a case filed under chapter 13 of this title during the 2-year period preceding the date of such order.

(g)(1) The court shall not grant a discharge under this section to a debtor unless after filing a petition the debtor has completed an instructional course concerning personal financial management described in section 111.

(2) Paragraph (1) shall not apply with respect to a debtor who is a person described in section 109(h)(4) or who resides in a district for which the United States trustee (or the bankruptcy administrator, if any) determines that the approved instructional courses are not adequate to service the additional individuals who would otherwise be required to complete such instructional course by reason of the requirements of paragraph (1).

(3) The United States trustee (or the bankruptcy administrator, if any) who makes a determination described in paragraph (2) shall review such determination not later than 1 year after the date of such determination, and not less frequently than annually thereafter.

(h) The court may not grant a discharge under this chapter unless the court after notice and a hearing held not more than 10 days before the date of the entry of the order granting the discharge finds that there is no reasonable cause to believe that—

(1) section 522(q)(1) may be applicable to the debtor; and

(2) there is pending any proceeding in which the debtor may be found guilty of a felony of the kind described in section 522(q)(1)(A) or liable for a debt of the kind described in section 522(q)(1)(B).

(Pub.L. 95–598, Nov. 6, 1978, 92 Stat. 2650; Pub.L. 98–353, Title III, § 532, July 10, 1984, 98 Stat. 389; Pub.L. 101–508, Title III, § 3007(b)(1), Nov. 5, 1990, 104 Stat. 1388–28; Pub.L. 101–581, §§ 2(b), 3, Nov. 15, 1990, 104 Stat. 2865; Pub.L. 101–647, Title XXXI, §§ 3102(b), 3103, Nov. 29, 1990, 104 Stat. 4916; Pub.L. 103–394, Title III, § 302, Title V, § 501(d)(38), Oct. 22, 1994, 108 Stat. 4132, 4147; Pub.L. 109–8, Title I, § 106(c), Title II, § 213(11), Title III, §§ 312(2), 314(b), 330(d), Title VII, § 707, Apr. 20, 2005, 119 Stat. 38, 53, 87, 88, 102, 126.)

HISTORICAL AND STATUTORY NOTES

Revision Notes and Legislative Reports

1978 Acts. The court is to enter a discharge, unless waived, as soon as practicable after completion of payments under the plan. The debtor is to be discharged of all debts provided for by the plan or disallowed under section 502, except a debt provided for under the plan the last payment on which was not due until after the completion of the plan, or a debt incurred for willful and malicious conversion of or injury to the property or person of another.

Subsection (b) is the successor to Bankruptcy Act Section [sic] 661 [Section 1061 of former title 11]. This subsection permits the bankruptcy judge to grant the debtor a discharge at any time after confirmation of a plan, if the court determines, after notice and hearing, that the failure to complete payments under the plan is due to circumstances for which the debtor should not justly be held accountable, the distributions made to each creditor under the plan equal in value the amount that would have been paid to the creditor had the estate been liquidated under chapter 7 of title 11 at the date of the hearing under this subsection, and that modification of the plan is impracticable. The discharge granted under subsection (b) relieves the debtor from all unsecured debts provided for by the plan or disallowed under section 502, except nondischargeable debts described in section 523(a) of title 11 or debts of the type covered by section 1322(b)(5).

Subsection (d) excepts from any chapter 13 discharge a debt based on an allowed section 1305(a)(2) postpetition claim, if prior trustee approval of the incurring of the debt was practicable but was not obtained.

A chapter 13 discharge obtained through fraud and before the moving party gained knowledge of the fraud may be revoked by the court under subsection (e), after notice and hearing, at the request of any party in interest made within 1 year after the discharge was granted. Senate Report No. 95–989.

1984 Acts. Statements by Legislative Leaders, see 1984 U.S.Code Cong. and Adm.News, p. 576.

1990 Acts. House Report No. 101–681(I), see 1990 U.S.Code Cong. and Adm.News, p. 6472.

Senate Report No. 101–434, see 1990 U.S.Code Cong. and Adm.News, p. 4065.

House Report No. 101–881, House Conference Report No. 101–964, and President's Signing Statement, see 1990 U.S.Code Cong. and Adm.News, p. 2017.

1994 Acts. House Report No. 103–835, see 1994 U.S. Code Cong. and Adm. News, p. 3340.

2005 Acts. House Report No. 109–31(Part I), see 2005 U.S. Code Cong. and Adm. News, p. 88.

Legislative Statements

Section 1328(a) adopts a provision contained in the Senate amendment permitting the court to approve a waiver of discharge by the debtor. It is anticipated that such a waiver must be in writing executed after the order for relief in a case under chapter 13.

References in Text

Chapter 7, 11, or 12 of this title, referred to in subsec. (f)(1), is 11 U.S.C.A. § 701 et seq., 11 U.S.C.A. § 1101 et seq., or 11 U.S.C.A. § 1201 et seq., respectively.

Chapter 13 of this title, referred to in subsec. (f)(2), is 11 U.S.C.A. § 1301 et seq.

Codifications

Pub.L. 101–581, §§ 2(b), 3(1) to (3) and Pub.L. 101–647, §§ 3102(b), 3103(1)–(3), contained identical amendments to subsec. (a)(2) and (a)(1)–(3) of this section.

Amendments by Pub.L. 101–581, § 2(b), and Pub.L. 101–647, § 3102(b), which both inserted "or 523(a)(9)" following "523(a)(5)", were incapable of literal execution in view of prior amendment by Pub.L. 101–508, which substituted "paragraph (5) or (8) of section 523(a)" for "section 523(a)(5)", thereby deleting language subsequently amended. See also 1990 Amendments note set out under this section.

Effective and Applicability Provisions

2005 Acts. Amendments Pub.L. 109–8 effective 180 days after Apr. 20, 2005, with amendments by sections 106(c), 213(11), 312(2), 314(b), and 707 of Pub.L. 109–8 not applicable with respect to cases commenced under this title before such effective date, except as otherwise provided, and amendment by section 330(d) of Pub.L. 109–8 applicable with respect to cases commenced under this title on or after Apr. 20, 2005, see Pub.L. 109–8, § 1501, set out as a note under 11 U.S.C.A. § 101.

1994 Acts. Amendments by Pub.L. 103–394 effective on Oct. 22, 1994, and not to apply with respect to cases commenced under Title 11 of the United States Code before Oct. 22, 1994, see section 702 of Pub.L. 103–394, set out as a note under section 101 of this title.

1990 Acts. Amendment by Pub.L. 101–647 effective Nov. 29, 1990, but not applicable with respect to cases commenced under this title before Nov. 29, 1990, see section 3104 of Pub.L. 101–647, set out as an Effective Date of 1990 Amendments note under section 523 of this title.

Amendment by Pub.L. 101–581 effective Nov. 15, 1990, but not applicable with respect to cases commenced under this title before Nov. 15, 1990, see section 4 of Pub.L. 101–581, set out as an Effective Date of 1990 Amendment note under section 523 of this title.

Section 3007(b)(2) of Pub.L. 101–508 provided that: "The amendment made by paragraph (1) [amending this section] shall not apply to any case under the provisions of title 11, United States Code, commenced before the date of the enactment of this Act [Nov. 5, 1990]."

Section 3008 of Pub.L. 101–508, which had provided that the amendment to this section by Pub.L. 101–508 was to cease to be effective on Oct. 1, 1996, was repealed by Pub.L. 102–325, Title XV, § 1558, July 23, 1992, 106 Stat. 841.

1984 Acts. Amendment by Pub.L. 98–353 effective with respect to cases filed 90 days after July 10, 1984, see section 552(a), formerly 553(a), of Pub.L. 98–353, set out as a note under section 101 of this title.

Separability of Provisions

If any provision of or amendment made by Pub.L. 103–394 or the application of such provision or amendment to any person or circumstance is held to be unconstitutional, the remaining provisions of and amendments made by Pub.L. 103–394 and the application of such provisions and amendments to any person or circumstance shall not be affected thereby, see section 701 of Pub.L. 103–394, set out as a note under section 101 of this title.

CROSS REFERENCES

Cancellation of indebtedness from discharged farm loans, see 12 USCA § 1150.

Discharge in—

Chapter seven cases, see 11 USCA § 727.

Chapter twelve cases, see 11 USCA § 1228.

Effect of, discharge, see 11 USCA § 524.

Exceptions to discharge, see 11 USCA § 523.

Nondischargeability of capital improvement loans for multifamily housing projects in proceedings under this section, see 12 USCA § 1715z–1a.

§ 1329. Modification of plan after confirmation

(a) At any time after confirmation of the plan but before the completion of payments under such plan, the plan may be modified, upon request of the debtor, the trustee, or the holder of an allowed unsecured claim, to—

(1) increase or reduce the amount of payments on claims of a particular class provided for by the plan;

(2) extend or reduce the time for such payments;

(3) alter the amount of the distribution to a creditor whose claim is provided for by the plan to the extent necessary to take account of any payment of such claim other than under the plan; or

(4) reduce amounts to be paid under the plan by the actual amount expended by the debtor to purchase health insurance for the debtor (and for any dependent of the debtor if such dependent does not otherwise have health insurance coverage) if the debtor documents the cost of such insurance and demonstrates that—

(A) such expenses are reasonable and necessary;

(B)(i) if the debtor previously paid for health insurance, the amount is not materially larger than the cost the debtor previously paid or the cost necessary to maintain the lapsed policy; or

(ii) if the debtor did not have health insurance, the amount is not materially larger than the reasonable cost that would be incurred by a debtor who purchases health insurance, who has similar income, expenses, age, and health status, and who lives in the same geographical location with the same number of dependents who do not otherwise have health insurance coverage; and

(C) the amount is not otherwise allowed for purposes of determining disposable income under section 1325(b) of this title;

and upon request of any party in interest, files proof that a health insurance policy was purchased.

(b)(1) Sections 1322(a), 1322(b), and 1323(c) of this title and the requirements of section 1325(a) of this title apply to any modification under subsection (a) of this section.

(2) The plan as modified becomes the plan unless, after notice and a hearing, such modification is disapproved.

(c) A plan modified under this section may not provide for payments over a period that expires after the applicable commitment period under section 1325(b)(1)(B) after the time that the first payment under the original confirmed plan was due, unless the court, for cause, approves a longer period, but the court may not approve a period that expires after five years after such time.

(Pub.L. 95–598, Nov. 6, 1978, 92 Stat. 2651; Pub.L. 98–353, Title III, §§ 319, 533, July 10, 1984, 98 Stat. 357, 389; Pub.L. 109–8, Title I, § 102(i), Title III, § 318(4), Apr. 20, 2005, 119 Stat. 34, 94.)

HISTORICAL AND STATUTORY NOTES

Revision Notes and Legislative Reports

1978 Acts. At any time prior to the completion of payments under a confirmed plan, the plan may be modified, after notice and hearing, to change the amount of payments to creditors or a particular class of creditors and to extend or reduce the payment period. A modified plan may not contain any provision which could not be included in an original plan as prescribed by section 1322. A modified plan may not call for payments to be made beyond four years as measured from the date of the commencement of payments under the original plan. Senate Report No. 95–989.

1984 Acts. Statements by Legislative Leaders, see 1984 U.S.Code Cong. and Adm.News, p. 576.

2005 Acts. House Report No. 109–31(Part I), see 2005 U.S. Code Cong. and Adm. News, p. 88.

Effective and Applicability Provisions

2005 Acts. Amendments by Pub.L. 109–8 effective, except as otherwise provided, 180 days after April 20, 2005, and inapplicable with respect to cases commenced under Title 11 before the effective date, see Pub.L. 109–8, § 1501, set out as a note under 11 U.S.C.A. § 101.

1984 Acts. Amendment by Pub.L. 98–353 effective with respect to cases filed 90 days after July 10, 1984, see section 552(a), formerly 553(a), of Pub.L. 98–353, set out as a note under section 101 of this title.

CROSS REFERENCES

Conversion or dismissal upon denial of confirmation of modified plan, see 11 USCA § 1307.

Duties of United States trustee, see 28 USCA § 586.

Modification of plan in—

Chapter eleven cases, see 11 USCA § 1127.

Chapter nine cases, see 11 USCA § 942.

Chapter twelve cases, see 11 USCA § 1229.

§ 1330. Revocation of an order of confirmation

(a) On request of a party in interest at any time within 180 days after the date of the entry of an order of confirmation under section 1325 of this title, and after notice and a hearing, the court may revoke such order if such order was procured by fraud.

(b) If the court revokes an order of confirmation under subsection (a) of this section, the court shall dispose of the case under section 1307 of this title, unless, within the time fixed by the court, the debtor proposes and the court confirms a modification of the plan under section 1329 of this title.

(Pub.L. 95–598, Nov. 6, 1978, 92 Stat. 2651.)

HISTORICAL AND STATUTORY NOTES

Revision Notes and Legislative Reports

1978 Acts. The court may revoke an order of confirmation procured by fraud, after notice and hearing, on application of a party in interest filed within 180 days after the entry of the order. Thereafter, unless a modified plan is confirmed, the court is to convert or dismiss the chapter 13 case as provided in section 1307. Senate Report No. 95–989.

Legislative Statements

Section 1331 of the House bill and Senate amendment is deleted in the House amendment.

Special tax provision: Section 1331 of title 11 of the House bill and the comparable provisions in sections 1322 and 1327(d) of the Senate amendment, pertaining to assessment and collection of taxes in wage earner plans, are deleted, and the governing rule is placed in section 505(c) of the House amendment. The provisions of both bills allowing assessment and collection of taxes after confirmation of the wage-earner plan are modified to allow assessment and collection after the court fixes the fact and amount of a tax liability, including administrative period taxes, regardless of whether this occurs before or after confirmation of the plan. The provision of the House bill limiting the collection of taxes to those assessed before one year after the filing of the petition is eliminated, thereby leaving the period of limitations on assessment of these nondischargeable tax liabilities the usual period provided by the Internal Revenue Code [Title 26].

CROSS REFERENCES

Conversion or dismissal upon revocation of order of confirmation, see 11 USCA § 1307.

Revocation of order of confirmation in—

Chapter eleven cases, see 11 USCA § 1144.

Chapter twelve cases, see 11 USCA § 1230.

CHAPTER 15—ANCILLARY AND OTHER CROSS–BORDER CASES

§ 1501. Purpose and scope of application

(a) The purpose of this chapter is to incorporate the Model Law on Cross–Border Insolvency so as to provide effective mechanisms for dealing with cases of cross-border insolvency with the objectives of—

(1) cooperation between—

(A) courts of the United States, United States trustees, trustees, examiners, debtors, and debtors in possession; and

(B) the courts and other competent authorities of foreign countries involved in cross-border insolvency cases;

(2) greater legal certainty for trade and investment;

(3) fair and efficient administration of cross-border insolvencies that protects the interests of all creditors, and other interested entities, including the debtor;

(4) protection and maximization of the value of the debtor's assets; and

(5) facilitation of the rescue of financially troubled businesses, thereby protecting investment and preserving employment.

(b) This chapter applies where—

(1) assistance is sought in the United States by a foreign court or a foreign representative in connection with a foreign proceeding;

(2) assistance is sought in a foreign country in connection with a case under this title;

(3) a foreign proceeding and a case under this title with respect to the same debtor are pending concurrently; or

(4) creditors or other interested persons in a foreign country have an interest in requesting the commencement of, or participating in, a case or proceeding under this title.

(c) This chapter does not apply to—

(1) a proceeding concerning an entity, other than a foreign insurance company, identified by exclusion in section 109(b);

(2) an individual, or to an individual and such individual's spouse, who have debts within the limits specified in section 109(e) and who are citizens of the United States or aliens lawfully admitted for permanent residence in the United States; or

(3) an entity subject to a proceeding under the Securities Investor Protection Act of 1970, a stockbroker subject to subchapter III of chapter 7 of this title, or a commodity broker subject to subchapter IV of chapter 7 of this title.

(d) The court may not grant relief under this chapter with respect to any deposit, escrow, trust fund, or other security required or permitted under any applicable State insurance law or regulation for the benefit of claim holders in the United States.

(Added Pub.L. 109–8, Title VIII, § 801(a), Apr. 20, 2005, 119 Stat. 135.)

HISTORICAL AND STATUTORY NOTES

Revision Notes and Legislative Reports

2005 Acts. House Report No. 109–31(Part I), see 2005 U.S. Code Cong. and Adm. News, p. 88.

References in Text

The Securities Investor Protection Act of 1970, referred to in subsec. (c)(3), is Pub.L. 91–598, Dec. 30, 1970, 84 Stat. 1636, also known as SIPA, which is classified principally to chapter 2B–1 of Title 15, 15 U.S.C.A. § 78aaa et seq.

Subchapter III of chapter 7 of this title, referred to in subsec. (c)(3), is 11 U.S.C.A. § 741 et seq.

Subchapter IV of chapter 7 of this title, referred to in subsec. (c)(3), is 11 U.S.C.A. § 761 et seq.

Effective and Applicability Provisions

2005 Acts. Amendments by Pub.L. 109–8 effective, except as otherwise provided, 180 days after April 20, 2005, and inapplicable with respect to cases commenced under Title 11 before the effective date, see Pub.L. 109–8, § 1501, set out as a note under 11 U.S.C.A. § 101.

SUBCHAPTER I—GENERAL PROVISIONS

§ 1502. Definitions

For the purposes of this chapter, the term—

(1) "debtor" means an entity that is the subject of a foreign proceeding;

(2) "establishment" means any place of operations where the debtor carries out a nontransitory economic activity;

(3) "foreign court" means a judicial or other authority competent to control or supervise a foreign proceeding;

(4) "foreign main proceeding" means a foreign proceeding pending in the country where the debtor has the center of its main interests;

(5) "foreign nonmain proceeding" means a foreign proceeding, other than a foreign main proceeding, pending in a country where the debtor has an establishment;

(6) "trustee" includes a trustee, a debtor in possession in a case under any chapter of this title, or a debtor under chapter 9 of this title;

(7) "recognition" means the entry of an order granting recognition of a foreign main proceeding or foreign nonmain proceeding under this chapter; and

(8) "within the territorial jurisdiction of the United States", when used with reference to property of a debtor, refers to tangible property located within the territory of the United States and intangible property deemed under applicable nonbankruptcy law to be located within that territory, including any property subject to attachment or garnishment that may properly be seized or garnished by an action in a Federal or State court in the United States.

(Added Pub.L. 109–8, Title VIII, § 801(a), Apr. 20, 2005, 119 Stat. 135.)

HISTORICAL AND STATUTORY NOTES

Revision Notes and Legislative Reports

2005 Acts. House Report No. 109–31(Part I), see 2005 U.S. Code Cong. and Adm. News, p. 88.

References in Text

Chapter 9 of this title, referred to in par. (6), is 11 U.S.C.A. § 901 et seq.

Effective and Applicability Provisions

2005 Acts. Amendments by Pub.L. 109–8 effective, except as otherwise provided, 180 days after April 20, 2005, and inapplicable with respect to cases commenced under Title 11 before the effective date, see Pub.L. 109–8, § 1501, set out as a note under 11 U.S.C.A. § 101.

§ 1503. International obligations of the United States

To the extent that this chapter conflicts with an obligation of the United States arising out of any treaty or other form of agreement to which it is a party with one or more other countries, the requirements of the treaty or agreement prevail.

(Added Pub.L. 109–8, Title VIII, § 801(a), Apr. 20, 2005, 119 Stat. 136.)

HISTORICAL AND STATUTORY NOTES

Revision Notes and Legislative Reports

2005 Acts. House Report No. 109–31(Part I), see 2005 U.S. Code Cong. and Adm. News, p. 88.

Effective and Applicability Provisions

2005 Acts. Amendments by Pub.L. 109–8 effective, except as otherwise provided, 180 days after April 20, 2005, and inapplicable with respect to cases commenced under Title 11 before the effective date, see Pub.L. 109–8, § 1501, set out as a note under 11 U.S.C.A. § 101.

§ 1504. Commencement of ancillary case

A case under this chapter is commenced by the filing of a petition for recognition of a foreign proceeding under section 1515.

(Added Pub.L. 109–8, Title VIII, § 801(a), Apr. 20, 2005, 119 Stat. 136.)

HISTORICAL AND STATUTORY NOTES

Revision Notes and Legislative Reports

2005 Acts. House Report No. 109–31(Part I), see 2005 U.S. Code Cong. and Adm. News, p. 88.

Effective and Applicability Provisions

2005 Acts. Amendments by Pub.L. 109–8 effective, except as otherwise provided, 180 days after April 20, 2005, and inapplicable with respect to cases commenced under Title 11 before the effective date, see Pub.L. 109–8, § 1501, set out as a note under 11 U.S.C.A. § 101.

§ 1505. Authorization to act in a foreign country

A trustee or another entity (including an examiner) may be authorized by the court to act in a foreign country on behalf of an estate created under section 541. An entity authorized to act under this section may act in any way permitted by the applicable foreign law.

(Added Pub.L. 109–8, Title VIII, § 801(a), Apr. 20, 2005, 119 Stat. 136.)

HISTORICAL AND STATUTORY NOTES

Revision Notes and Legislative Reports

2005 Acts. House Report No. 109–31(Part I), see 2005 U.S. Code Cong. and Adm. News, p. 88.

Effective and Applicability Provisions

2005 Acts. Amendments by Pub.L. 109–8 effective, except as otherwise provided, 180 days after April 20, 2005, and inapplicable with respect to cases commenced under Title 11 before the effective date, see Pub.L. 109–8, § 1501, set out as a note under 11 U.S.C.A. § 101.

§ 1506. Public policy exception

Nothing in this chapter prevents the court from refusing to take an action governed by this chapter if the action would be manifestly contrary to the public policy of the United States.

(Added Pub.L. 109–8, Title VIII, § 801(a), Apr. 20, 2005, 119 Stat. 136.)

HISTORICAL AND STATUTORY NOTES

Revision Notes and Legislative Reports

2005 Acts. House Report No. 109–31(Part I), see 2005 U.S. Code Cong. and Adm. News, p. 88.

Effective and Applicability Provisions

2005 Acts. Amendments by Pub.L. 109–8 effective, except as otherwise provided, 180 days after April 20, 2005, and inapplicable with respect to cases commenced under Title 11 before the effective date, see Pub.L. 109–8, § 1501, set out as a note under 11 U.S.C.A. § 101.

§ 1507. Additional assistance

(a) Subject to the specific limitations stated elsewhere in this chapter the court, if recognition is granted, may provide additional assistance to a foreign representative under this title or under other laws of the United States.

(b) In determining whether to provide additional assistance under this title or under other laws of the United States, the court shall consider whether such additional assistance, consistent with the principles of comity, will reasonably assure—

(1) just treatment of all holders of claims against or interests in the debtor's property;

(2) protection of claim holders in the United States against prejudice and inconvenience in the processing of claims in such foreign proceeding;

(3) prevention of preferential or fraudulent dispositions of property of the debtor;

(4) distribution of proceeds of the debtor's property substantially in accordance with the order prescribed by this title; and

(5) if appropriate, the provision of an opportunity for a fresh start for the individual that such foreign proceeding concerns.

(Added Pub.L. 109–8, Title VIII, § 801(a), Apr. 20, 2005, 119 Stat. 136.)

HISTORICAL AND STATUTORY NOTES

Revision Notes and Legislative Reports

2005 Acts. House Report No. 109–31(Part I), see 2005 U.S. Code Cong. and Adm. News, p. 88.

Effective and Applicability Provisions

2005 Acts. Amendments by Pub.L. 109–8 effective, except as otherwise provided, 180 days after April 20, 2005, and inapplicable with respect to cases commenced under Title 11 before the effective date, see Pub.L. 109–8, § 1501, set out as a note under 11 U.S.C.A. § 101.

§ 1508. Interpretation

In interpreting this chapter, the court shall consider its international origin, and the need to promote an application of this chapter that is consistent with the application of similar statutes adopted by foreign jurisdictions.

(Added Pub.L. 109–8, Title VIII, § 801(a), Apr. 20, 2005, 119 Stat. 137.)

HISTORICAL AND STATUTORY NOTES

Revision Notes and Legislative Reports

2005 Acts. House Report No. 109–31(Part I), see 2005 U.S. Code Cong. and Adm. News, p. 88.

Effective and Applicability Provisions

2005 Acts. Amendments by Pub.L. 109–8 effective, except as otherwise provided, 180 days after April 20, 2005, and inapplicable with respect to cases commenced under Title 11 before the effective date, see Pub.L. 109–8, § 1501, set out as a note under 11 U.S.C.A. § 101.

SUBCHAPTER II—ACCESS OF FOREIGN REPRESENTATIVES AND CREDITORS TO THE COURT

§ 1509. Right of direct access

(a) A foreign representative may commence a case under section 1504 by filing directly with the court a petition for recognition of a foreign proceeding under section 1515.

(b) If the court grants recognition under section 1517, and subject to any limitations that the court may impose consistent with the policy of this chapter—

(1) the foreign representative has the capacity to sue and be sued in a court in the United States;

(2) the foreign representative may apply directly to a court in the United States for appropriate relief in that court; and

(3) a court in the United States shall grant comity or cooperation to the foreign representative.

(c) A request for comity or cooperation by a foreign representative in a court in the United States other than the court which granted recognition shall be accompanied by a certified copy of an order granting recognition under section 1517.

(d) If the court denies recognition under this chapter, the court may issue any appropriate order necessary to prevent the foreign representative from obtaining comity or cooperation from courts in the United States.

(e) Whether or not the court grants recognition, and subject to sections 306 and 1510, a foreign representative is subject to applicable nonbankruptcy law.

(f) Notwithstanding any other provision of this section, the failure of a foreign representative to commence a case or to obtain recognition under this chapter does not affect any right the foreign representative may have to sue in a court in the United States to collect or recover a claim which is the property of the debtor.

(Added Pub.L. 109–8, Title VIII, § 801(a), Apr. 20, 2005, 119 Stat. 137.)

HISTORICAL AND STATUTORY NOTES

Revision Notes and Legislative Reports

2005 Acts. House Report No. 109–31(Part I), see 2005 U.S. Code Cong. and Adm. News, p. 88.

Effective and Applicability Provisions

2005 Acts. Amendments by Pub.L. 109–8 effective, except as otherwise provided, 180 days after April 20, 2005, and inapplicable with respect to cases commenced under Title 11 before the effective date, see Pub.L. 109–8, § 1501, set out as a note under 11 U.S.C.A. § 101.

§ 1510. Limited jurisdiction

The sole fact that a foreign representative files a petition under section 1515 does not subject the foreign representative to the jurisdiction of any court in the United States for any other purpose.

(Added Pub.L. 109–8, Title VIII, § 801(a), Apr. 20, 2005, 119 Stat. 138.)

HISTORICAL AND STATUTORY NOTES

Revision Notes and Legislative Reports

2005 Acts. House Report No. 109–31(Part I), see 2005 U.S. Code Cong. and Adm. News, p. 88.

Effective and Applicability Provisions

2005 Acts. Amendments by Pub.L. 109–8 effective, except as otherwise provided, 180 days after April 20, 2005, and inapplicable with respect to cases commenced under Title 11 before the effective date, see Pub.L. 109–8, § 1501, set out as a note under 11 U.S.C.A. § 101.

§ 1511. Commencement of case under section 301 or 303

(a) Upon recognition, a foreign representative may commence—

(1) an involuntary case under section 303; or

(2) a voluntary case under section 301 or 302, if the foreign proceeding is a foreign main proceeding.

(b) The petition commencing a case under subsection (a) must be accompanied by a certified copy of an order granting recognition. The court where the petition for recognition has been filed must be advised of the foreign representative's intent to commence a case under subsection (a) prior to such commencement.

(Added Pub.L. 109–8, Title VIII, § 801(a), Apr. 20, 2005, 119 Stat. 138.)

HISTORICAL AND STATUTORY NOTES

Revision Notes and Legislative Reports

2005 Acts. House Report No. 109–31(Part I), see 2005 U.S. Code Cong. and Adm. News, p. 88.

Effective and Applicability Provisions

2005 Acts. Amendments by Pub.L. 109–8 effective, except as otherwise provided, 180 days after April 20, 2005, and inapplicable with respect to cases commenced under Title 11 before the effective date, see Pub.L. 109–8, § 1501, set out as a note under 11 U.S.C.A. § 101.

§ 1512. Participation of a foreign representative in a case under this title

Upon recognition of a foreign proceeding, the foreign representative in the recognized proceeding is entitled to participate as a party in interest in a case regarding the debtor under this title.

(Added Pub.L. 109-8, Title VIII, § 801(a), Apr. 20, 2005, 119 Stat. 138.)

HISTORICAL AND STATUTORY NOTES

Revision Notes and Legislative Reports

2005 Acts. House Report No. 109-31(Part I), see 2005 U.S. Code Cong. and Adm. News, p. 88.

Effective and Applicability Provisions

2005 Acts. Amendments by Pub.L. 109-8 effective, except as otherwise provided, 180 days after April 20, 2005, and inapplicable with respect to cases commenced under Title 11 before the effective date, see Pub.L. 109-8, § 1501, set out as a note under 11 U.S.C.A. § 101.

§ 1513. Access of foreign creditors to a case under this title

(a) Foreign creditors have the same rights regarding the commencement of, and participation in, a case under this title as domestic creditors.

(b)(1) Subsection (a) does not change or codify present law as to the priority of claims under section 507 or 726, except that the claim of a foreign creditor under those sections shall not be given a lower priority than that of general unsecured claims without priority solely because the holder of such claim is a foreign creditor.

(2)(A) Subsection (a) and paragraph (1) do not change or codify present law as to the allowability of foreign revenue claims or other foreign public law claims in a proceeding under this title.

(B) Allowance and priority as to a foreign tax claim or other foreign public law claim shall be governed by any applicable tax treaty of the United States, under the conditions and circumstances specified therein.

(Added Pub.L. 109-8, Title VIII, § 801(a), Apr. 20, 2005, 119 Stat. 138.)

HISTORICAL AND STATUTORY NOTES

Revision Notes and Legislative Reports

2005 Acts. House Report No. 109-31(Part I), see 2005 U.S. Code Cong. and Adm. News, p. 88.

Effective and Applicability Provisions

2005 Acts. Amendments by Pub.L. 109-8 effective, except as otherwise provided, 180 days after April 20, 2005, and inapplicable with respect to cases commenced under Title 11 before the effective date, see Pub.L. 109-8, § 1501, set out as a note under 11 U.S.C.A. § 101.

§ 1514. Notification to foreign creditors concerning a case under this title

(a) Whenever in a case under this title notice is to be given to creditors generally or to any class or category of creditors, such notice shall also be given to the known creditors generally, or to creditors in the notified class or category, that do not have addresses in the United States. The court may order that appropriate steps be taken with a view to notifying any creditor whose address is not yet known.

(b) Such notification to creditors with foreign addresses described in subsection (a) shall be given individually, unless the court considers that, under the circumstances, some other form of notification would be more appropriate. No letter or other formality is required.

(c) When a notification of commencement of a case is to be given to foreign creditors, such notification shall—

(1) indicate the time period for filing proofs of claim and specify the place for filing such proofs of claim;

(2) indicate whether secured creditors need to file proofs of claim; and

(3) contain any other information required to be included in such notification to creditors under this title and the orders of the court.

(d) Any rule of procedure or order of the court as to notice or the filing of a proof of claim shall provide such additional time to creditors with foreign addresses as is reasonable under the circumstances.

(Added Pub.L. 109-8, Title VIII, § 801(a), Apr. 20, 2005, 119 Stat. 138.)

HISTORICAL AND STATUTORY NOTES

Revision Notes and Legislative Reports

2005 Acts. House Report No. 109-31(Part I), see 2005 U.S. Code Cong. and Adm. News, p. 88.

Effective and Applicability Provisions

2005 Acts. Amendments by Pub.L. 109-8 effective, except as otherwise provided, 180 days after April 20, 2005, and inapplicable with respect to cases commenced under Title 11 before the effective date, see Pub.L. 109-8, § 1501, set out as a note under 11 U.S.C.A. § 101.

SUBCHAPTER III—RECOGNITION OF A FOREIGN PROCEEDING AND RELIEF

§ 1515. Application for recognition

(a) A foreign representative applies to the court for recognition of a foreign proceeding in which the foreign representative has been appointed by filing a petition for recognition.

(b) A petition for recognition shall be accompanied by—

(1) a certified copy of the decision commencing such foreign proceeding and appointing the foreign representative;

(2) a certificate from the foreign court affirming the existence of such foreign proceeding and of the appointment of the foreign representative; or

(3) in the absence of evidence referred to in paragraphs (1) and (2), any other evidence acceptable to the court of the existence of such foreign proceeding and of the appointment of the foreign representative.

(c) A petition for recognition shall also be accompanied by a statement identifying all foreign proceedings with respect to the debtor that are known to the foreign representative.

(d) The documents referred to in paragraphs (1) and (2) of subsection (b) shall be translated into English. The court may require a translation into English of additional documents.

(Added Pub.L. 109–8, Title VIII, § 801(a), Apr. 20, 2005, 119 Stat. 139.)

HISTORICAL AND STATUTORY NOTES

Revision Notes and Legislative Reports

2005 Acts. House Report No. 109–31(Part I), see 2005 U.S. Code Cong. and Adm. News, p. 88.

Effective and Applicability Provisions

2005 Acts. Amendments by Pub.L. 109–8 effective, except as otherwise provided, 180 days after April 20, 2005, and inapplicable with respect to cases commenced under Title 11 before the effective date, see Pub.L. 109–8, § 1501, set out as a note under 11 U.S.C.A. § 101.

§ 1516. Presumptions concerning recognition

(a) If the decision or certificate referred to in section 1515(b) indicates that the foreign proceeding is a foreign proceeding and that the person or body is a foreign representative, the court is entitled to so presume.

(b) The court is entitled to presume that documents submitted in support of the petition for recognition are authentic, whether or not they have been legalized.

(c) In the absence of evidence to the contrary, the debtor's registered office, or habitual residence in the case of an individual, is presumed to be the center of the debtor's main interests.

(Added Pub.L. 109–8, Title VIII, § 801(a), Apr. 20, 2005, 119 Stat. 139.)

HISTORICAL AND STATUTORY NOTES

Revision Notes and Legislative Reports

2005 Acts. House Report No. 109–31(Part I), see 2005 U.S. Code Cong. and Adm. News, p. 88.

Effective and Applicability Provisions

2005 Acts. Amendments by Pub.L. 109–8 effective, except as otherwise provided, 180 days after April 20, 2005, and inapplicable with respect to cases commenced under Title 11 before the effective date, see Pub.L. 109–8, § 1501, set out as a note under 11 U.S.C.A. § 101.

§ 1517. Order granting recognition

(a) Subject to section 1506, after notice and a hearing, an order recognizing a foreign proceeding shall be entered if—

(1) such foreign proceeding for which recognition is sought is a foreign main proceeding or foreign nonmain proceeding within the meaning of section 1502;

(2) the foreign representative applying for recognition is a person or body; and

(3) the petition meets the requirements of section 1515.

(b) Such foreign proceeding shall be recognized—

(1) as a foreign main proceeding if it is pending in the country where the debtor has the center of its main interests; or

(2) as a foreign nonmain proceeding if the debtor has an establishment within the meaning of section 1502 in the foreign country where the proceeding is pending.

(c) A petition for recognition of a foreign proceeding shall be decided upon at the earliest possible time. Entry of an order recognizing a foreign proceeding constitutes recognition under this chapter.

(d) The provisions of this subchapter do not prevent modification or termination of recognition if it is shown that the grounds for granting it were fully or partially lacking or have ceased to exist, but in considering such action the court shall give due weight to possible prejudice to parties that have relied upon the order granting recognition. A case under this chapter may be closed in the manner prescribed under section 350.

(Added Pub.L. 109–8, Title VIII, § 801(a), Apr. 20, 2005, 119 Stat. 139.)

HISTORICAL AND STATUTORY NOTES

Revision Notes and Legislative Reports

2005 Acts. House Report No. 109–31(Part I), see 2005 U.S. Code Cong. and Adm. News, p. 88.

Effective and Applicability Provisions

2005 Acts. Amendments by Pub.L. 109–8 effective, except as otherwise provided, 180 days after April 20, 2005, and inapplicable with respect to cases commenced under Title 11 before the effective date, see Pub.L. 109–8, § 1501, set out as a note under 11 U.S.C.A. § 101.

§ 1518. Subsequent information

From the time of filing the petition for recognition of a foreign proceeding, the foreign representative shall file with the court promptly a notice of change of status concerning—

(1) any substantial change in the status of such foreign proceeding or the status of the foreign representative's appointment; and

(2) any other foreign proceeding regarding the debtor that becomes known to the foreign representative.

(Added Pub.L. 109–8, Title VIII, § 801(a), Apr. 20, 2005, 119 Stat. 140.)

HISTORICAL AND STATUTORY NOTES

Revision Notes and Legislative Reports

2005 Acts. House Report No. 109–31(Part I), see 2005 U.S. Code Cong. and Adm. News, p. 88.

Effective and Applicability Provisions

2005 Acts. Amendments by Pub.L. 109–8 effective, except as otherwise provided, 180 days after April 20, 2005, and inapplicable with respect to cases commenced under Title 11 before the effective date, see Pub.L. 109–8, § 1501, set out as a note under 11 U.S.C.A. § 101.

§ 1519. Relief that may be granted upon filing petition for recognition

(a) From the time of filing a petition for recognition until the court rules on the petition, the court may, at the request of the foreign representative, where relief is urgently needed to protect the assets of the debtor or the interests of the creditors, grant relief of a provisional nature, including—

(1) staying execution against the debtor's assets;

(2) entrusting the administration or realization of all or part of the debtor's assets located in the United States to the foreign representative or another person authorized by the court, including an examiner, in order to protect and preserve the value of assets that, by their nature or because of other circumstances, are perishable, susceptible to devaluation or otherwise in jeopardy; and

(3) any relief referred to in paragraph (3), (4), or (7) of section 1521(a).

(b) Unless extended under section 1521(a)(6), the relief granted under this section terminates when the petition for recognition is granted.

(c) It is a ground for denial of relief under this section that such relief would interfere with the administration of a foreign main proceeding.

(d) The court may not enjoin a police or regulatory act of a governmental unit, including a criminal action or proceeding, under this section.

(e) The standards, procedures, and limitations applicable to an injunction shall apply to relief under this section.

(f) The exercise of rights not subject to the stay arising under section 362(a) pursuant to paragraph (6), (7), (17), or (27) of section 362(b) or pursuant to section 362(n) shall not be stayed by any order of a court or administrative agency in any proceeding under this chapter.

(Added Pub.L. 109–8, Title VIII, § 801(a), Apr. 20, 2005, 119 Stat. 140.)

HISTORICAL AND STATUTORY NOTES

Revision Notes and Legislative Reports

2005 Acts. House Report No. 109–31(Part I), see 2005 U.S. Code Cong. and Adm. News, p. 88.

Effective and Applicability Provisions

2005 Acts. Amendments by Pub.L. 109–8 effective, except as otherwise provided, 180 days after April 20, 2005, and inapplicable with respect to cases commenced under Title 11 before the effective date, see Pub.L. 109–8, § 1501, set out as a note under 11 U.S.C.A. § 101.

§ 1520. Effects of recognition of a foreign main proceeding

(a) Upon recognition of a foreign proceeding that is a foreign main proceeding—

(1) sections 361 and 362 apply with respect to the debtor and the property of the debtor that is within the territorial jurisdiction of the United States;

(2) sections 363, 549, and 552 apply to a transfer of an interest of the debtor in property that is within the territorial jurisdiction of the United States to the same extent that the sections would apply to property of an estate;

(3) unless the court orders otherwise, the foreign representative may operate the debtor's business and may exercise the rights and powers of a trustee under and to the extent provided by sections 363 and 552; and

(4) section 552 applies to property of the debtor that is within the territorial jurisdiction of the United States.

(b) Subsection (a) does not affect the right to commence an individual action or proceeding in a foreign country to the extent necessary to preserve a claim against the debtor.

(c) Subsection (a) does not affect the right of a foreign representative or an entity to file a petition commencing a case under this title or the right of any party to file claims or take other proper actions in such a case.

(Added Pub.L. 109–8, Title VIII, § 801(a), Apr. 20, 2005, 119 Stat. 141.)

HISTORICAL AND STATUTORY NOTES

Revision Notes and Legislative Reports

2005 Acts. House Report No. 109–31(Part I), see 2005 U.S. Code Cong. and Adm. News, p. 88.

Effective and Applicability Provisions

2005 Acts. Amendments by Pub.L. 109–8 effective, except as otherwise provided, 180 days after April 20, 2005, and inapplicable with respect to cases commenced under Title 11 before the effective date, see Pub.L. 109–8, § 1501, set out as a note under 11 U.S.C.A. § 101.

§ 1521. Relief that may be granted upon recognition

(a) Upon recognition of a foreign proceeding, whether main or nonmain, where necessary to effectuate the purpose of this chapter and to protect the assets of the debtor or the interests of the creditors, the court may, at the request of the foreign representative, grant any appropriate relief, including—

(1) staying the commencement or continuation of an individual action or proceeding concerning the debtor's assets, rights, obligations or liabilities to the extent they have not been stayed under section 1520(a);

(2) staying execution against the debtor's assets to the extent it has not been stayed under section 1520(a);

(3) suspending the right to transfer, encumber or otherwise dispose of any assets of the debtor to the extent this right has not been suspended under section 1520(a);

(4) providing for the examination of witnesses, the taking of evidence or the delivery of information concerning the debtor's assets, affairs, rights, obligations or liabilities;

(5) entrusting the administration or realization of all or part of the debtor's assets within the territorial jurisdiction of the United States to the foreign representative or another person, including an examiner, authorized by the court;

(6) extending relief granted under section 1519(a); and

(7) granting any additional relief that may be available to a trustee, except for relief available under sections 522, 544, 545, 547, 548, 550, and 724(a).

(b) Upon recognition of a foreign proceeding, whether main or nonmain, the court may, at the request of the foreign representative, entrust the distribution of all or part of the debtor's assets located in the United States to the foreign representative or another person, including an examiner, authorized by the court, provided that the court is satisfied that the interests of creditors in the United States are sufficiently protected.

(c) In granting relief under this section to a representative of a foreign nonmain proceeding, the court must be satisfied that the relief relates to assets that, under the law of the United States, should be administered in the foreign nonmain proceeding or concerns information required in that proceeding.

(d) The court may not enjoin a police or regulatory act of a governmental unit, including a criminal action or proceeding, under this section.

(e) The standards, procedures, and limitations applicable to an injunction shall apply to relief under paragraphs (1), (2), (3), and (6) of subsection (a).

(f) The exercise of rights not subject to the stay arising under section 362(a) pursuant to paragraph (6), (7), (17), or (27) of section 362(b) or pursuant to section 362(n) shall not be stayed by any order of a court or administrative agency in any proceeding under this chapter.

(Added Pub.L. 109–8, Title VIII, § 801(a), Apr. 20, 2005, 119 Stat. 141.)

HISTORICAL AND STATUTORY NOTES

Revision Notes and Legislative Reports

2005 Acts. House Report No. 109–31(Part I), see 2005 U.S. Code Cong. and Adm. News, p. 88.

Effective and Applicability Provisions

2005 Acts. Amendments by Pub.L. 109–8 effective, except as otherwise provided, 180 days after April 20, 2005, and inapplicable with respect to cases commenced under Title 11 before the effective date, see Pub.L. 109–8, § 1501, set out as a note under 11 U.S.C.A. § 101.

§ 1522. Protection of creditors and other interested persons

(a) The court may grant relief under section 1519 or 1521, or may modify or terminate relief under subsection (c), only if the interests of the creditors and other interested entities, including the debtor, are sufficiently protected.

(b) The court may subject relief granted under section 1519 or 1521, or the operation of the debtor's business under section 1520(a)(3), to conditions it considers appropriate, including the giving of security or the filing of a bond.

(c) The court may, at the request of the foreign representative or an entity affected by relief granted under section 1519 or 1521, or at its own motion, modify or terminate such relief.

(d) Section 1104(d) shall apply to the appointment of an examiner under this chapter. Any examiner shall comply with the qualification requirements imposed on a trustee by section 322.

(Added Pub.L. 109–8, Title VIII, § 801(a), Apr. 20, 2005, 119 Stat. 142.)

HISTORICAL AND STATUTORY NOTES

Revision Notes and Legislative Reports

2005 Acts. House Report No. 109–31(Part I), see 2005 U.S. Code Cong. and Adm. News, p. 88.

Effective and Applicability Provisions

2005 Acts. Amendments by Pub.L. 109–8 effective, except as otherwise provided, 180 days after April 20, 2005, and inapplicable with respect to cases commenced under Title 11 before the effective date, see Pub.L. 109–8, § 1501, set out as a note under 11 U.S.C.A. § 101.

§ 1523. Actions to avoid acts detrimental to creditors

(a) Upon recognition of a foreign proceeding, the foreign representative has standing in a case concerning the debtor pending under another chapter of this title to initiate actions under sections 522, 544, 545, 547, 548, 550, 553, and 724(a).

(b) When a foreign proceeding is a foreign nonmain proceeding, the court must be satisfied that an action under subsection (a) relates to assets that, under United States law, should be administered in the foreign nonmain proceeding.

(Added Pub.L. 109–8, Title VIII, § 801(a), Apr. 20, 2005, 119 Stat. 142.)

HISTORICAL AND STATUTORY NOTES

Revision Notes and Legislative Reports

2005 Acts. House Report No. 109–31(Part I), see 2005 U.S. Code Cong. and Adm. News, p. 88.

Effective and Applicability Provisions

2005 Acts. Amendments by Pub.L. 109–8 effective, except as otherwise provided, 180 days after April 20, 2005, and inapplicable with respect to cases commenced under Title 11 before the effective date, see Pub.L. 109–8, § 1501, set out as a note under 11 U.S.C.A. § 101.

§ 1524. Intervention by a foreign representative

Upon recognition of a foreign proceeding, the foreign representative may intervene in any proceedings in a State or Federal court in the United States in which the debtor is a party.

(Added Pub.L. 109–8, Title VIII, § 801(a), Apr. 20, 2005, 119 Stat. 142.)

HISTORICAL AND STATUTORY NOTES

Revision Notes and Legislative Reports

2005 Acts. House Report No. 109–31(Part I), see 2005 U.S. Code Cong. and Adm. News, p. 88.

Effective and Applicability Provisions

2005 Acts. Amendments by Pub.L. 109–8 effective, except as otherwise provided, 180 days after April 20, 2005, and inapplicable with respect to cases commenced under Title 11 before the effective date, see Pub.L. 109–8, § 1501, set out as a note under 11 U.S.C.A. § 101.

SUBCHAPTER IV—COOPERATION WITH FOREIGN COURTS AND FOREIGN REPRESENTATIVES

§ 1525. Cooperation and direct communication between the court and foreign courts or foreign representatives

(a) Consistent with section 1501, the court shall cooperate to the maximum extent possible with a foreign court or a foreign representative, either directly or through the trustee.

(b) The court is entitled to communicate directly with, or to request information or assistance directly from, a foreign court or a foreign representative, subject to the rights of a party in interest to notice and participation.

(Added Pub.L. 109–8, Title VIII, § 801(a), Apr. 20, 2005, 119 Stat. 143.)

HISTORICAL AND STATUTORY NOTES

Revision Notes and Legislative Reports

2005 Acts. House Report No. 109–31(Part I), see 2005 U.S. Code Cong. and Adm. News, p. 88.

Effective and Applicability Provisions

2005 Acts. Amendments by Pub.L. 109–8 effective, except as otherwise provided, 180 days after April 20, 2005, and inapplicable with respect to cases commenced under Title 11 before the effective date, see Pub.L. 109–8, § 1501, set out as a note under 11 U.S.C.A. § 101.

§ 1526. Cooperation and direct communication between the trustee and foreign courts or foreign representatives

(a) Consistent with section 1501, the trustee or other person, including an examiner, authorized by the court, shall, subject to the supervision of the court, cooperate to the maximum extent possible with a foreign court or a foreign representative.

(b) The trustee or other person, including an examiner, authorized by the court is entitled, subject to the supervision of the court, to communicate directly with a foreign court or a foreign representative.

(Added Pub.L. 109–8, Title VIII, § 801(a), Apr. 20, 2005, 119 Stat. 143.)

HISTORICAL AND STATUTORY NOTES

Revision Notes and Legislative Reports

2005 Acts. House Report No. 109–31(Part I), see 2005 U.S. Code Cong. and Adm. News, p. 88.

Effective and Applicability Provisions

2005 Acts. Amendments by Pub.L. 109–8 effective, except as otherwise provided, 180 days after April 20, 2005, and inapplicable with respect to cases commenced under Title 11 before the effective date, see Pub.L. 109–8, § 1501, set out as a note under 11 U.S.C.A. § 101.

§ 1527. Forms of cooperation

Cooperation referred to in sections 1525 and 1526 may be implemented by any appropriate means, including—

(1) appointment of a person or body, including an examiner, to act at the direction of the court;

(2) communication of information by any means considered appropriate by the court;

(3) coordination of the administration and supervision of the debtor's assets and affairs;

(4) approval or implementation of agreements concerning the coordination of proceedings; and

(5) coordination of concurrent proceedings regarding the same debtor.

(Added Pub.L. 109–8, Title VIII, § 801(a), Apr. 20, 2005, 119 Stat. 143.)

HISTORICAL AND STATUTORY NOTES

Revision Notes and Legislative Reports

2005 Acts. House Report No. 109–31(Part I), see 2005 U.S. Code Cong. and Adm. News, p. 88.

Effective and Applicability Provisions

2005 Acts. Amendments by Pub.L. 109–8 effective, except as otherwise provided, 180 days after April 20, 2005, and inapplicable with respect to cases commenced under Title 11 before the effective date, see Pub.L. 109–8, § 1501, set out as a note under 11 U.S.C.A. § 101.

SUBCHAPTER V—CONCURRENT PROCEEDINGS

§ 1528. Commencement of a case under this title after recognition of a foreign main proceeding

After recognition of a foreign main proceeding, a case under another chapter of this title may be commenced only if the debtor has assets in the United States. The effects of such case shall be restricted to the assets of the debtor that are within the territorial jurisdiction of the United States and, to the extent necessary to implement cooperation and coordination under sections 1525, 1526, and 1527, to other assets of the debtor that are within the jurisdiction of the court under sections 541(a) of this title, and 1334(e) of title 28, to the extent that such other assets are not subject to the jurisdiction and control of a foreign proceeding that has been recognized under this chapter.

(Added Pub.L. 109–8, Title VIII, § 801(a), Apr. 20, 2005, 119 Stat. 143.)

HISTORICAL AND STATUTORY NOTES

Revision Notes and Legislative Reports

2005 Acts. House Report No. 109–31(Part I), see 2005 U.S. Code Cong. and Adm. News, p. 88.

Effective and Applicability Provisions

2005 Acts. Amendments by Pub.L. 109–8 effective, except as otherwise provided, 180 days after April 20, 2005, and inapplicable with respect to cases commenced under Title 11 before the effective date, see Pub.L. 109–8, § 1501, set out as a note under 11 U.S.C.A. § 101.

§ 1529. Coordination of a case under this title and a foreign proceeding

If a foreign proceeding and a case under another chapter of this title are pending concurrently regarding the same debtor, the court shall seek cooperation and coordination under sections 1525, 1526, and 1527, and the following shall apply:

(1) If the case in the United States pending at the time the petition for recognition of such foreign proceeding is filed—

(A) any relief granted under section 1519 or 1521 must be consistent with the relief granted in the case in the United States; and

(B) section 1520 does not apply even if such foreign proceeding is recognized as a foreign main proceeding.

(2) If a case in the United States under this title commences after recognition, or after the date of the filing of the petition for recognition, of such foreign proceeding—

(A) any relief in effect under section 1519 or 1521 shall be reviewed by the court and shall be modified or terminated if inconsistent with the case in the United States; and

(B) if such foreign proceeding is a foreign main proceeding, the stay and suspension referred to in section 1520(a) shall be modified or terminated if inconsistent with the relief granted in the case in the United States.

(3) In granting, extending, or modifying relief granted to a representative of a foreign nonmain proceeding, the court must be satisfied that the relief relates to assets that, under the laws of the United States, should be administered in the foreign nonmain proceeding or concerns information required in that proceeding.

(4) In achieving cooperation and coordination under sections 1528 and 1529, the court may grant any of the relief authorized under section 305.

(Added Pub.L. 109–8, Title VIII, § 801(a), Apr. 20, 2005, 119 Stat. 144.)

HISTORICAL AND STATUTORY NOTES

Revision Notes and Legislative Reports

2005 Acts. House Report No. 109–31(Part I), see 2005 U.S. Code Cong. and Adm. News, p. 88.

Effective and Applicability Provisions

2005 Acts. Amendments by Pub.L. 109–8 effective, except as otherwise provided, 180 days after April 20, 2005, and inapplicable with respect to cases commenced under Title 11

before the effective date, see Pub.L. 109–8, § 1501, set out as a note under 11 U.S.C.A. § 101.

§ 1530. Coordination of more than 1 foreign proceeding

In matters referred to in section 1501, with respect to more than 1 foreign proceeding regarding the debtor, the court shall seek cooperation and coordination under sections 1525, 1526, and 1527, and the following shall apply:

(1) Any relief granted under section 1519 or 1521 to a representative of a foreign nonmain proceeding after recognition of a foreign main proceeding must be consistent with the foreign main proceeding.

(2) If a foreign main proceeding is recognized after recognition, or after the filing of a petition for recognition, of a foreign nonmain proceeding, any relief in effect under section 1519 or 1521 shall be reviewed by the court and shall be modified or terminated if inconsistent with the foreign main proceeding.

(3) If, after recognition of a foreign nonmain proceeding, another foreign nonmain proceeding is recognized, the court shall grant, modify, or terminate relief for the purpose of facilitating coordination of the proceedings.

(Added Pub.L. 109–8, Title VIII, § 801(a), Apr. 20, 2005, 119 Stat. 144.)

HISTORICAL AND STATUTORY NOTES

Revision Notes and Legislative Reports

2005 Acts. House Report No. 109–31(Part I), see 2005 U.S. Code Cong. and Adm. News, p. 88.

Effective and Applicability Provisions

2005 Acts. Amendments by Pub.L. 109–8 effective, except as otherwise provided, 180 days after April 20, 2005, and inapplicable with respect to cases commenced under Title 11 before the effective date, see Pub.L. 109–8, § 1501, set out as a note under 11 U.S.C.A. § 101.

§ 1531. Presumption of insolvency based on recognition of a foreign main proceeding

In the absence of evidence to the contrary, recognition of a foreign main proceeding is, for the purpose of commencing a proceeding under section 303, proof that the debtor is generally not paying its debts as such debts become due.

(Added Pub.L. 109–8, Title VIII, § 801(a), Apr. 20, 2005, 119 Stat. 144.)

HISTORICAL AND STATUTORY NOTES

Revision Notes and Legislative Reports

2005 Acts. House Report No. 109–31(Part I), see 2005 U.S. Code Cong. and Adm. News, p. 88.

Effective and Applicability Provisions

2005 Acts. Amendments by Pub.L. 109–8 effective, except as otherwise provided, 180 days after April 20, 2005, and inapplicable with respect to cases commenced under Title 11 before the effective date, see Pub.L. 109–8, § 1501, set out as a note under 11 U.S.C.A. § 101.

§ 1532. Rule of payment in concurrent proceedings

Without prejudice to secured claims or rights in rem, a creditor who has received payment with respect to its claim in a foreign proceeding pursuant to a law relating to insolvency may not receive a payment for the same claim in a case under any other chapter of this title regarding the debtor, so long as the payment to other creditors of the same class is proportionately less than the payment the creditor has already received.

(Added Pub.L. 109–8, Title VIII, § 801(a), Apr. 20, 2005, 119 Stat. 145.)

HISTORICAL AND STATUTORY NOTES

Revision Notes and Legislative Reports

2005 Acts. House Report No. 109–31(Part I), see 2005 U.S. Code Cong. and Adm. News, p. 88.

Effective and Applicability Provisions

2005 Acts. Amendments by Pub.L. 109–8 effective, except as otherwise provided, 180 days after April 20, 2005, and inapplicable with respect to cases commenced under Title 11 before the effective date, see Pub.L. 109–8, § 1501, set out as a note under 11 U.S.C.A. § 101.

[§§ 15101 to 151326. Repealed. Pub.L. 99–554, Title II, § 231, Oct. 27, 1986, 100 Stat. 3103]

HISTORICAL AND STATUTORY NOTES

Section 15101, Pub.L. 95–598, Nov. 6, 1978, 92 Stat. 2652, defined terms "entity" and "governmental unit".

Section 15102, Pub.L. 95–598, Nov. 6, 1978, 92 Stat. 2652, set forth rule of construction.

Section 15103, Pub.L. 95–598, Nov. 6, 1978, 92 Stat. 2652; Pub.L. 98–353, Title III, §§ 311(b)(3), 318(b), July 10, 1984, 98 Stat. 355, 357, set forth applicability of subchapters and sections.

Section 15303, Pub.L. 95–598, Nov. 6, 1978, 92 Stat. 2653, set forth provisions relating to involuntary cases.

Section 15321, Pub.L. 95–598, Nov. 6, 1978, 92 Stat. 2653, related to eligibility to serve as trustee.

Section 15322, Pub.L. 95–598, Nov. 6, 1978, 92 Stat. 2653, related to qualifications of trustees.

Section 15324, Pub.L. 95–598, Nov. 6, 1978, 92 Stat. 2653, related to removal of trustee or examiner.

Section 15326, Pub.L. 95–598, Nov. 6, 1978, 92 Stat. 2653, related to limitation on compensation of trustees.

Section 15330, Pub.L. 95–598, Nov. 6, 1978, 92 Stat. 2653, set forth compensation of officers.

Section 15343, Pub.L. 95–598, Nov. 6, 1978, 92 Stat. 2653, related to examination of the debtor.

Section 15345, Pub.L. 95–598, Nov. 6, 1978, 92 Stat. 2654; Pub.L. 97–258, § 3(c), Sept. 13, 1982, 96 Stat. 1064, related to money of estates.

Section 15701, Pub.L. 95–598, Nov. 6, 1978, 92 Stat. 2654, related to appointment, etc., of interim trustee.

Section 15703, Pub.L. 95–598, Nov. 6, 1978, 92 Stat. 2654, related to successor trustee.

Section 15704, Pub.L. 95–598, Nov. 6, 1978, 92 Stat. 2655, related to duties of trustees.

Section 15727, Pub.L. 95–598, Nov. 6, 1978, 92 Stat. 2655, set forth provisions relating to discharge under section 727(a) of this title.

Section 151102, Pub.L. 95–598, Nov. 6, 1978, 92 Stat. 2655, set forth provisions relating to creditors' and equity security holders' committees.

Section 151104, Pub.L. 95–598, Nov. 6, 1978, 92 Stat. 2655, related to appointment of trustee or examiner in reorganization matters.

Section 151105, Pub.L. 95–598, Nov. 6, 1978, 92 Stat. 2656, related to termination of trustee's appointment.

Section 151163, Pub.L. 95–598, Nov. 6, 1978, 92 Stat. 2656, related to appointment of trustee.

Section 151302, Pub.L. 95–598, Nov. 6, 1978, 92 Stat. 2656; Pub.L. 98–353, Title III, §§ 311(b)(4), 534, July 10, 1984, 98 Stat. 355, 390, related to functions of trustee with respect to adjustment of debts of an individual with regular income.

Section 151326, Pub.L. 95–598, Nov. 6, 1978, 92 Stat. 2657, set forth provisions relating to payments.

Effective and Applicability Provisions of Repeal

Repeal of sections by Pub.L. 99–554 effective 30 days after Oct. 27, 1986, except as otherwise provided for, see section 302 of Pub.L. 99–554, set out as a note under section 581 of Title 28, Judiciary and Judicial Procedure.

Repeal of sections not applicable in or with respect to Northern District of Alabama until March 1, 1987, or the effective date of any election made under section 302(d)(3)(A) of Pub.L. 99–554, whichever occurs first, see section 302(d)(3)(H) of Pub.L. 99–554, set out as a note under section 581 of Title 28.

Pub.L. 95–598, Title IV, § 408(c), Nov. 6, 1978, 92 Stat. 2687, as amended Pub.L. 98–166, Title II, § 200, Nov. 28, 1983, 97 Stat. 1081; Pub.L. 98–353, Title III, § 323, July 10, 1984, 98 Stat. 358; Pub.L. 99–429, Sept. 30, 1986, 100 Stat. 985; Pub.L. 99–500, § 101(b) [Title II, § 200], Oct. 18, 1986, 100 Stat. 1783–39, 1783–45, and Pub.L. 99–591, § 101(b) [Title II, § 200], Oct. 30, 1986, 100 Stat. 3341–39, 3341–45; Pub.L. 99–554, Title III, § 307(a), Oct. 27, 1986, 100 Stat. 3125, which provided for the repeal of this chapter at a prospective date, was repealed by Pub.L. 99–554, Title III, § 307(b), Oct. 27, 1986, 100 Stat. 3125.

RELATED PROVISIONS
OF
U.S. CODE TITLES 18 AND 28

TITLE 18
CRIMES AND CRIMINAL PROCEDURE

CHAPTER 9—BANKRUPTCY

§ 151. Definition

As used in this chapter, the term "debtor" means a debtor concerning whom a petition has been filed under Title 11.

(June 25, 1948, c. 645, 62 Stat. 689; Nov. 6, 1978, Pub.L. 95–598, Title III, § 314(b)(1), 92 Stat. 2676; Sept. 13, 1994, Pub.L. 103–322, Title XXXIII, § 330008(5), 108 Stat. 2143.)

HISTORICAL AND STATUTORY NOTES

Revision Notes and Legislative Reports

1948 Acts. Based on § 52(f) of Title 11, U.S.C., 1940, ed., Bankruptcy (July 1, 1898, c. 541, § 29f as added June 22, 1938, c. 575, § 1, 52 Stat. 857).

Definition of "bankruptcy" was added to avoid repetitious references to said Title 11.

Minor changes in phraseology were made. 80th Congress House Report No. 304.

1994 Acts. House Report Nos. 103–324 and 103–489, and House Conference Report No. 103–711, see 1994 U.S. Code Cong. and Adm. News, p. 1801.

Effective and Applicability Provisions

1978 Acts. Amendment by Pub.L. 95–598 effective Oct. 1, 1979, see section 402(a) of Pub.L. 95–598, set out as a note preceding section 101 of Title 11, Bankruptcy.

Savings Provisions

Amendment by section 314 of Pub. L. 95–598 not to affect the application of this chapter to any act of any person (1) committed before Oct. 1, 1979, or (2) committed after Oct. 1, 1979, in connection with a case commenced before such date, see section 403(d) of Pub. L. 95–598, set out preceding section 101 of Title 11, Bankruptcy.

CROSS REFERENCES

Meaning of words and phrases in bankruptcy proceedings, see 11 USCA § 101.

§ 152. Concealment of assets; false oaths and claims; bribery

A person who—

(1) knowingly and fraudulently conceals from a custodian, trustee, marshal, or other officer of the court charged with the control or custody of property, or, in connection with a case under title 11, from creditors or the United States Trustee, any property belonging to the estate of a debtor;

(2) knowingly and fraudulently makes a false oath or account in or in relation to any case under title 11;

(3) knowingly and fraudulently makes a false declaration, certificate, verification, or statement under penalty of perjury as permitted under section 1746 of title 28, in or in relation to any case under title 11;

(4) knowingly and fraudulently presents any false claim for proof against the estate of a debtor, or uses any such claim in any case under title 11, in a personal capacity or as or through an agent, proxy, or attorney;

(5) knowingly and fraudulently receives any material amount of property from a debtor after the filing of a case under title 11, with intent to defeat the provisions of title 11;

(6) knowingly and fraudulently gives, offers, receives, or attempts to obtain any money or property, remuneration, compensation, reward, advantage, or promise thereof for acting or forbearing to act in any case under title 11;

(7) in a personal capacity or as an agent or officer of any person or corporation, in contemplation of a case under title 11 by or against the person or any other person or corporation, or with intent to defeat the provisions of title 11, knowingly and fraudulently transfers or conceals any of his property or the property of such other person or corporation;

(8) after the filing of a case under title 11 or in contemplation thereof, knowingly and fraudulently conceals, destroys, mutilates, falsifies, or makes a false entry in any recorded information (including books, documents, records, and papers) relating to the property or financial affairs of a debtor; or

(9) after the filing of a case under title 11, knowingly and fraudulently withholds from a custodian, trustee, marshal, or other officer of the court or a United States Trustee entitled to its possession, any recorded information (including books, documents, records, and papers) relating to the property or financial affairs of a debtor,

shall be fined under this title, imprisoned not more than 5 years, or both.

(June 25, 1948, c. 645, 62 Stat. 689; June 12, 1960, Pub.L. 86–519, § 2, 74 Stat. 217; Sept. 2, 1960, Pub.L. 86–701, 74 Stat. 753; Oct. 18, 1976, Pub.L. 94–550, § 4, 90 Stat. 2535; Nov. 6, 1978, Pub.L. 95–598, Title III, § 314(a), (c), 92 Stat. 2676, 2677; Nov. 18, 1988, Pub.L. 100–690, Title VII, § 7017, 102 Stat. 4395; Sept. 13, 1994, Pub.L. 103–322, Title XXXIII, § 330016(1)(K), 108 Stat. 2147; Oct. 22, 1994, Pub.L. 103–394, Title III, § 312(a)(1)(A), 108 Stat. 4138; Oct. 11, 1996, Pub.L. 104–294, Title VI, § 601(a)(1), 110 Stat. 3498.)

HISTORICAL AND STATUTORY NOTES

Revision Notes and Legislative Reports

1948 Acts. Based on § 52(b) of Title 11, U.S.C., 1940 ed., Bankruptcy (July 1, 1898, c. 541, § 29b, 30 Stat. 554; May 27, 1926, c. 406, § 11 (part), 44 Stat. 665; June 22, 1938, c. 575, § 1 (part), 52 Stat. 855).

Section was broadened to apply to one who gives or offers a bribe.

Minor changes were made in phraseology. 80th Congress House Report No. 304.

1960 Acts. Senate Report No. 1477, see 1960 U.S. Code Cong. and Adm. News, p. 2396.

Senate Report No. 974, see 1960 U.S. Code Cong. and Adm. News, p. 3307.

1976 Acts. House Report No. 94–1616, see 1976 U.S. Code Cong. and Adm. News, p. 5644.

1988 Acts. For Related Reports, see 1988 U.S. Code Cong. and Adm. News, p. 5937.

1994 Acts. House Report Nos. 103–324 and 103–489, and House Conference Report No. 103–711, see 1994 U.S. Code Cong. and Adm. News, p. 1801.

House Report No. 103–835, see 1994 U.S. Code Cong. and Adm. News, p. 3340.

1996 Acts. House Report No. 104–788, see 1996 U.S. Code Cong. and Adm. News, p. 4021.

Effective and Applicability Provisions

1994 Acts. Amendment by Pub.L. 103–394 effective on Oct. 22, 1994, and not to apply with respect to cases commenced under Title 11 of the United States Code before Oct. 22, 1994, see section 702 of Pub.L. 103–394, set out as a note under section 101 of Title 11, Bankruptcy.

1978 Acts. Amendment by Pub.L. 95–598 effective Oct. 1, 1979, see section 402(a) of Pub.L. 95–598, set out as a note preceding section 101 of Title 11, Bankruptcy.

Separability of Provisions

If any provision of or amendment made by Pub.L. 103–394 or the application of such provision or amendment to any person or circumstance is held to be unconstitutional, the remaining provisions of and amendments made by Pub.L. 103–394 and the application of such provisions and amendments to any person or circumstance shall not be affected thereby, see section 701 of Pub.L. 103–394, set out as a note under section 101 of Title 11, Bankruptcy.

Savings Provisions

Amendment by section 314 of Pub. L. 95–598 not to affect the application of this chapter to any act of any person (1) committed before Oct. 1, 1979, or (2) committed after Oct. 1, 1979, in connection with a case commenced before such date, see section 403(d) of Pub. L. 95–598, set out preceding section 101 of Title 11, Bankruptcy.

CROSS REFERENCES

Bankruptcy investigations; duties of United States attorney, see 18 USCA § 3057.

Discharges, refusal to grant when offense committed under this section, see 11 USCA § 727.

Examination of bankrupt, evidence as inadmissible in criminal proceedings, see 11 USCA § 521.

Limitation of prosecutions, see 18 USCA §§ 3282 and 3284.

§ 153. Embezzlement against estate

(a) Offense.—A person described in subsection (b) who knowingly and fraudulently appropriates to the person's own use, embezzles, spends, or transfers any property or secretes or destroys any document belonging to the estate of a debtor shall be fined under this title, imprisoned not more than 5 years, or both.

(b) Person to whom section applies.—A person described in this subsection is one who has access to property or documents belonging to an estate by virtue of the person's participation in the administration of the estate as a trustee, custodian, marshal, attorney, or other officer of the court or as an agent, employee, or other person engaged by such an officer to perform a service with respect to the estate.

(June 25, 1948, c. 645, 62 Stat. 690; Nov. 6, 1978, Pub.L. 95–598, Title III, § 314(a)(1), (d)(1), (2), 92 Stat. 2676, 2677; Sept. 13, 1994, Pub.L. 103–322, Title XXXIII, § 330016(1)(K), 108 Stat. 2147; Oct. 22, 1994, Pub.L. 103–394, Title III, § 312(a)(1)(A), 108 Stat. 4139; Oct. 11, 1996, Pub.L. 104–294, Title VI, § 601(a)(1), 110 Stat. 3498.)

HISTORICAL AND STATUTORY NOTES

Revision Notes and Legislative Reports

1948 Acts. Based on § 52(a) of Title 11, U.S.C., 1940 ed., Bankruptcy (July 1, 1898, c. 541, § 29a, 30 Stat. 554; May 27, 1926, c. 406, § 11 (part), 44 Stat. 665; June 22, 1938, c. 575, § 1 (part), 52 Stat. 855).

Minor changes were made in phraseology. 80th Congress House Report No. 304.

1960 Acts. Senate Report No. 1477, see 1960 U.S. Code Cong. and Adm. News, p. 2396.

Senate Report No. 974, see 1960 U.S. Code Cong. and Adm. News, p. 3307.

1994 Acts. House Report Nos. 103–324 and 103–489, and House Conference Report No. 103–711, see 1994 U.S. Code Cong. and Adm. News, p. 1801.

House Report No. 103–835, see 1994 U.S. Code Cong. and Adm. News, p. 3340.

1996 Acts. House Report No. 104–788, see 1996 U.S. Code Cong. and Adm. News, p. 4021.

Effective and Applicability Provisions

1994 Acts. Amendment by Pub.L. 103–394 effective on Oct. 22, 1994, and not to apply with respect to cases commenced under Title 11 of the United States Code before Oct. 22, 1994, see section 702 of Pub.L. 103–394, set out as a note under section 101 of Title 11, Bankruptcy.

1978 Acts. Amendment by Pub.L. 95–598 effective Oct. 1, 1979, see section 402(a) of Pub.L. 95–598, set out as a note preceding section 101 of Title 11, Bankruptcy.

Savings Provisions

Amendment by section 314 of Pub. L. 95–598 not to affect the application of this chapter to any act of any person (1) committed before Oct. 1, 1979, or (2) committed after Oct. 1, 1979, in connection with a case commenced before such date, see section 403(d) of Pub. L. 95–598, set out preceding section 101 of Title 11, Bankruptcy.

Separability of Provisions

If any provision of or amendment made by Pub.L. 103–394 or the application of such provision or amendment to any person or circumstance is held to be unconstitutional, the remaining provisions of and amendments made by Pub.L. 103–394 and the application of such provisions and amendments to any person or circumstance shall not be affected thereby, see section 701 of Pub.L. 103–394, set out as a note under section 101 of Title 11, Bankruptcy.

CROSS REFERENCES

Debts of bankrupt created by fraud, embezzlement, misappropriation or defalcation while acting as an officer or in any fiduciary capacity as not affected by a discharge, see 11 USCA § 523.

Embezzlement by court officers, generally, see 18 USCA § 645.

§ 154. Adverse interest and conduct of officers

A person who, being a custodian, trustee, marshal, or other officer of the court—

(1) knowingly purchases, directly or indirectly, any property of the estate of which the person is such an officer in a case under title 11;

(2) knowingly refuses to permit a reasonable opportunity for the inspection by parties in interest of the documents and accounts relating to the affairs of estates in the person's charge by parties when directed by the court to do so; or

(3) knowingly refuses to permit a reasonable opportunity for the inspection by the United States Trustee of the documents and accounts relating to the affairs of an estate in the person's charge,

shall be fined under this title and shall forfeit the person's office, which shall thereupon become vacant.

(June 25, 1948, c. 645, 62 Stat. 690; Nov. 6, 1978, Pub.L. 95–598, Title III, § 314(a)(2), (e)(1), (2), 92 Stat. 2676, 2677; Sept. 13, 1994, Pub.L. 103–322, Title XXXIII, § 330016(1)(G), 108 Stat. 2147; Oct. 22, 1994, Pub.L. 103–394, Title III, § 312(a)(1)(A), 108 Stat. 4139; Oct. 11, 1996, Pub.L. 104–294, Title VI, § 601(a)(1), 110 Stat. 3498.)

HISTORICAL AND STATUTORY NOTES

Revision Notes and Legislative Reports

1948 Acts. Based on § 52(c) of Title 11, U.S.C., 1940 ed., Bankruptcy (July 1, 1898, c. 541, § 29c, 30 Stat. 554; June 22, 1938, c. 575, § 1, (part), 52 Stat. 856).

Minor changes were made in phraseology. 80th Congress House Report No. 304.

1994 Acts. House Report Nos. 103–324 and 103–489, and House Conference Report No. 103–711, see 1994 U.S. Code Cong. and Adm. News, p. 1801.

House Report No. 103–835, see 1994 U.S. Code Cong. and Adm. News, p. 3340.

1996 Acts. House Report No. 104–788, see 1996 U.S. Code Cong. and Adm. News, p. 4021.

Effective and Applicability Provisions

1994 Acts. Amendment by Pub.L. 103–394 effective on Oct. 22, 1994, and not to apply with respect to cases commenced under Title 11 of the United States Code before Oct. 22, 1994, see section 702 of Pub.L. 103–394, set out as a note under section 101 of Title 11, Bankruptcy.

1978 Acts. Amendment by Pub.L. 95–598 effective Oct. 1, 1979, see section 402(a) of Pub.L. 95–598, set out as a note preceding section 101 of Title 11, Bankruptcy.

Savings Provisions

Amendment by section 314 of Pub. L. 95–598 not to affect the application of this chapter to any act of any person (1) committed before Oct. 1, 1979, or (2) committed after Oct. 1, 1979, in connection with a case commenced before such date, see section 403(d) of Pub. L. 95–598, set out preceding section 101 of Title 11, Bankruptcy.

Separability of Provisions

If any provision of or amendment made by Pub.L. 103–394 or the application of such provision or amendment to any person or circumstance is held to be unconstitutional, the remaining provisions of and amendments made by Pub.L. 103–394 and the application of such provisions and amendments to any person or circumstance shall not be affected thereby, see section 701 of Pub.L. 103–394, set out as a note under section 101 of Title 11, Bankruptcy.

§ 155. Fee agreements in cases under title 11 and receiverships

Whoever, being a party in interest, whether as a debtor, creditor, receiver, trustee or representative of any of them, or attorney for any such party in interest, in any receivership or case under title 11 in any United States court or under its supervision, knowingly and fraudulently enters into any agreement, express or implied, with another such party in interest or attorney for another such party in interest, for the purpose of fixing the fees or other compensation to be paid to any party in interest or to any attorney for any party in interest for services rendered in connection therewith, from the assets of the estate, shall be fined under this title or imprisoned not more than one year, or both.

(June 25, 1948, c. 645, 62 Stat. 690; May 24, 1949, c. 139, § 4, 63 Stat. 90; Nov. 6, 1978, Pub.L. 95–598, Title III, § 314(f)(1), (2) 92 Stat. 2677; Sept. 13, 1994, Pub.L. 103–322, Title XXXIII, § 330016(1)(K), 108 Stat. 2147.)

HISTORICAL AND STATUTORY NOTES

Revision Notes and Legislative Reports

1948 Acts. Based on § 572a of Title 28, U.S.C., 1940 ed., Judicial Code and Judiciary (Aug. 25, 1937, c. 777, 50 Stat. 810.

Words "upon conviction" were deleted as surplusage since punishment can be imposed only after a conviction.

A fine of "$5,000" was substituted for "$10,000" and "one year" for "five years", to reduce the offense to the grade of a misdemeanor and the punishment to an amount and term proportionate to the gravity of the offense.

Minor changes were made in phraseology. 80th Congress House Report No. 304.

1949 Acts. This amendment [see section 4] clarifies section 155 of Title 18, U.S.C., by restating the first paragraph thereof in closer conformity with the original law, as it existed at the time of the enactment of the revision of Title 18.

Senate Report No. 303 and House Report No. 352, see 1949 U.S. Code Cong. Service, p. 1248.

1994 Acts. House Report Nos. 103–324 and 103–489, and House Conference Report No. 103–711, see 1994 U.S. Code Cong. and Adm. News, p. 1801.

Effective and Applicability Provisions

1978 Acts. Amendment by Pub.L. 95–598 effective Oct. 1, 1979, see section 402(a) of Pub.L. 95–598, set out as a note preceding section 101 of Title 11, Bankruptcy.

Savings Provisions

Amendment by section 314 of Pub. L. 95–598 not to affect the application of this chapter to any act of any person (1) committed before Oct. 1, 1979, or (2) committed after Oct. 1, 1979, in connection with a case commenced before such date, see section 403(d) of Pub. L. 95–598, set out preceding section 101 of Title 11, Bankruptcy.

§ 156. Knowing disregard of bankruptcy law or rule

(a) Definitions.—In this section—

(1) the term "bankruptcy petition preparer" means a person, other than the debtor's attorney or an employee of such an attorney, who prepares for compensation a document for filing; and

(2) the term "document for filing" means a petition or any other document prepared for filing by a debtor in a United States bankruptcy court or a United States district court in connection with a case under title 11.

(b) Offense.—If a bankruptcy case or related proceeding is dismissed because of a knowing attempt by a bankruptcy petition preparer in any manner to disregard the requirements of title 11, United States Code, or the Federal Rules of Bankruptcy Procedure, the bankruptcy petition preparer shall be fined under this title, imprisoned not more than 1 year, or both.

(Added Pub.L. 103–394, Title III, § 312(a)(1)(B), Oct. 22, 1994, 108 Stat. 4140, and amended Pub.L. 109–8, Title XII, § 1220, Apr. 20, 2005, 119 Stat. 195.)

HISTORICAL AND STATUTORY NOTES

Revision Notes and Legislative Reports

1994 Acts. House Report No. 103–835, see 1994 U.S. Code Cong. and Adm. News, p. 3340.

2005 Acts. House Report No. 109–31(Part I), see 2005 U.S. Code Cong. and Adm. News, p. 88.

References in Text

The Federal Rules of Bankruptcy Procedure, referred to in subsec. (b), are set out in Title 11, Bankruptcy.

Effective and Applicability Provisions

2005 Acts. Except as otherwise provided, amendments by Pub.L. 109–8 effective 180 days after April 20, 2005, and inapplicable with respect to cases commenced under Title 11 before the effective date, see Pub.L. 109–8, § 1501, set out as a note under 11 U.S.C.A. § 101.

1994 Acts. Section effective on Oct. 22, 1994, and not to apply with respect to cases commenced under Title 11 of the United States Code before Oct. 22, 1994, see section 702 of Pub.L. 103–394, set out as a note under section 101 of Title 11, Bankruptcy.

Separability of Provisions

If any provision of or amendment made by Pub.L. 103–394 or the application of such provision or amendment to any person or circumstance is held to be unconstitutional, the remaining provisions of and amendments made by Pub.L. 103–394 and the application of such provisions and amendments to any person or circumstance shall not be affected thereby, see section 701 of Pub.L. 103–394, set out as a note under section 101 of Title 11, Bankruptcy.

§ 157. Bankruptcy fraud

A person who, having devised or intending to devise a scheme or artifice to defraud and for the purpose of executing or concealing such a scheme or artifice or attempting to do so—

(1) files a petition under title 11, including a fraudulent involuntary bankruptcy petition under section 303 of such title;

(2) files a document in a proceeding under title 11, including a fraudulent involuntary bankruptcy petition under section 303 of such title; or

(3) makes a false or fraudulent representation, claim, or promise concerning or in relation to a proceeding under title 11, including a fraudulent involuntary bankruptcy petition under section 303 of such title, at any time before or after the filing of the petition, or in relation to a proceeding falsely asserted to be pending under such title,

shall be fined under this title, imprisoned not more than 5 years, or both.

(Added Pub.L. 103–394, Title III, § 312(a)(1)(B), Oct. 22, 1994, 108 Stat. 4140, and amended Pub.L. 109–8, Title III, § 332(c), Apr. 20, 2005, 119 Stat. 103.)

HISTORICAL AND STATUTORY NOTES

Revision Notes and Legislative Reports

1994 Acts. House Report No. 103–835, see 1994 U.S. Code Cong. and Adm. News, p. 3340.

2005 Acts. House Report No. 109–31(Part I), see 2005 U.S. Code Cong. and Adm. News, p. 88.

Effective and Applicability Provisions

2005 Acts. Except as otherwise provided, amendments by Pub.L. 109–8 effective 180 days after April 20, 2005, and inapplicable with respect to cases commenced under Title 11 before the effective date, see Pub.L. 109–8, § 1501, set out as a note under 11 U.S.C.A. § 101.

1994 Acts. Section effective on Oct. 22, 1994, and not to apply with respect to cases commenced under Title 11 of the United States Code before Oct. 22, 1994, see section 702 of Pub.L. 103–394, set out as a note under section 101 of Title 11, Bankruptcy.

Separability of Provisions

If any provision of or amendment made by Pub.L. 103–394 or the application of such provision or amendment to any person or circumstance is held to be unconstitutional, the remaining provisions of and amendments made by Pub.L. 103–394 and the application of such provisions and amendments to any person or circumstance shall not be affected thereby, see section 701 of Pub.L. 103–394, set out as a note under section 101 of Title 11, Bankruptcy.

§ 158. Designation of United States attorneys and agents of the Federal Bureau of Investigation to address abusive reaffirmations of debt and materially fraudulent statements in bankruptcy schedules

(a) In general.—The Attorney General of the United States shall designate the individuals described in subsection (b) to have primary responsibility in carrying out enforcement activities in addressing violations of section 152 or 157 relating to abusive reaffirmations of debt. In addition to addressing the violations referred to in the preceding sentence, the individuals described under subsection (b) shall address violations of section 152 or 157 relating to materially fraudulent statements in bankruptcy schedules that are intentionally false or intentionally misleading.

(b) United States attorneys and agents of the Federal Bureau of Investigation.—The individuals referred to in subsection (a) are—

(1) the United States attorney for each judicial district of the United States; and

(2) an agent of the Federal Bureau of Investigation for each field office of the Federal Bureau of Investigation.

(c) Bankruptcy investigations.—Each United States attorney designated under this section shall, in addition to any other responsibilities, have primary responsibility for carrying out the duties of a United States attorney under section 3057.

(d) Bankruptcy procedures.—The bankruptcy courts shall establish procedures for referring any case that may contain a materially fraudulent statement in a bankruptcy schedule to the individuals designated under this section.

(Added Pub.L. 109–8, Title II, § 203(b)(1), Apr. 20, 2005, 119 Stat. 49.)

HISTORICAL AND STATUTORY NOTES

Revision Notes and Legislative Reports

2005 Acts. House Report No. 109–31(Part I), see 2005 U.S. Code Cong. and Adm. News, p. 88.

Effective and Applicability Provisions

2005 Acts. Except as otherwise provided, amendments by Pub.L. 109–8 effective 180 days after April 20, 2005, and inapplicable with respect to cases commenced under Title 11 before the effective date, see Pub.L. 109–8, § 1501, set out as a note under 11 U.S.C.A. § 101.

CHAPTER 73—OBSTRUCTION OF JUSTICE

§ 1519. Destruction, alteration, or falsification of records in Federal investigations and bankruptcy

Whoever knowingly alters, destroys, mutilates, conceals, covers up, falsifies, or makes a false entry in any record, document, or tangible object with the intent to impede, obstruct, or influence the investigation or proper administration of any matter within the jurisdiction of any department or agency of the United States or any case filed under title 11, or in relation to or contemplation of any such matter or case, shall be fined under this title, imprisoned not more than 20 years, or both.

(Added Pub.L. 107–204, Title VIII, § 802(a), July 30, 2002, 116 Stat. 800.)

HISTORICAL AND STATUTORY NOTES

Revision Notes and Legislative Reports

2002 Acts. House Conference Report No. 107–610 and Statement by President, see 2002 U.S. Code Cong. and Adm. News, p. 542.

CHAPTER 96—RACKETEER INFLUENCED AND CORRUPT ORGANIZATIONS

§ 1961. Definitions

As used in this chapter—

(1) "racketeering activity" means (A) any act or threat involving murder, kidnapping, gambling, arson, robbery, bribery, extortion, dealing in obscene matter, or dealing in a controlled substance or listed chemical (as defined in section 102 of the Controlled Substances Act), which is chargeable under State law and punishable by imprisonment for more than one year; (B) any act which is indictable under any of the following provisions of title 18, United States Code: Section 201 (relating to bribery), section 224 (relating to sports bribery), sections 471, 472, and 473 (relating to counterfeiting), section 659 (relating to theft from interstate shipment) if the act indictable under section 659 is felonious, section 664 (relating to embezzlement from pension and welfare funds), sections 891–894 (relating to extortionate credit transactions), section 1028 (relating to fraud and related activity in connection with identification documents), section 1029 (relating to fraud and related activity in connection with access devices), section 1084 (relating to the transmission of gambling information), section 1341 (relating to mail fraud), section 1343 (relating to wire fraud), section 1344 (relating to financial institution fraud), section 1425 (relating to the procurement of citizenship or nationalization unlawfully), section 1426 (relating to the reproduction of naturalization or citizenship papers), section 1427 (relating to the sale of naturalization or citizenship papers), sections 1461–1465 (relating to obscene matter), section 1503 (relating to obstruction of justice), section 1510 (relating to obstruction of criminal investigations), section 1511 (relating to the obstruction of State or local law enforcement), section 1512 (relating to tampering with a witness, victim, or an informant), section 1513 (relating to retaliating against a witness, victim, or an informant), section 1542 (relating to false statement in application and use of passport), section 1543 (relating to forgery or false use of passport), section 1544 (relating to misuse of passport), section 1546 (relating to fraud and misuse of visas, permits, and other documents), sections 1581–1592 (relating to peonage, slavery, and trafficking in persons).,[1] section 1951 (relating to interference with commerce, robbery, or extortion), section 1952 (relating to racketeering), section 1953 (relating to interstate transportation of wagering paraphernalia), section 1954 (relating to unlawful welfare fund payments), section 1955 (relating to the prohibition of illegal gambling businesses), section 1956 (relating to the laundering of monetary instruments), section 1957 (relating to engaging in monetary transactions in property derived from specified unlawful activity), section 1958 (relating to use of interstate commerce facilities in the commission of murder-for-hire), section 1960 (relating to illegal money transmitters), sections 2251, 2251A, 2252, and 2260 (relating to sexual exploitation of children), sections 2312 and 2313 (relating to interstate transportation of stolen motor vehicles), sections 2314 and 2315 (relating to interstate transportation of stolen property), section 2318 (relating to trafficking in counterfeit labels for phonorecords, computer programs or computer program documentation or packaging and copies of motion pictures or other audiovisual works), section 2319 (relating to criminal infringement of a copyright), section 2319A (relating to unauthorized fixation of and trafficking in sound recordings and music videos of live musical performances), section 2320 (relating to trafficking in goods or services bearing counterfeit marks), section 2321 (relating to trafficking in certain motor vehicles or motor vehicle parts), sections 2341–2346 (relating to trafficking in contraband cigarettes), sections 2421–24 (relating to white slave traffic), sections 175–178 (relating to biological weapons), sections 229–229F (relating to chemical weapons), section 831 (relating to nuclear materials), (C) any act which is indictable under title 29, United States

Code, section 186 (dealing with restrictions on payments and loans to labor organizations) or section 501(c) (relating to embezzlement from union funds), (D) any offense involving fraud connected with a case under title 11 (except a case under section 157 of this title), fraud in the sale of securities, or the felonious manufacture, importation, receiving, concealment, buying, selling, or otherwise dealing in a controlled substance or listed chemical (as defined in section 102 of the Controlled Substances Act), punishable under any law of the United States, (E) any act which is indictable under the Currency and Foreign Transactions Reporting Act, (F) any act which is indictable under the Immigration and Nationality Act, section 274 (relating to bringing in and harboring certain aliens), section 277 (relating to aiding or assisting certain aliens to enter the United States), or section 278 (relating to importation of alien for immoral purpose) if the act indictable under such section of such Act was committed for the purpose of financial gain, or (G) any act that is indictable under any provision listed in section 2332b(g)(5)(B);

(2) "State" means any State of the United States, the District of Columbia, the Commonwealth of Puerto Rico, any territory or possession of the United States, any political subdivision, or any department, agency, or instrumentality thereof;

(3) "person" includes any individual or entity capable of holding a legal or beneficial interest in property;

(4) "enterprise" includes any individual, partnership, corporation, association, or other legal entity, and any union or group of individuals associated in fact although not a legal entity;

(5) "pattern of racketeering activity" requires at least two acts of racketeering activity, one of which occurred after the effective date of this chapter and the last of which occurred within ten years (excluding any period of imprisonment) after the commission of a prior act of racketeering activity;

(6) "unlawful debt" means a debt (A) incurred or contracted in gambling activity which was in violation of the law of the United States, a State or political subdivision thereof, or which is unenforceable under State or Federal law in whole or in part as to principal or interest because of the laws relating to usury, and (B) which was incurred in connection with the business of gambling in violation of the law of the United States, a State or political subdivision thereof, or the business of lending money or a thing of value at a rate usurious under State or Federal law, where the usurious rate is at least twice the enforceable rate;

(7) "racketeering investigator" means any attorney or investigator so designated by the Attorney General and charged with the duty of enforcing or carrying into effect this chapter;

(8) "racketeering investigation" means any inquiry conducted by any racketeering investigator for the purpose of ascertaining whether any person has been involved in any violation of this chapter or of any final order, judgment, or decree of any court of the United States, duly entered in any case or proceeding arising under this chapter;

(9) "documentary material" includes any book, paper, document, record, recording, or other material; and

(10) "Attorney General" includes the Attorney General of the United States, the Deputy Attorney General of the United States, the Associate Attorney General of the United States, any Assistant Attorney General of the United States, or any employee of the Department of Justice or any employee of any department or agency of the United States so designated by the Attorney General to carry out the powers conferred on the Attorney General by this chapter. Any department or agency so designated may use in investigations authorized by this chapter either the investigative provisions of this chapter or the investigative power of such department or agency otherwise conferred by law.

(Added Pub.L. 91–452, Title IX, § 901(a), Oct. 15, 1970, 84 Stat. 941, and amended Pub.L. 95–575, § 3(c), Nov. 2, 1978, 92 Stat. 2465; Pub.L. 95–598, Title III, § 314(g), Nov. 6, 1978, 92 Stat. 2677; Pub.L. 98–473, Title II, §§ 901(g), 1020, Oct. 12, 1984, 98 Stat. 2136, 2143; Pub.L. 98–547, Title II, § 205, Oct. 25, 1984, 98 Stat. 2770; Pub.L. 99–570, Title XIII, § 1365(b), Oct. 27, 1986, 100 Stat. 3207–35; Pub.L. 99–646, § 50(a), Nov. 10, 1986, 100 Stat. 3605; Pub.L. 100–690, Title VII, §§ 7013, 7020(c), 7032, 7054, 7514, Nov. 18, 1988, 102 Stat. 4395, 4396, 4398, 4402, 4489; Pub.L. 101–73, Title IX, § 968, Aug. 9, 1989, 103 Stat. 506; Pub.L. 101–647, Title XXXV, § 3560, Nov. 29, 1990, 104 Stat. 4927; Pub.L. 103–322, Title IX, § 90104, Title XVI, § 160001(f), Title XXXIII, § 330021(1), Sept. 13, 1994, 108 Stat. 1987, 2037, 2150; Pub.L. 103–394, Title III, § 312(b), Oct. 22, 1994, 108 Stat. 4140; Pub.L. 104–132, Title IV, § 433, Apr. 24, 1996, 110 Stat. 1274; Pub.L. 104–153, § 3, July 2, 1996, 110 Stat. 1386; Pub.L. 104–208, Div. C, Title II, § 202, Sept. 30, 1996, 110 Stat. 3009–565; Pub.L. 104–294, Title VI, §§ 601(b)(3), (i)(3), 604(b)(6), Oct. 11, 1996, 110 Stat. 3499, 3501, 3506; Pub.L. 107–56, Title VIII, § 813, Oct. 26, 2001, 115 Stat. 382; Pub.L. 107–273, Div. B, Title IV, § 4005(f)(1), Nov. 2, 2002, 116 Stat. 1813; Pub.L. 108–193, § 5(b), Dec. 19, 2003, 117 Stat. 2879; Pub.L. 108–458, Title VI, § 6802(e), Dec. 17, 2004, 118 Stat. 3767; Pub.L. 109–164, Title I, § 103(c), Jan. 10, 2006, 119 Stat. 3563; Pub.L. 109–177, Title IV, § 403(a), Mar. 9, 2006, 120 Stat. 243.)

[1] So in original.

HISTORICAL AND STATUTORY NOTES

Revision Notes and Legislative Reports

1970 Acts. House Report No. 91–1549, see 1970 U.S. Code Cong. and Adm. News, p. 4007.

1978 Acts. Senate Report No. 95–962 and House Conference Report No. 95–1778, see 1978 U.S. Code Cong. and Adm. News, p. 5518.

1984 Acts. House Report No. 98–1030 and House Conference Report No. 98–1159, see 1984 U.S. Code Cong. and Adm. News, p. 3182.

House Report No. 98–1087, see 1984 U.S. Code Cong. and Adm. News, p. 4628.

1986 Acts. Statement by President, see 1986 U.S. Code Cong. and Adm. News, p. 5393.

House Report No. 99–797, see 1986 U.S. Code Cong. and Adm. News, p. 6138.

1988 Acts. For Related Reports, see 1988 U.S. Code Cong. and Adm. News, p. 5937.

1989 Acts. House Report No. 101–54(Parts I–VII) and House Conference Report No. 101–222, see 1989 Code Cong. and Adm. News, p. 86.

1990 Acts. House Report Nos. 101–681(Parts I and II), 101–736, Senate Report No. 101–460, and Statement by President, see 1990 U.S. Code Cong. and Adm. News, p. 6472.

1994 Acts. House Report Nos. 103–324, 103–489, and House Conference Report No. 103–711, see 1994 U.S. Code Cong. and Adm. News, p. 1801.

House Report No. 103–835, see 1994 U.S. Code Cong. and Adm. News, p. 3340.

1996 Acts. Senate Report No. 104–179 and House Conference Report No. 104–518, see 1996 U.S. Code Cong. and Adm. News, p. 924.

House Report No. 104–556, see 1996 U.S. Code Cong. and Adm. News, p. 1074.

House Report No. 104–788, see 1996 U.S. Code Cong. and Adm. News, p. 4021.

2002 Acts. House Conference Report No. 107–685 and Statement by President, see 2002 U.S. Code Cong. and Adm. News, p. 1120.

2003 Acts. House Report No. 108–264(Parts I and II), see 2003 U.S. Code Cong. and Adm. News, p. 2408.

2004 Acts. House Conference Report No. 108–796, see 2004 U.S. Code Cong. and Adm. News, p. 3178.

Statement by President, see 2004 U.S. Code Cong. and Adm. News, p. S51.

2006 Acts. House Report No. 109–317(Parts I and II), see 2005 U.S. Code Cong. and Adm. News, p. 1888.

Statement by President, see 2005 U.S. Code Cong. and Adm. News, p. S56.

House Conference Report No. 109–333, see 2006 U.S. Code Cong. and Adm. News, p. 184.

Statement by President, see 2006 U.S. Code Cong. and Adm. News, p. S7.

References in Text

Section 102 of the Controlled Substances Act, referred to in par. (1), is section 102 of Pub.L. 91–513, Title II, Oct. 27, 1970, 84 Stat. 1242, as amended, which is classified to section 802 of Title 21, Food and Drugs.

Sections 201, 224, 471, 472, 473, 659, 664, 891 to 894, 1028, 1029, 1084, 1341, 1343, 1344, 1461 to 1465, 1503, 1510, 1511, 1512, 1513, 1542, 1543, 1544, 1546, 1581 to 1591, 1951, 1952, 1953, 1954, 1955, 1956, 1957, 1958, 2251, 2252, 2312, 2313, 2314, 2315, 2321, 2341 to 2346, and 2421 to 2424 of title 18, United States Code, referred to in par. (1)(B), are sections 201, 224, 471, 472, 473, 659, 664, 891 to 894, 1028, 1029, 1084, 1341, 1343, 1344, 1461 to 1465, 1503, 1510, 1511, 1512, 1513, 1452, 1543, 1544, 1546, 1581 to 1591, 1951, 1952, 1953, 1954, 1955, 1956, 1957, 1958, 2251, 2252, 2312, 2313, 2314, 2315, 2321, 2341 to 2346, and 2421 to 2424 of this title, respectively.

The Currency and Foreign Transaction Reporting Act, as amended, referred to in par. (1)(E), was Pub.L. 91–508, Title II, Oct. 26, 1970, 84 Stat. 1118, which was classified generally to chapter 21 (section 1051 et seq.) of Title 31, Money and Finance prior to the revision of this title by Pub.L. 97–258, Sept. 12, 1982, 96 Stat. 995. For complete classification of this Act to the Code see section 5311 et seq. of revised Title 31 and Tables.

The Immigration and Nationality Act and such Act, referred to in par. (1)(F), is Act June 27, 1952, c. 477, 66 Stat. 163, as amended, which is classified principally to chapter 12 (section 1101 et seq.) of Title 8, Aliens and Nationality. Sections 274, 277 and 278 of such Act are classified to sections 1324, 1327 and 1328 of Title 8, respectively. For complete classification of this Act to the Code, see Tables.

The effective date of this chapter, referred to in par. (5), is Oct. 15, 1970.

Codifications

Section 5(b) of Pub.L. 108–193, which directed that paragraph (1)(A) of this section be amended by striking "sections 1581–1588 (relating to peonage and slavery)" and inserting "sections 1581–1591 (relating to peonage, slavery, and trafficking in persons)", was executed to paragraph (1)(B) of this section as the probable intent of Congress.

Effective and Applicability Provisions

2002 Acts. Amendment by section 4005(f)(1) of Pub.L. 107–273, as therein provided, effective Oct. 26, 2001, which is the date of enactment of Pub.L. 107–56, to which such amendment relates.

1996 Acts. Amendment by section 604 of Pub.L. 104–294 effective Sept. 13, 1994, see section 604(d) of Pub.L. 104–294, set out as a note under section 13 of this title.

1994 Acts. Amendment by Pub.L. 103–394 effective on Oct. 22, 1994, and not to apply with respect to cases commenced under Title 11 of the United States Code before Oct. 22, 1994, see section 702 of Pub.L. 103–394, set out as a note under section 101 of Title 11, Bankruptcy.

1978 Acts. Amendment by Pub.L. 95–598 effective Oct. 1, 1979, see section 402(a) of Pub.L. 95–598, set out as an Effective Date note preceding section 101 of Title 11, Bankruptcy.

Amendment by Pub.L. 95–575 effective Nov. 2, 1978, see section 4 of Pub.L. 95–575, set out as an Effective Date note under section 2341 of this title.

Severability of Provisions

If any provision of Division C of Pub.L. 104–208 or the application of such provision to any person or circumstances is held to be unconstitutional, the remainder of Division C of Pub.L. 104–208 and the application of the provisions of Division C of Pub.L. 104–208 to any person or circumstance not to be affected thereby, see section 1(e) of Pub.L. 104–208, set out as a note under section 1101 of Title 8, Aliens and Nationality.

Amendment by section 314 of Pub.L. 95–598 not to affect the application of chapter 9 [section 151 et seq.], chapter 96 [section 1961 et seq.], or section 2516, 3057, or 3284 of this title to any act of any person (1) committed before Oct. 1, 1979, or (2) committed after Oct. 1, 1979, in connection with a case commenced before such date, see section 403(d) of Pub.L. 95–598, set out preceding section 151 of this title.

If any provision of or amendment made by Pub.L. 103–394 or the application of such provision or amendment to any person or circumstance is held to be unconstitutional, the remaining provisions of and amendments made by Pub.L. 103–394 and the application of such provisions and amendments to any person or circumstance shall not be affected thereby, see section 701 of Pub.L. 103–394, set out as a note under section 101 of Title 11, Bankruptcy.

If any provision of Pub.L. 101–73 or the application thereof to any person or circumstance is held invalid, the remainder of Pub.L. 101–73 and the application of the provision to other persons not similarly situated or to other circumstances not to be affected thereby, see section 1221 of Pub.L. 101–73, set out as a note under section 1811 of Title 12, Banks and Banking.

Section 1301 of Pub.L. 91–452 provided that: "If the provisions of any part of this Act [see Short Title note set out above] or the application thereof to any person or circumstances be held invalid, the provisions of the other parts and their application to other persons or circumstances shall not be affected thereby."

Short Title

1984 Amendments. Pub.L. 98–473, Title II, § 301, Oct. 12, 1984, 98 Stat. 2040, provided that: "This title [probably means chapter III of title II of Pub.L. 98–473 which enacted sections 853, 854, and 970 of Title 21, Food and Drugs, and sections 1589, 1600, 1613a, and 1616 of Title 19, Customs Duties, amended section 1963 of this title and sections 1602, 1605, 1606, 1607, 1608, 1609, 1610, 1611, 1612, 1613, 1614, 1615, 1618, 1619, and 1644 of Title 19, sections 824, 848, and 881 of Title 21, and section 524 of Title 28, Judiciary and Judicial Procedure, and repealed section 7607 of Title 26, Internal Revenue Code] may be cited as the 'Comprehensive Forfeiture Act of 1984'."

1970 Acts. Section 1 of Pub.L. 91–452 provided in part that: "This Act [enacting sections 841 to 848, 1511, 1623, 1955, 1961 to 1968, 3331 to 3334, 3503, 3504, 3575 to 3578, and 6001 to 6005 of this title, and section 1826 of Title 28, Judiciary and Judicial Procedure, amending sections 835, 1073, 1505, 1954, 2424, 2516, 2517, 3148, 3486, and 3500 of this title, sections 15, 87f, 135c, 499m, and 2115 of Title 7, Agriculture, section 25 of Title 11, Bankruptcy, section 1820 of Title 12, Banks and Banking, sections 49, 77v, 78u, 79r, 80a–41, 80b–9, 155, 717m, 1271, and 1714 of Title 15, Commerce and Trade, section 825f of Title 16, Conservation, section 1333 of Title 19, Customs Duties, section 373 of Title 21, Food and Drugs, section 161 of Title 29, Labor, section 506 of Title 33, Navigation and Navigable Waters, sections 405 and 2201 of Title 42, The Public Health and Welfare, sections 157 and 362 of Title 45, Railroads, section 1124 of Title 46, Shipping, section 409 of Title 47, Telegraphs, Telephones, and Radio telegraphs, sections 9, 43, 46, 916, 1017, and 1484 of former Title 49, Transportation, section 792 of Title 50, War and National Defense, and sections 643a, 1152, 2026, and former section 2155 of Title 50, Appendix, repealing sections 837, 895, 1406, and 2514 of this title, sections 32 and 33 of Title 15; sections 4874 and 7493 of Title 26, Internal Revenue Code, section 827 of Title 46, sections 47 and 48 of former Title 49, and sections 121 to 144 of Title 50, enacting provisions set out as notes under this section and sections 841, 1511, 1955, preceding 3331, preceding 3481, 3504, and 6001 of this title, and repealing provisions set out as a note under section 2510 of this title] may be cited as the 'Organized Crime Control Act of 1970'."

This chapter is commonly known as the Racketeer Influenced and Corrupt Organizations Act or RICO.

President's Commission on Organized Crime; Taking of Testimony and Receipt of Evidence

Pub.L. 98–368, July 17, 1984, 98 Stat. 490, provided for the Commission established by Ex. Ord. No. 12435, formerly set out below, authority relating to taking of testimony, receipt of evidence, subpoena power, testimony of persons in custody, immunity, service of process, witness fees, access to other records and information, Federal protection for members and staff, closure of meetings, rules, and procedures, for the period of July 17, 1984, until the earlier of 2 years or the expiration of the Commission.

Congressional Statement of Findings and Purpose

Section 1 of Pub.L. 91–452 provided in part that: "The Congress finds that (1) organized crime in the United States is a highly sophisticated, diversified, and widespread activity that annually drains billions of dollars from America's economy by unlawful conduct and the illegal use of force, fraud, and corruption; (2) organized crime derives a major portion of its power through money obtained from such illegal endeavors as syndicated gambling, loan sharking, the theft and fencing of property, the importation and distribution of narcotics and other dangerous drugs, and other forms of social exploitation; (3) this money and power are increasingly used to infiltrate and corrupt legitimate business and labor unions and to subvert and corrupt our democratic processes; (4) organized crime activities in the United States weaken the stability of the Nation's economic system, harm innocent investors and competing organizations, interfere with free competition, seriously burden interstate and foreign commerce, threaten the domestic security, and undermine the general welfare of the Nation and its citizens; and (5) organized crime continues to grow because of defects in the evidence-gathering process of the law inhibiting the development of the legally admissible evidence necessary to bring criminal and other sanctions or remedies to bear the unlawful activities of those engaged in organized crime and because the sanctions and remedies available to the Government are unnecessarily limited in scope and impact.

"It is the purpose of this Act [see Short Title note above] to seek the eradication of organized crime in the United States by strengthening the legal tools in the evidence-gathering process, by establishing new penal prohibitions, and by providing enhanced sanctions and new remedies to deal with the unlawful activities of those engaged in organized crime."

Liberal Construction of Provisions; Supersedure of Federal or State Laws; Authority of Attorneys Representing United States

Section 904 of Pub.L. 91–452 provided that:

"(a) The provisions of this title [enacting this chapter and amending sections 1505, 2516, and 2517 of this title] shall be liberally construed to effectuate its remedial purposes.

"(b) Nothing in this title shall supersede any provision of Federal, State, or other law imposing criminal penalties or affording civil remedies in addition to those provided for in this title.

"(c) Nothing contained in this title shall impair the authority of any attorney representing the United States to—

"(1) lay before any grand jury impaneled by any district court of the United States any evidence concerning any alleged racketeering violation of law;

"(2) invoke the power of any such court to compel the production of any evidence before any such grand jury; or

"(3) institute any proceeding to enforce any order or process issued in execution of such power or to punish disobedience of any such order or process by any person."

EXECUTIVE ORDERS

EXECUTIVE ORDER NO. 12435

Ex. Ord. No. 12503, July 28, 1983, 48 F.R. 34723, as amended by Ex. Ord. No. 12507, March 22, 1985, 50 F.R. 11835, which related to the establishment, functions, administration and termination of the President's Commission on Organized Crime, was revoked by Ex. Ord. No. 12610, Sept. 30, 1987, 52 F.R. 36901.

CHAPTER 119—WIRE AND ELECTRONIC COMMUNICATIONS INTERCEPTION AND INTERCEPTION OF ORAL COMMUNICATIONS

§ 2516. Authorization for interception of wire, oral, or electronic communications

(1) The Attorney General, Deputy Attorney General, Associate Attorney General[1], or any Assistant Attorney General, any acting Assistant Attorney General, or any Deputy Assistant Attorney General or acting Deputy Assistant Attorney General in the Criminal Division or National Security Division specially designated by the Attorney General, may authorize an application to a Federal judge of competent jurisdiction for, and such judge may grant in conformity with section 2518 of this chapter an order authorizing or approving the interception of wire or oral communications by the Federal Bureau of Investigation, or a Federal agency having responsibility for the investigation of the offense as to which the application is made, when such interception may provide or has provided evidence of—

(a) any offense punishable by death or by imprisonment for more than one year under sections 2122 and 2274 through 2277 of title 42 of the United States Code (relating to the enforcement of the Atomic Energy Act of 1954), section 2284 of title 42 of the United States Code (relating to sabotage of nuclear facilities or fuel), or under the following chapters of this title: chapter 10 (relating to biological weapons)[2] chapter 37 (relating to espionage), chapter 55 (relating to kidnapping), chapter 90 (relating to protection of trade secrets), chapter 105 (relating to sabotage), chapter 115 (relating to treason), chapter 102 (relating to riots), chapter 65 (relating to malicious mischief), chapter 111 (relating to destruction of vessels), or chapter 81 (relating to piracy);

(b) a violation of section 186 or section 501(c) of title 29, United States Code (dealing with restrictions on payments and loans to labor organizations), or any offense which involves murder, kidnapping, robbery, or extortion, and which is punishable under this title;

(c) any offense which is punishable under the following sections of this title: section 37 (relating to violence at international airports), section 43 (relating to animal enterprise terrorism), section 81 (arson within special maritime and territorial jurisdiction), section 201 (bribery of public officials and witnesses), section 215 (relating to bribery of bank officials), section 224 (bribery in sporting contests), subsection (d), (e), (f), (g), (h), or (i) of section 844 (unlawful use of explosives), section 1032 (relating to concealment of assets), section 1084 (transmission of wagering information), section 751 (relating to escape), section 832 (relating to nuclear and weapons of mass destruction threats), section 842 (relating to explosive materials), section 930 (relating to possession of weapons in Federal facilities), section 1014 (relating to loans and credit applications generally; renewals and discounts), section 1114 (relating to officers and employees of the United States), section 1116 (relating to protection of foreign officials), sections 1503, 1512, and 1513 (influencing or injuring an officer, juror, or witness generally), section 1510 (obstruction of criminal investigations), section 1511 (obstruction of State or local law enforcement), section 1591 (sex trafficking of children by force, fraud, or coercion), section 1751 (Presidential and Presidential staff assassination, kidnapping, and assault), section 1951 (interference with commerce by threats or violence), section 1952 (interstate and foreign travel or transportation in aid of racketeering enterprises), section 1958 (relating to use of interstate commerce facilities in the commission of murder for hire), section 1959 (relating to violent crimes in aid of racketeering activity), section 1954 (offer, acceptance, or solicitation to influence operations of employee benefit plan), section 1955 (prohibition of business enterprises of gambling), section 1956 (laundering of monetary instruments), section 1957 (relating to engaging in monetary transactions in property derived from specified unlawful activity), section 659 (theft from interstate shipment), section 664 (embezzlement from pension and welfare funds), section 1343 (fraud by wire, radio, or television), section 1344 (relating to bank fraud), section 1992 (relating to terrorist attacks against mass transportation), sections 2251 and 2252 (sexual exploitation of children), section 2251A (selling or buying of children), section 2252A (relating to material constituting or containing child pornography), section 1466A (relating to child obscenity), section 2260 (production of sexually explicit depictions of a minor for importation into the United States), sections 2421, 2422, 2423, and 2425 (relating to transportation for illegal sexual activity and related crimes), sections 2312, 2313, 2314, and 2315 (interstate transportation of stolen property), section 2321 (relating to trafficking in certain motor vehicles or motor vehicle parts), section 2340A (relating to torture), section 1203 (relating to hostage taking), section 1029 (relating to fraud and related activity in connection with access devices), section 3146 (relating to penalty for failure to appear), section 3521(b)(3) (relating to witness relocation and assistance), section 32 (relating to destruction of aircraft or aircraft facilities), section 38 (relating to aircraft parts fraud), section 1963 (violations with respect to racketeer influenced and corrupt organizations), section 115 (relating to threatening or retaliating against a Federal official), section 1341 (relating to mail fraud), a felony violation of section 1030 (relating to computer fraud and abuse), section 351 (violations with respect to congressional, Cabinet, or Supreme Court assassinations, kidnapping, and assault), section 831 (relating to prohibited transactions involving nuclear materials), section 33 (relating to destruction of motor vehicles or motor vehicle facilities), section 175 (relating to biological weapons), section 175c (relating to variola virus), section 956 (conspiracy to harm persons or property overseas), section [3] a felony violation of section 1028 (relating to production of false identification documentation), section 1425 (relating to the procurement of citizenship or nationalization unlawfully), section 1426 (relating to the reproduction of naturalization or citizenship papers), section 1427 (relating to the sale of naturalization or citizenship papers), section 1541 (relating to passport issuance without authority), section 1542 (relating to false statements in passport applications), section 1543 (relating to forgery or false use of passports), section 1544 (relating to misuse of passports), or section 1546 (relating to fraud and misuse of visas, permits, and other documents);

(d) any offense involving counterfeiting punishable under section 471, 472, or 473 of this title;

(e) any offense involving fraud connected with a case under title 11 or the manufacture, importation, receiving, concealment, buying, selling, or otherwise dealing in narcotic drugs, marihuana, or other dangerous drugs, punishable under any law of the United States;

(f) any offense including extortionate credit transactions under sections 892, 893, or 894 of this title;

(g) a violation of section 5322 of title 31, United States Code (dealing with the reporting of currency transactions), or section 5324 of title 31, United States Code (relating to structuring transactions to evade reporting requirement prohibited);

(h) any felony violation of sections 2511 and 2512 (relating to interception and disclosure of certain communications and to certain intercepting devices) of this title;

(i) any felony violation of chapter 71 (relating to obscenity) of this title;

(j) any violation of section 60123(b) (relating to destruction of a natural gas pipeline), section 46502 (relating to aircraft piracy), the second sentence of section 46504 (relating to assault on a flight crew with dangerous weapon), or section 46505(b)(3) or (c) (relating to explosive or incendiary devices, or endangerment of human life, by means of weapons on aircraft) of title 49;

(k) any criminal violation of section 2778 of title 22 (relating to the Arms Export Control Act);

(*l*) the location of any fugitive from justice from an offense described in this section;

(m) a violation of section 274, 277, or 278 of the Immigration and Nationality Act (8 U.S.C. 1324, 1327, or 1328) (relating to the smuggling of aliens);

(n) any felony violation of sections 922 and 924 of title 18, United States Code (relating to firearms);

(*o*) any violation of section 5861 of the Internal Revenue Code of 1986 (relating to firearms);

(p) a felony violation of section 1028 (relating to production of false identification documents), section 1542 (relating to false statements in passport applications), section 1546 (relating to fraud and misuse of visas, permits, and other documents, [4] section 1028A (relating to aggravated identity theft)) [5] of this title or a violation of section 274, 277, or 278 of the Immigration and Nationality Act (relating to the smuggling of aliens); or [6]

(q) any criminal violation of section 229 (relating to chemical weapons): or sections [7] 2332, 2332a, 2332b, 2332d, 2332f, 2332g, 2332h [8] 2339, 2339A, 2339B, 2339C, or 2339D of this title (relating to terrorism);

(r) any criminal violation of section 1 (relating to illegal restraints of trade or commerce), 2 (relating to illegal monopolizing of trade or commerce), or 3 (relating to illegal restraints of trade or commerce in territories or the District of Columbia) of the Sherman Act (15 U.S.C. 1, 2, 3); or

(s) any conspiracy to commit any offense described in any subparagraph of this paragraph.

(2) The principal prosecuting attorney of any State, or the principal prosecuting attorney of any political subdivision thereof, if such attorney is authorized by a statute of that State to make application to a State court judge of competent jurisdiction for an order authorizing or approving the interception of wire, oral, or electronic communications, may apply to such judge for, and such judge may grant in conformity with section 2518 of this chapter and with the applicable State statute an order authorizing, or approving the interception of wire, oral, or electronic communications by investigative or law enforcement officers having responsibility for the investigation of the offense as to which the application is made, when such interception may provide or has provided evidence of the commission of the offense of murder, kidnapping, gambling, robbery, bribery, extortion, or dealing in narcotic drugs, marihuana or other dangerous drugs, or other crime dangerous to life, limb, or property, and punishable by imprisonment for more than one year, designated in any applicable State statute authorizing such interception, or any conspiracy to commit any of the foregoing offenses.

(3) Any attorney for the Government (as such term is defined for the purposes of the Federal Rules of Criminal Procedure) may authorize an application to a Federal judge of competent jurisdiction for, and such judge may grant, in conformity with section 2518 of this title, an order authorizing or approving the interception of electronic communications by an investigative or law enforcement officer having responsibility for the investigation of the offense as to which the application is made, when such interception may provide or has provided evidence of any Federal felony.

(Added Pub.L. 90–351, Title III, § 802, June 19, 1968, 82 Stat. 216, and amended Pub.L. 91–452, Title VIII, § 810, Title IX, § 902(a), Title XI, § 1103, Oct. 15, 1970, 84 Stat. 940, 947, 959; Pub.L. 91–644, Title IV, § 16, Jan. 2, 1971, 84 Stat. 1891; Pub.L. 95–598, Title III, § 314(h), Nov. 6, 1978, 92 Stat. 2677; Pub.L. 97–285, §§ 2(e), 4(e), Oct. 6, 1982, 96 Stat. 1220, 1221; Pub.L. 98–292, § 8, May 21, 1984, 98 Stat. 206; Pub.L. 98–473, Title II, § 1203(c), Oct. 12, 1984, 98 Stat. 2152; Pub.L. 99–508, Title I, §§ 101(c)(1)(A), 104, 105, Oct. 21, 1986, 100 Stat. 1851, 1855; Pub.L. 99–570, Title I, § 1365(c), Oct. 27, 1986, 100 Stat. 3207–35; Pub.L. 100–690, Title VI, § 6461, Title VII, §§ 7036, 7053(d), 7525, Nov. 18, 1988, 102 Stat. 4374, 4399, 4402, 4502; Pub.L. 101–298, § 3(b), May 22, 1990, 104 Stat. 203; Pub.L. 101–647, Title XXV, § 2531, Title XXXV, § 3568, Nov. 29, 1990, 104 Stat. 4879, 4928; Pub.L. 103–272, § 5(e)(11), July 5, 1994, 108 Stat. 1374; Pub.L. 103–322, Title XXXIII, §§ 330011(c)(1), (q)(1), (r), 330021(1), Sept. 13, 1994, 108 Stat. 2144, 2145, 2150; Pub.L. 103–414, Title II, § 208, Oct. 25, 1994, 108 Stat. 4292; Pub.L. 103–429, § 7(a)(4)(A), Oct. 31, 1994, 108 Stat. 4389; Pub.L. 104–132, Title IV, § 434, Apr. 24, 1996, 110 Stat. 1274; Pub.L. 104–208, Div. C, Title II, § 201, Sept. 30, 1996, 110 Stat. 3009–564; Pub.L. 104–287, § 6(a)(2), Oct. 11, 1996, 110 Stat. 3398; Pub.L. 104–294, Title I, § 102, Title VI, § 601(d), Oct. 11, 1996, 110 Stat. 3491, 3499; Pub.L. 105–318, § 6(b), Oct. 30, 1998, 112 Stat. 3011; Pub.L. 106–181, Title V, § 506(c)(2)(B), Apr. 5, 2000, 114 Stat. 139; Pub.L. 107–56, Title II, §§ 201, 202, Oct. 26, 2001, 115 Stat. 278; Pub.L. 107–197, Title III, § 301(a), June 25, 2002, 116 Stat. 728; Pub.L. 107–273, Div. B, Title IV, §§ 4002(c)(1), 4005(a)(1), Nov. 2, 2002, 116 Stat. 1808, 1812; Pub.L. 108–21, Title II, § 201, Apr. 30, 2003, 117 Stat. 659; Pub.L. 108–458, Title VI, § 6907, Dec. 17, 2004, 118 Stat. 3774; Pub.L. 109–162, Title XI, § 1171(b), Jan. 5, 2006, 119 Stat. 3123; Pub.L. 109–177, Title I, §§ 110(b)(3)(C), 113, Title V, § 506(a)(6), Mar. 9, 2006, 120 Stat. 208, 209, 248.)

1 See Codifications note set out under this section.

2 So in original. A comma probably should appear.

3 So in original. The word "section" probably should not appear.

4 So in original. Probably should read "other documents),".

5 So in original. The second closing parenthesis probably should not appear.

6 So in original. The word "or" probably should not appear.

7 So in original. Probably should be "weapons) or section".

8 So in original. A comma probably should appear.

HISTORICAL AND STATUTORY NOTES

Revision Notes and Legislative Reports

1968 Acts. Senate Report No. 90–1097, see 1968 U.S. Code Cong. and Adm. News, p. 2112.

1970 Acts. House Report No. 91–1549, see 1970 U.S. Code Cong. and Adm. News, p. 4007.

1971 Acts. Senate Report No. 91–1253 and Conference Report No. 91–1768, see 1970 U.S. Code Cong. and Adm. News, p. 5804.

1982 Acts. House Report No. 97–803, see 1982 U.S. Code Cong. and Adm. News, p. 2428.

1984 Acts. House Report No. 98–536, see 1984 U.S. Code Cong. and Adm. News, p. 492.

House Report No. 98–1030 and House Conference Report No. 98–1159, see 1984 U.S. Code Cong. and Adm. News, p. 3182.

1986 Acts. Senate Report No. 99–541, see 1986 U.S. Code Cong. and Adm. News, p. 3555.

Statement by President, see 1986 U.S. Code Cong. and Adm. News, p. 5393.

1988 Acts. For Related Reports, see 1988 U.S. Code Cong. and Adm. News, p. 5937.

1990 Acts. Senate Report No. 101–210, and Statement by President, see 1990 U.S. Code Cong. and Adm. News, p. 186.

1994 Acts. House Report No. 103–180, see 1994 U.S. Code Cong. and Adm. News, p. 818.

House Report Nos. 103–324, 103–489, and House Conference Report No. 103–711, see 1994 U.S. Code Cong. and Adm. News, p. 1801.

House Report No. 103–827, see 1994 U.S. Code Cong. and Adm. News, p. 3489.

House Report No. 103–831, see 1994 U.S. Code Cong. and Adm. News, p. 3579.

1996 Acts. Senate Report No. 104–179 and House Conference Report No. 104–518, see 1996 U.S. Code Cong. and Adm. News, p. 924.

House Report No. 104–573, see 1996 U.S. Code Cong. and Adm. News, p. 3831.

House Report No. 104–788, see 1996 U.S. Code Cong. and Adm. News, p. 4021.

1998 Acts. Statement by President, see 1998 U.S. Code Cong. and Adm. News, p. 709.

2000 Acts. House Conference Report No. 106–513 and Statement by President, see 2000 U.S. Code Cong. and Adm. News, p. 80.

2002 Acts. House Report No. 107–307 and Statement by President, see 2002 U.S. Code Cong. and Adm. News, p. 521.

House Conference Report No. 107–685 and Statement by President, see 2002 U.S. Code Cong. and Adm. News, p. 1120.

2003 Acts. House Conference Report No. 108–66 and Statement by President, see 2003 U.S. Code Cong. and Adm. News, p. 683.

2004 Acts. House Conference Report No. 108–796, see 2004 U.S. Code Cong. and Adm. News, p. 3178.

Statement by President, see 2004 U.S. Code Cong. and Adm. News, p. S51.

2006 Acts. House Report No. 109–233, see 2005 U.S. Code Cong. and Adm. News, p. 1636.

House Conference Report No. 109–333, see 2006 U.S. Code Cong. and Adm. News, p. 184.

Statement by President, see 2006 U.S. Code Cong. and Adm. News, p. S7.

References in Text

The Atomic Energy Act of 1954, referred to in par. (1)(a), is classified generally to 42 U.S.C.A. § 2011 et seq.

Chapters 10, 37, 55, 90, 105, 115, 102, 65, 111, and 81, referred to in par. (1)(a), are 18 U.S.C.A. §§ 175 et seq., 791 et seq., 1201 et seq., 1831 et seq., 2151 et seq., 2381 et seq., 2101 et seq., 1361 et seq., 2271 et seq., and 1651 et seq., respectively.

The Arms Export Control Act, referred to in par. (1)(k), is Pub.L. 90–629, Oct. 22, 1968, 82 Stat. 1320, as amended, which is classified generally to chapter 39 of Title 22, Foreign Relations and Intercourse (22 U.S.C.A. § 2751 et seq.). For complete classification of this Act to the Code, see Short Title note set out under 22 U.S.C.A. § 2751 and Tables.

Sections 274, 277, and 278 of the Immigration and Nationality Act, referred to in par. (1)(m) and (p), are sections 274, 277, and 278 of Act June 27, 1952, c. 477, 66 Stat. 163, as amended, which are classified to 8 U.S.C.A. §§ 1324, 1327, and 1328.

Sections 1, 2, or 3 of the Sherman Act, referred to in par. (1)(r), are sections 1, 2, or 3, of Act July 2, 1890, c. 647, 26 Stat. 209, also known as the Sherman Anti-Trust Act, which are classified to 15 U.S.C.A. § 1, 2, or 3.

Codifications

Pub.L. 98–473, § 1203(c)(4), which directed the amendment of the first par. of par. (1) by inserting "Deputy Attorney General, Associate Attorney General," after "Attorney General." was executed by making the insertion after the first reference to "Attorney General," to reflect the probable intent of Congress.

Section 102 of Pub.L. 104–294, which directed that par. (1)(c) of this section be amended by inserting "chapter 90 (relating to protection of trade secrets)," following "chapter 37 (relating to espionage),", could not be executed to text, as par. (1)(c) does not contain phrase "chapter 37 (relating to espionage),".

Amendment to par. (1)(c) by section 1365(c) of Pub.L. 99–570 was executed by inserting "section 1956 (laundering of monetary instruments), section 1957 (relating to engaging in monetary transactions in property derived from specified unlawful activity)," after "section 1955 (prohibition of business enterprises of gambling)," as the probable intent of Congress.

Amendment by section 601(d)(1) of Pub.L. 104–294, which directed that "or" be struck out after the semicolon in par. (1)(*l*), could not be executed in view of prior identical amendment by section 201(2) of Pub.L. 104–208.

Amendment by section 601(d)(2) of Pub.L. 104–294, which directed that "or" be substituted for "and" following the semicolon in par. (1)(n), could not be executed as the word "and" does not appear at the end of par. (1)(n). See also 2002 Amendments notes set out under this section.

Effective and Applicability Provisions

2002 Acts. Amendment made by section 4002(c)(1) of Pub.L. 107–273, as therein provided, effective Oct. 11, 1996, which is the date of enactment of Pub.L. 104–294, to which such amendment relates.

2000 Acts. Amendment by Pub.L. 106–181 applicable only to fiscal years beginning after September 30, 1999, see section 3 of Pub.L. 106–181, set out as a note under section 106 of Title 49.

1996 Acts. Section 6(a) of Pub.L. 104–287 provided in part that amendment by such section 6(a), amending this section and section 6101 of Title 31, Money and Finance, was effective July 5, 1994.

1994 Acts. Section 7(a) of Pub.L. 103–429 provided in part that amendment of this section by section 7(a) of Pub.L. 103–429 is effective July 5, 1994.

Section 330011(c)(1) of Pub.L. 103–322 provided in part that the amendment made by such section, amending section 3(b) of Pub.L. 101–298, was to take effect on the date on which section 3(b) of Pub.L. 101–298 took effect [section 3(b) of Pub.L. 101–298 took effect on the date of enactment of Pub.L. 101–298, which was approved May 22, 1990].

Section 330011(q)(1) of Pub.L. 103–322 provided in part that the amendment made by such section, repealing section 3568 of Pub.L. 101–647, was to take effect on the date section 3568 of Pub.L. 101–647 took effect [section 3568 of Pub.L.

101–647 took effect on the date of enactment of Pub.L. 101–647, which was approved Nov. 29, 1990].

Section 330011(r) of Pub.L. 103–322 provided in part that the amendment made by such section, amending language of section 2531(3) of Pub.L. 101–647, was to take effect on the date section 2531(3) of Pub.L. 101–647 took effect [section 2531(3) of Pub.L. 101–647 took effect on the date of enactment of Pub.L. 101–647, which was approved Nov. 29, 1990].

1986 Acts. Except as otherwise provided in section 111 of Pub.L. 99–508, amendment by Pub.L. 99–508 effective 90 days after Oct. 21, 1986, see section 111 of Pub.L. 99–508 set out as a note under section 2510 of this title.

1978 Acts. Amendment by Pub.L. 95–598 effective Oct. 1, 1979, see section 402(a) of Pub.L. 95–598, set out as a note preceding section 101 of Title 11, Bankruptcy.

Sunset Provisions

Provision that amendments by Pub.L. 107–56, Title II, Oct. 26, 2001, 115 Stat. 278, with certain exclusions, shall cease to have effect on March 10, 2006, except with respect to any particular foreign intelligence investigation that began before that date, or with respect to any particular offense or potential offense that began or occurred before that, such provisions to continue in effect, was repealed by Pub.L. 109–177, § 102(a), see Pub.L. 107–56, § 224, as amended, set out as a note under 18 U.S.C.A. § 2510.

Repeals

Section 3568 of Pub.L. 101–647, which made an identical amendment to par. (1)(j) of this section as did section 2531(3) of Pub.L. 101–647, was repealed by section 330011(q)(1) of Pub.L. 103–322.

Paragraph (2) of section 601(d) of Pub.L. 104–294, cited in the credit of this section, was repealed by section 4002(c)(1) of Pub.L. 107–273, effective Oct. 11, 1996.

Severability of Provisions

If any provision of Division C of Pub.L. 104–208 or the application of such provision to any person or circumstances is held to be unconstitutional, the remainder of Division C of Pub.L. 104–208 and the application of the provisions of Division C of Pub.L. 104–208 to any person or circumstance not to be affected thereby, see section 1(e) of Pub.L. 104–208, set out as a note under section 1101 of Title 8, Aliens and Nationality.

Amendment by section 314 of Pub.L. 95–598 not to affect the application of this section to any act of any person (1) committed before Oct. 1, 1979, or (2) committed after Oct. 1, 1979, in connection with a case commenced before such date, see section 403(d) of Pub.L. 95–598, set out preceding section 101 of Title 11, Bankruptcy.

CHAPTER 203—ARREST AND COMMITMENT

§ 3057. Bankruptcy investigations

(a) Any judge, receiver, or trustee having reasonable grounds for believing that any violation under chapter 9 of this title or other laws of the United States relating to insolvent debtors, receiverships or reorganization plans has been committed, or that an investigation should be had in connection therewith, shall report to the appropriate United States attorney all the facts and circumstances of the case, the names of the witnesses and the offense or offenses believed to have been committed. Where one of such officers has made such report, the others need not do so.

(b) The United States attorney thereupon shall inquire into the facts and report thereon to the judge, and if it appears probable that any such offense has been committed, shall without delay, present the matter to the grand jury, unless upon inquiry and examination he decides that the ends of public justice do not require investigation or prosecution, in which case he shall report the facts to the Attorney General for his direction.

(June 25, 1948, c. 645, 62 Stat. 818; May 24, 1949, c. 139, § 48, 63 Stat. 96; Nov. 6, 1978, Pub.L. 95–598, Title III, § 314(i), 92 Stat. 2677.)

HISTORICAL AND STATUTORY NOTES

Revision Notes and Legislative Reports

1948 Acts. Based on section 52(e)(1), (2) of Title 11, U.S.C., 1940 ed., Bankruptcy (July 1, 1898, c. 541, § 29e(1), (2), as added by May 27, 1926, c. 406, § 11, 44 Stat. 665, 666; June 22, 1938, c. 575, § 1, 52 Stat. 840, 856).

Remaining provisions of section 52 of Title 11, U.S.C., 1940 ed., Bankruptcy, constitute sections 151 to 154, and 3284 of this title.

The words "or laws relating to insolvent debtors, receiverships, or reorganization plans" were inserted to avoid reference to "Title 11".

Minor changes were made in phraseology.

1949 Acts. This section [section 48] clarifies the meaning of section 3057 of Title 18, U.S.C., by expressly limiting to laws "of the United States", violations of laws which are to be reported to the United States attorney.

Senate Report No. 303 and House Report No. 352, see 1949 U.S. Code Cong. Service, p. 1248.

1978 Acts. Senate Report No. 95–989 and House Report No. 95–595, see 1978 U.S. Code Cong. and Adm. News, p. 5787.

Effective and Applicability Provisions

1978 Acts. Amendment by Pub.L. 95–598 effective Oct. 1, 1979, see section 402(a) of Pub.L. 95–598, set out as an Effective Dates note preceding section 101 of Title 11, Bankruptcy.

Savings Provisions of Pub.L. 95–598

Amendment by section 314 of Pub.L. 95–598 not to affect the application of chapter 9 [§ 151 et seq.], chapter 96 [§ 1961 et seq.], or section 2516, 3057, or 3284 of this title to any act of any person (1) committed before Oct. 1, 1979, or (2) committed after Oct. 1, 1979, in connection with a case commenced before such date, see section 403(d) of Pub.L. 95–598, set out preceding section 151 of this title.

Transfer of Functions

All functions of all other officers of the Department of Justice and all functions of all agencies and employees of such Department were, with a few exceptions, transferred to the Attorney General, with power vested in him to authorize their performance or the performance of any of his functions by any of such officers, agencies, and employees, by Reorg. Plan No. 2, of 1950, §§ 1, 2, eff. May 24, 1950, 15 F.R. 3173, 64 Stat. 1261, set out in Appendix 1 to Title 5, Government Organization and Employees.

CHAPTER 213—LIMITATIONS

§ 3284. Concealment of bankrupt's assets

The concealment of assets of a debtor in a case under title 11 shall be deemed to be a continuing offense until the debtor shall have been finally discharged or a discharge denied, and the period of limitations shall not begin to run until such final discharge or denial of discharge.

(June 25, 1948, c. 645, 62 Stat. 828; Nov. 6, 1978, Pub.L. 95–598, Title III, § 314(k), 92 Stat. 2678.)

HISTORICAL AND STATUTORY NOTES

Revision Notes and Legislative Reports

1948 Acts. Based on section 52(d) of Title 11, U.S.C., 1940 ed., Bankruptcy (May 27, 1926, c. 406, § 11(d), 44 Stat. 665; June 22, 1938, c. 575, § 1, 52 Stat. 856).

The 3-year-limitation provision was omitted as unnecessary in view of the general statute, section 3282 of this title.

The words "or a discharge denied" and "or denial of discharge" were added on the recommendation of the Department of Justice to supply an omission in existing law.

Other subsections of said section 52 of Title 11, U.S.C., 1940 ed., are incorporated in sections 151–154 and 3057 of this title.

Other minor changes of phraseology were made.

1978 Acts. Senate Report No. 95–989 and House Report No. 95–595, see 1978 U.S. Code Cong. and Adm. News, p. 5787.

Effective and Applicability Provisions

1978 Acts. Amendment by Pub.L. 95–598 effective Oct. 1, 1979, see section 402(a) of Pub.L. 95–598, set out as an Effective Date note preceding section 101 of Title 11, Bankruptcy.

Savings Provisions

Amendment by section 314 of Pub.L. 95–598 not to affect the application of this section to any act of any person (1) committed before Oct. 1, 1979, or (2) committed after Oct. 1, 1979, in connection with a case commenced before such date, see section 403(d) of Pub.L. 95–598, set out preceding section 101 of Title 11, Bankruptcy.

CROSS REFERENCES

Bankruptcy investigations, see 18 USCA § 3057.

Five year limitation on offenses relating to bankruptcy, see 18 USCA § 3282.

Offenses relating to bankruptcy, see 18 USCA § 151 et seq.

TITLE 28
JUDICIARY AND JUDICIAL PROCEDURE

PART I—ORGANIZATION OF COURTS

CHAPTER 6—BANKRUPTCY JUDGES

[1] So in original. Does not conform to section catchline.

Effective and Applicability Provisions

2005 Acts. Amendments by Pub.L. 109–8, Title VI, § 601, effective 18 months after Apr. 20, 2005, see Pub.L. 109–8, § 601(c), set out as a note under 28 U.S.C.A. § 159.

Except as otherwise provided, amendments by Pub.L. 109–8 effective 180 days after April 20, 2005, and inapplicable with respect to cases commenced under Title 11 before the effective date, see Pub.L. 109–8, § 1501, set out as a note under 11 U.S.C.A. § 101.

§ 151. Designation of bankruptcy courts

In each judicial district, the bankruptcy judges in regular active service shall constitute a unit of the district court to be known as the bankruptcy court for that district. Each bankruptcy judge, as a judicial officer of the district court, may exercise the authority conferred under this chapter with respect to any action, suit, or proceeding and may preside alone and hold a regular or special session of the court, except as otherwise provided by law or by rule or order of the district court.

(Added Pub.L. 98–353, Title I, § 104(a), July 10, 1984, 98 Stat. 336.)

HISTORICAL AND STATUTORY NOTES

Revision Notes and Legislative Reports

1984 Acts. Statements by Legislative Leaders, see 1984 U.S.Code Cong. and Adm.News, p. 576.

Codifications

This section as added by Pub.L. 95–598, Title II, § 201(a), Nov. 6, 1978, 92 Stat. 2657, effective June 28, 1984, pursuant to Pub.L. 95–598, Title IV, § 402(b), Nov. 6, 1978, 92 Stat. 2682, as amended by Pub.L. 98–249, § 1(a), Mar. 31, 1984, 98 Stat. 116; Pub.L. 98–271, § 1(a), Apr. 30, 1984, 98 Stat. 163; Pub.L. 98–299, § 1(a), May 25, 1984, 98 Stat. 214; Pub.L. 98–325, § 1(a), June 20, 1984, 98 Stat. 268, set out as a note preceding section 101 of Title 11, Bankruptcy, read as follows:

§ 151. Creation and composition of bankruptcy courts

(a) There shall be in each judicial district, as an adjunct to the district court for such district, a bankruptcy court which shall be a court of record known as the United States Bankruptcy Court for the district.

(b) Each bankruptcy court shall consist of the bankruptcy judge or judges for the district in regular active service. Justices or judges designated and assigned shall be competent to sit as judges of the bankruptcy court.

(c) Except as otherwise provided by law, or rule or order of court, the judicial power of a bankruptcy court with respect to any action, suit or proceeding may be exercised by a single bankruptcy judge, who may preside alone and hold a regular or special session of court at the same time other sessions are held by other bankruptcy judges.

Section 402(b) of Pub.L. 95–598 was amended by section 113 of Pub.L. 98–353 by substituting "shall not be effective" for "shall take effect on June 28, 1984", thereby eliminating the addition of section 151 by section 201(a) of Pub.L. 95–598, effective June 27, 1984, pursuant to section 122(c) of Pub.L. 98–353, set out as an Effective and Applicability Provisions note under this section.

Section 121(a) of Pub.L. 98–353 directed that section 402(b) of Pub.L. 95–598 be amended by substituting "the date of enactment of the Bankruptcy Amendments and Federal Judgeship Act of 1984 [i.e. July 10, 1984]" for "June 28, 1984". This amendment was not executed in view of the prior amendment to section 402(b) of Pub.L. 95–598 by section 113 of Pub.L. 98–353.

Effective and Applicability Provisions

1984 Acts. Section 122 of Title I of Pub.L. 98–353 provided that:

"**(a)** Except as otherwise provided in this section, this title and the amendments made by this title [Title I of Pub.L. 98–353, enacting this chapter, and sections 1408 to 1412 and 1452 of this title, amending sections 372, 634, 957, 1334, 1360, and 1930 of this title, sections 8331, 8334, 8336, 8339, 8341, and 8344 of Title 5, Government Organization and Employees, and section 105 of Title 11, Bankruptcy, enacting provisions set out as notes preceding section 151 of this title and under sections 151, 152, 153, 634, and 1334 of this title and section 8331 of Title 5, amending provisions set out as notes preceding sections 151 and 1471 of this title and section 101 of Title 11, and repealing provisions set out as notes preceding this section and section 1471 of this title] shall take effect on the date of the enactment of this Act [July 10, 1984].

"(b) Section 1334(c)(2) of title 28, United States Code [section 1334(c)(2) of this title], and section 1411(a) of title 28, United States Code, as added by this Act [section 1411(a) of this title], shall not apply with respect to cases under title 11 of the United States Code [Title 11] that are pending on the date of enactment of this Act [July 10, 1984], or to proceedings arising in or related to such cases.

"(c) Sections 108(b) [enacting provisions set out as a note under section 634 of this title], 113 [amending section 402(b) of Pub.L. 95–598, set out as a note preceding section 101 of Title 11], and 121(e) [enacting provisions set out as a note preceding section 151 of this title] shall take effect on June 27, 1984."

Separability of Provisions

Section 119 of Pub.L. 98–353 provided that: "If any provision of this Act [see Short Title of 1984 Amendments note set out under this section] or the application thereof to any person or circumstance is held invalid, the remainder of this Act, or the application of that provision to persons or circumstances other than those as to which it is held invalid, is not affected thereby."

Short Title

1984 Amendments. Section 1 of Pub.L. 98–353 provided: That this Act [enacting this chapter and sections 1408 to 1412 and 1452 of this title and sections 557, 558, 559, and 1113 of Title 11, Bankruptcy, amending sections 44, 98, 131, 133, 371, 372, 634, 957, 1334, 1360, and 1930 of this title, sections 8331, 8334, 8336, 8339, 8341, 8344, 8701, 8706, 8714a, and 8714b of Title 5, Government Organization and Employees, and sections 101, 102, 103, 105, 108, 109, 303, 321, 322, 326, 327, 328, 329, 330, 342, 343, 345, 346, 349, 350, 361, 362, 363, 365, 366, 501, 502, 503, 505, 506, 507, 509, 510, 521, 522, 523, 524, 525, 541, 542, 543, 544, 545, 546, 547, 548, 549, 550, 552, 553, 554, 555, 702, 703, 704, 707, 723, 724, 725, 726, 727, 728, 741, 745, 752, 761, 763, 764, 765, 766, 901, 902, 903, 921, 922, 927, 943, 945, 1102, 1103, 1105, 1106, 1107, 1108, 1112, 1121, 1123, 1124, 1125, 1126, 1127, 1129, 1141, 1142, 1144, 1145, 1146, 1166, 1168, 1169, 1170, 1171, 1173, 1301, 1302, 1304, 1307, 1322, 1324, 1325, 1326, 1328, 1329, 15103, and 151302 of Title 11, Bankruptcy Rules 2002 and 3001, Title 11, and Bankruptcy Form No. 1, Title 11, enacting provisions set out as notes preceding section 151 of this title and under sections 44, 133, 151, 152, 153, 371, 634, 1334, and 2075 of this title, sections 8331 and 8706 of Title 5, and preceding section 101 and sections 101, 365, and 1113 of Title 11, amending provisions set out as notes preceding sections 151, 581 and 1471 of this title and section 101 of Title 11, and repealing provisions set out as notes preceding this section and section 1471 of this title] may be cited as the 'Bankruptcy Amendments and Federal Judgeship Act of 1984'."

§ 152. Appointment of bankruptcy judges

(a)(1) Each bankruptcy judge to be appointed for a judicial district, as provided in paragraph (2), shall be appointed by the court of appeals of the United States for the circuit in which such district is located. Such appointments shall be made after considering the recommendations of the Judicial Conference submitted pursuant to subsection (b). Each bankruptcy judge shall be appointed for a term of fourteen years, subject to the provisions of subsection (e). However, upon the expiration of the term, a bankruptcy judge may, with the approval of the judicial council of the circuit, continue to perform the duties of the office until the earlier of the date which is 180 days after the expiration of the term or the date of the appointment of a successor. Bankruptcy judges shall serve as judicial officers of the United States district court established under Article III of the Constitution.

(2) The bankruptcy judges appointed pursuant to this section shall be appointed for the several judicial districts as follows:

Districts	Judges
Alabama:	
Northern	5
Middle	2
Southern	2
Alaska	2
Arizona	7
Arkansas:	
Eastern and Western	3
California:	
Northern	9
Eastern	6
Central	21
Southern	4
Colorado	5
Connecticut	3
Delaware	1
District of Columbia	1
Florida:	
Northern	1
Middle	8
Southern	5
Georgia:	
Northern	8
Middle	3
Southern	2
Hawaii	1
Idaho	2
Illinois:	
Northern	10
Central	3
Southern	1
Indiana:	
Northern	3
Southern	4
Iowa:	
Northern	2
Southern	2
Kansas	4
Kentucky:	
Eastern	2
Western	3
Louisiana:	
Eastern	2
Middle	1

Districts	Judges
Western	3
Maine	2
Maryland	4
Massachusetts	5
Michigan:	
Eastern	4
Western	3
Minnesota	4
Mississippi:	
Northern	1
Southern	2
Missouri:	
Eastern	3
Western	3
Montana	1
Nebraska	2
Nevada	3
New Hampshire	1
New Jersey	8
New Mexico	2
New York:	
Northern	2
Southern	9
Eastern	6
Western	3
North Carolina:	
Eastern	2
Middle	2
Western	2
North Dakota	1
Ohio:	
Northern	8
Southern	7
Oklahoma:	
Northern	2
Eastern	1
Western	3
Oregon	5
Pennsylvania:	
Eastern	5
Middle	2
Western	4
Puerto Rico	2
Rhode Island	1
South Carolina	2
South Dakota	2
Tennessee:	
Eastern	3
Middle	3
Western	4
Texas:	
Northern	6
Eastern	2
Southern	6
Western	4
Utah	3
Vermont	1
Virginia:	
Eastern	5
Western	3
Washington:	
Eastern	2
Western	5
West Virginia:	
Northern	1
Southern	1
Wisconsin:	
Eastern	4
Western	2
Wyoming	1

(3) Whenever a majority of the judges of any court of appeals cannot agree upon the appointment of a bankruptcy judge, the chief judge of such court shall make such appointment.

(4) The judges of the district courts for the territories shall serve as the bankruptcy judges for such courts. The United States court of appeals for the circuit within which such a territorial district court is located may appoint bankruptcy judges under this chapter for such district if authorized to do so by the Congress of the United States under this section.

(b)(1) The Judicial Conference of the United States shall, from time to time, and after considering the recommendations submitted by the Director of the Administrative Office of the United States Courts after such Director has consulted with the judicial council of the circuit involved, determine the official duty stations of bankruptcy judges and places of holding court.

(2) The Judicial Conference shall, from time to time, submit recommendations to the Congress regarding the number of bankruptcy judges needed and the districts in which such judges are needed.

(3) Not later than December 31, 1994, and not later than the end of each 2–year period thereafter, the Judicial Conference of the United States shall conduct a comprehensive review of all judicial districts to assess the continuing need for the bankruptcy judges authorized by this section, and shall report to the Congress its findings and any recommendations for the elimination of any authorized position which can be eliminated when a vacancy exists by reason of resignation, retirement, removal, or death.

(c)(1) Each bankruptcy judge may hold court at such places within the judicial district, in addition to the official duty station of such judge, as the business of the court may require.

(2)(A) Bankruptcy judges may hold court at such places within the United States outside the judicial district as the nature of the business of the court may require, and upon such notice as the court orders, upon a finding by either the chief judge of the bankruptcy court (or, if the chief judge is unavailable, the most senior available bankruptcy judge) or by the judicial council of the circuit that, because of emergency conditions, no location within the district is reasonably available where the bankruptcy judges could hold court.

(B) Bankruptcy judges may transact any business at special sessions of court held outside the district pursuant to this paragraph that might be transacted at a regular session.

(C) If a bankruptcy court issues an order exercising its authority under subparagraph (A), the court—

(i) through the Administrative Office of the United States Courts, shall—

(I) send notice of such order, including the reasons for the issuance of such order, to the Committee on the Judiciary of the Senate and the Committee on the Judiciary of the House of Representatives; and

(II) not later than 180 days after the expiration of such court order submit a brief report to the Committee on the Judiciary of the Senate and the Committee on the Judiciary of the House of Representatives describing the impact of such order, including—

(aa) the reasons for the issuance of such order;

(bb) the duration of such order;

(cc) the impact of such order on litigants; and

(dd) the costs to the judiciary resulting from such order; and

(ii) shall provide reasonable notice to the United States Marshals Service before the commencement of any special session held pursuant to such order.

(d) With the approval of the Judicial Conference and of each of the judicial councils involved, a bankruptcy judge may be designated to serve in any district adjacent to or near the district for which such bankruptcy judge was appointed.

(e) A bankruptcy judge may be removed during the term for which such bankruptcy judge is appointed, only for incompetence, misconduct, neglect of duty, or physical or mental disability and only by the judicial council of the circuit in which the judge's official duty station is located. Removal may not occur unless a majority of all of the judges of such council concur in the order of removal. Before any order of removal may be entered, a full specification of charges shall be furnished to such bankruptcy judge who shall be accorded an opportunity to be heard on such charges.

(Added Pub.L. 98–353, Title I, § 104(a), July 10, 1984, 98 Stat. 336, and amended Pub.L. 99–554, Title I, § 101, Oct. 27, 1986, 100 Stat. 3088; Pub.L. 100–587, Nov. 3, 1988, 102 Stat. 2982; Pub.L. 101–650, Title III, § 304, Dec. 1, 1990, 104 Stat. 5105; Pub.L. 102–361, §§ 2, 4, Aug. 26, 1992, 106 Stat. 965, 966; Pub.L. 109–8, Title XII, § 1223(d), Apr. 20, 2005, 119 Stat. 198; Pub.L. 109–63, § 2(c), Sept. 9, 2005, 119 Stat. 1994.)

HISTORICAL AND STATUTORY NOTES

Revision Notes and Legislative Reports

1984 Acts. Statements by Legislative Leaders, see 1984 U.S. Code Cong. and Adm. News, p. 576.

1986 Acts. House Report No. 99–764 and House Conference Report No. 99–958, see 1986 U.S. Code Cong. and Adm. News, p. 5227.

1988 Acts. House Report No. 100–756, see 1988 U.S. Code Cong. and Adm. News, p. 3979.

1990 Acts. Senate Report No. 101–416, Related House Reports, and Statement by President, see 1990 U.S. Code Cong. and Adm. News, p. 6802.

1992 Acts. House Report No. 102–825, see 1992 U.S. Code Cong. and Adm. News, p. 855.

2005 Acts. House Report No. 109–31(Part I), see 2005 U.S. Code Cong. and Adm. News, p. 88.

Codifications

This section as added by Pub.L. 95–598, Title II, § 201(a), Nov. 6, 1978, 92 Stat. 2657, effective June 28, 1984, pursuant to Pub.L. 95–598, Title IV, § 402(b), Nov. 6, 1978, 92 Stat. 2682, as amended by Pub.L. 98–249, § 1(a), Mar. 31, 1984, 98 Stat. 116; Pub.L. 98–271, § 1(a), Apr. 30, 1984, 98 Stat. 163; Pub.L. 98–299, § 1(a), May 25, 1984, 98 Stat. 214; Pub.L. 98–325, § 1(a), June 20, 1984, 98 Stat. 268, set out as a note preceding section 101 of Title 11, Bankruptcy, read as follows:

"§ 152. Appointment of bankruptcy judges

"The President shall appoint, by and with the advice and consent of the Senate, bankruptcy judges for the several judicial districts. In each instance, the President shall give due consideration to the recommended nominee or nominees of the Judicial Council of the Circuit within which an appointment is to be made."

Section 402(b) of Pub.L. 95–598 was amended by section 113 of Pub.L. 98–353 by substituting "shall not be effective" for "shall take effect on June 28, 1984", thereby eliminating the addition of section 152 by section 201(a) of Pub.L. 95–598, effective June 27, 1984, pursuant to section 122(c) of Pub.L. 98–353, set out as an Effective and Applicability Provisions note under 28 U.S.C.A. § 151.

Section 121(a) of Pub.L. 98–353 directed that section 402(b) of Pub.L. 95–598 be amended by substituting "the date of enactment of the Bankruptcy Amendments and Federal Judgeship Act of 1984 [i.e. July 10, 1984]" for "June 28, 1984". This amendment was not executed in view of the prior amendment to section 402(b) of Pub.L. 95–598 by section 113 of Pub.L. 98–353.

Effective and Applicability Provisions

2005 Acts. Pub.L. 109–8, Title XII, § 1223(e), Apr. 20, 2005, 119 Stat. 198, provided that: "The amendments made by this section [amending this section and enacting provisions set out as notes under this section and 28 U.S.C.A. § 1] shall take effect on the date of the enactment of this Act [Apr. 20, 2005]."

Except as otherwise provided, amendments by Pub.L. 109–8 effective 180 days after April 20, 2005, and inapplicable with respect to cases commenced under Title 11 before the effective date, see Pub.L. 109–8, § 1501, set out as a note under 11 U.S.C.A. § 101.

1986 Acts. Amendment by Pub.L. 99–554 effective on Oct. 27, 1986, see section 302(b) of Pub.L. 99–554, set out as a note under section 581 of this title.

1984 Acts. Section effective July 10, 1984, see section 122(a) of Pub.L. 98–353, set out as a note under section 151 of this title.

Termination of Reporting Requirements

For termination of reporting provisions of subsec. (b)(2) of this section, effective May 15, 2000, see Pub.L. 104–66, § 3003, as amended, set out as a note under 31 U.S.C.A. § 1113, and the 16th item on page 12 of House Document No. 103–7.

Temporary Judgeships: Appointments, Vacancies, and Extensions

Pub.L. 109–8, Title XII, § 1223(b), (c), Apr. 20, 2005, 119 Stat. 196, 198, provided that:

"**(b) Temporary Judgeships.**—

"**(1) Appointments.**—The following bankruptcy judges shall be appointed in the manner prescribed in section 152(a)(1) of title 28, United States Code, for the appointment of bankruptcy judges provided for in section 152(a)(2) of such title:

"**(A)** One additional bankruptcy judge for the eastern district of California.

"**(B)** Three additional bankruptcy judges for the central district of California.

"**(C)** Four additional bankruptcy judges for the district of Delaware.

"**(D)** Two additional bankruptcy judges for the southern district of Florida.

"**(E)** One additional bankruptcy judge for the southern district of Georgia.

"**(F)** Three additional bankruptcy judges for the district of Maryland.

"**(G)** One additional bankruptcy judge for the eastern district of Michigan.

"**(H)** One additional bankruptcy judge for the southern district of Mississippi.

"**(I)** One additional bankruptcy judge for the district of New Jersey.

"**(J)** One additional bankruptcy judge for the eastern district of New York.

"**(K)** One additional bankruptcy judge for the northern district of New York.

"**(L)** One additional bankruptcy judge for the southern district of New York.

"**(M)** One additional bankruptcy judge for the eastern district of North Carolina.

"**(N)** One additional bankruptcy judge for the eastern district of Pennsylvania.

"**(O)** One additional bankruptcy judge for the middle district of Pennsylvania.

"**(P)** One additional bankruptcy judge for the district of Puerto Rico.

"**(Q)** One additional bankruptcy judge for the western district of Tennessee.

"**(R)** One additional bankruptcy judge for the eastern district of Virginia.

"**(S)** One additional bankruptcy judge for the district of South Carolina.

"**(T)** One additional bankruptcy judge for the district of Nevada.

"**(2) Vacancies.**—

"**(A) Districts with single appointments.**—Except as provided in subparagraphs (B), (C), (D), and (E), the first vacancy occurring in the office of bankruptcy judge in each of the judicial districts set forth in paragraph (1)—

"**(i)** occurring 5 years or more after the appointment date of the bankruptcy judge appointed under paragraph (1) to such office; and

"**(ii)** resulting from the death, retirement, resignation, or removal of a bankruptcy judge;

shall not be filled.

"**(B) Central district of California.**—The 1st, 2d, and 3d vacancies in the office of bankruptcy judge in the central district of California—

"**(i)** occurring 5 years or more after the respective 1st, 2d, and 3d appointment dates of the bankruptcy judges appointed under paragraph (1)(B); and

"**(ii)** resulting from the death, retirement, resignation, or removal of a bankruptcy judge;

shall not be filled.

"**(C) District of Delaware.**—The 1st, 2d, 3d, and 4th vacancies in the office of bankruptcy judge in the district of Delaware—

"**(i)** occurring 5 years or more after the respective 1st, 2d, 3d, and 4th appointment dates of the bankruptcy judges appointed under paragraph (1)(F); and

"**(ii)** resulting from the death, retirement, resignation, or removal of a bankruptcy judge;

shall not be filled.

"**(D) Southern district of Florida.**—The 1st and 2d vacancies in the office of bankruptcy judge in the southern district of Florida—

"**(i)** occurring 5 years or more after the respective 1st and 2d appointment dates of the bankruptcy judges appointed under paragraph (1)(D); and

"**(ii)** resulting from the death, retirement, resignation, or removal of a bankruptcy judge;

shall not be filled.

"**(E) District of Maryland.**—The 1st, 2d, and 3d vacancies in the office of bankruptcy judge in the district of Maryland—

"**(i)** occurring 5 years or more after the respective 1st, 2d, and 3d appointment dates of the bankruptcy judges appointed under paragraph (1)(F); and

"**(ii)** resulting from the death, retirement, resignation, or removal of a bankruptcy judge;

shall not be filled.

"**(c) Extensions.**—

"**(1) In general.**—The temporary office of bankruptcy judges authorized for the northern district of Alabama, the district of Delaware, the district of Puerto Rico, and the eastern district of Tennessee under paragraphs (1), (3), (7), and (9) of section 3(a) of the Bankruptcy Judgeship Act of 1992 (28 U.S.C. 152 note) are extended until the first vacancy occurring in the office of a bankruptcy judge in the applicable district resulting from the death, retirement, resignation, or removal of a bankruptcy judge and occurring 5 years after the date of the enactment of this Act [April 20, 2005].

"(2) **Applicability of other provisions.**—All other provisions of section 3 of the Bankruptcy Judgeship Act of 1992 (28 U.S.C. 152 note) remain applicable to the temporary office of bankruptcy judges referred to in this subsection."

[Amendments by Pub.L. 109–8, § 1223, effective Apr. 20, 2005, see Pub.L. 109–8, § 1223(e), set out as a note under this section.]

Temporary Appointment of Additional Judges

Section 3 of Pub.L. 102–361, as amended Pub.L. 104–317, Title III, § 307, Oct. 19, 1996, 110 Stat. 3852, provided that:

"**(a) Appointments.**—The following bankruptcy judges shall be appointed in the manner prescribed in section 152(a)(1) of title 28, United States Code [subsec. (a)(1) of this section]:

"(1) 1 additional bankruptcy judge for the northern district of Alabama.

"(2) 1 additional bankruptcy judge for the district of Colorado.

"(3) 1 additional bankruptcy judge for the district of Delaware.

"(4) 1 additional bankruptcy judge for the southern district of Illinois.

"(5) 1 additional bankruptcy judge for the district of New Hampshire.

"(6) 1 additional bankruptcy judge for the middle district of North Carolina.

"(7) 1 additional bankruptcy judge for the district of Puerto Rico.

"(8) 1 additional bankruptcy judge for the district of South Carolina.

"(9) 1 additional bankruptcy judge for the eastern district of Tennessee.

"(10) 1 additional bankruptcy judge for the western district of Texas.

"**(b) Vacancies.**—The first vacancy in the office of bankruptcy judge in each of the judicial districts set forth in subsection (a), resulting from the death, retirement, resignation, or removal of a bankruptcy judge, and occurring 5 years or more after the appointment date of the judge named to fill the temporary judgeship position shall not be filled. In the case of a vacancy resulting from the expiration of the term of a bankruptcy judge not described in the preceding sentence, that judge shall be eligible for reappointment as a bankruptcy judge in that district."

Appointment to Fill Vacancies; Nominations; Qualifications

Section 120 of Pub.L. 98–353, as amended Pub.L. 99–554, Title I, § 102, Oct. 22, 1986, 100 Stat. 3089; Pub.L. 104–317, Title III, § 303, Oct. 19, 1996, 110 Stat. 3852, provided that:

"(a)(1) Whenever a court of appeals is authorized to fill a vacancy that occurs on a bankruptcy court of the United States, such court of appeals shall appoint to fill that vacancy a person whose character, experience, ability, and impartiality qualify such person to serve in the Federal judiciary.

"(2) It is the sense of the Congress that the courts of appeals should consider for appointment under section 152 of title 28, United States Code [this section], to the first vacancy which arises after the date of the enactment of this Act [July 10, 1984] in the office of each bankruptcy judge, the bankruptcy judge who holds such office immediately before such vacancy arises, if such bankruptcy judge requests to be considered for such appointment.

"(3) When filling vacancies, the court of appeals may consider reappointing incumbent bankruptcy judges under procedures prescribed by regulations issued by the Judicial Conference of the United States.

"(b) The judicial council of the circuit involved shall assist the court of appeals by evaluating potential nominees and by recommending to such court for consideration for appointment to each vacancy on the bankruptcy court persons who are qualified to be bankruptcy judges under regulations prescribed by the Judicial Conference of the United States. In the case of the first vacancy which arises after the date of the enactment of this Act [July 10, 1984] in the office of each bankruptcy judge, such potential nominees shall include the bankruptcy judge who holds such office immediately before such vacancy arises, if such bankruptcy judge requests to be considered for such appointment and the judicial council determines that such judge is qualified under subsection (c) of this section to continue to serve. Such potential nominees shall receive consideration equal to that given all other potential nominees for such position. All incumbent nominees seeking reappointment thereafter may be considered for such a reappointment, pursuant to a majority vote of the judges of the appointing court of appeals, under procedures authorized under subsection (a)(3).

"(c) Before transmitting to the court of appeals the names of the persons the judicial council for the circuit deems best qualified to fill any existing vacancy, the judicial council shall have determined that—

"(1) public notice of such vacancy has been given and an effort has been made, in the case of each such vacancy, to identify qualified candidates, without regard to race, color, sex, religion, or national origin,

"(2) such persons are members in good standing of at least one State bar, the District of Columbia bar, or the bar of the Commonwealth of Puerto Rico, and members in good standing of every other bar of which they are members,

"(3) such persons possess, and have a reputation for, integrity and good character,

"(4) such persons are of sound physical and mental health,

"(5) such persons possess and have demonstrated commitment to equal justice under law,

"(6) such persons possess and have demonstrated outstanding legal ability and competence, as evidenced by substantial legal experience, ability to deal with complex legal problems, aptitude for legal scholarship and writing, and familiarity with courts and court processes, and

"(7) such persons [sic] demeanor, character, and personality indicate that they would exhibit judicial temperament if appointed to the position of United States bankruptcy judge."

Extension and Termination of Term of Office of Bankruptcy Judge and Part-Time Bankruptcy Judge Serving on July 10, 1984; Practice of Law by Part-Time Bankruptcy Judge

Section 106 of Pub.L. 98–353 provided that:

"**(a)** Notwithstanding section 152 of title 28, United States Code, as added by this Act [this section], the term of office of a bankruptcy judge who is serving on the date of enactment of this Act [July 10, 1984] is extended to and expires four years after the date such bankruptcy judge was last appointed to such office or on October 1, 1986, whichever is later.

"**(b)(1)** Notwithstanding section 153(a) of title 28, United States Code, as added by this Act [section 153(a) of this title], and notwithstanding subsection (a) of this section, a bankruptcy judge serving on a part-time basis on the date of enactment of this Act [July 10, 1984] may continue to serve on such basis for a period not to exceed two years from the date of enactment of this Act [July 10, 1984].

"**(2)** Notwithstanding the provisions of section 153(b) of title 28, United States Code [section 153(b) of this title], a bankruptcy judge serving on a part-time basis may engage in the practice of law but may not engage in any other practice, business, occupation, or employment inconsistent with the expeditious, proper, and impartial performance of such bankruptcy judge's duties as a judicial officer. The Judicial Conference of the United States may promulgate appropriate rules and regulations to implement this paragraph."

Extension and Termination of Term of Office of Part-Time Bankruptcy Judge Serving on July 2, 1986, In District of Oregon, Western District of Michigan, and Eastern District of Oklahoma

Pub.L. 99–349, Title I, July 2, 1986, 100 Stat. 718, provided that: "Notwithstanding the provisions of section 106(b)(1) of the Bankruptcy Amendments and Federal Judgeship Act of 1984 [section 106(b)(1) of Pub.L. 98–353, set out as a note under this section], a bankruptcy judge serving on a part-time basis on the date of enactment of this Act [July 2, 1986] may continue to serve as a part-time judge for such district until December 31, 1986, or until such time as a full-time bankruptcy judge for such district is appointed, whichever is earlier: *Provided,* That these provisions shall apply only to part-time bankruptcy judges serving in the district of Oregon, the western district of Michigan, and the eastern district of Oklahoma."

CROSS REFERENCES

Appeals, hearing of, see 28 USCA § 158.

Definition of Bankruptcy judge as including a judge appointed under this section for purposes of civil service retirement, see 5 USCA § 8331.

Removal of judges for disability to be in accordance with provisions of this section, see 28 USCA § 372.

Retirement of bankruptcy judges and magistrates, see 28 USCA § 377.

§ 153. Salaries; character of service

(a) Each bankruptcy judge shall serve on a full-time basis and shall receive as full compensation for his services, a salary at an annual rate that is equal to 92 percent of the salary of a judge of the district court of the United States as determined pursuant to section 135, to be paid at such times as the Judicial Conference of the United States determines.

(b) A bankruptcy judge may not engage in the practice of law and may not engage in any other practice, business, occupation, or employment inconsistent with the expeditious, proper, and impartial performance of such bankruptcy judge's duties as a judicial officer. The Conference may promulgate appropriate rules and regulations to implement this subsection.

(c) Each individual appointed under this chapter shall take the oath or affirmation prescribed by section 453 of this title before performing the duties of the office of bankruptcy judge.

(d) A bankruptcy judge appointed under this chapter shall be exempt from the provisions of subchapter I of chapter 63 of title 5.

(Added Pub.L. 98–353, Title I, § 104(a), July 10, 1984, 98 Stat. 338, and amended Pub.L. 100–202, § 101(a) [Title IV, § 408(a)], Dec. 22, 1987, 101 Stat. 1329–26; Pub.L. 100–702, Title X, § 1003(a)(1), Nov. 19, 1988, 102 Stat. 4665.)

HISTORICAL AND STATUTORY NOTES

Revision Notes and Legislative Reports

1984 Acts. Statements by Legislative Leaders, see 1984 U.S.Code Cong. and Adm.News, p. 576.

1988 Acts. House Report No. 100–889, see 1988 U.S.Code Cong. and Adm.News, p. 5982.

Codifications

This section as added by Pub.L. 95–598, Title II, § 201(a), Nov. 6, 1978, 92 Stat. 2657, effective June 28, 1984, pursuant to Pub.L. 95–598, Title IV, § 402(b), Nov. 6, 1978, 92 Stat. 2682, as amended by Pub.L. 98–249, § 1(a), Mar. 31, 1984, 98 Stat. 116; Pub.L. 98–271, § 1(a), Apr. 30, 1984, 98 Stat. 163; Pub.L. 98–299, § 1(a), May 25, 1984, 98 Stat. 214; Pub.L. 98–325, § 1(a), June 20, 1984, 98 Stat. 268, set out as a note preceding section 101 of Title 11, Bankruptcy, read as follows:

§ 153. Tenure and residence of bankruptcy judges

(a) Each bankruptcy judge shall hold office for a term of 14 years, but may continue to perform the duties of his office until his successor takes office, unless such office has been eliminated.

(b) Removal of a bankruptcy judge during the term for which he is appointed shall be only for incompetency, misconduct, neglect of duty, or physical or mental disability. Removal shall be by the judicial council of the circuit or circuits in which the bankruptcy judge serves, but removal may not occur unless a majority of all the judges of such circuit council or councils concur in the order of removal. Before any order of removal may be entered, a full specification of the charges shall be furnished to the bankruptcy judge, and he shall be accorded an opportunity to be heard on the charges. Any cause for removal of any bankruptcy judge coming to the knowledge of the Director of the Administrative Office of the United States Courts shall be reported by him to the chief judge of the circuit or circuits in which he serves, and a copy of the report shall at the same time be transmitted to the circuit council or councils and to the bankruptcy judge.

(c) Each bankruptcy judge shall reside in the district or one of the districts for which he is appointed, or within 20 miles of his official station.

(d) If the public interest and the nature of the business of a bankruptcy court require that a bankruptcy judge should maintain his abode at or near a particular part of the district the judicial council of the circuit may so declare and may make an appropriate order. If the bankruptcy judges of such a district are unable to agree as to which of them shall maintain his abode at or near the place or within the area specified in such an order the judicial council of the circuit may decide which of them shall do so.

Section 402(b) of Pub.L. 95–598 was amended by section 113 of Pub.L. 98–353 by substituting "shall not be effective" for "shall take effect on June 28, 1984", thereby eliminating the addition of section 153 by section 201(a) of Pub.L. 95–598, effective June 27, 1984, pursuant to section 122(c) of Pub.L. 98–353, set out as an Effective Date note under section 151 of this title.

Section 121(a) of Pub.L. 98–353 directed that section 402(b) of Pub.L. 95–598 be amended by substituting "the date of enactment of the Bankruptcy Amendments and Federal Judgeship Act of 1984 [i.e. July 10, 1984]" for "June 28, 1984". This amendment was not executed in view of the prior amendment to section 402(b) of Pub.L. 95–598 by section 113 of Pub.L. 98–353.

Effective and Applicability Provisions

1987 Acts. Section 101(a) [Title IV, § 408(d)] of Pub.L. 100–202 provided that: "This section [amending this section, section 634 of this title, and section 356 of Title 2, The Congress] shall become effective October 1, 1988, and any salary affected by the provisions of this section shall be adjusted at the beginning of the first applicable pay period commencing on or after such date of enactment [probably should read "such date", meaning Oct. 1, 1988]."

1984 Acts. Section effective July 10, 1984, see section 122(a) of Pub.L. 98–353, set out as a note under section 151 of this title.

Continuation of Salaries of Bankruptcy Judges in Effect on June 27, 1984

Section 105(a) of Pub.L. 98–353 provided that: "The salary of a bankruptcy judge in effect on June 27, 1984, shall remain in effect until changed as a result of a determination or adjustment made pursuant to section 153(a) of title 28, United States Code, as added by this Act [subsec. (a) of this section]."

Increase in Salaries

1988—Salaries of bankruptcy judges continued at $72,500 per annum by Ex. Ord. No. 12622, Dec. 31, 1987, 53 F.R. 222, formerly set out as a note under section 5332 of Title 5, Government Organization and Employees.

1987—Salaries of bankruptcy judges increased to $72,500 per annum, on recommendation of the President of the United States, see note set out under section 358 of Title 2, The Congress.

Salaries of bankruptcy judges increased to $70,500 effective on the first day of the first pay period beginning on or after January 1, 1987, by Ex. Ord. No. 12578, Dec. 31, 1986, 52 F.R. 505, formerly set out as a note under section 5332 of Title 5.

1985—Salaries of bankruptcy judges increased to $68,400 effective on the first day of the first pay period beginning on or after Jan. 1, 1985, by Ex. Ord. No. 12496, Dec. 28, 1984, 50 F.R. 211, as amended by Ex. Ord. No. 12540, Dec. 30, 1985, 51 F.R. 577, formerly set out as a note under section 5332 of Title 5.

1984—Salaries of bankruptcy judges (full-time) and bankruptcy judges (part-time) (maximum rate) increased to $66,100 and $33,100, respectively, effective on the first day of the first pay period beginning on or after Jan. 1, 1984, by Ex. Ord. No. 12456, Dec. 30, 1983, 49 F.R. 347, as amended Ex. Ord. No. 12477, May 23, 1984, 49 F.R. 22041; Ex. Ord. No. 12487, Sept. 14, 1984, 49 F.R. 36493, formerly set out as a note under section 5332 of Title 5.

1982—Salaries of bankruptcy judges and referees in bankruptcy (full-time), or referees in bankruptcy (part-time) (maximum rate) increased to $63,600 and $31,800, respectively, effective on the first day of the first pay period beginning on or after Oct. 1, 1982, by Ex. Ord. No. 12387, Oct. 8, 1982, 47 F.R. 44981, formerly set out as a note under section 5332 of Title 5, Government Organization and Employees. Ex. Ord. No. 12387 further provided that pursuant to section 101(e) of Pub.L. 97–276 funds are not available to pay a salary at a rate which exceeds the rate in effect on Sept. 30, 1982, which was $58,500 for bankruptcy judges and referees in bankruptcy (full-time), and $30,600 for referees in bankruptcy (part-time) (maximum rate).

Maximum rate payable to bankruptcy judges after Dec. 17, 1982, increased from $58,500 to $63,600, see Pub.L. 97–377, Title I, § 129(b)–(d), Dec. 21, 1982, 96 Stat. 1914, set out as a note under section 5318 of Title 5.

1981—Salaries of bankruptcy judges and referees in bankruptcy (full-time), or referees in bankruptcy (part-time) (maximum rate) increased to $61,200 and $30,600, respectively, effective on the first day of the first pay period beginning on or after Oct. 1, 1981, by Ex. Ord. No. 12330, Oct. 15, 1981, 46 F.R. 50921, formerly set out as a note under section 5332 of Title 5. Ex. Ord. No. 12330 further provided that pursuant to section 101(c) of Pub.L. 97–51 funds are not available to pay a salary at a rate which exceeds the rate in effect on Sept. 30, 1981, which was $51,167.50 for bankruptcy judges and referees in bankruptcy (full-time), and $25,583.75 for referees in bankruptcy (part-time) (maximum rate).

1980—Salaries of bankruptcy judges and referees in bankruptcy (full-time), or referees in bankruptcy (part-time) (maximum rate) increased to $58,400 and $29,200, respectively, effective on the first day of the first pay period beginning on or after Oct. 1, 1980, by Ex. Ord. No. 12248, Oct. 16, 1980, 45 F.R. 69199, formerly set out as a note under section 5332 of Title 5. Ex. Ord. No. 12248 further provided that pursuant to section 101(c) of Pub.L. 96–369 funds are not available to pay a salary which exceeds the rate in effect on Sept. 30, 1980, which was $51,167.50 for bankruptcy judges and referees in bankruptcy (full-time), and $25,583.75 for referees in bankruptcy (part-time) (maximum rate).

For limitations on use of funds for period Oct. 1, 1980 through June 5, 1981, appropriated by any Act to pay the salary or pay of any individual in legislative, executive, or judicial branch in position equal to or above level V of the Executive Schedule, see section 101(c) of Pub.L. 96–369 and section 101(c) of Pub.L. 96–536, set out as notes under section 5318 of Title 5.

1979—Salaries of bankruptcy judges increased to $53,500 effective on the first day of the first applicable pay period beginning on or after Oct. 1, 1979, by Ex. Ord. No. 12165, Oct. 9, 1979, 44 F.R. 58671, as amended by Ex. Ord. No. 12200, Mar. 12, 1980, 45 F.R. 16443, formerly set out as a note under section 5332 of Title 5. Ex. Ord. No. 12165 further provided that pursuant to Pub.L. 96–86 funds appropriated for fiscal year 1980 may not be used to pay a salary at a rate which exceeds an increase of 5.5 percent over the applicable rate payable for such position or office in effect on Sept. 30, 1978, which was $51,167.50 for bankruptcy judges.

Part–Time Bankruptcy Judges

For provision that notwithstanding subsecs. (a) and (b) of this section, a bankruptcy judge serving on a part-time basis on July 10, 1984, may continue to serve on such basis for two years from such date, and may engage in the practice of law, see section 106 of Pub.L. 98–353, set out as a note under section 152 of this title.

Transition Provisions

Section 1003(b) of Pub.L. 100–702 provided that:

"(1) If an individual who is exempted from the Leave Act by operation of amendments under this section [amending this section and sections 156, 631, 634, 712, 752, and 794 of this title] and who was previously subject to the provisions of subchapter I of chapter 63 of title 5, United States Code [section 6301 et seq. of Title 5, Government Organization and Employees], without a break in service, again becomes subject to this subchapter on completion of his service as an exempted officer, the unused annual leave and sick leave standing to his credit when he was exempted from this subchapter is deemed to have remained to his credit.

"(2) In computing an annuity under section 8339 of title 5, United States Code [section 8339 of Title 5], the total service of a person specified in paragraph (1) of this subsection who retired on an immediate annuity or dies leaving a survivor or survivors entitled to an annuity includes, without regard to the limitations imposed by subsection (f) of section 8339 of title 5, United States Code [section 8339(f) of Title 5], the days of unused sick leave standing to his credit when he was exempted from subchapter I of chapter 63 of title 5, United States Code [section 6301 et seq. of Title 5], except that these days will not be counted in determining average pay or annuity eligibility."

§ 154. Division of businesses; chief judge

(a) Each bankruptcy court for a district having more than one bankruptcy judge shall by majority vote promulgate rules for the division of business among the bankruptcy judges to the extent that the division of business is not otherwise provided for by the rules of the district court.

(b) In each district court having more than one bankruptcy judge the district court shall designate one judge to serve as chief judge of such bankruptcy court. Whenever a majority of the judges of such district court cannot agree upon the designation as chief judge, the chief judge of such district court shall make such designation. The chief judge of the bankruptcy court shall ensure that the rules of the bankruptcy court and of the district court are observed and that the business of the bankruptcy court is handled effectively and expeditiously.

(Added Pub.L. 98–353, Title I, § 104(a), July 10, 1984, 98 Stat. 339.)

HISTORICAL AND STATUTORY NOTES

Revision Notes and Legislative Reports

1984 Acts. Statements by Legislative Leaders, see 1984 U.S.Code Cong. and Adm.News, p. 576.

Codifications

This section as added by Pub.L. 95–598, Title II, § 201(a), Nov. 6, 1978, 92 Stat. 2657, effective June 28, 1984, pursuant to Pub.L. 95–598, Title IV, § 402(b), Nov. 6, 1978, 92 Stat. 2682, as amended by Pub.L. 98–249, § 1(a), Mar. 31, 1984, 98 Stat. 116; Pub.L. 98–271, § 1(a), Apr. 30, 1984, 98 Stat. 163; Pub.L. 98–299, § 1(a), May 25, 1984, 98 Stat. 214; Pub.L. 98–325, § 1(a), June 20, 1984, 98 Stat. 268, set out as a note preceding section 101 of Title 11, Bankruptcy, read as follows:

§ 154. Salaries of bankruptcy judges

Each judge of a bankruptcy court shall receive a salary at an annual rate of $50,000, subject to adjustment under section 225 of the Federal Salary Act of 1967 (2 U.S.C. 351–361), and section 461 of this title.

Section 402(b) of Pub.L. 95–598 was amended by section 113 of Pub.L. 98–353 by substituting "shall not be effective" for "shall take effect on June 28, 1984", thereby eliminating the addition of section 154 by section 201(a) of Pub.L. 95–598, effective June 27, 1984, pursuant to section 122(c) of Pub.L. 98–353, set out as an Effective Date note under section 151 of this title.

Section 121(a) of Pub.L. 98–353 directed that section 402(b) of Pub.L. 95–598 be amended by substituting "the date of enactment of the Bankruptcy Amendments and Federal Judgeship Act of 1984 [i.e. July 10, 1984]" for "June 28, 1984". This amendment was not executed in view of the prior amendment to section 402(b) of Pub.L. 95–598 by section 113 of Pub.L. 98–353.

Effective and Applicability Provisions

1984 Acts. Section effective July 10, 1984, see section 122(a) of Pub.L. 98–353, set out as a note under section 151 of this title.

§ 155. Temporary transfer of bankruptcy judges

(a) A bankruptcy judge may be transferred to serve temporarily as a bankruptcy judge in any judicial district other than the judicial district for which such bankruptcy judge was appointed upon the approval of the judicial council of each of the circuits involved.

(b) A bankruptcy judge who has retired may, upon consent, be recalled to serve as a bankruptcy judge in any judicial district by the judicial council of the circuit within which such district is located. Upon recall, a bankruptcy judge may receive a salary for such service in accordance with regulations promulgated by the Judicial Conference of the United States, subject to the restrictions on the payment of an annuity in section 377 of this title or in subchapter III of chapter 83, and chapter 84, of title 5 which are applicable to such judge.

(Added Pub.L. 98–353, Title I, § 104(a), July 10, 1984, 98 Stat. 339, and amended Pub.L. 99–651, Title II, § 202(a), Nov. 14, 1986, 100 Stat. 3648; Pub.L. 100–659, § 4(a), Nov. 15, 1988, 102 Stat. 3918.)

HISTORICAL AND STATUTORY NOTES

Revision Notes and Legislative Reports

1984 Acts. Statements by Legislative Leaders, see 1984 U.S.Code Cong. and Adm.News, p. 576.

1986 Acts. House Report No. 99–417, see 1986 U.S.Code Cong. and Adm.News, p. 6165.

1988 Acts. Senate Report No. 100–293, and House Conference Report No. 100–1072, see 1988 U.S.Code Cong. and Adm.News, p. 5564.

Codifications

This section as added by Pub.L. 95–598, Title II, § 201(a), Nov. 6, 1978, 92 Stat. 2658, effective June 28, 1984, pursuant to Pub.L. 95–598, Title IV, § 402(b), Nov. 6, 1978, 92 Stat. 2682, as amended by Pub.L. 98–249, § 1(a), Mar. 31, 1984, 98 Stat. 116; Pub.L. 98–271, § 1(a), Apr. 30, 1984, 98 Stat. 163; Pub.L. 98–299, § 1(a), May 25, 1984, 98 Stat. 214; Pub.L. 98–325, § 1(a), June 20, 1984, 98 Stat. 268, set out as a note preceding section 101 of Title 11, Bankruptcy, read as follows:

§ 155. Chief judge; precedence of bankruptcy judges

(a) In each district having more than one judge the bankruptcy judge in regular active service who is senior in commission and under seventy years of age shall be the chief judge of the bankruptcy court. If all the bankruptcy judges in regular active service are 70 years of age or older the youngest shall act as chief judge until a judge has been appointed and qualified who is under 70 years of age, but a judge may not act as chief judge until he has served as a bankruptcy judge for one year.

(b) The chief judge shall have precedence and preside at any session which he attends.

Other bankruptcy judges shall have precedence and preside according to the seniority of their commissions. Judges whose commissions bear the same date shall have precedence according to seniority in age.

(c) A judge whose commission extends over more than one district shall be junior to all bankruptcy judges except in the district in which he resided at the time he entered upon the duties of his office.

(d) If a chief judge desires to be relieved of his duties as chief judge while retaining his active status as a bankruptcy judge, he may so certify to the chief judge of the court of appeals for the circuit in which the bankruptcy judge serves, and thereafter the bankruptcy judge in active service next in precedence and willing to serve shall be designated by the chief judge of the court of appeals as the chief judge of the bankruptcy court.

(e) If a chief judge is temporarily unable to perform his duties as such, they shall be performed by the bankruptcy judge in active service, present in the district and able and qualified to act, who is next in precedence.

(f) Service as a referee in bankruptcy or as a bankruptcy judge under the Bankruptcy Act shall be taken into account in the determination of seniority of commission under this section.

Section 402(b) of Pub.L. 95–598 was amended by section 113 of Pub.L. 98–353 by substituting "shall not be effective" for "shall take effect on June 28, 1984", thereby eliminating the addition of section 155 by section 201(a) of Pub.L. 95–598, effective June 27, 1984, pursuant to section 122(c) of Pub.L. 98–353, set out as an Effective Date note under section 151 of this title.

Section 121(a) of Pub.L. 98–353 directed that section 402(b) of Pub.L. 95–598 be amended by substituting "the date of enactment of the Bankruptcy Amendments and Federal Judgeship Act of 1984 [i.e. July 10, 1984]" for "June 28, 1984". This amendment was not executed in view of the prior amendment to section 402(b) of Pub.L. 95–598 by section 113 of Pub.L. 98–353.

Effective and Applicability Provisions

1988 Acts. Amendment to this section by Pub.L. 100–659 to take effect on Nov. 15, 1988, and shall apply to bankruptcy judges and magistrates who retire on or after Nov. 15, 1988, with special election provisions for bankruptcy judges, etc., who left office on or after July 31, 1987, and before Nov. 15, 1988, see section 9 of Pub.L. 100–659, set out as a note under section 377 of this title.

1986 Acts. Section 203 of Title II of Pub.L. 99–651 provided that: "This title and the amendments made by this title [enacting section 375 of this title, and amending sections 155, 374, 631, 633, 636, and 797 of this title] take effect on January 1, 1987."

1984 Acts. Section effective July 10, 1984, see section 122(a) of Pub.L. 98–353, set out as a note under section 151 of this title.

CROSS REFERENCES

Recall of retired judges—

Generally, see 28 USCA § 375.

Actual abode deemed official station for purposes of residency, see 28 USCA § 374.

Practicing attorney not eligible for recall, see 28 USCA § 377.

§ 156. Staff; expenses

(a) Each bankruptcy judge may appoint a secretary, a law clerk, and such additional assistants as the Director of the Administrative Office of the United States Courts determines to be necessary. A law clerk appointed under this section shall be exempt from the provisions of subchapter I of chapter 63 of title 5, unless specifically included by the appointing judge or by local rule of court.

(b) Upon certification to the judicial council of the circuit involved and to the Director of the Administrative Office of the United States Courts that the number of cases and proceedings pending within the jurisdiction under section 1334 of this title within a judicial district so warrants, the bankruptcy judges for such district may appoint an individual to serve as clerk of such bankruptcy court. The clerk may appoint, with the approval of such bankruptcy judges, and in such number as may be approved by the Director, necessary deputies, and may remove such deputies with the approval of such bankruptcy judges.

(c) Any court may utilize facilities or services, either on or off the court's premises, which pertain to the provision of notices, dockets, calendars, and other administrative information to parties in cases filed under the provisions of title 11, United States Code, where the costs of such facilities or services are paid for out of the assets of the estate and are not charged to the United States. The utilization of such facilities or services shall be subject to such conditions and limitations as the pertinent circuit council may prescribe.

(d) No office of the bankruptcy clerk of court may be consolidated with the district clerk of court office without the prior approval of the Judicial Conference and the Congress.

(e) In a judicial district where a bankruptcy clerk has been appointed pursuant to subsection (b), the bankruptcy clerk shall be the official custodian of the records and dockets of the bankruptcy court.

(f) For purposes of financial accountability in a district where a bankruptcy clerk has been certified, such clerk shall be accountable for and pay into the Treasury all fees, costs, and other monies collected by such clerk except uncollected fees not required by an Act of Congress to be prepaid. Such clerk shall make returns thereof to the Director of the Administrative Office of the United States Courts and the Director of the Executive Office For United States Trustees, under regulations prescribed by such Directors.

(Added Pub.L. 98–353, Title I, § 104(a), July 10, 1984, 98 Stat. 339, and amended Pub.L. 99–554, Title I, §§ 103, 142, 144(a), Oct. 27, 1986, 100 Stat. 3090, 3096; Pub.L. 100–702, Title X, § 1003(a)(3), Nov. 19, 1988, 102 Stat. 4665.)

HISTORICAL AND STATUTORY NOTES

Revision Notes and Legislative Reports

1984 Acts. Statements by Legislative Leaders, see 1984 U.S. Code Cong. and Adm. News, p. 576.

1986 Acts. House Report No. 99–764 and House Conference Report No. 99–958, see 1986 U.S. Code Cong. and Adm. News, p. 5227.

1988 Acts. House Report No. 100–889, see 1988 U.S. Code Cong. and Adm. News, p. 5982.

Codifications

This section as added by Pub.L. 95–598, Title II, § 201(a), Nov. 6, 1978, 92 Stat. 2659, effective June 28, 1984, pursuant to Pub.L. 95–598, Title IV, § 402(b), Nov. 6, 1978, 92 Stat. 2682, as amended by Pub.L. 98–249, § 1(a), Mar. 31, 1984, 98 Stat. 116; Pub.L. 98–271, § 1(a), Apr. 30, 1984, 98 Stat. 163; Pub.L. 98–299, § 1(a), May 25, 1984, 98 Stat. 214; Pub.L. 98–325, § 1(a), June 20, 1984, 98 Stat. 268, set out as a note preceding section 101 of Title 11, Bankruptcy, read as follows:

§ 156. Division of business among bankruptcy judges

The business of a bankruptcy court having more than one judge shall be divided among the judges as provided by the rules and orders of the court.

The chief judge of the bankruptcy court shall be responsible for the observance of such rules and orders, and shall divide the business and assign the cases so far as such rules and orders do not otherwise prescribe.

If the bankruptcy judges in any district are unable to agree upon the adoption of rules or orders for that purpose the judicial council of the circuit shall make the necessary orders.

Section 402(b) of Pub.L. 95–598 was amended by section 113 of Pub.L. 98–353 by substituting "shall not be effective" for "shall take effect on June 28, 1984", thereby eliminating the addition of section 156 by section 201(a) of Pub.L. 95–598, effective June 27, 1984, pursuant to section 122(c) of Pub.L. 98–353, set out as an Effective Date note under section 151 of this title.

Section 121(a) of Pub.L. 98–353 directed that section 402(b) of Pub.L. 95–598 be amended by substituting "the date of enactment of the Bankruptcy Amendments and Federal Judgeship Act of 1984 [i.e. July 10, 1984]" for "June 28, 1984". This amendment was not executed in view of the prior amendment to section 402(b) of Pub.L. 95–598 by section 113 of Pub.L. 98–353.

Effective and Applicability Provisions

1986 Acts. Amendment of subsec. (d) by section 103 of Pub.L. 99–554 effective on Oct. 27, 1986, see section 302(b) of Pub.L. 99–554, set out as a note under section 581 of this title.

Enactment of subsecs. (e) and (f) by sections 142 and 144(a) of Pub.L. 99–554 effective 30 days after Oct. 27, 1986, except as otherwise provided for, see section 302(a) of Pub.L. 99–554, set out as a note under section 581 of this title.

1984 Acts. Section effective July 10, 1984, see section 122(a) of Pub.L. 98–353, set out as a note under section 151 of this title.

CROSS REFERENCES

Conversion fees in bankruptcy, see 28 USCA § 1930.

§ 157. Procedures

(a) Each district court may provide that any or all cases under title 11 and any or all proceedings arising under title 11 or arising in or related to a case under title 11 shall be referred to the bankruptcy judges for the district.

(b)(1) Bankruptcy judges may hear and determine all cases under title 11 and all core proceedings arising under title 11, or arising in a case under title 11, referred under subsection (a) of this section, and may enter appropriate orders and judgments, subject to review under section 158 of this title.

(2) Core proceedings include, but are not limited to—

(A) matters concerning the administration of the estate;

(B) allowance or disallowance of claims against the estate or exemptions from property of the estate, and estimation of claims or interests for the purposes of confirming a plan under chapter 11, 12, or 13 of title 11 but not the liquidation or estimation of contingent or unliquidated personal injury tort or wrongful death claims against the estate for purposes of distribution in a case under title 11;

(C) counterclaims by the estate against persons filing claims against the estate;

(D) orders in respect to obtaining credit;

(E) orders to turn over property of the estate;

(F) proceedings to determine, avoid, or recover preferences;

(G) motions to terminate, annul, or modify the automatic stay;

(H) proceedings to determine, avoid, or recover fraudulent conveyances;

(I) determinations as to the dischargeability of particular debts;

(J) objections to discharges;

(K) determinations of the validity, extent, or priority of liens;

(L) confirmations of plans;

(M) orders approving the use or lease of property, including the use of cash collateral;

(N) orders approving the sale of property other than property resulting from claims brought by the estate against persons who have not filed claims against the estate;

(O) other proceedings affecting the liquidation of the assets of the estate or the adjustment of the debtor-creditor or the equity security holder relationship, except personal injury tort or wrongful death claims; and

(P) recognition of foreign proceedings and other matters under chapter 15 of title 11.

(3) The bankruptcy judge shall determine, on the judge's own motion or on timely motion of a party, whether a proceeding is a core proceeding under this subsection or is a proceeding that is otherwise related to a case under title 11. A determination that a proceeding is not a core proceeding shall not be made solely on the basis that its resolution may be affected by State law.

(4) Non-core proceedings under section 157(b)(2)(B) of title 28, United States Code, shall not be subject to the mandatory abstention provisions of section 1334(c)(2).

(5) The district court shall order that personal injury tort and wrongful death claims shall be tried in the district court in which the bankruptcy case is pending, or in the district court in the district in which the claim arose, as determined by the district court in which the bankruptcy case is pending.

(c)(1) A bankruptcy judge may hear a proceeding that is not a core proceeding but that is otherwise related to a case under title 11. In such proceeding, the bankruptcy judge shall submit proposed findings of fact and conclusions of law to the district court, and any final order or judgment shall be entered by the district judge after considering the bankruptcy judge's proposed findings and conclusions and after reviewing de novo those matters to which any party has timely and specifically objected.

(2) Notwithstanding the provisions of paragraph (1) of this subsection, the district court, with the consent of all the parties to the proceeding, may refer a proceeding related to a case under title 11 to a bankruptcy judge to hear and determine and to enter appropriate orders and judgments, subject to review under section 158 of this title.

(d) The district court may withdraw, in whole or in part, any case or proceeding referred under this section, on its own motion or on timely motion of any party, for cause shown. The district court shall, on timely motion of a party, so withdraw a proceeding if the court determines that resolution of the proceeding requires consideration of both title 11 and other laws of the United States regulating organizations or activities affecting interstate commerce.

(e) If the right to a jury trial applies in a proceeding that may be heard under this section by a bankruptcy judge, the bankruptcy judge may conduct the jury trial if specially designated to exercise such jurisdiction by the district court and with the express consent of all the parties.

(Added Pub.L. 98-353, Title I, § 104(a), July 10, 1984, 98 Stat. 340, and amended Pub.L. 99-554, Title I, §§ 143, 144(b), Oct. 27, 1986, 100 Stat. 3096; Pub.L. 103-394, Title I, § 112, Oct. 22, 1994, 108 Stat. 4117; Pub.L. 109-8, Title VIII, § 802(c)(1), Apr. 20, 2005, 119 Stat. 145.)

HISTORICAL AND STATUTORY NOTES

Revision Notes and Legislative Reports

1984 Acts. Statements by Legislative Leaders, see 1984 U.S. Code Cong. and Adm. News, p. 576.

1986 Acts. House Report No. 99–764 and House Conference Report No. 99–958, see 1986 U.S. Code Cong. and Adm. News, p. 5227.

1994 Acts. House Report No. 103–835, see 1994 U.S. Code Cong. and Adm. News, p. 3340.

2005 Acts. House Report No. 109–31(Part I), see 2005 U.S. Code Cong. and Adm. News, p. 88.

References in Text

Chapter 11, 12, or 13 of title 11, referred to in subsec. (b)(2)(B), is 11 U.S.C.A. § 1101 et seq., 11 U.S.C.A. § 1201 et seq., or 11 U.S.C.A. § 1301 et seq., respectively.

Chapter 15 of title 11, referred to in subsec. (b)(2)(P), is 11 U.S.C.A. § 1501 et seq.

Codifications

This section as added by Pub.L. 95–598, Title II, § 201(a), Nov. 6, 1978, 92 Stat. 2659, effective June 28, 1984, pursuant to Pub.L. 95–598, Title IV, § 402(b), Nov. 6, 1978, 92 Stat. 2682, as amended by Pub.L. 98–249, § 1(a), Mar. 31, 1984, 98 Stat. 116; Pub.L. 98–271, § 1(a), Apr. 30, 1984, 98 Stat. 163; Pub.L. 98–299, § 1(a), May 25, 1984, 98 Stat. 214; Pub.L. 98–325, § 1(a), June 20, 1984, 98 Stat. 268, set out as a note preceding section 101 of Title 11, Bankruptcy, read as follows:

"**§ 157. Times of holding court**

"**(a)** The bankruptcy court at each designated location shall be deemed to be in continuous session on all business days throughout the year.

"**(b)** Each bankruptcy court may establish by local rule or order schedules of court sessions at designated places of holding court other than the headquarters office of the court. Such schedules may be pretermitted by order of the court.

"**(c)** Bankruptcy court may be held at any place within the territory served, in any case, on order of the bankruptcy court, for the convenience of the parties, on such notice as the bankruptcy court orders."

Section 402(b) of Pub.L. 95–598 was amended by section 113 of Pub.L. 98–353 by substituting "shall not be effective" for "shall take effect on June 28, 1984", thereby eliminating the addition of section 157 by section 201(a) of Pub.L. 95–598, effective June 27, 1984, pursuant to section 122(c) of Pub.L. 98–353, set out as an Effective Date note under section 151 of this title.

Section 121(a) of Pub.L. 98–353 directed that section 402(b) of Pub.L. 95–598 be amended by substituting "the date of enactment of the Bankruptcy Amendments and Federal Judgeship Act of 1984 [i.e. July 10, 1984]" for "June 28, 1984". This amendment was not executed in view of the prior amendment to section 402(b) of Pub.L. 95–598 by section 113 of Pub.L. 98–353.

Effective and Applicability Provisions

2005 Acts. Except as otherwise provided, amendments by Pub.L. 109–8 effective 180 days after April 20, 2005, and inapplicable with respect to cases commenced under Title 11 before the effective date, see Pub.L. 109–8, § 1501, set out as a note under 11 U.S.C.A. § 101.

1994 Acts. Amendment by Pub.L. 103–394 effective on Oct. 22, 1994, and not to apply with respect to cases commenced under Title 11 of the United States Code before Oct. 22, 1994, see section 702 of Pub.L. 103–394, set out as a note under section 101 of Title 11, Bankruptcy.

1986 Acts. Amendment by Pub.L. 99–554 effective 30 days after Oct. 27, 1986, except as otherwise provided for, see section 302(a) of Pub.L. 99–554, set out as a note under section 581 of this title.

1984 Acts. Section effective July 10, 1984, see section 122(a) of Pub.L. 98–353, set out as a note under section 151 of this title.

Separability of Provisions

If any provision of or amendment made by Pub.L. 103–394 or the application of such provision or amendment to any person or circumstance is held to be unconstitutional, the remaining provisions of and amendments made by Pub.L. 103–394 and the application of such provisions and amendments to any person or circumstance shall not be affected thereby, see section 701 of Pub.L. 103–394, set out as a note under section 101 of Title 11, Bankruptcy.

CROSS REFERENCES

Supplemental injunctions and power of district court to refer proceedings, see 11 USCA § 524.

§ 158. Appeals

(a) The district courts of the United States shall have jurisdiction to hear appeals [1]

(1) from final judgments, orders, and decrees;

(2) from interlocutory orders and decrees issued under section 1121(d) of title 11 increasing or reducing the time periods referred to in section 1121 of such title; and

(3) with leave of the court, from other interlocutory orders and decrees;

and, with leave of the court, from interlocutory orders and decrees, of bankruptcy judges entered in cases and proceedings referred to the bankruptcy judges under section 157 of this title. An appeal under this subsection shall be taken only to the district court for the judicial district in which the bankruptcy judge is serving.

(b)(1) The judicial council of a circuit shall establish a bankruptcy appellate panel service composed of bankruptcy judges of the districts in the circuit who are appointed by the judicial council in accordance with paragraph (3), to hear and determine, with the consent of all the parties, appeals under subsection (a) unless the judicial council finds that—

(A) there are insufficient judicial resources available in the circuit; or

(B) establishment of such service would result in undue delay or increased cost to parties in cases under title 11.

Not later than 90 days after making the finding, the judicial council shall submit to the Judicial Conference of the United States a report containing the factual basis of such finding.

(2)(A) A judicial council may reconsider, at any time, the finding described in paragraph (1).

(B) On the request of a majority of the district judges in a circuit for which a bankruptcy appellate panel service is established under paragraph (1), made after the expiration of the 1-year period beginning on the date such service is established, the judicial council of the circuit shall determine whether a circumstance specified in subparagraph (A) or (B) of such paragraph exists.

(C) On its own motion, after the expiration of the 3-year period beginning on the date a bankruptcy appellate panel service is established under paragraph (1), the judicial council of the circuit may determine whether a circumstance specified in subparagraph (A) or (B) of such paragraph exists.

(D) If the judicial council finds that either of such circumstances exists, the judicial council may provide for the completion of the appeals then pending before such service and the orderly termination of such service.

(3) Bankruptcy judges appointed under paragraph (1) shall be appointed and may be reappointed under such paragraph.

(4) If authorized by the Judicial Conference of the United States, the judicial councils of 2 or more circuits may establish a joint bankruptcy appellate panel comprised of bankruptcy judges from the districts within the circuits for which such panel is established, to hear and determine, upon the consent of all the parties, appeals under subsection (a) of this section.

(5) An appeal to be heard under this subsection shall be heard by a panel of 3 members of the bankruptcy appellate panel service, except that a member of such service may not hear an appeal originating in the district for which such member is appointed or designated under section 152 of this title.

(6) Appeals may not be heard under this subsection by a panel of the bankruptcy appellate panel service unless the district judges for the district in which the appeals occur, by majority vote, have authorized such service to hear and determine appeals originating in such district.

(c)(1) Subject to subsections (b) and (d)(2), each appeal under subsection (a) shall be heard by a 3-judge panel of the bankruptcy appellate panel service established under subsection (b)(1) unless—

(A) the appellant elects at the time of filing the appeal; or

(B) any other party elects, not later than 30 days after service of notice of the appeal;

to have such appeal heard by the district court.

(2) An appeal under subsections (a) and (b) of this section shall be taken in the same manner as appeals in civil proceedings generally are taken to the courts of appeals from the district courts and in the time provided by Rule 8002 of the Bankruptcy Rules.

(d)(1) The courts of appeals shall have jurisdiction of appeals from all final decisions, judgments, orders, and decrees entered under subsections (a) and (b) of this section.

(2)(A) The appropriate court of appeals shall have jurisdiction of appeals described in the first sentence of subsection (a) if the bankruptcy court, the district court, or the bankruptcy appellate panel involved, acting on its own motion or on the request of a party to the judgment, order, or decree described in such first sentence, or all the appellants and appellees (if any) acting jointly, certify that—

(i) the judgment, order, or decree involves a question of law as to which there is no controlling decision of the court of appeals for the circuit or of the Supreme Court of the United States, or involves a matter of public importance;

(ii) the judgment, order, or decree involves a question of law requiring resolution of conflicting decisions; or

(iii) an immediate appeal from the judgment, order, or decree may materially advance the progress of the case or proceeding in which the appeal is taken;

and if the court of appeals authorizes the direct appeal of the judgment, order, or decree.

(B) If the bankruptcy court, the district court, or the bankruptcy appellate panel—

(i) on its own motion or on the request of a party, determines that a circumstance specified in clause (i), (ii), or (iii) of subparagraph (A) exists; or

(ii) receives a request made by a majority of the appellants and a majority of appellees (if any) to make the certification described in subparagraph (A);

then the bankruptcy court, the district court, or the bankruptcy appellate panel shall make the certification described in subparagraph (A).

(C) The parties may supplement the certification with a short statement of the basis for the certification.

(D) An appeal under this paragraph does not stay any proceeding of the bankruptcy court, the district court, or the bankruptcy appellate panel from which the appeal is taken, unless the respective bankruptcy court, district court, or bankruptcy appellate panel, or the court of appeals in which the appeal in [2] pending, issues a stay of such proceeding pending the appeal.

(E) Any request under subparagraph (B) for certification shall be made not later than 60 days after the entry of the judgment, order, or decree.

(Added Pub.L. 98–353, Title I, § 104(a), July 10, 1984, 98 Stat. 341, and amended Pub.L. 101–650, Title III, § 305, Dec. 1, 1990, 104 Stat. 5105; Pub.L. 103–394, Title I, §§ 102, 104(c), (d), Oct. 22, 1994, 108 Stat. 4108–4110; Pub.L. 109–8, Title XII, § 1233(a), Apr. 20, 2005, 119 Stat. 202.)

1 So in original.

2 So in original. Probably should read "is".

HISTORICAL AND STATUTORY NOTES

Revision Notes and Legislative Reports

1984 Acts. Statements by Legislative Leaders, see 1984 U.S. Code Cong. and Adm. News, p. 576.

1990 Acts. Senate Report No. 101–416, Related House Reports, and Statement by President, see 1990 U.S. Code Cong. and Adm. News, p. 6802.

1994 Acts. House Report No. 103–835, see 1994 U.S. Code Cong. and Adm. News, p. 3340.

2005 Acts. House Report No. 109–31(Part I), see 2005 U.S. Code Cong. and Adm. News, p. 88.

Codifications

Amendment by section 102 of Pub.L. 103–394, which directed amendment of subsec. (a) by striking "from" the first place it appeared and all that followed through "decrees," and making a substitution for such language, was executed by striking through "decrees," the first place it appeared, as the probable intent of Congress.

This section (section 158) and section 159 as added by Pub.L. 95–598, Title II, § 201(a), Nov. 6, 1978, 92 Stat. 2659, and section 160, as added by Pub.L. 95–598, Title II, § 201(a), Nov. 6, 1978, 92 Stat. 2659, and amended Pub.L. 97–164, Title I, § 110(d), Apr. 2, 1982, 96 Stat. 29, effective June 28, 1984, pursuant to Pub.L. 95–598, Title IV, § 402(b), Nov. 6, 1978, 92 Stat. 2682, as amended by Pub.L. 98–249, § 1(a), Mar. 31, 1984, 98 Stat. 116; Pub.L. 98–271, § 1(a), Apr. 30, 1984, 98 Stat. 163; Pub.L. 98–299, § 1(a), May 25, 1984, 98 Stat. 214; Pub.L. 98–325, § 1(a), June 20, 1984, 98 Stat. 268, set out as a note preceding section 101 of Title II, Bankruptcy, read as follows:

"§ 158. Accommodations at places for holding court

"Court shall be held only at places where Federal quarters and accommodations are available, or suitable quarters and accommodations are furnished without cost to the United States. The foregoing restrictions shall not, however, preclude the Administrator of General Services, at the request of the Director of the Administrative Office of the United States Courts, from providing such court quarters and accommodations as the Administrator determines can appropriately be made available at places where court is authorized by law to be held, but only if such court quarters and accommodations have been approved as necessary by the judicial council of the appropriate circuit.

"§ 159. Vacant judgeship as affecting proceedings

"When the office of a bankruptcy judge becomes vacant, all pending process, pleadings and proceedings shall, when necessary, be continued by the clerk until a judge is appointed or designated to hold such court.

"§ 160. Appellate panels

"**(a)** If the circuit council of a circuit orders application of this section to a district within such circuit, the chief judge of each circuit shall designate panels of three bankruptcy judges to hear appeals from judgments, orders, and decrees of the bankruptcy court of the United States for such district. Except as provided in section 293(b) of this title, a panel shall be composed only of bankruptcy judges for districts located in the circuit in which the appeal arises. The chief judge shall designate a sufficient number of such panels so that appeals may be heard and disposed of expeditiously.

"**(b)** A panel designated under subsection (a) of this section may not hear an appeal from a judgment, order, or decree entered by a member of the panel.

"**(c)** When hearing an appeal, a panel designated under subsection (a) of this section shall sit at a place convenient to the parties to the appeal."

Section 402(b) of Pub.L. 95–598 was amended by section 113 of Pub.L. 98–353 by substituting "shall not be effective" for "shall take effect on June 28, 1984", thereby eliminating the additions of sections 158 to 160 by section 201(a) of Pub.L. 95–598, effective June 27, 1984, pursuant to section 122(c) of Pub.L. 98–353, set out as an Effective Date note under section 151 of this title.

Section 121(a) of Pub.L. 98–353 directed that section 402(b) of Pub.L. 95–598 be amended by substituting "the date of enactment of the Bankruptcy Amendments and Federal Judgeship Act of 1984 [i.e. July 10, 1984]" for "June 28, 1984". This amendment was not executed in view of the prior amendment to section 402(b) of Pub.L. 95–598 by section 113 of Pub.L. 98–353.

Effective and Applicability Provisions

2005 Acts. Except as otherwise provided, amendments by Pub.L. 109–8 effective 180 days after April 20, 2005, and inapplicable with respect to cases commenced under Title 11 before the effective date, see Pub.L. 109–8, § 1501, set out as a note under 11 U.S.C.A. § 101.

1994 Acts. Amendments by Pub.L. 103–394 effective on Oct. 22, 1994, and not to apply with respect to cases commenced under Title 11 of the United States Code before Oct. 22, 1994, see section 702 of Pub.L. 103–394, set out as a note under 11 U.S.C.A. § 101.

1984 Acts. Section effective July 10, 1984, see section 122(a) of Pub.L. 98–353, set out as a note under 28 U.S.C.A. § 151.

Separability of Provisions

If any provision of or amendment made by Pub.L. 103–394 or the application of such provision or amendment to any person or circumstance is held to be unconstitutional, the remaining provisions of and amendments made by Pub.L. 103–394 and the application of such provisions and amendments to any person or circumstance shall not be affected thereby, see section 701 of Pub.L. 103–394, set out as a note under 11 U.S.C.A. § 101.

Procedural Rules

Pub.L. 109–8, Title XII, § 1233(b), Apr. 20, 2005, 119 Stat. 203, provided that:

"**(1) Temporary application.**—A provision of this subsection shall apply to appeals under section 158(d)(2) of title 28, United States Code, until a rule of practice and procedure relating to such provision and such appeals is promulgated or amended under chapter 131 of such title [28 U.S.C.A. § 2071 et seq.].

"**(2) Certification.**—A district court, a bankruptcy court, or a bankruptcy appellate panel may make a certification under section 158(d)(2) of title 28, United States Code, only with respect to matters pending in the respective bankruptcy court, district court, or bankruptcy appellate panel.

"**(3) Procedure.**—Subject to any other provision of this subsection, an appeal authorized by the court of appeals under section 158(d)(2)(A) of title 28, United States Code, shall be taken in the manner prescribed in subdivisions (a)(1), (b), (c), and (d) of rule 5 of the Federal Rules of Appellate Procedure. For purposes of subdivision (a)(1) of rule 5—

"**(A)** a reference in such subdivision to a district court shall be deemed to include a reference to a bankruptcy court and a bankruptcy appellate panel, as appropriate; and

"**(B)** a reference in such subdivision to the parties requesting permission to appeal to be served with the petition shall be deemed to include a reference to the parties to the judgment, order, or decree from which the appeal is taken.

"**(4) Filing of petition with attachment.**—A petition requesting permission to appeal, that is based on a certification made under subparagraph (A) or (B) of section 158(d)(2) shall—

"**(A)** be filed with the circuit clerk not later than 10 days after the certification is entered on the docket of the bankruptcy court, the district court, or the bankruptcy appellate panel from which the appeal is taken; and

"**(B)** have attached a copy of such certification.

"**(5) References in rule 5.**—For purposes of rule 5 of the Federal Rules of Appellate Procedure—

"**(A)** a reference in such rule to a district court shall be deemed to include a reference to a bankruptcy court and to a bankruptcy appellate panel; and

"**(B)** a reference in such rule to a district clerk shall be deemed to include a reference to a clerk of a bankruptcy court and to a clerk of a bankruptcy appellate panel.

"**(6) Application of rules.**—The Federal Rules of Appellate Procedure [set out in Title 28, Judiciary and Judicial Procedure] shall apply in the courts of appeals with respect to appeals authorized under section 158(d)(2)(A), to the extent relevant and as if such appeals were taken from final judgments, orders, or decrees of the district courts or bankruptcy appellate panels exercising appellate jurisdiction under subsection (a) or (b) of section 158 of title 28, United States Code."

[Except as otherwise provided, amendments by Pub.L. 109–8 effective 180 days after April 20, 2005, and inapplicable with respect to cases commenced under Title 11 before the effective date, see Pub.L. 109–8, § 1501, set out as a note under 11 U.S.C.A. § 101.]

CROSS REFERENCES

Orders and decisions not reviewable under this section—

Abstention from exercising jurisdiction generally, see 28 USCA § 1334.

Dismissal or suspension of bankruptcy case on abstention grounds, see 11 USCA § 305.

Remand orders, see 28 USCA § 1452.

§ 159. Bankruptcy statistics

(a) The clerk of the district court, or the clerk of the bankruptcy court if one is certified pursuant to section 156(b) of this title, shall collect statistics regarding debtors who are individuals with primarily consumer debts seeking relief under chapters 7, 11, and 13 of title 11. Those statistics shall be in a standardized format prescribed by the Director of the Administrative Office of the United States Courts (referred to in this section as the "Director").

(b) The Director shall—

(1) compile the statistics referred to in subsection (a);

(2) make the statistics available to the public; and

(3) not later than July 1, 2008, and annually thereafter, prepare, and submit to Congress a report concerning the information collected under subsection (a) that contains an analysis of the information.

(c) The compilation required under subsection (b) shall—

(1) be itemized, by chapter, with respect to title 11;

(2) be presented in the aggregate and for each district; and

(3) include information concerning—

(A) the total assets and total liabilities of the debtors described in subsection (a), and in each category of assets and liabilities, as reported in the schedules prescribed pursuant to section 2075 of this title and filed by debtors;

(B) the current monthly income, average income, and average expenses of debtors as reported on the schedules and statements that each such debtor files under sections 521 and 1322 of title 11;

(C) the aggregate amount of debt discharged in cases filed during the reporting period, determined as the difference between the total amount of debt and obligations of a debtor reported on the schedules and the amount of such debt reported in categories which are predominantly nondischargeable;

(D) the average period of time between the date of the filing of the petition and the closing of the case for cases closed during the reporting period;

(E) for cases closed during the reporting period—

(i) the number of cases in which a reaffirmation agreement was filed; and

(ii)(I) the total number of reaffirmation agreements filed;

(II) of those cases in which a reaffirmation agreement was filed, the number of cases in which the debtor was not represented by an attorney; and

(III) of those cases in which a reaffirmation agreement was filed, the number of cases in which the reaffirmation agreement was approved by the court;

(F) with respect to cases filed under chapter 13 of title 11, for the reporting period—

(i)(I) the number of cases in which a final order was entered determining the value of property securing a claim in an amount less than the amount of the claim; and

(II) the number of final orders entered determining the value of property securing a claim;

(ii) the number of cases dismissed, the number of cases dismissed for failure to make payments under the plan, the number of cases refiled after dismissal, and the number of cases in which the plan was completed, separately itemized with respect to the number of modifications made before completion of the plan, if any; and

(iii) the number of cases in which the debtor filed another case during the 6-year period preceding the filing;

(G) the number of cases in which creditors were fined for misconduct and any amount of punitive damages awarded by the court for creditor misconduct; and

(H) the number of cases in which sanctions under rule 9011 of the Federal Rules of Bankruptcy Procedure were imposed against debtor's attorney or damages awarded under such Rule.

(Added Pub.L. 109–8, Title VI, § 601(a), Apr. 20, 2005, 119 Stat. 119.)

HISTORICAL AND STATUTORY NOTES

Revision Notes and Legislative Reports

2005 Acts. House Report No. 109–31(Part I), see 2005 U.S. Code Cong. and Adm. News, p. 88.

References in Text

Chapters 7 and 11 of title 11, referred to in subsec. (a), are 11 U.S.C.A. § 701 et seq. and 11 U.S.C.A. § 1101 et seq., respectively.

Chapter 13 of title 11, referred to in subsecs. (a) and (c)(3)(F), is 11 U.S.C.A. § 1301 et seq.

The Federal Rules of Bankruptcy Procedure, referred to in subsec. (c)(3)(H), are set out in Title 11.

Effective and Applicability Provisions

2005 Acts. Pub.L. 109–8, Title VI, § 601(c), Apr. 20, 2005, 119 Stat. 120, provided that: "The amendments made by this section [enacting this section] shall take effect 18 months after the date of enactment of this Act [April 20, 2005]."

Except as otherwise provided, amendments by Pub.L. 109–8 effective 180 days after April 20, 2005, and inapplicable with respect to cases commenced under Title 11 before the effective date, see Pub.L. 109–8, § 1501, set out as a note under 11 U.S.C.A. § 101.

CHAPTER 17—RESIGNATION AND RETIREMENT OF JUSTICES AND JUDGES

§ 372. Retirement for disability; substitute judge on failure to retire

(a) Any justice or judge of the United States appointed to hold office during good behavior who becomes permanently disabled from performing his duties may retire from regular active service, and the President shall, by and with the advice and consent of the Senate, appoint a successor.

Any justice or judge of the United States desiring to retire under this section shall certify to the President his disability in writing.

Whenever an associate justice of the Supreme Court, a chief judge of a circuit or the chief judge of the Court of International Trade, desires to retire under this section, he shall furnish to the President a certificate of disability signed by the Chief Justice of the United States.

A circuit or district judge, desiring to retire under this section, shall furnish to the President a certificate of disability signed by the chief judge of his circuit.

A judge of the Court of International Trade desiring to retire under this section, shall furnish to the President a certificate of disability signed by the chief judge of his court.

Each justice or judge retiring under this section after serving ten years continuously or otherwise shall, during the remainder of his lifetime, receive the salary of the office. A justice or judge retiring under this section who has served less than ten years in all shall, during the remainder of his lifetime, receive one-half the salary of the office.

(b) Whenever any judge of the United States appointed to hold office during good behavior who is eligible to retire under this section does not do so and a certificate of his disability signed by a majority of the members of the Judicial Council of his circuit in the case of a circuit or district judge, or by the Chief Justice of the United States in the case of the Chief Judge of the Court of International Trade, or by the chief judge of his court in the case of a judge of the Court of International Trade, is presented to the President and the President finds that such judge is unable to discharge efficiently all the duties of his office by reason of permanent mental or physical disability and that the appointment of an additional judge is necessary for the efficient dispatch of business, the President may make such appointment by and with the advice and consent of the Senate. Whenever any such additional judge is appointed, the vacancy subsequently caused by the death, resignation, or retirement of the disabled judge shall not be filled. Any judge whose disability causes the appointment of an additional judge shall, for purpose of precedence, service as chief judge, or temporary performance of the duties of that office, be treated as junior in commission to the other judges of the circuit, district, or court.

[(c) Repealed. Pub.L. 107–273, Div. C, Title I, § 11043(a)(1)(B), Nov. 2, 2002, 116 Stat. 1855]

(June 25, 1948, c. 646, 62 Stat. 903; May 24, 1949, c. 139, § 67, 63 Stat. 99; Feb. 10, 1954, c. 6, § 4(a), 68 Stat. 12; Sept. 2, 1957, Pub.L. 85–261, 71 Stat. 586; Oct. 10, 1980, Pub.L. 96–417, Title V, § 501(9), 94 Stat. 1742; Oct. 15, 1980, Pub.L. 96–458, § 3(a), (b), 94 Stat. 2036, 2040; Apr. 2, 1982, Pub.L. 97–164, Title I, § 112, 96 Stat. 29; July 10, 1984, Pub.L. 98–353, Title I, § 107, 98 Stat. 342; Nov. 19, 1988, Pub.L. 100–702, Title IV, § 403(c), 102 Stat. 4651; Dec. 1, 1990, Pub.L. 101–650, Title III, § 321, Title IV, § 402, 104 Stat. 5117, 5122; Oct. 29, 1992, Pub.L. 102–572, Title IX, § 902(b)(1), 106 Stat. 4516; Nov. 2, 2002, Pub.L. 107–273, Div. C, Title I, § 11043(a)(1), 116 Stat. 1855.)

HISTORICAL AND STATUTORY NOTES

Revision Notes and Legislative Reports

1948 Acts. Based on Title 28, U.S.C., 1940 ed., §§ 375b, 375c, and 375d (Aug. 5, 1939, c. 433, §§ 1 to 3, 53 Stat. 1204, 1205).

This section consolidates sections 375b, 375c, and 375d of Title 28, U.S.C., 1940 ed.

Said section 375e of Title 28, U.S.C., 1940 ed. providing that term "senior circuit judge" includes the Chief Justice of the United States Court of Appeals for the District of Columbia, and the term "judicial circuit" includes the District of Columbia, was omitted from this revision as unnecessary. Such district is included as a judicial circuit by section 41 of this title.

Words "justice or judge of the United States" were used to describe members of all courts who hold office during good behavior. (See reviser's note [now Revision Notes and Legislative Reports] under section 371 of this title.)

Term "chief judge" was substituted for "Chief Justice" of the Court of Claims, "presiding judge" of the Court of Customs and Patent Appeals and "senior circuit judge." (See reviser's note [now Revision Notes and Legislative Reports] under section 136 of this title.)

For clarity and convenience the requirement that certificates of disability be submitted "to the President," was made explicit.

The revised section requires a judge of the Customs Court to furnish a certificate of disability signed by the chief judge of his court, instead of by the chief judge of the Court of Customs and Patent Appeals as in said section 375c of Title 28, U.S.C., 1940 ed. This change insures signing of the certificate of disability by the chief judge possessing knowledge of the facts.

Changes were made in phraseology and arrangement. 80th Congress House Report No. 308.

1949 Acts. Subsection (a) of this section amends section 372 of Title 28, U.S.C., to express the requirement that appointment of successors to justices or judges must be made with confirmation by the Senate. Subsection (b) of this section clarifies the intent of section 372 of Title 28, U.S.C., and conforms with the language of section 371 of such title.

1954 Acts. House Report No. 1005 and Conference Report No. 1133, see 1954 U.S. Code Cong. and Adm. News p. 2006.

1957 Acts. Senate Report No. 1094, see 1957 U.S. Code Cong. and Adm. News, p. 1833.

1980 Acts. House Report No. 96–1235, see 1980 U.S. Code Cong. and Adm. News, p. 3729.

Senate Report No. 96–362, see 1980 U.S. Code Cong. and Adm. News, p. 4315.

1982 Acts. Senate Report No. 97–275, see 1982 U.S. Code Cong. and Adm. News, p. 11.

1984 Acts. Statements by Legislative Leaders, see 1984 U.S. Code Cong. and Adm. News, p. 576.

1988 Acts. House Report No. 100–889, see 1988 U.S. Code Cong. and Adm. News, p. 5982.

1990 Acts. Senate Report No. 101–416, related House Reports, and President's Signing Statement, see 1990 U.S. Code Cong. and Adm. News, p. 6802.

2002 Acts. House Conference Report No. 107–685 and Statement by President, see 2002 U.S. Code Cong. and Adm. News, p. 1120.

Effective and Applicability Provisions

1992 Acts. Amendment by Pub.L. 102–572 effective Oct. 29, 1992, see section 911 of Pub.L. 102–572, set out as a note under section 171 of this title.

1990 Acts. Amendment by section 402 of Pub.L. 101–650 effective 90 days after Dec. 1, 1990, see section 407 of Pub.L. 101–650, set out as a note under section 332 of this title.

1988 Acts. Amendment by Pub.L. 100–702 effective Dec. 1, 1988, see section 407 of Pub.L. 100–702, set out as a note under section 2071 of this title.

1984 Acts. Amendment by Pub.L. 98–353 effective July 10, 1984, see section 122(a) of Pub.L. 98–353, set out as a note under section 151 of this title.

1982 Acts. Amendment by Pub.L. 97–164 effective Oct. 1, 1982, see section 402 of Pub.L. 97–164, set out as a note under section 171 of this title.

1980 Acts. Amendment by Pub.L. 96–458 effective Oct. 1, 1981, see section 7 of Pub.L. 96–458, set out as a note under section 331 of this title.

Amendment by Pub.L. 96–417 effective on Nov. 1, 1980, and applicable with respect to civil actions pending on or commenced on or after such date, see section 701(a) of Pub.L. 96–417, as amended, set out as a note under section 251 of this title.

Change of Name

References to United States Claims Court deemed to refer to United States Court of Federal Claims and references to Claims Court deemed to refer to Court of Federal Claims, see section 902(b) of Pub.L. 102–572, set out as a note under section 171 of Title 28, Judiciary and Judicial Procedure.

"United States magistrate judge" substituted for "United States magistrate" in text pursuant to section 321 of Pub.L. 101–650, set out as a note under 28 U.S.C.A. § 631.

Transfer of Functions

Any reference in any provision of law enacted before Jan. 4, 1995, to a function, duty, or authority of the Clerk of the

House of Representatives treated as referring, with respect to that function, duty, or authority, to the officer of the House of Representatives exercising that function, duty, or authority, as determined by the Committee on House Oversight of the House of Representatives, see section 2(1) of Pub.L. 104–14, set out as a note preceding section 21 of Title 2, The Congress.

Computation of Judicial Service, District of Alaska

Inclusion of service as judge of the District Court for the Territory of Alaska in the computation of years of judicial service for judges of the United States District Court for the District of Alaska, see Pub.L. 89–70, July 8, 1965, 79 Stat. 213, set out as a note under section 371 of this title.

Extension of Time For Report by National Commission on Judicial Discipline and Removal

Pub.L. 102–368, Title I, Sept. 23, 1992, 106 Stat. 1118, provided in part that: "Notwithstanding the requirement of section 415 of Public Law 101–650 [set out as a note under this section] to submit the report mandated by said section not later than one year after the date of the Commission's first meeting, the National Commission on Judicial Discipline and Removal shall submit to each House of Congress, the Chief Justice of the United States, and the President, the report mandated in said section no later than August 1, 1993."

Judicial Service in Hawaii

Certain judicial service in Hawaii as included within computation of aggregate years of judicial service, see section 14(d) of Pub.L. 86–3, Mar. 18, 1959, 73 Stat. 10, set out as a note under section 371 of this title.

National Commission on Judicial Discipline and Removal

Subtitle II (sections 408 to 418) of Title IV of Pub.L. 101–650, as amended Pub.L. 102–198, § 8(a),(b)(2), Dec. 9, 1991, 105 Stat. 1625, 1626, provided that:

"Sec. 408. Short Title.

"This subtitle [subtitle II of Title IV of Pub.L. 101–650] may be cited as the 'National Commission on Judicial Discipline and Removal Act'.

"Sec. 409. Establishment.

"There is hereby established a commission to be known as the 'National Commission on Judicial Discipline and Removal' (hereinafter in this subtitle referred to as the 'Commission').

"Sec. 410. Duties of Commission.

"The duties of the Commission are—

"(1) to investigate and study the problems and issues involved in the tenure (including discipline and removal) of an article III judge;

"(2) to evaluate the advisability of proposing alternatives to current arrangements with respect to such problems and issues, including alternatives for discipline or removal of judges that would require amendment to the Constitution; and

"(3) to prepare and submit to the Congress, the Chief Justice of the United States, and the President a report in accordance with section 415.

"Sec. 411. Membership.

"**(a) Number and appointment.**—The Commission shall be composed of 13 members as follows:

"(1) Three appointed by the President pro tempore of the Senate.

"(2) Three appointed by the Speaker of the House of Representatives.

"(3) Three appointed by the Chief Justice of the United States.

"(4) Three appointed by the President.

"(5) One appointed by the Conference of Chief Justices of the States of the United States.

"**(b) Term.**—Members of the Commission shall be appointed for the life of the Commission.

"**(c) Quorum.**—Six members of the Commission shall constitute a quorum, but a lesser number may conduct meetings.

"**(d) Chairman.**—The members of the Commission shall select one of the members to be the Chairman.

"**(e) Vacancy.**—A vacancy on the Commission resulting from the death or resignation of a member shall not affect its powers and shall be filled in the same manner in which the original appointment was made.

"**(f) Continuation of membership.**—If any member of the Commission who was appointed to the Commission as a Member of Congress or as an officer or employee of a government leaves that office, or if any member of the Commission who was appointed from persons who are not officers or employees of a government becomes an officer or employee of a government, the member may continue as a member of the Commission for not longer than the 90–day period beginning on the date the member leaves that office or becomes such an officer or employee, as the case may be.

"Sec. 412. Compensation of the Commission.

"**(a) Pay.**—(1) Except as provided in paragraph (2), each member of the Commission who is not otherwise employed by the United States Government shall be entitled to receive the daily equivalent of the annual rate of basic pay payable for GS–18 of the General Schedule under section 5332 of title 5, United States Code [section 5332 of Title 5, Government Organization and Employees], for each day (including travel time) during which he or she is engaged in the actual performance of duties as a member of the Commission.

"(2) A member of the Commission who is an officer or employee of the United States Government shall serve without additional compensation.

"**(b) Travel.**—All members of the Commission shall be reimbursed for travel, subsistence, and other necessary expenses incurred by them in the performance of their duties.

"Sec. 413. Director and staff of Commission; experts and consultants.

"**(a) Director.**—The Commission shall, without regard to section 5311(b) of title 5, United States Code [section 5311(b) of Title 5], have a Director who shall be appointed by the Chairman and who shall be paid at a rate not to exceed the rate of basic pay payable for level V of the Executive Schedule under section 5316 of such title [section 5316 of Title 5].

"**(b) Staff.**—The Chairman of the Commission may appoint and fix the pay of such additional personnel as the Chairman finds necessary to enable the Commission to carry out its duties. Such personnel may be appointed without regard to the provisions of title 5, United States Code [Title 5], governing appointments in the competitive service, and may be paid without regard to the provisions of chapter 51 and subchapter III of chapter 53 of such title [section 5101 et seq. and section 5331 et seq. of Title 5] relating to classification and General Schedule pay rates, except that the annual rate of pay for any individual so appointed may not exceed a rate equal to the annual rate of basic pay payable for GS–18 of the General Schedule under section 5332 of such title [section 5332 of Title 5].

"(c) Experts and consultants.—The Commission may procure temporary and intermittent services of experts and consultants under section 3109(b) of title 5, United States Code [section 3109(b) of Title 5].

"Sec. 414. Powers of Commission.

"(a) Hearings and sessions.—The Commission or, on authorization of the Commission, a member of the Commission may, for the purpose of carrying out this subtitle, hold such hearings, sit and act at such times and places, take such testimony, and receive such evidence, as the Commission considers appropriate. The Commission may administer oaths or affirmations to witnesses appearing before it.

"(b) Obtaining official data.—The Commission may secure directly from any department, agency, or entity within the executive or judicial branch of the Federal Government information necessary to enable it to carry out this subtitle. Upon request of the Chairman of the Commission, the head of such department or agency shall furnish such information to the Commission.

"(c) Facilities and support services.—The Administrator of General Services shall provide to the Commission on a reimbursable basis such facilities and support services as the Commission may request. Upon request of the Commission, the head of any Federal agency is authorized to make any of the facilities and services of such agency available to the Commission to assist the Commission in carrying out its duties under this subtitle.

"(d) Expenditures and contracts.—The Commission or, on authorization of the Commission, a member of the Commission may make expenditures and enter into contracts for the procurement of such supplies, services, and property as the Commission or member considers appropriate for the purposes of carrying out the duties of the Commission. Such expenditures and contracts may be made only to such extent or in such amounts as are provided in appropriation Acts.

"(e) Mails.—The Commission may use the United States mails in the same manner and under the same conditions as other departments and agencies of the United States.

"(f) Gifts.—The Commission may accept, use, and dispose of gifts or donations of services or property.

"Sec. 415. Report.

"The Commission shall submit to each House of Congress, the Chief Justice of the United States, and the President a report not later than one year after the date of its first meeting. The report shall contain a detailed statement of the findings and conclusions of the Commission, together with its recommendations for such legislative or administrative action as it considers appropriate.

"Sec. 416. Termination.

"The Commission shall cease to exist on the date 30 days after the date it submits its report to the President and the Congress under section 415.

"Sec. 417. Authorization of appropriations.

"There is authorized to be appropriated the sum of $750,000 to carry out the provisions of this subtitle.

"Sec. 418. Effective date.

"This subtitle shall take effect on the date of the enactment of this Act [Dec. 1, 1990]."

[References in laws to the rates of pay for GS–16, 17, or 18, or to maximum rates of pay under the General Schedule, to be considered references to rates payable under specified sections of Title 5, Government Organization and Employees, see section 529 [Title I, § 101(c)(1)] of Pub.L. 101–509, set out in a note under section 5376 of Title 5.]

[For provisions extending the time for submission by the National Commission on Judicial Discipline and Removal of the report required by section 415 of Pub.L. 101–650, see Pub.L. 102–368, Title 1, Sept. 23, 1992, 106 Stat. 1118, set out as a note under this section.]

[For termination, effective May 15, 2000, of reporting provisions pertaining to the findings and conclusions of the Commission of Pub.L. 101–650, § 415 set out above, see Pub.L. 104–66, § 3003, as amended, set out as a note under 31 U.S.C.A. § 1113, and the 4th item on page 181 of House Document No. 103–7.]

CROSS REFERENCES

Assignment of retired justices or judges to active duty, see 28 USCA § 294.

Court of Federal Claims judges election of annuity payments upon retirement not entitled to receive annuity or salary in senior status under this section, see 28 USCA § 178.

Court of Veterans Appeals, applicability of this section in prescribing rules and establishing procedures for filing of complaints against any judge, see 38 USCA § 7253.

Duties of Director of Administrative Office of United States Courts, see 28 USCA § 604.

Employee defined as including retired judge under this section for purposes of life insurance for federal employees, see 5 USCA § 8701.

Judicial Conference of the United States, see 28 USCA § 331.

Justices and judges appointed to hold office during good behavior—

Court of Appeals, see USCA Const. Art. III § 1.

Court of International Trade, see 28 USCA § 252.

District Courts, see USCA Const. Art. III § 1.

Supreme Court, see USCA Const. Art. III § 1.

Thrift Savings Fund, see 5 USCA § 8440a.

CHAPTER 21—GENERAL PROVISIONS APPLICABLE TO COURTS AND JUDGES

§ 455. Disqualification of justice, judge, or magistrate judge

(a) Any justice, judge, or magistrate judge of the United States shall disqualify himself in any proceeding in which his impartiality might reasonably be questioned.

(b) He shall also disqualify himself in the following circumstances:

(1) Where he has a personal bias or prejudice concerning a party, or personal knowledge of disputed evidentiary facts concerning the proceeding;

(2) Where in private practice he served as lawyer in the matter in controversy, or a lawyer with whom he previously practiced law served during such association as a lawyer concerning the matter, or the judge or such lawyer has been a material witness concerning it;

(3) Where he has served in governmental employment and in such capacity participated as counsel, adviser or material witness concerning the proceeding or expressed an opinion concerning the merits of the particular case in controversy;

(4) He knows that he, individually or as a fiduciary, or his spouse or minor child residing in his household, has a financial interest in the subject matter in controversy or in a party to the proceeding, or any other interest that could be substantially affected by the outcome of the proceeding;

(5) He or his spouse, or a person within the third degree of relationship to either of them, or the spouse of such a person:

(i) Is a party to the proceeding, or an officer, director, or trustee of a party;

(ii) Is acting as a lawyer in the proceeding;

(iii) Is known by the judge to have an interest that could be substantially affected by the outcome of the proceeding;

(iv) Is to the judge's knowledge likely to be a material witness in the proceeding.

(c) A judge should inform himself about his personal and fiduciary financial interests, and make a reasonable effort to inform himself about the personal financial interests of his spouse and minor children residing in his household.

(d) For the purposes of this section the following words or phrases shall have the meaning indicated:

(1) "proceeding" includes pretrial, trial, appellate review, or other stages of litigation;

(2) the degree of relationship is calculated according to the civil law system;

(3) "fiduciary" includes such relationships as executor, administrator, trustee, and guardian;

(4) "financial interest" means ownership of a legal or equitable interest, however small, or a relationship as director, adviser, or other active participant in the affairs of a party, except that:

(i) Ownership in a mutual or common investment fund that holds securities is not a "financial interest" in such securities unless the judge participates in the management of the fund;

(ii) An office in an educational, religious, charitable, fraternal, or civic organization is not a "financial interest" in securities held by the organization;

(iii) The proprietary interest of a policyholder in a mutual insurance company, of a depositor in a mutual savings association, or a similar proprietary interest, is a "financial interest" in the organization only if the outcome of the proceeding could substantially affect the value of the interest;

(iv) Ownership of government securities is a "financial interest" in the issuer only if the outcome of the proceeding could substantially affect the value of the securities.

(e) No justice, judge, or magistrate judge shall accept from the parties to the proceeding a waiver of any ground for disqualification enumerated in subsection (b). Where the ground for disqualification arises only under subsection (a), waiver may be accepted provided it is preceded by a full disclosure on the record of the basis for disqualification.

(f) Notwithstanding the preceding provisions of this section, if any justice, judge, magistrate judge, or bankruptcy judge to whom a matter has been assigned would be disqualified, after substantial judicial time has been devoted to the matter, because of the appearance or discovery, after the matter was assigned to him or her, that he or she individually or as a fiduciary, or his or her spouse or minor child residing in his or her household, has a financial interest in a party (other than an interest that could be substantially affected by the outcome), disqualification is not required if the justice, judge, magistrate judge, bankruptcy judge, spouse or minor child, as the case may be, divests himself or herself of the interest that provides the grounds for the disqualification.

(June 25, 1948, c. 646, 62 Stat. 908; Dec. 5, 1974, Pub.L. 93–512, § 1, 88 Stat. 1609; Nov. 6, 1978, Pub.L. 95–598, Title II, § 214(a), (b), 92 Stat. 2661; Nov. 19, 1988, Pub.L. 100–702, Title X, § 1007, 102 Stat. 4667; Dec. 1, 1990, Pub.L. 101–650, Title III, § 321, 104 Stat. 5117.)

HISTORICAL AND STATUTORY NOTES

Revision Notes and Legislative Reports

1948 Acts. Based on Title 28, U.S.C., 1940 ed., § 24 (Mar. 3, 1911, c. 231, § 20, 36 Stat. 1090 [Derived from R.S. § 601]).

Section 24 of Title 28, U.S.C., 1940 ed., applied only to district judges. The revised section is made applicable to all justices and judges of the United States.

The phrase "in which he has a substantial interest" was substituted for "concerned in interest in any suit."

The provision of section 24 of Title 28, U.S.C., 1940 ed., as to giving notice of disqualification to the "senior circuit judge," and words "and thereupon such proceedings shall be had as are provided in sections 17 and 18 of this title," were omitted as unnecessary and covered by section 291 et seq. of this title relating to designation and assignment of judges. Such provision is not made by statute in case of disqualification or incapacity, for other cause. See sections 140, 143, and 144 of this title. If a judge or clerk of court is remiss in failing to notify the chief judge of the district or circuit, the judicial council of the circuit has ample power under section 332 of this title to apply a remedy.

Relationship to a party's attorney is included in the revised section as a basis of disqualification in conformity with the views of judges cognizant of the grave possibility of undesirable consequences resulting from a less inclusive rule.

Changes were made in phraseology. 80th Congress House Report No. 308.

1974 Acts. House Report No. 93–1453, see 1974 U.S.Code Cong. and Adm.News, p. 6351.

1978 Acts. Senate Report No. 95–989 and House Report No. 95–595, see 1978 U.S. Code Cong. and Adm. News, p. 5787.

1988 Acts. House Report No. 100–889, see 1988 U.S.Code Cong. and Adm.News, p. 5982.

Change of Name

"United States magistrate judge" substituted for "United States magistrate" in text pursuant to section 321 of Pub.L. 101–650, set out as a note under 28 U.S.C.A. § 631.

Effective and Applicability Provisions

1978 Acts. Amendment by Pub.L. 95–598 effective Oct. 1, 1979, see section 402(c) of Pub.L. 95–598, set out as a note preceding section 101 of Title 11, Bankruptcy. For procedures relating to bankruptcy matters during transition period, see note preceding section 151 of this title.

1974 Acts. Section 3 of Pub.L. 93–512 provided that: "This Act [amending this section] shall not apply to the trial of any proceeding commenced prior to the date of this Act [Dec. 5, 1974], nor to appellate review of any proceeding which was fully submitted to the reviewing court prior to the date of this Act."

CROSS REFERENCES

Application to other courts, see 28 USCA § 460.

Arbitrators subject to disqualification rules under this section, see 28 USCA § 656.

Bias or prejudice of judge, see 28 USCA § 144.

Disqualification of trial judge to hear appeal, see 28 USCA § 47.

United States Court of Veterans affairs, judges and proceedings of subject to this section, see 38 USCA § 7264.

PART II—DEPARTMENT OF JUSTICE

CHAPTER 39—UNITED STATES TRUSTEES

HISTORICAL AND STATUTORY NOTES

Effective and Applicability Provisions

2005 Acts. Except as otherwise provided, amendments by Pub.L. 109–8 effective 180 days after April 20, 2005, and inapplicable with respect to cases commenced under Title 11 before the effective date, see Pub.L. 109–8, § 1501, set out as a note under 11 U.S.C.A. § 101.

United States Trustee Pilot; Repeal of Bankruptcy Provisions Relating to United States Trustees

Pub.L. 95–598, Title IV, § 408, Nov. 6, 1978, 92 Stat. 2686, as amended Pub.L. 98–166, Title II, § 200, Nov. 28, 1983, 97 Stat. 1081; Pub.L. 98–353, Title III, § 323, July 10, 1984, 98 Stat. 358; Pub.L. 99–429, Sept. 30, 1986, 100 Stat. 985; Pub.L. 99–500, Title I, § 101(b) [Title II, § 200], Oct. 18, 1986, 100 Stat. 1783–39, 1783–45, and Pub.L. 99–591, Title I, § 101(b), [Title II, § 200], Oct. 30, 1986, 100 Stat. 3341–45; Pub.L. 99–554, Title III, § 307(a), Oct. 27, 1986, 100 Stat. 3125, which provided that the Attorney General conduct such studies and surveys as necessary to evaluate the needs, feasibility, and effectiveness of the United States trustee system, and report the result of such studies and surveys to the Congress, the President, and the Judicial Conference of the United States, beginning on or before January 3, 1980, and annually thereafter during the transition period; that not later than January 3, 1984, the Attorney General report to the Congress, the President, and the Judicial Conference of the United States, as to the feasibility, projected annual cost and effectiveness of the United States trustee system, as determined on the basis of the studies and surveys respecting the operation of the United States trustee system in the districts, together with recommendations as to the desirability and method of proceeding with implementation of the United States trustee system in all judicial districts of the United States; and that chapter 15 of title 11 of the United States Code [section 1501 et seq. of Title 11, Bankruptcy] and chapter 39 of title 28 of the United States Code [this chapter] are repealed, and all references to the United States trustee contained in title 28 of the United States Code [this title] are deleted, as of 30 days after the effective date of the

Bankruptcy Judges, United States Trustees, and Family Farmer Bankruptcy Act of 1986 [see section 302 of Pub.L. 99–554, set out as a note under 28 U.S.C.A. § 581], with service of any United States trustee, of any assistant United States trustee, and of any employee employed or appointed under the authority of such chapter 39 is terminated on such date, was repealed by Pub.L. 99–554, Title III, § 307(b), Oct. 27, 1986, 100 Stat. 3125 [set out as a note under 28 U.S.C.A. § 581].

§ 581. United States trustees

(a) The Attorney General shall appoint one United States trustee for each of the following regions composed of Federal judicial districts (without regard to section 451):

(1) The judicial districts established for the States of Maine, Massachusetts, New Hampshire, and Rhode Island.

(2) The judicial districts established for the States of Connecticut, New York, and Vermont.

(3) The judicial districts established for the States of Delaware, New Jersey, and Pennsylvania.

(4) The judicial districts established for the States of Maryland, North Carolina, South Carolina, Virginia, and West Virginia and for the District of Columbia.

(5) The judicial districts established for the States of Louisiana and Mississippi.

(6) The Northern District of Texas and the Eastern District of Texas.

(7) The Southern District of Texas and the Western District of Texas.

(8) The judicial districts established for the States of Kentucky and Tennessee.

(9) The judicial districts established for the States of Michigan and Ohio.

(10) The Central District of Illinois and the Southern District of Illinois; and the judicial districts established for the State of Indiana.

(11) The Northern District of Illinois; and the judicial districts established for the State of Wisconsin.

(12) The judicial districts established for the States of Minnesota, Iowa, North Dakota, and South Dakota.

(13) The judicial districts established for the States of Arkansas, Nebraska, and Missouri.

(14) The District of Arizona.

(15) The Southern District of California; and the judicial districts established for the State of Hawaii, and for Guam and the Commonwealth of the Northern Mariana Islands.

(16) The Central District of California.

(17) The Eastern District of California and the Northern District of California; and the judicial district established for the State of Nevada.

(18) The judicial districts established for the States of Alaska, Idaho (exclusive of Yellowstone National Park), Montana (exclusive of Yellowstone National Park), Oregon, and Washington.

(19) The judicial districts established for the States of Colorado, Utah, and Wyoming (including those portions of Yellowstone National Park situated in the States of Montana and Idaho).

(20) The judicial districts established for the States of Kansas, New Mexico, and Oklahoma.

(21) The judicial districts established for the States of Alabama, Florida, and Georgia and for the Commonwealth of Puerto Rico and the Virgin Islands of the United States.

(b) Each United States trustee shall be appointed for a term of five years. On the expiration of his term, a United States trustee shall continue to perform the duties of his office until his successor is appointed and qualifies.

(c) Each United States trustee is subject to removal by the Attorney General.

(Added Pub.L. 95–598, Title II, § 224(a), Nov. 6, 1978, 92 Stat. 2662, and amended Pub.L. 99–554, Title I, § 111(a) to (c), Oct. 27, 1986, 100 Stat. 3090, 3091.)

HISTORICAL AND STATUTORY NOTES

Revision Notes and Legislative Reports

1978 Acts. Senate Report No. 95–989 and House Report No. 95–595, see 1978 U.S. Code Cong. and Adm. News, p. 5787.

1986 Acts. House Report No. 99–764 and House Conference Report No. 99–958, see 1986 U.S. Code Cong. and Adm. News, p. 5227.

Codifications

Section 408(c) of Pub.L. 95–598, as amended, which provided for the repeal of this section and the deletion of any references to United States Trustees in this title at a prospective date, was repealed by section 307(b) of Pub.L. 99–554. See note set out preceding this section.

Effective and Applicability Provisions

1978 Acts. Section effective Oct. 1, 1979, see section 402(c) of Pub.L. 95–598, as amended, set out as a note preceding 11 U.S.C.A. § 101.

Short Title

1986 Amendments. Section 1 of Pub.L. 99–554 provided: "That this Act [enacting section 589a of this title and sections 307, and 1201 to 1231 of Title 11, Bankruptcy, amending sections 49, 96, 152, 156, 157, 528, 581, 582, 584 to 587, 604, 1334, and 1930 of this title and sections 101 to 103, 105, 108, 109, 303, 321, 322, 324, 326, 327, 329, 330, 341, 343, 345 to 348, 362 to 365, 502, 503, 521 to 524, 546 to 549, 554, 557, 701, 703 to 707, 724, 726 to 728, 743, 1102, 1104 to 1106, 1112, 1121, 1129, 1163, 1202, 1302, 1306, 1307, and 1324 to 1326 of Title

11, Bankruptcy Form No. 1, set out in the Appendix to Title 11, repealing sections 1201 to 1231 and 1501 to 151326 of Title 11, enacting provisions set out as notes under sections 581 and 589 of this title, amending provisions set out as a note under section 152 of this title and preceding section 581 of this title, and repealing provisions set out as notes under preceding section 581 of this title] may be cited as the 'Bankruptcy Judges, United States Trustees, and Family Farmer Bankruptcy Act of 1986'."

Bankruptcy Crimes

Pub.L. 109–162, Title XI, § 1175, Jan. 5, 2006, 119 Stat. 3125, provided that:

"The Director of the Executive Office for United States Trustees shall prepare an annual report to the Congress detailing—

"(1) the number and types of criminal referrals made by the United States Trustee Program;

"(2) the outcomes of each criminal referral;

"(3) for any year in which the number of criminal referrals is less than for the prior year, an explanation of the decrease; and

"(4) the United States Trustee Program's efforts to prevent bankruptcy fraud and abuse, particularly with respect to the establishment of uniform internal controls to detect common, higher risk frauds, such as a debtor's failure to disclose all assets."

CROSS REFERENCES

Appointment of acting United States trustee by Attorney General to serve until vacancy is filled by appointment under this section, see 28 USCA § 585.

§ 582. Assistant United States trustees

(a) The Attorney General may appoint one or more assistant United States trustees in any region when the public interest so requires.

(b) Each assistant United States trustee is subject to removal by the Attorney General.

(Added Pub.L. 95–598, Title II, § 224(a), Nov. 6, 1978, 92 Stat. 2663, and amended Pub.L. 99–554, Title I, § 111(d), Oct. 27, 1986, 100 Stat. 3091.)

HISTORICAL AND STATUTORY NOTES

Revision Notes and Legislative Reports

1978 Acts. Senate Report No. 95–989 and House Report No. 95–595, see 1978 U.S.Code Cong. and Adm.News, p. 5787.

1986 Acts. House Report No. 99–764 and House Conference Report No. 99–958, see 1986 U.S.Code Cong. and Adm.News, p. 5227.

Codifications

Section 408(c) of Pub.L. 95–598, as amended, which provided for the repeal of this section and the deletion of any references to United States Trustees in this title at a prospective date, was repealed by section 307(b) of Pub.L. 99–554. See note set out preceding section 581 of this title.

Effective and Applicability Provisions

1986 Acts. Amendment by Pub.L. 99–554 effective 30 days after Oct. 27, 1986, except as otherwise provided, see section 302(a) of Pub.L. 99–554, as amended, set out as a note under section 581 of this title.

1978 Acts. Section effective Oct. 1, 1979, see section 402(c) of Pub.L. 95–598, as amended, set out as a note preceding section 101 of Title 11, Bankruptcy.

Appointment of United States Trustees by Attorney General

Appointment of United States Trustees by the Attorney General of individuals otherwise qualified, serving as estate administrators under Title 11, Bankruptcy, before effective date of Pub.L. 99–554, see section 309 of Pub.L. 99–554, as amended; set out as a note under section 581 of this title.

§ 583. Oath of office

Each United States trustee and assistant United States trustee, before taking office, shall take an oath to execute faithfully his duties.

(Added Pub.L. 95–598, Title II, § 224(a), Nov. 6, 1978, 92 Stat. 2663.)

HISTORICAL AND STATUTORY NOTES

Revision Notes and Legislative Reports

1978 Acts. Senate Report No. 95–989 and House Report No. 95–595, see 1978 U.S.Code Cong. and Adm.News, p. 5787.

Codifications

Section 408(c) of Pub.L. 95–598, as amended, which provided for the repeal of this section and the deletion of any references to United States Trustees in this title at a prospective date, was repealed by section 307(b) of Pub.L. 99–554. See note set out preceding section 581 of this title.

Effective and Applicability Provisions

1978 Acts. Section effective Oct. 1, 1979, see section 402(c) of Pub.L. 95–598, as amended, set out as a note preceding section 101 of Title 11, Bankruptcy.

§ 584. Official stations

The Attorney General may determine the official stations of the United States trustees and assistant United States trustees within the regions for which they were appointed.

(Added Pub.L. 95–598, Title II, § 224(a), Nov. 6, 1978, 92 Stat. 2663, and amended Pub.L. 99–554, Title I, § 144(d), Oct. 27, 1986, 100 Stat. 3096.)

HISTORICAL AND STATUTORY NOTES

Revision Notes and Legislative Reports

1978 Acts. Senate Report No. 95–989 and House Report No. 95–595, see 1978 U.S.Code Cong. and Adm.News, p. 5787.

1986 Acts. House Report No. 99–764 and House Conference Report No. 99–958, see 1986 U.S.Code Cong. and Adm.News, p. 5227.

Codifications

Section 408(c) of Pub.L. 95–598, as amended, which provided for the repeal of this section and the deletion of any references to United States Trustees in this title at a prospective date, was repealed by section 307(b) of Pub.L. 99–554. See note set out preceding section 581 of this title.

Effective and Applicability Provisions

1986 Acts. Amendment by Pub.L. 99–554 effective 30 days after Oct. 27, 1986, except as otherwise provided, see section 302(a) of Pub.L. 99–554, as amended, set out as a note under section 581 of this title.

1978 Acts. Section effective Oct. 1, 1979, see section 402(c) of Pub.L. 95–598, as amended, set out as a note preceding section 101 of Title 11, Bankruptcy.

§ 585. Vacancies

(a) The Attorney General may appoint an acting United States trustee for a region in which the office of the United States trustee is vacant. The individual so appointed may serve until the date on which the vacancy is filled by appointment under section 581 of this title or by designation under subsection (b) of this section.

(b) The Attorney General may designate a United States trustee to serve in not more than two regions for such time as the public interest requires.

(Added Pub.L. 95–598, Title II, § 224(a), Nov. 6, 1978, 92 Stat. 2663, and amended Pub.L. 99–554, Title I, § 112, Oct. 27, 1986, 100 Stat. 3091.)

HISTORICAL AND STATUTORY NOTES

Revision Notes and Legislative Reports

1978 Acts. Senate Report No. 95–989 and House Report No. 95–595, see 1978 U.S. Code Cong. and Adm. News, p. 5787.

1986 Acts. House Report No. 99–764 and House Conference Report No. 99–958, see 1986 U.S. Code Cong. and Adm. News, p. 5227.

Codifications

Section 408(c) of Pub.L. 95–598, as amended, which provided for the repeal of this section and the deletion of any references to United States Trustees in this title at a prospective date, was repealed by section 307(b) of Pub.L. 99–554. See note set out preceding section 581 of this title.

Effective and Applicability Provisions

1986 Acts. Amendment by Pub.L. 99–554 effective 30 days after Oct. 27, 1986, except as otherwise provided, see section 302(a) of Pub.L. 99–554, as amended, set out as a note under section 581 of this title.

1978 Acts. Section effective Oct. 1, 1979, see section 402(c) of Pub.L. 95–598, as amended, set out as a note preceding section 101 of Title 11, Bankruptcy.

§ 586. Duties; supervision by Attorney General

(a) Each United States trustee, within the region for which such United States trustee is appointed, shall—

(1) establish, maintain, and supervise a panel of private trustees that are eligible and available to serve as trustees in cases under chapter 7 of title 11;

(2) serve as and perform the duties of a trustee in a case under title 11 when required under title 11 to serve as trustee in such a case;

(3) supervise the administration of cases and trustees in cases under chapter 7, 11, 12, 13, or 15 of title 11 by, whenever the United States trustee considers it to be appropriate—

(A)(i) reviewing, in accordance with procedural guidelines adopted by the Executive Office of the United States Trustee (which guidelines shall be applied uniformly by the United States trustee except when circumstances warrant different treatment), applications filed for compensation and reimbursement under section 330 of title 11; and

(ii) filing with the court comments with respect to such application and, if the United States Trustee considers it to be appropriate, objections to such application.[1]

(B) monitoring plans and disclosure statements filed in cases under chapter 11 of title 11 and filing with the court, in connection with hearings under sections 1125 and 1128 of such title, comments with respect to such plans and disclosure statements;

(C) monitoring plans filed under chapters 12 and 13 of title 11 and filing with the court, in connection with hearings under sections 1224, 1229, 1324, and 1329 of such title, comments with respect to such plans;

(D) taking such action as the United States trustee deems to be appropriate to ensure that all reports, schedules, and fees required to be filed under title 11 and this title by the debtor are properly and timely filed;

(E) monitoring creditors' committees appointed under title 11;

(F) notifying the appropriate United States attorney of matters which relate to the occurrence of any action which may constitute a crime under the laws of the United States and, on the request of the United States attorney, assisting the United States attorney in carrying out prosecutions based on such action;

(G) monitoring the progress of cases under title 11 and taking such actions as the United States trustee deems to be appropriate to prevent undue delay in such progress;

(H) in small business cases (as defined in section 101 of title 11), performing the additional duties specified in title 11 pertaining to such cases; and

(I) monitoring applications filed under section 327 of title 11 and, whenever the United States trustee deems it to be appropriate, filing with the court comments with respect to the approval of such applications;

(4) deposit or invest under section 345 of title 11 money received as trustee in cases under title 11;

(5) perform the duties prescribed for the United States trustee under title 11 and this title, and such duties consistent with title 11 and this title as the Attorney General may prescribe;

(6) make such reports as the Attorney General directs, including the results of audits performed under section 603(a) of the Bankruptcy Abuse Prevention and Consumer Protection Act of 2005;

(7) in each of such small business cases—

(A) conduct an initial debtor interview as soon as practicable after the date of the order for relief but before the first meeting scheduled under section 341(a) of title 11, at which time the United States trustee shall—

(i) begin to investigate the debtor's viability;

(ii) inquire about the debtor's business plan;

(iii) explain the debtor's obligations to file monthly operating reports and other required reports;

(iv) attempt to develop an agreed scheduling order; and

(v) inform the debtor of other obligations;

(B) if determined to be appropriate and advisable, visit the appropriate business premises of the debtor, ascertain the state of the debtor's books and records, and verify that the debtor has filed its tax returns; and

(C) review and monitor diligently the debtor's activities, to identify as promptly as possible whether the debtor will be unable to confirm a plan; and

(8) in any case in which the United States trustee finds material grounds for any relief under section 1112 of title 11, the United States trustee shall apply promptly after making that finding to the court for relief.

(b) If the number of cases under chapter 12 or 13 of title 11 commenced in a particular region so warrants, the United States trustee for such region may, subject to the approval of the Attorney General, appoint one or more individuals to serve as standing trustee, or designate one or more assistant United States trustees to serve in cases under such chapter. The United States trustee for such region shall supervise any such individual appointed as standing trustee in the performance of the duties of standing trustee.

(c) Each United States trustee shall be under the general supervision of the Attorney General, who shall provide general coordination and assistance to the United States trustees.

(d)(1) The Attorney General shall prescribe by rule qualifications for membership on the panels established by United States trustees under paragraph (a)(1) of this section, and qualifications for appointment under subsection (b) of this section to serve as standing trustee in cases under chapter 12 or 13 of title 11. The Attorney General may not require that an individual be an attorney in order to qualify for appointment under subsection (b) of this section to serve as standing trustee in cases under chapter 12 or 13 of title 11.

(2) A trustee whose appointment under subsection (a)(1) or under subsection (b) is terminated or who ceases to be assigned to cases filed under title 11, United States Code, may obtain judicial review of the final agency decision by commencing an action in the district court of the United States for the district for which the panel to which the trustee is appointed under subsection (a)(1), or in the district court of the United States for the district in which the trustee is appointed under subsection (b) resides, after first exhausting all available administrative remedies, which if the trustee so elects, shall also include an administrative hearing on the record. Unless the trustee elects to have an administrative hearing on the record, the trustee shall be deemed to have exhausted all administrative remedies for purposes of this paragraph if the agency fails to make a final agency decision within 90 days after the trustee requests administrative remedies. The Attorney General shall prescribe procedures to implement this paragraph. The decision of the agency shall be affirmed by the district court unless it is unreasonable and without cause based on the administrative record before the agency.

(e)(1) The Attorney General, after consultation with a United States trustee that has appointed an individual under subsection (b) of this section to serve as standing trustee in cases under chapter 12 or 13 of title 11, shall fix—

(A) a maximum annual compensation for such individual consisting of—

(i) an amount not to exceed the highest annual rate of basic pay in effect for level V of the Executive Schedule; and

(ii) the cash value of employment benefits comparable to the employment benefits provided by the United States to individuals who are employed by the United States at the same rate of basic pay to perform similar services during the same period of time; and

(B) a percentage fee not to exceed—

(i) in the case of a debtor who is not a family farmer, ten percent; or

(ii) in the case of a debtor who is a family farmer, the sum of—

(I) not to exceed ten percent of the payments made under the plan of such debtor, with respect to payments in an aggregate amount not to exceed $450,000; and

(II) three percent of payments made under the plan of such debtor, with respect to payments made after the aggregate amount of payments made under the plan exceeds $450,000;

based on such maximum annual compensation and the actual, necessary expenses incurred by such individual as standing trustee.

(2) Such individual shall collect such percentage fee from all payments received by such individual under plans in the cases under chapter 12 or 13 of title 11 for which such individual serves as standing trustee. Such individual shall pay to the United States trustee, and the United States trustee shall deposit in the United States Trustee System Fund—

(A) any amount by which the actual compensation of such individual exceeds 5 per centum upon all payments received under plans in cases under chapter 12 or 13 of title 11 for which such individual serves as standing trustee; and

(B) any amount by which the percentage for all such cases exceeds—

(i) such individual's actual compensation for such cases, as adjusted under subparagraph (A) of paragraph (1); plus

(ii) the actual, necessary expenses incurred by such individual as standing trustee in such cases. Subject to the approval of the Attorney General, any or all of the interest earned from the deposit of payments under plans by such individual may be utilized to pay actual, necessary expenses without regard to the percentage limitation contained in subparagraph (d)(1)(B) of this section.

(3) After first exhausting all available administrative remedies, an individual appointed under subsection (b) may obtain judicial review of final agency action to deny a claim of actual, necessary expenses under this subsection by commencing an action in the district court of the United States for the district where the individual resides. The decision of the agency shall be affirmed by the district court unless it is unreasonable and without cause based upon the administrative record before the agency.

(4) The Attorney General shall prescribe procedures to implement this subsection.

(f)(1) The United States trustee for each district is authorized to contract with auditors to perform audits in cases designated by the United States trustee, in accordance with the procedures established under section 603(a) of the Bankruptcy Abuse Prevention and Consumer Protection Act of 2005.

(2)(A) The report of each audit referred to in paragraph (1) shall be filed with the court and transmitted to the United States trustee. Each report shall clearly and conspicuously specify any material misstatement of income or expenditures or of assets identified by the person performing the audit. In any case in which a material misstatement of income or expenditures or of assets has been reported, the clerk of the district court (or the clerk of the bankruptcy court if one is certified under section 156(b) of this title) shall give notice of the misstatement to the creditors in the case.

(B) If a material misstatement of income or expenditures or of assets is reported, the United States trustee shall—

(i) report the material misstatement, if appropriate, to the United States Attorney pursuant to section 3057 of title 18; and

(ii) if advisable, take appropriate action, including but not limited to commencing an adversary proceeding to revoke the debtor's discharge pursuant to section 727(d) of title 11.

(Added Pub.L. 95–598, Title II, § 224(a), Nov. 6, 1978, 92 Stat. 2663, and amended Pub.L. 99–554, Title I, § 113, Oct. 27, 1986, 100 Stat. 3091; Pub.L. 101–509, Title V, § 529 [Title I, § 110(a)], Nov. 5, 1990, 104 Stat. 1427, 1452; Pub.L. 103–394, Title II, § 224(a), Title V, § 502, Oct. 22, 1994, 108 Stat. 4130, 4147; Pub.L. 109–8, Title IV, § 439, Title VI, § 603(b), Title VIII, § 802(c)(3), Title XII, § 1231, Apr. 20, 2005, 119 Stat. 113, 122, 146, 201.)

[1] So in original. The period probably should be a semicolon.

HISTORICAL AND STATUTORY NOTES

Revision Notes and Legislative Reports

1978 Acts. Senate Report No. 95–989 and House Report No. 95–595, see 1978 U.S. Code Cong. and Adm. News, p. 5787.

1986 Acts. House Report No. 99–764 and House Conference Report No. 99–958, see 1986 U.S. Code Cong. and Adm. News, p. 5227.

1994 Acts. House Report No. 103–835, see 1994 U.S. Code Cong. and Adm. News, p. 3340.

2005 Acts. House Report No. 109–31(Part I), see 2005 U.S. Code Cong. and Adm. News, p. 88.

References in Text

Chapter 12 or 13 of title 11, referred to in text, is 11 U.S.C.A. § 1201 et seq. or 11 U.S.C.A. § 1301 et seq., respectively.

Chapter 7, 11, 12, 13, or 15 of title 11, referred to in subsec. (a)(3), is 11 U.S.C.A. § 701 et seq., 11 U.S.C.A. § 1101 et seq., 11 U.S.C.A. § 1201 et seq., 11 U.S.C.A. § 1301 et seq., or 11 U.S.C.A. § 1501 et seq., respectively.

Level V of the Executive Schedule, referred to in subsec. (e)(1)(A)(i), is set out in section 5316 of Title 5, Government Organization and Employees.

Section 603(a) of the Bankruptcy Abuse Prevention and Consumer Protection Act of 2005, referred to in subsecs. (a)(6) and (f)(1), is Pub.L. 109–8, Title VII, § 603(a), Apr. 20, 2005, 119 Stat. 122, which is set out as a note under this section.

Codifications

Section 408(c) of Pub.L. 95–598, as amended, which provided for the repeal of this section and the deletion of any references to United States Trustees in this title at a prospective date, was repealed by section 307(b) of Pub.L. 99–554. See note set out preceding section 581 of this title.

Effective and Applicability Provisions

2005 Acts. Amendments by Pub.L. 109–8, § 603, effective 18 months after Apr. 20, 2005, see Pub.L. 109–8, § 603(e), set out as a note under 11 U.S.C.A. 521.

Except as otherwise provided, amendments by Pub.L. 109–8 effective 180 days after April 20, 2005, and inapplicable with respect to cases commenced under Title 11 before the effective date, see Pub.L. 109–8, § 1501, set out as a note under 11 U.S.C.A. § 101.

1994 Acts. Amendments by Pub.L. 103–394 effective on Oct. 22, 1994, and not to apply with respect to cases commenced under Title 11 of the United States Code before Oct. 22, 1994, see section 702 of Pub.L. 103–394, set out as a note under section 101 of Title 11, Bankruptcy.

1990 Acts. Amendment by Pub.L. 101–509 effective on such date as the President shall determine, but not earlier than 90 days, and not later than 180 days, after Nov. 5, 1990, see section 529 [Title III, § 305] of Pub.L. 101–509, set out as a note under section 5301 of Title 5, Government Organization and Employees. [See also related provisions in Ex. Ord. No. 12748, Feb. 1, 1991, 56 F.R. 4521, set out under that section.]

1986 Acts. Effective date and applicability of amendment by Pub.L. 99–554 dependent upon the judicial district involved, see section 302(d), (e) of Pub.L. 99–554, set out as a note under section 581 of this title.

1978 Acts. Section effective Oct. 1, 1979, see section 402(c) of Pub.L. 95–598, as amended, set out as a note preceding section 101 of Title 11, Bankruptcy.

Separability of Provisions

If any provision of or amendment made by Pub.L. 103–394 or the application of such provision or amendment to any person or circumstance is held to be unconstitutional, the remaining provisions of and amendments made by Pub.L. 103–394 and the application of such provisions and amendments to any person or circumstance shall not be affected thereby, see section 701 of Pub.L. 103–394, set out as a note under section 101 of Title 11, Bankruptcy.

Audit Procedures

Pub.L. 109–8, Title VI, § 603(a), Apr. 20, 2005, 119 Stat. 122, provided that:

"**(a) In general.**—

"**(1) Establishment of procedures.**—The Attorney General (in judicial districts served by United States trustees) and the Judicial Conference of the United States (in judicial districts served by bankruptcy administrators) shall establish procedures to determine the accuracy, veracity, and completeness of petitions, schedules, and other information that the debtor is required to provide under sections 521 and 1322 of title 11, United States Code, and, if applicable, section 111 of such title [11 U.S.C.A. § 111], in cases filed under chapter 7 or 13 of such title [11 U.S.C.A. § 701 or 1301 et seq.] in which the debtor is an individual. Such audits shall be in accordance with generally accepted auditing standards and performed by independent certified public accountants or independent licensed public accountants, provided that the Attorney General and the Judicial Conference, as appropriate, may develop alternative auditing standards not later than 2 years after the date of enactment of this Act [April 20, 2005].

"**(2) Procedures.**—Those procedures required by paragraph (1) shall—

"**(A)** establish a method of selecting appropriate qualified persons to contract to perform those audits;

"**(B)** establish a method of randomly selecting cases to be audited, except that not less than 1 out of every 250 cases in each Federal judicial district shall be selected for audit;

"**(C)** require audits of schedules of income and expenses that reflect greater than average variances from the statistical norm of the district in which the schedules were filed if those variances occur by reason of higher income or higher expenses than the statistical norm of the district in which the schedules were filed; and

"**(D)** establish procedures for providing, not less frequently than annually, public information concerning the aggregate results of such audits including the percentage of cases, by district, in which a material misstatement of income or expenditures is reported."

[Enactment of this note by Pub.L. 109–8, § 603, effective 18 months after Apr. 20, 2005, see Pub.L. 109–8, § 603(e), set out as a note under 11 U.S.C.A. § 521.]

[Except as otherwise provided, amendments by Pub.L. 109–8 effective 180 days after April 20, 2005, and inapplicable with respect to cases commenced under Title 11 before the effective date, see Pub.L. 109–8, § 1501, set out as a note under 11 U.S.C.A. § 101.]

Application to All Standing Trustees

Section 529 [Title I, § 110(b)] of Pub.L. 101–509 provided that: "The amendment made by subsection (a) [amending this section] shall apply to any trustee to whom the provisions of section 302(d)(3) of the Bankruptcy Judges, United States Trustees, and Family Farmer Bankruptcy Act of 1986 (Public Law 99–54 [Pub.L. 99–554]; 100 Stat. 3121) [set out in a note under section 581 of this title] apply."

CROSS REFERENCES

Appointment of disinterested person from panel of private trustees established under this section to serve as—

Interim trustee, see 11 USCA § 701.

Successor trustee, see 11 USCA § 703.

Appointment of standing trustee to serve in cases under—

Chapter thirteen of Bankruptcy, see 11 USCA § 1302.

Chapter twelve of Bankruptcy, see 11 USCA § 1202.

Compensation for services or reimbursement of expenses not allowable for standing trustee appointed under this section, see 11 USCA § 326.

Payments to standing trustee; percentage fee fixed under this section, see 11 USCA § 1326.

§ 587. Salaries

Subject to sections 5315 through 5317 of title 5, the Attorney General shall fix the annual salaries of United States trustees and assistant United States trustees at rates of compensation not in excess of the rate of basic compensation provided for Executive Level IV of the Executive Schedule set forth in section 5315 of title 5, United States Code.

(Added Pub.L. 95–598, Title II, § 224(a), Nov. 6, 1978, 92 Stat. 2664, and amended Pub.L. 99–554, Title I, § 114(a), Oct. 27, 1986, 100 Stat. 3093.)

HISTORICAL AND STATUTORY NOTES

Revision Notes and Legislative Reports

1978 Acts. Senate Report No. 95–989 and House Report No. 95–595, see 1978 U.S.Code Cong. and Adm.News, p. 5787.

1986 Acts. House Report No. 99–764 and House Conference Report No. 99–958, see 1986 U.S.Code Cong. and Adm.News, p. 5227.

Codifications

Section 408(c) of Pub.L. 95–598, as amended, which provided for the repeal of this section and the deletion of any references to United States Trustees in this title at a prospective date, was repealed by section 307(b) of Pub.L. 99–554. See note set out preceding section 581 of this title.

Effective and Applicability Provisions

1986 Acts. Amendment by Pub.L. 99–554 effective 30 days after Oct. 27, 1986, except as otherwise provided, see section 302(a) of Pub.L. 99–554, as amended, set out as a note under section 581 of this title.

1978 Acts. Section effective Oct. 1, 1979, see section 402(c) of Pub.L. 95–598, as amended, set out as a note preceding section 101 of Title 11, Bankruptcy.

§ 588. Expenses

Necessary office expenses of the United States trustee shall be allowed when authorized by the Attorney General.

(Added Pub.L. 95–598, Title II, § 224(a), Nov. 6, 1978, 92 Stat. 2664.)

HISTORICAL AND STATUTORY NOTES

Revision Notes and Legislative Reports

1978 Acts. Senate Report No. 95–989 and House Report No. 95–595, see 1978 U.S.Code Cong. and Adm.News, p. 5787.

Codifications

Section 408(c) of Pub.L. 95–598, as amended, which provided for the repeal of this section and the deletion of any references to United States Trustees in this title at a prospective date, was repealed by section 307(b) of Pub.L. 99–554. See note set out preceding section 581 of this title.

Effective and Applicability Provisions

1978 Acts. Section effective Oct. 1, 1979, see section 402(c) of Pub.L. 95–598, as amended, set out as a note preceding section 101 of Title 11, Bankruptcy.

§ 589. Staff and other employees

The United States trustee may employ staff and other employees on approval of the Attorney General.

(Added Pub.L. 95–598, Title II, § 224(a), Nov. 6, 1978, 92 Stat. 2664.)

HISTORICAL AND STATUTORY NOTES

Revision Notes and Legislative Reports

1978 Acts. Senate Report No. 95–989 and House Report No. 95–595, see 1978 U.S.Code Cong. and Adm.News, p. 5787.

Codifications

Section 408(c) of Pub.L. 95–598, as amended, which provided for the repeal of this section and the deletion of any references to United States Trustees in this title at a prospective date, was repealed by section 307(b) of Pub.L. 99–554. See note set out preceding section 581 of this title.

Effective and Applicability Provisions

1978 Acts. Section effective Oct. 1, 1979, see section 402(c) of Pub.L. 95–598, as amended, set out as a note preceding section 101 of Title 11, Bankruptcy.

Temporary Suspension of Limitation on Appointments

Pub.L. 99–554, Title I, § 114(b), Oct. 27, 1986, 100 Stat. 3093, provided that: "During the period beginning on the effective date of this Act [see section 302 of Pub.L. 99–554, as amended, set out as a note under section 581 of this title], and ending on October 1, 1989, the provisions of title 5 of the United States Code [Title 5, Government Organization and Employees] governing appointments in the competitive service shall not apply with respect to appointments under section 589 of title 28, United States Code [this section]."

§ 589a. United States Trustee System Fund

(a) There is hereby established in the Treasury of the United States a special fund to be known as the "United States Trustee System Fund" (hereinafter in this section referred to as the "Fund"). Monies in the Fund shall be available to the Attorney General without fiscal year limitation in such amounts as may be specified in appropriations Acts for the following purposes in connection with the operations of United States trustees—

(1) salaries and related employee benefits;

(2) travel and transportation;

(3) rental of space;

(4) communication, utilities, and miscellaneous computer charges;

(5) security investigations and audits;

(6) supplies, books, and other materials for legal research;

(7) furniture and equipment;

(8) miscellaneous services, including those obtained by contract; and

(9) printing.

(b) For the purpose of recovering the cost of services of the United States Trustee System, there shall be deposited as offsetting collections to the appropriation "United States Trustee System Fund", to remain available until expended, the following—

(1)(A) 40.46 percent of the fees collected under section 1930(a)(1)(A); and

(B) 28.33 percent of the fees collected under section 1930(a)(1)(B);

(2) 55 percent of the fees collected under section 1930(a)(3) of this title;

(3) one-half of the fees collected under section 1930(a)(4) of this title;

(4) one-half of the fees collected under section 1930(a)(5) of this title;

(5) 100 percent of the fees collected under section 1930(a)(6) of this title;

(6) three-fourths of the fees collected under the last sentence of section 1930(a) of this title;

(7) the compensation of trustees received under section 330(d) of title 11 by the clerks of the bankruptcy courts;

(8) excess fees collected under section 586(e)(2) of this title;

(9) interest earned on Fund investment; and

(10) fines imposed under section 110(l) of title 11, United States Code.

(c) Amounts in the Fund which are not currently needed for the purposes specified in subsection (a) shall be kept on deposit or invested in obligations of, or guaranteed by, the United States.

(d) The Attorney General shall transmit to the Congress, not later than 120 days after the end of each fiscal year, a detailed report on the amounts deposited in the Fund and a description of expenditures made under this section.

(e) There are authorized to be appropriated to the Fund for any fiscal year such sums as may be necessary to supplement amounts deposited under subsection (b) for the purposes specified in subsection (a).

(Added Pub.L. 99–554, Title I, § 115(a), Oct. 27, 1986, 100 Stat. 3094, and amended Pub.L. 101–162, Title IV, § 406(c), Nov. 21, 1989, 103 Stat. 1016; Pub.L. 102–140, Title I, § 111(b), (c), Oct. 28, 1991, 105 Stat. 795; Pub.L. 103–121, Title I, § 111(a)(2), (b)(2), (3), Oct. 27, 1993, 107 Stat. 1164; Pub.L. 104–91, Title I, § 101(a), Jan. 6, 1996, 110 Stat. 11, as amended Pub.L. 104–99, Title II, § 211, Jan. 26, 1996, 110 Stat. 37; Pub.L. 104–208, Div. A, Title I, § 101(a) [Title I, § 109(b)], Sept. 30, 1996, 110 Stat. 3009–18; Pub.L. 106–113, Div. B, § 1000(a)(1) [Title I, § 113], Nov. 29, 1999, 113 Stat. 1535, 1501A–6, 1501A–20; Pub.L. 109–8, Title III, § 325(b), Apr. 20, 2005, 119 Stat. 99; Pub.L. 109–13, Div. A, Title VI, § 6058(a), May 11, 2005, 119 Stat. 297; Pub.L. 110–161, Div. B, Title II, § 212(a), Dec. 26, 2007, 121 Stat. 1914.)

HISTORICAL AND STATUTORY NOTES

Revision Notes and Legislative Reports

1986 Acts. House Report No. 99–764 and House Conference Report No. 99–958, see 1986 U.S. Code Cong. and Adm. News, p. 5227.

1989 Acts. Statement by President, see 1989 U.S. Code Cong. and Adm. News, p. 733–3.

1999 Acts. Statement by President, see 1999 U.S. Code Cong. and Adm. News, p. 290.

2005 Acts. House Report No. 109–31(Part I), see 2005 U.S. Code Cong. and Adm. News, p. 88.

House Conference Report No. 109–72, see 2005 U.S. Code Cong. and Adm. News, p. 240.

2007 Acts. House Report No. 110–197, see 2007 U.S. Code Cong. and Adm. News, p. 661.

Statement by President, see 2007 U.S. Code Cong. and Adm. News, p. S34.

Codifications

Section 101(a) of Pub.L. 104–91, as amended by section 211 of Pub.L. 104–99, provided in part that section 111(b) and (c) of the General Provisions for the Department of Justice in Title I of the Departments of Commerce, Justice, and State, the Judiciary, and Related Agencies Appropriations Act, 1996 (H.R. 2076) as passed by the House of Representatives on Dec. 6, 1995, was enacted into permanent law. Such section 111(b) and (c) of H.R. 2076 amended subsecs. (b) and (f) of this section. See 1996 Amendments notes set out under this section.

Effective and Applicability Provisions

2005 Acts. Pub.L. 109–13, Div. A, Title VI, § 6058(b), May 11, 2005, 119 Stat. 297, provided that: "This section [amending this section and 28 U.S.C.A. § 1930, enacting provisions set out as a note under this section, and amending provisions set out as notes under this section and 28 U.S.C.A. §§ 1930 and 1931] and the amendment made by this section shall take effect immediately after the enactment of the Bankruptcy Abuse Prevention and Consumer Protection Act of 2005 [Pub.L. 109–8, approved Apr. 20, 2005]."

Except as otherwise provided, amendments by Pub.L. 109–8 effective 180 days after April 20, 2005, and inapplicable with respect to cases commenced under Title 11 before the effective date, see Pub.L. 109–8, § 1501, set out as a note under 11 U.S.C.A. § 101.

1999 Acts. Pub.L. 106–113, Div. B, § 1000(a)(1), [Title I, § 113], Nov. 29, 1999, 113 Stat. 1535, 1501A–20, provided in part that section 113 (amending this section and section 1930 of this title and provisions set out as a note under section 1931 of this title) is "[e]ffective 30 days after the enactment of this Act [Department of Commerce, Justice, and State, the Judiciary and Related Agencies Appropriations Act, 2000, Pub.L. 106–113, Div. B, § 1000(a)(1), Nov. 29, 1999, 113 Stat. 1535, 1501A–3; see Tables for complete classification]".

1996 Acts. Pub.L. 104–208, Div. A, Title I, § 101(a) [Title I, § 109(c)], Sept. 30, 1996, 110 Stat. 3009–19, provided that: "Notwithstanding any other provision of law or of this Act [Pub.L. 104–208, Sept. 30, 1996, 110 Stat. 3009, see Tables for classification] the amendments to 28 U.S.C. 589a [this section] made by subsection (b) of this section shall take effect upon enactment of this Act [probably means the date of enactment of Pub.L. 104–208, 110 Stat. 3009, which was approved Sept. 30, 1996]."

1993 Acts. Section 111(a) of Pub.L. 103–121 provided in part that amendment by section 111(a)(2) of Pub.L. 103–121, amending subsec. (b)(1) of this section, is effective 30 days after Oct. 27, 1993.

Section 111(b) of Pub.L. 103–121 provided in part that amendment by section 111(b)(2) and (3) of Pub.L. 103–121, amending subsecs. (b)(2) and (f)(1) of this section, is effective 30 days after Oct. 27, 1993.

1991 Acts. Section 111 of Pub.L. 102–140 provided that the amendment made by that section is effective 60 days after Oct. 28, 1991.

1986 Acts. Enactment by Pub.L. 99–554 effective 30 days after Oct. 27, 1986, except as otherwise provided, see section 302(a) of Pub.L. 99–554, as amended, set out as a note under section 581 of this title.

Sunset Provisions

Pub.L. 109–8, Title III, § 325(d), Apr. 20, 2005, 119 Stat. 99, as amended Pub.L. 109–13, Div. A, Title VI, § 6058(b), May 11, 2005, 119 Stat. 297, which set forth a two-year effective period for the original amendments by Pub.L. 109–8 to this section, has been omitted. The amendment by Pub.L. 109–13, § 6058(a), to Pub.L. 109–8, § 325, omitted this note in the reenactment of the section, to take effect immediately after the enactment of the Bankruptcy Abuse Prevention and Consumer Protection Act of 2005 [Pub.L. 109–8, Apr. 20, 2005, 119 Stat. 23], see Pub.L. 109–13, § 6058(b), set out as an Effective and Applicability Provisions note under this section.

Termination of Reporting Requirements

For termination of reporting provisions of this section, effective May 15, 2000, see Pub.L. 104–66, § 3003, as amended, set out as a note under 31 U.S.C.A. § 1113, and the 9th item on page 119 of House Document No. 103–7.

Reporting requirement of subsec. (d) of this section excepted from termination under Pub.L. 104–66, § 3003(a)(1), as amended, set out in a note under 31 U.S.C.A. § 1113, see Pub.L. 106–197, § 1, set out as a note under 31 U.S.C.A. § 1113.

CROSS REFERENCES

Compensation of Bankruptcy trustee to be deposited by clerk of bankruptcy court into Fund established by this section, see 11 USCA § 330.

§ 589b. Bankruptcy data

(a) Rules.—The Attorney General shall, within a reasonable time after the effective date of this section, issue rules requiring uniform forms for (and from time to time thereafter to appropriately modify and approve)—

(1) final reports by trustees in cases under chapters 7, 12, and 13 of title 11; and

(2) periodic reports by debtors in possession or trustees in cases under chapter 11 of title 11.

(b) Reports.—Each report referred to in subsection (a) shall be designed (and the requirements as to place and manner of filing shall be established) so as to facilitate compilation of data and maximum possible access of the public, both by physical inspection at one or more central filing locations, and by electronic access through the Internet or other appropriate media.

(c) Required information.—The information required to be filed in the reports referred to in subsection (b) shall be that which is in the best interests of debtors and creditors, and in the public interest in reasonable and adequate information to evaluate the efficiency and practicality of the Federal bankruptcy system. In issuing rules proposing the forms referred to in subsection (a), the Attorney General shall strike the best achievable practical balance between—

(1) the reasonable needs of the public for information about the operational results of the Federal bankruptcy system;

(2) economy, simplicity, and lack of undue burden on persons with a duty to file reports; and

(3) appropriate privacy concerns and safeguards.

(d) Final reports.—The uniform forms for final reports required under subsection (a) for use by trustees under chapters 7, 12, and 13 of title 11 shall, in addition to such other matters as are required by law or as the Attorney General in the discretion of the Attorney General shall propose, include with respect to a case under such title—

(1) information about the length of time the case was pending;

(2) assets abandoned;

(3) assets exempted;

(4) receipts and disbursements of the estate;

(5) expenses of administration, including for use under section 707(b), actual costs of administering cases under chapter 13 of title 11;

(6) claims asserted;

(7) claims allowed; and

(8) distributions to claimants and claims discharged without payment,

in each case by appropriate category and, in cases under chapters 12 and 13 of title 11, date of confirmation of the plan, each modification thereto, and defaults by the debtor in performance under the plan.

(e) Periodic reports.—The uniform forms for periodic reports required under subsection (a) for use by trustees or debtors in possession under chapter 11 of title 11 shall, in addition to such other matters as are required by law or as the Attorney General in the discretion of the Attorney General shall propose, include—

(1) information about the industry classification, published by the Department of Commerce, for the businesses conducted by the debtor;

(2) length of time the case has been pending;

(3) number of full-time employees as of the date of the order for relief and at the end of each reporting period since the case was filed;

(4) cash receipts, cash disbursements and profitability of the debtor for the most recent period and cumulatively since the date of the order for relief;

(5) compliance with title 11, whether or not tax returns and tax payments since the date of the order for relief have been timely filed and made;

(6) all professional fees approved by the court in the case for the most recent period and cumulatively since the date of the order for relief (separately reported, for the professional fees incurred by or on behalf of the debtor, between those that would have been incurred absent a bankruptcy case and those not); and

(7) plans of reorganization filed and confirmed and, with respect thereto, by class, the recoveries of the holders, expressed in aggregate dollar values and, in the case of claims, as a percentage of total claims of the class allowed.

(Added Pub.L. 109–8, Title VI, § 602(a), Apr. 20, 2005, 119 Stat. 120.)

HISTORICAL AND STATUTORY NOTES

Revision Notes and Legislative Reports

2005 Acts. House Report No. 109–31(Part I), see 2005 U.S. Code Cong. and Adm. News, p. 88.

References in Text

The effective date of this section, referred to in subsec. (a), means 180 days after April 20, 2005. See Pub.L. 109–8, § 1501, set out as an Effective and Applicability Provisions note for 2005 Acts under 11 U.S.C.A. § 101.

Chapters 7, 12, and 13 of title 11, referred to in subsecs. (a)(1) and (d), are 11 U.S.C.A. § 701 et seq., 11 U.S.C.A. § 1201 et seq., and 11 U.S.C.A. § 1301 et seq., respectively.

Chapter 11 of title 11, referred to in subsecs. (a)(2) and (e), is 11 U.S.C.A. § 1101 et seq.

Effective and Applicability Provisions

2005 Acts. Except as otherwise provided, amendments by Pub.L. 109–8 effective 180 days after April 20, 2005, and inapplicable with respect to cases commenced under Title 11 before the effective date, see Pub.L. 109–8, § 1501, set out as a note under 11 U.S.C.A. § 101.

PART III—COURT OFFICERS AND EMPLOYEES

CHAPTER 41—ADMINISTRATIVE OFFICE OF UNITED STATES COURTS

§ 604. Duties of Director generally

(a) The Director shall be the administrative officer of the courts, and under the supervision and direction of the Judicial Conference of the United States, shall:

(1) Supervise all administrative matters relating to the offices of clerks and other clerical and administrative personnel of the courts;

(2) Examine the state of the dockets of the courts; secure information as to the courts' need of assistance; prepare and transmit semiannually to the chief judges of the circuits, statistical data and reports as to the business of the courts;

(3) Submit to the annual meeting of the Judicial Conference of the United States, at least two weeks prior thereto, a report of the activities of the Administrative Office and the state of the business of the courts, together with the statistical data submitted to the chief judges of the circuits under paragraph (a)(2) of this section, and the Director's recommendations, which report, data and recommendations shall be public documents.

(4) Submit to Congress and the Attorney General copies of the report, data and recommendations required by paragraph (a)(3) of this section;

(5) Fix the compensation of clerks of court, deputies, librarians, criers, messengers, law clerks, secretaries, stenographers, clerical assistants, and other employees of the courts whose compensation is not otherwise fixed by law, and, notwithstanding any other provision of law, pay on behalf of Justices and judges of the United States appointed to hold office during good behavior magistrate judges appointed under section 631 of this title,,[1] aged 65 or over, any increases in the cost of Federal Employees' Group Life Insurance imposed after April 24, 1999, including any expenses generated by such payments, as authorized by the Judicial Conference of the United States;

(6) Determine and pay necessary office expenses of courts, judges, and those court officials whose expenses are by law allowable, and the lawful fees of United States magistrate judges;

(7) Regulate and pay annuities to widows and surviving dependent children of justices and judges of the United States, judges of the United States Court of Federal Claims, bankruptcy judges, United States magistrate judges, Directors of the Federal Judicial Center, and Directors of the Administrative Office, and necessary travel and subsistence expenses incurred by judges, court officers and em-

ployees, and officers and employees of the Administrative Office, and the Federal Judicial Center, while absent from their official stations on official business, without regard to the per diem allowances and amounts for reimbursement of actual and necessary expenses established by the Administrator of General Services under section 5702 of title 5, except that the reimbursement of subsistence expenses may not exceed that authorized by the Director for judges of the United States under section 456 of this title;

(8) Disburse appropriations and other funds for the maintenance and operation of the courts;

(9) Establish pretrial services pursuant to section 3152 of title 18, United States Code;

(10) (A) Purchase, exchange, transfer, distribute, and assign the custody of lawbooks, equipment, supplies, and other personal property for the judicial branch of Government (except the Supreme Court unless otherwise provided pursuant to paragraph (17)); (B) provide or make available readily to each court appropriate equipment for the interpretation of proceedings in accordance with section 1828 of this title; and (C) enter into and perform contracts and other transactions upon such terms as the Director may deem appropriate as may be necessary to the conduct of the work of the judicial branch of Government (except the Supreme Court unless otherwise provided pursuant to paragraph (17)), and contracts for nonpersonal services providing pretrial services, agencies for the interpretation of proceedings, and for the provision of special interpretation services pursuant to section 1828 of this title may be awarded without regard to section 3709 of the Revised Statutes of the United States (41 U.S.C. 5);

(11) Audit vouchers and accounts of the courts, the Federal Judicial Center, the offices providing pretrial services, and their clerical and administrative personnel;

(12) Provide accommodations for the courts, the Federal Judicial Center, the offices providing pretrial services and their clerical and administrative personnel;

(13) Lay before Congress, annually, statistical tables that will accurately reflect the business transacted by the several bankruptcy courts, and all other pertinent data relating to such courts;

(14) Pursuant to section 1827 of this title, establish a program for the certification and utilization of interpreters in courts of the United States;

(15) Pursuant to section 1828 of this title, establish a program for the provision of special interpretation services in courts of the United States;

(16) (A) In those districts where the Director considers it advisable based on the need for interpreters, authorize the full-time or part-time employment by the court of certified interpreters; (B) where the Director considers it advisable based on the need for interpreters, appoint certified interpreters on a full-time or part-time basis, for services in various courts when he determines that such appointments will result in the economical provision of interpretation services; and (C) pay out of moneys appropriated for the judiciary interpreters' salaries, fees, and expenses, and other costs which may accrue in accordance with the provisions of sections 1827 and 1828 of this title;

(17) In the Director's discretion, (A) accept and utilize voluntary and uncompensated (gratuitous) services, including services as authorized by section 3102(b) of title 5, United States Code; and (B) accept, hold, administer, and utilize gifts and bequests of personal property for the purpose of aiding or facilitating the work of the judicial branch of Government, but gifts or bequests of money shall be covered into the Treasury;

(18) Establish procedures and mechanisms within the judicial branch for processing fines, restitution, forfeitures of bail bonds or collateral, and assessments;

(19) Regulate and pay annuities to bankruptcy judges and United States magistrate judges in accordance with section 377 of this title and paragraphs (1)(B) and (2) of section 2(c) of the Retirement and Survivors' Annuities for Bankruptcy Judges and Magistrates Act of 1988;

(20) Periodically compile—

(A) the rules which are prescribed under section 2071 of this title by courts other than the Supreme Court;

(B) the rules which are prescribed under section 358 of this title; and

(C) the orders which are required to be publicly available under section 360(b) of this title;

so as to provide a current record of such rules and orders;

(21) Establish a program of incentive awards for employees of the judicial branch of the United States Government, other than any judge who is entitled to hold office during good behavior;

(22) Receive and expend, either directly or by transfer to the United States Marshals Service or other Government agency, funds appropriated for the procurement, installation, and maintenance of security equipment and protective services for the United States Courts in courtrooms and adjacent areas, including building ingress/egress control, inspection of packages, directed security patrols, and other similar activities;

(23) Regulate and pay annuities to judges of the United States Court of Federal Claims in accordance with section 178 of this title; and

(24) Perform such other duties as may be assigned to him by the Supreme Court or the Judicial Conference of the United States.

(b) The clerical and administrative personnel of the courts shall comply with all requests by the Director for information or statistical data as to the state of court dockets.

(c) Inspection of court dockets outside the continental United States may be made through United States officials residing within the jurisdiction where the inspection is made.

(d) The Director, under the supervision and direction of the conference, shall:

(1) supervise all administrative matters relating to the offices of the United States magistrate judges;

(2) gather, compile, and evaluate all statistical and other information required for the performance of his duties and the duties of the conference with respect to such officers;

(3) lay before Congress annually statistical tables and other information which will accurately reflect the business which has come before the various United States magistrate judges, including (A) the number of matters in which the parties consented to the exercise of jurisdiction by a magistrate judge, (B) the number of appeals taken pursuant to the decisions of magistrate judges and the disposition of such appeals, and (C) the professional background and qualifications of individuals appointed under section 631 of this title to serve as magistrate judges;

(4) prepare and distribute a manual, with annual supplements and periodic revisions, for the use of such officers, which shall set forth their powers and duties, describe all categories of proceedings that may arise before them, and contain such other information as may be required to enable them to discharge their powers and duties promptly, effectively, and impartially.

(e) The Director may promulgate appropriate rules and regulations approved by the conference and not inconsistent with any provision of law, to assist him in the performance of the duties conferred upon him by subsection (d) of this section. Magistrate judges shall keep such records and make such reports as are specified in such rules and regulations.

(f) The Director may make, promulgate, issue, rescind, and amend rules and regulations (including regulations prescribing standards of conduct for Administrative Office employees) as may be necessary to carry out the Director's functions, powers, duties, and authority. The Director may publish in the Federal Register such rules, regulations, and notices for the judicial branch of Government as the Director determines to be of public interest; and the Director of the Federal Register hereby is authorized to accept and shall publish such materials.

(g)(1) When authorized to exchange personal property, the Director may exchange or sell similar items and may apply the exchange allowance or proceeds of sale in such cases in whole or in part payment for the property acquired, but any transaction carried out under the authority of this subsection shall be evidenced in writing.

(2) The Director hereby is authorized to enter into contracts for public utility services and related terminal equipment for periods not exceeding ten years.

(3)(A) In order to promote the recycling and reuse of recyclable materials, the Director may provide for the sale or disposal of recyclable scrap materials from paper products and other consumable office supplies held by an entity within the judicial branch.

(B) The sale or disposal of recyclable materials under subparagraph (A) shall be consistent with the procedures provided in sections 541–555 of title 40 for the sale of surplus property.

(C) Proceeds from the sale of recyclable materials under subparagraph (A) shall be deposited as offsetting collections to the fund established under section 1931 of this title and shall remain available until expended to reimburse any appropriations for the operation and maintenance of the judicial branch.

(4) The Director is hereby authorized:

(A) to enter into contracts for the acquisition of severable services for a period that begins in one fiscal year and ends in the next fiscal year to the same extent as the head of an executive agency under the authority of section 2531 of title 41, United States Code;

(B) to enter into contracts for multiple years for the acquisition of property and services to the same extent as executive agencies under the authority of section 254c of title 41, United States Code; and

(C) to make advance, partial, progress or other payments under contracts for property or services to the same extent as executive agencies under the authority of section 255 of title 41, United States Code.

(h)(1) The Director shall, out of funds appropriated for the operation and maintenance of the courts, provide facilities and pay necessary expenses incurred by the judicial councils of the circuits and the Judicial Conference under chapter 16 of this title, including mileage allowance and witness fees, at the same rate as provided in section 1821 of this title. Administrative and professional assistance from the

Administrative Office of the United States Courts may be requested by each judicial council and the Judicial Conference for purposes of discharging their duties under chapter 16 of this title.

(2) The Director of the Administrative Office of the United States Courts shall include in his annual report filed with the Congress under this section a summary of the number of complaints filed with each judicial council under chapter 16 of this title, indicating the general nature of such complaints and the disposition of those complaints in which action has been taken.

(June 25, 1948, c. 646, 62 Stat. 914; Aug. 3, 1956, c. 944, § 3, 70 Stat. 1026; Dec. 20, 1967, Pub.L. 90–219, Title II, § 203, 81 Stat. 669; Oct. 17, 1968, Pub.L. 90–578, Title II, § 201, Title IV, § 402(b)(2), 82 Stat. 1114, 1118; Aug. 22, 1972, Pub.L. 92–397, § 4, 86 Stat. 580; Jan. 3, 1975, Pub.L. 93–619, Title II, § 204, 88 Stat. 2089; Oct. 28, 1978, Pub.L. 95–539, §§ 3, 4, 92 Stat. 2043; Nov. 6, 1978, Pub.L. 95–598, Title II, § 225, 92 Stat. 2664; Oct. 10, 1979, Pub.L. 96–82, § 5, 93 Stat. 645; Oct. 15, 1980, Pub.L. 96–458, § 5, 94 Stat. 2040; Dec. 12, 1980, Pub.L. 96–523, § 1(c)(1), 94 Stat. 3040; Sept. 27, 1982, Pub.L. 97–267, § 7, 96 Stat. 1139; Oct. 27, 1986, Pub.L. 99–554, Title I, § 116, 100 Stat. 3095; Dec. 11, 1987, Pub.L. 100–185, § 2, 101 Stat. 1279; Nov. 15, 1988, Pub.L. 100–659, § 6(a), 102 Stat. 3918; Nov. 19, 1988, Pub.L. 100–702, Title IV, § 402(a), Title X, §§ 1008, 1010, 1011, 1020(a)(2), 102 Stat. 4650, 4667, 4668, 4671; Oct. 30, 1990, Pub.L. 101–474, § 5(r), 104 Stat. 1101; Nov. 29, 1990, Pub.L. 101–647, Title XXV, § 2548, 104 Stat. 4888; Dec. 1, 1990, Pub.L. 101–650, Title III, §§ 306(e)(1), 321, 325(c)(1), 104 Stat. 5111, 5117, 5121; Oct. 29, 1992, Pub.L. 102–572, Title V, § 503, Title IX, § 902(b)(1), 106 Stat. 4513, 4516; Nov. 29, 1999, Pub.L. 106–113, § 1000(a)(1) [Title III, § 305], 113 Stat. 1535, 1501A–37; Nov. 13, 2000, Pub.L. 106–518, Title II, § 204, Title III, § 304(d), 114 Stat. 2414, 2418; Aug. 21, 2002, Pub.L. 107–217, § 3(g)(1), 116 Stat. 1299; Nov. 2, 2002, Pub.L. 107–273, Div. C, Title I, § 11043(e), 116 Stat. 1855; Nov. 30, 2005, Pub.L. 109–115, Div. A, Title IV, § 407(a), 119 Stat. 2470; Jan. 7, 2008, Pub.L. 110–177, Title V, § 502(a), 121 Stat. 2542.)

[1] So in original.

HISTORICAL AND STATUTORY NOTES

Revision Notes and Legislative Reports

1948 Acts. Based on sections 726–1 and 726a of Title 18, U.S.C., 1940 ed., Criminal Code and Criminal Procedure, and sections 1130(a), (b), and 1131 of Title 26, U.S.C., 1940 ed., Internal Revenue Code, Title 28, U.S.C., 1940 ed., §§ 9, 128, 222a, 245, 268a, 278a, 302–306, 374b, 446, 447, 450, 544, 545, 547, 557, 558, 560, 561, 561a, 562, 563, 565, 566, 595, and 596 and sections 11–204 and 11–403, District of Columbia Code, 1940 ed. (R.S. §§ 1075, 1085; Mar. 3, 1891, c. 517, §§ 2, 9, 26 Stat. 826, 829; Feb. 9, 1893, c. 74, § 4, 27 Stat. 435; July 30, 1894, c. 172, § 1, 28 Stat. 160; Mar. 3, 1901, c. 854, § 224, 31 Stat. 1224; June 30, 1902, c. 1329, 32 Stat. 528; Mar. 3, 1905, c. 1487, 33 Stat. 1259; Mar. 3, 1911, c. 231, § 5, 36 Stat. 1088; Mar. 3, 1911, c. 231, § 118a, as added June 17, 1930, c. 509, 46 Stat. 774; Mar. 3, 1911, c. 231, § 118b, as added Feb. 17, 1936, c. 75, 49 Stat. 1140; Mar. 3, 1911, c. 231, §§ 140, 163, 171, 189–193, 291, 36 Stat. 1136, 1140, 1141, 1143, 1167; Mar. 3, 1911, c. 231, §§ 304, 305, 308, as added Aug. 7, 1939, c. 501, § 1, 53 Stat. 1223; Aug. 23, 1912, c. 350, 37 Stat. 412; Feb. 26, 1919, c. 49, §§ 1, 2, 3, 4, 5, 7, 8, 40 Stat. 1182; July 19, 1919, c. 24, § 1, 41 Stat. 210; Nov. 4, 1919, c. 93, § 1, 41 Stat. 338; Feb. 11, 1921, c. 46, 41 Stat. 1099; Feb. 22, 1921, c. 70, § 7, 41 Stat. 1144; Mar. 4, 1921, c. 161, 41 Stat. 1412; June 1, 1922, c. 204, Title II, 42 Stat. 616; Jan. 3, 1923, c. 21, Title II, 42 Stat. 1084; Mar. 4, 1923, c. 265, 42 Stat. 1488; May 28, 1924, c. 204, Title II, 43 Stat. 221; Feb. 27, 1925, c. 364, Title II, 43 Stat. 1030; Apr. 29, 1926, c. 195, Title II, 44 Stat. 346, 347; May 21, 1928, c. 659, 45 Stat. 645; Mar. 2, 1929, c. 488, § 1, 45 Stat. 1475; June 16, 1930, c. 494, 46 Stat. 589; May 17, 1932, c. 190, 47 Stat. 158; June 25, 1936, c. 804, 49 Stat. 1921; Apr. 27, 1938, c. 180, Title II, § 1, 52 Stat. 264; Feb. 10, 1939, c. 2, §§ 1130(a), (b), 1131, 53 Stat. 162, 163; June 29, 1939, c. 248, Title II, 53 Stat. 902; May 14, 1940, c. 189, Titles III, IV, 54 Stat. 204, 209, 210; June 28, 1941, c. 258, Title IV, 55 Stat. 300–302; July 2, 1942, c. 472, Title IV, 56 Stat. 503, 504; June 28, 1943, c. 173, Title II, § 201, 57 Stat. 242, 243; June 26, 1944, c. 277, Title II, § 201, 58 Stat. 357; Dec. 7, 1944, c. 522, § 1, 58 Stat. 796; May 21, 1945, c. 129, Titles II, IV, 59 Stat. 184, 199; July 5, 1946, c. 541, Title IV, 60 Stat. 478, 479).

For purposes of uniformity, all provisions of law governing the regulation and allowance of office, travel, and subsistence expenses of all officers and employees of the courts, except those provisions relating to Supreme Court officers and employees, are incorporated in subsection (a)(6)(7) of this section. Likewise the provisions respecting the compensation of court officers and employees, except those of the Supreme Court, are incorporated in subsection (a)(5). In each instance the power to fix and determine such salaries and expenses is transferred to the Director of the Administrative Office of the United States Courts. This change is in conformity with the Administrative Office Act 1939 included in this chapter.

Compensation of bailiffs however is provided by sections 713 and 755 of this title and that of court reporters by section 753 of this title.

Salaries and travel expenses of Court of Claims Commissioners are covered by section 792 of this title.

The language "and the lawful fees of United States Commissioners" in subsection (a)(6) and "the offices of the United States Commissioners" in subsection (a)(9) is new. It conforms with sections 633, 636 and 639 of this title.

Subsection (a)(5)(7) covers the provisions of section 726–1 and 726a of Title 18, U.S.C., 1940 ed., which provided that probation officers' salaries, should not be less than $1,800 nor more than $3,600 per annum and their traveling expenses should not exceed more than 4 cents per mile.

Words, "and officers and employees of the Administrative Office" were added in subsection (a)(7) to expressly authorize travel and subsistence expenses of such officers and employees.

The power to fix such pay and allowances is transferred to the Director as above indicated, and conforms with the Administrative Office Act of 1939. For further explanation of the general supervision of probation officers, see reviser's note [now Revision Notes and Legislative Reports] under section 3654, H.Rept. to accompany H.R. 3190 for revision of Title 18, U.S.C.

Subsection (a)(8) covers the provisions of section 1131 of Title 26, U.S.C., 1940 ed. Such section 1131 authorized the Tax Court, successor to the Board of Tax Appeals, to make expenditures for personal services, rent, law books, reference books, periodicals, and provided that all expenditures should be paid out of appropriations for the Tax Court, on itemized vouchers approved by the court.

Two reference to "officials and employees covered by this chapter" were changed to "clerical and administrative personnel," following the language of paragraph (a)(1), conferring general power to supervise such personnel as respects administrative matters.

Similar language was used in paragraph (b) instead of "The clerks of the district courts, their deputies and assistants, and all other employees of said courts."

The provisions of section 374b of Title 28, U.S.C., 1940 ed., based on successive Acts relating to classification and compensation of secretaries and law clerks were omitted as temporary and unnecessary in revision, in view of subsection (a)(5) of this section under which the salaries of all personnel are necessarily limited by current appropriation Acts.

For increases in basic rates of compensation for other judicial officers and employees see, also, section 521 of Act June 30, 1945, c. 212.

The designation "senior circuit judges" was changed to "chief judges of the circuits" in conformity with section 45 of this title.

Provisions of section 11–204 of District of Columbia Code, 1940 ed., relating to appointment of clerk of the United States Court of Appeals for the District of Columbia, and deputy clerk, crier, and messenger thereof, and the provisions relating to accounting for fees, are incorporated in sections 711 and 713 of this title. Provisions of said section, requiring the clerk of such court to give bond, were omitted as covered by section 952 of this title. Provisions of said section, relating to regulation of clerk's fees by such court were omitted so as to render uniform the method of such regulation as prescribed by section 1913 of this title, and the provisions of said section, placing a maximum of five hundred dollars per year on the office expenditures of the clerk of such court, were omitted as inconsistent with this consolidated section.

For distribution of other provisions of sections on which this section is based, see Distribution Table.

Changes were made in phraseology and arrangement. 80th Congress House Report No. 308.

By Senate amendment, all provisions relating to the Tax Court were eliminated, therefore, as finally enacted, sections 1130(a)(b) and 1131 of Title 26 U.S.C., Internal Revenue Code [1940 ed.], did not constitute part of the source of this section. However, no change in the text of the section was necessary. See 80th Congress Senate Report No. 1559.

As finally enacted, part of Act July 9, 1947, c. 211, Title IV, 61 Stat. 304, 305, which was classified to Title 28 U.S.C., 1946 ed., § 374b, became one of the sources of this section and was accordingly included in the schedule of repeals by Senate amendment. See 80th Congress Senate Report No. 1559.

1956 Acts. House Report No. 2170 and Conference Report No. 2934, see 1956 U.S. Code Cong. and Adm. News, p. 4354.

1967 Acts. Senate Report No. 781 and Conference Report No. 996, see 1967 U.S. Code Cong. and Adm. News, p. 2402.

1968 Acts. House Report No. 1629, see 1968 U.S. Code Cong. and Adm. News, p. 4252.

1972 Acts. House Report No. 92–1148, see 1972 U.S. Code Cong. and Adm. News, p. 3007.

1975 Acts. House Report No. 93–1508, see 1974 U.S. Code Cong. and Adm. News, p. 7401.

1978 Acts. House Report No. 95–1687, see 1978 U.S. Code Cong. and Adm. News, p. 4652.

Senate Report No. 95–989 and House Report No. 95–595, see 1978 U.S. Code Cong. and Adm. News, p. 5787.

1979 Acts. Senate Report No. 96–74 and House Conference Report No. 96–444, see 1979 U.S. Code Cong. and Adm. News, p. 1469.

1980 Acts. Senate Report No. 96–362, see 1980 U.S. Code Cong. and Adm. News, p. 4315.

House Report No. 96–1279, see 1980 U.S. Code Cong. and Adm. News, p. 6530.

1982 Acts. Senate Report No. 97–77 and House Conference Report No. 97–792, see 1982 U.S. Code Cong. and Adm. News, p. 2377.

1986 Acts. House Report No. 99–764 and House Conference Report No. 99–958, see 1986 U.S. Code Cong. and Adm. News, p. 5227.

1987 Acts. House Report No. 100–390, see 1987 U.S. Code Cong. and Adm. News, p. 2137.

1988 Acts. Senate Report No. 100–293 and House Conference Report No. 100–1072, see 1988 U.S. Code Cong. and Adm. News, p. 5564.

House Report No. 100–889, see 1988 U.S. Code Cong. and Adm. News, p. 5982.

1990 Acts. House Report No. 101–770, see 1990 U.S. Code Cong. and Adm. News, p. 1709.

House Report No. 101–681(Part I), see 1990 U.S. Code Cong. and Adm. News, p. 6472.

Senate Report No. 101–416, Related House Reports, and President's Signing Statement, see 1990 U.S. Code Cong. and Adm. News, p. 6802.

1992 Acts. House Report No. 102–1006, see 1992 U.S. Code Cong. and Adm. News, p. 3921.

1999 Acts. Statement by President, see 1999 U.S. Code Cong. and Adm. News, p. 290.

2002 Acts. House Report No. 107–479, see 2002 U.S. Code Cong. and Adm. News, p. 827.

House Conference Report No. 107–685 and Statement by President, see 2002 U.S. Code Cong. and Adm. News, p. 1120.

2005 Acts. House Conference Report No. 109–307, see 2005 U.S. Code Cong. and Adm. News, p. 1260.

Statement by President, see 2005 U.S. Code Cong. and Adm. News, p. S42.

2008 Acts. House Report No. 110–218(Part I), see 2007 U.S. Code Cong. and Adm. News, p. 827.

References in Text

Section 2(c) of the Retirement and Survivors' Annuities for Bankruptcy Judges and Magistrates Act of 1988, referred to in subsec. (a)(19), is section 2(c) of Pub.L. 100–659, Nov. 15, 1988, 102 Stat. 3916, which is set out as a note under section 377 of this title.

Codifications

Pub.L. 101–650, § 306(e)(1)(A), directing amendment of Pub.L. 100–702, § 402(1), probably intended amendment of section 402(a)(1) of pub.L. 100–702, which provided for redesignation of subsec. (a)(19) to be subsec. (a)(23) of this section, redesignated as subsec. (a)(24) by Pub.L. 101–650, § 306(e)(1)(B)(ii).

Amendment by Pub.L. 109–115, Div. A, § 407(a), which directed that this section is amended by adding "section (4) at the end of section '(g)'" was executed by adding par. (4) to the end of subsec. (g), as the probable intent of Congress.

Effective and Applicability Provisions

2008 Acts. Pub.L. 110–177, Title V, § 502(c), Jan. 7, 2008, 121 Stat. 2542, provided that: "Subsection (b) [enacting provisions set out as a note under 5 U.S.C.A. § 8701] and the amendment made by subsection (a) [amending this section] shall apply with respect to any payment made on or after the first day of the first applicable pay period beginning on or after the date of enactment of this Act [Jan. 7, 2008]."

1992 Acts. Amendment by section 902(b)(1) of Pub.L. 102–572 effective Oct. 29, 1992, see section 911 of Pub.L. 102–572, set out as a note under section 171 of this title.

Amendment by Pub.L. 102–572 effective Jan. 1, 1993, see section 1101(a) of Pub.L. 102–572, set out as a note under section 905 of Title 2, The Congress.

1990 Acts. Amendment by section 306(e)(1) of Pub.L. 101–650 applicable to judges of, and senior judges in active service with, the United States Court of Federal Claims on or after Dec. 1, 1990, see section 306(f) of Pub.L. 101–650, set out as a note under section 8331 of Title 5, Government Organization and Employees.

1988 Acts. Amendment by section 402(a) of Pub.L. 100–702 effective Dec. 1, 1988, see section 407 of Pub.L. 100–702, set out as a note under section 2071 of this title.

Amendment to this section by Pub.L. 100–659 to take effect on Nov. 15, 1988, and shall apply to bankruptcy judges and magistrates who retire on or after Nov. 15, 1988, with special election provisions for bankruptcy judges, etc., who left office on or after July 31, 1987, and before Nov. 15, 1988, see section 9 of Pub.L. 100–659, set out as a note under section 377 of this title.

1986 Acts. Amendment by Pub.L. 99–554 effective 30 days after Oct. 27, 1986, except as otherwise provided, see section 302(a) of Pub.L. 99–554, as amended, set out as a note under section 581 of this title.

1980 Acts. Amendment by Pub.L. 96–523 effective sixty days after Dec. 12, 1980, see section 3 of Pub.L. 96–523, set out as a note under section 3102 of Title 5, Government Organization and Employees.

Amendment by Pub.L. 96–458 effective Oct. 1, 1981, see section 7 of Pub.L. 96–458, set out as a note under section 331 of this title.

1978 Acts. Amendment by Pub.L. 95–598 effective Oct. 1, 1979, see section 402(c) of Pub.L. 95–598, as amended, set out as a note preceding section 101 of Title 11, Bankruptcy.

Amendment by Pub.L. 95–539 effective Oct. 28, 1978, see section 10(a) of Pub.L. 95–539, set out as a note under section 602 of this title.

1968 Acts. Amendment by Pub.L. 90–578 effective Oct. 17, 1968, except when a later effective date is applicable, which is the earlier of date when implementation of amendment by appointment of magistrates and assumption of office takes place or third anniversary of enactment of Pub.L. 90–578 on Oct. 17, 1968, see section 403 of Pub.L. 90–578, set out as a note under section 631 of this title.

Termination of Authority

Pub.L. 109–115, Div. A, Title IV, § 407(c), Nov. 30, 2005, 119 Stat. 2471, provided that: "The authorities granted in this section [Pub.L. 109–115, Div. A, Title IV, § 407, 119 Stat. 2470, which amended subsec. (g)(4) of this section and 28 U.S.C.A. § 612] shall expire on September 30, 2010."

Termination of Reporting Requirements

For termination, effective May 15, 2000, of provisions in subsecs. (a)(4), (d)(3), and (h)(2) of this section relating to reporting certain information annually to Congress, see Pub.L. 104–66, § 3003, as amended, set out as a note under 31 U.S.C.A. § 1113 and page 12 of House Document No. 103–7.

Change of Name

References to United States Claims Court deemed to refer to United States Court of Federal Claims and references to Claims Court deemed to refer to Court of Federal Claims, see section 902(b) of Pub.L. 102–572, set out as a note under section 171 of Title 28, Judiciary and Judicial Procedure.

"United States magistrate judge" substituted for "United States magistrate" in text pursuant to section 321 of Pub.L. 101–650, set out as a note under 28 U.S.C.A. § 631. Previously, United States commissioners, referred to in text, were replaced by United States magistrates pursuant to Pub.L. 90–578, Oct. 17, 1968, 82 Stat. 1118. See chapter 43 of Title 28, 28 U.S.C.A. § 631 et seq.

Compensation and Appointment of Secretaries and Law Clerks

Provisions authorizing the appointment and compensation of secretaries and law clerks to circuit and district judges in such number and at such rates of compensation as may be determined by the Judicial Conference of the United States were contained in the following appropriation Acts:

Dec. 12, 1985, Pub.L. 99–180, Title IV, § 400, 99 Stat. 1154.

Aug. 30, 1984, Pub.L. 98–411, Title IV, § 400, 98 Stat. 1571.

Nov. 28, 1983, Pub.L. 98–166, Title IV, § 400, 97 Stat. 1099.

Dec. 21, 1982, Pub.L. 97–377, § 101(d) [S. 2956, Title IV, § 400], 96 Stat. 1866.

Dec. 15, 1981, Pub.L. 97–92, § 101(h) [incorporating Pub.L. 96–536, § 101(*o*); H.R. 7584, Title IV, § 400], 95 Stat. 1190.

Dec. 16, 1980, Pub.L. 96–536, § 101(*o*) [H.R. 7584, Title IV, § 400], 94 Stat. 3169.

Sept. 24, 1979, Pub.L. 96–68, Title IV, § 400, 93 Stat. 428.

Oct. 10, 1978, Pub.L. 95–431, Title IV, § 401, 92 Stat. 1037.

Aug. 2, 1977, Pub.L. 95–86, Title IV, § 401, 91 Stat. 435.

July 14, 1976, Pub.L. 94–362, Title IV, § 401, 90 Stat. 953.

Oct. 21, 1975, Pub.L. 94–121, Title IV, § 401, 89 Stat. 630.

Oct. 5, 1974, Pub.L. 93–433, Title IV, § 401, 88 Stat. 1202.

Nov. 27, 1973, Pub.L. 93–162, Title IV, § 401, 87 Stat. 651.

Oct. 25, 1972, Pub.L. 92–544, Title IV, § 401, 86 Stat. 1126.

Aug. 10, 1971, Pub.L. 92–77, Title IV, § 401, 85 Stat. 262.

Oct. 21, 1970, Pub.L. 91–472, Title IV, § 401, 84 Stat. 1056.

Dec. 24, 1969, Pub.L. 91–153, Title IV, § 401, 83 Stat. 419.

Aug. 9, 1968, Pub.L. 90–470, Title IV, § 401, 82 Stat. 685.

Nov. 8, 1967, Pub.L. 90–133, Title IV, § 401, 81 Stat. 427.

Nov. 8, 1966, Pub.L. 89–797, Title IV, § 401, 80 Stat. 1499.

Sept. 2, 1965, Pub.L. 89–164, Title IV, § 401, 79 Stat. 638.

Aug. 31, 1964, Pub.L. 88–527, Title IV, § 401, 78 Stat. 729.

Dec. 30, 1963, Pub.L. 88–245, Title IV, § 401, 77 Stat. 795.

Oct. 18, 1962, Pub.L. 87–843, Title IV, § 401, 76 Stat. 1099.

Sept. 21, 1961, Pub.L. 87–264, Title III, § 301, 75 Stat. 555.

Aug. 31, 1960, Pub.L. 86–678, Title III, § 301, 74 Stat. 566.

July 13, 1959, Pub.L. 86–84, Title III, § 301, 73 Stat. 192.

June 30, 1958, Pub.L. 85–474, Title III, § 301, 72 Stat. 254.

June 11, 1957, Pub.L. 85–40, Title III, § 301, 70 Stat. 65.

June 20, 1956, c. 414, Title III, § 301, 70 Stat. 310.

July 7, 1955, c. 279, Title III, § 301, 69 Stat. 276.

July 2, 1954, c. 455, Title II, § 201, 68 Stat. 410.

Aug. 1, 1953, c. 304, Title II, § 201, 67 Stat. 334.

July 10, 1952, c. 651, Title IV, § 401, 66 Stat. 569.

Oct. 22, 1951, c. 533, Title IV, § 401, 65 Stat. 596.

Sept. 6, 1950, c. 896, ch. III, Title IV, § 401, 64 Stat. 631.

Increases in Compensation Rates

Increases in rates of basic compensation fixed pursuant to subsec. (a)(5) of this section, see notes under section 603 of this title.

Limitation on Aggregate Salaries of Secretaries and Law Clerks

1967—Pub.L. 90–206, Title II, § 213(b), Dec. 16, 1967, 81 Stat. 635, provided that: "The limitations provided by applicable law on the effective date of this section [see Effective and Applicability Provisions of 1967 amendments note set out under section 5332 of Title 5, Government Organization and Employees] with respect to the aggregate salaries payable to secretaries and law clerks of circuit and district judges are hereby increased by amounts which reflect the respective applicable increases provided by section 202(a) of this title [amending section 5332(a) of Title 5] in corresponding rates of compensation for officers and employees subject to section 5332 of title 5, United States Code [section 5332 of Title 5]."

Section 213(b) of Pub.L. 90–206 effective as of the beginning of the first pay period which begins on or after Oct. 1, 1967, see section 220(a)(2) of Pub.L. 90–206, set out as a note under section 5332 of Title 5, Government Organization and Employees.

1966—Pub.L. 89–504, Title II, § 202(b), July 18, 1966, 80 Stat. 294, provided that: "The limitations provided by applicable law on the effective date of this section with respect to the aggregate salaries payable to secretaries and law clerks of circuit and district judges are hereby increased by amounts which reflect the respective applicable increases provided by section 102(a) of title I of this Act [amending section 1113(b) of former Title 5, Executive Departments and Government Officers and Employees] in corresponding rates of compensation for officers and employees subject to the Classification Act of 1949, as amended [chapter 51 and subchapter III of chapter 53 of Title 5, Government Organization and Employees]."

Provision effective the first day of the first pay period which begins on or after July 1, 1966, see section 203 of Pub.L. 89–504, set out as a note under section 603 of this title.

1965—Pub.L. 89–301, § 12(b), Oct. 29, 1965, 79 Stat. 1122, provided that: "The limitations provided by applicable law on the effective date of this section with respect to the aggregate salaries payable to secretaries and law clerks of circuit and district judges are hereby increased by amounts which reflect the respective applicable increases provided by section 2(a) of this Act [amending section 1113(b) of former Title 5, Executive Departments and Government Officers and Employees] in corresponding rates of compensation for officers and employees subject to the Classification Act of 1949, as amended [chapter 51 and subchapter III of chapter 53 of Title 5, Government Organization and Employees]."

1964—Pub.L. 88–426, Title IV, § 402(b), Aug. 14, 1964, 78 Stat. 433, provided that: "The limitations provided by applicable law on the effective date of this section with respect to the aggregate salaries payable to secretaries and law clerks of circuit and district judges are hereby increased by amounts which reflect the respective applicable increases provided by title I of this Act in corresponding rates of compensation for officers and employees subject to the Classification Act of 1949, as amended [chapter 51 and subchapter III of chapter 53 of Title 5, Government Organization and Employees]."

1962—Pub.L. 87–793, Title VI, § 1004(b), Oct. 11, 1962, 76 Stat. 866, provided that: "The limitations provided by applicable law on the effective date of this section with respect to the aggregate salaries payable to secretaries and law clerks of circuit and district judges are hereby increased by two amounts, the first amount to be effective for the period beginning as of the first day of the first pay period which begins on or after the date of enactment of this Act [Oct. 11, 1962], and ending immediately prior to the first day of the first pay period which begins on or after January 1, 1964, and the second amount to be effective on the first day of the first pay period which begins on or after January 1, 1964, and thereafter, which reflect the respective applicable increases provided by title II of this part in corresponding rates of compensation for officers and employees subject to the Classification Act of 1949, as amended [chapter 51 and subchapter III of chapter 53 of Title 5, Government Organization and Employees]."

1960—Pub.L. 86–568, Title I, § 116(b), July 1, 1960, 74 Stat. 303, provided that: "The limitations provided by applicable law on the effective date of this section with respect to the aggregate salaries payable to secretaries and law clerks of circuit and district judges are hereby increased by the amounts necessary to pay the additional basic compensation provided by this part."

Words "this part", referred to in section 116(b) of Pub.L. 86–568 [this note], means Part B of Pub.L. 86–568, which enacted section 932e of former Title 5, Executive Departments and Government Officers and Employees, amended section 753 of this title, sections 1113, 2091, 2252 and 3002 of former Title 5, sections 867 and 870 of Title 22, Foreign Relations and Intercourse, and sections 4103, 4107 and 4108 of Title 38, Veterans' Benefits and enacted notes set out under sections 603 and 604 of this title, sections 60a and 60f of Title 2, The Congress, sections 1113 and 2252 of former Title 5, section 590h of Title 16, Conservation, and section 867 of Title 22.

1958—Pub.L. 85–462, § 3(b), June 20, 1958, 72 Stat. 207, provided that: "The limitations of $13,485 and $18,010 with respect to the aggregate salaries payable to secretaries and law clerks of circuit and district judges, contained in the paragraph designated "Salaries of supporting personnel" in the Judiciary Appropriation Act, 1958 (71 Stat. 65; Public Law 85–49), or any subsequent appropriation Act, shall be increased by the amounts necessary to pay the additional basic compensation provided by this Act."

1955—Act June 28, 1955, c. 189, § 3(b), 69 Stat. 175, provided that: "The limitations of $10,560 and $14,355 with respect to the aggregate salaries payable to secretaries and law clerks of circuit and district judges, contained in the paragraph under the heading 'SALARIES OF SUPPORTING PERSONNEL' in the Judiciary Appropriation Act, 1955 (Public Law 470, Eighty-third Congress), or in any subsequent appropriation Act, shall be increased by the amounts necessary to pay the additional basic compensation provided by this Act."

1951—Act Oct. 24, 1951, c. 554, § 1(d), 65 Stat. 613, provided that: "The limitations of $9,600 and $13,050 with respect to the aggregate salaries payable to secretaries and law clerks of circuit and district judges, contained in the sixteenth paragraph under the head 'Miscellaneous salaries' in the Judiciary Appropriation Act, 1951 (Public Law 759, Eighty-first Congress), or in any subsequent appropriation Act, shall be increased by the amounts necessary to pay the additional basic compensation provided by this Act."

The particular paragraph of the "Judiciary Appropriation Act, 1951 (Public Law 759, Eighty-first Congress)", referred to in section 1(d) of Act Oct. 24, 1951, c. 554 [this note], is Act Sept. 6, 1950, c. 896, ch. III, Title IV, § 401 (part), 64 Stat. 631. The salary limitations therein, also referred to above, were identical with those in the Judiciary Appropriation Act, 1952 (Act Oct. 22, 1951, c. 533, Title IV, § 401 (part), 65 Stat. 596).

1970 Increase in Pay Rates of Judicial Branch Employees Whose Rates of Pay Are Fixed by Administrative Action

Adjustment of rates of pay of judicial branch employees whose rates of pay are fixed by administrative action by not to exceed the amounts of the adjustment for corresponding rates for employees subject to section 2(a) of Pub.L. 91–231, which raised corresponding rates by 6 percent, effective on the first day of the first pay period which begins on or after Dec. 27, 1969, see Pub.L. 91–231, set out as a note under section 5332 of Title 5, Government Organization and Employees.

Reports by Director of Administrative Office of United States Courts

For requirement that Director of Administrative Office of the United States Courts include statistical information about implementation of chapter 44 of this title in annual report under section 604(a)(3) of this title, see section 903(a) of Pub.L. 100–702, set out as a note under section 651 of this title.

Travel and Subsistence Expenses

Pub.L. 87–139, § 6, Aug. 14, 1961, 75 Stat. 340, provided that: "The Director of the Administrative Office of the United States Courts shall promulgate, in accordance with section 604(a)(7) and section 456 of title 28 of the United States Code [subsec. (a)(7) of this section and section 456 of this title], such regulations as he may deem necessary to effectuate the increases provided by this Act [amending section 553 of this title, section 68b of Title 2, The Congress, sections 73b–2, 836 and 837 of former Title 5, Executive Departments and Government Officers and Employees, and sections 287*o*, 287q and 1471 of Title 22, Foreign Relations and Intercourse]."

CROSS REFERENCES

Actual abode of recalled judge or magistrate deemed official station for purposes of this section, see 28 USCA § 374.

Annual report to Judicial Conference under this section to include administration and operation pretrial services for previous year, see 18 USCA § 3155.

Classification and general schedule pay rates, see 5 USCA §§ 5101 et seq. and 5331 et seq.

Duties of Supreme Court Marshal, see 28 USCA § 672.

Expenses of judges and United States attorneys, see 28 USCA §§ 456, 460, 549, and 566.

Juror travel allowance not to exceed maximum rate per mile that Director prescribes pursuant to this section, see 28 USCA § 1871.

Notification to Attorney General of receipt of payment of unpaid fines, see 18 USCA § 3612.

Office expenses of clerks of court, see 28 USCA § 961.

Overtime pay, see 5 USCA § 5541 et seq.

Specification by Director in payment of fine as provided under this section, see 18 USCA § 3611.

Supreme Court officers and employees; compensation and disbursement, see 28 USCA § 671 et seq.

CHAPTER 44—ALTERNATIVE DISPUTE RESOLUTION

§ 651. Authorization of alternative dispute resolution

(a) Definition.—For purposes of this chapter, an alternative dispute resolution process includes any process or procedure, other than an adjudication by a presiding judge, in which a neutral third party participates to assist in the resolution of issues in controversy, through processes such as early neutral evaluation, mediation, minitrial, and arbitration as provided in sections 654 through 658.

(b) Authority.—Each United States district court shall authorize, by local rule adopted under section 2071(a), the use of alternative dispute resolution processes in all civil actions, including adversary proceedings in bankruptcy, in accordance with this chapter, except that the use of arbitration may be authorized only as provided in section 654. Each United States district court shall devise and implement its own alternative dispute resolution program, by local rule adopted under section 2071(a), to encourage and promote the use of alternative dispute resolution in its district.

(c) Existing alternative dispute resolution programs.—In those courts where an alternative dispute resolution program is in place on the date of the enactment of the Alternative Dispute Resolution Act of 1998, the court shall examine the effectiveness of that program and adopt such improvements to the program as are consistent with the provisions and purposes of this chapter [28 U.S.C.A. § 651 et seq.].

(d) Administration of alternative dispute resolution programs.—Each United States district court shall designate an employee, or a judicial officer, who is knowledgeable in alternative dispute resolution practices and processes to implement, administer, oversee, and evaluate the court's alternative dispute resolution program. Such person may also be responsible for recruiting, screening, and training attorneys to serve as neutrals and arbitrators in the court's alternative dispute resolution program.

(e) Title 9 not affected.—This chapter [28 U.S.C.A. § 651 et seq.] shall not affect title 9, United States Code.

(f) Program support.—The Federal Judicial Center and the Administrative Office of the United States Courts are authorized to assist the district courts in the establishment and improvement of alternative dispute resolution programs by identifying particular practices employed in successful programs and providing additional assistance as needed and appropriate.

(Added Pub.L. 100–702, Title IX, § 901(a), Nov. 19, 1988, 102 Stat. 4659, and amended Pub.L. 105–315, § 3, Oct. 30, 1998, 112 Stat. 2993.)

HISTORICAL AND STATUTORY NOTES

Revision Notes and Legislative Reports

1988 Acts. House Report No. 100–889, see 1988 U.S. Code Cong. and Adm. News, p. 5982.

References in Text

The enactment of the Alternative Dispute Resolution Act of 1998, referred to in subsec. (c), is the enactment of Pub.L. 105–315, 112 Stat. 2993, which was approved Oct. 30, 1998.

Effective and Applicability Provisions

1988 Acts. Section 906 of Title IX of Pub.L. 100–702, as amended Pub.L. 103–192, § 1(a), Dec. 14, 1993, 107 Stat. 2292, which provided that, effective December 31, 1994, this chapter, as added by section 901 of Pub.L. 100–702, and the item relating to this chapter in the table of chapters at the beginning of part III of this title, were repealed, except that the provisions of this chapter were to continue to apply through final disposition of all actions in which referral to arbitration was made before the date of repeal, was itself repealed by Pub.L. 103–420, § 3(b), Oct. 25, 1994, 108 Stat. 4345.

Section 907 of Title IX of Pub.L. 100–702 provided that: "This title and the amendments made by this title [enacting this chapter, provisions set out as notes under this section and section 652 of this title] shall take effect 180 days after the date of enactment of this Act [Nov. 19, 1988]."

Findings and Declaration of Policy

Pub.L. 105–315, § 2, Oct. 30, 1998, 112 Stat. 2993, provided that:

"Congress finds that—

"(1) alternative dispute resolution, when supported by the bench and bar, and utilizing properly trained neutrals in a program adequately administered by the court, has the potential to provide a variety of benefits, including greater satisfaction of the parties, innovative methods of resolving disputes, and greater efficiency in achieving settlements;

"(2) certain forms of alternative dispute resolution, including mediation, early neutral evaluation, minitrials, and voluntary arbitration, may have potential to reduce the large backlog of cases now pending in some Federal courts throughout the United States, thereby allowing the courts to process their remaining cases more efficiently; and

"(3) the continued growth of Federal appellate court-annexed mediation programs suggests that this form of alternative dispute resolution can be equally effective in resolving disputes in the Federal trial courts; therefore, the district courts should consider including mediation in their local alternative dispute resolution programs."

Authorization of Appropriations

Pub.L. 105–315, § 11, Oct. 30, 1998, 112 Stat. 2998, provided that: "There are authorized to be appropriated for each fiscal year such sums as may be necessary to carry out chapter 44 of title 28, United States Code [28 U.S.C.A. § 651 et seq.], as amended by this Act [Alternative Dispute Resolution Act of 1998, Pub.L. 105–315, Oct. 30, 1998, 112 Stat. 2993, amending sections 651 to 658 of this title, amending a provision set out as a note under section 652 of this title, and enacting notes set out under this section]."

Section 905 of Title IX of Pub.L. 100–702, as amended Pub.L. 103–192, § 1(b), Dec. 14, 1993, 107 Stat. 2292; Pub.L. 103–420, § 3(a), Oct. 25, 1994, 108 Stat. 4345; Pub.L. 105–53, § 1, Oct. 6, 1997, 111 Stat. 1173, provided that: "There are authorized to be appropriated for each fiscal year to the judicial branch such sums as may be necessary to carry out the purposes of chapter 44 [this chapter], as added by section 901 of this Act. Funds appropriated under this section shall be allocated by the Administrative Office of the United States Courts to Federal judicial districts and the Federal Judicial Center. The funds so appropriated are authorized to remain available until expended."

Effect on Judicial Rulemaking Powers

Section 904 of Title IX of Pub.L. 100–702 provided that: "Nothing in this title [enacting this chapter and provisions set out as notes under this section and section 652 of this title], or in chapter 44 [this chapter], as added by section 901 of this Act, is intended to abridge, modify, or enlarge the rule making powers of the Federal judiciary."

Model Procedures

Section 902 of Title IX of Pub.L. 100–702 provided that: "The Judicial Conference of the United States may develop model rules relating to procedures for arbitration under chapter 44 [this chapter], as added by section 901 of this Act. No model rule may supersede any provision of such chapter 44, this title [enacting this chapter and provisions set out as notes under this section and section 652 of this title], or any law of the United States."

Reports by Director of Administrative Office of United States Courts and by Federal Judicial Center

Pub.L. 100–702, Title IX, § 903, Nov. 19, 1988, 102 Stat. 4663, provided that:

"**(a) Annual Report by Director of Administrative Office of the United States Courts.**—The Director of the Administrative Office of the United States Courts shall include in the annual report of the activities of the Administrative Office required under section 604(a)(3) [section 604(a)(3) of this title], statistical information about the implementation of chapter 44 [this chapter], as added by section 901 of this Act."

"**(b) Report by Federal Judicial Center.**—Not later than 5 years after the date of enactment of this Act [Nov. 19, 1988], the Federal Judicial Center, in consultation with the Director of the Administrative Office of the United States Courts, shall submit to the Congress a report on the implementation of chapter 44 [this chapter], as added by section 901 of this Act, which shall include the following:

"(1) A description of the arbitration programs authorized by such chapter, as conceived and as implemented in the judicial districts in which such programs are authorized.

"(2) A determination of the level of satisfaction with the arbitration programs in those judicial districts by a sampling of court personnel, attorneys, and litigants whose cases have been referred to arbitration.

"(3) A summary of those program features that can be identified as being related to program acceptance both within and across judicial districts.

"(4) A description of the levels of satisfaction relative to the cost per hearing of each program.

"(5) Recommendations to the Congress on whether to terminate or continue chapter 44, or alternatively, to enact an arbitration provision in title 28, United States Code [this title], authorizing arbitration in all Federal district courts."

[For termination, effective May 15, 2000, of reporting provisions of this note, see Pub.L. 104–66, § 3003, as amended, set out as a note under 31 U.S.C.A. § 1113, and the 11th item on page 12 of House Document No. 103–7.]

Treatment of Expired Provisions

Pub.L. 103–192, § 2, Dec. 14, 1993, 107 Stat. 2292, provided that: "Chapter 44 of title 28, United States Code [this chapter], and the item relating to that chapter in the table of chapters at the beginning of part III of such title [analysis preceding section 601 of this title], shall be effective on or after the date of the enactment of this Act [Dec. 14, 1993] as if such chapter and item had not been repealed by section 906 of the Judicial Improvements and Access to Justice Act [section 906 of Pub.L. 100–702, set out as an Effective Date of Repeal note under this section] as such section was in effect on the day before the date of the enactment of this Act [Dec. 14, 1993]."

§ 652. Jurisdiction

(a) Consideration of alternative dispute resolution in appropriate cases.—Notwithstanding any provision of law to the contrary and except as provided in subsections (b) and (c), each district court shall, by local rule adopted under section 2071(a), require that litigants in all civil cases consider the use of an alternative dispute resolution process at an appropriate stage in the litigation. Each district court shall provide litigants in all civil cases with at least one alternative dispute resolution process, including, but not limited to, mediation, early neutral evaluation, minitrial, and arbitration as authorized in sections 654 through 658. Any district court that elects to require the use of alternative dispute resolution in certain cases may do so only with respect to mediation, early neutral evaluation, and, if the parties consent, arbitration.

(b) Actions exempted from consideration of alternative dispute resolution.—Each district court may exempt from the requirements of this section specific cases or categories of cases in which use of alternative dispute resolution would not be appropriate. In defining these exemptions, each district court shall consult with members of the bar, including the United States Attorney for that district.

(c) Authority of the Attorney General.—Nothing in this section shall alter or conflict with the authority of the Attorney General to conduct litigation on behalf of the United States, with the authority of any Federal agency authorized to conduct litigation in the United States courts, or with any delegation of litigation authority by the Attorney General.

(d) Confidentiality provisions.—Until such time as rules are adopted under chapter 131 of this title [28 U.S.C.A. § 2071 et seq.] providing for the confidentiality of alternative dispute resolution processes under this chapter [28 U.S.C.A. § 651 et seq.], each district court shall, by local rule adopted under section 2071(a), provide for the confidentiality of the alternative dispute resolution processes and to prohibit disclosure of confidential dispute resolution communications.

(Added Pub.L. 100–702, Title IX, § 901(a), Nov. 19, 1988, 102 Stat. 4659, and amended Pub.L. 105–315, § 4, Oct. 30, 1998, 112 Stat. 2994.)

HISTORICAL AND STATUTORY NOTES

Revision Notes and Legislative Reports

1988 Acts. House Report No. 100–889, see 1988 U.S.Code Cong. and Adm.News, p. 5982.

Effective and Applicability Provisions

1988 Acts. Section 906 of Pub.L. 100–702, as amended, which provided that, effective Dec. 31, 1994, this section was repealed, with certain exceptions, was itself repealed by Pub.L. 103–420, § 3(b), Oct. 25, 1994, 108 Stat. 4345. See section 906 of Pub.L. 100–702, set out as a note under section 651 of this title.

Section effective 180 days after Nov. 19, 1988, see section 907 of Pub.L. 100–702, set out as a note under section 651 of this title.

Treatment of Expired Provisions

This section to continue to be effective on or after Dec. 14, 1993 as if it had not been repealed by section 906 of Pub.L. 100–702, as such section was in effect on the day before such date, see Treatment of Expired Provisions note set out under section 651 of this title.

Exception to Limitation on Money Damages

Section 901(c) of Pub.L. 100–702, which provided that notwithstanding this section a district court listed in section 658 of this title whose local rule on Nov. 19, 1988 provided for a limitation on money damages with respect to cases referred to arbitration of not more than $150,000 may continue to apply the higher limitation, was repealed by Pub.L. 105–315, § 12(a), Oct. 30, 1998, 112 Stat. 2998.

§ 653. Neutrals

(a) Panel of neutrals.—Each district court that authorizes the use of alternative dispute resolution processes shall adopt appropriate processes for making neutrals available for use by the parties for each category of process offered. Each district court shall promulgate its own procedures and criteria for the selection of neutrals on its panels.

(b) Qualifications and training.—Each person serving as a neutral in an alternative dispute resolution process should be qualified and trained to serve as a neutral in the appropriate alternative dispute resolution process. For this purpose, the district court may use, among others, magistrate judges who have been trained to serve as neutrals in alternative dispute resolution processes, professional neutrals from the private sector, and persons who have been trained to serve as neutrals in alternative dispute resolution processes. Until such time as rules are adopted under chapter 131 of this title [28 U.S.C.A. § 2071 et seq.] relating to the disqualification of neutrals, each district court shall issue rules under section 2071(a) relating to the disqualification of neutrals (including, where appropriate, disqualification under section 455 of this title, other applicable law, and professional responsibility standards).

(Added Pub.L. 100–702, Title IX, § 901(a), Nov. 19, 1988, 102 Stat. 4660, and amended Pub.L. 105–315, § 5, Oct. 30, 1998, 112 Stat. 2995.)

HISTORICAL AND STATUTORY NOTES

Revision Notes and Legislative Reports

1988 Acts. House Report No. 100–889, see 1988 U.S.Code Cong. and Adm. News, p. 5982.

Effective and Applicability Provisions

1988 Acts. Section 906 of Pub.L. 100–702, as amended, which provided that, effective Dec. 31, 1994, this section was repealed, with certain exceptions, was itself repealed by Pub.L. 103–420, § 3(b), Oct. 25, 1994, 108 Stat. 4345. See section 906 of Pub.L. 100–702, set out as a note under section 651 of this title.

Section effective 180 days after Nov. 19, 1988, see section 907 of Pub.L. 100–702, set out as a note under section 651 of this title.

Treatment of Expired Provisions

This section to continue to be effective on or after Dec. 14, 1993 as if it had not been repealed by section 906 of Pub.L. 100–702 as such section was in effect on the day before such date, see Treatment of Expired Provisions note set out under section 651 of this title.

§ 654. Arbitration

(a) Referral of actions to arbitration.—Notwithstanding any provision of law to the contrary and except as provided in subsections (a), (b), and (c) of section 652 and subsection (d) of this section, a district court may allow the referral to arbitration of any civil action (including any adversary proceeding in bankruptcy) pending before it when the parties consent, except that referral to arbitration may not be made where—

(1) the action is based on an alleged violation of a right secured by the Constitution of the United States;

(2) jurisdiction is based in whole or in part on section 1343 of this title; or

(3) the relief sought consists of money damages in an amount greater than $150,000.

(b) Safeguards in consent cases.—Until such time as rules are adopted under chapter 131 of this title relating to procedures described in this subsection, the district court shall, by local rule adopted under section 2071(a), establish procedures to ensure that any civil action in which arbitration by consent is allowed under subsection (a)—

(1) consent to arbitration is freely and knowingly obtained; and

(2) no party or attorney is prejudiced for refusing to participate in arbitration.

(c) Presumptions.—For purposes of subsection (a)(3), a district court may presume damages are not in excess of $150,000 unless counsel certifies that damages exceed such amount.

(d) Existing programs.—Nothing in this chapter is deemed to affect any program in which arbitration is conducted pursuant to section [1] title IX of the Judicial Improvements and Access to Justice Act (Public Law 100–702), as amended by section 1 of Public Law 105–53.

(Added Pub.L. 100–702, Title IX, § 901(a), Nov. 19, 1988, 102 Stat. 4660, and amended Pub.L. 105–315, § 6, Oct. 30, 1998, 112 Stat. 2995.)

[1] So in original. The word "section" probably should not appear.

HISTORICAL AND STATUTORY NOTES

Revision Notes and Legislative Reports

1988 Acts. House Report No. 100–889, see 1988 U.S. Code Cong. and Adm. News, p. 5982.

References in Text

Title IX of the Judicial Improvements and Access to Justice Act, referred to in subsec. (d), is Pub.L. 100–702, Title IX, Nov. 19, 1988, 102 Stat. 4663. See Codifications note under this section.

Codifications

Section title IX of the Judicial Improvements and Access to Justice Act, referred to in subsec. (d), probably should read section 905 of title IX of the Judicial Improvements and Access to Justice Act, which is Pub.L. 100–702, Title IX, § 905, Nov. 19, 1988, 102 Stat. 4663, set out as a note under section 651 of this title.

Effective and Applicability Provisions

1988 Acts. Section 906 of Pub.L. 100–702, as amended, which provided that, effective Dec. 31, 1994, this section was repealed, with certain exceptions, was itself repealed by Pub.L. 103–420, § 3(b), Oct. 25, 1994, 108 Stat. 4345. See section 906 of Pub.L. 100–702, set out as a note under section 651 of this title.

Section effective 180 days after Nov. 19, 1988, see section 907 of Pub.L. 100–702, set out as a note under section 651 of this title.

Treatment of Expired Provisions

This section to continue to be effective on or after Dec. 14, 1993 as if it had not been repealed by section 906 of Pub.L. 100–702 as such section was in effect on the day before such date, see Treatment of Expired Provisions note set out under section 651 of this title.

§ 655. Arbitrators

(a) Powers of arbitrators.—An arbitrator to whom an action is referred under section 654 shall have the power, within the judicial district of the district court which referred the action to arbitration—

(1) to conduct arbitration hearings;

(2) to administer oaths and affirmations; and

(3) to make awards.

(b) Standards for certification.—Each district court that authorizes arbitration shall establish standards for the certification of arbitrators and shall certify arbitrators to perform services in accordance with such standards and this chapter. The standards shall include provisions requiring that any arbitrator—

(1) shall take the oath or affirmation described in section 453; and

(2) shall be subject to the disqualification rules under section 455.

(c) Immunity.—All individuals serving as arbitrators in an alternative dispute resolution program under this chapter are performing quasi-judicial functions and are entitled to the immunities and protections that the law accords to persons serving in such capacity.

(Added Pub.L. 100–702, Title IX, § 901(a), Nov. 19, 1988, 102 Stat. 4661, and amended Pub.L. 105–315, § 7, Oct. 30, 1998, 112 Stat. 2996.)

HISTORICAL AND STATUTORY NOTES

Revision Notes and Legislative Reports

1988 Acts. House Report No. 100–889, see 1988 U.S.Code Cong. and Adm.News, p. 5982.

Effective and Applicability Provisions

1988 Acts. Section 906 of Pub.L. 100–702, as amended, which provided that, effective Dec. 31, 1994, this section was repealed, with certain exceptions, was itself repealed by Pub.L. 103–420, § 3(b), Oct. 25, 1994, 108 Stat. 4345. See section 906 of Pub.L. 100–702, set out as a note under section 651 of this title.

Section effective 180 days after Nov. 19, 1988, see section 907 of Pub.L. 100–702, set out as a note under section 651 of this title.

Treatment of Expired Provisions

This section to continue to be effective on or after Dec. 14, 1993 as if it had not been repealed by section 906 of Pub.L. 100–702 as such section was in effect on the day before such date, see Treatment of Expired Provisions note set out under section 651 of this title.

§ 656. Subpoenas

Rule 45 of the Federal Rules of Civil Procedure (relating to subpoenas) applies to subpoenas for the attendance of witnesses and the production of documentary evidence at an arbitration hearing under this chapter.

(Added Pub.L. 100–702, Title IX, § 901(a), Nov. 19, 1988, 102 Stat. 4662, and amended Pub.L. 105–315, § 8, Oct. 30, 1998, 112 Stat. 2996.)

HISTORICAL AND STATUTORY NOTES

Revision Notes and Legislative Reports

1988 Acts. House Report No. 100–889, see 1988 U.S.Code Cong. and Adm.News, p. 5982.

Effective and Applicability Provisions

1988 Acts. Section 906 of Pub.L. 100–702, as amended, which provided that, effective Dec. 31, 1994, this section was repealed, with certain exceptions, was itself repealed by Pub.L. 103–420, § 3(b), Oct. 25, 1994, 108 Stat. 4345. See section 906 of Pub.L. 100–702, set out as a note under section 651 of this title.

Section effective 180 days after Nov. 19, 1988, see section 907 of Pub.L. 100–702, set out as a note under section 651 of this title.

Treatment of Expired Provisions

This section to continue to be effective on or after Dec. 14, 1993 as if it had not been repealed by section 906 of Pub.L. 100–702 as such section was in effect on the day before such date, see Treatment of Expired Provisions note set out under section 651 of this title.

§ 657. Arbitration award and judgment

(a) Filing and effect of arbitration award.—An arbitration award made by an arbitrator under this chapter, along with proof of service of such award on the other party by the prevailing party or by the plaintiff, shall be filed promptly after the arbitration hearing is concluded with the clerk of the district court that referred the case to arbitration. Such award shall be entered as the judgment of the court after the time has expired for requesting a trial de novo. The judgment so entered shall be subject to the same provisions of law and shall have the same force and effect as a judgment of the court in a civil action, except that the judgment shall not be subject to review in any other court by appeal or otherwise.

(b) Sealing of arbitration award.—The district court shall provide, by local rule adopted under section 2071(a), that the contents of any arbitration award made under this chapter shall not be made known to any judge who might be assigned to the case until the district court has entered final judgment in the action or the action has otherwise terminated.

(c) Trial de novo of arbitration awards.—

(1) Time for filing demand.—Within 30 days after the filing of an arbitration award with a district court under subsection (a), any party may file a written demand for a trial de novo in the district court.

(2) Action restored to court docket.—Upon a demand for a trial de novo, the action shall be restored to the docket of the court and treated for all purposes as if it had not been referred to arbitration.

(3) Exclusion of evidence of arbitration.—The court shall not admit at the trial de novo any evidence that there has been an arbitration proceeding, the nature or amount of any award, or any other matter concerning the conduct of the arbitration proceeding, unless—

(A) the evidence would otherwise be admissible in the court under the Federal Rules of Evidence; or

(B) the parties have otherwise stipulated.

(Added Pub.L. 100–702, Title IX, § 901(a), Nov. 19, 1988, 102 Stat. 4662, and amended Pub.L. 105–315, § 9, Oct. 30, 1998, 112 Stat. 2997.)

HISTORICAL AND STATUTORY NOTES

Revision Notes and Legislative Reports

1988 Acts. House Report No. 100–889, see 1988 U.S. Code Cong. and Adm. News, p. 5982.

Effective and Applicability Provisions

1988 Acts. Section 906 of Pub.L. 100–702, as amended, which provided that, effective Dec. 31, 1994, this section was repealed, with certain exceptions, was itself repealed by Pub.L. 103–420, § 3(b), Oct. 25, 1994, 108 Stat. 4345. See section 906 of Pub.L. 100–702, set out as a note under section 651 of this title.

Section effective 180 days after Nov. 19, 1988, see section 907 of Pub.L. 100–702, set out as a note under section 651 of this title.

Treatment of Expired Provisions

This section to continue to be effective on or after Dec. 14, 1993 as if it had not been repealed by section 906 of Pub.L. 100–702 as such section was in effect on the day before such date, see Treatment of Expired Provisions note set out under section 651 of this title.

§ 658. Compensation of arbitrators and neutrals

(a) Compensation.—The district court shall, subject to regulations approved by the Judicial Conference of the United States, establish the amount of compensation, if any, that each arbitrator or neutral shall receive for services rendered in each case under this chapter.

(b) Transportation allowances.—Under regulations prescribed by the Director of the Administrative Office of the United States Courts, a district court may reimburse arbitrators and other neutrals for actual transportation expenses necessarily incurred in the performance of duties under this chapter.

(Added Pub.L. 100–702, Title IX, § 901(a), Nov. 19, 1988, 102 Stat. 4662, and amended Pub.L. 105–315, § 10, Oct. 30, 1998, 112 Stat. 2997.)

HISTORICAL AND STATUTORY NOTES

Effective and Applicability Provisions

1988 Acts. Section 906 of Pub.L. 100–702, as amended, which provided that, effective Dec. 31, 1994, this section was repealed, with certain exceptions, was itself repealed by Pub.L. 103–420, § 3(b), Oct. 25, 1994, 108 Stat. 4345. See section 906 of Pub.L. 100–702, set out as a note under section 651 of this title.

Section effective 180 days after Nov. 19, 1988, see section 907 of Pub.L. 100–702, set out as a note under section 651 of this title.

Treatment of Expired Provisions

This section to continue to be effective on or after Dec. 14, 1993 as if it had not been repealed by section 906 of Pub.L. 100–702 as such section was in effect on the day before such date, see Treatment of Expired Provisions note set out under section 651 of this title.

CHAPTER 57—GENERAL PROVISIONS APPLICABLE TO COURT OFFICERS AND EMPLOYEES

§ 959. Trustees and receivers suable; management; State laws

(a) Trustees, receivers or managers of any property, including debtors in possession, may be sued, without leave of the court appointing them, with respect to any of their acts or transactions in carrying on business connected with such property. Such actions shall be subject to the general equity power of such court so far as the same may be necessary to the ends of justice, but this shall not deprive a litigant of his right to trial by jury.

(b) Except as provided in section 1166 of title 11, a trustee, receiver or manager appointed in any cause pending in any court of the United States, including a debtor in possession, shall manage and operate the property in his possession as such trustee, receiver or manager according to the requirements of the valid laws of the State in which such property is situated, in the same manner that the owner or possessor thereof would be bound to do if in possession thereof.

(June 25, 1948, c. 646, 62 Stat. 926; Nov. 6, 1978, Pub.L. 95–598, Title II, § 235, 92 Stat. 2667.)

HISTORICAL AND STATUTORY NOTES

Revision Notes and Legislative Reports

1948 Acts. Based on Title 28, U.S.C., 1940 ed., §§ 124, 125 (Mar. 3, 1911, c. 231, §§ 65, 66, 36 Stat. 1104).

Section consolidates part of section 124 of Title 28, U.S.C., 1940 ed., with section 125 of the same title. The criminal penalty for violation of said section 124 is incorporated in section 1911 of Title 18, Crimes and Criminal Procedure (H.R. 1600, 80th Cong.).

Section was extended and made applicable to trustees and debtors in possession. The provision at the end of subsection (a) for preserving the right to a jury trial was added to clarify the intent of section 125 of Title 28, U.S.C., 1940 ed., as construed in *Vany v. Receiver of Toledo, St. L. and K.C.R.R. Co.,* C.C.1895, 67 F. 379.

Changes in phraseology were made. 80th Congress House Report No. 308.

1978 Acts. Senate Report No. 95–989 and House Report No. 95–595, see 1978 U.S.Code Cong. and Adm.News, p. 5787.

Effective and Applicability Provisions

1978 Acts. Amendment by Pub.L. 95–598 effective Oct. 1, 1979, see section 402(c) of Pub.L. 95–598, as amended, set out as a note preceding section 101 of Title 11, Bankruptcy.

CROSS REFERENCES

Capacity to sue or be sued, see Fed.Rules Civ.Proc. Rule 17, 28 USCA.

Mismanagement of property by receiver, criminal penalty, see 18 USCA § 1911.

Process and orders affecting property in different districts, see 28 USCA § 1692.

Receivers of property in different districts; jurisdiction, see 28 USCA § 754.

PART IV—JURISDICTION AND VENUE

§ 1334. Bankruptcy cases and proceedings

(a) Except as provided in subsection (b) of this section, the district courts shall have original and exclusive jurisdiction of all cases under title 11.

(b) Except as provided in subsection (e)(2), and notwithstanding any Act of Congress that confers exclusive jurisdiction on a court or courts other than the district courts, the district courts shall have original but not exclusive jurisdiction of all civil proceedings arising under title 11, or arising in or related to cases under title 11.

(c)(1) Except with respect to a case under chapter 15 of title 11, nothing in this section prevents a district court in the interest of justice, or in the interest of comity with State courts or respect for State law, from abstaining from hearing a particular proceeding arising under title 11 or arising in or related to a case under title 11.

(2) Upon timely motion of a party in a proceeding based upon a State law claim or State law cause of action, related to a case under title 11 but not arising under title 11 or arising in a case under title 11, with respect to which an action could not have been commenced in a court of the United States absent jurisdiction under this section, the district court shall abstain from hearing such proceeding if an action is commenced, and can be timely adjudicated, in a State forum of appropriate jurisdiction.

(d) Any decision to abstain or not to abstain made under subsection (c) (other than a decision not to abstain in a proceeding described in subsection (c)(2)) is not reviewable by appeal or otherwise by the court of appeals under section 158(d), 1291, or 1292 of this title or by the Supreme Court of the United States under section 1254 of this title. Subsection (c) and this subsection shall not be construed to limit the applicability of the stay provided for by section 362 of title 11, United States Code, as such section applies to an action affecting the property of the estate in bankruptcy.

(e) The district court in which a case under title 11 is commenced or is pending shall have exclusive jurisdiction—

(1) of all the property, wherever located, of the debtor as of the commencement of such case, and of property of the estate; and

(2) over all claims or causes of action that involve construction of section 327 of title 11, United States Code, or rules relating to disclosure requirements under section 327.

(June 25, 1948, c. 646, 62 Stat. 931; Nov. 6, 1978, Pub.L. 95–598, Title II, § 238(a), 92 Stat. 2667; July 10, 1984, Pub.L. 98–353, Title I, § 101(a), 98 Stat. 333; Oct. 27, 1986, Pub.L. 99–554, Title I, § 144(e), 100 Stat. 3096; Dec. 1, 1990, Pub.L. 101–650, Title III, § 309(b), 104 Stat. 5113; Oct. 22, 1994, Pub.L. 103–394, Title I, § 104(b), 108 Stat. 4109; Apr. 20, 2005, Pub.L. 109–8, Title III, § 324(a), Title VIII, § 802(c)(2), Title XII, § 1219, 119 Stat. 98, 145, 195.)

HISTORICAL AND STATUTORY NOTES

Revision Notes and Legislative Reports

1948 Acts. Based on Title 28, U.S.C., 1940 ed., §§ 41(19) and 371(6) (Mar. 3, 1911, c. 231, §§ 24, par. 19, 256, par. 6, 36 Stat. 1093, 1160).

Changes in phraseology were made.

1984 Acts. Statements by Legislative Leaders, see 1984 U.S. Code Cong. and Adm. News, p. 576.

1986 Acts. House Report No. 99–764 and House Conference Report No. 99–958, see 1986 U.S. Code Cong. and Adm. News, p. 5227.

1990 Acts. Senate Report No. 101–416, House Report Nos. 101–123, 101–512, 101–514, 101–734, and 101–735, and Statement by President, see 1990 U.S. Code Cong. and Adm. News, p. 6802.

1994 Acts. House Report No. 103–835, see 1994 U.S. Code Cong. and Adm. News, p. 3340.

2005 Acts. House Report No. 109–31(Part I), see 2005 U.S. Code Cong. and Adm. News, p. 88.

References in Text

Chapter 15 of title 11, referred to in subsec. (c), is 11 U.S.C.A. § 1501 et seq.

Codifications

This section was amended by Pub.L. 95–598, Title II, § 238(a), Nov. 6, 1978, 92 Stat. 2668, effective June 28, 1984, pursuant to Pub.L. 95–598, Title IV, § 402(b), Nov. 6, 1978, 92 Stat. 2682, as amended by Pub.L. 98–249, § 1(a), Mar. 31, 1984, 98 Stat. 116; Pub.L. 98–271, § 1(a), Apr. 30, 1984, 98 Stat. 163; Pub.L. 98–299, § 1(a), May 25, 1984, 98 Stat. 214; Pub.L. 98–325, § 1(a), June 20, 1984, 98 Stat. 268, set out as an Effective and Applicability Provisions note preceding section 101 of Title 11, Bankruptcy, to read as follows:

"§ 1334. Bankruptcy appeals

"**(a)** The district courts for districts for which panels have not been ordered appointed under section 160 of this title shall have jurisdiction of appeals from all final judgments, orders, and decrees of bankruptcy courts.

"**(b)** The district courts for such districts shall have jurisdiction of appeals from interlocutory orders and decrees of bankruptcy courts, but only by leave of the district court to which the appeal is taken.

"**(c)** A district court may not refer an appeal under that section to a magistrate or to a special master."

Section 402(b) of Pub.L. 95–598 was amended by section 113 of Pub.L. 98–353 by substituting "shall not be effective" for "shall take effect on June 28, 1984", thereby eliminating the amendment by section 238(a) of Pub.L. 95–598, effective June 27, 1984, pursuant to section 122(c) of Pub.L. 98–353, set out as an Effective and Applicability Provisions note under 28 U.S.C.A. § 151.

Section 121(a) of Pub.L. 98–353 directed that section 402(b) of Pub.L. 95–598 be amended by substituting "the date of enactment of the Bankruptcy Amendments and Federal Judgeship Act of 1984 [i.e. July 10, 1984]" for "June 28, 1984". This amendment was not executed in view of the prior amendment to section 402(b) of Pub.L. 95–598 by section 113 of Pub.L. 98–353.

Effective and Applicability Provisions

2005 Acts. Pub.L. 109–8, Title III, § 324(b), Apr. 20, 2005, 119 Stat. 98, provided that: "This section [amending subsecs. (b) and (e) of this section] shall only apply to cases filed after the date of enactment of this Act [Apr. 20, 2005]."

Except as otherwise provided, amendments by Pub.L. 109–8 effective 180 days after April 20, 2005, and inapplicable with respect to cases commenced under Title 11 before the effective date, see Pub.L. 109–8, § 1501, set out as a note under 11 U.S.C.A. § 101.

1994 Acts. Amendment by Pub.L. 103–394 effective on Oct. 22, 1994, and not to apply with respect to cases commenced under Title 11 of the United States Code before Oct. 22, 1994, see section 702 of Pub.L. 103–394, set out as a note under section 101 of Title 11, Bankruptcy.

1986 Acts. Amendment by Pub.L. 99–554 effective 30 days after Oct. 27, 1986, except as otherwise provided for, see section 302(a) of Pub.L. 99–554, as amended, set out as a note under section 581 of this title.

1984 Acts. Amendment by Pub.L. 98–353, except for subsec. (c)(2), effective July 10, 1984, see section 122(a) of Pub.L. 98–353, set out as a note under section 151 of this title.

Subsec. (c)(2) not applicable with respect to cases under Title 11, Bankruptcy, that are pending on July 10, 1984, or to proceedings arising in or related to such cases, see section 122(b) of Pub.L. 98–353, set out as a note under section 151 of this title.

Separability of Provisions

If any provision of or amendment made by Pub.L. 103–394 or the application of such provision or amendment to any person or circumstance is held to be unconstitutional, the remaining provisions of and amendments made by Pub.L. 103–394 and the application of such provisions and amendments to any person or circumstance shall not be affected thereby, see section 701 of Pub.L. 103–394, set out as a note under section 101 of Title 11, Bankruptcy.

Jurisdiction Over and Transfer of Bankruptcy Cases and Proceedings

Section 115 of Pub.L. 98–353 provided that:

"**(a)** On the date of the enactment of this Act [July 10, 1984] the appropriate district court of the United States shall have jurisdiction of—

"**(1)** cases, and matters and proceedings in cases, under the Bankruptcy Act [former Title 11, Bankruptcy] that are pending immediately before such date in the bankruptcy courts continued by section 404(a) of the Act of November 6, 1978 (Public Law 95–598; 92 Stat. 2687) [Pub.L. 95–598, Title IV, § 404(a), Nov. 6, 1978, 92 Stat. 2683, formerly set out as a note preceding section 151 of this title], and

"**(2)** cases under title 11 of the United States Code [Title 11, Bankruptcy], and proceedings arising under title 11 of the United States Code or arising in or related to cases under title 11 of the United States Code, that are pending immediately before such date in the bankruptcy courts continued by section 404(a) of the Act of November 6, 1978 (Public Law 95–598; 92 Stat. 2687).

"**(b)** On the date of the enactment of this Act [July 10, 1984], there shall be transferred to the appropriate district court of the United States appeals from final judgments, orders, and decrees of the bankruptcy courts pending immediately before such date in the bankruptcy appellate panels appointed under section 405(c) of the Act of November 6, 1978 (Public Law 95–598; 92 Stat. 2685) [formerly set out as a note preceding section 1471 of this title]."

CROSS REFERENCES

Appointment of clerk for bankruptcy court where warranted by number of cases and proceedings pending, see 28 USCA § 156.

Non-core proceedings not subject to mandatory abstention provisions, see 28 USCA § 157.

Removal of claims related to bankruptcy cases, see 28 USCA § 1452.

Venue, see 28 USCA §§ 1408 and 1409.

CHAPTER 87—DISTRICT COURTS; VENUE

CROSS REFERENCES

Criminal cases, venue, see 18 USCA § 3235 et seq.

Fair housing actions venue determined in accordance with this chapter, see 42 USCA § 3612.

Jurisdiction of district courts, see 28 USCA § 1331 et seq.

Process, see 28 USCA § 1691 et seq.

Venue, see Fed.Rules Cr.Proc. Rules 18 and 20 to 22, 18 USCA.

§ 1408. Venue of cases under title 11

Except as provided in section 1410 of this title, a case under title 11 may be commenced in the district court for the district—

(1) in which the domicile, residence, principal place of business in the United States, or principal assets in the United States, of the person or entity that is the subject of such case have been located for the one hundred and eighty days immediately preceding such commencement, or for a longer portion of such one-hundred-and-eighty-day period than the domicile, residence, or principal place of business, in the United States, or principal assets in the United States, of such person were located in any other district; or

(2) in which there is pending a case under title 11 concerning such person's affiliate, general partner, or partnership.

(Added Pub.L. 98–353, Title I, § 102(a), July 10, 1984, 98 Stat. 334.)

HISTORICAL AND STATUTORY NOTES

Revision Notes and Legislative Reports

1984 Acts. Statements by Legislative Leaders, see 1984 U.S. Code Cong. and Adm. News, p. 576.

Effective and Applicability Provisions

1984 Acts. Section effective July 10, 1984, see section 122(a) of Pub.L. 98–353, set out as a note under section 151 of this title.

§ 1409. Venue of proceedings arising under title 11 or arising in or related to cases under title 11

(a) Except as otherwise provided in subsections (b) and (d), a proceeding arising under title 11 or arising in or related to a case under title 11 may be commenced in the district court in which such case is pending.

(b) Except as provided in subsection (d) of this section, a trustee in a case under title 11 may commence a proceeding arising in or related to such case to recover a money judgment of or property worth less than $1,100 [1] or a consumer debt of less than $16,425 [1], or a debt (excluding a consumer debt) against a noninsider of less than $10,950 [1], only in the district court for the district in which the defendant resides.

(c) Except as provided in subsection (b) of this section, a trustee in a case under title 11 may commence a proceeding arising in or related to such case as statutory successor to the debtor or creditors under section 541 or 544(b) of title 11 in the district court for the district where the State or Federal court sits in which, under applicable nonbankruptcy venue provisions, the debtor or creditors, as the case may be, may have commenced an action on which such proceeding is based if the case under title 11 had not been commenced.

(d) A trustee may commence a proceeding arising under title 11 or arising in or related to a case under title 11 based on a claim arising after the commencement of such case from the operation of the business of the debtor only in the district court for the district where a State or Federal court sits in which, under applicable nonbankruptcy venue provisions, an action on such claim may have been brought.

(e) A proceeding arising under title 11 or arising in or related to a case under title 11, based on a claim arising after the commencement of such case from the operation of the business of the debtor, may be commenced against the representative of the estate in such case in the district court for the district where the State or Federal court sits in which the party commencing such proceeding may, under applicable nonbankruptcy venue provisions, have brought an action on such claim, or in the district court in which such case is pending.

(Added Pub.L. 98–353, Title I, § 102(a), July 10, 1984, 98 Stat. 334, and amended Pub.L. 109–8, Title IV, § 410, Apr. 20, 2005, 119 Stat. 106.)

[1] Dollar amount as adjusted by the Judicial Conference of the United States. See Adjustment of Dollar Amounts notes set out under this section and 11 U.S.C.A. § 104.

HISTORICAL AND STATUTORY NOTES

Revision Notes and Legislative Reports

1984 Acts. Statements by Legislative Leaders, see 1984 U.S. Code Cong. and Adm. News, p. 576.

2005 Acts. House Report No. 109–31(Part I), see 2005 U.S. Code Cong. and Adm. News, p. 88.

Effective and Applicability Provisions

2007 Acts. Increase of dollar amounts by Judicial Conference of the United States by notice published Feb. 14, 2007, 72 F.R. 7082 effective April 1, 2007, and increase not applicable to cases commenced before the effective date of the adjustments, i.e., April 1, 2007. See Adjustment of Dollar Amounts notes under 11 U.S.C.A. § 104 and this section.

2005 Acts. Except as otherwise provided, amendments by Pub.L. 109–8 effective 180 days after April 20, 2005, and inapplicable with respect to cases commenced under Title 11 before the effective date, see Pub.L. 109–8, § 1501, set out as a note under 11 U.S.C.A. § 101.

1984 Acts. Section effective July 10, 1984, see section 122(a) of Pub.L. 98–353, set out as a note under section 151 of this title.

Adjustment of Dollar Amounts

For adjustment of dollar amounts specified in subsec. (b) of this section by the Judicial Conference of the United States, effective Apr. 1, 2007, see note set out under 11 U.S.C.A. § 104.

By notice published Feb. 14, 2007, 72 F.R. 7082, the Judicial Conference of the United States adjusted the dollar amounts in provisions specified in subsec. (b) of this section, effective Apr. 1, 2007, as follows:

Adjusted $1,000 to $1,100.
Adjusted $15,000 to $16,425.
Adjusted $10,000 to $10,950.

§ 1410. Venue of cases ancillary to foreign proceedings

A case under chapter 15 of title 11 may be commenced in the district court of the United States for the district—

(1) in which the debtor has its principal place of business or principal assets in the United States;

(2) if the debtor does not have a place of business or assets in the United States, in which there is pending against the debtor an action or proceeding in a Federal or State court; or

(3) in a case other than those specified in paragraph (1) or (2), in which venue will be consistent with the interests of justice and the convenience of the parties, having regard to the relief sought by the foreign representative.

(Added Pub.L. 98–353, Title I, § 102(a), July 10, 1984, 98 Stat. 335, and amended Pub.L. 109–8, Title VIII, § 802(c)(4), Apr. 20, 2005, 119 Stat. 146.)

HISTORICAL AND STATUTORY NOTES

Revision Notes and Legislative Reports

1984 Acts. Statements by Legislative Leaders, see 1984 U.S. Code Cong. and Adm. News, p. 576.

2005 Acts. House Report No. 109–31(Part I), see 2005 U.S. Code Cong. and Adm. News, p. 88.

References in Text

Chapter 15 of title 11, referred to in text, is 11 U.S.C.A. § 1501 et seq.

Effective and Applicability Provisions

2005 Acts. Except as otherwise provided, amendments by Pub.L. 109–8 effective 180 days after April 20, 2005, and inapplicable with respect to cases commenced under Title 11 before the effective date, see Pub.L. 109–8, § 1501, set out as a note under 11 U.S.C.A. § 101.

1984 Acts. Section effective July 10, 1984, see section 122(a) of Pub.L. 98–353, set out as a note under section 151 of this title.

CROSS REFERENCES

Commencement of bankruptcy cases in district courts having venue except as provided by this section, see 28 USCA § 1408.

§ 1411. Jury trials

(a) Except as provided in subsection (b) of this section, this chapter and title 11 do not affect any right to trial by jury that an individual has under applicable nonbankruptcy law with regard to a personal injury or wrongful death tort claim.

(b) The district court may order the issues arising under section 303 of title 11 to be tried without a jury.

(Added Pub.L. 98–353, Title I, § 102(a), July 10, 1984, 98 Stat. 335.)

HISTORICAL AND STATUTORY NOTES

Revision Notes and Legislative Reports

1984 Acts. Statements by Legislative Leaders, see 1984 U.S. Code Cong. and Adm. News, p. 576.

Effective and Applicability Provisions

1984 Acts. Section, except subsec. (a), effective July 10, 1984, see section 122(a) of Pub.L. 98–353, set out as a note under section 151 of this title.

Subsec. (a) not applicable with respect to cases under Title 11, Bankruptcy, that are pending on July 10, 1984, or to proceedings arising in or related to such cases, see section 122(b) of Pub.L. 98–353, set out as a note under section 151 of this title.

§ 1412. Change of venue

A district court may transfer a case or proceeding under title 11 to a district court for another district, in the interest of justice or for the convenience of the parties.

(Added Pub.L. 98–353, Title I, § 102(a), July 10, 1984, 98 Stat. 335.)

HISTORICAL AND STATUTORY NOTES

Revision Notes and Legislative Reports

1984 Acts. Statements by Legislative Leaders, see 1984 U.S. Code Cong. and Adm. News, p. 576.

Effective and Applicability Provisions

1984 Acts. Section effective July 10, 1984, see section 122(a) of Pub.L. 98–353, set out as a note under section 151 of this title.

CHAPTER 89—DISTRICT COURTS; REMOVAL OF CASES FROM STATE COURTS

§ 1452. Removal of claims related to bankruptcy cases

(a) A party may remove any claim or cause of action in a civil action other than a proceeding before the United States Tax Court or a civil action by a governmental unit to enforce such governmental unit's police or regulatory power, to the district court for the district where such civil action is pending, if such district court has jurisdiction of such claim or cause of action under section 1334 of this title.

(b) The court to which such claim or cause of action is removed may remand such claim or cause of action on any equitable ground. An order entered under this subsection remanding a claim or cause of action, or a decision to not remand, is not reviewable by appeal or otherwise by the court of appeals under section 158(d), 1291, or 1292 of this title or by the Supreme Court of the United States under section 1254 of this title.

(Added Pub.L. 98–353, Title I, § 103(a), July 10, 1984, 98 Stat. 335, and amended Pub.L. 101–650, Title III, § 309(c), Dec. 1, 1990, 104 Stat. 5113.)

HISTORICAL AND STATUTORY NOTES

Revision Notes and Legislative Reports

1984 Acts. Statements by Legislative Leaders, see 1984 U.S. Code Cong. and Adm. News, p. 576.

1990 Acts. Senate Report No. 101–416, House Report Nos. 101–123, 101–512, 101–514, 101–734, and 101–735, and Statement by President, see 1990 U.S. Code Cong. and Adm. News, p. 6802.

Effective and Applicability Provisions

1984 Acts. Section effective July 10, 1984, see section 122(a) of Pub.L. 98–353, set out as a note under section 151 of this title.

CHAPTER 123—FEES AND COSTS

§ 1913. Courts of appeals

The fees and costs to be charged and collected in each court of appeals shall be prescribed from time to time by the Judicial Conference of the United States. Such fees and costs shall be reasonable and uniform in all the circuits.

(June 25, 1948, c. 646, 62 Stat. 954.)

JUDICIAL CONFERENCE SCHEDULE OF FEES

Court of Appeals Miscellaneous Fee Schedule

(Issued in accordance with 28 U.S.C. § 1913)

(Effective 01/01/2007)

The following are fees to be charged for services provided by the courts of appeals. No fees are to be charged for services rendered on behalf of the United States, with the exception of those specifically prescribed in items 2, 4 and 5. No fees under this schedule shall be charged to federal agencies or programs which are funded from judiciary appropriations, including, but not limited to, agencies, organizations, and individuals providing services authorized by the Criminal Justice Act, 18 U.S.C. § 3006A, and Bankruptcy Administrator programs.

(1) For docketing a case on appeal or review, or docketing any other proceeding, $450. A separate fee shall be paid by each party filing a notice of appeal in the district court, but parties filing a joint notice of appeal in the district court are required to pay only one fee. A docketing fee shall not be charged for the docketing of an application for the allowance of an interlocutory appeal under 28 U.S.C. § 1292(b), unless the appeal is allowed. A docketing fee shall not be charged for the docketing of a direct bankruptcy appeal or a direct bankruptcy cross appeal when the fee has been collected by the bankruptcy court in accordance with Item 15 or Item 21 of the Bankruptcy Court Miscellaneous Fee Schedule.

(2) For every search of the records of the court and certifying the results thereof, $26. This fee shall apply to services rendered on behalf of the United States if the information requested is available through electronic access.

(3) For certifying any document or paper, whether the certification is made directly on the document, or by separate instrument, $9.

(4) For reproducing any record or paper, 50 cents per page. This fee shall apply to paper copies made from either: (1) original documents; or (2) microfiche or microfilm reproductions of the original records. This fee shall apply to services rendered on behalf of the United States if the record or paper requested is available through electronic access.

(5) For reproduction of recordings of proceedings, regardless of the medium, $26, including the cost of materials. This fee shall apply to services rendered on behalf of the United States if the reproduction of the recording is available electronically.

(6) For reproduction of the record in any appeal in which the requirement of an appendix is dispensed with by any court of appeals pursuant to Rule 30(f), F.R.A.P., a flat fee of $71.

(7) For each microfiche or microfilm copy of any court record, where available, $5.

(8) For retrieval of a record from a Federal Records Center, National Archives, or other storage location removed from the place of business of the court, $45.

(9) For a check paid into the court which is returned for lack of funds, $45.

(10) Fees to be charged and collected for copies of opinions shall be fixed, from time to time, by each court, commensurate with the cost of printing.

(11) The court may charge and collect fees commensurate with the cost of providing copies of the local rules of court. The court may also distribute copies of the local rules without charge.

(12) The clerk shall assess a charge for the handling of registry funds deposited with the court, to be assessed from interest earnings and in accordance with the detailed fee schedule issued by the Director of the Administrative Office of the United States Courts.

(13) Upon the filing of any separate or joint notice of appeal or application for appeal from the Bankruptcy Appellate Panel, or notice of the allowance of an appeal from the Bankruptcy Appellate Panel, or of a writ of certiorari, $5 shall be paid by the appellant or petitioner.

(14) The court may charge and collect a fee of $200 per remote location for counsel's requested use of videoconferencing equipment in connection with each oral argument.

(15) For original admission of attorneys to practice, $150 each, including a certificate of admission. For a duplicate certificate of admission or certificate of good standing, $15.

ELECTRONIC PUBLIC ACCESS FEE SCHEDULE (eff. 3/11/2008)

As directed by Congress, the Judicial Conference has determined that the following fees are necessary to reimburse expenses incurred by the judiciary in providing electronic public access to court records. These fees shall apply to the United States unless otherwise stated. No fees under this schedule shall be charged to federal agencies or programs which are funded from judiciary appropriations, including, but not limited to, agencies, organizations, and individuals providing services authorized by the Criminal Justice Act, 18 U.S.C. § 3006A, and bankruptcy administrator programs.

I. For electronic access to court data via a federal judiciary Internet site: 8 cents per page, with the total for any document, docket sheet, or case-specific report not to exceed the fee for 30 pages—provided however that transcripts of federal court proceedings shall not be subject to the 30–page fee limit. Attorneys of record and parties in a case (including pro se litigants) receive one free electronic copy of all documents filed electronically, if receipt is required by law or directed by the filer. No fee is owed under this provision until an account holder accrues charges of more than $10 in a calendar year. Consistent with Judicial Conference policy, courts may, upon a showing of cause, exempt indigents, bankruptcy case trustees, individual researchers associated with educational institutions, courts, section 501(c)(3) not-for-profit organizations, court appointed pro bono attorneys, and pro bono ADR neutrals from payment of these fees. Courts must find that parties from the classes of persons or entities listed above seeking exemption have demonstrated that an exemption is necessary in order to avoid unreasonable burdens and to promote public access to information. Any user granted an exemption agrees not to sell for profit the data obtained as a result. Any transfer of data obtained as the result of a fee exemption is prohibited unless expressly authorized by the court. Exemptions may be granted for a definite period of time and may be revoked at the discretion of the court granting the exemption.

II. For printing copies of any record or document accessed electronically at a public terminal in the courthouse: 10 cents per page. This fee shall apply to services rendered on behalf of the United States if the record requested is remotely available through electronic access.

III. For every search of court records conducted by the PACER Service Center, $26 per name or item searched.

IV. For the PACER Service Center to reproduce on paper any record pertaining to a PACER account, if this information is remotely available through electronic access, 50 cents per page.

V. For a check paid to the PACER Service Center which is returned for lack of funds, $45.

JUDICIAL CONFERENCE POLICY NOTES

Courts should not exempt local, state or federal government agencies, members of the media, attorneys or others not members of one of the groups listed above. Exemptions should be granted as the exception, not the rule. A court may not use this exemption language to exempt all users. An exemption applies only to access related to the case or purpose for which it was given. The prohibition on transfer of information received without fee is not intended to bar a quote or reference to information received as a result of a fee exemption in a scholarly or other similar work.

The electronic public access fee applies to electronic court data viewed remotely from the public records of individual cases in the court, including filed documents and the docket sheet. Electronic court data may be viewed free at public terminals at the courthouse and courts may provide other local court information at no cost. Examples of information that can be provided at no cost include: local rules, court forms, news items, court calendars, opinions, and other information—such as court hours, court location, telephone listings—determined locally to benefit the public and the court.

Miscellaneous Fee Schedules

Registry Fund Fees

Effective June 12, 1989, a fee will be assessed for handling funds deposited in noncriminal proceedings with the court and held in interest bearing accounts or instruments pursuant to 28 U.S.C. § 2041 and Federal Rules of Civil Procedure rule 67. For new accounts, i.e., investments made on or after June 12, 1989, the fee will be equal to the first 45 days income earned on the deposit. Each subsequent deposit of new principal in the same case or proceeding will be subject to the fee. Reinvestment of prior deposits will not be subject to the fee. For existing accounts, i.e., investments held by the court prior to June 12, 1989, a fee will be assessed equal to the first 45 days of income earned beginning 30 days after June 12, 1989. Subsequent deposits of new principal in the same account will be subject to the fee. Subsequent reinvestment of existing deposits will not be subject to the fee.

The fee will apply only once to each sum deposited regardless of the length of time deposits are held and will not exceed income actually earned on the account.

The fee does not apply in the District Courts of Guam, Northern Mariana Islands, the Virgin Islands, the United States Claims Court, or other courts whose fees are not set under 28 U.S.C. §§ 1913, 1914, and 1930.

Registry Fund Fees—Item 12
(55 F.R. 42867, October 24, 1990)

Effective December 1, 1990, the registry fee assessment provisions were revised and converted from a one-time charge equal to all income earned in the first 45 days of the investment to a charge of 10 percent of the income earned while funds are held in the court registry. Additionally, the fee was extended to any funds placed in the court's registry and invested regardless of the nature of the action underlying the deposit.

The new method will not be applied on investments in cases from which a fee has been exacted based on the prior method (interest earned in the first 45 days the funds were invested or the first 45 days following July 12, 1989). The new method will also not be applied in cases where the investment instrument has a maturity date greater than one year, but where a fee under the prior method applies but has not been deducted.

The fee does not apply in the District Courts of Guam, the Northern Mariana Islands, the Virgin Islands, the United States Claims Court, or any other federal court whose fees are not set under 28 U.S.C. §§ 1913, 1914, and 1930.

Registry Fund Fees—Item 12
(56 F.R. 56356, November 4, 1991)

Effective February 3, 1992, the registry fee assessment provisions are revised and converted from a charge equal to 10 percent of the income earned while funds are held in the court's registry to a variable rate based on the amount deposited with the court and, in certain cases, the length of time funds are held in the court's registry.

The revised fee will be a fee of 10 percent of the total income received during each income period from investments of less than $100,000,000 of registry funds in income-bearing accounts. On investments exceeding $100,000,000 the 10 percent fee shall be reduced by one percent for each increment of $50,000,000 over the initial $100,000,000. For those deposits where funds are placed in the registry by court order for a time certain, for example, by the terms of an adjudicated trust, the fee will be further reduced. This further reduction will amount to 2.5 percent for each five-year interval or part thereof. The total minimum fee to be charged will be no less than two percent of the income on investments.

The following table sets out the fee schedule promulgated by this notice:

REGISTRY—SCHEDULE OF FEES

[% of income earned]

Amount of deposit *	0–5 yrs.	>5–10 yrs.	>10–15 yrs.	>15 yrs.
less than 100M	10	7.5	5.0	2.5
100M–<150M	9	6.5	4.0	2.0
150M–<200M	8	5.5	3.0	2.0
200M–<250M	7	4.5	2.0	2.0
250M–<300M	6	3.5	2.0	2.0

Amount of deposit *	0–5 yrs.	>5–10 yrs.	>10–15 yrs.	>15 yrs.
300M–<350M	5	2.5	2.0	2.0
350M–<400M	4	2.0	2.0	2.0
400M–<450M	3	2.0	2.0	2.0
over 450M	2	2.0	2.0	2.0

* Except where otherwise authorized by the Director, each deposit into any account is treated separately in determining the fee.

The new fee applies to all earnings applied to investments on and after the effective date of this change, except for earnings on investments in cases being administered under the provisions of the May 11, 1989 notice [54 FR 20407], i.e., to which the fee equal to the first 45 days income is applicable.

The fee, as modified herein, will continue to apply to any case where the court has authorized the investment of funds placed in its custody or held by it in trust in its registry regardless of the nature of the underlying action.

The fee does not apply in the District Court of Guam, the Northern Mariana Islands, the Virgin Islands, the United States Claims Court, or any other Federal court whose fees are not set under 28 U.S.C. §§ 1913, 1914, and 1930.

HISTORICAL AND STATUTORY NOTES

Revision Notes and Legislative Reports

1948 Acts. Based on Title 28, U.S.C., 1940 ed., § 543 (Mar. 3, 1891, c. 517, § 2, 26 Stat. 826; Feb. 19, 1897, c. 263, 29 Stat. 536; Sept. 27, 1944, c. 413, 58 Stat. 743).

Words "and in the United States Circuit Court of Appeals for the District of Columbia" were omitted as covered by "each court of appeals."

Judicial Conference of Senior Circuit Judges was changed to Judicial Conference "of the United States" in conformity with section 331 of this title.

Changes were made in phraseology. 80th Congress House Report No. 308.

Appeals Filed in Courts of Appeals

Pub.L. 109–171, Title X, § 10001(b), Feb. 8, 2006, 120 Stat. 183, provided that: "The $250 fee for docketing a case on appeal or review, or docketing any other proceeding, in a court of appeals, as prescribed by the Judicial Conference, effective as of January 1, 2005, under section 1913 of title 28, United States Code [this section], shall be increased to $450."

[This note effective 60 days after Feb. 8, 2006, see Pub.L. 109–171, § 10001(d), set out as a note under 28 U.S.C.A. § 1914]

Court Fees for Electronic Access to Information

Pub.L. 102–140, Title III, § 303, Oct. 28, 1991, 105 Stat. 810, as amended Pub.L. 104–317, Title IV, § 403(b), Oct. 19, 1996, 110 Stat. 3854; Pub.L. 107–347, Title II, § 205(e), Dec. 17, 2002, 116 Stat. 2915, provided that:

"**(a)** The Judicial Conference may, only to the extent necessary, prescribe reasonable fees, pursuant to sections 1913, 1914, 1926, 1930, and 1932 of title 28, United States Code [this section and sections 1914, 1926, 1930, and 1932 of this title], for collection by the courts under those sections for access to information available through automatic data processing equipment. These fees may distinguish between classes of persons, and shall provide for exempting persons or classes of persons from the fees, in order to avoid unreasonable burdens and to promote public access to such information. The Director of the Administrative Office of the United States Courts, under the direction of the Judicial Conference of the United States, shall prescribe a schedule of reasonable fees for electronic access to information which the Director is required to maintain and make available to the public.

"**(b)** The Judicial Conference and the Director shall transmit each schedule of fees prescribed under paragraph (a) to the Congress at least 30 days before the schedule becomes effective. All fees hereafter collected by the Judiciary under paragraph (a) as a charge for services rendered shall be deposited as offsetting collections to the Judiciary Automation Fund pursuant to 28 U.S.C. 612(c)(1)(A) [section 612(c)(1)(A) of this title] to reimburse expenses incurred in providing these services."

[Amendment by Pub.L. 107–347, § 205, effective 120 days after Dec. 17, 2002, see section 402(a) of Pub.L. 107–347, set out as a note under 44 U.S.C.A. § 3601.]

Similar provisions were contained in the following prior appropriation Act:

Pub.L. 101–515, Title IV, § 404, Nov. 5, 1990, 104 Stat. 2132.

CROSS REFERENCES

Fees for sales of copies of rules of various Courts of Appeals, see 28 USCA § 2077.

Power of Judicial Conference of the United States, see 28 USCA § 331.

§ 1930. Bankruptcy fees

(a) The parties commencing a case under title 11 shall pay to the clerk of the district court or the clerk of the bankruptcy court, if one has been certified pursuant to section 156(b) of this title, the following filing fees:

(1) For a case commenced under—

(A) chapter 7 of title 11, $245, and

(B) chapter 13 of title 11, $235.

(2) For a case commenced under chapter 9 of title 11, equal to the fee specified in paragraph (3) for filing a case under chapter 11 of title 11. The amount by which the fee payable under this paragraph exceeds $300 shall be deposited in the fund established under section 1931 of this title.

(3) For a case commenced under chapter 11 of title 11 that does not concern a railroad, as defined in section 101 of title 11, $1,000.

(4) For a case commenced under chapter 11 of title 11 concerning a railroad, as so defined, $1,000.

(5) For a case commenced under chapter 12 of title 11, $200.

(6) In addition to the filing fee paid to the clerk, a quarterly fee shall be paid to the United States trustee, for deposit in the Treasury, in each case under chapter 11 of title 11 for each quarter (including any fraction thereof) until the case is converted or dismissed, whichever occurs first. The fee shall be $325 for each quarter in which disbursements total less than $15,000; $650 for each quarter in which disbursements total $15,000 or more but less than $75,000; $975 for each quarter in which disbursements total $75,000 or more but less than $150,000; $1,625 for each quarter in which disbursements total $150,000 or more but less than $225,000; $1,950 for each quarter in which disbursements total $225,000 or more but less than $300,000; $4,875 for each quarter in which disbursements total $300,000 or more but less than $1,000,000; $6,500 for each quarter in which disbursements total $1,000,000 or more but less than $2,000,000; $9,750 for each quarter in which disbursements total $2,000,000 or more but less than $3,000,000; $10,400 for each quarter in which disbursements total $3,000,000 or more but less than $5,000,000; $13,000 for each quarter in which disbursements total $5,000,000 or more but less than $15,000,000; $20,000 for each quarter in which disbursements total $15,000,000 or more but less than $30,000,000; $30,000 for each quarter in which disbursements total more than $30,000,000. The fee shall be payable on the last day of the calendar month following the calendar quarter for which the fee is owed.

(7) In districts that are not part of a United States trustee region as defined in section 581 of this title, the Judicial Conference of the United States may require the debtor in a case under chapter 11 of title 11 to pay fees equal to those imposed by paragraph (6) of this subsection. Such fees shall be deposited as offsetting receipts to the fund established under section 1931 of this title and shall remain available until expended.

An individual commencing a voluntary case or a joint case under title 11 may pay such fee in installments. For converting, on request of the debtor, a case under chapter 7, or 13 of title 11, to a case under chapter 11 of title 11, the debtor shall pay to the clerk of the district court or the clerk of the bankruptcy court, if one has been certified pursuant to section 156(b) of this title, a fee of the amount equal to the difference between the fee specified in paragraph (3) and the fee specified in paragraph (1).

(b) The Judicial Conference of the United States may prescribe additional fees in cases under title 11 of the same kind as the Judicial Conference prescribes under section 1914(b) of this title.

(c) Upon the filing of any separate or joint notice of appeal or application for appeal or upon the receipt of any order allowing, or notice of the allowance of, an appeal or a writ of certiorari $5 shall be paid to the clerk of the court, by the appellant or petitioner.

(d) Whenever any case or proceeding is dismissed in any bankruptcy court for want of jurisdiction, such court may order the payment of just costs.

(e) The clerk of the court may collect only the fees prescribed under this section.

(f)(1) Under the procedures prescribed by the Judicial Conference of the United States, the district court or the bankruptcy court may waive the filing fee in a case under chapter 7 of title 11 for an individual if the court determines that such individual has income less than 150 percent of the income official poverty line (as defined by the Office of Management and Budget, and revised annually in accordance with section 673(2) of the Omnibus Budget Reconciliation Act of 1981) applicable to a family of the size involved and is unable to pay that fee in installments. For purposes of this paragraph, the term "filing fee" means the filing fee required by subsection (a), or any other fee prescribed by the Judicial Conference under subsections (b) and (c) that is payable to the clerk upon the commencement of a case under chapter 7.

(2) The district court or the bankruptcy court may waive for such debtors other fees prescribed under subsections (b) and (c).

(3) This subsection does not restrict the district court or the bankruptcy court from waiving, in accordance with Judicial Conference policy, fees prescribed under this section for other debtors and creditors.

(Added Pub.L. 95–598, Title II, § 246(a), Nov. 6, 1978, 92 Stat. 2671, and amended Pub.L. 98–353, Title I, § 111(a), (b), July 10, 1984, 98 Stat. 342; Pub.L. 99–500, Title I, § 101(b) [Title IV, § 407(b)], Oct. 18, 1986, 100 Stat. 1783–64; Pub.L. 99–554, Title I, §§ 117, 144(f), Oct. 27, 1986, 100 Stat. 3095, 3097; Pub.L. 99–591, Title I, § 101(b) [Title IV, § 407(b)], Oct. 30, 1986, 100 Stat. 3341–64; Pub.L. 101–162, Title IV, § 406(a), Nov. 21, 1989, 103 Stat. 1016; Pub.L. 102–140, Title I, § 111(a), Oct. 28, 1991, 105 Stat. 795; Pub.L. 103–121, Title I, § 111(a)(1), (b)(1), Oct. 27, 1993, 107 Stat. 1164; Pub.L. 104–91, Title I, § 101(a), Jan. 6, 1996, 110 Stat. 11; Pub.L. 104–99, Title II, § 211, Jan. 26, 1996, 110 Stat. 37; Pub.L. 104–208, Div. A, Title I, § 101(a) [Title I, § 109(a)], Sept. 30, 1996, 110 Stat. 3009–18; Pub.L. 106–113, Div. B, § 1000(a)(1) [Title I, § 113], Nov. 29, 1999, 113 Stat. 1535, 1501A–20; Pub.L. 106–518, Title I, §§ 103 to 105, Nov. 13, 2000, 114 Stat. 2411; Pub.L. 109–8, Title III, § 325(a), Title IV, § 418, Apr. 20, 2005, 119 Stat. 98, 108; Pub.L. 109–13, Div. A, Title VI, § 6058(a), May 11, 2005, 119 Stat. 297; Pub.L. 109–171, Title X, § 10101(a), Feb. 8, 2006, 120 Stat. 184; Pub.L. 110–161, Div. B, Title II, § 213(a), Dec. 26, 2007, 121 Stat. 1914.)

JUDICIAL CONFERENCE SCHEDULE OF FEES

Bankruptcy Court Miscellaneous Fee Schedule

(Issued in accordance with 28 U.S.C. § 1930(b))

(Effective 10/1/2008)

[The Judicial Conference of the United States at its session on March 7–9, 1979, set forth the schedule of fees to be charged in bankruptcy courts pursuant to this section. That schedule became effective on October 1, 1979. At its sessions in March and September 1980, March, 1981, March, 1987, and March and September, 1988, the Judicial Conference amended the schedule of fees. The Administrative Office of the United States Courts provided for Registry Fund Fees effective June 12, 1989. At its September, 1989 meeting, the Judicial Conference again amended the schedule of fees, such amendments effective pursuant to 1989 Judicial Conference Statement. The schedule of fees was again amended by the Judicial Conference at its March, 1990 and September, 1990 meetings. At its 1991 meeting, the Judicial Conference amended the schedule of fees to be effective Feb. 3, 1992. At its March 1991 meeting the Judicial Conference adopted Item 23 to be effective Oct. 19, 1992, with later implementation. At its September, 1992 meeting the Judicial Conference amended Item 8 to be effective Dec. 1, 1992. At its March, 1993 meeting the Judicial Conference amended its fee schedule effective May 6, 1993. At its September, 1993 meeting the Judicial Conference amended its fee schedule to be effective November 8, 1993. At its 1994 meeting, the Judicial Conference amended its fee schedule to be effective January 1, 1995. At its September, 1995 meeting the Judicial Conference amended its fee schedule to be effective November 9, 1995, and at its 1996 meetings it adopted amendments to be effective April 1, 1996 and October 28, 1996. At its 1997 meeting the Judicial Conference amended its fee schedule to be effective January 1, 1998. At its 1999 meeting the Judicial Conference amended its fee schedule to be effective October 1, 1999. The Judicial Conference subsequently adopted amendments to its fee schedule effective February 1, 2001. At its March 2001 meeting the Judicial Conference amended its fee schedule to be effective July 1, 2001. The Judicial Conference adopted amendments to its fee schedule effective January 1, 2002; and effective November 1, 2003. The Judicial Conference at its March 16, 2004 meeting adopted amendments to its fee schedule to be effective June 1, 2004. The Judicial Conference adopted amendments to its fee schedule effective January 1, 2005; and effective September 20, 2005; and effective October 17, 2005; and effective January 1, 2007; and effective October 1, 2008.]

The fees included in the Bankruptcy Court Miscellaneous Fee Schedule are to be charged for services provided by the bankruptcy courts.

- The United States should not be charged fees under this schedule, with the exception of those specifically prescribed in Items 1, 3 and 5 when the information requested is available through remote electronic access.
- Federal agencies or programs that are funded from judiciary appropriations (agencies, organizations, and individuals providing services authorized by the Criminal Justice Act, 18 U.S.C. § 3006A, and bankruptcy administrators) should not be charged any fees under this schedule.

(1) For reproducing any document, $.50 per page. This fee applies to services rendered on behalf of the United States if the document requested is available through electronic access.

(2) For certification of any document, $9.

For exemplification of any document, $18.

(3) For reproduction of an audio recording of a court proceeding, $26. This fee applies to services rendered on behalf of the United States if the recording is available electronically.

(4) For filing an amendment to the debtor's schedules, lists of creditors, or mailing list, $26, except:

- The bankruptcy judge may, for good cause, waive the charge in any case.
- This fee must not be charged if—
  - the amendment is to change the address of a creditor or an attorney for a creditor listed on the schedules; or
  - the amendment is to add the name and address of an attorney for a creditor listed on the schedules.

(5) For conducting a search of the bankruptcy court records, $26 per name or item searched. This fee applies to services rendered on behalf of the United States if the information requested is available through electronic access.

(6) For filing a complaint, $250, except:

- If the trustee or debtor-in-possession files the complaint, the fee should be paid by the estate, if there is an estate.
- This fee must not be charged if—
  - the debtor is the plaintiff; or
  - a child support creditor or representative files the complaint and submits the form required by § 304(g) of the Bankruptcy Reform Act of 1994.

(7) For filing any document that is not related to a pending case or proceeding, $39.

(8) Administrative fee for filing a case under Title 11 or when a motion to divide a joint case under Title 11 is filed, $39.

(9) For payment to trustees pursuant to 11 U.S.C. § 330(b)(2), a $15 fee applies in the following circumstances:

- For filing a petition under Chapter 7.
- For filing a motion to reopen a Chapter 7 case.
- For filing a motion to divide a joint Chapter 7 case.
- For filing a motion to convert a case to a Chapter 7 case.
- For filing a notice of conversion to a Chapter 7 case.

(10) In addition to any fees imposed under Item 9, above, the following fees must be collected:

- For filing a motion to convert a Chapter 12 case to a Chapter 7 case or a notice of conversion pursuant to 11 U.S.C. § 1208(a), $45.
- For filing a motion to convert a Chapter 13 case to a Chapter 7 case or a notice of conversion pursuant to 11 U.S.C. § 1307(a), $10.

The fee amounts in this item are derived from the fees prescribed in 28 U. S.C. § 1930(a).

If the trustee files the motion to convert, the fee is payable only from the estate that exists prior to conversion.

If the filing fee for the chapter to which the case is requested to be converted is less than the fee paid at the commencement of the case, no refund may be provided.

(11) For filing a motion to reopen, the following fees apply:

- For filing a motion to reopen a Chapter 7 case, $245.
- For filing a motion to reopen a Chapter 9 case, $1000.
- For filing a motion to reopen a Chapter 11 case, $1000.

• For filing a motion to reopen a Chapter 12 case, $200.

• For filing a motion to reopen a Chapter 13 case, $235.

• For filing a motion to reopen a Chapter 15 case, $1000.

The fee amounts in this item are derived from the fees prescribed in 28 U. S.C. § 1930(a).

The reopening fee must be charged when a case has been closed without a discharge being entered.

The court may waive this fee under appropriate circumstances or may defer payment of the fee from trustees pending discovery of additional assets. If payment is deferred, the fee should be waived if no additional assets are discovered.

The reopening fee must not be charged in the following situations:

• to permit a party to file a complaint to obtain a determination under Rule 4007(b); or

• when a debtor files a motion to reopen a case based upon an alleged violation of the terms of the discharge under 11 U.S.C. § 524.

(12) For retrieval of a record from a Federal Records Center, National Archives, or other storage location removed from the place of business of the court, $45.

(13) For a check paid into the court which is returned for lack of funds, $45.

(14) For filing an appeal or cross appeal from a final judgment, $250.

This fee is collected in addition to the statutory fee of $5 that is collected under 28 U.S.C. § 1930(c) when a notice of appeal is filed.

Parties filing a joint notice of appeal should pay only one fee.

If a trustee or debtor in possession is the appellant, the fee must be payable only from the estate and to the extent there is any estate realized.

Upon notice from the court of appeals that a direct appeal or direct cross appeal has been authorized, an additional fee of $200 must be collected.

(15) For filing a case under Chapter 15 of the Bankruptcy Code, $1000.

This fee is derived from and equal to the fee prescribed in 28 U.S.C. § 1930(a)(4) for filing a case commenced under Chapter 11 of Title 11.

(16) The court may charge and collect fees commensurate with the cost of providing copies of the local rules of court. The court may also distribute copies of the local rules without charge.

(17) The clerk shall assess a charge for the handling of registry funds deposited with the court, to be assessed from interest earnings and in accordance with the detailed fee schedule issued by the Director of the Administrative Office of the United States Courts.

(18) For filing a motion to divide a joint case filed under 11 U.S.C. § 302, the following fees apply:

• For filing a motion to divide a joint Chapter 7 case, $245.

• For filing a motion to divide a joint Chapter 11 case, $1000.

• For filing a motion to divide a joint Chapter 12 case, $200.

• For filing a motion to divide a joint Chapter 13 case, $235.

These fees are derived from and equal to the filing fees prescribed in 28 U.S.C. § 1930(a).

(19) For filing the following motions, $150:

• To terminate, annul, modify or condition the automatic stay;

• To compel abandonment of property of the estate pursuant to Rule 6007(b) of the Federal Rules of Bankruptcy Procedure; or

• To withdraw the reference of a case or proceeding under 28 U.S.C. § 157(d).

This fee must not be collected in the following situations:

• For a motion for relief from the co-debtor stay;

• For a stipulation for court approval of an agreement for relief from a stay; or

• For a motion filed by a child support creditor or its representative, if the form required by § 304(g) of the Bankruptcy Reform Act of 1994 is filed.

ELECTRONIC PUBLIC ACCESS FEE SCHEDULE (eff. 3/11/2008)

As directed by Congress, the Judicial Conference has determined that the following fees are necessary to reimburse expenses incurred by the judiciary in providing electronic public access to court records. These fees shall apply to the United States unless otherwise stated. No fees under this schedule shall be charged to federal agencies or programs which are funded from judiciary appropriations, including, but not limited to, agencies, organizations, and individuals providing services authorized by the Criminal Justice Act, 18 U.S.C. § 3006A, and bankruptcy administrator programs.

I. For electronic access to court data via a federal judiciary Internet site: 8 cents per page, with the total for any document, docket sheet, or case-specific report not to exceed the fee for 30 pages—provided however that transcripts of federal court proceedings shall not be subject to the 30–page fee limit. Attorneys of record and parties in a case (including pro se litigants) receive one free electronic copy of all documents filed electronically, if receipt is required by law or directed by the filer. No fee is owed under this provision until an account holder accrues charges of more than $10 in a calendar year. Consistent with Judicial Conference policy, courts may, upon a showing of cause, exempt indigents, bankruptcy case trustees, individual researchers associated with educational institutions, courts, section 501(c)(3) not-for-profit organizations, court appointed pro bono attorneys, and pro bono ADR neutrals from payment of these fees. Courts must find that parties from the classes of persons or entities listed above seeking exemption have demonstrated that an exemption is necessary in order to avoid unreasonable burdens and to promote public access to information. Any user granted an exemption agrees not to sell for profit the data obtained as a result. Any transfer of data obtained as the result of a fee exemption is prohibited unless expressly authorized by the court. Exemptions may be granted for a definite period of time and may be revoked at the discretion of the court granting the exemption.

II. For printing copies of any record or document accessed electronically at a public terminal in the courthouse: 10 cents per page. This fee shall apply to services rendered on behalf of the United States if the record requested is remotely available through electronic access.

III. For every search of court records conducted by the PACER Service Center, $26 per name or item searched.

IV. For the PACER Service Center to reproduce on paper any record pertaining to a PACER account, if this information is remotely available through electronic access, 50 cents per page.

V. For a check paid to the PACER Service Center which is returned for lack of funds, $45.

JUDICIAL CONFERENCE POLICY NOTES

Courts should not exempt local, state or federal government agencies, members of the media, attorneys or others not members of one of the groups listed above. Exemptions should be granted as the exception, not the rule. A court may not use this exemption language to exempt all users. An exemption applies only to access related to the case or purpose for which it was given. The prohibition on transfer of information received without fee is not intended to bar a quote or reference to information received as a result of a fee exemption in a scholarly or other similar work.

The electronic public access fee applies to electronic court data viewed remotely from the public records of individual cases in the court, including filed documents and the docket sheet. Electronic court data may be viewed free at public terminals at the courthouse and courts may provide other local court information at no cost. Examples of information that can be provided at no cost include: local rules, court forms, news items, court calendars, opinions, and other information—such as court hours, court location, telephone listings—determined locally to benefit the public and the court.

STATEMENT RESPECTING 1988 AMENDMENTS FROM ADMINISTRATIVE OFFICE OF UNITED STATES COURTS

The Director of the Administrative Office of the United States Courts in a memorandum to the Chief Judges of the United States Courts of Appeals, United States District Courts, and United States Bankruptcy Courts, dated April 19, 1988, provided in part that: "The amendment establishing a fee for filing a petition ancillary to a foreign proceeding under § 304 of the Bankruptcy Code will become effective May 1, 1988. The amendment expanding the exemption for services rendered 'to the United States' to include services rendered to bankruptcy administrators simply expresses a policy which has been in effect since the creation of the bankruptcy administrator program by Congress in the Bankruptcy Judges, United States Trustees and Family Farmer Bankruptcy Act of 1986. [Pub.L. No. 99–554, § 302(d)(3)(I).]"

Statement from 1989 Meeting of Judicial Conference

The Judicial Conference, at the September 20, 1989 meeting, provided in part that Item 21 takes effect on December 21, 1989. The Conference further provided that: "The remaining fees, Items 20 and 22, take effect on January 11, 1990, pending approval of the Appropriations Committees."

Registry Fund Fees—Item 19
(54 FR 20407, May 11, 1989)

Effective June 12, 1989, a fee will be assessed for handling funds deposited in noncriminal proceedings with the court and held in interest bearing accounts or instruments pursuant to 28 U.S.C. § 2041 and Federal Rules of Civil Procedure rule 67. For new accounts, i.e., investments made on or after June 12, 1989, the fee will be equal to the first 45 days income earned on the deposit. Each subsequent deposit of new principal in the same case or proceeding will be subject to the fee. Reinvestment of prior deposits will not be subject to the fee. For existing accounts, i.e., investments held by the court prior to June 12, 1989, a fee will be assessed equal to the first 45 days of income earned beginning 30 days after June 12, 1989. Subsequent deposits of new principal in the same account will be subject to the fee. Subsequent reinvestment of existing deposits will not be subject to the fee.

The fee will apply only once to each sum deposited regardless of the length of time deposits are held and will not exceed income actually earned on the account.

The fee does not apply in the District Courts of Guam, Northern Mariana Islands, the Virgin Islands, the United States Claims Court, or other courts whose fees are not set under 28 U.S.C. § 1930.

Registry Fund Fees—Item 19
(55 F.R. 42867, October 24, 1990)

Effective December 1, 1990, the registry fee assessment provisions were revised and converted from a one-time charge equal to all income earned in the first 45 days of the investment to a charge of 10 percent of the income earned while funds are held in the court registry. Additionally, the fee was extended to any funds placed in the court's registry and invested regardless of the nature of the action underlying the deposit.

The new method will not be applied on investments in cases from which a fee has been exacted based on the prior method (interest earned in the first 45 days the funds were invested or the first 45 days following July 12, 1989). The new method will also not be applied in cases where the investment instrument has a maturity date greater than one year, but where a fee under the prior method applies but has not been deducted.

The fee does not apply in the District Courts of Guam, the Northern Mariana Islands, the Virgin Islands, the United States Claims Court, or any other federal court whose fees are not set under 28 U.S.C. §§ 1913, 1914, and 1930.

Registry Fund Fees—Item 19
(56 F.R. 56356, November 4, 1991)

Effective February 3, 1992, the registry fee assessment provisions are revised and converted from a charge equal to 10 percent of the income earned while funds are held in the court's registry to a variable rate based on the amount deposited with the court and, in certain cases, the length of time funds are held in the court's registry.

The revised fee will be a fee of 10 percent of the total income received during each income period from investments of less than $100,000,000 of registry funds in income-bearing accounts. On investments exceeding $100,000,000 the 10 percent fee shall be reduced by one percent for each increment of $50,000,000 over the initial $100,000,000. For those deposits where funds are placed in the registry by court order for a time certain, for example, by the terms of an adjudicated trust, the fee will be further reduced. This further reduction will amount to 2.5 percent for each five-year interval or part thereof. The total minimum fee to be charged will be no less than two percent of the income on investments.

The following table sets out the fee schedule promulgated by this notice:

REGISTRY—SCHEDULE OF FEES

[% of income earned]

Amount of deposit *	0–5 yrs.	>5–10 yrs.	>10–15 yrs.	>15 yrs.
less than 100M	10	7.5	5.0	2.5
100M–<150M	9	6.5	4.0	2.0
150M–<200M	8	5.5	3.0	2.0
200M–<250M	7	4.5	2.0	2.0
250M–<300M	6	3.5	2.0	2.0
300M–<350M	5	2.5	2.0	2.0
350M–<400M	4	2.0	2.0	2.0
400M–<450M	3	2.0	2.0	2.0
over 450M	2	2.0	2.0	2.0

The new fee applies to all earnings applied to investments on and after the effective date of this change, except for earnings on investments in cases being administered under the provisions of the May 11, 1989 notice [54 FR 20407], i.e., to which the fee equal to the first 45 days income is applicable.

The fee, as modified herein, will continue to apply to any case where the court has authorized the investment of funds placed in its custody or held by it in trust in its registry regardless of the nature of the underlying action.

The fee does not apply in the District Court of Guam, the Northern Mariana Islands, the Virgin Islands, the United States Claims Court, or any other Federal court whose fees are not set under 28 U.S.C. §§ 1913, 1914, and 1930.

HISTORICAL AND STATUTORY NOTES

Revision Notes and Legislative Reports

1978 Acts. Senate Report No. 95–989 and House Report No. 95–595, see 1978 U.S. Code Cong. and Adm. News, p. 5787.

1984 Acts. Statements by Legislative Leaders, see 1984 U.S. Code Cong. and Adm. News, p. 576.

1986 Acts. House Report No. 99–764 and House Conference Report No. 99–958, see 1986 U.S. Code Cong. and Adm. News, p. 5227.

Statement by President, see 1986 U.S. Code Cong. and Adm. News, p. 5627.

1989 Acts. Statement by President, see 1989 U.S. Code Cong. and Adm. News, p. 733–3.

1991 Acts. Statement by President, see 1991 U.S. Code Cong. and Adm. News, p. 507.

1999 Acts. Statement by President, see 1999 U.S. Code Cong. and Adm. News, p. 290.

2005 Acts. House Report No. 109–31(Part I), see 2005 U.S. Code Cong. and Adm. News, p. 88.

House Conference Report No. 109–72, see 2005 U.S. Code Cong. and Adm. News, p. 240.

2006 Acts. House Conference Report No. 109–362, see 2006 U.S. Code Cong. and Adm. News, p. 3.

Statement by President, see 2006 U.S. Code Cong. and Adm. News, p. S3.

2007 Acts. House Report No. 110–197, see 2007 U.S. Code Cong. and Adm. News, p. 661.

Statement by President, see 2007 U.S. Code Cong. and Adm. News, p. S34.

References in Text

Chapter 7, 11, 12, or 13 of title 11, referred to in text, is 11 U.S.C.A. § 701 et seq., 11 U.S.C.A. § 1101 et seq., 11 U.S.C.A. § 1201 et seq., or 11 U.S.C.A. § 1301 et seq., respectively.

Section 673(2) of the Omnibus Budget Reconciliation Act of 1981, referred to in subsec. (f)(1), is Pub.L. 97–35, Title VI, § 673(2), Aug. 13, 1981, as added Pub.L. 105–285, Title II, § 201, Oct. 27, 1998, 112 Stat. 2729, which is classified to 42 U.S.C.A. § 9902(2).

Codifications

Pub.L. 99–591 is a corrected version of Pub.L. 99–500.

The Chapter 11 filing fee will not change from its current amount of $1,000. It appears that Congress intended to increase chapter 11 filing fees from $1,000 to $2,750. However, there is a drafting error in the language of the Deficit Reduction Act of 2005 which references the incorrect statutory subsection [Pub.L. 109–171, Title X, § 10101(a)(2), Feb. 8, 2006, 120 Stat. 184]. Thus, the chapter 11 fee, at this time, is unaltered. See 2006 Amendments note set out under this section.

Section 101(a) of Pub.L. 104–91, as amended by section 211 of Pub.L. 104–99, provided in part that section 111(a) of the General Provisions for the Department of Justice in Title I of the Departments of Commerce, Justice, and State, the Judiciary, and Related Agencies Appropriations Act, 1996 (H.R. 2076) as passed by the House of Representatives on Dec. 6, 1995, was enacted into permanent law. Such section 111(a) of H.R. 2076 amended subsec. (a)(6) of this section. See 1996 Amendments note set out under this section.

Effective and Applicability Provisions

2007 Acts. Pub.L. 110–161, Div. B, Title II, § 213(b), Dec. 26, 2007, 121 Stat. 1914, provided that: "This section and the amendment made by this section [amending this section] shall take effect January 1, 2008, or the date of the enactment of this Act [Dec. 26, 2007], whichever is later."

2006 Acts. Pub.L. 109–171, Title X, § 10101(c), Feb. 8, 2006, 120 Stat. 184, provided that: "This section and the amendments made by this section [amending this section and enacting provisions set out as a note under 28 U.S.C.A. § 1931] shall take effect 60 days after the date of the enactment of this Act [Feb. 8, 2006]."

2005 Acts. Amendment by Pub.L. 109–13, § 6058(a), amending Pub.L. 109–8, § 325, which amended this section, effective immediately after the enactment of the Bankruptcy Abuse Prevention and Consumer Protection Act of 2005 [Pub.L. 109–8, Apr. 20, 2005, 119 Stat. 23], see Pub.L. 109–13, § 6058(b), set out as a note under 28 U.S.C.A. § 589a.

Except as otherwise provided, amendments by Pub.L. 109–8 effective 180 days after April 20, 2005, and inapplicable with respect to cases commenced under Title 11 before the effective date, see Pub.L. 109–8, § 1501, set out as a note under 11 U.S.C.A. § 101.

1999 Acts. Amendment by Pub.L. 106–113, [§ 113], effective 30 days after Nov. 29, 1999, see Pub.L. 106–113, [§ 113], set out as a note under section 589a of this title.

1993 Acts. Section 111(a) of Pub.L. 103–121 provided in part that amendment by section 111(a)(1) of Pub.L. 103–121, amending subsec. (a)(1) of this section, is effective 30 days after Oct. 27, 1993.

Section 111(b) of Pub.L. 103–121 provided in part that amendment by section 111(b)(1) of Pub.L. 103–121, amending subsec. (a)(3) of this section, is effective 30 days after Oct. 27, 1993.

1991 Acts. Amendment by Pub.L. 102–140 effective 60 days after the date of the enactment of Pub.L. 102–140, which was approved Oct. 28, 1991, see section 111(a) of Pub.L. 102–140, set out as a note under section 589a of this title.

1986 Acts. Amendment by Pub.L. 99–554 effective 30 days after Oct. 27, 1986, except as otherwise provided for, see section 302(a) of Pub.L. 99–554, set out as a note under section 581 of this title.

Amendment by Pub.L. 99–554, § 117(4), not to become effective in or with respect to certain specified judicial districts until, or apply to cases while pending in such district before, the expiration of the 270-day period beginning 30 days after Oct. 27, 1986, or of the 30-day period beginning on the date the Attorney General certifies under section 303 of Pub.L. 99–554 the region specified in a paragraph of section 581(a) of Title 28, as amended by section 111(a) of Pub.L. 99–554, that includes such district, whichever occurs first, see section 302(d)(1) of Pub.L. 99–554, set out as a note under section 581 of this title.

Amendment by Pub.L. 99–554, § 117(4), not to become effective in or with respect to certain specified judicial districts until, or apply to cases while pending in such district before, the expiration of the 2-year period beginning 30 days after Oct. 27, 1986, or of the 30-day period beginning on the date the Attorney General certifies under section 303 of Pub.L. 99–554 the region specified in a paragraph of section 581(a) of Title 28, as amended by section 111(a) of Pub.L. 99–554, that includes such district, whichever occurs first, see section 302(d)(2) of Pub.L. 99–554, set out as a note under section 581 of this title.

Amendment by Pub.L. 99–554, § 117(4), not to become effective in or with respect to judicial districts established for the States of Alabama and North Carolina until, or apply to cases while pending in such district before, such district elects to be included in a bankruptcy region established in section 581(a) of Title 28, as amended by section 111(a) of Pub.L. 99–554, or Oct. 1, 2002, whichever occurs first, and, except as otherwise provided for, with respect to cases under chapters 7, 11, 12, and 13 of Title 11 commenced before 30 days after Oct. 27, 1986, and pending in a judicial district in the States of Alabama or North Carolina before any election made under section 302(d)(3)(A) of Pub.L. 99–554 by such district becomes effective or Oct. 1, 2002, whichever occurs first, amendments by Pub.L. 99–554 not to apply until Oct. 1, 2003, or the expiration of the 1-year period beginning on the date such election becomes effective, whichever occurs first, and further, in any judicial district in Alabama or North Carolina not making the election described in section 302(d)(3)(A) of Pub.L. 99–554, any person appointed under regulations issued by the Judicial Conference to administer estates in cases under Title 11 authorized to establish, etc., a panel of private trustees, and to supervise cases and trustees in cases under chapters 7, 11, 12, and 13 of Title 11, until amendments by sections 201 to 231 of Pub.L. 99–554 effective in such district, see section 302(d)(3)(A) to (F), (H), (I) of Pub.L. 99–554, set out as a note under section 581 of this title.

Deposit in the general receipts of the Treasury of funds collected as a result of the amendments made by section 117 of Pub.L. 99–554 in a judicial district in the States of Alabama or North Carolina under section 1930(a) of Title 28 before the date the amendments made by sections 201 to 231 of Pub.L. 99–554 take effect in such districts, and notwithstanding section 589a of Title 28, see section 302(d)(3)(G) of Pub.L. 99–554, set out as a note under section 581 of this title.

Amendment by Pub.L. 99–554, § 117(4), except as otherwise provided, with respect to cases under chapters 7, 11, 12, and 13 of Title 11 commenced before 30 days after Oct. 27, 1986, and pending in a judicial district referred to in section 581(a) of Title 28, as amended by section 111(a) of Pub.L. 99–554, for which a United States trustee is not authorized before 30 days after Oct. 27, 1986 to be appointed, not applicable until the expiration of the 3-year period beginning on Oct. 27, 1986, or of the 1-year period beginning on the date the Attorney General certifies under section 303 of Pub.L. 99–554 the region specified in a paragraph of such section 581(a) that includes, such district, whichever occurs first, see section 302(e)(1), (2) of Pub.L. 99–554, set out as a note under section 581 of this title.

Rule of construction regarding fees for cases under Title 11 for any conduct or period occurring before section 1930(a)(6) of Title 28 becomes effective in the district in which such case is pending, see section 302(e)(3) of Pub.L. 99–554, set out as a note under section 581 of this title.

1984 Acts. Amendment by Pub.L. 98–353 effective July 10, 1984, see section 122(a) of Pub.L. 98–353, set out as a note under section 151 of this title.

1979 Acts. Section effective Oct. 1, 1979, see section 402(c) of Pub.L. 95–598, set out as a note preceding section 101 of Title 11, Bankruptcy.

Use of Increased Receipts

Pub.L. 109–8, Title III, § 325(e), Apr. 20, 2005, 119 Stat. 99, which pertained to the use of increased receipts from fees under subsec. (a) of this section, was omitted in the general amendment of Pub.L. 109–8, § 325, by Pub.L. 109–13, Div. A, Title VI, § 6058(a), May 11, 2005, 119 Stat. 297. Such amendment by Pub.L. 109–13, § 6058(a), effective immediately after the enactment of the Bankruptcy Abuse Prevention and Consumer Protection Act of 2005 [Pub.L. 109–8, Apr. 20, 2005, 119 Stat. 23], see Pub.L. 109–13, § 6058(b), set out as a note under 28 U.S.C.A. § 589a.

[Except as otherwise provided, amendments by Pub.L. 109–8 effective 180 days after April 20, 2005, and inapplicable with respect to cases commenced under Title 11 before the effective date, see Pub.L. 109–8, § 1501, set out as a note under 11 U.S.C.A. § 101.]

Effective and Applicability Provisions of 1989 Amendments; Miscellaneous Fees

Section 406(a) of Pub.L. 101–162 provided in part that: "Pursuant to section 1930(b) of title 28 [subsec. (b) of this section] the Judicial Conference of the United States shall prescribe a fee of $60 on motions seeking relief from the automatic stay under 11 U.S.C. section 362(b) [section 362(b) of Title 11, Bankruptcy] and motions to compel abandonment of property of the estate. The fees established pursuant to the preceding two sentences shall take effect 30 days after the enactment of this Act [Nov. 21, 1989]."

Accrual and Payment of Quarterly Fees in Chapter 11 Cases After Jan. 27, 1996; Confirmation Status of Plans

Section 101(a) of Pub.L. 104–91, as amended Pub.L. 104–99, Title II, § 211, Jan. 26, 1996, 110 Stat. 37; Pub.L. 104–208, Div. A, Title I, § 101(a) [Title I, § 109(d)], Sept. 30, 1996, 110 Stat. 3009–19, provided, in part: "That, notwithstanding any other provision of law, the fees under 28 U.S.C. 1930(a)(6) [subsec. (a)(6) of this section] shall accrue and be payable from and after January 27, 1996, in all cases (including, without limitation, any cases pending as of that date), regardless of confirmation status of their plans."

Collection and Disposition of Fees in Bankruptcy Cases

Section 404(a) of Pub. L. 101–162 provided that: "For fiscal year 1990 and hereafter, such fees as shall be collected for the preparation and mailing of notices in bankruptcy cases as prescribed by the Judicial Conference of the United States pursuant to 28 U.S.C. 1930(b) [subsec. (b) of this section] shall be deposited to the 'Courts of Appeals, District Courts, and Other Judicial Services, Salaries and Expenses' appropriation to be used for salaries and other expenses incurred in providing these services."

Court Fees for Electronic Access to Information

Judicial Conference to prescribe reasonable fees for collection by courts under this section for access to information available through automatic data processing equipment and fees to be deposited in Judiciary Automation Fund, see section 303 of Pub.L. 102–140, set out as a note under section 1913 of this title.

Issuance of Notices to Creditors and Other Interested Parties

Section 403 of Pub.L. 101–162 provided that: "Notwithstanding any other provision of law, for fiscal year 1990 and hereafter, (a) The Administrative Office of the United States Courts, or any other agency or instrumentality of the United States, is prohibited from restricting solely to staff of the Clerks of the United States Bankruptcy Courts the issuance of notices to creditors and other interested parties. (b) The Administrative Office shall permit and encourage the preparation and mailing of such notices to be performed by or at the expense of the debtors, trustees or such other interested parties as the Court may direct and approve. (c) The Director of the Administrative Office of the United States Courts shall make appropriate provisions for the use of and accounting for any postage required pursuant to such directives."

Report on Bankruptcy Fees

Section 111(d) of Pub.L. 103–121 provided that:

"(1) **Report required.**—Not later than March 31, 1998, the Judicial Conference of the United States shall submit to the Committees on the Judiciary of the House of Representatives and the Senate, a report relating to the bankruptcy fee system and the impact of such system on various participants in bankruptcy cases.

"(2) **Contents of report.**—Such report shall include—

"(A)(i) an estimate of the costs and benefits that would result from waiving bankruptcy fees payable by debtors who are individuals, and

"(ii) recommendations regarding various revenue sources to offset the net cost of waiving such fees; and

"(B)(i) an evaluation of the effects that would result in cases under chapters 11 and 13 of title 11, United States Code [sections 1101 et seq. and 1301 et seq., respectively, of Title 11, Bankruptcy], from using a graduated bankruptcy fee system based on assets, liabilities, or both of the debtor, and

"(ii) recommendations regarding various methods to implement such a graduated bankruptcy fee system.

"(3) **Waiver of fees in selected districts.**—For purposes of carrying out paragraphs (1) and (2), the Judicial Conference of the United States shall carry out in not more than six judicial districts, throughout the 3–year period beginning on October 1, 1994, a program under which fees payable under section 1930 of title 28, United States Code [this section], may be waived in cases under chapter 7 of title 11, United States Code [section 701 et seq. of Title 11], for debtors who are individuals unable to pay such fees in installments.

"(4) **Study of graduated fee system.**—For purposes of carrying out paragraphs (1) and (2), the Judicial Conference of the United States shall carry out, in not fewer than six judicial districts, a study to estimate the results that would occur in cases under chapters 11 and 13 of title 11, United States Code [sections 1101 et seq. and 1301 et seq., respectively, of Title 11], if filing fees payable under section 1930 of title 28, United States Code [this section], were paid on a graduated scale based on assets, liabilities, or both of the debtor."

CROSS REFERENCES

Confirmation of reorganization plan contingent on payment of fees, see 11 USCA § 1129.

Recommendation for adjustment of dollar amounts of fees, see 11 USCA § 104.

United States Trustee System Fund, depositing of bankruptcy fees into Fund, see 28 USCA § 589a.

CHAPTER 131—RULES OF COURTS

§ 2075. Bankruptcy rules

The Supreme Court shall have the power to prescribe by general rules, the forms of process, writs, pleadings, and motions, and the practice and procedure in cases under title 11.

Such rules shall not abridge, enlarge, or modify any substantive right.

The Supreme Court shall transmit to Congress not later than May 1 of the year in which a rule prescribed under this section is to become effective a copy of the proposed rule. The rule shall take effect no earlier than December 1 of the year in which it is transmitted to Congress unless otherwise provided by law.

The bankruptcy rules promulgated under this section shall prescribe a form for the statement required under section 707(b)(2)(C) of title 11 and may provide general rules on the content of such statement.

(Added Pub.L. 88–623, § 1, Oct. 3, 1964, 78 Stat. 1001, and amended Pub.L. 95–598, Title II, § 247, Nov. 6, 1978, 92 Stat. 2672; Pub.L. 103–394, Title I, § 104(f), Oct. 22, 1994, 108 Stat. 4110; Pub.L. 109–8, Title XII, § 1232, Apr. 20, 2005, 119 Stat. 202.)

HISTORICAL AND STATUTORY NOTES

Revision Notes and Legislative Reports

1964 Acts. Senate Report No. 1561, see 1964 U.S. Code Cong. and Adm. News, p. 3804.

1978 Acts. Senate Report No. 95–989 and House Report No. 95–595, see 1978 U.S. Code Cong. and Adm. News, p. 5787.

1994 Acts. House Report No. 103–835, see 1994 U.S. Code Cong. and Adm. News, p. 3340.

2005 Acts. House Report No. 109–31(Part I), see 2005 U.S. Code Cong. and Adm. News, p. 88.

Effective and Applicability Provisions

2005 Acts. Except as otherwise provided, amendments by Pub.L. 109–8 effective 180 days after April 20, 2005, and inapplicable with respect to cases commenced under Title 11 before the effective date, see Pub.L. 109–8, § 1501, set out as a note under 11 U.S.C.A. § 101.

1994 Acts. Amendment by Pub.L. 103–394 effective on Oct. 22, 1994, and not to apply with respect to cases commenced under Title 11 of the United States Code before Oct. 22, 1994, see section 702 of Pub.L. 103–394, set out as a note under section 101 of Title 11, Bankruptcy.

1978 Acts. Amendment by Pub.L. 95–598 effective Nov. 6, 1978, see section 402(d) of Pub.L. 95–598, set out as a note preceding section 101 of Title 11, Bankruptcy.

Separability of Provisions

If any provision of or amendment made by Pub.L. 103–394 or the application of such provision or amendment to any person or circumstance is held to be unconstitutional, the remaining provisions of and amendments made by Pub.L. 103–394 and the application of such provisions and amendments to any person or circumstance shall not be affected thereby, see section 701 of Pub.L. 103–394, set out as a note under section 101 of Title 11, Bankruptcy.

Additional Rulemaking Power

Pub.L. 95–598, Title IV, § 410, Nov. 6, 1978, 92 Stat. 2687, provided that: "The Supreme Court may issue such additional rules of procedure, consistent with Acts of Congress, as may be necessary for the orderly transfer of functions and records and the orderly transition to the new bankruptcy court system created by this Act [see Tables for complete classification of Pub.L. 95–598]."

Applicability of Rules to Cases Under Title 11

Pub.L. 95–598, Title IV, § 405(d), Nov. 6, 1978, 92 Stat. 2685, provided that: "The rules prescribed under section 2075 of title 28 of the United States Code and in effect on September 30, 1979, shall apply to cases under title 11, to the extent not inconsistent with the amendments made by this Act, or with this Act [see Tables for complete classification of Pub.L. 95–598], until such rules are repealed or superseded by rules prescribed and effective under such section, as amended by section 248 of this Act."

Rules Promulgated by Supreme Court

Pub.L. 98–353, Title III, § 320, July 10, 1984, 98 Stat. 357, provided that: "The Supreme Court shall prescribe general rules implementing the practice and procedure to be followed under section 707(b) of title 11, United States Code [section 707(b) of Title 11, Bankruptcy]. Section 2075 of title 28, United States Code [this section], shall apply with respect to the general rules prescribed under this section."

*

BANKRUPTCY RULES

Amendments received to December 1, 2008

ORDER OF APRIL 26, 2004

1. That the Federal Rules of Bankruptcy Procedure be, and they hereby are, amended by including therein amendments to Bankruptcy Rules 1011, 2002, and 9014.

2. That the foregoing amendments to the Federal Rules of Bankruptcy Procedure shall take effect on December 1, 2004, and shall govern in all proceedings in bankruptcy cases thereafter commenced and, insofar as just and practicable, all proceedings then pending.

3. That THE CHIEF JUSTICE be, and hereby is, authorized to transmit to the Congress the foregoing amendments to the Federal Rules of Bankruptcy Procedure in accordance with the provisions of Section 2075 of Title 28, United States Code.

ORDER OF APRIL 25, 2005

1. That the Federal Rules of Bankruptcy Procedure be, and they hereby are, amended by including therein amendments to Bankruptcy Rules 1007, 2002, 3004, 3005, 7004, 9001, 9006, and 9036.

2. That the foregoing amendments to the Federal Rules of Bankruptcy Procedure shall take effect on December 1, 2005, and shall govern in all proceedings in bankruptcy cases thereafter commenced and, insofar as just and practicable, all proceedings then pending.

3. That THE CHIEF JUSTICE be, and hereby is, authorized to transmit to the Congress the foregoing amendments to the Federal Rules of Bankruptcy Procedure in accordance with the provisions of Section 2075 of Title 28, United States Code.

ORDER OF APRIL 12, 2006

1. That the Federal Rules of Bankruptcy Procedure be, and they hereby are, amended by including therein amendments to Bankruptcy Rules 1009, 5005, and 7004.

2. That the foregoing amendments to the Federal Rules of Bankruptcy Procedure shall take effect on December 1, 2006, and shall govern in all proceedings in bankruptcy cases thereafter commenced and, insofar as just and practicable, all proceedings then pending.

3. That THE CHIEF JUSTICE be, and hereby is, authorized to transmit to the Congress the foregoing amendments to the Federal Rules of Bankruptcy Procedure in accordance with the provisions of Section 2075 of Title 28, United States Code.

ORDER OF APRIL 30, 2007

1. That the Federal Rules of Bankruptcy Procedure be, and they hereby are, amended by including therein amendments to Bankruptcy Rules 1014, 3007, 4001, 6006, 7007.1, and new Rules 6003, 9005.1, and 9037.

2. That the foregoing amendments to the Federal Rules of Bankruptcy Procedure shall take effect on December 1, 2007, and shall govern in all proceedings in bankruptcy cases thereafter commenced and, insofar as just and practicable, all proceedings then pending.

3. That THE CHIEF JUSTICE be, and hereby is, authorized to transmit to the Congress the foregoing amendments to the Federal Rules of Bankruptcy Procedure in accordance with the provisions of Section 2075 of Title 28, United States Code.

ORDER OF APRIL 23, 2008

1. That the Federal Rules of Bankruptcy Procedure be, and they hereby are, amended by including therein amendments to Bankruptcy Rules 1005, 1006, 1007, 1009, 1010, 1011, 1015, 1017, 1019, 1020, 2002, 2003, 2007.1, 2015, 3002, 3003, 3016, 3017.1, 3019, 4002, 4003, 4004, 4006, 4007, 4008, 5001, 5003, 6004, 7012, 7022, 7023.1, 8001, 8003, 9006, 9009, and 9024, and new Rules 1021, 2007.2, 2015.1, 2015.2, 2015.3, 5008, and 6011.

2. That the foregoing amendments to the Federal Rules of Bankruptcy Procedure shall take effect on December 1, 2008, and shall govern in all proceedings in bankruptcy cases thereafter commenced and, insofar as just and practicable, all proceedings then pending.

3. That THE CHIEF JUSTICE be, and hereby is, authorized to transmit to the Congress the foregoing amendments to the Federal Rules of Bankruptcy Procedure in accordance with the provisions of Section 2075 of Title 28, United States Code.

Rule 1001. Scope of Rules and Forms; Short Title

The Bankruptcy Rules and Forms govern procedure in cases under title 11 of the United States Code.

The rules shall be cited as the Federal Rules of Bankruptcy Procedure and the forms as the Official Bankruptcy Forms. These rules shall be construed to secure the just, speedy, and inexpensive determination of every case and proceeding.

(As amended Mar. 30, 1987, eff. Aug. 1, 1987; Apr. 30, 1991, eff. Aug. 1, 1991.)

ADVISORY COMMITTEE NOTES

Section 247 of Public Law 95–598, 92 Stat. 2549 amended 28 U.S.C. § 2075 by omitting the last sentence. The effect of the amendment is to require that procedural rules promulgated pursuant to 28 U.S.C. § 2075 be consistent with the bankruptcy statute, both titles 11 and 28 U.S.C. Thus, although Rule 1001 sets forth the scope of the bankruptcy rules and forms, any procedural matters contained in title 11 or 28 U.S.C. with respect to cases filed under 11 U.S.C. would control. See 1 Collier, Bankruptcy ¶3.04[2][c] (15th ed. 1980).

28 U.S.C. § 151 establishes a United States Bankruptcy Court in each district as an adjunct to the district court. This provision does not, however, become effective until April 1, 1984. Public Law 95–598, § 402(b). From October 1, 1979 through March 31, 1984, the courts of bankruptcy as defined in § 1(10) of the Bankruptcy Act [former § 1(10) of this title], and created in § 2a of that Act [former § 11(a) of this title], continue to be the courts of bankruptcy. Public Law 95–598, § 404(a). From their effective date these rules and forms are to be applicable in cases filed under chapters 7, 9, 11 and 13 of title 11 regardless of whether the court is established by the Bankruptcy Act or by 28 U.S.C. § 151. Rule 9001 contains a broad and general definition of "bankruptcy court," "court" and "United States Bankruptcy Court" for this purpose.

"Bankruptcy Code" or "Code" as used in these rules means title 11 of the United States Code, the codification of the bankruptcy law. Public Law 95–598, § 101. See Rule 9001.

"Bankruptcy Act" as used in the notes to these rules means the Bankruptcy Act of 1898 as amended which was repealed by § 401(a) of Public Law 95–598.

These rules apply to all cases filed under the Code except as otherwise specifically stated.

The final sentence of the rule is derived from former Bankruptcy Rule 903. The objective of "expeditious and economical administration" of cases under the Code has frequently been recognized by the courts to be "a chief purpose of the bankruptcy laws." See Katchen v. Landy, 382 U.S. 323, 328 (1966); Bailey v. Glover, 88 U.S. (21 Wall.) 342, 346–47 (1874); Ex parte Christy, 44 U.S. (3 How.) 292, 312–14, 320–22 (1845). The rule also incorporates the wholesome mandate of the last sentence of Rule 1 of the Federal Rules of Civil Procedure. 2 Moore, Federal Practice ¶1.13 (2d ed. 1980); 4 Wright & Miller, Federal Practice and Procedure—Civil § 1029 (1969).

1987 Amendments

Title I of the Bankruptcy Amendments and Federal Judgeship Act of 1984, Pub.L. No. 98–353, 98 Stat. 333 (hereinafter the 1984 amendments), created a new bankruptcy judicial system in which the role of the district court was substantially increased. 28 U.S.C. § 1334 confers on the United States district courts original and exclusive jurisdiction over all cases under title 11 of the United States Code and original but not exclusive jurisdiction over civil proceedings arising under title 11 and civil proceedings arising in or related to a case under title 11.

Pursuant to 28 U.S.C. § 157(a) the district court may but need not refer cases and proceedings within the district court's jurisdiction to the bankruptcy judges for the district. Judgments or orders of the bankruptcy judges entered pursuant to 28 U.S.C. § 157(b)(1) and (c)(2) are subject to appellate review by the district courts or bankruptcy appellate panels under 28 U.S.C. § 158(a).

Rule 81(a)(1) F.R.Civ.P. provides that the civil rules do not apply to proceedings in bankruptcy, except as they may be made applicable by rules promulgated by the Supreme Court, *e.g.,* Part VII of these rules. This amended Bankruptcy Rule 1001 makes the Bankruptcy Rules applicable to cases and proceedings under title 11, whether before the district judges or the bankruptcy judges of the district.

1991 Amendments

The citation to these rules is amended to conform to the citation form of the Federal Rules of Civil Procedure, Federal Rules of Appellate Procedure, and Federal Rules of Criminal Procedure.

CROSS REFERENCES

Promulgation of bankruptcy rules by Supreme Court, see 28 USCA § 2075.

Scope of rules, see Federal Rules of Appellate Procedure Rule 1, 28 USCA.

Applicability of rules, see Fed.Rules Civ.Proc. Rule 81, 28 USCA.

Scope of rules, see Fed.Rules Civ.Proc. Rule 1, 28 USCA.

Applicability of rules, see Fed.Rules Evid. Rule 1101, 28 USCA.

Scope of rules, see Fed.Rules Evid. Rule 101, 28 USCA.

PART I—COMMENCEMENT OF CASE: PROCEEDINGS RELATING TO PETITION AND ORDER FOR RELIEF

Rule 1002. Commencement of Case

(a) Petition

A petition commencing a case under the Code shall be filed with the clerk.

(b) Transmission to United States trustee

The clerk shall forthwith transmit to the United States trustee a copy of the petition filed pursuant to subdivision (a) of this rule.

(As amended Mar. 30, 1987, eff. Aug. 1, 1987; Apr. 30, 1991, eff. Aug. 1, 1991.)

ADVISORY COMMITTEE NOTES

Under §§ 301–303 of the Code, a voluntary or involuntary case is commenced by filing a petition with the bankruptcy court. The voluntary petition may request relief under chapter 7, 9, 11, or 13 whereas an involuntary petition may be filed under only chapter 7 or 11. Section 109 of the Code specifies the types of debtors for whom the different forms of relief are available and § 303(a) indicates the persons against whom involuntary petitions may be filed.

The rule in subdivision (a) is in harmony with the Code in that it requires the filing to be with the bankruptcy court.

The number of copies of the petition to be filed is specified in this rule but a local rule may require additional copies. This rule provides for filing sufficient copies for the court's files and for the trustee in a chapter 7 or 13 case.

Official Form No. 1 may be used to seek relief voluntarily under any of the chapters. Only the original need be signed and verified, but the copies must be conformed to the original. See Rules 1008 and 9011(c). As provided in § 362(a) of the Code, the filing of a petition acts as a stay of certain acts and proceedings against the debtor, property of the debtor, and property of the estate.

ADVISORY COMMITTEE NOTES

1987 Amendments

Rules 1002(a), governing a voluntary petition, 1003(a), governing an involuntary petition, and 1003(e), governing a petition in a case ancillary to a foreign proceedings, are combined into this Rule 1002. If a bankruptcy clerk has been appointed for the district, the petition is filed with the bankruptcy clerk. Otherwise, the petition is filed with the clerk of the district court.

The elimination of the reference to the Official Forms of the petition is not intended to change the practice. Rule 9009 provides that the Official Forms "shall be observed and used" in cases and proceedings under the Code.

Subdivision (b) which provided for the distribution of copies of the petition to agencies of the United States has been deleted. Some of these agencies no longer wish to receive copies of the petition, while others not included in subdivision (b) have now requested copies. The Director of the Administrative Office will determine on an ongoing basis which government agencies will be provided a copy of the petition.

The number of copies of a petition that must be filed is a matter for local rule.

1991 Amendments

Subdivision (b) is derived from Rule X–1002(a). The duties of the United States trustee pursuant to the Code and 28 U.S.C. § 586(a) require that the United States trustee be apprised of the commencement of every case under chapters 7, 11, 12 and 13 and this is most easily accomplished by providing that office with a copy of the petition. Although 28 U.S.C. § 586(a) does not give the United States trustee an administrative role in chapter 9 cases, § 1102 of the Code requires the United States trustee to appoint committees and that section is applicable in chapter 9 cases pursuant to § 901(a). It is therefore appropriate that the United States trustee receive a copy of every chapter 9 petition.

Notwithstanding subdivision (b), pursuant to Rule 5005(b)(3), the clerk is not required to transmit a copy of the petition to the United States trustee if the United States trustee requests that it not be transmitted. Many rules require the clerk to transmit a certain document to the United States trustee, but Rule 5005(b)(3) relieves the clerk of that duty under this or any other rule if the United States trustee requests that such document not be transmitted.

CROSS REFERENCES

Commencement of voluntary cases, see 11 USCA § 301.

Debtors for whom relief available, see 11 USCA § 109.

Joint cases, see 11 USCA § 302.

Number of copies—

Involuntary petition, see Fed.Rules Bankr.Proc. Rule 1003, 11 USCA.

Schedules, statements, and lists, see Fed.Rules Bankr. Proc. Rule 1007, 11 USCA.

Signing and verification of petitions, see Fed.Rules Bankr. Proc. Rules 1008 and 9011, 11 USCA.

Stay of acts and proceedings against debtor and estate property, see 11 USCA § 362.

Rule 1003. Involuntary Petition

(a) Transferor or transferee of claim

A transferor or transferee of a claim shall annex to the original and each copy of the petition a copy of all documents evidencing the transfer, whether transferred unconditionally, for security, or otherwise, and a signed statement that the claim was not transferred for the purpose of commencing the case and setting forth the consideration for and terms of the transfer. An entity that has transferred or acquired a claim for the purpose of commencing a case for liquidation under chapter 7 or for reorganization under chapter 11 shall not be a qualified petitioner.

(b) Joinder of petitioners after filing

If the answer to an involuntary petition filed by fewer than three creditors avers the existence of 12 or more creditors, the debtor shall file with the answer a list of all creditors with their addresses, a brief statement of the nature of their claims, and the amounts thereof. If it appears that there are 12 or more creditors as provided in § 303(b) of the Code, the court shall afford a reasonable opportunity for other creditors to join in the petition before a hearing is held thereon.

(As amended Mar. 30, 1987, eff. Aug. 1, 1987.)

ADVISORY COMMITTEE NOTES

Subdivision (a). Official Form No. 11 (Involuntary Case: Creditors' Petition), is prescribed for use by petitioning creditors to have a debtor's assets liquidated under chapter 7 of the Code or the business reorganized under chapter 11. It contains the required allegations as specified in § 303(b) of the Code. Official Form 12 is prescribed for use by fewer than all the general partners to obtain relief for the partnership as governed by § 303(b)(3) of the Code and Rule 1004(b).

Although the number of copies to be filed is specified in Rule 1002, a local rule may require additional copies.

Only the original need be signed and verified, but the copies must be conformed to the original. See Rules 1008 and 9011(c). The petition must be filed with the bankruptcy court. This provision implements § 303(b) which provides that an involuntary case is commenced by filing the petition with the court.

As provided in § 362 of the Code, the filing of the petition acts as a stay of certain acts and proceedings against the debtor, the debtor's property and property of the estate.

Subdivision (c) retains the explicitness of former Bankruptcy Rule 104(d) that a transfer of a claim for the purpose of commencing a case under the Code is a ground for disqualification of a party to the transfer as a petitioner.

Section 303(b) "is not intended to overrule Bankruptcy Rule 104(d), which places certain restrictions on the transfer of claims for the purpose of commencing an involuntary case." House Report No. 95–595, 95th Cong., 1st Sess. (1977) 322; Senate Report No. 95–989, 95th Cong., 2d Sess. (1978) 33.

The subdivision requires disclosure of any transfer of the petitioner's claim as well as a transfer to the petitioner and applies to transfers for security as well as unconditional transfers. Cf. In re 69th & Crandon Bldg. Corp., 97 F.2d 392, 395 (7th Cir.), cert. denied, 305 U.S. 629 (1938), recognizing the right of a creditor to sign a bankruptcy petition notwithstanding a prior assignment of his claim for the purpose of security. This rule does not, however, qualify the requirement of § 303(b)(1) that a petitioning creditor must have a claim not contingent as to liability.

Subdivision (d). Section 303(c) of the Code permits a creditor to join in the petition at any time before the case is dismissed or relief is ordered. While this rule does not require the court to give all creditors notice of the petition, the list of creditors filed by the debtor affords a petitioner the information needed to enable him to give notice for the purpose of obtaining the co-petitioners required to make the petition sufficient. After a reasonable opportunity has been afforded other creditors to join in an involuntary petition, the hearing on the petition should be held without further delay.

Subdivision (e). This subdivision implements § 304. A petition for relief under § 304 may only be filed by a foreign representative who is defined in § 101(20) generally as a representative of an estate in a foreign proceeding. The term "foreign proceeding" is defined in § 101(19).

Section 304(b) permits a petition filed thereunder to be contested by a party in interest. Subdivision (e)(2) therefore requires that the summons and petition be served on any person against whom the relief permitted by § 304(b) is sought as well as on any other party the court may direct.

The rules applicable to the procedure when an involuntary petition is filed are made applicable generally when a case ancillary to a foreign proceeding is commenced. These rules include Rule 1010 with respect to issuance and service of a summons, Rule 1011 concerning responsive pleadings and motions, and Rule 1018 which makes various rules in Part VII applicable in proceedings on contested petitions.

The venue for a case ancillary to a foreign proceeding is provided in 28 U.S.C. § 1474.

1987 Amendments

The subject matter of subdivisions (a), (b), and (e) has been incorporated in Rules 1002, 1010, 1011, and 1018.

CROSS REFERENCES

Case ancillary to foreign proceeding—

Commencement of and contested petitions, see 11 USCA § 304.

Foreign proceeding and foreign representative defined, see 11 USCA § 101.

Debtors for whom relief available, see 11 USCA § 109.

Number of copies—

Voluntary petition, see Fed.Rules Bankr.Proc. Rule 1002, 11 USCA.

Requisite allegations and joinder of parties, see 11 USCA § 303.

Signing and verification of petitions, see Fed.Rules Bankr. Proc. Rules 1008 and 9011, 11 USCA.

Stay of acts and proceedings against debtor and estate property, see 11 USCA § 362.

Rule 1004. Involuntary Petition Against a Partnership

After filing of an involuntary petition under § 303(b)(3) of the Code, (1) the petitioning partners or other petitioners shall promptly send to or serve on each general partner who is not a petitioner a copy of the petition; and (2) the clerk shall promptly issue a summons for service on each general partner who is not a petitioner. Rule 1010 applies to the form and service of the summons.

(As amended Apr. 29, 2002, eff. Dec. 1, 2002.)

ADVISORY COMMITTEE NOTES

This rule is adapted from former Bankruptcy Rule 105 and complements §§ 301 and 303(b)(3) of the Code.

Subdivision (a) specifies that while all general partners must consent to the filing of a voluntary petition, it is not necessary that they all execute the petition. It may be executed and filed on behalf of the partnership by fewer than all.

Subdivision (b) implements § 303(b)(3) of the Code which provides that an involuntary petition may be filed by fewer than all the general partners or, when all the general partners are debtors, by a general partner, trustee of the partner or creditors of the partnership. Rule 1010, which governs service of a petition and summons in an involuntary case, specifies the time and mode of service on the partnership. When a petition is filed against a partnership under § 303(b)(3), this rule requires an additional service on the nonfiling general partners. It is the purpose of this subdivision to protect the interests of the nonpetitioning partners and the partnership.

2002 Amendments

Section 303(b)(3)(A) of the Code provides that fewer than all of the general partners in a partnership may commence an involuntary case against the partnership. There is no counterpart provision in the Code setting out the manner in which a partnership commences a voluntary case. The Supreme Court has held in the corporate context that applicable nonbankruptcy law determines whether authority exists for a particular debtor to commence a bankruptcy case. *See Price v. Gurney*, 324 U.S. 100 (1945). The lower courts have followed this rule in the partnership context as well. *See, e.g., Jolly v. Pittore*, 170 B.R. 793 (S.D.N.Y. 1994); *Union Planters National Bank v. Hunters Horn Associates*, 158 B.R. 729 (Bankr. M.D. Tenn. 1993); *In re Channel 64 Joint Venture*, 61 B.R. 255 (Bankr. S.D. Oh. 1986). Rule 1004(a) could be construed as requiring the consent of all of the general partners to the filing of a voluntary petition, even if fewer than all of the general partners would have the authority under applicable nonbankruptcy law to commence a bankruptcy case for the partnership. Since this is a matter of substantive law beyond the scope of these rules, Rule 1004(a) is deleted as is the designation of subdivision (b).

The rule is retitled to reflect that it applies only to involuntary petitions filed against partnerships.

Changes Made After Publication and Comments. No changes since publication.

CROSS REFERENCES

Commencement of—

Involuntary cases, see 11 USCA § 303.

Voluntary cases, see 11 USCA § 301.

Contested petition by general partners, see Fed.Rules Bankr.Proc. Rule 1011, 11 USCA.

No change in status for purposes of state or local income tax law, see 11 USCA § 346.

Person defined to include partnership, see 11 USCA § 101.

Rule 1004.1. Petition for an Infant or Incompetent Person

If an infant or incompetent person has a representative, including a general guardian, committee, conservator, or similar fiduciary, the representative may file a voluntary petition on behalf of the infant or incompetent person. An infant or incompetent person who does not have a duly appointed representative may file a voluntary petition by next friend or guardian ad litem. The court shall appoint a guardian ad litem for an infant or incompetent person who is a debtor and is not otherwise represented or shall make any other order to protect the infant or incompetent debtor.

(Added Apr. 29, 2002, eff. Dec. 1, 2002.)

ADVISORY COMMITTEE NOTES

2002 Adoption

This rule is derived from Rule 17(c) F.R. Civ. P. It does not address the commencement of a case filed on behalf of a missing person. *See, e.g., In re King*, 234 B.R. 515 (Bankr. D.N.M. 1999).

Changes Made After Publication and Comments. No changes were made.

Rule 1005. Caption of Petition

The caption of a petition commencing a case under the Code shall contain the name of the court, the title of the case, and the docket number. The title of the case shall include the following information about the debtor: name, employer identification number, last four digits of the social-security number or individual debtor's taxpayer-identification number, any other federal taxpayer-identification number, and all other names used within eight years before filing the petition. If the petition is not filed by the debtor, it shall include all names used by the debtor which are known to the petitioners.

(As amended Mar. 30, 1987, eff. Aug. 1, 1987; Mar. 27, 2003, eff. Dec. 1, 2003; Apr. 23, 2008, eff. Dec. 1, 2008.)

ADVISORY COMMITTEE NOTES

The title of the case should include all names used by the debtor, such as trade names, former married names and maiden name. See also Official Form No. 1 and the Advisory Committee Note to that Form. Additional names of the debtor are also required to appear in the caption of each notice to creditors. See Rule 2002(m).

2003 Amendments

The rule is amended to implement the Judicial Conference policy to limit the disclosure of a party's social security number and similar identifiers. Under the rule, as amended, only the last four digits of the debtor's social security number need be disclosed. Publication of the employer identification number does not present the same identity theft or privacy protection issues. Therefore, the caption must include the full employer identification number.

Debtors must submit with the petition a statement setting out their social security numbers. This enables the clerk to include the full social security number on the notice of the section 341 meeting of creditors, but the statement itself is not submitted in the case or maintained in the case file.

2008 Amendments

The rule is amended to require the disclosure of all names used by the debtor in the past eight years. Section 727(a)(8) was amended in 2005 to extend the time between chapter 7 discharges from six to eight years, and the rule is amended to implement that change. The rule also is amended to require the disclosure of the last four digits of an individual debtor's taxpayer-identification number. This truncation of the number applies only to individual debtors. This is consistent with the requirements of Rule 9037.

CROSS REFERENCES

Conformance of captions of creditor notices with this rule, see Fed.Rules Bankr.Proc. Rule 2002, 11 USCA.

General requirements of form for petition, see Fed.Rules Bankr.Proc. Rule 9004, 11 USCA.

Rule 1006. Filing Fee

(a) General requirement

Every petition shall be accompanied by the filing fee except as provided in subdivisions (b) and (c) of this rule. For the purpose of this rule, "filing fee" means the filing fee prescribed by 28 U.S.C. § 1930(a)(1)–(a)(5) and any other fee prescribed by the Judicial Conference of the United States under 28 U.S.C. § 1930(b) that is payable to the clerk upon the commencement of a case under the Code.

(b) Payment of filing fee in installments

(1) Application to pay filing fee in installments

A voluntary petition by an individual shall be accepted for filing if accompanied by the debtor's signed application, prepared as prescribed by the appropriate Official Form, stating that the debtor is unable to pay the filing fee except in installments.

(2) Action on application

Prior to the meeting of creditors, the court may order the filing fee paid to the clerk or grant leave to pay in installments and fix the number, amount and dates of payment. The number of installments shall not exceed four, and the final installment shall be payable not later than 120 days after filing the petition. For cause shown, the court may extend the time of any installment, provided the last installment is paid not later than 180 days after filing the petition.

(3) Postponement of attorney's fees

All installments of the filing fee must be paid in full before the debtor or chapter 13 trustee may make further payments to an attorney or any other person who renders services to the debtor in connection with the case.

(c) Waiver of filing fee

A voluntary chapter 7 petition filed by an individual shall be accepted for filing if accompanied by the debtor's application requesting a waiver under 28 U.S.C. § 1930(f), prepared as prescribed by the appropriate Official Form.

(As amended Mar. 30, 1987, eff. Aug. 1, 1987; Apr. 23, 1996, eff. Dec. 1, 1996; Apr. 23, 2008, eff. Dec. 1, 2008.)

ADVISORY COMMITTEE NOTES

1983 Enactments

28 U.S.C. § 1930 specifies the filing fees for petitions under chapters 7, 9, 11 and 13 of the Code. It also permits the payment in installments by individual debtors.

Subdivision (b) is adapted from former Bankruptcy Rule 107. The administrative cost of installments in excess of four is disproportionate to the benefits conferred. Prolonging the period beyond 180 days after the commencement of the case causes undesirable delays in administration. Paragraph (2) accordingly continues the imposition of a maximum of four on the number of installments and retains the maximum period of installment payments allowable on an original application at 120 days. Only in extraordinary cases should it be necessary to give an applicant an extension beyond the four months. The requirement of paragraph (3) that filing fees be paid in full before the debtor may pay an attorney for services in connection with the case codifies the rule declared in In re Latham, 271 Fed. 538 (N.D.N.Y.1921), and In re Darr, 232 Fed. 415 (N.D.Cal.1916).

1987 Amendments

Subdivision (b)(3) is expanded to prohibit payments by the debtor or the chapter 13 trustee not only to attorneys but to any person who renders services to the debtor in connection with the case.

1996 Amendments

The Judicial Conference prescribes miscellaneous fees pursuant to 28 U.S.C. § 1930(b). In 1992, a $30 miscellaneous administrative fee was prescribed for all chapter 7 and chapter 13 cases. The Judicial Conference fee schedule was amended in 1993 to provide that an individual debtor may pay this fee in installments.

Subdivision (a) of this rule is amended to clarify that every petition must be accompanied by any fee prescribed under 28 U.S.C. § 1930(b) that is required to be paid when a petition is filed, as well as the filing fee prescribed by 28 U.S.C. § 1930(a). By defining "filing fee" to include Judicial Conference fees, the procedures set forth in subdivision (b) for paying the filing fee in installments will also apply with respect to any Judicial Conference fee required to be paid at the commencement of the case.

GAP Report on Rule 1006. No changes since publication, except for a stylistic change in subdivision (a).

2008 Amendments

Subdivision (a) is amended to include a reference to new subdivision (c), which deals with fee waivers under 28 U.S.C. § 1930(f), which was added in 2005.

Subdivision (b)(1) is amended to delete the sentence requiring a disclosure that the debtor has not paid an attorney or other person in connection with the case. Inability to pay the filing fee in installments is one of the requirements for a fee waiver under the 2005 revisions to 28 U. S.C. § 1930(f). If the attorney payment prohibition were retained, payment of an attorney's fee would render many debtors ineligible for installment payments and thus enhance their eligibility for the fee waiver. The deletion of this prohibition from the rule, which was not statutorily required, ensures that debtors who have the financial ability to pay the fee in installments will do so rather than request a waiver.

Subdivision (b)(3) is amended in conformance with the changes to subdivision (b)(1) to reflect the 2005 amendments. The change is meant to clarify that subdivision (b)(3) refers to payments made after the debtor has filed the bankruptcy case and after the debtor has received permission to pay the fee in installments. Otherwise, the subdivision may conflict with the intent and effect of the amendments to subdivision (b)(1).

CROSS REFERENCES

District court; filing and miscellaneous fees; rules of court, see 28 USCA § 1914.

Enlargement of time for payment of filing fee installments permitted as limited under this rule, see Fed.Rules Bankr. Proc. Rule 9006, 11 USCA.

Specific amount of fee, see 28 USCA § 1930.

Rule 1007. Lists, Schedules, Statements, and Other Documents; Time Limits

(a) Corporate ownership statement, list of creditors and equity security holders, and other lists

(1) Voluntary case

In a voluntary case, the debtor shall file with the petition a list containing the name and address of each entity included or to be included on Schedules D, E, F, G, and H as prescribed by the Official Forms. If the debtor is a corporation, other than a governmental unit, the debtor shall file with the petition a corporate ownership statement containing the information described in Rule 7007.1. The debtor shall file a supplemental statement promptly upon any change in circumstances that renders the corporate ownership statement inaccurate.

(2) Involuntary case

In an involuntary case, the debtor shall file within 15 days after entry of the order for relief, a list containing the name and address of each entity included or to be included on Schedules D, E, F, G, and H as prescribed by the Official Forms.

(3) Equity security holders

In a chapter 11 reorganization case, unless the court orders otherwise, the debtor shall file within 15 days after entry of the order for relief a list of the debtor's equity security holders of each class showing the number and kind of interests registered in the name of each holder, and the last known address or place of business of each holder.

(4) Chapter 15 case

In addition to the documents required under § 1515 of the Code, a foreign representative filing a petition for recognition under chapter 15 shall file with the petition: (A) a corporate ownership statement containing the information described in Rule 7007.1; and (B) unless the court orders otherwise, a list containing the names and addresses of all persons or bodies authorized to administer foreign proceedings of the debtor, all parties to litigation pending in the United States in which the debtor is a party at the time of the filing of the petition, and all entities against whom provisional relief is being sought under § 1519 of the Code.

(5) Extension of time

Any extension of time for the filing of the lists required by this subdivision may be granted only on motion for cause shown and on notice to the United States trustee and to any trustee, committee elected under § 705 or appointed under § 1102 of the Code, or other party as the court may direct.

(b) Schedules, statements, and other documents required

(1) Except in a chapter 9 municipality case, the debtor, unless the court orders otherwise, shall file the following schedules, statements, and other documents, prepared as prescribed by the appropriate Official Forms, if any:

(A) schedules of assets and liabilities;

(B) a schedule of current income and expenditures;

(C) a schedule of executory contracts and unexpired leases;

(D) a statement of financial affairs;

(E) copies of all payment advices or other evidence of payment, if any, received by the debtor from an employer within 60 days before the filing of the petition, with redaction of all but the last four digits of the debtor's social-security number or individual taxpayer-identification number; and

(F) a record of any interest that the debtor has in an account or program of the type specified in § 521(c) of the Code.

(2) An individual debtor in a chapter 7 case shall file a statement of intention as required by § 521(a) of the Code, prepared as prescribed by the appropriate Official Form. A copy of the statement of intention shall be served on the trustee and the creditors named in the statement on or before the filing of the statement.

(3) Unless the United States trustee has determined that the credit counseling requirement of § 109(h) does not apply in the district, an individual debtor must file a statement of compliance with the credit counseling requirement, prepared as prescribed by the appropriate Official Form which must include one of the following:

(A) an attached certificate and debt repayment plan, if any, required by § 521(b);

(B) a statement that the debtor has received the credit counseling briefing required by § 109(h)(1) but does not have the certificate required by § 521(b);

(C) a certification under § 109(h)(3); or

(D) a request for a determination by the court under § 109(h)(4).

(4) Unless § 707(b)(2)(D) applies, an individual debtor in a chapter 7 case shall file a statement of current monthly income prepared as prescribed by the appropriate Official Form, and, if the current monthly income exceeds the median family income for the applicable state and household size, the information, including calculations, required by § 707(b), prepared as prescribed by the appropriate Official Form.

(5) An individual debtor in a chapter 11 case shall file a statement of current monthly income, prepared as prescribed by the appropriate Official Form.

(6) A debtor in a chapter 13 case shall file a statement of current monthly income, prepared as prescribed by the appropriate Official Form, and, if the current monthly income exceeds the median family income for the applicable state and household size, a calculation of disposable income made in accordance with § 1325(b)(3), prepared as prescribed by the appropriate Official Form.

(7) An individual debtor in a chapter 7 or chapter 13 case shall file a statement of completion of a course concerning personal financial management, prepared as prescribed by the appropriate Official Form. An individual debtor shall file the statement in a chapter 11 case in which § 1141(d)(3) applies.

(8) If an individual debtor in a chapter 11, 12, or 13 case has claimed an exemption under § 522(b)(3)(A) in property of the kind described in § 522(p)(1) with a value in excess of the amount set out in § 522(q)(1), the debtor shall file a statement as to whether there is any proceeding pending in which the debtor may be found guilty of a felony of a kind described in § 522(q)(1)(A) or found liable for a debt of the kind described in § 522(q)(1)(B).

(c) Time limits

In a voluntary case, the schedules, statements, and other documents required by subdivision (b)(1), (4), (5), and (6) shall be filed with the petition or within 15 days thereafter, except as otherwise provided in subdivisions (d), (e), (f), and (h) of this rule. In an involuntary case, the list in subdivision (a)(2), and the schedules, statements, and other documents required by subdivision (b)(1) shall be filed by the debtor within 15 days of the entry of the order for relief. In a voluntary case, the documents required by paragraphs (A), (C), and (D) of subdivision (b)(3) shall be filed with the petition. Unless the court orders otherwise, a debtor who has filed a statement under subdivision (b)(3)(B), shall file the documents required by subdivision (b)(3)(A) within 15 days of the order for relief. In a chapter 7 case, the debtor shall file the statement required by subdivision (b)(7) within 45 days after the first date set for the meeting of creditors under § 341 of the Code, and in a chapter 11 or 13 case no later than the date when the last payment was made by the debtor as required by the plan or the filing of a motion for a discharge under § 1141(d)(5)(B) or § 1328(b) of the Code. The court may, at any time and in its discretion, enlarge the time to file the statement required by subdivision (b)(7). The debtor shall file the statement required by subdivision (b)(8) no earlier than the date of the last payment made under the plan or the date of the filing of a motion for a discharge under §§ 1141(d)(5)(B), 1228(b), or 1328(b) of the Code. Lists, schedules, statements, and other documents filed prior to the conversion of a case to another chapter shall be deemed filed in the converted case unless the court directs otherwise. Except as provided in § 1116(3), any extension of time to file schedules, statements, and other documents required under this rule may be granted only on motion for cause shown and on notice to the United States trustee, any committee elected under § 705 or appointed under § 1102 of the Code, trustee, examiner, or other party as the court may direct. Notice of an extension shall be given to the United States trustee and to any committee, trustee, or other party as the court may direct.

(d) List of 20 largest creditors in chapter 9 municipality case or chapter 11 reorganization case

In addition to the list required by subdivision (a) of this rule, a debtor in a chapter 9 municipality case or a debtor in a voluntary chapter 11 reorganization case shall file with the petition a list containing the name, address and claim of the creditors that hold the 20 largest unsecured claims, excluding insiders, as prescribed by the appropriate Official Form. In an involuntary chapter 11 reorganization case, such list shall be filed by the debtor within 2 days after entry of the order for relief under § 303(h) of the Code.

(e) List in chapter 9 municipality cases

The list required by subdivision (a) of this rule shall be filed by the debtor in a chapter 9 municipality case within such time as the court shall fix. If a proposed plan requires a revision of assessments so that the proportion of special assessments or special taxes to be assessed against some real property will be different from the proportion in effect at the date the petition is filed, the debtor shall also file a list showing the name and address of each known holder of title, legal or equitable, to real property adversely affected. On motion for cause shown, the court may modify the requirements of this subdivision and subdivision (a) of this rule.

(f) Statement of social security number

An individual debtor shall submit a verified statement that sets out the debtor's social security number, or states that the debtor does not have a social security number. In a voluntary case, the debtor shall submit the statement with the petition. In an involuntary case, the debtor shall submit the statement within 15 days after the entry of the order for relief.

(g) Partnership and partners

The general partners of a debtor partnership shall prepare and file the list required under subdivision (a), the schedules of the assets and liabilities, schedule of current income and expenditures, schedule of executory contracts and unexpired leases, and statement of financial affairs of the partnership. The court may order any general partner to file a statement of personal assets and liabilities within such time as the court may fix.

(h) Interests acquired or arising after petition

If, as provided by § 541(a)(5) of the Code, the debtor acquires or becomes entitled to acquire any interest in property, the debtor shall within 10 days after the information comes to the debtor's knowledge or within such further time the court may allow, file a supplemental schedule in the chapter 7 liquidation case, chapter 11 reorganization case, chapter 12 family farmer's debt adjustment case, or chapter 13 individual debt adjustment case. If any of the property required to be reported under this subdivision is claimed by the debtor as exempt, the debtor shall claim the exemptions in the supplemental schedule. The duty to file a supplemental schedule in accordance with this subdivision continues notwithstanding the closing of the case, except that the schedule need not be filed in a chapter 11, chapter 12, or chapter 13 case with respect to property acquired after entry of the order confirming a chapter 11 plan or discharging the debtor in a chapter 12 or chapter 13 case.

(i) Disclosure of list of security holders

After notice and hearing and for cause shown, the court may direct an entity other than the debtor or trustee to disclose any list of security holders of the debtor in its possession or under its control, indicating the name, address and security held by any of them. The entity possessing this list may be required either to produce the list or a true copy thereof, or permit inspection or copying, or otherwise disclose the information contained on the list.

(j) Impounding of lists

On motion of a party in interest and for cause shown the court may direct the impounding of the lists filed under this rule, and may refuse to permit inspection by any entity. The court may permit inspection or use of the lists, however, by any party in interest on terms prescribed by the court.

(k) Preparation of list, schedules, or statements on default of debtor

If a list, schedule, or statement, other than a statement of intention, is not prepared and filed as required by this rule, the court may order the trustee, a petitioning creditor, committee, or other party to prepare and file any of these papers within a time fixed by the court. The court may approve reimbursement of the cost incurred in complying with such an order as an administrative expense.

(*l*) Transmission to United States trustee

The clerk shall forthwith transmit to the United States trustee a copy of every list, schedule, and statement filed pursuant to subdivision (a)(1), (a)(2), (b), (d), or (h) of this rule.

(m) Infants and incompetent persons

If the debtor knows that a person on the list of creditors or schedules is an infant or incompetent person, the debtor also shall include the name, address, and legal relationship of any person upon whom process would be served in an adversary proceeding against the infant or incompetent person in accordance with Rule 7004(b)(2).

(As amended Mar. 30, 1987, eff. Aug. 1, 1987; Apr. 30, 1991, eff. Aug. 1, 1991; Apr. 23, 1996, eff. Dec. 1, 1996; Apr. 23, 2001, eff. Dec. 1, 2001; Mar. 27, 2003, eff. Dec. 1, 2003; Apr. 25, 2005, eff. Dec. 1, 2005; Apr. 23, 2008, eff. Dec. 1, 2008.)

ADVISORY COMMITTEE NOTES

1983 Enactments

This rule is an adaptation of former Rules 108, 8–106, 10–108 and 11–11. As specified in the rule, it is applicable in all types of cases filed under the Code.

Subdivision (a) requires at least a list of creditors with their names and addresses to be filed with the petition. This list is needed for notice of the meeting of creditors (Rule 2002) and notice of the order for relief (§ 342 of the Code). The list will also serve to meet the requirements of § 521(1) of the Code. Subdivision (a) recognizes that it may be impossible to file the schedules required by § 521(1) and subdivision (b) of the rule at the time the petition is filed but in order for the case to proceed expeditiously and efficiently it is necessary that the clerk have the names and addresses of creditors. It should be noted that subdivision (d) of the rule requires a special list of the 20 largest unsecured creditors in chapter 9 and 11 cases. That list is for the purpose of selecting a committee of unsecured creditors.

Subdivision (b) is derived from former Rule 11–11 and conforms with § 521. This subdivision indicates the forms to be used. The court may dispense with the filing of schedules and the statement of affairs pursuant to § 521.

Subdivisions (c) and (f) specify the time periods for filing the papers required by the rule as well as the number of copies. The provisions dealing with an involuntary case are derived from former Bankruptcy Rule 108. Under the Code, a chapter 11 case may be commenced by an involuntary petition (§ 303(a)), whereas under the Act [former Title 11], a Chapter XI [former § 1101 et seq. of this title] case could have been commenced only by a voluntary petition. A motion for an extension of time to file the schedules and statements is required to be made on notice to parties, as the court may direct, including a creditors' committee if one has been appointed under § 1102 of the Code and a trustee or examiner if one has been appointed pursuant to § 1104 of the Code. Although written notice is preferable, it is not required by the rule; in proper circumstances the notice may be by telephone or otherwise.

Subdivision (d) is new and requires that a list of the 20 largest unsecured creditors, excluding insiders as defined in § 101(25) of the Code, be filed with the petition. The court, pursuant to § 1102 of the Code, is required to appoint a committee of unsecured creditors as soon as practicable after the order for relief. That committee generally is to consist of the seven largest unsecured creditors who are willing to serve. The list should, as indicated on Official Form No. 9, specify the nature and amount of the claim. It is important for the court to be aware of the different types of claims existing in the case and this form should supply such information.

Subdivision (e) applies only in chapter 9 municipality cases. It gives greater discretion to the court to determine the time for filing a list of creditors and any other matter related to the list. A list of creditors must at some point be filed since one is required by § 924 of the Code. When the plan affects special assessments, the definitions in § 902(2) and (3) for "special tax payer" and "special tax payer affected by the plan" become relevant.

Subdivision (g) is derived from former Rules 108(c) and 11–11. Nondebtor general partners are liable to the partnership's trustee for any deficiency in the partnership's estate to pay creditors in full as provided by § 723 of the Code. Subdivision (g) authorizes the court to require a partner to file a statement of personal assets and liabilities to provide the trustee with the relevant information.

Subdivision (h) is derived from former Bankruptcy Rule 108(e) for chapter 7, 11 and 13 purposes. It implements the provisions in and language of § 541(a)(5) of the Code.

Subdivisions (i) and (j) are adapted from §§ 165 and 166 of the Act [former §§ 565 and 566 of this title] and former Rule 10–108(b) and (c) without change in substance. The term "party in interest" is not defined in the Code or the rules, but reference may be made to § 1109(b) of the Code. In the context of this subdivision, the term would include the debtor, the trustee, any indenture trustee, creditor, equity security holder or committee appointed pursuant to § 1102 of the Code.

Subdivision (k) is derived from former Rules 108(d) and 10–108(a).

1987 Amendments

Subdivisions (b), (c), and (g) are amended to provide for the filing of a schedule of current income and current expenditures and the individual debtor's statement of intention. These documents are required by the 1984 amendments to § 521 of the Code. Official Form No. 6A is prescribed for use by an individual debtor for filing a schedule of current income and current expenditures in a chapter 7 or chapter 11 case. Although a partnership or corporation is also required by § 521(1) to file a schedule of current income and current expenditures, no Official Form is prescribed therefor.

The time for filing the statement of intention is governed by § 521(2)(A). A copy of the statement of intention must be served on the trustee and the creditors named in the statement within the same time. The provisions of subdivision (c) governing the time for filing when a chapter 11 or chapter 13 case is converted to a chapter 7 case have been omitted from subdivision (c) as amended. Filing after conversion is now governed exclusively by Rule 1019.

Subdivision (f) has been abrogated. The number of copies of the documents required by this rule will be determined by local rule.

Subdivision (h) is amended to include a direct reference to § 541(a)(5).

Subdivision (k) provides that the court may not order an entity other than the debtor to prepare and file the statement of intention.

1991 Amendments

References to Official Form numbers and to the Chapter 13 Statement are deleted and subdivision (b) is amended in anticipation of future revision and renumbering of the Official Forms. The debtor in a chapter 12 or chapter 13 case shall file the list, schedules and statements required in subdivisions (a)(1), (b)(1), and (h). It is expected that the information currently provided in the Chapter 13 Statement will be included in the schedules and statements as revised not later than the effective date of these rule amendments.

Subdivisions (a)(4) and (c) are amended to provide the United States trustee with notice of any motion to extend the time for the filing of any lists, schedules, or statements. Such notice enables the United States trustee to take appropriate steps to avoid undue delay in the administration of the case. See 28 U.S.C. § 586(a)(3)(G). Subdivisions (a)(4) and (c) are amended further to provide notice to committees elected under § 705 or appointed pursuant to § 1102 of the Code. Committees of retired employees appointed pursuant to § 1114 are not included.

The additions of references to unexpired leases in subdivisions (b)(1) and (g) indicate that the schedule requires the inclusion of unexpired leases as well as other executory contracts.

The words "with the court" in subdivisions (b)(1), (e), and (g) are deleted as unnecessary. See Rules 5005(a) and 9001(3).

Subdivision (*l*), which is derived from Rule X–1002(a), provides the United States trustee with the information required to perform certain administrative duties such as the appointment of a committee of unsecured creditors. In a chapter 7 case, the United States trustee should be aware of the debtor's intention with respect to collateral that secures a consumer debt so that the United States trustee may monitor the progress of the case. Pursuant to § 307 of the Code, the United States trustee has standing to raise, appear and be heard on issues and the lists, schedules and statements contain information that, when provided to the United States trustee, enable that office to participate effectively in the case. The United States trustee has standing to move to dismiss a chapter 7 or 13 case for failure to file timely the list, schedules or statement required by § 521(*l*) of the Code. See §§ 707(a)(3) and 1307(c)(9). It is therefore necessary for the United States trustee to receive notice of any extension of time to file such documents. Upon request, the United States trustee also may receive from the trustee or debtor in possession a list of equity security holders.

1996 Amendments

Subdivision (c) is amended to provide that schedules and statements filed prior to the conversion of a case to another chapter shall be deemed filed in the converted case, whether or not the case was a chapter 7 case prior to conversion. This amendment is in recognition of the 1991 amendments to the Official Forms that abrogated the Chapter 13 Statement and made the same forms for schedules and statements applicable in all cases.

This subdivision also contains a technical correction. The phrase "superseded case" creates the erroneous impression that conversion of a case results in a new case that is distinct from the original case. The effect of conversion of a case is governed by § 348 of the Code.

GAP Report on Rule 1007(c). No changes since publication, except for stylistic changes.

2001 Amendments

Subdivision (m) is added to enable the person required to mail notices under Rule 2002 to mail them to the appropriate guardian or other representative when the debtor knows that a creditor or other person listed is an infant or incompetent person.

The proper mailing address of the representative is determined in accordance with Rule 7004(b)(2), which requires mailing to the person's dwelling house or usual place of abode or at the place where the person regularly conducts a business or profession.

CHANGES MADE AFTER PUBLICATION AND COMMENTS

No changes were made.

2003 Amendments

This rule is amended to require the debtor to file a corporate ownership statement setting out the information described in Rule 7007.1. Requiring debtors to file the statement provides the court with an opportunity to make judicial disqualification determinations at the outset of the case. This could reduce problems later in the case by preventing the initial assignment of the case to a judge who holds a financial interest in a parent company of the debtor or some other entity that holds a significant ownership interest in the debtor. Moreover, by including the disclosure statement filing requirement at the commencement of the case, the debtor does not have to make the same disclosure filing each time it is involved in an adversary proceeding throughout the case. The debtor also must file supplemental statements as changes in ownership might arise.

The rule is amended to add a requirement that a debtor submit a statement setting out the debtor's social security number. The addition is necessary because of the corresponding amendment to Rule 1005 which now provides that the caption of the petition includes only the final four digits of the debtor's social security number. The debtor submits the statement, but it is not filed, nor is it included in the case file. The statement provides the information necessary to include on the service copy of the notice required under Rule 2002(a)(1). It will also provide the information to facilitate the ability of creditors to search the court record by a search of a social security number already in the creditor's possession.

2005 Amendments

Notice to creditors and other parties in interest is essential to the operation of the bankruptcy system. Sending notice requires a convenient listing of the names and addresses of the entities to whom notice must be sent, and virtually all of the bankruptcy courts have adopted a local rule requiring the submission of a list of these entities with the petition and in a particular format. These lists are commonly called the "mailing matrix."

Given the universal adoption of these local rules, the need for such lists in all cases is apparent. Consequently, the rule is amended to require the debtor to submit such a list at the commencement of the case. This list may be amended when necessary. See Rule 1009(a).

The content of the list is described by reference to Schedules D through H of the Official Forms rather than by reference to creditors or persons holding claims. The cross reference to the Schedules as the source of the names for inclusion in the list ensures that persons such as codebtors or nondebtor parties to executory contracts and unexpired leases will receive appropriate notices in the case.

While this rule renders unnecessary, in part, local rules on the subject, this rule does not direct any particular format or form for the list to take. Local rules still may govern those particulars of the list.

Subdivision (c) is amended to reflect that subdivision (a)(1) no longer requires the debtor to file a schedule of liabilities with the petition in lieu of a list of creditors. The filing of the list is mandatory, and subdivision (b) of the rule requires the filing of schedules. Thus, subdivision (c) no longer needs to account for the possibility that the debtor can delay filing a schedule of liabilities when the petition is accompanied by a list of creditors. Subdivision (c) simply addresses the situation in which the debtor does not file schedules or statements with the petition, and the procedure for seeking an extension of time for filing.

Other changes are stylistic.

2008 Amendments

The title of this rule is expanded to refer to "documents" in conformity with the 2005 amendments to § 521 and related provisions of the Bankruptcy Code that include a wider range of documentary requirements.

Subdivision (a) is amended to require that any foreign representative filing a petition for recognition to commence a case under chapter 15, which was added to the Code in 2005, file a list of entities with whom the debtor is engaged in litigation in the United States. The foreign representative filing the petition for recognition must also list any entities against whom provisional relief is being sought as well as all persons or bodies authorized to administer foreign proceedings of the debtor. This should ensure that entities most interested in the case, or their representatives, will receive notice of the petition under Rule 2002(q).

Subdivision (a)(4) is amended to require the foreign representative who files a petition for recognition under chapter 15 to file the documents described in § 1515 of the Code as well as a corporate ownership statement. The subdivision is also amended to identify the foreign representative in language that more closely follows the text of the Code. Former subdivision (a)(4) is renumbered as subdivision (a)(5) and stylistic changes were made to the subdivision.

Subdivision (b)(1) addresses schedules, statements, and other documents that the debtor must file unless the court orders otherwise and other than in a case under chapter 9. This subdivision is amended to include documentary requirements added by the 2005 amendments to § 521 that apply to the same group of debtors and have the same time limits as the existing requirements of (b)(1). Consistent with the E-Government Act of 2002, Pub. L. No. 107–347, the payment advices should be redacted before they are filed.

Subdivision (b)(2) is amended to conform to the renumbering of the subsections of § 521.

Subdivisions (b)(3) through (b)(8) are new and implement the 2005 amendments to the Code. Subdivision (b)(3) provides for the filing of a document relating to the credit counseling requirement provided by the 2005 amendments to § 109 in the context of an Official Form that warns the debtor of the consequences of failing to comply with the credit counseling requirement.

Subdivision (b)(4) addresses the filing of information about current monthly income, as defined in § 101, for certain chapter 7 debtors and, if required, additional calculations of expenses required by the 2005 amendments to § 707(b).

Subdivision (b)(5) addresses the filing of information about current monthly income, as defined in § 101, for individual chapter 11 debtors. The 2005 amendments to § 1129(a)(15) condition plan confirmation for individual debtors on the commitment of disposable income, as defined in § 1325(b)(2), which is based on current monthly income.

Subdivision (b)(6) addresses the filing of information about current monthly income, as defined in § 101, for chapter 13 debtors and, if required, additional calculations of expenses. These changes are necessary because the 2005 amendments to § 1325 require that the determination of disposable income begin with current monthly income.

Subdivision (b)(7) reflects the 2005 amendments to §§ 727 and 1328 of the Code that condition the receipt of a discharge on the completion of a personal financial management course, with certain exceptions. Certain individual chapter 11 debtors may also be required to complete a personal financial management course under § 727(a)(11) as incorporated by § 1141(d)(3)(C). To evidence compliance with that requirement, the subdivision requires the debtor to file the appropriate Official Form certifying that the debtor has completed the personal financial management course.

Subdivision (b)(8) requires an individual debtor in a case under chapter 11, 12, or 13 to file a statement that there are no reasonable grounds to believe that the restrictions on a homestead exemption as set out in § 522(q) of the Code are applicable. Sections 1141(d)(5)(C), 1228(f), and 1328(h) each provide that the court shall not enter a discharge order unless it finds that there is no reasonable cause to believe that § 522(q) applies. Requiring the debtor to submit a statement to that effect in cases under chapters 11, 12, and 13 in which an exemption is claimed in excess of the amount allowed under § 522(q)(1) provides the court with a basis to conclude, in the absence of any contrary information, that § 522(q) does not apply. Creditors receive notice under Rule 2002(f)(11) of the time to request postponement of the entry of the discharge to permit an opportunity to challenge the debtor's assertions in the Rule 1007(b)(8) statement in appropriate cases.

Subdivision (c) is amended to include time limits for the filing requirements added to subdivision (b) due to the 2005 amendments to the Code, and to make conforming amendments. Separate time limits are provided for the documentation of credit counseling and for the statement of the completion of the financial management course. While most documents relating to credit counseling must be filed with the voluntary petition, the credit counseling certificate and debt repayment plan can be filed within 15 days of the filing of a voluntary petition if the debtor files a statement under subdivision (b)(3)(B) with the petition. Sections 727(a)(11), 1141(d)(3), and 1328(g) of the Code require individual debtors to complete a personal financial management course prior to the entry of a discharge. The amendment allows the court to enlarge the deadline for the debtor to file the statement of completion. Because no party is harmed by the enlargement, no specific restriction is placed on the court's discretion to enlarge the deadline, even after its expiration.

Subdivision (c) of the rule is also amended to recognize the limitation on the extension of time to file schedules and statements when the debtor is a small business debtor. Section 1116(3), added to the Code in 2005, establishes a specific standard for courts to apply in the event that the debtor in possession or the trustee seeks an extension for filing these forms for a period beyond 30 days after the order for relief.

CROSS REFERENCES

Committee of seven unsecured creditors appointed in reorganization case, see 11 USCA § 1102.

Compliance with this rule upon conversion to liquidation case, see Fed.Rules Bankr.Proc. Rule 1019, 11 USCA.

Duty of debtor to—

- Inform trustee as to property location and name and address of money and property obligors, see Fed. Rules Bankr.Proc. Rule 4002, 11 USCA.
- Prepare and file schedule and statement, see 11 USCA § 521.

Enlargement of time for filing list of twenty largest unsecured creditors not permitted, see Fed.Rules Bankr.Proc. Rule 9006, 11 USCA.

Filing of proof of interest by equity security holder obviated by list filed by debtor, see Fed.Rules Bankr.Proc. Rule 3003, 11 USCA.

Immunity from self-incrimination, see 11 USCA § 344.

Insider for purposes of list of 20 unsecured claims defined, see 11 USCA § 101.

List of exempt property to be filed—

- By dependent of debtor, see Fed.Rules Bankr.Proc. Rule 4003, 11 USCA.
- With schedule of assets, see Fed.Rules Bankr.Proc. Rule 4003, 11 USCA.

Motions; form and service, see Fed.Rules Bankr.Proc. Rule 9013, 11 USCA.

Notice required for—

- Creditors' meetings, see Fed.Rules Bankr.Proc. Rule 2002, 11 USCA.
- Order for relief, see 11 USCA § 342.

Rule 1008. Verification of Petitions and Accompanying Papers

All petitions, lists, schedules, statements and amendments thereto shall be verified or contain an unsworn declaration as provided in 28 U.S.C. § 1746.

(As amended Apr. 30, 1991, eff. Aug. 1, 1991.)

ADVISORY COMMITTEE NOTES

This rule retains the requirement under the Bankruptcy Act [former Title 11] and rules that petitions and accompanying papers must be verified. Only the original need be signed and verified, but the copies must be conformed to the original. See Rule 9011(c).

The verification may be replaced by an unsworn declaration as provided in 28 U.S.C. § 1746. See also, Official Form No. 1 and Advisory Committee Note.

1991 Amendments

The amendments to this rule are stylistic.

CROSS REFERENCES

Signing and verification of papers, see Fed.Rules Bankr. Proc. Rule 9011, 11 USCA.

Rule 1009. Amendments of Voluntary Petitions, Lists, Schedules and Statements

(a) General right to amend

A voluntary petition, list, schedule, or statement may be amended by the debtor as a matter of course at any time before the case is closed. The debtor shall give notice of the amendment to the trustee and to any entity affected thereby. On motion of a party in interest, after notice and a hearing, the court may order any voluntary petition, list, schedule, or statement to be amended and the clerk shall give notice of the amendment to entities designated by the court.

(b) Statement of intention

The statement of intention may be amended by the debtor at any time before the expiration of the period provided in § 521(a) of the Code. The debtor shall give notice of the amendment to the trustee and to any entity affected thereby.

(c) Statement of social security number

If a debtor becomes aware that the statement of social security number submitted under Rule 1007(f) is incorrect, the debtor shall promptly submit an amended verified statement setting forth the correct social security number. The debtor shall give notice of the amendment to all of the entities required to be included on the list filed under Rule 1007(a)(1) or (a)(2).

(d) Transmission to United States trustee

The clerk shall promptly transmit to the United States trustee a copy of every amendment filed or submitted under subdivision (a), (b), or (c) of this rule.

(As amended Mar. 30, 1987, eff. Aug. 1, 1987; Apr. 30, 1991, eff. Aug. 1, 1991; Apr. 12, 2006, eff. Dec. 1, 2006; Apr. 23, 2008, eff. Dec. 1, 2008.)

ADVISORY COMMITTEE NOTES

This rule continues the permissive approach adopted by former Bankruptcy Rule 110 to amendments of voluntary petitions and accompanying papers. Notice of any amendment is required to be given to the trustee. This is particularly important with respect to any amendment of the schedule of property affecting the debtor's claim of exemptions. Notice of any amendment of the schedule of liabilities is to be given to any creditor whose claim is changed or newly listed.

The rule does not continue the provision permitting the court to order an amendment on its own initiative. Absent a request in some form by a party in interest, the court should not be involved in administrative matters affecting the estate.

If a list or schedule is amended to include an additional creditor, the effect on the dischargeability of the creditor's claim is governed by the provisions of § 523(a)(3) of the Code.

1987 Amendments

Subdivision (a) is amended to require notice and a hearing in the event a party in interest other than the debtor seeks to amend. The number of copies of the amendment will be determined by local rule of court.

Subdivision (b) is added to treat amendments of the statement of intention separately from other amendments. The intention of the individual debtor must be performed within 45 days of the filing of the statement, unless the court extends the period. Subdivision (b) limits the time for amendment to the time for performance under § 521(2)(B) of the Code or any extension granted by the court.

1991 Amendments

The amendments to subdivision (a) are stylistic.

Subdivision (c) is derived from Rule X–1002(a) and is designed to provide the United States trustee with current information to enable that office to participate effectively in the case.

2006 Amendments

Subdivision (c). Rule 2002(a)(1) provides that the notice of the § 341 meeting of creditors include the debtor's social security number. It provides creditors with the full number while limiting publication of the social security number otherwise to the final four digits of the number to protect the debtor's identity from others who do not have the same need for that information. If, however, the social security number that the debtor submitted under Rule 1007(f) is incorrect, then the only notice to the entities contained on the list filed under Rule 1007(a)(1) or (a)(2) would be incorrect. This amendment adds a new subdivision (c) that directs the debtor to submit a verified amended statement of social security number and to give notice of the new statement to all entities in the case who received the notice containing the erroneous social security number.

Subdivision (d). Former subdivision (c) becomes subdivision (d) and is amended to include new subdivision (c) amendments in the list of documents that the clerk must transmit to the United States trustee.

Other amendments are stylistic.

2008 Amendments

Subdivision (b) is amended to conform to the 2005 amendments to § 521 of the Code.

CROSS REFERENCES

Dischargeability of debts added to list or schedule, see 11 USCA § 523.

Motions; form and service, see Fed.Rules Bankr.Proc. Rule 9013, 11 USCA.

Amended and supplemental pleadings, see Fed.Rules Civ. Proc. Rule 15, 28 USCA.

Rule 1010. Service of Involuntary Petition and Summons; Petition for Recognition of a Foreign Nonmain Proceeding

(a) Service of involuntary petition and summons; service of petition for recognition of foreign nonmain proceeding

On the filing of an involuntary petition or a petition for recognition of a foreign nonmain proceeding, the clerk shall forthwith issue a summons for service. When an involuntary petition is filed, service shall be made on the debtor. When a petition for recognition of a foreign nonmain proceeding is filed, service shall be made on the debtor, any entity against whom provisional relief is sought under § 1519 of the Code, and on any other party as the court may direct. The summons shall be served with a copy of the petition in the manner provided for service of a summons and complaint by Rule 7004(a) or (b). If service cannot be so made, the court may order that the summons and petition be served by mailing copies to the party's last known address, and by at least one publication in a manner and form directed by the court. The summons and petition may be served on the party anywhere. Rule 7004(e) and Rule 4(*l*) F.R.Civ.P. apply when service is made or attempted under this rule.

(b) Corporate ownership statement

Each petitioner that is a corporation shall file with the involuntary petition a corporate ownership statement containing the information described in Rule 7007.1.

(As amended Mar. 30, 1987, eff. Aug. 1, 1987; Apr. 30, 1991, eff. Aug. 1, 1991; Apr. 22, 1993, eff. Aug. 1, 1993; Apr. 11, 1997, eff. Dec. 1, 1997; Apr. 23, 2008, eff. Dec. 1, 2008.)

ADVISORY COMMITTEE NOTES

This rule provides the procedure for service of the involuntary petition and summons. It does not deal with service of a summons and complaint instituting an adversary proceeding pursuant to Part VII.

While this rule is similar to former Bankruptcy Rule 111, it substitutes the clerk of the bankruptcy court for the clerk of the district court as the person who is to issue the summons.

The modes of service prescribed by the rule are personal or by mail, when service can be effected in one of these ways in the United States. Such service is to be made in the manner prescribed in adversary proceedings by Rule 7004(a) and (b). If service must be made in a foreign country, the mode of service is one of that set forth in Rule 4(i) F.R.Civ.P.

When the method set out in Rule 7004(a) and (b) cannot be utilized, service by publication coupled with mailing to the last known address is authorized. Cf. Rule 7004(c). The court determines the form and manner of publication as provided in Rule 9007. The publication need not set out the petition or the order directing service by publication. In order to apprise the debtor fairly, however, the publication should include all the information required to be in the summons by Official Form No. 13 and a notice indicating how service is being effected and how a copy of the petition may be obtained.

There are no territorial limits on the service authorized by this rule, which continues the practice under the former rules and Act. There must, however, be a basis for jurisdiction pursuant to § 109(a) of the Code for the court to order relief. Venue provisions are set forth in 28 U.S.C. § 1472.

Subdivision (f) of Rule 7004 and subdivisions (g) and (h) of Rule 4 F.R.Civ.P. govern time and proof of service and amendment of process or of proof of service.

Rule 1004 provides for transmission to nonpetitioning partners of a petition filed against the partnership by fewer than all the general partners.

1987 Amendments

The rule has been broadened to include service of a petition commencing a case ancillary to a foreign proceeding, previously included in Rule 1003(e)(2).

1991 Amendments

Reference to the Official Form number is deleted in anticipation of future revision and renumbering of the Official Forms.

Rule 4(g) and (h) F.R.Civ.P. made applicable by this rule refers to Rule 4(g) and (h) F.R.Civ.P. in effect on January 1, 1990, notwithstanding any subsequent amendment thereto. See Rule 7004(g).

1993 Amendments

This rule is amended to delete the reference to the Official Form. The Official Form for the summons was abrogated in 1991. Other amendments are stylistic and make no substantive change.

1997 Amendments

The amendments to this rule are technical, are promulgated solely to conform to changes in subdivision designations in Rule 4, F.R.Civ.P., and in Rule 7004, and are not intended to effectuate any material change in substance.

In 1996, the letter designation of subdivision (f) of Rule 7004 (Summons; Time Limit for Service) was changed to subdivision (e). In 1993, the provisions of Rule 4, F.R.Civ.P., relating to proof of service contained in Rule 4(g) (Return) and Rule 4(h) (Amendments), were placed in the new subdivision (*l*) of Rule 4 (Proof of Service). The technical amendments to Rule 1010 are designed solely to conform to these new subdivision designations.

The 1996 amendments to Rule 7004 and the 1993 amendments to Rule 4, F.R.Civ.P., have not affected the availability of service by first class mail in accordance with Rule 7004(b) for the service of a summons and petition in an involuntary case commenced under § 303 or an ancillary case commenced under § 304 of the Code.

GAP Report on Rule 1010. These amendments, which are technical and conforming, were not published for comment.

2008 Amendments

This rule is amended to implement the 2005 amendments to the Code, which repealed § 304 and replaced it with chapter 15 governing ancillary and other cross-border cases. Under chapter 15, a foreign representative commences a case by filing a petition for recognition of a pending foreign nonmain proceeding. The amendment requires service of the summons and petition on the debtor and any entity against whom the representative is seeking provisional relief. Until the court enters a recognition order under § 1517, no stay is in effect unless the court enters some form of provisional relief under § 1519. Thus, only those entities against whom specific provisional relief is sought need to be served. The court may, however, direct that service be made on additional entities as appropriate.

This rule does not apply to a petition for recognition of a foreign main proceeding.

The rule is also amended by renumbering the prior rule as subdivision (a) and adding a new subdivision (b) requiring any corporate creditor that files or joins an involuntary petition to file a corporate ownership statement.

CROSS REFERENCES

Applicability of this rule to—

Involuntary case ancillary to foreign proceeding, see Fed.Rules Bankr.Proc. Rule 1003, 11 USCA.

Involuntary partnership petitions, see Fed.Rules Bankr. Proc. Rule 1004, 11 USCA.

Form and manner of service by publication, see Fed.Rules Bankr.Proc. Rules 9007 and 9008, 11 USCA.

Jurisdictional basis for service, see 11 USCA § 109.

Process, see Fed.Rules Civ.Proc. Rule 4, 28 USCA.

Rule 1011. Responsive Pleading or Motion in Involuntary and Cross–Border Cases

(a) Who may contest petition

The debtor named in an involuntary petition, or a party in interest to a petition for recognition of a foreign proceeding, may contest the petition. In the case of a petition against a partnership under Rule 1004, a nonpetitioning general partner, or a person who is alleged to be a general partner but denies the allegation, may contest the petition.

(b) Defenses and objections; when presented

Defenses and objections to the petition shall be presented in the manner prescribed by Rule 12 F.R.Civ.P. and shall be filed and served within 20 days after service of the summons, except that if service is made by publication on a party or partner not residing or found within the state in which the court sits, the court shall prescribe the time for filing and serving the response.

(c) Effect of motion

Service of a motion under Rule 12(b) F.R.Civ.P. shall extend the time for filing and serving a responsive pleading as permitted by Rule 12(a) F.R.Civ.P.

(d) Claims against petitioners

A claim against a petitioning creditor may not be asserted in the answer except for the purpose of defeating the petition.

(e) Other pleadings

No other pleadings shall be permitted, except that the court may order a reply to an answer and prescribe the time for filing and service.

(f) Corporate ownership statement

If the entity responding to the involuntary petition or the petition for recognition of a foreign proceeding is a corporation, the entity shall file with its first appearance, pleading, motion, response, or other request addressed to the court a corporate ownership statement containing the information described in Rule 7007.1.

(As amended Mar. 30, 1987, eff. Aug. 1, 1987; Apr. 26, 2004, eff. Dec. 1, 2004; Apr 23, 2008, eff. Dec. 1, 2008.)

ADVISORY COMMITTEE NOTES

This rule is derived from former Bankruptcy Rule 112. A petition filed by fewer than all the general partners under Rule 1004(b) to have an order for relief entered with respect to the partnership is referred to as a petition against the partnership because of the adversary character of the proceeding it commences. Cf. § 303(b)(3) of the Code; 2 Collier Bankruptcy ¶303.05[5][a] (15th ed.1981); id. ¶¶18.33[2], 18.46 (14th ed.1966). One who denies an allegation of membership in the firm is nevertheless recognized as a party entitled to contest a petition filed against a partnership under subdivision (b) of Rule 1004 in view of the possible consequences to him of an order for relief against the entity alleged to include him as a member. See § 723 of the Code; Francis v. McNeal, 228 U.S. 695 (1913); Manson v. Williams, 213 U.S. 453 (1909); Carter v. Whisler, 275 Fed. 743, 746–747 (8th Cir.1921). The rule preserves the features of the former Act and Rule 112 and the Code permitting no response by creditors to an involuntary petition or petition against a partnership under rule 1004(b).

Subdivision (b): Rule 12 F.R.Civ.P. has been looked to by the courts as prescribing the mode of making a defense or objection to a petition in bankruptcy. See Fada of New York, Inc. v. Organization Service Co., Inc., 125 F.2d 120 (2d Cir.1942); In the Matter of McDougald, 17 F.R.D. 2, 5 (W.D.Ark.1955); In the Matter of Miller, 6 Fed.Rules Serv. 12f.26, Case No. 1 (N.D.Ohio 1942); Tatum v. Acadian Production Corp. of La., 35 F.Supp. 40, 50 (E.D.La.1940); 2 Collier, supra ¶303.07 (15th ed.1981); 2 id. at 134–40 (14th ed.1966). As pointed out in the Note accompanying former Bankruptcy rule 915 an objection that a debtor is neither entitled to the benefits of the Code nor amenable to an involuntary petition goes to jurisdiction of the subject matter and may be made at any time consistent with Rule 12(h)(3) F.R.Civ.P. Nothing in this rule recognizes standing in a creditor or any other person not authorized to contest a petition to raise an objection that a person eligible to file a voluntary petition cannot be the subject of an order for relief on an involuntary petition. See Seligson & King, Jurisdiction and Venue in Bankruptcy, 36 Ref.J. 36, 38–40 (1962).

As Collier has pointed out with respect to the Bankruptcy Act, "the mechanics of the provisions in § 18a and b relating to time for appearance and pleading are unnecessarily confusing. . . . It would seem, though, to be more straightforward to provide, as does Federal Rule 12(a), that the time to respond runs from the date of service rather than the date of issuance of process." 2 Collier, supra at 119. The time normally allowed for the service and filing of an answer or motion under Rule 1011 runs from the date of the issuance of the summons. Compare Rule 7012. Service of the summons and petition will ordinarily be made by mail under Rule 1010 and must be made within 10 days of the issuance of the summons under Rule 7004(e), which governs the time of service. When service is made by publication, the court should fix the time for service and filing of the response in the light of all the circumstances so as to afford a fair opportunity to the debtor to enter a defense or objection without unduly delaying the hearing on the petition. Cf. Rule 12(a) F.R.Civ.P.

Subdivision (c): Under subdivision (c), the timely service of a motion permitted by Rule 12(b), (e), (f), or (h) F.R.Civ.P. alters the time within which an answer must be filed. If the court denies a motion or postpones its disposition until trial on the merits, the answer must be served within 10 days after notice of the court's action. If the court grants a motion for a more definite statement, the answer may be served any time within 10 days after the service of the more definite statement.

Many of the rules governing adversary proceedings apply to proceedings on a contested petition unless the court otherwise directs as provided in Rule 1018. The specific provisions of this Rule 1011 or 7005, however, govern the filing of an answer or motion responsive to a petition. The rules of Part VII are adaptations of the corresponding Federal Rules of Civil Procedure, and the effect of Rule 1018 is thus to make the provisions of Civil Rules 5, 8, 9, 15, and 56, inter alia, generally applicable to the making of defenses and objections to the petition. Rule 1018 follows prior law and practice in this respect. See 2 Collier, Bankruptcy ¶¶18.39–18.41 (14th ed.1966).

Subdivision (d). This subdivision adopts the position taken in many cases that an affirmative judgment against a petitioning creditor cannot be sought by a counterclaim filed in an answer to an involuntary petition. See, e.g., Georgia Jewelers, Inc., v. Bulova Watch Co., 302 F.2d 362, 369–70 (5th Cir.1962); Associated Electronic Supply Co. of Omaha v. C.B.S. Electronic Sales Corp., 288 F.2d 683, 684–85 (8th Cir. 1961). The subdivision follows Harris v. Capehart-Farnsworth Corp., 225 F.2d 268 (8th Cir.1955), in permitting the debtor to challenge the standing of a petitioner by filing a counterclaim against him. It does not foreclose the court from rejecting a counterclaim that cannot be determined without unduly delaying the decision upon the petition. See In the Matter of Bichel Optical Laboratories, Inc., 299 F.Supp. 545 (D.Minn.1969).

Subdivision (e). This subdivision makes it clear that no reply needs to be made to an answer, including one asserting a counterclaim, unless the court orders otherwise.

1987 Amendments

The rule has been broadened to make applicable in ancillary cases the provisions concerning responsive pleadings to involuntary petitions.

2004 Amendments

The amendment to Rule 1004 that became effective on December 1, 2002, deleted former subdivision (a) of that rule leaving only the provisions relating to involuntary petitions against partnerships. The rule no longer includes subdivisions. Therefore, this technical amendment changes the reference to Rule 1004(b) to Rule 1004.

2008 Amendments

The rule is amended to reflect the 2005 amendments to the Code, which repealed § 304 and added chapter 15. Section 304 covered cases ancillary to foreign proceedings, while chapter 15 governs ancillary and other cross-border cases and introduces the concept of a petition for recognition of a foreign proceeding.

The rule is also amended in tandem with the amendment to Rule 1010 to require the parties responding to an involuntary petition and a petition for recognition of a foreign proceeding to file corporate ownership statements to assist the court in determining whether recusal is necessary.

CROSS REFERENCES

Applicability of this rule to involuntary case ancillary to foreign proceeding, see Fed.Rules Bankr.Proc. Rule 1003, 11 USCA.

Entry of default upon failure to plead within time, see Fed.Rules Bankr.Proc. Rule 1013, 11 USCA.

Motions; form and service, see Fed.Rules Bankr.Proc. Rule 9013, 11 USCA.

Responsive pleadings, see 11 USCA § 303.

Pleadings—

- Amended and supplemental, see Fed.Rules Civ.Proc. Rule 15, 28 USCA.
- Capacity, fraud, and other special matters, see Fed. Rules Civ.Proc. Rule 9, 28 USCA.
- General rules, see Fed.Rules Civ.Proc. Rule 8, 28 USCA.
- Service and filing, see Fed.Rules Civ.Proc. Rule 5, 28 USCA.

Summary judgment, see Fed.Rules Civ.Proc. Rule 56, 28 USCA.

Rule 1012. [Abrogated Mar. 30, 1987, eff. Aug. 1, 1987]

ADVISORY COMMITTEE NOTES

This rule is abrogated. The discovery rules apply whenever an involuntary petition is contested. Rule 1018.

Rule 1013. Hearing and Disposition of Petition in Involuntary Cases

(a) Contested petition

The court shall determine the issues of a contested petition at the earliest practicable time and forthwith enter an order for relief, dismiss the petition, or enter any other appropriate order.

(b) Default

If no pleading or other defense to a petition is filed within the time provided by Rule 1011, the court, on the next day, or as soon thereafter as practicable, shall enter an order for the relief requested in the petition.

(c) [Abrogated]

(As amended Apr. 30, 1991, eff. Aug. 1, 1991; Apr. 22, 1993, eff. Aug. 1, 1993.)

ADVISORY COMMITTEE NOTES

This rule is adapted from former Bankruptcy Rule 115(a) and (c) and applies in chapter 7 and 11 cases. The right to trial by jury under § 19a of the Bankruptcy Act [former § 42(a) of this title] has been abrogated and the availability of a trial by jury is within the discretion of the bankruptcy judge pursuant to 28 U.S.C. § 1480(b). Rule 9015 governs the demand for a jury trial.

Subdivision (b) of Rule 1013 is derived from former Bankruptcy Rule 115(c) and § 18(e) of the Bankruptcy Act [former § 41(e) of this title]. If an order for relief is not entered on default, dismissal will ordinarily be appropriate but the court may postpone definitive action. See also Rule 9024 with respect to setting aside an order for relief on default for cause.

Subdivision (e) of former Bankruptcy Rule 115 has not been carried over because its provisions are covered by § 303(i) of the Code.

1991 Amendments

Reference to the Official Form number is deleted in anticipation of future revision and renumbering of the Official Forms.

1993 Amendments

Subdivision (c) is abrogated because the official form for the order for relief was abrogated in 1991. Other amendments are stylistic and make no substantive change.

CROSS REFERENCES

Costs, counsel fees, expenses and damages upon dismissal of petition, see 11 USCA § 303.

Power of court to render judgments, see 11 USCA § 105.

Setting aside default for cause, see Fed.Rules Bankr.Proc. Rule 9024, 11 USCA.

Instructions to jury; objection, see Fed.Rules Civ.Proc. Rule 51, 28 USCA.

Juries of less than twelve; majority verdict, see Fed.Rules Civ.Proc. Rule 48, 28 USCA.

Jurors, see Fed.Rules Civ.Proc. Rule 47, 28 USCA.

Jury trial of right, see Fed.Rules Civ.Proc. Rule 38, 28 USCA.

Motion for directed verdict and for judgment notwithstanding verdict, see Fed.Rules Civ.Proc. Rule 50, 28 USCA.

Special verdicts and interrogatories, see Fed.Rules Civ. Proc. Rule 49, 28 USCA.

Trial by jury or by court, see Fed.Rules Civ.Proc. Rule 39, 28 USCA.

Rule 1014. Dismissal and Change of Venue

(a) Dismissal and Transfer of Cases

(1) Cases Filed in Proper District

If a petition is filed in the proper district, the court, on the timely motion of a party in interest or on its own motion, and after hearing on notice to the petitioners, the United States trustee, and other entities as directed by the court, may transfer the case to any other district if the court determines that the transfer is in the interest of justice or for the convenience of the parties.

(2) Cases Filed in Improper District

If a petition is filed in an improper district, the court, on the timely motion of a party in interest or on its own motion, and after hearing on notice to the petitioners, the United States trustee, and other entities as directed by the court, may dismiss the case or transfer it to any other district if the court determines that transfer is in the interest of justice or for the convenience of the parties.

(b) Procedure when petitions involving the same debtor or related debtors are filed in different courts

If petitions commencing cases under the Code are filed in different districts by or against (1) the same debtor, or (2) a partnership and one or more of its general partners, or (3) two or more general partners, or (4) a debtor and an affiliate, on motion filed in the district in which the petition filed first is pending and after hearing on notice to the petitioners, the United States trustee, and other entities as directed by the court, the court may determine, in the interest of justice or for the convenience of the parties, the district or districts in which the case or cases should proceed. Except as otherwise ordered by the court in the district in which the petition filed first is pending, the proceedings on the other petitions shall be stayed by the courts in which they have been filed until the determination is made.

(As amended Mar. 30, 1987, eff. Aug. 1, 1987; Apr. 30, 1991, eff. Aug. 1, 1991; Apr. 30, 2007, eff. Dec. 1, 2007.)

ADVISORY COMMITTEE NOTES

This rule is derived from former Bankruptcy Rule 116 which contained venue as well as transfer provisions. Public Law 95–598, however, placed the venue provisions in 28 U.S.C. § 1472, and no purpose is served by repeating them in this rule. Transfer of cases is provided in 28 U.S.C. § 1475 but this rule adds the procedure for obtaining transfer. Pursuant to 28 U.S.C. § 1472, proper venue for cases filed under the Code is either the district of domicile, residence, principal place of business, or location of principal assets for 180 days or the longer portion thereof immediately preceding the petition. 28 U.S.C. § 1475 permits the court to transfer a case in the interest of justice and for the convenience of the parties. If the venue is improper, the court may retain or transfer the case in the interest of justice and for the convenience of the parties pursuant to 28 U.S.C. § 1477.

Subdivision (a) of the rule is derived from former Bankruptcy Rule 116(b). It implements 28 U.S.C. §§ 1475 and 1477 and clarifies the procedure to be followed in requesting and effecting transfer of a case. Subdivision (a) protects the parties against being subjected to a transfer except on a timely motion of a party in interest. If the transfer would result in fragmentation or duplication of administration, increase expense, or delay closing the estate, such a factor would bear on the timeliness of the motion as well as on the propriety of the transfer under the standards prescribed in subdivision (a). Subdivision (a) of the rule requires the interest of justice and the convenience of the parties to be the grounds of any transfer of a case or of the retention of a case filed in an improper district as does 28 U.S.C. § 1477. Cf. 28 U.S.C. § 1404(a) (district court may transfer any civil action "[f]or the convenience of parties and witnesses, in the interest of justice"). It also expressly requires a hearing on notice to the petitioner or petitioners before the transfer of any case may be ordered. Under this rule, a motion by a party in interest is necessary. There is no provision for the court to act on its own initiative.

Subdivision (b) is derived from former Bankruptcy Rule 116(c). It authorizes the court in which the first petition is filed under the Code by or against a debtor to entertain a motion seeking a determination whether the case so commenced should continue or be transferred and consolidated or administered jointly with another case commenced by or against the same or related person in another court under a different chapter of the Code. Subdivision (b) is correlated with 28 U.S.C. § 1472 which authorizes petitioners to file cases involving a partnership and partners or affiliated debtors.

The reference in subdivision (b) to petitions filed "by" a partner or "by" any other of the persons mentioned is to be understood as referring to voluntary petitions. It is not the purpose of this subdivision to permit more than one case to be filed in the same court because a creditor signing an involuntary petition happens to be a partner, a partnership, or an affiliate of a debtor.

Transfers of adversary proceedings in cases under title 11 are governed by Rule 7087 and 28 U.S.C. § 1475.

1987 Amendments

Both paragraphs 1 and 2 of subdivision (a) are amended to conform to the standard for transfer in 28 U.S.C. § 1412. Formerly, 28 U.S.C. § 1477 authorized a court either to transfer or retain a case which had been commenced in a district where venue was improper. However, 28 U.S.C. § 1412, which supersedes 28 U.S.C. § 1477, authorizes only the transfer of a case. The rule is amended to delete the reference to retention of a case commenced in the improper district. Dismissal of a case commenced in the improper district as authorized by 28 U.S.C. § 1406 has been added to the rule. If a timely motion to dismiss for improper venue is not filed, the right to object to venue is waived.

The last sentence of the rule has been deleted as unnecessary.

1991 Amendments

Subdivision (b) is amended to provide that a motion for transfer of venue under this subdivision shall be filed in the district in which the first petition is pending. If the case commenced by the first petition has been transferred to another district prior to the filing of a motion to transfer a related case under this subdivision, the motion must be filed in the district to which the first petition had been transferred.

The other amendments to this rule are consistent with the responsibilities of the United States trustee in the supervision and administration of cases pursuant to 28 U.S.C. § 586(a)(3). The United States trustee may appear and be heard on issues relating to the transfer of the case or dismissal due to improper venue. See § 307 of the Code.

2007 Amendments

Courts have generally held that they have the authority to dismiss or transfer cases on their own motion. The amendment recognizes this authority and also provides that dismissal or transfer of the case may take place only after notice and a hearing.

Other amendments are stylistic.

CROSS REFERENCES

Change of venue, see 28 USCA § 1404.

Motions; form and service, see Fed.Rules Bankr.Proc. Rule 9013, 11 USCA.

Transfer of adversary proceeding, see Fed.Rules Bankr. Proc. Rule 7087, 11 USCA.

Rule 1015. Consolidation or Joint Administration of Cases Pending in Same Court

(a) Cases involving same debtor

If two or more petitions are pending in the same court by or against the same debtor, the court may order consolidation of the cases.

(b) Cases Involving Two or More Related Debtors

If a joint petition or two or more petitions are pending in the same court by or against (1) a husband and wife, or (2) a partnership and one or more of its general partners, or (3) two or more general partners, or (4) a debtor and an affiliate, the court may order a joint administration of the estates. Prior to entering an order the court shall give consideration to protecting creditors of different estates against potential conflicts of interest. An order directing joint administration of individual cases of a husband and wife shall, if one spouse has elected the exemptions under § 522(b)(2) of the Code and the other has elected the exemptions under § 522(b)(3), fix a reasonable time within which either may amend the election so that both shall have elected the same exemptions. The order shall notify the debtors that unless they elect the same exemptions within the time fixed by the court, they will be deemed to have elected the exemptions provided by § 522(b)(2).

(c) Expediting and protective orders

When an order for consolidation or joint administration of a joint case or two or more cases is entered pursuant to this rule, while protecting the rights of the parties under the Code, the court may enter orders as may tend to avoid unnecessary costs and delay.

(As amended Mar. 30, 1987, eff. Aug. 1, 1987; Apr. 23, 2008, eff. Dec. 1, 2008.)

ADVISORY COMMITTEE NOTES

Subdivision (a) of this rule is derived from former Bankruptcy Rule 117(a). It applies to cases when the same debtor is named in both voluntary and involuntary petitions, when husband and wife have filed a joint petition pursuant to § 302 of the Code, and when two or more involuntary petitions are filed against the same debtor. It also applies when cases are pending in the same court by virtue of a transfer of one or more petitions from another court. Subdivision (c) allows the court discretion regarding the order of trial of issues raised by two or more involuntary petitions against the same debtor.

Subdivision (b) recognizes the propriety of joint administration of estates in certain kinds of cases. The election or appointment of one trustee for two or more jointly administered estates is authorized by Rule 2009. The authority of the court to order joint administration under subdivision (b) extends equally to the situation when the petitions are filed under different sections, e.g., when one petition is voluntary and the other involuntary, and when all of the petitions are filed under the same section of the Code.

Consolidation of cases implies a unitary administration of the estate and will ordinarily be indicated under the circumstances to which subdivision (a) applies. This rule does not deal with the consolidation of cases involving two or more separate debtors. Consolidation of the estates of separate debtors may sometimes be appropriate, as when the affairs of an individual and a corporation owned or controlled by that individual are so intermingled that the court cannot separate their assets and liabilities. Consolidation, as distinguished from joint administration, is neither authorized nor prohibited by this rule since the propriety of consolidation depends on substantive considerations and affects the substantive rights of the creditors of the different estates. For illustrations of the substantive consolidation of separate estates, see Sampsell v. Imperial Paper & Color Corp., 313 U.S. 215 [61 S.Ct. 904, 85 L.Ed. 1293] (1941). See also Chemical Bank N.Y. Trust Co. v. Kheel, 369 F.2d 845 (2d Cir. 1966); Seligson & Mandell, Multi-Debtor Petition—Consolidation of Debtors and Due Process of Law, 73 Com. L.J. 341 (1968); Kennedy, Insolvency and the Corporate Veil in the United States in Proceedings of the 8th International Symposium on Comparative Law 232, 248–55 (1971).

Joint administration as distinguished from consolidation may include combining the estates by using a single docket for the matters occurring in the administration, including the listing of filed claims, the combining of notices to creditors of the different estates, and the joint handling of other purely administrative matters that may aid in expediting the cases and rendering the process less costly.

Subdivision (c) is an adaptation of the provisions of Rule 42(a) F.R.Civ.P. for the purposes of administration of estates under this rule. The rule does not deal with filing fees when an order for the consolidation of cases or joint administration of estates is made.

A joint petition of husband and wife, requiring the payment of a single filing fee, is permitted by § 302 of the Code. Consolidation of such a case, however, rests in the discretion of the court; see § 302(b) of the Code.

1987 Amendments

The amendment to subdivision (b) implements the provisions of § 522(b) of the Code, as enacted by the 1984 amendments.

2008 Amendments

The rule is amended to conform to the change in the numbering of § 522(b) of the Code that was made as a part of the 2005 amendments. Former subsections (b)(1) and (b)(2) of § 522 were renumbered as subsections (b)(2) and (b)(3), respectively. The rule is amended to make the parallel change.

CROSS REFERENCES

Election of trustees in liquidation cases when joint administration ordered, see Fed.Rules Bankr.Proc. Rule 2009, 11 USCA.

Joint cases, see 11 USCA § 302.

Consolidation, see Fed.Rules Civ.Proc. Rule 42, 28 USCA.

Rule 1016. Death or Incompetency of Debtor

Death or incompetency of the debtor shall not abate a liquidation case under chapter 7 of the Code. In such event the estate shall be administered and the case concluded in the same manner, so far as possible, as though the death or incompetency had not occurred. If a reorganization, family farmer's debt adjustment, or individual's debt adjustment case is pending under chapter 11, chapter 12, or chapter 13, the case may be dismissed; or if further administration is possible and in the best interest of the parties, the case may proceed and be concluded in the same manner, so far as possible, as though the death or incompetency had not occurred.

(As amended Apr. 30, 1991, eff. Aug. 1, 1991.)

ADVISORY COMMITTEE NOTES

This rule is derived from former Rules 118 and 11–16. In a chapter 11 reorganization case or chapter 13 individual's debt adjustment case, the likelihood is that the case will be dismissed.

1991 Amendments

This rule is amended to conform to 25 F.R.Civ.P. and to include chapter 12 cases.

CROSS REFERENCES

Exemptions, see 11 USCA § 522.

Property of estate, see 11 USCA § 541.

Rule 1017. Dismissal or Conversion of Case; Suspension

(a) Voluntary dismissal; dismissal for want of prosecution or other cause

Except as provided in §§ 707(a)(3), 707(b), 1208(b), and 1307(b) of the Code, and in Rule 1017(b), (c), and (e), a case shall not be dismissed on motion of the petitioner, for want of prosecution or other cause, or by consent of the parties, before a hearing on notice as provided in Rule 2002. For the purpose of the notice, the debtor shall file a list of creditors with their addresses within the time fixed by the court unless the list was previously filed. If the debtor fails to file the list, the court may order the debtor or another entity to prepare and file it.

(b) Dismissal for failure to pay filing fee

(1) If any installment of the filing fee has not been paid, the court may, after a hearing on notice to the debtor and the trustee, dismiss the case.

(2) If the case is dismissed or closed without full payment of the filing fee, the installments collected shall be distributed in the same manner and proportions as if the filing fee had been paid in full.

(c) Dismissal of voluntary chapter 7 or chapter 13 case for failure to timely file list of creditors, schedules, and statement of financial affairs

The court may dismiss a voluntary chapter 7 or chapter 13 case under § 707(a)(3) or § 1307(c)(9) after a hearing on notice served by the United States trustee on the debtor, the trustee, and any other entities as the court directs.

(d) Suspension

The court shall not dismiss a case or suspend proceedings under § 305 before a hearing on notice as provided in Rule 2002(a).

(e) Dismissal of an individual debtor's chapter 7 case, or conversion to a case under chapter 11 or 13, for abuse

The court may dismiss or, with the debtor's consent, convert an individual debtor's case for abuse under § 707(b) only on motion and after a hearing on notice to the debtor, the trustee, the United States trustee, and any other entity as the court directs.

(1) Except as otherwise provided in § 704(b)(2), a motion to dismiss a case for abuse under § 707(b) or (c) may be filed only within 60 days after the first date set for the meeting of creditors under § 341(a), unless, on request filed before the time has expired, the court for cause extends the time for filing the motion to dismiss. The party filing the motion shall set forth in the motion all matters to be considered at the hearing. In addition, a motion to dismiss under § 707(b)(1) and (3) shall state with particularity the circumstances alleged to constitute abuse.

(2) If the hearing is set on the court's own motion, notice of the hearing shall be served on the debtor no later than 60 days after the first date set for the meeting of creditors under § 341(a). The notice shall set forth all matters to be considered by the court at the hearing.

(f) Procedure for dismissal, conversion, or suspension

(1) Rule 9014 governs a proceeding to dismiss or suspend a case, or to convert a case to another chapter, except under §§ 706(a), 1112(a), 1208(a) or (b), or 1307(a) or (b).

(2) Conversion or dismissal under §§ 706(a), 1112(a), 1208(b), or 1307(b) shall be on motion filed and served as required by Rule 9013.

(3) A chapter 12 or chapter 13 case shall be converted without court order when the debtor files a notice of conversion under §§ 1208(a) or 1307(a). The filing date of the notice becomes the date of the conversion order for the purposes of applying § 348(c) and Rule 1019. The clerk shall promptly transmit a copy of the notice to the United States trustee.

(As amended Mar. 30, 1987, eff. Aug. 1, 1987; Apr. 30, 1991, eff. Aug. 1, 1991; Apr. 22, 1993, eff. Aug. 1, 1993; Apr. 29, 1999, eff. Dec. 1, 1999; Apr. 17, 2000, eff. Dec. 1, 2000; Apr. 23, 2008, eff. Dec. 1, 2008.)

ADVISORY COMMITTEE NOTES

Subdivision (a) of this rule is derived from former Bankruptcy Rule 120(a). While the rule applies to voluntary and involuntary cases, the "consent of the parties" referred to is that of petitioning creditors and the debtor in an involuntary case. The last sentence recognizes that the court should not be confined to petitioning creditors in its choice of parties on whom to call for assistance in preparing the list of creditors when the debtor fails to do so. This subdivision implements §§ 303(j), 707, 1112 and 1307 of the Code by specifying the manner of and persons to whom notice shall be given and requiring the court to hold a hearing on the issue of dismissal.

Subdivision (b) is derived from former Bankruptcy Rule 120(b). A dismissal under this subdivision can occur only when the petition has been permitted to be filed pursuant to Rule 1006(b). The provision for notice in paragraph (3) is correlated with the provision in Rule 4006 when there is a waiver, denial, or revocation of a discharge. As pointed out in the Note accompanying Rule 4008, the purpose of notifying creditors of a debtor that no discharge has been granted is to correct their assumption to the contrary so that they can take appropriate steps to protect their claims.

Subdivision (c) is new and specifies the notice required for a hearing on dismissal or suspension pursuant to § 305 of the Code. The suspension to which this subdivision refers is that of the case; it does not concern abstention of the court in hearing an adversary proceeding pursuant to 28 U.S.C. § 1478(b).

Subdivision (d). Any proceeding, whether by a debtor or other party, to dismiss or convert a case under §§ 706, 707, 1112, or 1307 is commenced by a motion pursuant to Rule 9014.

1987 Amendments

Subdivision (d) is amended to provide that dismissal or conversion pursuant to §§ 706(a), 707(b), 1112(a), and 1307(b) is not automatically a contested matter under Rule 9014. Conversion or dismissal under these sections is initiated by the filing and serving of a motion as required by Rule 9013. No hearing is required on these motions unless the court directs.

Conversion of a chapter 13 case to a chapter 7 case as authorized by § 1307(a) is accomplished by the filing of a notice of conversion. The notice of conversion procedure is modeled on the voluntary dismissal provision of Rule 41(a)(1) F.R.Civ.P. Conversion occurs on the filing of the notice. No court order is required.

Subdivision (e) is new and provides the procedure to be followed when a court on its own motion has made a preliminary determination that an individual debtor's chapter 7 case may be dismissed pursuant to § 707(b) of the Code, which was added by the 1984 amendments. A debtor's failure to attend the hearing is not a ground for dismissal pursuant to § 707(b).

1991 Amendments

Subdivision (a) is amended to clarify that all entities required to receive notice under Rule 2002, including but not limited to creditors, are entitled to the 20 day notice of the hearing to dismiss the case. The United States trustee receives the notice pursuant to Rule 2002(k).

The word "petition" is changed to "case" in subdivisions (a), (b), and (c) to conform to §§ 707, 930, 1112, 1208, and 1307.

Subdivision (d) is amended to conform to § 348(c) of the Code which refers to the "conversion order."

Subdivisions (a) and (d) are amended to provide procedures for dismissal or conversion of a chapter 12 case. Procedures for dismissal or conversion under § 1208(a) and (b) are the same as the procedures for dismissal or conversion of a chapter 13 case under § 1307(a) and (b).

Subdivision (e) is amended to conform to the 1986 amendment to § 707(b) of the Code which permits the United States trustee to make a motion to dismiss a case for substantial abuse. The time limit for such a motion is added by this subdivision. In general, the facts that are the basis for a motion to dismiss under § 707(b) exist at the time the case is commenced and usually can be discovered early in the case by reviewing the debtor's schedules and examining the debtor at the meeting of creditors. Since dismissal for substantial abuse has the effect of denying the debtor a discharge in the chapter 7 case based on matters which may be discovered early, a motion to dismiss under § 707(b) is analogous to an objection to discharge pursuant to Rule 4004 and, therefore, should be required to be made within a specified time period. If matters relating to substantial abuse are not discovered within the time period specified in subdivision (e) because of the debtor's false testimony, refusal to obey a court order, fraudulent schedules or other fraud, and the debtor receives a discharge, the debtor's conduct may constitute the basis for revocation of the discharge under § 727(d) and (e) of the Code.

1993 Amendments

Subdivision (d) is amended to clarify that the date of the filing of a notice of conversion in a chapter 12 or chapter 13 case is treated as the date of the conversion order for the purpose of applying Rule 1019. Other amendments are stylistic and make no substantive change.

1999 Amendments

Subdivision (b)(3), which provides that notice of dismissal for failure to pay the filing fee shall be sent to all creditors within 30 days after the dismissal, is deleted as unnecessary. Rule 2002(f) provides for notice to creditors of the dismissal of a case.

Rule 2002(a) and this rule currently require notice to all creditors of a hearing on dismissal of a voluntary chapter 7 case for the debtor's failure to file a list of creditors, schedules, and statement of financial affairs within the time provided in § 707(a)(3) of the Code. A new subdivision (c) is added to provide that the United States trustee, who is the only entity with standing to file a motion to dismiss under § 707(a)(3) or § 1307(c)(9), is required to serve the motion on only the debtor, the trustee, and any other entities as the court directs. This amendment, and the amendment to Rule 2002, will have the effect of avoiding the expense of sending notices of the motion to all creditors in a chapter 7 case.

New subdivision (f) is the same as current subdivision (d), except that it provides that a motion to suspend all proceedings in a case or to dismiss a case for substantial abuse of chapter 7 under § 707(b) is governed by Rule 9014.

Other amendments to this rule are stylistic or for clarification.

Gap Report on Rule 1017. No changes since publication, except for stylistic changes in Rule 1017(e) and (f).

2000 Amendments

This rule is amended to permit the court to grant a timely request filed by the United States trustee for an extension of time to file a motion to dismiss a chapter 7 case under § 707(b), whether the court rules on the request before or after the expiration of the 60–day period.

Reporter's Note on Text of Rule 1017(e). The above text of Rule 1017(e) is not based on the text of the rule in effect on this date. The above text embodies amendments that have been promulgated by the Supreme Court in April 1999 and, unless Congress acts with respect to the amendments, will become effective on December 1, 1999.

GAP Report on Rule 1017(e). No changes since publication.

2008 Amendments

Subdivision (e) is amended to implement the 2005 amendments to § 707 of the Code. These statutory amendments permit conversion of a chapter 7 case to a case under chapter 11 or 13, change the basis for dismissal or conversion from "substantial abuse" to "abuse," authorize parties other than the United States trustee to bring motions under § 707(b) under certain circumstances, and add § 707(c) to create an explicit ground for dismissal based on the request of a victim of a crime of violence or drug trafficking. The conforming amendments to subdivision (e) preserve the time limits already in place for § 707(b) motions, except to the extent that § 704(b)(2) sets the deadline for the United States trustee to act. In contrast to the grounds for a motion to dismiss under § 707(b)(2), which are quite specific, the grounds under § 707(b)(1) and (3) are very general. Therefore, to enable the debtor to respond, subdivision (e) requires that motions to dismiss under § 707(b)(1) and (3) state with particularity the circumstances alleged to constitute abuse.

CROSS REFERENCES

Conversion of—
- Individual debt adjustment case, see 11 USCA § 1307.
- Liquidation case, see 11 USCA § 706.
- Reorganization case, see 11 USCA § 1112.

Dismissal of—
- Individual debt adjustment case, see 11 USCA § 1307.
- Involuntary petition, see 11 USCA § 303.
- Liquidation case, see 11 USCA § 707.
- Reorganization case, see 11 USCA § 1112.

Enlargement of thirty-day period for notice of dismissal for failure to pay filing fee not permitted, see Fed.Rules Bankr.Proc. Rule 9006, 11 USCA.

Motions; form and service, see Fed.Rules Bankr.Proc. Rule 9013, 11 USCA.

Rule 1018. Contested Involuntary Petitions; Contested Petitions Commencing Ancillary Cases; Proceedings to Vacate Order for Relief; Applicability of Rules in Part VII Governing Adversary Proceedings

The following rules in Part VII apply to all proceedings relating to a contested involuntary petition, to proceedings relating to a contested petition commencing a case ancillary to a foreign proceeding, and to all proceedings to vacate an order for relief: Rules 7005, 7008–7010, 7015, 7016, 7024–7026, 7028–7037, 7052, 7054, 7056, and 7062, except as otherwise provided in Part I of these rules and unless the court otherwise directs. The court may direct that other rules in Part VII shall also apply. For the purposes of this rule a reference in the Part VII rules to adversary proceedings shall be read as a reference to proceedings relating to a contested involuntary petition, or contested ancillary petition, or proceedings to vacate an order for relief. Reference in the Federal Rules of Civil Procedure to the complaint shall be read as a reference to the petition.

(As amended Mar. 30, 1987, eff. Aug. 1, 1987.)

ADVISORY COMMITTEE NOTES

The rules in Part VII to which this rule refers are adaptations of the Federal Rules of Civil Procedure for the purpose of governing the procedure in adversary proceedings in cases under the Code. See the Note accompanying Rule 7001 infra. Because of the special need for dispatch and expedition in the determination of the issues in an involuntary petition, see Acme Harvester Co. v. Beekman Lumber Co., 222 U.S. 300, 309 (1911), the objective of some of the Federal Rules of Civil Procedure and their adaptations in Part VII to facilitate the settlement of multiple controversies involving many persons in a single lawsuit is not compatible with the exigencies of bankruptcy administration. See United States F. & G. Co. v. Bray, 225 U.S. 205, 218 (1912). For that reason Rules 7013, 7014 and 7018–7023 will rarely be appropriate in a proceeding on a contested petition.

Certain terms used in the Federal Rules of Civil Procedure have altered meanings when they are made applicable in cases under the Code by these rules. See Rule 9002 infra. This Rule 1018 requires that the terms "adversary proceedings" when used in the rules in Part VII and "complaint" when used in the Federal Rules of Civil Procedure be given altered meanings when they are made applicable to proceedings relating to a contested petition or proceedings to vacate any order for relief. A motion to vacate an order for relief, whether or not made on a petition that was or could have been contested, is governed by the rules in Part VII referred to in this Rule 1018.

1987 Amendments

Rule 1018 is amended to include within its terms a petition commencing an ancillary case when it is contested. This provision was formerly included in Rule 1003(e)(4).

Although this rule does not contain an explicit authorization for the entry of an order for relief when a debtor refuses to cooperate in discovery relating to a contested involuntary petition, the court has ample power under Rule 37(b) F.R.Civ.P., as incorporated by Rule 7037, to enter an order for relief under appropriate circumstances. Rule 37(b) authorizes the court to enter judgment by default or an order that "facts shall be taken as established."

CROSS REFERENCES

Applicability of this rule to involuntary case ancillary to foreign proceeding, see Fed.Rules Bankr.Proc. Rule 1003, 11 USCA.

Effect of amendment of Federal Rules of Civil Procedure, see Fed.Rules Bankr.Proc. Rule 9032, 11 USCA.

Rule 1019. Conversion of a Chapter 11 Reorganization Case, Chapter 12 Family Farmer's Debt Adjustment Case, or Chapter 13 Individual's Debt Adjustment Case to a Chapter 7 Liquidation Case

When a chapter 11, chapter 12, or chapter 13 case has been converted or reconverted to a chapter 7 case:

(1) Filing of lists, inventories, schedules, statements

(A) Lists, inventories, schedules, and statements of financial affairs theretofore filed shall be deemed to be filed in the chapter 7 case, unless the court directs otherwise. If they have not been previously filed, the debtor shall comply with Rule 1007 as if an order for relief had been entered on an involuntary petition on the date of the entry of the order directing that the case continue under chapter 7.

(B) If a statement of intention is required, it shall be filed within 30 days after entry of the order of conversion or before the first date set for the meeting of creditors, whichever is earlier. The court may grant an extension of time for cause only on written motion filed, or oral request made during a hearing, before the time has expired. Notice of an extension shall be given to the United States trustee and to any committee, trustee, or other party as the court may direct.

(2) New filing periods

A new time period for filing a motion under § 707(b) or (c), a claim, a complaint objecting to discharge, or a complaint to obtain a determination of dischargeability of any debt shall commence under Rules 1017, 3002, 4004, or 4007, but a new time period shall not commence if a chapter 7 case had been converted to a chapter 11, 12, or 13 case and thereafter reconverted to a chapter 7 case and the time for filing a motion under § 707(b) or (c), a claim, a complaint objecting to discharge, or a complaint to obtain a determination of the dischargeability of any debt, or any extension thereof, expired in the original chapter 7 case.

(3) Claims filed before conversion

All claims actually filed by a creditor before conversion of the case are deemed filed in the chapter 7 case.

(4) Turnover of records and property

After qualification of, or assumption of duties by the chapter 7 trustee, any debtor in possession or trustee previously acting in the chapter 11, 12, or 13 case shall, forthwith, unless otherwise ordered, turn over to the chapter 7 trustee all records and property of the estate in the possession or control of the debtor in possession or trustee.

(5) Filing final report and schedule of postpetition debts

(A) Conversion of Chapter 11 or Chapter 12 case

Unless the court directs otherwise, if a chapter 11 or chapter 12 case is converted to chapter 7, the debtor in possession or, if the debtor is not a debtor in possession, the trustee serving at the time of conversion, shall:

(i) not later than 15 days after conversion of the case, file a schedule of unpaid debts incurred after the filing of the petition and before conversion of the case, including the name and address of each holder of a claim; and

(ii) not later than 30 days after conversion of the case, file and transmit to the United States trustee a final report and account;

(B) Conversion of Chapter 13 case

Unless the court directs otherwise, if a chapter 13 case is converted to chapter 7,

(i) the debtor, not later than 15 days after conversion of the case, shall file a schedule of unpaid debts incurred after the filing of the petition and before conversion of the case, including the name and address of each holder of a claim; and

(ii) the trustee, not later than 30 days after conversion of the case, shall file and transmit to the United States trustee a final report and account;

(C) Conversion after confirmation of a plan

Unless the court orders otherwise, if a chapter 11, chapter 12, or chapter 13 case is converted to chapter 7 after confirmation of a plan, the debtor shall file:

(i) a schedule of property not listed in the final report and account acquired after the filing of the petition but before conversion, except if the case is converted from chapter 13 to chapter 7 and § 348(f)(2) does not apply;

(ii) a schedule of unpaid debts not listed in the final report and account incurred after confirmation but before the conversion; and

(iii) a schedule of executory contracts and unexpired leases entered into or assumed after the filing of the petition but before conversion.

(D) Transmission to United States trustee

The clerk shall forthwith transmit to the United States trustee a copy of every schedule filed pursuant to Rule 1019(5).

(6) Postpetition claims; preconversion administrative expenses; notice

A request for payment of an administrative expense incurred before conversion of the case is timely filed under § 503(a) of the Code if it is filed before conversion or a time fixed by the court. If the request is filed by a governmental unit, it is timely if it is filed before conversion or within the later of a time fixed by the court or 180 days after the date of the conversion. A claim of a kind specified in § 348(d) may be filed in accordance with Rules 3001(a)-(d) and 3002. Upon the filing of the schedule of unpaid debts incurred after commencement of the case and before conversion, the clerk, or some other person as the court may direct, shall give notice to those entities listed on the schedule of the time for filing a request for payment of an administrative expense and, unless a notice of insufficient assets to pay a dividend is mailed in accordance with Rule 2002(e), the time for filing a claim of a kind specified in § 348(d).

(7) [Abrogated]

(As amended Mar. 30, 1987, eff. Aug. 1, 1987; Apr. 30, 1991, eff. Aug. 1, 1991; Apr. 23, 1996, eff. Dec. 1, 1996; Apr. 11, 1997, eff. Dec. 1, 1997; Apr. 29, 1999, eff. Dec. 1, 1999; Apr. 23, 2008, eff. Dec. 1, 2008.)

ADVISORY COMMITTEE NOTES

1983 Enactments

This rule is derived from former Bankruptcy Rule 122 and implements § 348 of the Code. The rule applies to proceedings in a chapter 7 case following supersession of a case commenced under chapter 11 or 13, whether the latter was initiated by an original petition or was converted from a pending chapter 7 or another chapter case. The rule is not intended to invalidate any action taken in the superseded case before its conversion to chapter 7.

Paragraph (1). If requirements applicable in the superseded case respecting the filing of schedules of debts and property, or lists of creditors and inventory, and of statements of financial affairs have been complied with before the order directing conversion to liquidation, these documents will ordinarily provide all the information about the debts, property, financial affairs, and contracts of the debtor needed for the administration of the estate. If the information submitted in the superseded case is inadequate for the purposes of administration, however, the court may direct the preparation of further informational material and the manner and time of its submission pursuant to paragraph (1). If no schedules, lists, inventories, or statements were filed in the superseded case, this paragraph imposes the duty on the debtor to file schedules and a statement of affairs pursuant to Rule 1007 as if an involuntary petition had been filed on the date when the court directed the conversion of the case to a liquidation case.

Paragraphs (2) and (3). Paragraph (2) requires notice to be given to all creditors of the order of conversion. The notice is to be included in the notice of the meeting of creditors and Official Form No. 16 may be adapted for use. A meeting of creditors may have been held in the superseded case as required by § 341(a) of the Code but that would not dispense with the need to hold one in the ensuing liquidation case. Section 701(a) of the Code permits the court to appoint the trustee acting in the chapter 11 or 13 case as interim trustee in the chapter 7 case. Section 702(a) of the Code allows creditors to elect a trustee but only at the meeting of creditors held under § 341. The right to elect a trustee is not lost because the chapter 7 case follows a chapter 11 or 13 case. Thus a meeting of creditors is necessary. The date fixed for the meeting of creditors will control at least the time for filing claims pursuant to Rule 3002(c). That time will remain applicable in the ensuing chapter 7 case except as paragraph (3) provides, if that time had expired in an earlier chapter 7 case which was converted to the chapter 11 or 13 case, it is not revived in the subsequent chapter 7 case. The same is true if the time for filing a complaint objecting to discharge or to determine nondischargeability of a debt had expired. Paragraph (3), however, recognizes that such time may be extended by the court under Rule 4004 or 4007 on motion made within the original prescribed time.

Paragraph (4) renders it unnecessary to file anew claims that had been filed in the chapter 11 or 13 case before conversion to chapter 7.

Paragraph (5) contemplates that typically, after the court orders conversion of a chapter case to liquidation, a trustee under chapter 7 will forthwith take charge of the property of the estate and proceed expeditiously to liquidate it. The court may appoint the interim trustee in the chapter 7 case pursuant to § 701(a) of the Code. If creditors do not elect a trustee under § 702, the interim trustee becomes the trustee.

Paragraph (6) requires the trustee or debtor in possession acting in the chapter 11 or 13 case to file a final report and schedule of debts incurred in that case. This schedule will provide the information necessary for giving the notice required by paragraph (7) of the rule.

Paragraph (7) requires that claims that arose in the chapter 11 or 13 case be filed within 60 days after entry of the order converting the case to one under chapter 7. Claims not scheduled pursuant to paragraph (6) of the rule or arising from the rejection of an executory contract entered into during the chapter case may be filed within a time fixed by the court. Pursuant to § 348(c) of the Code, the conversion order is treated as the order for relief to fix the time for the trustee to assume or reject executory contracts under § 365(d).

Paragraph (8) permits the extension of the time for filing claims when claims are not timely filed but only with respect to any surplus that may remain in the estate. See also § 726(a)(2)(C) and (3) of the Code.

1987 Amendments

Paragraph (1) is amended to provide for the filing of a statement of intention in a case converted to chapter 7. Paragraph (1)(B) is added to provide for the filing of the statement of intention when a case is converted to chapter 7. The time for filing the statement of intention and for an extension of that time is governed by § 521(2)(A) of the Code. An extension of time for other required filings is governed by Rule 1007(c), which paragraph (1)(A) incorporates by reference. Because of the amendment to Rule 1007(c), the filing of new lists, schedules, and statements is now governed exclusively by Rule 1019(1).

Paragraph (3) of the rule is expanded to include the effect of conversion of a chapter 11 or 13 case to a chapter 7 case. On conversion of a case from chapter 11 or 13 to a chapter 7 case, parties have a new period within which to file claims or complaints relating to the granting of the discharge or the dischargeability of a debt. This amendment is consistent with the holding and reasoning of the court in *F & M Marquette Nat'l Bank v. Richards,* 780 F.2d 24 (8th Cir. 1985).

Paragraph (4) is amended to deal directly with the status of claims which are properly listed on the schedules filed in a chapter 11 case and deemed filed pursuant to § 1111(a) of the Code. Section 1111(a) is only applicable to the chapter 11 case. On conversion of the chapter 11 case to a chapter 7 case, paragraph (4) governs the status of claims filed in the chapter 11 case. The Third Circuit properly construed paragraph (4) as applicable to claims deemed filed in the superseded chapter 11 case. *In re Crouthamel Potato Chip Co.,* 786 F.2d 141 (3d Cir.1986).

The amendment to paragraph (4) changes that result by providing that only claims that are actually filed in the chapter 11 case are treated as filed in the superseding chapter 7 case. When chapter 11 cases are converted to chapter 7 cases, difficulties in obtaining and verifying the debtors' records are common. It is unfair to the chapter 7 trustee and creditors to require that they be bound by schedules which may not be subject to verification.

Paragraph (6) is amended to place the obligation on the chapter 13 debtor to file a schedule of unpaid debts incurred during the superseded chapter 13 case.

1991 Amendments

This rule is amended to include conversion of a case from chapter 12 to chapter 7 and to implement the United States trustee system.

The amendments to paragraph (1)(A) are stylistic. Reference to the statement of executory contracts is deleted to conform to the amendment to Rule 1007(b)(1) which changes the statement to a schedule of executory contracts and unexpired leases.

Paragraph (1)(B) is amended to enable the United States trustee to monitor the progress of the case and to take appropriate action to enforce the debtor's obligation to perform the statement of intention in a timely manner.

Paragraph (2) is deleted because notice of conversion of the case is required by Rules 1017(d), 2002(f)(2), and 9022. The United States trustee, who supervises trustees pursuant to 28 U.S.C. § 586(a), may give notice of the conversion to the trustee in the superseded case.

Paragraph (6), renumbered as paragraph (5), is amended to reduce to 15 days the time for filing a schedule of postpetition debts and requires inclusion of the name and address of each creditor in connection with the postpetition debt. These changes will enable the clerk to send postpetition creditors a timely notice of the meeting of creditors held pursuant to § 341(a) of the Code. The amendments to this paragraph also provide the United States trustee with the final report and account of the superseded case, and with a copy of every schedule filed after conversion of the case. Conversion to chapter 7 terminates the service of the trustee in the superseded case pursuant to § 348(e) of the Code. Sections 704(a)(9), 1106(a)(1), 1107(a), 1202(b)(1), 1203 and 1302(b)(1) of the Code require the trustee or debtor in possession to file a final report and account with the court and the United States trustee. The words "with the court" are deleted as unnecessary. See Rules 5005(a) and 9001(3).

Paragraph (7), renumbered as paragraph (6), is amended to conform the time for filing postpetition claims to the time for filing prepetition claims pursuant to paragraph (3) (renumbered as paragraph (2)) of this rule and Rule 3002(c). This paragraph is also amended to eliminate the need for a court order to provide notice of the time for filing claims. It is anticipated that this notice will be given together with the notice of the meeting of creditors. It is amended further to avoid the need to fix a time for filing claims arising under § 365(d) if it is a no asset case upon conversion. If assets become available for distribution, the court may fix a time for filing such claims pursuant to Rule 3002(c)(4).

The additions of references to unexpired leases in paragraph (1)(A) and in paragraphs (6) and (7) (renumbered as paragraphs (5) and (6)) are technical amendments to clarify that unexpired leases are included as well as other executory contracts.

1996 Amendments

Subdivision (7) is abrogated to conform to the abrogation of Rule 3002(c)(6).

GAP Report on Rule 1019. No changes were made to the text of the rule. The Committee Note was changed to conform to the proposed changes to Rule 3002 (see GAP Report on Rule 3002 below).

1997 Amendments

The amendments to subdivisions (3) and (5) are technical corrections and stylistic changes. The phrase "superseded case" is deleted because it creates the erroneous impression that conversion of a case results in a new case that is distinct from the original case. Similarly, the phrase "original petition" is deleted because it erroneously implies that there is a second petition with respect to a converted case. See § 348 of the Code.

GAP Report on Rule 1019. No changes to the published draft.

1999 Amendments

Paragraph (1)(B) is amended to clarify that a motion for an extension of time to file a statement of intention must be made by written motion filed before the time expires, or by oral request made at a hearing before the time expires.

Subdivision (6) is amended to provide that a holder of an administrative expense claim incurred after the commencement of the case, but before conversion to chapter 7, is required to file a request for payment under § 503(a) within a time fixed by the court, rather than a proof of claim under § 501 and Rules 3001(a)-(d) and 3002. The 180–day period applicable to governmental units is intended to conform to § 502(b)(9) of the Code and Rule 3002(c)(1). It is unnecessary for the court to fix a time for filing requests for payment if it appears that there are not sufficient assets to pay preconversion administrative expenses. If a time for filing a request for payment of an administrative expense is fixed by the court, it may be enlarged as provided in Rule 9006(b). If an administrative expense claimant fails to timely file the request, it may be tardily filed under § 503(a) if permitted by the court for cause.

The final sentence of Rule 1019(6) is deleted because it is unnecessary in view of the other amendments to this paragraph. If a party has entered into a postpetition contract or lease with the trustee or debtor that constitutes an administrative expense, a timely request for payment must be filed in accordance with this paragraph and § 503(b) of the Code. The time for filing a proof of claim in connection with the rejection of any other executory contract or unexpired lease is governed by Rule 3002(c)(4).

The phrase "including the United States, any state, or any subdivision thereof" is deleted as unnecessary. Other amendments to this rule are stylistic.

Gap Report on Rule 1019. The proposed amendments to Rule 1019(6) were changed to delete the deadline for filing requests for payment of preconversion administrative expenses that would be applicable in all cases, and to provide instead that the court may fix such a deadline. The committee note was revised to clarify that it is not necessary for the court to fix a deadline where there are insufficient assets to pay preconversion administrative expenses.

2008 Amendments

Subdivision (2) is amended to include a new filing period for motions under § 707(b) and (c) of the Code when a case is converted to chapter 7. The establishment of a deadline for filing such motions is not intended to express a position as to whether such motions are permitted under the Code.

CROSS REFERENCES

Appointment of interim trustee, see Fed.Rules Bankr.Proc. Rule 2001, 11 USCA.

Election of trustee, see 11 USCA § 702.

Enlargement of twenty-day period for notice of order of conversion to liquidation case not permitted, see Fed.Rules Bankr.Proc. Rule 9006, 11 USCA.

Failure to effect plan or substantial consummation of confirmed plan, see 11 USCA § 1112.

Meeting of creditors or equity security holders, see Fed. Rules Bankr.Proc. Rule 2003, 11 USCA.

Rule 1020. Small Business Chapter 11 Reorganization Case

(a) Small business debtor designation

In a voluntary chapter 11 case, the debtor shall state in the petition whether the debtor is a small business debtor. In an involuntary chapter 11 case, the debtor shall file within 15 days after entry of the order for relief a statement as to whether the debtor is a small business debtor. Except as provided in subdivision (c), the status of the case as a small business case shall be in accordance with the debtor's statement under this subdivision, unless and until the court enters an order finding that the debtor's statement is incorrect.

(b) Objecting to designation

Except as provided in subdivision (c), the United States trustee or a party in interest may file an objection to the debtor's statement under subdivision (a) no later than 30 days after the conclusion of the meeting of creditors held under § 341(a) of the Code, or within 30 days after any amendment to the statement, whichever is later.

(c) Appointment of committee of unsecured creditors

If a committee of unsecured creditors has been appointed under § 1102(a)(1), the case shall proceed as a small business case only if, and from the time when, the court enters an order determining that the committee has not been sufficiently active and representative to provide effective oversight of the debtor and that the debtor satisfies all the other requirements for being a small business. A request for a determination under this subdivision may be filed by the United States trustee or a party in interest only within a reasonable time after the failure of the committee to be sufficiently active and representative. The debtor may file a request for a determination at any time as to whether the committee has been sufficiently active and representative.

(d) Procedure for objection or determination

Any objection or request for a determination under this rule shall be governed by Rule 9014 and served on: the debtor; the debtor's attorney; the United States trustee; the trustee; any committee appointed under § 1102 or its authorized agent, or, if no committee of unsecured creditors has been appointed under § 1102, the creditors included on the list filed under Rule 1007(d); and any other entity as the court directs.

(Added Apr. 11, 1997, eff. Dec. 1, 1997; Apr. 23, 2008, eff. Dec. 1, 2008.)

ADVISORY COMMITTEE NOTES

1997 Amendments

This rule is designed to implement §§ 1121(e) and 1125(f), which were added to the Code by the Bankruptcy Reform Act of 1994.

GAP Report on Rule 1020. The phrase "or by a later date as the court, for cause, may fix" at the end of the published draft was deleted. The general provisions on reducing or extending time periods under Rule 9006 will be applicable.

2008 Amendments

Under the Code, as amended in 2005, there are no longer any provisions permitting or requiring a small business debtor to elect to be treated as a small business. Therefore, the election provisions in the rule are eliminated.

The 2005 amendments to the Code include several provisions relating to small business cases under chapter 11. Section 101 includes definitions of "small business debtor" and "small business case." The purpose of the new language in this rule is to provide a procedure for informing the parties, the United States trustee, and the court of whether the debtor is a small business debtor, and to provide procedures for resolving disputes regarding the proper characterization of the debtor. Because it is important to resolve such disputes early in the case, a time limit for objecting to the debtor's self-designation is imposed. Rule 9006(b)(1), which governs enlargement of time, is applicable to the time limits set forth in this rule.

An important factor in determining whether the debtor is a small business debtor is whether the United States trustee has appointed a committee of unsecured creditors under § 1102, and whether such a committee is sufficiently active and representative. Subdivision (c), relating to the appointment and activity of a committee of unsecured creditors, is designed to be consistent with the Code's definition of "small business debtor."

Rule 1021. Health Care Business Case

(a) Health care business designation

Unless the court orders otherwise, if a petition in a case under Chapter 7, chapter 9, or chapter 11 states that the debtor is a health care business, the case shall proceed as a case in which the debtor is a health care business.

(b) Motion

The United States trustee or a party in interest may file a motion to determine whether the debtor is a health care business. The motion shall be transmitted to the United States trustee and served on: the debtor; the trustee; any committee elected under § 705 or appointed under § 1102 of the Code or its authorized agent, or, if the case is a chapter 9 municipality case or a chapter 11 reorganization case and no committee of unsecured creditors has been appointed under § 1102, the creditors included on the list filed under Rule 1007(d); and any other entity as the court directs. The motion shall be governed by Rule 9014.

(Added Apr. 23, 2008, eff. Dec. 1, 2008.)

ADVISORY COMMITTEE NOTES

2008 Adoption

Section 101(27A) of the Code, added by the 2005 amendments, defines a health care business. This rule provides procedures for designating the debtor as a health care business. The debtor in a voluntary case, or petitioning creditors in an involuntary case, make that designation by checking the appropriate box on the petition. The rule also provides procedures for resolving disputes regarding the status of the debtor as a health care business.

PART II—OFFICERS AND ADMINISTRATION; NOTICES; MEETINGS; EXAMINATIONS; ELECTIONS; ATTORNEYS AND ACCOUNTANTS

Rule 2001. Appointment of Interim Trustee Before Order for Relief in a Chapter 7 Liquidation Case

(a) Appointment

At any time following the commencement of an involuntary liquidation case and before an order for relief, the court on written motion of a party in interest may order the appointment of an interim trustee under § 303(g) of the Code. The motion shall set forth the necessity for the appointment and may be granted only after hearing on notice to the debtor, the petitioning creditors, the United States trustee, and other parties in interest as the court may designate.

(b) Bond of movant

An interim trustee may not be appointed under this rule unless the movant furnishes a bond in an amount approved by the court, conditioned to indemnify the debtor for costs, attorney's fee, expenses, and damages allowable under § 303(i) of the Code.

(c) Order of Appointment

The order directing the appointment of an interim trustee shall state the reason the appointment is necessary and shall specify the trustee's duties.

(d) Turnover and report

Following qualification of the trustee selected under § 702 of the Code, the interim trustee, unless otherwise ordered, shall (1) forthwith deliver to the trustee all the records and property of the estate in possession or subject to control of the interim trustee and, (2) within 30 days thereafter file a final report and account.

(As amended Mar. 30, 1987, eff. Aug. 1, 1987; Apr. 30, 1991, eff. Aug. 1, 1991.)

ADVISORY COMMITTEE NOTES

This rule is adapted from former Bankruptcy Rule 201. See also former Chapter X Rule 10–201. In conformity with title 11 of the United States Code, this rule substitutes "interim trustee" for "receiver." Subdivision (a) and (e) of Rule 201 are not included because the provisions contained therein are found in detail in § 303(g) of the Code, or they are inconsistent with § 701 of the Code. Similarly, the provisions in Rule 201(d) relating to a debtor's counterbond are not included because of their presence in § 303(g).

Subdivision (a) makes it clear that the court may not on its own motion order the appointment of an interim trustee before an order for relief is entered. Appointment may be ordered only on motion of a party in interest.

Subdivision (b) requires those seeking the appointment of an interim trustee to furnish a bond. The bond may be the same one required of petitioning creditors under § 303(e) of the Code to indemnify the debtor for damages allowed by the court under § 303(i).

Subdivision (c) requires that the order specify which duties enumerated in § 303(g) shall be performed by the interim trustee. Reference should be made to Rule 2015 for additional duties required of an interim trustee including keeping records and filing periodic reports with the court.

Subdivision (d) requires turnover of records and property to the trustee selected under § 702 of the Code, after qualification. That trustee may be the interim trustee who becomes the trustee because of the failure of creditors to elect one under § 702(d) or the trustee elected by creditors under § 702(b), (c).

1991 Amendments

This rule is amended to conform to § 303(g) of the Code which provides that the United States trustee appoints the interim trustee. See Rule X–1003. This rule does not apply to the exercise by the court of the power to act sua sponte pursuant to § 105(a) of the Code.

CROSS REFERENCES

Duty to keep and file records and reports, see Fed.Rules Bankr.Proc. Rule 2015, 11 USCA.

Interim trustee, see 11 USCA § 701.

Motions; form and service, see Fed.Rules Bankr.Proc. Rule 9013, 11 USCA.

Security; proceedings against sureties, see Fed.Rules Bankr.Proc. Rule 9025, 11 USCA.

Rule 2002. Notices to Creditors, Equity Security Holders, Administrators in Foreign Proceedings, Persons Against Whom Provisional Relief is Sought in Ancillary and Other Cross–Border Cases, United States, and United States Trustee

(a) Twenty–day notices to parties in interest

Except as provided in subdivisions (h), (i), (*l*), (p), and (q) of this rule, the clerk, or some other person as the court may direct, shall give the debtor, the trustee, all creditors and indenture trustees at least 20 days' notice by mail of:

(1) the meeting of creditors under § 341 or § 1104(b) of the Code, which notice, unless the court orders otherwise, shall include the debtor's employer identification number, social security number, and any other federal taxpayer identification number;

(2) a proposed use, sale, or lease of property of the estate other than in the ordinary course of business, unless the court for cause shown shortens the time or directs another method of giving notice;

(3) the hearing on approval of a compromise or settlement of a controversy other than approval of an agreement pursuant to Rule 4001(d), unless the court for cause shown directs that notice not be sent;

(4) in a chapter 7 liquidation, a chapter 11 reorganization case, or a chapter 12 family farmer debt adjustment case, the hearing on the dismissal of the case or the conversion of the case to another chapter, unless the hearing is under § 707(a)(3) or § 707(b) or is on dismissal of the case for failure to pay the filing fee;

(5) the time fixed to accept or reject a proposed modification of a plan;

(6) a hearing on any entity's request for compensation or reimbursement of expenses if the request exceeds $1,000;

(7) the time fixed for filing proofs of claims pursuant to Rule 3003(c); and

(8) the time fixed for filing objections and the hearing to consider confirmation of a chapter 12 plan.

(b) Twenty–five–day notices to parties in interest

Except as provided in subdivision (*l*) of this rule, the clerk, or some other person as the court may direct, shall give the debtor, the trustee, all creditors and indenture trustees not less than 25 days notice by mail of the time fixed (1) for filing objections and the hearing to consider approval of a disclosure statement or, under § 1125(f), to make a final determination whether the plan provides adequate information so that a separate disclosure statement is not necessary; and (2) for filing objections and the hearing to consider confirmation of a chapter 9, chapter 11, or chapter 13 plan.

(c) Content of notice

(1) Proposed Use, Sale, or Lease of Property

Subject to Rule 6004, the notice of a proposed use, sale, or lease of property required by subdivision (a)(2) of this rule shall include the time and place of any public sale, the terms and conditions of any private sale and the time fixed for filing objections. The notice of a proposed use, sale, or lease of property, including real estate, is sufficient if it generally describes the property. The notice of a proposed sale or lease of personally identifiable information under § 363(b)(1) of the Code shall state whether the sale is consistent with any policy prohibiting the transfer of the information.

(2) Notice of hearing on compensation

The notice of a hearing on an application for compensation or reimbursement of expenses required by subdivision (a)(6) of this rule shall identify the applicant and the amounts requested.

(3) Notice of hearing on confirmation when plan provides for an injunction

If a plan provides for an injunction against conduct not otherwise enjoined under the Code, the notice required under Rule 2002(b)(2) shall:

(A) include in conspicuous language (bold, italic, or underlined text) a statement that the plan proposes an injunction;

(B) describe briefly the nature of the injunction; and

(C) identify the entities that would be subject to the injunction.

(d) Notice to equity security holders

In a chapter 11 reorganization case, unless otherwise ordered by the court, the clerk, or some other person as the court may direct, shall in the manner and form directed by the court give notice to all equity security holders of (1) the order for relief; (2) any meeting of equity security holders held pursuant to § 341 of the Code; (3) the hearing on the proposed sale of all or substantially all of the debtor's assets; (4) the hearing on the dismissal or conversion of a case to another chapter; (5) the time fixed for filing objections to and the hearing to consider approval of a disclosure statement; (6) the time fixed for filing objections to and the hearing to consider confirmation of a plan; and (7) the time fixed to accept or reject a proposed modification of a plan.

(e) Notice of no dividend

In a chapter 7 liquidation case, if it appears from the schedules that there are no assets from which a dividend can be paid, the notice of the meeting of creditors may include a statement to that effect; that it is unnecessary to file claims; and that if sufficient assets become available for the payment of a dividend, further notice will be given for the filing of claims.

(f) Other notices

Except as provided in subdivision (*l*) of this rule, the clerk, or some other person as the court may direct, shall give the debtor, all creditors, and indenture trustees notice by mail of:

(1) the order for relief;

(2) the dismissal or the conversion of the case to another chapter, or the suspension of proceedings under § 305;

(3) the time allowed for filing claims pursuant to Rule 3002;

(4) the time fixed for filing a complaint objecting to the debtor's discharge pursuant to § 727 of the Code as provided in Rule 4004;

(5) the time fixed for filing a complaint to determine the dischargeability of a debt pursuant to § 523 of the Code as provided in Rule 4007;

(6) the waiver, denial, or revocation of a discharge as provided in Rule 4006;

(7) entry of an order confirming a chapter 9, 11, or 12 plan;

(8) a summary of the trustee's final report in a chapter 7 case if the net proceeds realized exceed $1,500;

(9) a notice under Rule 5008 regarding the presumption of abuse;

(10) a statement under § 704(b)(1) as to whether the debtor's case would be presumed to be an abuse under § 707(b); and

(11) the time to request a delay in the entry of the discharge under §§ 1141(d)(5)(C), 1228(f), and 1328(h). Notice of the time fixed for accepting or rejecting a plan pursuant to Rule 3017(c) shall be given in accordance with Rule 3017(d).

(g) Addressing notices

(1) Notices required to be mailed under Rule 2002 to a creditor, indenture trustee, or equity security holder shall be addressed as such entity or an authorized agent has directed in its last request filed in the particular case. For the purposes of this subdivision—

(A) a proof of claim filed by a creditor or indenture trustee that designates a mailing address constitutes a filed request to mail notices to that address, unless a notice of no dividend has been given under Rule 2002(e) and a later notice of possible dividend under Rule 3002(c)(5) has not been given; and

(B) a proof of interest filed by an equity security holder that designates a mailing address constitutes a filed request to mail notices to that address.

(2) Except as provided in § 342(f) of the Code, if a creditor or indenture trustee has not filed a request designating a mailing address under Rule 2002(g)(1) or Rule 5003(e), the notices shall be mailed to the address shown on the list of creditors or schedule of liabilities, whichever is filed later. If an equity security holder has not filed a request designating a mailing address under Rule 2002(g)(1) or Rule 5003(e), the notices shall be mailed to the address shown on the list of equity security holders.

(3) If a list or schedule filed under Rule 1007 includes the name and address of a legal representative of an infant or incompetent person, and a person other than that representative files a request or proof of claim designating a name and mailing address that differs from the name and address of the representative included in the list or schedule, unless the court orders otherwise, notices under Rule 2002 shall be mailed to the representative included in the list or schedules and to the name and address designated in the request or proof of claim.

(4) Notwithstanding Rule 2002(g) (1) - (3), an entity and a notice provider may agree that when

the notice provider is directed by the court to give a notice, the notice provider shall give the notice to the entity in the manner agreed to and at the address or addresses the entity supplies to the notice provider. That address is conclusively presumed to be a proper address for the notice. The notice provider's failure to use the supplied address does not invalidate any notice that is otherwise effective under applicable law.

(5) A creditor may treat a notice as not having been brought to the creditor's attention under § 342(g)(1) only if, prior to issuance of the notice, the creditor has filed a statement that designates the name and address of the person or organizational subdivision of the creditor responsible for receiving notices under the Code, and that describes the procedures established by the creditor to cause such notices to be delivered to the designated person or subdivision.

(h) Notices to creditors whose claims are filed

In a chapter 7 case, after 90 days following the first date set for the meeting of creditors under § 341 of the Code, the court may direct that all notices required by subdivision (a) of this rule be mailed only to the debtor, the trustee, all indenture trustees, creditors that hold claims for which proofs of claim have been filed, and creditors, if any, that are still permitted to file claims by reason of an extension granted pursuant to Rule 3002(c)(1) or (c)(2). In a case where notice of insufficient assets to pay a dividend has been given to creditors pursuant to subdivision (e) of this rule, after 90 days following the mailing of a notice of the time for filing claims pursuant to Rule 3002(c)(5), the court may direct that notices be mailed only to the entities specified in the preceding sentence.

(i) Notices to committees

Copies of all notices required to be mailed pursuant to this rule shall be mailed to the committees elected under § 705 or appointed under § 1102 of the Code or to their authorized agents. Notwithstanding the foregoing subdivisions, the court may order that notices required by subdivision (a)(2), (3) and (6) of this rule be transmitted to the United States trustee and be mailed only to the committees elected under § 705 or appointed under § 1102 of the Code or to their authorized agents and to the creditors and equity security holders who serve on the trustee or debtor in possession and file a request that all notices be mailed to them. A committee appointed under § 1114 shall receive copies of all notices required by subdivisions (a)(1), (a)(5), (b), (f)(2), and (f)(7), and such other notices as the court may direct.

(j) Notices to the United States

Copies of notices required to be mailed to all creditors under this rule shall be mailed (1) in a chapter 11 reorganization case, to the Securities and Exchange Commission at any place the Commission designates, if the Commission has filed either a notice of appearance in the case or a written request to receive notices; (2) in a commodity broker case, to the Commodity Futures Trading Commission at Washington, D.C.; (3) in a chapter 11 case, to the Internal Revenue Service at its address set out in the register maintained under Rule 5003(e) for the district in which the case is pending; (4) if the papers in the case disclose a debt to the United States other than for taxes, to the United States attorney for the district in which the case is pending and to the department, agency, or instrumentality of the United States through which the debtor became indebted; or (5) if the filed papers disclose a stock interest of the United States, to the Secretary of the Treasury at Washington, D.C.

(k) Notices to United States trustee

Unless the case is a chapter 9 municipality case or unless the United States trustee requests otherwise, the clerk, or some other person as the court may direct, shall transmit to the United States trustee notice of the matters described in subdivisions (a)(2), (a)(3), (a)(4), (a)(8), (b), (f)(1), (f)(2), (f)(4), (f)(6), (f)(7), (f)(8), and (q) of this rule and notice of hearings on all applications for compensation or reimbursement of expenses. Notices to the United States trustee shall be transmitted within the time prescribed in subdivision (a) or (b) of this rule. The United States trustee shall also receive notice of any other matter if such notice is requested by the United States trustee or ordered by the court. Nothing in these rules requires the clerk or any other person to transmit to the United States trustee any notice, schedule, report, application or other document in a case under the Securities Investor Protection Act, 15 U.S.C. § 78aaa et. seq.

(*l*) Notice by publication

The court may order notice by publication if it finds that notice by mail is impracticable or that it is desirable to supplement the notice.

(m) Orders designating matter of notices

The court may from time to time enter orders designating the matters in respect to which, the entity to whom, and the form and manner in which notices shall be sent except as otherwise provided by these rules.

(n) Caption

The caption of every notice given under this rule shall comply with Rule 1005. The caption of every notice required to be given by the debtor to a creditor shall include the information required to be in the notice by § 342(c) of the Code.

(o) Notice of order for relief in consumer case

In a voluntary case commenced by an individual debtor whose debts are primarily consumer debts, the clerk or some other person as the court may direct shall give the trustee and all creditors notice by mail of the order for relief within 20 days from the date thereof.

(p) Notice to a creditor with a foreign address

(1) If, at the request of the United States trustee or a party in interest, or on its own initiative, the court finds that a notice mailed within the time prescribed by these rules would not be sufficient to give a creditor with a foreign address to which notices under these rules are mailed reasonable notice under the circumstances, the court may order that the notice be supplemented with notice by other means or that the time prescribed for the notice by mail be enlarged.

(2) Unless the court for cause orders otherwise, a creditor with a foreign address to which notices under this rule are mailed shall be given at least 30 days' notice of the time fixed for filing a proof of claim under Rule 3002(c) or Rule 3003(c).

(3) Unless the court for cause orders otherwise, the mailing address of a creditor with a foreign address shall be determined under Rule 2002(g).

(q) Notice of petition for recognition of foreign proceeding and of court's intention to communicate with foreign courts and foreign representatives

(1) Notice of Petition for Recognition

The clerk, or some other person as the court may direct, shall forthwith give the debtor, all persons or bodies authorized to administer foreign proceedings of the debtor, all entities against whom provisional relief is being sought under § 1519 of the Code, all parties to litigation pending in the United States in which the debtor is a party at the time of the filing of the petition, and such other entities as the court may direct, at least 20 days' notice by mail of the hearing on the petition for recognition of a foreign proceeding. The notice shall state whether the petition seeks recognition as a foreign main proceeding or foreign nonmain proceeding.

(2) Notice of Court's Intention to Communicate with Foreign Courts and Foreign Representatives.

The clerk, or some other person as the court may direct, shall give the debtor, all persons or bodies authorized to administer foreign proceedings of the debtor, all entities against whom provisional relief is being sought under § 1519 of the Code, all parties to litigation pending in the United States in which the debtor is a party at the time of the filing of the petition, and such other entities as the court may direct, notice by mail of the court's intention to communicate with a foreign court or foreign representative.

(As amended Pub.L. 98–91, § 2(a), Aug. 30, 1983, 97 Stat. 607; Pub.L. 98–353, Title III, § 321, July 10, 1984, 98 Stat. 357; Mar. 30, 1987, eff. Aug. 1, 1987; Apr. 30, 1991, eff. Aug. 1, 1991; Apr. 22, 1993, eff. Aug. 1, 1993; Apr. 23, 1996, eff. Dec. 1, 1996; Apr. 11, 1997, eff. Dec. 1, 1997; Apr. 29, 1999, eff. Dec. 1, 1999; Apr. 17, 2000, eff. Dec. 1, 2000; Apr. 23, 2001, eff. Dec. 1, 2001; Mar. 27, 2003, eff. Dec. 1, 2003; Apr. 26, 2004, eff. Dec. 1, 2004; Apr. 25, 2005, eff. Dec. 1, 2005; Apr. 23, 2008, eff. Dec. 1, 2008.)

ADVISORY COMMITTEE NOTES

1983 Enactments

Some of the notices required by this rule may be given either by the clerk or as the court may otherwise direct. For example, the court may order the trustee or debtor in possession to transmit one or more of the notices required by this rule, such as, notice of a proposed sale of property. See § 363(b) of the Code. When publication of notices is required or desirable, reference should be made to Rule 9008.

Notice of the order for relief is required to be given by § 342 of the Code and by subdivision (f)(1) of this rule. That notice may be combined with the notice of the meeting of creditors as indicated in Official Form No. 16, the notice and order of the meeting of creditors.

Subdivision (a) sets forth the requirement that 20 days notice be given of the significant events in a case under the Bankruptcy Code. The former Act and Rules provided a ten day notice in bankruptcy and Chapter XI [former § 701 et seq. of this title] cases, and a 20 day notice in a Chapter X [former § 501 et seq. of this title] case. This rule generally makes uniform the 20 day notice provision except that subdivision (b) contains a 25 day period for certain events in a chapter 9, 11, or 13 case. Generally, Rule 9006 permits reduction of time periods. Since notice by mail is complete on mailing, the requirement of subdivision (a) is satisfied if the notices are deposited in the mail at least 20 days before the event. See Rule 9006(e). The exceptions referred to in the introductory phrase include the modifications in the notice procedure permitted by subdivision (h) as to non-filing creditors, subdivision (i) as to cases where a committee is functioning, and subdivision (k) where compliance with subdivision (a) is impracticable.

The notice of a proposed sale affords creditors an opportunity to object to the sale and raise a dispute for the court's attention. Section 363(b) of the Code permits the trustee or debtor in possession to sell property, other than in the ordinary course of business, only after notice and hearing. If no objection is raised after notice, § 102(1) provides that there need not be an actual hearing. Thus, absent objection, there would be no court involvement with respect to a trustee's sale. Once an objection is raised, only the court may pass on it.

Prior to the Code the court could shorten the notice period for a proposed sale of property or dispense with notice. This subdivision (a), permits the 20 day period to be shortened in appropriate circumstances but the rule does not contain a provision allowing the court to dispense with notice. The rule is thus consistent with the Code, §§ 363(b) and 102(1)(A) of the Code. See 28 U.S.C. § 2075. It may be necessary, in certain circumstances, however, to use a method of notice other than mail. Subdivision (a)(2) vests the court with discretion, on cause shown, to order a different method. Reference should also be made to Rule 6004 which allows a different type of notice of proposed sales when the property is of little value.

Notice of the hearing on an application for compensation or reimbursement of expenses totalling $100 or less need not be given. In chapter 13 cases relatively small amounts are sometimes allowed for post-confirmation services and it would not serve a useful purpose to require advance notice.

Subdivision (b) is similar to subdivision (a) but lengthens the notice time to 25 days with respect to those events particularly significant in chapter 9, 11 and 13 cases. The additional time may be necessary to formulate objections to a disclosure statement or confirmation of a plan and preparation for the hearing on approval of the disclosure statement or confirmation. The disclosure statement and hearing thereon is only applicable in chapter 9 cases (§ 901(a) of the Code), and chapter 11 cases (§ 1125 of the Code).

Subdivision (c) specifies certain matters that should be included in the notice of a proposed sale of property and notice of the hearing on an application for allowances. Rule 6004 fixes the time within which parties in interest may file objections to a proposed sale of property.

Subdivision (d) relates exclusively to the notices given to equity security holders in chapter 11 cases. Under chapter 11, a plan may impair the interests of the debtor's shareholders or a plan may be a relatively simple restructuring of unsecured debt. In some cases, it is necessary that equity interest holders receive various notices and in other cases there is no purpose to be served. This subdivision indicates that the court is not mandated to order notices but rather that the matter should be treated with some flexibility. The court may decide whether notice is to be given and how it is to be given. Under § 341(b) of the Code, a meeting of equity security holders is not required in each case, only when it is ordered by the court. Thus subdivision (d)(2) requires notice only when the court orders a meeting.

In addition to the notices specified in this subdivision, there may be other events or matters arising in a case as to which equity security holders should receive notice. These are situations left to determination by the court.

Subdivision (e), authorizing a notice of the apparent insufficiency of assets for the payment of any dividend, is correlated with Rule 3002(c)(5), which provides for the issuance of an additional notice to creditors if the possibility of a payment later materializes.

Subdivision (f) provides for the transmission of other notices to which no time period applies. Clause (1) requires notice of the order for relief; this complements the mandate of § 342 of the Code requiring such notice as is appropriate of the order for relief. This notice may be combined with the notice of the meeting of creditors to avoid the necessity of more than one mailing. See Official Form No. 16, notice of meeting of creditors.

Subdivision (g) recognizes that an agent authorized to receive notices for a creditor may, without a court order, designate where notices to the creditor he represents should be addressed. Agent includes an officer of a corporation, an attorney at law, or an attorney in fact if the requisite authority has been given him. It should be noted that Official Forms Nos. 17 and 18 do not include an authorization of the holder of a power of attorney to receive notices for the creditor. Neither these forms nor this rule carries any implication that such an authorization may not be given in a power of attorney or that a request for notices to be addressed to both the creditor or his duly authorized agent may not be filed.

Subdivision (h). After the time for filing claims has expired in a chapter 7 case, creditors who have not filed their claims in accordance with Rule 3002(c) are not entitled to share in the estate except as they may come within the special provisions of § 726 of the Code or Rule 3002(c)(6). The elimination of notice to creditors who have no recognized stake in the estate may permit economies in time and expense. Reduction of the list of creditors to receive notices under this subdivision is discretionary. This subdivision does not apply to the notice of the meeting of creditors.

Subdivision (i) contains a list of matters of which notice may be given a creditors' committee or to its authorized agent in lieu of notice to the creditors. Such notice may serve every practical purpose of a notice to all the creditors and save delay and expense. In re Schulte-United, Inc., 59 F.2d 553, 561 (8th Cir.1932).

Subdivision (j). The premise for the requirement that the district director of internal revenue receive copies of notices that all creditors receive in a chapter 11 case is that every debtor is potentially a tax debtor of the United States. Notice to the district director alerts him to the possibility that a tax debtor's estate is about to be liquidated or reorganized and that the debtor may be discharged. When other indebtedness to the United States is indicated, the United States attorney is notified as the person in the best position to protect the interests of the government. In addition, the provision requires notice by mail to the head of any department, agency, or instrumentality of the United States through whose action the debtor became indebted to the United States. This rule is not intended to preclude a local rule from requiring a state or local tax authority to receive some or all of the notices to creditors under these rules.

Subdivision (k) specifies two kinds of situations in which notice by publication may be appropriate: (1) when notice by mail is impracticable; and (2) when notice by mail alone is less than adequate. Notice by mail may be impracticable when, for example, the debtor has disappeared or his records have been destroyed and the names and addresses of his creditors are unavailable, or when the number of creditors with nominal claims is very large and the estate to be distributed may be insufficient to defray the costs of issuing the notices. Supplementing notice by mail is also indicated when the debtor's records are incomplete or inaccurate and it is reasonable to believe that publication may reach some of the creditors who would otherwise be missed. Rule 9008 applies when the court directs notice by publication under this rule. Neither clause (2) of subdivision (a) nor subdivision (k) of this rule is concerned with the publication of advertisement to the general public of a sale of property of the estate at public auction under Rule 6004(b). See 3 Collier, Bankruptcy 522–23 (14th ed. 1971); 4B id. 1165–67 (1967); 2 id. ¶363.03 (15th ed. 1981).

Subdivision (m). Inclusion in notices to creditors of information as to other names used by the debtor as required by Rule 1005 will assist them in the preparation of their proofs of claim and in deciding whether to file a complaint objecting to the debtor's discharge. Additional names may be listed by the debtor on his statement of affairs when he did not file the petition. The mailing of notices should not be postponed to await a delayed filing of the statement of financial affairs.

1987 Amendments

Subdivision (a) is amended to provide that notice of a hearing on an application for compensation must be given only when the amount requested is in excess of $500.

Subdivision (d). A new notice requirement is added as clause (3). When a proposed sale is of all or substantially all of the debtor's assets, it is appropriate that equity security holders be given notice of the proposed sale. The clauses of subdivision (d) are renumbered to accommodate this addition.

Subdivision (f). Clause (7) is eliminated. Mailing of a copy of the discharge order is governed by Rule 4004(g).

Subdivision (g) is amended to relieve the clerk of the duty to mail notices to the address shown in a proof of claim when a notice of no dividend has been given pursuant to Rule 2002. This amendment avoids the necessity of the clerk searching proofs of claim which are filed in no dividend cases to ascertain whether a different address is shown.

Subdivision (n) was enacted by § 321 of the 1984 amendments.

1991 Amendments

Subdivision (a)(3) is amended to exclude compromise or settlement agreements concerning adequate protection or which modify or terminate the automatic stay, provide for use of cash collateral, or create a senior or equal lien on collateral to obtain credit. Notice requirements relating to approval of such agreements are governed by Rule 4001(d).

Subdivision (a)(5) is amended to include a hearing on dismissal or conversion of a chapter 12 case. This subdivision does not apply when a hearing is not required. It is also amended to avoid the necessity of giving notice to all creditors of a hearing on the dismissal of a consumer debtor's case based on substantial abuse of chapter 7. Such hearings on dismissal under § 707(b) of the Code are governed by Rule 1017(e).

Subdivision (a)(9) is added to provide for notice of the time fixed for filing objections and the hearing to consider confirmation of a plan in a chapter 12 case. Section 1224 of the Code requires "expedited notice" of the confirmation hearing in a chapter 12 case and requires that the hearing be concluded not later than 45 days after the filing of the plan unless the time is extended for cause. This amendment establishes 20 days as the notice period. The court may shorten this time on its own motion or on motion of a party in interest. The notice includes both the date of the hearing and the date for filing objections, and must be accompanied by a copy of the plan or a summary of the plan in accordance with Rule 3015(d).

Subdivision (b) is amended to delete as unnecessary the references to subdivisions (h) and (i).

Subdivision (d) does not require notice to equity security holders in a chapter 12 case. The procedural burden of requiring such notice is outweighed by the likelihood that all equity security holders of a family farmer will be informed of the progress of the case without formal notice. Subdivision (d) is amended to recognize that the United States trustee may convene a meeting of equity security holders pursuant to § 341(b).

Subdivision (f)(2) is amended and subdivision (f)(4) is deleted to require notice of any conversion of the case, whether the conversion is by court order or is effectuated by the debtor filing a notice of conversion pursuant to §§ 1208(a) or 1307(a). Subdivision (f)(8), renumbered (f)(7), is amended to include entry of an order confirming a chapter 12 plan. Subdivision (f)(9) is amended to increase the amount to $1,500.

Subdivisions (g) and (j) are amended to delete the words "with the court" and subdivision (i) is amended to delete the words "with the clerk" because these phrases are unnecessary. See Rules 5005(a) and 9001(3).

Subdivision (i) is amended to require that the United States trustee receive notices required by subdivision (a)(2), (3) and (7) of this rule notwithstanding a court order limiting such notice to committees and to creditors and equity security holders who request such notices. Subdivision (i) is amended further to include committees elected pursuant to § 705 of the Code and to provide that committees of retired employees appointed in chapter 11 cases receive certain notices.

Subdivision (k) is derived from Rule X–1008. The administrative functions of the United States trustee pursuant to 28 U.S.C. § 586(a) and standing to be heard on issues under § 307 and other sections of the Code require that the United States trustee be informed of developments and issues in every case except chapter 9 cases. The rule omits those notices described in subdivision (a)(1) because a meeting of creditors is convened only by the United States trustee, and those notices described in subdivision (a)(4) (date fixed for filing claims against a surplus), subdivision (a)(6) (time fixed to accept or reject proposed modification of a plan), subdivision (a)(8) (time fixed for filing proofs of claims in chapter 11 cases), subdivision (f)(3) (time fixed for filing claims in chapter 7, 12, and 13 cases), and subdivision (f)(5) (time fixed for filing complaint to determine dischargeability of debt) because these notices do not relate to matters that generally involve the United States trustee. Nonetheless, the omission of these notices does not prevent the United States trustee from receiving such notices upon request. The United States trustee also receives notice of hearings on applications for compensation or reimbursement without regard to the $500 limitation contained in subdivision (a)(7) of this rule. This rule is intended to be flexible in that it permits the United States trustee in a particular judicial district to request notices in certain categories, and to request not to receive notices in other categories, when the practice in that district makes that desirable.

1993 Amendments

Subdivision (j) is amended to avoid the necessity of sending an additional notice to the Washington, D.C. address of the Securities and Exchange Commission if the Commission prefers to have notices sent only to a local office. This change also clarifies that notices required to be mailed pursuant to this rule must be sent to the Securities and Exchange Commission only if it has filed a notice of appearance or has filed a written request. Other amendments are stylistic and make no substantive change.

1996 Amendments

Paragraph (a)(4) is abrogated to conform to the abrogation of Rule 3002(c)(6). The remaining paragraphs of subdivision (a) are renumbered, and references to these paragraphs contained in other subdivisions of this rule are amended accordingly.

Paragraph (f)(8) is amended so that a summary of the trustee's final account, which is prepared after distribution of property, does not have to be mailed to the debtor, all creditors, and indenture trustees in a chapter 7 case. Parties are sufficiently protected by receiving a summary of the trustee's final report that informs parties of the proposed distribution of property.

Subdivision (h) is amended (1) to provide that an order under this subdivision may not be issued if a notice of no dividend is given pursuant to Rule 2002(e) and the time for filing claims has not expired as provided in Rule 3002(c)(5); (2) to clarify that notices required to be mailed by subdivision (a) to parties other than creditors must be mailed to those entities despite an order issued pursuant to subdivision (h); (3) to provide that if the court, pursuant to Rule 3002(c)(1) or 3002(c)(2), has granted an extension of time to file a proof of claim, the creditor for whom the extension has been granted must continue to receive notices despite an order issued pursuant to subdivision (h); and (4) to delete references to subdivision (a)(4) and Rule 3002(c)(6), which have been abrogated.

Other amendments to this rule are stylistic.

GAP Report on Rule 2002. No changes since publication, except for stylistic changes and the correction of a typographical error in the committee note.

1997 Amendments

Paragraph (a)(1) is amended to include notice of a meeting of creditors convened under § 1104(b) of the Code for the purpose of electing a trustee in a chapter 11 case. The court for cause shown may order the 20–day period reduced pursuant to Rule 9006(c)(1).

Subdivision (n) is amended to conform to the 1994 amendment to § 342 of the Code. As provided in § 342(c), the failure of a notice given by the debtor to a creditor to contain the information required by § 342(c) does not invalidate the legal effect of the notice.

GAP Report on Rule 2002. No changes to the published draft.

1999 Amendments

Paragraph (a)(4) is amended to conform to the amendments to Rule 1017. If the United States trustee files a motion to dismiss a case for the debtor's failure to file the list of creditors, schedules, or the statement of financial affairs within the time specified in § 707(a)(3), the amendments to this rule and to Rule 1017 eliminate the requirement that all creditors receive notice of the hearing.

Paragraph (a)(4) is amended further to conform to Rule 1017(b), which requires that notice of the hearing on dismissal of a case for failure to pay the filing fee be served on only the debtor and the trustee.

Paragraph (f)(2) is amended to provide for notice of the suspension of proceedings under § 305.

Gap Report on Rule 2002. No changes since publication.

2000 Amendments

Paragraph(a)(6) is amended to increase the dollar amount from $500 to $1,000. The amount was last amended in 1987, when it was changed from $100 to $500. The amendment also clarifies that the notice is required only if a particular entity is requesting more than $1,000 as compensation or reimbursement of expenses. If several professionals are requesting compensation or reimbursement, and only one hearing will be held on all applications, notice under paragraph (a)(6) is required only with respect to the entities that have requested more than $1,000. If each applicant requests $1,000 or less, notice under paragraph (a)(6) is not required even though the aggregate amount of all applications to be considered at the hearing is more than $1,000.

If a particular entity had filed prior applications or had received compensation or reimbursement of expenses at an earlier time in the case, the amounts previously requested or awarded are not considered when determining whether the present application exceeds $1,000 for the purpose of applying this rule.

GAP Report on Rule 2002(a). No changes since publication.

2001 Amendments

Subdivision (c)(3) is added to assure that parties given notice of a hearing to consider confirmation of a plan under subdivision (b) are given adequate notice of an injunction provided for in the plan if it would enjoin conduct that is not otherwise enjoined by operation of the Code. The validity and effect of any injunction provided for in a plan are substantive law matters that are beyond the scope of these rules.

The notice requirement of subdivision (c)(3) is not applicable to an injunction contained in a plan if it is substantially the same as an injunction provided under the Code. For example, if a plan contains an injunction against acts to collect a discharged debt from the debtor, Rule 2002(c)(3) would not apply because that conduct would be enjoined under § 524(a)(2) upon the debtor's discharge. But if a plan provides that creditors will be enjoined from asserting claims against persons who are not debtors in the case, the notice of the confirmation hearing must include the information required under Rule 2002(c)(3) because that conduct would not be enjoined by operation of the Code. *See* § 524(e).

The requirement that the notice identify the entities that would be subject to the injunction requires only reasonable identification under the circumstances. If the entities that would be subject to the injunction cannot be identified by name, the notice may describe them by class or category if reasonable under the circumstances. For example, it may be sufficient for the notice to identify the entities as "all creditors of the debtor" and for the notice to be published in a manner that satisfies due process requirements.

Subdivision (g) has been revised to clarify that where a creditor or indenture trustee files both a proof of claim which includes a mailing address and a separate request designating a mailing address, the last paper filed determines the proper address. The amendments also clarify that a request designating a mailing address is effective only with respect to a particular case.

Under Rule 2002(g), a duly filed proof of claim is considered a request designating a mailing address if a notice of no dividend has been given under Rule 2002(e), but has been superseded by a subsequent notice of possible dividend under Rule 3002(c)(5). A duly filed proof of interest is considered a request designating a mailing address of an equity security holder.

Rule 2002(g)(3) is added to assure that notices to an infant or incompetent person under this rule are mailed to the appropriate guardian or other legal representative. Under Rule 1007(m), if the debtor knows that a creditor is an infant or incompetent person, the debtor is required to include in the list and schedule of creditors the name and address of the person upon whom process would be served in an adversary proceeding in accordance with Rule 7004(b)(2). If the infant or incompetent person, or another person, files a request or proof of claim designating a different name and mailing address, the notices would have to be mailed to both names and addresses until the court resolved the issue as to the proper mailing address.

The other amendments to Rule 2002(g) are stylistic.

CHANGES MADE AFTER PUBLICATION AND COMMENTS

In Rule 2002(c)(3), the word "highlighted" was replaced with "underlined" because highlighted documents are difficult to scan electronically for inclusion in the clerks' files. The Committee Note was revised to put in a more prominent position the statement that the validity and effect of any injunction provided for in a plan are substantive matters beyond the scope of the rules.

In Rule 2002(g), no changes were made.

2003 Amendments

Subdivision (a)(1) of the rule is amended to direct the clerk or other person giving notice of the § 341 or § 1104(b) meeting of creditors to include the debtor's full social security number on the notice. Official Form 9, the form of the notice of the meeting of creditors that will become a part of the court's file in the case, will include only the last four digits of the debtor's social security number. This rule, however, directs the clerk to include the full social security number on the notice that is served on the creditors and other identified parties, unless the court orders otherwise in a particular case. This will enable creditors and other parties in interest who are in possession of the debtor's social security number to verify the debtor's identity and proceed accordingly. The filed Official Form 9, however, will not include the debtor's full social security number. This will prevent the full social security number from becoming a part of the court's file in the case, and the number will not be included in the court's electronic records. Creditors who already have the debtor's social security number will be able to verify the existence of a case under the debtor's social security number, but any person searching the electronic case files without the number will not be able to acquire the debtor's social security number.

2004 Amendments

The rule is amended to reflect that the structure of the Internal Revenue Service no longer includes a District Director. Thus, rather than sending notice to the District Director, the rule now requires that the notices be sent to the location designated by the Service and set out in the register of addresses maintained by the clerk under Rule 5003(e). The other change is stylistic.

2005 Amendments

A new paragraph (g)(4) is inserted in the rule. The new paragraph authorizes an entity and a notice provider to agree that the notice provider will give notices to the entity at the address or addresses set out in their agreement. Rule 9001(9) sets out the definition of a notice provider.

The business of many entities is national in scope, and technology currently exists to direct the transmission of notice (both electronically and in paper form) to those entities in an accurate and much more efficient manner than by sending individual notices to the same creditor by separate mailings. The rule authorizes an entity and a notice provider to determine the manner of the service as well as to set the address or addresses to which the notices must be sent. For example, they could agree that all notices sent by the notice provider to the entity must be sent to a single, nationwide electronic or postal address. They could also establish local or regional addresses to which notices would be sent in matters pending in specific districts. Since the entity and notice provider also can agree on the date of the commencement of service under the agreement, there is no need to set a date in the rule after which notices would have to be sent to the address or addresses that the entity establishes. Furthermore, since the entity supplies the address to the notice provider, use of that address is conclusively presumed to be proper. Nonetheless, if that address is not used, the notice still may be effective if the notice is otherwise effective under applicable law. This is the same treatment given under Rule 5003(e) to notices sent to governmental units at addresses other than those set out in that register of addresses.

The remaining subdivisions of Rule 2002(g) continue to govern the addressing of a notice that is not sent pursuant to an agreement described in Rule 2002(g)(4).

2008 Amendments

Subdivision (b) is amended to provide for 25 days' notice of the time for the court to make a final determination whether the plan in a small business case can serve as a disclosure statement. Conditional approval of a disclosure statement in a small business case is governed by Rule 3017.1 and does not require 25 days' notice. The court may consider this matter in a hearing combined with the confirmation hearing in a small business case.

Because of the requirements of Rule 6004(g), subdivision (c)(1) is amended to require that a trustee leasing or selling personally identifiable information under § 363(b)(1)(A) or (B) of the Code, as amended in 2005, include in the notice of the lease or sale transaction a statement as to whether the lease or sale is consistent with a policy prohibiting the transfer of the information.

Subdivisions (f)(9) and (10) are new. They reflect the 2005 amendments to §§ 342(d) and 704(b) of the Code. Section 342(d) requires the clerk to give notice to creditors shortly after the commencement of the case as to whether a presumption of abuse exists. Subdivision (f)(9) adds this notice to the list of notices that the clerk must give. Subdivision (f)(10) implements the amendment to § 704(b), which requires the court to provide a copy to all creditors of a statement by the United States trustee or bankruptcy administrator as to whether the debtor's case would be presumed to be an abuse under § 707(b) not later than five days after receiving it.

Subdivision (f)(11) is also added to provide notice to creditors of the debtor's filing of a statement in a chapter 11, 12, or 13 case that there is no reasonable cause to believe that § 522(q) applies in the case. This allows a creditor who disputes that assertion to request a delay of the entry of the discharge in the case.

Subdivision (g)(2) of the rule is amended because the 2005 amendments to § 342(f) of the Code permit creditors in chapter 7 and 13 individual debtor cases to file a notice with any bankruptcy court of the address to which the creditor wishes all notices to be sent. The amendment to Rule 2002(g)(2) therefore only limits application of the subdivision when a creditor files a notice under § 342(f).

New subdivision (g)(5) implements § 342(g)(1) which was added to the Code in 2005. Section 342(g)(1) allows a creditor to treat a notice as not having been brought to the creditor's attention, and so potentially ineffective, until it is received by a person or organizational subdivision that the creditor has designated to receive notices under the Bankruptcy Code. Under that section, the creditor must have established reasonable procedures for such notices to be delivered to the designated person or subdivision. The rule provides that, in order to challenge a notice under § 342(g)(1), a creditor must have filed the name and address of the designated notice recipient, as well as a description of the procedures for directing notices to that recipient, prior to the time that the challenged notice was issued. The filing required by the rule may be made as part of a creditor's filing under § 342(f), which allows a creditor to file a notice of the address to be used by all bankruptcy courts or by particular bankruptcy courts to provide notice to the creditor in cases under chapters 7 and 13. Filing the name and address of the designated notice recipient and the procedures for directing notices to that recipient will reduce uncertainty as to the proper party for receiving notice and limit factual disputes as to whether a notice recipient has been designated and as to the nature of procedures adopted to direct notices to the recipient.

Subdivision (k) is amended to add notices given under subdivision (q) to the list of notices which must be served on the United States trustee.

Section 1514(d) of the Code, added by the 2005 amendments, requires that such additional time as is reasonable under the circumstances be given to creditors with foreign addresses with respect to notices and the filing of a proof of claim. Thus, subdivision (p)(1) is added to this rule to give the court flexibility to direct that notice by other means shall supplement notice by mail, or to enlarge the notice period, for creditors with foreign addresses. If cause exists, such as likely delays in the delivery of mailed notices in particular locations, the court may order that notice also be given by email, facsimile, or private courier. Alternatively, the court may enlarge the notice period for a creditor with a foreign address. It is expected that in most situations involving foreign creditors, fairness will not require any additional notice or extension of the notice period. This rule recognizes that the court has discretion to establish procedures to determine, on its own initiative, whether relief under subdivision (p) is appropriate, but that the court is not required to establish such procedures and may decide to act only on request of a party in interest.

Subdivision (p)(2) is added to the rule to grant creditors with a foreign address to which notices are mailed at least 30 days' notice of the time within which to file proofs of claims if notice is mailed to the foreign address, unless the court orders otherwise. If cause exists, such as likely delays in the delivery of notices in particular locations, the court may extend the notice period for creditors with foreign addresses. The court may also shorten the additional notice time if circumstances so warrant. For example, if the court in a chapter 11 case determines that supplementing the notice to a foreign creditor with notice by electronic means, such as email or facsimile, would give the creditor reasonable notice, the court may order that the creditor be given only 20 days' notice in accordance with Rule 2002(a)(7).

Subdivision (p)(3) is added to provide that the court may, for cause, override a creditor's designation of a foreign address under Rule 2002(g). For example, if a party in interest believes that a creditor has wrongfully designated a foreign address to obtain additional time when it has a significant presence in the United States, the party can ask the court to order that notices to that creditor be sent to an address other than the one designated by the foreign creditor.

Subdivision (q) is added to require that notice of the hearing on the petition for recognition of a foreign proceeding be given to the debtor, all administrators in foreign proceedings of the debtor, entities against whom provisional relief is sought, and entities with whom the debtor is engaged in litigation at the time of the commencement of the case. There is no need at this stage of the proceedings to provide notice to all creditors. If the foreign representative should take action to commence a case under another chapter of the Code, the rules governing those proceedings will operate to provide that notice is given to all creditors.

The rule also requires notice of the court's intention to communicate with a foreign court or foreign representative.

HISTORICAL NOTES

Effective and Applicability Provisions

1984 Acts. Amendment by Pub.L. 98–353 effective with respect to cases filed 90 days after July 10, 1984, see section 553 of Pub.L. 98–353, set out as a note under section 101 of this title.

1983 Acts. Section 1 of Pub.L. 98–91 provided: "That rule 2002(f) of the Bankruptcy Rules, as proposed by the United States Supreme Court in the order of April 25, 1983, of the court, shall take effect on August 1, 1983, except as otherwise provided in section 2 [amending subd. (f) of this rule and enacting a provision set out as a note below]."

Section 2(b) of Pub.L. 98–91 provided that: "The amendment made by subsection (a) [amending subd. (f) of this rule] shall take effect on August 1, 1983."

CROSS REFERENCES

Form and manner of publication of notices, see Fed.Rules Bankr.Proc. Rule 9008, 11 USCA.

General requirements of form for creditors' notices, see Fed.Rules Bankr.Proc. Rule 9004, 11 USCA.

Hearing on disclosure statement in municipality debt adjustment and reorganization cases, see Fed.Rules Bankr. Proc. Rule 3017, 11 USCA.

Notice by mail complete on mailing, see Fed.Rules Bankr. Proc. Rule 9006, 11 USCA.

Notice of—

Dismissal for failure to pay filing fees, see Fed.Rules Bankr.Proc. Rule 1017, 11 USCA.

Dividend and of time to file proof of claim in liquidation case, see Fed.Rules Bankr.Proc. Rule 3002, 11 USCA.

Hearing on compromise or settlement to creditors, debtor, indenture trustees, and others designated by court, see Fed.Rules Bankr.Proc. Rule 9019, 11 USCA.

Hearing on confirmation of individual debt adjustment plan to include plan or summary, see Fed.Rules Bankr.Proc. Rule 3015, 11 USCA.

Hearing on dismissal of case, see Fed.Rules Bankr.Proc. Rule 1017, 11 USCA.

Order of conversion to liquidation case, see Fed.Rules Bankr.Proc. Rule 1019, 11 USCA.

Time extended to file claims against surplus in converted liquidation case, see Fed.Rules Bankr.Proc. Rule 1019, 11 USCA.

Time fixed for filing complaint objecting to discharge in reorganization case, see Fed.Rules Bankr.Proc. Rule case, see Fed.Rules Bankr.Proc. Rule 4004, 11 USCA.

Time fixed for filing complaint to determine debt's dischargeability, see Fed.Rules Bankr.Proc. Rule 4007, 11 USCA.

Use, sale, or lease of property other than in ordinary course, see Fed.Rules Bankr.Proc. Rule 6004, 11 USCA.

Waiver, denial, or revocation of discharge, see Fed.Rules Bankr.Proc. Rule 4006, 11 USCA.

Reduction in time periods generally, see Fed.Rules Bankr.Proc. Rule 9006, 11 USCA.

Reduction in twenty-day period for notice to file claims not permitted—

Against surplus in estate in liquidation case, see Fed. Rules Bankr.Proc. Rule 9006, 11 USCA.

In municipality debt adjustment or reorganization cases, see Fed.Rules Bankr.Proc. Rule 9006, 11 USCA.

Review by court on plan's confirmation after notice and hearing pursuant to, see Fed.Rules Bankr.Proc. Rule 3020, 11 USCA.

Rule 2003. Meeting of Creditors or Equity Security Holders

(a) Date and place

Except as otherwise provided in § 341(e) of the Code, in a chapter 7 liquidation or a chapter 11 reorganization case, the United States trustee shall call a meeting of creditors to be held no fewer than 20 and no more than 40 days after the order for relief. In a chapter 12 family farmer's debt adjustment case, the United States trustee shall call a meeting of creditors to be held no fewer than 20 and no more than 35 days after the order for relief. In a chapter 13 individual's debt adjustment case, the United States trustee shall call a meeting of creditors to be held no fewer than 20 and no more than 50 days after the order for relief. If there is an appeal from or a motion to vacate the order for relief, or if there is a motion to dismiss the case, the United States trustee may set a later date for the meeting. The meeting may be held at a regular place for holding court or at any other place designated by the United States trustee within the district convenient for the parties in interest. If the United States trustee designates a place for the meeting which is not regularly staffed by the United States trustee or an assistant who may preside at the meeting, the meeting may be held not more than 60 days after the order for relief.

(b) Order of meeting

(1) Meeting of Creditors

The United States trustee shall preside at the meeting of creditors. The business of the meeting shall include the examination of the debtor under oath and, in a chapter 7 liquidation case, may include the election of a creditors' committee and, if the case is not under subchapter V of chapter 7, the election of a trustee. The presiding officer shall have the authority to administer oaths.

(2) Meeting of equity security holders

If the United States trustee convenes a meeting of equity security holders pursuant to § 341(b) of the Code, the United States trustee shall fix a date for the meeting and shall preside.

(3) Right to vote

In a chapter 7 liquidation case, a creditor is entitled to vote at a meeting if, at or before the meeting, the creditor has filed a proof of claim or a writing setting forth facts evidencing a right to vote pursuant to § 702(a) of the Code unless objection is made to the claim or the proof of claim is insufficient on its face. A creditor of a partnership may file a proof of claim or writing evidencing a right to vote for the trustee for the estate of a general partner notwithstanding that a trustee for the estate of the partnership has previously qualified. In the event of an objection to the amount or allowability of a claim for the purpose of voting, unless the court orders otherwise, the United States trustee shall tabulate the votes for each alternative presented by the dispute and, if resolution of such dispute is necessary to determine the result of the election, the tabulations for each alternative shall be reported to the court.

(c) Record of meeting

Any examination under oath at the meeting of creditors held pursuant to § 341(a) of the Code shall be recorded verbatim by the United States trustee using electronic sound recording equipment or other means of recording, and such record shall be preserved by the United States trustee and available for public access until two years after the conclusion of the meeting of creditors. Upon request of any entity, the United States trustee shall certify and provide a copy or transcript of such recording at the entity's expense.

(d) Report of election and resolution of disputes in a chapter 7 case

(1) Report of undisputed election

In a chapter 7 case, if the election of a trustee or a member of a creditors' committee is not disputed, the United States trustee shall promptly file a report of the election, including the name and address of the person or entity elected and a statement that the election is undisputed.

(2) Disputed election

If the election is disputed, the United States trustee shall promptly file a report stating that the election is disputed, informing the court of the nature of the dispute, and listing the name and address of any candidate elected under any alternative presented by the dispute. No later than the date on which the report is filed, the United States trustee shall mail a copy of the report to any party in interest that has made a request to receive a copy of the report. Pending disposition by the court of a disputed election for trustee, the interim trustee shall continue in office. Unless a motion for the resolution of the dispute is filed no later than 10 days after the United States trustee files a report of a disputed election for trustee, the interim trustee shall serve as trustee in the case.

(e) Adjournment

The meeting may be adjourned from time to time by announcement at the meeting of the adjourned date and time without further written notice.

(f) Special meetings

The United States trustee may call a special meeting of creditors on request of a party in interest or on the United States trustee's own initiative.

(g) Final meeting

If the United States trustee calls a final meeting of creditors in a case in which the net proceeds realized exceed $1,500, the clerk shall mail a summary of the trustee's final account to the creditors with a notice of the meeting, together with a statement of the amount of the claims allowed. The trustee shall attend the final meeting and shall, if requested, report on the administration of the estate.

(As amended Mar. 30, 1987, eff. Aug. 1, 1987; Apr. 30, 1991, eff. Aug. 1, 1991; Apr. 22, 1993, eff. Aug. 1, 1993; Apr. 29, 1999, eff. Dec. 1, 1999; Mar. 27, 2003, eff. Dec. 1, 2003; Apr. 23, 2008, eff. Dec. 1, 2008.)

ADVISORY COMMITTEE NOTES

Section 341(a) of the Code requires a meeting of creditors in a chapter 7, 11 or 13 case, and § 341(b) permits the court to order a meeting of equity security holders. A major change from prior law, however, prohibits the judge from attending or presiding over the meeting. Section 341(c).

This rule does not apply either in a case for the reorganization of a railroad or for the adjustment of debts of a municipality. Sections 1161 and 901 render §§ 341 and 343 inapplicable in these types of cases. Section 341 sets the requirement for a meeting of creditors and § 343 provides for the examination of the debtor.

Subdivision (a). The meeting is to be held between 20 and 40 days after the date of the order for relief. In a voluntary case, the date of the order for relief is the date of the filing of the petition (§ 301 of the Code); in an involuntary case, it is the date of an actual order (§ 303(i) of the Code).

Subdivision (b) provides flexibility as to who will preside at the meeting of creditors. The court may designate a person to serve as presiding officer, such as the interim trustee appointed under § 701 of the Code. If the court does not designate anyone, the clerk will preside. In either case, creditors may elect a person of their own choosing. In any event, the clerk may remain to record the proceedings and take appearances. Use of the clerk is not contrary to the legislative policy of § 341(c). The judge remains insulated from any information coming forth at the meeting and any information obtained by the clerk must not be relayed to the judge.

Although the clerk may preside at the meeting, the clerk is not performing any kind of judicial role, nor should the clerk give any semblance of performing such a role. It would be pretentious for the clerk to ascend the bench, don a robe or be addressed as "your honor". The clerk should not appear to parties or others as any type of judicial officer.

In a chapter 11 case, if a committee of unsecured creditors has been appointed pursuant to § 1102(a)(1) of the Code and a chairman has been selected, the chairman will preside or a person, such as the attorney for the committee, may be designated to preside by the chairman.

Since the judge must fix the bond of the trustee but cannot be present at the meeting, the rule allows the creditors to recommend the amount of the bond. They should be able to obtain relevant information concerning the extent of assets of the debtor at the meeting.

Paragraph (1) authorizes the presiding officer to administer oaths. This is important because the debtor's examination must be under oath.

Paragraph (3) of subdivision (b) has application only in a chapter 7 case. That is the only type of case under the Code that permits election of a trustee or committee. In all other cases, no vote is taken at the meeting of creditors. If it is necessary for the court to make a determination with respect to a claim, the meeting may be adjourned until the objection or dispute is resolved.

The second sentence recognizes that partnership creditors may vote for a trustee of a partner's estate along with the separate creditors of the partner. Although § 723(c) gives the trustee of a partnership a claim against a partner's estate for the full amount of partnership creditors' claims allowed, the purpose and function of this provision are to simplify distribution and prevent double proof, not to disfranchise partnership creditors in electing a trustee of an estate against which they hold allowable claims.

Subdivision (c) requires minutes and a record of the meeting to be maintained by the presiding officer. A verbatim record must be made of the debtor's examination but the rule is flexible as to the means used to record the examination.

Subdivision (d) recognizes that the court must be informed immediately about the election or nonelection of a trustee in a chapter 7 case. Pursuant to Rule 2008, the clerk officially informs the trustee of his election or appointment and how he is to qualify. The presiding person has no authority to resolve a disputed election.

For purposes of expediency, the results of the election should be obtained for each alternative presented by the dispute and immediately reported to the court. Thus, when an interested party presents the dispute to the court, its prompt resolution by the court will determine the dispute and a new or adjourned meeting to conduct the election may be avoided. The clerk is not an interested party.

A creditors' committee may be elected only in a chapter 7 case. In chapter 11 cases, a creditors' committee is appointed pursuant to § 1102.

While a final meeting is not required, Rule 2002(f)(10) provides for the trustee's final account to be sent to creditors.

1987 Amendments

Subdivision (a). Many courts schedule meetings of creditors at various locations in the district. Because the clerk must schedule meetings at those locations, an additional 20 days for scheduling the meetings is provided under the amended rule.

1991 Amendments

The amendment to subdivision (a) relating to the calling of the meeting of creditors in a chapter 12 case is consistent with the expedited procedures of chapter 12. Subdivision (a) is also amended to clarify that the United States trustee does not call a meeting of creditors in a chapter 9 case. Pursuant to § 901(a) of the Code, § 341 is inapplicable in chapter 9 cases. The other amendments to subdivisions (a), (b)(1), and (b)(2) and the additions of subdivisions (f) and (g) are derived from Rule X–1006 and conform to the 1986 amendments to § 341 of the Code. The second sentence of subdivision (b)(3) is amended because Rule 2009(e) is abrogated. Although the United States trustee fixes the date for the meeting, the clerk of the bankruptcy court transmits the notice of the meeting unless the court orders otherwise, as prescribed in Rule 2002(a)(1).

Pursuant to § 702 and § 705 of the Code, creditors may elect a trustee and a committee in a chapter 7 case. Subdivision (b) of this rule provides that the United States trustee shall preside over any election that is held under those sections. The deletion of the last sentence of subdivision (b)(1) does not preclude creditors from recommending to the United States trustee the amount of the trustee's bond when a trustee is elected. Trustees and committees are not elected in chapter 11, 12, and 13 cases.

If an election is disputed, the United States trustee shall not resolve the dispute. For purposes of expediency, the United States trustee shall tabulate the results of the election for each alternative presented by the dispute. However, if the court finds that such tabulation is not feasible under the circumstances, the United States trustee need not tabulate the votes. If such tabulation is feasible and if the disputed vote or votes would affect the result of the election, the tabulations of votes for each alternative presented by the dispute shall be reported to the court. If a motion is made for resolution of the dispute in accordance with subdivision (d) of this rule, the court will determine the issue and another meeting to conduct the election may not be necessary.

Subdivisions (f) and (g) are derived from Rule X–1006(d) and (e), except that the amount is increased to $1,500 to conform to the amendment to Rule 2002(f).

1993 Amendments

Subdivision (a) is amended to extend by ten days the time for holding the meeting of creditors in a chapter 13 case. This extension will provide more flexibility for scheduling the meeting of creditors. Other amendments are stylistic and make no substantive change.

1999 Amendments

Subdivision (d) is amended to require the United States trustee to mail a copy of a report of a disputed election to any party in interest that has requested a copy of it. Also, if the election is for a trustee, the rule as amended will give a party in interest ten days from the filing of the report, rather than from the date of the meeting of creditors, to file a motion to resolve the dispute.

The substitution of "United States trustee" for "presiding officer" is stylistic. Section 341(a) of the Code provides that the United States trustee shall preside at the meeting of creditors. Other amendments are designed to conform to the style of Rule 2007.1(b)(3) regarding the election of a trustee in a chapter 11 case.

Gap Report on Rule 2003. No changes since publication.

2003 Amendments

The rule is amended to reflect the enactment of subchapter V of chapter 7 of the Code governing multilateral clearing organization liquidations. Section 782 of the Code provides that the designation of a trustee or alternative trustee for the case is made by the Federal Reserve Board. Therefore, the meeting of creditors in those cases cannot include the election of a trustee.

2008 Amendments

If the debtor has solicited acceptances to a plan before commencement of the case, § 341(e), which was added to the Code by the 2005 amendments, authorizes the court, on request of a party in interest and after notice and a hearing, to order that a meeting of creditors not be convened. The rule is amended to recognize that a meeting of creditors might not be held in those cases.

CROSS REFERENCES

Affirmations, see Fed.Rules Bankr.Proc. Rule 9012, 11 USCA.

Election of creditors' committee in liquidation case, see 11 USCA § 705.

Eligibility to serve as and qualification of trustee, see 11 USCA §§ 321 and 322.

Enlargement of time not permitted—

Date of meeting of creditors, see Fed.Rules Bankr.Proc. Rule 9006, 11 USCA.

Motion for resolution of trustee election dispute, see Fed.Rules Bankr.Proc. Rule 9006, 11 USCA.

Holders of multiple proxies to file list of proxies to be voted, see Fed.Rules Bankr.Proc. Rule 2006, 11 USCA.

Inapplicability of this rule to—

Municipality debt adjustment case, see 11 USCA § 901.

Railroad reorganization case, see 11 USCA § 1161.

Interim trustee in liquidation case, see Fed.Rules Bankr. Proc. Rule 2001, 11 USCA, and 11 USCA § 701.

Motions; form and service, see Fed.Rules Bankr.Proc. Rule 9013, 11 USCA.

Reduction of twenty-day period for date of meeting of creditors not permitted, see Fed.Rules Bankr.Proc. Rule 9006, 11 USCA.

Selection and substitution of trustees, see Fed.Rules Bankr.Proc. Rules 2008 and 2012, 11 USCA.

Time for objections to property claimed to be exempt, see Fed.Rules Bankr.Proc. Rule 4003, 11 USCA.

Rule 2004. Examination

(a) Examination on motion

On motion of any party in interest, the court may order the examination of any entity.

(b) Scope of examination

The examination of an entity under this rule or of the debtor under § 343 of the Code may relate only to the acts, conduct, or property or to the liabilities and financial condition of the debtor, or to any matter which may affect the administration of the debtor's estate, or to the debtor's right to a discharge. In a family farmer's debt adjustment case under chapter 12, an individual's debt adjustment case under chapter 13, or a reorganization case under chapter 11 of the Code, other than for the reorganization of a railroad, the examination may also relate to the operation of any business and the desirability of its continuance, the source of any money or property acquired or to be acquired by the debtor for purposes of consummating a plan and the consideration given or offered therefor, and any other matter relevant to the case or to the formulation of a plan.

(c) Compelling attendance and production of documents

The attendance of an entity for examination and for the production of documents, whether the examination is to be conducted within or without the district in which the case is pending, may be compelled as provided in Rule 9016 for the attendance of a witness at a hearing or trial. As an officer of the court, an attorney may issue and sign a subpoena on behalf of the court for the district in which the examination is to be held if the attorney is admitted to practice in that court or in the court in which the case is pending.

(d) Time and place of examination of debtor

The court may for cause shown and on terms as it may impose order the debtor to be examined under this rule at any time or place it designates, whether within or without the district wherein the case is pending.

(e) Mileage

An entity other than a debtor shall not be required to attend as a witness unless lawful mileage and witness fee for one day's attendance shall be first tendered. If the debtor resides more than 100 miles from the place of examination when required to appear for an examination under this rule, the mileage allowed by law to a witness shall be tendered for any distance more than 100 miles from the debtor's residence at the date of the filing of the first petition commencing a case under the Code or the residence at the time the debtor is required to appear for the examination, whichever is the lesser.

(As amended Mar. 30, 1987, eff. Aug. 1, 1987; Apr. 30, 1991, eff. Aug. 1, 1991; Apr. 29, 2002, eff. Dec. 1, 2002.)

ADVISORY COMMITTEE NOTES

Subdivision (a) of this rule is derived from former Bankruptcy Rule 205(a). See generally 2 Collier, Bankruptcy ¶¶343.02, 343.08, 343.13 (15th ed. 1981). It specifies the manner of moving for an examination. The motion may be heard ex parte or it may be heard on notice.

Subdivision (b) is derived from former Bankruptcy Rules 205(d) and 11–26.

Subdivision (c) specifies the mode of compelling attendance of a witness or party for an examination and for the production of evidence under this rule. The subdivision is substantially declaratory of the practice that had developed under § 21a of the Act [former § 44(a) of this title]. See 2 Collier, supra ¶343.11.

This subdivision will be applicable for the most part to the examination of a person other than the debtor. The debtor is required to appear at the meeting of creditors for examination. The word "person" includes the debtor and this subdivision may be used if necessary to obtain the debtor's attendance for examination.

Subdivision (d) is derived from former Bankruptcy Rule 205(f) and is not a limitation on subdivision (c). Any person, including the debtor, served with a subpoena within the range of a subpoena must attend for examination pursuant to subdivision (c). Subdivision (d) applies only to the debtor and a subpoena need not be issued. There are no territorial limits on the service of an order on the debtor. See, e.g., In re Totem Lodge & Country Club, Inc., 134 F.Supp. 158 (S.D.N.Y.1955).

Subdivision (e) is derived from former Bankruptcy Rule 205(g). The lawful mileage and fee for attendance at a United States court as a witness are prescribed by 28 U.S.C. § 1821.

Definition of debtor. The word "debtor" as used in this rule includes the persons specified in the definition in Rule 9001(5).

Spousal privilege. The limitation on the spousal privilege formerly contained in § 21a of the Act [former § 44(a) of this title] is not carried over in the Code. For privileges generally, see Rule 501 of the Federal Rules of Evidence made applicable in cases under the Code by Rule 1101 thereof.

1991 Amendments

This rule is amended to allow the examination in a chapter 12 case to cover the same matters that may be covered in an examination in a chapter 11 or 13 case.

2002 Amendments

Subdivision (c) is amended to clarify that an examination ordered under Rule 2004(a) may be held outside the district in which the case is pending if the subpoena is issued by the court for the district in which the examination is to be held and is served in the manner provided in Rule 45 F.R.Civ.P., made applicable by Rule 9016.

The subdivision is amended further to clarify that, in addition to the procedures for the issuance of a subpoena set forth in Rule 45 F.R.Civ.P., an attorney may issue and sign a subpoena on behalf of the court for the district in which a Rule 2004 examination is to be held if the attorney is authorized to practice, even if admitted pro hac vice, either in the court in which the case is pending or in the court for the district in which the examination is to be held. This provision supplements the procedures for the issuance of a subpoena set forth in Rule 45(a)(3)(A) and (B) F.R.Civ.P. and is consistent with one of the purposes of the 1991 amendments to Rule 45, to ease the burdens of interdistrict law practice.

Changes Made After Publication and Comments. The typographical error was corrected, but no other changes were made.

CROSS REFERENCES

Allowances and travel expenses of witnesses, see 28 USCA § 1821.

Apprehension and removal of debtor to compel attendance for examination, see Fed.Rules Bankr.Proc. Rule 2005, 11 USCA.

Debtor as corporation or partnership for purposes of this rule, see Fed.Rules Bankr.Proc. Rule 9001, 11 USCA.

Duty of bankrupt to—

- Attend hearing on right to discharge, see 11 USCA § 524.
- Submit to examination, see Fed.Rules Bankr.Proc. Rule 4002, 11 USCA.

Duty of trustee to investigate debtor—

- Individual debt adjustment case, see 11 USCA § 1302.
- Liquidation case, see 11 USCA § 704.

Examination of debtor concerning compensation agreements with attorney, see Fed.Rules Bankr.Proc. Rule 2017, 11 USCA.

Immunity from self-incrimination, see 11 USCA § 344.

Motions; form and service, see Fed.Rules Bankr.Proc. Rule 9013, 11 USCA.

Subpoena, see Fed.Rules Civ.Proc. Rule 45, 28 USCA.

Privileges, see Fed.Rules Evid. Rule 501, 28 USCA.

Rule 2005. Apprehension and Removal of Debtor to Compel Attendance for Examination

(a) Order to compel attendance for examination

On motion of any party in interest supported by an affidavit alleging (1) that the examination of the debtor is necessary for the proper administration of the estate and that there is reasonable cause to believe that the debtor is about to leave or has left the debtor's residence or principal place of business to avoid examination, or (2) that the debtor has evaded service of a subpoena or of an order to attend for examination, or (3) that the debtor has willfully disobeyed a subpoena or order to attend for examination, duly served, the court may issue to the marshal, or some other officer authorized by law, an order directing the officer to bring the debtor before the court without unnecessary delay. If, after hearing, the court finds the allegations to be true, the court shall thereupon cause the debtor to be examined forthwith. If necessary, the court shall fix conditions for further examination and for the debtor's obedience to all orders made in reference thereto.

(b) Removal

Whenever any order to bring the debtor before the court is issued under this rule and the debtor is found in a district other than that of the court issuing the order, the debtor may be taken into custody under the order and removed in accordance with the following rules:

(1) If the debtor is taken into custody under the order at a place less than 100 miles from the place of issue of the order, the debtor shall be brought forthwith before the court that issued the order.

(2) If the debtor is taken into custody under the order at a place 100 miles or more from the place of issue of the order, the debtor shall be brought without unnecessary delay before the nearest available United States magistrate judge, bankruptcy judge, or district judge. If, after hearing, the magistrate judge, bankruptcy judge, or district judge finds that an order has issued under this rule and that the person in custody is the debtor, or if the person in custody waives a hearing, the magistrate judge, bankruptcy judge, or district judge shall order removal, and the person in custody shall be

released on conditions ensuring prompt appearance before the court that issued the order to compel the attendance.

(c) Conditions of release

In determining what conditions will reasonably assure attendance or obedience under subdivision (a) of this rule or appearance under subdivision (b) of this rule, the court shall be governed by the provisions and policies of title 18, U.S.C., § 3146(a) and (b).

(As amended Mar. 30, 1987, eff. Aug. 1, 1987; Apr. 22, 1993, eff. Aug. 1, 1993.)

ADVISORY COMMITTEE NOTES

This rule is derived from former Bankruptcy Rule 206. The rule requires the debtor to be examined as soon as possible if allegations of the movant for compulsory examination under this rule are found to be true after a hearing. Subdivision (b) includes in paragraphs (1) and (2) provisions adapted from subdivisions (a) and (b) of Rule 40 of the Federal Rules of Criminal Procedure, which governs the handling of a person arrested in one district on a warrant issued in another. Subdivision (c) incorporates by reference the features of subdivisions (a) and (b) of 18 U.S.C. § 3146, which prescribe standards, procedures and factors to be considered in determining conditions of release of accused persons in noncapital cases prior to trial. The word "debtor" as used in this rule includes the persons named in Rule 9001(5).

The affidavit required to be submitted in support of the motion may be subscribed by the unsworn declaration provided for in 28 U.S.C. § 1746.

1993 Amendments

Subdivision (b)(2) is amended to conform to § 321 of the Judicial Improvements Act of 1990, Pub. L. No. 101–650, which changed the title of "United States magistrate" to "United States magistrate judge." Other amendments are stylistic and make no substantive change.

Change of Name

United States magistrate appointed under section 631 of Title 28, Judiciary and Judicial Procedure, to be known as United States magistrate judge after Dec. 1, 1990, with any reference to United States magistrate or magistrate in Title 28, in any other Federal statute, etc., deemed a reference to United States magistrate judge appointed under section 631 of Title 28, see section 321 of Pub.L. 101–650, set out as a note under section 631 of Title 28.

CROSS REFERENCES

Debtor as corporation or partnership for purposes of this rule, see Fed.Rules Bankr.Proc. Rule 9001, 11 USCA.

Motions; form and service, see Fed.Rules Bankr.Proc. Rule 9013, 11 USCA.

Commitment to another district; removal, see Fed.Rules Cr.Proc. Rule 40, 18 USCA.

Rule 2006. Solicitation and Voting of Proxies in Chapter 7 Liquidation Cases

(a) Applicability

This rule applies only in a liquidation case pending under chapter 7 of the Code.

(b) Definitions

(1) Proxy

A proxy is a written power of attorney authorizing any entity to vote the claim or otherwise act as the owner's attorney in fact in connection with the administration of the estate.

(2) Solicitation of proxy

The solicitation of a proxy is any communication, other than one from an attorney to a regular client who owns a claim or from an attorney to the owner of a claim who has requested the attorney to represent the owner, by which a creditor is asked, directly or indirectly, to give a proxy after or in contemplation of the filing of a petition by or against the debtor.

(c) Authorized solicitation

(1) A proxy may be solicited only by (A) a creditor owning an allowable unsecured claim against the estate on the date of the filing of the petition; (B) a committee elected pursuant to § 705 of the Code; (C) a committee of creditors selected by a majority in number and amount of claims of creditors (i) whose claims are not contingent or unliquidated, (ii) who are not disqualified from voting under § 702(a) of the Code and (iii) who were present or represented at a meeting of which all creditors having claims of over $500 or the 100 creditors having the largest claims had at least five days notice in writing and of which meeting written minutes were kept and are available reporting the names of the creditors present or represented and voting and the amounts of their claims; or (D) a bona fide trade or credit association, but such association may solicit only creditors who were its members or subscribers in good standing and had allowable unsecured claims on the date of the filing of the petition.

(2) A proxy may be solicited only in writing.

(d) Solicitation not authorized

This rule does not permit solicitation (1) in any interest other than that of general creditors; (2) by or on behalf of any custodian; (3) by the interim trustee or by or on behalf of any entity not qualified to vote under § 702(a) of the Code; (4) by or on behalf of an attorney at law; or (5) by or on behalf of a transferee of a claim for collection only.

(e) Data required from holders of multiple proxies

At any time before the voting commences at any meeting of creditors pursuant to § 341(a) of the Code, or at any other time as the court may direct, a holder of two or more proxies shall file and transmit to the United States trustee a verified list of the proxies to be voted and a verified statement of the pertinent facts and circumstances in connection with the execution and delivery of each proxy, including:

(1) a copy of the solicitation;

(2) identification of the solicitor, the forwarder, if the forwarder is neither the solicitor nor the owner of the claim, and the proxyholder, including their connections with the debtor and with each other. If the solicitor, forwarder, or proxyholder is an association, there shall also be included a statement that the creditors whose claims have been solicited and the creditors whose claims are to be voted were members or subscribers in good standing and had allowable unsecured claims on the date of the filing of the petition. If the solicitor, forwarder, or proxyholder is a committee of creditors, the statement shall also set forth the date and place the committee was organized, that the committee was organized in accordance with clause (B) or (C) of paragraph (c)(1) of this rule, the members of the committee, the amounts of their claims, when the claims were acquired, the amounts paid therefor, and the extent to which the claims of the committee members are secured or entitled to priority;

(3) a statement that no consideration has been paid or promised by the proxyholder for the proxy;

(4) a statement as to whether there is any agreement and, if so, the particulars thereof, between the proxyholder and any other entity for the payment of any consideration in connection with voting the proxy, or for the sharing of compensation with any entity, other than a member or regular associate of the proxyholder's law firm, which may be allowed the trustee or any entity for services rendered in the case, or for the employment of any person as attorney, accountant, appraiser, auctioneer, or other employee for the estate;

(5) if the proxy was solicited by an entity other than the proxyholder, or forwarded to the holder by an entity who is neither a solicitor of the proxy nor the owner of the claim, a statement signed and verified by the solicitor or forwarder that no consideration has been paid or promised for the proxy, and whether there is any agreement, and, if so, the particulars thereof, between the solicitor or forwarder and any other entity for the payment of any consideration in connection with voting the proxy, or for sharing compensation with any entity, other than a member or regular associate of the solicitor's or forwarder's law firm which may be allowed the trustee or any entity for services rendered in the case, or for the employment of any person as attorney, accountant, appraiser, auctioneer, or other employee for the estate;

(6) if the solicitor, forwarder, or proxyholder is a committee, a statement signed and verified by each member as to the amount and source of any consideration paid or to be paid to such member in connection with the case other than by way of dividend on the member's claim.

(f) Enforcement of restrictions on solicitation

On motion of any party in interest or on its own initiative, the court may determine whether there has been a failure to comply with the provisions of this rule or any other impropriety in connection with the solicitation or voting of a proxy. After notice and a hearing the court may reject any proxy for cause, vacate any order entered in consequence of the voting of any proxy which should have been rejected, or take any other appropriate action.

(As amended Mar. 30, 1987, eff. Aug. 1, 1987; Apr. 30, 1991, eff. Aug. 1, 1991.)

ADVISORY COMMITTEE NOTES

This rule is a comprehensive regulation of solicitation and voting of proxies in liquidation cases. It is derived from former Bankruptcy Rule 208. The rule applies only in chapter 7 cases because no voting occurs, other than on a plan, in a chapter 11 case. Former Bankruptcy Rule 208 did not apply to solicitations of acceptances of plans.

Creditor control was a basic feature of the Act and is continued, in part, by the Code. Creditor democracy is perverted and the congressional objective frustrated, however, if control of administration falls into the hands of persons whose principal interest is not in what the estate can be made to yield to the unsecured creditors but in what it can yield to those involved in its administration or in other ulterior objectives.

Subdivision (b). The definition of proxy in the first paragraph of subdivision (b) is derived from former Bankruptcy Rule 208.

Subdivision (c). The purpose of the rule is to protect creditors against loss of control of administration of their debtors' estates to holders of proxies having interests that differ from those of the creditors. The rule does not prohibit solicitation but restricts it to those who were creditors at the commencement of the case or their freely and fairly selected representatives. The special role occupied by credit and trade associations is recognized in the last clause of subdivision (c)(1). On the assumption that members or subscribers may have affiliated with an association in part for the purpose of obtaining its services as a representative in liquidation proceedings, an established association is authorized to solicit its own members, or its regular customers or clients, who were creditors on the date of the filing of the petition. Although the association may not solicit nonmembers or nonsubscribers for proxies, it may sponsor a meeting of creditors at which a committee entitled to solicit proxies may be selected in accordance with clause (C) of subdivision (c)(1).

Under certain circumstances, the relationship of a creditor, creditors' committee, or association to the estate or the case may be such as to warrant rejection of any proxy solicited by such a person or group. Thus a person who is forbidden by the Code to vote his own claim should be equally disabled to solicit proxies from creditors. Solicitation by or on behalf of the debtor has been uniformly condemned, e.g., In re White,

15 F.2d 371 (9th Cir. 1926), as has solicitation on behalf of a preferred creditor, Matter of Law, 13 Am.B.R. 650 (S.D.Ill. 1905). The prohibition on solicitation by a receiver or his attorney made explicit by General Order 39 has been collaterally supported by rulings rejecting proxies solicited by a receiver in equity, In re Western States Bldg.-Loan Ass'n, 54 F.2d 415 (S.D.Cal.1931), and by an assignee for the benefit of creditors, Lines v. Falstaff Brewing Co., 233 F.2d 927 (9th Cir. 1956).

Subdivision (d) prohibits solicitation by any person or group having a relationship described in the preceding paragraph. It also makes no exception for attorneys or transferees of claims for collection. The rule does not undertake to regulate communications between an attorney and his regular client or between an attorney and a creditor who has asked the attorney to represent him in a proceeding under the Code, but any other communication by an attorney or any other person or group requesting a proxy from the owner of a claim constitutes a regulated solicitation. Solicitation by an attorney of a proxy from a creditor who was not a client prior to the solicitation is objectionable not only as unethical conduct as recognized by such cases as In the Matter of Darland Company, 184 F.Supp. 760 (S.D.Iowa 1960) but also and more importantly because the practice carries a substantial risk that administration will fall into the hands of those whose interest is in obtaining fees from the estate rather than securing dividends for creditors. The same risk attaches to solicitation by the holder of a claim for collection only.

Subdivision (e). The regulation of solicitation and voting of proxies is achieved by the rule principally through the imposition of requirements of disclosure on the holders of two or more proxies. The disclosures must be made to the clerk before the meeting at which the proxies are to be voted to afford the clerk or a party in interest an opportunity to examine the circumstances accompanying the acquisition of the proxies in advance of any exercise of the proxies. In the light of the examination the clerk or a party in interest should bring to the attention of the judge any question that arises and the judge may permit the proxies that comply with the rule to be voted and reject those that do not unless the holders can effect or establish compliance in such manner as the court shall prescribe. The holders of single proxies are excused from the disclosure requirements because of the insubstantiality of the risk that such proxies have been solicited, or will be voted, in an interest other than that of general creditors.

Every holder of two or more proxies must include in the submission a verified statement that no consideration has been paid or promised for the proxy, either by the proxyholder or the solicitor or any forwarder of the proxy. Any payment or promise of consideration for a proxy would be conclusive evidence of a purpose to acquire control of the administration of an estate for an ulterior purpose. The holder of multiple proxies must also include in the submission a verified statement as to whether there is any agreement by the holder, the solicitor, or any forwarder of the proxy for the employment of any person in the administration of an estate or for the sharing of any compensation allowed in connection with the administration of the estate. The provisions requiring these statements implement the policy of the Code expressed in § 504 as well as the policy of this rule to deter the acquisition of proxies for the purpose of obtaining a share in the outlays for administration. Finally the facts as to any consideration moving or promised to any member of a committee which functions as a solicitor, forwarder, or proxyholder must be disclosed by the proxyholder. Such information would be of significance to the court in evaluating the purpose of the committee in obtaining, transmitting, or voting proxies.

Subdivision (f) has counterparts in the local rules referred to in the Advisory Committee's Note to former Bankruptcy Rule 208. Courts have been accorded a wide range of discretion in the handling of disputes involving proxies. Thus the referee was allowed to reject proxies and to proceed forthwith to hold a scheduled election at the same meeting. E.g., In re Portage Wholesale Co., 183 F.2d 959 (7th Cir. 1950); In re McGill, 106 Fed. 57 (6th Cir. 1901); In re Deena Woolen Mills, Inc., 114 F.Supp. 260, 273 (D.Me. 1953); In re Finlay, 3 Am.B.R. 738 (S.D.N.Y.1900). The bankruptcy judge may postpone an election to permit a determination of issues presented by a dispute as to proxies and to afford those creditors whose proxies are rejected an opportunity to give new proxies or to attend an adjourned meeting to vote their own claims. Cf. In the Matter of Lenrick Sales, Inc., 369 F.2d 439, 442–43 (3d Cir.), cert. denied, 389 U.S. 822 (1967); In the Matter of Construction Supply Corp., 221 F.Supp. 124, 128 (E.D.Va.1963). This rule is not intended to restrict the scope of the court's discretion in the handling of disputes as to proxies.

1991 Amendments

This rule is amended to give the United States trustee information in connection with proxies so that the United States trustee may perform responsibilities as presiding officer at the § 341 meeting of creditors. See Rule 2003.

The words "with the clerk" are deleted as unnecessary. See Rules 5005(a) and 9001(3).

CROSS REFERENCES

Committee of unsecured creditors selected before order for relief, solicitation pursuant to this rule, see Fed.Rules Bankr.Proc. Rule 2007, 11 USCA.

Motions; form and service, see Fed.Rules Bankr.Proc. Rule 9013, 11 USCA.

Signing and verification of papers, see Fed.Rules Bankr. Proc. Rule 9011, 11 USCA.

Rule 2007. Review of Appointment of Creditors' Committee Organized Before Commencement of the Case

(a) Motion to review appointment

If a committee appointed by the United States trustee pursuant to § 1102(a) of the Code consists of the members of a committee organized by creditors before the commencement of a chapter 9 or chapter 11 case, on motion of a party in interest and after a hearing on notice to the United States trustee and other entities as the court may direct, the court may determine whether the appointment of the committee satisfies the requirements of § 1102(b)(1) of the Code.

(b) Selection of members of committee

The court may find that a committee organized by unsecured creditors before the commencement of a chapter 9 or chapter 11 case was fairly chosen if:

(1) it was selected by a majority in number and amount of claims of unsecured creditors who may vote under § 702(a) of the Code and were present in person or represented at a meeting of which all creditors having unsecured claims of over $1,000 or the 100 unsecured creditors having the largest claims had at least five days notice in writing, and of which meeting written minutes reporting the names of the creditors present or represented and voting and the amounts of their claims were kept and are available for inspection;

(2) all proxies voted at the meeting for the elected committee were solicited pursuant to Rule 2006 and the lists and statements required by subdivision (e) thereof have been transmitted to the United States trustee; and

(3) the organization of the committee was in all other respects fair and proper.

(c) Failure to comply with requirements for appointment

After a hearing on notice pursuant to subdivision (a) of this rule, the court shall direct the United States trustee to vacate the appointment of the committee and may order other appropriate action if the court finds that such appointment failed to satisfy the requirements of § 1102(b)(1) of the Code.

(As amended Mar. 30, 1987, eff. Aug. 1, 1987; Apr. 30, 1991, eff. Aug. 1, 1991.)

ADVISORY COMMITTEE NOTES

Section 1102(b)(1) of the Code permits the court to appoint as the unsecured creditors' committee, the committee that was selected by creditors before the order for relief. This provision recognizes the propriety of continuing a "prepetition" committee in an official capacity. Such a committee, however, must be found to have been fairly chosen and representative of the different kinds of claims to be represented.

Subdivision (a) does not necessarily require a hearing but does require a party in interest to bring to the court's attention the fact that a prepetition committee had been organized and should be appointed. An application would suffice for this purpose. Party in interest would include the committee, any member of the committee, or any of its agents acting for the committee. Whether or not notice of the application should be given to any other party is left to the discretion of the court.

Subdivision (b) implements § 1102(b)(1). The Code provision allows the court to appoint, as the official § 1102(a) committee, a "prepetition" committee if its members were fairly chosen and the committee is representative of the different kinds of claims. This subdivision of the rule indicates some of the factors the court may consider in determining whether the requirements of § 1102(b)(1) have been satisfied. In effect, the subdivision provides various factors which are similar to those set forth in Rule 2006 with respect to the solicitation and voting of proxies in a chapter 7 liquidation case.

1987 Amendments

The rule is amended to conform to the 1984 amendments to § 1102(b)(1) of the Code.

1991 Amendments

This rule is amended to conform to the 1986 amendments to § 1102(a). The United States trustee appoints committees pursuant to § 1102 in chapter 11 cases. Section 1102 is applicable in chapter 9 cases pursuant to § 901(a).

Although § 1102(b)(1) of the Code permits the United States trustee to appoint a prepetition committee as the statutory committee if its members were fairly chosen and it is representative of the different kinds of claims to be represented, the amendment to this rule provides a procedure for judicial review of the appointment. The factors that may be considered by the court in determining whether the committee was fairly chosen are not new. A finding that a prepetition committee has not been fairly chosen does not prohibit the appointment of some or all of its members to the creditors' committee. Although this rule deals only with judicial review of the appointment of prepetition committees, it does not preclude judicial review under Rule 2020 regarding the appointment of other committees.

CROSS REFERENCES

Representation of creditors and equity security holders in municipality debt adjustment and reorganization cases, see Fed.Rules Bankr.Proc. Rule 2019, 11 USCA.

Rule 2007.1. Appointment of Trustee or Examiner in a Chapter 11 Reorganization Case

(a) Order to appoint trustee or examiner

In a chapter 11 reorganization case, a motion for an order to appoint a trustee or an examiner under § 1104(a) or § 1104(c) of the Code shall be made in accordance with Rule 9014.

(b) Election of trustee

(1) Request for an election

A request to convene a meeting of creditors for the purpose of electing a trustee in a chapter 11 reorganization case shall be filed and transmitted to the United States trustee in accordance with Rule 5005 within the time prescribed by § 1104(b) of the Code. Pending court approval of the person elected, any person appointed by the United States trustee under § 1104(d) and approved in accordance with subdivision (c) of this rule shall serve as trustee.

(2) Manner of election and notice

An election of a trustee under § 1104(b) of the Code shall be conducted in the manner provided in Rules 2003(b)(3) and 2006. Notice of the meeting of creditors convened under § 1104(b) shall be given as provided in Rule 2002. The United States trustee shall preside at the meeting. A proxy for the purpose of voting in the election may be solicited only by a committee of creditors appointed under § 1102 of the Code or by any other party entitled to solicit a proxy pursuant to Rule 2006.

(3) Report of election and resolution of disputes.

(A) Report of undisputed election

If no dispute arises out of the election, the United States trustee shall promptly file a report certifying the election, including the name and address of the person elected and a statement that the election is undisputed. The report shall be accompanied by a verified statement of the person elected setting forth that person's connections with the debtor, creditors, any other party in interest, their respective attorneys and accountants, the United States trustee, or any person employed in the office of the United States trustee.

(B) Dispute arising out of an election

If a dispute arises out of an election, the United States trustee shall promptly file a report stating that the election is disputed, informing the court of the nature of the dispute, and listing the name and address of any candidate elected under any alternative presented by the dispute. The report shall be accompanied by a verified statement by each candidate elected under each alternative presented by the dispute, setting forth the person's connections with the debtor, creditors, any other party in interest, their respective attorneys and accountants, the United States trustee, or any person employed in the office of the United States trustee. Not later than the date on which the report of the disputed election is filed, the United States trustee shall mail a copy of the report and each verified statement to any party in interest that has made a request to convene a meeting under § 1104(b) or to receive a copy of the report, and to any committee appointed under § 1102 of the Code.

(c) Approval of appointment

An order approving the appointment of a trustee or an examiner under § 1104(d) of the Code shall be made on application of the United States trustee. The application shall state the name of the person appointed and, to the best of the applicant's knowledge, all the person's connections with the debtor, creditors, any other parties in interest, their respective attorneys and accountants, the United States trustee, or persons employed in the office of the United States trustee. The application shall state the names of the parties in interest with whom the United States trustee consulted regarding the appointment. The application shall be accompanied by a verified statement of the person appointed setting forth the person's connections with the debtor, creditors, any other party in interest, their respective attorneys and accountants, the United States trustee, or any person employed in the office of the United States trustee.

(Added Apr. 30, 1991, eff. Aug. 1, 1991; amended Apr. 11, 1997, eff. Dec. 1, 1997; Apr. 23, 2008, eff. Dec. 1, 2008.)

ADVISORY COMMITTEE NOTES

1991 Adoption

This rule is added to implement the 1986 amendments to § 1104 of the Code regarding the appointment of a trustee or examiner in a chapter 11 case. A motion for an order to appoint a trustee or examiner is a contested matter. Although the court decides whether the appointment is warranted under the particular facts of the case, it is the United States trustee who makes the appointment pursuant to § 1104(c) of the Code. The appointment is subject to approval of the court, however, which may be obtained by application of the United States trustee. Section 1104(c) of the Code requires that the appointment be made after consultation with parties in interest and that the person appointed be disinterested.

The requirement that connections with the United States trustee or persons employed in the United States trustee's office be revealed is not intended to enlarge the definition of "disinterested person" in § 101(13) of the Code, to supersede executive regulations or other laws relating to appointments by United States trustees, or to otherwise restrict the United States trustee's discretion in making appointments. This information is required, however, in the interest of full disclosure and confidence in the appointment process and to give the court all information that may be relevant to the exercise of judicial discretion in approving the appointment of a trustee or examiner in a chapter 11 case.

1997 Amendments

This rule is amended to implement the 1994 amendments to § 1104 of the Code regarding the election of a trustee in a chapter 11 case.

Eligibility for voting in an election for a chapter 11 trustee is determined in accordance with Rule 2003(b)(3). Creditors whose claims are deemed filed under § 1111(a) are treated for voting purposes as creditors who have filed proofs of claim.

Proxies for the purpose of voting in the election may be solicited only by a creditors' committee appointed under § 1102 or by any other party entitled to solicit proxies pursuant to Rule 2006. Therefore, a trustee or examiner who has served in the case, or a committee of equity security holders appointed under § 1102, may not solicit proxies.

The procedures for reporting disputes to the court derive from similar provisions in Rule 2003(d) applicable to chapter 7 cases. An election may be disputed by a party in interest or by the United States trustee. For example, if the United States trustee believes that the person elected is ineligible to serve as trustee because the person is not "disinterested," the United States trustee should file a report disputing the election.

The word "only" is deleted from subdivision (b), redesignated as subdivision (c), to avoid any negative inference with respect to the availability of procedures for obtaining review of the United States trustee's acts or failure to act pursuant to Rule 2020.

GAP Report on Rule 2007.1. The published draft of proposed new subdivision (b)(3) of Rule 2007.1, and the Committee Note, was substantially revised to implement Mr. Patchan's recommendations (described above), to clarify how a disputed election will be reported, and to make stylistic improvements.

2008 Amendments

Under § 1104(b)(2) of the Code, as amended in 2005, if an eligible, disinterested person is elected to serve as trustee in a chapter 11 case, the United States trustee is directed to file a report certifying the election. The person elected does not have to be appointed to the position. Rather, the filing of the report certifying the election itself constitutes the appointment. The section further provides that in the event of a dispute in the election of a trustee, the court must resolve the matter. The rule is amended to be consistent with § 1104(b)(2).

When the United States trustee files a report certifying the election of a trustee, the person elected must provide a verified statement, similar to the statement required of professional persons under Rule 2014, disclosing connections with parties in interest and certain other persons connected with the case. Although court approval of the person elected is not required, the disclosure of the person's connections will enable parties in interest to determine whether the person is disinterested.

Rule 2007.2. Appointment of Patient Care Ombudsman in a Health Care Business Case

(a) Order to appoint patient care ombudsman

In a chapter 7, chapter 9, or chapter 11 case in which the debtor is a health care business, the court shall order the appointment of a patient care ombudsman under § 333 of the Code, unless the court, on motion of the United States trustee or a party in interest filed no later than 20 days after the commencement of the case or within another time fixed by the court, finds that the appointment of a patient care ombudsman is not necessary under the specific circumstances of the case for the protection of patients.

(b) Motion for order to appoint ombudsman

If the court has found that the appointment of an ombudsman is not necessary, or has terminated the appointment, the court, on motion of the United States trustee or a party in interest, may order the appointment at a later time if it finds that the appointment has become necessary to protect patients.

(c) Notice of appointment

If a patient care ombudsman is appointed under § 333, the United States trustee shall promptly file a notice of the appointment, including the name and address of the person appointed. Unless the person appointed is a State Long–Term Care Ombudsman, the notice shall be accompanied by a verified statement of the person appointed setting forth the person's connections with the debtor, creditors, patients, any other party in interest, their respective attorneys and accountants, the United States trustee, and any person employed in the office of the United States trustee.

(d) Termination of appointment

On motion of the United States trustee or a party in interest, the court may terminate the appointment of a patient care ombudsman if the court finds that the appointment is not necessary to protect patients.

(e) Motion

A motion under this rule shall be governed by Rule 9014. The motion shall be transmitted to the United States trustee and served on: the debtor; the trustee; any committee elected under § 705 or appointed under § 1102 of the Code or its authorized agent, or, if the case is a chapter 9 municipality case or a chapter 11 reorganization case and no committee of unsecured creditors has been appointed under § 1102, on the creditors included on the list filed under Rule 1007(d); and such other entities as the court may direct.

(Added Apr. 23, 2008, eff. Dec. 1, 2008.)

ADVISORY COMMITTEE NOTES

2008 Adoption

Section 333 of the Code, added by the 2005 amendments, requires the court to order the appointment of a health care ombudsman within the first 30 days of a health care business case, unless the court finds that the appointment is not necessary for the protection of patients. The rule recognizes this requirement and provides a procedure by which a party may obtain a court order finding that the appointment of a patient care ombudsman is unnecessary. In the absence of a timely motion under subdivision (a) of this rule, the court will enter an order directing the United States trustee to appoint the ombudsman.

Subdivision (b) recognizes that, despite a previous order finding that a patient care ombudsman is not necessary, circumstances of the case may change or newly discovered evidence may demonstrate the necessity of an ombudsman to protect the interests of patients. In that event, a party may move the court for an order directing the appointment of an ombudsman.

When the appointment of a patient care ombudsman is ordered, the United States trustee is required to appoint a disinterested person to serve in that capacity. Court approval of the appointment is not required, but subdivision (c) requires the person appointed, if not a State Long–Term Care Ombudsman, to file a verified statement similar to the statement filed by professional persons under Rule 2014 so that parties in interest will have information relevant to disinterestedness. If a party believes that the person appointed is not disinterested, it may file a motion asking the court to find that the person is not eligible to serve.

Subdivision (d) permits parties in interest to move for the termination of the appointment of a patient care ombudsman. If the movant can show that there no longer is any need for the ombudsman, the court may order the termination of the appointment.

Rule 2008. Notice to Trustee of Selection

The United States trustee shall immediately notify the person selected as trustee how to qualify and, if applicable, the amount of the trustee's bond. A trustee that has filed a blanket bond pursuant to Rule 2010 and has been selected as trustee in a chapter 7, chapter 12, or chapter 13 case that does not notify the court and the United States trustee in writing of rejection of the office within five days after receipt of notice of selection shall be deemed to have accepted the office. Any other person selected as trustee shall notify the court and the United States trustee in writing of acceptance of the office within five days after receipt of notice of selection or shall be deemed to have rejected the office.

(As amended Mar. 30, 1987, eff. Aug. 1, 1987; Apr. 30, 1991, eff. Aug. 1, 1991.)

ADVISORY COMMITTEE NOTES

This rule is adapted from former Bankruptcy Rule 209(c). The remainder of that rule is inapplicable because its provisions are covered by §§ 701–703, 321 of the Code.

If the person selected as trustee accepts the office, he must qualify within five days after his selection, as required by § 322(a) of the Code.

In districts having a standing trustee for chapter 13 cases, a blanket acceptance of the appointment would be sufficient for compliance by the standing trustee with this rule.

1987 Amendments

The rule is amended to eliminate the need for a standing chapter 13 trustee or member of the panel of chapter 7 trustees to accept or reject an appointment.

1991 Amendments

The amendments to this rule relating to the United States trustee are derived from Rule X–1004(a) and conform to the 1986 amendments to the Code and 28 U.S.C. § 586 which provide that the United States trustee appoints and supervises trustees, and in a chapter 7 case presides over any election of a trustee. This rule applies when a trustee is either appointed or elected. This rule is also amended to provide for chapter 12 cases.

CROSS REFERENCES

Appointment of trustees—

Individual debt adjustment case, see 11 USCA § 1302.

Railroad reorganization case, see 11 USCA § 1163.

Reorganization case, see 11 USCA § 1104.

Bonds of trustees, see 11 USCA § 322.

Election of trustee in liquidation case, see 11 USCA § 702.

Eligibility to serve as trustee, see 11 USCA § 321.

Limited purpose of trustee appointed in municipality debt adjustment case, see 11 USCA § 926.

Representation of creditors and equity security holders in municipality debt adjustment and reorganization cases, see Fed.Rules Bankr.Proc. Rule 2019, 11 USCA.

Right of creditors to elect single trustee when joint administration ordered, see Fed.Rules Bankr.Proc. Rule 2009, 11 USCA.

Rule 2009. Trustees for Estates When Joint Administration Ordered

(a) Election of single trustee for estates being jointly administered

If the court orders a joint administration of two or more estates under Rule 1015(b), creditors may elect a single trustee for the estates being jointly administered, unless the case is under subchapter V of chapter 7 of the Code.

(b) Right of creditors to elect separate trustee

Notwithstanding entry of an order for joint administration under Rule 1015(b), the creditors of any debtor may elect a separate trustee for the estate of the debtor as provided in § 702 of the Code, unless the case is under subchapter V of chapter 7.

(c) Appointment of trustees for estates being jointly administered

(1) Chapter 7 liquidation cases

Except in a case governed by subchapter V of chapter 7, the United States trustee may appoint one or more interim trustees for estates being jointly administered in chapter 7 cases.

(2) Chapter 11 reorganization cases

If the appointment of a trustee is ordered, the United States trustee may appoint one or more trustees for estates being jointly administered in chapter 11 cases.

(3) Chapter 12 family farmer's debt adjustment cases

The United States trustee may appoint one or more trustees for estates being jointly administered in chapter 12 cases.

(4) Chapter 13 individual's debt adjustment cases

The United States trustee may appoint one or more trustees for estates being jointly administered in chapter 13 cases.

(d) Potential conflicts of interest

On a showing that creditors or equity security holders of the different estates will be prejudiced by conflicts of interest of a common trustee who has been elected or appointed, the court shall order the selection of separate trustees for estates being jointly administered.

(e) Separate accounts

The trustee or trustees of estates being jointly administered shall keep separate accounts of the property and distribution of each estate.

(As amended Mar. 30, 1987, eff. Aug. 1, 1987; Apr. 30, 1991, eff. Aug. 1, 1991; Mar. 27, 2003, eff. Dec. 1, 2003.)

ADVISORY COMMITTEE NOTES

This rule is applicable in chapter 7 cases and, in part, in chapter 11 and 13 cases. The provisions in subdivisions (a) and (b) concerning creditor election of a trustee apply only in a chapter 7 case because it is only pursuant to § 702 of the Code that creditors may elect a trustee. Subdivision (c) of the rule applies in chapter 11 and 13 as well as chapter 7 cases; pursuant to § 1104 of the Code, the court may order the appointment of a trustee on application of a party in interest and, pursuant to § 1163 of the Code, the court must appoint a trustee in a railroad reorganization case. Subdivision (c) should not be taken as an indication that more than one trustee may be appointed for a single debtor. Section 1104(c) permits only one trustee for each estate. In a chapter 13 case, if there is no standing trustee, the court is to appoint a person to serve as trustee pursuant to § 1302 of the Code. There is no provision for a trustee in a chapter 9 case, except for a very limited purpose; see § 926 of the Code.

This rule recognizes that economical and expeditious administration of two or more estates may be facilitated not only by the selection of a single trustee for a partnership and its partners, but by such selection whenever estates are being jointly administered pursuant to Rule 1015. See In the Matter of International Oil Co., 427 F.2d 186, 187 (2d Cir.1970). The rule is derived from former § 5c of the Act [former § 23(c) of this title] and former Bankruptcy Rule 210. The premise of § 5c of the Act was that notwithstanding the potentiality of conflict between the interests of the creditors of the partners and those of the creditors of the partnership, the conflict is not sufficiently serious or frequent in most cases to warrant the selection of separate trustees for the firm and the several partners. Even before the proviso was added to § 5c of the Act in 1938 to permit the creditors of a general partner to elect their separate trustee for his estate, it was held that the court had discretion to permit such an election or to make a separate appointment when a conflict of interest was recognized. In re Wood, 248 Fed. 246, 249–50 (6th Cir.), cert. denied, 247 U.S. 512 (1918); 4 Collier, Bankruptcy ¶723.04 (15th ed.1980). The rule retains in subdivision (e) the features of the practice respecting the selection of a trustee that was developed under § 5 of the Act [former § 23 of this title]. Subdivisions (a) and (c) permit the court to authorize election of a single trustee or to make a single appointment when joint administration of estates of other kinds of debtors is ordered, but subdivision (d) requires the court to make a preliminary evaluation of the risks of conflict of interest. If after the election or appointment of a common trustee a conflict of interest materializes, the court must take appropriate action to deal with it.

Subdivision (f) is derived from § 5e of the Act [former § 23(e) of this title] and former Bankruptcy Rule 210(f) and requires that the common trustee keep a separate account for each estate in all cases that are jointly administered.

1991 Amendments

One or more trustees may be appointed for estates being jointly administered in chapter 12 cases.

The amendments to this rule are derived from Rule X–1005 and are necessary because the United States trustee, rather than the court, has responsibility for appointing trustees pursuant to §§ 701, 1104, 1202, and 1302 of the Code.

If separate trustees are ordered for chapter 7 estates pursuant to subdivision (d), separate and successor trustees should be chosen as prescribed in § 703 of the Code. If the occasion for another election arises, the United States trustee should call a meeting of creditors for this purpose. An order to select separate trustees does not disqualify an appointed or elected trustee from serving for one of the estates.

Subdivision (e) is abrogated because the exercise of discretion by the United States trustee, who is in the Executive Branch, is not subject to advance restriction by rule of court. United States v. Cox, 342 F.2d 167 (5th Cir.1965), *cert. denied,* 365 U.S. 863 (1965); United States v. Frumento, 409 F.Supp. 136, 141 (E.D.Pa.), *aff'd,* 563 F.2d 1083 (3d Cir.1977), *cert. denied,* 434 U.S. 1072 (1977); see, Smith v. United States, 375 F.2d 243 (5th Cir.1967); House Report No. 95–595, 95th Cong., 1st Sess. 110 (1977). However, a trustee appointed by the United States trustee may be removed by the court for cause. See § 324 of the Code. Subdivision (d) of this rule, as amended, is consistent with § 324. Subdivision (f) is redesignated as subdivision (e).

2003 Amendments

The rule is amended to reflect the enactment of subchapter V of chapter 7 of the Code governing multilateral clearing organization liquidations. Section 782 of the Code provides that the designation of a trustee or alternative trustee for the case is made by the Federal Reserve Board. Therefore, neither the United States trustee nor the creditors can appoint or elect a trustee in these cases.

Other amendments are stylistic.

CROSS REFERENCES

Partnerships—

Commencement of involuntary cases, see 11 USCA § 303.

Person defined to include partnerships, see 11 USCA § 101.

Representation of creditors and equity security holders in municipality debt adjustment and reorganization cases, see Fed.Rules Bankr.Proc. Rule 2019, 11 USCA.

Rule 2010. Qualification by Trustee; Proceeding on Bond

(a) Blanket bond

The United States trustee may authorize a blanket bond in favor of the United States conditioned on the faithful performance of official duties by the trustee or trustees to cover (1) a person who qualifies as trustee in a number of cases, and (2) a number of trustees each of whom qualifies in a different case.

(b) Proceeding on bond

A proceeding on the trustee's bond may be brought by any party in interest in the name of the United States for the use of the entity injured by the breach of the condition.

(As amended Mar. 30, 1987, eff. Aug. 1, 1987; Apr. 30, 1991, eff. Aug. 1, 1991.)

ADVISORY COMMITTEE NOTES

Subdivisions (a) and (b). Subdivision (a) gives authority for approval by the court of a single bond to cover (1) a person who qualifies as trustee in a number of cases, and (2) a number of trustees each of whom qualifies in a different case. The cases need not be related in any way. Substantial economies can be effected if a single bond covering a number of different cases can be issued and approved at one time. When a blanket bond is filed, the trustee qualifies under subdivision (b) of the rule by filing an acceptance of the office.

Subdivision (c) prescribes the evidentiary effect of a certified copy of an order approving the trustee's bond given by a trustee under this rule or, when a blanket bond has been authorized, of a certified copy of acceptance. This rule supplements the Federal Rules of Evidence, which apply in bankruptcy cases. See Rule 1101 of the Federal Rules of Evidence. The order of approval should conform to Official Form No. 25. See, however, § 549(c) of the Code which provides only for the filing of the petition in the real estate records of serve as constructive notice of the pendency of the case. See also Rule 2011 which prescribes the evidentiary effect of a certificate that the debtor is a debtor in possession.

Subdivision (d) is derived from former Bankruptcy Rule 212(f). Reference should be made to § 322(a) and (d) of the Code which requires the bond to be filed with the bankruptcy court and places a two year limitation for the commencement of a proceeding on the bond. A bond filed under this rule should conform to Official Form No. 25. A proceeding on the bond of a trustee is governed by the rules in Part VII. See the Note accompanying Rule 7001. See also Rule 9025.

1987 Amendments

Subdivision (b) is deleted because of the amendment to Rule 2008.

1991 Amendments

This rule is amended to conform to the 1986 amendment of § 322 of the Code. The United States trustee determines the amount and sufficiency of the trustee's bond. The amendment to subdivision (a) is derived from Rule X–1004(b).

Subdivision (b) is abrogated because an order approving a bond is no longer necessary in view of the 1986 amendments to § 322 of the Code. Subdivision (c) is redesignated as subdivision (b).

CROSS REFERENCES

Proceeding on trustee's bond as exception to procedural rule of prosecution in name of real party in interest, see Fed.Rules Bankr.Proc. Rule 7017, 11 USCA.

Security; proceedings against sureties, see Fed.Rules Bankr.Proc. Rule 9025, 11 USCA.

Two-year limitations period on bond proceeding, see 11 USCA § 322.

Parties plaintiff and defendant; capacity, see Fed.Rules Civ.Proc. Rule 17, 28 USCA.

Security; proceedings against sureties, see Fed.Rules Civ. Proc. Rule 65.1, 28 USCA.

Rule 2011. Evidence of Debtor in Possession or Qualification of Trustee

(a) Whenever evidence is required that a debtor is a debtor in possession or that a trustee has qualified, the clerk may so certify and the certificate shall constitute conclusive evidence of that fact.

(b) If a person elected or appointed as trustee does not qualify within the time prescribed by § 322(a) of the Code, the clerk shall so notify the court and the United States trustee.

(As amended Apr. 30, 1991, eff. Aug. 1, 1991.)

ADVISORY COMMITTEE NOTES

This rule prescribes the evidentiary effect of a certificate issued by the clerk that the debtor is a debtor in possession. See Official Form No. 26. Only chapter 11 of the Code provides for a debtor in possession. See § 1107(a) of the Code. If, however, a trustee is appointed in the chapter 11 case, there will not be a debtor in possession. See §§ 1101(1), 1105 of the Code.

1991 Amendments

This rule is amended to provide a procedure for proving that a trustee has qualified in accordance with § 322 of the Code. *Subdivision (b)* is added so that the court and the United States trustee will be informed if the person selected as trustee pursuant to §§ 701, 702, 1104, 1202, 1302, or 1163 fails to qualify within the time prescribed in § 322(a).

CROSS REFERENCES

Debtor in possession for purposes of reorganization case defined as debtor except when trustee is serving, see 11 USCA § 1101.

Rule 2012. Substitution of Trustee or Successor Trustee; Accounting

(a) Trustee

If a trustee is appointed in a chapter 11 case or the debtor is removed as debtor in possession in a chapter 12 case, the trustee is substituted automatically for the debtor in possession as a party in any pending action, proceeding, or matter.

(b) Successor trustee

When a trustee dies, resigns, is removed, or otherwise ceases to hold office during the pendency of a case under the Code (1) the successor is automatically substituted as a party in any pending action, proceeding, or matter; and (2) the successor trustee shall prepare, file, and transmit to the United States trustee an accounting of the prior administration of the estate.

(As amended Mar. 30, 1987, eff. Aug. 1, 1987; Apr. 30, 1991, eff. Aug. 1, 1991.)

ADVISORY COMMITTEE NOTES

Paragraph (1) of this rule implements § 325 of the Code. It provides that a pending action or proceeding continues without abatement and that the trustee's successor is automatically substituted as a party whether it be another trustee or the debtor returned to possession, as such party.

Paragraph (2) places it within the responsibility of a successor trustee to file an accounting of the prior administration of the estate. If an accounting is impossible to obtain from the prior trustee because of death or lack of cooperation, prior reports submitted in the earlier administration may be updated.

1987 Amendments

Subdivision (a) is new. The subdivision provides for the substitution of a trustee appointed in a chapter 11 case for the debtor in possession in any pending litigation.

The original provisions of the rule are now in subdivision (b).

1991 Amendments

Subdivision (a) is amended to include any chapter 12 case in which the debtor is removed as debtor in possession pursuant to § 1204(a) of the Code.

Subdivision (b) is amended to require that the accounting of the prior administration which must be filed with the court is also transmitted to the United States trustee who is responsible for supervising the administration of cases and trustees. See 28 U.S.C. § 586(a)(3). Because a court order is not required for the appointment of a successor trustee, requiring the court to fix a time for filing the accounting is inefficient and unnecessary. The United States trustee has supervisory powers over trustees and may require the successor trustee to file the accounting within a certain time period. If the successor trustee fails to file the accounting within a reasonable time, the United States trustee or a party in interest may take appropriate steps including a request for an appropriate court order. See 28 U.S.C. § 586(a)(3)(G). The words "with the court" are deleted in subdivision (b)(2) as unnecessary. See Rules 5005(a) and 9001(3).

CROSS REFERENCES

Abatement of suit or proceeding upon death or removal of trustee, see 11 USCA § 325.

Election by creditors of successor trustee in liquidation case, see 11 USCA § 703.

Exception to procedural rule for substitution of parties, see Fed.Rules Bankr.Proc. Rule 7025, 11 USCA.

Power of court to remove trustee, see 11 USCA § 324.

Substitution of public officer on death or separation from office, see Fed.Rules Civ.Proc. Rule 25, 28 USCA.

Rule 2013. Public Record of Compensation Awarded to Trustees, Examiners, and Professionals

(a) Record to be kept

The clerk shall maintain a public record listing fees awarded by the court (1) to trustees and attorneys, accountants, appraisers, auctioneers and other professionals employed by trustees, and (2) to examiners. The record shall include the name and docket number of the case, the name of the individual or firm receiving the fee and the amount of the fee awarded. The record shall be maintained chronologically and shall be kept current and open to examination by the public without charge. "Trustees," as used in this rule, does not include debtors in possession.

(b) Summary of record

At the close of each annual period, the clerk shall prepare a summary of the public record by individual or firm name, to reflect total fees awarded during the preceding year. The summary shall be open to examination by the public without charge. The clerk shall transmit a copy of the summary to the United States trustee.

(As amended Mar. 30, 1987, eff. Aug. 1, 1987; Apr. 30, 1991, eff. Aug. 1, 1991.)

ADVISORY COMMITTEE NOTES

This rule is adapted from former Rule 213. The first sentence of that rule is omitted because of the provisions in 28 U.S.C. §§ 586 and 604(f) creating panels of private trustees.

The rule is not applicable to standing trustees serving in chapter 13 cases. See § 1302 of the Code.

A basic purpose of the rule is to prevent what Congress has defined as "cronyism." Appointment or employment, whether in a chapter 7 or 11 case, should not center among a small select group of individuals unless the circumstances are such that it would be warranted. The public record of appointments to be kept by the clerk will provide a means for monitoring the appointment process.

Subdivision (b) provides a convenient source for public review of fees paid from debtors' estates in the bankruptcy courts. Thus, public recognition of appointments, fairly distributed and based on professional qualifications and expertise, will be promoted and notions of improper favor dispelled. This rule is in keeping with the findings of the Congressional subcommittees as set forth in the House Report of the Committee on the Judiciary, No. 95–595, 95th Cong., 1st Sess. 89–99 (1977). These findings included the observations that there were frequent appointments of the same person, contacts developed between the bankruptcy bar and the courts, and an unusually close relationship between the bar and the judges developed over the years. A major purpose of the new statute is to dilute these practices and instill greater public confidence in the system. Rule 2013 implements that laudatory purpose.

1987 Amendments

In subdivisions (b) and (c) the word awarded is substituted for the word paid. While clerks do not know if fees are paid, they can determine what fees are awarded by the court.

1991 Amendments

Subdivision (a) is deleted. The matter contained in this subdivision is more properly left for regulation by the United States trustee. When appointing trustees and examiners and when monitoring applications for employment of auctioneers, appraisers and other professionals, the United States trustee should be sensitive to disproportionate or excessive fees received by any person.

Subdivision (b), redesignated as subdivision (a), is amended to reflect the fact that the United States trustee appoints examiners subject to court approval.

Subdivision (c), redesignated as subdivision (b), is amended to furnish the United States trustee with a copy of the annual summary which may assist that office in the performance of its responsibilities under 28 U.S.C. § 586 and the Code.

The rule is not applicable to standing trustees serving in chapter 12 cases. See § 1202 of the Code.

CROSS REFERENCES

Compensation of officers to reimburse actual and necessary services, see 11 USCA § 330.

Limitation on compensation of trustee, see 11 USCA § 326.

Rule 2014. Employment of Professional Persons

(a) Application for an order of employment

An order approving the employment of attorneys, accountants, appraisers, auctioneers, agents, or other professionals pursuant to § 327, § 1103, or § 1114 of the Code shall be made only on application of the trustee or committee. The application shall be filed and, unless the case is a chapter 9 municipality case, a copy of the application shall be transmitted by the applicant to the United States trustee. The application shall state the specific facts showing the necessity for the employment, the name of the person to be employed, the reasons for the selection, the professional services to be rendered, any proposed arrangement for compensation, and, to the best of the applicant's knowledge, all of the person's connections with the debtor, creditors, any other party in interest, their respective attorneys and accountants, the United States trustee, or any person employed in the office of the United States trustee. The application shall be accompanied by a verified statement of the person to be employed setting forth the person's connections with the debtor, creditors, any other party in interest, their respective attorneys and accountants, the United States trustee, or any person employed in the office of the United States trustee.

(b) Services rendered by member or associate of firm of attorneys or accountants

If, under the Code and this rule, a law partnership or corporation is employed as an attorney, or an accounting partnership or corporation is employed as an accountant, or if a named attorney or accountant is employed, any partner, member, or regular associate of the partnership, corporation or individual may act as attorney or accountant so employed, without further order of the court.

(As amended Mar. 30, 1987, eff. Aug. 1, 1987; Apr. 30, 1991, eff. Aug. 1, 1991.)

ADVISORY COMMITTEE NOTES

Subdivision (a) is adapted from the second sentence of former Bankruptcy Rule 215(a). The remainder of that rule is covered by § 327 of the Code.

Subdivision (b) is derived from former Bankruptcy Rule 215(f). The compensation provisions are set forth in § 504 of the Code.

1991 Amendments

This rule is amended to include retention of professionals by committees of retired employees pursuant to § 1114 of the Code.

The United States trustee monitors applications filed under § 327 of the Code and may file with the court comments with respect to the approval of such applications. See 28 U.S.C. § 586(a)(3)(H). The United States trustee also monitors creditors' committees in accordance with 28 U.S.C. § 586(a)(3)(E). The addition of the second sentence of subdivision (a) is designed to enable the United States trustee to perform these duties.

Subdivision (a) is also amended to require disclosure of the professional's connections with the United States trustee or persons employed in the United States trustee's office. This requirement is not intended to prohibit the employment of such persons in all cases or to enlarge the definition of "disinterested person" in § 101(13) of the Code. However, the court may consider a connection with the United States trustee's office as a factor when exercising its discretion. Also, this information should be revealed in the interest of full disclosure and confidence in the bankruptcy system, especially since the United States trustee monitors and may be heard on applications for compensation and reimbursement of professionals employed under this rule.

The United States trustee appoints committees pursuant to § 1102 of the Code which is applicable in chapter 9 cases under § 901. In the interest of full disclosure and confidence in the bankruptcy system, a connection between the United States trustee and a professional employed by the committee should be revealed in every case, including a chapter 9 case. However, since the United States trustee does not have any role in the employment of professionals in chapter 9 cases, it is not necessary in such cases to transmit to the United States trustee a copy of the application under subdivision (a) of this rule. See 28 U.S.C. § 586(a)(3)(H).

CROSS REFERENCES

Application for compensation or reimbursement, see Fed. Rules Bankr.Proc. Rule 2016, 11 USCA.

Compensation for services and reimbursement of costs, see 11 USCA § 503.

Compensation of professional persons—

Actual, necessary services, see 11 USCA § 330.

Limitation on, see 11 USCA § 328.

Sharing of, see 11 USCA § 504.

Rule 2015. Duty to Keep Records, Make Reports, and Give Notice of Case or Change of Status

(a) Trustee or debtor in possession

A trustee or debtor in possession shall:

(1) in a chapter 7 liquidation case and, if the court directs, in a chapter 11 reorganization case file and transmit to the United States trustee a complete inventory of the property of the debtor within 30 days after qualifying as a trustee or debtor in possession, unless such an inventory has already been filed;

(2) keep a record of receipts and the disposition of money and property received;

(3) file the reports and summaries required by § 704(8) of the Code which shall include a statement, if payments are made to employees, of the amounts of deductions for all taxes required to be withheld or paid for and in behalf of employees and the place where these amounts are deposited;

(4) as soon as possible after the commencement of the case, give notice of the case to every entity known to be holding money or property subject to withdrawal or order of the debtor, including every bank, savings or building and loan association, public utility company, and landlord with whom the debtor has a deposit, and to every insurance company which has issued a policy having a cash surrender value payable to the debtor, except that notice need not be given to any entity who has knowledge or has previously been notified of the case;

(5) in a chapter 11 reorganization case, on or before the last day of the month after each calendar quarter during which there is a duty to pay fees under 28 U.S.C. § 1930(a)(6), file and transmit to the United States trustee a statement of any disbursements made during that quarter and of any fees payable under 28 U.S.C. § 1930(a)(6) for that quarter; and

(6) in a chapter 11 small business case, unless the court, for cause, sets another reporting interval, file and transmit to the United States trustee for each calendar month after the order for relief, on the appropriate Official Form, the report required by § 308. If the order for relief is within the first 15 days of a calendar month, a report shall be filed for the portion of the month that follows the order for relief. If the order for relief is after the 15th day of a calendar month, the period for the remainder of the month shall be included in the report for the next calendar month. Each report shall be filed no later than 20 days after the last day of the calendar month following the month covered by the report. The obligation to file reports under this subparagraph terminates on the effective date of the plan, or conversion or dismissal of the case.

(b) Chapter 12 trustee and debtor in possession

In a chapter 12 family farmer's debt adjustment case, the debtor in possession shall perform the duties prescribed in clauses (2)-(4) of subdivision (a) of this rule and, if the court directs, shall file and transmit to the United States trustee a complete inventory of the property of the debtor within the time fixed by the court. If the debtor is removed as debtor in possession, the trustee shall perform the duties of the debtor in possession prescribed in this paragraph.

(c) Chapter 13 trustee and debtor

(1) Business cases

In a chapter 13 individual's debt adjustment case, when the debtor is engaged in business, the debtor shall perform the duties prescribed by clauses (2)-(4) of subdivision (a) of this rule and, if the court directs, shall file and transmit to the United States trustee a complete inventory of the property of the debtor within the time fixed by the court.

(2) Nonbusiness cases

In a chapter 13 individual's debt adjustment case, when the debtor is not engaged in business, the trustee shall perform the duties prescribed by clause (2) of subdivision (a) of this rule.

(d) Foreign representative

In a case in which the court has granted recognition of a foreign proceeding under chapter 15, the foreign representative shall file any notice required under § 1518 of the Code within 15 days after the date when the representative becomes aware of the subsequent information.

(e) Transmission of reports

In a chapter 11 case the court may direct that copies or summaries of annual reports and copies or summaries of other reports shall be mailed to the creditors, equity security holders, and indenture trustees. The court may also direct the publication of summaries of any such reports. A copy of every report or summary mailed or published pursuant to this subdivision shall be transmitted to the United States trustee.

(As amended Mar. 30, 1987, eff. Aug. 1, 1987; Apr. 30, 1991, eff. Aug. 1, 1991; Apr. 23, 1996, eff. Dec. 1, 1996; Apr. 29, 2002, eff. Dec. 1, 2002; Apr. 23, 2008, eff. Dec. 1, 2008.)

ADVISORY COMMITTEE NOTES

This rule combines the provisions found in former Rules 218, 10–208, 11–30 and 13–208 of the Rules of Bankruptcy Procedure. It specifies various duties which are in addition to those required by §§ 704, 1106, 1302 and 1304 of the Code.

In **subdivision (a)** the times permitted to be fixed by the court in clause (3) for the filing of reports and summaries may be fixed by local rule or order.

Subdivision (b). This subdivision prescribes duties on either the debtor or trustee in chapter 13 cases, depending on whether or not the debtor is engaged in business (§ 1304 of the Code). The duty of giving notice prescribed by subdivision (a)(4) is not included in a nonbusiness case because of its impracticability.

Subdivision (c) is derived from former Chapter X Rule 10–208(c) which, in turn, was derived from § 190 of the Act [former § 590 of this title]. The equity security holders to whom the reports should be sent are those of record at the time of transmittal of such reports.

1987 Amendments

Subdivision (a) is amended to add as a duty of the trustee or debtor in possession the filing of a notice of or a copy of the petition. The filing of such notice or a copy of the petition is essential to the protection of the estate from unauthorized post-petition conveyances of real property. Section 549(c) of the Code protects the title of a good faith purchaser for fair equivalent value unless the notice or copy of the petition is filed.

1991 Amendments

This rule is amended to provide the United States trustee with information needed to perform supervisory responsibilities in accordance with 28 U.S.C. § 586(a)(3) and to exercise the right to raise, appear and be heard on issues pursuant to § 307 of the Code.

Subdivision (a)(3) is amended to conform to the 1986 amendments to § 704(8) of the Code and the United States trustee system. It may not be necessary for the court to fix a time to file reports if the United States trustee requests that they be filed within a specified time and there is no dispute regarding such time.

Subdivision (a)(5) is deleted because the filing of a notice of or copy of the petition to protect real property against unauthorized postpetition transfers in a particular case is within the discretion of the trustee.

The new subdivision (a)(5) was added to enable the United States trustee, parties in interest, and the court to determine the appropriate quarterly fee required by 28 U.S.C. § 1930(a)(6). The requirements of subdivision (a)(5) should be satisfied whenever possible by including this information in other reports filed by the trustee or debtor in possession. Nonpayment of the fee may result in dismissal or conversion of the case pursuant to § 1112(b) of the Code.

Rule X–1007(b), which provides that the trustee or debtor in possession shall cooperate with the United States trustee by furnishing information that the United States trustee reasonably requires, is deleted as unnecessary. The deletion of Rule X–1007(b) should not be construed as a limitation of the powers of the United States trustee or of the duty of the trustee or debtor in possession to cooperate with the United States trustee in the performance of the statutory responsibilities of that office.

Subdivision (a)(6) is abrogated as unnecessary. See § 1106(a)(7) of the Code.

Subdivision (a)(7) is abrogated. The closing of a chapter 11 case is governed by Rule 3022.

New **subdivision (b),** which prescribes the duties of the debtor in possession and trustee in a chapter 12 case, does not prohibit additional reporting requirements pursuant to local rule or court order.

1996 Amendments

Subdivision (a)(1) provides that the trustee in a chapter 7 case and, if the court directs, the trustee or debtor in possession in a chapter 11 case, is required to file and transmit to the United States trustee a complete inventory of the debtor's property within 30 days after qualifying as trustee or debtor in possession, unless such an inventory has already been filed. Subdivisions (b) and (c) are amended to clarify that a debtor in possession and trustee in a chapter 12 case, and a debtor in a chapter 13 case where the debtor is engaged in business, are not required to file and transmit to the United States trustee a complete inventory of the property of the debtor unless the court so directs. If the court so directs, the court also fixes the time limit for filing and transmitting the inventory.

GAP Report on Rule 2015. No changes since publication, except for a stylistic change in the first sentence of the committee note.

2002 Amendments

Subdivision (a)(5) is amended to provide that the duty to file quarterly disbursement reports continues only so long as there is an obligation to make quarterly payments to the United States trustee under 28 U.S.C. § 1930(a)(6).

Other amendments are stylistic.

Changes Made After Publication and Comments. No changes were made.

2008 Amendments

Subparagraph (a)(6) implements § 308 of the Code, added by the 2005 amendments. That section requires small business chapter 11 debtors to file periodic financial and operating reports, and the rule sets the time for filing those reports and requires the use of an Official Form for the report. The obligation to file reports under this rule does not relieve the trustee or debtor of any other obligations to provide information or documents to the United States trustee.

The rule also is amended to fix the time for the filing of notices under § 1518, added to the Code in 2005. Former subdivision (d) is renumbered as subdivision (e).

CROSS REFERENCES

Duties of trustee—

Individual debt adjustment case, see 11 USCA § 1302.

Reorganization case, see 11 USCA § 1106.

Operation of business by debtor, see 11 USCA § 1304.

Public access to papers filed in case under this title, see 11 USCA § 107.

Rule 2015.1. Patient Care Ombudsman

(a) Reports

A patient care ombudsman, at least 10 days before making a report under § 333(b)(2) of the Code, shall give notice that the report will be made to the court, unless the court orders otherwise. The notice shall be transmitted to the United States trustee, posted conspicuously at the health care facility that is the subject of the report, and served on: the debtor; the trustee; all patients; and any committee elected under § 705 or appointed under § 1102 of the Code or its authorized agent, or, if the case is a chapter 9 municipality case or a chapter 11 reorganization case and no committee of unsecured creditors has been appointed under § 1102, on the creditors included on the list filed under Rule 1007(d); and such other entities as the court may direct. The notice shall state the date and time when the report will be made, the manner in which the report will be made, and, if the report is in writing, the name, address, telephone number, email address, and website, if any, of the person from whom a copy of the report may be obtained at the debtor's expense.

(b) Authorization to review confidential patient records

A motion by a patient care ombudsman under § 333(c) to review confidential patient records shall be governed by Rule 9014, served on the patient and any family member or other contact person whose name and address have been given to the trustee or the debtor for the purpose of providing information regarding the patient's health care, and transmitted to the United States trustee subject to applicable nonbankruptcy law relating to patient privacy. Unless the court orders otherwise, a hearing on the motion may not be commenced earlier than 15 days after service of the motion.

(Added Apr. 23, 2008, eff. Dec. 1, 2008.)

ADVISORY COMMITTEE NOTES

2008 Adoption

This rule is new and implements § 333 of the Code, added by the 2005 amendments. Subdivision (a) is designed to give parties in interest, including patients or their representatives, sufficient notice so that they will be able to review written reports or attend hearings at which reports are made. The rule permits a notice to relate to a single report or to periodic reports to be given during the case. For example, the ombudsman may give notice that reports will be made at specified intervals or dates during the case.

Subdivision (a) of the rule also requires that the notice be posted conspicuously at the health care facility in a place where it will be seen by patients and their families or others visiting the patients. This may require posting in common areas and patient rooms within the facility. Because health care facilities and the patients they serve can vary greatly, the locations of the posted notice should be tailored to the specific facility that is the subject of the report.

Subdivision (b) requires the ombudsman to notify the patient and the United States trustee that the ombudsman is seeking access to confidential patient records so that they will be able to appear and be heard on the matter. This procedure should assist the court in reaching its decision both as to access to the records and appropriate restrictions on that access to ensure continued confidentiality. Notices given under this rule are subject to the provisions of applicable federal and state law that relate to the protection of patients' privacy, such as the Health Insurance Portability and Accountability Act of 1996, Pub. L. No. 104–191 (HIPAA).

Rule 2015.2. Transfer of Patient in Health Care Business Case

Unless the court orders otherwise, if the debtor is a health care business, the trustee may not transfer a patient to another health care business under § 704(a)(12) of the Code unless the trustee gives at least 10 days' notice of the transfer to the patient care ombudsman, if any, the patient, and any family member or other contact person whose name and address have been given to the trustee or the debtor for the purpose of providing information regarding the patient's health care. The notice is subject to applicable nonbankruptcy law relating to patient privacy.

(Added Apr. 23, 2008, eff. Dec. 1, 2008.)

ADVISORY COMMITTEE NOTES

2008 Adoption

This rule is new. Section 704(a)(12), added to the Code by the 2005 amendments, authorizes the trustee to relocate patients when a health care business debtor's facility is in the process of being closed. The Code permits the trustee to take this action without the need for any court order, but the notice required by this rule will enable a patient care ombudsman appointed under § 333, or a patient who contends that the trustee's actions violate § 704(a)(12), to have those issues resolved before the patient is transferred.

This rule also permits the court to enter an order dispensing with or altering the notice requirement in proper circumstances. For example, a facility could be closed immediately, or very quickly, such that 10 days' notice would not be possible in some instances. In that event, the court may shorten the time required for notice.

Notices given under this rule are subject to the provisions of applicable federal and state law that relate to the protection of patients' privacy, such as the Health Insurance Portability and Accountability Act of 1996, Pub. L. No. 104–191 (HIPAA).

Rule 2015.3. Reports of Financial Information on Entities in Which a Chapter 11 Estate Holds a Controlling or Substantial Interest

(a) Reporting requirement

In a chapter 11 case, the trustee or debtor in possession shall file periodic financial reports of the value, operations, and profitability of each entity that is not a publicly traded corporation or a debtor in a case under title 11, and in which the estate holds a substantial or controlling interest. The reports shall be prepared as prescribed by the appropriate Official Form, and shall be based upon the most recent information reasonably available to the trustee or debtor in possession.

(b) Time for filing; service

The first report required by this rule shall be filed no later than five days before the first date set for the meeting of creditors under § 341 of the Code. Subsequent reports shall be filed no less frequently than every six months thereafter, until the effective date of a plan or the case is dismissed or converted. Copies of the report shall be served on the United States trustee, any committee appointed under § 1102 of the Code, and any other party in interest that has filed a request therefor.

(c) Presumption of substantial or controlling interest; judicial determination

For purposes of this rule, an entity of which the estate controls or owns at least a 20 percent interest, shall be presumed to be an entity in which the estate has a substantial or controlling interest. An entity in which the estate controls or owns less than a 20 percent interest shall be presumed not to be an entity in which the estate has a substantial or controlling interest. Upon motion, the entity, any holder of an interest therein, the United States trustee, or any other party in interest may seek to rebut either presumption, and the court shall, after notice and a hearing, determine whether the estate's interest in the entity is substantial or controlling.

(d) Modification of reporting requirement

The court may, after notice and a hearing, vary the reporting requirement established by subdivision (a) of this rule for cause, including that the trustee or debtor in possession is not able, after a good faith effort, to comply with those reporting requirements, or that the information required by subdivision (a) is publicly available.

(e) Notice and protective orders

No later than 14 days before filing the first report required by this rule, the trustee or debtor in possession shall send notice to the entity in which the estate has a substantial or controlling interest, and to all holders—known to the trustee or debtor in possession—of an interest in that entity, that the trustee or debtor in possession expects to file and serve financial information relating to the entity in accordance with this rule. The entity in which the estate has a substantial or controlling interest, or a person holding an interest in that entity, may request protection of the information under § 107 of the Code.

(f) Effect of request

Unless the court orders otherwise, the pendency of a request under subdivisions (c), (d), or (e) of this rule shall not alter or stay the requirements of subdivision (a).

(Added Apr. 23, 2008, eff. Dec. 1, 2008.)

ADVISORY COMMITTEE NOTES

2008 Adoption

This rule implements § 419 of the Bankruptcy Abuse Prevention and Consumer Protection Act of 2005 ("BAPCPA"). Reports are to be made on the appropriate Official Form. While § 419 of BAPCPA places the obligation to report upon the "debtor," this rule extends the obligation to include cases in which a trustee has been appointed. The court can order that the reports not be filed in appropriate circumstances, such as when the information that would be included in these reports is already available to interested parties.

Rule 2016. Compensation for Services Rendered and Reimbursement of Expenses

(a) Application for compensation or reimbursement

An entity seeking interim or final compensation for services, or reimbursement of necessary expenses, from the estate shall file an application setting forth a detailed statement of (1) the services rendered, time expended and expenses incurred, and (2) the amounts requested. An application for compensation shall include a statement as to what payments have theretofore been made or promised to the applicant for services rendered or to be rendered in any capacity whatsoever in connection with the case, the source of the compensation so paid or promised, whether any compensation previously received has been shared and whether an agreement or understanding exists between the applicant and any other entity for the sharing of compensation received or to be received for services rendered in or in connection with the case, and the particulars of any sharing of compensation or agreement or understanding therefor, except that details of any agreement by the applicant for the sharing of compensation as a member or regular associate of a firm of lawyers or accountants shall not be required. The requirements of this subdivision shall apply to an application for compensation for services rendered by an attorney or accountant even though the application is filed by a creditor or other entity. Unless the case is a chapter 9 municipality case, the applicant shall transmit to the United States trustee a copy of the application.

(b) Disclosure of compensation paid or promised to attorney for debtor

Every attorney for a debtor, whether or not the attorney applies for compensation, shall file and transmit to the United States trustee within 15 days after the order for relief, or at another time as the court may direct, the statement required by § 329 of the Code including whether the attorney has shared or agreed to share the compensation with any other entity. The statement shall include the particulars of any such sharing or agreement to share by the attorney, but the details of any agreement for the sharing of the compensation with a member or regular associate of the attorney's law firm shall not be required. A supplemental statement shall be filed and transmitted to the United States trustee within 15 days after any payment or agreement not previously disclosed.

(c) Disclosure of compensation paid or promised to bankruptcy petition preparer

Every bankruptcy petition preparer for a debtor shall file a declaration under penalty of perjury and transmit the declaration to the United States trustee within 10 days after the date of the filing of the petition, or at another time as the court may direct, as required by § 110(h)(1). The declaration must disclose any fee, and the source of any fee, received from or on behalf of the debtor within 12 months of the filing of the case and all unpaid fees charged to the debtor. The declaration must describe the services performed and documents prepared or caused to be prepared by the bankruptcy petition preparer. A supplemental statement shall be filed within 10 days after any payment or agreement not previously disclosed.

(As amended Mar. 30, 1987, eff. Aug. 1, 1987; Apr. 30, 1991, eff. Aug. 1, 1991; Mar. 27, 2003, eff. Dec. 1, 2003.)

ADVISORY COMMITTEE NOTES

This rule is derived from former Rule 219. Many of the former rule's requirements are, however, set forth in the Code. Section 329 requires disclosure by an attorney of transactions with the debtor, § 330 sets forth the bases for allowing compensation, and § 504 prohibits sharing of compensation. This rule implements those various provisions.

Subdivision (a) includes within its provisions a committee, member thereof, agent, attorney or accountant for the committee when compensation or reimbursement of expenses is sought from the estate.

Regular associate of a law firm is defined in Rule 9001(9) to include any attorney regularly employed by, associated with, or counsel to that law firm. Firm is defined in Rule 9001(6) to include a partnership or professional corporation.

1987 Amendments

Subdivision (a) is amended to change "person" to "entity." There are occasions in which a governmental unit may be entitled to file an application under this rule. The requirement that the application contain a "detailed statement of services rendered, time expended and expenses incurred" gives to the court authority to ensure that the application is both comprehensive and detailed. No amendments are made to delineate further the requirements of the application because the amount of detail to be furnished is a function of the nature of the services rendered and the complexity of the case.

Subdivision (b) is amended to require that the attorney for the debtor file the § 329 statement before the meeting of creditors. This will assist the parties in conducting the examination of the debtor. In addition, the amended rule requires the attorney to supplement the § 329 statement if an undisclosed payment is made to the attorney or a new or amended agreement is entered into by the debtor and the attorney.

1991 Amendments

Subdivision (a) is amended to enable the United States trustee to perform the duty to monitor applications for compensation and reimbursement filed under § 330 of the Code. See 28 U.S.C. § 586(a)(3)(A).

Subdivision (b) is amended to give the United States trustee the information needed to determine whether to request appropriate relief based on excessive fees under § 329(b) of the Code. See Rule 2017.

The words "with the court" are deleted in subdivisions (a) and (b) as unnecessary. See Rules 5005(a) and 9001(3).

2003 Amendments

This rule is amended by adding subdivision (c) to implement § 110(h)(1) of the Code.

HISTORICAL NOTES

Guidelines for Reviewing Applications for Compensation and Reimbursement of Expenses Filed Under 11 U.S.C. § 330

(a) General Information. (1) The Bankruptcy Reform Act of 1994 amended the responsibilities of the United States Trustees under 28 U.S.C. 586(a)(3)(A) to provide that, whenever they deem appropriate, United States Trustees will review applications for compensation and reimbursement of expenses under section 330 of the Bankruptcy Code, 11 U.S.C. 101, et seq. ("Code"), in accordance with procedural guidelines ("Guidelines") adopted by the Executive Office for United States Trustees ("Executive Office"). The following Guidelines have been adopted by the Executive Office and are to be uniformly applied by the United States Trustees except when circumstances warrant different treatment.

(2) The United States Trustees shall use these Guidelines in all cases commenced on or after October 22, 1994.

(3) The Guidelines are not intended to supersede local rules of court, but should be read as complementing the procedures set forth in local rules.

(4) Nothing in the Guidelines should be construed:

(i) To limit the United States Trustee's discretion to request additional information necessary for the review of a particular application or type of application or to refer any information provided to the United States Trustee to any investigatory or prosecutorial authority of the United States or a state;

(ii) To limit the United States Trustee's discretion to determine whether to file comments or objections to applications; or

(iii) To create any private right of action on the part of any person enforceable in litigation with the United States Trustee or the United States.

(5) Recognizing that the final authority to award compensation and reimbursement under section 330 of the Code is vested in the Court, the Guidelines focus on the disclosure of information relevant to a proper award under the law. In evaluating fees for professional services, it is relevant to consider various factors including the following: the time spent; the rates charged; whether the services were necessary to the administration of, or beneficial towards the completion of, the case at the time they were rendered; whether services were performed within a reasonable time commensurate with the complexity, importance, and nature of the problem, issue, or task addressed; and whether compensation is reasonable based on the customary compensation charged by comparably skilled practitioners in non-bankruptcy cases. The Guidelines thus reflect standards and procedures articulated in section 330 of the Code and Rule 2016 of the Federal Rules of Bankruptcy Procedure for awarding compensation to trustees and to professionals employed under section 327 or 1103. Applications that contain the information requested in these Guidelines will facilitate review by the Court, the parties, and the United States Trustee.

(6) Fee applications submitted by trustees are subject to the same standard of review as are applications of other professionals and will be evaluated according to the principles articulated in these Guidelines. Each United States Trustee should establish whether and to what extent trustees can deviate from the format specified in these Guidelines without substantially affecting the ability of the United States Trustee to review and comment on their fee applications in a manner consistent with the requirements of the law.

(b) Contents of Applications for Compensation and Reimbursement of Expenses. All applications should include sufficient detail to demonstrate compliance with the standards set forth in 11 U.S.C. § 330. The fee application should also contain sufficient information about the case and the applicant so that the Court, the creditors, and the United States Trustee can review it without searching for relevant information in other documents. The following will facilitate review of the application.

(1) Information about the Applicant and the Application. The following information should be provided in every fee application:

(i) Date the bankruptcy petition was filed, date of the order approving employment, identity of the party represented, date services commenced, and whether the applicant is seeking compensation under a provision of the Bankruptcy Code other than section 330.

(ii) Terms and conditions of employment and compensation, source of compensation, existence and terms controlling use of a retainer, and any budgetary or other limitations on fees.

(iii) Names and hourly rates of all applicant's professionals and paraprofessionals who billed time, explanation of any changes in hourly rates from those previously charged, and statement of whether the compensation is based on the customary compensation charged by comparably skilled practitioners in cases other than cases under title 11.

(iv) Whether the application is interim or final, and the dates of previous orders on interim compensation or reimbursement of expenses along with the amounts requested and the amounts allowed or disallowed, amounts of all previous payments, and amount of any allowed fees and expenses remaining unpaid.

(v) Whether the person on whose behalf the applicant is employed has been given the opportunity to review the application and whether that person has approved the requested amount.

(vi) When an application is filed less than 120 days after the order for relief or after a prior application to the Court, the date and terms of the order allowing leave to file at shortened intervals.

(vii) Time period of the services or expenses covered by the application.

(2) Case Status. The following information should be provided to the extent that it is known to or can be reasonably ascertained by the applicant:

(i) In a chapter 7 case, a summary of the administration of the case including all moneys received and disbursed in the case, when the case is expected to close, and, if applicant is seeking an interim award, whether it is feasible to make an interim distribution to creditors without prejudicing the rights of any creditor holding a claim of equal or higher priority.

(ii) In a chapter 11 case, whether a plan and disclosure statement have been filed and, if not yet filed, when the plan and disclosure statement are expected to be filed; whether all quarterly fees have been paid to the United States Trustee; and whether all monthly operating reports have been filed.

(iii) In every case, the amount of cash on hand or on deposit, the amount and nature of accrued unpaid administrative expenses, and the amount of unencumbered funds in the estate.

(iv) Any material changes in the status of the case that occur after the filing of the fee application should be raised, orally or in writing, at the hearing on the application or, if a hearing is not required, prior to the expiration of the time period for objection.

(3) Summary Sheet. All applications should contain a summary or cover sheet that provides a synopsis of the following information:

(i) Total compensation and expenses requested and any amount(s) previously requested;

(ii) Total compensation and expenses previously awarded by the court;

(iii) Name and applicable billing rate for each person who billed time during the period, and date of bar admission for each attorney;

(iv) Total hours billed and total amount of billing for each person who billed time during billing period; and

(v) Computation of blended hourly rate for persons who billed time during period, excluding paralegal or other paraprofessional time.

(4) **Project Billing Format.** (i) To facilitate effective review of the application, all time and service entries should be arranged by project categories. The project categories set forth in Exhibit A should be used to the extent applicable. A separate project category should be used for administrative matters and, if payment is requested, for fee application preparation.

(ii) The United States Trustee has discretion to determine that the project billing format is not necessary in a particular case or in a particular class of cases. Applicants should be encouraged to consult with the United States Trustee if there is a question as to the need for project billing in any particular case.

(iii) Each project category should contain a narrative summary of the following information:

(A) a description of the project, its necessity and benefit to the estate, and the status of the project including all pending litigation for which compensation and reimbursement are requested;

(B) identification of each person providing services on the project; and

(C) a statement of the number of hours spent and the amount of compensation requested for each professional and paraprofessional on the project.

(iv) Time and service entries are to be reported in chronological order under the appropriate project category.

(v) Time entries should be kept contemporaneously with the services rendered in time periods of tenths of an hour. Services should be noted in detail and not combined or "lumped" together, with each service showing a separate time entry; however, tasks performed in a project which total a de minimis amount of time can be combined or lumped together if they do not exceed .5 hours on a daily aggregate. Time entries for telephone calls, letters, and other communications should give sufficient detail to identify the parties to and the nature of the communication. Time entries for court hearings and conferences should identify the subject of the hearing or conference. If more than one professional from the applicant firm attends a hearing or conference, the applicant should explain the need for multiple attendees.

(5) **Reimbursement for Actual, Necessary Expenses.** Any expense for which reimbursement is sought must be actual and necessary and supported by documentation as appropriate. Factors relevant to a determination that the expense is proper include the following:

(i) Whether the expense is reasonable and economical. For example, first class and other luxurious travel mode or accommodations will normally be objectionable.

(ii) Whether the requested expenses are customarily charged to non-bankruptcy clients of the applicant.

(iii) Whether applicant has provided a detailed itemization of all expenses including the date incurred, description of expense (e.g., type of travel, type of fare, rate, destination), method of computation, and, where relevant, name of the person incurring the expense and purpose of the expense. Itemized expenses should be identified by their nature (e.g., long distance telephone, copy costs, messengers, computer research, airline travel, etc.) and by the month incurred. Unusual items require more detailed explanations and should be allocated, where practicable, to specific projects.

(iv) Whether applicant has prorated expenses where appropriate between the estate and other cases (e.g., travel expenses applicable to more than one case) and has adequately explained the basis for any such proration.

(v) Whether expenses incurred by the applicant to third parties are limited to the actual amounts billed to, or paid by, the applicant on behalf of the estate.

(vi) Whether applicant can demonstrate that the amount requested for expenses incurred in-house reflect the actual cost of such expenses to the applicant. The United States Trustee may establish an objection ceiling for any in-house expenses that are routinely incurred and for which the actual cost cannot easily be determined by most professionals (e.g., photocopies, facsimile charges, and mileage).

(vii) Whether the expenses appear to be in the nature nonreimbursable overhead. Overhead consists of all continuous administrative or general costs incident to the operation of the applicant's office and not particularly attributable to an individual client or case. Overhead includes, but is not limited to, word processing, proofreading, secretarial and other clerical services, rent, utilities, office equipment and furnishings, insurance, taxes, local telephones and monthly car phone charges, lighting, heating and cooling, and library and publication charges.

(viii) Whether applicant has adhered to allowable rates for expenses as fixed by local rule or order of the Court.

Exhibit A—Project Categories

Here is a list of suggested project categories for use in most bankruptcy cases. Only one category should be used for a given activity. Professionals should make their best effort to be consistent in their use of categories, whether within a particular firm or by different firms working on the same case. It would be appropriate for all professionals to discuss the categories in advance and agree generally on how activities will be categorized. This list is not exclusive. The application may contain additional categories as the case requires. They are generally more applicable to attorneys in chapter 7 and chapter 11, but may be used by all professionals as appropriate.

Asset Analysis and Recovery: Identification and review of potential assets including causes of action and non-litigation recoveries.

Asset Disposition: Sales, leases (§ 365 matters), abandonment and related transaction work.

Business Operations: Issues related to debtor-in-possession operating in chapter 11 such as employee, vendor, tenant issues and other similar problems.

Case Administration: Coordination and compliance activities, including preparation of statement of financial affairs; schedules; list of contracts; United States Trustee interim statements and operating reports; contacts with the United States Trustee; general creditor inquiries.

Claims Administration and Objections: Specific claim inquiries; bar date motions; analyses, objections and allowances of claims.

Employee Benefits/Pensions: Review issues such as severance, retention, 401K coverage and continuance of pension plan.

Fee/Employment Applicants: Preparation of employment and fee applications for self or others; motions to establish interim procedures.

Fee/Employment Objections: Review of and objections to the employment and fee applications of others.

Financing: Matters under §§ 361, 363 and 364 including cash collateral and secured claims; loan document analysis.

Litigation: There should be a separate category established for each matter (e.g., XYZ Litigation).

Meetings of Creditors: Preparing for and attending the conference of creditors, the § 341(a) meeting and other creditors' committee meetings.

Plan and Disclosure Statement: Formulation, presentation and confirmation; compliance with the plan confirmation order, related orders and rules; disbursement and case closing activities, except those related to the allowance and objections to allowance of claims.

Relief From Stay Proceedings: Matters relating to termination or continuation of automatic stay under § 362.

The following categories are generally more applicable to accountants and financial advisors, but may be used by all professionals as appropriate.

Accounting/Auditing: Activities related to maintaining and auditing books of account, preparation of financial statements and account analysis.

Business Analysis: Preparation and review of company business plan; development and review of strategies; preparation and review of cash flow forecasts and feasibility studies.

Corporate Finance: Review financial aspects of potential mergers, acquisitions and disposition of company or subsidiaries.

Data Analysis: Management information systems review, installation and analysis, construction, maintenance and reporting of significant case financial data, lease rejection, claims, etc.

Litigation Consulting: Providing consulting and expert witness services relating to various bankruptcy matters such as insolvency, feasibility, avoiding actions, forensic accounting, etc.

Reconstruction Accounting: Reconstructing books and records from past transactions and bringing accounting current.

Tax Issues: Analysis of tax issues and preparation of state and federal tax returns.

Valuation: Appraise or review appraisals of assets.

[61 FR 24890, May 17, 1996]

CROSS REFERENCES

Compensation of professional persons—

Actual, necessary services, see 11 USCA § 330.

Limitation on, see 11 USCA § 328.

Sharing of, see 11 USCA § 504.

Definition of—

Firm to include partnership or professional corporation, see Fed.Rules Bankr.Proc. Rule 9001, 11 USCA.

Regular associate to mean attorney employed by, associated with, as counsel to firm or individual, see Fed. Rules Bankr.Proc. Rule 9001, 11 USCA.

Employment of professional persons, see Fed.Rules Bankr. Proc. Rule 2014, 11 USCA.

Rule 2017. Examination of Debtor's Transactions with Debtor's Attorney

(a) Payment or transfer to attorney before order for relief

On motion by any party in interest or on the court's own initiative, the court after notice and a hearing may determine whether any payment of money or any transfer of property by the debtor, made directly or indirectly and in contemplation of the filing of a petition under the Code by or against the debtor or before entry of the order for relief in an involuntary case, to an attorney for services rendered or to be rendered is excessive.

(b) Payment or transfer to attorney after order for relief

On motion by the debtor, the United States trustee, or on the court's own initiative, the court after notice and a hearing may determine whether any payment of money or any transfer of property, or any agreement therefor, by the debtor to an attorney after entry of an order for relief in a case under the Code is excessive, whether the payment or transfer is made or is to be made directly or indirectly, if the payment, transfer, or agreement therefor is for services in any way related to the case.

(As amended Mar. 30, 1987, eff. Aug. 1, 1987; Apr. 30, 1991, eff. Aug. 1, 1991.)

ADVISORY COMMITTEE NOTES

This rule is derived from § 60d of the Act [former § 96(d) of this title] and former Bankruptcy Rule 220 and implements § 329 of the Code. Information required to be disclosed by the attorney for a debtor by § 329 of the Code and by the debtor in his Statement of Financial Affairs (Item #15 of Form No. 7, Item #20 of Form No. 8) will assist the court in determining whether to proceed under this rule. Section 60d was enacted in recognition of "the temptation of a failing debtor to deal too liberally with his property in employing counsel to protect him in view of financial reverses and probable failure." In re Wood & Henderson, 210 U.S. 246, 253 (1908). This rule, like § 60d of the Act and § 329 of the Code, is premised on the need for and appropriateness of judicial scrutiny of arrangements between a debtor and his attorney to protect the creditors of the estate and the debtor against overreaching by an officer of the court who is in a peculiarly advantageous position to impose on both the creditors and his client. 2 Collier, Bankruptcy ¶329.02 (15th ed. 1980); MacLachlan, Bankruptcy 318 (1956). Rule 9014 applies to any contested matter arising under this rule.

This rule is not to be construed to permit post-petition payments or transfers which may be avoided under other provisions of the Code.

1991 Amendments

This rule is amended to include within subdivision (a) a payment or transfer of property by the debtor to an attorney after the filing of an involuntary petition but before the order for relief. Any party in interest should be able to make a motion for a determination of whether such payment or transfer is excessive because the funds or property transferred may be property of the estate.

The United States trustee supervises and monitors the administration of bankruptcy cases other than chapter 9 cases and pursuant to § 307 of the Code may raise, appear and be heard on issues relating to fees paid to the debtor's attorney. It is consistent with that role to expect the United States trustee to review statements filed under Rule 2016(b) and to file motions relating to excessive fees pursuant to § 329 of the Code.

CROSS REFERENCES

Court filing of compensation paid or agreed to be paid, see 11 USCA § 329.

Motions; form and service, see Fed.Rules Bankr.Proc. Rule 9013, 11 USCA.

Proceedings under this rule as nonadversarial proceedings, see Fed.Rules Bankr.Proc. Rule 7001, 11 USCA.

Process; service of summons, complaint, see Fed.Rules Bankr.Proc. Rule 7004, 11 USCA.

Rule 2018. Intervention; Right to Be Heard

(a) Permissive intervention

In a case under the Code, after hearing on such notice as the court directs and for cause shown, the court may permit any interested entity to intervene generally or with respect to any specified matter.

(b) Intervention by Attorney General of a State

In a chapter 7, 11, 12, or 13 case, the Attorney General of a State may appear and be heard on behalf of consumer creditors if the court determines the appearance is in the public interest, but the Attorney General may not appeal from any judgment, order, or decree in the case.

(c) Chapter 9 municipality case

The Secretary of the Treasury of the United States may, or if requested by the court shall, intervene in a chapter 9 case. Representatives of the state in which the debtor is located may intervene in a chapter 9 case with respect to matters specified by the court.

(d) Labor unions

In a chapter 9, 11, or 12 case, a labor union or employees' association, representative of employees of the debtor, shall have the right to be heard on the economic soundness of a plan affecting the interests of the employees. A labor union or employees' association which exercises its right to be heard under this subdivision shall not be entitled to appeal any judgment, order, or decree relating to the plan, unless otherwise permitted by law.

(e) Service on entities covered by this rule

The court may enter orders governing the service of notice and papers on entities permitted to intervene or be heard pursuant to this rule.

(As amended Mar. 30, 1987, eff. Aug. 1, 1987; Apr. 30, 1991, eff. Aug. 1, 1991.)

ADVISORY COMMITTEE NOTES

This rule is derived from former Rules 8–210, 9–15 and 10–210 and it implements §§ 1109 and 1164 of the Code.

Pursuant to § 1109 of the Code, parties in interest have a right to be heard and the Securities and Exchange Commission may raise and be heard on any issue but it may not take an appeal. That section is applicable in chapter 9 cases (§ 901 of the Code) and in chapter 11 cases, including cases under subchapter IV thereof for the reorganization of a railroad.

In a railroad reorganization case under subchapter IV of chapter 11, § 1164 also gives the right to be heard to the Interstate Commerce Commission, the Department of Transportation and any state or local regulatory commission with jurisdiction over the debtor, but these entities may not appeal.

This rule does not apply in adversary proceedings. For intervention in adversary proceedings, see Rule 7024. The rules do not provide any right of compensation to or reimbursement of expenses for intervenors or others covered by this rule. Section 503(b)(3)(D) and (4) is not applicable to the entities covered by this rule.

Subdivision (a) is derived from former Chapter VIII Rule 8–210 and former Chapter X Rule 10–210. It permits intervention of an entity (see § 101(14), (21) of the Code) not otherwise entitled to do so under the Code or this rule. Such a party seeking to intervene must show cause therefor.

Subdivision (b) specifically grants the appropriate state's attorney General the right to appear and be heard on behalf of consumer creditors when it is in the public interest. See House Rep. No. 95–595, 95th Cong., 1st Sess. (1977) 189. While "consumer creditor" is not defined in the Code or elsewhere, it would include the type of individual entitled to priority under § 507(a)(5) of the Code, that is, an individual who has deposited money for the purchase, lease or rental of property or the purchase of services for the personal, family, or household use of the individual. It would also include individuals who purchased or leased property for such purposes in connection with which there may exist claims for breach of warranty.

This subdivision does not grant the Attorney General the status of party in interest. In other contexts, the Attorney General will, of course, be a party in interest as for example, in representing a state in connection with a tax claim.

Subdivision (c) recognizes the possible interests of the Secretary of the Treasury or of the state of the debtor's locale when a municipality is the debtor. It is derived from former Chapter IX Rule 9–15 and § 85(d) of the Act [former § 405(d) of this title].

Subdivision (d) is derived from former Chapter X Rule 10–210 which, in turn, was derived from § 206 of the Act [former § 606 of this title]. Section 206 has no counter-part in the Code.

Subdivision (e) is derived from former Chapter VIII Rule 8–210(d). It gives the court flexibility in directing the type of future notices to be given intervenors.

1987 Amendments

Subdivision (d) is amended to make it clear that the prohibition against appeals by labor unions is limited only to their participation in connection with the hearings on the plan as provided in subdivision (d). If a labor union would otherwise have the right to file an appeal or to be a party to an appeal, this rule does not preclude the labor union from exercising that right.

1991 Amendments

Subdivisions (b) and (d) are amended to include chapter 12.

CROSS REFERENCES

Consumer debt defined as debt primarily for personal, family, or household purpose, see 11 USCA § 101.

Definitions for purposes of this rule of—

Entity, see 11 USCA § 101.

Governmental unit, see 11 USCA § 101.

Person, see 11 USCA § 101.

Intervention of—

Department of Transportation, see 11 USCA § 1164.

Interstate Commerce Commission, see 11 USCA § 1164.

Party in interest, see 11 USCA § 1109.

Securities and Exchange Commission, see 11 USCA § 1109.

State or local regulatory commission, see 11 USCA § 1164.

Intervention in adversary proceedings, see Fed.Rules Bankr.Proc. Rule 7024, 11 USCA.

Rule 2019. Representation of Creditors and Equity Security Holders in Chapter 9 Municipality and Chapter 11 Reorganization Cases

(a) Data required

In a chapter 9 municipality or chapter 11 reorganization case, except with respect to a committee appointed pursuant to § 1102 or 1114 of the Code, every entity or committee representing more than one creditor or equity security holder and, unless otherwise directed by the court, every indenture trustee, shall file a verified statement setting forth (1) the name and address of the creditor or equity security holder; (2) the nature and amount of the claim or interest and the time of acquisition thereof unless it is alleged to have been acquired more than one year prior to the filing of the petition; (3) a recital of the pertinent facts and circumstances in connection with the employment of the entity or indenture trustee, and, in the case of a committee, the name or names of the entity or entities at whose instance, directly or indirectly, the employment was arranged or the committee was organized or agreed to act; and (4) with reference to the time of the employment of the entity, the organization or formation of the committee, or the appearance in the case of any indenture trustee, the amounts of claims or interests owned by the entity, the members of the committee or the indenture trustee, the times when acquired, the amounts paid therefor, and any sales or other disposition thereof. The statement shall include a copy of the instrument, if any, whereby the entity, committee, or indenture trustee is empowered to act on behalf of creditors or equity security holders. A supplemental statement shall be filed promptly, setting forth any material changes in the facts contained in the statement filed pursuant to this subdivision.

(b) Failure to comply; effect

On motion of any party in interest or on its own initiative, the court may (1) determine whether there has been a failure to comply with the provisions of subdivision (a) of this rule or with any other applicable law regulating the activities and personnel of any entity, committee, or indenture trustee or any other impropriety in connection with any solicitation and, if it so determines, the court may refuse to permit that entity, committee, or indenture trustee to be heard further or to intervene in the case; (2) examine any representation provision of a deposit agreement, proxy, trust mortgage, trust indenture, or deed of trust, or committee or other authorization, and any claim or interest acquired by any entity or committee in contemplation or in the course of a case under the Code and grant appropriate relief; and (3) hold invalid any authority, acceptance, rejection, or objection given, procured, or received by an entity or committee who has not complied with this rule or with § 1125(b) of the Code.

(As amended Mar. 30, 1987, eff. Aug. 1, 1987; Apr. 30, 1991, eff. Aug. 1, 1991.)

ADVISORY COMMITTEE NOTES

This rule is a comprehensive regulation of representation in chapter 9 municipality and in chapter 11 reorganization cases. It is derived from §§ 209 to 213 of the Act [former §§ 609 to 613 of this title] and former Chapter X Rule 10–211.

Subdivision (b) is derived from §§ 212, 213 of the Act [former §§ 612 and 613 of this title]. As used in clause (2), "other authorization" would include a power or warrant of attorney which are specifically mentioned in § 212 of the Act. This rule deals with representation provisions in mortgages, trust deeds, etc. to protect the beneficiaries from unfair practices and the like. It does not deal with the validation or invalidation of security interests generally. If immediate compliance is not possible, the court may permit a representative to be heard on a specific matter, but there is no implicit waiver of compliance on a permanent basis.

1991 Amendments

Subdivision (a) is amended to exclude from the requirements of this rule committees of retired employees appointed pursuant to § 1114 of the Code. The words "with the clerk" are deleted as unnecessary. See Rules 5005(a) and 9001(3).

CROSS REFERENCES

Appointment of creditors' committee organized before order for relief, see Fed.Rules Bankr.Proc. Rule 2007, 11 USCA.

Motions; form and service, see Fed.Rules Bankr.Proc. Rule 9013, 11 USCA.

Trustees for estates when joint administration ordered, see Fed.Rules Bankr.Proc. Rule 2009, 11 USCA.

Rule 2020. Review of Acts by United States Trustee

A proceeding to contest any act or failure to act by the United States trustee is governed by Rule 9014.

(Added Apr. 30, 1991, eff. Aug. 1, 1991.)

ADVISORY COMMITTEE NOTES

The United States trustee performs administrative functions, such as the convening of the meeting of creditors and the appointment of trustees and committees. Most of the acts of the United States trustee are not controversial and will go unchallenged. However, the United States trustee is not a judicial officer and does not resolve disputes regarding the propriety of its own actions. This rule, which is new, provides a procedure for judicial review of the United States trustee's acts or failure to act in connection with the administration of the case. For example, if the United States trustee schedules a § 341 meeting to be held 90 days after the petition is filed, and a party in interest wishes to challenge the propriety of that act in view of § 341(a) of the Code and Rule 2003 which requires that the meeting be held not more than 40 days after the order for relief, this rule permits the party to do so by motion.

This rule provides for review of acts already committed by the United States trustee, but does not provide for advisory opinions in advance of the act. This rule is not intended to limit the discretion of the United States trustee, provided that the United States trustee's act is authorized by, and in compliance with, the Code, title 28, these rules, and other applicable law.

PART III—CLAIMS AND DISTRIBUTION TO CREDITORS AND EQUITY INTEREST HOLDERS; PLANS

Rule 3001. Proof of Claim

(a) Form and content

A proof of claim is a written statement setting forth a creditor's claim. A proof of claim shall conform substantially to the appropriate Official Form.

(b) Who may execute

A proof of claim shall be executed by the creditor or the creditor's authorized agent except as provided in Rules 3004 and 3005.

(c) Claim based on a writing

When a claim, or an interest in property of the debtor securing the claim, is based on a writing, the original or a duplicate shall be filed with the proof of claim. If the writing has been lost or destroyed, a statement of the circumstances of the loss or destruction shall be filed with the claim.

(d) Evidence of perfection of security interest

If a security interest in property of the debtor is claimed, the proof of claim shall be accompanied by evidence that the security interest has been perfected.

(e) Transferred claim

(1) Transfer of claim other than for security before proof filed

If a claim has been transferred other than for security before proof of the claim has been filed, the proof of claim may be filed only by the transferee or an indenture trustee.

(2) Transfer of claim other than for security after proof filed

If a claim other than one based on a publicly traded note, bond, or debenture has been transferred other than for security after the proof of claim has been filed, evidence of the transfer shall be filed by the transferee. The clerk shall immediately notify the alleged transferor by mail of the filing of the evidence of transfer and that objection thereto, if any, must be filed within 20 days of the mailing of the notice or within any additional time allowed by the court. If the alleged transferor files a timely objection and the court finds, after notice and a hearing, that the claim has been transferred other than for security, it shall enter an order substituting the transferee for the transferor. If a timely objection is not filed by the alleged transferor, the transferee shall be substituted for the transferor.

(3) Transfer of claim for security before proof filed

If a claim other than one based on a publicly traded note, bond, or debenture has been transferred for security before proof of the claim has been filed, the transferor or transferee or both may file a proof of claim for the full amount. The proof shall be supported by a statement setting forth the terms of the transfer. If either the transferor or the transferee files a proof of claim, the clerk shall immediately notify the other by mail of the right to join in the filed claim. If both transferor and transferee file proofs of the same claim, the proofs shall be consolidated. If the transferor or transferee does not file an agreement regarding its relative rights respecting voting of the claim, payment of dividends thereon, or participation in the administration of the estate, on motion by a party in interest and after notice and a hearing, the court shall enter such orders respecting these matters as may be appropriate.

(4) Transfer of claim for security after proof filed

If a claim other than one based on a publicly traded note, bond, or debenture has been transferred for security after the proof of claim has been filed, evidence of the terms of the transfer shall be filed by the transferee. The clerk shall immediately notify the alleged transferor by mail of the filing of the evidence of transfer and that objection thereto, if any, must be filed within 20 days of the mailing of the notice or within any additional time allowed by the court. If a timely objection is filed by the alleged transferor, the court, after notice and a hearing, shall determine whether the claim has been transferred for security. If the transferor or transferee does not file an agreement regarding its relative rights respecting voting of the claim, payment of dividends thereon, or participation in the administration of the estate, on motion by a party in interest and after notice and a hearing, the court shall enter such orders respecting these matters as may be appropriate.

(5) Service of objection or motion; notice of hearing

A copy of an objection filed pursuant to paragraph (2) or (4) or a motion filed pursuant to paragraph (3) or (4) of this subdivision together with a notice of a hearing shall be mailed or otherwise delivered to the transferor or transferee, whichever is appropriate, at least 30 days prior to the hearing.

(f) Evidentiary effect

A proof of claim executed and filed in accordance with these rules shall constitute prima facie evidence of the validity and amount of the claim.

(g) [1] To the extent not inconsistent with the United States Warehouse Act or applicable State law, a warehouse receipt, scale ticket, or similar document of the type routinely issued as evidence of title by a grain storage facility, as defined in section 557 of title 11, shall constitute prima facie evidence of the validity and amount of a claim of ownership of a quantity of grain.

(As amended Pub.L. 98–353, Title III, § 354, July 10, 1984, 98 Stat. 361; Apr. 30, 1991, eff. Aug. 1, 1991.)

[1] So in original. Subsec. (g) was enacted without a catchline.

ADVISORY COMMITTEE NOTES

This rule is adapted from former Bankruptcy Rules 301 and 302. The Federal Rules of Evidence, made applicable to cases under the Code by Rule 1101, do not prescribe the evidentiary effect to be accorded particular documents. Subdivision (f) of this rule supplements the Federal Rules of Evidence as they apply to cases under the Code.

Subdivision (c). This subdivision is similar to former Bankruptcy Rule 302(c) and continues the requirement for the filing of any written security agreement and provides that the filing of a duplicate of a writing underlying a claim authenticates the claim with the same effect as the filing of the original writing. Cf. Rules 1001(4) and 1003 of F.R. of Evid. Subdivision (d) together with the requirement in the first sentence of subdivision (c) for the filing of any written security agreement, is designed to facilitate the determination whether the claim is secured and properly perfected so as to be valid against the trustee.

Subdivision (d). "Satisfactory evidence" of perfection, which is to accompany the proof of claim, would include a duplicate of an instrument filed or recorded, a duplicate of a certificate of title when a security interest is perfected by notation on such a certificate, a statement that pledged property has been in possession of the secured party since a specified date, or a statement of the reasons why no action was necessary for perfection. The secured creditor may not be required to file a proof of claim under this rule if he is not seeking allowance of a claim for a deficiency. But see § 506(d) of the Code.

Subdivision (e). The rule recognizes the differences between an unconditional transfer of a claim and a transfer for the purpose of security and prescribes a procedure for dealing with the rights of the transferor and transferee when the transfer is for security. The rule clarifies the procedure to be followed when a transfer precedes or follows the filing of the petition. The interests of sound administration are served by requiring the post-petition transferee to file with the proof of claim a statement of the transferor acknowledging the transfer and the consideration for the transfer. Such a disclosure will assist the court in dealing with evils that may arise out of post-bankruptcy traffic in claims against an estate. Monroe v. Scofield, 135 F.2d 725 (10th Cir. 1943); In re Philadelphia & Western Ry., 64 F.Supp. 738 (E.D.Pa.1946); cf. In re Latham Lithographic Corp., 107 F.2d 749 (2d Cir. 1939). Both paragraphs (1) and (3) of this subdivision, which deal with a transfer before the filing of a proof of claim, recognize that the transferee may be unable to obtain the required statement from the transferor, but in that event a sound reason for such inability must accompany the proof of claim filed by the transferee.

Paragraphs (3) and (4) clarify the status of a claim transferred for the purpose of security. An assignee for security has been recognized as a rightful claimant in bankruptcy. Feder v. John Engelhorn & Sons, 202 F.2d 411 (2d Cir. 1953). An assignor's right to file a claim notwithstanding the assignment was sustained in In re R & L Engineering Co.,

182 F.Supp. 317 (S.D.Cal.1960). Facilitation of the filing of proofs by both claimants as holders of interests in a single claim is consonant with equitable treatment of the parties and sound administration. See In re Latham Lithographic Corp., 107 F.2d 749 (2d Cir. 1939).

Paragraphs (2) and (4) of subdivision (e) deal with the transfer of a claim after proof has been filed. Evidence of the terms of the transfer required to be disclosed to the court will facilitate the court's determination of the appropriate order to be entered because of the transfer.

Paragraph (5) describes the procedure to be followed when an objection is made by the transferor to the transferee's filed evidence of transfer.

The United States Warehouse Act, referred to in subd. (g), is Part C of Act Aug. 11, 1916, c. 313, 39 Stat. 486, as amended, which is classified generally to chapter 10 (§ 241 et seq.) of Title 7, Agriculture. For complete classification of this Act to the Code, see section 241 of Title 7 and Tables.

1984 Amendments

Subdivision (g) was added by § 354 of the 1984 amendments.

Subd. (g). Pub.L. 98–353 added subd. (g).

1991 Amendments

Subdivision (a) is amended in anticipation of future revision and renumbering of the Official Forms.

Subdivision (e) is amended to limit the court's role to the adjudication of disputes regarding transfers of claims. If a claim has been transferred prior to the filing of a proof of claim, there is no need to state the consideration for the transfer or to submit other evidence of the transfer. If a claim has been transferred other than for security after a proof of claim has been filed, the transferee is substituted for the transferor in the absence of a timely objection by the alleged transferor. In that event, the clerk should note the transfer without the need for court approval. If a timely objection is filed, the court's role is to determine whether a transfer has been made that is enforceable under nonbankruptcy law. This rule is not intended either to encourage or discourage postpetition transfers of claims or to affect any remedies otherwise available under nonbankruptcy law to a transferor or transferee such as for misrepresentation in connection with the transfer of a claim. "After notice and a hearing" as used in subdivision (e) shall be construed in accordance with paragraph (5).

The words "with the clerk" in subdivision (e)(2) and (e)(4) are deleted as unnecessary. See Rules 5005(a) and 9001(3).

1984 Acts

Amendment by Pub.L. 98–353 effective with respect to cases filed 90 days after July 10, 1984, see section 553 of Pub.L. 98–353, set out as a note under section 101 of this title.

CROSS REFERENCES

Filed claims or interests deemed allowed, see 11 USCA § 502.

Filing of proofs of claims or interests, see 11 USCA § 501.

Notice to claimants in converted liquidation case, see Fed. Rules Bankr.Proc. Rule 1019, 11 USCA.

Admissibility of duplicates, see Fed.Rules Evid. Rule 1003, 28 USCA.

Rule 3002. Filing Proof of Claim or Interest

(a) Necessity for filing

An unsecured creditor or an equity security holder must file a proof of claim or interest for the claim or interest to be allowed, except as provided in Rules 1019(3), 3003, 3004, and 3005.

(b) Place of filing

A proof of claim or interest shall be filed in accordance with Rule 5005.

(c) Time for filing

In a chapter 7 liquidation, chapter 12 family farmer's debt adjustment, or chapter 13 individual's debt adjustment case, a proof of claim is timely filed if it is filed not later than 90 days after the first date set for the meeting of creditors called under § 341(a) of the Code, except as follows:

(1) A proof of claim filed by a governmental unit, other than for a claim resulting from a tax return filed under § 1308, is timely filed if it is filed not later than 180 days after the date of the order for relief. A proof of claim filed by a governmental unit for a claim resulting from a tax return filed under § 1308 is timely filed if it is filed no later than 180 days after the date of the order for relief or 60 days after the date of the filing of the tax return. The court may, for cause, enlarge the time for a governmental unit to file a proof of claim only upon motion of the governmental unit made before expiration of the period for filing a timely proof of claim.

(2) In the interest of justice and if it will not unduly delay the administration of the case, the court may extend the time for filing a proof of claim by an infant or incompetent person or the representative of either.

(3) An unsecured claim which arises in favor of an entity or becomes allowable as a result of a judgment may be filed within 30 days after the judgment becomes final if the judgment is for the recovery of money or property from that entity or denies or avoids the entity's interest in property. If the judgment imposes a liability which is not satisfied, or a duty which is not performed within such period or such further time as the court may permit, the claim shall not be allowed.

(4) A claim arising from the rejection of an executory contract or unexpired lease of the debtor may be filed within such time as the court may direct.

(5) If notice of insufficient assets to pay a dividend was given to creditors under Rule 2002(e), and subsequently the trustee notifies the court that payment of a dividend appears possible, the clerk shall give at least 90 days' notice by mail to creditors of that fact and of the date by which proofs of claim must be filed.

(6) If notice of the time to file a proof of claim has been mailed to a creditor at a foreign address, on motion filed by the creditor before or after the expiration of the time, the court may extend the time by not more than 60 days if the court finds that the notice was insufficient under the circumstances to give the creditor a reasonable time to file a proof of claim.

(As amended Mar. 30, 1987, eff. Aug. 1, 1987; Apr. 30, 1991, eff. Aug. 1, 1991; Apr. 23, 1996, eff. Dec. 1, 1996; Apr. 23, 2008, eff. Dec. 1, 2008.)

ADVISORY COMMITTEE NOTES

Subdivision (a) of this rule is substantially a restatement of the general requirement that claims be proved and filed. The exceptions refer to Rule 3003 providing for the filing of claims in chapter 9 and 11 cases, and to Rules 3004 and 3005 authorizing claims to be filed by the debtor or trustee and the filing of a claim by a contingent creditor of the debtor.

A secured claim need not be filed or allowed under § 502 or § 506(d) unless a party in interest has requested a determination and allowance or disallowance under § 502.

Subdivision (c) is adapted from former Bankruptcy Rule 302(e) but changes the time limits on the filing of claims in chapter 7 and 13 cases from six months to 90 days after the first date set for the meeting of creditors. The special rule for early filing by a secured creditor in a chapter 13 case, in former Rule 13–302(e)(1) is not continued.

Although the claim of a secured creditor may have arisen before the petition, a judgment avoiding the security interest may not have been entered until after the time for filing claims has expired. Under Rule 3002(c)(3) the creditor who did not file a secured claim may nevertheless file an unsecured claim within the time prescribed. A judgment does not become final for the purpose of starting the 30 day period provided for by paragraph (3) until the time for appeal has expired or, if an appeal is taken, until the appeal has been disposed of. In re Tapp, 61 F.Supp. 594 (W.D.Ky. 1945).

Paragraph (1) is derived from former Bankruptcy Rule 302(e). The governmental unit may move for an extension of the 90 day period. Pursuant to § 501(c) of the Code, if the government does not file its claim within the proper time period, the debtor or trustee may file on its behalf. An extension is not needed by the debtor or trustee because the right to file does not arise until the government's time has expired.

Paragraph (4) is derived from former chapter rules. See, e.g., Rule 11–33(a)(2)(B). In light of the reduced time it is necessary that a party with a claim arising from the rejection of an executory contract have sufficient time to file that claim. This clause allows the court to fix an appropriate time.

Paragraph (5) of subdivision (c) is correlated with the provision in Rule 2002(e) authorizing notification to creditors of estates from which no dividends are anticipated. The clause permits creditors who have refrained from filing claims after receiving notification to be given an opportunity to file when subsequent developments indicate the possibility of a dividend. The notice required by this clause must be given in the manner provided in Rule 2002. The information relating to the discovery of assets will usually be obtained by the clerk from the trustee's interim reports or special notification by the trustee.

Provision is made in Rule 2002(a) and (h) for notifying all creditors of the fixing of a time for filing claims against a surplus under paragraph (6). This paragraph does not deal with the distribution of the surplus. Reference must also be made to § 726(a)(2)(C) and (3) which permits distribution on late filed claims.

Paragraph (6) is only operative in a chapter 7 case. In chapter 13 cases, the plan itself provides the distribution to creditors which is not necessarily dependent on the size of the estate.

1987 Amendments

Subdivision (a) is amended by adding a reference to Rule 1019(4). Rule 1019(4) provides that claims actually filed by a creditor in a chapter 11 or 13 case shall be treated as filed in a superseding chapter 7 case. Claims deemed filed in a chapter 11 case pursuant to § 1111(a) of the Code are not considered as filed in a superseding chapter 7 case. The creditor must file a claim in the superseding chapter 7 case.

1991 Amendments

Subdivision (a) is amended to conform to the renumbering of subdivisions of Rule 1019. Subdivision (c) is amended to include chapter 12 cases. Subdivision (c)(4) is amended to clarify that it includes a claim arising from the rejection of an unexpired lease.

1996 Amendments

The amendments are designed to conform to §§ 502(b)(9) and 726(a) of the Code as amended by the Bankruptcy Reform Act of 1994.

The Reform Act amended § 726(a)(1) and added § 502(b)(9) to the Code to govern the effects of a tardily filed claim. Under § 502(b)(9), a tardily filed claim must be disallowed if an objection to the proof of claim is filed, except to the extent that a holder of a tardily filed claim is entitled to distribution under § 726(a)(1), (2), or (3).

The phrase "in accordance with this rule" is deleted from Rule 3002(a) to clarify that the effect of filing a proof of claim after the expiration of the time prescribed in Rule 3002(c) is governed by § 502(b)(9) of the Code, rather than by this rule.

Section 502(b)(9) of the Code provides that a claim of a governmental unit shall be timely filed if it is filed "before 180 days after the date of the order for relief" or such later time as the Bankruptcy Rules provide. To avoid any confusion as to whether a governmental unit's proof of claim is timely filed under § 502(b)(9) if it is filed on the 180th day after the order for relief, paragraph (1) of subdivision (c) provides that a governmental unit's claim is timely if it is filed not later than 180 days after the order for relief.

References to "the United States, a state, or subdivision thereof" in paragraph (1) of subdivision (c) are changed to "governmental unit" to avoid different treatment among foreign and domestic governments.

GAP Report on Rule 3002. After publication of the proposed amendments, the Bankruptcy Reform Act of 1994 amended sections 726 and 502(b) of the Code to clarify the rights of creditors who tardily file a proof of claim. In view of the Reform Act, proposed new subdivision (d) of Rule 3002 has been deleted from the proposed amendments because it is no longer necessary. In addition, subdivisions (a) and (c) have been changed after publication to clarify that the effect of tardily filing a proof of claim is governed by § 502(b)(9) of the Code, rather than by this rule.

The amendments to § 502(b) also provide that a governmental unit's proof of claim is timely filed if it is filed before 180 days after the order for relief. Proposed amendments to Rule 3002(c)(1) were added to the published amendments to conform to this statutory change and to avoid any confusion as to whether a claim by a governmental unit is timely if it is filed on the 180th day.

The committee note has been re-written to explain the rule changes designed to conform to the Reform Act.

2008 Amendments

Subdivision (c)(1) is amended to reflect the addition of § 1308 to the Bankruptcy Code in 2005. This provision requires that chapter 13 debtors file tax returns during the pendency of the case, and imposes bankruptcy-related consequences if debtors fail to do so. Subdivision (c)(1) provides additional time for governmental units to file a proof of claim for tax obligations with respect to tax returns filed during the pendency of a chapter 13 case. The amendment also allows the governmental unit to move for additional time to file a proof of claim prior to expiration of the applicable filing period.

Subdivision (c)(5) of the rule is amended to set a new period for providing notice to creditors that they may file a proof of claim in a case in which they were previously informed that there was no need to file a claim. Under Rule 2002(e), if it appears that there will be no distribution to creditors, the creditors are notified of this fact and are informed that if assets are later discovered and a distribution is likely that a new notice will be given to the creditors. This second notice is prescribed by Rule 3002(c)(5). The rule is amended to direct the clerk to give at least 90 days' notice of the time within which creditors may file a proof of claim. Setting the deadline in this manner allows the notices being sent to creditors to be more accurate regarding the deadline than was possible under the prior rule. The rule previously began the 90 day notice period from the time of the mailing of the notice, a date that could vary and generally would not even be known to the creditor. Under the amended rule, the notice will identify a specific bar date for filing proofs of claim thereby being more helpful to the creditors.

Subdivision (c)(6) is added to give the court discretion to extend the time for filing a proof of claim for a creditor who received notice of the time to file the claim at a foreign address, if the court finds that the notice was not sufficient, under the particular circumstances, to give the foreign creditor a reasonable time to file a proof of claim. This amendment is designed to comply with § 1514(d), added to the Code by the 2005 amendments, and requires that the rules and orders of the court provide such additional time as is reasonable under the circumstances for foreign creditors to file claims in cases under all chapters of the Code.

Other changes are stylistic.

CROSS REFERENCES

Filed claims or interests deemed allowed, see 11 USCA § 502.

Filing of—

Claims by debtor or trustee, see Fed.Rules Bankr.Proc. Rule 3004, 11 USCA.

Claims by guarantor, surety, indorser, or other codebtor, see Fed.Rules Bankr.Proc. Rule 3005, 11 USCA.

Proofs of claims or interests, see 11 USCA § 501.

Filing proof of claim in liquidation or individual debt adjustment case, ninety-day period—

Enlargement permitted as limited in this rule, see Fed. Rules Bankr.Proc. Rule 9006, 11 USCA.

Reduction not permitted, see Fed.Rules Bankr.Proc. Rule 9006, 11 USCA.

Motions; form and service, see Fed.Rules Bankr.Proc. Rule 9013, 11 USCA.

Notice by mail of time allowed to file claims, see Fed.Rules Bankr.Proc. Rule 2002, 11 USCA.

Time extended to file claims against surplus—

Converted liquidation case, see Fed.Rules Bankr.Proc. Rule 1019, 11 USCA.

Notice to creditors in liquidation case, see Fed.Rules Bankr.Proc. Rule 2002, 11 USCA.

Twenty-day notice of time to file claims against surplus, see Fed.Rules Bankr.Proc. Rule 2002, 11 USCA.

Rule 3003. Filing Proof of Claim or Equity Security Interest in Chapter 9 Municipality or Chapter 11 Reorganization Cases

(a) Applicability of rule

This rule applies in chapter 9 and 11 cases.

(b) Schedule of liabilities and list of equity security holders

(1) Schedule of liabilities

The schedule of liabilities filed pursuant to § 521(1) of the Code shall constitute prima facie evidence of the validity and amount of the claims of creditors, unless they are scheduled as disputed, contingent, or unliquidated. It shall not be necessary for a creditor or equity security holder to file a proof of claim or interest except as provided in subdivision (c)(2) of this rule.

(2) List of equity security holders

The list of equity security holders filed pursuant to Rule 1007(a)(3) shall constitute prima facie evidence of the validity and amount of the equity security interests and it shall not be necessary for the holders of such interests to file a proof of interest.

(c) Filing of proof of claim

(1) Who may file

Any creditor or indenture trustee may file a proof of claim within the time prescribed by subdivision (c)(3) of this rule.

(2) Who must file

Any creditor or equity security holder whose claim or interest is not scheduled or scheduled as disputed, contingent, or unliquidated shall file a proof of claim or interest within the time prescribed by subdivision (c)(3) of this rule; any creditor who fails to do so shall not be treated as a creditor with respect to such claim for the purposes of voting and distribution.

(3) Time for filing

The court shall fix and for cause shown may extend the time within which proofs of claim or interest may be filed. Notwithstanding the expiration of such time, a proof of claim may be filed to the extent and under the conditions stated in Rule 3002(c)(2), (c)(3), (c)(4), and (c)(6).

(4) Effect of filing claim or interest

A proof of claim or interest executed and filed in accordance with this subdivision shall supersede any scheduling of that claim or interest pursuant to § 521(a)(1) of the Code.

(5) Filing by indenture trustee

An indenture trustee may file a claim on behalf of all known or unknown holders of securities issued pursuant to the trust instrument under which it is trustee.

(d) Proof of right to record status

For the purposes of Rules 3017, 3018 and 3021 and for receiving notices, an entity who is not the record holder of a security may file a statement setting forth facts which entitle that entity to be treated as the record holder. An objection to the statement may be filed by any party in interest.

(As amended Mar. 30, 1987, eff. Aug. 1, 1987; Apr. 30, 1991, eff. Aug. 1, 1991; Apr. 23, 2008, eff. Dec. 1, 2008.)

ADVISORY COMMITTEE NOTES

Subdivision (a). This rule applies only in chapter 9 and chapter 11 cases. It is adapted from former Chapter X Rule 10–401 and provides an exception to the requirement for filing proofs of claim and interest as expressed in §§ 925 and 1111(a) of the Code.

Subdivision (b). This general statement implements §§ 925 and 1111(a) of the Code.

Subdivision (c). This subdivision permits, in paragraph (1), the filing of a proof of claim but does not make it mandatory. Paragraph (2) requires, as does the Code, filing when a claim is scheduled as disputed, contingent, or unliquidated as to amount. It is the creditor's responsibility to determine if the claim is accurately listed. Notice of the provision of this rule is provided for in Official Form No. 16, the order for the meeting of creditors. In an appropriate case the court may order creditors whose claims are scheduled as disputed, contingent, or unliquidated be notified of that fact but the procedure is left to the discretion of the court.

Subdivision (d) is derived from former Chapter X Rule 10–401(f).

Except with respect to the need and time for filing claims, the other aspects concerning claims covered by Rules 3001 and 3002 are applicable in chapter 9 and 11 cases.

Holders of equity security interests need not file proofs of interest. Voting and distribution participation is dependent on ownership as disclosed by the appropriate records of a transfer agent or the corporate or other business records at the time prescribed in Rules 3017 and 3021.

1991 Amendments

Paragraph (3) of subdivision (c) is amended to permit the late filing of claims by infants or incompetent persons under the same circumstances that permit late filings in cases under chapter 7, 12, or 13. The amendment also provides sufficient time in which to file a claim that arises from a postpetition judgment against the claimant for the recovery of money or property or the avoidance of a lien. It also provides for purposes of clarification that upon rejection of an executory contract or unexpired lease, the court shall set a time for filing a claim arising therefrom despite prior expiration of the time set for filing proofs of claim.

The caption of paragraph (4) of subdivision (c) is amended to indicate that it applies to a proof of claim.

2008 Amendments

Subdivision (c)(3) is amended to implement § 1514(d) of the Code, which was added by the 2005 amendments. It makes the new Rule 3002(c)(6) applicable in chapter 9 and chapter 11 cases. This change was necessary so that creditors with foreign addresses be provided such additional time as is reasonable under the circumstances to file proofs of claims.

CROSS REFERENCES

Acceptance or rejection of municipality debt adjustment or reorganization plan by obligor filing creditor's claim, see Fed.Rules Bankr.Proc. Rule 3005, 11 USCA.

Distribution under confirmed plan to indenture trustee filing under this rule, see Fed.Rules Bankr.Proc. Rule 3021, 11 USCA.

Exception to filing requirement for—

Municipality debt adjustment case, see 11 USCA § 925.

Reorganization case, see 11 USCA § 1111.

Filing of claims by—

Debtor or trustee, see Fed.Rules Bankr.Proc. Rule 3004, 11 USCA.

Guarantor, surety, indorser, or other codebtor, see Fed. Rules Bankr.Proc. Rule 3005, 11 USCA.

Twenty-day notice of time fixed to file proof of claim, see Fed.Rules Bankr.Proc. Rule 2002, 11 USCA.

Rule 3004. Filing of Claims by Debtor or Trustee

If a creditor does not timely file a proof of claim under Rule 3002(c) or 3003(c), the debtor or trustee may file a proof of the claim within 30 days after the expiration of the time for filing claims prescribed by Rule 3002(c) or 3003(c), whichever is applicable. The clerk shall forthwith give notice of the filing to the creditor, the debtor and the trustee.

(As amended Mar. 30, 1987, eff. Aug. 1, 1987; Apr. 25, 2005, eff. Dec. 1, 2005.)

ADVISORY COMMITTEE NOTES

This rule is adapted from former Bankruptcy Rule 303 but conforms with the changes made by § 501(c) of the Code. Rule 303 permitted only the filing of tax and wage claims by the debtor. Section 501(c) of the Code, however, permits the filing by the debtor or trustee on behalf of any creditor.

It is the policy of the Code that debtors' estates should be administered for the benefit of creditors without regard to the dischargeability of their claims. After their estates have been closed, however, discharged debtors may find themselves saddled with liabilities, particularly for taxes, which remain unpaid because of the failure of creditors holding nondischargeable claims to file proofs of claim and receive distributions thereon. The result is that the debtor is deprived of an important benefit of the Code without any fault or omission on the debtor's part and without any objective of the Code being served thereby.

Section 501(c) of the Code authorizes a debtor or trustee to file a proof of claim for any holder of a claim. Although all claims may not be nondischargeable, it may be difficult to determine, in particular, whether tax claims survive discharge. See Plumb, Federal Tax Liens and Priorities in Bankruptcy, 43 Ref.J. 37, 43–44 (1969); 1 Collier, Bankruptcy ¶17.14 (14th ed. 1967); 3 id. ¶523.06 (15th ed. 1979). To eliminate the necessity of the resolution of this troublesome issue, the option accorded the debtor by the Code does not depend on the nondischargeability of the claim. No serious administrative problems and no unfairness to creditors seemed to develop from adoption of Rule 303, the forerunner to § 501(c). The authority to file is conditioned on the creditor's failure to file the proof of claim on or before the first date set for the meeting of creditors, which is the date a claim must ordinarily be filed in order to be voted in a chapter 7 case. Notice to the creditor is provided to enable him to file a proof of claim pursuant to Rule 3002, which proof, when filed, would supersede the proof filed by the debtor or trustee. Notice to the trustee would serve to alert the trustee to the special character of the proof and the possible need for supplementary evidence of the validity and amount of the claim. If the trustee does not qualify until after a proof of claim is filed by the debtor pursuant to this rule, he should be notified as soon as practicable thereafter.

To the extent the claim is allowed and dividends paid thereon, it will be reduced or perhaps paid in full. If the claim is also filed pursuant to Rule 3005, only one distribution thereon may be made. As expressly required by Rule 3005 and by the purpose of this rule such distribution must diminish the claim.

1987 Amendments

Under the rule as amended, the debtor or trustee in a chapter 7 or 13 case has 120 days from the first date set for the meeting of creditors to file a claim for the creditor. During the first 90 days of that period the creditor in a Chapter 7 or 13 case may file a claim as provided by Rule 3002(c). If the creditor fails to file a claim, the debtor or trustee shall have an additional 30 days thereafter to file the claim. A proof of claim filed by a creditor supersedes a claim filed by the debtor or trustee only if it is timely filed within the 90 days allowed under Rule 3002(c).

2005 Amendments

The rule is amended to conform to § 501(c) of the Code. Under that provision, the debtor or trustee may file proof of a claim if the creditor fails to do so in a timely fashion. The rule previously authorized the debtor and the trustee to file a claim as early as the day after the first date set for the meeting of creditors under § 341(a). Under the amended rule, the debtor and trustee must wait until the creditor's opportunity to file a claim has expired. Providing the debtor and the trustee with the opportunity to file a claim ensures that the claim will participate in any distribution in the case. This is particularly important for claims that are nondischargeable.

Since the debtor and trustee cannot file a proof of claim until after the creditor's time to file has expired, the rule no longer permits the creditor to file a proof of claim that will supersede the claim filed by the debtor or trustee. The rule leaves to the courts the issue of whether to permit subsequent amendment of such proof of claim.

Other changes are stylistic.

CROSS REFERENCES

Exception to execution of proof of claim by creditor or agent, see Fed.Rules Bankr.Proc. Rule 3001, 11 USCA.

Filing of claims by debtor or trustee, see 11 USCA § 501.

Rule 3005. Filing of Claim, Acceptance, or Rejection By Guarantor, Surety, Indorser, or Other Codebtor

(a) Filing of claim

If a creditor does not timely file a proof of claim under Rule 3002(c) or 3003(c), any entity that is or may be liable with the debtor to that creditor, or who has secured that creditor, may file a proof of the claim within 30 days after the expiration of the time for filing claims prescribed by Rule 3002(c) or Rule 3003(c) whichever is applicable. No distribution shall be made on the claim except on satisfactory proof that the original debt will be diminished by the amount of distribution.

(b) Filing of acceptance or rejection; substitution of creditor

An entity which has filed a claim pursuant to the first sentence of subdivision (a) of this rule may file an acceptance or rejection of a plan in the name of the creditor, if known, or if unknown, in the entity's own name but if the creditor files a proof of claim within the time permitted by Rule 3003(c) or files a notice prior to confirmation of a plan of the creditor's intention to act in the creditor's own behalf, the creditor shall be substituted for the obligor with respect to that claim.

(As amended Mar. 30, 1987, eff. Aug. 1, 1987; Apr. 30, 1991, eff. Aug. 1, 1991; Apr. 25, 2005, eff. Dec. 1, 2005.)

ADVISORY COMMITTEE NOTES

This rule is adapted from former Rules 304 and 10–402. Together with § 501(b) of the Code, the rule makes clear that anyone who may be liable on a debt of the debtor, including a surety, guarantor, indorser, or other codebtor, is authorized to file in the name of the creditor of the debtor.

Subdivision (a). Rule 3002(c) provides the time period for filing proofs of claim in chapter 7 and 13 cases; Rule 3003(c) provides the time, when necessary, for filing claims in a chapter 9 or 11 case.

Subdivision (b). This subdivision applies in chapter 9 and 11 cases as distinguished from chapter 7 cases. It permits voting for or against a plan by an obligor who files a claim in place of the creditor.

1991 Amendments

The words "with the court" in subdivision (b) are deleted as unnecessary. See Rules 5005(a) and 9001(3).

2005 Amendments

The rule is amended to delete the last sentence of subdivision (a). The sentence is unnecessary because if a creditor has filed a timely claim under Rule 3002 or 3003(c), the codebtor cannot file a proof of such claim. The codebtor, consistent with § 501(b) of the Code, may file a proof of such claim only after the creditor's time to file has expired. Therefore, the rule no longer permits the creditor to file a superseding claim. The rule leaves to the courts the issue of whether to permit subsequent amendment of the proof of claim.

The amendment conforms the rule to § 501(b) by deleting language providing that the codebtor files proof of the claim in the name of the creditor.

Other amendments are stylistic.

CROSS REFERENCES

Exception to execution of proof of claim by creditor or agent, see Fed.Rules Bankr.Proc. Rule 3001, 11 USCA.

Rule 3006. Withdrawal of Claim; Effect on Acceptance or Rejection of Plan

A creditor may withdraw a claim as of right by filing a notice of withdrawal, except as provided in this rule. If after a creditor has filed a proof of claim an objection is filed thereto or a complaint is filed against that creditor in an adversary proceeding, or the creditor has accepted or rejected the plan or otherwise has participated significantly in the case, the creditor may not withdraw the claim except on order of the court after a hearing on notice to the trustee or debtor in possession, and any creditors' committee elected pursuant to § 705(a) or appointed pursuant to § 1102 of the Code. The order of the court shall contain such terms and conditions as the court deems proper. Unless the court orders otherwise, an authorized withdrawal of a claim shall constitute withdrawal of any related acceptance or rejection of a plan.

(As amended Apr. 30, 1991, eff. Aug. 1, 1991.)

ADVISORY COMMITTEE NOTES

This rule is derived from former Rules 305 and 10–404.

Since 1938 is has generally been held that Rule 41 F.R.Civ.P. governs the withdrawal of a proof of claim. In re Empire Coal Sales Corp., 45 F.Supp. 974, 976 (S.C.N.Y.), aff'd sub nom. Kleid v. Ruthbell Coal Co., 131 F.2d 372, 373 (2d Cir.1942); Kelso v. MacLaren, 122 F.2d 867, 870 (8th Cir.1941); In re Hills, 35 F.Supp. 532, 533 (W.D.Wash.1940). Accordingly the cited cases held that after an objection has been filed a proof of claim may be withdrawn only subject to approval by the court. This constitutes a restriction of the right of withdrawal as recognized by some though by no means all of the cases antedating the promulgation of the Federal Rules of Civil Procedure. See 3 Collier, Bankruptcy ¶57.12 (14th ed. 1961); Note, 20 Bost.U.L.Rev. 121 (1940).

The filing of a claim does not commence an adversary proceeding but the filing of an objection to the claim initiates a contest that must be disposed of by the court. This rule recognizes the applicability of the considerations underlying Rule 41(a) F.R.Civ.P. to the withdrawal of a claim after it has been put in issue by an objection. Rule 41(a)(2) F.R.Civ.P. requires leave of court to obtain dismissal over the objection of a defendant who has pleaded a counterclaim prior to the service of the plaintiff's motion to dismiss. Although the applicability of this provision to the withdrawal of a claim was assumed in Conway v. Union Bank of Switzerland, 204 F.2d 603, 608 (2d Cir.1953), Kleid v. Ruthbell Coal Co., supra, Kelso v. MacLaren, supra, and In re Hills, supra, this rule vests discretion in the court to grant, deny, or condition the request of a creditor to withdraw, without regard to whether the trustee has filed a merely defensive objection or a complaint seeking an affirmative recovery of money or property from the creditor.

A number of pre-1938 cases sustained denial of a creditor's request to withdraw proof of claim on the ground of estoppel or election of remedies. 2 Remington, Bankruptcy 186 (Henderson ed. 1956); cf. 3 Collier, supra ¶57.12, at 201 (1964). Voting a claim for a trustee was an important factor in the denial of a request to withdraw in Standard Varnish Works v. Haydock, 143 Fed. 318, 319–20 (6th Cir.1906), and In re Cann, 47 F.2d 661, 662 (W.D.Pa.1931). And it has frequently been recognized that a creditor should not be allowed to withdraw a claim after accepting a dividend. In re Friedmann, 1 Am.B.R. 510, 512 (Ref., S.D.N.Y.1899); 3 Collier 205 (1964); cf. In re O'Gara Coal Co., 12 F.2d 426, 429 (7th Cir.), cert. denied, 271 U.S. 683 (1926). It was held in Industrial Credit Co. v. Hazen, 222 F.2d 225 (8th Cir.1955), however, that although a claimant had participated in the first meeting of creditors and in the examination of witnesses, the creditor was entitled under Rule 41(a)(1) F.R.Civ.P. to withdraw the claim as of right by filing a notice of withdrawal before the trustee filed an objection under § 57g of the Act. While this rule incorporates the post-1938 case law referred to in the first paragraph of this note, it rejects the inference drawn in the Hazen case that Rule 41(a) F.R.Civ.P. supersedes the pre-1938 case law that vests discretion in the court to deny or restrict withdrawal of a claim by a creditor on the ground of estoppel or election of remedies. While purely formal or technical participation in a case by a creditor who has filed a claim should not deprive the creditor of the right to withdraw the claim, a creditor who has accepted a dividend or who has voted in the election of a trustee or otherwise participated actively in proceedings in a case should be permitted to withdraw only with the approval of the court on terms it deems appropriate after notice to the trustee. 3 Collier 205–06 (1964).

1991 Amendments

This amendment is stylistic. Notice of the hearing need not be given to committees of equity security holders appointed pursuant to § 1102 or committees of retired employees appointed pursuant to § 1114 of the Code.

CROSS REFERENCES

Dismissal of actions, see Fed.Rules Civ.Proc. Rule 41, 28 USCA.

Rule 3007. Objections to Claims

(a) Objections to Claims

An objection to the allowance of a claim shall be in writing and filed. A copy of the objection with notice of the hearing thereon shall be mailed or otherwise delivered to the claimant, the debtor or debtor in possession, and the trustee at least 30 days prior to the hearing.

(b) Demand for Relief Requiring an Adversary Proceeding

A party in interest shall not include a demand for relief of a kind specified in Rule 7001 in an objection to the allowance of a claim, but may include the objection in an adversary proceeding.

(c) Limitation on Joinder of Claims Objections

Unless otherwise ordered by the court or permitted by subdivision (d), objections to more than one claim shall not be joined in a single objection.

(d) Omnibus Objection

Subject to subdivision (e), objections to more than one claim may be joined in an omnibus objection if all the claims were filed by the same entity, or the objections are based solely on the grounds that the claims should be disallowed, in whole or in part, because:

(1) they duplicate other claims;

(2) they have been filed in the wrong case;

(3) they have been amended by subsequently filed proofs of claim;

(4) they were not timely filed;

(5) they have been satisfied or released during the case in accordance with the Code, applicable rules, or a court order;

(6) they were presented in a form that does not comply with applicable rules, and the objection states that the objector is unable to determine the validity of the claim because of the noncompliance;

(7) they are interests, rather than claims; or

(8) they assert priority in an amount that exceeds the maximum amount under § 507 of the Code.

(e) Requirements For Omnibus Objection

An omnibus objection shall:

(1) state in a conspicuous place that claimants receiving the objection should locate their names and claims in the objection;

(2) list claimants alphabetically, provide a cross-reference to claim numbers, and, if appropriate, list claimants by category of claims;

(3) state the grounds of the objection to each claim and provide a cross-reference to the pages in the omnibus objection pertinent to the stated grounds;

(4) state in the title the identity of the objector and the grounds for the objections;

(5) be numbered consecutively with other omnibus objections filed by the same objector; and

(6) contain objections to no more than 100 claims.

(f) Finality of Objection

The finality of any order regarding a claim objection included in an omnibus objection shall be determined as though the claim had been subject to an individual objection.

(As amended Apr. 30, 1991, eff. Aug. 1, 1991; Apr. 30, 2007, eff. Dec. 1, 2007.)

ADVISORY COMMITTEE NOTES

This rule is derived from § 47a(8) of the Act [former § 75(a)(8) of this title] and former Bankruptcy Rule 306. It prescribes the manner in which an objection to a claim shall be made and notice of the hearing thereon given to the claimant. The requirement of a writing does not apply to an objection to the allowance of a claim for the purpose of voting for a trustee or creditors' committee in a chapter 7 case. See Rule 2003.

The contested matter initiated by an objection to a claim is governed by rule 9014, unless a counterclaim by the trustee is joined with the objection to the claim. The filing of a counterclaim ordinarily commences an adversary proceeding subject to the rules in Part VII.

While the debtor's other creditors may make objections to the allowance of a claim, the demands of orderly and expeditious administration have led to a recognition that the right to object is generally exercised by the trustee. Pursuant to § 502(a) of the Code, however, any party in interest may object to a claim. But under § 704 the trustee, if any purpose would be served thereby, has the duty to examine proofs of claim and object to improper claims.

By virtue of the automatic allowance of a claim not objected to, a dividend may be paid on a claim which may thereafter be disallowed on objection made pursuant to this rule. The amount of the dividend paid before the disallowance in such event would be recoverable by the trustee in an adversary proceeding.

1991 Amendments

The words "with the court" are deleted as unnecessary. See Rules 5005(a) and 9001(3).

2007 Amendments

The rule is amended in a number of ways. First, the amendment prohibits a party in interest from including in a claim objection a request for relief that requires an adversary proceeding. A party in interest may, however, include an objection to the allowance of a claim in an adversary proceeding. Unlike a contested matter, an adversary proceeding requires the service of a summons and complaint, which puts the defendant on notice of the potential for an affirmative recovery. Permitting the plaintiff in the adversary proceeding to include an objection to a claim would not unfairly surprise the defendant as might be the case if the action were brought as a contested matter that included an action to obtain relief of a kind specified in Rule 7001.

The rule as amended does not require that a party include an objection to the allowance of a claim in an adversary proceeding. If a claim objection is filed separately from a related adversary proceeding, the court may consolidate the objection with the adversary proceeding under Rule 7042.

The rule also is amended to authorize the filing of a pleading that joins objections to more than one claim. Such filings present a significant opportunity for the efficient administration of large cases, but the rule includes restrictions on the use of these omnibus objections to ensure the protection of the due process rights of the claimants.

Unless the court orders otherwise, objections to more than one claim may be joined in a single pleading only if all of the claims were filed by the same entity, or if the objections are based solely on the grounds set out in subdivision (d) of the rule. Objections of the type listed in subdivision (d) often can be resolved without material factual or legal disputes. Objections to multiple claims permitted under the rule must comply with the procedural requirements set forth in subdivision (e). Among those requirements is the requirement in subdivision (e)(5) that these omnibus objections be consecutively numbered. Since these objections may not join more than 100 objections in any one omnibus objection, there may be a need for several omnibus objections to be filed in a particular case. Consecutive numbering of each omnibus objection and the identification of the objector in the title of the objection is essential to keep track of the objections on the court's docket. For example, the objections could be titled Debtor in Possession's First Omnibus Objection to Claims, Debtor in Possession's Second Omnibus Objection to Claims, Creditors' Committee's First Omnibus Objection to Claims, and so on. Titling the objections in this manner should avoid confusion and aid in tracking the objections on the docket.

Subdivision (f) provides that an order resolving an objection to any particular claim is treated, for purposes of finality, as if the claim had been the subject of an individual objection. A party seeking to appeal any such order is neither required, nor permitted, to await the court's resolution of all other joined objections. The rule permits the joinder of objections for convenience, and that convenience should not impede timely review of a court's decision with respect to each claim. Whether the court's action as to a particular objection is final, and the consequences of that finality, are not addressed by this amendment. Moreover, use of an omnibus objection generally does not preclude the objecting party from raising a subsequent objection to the claim on other grounds. See Restatement (Second) of Judgments § 26(1)(d) (1982) (generally applicable rule barring multiple actions based on same transaction or series of transactions is overridden when a statutory scheme permits splitting of claims).

CROSS REFERENCES

Allowance of claims or interests after objection, see 11 USCA § 502.

Contested matters, see Fed.Rules Bankr.Proc. Rule 9014, 11 USCA.

Duty of trustee to examine proofs of claims and to object to improper claims—

Individual debt adjustment case, see 11 USCA § 1302.

Liquidation case, see 11 USCA § 704.

Reorganization case, see 11 USCA § 1106.

Objection to claim for purpose of voting for trustee or creditors' committee in liquidation case, see Fed.Rules Bankr.Proc. Rule 2003, 11 USCA.

Rule 3008. Reconsideration of Claims

A party in interest may move for reconsideration of an order allowing or disallowing a claim against the estate. The court after a hearing on notice shall enter an appropriate order.

ADVISORY COMMITTEE NOTES

Section 502(j) of the Code deals only with the reconsideration of allowed claims as did former § 57k of the Act [former § 93(k) of this title] and General Order 21(b). It had sometimes been held that a referee had no jurisdiction to reconsider a disallowed claim, or the amount or priority of an allowed claim, at the instance of the claimant. See, e.g., In re Gouse, 7 F.Supp. 106 (M.D.Pa.1934); In re Tomlinson & Dye, Inc., 3 F.Supp. 800 (N.D.Okla.1933). This view disregarded § 2a(2) of the Act [former § 11(a)(2) of this title] and the "ancient and elementary power" of a referee as a court to reconsider orders. In re Pottasch Bros. Co., Inc., 79 F.2d 613, 616 (2d Cir.1935); Castaner v. Mora, 234 F.2d 710 (1st Cir.1956). This rule recognizes, as did former Bankruptcy Rule 307, the power of the court to reconsider an order of disallowance on appropriate motion.

Reconsideration of a claim that has been previously allowed or disallowed after objection is discretionary with the court. The right to seek reconsideration of an allowed claim, like the right to object to its allowance, is generally exercised by the trustee if one has qualified and is performing the duties of that office with reasonable diligence and fidelity. A request for reconsideration of a disallowance would, on the other hand, ordinarily come from the claimant.

A proof of claim executed and filed in accordance with the rules in this Part III is prima facie evidence of the validity and the amount of the claim notwithstanding a motion for reconsideration of an order of allowance. Failure to respond does not constitute an admission, though it may be deemed a consent to a reconsideration. In re Goble Boat Co., 190 Fed. 92 (N.D.N.Y.1911). The court may decline to reconsider an order of allowance or disallowance without notice to any adverse party and without affording any hearing to the movant. If a motion to reconsider is granted, notice and hearing must be afforded to parties in interest before the previous action in the claim taken in respect to the claim may be vacated or modified. After reconsideration, the court may allow or disallow the claim, increase or decrease the amount of a prior allowance, accord the claim a priority different from that originally assigned it, or enter any other appropriate order.

The rule expands § 502(j) which provides for reconsideration of an allowance only before the case is closed. Authorities have disagreed as to whether reconsideration may be had after a case has been reopened. Compare 3 Collier, Bankruptcy ¶57.23[4] (14th ed. 1964), see generally 3 id. ¶502.10 (15th ed. 1979), with 2 Remington, Bankruptcy 498 (Henderson ed. 1956). If a case is reopened as provided in § 350(b) of the Code, reconsideration of the allowance or disallowance of a claim may be sought and granted in accordance with this rule.

CROSS REFERENCES

Closing and reopening cases, see 11 USCA § 350.

Exception to procedural rule on new trials and amendment of judgments, see Fed.Rules Bankr.Proc. Rule 9023, 11 USCA.

Motions; form and service, see Fed.Rules Bankr.Proc. Rule 9013, 11 USCA.

Reconsideration of claim prior to closing of case, see 11 USCA § 502.

Rule 3009. Declaration and Payment of Dividends in a Chapter 7 Liquidation Case

In a chapter 7 case, dividends to creditors shall be paid as promptly as practicable. Dividend checks shall be made payable to and mailed to each creditor whose claim has been allowed, unless a power of attorney authorizing another entity to receive dividends has been executed and filed in accordance with Rule 9010. In that event, dividend checks shall be made payable to the creditor and to the other entity and shall be mailed to the other entity.

(As amended Mar. 30, 1987, eff. Aug. 1, 1987; Apr. 22, 1993, eff. Aug. 1, 1993.)

ADVISORY COMMITTEE NOTES

This rule is derived from former Rules 308 and 11–35(a). The preparation of records showing dividends declared and to whom payable is subject to prescription by the Director of the Administrative Office pursuant to Rule 5003(e). The rule governs distributions to creditors having priority as well as to general unsecured creditors. Notwithstanding the detailed statutory provisions regulating the declaration of dividends, a necessarily wide discretion over this matter has been recognized to reside in the court. See 3A Collier, Bankruptcy ¶65.03 (14th ed. 1975): 1 Proceedings of Seminar for Newly Appointed Referees in Bankruptcy 173 (1964). Although the rule leaves to the discretion of the court the amount and the times of dividend payments, it recognizes the creditors' right to as prompt payment as practicable.

The second and third sentences of the rule make explicit the method of payment of dividends and afford protection of the interests of the creditor and the holder of a power of attorney authorized to receive payment.

The rule does not permit variance at local option. This represents a marked change from former Bankruptcy Rule 308.

1993 Amendments

This rule is amended to delete the requirement that the court approve the amounts and times of distributions in chapter 7 cases. This change recognizes the role of the United States trustee in supervising trustees. Other amendments are stylistic and make no substantive change.

CROSS REFERENCES

Dividend records kept by clerk, see Fed.Rules Bankr.Proc. Rule 5003, 11 USCA.

Unclaimed dividends, see 11 USCA § 347.

Rule 3010. Small Dividends and Payments in Chapter 7 Liquidation, Chapter 12 Family Farmer's Debt Adjustment, and Chapter 13 Individual's Debt Adjustment Cases

(a) Chapter 7 cases

In a chapter 7 case no dividend in an amount less than $5 shall be distributed by the trustee to any creditor unless authorized by local rule or order of the court. Any dividend not distributed to a creditor shall be treated in the same manner as unclaimed funds as provided in § 347 of the Code.

(b) Chapter 12 and chapter 13 cases

In a chapter 12 or chapter 13 case no payment in an amount less than $15 shall be distributed by the trustee to any creditor unless authorized by local rule or order of the court. Funds not distributed because of this subdivision shall accumulate and shall be paid whenever the accumulation aggregates $15. Any funds remaining shall be distributed with the final payment.

(As amended Mar. 30, 1987, eff. Aug. 1, 1987; Apr. 30, 1991, eff. Aug. 1, 1991.)

ADVISORY COMMITTEE NOTES

This rule permits a court to eliminate the disproportionate expense and inconvenience incurred by the issuance of a dividend check of less than $5 (or $15 in a chapter 13 case). Creditors are more irritated than pleased to receive such small dividends, but the money is held subject to their specific request as are unclaimed dividends under § 347(a) of the Code. When the trustee deposits undistributed dividends pursuant to a direction in accordance with this rule the trustee should file with the clerk a list of the names and addresses, so far as known, of the persons entitled to the money so deposited and the respective amounts payable to them pursuant to Rule 3011. In a chapter 13 case, the small dividend will accumulate and will be payable at the latest, with the final dividend. Local rule or order may change the practice permitted in this rule and, in that connection, the order may be incorporated in the order confirming a chapter 13 plan.

1991 Amendments

Subdivision (b) is amended to include chapter 12 cases.

Rule 3011. Unclaimed Funds in Chapter 7 Liquidation, Chapter 12 Family Farmer's Debt Adjustment, and Chapter 13 Individual's Debt Adjustment Cases

The trustee shall file a list of all known names and addresses of the entities and the amounts which they are entitled to be paid from remaining property of the estate that is paid into court pursuant to § 347(a) of the Code.

(As amended Mar. 30, 1987, eff. Aug. 1, 1987; Apr. 30, 1991, eff. Aug. 1, 1991.)

ADVISORY COMMITTEE NOTES

This rule is derived from former Bankruptcy Rule 310. The operative provisions of that rule, however, are contained in § 347(a) of the Code, requiring the trustee to stop payment of checks remaining unpaid 90 days after distribution. The rule adds the requirement of filing a list of the names and addresses of the persons entitled to these dividends. This rule applies in a chapter 7 or 13 case but not in a chapter 9 or 11 case. The latter cases are governed by § 347(b) of the Code which provides for unclaimed distributions to be returned to the debtor or other entity acquiring the assets of the debtor.

1991 Amendments

The title of this rule is amended to include chapter 12 cases. The words "with the clerk" are deleted as unnecessary. See Rules 5005(a) and 9001(3).

CROSS REFERENCES

Treatment of small dividends as unclaimed funds, see Fed.Rules Bankr.Proc. Rule 3010, 11 USCA.

Rule 3012. Valuation of Security

The court may determine the value of a claim secured by a lien on property in which the estate has an interest on motion of any party in interest and after a hearing on notice to the holder of the secured claim and any other entity as the court may direct.

(As amended Mar. 30, 1987, eff. Aug. 1, 1987.)

ADVISORY COMMITTEE NOTES

Pursuant to § 506(a) of the Code, secured claims are to be valued and allowed as secured to the extent of the value of the collateral and unsecured, to the extent it is enforceable, for the excess over such value. The valuation of secured claims may become important in different contexts, e.g., to determine the issue of adequate protection under § 361, impairment under § 1124, or treatment of the claim in a plan pursuant to § 1129(b) of the Code. This rule permits the issue to be raised on motion by a party in interest. The secured creditor is entitled to notice of the hearing on the motion and the court may direct that others in the case also receive such notice.

An adversary proceeding is commenced when the validity, priority, or extent of a lien is at issue as prescribed by Rule 7001. That proceeding is relevant to the basis of the lien itself while valuation under Rule 3012 would be for the purposes indicated above.

CROSS REFERENCES

Definition of—

Lien, see 11 USCA § 101.

Security, see 11 USCA § 101.

Security interest, see 11 USCA § 101.

Determination of secured status, see 11 USCA § 506.

Motions; form and service, see Fed.Rules Bankr.Proc. Rule 9013, 11 USCA.

Rule 3013. Classification of Claims and Interests

For the purposes of the plan and its acceptance, the court may, on motion after hearing on notice as the court may direct, determine classes of creditors and equity security holders pursuant to §§ 1122, 1222(b)(1), and 1322(b)(1) of the Code.

(As amended Apr. 30, 1991, eff. Aug. 1, 1991.)

ADVISORY COMMITTEE NOTES

Sections 1122 and 1322(b)(1) set the standards for classifying claims and interests but provide that such classification is accomplished in the plan. This rule does not change the standards; rather it recognizes that it may be desirable or necessary to establish proper classification before a plan can be formulated. It provides for a court hearing on such notice as the court may direct.

1991 Amendments

This rule is amended to include chapter 12 cases.

CROSS REFERENCES

Motions; form and service, see Fed.Rules Bankr.Proc. Rule 9013, 11 USCA.

Rule 3014. Election Under § 1111(b) by Secured Creditor in Chapter 9 Municipality or Chapter 11 Reorganization Case

An election of application of § 1111(b)(2) of the Code by a class of secured creditors in a chapter 9 or 11 case may be made at any time prior to the conclusion of the hearing on the disclosure statement or within such later time as the court may fix. If the disclosure statement is conditionally approved pursuant to Rule 3017.1, and a final hearing on the disclosure statement is not held, the election of application of § 1111(b)(2) may be made not later than the date fixed pursuant to Rule 3017.1(a)(2) or another date the court may fix. The election shall be in writing and signed unless made at the hearing on the disclosure statement. The election, if made by the majorities required by § 1111(b)(1)(A)(i), shall be binding on all members of the class with respect to the plan.

(As amended Apr. 11, 1997, eff. Dec. 1, 1997)

ADVISORY COMMITTEE NOTES

Pursuant to § 1111(b)(1) of the Code, a nonrecourse secured loan is converted, automatically, into a recourse loan thereby entitling the creditor to an unsecured deficiency claim if the value of the collateral is less than the debt. The class, however, may retain the loan as a nonrecourse loan by electing application of § 1111(b)(2) by the majorities stated in § 1111(b)(1)(A)(i). That section does not specify any time periods for making the election.

Rule 3014 provides that if no agreement is negotiated, the election of § 1111(b)(2) of the Code may be made at any time prior to conclusion of the hearing on the disclosure statement. Once the hearing has been concluded, it would be too late for a secured creditor class to demand different treatment unless the court has fixed a later time. This would be the case if, for example, a public class of secured creditors should have an approved disclosure statement prior to electing under § 1111(b).

Generally it is important that the proponent of a plan ascertain the position of the secured creditor class before a plan is proposed. The secured creditor class must know the prospects of its treatment under the plan before it can intelligently determine its rights under § 1111(b). The rule recognizes that there may be negotiations between the proponent of the plan and the secured creditor leading to a representation of desired treatment under § 1111(b). If that treatment is approved by the requisite majorities of the class and culminates in a written, signed statement filed with the court, that statement becomes binding and the class may not thereafter demand different treatment under § 1111(b) with respect to that plan. The proponent of the plan is thus enabled to seek approval of the disclosure statement and transmit the plan for voting in anticipation of confirmation. Only if that plan is not confirmed may the class of secured creditors thereafter change its prior election.

While this rule and the Code refer to a class of secured creditors it should be noted that ordinarily each secured creditor is in a separate and distinct class. In that event, the secured creditor has the sole power to determine application of § 1111(b) with respect to that claim.

1997 Amendments

This amendment provides a deadline for electing application of § 1111(b)(2) in a small business case in which a conditionally approved disclosure statement is finally approved without a hearing.

GAP Report on Rule 3014. No changes to the published draft.

CROSS REFERENCES

Hearing on disclosure statement, see Fed.Rules Bankr. Proc. Rule 3017, 11 USCA.

Reduction of time for election pursuant to § 1111(b) not permitted, see Fed.Rules Bankr.Proc. Rule 9006, 11 USCA.

Rule 3015. Filing, Objection to Confirmation, and Modification of a Plan in a Chapter 12 Family Farmer's Debt Adjustment or a Chapter 13 Individual's Debt Adjustment Case

(a) Chapter 12 plan

The debtor may file a chapter 12 plan with the petition. If a plan is not filed with the petition, it shall be filed within the time prescribed by § 1221 of the Code.

(b) Chapter 13 plan

The debtor may file a chapter 13 plan with the petition. If a plan is not filed with the petition, it shall be filed within 15 days thereafter, and such time may not be further extended except for cause shown and on notice as the court may direct. If a case is converted to chapter 13, a plan shall be filed within 15 days thereafter, and such time may not be further extended except for cause shown and on notice as the court may direct.

(c) Dating

Every proposed plan and any modification thereof shall be dated.

(d) Notice and copies

The plan or a summary of the plan shall be included with each notice of the hearing on confirmation mailed pursuant to Rule 2002. If required by the court, the debtor shall furnish a sufficient number of copies to enable the clerk to include a copy of the plan with the notice of the hearing.

(e) Transmission to United States trustee

The clerk shall forthwith transmit to the United States trustee a copy of the plan and any modification thereof filed pursuant to subdivision (a) or (b) of this rule.

(f) Objection to confirmation; determination of good faith in the absence of an objection

An objection to confirmation of a plan shall be filed and served on the debtor, the trustee, and any other entity designated by the court, and shall be transmitted to the United States trustee, before confirmation of the plan. An objection to confirmation is governed by Rule 9014. If no objection is timely filed, the court may determine that the plan has been proposed in good faith and not by any means forbidden by law without receiving evidence on such issues.

(g) Modification of plan after confirmation

A request to modify a plan pursuant to § 1229 or § 1329 of the Code shall identify the proponent and shall be filed together with the proposed modification. The clerk, or some other person as the court may direct, shall give the debtor, the trustee, and all creditors not less than 20 days notice by mail of the time fixed for filing objections and, if an objection is filed, the hearing to consider the proposed modification, unless the court orders otherwise with respect to creditors who are not affected by the proposed modification. A copy of the notice shall be transmitted to the United States trustee. A copy of the proposed modification, or a summary thereof, shall be included with the notice. If required by the court, the proponent shall furnish a sufficient number of copies of the proposed modification, or a summary thereof, to enable the clerk to include a copy with each notice. Any objection to the proposed modification shall be filed and served on the debtor, the trustee, and any other entity designated by the court, and shall be transmitted to the United States trustee. An objection to a proposed modification is governed by rule 9014.

(As amended Apr. 30, 1991, eff. Aug. 1, 1991; Apr. 22, 1993, eff. Aug. 1, 1993)

ADVISORY COMMITTEE NOTES

Section 1321 provides only that the "debtor shall file a plan." No time periods are specified, nor is any other detail provided. The rule requires a chapter 13 plan to be filed either with the petition or within 15 days thereafter. The court may, for cause, extend the time. The rule permits a summary of the plan to be transmitted with the notice of the hearing on confirmation. The court may, however, require the plan itself to be transmitted and the debtor to supply enough copies for this purpose. In the former rules under Chapter XIII [former § 1001 et seq. of this title] the plan would accompany the notice of the first meeting of creditors. It is more important for the plan or a summary of its terms to be sent with the notice of the confirmation hearing. At that hearing objections to the plan will be heard by the court.

1991 Amendments

This rule is amended to include chapter 12 plans. Section 1221 of the Code requires the debtor to file a chapter 12 plan not later than 90 days after the order for relief, except that the court may extend the period if an extension is "substantially justified."

Subdivision (e) enables the United States trustee to monitor chapter 12 and chapter 13 plans pursuant to 28 U.S.C. § 586(a)(3)(C).

1993 Amendments

Subdivision (b) is amended to provide a time limit for filing a plan after a case has been converted to chapter 13. The substitution of "may" for "shall" is stylistic and makes no substantive change.

Subdivision (d) is amended to clarify that the plan or a summary of the plan must be included with each notice of the confirmation hearing in a chapter 12 case pursuant to Rule 2002(a).

Subdivision (f) is added to expand the scope of the rule to govern objections to confirmation in chapter 12 and chapter 13 cases. The subdivision also is amended to include a provision that permits the court, in the absence of an objection, to determine that the plan has been proposed in good faith and not by any means forbidden by law without the need to receive evidence on these issues. These matters are now governed by Rule 3020.

Subdivision (g) is added to provide a procedure for post-confirmation modification of chapter 12 and chapter 13 plans. These procedures are designed to be similar to the procedures for confirmation of plans. However, if no objection is filed with respect to a proposed modification of a plan after confirmation, the court is not required to hold a hearing. *See* § 1229(b)(2) and § 1329(b)(2) which provide that the plan as modified becomes the plan unless, after notice and a hearing, such modification is disapproved. *See* § 102(1). The notice of the time fixed for filing objections to the proposed modification should set a date for a hearing to be held in the event that an objection is filed.

Amendments to the title of this rule are stylistic and make no substantive change.

CROSS REFERENCES

Acceptance or rejection of plans, see Fed.Rules Bankr. Proc. Rule 3018, 11 USCA.

Deposit; confirmation of plan, see Fed.Rules Bankr.Proc. Rule 3020, 11 USCA.

Reduction of time for filing plan not permitted, see Fed. Rules Bankr.Proc. Rule 9006, 11 USCA.

Rule 3016. Filing of Plan and Disclosure Statement in a Chapter 9 Municipality or Chapter 11 Reorganization Case

(a) Identification of plan

Every proposed plan and any modification thereof shall be dated and, in a chapter 11 case, identified with the name of the entity or entities submitting or filing it.

(b) Disclosure statement

In a chapter 9 or 11 case, a disclosure statement under § 1125 of the Code or evidence showing compliance with § 1126(b) shall be filed with the plan or within a time fixed by the court, unless the plan is intended to provide adequate information under § 1125(f)(1). If the plan is intended to provide adequate information under § 1125(f)(1), it shall be so designated and Rule 3017.1 shall apply as if the plan is a disclosure statement.

(c) Injunction under a plan

If a plan provides for an injunction against conduct not otherwise enjoined under the Code, the plan and disclosure statement shall describe in specific and conspicuous language (bold, italic, or underlined text) all acts to be enjoined and identify the entities that would be subject to the injunction.

(d) Standard form small business disclosure statement and plan

In a small business case, the court may approve a disclosure statement and may confirm a plan that conform substantially to the appropriate Official Forms or other standard forms approved by the court.

(As amended Mar. 30, 1987, eff. Aug. 1, 1987; Apr. 30, 1991, eff. Aug. 1, 1991; Apr. 23, 1996, eff. Dec. 1, 1996; Apr. 23, 2001, eff. Dec. 1, 2001; Apr. 23, 2008, eff. Dec. 1, 2008.)

ADVISORY COMMITTEE NOTES

This rule implements the Code provisions concerning the filing of plans in chapters 9 and 11.

Chapter 9 Cases. Section 941 provides that the debtor may file a plan with the petition or thereafter but within a time fixed by the court. A rule, therefore, is unnecessary to specify the time for filing chapter 9 plans.

Chapter 11 Nonrailroad Cases. Section 1121 contains detailed provisions with respect to who may file a chapter 11 plan and, in part, the time period. Section 1121(a) permits a debtor to file a plan with the petition or at any time during the case. Section 1121(b) and (c) grants exclusive periods of 120 days and 180 days for the debtor to file and obtain acceptance of a plan. Failure to take advantage of these periods or the appointment of a trustee would permit other parties in interest to file a plan. These statutory provisions are not repeated in the rules.

Chapter 11 Railroad Cases. Pursuant to subchapter IV of chapter 11, § 1121 of the Code is applicable in railroad cases; see §§ 1161, 103(g). A trustee, however, is to be appointed in every case; thus, pursuant to § 1121(c), any party in interest may file a plan. See discussion of subdivision (a) of this rule, infra.

Subdivision (a). Section 1121(c), while permitting parties in interest a limited right to file plans, does not provide any time limitation. This subdivision sets as the deadline, the conclusion of the hearing on the disclosure statement. The court may, however, grant additional time. It is derived from former Chapter X Rule 10–301(c)(2) which used, as the cut-off time, the conclusion of the hearing on approval of a plan. As indicated, supra, § 1121(a) permits a debtor to file a plan at any time during the chapter 11 case. Under § 1121(c), parties other than a debtor may file a plan only after a trustee is appointed or the debtor's exclusive time expires.

Subdivision (b) requires plans to be properly identified.

Subdivision (c). This provision is new. In chapter 9 and 11 cases (including railroad reorganization cases) postpetition solicitation of votes on a plan requires transmittal of a disclosure statement, the contents of which have been approved by the court. See § 1125 of the Code. A prepetition solicitation must either have been in conformity with applicable nonbankruptcy law or, if none, the disclosure must have been of adequate information as set forth in § 1125 of the Code. See § 1126(b). Subdivision (c) of this rule provides the time for filing the disclosure statement or evidence of compliance with § 1126(b) which ordinarily will be with the plan but the court may allow a later time or the court may, pursuant to the last sentence, fix a time certain. Rule 3017 deals with the hearing on the disclosure statement. The disclosure statement, pursuant to § 1125 is to contain adequate information. "Adequate information" is defined in § 1125(a) as information that would permit a reasonable creditor or equity security holder to make an informed judgment on the plan.

1991 Amendments

Subdivision (a) is amended to enlarge the time for filing competing plans. A party in interest may not file a plan without leave of court only if an order approving a disclosure statement relating to another plan has been entered and a decision on confirmation of the plan has not been entered. This subdivision does not fix a deadline beyond which a debtor may not file a plan.

1996 Amendments

Section 1121(c) gives a party in interest the right to file a chapter 11 plan after expiration of the period when only the debtor may file a plan. Under § 1121(d), the exclusive period in which only the debtor may file a plan may be extended, but only if a party in interest so requests and the court, after notice and a hearing, finds cause for an extension. Subdivision (a) is abrogated because it could have the effect of extending the debtor's exclusive period for filing a plan without satisfying the requirements of § 1121(d). The abrogation of subdivision (a) does not affect the court's discretion with respect to the scheduling of hearings on the approval of disclosure statements when more than one plan has been filed.

The amendment to subdivision (c), redesignated as subdivision (b), is stylistic.

GAP Report on Rule 3016. No changes since publication, except for a stylistic change.

2001 Amendments

Subdivision (c) is added to assure that entities whose conduct would be enjoined under a plan, rather than by operation of the Code, are given adequate notice of the proposed injunction. The validity and effect of any injunction are substantive law matters that are beyond the scope of these rules.

Specific and conspicuous language is not necessary if the injunction contained in the plan is substantially the same as an injunction provided under the Code. For example, if a plan contains an injunction against acts to collect a discharged debt from the debtor, Rule 3016(c) would not apply because that conduct would be enjoined nonetheless under § 524(a)(2). But if a plan provides that creditors will be permanently enjoined from asserting claims against persons who are not debtors in the case, the plan and disclosure statement must highlight the injunctive language and comply with the requirements of Rule 3016(c). *See* § 524(e).

The requirement in this rule that the plan and disclosure statement identify the entities that would be subject to the injunction requires reasonable identification under the circumstances. If the entities that would be subject to the injunction cannot be identified by name, the plan and disclosure statement may describe them by class or category. For example, it may be sufficient to identify the subjects of the injunction as "all creditors of the debtor."

CHANGES MADE AFTER PUBLICATION AND COMMENTS

The word "highlighted" in the parenthesis was replaced with "underlined" because highlighted documents are difficult to scan electronically for inclusion in the clerks' files. The Committee Note was revised to put in a more prominent position the statement that the validity and effect of any injunction provided for in a plan are substantive matters beyond the scope of the rules. Other stylistic changes were made to the Committee Note.

2008 Amendments

Subdivision (b) is amended to recognize that, in 2005, § 1125(f)(1) was added to the Code to provide that the plan proponent in a small business case need not file a disclosure statement if the plan itself includes adequate information and the court finds that a separate disclosure statement is unnecessary. If the plan is intended to provide adequate information in a small business case, it may be conditionally approved as a disclosure statement under Rule 3017.1 and is subject to all other rules applicable to disclosure statements in small business cases.

Subdivision (d) is added to the rule to implement § 433 of the Bankruptcy Abuse Prevention and Consumer Protection Act of 2005 which requires the promulgation of Official Forms for plans and disclosure statements in small business cases. Section 1125(f)(2) of the Code provides that the court may approve a disclosure statement submitted on the appropriate Official Form or on a standard form approved by the court. The rule takes no position on whether a court may require a local standard form disclosure statement or plan of reorganization in lieu of the Official Forms.

Other amendments are stylistic.

CROSS REFERENCES

Filing of municipality debt adjustment plan, see 11 USCA § 941.

Hearing on disclosure statement, see Fed.Rules Bankr. Proc. Rule 3017, 11 USCA.

Rule 3017. Court Consideration of Disclosure Statement in a Chapter 9 Municipality or Chapter 11 Reorganization Case

(a) Hearing on disclosure statement and objections

Except as provided in Rule 3017.1, after a disclosure statement is filed in accordance with Rule 3016(b), the court shall hold a hearing on at least 25 days' notice to the debtor, creditors, equity security holders and other parties in interest as provided in Rule 2002 to consider the disclosure statement and any objections or modifications thereto. The plan and the disclosure statement shall be mailed with the notice of the hearing only to the debtor, any trustee or committee appointed under the Code, the Securities and Exchange Commission, and any party in interest who requests in writing a copy of the statement or plan. Objections to the disclosure statement shall be filed and served on the debtor, the trustee, any committee appointed under the Code, and any other entity designated by the court, at any time before the disclosure statement is approved or by an earlier date as the court may fix. In a chapter 11 reorganization case, every notice, plan, disclosure statement, and objection required to be served or mailed pursuant to this subdivision shall be transmitted to the United States trustee within the time provided in this subdivision.

(b) Determination on disclosure statement

Following the hearing the court shall determine whether the disclosure statement should be approved.

(c) Dates fixed for voting on plan and confirmation

On or before approval of the disclosure statement, the court shall fix a time within which the holders of claims and interests may accept or reject the plan and may fix a date for the hearing on confirmation.

(d) Transmission and notice to United States trustee, creditors and equity security holders

Upon approval of a disclosure statement,—[1]except to the extent that the court orders otherwise with respect to one or more unimpaired classes of creditors or equity security holders—the debtor in possession, trustee, proponent of the plan, or clerk as the court orders shall mail to all creditors and equity security holders, and in a chapter 11 reorganization case shall transmit to the United States trustee,

(1) the plan or a court-approved summary of the plan;

(2) the disclosure statement approved by the court;

(3) notice of the time within which acceptances and rejections of the plan may be filed; and

(4) any other information as the court may direct, including any court opinion approving the disclosure statement or a court-approved summary of the opinion.

In addition, notice of the time fixed for filing objections and the hearing on confirmation shall be mailed to all creditors and equity security holders in accordance with Rule 2002(b), and a form of ballot conforming to the appropriate Official Form shall be mailed to creditors and equity security holders entitled to vote on the plan. If the court opinion is not transmitted or only a summary of the plan is transmitted, the court opinion or the plan shall be provided on request of a party in interest at the plan proponent's expense. If the court orders that the disclosure statement and the plan or a summary of the plan shall not be mailed to any unimpaired class, notice that the class is designated in the plan as unimpaired and notice of the name and address of the person from whom the plan or summary of the plan and disclosure statement may be obtained upon request and at the plan proponent's expense, shall be mailed to members of the unimpaired class together with the notice of the time fixed for filing objections to and the hearing on confirmation. For the purposes of this subdivision, creditors and equity security holders shall include holders of stock, bonds, debentures, notes, and other securities of record on the date the order approving the disclosure statement is entered or another date fixed by the court, for cause, after notice and a hearing.

(e) Transmission to beneficial holders of securities

At the hearing held pursuant to subdivision (a) of this rule, the court shall consider the procedures for transmitting the documents and information required by subdivision (d) of this rule to beneficial holders of stock, bonds, debentures, notes, and other securities, determine the adequacy of the procedures, and enter any orders the court deems appropriate.

(f) Notice and transmission of documents to entities subject to an injunction under a plan

If a plan provides for an injunction against conduct not otherwise enjoined under the Code and an entity that would be subject to the injunction is not a creditor or equity security holder, at the hearing held under Rule 3017(a), the court shall consider procedures for providing the entity with:

(1) at least 25 days' notice of the time fixed for filing objections and the hearing on confirmation of the plan containing the information described in Rule 2002(c)(3); and

(2) to the extent feasible, a copy of the plan and disclosure statement.

(As amended Mar. 30, 1987, eff. Aug. 1, 1987; Apr. 30, 1991, eff. Aug. 1, 1991; Apr. 11, 1997, eff. Dec. 1, 1997; Apr. 23, 2001, eff. Dec. 1, 2001.)

1 So in original. The comma probably should not appear.

ADVISORY COMMITTEE NOTES

This rule is adapted from former Rule 10–303 which dealt with the approval of a Chapter X plan by the court. There is no requirement for plan approval in a chapter 9 or 11 case under the Code but there is the requirement that a disclosure statement containing adequate financial information be approved by the court after notice and a hearing before votes on a plan are solicited. Section 1125(b) of the Code is made applicable in chapter 9 cases by § 901(a). It is also applicable in railroad reorganization cases under subchapter IV of chapter 11; see § 1161 of the Code.

Subdivision (a) of this rule provides for the hearing on the disclosure statement. Thus, a hearing would be required in all cases; whether it may be ex parte would depend on the circumstances of the case, but a mere absence of objections would not eliminate the need for a hearing; see § 102(1) of the Code.

No provision similar to former Rule 10–303(f) is included. That subdivision together with former Rule 10–304 prohibited solicitation of votes until after entry of an order approving the plan. Section 1125(b) of the Code explicitly provides that votes on a plan may not be solicited until a disclosure statement approved by the court is transmitted. Pursuant to the change in rulemaking power, a comparable provision in this rule is unnecessary. 28 U.S.C. § 2075.

Copies of the disclosure statement and plan need not be mailed with the notice of the hearing or otherwise transmitted prior to the hearing except with respect to the parties explicitly set forth in the subdivision.

It should be noted that, by construction, the singular includes the plural. Therefore, the phrase "plan or plans" or "disclosure statement or statements" has not been used although the possibility of multiple plans and statements is recognized.

Subdivision (d) permits the court to require a party other than the clerk of the bankruptcy court to bear the responsibility for transmitting the notices and documents specified in the rule when votes on the plan are solicited. Ordinarily the person responsible for such mailing will be the proponent of the plan. In rare cases the clerk may be directed to mail these documents, particularly when the trustee would have the responsibility but there is insufficient money in the estate to enable the trustee to perform this task.

1987 Amendments

Subdivision (d). Section 1125(c) of the Code requires that the entire approved disclosure statement be provided in connection with voting on a plan. The court is authorized by § 1125(c) to approve different disclosure statements for different classes. Although the rule does not permit the mailing of a summary of the disclosure statement in place of the approved disclosure statement, the court may approve a summary of the disclosure statement to be mailed with the complete disclosure statement to those voting on the plan.

1991 Amendments

This rule is amended to enable the United States trustee to monitor and comment with regard to chapter 11 disclosure statements and plans. The United States trustee does not perform these functions in a chapter 9 municipal debt adjustment case. See 28 U.S.C. § 586(a)(3)(B).

Subdivision (d) is amended to give the court the discretion to direct that one or more unimpaired classes shall not receive disclosure statements, plans, or summaries of plans. Members of unimpaired classes are not entitled to vote on the plan. Although disclosure statements enable members of unimpaired classes to make informed judgments as to whether to object to confirmation because of lack of feasibility or other grounds, in an unusual case the court may direct that disclosure statements shall not be sent to such classes if to do so would not be feasible considering the size of the unimpaired classes and the expense of printing and mailing. In any event, all creditors are entitled to notice of the time fixed for filing objections and notice of the hearing to consider confirmation of the plan pursuant to Rule 2002(b) and the requirement of such notice may not be excused with respect to unimpaired classes. The amendment to subdivision (d) also ensures that the members of unimpaired classes who do not receive such documents will have sufficient information so that they may request these documents in advance of the hearing on confirmation. The amendment to subdivision (d) is not intended to give the court the discretion to dispense with the mailing of the plan and disclosure statement to governmental units holding claims entitled to priority under § 507(a)(7) because they may not be classified. See § 1123(a)(1).

The words "with the court" in subdivision (a) are deleted as unnecessary. See Rules 5005(a) and 9001(3). Reference to the Official Form number in subdivision (d) is deleted in anticipation of future revision and renumbering of the Official Forms.

Subdivision (e) is designed to ensure that appropriate measures are taken for the plan, disclosure statement, ballot and other materials which are required to be transmitted to creditors and equity security holders under this rule to reach the beneficial holders of securities held in nominee name. Such measures may include orders directing the trustee or debtor in possession to reimburse the nominees out of the funds of the estate for the expenses incurred by them in distributing materials to beneficial holders. In most cases, the plan proponent will not know the identities of the beneficial holders and therefore it will be necessary to rely on the nominal holders of the securities to distribute the plan materials to the beneficial owners.

1997 Amendments

Subdivision (a) is amended to provide that it does not apply to the extent provided in new Rule 3017.1, which applies in small business cases.

Subdivision (d) is amended to provide flexibility in fixing the record date for the purpose of determining the holders of securities who are entitled to receive documents pursuant to this subdivision. For example, if there may be a delay between the oral announcement of the judge's order approving the disclosure statement and entry of the order on the court docket, the court may fix the date on which the judge orally approves the disclosure statement as the record date so that the parties may expedite preparation of the lists necessary to facilitate the distribution of the plan, disclosure statement, ballots, and other related documents.

The court may set a record date pursuant to subdivision (d) only after notice and a hearing as provided in § 102(1) of the Code. Notice of a request for an order fixing the record date may be included in the notice of the hearing to consider approval of the disclosure statement mailed pursuant to Rule 2002(b).

If the court fixes a record date pursuant to subdivision (d) with respect to the holders of securities, and the holders are impaired by the plan, the judge also should order that the same record date applies for the purpose of determining eligibility for voting pursuant to Rule 3018(a).

Other amendments to this rule are stylistic.

GAP Report on Rule 3017. No changes to the published draft.

2001 Amendments

Subdivision (f) is added to assure that entities whose conduct would be enjoined under a plan, rather than by operation of the Code, and who will not receive the documents listed in subdivision (d) because they are neither creditors nor equity security holders, are provided with adequate notice of the proposed injunction. It does not address any substantive law issues relating to the validity or effect of any injunction provided under a plan, or any due process or other constitutional issues relating to notice. These issues are beyond the scope of these rules and are left for judicial determination.

This rule recognizes the need for adequate notice to subjects of an injunction, but that reasonable flexibility under the circumstances may be required. If a known and identifiable entity would be subject to the injunction, and the notice, plan, and disclosure statement could be mailed to that entity, the court should require that they be mailed at the same time that the plan, disclosure statement and related documents are mailed to creditors under Rule 3017(d). If mailing notices and other documents is not feasible because the entities subject to the injunction are described in the plan and disclosure statement by class or category and they cannot be identified individually by name and address, the court may require that notice under Rule 3017(f)(1) be published.

CHANGES MADE AFTER PUBLICATION AND COMMENTS

No changes were made in the text of the proposed amendments since publication. The Committee Note was revised to put in a more prominent position the statement that the rule does not address related substantive law issues which are beyond the scope of the rules.

CROSS REFERENCES

Acceptance or rejection of plan—

Eligible persons, see Fed.Rules Bankr.Proc. Rule 3018, 11 USCA.

Preference among more than one plan, see Fed.Rules Bankr.Proc. Rule 3018, 11 USCA.

Disclosure statement—

Different statements as between different classes of claims, see 11 USCA § 1125.

Right to be heard on adequacy of information, see 11 USCA § 1125.

Solicitation of plan's acceptance, see 11 USCA § 1125.

Notice of—

Time fixed for plan's acceptance or rejection in accord with this rule, see Fed.Rules Bankr.Proc. Rule 2002, 11 USCA.

Proof of right to record status filed by security holder, see Fed.Rules Bankr.Proc. Rule 3003, 11 USCA.

Rule 3017.1. Court Consideration of Disclosure Statement in a Small Business Case

(a) Conditional approval of disclosure statement

In a small business case, the court may, on application of the plan proponent or on its own initiative, conditionally approve a disclosure statement filed in accordance with Rule 3016. On or before conditional approval of the disclosure statement, the court shall:

(1) fix a time within which the holders of claims and interests may accept or reject the plan;

(2) fix a time for filing objections to the disclosure statement;

(3) fix a date for the hearing on final approval of the disclosure statement to be held if a timely objection is filed; and

(4) fix a date for the hearing on confirmation.

(b) Application of Rule 3017

Rule 3017(a), (b), (c), and (e) do not apply to a conditionally approved disclosure statement. Rule 3017(d) applies to a conditionally approved disclosure statement, except that conditional approval is considered approval of the disclosure statement for the purpose of applying Rule 3017(d).

(c) Final approval

(1) Notice

Notice of the time fixed for filing objections and the hearing to consider final approval of the disclosure statement shall be given in accordance with Rule 2002 and may be combined with notice of the hearing on confirmation of the plan.

(2) Objections

Objections to the disclosure statement shall be filed, transmitted to the United States trustee, and served on the debtor, the trustee, any committee appointed under the Code and any other entity designated by the court at any time before final approval of the disclosure statement or by an earlier date as the court may fix.

(3) Hearing

If a timely objection to the disclosure statement is filed, the court shall hold a hearing to consider final approval before or combined with the hearing on confirmation of the plan.

(Added Apr. 11, 1997, eff. Dec. 1, 1997. Amended Apr. 23, 2008, eff. Dec. 1, 2008.)

ADVISORY COMMITTEE NOTES

1997 Amendment

This rule is added to implement § 1125(f), which was added to the Code by the Bankruptcy Reform Act of 1994.

The procedures for electing to be considered a small business are set forth in Rule 1020. If the debtor is a small business and has elected to be considered a small business, § 1125(f) permits the court to conditionally approve a disclosure statement subject to final approval after notice and a hearing. If a disclosure statement is conditionally approved, and no timely objection to the disclosure statement is filed, it is not necessary for the court to hold a hearing on final approval.

GAP Report on Rule 3017.1. No changes to the published draft.

2008 Amendments

Section 101 of the Code, as amended in 2005, defines a "small business case" and "small business debtor," and eliminates any need to elect that status. Therefore, the reference in the rule to an election is deleted.

As provided in the amendment to Rule 3016(b), a plan intended to provide adequate information in a small business case under § 1125(f)(1) may be conditionally approved and is otherwise treated as a disclosure statement under this rule.

Rule 3018. Acceptance or Rejection of Plan in a Chapter 9 Municipality or a Chapter 11 Reorganization Case

(a) Entities entitled to accept or reject plan; time for acceptance or rejection

A plan may be accepted or rejected in accordance with § 1126 of the Code within the time fixed by the court pursuant to Rule 3017. Subject to subdivision (b) of this rule, an equity security holder or creditor whose claim is based on a security of record shall not be entitled to accept or reject a plan unless the equity security holder or creditor is the holder of record of the security on the date the order approving the disclosure statement is entered or on another date fixed by the court, for cause, after notice and a hearing. For cause shown, the court after notice and hearing may permit a creditor or equity security holder to change or withdraw an acceptance or rejection. Notwithstanding objection to a claim or interest, the court after notice and hearing may temporarily allow the claim or interest in an amount which the court deems proper for the purpose of accepting or rejecting a plan.

(b) Acceptances or rejections obtained before petition

An equity security holder or creditor whose claim is based on a security of record who accepted or rejected the plan before the commencement of the case shall not be deemed to have accepted or rejected the plan pursuant to § 1126(b) of the Code unless the equity security holder or creditor was the holder of record of the security on the date specified in the solicitation of such acceptance or rejection for the purposes of such solicitation. A holder of a claim or interest who has accepted or rejected a plan before the commencement of the case under the Code shall not be deemed to have accepted or rejected the plan if the court finds after notice and hearing that the plan was not transmitted to substantially all creditors and equity security holders of the same class, that an unreasonably short time was prescribed for such creditors and equity security holders to accept or reject the plan, or that the solicitation was not in compliance with § 1126(b) of the Code.

(c) Form of acceptance or rejection

An acceptance or rejection shall be in writing, identify the plan or plans accepted or rejected, be signed by the creditor or equity security holder or an authorized agent, and conform to the appropriate Official Form. If more than one plan is transmitted pursuant to Rule 3017, an acceptance or rejection may be filed by each creditor or equity security holder for any number of plans transmitted and if acceptances are filed for more than one plan, the creditor or equity security holder may indicate a preference or preferences among the plans so accepted.

(d) Acceptance or rejection by partially secured creditor

A creditor whose claim has been allowed in part as a secured claim and in part as an unsecured claim shall be entitled to accept or reject a plan in both capacities.

(As amended Mar. 30, 1987, eff. Aug. 1, 1987; Apr. 30, 1991, eff. Aug. 1, 1991; Apr. 22, 1993, eff. Aug. 1, 1993; Apr. 11, 1997, eff. Dec. 1, 1997.)

ADVISORY COMMITTEE NOTES

This rule applies in chapter 9, 11 and 13 cases under the Code. The references in the rule to equity security holders will not, however, be relevant in chapter 9 or 13 cases. The rule will be of little utility in a chapter 13 case because only secured creditors may be requested to vote on a plan; unsecured creditors are not entitled to vote; see § 1325(a)(4), (5) of the Code.

Subdivision (a) is derived from former Rule 10–305(a). It substitutes, in a reorganization case, entry of the order approving the disclosure statement for the order approving a plan in conformity with the differences between Chapter X [former § 501 et seq. of this title] and chapter 11. In keeping with the underlying theory, it continues to recognize that the lapse of time between the filing of the petition and entry of such order will normally be significant and, during that interim, bonds and equity interests can change ownership.

Subdivision (b) recognizes the former Chapter XI [former § 701 et seq. of this title] practice permitting a plan and acceptances to be filed with the petition, as does § 1126(b) of the Code. However, because a plan under chapter 11 may affect shareholder interests, there should be reference to a record date of ownership. In this instance the appropriate record date is that used in the prepetition solicitation materials because it is those acceptances or rejections which are being submitted to the court.

While § 1126(c), (d), and (e) prohibits use of an acceptance or rejection not procured in good faith, the added provision in subdivision (b) of the rule is somewhat more detailed. It would prohibit use of prepetition acceptances or rejections when some but not all impaired creditors or equity security holders are solicited or when they are not given a reasonable opportunity to submit their acceptances or rejections. This provision together with § 1126(e) gives the court the power to nullify abusive solicitation procedures.

Subdivision (c). It is possible that multiple plans may be before the court for confirmation. Pursuant to § 1129(c) of the Code, the court may confirm only one plan but is required to consider the preferences expressed by those accepting the plans in determining which one to confirm.

Subdivisions (d) and (e) of former Rule 10–305 are not continued since comparable provisions are contained in the statute; see § 1126(c), (d), (e).

It should be noted that while the singular "plan" is used throughout, by construction the plural is included; see § 102(7).

1991 Amendments

Subdivisions (a) and (b) are amended to delete provisions that duplicate § 1126 of the Code. An entity who is not a record holder of a security, but who claims that it is entitled to be treated as a record holder, may file a statement pursuant to Rule 3003(d).

Subdivision (a) is amended further to allow the court to permit a creditor or equity security holder to change or withdraw an acceptance or rejection for cause shown whether or not the time fixed for voting has expired.

Subdivision (b) is also amended to give effect to a prepetition acceptance or rejection if solicitation requirements were satisfied with respect to substantially all members of the same class, instead of requiring proper solicitation with respect to substantially all members of all classes.

Subdivision (c) is amended to delete the Official Form number in anticipation of future revision and renumbering of the Official Forms.

1993 Amendments

The title of this rule is amended to indicate that it applies only in a chapter 9 or a chapter 11 case. The amendment of the word "Plans" to "Plan" is stylistic.

1997 Amendments

Subdivision (a) is amended to provide flexibility in fixing the record date for the purpose of determining the holders of securities who are entitled to vote on the plan. For example, if there may be a delay between the oral announcement of the judge's decision approving the disclosure statement and entry of the order on the court docket, the court may fix the date on which the judge orally approves the disclosure statement as the record date for voting purposes so that the parties may expedite preparation of the lists necessary to facilitate the distribution of the plan, disclosure statement, ballots, and other related documents in connection with the solicitation of votes.

The court may set a record date pursuant to subdivision (a) only after notice and a hearing as provided in § 102(1) of the Code. Notice of a request for an order fixing the record date may be included in the notice of the hearing to consider approval of the disclosure statement mailed pursuant to Rule 2002(b).

If the court fixes the record date for voting purposes, the judge also should order that the same record date shall apply for the purpose of distributing the documents required to be distributed pursuant to Rule 3017(d).

GAP Report on Rule 3018. No changes to the published draft.

CROSS REFERENCES

Acceptance of altered or modified plan, see 11 USCA § 1127.

Disqualification of votes on acceptance in absence of good faith, see 11 USCA § 1126.

Filing of plan in—

Individual debt adjustment case, see Fed.Rules Bankr. Proc. Rule 3015, 11 USCA.

Municipality debt adjustment and reorganization cases, with disclosure statement, see Fed.Rules Bankr.Proc. Rule 3016, 11 USCA.

Proof of right to record status filed by security holder, see Fed.Rules Bankr.Proc. Rule 3003, 11 USCA.

Rule 3019. Modification of Accepted Plan in a Chapter 9 Municipality or a Chapter 11 Reorganization Case

(a) Modification of plan before confirmation

In a chapter 9 or chapter 11 case, after a plan has been accepted and before its confirmation, the proponent may file a modification of the plan. If the court finds after hearing on notice to the trustee, any committee appointed under the Code, and any other entity designated by the court that the proposed modification does not adversely change the treatment of the claim of any creditor or the interest of any equity security holder who has not accepted in writing the modification, it shall be deemed accepted by all creditors and equity security holders who have previously accepted the plan.

(b) Modification of plan after confirmation in individual debtor case

If the debtor is an individual, a request to modify the plan under § 1127(e) of the Code is governed by Rule 9014. The request shall identify the proponent and shall be filed together with the proposed modification. The clerk, or some other person as the court may direct, shall give the debtor, the trustee, and all creditors not less than 20 days' notice by mail of the time fixed to file objections and, if an objection is filed, the hearing to consider the proposed modification, unless the court orders otherwise with respect to creditors who are not affected by the proposed modification. A copy of the notice shall be transmitted to the United States trustee, together with a copy of the proposed modification. Any objection to the proposed modification shall be filed and served on the debtor, the proponent of the modification, the trustee, and any other entity designated by the court, and shall be transmitted to the United States trustee.

(As amended Mar. 30, 1987, eff. Aug. 1, 1987; Apr. 22, 1993, eff. Aug. 1, 1993; Apr. 23, 2008, eff. Dec. 1, 2008.)

ADVISORY COMMITTEE NOTES

This rule implements §§ 942, 1127 and 1323 of the Code. For example, § 1127 provides for modification before and after confirmation but does not deal with the minor modifications that do not adversely change any rights. The rule makes clear that a modification may be made, after acceptance of the plan without submission to creditors and equity security holders if their interests are not affected. To come within this rule, the modification should be one that does not change the rights of a creditor or equity security holder as fixed in the plan before modification.

1993 Amendments

This rule is amended to limit its application to chapter 9 and chapter 11 cases. Modification of plans after confirmation in chapter 12 and chapter 13 cases is governed by Rule 3015. The addition of the comma in the second sentence is stylistic and makes no substantive change.

2008 Amendments

The 2005 amendments to § 1127 of the Code provide for modification of a confirmed plan in an individual debtor chapter 11 case. Therefore, the rule is amended to establish the procedure for filing and objecting to a proposed modification of a confirmed plan.

CROSS REFERENCES

Acceptance or rejection of plans, see Fed.Rules Bankr. Proc. Rule 3018, 11 USCA.

Modification of plan in—

Individual debt adjustment case, see 11 USCA § 1323.

Municipality debt adjustment case, see 11 USCA § 942.

Reorganization case, see 11 USCA § 1127.

Rule 3020. Deposit; Confirmation of Plan in a Chapter 9 Municipality or Chapter 11 Reorganization Case

(a) Deposit

In a chapter 11 case, prior to entry of the order confirming the plan, the court may order the deposit with the trustee or debtor in possession of the consideration required by the plan to be distributed on confirmation. Any money deposited shall be kept in a special account established for the exclusive purpose of making the distribution.

(b) Objection to and hearing on confirmation in a Chapter 9 or Chapter 11 case

(1) Objection

An objection to confirmation of the plan shall be filed and served on the debtor, the trustee, the proponent of the plan, any committee appointed under the Code, and any other entity designated by the court, within a time fixed by the court. Unless the case is a chapter 9 municipality case, a copy of every objection to confirmation shall be transmitted by the objecting party to the United States trustee within the time fixed for filing objections. An objection to confirmation is governed by Rule 9014.

(2) Hearing

The court shall rule on confirmation of the plan after notice and hearing as provided in Rule 2002. If no objection is timely filed, the court may determine that the plan has been proposed in good faith and not by any means forbidden by law without receiving evidence on such issues.

(c) Order of confirmation

(1) The order of confirmation shall conform to the appropriate Official Form. If the plan provides for an injunction against conduct not otherwise enjoined under the Code, the order of confirmation shall (1) describe in reasonable detail all acts enjoined; (2) be specific in its terms regarding the injunction; and (3) identify the entities subject to the injunction.

(2) Notice of entry of the order of confirmation shall be mailed promptly to the debtor, the trustee, creditors, equity security holders, other parties in interest, and, if known, to any identified entity subject to an injunction provided for in the plan against conduct not otherwise enjoined under the Code.

(3) Except in a chapter 9 municipality case, notice of entry of the order of confirmation shall be transmitted to the United States trustee as provided in Rule 2002(k).

(d) Retained power

Notwithstanding the entry of the order of confirmation, the court may issue any other order necessary to administer the estate.

(e) Stay of confirmation order

An order confirming a plan is stayed until the expiration of 10 days after the entry of the order, unless the court orders otherwise.

(As amended Mar. 30, 1987, eff. Aug. 1, 1987; Apr. 30, 1991, eff. Aug. 1, 1991; Apr. 22, 1993, eff. Aug. 1, 1993; Apr. 29, 1999, eff. Dec. 1, 1999; Apr. 23, 2001, eff. Dec. 1, 2001.)

ADVISORY COMMITTEE NOTES

This rule is adapted from former Rules 10–307, 11–38, and 13–213. It applies to cases filed under chapters 9, 11 and 13. Certain subdivisions of the earlier rules have not been included, such as, a subdivision revesting title in the debtor because § 541 of the Code does not transfer title out of the debtor as did § 70a of the Bankruptcy Act [former § 110(a) of this title]; see also §§ 1141(b), 1327(b). Subdivision (b) of former Rule 13–213 is not included because its provisions are contained in the statute; see §§ 1322, 1325(b), 105.

Subdivision (a) gives discretion to the court to require in chapter 11 cases the deposit of any consideration to be distributed on confirmation. If money is to be distributed, it is to be deposited in a special account to assure that it will not be used for any other purpose. The Code is silent in chapter 11 with respect to the need to make a deposit or the person with whom any deposit is to be to made. Consequently, there is no statutory authority for any person to act in a capacity similar to the disbursing agent under former Chapter XI [former § 701 et seq. of this title] practice. This rule provides that only the debtor in possession or trustee should be appointed as the recipient of the deposit. Any consideration other than money, e.g., notes or stock may be given directly to the debtor in possession or trustee and need not be left in any kind of special account. In chapter 9 cases, § 944(b) provides for deposit with a disbursing agent appointed by the court of any consideration to be distributed under the plan.

Subdivision (d) clarifies the authority of the court to conclude matters pending before it prior to confirmation and to continue to administer the estate as necessary, e.g., resolving objections to claims.

1991 Amendments

The United States trustee monitors chapter 11, chapter 12, and chapter 13 plans and has standing to be heard regarding confirmation of a plan. See 28 U.S.C. § 586(a)(3). The amendments to subdivisions (b)(1) and (c) of this rule facilitate that role of the United States trustee. Subdivision (b)(1) is also amended to require service on the proponent of the plan of objections to confirmation. The words "with the court" in subdivision (b)(1) are deleted as unnecessary. See Rules 5005(a) and 9001(3).

In a chapter 12 case, the court is required to conduct and conclude the hearing on confirmation of the plan within the time prescribed in § 1224 of the Code.

Subdivision (c) is also amended to require that the confirmation order be mailed to the trustee. Reference to the Official Form number is deleted in anticipation of future revision and renumbering of the Official Forms.

1993 Amendments

This rule is amended to limit its application to chapter 9 and chapter 11 cases. The procedures relating to confirmation of plans in chapter 12 and chapter 13 cases are provided in rule 3015. Other amendments are stylistic and make no substantive change.

1999 Amendments

Subdivision (e) is added to provide sufficient time for a party to request a stay pending appeal of an order confirming a plan under chapter 9 or chapter 11 of the Code before the plan is implemented and an appeal becomes moot. Unless the court orders otherwise, any transfer of assets, issuance of securities, and cash distributions provided for in the plan may not be made before the expiration of the 10–day period. The stay of the confirmation order under subdivision (e) does not affect the time for filing a notice of appeal from the confirmation order in accordance with Rule 8002.

The court may, in its discretion, order that Rule 3020(e) is not applicable so that the plan may be implemented and distributions may be made immediately. Alternatively, the court may order that the stay under Rule 3020(e) is for a fixed period less than 10 days.

Gap Report on Rule 3020. No changes since publication.

2001 Amendments

Subdivision (c) is amended to provide notice to an entity subject to an injunction provided for in a plan against conduct not otherwise enjoined by operation of the Code. This requirement is not applicable to an injunction contained in a plan if it is substantially the same as an injunction provided under the Code. The validity and effect of any injunction provided for in a plan are substantive law matters that are beyond the scope of these rules.

The requirement that the order of confirmation identify the entities subject to the injunction requires only reasonable identification under the circumstances. If the entities that would be subject to the injunction cannot be identified by name, the order may describe them by class or category if reasonable under the circumstances. For example, it may be sufficient to identify the entities as "all creditors of the debtor."

CHANGES MADE AFTER PUBLICATION AND COMMENTS

No changes were made in the text of the proposed amendments. The Committee Note was revised to put in a more prominent position the statement that the validity and effect of injunctions provided for in plans is beyond the scope of the rules.

CROSS REFERENCES

Modification of accepted plan before confirmation, see Fed.Rules Bankr.Proc. Rule 3019, 11 USCA.

Rule 3021. Distribution Under Plan

Except as provided in Rule 3020(e), after a plan is confirmed, distribution shall be made to creditors whose claims have been allowed, to interest holders whose interests have not been disallowed, and to indenture trustees who have filed claims under Rule 3003(c)(5) that have been allowed. For purposes of this rule, creditors include holders of bonds, debentures, notes, and other debt securities, and interest holders include the holders of stock and other equity securities, of record at the time of commencement of distribution, unless a different time is fixed by the plan or the order confirming the plan.

(As amended Apr. 11, 1997, eff. Dec. 1, 1997; Apr. 29, 1999, eff. Dec. 1, 1999.)

ADVISORY COMMITTEE NOTES

This rule is derived from former Chapter X Rule 10–405(a). Subdivision (b) of that rule is covered by § 1143 of the Code.

1997 Amendments

This rule is amended to provide flexibility in fixing the record date for the purpose of making distributions to holders of securities of record. In a large case, it may be impractical for the debtor to determine the holders of record with respect to publicly held securities and also to make distributions to those holders at the same time. Under this amendment, the plan or the order confirming the plan may fix a record date for distributions that is earlier than the date on which distributions commence.

This rule also is amended to treat holders of bonds, debentures, notes, and other debt securities the same as any other creditors by providing that they shall receive a distribution only if their claims have been allowed. Finally, the amendments clarify that distributions are to be made to all interest holders—not only those that are within the definition of "equity security holders" under § 101 of the Code—whose interests have not been disallowed.

GAP Report on Rule 3021. No changes to the published draft.

1999 Amendments

This amendment is to conform to the amendments to Rule 3020 regarding the ten-day stay of an order confirming a plan in a chapter 9 or chapter 11 case. The other amendments are stylistic.

Gap Report on Rule 3021. No changes since publication.

CROSS REFERENCES

Disposition of unclaimed property, see 11 USCA § 347.

Power of court to require transfers of property, see 11 USCA § 1142.

Proof of right to record status filed by security holder, see Fed.Rules Bankr.Proc. Rule 3003, 11 USCA.

Time for surrender of security or performance of required act under reorganization plan, see 11 USCA § 1143.

Rule 3022. Final Decree in Chapter 11 Reorganization Case

After an estate is fully administered in a chapter 11 reorganization case, the court, on its own motion or on motion of a party in interest, shall enter a final decree closing the case.

(As amended Mar. 30, 1987, eff. Aug. 1, 1987; Apr. 30, 1991, eff. Aug. 1, 1991.)

ADVISORY COMMITTEE NOTES

Section 350 of the Code requires the court to close the case after the estate is fully administered and the trustee has been discharged. Section 1143 places a five year limitation on the surrender of securities when required for participation under a plan but this provision should not delay entry of the final decree.

1991 Amendments

Entry of a final decree closing a chapter 11 case should not be delayed solely because the payments required by the plan have not been completed. Factors that the court should consider in determining whether the estate has been fully administered include (1) whether the order confirming the plan has become final, (2) whether deposits required by the plan have been distributed, (3) whether the property proposed by the plan to be transferred has been transferred, (4) whether the debtor or the successor of the debtor under the plan has assumed the business or the management of the property dealt with by the plan, (5) whether payments under the plan have commenced, and (6) whether all motions, contested matters, and adversary proceedings have been finally resolved.

The court should not keep the case open only because of the possibility that the court's jurisdiction may be invoked in the future. A final decree closing the case after the estate is fully administered does not deprive the court of jurisdiction to enforce or interpret its own orders and does not prevent the court from reopening the case for cause pursuant to § 350(b) of the Code. For example, on motion of a party in interest, the court may reopen the case to revoke an order of confirmation procured by fraud under § 1144 of the Code. If the plan or confirmation order provides that the case shall remain open until a certain date or event because of the likelihood that the court's jurisdiction may be required for specific purposes prior thereto, the case should remain open until that date or event.

CROSS REFERENCES

Close of case after trustee's discharge, see 11 USCA § 350.

Surrender of security or performance of required act under reorganization plan, denial of distribution, see 11 USCA § 1143.

PART IV—THE DEBTOR: DUTIES AND BENEFITS

Rule 4001. Relief from Automatic Stay; Prohibiting or Conditioning the Use, Sale, or Lease of Property; Use of Cash Collateral; Obtaining Credit; Agreements

(a) Relief from stay; prohibiting or conditioning the use, sale, or lease of property

(1) Motion

A motion for relief from an automatic stay provided by the Code or a motion to prohibit or condition the use, sale, or lease of property pursuant to § 363(e) shall be made in accordance with Rule 9014 and shall be served on any committee elected pursuant to § 705 or appointed pursuant to § 1102 of the Code or its authorized agent, or, if the case is a chapter 9 municipality case or a chapter 11 reorganization case and no committee of unsecured creditors has been appointed pursuant to § 1102, on the creditors included on the list filed pursuant to Rule 1007(d), and on such other entities as the court may direct.

(2) Ex parte relief

Relief from a stay under § 362(a) or a request to prohibit or condition the use, sale, or lease of property pursuant to § 363(e) may be granted without prior notice only if (A) it clearly appears from specific facts shown by affidavit or by a verified motion that immediate and irreparable injury, loss, or damage will result to the movant before the adverse party or the attorney for the adverse party can be heard in opposition, and (B) the movant's attorney certifies to the court in writing the efforts, if any, which have been made to give notice and the reasons why notice should not be required. The party obtaining relief under this subdivision and § 362(f) or § 363(e) shall immediately give oral notice thereof to the trustee or debtor in possession and to the debtor and forthwith mail or otherwise transmit to such adverse party or parties a copy of the order granting relief. On two days notice to the party who obtained relief from the stay without notice or on shorter notice to that party as the court may prescribe, the adverse party may appear and move reinstatement of the stay or reconsideration of the order prohibiting or conditioning the use, sale, or lease of property. In that event, the court shall proceed expeditiously to hear and determine the motion.

(3) Stay of order

An order granting a motion for relief from an automatic stay made in accordance with Rule 4001(a)(1) is stayed until the expiration of 10 days after the entry of the order, unless the court orders otherwise.

(b) Use of cash collateral

(1) Motion; Service

(A) Motion

A motion for authority to use cash collateral shall be made in accordance with Rule 9014 and shall be accompanied by a proposed form of order.

(B) Contents

The motion shall consist of or (if the motion is more than five pages in length) begin with a concise statement of the relief requested, not to exceed five pages, that lists or summarizes, and sets out the location within the relevant documents of, all material provisions, including:

(i) the name of each entity with an interest in the cash collateral;

(ii) the purposes for the use of the cash collateral;

(iii) the material terms, including duration, of the use of the cash collateral; and

(iv) any liens, cash payments, or other adequate protection that will be provided to each entity with an interest in the cash collateral or, if no additional adequate protection is proposed, an explanation of why each entity's interest is adequately protected.

(C) Service

The motion shall be served on: (1) any entity with an interest in the cash collateral; (2) any committee elected under § 705 or appointed under § 1102 of the Code, or its authorized agent, or, if the case is a chapter 9 municipality case or a chapter 11 reorganization case and no committee of unsecured creditors has been appointed under § 1102, the creditors included on the list filed under Rule 1007(d); and (3) any other entity that the court directs.

(2) **Hearing**

The court may commence a final hearing on a motion for authorization to use cash collateral no earlier than 15 days after service of the motion. If the motion so requests, the court may conduct a preliminary hearing before such 15 day period expires, but the court may authorize the use of only that amount of cash collateral as is necessary to avoid immediate and irreparable harm to the estate pending a final hearing.

(3) **Notice**

Notice of hearing pursuant to this subdivision shall be given to the parties on whom service of the motion is required by paragraph (1) of this subdivision and to such other entities as the court may direct.

(c) **Obtaining credit**

(1) **Motion; Service**

(A) **Motion**

A motion for authority to obtain credit shall be made in accordance with Rule 9014 and shall be accompanied by a copy of the credit agreement and a proposed form of order.

(B) **Contents**

The motion shall consist of or (if the motion is more than five pages in length) begin with a concise statement of the relief requested, not to exceed five pages, that lists or summarizes, and sets out the location within the relevant documents of, all material provisions of the proposed credit agreement and form of order, including interest rate, maturity, events of default, liens, borrowing limits, and borrowing conditions. If the proposed credit agreement or form of order includes any of the provisions listed below, the concise statement shall also: briefly list or summarize each one; identify its specific location in the proposed agreement and form of order; and identify any such provision that is proposed to remain in effect if interim approval is granted, but final relief is denied, as provided under Rule 4001(c)(2). In addition, the motion shall describe the nature and extent of each provision listed below:

(**i**) a grant of priority or a lien on property of the estate under § 364(c) or (d);

(**ii**) the providing of adequate protection or priority for a claim that arose before the commencement of the case, including the granting of a lien on property of the estate to secure the claim, or the use of property of the estate or credit obtained under § 364 to make cash payments on account of the claim;

(**iii**) a determination of the validity, enforceability, priority, or amount of a claim that arose before the commencement of the case, or of any lien securing the claim;

(**iv**) a waiver or modification of Code provisions or applicable rules relating to the automatic stay;

(**v**) a waiver or modification of any entity's authority or right to file a plan, seek an extension of time in which the debtor has the exclusive right to file a plan, request the use of cash collateral under § 363(c), or request authority to obtain credit under § 364;

(**vi**) the establishment of deadlines for filing a plan of reorganization, for approval of a disclosure statement, for a hearing on confirmation, or for entry of a confirmation order;

(**vii**) a waiver or modification of the applicability of nonbankruptcy law relating to the perfection of a lien on property of the estate, or on the foreclosure or other enforcement of the lien;

(**viii**) a release, waiver, or limitation on any claim or other cause of action belonging to the estate or the trustee, including any modification of the statute of limitations or other deadline to commence an action;

(**ix**) the indemnification of any entity;

(**x**) a release, waiver, or limitation of any right under § 506(c); or

(**xi**) the granting of a lien on any claim or cause of action arising under §§ 544, 545, 547, 548, 549, 553(b), 723(a), or 724(a).

(C) **Service**

The motion shall be served on: (1) any committee elected under § 705 or appointed under § 1102 of the Code, or its authorized agent, or, if the case is a chapter 9 municipality case or a chapter 11 reorganization case and no committee of unsecured creditors has been appointed under § 1102, on the creditors included on the list filed under Rule 1007(d); and (2) on any other entity that the court directs.

(2) **Hearing**

The court may commence a final hearing on a motion for authority to obtain credit no earlier than 15 days after service of the motion. If the motion so requests, the court may conduct a hearing before such 15 day period expires, but the court may authorize the obtaining of credit only to the extent necessary to avoid immediate and irreparable harm to the estate pending a final hearing.

(3) Notice

Notice of hearing pursuant to this subdivision shall be given to the parties on whom service of the motion is required by paragraph (1) of this subdivision and to such other entities as the court may direct.

(d) Agreement relating to relief from the automatic stay, prohibiting or conditioning the use, sale, or lease of property, providing adequate protection, use of cash collateral, and obtaining credit

(1) Motion; Service

(A) Motion

A motion for approval of any of the following shall be accompanied by a copy of the agreement and a proposed form of order:

(i) an agreement to provide adequate protection;

(ii) an agreement to prohibit or condition the use, sale, or lease of property;

(iii) an agreement to modify or terminate the stay provided for in § 362;

(iv) an agreement to use cash collateral; or

(v) an agreement between the debtor and an entity that has a lien or interest in property of the estate pursuant to which the entity consents to the creation of a lien senior or equal to the entity's lien or interest in such property.

(B) Contents

The motion shall consist of or (if the motion is more than five pages in length) begin with a concise statement of the relief requested, not to exceed five pages, that lists or summarizes, and sets out the location within the relevant documents of, all material provisions of the agreement. In addition, the concise statement shall briefly list or summarize, and identify the specific location of, each provision in the proposed form of order, agreement, or other document of the type listed in subdivision (c)(1)(B). The motion shall also describe the nature and extent of each such provision.

(C) Service

The motion shall be served on: (1) any committee elected under § 705 or appointed under § 1102 of the Code, or its authorized agent, or, if the case is a chapter 9 municipality case or a chapter 11 reorganization case and no committee of unsecured creditors has been appointed under § 1102, on the creditors included on the list filed under Rule 1007(d); and (2) on any other entity the court directs.

(2) Objection

Notice of the motion and the time within which objections may be filed and served on the debtor in possession or trustee shall be mailed to the parties on whom service is required by paragraph (1) of this subdivision and to such other entities as the court may direct. Unless the court fixes a different time, objections may be filed within 15 days of the mailing of notice.

(3) Disposition; hearing

If no objection is filed, the court may enter an order approving or disapproving the agreement without conducting a hearing. If an objection is filed or if the court determines a hearing is appropriate, the court shall hold a hearing on no less than five days' notice to the objector, the movant, the parties on whom service is required by paragraph (1) of this subdivision and such other entities as the court may direct.

(4) Agreement in settlement of motion

The court may direct that the procedures prescribed in paragraphs (1), (2), and (3) of this subdivision shall not apply and the agreement may be approved without further notice if the court determines that a motion made pursuant to subdivisions (a), (b), or (c) of this rule was sufficient to afford reasonable notice of the material provisions of the agreement and opportunity for a hearing.

(As amended Mar. 30, 1987, eff. Aug. 1, 1987; Apr. 30, 1991, eff. Aug. 1, 1991; Apr. 29, 1999, eff. Dec. 1, 1999; Apr. 30, 2007, eff. Dec. 1, 2007.)

ADVISORY COMMITTEE NOTES

This rule implements § 362 of the Code which sets forth provisions regarding the automatic stay that arises on the filing of a petition. That section and this rule are applicable in chapter 7, 9, 11 and 13 cases. It also implements § 363(c)(2) concerning use of cash collateral.

Subdivision (a) transforms with respect to the automatic stay what was an adversary proceeding under the former rules to motion practice. The Code provides automatic stays in several sections, e.g., §§ 362(a), 1301(a), and in § 362(d) provides some grounds for relief from the stay. This rule specifies that the pleading seeking relief is by means of a motion. Thus the time period in Rule 7012 to answer a complaint would not be applicable and shorter periods may be fixed. Section 362(e) requires the preliminary hearing to be concluded within 30 days of its inception, rendering ordinary complaint and answer practice inappropriate.

This subdivision also makes clear that a motion under Rule 9014 is the proper procedure for a debtor to seek court permission to use cash collateral. See § 363(c)(2). Pursuant to Rule 5005, the motion should be filed in the court in which the case is pending. The court or local rule may specify the persons to be served with the motion for relief from the stay; see Rule 9013.

Subdivision (b) of the rule fills a procedural void left by § 362. Pursuant to § 362(e), the automatic stay is terminated 30 days after a motion for relief is made unless the court continues the stay as a result of a final hearing or, pending final hearing, after a preliminary hearing. If a preliminary hearing is held, § 362(e) requires the final hearing to be commenced within 30 days after the preliminary hearing. Although the expressed legislative intent is to require expeditious resolution of a secured party's motion for relief, § 362 is silent as to the time within which the final hearing must be concluded. Subdivision (b) imposes a 30 day deadline on the court to resolve the dispute.

At the final hearing, the stay is to be terminated, modified, annulled, or conditioned for cause, which includes, inter alia, lack of adequate protection; § 362(d). The burden of proving adequate protection is on the party opposing relief from the stay; § 362(g)(2). Adequate protection is exemplified in § 361.

Subdivision (c) implements § 362(f) which permits ex parte relief from the stay when there will be irreparable damage. This subdivision sets forth the procedure to be followed when relief is sought under § 362(f). It is derived from former Bankruptcy Rule 601(d).

1987 Amendments

The scope of this rule is expanded and the former subdivisions (a), (b) and (c) are now combined in subdivision (a). The new subdivision (a)(2) is amended to conform to the 1984 amendments to § 362(e) of the Code.

Subdivision (b) deals explicitly with the procedures which follow after a motion to use cash collateral is made and served. Filing shall be pursuant to Rule 5005. Service of the motion may be made by any method authorized by Rule 7004 and, if service is by mail, service is complete on mailing. Rule 9006(e). Under subdivision (b)(2), the court may commence a final hearing on the motion within 15 days of service. Rule 9006(f) does not extend this 15 day period when service of the motion is by mail because the party served is not required to act within the 15 day period. In addition to service of the motion, notice of the hearing must be given. Rule 9007 authorizes the court to direct the form and manner of giving notice that is appropriate to the circumstances.

Section 363(c)(3) authorizes the court to conduct a preliminary hearing and to authorize the use of cash collateral "if there is a reasonable likelihood that the trustee will prevail at a final hearing." Subdivision (b)(2) of the rule permits a preliminary hearing to be held earlier than 15 days after service. Any order authorizing the use of cash collateral shall be limited to the amount necessary to protect the estate until a final hearing is held.

The objective of subdivision (b) is to accommodate both the immediate need of the debtor and the interest of the secured creditor in the cash collateral. The time for holding the final hearing may be enlarged beyond the 15 days prescribed when required by the circumstances.

The motion for authority to use cash collateral shall include (1) the amount of cash collateral sought to be used; (2) the name and address of each entity having an interest in the cash collateral; (3) the name and address of the entity in control or having possession of the cash collateral; (4) the facts demonstrating the need to use the cash collateral; and (5) the nature of the protection to be provided those having an interest in the cash collateral. If a preliminary hearing is requested, the motion shall also include the amount of cash collateral sought to be used pending final hearing and the protection to be provided.

Notice of the preliminary and final hearings may be combined. This rule does not limit the authority of the court under § 363(c)(2)(B) and § 102(1).

Subdivision (c) is new. The service, hearing, and notice requirements are similar to those imposed by subdivision (b). The motion to obtain credit shall include the amount and type of the credit to be extended, the name and address of the lender, the terms of the agreement, the need to obtain the credit, and the efforts made to obtain credit from other sources. If the motion is to obtain credit pursuant to § 364(c) or (d), the motion shall describe the collateral, if any, and the protection for any existing interest in the collateral which may be affected by the proposed agreement.

Subdivision (d) is new. In the event the 15 day period for filing objections to the approval of an agreement of the parties described in this subdivision is too long, the parties either may move for a reduction of the period under Rule 9006(c)(1) or proceed under subdivision (b) or (c), if applicable. Rule 9006(c)(1) requires that cause be shown for the reduction of the period in which to object. In applying this criterion the court may consider the option of proceeding under subdivision (b) or (c) and grant a preliminary hearing and relief pending final hearing.

1991 Amendments

Subdivision (a) is expanded to include a request to prohibit or condition the use, sale, or lease of property as is necessary to provide adequate protection of a property interest pursuant to § 363(e) of the Code.

Notice of the motion for relief from the automatic stay or to prohibit or condition the use, sale, or lease of property must be served on the entities entitled to receive notice of a motion to approve an agreement pursuant to subdivision (d). If the movant and the adverse party agree to settle the motion and the terms of the agreement do not materially differ from the terms set forth in the movant's motion papers, the court may approve the agreement without further notice pursuant to subdivision (d)(4).

Subdivision (a)(2) is deleted as unnecessary because of § 362(e) of the Code.

Subdivisions (b)(1), (c)(1), and (d)(1) are amended to require service on committees that are elected in chapter 7 cases. Service on committees of retired employees appointed under § 1114 of the Code is not required. These subdivisions are amended further to clarify that, in the absence of a creditors' committee, service on the creditors included on the list filed pursuant to Rule 1007(d) is required only in chapter 9 and chapter 11 cases. The other amendments to subdivision (d)(1) are for consistency of style and are not substantive.

Subdivision (d)(4) is added to avoid the necessity of further notice and delay for the approval of an agreement in settlement of a motion for relief from an automatic stay, to prohibit or condition the use, sale, or lease of property, for use of cash collateral, or for authority to obtain credit if the entities entitled to notice have already received sufficient notice of the scope of the proposed agreement in the motion papers and have had an opportunity to be heard. For example, if a trustee makes a motion to use cash collateral and proposes in the original motion papers to provide adequate protection of the interest of the secured party by granting a lien on certain equipment, and the secured creditor subsequently agrees to terms that are within the scope of those proposed in the motion, the court may enter an order approving the agreement without further notice if the entities that received the original motion papers have had a reasonable opportunity to object to the granting of the motion to use cash collateral.

If the motion papers served under subdivision (a), (b), or (c) do not afford notice sufficient to inform the recipients of the material provisions of the proposed agreement and opportunity for a hearing, approval of the settlement agreement may not be obtained unless the procedural requirements of subdivision (d)(1), (d)(2), and (d)(3) are satisfied. If the 15 day period for filing objections to the approval of the settlement agreement is too long under the particular circumstances of the case, the court may shorten the time for cause under Rule 9006(c)(1).

1999 Amendments

Paragraph (a)(3) is added to provide sufficient time for a party to request a stay pending appeal of an order granting relief from an automatic stay before the order is enforced or implemented. The stay under paragraph (a)(3) is not applicable to orders granted ex parte in accordance with Rule 4001(a)(2).

The stay of the order does not affect the time for filing a notice of appeal in accordance with Rule 8002. While the enforcement and implementation of an order granting relief from the automatic stay is temporarily stayed under paragraph (a)(3), the automatic stay continues to protect the debtor, and the moving party may not foreclose on collateral or take any other steps that would violate the automatic stay.

The court may, in its discretion, order that Rule 4001(a)(3) is not applicable so that the prevailing party may immediately enforce and implement the order granting relief from the automatic stay. Alternatively, the court may order that the stay under Rule 4001(a)(3) is for a fixed period less than 10 days.

Gap Report on Rule 4001. No changes since publication.

2007 Amendments

The rule is amended to require that parties seeking authority to use cash collateral, to obtain credit, and to obtain approval of agreements to provide adequate protection, modify or terminate the stay, or to grant a senior or equal lien on property, submit with those requests a proposed order granting the relief, and that they provide more extensive notice to interested parties of a number of specified terms. The motion must either not exceed five pages in length, or, if it is longer, begin with a concise statement of five pages or less, that summarizes or lists the material provisions and which will assist the court and interested parties in understanding the nature of the relief requested. The concise statement must also set out the location within the documents of the summarized or listed provisions. The parties to agreements and lending offers frequently have concise summaries of their transactions that contain a list of the material provisions of the agreements, even if the agreements themselves are very lengthy. A similar summary should allow the court and interested parties to understand the relief requested.

In addition to the concise statement, the rule requires that motions under subdivisions (c) and (d) state whether the movant is seeking approval of any of the provisions listed in subdivision (c)(1)(B), and where those provisions are located in the documents. The rule is intended to enhance the ability of the court and interested parties to find and evaluate those provisions.

The rule also provides that any motion for authority to obtain credit must identify any provision listed in subdivision (c)(1)(B)(i)-(xi) that is proposed to remain effective if the court grants the motion on an interim basis under Rule 4001 (c)(2), but later denies final relief.

Other amendments are stylistic.

CROSS REFERENCES

Enlargement of thirty-day period after which stay will expire following commencement of final hearing not permitted, see Fed.Rules Bankr.Proc. Rule 9006, 11 USCA.

Extension of time for trustee to redeem debtor's property, see 11 USCA § 108.

Methods for providing adequate protection, see 11 USCA § 361.

Motions—

For relief from stay filed with court in which case is pending, see Fed.Rules Bankr.Proc. Rule 5005, 11 USCA.

Form and service, see Fed.Rules Bankr.Proc. Rule 9013, 11 USCA.

Signing and verification of papers, see Fed.Rules Bankr. Proc. Rule 9011, 11 USCA.

Stay of actions on claims against, codebtor in individual debt adjustment case, see 11 USCA § 1301.

Rule 4002. Duties of Debtor

(a) In general

In addition to performing other duties prescribed by the Code and rules, the debtor shall:

(1) attend and submit to an examination at the times ordered by the court;

(2) attend the hearing on a complaint objecting to discharge and testify, if called as a witness;

(3) inform the trustee immediately in writing as to the location of real property in which the debtor has an interest and the name and address of every person holding money or property subject to the debtor's withdrawal or order if a schedule of property has not yet been filed pursuant to Rule 1007;

(4) cooperate with the trustee in the preparation of an inventory, the examination of proofs of claim, and the administration of the estate; and

(5) file a statement of any change of the debtor's address.

(b) Individual debtor's duty to provide documentation

(1) Personal identification

Every individual debtor shall bring to the meeting of creditors under § 341:

(A) a picture identification issued by a governmental unit, or other personal identifying information that establishes the debtor's identity; and

(B) evidence of social-security number(s), or a written statement that such documentation does not exist.

(2) Financial information

Every individual debtor shall bring to the meeting of creditors under § 341, and make available to the trustee, the following documents or copies of them, or provide a written statement that the documentation does not exist or is not in the debtor's possession:

(A) evidence of current income such as the most recent payment advice;

(B) unless the trustee or the United States trustee instructs otherwise, statements for each of the debtor's depository and investment accounts, including checking, savings, and money market accounts, mutual funds and brokerage accounts for the time period that includes the date of the filing of the petition; and

(C) documentation of monthly expenses claimed by the debtor if required by § 707(b)(2)(A) or (B).

(3) Tax return

At least 7 days before the first date set for the meeting of creditors under § 341, the debtor shall provide to the trustee a copy of the debtor's federal income tax return for the most recent tax year ending immediately before the commencement of the case and for which a return was filed, including any attachments, or a transcript of the tax return, or provide a written statement that the documentation does not exist.

(4) Tax returns provided to creditors

If a creditor, at least 15 days before the first date set for the meeting of creditors under § 341, requests a copy of the debtor's tax return that is to be provided to the trustee under subdivision (b)(3), the debtor, at least 7 days before the first date set for the meeting of creditors under § 341, shall provide to the requesting creditor a copy of the return, including any attachments, or a transcript of the tax return, or provide a written statement that the documentation does not exist.

(5) Confidentiality of tax information

The debtor's obligation to provide tax returns under Rule 4002(b)(3) and (b)(4) is subject to procedures for safeguarding the confidentiality of tax information established by the Director of the Administrative Office of the United States Courts.

(As amended Mar. 30, 1987, eff. Aug. 1, 1987; Apr. 23, 2008, eff. Dec. 1, 2008.)

ADVISORY COMMITTEE NOTES

This rule should be read together with §§ 343 and 521 of the Code and Rule 1007, all of which impose duties on the debtor. Clause (3) of this rule implements the provisions of Rule 2015(a).

1987 Amendments

New clause (5) of the rule imposes on the debtor the duty to advise the clerk of any change of the debtor's address.

2008 Amendments

This rule is amended to implement § 521(a)(1)(B)(iv) and (e)(2), added to the Code by the 2005 amendments. These Code amendments expressly require the debtor to file with the court, or provide to the trustee, specific documents. The amendments to the rule implement these obligations and establish a time frame for creditors to make requests for a copy of the debtor's Federal income tax return. The rule also requires the debtor to provide documentation in support of claimed expenses under § 707(b)(2)(A) and (B).

Subdivision (b) of the rule is also amended to require the debtor to cooperate with the trustee by providing materials and documents necessary to assist the trustee in the performance of the trustee's duties. Nothing in the rule, however, is intended to limit or restrict the debtor's duties under § 521, or to limit the access of the Attorney General to any information provided by the debtor in the case. Subdivision (b)(2) does not require that the debtor create documents or obtain documents from third parties; rather, the debtor's obligation is to bring to the meeting of creditors under § 341 the documents which the debtor possesses. Under subdivision (b)(2)(B), the trustee or the United States trustee can instruct debtors that they need not provide the documents described in that subdivision. Under subdivisions (b)(3) and (b)(4), the debtor must obtain and provide copies of tax returns or tax transcripts to the appropriate person, unless no such documents exist. Any written statement that the debtor provides indicating either that documents do not exist or are not in the debtor's possession must be verified or contain an unsworn declaration as required under Rule 1008.

Because the amendment implements the debtor's duty to cooperate with the trustee, the materials provided to the trustee would not be made available to any other party in interest at the § 341 meeting of creditors other than the Attorney General. Some of the documents may contain otherwise private information that should not be disseminated. For example, pay stubs and financial account statements might include the social-security numbers of the debtor and the debtor's spouse and dependents, as well as the names of the debtor's children. The debtor should redact all but the last four digits of all social-security numbers and the names of any minors when they appear in these documents. This type of information would not usually be needed by creditors and others who may be attending the meeting. If a creditor perceives a need to review specific documents or other evidence, the creditor may proceed under Rule 2004.

Tax information produced under this rule is subject to procedures for safeguarding confidentiality established by the Director of the Administrative Office of the United States Courts.

CROSS REFERENCES

Debtor's duties to—

Appear at meeting of creditors, see 11 USCA § 343.

File list of creditors and assets, cooperate with trustee, and appear at discharge hearing, see 11 USCA § 521.

File lists, schedules, and statements, see Fed.Rules Bankr.Proc. Rule 1007, 11 USCA.

Keep records, make reports, and give notice, see Fed. Rules Bankr.Proc. Rule 2015, 11 USCA.

Immunity from self-incrimination, see 11 USCA § 344.

Rule 4003. Exemptions

(a) Claim of exemptions

A debtor shall list the property claimed as exempt under § 522 of the Code on the schedule of assets required to be filed by Rule 1007. If the debtor fails to claim exemptions or file the schedule within the time specified in Rule 1007, a dependent of the debtor may file the list within 30 days thereafter.

(b) Objecting to a claim of exemptions

(1) Except as provided in paragraphs (2) and (3), a party in interest may file an objection to the list of property claimed as exempt within 30 days after the meeting of creditors held under § 341(a) is concluded or within 30 days after any amendment to the list or supplemental schedules is filed, whichever is later. The court may, for cause, extend the time for filing objections if, before the time to object expires, a party in interest files a request for an extension.

(2) The trustee may file an objection to a claim of exemption at any time prior to one year after the closing of the case if the debtor fraudulently asserted the claim of exemption. The trustee shall deliver or mail the objection to the debtor and the debtor's attorney, and to any person filing the list of exempt property and that person's attorney.

(3) An objection to a claim of exemption based on § 522(q) shall be filed before the closing of the case. If an exemption is first claimed after a case is reopened, an objection shall be filed before the reopened case is closed.

(4) A copy of any objection shall be delivered or mailed to the trustee, the debtor and the debtor's attorney, and the person filing the list and that person's attorney.

(c) Burden of proof

In any hearing under this rule, the objecting party has the burden of proving that the exemptions are not properly claimed. After hearing on notice, the court shall determine the issues presented by the objections.

(d) Avoidance by debtor of transfers of exempt property

A proceeding by the debtor to avoid a lien or other transfer of property exempt under § 522(f) of the Code shall be by motion in accordance with Rule 9014. Notwithstanding the provisions of subdivision (b), a creditor may object to a motion filed under § 522(f) by challenging the validity of the exemption asserted to be impaired by the lien.

(As amended Mar. 30, 1987, eff. Aug. 1, 1987; Apr. 30, 1991, eff. Aug. 1, 1991; Apr. 17, 2000, eff. Dec. 1, 2000; Apr. 23, 2008, eff. Dec. 1, 2008.)

ADVISORY COMMITTEE NOTES

This rule is derived from § 522(*l*) of the Code and, in part, former Bankruptcy Rule 403. The Code changes the thrust of that rule by making it the burden of the debtor to list his exemptions and the burden of parties in interest to raise objections in the absence of which "the property claimed as exempt on such list is exempt;" § 522(*l*).

Subdivision (a). While § 522(*l*) refers to a list of property claimed as exempt, the rule incorporates such a list as part of Official Form No. 6, the schedule of the debtor's assets, rather than requiring a separate list and filing. Rule 1007, to which subdivision (a) refers, requires that schedule to be filed within 15 days after the order for relief, unless the court extends the time.

Section 522(*l*) also provides that a dependent of the debtor may file the list if the debtor fails to do so. Subdivision (a) of the rule allows such filing from the expiration of the debtor's time until 30 days thereafter. Dependent is defined in § 522(a)(1).

Subdivision (d) provides that a proceeding by the debtor, permitted by § 522(f) of the Code, is a contested matter rather than the more formal adversary proceeding. Proceedings within the scope of this subdivision are distinguished from proceedings brought by the trustee to avoid transfers. The latter are classified as adversary proceedings by Rule 7001.

1991 Amendments

Subdivision (b) is amended to facilitate the filing of objections to exemptions claimed on a supplemental schedule filed under Rule 1007(h).

2000 Amendments

This rule is amended to permit the court to grant a timely request for an extension of time to file objections to the list of claimed exemptions, whether the court rules on the request before or after the expiration of the 30–day period. The purpose of this amendment is to avoid the harshness of the present rule which has been construed to deprive a bankruptcy court of jurisdiction to grant a timely request for an extension if it has failed to rule on the request within the 30–day period. See *In re Laurain*, 113 F.3d 595 (6th Cir. 1997); *Matter of Stoulig*, 45 F.3d 957 (5th Cir. 1995); *In re Brayshaw*, 912 F.2d 1255 (10th Cir. 1990). The amendments clarify that the extension may be granted only for cause. The amendments also conform the rule to § 522(*l*) of the Code by recognizing that any party in interest may file an objection or request for an extension of time under this rule. Other amendments are stylistic.

GAP Report on Rule 4003(b). The words "trustee or creditor" were replaced by "party in interest" to conform to § 522(*l*) of the Bankruptcy Code which permits any party in interest to object to claimed exemptions. Style revisions also were made to the published draft.

2008 Amendments

Subdivision (b) is rewritten to include four paragraphs.

Subdivision (b)(2) is added to the rule to permit the trustee to object to an exemption at any time up to one year after the closing of the case if the debtor fraudulently claimed the exemption. Extending the deadline for trustees to object to an exemption when the exemption claim has been fraudulently made will permit the court to review and, in proper circumstances, deny improperly claimed exemptions, thereby protecting the legitimate interests of creditors and the bankruptcy estate. However, similar to the deadline set in § 727(e) of the Code for revoking a discharge which was fraudulently obtained, an objection to an exemption that was fraudulently claimed must be filed within one year after the closing of the case. Subdivision (b)(2) extends the objection deadline only for trustees.

Subdivision (b)(3) is added to the rule to reflect the addition of subsection (q) to § 522 of the Code by the 2005 Act. Section 522(q) imposes a $136,875 limit on a state homestead exemption if the debtor has been convicted of a felony or owes a debt arising from certain causes of action. Other revised provisions of the Code, such as § 727(a)(12) and § 1328(h), suggest that the court may consider issues relating to § 522(q) late in the case, and the 30–day period for objections would not be appropriate for this provision.

Subdivision (d) is amended to clarify that a creditor with a lien on property that the debtor is attempting to avoid on the grounds that the lien impairs an exemption may raise in defense to the lien avoidance action any objection to the debtor's claimed exemption. The right to object is limited to an objection to the exemption of the property subject to the lien and for purposes of the lien avoidance action only. The creditor may not object to other exemption claims made by the debtor. Those objections, if any, are governed by Rule 4003(b).

Other changes are stylistic.

CROSS REFERENCES

Automatic preservation of avoided property transfers for benefit of estate, see 11 USCA § 551.

Enlargement of thirty-day period for filing objections to property claimed as exempt permitted as limited in this rule, see Fed.Rules Bankr.Proc. Rule 9006, 11 USCA.

Motions; form and service, see Fed.Rules Bankr.Proc. Rule 9013, 11 USCA.

Proceedings to avoid transfers of exempt property as nonadversarial proceedings, see Fed.Rules Bankr.Proc. Rule 7001, 11 USCA.

Reduction of time to claim property as exempt by dependent not permitted, see Fed.Rules Bankr.Proc. Rule 9006, 11 USCA.

Right of debtor's redemption of personal property from lien securing dischargeable consumer debt, see 11 USCA § 722.

Rule 4004. Grant or Denial of Discharge

(a) Time for filing complaint objecting to discharge; notice of time fixed

In a chapter 7 liquidation case a complaint objecting to the debtor's discharge under § 727(a) of the Code shall be filed no later than 60 days after the first date set for the meeting of creditors under § 341(a). In a chapter 11 reorganization case, the complaint shall be filed no later than the first date set for the hearing on confirmation. At least 25 days' notice of the time so fixed shall be given to the United States trustee and all creditors as provided in Rule 2002(f) and (k), and to the trustee and the trustee's attorney.

(b) Extension of time

On motion of any party in interest, after hearing on notice, the court may for cause extend the time to file a complaint objecting to discharge. The motion shall be filed before the time has expired.

(c) Grant of discharge

(1) In a chapter 7 case, on expiration of the time fixed for filing a complaint objecting to discharge and the time fixed for filing a motion to dismiss the case under Rule 1017(e), the court shall forthwith grant the discharge unless:

(A) the debtor is not an individual;

(B) a complaint objecting to the discharge has been filed;

(C) the debtor has filed a waiver under § 727(a)(10);

(D) a motion to dismiss the case under § 707 is pending;

(E) a motion to extend the time for filing a complaint objecting to the discharge is pending;

(F) a motion to extend the time for filing a motion to dismiss the case under Rule 1017(e)(1) is pending;

(G) the debtor has not paid in full the filing fee prescribed by 28 U.S.C. § 1930(a) and any other fee prescribed by the Judicial Conference of the United States under 28 U.S.C. § 1930(b) that is payable to the clerk upon the commencement of a case under the Code, unless the court has waived the fees under 28 U.S.C. § 1930(f);

(H) the debtor has not filed with the court a statement of completion of a course concerning personal financial management as required by Rule 1007(b)(7);

(I) a motion to delay or postpone discharge under § 727(a)(12) is pending;

(J) a motion to enlarge the time to file a reaffirmation agreement under Rule 4008(a) is pending;

(K) a presumption has arisen under § 524(m) that a reaffirmation agreement is an undue hardship; or

(L) a motion is pending to delay discharge, because the debtor has not filed with the court all tax documents required to be filed under § 521(f).

(2) Notwithstanding Rule 4004(c)(1), on motion of the debtor, the court may defer the entry of an order granting a discharge for 30 days and, on motion within that period, the court may defer entry of the order to a date certain.

(3) If the debtor is required to file a statement under Rule 1007(b)(8), the court shall not grant a discharge earlier than 30 days after the statement is filed.

(d) Applicability of rules in Part VII

A proceeding commenced by a complaint objecting to discharge is governed by Part VII of these rules.

(e) Order of discharge

An order of discharge shall conform to the appropriate Official Form.

(f) Registration in other districts

An order of discharge that has become final may be registered in any other district by filing a certified copy of the order in the office of the clerk of that district. When so registered the order of discharge shall have the same effect as an order of the court of the district where registered.

(g) Notice of discharge

The clerk shall promptly mail a copy of the final order of discharge to those specified in subdivision (a) of this rule.

(As amended Mar. 30, 1987, eff. Aug. 1, 1987; Apr. 30, 1991, eff. Aug. 1, 1991; Apr. 23, 1996, eff. Dec. 1, 1996; Apr. 29, 1999, eff. Dec. 1, 1999; Apr. 17, 2000, eff. Dec. 1, 2000; Apr. 29, 2002, eff. Dec. 1, 2002; Apr. 23, 2008, eff. Dec. 1, 2008.)

ADVISORY COMMITTEE NOTES

This rule is adapted from former Bankruptcy Rule 404.

Subdivisions (a) and (b) of this rule prescribe the procedure for determining whether a discharge will be granted pursuant to § 727 of the Code. The time fixed by subdivision (a) may be enlarged as provided in subdivision (b).

The notice referred to in subdivision (a) is required to be given by mail and addressed to creditors as provided in Rule 2002.

An extension granted on a motion pursuant to subdivision (b) of the rule would ordinarily benefit only the movant, but its scope and effect would depend on the terms of the extension.

Subdivision (c). If a complaint objecting to discharge is filed, the court's grant or denial of the discharge will be entered at the conclusion of the proceeding as a judgment in accordance with Rule 9021. The inclusion of the clause in subdivision (c) qualifying the duty of the court to grant a discharge when a waiver has been filed is in accord with the construction of the Code. 4 Collier, Bankruptcy ¶727.12 (15th ed. 1979).

The last sentence of subdivision (c) takes cognizance of § 524(c) of the Code which authorizes a debtor to enter into enforceable reaffirmation agreements only prior to entry of the order of discharge. Immediate entry of that order after expiration of the time fixed for filing complaints objecting to discharge may render it more difficult for a debtor to settle pending litigation to determine the dischargeability of a debt and execute a reaffirmation agreement as part of a settlement.

Subdivision (d). An objection to discharge is required to be made by a complaint, which initiates an adversary proceeding as provided in Rule 7003. Pursuant to Rule 5005, the complaint should be filed in the court in which the case is pending.

Subdivision (e). Official Form No. 27 to which subdivision (e) refers, includes notice of the effects of a discharge specified in § 524(a) of the Code.

Subdivision (f). Registration may facilitate the enforcement of the order of discharge in a district other than that in which it was entered. See 2 Moore's Federal Practice ¶1.04[2] (2d ed. 1967). Because of the nationwide service of process authorized by Rule 7004, however, registration of the order of discharge is not necessary under these rules to enable a discharged debtor to obtain relief against a creditor proceeding anywhere in the United States in disregard of the injunctive provisions of the order of discharge.

Subdivision (g). Notice of discharge should be mailed promptly after the order becomes final so that creditors may be informed of entry of the order and of its injunctive provisions. Rule 2002 specifies the manner of the notice and persons to whom the notice is to be given.

1991 Amendments

This rule is amended to conform to § 727(c) which gives the United States trustee the right to object to discharge. This amendment is derived from Rule X–1008(a)(1) and is consistent with Rule 2002. The amendment to subdivision (c) is to prevent a timely motion to dismiss a chapter 7 case for substantial abuse from becoming moot merely because a discharge order has been entered. Reference to the Official Form number in subdivision (e) is deleted in anticipation of future revision and renumbering of the Official Forms.

1996 Amendments

Subsection (c) is amended to delay entry of the order of discharge if a motion pursuant to Rule 4004(b) to extend the time for filing a complaint objecting to discharge is pending. Also, this subdivision is amended to delay entry of the discharge order if the debtor has not paid in full the filing fee and the administrative fee required to be paid upon the commencement of the case. If the debtor is authorized to pay the fees in installments in accordance with Rule 1006, the discharge order will not be entered until the final installment has been paid.

The other amendments to this rule are stylistic.

GAP Report on Rule 4004. No changes have been made since publication, except for stylistic changes.

1999 Amendments

Subdivision (a) is amended to clarify that, in a chapter 7 case, the deadline for filing a complaint objecting to discharge under § 727(a) is 60 days after the first date set for the meeting of creditors, whether or not the meeting is held on that date. The time for filing the complaint is not affected by any delay in the commencement or conclusion of the meeting of creditors. This amendment does not affect the right of any party in interest to file a motion for an extension of time to file a complaint objecting to discharge in accordance with Rule 4004(b).

The substitution of the word "filed" for "made" in subdivision (b) is intended to avoid confusion regarding the time when a motion is "made" for the purpose of applying these rules. *See, e.g., In re Coggin*, 30 F.3d 1443 (11th Cir. 1994). As amended, this rule requires that a motion for an extension of time for filing a complaint objecting to discharge be *filed* before the time has expired.

Other amendments to this rule are stylistic.

Gap Report on Rule 4004. No changes since publication.

2000 Amendments

Subdivision (c) is amended so that a discharge will not be granted while a motion requesting an extension of time to file a motion to dismiss the case under § 707(b) is pending. Other amendments are stylistic.

GAP Report on Rule 4004(c). No changes since publication except for style revisions.

2002 Amendments

Subdivision (c)(1)(D) is amended to provide that the filing of a motion to dismiss under § 707 of the Bankruptcy Code postpones the entry of the discharge. Under the present version of the rule, only motions to dismiss brought under § 707(b) cause the postponement of the discharge. This amendment would change the result in cases such as *In re Tanenbaum*, 210 B.R. 182 (Bankr. D. Colo. 1997).

Changes Made After Publication and Comments. No changes were made.

2008 Amendments

Subdivision (c)(1)(G) is amended to reflect the fee waiver provision in 28 U.S.C. § 1930, added by the 2005 amendments.

Subdivision (c)(1)(H) is new. It reflects the 2005 addition to the Code of §§ 727(a)(11) and 1328(g), which require that individual debtors complete a course in personal financial management as a condition to the entry of a discharge. Including this requirement in the rule helps prevent the inadvertent entry of a discharge when the debtor has not complied with this requirement. If a debtor fails to file the required statement regarding a personal financial management course, the clerk will close the bankruptcy case without the entry of a discharge.

Subdivision (c)(1)(I) is new. It reflects the 2005 addition to the Code of § 727(a)(12). This provision is linked to § 522(q). Section 522(q) limits the availability of the homestead exemption for individuals who have been convicted of a felony or who owe a debt arising from certain causes of action within a particular time frame. The existence of reasonable cause to believe that § 522(q) may be applicable to the debtor constitutes grounds for withholding the discharge.

Subdivision (c)(1)(J) is new. It accommodates the deadline for filing a reaffirmation agreement established by Rule 4008(a).

Subdivision (c)(1)(K) is new. It reflects the 2005 revisions to § 524 of the Code that alter the requirements for approval of reaffirmation agreements. Section 524(m) sets forth circumstances under which a reaffirmation agreement is presumed to be an undue hardship. This triggers an obligation to review the presumption and may require notice and a hearing. Subdivision (c)(1)(J) has been added to prevent the discharge from being entered until the court approves or disapproves the reaffirmation agreement in accordance with § 524(m).

Subdivision (c)(1)(L) is new. It implements § 1228(a) of Public Law Number 109–8, an uncodified provision of the Bankruptcy Abuse Prevention and Consumer Protection Act of 2005, which prohibits entry of a discharge unless required tax documents have been provided to the court.

Subdivision (c)(3) is new. It postpones the entry of the discharge of an individual debtor in a case under chapter 11, 12, or 13 if there is a question as to the applicability of § 522(q) of the Code. The postponement provides an opportunity for a creditor to file a motion to limit the debtor's exemption under that provision.

Other changes are stylistic.

CROSS REFERENCES

Discharge—

Effect of, see 11 USCA § 524.

Exceptions to, see 11 USCA § 523.

Filing complaint to object to discharge, sixty-day period—

Enlargement permitted as limited in this rule, see Fed. Rules Bankr.Proc. Rule 9006, 11 USCA.

Reduction not permitted, see Fed.Rules Bankr.Proc. Rule 9006, 11 USCA.

Motions; form and service, see Fed.Rules Bankr.Proc. Rule 9013, 11 USCA.

Notice by mail—

Order of discharge, see Fed.Rules Bankr.Proc. Rule 2002, 11 USCA.

Time fixed to file complaint objecting to discharge, see Fed.Rules Bankr.Proc. Rule 2002, 11 USCA.

Time for filing complaint in reconverted liquidation case revived or extended as under this rule, see Fed.Rules Bankr. Proc. Rule 1019, 11 USCA.

Transfer of claim before or after proof of claim filed, see Fed.Rules Bankr.Proc. Rule 3001, 11 USCA.

Rule 4005. Burden of Proof in Objecting to Discharge

At the trial on a complaint objecting to a discharge, the plaintiff has the burden of proving the objection.

(As amended Mar. 30, 1987, eff. Aug. 1, 1987.)

ADVISORY COMMITTEE NOTES

This rule does not address the burden of going forward with the evidence. Subject to the allocation by the rule of the initial burden of producing evidence and the ultimate burden of persuasion, the rule leaves to the courts the formulation of rules governing the shift of the burden of going forward with the evidence in the light of considerations such as the difficulty of proving the nonexistence of a fact and of establishing a fact as to which the evidence is likely to be more accessible to the debtor than to the objector. See, e.g., In re Haggerty, 165 F.2d 977, 979–80 (2d Cir. 1948); Federal Provision Co. v. Ershowsky, 94 F.2d 574, 575 (2d Cir.1938); In re Riceputo, 41 F.Supp. 926, 927–28 (E.D.N.Y. 1941).

Rule 4006. Notice of No Discharge

If an order is entered: denying a discharge; revoking a discharge; approving a waiver of discharge; or, in the case of an individual debtor, closing the case without the entry of a discharge, the clerk shall promptly notify all parties in interest in the manner provided by Rule 2002.

(As amended Mar. 30, 1987, eff. Aug. 1, 1987; Apr. 23, 2008, eff. Dec. 1, 2008.)

ADVISORY COMMITTEE NOTES

The suspension by § 108(c) of the Code of the statute of limitations affecting any debt of a debtor terminates within 30 days after the debtor is denied a discharge or otherwise loses his right to a discharge. If, however, a debtor's failure to receive a discharge does not come to the attention of his creditors until after the statutes of limitations have run, the debtor obtains substantially the same benefits from his bankruptcy as a debtor who is discharged.

This rule requires the clerk to notify creditors if a debtor fails to obtain a discharge because a waiver of discharge was filed under § 727(a)(10) or as a result of an order denying or revoking the discharge under § 727(a) or (d).

2008 Amendments

This amendment was necessary because the 2005 amendments to the Code require that individual debtors in a chapter 7 or 13 case complete a course in personal financial management as a condition to the entry of a discharge. If the debtor fails to complete the course, the case may be closed and no discharge will be entered. Reopening the case is governed by § 350 and Rule 5010. The rule is amended to provide notice to parties in interest, including the debtor, that no discharge was entered.

CROSS REFERENCES

Notice by mail, see Fed.Rules Bankr.Proc. Rule 2002, 11 USCA.

Suspension of statute of limitations on debts of debtor, see 11 USCA § 108.

Rule 4007. Determination of Dischargeability of a Debt

(a) Persons entitled to file complaint

A debtor or any creditor may file a complaint to obtain a determination of the dischargeability of any debt.

(b) Time for commencing proceeding other than under § 523(c) of the Code

A complaint other than under § 523(c) may be filed at any time. A case may be reopened without payment of an additional filing fee for the purpose of filing a complaint to obtain a determination under this rule.

(c) Time for filing complaint under § 523(c) in a chapter 7 liquidation, chapter 11 reorganization, chapter 12 family farmer's debt adjustment case, or chapter 13 individual's debt adjustment case; notice of time fixed

Except as otherwise provided in subdivision (d), a complaint to determine the dischargeability of a debt under § 523(c) shall be filed no later than 60 days after the first date set for the meeting of creditors under § 341(a). The court shall give all creditors no less than 30 days' notice of the time so fixed in the manner provided in Rule 2002. On motion of a party in interest, after hearing on notice, the court may for cause extend the time fixed under this subdivision. The motion shall be filed before the time has expired.

(d) Time for filing complaint under § 523(a)(6) in a chapter 13 individual's debt adjustment case; notice of time fixed

On motion by a debtor for a discharge under § 1328(b), the court shall enter an order fixing the time to file a complaint to determine the dischargeability of any debt under § 523(a)(6) and shall give no less than 30 days' notice of the time fixed to all creditors in the manner provided in Rule 2002. On motion of any party in interest, after hearing on notice, the court may for cause extend the time fixed under this subdivision. The motion shall be filed before the time has expired.

(e) Applicability of rules in Part VII

A proceeding commenced by a complaint filed under this rule is governed by Part VII of these rules.

(As amended Mar. 30, 1987, eff. Aug. 1, 1987; Apr. 30, 1991, eff. Aug. 1, 1991; Apr. 29, 1999, eff. Dec. 1, 1999; Apr. 23, 2008, eff. Dec. 1, 2008.)

ADVISORY COMMITTEE NOTES

This rule prescribes the procedure to be followed when a party requests the court to determine dischargeability of a debt pursuant to § 523 of the Code.

Although a complaint that comes within § 523(c) must ordinarily be filed before determining whether the debtor will be discharged, the court need not determine the issues presented by the complaint filed under this rule until the question of discharge has been determined under Rule 4004. A complaint filed under this rule initiates an adversary proceeding as provided in Rule 7003.

Subdivision (b) does not contain a time limit for filing a complaint to determine the dischargeability of a type of debt listed as nondischargeable under § 523(a)(1), (3), (5), (7), (8), or (9). Jurisdiction over this issue on these debts is held concurrently by the bankruptcy court and any appropriate nonbankruptcy forum.

Subdivision (c) differs from subdivision (b) by imposing a deadline for filing complaints to determine the issue of dischargeability of debts set out in § 523(a)(2), (4) or (6) of the Code. The bankruptcy court has exclusive jurisdiction to determine dischargeability of these debts. If a complaint is not timely filed, the debt is discharged. See § 523(c).

Subdivision (e). The complaint required by this subdivision should be filed in the court in which the case is pending pursuant to Rule 5005.

1991 Amendments

Subdivision (a) is amended to delete the words "with the court" as unnecessary. See Rules 5005(a) and 9001(3).

Subdivision (c) is amended to apply in chapter 12 cases the same time period that applies in chapter 7 and 11 cases for filing a complaint under § 523(c) of the Code to determine dischargeability of certain debts. Under § 1228(a) of the Code, a chapter 12 discharge does not discharge the debts specified in § 523(a) of the Code.

1999 Amendments

Subdivision (c) is amended to clarify that the deadline for filing a complaint to determine the dischargeability of a debt under § 523(c) of the Code is 60 days after the first date set for the meeting of creditors, whether or not the meeting is held on that date. The time for filing the complaint is not affected by any delay in the commencement or conclusion of the meeting of creditors. This amendment does not affect the right of any party in interest to file a motion for an extension of time to file a complaint to determine the dischargeability of a debt in accordance with this rule.

The substitution of the word "filed" for "made" in the final sentences of subdivisions (c) and (d) is intended to avoid confusion regarding the time when a motion is "made" for the purpose of applying these rules. *See, e.g., In re Coggin,* 30 F.3d 1443 (11th Cir. 1994). As amended, these subdivisions require that a motion for an extension of time be *filed* before the time has expired.

The other amendments to this rule are stylistic.

Gap Report on Rule 4007. No changes since publication, except for stylistic changes in the heading of Rule 4007(d).

2008 Amendments

Subdivision (c) is amended because of the 2005 amendments to § 1328(a) of the Code. This revision expands the exceptions to discharge upon completion of a chapter 13 plan. Subdivision (c) extends to chapter 13 the same time limits applicable to other chapters of the Code with respect to the two exceptions to discharge that have been added to § 1328(a) and that are within § 523(c).

The amendment to subdivision (d) reflects the 2005 amendments to § 1328(a) that expands the exceptions to discharge upon completion of a chapter 13 plan, including two out of three of the provisions that fall within § 523(c). However, the 2005 revisions to § 1328(a) do not include a reference to § 523(a)(6), which is the third provision to which § 523(c) refers. Thus, subdivision (d) is now limited to that provision.

CROSS REFERENCES

Costs and attorney fees to consumer debtor upon discharge of debt, see 11 USCA § 523.

Effect of dismissal on dischargeability of debt, see 11 USCA § 349.

Filing complaint to determine dischargeability of debt, sixty-day period—

Enlargement permitted as limited in this rule, see Fed. Rules Bankr.Proc. Rule 9006, 11 USCA.

Reduction not permitted, see Fed.Rules Bankr.Proc. Rule 9006, 11 USCA.

Motions; form and service, see Fed.Rules Bankr.Proc. Rule 9013, 11 USCA.

Notice by mail of time fixed to file complaint, see Fed. Rules Bankr.Proc. Rule 2002, 11 USCA.

Time for filing complaint in reconverted liquidation case revived or extended as under this rule, see Fed.Rules Bankr. Proc. Rule 1019, 11 USCA.

Rule 4008. Filing of Reaffirmation Agreement; Statement in Support of Reaffirmation Agreement

(a) Filing of reaffirmation agreement

A reaffirmation agreement shall be filed no later than 60 days after the first date set for the meeting of creditors under § 341(a) of the Code. The court may, at any time and in its discretion, enlarge the time to file a reaffirmation agreement.

(b) Statement in support of reaffirmation agreement

The debtor's statement required under § 524(k)(6)(A) of the Code shall be accompanied by a statement of the total income and expenses stated on schedules I and J. If there is a difference between the total income and expenses stated on those schedules and the statement required under § 524(k)(6)(A), the statement required by this subdivision shall include an explanation of the difference.

(As amended Apr. 30, 1991, eff. Aug. 1, 1991; Apr. 23, 2008, eff. Dec. 1, 2008.)

ADVISORY COMMITTEE NOTES

Section 524(d) of the Code requires the court to hold a hearing to inform an individual debtor concerning the granting or denial of discharge and the law applicable to reaffirmation agreements.

The notice of the § 524(d) hearing may be combined with the notice of the meeting of creditors or entered as a separate order.

The expression "not more than" contained in the first sentence of the rule is for the explicit purpose of requiring the hearing to occur within that time period and cannot be extended.

1991 Amendments

This rule is changed to conform to § 524(d) of the Code as amended in 1986. A hearing under § 524(d) is not mandatory unless the debtor desires to enter into a reaffirmation agreement.

2008 Amendments

This rule is amended to establish a deadline for filing reaffirmation agreements. The Code sets out a number of prerequisites to the enforceability of reaffirmation agreements. Among those requirements, § 524(k)(6)(A) provides that each reaffirmation agreement must be accompanied by a statement indicating the debtor's ability to make the payments called for by the agreement. In the event that this statement reflects an insufficient income to allow payment of the reaffirmed debt, § 524(m) provides that a presumption of undue hardship arises, allowing the court to disapprove the reaffirmation agreement, but only after a hearing conducted prior to the entry of discharge. Rule 4004(c)(1)(K) accommodates this provision by delaying the entry of discharge where a presumption of undue hardship arises. However, in order for that rule to be effective, the reaffirmation agreement itself must be filed before the entry of discharge. Under Rule 4004(c)(1) discharge is to be entered promptly after the expiration of the time for filing a complaint objecting to discharge, which, under Rule 4004(a), is 60 days after the first date set for the meeting of creditors under § 341(a). Accordingly, that date is set as the deadline for filing a reaffirmation agreement.

Any party may file the agreement with the court. Thus, whichever party has a greater incentive to enforce the agreement usually will file it. In the event that the parties are unable to file a reaffirmation agreement in a timely fashion, the rule grants the court broad discretion to permit a late filing. A corresponding change to Rule 4004(c)(1)(J) accommodates such an extension by providing for a delay in the entry of discharge during the pendency of a motion to extend the time for filing a reaffirmation agreement.

Rule 4008 is also amended by deleting provisions regarding the timing of any reaffirmation and discharge hearing. As noted above, § 524(m) itself requires that hearings on undue hardship be conducted prior to the entry of discharge. In other respects, including hearings to approve reaffirmation agreements of unrepresented debtors under § 524(c)(6), the rule leaves discretion to the court to set the hearing at a time appropriate for the particular circumstances presented in the case and consistent with the scheduling needs of the parties.

CROSS REFERENCES

Confirmation of reorganization plan, see Fed.Rules Bankr. Proc. Rule 3020, 11 USCA.

Motions; form and service, see Fed.Rules Bankr.Proc. Rule 9013, 11 USCA.

PART V—BANKRUPTCY COURTS AND CLERKS

Rule 5001. Courts and Clerks' Offices

(a) Courts always open

The courts shall be deemed always open for the purpose of filing any pleading or other proper paper, issuing and returning process, and filing, making, or entering motions, orders and rules.

(b) Trials and hearings; orders in chambers

All trials and hearings shall be conducted in open court and so far as convenient in a regular court room. Except as otherwise provided in 28 U.S.C. § 152(c), all other acts or proceedings may be done or conducted by a judge in chambers and at any place either within or without the district; but no hearing, other than one ex parte, shall be conducted outside the district without the consent of all parties affected thereby.

(c) Clerk's office

The clerk's office with the clerk or a deputy in attendance shall be open during business hours on all days except Saturdays, Sundays and the legal holidays listed in Rule 9006(a).

(As amended Mar. 30, 1987, eff. Aug. 1, 1987; Apr. 30, 1991, eff. Aug. 1, 1991; Apr. 23, 2008, eff. Dec. 1, 2008.)

ADVISORY COMMITTEE NOTES

This rule is adapted from subdivisions (a), (b) and (c) of Rule 77 F.R.Civ.P.

1987 Amendments

Rule 9001, as amended, defines court to mean the bankruptcy judge or district judge before whom a case or proceeding is pending. Clerk means the bankruptcy clerk, if one has been appointed for the district; if a bankruptcy clerk has not been appointed, clerk means clerk of the district court.

1991 Amendments

Subdivision (c) is amended to refer to Rule 9006(a) for a list of legal holidays. Reference to F.R.Civ.P. is not necessary for this purpose.

2008 Amendments

The rule is amended to permit bankruptcy judges to hold hearings outside of the district in which the case is pending to the extent that the circumstances lead to the authorization of the court to take such action under the 2005 amendment to 28 U.S.C. § 152(c). Under that provision, bankruptcy judges may hold court outside of their districts in emergency situations and when the business of the court otherwise so requires. This amendment to the rule is intended to implement the legislation.

CROSS REFERENCES

Legal holiday defined, see Fed.Rules Bankr.Proc. Rule 9006, 11 USCA.

Rule 5002. Restrictions on Appointments

(a) Approval of appointment of relatives prohibited

The appointment of an individual as a trustee or examiner pursuant to § 1104 of the Code shall not be approved by the court if the individual is a relative of the bankruptcy judge approving the appointment or the United States trustee in the region in which the case is pending. The employment of an individual as attorney, accountant, appraiser, auctioneer, or other professional person pursuant to §§ 327, 1103, or 1114 shall not be approved by the court if the individual is a relative of the bankruptcy judge approving the employment. The employment of an individual as attorney, accountant, appraiser, auctioneer, or other professional person pursuant to §§ 327, 1103, or 1114 may be approved by the court if the individual is a relative of the United States trustee in the region in which the case is pending, unless the court finds that the relationship with the United States trustee renders the employment improper under the circumstances of the case. Whenever under this subdivision an individual may not be approved for appointment or employment, the individual's firm, partnership, corporation, or any other form of business association or relationship, and all members, associates and professional employees thereof also may not be approved for appointment or employment.

(b) Judicial determination that approval of appointment or employment is improper

A bankruptcy judge may not approve the appointment of a person as a trustee or examiner pursuant to § 1104 of the Code or approve the employment of a person as an attorney, accountant, appraiser, auctioneer, or other professional person pursuant to §§ 327, 1103, or 1114 of the Code if that person is or has been so connected with such judge or the United States trustee as to render the appointment or employment improper.

(As amended Apr. 29, 1985, eff. Aug. 1, 1985; Apr. 30, 1991, eff. Aug. 1, 1991.)

ADVISORY COMMITTEE NOTES

This rule is adapted from former Bankruptcy Rule 505(a). The scope of the prohibition on appointment or employment is expanded to include an examiner appointed under § 1104 of the Code and attorneys and other professional persons whose employment must be approved by the court under § 327 or § 1103.

The rule supplements two statutory provisions. Under 18 U.S.C. § 1910, it is a criminal offense for a judge to appoint a relative as a trustee and, under 28 U.S.C. § 458, a person may not be "appointed to or employed in any office or duty in any court" if he is a relative of any judge of that court. The rule prohibits the appointment or employment of a relative of a bankruptcy judge in a case pending before that bankruptcy judge or before other bankruptcy judges sitting within the district.

A relative is defined in § 101(34) of the Code to be an "individual related by affinity or consanguinity within the third degree as determined by the common law, or individual in a step or adoptive relationship within such third degree." Persons within the third degree under the common law system are as follows: first degree—parents, brothers and sisters, and children; second degree—grandparents, uncles and aunts, first cousins, nephews and nieces, and grandchildren; third degree—great grandparents, great uncles and aunts, first cousins once removed, second cousins, grand nephews and nieces, great grandchildren. Rule 9001 incorporates the definitions of § 101 of the Code.

In order for the policy of this rule to be meaningfully implemented, it is necessary to extend the prohibition against appointment or employment to the firm or other business association of the ineligible person and to those affiliated with the firm or business association. "Firm" is defined in Rule 9001 to include a professional partnership or corporation of attorneys or accountants. All other types of business and professional associations and relationships are covered by this rule.

1985 Amendments

The amended rule is divided into two subdivisions. Subdivision (a) applies to relatives of bankruptcy judges and subdivision (b) applies to persons who are or have been connected with bankruptcy judges. Subdivision (a) permits no judicial discretion; subdivision (b) allows judicial discretion. In both subdivisions of the amended rule "bankruptcy judge" has been substituted for "judge." The amended rule makes clear that it only applies to relatives of, or persons connected with, the bankruptcy judge. *See In re Hilltop Sand and Gravel, Inc.*, 35 B.R. 412 (N.D.Ohio 1983).

Subd. (a). The original rule prohibited all bankruptcy judges in a district from appointing or approving the employment of (i) a relative of any bankruptcy judge serving in the district, (ii) the firm or business association of any ineligible relative and (iii) any member or professional employee of the firm or business association of an ineligible relative. In addition, the definition of relative, the third degree relationship under the common law, is quite broad. The restriction on the employment opportunities of relatives of bankruptcy judges was magnified by the fact that many law and accounting firms have practices and offices spanning the nation.

Relatives are not eligible for appointment or employment when the bankruptcy judge to whom they are related makes the appointment or approves the employment. Canon 3(b)(4) of the Code of Judicial Conduct, which provides that the judge "shall exercise his power of appointment only on the basis of merit, avoiding nepotism and favoritism," should guide a bankruptcy judge when a relative of a judge of the same bankruptcy court is considered for appointment or employment.

Subd. (b), derived from clause (2) of the original rule, makes a person ineligible for appointment or employment if the person is so connected with a bankruptcy judge making the appointment or approving the employment as to render the appointment or approval of employment improper. The caption and text of the subdivision emphasize that application of the connection test is committed to the sound discretion of the bankruptcy judge who is to make the appointment or approve the employment. All relevant circumstances are to be taken into account by the court. The most important of those circumstances include: the nature and duration of the connection with the bankruptcy judge; whether the connection still exists, and, if not, when it was terminated; and the type of appointment or employment. These and other considerations must be carefully evaluated by the bankruptcy judge.

The policy underlying subdivision (b) is essentially the same as the policy embodied in the Code of Judicial Conduct. Canon 2 of the Code of Judicial Conduct instructs a judge to avoid impropriety and the appearance of impropriety, and Canon 3(b)(4) provides that the judge "should exercise his power of appointment only on the basis of merit, avoiding nepotism and favoritism." Subdivision (b) alerts the potential appointee or employee and party seeking approval of employment to consider the possible relevance or impact of subdivision (b) and indicates to them that appropriate disclosure must be made to the bankruptcy court before accepting appointment or employment. The information required may be made a part of the application for approval of employment. See Rule 2014(a).

Subdivision (b) departs from the former rule in an important respect: a firm or business association is not prohibited from appointment or employment merely because an individual member or employee of the firm or business association is ineligible under subdivision (b).

The emphasis given to the bankruptcy court's judicial discretion in applying subdivision (b) and the absence of a *per se* extension of ineligibility to the firm or business association or any ineligible individual complement the amendments to subdivision (a). The change is intended to moderate the prior limitation on the employment opportunities of attorneys, accountants and other professional persons who are or who have been connected in some way with the bankruptcy judge. For example, in all but the most unusual situations service as a law clerk to a bankruptcy judge is not the type of connection which alone precludes appointment or employment. Even if a bankruptcy judge determines that it is improper to appoint or approve the employment of a former law clerk in the period immediately after completion of the former law clerk's service with the judge, the firm which employs the former law clerk will, absent other circumstances, be eligible for employment. In each instance all the facts must be considered by the bankruptcy judge.

Subdivision (b) applies to persons connected with a bankruptcy judge. "Person" is defined in § 101 of the Bankruptcy Code to include an "individual, partnership and corporation." A partnership or corporation may be appointed or employed to serve in a bankruptcy case. If a bankruptcy judge is connected in some way with a partnership or corporation, it is necessary for the court to determine whether the appointment or employment of that partnership or corporation is proper.

The amended rule does not regulate professional relationships which do not require approval of a bankruptcy judge. Disqualification of the bankruptcy judge pursuant to 28 U.S.C. § 455 may, however, be appropriate. Under Rule 5004(a), a bankruptcy judge may find that disqualification from only some aspect of the case, rather than the entire case, is necessary. A situation may also arise in which the disqualifying circumstance only comes to light after services have been performed. Rule 5004(b) provides that if compensation from the estate is sought for these services, the bankruptcy judge is disqualified from awarding compensation.

1991 Amendments

The 1986 amendments to the Code provide that the United States trustee shall appoint trustees in chapter 7, chapter 12, and chapter 13 cases without the necessity of court approval. This rule is not intended to apply to the appointment of trustees in those cases because it would be inappropriate for a court rule to restrict in advance the exercise of discretion by the executive branch. See COMMITTEE NOTE to Rule 2009.

In chapter 11 cases, a trustee or examiner is appointed by the United States trustee after consultation with parties in interest and subject to court approval. Subdivision (a), as amended, prohibits the approval of the appointment of an individual as a trustee or examiner if the person is a relative of the United States trustee making the appointment or the bankruptcy judge approving the appointment.

The United States trustee neither appoints nor approves the employment of professional persons employed pursuant to §§ 327, 1103, or 1114 of the Code. Therefore, subdivision (a) is not a prohibition against judicial approval of employment of a professional person who is a relative of the United States trustee. However, the United States trustee monitors applications for compensation and reimbursement of expenses and may raise, appear and be heard on issues in the case. Employment of relatives of the United States trustee may be approved unless the court finds, after considering the relationship and the particular circumstances of the case, that the relationship would cause the employment to be improper. As used in this rule, "improper" includes the appearance of impropriety.

United States trustee is defined to include a designee or assistant United States trustee. See Rule 9001. Therefore, subdivision (a) is applicable if the person appointed as trustee or examiner or the professional to be employed is a relative of a designee of the United States trustee or any assistant United States trustee in the region in which the case is pending.

This rule is not exclusive of other laws or rules regulating ethical conduct. See, e.g., 28 CFR § 45.735–5.

CROSS REFERENCES

Appointment of trustee or examiner, see 11 USCA § 1104.

Definition of relative, see 11 USCA § 101.

Nepotism in appointment of receiver or trustee, see 18 USCA § 1910.

Relative of justice or judge ineligible to appointment, see 28 USCA § 458.

Rule 5003. Records Kept By the Clerk

(a) Bankruptcy dockets

The clerk shall keep a docket in each case under the Code and shall enter thereon each judgment, order, and activity in that case as prescribed by the Director of the Administrative Office of the United States Courts. The entry of a judgment or order in a docket shall show the date the entry is made.

(b) Claims register

The clerk shall keep in a claims register a list of claims filed in a case when it appears that there will be a distribution to unsecured creditors.

(c) Judgments and orders

The clerk shall keep, in the form and manner as the Director of the Administrative Office of the United States Courts may prescribe, a correct copy of every final judgment or order affecting title to or lien on real property or for the recovery of money or property, and any other order which the court may direct to be kept. On request of the prevailing party, a correct copy of every judgment or order affecting title to or lien upon real or personal property or for the recovery of money or property shall be kept and indexed with the civil judgments of the district court.

(d) Index of cases; certificate of search

The clerk shall keep indices of all cases and adversary proceedings as prescribed by the Director of the Administrative Office of the United States Courts. On request, the clerk shall make a search of any index and papers in the clerk's custody and certify whether a case or proceeding has been filed in or transferred to the court or if a discharge has been entered in its records.

(e) Register of mailing addresses of federal and state governmental units and certain taxing authorities

The United States or the state or territory in which the court is located may file a statement designating its mailing address. The United States, state, territory, or local governmental unit responsible for collecting taxes within the district in which the case is pending may also file a statement designating an address for service of requests under § 505(b) of the Code, and the designation shall describe where further information concerning additional requirements for filing such requests may be found. The clerk shall keep, in the form and manner as the Director of the Administrative Office of the United States Courts may prescribe, a register that includes the mailing addresses designated under the first sentence of this subdivision, and a separate register of the addresses designated for the service of requests under § 505(b) of the Code. The clerk is not required to include in any single register more than one mailing address for each department, agency, or instrumentality of the United States or the state or territory. If more than one address for a department, agency, or instrumentality is included in the register, the clerk shall also include information that would enable a user of the register to determine the circumstances when each address is applicable, and mailing notice to only one applicable address is sufficient to provide effective notice. The clerk shall update the register annually, effective January 2 of each year. The mailing address in the register is conclusively presumed to be a proper address for the governmental unit, but the failure to use that mailing address does not invalidate any notice that is otherwise effective under applicable law.

(f) Other books and records of the clerk

The clerk shall keep any other books and records required by the Director of the Administrative Office of the United States Courts.

(As amended Mar. 30, 1987, eff. Aug. 1, 1987; Apr. 17, 2000, Dec. 1, 2000; Apr. 23, 2008, eff. Dec. 1, 2008.)

ADVISORY COMMITTEE NOTES

This rule consolidates former Bankruptcy Rules 504 and 507. The record-keeping duties of the referee under former Bankruptcy Rule 504 are transferred to the clerk. Subdivisions (a), (c), (d) and (e) are similar to subdivisions (a)–(d) of Rule 79 F.R.Civ.P.

Subdivision (b) requires that filed claims be listed on a claims register only when there may be a distribution to unsecured creditors. Compilation of the list for no asset or nominal asset cases would serve no purpose.

Rule 2013 requires the clerk to maintain a public record of fees paid from the estate and an annual summary thereof.

Former Bankruptcy Rules 507(d) and 508, which made materials in the clerk's office and files available to the public, are not necessary because § 107 of the Code guarantees public access to files and dockets of cases under the Code.

1987 Amendments

Subdivision (a) has been made more specific.

Subdivision (c) is amended to require that on the request of the prevailing party the clerk of the district court shall keep and index bankruptcy judgments and orders affecting title to or lien upon real or personal property or for the recovery of money or property with the civil judgments of the district court. This requirement is derived from former Rule 9021(b). The Director of the Administrative Office will provide guidance to the bankruptcy and district court clerks regarding appropriate paperwork and retention procedures.

2000 Amendments

Subdivision (e) is added to provide a source where debtors, their attorneys, and other parties may go to determine whether the United States or the state or territory in which the court is located has filed a statement designating a mailing address for notice purposes. By using the address in the register—which must be available to the public—the sender is assured that the mailing address is proper. But the use of an address that differs from the address included in the register does not invalidate the notice if it is otherwise effective under applicable law.

The register may include a separate mailing address for each department, agency, or instrumentality of the United States or the state or territory. This rule does not require that addresses of municipalities or other local governmental units be included in the register, but the clerk may include them.

Although it is important for the register to be kept current, debtors, their attorneys, and other parties should be able to rely on mailing addresses listed in the register without the need to continuously inquire as to new or amended addresses. Therefore, the clerk must update the register, but only once each year.

To avoid unnecessary cost and burden on the clerk and to keep the register a reasonable length, the clerk is not required to include more than one mailing address for a particular agency, department, or instrumentality of the United States or the state or territory. But if more than one address is included, the clerk is required to include information so that a person using the register could determine when each address should be used. In any event, the inclusion of more than one address for a particular department, agency, or instrumentality does not impose on a person sending a notice the duty to send it to more than one address.

GAP Report on Rule 5003. No changes since publication.

2008 Amendments

The rule is amended to implement § 505(b)(1) of the Code added by the 2005 amendments, which allows a taxing authority to designate an address to use for the service of requests under that subsection. Under the amendment, the clerk is directed to maintain a separate register for mailing addresses of governmental units solely for the service of requests under § 505(b). This register is in addition to the register of addresses of governmental units already maintained by the clerk. The clerk is required to keep only one address for a governmental unit in each register.

CROSS REFERENCES

Books and records kept by Clerk and entries therein, see Fed.Rules Civ.Proc. Rule 79, 28 USCA.

Judgment effective when entered as provided in this rule, see Fed.Rules Bankr.Proc. Rule 9021, 11 USCA.

Public access to case dockets, see 11 USCA § 107.

Public record of estate fees to be kept by clerk, see Fed.Rules Bankr.Proc. Rule 2013, 11 USCA.

Rule 5004. Disqualification

(a) Disqualification of judge

A bankruptcy judge shall be governed by 28 U.S.C. § 455, and disqualified from presiding over the proceeding or contested matter in which the disqualifying circumstances [1] arises or, if appropriate, shall be disqualified from presiding over the case.

(b) Disqualification of judge from allowing compensation

A bankruptcy judge shall be disqualified from allowing compensation to a person who is a relative of the bankruptcy judge or with whom the judge is so connected as to render it improper for the judge to authorize such compensation.

(As amended Apr. 29, 1985, eff. Aug. 1, 1985; Mar. 30, 1987, eff. Aug. 1, 1987.)

[1] So in original. Probably should be "circumstance".

ADVISORY COMMITTEE NOTES

Subdivision (a). Disqualification of a bankruptcy judge is governed by 28 U.S.C. § 455. That section provides that the judge "shall disqualify himself in any proceeding in which his impartiality might reasonably be questioned" or under certain other circumstances. In a case under the Code it is possible that the disqualifying circumstance will be isolated to an adversary proceeding or contested matter. The rule makes it clear that when the disqualifying circumstance is limited in that way the judge need only disqualify himself from presiding over that adversary proceeding or contested matter.

It is possible, however, that even if the disqualifying circumstance arises in connection with an adversary proceeding, the effect will be so pervasive that disqualification from presiding over the case is appropriate. This distinction is consistent with the definition of "proceeding" in 28 U.S.C. § 455(d)(1).

Subdivision (b) precludes a bankruptcy judge from allowing compensation from the estate to a relative or other person closely associated with the judge. The subdivision applies where the judge has not appointed or approved the employment of the person requesting compensation. Perhaps the most frequent application of the subdivision will be in the allowance of administrative expenses under § 503(b)(3) to (5) of the Code. For example, if an attorney or accountant is retained by an indenture trustee who thereafter makes a substantial contribution in a chapter 11 case, the attorney or accountant may seek compensation under § 503(b)(4). If the attorney or accountant is a relative of or associated with the bankruptcy judge, the judge may not allow compensation to the attorney or accountant. Section 101(34) defines relative and Rule 9001 incorporates the definitions of the Code. See the Advisory Committee's Note to Rule 5002.

1987 Amendments

The rule is amended to be gender neutral. The bankruptcy judge before whom the matter is pending determines whether disqualification is required.

1985 Amendments

Subdivision (a) was affected by the Bankruptcy Amendments and Federal Judgeship Act of 1984, P.L. 98–353, 98 Stat. 333. The 1978 Bankruptcy Reform Act, P.L. 95–598, included bankruptcy judges in the definition of United States judges in 28 U.S.C. § 451 and they were therefore subject to the provisions of 28 U.S.C. § 455. This was to become effective on April 1, 1984, P.L. 95–598, § 404(b). Section 113 of P.L. 98–353, however, appears to have rendered the amendment to 28 U.S.C. § 451 ineffective. Subdivision (a) of the rule retains the substance and intent of the earlier draft by making bankruptcy judges subject to 28 U.S.C. § 455.

The word "associated" in subdivision (b) has been changed to "connected" in order to conform with Rule 5002(b).

CROSS REFERENCES

Definition of relative, see 11 USCA § 101.

Prohibited appointments, see Fed.Rules Bankr.Proc. Rule 5002, 11 USCA.

Rule 5005. Filing and Transmittal of Papers

(a) Filing

(1) Place of filing

The lists, schedules, statements, proofs of claim or interest, complaints, motions, applications, objections and other papers required to be filed by these rules, except as provided in 28 U.S.C. § 1409, shall be filed with the clerk in the district where the case under the Code is pending. The judge of that court may permit the papers to be filed with the judge, in which event the filing date shall be noted thereon, and they shall be forthwith transmitted to the clerk. The clerk shall not refuse to accept for filing any petition or other paper presented for the purpose of filing solely because it is not presented in proper form as required by these rules or any local rules or practices.

(2) Filing by electronic means

A court may by local rule permit or require documents to be filed, signed, or verified by electronic means that are consistent with technical standards, if any, that the Judicial Conference of the United States establishes. A local rule may require filing by electronic means only if reasonable exceptions are allowed. A document filed by electronic means in compliance with a local rule constitutes a written paper for the purpose of applying these rules, the Federal Rules of Civil Procedure made applicable by these rules, and § 107 of the Code.

(b) Transmittal to the United States trustee

(1) The complaints, motions, applications, objections and other papers required to be transmitted to the United States trustee by these rules shall be mailed or delivered to an office of the United States trustee, or to another place designated by the United States trustee, in the district where the case under the Code is pending.

(2) The entity, other than the clerk, transmitting a paper to the United States trustee shall promptly file as proof of such transmittal a verified statement identifying the paper and stating the date on which it was transmitted to the United States trustee.

(3) Nothing in these rules shall require the clerk to transmit any paper to the United States trustee if the United States trustee requests in writing that the paper not be transmitted.

(c) Error in filing or transmittal

A paper intended to be filed with the clerk but erroneously delivered to the United States trustee, the trustee, the attorney for the trustee, a bankruptcy judge, a district judge, the clerk of the bankruptcy appellate panel, or the clerk of the district court shall, after the date of its receipt has been noted thereon, be transmitted forthwith to the clerk of the bankruptcy court. A paper intended to be transmitted to the United States trustee but erroneously delivered to the clerk, the trustee, the attorney for the trustee, a bankruptcy judge, a district judge, the clerk of the bankruptcy appellate panel, or the clerk of the district court shall, after the date of its receipt has been noted thereon, be transmitted forthwith to the United States trustee. In the interest of justice, the court may order that a paper erroneously delivered shall be deemed filed with the clerk or transmitted to the United States trustee as of the date of its original delivery.

(As amended Mar. 30, 1987, eff. Aug. 1, 1987 ; Apr. 30, 1991, eff. Aug. 1, 1991; Apr. 22, 1993, eff. Aug. 1, 1993; Apr. 23, 1996, eff. Dec. 1, 1996; Apr. 12, 2006, eff. Dec. 1, 2006.)

ADVISORY COMMITTEE NOTES

Subdivision (a) is an adaptation of Rule 5(e) F.R.Civ.P. §§ 301–304 of the Code and Rules 1002 and 1003 require that cases under the Code be commenced by filing a petition "with the bankruptcy court." Other sections of the Code and other rules refer to or contemplate filing but there is no specific reference to filing with the bankruptcy court. For example, § 501 of the Code requires filing of proofs of claim and Rule 3016(c) requires the filing of a disclosure statement. This subdivision applies to all situations in which filing is required. Except when filing in another district is authorized by 28 U.S.C. § 1473, all papers, including complaints commencing adversary proceedings, must be filed in the court where the case under the Code is pending.

Subdivision (b) is the same as former Bankruptcy Rule 509(c).

1987 Amendments

Subdivision (a) is amended to conform with the 1984 amendments.

1991 Amendments

Subdivision (b)(1) is flexible in that it permits the United States trustee to designate a place or places for receiving papers within the district in which the case is pending. Transmittal of papers to the United States trustee may be accomplished by mail or delivery, including delivery by courier, and the technical requirements for service of process are not applicable. Although papers relating to a proceeding commenced in another district pursuant to 28 U.S.C. § 1409 must be filed with the clerk in that district, the papers required to be transmitted to the United States trustee must be mailed or delivered to the United States trustee in the district in which the case under the Code is pending. The United States trustee in the district in which the case is pending monitors the progress of the case and should be informed of all developments in the case wherever the developments take place.

Subdivision (b)(2) requires that proof of transmittal to the United States trustee be filed with the clerk. If papers are served on the United States trustee by mail or otherwise, the filing of proof of service would satisfy the requirements of this subdivision. This requirement enables the court to assure that papers are actually transmitted to the United States trustee in compliance with the rules. When the rules require that a paper be transmitted to the United States trustee and proof of transmittal has not been filed with the clerk, the court should not schedule a hearing or should take other appropriate action to assure that the paper is transmitted to the United States trustee. The filing of the verified statement with the clerk also enables other parties in interest to determine whether a paper has been transmitted to the United States trustee.

Subdivision (b)(3) is designed to relieve the clerk of any obligation under these rules to transmit any paper to the United States trustee if the United States trustee does not wish to receive it.

Subdivision (c) is amended to include the erroneous delivery of papers intended to be transmitted to the United States trustee.

1993 Amendments

Subdivision (a) is amended to conform to the 1991 amendment to Rule 5(e) F.R.Civ.P. It is not a suitable role for the office of the clerk to refuse to accept for filing papers not conforming to requirements of form imposed by these rules or by local rules or practices. The enforcement of these rules and local rules is a role for a judge. This amendment does not require the clerk to accept for filing papers sent to the clerk's office by facsimile transmission.

1996 Amendments

The rule is amended to permit, but not require, courts to adopt local rules that allow filing, signing, or verifying of documents by electronic means. However, such local rules must be consistent with technical standards, if any, promulgated by the Judicial Conference of the United States.

An important benefit to be derived by permitting filing by electronic means is that the extensive volume of paper received and maintained as records in the clerk's office will be reduced substantially. With the receipt of electronic data transmissions by computer, the clerk may maintain records electronically without the need to reproduce them in tangible paper form.

Judicial Conference standards governing the technological aspects of electronic filing will result in uniformity among judicial districts to accommodate an increasingly national bar. By delegating to the Judicial Conference the establishment and future amendment of national standards for electronic filing, the Supreme Court and Congress will be relieved of the burden of reviewing and promulgating detailed rules dealing with complex technological standards. Another reason for leaving to the Judicial Conference the formulation of technological standards for electronic filing is that advances in computer technology occur often, and changes in the technological standards may have to be implemented more frequently than would be feasible by rule amendment under the Rules Enabling Act process.

It is anticipated that standards established by the Judicial Conference will govern technical specifications for electronic data transmission, such as requirements relating to the formatting of data, speed of transmission, means to transmit copies of supporting documentation, and security of communication procedures. In addition, before procedures for electronic filing are implemented, standards must be established to assure the proper maintenance and integrity of the record and to provide appropriate access and retrieval mechanisms. These matters will be governed by local rules until system-wide standards are adopted by the Judicial Conference.

Rule 9009 requires that the Official Forms shall be observed and used "with alterations as may be appropriate." Compliance with local rules and any Judicial Conference standards with respect to the formatting or presentation of electronically transmitted data, to the extent that they do not conform to the Official Forms, would be an appropriate alteration within the meaning of Rule 9009.

These rules require that certain documents be in writing. For example, Rule 3001 states that a proof of claim is a "written statement." Similarly, Rule 3007 provides that an objection to a claim "shall be in writing." Pursuant to the new subdivision (a)(2), any requirement under these rules that a paper be written may be satisfied by filing the document by electronic means, notwithstanding the fact that the clerk neither receives nor prints a paper reproduction of the electronic data.

Section 107(a) of the Code provides that a "paper" filed in a case is a public record open to examination by an entity at reasonable times without charge, except as provided in § 107(b). The amendment to subdivision (a)(2) provides that an electronically filed document is to be treated as such a public record.

Although under subdivision (a)(2) electronically filed documents may be treated as written papers or as signed or verified writings, it is important to emphasize that such treatment is only for the purpose of applying these rules. In addition, local rules and Judicial Conference standards regarding verification must satisfy the requirements of 28 U.S.C. § 1746.

GAP Report on Rule 5005. No changes since publication.

2006 Amendments

Subdivision (a). Amended Rule 5005(a)(2) acknowledges that many courts have required electronic filing by means of a standing order, procedures manual, or local rule. These local practices reflect the advantages that courts and most litigants realize from electronic filings. Courts requiring electronic filing must make reasonable exceptions for persons for whom electronic filing of documents constitutes an unreasonable denial of access to the courts. Experience with the rule will facilitate convergence on uniform exceptions in an amended Rule 5005(a)(2).

Subdivision (c). The rule is amended to include the clerk of the bankruptcy appellate panel among the list of persons required to transmit to the proper person erroneously filed or transmitted papers. The amendment is necessary because the bankruptcy appellate panels were not in existence at the time of the original promulgation of the rule. The amendment also inserts the district judge on the list of persons required to transmit papers intended for the United States trustee but erroneously sent to another person. The district judge is included in the list of persons who must transmit papers to the clerk of the bankruptcy court in the first part of the rule, and there is no reason to exclude the district judge from the list of persons who must transmit erroneously filed papers to the United States trustee.

HISTORICAL NOTES

References in Text

The Federal Rules of Civil Procedure, referred to in subd. (a)(2), are set out in Title 28.

CROSS REFERENCES

Filing of pleadings and other papers with court, see Fed. Rules Civ.Proc. Rule 5, 28 USCA.

Rule 5006. Certification of Copies of Papers

The clerk shall issue a certified copy of the record of any proceeding in a case under the Code or of any paper filed with the clerk on payment of any prescribed fee.

(As amended Apr. 30, 1991, eff. Aug. 1, 1991.)

ADVISORY COMMITTEE NOTES

Fees for certification and copying are fixed by the Judicial Conference under 28 U.S.C. § 1930(b).

Rule 1101 F.R.Evid. makes the Federal Rules of Evidence applicable to cases under the Code. Rule 1005 F.R.Evid. allows the contents of an official record or of a paper filed with the court to be proved by a duly certified copy. A copy certified and issued in accordance with Rule 5006 is accorded authenticity by Rule 902(4) F.R.Evid.

CROSS REFERENCES

Public records, see Fed.Rules Evid. Rule 1005, 28 USCA.

Rule 5007. Record of Proceedings and Transcripts

(a) Filing of record or transcript

The reporter or operator of a recording device shall certify the original notes of testimony, tape recording, or other original record of the proceeding and promptly file them with the clerk. The person preparing any transcript shall promptly file a certified copy.

(b) Transcript fees

The fees for copies of transcripts shall be charged at rates prescribed by the Judicial Conference of the United States. No fee may be charged for the certified copy filed with the clerk.

(c) Admissibility of record in evidence

A certified sound recording or a transcript of a proceeding shall be admissible as prima facie evidence to establish the record.

(As amended Mar. 30, 1987, eff. Aug. 1, 1987; Apr. 30, 1991, eff. Aug. 1, 1991.)

ADVISORY COMMITTEE NOTES

This rule supplements 28 U.S.C. § 773. A record of proceedings before the bankruptcy judge is to be made whenever practicable. By whatever means the record is made, subdivision (a) requires that the preparer of the record certify and file the original notes, tape recording, or other form of sound recording of the proceedings. Similarly, if a transcript is requested, the preparer is to file a certified copy with the clerk.

Subdivision (b) is derived from 28 U.S.C. § 753(f).

Subdivision (c) is derived from former Bankruptcy Rule 511(c). This subdivision extends to a sound recording the same evidentiary status as a transcript under 28 U.S.C. § 773(b).

1991 Amendments

The words "with the clerk" in the final sentence of subdivision (a) are deleted as unnecessary. See Rules 5005(a) and 9001(3).

CROSS REFERENCES

Reporters, see 28 USCA § 753.

Stenographer; stenographic report or transcript as evidence, see Fed.Rules Civ.Proc. Rule 80, 28 USCA.

Rule 5008. Notice Regarding Presumption of Abuse in Chapter 7 Cases of Individual Debtors

If a presumption of abuse has arisen under § 707(b) in a chapter 7 case of an individual with primarily consumer debts, the clerk shall within 10 days after the date of the filing of the petition notify creditors of the presumption of abuse in accordance with Rule 2002. If the debtor has not filed a statement indicating whether a presumption of abuse has arisen, the clerk shall within 10 days after the date of the filing of the petition notify creditors that the debtor has not filed the statement and that further notice will be given if a later filed statement indicates that a presumption of abuse has arisen. If a debtor later files a statement indicating that a presumption of abuse has arisen, the clerk shall notify creditors of the presumption of abuse as promptly as practicable.

(Added Apr. 23, 2008, eff. Dec. 1, 2008.)

ADVISORY COMMITTEE NOTES

2008 Amendments

This rule is new. The 2005 amendments to § 342 of the Code require that clerks give written notice to all creditors not later than 10 days after the date of the filing of the petition that a presumption of abuse has arisen under § 707(b). A statement filed by the debtor will be the source of the clerk's information about the presumption of abuse. This rule enables the clerk to meet its obligation to send the notice within the statutory time period set forth in § 342. In the event that the court receives the debtor's statement after the clerk has sent the first notice, and the debtor's statement indicates a presumption of abuse, the rule requires that the clerk send a second notice.

Rule 5009. Closing Chapter 7 Liquidation, Chapter 12 Family Farmer's Debt Adjustment, and Chapter 13 Individual's Debt Adjustment Cases

If in a chapter 7, chapter 12, or chapter 13 case the trustee has filed a final report and final account and has certified that the estate has been fully administered, and if within 30 days no objection has been filed by the United States trustee or a party in interest, there shall be a presumption that the estate has been fully administered.

(As amended Apr. 30, 1991, eff. Aug. 1, 1991.)

ADVISORY COMMITTEE NOTES

This rule is the same as § 350(a) of the Code. An estate may be closed even though the period allowed by Rule 3002(c) for filing claims has not expired. The closing of a case may be expedited when a notice of no dividends is given under Rule 2002(e). Dismissal of a case for want of prosecution or failure to pay filing fees is governed by Rule 1017.

1991 Amendments

The final report and account of the trustee is required to be filed with the court and the United States trustee under §§ 704(9), 1202(b)(1), and 1302(b)(1) of the Code. This amendment facilitates the United States trustee's performance of statutory duties to supervise trustees and administer cases under chapters 7, 12, and 13 pursuant to 28 U.S.C. § 586. In the absence of a timely objection by the United States trustee or a party in interest, the court may discharge the trustee and close the case pursuant to § 350(a) without the need to review the final report and account or to determine the merits of the trustee's certification that the estate has been fully administered.

Rule 3022 governs the closing of chapter 11 cases.

CROSS REFERENCES

Debtor to succeed to any tax attributes of estate, see 11 USCA § 346.

Dismissal of case; suspension, see Fed.Rules Bankr.Proc. Rule 1017, 11 USCA.

Final decree, see Fed.Rules Bankr.Proc. Rule 3022, 11 USCA.

Postpetition transfers of estate property not avoidable by trustee after case closed, see 11 USCA § 549.

Scheduled property not administered before case closed deemed abandoned, see 11 USCA § 554.

Rule 5010. Reopening Cases

A case may be reopened on motion of the debtor or other party in interest pursuant to § 350(b) of the Code. In a chapter 7, 12, or 13 case a trustee shall not be appointed by the United States trustee unless the court determines that a trustee is necessary to protect the interests of creditors and the debtor or to insure efficient administration of the case.

(As amended Mar. 30, 1987, eff. Aug. 1, 1987; Apr. 30, 1991, eff. Aug. 1, 1991.)

ADVISORY COMMITTEE NOTES

Section 350(b) of the Code provides: "A case may be reopened in the court in which such case was closed to administer assets, to accord relief to the debtor, or for other cause."

Rule 9024, which incorporates Rule 60 F.R.Civ.P., exempts motions to reopen cases under the Code from the one year limitation of Rule 60(b).

Although a case has been closed the court may sometimes act without reopening the case. Under Rule 9024, clerical errors in judgments, orders, or other parts of the record or errors therein caused by oversight or omission may be corrected. A judgment determined to be non-dischargeable pursuant to Rule 4007 may be enforced after a case is closed by a writ of execution obtained pursuant to Rule 7069.

1987 Amendments

In order to avoid unnecessary cost and delay, the rule is amended to permit reopening of a case without the appointment of a trustee when the services of a trustee are not needed.

1991 Amendments

This rule is amended to conform to the 1986 amendments to the Code that give the United States trustee the duty to appoint trustees in chapter 7, 12 and 13 cases. See §§ 701, 702(d), 1202(a), and 1302(a) of the Code. In most reopened cases, a trustee is not needed because there are no assets to be administered. Therefore, in the interest of judicial economy, this rule is amended so that a motion will not be necessary unless the United States trustee or a party in interest seeks the appointment of a trustee in the reopened case.

CROSS REFERENCES

Motions; form and service, see Fed.Rules Bankr.Proc. Rule 9013, 11 USCA.

Relief from judgment or order, see Fed.Rules Bankr.Proc. Rule 9024, 11 USCA.

Rule 5011. Withdrawal and Abstention from Hearing a Proceeding

(a) Withdrawal

A motion for withdrawal of a case or proceeding shall be heard by a district judge.

(b) Abstention from hearing a proceeding

A motion for abstention pursuant to 28 U.S.C. § 1334(c) shall be governed by Rule 9014 and shall be served on the parties to the proceeding.

(c) Effect of filing of motion for withdrawal or abstention

The filing of a motion for withdrawal of a case or proceeding or for abstention pursuant to 28 U.S.C. § 1334(c) shall not stay the administration of the case or any proceeding therein before the bankruptcy judge except that the bankruptcy judge may stay, on such terms and conditions as are proper, proceedings pending disposition of the motion. A motion for a stay ordinarily shall be presented first to the bankruptcy judge. A motion for a stay or relief from a stay filed in the district court shall state why it has not been presented to or obtained from the bankruptcy judge. Relief granted by the district judge shall be on such terms and conditions as the judge deems proper.

(Added Mar. 30, 1987, eff. Aug. 1, 1987 and amended Apr. 30, 1991, eff. Aug. 1, 1991.)

ADVISORY COMMITTEE NOTES

Motions for withdrawal pursuant to 28 U.S.C. § 157(d) or abstention pursuant to 28 U.S.C. § 1334(c), like all other motions, are to be filed with the clerk as required by Rule 5005(a). If a bankruptcy clerk has been appointed for the district, all motions are filed with the bankruptcy clerk. The method for forwarding withdrawal motions to the district court will be established by administrative procedures.

Subdivision (a). Section 157(d) permits the district court to order withdrawal on its own motion or the motion of a party. Subdivision (a) of this rule makes it clear that the bankruptcy judge will not conduct hearings on a withdrawal motion. The withdrawal decision is committed exclusively to the district court.

Subdivision (b). A decision to abstain under 28 U.S.C. § 1334(c) is not appealable. The district court is vested originally with jurisdiction and the decision to relinquish that jurisdiction must ultimately be a matter for the district court. The bankruptcy judge ordinarily will be in the best position to evaluate the grounds asserted for abstention. This subdivision (b) provides that the initial hearing on the motion is before the bankruptcy judge. The procedure for review of the report and recommendation are governed by Rule 9033.

This rule does not apply to motions under § 305 of the Code for abstention from hearing a case. Judicial decisions will determine the scope of the bankruptcy judge's authority under § 305.

Subdivision (c). Unless the court so orders, proceedings are not stayed when motions are filed for withdrawal or for abstention from hearing a proceeding. Because of the district court's authority over cases and proceedings, the subdivision authorizes the district court to order a stay or modify a stay ordered by the bankruptcy judge.

1991 Amendments

Subdivision (b) is amended to delete the restriction that limits the role of the bankruptcy court to the filing of a report and recommendation for disposition of a motion for abstention under 28 U.S.C. § 1334(c)(2). This amendment is consistent with § 309(b) of the Judicial Improvements Act of 1990 which amended § 1334(c(2) so that it allows an appeal to the district court of a bankruptcy court's order determining an abstention motion. This subdivision is also amended to clarify that the motion is a contested matter governed by Rule 9014 and that it must be served on all parties to the proceeding with is the subject of the motion.

PART VI—COLLECTION AND LIQUIDATION OF THE ESTATE

Rule 6001. Burden of Proof as to Validity of Postpetition Transfer

Any entity asserting the validity of a transfer under § 549 of the Code shall have the burden of proof.

ADVISORY COMMITTEE NOTES

This rule is derived from former Bankruptcy Rule 603. The Act contained, in § 70d [former § 110(d) of this title], a provision placing the burden of proof on the same person as did Rule 603. The Code does not contain any directive with respect to the burden of proof. This omission, in all probability, resulted from the intention to leave matters affecting evidence to these rules. See H.Rep. No. 95–595, 95th Cong. 1st Sess. (1977) 293.

Rule 6002. Accounting by Prior Custodian of Property of the Estate

(a) Accounting required

Any custodian required by the Code to deliver property in the custodian's possession or control to the trustee shall promptly file and transmit to the United States trustee a report and account with respect to the property of the estate and the administration thereof.

(b) Examination of administration

On the filing and transmittal of the report and account required by subdivision (a) of this rule and after an examination has been made into the superseded administration, after notice and a hearing, the court shall determine the propriety of the administration, including the reasonableness of all disbursements.

(As amended Mar. 30, 1987, eff. Aug. 1, 1987; Apr. 30, 1991, eff. Aug. 1, 1991; Apr. 22, 1993, eff. Aug. 1, 1993.)

ADVISORY COMMITTEE NOTES

"Custodian" is defined in § 101(10) of the Code. The definition includes a trustee or receiver appointed in proceedings not under the Code, as well as an assignee for the benefit of creditors.

This rule prescribes the procedure to be followed by a custodian who under § 543 of the Code is required to deliver property to the trustee and to account for its disposition. The examination under subdivision (b) may be initiated (1) on the motion of the custodian required to account under subdivision (a) for an approval of his account and discharge thereon, (2) on the motion of, or the filing of an objection to the custodian's account by, the trustee or any other party in interest, or (3) on the court's own initiative. Rule 9014 applies to any contested matter arising under this rule.

Section 543(d) is similar to an abstention provision. It grants the bankruptcy court discretion to permit the custodian to remain in possession and control of the property. In that event, the custodian is excused from complying with § 543(a)(c) and thus would not be required to turn over the property to the trustee. When there is no duty to turn over to the trustee, Rule 6002 would not be applicable.

1991 Amendments

This rule is amended to enable the United States trustee to review, object to, or to otherwise be heard regarding the custodian's report and accounting. See §§ 307 and 543 of the Code.

1993 Amendments

Subdivision (b) is amended to conform to the language of § 102(1) of the Code.

CROSS REFERENCES

Accountability of prior custodians for estate property, see 11 USCA § 543.

Definition of custodian, see 11 USCA § 101.

Proceedings under this rule as nonadversarial proceedings, see Fed.Rules Bankr.Proc. Rule 7001, 11 USCA.

Property of estate, see 11 USCA § 541.

Rule 6003. Interim and Final Relief Immediately Following the Commencement of the Case—Applications for Employment; Motions for Use, Sale, or Lease of Property; and Motions for Assumption or Assignment of Executory Contracts

Except to the extent that relief is necessary to avoid immediate and irreparable harm, the court shall not, within 20 days after the filing of the petition, grant relief regarding the following:

(a) an application under Rule 2014;

(b) a motion to use, sell, lease, or otherwise incur an obligation regarding property of the estate, including a motion to pay all or part of a claim that arose before the filing of the petition, but not a motion under Rule 4001; and

(c) a motion to assume or assign an executory contract or unexpired lease in accordance with § 365.

(Added Apr. 30, 2007, eff. Dec. 1, 2007.)

ADVISORY COMMITTEE NOTES

2007 Adoption

There can be a flurry of activity during the first days of a bankruptcy case. This activity frequently takes place prior to the formation of a creditors' committee, and it also can include substantial amounts of materials for the court and parties in interest to review and evaluate. This rule is intended to alleviate some of the time pressures present at the start of a case so that full and close consideration can be given to matters that may have a fundamental impact on the case.

The rule provides that the court cannot grant relief on applications for the employment of professional persons, motions for the use, sale, or lease of property of the estate other than such a motion under Rule 4001, and motions to assume or assign executory contracts and unexpired leases for the first 20 days of the case, unless granting relief is necessary to avoid immediate and irreparable harm. This standard is taken from Rule 4001(b)(2) and (c)(2), and decisions under those provisions should provide guidance for the application of this provision.

This rule does not govern motions and applications made more than 20 days after the filing of the petition.

Rule 6004. Use, Sale, or Lease of Property

(a) Notice of proposed use, sale, or lease of property

Notice of a proposed use, sale, or lease of property, other than cash collateral, not in the ordinary course of business shall be given pursuant to Rule 2002(a)(2), (c)(1), (i), and (k) and, if applicable, in accordance with § 363(b)(2) of the Code.

(b) Objection to proposal

Except as provided in subdivisions (c) and (d) of this rule, an objection to a proposed use, sale, or lease of property shall be filed and served not less than five days before the date set for the proposed action or within the time fixed by the court. An objection to the proposed use, sale, or lease of property is governed by Rule 9014.

(c) Sale free and clear of liens and other interests

A motion for authority to sell property free and clear of liens or other interests shall be made in accordance with Rule 9014 and shall be served on the parties who have liens or other interests in the property to be sold. The notice required by subdivision (a) of this rule shall include the date of the hearing on the motion and the time within which objections may be filed and served on the debtor in possession or trustee.

(d) Sale of property under $2,500

Notwithstanding subdivision (a) of this rule, when all of the nonexempt property of the estate has an aggregate gross value less than $2,500, it shall be sufficient to give a general notice of intent to sell such property other than in the ordinary course of business to all creditors, indenture trustees, committees appointed or elected pursuant to the Code, the United States trustee and other persons as the court may direct. An objection to any such sale may be filed and served by a party in interest within 15 days of the mailing of the notice, or within the time fixed by the court. An objection is governed by Rule 9014.

(e) Hearing

If a timely objection is made pursuant to subdivision (b) or (d) of this rule, the date of the hearing thereon may be set in the notice given pursuant to subdivision (a) of this rule.

(f) Conduct of sale not in the ordinary course of business

(1) Public or private sale

All sales not in the ordinary course of business may be by private sale or by public auction. Unless it is impracticable, an itemized statement of the property sold, the name of each purchaser, and the price received for each item or lot or for the property as a whole if sold in bulk shall be filed on completion of a sale. If the property is sold by an auctioneer, the auctioneer shall file the statement, transmit a copy thereof to the United States trustee, and furnish a copy to the trustee, debtor in possession, or chapter 13 debtor. If the property is not sold by an auctioneer, the trustee, debtor in possession, or chapter 13 debtor shall file the statement and transmit a copy thereof to the United States trustee.

(2) Execution of instruments

After a sale in accordance with this rule the debtor, the trustee, or debtor in possession, as the case may be, shall execute any instrument necessary or ordered by the court to effectuate the transfer to the purchaser.

(g) Sale of personally identifiable information

(1) Motion

A motion for authority to sell or lease personally identifiable information under § 363(b)(1)(B) shall include a request for an order directing the United States trustee to appoint a consumer privacy ombudsman under § 332. Rule 9014 governs the motion which shall be served on: any committee elected under § 705 or appointed under § 1102 of the Code, or if the case is a chapter 11 reorganization case and no committee of unsecured creditors has been appointed under § 1102, on the creditors included on the list of creditors filed under Rule 1007(d); and on such other entities as the court may direct. The motion shall be transmitted to the United States trustee.

(2) Appointment

If a consumer privacy ombudsman is appointed under § 332, no later than 5 days before the hearing on the motion under § 363(b)(1)(B), the United States trustee shall file a notice of the appointment, including the name and address of the person appointed. The United States trustee's notice shall be accompanied by a verified statement of the person appointed setting forth the person's connections with the debtor, creditors, any other party in interest, their respective attorneys and accountants, the United States trustee, or any person employed in the office of the United States trustee.

(h) Stay of order authorizing use, sale, or lease of property

An order authorizing the use, sale, or lease of property other than cash collateral is stayed until the expiration of 10 days after entry of the order, unless the court orders otherwise.

(As amended Mar. 30, 1987, eff. Aug. 1, 1987; Apr. 30, 1991, eff. Aug. 1, 1991; Apr. 29, 1999, eff. Dec. 1, 1999; Apr. 23, 2008, eff. Dec. 1, 2008.)

ADVISORY COMMITTEE NOTES

Subdivisions (a) and (b). Pursuant to § 363(b) of the Code, a trustee or debtor in possession may use, sell, or lease property other than in the ordinary course of business only after notice and hearing. Rule 2002(a), (c) and (i) specifies the time when notice of sale is to be given, the contents of the notice and the persons to whom notice is to be given of sales of property. Subdivision (a) makes those provisions applicable as well to notices for proposed use and lease of property.

The Code does not provide the time within which parties may file objections to a proposed sale. Subdivision (b) of the rule requires the objection to be in writing and filed not less than five days before the proposed action is to take place. The objection should also be served within that time on the person who is proposing to take the action which would be either the trustee or debtor in possession. This time period is subject to change by the court. In some instances there is a need to conduct a sale in a short period of time and the court is given discretion to tailor the requirements to the circumstances.

Subdivision (c). In some situations a notice of sale for different pieces of property to all persons specified in Rule 2002(a) may be uneconomic and inefficient. This is particularly true in some chapter 7 liquidation cases when there is property of relatively little value which must be sold by the trustee. Subdivision (c) allows a general notice of intent to sell when the aggregate value of the estate's property is less than $2,500. The gross value is the value of the property without regard to the amount of any debt secured by a lien on the property. It is not necessary to give a detailed notice specifying the time and place of a particular sale. Thus, the requirements of Rule 2002(c) need not be met. If this method of providing notice of sales is used, the subdivision specifies that parties in interest may serve and file objections to the proposed sale of any property within the class and the time for service and filing is fixed at not later than 15 days after mailing the notice. The court may fix a different time. Subdivision (c) would have little utility in chapter 11 cases. Pursuant to Rule 2002(i), the court can limit notices of sale to the creditors' committee appointed under § 1102 of the Code and the same burdens present in a small chapter 7 case would not exist.

Subdivision (d). If a timely objection is filed, a hearing is required with respect to the use, sale, or lease of property. Subdivision (d) renders the filing of an objection tantamount to requesting a hearing so as to require a hearing pursuant to §§ 363(b) and 102(1)(B)(i).

Subdivision (e) is derived in part from former Bankruptcy Rule 606(b) but does not carry forward the requirement of that rule that court approval be obtained for sales of property. Pursuant to § 363(b) court approval is not required unless timely objection is made to the proposed sale. The itemized statement or information required by the subdivision is not necessary when it would be impracticable to prepare it or set forth the information. For example, a liquidation sale of retail goods although not in the ordinary course of business may be on a daily ongoing basis and only summaries may be available.

The duty imposed by paragraph (2) does not affect the power of the bankruptcy court to order third persons to execute instruments transferring property purchased at a sale under this subdivision. See, e.g., In re Rosenberg, 138 F.2d 409 (7th Cir. 1943).

1987 Amendments

Subdivision (a) is amended to conform to the 1984 amendments to § 363(b)(2) of the Code.

Subdivision (b) is amended to provide that an objection to a proposed use, sale, or lease of property creates a contested matter governed by Rule 9014. A similar amendment is made to subdivision (d), which was formerly subdivision (c).

Subdivision (c) is new. Section 363(f) provides that sales free and clear of liens or other interests are only permitted if one of the five statutory requirements is satisfied. Rule 9013 requires that a motion state with particularity the grounds relied upon by the movant. A motion for approval of a sale free and clear of liens or other interests is subject to Rule 9014, service must be made on the parties holding liens or other interests in the property, and notice of the hearing on the motion and the time for filing objections must be included in the notice given under subdivision (a).

1991 Amendments

This rule is amended to provide notice to the United States trustee of a proposed use, sale or lease of property not in the ordinary course of business. See Rule 2002(k). Subdivision (f)(1) is amended to enable the United States trustee to monitor the progress of the case in accordance with 28 U.S.C. § 586(a)(3)(G).

The words "with the clerk" in subdivision (f)(1) are deleted as unnecessary. See Rules 5005(a) and 9001(3).

1999 Amendments

Subdivision (g) is added to provide sufficient time for a party to request a stay pending appeal of an order authorizing the use, sale, or lease of property under § 363(b) of the Code before the order is implemented. It does not affect the time for filing a notice of appeal in accordance with Rule 8002.

Rule 6004(g) does not apply to orders regarding the use of cash collateral and does not affect the trustee's right to use, sell, or lease property without a court order to the extent permitted under § 363 of the Code.

The court may, in its discretion, order that Rule 6004(g) is not applicable so that the property may be used, sold, or leased immediately in accordance with the order entered by the court. Alternatively, the court may order that the stay under Rule 6004(g) is for a fixed period less than 10 days.

Gap Report on Rule 6004. No changes since publication.

2008 Amendments

The rule is amended by inserting a new subdivision (g) to implement §§ 332 and 363(b)(1)(B) of the Code, added by the 2005 amendments. This rule governs the proposed transfer of personally identifiable information in a manner inconsistent with any policy covering the transfer of the information. Rule 2002(c)(1) requires the seller to state in the notice of the sale or lease whether the transfer is consistent with and policy governing the transfer of the information.

Under § 332 of the Code, the consumer privacy ombudsman must be appointed at least five days prior to the hearing on a sale or lease of personally identifiable information. In an appropriate case, the consumer privacy ombudsman may seek a continuance of the hearing on the proposed sale to perform the tasks required of the ombudsman by § 332 of the Code.

Former subdivision (g) is redesignated as subdivision (h).

CROSS REFERENCES

Appraisers and auctioneers, see Fed.Rules Bankr.Proc. Rule 6005, 11 USCA.

Authorization to operate debtor's business—

Individual debt adjustment case, see 11 USCA § 1304.

Liquidation case, see 11 USCA § 721.

Reorganization case, see 11 USCA § 1108.

Twenty-day notice of property disposition to include certain information, see Fed.Rules Bankr.Proc. Rule 2002, 11 USCA.

Rule 6005. Appraisers and Auctioneers

The order of the court approving the employment of an appraiser or auctioneer shall fix the amount or rate of compensation. No officer or employee of the Judicial Branch of the United States or the United States Department of Justice shall be eligible to act as appraiser or auctioneer. No residence or licensing requirement shall disqualify an appraiser or auctioneer from employment.

(As amended Mar. 30, 1987, eff. Aug. 1, 1987; Apr. 30, 1991, eff. Aug. 1, 1991.)

ADVISORY COMMITTEE NOTES

This rule is derived from former Bankruptcy Rule 606(c) and implements § 327 of the Code. Pursuant to § 327, the trustee or debtor in possession may employ one or more appraisers or auctioneers, subject to court approval. This rule requires the court order approving such employment to fix the amount or rate of compensation. The second sentence of the former rule is retained to continue to safeguard against imputations of favoritism which detract from public confidence in bankruptcy administration. The final sentence is to guard against imposition of parochial requirements not warranted by any consideration having to do with sound bankruptcy administration.

Reference should also be made to Rule 2013(a) regarding the limitation on employment of appraisers and auctioneers, and Rule 2014(a) regarding the application for appointment of an appraiser or auctioneer.

CROSS REFERENCES

Employment—

Application for, see Fed.Rules Bankr.Proc. Rule 2014, 11 USCA.

Limitation on appointment, see Fed.Rules Bankr.Proc. Rule 2013, 11 USCA.

Professional persons, see 11 USCA § 327.

Sharing of compensation prohibited, see 11 USCA § 504.

Rule 6006. Assumption, Rejection or Assignment of an Executory Contract or Unexpired Lease

(a) Proceeding to assume, reject, or assign

A proceeding to assume, reject, or assign an executory contract or unexpired lease, other than as part of a plan, is governed by Rule 9014.

(b) Proceeding to require trustee to act

A proceeding by a party to an executory contract or unexpired lease in a chapter 9 municipality case, chapter 11 reorganization case, chapter 12 family farmer's debt adjustment case, or chapter 13 individual's debt adjustment case, to require the trustee, debtor in possession, or debtor to determine whether to assume or reject the contract or lease is governed by Rule 9014.

(c) Notice

Notice of a motion made pursuant to subdivision (a) or (b) of this rule shall be given to the other party to the contract or lease, to other parties in interest as the court may direct, and, except in a chapter 9 municipality case, to the United States trustee.

(d) Stay of order authorizing assignment

An order authorizing the trustee to assign an executory contract or unexpired lease under § 365(f) is stayed until the expiration of 10 days after the entry of the order, unless the court orders otherwise.

(e) Limitations

The trustee shall not seek authority to assume or assign multiple executory contracts or unexpired leases in one motion unless: (1) all executory contracts or unexpired leases to be assumed or assigned are between the same parties or are to be assigned to the same assignee; (2) the trustee seeks to assume, but not assign to more than one assignee, unexpired leases of real property; or (3) the court otherwise authorizes the motion to be filed. Subject to subdivision (f), the trustee may join requests for authority to reject multiple executory contracts or unexpired leases in one motion.

(f) Omnibus Motions

A motion to reject or, if permitted under subdivision (e), a motion to assume or assign multiple executory contracts or unexpired leases that are not between the same parties shall:

(1) state in a conspicuous place that parties receiving the omnibus motion should locate their names and their contracts or leases listed in the motion;

(2) list parties alphabetically and identify the corresponding contract or lease;

(3) specify the terms, including the curing of defaults, for each requested assumption or assignment;

(4) specify the terms, including the identity of each assignee and the adequate assurance of future performance by each assignee, for each requested assignment;

(5) be numbered consecutively with other omnibus motions to assume, assign, or reject executory contracts or unexpired leases; and

(6) be limited to no more than 100 executory contracts or unexpired leases.

(g) Finality of Determination

The finality of any order respecting an executory contract or unexpired lease included in an omnibus motion shall be determined as though such contract or lease had been the subject of a separate motion.

(As amended Mar. 30, 1987, eff. Aug. 1, 1987; Apr. 30, 1991, eff. Aug. 1, 1991; Apr. 22, 1993, eff. Aug. 1, 1993; Apr. 29, 1999, eff. Dec. 1, 1999; Apr. 30, 2007, eff. Dec. 1, 2007.)

ADVISORY COMMITTEE NOTES

Section 365(a) of the Code requires court approval for the assumption or rejection of an executory contract by the trustee or debtor in possession. The trustee or debtor in possession may also assign an executory contract, § 365(f)(1), but must first assume the contract, § 365(f)(2). Rule 6006 provides a procedure for obtaining court approval. It does not apply to the automatic rejection of contracts which are not assumed in chapter 7 liquidation cases within 60 days after the order for relief, or to the assumption or rejection of contracts in a plan pursuant to § 1123(b)(2) or § 1322(b)(7).

Subdivision (a) by referring to Rule 9014 requires a motion to be brought for the assumption, rejection, or assignment of an executory contract. Normally, the motion will be brought by the trustee, debtor in possession or debtor in a chapter 9 or chapter 13 case. The authorization to assume a contract and to assign it may be sought in a single motion and determined by a single order.

Subdivision (b) makes applicable the same motion procedure when the other party to the contract seeks to require the chapter officer to take some action. Section 365(d)(2) recognizes that this procedure is available to these contractual parties. This provision of the Code and subdivision of the rule apply only in chapter 9, 11 and 13 cases. A motion is not necessary in chapter 7 cases because in those cases a contract is deemed rejected if the trustee does not timely assume it.

Subdivision (c) provides for the court to set a hearing on a motion made under subdivision (a) or (b). The other party to the contract should be given appropriate notice of the hearing and the court may order that other parties in interest, such as a creditors' committee, also be given notice.

1987 Amendments

Subdivisions (a) and (b) are amended to conform to the 1984 amendment to § 365 of the Code, which governs assumption or rejection of time share interests.

Section 1113, governing collective bargaining agreements, was added to the Code in 1984. It sets out requirements that must be met before a collective bargaining agreement may be rejected. The application to reject a collective bargaining agreement referred to in § 1113 shall be made by motion. The motion to reject creates a contested matter under Rule 9014, and service is made pursuant to Rule 7004 on the representative of the employees. The time periods set forth in § 1113(d) govern the scheduling of the hearing and disposition of a motion to reject the agreement.

1991 Amendments

References to time share interests are deleted as unnecessary. Time share interests are within the scope of this rule to the extent that they are governed by § 365 of the Code.

Subdivision (b) is amended to include chapter 12 cases.

Subdivision (c) is amended to enable the United States trustee to appear and be heard on the issues relating to the assumption or rejection of executory contracts and unexpired leases. See §§ 307, 365, and 1113 of the Code.

1993 Amendments

This rule is amended to delete the requirement for an actual hearing when no request for a hearing is made. See rule 9014.

1999 Amendments

Subdivision (d) is added to provide sufficient time for a party to request a stay pending appeal of an order authorizing the assignment of an executory contract or unexpired lease under § 365(f) of the Code before the assignment is consummated. The stay under subdivision (d) does not affect the time for filing a notice of appeal in accordance with Rule 8002.

The court may, in its discretion, order that Rule 6006(d) is not applicable so that the executory contract or unexpired lease may be assigned immediately in accordance with the order entered by the court. Alternatively, the court may order that the stay under Rule 6006(d) is for a fixed period less than 10 days.

Gap Report on Rule 6006. No changes since publication.

2007 Amendments

The rule is amended to authorize the use of omnibus motions to reject multiple executory contracts and unexpired leases. In some cases there may be numerous executory contracts and unexpired leases, and this rule permits the combining of up to one hundred of these contracts and leases in a single motion to initiate the contested matter.

The rule also is amended to authorize the use of a single motion to assume or assign executory contracts and unexpired leases (i) when such contracts and leases are with a single nondebtor party, (ii) when such contracts and leases are being assigned to the same assignee, (iii) when the trustee proposes to assume, but not assign to more than one assignee, real property leases, or (iv) the court authorizes the filing of a joint motion to assume or to assume and assign executory contracts and unexpired leases under other circumstances that are not specifically recognized in the rule.

An omnibus motion to assume, assign, or reject multiple executory contracts and unexpired leases must comply with the procedural requirements set forth in subdivision (f) of the rule, unless the court orders otherwise. These requirements are intended to ensure that the nondebtor parties to the contracts and leases receive effective notice of the motion. Among those requirements is the requirement in subdivision (f)(5) that these motions be consecutively numbered (e.g., Debtor in Possession's First Omnibus Motion for Authority to Assume Executory Contracts and Unexpired Leases, Debtor in Possession's Second Omnibus Motion for Authority to Assume Executory Contracts and Unexpired Leases, etc.). There may be a need for several of these motions in a particular case. Numbering the motions consecutively is essential to keep track of these motions on the court's docket and should avoid confusion that might otherwise result from similar or identically-titled motions.

Subdivision (g) of the rule provides that the finality of any order respecting an executory contract or unexpired lease included in an omnibus motion shall be determined as though such contract or lease had been the subject of a separate motion. A party seeking to appeal any such order is neither required, nor permitted, to await the court's resolution of all other contracts or leases included in the omnibus motion to obtain appellate review of the order. The rule permits the listing of multiple contracts or leases for convenience, and that convenience should not impede timely review of the court's decision with respect to each contract or lease.

CROSS REFERENCES

Assumption or rejection of executory contracts by trustee, see 11 USCA § 365.

Commodity contracts—

Compliance by trustee with customer's instructions, see 11 USCA § 765.

Definition of, see 11 USCA § 761.

Treatment of customer property, see 11 USCA § 766.

Motions; form and service, see Fed.Rules Bankr.Proc. Rule 9013, 11 USCA.

Provisions in plan for assumption or rejection of certain executory contracts or unexpired leases, see 11 USCA §§ 1123 and 1322.

Rule 6007. Abandonment or Disposition of Property

(a) Notice of proposed abandonment or disposition; objections; hearing

Unless otherwise directed by the court, the trustee or debtor in possession shall give notice of a proposed abandonment or disposition of property to the United States trustee, all creditors, indenture trustees, and committees elected pursuant to § 705 or appointed pursuant to § 1102 of the Code. A party in interest may file and serve an objection within 15 days of the mailing of the notice, or within the time fixed by the court. If a timely objection is made, the court shall set a hearing on notice to the United States trustee and to other entities as the court may direct.

(b) Motion by party in interest

A party in interest may file and serve a motion requiring the trustee or debtor in possession to abandon property of the estate.

(c) [Abrogated]

(As amended Mar. 30, 1987, eff. Aug. 1, 1987; Apr. 30, 1991, eff. Aug. 1, 1991; Apr. 22, 1993, eff. Aug. 1, 1993.)

ADVISORY COMMITTEE NOTES

Sections 554 and 725 of the Code permit and require abandonment and disposition of property of the estate. Pursuant to § 554, the trustee may abandon property but only after notice and hearing. This section is applicable in chapter 7, 11 and 13 cases. Section 725 requires the trustee to dispose of property in which someone other than the estate has an interest, prior to final distribution. It applies only in chapter 7 cases. Notice and hearing are also required conditions. Section 102(1) provides that "notice and hearing" is construed to mean appropriate notice and an opportunity for a hearing. Neither § 554 nor § 725 specify to whom the notices are to be sent. This rule does not apply to § 554(c). Pursuant to that subsection, property is deemed abandoned if it is not administered. A hearing is not required by the statute.

Subdivision (a) requires the notices to be sent to all creditors, indenture trustees, and committees elected under § 705 or appointed under § 1102 of the Code. This may appear burdensome, expensive and inefficient but the subdivision is in keeping with the Code's requirement for notice and the Code's intent to remove the bankruptcy judge from undisputed matters. The burden, expense and inefficiency can be alleviated in large measure by incorporating the notice into or together with the notice of the meeting of creditors so that separate notices would not be required.

Subdivision (b) implements § 554(b) which specifies that a party in interest may request an order that the trustee abandon property. The rule specifies that the request be by motion and, pursuant to the Code, lists the parties who should receive notice.

Subdivision (c) requires a hearing when an objection under subdivision (a) is filed or a motion under subdivision (b) is made. Filing of an objection is sufficient to require a hearing; a separate or joined request for a hearing is unnecessary since the objection itself is tantamount to such a request.

1991 Amendments

This rule is amended to conform to the 1986 amendments to 28 U.S.C. § 586(a) and to the Code. The United States trustee monitors the progress of the case and has standing to raise, appear and be heard on the issues relating to the abandonment or other disposition of property. See §§ 307 and 554 of the Code. Committees of retired employees appointed under § 1114 are not entitled to notice under subdivision (a) of this rule.

1993 Amendments

This rule is amended to clarify that when a motion is made pursuant to subdivision (b), a hearing is not required if a hearing is not requested or if there is no opposition to the motion. *See* Rule 9014. Other amendments are stylistic and make no substantive change.

CROSS REFERENCES

Abandonment of property burdensome or of little value to estate, see 11 USCA § 554.

Abandonment of railroad line—

Authorization by court, see 11 USCA § 1170.

Provision of plan, see 11 USCA § 1172.

Disposition of property with lien in liquidation case, see 11 USCA § 725.

Motions; form and service, see Fed.Rules Bankr.Proc. Rule 9013, 11 USCA.

Rule 6008. Redemption of Property from Lien or Sale

On motion by the debtor, trustee, or debtor in possession and after hearing on notice as the court may direct, the court may authorize the redemption of property from a lien or from a sale to enforce a lien in accordance with applicable law.

ADVISORY COMMITTEE NOTES

This rule is derived from former Bankruptcy Rule 609. No provision in the Code addresses the trustee's right of redemption. Ordinarily the secured creditor should be given notice of the trustee's motion so that any objection may be raised to the proposed redemption.

The rule applies also to a debtor exercising a right of redemption pursuant to § 722. A proceeding under that section is governed by Rule 9014.

CROSS REFERENCES

Motions; form and service, see Fed.Rules Bankr.Proc. Rule 9013, 11 USCA.

Tangible personal property—

Enforceability of agreement between holder of claim and debtor having consideration based on dischargeable debt, see 11 USCA § 524.

Redemption of exempt or abandoned property from lien securing dischargeable consumer debt, see 11 USCA § 722.

Rule 6009. Prosecution and Defense of Proceedings by Trustee or Debtor in Possession

With or without court approval, the trustee or debtor in possession may prosecute or may enter an appearance and defend any pending action or proceeding by or against the debtor, or commence and prosecute any action or proceeding in behalf of the estate before any tribunal.

ADVISORY COMMITTEE NOTES

This rule is derived from former Bankruptcy Rule 610.

CROSS REFERENCES

Suspension of statutes of limitations, see 11 USCA § 108.

Voluntary or involuntary petition filed to operate as automatic stay on other proceedings, see 11 USCA § 362.

Rule 6010. Proceeding to Avoid Indemnifying Lien or Transfer to Surety

If a lien voidable under § 547 of the Code has been dissolved by the furnishing of a bond or other obligation and the surety thereon has been indemnified by the transfer of, or the creation of a lien upon, nonexempt property of the debtor, the surety shall be joined as a defendant in any proceeding to avoid the indemnifying transfer or lien. Such proceeding is governed by the rules in Part VII.

(As amended Apr. 30, 1991, eff. Aug. 1, 1991.)

ADVISORY COMMITTEE NOTES

This rule is derived from former Bankruptcy Rule 612.

1991 Amendments

This rule is amended to conform to § 550(a) of the Code which provides that the trustee may recover the property transferred in a voidable transfer. The value of the property may be recovered in lieu of the property itself only if the court so orders.

CROSS REFERENCES

Motions; form and service, see Fed.Rules Bankr.Proc. Rule 9013, 11 USCA.

Rule 6011. Disposal of Patient Records in Health Care Business Case

(a) Notice by publication under § 351(1)(A)

A notice regarding the claiming or disposing of patient records under § 351(1)(A) shall not identify any patient by name or other identifying information, but shall:

(1) identify with particularity the health care facility whose patient records the trustee proposes to destroy;

(2) state the name, address, telephone number, email address, and website, if any, of a person from whom information about the patient records may be obtained;

(3) state how to claim the patient records; and

(4) state the date by which patient records must be claimed, and that if they are not so claimed the records will be destroyed.

(b) Notice by mail under § 351(1)(B)

Subject to applicable nonbankruptcy law relating to patient privacy, a notice regarding the claiming or disposing of patient records under § 351(1)(B) shall, in addition to including the information in subdivision (a), direct that a patient's family member or other representative who receives the notice inform the patient of the notice. Any notice under this subdivision shall be mailed to the patient and any family member or other contact person whose name and address have been given to the trustee or the debtor for the purpose of providing information regarding the patient's health care, to the Attorney General of the State where the health care facility is located, and to any insurance company known to have provided health care insurance to the patient.

(c) Proof of compliance with notice requirement

Unless the court orders the trustee to file proof of compliance with § 351(1)(B) under seal, the trustee shall not file, but shall maintain, the proof of compliance for a reasonable time.

(d) Report of destruction of records

The trustee shall file, no later than 30 days after the destruction of patient records under § 351(3), a report certifying that the unclaimed records have been destroyed and explaining the method used to effect the destruction. The report shall not identify any patient by name or other identifying information.

(Added Apr. 23, 2008, eff. Dec. 1, 2008.)

ADVISORY COMMITTEE NOTES

2008 Adoption

This rule is new. It implements § 351(1), which was added to the Code by the 2005 amendments. That provision requires the trustee to notify patients that their patient records will be destroyed if they remain unclaimed for one year after the publication of a notice in an appropriate newspaper. The Code provision also requires that individualized notice be sent to each patient and to the patient's family member or other contact person.

The variety of health care businesses and the range of current and former patients present the need for flexibility in the creation and publication of the notices that will be given. Nevertheless, there are some matters that must be included in any notice being given to patients, their family members, and contact persons to ensure that sufficient information is provided to these persons regarding the trustee's intent to dispose of patient records. Subdivision (a) of this rule lists the minimum requirements for notices given under § 351(1)(A), and subdivision (b) governs the form of notices under § 351(1)(B). Notices given under this rule are subject to provisions under applicable federal and state law that relate to the protection of patients' privacy, such as the Health Insurance Portability and Accountability Act of 1996, Pub. L. No. 104–191 (HIPAA).

Subdivision (c) directs the trustee to maintain proof of compliance with § 351(1)(B), but because the proof of compliance may contain patient names that should or must remain confidential, it prohibits filing the proof of compliance unless the court orders the trustee to file it under seal.

Subdivision (d) requires the trustee to file a report with the court regarding the destruction of patient records. This certification is intended to ensure that the trustee properly completed the destruction process. However, because the report will be filed with the court and ordinarily will be available to the public under § 107, the names, addresses, and other identifying information of patients are not to be included in the report to protect patient privacy.

PART VII—ADVERSARY PROCEEDINGS

Rule 7001. Scope of Rules of Part VII

An adversary proceeding is governed by the rules of this Part VII. The following are adversary proceedings:

(1) a proceeding to recover money or property, other than a proceeding to compel the debtor to deliver property to the trustee, or a proceeding under § 554(b) or § 725 of the Code, Rule 2017, or Rule 6002;

(2) a proceeding to determine the validity, priority, or extent of a lien or other interest in property, other than a proceeding under Rule 4003(d);

(3) a proceeding to obtain approval under § 363(h) for the sale of both the interest of the estate and of a co-owner in property;

(4) a proceeding to object to or revoke a discharge;

(5) a proceeding to revoke an order of confirmation of a chapter 11, chapter 12, or chapter 13 plan;

(6) a proceeding to determine the dischargeability of a debt;

(7) a proceeding to obtain an injunction or other equitable relief, except when a chapter 9, chapter 11, chapter 12, or chapter 13 plan provides for the relief;

(8) a proceeding to subordinate any allowed claim or interest, except when a chapter 9, chapter 11, chapter 12, or chapter 13 plan provides for subordination;

(9) a proceeding to obtain a declaratory judgment relating to any of the foregoing; or

(10) a proceeding to determine a claim or cause of action removed under 28 U.S.C. § 1452.

(As amended Mar. 30, 1987, eff. Aug. 1, 1987; Apr. 30, 1991, eff. Aug. 1, 1991; Apr. 29, 1999, eff. Dec. 1, 1999.)

ADVISORY COMMITTEE NOTES

The rules in Part VII govern the procedural aspects of litigation involving the matters referred to in this Rule 7001. Under Rule 9014 some of the Part VII rules also apply to contested matters.

These Part VII rules are based on the premise that to the extent possible practice before the bankruptcy courts and the district courts should be the same. These rules either incorporate or are adaptations of most of the Federal Rules of Civil Procedure. Although the Part VII rules of the former Bankruptcy Rules also relied heavily on the F.R.Civ. P., the former Part VII rules departed from the civil practice in two significant ways: a trial or pretrial conference had to be scheduled as soon as the adversary proceeding was filed and pleadings had to be filed within periods shorter than those established by the F.R.Civ.P. These departures from the civil practice have been eliminated.

The content and numbering of these Part VII rules correlate to the content and numbering of the F.R.Civ.P. Most, but not all, of the F.R.Civ.P. have a comparable Part VII rule. When there is no Part VII rule with a number corresponding to a particular F.R.Civ.P., Parts V and IX of these rules must be consulted to determine if one of the rules in those parts deals with the subject. The list below indicates the F.R.Civ.P., or subdivision thereof, covered by a rule in either Part V or Part IX.

F.R.Civ.P.	Rule in Part V or IX
6	9006
7(b)	9013
10(a)	9004(b)
11	9011
38, 39	9015(a)–(e)
47–51	9015(f)
43, 44, 44.1	9017
45	9016
58	9021
59	9023
60	9024
61	9005
63	9028
77(a), (b), (c)	5001
77(d)	9022(d)
79(a)–(d)	5003
81(c)	9027
83	9029
92	9030

Proceedings to which the rules in Part VII apply directly include those brought to avoid transfers by the debtor under §§ 544, 545, 547, 548 and 549 of the Code; subject to important exceptions, proceedings to recover money or property; proceedings on bonds under Rules 5008(d) and 9025; proceedings under Rule 4004 to determine whether a discharge in a chapter 7 or 11 case should be denied because of an objection grounded on § 727 and proceedings in a chapter 7 or 13 case to revoke a discharge as provided in §§ 727(d) or 1328(e); and proceedings initiated pursuant to § 523(c) of the Code to determine the dischargeability of a particular debt. Those proceedings were classified as adversary proceedings under former Bankruptcy Rule 701.

Also included as adversary proceedings are proceedings to revoke an order of confirmation of a plan in a chapter 11 or 13 case as provided in §§ 1144 and 1330, to subordinate under § 510(c), other than as part of a plan, an allowed claim or interest, and to sell under § 363(h) both the interest of the estate and a co-owner in property.

Declaratory judgments with respect to the subject matter of the various adversary proceedings are also adversary proceedings.

Any claim or cause of action removed to a bankruptcy court pursuant to 28 U.S.C. § 1478 is also an adversary proceeding.

Unlike former Bankruptcy Rule 701, requests for relief from an automatic stay do not commence an adversary proceeding. Section 362(e) of the Code and Rule 4001 establish an expedited schedule for judicial disposition of requests for relief from the automatic stay. The formalities of the adversary proceeding process and the time for serving pleadings are not well suited to the expedited schedule. The motion practice prescribed in Rule 4001 is best suited to such requests because the court has the flexibility to fix hearing dates and other deadlines appropriate to the particular situation.

Clause (1) contains important exceptions. A person with an interest in property in the possession of the trustee or debtor in possession may seek to recover or reclaim that property under § 554(b) or § 725 of the Code. Since many attempts to recover or reclaim property under these two sections do not generate disputes, application of the formalities of the Part VII Rules is not appropriate. Also excluded from adversary proceedings is litigation arising from an examination under Rule 2017 of a debtor's payments of money or transfers of property to an attorney representing the debtor in a case under the Code or an examination of a superseded administration under Rule 6002.

Exemptions and objections thereto are governed by Rule 4003. Filing of proofs of claim and the allowances thereof are governed by Rules 3001–3005, and objections to claims are governed by Rule 3007. When an objection to a claim is joined with a demand for relief of the kind specified in this Rule 7001, the matter becomes an adversary proceeding. See Rule 3007.

1987 Amendment

Another exception is added to clause (1). A trustee may proceed by motion to recover property from the debtor.

1991 Amendment

Clauses (5) and (8) are amended to include chapter 12 plans.

1999 Amendments

This rule is amended to recognize that an adversary proceeding is not necessary to obtain injunctive or other equitable relief that is provided for in a plan under circumstances in which substantive law permits the relief. Other amendments are stylistic.

Gap Report on Rule 7001. No changes since publication, except for stylistic changes.

CROSS REFERENCES

Adversarial nature of proceeding—

Avoidance of indemnifying lien or transfer to surety, see Fed.Rules Bankr.Proc. Rule 6010, 11 USCA.

Commenced by complaint objecting to discharge, see Fed.Rules Bankr.Proc. Rule 4004, 11 USCA.

Commenced by complaint to obtain determination of debt's dischargeability, see Fed.Rules Bankr.Proc. Rule 4007, 11 USCA.

Joinder of objection to claim with demand for relief, see Fed.Rules Bankr.Proc. Rule 3007, 11 USCA.

Liability of sureties on bond or stipulation or other undertaking, see Fed.Rules Bankr.Proc. Rule 9025, 11 USCA.

Applicability of rules of this part to removed claim or cause of action, see Fed.Rules Bankr.Proc. Rule 9027, 11 USCA.

Contested matters, applicability of and notice to parties of applicability of rules of this part, see Fed.Rules Bankr.Proc. Rule 9014, 11 USCA.

Effect of amendment of Federal Rules of Civil Procedure, see Fed.Rules Bankr.Proc. Rule 9032, 11 USCA.

Meanings of words in Federal Rules of Civil Procedure when applicable, see Fed.Rules Bankr.Proc. Rule 9002, 11 USCA.

Rule 7002. References to Federal Rules of Civil Procedure

Whenever a Federal Rule of Civil Procedure applicable to adversary proceedings makes reference to another Federal Rule of Civil Procedure, the reference shall be read as a reference to the Federal Rule of Civil Procedure as modified in this Part VII.

ADVISORY COMMITTEE NOTES

Rules 5, 12, 13, 14, 25, 27, 30, 41 and 52 F.R.Civ.P. are made applicable to adversary proceedings by Part VII. Each of those rules contains a cross reference to another Federal Rule; however, the Part VII rule which incorporates the cross-referenced Federal Rule modifies the Federal Rule in some way. Under this Rule 7002 the cross reference is to the Federal Rule as modified by Part VII. For example, Rule 5 F.R.Civ.P., which is made applicable to adversary proceedings by Rule 7005, contains a reference to Rule 4 F.R.Civ.P. Under this Rule 7002, the cross reference is to Rule 4 F.R.Civ.P. as modified by Rule 7004.

Rules 7, 10, 12, 13, 14, 19, 22, 23.2, 24–37, 41, 45, 49, 50, 52, 55, 59, 60, 62 F.R.Civ.P. are made applicable to adversary proceedings by Part VII or generally to cases under the Code by Part IX. Each of those Federal Rules contains a cross reference to another Federal Rule which is not modified by the Part VII or Part IX rule which makes the cross-referenced Federal Rule applicable. Since the cross-referenced rule is not modified by a Part VII rule this Rule 7002 does not apply.

Rule 7003. Commencement of Adversary Proceeding

Rule 3 F.R.Civ.P. applies in adversary proceedings.

ADVISORY COMMITTEE NOTES

Rule 5005(a) requires that a complaint commencing an adversary proceeding be filed with the court in which the case under the Code is pending unless 28 U.S.C. § 1473 authorizes the filing of the complaint in another district.

CROSS REFERENCES

Complaint filed with court in which case is pending, see Fed.Rules Bankr.Proc. Rule 5005, 11 USCA.

Rule 7004. Process; Service of Summons, Complaint

(a) Summons; service; proof of service

(1) Except as provided in Rule 7004(a)(2), Rule 4(a), (b), (c)(1), (d)(1), (e)–(j), (*l*), and (m) F.R.Civ.P. applies in adversary proceedings. Personal service under Rule 4(e)–(j) F.R.Civ.P. may be made by any person at least 18 years of age who is not a party, and the summons may be delivered by the clerk to any such person.

(2) The clerk may sign, seal, and issue a summons electronically by putting an "s/" before the clerk's name and including the court's seal on the summons.

(b) Service by first class mail

Except as provided in subdivision (h), in addition to the methods of service authorized by Rule 4(e)—(j) F.R.Civ.P., service may be made within the United States by first class mail postage prepaid as follows:

(1) Upon an individual other than an infant or incompetent, by mailing a copy of the summons and complaint to the individual's dwelling house or usual place of abode or to the place where the individual regularly conducts a business or profession.

(2) Upon an infant or an incompetent person, by mailing a copy of the summons and complaint to the person upon whom process is prescribed to be served by the law of the state in which service is made when an action is brought against such a defendant in the courts of general jurisdiction of that state. The summons and complaint in that case shall be addressed to the person required to be served at that person's dwelling house or usual place of abode or at the place where the person regularly conducts a business or profession.

(3) Upon a domestic or foreign corporation or upon a partnership or other unincorporated association, by mailing a copy of the summons and complaint to the attention of an officer, a managing or general agent, or to any other agent authorized by appointment or by law to receive service of process and, if the agent is one authorized by statute to receive service and the statute so requires, by also mailing a copy to the defendant.

(4) Upon the United States, by mailing a copy of the summons and complaint addressed to the civil process clerk at the office of the United States attorney for the district in which the action is brought and by mailing a copy of the summons and complaint to the Attorney General of the United States at Washington, District of Columbia, and in any action attacking the validity of an order of an officer or an agency of the United States not made a party, by also mailing a copy of the summons and complaint to that officer or agency. The court shall allow a reasonable time for service pursuant to this

subdivision for the purpose of curing the failure to mail a copy of the summons and complaint to multiple officers, agencies, or corporations of the United States if the plaintiff has mailed a copy of the summons and complaint either to the civil process clerk at the office of the United States attorney or to the Attorney General of the United States.

(5) Upon any officer or agency of the United States, by mailing a copy of the summons and complaint to the United States as prescribed in paragraph (4) of this subdivision and also to the officer or agency. If the agency is a corporation, the mailing shall be as prescribed in paragraph (3) of this subdivision of this rule. The court shall allow a reasonable time for service pursuant to this subdivision for the purpose of curing the failure to mail a copy of the summons and complaint to multiple officers, agencies, or corporations of the United States if the plaintiff has mailed a copy of the summons and complaint either to the civil process clerk at the office of the United States attorney or to the Attorney General of the United States. If the United States trustee is the trustee in the case and service is made upon the United States trustee solely as trustee, service may be made as prescribed in paragraph (10) of this subdivision of this rule.

(6) Upon a state or municipal corporation or other governmental organization thereof subject to suit, by mailing a copy of the summons and complaint to the person or office upon whom process is prescribed to be served by the law of the state in which service is made when an action is brought against such a defendant in the courts of general jurisdiction of that state, or in the absence of the designation of any such person or office by state law, then to the chief executive officer thereof.

(7) Upon a defendant of any class referred to in paragraph (1) or (3) of this subdivision of this rule, it is also sufficient if a copy of the summons and complaint is mailed to the entity upon whom service is prescribed to be served by any statute of the United States or by the law of the state in which service is made when an action is brought against such a defendant in the court of general jurisdiction of that state.

(8) Upon any defendant, it is also sufficient if a copy of the summons and complaint is mailed to an agent of such defendant authorized by appointment or by law to receive service of process, at the agent's dwelling house or usual place of abode or at the place where the agent regularly carries on a business or profession and, if the authorization so requires, by mailing also a copy of the summons and complaint to the defendant as provided in this subdivision.

(9) Upon the debtor, after a petition has been filed by or served upon the debtor and until the case is dismissed or closed, by mailing a copy of the summons and complaint to the debtor at the address shown in the petition or to such other address as the debtor may designate in a filed writing.

(10) Upon the United States trustee, when the United States trustee is the trustee in the case and service is made upon the United States trustee solely as trustee, by mailing a copy of the summons and complaint to an office of the United States trustee or another place designated by the United States trustee in the district where the case under the Code is pending.

(c) Service by publication

If a party to an adversary proceeding to determine or protect rights in property in the custody of the court cannot be served as provided in Rule 4(e)-(j) F.R.Civ.P. or subdivision (b) of this rule, the court may order the summons and complaint to be served by mailing copies thereof by first class mail, postage prepaid, to the party's last known address, and by at least one publication in such manner and form as the court may direct.

(d) Nationwide service of process

The summons and complaint and all other process except a subpoena may be served anywhere in the United States.

(e) Summons: time limit for service within the United States

Service made under Rule 4(e), (g), (h)(1), (i), or (j)(2) F.R.Civ.P. shall be by delivery of the summons and complaint within 10 days after the summons is issued. If service is by any authorized form of mail, the summons and complaint shall be deposited in the mail within 10 days after the summons is issued. If a summons is not timely delivered or mailed, another summons shall be issued and served. This subdivision does not apply to service in a foreign country.

(f) Personal jurisdiction

If the exercise of jurisdiction is consistent with the Constitution and laws of the United States, serving a summons or filing a waiver of service in accordance with this rule or the subdivisions of Rule 4 F.R.Civ.P. made applicable by these rules is effective to establish personal jurisdiction over the person of any defendant with respect to a case under the Code or a civil proceeding arising under the Code, or arising in or related to a case under the Code.

(g) Service on debtor's attorney

If the debtor is represented by an attorney, whenever service is made upon the debtor under this Rule, service shall also be made upon the debtor's attorney by any means authorized under Rule 5(b) F. R. Civ. P.

(h) Service of process on an insured depository institution

Service on an insured depository institution (as defined in section 3 of the Federal Deposit Insurance Act) in a contested matter or adversary proceeding shall be made by certified mail addressed to an officer of the institution unless—

(1) the institution has appeared by its attorney, in which case the attorney shall be served by first class mail;

(2) the court orders otherwise after service upon the institution by certified mail of notice of an application to permit service on the institution by first class mail sent to an officer of the institution designated by the institution; or

(3) the institution has waived in writing its entitlement to service by certified mail by designating an officer to receive service.

(As amended Mar. 30, 1987, eff. Aug. 1, 1987; Apr. 30, 1991, eff. Aug. 1, 1991; Oct. 22, 1994, Pub.L. 103–394, Title I, § 114, 108 Stat. 4118; Apr. 23, 1996, eff. Dec. 1, 1996; Apr. 29, 1999, eff. Dec. 1, 1999; Apr. 25, 2005, eff. Dec. 1, 2005; Apr. 12, 2006, eff. Dec. 1, 2006.)

ADVISORY COMMITTEE NOTES

Subdivision (a) of the rule, by incorporation of Rule 4(a), (b), (d), (e) and (g)–(i) F.R.Civ.P., governs the mechanics of issuance of a summons and its form, the manner of service on parties and their representatives, and service in foreign countries.

Subdivision (b), which is the same as former Rule 704(c), authorizes service of process by first class mail postage prepaid. This rule retains the modes of service contained in former Bankruptcy Rule 704. The former practice, in effect since 1976, has proven satisfactory.

Subdivision (c) is derived from former Bankruptcy Rule 704(d)(2).

Subdivision (d). Nationwide service of process is authorized by subdivision (d).

Subdivision (e) authorizes service by delivery on individuals and corporations in foreign countries if the party to be served is the debtor or any person required to perform the duties of the debtor and certain other persons, the adversary proceeding involves property in the custody of the bankruptcy court, or if federal or state law authorizes such service in a foreign country.

Subdivision (f). The requirement of former Bankruptcy Rule 704 that the summons be served within 10 days is carried over into these rules by subdivision (f).

1987 Amendment

Subdivision (a) is amended to make Rule 4(j) F.R.Civ.P. applicable to service of the summons. If service is not completed within 120 days of the filing of the complaint, the complaint may be dismissed.

Technical amendments are made to subdivisions (a), (b), (e), and (f) to conform to recent amendments to Rule 4 F.R.Civ.P.

1991 Amendment

The United States trustee may serve as trustee in a case pursuant to 28 U.S.C. § 586(a)(2) and §§ 701(a)(2), 1202(a), and 1302(a) of the Code. This rule is amended to avoid the necessity of mailing copies of a summons and complaint or other pleadings to the Attorney General and to the United States attorney when service on the United States trustee is required only because the United States trustee is acting as a case trustee. For example, a proceeding commenced by a creditor to dismiss a case for unreasonable delay under § 707(a) is governed by Rule 9014 which requires service on the trustee pursuant to the requirements of Rule 7004 for the service of a summons and complaint. The Attorney General and the United States attorney would have no interest in receiving a copy of the motion to dismiss. Mailing to the office of the United States trustee when acting as the case trustee is sufficient in such cases.

The words "with the court" in subdivision (b)(9) are deleted as unnecessary. See Rules 5005(a) and 9001(3).

The new paragraph (10) of subdivision (b) does not affect requirements for service of process on the United States trustee when sued or otherwise a party to a litigation unrelated to its capacity as a trustee. If a proceeding is commenced against the United States trustee which is unrelated to the United States trustee's role as trustee, the requirements of paragraph (5) of subdivision (b) of this rule would apply.

Subdivision (g) is added in anticipation of substantial amendment to, and restructuring of subdivisions of, Rule 4 F.R.Civ.P. Any amendment to Rule 4 will not affect service in bankruptcy cases and proceedings until further amendment to the Bankruptcy Rules. On January 1, 1990, Rule 4 F.R.Civ.P. read as follows:

Rule 4 F.R.Civ.P.

PROCESS

(a) Summons: issuance. Upon the filing of the complaint the clerk shall forthwith issue a summons and deliver the summons of the plaintiff or the plaintiff's attorney, who shall be responsible for prompt service of the summons and a copy of the complaint. Upon request of the plaintiff separate or additional summons shall issue against any defendants.

(b) Same: form. The summons shall be signed by the clerk, be under the seal of the court, contain the name of the court and the names of the parties, be directed to the defendant, state the name and address of the plaintiff's attorney, if any, otherwise the plaintiff's address, and the time within which these rules require the defendant to appear and defend, and shall notify the defendant that in case of the defendant's failure to do so judgment by default will be rendered against the defendant for the relief demanded in the complaint. When, under Rule 4(e), service is made pursuant to a statute or rule of court of a state, the summons, or notice, or order in lieu of summons shall correspond as nearly as may be to that required by the statute or rule.

(c) Service

(1) [Not applicable.]

(2)(A) [Not applicable.]

(B) [Not applicable.]

(C) A summons and complaint may be served upon a defendant of any class referred to in paragraph (1) or (3) of subdivision (d) of this rule—

(i) pursuant to the law of the State in which the district court held for the service of summons or other like process upon such defendant in an action brought in the courts of general jurisdiction of that State, or

(ii) [Not applicable.]

(D) [Not applicable.]

(E) [Not applicable.]

(3) [Not applicable.]

(d) Summons and complaint: person to be served. The summons and complaint shall be served together. The plaintiff shall furnish the person making service with such copies as are necessary. Service shall be made as follows:

(1) Upon an individual other than an infant or an incompetent person, by delivering a copy of the summons and of the complaint to the individual personally or by leaving copies thereof at the individual's dwelling house or usual place of abode with some person of suitable age and discretion then residing therein or by delivering a copy of the summons and of the complaint to an agent authorized by appointment or by law to receive service of process.

(2) Upon an infant or an incompetent person, by serving the summons and complaint in the manner prescribed by the law of the state in which the service is made for the service of summons or other like process upon any such defendant in an action brought in the courts of general jurisdiction of that state.

(3) Upon a domestic or foreign corporation or upon a partnership or other unincorporated association which the subject to suit under a common name, by delivering a copy of the summons and of the complaint to an officer, a managing or general agent, or to any other agent authorized by appointment or by law to receive service of process and, if the agent is one authorized by statute to receive service and the statute so requires, by also mailing a copy to the defendant.

(4) Upon the United States, by delivering a copy of the summons and of the complaint to the United States attorney for the district in which the action is brought or to an assistant United States attorney or clerical employee designated by the United States attorney in a writing filed with the clerk of the court and by sending a copy of the summons and of the complaint by registered or certified mail to the Attorney General of the United States at Washington, District of Columbia, and in any action attacking the validity of an order of an officer or agency of the United States not made a party, by also sending a copy of the summons and of the complaint by registered or certified mail to such officer or agency.

(5) Upon an officer or agency of the United States, by serving the United States and by sending a copy of the summons and of the complaint by registered or certified mail to such officer or agency. If the agency is a corporation the copy shall be delivered as provided in paragraph (3) of this subdivision of this rule.

(6) Upon a state or municipal corporation or other governmental organization thereof subject to suit, by delivering a copy of the summons and of the complaint to the chief executive officer thereof or by serving the summons and complaint in the manner prescribed by the law of that state for the service of summons or other like process upon any such defendant.

(e) Summons: service upon party not inhabitant of or found within state. Whenever a statute of the United States or an order of court thereunder provides for service of a summons, or of a notice, or of an order in lieu of summons upon a party not an inhabitant of or found within the state in which the district court is held, service may be made under the circumstances and in the manner prescribed by the statute or order, or, if there is no provision therein prescribing the manner of service, in a manner stated in this rule. Whenever a statute or rule of court of the state in which the district court is held provides (1) for service of a summons, or of a notice, or of an order in lieu of summons upon a party not an inhabitant of or found within the state, or (2) for service upon or notice to such a party to appear and respond or defend in an action by reason of the attachment or garnishment or similar seizure of the party's property located within the state, service may in either case be made under the circumstances and in the manner prescribed in the statute or rule.

(f) [Not applicable.]

(g) Return. The person serving the process shall make proof of service thereof to the court promptly and in any event within the time during which the person served must respond to the process. If service is made by a person other than a United States marshal or deputy United States marshal, such person shall make affidavit thereof. If service is made under subdivision (c)(2)(C)(ii) of this rule, return shall be made by the sender's filing with the court the acknowledgement received pursuant to such subdivision. Failure to make proof of service does not affect the validity of the service.

(h) Amendment. At any time in its discretion and upon such terms as it deems just, the court may allow any process or proof of service thereof to be amended, unless it clearly appears that material prejudice would result to the substantial rights of the party against whom the process issued.

(i) Alternative provisions for service in a foreign country.

(1) Manner. When the federal or state law referred to in subdivision (e) of this rule authorizes service upon a party not an inhabitant of or found within the state in which the district court is held, and service is to be effected upon the party in a foreign country, it is also sufficient if service of the summons and complaint is made: (A) in the manner prescribed by the law of the foreign country for service in that country in an action in any of its courts of general jurisdiction; or (B) as directed by the foreign authority in response to a letter rogatory, when service in either case is reasonably calculated to give actual notice; or (C) upon an individual, by delivery to the individual personally, and upon a corporation or partnership or association, by delivery to an officer, a managing or general agent; or (D) by any form of mail, requiring a signed receipt, to be addressed and dispatched by the clerk of the court to the party to be served; or (E) above may be made by any person who is not a party and is not less than 18 years of age or who is designated by order of the district court or by the foreign court. On request, the clerk shall deliver the summons to the plaintiff for trans-

mission to the person or the foreign court or officer who will make the service.

(2) Return. Proof of service may be made as prescribed by subdivision (g) of this rule, or by the law of the foreign country, or by order of the court. When service is made pursuant to subparagraph (1)(D) of this subdivision, proof of service shall include a receipt signed by the addressee or other evidence of delivery to the addressee satisfactory to the court.

(j) Summons: time limit for service. If a service of the summons and complaint is not made upon a defendant within 120 days after the filing of the complaint and the party on whose behalf such service was required cannot show good cause why such service was not made within that period, the action shall be dismissed as to that defendant without prejudice upon the court's own initiative with notice to such party or upon motion. This subdivision shall not apply to service in a foreign country pursuant to subdivision (i) of this rule.

1996 Amendments

The purpose of these amendments is to conform the rule to the 1993 revisions of Rule 4 F.R.Civ.P. and to make stylistic improvements. Rule 7004, as amended, continues to provide for service by first class mail as an alternative to the methods of personal service provided in Rule 4 F.R.Civ.P., except as provided in the new subdivision (h).

Rule 4(d)(2) F.R.Civ.P. provides a procedure by which the plaintiff may request by first class mail that the defendant waive service of the summons. This procedure is not applicable in adversary proceedings because it is not necessary in view of the availability of service by mail pursuant to Rule 7004(b). However, if a written waiver of service of a summons is made in an adversary proceeding, Rule 4(d)(1) F.R.Civ.P. applies so that the defendant does not thereby waive any objection to the venue or the jurisdiction of the court over the person of the defendant.

Subdivisions (b)(4) and (b)(5) are amended to conform to the 1993 amendments to Rule 4(i)(3) F.R.Civ.P., which protect the plaintiff from the hazard of losing a substantive right because of failure to comply with the requirements of multiple service when the United States or an officer, agency, or corporation of the United States is a defendant. These subdivisions also are amended to require that the summons and complaint be addressed to the civil process clerk at the office of the United States attorney.

Subdivision (e), which has governed service in a foreign country, is abrogated and Rule 4(f) and (h)(2) F.R.Civ.P., as substantially revised in 1993, are made applicable in adversary proceedings.

The new subdivision (f) is consistent with the 1993 amendments to F.R.Civ.P. 4(k)(2). It clarifies that service or filing a waiver of service in accordance with this rule or the applicable subdivisions of F.R.Civ.P. 4 is sufficient to establish personal jurisdiction over the defendant. See the committee note to the 1993 amendments to Rule 4 F.R.Civ.P.

Subdivision (g) is abrogated. This subdivision was promulgated in 1991 so that anticipated revisions to Rule 4 F.R.Civ.P. would not affect service of process in adversary proceedings until further amendment to Rule 7004.

Subdivision (h) and the first phrase of subdivision (b) were added by § 114 of the Bankruptcy Reform Act of 1994, Pub.L. No. 103–394, 108 Stat. 4106.

GAP Report on Rule 7004. After publication of the proposed amendments, Rule 7004(b) was amended and Rule 7004(h) was added by the Bankruptcy Reform Act of 1994 to provide for service by certified mail on an insured depository institution. The above draft includes those statutory amendments (without underlining new language or striking former language). No other changes have been made since publication, except for stylistic changes.

1999 Amendments

Subdivision (e) is amended so that the ten-day time limit for service of a summons does not apply if the summons is served in a foreign country.

Gap Report on Rule 7004. No changes since publication.

2005 Amendments

This amendment specifically authorizes the clerk to issue a summons electronically. In some bankruptcy cases the trustee or debtor in possession may commence hundreds of adversary proceedings simultaneously, and permitting the electronic signing and sealing of the summonses for those proceedings increases the efficiency of the clerk's office without any negative impact on any party. The rule only authorizes electronic issuance of the summons. It does not address the service requirements for the summons. Those requirements are set out elsewhere in Rule 7004, and nothing in Rule 7004(a)(2) should be construed as authorizing electronic service of a summons.

2006 Amendments

Under current Rule 7004, an entity may serve a summons and complaint upon the debtor by personal service or by mail. If the entity chooses to serve the debtor by mail, it must also serve a copy of the summons and complaint on the debtor's attorney by mail. If the entity effects personal service on the debtor, there is no requirement that the debtor's attorney also be served.

Subdivision (b)(9). The rule is amended to delete the reference in subdivision (b)(9) to the debtor's address as set forth in the statement of financial affairs. In 1991, the Official Form of the statement of financial affairs was revised and no longer includes a question regarding the debtor's current residence. Since that time, Official Form 1, the petition, has required the debtor to list both the debtor's residence and mailing address. Therefore, the subdivision is amended to delete the statement of financial affairs as a document that might contain an address at which the debtor can be served.

Subdivision (g). The rule is amended to require service on the debtor's attorney whenever the debtor is served with a summons and complaint. The amendment makes this change by deleting that portion of Rule 7004(b)(9) that requires service on the debtor's attorney when the debtor is served by mail, and relocates the obligation to serve the debtor's attorney into new subdivision (g). Service on the debtor's attorney is not limited to mail service, but may be accomplished by any means permitted under Rule 5(b) F. R. Civ. P.

HISTORICAL NOTES

References in Text

Section 3 of the Federal Deposit Insurance Act, referred to in subd. (h), is Act Sept. 21, 1950, c. 967, § 2[3], 64 Stat. 873, as amended, which is classified to section 1813 of Title 12, Banks and Banking.

Effective Date

1994 Acts. Amendment by Pub.L. 103–394 effective on Oct. 22, 1994, and not to apply with respect to cases commenced under Title 11 of the United States Code before Oct. 22, 1994, see section 702 of Pub.L. 103–394, set out as a note under section 101 of Title 11, Bankruptcy.

Separability of Provisions

If any provision of or amendment made by Pub.L. 103–394 or the application of such provision or amendment to any person or circumstance is held to be unconstitutional, the remaining provisions of and amendments made by Pub.L. 103–394 and the application of such provisions and amendments to any person or circumstance shall not be affected thereby, see section 701 of Pub.L. 103–394, set out as a note under section 101 of Title 11, Bankruptcy.

Legislative History

For legislative history and purpose of Pub.L. 103–394, see 1994 U.S. Code Cong. and Adm. News, p. 3340.

CROSS REFERENCES

Contested matters, request for relief by motion served in manner provided in this rule, see Fed.Rules Bankr.Proc. Rule 9014, 11 USCA.

Form of pleadings, see Fed.Rules Bankr.Proc. Rule 7010, 11 USCA.

Service of—

Motion for substitution of parties, see Fed.Rules Bankr. Proc. Rule 7025, 11 USCA.

Notice of depositions before adversary proceedings or pending appeal, see Fed.Rules Bankr.Proc. Rule 7027, 11 USCA.

Pleadings and other papers, see Fed.Rules Bankr.Proc. Rule 7005, 11 USCA.

Summons and involuntary petition—

Manner of service, see Fed.Rules Bankr.Proc. Rule 1010, 11 USCA.

Time limitations, see Fed.Rules Bankr.Proc. Rule 1010, 11 USCA.

Rule 7005. Service and Filing of Pleadings and Other Papers

Rule 5 F.R.Civ.P. applies in adversary proceedings.

ADVISORY COMMITTEE NOTES

Rule 5 F.R.Civ.P. refers to Rule 4 F.R.Civ.P. Pursuant to Rule 7002 this reference is to Rule 4 F.R.Civ.P. as incorporated and modified by Rule 7004.

CROSS REFERENCES

Applicability of this rule in proceedings on contested involuntary petition and to vacate order for relief, see Fed.Rules Bankr.Proc. Rule 1018, 11 USCA.

Form of pleadings, see Fed.Rules Bankr.Proc. Rule 7010, 11 USCA.

Service of—

Motion for substitution, see Fed.Rules Bankr.Proc. Rule 7025, 11 USCA.

Motion to intervene, see Fed.Rules Bankr. Proc. Rule 7024, 11 USCA.

Notice of judgment or order, see Fed.Rules Bankr.Proc. Rule 9022, 11 USCA.

Requests for depositions and discovery, see Fed.Rules Bankr.Proc. Rule 7027 et seq., 11 USCA.

Rule 7007. Pleadings Allowed

Rule 7 F.R.Civ.P. applies in adversary proceedings.

CROSS REFERENCES

Amended and supplemental pleadings, see Fed.Rules Bankr.Proc. Rule 7015, 11 USCA.

Counterclaim and cross-claim, see Fed.Rules Bankr.Proc. Rule 7013, 11 USCA.

Form of pleadings, see Fed.Rules Bankr.Proc. Rule 7010, 11 USCA.

Service and filing of pleadings and other papers, see Fed.Rules Bankr.Proc. Rule 7005, 11 USCA.

Third-party practice, see Fed.Rules Bankr.Proc. Rule 7014, 11 USCA.

Rule 7007.1. Corporate Ownership Statement

(a) Required disclosure

Any corporation that is a party to an adversary proceeding, other than the debtor or a governmental unit, shall file two copies of a statement that identifies any corporation, other than a governmental unit, that directly or indirectly owns 10% or more of any class of the corporation's equity interests, or states that there are no entities to report under this subdivision.

(b) Time for Filing

A party shall file the statement required under Rule 7007.1(a) with its first appearance, pleading, motion, response, or other request addressed to the court. A party shall file a supplemental statement promptly upon any change in circumstances that this rule requires the party to identify or disclose.

(Added Mar. 27, 2003, eff. Dec. 1, 2003. As amended Apr. 30, 2007, eff. Dec. 1, 2007.)

ADVISORY COMMITTEE NOTES

2003 Adoption

This rule is derived from Rule 26.1 of the Federal Rules of Appellate Procedure. The information that parties shall supply will support properly informed disqualification decisions in situations that call for automatic disqualification under Canon 3C(1)(c) of the Code of Conduct for United States Judges. This rule does not cover all of the circumstances that may call for disqualification under the subjective financial interest standard of Canon 3C, and does not deal at all with other circumstances that may call for disqualification. Nevertheless, the required disclosures are calculated to reach the majority of circumstances that are likely to call for disqualification under Canon 3C(1)(c).

The rule directs nongovernmental corporate parties to list those corporations that hold significant ownership interests in them. This includes listing membership interests in limited liability companies and similar entities that fall under the definition of a corporation in Bankruptcy Code § 101.

Under subdivision (b), parties must file the statement with the first document that they file in any adversary proceeding. The rule also requires parties and other persons to file supplemental statements promptly whenever changed circumstances require disclosure of new or additional information.

The rule does not prohibit the adoption of local rules requiring disclosures beyond those called for in Rule 7007.1.

2007 Amendments

The rule is amended to clarify that a party must file a corporate ownership statement with its initial paper filed with the court in an adversary proceeding. The party's initial filing may be a document that is not a "pleading" as defined in Rule 7 F. R. Civ. P., which is made applicable in adversary proceedings by Rule 7007. The amendment also brings Rule 7007.1 more closely in line with Rule 7.1 F. R. Civ. P.

Rule 7008. General Rules of Pleading

(a) Applicability of Rule 8 F.R.Civ.P.

Rule 8 F.R.Civ.P. applies in adversary proceedings. The allegation of jurisdiction required by Rule 8(a) shall also contain a reference to the name, number, and chapter of the case under the Code to which the adversary proceeding relates and to the district and division where the case under the Code is pending. In an adversary proceeding before a bankruptcy judge, the complaint, counterclaim, cross-claim, or third-party complaint shall contain a statement that the proceeding is core or non-core and, if non-core, that the pleader does or does not consent to entry of final orders or judgment by the bankruptcy judge.

(b) Attorney's fees

A request for an award of attorney's fees shall be pleaded as a claim in a complaint, cross-claim, third-party complaint, answer, or reply as may be appropriate.

(As amended Mar. 30, 1987, eff. Aug. 1, 1987.)

ADVISORY COMMITTEE NOTES

1987 Amendment

Proceedings before a bankruptcy judge are either core or non-core. 28 U.S.C. § 157. A bankruptcy judge may enter a final order or judgment in a core proceeding. In a non-core proceeding, absent consent of the parties, the bankruptcy judge may not enter a final order or judgment but may only submit proposed findings of fact and conclusions of law to the district judge who will enter the final order or judgment. 28 U.S.C. § 157(c)(1). The amendment to subdivision (a) of this rule requires an allegation as to whether a proceeding is core or non-core. A party who alleges that the proceeding is non-core shall state whether the party does or does not consent to the entry of a final order or judgment by the bankruptcy judge. Failure to include the statement of consent does not constitute consent. Only express consent in the pleadings or otherwise is effective to authorize entry of a final order or judgment by the bankruptcy judge in a non-core proceeding. Amendments to Rule 7012 require that the defendant admit or deny the allegation as to whether the proceeding is core or non-core.

CROSS REFERENCES

Amended and supplemental pleadings, see Fed.Rules Bankr.Proc. Rule 7015, 11 USCA.

Applicability of this rule in proceedings on contested involuntary petition and to vacate order for relief, see Fed.Rules Bankr.Proc. Rule 1018, 11 USCA.

Defenses and objections, see Fed.Rules Bankr.Proc. Rule 7012, 11 USCA.

Joinder of claims and remedies, see Fed.Rules Bankr.Proc. Rule 7013, 11 USCA.

Rule 7009. Pleading Special Matters

Rule 9 F.R.Civ.P. applies in adversary proceedings.

CROSS REFERENCES

Applicability of this rule in proceedings on contested involuntary petition and to vacate order for relief, see Fed.Rules Bankr.Proc. Rule 1018, 11 USCA.

Parties plaintiff and defendant; capacity, see Fed.Rules Bankr.Proc. Rule 7017, 11 USCA.

Pleading affirmative defenses, see Fed.Rules Bankr.Proc. Rule 7008, 11 USCA.

Rule 7010. Form of Pleadings

Rule 10 F.R.Civ.P. applies in adversary proceedings, except that the caption of each pleading in such a proceeding shall conform substantially to the appropriate Official Form.

(As amended Apr. 30, 1991, eff. Aug. 1, 1991.)

ADVISORY COMMITTEE NOTES

1991 Amendment

Reference to the Official Form number is deleted in anticipation of future revision and renumbering of the Official Forms.

CROSS REFERENCES

Applicability of this rule in proceedings on contested involuntary petition and to vacate order for relief, see Fed.Rules Bankr.Proc. Rule 1018, 11 USCA.

General requirements of form for adversarial pleading or paper, see Fed.Rules Bankr.Proc. Rule 9004, 11 USCA.

Rule 7012. Defenses and Objections—When and How Presented—By Pleading or Motion—Motion for Judgment on the Pleadings

(a) When presented

If a complaint is duly served, the defendant shall serve an answer within 30 days after the issuance of the summons, except when a different time is prescribed by the court. The court shall prescribe the time for service of the answer when service of a complaint is made by publication or upon a party in a foreign country. A party served with a pleading stating a cross-claim shall serve an answer thereto within 20 days after service. The plaintiff shall serve a reply to a counterclaim in the answer within 20 days after service of the answer or, if a reply is ordered by the court, within 20 days after service of the order, unless the order otherwise directs. The United States or an officer or agency thereof shall serve an answer to a complaint within 35 days after the issuance of the summons, and shall serve an answer to a cross-claim, or a reply to a counterclaim, within 35 days after service upon the United States attorney of the pleading in which the claim is asserted. The service of a motion permitted under this rule alters these periods of time as follows, unless a different time is fixed by order of the court: (1) if the court denies the motion or postpones its disposition until the trial on the merits, the responsive pleading shall be served within 10 days after notice of the court's action; (2) if the court grants a motion for a more definite statement, the responsive pleading shall be served within 10 days after the service of a more definite statement.

(b) Applicability of Rule 12(b)–(i) F.R.Civ.P.

Rule 12(b)–(i) F.R.Civ.P. applies in adversary proceedings. A responsive pleading shall admit or deny an allegation that the proceeding is core or non-core. If the response is that the proceeding is non-core, it shall include a statement that the party does or does not consent to entry of final orders or judgment by the bankruptcy judge. In non-core proceedings final orders and judgments shall not be entered on the bankruptcy judge's order except with the express consent of the parties.

(b) Applicability of Rule 12(b)–(h) F.R.Civ.P.

Rule 12(b)–(h) F.R.Civ.P. applies in adversary proceedings. A responsive pleading shall admit or deny an allegation that the proceeding is core or non-core. If the response is that the proceeding is non-core, it shall include a statement that the party does or does not consent to entry of final orders or judgment by the bankruptcy judge. In non-core proceedings final orders and judgments shall not be entered on the bankruptcy judge's order except with the express consent of the parties.

(As amended Mar. 30, 1987, eff. Aug. 1, 1987; Apr. 23, 2008, eff. Dec. 1, 2008.)

ADVISORY COMMITTEE NOTES

Subdivision (a) continues the practice of former Bankruptcy Rule 712(a) by requiring that the answer to a complaint be filed within 30 days after the issuance of the summons. Under Rule 7004(f), the summons must be served within 10 days of issuance. The other pleading periods in adversary proceedings are the same as those in civil actions before the district courts, except that the United States is allowed 35 rather than 60 days to respond.

Rule 12(b)(7) and (h)(2) F.R.Civ.P. refers to Rule 19 F.R.Civ.P. Pursuant to Rule 7002 these references are to Rule 19 F.R.Civ.P. as incorporated and modified by Rule 7019.

1987 Amendment

The amendment to subdivision (b) requires a response to the allegation that the proceeding is core or non-core. A final order of judgment may not be entered in a non-core proceeding heard by a bankruptcy judge unless all parties expressly consent. 28 U.S.C. § 157(c).

2008 Amendments

The rule is amended to conform to the changes made to the Federal Rules of Civil Procedure through the restyling of those rules effective on December 1, 2007.

CROSS REFERENCES

Averments of defense in separate statements, see Fed. Rules Bankr.Proc. Rule 7010, 11 USCA.

Counterclaim and cross-claim, see Fed.Rules Bankr.Proc. Rule 7013, 11 USCA.

Defenses of third-party defendant, see Fed.Rules Bankr. Proc. Rule 7014, 11 USCA.

Pleadings allowed, see Fed.Rules Bankr.Proc. Rule 7007, 11 USCA.

Removed actions, see Fed.Rules Bankr.Proc. Rule 9027, 11 USCA.

Waiver of sovereign immunity, see 11 USCA § 106.

Rule 7013. Counterclaim and Cross-Claim

Rule 13 F.R.Civ.P. applies in adversary proceedings, except that a party sued by a trustee or debtor in possession need not state as a counterclaim any claim that the party has against the debtor, the debtor's property, or the estate, unless the claim arose after the entry of an order for relief. A trustee or debtor in possession who fails to plead a counterclaim through oversight, inadvertence, or excusable neglect, or when justice so requires, may by leave of court amend the pleading, or commence a new adversary proceeding or separate action.

(As amended Mar. 30, 1987, eff. Aug. 1, 1987.)

ADVISORY COMMITTEE NOTES

Rule 13(h) F.R.Civ.P. refers to Rule 19 F.R.Civ.P. Pursuant to Rule 7002 this reference is to Rule 19 F.R.Civ.P. as incorporated and modified by Rule 7019.

CROSS REFERENCES

Amended and supplemental pleadings, see Fed.Rules Bankr.Proc. Rule 7015, 11 USCA.

Counterclaims and cross-claims of third-party defendant, see Fed.Rules Bankr.Proc. Rule 7014, 11 USCA.

Default judgment against counterclaimants and cross-claimants, see Fed.Rules Bankr.Proc. Rule 7055, 11 USCA.

Dismissal of counterclaims and cross-claims, see Fed.Rules Bankr.Proc. Rule 7041, 11 USCA.

Separate trial of counterclaims and cross-claims, see Fed. Rules Bankr.Proc. Rule 7042, 11 USCA.

Rule 7014. Third-Party Practice

Rule 14 F.R.Civ.P. applies in adversary proceedings.

ADVISORY COMMITTEE NOTES

This rule does not purport to deal with questions of jurisdiction. The scope of the jurisdictional grant under 28 U.S.C. § 1471 and whether the doctrines of pendent or ancillary jurisdiction are applicable to adversary proceedings will be determined by the courts.

Rule 14 F.R.Civ.P. refers to Rules 12 and 13 F.R.Civ.P. Pursuant to Rule 7002 those references are to Rules 12 and 13 as incorporated and modified by Rules 7012 and 7013.

CROSS REFERENCES

Default judgment against third-party plaintiff, see Fed. Rules Bankr.Proc. Rule 7055, 11 USCA.

Joinder of claims, see Fed.Rules Bankr.Proc. Rule 7018, 11 USCA.

Requisites of pleading, see Fed.Rules Bankr.Proc. Rule 7008, 11 USCA.

Separate trial of third-party claim, see Fed.Rules Bankr. Proc. Rule 7042, 11 USCA.

Rule 7015. Amended and Supplemental Pleadings

Rule 15 F.R.Civ.P. applies in adversary proceedings.

CROSS REFERENCES

Amendments to pleadings considered at pre-trial conference, see Fed.Rules Bankr.Proc. Rule 7016, 11 USCA.

Applicability of this rule in proceedings on contested involuntary petition and to vacate order for relief, see Fed.Rules Bankr.Proc. Rule 1018, 11 USCA.

Substitution of parties, see Fed.Rules Bankr.Proc. Rule 7025, 11 USCA.

Rule 7016. Pre-Trial Procedure; Formulating Issues

Rule 16 F.R.Civ.P. applies in adversary proceedings.

CROSS REFERENCES

Amended and supplemental pleadings, see Fed.Rules Bankr.Proc. Rule 7015, 11 USCA.

Applicability of this rule in proceedings on contested involuntary petition and to vacate order for relief, see Fed.Rules Bankr.Proc. Rule 1018, 11 USCA.

Preliminary hearing before trial to determine merit of defenses, see Fed.Rules Bankr.Proc. Rule 7012, 11 USCA.

Rule 7017. Parties Plaintiff and Defendant; Capacity

Rule 17 F.R.Civ.P. applies in adversary proceedings, except as provided in Rule 2010(b).

(As amended Apr. 30, 1991, eff. Aug. 1, 1991.)

ADVISORY COMMITTEE NOTES

Rules 2010(d) and 5008(d), which implement §§ 322 and 345 of the Code, authorize a party in interest to prosecute a claim on the bond of a trustee or depository in the name of the United States.

1991 Amendment

Reference to Rule 5008(d) is deleted because of the abrogation of Rule 5008.

CROSS REFERENCES

Bond requirement for deposit or investment by trustee of estate money, see 11 USCA § 345.

Filing by trustee of bond in favor of United States as qualification to serve, see 11 USCA § 322.

Service upon infants or incompetent persons of—

- Notice of application for depositions before adversary proceedings or pending appeal, see Fed.Rules Bankr. Proc. Rule 7027, 11 USCA.
- Summons and complaint, see Fed.Rules Bankr.Proc. Rule 7004, 11 USCA.

Rule 7018. Joinder of Claims and Remedies

Rule 18 F.R.Civ.P. applies in adversary proceedings.

CROSS REFERENCES

Joinder of parties—

- Misjoinder and non-joinder, see Fed.Rules Bankr.Proc. Rule 7021, 11 USCA.
- Permissive joinder, see Fed.Rules Bankr.Proc. Rule 7020, 11 USCA.
- Persons needed for just determination, see Fed.Rules Bankr.Proc. Rule 7019, 11 USCA.

Rule 7019. Joinder of Persons Needed for Just Determination

Rule 19 F.R.Civ.P. applies in adversary proceedings, except that (1) if an entity joined as a party raises the defense that the court lacks jurisdiction over the subject matter and the defense is sustained, the court shall dismiss such entity from the adversary proceeding and (2) if an entity joined as a party properly and timely raises the defense of improper venue, the court shall determine, as provided in 28 U.S.C. § 1412, whether that part of the proceeding involving the joined party shall be transferred to another district, or whether the entire adversary proceeding shall be transferred to another district.

(As amended Mar. 30, 1987, eff. Aug. 1, 1987.)

ADVISORY COMMITTEE NOTES

This rule addresses a situation different from that encountered by the district court when its jurisdiction is based on diversity of citizenship under 28 U.S.C. § 1332. Joining of a party whose citizenship is the same as that of an adversary destroys the district court's jurisdiction over the entire civil action but under 28 U.S.C. § 1471 the attempted joinder of such a person would not affect the bankruptcy court's jurisdiction over the original adversary proceeding.

1987 Amendment

The rule is amended to delete the reference to retention of the adversary proceeding if venue is improper. See 28 U.S.C. § 1412.

CROSS REFERENCES

Additional parties for determination of counterclaim or cross-claim, see Fed.Rules Bankr.Proc. Rule 7013, 11 USCA.

Exception to procedural rule on transfer by court of adversary proceeding, see Fed.Rules Bankr.Proc. Rule 7087, 11 USCA.

Parties—

Permissive joinder, see Fed.Rules Bankr.Proc. Rule 7020, 11 USCA.

Substitution of, see Fed.Rules Bankr.Proc. Rule 7025, 11 USCA.

Rule 7020. Permissive Joinder of Parties

Rule 20 F.R.Civ.P. applies in adversary proceedings.

CROSS REFERENCES

Additional parties for determination of counterclaim or cross-claim, see Fed.Rules Bankr.Proc. Rule 7013, 11 USCA.

Parties—

Joinder of persons needed for just determination, see Fed.Rules Bankr.Proc. Rule 7019, 11 USCA.

Substitution of, see Fed.Rules Bankr.Proc. Rule 7025, 11 USCA.

Rule 7021. Misjoinder and Non-Joinder of Parties

Rule 21 F.R.Civ.P. applies in adversary proceedings.

CROSS REFERENCES

Applicability of this rule in contested matters not otherwise provided for, see Fed.Rules Bankr.Proc. Rule 9014, 11 USCA.

Judgment on counterclaim or cross-claim rendered in separate trials, see Fed.Rules Bankr.Proc. Rule 7013, 11 USCA.

Separate trials—

In furtherance of convenience or to avoid prejudice, see Fed.Rules Bankr.Proc. Rule 7042, 11 USCA.

Of parties joined permissively, see Fed.Rules Bankr. Proc. Rule 7020, 11 USCA.

Rule 7022. Interpleader

Rule 22(a) F.R.Civ.P. applies in adversary proceedings. This rule supplements—and does not limit—the joinder of parties allowed by Rule 7020.

(As amended Apr. 23, 2008, eff. Dec. 1, 2008.)

ADVISORY COMMITTEE NOTES

2008 Amendments

The rule is amended to conform to the changes made to the Federal Rules of Civil Procedure through the restyling of those rules effective on December 1, 2007.

CROSS REFERENCES

Preliminary injunction in interpleader actions, see Fed. Rules Bankr.Proc. Rule 7065, 11 USCA.

Rule 7023. Class proceedings

Rule 23 F.R.Civ.P. applies in adversary proceedings.

CROSS REFERENCES

Exception of class actions from procedural rule of necessary joinder of parties, see Fed.Rules Bankr.Proc. Rule 7019, 11 USCA.

Rule 7023.1. Derivative Actions

Rule 23.1 F.R.Civ.P. applies in adversary proceedings.

(As amended Apr. 23, 2008, eff. Dec. 1,2008.)

ADVISORY COMMITTEE NOTES

2008 Amendments

The rule is amended to conform to the changes made to the Federal Rules of Civil Procedure through the restyling of those rules effective on December 1, 2007.

CROSS REFERENCES

Actions relating to unincorporated associations, see Fed. Rules Bankr.Proc. Rule 7023.1, 11 USCA.

Rule 7023.2. Adversary Proceedings Relating to Unincorporated Associations

Rule 23.2 F.R.Civ.P. applies in adversary proceedings.

CROSS REFERENCES

Capacity of unincorporated association to sue or be sued, see Fed.Rules Bankr.Proc. Rule 7017, 11 USCA.

Derivative actions by shareholders, see Fed.Rules Bankr. Proc. Rule 7023.1, 11 USCA.

Rule 7024. Intervention

Rule 24 F.R.Civ.P. applies in adversary proceedings.

ADVISORY COMMITTEE NOTES

A person may seek to intervene in the case under the Code or in an adversary proceeding relating to the case under the Code. Intervention in a case under the Code is governed by Rule 2018 and intervention in an adversary proceeding is governed by this rule. Intervention in a case and intervention in an adversary proceeding must be sought separately.

CROSS REFERENCES

Applicability of this rule in proceedings on contested involuntary petition and to vacate order for relief, see Fed.Rules Bankr.Proc. Rule 1018, 11 USCA.

Intervention in case under this title, see Fed.Rules Bankr. Proc. Rule 2018, 11 USCA.

Rule 7025. Substitution of Parties

Subject to the provisions of Rule 2012, Rule 25 F.R.Civ.P. applies in adversary proceedings.

ADVISORY COMMITTEE NOTES

Rule 25 F.R.Civ.P. refers to Rule 4 F.R.Civ.P. Pursuant to Rule 7002 that reference is to Rule 4 as incorporated and modified by Rule 7004.

CROSS REFERENCES

Applicability of this rule in—

Contested matters not otherwise provided for, see Fed. Rules Bankr.Proc. Rule 9014, 11 USCA.

Proceedings on contested involuntary petition and to vacate order for relief, see Fed.Rules Bankr.Proc. Rule 1018, 11 USCA.

Right to use depositions previously taken, see Fed.Rules Bankr.Proc. Rule 7026, 11 USCA.

Rule 7026. General Provisions Governing Discovery

Rule 26 F.R.Civ.P. applies in adversary proceedings.

CROSS REFERENCES

Applicability of this rule in—

Contested matters not otherwise provided for, see Fed. Rules Bankr.Proc. Rule 9014, 11 USCA.

Proceedings on contested involuntary petition and to vacate order for relief, see Fed.Rules Bankr.Proc. Rule 1018, 11 USCA.

Failure to make discovery; sanctions, see Fed.Rules Bankr.Proc. Rule 7037, 11 USCA.

Subpoena for taking depositions; place of examination, see Fed.Rules Bankr.Proc. Rule 9016, 11 USCA.

Rule 7027. Depositions Before Adversary Proceedings or Pending Appeal

Rule 27 F.R.Civ.P. applies to adversary proceedings.

ADVISORY COMMITTEE NOTES

Rule 27(a)(2) F.R.Civ.P. refers to Rule 4 F.R.Civ.P. Pursuant to Rule 7002 the reference is to Rule 4 F.R.Civ.P. as incorporated and modified by Rule 7004.

CROSS REFERENCES

Applicability of this rule in contested matters not otherwise provided for, see Fed.Rules Bankr.Proc. Rule 9014, 11 USCA.

Rule 7028. Persons Before Whom Depositions May be Taken

Rule 28 F.R.Civ.P. applies in adversary proceedings.

CROSS REFERENCES

Affirmations, see Fed.Rules Bankr.Proc. Rule 9012, 11 USCA.

Applicability of this rule in—

Contested matters not otherwise provided for, see Fed. Rules Bankr.Proc. Rule 9014, 11 USCA.

Proceedings on contested involuntary petition and to vacate order for relief, see Fed.Rules Bankr.Proc. Rule 1018, 11 USCA.

Rule 7029. Stipulations Regarding Discovery Procedure

Rule 29 F.R.Civ.P. applies in adversary proceedings.

CROSS REFERENCES

Applicability of this rule in—

Contested matters not otherwise provided for, see Fed. Rules Bankr.Proc. Rule 9014, 11 USCA.

Proceedings on contested involuntary petition and to vacate order for relief, see Fed.Rules Bankr.Proc. Rule 1018, 11 USCA.

Rule 7030. Depositions Upon Oral Examination

Rule 30 F.R.Civ.P. applies in adversary proceedings.

ADVISORY COMMITTEE NOTES

Rule 30 F.R.Civ.P. refers to Rule 4 F.R.Civ.P. Pursuant to Rule 7002 that reference is a reference to Rule 4 F.R.Civ.P. as incorporated and modified by Rule 7004.

CROSS REFERENCES

Applicability of this rule in—

Contested matters not otherwise provided for, see Fed. Rules Bankr.Proc. Rule 9014, 11 USCA.

Proceedings on contested involuntary petition and to vacate order for relief, see Fed.Rules Bankr.Proc. Rule 1018, 11 USCA.

Failure to make discovery; sanctions, see Fed.Rules Bankr.Proc. Rule 7037, 11 USCA.

Subpoena for taking depositions; place of examination, see Fed.Rules Bankr.Proc. Rule 9016, 11 USCA.

Rule 7031. Deposition Upon Written Questions

Rule 31 F.R.Civ.P. applies in adversary proceedings.

CROSS REFERENCES

Applicability of this rule in—

Contested matters not otherwise provided for, see Fed. Rules Bankr.Proc. Rule 9014, 11 USCA.

Proceedings on contested involuntary petition and to vacate order for relief, see Fed.Rules Bankr.Proc. Rule 1018, 11 USCA.

Failure to make discovery; sanctions, see Fed.Rules Bankr.Proc. Rule 7037, 11 USCA.

Rule 7032. Use of Depositions in Adversary Proceedings

Rule 32 F.R.Civ.P. applies in adversary proceedings.

CROSS REFERENCES

Applicability of this rule in—

Contested matters not otherwise provided for, see Fed. Rules Bankr.Proc. Rule 9014, 11 USCA.

Proceedings on contested involuntary petition and to vacate order for relief, see Fed.Rules Bankr.Proc. Rule 1018, 11 USCA.

Rule 7033. Interrogatories to Parties

Rule 33 F.R.Civ.P. applies in adversary proceedings.

CROSS REFERENCES

Applicability of this rule in—

Contested matters not otherwise provided for, see Fed. Rules Bankr.Proc. Rule 9014, 11 USCA.

Proceedings on contested involuntary petition and to vacate order for relief, see Fed.Rules Bankr.Proc. Rule 1018, 11 USCA.

Failure to make discovery; sanctions, see Fed.Rules Bankr.Proc. Rule 7037, 11 USCA.

Rule 7034. Production of Documents and Things and Entry Upon Land for Inspection and Other Purposes

Rule 34 F.R.Civ.P. applies in adversary proceedings.

CROSS REFERENCES

Applicability of this rule in—

Contested matters not otherwise provided for, see Fed. Rules Bankr.Proc. Rule 9014, 11 USCA.

Proceedings on contested involuntary petition and to vacate order for relief, see Fed.Rules Bankr.Proc. Rule 1018, 11 USCA.

Failure to make discovery; sanctions, see Fed.Rules Bankr.Proc. Rule 7037, 11 USCA.

Subpoena for production of documentary evidence, see Fed.Rules Bankr.Proc. Rule 9016, 11 USCA.

Rule 7035. Physical and Mental Examination of Persons

Rule 35 F.R.Civ.P. applies in adversary proceedings.

CROSS REFERENCES

Applicability of this rule in—

Contested matters not otherwise provided for, see Fed. Rules Bankr.Proc. Rule 9014, 11 USCA.

Proceedings on contested involuntary petition and to vacate order for relief, see Fed.Rules Bankr.Proc. Rule 1018, 11 USCA.

Failure to make discovery; sanctions, see Fed.Rules Bankr.Proc. Rule 7037, 11 USCA.

Rule 7036. Requests for Admission

Rule 36 F.R.Civ.P. applies in adversary proceedings.

CROSS REFERENCES

Applicability of this rule in—

Contested matters not otherwise provided for, see Fed. Rules Bankr.Proc. Rule 9014, 11 USCA.

Proceedings on contested involuntary petition and to vacate order for relief, see Fed.Rules Bankr.Proc. Rule 1018, 11 USCA.

Pre-trial conference to obtain admissions of facts and documents, see Fed.Rules Bankr.Proc. Rule 7016, 11 USCA.

Rule 7037. Failure to Make Discovery: Sanctions

Rule 37 F.R.Civ.P. applies in adversary proceedings.

CROSS REFERENCES

Applicability of this rule in—

Contested matters not otherwise provided for, see Fed. Rules Bankr.Proc. Rule 9014, 11 USCA.

Proceedings on contested involuntary petition and to vacate order for relief, see Fed.Rules Bankr.Proc. Rule 1018, 11 USCA.

Rule 7040. Assignment of Cases for Trial

Rule 40 F.R.Civ.P. applies in adversary proceedings.

CROSS REFERENCES

Local bankruptcy rules on practice and procedure not inconsistent with these rules, see Fed.Rules Bankr.Proc. Rule 9029, 11 USCA.

Rule 7041. Dismissal of Adversary Proceedings

Rule 41 F.R.Civ.P. applies in adversary proceedings, except that a complaint objecting to the debtor's discharge shall not be dismissed at the plaintiff's instance without notice to the trustee, the United States trustee, and such other persons as the court may direct, and only on order of the court containing terms and conditions which the court deems proper.

(As amended Apr. 30, 1991, eff. Aug. 1, 1991.)

ADVISORY COMMITTEE NOTES

Dismissal of a complaint objecting to a discharge raises special concerns because the plaintiff may have been induced to dismiss by an advantage given or promised by the debtor or someone acting in his interest. Some courts by local rule or order have required the debtor and his attorney or the plaintiff to file an affidavit that nothing has been promised to the plaintiff in consideration of the withdrawal of the objection. By specifically authorizing the court to impose conditions in the order of dismissal this rule permits the continuation of this salutary practice.

Rule 41 F.R.Civ.P. refers to Rule 19 F.R.Civ.P. Pursuant to Rule 7002 that reference is to Rule 19 F.R.Civ.P. as incorporated and modified by Rule 7019.

1991 Amendment

The United States trustee has standing to object to the debtor's discharge pursuant to § 727(c) and may have refrained from commencing an adversary proceeding objecting to discharge within the time limits provided in Rule 4004 only because another party commenced such a proceeding. The United States trustee may oppose dismissal of the original proceeding.

The rule is also amended to clarify that the court may direct that other persons receive notice of a plaintiff's motion to dismiss a complaint objecting to discharge.

CROSS REFERENCES

Applicability of this rule in contested matters not otherwise provided for, see Fed.Rules Bankr.Proc. Rule 9014, 11 USCA.

Findings by court necessary when judgment rendered on merits of motion to dismiss after trial on facts, see Fed.Rules Bankr.Proc. Rule 7052, 11 USCA.

Sanction for failure to attend deposition, to answer interrogatories, or to respond to inspection request, see Fed. Rules Bankr.Proc. Rule 7037, 11 USCA.

Rule 7042. Consolidation of Adversary Proceedings; Separate Trials

Rule 42 F.R.Civ.P. applies in adversary proceedings.

CROSS REFERENCES

Applicability of this rule in contested matters not otherwise provided for, see Fed.Rules Bankr.Proc. Rule 9014, 11 USCA.

Separate trials—

Joinder of party against whom no claim exists, see Fed.Rules Bankr.Proc. Rule 7020, 11 USCA.

Separate judgments rendered on counterclaim or cross-claim, see Fed.Rules Bankr.Proc. Rule 7013, 11 USCA.

Rule 7052. Findings by the Court

Rule 52 F.R.Civ.P. applies in adversary proceedings.

ADVISORY COMMITTEE NOTES

Rule 52(a) F.R.Civ.P. refers to Rule 12 F.R.Civ.P. Pursuant to Rule 7002 this reference is to Rule 12 F.R.Civ.P. as incorporated and modified by Rule 7012.

CROSS REFERENCES

Amendment of findings—

On motion for new trial, see Fed.Rules Bankr.Proc. Rule 9023, 11 USCA.

Stay of proceedings to enforce judgment pending disposition of motion to amend, see Fed.Rules Bankr.Proc. Rule 7062, 11 USCA.

Applicability of this rule in—

Contested matters not otherwise provided for, see Fed. Rules Bankr.Proc. Rule 9014, 11 USCA.

Proceedings on contested involuntary petition and to vacate order for relief, see Fed.Rules Bankr.Proc. Rule 1018, 11 USCA.

Effect of motion to amend or to add fact findings on time for appeal, see Fed.Rules Bankr.Proc. Rule 8002, 11 USCA.

Enlargement of ten-day period for motion to amend findings of court not permitted, see Fed.Rules Bankr.Proc. Rule 9006, 11 USCA.

Rule 7054. Judgments; Costs

(a) Judgments

Rule 54(a)–(c) F.R.Civ.P. applies in adversary proceedings.

(b) Costs

The court may allow costs to the prevailing party except when a statute of the United States or these rules otherwise provides. Costs against the United States, its officers and agencies shall be imposed only to the extent permitted by law. Costs may be taxed by the clerk on one day's notice; on motion served within five days thereafter, the action of the clerk may be reviewed by the court.

CROSS REFERENCES

Amendment or alteration—

Stay of proceedings pending disposition of motion for, see Fed.Rules Bankr.Proc. Rule 7062, 11 USCA.

Time for service of motion, see Fed.Rules Bankr.Proc. Rule 9023, 11 USCA.

Applicability of this rule in—

Contested matters not otherwise provided for, see Fed. Rules Bankr.Proc. Rule 9014, 11 USCA.

Proceedings on contested involuntary petition and to vacate order for relief, see Fed.Rules Bankr.Proc. Rule 1018, 11 USCA.

Entry of judgment, district court record of judgment, see Fed.Rules Bankr.Proc. Rule 9021, 11 USCA.

Relief from judgment or order, see Fed.Rules Bankr.Proc. Rule 9024, 11 USCA.

Rule 7055. Default

Rule 55 F.R.Civ.P. applies in adversary proceedings.

CROSS REFERENCES

Applicability of this rule in contested matters not otherwise provided for, see Fed.Rules Bankr.Proc. Rule 9014, 11 USCA.

Demand for judgment, see Fed.Rules Bankr.Proc. Rule 7054, 11 USCA.

Rule 7056. Summary Judgment

Rule 56 F.R.Civ.P. applies in adversary proceedings.

CROSS REFERENCES

Applicability of this rule in—

Contested matters, not otherwise provided for, see Fed. Rules Bankr.Proc. Rule 9014, 11 USCA.

Proceedings on contested involuntary petition and to vacate order for relief, see Fed.Rules Bankr.Proc. Rule 1018, 11 USCA.

Rule 7062. Stay of Proceedings to Enforce a Judgment

Rule 62 F.R.Civ.P. applies in adversary proceedings.

(As amended Apr. 30, 1991, eff. Aug. 1, 1991; Apr. 29, 1999, eff. Dec. 1, 1999.)

ADVISORY COMMITTEE NOTES

The additional exceptions set forth in this rule make applicable to those matters the consequences contained in Rule 62(c) and (d) with respect to orders in actions for injunctions.

1991 Amendment

This rule is amended to include as additional exceptions to Rule 62(a) an order granting relief from the automatic stay of actions against codebtors provided by § 1201 of the Code, the sale or lease of property of the estate under § 363, and the assumption or assignment of an executory contract under § 365.

1999 Amendments

The additional exceptions to Rule 62(a) consist of orders that are issued in contested matters. These exceptions are deleted from this rule because of the amendment to Rule 9014 that renders this rule inapplicable in contested matters unless the court orders otherwise. See also the amendments to Rules 3020, 3021, 4001, 6004, and 6006 that delay the implementation of certain types of orders for a period of ten days unless the court otherwise directs.

Gap Report on Rule 7062. No changes since publication.

CROSS REFERENCES

Applicability of this rule in—

Contested matters not otherwise provided for, see Fed. Rules Bankr.Proc. Rule 9014, 11 USCA.

Proceedings on contested involuntary petition and to vacate order for relief, see Fed.Rules Bankr.Proc. Rule 1018, 11 USCA.

Effect of entry of judgment on availability of relief under this rule, see Fed.Rules Bankr.Proc. Rule 9021, 11 USCA.

Power of court to suspend or to order continuation of other proceedings pending appeal, see Fed.Rules Bankr.Proc. Rule 8005, 11 USCA.

Security; proceedings against sureties, see Fed.Rules Bankr.Proc. Rule 9025, 11 USCA.

Stay of new proceedings until payment of costs of previously dismissed action, see Fed.Rules Bankr.Proc. Rule 7041, 11 USCA.

Rule 7064. Seizure of Person or Property

Rule 64 F.R.Civ.P. applies in adversary proceedings.

CROSS REFERENCES

Applicability of this rule in contested matters not otherwise provided for, see Fed.Rules Bankr.Proc. Rule 9014, 11 USCA.

Writ of attachment or sequestration issued against property ordered by judgment to be conveyed, see Fed.Rules Bankr.Proc. Rule 7070, 11 USCA.

Rule 7065. Injunctions

Rule 65 F.R.Civ.P. applies in adversary proceedings, except that a temporary restraining order or preliminary injunction may be issued on application of a debtor, trustee, or debtor in possession without compliance with Rule 65(c).

CROSS REFERENCES

Injunction pending appeal of interlocutory or final judgment concerning injunction, see Fed.Rules Bankr.Proc. Rule 7062, 11 USCA.

Security; proceedings against sureties, see Fed.Rules Bankr.Proc. Rule 9025, 11 USCA.

Signing and verification of papers, see Fed.Rules Bankr. Proc. Rule 9011, 11 USCA.

Rule 7067. Deposit in Court

Rule 67 F.R.Civ.P. applies in adversary proceedings.

Rule 7068. Offer of Judgment

Rule 68 F.R.Civ.P. applies in adversary proceedings.

Rule 7069. Execution

Rule 69 F.R.Civ.P. applies in adversary proceedings.

CROSS REFERENCES

Applicability of this rule in contested matters not otherwise provided for, see Fed.Rules Bankr.Proc. Rule 9014, 11 USCA.

Effect of entry of judgment on availability of process to enforce judgment, see Fed.Rules Bankr.Proc. Rule 9021, 11 USCA.

Writ of execution to enforce judgment to deliver possession of property, see Fed.Rules Bankr.Proc. Rule 7070, 11 USCA.

Rule 7070. Judgment for Specific Acts; Vesting Title

Rule 70 F.R.Civ.P. applies in adversary proceedings and the court may enter a judgment divesting the title of any party and vesting title in others whenever the real or personal property involved is within the jurisdiction of the court.

(As amended Mar. 30, 1987, eff. Aug. 1, 1987.)

ADVISORY COMMITTEE NOTES

1987 Amendment

The reference to court is used in the amendment because the district court may preside over an adversary proceeding.

CROSS REFERENCES

Effect of entry of judgment on availability of relief under this rule, see Fed.Rules Bankr.Proc. Rule 9021, 11 USCA.

Rule 7071. Process in Behalf of and Against Persons Not Parties

Rule 71 F.R.Civ.P. applies in adversary proceedings.

CROSS REFERENCES

Applicability of this rule in contested matters not otherwise provided for, see Fed.Rules Bankr.Proc. Rule 9014, 11 USCA.

Rule 7087. Transfer of Adversary Proceeding

On motion and after a hearing, the court may transfer an adversary proceeding or any part thereof to another district pursuant to 28 U.S.C. § 1412, except as provided in Rule 7019(2).

(As amended Mar. 30, 1987, eff. Aug. 1, 1987.)

ADVISORY COMMITTEE NOTES

1987 Amendment

The reference to the venue section of title 28 is amended to conform to the 1984 amendments to title 28.

PART VIII—APPEALS TO DISTRICT COURT OR BANKRUPTCY APPELLATE PANEL

Rule 8001. Manner of Taking Appeal; Voluntary Dismissal; Certification to Court of Appeals

(a) Appeal as of right; how taken

An appeal from a judgment, order, or decree of a bankruptcy judge to a district court or bankruptcy appellate panel as permitted by 28 U.S.C. § 158(a)(1) or (a)(2) shall be taken by filing a notice of appeal with the clerk within the time allowed by Rule 8002. An appellant's failure to take any step other than timely filing a notice of appeal does not affect the validity of the appeal, but is ground only for such action as the district court or bankruptcy appellate panel deems appropriate, which may include dismissal of the appeal. The notice of appeal shall (1) conform substantially to the appropriate Official Form, (2) contain the names of all parties to the judgment, order, or decree appealed from and the names, addresses, and telephone numbers of their respective attorneys, and (3) be accompanied by the prescribed fee. Each appellant shall file a sufficient number of copies of the notice of appeal to enable the clerk to comply promptly with Rule 8004.

(b) Appeal by leave; how taken

An appeal from an interlocutory judgment, order, or decree of a bankruptcy judge as permitted by 28 U.S.C. § 158(a)(3) shall be taken by filing a notice of appeal, as prescribed in subdivision (a) of this rule, accompanied by a motion for leave to appeal prepared in accordance with Rule 8003 and with proof of service in accordance with Rule 8008.

(c) Voluntary dismissal

(1) Before docketing

If an appeal has not been docketed, the appeal may be dismissed by the bankruptcy judge on the filing of a stipulation for dismissal signed by all the parties, or on motion and notice by the appellant.

(2) After docketing

If an appeal has been docketed and the parties to the appeal sign and file with the clerk of the district court or the clerk of the bankruptcy appellate panel an agreement that the appeal be dismissed and pay any court costs or fees that may be due, the clerk of the district court or the clerk of the bankruptcy appellate panel shall enter an order dismissing the appeal. An appeal may also be dismissed on motion of the appellant on terms and conditions fixed by the district court or bankruptcy appellate panel.

(d) [Abrogated]

(e) Election to have appeal heard by district court instead of bankruptcy appellate panel; withdrawal of election

(1) Separate writing for election

An election to have an appeal heard by the district court under 28 U.S.C. § 158(c)(1) may be made only by a statement of election contained in a separate writing filed within the time prescribed by 28 U.S.C. § 158(c)(1).

(2) Withdrawal of election

A request to withdraw the election may be filed only by written stipulation of all the parties to the appeal or their attorneys of record. Upon such a stipulation, the district court may either transfer the appeal to the bankruptcy appellate panel or retain the appeal in the district court.

(f) Certification for direct appeal to court of appeals

(1) Timely appeal required

A certification of a judgment, order, or decree of a bankruptcy court to a court of appeals under 28 U.S.C. § 158(d)(2) shall not be effective until a timely appeal has been taken in the manner required by subdivisions (a) or (b) of this rule and the notice of appeal has become effective under Rule 8002.

(2) Court where certification made and filed

A certification that a circumstance specified in 28 U.S.C. § 158(d)(2)(A)(i)–(iii) exists shall be filed in the court in which a matter is pending for purposes of 28 U.S.C. § 158(d)(2) and this rule. A matter is pending in a bankruptcy court until the docketing, in accordance with Rule 8007(b), of an appeal taken under 28 U.S.C. § 158(a)(1) or (2), or the grant of leave to appeal under 28 U.S.C. § 158(a)(3). A matter is pending in a district court or bankruptcy appellate panel after the docketing, in accordance with Rule 8007(b), of an appeal taken under 28 U.S.C. § 158(a)(1) or (2), or the grant of leave to appeal under 28 U.S.C. § 158(a)(3).

(A) Certification by court on request or court's own initiative

(i) Before docketing or grant of leave to appeal

Only a bankruptcy court may make a certification on request or on its own initiative while the matter is pending in the bankruptcy court.

(ii) After docketing or grant of leave to appeal

Only the district court or bankruptcy appellate panel involved may make a certification on request of the parties or on its own initiative while the matter is pending in the district court or bankruptcy appellate panel.

(B) Certification by all appellants and appellees acting jointly

A certification by all the appellants and appellees, if any, acting jointly may be made by filing the appropriate Official Form with the clerk of the court in which the matter is pending. The certification may be accompanied by a short statement of the basis for the certification, which may include the information listed in subdivision (f)(3)(C) of this rule.

(3) Request for certification; filing; service; contents

(A) A request for certification shall be filed, within the time specified by 28 U.S.C. § 158(d)(2), with the clerk of the court in which the matter is pending.

(B) Notice of the filing of a request for certification shall be served in the manner required for service of a notice of appeal under Rule 8004.

(C) A request for certification shall include the following:

(i) the facts necessary to understand the question presented;

(ii) the question itself;

(iii) the relief sought;

(iv) the reasons why the appeal should be allowed and is authorized by statute or rule, including why a circumstance specified in 28 U.S.C. § 158(d)(2)(A)(i)–(iii) exists; and

(v) an attached copy of the judgment, order, or decree complained of and any related opinion or memorandum.

(D) A party may file a response to a request for certification or a cross request within 10 days after the notice of the request is served, or another time fixed by the court.

(E) Rule 9014 does not govern a request, cross request, or any response. The matter shall be submitted without oral argument unless the court otherwise directs.

(F) A certification of an appeal under 28 U.S.C. § 158(d)(2) shall be made in a separate document served on the parties.

(4) Certification on court's own initiative

(A) A certification of an appeal on the court's own initiative under 28 U.S.C. § 158(d)(2) shall be made in a separate document served on the parties in the manner required for service of a notice of appeal under Rule 8004. The certification shall be accompanied by an opinion or memorandum that contains the information required by subdivision (f)(3)(C)(i)–(iv) of this rule.

(B) A party may file a supplementary short statement of the basis for certification within 10 days after the certification.

(5) Duties of parties after certification

A petition for permission to appeal in accordance with F. R. App. P. 5 shall be filed no later than 30 days after a certification has become effective as provided in subdivision (f)(1).

(As amended Mar. 30, 1987, eff. Aug. 1, 1987; Apr. 30, 1991, eff. Aug. 1, 1991; Apr. 11, 1997, eff. Dec. 1, 1997; Apr. 23, 2008, eff. Dec. 1, 2008.)

ADVISORY COMMITTEE NOTES

These rules in Part VIII apply only to appeals to the district courts or bankruptcy appellate panels. Subsequent appeals to the courts of appeals, or direct appeals by agreement of the parties under 28 U.S.C. § 1293(b), are governed by Federal Rules of Appellate Procedure.

Subdivisions (a) and (b) require that a notice of appeal be filed whenever a litigant seeks to secure appellate review by the district court or bankruptcy appellate panel. An appeal from an interlocutory order which will be heard only if leave is granted under 28 U.S.C. §§ 1334(b) or 1482(b) is taken by filing a notice of appeal accompanied by a motion for leave to appeal which complies with the requirements set forth in Rule 8003. Rule 8003 also governs other aspects of interlocutory appeals.

Subdivision (c) is an adaptation of Rule 42 F.R.App.P.

Subdivision (d) deals with the situation in which an appellant perfects an appeal to the district court or a bankruptcy appellate panel and also a direct appeal pursuant to 28 U.S.C. § 1293(b) to the court of appeals. This subdivision provides that once the appeal to the court of appeals is taken, a notice of appeal to the district court or bankruptcy appellate panel shall be dismissed and, if the first appeal is to the district court or bankruptcy appellate panel, the first appeal shall be dismissed. Paragraph (3) gives an appellant or cross appellant an opportunity to file an appeal to the district court or bankruptcy appellate panel if the court of appeals dismisses the direct appeal because the judgment, order, or decree appealed from is not final. Since the court of appeals has determined the judgment, order, or decree is not final, the new appeal is an appeal for which leave is necessary.

1987 Amendment

Subdivisions (a) and (b) are amended to conform to the 1984 amendments.

Subdivision (d) is abrogated because there is no direct appeal to the court of appeals under 28 U.S.C. § 158, as enacted by the 1984 amendments.

Subdivision (e) is new. Section 158(b)(1) of title 28 authorizes the circuit councils to establish bankruptcy appellate panels. Appeals may not be heard by these panels unless the district court authorizes the referral and all parties to the appeal consent. This rule requires that the parties consent to such an appeal; however, the method of consenting to an appeal may be the subject of a rule promulgated by a circuit council under Rule 8018.

1991 Amendment

Reference to the Official Form number is deleted in anticipation of future revision and renumbering of the Official Forms.

1997 Amendment

This rule is amended to conform to the Bankruptcy Reform Act of 1994 which amended 28 U.S.C. § 158. As amended, a party may—without obtaining leave of the court—appeal from an interlocutory order or decree of the bankruptcy court issued under § 1121(d) of the Code increasing or reducing the time periods referred to in § 1121.

Subdivision (e) is amended to provide the procedure for electing under 28 U.S.C. § 158(c)(1) to have an appeal heard by the district court instead of the bankruptcy appellate panel service. This subdivision is applicable only if a bankruptcy appellate panel service is authorized under 28 U.S.C. § 158(b) to hear the appeal.

GAP Report on Rule 8001. The heading of subdivision (e) is amended to clarify that it applies to the election to have an appeal heard by the district court instead of the BAP. The final paragraph of the Committee Note is revised to clarify that subdivision (e) is applicable only if a BAP is authorized to hear the appeal.

2008 Amendments

Subdivision (e) is amended by redesignating the subdivision as (e)(1) and adding new subdivision (e)(2). Subdivision (e)(2) explicitly recognizes the district court's authority to transfer an appeal to the bankruptcy appellate panel on two conditions: first, all of the parties to the appeal must have agreed to request the withdrawal of the election to have the district court hear the appeal; and, second, the district court must decide whether to grant the request for withdrawal. The district court has discretion either to keep the case or transfer it to the bankruptcy appellate panel, which will prevent strategic behavior by parties and avoid the wasting of judicial resources.

Subdivision (f) is added to the rule to implement the 2005 amendments to 28 U.S.C. § 158(d). That section authorizes appeals directly to the court of appeals, with that court's consent, upon certification that a ground for the appeal exists under § 158(d)(2)(A)(i)–(iii). Certification can be made by the court on its own initiative under subdivision (f)(4), or in response to a request of a party or a majority of the appellants and appellees (if any) under subdivision (f)(3). Certification also can be made by all of the appellants and appellees under subdivision (f)(2)(B). Under subdivision (f)(1), certification is effective only when a timely appeal is commenced under subdivision (a) or (b), and a notice of appeal has been timely filed under Rule 8002. These actions will provide sufficient notice of the appeal to the circuit clerk, so the rule dispenses with the uncodified temporary procedural requirements set out in § 1233(b)(4) of the Bankruptcy Abuse Prevention and Consumer Protection Act of 2005, Pub. L. No. 109–8.

The rule adopts a bright-line test for identifying the court in which a matter is pending. Under subdivision (f)(2), the bright-line chosen is the "docketing" under Rule 8007(b) of an appeal of an interlocutory order or decree under 28 U.S.C. § 158(a)(2) or a final judgment, order or decree under 28 U.S.C. § 158(a)(1), or the granting of leave to appeal any other interlocutory judgment, order or decree under 28 U.S.C. § 158(a)(3), whichever is earlier.

To ensure that parties are aware of a certification, the rule requires either that it be made on the Official Form (if being made by all of the parties to the appeal) or on a separate document (whether the certification is made on the court's own initiative or in response to a request by a party). This is particularly important because the rule adopts the bankruptcy practice established by Rule 8001(a) and (b) of requiring a notice of appeal in every instance, including interlocutory orders, of appeals from bankruptcy court orders, judgments, and decrees. Because this requirement is satisfied by filing the notice of appeal that takes the appeal to the district court or bankruptcy appellate panel in the first instance, the rule does not require a separate notice of appeal if a certification occurs after a district court or bankruptcy appellate panel decision.

A certification under subdivision (f)(1) does not place the appeal in the circuit court. Rather, the court of appeals must first authorize the direct appeal. Subdivision (f)(5) therefore provides that any party intending to pursue the appeal in the court of appeals must seek that permission under Rule 5 of the Federal Rules of Appellate Procedure. Subdivision (f)(5) requires that the petition for permission to appeal be filed within 30 days after an effective certification.

CROSS REFERENCES

Appeals as of right, when taken, see Federal Rules of Appellate Procedure Rule 3, 28 USCA.

Effect of clerk's retention and indexing of judgment on appealability and proceedings on appeal, see Fed.Rules Bankr.Proc. Rule 9021, 11 USCA.

Suspension of this rule, see Fed.Rules Bankr.Proc. Rule 8019, 11 USCA.

Time to file and to serve items of record and statement of issues on appeal, see Fed.Rules Bankr.Proc. Rule 8006, 11 USCA.

Voluntary dismissal, see Federal Rules of Appellate Procedure Rule 42, 28 USCA.

Rule 8002. Time for Filing Notice of Appeal

(a) Ten-day period

The notice of appeal shall be filed with the clerk within 10 days of the date of the entry of the judgment, order, or decree appealed from. If a timely notice of appeal is filed by a party, any other party may file a notice of appeal within 10 days of the date on which the first notice of appeal was filed, or within the time otherwise prescribed by this rule, whichever period last expires. A notice of appeal filed after the announcement of a decision or order but before entry of the judgment, order, or decree shall be treated as filed after such entry and on the day thereof. If a notice of appeal is mistakenly filed with the district court or the bankruptcy appellate panel, the clerk of the district court or the clerk of the bankruptcy appellate panel shall note thereon the date on which it was received and transmit it to the clerk and it shall be deemed filed with the clerk on the date so noted.

(b) Effect of motion on time for appeal

If any party makes a timely motion of a type specified immediately below, the time for appeal for all parties runs from the entry of the order disposing of the last such motion outstanding. This provision applies to a timely motion:

(1) to amend or make additional findings of fact under Rule 7052, whether or not granting the motion would alter the judgment;

(2) to alter or amend the judgment under Rule 9023;

(3) for a new trial under Rule 9023; or

(4) for relief under Rule 9024 if the motion is filed no later than 10 days after the entry of judgment. A notice of appeal filed after announcement or entry of the judgment, order, or decree but before disposition of any of the above motions is ineffective to appeal from the judgment, order, or decree, or part thereof, specified in the notice of appeal, until the entry of the order disposing of the last such motion outstanding. Appellate review of an order disposing of any of the above motions requires the party, in compliance with Rule 8001, to amend a previously filed notice of appeal. A party intending to challenge an alteration or amendment of the judgment, order, or decree shall file a notice, or an amended notice, of appeal within the time prescribed by this Rule 8002 measured from the entry of the order disposing of the last such motion outstanding. No additional fees will be required for filing an amended notice.

(c) Extension of time for appeal

(1) The bankruptcy judge may extend the time for filing the notice of appeal by any party, unless the judgment, order, or decree appealed from:

(A) grants relief from an automatic stay under § 362, § 922, § 1201, or § 1301;

(B) authorizes the sale or lease of property or the use of cash collateral under § 363;

(C) authorizes the obtaining of credit under § 364;

(D) authorizes the assumption or assignment of an executory contract or unexpired lease under § 365;

(E) approves a disclosure statement under § 1125; or

(F) confirms a plan under § 943, § 1129, § 1225, or § 1325 of the Code.

(2) A request to extend the time for filing a notice of appeal must be made by written motion filed before the time for filing a notice of appeal has expired, except that such a motion filed not later than 20 days after the expiration of the time for filing a notice of appeal may be granted upon a showing of excusable neglect. An extension of time for filing a notice of appeal may not exceed 20 days from the expiration of the time for filing a notice of appeal otherwise prescribed by this rule or 10 days from the date of entry of the order granting the motion, whichever is later.

(As amended Mar. 30, 1987, eff. Aug. 1, 1987; Apr. 30, 1991, eff. Aug. 1, 1991; Apr. 29, 1994, eff. Aug. 1, 1994; Apr. 11, 1997, eff. Dec. 1, 1997.)

ADVISORY COMMITTEE NOTES

This rule is an adaptation of Rule 4(a) F.R.App.P. The time to appeal from a judgment, order, or decree of a bankruptcy judge is 10 days, rather than the 30 days provided for in the civil practice. The shortened time is specified in order to obtain prompt appellate review, often important to the administration of a case under the Code. If a timely notice of appeal is filed, other parties have an additional 10 days within which to file a notice of appeal. A notice of appeal filed within the additional 10 day period by an appellee is a cross appeal, but there is a separate appeal if a non-appellee files a notice of appeal within that 10 day period. The district courts and bankruptcy appellate panels have inherent authority to consolidate appeals.

Subdivision (b) is essentially the same as Rule 4(a)(4) of the F.R.App.P.

Subdivision (c) is similar to former Bankruptcy Rule 802(c). To expedite the disposition of appeals the maximum extension of time is 20 days instead of the 30 days provided by Rule 4(a)(5) of the F.R.App.P. Subject to the exceptions set forth in subdivision (c), the court may extend the time for taking an appeal when a motion for extension is filed after the expiration of the original 10 day period but no later than 20 days after the expiration of the original 10 day period. Orders of the bankruptcy court relating to the sale of property, extension of credit, confirmation of a plan, dismissal or conversion of the case, and approval of the disclosure statement are of such significance to the administration of the case, the parties in interest, and third parties that this subdivision requires that either an appeal or a motion for extension be filed within the original 10 day period.

If a timely notice of appeal is not filed, no appeal may be taken later. Former Bankruptcy Rule 803, which provided that a referee's judgment became final when the appeal period expired, has been omitted as unnecessary.

1991 Amendment

Subdivision (a) is amended to conform to F.R.App.P. 4(a)(2) which is designed to avoid the loss of the right to appeal when a notice of appeal is filed prematurely.

Subdivision (b)(1) is deleted because Rule 9015 was abrogated in 1987.

1994 Amendments

These amendments are intended to conform to the 1993 amendments to F.R.App.P. 4(a)(4) and 6(b)(2)(i).

This rule as amended provides that a notice of appeal filed before the disposition of a specified postjudgment motion will become effective upon disposition of the motion. A notice filed before the filing of one of the specified motions or after the filing of a motion but before disposition of the motion is, in effect, suspended until the motion is disposed of, whereupon, the previously filed notice effectively places jurisdiction in the district court or bankruptcy appellate panel.

Because a notice of appeal will ripen into an effective appeal upon disposition of a postjudgment motion, in some instances there will be an appeal from a judgment that has been altered substantially because the motion was granted in whole or in part. The appeal may be dismissed for want of prosecution when the appellant fails to meet the briefing schedule. But, the appellee may also move to strike the appeal. When responding to such a motion, the appellant would have an opportunity to state that, even though some relief sought in a postjudgment motion was granted, the appellant still plans to pursue the appeal. Because the appellant's response would provide the appellee with sufficient notice of the appellant's intentions, the rule does not require an additional notice of appeal in that situation.

The amendment provides that a notice of appeal filed before the disposition of a postjudgment tolling motion is sufficient to bring the judgment, order, or decree specified in the original notice of appeal to the district court or bankruptcy appellate panel. If the judgment is altered upon disposition of a postjudgment motion, however, and if a party who has previously filed a notice of appeal wishes to appeal from the disposition of the motion, the party must amend the notice to so indicate. When a party files an amended notice, no additional fees are required because the notice is an amendment of the original and not a new notice of appeal.

Subdivision (b) is also amended to include, among motions that extend the time for filing a notice of appeal, a motion under Rule 9024 that is filed within 10 days after entry of a judgment. The addition of this motion conforms to a similar amendment to F.R.App.P. 4(a)(4) made in 1993, except that a Rule 9024 motion does not toll the time to appeal unless it is filed within the 10-day period. The reason for providing that the motion extends the time to appeal only if it is filed within the 10-day period is to enable the court and the parties in interest to determine solely from the court records whether the time to appeal has been extended by a motion for relief under Rule 9024.

1997 Amendment

Subdivision (c) is amended to provide that a request for an extension of time to file a notice of appeal must be filed within the applicable time period. This amendment will avoid uncertainty as to whether the mailing of a motion or an oral request in court is sufficient to request an extension of time, and will enable the court and the parties in interest to determine solely from the court records whether a timely request for an extension has been made.

The amendments also give the court discretion to permit a party to file a notice of appeal more than 20 days after expiration of the time to appeal otherwise prescribed, but only if the motion was timely filed and the notice of appeal is filed within a period not exceeding 10 days after entry of the order extending the time. This amendment is designed to protect parties that file timely motions to extend the time to appeal from the harshness of the present rule as demonstrated in In re Mouradick, 13 F.3d 326 (9th Cir.1994), where the court held that a notice of appeal filed within the 3–day period expressly prescribed by an order granting a timely motion for an extension of time did not confer jurisdiction on the appellate court because the notice of appeal was not filed within the 20–day period specified in subdivision (c).

The subdivision is amended further to prohibit any extension of time to file a notice of appeal—even if the motion for an extension is filed before the expiration of the original time to appeal—if the order appealed from grants relief from the automatic stay, authorizes the sale or lease of property, use of cash collateral, obtaining of credit, or assumption or assignment of an executory contract or unexpired lease under § 365, or approves a disclosure statement or confirms a plan. These types of orders are often relied upon immediately after they are entered and should not be reviewable on appeal after the expiration of the original appeal period under Rule 8002(a) and (b).

GAP Report on Rule 8002. No changes to the published draft.

CROSS REFERENCES

Appeal as of right, how taken, see Fed.Rules Bankr.Proc. Rule 8001, 11 USCA.

Appeals as of right, when taken, see Federal Rules of Appellate Procedure Rule 4, 28 USCA.

Filing notice of appeal, ten-day period—

Enlargement permitted as limited in this rule, see Fed. Rules Bankr.Proc. Rule 9006, 11 USCA.

Reduction not permitted, see Fed.Rules Bankr.Proc. Rule 9006, 11 USCA.

Lack of notice of judgment has no affect on time to appeal nor relief from failure to appeal except as permitted in this rule, see Fed.Rules Bankr.Proc. Rule 9022, 11 USCA.

Suspension of this rule, see Fed.Rules Bankr.Proc. Rule 8019, 11 USCA.

Rule 8003. Leave to Appeal

(a) Content of motion; answer

A motion for leave to appeal under 28 U.S.C. § 158(a) shall contain: (1) a statement of the facts necessary to an understanding of the questions to be presented by the appeal; (2) a statement of those questions and of the relief sought; (3) a statement of the reasons why an appeal should be granted; and (4) a copy of the judgment, order, or decree complained of and of any opinion or memorandum relating thereto. Within 10 days after service of the motion, an adverse party may file with the clerk an answer in opposition.

(b) Transmittal; determination of motion

The clerk shall transmit the notice of appeal, the motion for leave to appeal and any answer thereto to the clerk of the district court or the clerk of the bankruptcy appellate panel as soon as all parties have filed answers or the time for filing an answer has expired. The motion and answer shall be submitted without oral argument unless otherwise ordered.

(c) Appeal improperly taken regarded as a motion for leave to appeal

If a required motion for leave to appeal is not filed, but a notice of appeal is timely filed, the district court or bankruptcy appellate panel may grant leave to appeal or direct that a motion for leave to appeal be filed. The district court or the bankruptcy appellate panel may also deny leave to appeal but in so doing shall consider the notice of appeal as a motion for leave to appeal. Unless an order directing that a motion for leave to appeal be filed provides otherwise, the motion shall be filed within 10 days of entry of the order.

(d) Requirement of leave to appeal

If leave to appeal is required by 28 U.S.C. § 158(a) and has not earlier been granted, the authorization of a direct appeal by a court of appeals under 28 U.S.C. § 158(d)(2) shall be deemed to satisfy the requirement for leave to appeal.

(As amended Mar. 30, 1987, eff. Aug. 1, 1987; Apr. 23, 2008, eff. Dec. 1, 2008.)

ADVISORY COMMITTEE NOTES

Subdivisions (a) and (b) of this rule are derived from Rules 5 and 6 F.R.App.P. The motion for leave to appeal is addressed to the district court or the bankruptcy appellate panel, although filed with the clerk of the bankruptcy court.

Subdivision (c) provides that if a party mistakenly believes the order appealed from is final and files only a notice of appeal, the appeal is not automatically dismissed. The district court or bankruptcy appellate panel has the options to direct that a motion be filed, to decide exclusively on the papers already filed to grant leave to appeal, or to deny leave to appeal. Cf. 28 U.S.C. § 2103.

2008 Amendments

The rule is amended to add subdivision (d) to solve the jurisdictional problem that could otherwise ensue when a district court or bankruptcy appellate panel has not granted leave to appeal under 28 U.S.C. § 158(a)(3). If the court of appeals accepts the appeal, the requirement of leave to appeal is deemed satisfied. However, if the court of appeals does not authorize a direct appeal, the question of whether to grant leave to appeal remains a matter to be resolved by the district court or the bankruptcy appellate panel.

CROSS REFERENCES

Appeal—

After dismissal of direct appeal by court of appeals, when taken, see Fed.Rules Bankr.Proc. Rule 8001, 11 USCA.

By leave, how taken, see Fed.Rules Bankr.Proc. Rule 8001, 11 USCA.

Effect of clerk's retention and indexing of judgment on appealability and proceedings on appeal, see Fed.Rules Bankr.Proc. Rule 9021, 11 USCA.

Rule 8004. Service of the Notice of Appeal

The clerk shall serve notice of the filing of a notice of appeal by mailing a copy thereof to counsel of record of each party other than the appellant or, if a party is not represented by counsel, to the party's last known address. Failure to serve notice shall not affect the validity of the appeal. The clerk shall note on each copy served the date of the filing of the notice of appeal and shall note in the docket the names of the parties to whom copies are mailed and the date of the mailing. The clerk shall forthwith transmit to the United States trustee a copy of the notice of appeal, but failure to transmit such notice shall not affect the validity of the appeal.

(As amended Mar. 30, 1987, eff. Aug. 1, 1987; Apr. 30, 1991, eff. Aug. 1, 1991.)

ADVISORY COMMITTEE NOTES

This rule is an adaptation of Rule 3(d) F.R.App.P.

1991 Amendment

This rule is amended to keep the United States trustee informed of the progress of the case.

CROSS REFERENCES

Appeals as of right, how taken, see Federal Rules of Appellate Procedure Rule 3, 28 USCA.

Filing by appellant of sufficient number of copies of notice of appeal, see Fed.Rules Bankr.Proc. Rule 8001, 11 USCA.

Notice of appeal under 28 U.S.C. § 158(a) or (b) from a judgment, order, or decree of a Bankruptcy Judge, see Official Bankr. Form 17, 11 USCA.

Rule 8005. Stay Pending Appeal

A motion for a stay of the judgment, order, or decree of a bankruptcy judge, for approval of a supersedeas bond, or for other relief pending appeal must ordinarily be presented to the bankruptcy judge in the first instance. Notwithstanding Rule 7062 but subject to the power of the district court and the bankruptcy appellate panel reserved hereinafter, the bankruptcy judge may suspend or order the continuation of other proceedings in the case under the Code or make any other appropriate order during the pendency of an appeal on such terms as will protect the rights of all parties in interest. A motion for such relief, or for modification or termination of relief granted by a bankruptcy judge, may be made to the district court or the bankruptcy appellate panel, but the motion shall show why the relief, modification, or termination was not obtained from the bankruptcy judge. The district court or the bankruptcy appellate panel may condition the relief it grants under this rule on the filing of a bond or other appropriate security with the bankruptcy court. When an appeal is taken by a trustee, a bond or other appropriate security may be required, but when an appeal is taken by the United States or an officer or agency thereof or by direction of any department of the Government of the United States a bond or other security shall not be required.

(As amended Mar. 30, 1987, eff. Aug. 1, 1987.)

ADVISORY COMMITTEE NOTES

The first, third, and fourth sentences of this rule are adaptations of Rule 8(a) and (b) F.R.App.P. The second sentence of the rule is derived from § 39(c) of the Bankruptcy Act [former § 67(c) of this title] and confers on the bankruptcy judge discretion respecting the stay or continuation of other proceedings in the case while an appeal is pending.

The last sentence of the rule, which specifically subjects a trustee to the same kind of security requirements as other litigants, is derived from former Bankruptcy Rule 805. The exemption of the United States from the bond or security requirements is the same as the exemption contained in Rule 62(e) F.R.Civ.P.

Sections 363(m) and 364(e) of the Code provide that unless an order approving a sale of property, or authorizing the obtaining of credit or the incurring of debt is stayed pending appeal, the sale of property to a good faith purchaser or a good faith extension of credit, with or without any priority or lien, shall not be affected by the reversal or modification of such order on appeal, whether or not the purchaser or creditor knows of the pendency of the appeal.

CROSS REFERENCES

Effect of clerk's retention and indexing of judgment on appealability and proceedings on appeal, see Fed.Rules Bankr.Proc. Rule 9021, 11 USCA.

Security; proceedings against sureties, see Fed.Rules Bankr.Proc. Rule 9025, 11 USCA.

Stay of proceedings to enforce judgment, see Fed.Rules Bankr.Proc. Rule 7062, 11 USCA.

Rule 8006. Record and Issues on Appeal

Within 10 days after filing the notice of appeal as provided by Rule 8001(a), entry of an order granting leave to appeal, or entry of an order disposing of the last timely motion outstanding of a type specified in Rule 8002(b), whichever is later, the appellant shall file with the clerk and serve on the appellee a designation of the items to be included in the record on appeal and a statement of the issues to be presented. Within 10 days after the service of the appellant's statement the appellee may file and serve on the appellant a designation of additional items to be included in the record on appeal and, if the appellee has filed a cross appeal, the appellee as cross appellant shall file and serve a statement of the issues to be presented on the cross appeal and a designation of additional items to be included in the record. A cross appellee may, within 10 days of service of the cross appellant's statement, file and serve on the cross appellant a designation of additional items to be included in the record. The record on appeal shall include the items so designated by the parties, the notice of appeal, the judgment, order, or decree appealed from, and any opinion, findings of fact, and conclusions of law of the court. Any party filing a designation of the items to be included in the record shall provide to the clerk a copy of the items designated or, if the party fails to provide the copy, the clerk shall prepare the copy at the party's expense. If the record designated by any party includes a transcript of any proceeding or a part thereof, the party shall, immediately after filing the designation, deliver to the reporter and file with the clerk a written request for the transcript and make satisfactory arrangements for payment of its cost. All parties shall take any other action necessary to enable the clerk to assemble and transmit the record.

(As amended Mar. 30, 1987, eff. Aug. 1, 1987; Apr. 30, 1991, eff. Aug. 1, 1991; Apr. 29, 1994, eff. Aug. 1, 1994.)

ADVISORY COMMITTEE NOTES

This rule is an adaptation of Rule 10(b) F.R.App.P. The last sentence of the rule is derived from Rule 11(a) F.R.App.P.

1991 Amendment

The seven-day time periods are changed to 10 days to conform to Rule 75(b)(2) F.R.Civ.P. and Rule 10(b)(3) F.R.App.P. The amendment requiring a party to provide a copy of the items designated for the record is to facilitate the amendments to Rule 8007 providing for retention by the bankruptcy clerk of the original record.

1994 Amendments

The amendment to the first sentence of this rule is made together with the amendment to Rule 8002(b), which provides, in essence, that certain specified postjudgment motions suspend a filed notice of appeal until the disposition of the last of such motions. The purpose of this amendment is to suspend the 10-day period for filing and serving a designation of the record and statement of the issues if a timely postjudgment motion is made and a notice of appeal is suspended under Rule 8002(b). The 10-day period set forth in the first sentence of this rule begins to run when the order disposing of the last of such postjudgment motions outstanding is entered. The other amendments to this rule are stylistic.

CROSS REFERENCES

Effect of clerk's retention and indexing of judgment on appealability and proceedings on appeal, see Fed.Rules Bankr.Proc. Rule 9021, 11 USCA.

Record on appeal for all purposes, see Fed.Rules Bankr. Proc. Rule 8007, 11 USCA.

Record on appeal, see Federal Rules of Appellate Procedure Rule 10, 28 USCA.

Transmission of record on appeal, see Federal Rules of Appellate Procedure Rule 11, 28 USCA.

Rule 8007. Completion and Transmission of the Record; Docketing of the Appeal

(a) Duty of reporter to prepare and file transcript

On receipt of a request for a transcript, the reporter shall acknowledge on the request the date it was received and the date on which the reporter expects to have the transcript completed and shall transmit the request, so endorsed, to the clerk or the clerk of the bankruptcy appellate panel. On completion of the transcript the reporter shall file it with the clerk and, if appropriate, notify the clerk of the bankruptcy appellate panel. If the transcript cannot be completed within 30 days of receipt of the request the reporter shall seek an extension of time from the clerk or the clerk of the bankruptcy appellate panel and the action of the clerk shall be entered in the docket and the parties notified. If the reporter does not file the transcript within the time allowed, the clerk or the clerk of the bankruptcy appellate panel shall notify the bankruptcy judge.

(b) Duty of clerk to transmit copy of record; docketing of appeal

When the record is complete for purposes of appeal, the clerk shall transmit a copy thereof forthwith to the clerk of the district court or the clerk of the bankruptcy appellate panel. On receipt of the transmission the clerk of the district court or the clerk of the bankruptcy appellate panel shall enter the appeal in the docket and give notice promptly to all parties to the judgment, order, or decree appealed from of the date on which the appeal was docketed. If the bankruptcy appellate panel directs that additional copies of the record be furnished, the clerk of the bankruptcy appellate panel shall notify the appellant and, if the appellant fails to provide the copies, the clerk shall prepare the copies at the expense of the appellant.

(c) Record for preliminary hearing

If prior to the time the record is transmitted a party moves in the district court or before the bankruptcy appellate panel for dismissal, for a stay pending appeal, for additional security on the bond on appeal or on a supersedeas bond, or for any intermediate order, the clerk at the request of any party to the appeal shall transmit to the clerk of the district court or the clerk of the bankruptcy appellate panel a copy of the parts of the record as any party to the appeal shall designate.

(As amended Mar. 30, 1987, eff. Aug. 1, 1987; Apr. 30, 1991, eff. Aug. 1, 1991.)

ADVISORY COMMITTEE NOTES

Subdivision (a) is an adaptation of Rule 11(b) F.R.App.P.

Subdivision (b) is similar to former Bankruptcy Rule 807. The duty of the clerk of the bankruptcy court to transmit the record as soon as the record is complete is derived from the second paragraph of Rule 11(b) F.R.App.P. The last sentence of the subdivision applies to appeals to bankruptcy appellate panels. Additional copies of the record may be needed when the appendix to the brief required under Rule 8009(b) is not adequate in the judgment of the bankruptcy appellate panel for disposition of the appeal. If additional copies are required, the appellant will arrange for the production of the copies; if the appellant fails to do so, the clerk of the bankruptcy appellate panel shall prepare the copies at the expense of the appellant.

Subdivision (c) is derived from subdivisions (c), (e) and (f) of Rule 11 F.R.App.P. and subdivision (d) is essentially the same as Rule 11(b) F.R.App.P.

1991 Amendment

This rule is amended to require that the bankruptcy clerk retain the original record and transmit a copy of the record to the clerk of the district court or bankruptcy appellate panel. Transmission of the original documents may cause disruption in the continuing administration of the case in the bankruptcy court.

CROSS REFERENCES

Docketing of appeal and filing of record, see Federal Rules of Appellate Procedure Rule 12, 28 USCA.

Effect of clerk's retention and indexing of judgment on appealability and proceedings on appeal, see Fed.Rules Bankr.Proc. Rule 9021, 11 USCA.

Time for filing and service of briefs, see Fed.Rules Bankr. Proc. Rule 8009, 11 USCA.

Transmission of record, see Federal Rules of Appellate Procedure Rule 11, 28 USCA.

Rule 8008. Filing and Service

(a) Filing

Papers required or permitted to be filed with the clerk of the district court or the clerk of the bankruptcy appellate panel may be filed by mail addressed to the clerk, but filing is not timely unless the papers are received by the clerk within the time fixed for filing, except that briefs are deemed filed on the day of mailing. An original and one copy of all papers shall be filed when an appeal is to the district court; an original and three copies shall be filed when an appeal is to a bankruptcy appellate panel. The district court or bankruptcy appellate panel may require that additional copies be furnished. Rule 5005(a)(2) applies to papers filed with the clerk of the district court or the clerk of the bankruptcy appellate panel if filing by electronic means is authorized by local rule promulgated pursuant to Rule 8018.

(b) Service of all papers required

Copies of all papers filed by any party and not required by these rules to be served by the clerk of the district court or the clerk of the bankruptcy appellate panel shall, at or before the time of filing, be served by the party or a person acting for the party on all other parties to the appeal. Service on a party represented by counsel shall be made on counsel.

(c) Manner of service

Service may be personal or by mail. Personal service includes delivery of the copy to a clerk or other responsible person at the office of counsel. Service by mail is complete on mailing.

(d) Proof of service

Papers presented for filing shall contain an acknowledgment of service by the person served or proof of service in the form of a statement of the date and manner of service and of the names of the persons served, certified by the person who made service. The clerk of the district court or the clerk of the bankruptcy appellate panel may permit papers to be filed without acknowledgment or proof of service but shall require the acknowledgment or proof of service to be filed promptly thereafter.

(As amended Mar. 30, 1987, eff. Aug. 1, 1987; Apr. 23, 1996, eff. Dec. 1, 1996.)

ADVISORY COMMITTEE NOTES

This rule is an adaptation of Rule 25 F.R.App.P. Motions, briefs, appendices when required, statements, and any other filed paper must be accompanied by the specified number of copies. Rules 8001 and 8004 govern the number of copies of the notice of appeal which must be filed.

1996 Amendment

This rule is amended to permit, but not require, district courts and, where bankruptcy appellate panels have been authorized, circuit councils to adopt local rules that allow filing of documents by electronic means, subject to the limitations contained in Rule 5005(a)(2). See the committee note to the amendments to Rule 5005. Other amendments to this rule are stylistic.

GAP Report on Rule 8008. No changes since publication, except for stylistic changes.

CROSS REFERENCES

Appeal—

After dismissal of direct appeal by court of appeals, when taken, see Fed.Rules Bankr.Proc. Rule 8001, 11 USCA.

By leave, how taken, see Fed.Rules Bankr.Proc. Rule 8001, 11 USCA.

Filing and service of papers, see Federal Rules of Appellate Procedure Rule 25, 28 USCA.

Manner and proof of service of emergency motions, see Fed.Rules Bankr.Proc. Rule 8011, 11 USCA.

Rule 8009. Briefs and Appendix; Filing and Service

(a) Briefs

Unless the district court or the bankruptcy appellate panel by local rule or by order excuses the filing of briefs or specifies different time limits:

(1) The appellant shall serve and file a brief within 15 days after entry of the appeal on the docket pursuant to Rule 8007.

(2) The appellee shall serve and file a brief within 15 days after service of the brief of appellant. If the appellee has filed a cross appeal, the brief of the appellee shall contain the issues and argument pertinent to the cross appeal, denominated as such, and the response to the brief of the appellant.

(3) The appellant may serve and file a reply brief within 10 days after service of the brief of the appellee, and if the appellee has cross-appealed, the appellee may file and serve a reply brief to the response of the appellant to the issues presented in the cross appeal within 10 days after service of the reply brief of the appellant. No further briefs may be filed except with leave of the district court or the bankruptcy appellate panel.

(b) Appendix to brief

If the appeal is to a bankruptcy appellate panel, the appellant shall serve and file with the appellant's brief excerpts of the record as an appendix, which shall include the following:

(1) The complaint and answer or other equivalent pleadings;

(2) Any pretrial order;

(3) The judgment, order, or decree from which the appeal is taken;

(4) Any other orders relevant to the appeal;

(5) The opinion, findings of fact, or conclusions of law filed or delivered orally by the court and citations of the opinion if published;

(6) Any motion and response on which the court rendered decision;

(7) The notice of appeal;

(8) The relevant entries in the bankruptcy docket; and

(9) The transcript or portion thereof, if so required by a rule of the bankruptcy appellate panel.

An appellee may also serve and file an appendix which contains material required to be included by the appellant but omitted by appellant.

(As amended Mar. 30, 1987, eff. Aug. 1, 1987.)

ADVISORY COMMITTEE NOTES

Subdivision (a) of this rule is adapted from Rules 28(a) and 31(a) F.R.App.P. The introductory clause of the rule recognizes the desirability of allowing local and individual variation in the filing of briefs. The numbered paragraphs prescribe shorter periods than the corresponding periods allowed by Rule 31(a) F.R.App.P.

Subdivision (b), which is similar to an interim rule for bankruptcy appellate panels promulgated by the Ninth Circuit, applies only when an appeal is to an appellate panel. The appellant must prepare an appendix to the brief which contains the documents relevant to the appeal. With the appendix available to each member of the appellate panel, it is unlikely that multiple copies of the record will be necessary. The last sentence of the subdivision enables the appellee to correct an omission of the appellant.

Rule 30 F.R.App.P., which governs the preparation of the appendix in appeals taken to the courts of appeals, specifies fewer documents which must be included in the appendix but permits the parties to include any other material.

1987 Amendment

The amendment to Rule 8007(c) permits a rule of the bankruptcy appellate panel to provide that the record is to be retained rather than transmitted. The new paragraph (9) of subdivision (b) of this rule complements Rule 8007(c) by authorizing a rule of the panel to require inclusion of the transcript or a portion thereof in the appendix.

Rule 8010. Form of Briefs; Length

(a) Form of briefs

Unless the district court or the bankruptcy appellate panel by local rule otherwise provides, the form of brief shall be as follows:

(1) **Brief of the appellant.** The brief of the appellant shall contain under appropriate headings and in the order here indicated:

(A) A table of contents, with page references, and a table of cases alphabetically arranged, statutes and other authorities cited, with references to the pages of the brief where they are cited.

(B) A statement of the basis of appellate jurisdiction.

(C) A statement of the issues presented and the applicable standard of appellate review.

(D) A statement of the case. The statement shall first indicate briefly the nature of the case, the course of the proceedings, and the disposition in the court below. There shall follow a statement of the facts relevant to the issues presented for review, with appropriate references to the record.

(E) An argument. The argument may be preceded by a summary. The argument shall contain the contentions of the appellant with respect to the issues presented, and the reasons therefor, with citations to the authorities, statutes and parts of the record relied on.

(F) A short conclusion stating the precise relief sought.

(2) **Brief of the appellee.** The brief of the appellee shall conform to the requirements of paragraph (1)(A)–(E) of this subdivision, except that a statement of the basis of appellate jurisdiction, of the issues, or of the case need not be made unless the appellee is dissatisfied with the statement of the appellant.

(b) Reproduction of statutes, rules, regulations, or similar material

If determination of the issues presented requires reference to the Code or other statutes, rules, regulations, or similar material, relevant parts thereof shall be reproduced in the brief or in an addendum or they may be supplied to the court in pamphlet form.

(c) Length of briefs

Unless the district court or the bankruptcy appellate panel by local rule or order otherwise provides, principal briefs shall not exceed 50 pages, and reply briefs shall not exceed 25 pages, exclusive of pages containing the table of contents, tables of citations and any addendum containing statutes, rules, regulations, or similar material.

ADVISORY COMMITTEE NOTES

This rule is derived from subdivisions (a), (b), (c), and (f) of Rule 28 F.R.App.P.

When an appeal is to a bankruptcy appellate panel and an appendix is filed pursuant to Rule 8009(b) and reference is made in a brief to parts of the record included in the appendix, the reference should be to the appropriate pages of the appendix at which those parts appear.

CROSS REFERENCES

Briefs, see Federal Rules of Appellate Procedure Rule 28, 28 USCA.

Rule 8011. Motions

(a) Content of motions; response; reply

A request for an order or other relief shall be made by filing with the clerk of the district court or the clerk of the bankruptcy appellate panel a motion for such order or relief with proof of service on all other parties to the appeal. The motion shall contain or be accompanied by any matter required by a specific provision of these rules governing such a motion, shall state with particularity the grounds on which it is based, and shall set forth the order or relief sought. If a motion is supported by briefs, affidavits or other papers, they shall be served and filed with the motion. Any party may file a response in opposition to a motion other than one for a procedural order within seven days after service of the motion, but the district court or the bankruptcy appellate panel may shorten or extend the time for responding to any motion.

(b) Determination of motions for procedural orders

Notwithstanding subdivision (a) of this rule, motions for procedural orders, including any motion under Rule 9006, may be acted on at any time, without awaiting a response thereto and without hearing. Any party adversely affected by such action may move for reconsideration, vacation, or modification of the action.

(c) Determination of all motions

All motions will be decided without oral argument unless the court orders otherwise. A motion for a stay, or for other emergency relief may be denied if not presented promptly.

(d) Emergency motions

Whenever a movant requests expedited action on a motion on the ground that, to avoid irreparable harm, relief is needed in less time than would normally be required for the district court or bankruptcy appellate panel to receive and consider a response, the word "Emergency" shall precede the title of the motion. The motion shall be accompanied by an affidavit setting forth the nature of the emergency. The motion shall state whether all grounds advanced in support thereof were submitted to the bankruptcy judge and, if any grounds relied on were not submitted, why the motion should not be remanded to the bankruptcy judge for reconsideration. The motion shall include the office addresses and telephone numbers of moving and opposing counsel and shall be served pursuant to Rule 8008. Prior to filing the motion, the movant shall make every practicable effort to notify opposing counsel in time for counsel to respond to the motion. The affidavit accompanying the motion shall also state when and how opposing counsel was notified or if opposing counsel was not notified why it was not practicable to do so.

(e) Power of a single judge to entertain motions

A single judge of a bankruptcy appellate panel may grant or deny any request for relief which under these rules may properly be sought by motion, except that a single judge may not dismiss or otherwise decide an appeal or a motion for leave to appeal. The action of a single judge may be reviewed by the panel.

ADVISORY COMMITTEE NOTES

Subdivisions (a), (b) and (e) of this rule conform substantially to subdivisions (a), (b) and (c) of Rule 27 F.R.App.P. Subdivisions (c) and (d) are taken from Rule 13(c) and (d) of the Rules of the First Circuit governing appeals to bankruptcy appellate panels.

CROSS REFERENCES

Motions, see Federal Rules of Appellate Procedure Rule 27, 28 USCA.

Signing and verification of papers, see Fed.Rules Bankr. Proc. Rule 9011, 11 USCA.

Rule 8012. Oral Argument

Oral argument shall be allowed in all cases unless the district judge or the judges of the bankruptcy appellate panel unanimously determine after examination of the briefs and record, or appendix to the brief, that oral argument is not needed. Any party shall have an opportunity to file a statement setting forth the reason why oral argument should be allowed.

Oral argument will not be allowed if (1) the appeal is frivolous; (2) the dispositive issue or set of issues has been recently authoritatively decided; or (3) the facts and legal arguments are adequately presented in the briefs and record and the decisional process would not be significantly aided by oral argument.

ADVISORY COMMITTEE NOTES

This rule is derived from Rule 34(a) F.R.App.P. The other details of oral argument which are covered by the remaining subdivisions of Rule 34 F.R.App.P. are not in these rules and are left to local rule or order of the court.

CROSS REFERENCES

Oral argument, see Federal Rules of Appellate Procedure Rule 34, 28 USCA.

Rule 8013. Disposition of Appeal; Weight Accorded Bankruptcy Judge's Findings of Fact

On an appeal the district court or bankruptcy appellate panel may affirm, modify, or reverse a bankruptcy judge's judgment, order, or decree or remand with instructions for further proceedings. Findings of fact, whether based on oral or documentary evidence, shall not be set aside unless clearly erroneous, and due

regard shall be given to the opportunity of the bankruptcy court to judge the credibility of the witnesses.
(As amended Mar. 30, 1987, eff. Aug. 1, 1987.)

ADVISORY COMMITTEE NOTES

This rule accords to the findings of a bankruptcy judge the same weight given the findings of a district judge under Rule 52 F.R.Civ.P. See also Rules 7052(a) and 9014.

1987 Amendment

The amendment to this rule conforms the appellate review standard to Rule 52 F.R.Civ.P., as amended in August 1985.

CROSS REFERENCES

Findings by court, see Fed.Rules Bankr.Proc. Rule 7052, 11 USCA.

Findings by court, see Fed.Rules Civ.Proc. Rule 52, 28 USCA.

Suspension of this rule, see Fed.Rules Bankr.Proc. Rule 8019, 11 USCA.

Rule 8014. Costs

Except as otherwise provided by law, agreed to by the parties, or ordered by the district court or the bankruptcy appellate panel, costs shall be taxed against the losing party on an appeal. If a judgment is affirmed or reversed in part, or is vacated, costs shall be allowed only as ordered by the court. Costs incurred in the production of copies of briefs, the appendices, and the record and in the preparation and transmission of the record, the cost of the reporter's transcript, if necessary for the determination of the appeal, the premiums paid for cost of supersedeas bonds or other bonds to preserve rights pending appeal and the fee for filing the notice of appeal shall be taxed by the clerk as costs of the appeal in favor of the party entitled to costs under this rule.
(As amended Mar. 30, 1987, eff. Aug. 1, 1987.)

ADVISORY COMMITTEE NOTES

This rule is an adaptation of Rule 39(a), (c) and (e) of the F.R.App.P. Under this rule all costs are taxed by the clerk of the bankruptcy court.

CROSS REFERENCES

Costs, see Federal Rules of Appellate Procedure Rule 39, 28 USCA.

Rule 8015. Motion for Rehearing

Unless the district court or the bankruptcy appellate panel by local rule or by court order otherwise provides, a motion for rehearing may be filed within 10 days after entry of the judgment of the district court or the bankruptcy appellate panel. If a timely motion for rehearing is filed, the time for appeal to the court of appeals for all parties shall run from the entry of the order denying rehearing or the entry of a subsequent judgment.
(As amended Mar. 30, 1987, eff. Aug. 1, 1987.)

ADVISORY COMMITTEE NOTES

This is an adaptation of the first sentence of Rule 40(a) F.R.App.P. The filing of a motion for rehearing does not toll the time for taking an appeal to the court of appeals from the district court or the bankruptcy appellate panel. Appeals from a district court or a bankruptcy appellate panel are to the appropriate court of appeals. Under Rule 4(a)(4) F.R.App.P. the filing of post-trial motions in the district court has the effect of vitiating any prior notice of appeal and, on the district court's disposition of those post-trial motions, a new appeal period starts. Rule 4 F.R.App.P. does not, however, contain any provision which stays or otherwise alters the time for taking an appeal to the court of appeals when a motion for rehearing is filed under Rule 8015 with the district court or bankruptcy appellate panel.

1987 Amendment

The amendment, which is derived from Rule 8002(b), Rule 4(a)(4) F.R.App.P., and Rule 11.1 Sup.Ct.R., clarifies the effect of the filing of a timely motion for rehearing. If a timely motion is filed, the appeal period to the court of appeals begins to run on the entry of an order denying the motion or the entry of a subsequent judgment.

CROSS REFERENCES

Petition for rehearing, see Federal Rules of Appellate Procedure Rule 40, 28 USCA.

Rule 8016. Duties of Clerk of District Court and Bankruptcy Appellate Panel

(a) Entry of judgment

The clerk of the district court or the clerk of the bankruptcy appellate panel shall prepare, sign and enter the judgment following receipt of the opinion of the court or the appellate panel or, if there is no opinion, following the instruction of the court or the appellate panel. The notation of a judgment in the docket constitutes entry of judgment.

(b) Notice of orders or judgments; return of record

Immediately on the entry of a judgment or order the clerk of the district court or the clerk of the bankruptcy appellate panel shall transmit a notice of the entry to each party to the appeal, to the United States trustee, and to the clerk, together with a copy of any opinion respecting the judgment or order, and shall make a note of the transmission in the docket. Original papers transmitted as the record on appeal shall be returned to the clerk on disposition of the appeal.
(As amended Mar. 30, 1987, eff. Aug. 1, 1987; Apr. 30, 1991, eff. Aug. 1, 1991.)

ADVISORY COMMITTEE NOTES

Subdivision (a) of this rule is adapted from Rule 36 F.R.App.P. Subdivision (b) is similar to subdivisions (c) and (d) of Rule 45 F.R.App.P.

1991 Amendment

Subdivision (b) is amended to enable the United States trustee to monitor the progress of the case. The requirements of this subdivision apply to an order of the district court or bankruptcy appellate panel staying its judgment pending appeal to the court of appeals pursuant to Rule 8017(b).

CROSS REFERENCES

Duties of clerks, see Federal Rules of Appellate Procedure Rule 45, 28 USCA.

Entry of judgment, see Federal Rules of Appellate Procedure Rule 36, 28 USCA.

Rule 8017. Stay of Judgment of District Court or Bankruptcy Appellate Panel

(a) Automatic stay of judgment on appeal

Judgments of the district court or the bankruptcy appellate panel are stayed until the expiration of 10 days after entry, unless otherwise ordered by the district court or the bankruptcy appellate panel.

(b) Stay pending appeal to the court of appeals

On motion and notice to the parties to the appeal, the district court or the bankruptcy appellate panel may stay its judgment pending an appeal to the court of appeals. The stay shall not extend beyond 30 days after the entry of the judgment of the district court or the bankruptcy appellate panel unless the period is extended for cause shown. If before the expiration of a stay entered pursuant to this subdivision there is an appeal to the court of appeals by the party who obtained the stay, the stay shall continue until final disposition by the court of appeals. A bond or other security may be required as a condition to the grant or continuation of a stay of the judgment. A bond or other security may be required if a trustee obtains a stay but a bond or security shall not be required if a stay is obtained by the United States or an officer or agency thereof or at the direction of any department of the Government of the United States.

(c) Power of court of appeals not limited

This rule does not limit the power of a court of appeals or any judge thereof to stay proceedings during the pendency of an appeal or to suspend, modify, restore, or grant an injunction during the pendency of an appeal or to make any order appropriate to preserve the status quo or the effectiveness of the judgment subsequently to be entered.

ADVISORY COMMITTEE NOTES

This rule is derived from Rule 62 F.R.Civ.P. and Rule 41 F.R.App. P.

Subdivision (a) accords to the parties to an appeal 10 days within which to decide whether to pursue an appeal to the court of appeals. In ordinary civil litigation there is a similar opportunity. Rule 62(a) F.R.Civ.P. automatically stays enforcement of a district court's judgment in a civil action and Rule 41(a) F.R.App.P. provides that the mandate of the court of appeals shall not issue for 21 days, unless the court otherwise directs. The district court or bankruptcy appellate panel may reduce the 10 day period of this subdivision.

Subdivision (b) vests in the district courts and the bankruptcy appellate panels the same authority the courts of appeals have under Rule 41(b) F.R.App.P. to stay their judgments pending appeal. Perfection of an appeal to the court of appeals while a stay entered by the district court or bankruptcy appellate panel is in effect results in the automatic continuation of that stay during the course of the appeal in the court of appeals.

Subdivision (c) is the same as Rule 62(g) F.R.Civ.P.

CROSS REFERENCES

Stay of mandate, see Federal Rules of Appellate Procedure Rule 41, 28 USCA.

Rule 8018. Rules by Circuit Councils and District Courts; Procedure When There is No Controlling Law

(a) Local Rules by Circuit Councils and District Courts

(1) Circuit councils which have authorized bankruptcy appellate panels pursuant to 28 U.S.C. § 158(b) and the district courts may, acting by a majority of the judges of the council or district court, make and amend rules governing practice and procedure for appeals from orders or judgments of bankruptcy judges to the respective bankruptcy appellate panel or district court consistent with—but not duplicative of—Acts of Congress and the rules of this Part VIII. Local rules shall conform to any uniform numbering system prescribed by the Judicial Conference of the United States. Rule 83 F.R.Civ.P. governs the procedure for making and amending rules to govern appeals.

(2) A local rule imposing a requirement of form shall not be enforced in a manner that causes a party to lose rights because of a nonwillful failure to comply with the requirement.

(b) Procedure When There is No Controlling Law. A bankruptcy appellate panel or district judge may regulate practice in any manner consistent with federal law, these rules, Official Forms, and local rules of the circuit council or district court. No sanction or other disadvantage may be imposed for noncompliance with any requirement not in federal law, federal rules, Official Forms, or the local rules of the circuit council or district court unless the alleged violator has been furnished in the particular case with actual notice of the requirement.

(As amended Mar. 30, 1987, eff. Aug. 1, 1987; Apr. 27, 1995, eff. Dec. 1, 1995.)

ADVISORY COMMITTEE NOTES

This rule is similar to Rule 47 F.R.App.P. and Rule 83 F.R.Civ.P. Local rules governing procedure before the bankruptcy courts may be promulgated under Rule 9028.

1987 Amendment

Rule 83 F.R.Civ.P. was amended in August 1985 to require greater participation by the public in the rule making process. The amendment to Rule 8018 incorporates Rule 83 F.R.Civ.P. Under 28 U.S.C. § 158(b)(2), appeals may be taken to a bankruptcy appellate panel only if the district court so authorizes. If a district court does not authorize appeals to the bankruptcy appellate panel, appeals will be to the district court. This rule is amended to authorize district courts to promulgate rules for appeals.

1995 Amendments

The amendments to this rule conform to the amendments to Rule 9029. See Committee Note to the amendments to Rule 9029.

CROSS REFERENCES

Promulgation of local rules governing bankruptcy procedure, see Fed.Rules Bankr.Proc. Rule 9029, 11 USCA.

Rules by courts of appeals, see Federal Rules of Appellate Procedure Rule 47, 28 USCA.

Rule 8019. Suspension of Rules in Part VIII

In the interest of expediting decision or for other cause, the district court or the bankruptcy appellate panel may suspend the requirements or provisions of the rules in Part VIII, except Rules 8001, 8002, and 8013, and may order proceedings in accordance with the direction.

(As amended Mar. 30, 1987, eff. Aug. 1, 1987.)

ADVISORY COMMITTEE NOTES

This rule is derived from Rule 2 F.R.App.P.

CROSS REFERENCES

Suspension of rules, see Federal Rules of Appellate Procedure Rule 2, 28 USCA.

Rule 8020. Damages and Costs for Frivolous Appeal

If a district court or bankruptcy appellate panel determines that an appeal from an order, judgment, or decree of a bankruptcy judge is frivolous, it may, after a separately filed motion or notice from the district court or bankruptcy appellate panel and reasonable opportunity to respond, award just damages and single or double costs to the appellee.

(Added Apr. 11, 1997, eff. Dec. 1, 1997.)

ADVISORY COMMITTEE NOTES

1997 Amendment

This rule is added to clarify that a district court hearing an appeal, or a bankruptcy appellate panel, has the authority to award damages and costs to an appellee if it finds that the appeal is frivolous. By conforming to the language of Rule 38 F.R.App.P., this rule recognizes that the authority to award damages and costs in connection with frivolous appeals is the same for district courts sitting as appellate courts, bankruptcy appellate panels, and courts of appeals.

GAP Report on Rule 8020. No changes to the published draft.

PART IX—GENERAL PROVISIONS

Rule 9001. General Definitions

The definitions of words and phrases in § 101, § 902 and § 1101 and the rules of construction in § 102 of the Code govern their use in these rules. In addition, the following words and phrases used in these rules have the meanings indicated:

(1) "Bankruptcy clerk" means a clerk appointed pursuant to 28 U.S.C. § 156(b).

(2) "Bankruptcy Code" or "Code" means title 11 of the United States Code.

(3) "Clerk" means bankruptcy clerk, if one has been appointed, otherwise clerk of the district court.

(4) "Court" or "judge" means the judicial officer before whom a case or proceeding is pending.

(5) "Debtor." When any act is required by these rules to be performed by a debtor or when it is necessary to compel attendance of a debtor for examination and the debtor is not a natural person: (A) if the debtor is a corporation, "debtor" includes, if designated by the court, any or all of its officers, members of its board of directors or trustees or of a similar controlling body, a controlling stockholder or member, or any other person in control; (B) if the debtor is a partnership, "debtor" includes any or all of its general partners or, if designated by the court, any other person in control.

(6) "Firm" includes a partnership or professional corporation of attorneys or accountants.

(7) "Judgment" means any appealable order.

(8) "Mail" means first class, postage prepaid.

(9) "Notice provider" means any entity approved by the Administrative Office of the United States Courts to give notice to creditors under Rule 2002(g)(4).

(10) "Regular associate" means any attorney regularly employed by, associated with, or counsel to an individual or firm.

(11) "Trustee" includes a debtor in possession in a chapter 11 case.

(12) "United States trustee" includes an assistant United States trustee and any designee of the United States trustee.

(As amended Mar. 30, 1987, eff. Aug. 1, 1987; Apr. 30, 1991, eff. Aug. 1, 1991; Apr. 25, 2005, eff. Dec. 1, 2005.)

ADVISORY COMMITTEE NOTES

1987 Amendment

The terms "bankruptcy clerk" and "clerk" have been defined to reflect that unless otherwise stated, for the purpose of these rules, the terms are meant to identify the court officer for the bankruptcy records. If a bankruptcy clerk is appointed, all filings are made with the bankruptcy clerk. If one has not been appointed, all filings are with the clerk of the district court. Rule 5005.

The rule is also amended to include a definition of "court or judge." Since a case or proceeding may be before a bankruptcy judge or a judge of the district court, "court or judge" is defined to mean the judicial officer before whom the case or proceeding is pending.

1991 Amendment

Section 582 of title 28 provides that the Attorney General may appoint one or more assistant United States trustees in any region when the public interest so requires. This rule is amended to clarify that an assistant United States trustee, as well as any designee of the United States trustee, is included within the meaning of "United States trustee" in the rules.

2005 Amendments

The rule is amended to add the definition of a notice provider and to renumber the final three definitions in the rule. A notice provider is an entity approved by the Administrative Office of the United States Courts to enter into agreements with entities to give notice to those entities in the form and manner agreed to by those parties. The new definition supports the amendment to Rule 2002(g)(4) that authorizes a notice provider to give notices under Rule 2002.

Many entities conduct business on a national scale and receive vast numbers of notices in bankruptcy cases throughout the country.Those entities can agree with a notice provider to receive their notices in a form and at an address or addresses that the creditor and notice provider agree upon. There are processes currently in use that provide substantial assurance that notices are not misdirected. Any notice provider would have to demonstrate to the Administrative Office of the United States Courts that it could provide the service in a manner that ensures the proper delivery of notice to creditors. Once the Administrative Office of the United States Courts approves the notice provider to enter into agreements with creditors, the notice provider and other entities can establish the relationship that will govern the delivery of notices in cases as provided in Rule 2002(g)(4).

HISTORICAL NOTES

References in Text

Bankruptcy Act of 1898 as amended, referred to in par. (10), is Act July 1, 1898, c. 541, 30 Stat. 544, which was classified to former § 1 et seq. of this title.

Sections 1(10) and 2a of the Act, referred to in par. (2), are §§ 1(10) and 2a of the Bankruptcy Act as amended, which were classified to former §§ 1(10) and 11(a) of this title.

CROSS REFERENCES

Clerk defined, see Fed.Rules Bankr.Proc. Rule 9002, 11 USCA.

Judgment defined, see Fed.Rules Bankr.Proc. Rules 7054 and 9002, 11 USCA.

Rule 9002. Meanings of Words in the Federal Rules of Civil Procedure When Applicable to Cases Under The Code

The following words and phrases used in the Federal Rules of Civil Procedure made applicable to cases under the Code by these rules have the meanings indicated unless they are inconsistent with the context:

(1) "Action" or "civil action" means an adversary proceeding or, when appropriate, a contested petition, or proceedings to vacate an order for relief or to determine any other contested matter.

(2) "Appeal" means an appeal as provided by 28 U.S.C. § 158.

(3) "Clerk" or "clerk of the district court" means the court officer responsible for the bankruptcy records in the district.

(4) "District court," "trial court," "court," "district judge," or "judge" means bankruptcy judge if the case or proceeding is pending before a bankruptcy judge.

(5) "Judgment" includes any order appealable to an appellate court.

(As amended Mar. 30, 1987, eff. Aug. 1, 1987; Apr. 22, 1993, eff. Aug. 1, 1993.)

ADVISORY COMMITTEE NOTES

1993 Amendments

This rule is revised to include the words "district judge" in anticipation of amendments to the Federal Rules of Civil Procedure.

CROSS REFERENCES

Contested matters, see Fed.Rules Bankr.Proc. Rule 9014, 11 USCA.

Judgment defined, see Fed.Rules Civ.Proc. Rule 54, 28 USCA.

One form of action, see Fed.Rules Civ.Proc. Rule 2, 28 USCA.

Procedural rules which govern adversary proceedings, see Fed.Rules Bankr.Proc. Rule 7001 et seq., 11 USCA.

Rule 9003. Prohibition of Ex Parte Contacts

(a) General prohibition

Except as otherwise permitted by applicable law, any examiner, any party in interest, and any attorney, accountant, or employee of a party in interest shall refrain from ex parte meetings and communications with the court concerning matters affecting a particular case or proceeding.

(b) United States trustee

Except as otherwise permitted by applicable law, the United States trustee and assistants to and employees or agents of the United States trustee shall refrain from ex parte meetings and communications with the court concerning matters affecting a particular case or proceeding. This rule does not preclude communications with the court to discuss general problems of administration and improvement of bankruptcy administration, including the operation of the United States trustee system.

(As amended Mar. 30, 1987, eff. Aug. 1, 1987; Apr. 30, 1991, eff. Aug. 1, 1991.)

ADVISORY COMMITTEE NOTES

This rule regulates the actions of parties in interest and their attorneys or others employed by parties in interest. This regulation of the conduct of parties in interest and their representative is designed to insure that the bankruptcy system operates fairly and that no appearance of unfairness is created. See H.Rep. No. 95–595, 95th Cong., 1st Sess. 95 et seq. (1977).

This rule is not a substitute for or limitation of any applicable canon of professional responsibility or judicial conduct. See, e.g., Canon 7, EC7–35, Disciplinary Rule 7–110(B) of the Code of Professional Responsibility: "Generally, in adversary proceedings a lawyer should not communicate with a judge relative to a matter pending before, or which is to be brought before, a tribunal over which he presides in circumstances which might have the effect or give the appearance of granting undue advantage to one party;" and Canon 3A(4) of the Code of Judicial Conduct: "A judge should . . . neither initiate nor consider ex parte or other communications concerning a pending or impending proceeding."

1987 Amendments

This rule is amended to apply to both the bankruptcy judges and the district judges of the district.

1991 Amendments

Subdivision (a) is amended to extend to examiners the prohibition on ex parte meetings and communications with the court.

Subdivision (b) is derived from Rule X–1010.

CROSS REFERENCES

Disqualification of judge, see Fed.Rules Bankr.Proc. Rule 5004, 11 USCA.

Rule 9004. General Requirements of Form

(a) Legibility; abbreviations

All petitions, pleadings, schedules and other papers shall be clearly legible. Abbreviations in common use in the English language may be used.

(b) Caption

Each paper filed shall contain a caption setting forth the name of the court, the title of the case, the bankruptcy docket number, and a brief designation of the character of the paper.

ADVISORY COMMITTEE NOTES

Subdivision (b). Additional requirements applicable to the caption for a petition are found in Rule 1005, to the caption for notices to creditors in Rule 2002(m), and to the caption for a pleading or other paper filed in an adversary proceeding in Rule 7010. Failure to comply with this or any other rule imposing a merely formal requirement does not ordinarily result in the loss of rights. See Rule 9005.

Rule 9005. Harmless Error

Rule 61 F.R.Civ.P. applies in cases under the Code. When appropriate, the court may order the correction of any error or defect or the cure of any omission which does not affect substantial rights.

Rule 9005.1. Constitutional Challenge to a Statute—Notice, Certification, and Intervention

Rule 5.1 F.R.Civ.P. applies in cases under the Code.

(Added Apr. 30, 2007, eff. Dec. 1, 2007.)

ADVISORY COMMITTEE NOTES

2007 Adoption

The rule is added to adopt the new rule added to the Federal Rules of Civil Procedure. The new Civil Rule replaces Rule 24(c) F. R. Civ. P., so the cross reference to Civil Rule 24 contained in Rule 7024 is no longer sufficient to bring the provisions of new Civil Rule 5.1 into adversary proceedings. This rule also makes Civil Rule 5.1 applicable to all contested matters and other proceedings within the bankruptcy case.

Rule 9006. Time

(a) Computation

In computing any period of time prescribed or allowed by these rules or by the Federal Rules of Civil Procedure made applicable by these rules, by the local rules, by order of court, or by any applicable statute, the day of the act, event, or default from which the designated period of time begins to run shall not be included. The last day of the period so computed shall be included, unless it is a Saturday, a Sunday, or a legal holiday, or, when the act to be done is the filing of a paper in court, a day on which weather or other conditions have made the clerk's office inaccessible, in which event the period runs until the end of the next day which is not one of the aforementioned days. When the period of time prescribed or allowed is less than 8 days, intermediate Saturdays, Sundays, and legal holidays shall be excluded in the computation. As used in this rule and in Rule 5001(c), "legal holiday" includes New Year's Day, Birthday of Martin Luther King, Jr., Washington's Birthday, Memorial Day, Independence Day, Labor Day, Columbus Day, Veterans Day, Thanksgiving Day, Christmas Day, and any other day appointed as a holiday by the President or the Congress of the United States, or by the state in which the court is held.

(b) Enlargement

(1) In general

Except as provided in paragraphs (2) and (3) of this subdivision, when an act is required or allowed to be done at or within a specified period by these rules or by a notice given thereunder or by order of court, the court for cause shown may at any time in its discretion (1) with or without motion or notice order the period enlarged if the request therefor is made before the expiration of the period originally prescribed or as extended by a previous order or (2) on motion made after the expiration of the specified period permit the act to be done where the failure to act was the result of excusable neglect.

(2) Enlargement not permitted

The court may not enlarge the time for taking action under Rules 1007(d), 2003(a) and (d), 7052, 9023, and 9024.

(3) Enlargement governed by other rules

The court may enlarge the time for taking action under Rules 1006(b)(2), 1017(e), 3002(c), 4003(b), 4004(a), 4007(c), 4008(a), 8002, and 9033, only to the extent and under the conditions stated in those rules. In addition, the court may enlarge the time to file the statement required under Rule 1007(b)(7), and to file schedules and statements in a small business case under § 1116(3) of the Code, only to the extent and under the conditions stated in Rule 1007(c).

(c) Reduction

(1) In general

Except as provided in paragraph (2) of this subdivision, when an act is required or allowed to be done at or within a specified time by these rules or by a notice given thereunder or by order of court, the court for cause shown may in its discretion with or without motion or notice order the period reduced.

(2) Reduction not permitted

The court may not reduce the time for taking action under Rules 2002(a)(7), 2003(a), 3002(c), 3014, 3015, 4001(b)(2), (c)(2), 4003(a), 4004(a), 4007(c), 4008(a), 8002, and 9033(b). In addition, the court may not reduce the time under Rule 1007(c) to file the statement required by Rule 1007(b)(7).

(d) For motions—affidavits

A written motion, other than one which may be heard ex parte, and notice of any hearing shall be served not later than five days before the time specified for such hearing, unless a different period is fixed by these rules or by order of the court. Such an order may for cause shown be made on ex parte application. When a motion is supported by affidavit, the affidavit shall be served with the motion; and, except as otherwise provided in Rule 9023, opposing affidavits may be served not later than one day before the hearing, unless the court permits them to be served at some other time.

(e) Time of service

Service of process and service of any paper other than process or of notice by mail is complete on mailing.

(f) Additional time after service by mail or under Rule 5(b)(2)(C) or (D) F.R.Civ.P.

When there is a right or requirement to act or undertake some proceedings within a prescribed period after service and that service is by mail or under Rule 5 (b)(2)(C) or (D) F. R. Civ. P., three days are added after the prescribed period would otherwise expire under Rule 9006(a).

(g) Grain storage facility cases

This rule shall not limit the court's authority under § 557 of the Code to enter orders governing procedures in cases in which the debtor is an owner or operator of a grain storage facility.

(As amended Mar. 30, 1987, eff. Aug. 1, 1987; Apr. 25, 1989, eff. Aug. 1, 1989; Apr. 30, 1991, eff. Aug. 1, 1991; Apr. 23, 1996, eff. Dec. 1, 1996; Apr. 29, 1999, eff. Dec. 1, 1999; Apr. 23, 2001, eff. Dec. 1, 2001; Apr. 25, 2005, eff. Dec. 1, 2005; Apr. 23, 2008, eff. Dec. 1, 2008.)

ADVISORY COMMITTEE NOTES

Subdivision (a). This rule is an adaptation of Rule 6 F.R.Civ.P. It governs the time for acts to be done and proceedings to be had in cases under the Code and any litigation arising therein.

Subdivision (b) is patterned after Rule 6(b) F.R.Civ.P. and Rule 26(b) F.R.App.P.

Paragraph (1) of this subdivision confers on the court discretion generally to authorize extensions of time for doing acts required or allowed by these rules or orders of court. The exceptions to this general authority to extend the time are contained in paragraphs (2) and (3).

In the interest of prompt administration of bankruptcy cases certain time periods may not be extended. Paragraph (2) lists the rules which establish time periods which may not be extended: Rule 1007(d), time for filing a list of 20 largest creditors; Rule 1017(b)(3), 30 day period for sending notice of dismissal for failure to pay the filing fee; Rule 1019(2), 20 day period for notice of conversion to a chapter 7 case; Rule 2003(a), meeting of creditors not more than 40 days after order for relief; Rule 2003(d), 10 days for filing a motion for resolution of an election dispute; Rule 3014, time for the § 1111(b)(2) election; Rule 4001(b), expiration of stay 30 days following the commencement of final hearing; Rule 7052(b), 10 day period to move to amend findings of fact; Rule 9015(f), 20 day period to move for judgment notwithstanding the verdict; Rule 9023, 10 day period to move for a new trial; and Rule 9024, time to move for relief from judgment.

Many rules which establish a time for doing an act also contain a specific authorization and standard for granting an extension of time and, in some cases, limit the length of an extension. In some instances it would be inconsistent with the objective of the rule and sound administration of the case to permit extension under Rule 9006(b)(1), but with respect to the other rules it is appropriate that the power to extend time be supplemented by Rule 9006(b)(1). Unless a rule which contains a specific authorization to extend time is listed in paragraph (3) of this subdivision, an extension of the time may be granted under paragraph (1) of this subdivision. If a rule is included in paragraph (3) an extension may not be granted under paragraph (1). The following rules are listed in paragraph (3): Rule 1006(b)(2), time for paying the filing fee in installments; Rule 3002(c), 90 day period for filing a claim in a chapter 7 or 13 case; Rule 4003(b), 30 days for filing objections to a claim of exemptions; Rule 4004(a), 60 day period to object to a discharge; Rule 4007(b), 60 day period to file a dischargeability complaint; and Rule 8002, 10 days for filing a notice of appeal.

Subdivision (c). Paragraph (1) of this subdivision authorizes the reduction of the time periods established by these rules or an order of the court. Excluded from this general authority are the time periods established by the rules referred to in paragraph (2) of the subdivision: Rule 2002(a) and (b), 20 day and 25 day notices of certain hearings and actions in the case; Rule 2003(a), meeting of creditors to be not less than 20 days after the order for relief; Rule 3002(c), 90 days for filing a claim in a chapter 7 or 13 case; Rule 3014, time for § 1111(b)(2) election; Rule 3015, 10 day period after filing of petition to file a chapter 13 plan; Rule 4003(a), 15 days for a dependent to claim exemptions; Rule 4004(a), 60 day period to object to a discharge; Rule 4007(c), 60 day period to file a dischargeability complaint; and Rule 8002, 10 days for filing a notice of appeal. Reduction of the time periods fixed in the rules referred to in this subdivision would be inconsistent with the purposes of those rules and would cause harmful uncertainty.

[The Advisory Committee Note for subd. (c) above states that Rule 2002(a) and (b) are excluded from the general authority for the reduction of time periods while the text of subd. (c)(2) specifies that only Rule 2002(a)(4) and (a)(8) are excluded.]

Subdivision (d) is derived from Rule 6(d) F.R.Civ.P. The reference is to Rule 9023 instead of to Rule 59(c) F.R.Civ.P. because Rule 9023 incorporates Rule 59 F.R.Civ.P. but excepts therefrom motions to reconsider orders allowing and disallowing claims.

Subdivision (f) is new and is the same as Rule 6(e) F.R.Civ.P.

1987 Amendment

Subdivision (a) is amended to conform to the 1984 amendments to Rule 6 F.R.Civ.P.

Subdivision (b). The reference to Rule 4001(b) in paragraph (3) is deleted because of the amendments made to Rule 4001. Rule 9033, which is new, contains specific provisions governing the extension of time to file objections to proposed findings of fact and conclusions of law. Rule 9033 is added to the rules referred to in paragraph (3).

Subdivision (c). Rule 4001(b)(2) and (c)(2) provide that a final hearing on a motion to use cash collateral or a motion for authority to obtain credit may be held no earlier than 15 days after the filing of the motion. These two rules are added to paragraph (2) to make it clear that the 15 day period may not be reduced. Rule 9033 is also added to paragraph (2).

Subdivision (g) is new. Under § 557 of the Code, as enacted by the 1984 amendments, the court is directed to expedite grain storage facility cases. This subdivision makes it clear this rule does not limit the court's authority under § 557.

The original Advisory Committee Note to this rule included the 25 day notice period of Rule 2002(b) as a time period which may not be reduced under Rule 9006(C)(2). This was an error.

1989 Amendment

Prior to 1987, subdivision (a) provided that intermediate weekends and legal holidays would not be counted in the computation of a time period if the prescribed or allowed time was less than 7 days. This rule was amended in 1987 to conform to Fed. R. Civ. P. 6(a) which provides for the exclusion of intermediate weekends and legal holidays if the time prescribed or allowed is less than 11 days. An undesirable result of the 1987 amendment was that 10-day time periods prescribed in the interest of prompt administration of bankruptcy cases were extended to at least 14 calendar days.

As a result of the present amendment, 10-day time periods prescribed or allowed will no longer be extended to at least 14 calendar days because of intermediate weekends and legal holidays.

1991 Amendment

As a result of the 1989 amendment to this rule, the method of computing time under subdivision (a) is not the same as the method of computing time under Rule 6(a) F.R.Civ.P. Subdivision (a) is amended to provide that it governs the computation of time periods prescribed by the Federal Rules of Civil Procedure when the Bankruptcy Rules make a civil rule applicable to a bankruptcy case or proceeding.

Subdivision (b)(2) is amended because of the deletion of Rule 1019(2). Reference to Rule 9015(f) is deleted because of the abrogation of Rule 9015 in 1987.

Subdivision (b)(3) is amended to limit the enlargement of time regarding dismissal of a chapter 7 case for substantial abuse in accordance with Rule 1017(e).

1996 Amendment

Subdivision (c)(2) is amended to conform to the abrogation of Rule 2002(a)(4) and the renumbering of Rule 2002(a)(8) to Rule 2002(a)(7).

GAP Report on Rule 9006. No changes since publication, except for a stylistic change.

1999 Amendments

Rule 9006(b)(2) is amended to conform to the abrogation of Rule 1017(b)(3).

Gap Report on Rule 9006. The proposed amendment to Rule 9006(b)(2) has been added as a technical change to conform to the abrogation of Rule 1017(b)(3). The proposed amendment to Rule 9006(c)(2), providing that the time under Rule 1019(6) to file a request for payment of an administrative expense after a case is converted to chapter 7 could not be reduced by the court, was deleted. The proposed amendments to Rule 1019(6) have been changed so that the court will fix the time for filing the request for payment. Since the court will fix the time limit, the court should have the power to reduce it. See Gap Report to Rule 1019(6).

2001 Amendments

Rule 5(b) F. R. Civ. P., which is made applicable in adversary proceedings by Rule 7005, is being restyled and amended to authorize service by electronic means—or any other means not otherwise authorized under Rule 5(b)—if consent is obtained from the person served. The amendment to Rule 9006(f) is intended to extend the three-day "mail rule" to service under Rule 5(b)(2)(D), including service by electronic means. The three-day rule also will apply to service under Rule 5(b)(2)(C) F. R. Civ. P. when the person served has no known address and the paper is served by leaving a copy with the clerk of the court.

CHANGES MADE AFTER PUBLICATION AND COMMENTS

No changes were made.

2005 Amendments

Rule 9006(f) is amended, consistent with a corresponding amendment to Rule 6 (e) of the F.R. Civ. P, to clarify the method of counting the number of days to respond after service either by mail or under Civil Rule 5(b)(2)(C) or (D). Three days are added after the prescribed period expires. If, before the application of Rule 9006(f), the prescribed period is less than 8 days, intervening Saturdays, Sundays, and legal holidays are excluded from the calculation under Rule 9006(a). Some illustrations may be helpful.

Under existing Rule 9006(a), assuming that there are no legal holidays and that a response is due in seven days, if a paper is filed on a Monday, the seven day response period commences on Tuesday and concludes on Wednesday of the next week. Adding three days to the end of the period would extend it to Saturday, but because the response period ends on a weekend, the response day would be the following Monday, two weeks after the filing of the initial paper. If the paper is filed on a Tuesday, the seven-day response period would end on the following Thursday, and the response time would also be the following Monday. If the paper is mailed on a Wednesday, the initial seven-day period would expire nine days later on a Friday, but the response would again be due on the following Monday because of Rule 9006(f). If the paper is mailed on a Thursday, however, the seven day period ends on Monday, eleven days after the mailing of the service because of the exclusion of the two intervening Saturdays and Sundays. The response is due three days later on the following Thursday. If the paper is mailed on a Friday, the seven day period would conclude on a Tuesday, and the response is due three days later on a Friday.

No other change in the system of counting time is intended.

Other changes are stylistic.

2008 Amendments

Subdivision (b)(3) is amended to implement § 1116(3) of the Code, as amended by the 2005 amendments, which places specific limits on the extension of time for filing schedules and statements of financial affairs in a small business case.

Subdivisions (b)(3) and (c)(2) are amended to provide that enlargement or reduction of the time to file the statement of completion of a personal financial management course required by Rule 1007(b)(7) are governed by Rule 1007(c). Likewise, the amendments to subdivisions (b)(3) and (c)(2) recognize that the enlargement of time to file a reaffirmation agreement is governed by Rule 4008(a), and that reduction of the time provided under that rule is not permitted.

Other amendments are stylistic.

CROSS REFERENCES

Completion of service by mail upon mailing, see Fed.Rules Civ.Proc. Rule 5, 28 USCA.

Computation and extension of time, see Federal Rules of Appellate Procedure Rule 26, 28 USCA.

Motions—

Form and service, see Fed.Rules Bankr.Proc. Rule 9013, 11 USCA.

On appeal to district court or bankruptcy appellate panel acted upon without hearing at any time, see Fed.Rules Bankr.Proc. Rule 8011, 11 USCA.

Time, see Fed.Rules Civ.Proc. Rule 6, 28 USCA.

HISTORICAL AND STATUTORY NOTES

References in Text

The Federal Rules of Civil Procedure, referred to in subds. (a) and (f), are set out in the Appendix to Title 28.

Rule 9007. General Authority to Regulate Notices

When notice is to be given under these rules, the court shall designate, if not otherwise specified herein, the time within which, the entities to whom, and the form and manner in which the notice shall be given. When feasible, the court may order any notices under these rules to be combined.

(As amended Mar. 30, 1987, eff. Aug. 1, 1987.)

CROSS REFERENCES

Construction of phrase "after notice and a hearing", see 11 USCA § 102.

Notice as is appropriate of order for relief, see 11 USCA § 342.

Rule 9008. Service or Notice by Publication

Whenever these rules require or authorize service or notice by publication, the court shall, to the extent not otherwise specified in these rules, determine the form and manner thereof, including the newspaper or other medium to be used and the number of publications.

CROSS REFERENCES

Construction of phrase "after notice and a hearing", see 11 USCA § 102.

Notice as is appropriate of order for relief, see 11 USCA § 342.

Rule 9009. Forms

Except as otherwise provided in Rule 3016(d), the Official Forms prescribed by the Judicial Conference of the United States shall be observed and used with alterations as may be appropriate. Forms may be combined and their contents rearranged to permit economies in their use. The Director of the Administrative Office of the United States Courts may issue additional forms for use under the Code. The forms shall be construed to be consistent with these rules and the Code.

(As amended Apr. 30, 1991, eff. Aug. 1, 1991; Apr. 23, 2008, eff. Dec. 1, 2008.)

ADVISORY COMMITTEE NOTES

The rule continues the obligatory character of the Official Forms in the interest of facilitating the processing of the paperwork of bankruptcy administration, but provides that Official Forms will be prescribed by the Judicial Conference of the United States. The Supreme Court and the Congress will thus be relieved of the burden of considering the large number of complex forms used in bankruptcy practice. The use of the Official Forms has generally been held subject to a "rule of substantial compliance" and some of these rules, for example Rule 1002, specifically state that the filed document need only "conform substantially" to the Official Form. See also Rule 9005. The second sentence recognizes the propriety of combining and rearranging Official Forms to take advantage of technological developments and resulting economies.

The Director of the Administrative Office is authorized to issue additional forms for the guidance of the bar.

1991 Amendment

Rule 9029 is amended to clarify that local court rules may not prohibit or limit the use of the Official Forms.

2008 Amendments

The rule is amended to provide that a plan proponent in a small business chapter 11 case need not use an Official Form of a plan of reorganization and disclosure statement. The use of those forms is optional, and under Rule 3016(d) the proponent may submit a plan and disclosure statement in those cases that does not conform to the Official Forms.

CROSS REFERENCES

Correction of harmless errors or cure of harmless omissions, see Fed.Rules Bankr.Proc. Rule 9005, 11 USCA.

Rule 9010. Representation and Appearances; Powers of Attorney

(a) Authority to act personally or by attorney

A debtor, creditor, equity security holder, indenture trustee, committee or other party may (1) appear in a case under the Code and act either in the entity's own behalf or by an attorney authorized to practice in the court, and (2) perform any act not constituting the practice of law, by an authorized agent, attorney in fact, or proxy.

(b) Notice of appearance

An attorney appearing for a party in a case under the Code shall file a notice of appearance with the attorney's name, office address and telephone number, unless the attorney's appearance is otherwise noted in the record.

(c) Power of attorney

The authority of any agent, attorney in fact, or proxy to represent a creditor for any purpose other than the execution and filing of a proof of claim or the acceptance or rejection of a plan shall be evidenced by a power of attorney conforming substantially to the appropriate Official Form. The execution of any such power of attorney shall be acknowledged before one of the officers enumerated in 28 U.S.C. § 459, § 953, Rule 9012, or a person authorized to administer oaths under the laws of the state where the oath is administered.

(As amended Mar. 30, 1987, eff. Aug. 1, 1987; Apr. 30, 1991, eff. Aug. 1, 1991.)

ADVISORY COMMITTEE NOTES

This rule is substantially the same as former Bankruptcy Rule 910 and does not purport to change prior holdings prohibiting a corporation from appearing pro se. See In re Las Colinas Development Corp., 585 F.2d 7 (1st Cir.1978).

1987 Amendment

Subdivision (c) is amended to include a reference to Rule 9012 which is amended to authorize a bankruptcy judge or clerk to administer oaths.

1991 Amendment

References to Official Form numbers in subdivision (c) are deleted in anticipation of future revision and renumbering of the Official Forms.

CROSS REFERENCES

Ex parte relief from automatic stay, see Fed.Rules Bankr. Proc. Rule 4001, 11 USCA.

Payment of dividends to persons authorized to receive them by power of attorney executed and filed in accordance with this rule, see Fed.Rules Bankr.Proc. Rule 3009, 11 USCA.

Rule 9011. Signing of Papers; Representations to the Court; Sanctions; Verification and Copies of Papers

(a) Signing of papers

Every petition, pleading, written motion, and other paper, except a list, schedule, or statement, or amendments thereto, shall be signed by at least one attorney of record in the attorney's individual name. A party who is not represented by an attorney shall sign all papers. Each paper shall state the signer's address and telephone number, if any. An unsigned paper shall be stricken unless omission of the signature is corrected promptly after being called to the attention of the attorney or party.

(b) Representations to the court

By presenting to the court (whether by signing, filing, submitting, or later advocating) a petition, pleading, written motion, or other paper, an attorney or unrepresented party is certifying that to the best of the person's knowledge, information, and belief, formed after an inquiry reasonable under the circumstances,—[1]

(1) it is not being presented for any improper purpose, such as to harass or to cause unnecessary delay or needless increase in the cost of litigation;

(2) the claims, defenses, and other legal contentions therein are warranted by existing law or by a nonfrivolous argument for the extension, modification, or reversal of existing law or the establishment of new law;

(3) the allegations and other factual contentions have evidentiary support or, if specifically so identified, are likely to have evidentiary support after a reasonable opportunity for further investigation or discovery; and

(4) the denials of factual contentions are warranted on the evidence or, if specifically so identified, are reasonably based on a lack of information or belief.

(c) Sanctions

If, after notice and a reasonable opportunity to respond, the court determines that subdivision (b) has been violated, the court may, subject to the conditions stated below, impose an appropriate sanction upon the attorneys, law firms, or parties that have violated subdivision (b) or are responsible for the violation.

(1) How initiated

(A) By motion

A motion for sanctions under this rule shall be made separately from other motions or requests and shall describe the specific conduct alleged to violate subdivision (b). It shall be served as provided in Rule 7004. The motion for sanctions may not be filed with or presented to the court unless, within 21 days after service of the motion (or such other period as the court may prescribe), the challenged paper, claim, defense, contention, allegation, or denial is not withdrawn or appropriately corrected, except that this limitation shall not apply if the conduct alleged is the filing of a petition in violation of subdivision (b). If warranted, the court may award to the party prevailing on the motion the reasonable expenses and attorney's fees incurred in presenting or opposing the motion. Absent exceptional circumstances, a law firm shall be held jointly responsible for violations committed by its partners, associates, and employees.

(B) On court's initiative

On its own initiative, the court may enter an order describing the specific conduct that appears to violate subdivision (b) and directing an attorney, law firm, or party to show cause why it has not violated subdivision (b) with respect thereto.

(2) Nature of sanction; limitations

A sanction imposed for violation of this rule shall be limited to what is sufficient to deter repetition of such conduct or comparable conduct by others similarly situated. Subject to the limitations in subparagraphs (A) and (B), the sanction may consist of, or include, directives of a nonmonetary nature, an order to pay a penalty into court, or, if imposed on motion and warranted for effective deterrence, an order directing payment to the movant of some or all of the reasonable attorneys' fees and other expenses incurred as a direct result of the violation.

(A) Monetary sanctions may not be awarded against a represented party for a violation of subdivision (b)(2).

(B) Monetary sanctions may not be awarded on the court's initiative unless the court issues its order to show cause before a voluntary dismissal or settlement of the claims made by or against the party which is, or whose attorneys are, to be sanctioned.

(3) Order

When imposing sanctions, the court shall describe the conduct determined to constitute a violation of this rule and explain the basis for the sanction imposed.

(d) Inapplicability to discovery

Subdivisions (a) through (c) of this rule do not apply to disclosures and discovery requests, responses, objections, and motions that are subject to the provisions of Rules 7026 through 7037.

(e) Verification

Except as otherwise specifically provided by these rules, papers filed in a case under the Code need not be verified. Whenever verification is required by these rules, an unsworn declaration as provided in 28 U.S.C. § 1746 satisfies the requirement of verification.

(f) Copies of signed or verified papers

When these rules require copies of a signed or verified paper, it shall suffice if the original is signed or verified and the copies are conformed to the original.

(As amended Mar. 30, 1987, eff. Aug. 1, 1987; Apr. 30, 1991, eff. Aug. 1, 1991; Apr. 11, 1997, eff. Dec. 1, 1997.)

[1] So in original. The comma probably should not appear.

ADVISORY COMMITTEE NOTES

Subdivision (a). Excepted from the papers which an attorney for a debtor must sign are lists, schedules, statements of financial affairs, statements of executory contracts, Chapter 13 Statements and amendments thereto. Rule 1008 requires that these documents be verified by the debtor. Although the petition must also be verified, counsel for the debtor must sign the petition. See Official Form No. 1. An unrepresented party must sign all papers.

The last sentence of this subdivision authorizes a broad range of sanctions.

The word "document" is used in this subdivision to refer to all papers which the attorney or party is required to sign.

Subdivision (b) extends to all papers filed in cases under the Code the policy of minimizing reliance on the formalities of verification which is reflected in the third sentence of Rule 11 F.R.Civ.P. The second sentence of subdivision (b) permits the substitution of an unsworn declaration for the verification. See 28 U.S.C. § 1746. Rules requiring verification or an affidavit are as follows: Rule 1008, petitions, schedules, statements of financial affairs, Chapter 13 Statements and amendments; Rule 2006(e), list of multiple proxies and statement of facts and circumstances regarding their acquisition; Rule 4001(c), motion for ex parte relief from stay; Rule 7065, incorporating Rule 65(b) F.R.Civ.P. governing issuance of temporary restraining order; Rule 8011(d), affidavit in support of emergency motion on appeal.

1987 Amendment

The statement of intention of the debtor under § 521(2) of the Code is added to the documents which counsel is not required to sign.

1991 Amendment

Subdivision (a) is amended to conform to Rule 11 F.R.Civ.P. where appropriate, but also to clarify that it applies to the unnecessary delay or needless increase in the cost of the administration of the case. Deletion of the references to specific statements that are excluded from the scope of this subdivision is stylistic. As used in subdivision (a) of this rule, "statement" is limited to the statement of financial affairs and the statement of intention required to be filed under Rule 1007. Deletion of the reference to the Chapter 13 Statement is consistent with the amendment to Rule 1007(b).

1997 Amendment

This rule is amended to conform to the 1993 changes to F.R.Civ.P. 11. For an explanation of these amendments, see the advisory committee note to the 1993 amendments to F.R.Civ.P. 11.

The "safe harbor" provision contained in subdivision (c)(1)(A), which prohibits the filing of a motion for sanctions unless the challenged paper is not withdrawn or corrected within a prescribed time after service of the motion, does not apply if the challenged paper is a petition. The filing of a petition has immediate serious consequences, including the imposition of the automatic stay under § 362 of the Code, which may not be avoided by the subsequent withdrawal of the petition. In addition, a petition for relief under chapter 7 or chapter 11 may not be withdrawn unless the court orders dismissal of the case for cause after notice and a hearing.

GAP Report on Rule 9011. The proposed amendments to subdivision (a) were revised to clarify that a party not represented by an attorney must sign lists, schedules, and statements, as well as other papers that are filed.

CROSS REFERENCES

Affidavit in support of—
- Complaint seeking temporary restraining order, see Fed.Rules Bankr.Proc. Rule 7065, 11 USCA.
- Emergency motion on appeal, see Fed.Rules Bankr. Proc. Rule 8011, 11 USCA.
- Motion for ex parte relief from stay, see Fed.Rules Bankr.Proc. Rule 4001, 11 USCA.

Verification of—
- Complaint seeking temporary restraining order, see Fed.Rules Bankr.Proc. Rule 7065, 11 USCA.
- List of multiple proxies and acquisition statement, see Fed.Rules Bankr.Proc. Rule 2006, 11 USCA.
- Motions for ex parte relief from stay, see Fed.Rules Bankr.Proc. Rule 4001, 11 USCA.
- Petitions and accompanying papers, see Fed.Rules Bankr.Proc. Rule 1008, 11 USCA.

Pleadings allowed; form of motions, see Fed.Rules Civ. Proc. Rule 7, 28 USCA.

Signing of pleadings, see Fed.Rules Civ.Proc. Rule 11, 28 USCA.

Statements in pleadings subject to obligations set forth in rule 11, see Fed.Rules Civ.Proc. Rule 8, 28 USCA.

Rule 9012. Oaths and Affirmations

(a) Persons authorized to administer oaths

The following persons may administer oaths and affirmations and take acknowledgments: a bankruptcy judge, clerk, deputy clerk, United States trustee, officer authorized to administer oaths in proceedings before the courts of the United States or under the laws of the state where the oath is to be taken, or a diplomatic or consular officer of the United States in any foreign country.

(b) Affirmation in lieu of oath

When in a case under the Code an oath is required to be taken, a solemn affirmation may be accepted in lieu thereof.

(As amended Mar. 30, 1987, eff. Aug. 1, 1987; Apr. 30, 1991, eff. Aug. 1, 1991.)

ADVISORY COMMITTEE NOTES

This rule is derived from Rule 43(d) F.R.Civ.P.

The provisions of former Bankruptcy Rule 912(a) relating to who may administer oaths have been deleted as unnecessary. Bankruptcy judges and the clerks and deputy clerks of bankruptcy courts are authorized by statute to administer oaths and affirmations and to take acknowledgments. 28 U.S.C. §§ 459, 953. A person designated to preside at the meeting of creditors has authority under Rule 2003(b)(1) to administer the oath. Administration of the oath at a deposition is governed by Rule 7028.

1987 Amendment

Subdivision (a) has been added to the rule to authorize bankruptcy judges and clerks to administer oaths.

1991 Amendment

This rule is amended to conform to the 1986 amendment to § 343 which provides that the United States trustee may administer the oath to the debtor at the § 341 meeting. This rule also allows the United States trustee to administer oaths and affirmations and to take acknowledgments in other situations. This amendment also affects Rule 9010(c) relating to the acknowledgment of a power of attorney. The words "United States trustee" include a designee of the United States trustee pursuant to Rule 9001 and § 102(9) of the Code.

CROSS REFERENCES

Acknowledgment of power of attorney, see Fed.Rules Bankr.Proc. Rule 9010, 11 USCA.

Administration of oaths and acknowledgments by—

Clerks of court, see 28 USCA § 953.

Justices or judges, see 28 USCA § 459.

Affirmation in lieu of oath, see Fed.Rules Civ.Proc. Rule 43, 28 USCA.

Oath defined to include affirmation, see 1 USCA § 1.

Oath or affirmation of witnesses, see Fed.Rules Evid. Rule 603, 28 USCA.

Rule 9013. Motions: Form and Service

A request for an order, except when an application is authorized by these rules, shall be by written motion, unless made during a hearing. The motion shall state with particularity the grounds therefor, and shall set forth the relief or order sought. Every written motion other than one which may be considered ex parte shall be served by the moving party on the trustee or debtor in possession and on those entities specified by these rules or, if service is not required or the entities to be served are not specified by these rules, the moving party shall serve the entities the court directs.

(As amended Mar. 30, 1987, eff. Aug. 1, 1987.)

ADVISORY COMMITTEE NOTES

This rule is derived from Rule 5(a) and Rule 7(b)(1) F.R.Civ.P. Except when an application is specifically authorized by these rules, for example an application under Rule 2014 for approval of the employment of a professional, all requests for court action must be made by motion.

Rule 9014. Contested Matters

(a) Motion. In a contested matter not otherwise governed by these rules, relief shall be requested by motion, and reasonable notice and opportunity for hearing shall be afforded the party against whom relief is sought. No response is required under this rule unless the court directs otherwise.

(b) Service. The motion shall be served in the manner provided for service of a summons and complaint by Rule 7004. Any paper served after the motion shall be served in the manner provided by Rule 5(b) F. R. Civ. P.

(c) Application of Part VII rules. Except as otherwise provided in this rule, and unless the court directs otherwise, the following rules shall apply: 7009, 7017, 7021, 7025, 7026, 7028–7037, 7041, 7042, 7052, 7054–7056, 7064, 7069, and 7071. The following subdivisions of Fed. R. Civ. P. 26, as incorporated by Rule 7026, shall not apply in a contested matter unless the court directs otherwise: 26(a)(1) (mandatory disclosure), 26(a)(2) (disclosures regarding expert testimony) and 26(a)(3) (additional pre-trial disclosure), and 26(f) (mandatory meeting before scheduling conference/ discovery plan). An entity that desires to perpetuate testimony may proceed in the same manner as provided in Rule 7027 for the taking of a deposition before an adversary proceeding. The court may at any stage in a particular matter direct that one or more of the other rules in Part VII shall apply. The court shall give the parties notice of any order issued under this paragraph to afford them a reasonable opportunity to comply with the procedures prescribed by the order.

(d) Testimony of witnesses. Testimony of witnesses with respect to disputed material factual issues shall be taken in the same manner as testimony in an adversary proceeding.

(e) Attendance of witnesses. The court shall provide procedures that enable parties to ascertain at a reasonable time before any scheduled hearing whether the hearing will be an evidentiary hearing at which witnesses may testify.

(As amended Mar. 30, 1987, eff. Aug. 1, 1987; Apr. 29, 1999, eff. Dec. 1, 1999; Apr. 29, 2002, eff. Dec. 1, 2002; Apr. 26, 2004, eff. Dec. 1, 2004.)

ADVISORY COMMITTEE NOTES

Rules 1017(d), 3020(b)(1), 4001(a), 4003(d), and 6006(a), which govern respectively dismissal or conversion of a case, objections to confirmation of a plan, relief from the automatic stay and the use of cash collateral, avoidance of a lien under § 522(f) of the Code, and the assumption or rejection of executory contracts or unexpired leases, specifically provide that litigation under those rules shall be as provided in Rule 9014. This rule also governs litigation in other contested matters.

Whenever there is an actual dispute, other than an adversary proceeding, before the bankruptcy court, the litigation to resolve that dispute is a contested matter. For example, the filing of an objection to a proof of claim, to a claim of exemption, or to a disclosure statement creates a dispute which is a contested matter. Even when an objection is not formally required, there may be a dispute. If a party in interest opposes the amount of compensation sought by a professional, there is a dispute which is a contested matter.

When the rules of Part VII are applicable to a contested matter, reference in the Part VII rules to adversary proceedings is to be read as a reference to a contested matter. See Rule 9002(1).

1999 Amendments

This rule is amended to delete Rule 7062 from the list of Part VII rules that automatically apply in a contested matter.

Rule 7062 provides that Rule 62 F.R.Civ.P., which governs stays of proceedings to enforce a judgment, is applicable in adversary proceedings. The provisions of Rule 62, including the ten-day automatic stay of the enforcement of a judgment provided by Rule 62(a) and the stay as a matter of right by posting a supersedeas bond provided in Rule 62(d), are not appropriate for most orders granting or denying motions governed by Rule 9014.

Although Rule 7062 will not apply automatically in contested matters, the amended rule permits the court, in its discretion, to order that Rule 7062 apply in a particular matter, and Rule 8005 gives the court discretion to issue a stay or any other appropriate order during the pendency of an appeal on such terms as will protect the rights of all parties in interest. In addition, amendments to Rules 3020, 4001, 6004, and 6006 automatically stay certain types of orders for a period of ten days, unless the court orders otherwise.

Gap Report on Rule 9014. No changes since publication.

2002 Amendments

The list of Part VII rules that are applicable in a contested matter is extended to include Rule 7009 on pleading special matters, and Rule 7017 on real parties in interest, infants and incompetent persons, and capacity. The discovery rules made applicable in adversary proceedings apply in contested matters unless the court directs otherwise.

Subdivision (b) is amended to permit parties to serve papers, other than the original motion, in the manner provided in Rule 5(b) F.R. Civ.P. When the court requires a response to the motion, this amendment will permit service of the response in the same manner as an answer is served in an adversary proceeding.

Subdivision (d) is added to clarify that if the motion cannot be decided without resolving a disputed material issue of fact, an evidentiary hearing must be held at which testimony of witnesses is taken in the same manner as testimony is taken in an adversary proceeding or at a trial in a district court civil case. Rule 43(a), rather than Rule 43(e), F.R. Civ.P. would govern the evidentiary hearing on the factual dispute. Under Rule 9017, the Federal Rules of Evidence also apply in a contested matter. Nothing in the rule prohibits a court from resolving any matter that is submitted on affidavits by agreement of the parties.

Subdivision (e). Local procedures for hearings and other court appearances in a contested matter vary from district to district. In some bankruptcy courts, an evidentiary hearing at which witnesses may testify usually is held at the first court appearance in the contested matter. In other courts, it is customary for the court to delay the evidentiary hearing on disputed factual issues until some time after the initial hearing date. In order to avoid unnecessary expense and inconvenience, it is important for attorneys to know whether they should bring witnesses to a court appearance. The purpose of the final sentence of this rule is to require that the court provide a mechanism that will enable attorneys to know at a reasonable time before a scheduled hearing whether it will be necessary for witnesses to appear in court on that particular date.

Other amendments to this rule are stylistic.

Changes Made After Publication and Comments: The Advisory Committee made two changes to subdivision (d) after considering the comments received addressing the proposed rule. First, the word "material" is inserted to make explicit that which was implied in the published version of the proposed rule. Second, the reference to F.R.Civ.P. 43(a) was removed. The purpose of proposed subdivision (d) was to recognize that testimony should be taken in the same manner in both contested matters and adversary proceedings. The revision to the published rule states this more directly.

The Committee Note was amended to reflect the changes made in the text of the rule.

2004 Amendments

The rule is amended to provide that the mandatory disclosure requirements of Fed. R. Civ. P. 26, as incorporated by Rule 7026, do not apply in contested matters. The typically short time between the commencement and resolution of most contested matters makes the mandatory disclosure provisions of Rule 26 ineffective. Nevertheless, the court may by local rule or by order in a particular case provide that these provisions of the rule apply in a contested matter.

HISTORICAL AND STATUTORY NOTES

References in Text

The Federal Rules of Civil Procedure, referred to in subds. (b) and (c), are set out in the Appendix to Title 28.

CROSS REFERENCES

Contested matters—

Assumption, rejection, or assignment of executory contract or unexpired lease, or proceeding to require trustee to act, see Fed.Rules Bankr.Proc. Rule 6006, 11 USCA.

Avoidance by debtor of transfers of exempt property, see Fed.Rules Bankr.Proc. Rule 4003, 11 USCA.

Dismissal or conversion to another chapter, see Fed. Rules Bankr.Proc. Rule 1017, 11 USCA.

Objection to confirmation of plan, see Fed.Rules Bankr. Proc. Rule 3020, 11 USCA.

Relief from automatic stay, see Fed.Rules Bankr.Proc. Rule 4001, 11 USCA.

Request for use of cash collateral, see Fed.Rules Bankr. Proc. Rule 4001, 11 USCA.

Effect of amendment of Federal Rules of Civil Procedure, see Fed.Rules Bankr.Proc. Rule 9032, 11 USCA.

Meanings of words in Federal Rules of Civil Procedure when applicable, see Fed.Rules Bankr.Proc. Rule 9002, 11 USCA.

Motions; form and service, see Fed.Rules Bankr.Proc. Rule 9013, 11 USCA.

Rule 9015. Jury Trials

(a) Applicability of certain Federal Rules of Civil Procedure

Rules 38, 39, and 47–51 F.R.Civ.P., and Rule 81(c) F.R.Civ.P. insofar as it applies to jury trials, apply in cases and proceedings, except that a demand made pursuant to Rule 38(b) F.R.Civ.P. shall be filed in accordance with Rule 5005.

(b) Consent to have trial conducted by bankruptcy judge

If the right to a jury trial applies, a timely demand has been filed pursuant to Rule 38(b) F.R.Civ.P., and the bankruptcy judge has been specially designated to conduct the jury trial, the parties may consent to have a jury trial conducted by a bankruptcy judge under 28 U.S.C. § 157(e) by jointly or separately filing a statement of consent within any applicable time limits specified by local rule.

(Added Apr. 11, 1997, eff. Dec. 1, 1997)

ADVISORY COMMITTEE NOTES

1987 Abrogation

Former section 1480 of title 28 preserved a right to trial by jury in any case or proceeding under title 11 in which jury trial was provided by statute. Rule 9015 provided the procedure for jury trials in bankruptcy courts. Section 1480 was repealed. Section 1411 added by the 1984 amendments affords a jury trial only for personal injury or wrongful death claims, which 28 U.S.C. § 157(b)(5) requires be tried in the district court. Nevertheless, Rule 9015 has been cited as conferring a right to jury trial in other matters before bankruptcy judges. In light of the clear mandate of 28 U.S.C. § 2075 that the "rules shall not abridge, enlarge, or modify any substantive right," Rule 9015 is abrogated. In the event the courts of appeals or the Supreme Court define a right to jury trial in any bankruptcy matters, a local rule in substantially the form of Rule 9015 can be adopted pending amendment of these rules.

1997 Amendment

This rule provides procedures relating to jury trials. This rule is not intended to expand or create any right to trial by jury where such right does not otherwise exist.

GAP Report on Rule 9015. No changes to the published draft.

Rule 9016. Subpoena

Rule 45 F.R.Civ.P. applies in cases under the Code.

(As amended Mar. 30, 1987, eff. Aug. 1, 1987.)

ADVISORY COMMITTEE NOTES

Although Rule 7004(d) authorizes nationwide service of process, Rule 45 F.R.Civ.P. limits the subpoena power to the judicial district and places outside the district which are within 100 miles of the place of trial or hearing.

CROSS REFERENCES

Compelling attendance of witnesses by use of subpoena—

Deposition upon oral examination, see Fed.Rules Bankr. Proc. Rule 7030, 11 USCA.

Deposition upon written questions, see Fed.Rules Bankr. Proc. Rule 7031, 11 USCA.

Examination of debtor—

Apprehension and removal of debtor to compel attendance, see Fed.Rules Bankr.Proc. Rule 2005, 11 USCA.

Compelling attendance for examination and production of documentary evidence, see Fed.Rules Bankr.Proc. Rule 2004, 11 USCA.

Rule 9017. Evidence

The Federal Rules of Evidence and Rules 43, 44 and 44.1 F.R.Civ.P. apply in cases under the Code.

ADVISORY COMMITTEE NOTES

Sections 251 and 252 of Public Law 95–598, amended Rule 1101 of the Federal Rules of Evidence to provide that the Federal Rules of Evidence apply in bankruptcy courts and to any case or proceeding under the Code. Rules 43, 44 and 44.1 of the F.R.Civ.P., which supplement the Federal Rules of Evidence, are by this rule made applicable to cases under the Code.

Examples of bankruptcy rules containing matters of an evidentiary nature are: Rule 2011, evidence of debtor retained in possession; Rule 3001(f), proof of claim constitutes prima facie evidence of the amount and validity of a claim; and Rule 5007(c), sound recording of court proceedings constitutes the record of the proceedings.

CROSS REFERENCES

Applicability of rules to proceedings and cases under this title, see Fed.Rules Evid. Rule 1101, 28 USCA.

Rule 9018. Secret Confidential, Scandalous, or Defamatory Matter

On motion or on its own initiative, with or without notice, the court may make any order which justice requires (1) to protect the estate or any entity in respect of a trade secret or other confidential research, development, or commercial information, (2) to protect any entity against scandalous or defamatory matter contained in any paper filed in a case under the Code, or (3) to protect governmental matters that are made confidential by statute or regulation. If an order is entered under this rule without notice, any entity affected thereby may move to vacate or modify the order, and after a hearing on notice the court shall determine the motion.

(As amended Mar. 30, 1987, eff. Aug. 1, 1987.)

ADVISORY COMMITTEE NOTES

This rule provides the procedure for invoking the court's power under § 107 of the Code.

CROSS REFERENCES

Motion to strike scandalous matter, see Fed.Rules Civ. Proc. Rule 12, 28 USCA.

Motions; form and service, see Fed.Rules Bankr.Proc. Rule 9013, 11 USCA.

Protective orders, see Fed.Rules Civ.Proc. Rule 26, 28 USCA.

Rule 9019. Compromise and Arbitration

(a) Compromise

On motion by the trustee and after notice and a hearing, the court may approve a compromise or settlement. Notice shall be given to creditors, the United States trustee, the debtor, and indenture trustees as provided in Rule 2002 and to any other entity as the court may direct.

(b) Authority to compromise or settle controversies within classes

After a hearing on such notice as the court may direct, the court may fix a class or classes of controversies and authorize the trustee to compromise or settle controversies within such class or classes without further hearing or notice.

(c) Arbitration

On stipulation of the parties to any controversy affecting the estate the court may authorize the matter to be submitted to final and binding arbitration.

(As amended Mar. 30, 1987, eff. Aug. 1, 1987; Apr. 30, 1991, eff. Aug. 1, 1991; Apr. 22, 1993, eff. Aug. 1, 1993.)

ADVISORY COMMITTEE NOTES

Subdivisions (a) and (c) of this rule are essentially the same as the provisions of former Bankruptcy Rule 919 and subdivision (b) is the same as former Rule 8–514(b), which was applicable to railroad reorganizations. Subdivision (b) permits the court to deal efficiently with a case in which there may be a large number of settlements.

1991 Amendment

This rule is amended to enable the United States trustee to object or otherwise be heard in connection with a proposed compromise or settlement and otherwise to monitor the progress of the case.

1993 Amendments

Subdivision (a) is amended to conform to the language of § 102(1) of the Code. Other amendments are stylistic and make no substantive change.

CROSS REFERENCES

Motions; form and service, see Fed.Rules Bankr.Proc. Rule 9013, 11 USCA.

Rule 9020. Contempt Proceedings

Rule 9014 governs a motion for an order of contempt made by the United States trustee or a party in interest.

(As amended Mar. 30, 1987, eff. Aug. 1, 1987; Apr. 30, 1991, eff. 1, 1991; Apr. 23, 2001, eff. Dec. 1, 2001.)

ADVISORY COMMITTEE NOTES

Section 1481 of Title 28 provides that a bankruptcy court "may not . . . punish a criminal contempt not committed in the presence of the judge of the court or warranting a punishment of imprisonment." Rule 9020 does not enlarge the power of bankruptcy courts.

Subdivision (a) is adapted from former Bankruptcy Rule 920 and Rule 42 F.R.Crim.P. Paragraph (1) of the subdivision permits summary imposition of punishment for contempt if the conduct is in the presence of the court and is of such nature that the conduct "obstruct[s] the administration of justice." See 18 U.S.C. § 401(a). Cases interpreting Rule 42(a) F.R.Crim.P. have held that when criminal contempt is in question summary disposition should be the exception: summary disposition should be reserved for situations where it is necessary to protect the judicial institution. 3 Wright, Federal Practice & Procedure—Criminal § 707 (1969). Those cases are equally pertinent to the application of this rule and, therefore, contemptuous conduct in the presence of the judge may often be punished only after the notice and hearing requirements of subdivision (b) are satisfied.

If the bankruptcy court concludes it is without power to punish or to impose the proper punishment for conduct which constitutes contempt, subdivision (a)(3) authorizes the bankruptcy court to certify the matter to the district court.

Subdivision (b) makes clear that when a person has a constitutional or statutory right to a jury trial in a criminal contempt matter this rule in no way affects that right. See Frank v. United States, 395 U.S. 147 (1969).

The Federal Rules of Civil Procedure do not specifically provide the procedure for the imposition of civil contempt sanctions. The decisional law governing the procedure for imposition of civil sanctions by the district courts will be equally applicable to the bankruptcy courts.

1987 Amendment

The United States Bankruptcy Courts, as constituted under the Bankruptcy Reform Act of 1978, were courts of law, equity, and admiralty with an inherent contempt power, but former 28 U.S.C. § 1481 restricted the criminal contempt power of bankruptcy judges. Under the 1984 amendments, bankruptcy judges are judicial officers of the district court, 28 U.S.C. §§ 151, 152(a)(1). There are no decisions by the courts of appeals concerning the authority of bankruptcy judges to punish for either civil or criminal contempt under the 1984 amendments. This rule, as amended, recognizes that bankruptcy judges may not have the power to punish for contempt.

Sound judicial administration requires that the initial determination of whether contempt has been committed should be made by the bankruptcy judge. If timely objections are not filed to the bankruptcy judge's order, the order has the same force and effect as an order of the district court. If objections are filed within 10 days of service of the order, the district court conducts a de novo review pursuant to Rule 9033 and any order of contempt is entered by the district court on completion of the court's review of the bankruptcy judge's order.

1991 Amendments

The words "with the clerk" in subdivision (c) are deleted as unnecessary. See Rules 5005(a) and 9001(3).

2001 Amendments

The amendments to this rule cover a motion for an order of contempt filed by the United States trustee or a party in interest. This rule, as amended, does not address a contempt proceeding initiated by the court sua sponte.

Whether the court is acting on motion under this rule or is acting sua sponte, these amendments are not intended to extend, limit, or otherwise affect either the contempt power of a bankruptcy judge or the role of the district judge regarding contempt orders. Issues relating to the contempt power of bankruptcy judges are substantive and are left to statutory and judicial development, rather than procedural rules.

This rule, as amended in 1987, delayed for ten days from service the effectiveness of a bankruptcy judge's order of contempt and rendered the order subject to de novo review by the district court. These limitations on contempt orders were added to the rule in response to the Bankruptcy Amendments and Federal Judgeship Act of 1984, Pub. L. No. 98–353, 98 Stat. 333, which provides that bankruptcy judges are judicial officers of the district court, but does not specifically mention contempt power. *See* 28 U.S.C. § 151. As explained in the committee note to the 1987 amendments to this rule, no decisions of the courts of appeals existed concerning the authority of a bankruptcy judge to punish for either civil or criminal contempt under the 1984 Act and, therefore, the rule as amended in 1987 "recognizes that bankruptcy judges may not have the power to punish for contempt." Committee Note to 1987 Amendments to Rule 9020.

Since 1987, several courts of appeals have held that bankruptcy judges have the power to issue civil contempt orders. *See, e.g., Matter of Terrebonne Fuel and Lube, Inc.*, 108 F.3d 609 (5th Cir. 1997); *In re Rainbow Magazine, Inc.*, 77 F.3d 278 (9th Cir. 1996). Several courts have distinguished between a bankruptcy judge's civil contempt power and criminal contempt power. *See, e.g., Matter of Terrebonne Fuel and Lube, Inc.*, 108 F.3d at 613, n. 3 ("[a]lthough we find that bankruptcy judge's [sic] can find a party in civil contempt, we must point out that bankruptcy courts lack the power to hold persons in criminal contempt."). For other decisions regarding criminal contempt power, *see, e.g., In re Ragar*, 3 F.3d 1174 (8th Cir. 1993); *Matter of Hipp, Inc.*, 895 F.2d 1503 (5th Cir. 1990). To the extent that Rule 9020, as amended in 1987, delayed the effectiveness of civil contempt orders and required de novo review by the district court, the rule may have been unnecessarily restrictive in view of judicial decisions recognizing that bankruptcy judges have the power to hold parties in civil contempt.

Subdivision (d), which provides that the rule shall not be construed to impair the right to trial by jury, is deleted as unnecessary and is not intended to deprive any party of the right to a jury trial when it otherwise exists.

CHANGES MADE AFTER PUBLICATION AND COMMENTS

No changes were made in the text of the proposed amendments. Stylistic changes were made to the Committee Note.

CROSS REFERENCES

Contempts, see 18 USCA §§ 401 et seq. and 3691 et seq.

Criminal contempt, see Fed.Rules Cr.Proc. Rule 42, 18 USCA.

Power of court to punish persons for contempts, see 11 USCA § 105.

Rule 9021. Entry of Judgment

Except as otherwise provided herein, Rule 58 F.R.Civ.P. applies in cases under the Code. Every judgment entered in an adversary proceeding or contested matter shall be set forth on a separate document. A judgment is effective when entered as provided in Rule 5003. The reference in Rule 58 F.R.Civ.P. to Rule 79(a) F.R.Civ.P. shall be read as a reference to Rule 5003 of these rules.

(As amended Mar. 30, 1987, eff. Aug. 1, 1987.)

ADVISORY COMMITTEE NOTES

Subdivision (a). This rule is derived from Rule 58 F.R.Civ.P. The requirement that a judgment entered in an adversary proceeding or contested matter be set forth on a separate document is to eliminate uncertainty as to whether an opinion or memorandum of the court is a judgment. There is no sound reason to require that every order in a case under the Code be evidenced by a separate document.

Subdivision (b) establishes a procedure for entering a judgment of a bankruptcy court for the recovery of money or property in an index of judgments kept by the clerk of the district court. It clarifies the availability of the same remedies for the enforcement of a bankruptcy court judgment as those provided for the enforcement of a district court judgment. See 28 U.S.C. §§ 1961–63. When indexed in accordance with subdivision (b) of this rule a judgment of the bankruptcy court may be found by anyone searching for liens of record in the judgment records of the district court. Certification of a copy of the judgment to the clerk of the district court provides a basis for registration of the judgment pursuant to 28 U.S.C. § 1963 in any other district. When so registered, the judgment may be enforced by issuance of execution and orders for supplementary proceedings that may be served anywhere within the state where the registering court sits. See 7 Moore, Federal Practice 2409–11 (2d ed. 1971). The procedures available in the district court are not exclusive, however, and the holder of a judgment entered by the bankruptcy court may use the remedies under Rules 7069 and 7070 even if the judgment is indexed by the clerk of the district court.

Subdivision (c) makes it clear that when a district court hears a matter reserved to it by 28 U.S.C. §§ 1471, 1481, its judgments are entered in the district court's civil docket and in the docket of the bankruptcy court. When the district court acts as an appellate court, Rule 8016(a) governs the entry of judgments on appeal.

1987 Amendment

Former subdivision (a) was derived from Rule 58 F.R.Civ.P. As amended, Rule 9021 adopts Rule 58. The reference in Rule 58 to Rule 79(a) F.R.Civ.P. is to be read as a reference to Rule 5003.

CROSS REFERENCES

Entry of judgment, see Fed.Rules Civ.Proc. Rule 58, 28 USCA.

Entry of judgment on appeal, see Fed.Rules Bankr.Proc. Rule 8016, 11 USCA.

Findings by court, see Fed.Rules Bankr.Proc. Rule 7052, 11 USCA.

Judgments rendered by district court—

Effect as lien on local property, see 28 USCA § 1962.

Interest allowed on money judgment, see 28 USCA § 1961.

Registration of final judgments in other districts, see 28 USCA § 1963.

Rule 9022. Notice of Judgment or Order

(a) Judgment or order of bankruptcy judge

Immediately on the entry of a judgment or order the clerk shall serve a notice of entry in the manner provided in Rule 5(b) F. R. Civ. P. on the contesting parties and on other entities as the court directs. Unless the case is a chapter 9 municipality case, the clerk shall forthwith transmit to the United States trustee a copy of the judgment or order. Service of the notice shall be noted in the docket. Lack of notice of the entry does not affect the time to appeal or relieve or authorize the court to relieve a party for failure to appeal within the time allowed, except as permitted in Rule 8002.

(b) Judgment or order of district judge

Notice of a judgment or order entered by a district judge is governed by Rule 77(d) F.R.Civ.P. Unless the case is a chapter 9 municipality case, the clerk shall forthwith transmit to the United States trustee a copy of a judgment or order entered by a district judge.

(As amended Mar. 30, 1987, eff. Aug. 1, 1987; Apr. 30, 1991, eff. Aug. 1, 1991; Apr. 23, 2001, eff. Dec. 1, 2001.)

ADVISORY COMMITTEE NOTES

Subdivision (a) of this rule is an adaptation of Rule 77(d) F.R.Civ.P.

Subdivision (b) complements Rule 9021(b). When a district court acts as an appellate court, Rule 8016(b) requires the clerk to give notice of the judgment on appeal.

1991 Amendments

This rule is amended to enable the United States trustee to be informed of all developments in the case so that administrative and supervisory functions provided in 28 U.S.C. § 586(a) may be performed.

2001 Amendments

Rule 5(b) F. R. Civ. P., which is made applicable in adversary proceedings by Rule 7005, is being restyled and amended to authorize service by electronic means—or any other means not otherwise authorized under Rule 5(b)—if consent is obtained from the person served. The amendment to Rule 9022(a) authorizes the clerk to serve notice of entry of a judgment or order by electronic means if the person served consents, or to use any other means of service authorized under Rule 5(b), including service by mail. This amendment conforms to the amendments made to Rule 77(d) F.R. Civ. P.

CHANGES MADE AFTER PUBLICATION AND COMMENTS

No changes were made.

CROSS REFERENCES

Entry of judgment; district court record of judgment, see Fed.Rules Bankr.Proc. Rule 9021, 11 USCA.

Notice of judgment on appeal, see Fed.Rules Bankr.Proc. Rule 8016, 11 USCA.

Rule 9023. New Trials; Amendment of Judgments

Rule 59 F.R.Civ.P. applies in cases under the Code, except as provided in Rule 3008.

ADVISORY COMMITTEE NOTES

Rule 59 F.R.Civ.P. regulates motions for a new trial and amendment of judgment. Those motions must be served within 10 days of the entry of judgment. No similar time limit is contained in Rule 3008 which governs reconsideration of claims.

CROSS REFERENCES

Amendment of findings by court, see Fed.Rules Bankr. Proc. Rule 7052, 11 USCA.

Effect of motion under this rule on time for appeal, see Fed.Rules Bankr.Proc. Rule 8002, 11 USCA.

Enlargement of ten-day period for motion for new trial not permitted, see Fed.Rules Bankr.Proc. Rule 9006, 11 USCA.

Time for service of opposing affidavits to motion for new trial, see Fed.Rules Bankr.Proc. Rule 9006, 11 USCA.

Rule 9024. Relief from Judgment or Order

Rule 60 F.R.Civ.P. applies in cases under the Code except that (1) a motion to reopen a case under the Code or for the reconsideration of an order allowing or disallowing a claim against the estate entered without a contest is not subject to the one year limitation prescribed in Rule 60(c), (2) a complaint to revoke a discharge in a chapter 7 liquidation case may be filed only within the time allowed by § 727(e) of the Code, and (3) a complaint to revoke an order confirming a plan may be filed only within the time allowed by § 1144, § 1230, or § 1330.

(As amended Apr. 30, 1991, eff. Aug. 1, 1991; Apr. 23, 2008, eff. Dec. 1, 2008.)

ADVISORY COMMITTEE NOTES

Motions to reopen cases are governed by Rule 5010. Reconsideration of orders allowing and disallowing claims is governed by Rule 3008. For the purpose of this rule all orders of the bankruptcy court are subject to Rule 60 F.R.Civ.P.

Pursuant to § 727(e) of the Code a complaint to revoke a discharge must be filed within one year of the entry of the discharge or, when certain grounds of revocation are asserted, the later of one year after the entry of the discharge or the date the case is closed. Under § 1144 and § 1330 of the Code a party must file a complaint to revoke an order confirming a chapter 11 or 13 plan within 180 days of its entry. Clauses (2) and (3) of this rule make it clear that the time periods established by §§ 727(e), 1144 and 1330 of the Code may not be circumvented by the invocation of F.R.Civ.P. 60(b).

1991 Amendment

Clause (3) is amended to include a reference to § 1230 of the Code which contains time limitations relating to revocation of confirmation of a chapter 12 plan. The time periods prescribed by § 1230 may not be circumvented by the invocation of F.R.Civ.P. 60(b).

2008 Amendments

The rule is amended to conform to the changes made to the Federal Rules of Civil Procedure through the restyling of those rules effective on December 1, 2007.

CROSS REFERENCES

Enlargement of time for motion for relief from judgment or order not permitted, see Fed.Rules Bankr.Proc. Rule 9006, 11 USCA.

Motions; form and service, see Fed.Rules Bankr.Proc. Rule 9013, 11 USCA.

Reconsideration of allowance or disallowance of claims, see Fed.Rules Bankr.Proc. Rule 3008, 11 USCA.

Reopening cases, see Fed.Rules Bankr.Proc. Rule 5010, 11 USCA.

Revocation of discharges under individual debt adjustment plan, see 11 USCA § 1328.

Setting aside judgment by default, see Fed.Rules Bankr. Proc. Rule 7055, 11 USCA.

Rule 9025. Security: Proceedings Against Sureties

Whenever the Code or these rules require or permit the giving of security by a party, and security is given in the form of a bond or stipulation or other undertaking with one or more sureties, each surety submits to the jurisdiction of the court, and liability may be determined in an adversary proceeding governed by the rules in Part VII.

ADVISORY COMMITTEE NOTES

This rule is an adaptation of Rule 65.1 F.R.Civ.P. and applies to any surety on a bond given pursuant to § 303(e) of the Code, Rules 2001, 2010, 5008, 7062, 7065, 8005, or any other rule authorizing the giving of such security.

CROSS REFERENCES

Bonds—

Deposit or investment by trustee of money of estates, see 11 USCA § 345.

Indemnification bond in involuntary cases, see 11 USCA § 303.

Qualification to serve as trustee, see 11 USCA § 322.

Enforcement of bond or undertaking on injunction against surety, see Fed.Rules Bankr.Proc. Rule 7065, 11 USCA.

Security; proceedings against sureties, see Fed.Rules Civ. Proc. Rule 65.1, 28 USCA.

Security defined, see 11 USCA § 101.

Rule 9026. Exceptions Unnecessary

Rule 46 F.R.Civ.P. applies in cases under the Code.

Rule 9027. Removal

(a) Notice of removal

(1) Where filed; form and content

A notice of removal shall be filed with the clerk for the district and division within which is located the state or federal court where the civil action is pending. The notice shall be signed pursuant to Rule 9011 and contain a short and plain statement of the facts which entitle the party filing the notice to remove, contain a statement that upon removal of the claim or cause of action the proceeding is core or non-core and, if non-core, that the party filing the notice does or does not consent to entry of final orders or judgment by the bankruptcy judge, and be accompanied by a copy of all process and pleadings.

(2) Time for filing; civil action initiated before commencement of the case under the code

If the claim or cause of action in a civil action is pending when a case under the Code is commenced, a notice of removal may be filed only within the longest of (A) 90 days after the order for relief in the case under the Code, (B) 30 days after entry of an order terminating a stay, if the claim or cause of action in a civil action has been stayed under § 362 of the Code, or (C) 30 days after a trustee qualifies in a chapter 11 reorganization case but not later than 180 days after the order for relief.

(3) Time for filing; civil action initiated after commencement of the case under the Code

If a claim or cause of action is asserted in another court after the commencement of a case under the Code, a notice of removal may be filed with the clerk only within the shorter of (A) 30 days after receipt, through service or otherwise, of a copy of the initial pleading setting forth the claim or cause of action sought to be removed, or (B) 30 days after receipt of the summons if the initial pleading has been filed with the court but not served with the summons.

(b) Notice

Promptly after filing the notice of removal, the party filing the notice shall serve a copy of it on all parties to the removed claim or cause of action.

(c) Filing in non-bankruptcy court

Promptly after filing the notice of removal, the party filing the notice shall file a copy of it with the clerk of the court from which the claim or cause of action is removed. Removal of the claim or cause of action is effected on such filing of a copy of the notice of removal. The parties shall proceed no further in that court unless and until the claim or cause of action is remanded.

(d) Remand

A motion for remand of the removed claim or cause of action shall be governed by Rule 9014 and served on the parties to the removed claim or cause of action.

(e) Procedure after removal

(1) After removal of a claim or cause of action to a district court the district court or, if the case under the Code has been referred to a bankruptcy judge of the district, the bankruptcy judge, may issue all necessary orders and process to bring before it all proper parties whether served by process issued by the court from which the claim or cause of action was removed or otherwise.

(2) The district court or, if the case under the Code has been referred to a bankruptcy judge of the district, the bankruptcy judge, may require the party filing the notice of removal to file with the clerk copies of all records and proceedings relating to the claim or cause of action in the court from which the claim or cause of action was removed.

(3) Any party who has filed a pleading in connection with the removed claim or cause of action, other than the party filing the notice of removal, shall file a statement admitting or denying any allegation in the notice of removal that upon removal of the claim or cause of action the proceeding is core or non-core. If the statement alleges that the proceeding is non-core, it shall state that the party does or does not consent to entry of final orders or judgment by the bankruptcy judge. A statement required by this paragraph shall be signed pursuant to Rule 9011 and shall be filed not later than 10 days after the filing of the notice of removal. Any party who files a statement pursuant to this paragraph shall mail a copy to every other party to the removed claim or cause of action.

(f) Process after removal

If one or more of the defendants has not been served with process, the service has not been perfected prior to removal, or the process served proves to be defective, such process or service may be completed or new process issued pursuant to Part VII of these rules. This subdivision shall not deprive any defendant on whom process is served after removal of the defendant's right to move to remand the case.

(g) Applicability of Part VII

The rules of Part VII apply to a claim or cause of action removed to a district court from a federal or state court and govern procedure after removal. Repleading is not necessary unless the court so orders. In a removed action in which the defendant has not answered, the defendant shall answer or present the other defenses or objections available under the rules of Part VII within 20 days following the receipt through service or otherwise of a copy of the initial pleading setting forth the claim for relief on which the action or proceeding is based, or within 20 days following the service of summons on such initial pleading, or within five days following the filing of the notice of removal, whichever period is longest.

(h) Record supplied

When a party is entitled to copies of the records and proceedings in any civil action or proceeding in a federal or a state court, to be used in the removed civil action or proceeding, and the clerk of the federal or state court, on demand accompanied by payment or tender of the lawful fees, fails to deliver certified copies, the court may, on affidavit reciting the facts, direct such record to be supplied by affidavit or otherwise. Thereupon the proceedings, trial and judgment may be had in the court, and all process awarded, as if certified copies had been filed.

(i) Attachment or sequestration; securities

When a claim or cause of action is removed to a district court, any attachment or sequestration of property in the court from which the claim or cause of action was removed shall hold the property to answer the final judgment or decree in the same manner as the property would have been held to answer final judgment or decree had it been rendered by the court from which the claim or cause of action was removed. All bonds, undertakings, or security given by either party to the claim or cause of action prior to its removal shall remain valid and effectual notwithstanding such removal. All injunctions issued, orders entered and other proceedings had prior to removal shall remain in full force and effect until dissolved or modified by the court.

(As amended Mar. 30, 1987, eff. Aug. 1, 1987; Apr. 30, 1991, eff. Aug. 1, 1991; Apr. 29, 2002, eff. Dec. 1, 2002.)

ADVISORY COMMITTEE NOTES

Under 28 U.S.C. § 1478(a) "any claim or cause of action in a civil action, other than a proceeding before the United States Tax Court or a civil action by a Government unit to enforce [a] . . . regulatory or police power" may be removed "if the bankruptcy courts have jurisdiction over such claim or cause of action." This rule specifies how removal is accomplished, the procedure thereafter, and the procedure to request remand of the removed claim or cause of action. If the claim or cause of action which is removed to the bankruptcy court is subject to the automatic stay of § 362 of the Code, the litigation may not proceed in the bankruptcy court until relief from the stay is granted.

The subdivisions of this rule conform substantially to 28 U.S.C. §§ 1446–1450 and Rule 81(a) F.R.Civ.P. pertaining to removal to the district courts.

Subdivision (a)(1) is derived from 28 U.S.C. § 1446(a).

Subdivisions (a)(2) and (a)(3) are derived from paragraphs one and two of 28 U.S.C. § 1446(b). Timely exercise of the right to remove is as important in bankruptcy cases as in removals from a state court to a district court.

Subdivision (a)(2) governs the situation in which there is litigation pending and a party to the litigation becomes a debtor under the Code. Frequently, removal would be of little utility in such cases because the pending litigation will be stayed by § 362(a) on commencement of the case under the Code. As long as the stay remains in effect there is no reason to impose a time limit for removal to the bankruptcy court and, therefore, clause (B) of subdivision (a)(2) provides that a removal application may be filed within 30 days of entry of an order terminating the stay. Parties to stayed litigation will not be required to act immediately on commencement of a case under the Code to protect their right to remove. If the pending litigation is not stayed by § 362(a) of the Code, the removal application must ordinarily be filed within 90 days of the order for relief. Clause (C) contains an alternative period for a chapter 11 case. If a trustee is appointed, the removal application may be filed within 30 days of the trustee's qualification, provided that the removal application is filed not more than 180 days after the order for relief.

The removal application must be filed within the longest of the three possible periods. For example, in a chapter 11 case if the 90 day period expires but a trustee is appointed shortly thereafter, the removal application may be filed within 30 days of the trustee's qualification but not later than 180 days after the order for relief. Nevertheless, if the claim or cause of action in the civil action is stayed under § 362, the application may be filed after the 180 day period expires, provided the application is filed within 30 days of an order terminating the stay.

Subdivision (a)(3) applies to the situation in which the case under the Code is pending when the removable claim or cause of action is asserted in a civil action initiated in other than the bankruptcy court. The time for filing the application for removal begins to run on receipt of the first pleading containing the removable claim or cause of action. Only litigation not stayed by the code or by court order may properly be initiated after the case under the Code is commenced. See e.g., § 362(a).

Subdivision (b). With one exception, this subdivision is the same as 28 U.S.C. § 1446(d). The exemption from the bond requirement is enlarged to include a trustee or debtor in possession. Complete exemption from the bond requirement for removal is appropriate because of the limited resources which may be available at the beginning of a case and the small probability that an action will be improperly removed.

Recovery on the bond is permitted only when the removal was improper. If the removal is proper but the bankruptcy court orders the action remanded on equitable grounds, 28 U.S.C. § 1478(b), there is no recovery on the bond.

Subdivisions (c) and (d) are patterned on 28 U.S.C. § 1446(e).

Subdivision (e). There is no provision in the Federal Rules of Civil Procedure for seeking remand. The first sentence of this subdivision requires that a request for remand be by motion and that the moving party serve all other parties; however, no hearing is required. In recognition of the intrusion of the removal practice on the state and federal courts from which claims or causes of action are removed, the subdivision directs the bankruptcy court to decide remand motions as soon as practicable. The last sentence of this subdivision is derived from 28 U.S.C. § 1446(c).

Subdivisions (f) and (g), with appropriate changes to conform them to the bankruptcy context, are the same as 28 U.S.C. § 1447(a) and (b) and 28 U.S.C. § 1448, respectively.

Subdivisions (h) and (i) are taken from Rule 81(c) F.R.Civ.P.

Subdivisions (j) and (k) are derived from 28 U.S.C. § 1449 and § 1450, respectively.

Remand orders of bankruptcy judges are not appealable. 28 U.S.C. § 1478(b).

This rule does not deal with the question whether a single plaintiff or defendant may remove a claim or cause of action if there are two or more plaintiffs or defendants. See 28 U.S.C. § 1478.

1987 Amendment

Section 1452 of title 28, with certain exceptions, provides for removal of claims or causes of action in civil actions pending in state or federal courts when the claim or cause of action is within the jurisdiction conferred by 28 U.S.C. § 1334. An order granting or denying a motion for remand is not appealable. 28 U.S.C. § 1452(b). Under subdivision (e), as amended, the district court must enter the order on the remand motion; however, the bankruptcy judge conducts the initial hearing on the motion and files a report and recommendation. The parties may file objections. Review of the report and recommendation is pursuant to Rule 9033.

Subdivision (f) has been amended to provide that if there has been a referral pursuant to 28 U.S.C. § 157(a) the bankruptcy judge will preside over the removed civil action.

Subdivision (i) has been abrogated consistent with the abrogation of Rule 9015.

1991 Amendment

The abrogation of subdivision (b) is consistent with the repeal of 28 U.S.C. § 1446(d). The changes substituting the notice of removal for the application for removal conform to the 1988 amendments to 28 U.S.C. § 1446.

Rules 7008(a) and 7012(b) were amended in 1987 to require parties to allege in pleadings whether a proceeding is core or non-core and, if non-core, whether the parties consent to the entry of final orders or judgment by the bankruptcy judge. Subdivision (a)(1) is amended and subdivision (f)(3) is added to require parties to a removed claim or cause of action to make the same allegations. The party filing the notice of removal must include the allegation in the notice and the other parties who have filed pleadings must respond to the allegation in a separate statement filed within 10 days after removal. However, if a party to the removed claim or cause of action has not filed a pleading prior to removal, there is no need to file a separate statement under subdivision (f)(3) because the allegation must be included in the responsive pleading filed pursuant to Rule 7012(b).

Subdivision (e), redesignated as subdivision (d), is amended to delete the restriction that limits the role of the bankruptcy court to the filing of a report and recommendation for disposition of a motion for remand under 28 U.S.C. § 1452(b). This amendment is consistent with § 309(c) of the Judicial Improvements Act of 1990, which amended § 1452(b) so that it allows an appeal to the district court of a bankruptcy court's order determining a motion for remand. This subdivision is also amended to clarify that the motion is a contested matter governed by Rule 9014. The words "filed with the clerk" are deleted as unnecessary. See Rules 5005(a) and 9001(3).

2002 Amendments

Subdivision (a)(3) is amended to clarify that if a claim or cause of action is initiated after the commencement of a bankruptcy case, the time limits for filing a notice of removal of the claim or cause of action apply whether the case is still pending or has been suspended, dismissed, or closed.

Changes Made After Publication and Comments: No changes were made.

CROSS REFERENCES

Removed actions, see Fed.Rules Civ.Proc. Rule 81, 28 USCA.

Removal of actions, see 28 USCA §§ 1446 to 1450.

Rule 9028. Disability of a Judge

Rule 63 F.R.Civ.P. applies in cases under the Code.

(As amended Mar. 30, 1987, eff. Aug. 1, 1987.)

ADVISORY COMMITTEE NOTES

This rule is an adaptation of Rule 63 F.R.Civ.P.

1987 Amendment

Rule 9028 has been changed to adopt the procedures contained in Rule 63 of the Federal Rules of Civil Procedure for substituting a judge in the event of disability.

CROSS REFERENCES

Disability of judge, see Fed.Rules Civ.Proc. Rule 63, 28 USCA.

Rule 9029. Local Bankruptcy Rules; Procedure When There is No Controlling Law

(a) Local Bankruptcy Rules

(1) Each district court acting by a majority of its district judges may make and amend rules governing practice and procedure in all cases and proceedings within the district court's bankruptcy jurisdiction which are consistent with—but not duplicative of—Acts of Congress and these rules and which do not prohibit or limit the use of the Official Forms. Rule 83 F.R.Civ.P. governs the procedure for making local rules. A district court may authorize the bankruptcy judges of the district, subject to any limitation or condition it may prescribe and the requirements of 83 F.R.Civ.P., to make and amend rules of practice and procedure which are consistent with—but not duplicative of—Acts of Congress and these rules and which do not prohibit or limit the use of the Official Forms. Local rules shall conform to any uniform numbering system prescribed by the Judicial Conference of the United States.

(2) A local rule imposing a requirement of form shall not be enforced in a manner that causes a party to lose rights because of a nonwillful failure to comply with the requirement.

(b) Procedure When There is No Controlling Law. A judge may regulate practice in any manner consistent with federal law, these rules, Official Forms, and local rules of the district. No sanction or other disadvantage may be imposed for noncompliance with any requirement not in federal law, federal rules, Official Forms, or the local rules of the district unless the alleged violator has been furnished in the particular case with actual notice of the requirement.

(As amended Mar. 30, 1987, eff. Aug. 1, 1987; Apr. 30, 1991, eff. Aug. 1, 1991; Apr. 27, 1995, eff. Dec. 1, 1995.)

ADVISORY COMMITTEE NOTES

This rule is an adaptation of Rule 83 F.R.Civ.P. and Rule 57(a) F.R.Crim.P. Under this rule bankruptcy courts may make local rules which govern practice before those courts. Circuit councils and district courts are authorized by Rule 8018 to make local rules governing appellate practice.

1987 Amendment

Rule 9029 is amended to authorize the district court to promulgate local rules governing bankruptcy practice. This rule, as amended, permits the district court to authorize the bankruptcy judges to promulgate or recommend local rules for adoption by the district court.

Effective August 1, 1985, Rule 83 F.R.Civ.P., governing adoption of local rules, was amended to achieve greater participation by the bar, scholars, and the public in the rule making process; to authorize the judicial council to abrogate local rules; and to make certain that single-judge standing orders are not inconsistent with these rules or local rules. Rule 9029 has been amended to incorporate Rule 83. The term "court" in the last sentence of the rule includes the judges of the district court and the bankruptcy judges of the district. Rule 9001(4).

1991 Amendments

This rule is amended to make it clear that the Official Forms must be accepted in every bankruptcy court.

1995 Amendments

Subdivision (a). This rule is amended to reflect the requirement that local rules be consistent not only with applicable national rules but also with Acts of Congress. The amendment also states that local rules should not repeat applicable national rules and Acts of Congress.

The amendment also requires that the numbering of local rules conform with any uniform numbering system that may be prescribed by the Judicial Conference. Lack of uniform numbering might create unnecessary traps for counsel and litigants. A uniform numbering system would make it easier for an increasingly national bar and for litigants to locate a local rule that applies to a particular procedural issue.

Paragraph (2) of subdivision (a) is new. Its aim is to protect against loss of rights in the enforcement of local rules relating to matters of form. For example, a party should not be deprived of a right to a jury trial because its attorney, unaware of—or forgetting—a local rule directing that jury demands be noted in the caption of the case, includes a jury demand only in the body of the pleading. The proscription of paragraph (2) is narrowly drawn—covering only violations that are not willful and only those involving local rules directed to matters of form. It does not limit the court's power to impose substantive penalties upon a party if it or its attorney stubbornly or repeatedly violates a local rule, even one involving merely a matter of form. Nor does it affect the court's power to enforce local rules that involve more than mere matters of form—for example, a local rule requiring that a party demand a jury trial within a specified time period to avoid waiver of the right to a trial by jury.

Subdivision (b). This rule provides flexibility to the court in regulating practice when there is no controlling law. Specifically, it permits the court to regulate practice in any manner consistent with federal law, with rules adopted under 28 U.S.C. § 2075, with Official Forms, and with the district's local rules.

This rule recognizes that courts rely on multiple directives to control practice. Some courts regulate practice through the published Federal Rules and the local rules of the court. Some courts also have used internal operating procedures, standing orders, and other internal directives. Although such directives continue to be authorized, they can lead to problems. Counsel or litigants may be unaware of various directives. In addition, the sheer volume of directives may impose an unreasonable barrier. For example, it may be difficult to obtain copies of the directives. Finally, counsel or litigants may be unfairly sanctioned for failing to comply with a directive. For these reasons, the amendment to this rule disapproves imposing any sanction or other disadvantage on a person for noncompliance with such an internal directive, unless the alleged violator has been furnished in a particular case with actual notice of the requirement.

There should be no adverse consequence to a party or attorney for violating special requirements relating to practice before a particular judge unless the party or attorney has actual notice of those requirements. Furnishing litigants with a copy outlining the judge's practices—or attaching instructions to a notice setting a case for conference or trial—would suffice to give actual notice, as would an order in a case specifically adopting by reference a judge's standing order and indicating how copies can be obtained.

CROSS REFERENCES

Local rules to govern appellate practice, see Fed.Rules Bankr.Proc. Rule 8018, 11 USCA.

Rules by district courts, see Fed.Rules Civ.Proc. Rule 83, 28 USCA.

Rules by district courts, see Fed.Rules Cr.Proc. Rule 57, 18 USCA.

Rule 9030. Jurisdiction and Venue Unaffected

These rules shall not be construed to extend or limit the jurisdiction of the courts or the venue of any matters therein.

(As amended Mar. 30, 1987, eff. Aug. 1, 1987.)

ADVISORY COMMITTEE NOTES

The rule is an adaptation of Rule 82 F.R.Civ.P.

CROSS REFERENCES

Jurisdiction and venue unaffected, see Fed.Rules Civ.Proc. Rule 82, 28 USCA.

Power of Supreme Court to prescribe bankruptcy rules, see 28 USCA § 2075.

Rule 9031. Masters Not Authorized

Rule 53 F.R.Civ.P. does not apply in cases under the Code.

ADVISORY COMMITTEE NOTES

This rule precludes the appointment of masters in cases and proceedings under the Code.

Rule 9032. Effect of Amendment of Federal Rules of Civil Procedure

The Federal Rules of Civil Procedure which are incorporated by reference and made applicable by these rules shall be the Federal Rules of Civil Procedure in effect on the effective date of these rules and as thereafter amended, unless otherwise provided by such amendment or by these rules.

(As amended Apr. 30, 1991, eff. Aug. 1, 1991.)

ADVISORY COMMITTEE NOTES

1991 Amendment

This rule is amended to provide flexibility so that the Bankruptcy Rules may provide that subsequent amendments to a Federal Rule of Civil Procedure made applicable by these rules are not effective with regard to Bankruptcy Code cases or proceedings. For example, in view of the anticipated amendments to, and restructuring of, Rule 4 F.R.Civ.P., Rule 7004(g) will prevent such changes from affecting Bankruptcy Code cases until the Advisory Committee on Bankruptcy Rules has an opportunity to consider such amendments and to make appropriate recommendations for incorporating such amendments into the Bankruptcy Rules.

Rule 9033. Review of Proposed Findings of Fact and Conclusions of Law in Non-Core Proceedings

(a) Service

In non-core proceedings heard pursuant to 28 U.S.C. § 157(c)(1), the bankruptcy judge shall file proposed findings of fact and conclusions of law. The clerk shall serve forthwith copies on all parties by mail and note the date of mailing on the docket.

(b) Objections: time for filing

Within 10 days after being served with a copy of the proposed findings of fact and conclusions of law a party may serve and file with the clerk written objections which identify the specific proposed findings or conclusions objected to and state the grounds for such objection. A party may respond to another party's objections within 10 days after being served with a copy thereof. A party objecting to the bankruptcy judge's proposed findings or conclusions shall arrange promptly for the transcription of the record, or such portions of it as all parties may agree upon or the bankruptcy judge deems sufficient, unless the district judge otherwise directs.

(c) Extension of time

The bankruptcy judge may for cause extend the time for filing objections by any party for a period not to exceed 20 days from the expiration of the time otherwise prescribed by this rule. A request to extend the time for filing objections must be made before the time for filing objections has expired, except that a request made no more than 20 days after the expiration of the time for filing objections may be granted upon a showing of excusable neglect.

(d) Standard of review

The district judge shall make a de novo review upon the record or, after additional evidence, of any portion of the bankruptcy judge's findings of fact or conclusions of law to which specific written objection has been made in accordance with this rule. The district judge may accept, reject, or modify the proposed findings of fact or conclusions of law, receive further evidence, or recommit the matter to the bankruptcy judge with instructions.

(Added Mar. 30, 1987, eff. Aug. 1, 1987.)

ADVISORY COMMITTEE NOTES

Section 157(c)(1) of title 28 requires a bankruptcy judge to submit proposed findings of fact and conclusions of law to the district court when the bankruptcy judge has heard a non-core proceeding. This rule, which is modeled on Rule 72 F.R.Civ.P., provides the procedure for objecting to, and for review by, the district court of specific findings and conclusions.

Subdivision (a) requires the clerk to serve a copy of the proposed findings and conclusions on the parties. The bankruptcy clerk, or the district court clerk if there is no bankruptcy clerk in the district, shall serve a copy of the proposed findings and conclusions on all parties.

Subdivision (b) is derived from Rule 72(b) F.R.Civ.P. which governs objections to a recommended disposition by a magistrate.

Subdivision (c) is similar to Rule 8002(c) of the Bankruptcy Rules and provides for granting of extensions of time to file objections to proposed findings and conclusions.

Subdivision (d) adopts the de novo review provisions of Rule 72(b) F.R.Civ.P.

Rule 9034. Transmittal of Pleadings, Motion Papers, Objections, and Other Papers to the United States Trustee

Unless the United States trustee requests otherwise or the case is a chapter 9 municipality case, any entity that files a pleading, motion, objection, or similar paper relating to any of the following matters shall transmit a copy thereof to the United States trustee within the time required by these rules for service of the paper:

(a) a proposed use, sale, or lease of property of the estate other than in the ordinary course of business;

(b) the approval of a compromise or settlement of a controversy;

(c) the dismissal or conversion of a case to another chapter;

(d) the employment of professional persons;

(e) an application for compensation or reimbursement of expenses;

(f) a motion for, or approval of an agreement relating to, the use of cash collateral or authority to obtain credit;

(g) the appointment of a trustee or examiner in a chapter 11 reorganization case;

(h) the approval of a disclosure statement;

(i) the confirmation of a plan;

(j) an objection to, or waiver or revocation of, the debtor's discharge;

(k) any other matter in which the United States trustee requests copies of filed papers or the court orders copies transmitted to the United States trustee.

(Added Apr. 30, 1991, eff. Aug. 1, 1991.)

ADVISORY COMMITTEE NOTES

Section 307 of the Code gives the United States trustee the right to appear and be heard on issues in cases and proceedings under the Code. This rule is intended to keep the United States trustee informed of certain developments and disputes in which the United States may wish to be heard. This rule, which derives from Rule X-1008, also enables the United States trustee to monitor the progress of the case in accordance with 28 U.S.C. § 586(a). The requirement to transmit copies of certain pleadings, motion papers and other documents is intended to be flexible in that the United States trustee in a particular judicial district may request copies of papers in certain categories, and may request not to receive copies of documents in other categories, when the practice in that district makes that desirable. When the rules require that a paper be served on particular parties, the time period in which service is required is also applicable to transmittal to the United States trustee.

Although other rules require that certain notices be transmitted to the United States trustee, this rule goes further in that it requires the transmittal to the United States trustee of other papers filed in connection with these matters. This rule is not an exhaustive list of the matters of which the United States trustee may be entitled to receive notice.

Rule 9035. Applicability of Rules in Judicial Districts in Alabama and North Carolina

In any case under the Code that is filed in or transferred to a district in the State of Alabama or the State of North Carolina and in which a United States trustee is not authorized to act, these rules apply to the extent that they are not inconsistent with any federal statute effective in the case.

(Added Apr. 30, 1991, eff. Aug. 1, 1991; amended Apr. 11, 1997, eff. Dec. 1, 1997.)

ADVISORY COMMITTEE NOTES

Section 302(d)(3) of the Bankruptcy Judges, United States Trustees, and Family Farmer Bankruptcy Act of 1986 provides that amendments to the Code relating to United States trustees and quarterly fees required under 28 U.S.C. § 1930(a)(6) do not become effective in any judicial district in the States of Alabama and North Carolina until the district elects to be included in the United States trustee system, or October 1, 1992, whichever occurs first, unless Congress extends the deadline. If the United States trustee system becomes effective in these districts, the transition provisions in the 1986 Act will govern the application of the United States trustee amendments to cases that are pending at that time. See § 302(d)(3)(F). The statute, and not the bankruptcy court, determines whether a United States trustee is authorized to act in a particular case.

Section 302(d)(3)(I) of the 1986 Act authorizes the Judicial Conference of the United States to promulgate regulations governing the appointment of bankruptcy administrators to supervise the administration of estates and trustees in cases in the districts in Alabama and North Carolina until the provisions of the Act relating to the United States trustee take effect in these districts. Pursuant to this authority, in September 1987, the Judicial Conference promulgated regulations governing the selection and appointment of bankruptcy administrators and regulations governing the establishment, duties, and functions of bankruptcy administrators. Guidelines relating to the bankruptcy administrator program have been prescribed by the Director of the Administrative Office of the United States Courts.

Many of these rules were amended to implement the United States trustee system in accordance with the 1986 Act. Since the provisions of the 1986 Act relating to the United States trustee system are not effective in cases in Alabama and North Carolina in which a bankruptcy administrator is serving, rules referring to United States trustees are at least partially inconsistent with the provisions of the Bankruptcy Code and title 28 of the United States Code effective in such cases.

In determining the applicability of these rules in cases in Alabama and North Carolina in which a United States trustee is not authorized to act, the following guidelines should be followed:

(1) The following rules do not apply because they are inconsistent with the provisions of the Code or title 28 in these cases: 1002(b), 1007(1), 1009(c), 2002(k), 2007.1(b), 2015(a)(6), 2020, 3015(b), 5005(b), 7004(b)(10), 9003(b), and 9034.

(2) The following rules are partially inconsistent with the provisions of the Code effective in these cases and, therefore, are applicable with the following modifications:

(a) **Rule 2001(a) and (c)**—The court, rather than the United States trustee, appoints the interim trustee.

(b) **Rule 2003**—The duties of the United States trustee relating to the meeting of creditors or equity security holders are performed by the officer determined in accordance with regulations of the Judicial Conference, guidelines of the Director of the Administrative Office, local rules or court orders.

(c) **Rule 2007**—The court, rather than the United States trustee, appoints committees in chapter 9 and chapter 11 cases.

(d) **Rule 2008**—The bankruptcy administrator, rather than the United States trustee, informs the trustee of how to qualify.

(e) **Rule 2009(c) and (d)**—The court, rather than the United States trustee, appoints interim trustees in chapter 7 cases and trustees in chapter 11, 12 and 13 cases.

(f) **Rule 2010**—The court, rather than the United States trustee, determines the amount and sufficiency of the trustee's bond.

(g) **Rule 5010**—The court, rather than the United States trustee, appoints the trustee when a case is reopened.

(3) All other rules are applicable because they are consistent with the provisions of the Code and title 28 effective in these cases, except that any reference to the United States trustee is not applicable and should be disregarded.

Many of the amendments to the rules are designed to give the United States trustee, a member of the Executive Branch, notice of certain developments and copies of petitions, schedules, pleadings, and other papers. In contrast, the bankruptcy administrator is an officer in the Judicial Branch and matters relating to notice of developments and access to documents filed in the clerk's office are governed by regulations of the Judicial Conference of the United States, guidelines of the Administrative Office of the United States Courts, local rules, and court orders. Also, requirements for disclosure of connections with the bankruptcy administrator in applications for employment of professional persons, restrictions on appointments of relatives of bankruptcy administrators, effects of erroneously filing papers with the bankruptcy administrator, and other matters not covered by these rules may be governed by regulations of the Judicial Conference, guidelines of the Director of the Administrative Office, local rules, and court orders.

This rule will cease to have effect if a United States trustee is authorized in every case in the districts in Alabama and North Carolina.

1997 Amendment

Certain statutes that are not codified in title 11 or title 28 of the United States Code, such as § 105 of the Bankruptcy Reform Act of 1994, Pub.L. 103–394, 108 Stat. 4106, relate to bankruptcy administrators in the judicial districts of North Carolina and Alabama. This amendment makes it clear that the Bankruptcy Rules do not apply to the extent that they are inconsistent with these federal statutes.

GAP Report on Rule 9035. No changes to the published draft.

Rule 9036. Notice by electronic transmission

Whenever the clerk or some other person as directed by the court is required to send notice by mail and the entity entitled to receive the notice requests in writing that, instead of notice by mail, all or part of the information required to be contained in the notice be sent by a specified type of electronic transmission, the court may direct the clerk or other person to send the information by such electronic transmission. Notice by electronic means is complete on transmission.
(Added Apr. 22, 1993, eff. Aug. 1, 1993; amended Apr. 25, 2005, eff. Dec. 1, 2005.)

ADVISORY COMMITTEE NOTES

1993 Amendments

This rule is added to provide flexibility for banks, credit card companies, taxing authorities, and other entities that ordinarily receive notices by mail in a large volume of bankruptcy cases, to arrange to receive by electronic transmission all or part of the information required to be contained in such notices.

The use of electronic technology instead of mail to send information to creditors and interested parties will be more convenient and less costly for the sender and the receiver. For example, a bank that receives by mail, at different locations, notices of meetings of creditors pursuant to Rule 2002(a) in thousands of cases each year may prefer to receive only the vital information ordinarily contained in such notices by electronic transmission to one computer terminal.

The specific means of transmission must be compatible with technology available to the sender and the receiver. Therefore, electronic transmission of notices is permitted only upon request of the entity entitled to receive the notice, specifying the type of electronic transmission, and only if approved by the court.

Electronic transmission pursuant to the rule completes the notice requirements. The creditor or interested party is not thereafter entitled to receive the relevant notice by mail.

2005 Amendments

The rule is amended to delete the requirement that the sender of an electronic notice must obtain electronic confirmation that the notice was received. The amendment provides that notice is complete upon transmission. When the rule was first promulgated, confirmation of receipt of electronic notices was commonplace. In the current electronic environment, very few internet service providers offer the confirmation of receipt service. Consequently, compliance with the rule may be impossible, and the rule could discourage the use of electronic noticing.

Confidence in the delivery of email text messages now rivals or exceeds confidence in the delivery of printed materials. Therefore, there is no need for confirmation of receipt of electronic messages just as there is no such requirement for paper notices.

Rule 9037. Privacy Protection For Filings Made with the Court

(a) Redacted Filings

Unless the court orders otherwise, in an electronic or paper filing made with the court that contains an individual's social-security number, taxpayer-identification number, or birth date, the name of an individual, other than the debtor, known to be and identified as a minor, or a financial-account number, a party or nonparty making the filing may include only:

(1) the last four digits of the social-security number and taxpayer-identification number;

(2) the year of the individual's birth;

(3) the minor's initials; and

(4) the last four digits of the financial-account number.

(b) Exemptions from the Redaction Requirement

The redaction requirement does not apply to the following:

(1) a financial-account number that identifies the property allegedly subject to forfeiture in a forfeiture proceeding;

(2) the record of an administrative or agency proceeding unless filed with a proof of claim;

(3) the official record of a state-court proceeding;

(4) the record of a court or tribunal, if that record was not subject to the redaction requirement when originally filed;

(5) a filing covered by subdivision (c) of this rule; and

(6) a filing that is subject to § 110 of the Code.

(c) Filings Made Under Seal

The court may order that a filing be made under seal without redaction. The court may later unseal the filing or order the entity that made the filing to file a redacted version for the public record.

(d) Protective Orders

For cause, the court may by order in a case under the Code:

(1) require redaction of additional information; or

(2) limit or prohibit a nonparty's remote electronic access to a document filed with the court.

(e) Option for Additional Unredacted Filing Under Seal

An entity making a redacted filing may also file an unredacted copy under seal. The court must retain the unredacted copy as part of the record.

(f) Option for Filing a Reference List

A filing that contains redacted information may be filed together with a reference list that identifies each item of redacted information and specifies an appropriate identifier that uniquely corresponds to each item listed. The list must be filed under seal and may be amended as of right. Any reference in the case to a listed identifier will be construed to refer to the corresponding item of information.

(g) Waiver of Protection of Identifiers

An entity waives the protection of subdivision (a) as to the entity's own information by filing it without redaction and not under seal.

(Added Apr. 30, 2007, eff. Dec. 1, 2007.)

ADVISORY COMMITTEE NOTES

2007 Adoption

The rule is adopted in compliance with section 205(c)(3) of the E–Government Act of 2002, Public Law No. 107–347. Section 205(c)(3) requires the Supreme Court to prescribe rules "to protect privacy and security concerns relating to electronic filing of documents and the public availability . . . of documents filed electronically." The rule goes further than the E–Government Act in regulating paper filings even when they are not converted to electronic form, but the number of filings that remain in paper form is certain to diminish over time. Most districts scan paper filings into the electronic case file, where they become available to the public in the same way as documents initially filed in electronic form. It is electronic availability, not the form of the initial filing, that raises the privacy and security concerns addressed in the E–Government Act.

The rule is derived from and implements the policy adopted by the Judicial Conference in September 2001 to address the privacy concerns resulting from public access to electronic case files. *See* http://www.privacy.uscourts.gov/Policy.htm. The Judicial Conference policy is that documents in case files generally should be made available electronically to the same extent they are available at the courthouse, provided that certain "personal data identifiers" are not included in the public file.

While providing for the public filing of some information, such as the last four digits of an account number, the rule does not intend to establish a presumption that this information never could or should be protected. For example, it may well be necessary in individual cases to prevent remote access by nonparties to any part of an account number or social-security number. It may also be necessary to protect information not covered by the redaction requirement—such as driver's license numbers and alien registration numbers—in a particular case. In such cases, protection may be sought under subdivision (c) or (d). Moreover, the rule does not affect the protection available under other rules, such as Rules 16 and 26(c) of the Federal Rules of Civil Procedure, or under other sources of protective authority.

Any personal information not otherwise protected by sealing or redaction will be made available over the internet. Counsel should therefore notify clients of this fact so that an informed decision may be made on what information is to be included in a document filed with the court.

An individual debtor's full social-security number or taxpayer-identification number is included on the notice of the § 341 meeting of creditors sent to creditors. Of course, that is not filed with the court, see Rule 1007(f) (the debtor "submits" this information), and the copy of the notice that is filed with the court does not include the full social-security number or taxpayer-identification number. Thus, since the full social-security number or taxpayer-identification number is not filed with the court, it is not available to a person searching that record.

The clerk is not required to review documents filed with the court for compliance with this rule. As subdivision (a) recognizes, the responsibility to redact filings rests with counsel, parties, and others who make filings with the court.

Subdivision (d) recognizes the court's inherent authority to issue a protective order to prevent remote access to private or sensitive information and to require redaction of material in addition to that which would be redacted under subdivision (a) of the rule. These orders may be issued whenever necessary either by the court on its own motion, or on motion of a party in interest.

Subdivision (e) allows an entity that makes a redacted filing to file an unredacted document under seal. This provision is derived from section 205(c)(3)(iv) of the E–Government Act. Subdivision (f) allows the option to file a reference list of redacted information. This provision is derived from section 205(c)(3)(v) of the E–Government Act, as amended in 2004.

In accordance with the E–Government Act, subdivision (f) of the rule refers to "redacted" information. The term "redacted" is intended to govern a filing that is prepared with abbreviated identifiers in the first instance, as well as a filing in which a personal identifier is edited after its preparation.

Subdivision (g) allows an entity to waive the protections of the rule as to that entity's own information by filing it in unredacted form. An entity may elect to waive the protection if, for example, it is determined that the costs of redaction outweigh the benefits to privacy. As to financial account numbers, the instructions to Schedules E and F of Official Form 6 note that the debtor may elect to include the complete account number on those schedules rather than limit the number to the final four digits. Including the complete number would operate as a waiver by the debtor under subdivision (g) as to the full information that the debtor set out on those schedules. The waiver operates only to the extent of the information that the entity filed without redaction. If an entity files an unredacted identifier by mistake, it may seek relief from the court.

Trial exhibits are subject to the redaction requirements of Rule 9037 to the extent they are filed with the court. Trial exhibits that are not initially filed with the court must be redacted in accordance with this rule if and when they are filed as part of an appeal or for other reasons.

PART X—UNITED STATES TRUSTEES [ABROGATED]

[Rules X–1001 to X–1010. Abrogated Apr. 30, 1991, eff. Aug. 1, 1991]

*

INTERIM AMENDMENTS TO THE FEDERAL BANKRUPTCY RULES

[The following amendments to the Federal Rules of Bankruptcy Procedure took effect on December 1, 2008:

Bankruptcy Rules 1005, 1006, 1007, 1009, 1010, 1011, 1015, 1017, 1019, 1020, 2002, 2003, 2007.1, 2015, 3002, 3003, 3016, 3017.1, 3019, 4002, 4003, 4004, 4006, 4007, 4008, 5001, 5003, 6004, 7012, 7022, 7023.1, 8001, 8003, 9006, 9009, and 9024, and new Bankruptcy Rules 1021, 2007.2, 2015.1, 2015.2, 2015.3, 5008, and 6011.

These amendments implement the Bankruptcy Abuse Prevention and Consumer Protection Act of 2005 (Pub. L. No. 109-08, 119 Stat. 23).

With the exception of Interim Rule 5012 (reproduced below), the amendments to the Federal Rules of Bankruptcy Procedure supersede the Interim Bankruptcy Rules adopted generally by bankruptcy courts as local rules in October 2005.]

Rule 5012. Communication and Cooperation with Foreign Courts and Foreign Representatives

Except for communications for scheduling and administrative purposes, the court in any case commenced by a foreign representative shall give at least 20 days' notice of its intent to communicate with a foreign court or a foreign representative. The notice shall identify the subject of the anticipated communication and shall be given in the manner provided by Rule 2002(q). Any entity that wishes to participate in the communication shall notify the court of its intention not later than 5 days before the scheduled communication.

COMMITTEE NOTE

This rule is new. It implements § 1525 which was added to the Code in 2005. The rule provides an opportunity for parties in the case to take appropriate action prior to the communication between courts or between the court and a foreign representative to establish procedures for the manner of the communication and the right to participate in the communication. Participation in the communication includes both active and passive participation. Parties wishing to participate must notify the court at least 5 days before the hearing so that ample time exists to make arrangements necessary to permit the participation.

*

OFFICIAL AND PROCEDURAL BANKRUPTCY FORMS

Amendments received to December 1, 2008

OFFICIAL FORMS

Form 1. Voluntary Petition

B1 (Official Form 1) (01/08)

United States Bankruptcy Court | **Voluntary Petition**

Name of Debtor (if individual, enter Last, First, Middle):	Name of Joint Debtor (Spouse) (Last, First, Middle):
All Other Names used by the Debtor in the last 8 years (include married, maiden, and trade names):	All Other Names used by the Joint Debtor in the last 8 years (include married, maiden, and trade names):
Last four digits of Soc. Sec. or Individual-Taxpayer I.D. (ITIN) No./Complete EIN (if more than one, state all):	Last four digits of Soc. Sec. or Individual-Taxpayer I.D. (ITIN) No./Complete EIN (if more than one, state all):
Street Address of Debtor (No. and Street, City, and State): ZIP CODE	Street Address of Joint Debtor (No. and Street, City, and State): ZIP CODE
County of Residence or of the Principal Place of Business:	County of Residence or of the Principal Place of Business:
Mailing Address of Debtor (if different from street address): ZIP CODE	Mailing Address of Joint Debtor (if different from street address): ZIP CODE

Location of Principal Assets of Business Debtor (if different from street address above):

ZIP CODE

Type of Debtor
(Form of Organization)
(Check **one** box.)

☐ Individual (includes Joint Debtors) *See Exhibit D on page 2 of this form.*
☐ Corporation (includes LLC and LLP)
☐ Partnership
☐ Other (If debtor is not one of the above entities, check this box and state type of entity below.)

Nature of Business
(Check **one** box).

☐ Health Care Business
☐ Single Asset Real Estate as defined in 11 U.S.C. § 101(51B)
☐ Railroad
☐ Stockbroker
☐ Commodity Broker
☐ Clearing Bank
☐ Other

Tax–Exempt Entity
(Check box, if applicable.)

☐ Debtor is a tax-exempt organization under Title 26 of the United States Code (the Internal Revenue Code).

Chapter of Bankruptcy Code Under Which the Petition is Filed
(Check **one** box.)

☐ Chapter 7
☐ Chapter 9
☐ Chapter 11
☐ Chapter 12
☐ Chapter 13
☐ Chapter 15 Petition for Recognition of a Foreign Main Proceeding
☐ Chapter 15 Petition for Recognition of a Foreign Nonmain Proceeding

Nature of Debts
(Check one box.)

☐ Debts are primarily consumer debts, defined in 11 U.S.C. § 101(8) as "incurred by an individual primarily for a personal, family, or household purpose."
☐ Debts are primarily business debts.

Filing Fee
(Check one box.)

☐ Full Filing Fee attached.

☐ Filing Fee to be paid in installments (applicable to individuals only). Must attach signed application for the court's consideration certifying that the debtor is unable to pay fee except in installments. Rule 1006(b). See Official Form 3A.

☐ Filing Fee waiver requested (applicable to chapter 7 individuals only). Must attach signed application for the court's consideration. See Official Form 3B.

Chapter 11 Debtors

Check one box:
☐ Debtor is a small business debtor as defined in 11 U.S.C. § 101(51D).
☐ Debtor is not a small business debtor as defined in 11 U.S.C. § 101(51D).

Check if:

☐ Debtor's aggregate noncontingent liquidated debts (excluding debts owed to insiders or affiliates) are less than $2,190,000.

Check all applicable boxes:
☐ A plan is being filed with this petition.
☐ Acceptances of the plan were solicited prepetition from one or more classes of creditors, in accordance with 11 U.S.C. § 1126(b).

Statistical/Administrative Information

☐ Debtor estimates that funds will be available for distribution to unsecured creditors.
☐ Debtor estimates that, after any exempt property is excluded and administrative expenses paid, there will be no funds available for distribution to unsecured creditors.

THIS SPACE FOR COURT USE ONLY

Estimated Number of Creditors

☐	☐	☐	☐	☐	☐
1–49	50–99	100–199	200–999	1,000–5,000	5,001–10,000
☐ 10,001–25,000	☐ 25,001–50,000	☐ 50,001–100,000	☐ Over 100,000		

Estimated Assets					
☐ $0 to $50,000	☐ $50,001 to $100,000	☐ $100,001 to $500,000	☐ $500,001 to $1 million	☐ $1,000,001 to $10 million	☐ $10,000,001 to $50 million
☐ $50,000,001 to $100 million	☐ $100,000,001 to $500 million	☐ $500,000,001 to $1 billion	☐ More than $1 billion		

Estimated Liabilities					
☐ $0 to $50,000	☐ $50,001 to $100,000	☐ $100,001 to $500,000	☐ $500,001 to $1 million	☐ $1,000,001 to $10 million	☐ $10,000,001 to $50 million
☐ $50,000,001 to $100 million	☐ $100,000,001 to $500 million	☐ $500,000,001 to $1 billion	☐ More than $1 billion		

B1 (Official Form 1) (01/08) Page 2

Voluntary Petition *(This page must be completed and filed in every case.)*	Name of Debtor(s):	
All Prior Bankruptcy Cases Filed Within Last 8 Years (If more than two, attach additional sheet.)		
Location Where Filed:	Case Number:	Date Filed:
Location Where Filed:	Case Number:	Date Filed:
Pending Bankruptcy Case Filed by any Spouse, Partner, or Affiliate of this Debtor (If more than one, attach additional sheet)		
Name of Debtor:	Case Number:	Date Filed:
District:	Relationship:	Judge:

Exhibit A

(To be completed if debtor is required to file periodic reports (e.g., forms 10K and 10Q) with the Securities and Exchange Commission pursuant to Section 13 or 15(d) of the Securities Exchange Act of 1934 and is requesting relief under chapter 11.)

☐ Exhibit A is attached and made a part of this petition.

Exhibit B

(To be completed if debtor is an individual whose debts are primarily consumer debts.)

I, the attorney for the petitioner named in the foregoing petition, declare that I have informed the petitioner that [he or she] may proceed under chapter 7, 11, 12, or 13 of title 11, United States Code, and have explained the relief available under each such chapter. I further certify that I have delivered to the debtor the notice required by 11 U.S.C. § 342(b).

X ______________________________

Signature of Attorney for Debtor(s) (Date)

Exhibit C

Does the debtor own or have possession of any property that poses or is alleged to pose a threat of imminent and identifiable harm to public health or safety?

☐ Yes, and Exhibit C is attached and made a part of this petition.

☐ No.

Exhibit D

(To be completed by every individual debtor. If a joint petition is filed, each spouse must complete and attach a separate Exhibit D.)

☐ Exhibit D completed and signed by the debtor is attached and made a part of this petition.

If this is a joint petition:

☐ Exhibit D also completed and signed by the joint debtor is attached and made a part of this petition.

Information Regarding the Debtor—Venue

(Check any applicable box.)

☐ Debtor has been domiciled or has had a residence, principal place of business, or principal assets in this District for 180 days immediately preceding the date of this petition or for a longer part of such 180 days than in any other District.

☐ There is a bankruptcy case concerning debtor's affiliate, general partner, or partnership pending in this District.

☐ Debtor is a debtor in a foreign proceeding and has its principal place of business or principal assets in the United States in this District, or has no principal place of business or assets in the United States but is a defendant in an action or proceeding [in a federal or state court] in this District, or the interests of the parties will be served in regard to the relief sought in this District.

Certification by a Debtor Who Resides as a Tenant of Residential Property

(Check all applicable boxes.)

☐ Landlord has a judgment against the debtor for possession of debtor's residence. (If box checked, complete the following.)

____

(Name of landlord that obtained judgment)

____

(Address of landlord)

☐ Debtor claims that under applicable nonbankruptcy law, there are circumstances under which the debtor would be permitted to cure the entire monetary default that gave rise to the judgment for possession, after the judgment for possession was entered, and

☐ Debtor has included with this petition the deposit with the court of any rent that would become due during the 30-day period after the filing of the petition.

☐ Debtor certifies that he/she has served the Landlord with this certification. (11 U.S.C. § 362(*l*)).

B1 (Official Form 1) (01/08) Page 3

Voluntary Petition *(This page must be completed and filed in every case)*	Name of Debtor(s):

Signatures

Signature(s) of Debtor(s) (Individual/Joint)

I declare under penalty of perjury that the information provided in this petition is true and correct.

[If petitioner is an individual whose debts are primarily consumer debts and has chosen to file under chapter 7] I am aware that I may proceed under chapter 7, 11, 12 or 13 of title 11, United States Code, understand the relief available under each such chapter, and choose to proceed under chapter 7.

[If no attorney represents me and no bankruptcy petition preparer signs the petition] I have obtained and read the notice required by 11 U.S.C. § 342(b).

I request relief in accordance with the chapter of title 11, United States Code, specified in this petition.

X____________________
Signature of Debtor

X____________________
Signature of Joint Debtor

____
Telephone Number (If not represented by attorney)

____
Date

Signature of a Foreign Representative

I declare under penalty of perjury that the information provided in this petition is true and correct, that I am the foreign representative of a debtor in a foreign proceeding, and that I am authorized to file this petition.

(Check only **one** box.)

☐ I request relief in accordance with chapter 15 of title 11, United States Code. Certified copies of the documents required by 11 U.S.C. § 1515 are attached.

☐ Pursuant to 11 U.S.C. § 1511, I request relief in accordance with the chapter of title 11 specified in this petition. A certified copy of the order granting recognition of the foreign main proceeding is attached.

X____________________
(Signature of Foreign Representative)

____
(Printed Name of Foreign Representative)

____
Date

Signature of Attorney *

X____________________
Signature of Attorney for Debtor(s)

____
Printed Name of Attorney for Debtor(s)

____
Firm Name

____
Address

____

____

____
Telephone Number

____
Date

* In a case in which § 707(b)(4)(D) applies, this signature also constitutes a certification that the attorney has no knowledge after an inquiry that the information in the schedules is incorrect.

Signature of Non-Attorney Bankruptcy Petition Preparer

I declare under penalty of perjury that: (1) I am a bankruptcy petition preparer as defined in 11 U.S.C. § 110; (2) I prepared this document for compensation and have provided the debtor with a copy of this document and the notices and information required under 11 U.S.C. §§ 110(b), 110(h), and 342(b); and, (3) if rules or guidelines have been promulgated pursuant to 11 U.S.C. § 110(h) setting a maximum fee for services chargeable by bankruptcy petition preparers, I have given the debtor notice of the maximum amount before preparing any document for filing for a debtor or accepting any fee from the debtor, as required in that section. Official Form 19 is attached.

____
Printed Name and title, if any, of Bankruptcy Petition Preparer

____
Social-Security number (If the bankruptcy petition preparer is not an individual, state the Social-Security number of the officer, principal, responsible person or partner of the bankruptcy petition preparer.) (Required by 11 U.S.C. § 110.)

____
Address

____

X____________________

____
Date

Signature of bankruptcy petition preparer or officer, principal, responsible person, or partner whose Social-Security number is provided above.

Names and Social-Security numbers of all other individuals who prepared or assisted in preparing this document unless the bankruptcy petition preparer is not an individual:

If more than one person prepared this document, attach additional sheets conforming to the appropriate official form for each person.

A bankruptcy petition preparer's failure to comply with the provisions of title 11 and the Federal Rules of Bankruptcy Procedure may result in fines or imprisonment or both. 11 U.S.C. § 110; 18 U.S.C. § 156.

Signature of Debtor (Corporation/Partnership)

I declare under penalty of perjury that the information provided in this petition is true and correct, and that I have been authorized to file this petition on behalf of the debtor.

The debtor requests relief in accordance with the chapter of title 11, United States Codes, specified in this petition.

X____________________
Signature of Authorized Individual

____
Printed Name of Authorized Individual

____
Title of Authorized Individual

____
Date

Form B1, Exh. A (9/97)

Exhibit "A"

[If debtor is required to file periodic reports (e.g., forms 10K and 10Q) with the Securities and Exchange Commission pursuant to Section 13 or 15(d) of the Securities Exchange Act of 1934 and is requesting relief under chapter 11 of the Bankruptcy Code, this Exhibit "A" shall be completed and attached to the petition.]

United States Bankruptcy Court

__________ District Of __________

In re ______________________________, Case No. ________________________
Debtor

Chapter 11

EXHIBIT "A" TO VOLUNTARY PETITION

1. If any of the debtor's securities are registered under Section 12 of the Securities Exchange Act of 1934, the SEC file number is __________.

2. The following financial data is the latest available information and refers to the debtor's condition on __________.

			Approximate number of holders
a.	Total assets	$__________	
b.	Total debts (including debts listed in 2.c., below)	$__________	
c.	Debt securities held by more than 500 holders.		
	secured ☐ unsecured ☐ subordinated ☐	$__________	__________
	secured ☐ unsecured ☐ subordinated ☐	$__________	__________
	secured ☐ unsecured ☐ subordinated ☐	$__________	__________
	secured ☐ unsecured ☐ subordinated ☐	$__________	__________
	secured ☐ unsecured ☐ subordinated ☐	$__________	__________
d.	Number of shares of preferred stock	__________	__________
e.	Number of shares common stock	__________	__________

Comments, if any: ______________________________

3. Brief description of debtor's business: ____________________

4. List the names of any person who directly or indirectly owns, controls, or holds, with power to vote, 5% or more of the voting securities of debtor: ____________________

Form B1, Exhibit C
(9/01)

Exhibit "C"

[If, to the best of the debtor's knowledge, the debtor owns or has possession of property that poses or is alleged to pose a threat of imminent and identifiable harm to the public health or safety, attach exhibit "C" to the petition.]

United States Bankruptcy Court
________ District Of ________

In re ________________________, Case No. ________________
Debtor

Chapter ________________

EXHIBIT "C" TO VOLUNTARY PETITION

1. Identify and briefly describe all real or personal property owned by or in possession of the debtor that, to the best of the debtor's knowledge, poses or is alleged to pose a threat of imminent and identifiable harm to the public health or safety (attach additional sheets if necessary):

....
....
....
....

2. With respect to each parcel of real property or item of personal property identified in question 1, describe the nature and location of the dangerous condition, whether environmental or otherwise, that poses or is alleged to pose a threat of imminent and identifiable harm to the public health or safety (attach additional sheets if necessary):

....
....
....
....

Official Form 1, Exhibit D (12/08)

UNITED STATES BANKRUPTCY COURT

In re____________________________ Case No. ______________________
Debtor (*if known*)

EXHIBIT D — INDIVIDUAL DEBTOR'S STATEMENT OF COMPLIANCE WITH CREDIT COUNSELING REQUIREMENT

Warning: You must be able to check truthfully one of the five statements regarding credit counseling listed below. If you cannot do so, you are not eligible to file a bankruptcy case, and the court can dismiss any case you do file. If that happens, you will lose whatever filing fee you paid, and your creditors will be able to resume collection activities against you. If your case is dismissed and you file another bankruptcy case later, you may be required to pay a second filing fee and you may have to take extra steps to stop creditors' collection activities.

Every individual debtor must file this Exhibit D. If a joint petition is filed, each spouse must complete and file a separate Exhibit D. Check one of the five statements below and attach any documents as directed.

☐ 1. Within the 180 days **before the filing of my bankruptcy case,** I received a briefing from a credit counseling agency approved by the United States trustee or bankruptcy administrator that outlined the opportunities for available credit counseling and assisted me in performing a related budget analysis, and I have a certificate from the agency describing the services provided to me. *Attach a copy of the certificate and a copy of any debt repayment plan developed through the agency.*

☐ 2. Within the 180 days **before the filing of my bankruptcy case**, I received a briefing from a credit counseling agency approved by the United States trustee or bankruptcy administrator that outlined the opportunities for available credit counseling and assisted me in performing a related budget analysis, but I do not have a certificate from the agency describing the services provided to me. *You must file a copy of a certificate from the agency describing the services provided to you and a copy of any debt repayment plan developed through the agency no later than 15 days after your bankruptcy case is filed.*

☐ 3. I certify that I requested credit counseling services from an approved agency but was unable to obtain the services during the five days from the time I made my request, and the following exigent circumstances merit a temporary waiver of the credit counseling requirement so I can file my bankruptcy case now. *[Summarize exigent circumstances here.]* __________
____

If your certification is satisfactory to the court, you must still obtain the credit counseling briefing within the first 30 days after you file your bankruptcy petition and promptly file a certificate from the agency that provided the counseling, together with a copy of any debt management plan developed through the agency. Failure to fulfill these requirements may result in dismissal of you case. Any extension of the 30–day deadline can be granted only for cause and is limited to a maximum of 15 days. Your case may also be dismissed if the court is not satisfied with your reasons for filing your bankruptcy case without first receiving a credit counseling briefing.

☐ 4. I am not required to receive a credit counseling briefing because of: *[Check the applicable statement.] [Must be accompanied by a motion for determination by the court.]*

☐ Incapacity. (Defined in 11 U.S.C. § 109(h)(4) as impaired by reason of mental illness or mental deficiency so as to be incapable of realizing and making rational decisions with respect to financial responsibilities.);

☐ Disability. (Defined in 11 U.S.C. § 109(h)(4) as physically impaired to the extent of being unable, after reasonable effort, to participate in a credit counseling briefing in person, by telephone, or through the Internet.);

☐ Active military duty in a military combat zone.

☐ 5. The United States trustee or bankruptcy administrator has determined that the credit counseling requirement of 11 U.S.C. § 109(h) does not apply in this district.

I certify under penalty of perjury that the information provided above is true and correct.

Signature of Debtor: ____________________

Date: _________________

(Added Aug. 1, 1991, and amended Mar. 16, 1993; Mar. 1995; Oct. 1, 1997; Dec. 1, 2001; Dec. 1, 2002; Dec. 1, 2003; Aug. 11, 2005, eff. Oct. 17, 2005; Oct. 12, 2006; April 1, 2007; revised eff. Dec. 1, 2007; Jan., 2008; Dec. 1, 2008.)

ADVISORY COMMITTEE NOTES

1991 Enactment

Form 1, the Voluntary Petition, is to be used to commence a voluntary case under chapter 7, 11, 12, or 13 of the Bankruptcy Code. A chapter 9 petition requires other allegations, (see § 109(c) of the Code), but this form may be adapted for such use. The form also may be adapted for use in filing a petition ancillary to a foreign proceeding under § 304 of the Code.

The form departs from the traditional format of a captioned pleading. All of the elements of the caption prescribed in Rule 1005 have been retained. Their placement on the page, however, has been changed to make the form compatible with electronic data processing by the clerk. The form of the caption of the case for use in other documents, formerly incorporated in Official Form No. 1, has been made a separate Form 16A.

All names used by the debtor, including trade names, names used in doing business, married names, and maiden names should be furnished in the spaces provided. If there is not sufficient room for all such names on the form itself, the list should be continued on an additional sheet attached to the petition. A complete list will enable creditors to identify the debtor properly when they receive notices and orders.

Redesign of this form into a box format also is intended to provide the court, the United States trustee, and other interested parties with as much information as possible during the 15–day period provided by Rule 1007(c), when schedules and statements may not have been filed. The box format separates into categories the data provided by the debtor, and enables the form to be used by all voluntary debtors in all chapters.

For the first time, the form requires both a street address and any separate mailing address, as well as any separate addresses used by a joint debtor. Disclosure of prior bankruptcies is new to the petition but formerly was required in the statement of financial affairs; its inclusion in the petition is intended to alert the trustee to cases in which an objection to discharge pursuant to § 727(a)(8) or (a)(9) or a motion to dismiss under § 109(g) may be appropriate. The information about pending related cases, also new to the petition, signals the clerk to assign the case to the judge to whom any related case has been assigned.

Rule 1008 requires all petitions to be verified or contain an unsworn declaration as provided in 28 U.S.C. § 1746. The unsworn declaration on page two of the petition conforms with 28 U.S.C. § 1746, which permits the declaration to be made in the manner indicated with the same force and effect as a sworn statement. The form may be adapted for use outside the United States by adding the words "under the laws of the United States" after the word "perjury."

Exhibit "A," to be attached to the petition of a corporate debtor, is for the purpose of supplying the Securities and Exchange Commission with information it needs at the beginning stages of a chapter 11 case in order to determine how actively to monitor the proceedings. Exhibit "B" was added by § 322 of Pub.L. No. 98–353, the Bankruptcy Amendments and Federal Judgeship Act of 1984. The references to chapters 11 and 12 of the Code found in Exhibit "B" and its related allegations were added by § 283(aa) of the 1986 amendments, (Pub.L. No. 99–554). This exhibit has been included in the form of the petition.

The form effects a merger of the petition and the bankruptcy cover sheet to assist the clerk in providing the statistical information required by the Director of the Administrative Office of the United States Courts pursuant to the Congressional reporting mandates of 28 U.S.C. § 604. The Director is authorized to change the particulars of the statistical portion of the form as needed in the performance of these statutory duties.

1993 Amendment

The form has been amended to require a debtor not represented by an attorney to provide a telephone number so that court personnel, the trustee, other parties in the case, and their attorneys can contact the debtor concerning matters in the case.

1995 Amendment

The form is amended to provide space for signing by a "bankruptcy petition preparer," as required under section 110 of the Code, which was added by the Bankruptcy Reform Act of 1994. In addition to signing, a bankruptcy petition preparer is required by section 110 to disclose the information requested. All signatories of Form 1 are requested to provide the clerk's office with a telephone number.

A chapter 11 debtor that qualifies as a "small business" under section 101 of the Code, as amended by the 1994 Act, may elect special, expedited treatment under amendments made to chapter 11 by the 1994 Act. The court may order that a creditors committee not be appointed in a small business case. Accordingly, the first page of the petition is amended to require a small business filing under chapter 11 to identify itself. The petition also is amended to offer a small business chapter 11 debtor an opportunity to exercise its right to elect to be considered a small business at the commencement of the case.

Several clarifying and technical amendments also have been made to indicate that a debtor is to check only one box with respect to "Type of Debtor" and "Nature of Debt," to clarify the intent that the individual signing on behalf of a corporation or partnership is authorized to file the petition, and to require a debtor to represent that it is eligible for relief under the chapter of title 11 specified in the petition.

1997 Amendment

The form has been substantially amended to simplify its format and make the form easier to complete correctly. The Latin phrase "In re" has been deleted as unnecessary. The amount of information requested in the boxes labeled "Type of Debtor" and "Nature of Debt" has been reduced, and the reporting by a corporation of whether it is a publicly held entity has been moved to Exhibit "A" of the petition. The box labeled "Representation by Attorney" has been deleted; the information it contained is requested in the signature boxes on the second page of the form.

In the statistical information section, the labels on the ranges of estimated assets and liabilities have been rewritten to improve the accuracy of reporting. The asset/liability range of $10 million to $100 million has been divided into two categories to promote better statistical reporting of the business cases. Requests for information in chapter 11 and chapter 12 cases concerning the number of the debtor's employees and equity security holders have been deleted.

The second page of the form has been simplified so that a debtor need only sign the petition once. The request for information concerning the filing of a plan has been deleted.

Exhibit "A" has been simplified. In addition, the category of chapter 11 debtors required to file Exhibit "A" is modified to include a corporation, partnership, or other entity, but only if the debtor has issued publicly-traded equity securities or debt instruments. Most small corporations will not be required to file Exhibit "A."

2001 Amendment

The form has been amended to require the debtor to disclose whether the debtor owns or has possession of any property that poses or is alleged to pose a threat of imminent and identifiable harm to public health or safety. If any such property exists, the debtor must complete and attach Exhibit "C" describing the property, its location, and the potential danger it poses. Exhibit "C" will alert the United States trustee and any person selected as trustee that immediate precautionary action may be necessary.

2002 Amendment

The form has been amended to provide a checkbox for designating a clearing bank case filed under subchapter V of chapter 7 of the Code enacted by § 112 of Pub. L. No. 106–554 (December 21, 2000).

2003 Amendment

The form has been amended to require the debtor to disclose only the last four digits of the debtor's Social Security or other Taxpayer Identification number. Those four digits will provide creditors with sufficient information to identify the debtor accurately while affording greater privacy to the debtor. Pursuant to § 110(c) of the Bankruptcy Code, the certification by a non-attorney bankruptcy petition preparer continues to require a petition preparer to provide the full Social Security number of the individual who actually prepares the document.

2005 Amendments

The form is amended to implement amendments to the Bankruptcy Code contained in the Bankruptcy Abuse Prevention and Consumer Protection Act of 2005, Pub. L. No. 109–8, 119 Stat. 23 (April 20, 2005). The period for which the debtor must provide all names used and information about any prior bankruptcy cases is now eight years to match the required time between the granting of discharges to the same debtor in § 727(a)(8) of the Code as amended in 2005. The box indicating the debtor's selection of a chapter under which to file the case has been amended to delete "Sec. 304—Case ancillary to foreign proceeding" and replace it with "Chapter 15 Petition for Recognition of a Foreign Main Proceeding" and "Chapter 15 Petition for Recognition of a Foreign Nonmain Proceeding" reflecting the 2005 repeal of § 304 and enactment of chapter 15 of the Code. A statement of venue to be used in a chapter 15 case also has been added.

The section of the form labeled "Type of Debtor" has been revised and subtitled "Form of Organization." This section is revised to make it clear that a limited liability corporation ("LLC") and limited liability partnership ("LLP") should identify itself as a "corporation." A new section titled "Nature of Business" has been created that includes both existing check boxes that identify certain types of debtors for which the Bankruptcy Code provides special treatment, such as stockbrokers and railroads, and a new checkbox for a "health care business" for which the 2005 amendments to the Code include specific requirements. This section of the form also contains checkboxes for single asset real estate debtors and nonprofit organizations which will be used by trustees and creditors and by the Director of the Administrative Office of the United States Courts in preparing statistical reports and analyses. The statistical section of the form also is amended to provide more detail concerning the number of creditors in a case. A check box also has been added for a debtor to indicate that the debtor is applying for a waiver of the filing fee, to implement the 2005 enactment of 28 U.S.C. § 1930(f) authorizing the bankruptcy court to waive the filing fee in certain circumstances.

Although the 2005 Act eliminated an eligible debtor's option to elect to be treated as a "small business" in a chapter 11 case, new provisions for such debtors added to the Code in 2005 make it desirable to identify eligible debtors at the outset of the case. Accordingly, the section of the form labeled "Chapter 11 Small Business" has been revised and renamed "Chapter 11 Debtors" for this purpose. Chapter 11 debtors that meet the definition of "small business debtor" in § 101 of the Code are directed to identify themselves in this section of the form. In addition, chapter 11 debtors whose aggregate noncontingent debts owed to non-insiders or affiliates are less than $2 million are directed to identify themselves in this section.

A space is provided for individuals to certify that they have received budget and credit counseling prior to filing, as required by § 109(h) which was added to the Code in 2005, or to request a waiver of the requirement. Space also is provided for a debtor who is a tenant of residential real property to state whether the debtor's landlord has a judgment against the debtor for possession of the premises, whether under applicable nonbankruptcy law the debtor would be permitted to cure the monetary default, and whether the debtor has made the appropriate deposit with the court. This addition to the form implements § 362(l) which was added to the Code in 2005.

The signature sections and the declaration under penalty of perjury by an individual debtor concerning the notice received about bankruptcy relief, the declaration under penalty of perjury by a bankruptcy petition preparer, and the declaration and certification by an attorney all are amended to include new material mandated by the 2005 Act. A signature section also is provided for a representative of a foreign proceeding.

2006 Amendment

Page one of the form is amended in several ways to assist the courts in evaluating their workload and fulfilling the statistical reporting requirements of 28 U.S.C. § 159. Section 159 was enacted as part of the Bankruptcy Abuse Prevention and Consumer Protection Act of 2005 (BAPCPA), Pub.L. No. 109-8 and takes effect October 17, 2006. Accordingly, in the section of the form labeled "Nature of Business," the instruction is amended to specify that only one box should be checked and only if the debtor is any of the entities listed. The "nonprofit" choice is separated into a discrete section and the language amended to the more precise "tax-exempt."

In addition, the section labeled "Type of Debtor" is amended to include, below the checkbox for "Individual or Joint," a direction to "See Exhibit D on page 2 of this form." Exhibit D replaces the certification concerning prepetition credit counseling and is described below. The section labeled "Nature of Debts" is amended to state the statutory definition of a "consumer debt" and to modify both the consumer and business categories by adding the word "primarily" to both make it clearer to individual debtors that "business" may be the more appropriate choice if personal debts have been incurred to finance a business venture.

In the section labeled "Chapter 11 Debtors," the language concerning whether the debtor owes less than $2 million is re-styled for clarity. This section also is augmented to provide the court with notice when a case if [sic] filed as a "prepackaged" chapter 11 reorganization case. Two checkboxes are offered, using language adapted from § 1126(b) of the Code. Lastly, the information requested concerning estimated assets and liabilities is abbreviated, with the number of ranges reduced and the scope of each range amended. Statistical reports now will be derived from actual dollar amounts of assets and liabilities as shown on the debtor's schedules. The information on the petition, accordingly, is for case management and public information purposes only.

Exhibit D replaces the section formerly labeled "Certification Concerning Debt Counseling by Individual/Joint Debtor(s)." Early cases decided under the 2005 amendments to the Bankruptcy Code indicate that individual debtors may not be aware of the requirements to obtain prepetition credit counseling, the few and very narrow exceptions to that requirement, or the potentially dire consequences to their efforts to obtain bankruptcy relief if they fail to complete the requirement. Accordingly, page 2 of the petition instructs individual debtors to attach a completed Exhibit D and makes it clear that each spouse in a joint case must complete and attach a separate Exhibit D. Exhibit D itself includes a warning about the requirement to obtain counseling and the consequences of failing to fulfill this requirement. It further provides checkboxes and instructions concerning the additional documents that are required in particular circumstances, in order to minimize the number of cases which the court must dismiss for ineligibility.

2005–2007 Amendments

(The 2005-2007 Committee Note incorporates Committee Notes previously published in 2005 and 2006.)

The form is amended to implement amendments to the Bankruptcy Code contained in the Bankruptcy Abuse Prevention and Consumer Protection Act of 2005, Pub. L. No. 109–8, 119 Stat. 23 (April 20, 2005)("BAPCPA"). The period for which the debtor must provide all names used and information about any prior bankruptcy cases is now eight years to match the required time between the granting of discharges to the same debtor in § 727(a)(8) of the Code as amended in 2005. In conformity with Rule 9037, the debtor is directed to provide only the last four digits of any individual's tax-identification number.

The box indicating the debtor's selection of a chapter under which to file the case has been amended to delete "Sec. 304—Case ancillary to foreign proceeding" and replace it with "Chapter 15 Petition for Recognition of a Foreign Main Proceeding" and "Chapter 15 Petition for Recognition of a Foreign Nonmain Proceeding" reflecting the 2005 repeal of § 304 and enactment of chapter 15 of the Code. A statement of venue to be used in a chapter 15 case also is added on page 2 of the form.

The section labeled "Type of Debtor" is amended to include, below the checkbox for "Individual or Joint," a direction to "See Exhibit D on page 2 of this form." This addition alerts individual debotrs that Exhibit D on page 2 of the form applies to them. Exhibit D, more fully described below, addresses the prepetition credit counseling requirements added to the Code by BAPCPA. The subtitle, "Form of Organization," is added, and this section also is revised to make clear that a limited liability corporation ("LLC") or limited liability partnership ("LLP") should identify itself as a "corporation."

The form is also amended in several ways to assist the courts in evaluating their workload and fulfilling the statistical reporting requirements of 28 U.S.C. § 159, enacted as part of BAPCPA. Accordingly, a new section of the form labeled "Nature of Business," is added that contains both existing checkboxes that identify certain types of debtors for which the Bankruptcy Code provides special treatment, such as stockbrokers and railroads, and a new checkbox for a "health care business" for which the 2005 amendments to the Code include specific requirements. This section of the form also contains checkboxes for single asset real estate debtors, so they can be identified at the time of filing. All other businesses will mark the checkbox "Other." Another new section titled "Tax-Exempt Entity" contains a checkbox to be used by qualified organizations. The Judicial Conference of the United States and the Administrative Office of the United States Courts will use this information in preparing statistical reports and analyses for Congress.

A checkbox also is added for an individual debtor to indicate that the debtor is applying for a waiver of the filing fee, to implement the 2005 enactment of 29 U.S.C. § 1930(f) authorizing the bankruptcy court to waive the filing fee in certain circumstances. The description directs the debtor to the Official Form for the application that must be filed for the court's consideration.

The section labeled "Nature of Debts" is amended to state the statutory definition of a "consumer debt" and to modify both the consumer and business categories by adding the word "primarily" to both choices to make it clearer to individual debtors that "business" may be the appropriate choice if personal debts have been incurred to finance a business venture.

Although the 2005 Act eliminated from the Code any option to be treated as a "small business" in a chapter 11 case, new provisions for "small business" debtors added by BAPCPA make it desirable to identify eligible debtors at the outset of the case. Accordingly, the section of the form labeled "Chapter 11 Small Business" is revised and renamed "Chapter 11 Debtors" for this purpose. Chapter 11 debtors that meet the definition of "small business debtor" in § 101 of the Code are directed to identify themselves in this section of the form. Chapter 11 debtors whose aggregate noncontingent debts owed to non-insiders or affiliates are less than $2,190,000 are directed to identify themselves in this section. A third part of this section attempts to identify chapter 11 cases that are filed as pre-packaged cases, using criteria taken from § 1126(b) of the Code. Identifying "pre-packs" at filing will assist judges and court staff to manage these cases appropriately.

The statistical information concerning the number of creditors and estimated assets and liabilities is revised to provide more detail.

BAPCPA also added a new § 109(h) to the Code. To implement this provision, a section labeled "Exhibit D" is inserted on page 2 of the form, and a separate Exhibit D is added. These additions will enable individual debtors to certify that they have received budget and credit counseling prior to filing, as required by § 109(h), or request a temporary waiver of, or exemption from, the requirement, if they meet the statutory requirements for such relief. Exhibit D includes directions to attach required documentation or, if the debtor requests a temporary waiver or an exemption, a motion for a determination by the court. Exhibit D also states the requirement that all individual debtors must obtain a briefing from an approved credit counseling agency before filing a bankruptcy case, unless one of the very limited exceptions applies, and further states the consequences that may be faced by any debtor who fails to comply.

Space is provided on page 2 for a debtor who is a tenant of residential real property to state whether the debtor's landlord has a judgment against the debtor for possession of the premises, whether under applicable nonbankruptcy law the debtor would be permitted to cure the monetary default, and whether the debtor has made the appropriate deposit with the court. This addition to the form implements § 362(*l*) which was added to the Code in 2005. And a box is provided that allows the debtor to certify that s/he has served the landlord with the certification as required by § 362(*l*)(1).

The signature sections and the declaration under penalty of perjury by an individual debtor concerning the notice received about bankruptcy relief, the declaration under penalty of perjury by a bankruptcy petition preparer, and the attorney signature box are amended to include new material mandated by the 2005 Act. The attorney signature box is also amended to remind the attorney that in a case in which § 707(b)(4)(D) applies, that the signature constitutes a certification that the attorney has no knowledge after an inquiry that the information in the schedules filed with the petition is incorrect. A signature section also is provided for a representative of a foreign proceeding.

2008 Amendments

Paragraph 3 of Exhibit D is amended to delete any reference to a requirement that a debtor file a motion with the court to obtain an order approving a request for the postponement of the debtor's obligation to obtain a credit counseling briefing prior to the commencement of the case. The paragraph immediately following numbered paragraph 3 is also amended to reflect the deletion of the need for a separate motion beyond the completion of the certification itself. That paragraph continues to warn the debtor that the case may be dismissed if the court does not find that a postponement is warranted. It also advises the debtor that, even if the court concludes that postponement of the obligation is appropriate, the debtor still must complete the briefing within the time allowed under the Code.

HISTORICAL NOTES

Effective and Applicability Provisions

1997 Acts. Order amending official forms dated Oct. 1, 1997, effective immediately, with mandatory use starting March 1, 1998.

Form 2. Declaration Under Penalty of Perjury on Behalf of a Corporation or Partnership

Official Form 2

6/90

I, [the president *or* other officer *or* an authorized agent of the corporation] [*or* a member *or* an authorized agent of the partnership] named as the debtor in this case, declare under penalty of perjury that I have read the foregoing [list *or* schedule *or* amendment *or* other document (describe)] and that it is true and correct to the best of my information and belief.

Date ______________________

Signature ______________________

____
(Print Name and Title)

(Added Aug. 1, 1991.)

ADVISORY COMMITTEE NOTES

This form is derived from former Official Form No. 4.

Rule 1008 requires that all petitions, lists, schedules, statements, and amendments thereto be verified or contain an unsworn declaration conforming with 28 U.S.C. § 1746. This form or adaptations of the form have been incorporated into the official forms of the petitions, schedules, and statement of financial affairs. See Official Forms 1, 5, 6, and 7. The form has been amended for use in connection with other papers required by these rules to be verified or contain an unsworn declaration.

Form 3A. Application and Order to Pay Filing Fee in Installments

B3A (Official Form 3A)(12/07)

United States Bankruptcy Court
__________ District Of __________

In re ______________________________, Case No. ______________________
Debtor

Chapter ______________________

APPLICATION TO PAY FILING FEE IN INSTALLMENTS

1. In accordance with Fed. R. Bankr. P. 1006, I apply for permission to pay the filing fee amounting to $ _______ in installments.

2. I am unable to pay the filing fee except in installments.

3. Until the filing fee is paid in full, I will not make any additional payment or transfer any additional property to an attorney or any other person for services in connection with this case.

4. I propose the following terms for the payment of the Filing Fee.*

$ _______________ Check one ☐ With the filing of the petition, or
☐ On or before _______________

$ _______________ on or before _______________

$ _______________ on or before _______________

$ _______________ on or before _______________

* The number of installments proposed shall not exceed four (4), and the final installment shall be payable not later than 120 days after filing the petition. For cause shown, the court may extend the time of any installment, provided the last installment is paid not later than 180 days after filing the petition. Fed. R. Bankr. P. 1006(b)(2).

5. I understand that if I fail to pay any installment when due, my bankruptcy case may be dismissed and I may not receive a discharge of my debts.

_______________________________ _______________________________
Signature of Attorney Date Signature of Debtor Date
(In a joint case, both spouses must sign.)

_______________________________ _______________________________
Name of Attorney Signature of Joint Debtor (if any) Date

DECLARATION AND SIGNATURE OF NON–ATTORNEY BANKRUPTCY PETITION PREPARER (See 11 U.S.C. § 110)

I declare under penalty of perjury that: (1) I am a bankruptcy petition preparer as defined in 11 U.S.C. § 110; (2) I prepared this document for compensation and have provided the debtor with a copy of this document and the notices and information required under 11 U.S.C. §§ 110(b), 110(h), and 342(b); (3) if rules or guidelines have been promulgated pursuant to 11 U.S. C. § 110(h) setting a maximum fee for services chargeable by bankruptcy petition preparers, I have given the debtor notice of the maximum amount before preparing any document for filing for a debtor or accepting any fee from the debtor, as required under that section; and (4) I will not accept any additional money or other property from the debtor before the filing fee is paid in full.

_______________________________________ ________________________
Printed or Typed Name and Title, if any, of Bankruptcy Petition Preparer — Social Security No. (Required by 11 U.S.C. § 110.)

If the bankruptcy petition preparer is not an individual, state the name, title (if any), address, and social security number of the officer, principal, responsible person, or partner who signs the document.

____

____
Address

x _______________________________________ ________________________
Signature of Bankruptcy Petition Preparer — Date

Names and Social Security numbers of all other individuals who prepared or assisted in preparing this document, unless the bankruptcy petition preparer is not an individual:

If more than one person prepared this document, attach additional signed sheets conforming to the appropriate Official Form for each person. A bankruptcy petition preparer's failure to comply with the provisions of title 11 and the Federal Rules of Bankruptcy Procedure may result in fines or imprisonment or both. 11 U.S.C. § 110; 18 U.S.C. § 156.

B3A (Official Form 3A) (12/07) - Cont.

United States Bankruptcy Court

________ District Of ________

In re ________________________, Case No. ________________

Debtor

Chapter ____________

ORDER APPROVING PAYMENT OF FILING FEE IN INSTALLMENTS

☐ IT IS ORDERED that the debtor(s) may pay the filing fee in installments on the terms proposed in the foregoing application.

☐ IT IS ORDERED that the debtor(s) shall pay the filing fee according to the following terms:

$ ________ Check one ☐ With the filing of the petition, or ☐ On or before ________

$ ________ on or before ________

$ ________ on or before ________

$ ________ on or before ________

☐ IT IS FURTHER ORDERED that until the filing fee is paid in full the debtor(s) shall not make any additional payment or transfer any additional property to an attorney or any other person for services in connection with this case.

BY THE COURT

Date: ________ ________________

United States Bankruptcy Judge

(Added Aug. 1, 1991, and amended Mar. 1995; Oct. 1, 1997; Dec. 1, 2003; Aug. 11, 2005, eff. Oct. 17, 2005; Dec. 1, 2007.)

ADVISORY COMMITTEE NOTES

This form is derived from former Official Form No. 2.

A statement that the applicant is unable to pay the filing fee except in installments has been added as required by Rule 1006(b).

1995 Amendment

This form is a "document for filing" that may be prepared by a "bankruptcy petition preparer" as defined in 11 U.S.C. § 110, which was added to the Code by the Bankruptcy Reform Act of 1994; accordingly, a signature line is provided for such preparer. In addition to signing, a bankruptcy petition preparer is required by section 110 to disclose the information requested. A signature line for a debtor's attorney also is added, as required by Rule 9011.

1997 Amendment

The form has been reorganized and the paragraphs numbered. The debtor's certification concerning payment for services in the case has been placed ahead of the statement of proposed terms for installment payment of court fees. Acknowledgement by the debtor of the potential consequences of failure to pay any installment when due has been added. (See 11 U.S.C. § 707(a)(2).) The language of the form also has been changed to conform to Rule 1006 and to clarify that a debtor is not disqualified from paying the filing fee in installments because the debtor has paid money to a bankruptcy petition preparer.

2003 Amendment

Pursuant to § 110(c) of the Bankruptcy Code, the certification by a non-attorney bankruptcy petition preparer continues to require a petition preparer to provide the full Social Security number of the individual who actually prepares the document pursuant to § 110(c) of the Code.

2005 Amendment

The form is amended to direct the debtor to state that, until the filing fee is paid in full, the debtor will not make any additional payment or transfer any additional property to an attorney or any other person for services in connection with the case. The declaration and certification by a non-attorney bankruptcy petition preparer in the form are amended to include material mandated by § 110 of the Code as amended by the Bankruptcy Abuse Prevention and Consumer Protection Act of 2005, Pub. L. No. 109—8, 119 Stat. 23 (April 20, 2005). The certification by a non-attorney bankruptcy petition preparer is re-named a declaration and also is revised to include material mandated by § 110 of the Code as amended in 2005. The order is amended to provide space for the court to set forth a payment schedule other than the one proposed by the debtor.

2005–2007 Amendments

(The 2005-2007 Committee Note incorporates the Committee Note previously published in 2005.)

The form is amended to direct the debtor to state that, until the filing fee is paid in full, the debtor will not make any additional payment or transfer any additional property to an attorney or any other person for services in connection with the case. The declaration and certification by a non-attorney bankruptcy petition preparer in the form are amended to include material mandated by § 110 of the Code as amended by the Bankruptcy Abuse Prevention and Consumer Protection Act of 2005, Pub. L. No. 109-8, 119 Stat. 23 (April 20, 2005). The certification by a non-attorney bankruptcy petition preparer is re-named a declaration and also is revised to include material mandated by § 110 of the Code as amended in 2005. The order is amended to provide space for the court to set forth a payment schedule other than the one proposed by the debtor.

HISTORICAL NOTES

Effective and Applicability Provisions

1997 Acts. Order amending official forms dated Oct. 1, 1997, effective immediately, with mandatory use starting March 1, 1998.

Form 3B. Application for Waiver of the Chapter 7 Filing Fee for Individuals Who Cannot Pay the Filing Fee in Full or in Installments

B3B (Official Form 3B)(12/07)

APPLICATION FOR WAIVER OF THE CHAPTER 7 FILING FEE FOR INDIVIDUALS WHO CANNOT PAY THE FILING FEE IN FULL OR IN INSTALLMENTS

The court fee for filing a case under chapter 7 of the Bankruptcy Code is $299.

If you cannot afford to pay the full fee at the time of filing, you may apply to pay the fee in installments. A form, which is available from the bankruptcy clerk's office, must be completed to make that application. If your application to pay in installments is approved, you will be permitted to file your petition, generally completing payment of the fee over the course of four to six months.

If you cannot afford to pay the fee either in full at the time of filing or in installments, you may request a waiver of the filing fee by completing this application and filing it with the Clerk of Court. A judge will decide whether you have to pay the fee. By law, the judge may waive the fee only if your income is less than 150 percent of the official poverty line applicable to your family size and you are unable to pay the fee in installments. You may obtain information about the poverty guidelines at www.uscourts.gov or in the bankruptcy clerk's office.

Required information. Complete all items in the application, and attach requested schedules. Then sign the application on the last page. If you and your spouse are filing a joint bankruptcy petition, you both must provide information as requested and sign the application.

B3B (Official Form 3B) (12/07) - Cont.

United States Bankruptcy Court
__________ District of __________

In re: ______________________ Case No. ______________
Debtor(s) (if known)

APPLICATION FOR WAIVER OF THE CHAPTER 7 FILING FEE FOR INDIVIDUALS WHO CANNOT PAY THE FILING FEE IN FULL OR IN INSTALLMENTS

Part A. Family Size and Income

1. Including yourself, your spouse, and dependents you have listed or will list on Schedule I (Current Income of Individual Debtors(s)), how many people are in your family? (Do not include your spouse if you are separated AND are not filing a joint petition.) ________

2. Restate the following information that you provided, or will provide, on Line 16 of Schedule I. Attach a completed copy of Schedule I, if it is available.

   Total Combined Monthly Income (Line 16 of Schedule I): $ ________

3. State the monthly net income, if any, of dependents included in Question 1 above. Do not include any income already reported in Item 2. If none, enter $0.

   $ ________

4. Add the "Total Combined Monthly Income" reported in Question 2 to your dependents' monthly net income from Question 3.

   $ ________

5. Do you expect the amount in Question 4 to increase or decrease by more than 10% during the next 6 months? Yes ________ No ________

   If yes, explain.

Part B: Monthly Expenses

6. EITHER (a) attach a completed copy of Schedule J (Schedule of Monthly Expenses), and state your total monthly expenses reported on Line 18 of that Schedule, OR (b) if you have not yet completed Schedule J, provide an estimate of your total monthly expenses.

   $ ________

7. Do you expect the amount in Question 6 to increase or decrease by more than 10% during the next 6 months? Yes ________ No ________
   If yes, explain.

Part C. Real and Personal Property

EITHER (1) attach completed copies of Schedule A (Real Property) and Schedule B (Personal Property), OR (2) if you have not yet completed those schedules, answer the following questions.

8. State the amount of cash you have on hand: $ ________
9. State below any money you have in savings, checking, or other accounts in a bank or other financial institution.

Bank or Other Financial Institution:	Type of Account such as savings, checking, CD:	Amount:
________	________	$ ________
________	________	$ ________

10. State below the assets owned by you. **Do not list ordinary household furnishings and clothing.**

Home — Address: ______ ______ — Value: $ ______ — Amount owed on mortgages and liens: $ ______

Other real estate — Address: ______ ______ — Value: $ ______ — Amount owed on mortgages and liens: $ ______

Motor vehicle — Model/Year: ______ ______ — Value: $ ______ — Amount owed: $ ______

Motor vehicle — Model/Year: ______ ______ — Value: $ ______ — Amount owed: $ ______

Other — Description ______ ______ — Value: $ ______ — Amount owed: $ ______

11. State below any person, business, organization, or governmental unit that owes you money and the amount that is owed.

Name of Person, Business, or Organization that Owes You Money	Amount Owed
______	$ ______
______	$ ______

Part D. Additional Information.

12. Have you paid an **attorney** any money for services in connection with this case, including the completion of this form, the bankruptcy petition, or schedules? Yes ______ No ______
If yes, how much have you paid? $ __
13. Have you promised to pay or do you anticipate paying an **attorney** in connection with your bankruptcy case? Yes ______ No ______
If yes, how much have you promised to pay or do you anticipate paying? $ __
14. Have you paid **anyone other than an attorney** (such as a bankruptcy petition preparer, paralegal, typing service, or another person) any money for services in connection with this case, including the completion of this form, the bankruptcy petition, or schedules? Yes ______ No ______
If yes, how much have you paid? $ __
15. Have you promised to pay or do you anticipate paying **anyone other than an attorney** (such as a bankruptcy petition preparer, paralegal, typing service, or another person) any money for services in connection with this case, including the completion of this form, the bankruptcy petition, or schedules?
Yes ______ No ______
If yes, how much have you promised to pay or do you anticipate paying? $ __
16. Has anyone paid an attorney or other person or service in connection with this case, on your behalf?
Yes ______ No ______
If yes, explain.
17. Have you previously filed for bankruptcy relief during the past eight years? Yes ______ No ______

Case Number (if known)	Year filed	Location of filing	Did you obtain a discharge? (if known)
______	____	______	Yes ____ No ____ Don't know ____
______	____	______	Yes ____ No ____ Don't know ____

18. Please provide any other information that helps to explain why you are unable to pay the filing fee in installments.

19. I (we) declare under penalty of perjury that I (we) cannot currently afford to pay the filing fee in full or in installments and that the foregoing information is true and correct.

Executed on: ______________ ______________________
Date Signature of Debtor

______________ ______________________
Date Signature of Co-debtor

DECLARATION AND SIGNATURE OF BANKRUPTCY PETITION PREPARER (See 11 U.S.C. § 110)

I declare under penalty of perjury that: (1) I am a bankruptcy petition preparer as defined in 11 U.S.C. § 110; (2) I prepared this document for compensation and have provided the debtor with a copy of this document and the notices and information required under 11 U.S.C. §§ 110(b), 110(h), and 342(b); and (3) if rules or guidelines have been promulgated pursuant to 11 U.S.C. § 110(h) setting a maximum fee for services chargeable by bankruptcy petition preparers, I have given the debtor notice of the maximum amount before preparing any document for filing for a debtor or accepting any fee from the debtor, as required under that section.

______________________ ______________________
Printed or Typed Name and Title, if any, of Bankruptcy Petition Preparer

Social Security No. (Required by 11 U.S.C. § 110.)

If the bankruptcy petition preparer is not an individual, state the name, title (if any), address, and social security number of the officer, principal, responsible person, or partner who signs the document.

____

____
Address

x______________________ ______________________
Signature of Bankruptcy Petition Preparer Date

Names and Social-Security numbers of all other individuals who prepared or assisted in preparing this document, unless the bankruptcy petition preparer is not an individual:

If more than one person prepared this document, attach additional signed sheets conforming to the appropriate Official Form for each person.

A bankruptcy petition preparer's failure to comply with the provisions of title 11 and the Federal Rules of Bankruptcy Procedure may result in fines or imprisonment or both. 11 U.S.C. § 110; 18 U.S.C. § 156.

B3B (Official Form 3B) (12/07) - Cont.

United States Bankruptcy Court
__________ District of __________

In re: ____________________________ Case No. ___________________________
Debtor(s)

ORDER ON DEBTOR'S APPLICATION FOR WAIVER OF THE CHAPTER 7 FILING FEE

Upon consideration of the debtor's "Application for Waiver of the Chapter 7 Filing Fee," the court orders that the application be:

[ ] GRANTED.

This order is subject to being vacated at a later time if developments in the administration of the bankruptcy case demonstrate that the waiver was unwarranted.

[ ] DENIED.

The debtor shall pay the chapter 7 filing fee according to the following terms:

$___ on or before __________
$___ on or before __________
$___ on or before __________
$___ on or before __________

Until the filing fee is paid in full, the debtor shall not make any additional payment or transfer any additional property to an attorney or any other person for services in connection with this case.

IF THE DEBTOR FAILS TO TIMELY PAY THE FILING FEE IN FULL OR TO TIMELY MAKE INSTALLMENT PAYMENTS, THE COURT MAY DISMISS THE DEBTOR'S CHAPTER 7 CASE.

[ ] SCHEDULED FOR HEARING.

A hearing to consider the debtor's "Application for Waiver of the Chapter 7 Filing Fee" shall be held on __________ at ___ am/pm at ____________________________.

(address of courthouse)

IF THE DEBTOR FAILS TO APPEAR AT THE SCHEDULED HEARING, THE COURT MAY DEEM SUCH FAILURE TO BE THE DEBTOR'S CONSENT TO THE ENTRY OF AN ORDER DENYING THE FEE WAIVER APPLICATION BY DEFAULT.

BY THE COURT:

DATE: __________________ ____________________________
United States Bankruptcy Judge

(Added Aug. 11, 2005, eff. Oct. 17, 2005. Amended Apr. 9, 2006; Dec. 1, 2007.)

ADVISORY COMMITTEE NOTES

2005 Amendment

This form is new. 28 U.S.C. § 1930(f), enacted as part of the Bankruptcy Abuse and Consumer Protection Act of 2005, Pub. L. No. 109–8, 119 Stat. 23 (April 20, 2005), provides that "under procedures prescribed by the Judicial Conference of the United States, the district court or the bankruptcy court may waive the filing fee in a case under chapter 7 of title 11 for an individual if the court determines that such individual has income less than 150 percent of the income official poverty line ... applicable to a family of the size involved and is unable to pay that fee in installments." To implement this provision, Interim Rule 1006 adds a new subdivision (c). Official Form 3B is the form referenced in that subdivision, and is to be used by individual chapter 7 debtors when applying for a waiver of the filing fee. A corresponding standard order also is included.

2005–2007 Amendments

(The 2005-2007 Committee Note incorporates the Committee Note previously published in 2005.)

This form is new. 28 U.S.C. § 1930(f), enacted as part of the Bankruptcy Abuse and Consumer Protection Act of 2005, Pub. L. No. 109-8, 119 Stat. 23 (April 20, 2005), provides that "under procedures prescribed by the Judicial Conference of the United States, the district court or the bankruptcy court may waive the filing fee in a case under chapter 7 of title 11 for an individual if the court determines that such individual has income less than 150 percent of the income official poverty line . . . applicable to a family of the size involved and is unable to pay that fee in installments." To implement this provision, Fed. R. Bankr. P.1006 adds a new subdivision (c). Official Form 3B is the form referenced in that subdivision, and is to be used by individual chapter 7 debtors when applying for a waiver of the filing fee. A corresponding standard order also is included.

Form 4. List of Creditors Holding 20 Largest Unsecured Claims

B4 (Official Form 4) (12/07)

United States Bankruptcy Court
__________ District Of __________

In re __________________________, Case No. __________
Debtor
Chapter __________

LIST OF CREDITORS HOLDING 20 LARGEST UNSECURED CLAIMS

Following is the list of the debtor's creditors holding the 20 largest unsecured claims. The list is prepared in accordance with Fed. R. Bankr. P. 1007(d) for filing in this chapter 11 [*or* chapter 9] case. The list does not include (1) persons who come within the definition of "insider" set forth in 11 U.S.C. § 101, or (2) secured creditors unless the value of the collateral is such that the unsecured deficiency places the creditor among the holders of the 20 largest unsecured claims. If a minor child is one of the creditors holding the 20 largest unsecured claims, state the child's initials and the name and address of the child's parent or guardian, such as "A.B., a minor child, by John Doe, guardian." Do not disclose the child's name. See 11 U.S.C. § 112 and Fed. R. Bankr. P. 1007(m).

(1)	(2)	(3)	(4)	(5)
Name of creditor and complete mailing address including zip code	*Name, telephone number and complete mailing address, including zip code, of employee, agent, or department of creditor familiar with claim who may be contacted*	*Nature of claim (trade debt, bank loan, government contract, etc.)*	*Indicate if claim is contingent, unliquidated, disputed or subject to setoff*	*Amount of claim [if secured also state value of security]*

Date: ____________________

____
Debtor

[Declaration as in Form 2]

(Added Aug. 1, 1991, and amended Mar. 16, 1993; Aug. 11, 2005, eff. Oct. 17, 2005; Dec. 1, 2007.)

ADVISORY COMMITTEE NOTES

1991 Enactment

This form is derived from former Official Form No. 9.

In conformity with Rule 1007(d) and in recognition of the notice function served by this list under Rule 4001, governmental units must be listed if they are among the creditors holding the 20 largest claims.

Rule 1008 requires all lists to be verified or contain an unsworn declaration conforming with 28 U.S.C. § 1746.

1993 Amendment

The form has been amended to delete reference to the specific subsection of 11 U.S.C. § 101 in connection with the definition of the term "insider." Section 101 of the Bankruptcy Code contains numerous definitions, and statutory amendments from time to time have resulted in the renumbering of many of its subsections. The more general reference will avoid the necessity to amend the form further in the event of future amendments to § 101.

2005 Amendment

The form is amended to direct that the name of any minor child not be disclosed. The amendment implements § 112 of the Code, which was added by the Bankruptcy Abuse Prevention and Consumer Protection Act of 2005, Pub. L. No. 109–8, 119 Stat. 23 (April 20, 2005).

2005–2007 Amendments

(The 2005-2007 Committee Note incorporates Committee Notes previously published in 2005.)

The form is amended to direct that the name of any minor child not be disclosed. The amendment implements § 112 of the Code, which was added by the Bankruptcy Abuse Prevention and Consumer Protection Act of 2005, Pub. L. No. 109-8, 119 Stat. 23 (April 20, 2005). In addition, the form is amended to add to the reference to Rule 1007(m) a direction to include for noticing purposes the name, address, and legal relationship to the child of "a person described" in that rule. Rule 1007(m) requires the person named to be someone on whom process would be served in an adversary proceeding against the child.

Form 5. Involuntary Petition

B5 (Official Form 5) (12/07)

United States Bankruptcy Court
_______ District of _______

INVOLUNTARY PETITION

IN RE (Name of Debtor—If Individual: Last, First, Middle)

ALL OTHER NAMES used by debtor in the last 8 years (Include married, maiden, and trade names.)

Last four digits of Social-Security or other Individual's Tax-I.D. No./Complete EIN (If more than one, state all.):

STREET ADDRESS OF DEBTOR (No. and street, city, state, and zip code)

MAILING ADDRESS OF DEBTOR (If different from street address)

COUNTY OF RESIDENCE OR PRINCIPAL PLACE OF BUSINESS

ZIP CODE

ZIP CODE

LOCATION OF PRINCIPAL ASSETS OF BUSINESS DEBTOR (If different from previously listed addresses)

CHAPTER OF BANKRUPTCY CODE UNDER WHICH PETITION IS FILED

☐ Chapter 7 ☐ Chapter 11

INFORMATION REGARDING DEBTOR (Check applicable boxes)

Nature of Debts (Check one box.)

Petitioners believe:

☐ Debts are primarily consumer debts

☐ Debts are primarily business debts

Type of Debtor (Form of Organization)

☐ Individual (Includes Joint Debtor)
☐ Corporation (Includes LLC and LLP)
☐ Partnership
☐ Other (If debtor is not one of the above entities, check this box and state type of entity below.)

____

Nature of Business (Check one box.)

☐ Health Care Business
☐ Single Asset Real Estate as defined in 11 U.S.C. § 101(51)(B)
☐ Railroad
☐ Stockbroker
☐ Commodity Broker
☐ Clearing Bank
☐ Other

VENUE

☐ Debtor has been domiciled or has had a residence, principal place of business, or principal assets in the District for 180 days immediately preceding the date of this petition or for a longer part of such 180 days than in any other District.

☐ A bankruptcy case concerning debtor's affiliate, general partner or partnership is pending in this District.

FILING FEE (Check one box)

☐ Full Filing Fee attached

☐ Petitioner is a child support creditor or its representative, and the form specified in § 304(g) of the Bankruptcy Reform Act of 1994 is attached.

[If a child support creditor or its representative is a petitioner, and if the petitioner files the form specified in § 304(g) of the Bankruptcy Reform Act of 1994, no fee is required.]

PENDING BANKRUPTCY CASE FILED BY OR AGAINST ANY PARTNER OR AFFILIATE OF THIS DEBTOR (Report information for any additional cases on attached sheets.)

Name of Debtor	Case Number	Date
Relationship	District	Judge

ALLEGATIONS
(Check applicable boxes)

1. ☐ Petitioner(s) are eligible to file this petition pursuant to 11 U.S.C. § 303(b).
2. ☐ The debtor is a person against whom an order for relief may be entered under title 11 of the United States Code.

3. a. ☐ The debtor is generally not paying such debtor's debts as they become due, unless such debts are the subject of a bona fide dispute as to liability or amount;

or

b. ☐ Within 120 days preceding the filing of this petition, a custodian, other than a trustee, receiver, or agent appointed or authorized to take charge of less than substantially all of the property of the debtor for the purpose of enforcing a lien against such property, was appointed or took possession.

COURT USE ONLY

B5 (Official Form 5) (12/07) - Page 2

Name of Debtor ______________

Case No. ______________

TRANSFER OF CLAIM

☐ Check this box if there has been a transfer of any claim against the debtor by or to any petitioner. Attach all documents that evidence the transfer and any statements that are required under Bankruptcy Rule 1003(a).

REQUEST FOR RELIEF

Petitioner(s) request that an order for relief be entered against the debtor under the chapter of title 11, United States Code, specified in this petition. If any petitioner is a foreign representative appointed in a foreign proceeding, a certified copy of the order of the court granting recognition is attached.

Petitioner(s) declare under penalty of perjury that the foregoing is true and correct according to the best of their knowledge, information, and belief.

X______________ Signature of Petitioner or Representative (State title) ______________ Name of Petitioner Date Signed Name & Mailing Address of Individual Signing in Representative Capacity ______________	X______________ Signature of Attorney Date ______________ Name of Attorney Firm (If any) ______________ Address ______________ Telephone No.
X______________ Signature of Petitioner or Representative (State title) ______________ Name of Petitioner Date Signed Name & Mailing Address of Individual Signing in Representative Capacity ______________	X______________ Signature of Attorney Date ______________ Name of Attorney Firm (If any) ______________ Address ______________ Telephone No.
X______________ Signature of Petitioner or Representative (State title) ______________ Name of Petitioner Date Signed Name & Mailing Address of Individual Signing in Representative Capacity ______________	X______________ Signature of Attorney Date ______________ Name of Attorney Firm (If any) ______________ Address ______________ Telephone No.

PETITIONING CREDITORS

Name and Address of Petitioner	Nature of Claim	Amount of Claim
Name and Address of Petitioner	Nature of Claim	Amount of Claim
Name and Address of Petitioner	Nature of Claim	Amount of Claim
Note: If there are more than three petitioners, attach additional sheets with the statement under penalty of perjury, each petitioner's signature under the statement and the name of attorney and petitioning creditor information in the format above.		Total Amount of Petitioners' Claims

_____ continuation sheets attached

(Added Aug. 1, 1991; and amended Dec. 1, 2002; Dec. 1, 2003; Aug. 11, 2005, eff. Oct. 17, 2005; Oct. 12 2006; Dec. 1, 2007.)

ADVISORY COMMITTEE NOTES

1991 Amendment

This form has been redesigned in a box format similar to that of Form 1. See Advisory Committee Note to Form 1.

The allegations required under § 303 are grouped together, and a separate section has been provided for additional allegations based upon the prohibitions and requirements set forth in Rule 1003(a) concerning transfer of claims by petitioning creditors. Petitioners may wish to supplement the allegations set forth in the form with a further statement of facts. Additional information concerning any allegation can be requested by the debtor as part of the discovery process.

Each petitioning creditor, by signing on the line provided, signs both the petition and the unsworn declaration which 28 U.S.C. § 1746 permits instead of verification. The addresses as well as the names of individuals signing the petition in a representative capacity are required, together with disclosure of which petitioner is represented by each signatory.

This form is intended to be used in every involuntary case, including that of a partnership. The separate form for a petition by a partner has been abrogated. Pursuant to § 303(b)(3)(A) of the Code, a petition by fewer than all of the general partners seeking an order for relief with respect to the partnership is treated as an involuntary petition. Such a petition is adversarial in character because not all of the partners are joining in the petition.

Section 303(b)(3)(B) permits a petition against the partnership if relief has been ordered under the Code with respect to all of the general partners. In that event, the petition may be filed by a general partner, a trustee of a general partner's estate, or a creditor of the partnership. This form may be adapted for use in that type of case.

28 U.S.C. § 1408(1) specifies the proper venue alternatives for all persons, including partnerships, as domicile, residence, principal place of business, or location of principal assets. Venue also may be based on a pending case commenced by an affiliate, general partner, or partnership pursuant to 28 U.S.C. § 1408(2). Both options are set forth in the block labeled "Venue."

28 U.S.C. § 1746 permits the unsworn declaration instead of a verification. See Committee Note to Form 2.

1992 Amendment

The form has been amended to require the dating of signatures.

2002 Amendment

The form is amended to give notice that no filing fee is required if a child support creditor or its representative is a petitioner, and if the petitioner also files a form detailing the child support debt, its status, and other characteristics, as specified in § 304(g) of the Bankruptcy Reform Act of 1994, Pub. L. No. 103–394, 108 Stat. 4106 (Oct. 22, 1994).

2003 Amendment

The form is amended to require the petitioner to disclose the debtor's employer identification number, if any, and only the last four digits of the debtor's social security number to afford greater privacy to the individual debtor, whose bankruptcy case records may be available on the Internet. The form also is amended to delete the request for information concerning the "Type of Business," as this data no longer is collected for statistical purposes.

2005 Amendment

The form has been amended to delete statistical information no longer required and to add "as to liability or amount" to the language concerning debts that are the subject of a bona fide dispute, in conformity with § 303 of the Code as amended by the Bankruptcy Abuse Prevention and Consumer Protection Act of 2005, Pub. L. No. 109—8, 119 Stat. 23 (April 20, 2005). The petitioning creditors must now provide, to the extent known to them, all other names used by the debtor during the 8 years, rather than 6 years, before the filing of the petition. A new check box is provided for the petitioning creditors to identify the debtor that is a "health care business" as defined in § 101 of the Code, thereby alerting the court and the United States trustee of the necessity under § 332 to appoint an ombudsman to represent the interests of the patients of the health care business. These amendments also implement the 2005 amendments to the Code. A new checkbox also is provided for a "clearing bank," which may become a debtor upon the filing of a petition at the direction of the Board of Governors of the Federal Reserve System; this addition conforms to an amendment to § 109(b)(2) of the Code which was enacted in 2000.

2006 Amendment

The section of the form labeled "Information Regarding Debtor" is amended to facilitate, to the extent available in an involuntary case, the collection of the same statistical information that is requested in a voluntary case. Accordingly, information about whether the debtor is an individual, a corporation, or some other type of entity is separated from the checklist of types of debtors, such as health care businesses and railroads, concerning which the Code provides for specialized treatment.

2005–2007 Amendments

(The 2005-2007 Committee Note incorporates Committee Notes previously published in 2005 and 2006.)

The form has been amended to delete statistical information about the debtor that no longer is required, and to substitute checkboxes similar to those on the voluntary petition form. The form also is amended to add "as to liability or amount" to the language concerning debts that are the subject of a bona fide dispute, in conformity with § 303 of the Code as amended by the Bankruptcy Abuse Prevention and Consumer Protection Act of 2005, Pub. L. No. 109-8, 119 Stat. 23 (April 20, 2005). The petitioning creditors must now provide, to the extent known to them, all other names used by the debtor during the 8 years, rather than 6 years, before the filing of the petition. In conformity with Rule 9037, the petitioning creditors are directed to provide only the last four digits of any individual's tax-identification number. A new checkbox is provided for the petitioning creditors to identify the debtor that is a "health care business" as defined in § 101 of the Code, thereby alerting the court and the United States trustee of the necessity under § 333 of the Code to appoint an ombudsman to represent the interests of the patients of the health care business. These amendments also implement the 2005 amendments to the Code. A new checkbox also is provided for a "clearing bank," which may become a debtor upon the filing of a petition at the direction of the Board of Governors of the Federal Reserve System; this addition conforms to an amendment to § 109(b)(2) of the Code, which was enacted in 2000.

Form 6. Schedules

B6 Cover (Form 6 Cover) (12/07)

Summary of Schedules
Statistical Summary of Certain Liabilities and Related Data (28 U.S.C. § 159)

Schedule A—Real Property
Schedule B—Personal Property
Schedule C—Property Claimed as Exempt
Schedule D—Creditors Holding Secured Claims
Schedule E—Creditors Holding Unsecured Priority Claims
Schedule F—Creditors Holding Unsecured Nonpriority Claims
Schedule G—Executory Contracts and Unexpired Leases
Schedule H—Codebtors
Schedule I—Current Income of Individual Debtor(s)
Schedule J—Current Expenditures of Individual Debtor(s)
Unsworn Declaration under Penalty of Perjury

GENERAL INSTRUCTIONS: The first page of the debtor's schedules and the first page of any amendments thereto must contain a caption as in Form 16B. Subsequent pages should be identified with the debtor's name and case number. If the schedules are filed with the petition, the case number should be left blank

Schedules D, E, and F have been designed for the listing of each claim only once. Even when a claim is secured only in part or entitled to priority only in part, it still should be listed only once. A claim which is secured in whole or in part should be listed on Schedule D only, and a claim which is entitled to priority in whole or in part should be listed on Schedule E only. Do not list the same claim twice. If a creditor has more than one claim, such as claims arising from separate transactions, each claim should be scheduled separately.

Review the specific instructions for each schedule before completing the schedule.

B6 Summary (Official Form 6—Summary) (12/07)

United States Bankruptcy Court

__________ District Of __________

In re _____________________________________, Case No. ______________________________

Debtor

Chapter ______________________________

SUMMARY OF SCHEDULES

Indicate as to each schedule whether that schedule is attached and state the number of pages in each. Report the totals from Schedules A, B, D, E, F, I, and J in the boxes provided. Add the amounts from Schedules A and B to determine the total amount of the debtor's assets. Add the amounts of all claims from Schedules D, E, and F to determine the total amount of the debtor's liabilities. Individual debtors also must complete the "Statistical Summary of Certain Liabilities and Related Data" if they file a case under chapter 7, 11, or 13.

NAME OF SCHEDULE	ATTACHED (YES/NO)	NO. OF SHEETS	ASSETS	LIABILITIES	OTHER
A—Real Property			$		
B—Personal Property			$		
C—Property Claimed As Exempt					
D—Creditors Holding Secured Claims				$	
E—Creditors Holding Unsecured Priority Claims (Total of Claims on Schedule E)				$	
F—Creditors Holding Unsecured Nonpriority Claims				$	
G—Executory Contracts and Unexpired Leases					
H—Codebtors					
I—Current Income of Individual Debtor(s)					$
J—Current Expenditures of Individual Debtor(s)					$
TOTAL			$	$	

B6 Summary (Official Form 6—Summary) (12/07)

United States Bankruptcy Court
__________ District Of __________

In re ______________________________________, Case No. ______________________
Debtor
Chapter ______________________

STATISTICAL SUMMARY OF CERTAIN LIABILITIES AND RELATED DATA (28 U.S.C. § 159)

If you are an individual debtor whose debts are primarily consumer debts, as defined in § 101(8) of the Bankruptcy Code (11 U.S.C. § 101(8)), filing a case under chapter 7, 11 or 13, you must report all information requested below.

☐ Check this box if you are an individual debtor whose debts are NOT primarily consumer debts. You are not required to report any information here.

This information is for statistical purposes only under 28 U.S.C. § 159.

Summarize the following types of liabilities, as reported in the Schedules, and total them.

Type of Liability	**Amount**	
Domestic Support Obligations (from Schedule E)	$	
Taxes and Certain Other Debts Owed to Governmental Units (from Schedule E)	$	
Claims for Death or Personal Injury While Debtor Was Intoxicated (from Schedule E) (whether disputed or undisputed)	$	
Student Loan Obligations (from Schedule F)	$	
Domestic Support, Separation Agreement, and Divorce Decree Obligations Not Reported on Schedule E	$	
Obligations to Pension or Profit-Sharing, and Other Similar Obligations (from Schedule F)	$	
TOTAL	$	
State the following:		
Average Income (from Schedule I, Line 16)	$	
Average Expenses (from Schedule J, Line 18)	$	
Current Monthly Income (from Form 22A Line 12; **OR**, Form 22B Line 11; **OR**, Form 22C Line 20)	$	
State the following:		
1. Total from Schedule D, "UNSECURED PORTION, IF ANY" column		$
2. Total from Schedule E, "AMOUNT ENTITLED TO PRIORITY" column.	$	
3. Total from Schedule E, "AMOUNT NOT ENTITLED TO PRIORITY, IF ANY" column		$
4. Total from Schedule F		$
5. Total of non-priority unsecured debt (sum of 1, 3, and 4)		$

B6A (Official Form 6A) (12/07)

In re ______________________________, Case No. ______________________,
Debtor (If known)

SCHEDULE A—REAL PROPERTY

Except as directed below, list all real property in which the debtor has any legal, equitable, or future interest, including all property owned as a cotenant, community property, or in which the debtor has a life estate. Include any property in which the debtor holds rights and powers exercisable for the debtor's own benefit. If the debtor is married, state whether husband, wife, or both own the property by placing an "H," "W," "J," or "C" in the column labeled "Husband, Wife, Joint, or Community." If the debtor holds no interest in real property, write "None" under "Description and Location of Property."

Do not include interests in executory contracts and unexpired leases on this schedule. List them in Schedule G—Executory Contracts and Unexpired Leases.

If an entity claims to have a lien or hold a secured interest in any property, state the amount of the secured claim. See Schedule D. If no entity claims to hold a secured interest in the property, write "None" in the column labeled "Amount of Secured Claim."

If the debtor is an individual or if a joint petition is filed, state the amount of any exemption claimed in the property only in Schedule C—Property Claimed as Exempt.

DESCRIPTION AND LOCATION OF PROPERTY	NATURE OF DEBTOR'S INTEREST IN PROPERTY	HUSBAND WIFE JOINT OR COMMUNITY	CURRENT VALUE OF DEBTOR'S INTEREST IN PROPERTY, WITHOUT DEDUCTING ANY SECURED CLAIM OR EXEMPTION	AMOUNT OF SECURED CLAIM
		Total ►	$	

(Report also on Summary of Schedules.)

B6B (Official Form 6B) (12/07)

In re __________________________, Case No. ____________________
Debtor (If known)

SCHEDULE B—PERSONAL PROPERTY

Except as directed below, list all personal property of the debtor of whatever kind. If the debtor has no property in one or more of the categories, place an "x" in the appropriate position in the column labeled "None." If additional space is needed in any category, attach a separate sheet properly identified with the case name, case number, and the number of the category. If the debtor is married, state whether the husband, wife, both, or the marital community own the property by placing an "H," "W," "J," or "C" in the column labeled "Husband, Wife, Joint, or Community." If the debtor is an individual or a joint petition is filed, state the amount of any exemptions claimed only in Schedule C—Property Claimed as Exempt.

Do not list interests in executory contracts and unexpired leases on this schedule. List them in Schedule G—Executory Contracts and Unexpired Leases.

If the property is being held for the debtor by someone else, state that person's name and address under "Description and Location of Property." If the property is being held for a minor child, simply state the child's initials and the name and address of the child's parent or guardian, such as "A.B., a minor child, by John Doe, guardian." Do not disclose the child's name. See, 11 U.S.C. § 112 and Fed. R. Bankr. P. 1007(m).

B6B (Official Form 6B) (12/07)—Cont.

TYPE OF PROPERTY	NONE	DESCRIPTION AND LOCATION OF PROPERTY	HUSBAND WIFE JOINT OR COMMUNITY	CURRENT VALUE OF DEBTOR'S INTEREST IN PROPERTY, WITHOUT DEDUCTING ANY SECURED CLAIM OR EXEMPTION
1. Cash on hand.				
2. Checking, savings or other financial accounts, certificates of deposit, or shares in banks, savings and loan, thrift, building and loan, and homestead associations, or credit unions, brokerage houses, or cooperatives.				
3. Security deposits with public utilities, telephone companies, landlords, and others.				
4. Household goods and furnishings, including audio, video, and computer equipment.				
5. Books; pictures and other art objects; antiques; stamp, coin, record, tape, compact disc, and other collections or collectibles.				
6. Wearing apparel.				
7. Furs and jewelry.				
8. Firearms and sports, photographic, and other hobby equipment.				
9. Interests in insurance policies. Name insurance company of each policy and itemize surrender or refund value of each.				
10. Annuities. Itemize and name each issuer.				
11. Interests in an education IRA as defined in 26 U.S.C. § 530(b)(1) or under a qualified State tuition plan as defined in 26 U.S.C. § 529(b)(1). Give particulars. (File separately the record(s) of any such interest(s). 11 U.S.C. § 521(c)).				

B6B (Official Form 6B) (12/07) - Cont.

In re ______________________________, Case No. ______________________,
Debtor (If known)

SCHEDULE B-PERSONAL PROPERTY
(Continuation Sheet)

TYPE OF PROPERTY	NONE	DESCRIPTION AND LOCATION OF PROPERTY	HUSBAND, WIFE, JOINT, OR COMMUNITY	CURRENT VALUE OF DEBTOR'S INTEREST IN PROPERTY, WITHOUT DEDUCTING ANY SECURED CLAIM OR EXEMPTION
12. Interests in IRA, ERISA, Keogh, or other pension or profit sharing plans. Give particulars.				
13. Stock and interests in incorporated and unincorporated businesses. Itemize.				
14. Interests in partnerships or joint ventures. Itemize.				
15. Government and corporate bonds and other negotiable and nonnegotiable instruments.				
16. Accounts receivable.				
17. Alimony, maintenance, support, and property settlements to which the debtor is or may be entitled. Give particulars.				
18. Other liquidated debts owed to debtor including tax refunds. Give particulars.				
19. Equitable or future interests, life estates, and rights or powers exercisable for the benefit of the debtor other than those listed in Schedule A— Real Property.				
20. Contingent and noncontingent interests in estate of a decedent, death benefit plan, life insurance policy, or trust.				
21. Other contingent and unliquidated claims of every nature, including tax refunds, counterclaims of the debtor, and rights to setoff claims. Give estimated value of each.				
22. Patents, copyrights, and other intellectual property. Give particulars.				
23. Licenses, franchises, and other general intangibles. Give particulars.				

B6B (Official Form 6B) (12/07)—Cont.

In re ____________________, Case No.____________________,
Debtor (If known)

SCHEDULE B-PERSONAL PROPERTY
(Continuation Sheet)

TYPE OF PROPERTY	NONE	DESCRIPTION AND LOCATION OF PROPERTY	HUSBAND, WIFE, JOINT, OR COMMUNITY	CURRENT VALUE OF DEBTOR'S INTEREST IN PROPERTY, WITHOUT DEDUCTING ANY SECURED CLAIM OR EXEMPTION
24. Customer lists or other compilations containing personally identifiable information (as defined in 11 U.S.C. § 101(41A)) provided to the debtor by individuals in connection with obtaining a product or service from the debtor primarily for personal, family, or household purposes.				
25. Automobiles, trucks, trailers, and other vehicles and accessories.				
26. Boats, motors, and accessories.				
27. Aircraft and accessories.				
28. Office equipment, furnishings, and supplies.				
29. Machinery, fixtures, equipment, and supplies used in business.				
30. Inventory.				
31. Animals.				
32. Crops—growing or harvested. Give particulars.				
33. Farming equipment and implements.				
34. Farm supplies, chemicals, and feed.				
35. Other personal property of any kind not already listed. Itemize.				

___ continuation sheets attached Total ▶ $

(Include amounts from any continuation sheets attached. Report total also on Summary of Schedules.)

B6C (Official Form 6C) (12/07)

In re ______________________, Case No. ______________________,
Debtor (If known)

SCHEDULE C—PROPERTY CLAIMED AS EXEMPT

Debtor claims the exemptions to which debtor is entitled under:
(Check one box)
☐ 11 U.S.C. § 522(b)(2)
☐ 11 U.S.C. § 522(b)(3)

☐ Check if debtor claims a homestead exemption that exceeds $136,875.

DESCRIPTION OF PROPERTY	SPECIFY LAW PROVIDING EACH EXEMPTION	VALUE OF CLAIMED EXEMPTION	CURRENT VALUE OF PROPERTY WITHOUT DEDUCTING EXEMPTION

B6D (Official Form 6D) (12/07)

In re ______________________________________, Case No. _______________________________,
Debtor (If known)

SCHEDULE D—CREDITORS HOLDING SECURED CLAIMS

State the name, mailing address, including zip code, and last four digits of any account number of all entities holding claims secured by property of the debtor as of the date of filing of the petition. The complete account number of any account the debtor has with the creditor is useful to the trustee and the creditor and may be provided if the debtor chooses to do so. List creditors holding all types of secured interests such as judgment liens, garnishments, statutory liens, mortgages, deeds of trust, and other security interests.

List creditors in alphabetical order to the extent practicable. If a minor child is the creditor, state the child's initials and the name and address of the child's parent or guardian, such as "A.B., a minor child, by John Doe, guardian." Do not disclose the child's name. See, 11 U.S.C. § 112 and Fed. R. Bankr. P. 1007(m). If all secured creditors will not fit on this page, use the continuation sheet provided.

If any entity other than a spouse in a joint case may be jointly liable on a claim, place an "X" in the column labeled "Codebtor," include the entity on the appropriate schedule of creditors, and complete Schedule H—Codebtors. If a joint petition is filed, state whether the husband, wife, both of them, or the marital community may be liable on each claim by placing an "H," "W," "J," or "C" in the column labeled "Husband, Wife, Joint, or Community."

If the claim is contingent, place an "X" in the column labeled "Contingent." If the claim is unliquidated, place an "X" in the column labeled "Unliquidated." If the claim is disputed, place an "X" in the column labeled "Disputed." (You may need to place an "X" in more than one of these three columns.)

Total the columns labeled "Amount of Claim Without Deducting Value of Collateral" and "Unsecured Portion, if Any" in the boxes labeled "Total(s)" on the last sheet of the completed schedule. Report the total from the column labeled "Amount of Claim Without Deducting Value of Collateral" also on the Summary of Schedules and, if the debtor is an individual with primarily consumer debts, report the total from the column labeled "Unsecured Portion, if Any" on the Statistical Summary of Certain Liabilities and Related Data.

☐ Check this box if debtor has no creditors holding secured claims to report on this Schedule D.

B6D (Official Form 6D) (12/07)—Cont.

CREDITOR'S NAME AND MAILING ADDRESS INCLUDING ZIP CODE AND AN ACCOUNT NUMBER *(See Instructions Above.)*	CODEBTOR	HUSBAND, WIFE, JOINT, OR COMMUNITY	DATE CLAIM WAS INCURRED, NATURE OF LIEN, AND DESCRIPTION AND VALUE OF PROPERTY SUBJECT TO LIEN	CONTINGENT	UNLIQUIDATED	DISPUTED	AMOUNT OF CLAIM WITHOUT DEDUCTING VALUE OF COLLATERAL	UNSECURED PORTION, IF ANY
ACCOUNT NO.			VALUE $					
ACCOUNT NO.			VALUE $					
ACCOUNT NO.			VALUE $					
ACCOUNT NO.			VALUE $					
___continuation sheets attached			Subtotal ▶ (Total of this page)				$	$
			Total ▶ (Use only on last page)				$	$
							(Report also on Summary of Schedules.)	(If applicable, report also on Statistical Summary of Certain Liabilities and Related Data.)

B6D (Official Form 6D) (12/07)- Cont.

In re ______________________________, Case No. ______________________,
Debtor (If known)

SCHEDULE D—CREDITORS HOLDING SECURED CLAIMS

(Continuation Sheet)

CREDITOR'S NAME AND MAILING ADDRESS INCLUDING ZIP CODE AND AN ACCOUNT NUMBER *(See Instructions Above)*	CODEBTOR	HUSBAND, WIFE, JOINT, OR COMMUNITY	DATE CLAIM WAS INCURRED, NATURE OF LIEN, AND DESCRIPTION AND VALUE OF PROPERTY SUBJECT TO LIEN	CONTINGENT	UNLIQUIDATED	DISPUTED	AMOUNT OF CLAIM WITHOUT DEDUCTING VALUE OF COLLATERAL	UNSECURED PORTION, IF ANY
ACCOUNT NO.			VALUE $					
ACCOUNT NO.			VALUE $					
ACCOUNT NO.			VALUE $					
ACCOUNT NO.			VALUE $					
ACCOUNT NO.			VALUE $					
Sheet no. __ of __ continuation sheets attached to Schedule of Creditors Holding Secured Claims			Subtotal(s) ▶ (Total(s) of this page(s))				$	$
			Total(s) ▶ (Use only on last page)				$	$
							(Report also on Summary of Schedules.)	(If applicable, report also on Statistical Summary of Certain Liabilities and Related Data.)

B6E (Official Form 6E) (12/07)

In re ______________________________, Case No. ____________________,
Debtor (if known)

SCHEDULE E—CREDITORS HOLDING UNSECURED PRIORITY CLAIMS

A complete list of claims entitled to priority, listed separately by type of priority, is to be set forth on the sheets provided. Only holders of unsecured claims entitled to priority should be listed in this schedule. In the boxes provided on the attached sheets, state the name, mailing address, including zip code, and last four digits of the account number, if any, of all entities holding priority claims against the debtor or the property of the debtor, as of the date of the filing of the petition. Use a separate continuation sheet for each type of priority and label each with the type of priority.

The complete account number of any account the debtor has with the creditor is useful to the trustee and the creditor and may be provided if the debtor chooses to do so. If a minor child is a creditor, state the child's initials and the name and address of the child's parent or guardian, such as "A.B., a minor child, by John Doe, guardian." Do not disclose the child's name. See, 11 U.S.C. § 112 and Fed.R.Bankr.P. 1007(m).

If any entity other than a spouse in a joint case may be jointly liable on a claim, place an "X" in the column labeled "Codebtor," include the entity on the appropriate schedule of creditors, and complete Schedule H–Codebtors. If a joint petition is filed, state whether the husband, wife, both of them, or the marital community may be liable on each claim by placing an "H,""W,""J," or "C" in the column labeled "Husband, Wife, Joint, or Community." If the claim is contingent, place an "X" in the column labeled "Contingent." If the claim is unliquidated, place an "X" in the column labeled "Unliquidated." If the claim is disputed, place an "X" in the column labeled "Disputed." (You may need to place an "X" in more than one of these three columns.)

Report the total of claims listed on each sheet in the box labeled "Subtotals" on each sheet. Report the total of all claims listed on this Schedule E in the box labeled "Total" on the last sheet of the completed schedule. Report this total also on the Summary of Schedules.

Report the total of amounts entitled to priority listed on each sheet in the box labeled "Subtotals" on each sheet. Report the total of all amounts entitled to priority listed on this Schedule E in the box labeled "Totals" on the last sheet of the completed schedule. Individual debtors with primarily consumer debts report this total also on the Statistical Summary of Certain Liabilities and Related Data.

Report the total of amounts not entitled to priority listed on each sheet in the box labeled "Subtotals" on each sheet. Report the total of all amounts not entitled to priority listed on this Schedule E in the box labeled "Totals" on the last sheet of the completed schedule. Individual debtors with primarily consumer debts report this total also on the Statistical Summary of Certain Liabilities and Related Data.

☐ Check this box if debtor has no creditors holding unsecured priority claims to report on this Schedule E.

TYPES OF PRIORITY CLAIMS (Check the appropriate box(es) below if claims in that category are listed on the attached sheets.)

☐ **Domestic Support Obligations**

Claims for domestic support that are owed to or recoverable by a spouse, former spouse, or child of the debtor, or the parent, legal guardian, or responsible relative of such a child, or a governmental unit to whom such a domestic support claim has been assigned to the extent provided in 11 U.S.C. § 507(a)(1).

☐ **Extensions of credit in an involuntary case**

Claims arising in the ordinary course of the debtor's business or financial affairs after the commencement of the case but before the earlier of the appointment of a trustee or the order for relief. 11 U.S.C. § 507(a)(3).

☐ **Wages, salaries, and commissions**

Wages, salaries, and commissions, including vacation, severance, and sick leave pay owing to employees and commissions owing to qualifying independent sales representatives up to $10,950* per person earned within 180 days immediately preceding the filing of the original petition, or the cessation of business, whichever occurred first, to the extent provided in 11 U.S.C. § 507(a)(4).

☐ **Contributions to employee benefit plans**

Money owed to employee benefit plans for services rendered within 180 days immediately preceding the filing of the original petition, or the cessation of business, whichever occurred first, to the extent provided in 11 U.S.C. § 507(a)(5).

☐ **Certain farmers and fishermen**

Claims of certain farmers and fishermen, up to $5,400* per farmer or fisherman, against the debtor, as provided in 11 U.S.C. § 507(a)(6).

☐ **Deposits by individuals**

Claims of individuals up to $2,425* for deposits for the purchase, lease, or rental of property or services for personal, family, or household use, that were not delivered or provided. 11 U.S.C. § 507(a)(7).

☐ **Taxes and Certain Other Debts Owed to Governmental Units**

Taxes, customs duties, and penalties owing to federal, state, and local governmental units as set forth in 11 U.S.C. § 507(a)(8).

☐ **Commitments to Maintain the Capital of an Insured Depository Institution**

Claims based on commitments to the FDIC, RTC, Director of the Office of Thrift Supervision, Comptroller of the Currency, or Board of Governors of the Federal Reserve System, or their predecessors or successors, to maintain the capital of an insured depository institution. 11 U.S.C. § 507(a)(9).

☐ **Claims for Death or Personal Injury While Debtor Was Intoxicated**

Claims for death or personal injury resulting from the operation of a motor vehicle or vessel while the debtor was intoxicated from using alcohol, a drug, or another substance. 11 U.S.C. § 507(a)(10).

* Amounts are subject to adjustment on April 1, 2010, and every three years thereafter with respect to cases commenced on or after the date of adjustment.

__________ continuation sheets attached

B6E (Official Form 6E) (12/07) - Cont.

In re ________________________, Case No. ____________________,
Debtor (If known)

SCHEDULE E—CREDITORS HOLDING UNSECURED PRIORITY CLAIMS

(Continuation Sheet)

Type of Priority for Claims Listed on This Sheet

CREDITOR'S NAME, MAILING ADDRESS INCLUDING ZIP CODE, AND ACCOUNT NUMBER *(See instructions above.)*	CODEBTOR	HUSBAND, WIFE, JOINT, OR COMMUNITY	DATE CLAIM WAS INCURRED AND CONSIDERATION FOR CLAIM	CONTINGENT	UNLIQUIDATED	DISPUTED	AMOUNT OF CLAIM	AMOUNT ENTITLED TO PRIORITY	AMOUNT NOT ENTITLED TO PRIORITY, IF ANY
Account No.									
Account No.									
Account No.									
Account No.									
Account No.									

Sheet no. __ of __ continuation sheets attached to Schedule of Creditors Holding Priority Claims

Subtotals ▶ (Totals of this page)	$	$	
Total ▶ (Use only on last page of the completed Schedule E. Report also on the Summary of Schedules.)	$		
Totals ▶ (Use only on last page of the completed Schedule E. If applicable, report also on the Statistical Summary of Certain Liabilities and Related Data.)		$	$

B6F (Official Form 6F) (12/07)

In re ______________________________, Debtor   Case No. ______________________, (if known)

SCHEDULE F—CREDITORS HOLDING UNSECURED NONPRIORITY CLAIMS

State the name, mailing address, including zip code, and last four digits of any account number, of all entities holding unsecured claims without priority against the debtor or the property of the debtor, as of the date of filing of the petition. The complete account number of any account the debtor has with the creditor is useful to the trustee and the creditor and may be provided if the debtor chooses to do so. If a minor child is a creditor, state the child's initials and the name and address of the child's parent or guardian, such as "A.B., a minor child, by John Doe, guardian." Do not disclose the child's name. See, 11 U.S.C. § 112 and Fed.R.Bankr.P. 1007(m). Do not include claims listed in Schedules D and E. If all creditors will not fit on this page, use the continuation sheet provided.

If any entity other than a spouse in a joint case may be jointly liable on a claim, place an "X" in the column labeled "Codebtor," include the entity on the appropriate schedule of creditors, and complete Schedule H—Codebtors. If a joint petition is filed, state whether the husband, wife, both of them, or the marital community may be liable on each claim by placing an "H," "W," "J," or "C" in the column labeled "Husband, Wife, Joint, or Community."

If the claim is contingent, place an "X" in the column labeled "Contingent." If the claim is unliquidated, place an "X" in the column labeled "Unliquidated." If the claim is disputed, place an "X" in the column labeled "Disputed." (You may need to place an "X" in more than one of these three columns.)

Report the total of all claims listed on this schedule in the box labeled "Total" on the last sheet of the completed schedule. Report this total also on the Summary of Schedules and, if the debtor is an individual with primarily consumer debts, report this total also on the Statistical Summary of Certain Liabilities and Related Data.

☐ Check this box if debtor has no creditors holding unsecured claims to report on this Schedule F.

CREDITOR'S NAME, MAILING ADDRESS INCLUDING ZIP CODE, AND ACCOUNT NUMBER (See instructions above.)	CODEBTOR	HUSBAND WIFE JOINT OR COMMUNITY	DATE CLAIM WAS INCURRED AND CONSIDERATION FOR CLAIM. IF CLAIM IS SUBJECT TO SETOFF, SO STATE.	CONTINGENT	UNLIQUIDATED	DISPUTED	AMOUNT OF CLAIM
ACCOUNT NO.							
ACCOUNT NO.							
ACCOUNT NO.							
ACCOUNT NO.							

____ continuation sheets attached

Subtotal ▶ $

Total ▶ $

(Use only on last page of the completed Schedule F.)
(Report also on Summary of Schedule and, if applicable, on the Statistical Summary of Certain Liabilities and Related Data.)

B6F (Official Form 6F) (12/07) — Cont.

In re ______________________, Case No. ______________________,
Debtor (If known)

SCHEDULE F—CREDITORS HOLDING UNSECURED NONPRIORITY CLAIMS

(Continuation Sheet)

CREDITOR'S NAME, MAILING ADDRESS INCLUDING ZIP CODE, AND ACCOUNT NUMBER (See instructions above.)	CODEBTOR	HUSBAND, WIFE, JOINT, OR COMMUNITY	DATE CLAIM WAS INCURRED AND CONSIDERATION FOR CLAIM. IF CLAIM IS SUBJECT TO SETOFF, SO STATE.	CONTINGENT	UNLIQUIDATED	DISPUTED	AMOUNT OF CLAIM
ACCOUNT NO.							
ACCOUNT NO.							
ACCOUNT NO.							
ACCOUNT NO.							
ACCOUNT NO.							

Sheet no. ___ of ___ continuation sheets attached to Schedule of Creditors Holding Unsecured Nonpriority Claims

Subtotal ▶ $

Total ▶ $
(Use only on last page of the completed Schedule F.)
(Report also on Summary of Schedules and, if applicable on the Statistical Summary of Certain Liabilities and Related Data.)

B6G (Official Form 6G) (12/07)

In re ______________________________, Case No. ______________________
Debtor (If known)

SCHEDULE G—EXECUTORY CONTRACTS AND UNEXPIRED LEASES

Describe all executory contracts of any nature and all unexpired leases of real or personal property. Include any timeshare interests. State nature of debtor's interest in contract, i.e., "Purchaser," "Agent," etc. State whether debtor is the lessor or lessee of a lease. Provide the names and complete mailing addresses of all other parties to each lease or contract described. If a minor child is a party to one of the leases or contracts, state the child's initials and the name and address of the child's parent or guardian, such as "A.B., a minor child, by John Doe, guardian." Do not disclose the child's name. See, 11 U.S.C. § 112 and Fed. R. Bankr. P. 1007(m).

☐ Check this box if debtor has no executory contracts or unexpired leases.

NAME AND MAILING ADDRESS, INCLUDING ZIP CODE, OF OTHER PARTIES TO LEASE OR CONTRACT.	DESCRIPTION OF CONTRACT OR LEASE AND NATURE OF DEBTOR'S INTEREST, STATE WHETHER LEASE IS FOR NONRESIDENTIAL REAL PROPERTY, STATE CONTRACT NUMBER OF ANY GOVERNMENT CONTRACT.

B6H (Official Form B6H) (12/07)

In re ______________________________, Case No. ______________________
Debtor (if known)

SCHEDULE H—CODEBTORS

Provide the information requested concerning any person or entity, other than a spouse in a joint case, that is also liable on any debts listed by the debtor in the schedules of creditors. Include all guarantors and co-signers. If the debtor resides or resided in a community property state, commonwealth, or territory (including Alaska, Arizona, California, Idaho, Louisiana, Nevada, New Mexico, Puerto Rico, Texas, Washington, or Wisconsin) within the eight-year period immediately preceding the commencement of the case, identify the name of the debtor's spouse and of any former spouse who resides or resided with the debtor in the community property state, commonwealth, or territory. Include all names used by the nondebtor spouse during the eight years immediately preceding the commencement of this case. If a minor child is a codebtor or a creditor, state the child's initials and the name and address of the child's parent or guardian, such as "A.B., a minor child, by John Doe, guardian." Do not disclose the child's name. See, 11 U.S.C. § 112 and Fed. Bankr. P. 1007(m).

☐ Check this box if debtor has no codebtors.

NAME AND ADDRESS OF CODEBTOR	NAME AND ADDRESS OF CREDITOR

B6I (Official Form 6I (12/07)

In re ______________________, Case No. ______________________,
Debtor (if known)

SCHEDULE I—CURRENT INCOME OF INDIVIDUAL DEBTOR(S)

The column labeled "Spouse" must be completed in all cases filed by joint debtors and by every married debtor, whether or not a joint petition is filed, unless the spouses are separated and a joint petition is not filed. Do not state the name of any minor child. The average monthly income calculated on this form may differ from the current monthly income calculated on Form 22A, 22B, or 22C.

Debtor's Marital Status:	DEPENDENTS OF DEBTOR AND SPOUSE	
	RELATIONSHIP(S):	AGE(S):
Employment:	DEBTOR	SPOUSE
Occupation		
Name of Employer		
How long employed		
Address of Employer		

INCOME: (Estimate of average or projected monthly income at time case filed)	DEBTOR	SPOUSE
1. Monthly gross wages, salary, and commissions (Prorate if not paid monthly)	$	$
2. Estimate monthly overtime	$	$
3. SUBTOTAL	$	$
4. LESS PAYROLL DEDUCTIONS		
a. Payroll taxes and social security	$	$
b. Insurance	$	$
c. Union dues	$	$
d. Other (Specify): ____________	$	$
5. SUBTOTAL OF PAYROLL DEDUCTIONS	$	$
6. TOTAL NET MONTHLY TAKE HOME PAY	$	$
7. Regular income from operation of business or profession or farm. (Attach detailed statement)	$	$
8. Income from real property	$	$
9. Interest and dividends	$	$
10. Alimony, maintenance or support payments payable to the debtor for the debtor's use or that of dependents listed above.	$	$
11. Social security or government assistance (Specify): ____________	$	$
12. Pension or retirement income	$	$
13. Other monthly income (Specify): ____________	$	$
14. SUBTOTAL OF LINES 7 THROUGH 13	$	$
15. AVERAGE MONTHLY INCOME (Add amounts on lines 6 and 14)	$	$
16. COMBINED AVERAGE MONTHLY INCOME: (Combine column totals from line 15)	$	$

(Report also on Summary of Schedules and, if applicable, on Statistical Summary of Certain Liabilities and Related Data)

17. Describe any increase or decrease in income reasonably anticipated to occur within the year following the filing of this document:

____

____

B6J (Official Form 6J) (12/07)

In re ______________________________, Case No. ______________________,
Debtor (if known)

SCHEDULE J—CURRENT EXPENDITURES OF INDIVIDUAL DEBTOR(S)

Complete this schedule by estimating the average or projected monthly expenses of the debtor and the debtor's family at time case filed. Prorate any payments made bi-weekly, quarterly, semi-annually, or annually to show monthly rate. The average monthly expenses calculated on this form may differ from the deductions from income allowed on Form 22A or 22C.

☐ Check this box if a joint petition is filed and debtor's spouse maintains a separate household. Complete a separate schedule of expenditures labeled "Spouse."

1. Rent or home mortgage payment (include lot rented for mobile home) $__________
   a. Are real estate taxes included? Yes ________ No ________
   b. Is property insurance included? Yes ________ No ________
2. Utilities: a. Electricity and heating fuel $__________
   b. Water and sewer $__________
   c. Telephone $__________
   d. Other ______________________ $__________
3. Home maintenance (repairs and upkeep) $__________
4. Food $__________
5. Clothing $__________
6. Laundry and dry cleaning $__________
7. Medical and dental expenses $__________
8. Transportation (not including car payments) $__________
9. Recreation, clubs and entertainment, newspapers, magazines, etc. $__________
10. Charitable contributions $__________
11. Insurance (not deducted from wages or included in home mortgage payments)
    a. Homeowner's or renter's $__________
    b. Life $__________
    c. Health $__________
    d. Auto $__________
    e. Other ______________________ $__________
12. Taxes (not deducted from wages or included in home mortgage payments) (Specify) ______________________ $__________
13. Installment payments: (In chapter 11, 12, and 13 cases, do not list payments to be included in the plan)
    a. Auto $__________
    b. Other ______________________ $__________
    c. Other ______________________ $__________
14. Alimony, maintenance, and support paid to others $__________
15. Payments for support of additional dependents not living at your home $__________
16. Regular expenses from operation of business, profession, or farm (attach detailed statement) $__________
17. Other ______________________ $__________
18. AVERAGE MONTHLY EXPENSES (Total lines 1-17. Report also on Summary of Schedules and, if applicable, on the Statistical Summary of Certain Liabilities and Related Data.) $__________
19. Describe any increase or decrease in expenditures reasonably anticipated to occur within the year following the filing of this document:
    ____
20. STATEMENT OF MONTHLY NET INCOME
    a. Average monthly income from Line 15 of Schedule I $__________
    b. Average monthly expenses from Line 18 above $__________
    c. Monthly net income (a. minus b.) $__________

B6 Declaration (Official Form 6—Declaration) (12/07)

In re ______________________________, Case No. ______________________________
Debtor (if known)

DECLARATION CONCERNING DEBTOR'S SCHEDULES

DECLARATION UNDER PENALTY OF PERJURY BY INDIVIDUAL DEBTOR

I declare under penalty of perjury that I have read the foregoing summary and schedules, consisting of ______ sheets, and that they are true and correct to the best of my knowledge, information, and belief.

Date: ______________________________ Signature: ______________________________
Debtor

Date: ______________________________ Signature: ______________________________
(Joint Debtor, if any)

[If joint case, both spouses must sign.]

DECLARATION AND SIGNATURE OF NON-ATTORNEY BANKRUPTCY PETITION PREPARER (See 11 U.S.C. § 110)

I declare under penalty of perjury that: (1) I am a bankruptcy petition preparer as defined in 11 U.S.C. § 110; (2) I prepared this document for compensation and have provided the debtor with a copy of this document and the notices and information required under 11 U.S.C. §§ 110(b), 110(h) and 342(b); and, (3) if rules or guidelines have been promulgated pursuant to 11 U.S.C. § 110(h) setting a maximum fee for services chargeable by bankruptcy petition preparers, I have given the debtor notice of the maximum amount before preparing any document for filing for a debtor or accepting any fee from the debtor, as required by that section.

______________________________ ______________________________
Printed or Typed Name and Title, if any, of Bankruptcy Petition Preparer — Social Security No. *(Required by 11 U.S.C. § 110.)*

If the bankruptcy petition preparer is not an individual, state the name, title (if any), address, and social security number of the officer, principal, responsible person, or partner who signs this document.

____

____

____
Address

X______________________________ ______________________________
Signature of Bankruptcy Petition Preparer — Date

Names and Social Security numbers of all other individuals who prepared or assisted in preparing this document, unless the bankruptcy petition preparer is not an individual:

If more than one person prepared this document, attach additional signed sheets conforming to the appropriate Official Form for each person.

A bankruptcy petition preparer's failure to comply with the provisions of title 11 and the Federal Rules of Bankruptcy Procedure may result in fines or imprisonment or both. 11 U.S.C. § 110; 18 U.S.C. § 156.

DECLARATION UNDER PENALTY OF PERJURY ON BEHALF OF A CORPORATION OR PARTNERSHIP

I, the ______________________ [the president or other officer or an authorized agent of the corporation or a member or an authorized agent of the partnership] of the ______________________ [corporation or partnership] named as debtor in this case, declare under penalty of perjury that I have read the foregoing summary and schedules, consisting of _____ sheets *(total shown on summary page plus 1)*, and that they are true and correct to the best of my knowledge, information, and belief.

Date ______________

Signature:______________________________

____

[Print or type name of individual signing on behalf of debtor.]

[An individual signing on behalf of a partnership or corporation must indicate position or relationship to debtor.]

Penalty for making a false statement or concealing property: Fine of up to $500,000 or imprisonment for up to 5 years or both. 18 U.S.C. §§ 152 and 3571.

(Added Aug. 1, 1991, and amended Mar. 16, 1993; Mar. 1995; Oct. 1, 1997; April 1, 1998; Dec. 1, 2003; April 1, 2004; Apr. 25, 2005, eff. Dec. 1, 2005; Aug. 11, 2005, eff. Oct. 17, 2005; Oct. 11, 2006; April 1, 2007; Dec. 2007.)

ADVISORY COMMITTEE NOTES

1991 Enactment

These schedules shall be used to comply with § 521(1) of the Code and Rule 1007(b). Schedules A, B, D, E, and F constitute the schedule of assets and liabilities. Schedules I and J constitute a schedule of current income and current expenditures for individual and joint debtors. Two new schedules have been created, Schedule G—Executory Contracts and Unexpired Leases, and Schedule H—Codebtors.

The order of the schedules has been arranged with the summary sheet in front and with the schedules of assets appearing first, followed by the schedules of liabilities. This structure corresponds to the customary pattern by which trustees and creditors review these documents and to the format of the accounting profession for balance sheets.

The schedules require a complete listing of assets and liabilities but leave many of the details to investigation by the trustee. Instructions in the former schedules to provide details concerning "written instruments" relating to the debtor's property or debts have been deleted. Section 521(3) of the Code requires the debtor to cooperate with the trustee, who can administer the estate more effectively by requesting any documents from the debtor rather than relying on descriptions in the schedules which may prove to be inaccurate.

Leasehold interests in both real and personal property are to be reported in Schedule G—Executory Contracts and Unexpired Leases. This information should not be repeated in the schedules of assets.

Generally in these schedules, a creditor's claim will be listed only once, even if the claim is secured only in part, or is entitled only in part to priority under § 507(a) of the Code, with the remainder of the claim to be treated as a general unsecured claim. For example, a partially secured creditor whose claim is reported in Schedule D—Creditors Holding Secured Claims will be listed together with the value of the property securing the claim and a notation of the amount of any unsecured portion of the claim. Information concerning the unsecured portion should not be repeated in Schedule F—Creditors Holding Nonpriority Unsecured Claims. Any resulting overstatement of the amounts owed on secured and priority claims as reported on the summary sheet is offset by a corresponding understatement of the amount owed on unsecured claims.

If a debtor has no property or no creditors in a particular category, an affirmative statement to that effect is required. Married debtors should indicate whether property is jointly or separately owned and whether spouses are jointly or separately liable for debts, using the columns provided in the schedules.

Former "Schedule B–3. Property not otherwise scheduled," has been deleted and its two questions moved. Schedule B—Personal Property now includes at item 33, "Other personal property of any kind not already listed." The only other question on former Schedule B–3 concerned assignments for the benefit of creditors; it has been moved to the Statement of Financial Affairs.

Schedule A—Real Property. Instructions at the top of the form indicate the scope of the interests in property to be reported on the schedule. Leasehold interests of the debtor are not reported here but on the Schedule of Executory Contracts and Unexpired Leases. The trustee will request copies of deeds or other instruments necessary to the administration of the estate.

Schedule B—Personal Property. This schedule is to be used for reporting all of the debtor's interests in personal property except leases and executory contracts, which are to be listed on the Schedule of Executory Contracts and Unexpired Leases. Several new categories of property have been added to the schedule, *i.e.*, aircraft, and interests in IRA, ERISA, Keogh, or other pension or profit-sharing plans. To minimize the potential for concealment of assets, the debtor must declare whether the debtor has any property in each category on the schedule. The trustee can request copies of any documents concerning the debtor's property necessary to the administration of the estate.

Schedule C—Property Claimed as Exempt. The form of the schedule has been modified to eliminate duplication of information provided elsewhere. The location of property, for example, which formerly was required here, is disclosed in the schedules of real and personal property. The requirement that the debtor state the present use of the property also has been eliminated as best left to inquiry by the trustee. Exemptions in some states are granted by constitutional provisions; accordingly, the requirement that the debtor state the "statute" creating an exemption has been changed to request a statement of the relevant "law."

This schedule adds a new requirement that the debtor state the market value of the property in addition to the amount claimed as exempt.

Schedule D—Creditors Holding Secured Claims. Schedules D, E, and F have been redesigned with address boxes sized to match the number of characters which can be accommodated on the computerized noticing systems used by the courts. The size also closely approximates that of standard mailing labels. Space is designated at the top of the box for the debtor's account number with the creditor. The design of the form is intended to reduce the volume of misdirected creditor mail.

The form requires the debtor to state affirmatively that a claim is disputed, unliquidated, or contingent. The existence of any type of codebtor is to be disclosed, but details are to be provided in Schedule H, as they are not needed here. Duplication of information also has been kept to a minimum by deleting requests that the debtor indicate on this schedule whether a debt has been reduced to judgment and the date on which a creditor repossessed any collateral. Requests for details concerning negotiable instruments and the consideration for a claim, formerly part of the schedule, are left to the trustee's inquiries.

Schedule E—Creditors Holding Unsecured Priority Claims. The schedule lists all of the types of claims entitled to priority and requires the debtor to indicate the existence of claims in each category. Continuation sheets are provided. The type of priority claim is to be noted at the top of the continuation sheet, and each type must be reported on a separate sheet. This schedule also requires the debtor to indicate the existence of any codebtors. As in Schedule D—Creditors Holding Secured Claims, requests for information concerning judgments and negotiable instruments have been deleted.

Schedule F—Creditors Holding Unsecured Nonpriority Claims. This schedule has been revised generally in conformity with the other schedules of creditors. If a claim is subject to setoff, the debtor is required to so state.

Schedule G—Executory Contracts and Unexpired Leases. Rule 1007(b) requires the debtor to file a schedule of executory contracts and unexpired leases, unless the court orders otherwise. All unexpired leases of either real or personal property are to be reported on this schedule. The schedule also requires the debtor to disclose specific information to assist the trustee in identifying leases which must be assumed within 60 days after the order for relief or be deemed rejected under § 365(d) of the Code.

Schedule H—Schedule of Codebtors. This schedule is designed to provide the trustee and creditors with information about codebtors of all types other than spouses in joint cases. The completed schedule provides information concerning non-debtor parties, such as guarantors and non-debtor spouses having an interest in property as tenants by the entirety. In chapter 12 and chapter 13 cases, the completed schedule also indicates those persons who may be entitled to certain protections from creditor action under §§ 1201 and 1301 of the Code.

Schedule I—Schedule of Current Income of Individual Debtor(s) and Schedule J—Schedule of Current Expenditures of Individual Debtor(s). Former Official Form No. 6A has been divided into a schedule of current income and a separate schedule of current expenditures. The language is substantially the same as in former Official Form No. 6A. In light of the abrogation of Official Form No. 10, the Chapter 13 Statement, style changes have been made so that these schedules can be used by individual and joint debtors in all chapters.

1993 Amendment

Schedule E (Creditors Holding Unsecured Priority Claims) has been changed to conform to the statutory amendment that added subsection (a)(8) to § 507 of the Code. Pub.L. No. 101–647, (Crime Control Act of 1990), added the new subsection, which had the effect of creating an eighth priority for claims of certain governmental units based on commitments to maintain the capital of an insured depository institution.

1995 Amendment

Schedule E—Creditors Holding Unsecured Priority Claims is amended to add the new seventh priority afforded to debts for alimony, maintenance, or support of a spouse, former spouse, or child of the debtor by the Bankruptcy Reform Act of 1994. Statutory references are amended to conform to the paragraph numbers of section 507(a) of the Code as renumbered by the 1994 Act. Schedule E also is amended to add commissions owed to certain independent sales representatives and to raise the maximum dollar amounts for certain priorities in accordance with amendments made by the 1994 Act to section 507(a) of the Code. The 1994 Act also amended section 104 of the Code to provide for future adjustment of the maximum dollar amounts specified in section 507(a) to be made by administrative action at three-year intervals to reflect changes in the consumer price index. Schedule E is amended to give notice that these dollar amounts are subject to change without formal amendment to the official form.

The Schedules are a "document for filing" that may be prepared by a "bankruptcy petition preparer" as defined in 11 U.S.C. § 110, which was added to the Code by the 1994 Act; accordingly, a signature line for such preparer is added. In addition to signing, a bankruptcy petition preparer is required by section 110 to disclose the information requested.

1997 Amendment

The form is amended to add to the column labels a reference to community liability for claims. The amendment is technical and corrects an editorial oversight.

2003 Amendment

The instructions to Schedule D (Creditors Holding Secured Claims), Schedule E (Creditors Holding Unsecured Priority Claims), and Schedule F (Creditors Holding Unsecured Nonpriority Claims) are amended to inform the debtor that the debtor's account number with a listed creditor is useful to the trustee and to the creditor and should be provided whenever practicable, but not require the number to be provided. Schedule I (Current Income of Individual Debtor(s)) is amended to provide greater privacy to minors and other dependents of the debtor by deleting the requirement that the debtor disclose their names. Pursuant to § 110(c) of the Bankruptcy Code, the certification by a non-attorney bankruptcy petition preparer requires a petition preparer to provide the full Social Security number of the individual who actually prepares the document.

2005 Amendment

The forms of the Schedules of Assets and Liabilities are amended to implement the provisions of the Bankruptcy Abuse Prevention and Consumer Protection Act of 2005, Pub. L. No. 109—8, 119 Stat. 23, (April 20, 2005). An amendment that directs the debtor to avoid disclosing the name of any minor child occurs in several of the schedules in conformity with § 112 which was added to the Code in 2005. Section 112 provides for the debtor to provide the name of any minor child confidentially to the court, should the trustee need the information to evaluate properly the information filed by the debtor.

The "Statistical Summary of Certain Liabilities" is added to collect information needed to prepare statistical reports required under 28 U.S.C. § 159, which was enacted as part of the 2005 Act.

Schedules A, B, C, and D are amended to delete the word "market" from the columns in which the debtor reports the value of various kinds of property. Amendments to § 506 of the Code enacted in 2005 specify that "replacement value" must be used in connection with certain property. The schedules no longer specify "market" value and permit the debtor to choose the appropriate one, whether that be replacement, market, or some other value. Valuation of property, generally, is the subject of extensive provisions in the Code, and the deletion of the word "market" from the determinations of value to be made by the debtor on the schedules is intended to remove any inference about choice of valuation standard. This deletion simply indicates that the form takes no position on which Code provision or valuation standard may be applicable in any instance.

The following paragraphs describe changes that are specific to each schedule.

Schedule B—Personal Property is amended to require the debtor to list any interests in an education IRA, as § 541(b)(5), added to the Code in 2005, makes special provision for them. The schedule also is amended to require the debtor to disclose the existence of any customer lists or other compilations containing personally identifiable information provided by an individual to the debtor in connection with obtaining a product or service from the debtor for personal, family, or household purposes. This amendment implements § 332, which was added to the Code in 2005.

Schedule C—Property Claimed as Exempt is amended to delete descriptive information concerning the length of domicile required for the debtor to qualify to claim certain exemptions. Any summary of the amendments enacted in 2005 to § 522 of the Code concerning these requirements might inadvertently cause the debtor to lose important rights. Accordingly, the form now directs the debtor to indicate whether exemptions are being claimed under § 522(b)(2) or § 522(b)(3) and whether the debtor claims a homestead exemption that exceeds $125,000.

Schedule E—Creditors Holding Unsecured Priority Claims is amended to implement the changes in priority to which a claim may be entitled under 11 U.S.C. § 507 as amended by the 2005 Act and to add the new priority included in the Reform Act for claims for death or personal injury while the debtor was intoxicated. "Subtotal" and "Total" boxes have been added to the column labeled "Amount Entitled to Priority" to assist the individual debtor to complete the Means Test form.

Schedule G—Executory Contracts and Unexpired Leases is amended by deleting the note to the debtor advising that parties listed on this schedule may not receive notice of the filing of the bankruptcy case unless they also are listed on one of the schedules of liabilities. The better practice is for all parties to transactions with the debtor to receive notice of the filing of the case, and an amendment to Rule 1007 requiring the debtor to provide a mailing list that includes these parties is scheduled to take effect December 1, 2005.

Schedule H—Codebtors is amended to add specifics about community property jurisdictions in connection with the requirement to provide the name of any spouse of a debtor who resides or resided in a community property jurisdiction. This amendment also mirrors amendments made in 1997 to Official Form 7, the Statement of Financial Affairs, and will assure that these codebtors receive notice of the filing of the bankruptcy case. The form also is amended to extend from six years to eight years the time period for which this information is reported pursuant to the 2005 amendments to § 727(a)(8) of the Code.

Schedule I—Current Income of Individual Debtor(s) is amended to require the income of a nondebtor spouse to be reported in cases filed under chapters 7 and 11. Line numbers have been added to assist the debtor in calculating and reporting totals. A new subtotal line for income from sources other than as an employee and a new "total monthly income" line provide for this form to be used in conjunction with Schedule J to satisfy the requirements of § 521(a)(1)(B)(v), which was added to the Code in 2005. The form also has been revised to provide the statement concerning any anticipated increase or decrease in income required in § 521(a)(1)(B)(vi), which also was added to the Code in 2005.

Schedule J—Current Expenditures of Individual Debtor(s). A direction has been added to require the debtor to report any increase or decrease in expenses anticipated to occur within the year following the filing of the document, as required by § 521(a)(1)(B)(vi), which was added to the Code in 2005. The form also is amended to provide, in conjunction with Schedule I, a statement of monthly net income, itemized to show how the amount is calculated, as required by § 522(a)(1)(B)(v), which was added to the Code in 2005.

Declaration Concerning Debtor's Schedules. The declaration by a non-attorney bankruptcy petition preparer is amended to include material mandated by § 110 of the Code as amended in 2005.

2006 Amendments

In order to comply fully with the statistical reporting requirements of 28 U.S.C. § 159, which was enacted as part of the 2005 Act and takes effect in October 2006, the "Statistical Summary of Certain Liabilities" is renamed "Statistical Summary of Certain Liabilities and Related Data," and additional information is required to be stated there. Collecting in one place the bulk of the information to be used in the reports required under 28 U.S.C. § 159 will assist the courts and the Director of the Administrative Office of the United States Courts to fulfill their statutory responsibilities.

Schedule D is amended to provide for creating a total of any unsecured amounts (amounts that exceed the value of the collateral) owed to creditors holding secured claims, and for stating this amount on the Statistical Summary of Certain Liabilities and Related Data.

Schedule E is amended to provide for creating totals of the amounts entitled to priority and of any amounts that exceed the statutory limits on certain priorities and to direct the debtor to report these amounts on the Statistical Summary of Certain Liabilities and Related Data. Schedule F is amended to direct the debtor to report the total of this schedule both on the Summary of Schedules and on the Statistical Summary of Certain Liabilities.

The statistical reports required under 28 U.S.C. § 159 must include "the current monthly income, average income, and average expenses" of individual debtors with primarily consumer debts as reported on the schedules filed by those debtors. Accordingly, Schedules I and J, on which debtors already are directed to report average income and average expenses are amended to label the totals arrived at by completing the schedules as " average monthly income" and "average monthly expenses." These amendments make no substantive changes, simply conforming the terminology on these schedules to that used in § 159.

The amount of the debtor's current monthly income, which also is required by § 159, is derived from Official Forms 22A, 22B, or 22C, depending on the chapter under which the debtor files. This amount is included on the Statistical Summary of Certain Liabilities and Related Data as a convenience to make reports under § 159 easier to compile.

The declaration Concerning Debtor's Schedules is amended in the section designated for signing and verifying by an individual or joint debtor. The amendment accommodates the requirement that individual debtors must complete both the Summary of Schedules and the Statistical Summary of Certain Liabilities and Related Data by directing the debtor to state number of pages being verified as the number of sheets in the completed schedules "plus 2."

2005–2007 Amendments

(The 2005–2007 Committee Note incorporates Committee Notes previously published in 2005 and 2006.)

The forms of the Schedules of Assets and Liabilities are amended to implement the provisions of the Bankruptcy Abuse Prevention and Consumer Protection Act of 2005, Pub. L. No. 109–8, 119 Stat. 23, (April 20, 2005) ("BAPCPA"). An amendment that directs the debtor to avoid disclosing the name and address of any minor child occurs in Schedules B, D, E, F, G, and H in conformity with § 112 which was added to the Code in 2005. Section 112 provides for the debtor to furnish the name of any minor child confidentially to the court, should the trustee need the information to evaluate properly the information filed by the debtor. In addition, those schedules are amended to add to the reference to Rule 1007(m), with respect to a minor child, a direction to include for noticing purposes the name, address, and legal relationship to the child of "a person described" in that rule. Rule 1007(m) requires the person named to be someone on whom process would be served in an adversary proceeding against the child.

The "Statistical Summary of Certain Liabilities and Related Data" is added to collect from individual debtors with primarily consumer debts the information needed to prepare statistical reports required under 28 U.S.C. § 159, which was enacted as part of BAPCPA. Collecting the bulk of the information to be used in these statistical reports in the Summary of Schedules and the statistical summary will assist the courts and the Director of the Administrative

Office to fulfil their statutory responsibilities. Schedules D and E are amended to provide additional totals and, together with Schedule F, to direct debtors who must complete statistical summary to report total amounts there. Similarly, Schedules I and J are amended to conform their terminology to that used in 28 U.S.C. § 159 and direct debtors who must complete the statistical summary to report the specific amounts there.

Schedules A, B, C, and D are amended to delete the word "market" from the columns in which the debtor reports the value of various kinds of property. Amendments to § 506 of the Code enacted in 2005 specify that "replacement value" must be used in connection with certain property. The schedules no longer specify "market" value and permit the debtor to choose the appropriate one, whether that be replacement, market, or some other value. Valuation of property, generally, is the subject of extensive provisions in the Code, and the deletion of the word "market" from the determination of value to be made by the debtor on the schedules is intended to remove any inference about choice of valuation standard. This deletion simply indicates that the form takes no position on which Code provision or valuation standard may be applicable in any particular instance.

The following paragraphs describe changes that are specific to each schedule:

Schedule B—Personal Property is amended to require the debtor to list any interests in an education IRA, because § 541(b)(5), added to the Code in 2005, makes special provision for them. The schedule is also amended to require the debtor to disclose the existence of any customer lists or other compilations containing personally identifiable information provided by an individual to the debtor in connection with obtaining a product or service from the debtor for personal, family, or household purposes. This amendment implements § 332, which was added to the Code by BAPCPA in 2005.

Schedule C—Property claimed as Exempt is amended to delete descriptive information concerning the length of domicile required for the debtor to qualify to claim certain exemptions. Any summary of the BAPCPA amendments to § 522 of the Code concerning these requirements might inadvertently cause the debtor to lose important rights. Accordingly, the form now directs the debtor to indicate whether exemptions are being claimed under § 522(b)(2) or § 522(b)(3) and whether the debtor claims a homestead exemption that exceeds $136,875.

Schedule D—Creditors Holding Secured Claims is amended to provide for creating a total of any unsecured amounts (amounts that exceed the value of the collateral) owed to creditors holding secured claims. In addition to facilitating statistical reporting, providing a breakdown of the amounts owed to creditors listed on this schedule will assist the individual debtor in completing the means test calculation under § 707(b)(2)(A)(i) of the Code.

Schedule E—Creditors Holding Unsecured Priority Claims is amended to implement the changes in priority to which a claim may be entitled under 11 U.S.C. § 507 as amended by BAPCPA and to add the new priority included in the 2005 Act for claims for death or personal injury while the debtor was intoxicated. "Subtotal" and "Total" boxes have been added to the columns labeled "Amount Not Entitled to Priority" for statistical reporting purposes and to assist the individual debtor in completing the means test calculation under § 707(b)(2)(A)(i) of the Code.

Schedule H—Codebtors is amended to add specifics about community property jurisdictions in connection with the requirement to provide the name of any spouse of a debtor who resides or resided in a community property jurisdiction. This amendment also mirrors amendments made in 1997 to Official Form 7, the Statement of Financial Affairs, and will assure that these codebtors receive notice of the filing of the bankruptcy case. The form also is amended to extend from six years to eight years the time period for which this information is reported pursuant to the 2005 amendments to § 727(a)(8) of the Code

Schedule I—Current Income of Individual Debtor(s) is amended to make it clear that "every" married debtor must either provide income information for both spouses, unless the spouses are separated and a joint petition is not filed. The description of the income to be reported is revised to clarify that the purpose of this schedule is to obtain information about actual income on the date the bankruptcy is filed and which a debtor reasonably expects in the future in contrast to the debtor's "current monthly income" as defined in § 101(10A) and reported on Form 22A, 22B, or 22C. And a statement included at the top of the form also explains that the income calculated this form may be different than the current monthly income. Line numbers have been added to assist the debtor in calculating and reporting totals. A new subtotal line for income from sources other than as an employee and a new "average monthly income" line will enable this form to be used in conjunction with Schedule J to satisfy the requirements of § 521(a)(1)(B)(v), which was added to the Code by BAPCPA. New statistical reporting requirements in 28 U.S.C. § 159 also require "average monthly income". In addition, the form is revised to provide the statement concerning any anticipated increase or decrease in income required in § 521(a)(1)(B)(vi), also added to the Code in 2005.

Schedule J—Current Expenditures of Individual Debtor(s). In conjunction with amendments to Schedule I, the form is amended to provide for reporting the debtor's actual "average monthly expenses," as required by 28 U.C.S. § 159 and a statement of monthly net income, itemized to show how the amount is calculated, as required by § 522(a)(1)(B)(v), which was added to the Code by BAPCPA in 2005. In addition, line numbers have been inserted and the description of expenses revised to make it clear than the purpose of this schedule is to obtain information about a debtor's actual and reasonable foreseeable expenses on the date the bankruptcy case id filed. And a statement similar to the statement at the top of Schedule I explains that the expenses calculated on the form may differ from the expenses calculated on Forms 22A or 22C. A direction has been added to require the debtor to report any increase or decrease in expenses anticipated to occur within the year following the filing of the document, as required by § 521(a)(1)(B)(vi), which also was added to the Code in 2005.

Declaration Concerning Debtor's Schedules. The declaration by individual or joint debtors is amended to require the debtor to merely state the total number of pages being verified. The declaration and signature of any non-attorney bankruptcy petition preparer is amended to include material mandated by § 110 of the Code as amended in 2005.

HISTORICAL NOTES

Effective and Applicability Provisions

1998 Acts. Memorandum amending official forms dated March 17, 1998, effective April 1, 1998, and applicable to cased filed on of after such date.

1997 Acts. Order amending official forms dated Oct. 1, 1997, effective immediately, with mandatory use starting March 1, 1998.

Form 7. Statement of Financial Affairs

B7 (Official Form 7) (12/07)

UNITED STATES BANKRUPTCY COURT

_________ DISTRICT OF _________

In re:______________________________, Case No.____________________
Debtor (If known)

STATEMENT OF FINANCIAL AFFAIRS

This statement is to be completed by every debtor. Spouses filing a joint petition may file a single statement on which the information for both spouses is combined. If the case is filed under chapter 12 or chapter 13, a married debtor must furnish information for both spouses whether or not a joint petition is filed, unless the spouses are separated and a joint petition is not filed. An individual debtor engaged in business as a sole proprietor, partner, family farmer, or self-employed professional, should provide the information requested on this statement concerning all such activities as well as the individual's personal affairs. To indicate payments, transfers and the like to minor children, state the child's initials and the name and address of the child's parent or guardian, such as "A.B., a minor child, by John Doe, guardian." Do not disclose the child's name. See, 11 U.S.C. § 112 and Fed. R. Bankr. P. 1007(m).

Questions 1–18 are to be completed by all debtors. Debtors that are or have been in business, as defined below, also must complete Questions 19–25. **If the answer to an applicable question is "None," mark the box labeled "None."** If additional space is needed for the answer to any question, use and attach a separate sheet properly identified with the case name, case number (if known), and the number of the question.

DEFINITIONS

"In business." A debtor is "in business" for the purpose of this form if the debtor is a corporation or partnership. An individual debtor is "in business" for the purpose of this form if the debtor is or has been, within six years immediately preceding the filing of this bankruptcy case, any of the following: an officer, director, managing executive, or owner of 5 percent or more of the voting or equity securities of a corporation; a partner, other than a limited partner, of a partnership; a sole proprietor or self-employed full-time or part-time. An individual debtor also may be "in business" for the purpose of this form if the debtor engages in a trade, business, or other activity, other than as an employee, to supplement income from the debtor's primary employment.

"Insider." The term "insider" includes but is not limited to: relatives of the debtor; general partners of the debtor and their relatives; corporations of which the debtor is an officer, director, or person in control; officers, directors, and any owner of 5 percent or more of the voting or equity securities of a corporate debtor and their relatives; affiliates of the debtor and insiders of such affiliates; any managing agent of the debtor. 11 U.S.C. § 101.

---

1. Income from employment or operation of business

None ☐ State the gross amount of income the debtor has received from employment, trade, or profession, or from operation of the debtor's business, including part-time activities either as an employee or in independent trade or business, from the beginning of this calendar year to the date this case was commenced. State also the gross amounts received during the **two years** immediately preceding this calendar year. (A debtor that maintains, or has maintained, financial records on the basis of a fiscal rather than a calendar year may report fiscal year income.

Identify the beginning and ending dates of the debtor's fiscal year.) If a joint petition is filed, state income for each spouse separately. (Married debtors filing under chapter 12 or chapter 13 must state income of both spouses whether or not a joint petition is filed, unless the spouses are separated and a joint petition is not filed.)

AMOUNT SOURCE

---

2. Income other than from employment or operation of business

None ☐ State the amount of income received by the debtor other than from employment, trade, profession, operation of the debtor's business during the **two years** immediately preceding the commencement of this case. Give particulars. If a joint petition is filed, state income for each spouse separately. (Married debtors filing under chapter 12 or chapter 13 must state income for each spouse whether or not a joint petition is filed, unless the spouses are separated and a joint petition is not filed.)

AMOUNT SOURCE

---

3. Payments to creditors

Complete a. or b., as appropriate, and c.

None ☐ a. *Individual or joint debtor(s) with primarily consumer debts:* List all payments on loans, installment purchases of goods or services, and other debts to any creditor made within **90 days** immediately preceding the commencement of this case unless the aggregate value of all property that constitutes or is affected by such transfer is not less than $600. Indicate with an asterisk (*) any payments that were made to a creditor on account of a domestic support obligation or as part of an alternative repayment schedule under a plan by an approved nonprofit budgeting and credit counseling agency. (Married debtors filing under chapter 12 or chapter 13 must include payments by either or both spouses whether or not a joint petition is filed, unless the spouses are separated and a joint petition is not filed.)

NAME AND ADDRESS OF CREDITOR	DATES OF PAYMENTS	AMOUNT PAID	AMOUNT STILL OWING

None ☐ b. *Debtor whose debts are not primarily consumer debts:* List each payment or other transfer to any creditor made within **90** days immediately preceding the commencement of the case unless the aggregate value of all property that constitutes or is affected by such transfer is not less than $5,475. If the debtor is an individual, indicate with an asterisk (*) any payments that were made to a creditor on account of a domestic support obligation or as part of an alternative repayment schedule under a plan by an approved nonprofit budgeting and credit counseling agency. (Married debtors filing under chapter 12 or chapter 13 must include payments and other transfers by either or both spouses whether or not a joint petition is filed, unless the spouses are separated and a joint petition is not filed.)

Complete Annotation Materials, see Title 11 U.S.C.A.

NAME AND ADDRESS OF CREDITOR	DATES OF PAYMENTS/ TRANSFERS	AMOUNT PAID OR VALUE OF TRANSFERS	AMOUNT STILL OWING

None ☐ c. *All debtors:* List all payments made within **one year** immediately preceding the commencement of this case to or for the benefit of creditors who are or were insiders. (Married debtors filing under chapter 12 or chapter 13 must include payments by either or both spouses whether or not a joint petition is filed, unless the spouses are separated and a joint petition is not filed.)

NAME AND ADDRESS OF CREDITOR AND RELATIONSHIP TO DEBTOR	DATE OF PAYMENT	AMOUNT PAID	AMOUNT STILL OWING

4. Suits and administrative proceedings, executions, garnishments and attachments

None ☐ a. List all suits and administrative proceedings to which the debtor is or was a party within **one year** immediately preceding the filing of this bankruptcy case. (Married debtors filing under chapter 12 or chapter 13 must include information concerning either or both spouses whether or not a joint petition is filed, unless the spouses are separated and a joint petition is not filed.)

CAPTION OF SUIT AND CASE NUMBER	NATURE OF PROCEEDING	COURT OR AGENCY AND LOCATION	STATUS OR DISPOSITION

None ☐ b. Describe all property that has been attached, garnished or seized under any legal or equitable process within **one year** immediately preceding the commencement of this case. (Married debtors filing under chapter 12 or chapter 13 must include information concerning property of either or both spouses whether or not a joint petition is filed, unless the spouses are separated and a joint petition is not filed.)

NAME AND ADDRESS OF PERSON FOR WHOSE BENEFIT PROPERTY WAS SEIZED	DATE OF SEIZURE	DESCRIPTION AND VALUE OF PROPERTY

5. Repossessions, foreclosures and returns

None ☐ List all property that has been repossessed by a creditor, sold at a foreclosure sale, transferred through a deed in lieu of foreclosure or returned to the seller, within **one year** immediately preceding the commencement of this case. (Married debtors filing under chapter 12 or chapter 13 must include information concerning property of either or both spouses whether or not a joint petition is filed, unless the spouses are separated and a joint petition is not filed.)

NAME AND ADDRESS OF CREDITOR OR SELLER	DATE OF REPOSSESSION, FORECLOSURE SALE, TRANSFER OR RETURN	DESCRIPTION AND VALUE OF PROPERTY

---

6. Assignments and receiverships

None ☐ a. Describe any assignment of property for the benefit of creditors made within **120 days** immediately preceding the commencement of this case. (Married debtors filing under chapter 12 or chapter 13 must include any assignment by either or both spouses whether or not a joint petition is filed, unless the spouses are separated and a joint petition is not filed.)

NAME AND ADDRESS OF ASSIGNEE	DATE OF ASSIGNMENT	TERMS OF ASSIGNMENT OR SETTLEMENT

None ☐ b. List all property which has been in the hands of a custodian, receiver, or court-appointed official within **one year** immediately preceding the commencement of this case. (Married debtors filing under chapter 12 or chapter 13 must include information concerning property of either or both spouses whether or not a joint petition is filed, unless the spouses are separated and a joint petition is not filed.)

NAME AND ADDRESS OF CUSTODIAN	NAME AND LOCATION OF COURT CASE TITLE & NUMBER	DATE OF ORDER	DESCRIPTION AND VALUE OF PROPERTY

---

7. Gifts

None ☐ List all gifts or charitable contributions made within **one year** immediately preceding the commencement of this case except ordinary and usual gifts to family members aggregating less than $200 in value per individual family member and charitable contributions aggregating less than $100 per recipient. (Married debtors filing under chapter 12 or chapter 13 must include gifts or contributions by either or both spouses whether or not a joint petition is filed, unless the spouses are separated and a joint petition is not filed.)

NAME AND ADDRESS OF PERSON OR ORGANIZATION	RELATIONSHIP TO DEBTOR, IF ANY	DATE OF GIFT	DESCRIPTION AND VALUE OF GIFT

---

8. Losses

None ☐ List all losses from fire, theft, other casualty or gambling within **one year** immediately preceding the commencement of this case **or since the commencement of this case.** (Married debtors filing under chapter 12 or chapter 13 must include losses by either or both spouses whether or not a joint petition is filed, unless the spouses are separated and a joint petition is not filed.)

DESCRIPTION AND VALUE OF PROPERTY	DESCRIPTION OF CIRCUMSTANCES AND, IF LOSS WAS COVERED IN WHOLE OR IN PART BY INSURANCE, GIVE PARTICULARS	DATE OF LOSS

9. Payments related to debt counseling or bankruptcy

None ☐ List all payments made or property transferred by or on behalf of the debtor to any persons, including attorneys, for consultation concerning debt consolidation, relief under the bankruptcy law or preparation of a petition in bankruptcy within **one year** immediately preceding the commencement of this case.

NAME AND ADDRESS OF PAYEE	DATE OF PAYMENT, NAME OF PAYOR IF OTHER THAN DEBTOR	AMOUNT OF MONEY OR DESCRIPTION AND VALUE OF PROPERTY

10. Other transfers

None ☐ a. List all other property, other than property transferred in the ordinary course of the business or financial affairs of the debtor, transferred either absolutely or as security within **two years** immediately preceding the commencement of this case. (Married debtors filing under chapter 12 or chapter 13 must include transfers by either or both spouses whether or not a joint petition is filed, unless the spouses are separated and a joint petition is not filed.)

NAME AND ADDRESS OF TRANSFEREE, RELATIONSHIP TO DEBTOR	DATE	DESCRIBE PROPERTY TRANSFERRED AND VALUE RECEIVED

None ☐ b. List all property transferred by the debtor within **ten years** immediately preceding the commencement of this case to a self-settled trust or similar device of which the debtor is a beneficiary.

NAME OF TRUST OR OTHER DEVICE	DATES(S) OF TRANSFER(S)	AMOUNT OF MONEY OR DESCRIPTION AND VALUE OF PROPERTY OR DEBTOR'S INTEREST IN PROPERTY

11. Closed financial accounts

None ☐ List all financial accounts and instruments held in the name of the debtor or for the benefit of the debtor which were closed, sold, or otherwise transferred within **one year** immediately preceding the commencement of this case. Include checking, savings, or other financial accounts, certificates of deposit, or other instruments; shares and share accounts held in banks, credit unions, pension funds, cooperatives, associations, brokerage houses and other financial institutions.

(Married debtors filing under chapter 12 or chapter 13 must include information concerning accounts or instruments held by or for either or both spouses whether or not a joint petition is filed, unless the spouses are separated and a joint petition is not filed.)

NAME AND ADDRESS OF INSTITUTION	TYPE OF ACCOUNT, LAST FOUR DIGITS OF ACCOUNT NUMBER, AND AMOUNT OF FINAL BALANCE	AMOUNT AND DATE OF SALE OR CLOSING

12. Safe deposit boxes

None ☐ List each safe deposit or other box or depository in which the debtor has or had securities, cash, or other valuables within **one year** immediately preceding the commencement of this case. (Married debtors filing under chapter 12 or chapter 13 must include boxes or depositories of either or both spouses whether or not a joint petition is filed, unless the spouses are separated and a joint petition is not filed.)

NAME AND ADDRESS OF BANK OR OTHER DEPOSITORY	NAMES AND ADDRESSES OF THOSE WITH ACCESS TO BOX OR DEPOSITORY	DESCRIPTION OF CONTENTS	DATE OF TRANSFER OR SURRENDER, IF ANY

13. Setoffs

None ☐ List all setoffs made by any creditor, including a bank, against a debt or deposit of the debtor within **90 days** preceding the commencement of this case. (Married debtors filing under chapter 12 or chapter 13 must include information concerning either or both spouses whether or not a joint petition is filed, unless the spouses are separated and a joint petition is not filed.)

NAME AND ADDRESS OF CREDITOR	DATE OF SETOFF	AMOUNT OF SETOFF

14. Property held for another person

None ☐ List all property owned by another person that the debtor holds or controls.

NAME AND ADDRESS OF OWNER	DESCRIPTION AND VALUE OF PROPERTY	LOCATION OF PROPERTY

15. Prior address of debtor

None ☐ If debtor has moved within **three years** immediately preceding the commencement of this case, list all premises which the debtor occupied during that period and vacated prior to the commencement of this case. If a joint petition is filed, report also any separate address of either spouse.

ADDRESS	NAME USED	DATES OF OCCUPANCY

16. Spouses and Former Spouses

None ☐ If the debtor resides or resided in a community property state, commonwealth, or territory (including Alaska, Arizona, California, Idaho, Louisiana, Nevada, New Mexico, Puerto Rico, Texas, Washington, or Wisconsin) within **eight years** immediately preceding the commencement of the case, identify the name of the debtor's spouse and of any former spouse who resides or resided with the debtor in the community property state.

NAME

17. Environmental Information

For the purpose of this question, the following definitions apply:

"Environmental Law" means any federal, state, or local statute or regulation regulating pollution, contamination, releases of hazardous or toxic substances, wastes or material into the air, land, soil, surface water, groundwater, or other medium, including, but not limited to, statutes or regulations regulating the cleanup of these substances, wastes, or material.

"Site" means any location, facility, or property as defined under any Environmental Law, whether or not presently or formerly owned or operated by the debtor, including, but not limited to, disposal sites.

"Hazardous Material" means anything defined as a hazardous waste, hazardous substance, toxic substance, hazardous material, pollutant, or contaminant or similar term under an Environmental Law.

None ☐ a. List the name and address of every site for which the debtor has received notice in writing by a governmental unit that it may be liable or potentially liable under or in violation of an Environmental Law. Indicate the governmental unit, the date of the notice, and, if known, the Environmental Law:

SITE NAME AND ADDRESS	NAME AND ADDRESS OF GOVERNMENTAL UNIT	DATE OF NOTICE	ENVIRONMENTAL LAW

None ☐ b. List the name and address of every site for which the debtor provided notice to a governmental unit of a release of Hazardous Material. Indicate the governmental unit to which the notice was sent and the date of the notice.

SITE NAME AND ADDRESS	NAME AND ADDRESS OF GOVERNMENTAL UNIT	DATE OF NOTICE	ENVIRONMENTAL LAW

None ☐ c. List all judicial or administrative proceedings, including settlements or orders, under any Environmental Law with respect to which the debtor is or was a party. Indicate the name and address of the governmental unit that is or was a party to the proceeding, and the docket number.

NAME AND ADDRESS OF GOVERNMENTAL UNIT	DOCKET NUMBER	STATUS OR DISPOSITION

18. Nature, location and name of business

None ☐ a. *If the debtor is an individual*, list the names, addresses, taxpayer identification numbers, nature of the businesses, and beginning and ending dates of all businesses in which the debtor was an officer, director, partner, or managing executive of a corporation, partner in a partnership, sole proprietor, or was self-employed in a trade, profession, or other activity either full- or part-time within **six years** immediately preceding the commencement of this case, or in which the debtor owned 5 percent or more of the voting or equity securities within **six years** immediately preceding the commencement of this case.

If the debtor is a partnership, list the names, addresses, taxpayer identification numbers, nature of the businesses, and beginning and ending dates of all businesses in which the debtor was a partner or owned 5 percent or more of the voting or equity securities, within **six years** immediately preceding the commencement of this case.

If the debtor is a corporation, list the names, addresses, taxpayer identification numbers, nature of the businesses, and beginning and ending dates of all businesses in which the debtor was a partner or owned 5 percent or more of the voting or equity securities within **six years** immediately preceding the commencement of this case.

NAME	LAST FOUR DIGITS OF SOCIAL-SECURITY OR OTHER INDIVIDUAL TAXPAYER–I.D. NO. (ITIN)/ COMPLETE EIN	ADDRESS	NATURE OF BUSINESS	BEGINNING AND ENDING DATES

None ☐ b. Identify any business listed in response to subdivision a., above, that is "single asset real estate" as defined in 11 U.S.C. § 101.

NAME	ADDRESS

The following questions are to be completed by every debtor that is a corporation or partnership and by any individual debtor who is or has been, within **six years** immediately preceding the commencement of this case, any of the following: an officer, director, managing executive, or owner of more than 5 percent of the voting or equity securities of a corporation; a partner, other than a limited partner, of a partnership, a sole proprietor, or self-employed in a trade, profession, or other activity, either full- or part-time.

*(An individual or joint debtor should complete this portion of the statement **only** if the debtor is or has been in business, as defined above, within six years immediately preceding the commencement of this case. A debtor who has not been in business within those six years should go directly to the signature page.)*

19. Books, records and financial statements

None ☐ a. List all bookkeepers and accountants who within **two years** immediately preceding the filing of this bankruptcy case kept or supervised the keeping of books of account and records of the debtor.

NAME AND ADDRESS	DATES SERVICES RENDERED

None ☐ b. List all firms or individuals who within **two years** immediately preceding the filing of this bankruptcy case have audited the books of account and records, or prepared a financial statement of the debtor.

NAME	ADDRESS	DATES SERVICES RENDERED

None ☐ c. List all firms or individuals who at the time of the commencement of this case were in possession of the books of account and records of the debtor. If any of the books of account and records are not available, explain.

NAME	ADDRESS

None ☐ d. List all financial institutions, creditors and other parties, including mercantile and trade agencies, to whom a financial statement was issued by the debtor within **two years** immediately preceding the commencement of this case.

NAME AND ADDRESS	DATE ISSUED

20. Inventories

None ☐ a. List the dates of the last two inventories taken of your property, the name of the person who supervised the taking of each inventory, and the dollar amount and basis of each inventory.

DATE OF INVENTORY	INVENTORY SUPERVISOR	DOLLAR AMOUNT OF INVENTORY (Specify cost, market or other basis)

None ☐ b. List the name and address of the person having possession of the records of each of the two inventories reported in a., above.

DATE OF INVENTORY	NAME AND ADDRESSES OF CUSTODIAN OF INVENTORY RECORDS

21. Current Partners, Officers, Directors and Shareholders

None ☐ a. If the debtor is a partnership, list the nature and percentage of partnership interest of each member of the partnership.

NAME AND ADDRESS	NATURE OF INTEREST	PERCENTAGE OF INTEREST

None ☐ b. If the debtor is a corporation, list all officers and directors of the corporation, and each stockholder who directly or indirectly owns, controls, or holds 5 percent or more of the voting or equity securities of the corporation.

NAME AND ADDRESS	TITLE	NATURE AND PERCENTAGE OF STOCK OWNERSHIP

22. Former partners, officers, directors and shareholders

None ☐ a. If the debtor is a partnership, list each member who withdrew from the partnership within **one year** immediately preceding the commencement of this case.

NAME	ADDRESS	DATE OF WITHDRAWAL

None ☐ b. If the debtor is a corporation, list all officers, or directors whose relationship with the corporation terminated within **one year** immediately preceding the commencement of this case.

NAME AND ADDRESS	TITLE	DATE OF TERMINATION

23. Withdrawals from a partnership or distributions by a corporation

None ☐ If the debtor is a partnership or corporation, list all withdrawals or distributions credited or given to an insider, including compensation in any form, bonuses, loans, stock redemptions, options exercised and any other perquisite during **one year** immediately preceding the commencement of this case.

NAME & ADDRESS OF RECIPIENT, RELATIONSHIP TO DEBTOR	DATE AND PURPOSE OF WITHDRAWAL	AMOUNT OF MONEY OR DESCRIPTION AND VALUE OF PROPERTY

24. Tax Consolidation Group.

None ☐ If the debtor is a corporation, list the name and federal taxpayer identification number of the parent corporation of any consolidated group for tax purposes of which the debtor has been a member at any time within **six years** immediately preceding the commencement of the case.

NAME OF PARENT CORPORATION	TAXPAYER–IDENTIFICATION NUMBER (EIN)

25. Pension Funds.

None ☐ If the debtor is not an individual, list the name and federal taxpayer identification number of any pension fund to which the debtor, as an employer, has been responsible for contributing at any time within **six years** immediately preceding the commencement of the case.

NAME OF PENSION FUND	TAXPAYER–IDENTIFICATION NUMBER (EIN)

* * * * * *

[If completed by an individual or individual and spouse]

I declare under penalty of perjury that I have read the answers contained in the foregoing statement of financial affairs and any attachments thereto and that they are true and correct.

Date ________________ Signature of Debtor ________________________

Date ________________ Signature of Joint Debtor (if any) ________________________

[If completed on behalf of a partnership or corporation]

I, declare under penalty of perjury that I have read the answers contained in the foregoing statement of financial affairs and any attachments thereto and that they are true and correct to the best of my knowledge, information and belief.

Date ________________ Signature ________________________

____
Print Name and Title

[An individual signing on behalf of a partnership or corporation must indicate position or relationship to debtor.]

_________ continuation sheets attached

Penalty for making a false statement: Fine of up to $500,000 or imprisonment for up to 5 years, or both. 18 U.S.C. §§ 152 and 3571

DECLARATION AND SIGNATURE OF NON–ATTORNEY BANKRUPTCY PETITION PREPARER (See 11 U.S.C. § 110)

I declare under penalty of perjury that: (1) I am a bankruptcy petition preparer as defined in 11 U.S.C. § 110; (2) I prepared this document for compensation and have provided the debtor with a copy of this document and the notices and information required under 11 U.S.C. §§ 110(b), 110(h), and 342(b); and, (3) if rules or guidelines have been promulgated pursuant to 11 U.S.C. § 110(h) setting a maximum fee for services chargeable by bankruptcy petition preparers, I have given the debtor notice of the maximum amount before preparing any document for filing for a debtor or accepting any fee from the debtor, as required by that section.

________________________________ ________________

Printed or Typed Name and Title, if any, of Bankruptcy Petition Preparer — Social Security No. (Required by 11 U.S.C. § 110.)

If the bankruptcy petition preparer is not an individual, state the name, title (if any), address, and social security number of the officer, principal, responsible person, or partner who signs this document.

____

____

Address

X ________________________________ ________________

Signature of Bankruptcy Petition Preparer — Date

Names and Social Security numbers of all other individuals who prepared or assisted in preparing this document unless the bankruptcy petition preparer is not an individual:

If more than one person prepared this document, attach additional signed sheets conforming to the appropriate Official Form for each person.

A bankruptcy petition preparer's failure to comply with the provisions of title 11 and the Federal Rules of Bankruptcy Procedure may result in fines or imprisonment or both. 18 U.S.C. § 156.

(Added Aug. 1, 1991, and amended Mar. 16, 1993; Mar. 1995; Sept. 2000; Dec. 1, 2003; Aug. 11, 2005, eff. Oct. 17, 2005; April 1, 2007.)

ADVISORY COMMITTEE NOTES

1991 Enactment

This form consolidates questions from former Official Forms No. 7, No. 8, and No. 10. This form is to be completed by all debtors. An individual debtor engaged in business as a sole proprietor, partner, family farmer, or self-employed professional should provide the information requested on this statement concerning all such activities as well as the individual's personal affairs.

The Chapter 13 Statement, former Official Form No. 10, has been abrogated. Chapter 13 debtors are to complete this statement and the schedules prescribed in Official Form 6.

All questions have been converted to affirmative directions to furnish information, and each question must be answered. If the answer is "none," or the question is not applicable, the debtor is required to so state by marking the box labeled "None" provided at each question.

See Committee Note to Form 2 for a discussion of the unsworn declaration at the end of this form.

1993 Amendment

The form has been amended in two ways. In the second paragraph of the instructions, the third sentence has been deleted to clarify that only a debtor that is or has been in business as defined in the form should answer Questions 16–21. In addition, administrative proceedings have been added to the types of legal actions to be disclosed in Question 4.a.

1995 Amendment

This form is a "document for filing" that may be prepared by a "bankruptcy petition preparer" as defined in 11 U.S.C. § 110, which was added to the Code by the Bankruptcy Reform Act of 1994; accordingly, a signature line for such preparer is added. In addition to signing, a bankruptcy petition preparer is required by section 110 to disclose the information requested.

2003 Amendment

The form has been amended to require the debtor to disclose only the last four digits of the debtor's Social Security or other Taxpayer Identification number. Those four digits will provide creditors with sufficient information to identify the debtor accurately while affording greater privacy to the debtor. In addition, those items that require the listing of any account number have been amended to specify that only the last four digits must be disclosed.

Pursuant to § 110(c) of the Bankruptcy Code, the certification by a non-attorney bankruptcy petition preparer continues to require a petition preparer to provide the full Social Security number of the individual who actually prepares the document.

2005 Amendment

The form is amended in several ways to reflect changes in the Bankruptcy Code made by the Bankruptcy Abuse Prevention and Consumer Protection Act of 2005, Pub. L. No. 109–8, 119 Stat. 23 (April 20, 2005). A new sentence in the introduction advises the debtor not to disclose the name and address of any minor child.

The definition of "in business" is amended in the introductory section and in Question 1 and Question 18 to clarify that various part-time activities can result in the debtor being "in business" for purposes of the form.

Question 1 is amended to specify that, in addition to the income from the debtor's primary employment, the debtor must include income from part-time activities either as an employee or from self-employment. The debtor now also will report the source of all income from employment or operation of a business, even if there is only one source, in order to assist the trustee in reviewing the pay stubs, etc., filed by the debtor in the case.

Question 3 is amended to accommodate amendments to § 547(c) of the Code enacted in 2005 which exempt from recovery by the trustee payments by a debtor for a domestic support obligation or as part of an alternative repayment schedule negotiated by an approved nonprofit budgeting and credit counseling agency. In addition, Question 3 now requires a debtor with primarily non-consumer debts to report only those transfers that aggregate more than $5,000 to any creditor in the 90–day period prior to the filing of the petition, as a result of the addition of § 547(c)(9) to the Code in 2005.

In Question 10, the extension of the reachback period for transfers from one year to two years reflects the 2005 amendment to § 548(a)(1) of the Code to permit a trustee to avoid a fraudulent transfer made by the debtor within two years of the date of the filing of the petition. Question 10 also is amended to implement new § 548(e) added to the Code in 2005 to require the debtor to disclose all transfers to any self-settled asset protection trust within the ten years before the filing of the petition.

Question 15 is amended to extend from two years to three years the prepetition time period for which the debtor must disclose the addresses of all premises occupied by the debtor. This information will assist the trustee, the United States trustee, and the court to ascertain whether any homestead exemption asserted by the debtor is properly claimed under § 522(v)(3)(A) as amended, and §§ 522(p) and (q) as added to the Code in 2005.

The form also is amended to extend from six years to eight years the period before the filing of the petition concerning which the debtor is required to disclose the name of the debtor's spouse or of any former spouse who resides or resided with the debtor in a community property state. In addition, the certification by a non-attorney bankruptcy petition preparer is renamed a "declaration" and is amended to include material mandated by 11 U.S.C. § 110 as amended by the 2005 Act.

2005-2007 Amendments

(The 2005-2007 Committee Note incorporates the Committee Note previously published in 2005.)

The form is amended in several ways to reflect changes in the Bankruptcy Code made by the Bankruptcy Abuse Prevention and Consumer Protection Act of 2005, Pub. L. No. 109–8, 119 Stat. 23 (April 20, 2005). A new sentence in the introduction advises the debtor not to disclose the name and address of any minor child in conformity with § 112, which was added to the Code by the 2005 Act. In addition, the form is amended to add the reference to Rule 1007(m) with respect to a minor child a direction to include for purposes the name, address, and legal relationship to the child of "a person described" in that rule. Rule 1007(m) requires the person named to be someone on whom process would be served in an adversary proceeding against the child.

The definition of "in business" is amended in the introductory section and in Question 1 and Question 18 to clarify that various part-time activities can result in the debtor being "in business" for purposes of the form.

Question 1 is amended to specify that, in addition to the income from the debtor's primary employment, the debtor must include income from part-time activities either as an employee or from self-employment. The debtor now also will report the source of all income from employment or operation of a business, even if there is only one source, in order to assist the trustee in reviewing the pay stubs, etc., filed by the debtor in the case.

Question 3 is amended to accommodate amendments to § 547(c) of the Code enacted in 2005 which exempt from recovery by the trustee payments by a debtor for a domestic support obligation or as part of an alternative repayment schedule negotiated by an approved nonprofit budgeting and credit counseling agency. In addition, Question 3 now requires a debtor with primarily non-consumer debts to report only those transfers that aggregate more than $5,475 to any creditor in the 90–day period prior to the filing of the petition, as a result of the addition of § 547(c)(9) to the Code in 2005. In addition, the language of the question is revised for clarity

In Question 10, the extension of the reachback period for transfers from one year to two years reflects the 2005 amendment to § 548(a)(1) of the Code to permit a trustee to avoid a fraudulent transfer made by the debtor within two years before the date of the filing of the petition. Question 10 also is amended to implement new § 548(e) added to the Code in 2005 to require the debtor to disclose all transfers to any self-settled asset protection trust within the ten years before the filing of the petition.

Question 15 is amended to extend from two years to three years the prepetition time period for which the debtor must disclose the addresses of all premises occupied by the debtor. This information will assist the trustee, the United States trustee, and the court to ascertain whether any homestead exemption asserted by the debtor is properly claimed under § 522(b)(3)(A) as amended, and §§ 522(p) and (q) as added to the Code in 2005.

The form also is amended to extend from six years to eight years the period before the filing of the petition concerning which the debtor is required to disclose the name of the debtor's spouse or of any former spouse who resides or resided with the debtor in a community property state. In addition, the certification by a non-attorney bankruptcy petition preparer is renamed a "declaration" and is amended to include material mandated by 11 U.S.C. § 110 as amended by the 2005 Act.

Form 8. Individual Debtor's Statement of Intention

B8 (Official Form 8) (12/08)

UNITED STATES BANKRUPTCY COURT

In re ______________________, Case No. ____________
Debtor Chapter 7

CHAPTER 7 INDIVIDUAL DEBTOR'S STATEMENT OF INTENTION

PART A—Debts secured by property of the estate. *(Part A must be fully completed for **EACH** debt which is secured by property of the estate. Attach additional pages if necessary.)*

Property No. 1	
Creditor's Name:	**Describe Property Securing Debt:**

Property will be *(check one)*:
☐ Surrendered ☐ Retained

If retaining the property, I intend to *(check at least one)*:
☐ Redeem the property
☐ Reaffirm the debt
☐ Other. Explain ____________ (for example, avoid lien using 11 U.S.C. § 522(f)).

Property is *(check one)*:
☐ Claimed as exempt ☐ Not claimed as exempt

Property No. 2 *(if necessary)*	
Creditor's Name:	**Describe Property Securing Debt:**

Property will be *(check one)*:
☐ Surrendered ☐ Retained

If retaining the property, I intend to *(check at least one)*:
☐ Redeem the property
☐ Reaffirm the debt
☐ Other. Explain ______ (for example, avoid lien using 11 U.S.C. § 522(f)).

Property is *(check one)*:
☐ Claimed as exempt ☐ Not claimed as exempt

Property No.	
Creditor's Name:	**Describe Property Securing Debt:**

Property will be *(check one)*:
☐ Surrendered ☐ Retained

If retaining the property, I intend to *(check at least one)*:
☐ Redeem the property
☐ Reaffirm the debt
☐ Other. Explain ______ (for example, avoid lien using 11 U.S.C. § 522(f)).

Property is *(check one)*:	
☐ Claimed as exempt	☐ Not claimed as exempt

PART B—Personal property subject to unexpired leases. *(All three columns of Part B must be completed for each unexpired lease. Attach additional pages if necessary.)*

Property No. 1		
Lessor's Name:	**Describe Leased Property:**	Lease will be Assumed pursuant to 11 U.S.C. § 365(p)(2): ☐ YES ☐ NO

Property No. 2 *(if necessary)*		
Lessor's Name:	**Describe Leased Property:**	Lease will be Assumed pursuant to 11 U.S.C. § 365(p)(2): ☐ YES ☐ NO

Property No. 3 *(if necessary)*		
Lessor's Name:	**Describe Leased Property:**	Lease will be Assumed pursuant to 11 U.S.C. § 365(p)(2): ☐ YES ☐ NO

Property No.		
Lessor's Name:	**Describe Leased Property:**	Lease will be Assumed pursuant to 11 U.S.C. § 365(p)(2): ☐ YES ☐ NO

Property No.		
Lessor's Name:	**Describe Leased Property:**	Lease will be Assumed pursuant to 11 U.S.C. § 365(p)(2): ☐ YES ☐ NO

___ continuation sheets attached *(if any)*

I declare under penalty of perjury that the above indicates my intention as to any property of my estate securing a debt and/or personal property subject to an unexpired lease.

Date: ______________

____
Signature of Debtor

____
Signature of Joint Debtor

(Added Aug. 1, 1991; and amended Mar. 1995; Oct. 1, 1997; Dec. 1, 2003; Aug. 11, 2005, eff. Oct. 17, 2005; Dec. 1, 2008.)

ADVISORY COMMITTEE NOTES

This form is derived from former Official Form No. 8A. Rule 1007(b)(2) requires the debtor to serve a copy of this statement on the trustee and all creditors named in the statement. In a joint case, if the property and debts of both debtors are the same, the form may be adapted for joint use. If joint debtors have separate debts, however, each debtor must use a separate form.

1995 Amendment

This form is a "document for filing" that may be prepared by a "bankruptcy petition preparer" as defined in 11 U.S.C. § 110, which was added to the Code by the Bankruptcy Reform Act of 1994; accordingly, a signature line for such preparer is added. In addition to signing, a bankruptcy petition preparer is required by section 110 to disclosure the information requested.

1997 Amendment

This form is amended to conform more closely to the language of the Bankruptcy Code. The amendments also make clear that the form is not intended to take a position regarding whether the options stated on the form are the only choices available to the debtor. Compare *Lowry Feder-*

al Credit Union v. West, 882 F.2d 1543 (10th Cir. 1989), with *In re Taylor*, 3 F.3d 1512 (11th Cir. 1993).

2003 Amendment

Pursuant to § 110(c) of the Bankruptcy Code, the certification by a non-attorney bankruptcy petition preparer continues to require a petition preparer to provide the full Social Security number of the individual who actually prepares the document.

2005 Amendment

The form is amended to conform to § 521(a)(6), which was added to the Code by the Bankruptcy Abuse Prevention and Consumer Protection Act of 2005, Pub. L. No. 109–8, 119 Stat. 23 (April 20, 2005), by adding a section covering personal property subject to an unexpired lease and an option labeled "lease will be assumed pursuant to 11 U.S.C. § 362(h)(1)(A)" to the choices a debtor may make. The certification by a non-attorney bankruptcy petition preparer in the form is renamed a "declaration" and is amended to include material mandated by the 2005 amendments to § 110 of the Code.

2008 Amendments

The form is amended to conform to § 362(h), which was added to the Code, and § 521(a)(2), which was amended, by the Bankruptcy Abuse Prevention and Consumer Protection Act of 2005, Pub. L. No. 109–8, 119 Stat. 23 (April 20, 2005), by expanding the questions directed to the debtor regarding leased personal property and property subject to security interests. The form is also amended and reformatted to require the debtor to complete a series of statements describing the property and setting out what actions the debtor intends to take for each listed asset. The amended form is intended to elicit more complete information about the debtor's intentions with regard to property subject to security interests and personal property leases than has been obtained under the current version of the form.

In addition, the form is amended to specify that the debtor's signature is a declaration under penalty of perjury, as required by Rule 1008, and to provide space for the codebtor's signature. A continuation page has been provided for use if necessary. The Declaration of Non–Attorney Bankruptcy Petition Preparer has been deleted from the form as duplicative of Form 19, Declaration and Signature of Non–Attorney Bankruptcy Petition Preparer. Form 19 contains both the petition preparer's declaration and signature and the notice the petition preparer is required to give to the debtor under § 110 of the Code.

HISTORICAL NOTES

Effective and Applicability Provisions

1997 Acts. Order amending official forms dated Oct. 1, 1997, effective immediately, with mandatory use starting March 1, 1998.

Form 9. Notice of Commencement of Case Under the Bankruptcy Code, Meeting of Creditors, and Deadlines

9A .... Chapter 7, Individual/Joint, No-Asset Case
9B .... Chapter 7, Corporation/Partnership, No-Asset Case
9C .... Chapter 7, Individual/Joint, Asset Case
9D .... Chapter 7, Corporation/Partnership, Asset Case
9E .... Chapter 11, Individual/Joint Case
9E(Alt.) ... Chapter 11, Individual/Joint Case
9F .... Chapter 11, Corporation/Partnership Case
9F(Alt.) ... Chapter 11, Corporation/Partnership Case
9G .... Chapter 12, Individual/Joint Case
9H .... Chapter 12, Corporation/Partnership Case
9I .... Chapter 13, Individual/Joint Case

B9A (Official Form 9A) (Chapter 7 Individual or Joint Debtor No Asset Case) (12/08)

UNITED STATES BANKRUPTCY COURT _______ **District of** _______

Notice of
Chapter 7 Bankruptcy Case, Meeting of Creditors, & Deadlines

[A chapter 7 bankruptcy case concerning the debtor(s) listed below was filed on _______ (date).]
or [A bankruptcy case concerning the debtor(s) listed below was originally filed under chapter _______ on _______ (date) and was converted to a case under chapter 7 on _______ (date).]

You may be a creditor of the debtor. **This notice lists important deadlines.** You may want to consult an attorney to protect your Rights. All documents filed in the case may be inspected at the bankruptcy clerk's office at the address listed below. NOTE: The staff of the bankruptcy clerk's office cannot give legal advice.

See Reverse Side For Important Explanations

Debtor(s) (name(s) and address):	Case Number:
	Last four digits of Social Security or Individual Taxpayer ID (ITIN) No(s)./Complete EIN:
All other names used by the Debtor(s) in the last 8 years (include married, maiden, and trade names):	Bankruptcy Trustee (name and address):
Attorney for Debtor(s) (name and address): Telephone number:	Telephone number:

Meeting of Creditors

Date: / / Time: ( ) A.M. ( ) P.M. Location:

Presumption of Abuse under 11 U.S.C. § 707(b)
See "Presumption of Abuse" on the reverse side.

Depending on the documents filed with the petition, one of the following statements will appear.

The presumption of abuse does not arise.
Or
The presumption of abuse arises.
Or
Insufficient information has been filed to date to permit the clerk to make any determination concerning the presumption of abuse. If more complete information, when filed, shows that the presumption has arisen, creditors will be notified.

Deadlines:
Papers must be *received* by the bankruptcy clerk's office by the following deadlines:

Deadline to File a Complaint Objecting to Discharge of the Debtor or to Determine Dischargeability of Certain Debts:

Deadline to Object to Exemptions:
Thirty (30) days after the *conclusion* of the meeting of creditors.

Creditors May Not Take Certain Actions:
In most instances, the filing of the bankruptcy case automatically stays certain collection and other actions against the debtor and the debtor's property. Under certain circumstances, the stay may be limited to 30 days or not exist at all, although the debtor can request the court to extend or impose a stay. If you attempt to collect a debt or take other action in violation of the Bankruptcy Code, you may be penalized. Consult a lawyer to determine your rights in this case.

Please Do Not File A Proof of Claim Unless You Receive a Notice To Do So.

Foreign Creditors:
A creditor to whom this notice is sent at a foreign address should read the information under "Do Not File a Proof of Claim at This Time" on the reverse side.

Address of the Bankruptcy Clerk's Office:	**For the Court:**
Telephone number:	Clerk of the Bankruptcy Court:
Hours Open:	Date:

EXPLANATIONS

B9A (Official Form 9A) (12/08)

Filing of Chapter 7 Bankruptcy Case	A bankruptcy case under Chapter 7 of the Bankruptcy Code (title 11, United States Code) has been filed in this court by or against the debtor(s) listed on the front side, and an order for relief has been entered.
Legal Advice	The staff of the bankruptcy clerk's office cannot give legal advice. Consult a lawyer to determine your rights in this case.
Creditors Generally May Not Take Certain Actions	Prohibited collection actions are listed in Bankruptcy Code § 362. Common examples of prohibited actions include contacting the debtor by telephone, mail, or otherwise to demand repayment; taking actions to collect money or obtain property from the debtor; repossessing the debtor's property; starting or continuing lawsuits or foreclosures; and garnishing or deducting from the debtor's wages. Under certain circumstances, the stay may be limited to 30 days or not exist at all, although the debtor can request the court to extend or impose a stay.
Presumption of Abuse	If the presumption of abuse arises, creditors may have the right to file a motion to dismiss the case under § 707(b) of the Bankruptcy Code. The debtor may rebut the presumption by showing special circumstances.
Meeting of Creditors	A meeting of creditors is scheduled for the date, time, and location listed on the front side. *The debtor (both spouses in a joint case) must be present at the meeting to be questioned under oath by the trustee and by creditors.* Creditors are welcome to attend, but are not required to do so. The meeting may be continued and concluded at a later date without further notice.
Do Not File a Proof of Claim at This Time	There does not appear to be any property available to the trustee to pay creditors. *You therefore should not file a proof of claim at this time.* If it later appears that assets are available to pay creditors, you will be sent another notice telling you that you may file a proof of claim, and telling you the deadline for filing your proof of claim. If this notice is mailed to a creditor at a foreign address, the creditor may file a motion requesting the court to extend the deadline.
Discharge of Debts	The debtor is seeking a discharge of most debts, which may include your debt. A discharge means that you may never try to collect the debt from the debtor. If you believe that the debtor is not entitled to receive a discharge under Bankruptcy Code § 727(a) *or* that a debt owed to you is not dischargeable under Bankruptcy Code § 523(a)(2), (4), or (6), you must start a lawsuit by filing a complaint in the bankruptcy clerk's office by the "Deadline to File a Complaint Objecting to Discharge of the Debtor or to Determine Dischargeability of Certain Debts" listed on the front side. The bankruptcy clerk's office must receive the complaint and any required filing fee by that Deadline.
Exempt Property	The debtor is permitted by law to keep certain property as exempt. Exempt property will not be sold and distributed to creditors. The debtor must file a list of all property claimed as exempt. You may inspect that list at the bankruptcy clerk's office. If you believe that an exemption claimed by the debtor is not authorized by law, you may file an objection to that exemption. The bankruptcy clerk's office must receive the objections by the "Deadline to Object to Exemptions" listed on the front side.
Bankruptcy Clerk's Office	Any paper that you file in this bankruptcy case should be filed at the bankruptcy clerk's office at the address listed on the front side. You may inspect all papers filed, including the list of the debtor's property and debts and the list of the property claimed as exempt, at the bankruptcy clerk's office.
Foreign Creditors	Consult a lawyer familiar with United States bankruptcy law if you have any questions regarding your rights in this case.

Refer To Other Side For Important Deadlines and Notices

B9B (Official Form 9B) (Chapter 7 Corporation/Partnership No Asset Case) (12/08)

UNITED STATES BANKRUPTCY COURT ________ District of ________

Notice of
Chapter 7 Bankruptcy Case, Meeting of Creditors, & Deadlines

[A chapter 7 bankruptcy case concerning the debtor(s) listed below was filed on ______ (date).]
or [A bankruptcy case concerning the debtor(s) listed below was originally filed under chapter ________ on ________ (date) and was converted to a case under chapter 7 on ________ (date).]

You may be a creditor of the debtor. **This notice lists important deadlines.** You may want to consult an attorney to protect your Rights. All documents filed in the case may be inspected at the bankruptcy clerk's office at the address listed below. NOTE: The staff of the bankruptcy clerk's office cannot give legal advice.

See Reverse Side For Important Explanations

Debtor(s) (name(s) and address):	Case Number:
	Last four digits of Social Security or Individual Taxpayer ID (ITIN) No(s)./Complete EIN:
All other names used by the debtor(s) in the last 8 years (include trade names):	Bankruptcy Trustee (name and address):
Attorney for Debtor(s) (name and address): Telephone number:	Telephone number:

Meeting of Creditors

Date: / / Time: ( ) A.M. ( ) P.M. Location:

Creditors May Not Take Certain Actions:

In most instances, the filing of the bankruptcy case automatically stays certain collection and other actions against the debtor and the debtor's property. Under certain circumstances, the stay may be limited to 30 days or not exist at all, although the debtor can request the court to extend or impose a stay. If you attempt to collect a debt or take other action in violation of the Bankruptcy Code, you may be penalized. Consult a lawyer to determine your rights in this case.

Please Do Not File A Proof of Claim Unless You Receive a Notice To Do So.

Foreign Creditors:

A creditor to whom this notice is sent at a foreign address should read the information under "Do Not File a Proof of Claim at This Time" on the reverse side.

Address of the Bankruptcy Clerk's Office:	**For the Court:**
	Clerk of the Bankruptcy Court:
Telephone number:	
Hours Open:	Date:

EXPLANATIONS

B9B (Official Form 9B) (12/08)

Filing of Chapter 7 Bankruptcy Case	A bankruptcy case under Chapter 7 of the Bankruptcy Code (title 11, United States Code) has been filed in this court by or against the debtor(s) listed on the front side, and an order for relief has been entered.
Legal Advice	The staff of the bankruptcy clerk's office cannot give legal advice. Consult a lawyer to determine your rights in this case.
Creditors Generally May Not Take Certain Actions	Prohibited collection actions are listed in Bankruptcy Code § 362. Common examples of prohibited actions include contacting the debtor by telephone, mail, or otherwise to demand repayment; taking actions to collect money or obtain property from the debtor; repossessing the debtor's property; and starting or continuing lawsuits or foreclosures. Under certain circumstances, the stay may be limited to 30 days or not exist at all, although the debtor can request the court to extend or impose a stay.
Meeting of Creditors	A meeting of creditors is scheduled for the date, time, and location listed on the front side. *The debtor's representative must be present at the meeting to be questioned under oath by the trustee and by creditors.* Creditors are welcome to attend, but are not required to do so. The meeting may be continued and concluded at a later date without further notice.
Do Not File a Proof of Claim at This Time	There does not appear to be any property available to the trustee to pay creditors. *You therefore should not file a proof of claim at this time.* If it later appears that assets are available to pay creditors, you will be sent another notice telling you that you may file a proof of claim, and telling you the deadline for filing your proof of claim. If this notice is mailed to a creditor at a foreign address, the creditor may file a motion requesting the court to extend the deadline.
Bankruptcy Clerk's Office	Any paper that you file in this bankruptcy case should be filed at the bankruptcy clerk's office at the address listed on the front side. You may inspect all papers filed, including the list of the debtor's property and debts and the list of the property claimed as exempt, at the bankruptcy clerk's office.
Foreign Creditors	Consult a lawyer familiar with United States bankruptcy law if you have any questions regarding your rights in this case.

Refer To Other Side For Important Deadlines and Notices

B9C (Official Form 9C) (Chapter 7 Individual or Joint Debtor Asset Case) (12/08)

UNITED STATES BANKRUPTCY COURT ________ **District of** ________

Notice of
Chapter 7 Bankruptcy Case, Meeting of Creditors, & Deadlines

[A chapter 7 bankruptcy case concerning the debtor(s) listed below was filed on ______ (date).]
or [A bankruptcy case concerning the debtor(s) listed below was originally filed under chapter ________ on ________ (date) and was converted to a case under chapter 7 on ________ (date).]

You may be a creditor of the debtor. **This notice lists important deadlines.** You may want to consult an attorney to protect your Rights. All documents filed in the case may be inspected at the bankruptcy clerk's office at the address listed below. NOTE: The staff of the bankruptcy clerk's office cannot give legal advice.

See Reverse Side For Important Explanations

Debtor(s) (name(s) and address):	Case Number:
	Last four digits of Social Security or Individual Taxpayer ID (ITIN) No(s)./Complete EIN:
All other names used by the Debtor(s) in the last 8 years (include married, maiden, and trade names):	Bankruptcy Trustee (name and address):
Attorney for Debtor(s) (name and address): Telephone number:	Telephone number:

Meeting of Creditors

Date: / / Time: ( ) A.M. ( ) P.M. Location:

Presumption of Abuse under 11 U.S.C. § 707(b)
See "Presumption of Abuse" on the reverse side.

Depending on the documents filed with the petition, one of the following statements will appear.

The presumption of abuse does not arise.
Or
The presumption of abuse arises.
Or
Insufficient information has been filed to date to permit the clerk to make any determination concerning the presumption of abuse. If more complete information, when filed, shows that the presumption has arisen, creditors will be notified.

Deadlines:
Papers must be *received* by the bankruptcy clerk's office by the following deadlines:

Deadline to File a Proof of Claim:
For all creditors (except a governmental unit): For a governmental unit:

Foreign Creditors:
A creditor to whom this notice is sent at a foreign address should read the information under "Claims" on the reverse side.

Deadline to File a Complaint Objecting to Discharge of the Debtor or to Determine Dischargeability of Certain Debts:

Deadline to Object to Exemptions:
Thirty (30) days after the *conclusion* of the meeting of creditors.

Creditors May Not Take Certain Actions:
In most instances, the filing of the bankruptcy case automatically stays certain collection and other actions against the debtor and the debtor's property. Under certain circumstances, the stay may be limited to 30 days or not exist at all, although the debtor can request the court to extend or impose a stay. If you attempt to collect a debt or take other action in violation of the Bankruptcy Code, you may be penalized. Consult a lawyer to determine your rights in this case.

Address of the Bankruptcy Clerk's Office:	For the Court:
	Clerk of the Bankruptcy Court:
Telephone number:	
Hours Open:	Date:

EXPLANATIONS

B9C (Official Form 9C) (12/08)

Filing of Chapter 7 Bankruptcy Case	A bankruptcy case under Chapter 7 of the Bankruptcy Code (title 11, United States Code) has been filed in this court by or against the debtor(s) listed on the front side, and an order for relief has been entered.
Legal Advice	The staff of the bankruptcy clerk's office cannot give legal advice. Consult a lawyer to determine your rights in this case.
Creditors Generally May Not Take Certain Actions	Prohibited collection actions are listed in Bankruptcy Code § 362. Common examples of prohibited actions include contacting the debtor by telephone, mail, or otherwise to demand repayment; taking actions to collect money or obtain property from the debtor; repossessing the debtor's property; starting or continuing lawsuits or foreclosures; and garnishing or deducting from the debtor's wages. Under certain circumstances, the stay may be limited to 30 days or not exist at all, although the debtor can request the court to extend or impose a stay.
Meeting of Creditors	A meeting of creditors is scheduled for the date, time, and location listed on the front side. *The debtor (both spouses in a joint case) must be present at the meeting to be questioned under oath by the trustee and by creditors.* Creditors are welcome to attend, but are not required to do so. The meeting may be continued and concluded at a later date without further notice.
Claims	A Proof of Claim is a signed statement describing a creditor's claim. If a Proof of Claim form is not included with this notice, you can obtain one at any bankruptcy clerk's office. A secured creditor retains rights in its collateral regardless of whether that creditor files a Proof of Claim. If you do not file a Proof of Claim by the "Deadline to File a Proof of Claim" listed on the front side, you might not be paid any money on your claim from other assets in the bankruptcy case. To be paid you must file a Proof of Claim even if your claim is listed in the schedules filed by the debtor. Filing a Proof of Claim submits the creditor to the jurisdiction of the bankruptcy court, with consequences a lawyer can explain. For example, a secured creditor who files a Proof of Claim may surrender important nonmonetary rights, including the right to a jury trial. **Filing Deadline for a Foreign Creditor:** The deadlines for filing claims set forth on the front of this notice apply to all creditors. If this notice has been mailed to a creditor at a foreign address, the creditor may file a motion requesting the court to extend the deadline.
Discharge of Debts	The debtor is seeking a discharge of most debts, which may include your debt. A discharge means that you may never try to collect the debt from the debtor. If you believe that the debtor is not entitled to receive a discharge under Bankruptcy Code § 727(a) *or* that a debt owed to you is not dischargeable under Bankruptcy Code § 523(a)(2), (4), or (6), you must start a lawsuit by filing a complaint in the bankruptcy clerk's office by the "Deadline to File a Complaint Objecting to Discharge of the Debtor or to Determine Dischargeability of Certain Debts" listed on the front side. The bankruptcy clerk's office must receive the complaint and any required filing fee by that Deadline.
Exempt Property	The debtor is permitted by law to keep certain property as exempt. Exempt property will not be sold and distributed to creditors. The debtor must file a list of all property claimed as exempt. You may inspect that list at the bankruptcy clerk's office. If you believe that an exemption claimed by the debtor is not authorized by law, you may file an objection to that exemption. The bankruptcy clerk's office must receive the objections by the "Deadline to Object to Exemptions" listed on the front side.
Presumption of Abuse	If the presumption of abuse arises, creditors may have the right to file a motion to dismiss the case under § 707(b) of the Bankruptcy Code. The debtor may rebut the presumption by showing special circumstances.
Bankruptcy Clerk's Office	Any paper that you file in this bankruptcy case should be filed at the bankruptcy clerk's office at the address listed on the front side. You may inspect all papers filed, including the list of the debtor's property and debts and the list of the property claimed as exempt, at the bankruptcy clerk's office.
Liquidation of the Debtor's Property and Payment of Creditors' Claims	The bankruptcy trustee listed on the front of this notice will collect and sell the debtor's property that is not exempt. If the trustee can collect enough money, creditors may be paid some or all of the debts owed to them, in the order specified by the Bankruptcy Code. To make sure you receive any share of that money, you must file a Proof of Claim, as described above.
Foreign Creditors	Consult a lawyer familiar with United States bankruptcy law if you have any questions regarding your rights in this case.

Refer To Other Side For Important Deadlines and Notices

B9D (Official Form 9D) (Chapter 7 Corporation/Partnership Asset Case) (12/08)

UNITED STATES BANKRUPTCY COURT ________ **District of** ________

Notice of
Chapter 7 Bankruptcy Case, Meeting of Creditors, & Deadlines

[A chapter 7 bankruptcy case concerning the debtor(s) listed below was filed on _____ (date).]
or [A bankruptcy case concerning the debtor(s) listed below was originally filed under chapter ______ on ______ (date) and was converted to a case under chapter 7 on ______ (date).]

You may be a creditor of the debtor. **This notice lists important deadlines.** You may want to consult an attorney to protect your Rights. All documents filed in the case may be inspected at the bankruptcy clerk's office at the address listed below. NOTE: The staff of the bankruptcy clerk's office cannot give legal advice.

See Reverse Side For Important Explanations

Debtor(s) (name(s) and address):	Case Number:
	Last four digits of Social Security or Individual Taxpayer ID (ITIN) No(s)./Complete EIN:
All other names used by the Debtor(s) in the last 8 years (include trade names):	Bankruptcy Trustee (name and address):
Attorney for Debtor(s) (name and address): Telephone number:	Telephone number:

Meeting of Creditors

Date: / / Time: ( ) A.M. ( ) P.M. Location:

Deadline to File a Proof of Claim:

Papers must be *received* by the bankruptcy clerk's office by the following deadlines:

For all creditors (except a governmental unit): For a governmental unit:

Foreign Creditors:
A creditor to whom this notice is sent at a foreign address should read the information under "Claims" on the reverse side.

Creditors May Not Take Certain Actions:

In most instances, the filing of the bankruptcy case automatically stays certain collection and other actions against the debtor and the debtor' s property. Under certain circumstances, the stay may be limited to 30 days or not exist at all, although the debtor can request the court to extend or impose a stay. If you attempt to collect a debt or take other action in violation of the Bankruptcy Code, you may be penalized. Consult a lawyer to determine your rights in this case.

Address of the Bankruptcy Clerk's Office:	**For the Court:**
Telephone number:	Clerk of the Bankruptcy Court:
Hours Open:	Date:

EXPLANATIONS

B9D (Official Form 9D) (12/08)

Filing of Chapter 7 Bankruptcy Case	A bankruptcy case under Chapter 7 of the Bankruptcy Code (title 11, United States Code) has been filed in this court by or against the debtor(s) listed on the front side, and an order for relief has been entered.
Legal Advice	The staff of the bankruptcy clerk's office cannot give legal advice. Consult a lawyer to determine your rights in this case.
Creditors Generally May Not Take Certain Actions	Prohibited collection actions are listed in Bankruptcy Code § 362. Common examples of prohibited actions include contacting the debtor by telephone, mail, or otherwise to demand repayment; taking actions to collect money or obtain property from the debtor; repossessing the debtor's property; and starting or continuing lawsuits or foreclosures. Under certain circumstances, the stay may be limited to 30 days or not exist at all, although the debtor can request the court to extend or impose a stay.
Meeting of Creditors	A meeting of creditors is scheduled for the date, time, and location listed on the front side. *The debtor's representative must be present at the meeting to be questioned under oath by the trustee and by creditors.* Creditors are welcome to attend, but are not required to do so. The meeting may be continued and concluded at a later date without further notice.
Claims	A Proof of Claim is a signed statement describing a creditor's claim. If a Proof of Claim form is not included with this notice, you can obtain one at any bankruptcy clerk's office. A secured creditor retains rights in its collateral regardless of whether that creditor files a Proof of Claim. If you do not file a Proof of Claim by the "Deadline to File a Proof of Claim" listed on the front side, you might not be paid any money on your claim from other assets in the bankruptcy case. To be paid, you must file a Proof of Claim even if your claim is listed in the schedules filed by the debtor. Filing a Proof of Claim submits the creditor to the jurisdiction of the bankruptcy court, with consequences a lawyer can explain. For example, a secured creditor who files a Proof of Claim may surrender important nonmonetary rights, including the right to a jury trial. **Filing Deadline for a Foreign Creditor:** The deadlines for filing claims set forth on the front of this notice apply to all creditors. If this notice has been mailed to a creditor at a foreign address, the creditor may file a motion requesting the court to extend the deadline.
Liquidation of the Debtor's Property and Payment of Creditors' Claims	The bankruptcy trustee listed on the front of this notice will collect and sell the debtor's property that is not exempt. If the trustee can collect enough money, creditors may be paid some or all of the debts owed to them, in the order specified by the Bankruptcy Code. To make sure you receive any share of that money, you must file a Proof of Claim, as described above.
Bankruptcy Clerk's Office	Any paper that you file in this bankruptcy case should be filed at the bankruptcy clerk's office at the address listed on the front side. You may inspect all papers filed, including the list of the debtor's property and debts and the list of the property claimed as exempt, at the bankruptcy clerk's office.
Foreign Creditors	Consult a lawyer familiar with United States bankruptcy law if you have any questions regarding your rights in this case.

Refer To Other Side For Important Deadlines and Notices

B9E (Official Form 9E) (Chapter 11 Individual or Joint Debtor Case) (12/08)

UNITED STATES BANKRUPTCY COURT ________ **District of** ________

Notice of
Chapter 11 Bankruptcy Case, Meeting of Creditors, & Deadlines

[A chapter 11 bankruptcy case concerning the debtor(s) listed below was filed on ______ (date).]
or [A bankruptcy case concerning the debtor(s) listed below was originally filed under chapter ______ on ______ (date) and was converted to a case under chapter 11 on ______ (date).]

You may be a creditor of the debtor. **This notice lists important deadlines.** You may want to consult an attorney to protect your rights. All documents filed in the case may be inspected at the bankruptcy clerk's office at the address listed below.
NOTE: The staff of the bankruptcy clerk's office cannot give legal advice.

See Reverse Side For Important Explanations

Debtor(s) (name(s) and address):	Case Number:
	Last four digits of Social Security or Individual Taxpayer ID (ITIN) No(s)./Complete EIN:
All other names used by the Debtor(s) in the last 8 years (include married, maiden, and trade names):	Attorney for Debtor(s) (name and address): Telephone number:

Meeting of Creditors

Date: / / Time: ( ) A.M. ( ) P.M. Location:

Deadlines:
Papers must be *received* by the bankruptcy clerk's office by the following deadlines:

Deadline to File a Proof of Claim:
Notice of deadline will be sent at a later time.

Foreign Creditors:
A creditor to whom this notice is sent at a foreign address should read the information under "Claims" on the reverse side.

Deadline to File a Complaint to Determine Dischargeability of Certain Debts:

Deadline to File a Complaint Objecting to Discharge of the Debtor:

First date set for hearing on confirmation of plan
Notice of that date will be sent at a later time.

Deadline to Object to Exemptions:

Thirty (30) days after the *conclusion* of the meeting of creditors.

Creditors May Not Take Certain Actions:

In most instances, the filing of the bankruptcy case automatically stays certain collection and other actions against the debtor and the debtor's property. Under certain circumstances, the stay may be limited to 30 days or not exist at all, although the debtor can request the court to extend or impose a stay. If you attempt to collect a debt or take other action in violation of the Bankruptcy Code, you may be penalized. Consult a lawyer to determine your rights in this case.

Address of the Bankruptcy Clerk's Office:	**For the Court:**
Telephone number:	Clerk of the Bankruptcy Court:
Hours Open:	Date:

EXPLANATIONS

B9E (Official Form 9E) (12/08)

Filing of Chapter 11 Bankruptcy Case	A bankruptcy case under Chapter 11 of the Bankruptcy Code (title 11, United States Code) has been filed in this court by or against the debtor(s) listed on the front side, and an order for relief has been entered. Chapter 11 allows a debtor to reorganize or liquidate pursuant to a plan. A plan is not effective unless confirmed by the court. You may be sent a copy of the plan and a disclosure statement telling you about the plan, and you might have the opportunity to vote on the plan. You will be sent notice of the date of the confirmation hearing, and you may object to confirmation of the plan and attend the confirmation hearing. Unless a trustee is serving, the debtor will remain in possession of the debtor's property and may continue to operate any business.
Legal Advice	The staff of the bankruptcy clerk's office cannot give legal advice. Consult a lawyer to determine your rights in this case.
Creditors Generally May Not Take Certain Actions	Prohibited collection actions are listed in Bankruptcy Code § 362. Common examples of prohibited actions include contacting the debtor by telephone, mail, or otherwise to demand repayment; taking actions to collect money or obtain property from the debtor; repossessing the debtor's property; starting or continuing lawsuits or foreclosures; and garnishing or deducting from the debtor's wages. Under certain circumstances, the stay may be limited to 30 days or not exist at all, although the debtor can request the court to extend or impose a stay.
Meeting of Creditors	A meeting of creditors is scheduled for the date, time, and location listed on the front side. *The debtor (both spouses in a joint case) must be present at the meeting to be questioned under oath by the trustee and by creditors.* Creditors are welcome to attend, but are not required to do so. The meeting may be continued and concluded at a later date without further notice. The court, after notice and a hearing, may order that the United States trustee not convene the meeting if the debtor has filed a plan for which the debtor solicited acceptances before filing the case.
Claims	A Proof of Claim is a signed statement describing a creditor's claim. If a Proof of Claim form is not included with this notice, you can obtain one at any bankruptcy clerk's office. You may look at the schedules that have been or will be filed at the bankruptcy clerk's office. If your claim is scheduled and is *not* listed as disputed, contingent, or unliquidated, it will be allowed in the amount scheduled unless you filed a Proof of Claim or you are sent further notice about the claim. Whether or not your claim is scheduled, you are permitted to file a Proof of Claim. If your claim is not listed at all *or* if your claim is listed as disputed, contingent, or unliquidated, then you must file a Proof of Claim or you might not be paid any money on your claim and may be unable to vote on a plan. The court has not yet set a deadline to file a Proof of Claim. If a deadline is set, you will be sent another notice. A secured creditor retains rights in its collateral regardless of whether that creditor files a Proof of Claim. Filing a Proof of Claim submits the creditor to the jurisdiction of the bankruptcy court, with consequences a lawyer can explain. For example, a secured creditor who files a Proof of Claim may surrender important nonmonetary rights, including the right to a jury trial. **Filing Deadline for a Foreign Creditor:** The deadlines for filing claims set forth on the front of this notice apply to all creditors. If this notice has been mailed to a creditor at a foreign address, the creditor may file a motion requesting the court to extend the deadline.
Discharge of Debts	Confirmation of a chapter 11 plan may result in a discharge of debts, which may include all or part of your debt. *See* Bankruptcy Code § 1141(d). Unless the court orders otherwise, however, the discharge will not be effective until completion of all payments under the plan. A discharge means that you may never try to collect the debt from the debtor except as provided in the plan. If you believe that a debt owed to you is not dischargeable under Bankruptcy Code § 523(a)(2), (4), or (6), you must start a lawsuit by filing a complaint in the bankruptcy clerk's office by the "Deadline to File a Complaint to Determine Dischargeability of Certain Debts" listed on the front side. The bankruptcy clerk's office must receive the complaint and any required filing fee by that Deadline. If you believe that the debtor is not entitled to receive a discharge under Bankruptcy Code § 1141(d)(3), you must file a complaint with the required filing fee in the bankruptcy clerk's office not later than the first date set for the hearing on confirmation of the plan. You will be sent another notice informing you of that date.
Exempt Property	The debtor is permitted by law to keep certain property as exempt. Exempt property will not be sold and distributed to creditors, even if the debtor's case is converted to chapter 7. The debtor must file a list of property claimed as exempt. You may inspect that list at the bankruptcy clerk's office. If you believe that an exemption claimed by the debtor is not authorized by law, you may file an objection to that exemption. The bankruptcy clerk's office must receive the objection by the "Deadline to Object to Exemptions" listed on the front side.
Bankruptcy Clerk's Office	Any paper that you file in this bankruptcy case should be filed at the bankruptcy clerk's office at the address listed on the front side. You may inspect all papers filed, including the list of the debtor's property and debts and the list of the property claimed as exempt, at the bankruptcy clerk's office.

Foreign Creditors	Consult a lawyer familiar with United States bankruptcy law if you have any questions regarding your rights in this case.

Refer To Other Side For Important Deadlines and Notices

B9E ALT (Official Form 9E ALT) (Chapter 11 Individual or Joint Debtor Case) (12/08)

UNITED STATES BANKRUPTCY COURT ________ **District of** ________

Notice of
Chapter 11 Bankruptcy Case, Meeting of Creditors, & Deadlines

[A chapter 11 bankruptcy case concerning the debtor(s) listed below was filed on ______ (date).]
or [A bankruptcy case concerning the debtor(s) listed below was originally filed under chapter ________ on ________ (date) and was converted to a case under chapter 11 on ________ (date).]

You may be a creditor of the debtor. **This notice lists important deadlines.** You may want to consult an attorney to protect your rights. All documents filed in the case may be inspected at the bankruptcy clerk's office at the address listed below.
NOTE: The staff of the bankruptcy clerk's office cannot give legal advice.

See Reverse Side For Important Explanations

Debtor(s) (name(s) and address):	Case Number:
	Last four digits of Social Security or Individual Taxpayer ID (ITIN) No(s)./Complete EIN:
All other names used by the Debtor(s) in the last 8 years (include married, maiden, and trade names):	Attorney for Debtor(s) (name and address): Telephone number:

Meeting of Creditors

Date: / / Time: ( ) A.M. ( ) P.M. Location:

Deadlines:

Papers must be *received* by the bankruptcy clerk's office by the following deadlines:

Deadline to File a Proof of Claim:

For all creditors (except governmental unit): For a governmental unit:

Foreign Creditors:

A creditor to whom this notice is sent at a foreign address should read the information under "Claims" on the reverse side.

Deadline to File a Complaint to Determine Dischargeability of Certain Debts:

Deadline to File a Complaint Objecting to Discharge of the Debtor:

First date set for hearing on confirmation of plan
Notice of that date will be sent at a later time.

Deadline to Object to Exemptions:

Thirty (30) days after the *conclusion* of the meeting of creditors.

Creditors May Not Take Certain Actions:

In most instances, the filing of the bankruptcy case automatically stays certain collection and other actions against the debtor and the debtor's property. Under certain circumstances, the stay may be limited to 30 days or not exist at all, although the debtor can request the court to extend or impose a stay. If you attempt to collect a debt or take other action in violation of the Bankruptcy Code, you may be penalized. Consult a lawyer to determine your rights in this case.

Address of the Bankruptcy Clerk's Office:	For the Court:
	Clerk of the Bankruptcy Court:
Telephone number:	
Hours Open:	Date:

EXPLANATIONS

B9E ALT (Official Form 9E ALT) (12/08)

Filing of Chapter 11 Bankruptcy Case	A bankruptcy case under Chapter 11 of the Bankruptcy Code (title 11, United States Code) has been filed in this court by or against the debtor(s) listed on the front side, and an order for relief has been entered. Chapter 11 allows a debtor to reorganize or liquidate pursuant to a plan. A plan is not effective unless confirmed by the court. You may be sent a copy of the plan and a disclosure statement telling you about the plan, and you might have the opportunity to vote on the plan. You will be sent notice of the date of the confirmation hearing, and you may object to confirmation of the plan and attend the confirmation hearing. Unless a trustee is serving, the debtor will remain in possession of the debtor's property and may continue to operate any business.
Legal Advice	The staff of the bankruptcy clerk's office cannot give legal advice. Consult a lawyer to determine your rights in this case.
Creditors Generally May Not Take Certain Actions	Prohibited collection actions are listed in Bankruptcy Code § 362. Common examples of prohibited actions include contacting the debtor by telephone, mail, or otherwise to demand repayment; taking actions to collect money or obtain property from the debtor; repossessing the debtor's property; starting or continuing lawsuits or foreclosures; and garnishing or deducting from the debtor's wages. Under certain circumstances, the stay may be limited to 30 days or not exist at all, although the debtor can request the court to extend or impose a stay.
Meeting of Creditors	A meeting of creditors is scheduled for the date, time, and location listed on the front side. *The debtor (both spouses in a joint case) must be present at the meeting to be questioned under oath by the trustee and by creditors.* Creditors are welcome to attend, but are not required to do so. The meeting may be continued and concluded at a later date without further notice. The court, after notice and a hearing, may order that the United States trustee not convene the meeting if the debtor has filed a plan for which the debtor solicited acceptances before filing the case.
Claims	A Proof of Claim is a signed statement describing a creditor's claim. If a Proof of Claim form is not included with this notice, you can obtain one at any bankruptcy clerk's office. You may look at the schedules that have been or will be filed at the bankruptcy clerk's office. If your claim is scheduled and is *not* listed as disputed, contingent, or unliquidated, it will be allowed in the amount scheduled unless you filed a Proof of Claim or you are sent further notice about the claim. Whether or not your claim is scheduled, you are permitted to file a Proof of Claim. If your claim is not listed at all *or* if your claim is listed as disputed, contingent, or unliquidated, then you must file a Proof of Claim by the "Deadline to File a Proof of Claim" listed on the front side or you might not be paid any money on your claim and may be unable to vote on a plan. A secured creditor retains rights in its collateral regardless of whether that creditor files a Proof of Claim. Filing a Proof of Claim submits the creditor to the jurisdiction of the bankruptcy court, with consequences a lawyer can explain. For example, a secured creditor who files a Proof of Claim may surrender important nonmonetary rights, including the right to a jury trial. **Filing Deadline for a Foreign Creditor:** The deadlines for filing claims set forth on the front of this notice apply to all creditors. If this notice has been mailed to a creditor at a foreign address, the creditor may file a motion requesting the court to extend the deadline.
Discharge of Debts	Confirmation of a chapter 11 plan may result in a discharge of debts, which may include all or part of your debt. *See* Bankruptcy Code § 1141(d). Unless the court orders otherwise, however, the discharge will not be effective until completion of all payments under the plan. A discharge means that you may never try to collect the debt from the debtor except as provided in the plan. If you believe that a debt owed to you is not dischargeable under Bankruptcy Code § 523(a)(2), (4), or (6), you must start a lawsuit by filing a complaint in the bankruptcy clerk's office by the "Deadline to File a Complaint to Determine Dischargeability of Certain Debts" listed on the front side. The bankruptcy clerk's office must receive the complaint and any required filing fee by that Deadline. If you believe that the debtor is not entitled to receive a discharge under Bankruptcy Code § 1141(d)(3), you must file a complaint with the required filing fee in the bankruptcy clerk's office not later than the first date set for the hearing on confirmation of the plan. You will be sent another notice informing you of that date.
Exempt Property	The debtor is permitted by law to keep certain property as exempt. Exempt property will not be sold and distributed to creditors, even if the debtor's case is converted to chapter 7. The debtor must file a list of property claimed as exempt. You may inspect that list at the bankruptcy clerk's office. If you believe that an exemption claimed by the debtor is not authorized by law, you may file an objection to that exemption. The bankruptcy clerk's office must receive the objection by the "Deadline to Object to Exemptions" listed on the front side.
Bankruptcy Clerk's Office	Any paper that you file in this bankruptcy case should be filed at the bankruptcy clerk's office at the address listed on the front side. You may inspect all papers filed, including the list of the debtor's property and debts and the list of the property claimed as exempt, at the bankruptcy clerk's office.

Foreign Creditors	Consult a lawyer familiar with United States bankruptcy law if you have any questions regarding your rights in this case.

Refer To Other Side For Important Deadlines and Notices

B9F (Official Form 9F) (Chapter 11 Corporation/Partnership Case) (12/08)

UNITED STATES BANKRUPTCY COURT ______ District of ______

Notice of
Chapter 11 Bankruptcy Case, Meeting of Creditors, & Deadlines

[A chapter 11 bankruptcy case concerning the debtor(s) listed below was filed on ______ (date).]
or [A bankruptcy case concerning the debtor(s) listed below was originally filed under chapter ______ on ______ (date) and was converted to a case under chapter 11 on ______ (date).]

You may be a creditor of the debtor. **This notice lists important deadlines.** You may want to consult an attorney to protect your rights. All documents filed in the case may be inspected at the bankruptcy clerk's office at the address listed below.
NOTE: The staff of the bankruptcy clerk's office cannot give legal advice.

See Reverse Side For Important Explanations

Debtor(s) (name(s) and address):	Case Number:
	Last four digits of Social Security or Individual Taxpayer ID (ITIN) No(s)./Complete EIN:
All other names used by the Debtor(s) in the last 8 years (include trade names): Telephone number:	Attorney for Debtor(s) (name and address): Telephone number:

Meeting of Creditors:

Date: / / Time: ( ) A.M. ( ) P.M. Location:

Deadline to File a Proof of Claim:

Proof of Claim must be *received* by the bankruptcy clerk's office by the following deadline:

Notice of deadline will be sent at a later time.

Foreign Creditors:

A creditor to whom this notice is sent at a foreign address should read the information under "Claims" on the reverse side.

Deadline to File a Complaint to Determine Dischargeability of Certain Debts:

Creditors May Not Take Certain Actions:

In most instances, the filing of the bankruptcy case automatically stays certain collection and other actions against the debtor and the debtor's property. Under certain circumstances, the stay may be limited to 30 days or not exist at all, although the debtor can request the court to extend or impose a stay. If you attempt to collect a debt or take other action in violation of the Bankruptcy Code, you may be penalized. Consult a lawyer to determine your rights in this case.

Address of the Bankruptcy Clerk's Office:	**For the Court:**
Telephone number:	Clerk of the Bankruptcy Court:
Hours Open:	Date:

EXPLANATIONS

B9F (Official Form 9F) (12/08)

Filing of Chapter 11 Bankruptcy Case	A bankruptcy case under Chapter 11 of the Bankruptcy Code (title 11, United States Code) has been filed in this court by or against the debtor(s) listed on the front side, and an order for relief has been entered. Chapter 11 allows a debtor to reorganize or liquidate pursuant to a plan. A plan is not effective unless confirmed by the court. You may be sent a copy of the plan and a disclosure statement telling you about the plan, and you might have the opportunity to vote on the plan. You will be sent notice of the date of the confirmation hearing, and you may object to confirmation of the plan and attend the confirmation hearing. Unless a trustee is serving, the debtor will remain in possession of the debtor's property and may continue to operate any business.
Legal Advice	The staff of the bankruptcy clerk's office cannot give legal advice. Consult a lawyer to determine your rights in this case.
Creditors Generally May Not Take Certain Actions	Prohibited collection actions are listed in Bankruptcy Code § 362. Common examples of prohibited actions include contacting the debtor by telephone, mail, or otherwise to demand repayment; taking actions to collect money or obtain property from the debtor; repossessing the debtor's property; and starting or continuing lawsuits or foreclosures. Under certain circumstances, the stay may be limited to 30 days or not exist at all, although the debtor can request the court to extend or impose a stay.
Meeting of Creditors	A meeting of creditors is scheduled for the date, time, and location listed on the front side. *The debtor's representative must be present at the meeting to be questioned under oath by the trustee and by creditors.* Creditors are welcome to attend, but are not required to do so. The meeting may be continued and concluded at a later date without further notice. The court, after notice and a hearing, may order that the United States trustee not convene the meeting if the debtor has filed a plan for which the debtor solicited acceptances before filing the case.
Claims	A Proof of Claim is a signed statement describing a creditor's claim. If a Proof of Claim form is not included with this notice, you can obtain one at any bankruptcy clerk's office. You may look at the schedules that have been or will be filed at the bankruptcy clerk's office. If your claim is scheduled and is *not* listed as disputed, contingent, or unliquidated, it will be allowed in the amount scheduled unless you filed a Proof of Claim or you are sent further notice about the claim. Whether or not your claim is scheduled, you are permitted to file a Proof of Claim. If your claim is not listed at all *or* if your claim is listed as disputed, contingent, or unliquidated, then you must file a Proof of Claim or you might not be paid any money on your claim and may be unable to vote on a plan. The court has not yet set a deadline to file a Proof of Claim. If a deadline is set, you will be sent another notice. A secured creditor retains rights in its collateral regardless of whether that creditor files a Proof of Claim. Filing a Proof of Claim submits the creditor to the jurisdiction of the bankruptcy court, with consequences a lawyer can explain. For example, a secured creditor who files a Proof of Claim may surrender important nonmonetary rights, including the right to a jury trial. **Filing Deadline for a Foreign Creditor:** The deadline for filing claims set forth on the front of this notice apply to all creditors. If this notice has been mailed to a creditor at a foreign address, the creditor may file a motion requesting the court to extend the deadline.
Discharge of Debts	Confirmation of a chapter 11 plan may result in a discharge of debts, which may include all or part of your debt. *See* Bankruptcy Code § 1141(d). A discharge means that you may never try to collect the debt from the debtor, except as provided in the plan. If you believe that a debt owed to you is not dischargeable under Bankruptcy Code § 1141(d)(6)(A), you must start a lawsuit by filing a complaint in the bankruptcy clerk's office by the "Deadline to File a Complaint to Determine Dischargeability of Certain Debts" listed on the front side. The bankruptcy clerk's office must receive the complaint and any required filing fee by that deadline.
Bankruptcy Clerk's Office	Any paper that you file in this bankruptcy case should be filed at the bankruptcy clerk's office at the address listed on the front side. You may inspect all papers filed, including the list of the debtor's property and debts and the list of the property claimed as exempt, at the bankruptcy clerk's office.
Foreign Creditors	Consult a lawyer familiar with United States bankruptcy law if you have any questions regarding your rights in this case.

Refer To Other Side For Important Deadlines and Notices

B9F ALT (Official Form 9F ALT) (Chapter 11 Corporation/Partnership Case) (12/08)

UNITED STATES BANKRUPTCY COURT ________ **District of** ________

Notice of
Chapter 11 Bankruptcy Case, Meeting of Creditors, & Deadlines

[A chapter 11 bankruptcy case concerning the debtor(s) listed below was filed on ______ (date).]
or [A bankruptcy case concerning the debtor(s) listed below was originally filed under chapter ________ on ________ (date) and was converted to a case under chapter 11 on ________ (date).]

You may be a creditor of the debtor. **This notice lists important deadlines.** You may want to consult an attorney to protect your rights. All documents filed in the case may be inspected at the bankruptcy clerk's office at the address listed below.
NOTE: The staff of the bankruptcy clerk's office cannot give legal advice.

See Reverse Side For Important Explanations

Debtor(s) (name(s) and address):	Case Number: Last four digits of Social-Security or Individual Taxpayer-ID (ITIN) No(s)./Complete EIN:
All other names used by the Debtor(s) in the last 8 years (include trade names):	Attorney for Debtor(s) (name and address): Telephone number:

Meeting of Creditors

Date: / / Time: ( ) A.M. ( ) P.M. Location:

Deadlines to File a Proof of Claim:

Proof of Claim must be *received* by the bankruptcy clerk's office by the following deadline:

For all creditors (except a governmental unit): For a governmental unit:

Foreign Creditors:

A creditor to whom this notice is sent at a foreign address should read the information under "Claims" on the reverse side.

Deadline to File a Complaint to Determine Dischargeability of Certain Debts:

Creditors May Not Take Certain Actions:

In most instances, the filing of the bankruptcy case automatically stays certain collection and other actions against the debtor and the debtor's property. Under certain circumstances, the stay may be limited to 30 days or not exist at all, although the debtor can request the court to extend or impose a stay. If you attempt to collect a debt or take other action in violation of the Bankruptcy Code, you may be penalized. Consult a lawyer to determine your rights in this case.

Address of the Bankruptcy Clerk's Office: Telephone number:	**For the Court:** Clerk of the Bankruptcy Court:
Hours Open:	Date:

EXPLANATIONS

B9F ALT (Official Form 9F ALT) (12/08)

Filing of Chapter 11 Bankruptcy Case	A bankruptcy case under Chapter 11 of the Bankruptcy Code (title 11, United States Code) has been filed in this court by or against the debtor(s) listed on the front side, and an order for relief has been entered. Chapter 11 allows a debtor to reorganize or liquidate pursuant to a plan. A plan is not effective unless confirmed by the court. You may be sent a copy of the plan and a disclosure statement telling you about the plan, and you might have the opportunity to vote on the plan. You will be sent notice of the date of the confirmation hearing, and you may object to confirmation of the plan and attend the confirmation hearing. Unless a trustee is serving, the debtor will remain in possession of the debtor's property and may continue to operate any business.
Legal Advice	The staff of the bankruptcy clerk's office cannot give legal advice. Consult a lawyer to determine your rights in this case.
Creditors Generally May Not Take Certain Actions	Prohibited collection actions are listed in Bankruptcy Code § 362. Common examples of prohibited actions include contacting the debtor by telephone, mail, or otherwise to demand repayment; taking actions to collect money or obtain property from the debtor; repossessing the debtor's property; and starting or continuing lawsuits or foreclosures. Under certain circumstances, the stay may be limited to 30 days or not exist at all, although the debtor can request the court to extend or impose a stay.
Meeting of Creditors	A meeting of creditors is scheduled for the date, time, and location listed on the front side. *The debtor's representative must be present at the meeting to be questioned under oath by the trustee and by creditors.* Creditors are welcome to attend, but are not required to do so. The meeting may be continued and concluded at a later date without further notice. The court, after notice and a hearing, may order that the United States trustee not convene the meeting if the debtor has filed a plan for which the debtor solicited acceptances before filing the case.
Claims	A Proof of Claim is a signed statement describing a creditor's claim. If a Proof of Claim form is not included with this notice, you can obtain one at any bankruptcy clerk's office. You may look at the schedules that have been or will be filed at the bankruptcy clerk's office. If your claim is scheduled and is *not* listed as disputed, contingent, or unliquidated, it will be allowed in the amount scheduled unless you filed a Proof of Claim or you are sent further notice about the claim. Whether or not your claim is scheduled, you are permitted to file a Proof of Claim. If your claim is not listed at all *or* if your claim is listed as disputed, contingent, or unliquidated, then you must file a Proof of Claim by the "Deadline to File Proof of Claim" listed on the front side, or you might not be paid any money on your claim and may be unable to vote on a plan. A secured creditor retains rights in its collateral regardless of whether that creditor files a Proof of Claim. Filing a Proof of Claim submits the creditor to the jurisdiction of the bankruptcy court, with consequences a lawyer can explain. For example, a secured creditor who files a Proof of Claim may surrender important nonmonetary rights, including the right to a jury trial. **Filing Deadline for a Foreign Creditor:** The deadlines for filing claims set forth on the front of this notice apply to all creditors. If this notice has been mailed to a creditor at a foreign address, the creditor may file a motion requesting the court to extend the deadline.
Discharge of Debts	Confirmation of a chapter 11 plan may result in a discharge of debts, which may include all or part of your debt. *See* Bankruptcy Code § 1141(d). A discharge means that you may never try to collect the debt from the debtor, except as provided in the plan. If you believe that a debt owed to you is not dischargeable under Bankruptcy Code § 1141(d)(6)(A), you must start a lawsuit by filing a complaint in the bankruptcy clerk's office by the "Deadline to File a Complaint to Determine Dischargeability of Certain Debts" listed on the front side. The bankruptcy clerk's office must receive the complaint and any required filing fee by that deadline.
Bankruptcy Clerk's Office	Any paper that you file in this bankruptcy case should be filed at the bankruptcy clerk's office at the address listed on the front side. You may inspect all papers filed, including the list of the debtor's property and debts and the list of the property claimed as exempt, at the bankruptcy clerk's office.
Foreign Creditors	Consult a lawyer familiar with United States bankruptcy law if you have any questions regarding your rights in this case.

Refer To Other Side For Important Deadlines and Notices

B9G (Official Form 9G) (Chapter 12 Individual or Joint Debtor Family Farmer or Family Fisherman) (12/08)

UNITED STATES BANKRUPTCY COURT ________ **District of** ________

Notice of
Chapter 12 Bankruptcy Case, Meeting of Creditors, & Deadlines

[The debtor(s) listed below filed a chapter 12 bankruptcy case on ________________ (date).]
or [A bankruptcy case concerning the debtor(s) listed below was originally filed under chapter ________ on ________ (date) and was converted to a case under chapter 12 on ________ (date).]

You may be a creditor of the debtor. **This notice lists important deadlines.** You may want to consult an attorney to protect your rights. All documents filed in the case may be inspected at the bankruptcy clerk's office at the address listed below.

NOTE: The staff of the bankruptcy clerk's office cannot give legal advice.

See Reverse Side For Important Explanations

Debtor(s) (name(s) and address):	Case Number:
	Last four digits of Social-Security or Individual Taxpayer-ID (ITIN) No(s)./Complete EIN:
All other names used by the Debtor(s) in the last 8 years (include married, maiden, and trade names):	Bankruptcy Trustee (name and address):
Attorney for Debtor(s) (name and address): Telephone number:	Telephone number:

Meeting of Creditors

Date: / / Time: ( ) A.M. ( ) P.M. Location:

Deadlines

Papers must be *received* by the bankruptcy clerk's office by the following deadlines:

Deadline to File a Proof of Claim:

For all creditors (except a governmental unit): For a governmental unit:

Foreign Creditors:

A creditor to whom this notice is sent at a foreign address should read the information under "Claims" on the reverse side.

Deadline to File a Complaint to Determine Dischargeability of Certain Debts:

Deadline to Object to Exemptions:

Thirty (30) days after the *conclusion* of the meeting of creditors.

Filing of Plan, Hearing on Confirmation of Plan

[The debtor has filed a plan. The plan or a summary of the plan is enclosed. The hearing on confirmation will be held:
Date: ____________ Time: ________ Location: ________________]

or [The debtor has filed a plan. The plan or a summary of the plan and notice of confirmation hearing will be sent separately.]

or [The debtor has not filed a plan as of this date. You will be sent separate notice of the hearing on confirmation of the plan.]

Creditors May Not Take Certain Actions:

In most instances, the filing of the bankruptcy case automatically stays certain collection and other actions against the debtor, the debtor's property, and certain codebtors. Under certain circumstances, the stay may be limited to 30 days or not exist at all, although the debtor can request the court to extend or impose a stay. If you attempt to collect a debt or take other action in violation of the Bankruptcy Code, you may be penalized. Consult a lawyer to determine your rights in this case.

Address of the Bankruptcy Clerk's Office: Telephone number:	For the Court: Clerk of the Bankruptcy Court:
Hours Open:	Date:

B9G (Official Form 9G) (12/08)

EXPLANATIONS

Filing of Chapter 12 Bankruptcy Case	A bankruptcy case under Chapter 12 of the Bankruptcy Code (title 11, United States Code) has been filed in this court by the debtor(s) listed on the front side, and an order for relief has been entered. Chapter 12 allows family farmers and family fishermen to adjust their debts pursuant to a plan. A plan is not effective unless confirmed by the court. You may object to confirmation of the plan and appear at the confirmation hearing. A copy or summary of the plan [is included with this notice] *or* [will be sent to you later], and [the confirmation hearing will be held on the date indicated on the front of this notice] *or* [you will be sent notice of the confirmation hearing]. The debtor will remain in possession of the debtor's property and may continue to operate the debtor's business unless the court orders otherwise.
Legal Advice	The staff of the bankruptcy clerk's office cannot give legal advice. Consult a lawyer to determine your rights in this case.
Creditors Generally May Not Take Certain Actions	Prohibited collection actions against the debtor and certain codebtors are listed in Bankruptcy Code § 362 and § 1201. Common examples of prohibited actions include contacting the debtor by telephone, mail, or otherwise to demand repayment; taking actions to collect money or obtain property from the debtor; repossessing the debtor's property; starting or continuing lawsuits or foreclosures; and garnishing or deducting from the debtor's wages. Under certain circumstances, the stay may be limited in duration or not exist at all, although the debtor may have the right to request the court to extend or impose a stay.
Meeting of Creditors	A meeting of creditors is scheduled for the date, time, and location listed on the front side. *The debtor (both spouses in a joint case) must be present at the meeting to be questioned under oath by the trustee and by creditors.* Creditors are welcome to attend, but are not required to do so. The meeting may be continued and concluded at a later date without further notice.
Claims	A Proof of Claim is a signed statement describing a creditor's claim. If a Proof of Claim form is not included with this notice, you can obtain one at any bankruptcy clerk's office. A secured creditor retains rights in its collateral regardless of whether that creditor files a Proof of Claim. If you do not file a Proof of Claim by the "Deadline to File a Proof of Claim" listed on the front side, you might not be paid any money on your claim from other assets in the bankruptcy case. To be paid you must file a Proof of Claim even if your claim is listed in the schedules filed by the debtor. Filing a Proof of Claim submits the creditor to the jurisdiction of the bankruptcy court, with consequences a lawyer can explain. For example, a secured creditor who files a Proof of Claim may surrender important nonmonetary rights, including the right to a jury trial. **Filing Deadline for a Foreign Creditor:** The deadlines for filing claims set forth on the front of this notice apply to all creditors. If this notice has been mailed to a creditor at a foreign address, the creditor may file a motion requesting the court to extend the deadline.
Discharge of Debts	The debtor is seeking a discharge of most debts, which may include your debt. A discharge means that you may never try to collect the debt from the debtor. If you believe that a debt owed to you is not dischargeable under Bankruptcy Code § 523(a)(2), (4), or (6), you must start a lawsuit by filing a complaint in the bankruptcy clerk's office by the "Deadline to File a Complaint to Determine Dischargeability of Certain Debts" listed on the front side. The bankruptcy clerk's office must receive the complaint and any required filing fee by that Deadline.
Exempt Property	The debtor is permitted by law to keep certain property as exempt. Exempt property will not be sold and distributed to creditors, even if the debtor's case is converted to chapter 7. The debtor must file a list of all property claimed as exempt. You may inspect that list at the bankruptcy clerk's office. If you believe that an exemption claimed by the debtor is not authorized by law, you may file an objection to that exemption. The bankruptcy clerk's office must receive the objection by the "Deadline to Object to Exemptions" listed on the front side.
Bankruptcy Clerk's Office	Any paper that you file in this bankruptcy case should be filed at the bankruptcy clerk's office at the address listed on the front side. You may inspect all papers filed, including the list of the debtor's property and debts and the list of the property claimed as exempt, at the bankruptcy clerk's office.
Foreign Creditors	Consult a lawyer familiar with United States bankruptcy law if you have any questions regarding your rights in this case.

Refer To Other Side For Important Deadlines and Notices

B9H (Official Form 9H) (Chapter 12 Corporation/Partnership Family Farmer or Family Fisherman) (12/08)

UNITED STATES BANKRUPTCY COURT ________ **District of** ________

Notice of
Chapter 12 Bankruptcy Case, Meeting of Creditors, & Deadlines

[The debtor [corporation] *or* [partnership] listed below filed a chapter 12 bankruptcy case on ______ (date).]
or [A bankruptcy case concerning the debtor [corporation] *or* [partnership] listed below was originally filed under chapter ________ on ________ (date) and was converted to a case under chapter 12 on ________ (date).]

You may be a creditor of the debtor. **This notice lists important deadlines.** You may want to consult an attorney to protect your rights. All documents filed in the case may be inspected at the bankruptcy clerk's office at the address listed below.
NOTE: The staff of the bankruptcy clerk's office cannot give legal advice.

See Reverse Side For Important Explanations

Debtor(s) (name(s) and address):	Case Number:
	Last four digits of Social-Security or Individual Taxpayer-ID (ITIN) No(s)./Complete EIN:
All other names used by the Debtor(s) in the last 8 years (include trade names):	Bankruptcy Trustee (name and address):
Attorney for Debtor(s) (name and address): Telephone number:	Telephone number:

Meeting of Creditors

Date: / / Time: ( ) A.M. ( ) P.M. Location:

Deadlines:

Papers must be *received* by the bankruptcy clerk's office by the following deadlines:

Deadline to File a Proof of Claim:

For all creditors (except a governmental unit): For a governmental unit:

Foreign Creditors:
A creditor to whom this notice is sent at a foreign address should read the information under "Claims" on the reverse side.

Deadline to File a Complaint to Determine Dischargeability of Certain Debts:

Filing of Plan, Hearing on Confirmation of Plan

[The debtor has filed a plan. The plan or a summary of the plan is enclosed. The hearing on confirmation will be held:
Date: ____________ Time: ________ Location: ____________________]
or [The debtor has filed a plan. The plan or a summary of the plan and notice of confirmation hearing will be sent separately.]
or [The debtor has not filed a plan as of this date. You will be sent separate notice of the hearing on confirmation of the plan.]

Creditors May Not Take Certain Actions:

In most instances, the filing of the bankruptcy case automatically stays certain collection and other actions against the debtor and the debtor's property. Under certain circumstances, the stay may be limited to 30 days or not exist at all, although the debtor can request the court to extend or impose a stay. If you attempt to collect a debt or take other action in violation of the Bankruptcy Code, you may be penalized. Consult a lawyer to determine your rights in this case.

Address of the Bankruptcy Clerk's Office:	For the Court:
Telephone number:	Clerk of the Bankruptcy Court:
Hours Open:	Date:

EXPLANATIONS

B9H (Official Form 9H) (12/08)

Filing of Chapter 12 Bankruptcy Case	A bankruptcy case under Chapter 12 of the Bankruptcy Code (title 11, United States Code) has been filed in this court by the debtor listed on the front side, and an order for relief has been entered. Chapter 12 allows family farmers and family fishermen to adjust their debts pursuant to a plan. A plan is not effective unless confirmed by the court. You may object to confirmation of the plan and appear at the confirmation hearing. A copy or summary of the plan [is included with this notice] *or* [will be sent to you later], and [the confirmation hearing will be held on the date indicated on the front of this notice] *or* [you will be sent notice of the confirmation hearing]. The debtor will remain in possession of the debtor's property and may continue to operate the debtor's business unless the court orders otherwise.
Legal Advice	The staff of the bankruptcy clerk's office cannot give legal advice. Consult a lawyer to determine your rights in this case.
Creditors Generally May Not Take Certain Actions	Prohibited collection actions against the debtor and certain codebtors are listed in Bankruptcy Code § 362 and § 1201. Common examples of prohibited actions include contacting the debtor by telephone, mail, or otherwise to demand repayment; taking actions to collect money or obtain property from the debtor; repossessing the debtor's property; and starting or continuing lawsuits or foreclosures. Under certain circumstances, the stay may be limited in duration or not exist at all, although the debtor may have the right to request the court to extend or impose a stay.
Meeting of Creditors	A meeting of creditors is scheduled for the date, time, and location listed on the front side. *The debtor's representative must be present at the meeting to be questioned under oath by the trustee and by creditors.* Creditors are welcome to attend, but are not required to do so. The meeting may be continued and concluded at a later date without further notice.
Claims	A Proof of Claim is a signed statement describing a creditor's claim. If a Proof of Claim form is not included with this notice, you can obtain one at any bankruptcy clerk's office. A secured creditor retains rights in its collateral regardless of whether that creditor files a Proof of Claim. If you do not file a Proof of Claim by the "Deadline to File a Proof of Claim" listed on the front side, you might not be paid any money on your claim from other assets in the bankruptcy case. To be paid you must file a Proof of Claim even if your claim is listed in the schedules filed by the debtor. Filing a Proof of Claim submits the creditor to the jurisdiction of the bankruptcy court, with consequences a lawyer can explain. For example, a secured creditor who files a Proof of Claim may surrender important nonmonetary rights, including the right to a jury trial. **Filing Deadline for a Foreign Creditor:** The deadlines for filing claims set forth on the front of this notice apply to all creditors. If this notice has been mailed to a creditor at a foreign address, the creditor may file a motion requesting the court to extend the deadline.
Discharge of Debts	The debtor is seeking a discharge of most debts, which may include your debt. A discharge means that you may never try to collect the debt from the debtor. If you believe that a debt owed to you is not dischargeable under Bankruptcy Code § 523(a)(2), (4), or (6), you must start a lawsuit by filing a complaint in the bankruptcy clerk's office by the "Deadline to File a Complaint to Determine Dischargeability of Certain Debts" listed on the front side. The bankruptcy clerk's office must receive the complaint and any required filing fee by that Deadline.
Bankruptcy Clerk's Office	Any paper that you file in this bankruptcy case should be filed at the bankruptcy clerk's office at the address listed on the front side. You may inspect all papers filed, including the list of the debtor's property and debts and the list of the property claimed as exempt, at the bankruptcy clerk's office.
Foreign Creditors	Consult a lawyer familiar with United States bankruptcy law if you have any questions regarding your rights in this case.

Refer To Other Side For Important Deadlines and Notices

B9I (Official Form 9I) (Chapter 13 Case) (12/08)

UNITED STATES BANKRUPTCY COURT ________ District of ________

Notice of
Chapter 13 Bankruptcy Case, Meeting of Creditors, & Deadlines

[The debtor(s) listed below filed a chapter 13 bankruptcy case on ____________________ (date).]
or [A bankruptcy case concerning the debtor(s) listed below was originally filed under chapter ________ on ________ (date) and was converted to a case under chapter 13 on ________ (date).]

You may be a creditor of the debtor. **This notice lists important deadlines.** You may want to consult an attorney to protect your rights. All documents filed in the case may be inspected at the bankruptcy clerk's office at the address listed below.
NOTE: The staff of the bankruptcy clerk's office cannot give legal advice.

See Reverse Side For Important Explanations

Debtor(s) (name(s) and address):	Case Number:
	Last four digits of Social-Security or Individual Taxpayer ID (ITIN) No(s)./Complete EIN:
All other names used by the Debtor(s) in the last 8 years (include married, maiden, and trade names): maiden, and trade names:	Bankruptcy Trustee (name and address):
Attorney for Debtor(s) (name and address): Telephone number:	Telephone number:

Meeting of Creditors

Date: / / Time: ( ) A.M. ( ) P.M. Location:

Deadlines:
Papers must be *received* by the bankruptcy clerk's office by the following deadlines:

Deadline to File a Proof of Claim:
For all creditors (except a governmental unit): For a governmental unit (except as otherwise provided in Fed.R.Bankr.P. 3002(c)(1)):

Foreign Creditors:
A creditor to whom this notice is sent at a foreign address should read the information under "Claims" on the reverse side.

Deadline to Object to Exemptions:
Thirty (30) days after the *conclusion* of the meeting of creditors.

Filing of Plan, Hearing on Confirmation of Plan

[The debtor has filed a plan. The plan or a summary of the plan is enclosed. The hearing on confirmation will be held:
Date: ____________ Time: ________ Location: ____________________]

or [The debtor has filed a plan. The plan or a summary of the plan and notice of confirmation hearing will be sent separately.]

or [The debtor has not filed a plan as of this date. You will be sent separate notice of the hearing on confirmation of the plan.]

Creditors May Not Take Certain Actions:
In most instances, the filing of the bankruptcy case automatically stays certain collection and other actions against the debtor, the debtor's property, and certain codebtors. Under certain circumstances, the stay may be limited to 30 days or not exist at all, although the debtor can request the court to extend or impose a stay. If you attempt to collect a debt or take other action in violation of the Bankruptcy Code, you may be penalized. Consult a lawyer to determine your rights in this case.

Address of the Bankruptcy Clerk's Office:	For the Court:
Telephone number:	Clerk of the Bankruptcy Court:
Hours Open:	Date:

EXPLANATIONS

B9I (Official Form 9I) (12/08)

Filing of Chapter 13 Bankruptcy Case	A bankruptcy case under Chapter 13 of the Bankruptcy Code (title 11, United States Code) has been filed in this court by the debtor(s) listed on the front side, and an order for relief has been entered. Chapter 13 allows an individual with regular income and debts below a specified amount to adjust debts pursuant to a plan. A plan is not effective unless confirmed by the bankruptcy court. You may object to confirmation of the plan and appear at the confirmation hearing. A copy or summary of the plan [is included with this notice] *or* [will be sent to you later], and [the confirmation hearing will be held on the date indicated on the front of this notice] *or* [you will be sent notice of the confirmation hearing]. The debtor will remain in possession of the debtor's property and may continue to operate the debtor's business, if any, unless the court orders otherwise.
Legal Advice	The staff of the bankruptcy clerk's office cannot give legal advice. Consult a lawyer to determine your rights in this case.
Creditors Generally May Not Take Certain Actions	Prohibited collection actions against the debtor and certain codebtors are listed in Bankruptcy Code § 362 and § 1301. Common examples of prohibited actions include contacting the debtor by telephone, mail, or otherwise to demand repayment; taking actions to collect money or obtain property from the debtor; repossessing the debtor's property; starting or continuing lawsuits or foreclosures; and garnishing or deducting from the debtor's wages. Under certain circumstances, the stay may be limited to 30 days or not exist at all, although the debtor can request the court to exceed or impose a stay.
Meeting of Creditors	A meeting of creditors is scheduled for the date, time, and location listed on the front side. *The debtor (both spouses in a joint case) must be present at the meeting to be questioned under oath by the trustee and by creditors.* Creditors are welcome to attend, but are not required to do so. The meeting may be continued and concluded at a later date without further notice.
Claims	A Proof of Claim is a signed statement describing a creditor's claim. If a Proof of Claim form is not included with this notice, you can obtain one at any bankruptcy clerk's office. A secured creditor retains rights in its collateral regardless of whether that creditor files a Proof of Claim. If you do not file a Proof of Claim by the "Deadline to File a Proof of Claim" listed on the front side, you might not be paid any money on your claim from other assets in the bankruptcy case. To be paid you must file a Proof of Claim even if your claim is listed in the schedules filed by the debtor. Filing a Proof of Claim submits the creditor to the jurisdiction of the bankruptcy court, with consequences a lawyer can explain. For example, a secured creditor who files a Proof of Claim may surrender important nonmonetary rights, including the right to a jury trial. **Filing Deadline for a Foreign Creditor:** The deadlines for filing claims set forth on the front of this notice apply to all creditors. If this notice has been mailed to a creditor at a foreign address, the creditor may file a motion requesting the court to extend the deadline.
Discharge of Debts	The debtor is seeking a discharge of most debts, which may include your debt. A discharge means that you may never try to collect the debt from the debtor. If you believe that a debt owed to you is not dischargeable under Bankruptcy Code § 523(a)(2) or (4), you must start a lawsuit by filing a complaint in the bankruptcy clerk's office by the "Deadline to File a Complaint to Determine Dischargeability of Certain Debts" listed on the front side. The bankruptcy clerk's office must receive the complaint and any required filing fee by that deadline.
Exempt Property	The debtor is permitted by law to keep certain property as exempt. Exempt property will not be sold and distributed to creditors, even if the debtor's case is converted to chapter 7. The debtor must file a list of all property claimed as exempt. You may inspect that list at the bankruptcy clerk's office. If you believe that an exemption claimed by the debtor is not authorized by law, you may file an objection to that exemption. The bankruptcy clerk's office must receive the objection by the "Deadline to Object to Exemptions" listed on the front side.
Bankruptcy Clerk's Office	Any paper that you file in this bankruptcy case should be filed at the bankruptcy clerk's office at the address listed on the front side. You may inspect all papers filed, including the list of the debtor's property and debts and the list of the property claimed as exempt, at the bankruptcy clerk's office.
Foreign Creditors	Consult a lawyer familiar with United States bankruptcy law if you have any questions regarding your rights in this case.

Refer To Other Side For Important Deadlines and Notices

(Added Aug. 1, 1991, and amended Mar. 16, 1993; Mar. 1995; Oct. 1, 1997; Dec. 1, 2003; Aug. 11, 2005, eff. Oct. 17, 2005; Oct. 2006; Dec. 1, 2007; Dec. 1, 2008.)

ADVISORY COMMITTEE NOTES

1991 Enactment

The form has been redesigned to facilitate electronic generation of notice to creditors concerning the filing of the petition, the meeting of creditors, and important deadlines in the case. Adoption of a box format, with significant dates highlighted, is intended to assist creditors who may be unfamiliar with bankruptcy cases to understand the data provided. Nine variations of the form, designated 9A through 9I, have been created to meet the specialized notice requirements for chapters 7, 11, 12, and 13, asset and no-asset cases, and the various types of debtors.

1992 Amendment

Forms 9B, 9D, 9F, and 9H are amended to make a technical correction in the reference to Rule 9001(5). Form 9H also contains a technical correction deleting the reference to a compliant objecting to discharge of the debtor.

1993 Amendment

The title page of the form has been amended to conform to the headings used on Forms 9A–9I. Alternate versions of Form 9E and Form 9F have been added for the convenience of districts that routinely set a deadline for filing claims in a chapter 11 case. When a creditor receives the alternate form in a case, the box labeled "Filing Claims" will contain information about the bar date as follows: "Deadline for filing a claim: (date) ." If no deadline is set in a particular case, either the court will use Form 9E or Form 9F, as appropriate, or the alternate form will be used with the following sentence appearing in the box labeled "Filing Claims": "When the court sets a deadline for filing claims, creditors will be notified."

1995 Amendment

The form is amended to provide notice of the claims filing period provided to "a governmental unit" by section 502(b)(9) of the Code as amended by the Bankruptcy Reform Act of 1994. A court that routinely sets a deadline for filing proofs of claim at the outset of chapter 11 cases and, accordingly, uses Form 9E(Alt.) or Form 9F(Alt.) retains the option in any case in which no deadlines actually are set to substitute a message stating that creditors will be notified if the court fixes a deadline.

The form also is amended to add, in the paragraph labeled "Discharge of Debts," a reference to dischargeability actions under section 523(a)(15) of the Code, which was added by the 1994 Act.

1997 Amendment

Forms 9A – 9I (and the alternate versions of Forms 9E and 9F) have been amended, redesigned, and rewritten. Minor conforming changes have been made to respond to amendments made in the Bankruptcy Reform Act of 1994: the longer claims filing period for governmental units in section 502(b)(9) of the Code (see Forms 9C, 9D, 9E(Alt.), 9F(Alt.), 9G, 9H, and 9I); and a reference to dischargeability actions under section 523(a)(15) (see Forms 9A, 9C, 9E, and 9E(Alt.), 9G, and 9H). All of the forms have been substantially revised to make them easier to read and understand. The titles have been simplified. Recipients are told why they are receiving the notice. Explanations are provided on the back of the form and are set in larger type. Plain English is used. Deadlines are highlighted on the front of the form. Recipients are told that papers must be received by the bankruptcy clerk's office by the applicable deadline. The box for the trustee has been deleted from the chapter 11 notices (Forms 9E and 9F and the alternates). Various alternatives are set out in brackets in many of the forms, permitting each bankruptcy clerk's office to tailor the forms even more precisely to fit the needs of a particular case. The court may use blank spaces on the form to include additional information applicable to the particular district.

2003 Amendment

The form is amended to add to the information provided to creditors, the trustee and the United States trustee, all the names used by the debtor during the six years prior to the filing of the petition. The form includes the debtor's full employer identification number, if any, as well as the last four digits of the debtor's social security number. Rule 2002(a)(1) also is amended to direct the clerk to include the debtor's full social security number and employer identification number on the notices served on the United States trustee, the trustee, and creditors. This will enable creditors to identify the debtor accurately. The copy of Official Form 9 included in the case file, however, will show only the last four digits of the debtor's social security number. This should afford greater privacy to the individual debtor, whose bankruptcy case records may be available on the Internet.

2005 Amendment

The form is amended in a variety of ways to implement the provisions of the Bankruptcy Abuse Prevention and Consumer Protection Act of 2005, Pub. L. No. 109–8, 119 Stat. 23 (April 20, 2005). All versions of the form are amended to advise creditors to consult an attorney concerning what rights they may have in the specific case. All versions of the form are also amended to provide information about filing claims to creditors with foreign addresses and to advise those creditors to consult a lawyer familiar with United States bankruptcy law regarding any questions they may have about their rights in a particular case. These amendments implement § 1514, which was added to the Code in 2005.

Forms 9A and 9C are amended to include a box in which the clerk can notify creditors in a chapter 7 case filed by an individual with primarily consumer debts whether the presumption of abuse has arisen under § 707(b) of the Code as amended in 2005. Under § 342(d) of the Code, the clerk has a duty to notify creditors concerning the presumption within ten days of the filing of the petition. If cases in which the debtor does not file Official Form 22A with the petition, the forms provide for the clerk to state that insufficient information has been filed, and to inform creditors that if later-filed information indicates that the presumption arises, creditors will be sent another notice.

In cases involving serial filers (debtors who have filed more than one case within a specified period), the automatic stay provided by § 362(a) of the Code as amended in 2005 may not apply or may be limited in duration, unless the stay is extended or imposed by court order. The form contains a general statement alerting debtors to this possibility.

Section 1514, added to the Code in 2005, also requires that a secured creditor with a foreign address be advised whether the creditor is required to file a proof of claim, and Forms 9B, 9D, 9E, 9E (Alt.), 9F, 9F (Alt.), 9G, 9H, and 9I are amended to include general information addressing that question. Forms 9E, 9E (Alt.), 9F, and 9F (Alt.) also are amended to inform creditors that in a case in which the debtor has filed a plan for which it has solicited acceptances before filing the case, the court may, after notice and a hearing, order that the United States trustee not convene a meeting of creditors.

Forms 9E and 9E Alt. are amended to state that, unless the court orders otherwise, an individual chapter 11 debtor's discharge is not effective until completion of all payments under the plan, as provided in § 1141(d)(5) which was added to the Code in 2005. Forms 9F and 9F (Alt.) are amended to include a deadline to file a complaint to determine the dischargeability of a debt, in conformity with § 1141(d)(6) which was added to the Code in 2005.

Form 9I is amended to include a deadline to file a complaint to determine the dischargeability of certain debts. This amendment implements 2005 amendment to § 1328(a)(1) of the Code.

2006 Amendment

Forms 9G and 9H are amended to add "family fisherman" to the title and to the description of chapter 12. The 2005 amendments to the Code added a "family fisherman," as defined in § 101(19A), to the persons eligible to file a bankruptcy case under chapter 12. Form 9I is amended to provide general notice to parties in interest of the potential for a claim to be filed late in the case.

2005–2007 Amendments

(The 2005-2007 Committee Note incorporates Committee Notes previously published in 2005 and 2006.)

The form is amended in a variety of ways to implement the provisions of the Bankruptcy Abuse Prevention and Consumer Protection Act of 2005, Pub. L. No. 109-8, 119 Stat. 23 (April 20, 2005). All versions of the form are amended to advise creditors to consult an attorney concerning what rights they may have in the specific case. All versions of the form also are amended to provide to creditors with foreign addresses information about filing claims and to advise those creditors to consult a lawyer familiar with United States bankruptcy law regarding any questions they may have about their rights in a particular case. These amendments implement § 1514, which was added to the Code in 2005.

Forms 9A and 9C are amended to include a box in which the clerk can notify creditors in a chapter 7 case filed by an individual with primarily consumer debts if the presumption of abuse has arisen under § 707(b) of the Code as amended in 2005. Under § 342(d) of the Code, the clerk has a duty to notify creditors concerning the presumption within ten days of the filing of the petition. In cases in which the debtor does not file Official Form 22A with the petition, the forms provide for the clerk to state that insufficient information has been filed, and to inform creditors that if later-filed information indicates that the presumption arises, creditors will be sent another notice. Forms 9G and 9H are amended to add "family fishermen" to the notices used in chapter 12 cases, in conformity with the 2005 amendments to the Code extending the provisions of chapter 12 to family fishermen.

In cases involving serial filers (debtors who have filed more than one case within a specified period), the automatic stay provided by § 362(a) of the Code as amended in 2005 may not apply or may be limited in duration, unless the stay is extended or imposed by court order. The form contains a general statement alerting debtors to this possibility.

Section 1514, added to the Code in 2005, also requires that a secured creditor with a foreign address be advised whether the creditor is required to file a proof of claim, and Forms 9B, 9D, 9E, 9E (Alt.), 9F, 9F (Alt.), 9G, 9H, and 9I are amended to include general information addressing that question. Forms 9E, 9E (Alt.), 9F, and 9F (Alt.) also are amended to inform creditors that in a case in which the debtor has filed a plan for which it has solicited acceptances before filing the case, the court may, after notice and a hearing, order that the United States trustee not convene a meeting of creditors.

Forms 9E and 9E (Alt.) are amended to state that, unless the court orders otherwise, an individual chapter 11 debtor's discharge is not effective until completion of all payments under the plan, as provided in § 1141(d)(5) which was added to the Code in 2005. Forms 9F and 9F (Alt.) are amended to include a deadline to file a complaint to determine the dischargeability of a debt, in conformity with § 1141(d)(6), which also was added to the Code in 2005.

Form 9I is amended to include a deadline to file a complaint to determine the dischargeability of certain debts. This amendment implements a 2005 amendment to § 1328(a) of the Code.

In addition, all versions of the form are amended to provide to the public only the last four digits of any individual debtor's taxpayer-identification number. This amendment implements Rule 9037.

HISTORICAL NOTES

Effective and Applicability Provisions

1997 Acts. Order amending official forms dated Oct. 1, 1997, effective immediately, with mandatory use starting March 1, 1998.

Form 10. Proof of Claim

B10 (Official Form 10) (12/08)

UNITED STATES BANKRUPTCY COURT | PROOF OF CLAIM

Name of Debtor: | Case Number:

NOTE: *This form should not be used to make a claim for an administrative expense arising after the commencement of the case. A request for payment of an administrative expense may be filed pursuant to 11 U.S.C. § 503.*

Name of Creditor (the person or other entity to whom the debtor owes money or property):

Name and address where notices should be sent:

Telephone number:

☐ Check this box to indicate that this claim amends a previously filed claim.

Court Claim Number:________
(If known)

Filed on:________

Name and address where payment should be sent (if different from above):

Telephone number:

☐ Check this box if you are aware that anyone else has filed a proof of claim relating to your claim. Attach copy of statement giving particulars.

☐ Check this box if you are the debtor or trustee in this case.

1. **Amount of Claim as of Date Case Filed:** $________

If all or part of your claim is secured, complete item 4 below; however, if all of your claim is unsecured, do not complete item 4.
If all or part of your claim is entitled to priority, complete item 5.

☐ Check this box if claim includes interest or other charges in addition to the principal amount of claim. Attach itemized statement of interest or charges.

2. **Basis for Claim:** ________
(See instruction #2 on reverse side.)

3. **Last four digits of any number by which creditor identifies debtor:**________

3a. **Debtor may have scheduled account as:** ________
(See instruction #3a on reverse side.)

4. **Secured Claim** (See instruction #4 on reverse side.)
Check the appropriate box if your claim is secured by a lien on property or a right of setoff and provide the requested information.

Nature of property or right of setoff: ☐ Real Estate ☐ Motor Vehicle ☐ Other
Describe:

Value of Property: $___ **Annual Interest Rate**___%

Amount of arrearage and other charges as of time case filed included in secured claim,

if any: $___ **Basis for perfection:** ___

Amount of Secured Claim: $___ **Amount Unsecured:** $___

6. **Credits:** The amount of all payments on this claim has been credited for the purpose of making this proof of claim.

5. **Amount of Claim Entitled to Priority under 11 U.S.C. § 507(a). If any portion of your claim falls in one of the following categories, check the box and state the amount.**

Specify the priority of the claim.

☐ Domestic support obligations under 11 U.S.C. § 507(a)(1)(A) or (a)(1)(B).

☐ Wages, salaries, or commissions (up to $10,950*) earned within 180 days before filing of the bankruptcy petition or cessation of the debtor's business, whichever is earlier–11 U.S.C. § 507(a)(4).

☐ Contributions to an employee benefit plan–11 U.S.C. § 507(a)(5).

☐ Up to $2,425* of deposits toward purchase, lease, or rental of property or services for personal, family, or household use—11 U.S.C. § 507(a)(7).

☐ Taxes or penalties owed to governmental units–11 U.S.C. § 507(a)(8).

☐ Other–Specify applicable paragraph of 11 U.S.C. § 507 (a)(__).

7. **Documents:** Attach redacted copies of any documents that support the claim, such as promissory notes, purchase orders, invoices, itemized statements of running accounts, contracts, judgments, mortgages, and security agreements. You may also attach a summary. Attach redacted copies of documents providing evidence of perfection of a security interest. You may also attach a summary. (*See definition of "redacted" on reverse side.*) DO NOT SEND ORIGINAL DOCUMENTS. ATTACHED DOCUMENTS MAY BE DESTROYED AFTER SCANNING. If the documents are not available, please explain:	**Amount entitled to priority:** $ ____________ **Amounts are subject to adjustment on 4/1/10 and every 3 years thereafter with respect to cases commenced on or after the date of adjustment.*
Date: — **Signature:** The person filing this claim must sign it. Sign and print name and title, if any, of the creditor or other person authorized to file this claim and state address and telephone number if different from the notice address above. Attach copy of power of attorney, if any.	FOR COURT USE ONLY

Penalty for presenting fraudulent claim: Fine of up to $500,000 or imprisonment for up to 5 years, or both. 18 U.S.C. §§ 152 and 3571.

B10 (Official Form 10) (12/07)—Cont.

INSTRUCTIONS FOR PROOF OF CLAIM FORM

The instructions and definitions below are general explanations of the law. In certain circumstances, such as bankruptcy cases not filed voluntarily by the debtor, there may be exceptions to these general rules.

Items to be completed in Proof of Claim form

Court, Name of Debtor, and Case Number:
Fill in the federal judicial district where the bankruptcy case was filed (for example, Central District of California), the bankruptcy debtor's name, and the bankruptcy case number. If the creditor received a notice of the case from the bankruptcy court, all of this information is located at the top of the notice.

Creditor's Name and Address:
Fill in the name of the person or entity asserting a claim and the name and address of the person who should receive notices issued during the bankruptcy case. A separate space is provided for the payment address if it differs from the notice address. The creditor has a continuing obligation to keep the court informed of its current address. See Federal Rule of Bankruptcy Procedure (FRBP) 2002(g).

1. **Amount of Claim as of Date Case Filed:**
State the total amount owed to the creditor on the date of the Bankruptcy filing. Follow the instructions concerning whether to complete items 4 and 5. Check the box if interest or other charges are included in the claim.

2. **Basis for Claim:**
State the type of debt or how it was incurred. Examples include goods sold, money loaned, services performed, personal injury/wrongful death, car loan, mortgage note, and credit card. If the claim is based on the delivery of health care goods or services, limit the disclosure of the goods or services so as to avoid embarrassment or the disclosure of confidential health care information. You may be required to provide additional disclosure if the trustee or another party in interest files an objection to your claim.

3. **Last Four Digits of Any Number by Which Creditor Identifies Debtor:**
State only the last four digits of the debtor's account or other number used by the creditor to identify the debtor.

3a. Debtor May Have Scheduled Account As:
Use this space to report a change in the creditor's name, a transferred claim, or any other information that clarifies a difference between this proof of claim and the claim as scheduled by the debtor.

4. **Secured Claim:**
Check the appropriate box and provide the requested information if the claim is fully or partially secured. Skip this section if the claim is entirely unsecured. (See DEFINITIONS, below.) State the type and the value of property that secures the claim, attach copies of lien documentation, and state annual interest rate and the amount past due on the claim as of the date of the bankruptcy filing.

5. **Amount of Claim Entitled to Priority Under 11 U.S.C. § 507(a).**
If any portion of your claim falls in one or more of the listed categories, check the appropriate box(es) and state the amount entitled to priority. (See DEFINITIONS, below.) A claim may be partly priority and partly non-priority. For example, in some of the categories, the law limits the amount entitled to priority.

6. **Credits:**
An authorized signature on this proof of claim serves as an acknowledgment that when calculating the amount of the claim, the creditor gave the debtor credit for any payments received toward the debt.

7. **Documents:**
Attach to this proof of claim form redacted copies documenting the existence of the debt and of any lien securing the debt. You may also attach a summary. You must also attach copies of documents that evidence perfection of any security interest. You may also attach a summary. FRBP 3001(c) and (d). Do not send original documents, as attachments may be destroyed after scanning.

Date and Signature:
The person filing this proof of claim must sign and date it. FRBP 9011. If the claim is filed electronically, FRBP 5005(a)(2), authorizes courts to establish local rules specifying what constitutes a signature. Print the name and title, if any, of the creditor or other person authorized to file this claim. State the filer's address and telephone number if it differs from the address given on the top of the form for purposes of receiving notices. Attach a complete copy of any power of attorney. Criminal penalties apply for making a false statement on a proof of claim.

DEFINITIONS

Debtor
A debtor is the person, corporation, or other entity that has filed a bankruptcy case.

Creditor
A creditor is the person, corporation, or other entity owed a debt by the debtor on the date of the bankruptcy filing.

Claim
A claim is the creditor's right to receive payment on a debt that was owed by the debtor on the date of the bankruptcy filing. See 11 U.S.C. § 101(5). A claim may be secured or unsecured.

Proof of Claim
A proof of claim is a form used by the creditor to indicate the amount of the debt owed by the debtor on the date of the bankruptcy filing. The creditor must file the form with the clerk of the same bankruptcy court in which the bankruptcy case was filed.

Secured Claim Under 11 U.S.C. § 506(a)
A secured claim is one backed by a lien on property of the debtor. The claim is secured so long as the creditor has the right to be paid from the property prior to other creditors. The amount of the secured claim cannot exceed the value of the property. Any amount owed to the creditor in excess of the value of the property is an unsecured claim. Examples of liens on property include a mortgage on real estate or a security interest in a car. A lien may be voluntarily granted by a debtor or may be obtained through a court proceeding. In some states, a court judgment is a lien. A claim also may be secured if the creditor owes the debtor money (has a right to setoff).

Unsecured Claim
An unsecured claim is one that does not meet the requirements of a secured claim. A claim may be partly unsecured if the amount of the claim exceeds the value of the property on which the creditor has a lien.

Claim Entitled to Priority Under 11 U.S.C. § 507(a)
Priority claims are certain categories of unsecured claims that are paid from the available money or property in a bankruptcy case before other unsecured claims.

Redacted
A document has been redacted when the person filing it has masked, edited out, or otherwise deleted, certain information. A creditor should redact and use only the last four digits of any social-security, individual's tax-identification, or financial-account number, all but the initials of a minor's name and only the year of any person's date of birth.

Evidence of Perfection
Evidence of perfection may include a mortgage, lien, certificate of title, financing statement, or other document showing that the lien has been filed or recorded.

INFORMATION

Acknowledgment of Filing of Claim
To receive acknowledgment of your filing, you may either enclose a stamped self-addressed envelope and a copy of this proof of claim or you may access the court's PACER system (www.pacer.psc.uscourts.gov) for a small fee to view your filed proof of claim.

Offers to Purchase a Claim
Certain entities are in the business of purchasing claims for an amount less than the face value of the claims. One or more of these entities may contact the creditor and offer to purchase the claim. Some of the written communications from these entities may easily be confused with official court documentation or communications from the debtor. These entities do not represent the bankruptcy court or the debtor. The creditor has no obligation to sell its claim. However, if the creditor decides to sell its claim, any transfer of such claim is subject to FRBP 3001(e), any applicable provisions of the Bankruptcy Code (11 U.S.C. § 101 *et seq.*), and any applicable orders of the bankruptcy court.

(Added Aug. 1, 1991, and amended Mar. 16, 1993; Mar. 1995; July, 1995; Oct. 1, 1997; April 1, 1998; Dec. 1, 2003; April 1, 2004; Aug. 11, 2005, eff. Oct. 17, 2005; April 1, 2007; Dec. 1, 2007; Dec. 1, 2008.)

ADVISORY COMMITTEE NOTES

1991 Enactment

This form replaces former Official Forms No. 19, No. 20, and No. 21. The box format and simplified language are intended to facilitate completion of the form.

The form directs the claimant to attach documents to support the claim or, if voluminous, a summary of such documents. These include any security agreement (if not included in the writing on which the claim is founded), and evidence of perfection of any security interest. See Committee Note to Rule 3001(d) concerning satisfactory evidence of perfection. If the claim includes prepetition interest or other charges such as attorney fees, a statement giving a detailed breakdown of the elements of the claim is required.

Rule 2002(g) requires the clerk to update the mailing list in the case by substituting the address provided by a creditor on a proof of claim, if that address is different from the one supplied by the debtor. The form contains checkboxes to assist the clerk in performing this duty. The form also alerts the trustee when the claim is an amendment to or replacement for an earlier claim.

1993 Amendment

The form has been amended to accommodate inclusion of the priority afforded in § 507(a)(8) of the Code, which was added by Pub.L. No. 101–647, (Crime Control Act of 1990), and to avoid the necessity of further amendment to the form if other priorities are added to § 507(a) in the future. In addition, sections 4 and 5 of the form have been amended to clarify that only prepetition arrearages and charges are to be included in the amount of the claim.

1995 Amendment

The form is amended to add the seventh priority granted by the Bankruptcy Reform Act of 1994 to debts for alimony, maintenance, or support of a spouse, former spouse, or child of the debtor. The form also amends the Code reference to the priority afforded to tax debts and the dollar maximums for the priorities granted to wages and customer deposits in conformity with amendments made by the 1994 Act to section 507(a) of the Code. The 1994 Act also amended section 104 of the Code to provide for future adjustment of the dollar amounts specified in section 507(a) to be made by administrative action at three-year intervals to reflect changes in the consumer price index. The form is amended to include notice that these dollar amounts are subject to change without formal amendment to the official form.

1997 Amendment

Numbered sections 4. and 5. of the form have been reformatted to eliminate redundant information and make it easier to complete the form correctly. A creditor will report the total amount of the claim first, and will report only that amount unless the claim is secured by collateral or entitled to a priority under § 507 of the Code.

Explanatory definitions and instructions for completing the form also have been added.

2003 Amendment

The form has been amended to require a wage, salary, or other compensation creditor to disclose only the last four digits of the creditor's Social Security number to afford greater privacy to the creditor. A trustee can request the full information necessary for tax withholding and reporting at the time the trustee makes a distribution to creditors.

2005 Amendment

The form is amended to conform to changes in the priority afforded the claims of certain creditors in § 507(a) of the Code as amended by the Bankruptcy Abuse Prevention and Consumer Protection Act of 2005, Pub. L. No. 109–8, 119 Stat. 23 (April 20, 2005).

2005-2007 Amendments

(The 2005-2007 Committee Note incorporates Committee Notes previously published in 2005.)

The form is amended to conform to changes in the priority afforded the claims of certain creditors in § 507(a) of the Code as amended by the Bankruptcy Abuse Prevention and Consumer Protection Act of 2005, Pub. L. No. 109-8, 119 Stat. 23 (April 20, 2005).

In addition, the form and its instructions are amended in several respects based on the experiences of creditors and trustees in using it and on the technological changes that have occurred in the courts' processing of claims. A definition of the word "redacted" has been added in conformity with Rule 9037.

The creditor now has a space in which to provide a separate payment address if different from the creditor's address for receiving notices in the case. The checkboxes for indicating that the creditor's address provided on the proof of claim is a new address, and that the creditor never received any notices from the court in the case have been deleted. The computer systems now used by the courts make it unnecessary for a creditor to "flag" a new address or call attention to the fact that the creditor is making its first appearance in the case. In place of the deleted items is a new checkbox to be used when a debtor or a trustee files a proof of claim for a creditor; it will alert the clerk to send the notice required by Rule 3004. The box for indicating whether the claim replaces a previously filed claim also has been deleted as no longer necessary in light of the 2005 amendments to Rules 3004 and 3005. The creditor simply will amend the claim filed by the other party.

Requests for the creditor to state the date on which the debt was incurred and the date on which any court judgment concerning the debt was obtained have been deleted, based on reports from trustees that they rely on the documents supporting the claim for this information. The checkboxes for stating the basis for the creditor's claim have been replaced with a blank in which the creditor is to provide this information. Examples of the most common categories, based on the former checkboxes, can be found in the instructions on the form. The request to state the account number by which the creditor identifies the debtor has been moved to paragraph 3 of the form and has been revised to request only the last four digits of the number, in conformity with Rule 9037. In addition, a new paragraph 3a gives the creditor a place to notify the trustee and the court of any change in the creditor's name, or that the claim has been transferred, or to provide any other information to clarify a difference between the proof of claim and the creditor's claim as scheduled by the debtor.

The adjective "total" is deleted from the sections of the form where the creditor states the amount of the claim and the creditor now simply reports the amount of the claim. If the claim is a general unsecured claim, no further details are stated on the form, although a creditor still must attach a copy of any writing on which the claim is based, as required by Rule 3001(c), and must attach a statement itemizing any interest or other charges (in addition to the principal) that are included in the claim. If the claim or any part of it is secured or entitled to priority under § 507(a) of the Code, the creditor is directed to provide details in the appropriate sections of the form. The creditor now states the amount to be afforded priority only once, in the section of the form designated for describing the specific priority being asserted. The introductory language in the section where the creditor describes any priority to which it is entitled has been revised for clarity. The word "collateral" has been replaced with the less colloquial and more accurate phrase "lien on property" throughout the form.

Information about obtaining acknowledgment from the court of the filing of the proof of claim is revised and moved to a new section on the reverse side called "Information." This new section also alerts a creditor to the possibility that it may be approached about selling its claim, advises that the court has no role in any such solicitations, and states that a creditor is under no obligation to accept any offer to purchase its claim. A new instruction is added about signing a proof of claim. This instruction includes citations to Rules 9011 and 5005(a)(2) concerning signature requirements in an electronic filing environment.

Finally, all of the definitions and instructions on the reverse side of the form are amended generally to reflect the deletions, additions, and other changes made on page 1. These include a reminder to the creditor to keep the court informed of any changes in its address. The instructions now appear at the top of the page, and the text is revised both to reflect the substantive changes to the form and to improve the clarity and style of this explanatory material.

2008 Amendment

The form is amended at box seven on page one, and instructions two and seven on page two, to instruct the claimant that the information contained in or attached to a claim based on the delivery of health care goods or services should be limited so as to avoid embarrassment or the unnecessary disclosure of confidential information. The claimant is informed that additional disclosure may be required if the trustee or another party in interest objects to the claim.

Page two of the form is also amended to revise slightly the definitions of "creditor" and "claim" to conform more closely to the definitions of those terms in the Code.

HISTORICAL NOTES

Effective and Applicability Provisions

1998 Acts. Memorandum amending official forms dated March 17, 1998, effective April 1, 1998, and applicable to cases filed on or after such date.

1997 Acts. Order amending official forms dated Oct. 1, 1997, effective immediately, with mandatory use starting March 1, 1998.

[Form 11. Omitted. See Form 5.]

Form 11A. General Power of Attorney

Official Form 11A
6/90

United States Bankruptcy Court
_______ District Of _______

In re ______________________________, Case No. ______________________
Debtor

Chapter ______________________

GENERAL POWER OF ATTORNEY

To ____ of *
____, and
_______________________________________ of * ___________________.

The undersigned claimant hereby authorizes you, or any one of you, as attorney in fact for the undersigned and with full power of substitution, to vote on any question that may be lawfully submitted to creditors of the debtor in the above-entitled case; [*if appropriate*] to vote for a trustee of the estate of the debtor and for a committee of creditors; to receive dividends; and in general to perform any act not constituting the practice of law for the undersigned in all matters arising in this case.

Dated: ____________________

Signed: ______________________________

By ________________________
as ________________________

Address: ______________________________
____

[*If executed by an individual*] Acknowledged before me on ____________________.

[*If executed on behalf of a partnership*] Acknowledged before me on ____________________, by ______________________________, who says that he [*or* she] is a member of the partnership named above and is authorized to execute this power of attorney in its behalf.

[*If executed on behalf of a corporation*] Acknowledged before me on ____________________, by ______________________________, who says that he [*or* she] is ____________________ of the corporation named above and is authorized to execute this power of attorney in its behalf.

____
____
[Official character.]

(Added Aug. 1, 1991.)

* State mailing address.

ADVISORY COMMITTEE NOTES

This form previously was numbered Official Form No. 17.

Form 11B. Special Power of Attorney

Official Form 11B
6/90

United States Bankruptcy Court
______ District Of ______

In re ______________________________, Case No. ____________________
Debtor

Chapter ____________________

SPECIAL POWER OF ATTORNEY

To ____________________________ of * ______________________________, and ______________________________ of * ____________________.

The undersigned claimant hereby authorizes you, or any one of you, as attorney in fact for the undersigned [*if desired:* and with full power of substitution,] to attend the meeting of creditors of the debtor or any adjournment thereof, and to vote in my behalf on any question that may be lawfully submitted to creditors at such meeting or adjourned meeting, and for a trustee or trustees of the estate of the debtor.

Dated: ____________________

Signed: ____________________________
By __________________________
as __________________________
Address: ____________________________
____

[*If executed by an individual*] Acknowledged before me on __________________.

[*If executed on behalf of a partnership*] Acknowledged before me __________________, by ____________________________, who says that he [*or* she] is a member of the partnership named above and is authorized to execute this power of attorney in its behalf.

[*If executed on behalf of a corporation*] Acknowledged before me on __________________, by ________________________, who says that he [*or* she] is ________________________ of the corporation named above and is authorized to execute this power of attorney in its behalf.

____
____
[*Official character.*]

(Added Aug. 1, 1991.)

* State mailing address.

ADVISORY COMMITTEE NOTES

This form previously was numbered Official Form No. 18.

Form 12. Order and Notice for Hearing on Disclosure Statement

Official Form 12
12/03

[Caption as in Form 16A]

ORDER AND NOTICE FOR HEARING ON DISCLOSURE STATEMENT

To the debtor, its creditors, and other parties in interest:

A disclosure statement and a plan under chapter 11 [*or* chapter 9] of the Bankruptcy Code having been filed by ____________________ on ____________________,

IT IS ORDERED and notice is hereby given, that:

1. The hearing to consider the approval of the disclosure statement shall be held at: ____________________, on ____________________, at __________ o'clock __.m.

2. ____________________ is fixed as the last day for filing and serving in accordance with Fed.R.Bankr.P. 3017(a) written objections to the disclosure statement.

3. Within __________ days after entry of this order, the disclosure statement and plan shall be distributed in accordance with Fed.R.Bankr.P. 3017(a).

4. Requests for copies of the disclosure statement and plan shall be mailed to the debtor in possession [*or* trustee *or* debtor *or* ____________________] at * ____.

Dated: ____________________

BY THE COURT

____

United States Bankruptcy Judge

(Added Aug. 1, 1991, and amended Dec. 2003.)

* State mailing address

ADVISORY COMMITTEE NOTES

1991 Enactment

This form previously was numbered Official Form No. 28. The form is related to Rule 3017(a). Section 1125 of the Code requires court approval of a disclosure statement before votes may be solicited for or against a plan in either chapter 11 reorganization or chapter 9 municipality cases.

Objections to the disclosure statement may be filed. Rule 3017(a) specifies that the court may fix a time for the filing of objections or they can be filed at any time prior to approval of the statement.

Rule 3017(a) also specifies the persons who are to receive copies of the statement and plan prior to the hearing. These documents will not be sent to all parties in interest because at this stage of the case it could be unnecessarily expensive and confusing. However, any party in interest may request copies. The request should be made in writing (Rule 3017(a)), and sent to the person mailing the statement and plan which, as the form indicates, would usually be the proponent of the plan.

This form may be adapted for use if more than one disclosure statement is to be considered by the court.

Form 13. Order Approving Disclosure Statement and Fixing Time for Filing Acceptances or Rejections of Plan, Combined with Notice Thereof

Official Form 13
12/03

[Caption as in Form 16A]

ORDER APPROVING DISCLOSURE STATEMENT AND FIXING TIME FOR FILING ACCEPTANCES OR REJECTIONS OF PLAN, COMBINED WITH NOTICE THEREOF

A disclosure statement under chapter 11 of the Bankruptcy Code having been filed by ________________, on ________ [*if appropriate,* and by ________________, on ________], referring to a plan under chapter 11 of the Code filed by ________________, on ________ [*if appropriate,* and by ________________, on ________ respectively] [*if appropriate,* as modified by a modification filed on ________]; and

It having been determined after hearing on notice that the disclosure statement [*or* statements] contain[s] adequate information:

IT IS ORDERED, and notice is hereby given, that:

A. The disclosure statement filed by ________________ dated ________ [*if appropriate,* and by ________________, dated ________ is [are] approved.

B. ________________ is fixed as the last day for filing written acceptances or rejections of the plan [*or* plans] referred to above.

C. Within ________ days after the entry of this order, the plan [*or* plans] *or* a summary *or* summaries thereof approved by the court, [and [*if appropriate*] a summary approved by the court of its opinion, if any, dated ________, approving the disclosure statement [*or* statements]], the disclosure statement [*or* statements], and a ballot conforming to Official Form 14 shall be mailed to creditors, equity security holders, and other parties in interest, and shall be transmitted to the United States trustee, as provided in Fed.R.Bankr.P. 3017(d).

D. If acceptances are filed for more than one plan, preferences among the plans so accepted may be indicated.

E. *[If appropriate]* ________________________________ is fixed for the hearing on confirmation of the plan [*or* plans].

F. *[If appropriate]* ________________ is fixed as the last day for filing and serving pursuant to Fed.R.Bankr.P. 3020(b)(1) written objections to confirmation of the plan.

Dated: ________________

BY THE COURT

____
United States Bankruptcy Judge

[If the court directs that a copy of the opinion should be transmitted in lieu of or in addition to the summary thereof, the appropriate change should be made in paragraph C of this order.]

(Added Aug. 1, 1991, and amended Dec. 2003.)

ADVISORY COMMITTEE NOTES

1991 Enactment

This form is derived from former Official Form No. 29. The form may be adapted for use if more than one disclosure statement is approved by the court.

Form 14. Class *[ ]* Ballot for Accepting or Rejecting Plan of Reorganization

Official Form 14

(12/03)

[Caption as in Form 16A]

CLASS *[ ]* BALLOT FOR ACCEPTING OR REJECTING PLAN OF REORGANIZATION

[Proponent] filed a plan of reorganization dated *[Date]* (the "Plan") for the Debtor in this case. The Court has *[conditionally]* approved a disclosure statement with respect to the Plan (the "Disclosure Statement"). The Disclosure Statement provides information to assist you in deciding how to vote your ballot. If you do not have a Disclosure Statement, you may obtain a copy from *[name, address, telephone number and telecopy number of proponent/proponent's attorney.]* Court approval of the disclosure statement does not indicate approval of the Plan by the Court.

You should review the Disclosure Statement and the Plan before you vote. You may wish to seek legal advice concerning the Plan and your classification and treatment under the Plan. Your *[claim] [equity interest]* has been placed in class *[ ]* under the Plan. If you hold claims or equity interests in more than one class, you will receive a ballot for each class in which you are entitled to vote.

If your ballot is not received by *[name and address of proponent's attorney or other appropriate address]* on or before *[date]*, and such deadline is not extended, your vote will not count as either an acceptance or rejection of the Plan.

If the Plan is confirmed by the Bankruptcy Court it will be binding on you whether or not you vote.

ACCEPTANCE OR REJECTION OF THE PLAN

[At this point the ballot should provide for voting by the particular class of creditors or equity holders receiving the ballot using one of the following alternatives;]

[If the voter is the holder of a secured, priority, or unsecured nonpriority claim:]

The undersigned, the holder of a Class *[ ]* claim against the Debtor in the unpaid amount of Dollars ($)

[or, if the voter is the holder of a bond, debenture, or other debt security:]

The undersigned, the holder of a Class *[ ]* claim against the Debtor, consisting of Dollars ($) principal amount of *[describe bond, debenture, or other debt security]* of the Debtor (For purposes of this Ballot, it is not necessary and you should not adjust the principal amount for any accrued or unmatured interest.)

Official Form 14 continued
(12/03)

[or, if the voter is the holder of an equity interest:]

The undersigned, the holder of Class *[ ]* equity interest in the Debtor, consisting of _____ shares or other interests of *[describe equity interest]* in the Debtor

[In each case, the following language should be included:]

(Check one box only)

[ ] ACCEPTS THE PLAN [ ] REJECTS THE PLAN

Dated: ____________

Print or type name: ____________

Signature: ____________

Title (if corporation or partnership) ____________

Address: ____________

____

RETURN THIS BALLOT TO:

[Name and address of proponent's attorney or other appropriate address]

(Added Aug. 1, 1991, and amended Oct. 1, 1997; Dec. 2003.)

ADVISORY COMMITTEE NOTES

1991 Enactment

This form is derived from former Official Form No. 30. The form has been amended to facilitate the voting of a debtor's shares held in "street name." The form may be adapted to designate the class in which each ballot is to be tabulated. It is intended that a separate ballot will be provided for each class in which a holder may vote.

1997 Amendment

The form has been substantially amended to simplify its format and make it easier to complete correctly.

Directions or blanks for proponent to complete the text of the ballot are in italics and enclosed within brackets. A ballot should include only the applicable language from the alternatives shown on this form and should be adapted to the particular requirements of the case.

If the plan provides for creditors in a class to have the right to reduce their claims so as to qualify for treatment given to creditors whose claims do not exceed a specified amount, the ballot should make provisions for the exercise of that right. See section 1122(b) of the Code.

If debt or equity securities are held in the name of a broker/dealer or nominee, the ballot should require the furnishing of sufficient information to assure that duplicate ballots are not submitted and counted and that ballots submitted by a broker/dealer or nominee reflect the votes of the beneficial holders of such securities. See Rule 3017(e).

In the event that more than one plan of reorganization is to be voted upon, the form of ballot will need to be adapted to permit holders of claims or equity interests (a) to accept or reject each plan being proposed, and (b) to indicate preferences among the competing plans. See section 1129(c) of the Code.

HISTORICAL NOTES

Effective and Applicability Provisions

1997 Acts. Order amending official forms dated Oct. 1, 1997, effective immediately, with mandatory use starting March 1, 1998.

Form 15. Order Confirming Plan

Form B15
(Rev. 12/01)

[Caption as in Form 16A]

ORDER CONFIRMING PLAN

The plan under chapter 11 of the Bankruptcy Code filed by ________, on ________ [*if applicable*, as modified by a modification filed on ________,] or a summary thereof, having been transmitted to creditors and equity security holders; and

It having been determined after hearing on notice that the requirements for confirmation set forth in 11 U.S.C. § 1129(a) [*or, if appropriate*, 11 U.S.C. § 1129(b)] have been satisfied;

IT IS ORDERED that:

The plan filed by ________, on ________, *[If appropriate, include dates and any other pertinent details of modifications to the plan]* is confirmed. *[If the plan provides for an injunction against conduct not otherwise enjoined under the Code, include the information required by Rule 3020.]*

A copy of the confirmed plan is attached.

Dated: ________________

BY THE COURT

____
United States Bankruptcy Judge

(Added Aug. 1, 1991, and amended Dec. 1, 2001.)

ADVISORY COMMITTEE NOTES

This form is derived from former Official Form No. 31. The form has been simplified to avoid the necessity of repeating the statutory requirements of 11 U.S.C. § 1129(a). In the case of an individual chapter 11 debtor, Form 18 may be adapted for use together with this form.

Form 16A. Caption (Full)

B16A (Official Form 16A) (12/07)

United States Bankruptcy Court
__________ District Of __________

In re ____,)
[Set forth here all names including married, maiden, and trade names used by debtor within last 8 years.])
Debtor) Case No. ____________

Address ____)
____) Chapter ________

Last four digits of Social-Security or Individual Taxpayer-Identification (ITIN) No(s)., (if any): ________________)
____)
Employer Tax-Identification (EIN) No(s). (if any): ________________)
____)

[Designation of Character of Paper]

(Added Aug. 1, 1991; and amended Mar. 1995; Dec. 1, 2003; Aug. 11, 2005, eff. Oct. 17, 2005; Dec. 1, 2007.)

ADVISORY COMMITTEE NOTES

1991 Enactment

This form has been transferred from former Official Form No. 1, which included the form of caption for the case. Rule 9004(b) requires a caption to set forth the title of the case. Rule 1005 provides that the title of the case shall include the debtor's name, all other names used by the debtor within six years before the commencement of the case, and the debtor's social security and tax identification numbers. This form of caption is prescribed for use on the petition, the notice of the meeting of creditors, the order of discharge, and the documents relating to a chapter 11 plan, (Official Forms 1, 9, 12, 13, 14, 15, and 18). See Rule 2002(m). In the petition, (Official Form 1), and the notice of the meeting of creditors, (Official Form 9), the information required by Rule 1005 appears in a block format. A notation of the chapter of the Bankruptcy Code under which the case is proceeding has been added to the form.

1995 Amendment

The form is amended to provide for the debtor's address to appear in the caption in furtherance of the duty of the debtor to include this information on every notice given by the debtor. The Bankruptcy Reform Act of 1994 amended section 342 of the Code to add this requirement.

2003 Amendment

The form has been amended to require disclosure of only the last four digits of the debtor's Social Security or other Taxpayer Identification number. Those four digits will provide creditors with sufficient information to identify the debtor accurately while affording greater privacy to the debtor.

2005 Amendment

The form is amended to require that the title of the case include all names used by the debtor within the last eight years in conformity with § 727(a)(8) as amended by the Bankruptcy Abuse Prevention and Consumer Protection Act of 2005, Pub. L. No. 109–8, 119 Stat. 23 (April 20, 2005), extending from six years to eight years the period during which a debtor is barred from receiving successive discharges.

2005–2007 Amendments

(The 2005-2007 Committee Note incorporates the Committee Note previously published in 2005.)

The form is amended to require that the title of the case include all names used by the debtor within the last eight years in conformity with § 727(a)(8) as amended by the Bankruptcy Abuse Prevention and Consumer Protection Act of 2005, Pub. L. No. 109–8, 119 Stat. 23 (April 20, 2005), extending from six years to eight years the period during which a debtor is barred from receiving successive discharges. In conformity with Rule 9037, the filer is directed to provide only the last four digits of any individual debtor's taxpayer-identification number.

Form 16B. Caption (Short Title)

Official Form 16B
12/94

(May be used if 11 U.S.C. § 342(c) is not applicable)

United States Bankruptcy Court
______ District Of ______

In re ____________________________,
Debtor

Case No. ________________________
Chapter _________________________

[Designation of Character of Paper]

(Added Aug. 1, 1991; and amended Mar. 1995.)

ADVISORY COMMITTEE NOTES

This form of caption is prescribed for general use in filing papers in a case under the Bankruptcy Code. Rule 9004(b) requires a caption to set forth the title of the case, and Rule 1005 specifies that the title must include all names used by the debtor within six years before the commencement of the case and the debtor's social security and tax identification numbers. This information is necessary in the petition, the notice of the meeting of creditors, the order of discharge, and the documents relating to the plan in chapter 11 cases. See Rule 2002(m) and Official Form 16A. In other notices, motions, applications, and papers filed in a case, however, a short title containing simply the name of the debtor or joint debtors may be used. Additional names, such as any under which the debtor has engaged in business, may be included in the short title as needed.

1995 Amendment

The title of this form is amended to specify that it can be used when section 342(c) of the Code, as added by the Bankruptcy Reform Act of 1994, is not applicable.

Form 16C. Caption of Complaint in Adversary Proceeding Filed by a Debtor [Abrogated]

ADVISORY COMMITTEE NOTES

This form previously was numbered Official Form No. 34. A notation of the chapter of the Bankruptcy Code under which the case is proceeding has been added to the form. Rule 7010 refers to this form as providing the caption of a pleading in an adversary proceeding.

1995 Amendment

The form is amended to conform to the amendments made to section 342 of the Code by the Bankruptcy Reform Act of 1994.

2003 Amendment

The form is abrogated. An amendment to Official Form 16A directs that only the last four digits of the debtor's Social Security number should appear in a caption. Section 342(c) of the Bankruptcy Code continues to require the debtor to provide a creditor with the debtor's name, address, and taxpayer identification number on any notice the debtor is required to give to the creditor. An individual debtor can fulfill this requirement by including the debtor's Social Security account number on only the creditor's copy of any notice or summons the debtor may serve on the creditor.

Form 16D. Caption for Use in Adversary Proceeding

Form B16D
12/04

United States Bankruptcy Court
______ District Of ______

In re ________________________,	)	
Debtor	)	Case No. ________________
	)	
____________________________,	)	Chapter ________________
Plaintiff	)	
	)	
v.	)	
	)	
____________________________,	)	Adv. Proc. No. ________________
Defendant	)	

COMPLAINT [*or* other Designation]

[If in a Notice of Appeal (see Form 17) or other notice filed and served by a debtor, this caption must be altered to include the debtor's address and Employer's Tax Identification Number(s) or last four digits of Social Security Number(s) as in Form 16A.]

(Added Mar. 1995, and amended Dec. 1, 2004)

ADVISORY COMMITTEE NOTES

This form of caption may be used in an adversary proceeding when section 342(c) of the Code, as added by the Bankruptcy Reform Act of 1994, is not applicable.

Form 17. Notice of Appeal Under 28 U.S.C. § 158(a) or (b) From a Judgment, Order, or Decree of a Bankruptcy Judge

Official Form 17
(12/04)

United States Bankruptcy Court
______ District Of ______

In re ________________________________, Case No. ____________________________
Debtor

Chapter ____________________________

[Caption as in Form 16A, 16B, or 16D, as appropriate]

NOTICE OF APPEAL

____________________, the plaintiff [*or* defendant *or* other party] appeals under 28 U.S.C. § 158(a) or (b) from the judgment, order, or decree of the bankruptcy judge (describe) entered in this adversary proceeding [*or other proceeding, describe type*] on the ______ day of __(month)__, __(year)__.

The names of all parties to the judgment, order, or decree appealed from and the names, addresses, and telephone numbers of their respective attorneys are as follows:

Dated: ________________

Signed: __________________________________
Attorney for Appellant (or Appellant, if not represented by an Attorney)

Attorney Name: ________________________________

Address: ________________________________
____

Telephone No: ________________________________

If a Bankruptcy Appellate Panel Service is authorized to hear this appeal, each party has a right to have the appeal heard by the district court. The appellant may exercise this right only by filing a separate statement of election at the time of the filing of this notice of appeal. Any other party may elect, within the time provided in 28 U.S.C. § 158(c), to have the appeal heard by the district court.

If a child support creditor or its representative is the appellant, and if the child support creditor or its representative files the form specified in § 304(g) of the Bankruptcy Reform Act of 1994, no fee is required.

(Added Aug. 1, 1991; and amended Mar. 1995; Oct. 1, 1997; Dec. 1, 2002; Dec. 1, 2004.)

ADVISORY COMMITTEE NOTES

This form is derived from former Official Form No. 35. The form has been amended to indicate that a final order may be entered other than in an adversary proceeding.

1995 Amendment

The form is amended to reflect the amendments to 28 U.S.C. § 158 concerning bankruptcy appellate panels made by the Bankruptcy Reform Act of 1994. Section 158(d) requires an appellant who elects to appeal to a district court rather than a bankruptcy appellate panel to do so "at the time of filing the appeal."

The 1994 Act also amended 28 U.S.C. § 158(a) to permit immediate appeal of interlocutory orders increasing or reducing a chapter 11 debtor's exclusive period to file a plan under section 1121 of the Code. The form is amended to provide appropriate flexibility.

1997 Amendment

The form has been amended to conform to Rule 8001(a), which requires the notice to contain the names of all parties to the judgment, order, or decree appealed from the names, addresses, and telephone numbers of their respective attorneys. A party filing a notice of appeal pro se should provide equivalent information.

2002 Amendment

The form is amended to give notice that no filing fee is required if a child support creditor or its representative is the appellant, and if the child support creditor or its representative files a form detailing the child support debt, its status, and other characteristics, as specified in § 304(g) of the Bankruptcy Reform Act of 1994, Pub. L. No. 103–396, 108 Stat. 4106 (Oct. 22, 1994).

HISTORICAL NOTES

Effective and Applicability Provisions

1997 Acts. Order amending official forms dated Oct. 1, 1997, effective immediately, with mandatory use starting March 1, 1998.

Form 18. Discharge of Debtor in a Chapter 7 Case

B18 (Official Form 18) (12/07)

United States Bankruptcy Court
__________ District Of __________

In re ____,)
[Set forth here all names including married, maiden, and trade names used by debtor within last 8 years.])
Debtor) Case No. __________
)
Address ____)
____) Chapter 7
)
Last four digits of Social-Security or other Individual Taxpayer-Identification No(s). (if any): ________________)
____)
Employer Tax-Identification No(s). (EIN) [if any]: ________________)
____)

DISCHARGE OF DEBTOR

It appearing that the debtor is entitled to a discharge, **IT IS ORDERED:** The debtor is granted a discharge under section 727 of title 11, United States Code, (the Bankruptcy Code).

Dated: ____________________

BY THE COURT

____
United States Bankruptcy Judge

SEE THE BACK OF THIS ORDER FOR IMPORTANT INFORMATION.

B18 (Official Form 18) (12/07) - Cont.

EXPLANATION OF BANKRUPTCY DISCHARGE IN A CHAPTER 7 CASE

This court order grants a discharge to the person named as the debtor. It is not a dismissal of the case and it does not determine how much money, if any, the trustee will pay to creditors.

Collection of Discharged Debts Prohibited

The discharge prohibits any attempt to collect from the debtor a debt that has been discharged. For example, a creditor is not permitted to contact a debtor by mail, phone, or otherwise, to file or continue a lawsuit, to attach wages or other property, or to take any other action to collect a discharged debt from the debtor. *[In a case involving community property:* There are also special rules that protect certain community property owned by the debtor's spouse, even if that spouse did not file a bankruptcy case.] A creditor who violates this order can be required to pay damages and attorney's fees to the debtor.

However, a creditor may have the right to enforce a valid lien, such as a mortgage or security interest, against the debtor's property after the bankruptcy, if that lien was not avoided or eliminated in the bankruptcy case. Also, a debtor may voluntarily pay any debt that has been discharged.

Debts That are Discharged

The chapter 7 discharge order eliminates a debtor's legal obligation to pay a debt that is discharged. Most, but not all, types of debts are discharged if the debt existed on the date the bankruptcy case was filed. (If this case was begun under a different chapter of the Bankruptcy Code and converted to chapter 7, the discharge applies to debts owed when the bankruptcy case was converted.)

Debts that are Not Discharged.

Some of the common types of debts which are not discharged in a chapter 7 bankruptcy case are:

a. Debts for most taxes;

b. Debts incurred to pay nondischargeable taxes;

c. Debts that are domestic support obligations;

d. Debts for most student loans;

e. Debts for most fines, penalties, forfeitures, or criminal restitution obligations;

f. Debts for personal injuries or death caused by the debtor's operation of a motor vehicle, vessel, or aircraft while intoxicated;

g. Some debts which were not properly listed by the debtor;

h. Debts that the bankruptcy court specifically has decided or will decide in this bankruptcy case are not discharged;

i. Debts for which the debtor has given up the discharge protections by signing a reaffirmation agreement in compliance with the Bankruptcy Code requirements for reaffirmation of debts; and

j. Debts owed to certain pension, profit sharing, stock bonus, other retirement plans, or to the Thrift Savings Plan for federal employees for certain types of loans from these plans.

This information is only a general summary of the bankruptcy discharge. There are exceptions to these general rules. Because the law is complicated, you may want to consult an attorney to determine the exact effect of the discharge in this case.

(Added Aug. 1, 1991; and amended Mar. 1995; Oct. 1, 1997; Aug. 11, 2005, eff. Oct. 17, 2005; Dec. 1, 2007.)

ADVISORY COMMITTEE NOTES

1991 Enactment

This form previously was numbered Official Form No. 27. The form has been revised to accommodate cases commenced by the filing of either a voluntary or an involuntary petition.

1995 Amendment

The form is amended to include debts described in section 523(a)(15) of the Code, which was added by the Bankruptcy Reform Act of 1994, in the list of debts discharged unless determined by the court to be nondischargeable.

1997 Amendment

The discharge order has been simplified by deleting paragraphs which had detailed some, but not all, of the effects of the discharge. These paragraphs have been replaced with a plain English explanation of the discharge. This explanation is to be printed on the reverse of the order, to increase understanding of the bankruptcy discharge among creditors and debtors. The bracketed sentence in the second paragraph should be included when the case involves community property.

2005 Amendment

The form is amended to require that the title of the case include all names used by the debtor within the eight years prior to the filing of the petition in the case in conformity with § 727(a)(8) as amended by the Bankruptcy Abuse Prevention and Consumer Protection Act of 2005, Pub. L. No. 109–8, 119 Stat. 23 (April 20, 2005), extending from six years to eight years the period during which a debtor is barred from receiving successive discharges. The explanation part of the form is amended to include additional types of debts that are not discharged under § 523(a) as amended in 2005 and to revise certain terminology in conformity with provisions of the 2005 Act.

2005–2007 Amendments

(The 2005–2007 Committee Note incorporates the Committee Note previously published in 2005.)

The form is amended to require that the title of the case include all names used by the debtor within the eight years prior to the filing of the petition in the case in conformity with § 727(a)(8) as amended by the Bankruptcy Abuse Prevention and Consumer Protection Act of 2005, Pub. L. No. 109-8, 119 Stat. 23 (April 20, 2005), extending from six years to eight years the period during which a debtor is barred from receiving successive discharges. The explanation part of the form is amended to include additional types of debts that are not discharged under § 523(a), as amended in 2005, and to revise certain terminology in conformity with provisions of the 2005 Act. In conformity with Rule 9037 and Official Form 16A, the caption also is amended to provide only the last four digits of any individual debtor's taxpayer-identification number.

HISTORICAL NOTES

Effective and Applicability Provisions

1997 Acts. Order amending official forms dated Oct. 1, 1997, effective immediately, with mandatory use starting March 1, 1998.

Form 19. Declaration and Signature of Non–Attorney Bankruptcy Petition Preparer

B19 (Official Form 19) (12/07)

United States Bankruptcy Court
__________ District Of __________

In re __________________________________,
Debtor

Case No. ____________________

Chapter ________

DECLARATION AND SIGNATURE OF NON–ATTORNEY BANKRUPTCY PETITION PREPARER (*See* 11 U.S.C. § 110)

I declare under penalty of perjury that:

(1) I am a bankruptcy petition preparer as defined in 11 U.S.C. § 110;

(2) I prepared the accompanying document(s) listed below for compensation and have provided the debtor with a copy of the document(s) and the attached notice as required by 11 U.S.C. §§ 110(b), 110(h), and 342 (b); and

(3) if rules or guidelines have been promulgated pursuant to 11 U.S.C. § 110(h) setting a maximum fee for services chargeable by bankruptcy petition preparers, I have given the debtor notice of the maximum amount before preparing any document for filing for a debtor or accepting any fee from the debtor, as required by that section.

Accompanying documents:
____
____
____
____
____

Printed or Typed Name and Title, if any, of Bankruptcy Petition Preparer:
____

Social-Security No. of Bankruptcy Petition Preparer (Required by 11 U.S.C. § 110):
____

If the bankruptcy petition preparer is not an individual, state the name, title (if any), address, and social-security number of the officer, principal, responsible person or partner who signs this document.

____
____
____
Address

X______________________________ _______________
Signature of Bankruptcy Petition Preparer Date

Names and Social-Security numbers of all other individuals who prepared or assisted in preparing this document, unless the bankruptcy petition preparer is not an individual:

If more than one person prepared this document, attach additional signed sheets conforming to the appropriate Official Form for each person.

A bankruptcy petition preparer's failure to comply with the provisions of title 11 and the Federal Rules of Bankruptcy Procedure may result in fines or imprisonment or both. 11 U.S.C. § 110; 18 U.S.C. § 156.

B19 (Official Form 19) (12/07) - Cont.

NOTICE TO DEBTOR BY NON–ATTORNEY BANKRUPTCY PETITION PREPARER

[Must be filed with any document(s) prepared by a bankruptcy petition preparer]

I am a bankruptcy petition preparer. I am not an attorney and may not practice law or give legal advice. Before preparing any document for filing as defined in § 110(a)(2) of the Bankruptcy Code or accepting any fees, I am required by law to provide you with this notice concerning bankruptcy petition preparers. Under the law, § 110 of the Bankruptcy Code (11 U.S.C. § 110), I am forbidden to offer you any legal advice, including advice about any of the following:

- whether to file a petition under the Bankruptcy Code (11 U.S.C. § 101 et seq.);
- whether commencing a case under chapter 7, 11, 12, or 13 is appropriate;
- whether your debts will be eliminated or discharged in a case under the Bankruptcy Code;
- whether you will be able to retain your home, car, or other property after commencing a case under the Bankruptcy Code;
- the tax consequences of a case brought under the Bankruptcy Code;
- the dischargeability of tax claims;
- whether you may or should promise to repay debts to a creditor or enter into a reaffirmation agreement with a creditor to reaffirm a debt;
- how to characterize the nature of your interests in property or your debts; or
- bankruptcy procedure and rights.

[The notice may provide additional examples of legal advice that a bankruptcy petition preparer is not authorized to give.]

In addition, under 11 U.S.C. § 110(h), the Supreme Court or the Judicial Conference of the United States may promulgate rules or guidelines setting a maximum allowable fee chargeable by a bankruptcy petition preparer. As required by law, I have notified you of this maximum allowable fee, if any, before preparing any document for filing or accepting any fee from you.

______________________________ ______________________________

Signature of Debtor Date Joint Debtor (if any) Date

[In a joint case, both spouses must sign.]

(Added Mar. 1995; and amended Dec. 1, 2003; Aug. 11, 2005, eff. Oct. 17, 2005; Dec. 1, 2007.)

ADVISORY COMMITTEE NOTES

1995 Amendment

This form is new. The Bankruptcy Reform Act of 1994 requires a "bankruptcy petition preparer," as defined in 11 U.S.C. § 110, to sign any "document for filing" that the bankruptcy petition preparer prepares for compensation on behalf of a debtor, to disclose on the document certain information, and to provide the debtor with a copy of the document. This form or adaptations of this form have been incorporated into the official forms of the voluntary petition, the schedules, the statement of financial affairs, and other official forms that typically would be prepared for a debtor by a bankruptcy petition preparer. This form is to be used in connection with any other document that a bankruptcy petition preparer prepares for filing by a debtor in a bankruptcy case.

2003 Amendment

Pursuant to § 110(c) of the Bankruptcy Code, the certification by a non-attorney bankruptcy petition preparer continues to require a petition preparer to provide the full Social

Security number of the individual who actually prepares the document.

2005 Amendment

The certification by a non-attorney bankruptcy petition preparer in this form is renamed a "declaration" and is amended to include material mandated by amendments to § 110 of the Code in the Bankruptcy Abuse Prevention and Consumer Protection Act of 2005, Pub. L. No. 109–8, 119 Stat. 23 (April 20, 2005).

2005-2007 Amendments

(The 2005–2007 Committee Note incorporates the Committee Notes to Forms 19A and 19B previously published in 2005.)

This form is new. It is derived from form 19B and replaces forms 19A and 19B (which forms are abrogated). The form contains the notice a bankruptcy petition preparer is required to give to a debtor under § 110 of the Code as amended by the Bankruptcy Abuse Prevention and Consumer Protection Act of 2005, Pub. L. No. 109-8, 119 Stat. 23 (April 20, 2005), and the bankruptcy petition preparer's signed declaration (also required by § 110 of the Code) that the notice was given to the debtor.

The notice states, in language mandated in the 2005 Act, that the bankruptcy petition preparer is not an attorney and must not give legal advice. The notice also includes examples of advice a bankruptcy petition preparer may not give that are taken from § 110(e)(2) of the Code.

Although space is provided in the declaration to list multiple documents prepared for a single filing, a new form 19 must be completed and accompany subsequent filings. For example, one form 19 listing all forms prepared by the bankruptcy petition preparer would be filed with the debtor's petition package. Another form 19 would be required if the debtor files amended schedules later in the case that were prepared by the bankruptcy petition preparer.

The form must be signed by the debtor and the bankruptcy petition preparer where indicated, and must be filed with each document for filing prepared by the bankruptcy petition preparer.

Form 20A. Notice of Motion or Objection

Official Form 20A
(12/03)

United States Bankruptcy Court
________ District Of ________

In re __________________________________,)
[Set forth here all names including married, maiden, and trade names used by debtor within last 6[1] years.])
Debtor) Case No. _______
)
Address __________________________________)
)
__________________________________) Chapter _______
)
Employer's Tax Identification (EIN) No(s). *[if any]*: ___)
Last Four Digits of Social Security No(s).: _________)
____)

NOTICE OF [MOTION TO] [OBJECTION TO]

________________ has filed papers with the court to [relief sought in motion or objection].

Your rights may be affected. You should read these papers carefully and discuss them with your attorney, if you have one in this bankruptcy case. (If you do not have an attorney, you may wish to consult one.)

If you do not want the court to [relief sought in motion or objection], or if you want the court to consider your views on the [motion] [objection], then on or before (date), you or your attorney must:

[File with the court a written request for a hearing {*or, if the court requires a written response*, an answer, explaining your position} at:

{address of the bankruptcy clerk's office}

If you mail your {request} {response} to court for filing, you must mail it early enough so the court will **receive** it on or before the date stated above. You must also mail a copy to:

{movant's attorney's name and address}

{names and addresses of others to be served}]

[Attend the hearing scheduled to be held on (date), (year), at ___ a.m./p.m. in Courtroom _____, United States Bankruptcy Court, {address}.]

[Other steps required to oppose a motion or objection under local rule or court order.]

If you or your attorney do not take these steps, the court may decide that you do not oppose the relief sought in the motion or objection and may enter an order granting that relief.

Date: ________________ Signature: ____________________
Name:
Address:

(Added Oct. 1, 1997, and amended Dec. 2003.)

[1] So in original. Probably should now read "8" years.

ADVISORY COMMITTEE NOTES

1997 Enactment

These forms are new. They are intended to provide uniform, plain English explanations to parties regarding what they must do to respond in certain contested matters which occur frequently in bankruptcy cases. Such explanations have been given better in some courts than in others. The forms are intended to make bankruptcy proceedings more fair, equitable, and efficient, by aiding parties, who sometimes do not have counsel, in understanding the applicable rules. It is hoped that use of these forms also will decrease the number of inquiries to bankruptcy clerks' offices.

These notices will be sent by the movant unless local rules provide for some other entity to give notice.

These forms are not intended to dictate the specific procedures to be used by different bankruptcy courts. The forms contain optional language that can be used or adapted, depending on local procedures. Similarly, the signature line will be adapted to identify the actual sender of the notice in each circumstance. All adaptations of the form should carry out the intent to give notice of applicable procedures in easily understood language.

HISTORICAL NOTES

Effective and Applicability Provisions

1997 Acts. Order amending official forms dated Oct. 1, 1997, effective immediately, with mandatory use starting March 1, 1998.

Form 20B. Notice of Objection to Claim

Official Form 20B

(12/03)

United States Bankruptcy Court

__________ District Of __________

In re ____,)
[Set forth here all names including married, maiden, and trade names used by debtor within last 6[1] years.])
Debtor) Case No. ________

Address ____)

____) Chapter ________

Employer's Tax Identification (EIN) No(s). *[if any]*: ___)
____)

NOTICE OF OBJECTION TO CLAIM

____________________ has filed an objection to your claim in this bankruptcy case.

Your claim may be reduced, modified, or eliminated. You should read these papers carefully and discuss them with your attorney, if you have one.

If you do not want the court to eliminate or change your claim, then on or before (date), you or your lawyer must:

{If required by local rule or court order.}

[File with the court a written response to the objection, explaining your position, at:

{address of the bankruptcy clerk's office}

If you mail your response to the court for filing, you must mail it early enough so that the court will **receive** it on or before the date stated above.

You must also mail a copy to:

{objector's attorney's name and address}

{names and addresses of others to be served}]

Attend the hearing on the objection, scheduled to be held on (date), (year), at ___ a.m./p.m. in Courtroom _____, United States Bankruptcy Court, {address}.

If you or your attorney do not take these steps, the court may decide that you do not oppose the objection to your claim.

Date: __________________ Signature: ______________________
Name:
Address:

(Added Oct. 1, 1997, and amended Dec. 2003.)

1 So in original. Probably should now read "8" years.

ADVISORY COMMITTEE NOTES

1997 Enactment

These forms are new. They are intended to provide uniform, plain English explanations to parties regarding what they must do to respond in certain contested matters which occur frequently in bankruptcy cases. Such explanations have been given better in some courts than in others. The forms are intended to make bankruptcy proceedings more fair, equitable, and efficient, by aiding parties, who sometimes do not have counsel, in understanding the applicable rules. It is hoped that use of these forms also will decrease the number of inquiries to bankruptcy clerks' offices.

These notices will be sent by the movant unless local rules provide for some other entity to give notice.

These forms are not intended to dictate the specific procedures to be used by different bankruptcy courts. The forms contain optional language that can be used or adapted, depending on local procedures. Similarly, the signature line will be adapted to identify the actual sender of the notice in each circumstance. All adaptations of the form should carry out the intent to give notice of applicable procedures in easily understood language.

HISTORICAL NOTES

Effective and Applicability Provisions

1997 Acts. Order amending official forms dated Oct. 1, 1997, effective immediately, with mandatory use starting March 1, 1998.

Form 21. Statement of Social-Security Number or Individual Taxpayer-Identification Number (ITIN)

B21 (Official Form 21) (12/07)

United States Bankruptcy Court
_________ District Of _________

In re ____________________________________,)
[Set forth here all names including married, maiden, and trade names used by debtor within last 8 years.])
Debtor) Case No. __________
)
Address)
____________________________________) Chapter __________
)
Last four digits of Social-Security or Individual Taxpayer-Identification (ITIN) No(s)., (if any):)
Employer Tax-Identification (EIN) No(s). (if any):)

STATEMENT OF SOCIAL-SECURITY NUMBER(S)
*(or other Individual Taxpayer-Identification Number(s) (ITIN(s))**

1. Name of Debtor (Last, First, Middle): ______________________
(Check the appropriate box and, if applicable, provide the required information.)

☐ Debtor has a Social-Security Number and it is: ___-__-____
(If more than one, state all.)

☐ Debtor does not have a Social-Security Number but has an Individual Taxpayer-Identification Number (ITIN), and it is: ______________________.
(If more than one, state all.)

☐ Debtor does not have either a Social-Security Number or an Individual Taxpayer-Identification Number (ITIN).

2. Name of Joint Debtor (enter Last, First, Middle): ______________________
(Check the appropriate box and, if applicable, provide the required information.)

☐ Joint Debtor has a Social-Security Number and it is: ___-__-____
(If more than one, state all.)

☐ Joint Debtor does not have a Social-Security Number but has an Individual Taxpayer-Identification Number (ITIN) and it is: ______________________.
(If more than one, state all.)

☐ Joint Debtor does not have either a Social-Security Number or an Individual Taxpayer-Identification Number (ITIN).

I declare under penalty of perjury that the foregoing is true and correct.

X ____
Signature of Debtor Date

X ____
Signature of Joint Debtor Date

**Joint debtors must provide information for both spouses.*
Penalty for making a false statement: Fine of up to $250,000 or up to 5 years imprisonment or both. 18 U.S.C. §§ 152 and 3571.
(Added Oct. 14, 2003, eff. Dec. 1, 2003; Dec. 1, 2007.)

ADVISORY COMMITTEE NOTES

2003 Enactment

The form implements Rule 1007(f), which requires a debtor to submit a statement under penalty of perjury setting out the debtor's Social Security number. The form is necessary because Rule 1005 provides that the caption of the petition includes only the final four digits of the debtor's Social Security number. The statement provides the information necessary for the clerk to include the debtor's full Social Security number on the notice of the meeting of creditors, as required under Rule 2002(a)(1). Creditors in a case, along with the trustee and United States trustee or bankruptcy administrator, will receive the full Social Security number on their copy of the notice of the meeting of creditors. The copy of that notice which goes into the court file will show only the last four digits of the number.

2007 Amendment

The form is amended to direct an individual debtor who does not have a social-security number but has another government-issued individual taxpayer-identification number to furnish that number to the court. In light of the new Rule 9037 which limits public disclosure to all but the last four digits of any individual taxpayer-identification number, the amendment to this form will ensure that the court and creditors can properly identify a debtor who does not have a social-security number.

Form 22. Statement of Current Monthly Income

B 22A (Official Form 22A) (Chapter 7) (01/08)

In re ______________________ Debtor(s)	According to the calculations required by this statement: ☐ **The presumption arises.** ☐ **The presumption does not arise.** (Check the box as directed in Parts I, III, and VI of this statement)

Case Number: ______________________ (If known)

CHAPTER 7 STATEMENT OF CURRENT MONTHLY INCOME AND MEANS–TEST CALCULATION

In addition to Schedules I and J, this statement must be completed by every individual chapter 7 debtor, whether or not filing jointly. Joint debtors may complete one statement only.

	Part I. EXCLUSION FOR DISABLED VETERANS AND NON–CONSUMER DEBTORS
1A	If you are a disabled veteran described in the Veteran's Declaration in this Part I, (1) check the box at the beginning of the Veteran's Declaration, (2) check the box for "The presumption does not arise" at the top of this statement, and (3) complete the verification in Part VIII. Do not complete any of the remaining parts of this statement. ☐ **Veteran's Declaration.** By checking this box, I declare under penalty of perjury that I am a disabled veteran (as defined in 38 U.S.C. § 3741(1)) whose indebtedness occurred primarily during a period in which I was on active duty (as defined in 10 U.S.C. § 101(d)(1)) or while I was performing a homeland defense activity (as defined in 32 U.S.C. § 901(1)).
1B	If your debts are not primarily consumer debts, check the box below and complete the verification in Part VIII. Do not complete any of the remaining parts of this statement. ☐ **Declaration of non-consumer debts.** By checking this box, I declare that my debts are not primarily consumer debts.

	Part II. CALCULATION OF MONTHLY INCOME FOR § 707(b)(7) EXCLUSION		
2	**Marital/filing status.** Check the box that applies and complete the balance of this part of this statement as directed. a. ☐ Unmarried. **Complete only Column A ("Debtor's Income") for Lines 3–11.** b. ☐ Married, not filing jointly, with declaration of separate households. By checking this box, debtor declares under penalty of perjury: "My spouse and I are legally separated under applicable non-bankruptcy law or my spouse and I are living apart other than for the purpose of evading the requirements of § 707(b)(2)(A) of the Bankruptcy Code." **Complete only Column A ("Debtor's Income") for Lines 3–11.** c. ☐ Married, not filing jointly, without the declaration of separate households set out in Line 2.b above. **Complete both Column A ("Debtor's Income") and Column B ("Spouse's Income") for Lines 3–11.** d. ☐ Married, filing jointly. **Complete both Column A ("Debtor's Income") and Column B ("Spouse's Income") for Lines 3–11.**		
	All figures must reflect average monthly income received from all sources, derived during the six calendar months prior to filing the bankruptcy case, ending on the last day of the month before the filing. If the amount of monthly income varied during the six months, you must divide the six-month total by six, and enter the result on the appropriate line.	**Column A Debtor's Income**	**Column B Spouse's Income**
3	**Gross wages, salary, tips, bonuses, overtime, commissions.**	$	$
4	**Income from the operation of a business, profession, or farm.** Subtract Line b from Line a and enter the difference in the appropriate column(s) of Line 4. If you operate more than one business, profession or farm, enter aggregate numbers and provide details on an attachment. Do not enter a number less than zero. **Do not include any part of the business expenses entered on Line b as a deduction in Part V.** a. Gross receipts — $ b. Ordinary and necessary business expenses — $ c. Business income — Subtract Line b from Line a	$	$
5	**Rent and other real property income.** Subtract Line b from Line a and enter the difference in the appropriate column(s) of Line 5. Do not enter a number less than zero. **Do not include any part of the operating expenses entered on Line b as a deduction in Part V.** a. Gross receipts — $ b. Ordinary and necessary operating expenses — $ c. Rent and other real property income — Subtract Line b from Line a	$	$
6	**Interest, dividends and royalties.**	$	$
7	**Pension and retirement income.**	$	$
8	**Any amounts paid by another person or entity, on a regular basis, for the household expenses of the debtor or the debtor's dependents, including child support paid for that purpose.** Do not include alimony or separate maintenance payments or amounts paid by your spouse if Column B is completed.	$	$
9	**Unemployment compensation.** Enter the amount in the appropriate column(s) of Line 9. However, if you contend that unemployment compensation received by you or your spouse was a benefit under the Social Security Act, do not list the amount of such compensation in Column A or B, but instead state the amount in the space below: Unemployment compensation claimed to		

	be a benefit under the Social Security Act | Debtor $____ | Spouse $____	$	$
10	**Income from all other sources.** Specify source and amount. If necessary, list additional sources on a separate page. **Do not include alimony or separate maintenance payments paid by your spouse if Column B is completed, but include all other payments of alimony or separate maintenance. Do not include** any benefits received under the Social Security Act or payments received as a victim of a war crime, crime against humanity, or as a victim of international or domestic terrorism. a. ____ $ b. ____ $ Total and enter on Line 10	$	$
11	**Subtotal of Current Monthly Income for § 707(b)(7).** Add Lines 3 thru 10 in Column A, and, if Column B is completed, add Lines 3 through 10 in Column B. Enter the total(s).	$	$
12	**Total Current Monthly Income for § 707(b)(7).** If Column B has been completed, add Line 11, Column A to Line 11, Column B, and enter the total. If Column B has not been completed, enter the amount from Line 11, Column A.	$	

	Part III. APPLICATION OF § 707(b)(7) EXCLUSION	
13	**Annualized Current Monthly Income for § 707(b)(7).** Multiply the amount from Line 12 by the number 12 and enter the result.	$
14	**Applicable median family income.** Enter the median family income for the applicable state and household size. (This information is available by family size at www.usdoj.gov/ust/ or from the clerk of the bankruptcy court.) a. Enter debtor's state of residence: ________ b. Enter debtor's household size: ________	$
15	**Application of Section 707(b)(7).** Check the applicable box and proceed as directed. ☐ **The amount on Line 13 is less than or equal to the amount on Line 14.** Check the box for "The presumption does not arise" at the top of page 1 of this statement, and complete Part VIII; do not complete Parts IV, V, VI or VII. ☐ **The amount on Line 13 is more than the amount on Line 14.** Complete the remaining parts of this statement.	

Complete Parts IV, V, VI, and VII of this statement only if required. (See Line 15.)

	Part IV. CALCULATION OF CURRENT MONTHLY INCOME FOR § 707(b)(2)	
16	**Enter the amount from Line 12.**	$
17	**Marital adjustment.** If you checked the box at Line 2.c, enter on Line 17 the total of any income listed in Line 11, Column B that was NOT paid on a regular basis for the household expenses of the debtor or the debtor's dependents. Specify in the lines below the basis for excluding the Column B income (such as payment of the spouse's tax liability or the spouse's support of persons other than the debtor or the debtor's dependents) and the amount of income devoted to each purpose. If necessary, list additional adjustments on a separate page. If you did not check box at Line 2.c, enter zero. a. ____ $ b. ____ $ c. ____ $ Total and enter on Line 17	$
18	**Current monthly income for § 707(b)(2).** Subtract Line 17 from Line 16 and enter the result.	$

	Part V. CALCULATION OF DEDUCTIONS FROM INCOME	
	Subpart A: Deductions under Standards of the Internal Revenue Service (IRS)	
19A	**National Standards: food, clothing, and other items.** Enter in Line 19A the "Total" amount from IRS National Standards for Food, Clothing and Other Items for the applicable household size. (This information is available at www.usdoj.gov/ust/ or from the clerk of the bankruptcy court.)	$
19B	**National Standards: health care.** Enter in Line a1 below the amount from IRS National Standards for Out-of-Pocket Health Care for persons under 65 years of age, and in Line a2 the IRS National Standards for Out-of-Pocket Health Care for persons 65 years of age or older. (This information is available at www.usdoj.gov/ust/ or from the clerk of the bankruptcy court.) Enter in Line b1 the number of members of your household who are under 65 years of age, and enter in Line b2 the number of members of your household who are 65 years of age or older. (The total number of household members must be the same as the number stated in Line 14b.) Multiply Line a1 by Line b1 to obtain a total amount for household members under 65, and enter the result in Line c1. Multiply Line a2 by Line b2 to obtain a total amount for household members 65 and older, and enter the result in Line c2. Add Lines c1 and c2 to obtain a total health care amount, and enter the result in Line 19B. **Household members under 65 years of age** | **Household members 65 years of age or older** a1. Allowance per member | a2. Allowance per member b1. Number of members | b2. Number of members c1. Subtotal | c2. Subtotal	$
20A	**Local Standards: housing and utilities; non-mortgage expenses.** Enter the amount of the IRS Housing and Utilities Standards; non-mortgage expenses for the applicable county and household size. (This information is available at www.usdoj.gov/ust/ or from the clerk of the bankruptcy court).	$
20B	**Local Standards: housing and utilities; mortgage/rent expense.** Enter, in Line a below, the amount of the IRS Housing and Utilities Standards; mortgage/rent expense for your county and household size (this information is available at www.usdoj.gov/ust/ or from the clerk of the bankruptcy court); enter on Line b the total of the Average Monthly Payments for any debts secured by your home, as stated in Line 42; subtract Line b from Line a and enter the result in Line 20B. **Do not enter an amount less than zero.** a. IRS Housing and Utilities Standards; mortgage/rental expense | $ b. Average Monthly Payment for any debts secured by your home, if any, as stated in Line 42 | $	

	c. Net mortgage/rental expense — Subtract Line b from Line a.	$
21	**Local Standards: housing and utilities; adjustment.** if you contend that the process set out in Lines 20A and 20B does not accurately compute the allowance to which you are entitled under the IRS Housing and Utilities Standards, enter any additional amount to which you contend you are entitled, and state the basis for your contention in the space below: ___	$
22A	**Local Standards: transportation; vehicle operation/public transportation expense.** You are entitled to an expense allowance in this category regardless of whether you pay the expenses of operating a vehicle and regardless of whether you use public transportation. Check the number of vehicles for which you pay the operating expenses or for which the operating expenses are included as a contribution to your household expenses in Line 8. □ 0 □ 1 □ 2 or more. If you checked 0, enter on Line 22A the "Public Transportation" amount from IRS Local Standards: Transportation. If you checked 1 or 2 or more, enter on Line 22A the "Operating Costs" amount from IRS Local Standards: Transportation for the applicable number of vehicles in the applicable Metropolitan Statistical Area or Census Region. (These amounts are available at www.usdoj.gov/ust/ or from the clerk of the bankruptcy court.)	$
22B	**Local Standards: transportation; additional public transportation expense.** If you pay the operating expenses for a vehicle and also use public transportation, and you contend that you are entitled to an additional deduction for your public transportation expenses, enter on Line 22B the "Public Transportation" amount from IRS Local Standards: Transportation. (This amount is available at www.usdoj.gov/ust/ or from the clerk of the bankruptcy court.)	$
23	**Local Standards: transportation ownership/lease expense; Vehicle 1.** Check the number of vehicles for which you claim an ownership/lease expense. (You may not claim an ownership/lease expense for more than two vehicles.) □ 1 □ 2 or more. Enter, in Line a below, the "Ownership Costs" for "One Car" from the IRS Local Standards: Transportation (available at www.usdoj.gov/ust/ or from the clerk of the bankruptcy court); enter in Line b the total of the Average Monthly Payments for any debts secured by Vehicle 1, as stated in Line 42; subtract Line b from Line a and enter the result in Line 23. **Do not enter an amount less than zero.** a. IRS Transportation Standards, Ownership Costs — $ b. Average Monthly Payment for any debts secured by Vehicle 1, as stated in Line 42 — $ c. Net ownership/lease expense for Vehicle 1 — Subtract Line b from Line a.	$
24	**Local Standards: transportation ownership/lease expense; Vehicle 2.** Complete this Line only if you checked the "2 or more" Box in Line 23. Enter, in Line a below, the amount of the "Ownership Costs" for "One Car" from the IRS Local Standards: Transportation (available at www.usdoj.gov/ust/ or from the clerk of the bankruptcy court); enter in Line b the total of the Average Monthly Payments for any debts secured by Vehicle 2, as stated in Line 42; subtract Line b from Line a and enter the result in Line 24. **Do not enter an amount less than zero.** a. IRS Transportation Standards, Ownership Costs — $ b. Average Monthly Payment for any debts secured by Vehicle 2, as stated in Line 42 — $ c. Net ownership/lease expense for Vehicle 2 — Subtract Line b from Line a.	$
25	**Other Necessary Expenses: taxes.** Enter the total average monthly expense that you actually incur for all federal, state and local taxes, other than real estate and sales taxes, such as income taxes, self-employment taxes, social-security taxes, and Medicare taxes. **Do not include real estate or sales taxes.**	$
26	**Other Necessary Expenses: involuntary deductions for employment.** Enter the total average monthly payroll deductions that are required for your employment, such as retirement contributions, union dues, and uniform costs. **Do not include discretionary amounts, such as voluntary 401(k) contributions.**	$
27	**Other Necessary Expenses: life insurance.** Enter total average monthly premiums that you actually pay for term life insurance for yourself. **Do not include premiums for insurance on your dependents, for whole life or for any other form of insurance.**	$
28	**Other Necessary Expenses: court-ordered payments.** Enter the total monthly amount that you are required to pay pursuant to the order of a court or administrative agency, such as spousal or child support payments. **Do not include payments on past due obligations included in Line 44.**	$
29	**Other Necessary Expenses: education for employment or for a physically or mentally challenged child.** Enter the total average monthly amount that you actually expend for education that is a condition of employment and for education that is required for a physically or mentally challenged dependent child for whom no public education providing similar services is available.	$
30	**Other Necessary Expenses: childcare.** Enter the total average monthly amount that you actually expend on childcare—such as baby-sitting, day care, nursery and preschool. **Do not include other educational payments.**	$
31	**Other Necessary Expenses: health care.** Enter the average monthly amount that you actually expend on health care that is required for the health and welfare of yourself or your dependents, that is not reimbursed by insurance or paid by a health savings account, and that is in excess of the amount entered in Line 19B. **Do not include payments for health insurance or health savings accounts listed in Line 34.**	$
32	**Other Necessary Expenses: telecommunication services.** Enter the total average monthly amount that you actually pay for telecommunication services other than your basic home telephone and cell phone service—such as pagers, call waiting, caller ID, special long distance, or internet service—to the extent necessary for your health and welfare or that of your dependents. **Do not include any amount previously deducted.**	$
33	**Total Expenses Allowed under IRS Standards.** Enter the total of Lines 19 through 32.	$
	Subpart B: Additional Living Expense Deductions **Note: Do not include any expenses that you have listed in Lines 19–32**	

34 **Health Insurance, Disability Insurance, and Health Savings Account Expenses.** List the monthly expenses in the categories set out in lines a–c below that are reasonably necessary for yourself, your spouse, or your dependents.

a.	Health Insurance	$
b.	Disability Insurance	$
c.	Health Savings Account	$

Total and enter on Line 34 $

If you do not actually expend this total amount, state your actual total average monthly expenditures in the space below:

$ ________

35 **Continued contributions to the care of household or family members.** Enter the total average actual monthly expenses that you will continue to pay for the reasonable and necessary care and support of an elderly, chronically ill, or disabled member of your household or member of your immediate family who is unable to pay for such expenses. $

36 **Protection against family violence.** Enter the total average reasonably necessary monthly expenses that you actually incurred to maintain the safety of your family under the Family Violence Prevention and Services Act or other applicable federal law. The nature of these expenses is required to be kept confidential by the court. $

37 **Home energy costs.** Enter the total average monthly amount, in excess of the allowance specified by IRS Local Standards for Housing and Utilities, that you actually expend for home energy costs. **You must provide your case trustee with documentation of your actual expenses, and you must demonstrate that the additional amount claimed is reasonable and necessary.** $

38 **Education expenses for dependent children less than 18.** Enter the total average monthly expenses that you actually incur, not to exceed $137.50 per child, for attendance at a private or public elementary or secondary school by your dependent children less than 18 years of age. **You must provide your case trustee with documentation of your actual expenses, and you must explain why the amount claimed is reasonable and necessary and not already accounted for in the IRS Standards.** $

39 **Additional food and clothing expense.** Enter the total average monthly amount by which your food and clothing expenses exceed the combined allowances for food and clothing (apparel and services) in the IRS National Standards, not to exceed 5% of those combined allowances. (This information is available at www.usdoj.gov/ust/ or from the clerk of the bankruptcy court.) **You must demonstrate that the additional amount claimed is reasonable and necessary.** $

40 **Continued charitable contributions.** Enter the amount that you will continue to contribute in the form of cash or financial instruments to a charitable organization as defined in 26 U.S.C. § 170(c)(1)–(2). $

41 **Total Additional Expense Deductions under § 707(b).** Enter the total of Lines 34 through 40 $

Subpart C: Deductions for Debt Payment

42 **Future payments on secured claims.** For each of your debts that is secured by an interest in property that you own, list the name of the creditor, identify the property securing the debt, state the Average Monthly Payment, and check whether the payment includes taxes or insurance. The Average Monthly Payment is the total of all amounts scheduled as contractually due to each Secured Creditor in the 60 months following the filing of the bankruptcy case, divided by 60. If necessary, list additional entries on a separate page. Enter the total of the Average Monthly Payments on Line 42.

	Name of Creditor	Property Securing the Debt	Average Monthly Payment	Does payment include taxes or insurance?
a.			$	☐ yes ☐ no
b.			$	☐ yes ☐ no
c.			$	☐ yes ☐ no
			Total: Add Lines a, b and c	

$

43 **Other payments on secured claims.** If any of the debts listed in Line 42 are secured by your primary residence, a motor vehicle, or other property necessary for your support or the support of your dependents, you may include in your deduction 1/60th of any amount (the “cure amount”) that you must pay the creditor in addition to the payments listed in Line 42, in order to maintain possession of the property. The cure amount would include any sums in default that must be paid in order to avoid repossession or foreclosure. List and total any such amounts in the following chart. If necessary, list additional entries on a separate page.

	Name of Creditor	Property Securing the Debt	1/60th of the Cure Amount
a.			$
b.			$
c.			$
			Total: Add Lines a, b and c

$

44 **Payments on prepetition priority claims.** Enter the total amount, divided by 60, of all priority claims, such as priority tax, child support and alimony claims, for which you were liable at the time of your bankruptcy filing. **Do not include current obligations, such as those set out in Line 28.** $

45 **Chapter 13 administrative expenses.** If you are eligible to file a case under chapter 13, complete the following chart, multiply the amount in line a by the amount in line b, and enter the resulting administrative expense.

a.	Projected average monthly chapter 13 plan payment.	$
b.	Current multiplier for your district as determined under schedules issued by the Executive Office for United States Trustees. (This information is available at www.usdoj.gov/ust/ or from the clerk of the bankruptcy court.)	x
c.	Average monthly administrative expense of chapter 13 case	Total: Multiply Lines a and b

$

46 **Total Deductions for Debt Payment.** Enter the total of Lines 42 through 45. $

Subpart D: Total Deductions from Income

47	**Total of all deductions allowed under § 707(b)(2).** Enter the total of Lines 33, 41, and 46.	$

Part VI. DETERMINATION OF § 707(b)(2) PRESUMPTION		
48	**Enter the amount from Line 18 (Current monthly income for § 707(b)(2))**	$
49	**Enter the amount from Line 47 (Total of all deductions allowed under § 707(b)(2))**	$
50	**Monthly disposable income under § 707(b)(2).** Subtract Line 49 from Line 48 and enter the result	$
51	**60-month disposable income under § 707(b)(2).** Multiply the amount in Line 50 by the number 60 and enter the result.	$
52	**Initial presumption determination.** Check the applicable box and proceed as directed. ☐ **The amount on Line 51 is less than $6,575** Check the box for "The presumption does not arise" at the top of page 1 of this statement, and complete the verification in Part VIII. Do not complete the remainder of Part VI. ☐ **The amount set forth on Line 51 is more than $10,950.** Check the box for "The presumption arises" at the top of page 1 of this statement, and complete the verification in Part VIII. You may also complete Part VII. Do not complete the remainder of Part VI. ☐ **The amount on Line 51 is at least $6,575, but not more than $10,950.** Complete the remainder of Part VI (Lines 53 through 55).	
53	**Enter the amount of your total non-priority unsecured debt**	$
54	**Threshold debt payment amount.** Multiply the amount in Line 53 by the number 0.25 and enter the result.	$
55	**Secondary presumption determination.** Check the applicable box and proceed as directed. ☐ **The amount on Line 51 is less than the amount on Line 54.** Check the box for "The presumption does not arise" at the top of page 1 of this statement, and complete the verification in Part VIII. ☐ **The amount on Line 51 is equal to or greater than the amount on Line 54.** Check the box for "The presumption arises" at the top of page 1 of this statement, and complete the verification in Part VIII. You may also complete Part VII.	

Part VII: ADDITIONAL EXPENSE CLAIMS

56 **Other Expenses.** List and describe any monthly expenses, not otherwise stated in this form, that are required for the health and welfare of you and your family and that you contend should be an additional deduction from your current monthly income under § 707(b)(2)(A)(ii)(I). If necessary, list additional sources on a separate page. All figures should reflect your average monthly expense for each item. Total the expenses.

	Expense Description	Monthly Amount
a.		$
b.		$
c.		$
	Total: Add Lines a, b, and c	$

Part VIII: VERIFICATION

57 I declare under penalty of perjury that the information provided in this statement is true and correct. *(If this is a joint case, both debtors must sign.)*

Date: ____________________ Signature: ____________________
(Debtor)

Date: ____________________ Signature: ____________________
(Joint Debtor, if any)

B22B (Official Form 22B) (Chapter 11) (01/08)

In re ______________________
Debtor(s)

Case Number: ______________________
(If known)

CHAPTER 11 STATEMENT OF CURRENT MONTHLY INCOME

In addition to Schedules I and J, this statement must be completed by every individual chapter 11 debtor, whether or not filing jointly. Joint debtors may complete one statement only.

	Part I. CALCULATION OF CURRENT MONTHLY INCOME		
1	**Marital/filing status.** Check the box that applies and complete the balance of this part of this statement as directed. a. ☐ Unmarried. **Complete only Column A ("Debtor's Income") for Lines 2–10.** b. ☐ Married, not filing jointly. **Complete only Column A (" Debtor's Income") for Lines 2–10.** c. ☐ Married, filing jointly. **Complete both Column A ("Debtor's Income") and Column B ("Spouse's Income") for Lines 2–10.**		
	All figures must reflect average monthly income received from all sources, derived during the six calendar months prior to filing the bankruptcy case, ending on the last day of the month before the filing. If the amount of monthly income varied during the six months, you must divide the six-month total by six, and enter the result on the appropriate line.	**Column A Debtor's Income**	**Column B Spouse's Income**
2	**Gross wages, salary, tips, bonuses, overtime, commissions.**	$	$
3	**Net income from the operation of a business, profession, or farm.** Subtract Line b from Line a and enter the difference in the appropriate column(s) Line 3. If more than one business, profession or farm, enter aggregate numbers and provide details on an attachment. Do not enter a number less than zero. a. Gross receipts $ b. Ordinary and necessary operating expenses $ c. Business income Subtract Line b from Line a	$	$
4	**Net rental and other real property income.** Subtract Line b from Line a and enter the difference in the appropriate column(s) of Line 4. Do not enter a number less than zero. a. Gross receipts $ b. Ordinary and necessary operating expenses $ c. Rent and other real property income Subtract Line b from Line a	$	$
5	**Interest, dividends, and royalties.**	$	$
6	**Pension and retirement income.**	$	$
7	**Any amounts paid by another person or entity, on a regular basis, for the household expenses of the debtor or the debtor's dependents, including child support paid for that purpose.** Do not include alimony or separate maintenance payments or amounts paid by the debtor's spouse if Column B is completed.	$	$
8	**Unemployment compensation.** Enter the amount in the appropriate column(s) of Line 8. However, if you contend that unemployment compensation received by you or your spouse was a benefit under the Social Security Act, do not list the amount of such compensation in Column A or B, but instead state the amount in the space below: Unemployment compensation claimed to be a benefit under the Social Security Act Debtor $ ___ Spouse $ ___	$	$
9	**Income from all other sources.** Specify source and amount. If necessary, list additional sources on a separate page. Total and enter on Line 9. **Do not include alimony or separate maintenance payments paid by your spouse if Column B is completed, but include all other payments of alimony or separate maintenance. Do not include** any benefits received under the Social Security Act or payments received as a victim of a war crime, crime against humanity, or as a victim of international or domestic terrorism. a. $ b. $	$	$
10	**Subtotal of current monthly income.** Add Lines 2 thru 9 in Column A, and, if Column B is completed, add Lines 2 through 9 in Column B. Enter the total(s).	$	$
11	**Total current monthly income.** If Column B has been completed, add Line 10, Column A to Line 10, Column B, and enter the total. If Column B has not been completed, enter the amount from Line 10, Column A.	$	

	Part II: VERIFICATION
12	I declare under penalty of perjury that the information provided in this statement is true and correct. *(If this a joint case, both debtors must sign.)* Date: ______________ Signature: ______________ (Debtor) Date: ______________ Signature: ______________ (Joint Debtor, if any)

B22C (Official Form 22C) (Chapter 13) (01/08)

In re ______________________ Debtor(s)

Case Number: ______________________ (If known)

According to the calculations required by this statement:
☐ **The applicable commitment period is 3 years.**
☐ **The applicable commitment period is 5 years.**
☐ **Disposable income is determined under § 1325(b)(3).**
☐ **Disposable income is not determined under § 1325(b)(3).**
(Check the boxes as directed in Lines 17 and 23 of this statement.)

CHAPTER 13 STATEMENT OF CURRENT MONTHLY INCOME AND CALCULATION OF COMMITMENT PERIOD AND DISPOSABLE INCOME

In addition to Schedules I and J, this statement must be completed by every individual Chapter 13 debtor, whether or not filing jointly. Joint debtors may complete one statement only.

Part I. REPORT OF INCOME			
1	**Marital/filing status.** Check the box that applies and complete the balance of this part of this statement as directed. a. ☐ Unmarried. **Complete only Column A ("Debtor's Income") for Lines 2–10.** b. ☐ Married. **Complete both Column A ("Debtor's Income") and Column B ("Spouse's Income") for Lines 2–10.**		
	All figures must reflect average monthly income received from all sources, derived during the six calendar months prior to filing the bankruptcy case, ending on the last day of the month before the filing. If the amount of monthly income varied during the six months, you must divide the six-month total by six, and enter the result on the appropriate line.	**Column A Debtor's Income**	**Column B Spouse's Income**
2	**Gross wages, salary, tips, bonuses, overtime, commissions.**	$	$
3	**Income from the operation of a business, profession, or farm.** Subtract Line b from Line a and enter the difference in the appropriate column(s) of Line 3. If you operate more than one business, profession or farm, enter aggregate numbers and provide details on an attachment. Do not enter a number less than zero. **Do not include any part of the business expenses entered on Line b as a deduction in Part IV.** a. Gross receipts — $ b. Ordinary and necessary business expenses — $ c. Business income — Subtract Line b from Line a	$	$
4	**Rent and other real property income.** Subtract Line b from Line a and enter the difference in the appropriate column(s) of Line 4. Do not enter a number less than zero. **Do not include any part of the operating expenses entered on Line b as a deduction in Part IV.** a. Gross receipts — $ b. Ordinary and necessary operating expenses — $ c. Rent and other real property income — Subtract Line b from Line a	$	$
5	**Interest, dividends, and royalties.**	$	$
6	**Pension and retirement income.**	$	$
7	**Any amounts paid by another person or entity, on a regular basis, for the household expenses of the debtor or the debtor's dependents, including child support paid for that purpose..** Do not include alimony or separate maintenance payments or amounts paid by the debtor's spouse.	$	$
8	**Unemployment compensation.** Enter the amount in the appropriate column(s) of Line 8. However, if you contend that unemployment compensation received by you or your spouse was a benefit under the Social Security Act, do not list the amount of such compensation in Column A or B, but instead state the amount in the space below: Unemployment compensation claimed to be a benefit under the Social Security Act — Debtor $ ___ Spouse $ ___	$	$
9	**Income from all other sources.** Specify source and amount. If necessary, list additional sources on a separate page. Total and enter on Line 9. **Do not include alimony or separate maintenance payments paid by your spouse, but include all other payments of alimony or separate maintenance. Do not include** any benefits received under the Social Security Act or payments received as a victim of a war crime, crime against humanity, or as a victim of international or domestic terrorism. a. ______ $ b. ______ $	$	$
10	**Subtotal.** Add Lines 2 thru 9 in Column A, and, if Column B is completed, add Lines 2 through 9 in Column B. Enter the total(s).	$	$
11	**Total.** If Column B has been completed, add Line 10, Column A to Line 10, Column B, and enter the total. If Column B has not been completed, enter the amount from Line 10, Column A.	$	

Part II. CALCULATION OF § 1325(b)(4) COMMITMENT PERIOD		
12	**Enter the amount from Line 11.**	
13	**Marital adjustment.** If you are married, but are not filing jointly with your spouse, AND if you contend that calculation of the commitment period under § 1325(b)(4) does not require inclusion of the income of your spouse, enter on Line 13 the amount of the income listed in Line 10, Column B that was NOT paid on a regular basis for the household expenses of you or your dependents and specify, in the lines below, the basis	

	for excluding this income (such as payment of the spouse's tax liability or the spouse's support of persons other than the debtor or the debtor's dependents) and the amount of income devoted to each purpose. If necessary, list additional adjustments on a separate page. If the conditions for entering this adjustment do not apply, enter zero. a. ____ $ b. ____ $ c. ____ $ Total and enter on Line 13	$
14	**Subtract Line 13 from Line 12 and enter the result.**	$
15	**Annualized current monthly income for § 1325(b)(4).** Multiply the amount from Line 14 by the number 12 and enter the result.	$
16	**Applicable median family income.** Enter the median family income for applicable state and household size. (This information is available by family size at www.usdoj.gov/ust/ or from the clerk of the bankruptcy court.) a. Enter debtor's state of residence: ______ b. Enter debtor's household size: ______	$
17	**Application of § 1325(b)(4).** Check the applicable box and proceed as directed. ☐ **The amount on Line 15 is less than the amount on Line 16.** Check the box for "The applicable commitment period is 3 years" at the top of page 1 of this statement and continue with this statement. ☐ **The amount on Line 15 is not less than the amount on Line 16.** Check the box for "The applicable commitment period is 5 years" at the top of page 1 of this statement and continue with this statement.	

	Part III. APPLICATION OF § 1325(b)(3) FOR DETERMINING DISPOSABLE INCOME	
18	**Enter the amount from Line 11.**	$
19	**Marital adjustment.** If you are married, but are not filing jointly with your spouse, enter on Line 19 the total of any income listed in Line 10, Column B that was NOT paid on a regular basis for the household expenses of the debtor or the debtor's dependents. Specify in the lines below the basis for excluding the Column B income (such as payment of the spouse's tax liability or the spouse's support of persons other than the debtor or the debtor's dependents) and the amount of income devoted to each purpose. If necessary, list additional adjustments on a separate page. If the conditions for entering this adjustment do not apply, enter zero. a. ____ $ b. ____ $ c. ____ $ Total and enter on Line 19.	$
20	**Current monthly income for § 1325(b)(3).** Subtract Line 19 from Line 18 and enter the result.	$
21	**Annualized current monthly income for § 1325(b)(3).** Multiply the amount from Line 20 by the number 12 and enter the result.	$
22	**Applicable median family income.** Enter the amount from Line 16.	$
23	**Application of § 1325(b)(3).** Check the applicable box and proceed as directed. ☐ **The amount on Line 21 is more than the amount on Line 22.** Check the box for "Disposable income is determined under § 1325(b)(3)" at the top of page 1 of this statement and complete the remaining parts of this statement. ☐ **The amount on Line 21 is not more than the amount on Line 22.** Check the box for "Disposable income is not determined under § 1325(b)(3)" at the top of page 1 of this statement and complete Part VII of this statement. **Do not complete Parts IV, V, or VI.**	

	Part IV. CALCULATION OF DEDUCTIONS FROM INCOME	
	Subpart A: Deductions under Standards of the Internal Revenue Service (IRS)	
24A	**National Standards: food, apparel and services, housekeeping supplies, personal care, and miscellaneous.** Enter in Line 24A the "Total" amount from IRS National Standards for Allowable Living Expenses for the applicable household size. (This information is available at www.usdoj.gov/ust/ or from the clerk of the bankruptcy court.)	$
24B	**National Standards: health care.** Enter in Line a1 below the amount from IRS National Standards for Out-of-Pocket Health Care for persons under 65 years of age, and in Line a2 the IRS National Standards for Out-of-Pocket Health Care for persons 65 years of age or older. (This information is available at www.usdoj.gov/ust/ or from the clerk of the bankruptcy court.) Enter in Line b1 the number of members of your household who are under 65 years of age, and enter in Line b2 the number of members of your household who are 65 years of age or older. (The total number of household members must be the same as the number stated in Line 16b.) Multiply Line a1 by Line b1 to obtain a total amount for household members under 65, and enter the result in Line c1. Multiply Line a2 by Line b2 to obtain a total amount for household members 65 and older, and enter the result in Line c2. Add Lines c1 and c2 to obtain a total health care amount, and enter the result in Line 24B. **Household members under 65 years of age**: a1. Allowance per member; b1. Number of members; c1. Subtotal **Household members 65 years of age or older**: a2. Allowance per member; b2. Number of members; c2. Subtotal	$
25A	**Local Standards: housing and utilities; non-mortgage expenses.** Enter the amount of the IRS Housing and Utilities Standards; non-mortgage expenses for the applicable county and household size. (This information is available at www.usdoj.gov/ust/ or from the clerk of the bankruptcy court).	$
	Local Standards: housing and utilities; mortgage/rent expense. Enter, in Line a below, the amount of the IRS Housing and Utilities Standards; mortgage/rent expense for your county and household size (this information is available at www.usdoj.gov/ust/ or from the clerk of the bankruptcy court); enter on Line b the total of the Average Monthly Payments for any debts secured by your home, as stated in Line 47; subtract Line b from Line a and enter the result in Line 25B. **Do not enter an amount less than zero.**	

25B	a.	IRS Housing and Utilities Standards; mortgage/rent expense	$	
	b.	Average Monthly Payment for any debts secured by your home, if any, as stated in Line 47	$	
	c.	Net mortgage/rental expense	Subtract Line b from Line a.	$
26	**Local Standards: housing and utilities; adjustment.** If you contend that the process set out in Lines 25A and 25B does not accurately compute the allowance to which you are entitled under the IRS Housing and Utilities Standards, enter any additional amount to which you contend you are entitled, and state the basis for your contention in the space below: ______ ______			$
27A	**Local Standards: transportation; vehicle operation/public transportation expense.** You are entitled to an expense allowance in this category regardless of whether you pay the expenses of operating a vehicle and regardless of whether you use public transportation. Check the number of vehicles for which you pay the operating expenses or for which the operating expenses are included as a contribution to your household expenses in Line 7. ☐ 0 ☐ 1 ☐ 2 or more. If you checked 0, enter on Line 27A the "Public Transportation" amount from IRS Local Standards: Transportation. If you checked 1 or 2 or more, enter on Line 27A the "Operating Costs" amount from IRS Local Standards: Transportation for the applicable number of vehicles in the applicable Metropolitan Statistical Area or Census Region. (These amounts are available at www.usdoj.gov/ust/ or from the clerk of the bankruptcy court.)			$
27B	**Local Standards: transportation; additional public transportation expense.** If you pay the operating expenses for a vehicle and also use public transportation, and you contend that you are entitled to an additional deduction for your public transportation expenses, enter on Line 27B the "Public Transportation" amount from IRS Local Standards: Transportation. (This amount is available at www.usdoj.gov/ust/ or from the clerk of the bankruptcy court.)			$
28	**Local Standards: transportation ownership/lease expense; Vehicle 1.** Check the number of vehicles for which you claim an ownership/lease expense. (You may not claim an ownership/lease expense for more than two vehicles.) ☐ 1 ☐ 2 or more. Enter, in Line a below, the "Ownership Costs" for "One Car" from the IRS Local Standards: Transportation (available at www.usdoj.gov/ust/ or from the clerk of the bankruptcy court); enter in Line b the total of the Average Monthly Payments for any debts secured by Vehicle 1, as stated in Line 47; subtract Line b from Line a and enter the result in Line 28. **Do not enter an amount less than zero.**			
	a.	IRS Transportation Standards, Ownership Costs	$	
	b.	Average Monthly Payment for any debts secured by Vehicle 1, as stated in Line 47	$	
	c.	Net ownership/lease expense for Vehicle 1	Subtract Line b from Line a.	$
29	**Local Standards: transportation ownership/lease expense; Vehicle 2.** Complete this Line only if you checked the "2 or more" Box in Line 28. Enter, in Line a below, the "Ownership Costs" for "One Care" from the IRS Local Standards: Transportation (available at www.usdoj.gov/ust/ or from the clerk of the bankruptcy court); enter in Line b the total of the Average Monthly Payments for any debts secured by Vehicle 2, as stated in Line 47; subtract Line b from Line a and enter the result in Line 29. **Do not enter an amount less than zero.**			
	a.	IRS Transportation Standards, Ownership Costs	$	
	b.	Average Monthly Payment for any debts secured by Vehicle 2, as stated in Line 47	$	
	c.	Net ownership/lease expense for Vehicle 2	Subtract Line b from Line a.	$
30	**Other Necessary Expenses: taxes.** Enter the total average monthly expense that you actually incur for all federal, state, and local taxes, other than real estate and sales taxes, such as income taxes, self-employment taxes, social-security taxes, and Medicare taxes. **Do not include real estate or sales taxes.**			$
31	**Other Necessary Expenses: involuntary deductions for employment.** Enter the total average monthly deductions that are required for your employment, such as mandatory retirement contributions, union dues, and uniform costs. **Do not include discretionary amounts, such as voluntary 401(k) contributions.**			$
32	**Other Necessary Expenses: life insurance.** Enter total average monthly premiums that you actually pay for term life insurance for yourself. **Do not include premiums for insurance on your dependents, for whole life or for any other form of insurance.**			$
33	**Other Necessary Expenses: court-ordered payments.** Enter the total monthly amount that you are required to pay pursuant to the order of a court or administrative agency, such as spousal or child support payments. **Do not include payments on past due obligations included in Line 49.**			$
34	**Other Necessary Expenses: education for employment or for a physically or mentally challenged child.** Enter the total average monthly amount that you actually expend for education that is a condition of employment and for education that is required for a physically or mentally challenged dependent child for whom no public education providing similar services is available.			
35	**Other Necessary Expenses: childcare.** Enter the total average monthly amount that you actually expend on childcare—such as baby-sitting, day care, nursery and preschool. **Do not include other educational payments.**			$
36	**Other Necessary Expenses: health care.** Enter the total average monthly amount that you actually expend on health care that is required for the health and welfare of yourself or your dependents, that is not reimbursed by insurance or paid by a health savings account, and that is in excess of the amount entered in line 24B. **Do not include payments for health insurance or health savings accounts listed in Line 39.**			$
37	**Other Necessary Expenses: telecommunication services.** Enter the total average monthly amount that you actually pay for telecommunication services other than your basic home telephone and cell phone service—such as pagers, call waiting, caller ID, special long distance, or internet service—to the extent necessary for your health and welfare or that of your dependents. **Do not include any amount previously deducted.**			$
38	**Total Expenses Allowed under IRS Standards.** Enter the total of Lines 24 through 37			$
	Subpart B: Additional Living Expense Deductions			

Note: Do not include any expenses that you have listed in Lines 24–37

39	**Health Insurance, Disability Insurance, and Health Savings Account Expenses.** List the monthly expenses in the categories set out in lines a–c below that are reasonably necessary for yourself, your spouse, or your dependents.	

a.	Health Insurance	$
b.	Disability Insurance	$
c.	Health Savings Account	$

	Total and enter on Line 39	$
	If you do not actually expend this total amount, state your actual total average monthly expenditures in the space below: $ ________	
40	**Continued contributions to the care of household or family members.** Enter the total average actual monthly expenses that you will continue to pay for the reasonable and necessary care and support of an elderly, chronically ill, or disabled member of your household or member of your immediate family who is unable to pay for such expenses. **Do not include payments listed in Line 34.**	$
41	**Protection against family violence.** Enter the total average reasonably necessary monthly expenses that you actually incur to maintain the safety of your family under the Family Violence Prevention and Services Act or other applicable federal law. The nature of these expenses is required to be kept confidential by the court.	$
42	**Home energy costs.** Enter the total average monthly amount, in excess of the allowance specified by IRS Local Standards for Housing and Utilities, that you actually expend for home energy costs. **You must provide your case trustee with documentation of your actual expenses, and you must demonstrate that the additional amount claimed is reasonable and necessary.**	$
43	**Education expenses for dependent children under 18.** Enter the total average monthly expenses that you actually incur, not to exceed $137.50 per child, for attendance at a private or public elementary or secondary school by your dependent children less than 18 years of age. **You must provide your case trustee with documentation of your actual expenses, and you must explain why the amount claimed is reasonable and necessary and not already accounted for in the IRS Standards.**	$
44	**Additional food and clothing expense.** Enter the total average monthly amount by which your food and clothing expenses exceed the combined allowances for food and clothing (apparel and services) in the IRS National Standards, not to exceed 5% of those combined allowances. (This information is available at www.usdoj.gov/ust/ or from the clerk of the bankruptcy court.) **You must demonstrate that the additional amount claimed is reasonable and necessary.**	$
45	**Charitable contributions.** Enter the amount reasonably necessary for you to expend each month on charitable contributions in the form of cash or financial instruments to a charitable organization as defined in 26 U.S.C. § 170(c)(1)–(2). **Do not include any amount in excess of 15% of your gross monthly income.**	$
46	**Total Additional Expense Deductions under § 707(b).** Enter the total of Lines 39 through 45.	$

Subpart C: Deductions for Debt Payment

47	**Future payments on secured claims.** For each of your debts that is secured by an interest in property that you own, list the name of the creditor, identify the property securing the debt, and state the Average Monthly Payment, and check whether the payment includes taxes or insurance. The Average Monthly Payment is the total of all amounts scheduled as contractually due to each Secured Creditor in the 60 months following the filing of the bankruptcy case, divided by 60. If necessary, list additional entries on a separate page. Enter the total of the Average Monthly Payments on Line 47.	

	Name of Creditor	Property Securing the Debt	Average Monthly Payment	Does payment include taxes or insurance?
a.			$	☐ yes ☐ no
b.			$	☐ yes ☐ no
c.			$	☐ yes ☐ no
			Total: Add Lines a, b, and c	$

48	**Other payments on secured claims.** If any of the debts listed in Line 47 are secured by your primary residence, a motor vehicle, or other property necessary for your support or the support of your dependents, you may include in your deduction 1/60th of any amount (the "cure amount") that you must pay the creditor in addition to the payments listed in Line 47, in order to maintain possession of the property. The cure amount would include any sums in default that must be paid in order to avoid repossession or foreclosure. List and total any such amounts in the following chart. If necessary, list additional entries on a separate page.	

	Name of Creditor	Property Securing the Debt	1/60th of the Cure Amount
a.			$
b.			$
c.			$
			Total: Add Lines a, b, and c — $

49	**Payments on prepetition priority claims.** Enter the total amount, divided by 60, of all priority claims, such as priority tax, child support and alimony claims, for which you were liable at the time of your bankruptcy filing. **Do not include current obligations, such as those set out in Line 33.**	$
50	**Chapter 13 administrative expenses.** Multiply the amount in Line a by the amount in Line b, and enter the resulting administrative expense.	

a.	Projected average monthly chapter 13 plan payment.	$
b.	Current multiplier for your district as determined under schedules issued by the Executive Office for United States Trustees. (This information is available at www.usdoj.gov/ust/ or from the clerk of the bankruptcy court.)	x
c.	Average monthly administrative expense of chapter 13 case	Total: Multiply Lines a and b — $

51	**Total Deductions for Debt Payment.** Enter the total of Lines 47 through 50.	$

Subpart D: Total Deductions from Income

52	**Total of all deductions from income.** Enter the total of Lines 38, 46, and 51.	$

	Part V. DETERMINATION OF DISPOSABLE INCOME UNDER § 1325(b)(2)	
53	**Total current monthly income.** Enter the amount from Line 20.	$
54	**Support income.** Enter the monthly average of any child support payments, foster care payments, or disability payments for a dependent child, reported in Part I, that you received in accordance with applicable nonbankruptcy law, to the extent reasonably necessary to be expended for such child.	$
55	**Qualified retirement deductions.** Enter the monthly total of (a) all amounts withheld by your employer from wages as contributions for qualified retirement plans, as specified in § 541(b)(7) and (b) all required repayments of loans from retirement plans, as specified in § 362(b)(19).	$
56	**Total of all deductions allowed under § 707(b)(2).** Enter the amount from Line 52.	$
57	**Deduction for special circumstances.** If there are special circumstances that justify additional expenses for which there is no reasonable alternative, describe the special circumstances and the resulting expenses in lines a–c below. If necessary, list additional entries on a separate page. Total the expenses and enter the total in Line 57. **You must provide your case trustee with documentation of these expenses and you must provide a detailed explanation of the special circumstances that make such expenses necessary and reasonable.** Nature of special circumstances — Amounts of expense a. — $ b. — $ c. — $ Total: Add Lines a, b, and c	$
58	**Total adjustments to determine disposable income.** Add the amounts on Lines 54, 55, 56, and 57 and enter the result.	$
59	**Monthly Disposable Income Under § 1325(b)(2).** Subtract Line 58 from Line 53 and enter the result.	$

	Part VI: ADDITIONAL EXPENSE CLAIMS
60	**Other Expenses.** List and describe any monthly expenses, not otherwise stated in this form, that are required for the health and welfare of you and your family and that you contend should be an additional deduction from your current monthly income under § 707(b)(2)(A)(ii)(I). If necessary, list additional sources on a separate page. All figures should reflect your average monthly expense for each item. Total the expenses. Expense Description — Monthly Amount a. — $ b. — $ c. — $ Total: Add Lines a, b, and c — $

	Part VII: VERIFICATION
61	I declare under penalty of perjury that the information provided in this statement is true and correct. *(If this is a joint case, both debtors must sign.)* Date: ________ Signature: ________ (Debtor) Date: ________ Signature: ________ (Joint Debtor, if any)

(Added Aug. 11, 2005, eff. Oct. 17, 2005 and amended Apr. 1, 2007; January, 2008.)

ADVISORY COMMITTEE NOTES

2005 Amendment

A. Overview

Among the changes introduced by the Bankruptcy Abuse Prevention and Consumer Protection Act of 2005 are interlocking provisions defining "current monthly income" and establishing a means test to determine whether relief under Chapter 7 should be presumed abusive. Current monthly income ("CMI") is defined in § 101(10A) of the Code, and the means test is set out in § 707(b)(2). These provisions have a variety of applications. In Chapter 7, if the debtor's CMI exceeds a defined level the debtor is subject to the means test, and § 707(b)(2)(C) specifically requires debtors to file a statement of CMI and calculations to determine the applicability of the means test presumption. In Chapters 11 and 13, CMI provides the starting point for determining the disposable income that must be contributed to payments of unsecured creditors. Moveover, Chapter 13 debtors with CMI above defined levels are required by § 1325(b)(3) to complete the means test in order to determine the amount of their monthly disposable income, and pursuant to § 1325(b)(4), the level of CMI determines the "applicable commitment period" over which projected disposable income must be paid to unsecured creditors.

To provide for the reporting and calculation of CMI and for the completion of the means test where required, three separate official forms have been created—one for Chapter 7, one for Chapter 11, and one for Chapter 13. This note first describes the calculation of CMI that is common to all three of the forms, next describes the means test as set out in the Chapter 7 and 13 forms, and finally addresses particular issues that are unique to each of the separate forms.

B. Calculation of CMI

Although Chapters 7, 11, and 13 use CMI for different purposes, the basic computation is the same in each. As defined in § 101(10A), CMI is the monthly average of certain income that the debtor (and in a joint case, the debtor's spouse) received in the six calendar months before the bankruptcy filing. The definition includes in this average (1) income from all sources, whether or not taxable, and (2) any amount paid by an entity other than the debtor (or the debtor's spouse in a joint case) on a regular basis for the household expenses of the debtor, the debtor's dependents, and (in a joint case) the debtor's spouse if not otherwise a dependent. At the same time, the definition excludes from the averaged income "benefits received under the Social Security Act" and certain payments to victims of terrorism, war crimes, and crimes against humanity.

Each of the forms provide for reporting income items constituting CMI. The items are reported in a set of entry lines—Part II of the Chapter 7 form and Part I of the forms for Chapter 11 and Chapter 13—that include separate columns for reporting income of the debtor and of the debtor's spouse. The first of these entry lines includes a set of instructions and check boxes indicating when the "debtor's spouse" column must be completed. The instructions also direct the required averaging of reported income.

The subsequent entry lines specify several common types of income and are followed by a "catch-all" line for other income. The specific entry lines address (a) gross wages; (b) business income; (c) rental income; (d) interest, dividends, and royalties; (e) pension and retirement income; (f) regular contributions to the debtor's household expenses; and (g) unemployment compensation. Gross wages (before taxes) are required to be entered. Consistent with usage in the Internal Revenue Manual and the American Community Survey of the Census Bureau, business and rental income is defined as gross receipts less ordinary and necessary expenses. Unemployment compensation is given special treatment. Because the federal government provides funding for the state unemployment compensation under the Social Security Act, there may be a dispute about whether unemployment compensation is a "benefit received under the Social Security Act." The forms take no position on the merits of this argument, but give debtors the option of reporting unemployment compensation separately from the CMI calculation. This separate reporting allows parties in interest to determine the materiality of an exclusion of unemployment compensation and to challenge it. The forms provide for totaling the income lines.

C. The means test: deductions from current monthly income (CMI)

The means test operates by deducting from CMI defined allowances for living expenses and payment of secured and priority debt, leaving disposable income presumptively available to pay unsecured non-priority debt. These deductions from CMI under are set out in § 707(b)(2)(A)(ii)–(iv). The forms for Chapter 7 and Chapter 13 have identical sections (Parts V and III, respectively) for calculating these deductions. The calculations are divided into subparts reflecting three different kinds of allowed deductions.

1. Deductions under IRS standards

Subpart A deals with deductions from CMI, set out in § 707(b)(2)(A)(ii), for "the debtor's applicable monthly expense amounts specified under the National Standards and Local Standards, and the debtor's actual monthly expenses for the categories specified as Other Necessary Expenses issued by the Internal Revenue Service for the area in which the debtor resides." The forms provide entry lines for each of the specified expense deductions under the IRS standards, and instructions on the entry lines identify the website of the U.S. Trustee Program, where the relevant IRS allowances can be found. As with all of the deductions in § 707(b)(2)(A)(ii), deductions under the IRS standards are subject to the proviso that they not include "any payments for debts."

The IRS National Standards provide a single allowance for food, clothing, household supplies, personal care, and miscellany, depending on income and household size. The forms contain an entry line for the applicable allowance.

The IRS Local Standards provide one set of deductions for housing and utilities and another set for transportation expenses, with different amounts for different areas of the country, depending on the size of the debtor's family and the number of debtor's vehicles. Each of the amount specified in the Local Standards are treated by the IRS as a cap on actual expenses, but because § 707(b)(2)(A)(ii) provides for deductions in the "amounts specified under the . . . Local Standards," the forms treat these amounts as allowed deductions. The forms again direct debtors to the website of the U.S. Trustee Program to obtain the appropriate allowances.

The Local Standards for housing and utilities, as published by the IRS for its internal purposes, present single amounts covering all housing expenses; however, for bankruptcy purposes, the IRS has separated these amounts into a non-mortgage component and a mortgage/rent component. The non-mortgage component covers a variety of expenses involved in maintaining a residence, such as utilities, repairs and maintenance. The mortgage/rent component covers the cost of acquiring the residence. For homeowners with mortgages, the mortgage/rent component involves debt payment, since the cost of a mortgage is part of the allowance. Accordingly, the forms require debtors to deduct from the mortgage/rent component their average monthly mortgage payment (including required payments for taxes and insurance), up to the full amount of the IRS mortgage/rent component, and instruct debtors that this average monthly payment is the one reported on the separate line of the forms for deductions of secured debt under § 707(b)(2)(A)(iii). The forms allow debtors to challenge appropriateness of this method of computing the Local Standards allowance for housing and utilities and to claim any additional housing allowance to which they contend they are entitled, but the forms require specification of the basis for such a contention.

The IRS issues Local Standards for transportation in two components for its internal purposes as well as for bankruptcy: one component covers vehicle operation/public transportation expense and the other ownership/lease expense. The amount of the vehicle operation/public transportation allowance depends on the number of vehicles the debtor operates, with debtors who do not operate vehicles being given a public transportation allowance. The instruction for this line item makes it clear that every debtor is thus entitled to some transportation expense allowance. No debt payment is involved in this allowance. The ownership/lease component, on the other hand, may involve debt payment. Accordingly, the forms require debtors to reduce the allowance for ownership/lease expense by the average monthly loan payment amount (principal and interest), up to the full amount the IRS ownership/lease expense amount. This average payment is as reported on the separate line of the forms for deductions of secured debt under § 707(b)(2)(A)(iii).

The IRS does not set out specific dollar allowances for "Other Necessary Expenses." Rather, it specifies a number of categories for such expenses, and describes the nature of the expenses that may be deducted in each of these categories. Section 707(b)(2)(A)(ii) allows a deduction for the debtor's actual expenses in these specified categories, subject to its requirement that payment of debt not be included. Several of the IRS categories deal with debt repayment and so are not included in the forms. Several other categories deal with expense items that are more expansively addressed by specific statutory allowances. Subpart A sets out the remaining categories of "Other Necessary Expenses" in individual entry lines. Instructions in these entry lines reflect limitations imposed by the IRS and the need to avoid inclusion of items deducted elsewhere on the forms.

Subpart A concludes with a subtotal of the deductions allowed under the IRS standards.

2. Additional statutory expense deductions

In addition to the expense deductions allowed under the IRS standards, the means test makes provision—in subclauses (I), (II), (IV), and (V) of § 707(b)(2)(A)(ii)—for six special expense deductions. Each of these additional expense items is set out on a separate entry line in Subpart B, introduced by an instruction that there should not be double counting of any expense already included in the IRS deductions. Contributions to tax-exempt charities provide another statutory expense deduction. Section 1325(b)(2)(A)(ii) expressly allows a deduction from CMI for such contributions (up to 15% of the debtor's gross income), and § 707(b)(1) provides that in considering whether a Chapter 7 filing is an abuse, the court may not take into consideration "whether a debtor ... continues to make [tax-exempt] charitable contributions." Accordingly, Subpart B also includes an entry line for charitable contributions. The subpart concludes with a subtotal of the additional statutory expense deductions.

3. Deductions for payment of debt

Subpart C of the forms deals with the means test's deductions from CMI for payment of secured and priority debt, as well as a deduction for administrative fees that would be incurred if the debtor paid debts through a Chapter 13 plan. In accord with § 707(b)(2)(A)(iii), the deduction for secured debt is divided into two entry lines—one for payments that are contractually due during the 60 months following the bankruptcy filing, the other for amounts needed to retain necessary collateral securing debts in default. In each situation, the instructions for the entry lines require dividing the total payment amount by 60, as the statute directs. Priority debt, deductible pursuant to § 707(b)(2)(A)(iv), is treated on a single entry line, also requiring division by 60. The defined deduction for the expenses of administering a Chapter 13 plan is allowed by § 707(b)(2)(A)(ii)(III) only for debtors eligible for Chapter 13. The forms treat this deduction in an entry line requiring the eligible debtor to state the amount of the prospective Chapter 13 plan payment and multiply that payment amount by the percentage fee established for the debtor's district by the Executive Office for United States Trustees. The forms refer debtors to the website of the U.S. Trustee Program to obtain this percentage fee. The subpart concludes with a subtotal of debt payment deductions.

4. Total deductions

Finally, the forms direct that the subtotals from Subparts A, B, and C be added together to arrive at the total of allowed deductions from CMI under the means test.

5. Additional claimed deductions

The forms do not provide for means test deductions from CMI for expenses in categories that are not specifically identified as "Other Necessary Expenses" in the Internal Revenue Manual. However, debtors may wish to claim expenses that do not fall within the categories listed as "Other Necessary Expenses" in the forms. Part VII of the Chapter 7 form and Part VI of the Chapter 13 form provide for such expenses to be identified and totaled. Although expenses listed in these sections are not deducted from CMI for purposes of the means test calculation, the listing provides a basis for debtors to assert that these expenses should be deducted from CMI under § 707(b)(2)(A)(ii)(I), and that the results of the forms' calculation should therefore by modified.

D. The chapter-specific forms

1. Chapter 7

The Chapter 7 form has several unique aspects. The form includes, in the upper right corner of the first page, a check box directing the debtor to state whether or not the calculations required by the form result in a presumption of abuse. The debtor is not bound by this statement and may argue, in response to a motion brought under § 707(b)(1), that there should be no presumption despite the calculations required by the form. The check box is intended to give clerks of court a conspicuous indication of the cases for which they are required to provide notice of a presumption of abuse pursuant to § 342(d).

Part I of the form implements the provision of § 707(b)(2)(D) that excludes certain disabled veterans from all means testing, making it unnecessary to compute the CMI of such veterans. Debtors who declare under penalty of the perjury that they are disabled veterans within the statutory definition are directed to verify their declaration in Part VII, to check the "no presumption" box at the beginning of the form, and to disregard the remaining parts of the form.

Part II of the form is the computation of CMI. Section 707(b)(7) eliminates standing to assert the means test's presumption of abuse if the debtor's annualized CMI does not exceed a defined median state income. For this purpose, the statute directs that CMI of the debtor's spouse be combined with the debtor's CMI even if the debtor's spouse is not a joint debtor, unless the debtor declares under penalty of perjury that the spouses are legally separated or living separately other than for purposes of evading the means test. Accordingly, the calculation of CMI in Part II directs a computation of the CMI of the debtor's spouse not only in joint cases, but also in cases of married debtors who do not make the specified declaration, and the CMI of both spouses in these cases is combined for purposes of determining standing under § 707(b)(7).

Part III of the form provides for the comparison of the debtor's CMI for purposes of § 707(b)(7) to the applicable state median income. It then directs debtors whose income does not exceed the applicable median to verify the form, to check the "no presumption" box at the beginning of the form, and not to complete the remaining parts of the form. Debtors whose CMI does exceed the applicable state median are required to complete the remaining parts of the form.

Part IV of the form provides for an adjustment to the CMI of a married debtor, not filing jointly, whose spouse's CMI was combined with the debtor's for purposes of determining standing to assert the means test presumption. The means test itself does not charge a married debtor in a non-joint case with the income of the non-filing spouse, but rather only with contributions made by that spouse to the household expenses of the debtor or the debtor's dependents, as provided in the definition of CMI in § 101(10)(A). Accordingly, Part IV calls for the combined CMI of Part II to be reduced by the amount of the non-filing spouse's income that was not contributed to the household expenses of the debtor or the debtor's dependents.

Part V of the form provides for a calculation of the means test's deductions from the debtor's CMI, as described above.

Part VI provides for a determination of whether the debtor's CMI, less the allowed deductions, gives rise to a presumption of abuse under 707(b)(2)(A). Depending on the outcome of this determination, the debtor is directed to check the appropriate box at the beginning of the form and to sign the verification in Part VIII. Part VII allows the debtor to claim additional deductions, as discussed above.

2. Chapter 11

The Chapter 11 form is the simplest of the three, since the means-test deductions of § 707(b)(2) are not employed in determining the extent of an individual Chapter 11 debtor's disposable income. Section 1129(a)(15) requires payments of disposable income "as defined in section 1325(b)(2)," and that paragraph allows calculation of disposable income under judicially-determined standards, rather than pursuant to the means test deductions, specified for higher income Chapter 13 debtors by § 1325(b)(3). However, § 1325(b)(2) does require that CMI be used as the starting point in the judicial determination of disposable income, and so the Chapter 11 form requires this calculation (in Part I of the form), as described above, together with a verification (in Part II).

3. Chapter 13

Like the Chapter 7 form, the form for Chapter 13 debtors contains a number of special provisions. The upper right corner of the first page includes check boxes requiring the debtor to state whether, under the calculations required by the statement, the applicable commitment period under § 1325(b)(4) is three years or five years and whether the means test deductions are required by § 1325(b)(3) to be used in determining the debtor's disposable income. The check box is intended to inform standing trustees and other interested parties about these items, but does not prevent the debtor from arguing that the calculations required by the form do not accurately reflect the debtor's disposable income.

Part I of the form is a report of income to be used for determining CMI. Section 1325(b)(4) imposes a five-year applicable commitment period—rather than a three-year period—if the debtor's annualized CMI is not less that a defined median state income. For this purpose, as under § 707(b)(4), the CMI of the debtor's spouse is required by the statute to be combined with the debtor's CMI, and there is no exception for spouses who are legally separated or living separately. Accordingly, the report of income in Part I directs a combined reporting of the income of both spouses in all cases of married debtors.

Part II of the form computes the applicable commitment period by annualizing the income calculated in Part I and comparing it to the applicable state median. The form allows debtors to contend that the income of a non-filing spouse should not be treated as CMI and permits debtors to claim a deduction for any income of a non-filing spouse to the extent that this income was not contributed to the household expenses of the debtor or the debtor's dependents. The debtor is directed to check the appropriate box at the beginning of the form, stating the applicable commitment period.

Part III of the form compares the debtor's CMI to the applicable state median, allowing a determination of whether the means-test deductions must be used, pursuant to § 1325(b)(3), in calculating disposable income. For this purpose, since § 1325(b)(3) does not provide for including the income of the debtor's spouse, the form directs a deduction of the income of a non-filing spouse that is not contributed to the household expenses of the debtor or the debtor's dependents. Again, the debtor is directed to check the appropriate box at the beginning of the form, indicating whether the means test deductions are applicable. If so, the debtor is directed to complete the remainder of the form. If not, the debtor is directed to complete the verification in Part VII but not complete the other parts of the form.

Part IV provides for calculation of the means-test deductions provided in § 707(b)(2), described above, as incorporated by § 1325(b)(3) for debtors with CMI above the applicable state median.

Part V provides for three adjustments required by special provisions affecting disposable income in Chapter 13. First, § 1325(b)(2) itself excludes from the CMI used in determining disposable income certain "child support payments, foster care payments, [and] disability payments for a dependent child." Because payments of this kind are included in the definition of CMI in § 101(10A), a line entry for deduction of these payments is provided. Second, a line entry is provided for deduction of contributions by the debtor to certain retirement plans, listed in § 541(b)(7)(B), since that provision states that such contributions "shall not constitute disposable income, as defined in section 1325(b)." Third, the same line entry also allows a deduction from disposable income for payments on loans from retirement accounts that are excepted from the automatic stay by § 362(b)(19), since § 1322(f) provides that for a "loan described in section 362(b)(19) . . . any amounts required to repay such loan shall not constitute 'disposable income' under section 1325."

The Chapter 13 form does not provide a deduction from disposable income for the Chapter 13 debtor's anticipated attorney fees. There is no specific statutory allowance for such a deduction, and none appears necessary. Section 1325(b)(1)(B) requires that disposable income contributed to a Chapter 13 plan be used to pay "unsecured creditors." A debtor's attorney who has not taken a security interest in the debtor's property is an unsecured creditor who may be paid from disposable income.

Part VI of the form allows the debtor to claim additional deductions, as described above, and Part VII is the verification.

2006 Amendment

Forms 22A, Line 43, and Form 22C, Line 48, are amended to delete the phrase "in default" with respect to "Other payments on secured claims." A debtor may be required to make other payments to the creditor even when the debt is not in default, such as to retain collateral. Form 22C, Line 17, also is amended to require all chapter 13 debtors, including those whose income falls below the applicable median income, to determine their disposable income under § 1325(b)(3) of the Code by completing Part III of the form.

Both forms contain stylistic amendments to conform the wording more closely to that used in the 2005 Act.

2005–2008 Amendment

(The 2005–2007 Committee Note incorporates Committee Notes previously published in 2005 and 2006.)

A. Overview

Among the changes introduced by the Bankruptcy Abuse Prevention and Consumer Protection Act of 2005 was a set of interlocking provisions defining "current monthly income" and establishing a means test to determine whether relief under Chapter 7 should be presumed abusive. Current monthly income ("CMI") is defined in § 101(10A) of the Code, and the means test is set out in § 707(b)(2). These provisions have a variety of applications. In Chapter 7, if the debtor's CMI exceeds a defined level the debtor is subject to the means test, and § 707(b)(2)(C) specifically requires debtors to file a statement of CMI and calculations to determine the applicability of the means test presumption. In Chapters 11 and 13, CMI provides the starting point for determining the disposable income that debtors may be required to pay to unsecured creditors. Moreover, Chapter 13 debtors with CMI above defined median income levels are required by § 1325(b)(3) to use the deductions from income prescribed by the means test in order to determine what part of their income is "disposable," and pursuant to § 1325(b)(4), the level of CMI determines the "applicable commitment period" over which projected disposable income must be paid to unsecured creditors.

To provide for the reporting and calculation of CMI and for the completion of the means test where required, three separate official forms have been created—one for Chapter 7, one for Chapter 11, and one for Chapter 13. This note first describes the calculation of CMI that is common to all three of the forms, next describes the means test deductions set out in the Chapter 7 and 13 forms, and finally addresses particular issues that are unique to each of the separate forms.

B. Calculation of CMI

Although Chapters 7, 11, and 13 use CMI for different purposes, the basic computation is the same in each. As defined in § 101(10A), CMI is the monthly average of certain income that the debtor (and in a joint case, the debtor's spouse) received in the six calendar months before the bankruptcy filing. The definition includes in this average (1) income from all sources, whether or not taxable, and (2) any amount paid by an entity other than the debtor (or the debtor's spouse in a joint case) on a regular basis for the household expenses of the debtor, the debtor's dependents, and (in a joint case) the debtor's spouse if not otherwise a dependent. At the same time, the definition excludes from the averaged income "benefits received under the Social Security Act" and certain payments to victims of terrorism, war crimes, and crimes against humanity.

Each of the three forms provides for reporting income items constituting CMI. The items are reported in a set of entry lines—Part II of the form for Chapter 7 and Part I of the forms for Chapter 11 and Chapter 13—that include separate columns for reporting income of the debtor and of the debtor's spouse. The first of these entry lines includes a set of instructions and check boxes indicating when the "debtor's spouse" column must be completed. The instructions also direct the required averaging of reported income.

The subsequent entry lines for income reporting specify several common types of income and are followed by a "catch-all" line for other income. The entry lines address (a) gross wages; (b) business income; (c) rental income; (d) interest, dividends, and royalties; (e) pension and retirement income; (f) regular payments of the household expenses of the debtor or the debtor's dependents; (g) unemployment compensation, and (h) all other forms of income (the "catch-all" line).

Gross wages (before taxes) are required to be entered. However, consistent with usage in the Internal Revenue Manual and the American Community Survey of the Census Bureau, business and rental income are defined as gross receipts less ordinary and necessary expenses.

Unemployment compensation is given special treatment. Because the federal government provides funding for state unemployment compensation under the Social Security Act, there may be a dispute about whether unemployment compensation is a "benefit received under the Social Security Act." The forms take no position on the merits of this argument, but give debtors the option of reporting unemployment compensation separately from the CMI calculation. This separate reporting allows parties in interest to determine the materiality of an exclusion of unemployment compensation and to challenge it.

Alimony and child support are also given special treatment. Child support is not generally considered "income" to the recipient. See 26 U.S.C. § 71(c). Thus, child support is only part of CMI if it is paid on a regular basis for the household expenses of the debtor or the debtor's dependents. On the other hand, alimony and other forms of spousal support are considered income to the recipient, and thus are within CMI regardless of the regularity and use of the payments. To address this distinction, the instruction in the entry line for regular payments of household expenses directs that the entry include regular child support payments used for household expenses of the debtor or the debtor's dependents, and the instruction for the "catch-all" line directs inclusion of all spousal support payments that are not otherwise reported as spousal income.

The forms provide for totaling the income reporting lines.

C. The means test: deductions from current monthly income

The means test operates by deducting from CMI defined allowances for living expenses and payment of secured and priority debt, leaving disposable income presumptively available to pay unsecured non-priority debt. These deductions from CMI are set out in the Code at § 707(b)(2)(A)(ii)-(iv). The forms for Chapter 7 and Chapter 13 have similar sections (Parts V and IV, respectively) for calculating these deductions. The calculations are divided into subparts reflecting three different kinds of allowed deductions.

1. Deductions under IRS standards

Subpart A deals with deductions from CMI, set out in § 707(b)(2)(A)(ii), for "the debtor's applicable monthly expense amounts specified under the National Standards and Local Standards, and the debtor's actual monthly expenses for the categories specified as Other Necessary Expenses issued by the Internal Revenue Service for the area in which the debtor resides." The forms provide entry lines for each of the specified expense deductions under the IRS standards, and instructions on the entry lines identify the website of the U.S. Trustee Program, where the relevant IRS allowances can be found. As with all of the deductions in § 707(b)(2)(A)(ii), deductions under the IRS standards are subject to the proviso that they not include "any payments for debts."

National Standards. The IRS National Standards provide a single allowance for food, clothing, household supplies, personal care, and miscellany, depending on household size, which can be entered directly from a table supplied by the IRS. There is also a National Standard for out-of-pocket health care expenses, which provides two different per-person allowances, depending on age group: the allowance for persons 65 or older is greater than the allowance for those under 65. Accordingly, the forms direct debtors to compute the National Standard allowance for health care by first multiplying each of the two age-group allowances by the number of household members within that age group and then adding subtotals for the two age groups to obtain the total allowance.

Local Standards. The IRS Local Standards provide one set of deductions for housing and utilities and another set for transportation expenses, with different amounts for different areas of the country, depending on the size of the debtor's household and the number of the debtor's vehicles. Each of the amounts specified in the Local Standards are treated by the IRS as a cap on actual expenses, but because § 707(b)(2)(A)(ii) provides for deductions in the "amounts specified under the . . . Local Standards," the forms treat these amounts as allowed deductions.

The Local Standards for housing and utilities, as published by the IRS for its internal purposes, present single amounts covering all housing expenses; however, for bankruptcy purposes, the IRS has provided the Executive Office for United States Trustees with information allowing a division of these amounts into a non-mortgage component and a mortgage/rent component. The non-mortgage component covers a variety of expenses involved in maintaining a residence, such as utilities, repairs and maintenance. The mortgage/rent component covers the cost of acquiring the residence. The forms take no position on the question of whether the debtor must actually be making payments on a home in order to claim a mortgage/rent allowance. For homeowners with mortgages, the mortgage/rent allowance involves debt payment, since the cost of a mortgage is the basis for the allowance. Accordingly, the forms require debtors to deduct from the mortgage/rent allowance their average monthly mortgage payment, up to the full amount of the IRS mortgage/rent allowance, and instruct debtors that this average monthly payment is the one reported on the separate line of the forms for deductions of secured debt under § 707(b)(2)(a)(iii). The forms allow debtors to challenge the appropriateness of this method of computing the Local Standards allowance for housing and utilities and to claim any additional housing allowance to which they contend they are entitled, but the forms require specification of the basis for such a contention.

The IRS issues Local Standards for transportation in two components for its internal purposes as well as for bankruptcy: one component covers vehicle operation/public transportation expense and the other ownership/lease expense. The amount of the vehicle operation/public transportation allowance depends on the number of vehicles the debtor operates; debtors who do not operate vehicles are given a public transportation allowance, regardless of whether they actually use public transportation. It is not clear whether the public transportation allowance may also be claimed by debtors who do make use of public transportation but also operate vehicles. The forms permit debtors to claim both a public transportation and vehicle operating allowance, but take no position as to whether it is appropriate to claim both allowances. No debt payment is involved in the vehicle operation/public transportation component of the Local Standards for transportation.

The ownership/lease component, on the other hand, may involve debt payment. Accordingly, the forms require debtors to reduce the allowance for ownership/lease expense by the average monthly loan payment amount (principal and interest), up to the full amount of the IRS ownership/lease expense amount. This average payment is as reported on the separate line of the forms for deductions of secured debt under § 707(b)(2)(a)(iii). The forms take no position on the question of whether the debtor must actually be making payments on a vehicle in order to claim the ownership/lease allowance.

Other Necessary Expenses. The IRS does not set out specific dollar allowances for "Other Necessary Expenses." Rather, it specifies a number of categories for such expenses, and describes the nature of the expenses that may be deducted in each of these categories. Section 707(b)(2)(a)(ii) allows a deduction for the debtor's actual expenses in these specified categories, subject to its requirement that payment of debt not be included. Several of the IRS categories deal with debt repayment and so are not included in the forms. Several other categories deal with expense items that are more expansively addressed by specific statutory allowances. Subpart A sets out the remaining categories of "Other Necessary Expenses" in individual entry lines. Instructions in these entry lines reflect limitations imposed by the IRS and the need to avoid inclusion of items deducted elsewhere on the forms.

Subpart A concludes with a subtotal of the deductions allowed under the IRS standards.

2. Additional statutory expense deductions

In addition to the expense deductions allowed under the IRS standards, the means test makes provision—in subclauses (I), (II), (IV), and (V) of § 707(b)(2)(A)(ii)—for six special expense deductions. Each of these additional expense items is set out on a separate entry line in Subpart B, introduced by an instruction that tracks the statutory language and provides that there should not be double counting of any expense already included in the IRS deductions.

One of these special expense deductions presents a problem of statutory construction. Section 707(b)(2)A)(ii)(I), after directing the calculation of the debtor's monthly expenses under the IRS standards, states, "Such expenses shall include reasonably necessary health insurance, disability insurance, and health saving account expenses . . . ." There is no express statutory limitation to expenses actually incurred by the debtor, and so the provision appears to allow a reasonable "monthly expense" deduction for health and disability insurance or a health savings account even if the debtor does not make such payments, similar to the way in which the National Standards give an allowance for food, clothing and personal care expenses without regard to the debtor's actual expenditures. However, the statutory language might also be read as providing that the debtor's "Other Necessary Expenses" should include reasonable insurance and health savings account payments. Since "Other Necessary Expenses" are limited to actual expenditures, such a limitation could be implied here. The forms deal with this ambiguity by allowing the debtor to claim a deduction for reasonable insurance and health savings account expenses even if not made, but also require a statement of the amount actually expended in these categories, thus allowing a challenge by any party who believes that only actual expenditures are properly deductible.

Contributions to tax-exempt charities provide another statutory expense deduction. Section 707(b)(1) provides that in considering whether a Chapter 7 filing is an abuse, the court may not take into consideration "whether a debtor . . . continues to make [tax-exempt] charitable contributions." Section 1325(b)(2)(A)(ii) expressly allows a deduction from CMI for such contributions that are "reasonably necessary" (up to 15% of the debtor's gross income), and the Religious Liberty and Charitable Donation Clarification Act of 2005 added language to § 1325(b)(3) to provide the same deduction for above-median income debtors whose disposable income is determined using means test deductions. Accordingly, Subpart B of both the Chapter 7 and Chapter 13 forms includes an entry line for charitable contributions, employing the different statutory deductions allowed in each context.

The Subpart B concludes with a subtotal of the additional statutory expense deductions.

3. Deductions for payment of debt

Subpart C deals with the means test's deductions from CMI for payment of secured and priority debt, as well as a deduction for administrative fees that would be incurred if the debtor paid debts through a Chapter 13 plan.

In accord with § 707(b)(2)(A)(iii), the deduction for secured debt is divided into two entry lines—one for payments that are contractually due during the 60 months following the bankruptcy filing, the other for amounts needed to retain necessary collateral securing debts in default. In each situation, the instructions for the entry lines require dividing the total payment amount by 60, as the statute directs. The forms recognize another ambiguity in this connection: "payments contractually due" might either be understood as limited to payments of principal and interest (payable to secured creditor) or, in the context of a mortgage with an escrow, might be understood as including payments of property taxes and insurance (ultimately paid to taxing bodies and insurers, but initially payable to the mortgagee). The forms require the debtor to specify whether the amount deducted includes taxes and insurance, allowing a party in interest to inquire into the deduction and raise an objection.

Priority debt, deductible pursuant to § 707(b)(2)(A)(iv), is treated on a single entry line, also requiring division by 60. The instruction for this line makes clear that only past due priority debt—not anticipated debts—should be included. Thus, future support or tax obligations, and future fees that might be payable to a Chapter 13 debtor's attorney, are not included.

The defined deduction for the expenses of administering a Chapter 13 plan is allowed by § 707(b)(2)(A)(ii)(III) only for debtors eligible for Chapter 13. The forms treat this deduction in an entry line requiring the eligible debtor to state the amount of the prospective Chapter 13 plan payment and multiply that payment amount by the percentage fee established for the debtor's district by the Executive Office for United States Trustees. The forms refer debtors to the website of the U.S. Trustee Program to obtain this percentage fee.

The subpart concludes with a subtotal of debt payment deductions.

4. Total deductions

Finally, the forms direct that the subtotals from Subparts A, B, and C be added together to arrive at the total of allowed deductions from CMI under the means test.

5. Additional claimed deductions

The forms do not provide for means test deductions from CMI for expenses in categories that are not specifically identified as "Other Necessary Expenses" in the Internal Revenue Manual. However, debtors may wish to claim expenses that do not fall within the categories listed as "Other Necessary Expenses" in the forms. Part VII of the Chapter 7 form and Part VI of the Chapter 13 form provide for such expenses to be identified and totaled. Although expenses listed in these sections are not deducted from CMI for purposes of the means test calculation, the listing provides a basis for debtors to assert that these expenses should be deducted from CMI under § 707(b)(2)(A)(ii)(I), and that the results of the forms' calculation should therefore be modified.

D. The chapter-specific forms

1. Chapter 7

The Chapter 7 form has several unique aspects. The form includes, in the upper right corner of the first page, a check box directing the debtor to state whether or not the calculations required by the form result in a presumption of abuse. The debtor is not bound by this statement and may argue, in response to a motion brought under § 707(b)(1), that there should be no presumption despite the calculations required by the form. The check box is intended to give clerks of court a conspicuous indication of the cases for which they are required to provide notice of a presumption of abuse pursuant to § 342(d).

Part I implements the provision of § 707(b)(2)(D) that excludes certain disabled veterans from all means testing, making it unnecessary to compute the CMI of such veterans. Debtors who declare under penalty of perjury that they are disabled veterans within the statutory definition are directed to verify their declaration in Part VII, to check the "no presumption" box at the beginning of the form, and to disregard the remaining parts of the form.

Part I also provides an exclusion for debtors who do not have primarily consumer debts. These debtors are not subject to any of the provisions of § 707(b)—including the requirement of § 707(b)(2)(C) for filing a CMI statement—since § 707(b) applies, by its terms, only to "an individual debtor . . . whose debts are primarily consumer debts." However, a debtor may be found to have asserted nonconsumer status incorrectly. Unless such a debtor has filed the CMI form within the 45 days after filing the case, the case could be subject to automatic dismissal under § 521(i). To avoid this possibility, debtors asserting principally non-consumer status may complete the appropriate portions of Part I, claim an exclusion from the balance of the form, and promptly file the form. If it is subsequently determined that the debtor does have primarily consumer debts, the form will have been filed within the deadline established by § 521(i), and can be amended to include the necessary CMI and means test information.

Part II computes CMI for purposes of the safe harbor of § 707(b)(7). Section 707(b)(7) prohibits a motion to dismiss based on the means test's presumption of abuse if the debtor's annualized CMI does not exceed a defined median state income. For this purpose, the statute directs that CMI of the debtor's spouse be combined with the debtor's CMI even if the debtor's spouse is not a joint debtor, unless the debtor declares under penalty of perjury that the spouses are legally separated or living separately other than for purposes of evading the means test. Accordingly, the calculation of CMI in Part II directs a computation of the CMI of the debtor's spouse not only in joint cases, but also in cases of married debtors who do not make the specified declaration, and the CMI of both spouses in these cases is combined for purposes of determining standing under § 707(b)(7).

Part III compares the debtor's CMI to the applicable state median income for purposes of § 707(b)(7). It then directs debtors whose income does not exceed the applicable median to verify the form, to check the "no presumption" box at the beginning of the form, and not to complete the remaining parts of the form. Debtors whose CMI does exceed the applicable state median are required to complete the remaining parts of the form.

Part IV adjusts the CMI of a married debtor, not filing jointly, whose spouse's CMI was combined with the debtor's in Part II. The means test itself does not charge a married debtor in a non-joint case with the income of the non-filing spouse, but only with payments regularly made by that spouse for the household expenses of the debtor or the debtor's dependents, as provided in the definition of CMI in § 101(10A). Accordingly, Part IV calls for the combined CMI of Part II to be reduced by the amount of the non-filing spouse's income that was not regularly paid for the household expenses of the debtor or the debtor's dependents. The form requires that the alternative uses of the spouse's income be specified.

Part V of the form provides for a calculation of the means test's deductions from the debtor's CMI, as described above in § C.

Part VI provides for a determination of whether the debtor's CMI, less the allowed deductions, gives rise to a presumption of abuse under § 707(b)(2)(A). Depending on the outcome of this determination, the debtor is directed to check the appropriate box at the beginning of the form and to sign the verification in Part VIII. Part VII allows the debtor to claim additional deductions, as discussed above in § C.5.

2. Chapter 11

The Chapter 11 form is the simplest of the three, since the means-test deductions of § 707(b)(2) are not employed in determining the extent of an individual Chapter 11 debtor's disposable income. Section 1129(a)(15) requires payments of disposable income "as defined in section 1325(b)(2)," and that paragraph allows calculation of disposable income under judicially-determined standards, rather than pursuant to the means test deductions, specified for higher income Chapter 13 debtors by § 1325(b)(3). However, § 1325(b)(2) does require that CMI be used as the starting point in the judicial determination of disposable income, and so the Chapter 11 form requires this calculation (in Part I of the form), as described above, together with a verification (in Part II).

3. Chapter 13

Like the Chapter 7 form, the form for Chapter 13 debtors contains a number of special provisions. The upper right corner of the first page includes check boxes requiring the debtor to state whether, under the calculations required by the statement, the applicable commitment period under § 1325(b)(4) is three years or five years and whether § 1325(b)(3) requires the means-test deductions to be used in determining the debtor's disposable income. The check box is intended to inform standing trustees and other interested parties about these items, but does not prevent the debtor from arguing that the calculations required by the form do not accurately reflect the debtor's disposable income.

Part I is a report of income to be used for determining CMI. In the absence of full payment of allowed unsecured claims, § 1325(b)(4) imposes a five-year applicable commitment period—rather than a three-year period—if the debtor's annualized CMI is not less than a defined median state income. For this purpose, as under § 707(b)(7), § 1325(b)(4) requires that the CMI of the debtor's spouse be combined with the debtor's CMI, but, unlike § 707(b)(7), no exception is made for spouses who are legally separated or living separately. Accordingly, the report of income in Part I directs a combined reporting of the income of both spouses in all cases of married debtors.

Part II computes the applicable commitment period by annualizing the income calculated in Part I and comparing it to the applicable state median. The form allows debtors to contend that the income of a non-filing spouse should not be treated as CMI and permits debtors to claim a deduction for any income of a non-filing spouse to the extent that this income was not regularly paid for the household expenses of the debtor or the debtor's dependents (with the alternative uses specified). The debtor is directed to check the appropriate box at the beginning of the form, stating the applicable commitment period. The check box does not prevent a debtor from proposing an applicable commitment period of less than three or five years in conjunction with a plan that pays all allowed unsecured claims in full.

Part III compares the debtor's CMI to the applicable state median, allowing a determination of whether the means-test deductions must be used, pursuant to § 1325(b)(3), in calculating disposable income. For this purpose, since § 1325(b)(3) does not provide for including the income of the debtor's spouse, the form directs a deduction of the income of a nonfiling spouse that was not contributed to the household expenses of the debtor or the debtor's dependents. Again, the debtor is directed to check the appropriate box at the beginning of the form, indicating whether the means test deductions are applicable. If so, the debtor is directed to complete the remainder of the form. If not, the debtor is directed to complete the verification in Part VII but not complete the other parts of the form.

Part IV provides for calculation of the means-test deductions provided in § 707(b)(2), described above in § C, as incorporated by § 1325(b)(3) for debtors with CMI above the applicable state median.

Part V provides for four adjustments required by special provisions affecting disposable income in Chapter 13. First, § 1325(b)(2) itself excludes from the CMI used in determining disposable income certain "child support payments, foster care payments, [and] disability payments for a dependent child." Because payments of this kind are included in the definition of CMI in § 101(10A), a line entry for deduction of these payments is provided. Second, a line entry is provided for deduction of contributions by the debtor to certain retirement plans, listed in § 541(b)(7)(B), since that provision states that such contributions "shall not constitute disposable income, as defined in section 1325(b)." Third, the same line entry also allows a deduction from disposable income for payments on loans from retirement accounts that are excepted from the automatic stay by § 362(b)(19), since § 1322(f) provides that for a "loan described in section 362(b)(19) . . . any amounts required to repay such loan shall not constitute 'disposable income' under section 1325." Finally, § 1325(b)(3) requires that deductions from income for above-median income debtors be determined not only in accordance with the means test deductions, set out in subparagraph (A) of § 707(b)(2), but also in accordance with subparagraph (B), which sets out the grounds for rebutting a presumption of abuse based on a demonstration of additional expenses justified by special circumstances. Part V includes an entry line for such additional expenses, with a warning that the debtor will be required (as provided by § 707(b)(2)(B)) to document the expenses and provide a detailed explanation of the special circumstances that make them reasonable and necessary.

The Chapter 13 form does not provide a deduction from disposable income for the Chapter 13 debtor's anticipated attorney fees. No specific statutory allowance for such a deduction exists, and none appears necessary. Section 1325(b)(1)(B) requires that disposable income contributed to a Chapter 13 plan be used to pay "unsecured creditors." A debtor's attorney who has not taken a security interest in the debtor's property is an unsecured creditor who may be paid from disposable income.

Part VI allows the debtor to declare expenses not allowed under the form without deducting them from CMI, as described above in § C.5.

Form 23. Debtor's Certification of Completion of Postpetition Instructional Course Concerning Personal Financial Management

B23 (Official Form 23) (12/08)

United States Bankruptcy Court

In re ______________________________,
Debtor

Case No. ______________

Chapter ________

DEBTOR'S CERTIFICATION OF COMPLETION OF POSTPETITION INSTRUCTIONAL COURSE CONCERNING PERSONAL FINANCIAL MANAGEMENT

Every individual debtor in a chapter 7, chapter 11 in which § 1141(d)(3) applies, or chapter 13 case must file this certification. If a joint petition is filed, each spouse must complete and file a separate certification. Complete one of the following statements and file by the deadline stated below:

☐ I, ______________________________, the debtor in the above-
(Printed Name of Debtor)

styled case, hereby certify that on __________ I completed an instructional
(Date)

course in personal financial management provided by ______________________,
(Name of Provider)

an approved personal financial management provider.

Certificate No. (if any): ______________

☐ I, ______________________________, the debtor in the above-
(Printed Name of Debtor)

styled case, hereby certify that no personal financial management course is required because of *[Check the appropriate box.]*:

☐ Incapacity or disability, as defined in 11 U.S.C. § 109(h);
☐ Active military duty in a military combat zone; or
☐ Residence in a district in which the United States trustee (or bankruptcy administrator) has determined that the approved instructional courses are not adequate at this time to serve the additional individuals who would otherwise be required to complete such courses.

Signature of Debtor: ______________

Date: ______________

Instructions: Use this form only to certify whether you completed a course in personal financial management. (Fed.R.Bankr.P. 1007(b)(7).) Do NOT use this form to file the certificate given to you by your prepetition credit counseling provider and do NOT include with the petition when filing your case.

Filing Deadlines: In a chapter 7 case, file within 45 days of the first date set for the meeting of creditors under § 341 of the Bankruptcy Code. In a chapter 11 or 13 case, file no later than the last payment made by the debtor as required by the plan or the filing of a motion for a discharge under § 1141(d)(5)B) or § 1328(b) of the Code. (See Fed.R.Bankr.P. 1007(c).)

(Added Aug. 11, 2005, eff. Oct. 17, 2005; Oct. 11, 2006; Dec. 1, 2007; Dec. 1, 2008.)

ADVISORY COMMITTEE NOTES

2005 Amendment

The form is new. Sections 727(a)(11) and 1328(g)(1), which were added to the Code by the Bankruptcy Abuse Prevention and Consumer Protection Act of 2005, Pub. L. No. 109–8, 119 Stat. 23 (April 20, 2005), require the debtor to complete an instructional course concerning personal financial management as a condition for receiving a discharge. The completed form, when filed by the debtor, will signal the clerk that this condition has been satisfied.

2006 Amendment

The form is amended to direct each individual debtor, including both spouses in a joint case, to file a separate certification and to provide the certificate number of the certificate of completion issued to the debtor by the approved personal financial management counselor. The form also is amended to include the deadlines for filing the certification in cases under chapters 7 and 13 and to instruct the debtor that the form is not to be used to file the certificate provided by the debtor's prepetition credit counselor.

2005-2007 Amendments

(The 2005–2007 Committee Note incorporates Committee Notes previously published in 2005 and 2006.)

The form was issued in 2005. Sections 727(a)(11), 1141(d)(3) and 1328(g)(1), which were added to the Code by the Bankruptcy Abuse Prevention and Consumer Protection Act of 2005, Pub. L. No. 109–8, 119 Stat. 23 (April 20, 2005), require individual debtors to complete an instructional course concerning personal financial management as a condition for receiving a discharge. The completed form will signal the clerk that this condition has been satisfied. Each individual debtor, including both spouses in a joint case, must file a separate certification and provide the certificate of completion issued to the debtor by the approved personal financial management counselor. Instructions are included that state the deadlines for filing the certification in chapter 7, chapter 11 in which § 1141(d)(3) applies, and chapter 13 cases, and remind the debtor that the form is not to be used for filing a certification of prepetition credit counseling.

Form 24. Certification to Court of Appeals by all Parties

B24 (Official Form 24) (12/07)

[Caption as described in Fed. R. Bankr. P. 7010 or 9004(b), as applicable.]

CERTIFICATION TO COURT OF APPEALS BY ALL PARTIES

A notice of appeal having been filed in the above-styled matter on _________ *[Date]*, _________, _________, and _________, [*Names of all the appellants and all the appellees, if any]*, who are all the appellants [and all the appellees] hereby certify to the court under 28 U.S.C. § 158(d)(2)(A) that a circumstance specified in 28 U.S.C. § 158(d)(2) exists as stated below.

Leave to appeal in this matter [___] is [___] is not required under 28 U.S.C. § 158(a).

[If from a final judgment, order, or decree] This certification arises in an appeal from a final judgment, order, or decree of the United States Bankruptcy Court for the _________ District of _________ entered on _________ *[Date]*.

[If from an interlocutory order or decree] This certification arises in an appeal from an interlocutory order or decree, and the parties hereby request leave to appeal as required by 28 U.S.C. § 158(a).

[The certification shall contain one or more of the following statements, as is appropriate to the circumstances.]

The judgment, order, or decree involves a question of law as to which there is no controlling decision of the court of appeals for this circuit or of the Supreme Court of the United States, or involves a matter of public importance.

Or

The judgment, order, or decree involves a question of law requiring resolution of conflicting decisions.

Or

An immediate appeal from the judgment, order, or decree may materially advance the progress of the case or proceeding in which the appeal is taken.

[The parties may include or attach the information specified in Rule 8001(f)(3)(C).]

Signed: *[If there are more than two signatories, all must sign and provide the information requested below. Attach additional signed sheets if needed.]*

_________________________	_________________________
Attorney for Appellant (or Appellant, if not represented by an attorney)	Attorney for Appellee (or Appellee if not represented by an attorney)
_________________________	_________________________
Printed Name of Signer	Printed Name of Signer
_________________________	_________________________
_________________________	_________________________
Address	Address
_________________________	_________________________
Telephone No.	Telephone No.
_________________________	_________________________
Date	Date

(Added Aug. 11, 2005, eff. Oct. 17, 2005; Dec. 1, 2007.)

ADVISORY COMMITTEE NOTES

2005 Amendment

This form is new. Rule 8001, as amended in 2005, requires that any certification of an appeal, bankruptcy court judgment, order, or decree directly to the United States Court of Appeals by all the appellants and appellees (if any) acting jointly be filed on this form.

2005-2007 Amendments

(The 2005–2007 Committee Note incorporates the Committee Note previously published in 2005.)

This form was issued in 2005. Rule 8001 requires that any certification of an appeal, bankruptcy court judgment, order, or decree directly to the United States Court of Appeals by all the appellants and appellees (if any) acting jointly be filed on this form.

Form 25A. Small Business Case Under Chapter 11

B25A (Official Form 25A) (12/08)

United States Bankruptcy Court
__________ District of __________

In re ______________________________, Case No. ______________________
Debtor

Small Business Case under Chapter 11

[NAME OF PROPONENT]'S PLAN OF REORGANIZATION, DATED [INSERT DATE]

ARTICLE I
SUMMARY

This Plan of Reorganization (the "Plan") under chapter 11 of the Bankruptcy Code (the "Code") proposes to pay creditors of [insert the name of the debtor] (the "Debtor") from [specify sources of payment, such as an infusion of capital, loan proceeds, sale of assets, cash flow from operations, or future income].

This Plan provides for __________ classes of secured claims; __________ classes of unsecured claims; and __________ classes of equity security holders. Unsecured creditors holding allowed claims will receive distributions, which the proponent of this Plan has valued at approximately ___ cents on the dollar. This Plan also provides for the payment of administrative and priority claims [if payment is not in full on the effective date of this Plan with respect to any such claim (to the extent permitted by the Code or the claimant's agreement), identify such claim and briefly summarize the proposed treatment.]

All creditors and equity security holders should refer to Articles III through VI of this Plan for information regarding the precise treatment of their claim. A disclosure statement that provides more detailed information regarding this Plan and the rights of creditors and equity security holders has been circulated with this Plan. **Your rights may be affected. You should read these papers carefully and discuss them with your attorney, if you have one. (If you do not have an attorney, you may wish to consult one.)**

ARTICLE II
CLASSIFICATION OF CLAIMS AND INTERESTS

2.01 Class 1. All allowed claims entitled to priority under § 507 of the Code (except administrative expense claims under § 507(a)(2), ["gap" period claims in an involuntary case under § 507(a)(3),] and priority tax claims under § 507(a)(8)).

2.02 Class 2. The claim of __________________, to the extent allowed as a secured claim under § 506 of the Code. [Add other classes of secured creditors, if any. Note: Section 1129(a)(9)(D) of the Code provides that a secured tax claim which would otherwise meet the description of a priority tax claim under § 507(a)(8) of the Code is to be paid in the same manner and over the same period as prescribed in § 507(a)(8).]

2.03 Class 3. All unsecured claims allowed under § 502 of the Code.

[Add other classes of unsecured claims, if any.]

2.04 Class 4. Equity interests of the Debtor. [If the Debtor is an individual, change this heading to "The interests of the individual Debtor in property of the estate."]

ARTICLE III

TREATMENT OF ADMINISTRATIVE EXPENSE CLAIMS, U.S. TRUSTEES FEES, AND PRIORITY TAX CLAIMS

3.01 Unclassified Claims. Under section § 1123(a)(1), administrative expense claims, ["gap" period claims in an involuntary case allowed under § 502(f) of the Code,] and priority tax claims are not in classes.

3.02 Administrative Expense Claims. Each holder of an administrative expense claim allowed under § 503 of the Code [, and a "gap" claim in an involuntary case allowed under § 502(f) of the Code,] will be paid in full on the effective date of this Plan (as defined in Article VII), in cash, or upon such other terms as may be agreed upon by the holder of the claim and the Debtor.

3.03 Priority Tax Claims. Each holder of a priority tax claim will be paid [specify terms of treatment consistent with § 1129(a)(9)(C) of the Code].

3.04 United States Trustee Fees. All fees required to be paid by 28 U.S.C. § 1930(a)(6) (U.S. Trustee Fees) will accrue and be timely paid until the case is closed, dismissed, or converted to another chapter of the Code. Any U.S. Trustee Fees owed on or before the effective date of this Plan will be paid on the effective date.

ARTICLE IV

TREATMENT OF CLAIMS AND INTERESTS UNDER THE PLAN

4.01 Claims and interests shall be treated as follows under this Plan:

Class	Impairment	Treatment
Class 1—Priority Claims	[State whether impaired or unimpaired.]	[Insert treatment of priority claims in this Class, including the form, amount and timing of distribution, if any. For example: "Class 1 is unimpaired by this Plan, and each holder of a Class 1 Priority Claim will be paid in full, in cash, upon the later of the effective date of this Plan as defined in Article VII, or the date on which such claim is allowed by a final non-appealable order. Except: ______."]
Class 2—Secured Claim of [Insert name of secured creditor.]	[State whether impaired or unimpaired.]	[Insert treatment of secured claim in this Class, including the form, amount and timing of distribution, if any.] [Add class[es] of secured claims if applicable]
Class 3—General Unsecured Creditors	[State whether impaired or unimpaired.]	[Insert treatment of unsecured creditors in this Class, including the form, amount and timing of distribution, if any.] [Add administrative convenience class if applicable]
Class 4—Equity Security Holders of the Debtor	[State whether impaired or unimpaired.]	[Insert treatment of equity security holders in this Class, including the form, amount and timing of distribution, if any.]

ARTICLE V

ALLOWANCE AND DISALLOWANCE OF CLAIMS

5.01 Disputed Claim. A disputed claim is a claim that has not been allowed or disallowed [by a final non-appealable order], and as to which either: (i) a proof of claim has been filed or deemed filed, and the Debtor or another party in interest has filed an objection; or (ii) no proof of claim has been filed, and the Debtor has scheduled such claim as disputed, contingent, or unliquidated.

5.02 Delay of Distribution on a Disputed Claim. No distribution will be made on account of a disputed claim unless such claim is allowed [by a final non-appealable order].

5.03 Settlement of Disputed Claims. The Debtor will have the power and authority to settle and compromise a disputed claim with court approval and compliance with Rule 9019 of the Federal Rules of Bankruptcy Procedure.

ARTICLE VI

PROVISIONS FOR EXECUTORY CONTRACTS AND UNEXPIRED LEASES

6.01 Assumed Executory Contracts and Unexpired Leases.

(a) The Debtor assumes the following executory contracts and/or unexpired leases effective upon the [Insert "effective date of this Plan as provided in Article VII," "the date of the entry of the order confirming this Plan," or other applicable date]:

[List assumed executory contracts and/or unexpired leases.]

(b) The Debtor will be conclusively deemed to have rejected all executory contracts and/or unexpired leases not expressly assumed under section 6.01(a) above, or before the date of the order confirming this Plan, upon the [Insert "effective date of this Plan," "the date of the entry of the order confirming this Plan," or other applicable date]. A proof of a claim arising from the rejection of an executory contract or unexpired lease under this section must be filed no later than ________ (___) days after the date of the order confirming this Plan.

ARTICLE VII

MEANS FOR IMPLEMENTATION OF THE PLAN

[Insert here provisions regarding how the plan will be implemented as required under § 1123(a)(5) of the Code. For example, provisions may include those that set out how the plan will be funded, as well as who will be serving as directors, officers or voting trustees of the reorganized debtor.]

ARTICLE VIII

GENERAL PROVISIONS

8.01 Definitions and Rules of Construction. The definitions and rules of construction set forth in §§ 101 and 102 of the Code shall apply when terms defined or construed in the Code are used in this Plan, and they are supplemented by the following definitions: [Insert additional definitions if necessary].

8.02 Effective Date of Plan. The effective date of this Plan is the eleventh business day following the date of the entry of the order of confirmation. But if a stay of the confirmation order is in effect on that date, the effective date will be the first business day after that date on which no stay of the confirmation order is in effect, provided that the confirmation order has not been vacated.

8.03 Severability. If any provision in this Plan is determined to be unenforceable, the determination will in no way limit or affect the enforceability and operative effect of any other provision of this Plan.

8.04 Binding Effect. The rights and obligations of any entity named or referred to in this Plan will be binding upon, and will inure to the benefit of the successors or assigns of such entity.

8.05 Captions. The headings contained in this Plan are for convenience of reference only and do not affect the meaning or interpretation of this Plan.

[8.06 Controlling Effect. Unless a rule of law or procedure is supplied by federal law (including the Code or the Federal Rules of Bankruptcy Procedure), the laws of the State of ________ govern this Plan and any agreements, documents, and instruments executed in connection with this Plan, except as otherwise provided in this Plan.]

[8.07 Corporate Governance. [If the Debtor is a corporation include provisions required by § 1123(a)(6) of the Code.]]

ARTICLE IX
DISCHARGE

[If the Debtor is not entitled to discharge under 11 U.S.C. § 1141(d)(3) change this heading to "**NO DISCHARGE OF DEBTOR.**"]

9.01. **[Option 1—If Debtor is an individual and § 1141(d)(3) is not applicable]**

Discharge. Confirmation of this Plan does not discharge any debt provided for in this Plan until the court grants a discharge on completion of all payments under this Plan, or as otherwise provided in § 1141(d)(5) of the Code. The Debtor will not be discharged from any debt excepted from discharge under § 523 of the Code, except as provided in Rule 4007(c) of the Federal Rules of Bankruptcy Procedure.

[Option 2—If the Debtor is a partnership and section 1141(d)(3) of the Code is not applicable]

Discharge. On the confirmation date of this Plan, the debtor will be discharged from any debt that arose before confirmation of this Plan, subject to the occurrence of the effective date, to the extent specified in § 1141(d)(1)(A) of the Code. The Debtor will not be discharged from any debt imposed by this Plan.

[Option 3—If the Debtor is a corporation and § 1141(d)(3) is not applicable]

Discharge. On the confirmation date of this Plan, the debtor will be discharged from any debt that arose before confirmation of this Plan, subject to the occurrence of the effective date, to the extent specified in § 1141(d)(1)(A) of the Code, except that the Debtor will not be discharged of any debt: (i) imposed by this Plan; (ii) of a kind specified in § 1141(d)(6)(A) if a timely complaint was filed in accordance with Rule 4007(c) of the Federal Rules of Bankruptcy Procedure; or (iii) of a kind specified in § 1141(d)(6)(B).

[Option 4—If § 1141(d)(3) is applicable]

No Discharge. In accordance with § 1141(d)(3) of the Code, the Debtor will not receive any discharge of debt in this bankruptcy case.

ARTICLE X
OTHER PROVISIONS

[Insert other provisions, as applicable.]

Respectfully submitted,

By: ________________________________

The Plan Proponent

By: ________________________________

Attorney for the Plan Proponent

Instructions for Small Business Plan of Reorganization Form

BACKGROUND AND GENERAL INSTRUCTIONS

1. This small business chapter 11 plan of reorganization form is promulgated pursuant to § 433 of the Bankruptcy Abuse Prevention and Consumer Protection Act of 2005. It may be used in cases where the debtor (whether an individual or an artificial entity) is a small business debtor under § 101(51D) of

the Code. This form is intended to be used in conjunction with the small business chapter 11 disclosure statement form (Official Form 25B). Because the type of debtor and the details of the proposed plan will vary from case to case, this form is intended to provide an illustrative format, rather than a specific prescription for the language or content of a plan in any particular case.

2. Some language in this form appears in brackets. The bracketed language sometimes instructs the plan's proponent to provide certain information and sometimes provides optional or alternative language that should be used when and where appropriate. Proponents should make the necessary insertions and/or delete inapplicable language.

SPECIFIC INSTRUCTIONS

SUMMARY

3. The first article should provide a summary of the debtor's proposed plan. It should describe the manner in which the plan will be consummated and the source of funds for payments to be made under the plan. These sources might include an infusion of capital, loan proceeds, sale of assets, cash flow from operations, or future income. The summary should also describe the treatment of the various classes of claimants under the plan.

CLASSIFICATION OF CLAIMS AND INTERESTS

4. The second article describes each class of claimants that will receive a distribution under the plan. The first class consists of claimants entitled to priority pursuant to § 507 of the Code other than those entitled to priority under § 507(a)(2), (3), or (8). The next class or group of classes consists of creditor(s) with allowed secured claims. Secured creditors are usually classified individually, with each secured creditor being placed in its own separate class. Classes of secured creditors should be added as necessary. Next, unsecured claimants, not entitled to priority, should be classified. The proponent may, to the extent allowed by law, create additional classes of unsecured claims, including an administrative convenience class pursuant to § 1122(b) of the Code. The last class consists of equity security holders of the debtor. If the debtor is an individual, this class consists of the interests of the individual Debtor in property of the estate.

TREATMENT OF ADMINISTRATIVE EXPENSE CLAIMS, U.S. TRUSTEES FEES, AND PRIORITY TAX CLAIMS

5. The treatment of certain claims, such as administrative expense claims, allowed under § 503 of the Code, and priority tax claims, allowed under § 507(a)(8) of the Code, is statutorily specified. These claims are not, therefore, placed into classes. Their treatment is described in the third article.

TREATMENT OF CLAIMS AND INTERESTS UNDER THE PLAN

6. The fourth article specifies the treatment accorded the various classes of claims and interests provided for under the plan.

7. Priority claimants other than those allowed under §§ 503 and 507(a)(8) must be classified and paid in full under the plan unless the claimant agrees otherwise.

8. Each secured creditor is generally placed in its own class, with a particular treatment specified for that class. Section 1129(a)(9)(D) of the Code provides that a secured tax claim which would otherwise meet the description of a priority tax claim under § 507(a)(8) of the Code is to be paid in the same manner and over the same period as prescribed in § 507(a)(8).

9. The plan should describe the treatment of the general unsecured claims. An administrative convenience class may be created pursuant to § 1122(b) of

the Code, and other classes of unsecured claims may be created to the extent permitted by applicable law.

10. Finally, the plan should describe the treatment of equity securities.

ALLOWANCE AND DISALLOWANCE OF CLAIMS

11. The fifth article addresses the treatment of disputed claims. A "disputed claim" is a claim that has not been allowed or disallowed. No distribution will be made on account of a disputed claim unless such claim is allowed. The debtor will have the power and authority to settle and compromise a disputed claim with court approval and compliance with Rule 9019.

PROVISIONS FOR EXECUTORY CONTRACTS AND UNEXPIRED LEASES

12. The sixth article deals with executory contracts and unexpired leases. The plan proponent should list all executory contracts and unexpired leases that it has already assumed, or which it intends to assume under the plan. All other executory contracts will be deemed rejected.

13. The seventh article describes how the plan will be implemented. It should indicate the source of any funds that will be used to pay claims and interests under the plan, and it should also list the persons who will be serving as the management of the debtor after the plan is confirmed.

GENERAL PROVISIONS

14. The eighth article provides certain general provisions. Definitions from the Code are incorporated by reference, and any other definitions required by the plan should be listed in section 7.01 of the plan. If a governing law clause is desired, it should be included here, and if the debtor is a corporation, provisions required by § 1123(a)(6) of the Code should be included.

DISCHARGE

15. The ninth article describes the effect of discharge under the plan. When and whether the debtor is entitled to a discharge will depend, among other things, upon whether the debtor is an individual, partnership, or corporation, and whether the debtor is continuing in business after consummation of the plan. The proponent should choose the appropriate language from the options provided.

OTHER PROVISIONS

16. To the extent that other provisions, not provided in the plan, are desired, they should be placed in the tenth article.

(Added Dec. 1, 2008.)

ADVISORY COMMITTEE NOTES

2008 Enactment

This form is new. It implements § 433 of the Bankruptcy Abuse Prevention and Consumer Protection Act of 2005, Pub. L. No. 109–8, 119 Stat. 23 (April 20, 2005). This form for a small business chapter 11 plan of reorganization may be used in cases where the debtor (whether an individual or an artificial entity) is a small business debtor under § 101(51D) of the Code. The form is intended to be used in conjunction with the small business chapter 11 disclosure statement form (Official Form 25B).

Because the type of debtor and the details of the proposed plan of reorganization may vary, the form is intended to provide an illustrative format, rather than a specific prescription for the language or content of a plan in any particular case. The form includes instructions and examples of the types of information needed to complete it.

Form 25B. Disclosure Statement—Small Business Case Under Chapter 11

B25B (Official Form 25B) (12/08)

United States Bankruptcy Court
________ District of ________

In re ____________________, Case No. ____________________
Debtor

Small Business Case under Chapter 11

[NAME OF PLAN PROPONENT]'S DISCLOSURE STATEMENT, DATED [INSERT DATE]

Table of Contents

[Insert when text is finalized]

I. INTRODUCTION

This is the disclosure statement (the "Disclosure Statement") in the small business chapter 11 case of ________ (the "Debtor"). This Disclosure Statement contains information about the Debtor and describes the [insert name of plan] (the "Plan") filed by [the Debtor] on [insert date]. A full copy of the Plan is attached to this Disclosure Statement as Exhibit A. ***Your rights may be affected. You should read the Plan and this Disclosure Statement carefully and discuss them with your attorney. If you do not have an attorney, you may wish to consult one.***

The proposed distributions under the Plan are discussed at pages ___—___ of this Disclosure Statement. [General unsecured creditors are classified in Class ___, and will receive a distribution of ___ % of their allowed claims, to be distributed as follows _________.]

A. Purpose of This Document.

This Disclosure Statement describes:

- The Debtor and significant events during the bankruptcy case,
- How the Plan proposes to treat claims or equity interests of the type you hold (*i.e.*, what you will receive on your claim or equity interest if the plan is confirmed),
- Who can vote on or object to the Plan,
- What factors the Bankruptcy Court (the "Court") will consider when deciding whether to confirm the Plan,
- Why [the Proponent] believes the Plan is feasible, and how the treatment of your claim or equity interest under the Plan compares to what you would receive on your claim or equity interest in liquidation, and
- The effect of confirmation of the Plan.

Be sure to read the Plan as well as the Disclosure Statement. This Disclosure Statement describes the Plan, but it is the Plan itself that will, if confirmed, establish your rights.

B. Deadlines for Voting and Objecting; Date of Plan Confirmation Hearing.

The Court has not yet confirmed the Plan described in this Disclosure Statement. This section describes the procedures pursuant to which the Plan will or will not be confirmed.

1. *Time and Place of the Hearing to [Finally Approve This Disclosure Statement and] Confirm the Plan.*

The hearing at which the Court will determine whether to [finally approve this Disclosure Statement and] confirm the Plan will take place on [insert date], at [insert time], in Courtroom ___, at the [Insert Courthouse Name, and Full Court Address, City, State, Zip Code].

2. *Deadline For Voting to Accept or Reject the Plan.*

If you are entitled to vote to accept or reject the plan, vote on the enclosed ballot and return the ballot in the enclosed envelope to [insert address]. See section IV.A. below for a discussion of voting eligibility requirements.

Your ballot must be received by [insert date] or it will not be counted.

3. *Deadline For Objecting to the [Adequacy of Disclosure and] Confirmation of the Plan.*

Objections to [this Disclosure Statement or to] the confirmation of the Plan must be filed with the Court and served upon [insert entities] by [insert date].

4. *Identity of Person to Contact for More Information.*

If you want additional information about the Plan, you should contact [insert name and address of representative of plan proponent].

C. Disclaimer.

The Court has [conditionally] approved this Disclosure Statement as containing adequate information to enable parties affected by the Plan to make an informed judgment about its terms. The Court has not yet determined whether the Plan meets the legal requirements for confirmation, and the fact that the Court has approved this Disclosure Statement does not constitute an endorsement of the Plan by the Court, or a recommendation that it be accepted. [The Court's approval of this Disclosure Statement is subject to final approval at the hearing on confirmation of the Plan. Objections to the adequacy of this Disclosure Statement may be filed until ________.]

II. BACKGROUND

A. Description and History of the Debtor's Business.

The Debtor is a [corporation, partnership, etc.]. Since [insert year operations commenced], the Debtor has been in the business of ________. [Describe the Debtor's business].

B. Insiders of the Debtor.

[Insert a detailed list of the names of Debtor's insiders as defined in § 101(31) of the United States Bankruptcy Code (the "Code") and their relationship to the Debtor. For each insider, list all compensation paid by the Debtor or its affiliates to that person or entity during the two years prior to the commencement of the Debtor's bankruptcy case, as well as compensation paid during the pendency of this chapter 11 case.]

C. Management of the Debtor Before and During the Bankruptcy.

During the two years prior to the date on which the bankruptcy petition was filed, the officers, directors, managers or other persons in control of the Debtor (collectively the "Managers") were [List the Managers of the Debtor prior to the petition date].

The Managers of the Debtor during the Debtor's chapter 11 case have been: [List Managers of the Debtor during the Debtor's chapter 11 case.]

After the effective date of the order confirming the Plan, the directors, officers, and voting trustees of the Debtor, any affiliate of the Debtor participating in a joint Plan with the Debtor, or successor of the Debtor under the Plan (collectively the "Post Confirmation Managers"), will be: [List Post Confirmation Managers of the Debtor.] The responsibilities and compensation of these Post Confirmation Managers are described in section ___ of this Disclosure Statement.

D. Events Leading to Chapter 11 Filing.

[Describe the events that led to the commencement of the Debtor's bankruptcy case.]

E. Significant Events During the Bankruptcy Case.

[Describe significant events during the Debtor's bankruptcy case:

- Describe any asset sales outside the ordinary course of business, debtor in possession financing, or cash collateral orders.
- Identify the professionals approved by the court.
- Describe any adversary proceedings that have been filed or other significant litigation that has occurred (including contested claim disallowance proceedings), and any other significant legal or administrative proceedings that are pending or have been pending during the case in a forum other than the Court.
- Describe any steps taken to improve operations and profitability of the Debtor.
- Describe other events as appropriate.]

F. Projected Recovery of Avoidable Transfers [Choose the option that applies].

[Option 1—If the Debtor does not intend to pursue avoidance actions]

The Debtor does not intend to pursue preference, fraudulent conveyance, or other avoidance actions.

[Option 2—If the Debtor intends to pursue avoidance actions]

The Debtor estimates that up to $ ___ may be realized from the recovery of fraudulent, preferential or other avoidable transfers. While the results of litigation cannot be predicted with certainty and it is possible that other causes of action may be identified, the following is a summary of the preference, fraudulent conveyance and other avoidance actions filed or expected to be filed in this case:

Transaction	Defendant	Amount Claimed

[Option 3—If the Debtor does not yet know whether it intends to pursue avoidance actions]

The Debtor has not yet completed its investigation with regard to prepetition transactions. If you received a payment or other transfer within 90 days of the bankruptcy, or other transfer avoidable under the Code, the Debtor may seek to avoid such transfer.

G. Claims Objections.

Except to the extent that a claim is already allowed pursuant to a final non-appealable order, the Debtor reserves the right to object to claims. Therefore, even if your claim is allowed for voting purposes, you may not be entitled to a distribution if an objection to your claim is later upheld. The procedures for resolving disputed claims are set forth in Article V of the Plan.

H. Current and Historical Financial Conditions.

The identity and fair market value of the estate's assets are listed in Exhibit B. [Identify source and basis of valuation.]

The Debtor's most recent financial statements [if any] issued before bankruptcy, each of which was filed with the Court, are set forth in Exhibit C.

[The most recent post-petition operating report filed since the commencement of the Debtor's bankruptcy case are set forth in Exhibit D.] [A summary of the Debtor's periodic operating reports filed since the commencement of the Debtor's bankruptcy case is set forth in Exhibit D.]

III. SUMMARY OF THE PLAN OF REORGANIZATION AND TREATMENT OF CLAIMS AND EQUITY INTERESTS

A. What is the Purpose of the Plan of Reorganization?

As required by the Code, the Plan places claims and equity interests in various classes and describes the treatment each class will receive. The Plan also states whether each class of claims or equity interests is impaired or unimpaired. If the Plan is confirmed, your recovery will be limited to the amount provided by the Plan.

B. Unclassified Claims.

Certain types of claims are automatically entitled to specific treatment under the Code. They are not considered impaired, and holders of such claims do not vote on the Plan. They may, however, object if, in their view, their treatment under the Plan does not comply with that required by the Code. As such, the Plan Proponent has *not* placed the following claims in any class:

1. *Administrative Expenses.*

Administrative expenses are costs or expenses of administering the Debtor's chapter 11 case which are allowed under § 507(a)(2) of the Code. Administrative expenses also include the value of any goods sold to the Debtor in the ordinary course of business and received within 20 days before the date of the bankruptcy petition. The Code requires that all administrative expenses be paid on the effective date of the Plan, unless a particular claimant agrees to a different treatment.

The following chart lists the Debtor's estimated administrative expenses, and their proposed treatment under the Plan:

Type	Estimated Amount Owed	Proposed Treatment
Expenses Arising in the Ordinary Course of Business After the Petition Date		Paid in full on the effective date of the Plan, or according to terms of obligation if later
The Value of Goods Received in the Ordinary Course of Business Within 20 Days Before the Petition Date		Paid in full on the effective date of the Plan, or according to terms of obligation if later
Professional Fees, as approved by the Court.		Paid in full on the effective date of the Plan, or according to separate written agreement, or according to court order if such fees have not been approved by the Court on the effective date of the Plan
Clerk's Office Fees		Paid in full on the effective date of the Plan
Other administrative expenses		Paid in full on the effective date of the Plan or according to separate written agreement
Office of the U.S. Trustee Fees		Paid in full on the effective date of the Plan
TOTAL		

2. *Priority Tax Claims.*

Priority tax claims are unsecured income, employment, and other taxes described by § 507(a)(8) of the Code. Unless the holder of such a § 507(a)(8) priority tax claim agrees otherwise, it must receive the present value of such claim, in regular installments paid over a period not exceeding 5 years from the order of relief.

The following chart lists the Debtor's estimated § 507(a)(8) priority tax claims and their proposed treatment under the Plan:

Description (name and type of tax)	Estimated Amount Owed	Date of Assessment	Treatment
			Pmt interval = [Monthly] payment = Begin date = End date = Interest Rate % = Total Payout Amount = $
			Pmt interval = [Monthly] payment = Begin date = End date = Interest Rate % = Total Payout Amount = $

C. Classes of Claims and Equity Interests.

The following are the classes set forth in the Plan, and the proposed treatment that they will receive under the Plan:

1. *Classes of Secured Claims.*

Allowed Secured Claims are claims secured by property of the Debtor's bankruptcy estate (or that are subject to setoff) to the extent allowed as secured claims under § 506 of the Code. If the value of the collateral or setoffs securing the creditor's claim is less than the amount of the creditor's allowed claim, the deficiency will [be classified as a general unsecured claim].

The following chart lists all classes containing Debtor's secured prepetition claims and their proposed treatment under the Plan:

Class #	Description	Insider? (Yes or No)	Impairment	Treatment
	Secured claim of: Name = Collateral description = Allowed Secured Amount = $____ Priority of lien = Principal owed = $____ Pre-pet. arrearage = $____ Total claim = $____		[State whether impaired or unimpaired]	[Monthly] Pmt = Pmts Begin = Pmts End = [Balloon pmt] = Interest rate % = Treatment of Lien = [Additional payment required to cure defaults] =
	Secured claim of: Name = Collateral description = Allowed Secured Amount = $____ Priority of lien =		[State whether impaired or unimpaired]	Monthly Pmt = Pmts Begin = Pmts End = [Balloon pmt] = Interest rate %

Class #	Description	Insider? (Yes or No)	Impairment	Treatment
	Principal owed = $____ Pre-pet. arrearage = $____ Total claim = $____			= Treatment of Lien = [Additional payment required to cure defaults] =

2. *Classes of Priority Unsecured Claims.*

Certain priority claims that are referred to in §§ 507(a)(1), (4), (5), (6), and (7) of the Code are required to be placed in classes. The Code requires that each holder of such a claim receive cash on the effective date of the Plan equal to the allowed amount of such claim. However, a class of holders of such claims may vote to accept different treatment.

The following chart lists all classes containing claims under §§ 507(a)(1), (4), (5), (6), and (a)(7) of the Code and their proposed treatment under the Plan:

Class #	Description	Impairment	Treatment
	Priority unsecured claim pursuant to Section [insert] Total amt of claims = $	[State whether impaired or unimpaired]	
	Priority unsecured claim pursuant to Section [insert] Total amt of claims = $	[State whether impaired or unimpaired]	

3. *Class[es] of General Unsecured Claims.*

General unsecured claims are not secured by property of the estate and are not entitled to priority under § 507(a) of the Code. [Insert description of § 1122(b) convenience class if applicable.]

The following chart identifies the Plan's proposed treatment of Class[es] ___ through ___, which contain general unsecured claims against the Debtor:

Class #	Description	Impairment	Treatment
	[1122(b) Convenience Class]	[State whether impaired or unimpaired]	[Insert proposed treatment, such as "Paid in full in cash on effective date of the Plan or when due under contract or applicable nonbankruptcy law"]
	General Unsecured Class	[State whether impaired or unimpaired]	Monthly Pmt = Pmts Begin = Pmts End = [Balloon pmt] = Interest rate % from [date] =

Class #	Description	Impairment	Treatment
			Estimated = percent of claim paid

4. *Class[es] of Equity Interest Holders.*

Equity interest holders are parties who hold an ownership interest (i.e., equity interest) in the Debtor. In a corporation, entities holding preferred or common stock are equity interest holders. In a partnership, equity interest holders include both general and limited partners. In a limited liability company ("LLC"), the equity interest holders are the members. Finally, with respect to an individual who is a debtor, the Debtor is the equity interest holder.

The following chart sets forth the Plan's proposed treatment of the class[es] of equity interest holders: [There may be more than one class of equity interests in, for example, a partnership case, or a case where the prepetition debtor had issued multiple classes of stock.]

Class #	Description	Impairment	Treatment
	Equity interest holders	[State whether impaired or unimpaired]	

D. Means of Implementing the Plan.

1. *Source of Payments.*

Payments and distributions under the Plan will be funded by the following: [Describe the source of funds for payments under the Plan.]

2. *Post-confirmation Management.*

The Post–Confirmation Managers of the Debtor, and their compensation, shall be as follows:

Name	Affiliations	Insider (yes or no)?	Position	Compensation

E. Risk Factors.

The proposed Plan has the following risks:

[List all risk factors that might affect the Debtor's ability to make payments and other distributions required under the Plan.]

F. Executory Contracts and Unexpired Leases.

The Plan, in Exhibit 5.1, lists all executory contracts and unexpired leases that the Debtor will assume under the Plan. Assumption means that the Debtor has elected to continue to perform the obligations under such contracts and unexpired leases, and to cure defaults of the type that must be cured under the Code, if any. Exhibit 5.1 also lists how the Debtor will cure and compensate the other party to such contract or lease for any such defaults.

If you object to the assumption of your unexpired lease or executory contract, the proposed cure of any defaults, or the adequacy of assurance of performance, you must file and serve your objection to the Plan within the deadline for objecting to the confirmation of the Plan, unless the Court has set an earlier time.

All executory contracts and unexpired leases that are not listed in Exhibit 5.1 will be rejected under the Plan. Consult your adviser or attorney for more specific information about particular contracts or leases.

If you object to the rejection of your contract or lease, you must file and serve your objection to the Plan within the deadline for objecting to the confirmation of the Plan.

[***The Deadline for Filing a Proof of Claim Based on a Claim Arising from the Rejection of a Lease or Contract Is ___.*** Any claim based on the rejection of a contract or lease will be barred if the proof of claim is not timely filed, unless the Court orders otherwise.]

G. Tax Consequences of Plan.

Creditors and Equity Interest Holders Concerned with How the Plan May Affect Their Tax Liability Should Consult with Their Own Accountants, Attorneys, And/Or Advisors.

The following are the anticipated tax consequences of the Plan: [List the following general consequences as a minimum: (1) Tax consequences to the Debtor of the Plan; (2) General tax consequences on creditors of any discharge, and the general tax consequences of receipt of plan consideration after confirmation.]

IV. CONFIRMATION REQUIREMENTS AND PROCEDURES

To be confirmable, the Plan must meet the requirements listed in §§ 1129(a) or (b) of the Code. These include the requirements that: the Plan must be proposed in good faith; at least one impaired class of claims must accept the plan, without counting votes of insiders; the Plan must distribute to each creditor and equity interest holder at least as much as the creditor or equity interest holder would receive in a chapter 7 liquidation case, unless the creditor or equity interest holder votes to accept the Plan; and the Plan must be feasible. These requirements are not the only requirements listed in § 1129, and they are not the only requirements for confirmation.

A. Who May Vote or Object.

Any party in interest may object to the confirmation of the Plan if the party believes that the requirements for confirmation are not met.

Many parties in interest, however, are not entitled to vote to accept or reject the Plan. A creditor or equity interest holder has a right to vote for or against the Plan only if that creditor or equity interest holder has a claim or equity interest that is both (1) allowed or allowed for voting purposes and (2) impaired.

In this case, the Plan Proponent believes that classes ___ are impaired and that holders of claims in each of these classes are therefore entitled to vote to accept or reject the Plan. The Plan Proponent believes that classes ___ are unimpaired and that holders of claims in each of these classes, therefore, do not have the right to vote to accept or reject the Plan.

1. *What Is an Allowed Claim or an Allowed Equity Interest?*

Only a creditor or equity interest holder with an allowed claim or an allowed equity interest has the right to vote on the Plan. Generally, a claim or equity interest is allowed if either (1) the Debtor has scheduled the claim on the Debtor's schedules, unless the claim has been scheduled as disputed, contingent, or unliquidated, or (2) the creditor has filed a proof of claim or equity interest, unless an objection has been filed to such proof of claim or equity interest. When a claim or equity interest is not allowed, the creditor or equity interest holder holding the claim or equity interest cannot vote unless the Court, after notice and hearing, either overrules the objection or allows the claim or equity interest for voting purposes pursuant to Rule 3018(a) of the Federal Rules of Bankruptcy Procedure.

The deadline for filing a proof of claim in this case was ___.

[If applicable—The deadline for filing objections to claims is ___.]

2. *What Is an Impaired Claim or Impaired Equity Interest?*

As noted above, the holder of an allowed claim or equity interest has the right to vote only if it is in a class that is *impaired* under the Plan. As provided in § 1124 of the Code, a class is considered impaired if the Plan alters the legal, equitable, or contractual rights of the members of that class.

3. *Who is **Not** Entitled to Vote.*

The holders of the following five types of claims and equity interests are *not* entitled to vote:

- holders of claims and equity interests that have been disallowed by an order of the Court;

- holders of other claims or equity interests that are not "allowed claims" or "allowed equity interests" (as discussed above), unless they have been "allowed" for voting purposes.

- holders of claims or equity interests in unimpaired classes;

- holders of claims entitled to priority pursuant to §§ 507(a)(2), (a)(3), and (a)(8) of the Code; and

- holders of claims or equity interests in classes that do not receive or retain any value under the Plan;

- administrative expenses.

Even If You Are Not Entitled to Vote on the Plan, You Have a Right to Object to the Confirmation of the Plan [and to the Adequacy of the Disclosure Statement].

4. *Who Can Vote in More Than One Class.*

A creditor whose claim has been allowed in part as a secured claim and in part as an unsecured claim, or who otherwise hold claims in multiple classes, is entitled to accept or reject a Plan in each capacity, and should cast one ballot for each claim.

B. Votes Necessary to Confirm the Plan.

If impaired classes exist, the Court cannot confirm the Plan unless (1) at least one impaired class of creditors has accepted the Plan without counting the votes of any insiders within that class, and (2) all impaired classes have voted to accept the Plan, unless the Plan is eligible to be confirmed by "cram down" on non-accepting classes, as discussed later in Section [B.2.].

1. *Votes Necessary for a Class to Accept the Plan.*

A class of claims accepts the Plan if both of the following occur: (1) the holders of more than one-half (1/2) of the allowed claims in the class, who vote, cast their votes to accept the Plan, and (2) the holders of at least two-thirds (2/3) in dollar amount of the allowed claims in the class, who vote, cast their votes to accept the Plan.

A class of equity interests accepts the Plan if the holders of at least two-thirds (2/3) in amount of the allowed equity interests in the class, who vote, cast their votes to accept the Plan.

2. *Treatment of Nonaccepting Classes.*

Even if one or more impaired classes reject the Plan, the Court may nonetheless confirm the Plan if the nonaccepting classes are treated in the manner prescribed by § 1129(b) of the Code. A plan that binds nonaccepting classes is commonly referred to as a "cram down" plan. The Code allows the Plan to bind nonaccepting classes of claims or equity interests if it meets all the requirements for consensual confirmation except the voting requirements of § 1129(a)(8) of the Code, does not "discriminate unfairly," and is "fair and equitable" toward each impaired class that has not voted to accept the Plan.

You should consult your own attorney if a "cramdown" confirmation will affect your claim or equity interest, as the variations on this general rule are numerous and complex.

C. Liquidation Analysis.

To confirm the Plan, the Court must find that all creditors and equity interest holders who do not accept the Plan will receive at least as much under the Plan as such claim and equity interest holders would receive in a chapter 7 liquidation. A liquidation analysis is attached to this Disclosure Statement as Exhibit E.

D. Feasibility.

The Court must find that confirmation of the Plan is not likely to be followed by the liquidation, or the need for further financial reorganization, of the Debtor or any successor to the Debtor, unless such liquidation or reorganization is proposed in the Plan.

1. *Ability to Initially Fund Plan.*

The Plan Proponent believes that the Debtor will have enough cash on hand on the effective date of the Plan to pay all the claims and expenses that are entitled to be paid on that date. Tables showing the amount of cash on hand on the effective date of the Plan, and the sources of that cash are attached to this disclosure statement as Exhibit F.

2. *Ability to Make Future Plan Payments And Operate Without Further Reorganization.*

The Plan Proponent must also show that it will have enough cash over the life of the Plan to make the required Plan payments.

The Plan Proponent has provided projected financial information. Those projections are listed in Exhibit G.

The Plan Proponent's financial projections show that the Debtor will have an aggregate annual average cash flow, after paying operating expenses and post-confirmation taxes, of $___-___. The final Plan payment is expected to be paid on ___.

[Summarize the numerical projections, and highlight any assumptions that are not in accord with past experience. Explain why such assumptions should now be made.]

You Should Consult with Your Accountant or other Financial Advisor If You Have Any Questions Pertaining to These Projections.

V. EFFECT OF CONFIRMATION OF PLAN

A. DISCHARGE OF DEBTOR. [If the Debtor is not entitled to discharge pursuant to 11 U.S.C. § 1141(d)(3) change this heading to "**NO DISCHARGE OF DEBTOR.**"]

[Option 1—If Debtor is an individual and § 1141(d)(3) is not applicable]

Discharge. Confirmation of the Plan does not discharge any debt provided for in the Plan until the court grants a discharge on completion of all payments under the Plan, or as otherwise provided in § 1141(d)(5) of the Code. Debtor will not be discharged from any debt excepted from discharge under § 523 of the Code, except as provided in Rule 4007(c) of the Federal Rules of Bankruptcy Procedure.

[Option 2—If the Debtor is a partnership and § 1141(d)(3) of the Code is not applicable]

Discharge. On the effective date of the Plan, the Debtor shall be discharged from any debt that arose before confirmation of the Plan, subject to the occurrence of the effective date, to the extent specified in § 1141(d)(1)(A) of the Code. However, the Debtor shall not be discharged from any debt imposed by the Plan. After the effective date of the Plan your claims against the Debtor will be limited to the debts imposed by the Plan.

[Option 3—If the Debtor is a corporation and § 1141(d)(3) is not applicable]

Discharge. On the effective date of the Plan, the Debtor shall be discharged from any debt that arose before confirmation of the Plan, subject to the occurrence of the effective date, to the extent specified in § 1141(d)(1)(A) of the Code, except that the Debtor shall not be discharged of any debt (i) imposed by the Plan, (ii) of a kind specified in § 1141(d)(6)(A) if a timely complaint was filed in accordance with Rule 4007(c) of the Federal Rules of Bankruptcy Procedure, or (iii) of a kind specified in § 1141(d)(6)(B). After the effective date of the Plan your claims against the Debtor will be limited to the debts described in clauses (i) through (iii) of the preceding sentence.

[Option 4—If § 1141(d)(3) is applicable]

No Discharge. In accordance with § 1141(d)(3) of the Code, the Debtor will not receive any discharge of debt in this bankruptcy case.

B. Modification of Plan.

The Plan Proponent may modify the Plan at any time before confirmation of the Plan. However, the Court may require a new disclosure statement and/or revoting on the Plan.

[If the Debtor is not an individual, add the following: "The Plan Proponent may also seek to modify the Plan at any time after confirmation only if (1) the Plan has not been substantially consummated *and* (2) the Court authorizes the proposed modifications after notice and a hearing."]

[If the Debtor is an individual, add the following: "Upon request of the Debtor, the United States trustee, or the holder of an allowed unsecured claim, the Plan may be modified at any time after confirmation of the Plan but before the completion of payments under the Plan, to (1) increase or reduce the amount of payments under the Plan on claims of a particular class, (2) extend or reduce the time period for such payments, or (3) alter the amount of distribution to a creditor whose claim is provided for by the Plan to the extent necessary to take account of any payment of the claim made other than under the Plan."]

C. Final Decree.

Once the estate has been fully administered, as provided in Rule 3022 of the Federal Rules of Bankruptcy Procedure, the Plan Proponent, or such other party as the Court shall designate in the Plan Confirmation Order, shall file a motion with the Court to obtain a final decree to close the case. Alternatively, the Court may enter such a final decree on its own motion.

VI. OTHER PLAN PROVISIONS

[Insert other provisions here, as necessary and appropriate.]

____

[Signature of the Plan Proponent]

____

[Signature of the Attorney for the Plan Proponent]

EXHIBITS

Exhibit A—Copy of Proposed Plan of Reorganization

Exhibit B—Identity and Value of Material Assets of Debtor

Exhibit C—Prepetition Financial Statements (to be taken from those filed with the court)

Exhibit D—[Most Recently Filed Postpetition Operating Report][Summary of Postpetition Operating Reports]

Exhibit E—Liquidation Analysis

Plan Proponent's Estimated Liquidation Value of Assets

Assets	
a. Cash on hand	$
b. Accounts receivable	$
c. Inventory	$
d. Office furniture & equipment	$
e. Machinery & equipment	$
f. Automobiles	$
g. Building & Land	$
h. Customer list	$
i. Investment property (such as stocks, bonds or other financial assets)	$
j. Lawsuits or other claims against third-parties	$
k. Other intangibles (such as avoiding powers actions)	$
Total Assets at Liquidation Value	$
Less: Secured creditors' recoveries	$
Less: Chapter 7 trustee fees and expenses	$
Less: Chapter 11 administrative expenses	$
Less: Priority claims, excluding administrative expense claims	$
[Less: Debtor's claimed exemptions]	$
(1) Balance for unsecured claims	$
(2) Total dollar amount of unsecured claims	$
Percentage of Claims Which Unsecured Creditors Would Receive Or Retain in a Chapter 7 Liquidation:	$
Percentage of Claims Which Unsecured Creditors Will Receive or Retain under the Plan:	___% [Divide (1) by (2)]
	___%

Exhibit F—Cash on Hand on the Effective Date of the Plan

Cash on hand on effective date of the Plan:	$
Less –	
Amount of administrative expenses payable on effective date of the Plan	-
Amount of statutory costs and charges	-
Amount of cure payments for executory contracts	-
Other Plan Payments due on effective date of the Plan	-
Balance after paying these amounts...............	$

The sources of the cash Debtor will have on hand by the effective date of the Plan are estimated as follows:

$	Cash in Debtor's bank account now
+	Additional cash Debtor will accumulate from net earnings between now and effective date of the Plan [state the basis for such projections]
+	Borrowing [separately state terms of repayment]
+	Capital Contributions
+	Other
$	Total [This number should match "cash on hand" figure noted above]

Exhibit G—Projections of Cash Flow and Earnings for Post–Confirmation Period

Instructions for Form Disclosure Statement

BACKGROUND AND GENERAL INSTRUCTIONS

1. This small business chapter 11 disclosure statement form is promulgated pursuant to § 433 of the Bankruptcy Abuse Prevention and Consumer Protection Act of 2005. This form may be used in cases where the debtor (whether an individual or an artificial entity) is a small business debtor within the meaning of § 101(51D) of the Code. This form provides a format for disseminating to parties in interest information about the plan of reorganization in a debtor's small business chapter 11 case, so that those parties can make reasonably informed judgments whether to accept, reject or object to the plan. Because the relevant legal requirements for and effects of a plan's confirmation may vary depending on the nature of the debtor, and because the details of any proposed reorganization necessarily vary, this form is intended to provide a format for disclosure, rather than a specific prescription for the language or content of a disclosure statement in any particular case. The form highlights the factual and legal disclosures required by § 1125 of the Code in connection with the plan's confirmation. It is not intended to restrict the plan's proponent from providing additional information where that would be useful.

2. Proponents are encouraged to present material information in as clear a fashion as possible, including, where feasible, in an accompanying executive

summary, approved by the court, that highlights particular creditors' or interest holders' voting status and treatment under the plan.

3. Some language in this form appears in brackets. The bracketed language sometimes instructs the plan's proponent to provide certain information, and sometimes provides optional or alternative language that should be used when and where appropriate. Proponents should make the necessary insertions and/or delete inapplicable language.

SPECIFIC INSTRUCTIONS

INTRODUCTORY SECTION

4. The introductory section describes the purpose of the disclosure statement, provides procedural information regarding confirmation of the plan, including where to obtain additional information, indicates whether particular claimants or interest holders will be entitled to vote on the plan, and details the procedures and deadlines for filing objections to confirmation of the plan. A copy of the plan should be attached to the debtor's disclosure statement as Exhibit A. Where the proposed distribution to unsecured creditors and other classes can be succinctly summarized, describe that distribution in the second introductory paragraph.

5. In some cases, the court will approve the debtor's disclosure statement prior to solicitation of acceptance or rejection of the plan. See Rule 3017. In other cases, the court may conditionally approve the disclosure statement, and combine the hearing on the adequacy of disclosure and the hearing on confirmation of the plan into one hearing. See Rule 3017.1. Use the bracketed language as appropriate in subsections I.B. and I.C.

BACKGROUND SECTION

6. The second part of disclosure statement provides a history of the debtor's business, both before and during the debtor's bankruptcy case. In this section, the plan proponent should describe the debtor's business, the events that led to the filing of the debtor's bankruptcy petition, and the key events in the debtor's bankruptcy case, and identify the people who managed the debtor during the case and who will manage the debtor after the plan is confirmed. The proponent should disclose its intentions with regard to, and the status of, avoidance actions. If the debtor or proponent intends to bring an avoidance action against a particular creditor or equity interest holder, the disclosure statement should disclose this fact so that the creditor or equity interest holder can use that information to determine the value of its claim or interest when considering whether to accept or reject the plan. If the debtor or plan proponent is uncertain as to what avoidance actions might be brought, that fact should be disclosed as well, so that claimants and equity interest holders can take that information into account, as well, when considering whether to accept or reject the plan.

7. A schedule of the debtor's material assets, along with the basis for their valuation should be attached to the debtor's disclosure statement as Exhibit B. Under § 1116 of the Code, the debtor must also file its most recent prepetition financial statements with the petition. These financial statements should be attached to the debtor's disclosure statement as Exhibit C.

8. Sections 434 and 435 of the Bankruptcy Abuse Prevention and Consumer Protection Act of 2005, and § 308 of the Code require the debtor to file periodic operating reports with the court. The most recent such reports, or a summary of the filed reports, should be attached to the debtor's disclosure statement as Exhibit D.

SUMMARY OF PLAN

9. The third part of the disclosure statement describes the treatment of various creditors and equity interest holders who will receive distributions

under the plan. Because the treatment of certain claims, such as administrative expense claims, allowed under § 503 of the Code, and priority tax claims, allowed under § 507(a)(8) of the Code, is statutorily specified, these claims are not placed into classes. Secured creditors are generally each placed in their own class, with the particular treatment specified for that class. Section 1129(a)(9)(D) of the Code provides that a secured tax claim which would otherwise meet the description of a priority tax claim under § 507(a)(8) of the Code is to be paid in the same manner and over the same period as prescribed in § 507(a)(8) of the Code. While it is not required, the proponent may, where applicable, wish to classify claims under § 507(a)(9) and (10) of the Code. Finally, the disclosure statement should describe the treatment of the general unsecured claimants and equity interest holders. An administrative convenience class may be created pursuant to § 1122(b) of the Code, and other classes of unsecured claims may be created to the extent permitted by applicable case law. Also, while the suggested language of the form contemplates that plan distributions will be in the form of monthly payments, other forms of consideration are permitted and this section of the disclosure statement should be modified to describe clearly the form(s), methods and timing of payments to be made under the particular plan.

10. The disclosure statement should also detail the sources of funds for payments to be made under the plan. These should include the sources of funds for payments to be made on the effective date of the plan (detailed in Exhibit F), and the source of payments that will be made over the life of the plan. The description should be supported by projections about the income and profitability of the debtor. The plan proponent must also fully describe post-confirmation management, as required by § 1129(a)(5) of the Code. The disclosure statement should also describe any risk factors that might influence the debtor's ability to complete the payments or affect the value of the distributions provided for under the plan. Also, the disclosure statement should list any material executory contracts that will be assumed pursuant to the plan, as well as any material contracts that will be rejected. To the extent possible, the tax consequences of the plan should also be summarized.

CONFIRMATION REQUIREMENTS AND PROCEDURES SECTION

11. The fourth part of the disclosure statement sets forth the procedures and requirements for confirmation. In this regard, the disclosure statement should inform creditors and equity interest holders of (1) which class they are in, (2) whether they are entitled to vote, and (3) the amount of their claim allowed for voting purposes. This may be accomplished in the disclosure statement itself or, as noted above, in a summary statement, approved by the court, and sent to the parties in interest along with the disclosure statement. A liquidation analysis of the debtor should be attached to the disclosure statement as Exhibit E. As noted above, the sources of funds for payments to be made on the effective date of the plan should be detailed in Exhibit F, and projections about the profitability and cash flow of the debtor's business after confirmation should be attached to the disclosure statement as Exhibit G.

EFFECT OF PLAN CONFIRMATION

12. The fifth part of the disclosure statement describes the effect of plan confirmation. The language used here should be chosen with care, as the effect of confirmation differs depending on whether the debtor is an individual, partnership, or corporation, and on whether the debtor will continue in business post-confirmation or will, instead, be liquidated.

13. If the plan provides that, after its confirmation, property of the estate will vest in and be distributed by someone other than the debtor, the disclosure statement should identify any such property and the person in whom the property will vest.

OTHER PROVISIONS

14. Other provisions may be added in Part VI as desired and appropriate.
(Added Dec. 1, 2008.)

ADVISORY COMMITTEE NOTES

2008 Enactment

This form is new. It implements § 433 of the Bankruptcy Abuse Prevention and Consumer Protection Act of 2005, Pub. L. No. 109–8, 119 Stat. 23 (April 20, 2005), which provides for an official form for a disclosure statement that may be used in cases where the debtor (whether an individual or an artificial entity) is a small business debtor under § 101(51D) of the Code. The form provides a format for disseminating information to parties in interest about the plan of reorganization in a small business debtor's chapter 11 case, so that a party can make a reasonably informed judgment whether to accept, reject, or object to a proposed plan of reorganization or liquidation.

The form is intended to be used in conjunction with the form small business chapter 11 plan (Official Form 25A). As required by § 433 of the 2005 Act, the form seeks to strike a practical balance between the reasonable needs of the courts, the United States trustee, creditors, and other parties in interest for reasonably complete information, on the one hand, and economy and simplicity for debtors, on the other. The form includes instructions and examples of the types of information needed to complete it.

Because the relevant legal requirements for, and effect of, a plan's confirmation may vary depending on the nature of the debtor and the details of the proposed plan, this form is intended to provide an illustrative format for disclosure, rather than a specific prescription for the language or content of a particular disclosure statement. The form highlights the factual and legal disclosures required for adequate disclosure under § 1125 of the Code. The form is not intended to restrict a plan proponent from providing additional information where that would be useful. Plan proponents are encouraged to present material information in as clear a manner as possible, including, where feasible, by providing an accompanying executive summary, approved by the court, that highlights particular creditors' or interest holders' voting status and treatment under the plan.

Rule 3016 specifies the manner in which the disclosure statement is to be filed. Rule 3017 specifies the manner in which the court will consider it. Rule 3017.1 specifies special procedures for the court's conditional approval of a disclosure statement in a small business case.

Form 25C. Small Business Monthly Operating Report

B 25C (Official Form 25C) (12/08)

UNITED STATES BANKRUPTCY COURT
________ DISTRICT OF ________

In re ______________________, Case No. ______________
Debtor

Small Business Case under Chapter 11

SMALL BUSINESS MONTHLY OPERATING REPORT

Month: ______________ Date filed: ______________

Line of Business: ______________ NAISC Code: ______________

IN ACCORDANCE WITH TITLE 28, SECTION 1746, OF THE UNITED STATES CODE, I DECLARE UNDER PENALTY OF PERJURY THAT I HAVE EXAMINED THE FOLLOWING SMALL BUSINESS MONTHLY OPERATING REPORT AND THE ACCOMPANYING ATTACHMENTS AND, TO THE BEST OF MY KNOWLEDGE, THESE DOCUMENTS ARE TRUE, CORRECT AND COMPLETE.

RESPONSIBLE PARTY:

____
Original Signature of Responsible Party

____
Printed Name of Responsible Party

Questionnaire: *(All questions to be answered on behalf of the debtor.)*	**Yes**	**No**
1. IS THE BUSINESS STILL OPERATING?	☐	☐
2. HAVE YOU PAID ALL YOUR BILLS ON TIME THIS MONTH?	☐	☐
3. DID YOU PAY YOUR EMPLOYEES ON TIME?	☐	☐
4. HAVE YOU DEPOSITED ALL THE RECEIPTS FOR YOUR BUSINESS INTO THE DIP ACCOUNT THIS MONTH?	☐	☐
5. HAVE YOU FILED ALL OF YOUR TAX RETURNS AND PAID ALL OF YOUR TAXES THIS MONTH	☐	☐
6. HAVE YOU TIMELY FILED ALL OTHER REQUIRED GOVERNMENT FILINGS?	☐	☐
7. HAVE YOU PAID ALL OF YOUR INSURANCE PREMIUMS THIS MONTH?	☐	☐
8. DO YOU PLAN TO CONTINUE TO OPERATE THE BUSINESS NEXT MONTH?	☐	☐
9. ARE YOU CURRENT ON YOUR QUARTERLY FEE PAYMENT TO THE U.S. TRUSTEE?	☐	☐
10. HAVE YOU PAID ANYTHING TO YOUR ATTORNEY OR OTHER PROFESSIONALS THIS MONTH?	☐	☐

Questionnaire: *(All questions to be answered on behalf of the debtor.)*	**Yes**	**No**
11. DID YOU HAVE ANY UNUSUAL OR SIGNIFICANT UNANTICIPATED EXPENSES THIS MONTH?	☐	☐
12. HAS THE BUSINESS SOLD ANY GOODS OR PROVIDED SERVICES OR TRANSFERRED ANY ASSETS TO ANY BUSINESS RELATED TO THE DIP IN ANY WAY?	☐	☐
13. DO YOU HAVE ANY BANK ACCOUNTS OPEN OTHER THAN THE DIP ACCOUNT?	☐	☐
14. HAVE YOU SOLD ANY ASSETS OTHER THAN INVENTORY THIS MONTH?	☐	☐
15. DID ANY INSURANCE COMPANY CANCEL YOUR POLICY THIS MONTH?	☐	☐
16. HAVE YOU BORROWED MONEY FROM ANYONE THIS MONTH?	☐	☐
17. HAS ANYONE MADE AN INVESTMENT IN YOUR BUSINESS THIS MONTH?	☐	☐
18. HAVE YOU PAID ANY BILLS YOU OWED BEFORE YOU FILED BANKRUPTCY?	☐	☐

TAXES

DO YOU HAVE ANY PAST DUE TAX RETURNS OR PAST DUE POST–PETITION TAX OBLIGATIONS?	☐	☐

IF YES, PLEASE PROVIDE A WRITTEN EXPLANATION INCLUDING WHEN SUCH RETURNS WILL BE FILED, OR WHEN SUCH PAYMENTS WILL BE MADE AND THE SOURCE OF THE FUNDS FOR THE PAYMENT.

(Exhibit A)

INCOME

PLEASE SEPARATELY LIST ALL OF THE INCOME YOU RECEIVED FOR THE MONTH. THE LIST SHOULD INCLUDE ALL INCOME FROM CASH AND CREDIT TRANSACTIONS. *(THE U.S. TRUSTEE MAY WAIVE THIS REQUIREMENT.)*

TOTAL INCOME $ ____________

SUMMARY OF CASH ON HAND

Cash on Hand at Start of Month $ ____________

Cash on Hand at End of Month $ ____________

PLEASE PROVIDE THE TOTAL AMOUNT OF CASH CURRENTLY AVAILABLE TO YOU

TOTAL $ ____________

(Exhibit B)

EXPENSES

PLEASE SEPARATELY LIST ALL EXPENSES PAID BY CASH OR BY CHECK FROM YOUR BANK ACCOUNTS THIS MONTH. INCLUDE THE DATE PAID, WHO WAS PAID THE MONEY, THE PURPOSE AND THE AMOUNT. *(THE U.S. TRUSTEE MAY WAIVE THIS REQUIREMENT.)*

TOTAL EXPENSES $ ________

(Exhibit C)

CASH PROFIT

INCOME FOR THE MONTH *(TOTAL FROM EXHIBIT B)* $ ________

EXPENSES FOR THE MONTH *(TOTAL FROM EXHIBIT C)* $ ________

(Subtract Line C from Line B) **CASH PROFIT FOR THE MONTH** $ ________

UNPAID BILLS

PLEASE ATTACH A LIST OF ALL DEBTS (INCLUDING TAXES) WHICH YOU HAVE INCURRED SINCE THE DATE YOU FILED BANKRUPTCY BUT HAVE NOT PAID. THE LIST MUST INCLUDE THE DATE THE DEBT WAS INCURRED, WHO IS OWED THE MONEY, THE PURPOSE OF THE DEBT AND WHEN THE DEBT IS DUE. *(THE U.S. TRUSTEE MAY WAIVE THIS REQUIREMENT.)*

TOTAL PAYABLES $ ________

(Exhibit D)

MONEY OWED TO YOU

PLEASE ATTACH A LIST OF ALL AMOUNTS OWED TO YOU BY YOUR CUSTOMERS FOR WORK YOU HAVE DONE OR THE MERCHANDISE YOU HAVE SOLD. YOU SHOULD INCLUDE WHO OWES YOU MONEY, HOW MUCH IS OWED AND WHEN IS PAYMENT DUE. *(THE U.S. TRUSTEE MAY WAIVE THIS REQUIREMENT.)*

TOTAL RECEIVABLES $ ________

(Exhibit E)

BANKING INFORMATION

PLEASE ATTACH A COPY OF YOUR LATEST BANK STATEMENT FOR EVERY ACCOUNT YOU HAVE AS OF THE DATE OF THIS FINANCIAL REPORT OR HAD DURING THE PERIOD COVERED BY THIS REPORT.

(Exhibit F)

EMPLOYEES

NUMBER OF EMPLOYEES WHEN THE CASE WAS FILED? ________

NUMBER OF EMPLOYEES AS OF THE DATE OF THIS MONTHLY REPORT? ____________

PROFESSIONAL FEES

BANKRUPTCY RELATED:

PROFESSIONAL FEES RELATING TO THE BANKRUPTCY CASE PAID DURING THIS REPORTING PERIOD? $ ____________

TOTAL PROFESSIONAL FEES RELATING TO THE BANKRUPTCY CASE PAID SINCE THE FILING OF THE CASE? $ ____________

NON-BANKRUPTCY RELATED:

PROFESSIONAL FEES NOT RELATING TO THE BANKRUPTCY CASE PAID DURING THIS REPORTING PERIOD? $ ____________

TOTAL PROFESSIONAL FEES NOT RELATING TO THE BANKRUPTCY CASE PAID SINCE THE FILING OF THE CASE? $ ____________

PROJECTIONS

COMPARE YOUR ACTUAL INCOME AND EXPENSES TO THE PROJECTIONS FOR THE FIRST 180 DAYS OF YOUR CASE PROVIDED AT THE INITIAL DEBTOR INTERVIEW.

	Projected	Actual	Difference
INCOME	$ ____________	$ ____________	$ ____________
EXPENSES	$ ____________	$ ____________	$ ____________
CASH PROFIT	$ ____________	$ ____________	$ ____________

TOTAL PROJECTED INCOME FOR THE NEXT MONTH: $ ____________
TOTAL PROJECTED EXPENSES FOR THE NEXT MONTH: $ ____________
TOTAL PROJECTED CASH PROFIT FOR THE NEXT MONTH: $ ____________

ADDITIONAL INFORMATION

PLEASE ATTACH ALL FINANCIAL REPORTS INCLUDING AN INCOME STATEMENT AND BALANCE SHEET WHICH YOU PREPARE INTERNALLY.
(Added Dec. 1, 2008.)

ADVISORY COMMITTEE NOTES

2008 Enactment

This form is new. It implements §§ 434 and 435 of the Bankruptcy Abuse Prevention and Consumer Protection Act of 2005, Pub. L. No. 109–8, 119 Stat. 23 (April 20, 2005), which provided for rules and an official form to assist small business debtors in chapter 11 cases to fulfill their responsibilities under § 308 of the Code, a provision added by the 2005 Act. The form directs the debtor to disclose the information required under § 308 and resembles those developed earlier by the United States trustees for use in supervising debtors in possession in chapter 11 cases.

Form 26. Periodic Report Regarding Value, Operations and Profitability of Entities in Which the Estate Holds a Substantial or Controlling Interest

B26 (Official Form 26) (12/08)

United States Bankruptcy Court
__________ District of __________

In re ______________________________, Case No. ____________________

Debtor Chapter 11

PERIODIC REPORT REGARDING VALUE, OPERATIONS AND PROFITABILITY OF ENTITIES IN WHICH THE ESTATE OF [NAME OF DEBTOR] HOLDS A SUBSTANTIAL OR CONTROLLING INTEREST

This is the report as of __________ on the value, operations and profitability of those entities in which the estate holds a substantial or controlling interest, as required by Bankruptcy Rule 2015.3. The estate of [Name of Debtor] holds a substantial or controlling interest in the following entities:

Name of Entity	Interest of the Estate	Tab #

This periodic report (the "Periodic Report") contains separate reports ("Entity Reports") on the value, operations, and profitability of each entity listed above.

Each Entity Report shall consist of three exhibits. Exhibit A contains a valuation estimate for the entity as of a date not more than two years prior to the date of this report. It also contains a description of the valuation method used. Exhibit B contains a balance sheet, a statement of income (loss), a statement of cash flows, and a statement of changes in shareholders' or partners' equity (deficit) for the period covered by the Entity Report, along with summarized footnotes. Exhibit C contains a description of the entity's business operations.

THIS REPORT MUST BE SIGNED BY A REPRESENTATIVE OF THE TRUSTEE OR DEBTOR IN POSSESSION.

The undersigned, having reviewed the above listing of entities in which the estate of [Debtor] holds a substantial or controlling interest, and being familiar with the Debtor's financial affairs, verifies under the penalty of perjury that the listing is complete, accurate and truthful to the best of his/her knowledge.

Date: ______________________________

____
Signature of Authorized Individual

____
Name of Authorized Individual

____
Title of Authorized Individual

[If the Debtor is an individual or in a joint case]

Signature(s) of Debtor(s) (Individual/Joint)

____
Signature of Debtor

____

Signature of Joint Debtor

Exhibit A

Valuation Estimate for [Name of Entity]

[Provide a statement of the entity's value and the value of the estate's interest in the entity, including a description of the basis for the valuation, the date of the valuation and the valuation method used. This valuation must be no more than two years old. Indicate the source of this information.]

Exhibit B

Financial Statements for [Insert Name of Entity]

Exhibit B–1

Balance Sheet for [Name of Entity]

As of [date]

[Provide a balance sheet dated as of the end of the most recent six-month period of the current fiscal year and as of the end of the preceding fiscal year. Indicate the source of this information.]

Exhibit B–2

Statement of Income (Loss) for [Name of Entity]

Period ending [date]

[Provide a statement of income (loss) for the following periods:

(i) For the initial report:

a. the period between the end of the preceding fiscal year and the end of the most recent six-month period of the current fiscal year; and

b. the prior fiscal year.

(ii) For subsequent reports, since the closing date of the last report.

Indicate the source of this information.]

Exhibit B–3

Statement of Cash Flows for [Name of Entity]

For the period ending [date]

[Provide a statement of changes in cash flows for the following periods:

(i) For the initial report:

a. the period between the end of the preceding fiscal year and the end of the most recent six-month period of the current fiscal year; and

b. the prior fiscal year.

(ii) For subsequent reports, since the closing date of the last report.

Indicate the source of this information.]

Exhibit B–4

Statement of Changes in Shareholders'/Partners' Equity (Deficit) for [Name Of Entity]

period ending [date]

[Provide a statement of changes in shareholders'/partners' equity (deficit) for the following periods:

(i) For the initial report:

a. the period between the end of the preceding fiscal year and the end of the most recent six-month period of the current fiscal year; and

b. the prior fiscal year.

(ii) For subsequent reports, since the closing date of the last report.

Indicate the source of this information.]

Exhibit C

Description of Operations for [name of entity]

[Describe the nature and extent of the estate's interest in the entity.

Describe the business conducted and intended to be conducted by the entity, focusing on the entity's dominant business segment(s). Indicate the source of this information.]

Instructions for Periodic Report Concerning Related Entities

General Instructions

1. This form periodic report ("Periodic Report") on value, profitability, and operations of entities in which the estate holds a substantial or controlling interest (the "Form") implements § 419 of the Bankruptcy Abuse Prevention and Consumer Protection Act of 2005, Pub. L. No. 19–8, 119 Stat. 23 (April 20, 2005)("BAPCPA"). This Form should be used when required by Fed. R. Bankr. P. 2015.3, with such variations as may be approved by the court pursuant to subdivisions (d) and (e) of that rule.

2. In a chapter 11 case, the trustee or debtor in possession shall file Periodic Reports of the value, operations, and profitability of each entity that is not also a debtor in a case under title 11, and in which the estate holds a substantial or controlling interest. The reports shall be prepared as prescribed by this Form, and shall be based upon the most recent information reasonably available to the trustee or debtor in possession.

3. Rule 2015.3 provides that, where the estate controls or owns at least a 20 percent interest of an entity, the estate's interest is presumed to be substantial or controlling. Where the estate controls or owns less than a 20 percent interest, the rule presumes that the estate's interest is not substantial or controlling. The question of substantial or controlling interest is, however, a factual one to be decided in each case.

4. The first Periodic Report required by subdivision (a) of Rule 2015.3 shall be filed no later than five days before the first date set for the meeting of creditors under § 341 of the Code. Subsequent Periodic Reports shall be filed no less frequently than every six months thereafter, until a plan of reorganization becomes effective or the case is closed, dismissed, or converted. Copies of the Periodic Report shall be served on the U.S. Trustee, any committee appointed under § 1102 of the Code, and any other party in interest that has filed a request therefor.

5. The source of the information contained in each Periodic Report shall be indicated.

Specific Instructions

6. Each entity subject to the reporting requirement of Rule 2015.3 shall be listed in the table contained on the first page of the form. Reports for each such entity shall be placed behind separate tabs, and each such report shall consist of three exhibits. Exhibit A shall provide valuation information; Exhibit B shall provide financial statements; and Exhibit C shall provide a description of operations.

Instructions for Exhibit A—Valuation

7. Provide a statement of the entity's value and the value of the estate's interest in the entity, including a description of the basis for the valuation, the date of the valuation, the valuation method used and the source or preparer of the information. This valuation must be no more than two years old.

Instructions for Exhibit B—Financial Statements and Profitability

8. The financial statements may be unaudited. The financial statements should be prepared in accordance with generally accepted accounting principles in the United States ("USGAAP"); deviations, if any from USGAAP, shall be disclosed. Indicate the source or preparer of the information.

9. Exhibit B shall include the following financial statements, and shall indicate the source of the information presented:

(a) A balance sheet dated as of the end of the most recent six-month period of the current fiscal year and as of the end of the preceding fiscal year.

(b) A statement of income (loss) for the following periods:

(i) For the initial report:

a. the period between the end of the preceding fiscal year and the end of the most recent six-month period of the current fiscal year; and

b. the prior fiscal year.

(ii) For subsequent reports, since the closing date of the last report.

(c) A statement of changes in cash flows for the following periods:

(i) For the initial report:

a. the period between the end of the preceding fiscal year and the end of the most recent six-month period of the current fiscal year; and

b. the prior fiscal year.

(ii) For subsequent reports, since the closing date of the last report.

(d) A statement of changes in shareholders'/partners' equity (deficit) for the following periods:

(i) For the initial report:

a. the period between the end of the preceding fiscal year and the end of the most recent six-month period of the current fiscal year; and

b. the prior fiscal year.

(ii) For subsequent reports, since the closing date of the last report.

10. The balance sheet contained in Exhibit B–1 may include only major captions with the exception of inventories. Data as to raw materials, work in process, and finished goods inventories should be included either on the face of the balance sheet or in the notes to the financial statements, if applicable. Where any major balance sheet caption is less than 10% of total assets, the caption may be combined with others. An illustrative example of such a balance sheet is set forth below:

XYZ Company
Balance Sheet
As of ________

Assets	Year to date	Prior Fiscal Year
Cash and cash items	________	________
Marketable securities	________	________
Accounts and notes receivable (non-affiliates), net of allowances	________	________
Accounts due from affiliates	________	________
Inventories		
Raw materials	________	________
Work in Process	________	________
Finished goods	________	________
Long-term contract costs	________	________
Supplies	________	________
LIFO reserve	________	________
Total inventories	________	________
Prepaid expenses	________	________
Other current assets	________	________

Assets	Year to date	Prior Fiscal Year
Total current assets		
Securities of affiliates		
Indebtedness of affiliates (non-current)		
Other investments		
Property, plant and equipment, net of accumulated depreciation and amortization		
Intangible assets		
Other assets		
Total Assets		

Liabilities and Shareholders'/Partners' Equity	Year to date	Prior Fiscal Year
Accounts and notes payable (non-affiliates)		
Payables to affiliates		
Other current liabilities		
Total current liabilities		
Bonds, mortgages, and other long-term debt, including capitalized leases		
Indebtedness to affiliates (non-current)		
Other liabilities		
Commitments and contingencies		
Deferred credits		
Minority interests in consolidated subsidiaries		
Preferred stock subject to mandatory redemption or whose redemption is outside the control of the issuer		
Total liabilities		
Shareholders' equity		
Total liabilities and shareholders'/partners' equity		

11. The statement of income (loss) contained in Exhibit B–2 should also include major captions. When any major statement of income (loss) caption is less than 15% of net income (loss) for the most recent fiscal year, the caption may be combined with others. Notwithstanding these tests, de minimis amounts need not be shown separately. An illustrative example of such a statement of income (loss) is set forth below:

XYZ Company
Statement of income (loss)
For the periods ending ________

	Year to date	Prior Fiscal Year
Net sales and gross revenues		
Costs and expenses applicable to sales and revenues		
Gross profit		
Selling, general, and administrative expenses		
Provision for doubtful accounts		
Other general expenses		
Operating income (loss)		
Non-operating income (loss)		
Interest and amortization of debt discount		
Non-operating expenses		
Income or loss before income tax expense		
Income tax expense		
Minority interest in income of consolidated subsidiaries		
Equity in earnings of unconsolidated subsidiaries and 50 per cent or less owned persons		
Income or loss from continuing operations		

	Year to date	Prior Fiscal Year
Discontinued operations		
Income or loss before extraordinary items and cumulative effects of changes in accounting principles		
Extraordinary items, net of tax		
Cumulative effects of changes in accounting principles		
Net income (loss)		
Earnings per share data		

12. The statement of cash flows in Exhibit B–3 may be abbreviated, starting with a single figure of funds provided by operations and showing other changes individually only when they exceed 10% of the average of funds provided by operations for the most recent fiscal year. Notwithstanding this test, de minimis amounts need not be shown separately. An illustrative example of such a statement of cash flows is set forth below:

XYZ Company
Statement of cash flows
For the periods ending ________

	Year to date	Prior Fiscal Year
Net cash provided (used) by operating activities		
Cash flows from investing activities		
Capital expenditures		
Sale of ____________________		
Other (describe)		
Net cash provided (used) in investing activities		
Cash flows provided (used) by financing activities		
Net borrowings under line-of-credit		
Principal payments under capital leases		
Proceeds from issuance of long-term debt		
Proceeds from sale of stock		
Dividends paid/Partner Distributions		
Net cash provided (used) in financing activities		
Net increase (decrease) in cash and cash equivalents		
Cash and cash equivalents		
Beginning of period		
End of period		

13. Subject to paragraph 11 above, an illustrative example of such a statement of changes in shareholders'/partners' equity in Exhibit B–4 is set forth below:

XYZ Company
Statement of changes in shareholders'/partners' equity (deficit)
For the periods ending

	Year to date	Prior Fiscal Year
Balance, beginning of period		
Comprehensive net income		
Net income		
Other comprehensive income, net of tax		
Unrealized gains (losses) on securities		
Foreign translation adjustments		
Minimum pension liability adjustment		
Issuance of stock		
Dividends paid		
Balance, end of period		

14. The financial information in the financial statements shall include disclosures either on the face of the statements or in accompanying footnotes sufficient to make the information not misleading. Disclosures should encompass, but not be limited to, for example, accounting principles and practices; estimates inherent in the preparation of financial statements; status of long-term contracts; capitalization including significant borrowings or modification of existing financing arrangements; and the reporting entity resulting from business combinations or dispositions. Where material contingencies exist, disclosure of such matters shall be provided.

15. If appropriate, the statement of income (loss) should show earnings (loss) per share and dividends declared per share applicable to common stock. The basis of the earnings per share computation should be stated together with the number of shares used in the computation.

16. In addition to the financial statements required above, entities in the development stage should provide the cumulative financial statements (condensed to the same degree as allowed above) and disclosures required by Statement of Financial Accounting Standards No. 7, "Accounting and Reporting by Development Stage Enterprises," to the date of the latest balance sheet presented.

Instructions for Exhibit C—Description of Operations

17. The description of operations contained in Exhibit C of this Form should describe the nature and extent of the estate's interest in the entity, as well as the business conducted by and intended to be conducted by the entity, focusing on the entity's dominant business segment(s) including, but not limited to the following as applicable:

· Principal product produced or services rendered and methods of distribution

· Description of the status of a new product or segment if a public announcement has been made or information publicly disseminated

· Sources and availability of raw materials

· Any significant patents, trademarks, licenses, franchises, and concessions held

· Seasonality of the business

· Dependence upon a single customer or a few customers

· Dollar amount of backlog orders believed to be firm

· Exposure to renegotiation or redetermination or termination of significant contracts

· Competitive conditions facing the entity

· Description of properties owned

· Significant legal proceedings

· Material purchase commitments

· Identified trends events or uncertainties that are likely to have a material impact on the entity's short-term liquidity, net sales, or income from continuing operations

18. The source preparer of the information should be indicated.

(Added Dec. 1, 2008.)

ADVISORY COMMITTEE NOTES

2008 Enactment

This form is new. It implements § 419 of the Bankruptcy Abuse Prevention and Consumer Protection Act of 2005, Pub. L. No. 109–8, 119 Stat. 23 (April 20, 2005), which requires a chapter 11 debtor to file periodic reports on the profitability of any entities in which the estate holds a substantial or controlling interest. The form is to be used when required by Bankruptcy Rule 2015.3, with such variations as may be approved by the court pursuant to subdivisions (d) and (e) of that rule. The form includes instructions and examples of the types of information needed to complete it.

PROCEDURAL FORMS

B13S (Form 13S) (08/07)

Form No. B 13S
United States Bankruptcy Court
__________ District Of __________

In re ______________________________

Debtor *
Address: ______________________________
____
Last four digits of Social-Security or Individual Taxpayer-Identification (ITIN) No(s).,(if any): ______________
Employer's Tax Identification (EIN) No(s). (if any): ______________

Case No. __________

Chapter 11
(Small Business)

ORDER CONDITIONALLY APPROVING DISCLOSURE STATEMENT, FIXING TIME FOR FILING ACCEPTANCES OR REJECTIONS OF THE PLAN, AND FIXING THE TIME FOR FILING OBJECTIONS TO THE DISCLOSURE STATEMENT AND TO THE CONFIRMATION OF THE PLAN, COMBINED WITH NOTICE THEREOF AND OF THE HEARING ON FINAL APPROVAL OF THE DISCLOSURE STATEMENT AND THE HEARING ON CONFIRMATION OF THE PLAN

A disclosure statement under chapter 11 of the Bankruptcy Code having been filed by ______________ on __________ with respect to a plan under chapter 11 of the Code filed by __________ on __________; and the debtor being a small business debtor:

IT IS ORDERED, and notice is hereby given, that:

A. The disclosure statement filed by __________ is conditionally approved.

B. __________ is fixed as the last day for filing written acceptances or rejections of the plan referred to above.

C. Within _____ days after the entry of this order, the plan, the disclosure statement and a ballot conforming to Official Form 14 shall be mailed to creditors, equity security holders, and other parties in interest, and shall be transmitted to the United States trustee.

D. ______________ is fixed for the hearing on final approval of the disclosure statement (if a written objection has been timely filed) and for the hearing on confirmation of the plan.

E. __________ is fixed as the last day for filing and serving written objections to the disclosure statement and confirmation of the plan.

Dated: ______________________

BY THE COURT

____
United States Bankruptcy Judge

* *Set forth all names, including trade names, used by the debtor(s) within the last 8 years. For joint debtors, set forth the last four digits of both social-security numbers or individual taxpayer-identification numbers.*

(Added Dec. 1994; revised effective August 1, 2007.)

Form B 15S. Order Approving Disclosure Statement and Confirming Plan

B15S (Form 15S) (08/07)

Form B 15S

United States Bankruptcy Court

__________ District Of __________

In re __________________________________
Debtor *
Address: ____________________________
____
Last four digits of Social-Security or Individual Taxpayer-Identification (ITIN) No(s)., (if any): ____________________
Employer Tax-Identification (EIN) No(s). (if any): ____________________________

Case No. __________

Chapter 11
(Small Business)

ORDER APPROVING DISCLOSURE STATEMENT AND CONFIRMING PLAN

The plan under chapter 11 of the Bankruptcy Code filed by __________, on __________ having been transmitted to creditors and equity security holders together with a copy of the disclosure statement conditionally approved by court on __________; and

It having been determined after notice and a hearing that the requirements for final approval of the disclosure statement have been satisfied, and it having been determined after a hearing on notice that the requirements for confirmation of the plan under 11 U.S.C. § 1129 have been satisfied;

IT IS ORDERED that:

The disclosure statement filed by __________ on __________ is finally approved, and

The plan filed by __________, on __________, *[If appropriate, include dates and any other pertinent details of modifications to the plan]* is confirmed.

A copy of the confirmed plan is attached.

Dated: ____________________________

BY THE COURT

____
United States Bankruptcy Judge.

** Set forth all names, including trade names, used by the debtor(s) within the last 8 years. For joint debtors, set forth the last four digits of both social-security numbers or individual taxpayer-identification numbers.*

(Added Dec. 1994; revised effective August 1, 2007.)

Form B 18F. Discharge of Debtor After Completion of Chapter 12 Plan

B18F (Form 18F) (08/07)

United States Bankruptcy Court
_______ District Of _______

In re ______________________________ Case No. __________
Debtor*
Address: ______________________________ Chapter 12
____

Last four digits of Social-Security or Individual Taxpayer-Identification (ITIN) No(s)., (if any): ______________
Employer Tax Identification (EIN) No(s). (if any): ______________

DISCHARGE OF DEBTOR AFTER COMPLETION OF CHAPTER 12 PLAN

It appearing that the debtor is entitled to a discharge,

IT IS ORDERED:

The debtor is granted a discharge under section 1228(a) of title 11, United States Code, (the Bankruptcy Code).

BY THE COURT

Dated: ______________________ ______________________
United States Bankruptcy Judge

SEE THE BACK OF THIS ORDER FOR IMPORTANT INFORMATION.

* *Set forth all names, including trade names, used by the debtor(s) within the last 8 years. For joint debtors, set forth the last four digits of both social-security numbers or individual taxpayer-identification numbers.*

Form 18F (08/07)

EXPLANATION OF BANKRUPTCY DISCHARGE IN A CHAPTER 12 CASE

This court order grants a discharge to the person named as the debtor after the debtor has fulfilled all requirements under the chapter 12 plan. It is not a dismissal of the case.

Collection of Discharged Debts Prohibited

The discharge prohibits any attempt to collect from the debtor a debt that has been discharged. For example, a creditor is not permitted to contact a debtor by mail, phone, or otherwise, to file or continue a lawsuit, to attach wages or other property, or to take any other action to collect a discharged debt from the debtor. *[In a case involving community property:* There are also special rules that protect certain community property owned by the debtor's spouse, even if that spouse did not file a bankruptcy case.] A creditor who violates this order can be required to pay damages and attorney's fees to the debtor.

However, a creditor may have the right to enforce a valid lien, such as a mortgage or security interest, against the debtor's property after the bankruptcy, if that lien was not avoided or eliminated in the bankruptcy case. Also, a debtor may voluntarily pay any debt that has been discharged.

Debts That are Discharged

The chapter 12 discharge order eliminates a debtor's legal obligation to pay a debt that is discharged. Most, but not all, types of debts are discharged if the debt is provided for by the chapter 12 plan or is disallowed by the court pursuant to section 502 of the Bankruptcy Code.

Debts that are Not Discharged.

Some of the common types of debts which are not discharged in a chapter 12 bankruptcy case are:

a. Debts for most taxes; and, in a case filed on or after October 17, 2005, debts incurred to pay nondischargeable taxes;

b. Debts that are domestic support obligations;

c. Debts for most student loans;

d. Debts provided for under sections 1222(b)(5) or (b)(9) of the Bankruptcy Code and on which the last payment or other transfer is due after the date on which the final payment under the plan was due;

e. Debts for most fines, penalties, forfeitures, or criminal restitution obligations;

f. Debts for personal injuries or death caused by the debtor's operation of a motor vehicle, vessel, or aircraft while intoxicated;

g. Some debts which were not properly listed by the debtor;

h. Debts that the bankruptcy court specifically has decided or will decide in this bankruptcy case are not discharged; and

i. Debts owed to certain pension, profit sharing, stock bonus, other retirement plans, or to the Thrift Savings Plan for federal employees for certain types of loans from these plans (in a case filed on or after October 17, 2005).

This information is only a general summary of the bankruptcy discharge. There are exceptions to these general rules. Because the law is complicated, you may want to consult an attorney to determine the exact effect of the discharge in this case.

(Revised effective August 1, 2007.)

Form B 18FH. Discharge of Debtor Before Completion of Chapter 12 Plan

B18FH (Form 18FH) (08/07)

United States Bankruptcy Court

_____ District Of _____

In re ______________________ Case No. _______
Debtor*

Address: ______________________ Chapter 12

____

Last four digits of Social-Security or Individual Taxpayer-Identification (ITIN) No(s)., (if any): ______________

Employer Tax-Identification (EIN) No(s). (if any): ______________

____

DISCHARGE OF DEBTOR BEFORE COMPLETION OF CHAPTER 12 PLAN

It appearing that the debtor is entitled to a discharge,

IT IS ORDERED:

The debtor is granted a discharge under section 1228(b) of title 11, United States Code, (the Bankruptcy Code).

BY THE COURT

Dated: ______________________ ______________________
United States Bankruptcy Judge

SEE THE BACK OF THIS ORDER FOR IMPORTANT INFORMATION.

____

* *Set forth all names, including trade names, used by the debtor(s) within the last 8 years. For joint debtors, set forth the last four digits of both social-security numbers or individual taxpayer-identification numbers.*

Form 18FH (08/07)

EXPLANATION OF BANKRUPTCY DISCHARGE BEFORE COMPLETION OF PLAN PAYMENTS IN A CHAPTER 12 CASE

This court order grants a discharge to the person named as the debtor. After notice and a hearing, the court has determined that the debtor is entitled to a discharge pursuant to section 1228(b) of the Bankruptcy Code without completing all of the requirements under the chapter 12 plan. Because this discharge is granted pursuant to the hardship provisions of section 1228(b), it is referred to as a chapter 12 "hardship discharge." This order is not the dismissal of the case.

Collection of Discharged Debts Prohibited

The discharge prohibits any attempt to collect from the debtor a debt that has been discharged. For example, a creditor is not permitted to contact a debtor by mail, phone, or otherwise, to file or continue a lawsuit, to attach wages or other property, or to take any other action to collect a discharged debt from the debtor. *[In a case involving community property:* There are also special rules that protect certain community property owned by the debtor's spouse, even if that spouse did not file a bankruptcy case.] A creditor who violates this order can be required to pay damages and attorney's fees to the debtor.

However, a creditor may have the right to enforce a valid lien, such as a mortgage or security interest, against the debtor's property after the bankruptcy, if that lien was not avoided or eliminated in the bankruptcy case. Also, a debtor may voluntarily pay any debt that has been discharged.

Debts That are Discharged

The chapter 12 "hardship discharge" eliminates a debtor's legal obligation to pay a debt that is discharged. Most, but not all, types of debts are discharged if the debt is provided for by the chapter 12 plan or is disallowed by the court pursuant to section 502 of the Bankruptcy Code.

Debts That are Not Discharged.

Some of the common types of debts which are not eliminated by in a chapter 12 "hardship discharge" are:

a. Debts for most taxes; and, in a case filed on or after October 17, 2005, debts incurred to pay nondischargeable taxes;

b. Debts that are domestic support obligations;

c. Debts for most student loans;

d. Debts provided for under sections 1222(b)(5) or (b)(9) of the Bankruptcy Code and on which the last payment or other transfer is due after the date on which the final payment under the plan was due;

e. Debts for most fines, penalties, forfeitures, or criminal restitution obligations;

f. Debts for personal injuries or death caused by the debtor's operation of a motor vehicle, vessel, or aircraft while intoxicated;

g. Some debts which were not properly listed by the debtor;

h. Debts that the bankruptcy court specifically has decided or will decide in this bankruptcy case are not discharged;

i. Debts for which the debtor has given up the discharge protections by signing a reaffirmation agreement in compliance with the Bankruptcy Code requirements for reaffirmation of debts; and

j. Debts owed to certain pension, profit sharing, stock bonus, other retirement plans, or to the Thrift Savings Plan for federal employees for certain types of loans from these plans (in a case filed on or after October 17, 2005).

This information is only a general summary of the bankruptcy discharge. There are exceptions to these general rules. Because the law is complicated, you may want to consult an attorney to determine the exact effect of the discharge in this case.

(Revised effective August 1, 2007.)

Form B 18J. Discharge of Joint Debtors

B 18J (Form 18J) (08/07)

United States Bankruptcy Court

______ District Of ______

In re ____________________________ Case No. ________

Debtor*

____

Joint Debtor

Address: ________________________ Chapter 7

____

Last four digits of Social-Security or Individual Taxpayer-Identification (ITIN) No(s)., (if any):

(Debtor)____________

(Joint Debtor)____________

Employer Tax-Identification (EIN) No(s). (if any): ________________________

____

DISCHARGE OF JOINT DEBTORS

It appearing that the debtors are entitled to a discharge,

IT IS ORDERED:

The debtor is granted a discharge under section 727 of title 11, United States Code, (the Bankruptcy Code).

BY THE COURT

Dated: ________________________ ____________________________

United States Bankruptcy Judge

SEE THE BACK OF THIS ORDER FOR IMPORTANT INFORMATION.

* *Set forth all names, including trade names, used by the debtors within the last 8 years. Set forth the last four digits of both debtor's social-security numbers or individual taxpayer-identification numbers.*

Form 18J (08/07)

EXPLANATION OF BANKRUPTCY DISCHARGE IN A JOINT CHAPTER 7 CASE

This court order grants a discharge to the persons named as the debtors. It is not a dismissal of the case and it does not determine how much money, if any, the trustee will pay to creditors.

Collection of Discharged Debts Prohibited

The discharge prohibits any attempt to collect from the debtors a debt that has been discharged. For example, a creditor is not permitted to contact a debtor by mail, phone, or otherwise, to file or continue a lawsuit, to attach wages or other property, or to take any other action to collect a discharged debt from the debtors. A creditor who violates this order can be required to pay damages and attorney's fees to the debtors.

However, a creditor may have the right to enforce a valid lien, such as a mortgage or security interest, against the debtors' property after the bankruptcy, if that lien was not avoided or eliminated in the bankruptcy case. Also, a debtor may voluntarily pay any debt that has been discharged.

Debts That are Discharged

The chapter 7 discharge order eliminates a debtor's legal obligation to pay a debt that is discharged. Most, but not all, types of debts are discharged if the debt existed on the date the bankruptcy case was filed. (If this case was begun under a different chapter of the Bankruptcy Code and converted to chapter 7, the discharge applies to debts owed when the bankruptcy case was converted.)

Debts That are Not Discharged.

Some of the common types of debts which are not discharged in a chapter 7 bankruptcy case are:

a. Debts for most taxes;

b. Debts incurred to pay nondischargeable taxes (in a case filed on or after October 17, 2005);

c. Debts that are domestic support obligations;

d. Debts for most student loans;

e. Debts for most fines, penalties, forfeitures, or criminal restitution obligations;

f. Debts for personal injuries or death caused by the debtor's operation of a motor vehicle, vessel, or aircraft while intoxicated;

g. Some debts which were not properly listed by the debtors;

h. Debts that the bankruptcy court specifically has decided or will decide in this bankruptcy case are not discharged;

i. Debts for which the debtor has given up the discharge protections by signing a reaffirmation agreement in compliance with the Bankruptcy Code requirements for reaffirmation of debts; and

j. Debts owed to certain pension, profit sharing, stock bonus, other retirement plans, or to the Thrift Savings Plan for federal employees for certain types of loans from these plans (in a case filed on or after October 17, 2005).

This information is only a general summary of the bankruptcy discharge. There are exceptions to these general rules. Because the law is complicated, you may want to consult an attorney to determine the exact effect of the discharge in this case.

(Added Dec. 1994: revised effective August 1, 2007.)

Form B 18JO. Discharge of One Joint Debtor

B 18JO (Form 18JO) (08/07)

United States Bankruptcy Court

______ District Of ______

In re ______________________________ Case No. ________

Debtor*

____

Joint Debtor

Address: __________________________ Chapter 7

____

Last four digits of Social-Security or Individual Taxpayer-Identification (ITIN) Nos., (if any):

(Debtor)______________

(Joint Debtor)______________

Employer Tax-Identification (EIN) No(s). (if any): __________________________

____

DISCHARGE OF ONE JOINT DEBTOR

It appearing that ____________________ ** is entitled to a discharge,

IT IS ORDERED: ____________________ ** is granted a discharge under section 727 of title 11, United States Code, (the Bankruptcy Code).

BY THE COURT

Dated: ________________________ ______________________________

United States Bankruptcy Judge

SEE THE BACK OF THIS ORDER FOR IMPORTANT INFORMATION.

---

* *Set forth all names, including trade names, used by the debtors within the last 8 years. Set forth the last four digits of both debtor's social-security numbers or individual taxpayer-identification numbers.*

** *When only one of the debtors in a joint case is discharged, state here the name of the individual debtor being discharged.*

Form 18JO (08/07)

EXPLANATION OF BANKRUPTCY DISCHARGE IN A CHAPTER 7 CASE

This court order grants a discharge to the person named in the order. It is not a dismissal of the case and it does not determine how much money, if any, the trustee will pay to creditors.

Collection of Discharged Debts Prohibited

The discharge prohibits any attempt to collect from the named debtor a debt that has been discharged. For example, a creditor is not permitted to contact a discharged debtor by mail, phone, or otherwise, to file or continue a lawsuit, to attach wages or other property, or to take any other action to collect a discharged debt from the named debtor. A creditor who violates this order can be required to pay damages and attorney's fees to the discharged debtor.

However, a creditor may have the right to enforce a valid lien, such as a mortgage or security interest, against the discharged debtor's property after the bankruptcy, if that lien was not avoided or eliminated in the bankruptcy case. Also, a debtor may voluntarily pay any debt that has been discharged.

Debts That are Discharged

The chapter 7 discharge order eliminates a debtor's legal obligation to pay a debt that is discharged. Most, but not all, types of debts are discharged if the debt existed on the date the bankruptcy case was filed. (If this case was begun under a different chapter of the Bankruptcy Code and converted to chapter 7, the discharge applies to debts owed when the bankruptcy case was converted.)

Debts That are Not Discharged.

Some of the common types of debts which are not discharged in a chapter 7 bankruptcy case are:

a. Debts for most taxes;

b. Debts incurred to pay nondischargeable taxes (in a case filed on or after October 17, 2005);

c. Debts that are domestic support obligations;

d. Debts for most student loans;

e. Debts for most fines, penalties, forfeitures, or criminal restitution obligations;

f. Debts for personal injuries or death caused by the debtor's operation of a motor vehicle, vessel, or aircraft while intoxicated;

g. Some debts which were not properly listed by the debtor;

h. Debts that the bankruptcy court specifically has decided or will decide in this bankruptcy case are not discharged;

i. Debts for which the debtor has given up the discharge protections by signing a reaffirmation agreement in compliance with the Bankruptcy Code requirements for reaffirmation of debts; and

j. Debts owed to certain pension, profit sharing, stock bonus, other retirement plans, or to the Thrift Savings Plan for federal employees for certain types of loans from these plans (in a case filed on or after October 17, 2005).

This information is only a general summary of the bankruptcy discharge. There are exceptions to these general rules. Because the law is complicated, you may want to consult an attorney to determine the exact effect of the discharge in this case.

(Added Dec. 1994: revised effective August 1, 2007.)

Form B 18W. Discharge of Debtor After Completion of Chapter 13 Plan

B 18W (Form 18W) (08/07)

United States Bankruptcy Court

______ District Of ______

In re ____________________ Case No. ________
Debtor*

Address: ____________________ Chapter 13
____

Last four digits of Social-Security or Individual Taxpayer-Identification (ITIN) No(s)., (if any): ______________
Employer Tax-Identification (EIN) No(s). (if any): ______________

DISCHARGE OF DEBTOR AFTER COMPLETION OF CHAPTER 13 PLAN

It appearing that the debtor is entitled to a discharge,

IT IS ORDERED:

The debtor is granted a discharge under section 1328(a) of title 11, United States Code, (the Bankruptcy Code).

BY THE COURT

Dated: ________________ ________________
United States Bankruptcy Judge

SEE THE BACK OF THIS ORDER FOR IMPORTANT INFORMATION.

* *Set forth all names, including trade names, used by the debtor(s) within the last 8 years. For joint debtors, set forth the last four digits of both social-security numbers or individual taxpayer-identification numbers.*

Form 18W (08/07)

EXPLANATION OF BANKRUPTCY DISCHARGE
IN A CHAPTER 13 CASE

This court order grants a discharge to the person named as the debtor after the debtor has completed all payments under the chapter 13 plan. It is not a dismissal of the case.

Collection of Discharged Debts Prohibited

The discharge prohibits any attempt to collect from the debtor a debt that has been discharged. For example, a creditor is not permitted to contact a debtor by mail, phone, or otherwise, to file or continue a lawsuit, to attach wages or other property, or to take any other action to collect a discharged debt from the debtor. *[In a case involving community property:* There are also special rules that protect certain community property owned by the debtor's spouse, even if that spouse did not file a bankruptcy case.] A creditor who violates this order can be required to pay damages and attorney's fees to the debtor.

However, a creditor may have the right to enforce a valid lien, such as a mortgage or security interest, against the debtor's property after the bankruptcy, if that lien was not avoided or eliminated in the bankruptcy case. Also, a debtor may voluntarily pay any debt that has been discharged.

Debts That are Discharged

The chapter 13 discharge order eliminates a debtor's legal obligation to pay a debt that is discharged. Most, but not all, types of debts are discharged if the debt is provided for by the chapter 13 plan or is disallowed by the court pursuant to section 502 of the Bankruptcy Code.

Debts That are Not Discharged.

Some of the common types of debts which are not discharged in a chapter 13 bankruptcy case are:

a. Domestic support obligations;

b. Debts for most student loans;

c. Debts for most fines, penalties, forfeitures, or criminal restitution obligations;

d. Debts for personal injuries or death caused by the debtor's operation of a motor vehicle, vessel, or aircraft while intoxicated;

e. Debts for restitution, or damages, awarded in a civil action against the debtor as a result of malicious or willful injury by the debtor that caused personal injury to an individual or the death of an individual (in a case filed on or after October 17, 2005);

f. Debts provided for under section 1322(b)(5) of the Bankruptcy Code and on which the last payment is due after the date on which the final payment under the plan was due;

g. Debts for certain consumer purchases made after the bankruptcy case was filed if prior approval by the trustee of the debtor's incurring the debt was practicable but was not obtained;

h. Debts for certain taxes to the extent not paid in full under the plan (in a case filed on or after October 17, 2005); and

i. Some debts which were not properly listed by the debtor (in a case filed on or after October 17, 2005).

This information is only a general summary of the bankruptcy discharge. There are exceptions to these general rules. Because the law is complicated, you may want to consult an attorney to determine the exact effect of the discharge in this case.

(Revised effective August 1, 2007.)

Form B 18WH. Discharge of Debtor Before Completion of Chapter 13 Plan

B 18WH (Form 18WH) (08/07)

United States Bankruptcy Court

______ District Of ______

In re ______________________________ Case No. __________

Debtor*

Address: ______________________________ Chapter 13

____

Last four digits of Social-Security or Individual Taxpayer-Identification (ITIN) No(s)., (if any): ____________________
Employer Tax-Identification (EIN) No(s). (if any): ____________________________

DISCHARGE OF DEBTOR BEFORE COMPLETION OF CHAPTER 13 PLAN

It appearing that the debtor is entitled to a discharge,

IT IS ORDERED:

The debtor is granted a discharge under section 1328(b) of title 11, United States Code, (the Bankruptcy Code).

BY THE COURT

Dated: ____________________________ ________________________________

United States Bankruptcy Judge

SEE THE BACK OF THIS ORDER FOR IMPORTANT INFORMATION.

* *Set forth all names, including trade names, used by the debtor(s) within the last 8 years. For joint debtors, set forth the last four digits of both social-security numbers or individual taxpayer-identification numbers.*

Form 18WH (08/07)

EXPLANATION OF BANKRUPTCY DISCHARGE IN A CHAPTER 13 CASE BEFORE COMPLETION OF PLAN PAYMENTS

This court order grants a discharge to the person named as the debtor. After notice and a hearing, the court has determined that the debtor is entitled to a discharge pursuant to section 1328(b) of the Bankruptcy Code without completing all of the payments under the chapter 13 plan. Because this discharge is granted pursuant to the hardship provisions of section 1328(b), it is referred to as a chapter 13 "hardship discharge." This order is not the dismissal of the case.

Collection of Discharged Debts Prohibited

The discharge prohibits any attempt to collect from the debtor a debt that has been discharged. For example, a creditor is not permitted to contact a debtor by mail, phone, or otherwise, to file or continue a lawsuit, to attach wages or other property, or to take any other action to collect a discharged debt from the debtor. *[In a case involving community property:* There are also special rules that protect certain community property owned by the debtor's spouse, even if that spouse did not file a bankruptcy case.] A creditor who violates this order can be required to pay damages and attorney's fees to the debtor.

However, a creditor may have the right to enforce a valid lien, such as a mortgage or security interest, against the debtor's property after the bankruptcy, if that lien was not avoided or eliminated in the bankruptcy case. Also, a debtor may voluntarily pay any debt that has been discharged.

Debts That Are Discharged

The chapter 13 "hardship discharge" order eliminates a debtor's legal obligation to pay a debt that is discharged. Most, but not all, types of debts are discharged if the debt is provided for by the chapter 13 plan or is disallowed by the court pursuant to section 502 of the Bankruptcy Code.

Debts That are Not Discharged.

Some of the common types of debts which are not eliminated by a chapter 13 "hardship discharge" are:

a. Domestic support obligations;

b. Debts for most taxes; and, in a case filed on or after October 17, 2005, debts incurred to pay nondischargeable taxes;

c. Debts for most student loans;

d. Debts provided for under section 1322(b)(5) of the Bankruptcy Code and on which the last payment is due after the date on which the final payment under the plan was due;

e. Debts for certain consumer purchases made after the bankruptcy case was filed if prior approval by the trustee of the debtor's incurring the debt was practicable but was not obtained;

f. Debts for most fines, penalties, forfeitures, or criminal restitution obligations;

g. Debts for personal injuries or death caused by the debtor's operation of a motor vehicle, vessel, or aircraft while intoxicated;

h. Some debts which were not properly listed by the debtor;

i. Debts that the bankruptcy court specifically has decided or will decide in this bankruptcy case are not discharged;

j. Debts for which the debtor has given up the discharge protections by signing a reaffirmation agreement in compliance with the Bankruptcy Code requirements for reaffirmation of debts; and,

k. Debts owed to certain pension, profit sharing, stock bonus, other retirement plans, or to the Thrift Savings Plan for federal employees for certain types of loans from these plans (in a case filed on or after October 17, 2005).

This information is only a general summary of the bankruptcy discharge. There are exceptions to these general rules. Because the law is complicated, you may want to consult an attorney to determine the exact effect of the discharge in this case.

(Revised effective August 1, 2007.)

Form B 104. Adversary Proceeding Cover Sheet

Form No. B 104

B 104 (Form 104) (08/07)

ADVERSARY PROCEEDING COVER SHEET (Instructions on Reverse)	ADVERSARY PROCEEDING NUMBER (Court Use Only)
PLAINTIFFS	**DEFENDANTS**
ATTORNEYS (Firm Name, Address, and Telephone No.)	**ATTORNEYS** (If Known)
PARTY (Check One Box Only) ☐ Debtor ☐ U.S. Trustee/Bankruptcy Admin ☐ Creditor ☐ Other ☐ Trustee	**PARTY** (Check One Box Only) ☐ Debtor ☐ U.S. Trustee/Bankruptcy Admin ☐ Creditor ☐ Other ☐ Trustee

CAUSE OF ACTION (WRITE A BRIEF STATEMENT OF CAUSE OF ACTION, INCLUDING ALL U.S. STATUTES INVOLVED)

NATURE OF SUIT

(Number up to five (5) boxes starting with lead cause of action as 1, first alternative cause as 2, second alternative cause as 3, etc.)

FRBP 7001(1)—Recovery of Money/Property

☐ 11–Recovery of money/property—§ 542 turnover of property

☐ 12–Recovery of money/property—§ 547 preference

☐ 13–Recovery of money/property—§ 548 fraudulent transfer

☐ 14–Recovery of money/property—other

FRBP 7001(2)—Validity, Priority or Extent of Lien

☐ 21–Validity, priority or extent of lien or other interest in property

FRBP 7001(3)—Approval of Sale of Property

☐ 31–Approval of sale of property of estate and of a co–owner—§ 363(h)

FRBP 7001(4)—Objection/Revocation of Discharge

☐ 41–Objection / revocation of discharge—§ 727(c),(d),(e)

FRBP 7001(5)—Revocation of Confirmation

☐ 51–Revocation of confirmation

FRBP 7001(6)—Dischargeability

☐ 66–Dischargeability—§ 523(a)(1),(14),(14A) priority tax claims

☐ 62–Dischargeability—§ 523(a)(2), false pretenses, false representation, actual fraud

(continued next column)

FRBP 7001(6)—Dischargeability (continued)

☐ 67–Dischargeability—§ 523(a)(4), fraud as fiduciary, embezzlement, larceny

☐ 61–Dischargeability—§ 523(a)(5), domestic support

☐ 68–Dischargeability—§ 523(a)(6), willful and malicious injury

☐ 63–Dischargeability—§ 523(a)(8), student loan

☐ 64–Dischargeability—§ 523(a)(15), divorce or separation obligation (other than domestic support)

☐ 65–Dischargeability—other

FRBP 7001(7)—Injunctive Relief

☐ 71–Injunctive relief—imposition of stay

☐ 72–Injunctive relief—other

FRBP 7001(8) Subordination of Claim or Interest

☐ 81–Subordination of claim or interest

FRBP 7001(9) Declaratory Judgment

☐ 91–Declaratory judgment

FRBP 7001(10) Determination of Removed Action

☐ 01–Determination of removed claim or cause

Other

☐ SS–SIPA Case—15 U.S.C. §§ 78aaa *et.seq.*

☐ 02–Other (e.g. other actions that would have been brought in state court if unrelated to bankruptcy case)

☐ Check if this case involves a substantive issue of state law	☐ Check if this is asserted to be a class action under FRCP 23
☐ Check if a jury trial is demanded in complaint	Demand $

Other Relief Sought

BANKRUPTCY CASE IN WHICH THIS ADVERSARY PROCEEDING ARISES		
NAME OF DEBTOR		BANKRUPTCY CASE NO.
DISTRICT IN WHICH CASE IS PENDING	DIVISION OFFICE	NAME OF JUDGE

RELATED ADVERSARY PROCEEDING (IF ANY)		
PLAINTIFF	DEFENDANT	ADVERSARY PROCEEDING NO.
DISTRICT IN WHICH ADVERSARY IS PENDING	DIVISION OFFICE	NAME OF JUDGE
SIGNATURE OF ATTORNEY (OR PLAINTIFF)		
DATE	PRINT NAME OF ATTORNEY (OR PLAINTIFF)	

INSTRUCTIONS

The filing of a bankruptcy case creates an "estate" under the jurisdiction of the bankruptcy court which consists of all of the property of the debtor, wherever that property is located. Because the bankruptcy estate is so extensive and the jurisdiction of the court so broad, there may be lawsuits over the property or property rights of the estate. There also may be lawsuits concerning the debtor's discharge. If such a lawsuit is filed in a bankruptcy court, it is called an adversary proceeding.

A party filing an adversary proceeding must also must complete and file Form 104, the Adversary Proceeding Cover Sheet, unless the party files the adversary proceeding electronically through the court's Case Management/Electronic Case Filing system (CM/ECF). (CM/ECF captures the information on Form 104 as part of the filing process.) When completed, the cover sheet summarizes basic information on the adversary proceeding. The clerk of court needs the information to process the adversary proceeding and prepare required statistical reports on court activity.

The cover sheet and the information contained on it do not replace or supplement the filing and service of pleadings or other papers as required by law, the Bankruptcy Rules, or the local rules of court. The cover sheet, which is largely self-explanatory, must be completed by the plaintiff's attorney (or by the plaintiff if the plaintiff is not represented by an attorney). A separate cover sheet must be submitted to the clerk for each complaint filed.

Plaintiffs and **Defendants.** Give the names of the plaintiffs and the defendants exactly as they appear on the complaint.

Attorneys. Give the names and addresses of the attorneys, if known.

Party. Check the most appropriate box in the first column for the plaintiffs and in the second column for the defendants.

Demand. Enter the dollar amount being demanded in the complaint.

Signature. This cover sheet must be signed by the attorney of record in the box on the second page of the form. If the plaintiff is represented by a law firm, a member of the firm must sign. If the plaintiff is pro se, that is, not represented by an attorney, the plaintiff must sign.

(Added Feb., 1992 and amended Oct. 2006; revised effective August 1, 2007.)

Form B 131. Exemplification Certificate

Form No. B 131
EXEMPLIFICATION CERTIFICATE

B 131
(9/94)

United States Bankruptcy Court

______ District of ______

In re

Case No.

Debtor

EXEMPLIFICATION CERTIFICATE

I, ______________, clerk of the bankruptcy court for this district and keeper of the records and seal of the court, certify that the documents attached are true copies of

now remaining among the records of the court. In testimony of this statement, I sign my name, and affix the seal of this court at ______________, in the State of ______________, this ______________.

[Seal of Court] ________________________
Clerk of the Bankruptcy Court

I, ______________, bankruptcy judge for this district certify that ______________ is and was at the date of the above certificate clerk of the bankruptcy court for this district, duly appointed and sworn, and keeper of the records and seal of the court, and that the above certificate of the clerk and the clerk's attestation are in due form of law.

______________ ________________________
Date *Bankruptcy Judge*

I, ______________, clerk of the bankruptcy court for this district and keeper of the seal of the court, certify that the Honorable ______________ is and was on the date of the above certificate a judge of this court, duly appointed and sworn; and that I am well acquainted with this handwriting and official signature and know and certify the signature written above to be that of the judge.

In testimony of this statement, I sign my name, and affix the seal of the court at ______________, in the State of ______________, this ______________.

[Seal of Court] ________________________
Clerk of the Bankruptcy Court

(Added Sept. 1988.)

Form B 132. Application for Search of Bankruptcy Records

Form No. B 132
APPLICATION FOR SEARCH OF BANKRUPTCY RECORDS

B 132
(11/03)

United States Bankruptcy Court

______ District of ______

APPLICATION FOR SEARCH OF BANKRUPTCY RECORDS

Name of individual or business that is the subject of the search:	Social Security No. or Employer Tax I.D. No. of Subject:

Please search your records for the following information regarding the individual or business named above:

☐ pending or closed bankruptcy cases in this district;
☐ pending or closed adversary proceedings;
☐ judgments/evidence of satisfaction of judgments; and
☐ other [describe briefly]

Please search for the period from ____________________ to ____________________.

A fee of $26.00 is charged for each name or item searched. Payment by check or money order must be enclosed.
Please do not send cash through the mail.

Name, address, and phone number of the person requesting the search:

CERTIFICATE OF SEARCH

The undersigned clerk hereby certifies the following results of a diligent search of the records of the court:
[Check only the items for which a search was requested and a fee paid.]

A. Bankruptcy Cases:
1. ☐ None found.
2. ☐ Case filed on ________.
(date)

☐ Voluntary ☐ Involuntary
☐ Pending ☐ Closed on ________.
(date)

☐ Discharge granted on ________.
(date)

B. Adversary Proceedings:
1. ☐ None found.
2. ☐ Subject is a party to the following proceeding:

________________ v. ________________
(Plaintiff) (Defendant)

Adversary Proceeding Number ____, filed on ____.
(date)

☐ Pending ☐ Closed on ________.
(date)

Disposition: ☐ Dismissed on ________________
(date)

☐ Final Judgment entered on ____
(date)

Case Number of Related Bankruptcy Case ______.

____
Clerk of the Bankruptcy Court

________________ By: ________________________
Date Deputy Clerk

(Added Sept. 1988, and amended Oct. 27, 2003, eff. Nov. 1, 2003.)

Form B 133. Claims Register

B 133
(1/88)

CLAIMS REGISTER

Page No. ______

NAME OF DEBTOR		CASE NUMBER
NAME AND ADDRESS OF CLAIMANT (AND NAME AND ADDRESS) OF ATTORNEY, IF ANY)	AMOUNT OF CLAIMS FILED AND ALLOWED	REMARKS
CLAIM NO. ______ DATE FILED ______	FILED $ ______ ALLOWED $	
CLAIM NO. ______ DATE FILED ______	FILED $ ______ ALLOWED $	
CLAIM NO. ______ DATE FILED ______	FILED $ ______ ALLOWED $	
CLAIM NO. ______ DATE FILED ______	FILED $ ______ ALLOWED $	
CLAIM NO. ______ DATE FILED ______	FILED $ ______ ALLOWED $	
CLAIM NO. ______ DATE FILED ______	FILED $ ______ ALLOWED $	
CLAIM NO. ______ DATE FILED ______	FILED $ ______ ALLOWED $	
CLAIM NO. ______ DATE FILED ______	FILED $ ______ ALLOWED $	
CLAIM NO. ______ DATE FILED ______	FILED $ ______ ALLOWED $	

Form B 200. Required Lists, Schedules, Statements, and Fees

UNITED STATES BANKRUPTCY COURT

B 200 (04/08)

REQUIRED LISTS, SCHEDULES, STATEMENTS, AND FEES

Voluntary Chapter 7 Case

☐ **Filing Fee of $245.**
If the fee is to be paid in installments or the debtor requests a waiver of the fee, the debtor must be an individual and must file a signed application for court approval. Official Form 3A or 3B and Fed.R.Bankr.P. 1006(b) & (c)

☐ **Administrative fee of $39 and trustee surcharge of $15.**
If the debtor is an individual and the court grants the debtor's request, these fees are payable in installments or may be waived.

☐ **Voluntary Petition (Official Form 1).**
Names and addresses of all creditors of the debtor.
Must be filed **WITH** the petition. Fed.R.Bankr.P. 1007(a)(1).

☐ **Notice to Individual Debtor with Primarily Consumer Debts under 11 U.S.C. § 342(b) (Director's Form 201),** if applicable.
Required if the debtor is an individual with primarily consumer debts. The notice must be **GIVEN** to the debtor before the petition is filed. Certification that the notice has been given must be **FILED** with the petition or within 15 days. 11 U.S.C. §§ 342(b), 521(a)(1)(B)(iii), 707(a)(3). Official Form 1 contains spaces for the certification.

☐ **Notice to debtor by "bankruptcy petition preparer" (Official Form 19).**
Required if a "bankruptcy petition preparer" prepares the petition. Must be submitted **WITH** the petition. 11 U.S.C. § 110(b)(2).

☐ **Statement of Social Security Number (Official Form 21).**
Required if the debtor is an individual. Must be submitted **WITH** the petition. Fed.R.Bankr.P. 1007(f).

☐ **Individual Debtor's Statement of Compliance with Credit Counseling Requirement (Exhibit D to Official Form 1).**
Certificate of Credit Counseling and Debt Repayment Plan, if applicable
Section 109(h)(3) certification and motion or § 109(h)(4) request), if applicable.
Exhibit D is required if the debtor is an individual. Exhibit D must be filed **WITH** the petition. If applicable, the Certificate of Credit Counseling and Debt Repayment Plan must be filed with the petition or within 15 days. If applicable, the § 109(h)(3) certification and motion or the § 109(h)(4) request must be filed **WITH** the petition. Fed.R.Bankr.P. 1007(b)(3) & (c).

☐ **Statement disclosing compensation paid or to be paid to a "bankruptcy petition preparer" (Director's Form 280).**
Required if a "bankruptcy petition preparer" prepares the petition. Must be submitted **WITH** the petition. 11 U.S.C. § 110(h)(2).

☐ **Statement of current monthly income, etc. (Official Form 22A).**
Required if the debtor is an individual. Must be filed with the petition or within 15 days. Fed.R.Bankr.P. 1007(b) & (c).

☐ **Schedules of assets and liabilities (Official Form 6).**
Must be filed with the petition or within 15 days. Fed.R.Bankr.P. 1007(b) & (c).

☐ **Schedule of executory contracts and unexpired leases (Schedule G of Official Form 6).**

B 200 (04/08) **REQUIRED LISTS, SCHEDULES, STATEMENTS, AND FEES**

Must be filed with the petition or within 15 days. Fed.R.Bankr.P. 1007(b) & (c).

☐ **Schedules of current income and expenditures.**
All debtors must file these schedules. If the debtor is an individual, Schedules I and J of Official Form 6 must be used for this purpose. Must be filed with the petition or within 15 days. 11 U.S.C. § 521(1) and Fed.R.Bankr.P. 1007(b) & (c).

☐ **Statement of financial affairs (Official Form 7).**
Must be filed with the petition or within 15 days. Fed.R.Bankr.P. 1007(b) & (c).

☐ **Copies of all payment advices or other evidence of payment received by the debtor from any employer within 60 days before the filing of the petition.**
Required if the debtor is an individual. Must be filed with the petition or within 15 days. Fed.R.Bankr.P. 1007(b) & (c).

☐ **Statement of intention regarding secured property and unexpired leases (Official Form 8).**
Required **ONLY** if the debtor is an individual and the schedules of assets and liabilities contain debts secured by property of the estate or personal property subject to an unexpired lease. Must be filed within 30 days or by the date set for the Section 341 meeting of creditors, whichever is **earlier.** 11 U.S.C. §§ 362(h).and 521(2).

☐ **Statement disclosing compensation paid or to be paid to the attorney for the debtor (Director's Form 203).**
Required if the debtor is represented by an attorney. Must be filed within 15 days or any other date set by the court. 11 U.S.C. § 329 and Fed.R.Bankr.P. 2016(b).

☐ **Certification of Completion of Instructional Course Concerning Financial Management (Official Form 23),** if applicable.
Required if the debtor is an individual. Must be filed within 45 days of the first date set for the meeting of creditors. 11 U.S.C. § 727(a)(11) and Fed.R.Bankr.P. 1007(b)(7) & (c).

B 200 *continued*
(04/08) **REQUIRED LISTS, SCHEDULES, STATEMENTS, AND FEES**

Voluntary Chapter 11 Case

☐ **Filing fee of $1,000.**
If the fee is to be paid in installments, the debtor must be an individual and must file a signed application for court approval. Official Form 3A and Fed.R.Bankr.P. 1006(b).

☐ **Administrative fee of $39.**
If the debtor is an individual and the court grants the debtor's request, this fee is payable in installments.

☐ **Voluntary Petition (Official Form 1).**
Names and addresses of all creditors of the debtor.
Must be filed **WITH** the petition. Fed.R.Bankr.P. 1007(a)(1).

☐ **Notice to Individual Debtor with Primarily Consumer Debts under 11 U.S.C. § 342(b) (Director's Form 201),** if applicable.
Required if the debtor is an individual with primarily consumer debts. The notice must be **GIVEN** to the debtor before the petition is filed.
Certification that the notice has been given must be **FILED** with the petition or within 15 days. 11 U.S.C. §§ 342(b), 521(a)(1)(B)(iii), 1112(e). Official Form 1 contains spaces for the certification.

☐ **Notice to debtor by "bankruptcy petition preparer" (Official Form 19).**
Required if a "bankruptcy petition preparer" prepares the petition. Must be submitted **WITH** the petition. 11 U.S.C. § 110(b)(2).

☐ **Statement of Social Security Number (Official Form 21).**
Required if the debtor is an individual. Must be submitted **WITH** the petition. Fed.R.Bankr.P. 1007(f).

☐ **Individual Debtor's Statement of Compliance with Credit Counseling Requirement (Exhibit D to Official Form 1).**
Certificate of Credit Counseling and Debt Repayment Plan, if applicable.
Section 109(h)(3) certification and motion or § 109(h)(4) request), if applicable.
Required if the debtor is an individual. Exhibit D must be filed **WITH** the petition. If applicable, the Certificate of Credit Counseling and Debt Repayment Plan must be filed with the petition or within 15 days. If applicable, the § 109(h)(3) certification and motion or the § 109(h)(4) request must be filed **WITH** the petition. Fed.R.Bankr.P. 1007(b)(3) & (c).

☐ **Statement disclosing compensation paid or to be paid to a "bankruptcy petition preparer" (Director's Form 280).**
Required if a "bankruptcy petition preparer" prepares the petition. Must be submitted **WITH** the petition. 11 U.S.C. § 110(h)(2).

☐ **Statement of current monthly income (Official Form 22B).**
Required if the debtor is an individual. Must be filed with the petition or within 15 days. Fed.R.Bankr.P. 1007(b) & (c).

☐ **List of Creditors holding the 20 largest unsecured claims (Official Form 4).**
Must be filed **WITH** the petition. Fed.R.Bankr.P. 1007(d).

☐ **Names and addresses of equity security holders of the debtor.**
Must be filed the petition or within 15 days, unless the court orders otherwise. Fed.R.Bankr.P. 1007(a)(3).

☐ **Schedules of assets and liabilities (Official Form 6).**

B 200 *continued*
(04/08) **REQUIRED LISTS, SCHEDULES, STATEMENTS, AND FEES**

Must be filed with the petition or within 15 days. Fed.R.Bankr.P. 1007(b) & (c).

☐ **Schedule of executory contracts and unexpired leases (Schedule G of Official Form 6).**
Must be filed with the petition or within 15 days. Fed.R.Bankr.P. 1007(b) & (c).

☐ **Schedules of current income and expenditures.**
All debtors must file these schedules. If the debtor is an individual, Schedules I and J of Official Form 6 must be used for this purpose.
Must be filed with the petition or within 15 days. 11 U.S.C. § 521(1) and Fed.R.Bankr.P. 1007(b) & (c).

☐ **Statement of financial affairs (Official Form 7).**
Must be filed with the petition or within 15 days. Fed.R.Bankr.P. 1007(b) & (c).

☐ **Copies of all payment advices or other evidence of payment received by debtor from any employer within 60 days before the filing of the petition.**
Required if the debtor is an individual. Must be filed **WITH** the petition or within 15 days. Fed.R.Bankr.P. 1007(b) & (c).

☐ **Statement disclosing compensation paid or to be paid to the attorney for the debtor (Director's Form 203),** if applicable.
Required if the debtor is represented by an attorney. Must be filed within 15 days or any other date set by the court. 11 U.S.C. § 329 and Fed.R.Bankr.P. 2016(b).

Notice: Under 28 U.S.C. § 1930(a) the debtor, or trustee if one is appointed, is required also to pay a fee to the United States trustee at the conclusion of each calendar quarter until the case is dismissed or converted to another chapter. The amount to be paid is:

$ 325 if disbursements total less than $15,000;
$ 650 if disbursements total between $15,000 and $75,000;
$ 975 if disbursements total between $75,000 and $150,000;
$1,625 if disbursements total between $150,000 and $225,000;
$1,950 if disbursements total between $225,000 and $300,000;
$4,875 if disbursements total between $300,000 and $1 million;
$ 6,500 if disbursements total between $1 million and $2 million;
$ 9,750 if disbursements total between $2 million and $3 million;
$$10,400 if disbursements total between $3 million and $5 million;
$13,000 if disbursements total between $5 million and $15 million;
$20,000 if disbursements total between $15 million and $30 million;
$30,000 if disbursements total more than $30 million.

B 200 *continued*

(04/08) **REQUIRED LISTS, SCHEDULES, STATEMENTS, AND FEES**

Chapter 12 Case

☐ **Filing Fee of $200.**
If the fee is to be paid in installments, the debtor must be an individual and must file a signed application for court approval. Official Form 3A and Fed.R.Bankr.P. 1006(b).

☐ **Administrative fee of $39.**
If the debtor is an individual and the court grants the debtor's request, this fee is payable in installments.

☐ **Voluntary petition (Official Form 1).**
Names and addresses of all creditors of the debtor.
Must be filed **WITH** the petition. Fed.R.Bankr.P. 1007(a)(a)(1)

☐ **Notice to Individual Debtor with Primarily Consumer Debts under 11 U.S.C. § 342(b) (Director's Form 201),** if applicable.
Required if the debtor is an individual with primarily consumer debts. The notice must be **GIVEN** to the debtor before the petition is filed.
Certification that the notice has been given must be **FILED** with the court in a timely manner. 11 U.S.C. §§ 342(b), 521(a)(1)(B)(iii). Official Form 1 contains spaces for the certification.

☐ **Notice to debtor by "bankruptcy petition preparer," (Official Form 19).**
Required if a "bankruptcy petition preparer" prepares the petition. Must be submitted **WITH** the petition. 11 U.S.C. § 110(b)(2).

☐ **Statement of Social Security Number (Official Form 21).**
Required if the debtor is an individual. Must be submitted **WITH** the petition. Fed.R.Bankr.P. 1007(f).

☐ **Individual Debtor's Statement of Compliance with Credit Counseling Requirement (Exhibit D to Official Form 1).**
Certificate of Credit Counseling and Debt Repayment Plan, if applicable.
Section 109(h)(3) certification and motion or § 109(h)(4) request)., if applicable.
Required if the debtor is an individual. Exhibit D must be filed **WITH** the petition. If applicable, the Certificate of Credit Counseling and Debt Repayment Plan must be filed with the petition or within 15 days. If applicable, the § 109(h)(3) certification and motion or the § 109(h)(4) request must be filed **WITH** the petition. Fed.R.Bankr.P. 1007(b)(3) & (c).

☐ **Statement disclosing compensation paid or to be paid to a "bankruptcy petition preparer" (Director's Form 280).**
Required if a "bankruptcy petition preparer" prepares the petition. Must be submitted **WITH** the petition. 11 U.S.C. § 110(h)(2).

☐ **Schedules of assets and liabilities (Official Form 6).**
Must be filed with the petition or within 15 days. Fed.R.Bankr.P. 1007(b) & (c).

☐ **Schedule of executory contracts and unexpired leases (Schedule G of Official Form 6).**
Must be filed with the petition or within 15 days. Fed.R.Bankr.P. 1007(b) & (c).

☐ **Schedules of current income and expenditures.**
All debtors must file these schedules. If the debtor is an individual, Schedule I and J of Official Form 6 must be used for this purpose. Must be filed with the

B 200 *continued*
(04/08) **REQUIRED LISTS, SCHEDULES, STATEMENTS, AND FEES**

petition or within 15 days. 11 U.S.C. § 521(1) and Fed.R.Bankr.P. 1007(b) & (c).

☐ **Statement of financial affairs (Official Form 7).**
Must be filed with the petition or within 15 days. Fed.R.Bankr.P. 1007(b) & (c).

☐ **Copies of all payment advices or other evidence of payment received by the debtor from any employer within 60 days before the filing of the petition if the debtor is an individual.** Must be filed with the petition or within 15 days. Fed.R.Bankr.P. 1007(b) & (c).

☐ **Statement disclosing compensation paid or to be paid to the attorney for the debtor (Director's Form 203),** if applicable.
Must be filed within 15 days or any other date set by the court. 11 U.S.C. § 329 and Fed.R.Bankr.P. 2016(b).

☐ **Chapter 12 Plan.**
Must be filed within 90 days. 11 U.S.C. § 1221.

B 200 *continued*
(04/08) **REQUIRED LISTS, SCHEDULES, STATEMENTS, AND FEES**

Chapter 13 Case

☐ **Filing fee of $235.**
If the fee is to be paid in installments, the debtor must file a signed application for court approval. Official Form 3A and Fed.R.Bankr.P. 1006(b).

☐ **Administrative fee of $39.**
If the court grants the debtor's request, this fee is payable in installments.

☐ **Voluntary Petition (Official Form 1).**
Names and addresses of all creditors of the debtor.
Must be filed **WITH** the petition. Fed.R.Bankr.P. 1007(a)(1).

☐ **Notice to Individual Debtor with Primarily Consumer Debts under 11 U.S.C. § 342(b) (Director's Form 201),** if applicable.
Required if the debtor is an individual with primarily consumer debts. The notice must be **GIVEN** to the debtor before the petition is filed.
Certification that the notice has been given must be **FILED** with the petition or within 15 days. 11 U.S.C. §§ 342(b), 521(a)(1)(B)(iii), 1307(c)(9). Official Form 1 contains spaces for the certification.

☐ **Notice to debtor by "bankruptcy petition preparer," (Official Form 19).**
Required if a "bankruptcy petition preparer" prepares the petition. Must be submitted **WITH** the petition. 11 U.S.C. § 110(b)(2).

☐ **Statement of Social Security Number (Official Form 21).**
Must be submitted **WITH** the petition. Fed.R.Bankr.P. 1007(f).

☐ **Individual Debtor's Statement of Compliance with Credit Counseling Requirement (Exhibit D to Official Form 1).**
Certificate of Credit Counseling and Debt Repayment Plan, if applicable.
Section 109(h)(3) certification and motion or § 109(h)(4) request)., if applicable.
Exhibit D must be filed **WITH** the petition. If applicable, the Certificate of Credit Counseling and Debt Repayment Plan must be filed with the petition or within 15 days. If applicable, the § 109(h)(3) certification and motion or the § 109(h)(4) request must be filed **WITH** the petition. Fed.R.Bankr.P. 1007(b)(3) & (c).

☐ **Statement disclosing compensation paid or to be paid to a "bankruptcy petition preparer" (Director's Form 280).**
Required if a "bankruptcy petition preparer" prepares the petition. Must be submitted **WITH** the petition. 11 U.S.C. § 110(h)(2).

☐ **Statement of current monthly income, etc. (Official Form 22C).**
Must be filed with the petition or within 15 days. Fed.R.Bankr.P. 1007.

☐ **Schedules of assets and liabilities (Official Form 6).**
Must be filed with the petition or within 15 days. Fed.R.Bankr.P. 1007(b) & (c).

☐ **Schedule of executory contracts and unexpired leases (Schedule G of Official Form 6).**
Must be filed with the petition or within 15 days. Fed.R.Bankr.P. 1007(b) & (c).

☐ **Schedules of current income and expenditures (Schedules I and J of Official Form 6).**
Must be filed with the petition or within 15 days. 11 U.S.C. § 521(1) and Fed.R.Bankr.P. 1007(b) & (c).

B 200 *continued*
(04/08) **REQUIRED LISTS, SCHEDULES, STATEMENTS, AND FEES**

☐ **Statement of financial affairs (Official Form 7).**
Must be filed with the petition or within 15 days. Fed.R.Bankr.P. 1007(b) & (c).

☐ **Copies of all payment advices or other evidence of payment received by the debtor from any employer within 60 days before the filing of the petition.**
Must be filed with the petition or within 15 days. Fed.R.Bankr. P. 1007(b) & (c).

☐ **Chapter 13 Plan.**
Must be filed with the petition or within 15 days. Fed.R.Bankr.P. 3015.

☐ **Statement disclosing compensation paid or to be paid to the attorney for the debtor (Director's Form 203),** if applicable.
Must be filed within 15 days or any other date set by the court. 11 U.S.C. § 329 and Fed.R.Bankr.P. 2016(b).

☐ **Certificate of Completion of Instructional Course Concerning Financial Management (Official Form 23).**
Must be filed no later than the date of the last payment made under the plan or the date of the filing of a motion for a discharge under § 1328(b). 11 U.S.C. § 1328(g)(1) and Fed.R.Bankr.P. 1007(b)(7) & (c).

(Added Sept. 1988, and amended Jan. 1993; Jan. 1995; Oct. 27, 2003 eff. Nov. 1, 2003; Oct. 17, 2005; Apr. 9, 2006; Oct. 11, 2006; Jan., 2008; April 2008.)

HISTORICAL NOTES

Source of Form

This Procedural Form is included as Form B 200 of the Bankruptcy Forms Manual, Volume II, "Forms and Instructions for the Public", issued by the Administrative Office of the United States Courts in September 1988.

Form B 201. Notice to Consumer Debtor(s) under § 342(b) of the Bankruptcy Code

UNITED STATES BANKRUPTCY COURT

NOTICE TO INDIVIDUAL CONSUMER DEBTOR UNDER § 342(b) OF THE BANKRUPTCY CODE

In accordance with § 342(b) of the Bankruptcy Code, this notice to individuals with primarily consumer debts: (1) Describes briefly the services available from credit counseling services; (2) Describes briefly the purposes, benefits and costs of the four types of bankruptcy proceedings you may commence; and (3) Informs you about bankruptcy crimes and notifies you that the Attorney General may examine all information you supply in connection with a bankruptcy case. You are cautioned that bankruptcy law is complicated and not easily described. Thus, you may wish to seek the advice of an attorney to learn of your rights and responsibilities should you decide to file a petition. Court employees cannot give you legal advice.

Notices from the bankruptcy court are sent to the mailing address you list on your bankruptcy petition. In order to ensure that you receive information about events concerning your case, Bankruptcy Rule 4002 requires that you notify the court of any changes in your address. If you are filing a joint case (a single bankruptcy case for two individuals married to each other), and each spouse lists the same mailing address on the bankruptcy petition, you and your spouse will generally receive a single copy of each notice mailed from the bankruptcy court in a jointly-addressed envelope, unless you file a statement with the court requesting that each spouse receive a separate copy of all notices.

1. Services Available from Credit Counseling Agencies

With limited exceptions, § 109(h) of the Bankruptcy Code requires that all individual debtors who file for bankruptcy relief on or after October 17, 2005, receive a briefing that outlines the available opportunities for credit counseling and provides assistance in performing a budget analysis. The briefing must be given within 180 days **before** the bankruptcy filing. The briefing may be provided individually or in a group (including briefings conducted by telephone or on the Internet) and must be provided by a nonprofit budget and credit counseling agency approved by the United States trustee or bankruptcy administrator. The clerk of the bankruptcy court has a list that you may consult of the approved budget and credit counseling agencies. Each debtor in a joint case must complete the briefing.

In addition, after filing a bankruptcy case, an individual debtor generally must complete a financial management instructional course before he or she can receive a discharge. The clerk also has a list of approved financial management instructional courses. Each debtor in a joint case must complete the course.

2. **The Four Chapters of the Bankruptcy Code Available to Individual Consumer Debtors**

Chapter 7: Liquidation ($245 filing fee, $39 administrative fee, $15 trustee surcharge: Total fee $299)

1. Chapter 7 is designed for debtors in financial difficulty who do not have the ability to pay their existing debts. Debtors whose debts are primarily consumer debts are subject to a "means test" designed to determine whether the case should be permitted to proceed under chapter 7. If your income is greater than the median income for your state of residence and family size, in some cases, creditors have the right to file a motion requesting that the court dismiss your case under § 707(b) of the Code. It is up to the court to decide whether the case should be dismissed.

2. Under chapter 7, you may claim certain of your property as exempt under governing law. A trustee may have the right to take possession of and

sell the remaining property that is not exempt and use the sale proceeds to pay your creditors.

3. The purpose of filing a chapter 7 case is to obtain a discharge of your existing debts. If, however, you are found to have committed certain kinds of improper conduct described in the Bankruptcy Code, the court may deny your discharge and, if it does, the purpose for which you filed the bankruptcy petition will be defeated.

4. Even if you receive a general discharge, some particular debts are not discharged under the law. Therefore, you may still be responsible for most taxes and student loans; debts incurred to pay nondischargeable taxes; domestic support and property settlement obligations; most fines, penalties, forfeitures, and criminal restitution obligations; certain debts which are not properly listed in your bankruptcy papers; and debts for death or personal injury caused by operating a motor vehicle, vessel, or aircraft while intoxicated from alcohol or drugs. Also, if a creditor can prove that a debt arose from fraud, breach of fiduciary duty, or theft, or from a willful and malicious injury, the bankruptcy court may determine that the debt is not discharged.

Chapter 13: Repayment of All or Part of the Debts of an Individual with Regular Income ($235 filing fee, $39 administrative fee: Total fee $274)

1. Chapter 13 is designed for individuals with regular income who would like to pay all or part of their debts in installments over a period of time. You are only eligible for chapter 13 if your debts do not exceed certain dollar amounts set forth in the Bankruptcy Code.

2. Under chapter 13, you must file with the court a plan to repay your creditors all or part of the money that you owe them, using your future earnings. The period allowed by the court to repay your debts may be three years or five years, depending upon your income and other factors. The court must approve your plan before it can take effect.

3. After completing the payments under your plan, your debts are generally discharged except for domestic support obligations; most student loans; certain taxes; most criminal fines and restitution obligations; certain debts which are not properly listed in your bankruptcy papers; certain debts for acts that caused death or personal injury; and certain long term secured obligations.

Chapter 11: Reorganization ($1000 filing fee, $39 administrative fee: Total fee $1039)

Chapter 11 is designed for the reorganization of a business but is also available to consumer debtors. Its provisions are quite complicated, and any decision by an individual to file a chapter 11 petition should be reviewed with an attorney.

Chapter 12: Family Farmer or Fisherman ($200 filing fee, $39 administrative fee: Total fee $239)

Chapter 12 is designed to permit family farmers and fishermen to repay their debts over a period of time from future earnings and is similar to chapter 13. The eligibility requirements are restrictive, limiting its use to those whose income arises primarily from a family-owned farm or commercial fishing operation.

3. Bankruptcy Crimes and Availability of Bankruptcy Papers to Law Enforcement Officials

A person who knowingly and fraudulently conceals assets or makes a false oath or statement under penalty of perjury, either orally or in writing, in connection with a bankruptcy case is subject to a fine, imprisonment, or both. All information supplied by a debtor in connection with a bankruptcy case is subject to examination by the Attorney General acting through the Office of the United States Trustee, the Office of the United States Attorney, and other components and employees of the Department of Justice.

WARNING: Section 521(a)(1) of the Bankruptcy Code requires that you promptly file detailed information regarding your creditors, assets, liabilities, income, expenses and general financial condition. Your bankruptcy case may be dismissed if this information is not filed with the court within the time deadlines set by the Bankruptcy Code, the Bankruptcy Rules, and the local rules of the court.

Certificate of [Non-Attorney] Bankruptcy Petition Preparer

I, the [non-attorney] bankruptcy petition preparer signing the debtor's petition, hereby certify that I delivered to the debtor this notice required by § 342(b) of the Bankruptcy Code.

____
Printed name and title, if any, of Bankruptcy Petition Preparer

Address:
____

X_____________________________
Signature of Bankruptcy Petition Preparer or officer, principal, responsible person, or partner whose Social Security number is provided above.

____
Social Security number (If the bankruptcy petition preparer is not an individual, state the Social Security number of the officer, principal, responsible person, or partner of the bankruptcy petition preparer.) (Required by 11 U.S.C. § 110.)

Certificate of the Debtor

I (We), the debtor(s), affirm that I (we) have received and read this notice.

____
Printed Name(s) of Debtor(s)

Case No. (if known) ____________

X_____________________________
Signature of Debtor Date

X_____________________________
Signature of Joint Debtor (if any) Date

(Added Sept. 1988, and amended Jan. 1993; Jan. 1995; Oct. 27, 2003, eff. Nov. 1, 2003; Oct. 17, 2005; Apr. 9, 2006; Dec. 1, 2008.)

HISTORICAL NOTES

Source of Form

This Procedural Form is included as Form B 201 of the Bankruptcy Forms Manual, Volume II, "Forms and Instructions for the Public", issued by the Administrative Office of the United States Courts in September 1988.

Form B 202. Statement of Military Service

B 202 (Form 202) (08/07)

United States Bankruptcy Court
______ District of ______

In re ____________________ Case Number ____________________

Chapter ____________________

STATEMENT OF MILITARY SERVICE

The Servicemembers' Civil Relief Act of 2003, Pub.L. No. 108-189, provides for the temporary suspension of certain judicial proceedings or transactions that may adversely affect military servicemembers, their dependents, and others. Each party to a bankruptcy case who might be eligible for relief under the act should complete this form and file it with the Bankruptcy Court.

IDENTIFICATION OF SERVICEMEMBER

☐ Self (Debtor, Codebtor, Creditor, Other)
☐ Non-Filing Spouse of Debtor (name) ____________________
☐ Other (Name of servicemember) ____________________
(Relationship of filer to servicemember) ____________________
(Type of liability) ____________________

TYPE OF MILITARY SERVICE

U.S. Armed Forces (Army, Navy, Air Force, Marine Corps, or Coast Guard) or commissioned officer of the Public Health Service or the National Oceanic and Atmospheric Administration (specify type of service) ____________________
☐ Active Service since ____________________ (date)
☐ Inductee ordered to report on ____________________ (date)
☐ Retired/Discharged ____________________ (date)

U.S. Military Reserves and National Guard
☐ Active Service since ____________________ (date)
☐ Impending Active Service-orders postmarked ____________________ (date)
Ordered to report on ____________________ (date)
☐ Retired/Discharged ____________________ (date)

U.S. Citizen Serving with U.S. ally in war or military action (specify ally and war or action)
____
☐ Active Service since ____________________ (date)
☐ Retired/Discharged ____________________ (date)

DEPLOYMENT

☐ Servicemember deployed overseas on ____________________ (date)
Anticipated completion of overseas tour-of-duty ____________________ (date)

SIGNATURE

______________________________ ______________________________
Date

____
(print name)

This statement is for information use only. Filing this statement with the Bankruptcy Court does not constitute an application for or invoke the benefits and relief available under the Servicemembers' Civil Relief Act of 2003.
(Revised effective August 1, 2007.)

Form No. B 203
DISCLOSURE OF COMPENSATION OF ATTORNEY FOR DEBTOR

B 203
(12/94)

United States Bankruptcy Court

______ District of ______

In re

Case No. ____________

Debtor

Chapter ____________

DISCLOSURE OF COMPENSATION OF ATTORNEY FOR DEBTOR

1. Pursuant to 11 U.S.C. § 329(a) and Fed. Bankr. P. 2016(b), I certify that I am the attorney for the above-named debtor(s) and that compensation paid to me within one year before the filing of the petition in bankruptcy, or agreed to be paid to me, for services rendered or to be rendered on behalf of the debtor(s) in contemplation of or in connection with the bankruptcy case is as follows:
   For legal services, I have agreed to accept .... $______
   Prior to the filing of this statement I have received .... $______
   Balance Due .... $______
2. The source of the compensation paid to me was:
   ☐ Debtor ☐ Other (specify)
3. The source of compensation to be paid to me is:
   ☐ Debtor ☐ Other (specify)
4. ☐ I have not agreed to share the above-disclosed compensation with any other person unless they are members and associates of my law firm.
   ☐ I have agreed to share the above-disclosed compensation with a person or persons who are not members or associates of my law firm. A copy of the agreement, together with a list of the names of the people sharing in the compensation, is attached.
5. In return for the above-disclosed fee, I have agreed to render legal service for all aspects of the bankruptcy case, including:
   a. Analysis of the debtor's financial situation, and rendering advice to the debtor in determining whether to file a petition in bankruptcy;
   b. Preparation and filing of any petition, schedules, statement of affairs and plan which may be required;
   c. Representation of the debtor at the meeting of creditors and confirmation hearing, and any adjourned hearings thereof;

B 203
(12/94)

DISCLOSURE OF COMPENSATION OF ATTORNEY FOR DEBTOR (Continued)

d. Representation of the debtor in adversary proceedings and other contested bankruptcy matters;

e. [Other provisions as needed]

6. By agreement with the debtor(s), the above-disclosed fee does not include the following services:

CERTIFICATION

I certify that the foregoing is a complete statement of any agreement or arrangement for payment to me for representation of the debtor(s) in this bankruptcy proceeding.

________________________ ________________________
Date *Signature of Attorney*

____
Name of law firm

(Added Sept. 1988.)

B 204 (Form 204) (08/07)

Form No. B 204

NOTICE OF NEED TO FILE PROOF OF CLAIM DUE TO RECOVERY OF ASSETS

United States Bankruptcy Court

______ District Of ______

In re ______________________________
Debtor*
Address: ______________________________
____
Last four digits of Social-Security or Individual Taxpayer-Identification (ITIN) No(s)., (if any): ________________
Employer Tax-Identification (EIN) No(s). (if any): ________________

Case No. ______

Chapter ______

NOTICE OF NEED TO FILE PROOF OF CLAIM DUE TO RECOVERY OF ASSETS

NOTICE IS GIVEN THAT:

The initial notice in this case instructed creditors that it was not necessary to file a proof of claim. Since that notice was sent, assets have been recovered by the trustee.

Creditors who wish to share in any distribution of funds must file a proof of claim with the clerk of the bankruptcy court at the address below on or before.

Date:

Creditors who do not file a proof of claim on or before this date might not share in any distribution from the debtor's estate.

The proof of claim form is attached to this notice. It may be filed by regular mail. To receive acknowledgment of your filing, you may either enclose a stamped self-addressed envelope and a copy of this proof of claim or you may access the court's PACER system (www.pacer.psc.uscourts.gov) to view your filed proof of claim.

There is no fee for filing the proof of claim.

Any creditor who has filed a proof of claim already need not file another proof of claim.

Address of the Bankruptcy Court

____
Clerk of the Bankruptcy Court

By: ______________________________
Deputy Clerk

Date: ______________________________

* *Set forth all names, including trade names, used by the debtor(s) within the last 8 years. For joint debtors, set forth the last four digits of both social-security numbers or individual taxpayer-identification numbers.*

(Added Sept. 1988; revised effective August 1, 2007.)

HISTORICAL NOTES

Source of Form

This Procedural Form is included as Form B 204 of the Bankruptcy Forms Manual, Volume II, "Forms and Instructions for the Public", issued by the Administrative Office of the United States Courts in September 1988.

Form No. B 205
NOTICE TO CREDITORS AND OTHER PARTIES IN INTEREST

B 205 (Form 205) (08/07)

United States Bankruptcy Court

______ District of ______

In re ______________________________
Debtor *
Address: __________________________
____
Last four digits of Social-Security or Individual Taxpayer-Identification (ITIN) No(s)., (if any): __________
Employer Tax-Identification (EIN) No(s). (if any): __________________
____

Case No. __________

Chapter __________

NOTICE TO CREDITORS AND OTHER PARTIES IN INTEREST

Notice is given that:

____
Clerk of the Bankruptcy Court

By: __________________________
Deputy Clerk

Date: __________________________

---

* *Set forth all names, including trade names, used by the debtor(s) within the last 8 years. For joint debtors, set forth the last four digits of both social-security numbers or individual taxpayer-identification numbers%.*

(Added Sept. 1988; revised effective August 1, 2007.)

Form No. B 206
CERTIFICATE OF COMMENCEMENT OF CASE

B206 (Form 206) (08/07)

United States Bankruptcy Court

______ District of ______

In re ________________________ Case No. __________

Debtor* Chapter __________

Address: ____________________

____

Last four digits of Social-Security or Individual Taxpayer-Identification (ITIN) No(s)., (if any): __________
Employer Tax-Identification (EIN) No(s).(if any): __________

CERTIFICATE OF COMMENCEMENT OF CASE

I certify that on ______________________________,
(date)

☐ the above named debtor filed a petition requesting relief under chapter ______ of the Bankruptcy Code (title 11 of the United States Code), or

☐ a petition was filed against the above named debtor under chapter ______ of the Bankruptcy Code (title 11 of the United States Code), and

☐ that as of the date below the case has not been dismissed.

____
Clerk of the Bankruptcy Court

By: ____________________
Deputy Clerk

Date: ____________________

* *Set forth all names, including trade names, used by the debtor(s) within the last 8 years. For joint debtors, set forth the last four digits of both social-security numbers or individual taxpayer-identification numbers.*

(Revised effective August 1, 2007.)

Form No. B 207
CERTIFICATE OF RETENTION OF DEBTOR IN POSSESSION

B207 (Form 207) (08/07)

United States Bankruptcy Court

______ **District of** ______

In re ________________________ Case No. __________
Debtor*

Address: ________________________ Chapter __________
____

Last four digits of Social-Security or Individual Taxpayer-Identification (ITIN) No(s)., (if any): _
Employer Tax-Identification (EIN) No(s). (if any): ________________________
____

CERTIFICATE OF RETENTION OF DEBTOR IN POSSESSION

I hereby certify that the above-named debtor continues in possession of its estate as debtor in possession, no trustee having been appointed.

____
Clerk of the Bankruptcy Court

Date: ______________ By: ________________________
Deputy Clerk

* *Set forth all names, including trade names, used by the debtor(s) within the last 8 years. For joint debtors, set forth the last four digits of both social-security numbers or individual taxpayer-identification numbers.*

(Revised effective August 1, 2007.)

Form B 210. Transfer of Claim Other Than for Security

B 210A (10/06)

United States Bankruptcy Court

______ District Of ______

In re ______________________________, Case No. __________

TRANSFER OF CLAIM OTHER THAN FOR SECURITY

A CLAIM HAS BEEN FILED IN THIS CASE or deemed filed under 11 U.S.C. § 1111(a). Transferee hereby gives evidence and notice pursuant to Rule 3001(e)(2), Fed. R. Bankr. P., of the transfer, other than for security, of the claim referenced in this evidence and notice.

______________________________ Name of Transferee	______________________________ Name of Transferor
Name and Address where notices to transferee should be sent:	Court Claim # (if known): __________ Amount of Claim: __________ Date Claim Filed: __________
Phone: ____________________ Last Four Digits of Acct #: __________	Phone: ____________________ Last Four Digits of Acct. #: __________

Name and Address where transferee payments should be sent (if different from above):

Phone: ____________________
Last Four Digits of Acct #: __________

I declare under penalty of perjury that the information provided in this notice is true and correct to the best of my knowledge and belief.

By: ______________________________ Date: ____________________
Transferee/Transferee's Agent

Penalty for making a false statement: Fine of up to $500,000 or imprisonment for up to 5 years, or both. 18 U.S.C. §§ 152 & 3571.

B 210B (10/06)

United States Bankruptcy Court
______ District Of ______

In re ______________________________, Case No. __________

NOTICE OF TRANSFER OF CLAIM OTHER THAN FOR SECURITY

Claim No. __________ (if known) was filed or deemed filed under 11 U.S.C. § 1111(a) in this case by the alleged transferor. As evidence of the transfer of that claim, the transferee filed a Transfer of Claim Other than for Security in the clerk's office of this court on __________(date).

______________________________	______________________________
Name of Alleged Transferor	Name of Transferee
Address of Alleged Transferor:	Address of Transferee:

—DEADLINE TO OBJECT TO TRANSFER—

The alleged transferor of the claim is hereby notified that objections must be filed with the court within twenty (20) days of the mailing of this notice. If no objection is timely received by the court, the transferee will be substituted as the original claimant without further order of the court.

Date: ______________ ______________________________
CLERK OF THE COURT

Form No. B 230A
ORDER CONFIRMING CHAPTER 12 PLAN

B 230A (Form 230A) (08/07)

United States Bankruptcy Court
______ District Of ______

In re ____________________ Case No. ____________
Debtor*

Address: ________________ Chapter 12
____

Last four digits of Social-Security or Individual Taxpayer-Identification (ITIN) No(s)., (if any): ____________
Employer Tax-Identification (EIN) No(s). (if any): ____________
____

ORDER CONFIRMING CHAPTER 12 PLAN

The debtor's plan was filed on ________, and was modified on
(date)
________.
(date)

The plan or a summary of the plan was transmitted to creditors pursuant to Bankruptcy Rule 3015. The court finds that the plan meets the requirements of 11 U.S.C. § 1225.

IT IS ORDERED THAT:

The debtor's chapter 12 plan is confirmed, with the following provisions:

1. Payments:
   Amount of each payment: $________
   Due date of each payment: ☐ the ____ day of each month, or
   ☐ ________________
   Period of payments: ☐ ________ months,
   ☐ until a ____ % dividend is paid to creditors holding allowed unsecured claims, or
   ☐ ________________
   Payable to:
   __________ Standing Trustee
   ____
   ____
   ____
   ____

2. Attorney's Fees:
   The debtor's attorney is awarded a fee in the amount of $________, of which $________ is due and payable from the estate.

3. [Other provisions as needed]

________________ ________________
Date *Bankruptcy Judge*

* *Set forth all names, including trade names, used by the debtor(s) within the last 8 years. For joint debtors, set forth the last four digits of both social-security numbers or individual taxpayer-identification numbers.*

(Added Sept. 1988; revised effective August 1, 2007.)

Form No. B 230B
ORDER CONFIRMING CHAPTER 13 PLAN

B 230B (Form 230B) (08/07)

United States Bankruptcy Court

__________ District of __________

In re ____________________
Debtor*

Case No. __________

Chapter 13

Address: ______________________________
____

Last four digits of Social-Security or Individual Taxpayer-Identification (ITIN) No(s)., (if any): _
Employer Tax-Identification (EIN) No(s). (if any): ______________________________
____

ORDER CONFIRMING CHAPTER 13 PLAN

The debtor's plan was filed on ________ *(date)*, and was modified on ______ *(date)*. The plan or a summary of the plan was transmitted to the creditors pursuant to Bankruptcy Rule 3015. The court finds that the plan meets the requirements of 11 U.S.C. § 1325.

IT IS ORDERED THAT:

The debtor's chapter 13 plan is confirmed, with the following provisions:

1. Payments:
   Amount of each payment: $________
   Due date of each payment: ☐ the ___ day of each month, or
   ☐ ______________________________
   Period of payments: ☐ ___ months,
   ☐ until a ___% dividend is paid to creditors holding allowed unsecured claims, or
   ☐ ______________________________

   Payable to:

   __________Standing Trustee
   ____
   ____
   ____

2. Attorney's Fees:
   The debtor's attorney is awarded a fee in the amount of $________, of which $________ is due and payable from the estate.

3. [Other provisions as needed]

____________________ ______________________________
Date *Bankruptcy Judge*

* *Set forth all names, including trade names, used by the debtor(s) within the last 8 years. For joint debtors, set forth the last four digits of both social-security numbers or individual taxpayer-identification numbers.*

(Added Sept. 1988; revised effective August 1, 2007.)

Form No. B 231A

ORDER FIXING TIME TO OBJECT TO PROPOSED MODIFICATION OF CONFIRMED CHAPTER 12 PLAN

B 231A (Form 231A) (08/07)

United States Bankruptcy Court

______ District of ______

In re ________________________________Case No. __________
Debtor*
Address: ________________________________Chapter __________
____
Last four digits of Social-Security or Individual Taxpayer-Identification (ITIN) No(s)., (if any): _
Employer Tax-Identification (EIN) No(s). (if any): ________________________________
____

ORDER FIXING TIME TO OBJECT TO PROPOSED MODIFICATION OF CONFIRMED CHAPTER 12 PLAN

To the debtor, trustee and creditors:

__________________ filed a proposed modification of the confirmed plan on ______.
(date)

A copy of the proposed modification is attached.

IT IS ORDERED AND NOTICE IS GIVEN THAT:

1. The last day for filing a written objection to the proposed modification is:

Date:

2. The proponent of the proposed modification is directed to serve a copy or summary of the proposed modification of the plan, together with a copy of this order, on the debtor, the trustee, the United States trustee, and all creditors no later than 20 days before the date set forth above.
3. Any objection to the proposed modification shall be filed and served on the debtor, the trustee, the United States trustee, and all creditors.

4. If an objection is filed, a hearing to consider the proposed modification will be held at:

Address	Room
	Date and Time

If no objection is filed, the court may not hold a hearing.

Date: ______________________ BY THE COURT

____
United States Bankruptcy Judge

---

* *Set forth all names, including trade names, used by the debtor(s) within the last 8 years. For joint debtors, set forth the last four digits of both social-security numbers or individual taxpayer-identification numbers.*

(Added Sept. 1988; revised effective August 1, 2007.)

Form No. B 231B
ORDER FIXING TIME TO OBJECT TO PROPOSED MODIFICATION OF CONFIRMED CHAPTER 13 PLAN

B 231B (Form 231B) (08/07)

United States Bankruptcy Court

______ District of ______

In re ______________________________________ Case No. __________
Debtor*
Address: ______________________________________ Chapter __________
____
Last four digits of Social-Security or Individual Taxpayer-Identification (ITIN) No(s)., (if any): _
Employer Tax-Identification (EIN) No(s). (if any): ________________________________
____

ORDER FIXING TIME TO OBJECT TO PROPOSED MODIFICATION OF CONFIRMED CHAPTER 13 PLAN

To the debtor, trustee, and creditors:
__________ filed a proposed modification of the confirmed plan on ______ (date).
A copy of the proposed modification is attached.

IT IS ORDERED AND NOTICE IS GIVEN THAT:

1. The last day for filing a written objection to the proposed modification is:

Date:

2. The proponent of the proposed modification is directed to serve a copy or summary of the proposed modification of the plan, together with a copy of this order, on the debtor, the trustee, the United States trustee, and all creditors no later than 20 days before the date set forth above.
3. Any objection to the proposed modification shall be filed and served on the debtor, the trustee, the United States trustee, and all creditors.
4. If an objection is filed, a hearing to consider the proposed modification will be held at:

Address	Room
	Date and Time

If no objection is filed, the court may not hold a hearing.

Date ____________________________ BY THE COURT

____
United States Bankruptcy Judge

---

* *Set forth all names, including trade names, used by the debtor(s) within the last 8 years. For joint debtors, set forth the last four digits of both social-security numbers or individual taxpayer-identification numbers.*

(Added Sept. 1988; revised effective August 1, 2007.)

Form B 240A. Reareaffirmation Agreement

Form 240A - Reaffirmation Agreement
(1/07)

☐ Presumption of Undue Hardship
☐ No Presumption of Undue Hardship
(Check box as directed in Part D: Debtor's Statement in Support of Reaffirmation Agreement.)

UNITED STATES BANKRUPTCY COURT
______________ District of ______________

In re ________________________, Case No. __________
Debtor Chapter __________

REAFFIRMATION AGREEMENT

[Indicate all documents included in this filing by checking each applicable box.]

☐ Part A: Disclosures, Instructions, and Notice to Debtor (pages 1—5)

☐ Part B: Reaffirmation Agreement

☐ Part C: Certification by Debtor's Attorney

☐ Part D: Debtor's Statement in Support of Reaffirmation Agreement

☐ Part E: Motion for Court Approval

*[**Note:** Complete Part E only if debtor was not represented by an attorney during the course of negotiating this agreement.* ***Note also:*** *If you complete Part E, you must prepare and file Form 240B—Order on Reaffirmation Agreement.]*

Name of Creditor: ______________________________

☐ *[Check this box if]* Creditor is a Credit Union as defined in § 19(b)(1)(a)(iv) of the Federal Reserve Act

PART A: DISCLOSURE STATEMENT, INSTRUCTIONS AND NOTICE TO DEBTOR

1. DISCLOSURE STATEMENT.

Before Agreeing to Reaffirm a Debt, Review These Important Disclosures:

SUMMARY OF REAFFIRMATION AGREEMENT

This Summary is made pursuant to the requirements of the Bankruptcy Code.

AMOUNT REAFFIRMED

The amount of debt you have agreed to reaffirm: $ __________

The amount of debt you have agreed to reaffirm includes all fees and costs (if any) that have accrued as of the date of this disclosure. Your credit agreement may obligate you to pay additional amounts which may come due after the date of this disclosure. Consult your credit agreement.

ANNUAL PERCENTAGE RATE

[The annual percentage rate can be disclosed in different ways, depending on the type of debt.]

a. If the debt is an extension of "credit" under an "open end credit plan," as those terms are defined in § 103 of the Truth in Lending Act, such as a credit card, the creditor may disclose the annual percentage rate shown in (i) below or, to the extent this rate is not readily available or not applicable, the simple interest rate shown in (ii) below, or both.

(i) The Annual Percentage Rate disclosed, or that would have been disclosed, to the debtor in the most recent periodic statement prior to entering into the reaffirmation agreement described in Part B below or, if no such periodic statement was given to the debtor during the prior six months, the annual percentage rate as it would have been so disclosed at the time of the disclosure statement: ___ %.

--- *And/Or* ---

(ii) The simple interest rate applicable to the amount reaffirmed as of the date this disclosure statement is given to the debtor: ___ %. If different simple interest rates apply to different balances included in the amount reaffirmed,
the amount of each balance and the rate applicable to it are:

$ __________ @ _________ %;
$ __________ @ _________ %;
$ __________ @ _________ %.

b. If the debt is an extension of credit other than under than an open end credit plan, the creditor may disclose the annual percentage rate shown in (I) below, or, to the extent this rate is not readily available or not applicable, the simple interest rate shown in (ii) below, or both.

(i) The Annual Percentage Rate under § 128(a)(4) of the Truth in Lending Act, as disclosed to the debtor in the most recent disclosure statement given to the debtor prior to entering into the reaffirmation agreement with respect to the debt or, if no such disclosure statement was given to the debtor, the annual percentage rate as it would have been so disclosed: ___ %.

--- And/Or ---

(ii) The simple interest rate applicable to the amount reaffirmed as of the date this disclosure statement is given to the debtor: ___ %. If different simple interest rates apply to different balances included in the amount reaffirmed, the amount of each balance and the rate applicable to it are:

$ __________ @ _________ %;
$ __________ @ _________ %;
$ __________ @ _________ %.

c. If the underlying debt transaction was disclosed as a variable rate transaction on the most recent disclosure given under the Truth in Lending Act:

The interest rate on your loan may be a variable interest rate which changes from time to time, so that the annual percentage rate disclosed here may be higher or lower.

d. If the reaffirmed debt is secured by a security interest or lien, which has not been waived or determined to be void by a final order of the court, the following items or types of items of the debtor's goods or property remain subject to such security interest or lien in connection with the debt or debts being reaffirmed in the reaffirmation agreement described in Part B.

Item or Type of Item	Original Purchase Price or Original Amount of Loan

<u>Optional</u> --- *At the election of the creditor, a repayment schedule using one or a combination of the following may be provided:*

<u>Repayment Schedule:</u>

Your first payment in the amount of $ ___ is due on _________ (date), but the future payment amount may be different. Consult your reaffirmation agreement or credit agreement, as applicable.

--- *Or* ---

Your payment schedule will be: ___ (number) payments in the amount of $ ___ each, payable (monthly, annually, weekly, etc.) on the ___ (day) of each ___ (week, month, etc.), unless altered later by mutual agreement in writing.

--- *Or* ---

A reasonably specific description of the debtor's repayment obligations to the extent known by the creditor or creditor's representative.

2. **INSTRUCTIONS AND NOTICE TO DEBTOR**

Reaffirming a debt is a serious financial decision. The law requires you to take certain steps to make sure the decision is in your best interest. If these steps are not completed, the reaffirmation agreement is not effective, even though you have signed it.

1. Read the disclosures in this Part A carefully. Consider the decision to reaffirm carefully. Then, if you want to reaffirm, sign the reaffirmation agreement in Part B (or you may use a separate agreement you and your creditor agree on).

2. Complete and sign Part D and be sure you can afford to make the payments you are agreeing to make and have received a copy of the disclosure statement and a completed and signed reaffirmation agreement.

3. If you were represented by an attorney during the negotiation of your reaffirmation agreement, the attorney must have signed the certification in Part C.

4. If you were not represented by an attorney during the negotiation of your reaffirmation agreement, you must have completed and signed Part E.

5. The original of this disclosure must be filed with the court by you or your creditor. If a separate reaffirmation agreement (other than the one in Part B) has been signed, it must be attached.

6. <u>If the creditor is not a Credit Union</u> and you were represented by an attorney during the negotiation of your reaffirmation agreement, your reaffirmation agreement becomes effective upon filing with the court unless the reaffirmation is presumed to be an undue hardship as explained in Part D. <u>If the creditor is a Credit Union</u> and you were represented by an attorney during the negotiation of your reaffirmation agreement, your reaffirmation agreement becomes effective upon filing with the court.

7. If you were not represented by an attorney during the negotiation of your reaffirmation agreement, it will not be effective unless the court approves it. The court will notify you and the creditor of the hearing on your reaffirmation agreement. You must attend this hearing in bankruptcy court where the judge will review your reaffirmation agreement. The bankruptcy court must approve your reaffirmation agreement as consistent with your best interests, except that no court approval is required if your reaffirmation agreement is for a consumer debt secured by a mortgage, deed of trust, security deed, or other lien on your real property, like your home.

YOUR RIGHT TO RESCIND (CANCEL) YOUR REAFFIRMATION AGREEMENT

You may rescind (cancel) your reaffirmation agreement at any time before the bankruptcy court enters a discharge order, or before the expiration of the 60–day period that begins on the date your reaffirmation agreement is filed with the court, whichever occurs later. To rescind (cancel) your reaffirmation agreement, you must notify the creditor that your reaffirmation agreement is rescinded (or canceled).

Frequently Asked Questions:

What are your obligations if you reaffirm the debt? A reaffirmed debt remains your personal legal obligation. It is not discharged in your bankruptcy case. That means that if you default on your reaffirmed debt after your bankruptcy case is over, your creditor may be able to take your property or your wages. Otherwise, your obligations will be determined by the reaffirmation agreement which may have changed the terms of the original agreement. For example, if you are reaffirming an open end credit agreement, the creditor may be permitted by that agreement or applicable law to change the terms of that agreement in the future under certain conditions.

Are you required to enter into a reaffirmation agreement by any law? No, you are not required to reaffirm a debt by any law. Only agree to reaffirm a debt if it is in your best interest. Be sure you can afford the payments you agree to make.

What if your creditor has a security interest or lien? Your bankruptcy discharge does not eliminate any lien on your property. A "lien" is often referred to as a security interest, deed of trust, mortgage or security deed. Even if you do not reaffirm and your personal liability on the debt is discharged, because of the lien your creditor may still have the right to take the security property if you do not pay the debt or default on it. If the lien is on an item of personal property that is exempt under your State's law or that the trustee has abandoned, you may be able to redeem the item rather than reaffirm the debt. To redeem, you make a single payment to the creditor equal to the current value of the security property, as agreed by the parties or determined by the court.

NOTE: When this disclosure refers to what a creditor "may" do, it does not use the word "may" to give the creditor specific permission. The word "may" is used to tell you what might occur if the law permits the creditor to take the action. If you have questions about your reaffirming a debt or what the law requires, consult with the attorney who helped you negotiate this agreement reaffirming a debt. If you don't have an attorney helping you, the judge will explain the effect of your reaffirming a debt when the hearing on the reaffirmation agreement is held.

PART B: REAFFIRMATION AGREEMENT.

I (we) agree to reaffirm the debts arising under the credit agreement described below.

1. Brief description of credit agreement:

2. Description of any changes to the credit agreement made as part of this reaffirmation agreement:

SIGNATURE(S):

Borrower: Accepted by creditor:

(Print Name)	(Printed Name of Creditor)
(Signature)	(Address of Creditor)
Date:	(Signature)
Co–borrower, if also reaffirming these debts:	(Printed Name and Title of Individual Signing for Creditor)
(Print Name)	
(Signature)	Date of creditor acceptance:
Date:	

PART C: CERTIFICATION BY DEBTOR'S ATTORNEY (IF ANY).

[To be filed only if the attorney represented the debtor during the course of negotiating this agreement.]

I hereby certify that (1) this agreement represents a fully informed and voluntary agreement by the debtor; (2) this agreement does not impose an undue hardship on the debtor or any dependent of the debtor; and (3) I have fully advised the debtor of the legal effect and consequences of this agreement and any default under this agreement.

☐ *[Check box, if applicable and the creditor is not a Credit Union.]* A presumption of undue hardship has been established with respect to this agreement. In my opinion, however, the debtor is able to make the required payment.

Printed Name of Debtor's Attorney: ____________

Signature of Debtor's Attorney: ____________

Date: ____________

PART D: DEBTOR'S STATEMENT IN SUPPORT OF REAFFIRMATION AGREEMENT

*[Read and complete sections 1 and 2, **OR**, if the creditor is a Credit Union and the debtor is represented by an attorney, read section 3. Sign the appropriate signature line(s) and date your signature. If you complete sections 1 and 2 **and** your income less monthly expenses does not leave enough to make the payments under this reaffirmation agreement, check the box at the top of page 1 indicating "Presumption of Undue Hardship." Otherwise, check the box at the top of page 1 indicating "No Presumption of Undue Hardship"]*

1. I believe this reaffirmation agreement will not impose an undue hardship on my dependents or me. I can afford to make the payments on the reaffirmed debt because my monthly income (take home pay plus any other income received) is $ ___, and my actual current monthly expenses including monthly payments on post-bankruptcy debt and other reaffirmation agreements total $ ___, leaving $ ___ to make the required payments on this reaffirmed debt.

I understand that if my income less my monthly expenses does not leave enough to make the payments, this reaffirmation agreement is presumed to be an undue hardship on me and must be reviewed by the court. However, this presumption may be overcome if I explain to the satisfaction of the court how I can afford to make the payments here: ______________________________.

____

____

(Use an additional page if needed for a full explanation.)

2. I received a copy of the Reaffirmation Disclosure Statement in Part A and a completed and signed reaffirmation agreement.

Signed: ____________________

(Debtor)

____

(Joint Debtor, if any)

Date: ____________________

— Or —

[If the creditor is a Credit Union and the debtor is represented by an attorney]

3. I believe this reaffirmation agreement is in my financial interest. I can afford to make the payments on the reaffirmed debt. I received a copy of the Reaffirmation Disclosure Statement in Part A and a completed and signed reaffirmation agreement.

Signed: ____________________

(Debtor)

____

(Joint Debtor, if any)

Date: ____

PART E: MOTION FOR COURT APPROVAL

[To be completed and filed only if the debtor is not represented by an attorney during the course of negotiating this agreement.]

MOTION FOR COURT APPROVAL OF REAFFIRMATION AGREEMENT

I (we), the debtor(s), affirm the following to be true and correct:

I am not represented by an attorney in connection with this reaffirmation agreement.

I believe this reaffirmation agreement is in my best interest based on the income and expenses I have disclosed in my Statement in Support of this reaffirmation agreement, and because (provide any additional relevant reasons the court should consider):

Therefore, I ask the court for an order approving this reaffirmation agreement under the following provisions (*check all applicable boxes)*:

☐ 11 U.S.C. § 524(c)(6) (debtor is not represented by an attorney during the course of the negotiation of the reaffirmation agreement)

☐ 11 U.S.C. § 524(m) (presumption of undue hardship has arisen because monthly expenses exceed monthly income)

Signed: ____________________
(Debtor)

____
(Joint Debtor, if any)

Date: ____________________

(Added Jan. 2007.)

Form B 240B. Order on Reafﬁrmation Agreement

Form 240B–Order on Reaffirmation Agreement (1/07)

United States Bankruptcy Court
_______________ District of _______________

In re _______________________________, Debtor
Case No. _______________
Chapter _______________

ORDER ON REAFFIRMATION AGREEMENT

The debtor(s) _______________ (Name(s) of debtor(s)) has (have) filed a motion for approval of the reaffirmation agreement dated _______________ (Date of agreement) made between the debtor(s) and _______________ (Name of creditor). The court held the hearing required by 11 U.S.C. § 524(d) on notice to the debtor(s) and the creditor on _______________ (Date).

COURT ORDER:

☐ The court grants the debtor's motion under 11 U.S.C. § 524(c)(6)(A) and approves the reaffirmation agreement described above as not imposing an undue hardship on the debtor(s) or a dependent of the debtor(s) and as being in the best interest of the debtor(s).

☐ The court grants the debtor's motion under 11 U.S.C. § 524(k)(8) and approves the reaffirmation agreement described above.

☐ The court does not disapprove the reaffirmation agreement under 11 U.S.C. § 524(m).

☐ The court disapproves the reaffirmation agreement under 11 U.S.C. § 524(m).

☐ The court does not approve the reaffirmation agreement.

BY THE COURT

Date: _______________

____
United States Bankruptcy Judge

(Added Jan. 2007.)

Form No. B 250A
SUMMONS IN AN ADVERSARY PROCEEDING

B 250A
(8/96)

United States Bankruptcy Court
______ District of ______

In re ____________________________,)
Debtor) Case No. ________
) Chapter ________
____________________________,)
Plaintiff)
v.)
____________________________,) Adv. Proc. No. ______
Defendant)

SUMMONS IN AN ADVERSARY PROCEEDING

YOU ARE SUMMONED and required to file a motion or answer to the complaint which is attached to this summons with the clerk of the bankruptcy court within 30 days after the date of issuance of this summons, except that the United States and its offices and agencies shall file a motion or answer to the complaint within 35 days.

Address of Clerk

At the same time, you must also serve a copy of the motion or answer upon the plaintiff's attorney.

Name and Address of Plaintiff's Attorney

If you make a motion, your time to answer is governed by Fed. R. Bankr. P. 7012.

IF YOU FAIL TO RESPOND TO THIS SUMMONS, YOUR FAILURE WILL BE DEEMED TO BE YOUR CONSENT TO ENTRY OF A JUDGMENT BY THE BANKRUPTCY COURT AND JUDGMENT BY DEFAULT MAY BE TAKEN AGAINST YOU FOR THE RELIEF DEMANDED IN THE COMPLAINT.

____
Clerk of the Bankruptcy Court

________________ By: ________________________
Date Deputy Clerk

CERTIFICATE OF SERVICE

I, ____________________, certify that I am, and at all times
(name)
during the service of process was, not less than 18 years of age and not a party to the matter concerning which service of process was

made. I further certify that the service of this summons and a copy of the complete was made ______________ by:
(date)

☐ Mail Service: Regular, first class United States mail, postage fully pre-paid, addressed to:

☐ Personal Service: By leaving the process with defendant or with an officer or agent of defendant at:

☐ Residence Service: By leaving the process with the following adult at:

☐ Certified Mail Service on an Insured Depository Institution: By sending the process by certified mail addressed to the following officer of the defendant at:

☐ Publication: The defendant was served as follows: [Describe briefly]

☐ State Law: The defendant was served pursuant to the laws of the State of __________________, as follows: [Describe briefly]
(name of state)

Under penalty of perjury, I declare that the foregoing is true and correct.

______________________ ______________________________________
Date Signature

Print Name		
Business Address		
City	State	Zip

(Added Sept. 1988.)

Form No. B 250B
SUMMONS AND NOTICE OF PRETRIAL CONFERENCE IN AN ADVERSARY PROCEEDING

B 250B
(8/96)

United States Bankruptcy Court

______ District of ______

In re ________________________, Debtor	)	Case No. ________
________________________, Plaintiff	)	Chapter ________
v.	)	
________________________, Defendant	)	Adv. Proc. No. ______

SUMMONS AND NOTICE OF PRETRIAL CONFERENCE IN AN ADVERSARY PROCEEDING

YOU ARE SUMMONED and required to file a motion or answer to the complaint which is attached to this summons with the clerk of the bankruptcy court within 30 days after the date of issuance of this summons, except that the United States and its offices and agencies shall file a motion or answer to the complaint within 35 days.

Address of Clerk

At the same time, you must also serve a copy of the motion or answer upon the plaintiff's attorney.

Name and Address of Plaintiff's Attorney

If you make a motion, your time to answer is governed by Fed. R. Bankr. P. 7012.

YOU ARE NOTIFIED that a pretrial conference of the proceeding commenced by the filing of the complaint will be held at the following time and place.

Address	Room
	Date and Time

IF YOU FAIL TO RESPOND TO THIS SUMMONS, YOUR FAILURE WILL BE DEEMED TO BE YOUR CONSENT TO ENTRY OF A JUDGMENT BY THE BANKRUPTCY COURT AND JUDGMENT BY DEFAULT MAY BE TAKEN AGAINST YOU FOR THE RELIEF DEMANDED IN THE COMPLAINT.

____
Clerk of the Bankruptcy Court

__________________ By: ______________________________
Date Deputy Clerk

CERTIFICATE OF SERVICE

I, ______________________, certify that I am, and at all times
(name)
during the service of process was, not less than 18 years of age and not a party to the matter concerning which service of process was made. I further certify that the service of this summons and a copy of the complaint was made ____________ by:
(date)

☐ Mail Service: Regular, first class United States mail, postage fully pre-paid, addressed to:

☐ Personal Service: By leaving the process with defendant or with an officer or agent of defendant at:

☐ Residence Service: By leaving the process with the following adult at:

☐ Certified Mail Service on an Insured Depository Institution: By sending the process by certified mail addressed to the following officer of the defendant at:

☐ Publication: The defendant was served as follows: [Describe briefly]

☐ State Law: The defendant was served pursuant to the laws of the State of ______________, as follows: [Describe briefly]
(name of state)

Under penalty of perjury, I declare that the foregoing is true and correct.

__________________ ______________________________
Date Signature

Print Name		
Business Address		
City	State	Zip

(Added Sept. 1988.)

Form No. B 250C
SUMMONS AND NOTICE OF TRIAL IN AN ADVERSARY PROCEEDING

B 250C
(8/96)

United States Bankruptcy Court

______ District of ______

In re ____,	)	
Debtor	)	Case No. __________
	)	
	)	Chapter __________
____,	)	
Plaintiff	)	
	)	
v.	)	
____,	)	Adv. Proc. No. ______
Defendant	)	

SUMMONS AND NOTICE OF TRIAL IN AN ADVERSARY PROCEEDING

YOU ARE SUMMONED and required to file a motion or answer to the complaint which is attached to this summons with the clerk of the bankruptcy court within 30 days after the date of issuance of this summons, except that the United States and its offices and agencies shall file a motion or answer to the complaint within 35 days.

Address of Clerk

At the same time, you must also serve a copy of the motion or answer upon the plaintiff's attorney.

Name and Address of Plaintiff's Attorney

If you make a motion, your time to answer is governed by Fed. R. Bankr. P. 7012. YOU ARE NOTIFIED that a trial of the proceeding commenced by the filing of the complaint will be held at the following time and place.

Address	Room
	Date and Time

IF YOU FAIL TO RESPOND TO THIS SUMMONS, YOUR FAILURE WILL BE DEEMED TO BE YOUR CONSENT TO ENTRY OF A JUDGMENT BY THE BANKRUPTCY COURT AND JUDGMENT BY DEFAULT MAY BE TAKEN AGAINST YOU FOR THE RELIEF DEMANDED IN THE COMPLAINT.

____
Clerk of the Bankruptcy Court

________________ By: __________________________
Date Deputy Clerk

CERTIFICATE OF SERVICE

I, ____________________ (name), certify that I am, and at all times during the service of process was, not less than 18 years of age and not a party to the matter concerning which service of process was made. I further certify that the service of this summons and a copy of the complaint was made __________ (date) by:

☐ Mail Service: Regular, first class United States mail, postage fully pre-paid, addressed to:

☐ Personal Service: By leaving the process with defendant or with an officer or agent of defendant at:

☐ Residence Service: By leaving the process with the following adult at:

☐ Certified Mail Service on an Insured Depository Institution: By sending the process by certified mail addressed to the following officer of the defendant at:

☐ Publication: The defendant was served as follows: [Describe briefly]

☐ State Law: The defendant was served pursuant to the laws of the State of ________________, as follows: [Describe briefly]
(name of state)

Under penalty of perjury, I declare that the foregoing is true and correct.

________________ ________________________
Date Signature

Print Name		
Business Address		
City	State	Zip

(Added Sept. 1988.)

Form No. B 250D
THIRD–PARTY SUMMONS

B 250D
(8/96)

United States Bankruptcy Court

______ District of ______

In re	______________________________, Debtor	)	Case No. ______
		)	Chapter ______
	______________________________, Plaintiff	)	
	v.	)	
	______________________________, Defendant and Third–Party Plaintiff	)	Adv. Proc. No. ___
	______________________________, Third–Party Defendant	)	

THIRD–PARTY SUMMONS

YOU ARE SUMMONED and required to file a motion or answer to the third-party complaint which is attached to this summons with the clerk of the bankruptcy court within 30 days after the date of issuance of this summons, except that the United States and its offices and agencies shall file a motion or answer to the complaint within 35 days.

Address of Clerk

At the same time, you must also serve a copy of the motion or answer upon the plaintiff's attorney.

Name and Address of Plaintiff's Attorney

At the same time, you must also serve a copy of the motion or answer upon Defendant and Third–Party Plaintiff's Attorney.

Name and Address of Defendant and Third-Party Plaintiff's Attorney

If you make a motion, your time to answer is governed by Fed. R. Bankr. P. 7012. If you are also being served with a copy of the complaint of the plaintiff you have the option of not answering the plaintiff's complaint **unless** this is an admiralty or maritime action subject to the provisions of Fed. R. Civ. P. 9(h) and 14(c), in which case you are required to file a motion or an answer to both the plaintiff's complaint and the third-party complaint, and to serve a copy of your motion or answer upon the appropriate parties.

IF YOU FAIL TO RESPOND TO THIS SUMMONS, YOUR FAILURE WILL BE DEEMED TO BE YOUR CONSENT TO ENTRY OF A JUDGMENT BY THE BANKRUPTCY COURT AND JUDGMENT BY DEFAULT MAY BE TAKEN AGAINST YOU FOR THE RELIEF DEMANDED IN THE THIRD–PARTY COMPLAINT.

____
Clerk of the Bankruptcy Court

________________ By: ________________________
Date *Deputy Clerk*

CERTIFICATE OF SERVICE

I, ____________________ (name), certify that I am, and at all times during the service of process was, not less than 18 years of age and not a party to the matter concerning which service of process was made. I further certify that the service of this summons and a copy of the complaint was made __________ (date) by:

☐ Mail service: Regular, first class United States mail, postage fully pre-paid, addressed to:

☐ Personal Service: By leaving the process with defendant or with an officer or agent of defendant at:

☐ Residence Service: By leaving the process with the following adult at:

☐ Certified Mail Service on an Insured Depository Institution: By sending the process by certified mail addressed to the following officer of the defendant at:

☐ Publication: The defendant was served as follows: [Describe briefly]

☐ State Law: The defendant was served pursuant to the laws of the State of ______________ (name of state), as follows: [Describe briefly]

Under penalty of perjury, I declare that the foregoing is true and correct.

____________________ ______________________________________

Date Signature

Print Name		
Business Address		
City	State	Zip

(Added Sept. 1988.)

Form No. B 250E
SUMMONS TO DEBTOR IN INVOLUNTARY CASE

B250E
(6/91)

United States Bankruptcy Court
______ District Of ______

In re ______________________, Case No. __________
Debtor

Chapter __________

SUMMONS TO DEBTOR IN INVOLUNTARY CASE

To the above named debtor:

A petition under title 11, United States Code was filed against you on __________ (date) in this bankruptcy court, requesting an order for relief under chapter ______ of the Bankruptcy Code (title 11 of the United States Code).

YOU ARE SUMMONED and required to file with the clerk of the bankruptcy court a motion or answer to the petition within 20 days after the service of this summons. A copy of the petition is attached.

Address of Clerk

At the same time, you must also serve a copy of your motion or answer on petitioner's attorney.

Name and Address of Petitioner's Attorney

If you make a motion, your time to serve an answer is governed by Federal Rule of Bankruptcy Procedure 1011(c).
If you fail to respond to this summons, the order for relief will be entered.

____
Clerk of the Bankruptcy Court

__________________ By: ____________________________

Date Deputy Clerk

**Set forth all names, including trade names, used by the debtor within the last 6 years. (Fed. R. Bankr. P. 1005).*

Case No. __________

CERTIFICATE OF SERVICE

I,
of**
certify:

That I am, and at all times hereinafter mentioned was, more than 18 years of age;

That on the day of , 19
I served a copy of the within summons, together with the petition filed in this case, on

the debtor in this case, by *[describe here the mode of service]*

the said debtor at

I certify under penalty of perjury that the foregoing is true and correct.

Executed on __________________ __________________

[Date] *[Signature]*

** *State mailing address.*

Form No. B 253
ORDER FOR RELIEF IN AN INVOLUNTARY CASE

Form 253
(08/07)

United States Bankruptcy Court

______ District of ______

In re ____________________________________ Case No. __________
Debtor*
Address: ____________________________________ Chapter __________
____

Last four digits of Social-Security or Individual Taxpayer-Identification (ITIN) No(s)., (if any): _
Employer Tax-Identification (EIN) No(s). (if any): ____________________________________
____

ORDER FOR RELIEF IN AN INVOLUNTARY CASE

On consideration of the petition filed on __________(date) against *(date)* the above-named debtor, an order for relief under chapter ______ of the Bankruptcy Code (title 11 of the United States Code) is granted.

Date ______________ BY THE COURT

____
United States Bankruptcy Judge

* *Set forth all names, including trade names, used by the debtor(s) within the last 8 years. For joint debtors, set forth the last four digits of both social-security numbers or individual taxpayer-identification numbers.*

(Revised effective August 1, 2007.)

Form No. B 254
SUBPOENA FOR RULE 2004 EXAMINATION

Form 254–Subpoena for Rule 2004 Examination (12/06)

United States Bankruptcy Court

_______ District of _______

In re ______________________, Debtor

SUBPOENA FOR RULE 2004 EXAMINATION
Case No. * ______________________

To: ______________________

Chapter ______________________

☐ **YOU ARE COMMANDED to appear and testify at an examination under Rule 2004, Federal Rules of Bankruptcy Procedure, at the place, date, and time specified below. A copy of the court order authorizing the examination is attached.**

PLACE OF TESTIMONY	DATE AND TIME

☐ **YOU ARE COMMANDED to produce and permit inspection and copying of the following documents or objects at the place, date, and time specified below (list documents or objects):**

PLACE	DATE AND TIME

ISSUING OFFICER SIGNATURE AND TITLE	DATE
ISSUING OFFICER'S NAME, ADDRESS, AND PHONE NUMBER	

* If the bankruptcy case is pending in a district other than the district in which the subpoena is issued, state the district under the case number.

Form 254–Subpoena for Rule 2004 Examination (12/06)

PROOF OF SERVICE

DATE PLACE

SERVED

SERVED ON (PRINT NAME) MANNER OF SERVICE

SERVED BY (PRINT NAME) TITLE

DECLARATION OF SERVER

I declare under penalty of perjury under the laws of the United States of America that the foregoing information contained in the Proof of Service is true and correct.

Executed on ____________________

DATE SIGNATURE OF SERVER

ADDRESS OF SERVER

Rule 45, Federal Rules of Civil Procedure, Subdivisions (c), (d), and (e), as amended on December 1, 2006, made applicable in cases under the Bankruptcy Code by Rule 9016, Federal Rules of Bankruptcy Procedure:

(c) PROTECTION OF PERSONS SUBJECT TO SUBPOENAS.

(1) A party or an attorney responsible for the issuance and service of a subpoena shall take reasonable steps to avoid imposing undue burden or expense on a person subject to that subpoena. The court on behalf of which the subpoena was issued shall enforce this duty and impose upon the party or attorney in breach of this duty an appropriate sanction, which may include, but is not limited to, lost earnings and a reasonable attorney's fee.

(2)(A) A person commanded to produce and permit inspection, copying, testing, or sampling of designated electronically stored information, books, papers, documents or tangible things, or inspection of premises need not appear in person at the place of production or inspection unless commanded to appear for deposition, hearing or trial.

(B) Subject to paragraph (d)(2) of this rule, a person commanded to produce and permit inspection, copying, testing, or sampling may, within 14 days after service of the subpoena or before the time specified for compliance if such time is less than 14 days after service, serve upon the party or attorney designated in the subpoena written objection to producing any or all of the designated materials or inspection of the premises—or to producing electronically stored information in the form or forms requested. If objection is made, the party serving the subpoena shall not be entitled to inspect, copy, test, or sample the materials or inspect the premises except pursuant to an order of the court by which the subpoena was issued. If objection has been made, the party serving the subpoena may, upon notice to the person commanded to produce, move at any time for an order to compel the production, inspection, copying, testing, or sampling. Such an order to compel shall protect any person who is not a party or an officer of a party from significant expense resulting from the inspection, copying, testing, or sampling commanded.

(3)(A) On timely motion, the court by which a subpoena was issued shall quash or modify the subpoena if it

(i) fails to allow reasonable time for compliance;

(ii) requires a person who is not a party or an officer of a party to travel to a place more than 100 miles from the place where that person resides, is employed or regularly transacts business in person, except that, subject to the provisions of clause (c)(3)(B)(iii) of this rule, such a person may in order to attend trial be commanded to travel from any such place within the state in which the trial is held;

(iii) requires disclosure of privileged or other protected matter and no exception or waiver applies; or

(iv) subjects a person to undue burden.

(B) If a subpoena

(i) requires disclosure of a trade secret or other confidential research, development, or commercial information, or

(ii) requires disclosure of an unretained expert's opinion or information not describing specific events or occurrences in dispute and resulting from the expert's study made not at the request of any party, or

(iii) requires a person who is not a party or an officer of a party to incur substantial expense to travel more than 100 miles to attend trial, the court may, to protect a person subject to or affected by the subpoena, quash or modify the subpoena or, if the party in whose behalf the subpoena is issued shows a substantial need for the testimony or material that cannot be otherwise met without undue hardship and assures that the person to whom the subpoena is addressed will be reasonably compensated, the court may order appearance or production only upon specified conditions.

(d) DUTIES IN RESPONDING TO SUBPOENA.

(1)(A) A person responding to a subpoena to produce documents shall produce them as they are kept in the usual course of business or shall organize and label them to correspond with the categories in the demand.

(B) If a subpoena does not specify the form or forms for producing electronically stored information, a person responding to a subpoena must produce the information in a form or forms in which the person ordinarily maintains it or in a form or forms that are reasonably usable.

(C) A person responding to a subpoena need not produce the same electronically stored information in more than one form.

(D) A person responding to a subpoena need not provide discovery of electronically stored information from sources that the person identifies as not reasonably accessible because of undue burden or cost. On motion to compel discovery or to quash, the person from whom discovery is sought must show that the information sought is not reasonably accessible because of undue burden or cost. If that showing is made, the court may nonetheless order discovery from such sources if the requesting party shows good cause, considering the limitations of Rule 26(b)(2)(C). The court may specify conditions for the discovery.

(2)(A) When information subject to a subpoena is withheld on a claim that it is privileged or subject to protection as trial-preparation materials, the claim shall be made expressly and shall be supported by a description of the nature of the documents, communications, or things not produced that is sufficient to enable the demanding party to contest the claim.

(B) If information is produced in response to a subpoena that is subject to a claim of privilege or of protection as trial-preparation material, the person making the claim may notify any party that received the information of the claim and the basis for it. After being notified, a party must promptly return, sequester, or destroy the specified information and any copies it has and may not use or disclose the information until the claim is resolved. A receiving party may promptly present the information to the court under seal for a determination of the claim. If the receiving party disclosed the information before being notified, it must take reasonable steps to retrieve it. The person who produced the information must preserve the information until the claim is resolved.

(e) CONTEMPT. Failure of any person without adequate excuse to obey a subpoena served upon that person may be deemed a contempt of the court from which the subpoena issued. An adequate cause for failure to obey exists when a subpoena purports to require a nonparty to attend or produce at a place not within the limits provided by clause (ii) of subparagraph (c)(3)(A).

Form No. B 255
SUBPOENA IN AN ADVERSARY PROCEEDING

Form 255–Subpoena in an Adversary Proceeding (12/06)

United States Bankruptcy Court

______ District of ______

In re	_______________, Debtor	**SUBPOENA IN AN ADVERSARY PROCEEDING**
	_______________, Plaintiff	Case No. * ________
	v.	Chapter __________
	_______________, Defendant	
To:	_______________	Adv. Proc. No. * ________

☐ YOU ARE COMMANDED to appear in the United States Bankruptcy Court at the place, date, and time specified below to testify in the above adversary proceeding.

PLACE OF TESTIMONY	COURTROOM
	DATE AND TIME

☐ YOU ARE COMMANDED to appear at the place, date, and time specified below to testify at the taking of a deposition in the above adversary proceeding.

PLACE OF DEPOSITION	DATE AND TIME

☐ YOU ARE COMMANDED to produce and permit inspection and copying of the following documents or objects at the place, date, and time specified below (list documents or objects):

PLACE	DATE AND TIME

☐ YOU ARE COMMANDED to permit inspection of the following premises at the date and time specified below.

PREMISES	DATE AND TIME

Any organization not a party to this adversary proceeding that is subpoenaed for the taking of a deposition shall designate one or more officers, directors, or managing agents, or other persons who consent to testify on its behalf, and may set forth, for each person designated, the matters on which the person will testify. Rule 30(b)(6), Federal Rules of Civil Procedure, made applicable in adversary proceedings by Rule 7030, Federal Rules of Bankruptcy Procedure.

ISSUING OFFICER SIGNATURE AND TITLE (INDICATE IF ATTORNEY FOR PLAINTIFF OR DEFENDANT)	DATE
ISSUING OFFICER'S NAME, ADDRESS, AND PHONE NUMBER	

* If the bankruptcy case or the adversary proceeding is pending in a district other than the district in which the subpoena is issued, state the district under the case number or adversary proceeding number.

Form 255—Subpoena in an Adversary Proceeding (12/06)

PROOF OF SERVICE

	DATE	PLACE
SERVED		

SERVED ON (PRINT NAME) MANNER OF SERVICE

SERVED BY (PRINT NAME) TITLE

DECLARATION OF SERVER

I declare under penalty of perjury under the laws of the United States of America that the foregoing information contained in the Proof of Service is true and correct.

Executed on ________________ ________________________

DATE SIGNATURE OF SERVER

____

ADDRESS OF SERVER

____

Rule 45, Federal Rules of Civil Procedure, Subdivisions (c), (d), and (e), as amended on December 1, 2006, made applicable in cases under the Bankruptcy Code by Rule 9016, Federal Rules of Bankruptcy Procedure:

(c) PROTECTION OF PERSONS SUBJECT TO SUBPOENAS.

(1) A party or an attorney responsible for the issuance and service of a subpoena shall take reasonable steps to avoid imposing undue burden or expense on a person subject to that subpoena. The court on behalf of which the subpoena was issued shall enforce this duty and impose upon the party or attorney in breach of this duty an appropriate sanction, which may include, but is not limited to, lost earnings and a reasonable attorney's fee.

(2)(A) A person commanded to produce and permit inspection, copying, testing, or sampling of designated electronically stored information, books, papers, documents or tangible things, or inspection of premises need not appear in person at the place of production or inspection unless commanded to appear for deposition, hearing or trial.

(B) Subject to paragraph (d)(2) of this rule, a person commanded to produce and permit inspection, copying, testing, or sampling may, within 14 days after service of the subpoena or before the time specified for compliance if such time is less than 14 days after service, serve upon the party or attorney designated in the subpoena written objection to producing any or all of the designated materials or inspection of the premises—or to producing electronically stored information in the form or forms requested. If objection is made, the party serving the subpoena shall not be entitled to inspect, copy, test, or sample the materials or inspect the premises except pursuant to an order of the court by which the subpoena was issued. If objection has been made, the party serving the subpoena may, upon notice to the person commanded to produce, move at any time for an order to compel the production, inspection, copying, testing, or sampling. Such an order to compel shall protect any person who is not a party or an officer of a party from significant expense resulting from the inspection, copying, testing, or sampling commanded.

(3)(A) On timely motion, the court by which a subpoena was issued shall quash or modify the subpoena if it

(i) fails to allow reasonable time for compliance;

(ii) requires a person who is not a party or an officer of a party to travel to a place more than 100 miles from the place where that person resides, is employed or regularly transacts business in person, except that, subject to the provisions of clause (c)(3)(B)(iii) of this rule, such a person may in order to attend trial be commanded to travel from any such place within the state in which the trial is held;

(iii) requires disclosure of privileged or other protected matter and no exception or waiver applies; or

(iv) subjects a person to undue burden.

(B) If a subpoena

(i) requires disclosure of a trade secret or other confidential research, development, or commercial information, or

(ii) requires disclosure of an unretained expert's opinion or information not describing specific events or occurrences in dispute and resulting from the expert's study made not at the request of any party, or

(iii) requires a person who is not a party or an officer of a party to incur substantial expense to travel more than 100 miles to attend trial, the court may, to protect a person subject to or affected by the subpoena, quash or modify the subpoena or, if the party in whose behalf the subpoena is issued shows a substantial need for the testimony or material that cannot be otherwise met without undue hardship and assures that the person to whom the subpoena is addressed will be reasonably compensated, the court may order appearance or production only upon specified conditions.

(d) DUTIES IN RESPONDING TO SUBPOENA.

(1)(A) A person responding to a subpoena to produce documents shall produce them as they are kept in the usual course of business or shall organize and label them to correspond with the categories in the demand.

(B) If a subpoena does not specify the form or forms for producing electronically stored information, a person responding to a subpoena must produce the information in a form or forms in which the person ordinarily maintains it or in a form or forms that are reasonably usable.

(C) A person responding to a subpoena need not produce the same electronically stored information in more than one form.

(D) A person responding to a subpoena need not provide discovery of electronically stored information from sources that the person identifies as not reasonably accessible because of undue burden or cost. On motion to compel discovery or to quash, the person from whom discovery is sought must show that the information sought is not reasonably accessible because of undue burden or cost. If that showing is made, the court may nonetheless order discovery from such sources if the requesting party shows good cause, considering the limitations of Rule 26(b)(2)(C). The court may specify conditions for the discovery.

(2)(A) When information subject to a subpoena is withheld on a claim that it is privileged or subject to protection as trial-preparation materials, the claim shall be made expressly and shall be supported by a description of the nature of the documents, communications, or things not produced that is sufficient to enable the demanding party to contest the claim.

(B) If information is produced in response to a subpoena that is subject to a claim of privilege or of protection as trial-preparation material, the person making the claim may notify any party that received the information of the claim and the basis for it. After being notified, a party must promptly return, sequester, or destroy the specified information and any copies it has and may not use or disclose the information until the claim is resolved. A receiving party may promptly present the information to the court under seal for a determination of the claim. If the receiving party disclosed the information before being notified, it must take reasonable steps to retrieve it. The person who produced the information must preserve the information until the claim is resolved.

(e) CONTEMPT. Failure of any person without adequate excuse to obey a subpoena served upon that person may be deemed a contempt of the court from which the subpoena issued. An adequate cause for failure to obey exists when a subpoena purports to require a nonparty to attend or produce at a place not within the limits provided by clause (ii) of subparagraph (c)(3)(A).

Form No. B 256
SUBPOENA IN A CASE UNDER THE BANKRUPTCY CODE

Form 256—Subpoena in a Case under the Bankruptcy Code (12/06)

United States Bankruptcy Court

______ District of ______

In re ______________, Debtor

SUBPOENA IN A CASE UNDER THE BANKRUPTCY CODE

Case No. * ______________

To: ______________

Chapter ______________

☐ YOU ARE COMMANDED to appear in the United States Bankruptcy Court at the place, date, and time specified below to testify in the above case.

PLACE OF TESTIMONY	COURTROOM
	DATE AND TIME

☐ YOU ARE COMMANDED to appear at the place, date, and time specified below to testify at the taking of a deposition in the above case.

PLACE OF DEPOSITION	DATE AND TIME

☐ YOU ARE COMMANDED to produce and permit inspection and copying of the following documents or objects at the place, date, and time specified below (list documents or objects):

PLACE	DATE AND TIME

☐ YOU ARE COMMANDED to permit inspection of the following premises at the date and time specified below.

PREMISES	DATE AND TIME

Any organization not a party to this proceeding that is subpoenaed for the taking of a deposition shall designate one or more officers, directors, or managing agents, or other persons who consent to testify on its behalf, and may set forth, for each person designated, the matters on which the person will testify. Rule 30(b)(6), Federal Rules of Civil Procedure, made applicable in bankruptcy cases and proceedings by Rules 1018, 7030, and 9014, Federal Rules of Bankruptcy Procedure.

ISSUING OFFICER SIGNATURE AND TITLE	DATE

ISSUING OFFICER'S NAME, ADDRESS,
AND PHONE NUMBER

* If the bankruptcy case is pending in a district other than the district in which the subpoena is issued, state the district under the case number.

Form 256—Subpoena in a Case under the Bankruptcy Code (12/06)

PROOF OF SERVICE

	DATE	PLACE
SERVED		

SERVED ON (PRINT NAME) MANNER OF SERVICE

SERVED BY (PRINT NAME) TITLE

DECLARATION OF SERVER

I declare under penalty of perjury under the laws of the United States of America that the foregoing information contained in the Proof of Service is true and correct.

Executed on ______________ ______________________
DATE SIGNATURE OF SERVER

____
ADDRESS OF SERVER

Rule 45, Federal Rules of Civil Procedure, Subdivisions (c), (d), and (e), as amended on December 1, 2006, made applicable in cases under the Bankruptcy Code by Rule 9016, Federal Rules of Bankruptcy Procedure:

(c) PROTECTION OF PERSONS SUBJECT TO SUBPOENAS.

(1) A party or an attorney responsible for the issuance and service of a subpoena shall take reasonable steps to avoid imposing undue burden or expense on a person subject to that subpoena. The court on behalf of which the subpoena was issued shall enforce this duty and impose upon the party or attorney in breach of this duty an appropriate sanction, which may include, but is not limited to, lost earnings and a reasonable attorney's fee.

(2)(A) A person commanded to produce and permit inspection, copying, testing, or sampling of designated electronically stored information, books, papers, documents or tangible things, or inspection of premises need not appear in person at the place of production or inspection unless commanded to appear for deposition, hearing or trial.

(B) Subject to paragraph (d)(2) of this rule, a person commanded to produce and permit inspection, copying, testing, or sampling may, within 14 days after service of the subpoena or before the time specified for compliance if such time is less than 14 days after service, serve upon the party or attorney designated in the subpoena written objection to producing any or all of the designated materials or inspection of the premises—or to producing electronically stored information in the form or forms requested. If objection is made, the party serving the subpoena shall not be entitled to inspect, copy, test, or sample the materials or inspect the premises except pursuant to an order of the court by which the subpoena was issued. If objection has been made, the party serving the subpoena may, upon notice to the person commanded to produce, move at any time for an order to compel the production, inspection, copying, testing, or sampling. Such an order to compel shall protect any person who is not a party or an officer of a party from significant expense resulting from the inspection, copying, testing, or sampling commanded.

(3)(A) On timely motion, the court by which a subpoena was issued shall quash or modify the subpoena if it

(i) fails to allow reasonable time for compliance;

(ii) requires a person who is not a party or an officer of a party to travel to a place more than 100 miles from the place where that person resides, is employed or regularly transacts business in person, except that, subject to the provisions of clause (c)(3)(B)(iii) of this rule, such a person may in order to attend trial be commanded to travel from any such place within the state in which the trial is held;

(iii) requires disclosure of privileged or other protected matter and no exception or waiver applies; or

(iv) subjects a person to undue burden.

(B) If a subpoena

(i) requires disclosure of a trade secret or other confidential research, development, or commercial information, or

(ii) requires disclosure of an unretained expert's opinion or information not describing specific events or occurrences in dispute and resulting from the expert's study made not at the request of any party, or

(iii) requires a person who is not a party or an officer of a party to incur substantial expense to travel more than 100 miles to attend trial, the court may, to protect a person subject to or affected by the subpoena, quash or modify the subpoena or, if the party in whose behalf the subpoena is issued shows a substantial need for the testimony or material that cannot be otherwise met without undue hardship and assures that the person to whom the subpoena is addressed will be reasonably compensated, the court may order appearance or production only upon specified conditions.

(d) DUTIES IN RESPONDING TO SUBPOENA.

(1)(A) A person responding to a subpoena to produce documents shall produce them as they are kept in the usual course of business or shall organize and label them to correspond with the categories in the demand.

(B) If a subpoena does not specify the form or forms for producing electronically stored information, a person responding to a subpoena must produce the information in a form or forms in which the person ordinarily maintains it or in a form or forms that are reasonably usable.

(C) A person responding to a subpoena need not produce the same electronically stored information in more than one form.

(D) A person responding to a subpoena need not provide discovery of electronically stored information from sources that the person identifies as not reasonably accessible because of undue burden or cost. On motion to compel discovery or to quash, the person from whom discovery is sought must show that the information sought is not reasonably accessible because of undue burden or cost. If that showing is made, the court may nonetheless order discovery from such sources if the requesting party shows good cause, considering the limitations of Rule 26(b)(2)(C). The court may specify conditions for the discovery.

(2)(A) When information subject to a subpoena is withheld on a claim that it is privileged or subject to protection as trial-preparation materials, the claim shall be made expressly and shall be supported by a description of the nature of the documents, communications, or things not produced that is sufficient to enable the demanding party to contest the claim.

(B) If information is produced in response to a subpoena that is subject to a claim of privilege or of protection as trial-preparation material, the person making the claim may notify any party that received the information of the claim and the basis for it. After being notified, a party must promptly return, sequester, or destroy the specified information and any copies it has and may not use or disclose the information until the claim is resolved. A receiving party may promptly present the information to the court under seal for a determination of the claim. If the receiving party disclosed the information before being notified, it must take reasonable steps to retrieve it. The person who produced the information must preserve the information until the claim is resolved.

(e) CONTEMPT. Failure of any person without adequate excuse to obey a subpoena served upon that person may be deemed a contempt of the court from which the subpoena issued. An adequate cause for failure to obey exists when a subpoena purports to require a nonparty to attend or produce at a place not within the limits provided by clause (ii) of subparagraph (c)(3)(A).

Form No. B 260
ENTRY OF DEFAULT

B 260
(1/96)

United States Bankruptcy Court

______ District of ______

In re ________________________________, Debtor	)	Case No. ____________
	)	Chapter ____________
________________________________ Plaintiff	)	
v.	)	
________________________________, Defendant	)	Adv. Proc. No. ____________

ENTRY OF DEFAULT

It appears from the record that the following defendant failed to plead or otherwise defend in this case as required by law.

Name:

Therefore, default is entered against the defendant as authorized by Federal Rule of Bankruptcy Procedure 7055.

____
Clerk of the Bankruptcy Court

________________________ By: ________________________
Date Deputy Clerk

(Added Sept. 1988.)

Form No. B 261A
JUDGMENT BY DEFAULT

B 261A
(8/96)

United States Bankruptcy Court

_______ District Of _______

In re ______________________, Debtor	)	Case No. ______________
	)	Chapter ______________
______________________, Plaintiff	)	
v.	)	
______________________, Defendant	)	Adv. Proc. No. ______________

JUDGMENT BY DEFAULT

Default was entered against defendant ______________________________ (name) on ______________ (date). The plaintiff has requested entry of judgment by default and has filed an affidavit of the amount due and stating that this defendant is not in the military service.

Furthermore, it appears from the record that this defendant is not an infant or incompetent person. Therefore, pursuant to Fed. R. Civ. P. 55(b)(1), as incorporated by Fed. R. Bankr. P. 7055, judgment is entered against this defendant in favor of the plaintiff as follows:

______________________ (Date)

______________________________ (Clerk of the Bankruptcy Court)

Form No. B 261B
JUDGMENT BY DEFAULT

B 261B
(8/96)

United States Bankruptcy Court

______ District Of ______

In re ______________________________, Debtor	))	Case No. ______________
	))	Chapter ______________
______________________________, Plaintiff	))	
v.	))	
______________________________, Defendant	))	Adv. Proc. No. __________

JUDGMENT BY DEFAULT

Default was entered against defendant ______________________________
(name)
on ______________. Therefore, on motion of the plaintiff, judgment is entered
(date)
against that defendant in favor of the plaintiff as follows.

IT IS ORDERED THAT:

______________________ (Date)

______________________________ (Bankruptcy Judge)

Form No. B 262
NOTICE OF ENTRY OF JUDGMENT

B 262
(1/88)

United States Bankruptcy Court

______ District of ______

In re ______________________________,	)	
Debtor	)	Case No. ______________
	)	
______________________________,	)	Chapter ______________
Plaintiff	)	
	)	
	)	
	)	
v.	)	
	)	
______________________________,	)	Adv. Proc. No. __________
Defendant	)	

NOTICE OF ENTRY OF JUDGMENT

On ____________, the following order (judgment) was entered on the docket:
(date)

I certify that on this date a copy of this notice was mailed to the following:

____
Clerk of the Bankruptcy Court

______________________________ By: ______________________________
Date Deputy Clerk

(Added Sept. 1988.)

Form No. B 263
BILL OF COSTS

B 263
(9/94)

United States Bankruptcy Court

________ District of ________

In re ____________________,) Case No. ________
Debtor)
) Chapter ________
____________________,)
Plaintiff)
)
v.)
)
____________________,) Adv. Proc. No. ________
Defendant)

BILL OF COSTS

Notice is given that the following Bill of Costs will be presented to the bankruptcy clerk at the following place and time:

Address	Room
	Date and Time

Judgment was entered in the above entitled action on ________ (date)

against ________.

The clerk of the bankruptcy court is requested to tax the following as costs:

Fees of the clerk .... $________
Fees for service of summons and complaint .... $________
Fees of the court reporter for any and all part of the transcript necessarily obtained for use in the case .... $________
Fees and disbursements for printing .... $________
Fees for witnesses (itemized on reverse) .... $________
Fees for exemplifications and copies of papers necessarily obtained for use in this case .... $________
Docket fees under 28 U.S.C. § 1923 .... $________
Costs incident to taking of depositions .... $________
Costs as shown on Mandate of appellate court .... $________
Other costs [Please itemize] .... $________
$________
$________
Total $________

DECLARATION

I, attorney for ____________________ *(name of party)* declare under penalties of perjury that the foregoing costs are correct and were necessarily incurred in this action, that the services for which fees have been charged were actually and necessarily performed, and that a copy of this Bill of Costs was mailed this day with postage fully prepaid to:

____

Name and Address of Judgment Debtor

____

______________________ ______________________

Date *Signature of Attorney*

COSTS ARE TAXED IN THE FOLLOWING AMOUNT AND INCLUDED IN THE JUDGMENT: $______________

____

Clerk of the Bankruptcy Court

______________________ By: ______________________

Date *Deputy Clerk*

B 263
(9/94)

WITNESS FEES (computation, cf. 28 U.S.C. 1821 for statutory fees)

NAME AND RESIDENCE	ATTENDANCE Days	ATTENDANCE Total Cost	SUBSISTENCE Days	SUBSISTENCE Total Cost	MILEAGE Miles	MILEAGE Total Cost	Total Cost Each Witness
						TOTAL	

NOTICE

Section 1924, Title 28, U.S. Code provides:

"Before any bill of costs is taxed, the party claiming any item of cost or disbursement shall attach thereto an affidavit, made by himself or by his duly authorized attorney or agent having knowledge of the facts, that such item is correct and has been necessarily incurred in the case and that the services for which fees have been charged were actually and necessarily performed."

Section 1920 of Title 28 reads in part as follows:

"A bill of costs shall be filed in the case and, upon allowance, included in the judgment or decree."

Section 1920 of Title 28 reads in part as follows:

Rule 7054(b)

"COSTS. The court may allow costs to the prevailing party except when a statute of the United States or these rules otherwise provides. Costs against the United States, its officers and agencies shall be imposed only to the extent permitted by law. Costs may be taxed by the clerk on one day's notice; on motion served within five days thereafter, the action of the clerk may be reviewed by the court."

Rule 9006(f)

"ADDITIONAL TIME AFTER SERVICE BY MAIL. When there is a right or requirement to do some act or undertake some proceedings within a prescribed period after service of a notice or other paper and the notice or paper other than process is served by mail, three days shall be added to the prescribed period."

Rule 9021, incorporating Federal Rule of Civil Procedure 58

"Entry of the judgment shall not be delayed . . . in order to tax costs."

(Added Sept. 1988.)

Form No. B 264
WRIT OF EXECUTION TO THE UNITED STATES MARSHAL

B 264
(1/96)
United States Bankruptcy Court

__________ **District of** __________

In re ______________________, Debtor	Case No. __________
	Chapter __________
______________________, Plaintiff	
v.	
______________________, Defendant	Adv. Proc. No. __________

WRIT OF EXECUTION TO THE UNITED STATES MARSHAL

Name and Address of Judgment Creditor	Amount of Judgment: $__________
vs.	Other Costs: $__________
Name and Address of Judgment Debtor	Date of Entry of Judgment: __________

TO THE UNITED STATES MARSHAL FOR THE __________ DISTRICT OF __________:

You are directed to levy upon the property of the above named judgment debtor to satisfy a money judgment in accordance with the attached instructions.

TO THE JUDGMENT DEBTOR:

You are notified that federal and state exemptions may be available to you and that you have a right to seek a court order releasing as exempt any property specified in the marshal's schedule from the levy.

__________________ Date

__________________ Clerk of the Bankruptcy Court

(Added Sept. 1988.)

Form No. B 265
CERTIFICATION OF JUDGMENT FOR REGISTRATION IN ANOTHER DISTRICT

B 265
(8/96)
United States Bankruptcy Court

_________ **District of** _________

In re ______________________,) Case No. __________
Debtor)
) Chapter __________
______________________,)
Plaintiff)
)
v.)
)
______________________,) Adv. Proc. No. __________
Defendant)

CERTIFICATION OF JUDGMENT FOR REGISTRATION IN ANOTHER DISTRICT

I, clerk of the United States Bankruptcy Court, do certify that the attached judgment is a true and correct copy of the original judgment entered in this proceeding on ______________________
(date)
as it appears in the records of this court, and that:

☐ No notice of appeal from this judgment has been filed, and no motion of the kind set forth in Federal Rule of Civil Procedure 60, as made applicable by Federal Rule of Bankruptcy Procedure 9024, has been filed.

☐ No notice of appeal from this judgment has been filed, and any motions of the kind set forth in Federal Rule of Civil Procedure 60, as made applicable by Federal Rule of Bankruptcy Procedure 9024, have been disposed of, the latest order disposing of such a motion having been entered on __________.
(date)

☐ An appeal was taken from this judgment, and the judgment was affirmed by mandate of the ______________________
(name of court)
issued on __________.
(date)

☐ An appeal was taken from this judgment, and the appeal was dismissed by order entered on __________.
(date)

____
Clerk of the Bankruptcy Court

______________________ By: ______________________
Date Deputy Clerk

(Added Sept. 1988.)

Form No. B 270

NOTICE OF FILING OF FINAL REPORT OF TRUSTEE, OF HEARING ON APPLICATIONS FOR COMPENSATION [AND OF HEARING ON ABANDONMENT OF PROPERTY BY THE TRUSTEE]

B270 (Form 270) (08/07)

United States Bankruptcy Court

______ District of ______

In re ____________________________________ Case No. __________
Debtor*

Address: ____________________________________ Chapter __________
____

Last four digits of Social-Security or Individual Taxpayer-Identification (ITIN) No(s)., (if any): _ Employer Tax-Identification (EIN) No(s). (if any): ________________________________
____

NOTICE OF FILING OF FINAL REPORTS OF TRUSTEE, OF HEARING ON APPLICATIONS FOR COMPENSATION [AND OF HEARING ON ABANDONMENT OF PROPERTY BY THE TRUSTEE]

TO THE CREDITORS:

1. NOTICE IS GIVEN that the final report of the trustee in this case has been filed and a hearing will be held by the court at the following place and time.

Address	Room
	Date and Time

2. The hearing will be held for the purpose of examining the final report of the trustee, acting on applications for compensation, and transacting such other business as may properly come before the court. ATTENDANCE BY THE DEBTOR AND THE CREDITORS IS WELCOMED BUT IS NOT REQUIRED.

3. The following applications for compensation have been filed:

Applicants	Commissions or Fees	Expenses
______________________ Trustee	$__________	$__________
______________________ Attorney for Trustee	$__________	$__________
______________________	$__________	$__________
______________________	$__________	$__________
______________________	$__________	$__________
______________________	$__________	$__________

(Continued on reverse side)

** Set forth all names, including trade names, used by the debtor(s) within the last 8 years. For joint debtors, set forth the last four digits of both social-security numbers or individual taxpayer-identification numbers.*

B270 (Form 270) (08/07)–Cont., page 2

4. The trustee's account shows total
receipt of $____________
and total disbursements of $____________
for a balance on hand of $____________

5. In addition to the commissions and fees that may be allowed by the court, liens and priority claims which must be paid in advance of general creditors have been allowed in the total amount of

$____________

General unsecured claims have been allowed in the amount of $____________

6. ☐ The debtor has been discharged.
☐ The debtor has not been discharged.

7. ☐ The trustee's application to abandon the following property will be heard and acted upon.

____
Clerk of the Bankruptcy Court

By: ________________________
Deputy Clerk

Date: ________________________

Form No. B 271
FINAL DECREE

B271 (8/06)

United States Bankruptcy Court

__________ District of __________

In re ______________________________, Case No. ________
(Debtor(s)

Last four digits of Social Security No(s).:
Employer's Tax Identification (EID) No(s).[if any]:

FINAL DECREE

The estate of the above named debtor has been fully administered.

☐ The deposit required by the plan has been distributed.

IT IS ORDERED THAT:

☐ ____
(name of trustee)
is discharged as trustee of the estate of the above-named debtor;

☐ the chapter ____ case of the above-named debtor is closed; and

☐ [other provisions as needed]

Date:________________ ____________________________
United States Bankruptcy Judge

Set forth all names, including trade names, used by the debtor within the last 8 years. For joint debtors set forth both social security numbers.

B 280
(10/05)

Form No. B 280

DISCLOSURE OF COMPENSATION OF BANKRUPTCY PETITION PREPARER

United States Bankruptcy Court

________ District Of ________

In re __________________________
Debtor

Case No. ________

Chapter ________

DISCLOSURE OF COMPENSATION OF BANKRUPTCY PETITION PREPARER

[Must be filed with the petition if a bankruptcy petition preparer prepares the petition. 11 U.S.C. § 110(h)(2).]

1. Under 11 U.S.C. § 110(h), I declare under penalty of perjury that I am not an attorney or employee of an attorney, that I prepared or caused to be prepared one or more documents for filing by the above-named debtor(s) in connection with this bankruptcy case, and that compensation paid to me within one year before the filing of the bankruptcy petition, or agreed to be paid to me, for services rendered on behalf of the debtor(s) in contemplation of or in connection with the bankruptcy case is as follows:

For document preparation services I have agreed to accept .... $________
Prior to the filing of this statement I have received .... $________
Balance Due .... $________

2. I have prepared or caused to be prepared the following documents (itemize):

and provided the following services (itemize):

3. The source of the compensation paid to me was:

☐ Debtor ☐ Other (specify)

4. The source of compensation to be paid to me is:

☐ Debtor ☐ Other (specify)

5. The foregoing is a complete statement of any agreement or arrangement for payment to me for preparation of the petition filed by the debtor(s) in this bankruptcy case.

6. To my knowledge no other person has prepared for compensation a document for filing in connection with this bankruptcy case except as listed below:

NAME SOCIAL SECURITY NUMBER

x____________________ ____________________ ________
Signature — Social Security number of bankruptcy petition preparer (If the bankruptcy petition preparer is not an individual, state the Social Security number of the officer, principal, responsible person or partner of the bankruptcy petition preparer.) (Required by 11 U.S.C. § 110.) — Date

____
Printed name and title, if any, of Bankruptcy Petition Preparer

Address: ____________________

____

....

A bankruptcy petition preparer's failure to comply with the provisions of title 11 and the Federal Rules of Bankruptcy Procedure may result in fines or imprisonment or both. 11 U.S.C. § 110; 18 U.S.C. § 156.

(Added Dec. 1994 and amended Oct. 17, 2005.)

Form No. B 281
APPEARANCE OF CHILD SUPPORT CREDITOR OR REPRESENTATIVE

B281
(08/06)

UNITED STATES BANKRUPTCY COURT

_______ DISTRICT OF ______

In re ___________________________, Case No. __________
Debtor(s)

APPEARANCE OF CHILD SUPPORT CREDITOR * OR REPRESENTATIVE

I certify under penalty of perjury that I am a child support creditor * of the above-named debtor, or the authorized representative of such child support creditor, with respect to the child support obligation which is set out below.

Name:
Organization:
Address:

Telephone Number:

____________________ X ______________________________
Date Child Support Creditor * or Authorized Representative

Summary of Child Support Obligation

Amount in arrears:

$ ____________________________

Amount currently due per week or per month: on a continuing basis:

$ ____________________________
(per week) (per month)

If Child Support has been assigned:

Amount of Support which is owed under assignments:

$ __________________

Amount owed primary child support creditor (balance not assigned):

$ __________________

Attach an itemized statement of account. Do not disclose the name of a minor child. See 11 U.S.C. § 112. If a social security number or a taxpayer identification number is included, set out only the last four digits of the number. Judicial Conference Policy(09/01).

(Added Dec. 1994, and amended Aug. 2006.)

* Child support creditor includes both creditor to whom the debtor has a primary obligation to pay child support as well as any entity to whom such support has been assigned, if pursuant to Section 402(a)(26) of the Social Security Act or if such debt has been assigned to the Federal Government or to any State or political subdivision of a State.

B 283 (12/08)

Form No. B 283
United States Bankruptcy Court
_________ District Of _________

In re ______________________________ Case No. _________
Debtor

CHAPTER 13 DEBTOR'S CERTIFICATIONS REGARDING DOMESTIC SUPPORT OBLIGATIONS AND SECTION 522(q)

Part I. Certification Regarding Domestic Support Obligations (check no more than one)

Pursuant to 11 U.S.C. Section 1328(a), I certify that:

☐ I owed no domestic support obligation when I filed my bankruptcy petition, and I have not been required to pay any such obligation since then.

☐ I am or have been required to pay a domestic support obligation. I have paid all such amounts that my chapter 13 plan required me to pay. I have also paid all such amounts that became due between the filing of my bankruptcy petition and today.

Part II. If you checked the second box, you must provide the information below.

My current address: ______________________________

My current employer and my employer's address: ______________________________

____

Part III. Certification Regarding Section 522(q) (check no more than one)

Pursuant to 11 U.S.C. Section 1328(h), I certify that:

☐ I have not claimed an exemption pursuant to § 522(b)(3) and state or local law (1) in property that I or a dependent of mine uses as a residence, claims as a homestead, or acquired as a burial plot, as specified in § 522(p)(1), and (2) that exceeds $136,875* in value in the aggregate.

☐ I have claimed an exemption in property pursuant to § 522(b)(3) and state or local law (1) that I or a dependent of mine uses as a residence, claims as a homestead, or acquired as a burial plot, as specified in § 522(p)(1), and (2) that exceeds $136,875* in value in the aggregate.

**Amounts are subject to adjustment on 4/1/10 and every 3 years thereafter with respect to cases commenced on or after the date of adjustment.*

Part IV. Debtor's Signature

I certify under penalty of perjury that the information provided in these certifications is true and correct to the best of my knowledge and belief.

Executed on ______________ ______________________________
Date Debtor

(Added Dec. 2008.)

FEDERAL
RULES OF CIVIL PROCEDURE
FOR THE
UNITED STATES DISTRICT COURTS

Amendments received to December 1, 2008

RULES OF CIVIL PROCEDURE

TIME TABLE FOR LAWYERS IN FEDERAL CIVIL CASES

Amended to December 1, 2007

This Time Table, prepared by the Publisher's editorial staff as a guide to the user, indicates the time for each of the steps of a civil action as provided by the Federal Rules of Civil Procedure and the Federal Rules of Appellate Procedure. Certain steps governed by statute and by the Rules of the Supreme Court are also listed. *The user should always consult the actual text of the rule or statute.* Usually the periods permitted for each of these steps may be enlarged by the court in its discretion. In some cases no enlargement is permitted. Citations to supporting authority are in the form "Civ.R. ———" for the Rules of Civil Procedure; "App.R. ———" for the Rules of Appellate Procedure; "28 U.S.C.A. § ———" for statutes; and "Supreme Court Rule ———".

ADMISSIONS

Requests for admissions, service of	On any other party a written request, for purposes of the pending action only. Civ.R. 36(a)(1).
Response to requested admissions	Written answers or objections must be served within 30 days after service of the request, or a shorter or longer time as may be stipulated to under Civ.R. 29 or be ordered by the court. Civ.R. 36(a).
ALTERNATE jurors	The institution of the alternate juror has been abolished. Civ.R. 47, 1991 Advisory Committee note, subd. (b).
ANSWER	**See, also, "Responsive Pleadings", this table.**
To complaint	Service within 20 days after being served with summons and complaint unless another time is specified by Civ.R. 12 or a federal statute. Civ.R. 12(a)(1)(A)(i). Service within 60 days after date request is sent for waiver of service of summons or within 90 days after that date if defendant was addressed outside any judicial district of the United States unless another time is specified by Civ.R. 12 or a federal statute. Civ.R. 12(a)(1)(A)(ii). Service within 60 days after service on the United States attorney, in action against the United States, a United States agency, or a United States officer or employee sued only in an official capacity. Civ.R. 12(a)(2). Service within 60 days after service on the officer or employee or service on the United States attorney, whichever is later, in an action against a United States officer or employee sued in an indi-

ANSWER	**See, also, "Responsive Pleadings", this table.**
	vidual capacity in connection with duties performed on the United States' behalf. Civ.R. 12(a)(3).
	The time for responsive pleading is altered by service of Civ.R. 12 motions. See "Responsive Pleadings", this table.
To counterclaim or cross-claim	
	Service within 20 days after being served with the pleading stating the counterclaim or cross-claim. Civ.R. 12(a)(1)(B).
	60 days for United States, United States agency, or United States officer or employee. Civ.R. 12(a)(2), (3).
	The time for responsive pleading is altered by service of Civ.R. 12(a) motions, see "Responsive Pleadings", this table.
To notice of condemnation	Service within 20 days after service of notice. Civ.R. 71A(e).
Removed actions	20 days after receipt of copy of initial pleading stating the claim for relief, or 20 days after service of summons for an initial pleading on file at time of service, or 5 days after filing of notice of removal, whichever is longest. Civ.R. 81(c).
Proceedings to cancel certificates of citizenship under 8 U.S.C.A. § 1451	60 days after service of petition. Civ.R. 81(a)(3).
ANSWERS (or objections) to interrogatories to party	
	Service within 30 days after service of the interrogatories. A shorter or longer time may be stipulated to under Civ.R. 29 or be ordered by the court. Civ.R. 33(b)(2).
APPEAL	
As of right	30 days from entry of judgment or order. App.R. 4(a)(1)(A).
	60 days in cases in which the United States or its officers, agencies are parties. App.R. 4(a)(1)(B).
	60 days in cases in which the United States or its officers, agencies are parties. App.R. 4(a)(1)(B).
	Entry of a judgment or order in the civil docket under Civ.R. 79(a) is entry for purposes of App.R. 4, unless Civ.R. 58(a)(1) requires a separate document, in which case entry occurs when the judgment or order is entered under Civ.R. 79(a) and either the judgment or order is set forth on a separate document, or 150 days have run from entry of the judgment or order in the civil docket. App.R. 4(a)(7)(A).
	If any party files a timely motion of a type specified below, time for appeal for all parties runs from

APPEAL

entry of order disposing of last such motion outstanding. App.R. 4(a)(4).

(1) motion for judgment under Civ.R. 50(b);
(2) Motion under Civ.R. 52(b) to amend or make additional findings of fact, whether or not granting the motion would alter the judgement;
(3) motion under Civ.R. 59 to alter or amend judgment;
(4) Motion under Civ.R. 54 for attorney's fees if time to appeal extended under Civ.R. 58.
(5) Motion under Civ.R. 59 for new trial.
(6) Motion for relief under Civ.R. 60 if motion filed no later than 10 days after entry of judgement.

App.R. 4(a)(4).

District court may extend for excusable neglect or good cause upon motion filed not later than 30 days after expiration of time prescribed by App.R. 4(a); no extension to exceed 30 days past prescribed time or 10 days from entry of order granting motion, whichever occurs later. App.R. 4(a)(5).

By other parties, within 14 days of filing of first notice of appeal, or within the time otherwise prescribed by App.R. 4(a), whichever last expires. App.R. 4(a)(3).

By permission — Petition filed with circuit clerk with proof of service within time specified by statute or rule authorizing the appeal, or if no such time is specified, within the time provided by App.R. 4(a) for filing a notice of appeal. App.R. 5(a).

Bankruptcy — If a motion for rehearing under Bankruptcy Rule 8015 is filed in a district court or in a bankruptcy appellate panel, time for appeal to court of appeals runs from entry of order disposing of motion. App.R. 6(b)(2)(A).

Class actions — Within 10 days after entry of order of district court granting or denying class action certification. Civ.R. 23(f).

Inmates — A notice of appeal is timely filed if deposited in the institution's internal mail system on or before the last day for filing. App.R. 4(c), 25(a).

Representation statement — Within 10 days after filing notice of appeal unless court of appeals designates another time, attorney who filed notice shall file with the circuit clerk a statement naming each party represented on appeal by that attorney. App.R. 12(b).

Entry of judgment or order, notice of — Lack of notice of entry by clerk does not affect time to appeal or relieve or authorize court to relieve party for failure to appeal within time allowed, except as allowed by App.R. 4(a). Civ.R. 77(d).

Record (Appellant) — Within 10 days after filing notice of appeal or entry of an order disposing of last timely remaining motion specified in App.R. 4(a)(4)(A), whichever is

APPEAL

	later: Appellant to place written order for transcript and file copy of order with clerk; if none to be ordered, file a certificate to that effect; unless entire transcript to be included, file a statement of issues and serve appellee a copy of order or certificate and of statement. App.R. 10(b).
Record (Appellee)	Within 10 days after service of appellant's order or certificate and statement, appellee to file and serve on appellant a designation of additional parts of transcript to be included. Unless within 10 days after designation appellant has ordered such parts and so notified appellee, appellee may within following 10 days either order the parts or move in district court for order requiring appellant to do so. App.R. 10(b).
Record (costs)	At time of ordering, party to make satisfactory arrangements with reporter for payment of cost of transcript. App.R. 10(b)(4).
Record (Reporter)	If transcript cannot be completed within 30 days of receipt of order, reporter shall request extension of time from circuit clerk. App.R. 11(b).
Stay of proceedings to enforce judgment	Effective when supersedeas bond is approved by court. Civ.R. 62(d).
	Supersedeas bond may be given upon or after filing notice of appeal or after obtaining the order allowing appeal. Civ.R. 62(d).
Briefs	Appellant must serve and file a brief within 40 days after the record is filed. Appellee must serve and file a brief within 30 days after service of the appellant's brief. A reply brief may be filed within 14 days after service of appellee's brief and, except for good cause shown, at least 3 days before argument. A court of appeals may shorten the times allowed for briefs either by local rule for all cases or by order for a particular case. App.R. 31(a).
Transcripts	See "RECORD", ante, this heading.
Tax Court decisions	Review must be obtained by filing a notice of appeal with the Tax Court clerk within 90 days after entry of decision. If a timely notice of appeal is filed by one party, any other party may take an appeal by filing a notice of appeal within 120 days after entry of decision by the Tax Court. If timely motion made to vacate or revise decision, time to file notice of appeal runs from entry of order disposing of motion or entry of new decision, whichever is later. App.R. 13(a).

APPEAL from magistrate judge to district judge under 28 U.S.C.A. § 636(c)(4) and Civ.R. 73(d)

Notice of Appeal	[This Rule provided as follows, prior to its abrogation:] Filed with clerk of district court within 30 days of entry of judgment. Within 60 days if United States or officer or agency thereof is a

APPEAL from magistrate judge to district judge under 28 U.S.C.A. § 636(c)(4) and Civ.R. 73(d)

party. Within 15 days after entry of an interlocutory decision or order. Civ.R. 74(a) [Civ.R. 74 abrogated eff. Dec. 1, 1997].

[This Rule provided as follows, prior to its abrogation:] When timely notice is filed by a party, any other party may file notice within 14 days thereafter or within time otherwise prescribed by Civ.R. 74(a), whichever period last expires. Civ.R. 74(a) [Civ.R. 74 abrogated eff. Dec. 1, 1997].

[This Rule provided as follows, prior to its abrogation:] Upon showing of excusable neglect, time for filing may be extended on motion filed not later than 20 days from expiration of time for filing. Civ.R. 74(a) [Civ.R. 74 abrogated eff. Dec. 1, 1997].

Running of time for filing terminated as to all parties by timely filing of any of the following motions with the magistrate judge by any party, and the full time for appeal from judgment entered commences to run anew from entry of any of the following orders:

(1) granting or denying motion for judgment under Civ.R. 50(b);

(2) granting or denying motion under Civ.R. 52(b) to amend or make additional findings of fact;

(3) granting or denying motion under Civ.R. 59 to alter or amend judgment;

(4) denying motion for new trial under Civ.R. 59. Civ.R. 74(a) [prior to its abrogation] [Civ.R. 74 abrogated eff. Dec. 1, 1997.]

Joint statement of case — Parties could file in lieu of record within 10 days after filing of notice of appeal, under provisions of this rule prior to its abrogation. Civ.R. 75(b)(1) [Civ.R. 75 abrogated eff. Dec. 1, 1997].

Transcript — Within 10 days after filing notice of appeal appellant to make arrangements for production. Unless entire transcript is to be included, description of parts appellant intends to present must be served on the appellee and filed by the appellant within the 10 day period. If appellee deems transcript of other parts to be necessary, designation of additional parts to be included must be served on the appellant and filed within 10 days after service of appellant's statement. Civ.R. 75(b)(2) [Civ.R. 75 abrogated eff. Dec. 1, 1997].

Statement in lieu of transcript — If no record is available for transcription, parties must file a statement of evidence in lieu of transcript within 10 days after filing of notice of appeal. Civ.R. 75(b)(3) [Civ.R. 75 abrogated eff. Dec. 1, 1997].

APPEAL from magistrate judge to district judge under 28 U.S.C.A. § 636(c)(4) and Civ.R. 73(d)	
Briefs	Appellant to serve and file within 20 days after the filing of transcript, statement of case, or statement of evidence. Civ.R. 75(c)(1) [Civ.R. 75 abrogated eff. Dec. 1, 1997].
	Appellee to serve and file within 20 days after service of appellant's brief. Civ.R. 75(c)(2) [Civ.R. 75 abrogated eff. Dec. 1, 1997].
	Appellant may serve and file reply brief within 10 days after service of appellee's brief. Civ.R. 75(c)(3) [Civ.R. 75 abrogated eff. Dec. 1, 1997].
	If appellee files a cross-appeal, appellee may file a reply brief within 10 days after service of the reply brief of the appellant. Civ.R. 75(c)(4) [Civ.R. 75 abrogated eff. Dec. 1, 1997].
Stay of judgments	Decision of district judge stayed for 10 days during which term a party may petition for rehearing. Civ.R. 76(b) [Civ.R. 76 abrogated eff. Dec. 1, 1997].
APPEAL from magistrate judge under 28 U.S.C.A. § 636(c)(3)	Appeal to court of appeals in identical fashion as appeals from other judgments of district courts. App.R. 3.1. [App.R. 3.1 abrogated eff. Dec. 1, 1998].
APPEAL to Supreme Court	
Direct appeals	30 days after entry of interlocutory or final order, decree or judgment holding Act of Congress unconstitutional under circumstances provided by 28 U.S.C.A. §§ 1252, and 1253. 28 U.S.C.A. § 2101(a), as amended by Act May 24, 1949, c. 139, § 106, 63 Stat. 104. [28 U.S.C.A. § 1252 was repealed and 28 U.S.C.A. § 2101(a) was amended by Pub.L. 100–352, §§ 1, 5(b), June 27, 1988, 102 Stat. 662, 663, respectively. For effective date and applicability to cases, see section 7 of Pub.L. 100–352, set out as 28 U.S.C.A. § 1254 note.]
	30 days from interlocutory judgment, order, or decree in any other direct appeal authorized by law from decision of district court. 28 U.S.C.A. § 2101(b).
	60 days from final judgment, order, or decree in any other direct appeal authorized by law from decision of district court. 28 U.S.C.A. § 2101(b).
Other appeals and certiorari	90 days after entry of judgment or decree; justice of Supreme Court for good cause shown may extend time for applying for writ of certiorari for period not exceeding 60 days. 28 U.S.C.A. § 2101(c).
Briefs supporting certiorari	No separate brief supporting petition for certiorari shall be filed; See Supreme Court Rule 14.2.

APPEAL to Supreme Court	
Brief opposing certiorari	30 days after case is placed on the docket unless time is extended by Court or a Justice or by the Clerk; See Supreme Court Rule 15.3.
Brief on merits on appeal or certiorari	By appellant or petitioner, filed within 45 days of the order granting the writ of certiorari or the order noting probable jurisdiction or postponing consideration of jurisdiction; see Supreme Court Rule 25.1.
	By appellee or respondent, filed within 35 days after the brief for the appellant or petitioner is filed; see Supreme Court Rule 25.2.
	Reply brief, if any, filed within 35 days after the brief for appellee or respondent is filed, but any reply brief must actually be received by Clerk not later than one week before the date of oral argument. See Supreme Court Rule 25.3.
Stay of mandate pending petition for certiorari	A stay of mandate pending filing a petition to the Supreme Court for certiorari must not exceed 90 days unless the period is extended for good cause or unless during the period of stay, the party who obtained the stay files a petition for the writ and so notifies the circuit clerk in writing in which case the stay will continue until final disposition by the Supreme Court. The court of appeals must issue the mandate immediately when a copy of the Supreme Court order denying the petition for writ of certiorari is filed. App.R. 41(d)(2).
ATTORNEY'S fees	See "Costs", this table.
BILL of particulars	Abolished. See Civ.R. 12(e), as amended in 1948. See, however, "More definite statement", this table.
CLASS actions	
Certification	At an early practicable time after a person sues or is sued as a class representative, the court must determine by order whether to certify the action as a class action. Civ.R. 23(c)(1)(A).
Settlement, voluntary dismissal, or compromise	Approval by court of settlement, voluntary dismissal, or compromise that would bind class members only after hearing and on finding that it is fair, reasonable, and adequate. Civ.R. 23(e)(2).
Attorney's fees	Claim for award of attorney's fees and nontaxable costs must be made by motion under Civ.R. 54(d)(2) subject to Civ.R. 23(h) at a time the court sets. Notice of motion must be served on all parties and, for motions by class counsel, directed to class members in a reasonable manner. Civ.R. 23(h)(1).
CLERICAL mistakes and mistakes of oversight or omission in judgments, orders, or record	May be corrected whenever found, on motion or on court's own, with or without notice; but after appeal docketed and while pending, may be corrected only with appellate court's leave. Civ.R. 60(a).
COMPLAINT	Filing commences action—must be served with summons. Civ.R. 3, 4(c)(1).

Service of summons and complaint within 120 days after filing. Civ.R. 4(m).

COMPUTATION of time

Exclude day of the act, event, or default that begins the time period. Exclude intermediate Saturdays, Sundays, and legal holidays when the period is less than 11 days. Include last day of the period unless it is a Saturday, Sunday, legal holiday, or, if act to be done is filing a paper in court, a day on which weather or other conditions make the clerk's office inaccessible. When the last day is excluded, the period runs until the end of the next day that is not a Saturday, Sunday, legal holiday, or day when the clerk's office is inaccessible. Civ.R. 6(a).

Intermediate Saturdays, Sundays, and legal holidays are excluded when the period is less than 11 days. Civ.R. 6(a).

Exclude day of the act, event, or default that begins the period. Exclude intermediate Saturdays, Sundays, and legal holidays when the period is less than 11 days, unless stated in calendar days. Include last day of the period unless it is a Saturday, Sunday, legal holiday, or, if the act to be done is filing a paper in court, a day on which weather or other conditions make the clerk's office inaccessible. App.R. 26(a).

Intermediate Saturdays, Sundays, and legal holidays are excluded when the period is less than 11 days, unless stated in calendar days. App.R. 26(a).

Service by mail is complete upon mailing. Civ.R. 5(b).

Service by mail or by commercial carrier is complete upon mailing or delivery to the carrier. App.R. 25(c).

Service under Civ.R. 5(b)(2)(C), (D), (E), or (F) adds three days after the period would otherwise expire under Civ.R. 6(a). Civ.R. 6(d).

When a party is required or permitted to act within a prescribed period after service of a paper upon that party, three calendar days are added to the period unless the paper is delivered on the date of service stated in the proof of service. A paper served electronically is not treated as delivered on the date of service stated in the proof of service. App.R. 26(c).

Legal holidays are defined by Civ.R. 6(a)(4) and App.R. 26(a)(4).

Supreme Court matters—See Supreme Court Rule 30.

CONDEMNATION of property

Answer to notice of condemnation — 20 days after service of notice. Civ.R. 71A(e).

CORPORATE DISCLOSURE	Nongovernmental corporate parties must file, with first appearance, pleading, motion, response, or other request addressed to the court, statement identifying any parent corporation and any publicly held corporation owning 10% or more of its stock or stating that there is no such corporation. Party must promptly file supplemental statement if any required information changes. Civ.R. 7.1.
COSTS	
	Taxation on 1 day's notice. Review taxation of costs on motion served within the next 5 days. Civ.R. 54(d)(1).
	Failure, without good cause, to sign and return requested waiver of service of summons and to return waiver within a reasonable time which must be at least 30 days after request is sent or at least 60 days if sent to a defendant outside any judicial district of the United States. Civ.R. 4(d).
Attorney's fees and related nontaxable expenses	Motion filed no later than 14 days after entry of judgement. Civ.R. 54(d)(2)(B).
CROSS APPEAL	
Optional appeal from magistrate judge to district judge	Appellee may file reply brief within 10 days after service of reply brief of appellant. Civ.R. 75(c)(4) [Civ.R. 75 abrogated eff. Dec. 1, 1997].
Appellate rules	Within 14 days of filing of first notice of appeal or within the time otherwise prescribed by App.R. 4(a), whichever period ends later. App.R. 4(a)(3).
Inmates	Within 14 days after date when first notice of appeal was filed, or within the time otherwise prescribed by App.R. 4(a), whichever period ends later. The 14 day period runs from date district court dockets first notice of appeal. App.R. 4(a)(3), (c).
DEFAULT	
Entry by clerk	No time stated. Civ.R. 55(b).
Entry by court	If party against whom default judgment is sought has appeared personally or by representative, that party or its representative must be served with written notice of application for default judgment at least 3 days before the hearing on such application. Civ.R. 55(b).
DEFENSES and objections, presentation of	
By pleading	See "Answer", this table.
By motion	Motion must be made before pleading if responsive pleading is allowed. Civ.R. 12(b).
At trial	Opposing party may assert at trial any defense to claim for relief to which such party is not required to serve responsive pleading. Civ.R. 12(b).
Motion affects time for responsive pleading	Service of motion under Civ.R. 12 alters times for responsive pleading. See "Responsive Pleadings", this table.

DEMURRERS	Abolished. Civ.R. 7, 20007 Advisory Committee note, relating to Civ.R. 7(c).
DEPOSITIONS	See, also, "Interrogatories to parties", "Depositions on written questions", this table.
Notice of filing	Promptly. Civ.R. 30(f)(4) and Civ.R. 31(c)(2).
Notice of taking	Reasonable written notice to every other party. Civ.R. 30(b)(1).
Objections	As to admissibility, objection may be made at hearing or trial, but subject to Civ.R. 28(b) and 32(d)(3). Civ.R. 32(b).
	As to errors or irregularities in the notice, service promptly. Civ.R. 32(d)(1).
	As to disqualification of officer, objection made before deposition begins or promptly after the basis for disqualification becomes known or could have been known with reasonable diligence. Civ.R. 32(d)(2).
	As to competence of deponent or competence, relevance, or materiality of testimony—not waived by failure to make the objection before or during deposition, unless the ground might have been corrected at that time. Civ.R. 32(d)(3)(A).
	As to errors and irregularities at oral examination in manner of taking deposition, in the form of questions or answers, in the oath or affirmation, or in conduct of parties, and other errors that might have been corrected at that time, objection timely made during deposition. Civ.R. 32(d)(3)(B).
	As to form of written questions under Civ.R. 31—service within time allowed for serving responsive questions or, if recross-question, within 5 days after being served with it. Civ.R. 32(d)(3)(C).
	As to completion and return (transcription, signing, certification, sealing, endorsing, sending, or otherwise)—motion to suppress made promptly after error or irregularity becomes known or, with reasonable diligence, could have been known. Civ.R. 32(d)(4).
Protective orders	Subsequent to certification that movant has in good faith conferred or attempted to confer with other affected parties to resolve dispute without court action. Civ.R. 26(c)(1).
Motion to terminate or limit examination	Any time during a deposition. Civ.R. 30(d)(3).

Perpetuate testimony pending appeal	Motion in court where judgment was rendered on same notice and service as if action was pending in district court. Civ.R. 27(b).
Perpetuate testimony before action	Service of notice and petition at least 20 days before date of hearing. Civ.R. 27(a)(2).
Taking	Time specified in the notice of taking. Civ. R. 30(b)(1). Prior notice by a party to deponent and other parties to designate another method for recording deponent's testimony in addition to method specified in original notice. Civ.R. 30(b)(3).
Review of transcript or recording	Request by a party or deponent before completion of deposition. Deponent has 30 days after notice of availability of transcript or recording to review and to sign statement listing changes and reasons for making them. Civ.R. 30(e).
When taken	After parties have conferred as required by Civ.R. 26(f), except in proceeding exempted from initial disclosure under Civ.R. 26(a)(1)(B), or when authorized by rules, stipulation, or court order. Civ.R. 26(d).
DEPOSITIONS on written questions	See, also, "Depositions", "Interrogatories to parties", this table.
When taken	After parties have conferred as required by Civ.R. 26(f), except in proceeding exempted from initial disclosure under Civ.R. 26(a)(1)(B), or when authorized by rules, stipulation, or court order. Civ.R. 26(d).
Cross questions	Service within 14 days after service of the notice and direct questions. Court may extend or shorten time. Civ.R. 31(a)(5).
Redirect questions	Service within 7 days after being served with cross questions. Court may extend or shorten time. Civ.R. 31(a)(5).
Recross questions	Service within 7 days after service with redirect questions. Court may extend or shorten time. Civ.R. 31(a)(5).
Notice of filing of deposition	Promptly. Civ.R. 31(c).
Objections to form	Service within the time for serving responsive questions or, if question is a recross-question, within 5 days after being served with it. Civ.R. 32(d)(3)(C).
DISCOVERY	See, also, "Admissions", "Depositions", "Depositions on written questions", "Interrogatories to parties", "Production of documents", this Table.

DISCOVERY

Discovery Conference

Except in exempted proceedings or when otherwise ordered, as soon as practicable and at least 21 days before a scheduling conference is to be held or a scheduling order is due under Civ.R. 16(b), the parties must confer to consider the nature and basis of their claims, defenses, and possibility of settling or resolving the case, to make or arrange for disclosures required by Civ.R. 26(a)(1), to discuss any issues about preserving discoverable information, and to develop a proposed discovery plan. A written report outlining the plan is to be submitted to the court within 14 days after the conference. Civ.R. 26(f); See, also, Civ.R. 26(d).

Without awaiting a discovery request and at or within 14 days after the parties' Civ.R. 26(f) conference, a party must provide information specified in Civ.R. 26(a)(1)(A). Disclosure of expert testimony under Civ.R. 26(a)(2), in absence of court order or stipulation, is to be made at least 90 days before trial date or date case is to be ready for trial or if evidence intended solely to contradict or rebut evidence on same subject matter identified by another party under Civ.R. 26(a)(2)(B), within 30 days after the other party's disclosure. Civ.R. 26(a)(2)(C). Disclosures under Civ.R. 26(a)(1) or (2), depositions, interrogatories, requests for documents or tangible things or to permit entry onto land, and requests for admission must not be filed until used in the proceeding or court orders filing. Civ.R. 5(d).

Identification of witnesses, documents, exhibits, including summaries of other evidence, and designation of witnesses whose testimony is expected to be presented by deposition with a transcript of pertinent testimony if deposition is not taken stenographically to be provided to other parties at least 30 days before trial unless otherwise directed by court. Within 14 days thereafter, unless court sets different time, a party may serve and promptly file objections. Civ.R. 26(a)(3).

DISMISSAL for lack of subject-matter jurisdiction

Any time. Civ.R. 12(h)(3).

DISMISSAL by plaintiff voluntarily without court order

By filing notice of dismissal before service of answer or motion for summary judgment. Civ.R. 41(a)(1).

DISMISSAL of counterclaim, crossclaim or third-party claim, voluntary

Before service of responsive pleading, or if none, before introduction of evidence at trial or hearing. Civ.R. 41(c).

DISMISSAL without prejudice

Service of summons and complaint not made within 120 days after filing of complaint. Civ.R. 4(m).

DOCUMENTS, Production of

See "Production of documents", this Table.

ENLARGEMENT of time generally

Act may or must be done within specified time	Court for good cause may extend time (1) with or without motion or notice if court acts, or if request is made, before the original time or its extension expires, or (2) on motion made after the time has expired if party failed to act because of excusable neglect; but court may not extend time for taking any action under Civ.R. 50(b) and (d), 52(b), 59(b), (d) and (e), and 60(b), except as those rules allow. Civ.R. 6(b).
Affidavits in opposition, service	At least 1 day before the hearing, unless court permits service at another time, except as Civ.R. 59(c) provides otherwise. Civ.R. 6(c)(2).
Hearing of motions and defenses	Heard and decided before trial unless court orders deferral until trial. Civ.R. 12(i).
Service under Rule 5(b)(2)(C), (D), (E), or (F)	Adds three days after which the prescribed period after service would otherwise expire under Civ.R. 6(a). Civ.R. 6(d). When a party is required or permitted to act within a prescribed period after service of a paper upon that party, three calendar days are added to the period unless the paper is delivered on the date of service stated in the proof of service. A paper served electronically is not treated as delivered on the day of service stated in the proof of service. App.R. 26(c).
Injunction—temporary restraining order	May be extended 10 days by order of court or for a longer period by consent of party against whom order is directed. Civ.R. 65(b).
Response to request for admissions	Time may be lengthened or shortened by court or as the parties may stipulate to under Civ.R. 29. Civ.R. 36(a).
Optional appeal from magistrate judge to district judge	Upon showing of excusable neglect, time to file notice of appeal may be extended upon motion filed not later than 20 days from expiration of time for filing. Civ.R. 74(a) [Civ.R. 74 abrogated eff. Dec. 1, 1997].
Motion for judgment as a matter of law	No enlargement of the 10 day period except to the extent and under conditions stated in Civ.R. 50(b). Civ.R. 6(b).
Findings by the court, amendment of or make additional findings	No enlargement of the 10 day period except to the extent and under conditions stated in Civ.R. 52(b). Civ.R. 6(b).
Motion for new trial	No enlargement of the 10 day period except to the extent and under conditions stated in Civ.R. 50(d), 59(b), (d), and (e). Civ.R. 6(b).
Motion for relief from judgment or order	No enlargement of the 1 year period except to the extent and under conditions stated in Civ.R. 60(b). Civ.R. 6(b).

ENLARGEMENT of time generally

Appellate rules — Court for good cause may extend time prescribed by App.Rules or by its order to perform any act or may permit act to be done after expiration of such time; but court may not extend time for filing notice of appeal, or petition for permission to appeal a notice of appeal from or a petition to enjoin, set aside, suspend, modify, enforce or otherwise review an order of an administrative agency, board, commission or officer of the United States, unless specifically authorized by law. App.R. 26(b).

Supreme Court matters, depositions — See Supreme Court Rule 30.

EXCEPTIONS for insufficiency of pleadings — Abolished. Civ.R. 7, 2007 Advisory Committee note, relating to Civ.R. 7(c).

EXECUTION

Stay — Automatically: No execution may issue, nor may proceedings be taken to enforce, until expiration of 10 days after entry of judgment; exceptions—injunctions, receiverships, and patent accountings. Civ.R. 62(a).

Stay according to state law. Civ.R. 62(f).

Motion for new trial or for judgment. Civ.R. 62(b).

Stay in favor of government. Civ.R. 62(e).

Supersedeas on appeal. Civ.R. 62(d).

Stay of judgment as to multiple claims or multiple parties. Civ.R. 62(h).

Stay of judgment pending appeal from magistrate judge to district judge. Civ.R. 74(c). Stay of decision of district judge for 10 days during which time a party may petition for rehearing. Civ.R. 76(b) [Civ.R. 74 and 76 abrogated eff. Dec. 1, 1997].

FILING papers

Filing complaint commences civil action. Civ.R. 3.

Constitutional challenge to a statute. Civ.R. 5.1.

Service of summons and complaint within 120 days after filing of complaint. Civ.R. 4(m).

Any paper after complaint that is required to be served, together with certificate of service, must be filed within reasonable time after service. Civ.R. 5(d).

Any paper after complaint that is required to be served, together with certificate of service, must be filed with clerk unless judge agrees to accept it for filing. Civ.R. 5(d).

Local court rules may allow papers to be filed, signed, or verified by electronic means if consistent with technical standards of Judicial Conference of the United States. A local rule requirement of electronic filing must allow reasonable exceptions.

FILING papers

The clerk must not refuse for filing any paper solely because it is not in the form prescribed by Rules of Civil Procedure or a local rule or practice. Civ.R. 5(d).

Any paper after the complaint required to be served, together with a certificate of service, must be filed with the court within a reasonable time after service. Civ.R. 5(d).

FINDINGS

Motion to amend — 10 days after entry of judgment. Civ.R. 52(b). Exception from general rule relating to enlargement. Civ.R. 6(b).

FOREIGN law — Notice by pleading or other writing required of party intending to raise an issue concerning the law of a foreign country. Civ.R. 44.1.

HEARING of motions

A court may establish regular times and places for oral hearings on motions; by rule or order court may provide for submitting and determining motions on briefs, without oral hearings. Civ.R. 78.

Service of notice at least 5 days before time specified for hearing unless motion may be heard ex parte, or otherwise these rules or a court order set a different time. Civ.R. 6(c).

Hearing of certain motions and defenses before trial on application of any party unless court orders deferral until trial. Civ.R. 12(i).

HOLIDAYS

New Year's Day, Birthday of Martin Luther King, Jr., Washington's Birthday, Memorial Day, Independence Day, Labor Day, Columbus Day, Veterans' Day, Thanksgiving Day, Christmas Day, and any other day declared a holiday by the President, Congress or the state in which is located either the district court that rendered the challenged judgment or order, or the circuit clerk's principal office. Civ.R. 6(a); App.R. 26(a).

Exclusion in computation of time. Civ.R. 6(a); App.R. 26(a).

INJUNCTION (Temporary restraining order granted without notice)

Order must state date and hour of issuance, promptly filed in clerk's office, and entered in the record. Civ.R. 65(b).

Expiration within the time after entry, not to exceed 10 days, that court sets, unless before that time the court for good cause extends the order for like period or, with consent of party against whom order is directed, for longer period. Civ.R. 65(b).

Motion for preliminary injunction must be set for hearing at earliest possible time—takes precedence

INJUNCTION (Temporary restraining order granted without notice)	
	over all matters except older ones of same character. Civ.R. 65(b).
	Motion for dissolution or modification on 2 days' notice or shorter notice set by the court; court must then hear and decide motion as promptly as justice requires. Civ.R. 65(b).
INSTRUCTIONS	
Requests	At close of evidence or at an earlier reasonable time that the court orders. After close of evidence for issues that could not reasonably have been anticipated at an earlier time for requests, and untimely requests for instructions on any issue with the court's permission. Civ.R. 51(a).
Proposed	Court must inform parties before instructing jury and before final argument, and give parties opportunity to object before instructions and arguments are delivered. Civ.R. 51(b)(1), (2).
Time of	Court may instruct jury at any time before jury is discharged. Civ.R. 51(b)(3).
Objections	For parties informed of instructions or actions on requests before the jury is instructed and before final jury arguments, at opportunity for objection provided under Civ.R. 51(b)(2). For parties not informed of instructions or actions on requests before time for objection under Civ.R. 51(b)(2), promptly after learning that instruction or request will be, or has been, given or refused. Civ.R. 51(c).
INTERROGATORIES to parties	
	See, also, "Depositions", "Depositions on written questions", this table.
	Service after parties have conferred pursuant to Civ.R. 26(f). Civ.R. 26(d), 33(a).
Answers or objections	
	Service within 30 days after service of the interrogatories. A shorter or longer time may be stipulated to or ordered by the court. Civ.R. 33(b)(3).
INTERVENTION	
	Upon timely motion. Civ.R. 24(a), (b).
	Person desiring to intervene shall serve a motion to intervene upon the parties as provided in Civ.R. 5. Civ.R. 24(c).
JUDGMENT or order	
Alter or amend judgment, motion to	Shall be filed not later than 10 days after entry of judgment. Civ.R. 59(e). Exception to general rule, relating to enlargement. Civ.R. 6(b).
Clerical mistakes, or from oversight or omission	May be corrected any time; but after an appeal has been docketed in appellate court and while appeal pending may be corrected only with leave of appellate court. Civ.R. 60(a).

JUDGMENT or order

Default	See "Default", this table.
Renewal of motion for judgment after trial	Not later than 10 days after entry of judgment. Exception from general rule relating to enlargement. Civ.R. 6(b).
Entry of judgment	Subject to Civ.R. 54(b), promptly by clerk without awaiting the court's direction, unless court orders otherwise, upon general verdict of jury or upon court decision that a party shall recover only a sum certain or costs or that all relief shall be denied. Promptly approved form of judgment by court, promptly entered by clerk, upon special verdict or general verdict with answers to written questions, or upon court decision granting other relief. Entry may not be delayed in order to tax costs or award fees. Civ.R. 58(b), (e).
	Time of entry—Entry of a judgment if separate document is not required when judgment is entered in the civil docket under Civ.R. 79(a). If separate document is required, when the judgment is entered in the civil docket under Civ.R. 79(a) and either the judgment is set forth in a separate document, or 150 days have run from entry of the judgment in the civil docket, whichever is earlier. Civ.R. 58(c).
Entry, notice of	Immediately after entry, clerk must serve notice thereof as provided in Civ.R. 5(b) and record service on the docket. Any party may in addition serve a notice of such entry in manner provided in Civ.R. 5(b) for service of papers. Civ.R. 77(d).
	Lack of notice of entry by clerk does not affect time for appeal or relieve or authorize court to relieve party for failure to appeal within time allowed, except as allowed by App.R. 4(a). Civ.R. 77(d).
Offer of judgment	Service more than 10 days before trial begins. Civ.R. 68.
	Acceptance, written notice of—service within 10 days after service of offer. Civ.R. 68.
On pleadings, motion for judgment	After pleadings are closed but early enough not to delay the trial. Civ.R. 12(c).
Relief from, on grounds stated in Rule 60(b)	Motion within a reasonable time and not more than 1 year after entry of judgment or order or the date of the proceeding, for following grounds: (1) mistake, inadvertence, surprise, or excusable neglect; (2) newly discovered evidence; (3) fraud, misrepresentation, or other misconduct. Civ.R. 60(b), (c). Exception from general rule relating to enlargement. Civ.R. 6(b).
	Motion within a reasonable time, for following grounds: (1) judgment void, (2) judgment satisfied, released, or discharged, (3) prior underlying judgment reversed or otherwise vacated, (4) no longer

JUDGMENT or order	equitable that judgment have prospective application, (5) any other reason justifying relief. Civ.R. 60(b). Exception from general rule relating to enlargement. Civ.R. 6(b).
Stay	See "Execution", this table.
Summary judgment	See "Summary Judgment", this table.
JURORS	The institution of the alternate juror has been abolished. Civ.R. 47, 1991 Advisory Committee note, subd. (b).
JURY trial	
Demand	Service any time after commencement of action and not later than 10 days after service of last pleading directed to the triable issue. Civ.R. 38(b).
	Adverse party may serve demand for jury trial within 10 days after service of first demand or within a shorter time ordered by the court. Civ.R. 38(c).
Removed actions	If at the time of removal all necessary pleadings have been served, demand for jury trial may be served:
	By petitioner, 10 days after the notice of removal is filed;
	By another party, within 10 days after service on party of the notice of filing the petition. Civ.R. 81(c).
	Demand after removal not necessary in either of two instances: (1) before removal, party has made express demand in accordance with state law; (2) state law does not require express demands and court does not order otherwise. Civ.R. 81(c).
LEGAL HOLIDAY	See "Holidays", this table.
MAGISTRATE JUDGES	
Trial by consent	Consent of parties to magistrate judge's authority to be exercised by filing statement consenting to the referral. Civ.R. 73(b).
Pretrial matters	Objections of parties to order disposing of matter not dispositive of claim or defense to be served and filed within 10 days after being served with copy of order. Civ.R. 72(a).
	Clerk to promptly mail copies to all parties of recommendation of magistrate judge for disposition of matter dispositive of claim or defense of a party or prisoner petition. Specific written objections to recommended disposition may be served and filed within 10 days after service. Response to objections may be made within 10 days after being served with copy. Civ.R. 72(b).

MAIL	Service under Rule 5(b)(2)(C), (D), (E), or (F) adds 3 days after a prescribed period after service would otherwise expire under Civ.R. 6(a). Civ.R. 6(d). When a party is required or permitted to act within a prescribed period after service of a paper upon that party, three calendar days are added to the period unless the paper is delivered on the date of service stated in the proof of service. A paper served electronically is not treated as delivered on the day of service stated in the proof of service. App.R. 26(c). A brief or appendix is timely filed if on or before the last day for filing it is mailed First-Class or other class at least as expeditious, postage prepaid, or dispatched for delivery within three calendar days by a third-party commercial carrier. App.R. 25(a)(2)(B).
MASTERS	
Order appointing master	Court may issue only after master has filed affidavit disclosing whether there is any ground for disqualification under 28 U.S.C. § 455 and, if ground is disclosed, after parties with court's approval waive the disqualification. Civ.R. 53(b)(3).
Amendment of order appointing	Order appointing master may be amended at any time after notice to parties, and opportunity to be heard. Civ.R. 53(b)(4).
Order of master	A master who issues an order must file the order and promptly serve a copy on each party. The clerk must enter the order on the docket. Civ.R. 53(d).
Report of master	Master must report to court as required by appointing order. The master must file the report and promptly serve a copy on each party unless the court orders otherwise. Civ.R. 53(e).
	In acting on, the court must give parties notice and an opportunity to be heard. Civ.R. 53(f)(1).
	A party may file objections or motion to adopt or modify no later than 20 days from the time the master's order, report, or recommendations are served, unless the court sets a different time. Civ.R. 53(f)(2).
Compensation of master	The court must fix the master's compensation before or after judgment on the basis and terms stated in the appointing order but the court may set a new basis and terms after notice and opportunity to be heard. Civ.R. 53(g)(1)
MORE DEFINITE STATEMENT	
Furnished	Must be furnished within 10 days after notice of order or other time fixed by court or court may strike pleading or issue any other appropriate order. Civ.R. 12(e).
Motion for	Must be made before responsive pleading is filed. Civ.R. 12(e).

MOTIONS, notices, and affidavits	
	See, also, specific headings, this table.
In general	A written motion, supporting affidavits, and notice of hearing thereof—service at least 5 days before time specified for hearing unless motion may be heard ex parte, or a different time is fixed by rule or by order of court. Civ.R. 6(c).
	Opposing affidavits must be served at least one day before hearing, unless court permits otherwise. Civ.R. 6(c).
	Pleading, written motion, or other paper not signed by attorney or party shall be stricken unless omission of signature is corrected promptly after being called to attention of attorney or party. Civ.R. 11(a).
NEW TRIAL	
Motion and affidavits	Motion shall be filed not later than 10 days after entry of judgment. Civ.R. 59(b). Exception from general rule relating to enlargement. Civ.R. 6(b). If motion based on affidavits, they must be filed with motion. Civ.R. 59(c).
Opposing affidavits	Shall be filed within 10 days of service of motion for new trial; period may be extended up to 20 days either by court for good cause shown or by parties by stipulation. Civ.R. 59(c).
Initiative of court	Not later than 10 days after entry of judgment, court may order new trial for any reason that would justify granting one on a party's motion. Civ.R. 59(d). Exception to general rule relating to enlargement. Civ.R. 6(b).
	After giving parties notice and opportunity to be heard, court may grant a timely motion for new trial, for reason not stated in the motion. Civ.R. 59(d). Exception to general rule relating to enlargement. Civ.R. 6(b).
Judgment as a matter of law	Party against whom judgment as a matter of law is rendered shall file a motion for a new trial under Civ.R. 59 no later than 10 days after entry of the judgment. Civ.R. 50(d).
OBJECTIONS to orders or rulings of court	
	At time ruling or order of court is requested or made; if party has no opportunity to object to ruling or order at time it is made, absence of objection does not prejudice the party. Civ.R. 46.
Pretrial matters referred to magistrate judge	Objections of parties to order disposing of matter not dispositive of claim or defense to be served and filed within 10 days after being served with copy of order. Civ.R. 72(a).
	Specific written objections to recommended disposition of matter dispositive of claim or defense of a party may be served or filed within 10 days after

OBJECTIONS to orders or rulings of court	
	service. Response to objections may be made within 10 days after being served with copy. Civ.R. 72(b).
OFFER of judgment	
	Must be served more than 10 days before trial. Civ.R. 68(a).
	Acceptance must be served within 10 days after service of offer. Civ.R. 68(a).
ORDERS	See Judgment or order.
PARTICULARS, Bill of	Abolished. Civ.R. 12(e), as amended in 1948. See, however, "More definite statement", this table.
PLEADINGS	
Amendment of	Once as matter of course before responsive pleading served or within 20 days after serving the pleading if no response is allowed and action is not yet on trial calendar. Civ.R. 15(a).
	By leave of court or written consent of opposing parties, at any time. Civ.R. 15(a).
	During trial or after judgment to conform to evidence or to raise an unpleaded issue, but tried by express or implied consent of parties. Civ.R. 15(b).
Supplemental	Upon motion of party—court may upon reasonable notice permit service of supplemental pleading setting out transactions, etc., that happened after the date of pleading sought to be supplemented. Civ.R. 15(d).
	Opposing party plead to supplemental pleading—court may so order, within a specified time. Civ.R. 15(d).
Allegations of time	Such allegations are material when testing the sufficiency of a pleading. Civ.R. 9(f).
Judgment on, motion for	After pleadings are closed but early enough not to delay the trial. Civ.R. 12(c).
Striking of matter from	Motion made before responding to a pleading or, if no responsive pleading allowed, within 20 days after service of pleading. Civ.R. 12(f).
	On court's own initiative at any time. Civ.R. 12(f).
Signing of	
	Pleading, written motion, or other paper not signed by attorney or party must be stricken unless omission of signature is corrected promptly after being called to attention of attorney or party. Civ.R. 11(a).
PLEAS	Abolished. Civ.R. 7, 2007 Advisory Committee note, relating to Civ.R. 7(c).
PRETRIAL conferences	

	Scheduling order to issue as soon as practicable but in any event within the earlier of 120 days after complaint served on defendant or 90 days after appearance of any defendant. Civ.R. 16(b).
PROCESS	See "Summons", this Table.
PRODUCTION of documents	
Request for, service of	Within the scope of Civ.R. 26(b). Civ.R. 34(a).
Response to request	Within 30 days after service of the request. A shorter or longer time may be ordered by court or stipulated to under Civ.R. 29. Civ.R. 34(b).
Time of inspection	The request must specify a reasonable time. Civ.R. 34(b).
Subpoena	See "Subpoena", this table.
REHEARING	
Petition for panel rehearing	Petitions for panel rehearings may be filed within 14 days after entry of judgement unless the time is shortened or extended by order or local rule. In all civil cases in which the United States or its agency or officer thereof is a party, the time within which any party may seek a rehearing shall be 45 days after entry of judgement unless the time is shortened or extended by order. App.R. 40(a).
Issuance of mandate	The mandate of the court must issue 7 calendar days after the time to file a petition for rehearing expires, or 7 calendar days after entry of an order denying a timely petition for panel rehearing, petition for rehearing en banc, or motion for stay of mandate, whichever is later. The court may shorten or extend the time. The timely filing of a petition for panel rehearing, petition for rehearing en banc, or motion for stay of mandate, stays the mandate until disposition of the petition or motion, unless the court orders otherwise. App.R. 41(b), (d)(1).
REMOVED actions	
Answers and defenses	Within 20 days after the receipt through service or otherwise of a copy of the initial pleading setting forth the claim for relief upon which the action or proceeding is based, or within 20 days after the service of summons for an initial pleading on file at the time of service, or within 5 days after filing of the notice for removal, whichever period is longest. Civ.R. 81(c).
Demand for jury trial	Demand after removal not necessary in either of two instances: (1) before removal, party has made express demand in accordance with state law; (2) state law does not require express demands and court does not direct otherwise. Civ.R. 81(c).
Notice of removal	Within 30 days after receipt through service or otherwise of a copy of the initial pleading setting forth the claim for relief upon which the action or proceeding is based, or within 30 days after service of summons if such initial pleading has then been filed in court and is not required to be served on

REMOVED actions	defendant, whichever period is shorter. 28 U.S.C.A. § 1446(b).
	If the case stated by the initial pleading is not removable, a notice of removal may be filed within 30 days after receipt by the defendant, through service or otherwise, of a copy of an amended pleading, motion, order or other paper from which it may first be ascertained that the case is one which is or has become removable. 28 U.S.C.A. § 1446(b).
	A case may not be removed on the basis of jurisdiction conferred by 28 U.S.C.A. § 1332 more than one year after action's commencement. 28 U.S.C.A. § 1446(b).
REPLY	See, also, "Responsive pleadings", this table.
To answer	If ordered by court. Civ.R. 7(a). Service within 20 days after service of order, unless order specifies a different time. Civ.R. 12(a).
To counterclaim or cross-claim	Service within 20 days after service of pleading that states the counterclaim or crossclaim. Civ.R. 12(a).
	United States or agency or officer or employee thereof sued only in an official capacity shall serve reply within 60 days after service on U.S. attorney. Civ.R. 12(a).
	United States officer or employee sued in an individual capacity in connection with duties performed on the United States' behalf shall serve reply within 60 days after service on officer or employee or service on the United States attorney, whichever is later. Civ.R. 12(a).
Alteration of time by service of Civ.R. 12 motion	See "Responsive pleadings", this table.
RESPONSIVE PLEADINGS	See, also, "Answer", "Reply", this table.
To amend pleading	Within 10 days after service of amended pleading or within time remaining for response to original pleading, whichever is later, unless court otherwise orders. Civ.R. 15(a).
To supplemental pleading	As ordered by court. Civ.R. 15(d).
Alteration of time by service of Civ.R. 12 motion	Service of motion permitted under Civ.R. 12 alters times for responsive pleadings as follows unless different time fixed by court: (1) if court denies motion or postpones its disposition until trial, service of responsive pleading within 10 days after notice of the court's action; (2) if court grants motion for more definite statement, service of responsive pleading within 10 days after service of the more definite statement. Civ.R. 12(a)(4).

RESTRAINING order, temporary, without notice	See "Injunction", this table.
RETURN	
	The court may allow a summons or proof of service to be amended. Civ.R. 4(a) & (*l*).
	Proof of service must be made to the court by server's affidavit, except for service by United States marshal or deputy marshal. Civ.R. 4(*l*).
SANCTIONS	Presentation to court of a pleading, written motion, or other paper is a certification under Civ.R. 11(b). If after notice and reasonable opportunity to respond, court determines that Civ.R. 11(b) was violated, sanctions may be imposed by a motion for sanctions which must not be filed or presented to court unless, within 21 days after service of the motion or another time period set by the court, the challenged matter is not withdrawn or corrected. Civ.R. 11(c). Sanctions are inapplicable to disclosures and discovery. Civ.R. 11(d).
SATURDAYS AND SUNDAYS, LEGAL HOLIDAYS	Exclusion in computation of time when period is less than 11 days. Civ.R. 6(a); App.R. 26(a).
STAY or supersedeas	See "Appeal", "Execution", this table.
SUBPOENA	
Objection	Before the earlier of 14 days after service of the subpoena or the time specified for compliance, service on the party or attorney designated in the subpoena written objection to production of any or all of the designated materials or of the premises. Civ.R. 45(c)(2)(B).
Motion to compel production	If objection has been made, the party serving the subpoena may, on notice to the person commanded to produce, move at any time for an order to compel the production or inspection. Civ.R. 45(c)(2)(B).
Motion to quash	The court by which a subpoena was issued must quash or modify the subpoena on timely motion under certain circumstances. Civ.R. 45(c)(3)(A).
Witnesses, documentary evidence, etc.	Subpoena specifies time for attendance and giving of testimony or to produce and permit inspection, copying, testing, or sampling of designated documents, electronically stored information, or tangible things in the possession, custody or control of that person, or to permit inspection of premises. Civ.R. 45(a)(1)(A), (C).
SUBSTITUTION of parties	
	In cases of death, incompetency, or transfer of interest—motion to substitute, together with notice of hearing, served on parties as provided in Civ.R. 5 and on nonparties in manner provided in Civ.R. 4 for service of a summons. Civ.R. 25(a), (b), (c).

SUBSTITUTION of parties	Dismissal as to deceased party unless motion for substitution is made within 90 days after service of a statement noting the death. Civ.R. 25(a).
	Successor of public officer substituted automatically. Court may order substitution at any time, but absence of order does not affect substitution. Civ.R. 25(d).
SUMMARY JUDGMENT, motion for	
Claimant	May move at any time after 20 days have passed from commencement of action or after service of motion for summary judgment by opposing party. Civ.R. 56(a).
Defending party	May move at any time. Civ.R. 56(b).
Service	Service of motion at least 10 days before the day set for hearing. Civ.R. 56(c).
	Service of opposing affidavits before the hearing day. Civ.R. 56(c).
SUMMONS	Served with a copy of complaint. Civ.R. 4(c)(1). If not served within 120 days after filing complaint, court must dismiss action without prejudice, order service be made within a specified time, or extend time for service. Civ.R. 4(m).
	Proof of service must be made to the court by server's affidavit, except for service by United States marshal or deputy marshal. Civ.R. 4(*l*).
	Service by any nonparty at least 18, a United States marshal, deputy marshal, or other person specially appointed by the court. Civ.R. 4(c)(2), (3).
SUPPLEMENTAL pleadings	See "Pleadings", this table.
SUPERSEDEAS or stay	See "Appeal", "Execution", this table.
TERM	Every district court considered always open. Civ.R. 77(a).
	Terms of court have been abolished. 28 U.S.C.A. §§ 138–141, as amended by Pub.L. 88–139, Oct. 16, 1963, 77 Stat. 248.
THIRD–PARTY practice	Third-party plaintiff need not obtain leave if third-party plaintiff files third-party complaint not later than 10 days after serving the original answer. Civ.R. 14(a).
VERDICT	
Renewal of motion for judgment after trial	Movant may renew motion for judgment as a matter of law by filing a motion no later than 10 days after the entry of judgment or — if the motion addresses a jury issue not decided by a verdict — no later than 10 days after the jury was discharged. Civ.R. 50(b).

VERDICT

	Exception from general rule relating to enlargement. Civ.R. 6(b).
New trial where judgment as a matter of law rendered	Party against whom judgment as a matter of law is rendered must file a motion for a new trial under Civ.R. 59 no later than 10 days after entry of the judgment. Civ.R. 50(d).

EQUITY RULES REFERENCE TABLE

The Federal Rules of Civil Procedure supplant the Equity Rules since in general they cover the field now covered by the Equity Rules and the Conformity Act (former section 724 of this title).

This table shows the Equity Rules to which references are made in the notes to the Federal Rules of Civil Procedure.

Equity Rules	Federal Rules of Civil Procedure
1	77
2	77
3	79
4	77
5	77
6	78
7	4, 70
8	6, 70
9	70
10	18, 54
11	71
12	3, 4, 5, 12, 55
13	4
14	4
15	4, 45
16	6, 55
17	55
18	7, 8
19	1, 15, 61
20	12
21	11, 12
22	1
23	1, 39
24	11
25	8, 9, 10, 19
26	18, 20, 82
27	23
28	15
29	7, 12, 42, 55
30	8, 13, 82
31	7, 8, 12, 55
32	15
33	7, 12
34	15
35	15
36	11
37	17, 19, 20, 24
38	23
39	19
40	20
41	17
42	19, 20
43	12, 21
44	12, 21
45	25
46	43, 61
47	26
48	43
49	53
50	30, 80
51	30, 53
52	45, 53
53	53
54	26
55	30
56	40
57	40
58	26, 33, 34, 36
59	53
60	53
61	53
61½	53
62	53
63	53
64	26
65	53
66	53
67	53
68	53
69	59
70	17
70½	52
71	54
72	60, 61
73	65
74	62
75	75
76	75
77	76
78	43
79	83
80	6
81	86

ORDERS OF THE SUPREME COURT OF THE UNITED STATES ADOPTING AND AMENDING RULES

ORDER OF DECEMBER 20, 1937

It is ordered that Rules of Procedure for the District Courts of the United States be adopted pursuant to Section 2 of the Act of June 19, 1934, Chapter 651 (48 Stat. 1064), and the Chief Justice is authorized and directed to transmit the Rules as adopted to the Attorney General and to request him, as provided in that section, to report these Rules to the Congress at the beginning of the regular session in January next. MR. JUSTICE BRANDEIS states that he does not approve of the adoption of the Rules.

ORDER OF DECEMBER 28, 1939

1. That the first sentence of Rule 81(a)(6) of the Rules of Civil Procedure be amended so as to read as follows:

"(6) These rules do not apply to proceedings under the Act of September 13, 1888, c. 1015, § 13 (25 Stat. 479) as amended, U.S.C., Title 8, § 282, 8 U.S.C.A. § 282, relating to deportation of Chinese; they apply to proceedings for enforcement or review of compensation orders under the Longshoremen's and Harbor Workers' Compensation Act, Act of March 4, 1927, c. 509, §§ 18, 21 (44 Stat. 1434, 1436), U.S.C., Title 33, §§ 918, 921, 33 U.S.C.A. §§ 918, 921, except to the extent that matters of procedure are provided for in that Act".

2. Effective Date. That the foregoing amendment take effect on the day which is three months subsequent to the adjournment of the second regular session of the 76th Congress, but if that day is prior to September 1, 1940, then this amendment shall take effect on September 1, 1940. This amendment governs all proceedings in actions brought after it takes effect and also all further proceedings in actions then pending, except to the extent that in the opinion of the Court its application in a particular action pending when the amendment takes effect would not be feasible or would work injustice, in which event the former procedure applies.

3. That THE CHIEF JUSTICE be authorized to transmit this amendment to the Attorney General with the request that he report it to the Congress at the beginning of the regular session in January, 1940.

MR. JUSTICE BLACK does not approve of the adoption of this amendment.

ORDER OF DECEMBER 27, 1946

1. That subdivisions (a) and (b) of Rule 80 of the Rules of Civil Procedure be, and they hereby are, abrogated.

2. That Rules 6, 7, 12, 13, 14, 17, 24, 26, 27, 28, 33, 34, 36, 41, 45, 52, 54, 56, 58, 59, 60, 62, 65, 66, 68, 73, 75, 77, 79, 81, 84, and 86 of the Rules of Civil Procedure and Forms Nos. 17, 20, 22, and 25, be, and they hereby are, amended as hereinafter set forth.

[See the amendments made thereby under the respective rules and forms, post.]

3. That THE CHIEF JUSTICE be authorized to transmit these amendments to the Attorney General with the request that he report them to the Congress at the beginning of the regular session in January, 1947.

MR. JUSTICE FRANKFURTER joins in approval of the proposed amendments essentially because of his confidence in the informed judgment of the Advisory Committee on Rules of Civil Procedure.

ORDER OF DECEMBER 29, 1948

1. That the title "Rules of Civil Procedure for the District Courts of the United States" be amended to read "Rules of Civil Procedure for the United States District Courts".

2. That Rules 1, 17, 22, 24, 25, 27, 37, 45, 57, 60, 62, 65, 66, 67, 69, 72, 73, 74, 75, 76, 79, 81, 82, and 86 of the Rules of Civil Procedure and Forms Nos. 1, 19, 22, 23, and 27, be, and they hereby are, amended as hereinafter set forth.

[See the amendments made thereby under the respective rules and forms, post.]

3. That THE CHIEF JUSTICE be authorized to transmit these amendments to the Attorney General with the request that he report them to the Congress at the beginning of the regular session in January, 1949.

ORDER OF APRIL 30, 1951

1. That paragraph (7) of Rule 81(a) of the Rules of Civil Procedure, be, and it hereby is, abrogated.

2. That the Rules of Civil Procedure be, and they hereby are, amended by including therein a rule to govern condemnation cases in the United States District Courts, numbered 71A, as follows:

[See text of Rule 71A, post.]

3. Effective Date. That this Rule 71A and the amendment to Rule 81(a) will take effect on August 1, 1951. Rule 71A governs all proceedings in actions brought after it takes effect and also all further proceedings in actions then pending, except to the extent that in the opinion of the court its application in a particular action pending when the rule takes effect would not be feasible or would work injustice, in which event the former procedure applies.

4. That Forms Nos. 28 and 29 be, and they hereby are, approved and added to the Appendix of Forms to the Rules of Civil Procedure. The forms read respectively as follows:

[See text of Forms 28 and 29, post.]

5. That THE CHIEF JUSTICE be authorized to transmit these amendments to the Congress on or before May 1, 1951.

ORDER OF APRIL 17, 1961

1. That Rules 25, 54, 62 and 86 of the Rules of Civil Procedure and Forms Nos. 2 and 19, be, and they hereby are, amended as hereinafter set forth:

[See the amendments made thereby under the respective rules and forms, post.]

2. That THE CHIEF JUSTICE be authorized to transmit these amendments to Congress in accordance with the provisions of Title 28, U.S.C., Sec. 2072.

3. MR. JUSTICE BLACK does not join in approval of the Rules because he believes that it would be better for Congress to act directly by legislation on the matters treated by the Rules.

4. MR. JUSTICE DOUGLAS filed the following statement:

"Most of the proposed changes in the Rules of Civil Procedure are picayune and harmless, yet hardly worth making apart from any overall revision of the Rules. The change in Rule 25 of the Rules of Civil Procedure is, however, a major one; and it seems to me unwise. The policy that a cabinet officer under one administration pursues is often not the policy of the next administration. I would not make the contrary assumption, as does the proposed change. I think the ends served by *Snyder v. Buck*, 340 U.S. 15, 71 S.Ct. 93, 95 L.Ed. 15, are proper ones. The Rule in its present form leaves the burden on the claimant who challenges a particular government policy to re-establish that the controversy he had with a predecessor is a live one as respects the successor. The burden should rest there, not with the newcomer to office.

"The critical language in Rule 25(d) that is changed by the proposed amendment derived from 28 U.S.C. § 780 which the Revised Code dropped in 1949 because it had been incorporated in Rule 25(d). See 28 U.S.C., p. XXIX. The history of § 780 is reviewed in *Snyder v. Buck*, supra, pp. 18–19.

"Congress dealt with the matter beginning with the Act of February 8, 1899, 30 Stat. 822. The care with which it approached the problem is shown in H.R.Rep. No. 960, 55th Cong., 2d Sess., p. 2, where it is said:

"'A mandamus proceeding against an officer is based upon the claim that he is personally refusing to perform some duty which the law requires of him in his official character, and if decided against him he is properly liable, personally, for all cost of the proceeding, but if he vacates the office before a decision, it might seem harsh to compel his successor to become a party to the suit and to the costs already accrued without having been guilty of any personal neglect of the official duty involved in the proceeding; but to provide against this seeming harshness your committee propose to amend the bill so as to give the succeeding official an opportunity to perform the official act involved in the proceeding and thereby prevent the survival of the action against himself, and if he fails to do so, he can not then complain of being mulct in costs accruing against his predecessor.'

"The provision of § 780 that the action might be continued against the successor in office on the requisite showing within the stated period was added by § 11 of the Judiciary Act of 1925. 43 Stat. 936, 941. The last word Congress spoke on the matter reflected the views in a Report submitted by Chief Justice Taft dated March 11, 1922, which explained § 11 in the following words:

"'It will be noted ..... that the provision is not mandatory, but leaves it to the sound discretion of the court to determine whether there is a substantial need for continuing the cause and obtaining an adjudication of the questions involved. This will tend to restrict the exercise of the right to cases which have a sound basis.' This language was repeated in the Senate Committee Print, 68th Cong., 1st Sess., of A General Review of H.R. 10479, 67th Cong., p. 16. The language so carefully tailored by Congress is now rejected by the professional group who constitute our advisors in these matters. I do not think we should allow a known and established congressional policy to be so readily abrogated.

"We said in *Snyder v. Buck*, supra, p. 20, that if Rule 25(d) is to be amended in the manner then urged and now adopted 'the amending process is available.' Where we have a matter so heavily encrusted with legislative policy, I think any change should be left to Congress.

"I, therefore, dissent from the submission to Congress of the proposed amendments to Rule 25 of the Rules of Civil Procedure under 28 U.S.C. § 2072. For under that Act the Rules submitted become effective at the expiration of a 90–day period, unless Congress takes contrary action. This machinery seems therefore, inappropriate to me for effecting such a basic change in congressional policy as the proposed Rule 25(d) achieves."

ORDER OF JANUARY 21, 1963

1. That the Rules of Civil Procedure be, and they hereby are, amended by including therein Forms Number 30, 31 and 32, and the amendments to Rules 4, 5, 6, 7, 12, 13, 14, 15, 24, 25, 26, 28, 30, 41, 49, 50, 52, 56, 58, 71A, 77, 79, 81, and 86 and to Forms Number 3, 4, 5, 6, 7, 8, 9, 10, 11, 12, 13, 16, 18, 21, 22–A and 22–B, as hereinafter set forth:

[See additions and amendments made thereby under the respective rules and forms, post.]

2. That THE CHIEF JUSTICE be authorized to transmit these amendments to Congress in accordance with the provisions of Title 28, U.S.C., Sec. 2072.

MR. JUSTICE BLACK and MR. JUSTICE DOUGLAS are opposed to the submission of these rules [1] to the Congress under a statute which permits them to "take effect" and to repeal "all laws in conflict with such rules" without requiring any affirmative consideration, action, or approval of the rules by Congress or by the President.[2] We believe that while some of the Rules of Civil Procedure are simply housekeeping details,[3] many determine matters so substantially affecting the rights of litigants in law suits that in practical effect they are the equivalent of new legislation which, in our judgment, the Constitution requires to be initiated in and enacted by the Congress [4] and approved by the President.[5] The Constitution, as we read it, provides that all laws shall be enacted by the House, the Senate, and the President, not by the mere failure of Congress to reject proposals of an outside agency. Even were there not this constitutional limitation, the authorizing statute itself qualifies this Court's power by imposing upon it a solemn responsibility not to submit rules that "abridge, enlarge or modify any substantive right" and by specifically charging the Court with the duty to "preserve the right to trial by jury as at common law and as declared by the Seventh Amendment to the Constitution." [6] Our chief objections to the rules relate essentially to the fact that many of their provisions do "abridge, enlarge or modify" substantive rights and do not "preserve the right to trial by jury" but actually encroach upon it.

(1)(a) Rule 50(a) is amended by making the order of a judge granting a motion for a directed verdict effective without submitting the question to the jury at all. It was pointed out in *Galloway v. United States,* 319 U.S. 372, 396, 401–407, 63 S.Ct. 1077, 87 L.Ed. 1458 (dissenting opinion), how judges have whittled away or denied the right of trial by jury through the devices of directed verdicts and judgments notwithstanding verdicts. Although the amendment here is not itself a momentous one, it gives formal sanction to the process by which the courts have been wresting from juries the power to render verdicts. Since we do not approve of this sapping of the Seventh Amendment's guarantee of a jury trial, we cannot join even this technical *coup de grace.*

(b) The proposed amendment to 50(c) in practical effect vests appellate courts with more power than they have had to grant or deny new trials. The Court in *Cone v. West Virginia Pulp & Paper Co.,* 330 U.S. 212, 217–218, 67 S.Ct. 752, 91 L.Ed. 849, and *Globe Liquor Co. v. San Roman,* 332 U.S. 571, 68 S.Ct. 246, 92 L.Ed. 177, refused to construe the federal rules then existing to allow Courts of Appeals to interfere with trial judges' discretion to grant new trials. To the extent that jury verdicts are to be set aside and new trials granted, we believe that those who hear the evidence, the trial judges, are the ones who should primarily exercise such discretion.

(c) The proposed amendment to Rule 56(e) imposes additional burdens upon litigants to protect against summary judgments rendered without hearing evidence on the part of witnesses who are confronted by the persons against whom they testify so that these persons can subject the witnesses to cross-examination. The summary judgment procedure, while justified in some cases, is made a handy instrument to let judges rather than juries try law suits and to let those judges try cases not on evidence of witnesses subjected to cross-examination but on ex parte affidavits obtained by parties. Most trial lawyers would agree, we think, that a litigant can frequently obtain in an actual trial favorable testimony which could not have been secured by affidavits or even by depositions.

(d) If there are to be amendments, Rule 49 should be repealed. That rule authorizes judges to require juries to return "only a special verdict in the form of a special written finding upon each issue of fact" or to answer "written interrogatories upon one or more issues of fact the decision of which is necessary to a verdict" in addition to rendering the general verdict. Such devices are used to impair or wholly take away the power of a jury to render a general verdict. One of the ancient, fundamental reasons for having general jury verdicts was to preserve the right of trial by jury as an indispensable part of a free government. Many of the most famous constitutional controversies in England revolved around litigants' insistence, particularly in seditious libel cases, that a jury had the right to render a general verdict without being compelled to return a number of subsidiary findings to support its general verdict. Some English jurors had to go to jail because they insisted upon their right to render general verdicts over the repeated commands of tyrannical judges not to do so. Rule 49 is but another means utilized by courts to weaken the constitutional power of juries and to vest judges with more power to decide cases according to their own judgments. A scrutiny of the special verdict and written interrogatory cases in appellate courts will show the confusion that necessarily results from the employment of these devices and the ease with which judges can use them to take away the right to trial by jury. We believe that Rule 49 be repealed, not amplified.

(2) There is a proposal to amend Rule 41, which provides for dismissal of actions. We believe that, if the Rules are to be changed, a major amendment to this rule is required in the interest of justice. Before dismissing a plaintiff's action for failure of his lawyer to prosecute, the trial judge should be required to have notice served on the plaintiff himself. The hardship that can result from the absence of such requirement is shown by *Link v. Wabash R. Co.*, 370 U.S. 626, 82 S.Ct. 1386, 8 L.Ed.2d 734. Link's lawyer failed to appear in response to a judge's order for a pre-trial conference, and the judge dismissed the case. As pointed out in the dissent, plaintiff had been severely injured, and a fair system of justice should not have penalized him because his lawyer, through neglect or any other reason, failed to appear when ordered. It would do a defendant no injury for the court to refuse to dismiss any apparently bona fide case until the plaintiff has actually had notice that some failure of his lawyer has irked the judge.

(3) MR. JUSTICE BLACK and MR. JUSTICE DOUGLAS object to the changes in Rule 4, which for the first time permit a Federal District Court to obtain jurisdiction over a defendant by service of process outside the state or over his property by garnishment or attachment, under the circumstances and in the manner prescribed by state law. Those changes will apparently have little effect insofar as "federal question" litigation is concerned, since 28 U.S.C. § 1391(b) requires such suits to be brought "only in the judicial district where all defendants reside. . . ." Diversity actions, however, may be greatly increased, for the effect of proposed 4(e) is not limited to suits authorized by such statutes as the Federal Interpleader Act, 28 U.S.C. § 1335. See Advisory Committee Rept., 5–8; 28 U.S.C. § 1391(a); Fed.Rules Civ. Proc. 1. We see no justification for an increase in the number of diversity cases. We also see no reason why the extent of a Federal District Court's personal jurisdiction should depend upon the existence or nonexistence of a state "long-arm" statute. Moreover, at present a state court action commenced by attachment or garnishment can get into a District Court only if a nonresident defendant chooses to appear and remove the case, see 28 U.S.C. § 1441, and there is no good reason, absent a congressional finding, why this should be changed.

Instead of recommending changes to the present Rules, we recommend that the statute authorizing this Court to prescribe Rules of Civil Procedure, if it is to remain a law, be amended to place the responsibility upon the Judicial Conference rather than upon this Court. Since the statute was first enacted in 1934, 48 Stat. 1064, the Judicial Conference has been enlarged and improved and is now very active in its surveillance of the work of the federal courts and in recommending appropriate legislation to Congress. The present Rules produced under 28 U.S.C. § 2072 are not prepared by us but by Committees of the Judicial Conference designated by the Chief Justice, and before coming to us they are approved by the Judicial Conference pursuant to 28 U.S.C. § 331.[7] The Committees and the Conference are composed of able and distinguished members and they render a high public service. It is they, however, who do the work, not we, and the rules have only our imprimatur. The only contribution that we actually make is an occasional exercise of a veto power. If the rule-making for Federal District Courts is to continue under the present plan, we believe that the Supreme Court should not have any part in the task; rather, the statute should be amended to substitute the Judicial Conference. The Judicial Conference can participate more actively in fashioning the rules and affirmatively contribute to their content and design better than we can. Transfer of the function to the Judicial Conference would relieve us of the embarrassment of having to sit in judgment on the constitutionality of rules which we have approved and which as applied in given situations might have to be declared invalid.

1 See our earlier statements in 368 U.S. 1012–1014 and 346 U.S. 946–947.

2 28 U.S.C. § 2072 gives this Court the power to prescribe rules of practice and procedure for Federal District Courts and further provides that such rules

"shall not take effect until they have been reported to Congress by THE CHIEF JUSTICE at or after the beginning of a regular session thereof but not later than the first day of May, and until the expiration of ninety days after they have been thus reported.

"All laws in conflict with such rules shall be of no further force or effect after such rules have taken effect."

3 See 368 U.S. 1012.

4 "All legislative Powers herein granted shall be vested in a Congress of the United States, which shall consist of a Senate and House of Representatives." U.S. Const., Art. I, § 1.

5 Every Bill which shall have passed the House of Representatives and the Senate, shall, before it becomes a Law, be presented to the President of the United States; ...." U.S. Const., Art. I, § 7.

6 28 U.S.C. § 2072.

7 "The Conference shall also carry on a continuous study of the operation and effect of the general rules of practice and procedure now or hereafter in use as prescribed by the Supreme Court for the other courts of the United States pursuant to law. Such changes in and additions to those rules as the Conference may deem desirable to promote simplicity in procedure, fairness in administration, the just determination of litigation, and the elimination of unjustifiable expense and delay shall be recommended by the Conference from time to time to the Supreme Court for its consideration and adoption, modification or rejection, in accordance with law."

ORDER OF FEBRUARY 28, 1966

1. That the Rules of Civil Procedure for the United States District Courts be, and they hereby are, amended by including therein Rules 23.1, 23.2, 44.1 and 65.1, Supplemental Rules A, B, C, D, E and F for Certain Admiralty and Maritime Claims, and amendments to Rules 1, 4, 8, 9, 12, 13, 14, 15, 17, 18, 19, 20, 23, 24, 26, 38, 41, 42, 43, 44, 47, 53, 59, 65, 68, 73, 74, 75, 81 and 82, and to Forms 2 and 15, as hereinafter set forth:

[See added, amended and supplemental Rules and Forms, post.]

2. That the foregoing amendments and additions to the Rules of Civil Procedure shall take effect on July 1, 1966, and shall govern all proceedings in actions brought thereafter and also in all further proceedings in actions then pending, except to the extent that in the opinion of the court their application in a particular action then pending would not be feasible or would work injustice, in which event the former procedure applies.

3. That THE CHIEF JUSTICE be, and he hereby is, authorized to transmit to the Congress the foregoing amendments and additions to the Rules of Civil Procedure in accordance with the provisions of Title 28, U.S.C., §§ 2072 and 2073.

4. That: (a) subdivision (c) of Rule 6 of the Rules of Civil Procedure for the United States District Courts promulgated by this court on December 20, 1937, effective September 16, 1938; (b) Rule 2 of the Rules for Practice and Procedure under section 25 of An Act to amend and consolidate the Acts respecting copyright, approved March 4, 1909, promulgated by this court on June 1, 1909, effective July 1, 1909; and (c) the Rules of Practice in Admiralty and Maritime Cases, promulgated by this court on December 6, 1920, effective March 7, 1921, as revised, amended and supplemented, be, and they hereby are, rescinded, effective July 1, 1966.

MR. JUSTICE BLACK, dissenting.

The Amendments to the Federal Rules of Civil and Criminal Procedure today transmitted to the Congress are the work of very capable advisory committees. Those committees, not the Court, wrote the rules. Whether by this transmittal the individual members of the Court who voted to transmit the rules intended to express approval of the varied policy decisions the rules embody I am not sure. I am reasonably certain, however, that the Court's transmittal does not carry with it a decision that the amended rules are all constitutional. For such a decision would be the equivalent of an advisory opinion which, I assume the Court would unanimously agree, we are without constitutional power to give. And I agree with my Brother DOUGLAS that some of the proposed criminal rules go to the very border line if they do not actually transgress the constitutional right of a defendant not to be compelled to be a witness against himself. This phase of the criminal rules in itself so infects the whole collection of proposals that, without mentioning other objections, I am opposed to transmittal of the proposed amendments to the criminal rules.

I am likewise opposed to transmittal of the proposed revision of the civil rules. In the first place I think the provisions of 28 U.S.C. § 2072 (1964 ed.), under which these rules are transmitted and the corresponding section, 18 U.S.C. § 3771 (1964 ed.), relating to the criminal rules, both of which provide for giving transmitted rules the effect of law as though they had been properly enacted by Congress are unconstitutional for reasons I have previously stated.[1] And in prior dissents I have stated some of the basic reasons for my objections to repeated rules revisions [2] that tend to upset established meanings and need not repeat those grounds of objection here. The confusion created by the adoption of the present rules, over my objection, has been partially dispelled by judicial interpretations of them by this Court and others. New rules and extensive amendments to present rules will mean renewed confusion resulting in new challenges and new reversals and prejudicial "pretrial" dismissals of cases before a trial on the merits for failure of lawyers to understand and comply with new rules of uncertain meaning. Despite my continuing objection to the old rules, it seems to me that since they have at least gained some degree of certainty it would be wiser to "bear those ills we have than fly to others we know not of," unless, of course, we are reasonably sure that the proposed reforms of the old rules are badly needed. But I am not. The new proposals, at least some of them, have, as I view them, objectionable possibilities that cause me to believe our judicial system could get along much better without them.

The momentum given the proposed revision of the old rules by this Court's transmittal makes it practically certain that Congress, just as has this Court, will permit the rules to take effect exactly as they were written by the Advisory Committee on Rules. Nevertheless, I am including here a memorandum I submitted to the Court expressing objections to the Committee's proposals and suggesting changes should they be transmitted. These suggestions chiefly center around rules that grant broad discretion to trial judges with reference to class suits, pretrial procedures, and dismissal of cases with prejudice. Cases coming before the federal courts over the years now filling nearly 40 volumes of Federal Rules Decisions show an accumulation of grievances by lawyers and litigants about the way many trial judges exercise their almost unlimited discretionary powers to use pretrial procedures to dismiss cases without trials. In fact, many of these cases indicate a belief of many judges and legal commentators that the cause of justice is best served in the long run not by trials on the merits but by summary dismissals based on out of court affidavits, pretrial depositions, and other pretrial techniques. My belief is that open court trials on the merits where litigants have the right to prove their case or defense best comports with due process of law.

The proposed rules revisions, instead of introducing changes designed to prevent the continued abuse of pretrial power to dismiss cases summarily without trials, move in the opposite direction. Of course, each such dismissal results in removal of one more case from our congested court dockets, but that factor should not weigh more heavily in our system of justice than assuring a full-fledged due process trial of every bona fide lawsuit brought to vindicate an honest, substantial claim. It is to protect this ancient right of a person to have his case tried rather than summarily thrown out of court that I suggested to the Court that it recommend changes in the Committee's proposals of the nature set out in the following memorandum.

"Dear Brethren:

"I have gone over all the proposed amendments carefully and while there are probably some good suggestions, it is my belief that the bad results that can come from the adoption of these amendments predominate over any good they can bring about. I particularly think that every member of the Court should examine with great care the amendments relating to class suits. It seems to me that they place too much power in the hands of the trial judges and that the rules might almost as well simply provide that 'class suits can be maintained either for or against particular groups whenever in the discretion of a judge he thinks it is wise.' The power given to the judge to dismiss such suits or to divide them up into groups at will subjects members of classes to dangers that could not follow from carefully prescribed legal standards enacted to control class suits.

"In addition, the rules as amended, in my judgment, greatly aggravate the evil of vesting judges with practically uncontrolled power to dismiss with prejudice cases brought by plaintiffs or defenses interposed by defendants. The power to dismiss a plaintiff's case or to render judgments by default against defendants can work great harm to both parties. There are many inherent urges in existence which may subconsciously incline a judge towards disposing of the cases before him without having to go through the burden of a trial. Mr. Chief Justice White, before he became Chief Justice, wrote an opinion in the case of *Hovey v. Elliott,* 167 U.S. 409 [17 S.Ct. 841, 42 L.Ed. 215], which pointed out grave constitutional questions raised by attempting to punish the parties by depriving them of the right to try their law suits or to defend against law suits brought against them by others.

"Rule 41 entitled 'Dismissal of Actions' points up the great power of judges to dismiss actions and provides an automatic method under which a dismissal must be construed as a dismissal 'with prejudice' unless the judge specifically states otherwise. For that reason I suggest to the Conference that if the Rules are accepted, including that one, the last sentence of Rule 41(b) be amended so as to provide that a simple order of dismissal by a judge instead of operating 'as an adjudication upon the merits,' as the amended rule reads, shall provide that such a dismissal 'does not operate as an adjudication upon the merits.'

"As a further guarantee against oppressive dismissals I suggest the addition of the following as subdivision (c) of Rule 41.

" 'No plaintiff's case shall be dismissed or defendant's right to defend be cut off because of the neglect, misfeasance, malfeasance, or failure of their counsel to obey any order of the court, until and unless such plaintiff or defendant shall have been personally served with notice of their counsel's delinquency, and not then unless the parties themselves do or fail to do something on their own part that can legally justify dismissal of the plaintiff's case or of the defendant's defense.'

"This proposed amendment is suggested in order to protect litigants, both plaintiffs and defendants, against being thrown out of court as a penalty for their lawyer's neglect or misconduct. The necessity for such a rule is shown, I think, by the dismissal in the plaintiff's case in *Link v. Wabash R. Co.,* 370 U.S. 626 [82 S.Ct. 1386, 8 L.Ed.2d 734]. The usual argument against this suggestion is that a party to a law suit hires his lawyer and should therefore be responsible for everything his lawyer does in the conduct of his case. This may be a good argument with reference to affluent litigants who not only know the best lawyers but are able to hire them. It is a wholly unrealistic argument, however, to make with reference to individual persons who do not know the ability of various lawyers or who are not financially able to hire those at the top of the bar and who are compelled to rely on the assumption that a lawyer licensed by the State is competent. It seems to me to be an uncivilized practice to punish clients by throwing their cases out of court because of their lawyers' conduct. It may be supportable by good, sound, formal logic but I think has no support whatever in a procedural system supposed to work as far as humanly possible to the end of obtaining equal and exact justice.

"For all the reasons stated above and in my previous objections to the transmittals of rules I dissent from the transmittals here."

[1] In a statement accompanying a previous transmittal of the civil rules, MR. JUSTICE DOUGLAS and I said:

"MR. JUSTICE BLACK and MR. JUSTICE DOUGLAS are opposed to the submission of these rules to the Congress under a statute which permits them to 'take effect' and to repeal 'all laws in conflict with such rules' without requiring any affirmative consideration, action, or approval of the rules by Congress or by the President. We believe that while some of the Rules of Civil Procedure are simply housekeeping details, many determine matters so substantially affecting the rights of litigants in lawsuits that in practical effect they are the equivalent of new legislation which, in our judgment, the Constitution requires to be initiated in and enacted by the Congress and approved by the President. The Constitution, as we read it, provides that all laws shall be enacted by the House, the Senate, and the President, not by the mere failure of Congress to reject proposals of an outside agency. * * *" (Footnotes omitted.) 374 U.S. 865–866.

[2] 346 U.S. 946, 374 U.S. 865. And see 368 U.S. 1011 and 1012.

MR. JUSTICE DOUGLAS, dissenting in part.

I reiterate today what I stated on an earlier occasion (374 U.S. 865, 869–870) (statement of Black and Douglas, JJ.), that the responsibility for promulgating Rules of the kind we send to Congress today should rest with the Judicial Conference and not the Court. It is the Judicial Conference, not the Court, which appoints the Advisory Committee on Criminal Rules which makes the actual recommendations.[1] Members of the Judicial Conference, being in large part judges of the lower courts and attorneys who are using the Rules day in and day out, are in a far better position to make a practical judgment upon their utility or inutility than we.

But since under the statute [2] the Rules go to Congress only on the initiative of the Court, I cannot be only a conduit. I think that placing our imprimatur on the amendments to the Rules entails a large degree of responsibility of judgment concerning them. Some of the criminal Rules which we forward to Congress today are very bothersome—not in the sense that they may be unwieldy or unworkable—but in the sense that they may entrench on important constitutional rights of defendants.

In my judgment, the amendments to Rule 16 dealing with discovery require further reflection. To the extent that they expand the defendant's opportunities for discovery, they accord with the views of a great many commentators who have concluded that a civilized society ought not to tolerate the conduct of a criminal prosecution as a "game." [3] But the proposed changes in the Rule go further. Rule 16(c) would permit a trial judge to condition granting the defendant discovery on the defendant's willingness to permit the prosecution to discover "scientific or medical reports, books, papers, documents, tangible objects, or copies or portions thereof" which (1) are in the defendant's possession; (2) he intends to produce at trial; and (3) are shown to be material to the preparation of the prosecution's case.[4]

The extent to which a court may compel the defendant to disclose information or evidence pertaining to his case without infringing the privilege against self-incrimination is a source of current controversy among judges, prosecutors, defense lawyers, and other legal commentators. A distinguished state court has concluded—although not without a strong dissent—that the privilege is not violated by discovery of the names of expert medical witnesses whose appearance at trial is contemplated by the defense.[5] I mean to imply no views on the point, except to note that a serious constitutional question lurks here.

The prosecution's opportunity to discover evidence in the possession of the defense is somewhat limited in the proposal with which we deal in that it is tied to the exercise by the defense of the right to discover from the prosecution. But *if* discovery, by itself, of information in the possession of the defendant would violate the privilege against self-incrimination, is it any less a violation if conditioned on the defendant's exercise of the opportunity to discover evidence? May benefits be conditioned on the abandonment of constitutional rights? See, e.g., *Sherbert v. Verner,* 374 U.S. 398, 403–406, 83 S.Ct. 1790, 1793–1795, 10 L.Ed.2d 965. To deny a defendant the opportunity to discovery—an opportunity not withheld from defendants who agree to prosecutorial discovery or from whom discovery is not sought—merely because the defendant chooses to exercise the constitutional right to refrain from self-incrimination arguably imposes a penalty upon the exercise of that fundamental privilege. It is said, however, that fairness may require disclosure by a defendant who obtains information from the prosecution.

Perhaps—but the proposed rule establishes no such standards. Its application is mechanical: if the defendant is allowed discovery, so, too, is the prosecution. No requirement is imposed, for example, that the subject matter of the material sought to be discovered by the prosecution be limited to that relating to the subject of the defendant's discovery.

The proposed addition of Rule 17.1 also suggests difficulties, perhaps of constitutional dimension. This rule would establish a pretrial conference procedure. The language of the rule and the Advisory Committee's comments suggest that under some circumstances, the conference might even take place in the absence of the defendant! Cf. *Lewis v. United States,* 146 U.S. 370, 13 S.Ct. 136, 36 L.Ed. 1011; Fed.Rules Crim.Proc. Rule 43.

The proposed amendment to Rule 32(c)(2) states that the trial judge "may" disclose to the defendant or his counsel the contents of a presentence report on which he is relying in fixing sentence. The imposition of sentence is of critical importance to a man convicted of crime. Trial judges need presentence reports so that they may have at their disposal the fullest possible information. See *Williams v. People of State of New York,* 337 U.S. 241, 69 S.Ct. 1079, 93 L.Ed. 1337. But while the formal rules of evidence do not apply to restrict the factors which the sentencing judge may consider, fairness would, in my opinion, require that the defendant be advised of the facts—perhaps very damaging to him—on which the judge intends to rely. The presentence report may be inaccurate, a flaw which may be of constitutional dimension. Cf. *Townsend v. Burke,* 334 U.S. 736, 68 S.Ct. 1252, 92 L.Ed. 1690. It may exaggerate the gravity of the defendant's prior offenses. The investigator may have made an incomplete investigation. See Tappan, Crime, Justice and Correction 556 (1960). There may be countervailing factors not disclosed by the probation report. In many areas we can rely on the sound exercise of discretion by the trial judge; but how can a judge know whether or not the presentence report calls for a reply by the defendant? Its faults may not appear on the face of the document.

Some States require full disclosure of the report to the defense.[6] The proposed Model Penal Code takes the middle-ground and requires the sentencing judge to disclose to the defense the factual contents of the report so that there is an opportunity to reply.[7] Whatever should be the rule for the federal courts, it ought not to be one which permits a judge to impose sentence on the basis of information of which the defendant may be unaware and to which he has not been afforded an opportunity to reply.

I do not think we should approve Rule 16, 17.1, and 32(c)(2). Instead, we should refer them back to the Judicial Conference and the Advisory Committee for further consideration and reflection, where I believe they were approved only by the narrowest majority.

WILLIAM O. DOUGLAS.

1 28 U.S.C. § 331 (1964 ed.) which establishes the Judicial Conference of the United States, provides that the Conference shall "carry on a continuous study of the operation and effect of the general rules of practice and procedure * * * prescribed by the Supreme Court * * *." The Conference has resolved that a standing Committee on Rules of Practice and Procedure be appointed by the Chief Justice and that, in addition, five advisory committees be established to recommend to the Judicial Conference changes in the rules of practice and procedure for the federal courts. See Annual Report of the Proceedings of the Judicial Conference of the United States 6–7 (1958).

2 18 U.S.C. § 3771 (1964 ed.).

3 See, e.g., Brennan, The Criminal Prosecution: Sporting Event or Quest for Truth?, 1963 Wash.U.L.Q. 279; Louisell, Criminal Discovery: Dilemma Real or Apparent?, 49 Calif.L.Rev. 56 (1961); Traynor, Ground Lost and Found in Criminal Discovery, 39 N.Y.U.L.Rev. 228 (1964).

4 The proposed rule explicitly provides that the prosecution may not discover nonmedical documents or reports "made by the defendant, or his attorneys or agents in connection with the investigation or defense of the case, or of statements made by the defendant, or by government or defense witnesses, or by prospective government or defense witnesses, to the defendant, his agents or attorneys."

5 *Jones v. Superior Court of Nevada County,* 58 Cal.2d 56, 22 Cal. Rptr. 879, 372 P.2d 919, 96 A.L.R.2d 1213. See Comment, 51 Calif.L.Rev. 135; Note, 76 Harv.L.Rev. 838 (1963). The case is more extensively treated in Louisell, Criminal Discovery and Self-Incrimination, 53 Calif.L.Rev. 89 (1965).

6 E.g., Calif.Penal Code § 1203.

7 Model Penal Code § 7.07(5) (Proposed Official Draft, 1962). The Code provides that the sources of confidential information need not be disclosed. "Less disclosure than this hardly comports with elementary fairness." Comment to § 7.07 (Tent.Draft No. 2, 1954), at 55. A discarded draft of the amendment to Fed.Rules Crim.Proc.Rule 32 would have allowed disclosure to defense counsel of the report, from which the confidential sources would be removed. A defendant not represented by counsel would be told of the "essential facts" in the report. See 8 Moore's Federal Practice ¶¶ 32.03[4], 32.09 (1965).

ORDER OF DECEMBER 4, 1967

1. That the following rules, to be known as the Federal Rules of Appellate Procedure, be, and they hereby are, prescribed, pursuant to sections 3771 and 3772 of Title 18, United States Code, and sections 2072 and 2075 of Title 28, United States Code, to govern the procedure in appeals to United States courts of appeals from the United States district courts, in the review by United States courts of appeals of decisions of the Tax Court of the United States, in proceedings in the United States courts of appeals for the review or enforcement of orders of administrative agencies, boards, commissions and officers, and in applications for writs or other relief which a United States court of appeals or judge thereof is competent to give:

[See text of Rules of Appellate Procedure, post.]

2. That the foregoing rules shall take effect on July 1, 1968, and shall govern all proceedings in appeals and petitions for review or enforcement of orders thereafter brought and in all such proceedings then pending, except to the extent that in the opinion of the court of appeals their application in a particular proceeding then pending would not be feasible or would work injustice, in which case the former procedure may be followed.

3. That Rules 6, 9, 41, 77 and 81 of the Rules of Civil Procedure for the United States District Courts be, and they hereby are, amended, effective July 1, 1968, as hereinafter set forth:

[See the amendments made thereby under the respective rules, post.]

4. That the chapter heading "IX. APPEALS", all of Rules 72, 73, 74, 75 and 76 of the Rules of Civil Procedure for the United States District Courts, and Form 27 annexed to the said rules, be, and they hereby are, abrogated, effective July 1, 1968.

[Paragraphs 5 and 6 of the order pertain to certain Rules of Criminal Procedure for the United States District Courts and to certain Forms annexed to the said rules. For text, see Pamphlet containing Federal Rules of Criminal Procedure.]

7. That THE CHIEF JUSTICE be, and he hereby is, authorized to transmit to the Congress the foregoing new rules and amendments to and abrogation of existing rules, in accordance with the provisions of Title 18, U.S.C., § 3771, and Title 28, U.S.C., §§ 2072 and 2075.

ORDER OF MARCH 30, 1970

1. That subdivision (a) of Rule 5, subdivision (h) of Rule 9 and Rules 26, 29, 30, 31, 32, 33, 34, 35, 36 and 37, and subdivision (d) of Rule 45, subdivision (a) of Rule 69, and Form 24 of the Rules of Civil Procedure for the United States District Courts be, and they hereby are, amended to read as follows:

[See the amendments made thereby under the respective rules and forms, post.]

2. That the foregoing amendments to the Rules of Civil Procedure shall take effect on July 1, 1970, and shall govern all proceedings in actions brought thereafter and also in all further proceedings in actions then pending, except to the extent that in the opinion of the court their application in a particular action then pending would not be feasible or would work injustice, in which event the former procedure applies.

3. That THE CHIEF JUSTICE be, and he hereby is, authorized to transmit to the Congress the foregoing amendments to the Rules of Civil Procedure in accordance with the provisions of Title 28, U.S.C. § 2072.

MR. JUSTICE BLACK and MR. JUSTICE DOUGLAS disapprove of the Amendments to the Federal Rules of Civil Procedure relating to Discovery, and dissent from the action of the Court in transmitting them to the Congress.

ORDER OF MARCH 1, 1971

1. That subdivision (a) of Rule 6, paragraph (4) of subdivision (a) of Rule 27, paragraph (6) of subdivision (b) of Rule 30, subdivision (c) of Rule 77, and paragraph (2) of subdivision (a) of Rule 81 of the Federal Rules of Civil Procedure be, and they hereby are, amended, effective July 1, 1971, to read as follows:

[See amendments made thereby under the respective rules, post.]

2. [*Certain Rules of Criminal Procedure for the United States District Courts amended*].

3. That subdivision (a) of Rule 26 and subdivision (a) of Rule 45 of the Federal Rules of Appellate Procedure be, and they hereby are, amended, effective July 1, 1971, to read as follows:

[See amendments made thereby under the respective Rules of Appellate Procedure, post.]

4. That THE CHIEF JUSTICE be, and he hereby is, authorized to transmit to the Congress the foregoing amendments to the Rules of Civil, Criminal and Appellate Procedure, in accordance with the provisions of Title 18 U.S.C. § 3771, and Title 28 U.S.C. §§ 2072 and 2075.

MR. JUSTICE BLACK and MR. JUSTICE DOUGLAS dissent.

ORDER OF NOVEMBER 20, 1972

1. That the rules hereinafter set forth, to be known as the Federal Rules of Evidence, be, and they hereby are, prescribed pursuant to Sections 3402, 3771, and 3772, Title 18, United States Code, and Sections 2072 and 2075, Title 28, United States Code, to govern procedure, in the proceedings and to the extent set forth therein, in the United States courts of appeals, the United States district courts, the District Court for the District of the Canal Zone and the district courts of Guam and the Virgin Islands, and before United States magistrates.

2. That the aforementioned Federal Rules of Evidence shall take effect on July 1, 1973, and shall be applicable to actions and proceedings brought thereafter and also to further procedure in actions and proceedings then pending, except to the extent that in the opinion of the court their application in a particular action or proceeding then pending would not be feasible or would work injustice in which event the former procedure applies.

3. That subdivision (c) of Rule 30 and Rules 43 and 44.1 of the Federal Rules of Civil Procedure be, and they hereby are, amended, effective July 1, 1973, to read as hereinafter set forth:

[See amendments made thereby under the respective rules, post.]

4. That subdivision (c) of Rule 32 of the Federal Rules of Civil Procedure be, and it hereby is, abrogated, effective July 1, 1973.

5. *[Certain Rules of Criminal Procedure for the United States District Courts amended].*

6. That THE CHIEF JUSTICE be, and he hereby is, authorized to transmit the foregoing new rules and amendments to and abrogation of existing rules to the Congress at the beginning of its next regular session, in accordance with the provisions of Title 18 U.S.C. § 3771 and Title 28 U.S.C. §§ 2072 and 2075.

ORDER OF DECEMBER 18, 1972

1. That Rule 43 of the Federal Rules of Civil Procedure, as amended by Order of this Court entered November 20, 1972, be, and it hereby is, further amended, effective July 1, 1973, to read as follows:

[See amendment made thereby under Rule 43 post.]

2. That THE CHIEF JUSTICE be, and he hereby is, authorized to transmit the foregoing amendment of Rule 43 of the Federal Rules of Civil Procedure to the Congress at the beginning of its next regular session in accordance with the provisions of Title 28, U.S.C. § 2072.

CONGRESSIONAL ACTION ON PROPOSED RULES OF EVIDENCE AND 1972 AMENDMENTS TO FEDERAL RULES OF CIVIL PROCEDURE AND FEDERAL RULES OF CRIMINAL PROCEDURE

Pub.L. 93–12, Mar. 30, 1973, 87 Stat. 9, provided: "That notwithstanding any other provisions of law, the Rules of Evidence for United States Courts and Magistrates, the Amendments to the Federal Rules of Civil Procedure, and the Amendments to the Federal Rules of Criminal Procedure, which are embraced by the orders entered by the Supreme Court of the United States on Monday, November 20, 1972, and Monday, December 18, 1972, shall have no force or effect except to the extent, and with such amendments, as they may be expressly approved by Act of Congress."

Pub.L. 93–595, § 3, Jan. 2, 1975, 88 Stat. 1959, provided that: "The Congress expressly approves the amendments to the Federal Rules of Civil Procedure, and the amendments to the Federal Rules of Criminal Procedure, which are embraced by the orders entered by the Supreme Court of the United States on November 20, 1972, and December 18, 1972, and such amendments shall take effect on the one hundred and eightieth day beginning after the date of the enactment of this Act [Jan. 2, 1975]."

ORDER OF APRIL 26, 1976

1. That the rules and forms governing proceedings in the United States District Courts under Section 2254 and Section 2255 of Title 28, United States Code, as approved by the Judicial Conference of the United States be, and they hereby are, prescribed pursuant to Section 2072 of Title 28, United States Code and Sections 3771 and 3772 of Title 18, United States Code.

2. That the aforementioned rules and forms shall take effect August 1, 1976, and shall be applicable to all proceedings then pending except to the extent that in the opinion of the court their application in a particular proceeding would not be feasible or would work injustice.

3. That THE CHIEF JUSTICE be, and he hereby is, authorized to transmit the aforementioned rules and forms governing Section 2254 and Section 2255 proceedings to the Congress in accordance with the provisions of Section 2072 of Title 28 and Sections 3771 and 3772 of Title 18, United States Code.

CONGRESSIONAL ACTION ON PROPOSED RULES AND FORMS GOVERNING PROCEEDINGS UNDER 28 U.S.C. §§ 2254 AND 2255

Pub.L. 94–349, § 2, July 8, 1976, 90 Stat. 822, provided: "That, notwithstanding the provisions of section 2072 of title 28 of the United States Code, the rules and forms governing section 2254 cases in the United States district courts and the rules and forms governing section 2255 proceedings in the United States district courts which are embraced by the order entered by the United States Supreme Court on April 26, 1976, and which were transmitted to the Congress on or about April 26, 1976, shall not take effect until thirty days after the adjournment sine die of the 94th Congress, or until and to the extent approved by Act of Congress, whichever is earlier."

Pub.L. 94–426, § 1, Sept. 28, 1976, 90 Stat. 1334, provided: "That the rules governing section 2254 cases in the United States district courts and the rules governing section 2255 proceedings for the United States district courts, as proposed by the United States Supreme Court, which were delayed by the Act entitled 'An Act to delay the effective date of certain proposed amendments to the Federal Rules of Criminal Procedure and certain other rules promulgated by the United States Supreme Court' (Public Law 94–349), are approved with the amendments set forth in section 2 of this Act and shall take effect as so amended, with respect to petitions under section 2254 and motions under section 2255 of title 28 of the United States Code filed on or after February 1, 1977."

ORDER OF APRIL 29, 1980

1. That the Federal Rules of Civil Procedure be, and they hereby are, amended by including therein amendments to Rules 4, 5, 26, 28, 30, 32, 33, 34, 37 and 45 as hereinafter set forth:

[See amendments made thereby under respective rules, post.]

2. That the foregoing amendments to the Federal Rules of Civil Procedure shall take effect on August 1, 1980, and shall govern all civil proceedings thereafter commenced and, insofar as just and practicable, all proceedings then pending.

3. That subsection (e) of Rule 37 of the Federal Rules of Civil Procedure is hereby abrogated, effective August 1, 1980.

4. That THE CHIEF JUSTICE be, and he hereby is, authorized to transmit to the Congress the foregoing amendments to the Federal Rules of Civil Procedure in accordance with the provisions of Section 2072 of Title 28, United States Code.

MR. JUSTICE POWELL, with whom MR. JUSTICE STEWART and MR. JUSTICE REHNQUIST join, filed a dissenting statement.

I dissent from the Court's adoption of the amendments to Federal Rules of Civil Procedure 26, 33, 34, and 37—the cluster of Rules authorizing and regulating discovery generally, interrogatories, production of documents, and sanctions for failure to make discovery. These amendments are not inherently objectionable. Indeed, they represent the culmination of several years' work by the Judicial Conference's distinguished and conscientious Standing Committee on Rules of Practice and Procedure and Advisory Committee on Civil Rules.[1] But the changes embodied in the amendments fall short of those needed to accomplish reforms in civil litigation that are long overdue.

The American Bar Association proposed significant and substantial reforms.[2] Although the Standing Committee initially favored most of these proposals, it ultimately rejected them in large part. The ABA now accedes to the Standing Committee's amendments because they make some improvements, but the most recent report of the ABA Section of Litigation makes clear that the "serious and widespread abuse of discovery" will remain largely uncontrolled.[3] There are wide differences of opinion within the profession as to the need for reform. The bench and the bar are familiar with the existing Rules, and it often is said that the bar has a vested interest in maintaining the status quo. I imply no criticism of the bar or the Standing Committee when I suggest that the present recommendations reflect a compromise as well as the difficulty of framing satisfactory discovery Rules. But whatever considerations may have prompted the Committee's final decision, I doubt that many judges or lawyers familiar with the proposed amendments believe they will have an appreciable effect on the acute problems associated with discovery. The Court's adoption of these inadequate changes could postpone effective reform for another decade.

When the Federal Rules first appeared in 1938, the discovery provisions properly were viewed as a constructive improvement. But experience under the discovery Rules demonstrates that "not infrequently [they have been] exploited to the disadvantage of justice." *Herbert v. Lando,* 441 U.S. 153, 179 (1979) (POWELL, J., concurring). Properly limited and controlled discovery is necessary in most civil litigation. The present Rules, however, invite discovery of such scope and duration that district judges often cannot keep the practice within reasonable bounds.[4] Even in a relatively simple case, discovery through depositions, interrogatories, and demands for documents may take weeks. In complex litigation, discovery can continue for years. One must doubt whether empirical evidence would demonstrate that untrammeled discovery actually contributes to the just resolution of disputes. If there is disagreement about that, there is none whatever about the effect of discovery practices upon the average citizen's ability to afford legal remedies.

Delay and excessive expense now characterize a large percentage of all civil litigation. The problems arise in significant part, as every judge and litigator knows, from abuse of the discovery procedures available under the Rules.[5] Indeed, the National Conference on the Causes of Popular Dissatisfaction with the Administration of Justice, led by THE CHIEF JUSTICE,[6] identified "Abuse in the use of discovery [as] a major concern" within our legal system.[7] Lawyers devote an enormous number of "chargeable hours" to the practice of discovery. We may assume that discovery usually is conducted in good faith. Yet all too often discovery practices enable the party with greater financial resources to prevail by exhausting the resources of a weaker opponent. The mere threat of delay or unbearable expense denies justice to many actual or prospective litigants. Persons or businesses of comparatively limited means settle unjust claims and relinquish just claims simply because they cannot afford to litigate.[8] Litigation costs have become intolerable, and they cast a lengthening shadow over the basic fairness of our legal system.

I reiterate that I do not dissent because the modest amendments recommended by the Judicial Conference are undesirable. I simply believe that Congress' acceptance of these tinkering changes will delay for years the adoption of genuinely effective reforms. The process of change, as experience teaches, is tortuous and contentious. Favorable congressional action on these amendments will create complacency and encourage inertia. Meanwhile, the discovery Rules will continue to deny justice to those least able to bear the burdens of delay, escalating legal fees, and rising court costs.

The amendments to Rules 26, 33, 34, and 37 recommended by the Judicial Conference should be rejected, and the Conference should be directed to initiate a thorough reexamination of the discovery Rules that have become so central to the conduct of modern civil litigation.

1 This Court's role in the rulemaking process is largely formalistic. Standing and advisory committees of the Judicial Conference make the initial studies, invite comments on their drafts, and prepare the Rules. Both the Judicial Conference and this Court necessarily rely upon the careful work of these committees. Congress should bear in mind that our approval of proposed Rules is more a certification that they are the products of proper procedures than a considered judgment on the merits of the proposals themselves. See generally 409 U.S. 1132, 1133 (1973) (DOUGLAS, J., dissenting from adoption of Federal Rules of Evidence); 383 U.S. 1032 (1966) (BLACK, J., dissenting from adoption of amendment to civil rules); 374 U.S. 865, 869–870 (1963) (statement of BLACK and DOUGLAS, JJ., upon adoption of amendments to Federal Rules of Civil Procedure).

2 American Bar Association, Report of the Section of Litigation Special Committee for the Study of Discovery Abuse (App.Draft 1977).

3 ABA Section of Litigation, Second Report of the Special Committee for the Study of Discovery Abuse, 5 (1980).

4 MR. JUSTICE WHITE, writing for the Court, recently reminded the federal courts that "the discovery provisions ... are subject to the injunction of Rule 1 that they be 'construed to secure the just, *speedy,* and *inexpensive* determination of every action.'" *Herbert v. Lando,* 441 U.S. 153, 177 (1979).

In his most recent Annual Report on the State of the Judiciary, THE CHIEF JUSTICE declared that "[t]he responsibility for control [of pretrial process] rests on both judges and lawyers. Where existing rules and statutes permit abuse, they must be changed. Where the power lies with judges to prevent or correct abuse and misuse of the system, judges must act." Address to American Bar Association Mid-Year Meeting, 6 (Feb. 3, 1980).

5 Writing from his wide experience as a judge, practicing lawyer, and Attorney General, Griffin B. Bell advised the Standing Committee that "the scope of discovery is far too broad and that excessive discovery has significantly contributed to the delays, complexity and high cost of civil litigation in the federal courts." Letter to The Honorable Roszel C. Thomsen, Chairman of the Committee on Rules of Practice and Procedure of the Judicial Conference, 1 (June 27, 1978).

6 THE CHIEF JUSTICE'S keynote address to this distinguished assembly, popularly known as the Pound Conference, recognized that discovery processes "are being misused and abused." See Burger, Agenda for 2000 A.D.—A Need for Systematic Anticipation, 70 F.R.D. 83, 95–96 (1976).

7 See Erickson, The Pound Conference Recommendations: A Blueprint for the Justice System in the Twenty-first Century, 76 F.R.D. 277, 288 (1978); ABA, Report of Pound Conference Follow-up Task Force, 74 F.R.D. 159, 171–192 (1976).

8 "The principal function of procedural rules," as MR. JUSTICE BLACK observed in another context, "should be to serve as useful guides to help, not hinder, persons who have a legal right to bring their problems before the courts." 346 U.S. 946 (1954) (separate statement upon adoption of revised Supreme Court Rules).

ORDER OF APRIL 28, 1983

1. That the Federal Rules of Civil Procedure be, and they hereby are, amended by including therein new Rules 26(g), 53(f), 72 through 76 and new Official Forms 33 and 34, and amendments to Rules 6(b), 7(b), 11, 16, 26(a) and (b), 52(a), 53(a), (b) and (c) and 67, as hereinafter set forth:

[See additions and amendments made thereby under respective rules and forms, post.]

2. That the foregoing additions and amendments to the Federal Rules of Civil Procedure shall take effect on August 1, 1983 and shall govern all civil proceedings thereafter commenced and, insofar as just and practicable, in proceedings then pending.

3. That THE CHIEF JUSTICE be, and he hereby is, authorized to transmit to the Congress the foregoing additions to and changes in the Federal Rules of Civil Procedure in accordance with the provisions of Section 2072 of Title 28, United States Code.

ORDER OF APRIL 29, 1985

1. That the Federal Rules of Civil Procedure for the United States District Courts be, and they hereby are, amended by including therein a new Rule E(4)(f) to the Supplemental Rules for Certain Admiralty and Maritime Claims; amendments to Rules 6(a), 45(d)(2), 52(a), 71A(h) and 83; amendments to Supplemental Admiralty Rules B(1) and C(3); and amendments to Official Form 18–A, as hereinafter set forth:

[See additions and amendments made thereby under respective rules and forms, post.]

2. That the foregoing addition to and changes in the Federal Rules of Civil Procedure, the Supplemental Rules for Certain Admiralty and Maritime Claims, and the Official Form shall take effect on August 1, 1985 and shall govern all proceedings in civil actions thereafter commenced and, insofar as just and practicable, all proceedings in civil actions then pending.

3. That THE CHIEF JUSTICE be, and he hereby is, authorized to transmit to the Congress the foregoing addition to and changes in the rules of civil procedure in accordance with the provisions of Section 2072 of Title 28, United States Code.

ORDER OF MARCH 2, 1987

1. That the Federal Rules of Civil Procedure and the Supplemental Rules for Certain Admiralty and Maritime Claims be, and they hereby are, amended by including therein amendments to Civil Rules 4, 5, 6, 8, 9, 11, 12, 13, 14, 15, 16, 17, 18, 19, 20, 22, 23, 23.1, 24, 25, 26, 27, 28, 30, 31, 32, 34, 35, 36, 37 38, 41, 43, 44, 44.1, 45, 46, 49, 50, 51, 53, 54, 55, 56, 60, 62, 63, 65, 65.1, 68, 69, 71, 71A, 73, 75, 77, 78, 81, and to the Supplemental Rules for Certain Admiralty and Maritime Claims, Rules B, C, E, and F, as hereinafter set forth:

[See amendments made thereby under respective rules, post.]

2. That the foregoing amendments to the Federal Rules of Civil Procedure and the Supplemental Rules for Certain Admiralty and Maritime Claims shall take effect on August 1, 1987.

3. That THE CHIEF JUSTICE be, and he hereby is, authorized to transmit to the Congress the foregoing amendments in accordance with the provisions of Section 2072 of Title 28, United States Code.

ORDER OF APRIL 25, 1988

1. That the Federal Rules of Civil Procedure be, and they hereby are, amended by including therein amendments to Civil Rules 17 and 71, as hereinafter set forth:

[See amendments made thereby under respective rules, post.]

2. That the foregoing amendments to the Federal Rules of Civil Procedure shall take effect on August 1, 1988.

3. That THE CHIEF JUSTICE be, and he hereby is, authorized to transmit to the Congress the foregoing amendments in accordance with the provisions of Section 2072 of Title 28, United States Code.

ORDER OF APRIL 30, 1991

1. That the Federal Rules of Civil Procedure for the United States District Courts be, and they hereby are, amended by including therein new chapter headings VIII and IX, amendments to Rules C and E of the Supplemental Rules for Certain Admiralty and Maritime Claims, new Forms 1A and 1B to the Appendix of Forms, the abrogation of Form 18A, and amendments to Civil Rules 5, 15, 24, 34, 35, 41, 44, 45, 47, 48, 50, 52, 53, 63, 72, and 77, as hereinafter set forth.

[See additions and amendments made thereby under respective rules and forms, post.]

2. That the foregoing additions to and changes in the Federal Rules of Civil Procedure, the Supplemental Rules for Certain Admiralty and Maritime Claims, and the Civil Forms shall take effect on December 1, 1991, and shall govern all proceedings in civil actions thereafter commenced and, insofar as just and practicable, all proceedings in civil actions then pending.

3. That THE CHIEF JUSTICE be, and hereby is, authorized to transmit to the Congress the foregoing addition to and changes in the Rules of Civil Procedure in accordance with the provisions of Section 2072 of Title 28, United States Code.

[Congress may postpone the proposed rule and form additions and amendments effective December 1, 1991, may decline to approve such additions and amendments, or may make changes to the additions and amendments.]

ORDER OF APRIL 22, 1993

1. That the Federal Rules of Civil Procedure for the United States District Courts be, and they hereby are, amended by including therein amendments to Civil Rules 1, 4, 5, 11, 12, 15, 16, 26, 28, 29, 30, 31, 32, 33, 34, 36, 37, 38, 50, 52, 53, 54, 58, 71A, 72, 73, 74, 75, and 76, and new Rule 4.1, and abrogation of Form 18–A, and amendments to Forms 2, 33, 34, and 34A, and new Forms 1A, 1B, and 35.

[See amendments made thereby under respective rules and forms, post.]

2. That the foregoing amendments to the Federal Rules of Civil Procedure shall take effect on December 1, 1993, and shall govern all proceedings in civil cases thereafter commenced and, insofar as just and practicable, all proceedings in civil cases then pending.

3. That THE CHIEF JUSTICE be, and he hereby is, authorized to transmit to the Congress the foregoing amendments to the Federal Rules of Civil Procedure in accordance with the provisions of Section 2072 of Title 23, United States Code.

ORDER OF APRIL 27, 1995

1. That the Federal Rules of Civil Procedure for the United States District Courts be, and they hereby are, amended by including therein amendments to Civil Rules 50, 52, 59, and 83.

[See amendments made thereby under respective rules, post.]

2. That the foregoing amendments to the Federal Rules of Civil Procedure shall take effect on December 1, 1995, and shall govern all proceedings in civil cases thereafter commenced and, insofar as just and practicable, all proceedings in civil cases then pending.

3. That THE CHIEF JUSTICE be, and hereby is, authorized to transmit to the Congress the foregoing amendments to the Federal Rules of Civil Procedure in accordance with the provisions of Section 2072 of Title 28, United States Code.

ORDER OF APRIL 23, 1996

1. That the Federal Rules of Civil Procedure for the United States District Courts be, and they hereby are, amended by including therein amendments to Civil Rules 5 and 43.

[See amendments made thereby under respective rules, post]

2. That the foregoing amendments to the Federal Rules of Civil Procedure shall take effect on December 1, 1996, and shall govern all proceedings in civil cases thereafter commenced and, insofar as just and practicable, all proceedings in civil cases then pending.

3. That THE CHIEF JUSTICE be, and hereby is, authorized to transmit to the Congress the foregoing amendments to the Federal Rules of Civil Procedure in accordance with the provisions of Section 2072 of Title 28, United States Code.

ORDER OF APRIL 11, 1997

1. That the Federal Rules of Civil Procedure for the United States District Courts be, and they hereby are, amended by including therein amendments to Civil Rules 9 and 73, and abrogation of Rules 74, 75, and 76, and amendments to Forms 33 and 34.

[See amendments made thereby under respective rules, post]

2. That the foregoing amendments to the Federal Rules of Civil Procedure shall take effect on December 1, 1997, and shall govern all proceedings in civil cases thereafter commenced and, insofar as just and practicable, all proceedings in civil cases then pending.

3. That THE CHIEF JUSTICE be, and hereby is, authorized to transmit to the Congress the foregoing amendments to the Federal Rules of Civil Procedure in accordance with the provisions of Section 2072 of Title 28, United States Code.

ORDER OF APRIL 24, 1998

1. That the Federal Rules of Civil Procedure for the United States District Courts be, and they hereby are, amended by including therein a new Civil Rule 23(f).

[See amendments made thereby under respective rules, post]

2. That the foregoing amendments to the Federal Rules of Civil Procedure shall take effect on December 1, 1998, and shall govern all proceedings in civil cases thereafter commenced and, insofar as just and practicable, all proceedings in civil cases then pending.

3. That THE CHIEF JUSTICE be, and hereby is, authorized to transmit to the Congress the foregoing amendments to the Federal Rules of Civil Procedure in accordance with the provisions of Section 2072 of Title 28, United States Code.

ORDER OF APRIL 26, 1999

1. That the Federal Rules of Civil Procedure for the United States District Courts be, and they hereby are, amended by including therein amendments to Civil Rule 6(b) and Form 2.

[See amendments made thereby under respective rules, post.]

2. That the foregoing amendments to the Federal Rules of Civil Procedure shall take effect on December 1, 1999, and shall govern all proceedings in civil cases thereafter commenced and, insofar as just and practicable, all proceedings in civil cases then pending.

3. That THE CHIEF JUSTICE be, and hereby is, authorized to transmit to the Congress the foregoing amendments to the Federal Rules of Civil Procedure in accordance with the provisions of Section 2072 of Title 28, United States Code.

ORDER OF APRIL 17, 2000

1. That the Federal Rules of Civil Procedure for the United States District Courts be, and they hereby are, amended by including therein amendments to Civil Rules 4, 5, 12, 14, 26, 30, and 37 and to Rules B, C, and E of the Supplemental Rules for Certain Admiralty and Maritime Claims.

[See amendments made thereby under respective rules, post.]

2. That the foregoing amendments to the Federal Rules of Civil Procedure and the Supplemental Rules for Certain Admiralty and Maritime Claims shall take effect on December 1, 2000, and shall govern all proceedings in civil cases thereafter commenced and, insofar as just and practicable, all proceedings in civil cases then pending.

3. That THE CHIEF JUSTICE be, and hereby is, authorized to transmit to the Congress the foregoing amendments to the Federal Rules of Civil Procedure in accordance with the provisions of Section 2072 of Title 28, United States Code.

ORDER OF APRIL 23, 2001

1. That the Federal Rules of Civil Procedure be, and they hereby are, amended by including therein amendments to Civil Rules 5, 6, 65, 77, 81, and 82.

[See amendments made thereby under respective rules, post.]

2. That the foregoing amendments to the Federal Rules of Civil Procedure shall take effect on December 1, 2001, and shall govern in all proceedings in civil cases thereafter commenced and, insofar as just and practicable, all proceedings then pending.

3. That THE CHIEF JUSTICE be, and hereby is, authorized to transmit to the Congress the foregoing amendments to the Federal Rules of Civil Procedure in accordance with the provisions of Section 2072 of Title 28, United States Code.

4. That the Rules for Practice and Procedure under section 25 of An Act To Amend and Consolidate the Acts Respecting Copyright, approved March 4, 1909, promulgated by this Court on June 1, 1909, effective July 1, 1909, as revised, be, and they hereby are, abrogated, effective December 1, 2001.

ORDER OF APRIL 29, 2002

1. That the Federal Rules of Civil Procedure be, and they hereby are, amended by including therein amendments to Civil Rules 54, 58, and 81, and a new Rule 7.1, and Rule C of Supplemental Rules for Certain Admiralty and Maritime Claims.

[See amendments made thereby under respective rules, post.]

2. That the foregoing amendments to the Federal Rules of Civil Procedure shall take effect on December 1, 2002, and shall govern in all proceedings in civil cases thereafter commenced and, insofar as just and practicable, all proceedings then pending.

3. That the CHIEF JUSTICE be, and hereby is, authorized to transmit to the Congress the foregoing amendments to the Federal Rules of Civil Procedure in accordance with the provisions of Section 2072 of Title 28, United States Code.

ORDER OF MARCH 27, 2003

1. That the Federal Rules of Civil Procedure be, and they hereby are, amended by including therein amendments to Civil Rules 23, 51, 53, 54, and 71A.

[See amendments made thereby under respective rules and forms, post.]

2. That Forms 19, 31, and 32 in the Appendix to the Federal Rules of Civil Procedure be, and they hereby are, amended by replacing all references to "19__" with references to "20__."

3. That the foregoing amendments to the Federal Rules of Civil Procedure shall take effect on December 1, 2003, and shall govern in all proceedings in civil cases thereafter commenced and, insofar as just and practicable, all proceedings then pending.

4. That the CHIEF JUSTICE be, and hereby is, authorized to transmit to the Congress the foregoing amendments to the Federal Rules of Civil Procedure in accordance with the provisions of Section 2072 of Title 28, United States Code.

ORDER OF APRIL 25, 2005

1. That the Federal Rules of Civil Procedure be, and they hereby are, amended by including therein the amendments to Civil Rules 6, 27, and 45, and to Rules B and C of the Supplemental Rules for Certain Admiralty and Maritime Claims.

[See amendments made thereby under respective rules and forms, post.]

2. That the foregoing amendments to the Federal Rules of Civil Procedure and the Supplemental Rules for Certain Admiralty and Maritime Claims shall take effect on December 1, 2005, and shall govern in all proceedings thereafter commenced and, insofar as just and practicable, all proceedings then pending.

3. That the CHIEF JUSTICE be, and hereby is, authorized to transmit to the Congress the foregoing amendments to the Federal Rules of Civil Procedure in accordance with the provisions of Section 2072 of Title 28, United States Code.

ORDER OF APRIL 12, 2006

1. That the Federal Rules of Civil Procedure be, and they hereby are, amended by including therein the amendments to Civil Rules 5, 9, 14, 16, 24, 26, 33, 34, 37, 45, 50, and 65.1; Form 35; and new Rule 5.1.

2. That the Supplemental Rules for Admiralty or Maritime Claims and Asset Forfeiture Actions be, and they hereby are, amended by including therein the amendments to Rules A, C, and E, and new Rule G.

[See amendments made thereby under respective rules and forms, post.]

3. That the foregoing amendments to the Federal Rules of Civil Procedure and the Supplemental Rules for Admiralty or Maritime Claims and Asset Forfeiture Actions shall take

effect on December 1, 2006, and shall govern in all proceedings thereafter commenced and, insofar as just and practicable, all proceedings then pending.

4. That THE CHIEF JUSTICE be, and hereby is, authorized to transmit to the Congress the foregoing amendments to the Federal Rules of Civil Procedure in accordance with the provisions of Section 2072 of Title 28, United States Code.

ORDER OF APRIL 30, 2007

1. That the Federal Rules of Civil Procedure be, and they hereby are, amended by including therein the amendments to Civil Rules 1 through 86 and new Rule 5.2.

2. That Forms 1 through 35 in the Appendix to the Federal Rules of Civil Procedure be, and they hereby are, amended to become restyled Forms 1 through 82.

[See amendments made thereby under respective rules and forms, post.]

3. That the foregoing amendments to the Federal Rules of Civil Procedure shall take effect on December 1, 2007, and shall govern in all proceedings thereafter commenced and, insofar as just and practicable, all proceedings then pending.

4. That THE CHIEF JUSTICE be, and hereby is, authorized to transmit to the Congress the foregoing amendments to the Federal Rules of Civil Procedure in accordance with the provisions of Section 2072 of Title 28, United States Code.

ORDER OF APRIL 23, 2008

1. That the Supplemental Rules for Admiralty or Maritime Claims and Asset Forfeiture Actions be, and they hereby are, amended by including therein the amendment to Rule C.

[See amendment made thereby under Rule C post.]

2. That the foregoing amendment to the Supplemental Rules for Admiralty or Maritime Claims and Asset Forfeiture Actions shall take effect on December 1, 2008, and shall govern in all proceedings thereafter commenced and, insofar as just and practicable, all proceedings then pending.

3. That THE CHIEF JUSTICE be, and hereby is, authorized to transmit to the Congress the foregoing amendment to the Supplemental Rules for Admiralty or Maritime Claims and Asset Forfeiture Actions in accordance with the provisions of Section 2072 of Title 28, United States Code.

HISTORICAL NOTES

The original Rules of Civil Procedure for the District Courts were adopted by order of the Supreme Court on Dec. 20, 1937, transmitted to Congress by the Attorney General on Jan. 3, 1938, and became effective on Sept. 16, 1938.

The Rules have been amended Dec. 28, 1939, eff. Apr. 3, 1941; Dec. 27, 1946, eff. Mar. 19, 1948; Dec. 29, 1948, eff. Oct. 20, 1949; Apr. 30, 1951, eff. Aug. 1, 1951; Apr. 17, 1961, eff. July 19, 1961; Jan. 21, 1963, eff. July 1, 1963; Feb. 28, 1966, eff. July 1, 1966; Dec. 4, 1967, eff. July 1, 1968; Mar. 30, 1970, eff. July 1, 1970; Mar. 1, 1971, eff. July 1, 1971; Nov. 20, 1972, and Dec. 18, 1972, eff. July 1, 1975; Apr. 29, 1980, eff. Aug. 1, 1980; Oct. 21, 1980, Pub.L. 96–481, Title II, § 205(a), (b), 94 Stat. 2330; Jan. 12, 1983, Pub.L. 97–462, §§ 2–4, 96 Stat. 2527–2530, eff. Feb. 26, 1983; Apr. 28, 1983, eff. Aug. 1, 1983; Apr. 29, 1985, eff. Aug. 1, 1985; Mar. 2, 1987, eff. Aug. 1, 1987; Apr. 25, 1988, eff. Aug. 1, 1988; Nov. 18, 1988, Pub.L. 100–690, Title VII, §§ 7047(b), 7049, 7050, 102 Stat. 4401; Apr. 30, 1991, eff. Dec. 1, 1991; Apr. 22, 1993, eff. Dec. 1, 1993; Apr. 27, 1995, eff. Dec. 1, 1995; Apr. 23, 1996, eff. Dec. 1, 1996; Apr. 11, 1997, eff. Dec. 1, 1997 Apr. 24, 1998, eff. Dec. 1, 1998; Apr. 26, 1999, eff. Dec. 1, 1999; Apr. 17, 2000, eff. Dec. 1, 2000; Apr. 23, 2001, eff. Dec. 1, 2001; Apr. 29, 2002, eff. Dec. 1, 2002; Mar. 27, 2003, eff. Dec. 1, 2003; Apr. 25, 2005, eff. Dec. 1, 2005; Apr. 12, 2006, eff. Dec. 1, 2006; Apr. 30, 2007, eff. Dec. 1, 2007; April 23, 2008, eff. Dec. 1, 2008, absent contrary Congressional action.

CROSS REFERENCES

Procedure in original actions in Supreme Court of United States, U.S.Sup. Ct. Rule 17, 28 USCA.

TITLE I. SCOPE OF RULES; FORM OF ACTION

Rule 1. Scope and Purpose

These rules govern the procedure in all civil actions and proceedings in the United States district courts, except as stated in Rule 81. They should be construed and administered to secure the just, speedy, and inexpensive determination of every action and proceeding.

(Amended December 29, 1948, effective October 20, 1949; February 28, 1966, effective July 1, 1966; April 22, 1993, effective December 1, 1993; April 30, 2007, effective December 1, 2007.)

ADVISORY COMMITTEE NOTES

1937 Adoption

1. Rule 81 states certain limitations in the application of these rules to enumerated special proceedings.

2. The expression "district courts of the United States" appearing in the statute authorizing the Supreme Court of the United States to promulgate rules of civil procedure does not include the district courts held in the territories and insular possessions. See *Mookini et al. v. United States,* 1938, 58 S.Ct. 543, 303 U.S. 201, 82 L.Ed. 748.

3. These rules are drawn under the authority of the Act of June 19, 1934, U.S.C., Title 28, § 723b [see 2072] (Rules in actions at law; Supreme Court authorized to make), and § 723c [see 2072] (Union of equity and action at law rules; power of Supreme Court) and also other grants of rule making power to the Court. See Clark and Moore, *A New Federal Civil Procedure—I. The Background,* 44 Yale L.J. 387, 391 (1935). Under § 723b after the rules have taken effect all laws in conflict therewith are of no further force or effect. In accordance with § 723c the Court has united the general rules prescribed for cases in equity with those in actions at law so as to secure one form of civil action and procedure for both. See Rule 2 (One Form of Action). For the former practice in equity and at law see U.S.C.A., Title 28, §§ 723 and 730 [see 2071 et seq.] (conferring power on the Supreme Court to make rules of practice in equity) and the [former] Equity Rules promulgated thereunder; U.S.C., Title 28, [former] § 724 (Conformity act); [former] Equity Rule 22 (Action at Law Erroneously Begun as Suit in Equity—Transfer); [former] Equity Rule 23 (Matters Ordinarily Determinable at Law When Arising in Suit in Equity to be Disposed of Therein); U.S.C., Title 28, [former] §§ 397 (Amendments to pleadings when case brought to wrong side of court), and 398 (Equitable defenses and equitable relief in actions at law).

4. With the second sentence compare U.S.C., Title 28, [former] §§ 777 (Defects of form; amendments), [former] 767 (Amendment of process); [former] Equity Rule 19 (Amendments Generally).

1948 Amendment

The amendment effective Oct. 20, 1949, substituted the words "United States district courts" for the words "district courts of the United States."

1966 Amendment

This is the fundamental change necessary to effect unification of the civil and admiralty procedure. Just as the 1938 rules abolished the distinction between actions at law and suits in equity, this change would abolish the distinction between civil actions and suits in admiralty. See also Rule 81.

1993 Amendments

The purpose of this revision, adding the words "and administered" to the second sentence, is to recognize the affirmative duty of the court to exercise the authority conferred by these rules to ensure that civil litigation is resolved not only fairly, but also without undue cost or delay. As officers of the court, attorneys share this responsibility with the judge to whom the case is assigned.

2007 Amendment

The language of Rule 1 has been amended as part of the general restyling of the Civil Rules to make them more easily understood and to make style and terminology consistent throughout the rules. These changes are intended to be stylistic only.

The merger of law, equity, and admiralty practice is complete. There is no need to carry forward the phrases that initially accomplished the merger.

The former reference to "suits of a civil nature" is changed to the more modern "civil actions and proceedings." This change does not affect such questions as whether the Civil Rules apply to summary proceedings created by statute. *See SEC v. McCarthy*, 322 F.3d 650 (9th Cir. 2003); *see also New Hampshire Fire Ins. Co. v. Scanlon*, 362 U.S. 404 (1960).

The Style Project

The Civil Rules are the third set of the rules to be restyled. The restyled Rules of Appellate Procedure took effect in 1998. The restyled Rules of Criminal Procedure took effect in 2002. The restyled Rules of Civil Procedure apply the same general drafting guidelines and principles used in restyling the Appellate and Criminal Rules.

1. General Guidelines

Guidance in drafting, usage, and style was provided by Bryan Garner, *Guidelines for Drafting and Editing Court Rules*, Administrative Office of the United States Courts (1996) and Bryan Garner, *Dictionary of Modern Legal Usage* (2d ed. 1995). *See also* Joseph Kimble, *Guiding Principles for Restyling the Civil Rules*, in *Preliminary Draft of Proposed Style Revision of the Federal Rules of Civil Procedure*, at x (Feb. 2005) (available at http://www.uscourts.gov/rules/Prelim_draft_proposed_pt1.pdf).

2. Formatting Changes

Many of the changes in the restyled Civil Rules result from using format to achieve clearer presentation. The rules are broken down into constituent parts, using progressively indented subparagraphs with headings and substituting vertical for horizontal lists. "Hanging indents" are used throughout. These formatting changes make the structure of the rules graphic and make the restyled rules easier to read and understand even when the words are not changed. Rule 14(a) illustrates the benefits of formatting changes.

3. Changes to Reduce Inconsistent, Ambiguous, Redundant, Repetitive, or Archaic Words

The restyled rules reduce the use of inconsistent terms that say the same thing in different ways. Because different words are presumed to have different meanings, such inconsistencies can result in confusion. The restyled rules reduce inconsistencies by using the same words to express the same meaning. For example, consistent expression is achieved without affecting meaning by the changes from "infant" in many rules to "minor" in all rules; from "upon motion or on its own initiative" in Rule 4(m) and variations in many other rules to "on motion or on its own"; and from "deemed" to "considered" in Rules 5(c), 12(e), and elsewhere. Some variations of expression have been carried forward when the context made that appropriate. As an example, "stipulate," "agree," and "consent" appear throughout the rules, and "written" qualifies these words in some places but not others. The number of variations has been reduced, but at times the former words were carried forward. None of the changes, when made, alters the rule's meaning.

The restyled rules minimize the use of inherently ambiguous words. For example, the word "shall" can mean "must," "may," or something else, depending on context. The potential for confusion is exacerbated by the fact that "shall" is no longer generally used in spoken or clearly written English. The restyled rules replace "shall" with "must," "may," or "should," depending on which one the context and established interpretation make correct in each rule.

The restyled rules minimize the use of redundant "intensifiers." These are expressions that attempt to add emphasis, but instead state the obvious and create negative implications for other rules. "The court in its discretion may" becomes "the court may"; "unless the order expressly directs otherwise" becomes "unless the court orders otherwise." The absence of intensifiers in the restyled rules does not change their substantive meaning. For example, the absence of the word "reasonable" to describe the written notice of foreign law required in Rule 44.1 does not mean that "unreasonable" notice is permitted.

The restyled rules also remove words and concepts that are outdated or redundant. The reference to "at law or in equity" in Rule 1 has become redundant with the merger of law and equity. Outdated words and concepts include the reference to "demurrers, pleas, and exceptions" in Rule 7(c); the reference to "mesne" process in Rule 77(c); and the reference in Rule 81(f) to a now-abolished official position.

The restyled rules remove a number of redundant cross-references. For example, Rule 8(b) states that a general denial is subject to the obligations of Rule 11, but all pleadings are subject to Rule 11. Removing such cross-references does not defeat application of the formerly cross-referenced rule.

4. Rule Numbers

The restyled rules keep the same rule numbers to minimize the effect on research. Subdivisions have been rearranged within some rules to achieve greater clarity and simplicity. The only change that moves one part of a rule to another is the transfer of former Rule 25(d)(2) to Rule 17(d). The restyled rules include a comparison chart to make it easy to identify transfers of provisions between subdivisions and redesignations of some subdivisions.

5. Other Changes

The style changes to the rules are intended to make no changes in substantive meaning. A very small number of minor technical amendments that arguably do change meaning were approved separately from the restyled rules, but become effective at the same time. An example is adding "e-mail address" to the information that must be included in pleadings. These minor changes occur in Rules 4(k), 9(h), 11(a), 14(b), 16(c)(1), 26(g)(1), 30(b), 31, 40, 71.1, and 78.

CROSS REFERENCES

Jurisdiction and venue as unaffected by these rules, see Fed.Rules Civ.Proc. Rule 82, 28 USCA.

Puerto Rico, governed by the rules as District Courts, see 28 USCA § 119.

Rule 2. One Form of Action

There is one form of action—the civil action.

(Amended April 30, 2007, effective December 1, 2007.)

ADVISORY COMMITTEE NOTES

1937 Adoption

1. This rule modifies U.S.C., Title 28, [former] § 384 (Suits in equity, when not sustainable). U.S.C., Title 28, §§ 723 and 730 [sec. 2071, et seq.] (conferring power on the Supreme Court to make rules of practice in equity), are unaffected in so far as they relate to the rule making power in admiralty. These sections, together with § 723b [sec. 2072] (Rules in actions at law; Supreme Court authorized to make) are continued in so far as they are not inconsistent with § 2072, formerly § 723c (Union of equity and action at law rules; power of Supreme Court). See Note 3 to Rule 1. U.S.C., Title 28, [former] §§ 724 (Conformity act), 397 (Amendments to pleadings when case brought to wrong side of court) and 398 (Equitable defenses and equitable relief in actions at law) are superseded.

2. Reference to actions at law or suits in equity in all statutes should now be treated as referring to the civil action prescribed in these rules.

3. This rule follows in substance the usual introductory statements to code practices which provide for a single action and mode of procedure, with abolition of forms of action and procedural distinctions. Representative statutes are N.Y. Code 1848 (Laws 1848, ch. 379) § 62; N.Y.C.P.A. (1937) § 8; Calif.Code Civ.Proc. (Deering, 1937) § 307; 2 Minn.Stat.Ann. 1945 § 540.01; 2 Wash.Rev.Stat.Ann. (Remington, 1932) §§ 153, 255.

2007 Amendment

The language of Rule 2 has been amended as part of the general restyling of the Civil Rules to make them more easily understood and to make style and terminology consistent throughout the rules. These changes are intended to be stylistic only.

CROSS REFERENCES

Injunctions, see Fed.Rules Civ.Proc. Rule 65, 28 USCA.

Joinder of claims and remedies, see Fed.Rules Civ.Proc. Rule 18, 28 USCA.

Receivers, see Fed.Rules Civ.Proc. Rule 66, 28 USCA.

TITLE II. COMMENCING AN ACTION; SERVICE OF PROCESS, PLEADINGS, MOTIONS, AND ORDERS

Rule 3. Commencing an Action

A civil action is commenced by filing a complaint with the court.

(Amended April 30, 2007, effective December 1, 2007.)

ADVISORY COMMITTEE NOTES

1937 Adoption

1. Rule 5(e) defines what constitutes filing with the court.

2. This rule governs the commencement of all actions, including those brought by or against the United States or an officer or agency thereof, regardless of whether service is to be made personally pursuant to Rule 4(d), or otherwise pursuant to Rule 4(e).

3. With this rule compare [former] Equity Rule 12 (Issue of Subpoena—Time for Answer) and the following statutes (and other similar statutes) which provide a similar method for commencing an action:

U.S.C., Title 28:

§ 45 [former] (District courts; practice and procedure in certain cases under interstate commerce laws).

§ 762 [see 1402] (Petition in suit against United States).

§ 766 [see 2409] (Partition suits where United States is tenant in common or joint tenant).

4. This rule provides that the first step in an action is the filing of the complaint. Under Rule 4(a) this is to be followed forthwith by issuance of a summons and its delivery to an officer for service. Other rules providing for dismissal for failure to prosecute suggest a method available to attack unreasonable delay in prosecuting an action after it has been commenced. When a Federal or State statute of limitations is pleaded as a defense, a question may arise under this rule whether the mere filing of the complaint stops the running of the statute, or whether any further step is required, such as, service of the summons and complaint or their delivery to the marshal for service. The answer to this question may depend on whether it is competent for the Supreme Court, exercising the power to make rules of procedure without affecting substantive rights, to vary the operation of statutes of limitations. The requirement of rule 4(a) that the clerk shall forthwith issue the summons and deliver it to the marshal for service will reduce the chances of such a question arising.

2007 Amendments

The caption of Rule 3 has been amended as part of the general restyling of the Civil Rules to make them more easily understood and to make style and terminology consistent throughout the rules. These changes are intended to be stylistic only.

CROSS REFERENCES

Filing with the court defined, see Fed.Rules Civ.Proc. Rule 5, 28 USCA.

Rule 4. Summons

(a) Contents; Amendments.

(1) ***Contents.*** A summons must:

(A) name the court and the parties;

(B) be directed to the defendant;

(C) state the name and address of the plaintiff's attorney or—if unrepresented—of the plaintiff;

(D) state the time within which the defendant must appear and defend;

(E) notify the defendant that a failure to appear and defend will result in a default judgment against the defendant for the relief demanded in the complaint;

(F) be signed by the clerk; and

(G) bear the court's seal.

(2) ***Amendments.*** The court may permit a summons to be amended.

(b) Issuance. On or after filing the complaint, the plaintiff may present a summons to the clerk for signature and seal. If the summons is properly completed, the clerk must sign, seal, and issue it to the plaintiff for service on the defendant. A summons—or a copy of a summons that is addressed to multiple defendants—must be issued for each defendant to be served.

(c) Service.

(1) ***In General.*** A summons must be served with a copy of the complaint. The plaintiff is responsible for having the summons and complaint served within the time allowed by Rule 4(m) and must furnish the necessary copies to the person who makes service.

(2) ***By Whom.*** Any person who is at least 18 years old and not a party may serve a summons and complaint.

(3) ***By a Marshal or Someone Specially Appointed.*** At the plaintiff's request, the court may order that service be made by a United States marshal or deputy marshal or by a person specially appointed by the court. The court must so order if the plaintiff is authorized to proceed in forma pauperis under 28 U.S.C. § 1915 or as a seaman under 28 U.S.C. § 1916.

(d) Waiving Service.

(1) ***Requesting a Waiver.*** An individual, corporation, or association that is subject to service under Rule 4(e), (f), or (h) has a duty to avoid unnecessary expenses of serving the summons. The plaintiff may notify such a defendant that an action has been commenced and request that the defendant waive service of a summons. The notice and request must:

(A) be in writing and be addressed:

(i) to the individual defendant; or

(ii) for a defendant subject to service under Rule 4(h), to an officer, a managing or general agent, or any other agent authorized by appointment or by law to receive service of process;

(B) name the court where the complaint was filed;

(C) be accompanied by a copy of the complaint, two copies of a waiver form, and a prepaid means for returning the form;

(D) inform the defendant, using text prescribed in Form 5, of the consequences of waiving and not waiving service;

(E) state the date when the request is sent;

(F) give the defendant a reasonable time of at least 30 days after the request was sent—or at least 60 days if sent to the defendant outside any judicial district of the United States—to return the waiver; and

(G) be sent by first-class mail or other reliable means.

(2) ***Failure to Waive.*** If a defendant located within the United States fails, without good cause, to sign and return a waiver requested by a plaintiff located within the United States, the court must impose on the defendant:

(A) the expenses later incurred in making service; and

(B) the reasonable expenses, including attorney's fees, of any motion required to collect those service expenses.

(3) ***Time to Answer After a Waiver.*** A defendant who, before being served with process, timely returns a waiver need not serve an answer to the complaint until 60 days after the request was sent—or until 90 days after it was sent to the defendant outside any judicial district of the United States.

(4) ***Results of Filing a Waiver.*** When the plaintiff files a waiver, proof of service is not required and these rules apply as if a summons and complaint had been served at the time of filing the waiver.

(5) ***Jurisdiction and Venue Not Waived.*** Waiving service of a summons does not waive any objection to personal jurisdiction or to venue.

(e) Serving an Individual Within a Judicial District of the United States. Unless federal law provides otherwise, an individual—other than a minor, an incompetent person, or a person whose waiver has been filed—may be served in a judicial district of the United States by:

(1) following state law for serving a summons in an action brought in courts of general jurisdiction in the state where the district court is located or where service is made; or

(2) doing any of the following:

(A) delivering a copy of the summons and of the complaint to the individual personally;

(B) leaving a copy of each at the individual's dwelling or usual place of abode with someone of suitable age and discretion who resides there; or

(C) delivering a copy of each to an agent authorized by appointment or by law to receive service of process.

(f) Serving an Individual in a Foreign Country. Unless federal law provides otherwise, an individual—other than a minor, an incompetent person, or a person whose waiver has been filed—may be served at a place not within any judicial district of the United States:

(1) by any internationally agreed means of service that is reasonably calculated to give notice, such as those authorized by the Hague Convention on the Service Abroad of Judicial and Extrajudicial Documents;

(2) if there is no internationally agreed means, or if an international agreement allows but does not specify other means, by a method that is reasonably calculated to give notice:

(A) as prescribed by the foreign country's law for service in that country in an action in its courts of general jurisdiction;

(B) as the foreign authority directs in response to a letter rogatory or letter of request; or

(C) unless prohibited by the foreign country's law, by:

(i) delivering a copy of the summons and of the complaint to the individual personally; or

(ii) using any form of mail that the clerk addresses and sends to the individual and that requires a signed receipt; or

(3) by other means not prohibited by international agreement, as the court orders.

(g) Serving a Minor or an Incompetent Person. A minor or an incompetent person in a judicial district of the United States must be served by following state law for serving a summons or like process on such a defendant in an action brought in the courts of general jurisdiction of the state where service is made. A minor or an incompetent person who is not within any judicial district of the United States must be served in the manner prescribed by Rule 4(f)(2)(A), (f)(2)(B), or (f)(3).

(h) Serving a Corporation, Partnership, or Association. Unless federal law provides otherwise or the defendant's waiver has been filed, a domestic or foreign corporation, or a partnership or other unincorporated association that is subject to suit under a common name, must be served:

(1) in a judicial district of the United States:

(A) in the manner prescribed by Rule 4(e)(1) for serving an individual; or

(B) by delivering a copy of the summons and of the complaint to an officer, a managing or general agent, or any other agent authorized by appointment or by law to receive service of process and—if the agent is one authorized by statute and the statute so requires—by also mailing a copy of each to the defendant; or

(2) at a place not within any judicial district of the United States, in any manner prescribed by Rule 4(f) for serving an individual, except personal delivery under (f)(2)(C)(i).

(i) Serving the United States and Its Agencies, Corporations, Officers, or Employees.

(1) ***United States.*** To serve the United States, a party must:

(A)(i) deliver a copy of the summons and of the complaint to the United States attorney for the district where the action is brought—or to an assistant United States attorney or clerical employee whom the United States attorney designates in a writing filed with the court clerk—or

(ii) send a copy of each by registered or certified mail to the civil-process clerk at the United States attorney's office;

(B) send a copy of each by registered or certified mail to the Attorney General of the United States at Washington, D.C.; and

(C) if the action challenges an order of a nonparty agency or officer of the United States, send a copy of each by registered or certified mail to the agency or officer.

(2) ***Agency; Corporation; Officer or Employee Sued in an Official Capacity.*** To serve a United States agency or corporation, or a United States officer or employee sued only in an official capacity, a party must serve the United States and also send a copy of the summons and of the complaint by registered or certified mail to the agency, corporation, officer, or employee.

(3) ***Officer or Employee Sued Individually.*** To serve a United States officer or employee sued in an individual capacity for an act or omission occurring in connection with duties performed on the United States' behalf (whether or not the officer or employee is also sued in an official capacity), a party must serve the United States and also serve the officer or employee under Rule 4(e), (f), or (g).

(4) ***Extending Time.*** The court must allow a party a reasonable time to cure its failure to:

(A) serve a person required to be served under Rule 4(i)(2), if the party has served either the United States attorney or the Attorney General of the United States; or

(B) serve the United States under Rule 4(i)(3), if the party has served the United States officer or employee.

(j) Serving a Foreign, State, or Local Government.

(1) ***Foreign State.*** A foreign state or its political subdivision, agency, or instrumentality must be served in accordance with 28 U.S.C. § 1608.

(2) ***State or Local Government.*** A state, a municipal corporation, or any other state-created governmental organization that is subject to suit must be served by:

(A) delivering a copy of the summons and of the complaint to its chief executive officer; or

(B) serving a copy of each in the manner prescribed by that state's law for serving a summons or like process on such a defendant.

(k) Territorial Limits of Effective Service.

(1) ***In General.*** Serving a summons or filing a waiver of service establishes personal jurisdiction over a defendant:

(A) who is subject to the jurisdiction of a court of general jurisdiction in the state where the district court is located;

(B) who is a party joined under Rule 14 or 19 and is served within a judicial district of the United States and not more than 100 miles from where the summons was issued; or

(C) when authorized by a federal statute.

(2) ***Federal Claim Outside State–Court Jurisdiction.*** For a claim that arises under federal law, serving a summons or filing a waiver of service establishes personal jurisdiction over a defendant if:

(A) the defendant is not subject to jurisdiction in any state's courts of general jurisdiction; and

(B) exercising jurisdiction is consistent with the United States Constitution and laws.

(*l*) Proving Service.

(1) ***Affidavit Required.*** Unless service is waived, proof of service must be made to the court. Except for service by a United States marshal or deputy marshal, proof must be by the server's affidavit.

(2) ***Service Outside the United States.*** Service not within any judicial district of the United States must be proved as follows:

(A) if made under Rule 4(f)(1), as provided in the applicable treaty or convention; or

(B) if made under Rule 4(f)(2) or (f)(3), by a receipt signed by the addressee, or by other evidence satisfying the court that the summons and complaint were delivered to the addressee.

(3) ***Validity of Service; Amending Proof.*** Failure to prove service does not affect the validity of service. The court may permit proof of service to be amended.

(m) Time Limit for Service. If a defendant is not served within 120 days after the complaint is filed, the court—on motion or on its own after notice to the plaintiff—must dismiss the action without prejudice against that defendant or order that service be made within a specified time. But if the plaintiff shows good cause for the failure, the court must extend the time for service for an appropriate period. This subdivision (m) does not apply to service in a foreign country under Rule 4(f) or 4(j)(1).

(n) Asserting Jurisdiction over Property or Assets.

(1) ***Federal Law.*** The court may assert jurisdiction over property if authorized by a federal statute. Notice to claimants of the property must be given as provided in the statute or by serving a summons under this rule.

(2) ***State Law.*** On a showing that personal jurisdiction over a defendant cannot be obtained in the district where the action is brought by reasonable efforts to serve a summons under this rule, the court may assert jurisdiction over the defendant's assets found in the district. Jurisdiction is acquired by seizing the assets under the circumstances and in the manner provided by state law in that district.

(Amended January 21, 1963, effective July 1, 1963; February 28, 1966, effective July 1, 1966; April 29, 1980, effective August 1, 1980; amended by Pub.L. 97-462, § 2, January 12, 1983, 96 Stat. 2527, effective 45 days after January 12, 1983; amended March 2, 1987, effective August 1, 1987; April 22, 1993, effective December 1, 1993; April 17, 2000, effective December 1, 2000; April 30, 2007, effective December 1, 2007.)

ADVISORY COMMITTEE NOTES

1937 Adoption

Note to Subdivision (a). With the provision permitting additional summons upon request of the plaintiff, compare former Equity Rule 14 (Alias Subpoena) and the last sentence of former Equity Rule 12 (Issue of Subpoena—Time for Answer).

Note to Subdivision (b). This rule prescribes a form of summons which follows substantially the requirements stated in former Equity Rules 12 (Issue of Subpoena—Time for Answer) and 7 (Process, Mesne and Final).

U.S.C., Title 28, § 721 [now 1691] (Sealing and testing of writs) is substantially continued insofar as it applies to a summons, but its requirements as to teste of process are superseded. U.S.C., Title 28, [former] § 722 (Teste of process, day of) is superseded.

See Rule 12(a) for a statement of the time within which the defendant is required to appear and defend.

Note to Subdivision (c). This rule does not affect U.S.C., Title 28, § 503 [see 566], as amended June 15, 1935 (Marshals; duties) and such statutes as the following insofar as they provide for service of process by a marshal, but modifies them in so far as they may imply service by a marshal only:

U.S.C., Title 15:

§ 5 (Bringing in additional parties) (Sherman Act)

§ 10 (Bringing in additional parties)

§ 25 (Restraining violations; procedure)

U.S.C., Title 28:

§ 45 [former] (Practice and procedure in certain cases under the interstate commerce laws)

Compare [former] Equity Rule 15 (Process, by Whom Served).

Note to Subdivision (d). Under this rule the complaint must always be served with the summons.

Paragraph (1). For an example of a statute providing for service upon an agent of an individual see U.S.C., Title 28, § 109 [now 1400, 1694] (Patent cases).

Paragraph (3). This enumerates the officers and agents of a corporation or of a partnership or other unincorporated association upon whom service of process may be made, and permits service of process only upon the officers, managing or general agents, or agents authorized by appointment or by law, of the corporation, partnership or unincorporated association against which the action is brought. See *Christian v. International Ass'n of Machinists,* 7 F.(2d) 481 (D.C.Ky. 1925) and *Singleton v. Order of Railway Conductors of America,* 9 F.Supp. 417 (D.C.Ill.1935). Compare *Operative Plasterers' and Cement Finishers' International Ass'n of the United States and Canada v. Case,* 93 F.(2d) 56 (App.D.C. 1937).

For a statute authorizing service upon a specified agent and requiring mailing to the defendant, see U.S.C., Title 6, § 7 (Surety companies as sureties; appointment of agents; service of process).

Paragraphs (4) and (5) provide a uniform and comprehensive method of service for all actions against the United States or an officer or agency thereof. For statutes providing for such service, see U.S.C., Title 7, §§ 217 (Proceedings for suspension of orders) 499k (Injunctions; application of injunction laws governing orders of Interstate Commerce Commission), 608c(15)(B) (Court review of ruling of Secretary of Agriculture), and 855 (making § 608c(15)(B) applicable to orders of the Secretary of Agriculture as to handlers of anti-hog-cholera serum and hog-cholera virus); U.S.C., Title 26, § 3679, (Bill in chancery to clear title to realty on which the United States has a lien for taxes); U.S.C., Title 28, former §§ 45, (District Courts; practice and procedure in certain cases under the interstate commerce laws), [former] 763 (Petition in suit against the United States; service; appearance by district attorney), 766 [now 2409] (Partition suits where United States is tenant in common or joint tenant), 902 [now 2410] (Foreclosure of mortgages or other liens on property in which the United States has an interest). These and similar statutes are modified in so far as they prescribe a different method of service or dispense with the service of a summons.

For the [former] Equity Rule on service, see [former] Equity Rule 13, Manner of Serving Subpoena.

Note to Subdivision (e). The provisions for the service of a summons or of notice or of an order in lieu of summons contained in U.S.C., Title 8, § 405 (Cancellation of certificates of citizenship fraudulently or illegally procured) (service by publication in accordance with State law); U.S.C., Title 28, § 118 [now 1655] (Absent defendants in suits to enforce liens); U.S.C., Title 35, § 72a [now 146, 291] (Jurisdiction of District Court of United States for the District of Columbia in certain equity suits where adverse parties reside elsewhere) (service by publication against parties residing in foreign countries); U.S.C., Title 38, § 445 [now 784] (Action against the United States on a veteran's contract of insurance) (parties not inhabitants of or not found within the district may be served with an order of the court, personally or by publication) and similar statutes are continued by this rule. Title 24, § 378 [now title 13, § 336] of the Code of the District of Columbia (Publication against non-resident; those absent for six months; unknown heirs or devisees; for divorce or in rem; actual service beyond District) is continued by this rule.

Note to Subdivision (f). This rule enlarges to some extent the present rule as to where service may be made. It does not, however, enlarge the jurisdiction of the district courts.

U.S.C., Title 28, §§ 113 [now 1392] (Suits in States containing more than one district) (where there are two or more defendants residing in different districts), [former] 115 (Suits of a local nature), 116 [now 1392] (Property in different districts in same state), [former] 838 (Executions run in all districts of state); U.S.C., Title 47, § 13 (Action for damages against a railroad or telegraph company whose officer or agent in control of a telegraph line refuses or fails to operate such line in a certain manner—"upon any agent of the company found in such state"); U.S.C., Title 49, § 321(c) [now 10330(b)] (Requiring designation of a process agent by interstate motor carriers and in case of failure so to do, service may be made upon any agent in the state) and similar statutes, allowing the running of process throughout a state, are substantially continued.

U.S.C., Title 15, §§ 5 (Bringing in additional parties) (Sherman Act), 25 (Restraining violations; procedure); U.S.C., Title 28, §§ 44 [now 2321] (Procedure in certain cases under interstate commerce laws; service of processes of court), 117 [now 754, 1692] (Property in different states in same circuit; jurisdiction of receiver), 839 [now 2413] (Executions; run in every State and Territory) and similar statutes, providing for the running of process beyond the territorial limits of a State, are expressly continued.

Note to Subdivision (g). With the second sentence compare [former] Equity Rule 15, (Process, by Whom Served).

Note to Subdivision (h). This rule substantially continues U.S.C., Title 28, [former] § 767 (Amendment of process).

1963 Amendment

Subdivision (b). Under amended subdivision (e) of this rule, an action may be commenced against a nonresident of the State in which the district court is held by complying with State procedures. Frequently the form of the summons or notice required in these cases by State law differs from the Federal form of summons described in present subdivision (b) and exemplified in Form 1. To avoid confusion, the amendment of subdivision (b) states that a form of summons or notice, corresponding "as nearly as may be" to the State form, shall be employed. See also a corresponding amendment of Rule 12(a) with regard to the time to answer.

Subdivision (d)(4). This paragraph, governing service upon the United States, is amended to allow the use of certified mail as an alternative to registered mail for sending copies of the papers to the Attorney General or to a United States officer or agency. Cf. N.J. Rule 4:5–2. See also the amendment of Rule 30(f)(1).

Subdivision (d)(7). Formerly a question was raised whether this paragraph, in the context of the rule as a whole, authorized service in original Federal actions pursuant to State statutes permitting service on a State official as a means of bringing a nonresident motorist defendant into court. It was argued in *McCoy v. Siler,* 205 F.2d 498, 501–2 (3d Cir.) (concurring opinion), cert. denied, 346 U.S. 872, 74 S.Ct. 120, 98 L.Ed. 380 (1953), that the effective service in those cases occurred not when the State official was served but when notice was given to the defendant outside the State, and that subdivision (f) (Territorial limits of effective service), as then worded, did not authorize out-of-State service. This contention found little support. A considerable number of cases held the service to be good, either by fixing upon the service on the official within the State as the effective service, thus satisfying the wording of subdivision (f) as it then stood, see *Holbrook v. Cafiero,* 18 F.R.D. 218 (D.Md. 1955); *Pasternack v. Dalo,* 17 F.R.D. 420 (W.D.Pa.1955); *Super Prods. Corp. v. Parkin,* 20 F.R.D. 377 (S.D.N.Y.1957), or by reading paragraph (7) as not limited by subdivision (f). See *Giffin v. Ensign,* 234 F.2d 307 (3d Cir. 1956); 2 Moore's *Federal Practice,* ¶4.19 (2d ed. 1948); 1 Barron & Holtzoff, *Federal Practice & Procedure* § 182.1 (Wright ed. 1960); Comment, 27 U. of Chi.L.Rev. 751 (1960). See also *Olberding v. Illinois Central R.R.,* 201 F.2d 582 (6th Cir.), rev'd on other grounds, 346 U.S. 338, 74 S.Ct. 83, 98 L.Ed. 39 (1953); *Feinsinger v. Bard,* 195 F.2d 45 (7th Cir. 1952).

An important and growing class of State statutes base personal jurisdiction over nonresidents on the doing of acts or on other contacts within the State, and permit notice to be given the defendant outside the State without any requirement of service on a local State official. See, e.g., Ill.Ann. Stat., c. 110, §§ 16, 17 (Smith–Hurd 1956); Wis.Stat. § 262.06 (1959). This service, employed in original Federal actions pursuant to paragraph (7), has also been held proper. See *Farr & Co. v. Cia. Intercontinental de Nav. de Cuba,* 243 F.2d 342 (2d Cir. 1957); *Kappus v. Western Hills Oil, Inc.,* 24 F.R.D. 123 (E.D.Wis.1959); *Star v. Rogalny,* 162 F.Supp. 181 (E.D.Ill.1957). It has also been held that the clause of paragraph (7) which permits service "in the manner prescribed by the law of the state," etc., is not limited by subdivision (c) requiring that service of all process be made by certain designated persons. See *Farr & Co. v. Cia. Intercontinental de Nav. de Cuba, supra.* But *cf. Sappia v. Lauro Lines,* 130 F.Supp. 810 (S.D.N.Y.1955).

The salutary results of these cases are intended to be preserved. See paragraph (7), with a clarified reference to State law, and amended subdivisions (e) and (f).

Subdivision (e). For the general relation between subdivisions (d) and (e), see 2 Moore, supra, ¶4.32.

The amendment of the first sentence inserting the word "thereunder" supports the original intention that the "order of court" must be authorized by a specific United States statute. See 1 Barron & Holtzoff, supra, at 731. The clause added at the end of the first sentence expressly adopts the view taken by commentators that, if no manner of service is prescribed in the statute or order, the service may be made in a manner stated in Rule 4. See 2 Moore, supra, ¶4.32, at 1004; Smit, *International Aspects of Federal Civil Procedure,* 61 Colum.L.Rev. 1031, 1036–39 (1961). But see Commentary, 5 Fed. Rules Serv. 791 (1942).

Examples of the statutes to which the first sentence relates are 28 U.S.C. § 2361 (Interpleader; process and procedure); 28 U.S.C. § 1655 (Lien enforcement; absent defendants).

The second sentence, added by amendment, expressly allows resort in original Federal actions to the procedures provided by State law for effecting service on nonresident parties (as well as on domiciliaries not found within the State). See, as illustrative, the discussion under amended subdivision (d)(7) of service pursuant to State nonresident motorist statutes and other comparable State statutes. Of particular interest is the change brought about by the reference in this sentence to State procedures for commencing actions against nonresidents by attachment and the like, accompanied by notice. Although an action commenced in a State court by attachment may be removed to the Federal court if ordinary conditions for removal are satisfied, see 28 U.S.C. § 1450; *Rorick v. Devon Syndicate, Ltd.*, 307 U.S. 299, 59 S.Ct. 877, 83 L.Ed. 1303 (1939); *Clark v. Wells*, 203 U.S. 164, 27 S.Ct. 43, 51 L.Ed. 138 (1906), there has heretofore been no provision recognized by the courts for commencing an original Federal civil action by attachment. See Currie, *Attachment and Garnishment in the Federal Courts*, 59 Mich.L.Rev. 337 (1961), arguing that this result came about through historical anomaly. Rule 64, which refers to attachment, garnishment, and similar procedures under State law, furnishes only provisional remedies in actions otherwise validly commenced. See *Big Vein Coal Co. v. Read*, 229 U.S. 31, 33 S.Ct. 694, 57 L.Ed. 1053 (1913); *Davis v. Ensign-Bickford Co.*, 139 F.2d 624 (8th Cir. 1944); 7 Moore's *Federal Practice* ¶64.05 (2d ed. 1954); 3 Barron & Holtzoff, *Federal Practice & Procedure* § 1423 (Wright ed. 1958); but cf. Note, 13 So.Calif.L.Rev. 361 (1940). The amendment will now permit the institution of original Federal actions against nonresidents through the use of familiar State procedures by which property of these defendants is brought within the custody of the court and some appropriate service is made upon them.

The necessity of satisfying subject-matter jurisdictional requirements and requirements of venue will limit the practical utilization of these methods of effecting service. Within those limits, however, there appears to be no reason for denying plaintiffs means of commencing actions in Federal courts which are generally available in the State courts. See 1 Barron & Holtzoff, supra, at 374–80; Nordbye, *Comments on Proposed Amendments to Rules of Civil Procedure for the United States District Courts*, 18 F.R.D. 105, 106 (1956); Note, 34 Corn.L.Q. 103 (1948); Note, 13 So.Calif.L.Rev. 361 (1940).

If the circumstances of a particular case satisfy the applicable Federal law (first sentence of Rule 4(e), as amended) and the applicable State law (second sentence), the party seeking to make the service may proceed under the Federal or the State law, at his option.

See also amended Rule 13(a), and the Advisory Committee's Note thereto.

Subdivision (f). The first sentence is amended to assure the effectiveness of service outside the territorial limits of the State in all the cases in which any of the rules authorize service beyond those boundaries. Besides the preceding provisions of Rule 4, see Rule 71A(d)(3). In addition, the new second sentence of the subdivision permits effective service within a limited area outside the State in certain special situations, namely, to bring in additional parties to a counterclaim or cross-claim (Rule 13 (h)), impleaded parties (Rule 14), and indispensable or conditionally necessary parties to a pending action (Rule 19); and to secure compliance with an order of commitment for civil contempt. In those situations effective service can be made at points not more than 100 miles distant from the courthouse in which the action is commenced, or to which it is assigned or transferred for trial.

The bringing in of parties under the 100-mile provision in the limited situations enumerated is designed to promote the objective of enabling the court to determine entire controversies. In the light of present-day facilities for communication and travel, the territorial range of the service allowed, analogous to that which applies to the service of a subpoena under Rule 45(e)(1), can hardly work hardship on the parties summoned. The provision will be especially useful in metropolitan areas spanning more than one State. Any requirements of subject-matter jurisdiction and venue will still have to be satisfied as to the parties brought in, although these requirements will be eased in some instances when the parties can be regarded as "ancillary." See *Pennsylvania R.R. v. Erie Avenue Warehouse Co.*, 5 F.R.Serv.2d 14a.62, Case 2 (3d Cir.1962); *Dery v. Wyer*, 265 F.2d 804 (2d Cir.1959); *United Artists Corp. v. Masterpiece Productions, Inc.*, 221 F.2d 213 (2d Cir.1955); *Lesnik v. Public Industrials Corp.*, 144 F.2d 968 (2d Cir.1944); *Vaughn v. Terminal Transp. Co.*, 162 F.Supp. 647 (E.D.Tenn.1957); and compare the fifth paragraph of the Advisory Committee's Note to Rule 4(e), as amended. The amendment is but a moderate extension of the territorial reach of Federal process and has ample practical justification. See 2 Moore, supra, § 4.01[13] (Supp. 1960); 1 Barron & Holtzoff, supra, § 184; Note, 51 Nw. U.L.Rev. 354 (1956). But cf. Nordbye, *Comments on Proposed Amendments to Rules of Civil Procedure for the United States District Courts*, 18 F.R.D. 105, 106 (1956).

As to the need for enlarging the territorial area in which orders of commitment for civil contempt may be served, see *Graber v. Graber*, 93 F.Supp. 281 (D.D.C.1950); *Teele Soap Mfg. Co. v. Pine Tree Products Co., Inc.*, 8 F.Supp. 546 (D.N.H.1934); *Mitchell v. Dexter*, 244 Fed. 926 (1st Cir. 1917); *In re Graves*, 29 Fed. 60 (N.D.Iowa 1886).

As to the Court's power to amend subdivisions (e) and (f) as here set forth, see *Mississippi Pub. Corp. v. Murphree*, 326 U.S. 438, 66 S.Ct. 242, 90 L.Ed. 185 (1946).

Subdivision (i). The continual increase of civil litigation having international elements makes it advisable to consolidate, amplify, and clarify the provisions governing service upon parties in foreign countries. See generally Jones, *International Judicial Assistance: Procedural Chaos and a Program for Reform*, 62 Yale L.J. 515 (1953); Longley, *Serving Process, Subpoenas and Other Documents in Foreign Territory*, Proc.A.B.A., Sec.Int'l & Comp.L. 34 (1959); Smit, *International Aspects of Federal Civil Procedure*, 61 Colum.L.Rev. 1031 (1961).

As indicated in the opening lines of new subdivision (i), referring to the provisions of subdivision (e), the authority for effecting foreign service must be found in a statute of the United States or a statute or rule of court of the State in which the district court is held providing in terms or upon proper interpretation for service abroad upon persons not inhabitants of or found within the State. See the Advisory Committee's Note to amended Rule 4(d)(7) and Rule 4(e). For examples of Federal and State statutes expressly authorizing such service, see 8 U.S.C. § 1451(b); 35 U.S.C. §§ 146, 293; Me.Rev.Stat., ch. 22, § 70 (Supp.1961); Minn.Stat.Ann. § 303.13 (1947); N.Y.Veh. & Tfc.Law § 253. Several decisions have construed statutes to permit service in foreign countries, although the matter is not expressly mentioned in the statutes. See, e.g., *Chapman v. Superior Court,* 162 Cal.App.2d 421, 328 P.2d 23 (Dist.Ct.App.1958); *Sperry v. Fliegers,* 194 Misc. 438, 86 N.Y.S.2d 830 (Sup.Ct.1949); *Ewing v. Thompson,* 233 N.C. 564, 65 S.E.2d 17 (1951); *Rushing v. Bush,* 260 S.W.2d 900 (Tex.Ct.Civ.App.1953). Federal and State statutes authorizing service on nonresidents in such terms as to warrant the interpretation that service abroad is permissible include 15 U.S.C. §§ 77v(a), 78aa, 79y; 28 U.S.C. § 1655; 38 U.S.C. § 784(a); Ill.Ann.Stat., c. 110, §§ 16, 17 (Smith–Hurd 1956); Wis.Stat. § 262.06 (1959).

Under subdivisions (e) and (i), when authority to make foreign service is found in a Federal statute or statute or rule of court of a State, it is always sufficient to carry out the service in the manner indicated therein. Subdivision (i) introduces considerable further flexibility by permitting the foreign service and return thereof to be carried out in any of a number of other alternative ways that are also declared to be sufficient. Other aspects of foreign service continue to be governed by the other provisions of Rule 4. Thus, for example, subdivision (i) effects no change in the form of the summons, or the issuance of separate or additional summons, or the amendment of service.

Service of process beyond the territorial limits of the United States may involve difficulties not encountered in the case of domestic service. Service abroad may be considered by a foreign country to require the performance of judicial, and therefore, "sovereign," acts within its territory, which that country may conceive to be offensive to its policy or contrary to its law. See Jones, supra, at 537. For example, a person not qualified to serve process according to the law of the foreign country may find himself subject to sanctions if he attempts service therein. See Inter-American Juridical Committee, *Report on Uniformity of Legislation on International Cooperation in Judicial Procedures* 20 (1952). The enforcement of a judgment in the foreign country in which the service was made may be embarrassed or prevented if the service did not comport with the law of that country. See ibid.

One of the purposes of subdivision (i) is to allow accommodation to the policies and procedures of the foreign country. It is emphasized, however, that the attitudes of foreign countries vary considerably and that the question of recognition of United States judgments abroad is complex. Accordingly, if enforcement is to be sought in the country of service, the foreign law should be examined before a choice is made among the methods of service allowed by subdivision (i).

Subdivision (i)(1). Subparagraph (a) of paragraph (1), permitting service by the method prescribed by the law of the foreign country for service on a person in that country in a civil action in any of its courts of general jurisdiction, provides an alternative that is likely to create least objection in the place of service and also is likely to enhance the possibilities of securing ultimate enforcement of the judgment abroad. See *Report on Uniformity of Legislation on International Cooperation in Judicial Procedures,* supra.

In certain foreign countries service in aid of litigation pending in other countries can lawfully be accomplished only upon request to the foreign courts, which in turn directs the service to be made. In many countries this has long been a customary way of accomplishing the service. See *In re Letters Rogatory out of First Civil Court of City of Mexico,* 261 Fed. 652 (S.D.N.Y.1919); Jones, supra, at 543; Comment, 44 Colum.L.Rev. 72 (1944); Note 58 Yale L.J. 1193 (1949). Subparagraph (B) of paragraph (1), referring to a letter rogatory, validates this method. A proviso, applicable to this subparagraph and the preceding one, requires, as a safeguard, that the service made shall be reasonably calculated to give actual notice of the proceedings to the party. See *Milliken v. Meyer,* 311 U.S. 457, 61 S.Ct. 339, 85 L.Ed. 278 (1940).

Subparagraph (C) of paragraph (1), permitting foreign service by personal delivery on individuals and corporations, partnerships, and associations, provides for a manner of service that is not only traditionally preferred, but also is most likely to lead to actual notice. Explicit provision for this manner of service was thought desirable because a number of Federal and State statutes permitting foreign service do not specifically provide for service by personal delivery abroad, see e.g., 35 U.S.C. §§ 146, 293; 46 U.S.C. § 1292; Calif.Ins.Code § 1612; N.Y.Veh. & Tfc. Law § 253, and it also may be unavailable under the law of the country in which the service is made.

Subparagraph (D) of paragraph (1), permitting service by certain types of mail, affords a manner of service that is inexpensive and expeditious, and requires a minimum of activity within the foreign country. Several statutes specifically provide for service in a foreign country by mail, e.g., Hawaii Rev.Laws §§ 230–31, 230–32 (1955); Minn.Stat.Ann. § 303.13 (1947); N.Y.Civ.Prac.Act, § 229–b; N.Y.Veh. & Tfc. Law § 253, and it has been sanctioned by the courts even in the absence of statutory provision specifying that form of service. *Zurini v. United States,* 189 F.2d 722 (8th Cir. 1951); *United States v. Cardillo,* 135 F.Supp. 798 (W.D.Pa. 1955); *Autogiro Co. v. Kay Gyroplanes, Ltd.,* 55 F.Supp. 919 (D.D.C.1944). Since the reliability of postal service may vary from country to country, service by mail is proper only when it is addressed to the party to be served and a form of mail requiring a signed receipt is used. An additional safeguard is provided by the requirement that the mailing be attended to by the clerk of the court. See also the provisions of paragraph (2) of this subdivision (i) regarding proof of service by mail.

Under the applicable law it may be necessary, when the defendant is an infant or incompetent person, to deliver the summons and complaint to a guardian, committee, or similar fiduciary. In such a case it would be advisable to make service under subparagraph (A), (B), or (E).

Subparagraph (E) of paragraph (1) adds flexibility by permitting the court by order to tailor the manner of service to fit the necessities of a particular case or the peculiar requirements of the law of the country in which the service is to be made. A similar provision appears in a number of statutes, e.g., 35 U.S.C. §§ 146, 293; 38 U.S.C. § 784(a); 46 U.S.C. § 1292.

The next-to-last sentence of paragraph (1) permits service under (C) and (E) to be made by any person who is not a party and is not less than 18 years of age or who is designated by court order or by the foreign court. Cf. Rule 45(c); N.Y.Civ.Prac.Act §§ 233, 235. This alternative increases the possibility that the plaintiff will be able to find a process server who can proceed unimpeded in the foreign country; it also may improve the changes of enforcing the judgment in the country of service. Especially is this alternative valuable when authority for the foreign service is found in a statute or rule of court that limits the group of eligible process servers to designated officials or special appointees who, because directly connected with another "sovereign," may be particularly offensive to the foreign country. See generally Smit, supra, at 1040–41. When recourse is had to subparagraph (A) or (B) the identity of the process server always will be determined by the law of the foreign country in which the service is made.

The last sentence of paragraph (1) sets forth an alternative manner for the issuance and transmission of the summons for service. After obtaining the summons from the clerk, the plaintiff must ascertain the best manner of delivering the summons and complaint to the person, court, or officer who will make the service. Thus the clerk is not burdened with the task of determining who is permitted to serve process under the law of a particular country or the appropriate governmental or nongovernmental channel for forwarding a letter rogatory. Under (D), however, the papers must always be posted by the clerk.

Subdivision (i)(2). When service is made in a foreign country, paragraph (2) permits methods for proof of service in addition to those prescribed by subdivision (g). Proof of service in accordance with the law of the foreign country is permitted because foreign process servers, unaccustomed to the form or the requirement of return of service prevalent in the United States, have on occasion been unwilling to execute the affidavit required by Rule 4(g). See Jones, supra, at 537; Longley, supra, at 35. As a corollary of the alternate manner of service in subdivision (i)(1)(E), proof of service as directed by order of the court is permitted. The special provision for proof of service by mail is intended as an additional safeguard when that method is used. On the type of evidence of delivery that may be satisfactory to a court in lieu of a signed receipt, see *Aero Associates, Inc. v. La Metropolitana*, 183 F.Supp. 357 (S.D.N.Y.1960).

1966 Amendment

The wording of Rule 4(f) is changed to accord with the amendment of Rule 13(h) referring to Rule 19 as amended.

1980 Amendment

Subdivision (a). This is a technical amendment to conform this subdivision with the amendment of subdivision (c).

Subdivision (c). The purpose of this amendment is to authorize service of process to be made by any person who is authorized to make service in actions in the courts of general jurisdiction of the state in which the district court is held or in which service is made.

There is a troublesome ambiguity in Rule 4. Rule 4(c) directs that all process is to be served by the marshal, by his deputy, or by a person specially appointed by the court. But Rule 4(d)(7) authorizes service in certain cases "in the manner prescribed by the law of the state in which the district court is held. . . . ." And Rule 4(e), which authorizes service beyond the state and service in quasi in rem cases when state law permits such service, directs that "service may be made . . . under the circumstances and in the manner prescribed in the [state] statute or rule." State statutes and rules of the kind referred to in Rule 4(d)(7) and Rule 4(e) commonly designate the persons who are to make the service provided for, e.g., a sheriff or a plaintiff. When that is so, may the persons so designated by state law make service, or is service in all cases to be made by a marshal or by one specially appointed under present Rule 4(c)? The commentators have noted the ambiguity and have suggested the desirability of an amendment. See 2 Moore's *Federal Practice* ¶4.08 (1974); Wright & Miller, *Federal Practice and Procedure:* Civil § 1092 (1969). And the ambiguity has given rise to unfortunate results. See *United States for the use of Tanos v. St. Paul Mercury Ins. Co.*, 361 F.2d 838 (5th Cir. 1966); *Veeck v. Commodity Enterprises, Inc.*, 487 F.2d 423 (9th Cir.1973).

The ambiguity can be resolved by specific amendments to Rules 4(d)(7) and 4(e), but the Committee is of the view that there is no reason why Rule 4(c) should not generally authorize service of process in all cases by anyone authorized to make service in the courts of general jurisdiction of the state in which the district court is held or in which service is made. The marshal continues to be the obvious, always effective officer for service of process.

1987 Amendment

The amendments are technical. No substantive change is intended.

1993 Amendments

SPECIAL NOTE: Mindful of the constraints of the Rules Enabling Act, the Committee calls the attention of the Supreme Court and Congress to new subdivision (k)(2). Should this limited extension of service be disapproved, the Committee nevertheless recommends adoption of the balance of the rule, with subdivision (k)(1) becoming simply subdivision (k). The Committee Notes would be revised to eliminate references to subdivision (k)(2).

Purposes of Revision. The general purpose of this revision is to facilitate the service of the summons and complaint. The revised rule explicitly authorizes a means for service of the summons and complaint on any defendant. While the methods of service so authorized always provide appropriate notice to persons against whom claims are made, effective service under this rule does not assure that personal jurisdiction has been established over the defendant served.

First, the revised rule authorizes the use of any means of service provided by the law not only of the forum state, but also of the state in which a defendant is served, unless the defendant is a minor or incompetent.

Second, the revised rule clarifies and enhances the cost-saving practice of securing the assent of the defendant to dispense with actual service of the summons and complaint. This practice was introduced to the rule in 1983 by an act of Congress authorizing "service-by-mail," a procedure that effects economic service with cooperation of the defendant. Defendants that magnify costs of service by requiring expensive service not necessary to achieve full notice of an action brought against them are required to bear the wasteful costs. This provision is made available in actions against defendants who cannot be served in the districts in which the actions are brought.

Third, the revision reduces the hazard of commencing an action against the United States or its officers, agencies, and corporations. A party failing to effect service on all the offices of the United States as required by the rule is assured adequate time to cure defects in service.

Fourth, the revision calls attention to the important effect of the Hague Convention and other treaties bearing on service of documents in foreign countries and favors the use of internationally agreed means of service. In some respects, these treaties have facilitated service in foreign countries but are not fully known to the bar.

Finally, the revised rule extends the reach of federal courts to impose jurisdiction over the person of all defendant against whom federal law claims are made and who can be constitutionally subjected to the jurisdiction of the courts of the United States. The present territorial limits on the effectiveness of service to subject a defendant to the jurisdiction of the court over the defendant's person are retained for all actions in which there is a state in which personal jurisdiction can be asserted consistently with state law and the Fourteenth Amendment. A new provision enables district courts to exercise jurisdiction, if permissible under the Constitution and not precluded by statute, when a federal claim is made against a defendant not subject to the jurisdiction of any single state.

The revised rule is reorganized to make its provisions more accessible to those not familiar with all of them. Additional subdivisions in this rule allow for more captions; several overlaps among subdivisions are eliminated; and several disconnected provisions are removed, to be relocated in a new Rule 4.1.

The Caption of the Rule. Prior to this revision, Rule 4 was entitled "Process" and applied to the service of not only the summons but also other process as well, although these are not covered by the revised rule. Service of process in eminent domain proceedings is governed by Rule 71A. Service of a subpoena is governed by Rule 45, and service of papers such as orders, motions, notices, pleadings, and other documents is governed by Rule 5.

The revised rule is entitled "Summons" and applies only to that form of legal process. Unless service of the summons is waived, a summons must be served whenever a person is joined as a party against whom a claim is made. Those few provisions of the former rule which relate specifically to service of process other than a summons are relocated in Rule 4.1 in order to simplify the text of this rule.

Subdivision (a). Revised subdivision (a) contains most of the language of the former subdivision (b). The second sentence of the former subdivision (b) has been stricken, so that the federal court summons will be the same in all cases. Few states now employ, distinctive requirements of form for a summons and the applicability of such a requirement in federal court can only serve as a trap for an unwary party or attorney. A sentence is added to this subdivision authorizing an amendment of a summons. This sentence replaces the rarely used former subdivision 4(h). See 4A Wright & Miller, Federal Practice and Procedure § 1131 (2d ed. 1987).

Subdivision (b). Revised subdivision (b) replaces the former subdivision (a). The revised text makes clear that the responsibility for filling in the summons falls on the plaintiff, not the clerk of the court. If there are multiple defendants, the plaintiff may secure issuance of a summons for each defendant, or may serve copies of a single original bearing the names of multiple defendants if the addressee of the summons is effectively identified.

Subdivision (c). Paragraph (1) of revised subdivision (c) retains language from the former subdivision (d)(1). Paragraph (2) retains language from the former subdivision (a), and adds an appropriate caution regarding the time limit for service set forth in subdivision (m).

The 1983 revision of Rule 4 relieved the marshals' offices of much of the burden of serving the summons. Subdivision (c) eliminates the requirement for service by the marshal's office in actions in which the party seeking service is the United States. The United States, like other civil litigants, is now permitted to designate any person who is 18 years of age and not a party to serve its summons.

The court remains obligated to appoint a marshal, a deputy, or some other person to effect service of a summons in two classes of cases specified by statute: actions brought in forma pauperis or by a seaman. 28 U.S.C. §§ 1915, 1916. The court also retains discretion to appoint a process server on motion of a party. If a law enforcement presence appears to be necessary or advisable to keep the peace, the court should appoint a marshal or deputy or other official person to make the service. The Department of Justice may also call upon the Marshals Service to perform services in actions brought by the United States. 28 U.S.C. § 651.

Subdivision (d). This text is new, but is substantially derived from the former subdivisions (c)(2)(C) and (D), added to the rule by Congress in 1983. The aims of the provision are to eliminate the costs of service of a summons on many parties and to foster cooperation among adversaries and counsel. The rule operates to impose upon the defendant those costs that could have been avoided if the defendant had cooperated reasonably in the manner prescribed. This device is useful in dealing with defendants who are furtive, who reside in places not easily reached by process servers, or who are outside the United States and can be served only at substantial and unnecessary expense. Illustratively, there is no useful purpose achieved by requiring a plaintiff to comply with all the formalities of service in a foreign country, including costs of translation, when suing a defendant manufacturer, fluent in English, whose products are widely distributed in the United States. See Bankston v. Toyota Motor Corp., 889 F.2d 172 (8th Cir.1989).

The former text described this process as service-by-mail. This language misled some plaintiffs into thinking that service could be effected by mail without the affirmative cooperation of the defendant. E.g., Gulley v. Mayo Foundation, 886 F.2d 161 (8th Cir.1989). It is more accurate to describe the communication sent to the defendant as a request for a waiver of formal service.

The request for waiver of service may be sent only to defendants subject to service under subdivision (e), (f), or (h). The United States is not expected to waive service for the reason that its mail receiving facilities are inadequate to assure that the notice is actually received by the correct person in the Department of Justice. The same principle is applied to agencies, corporations, and officers of the United States and to other governments and entities subject to service under subdivision (j). Moreover, there are policy reasons why governmental entities should not be confronted with the potential for bearing costs of service in cases in which they ultimately prevail. Infants or incompetent persons likewise are not called upon to waive service because, due to their presumed inability to understand the request and its consequences, they must generally be served through fiduciaries.

It was unclear whether the former rule authorized, mailing of a request for "acknowledgement of service" to defendants outside the forum state. See 1 R. Casad, Jurisdiction in Civil Actions (2d Ed.) 5–29, 30 (1991) and cases cited. But, as Professor Casad observed, there was no reason not to employ this device in an effort to obtain service outside the state, and there are many instances in which it was in fact so used, with respect both to defendants within the United States and to defendants in other countries.

The opportunity for waiver has distinct advantages to a foreign defendant. By waiving service, the defendant can reduce the costs that may ultimately be taxed against it if unsuccessful in the lawsuit, including the sometimes substantial expense of translation that may be wholly unnecessary for defendants fluent in English. Moreover, a foreign defendant that waives service is afforded substantially more time to defend against the action than if it had been formally served: under Rule 12, a defendant ordinarily has only 20 days after service in which to file its answer or raise objections by motion, but by signing a waiver it is allowed 90 days after the date the request for waiver was mailed in which to submit its defenses. Because of the additional time needed for mailing and the unreliability of some foreign mail services, a period of 60 days (rather than the 30 days required for domestic transmissions) is provided for a return of a waiver sent to a foreign country.

It is hoped that, since transmission of the notice and waiver forms is a private nonjudicial act, does not purport to effect service, and is not accompanied by any summons or directive from a court, use of the procedure will not offend foreign sovereignties, even those that have withheld their assent to formal service by mail or have objected to the "service-by-mail" provisions of the former rule. Unless the addressee consents, receipt of the request under the revised rule does not give rise to any obligation to answer the lawsuit, does not provide a basis for default judgment, and does not suspend the statute of limitations in those states where the period continues to run until service. Nor are there any adverse consequences to a foreign defendant, since the provisions for shifting the expense of service to a defendant that declines to waive service apply only if the plaintiff and defendant are both located in the United States.

With respect to a defendant located in a foreign country like the United Kingdom, which accepts documents in English, whose Central Authority acts promptly in effecting service, and whose policies discourage its residents from waiving formal service, there will be little reason for a plaintiff to send the notice and request under subdivision (d) rather than use convention methods. On the other hand, the procedure offers significant potential benefits to a plaintiff when suing a defendant that, though fluent in English, is located in a country where, as a condition to formal service under a convention, documents must be translated into another language or where formal service will be otherwise costly or time-consuming.

Paragraph (1) is explicit that a timely waiver of service of a summons does not prejudice the right of a defendant to object by means of a motion authorized by Rule 12(b)(2) to the absence of jurisdiction over the defendant's person, or to assert other defenses that may be available. The only issues eliminated are those involving the sufficiency of the summons or the sufficiency of the method by which it is served.

Paragraph (2) states what the present rule implies: the defendant has a duty to avoid costs associated with the service of a summons not needed to inform the defendant regarding the commencement of an action. The text of the rule also sets forth the requirements for a Notice and Request for Waiver sufficient to put the cost-shifting provision in place. These requirements are illustrated in Forms 1A and 1B, which replace the former Form 18–A.

Paragraph (2)(A) is explicit that a request for waiver of service by a corporate defendant must be addressed to a person qualified to receive service. The general mail rooms of large organizations cannot be required to identify the appropriate individual recipient for an institutional summons.

Paragraph (2)(B) permits the use of alternatives to the United States mails in sending the Notice and Request. While private messenger services or electronic communications may be more expensive than the mail, they may be equally reliable and on occasion more convenient to the parties. Especially with respect to transmissions to foreign countries, alternative means may be desirable, for in some countries facsimile transmission is the most efficient and economical means of communication. If electronic means such as facsimile transmission are employed, the sender should maintain a record of the transmission to assure proof of transmission if receipt is denied, but a party receiving such a transmission has a duty to cooperate and cannot avoid liability for the resulting cost of formal service if the transmission is prevented at the point of receipt.

A defendant failing to comply with a request for waiver shall be given an opportunity to show good cause for the failure, but sufficient cause should be rare. It is not a good cause for failure to waive service that the claim is unjust or that the court lacks jurisdiction. Sufficient cause not to shift the cost of service would exist, however, if the defendant did not receive the request or was insufficiently literate in English to understand it. It should be noted that the provisions for shifting the cost of service apply only if the plaintiff and the defendant are both located in the United States, and accordingly a foreign defendant need not show "good cause" for its failure to waive service.

Paragraph (3) extends the time for answer if, before being served with process, the defendant waives formal service. The extension is intended to serve as an inducement to waive service and to assure that a defendant will not gain any delay be declining to waive service and thereby causing the additional time needed to effect service. By waiving service, a defendant is not called upon to respond to the complaint until 60 days from the date the notice was sent to it—90 days if the notice was sent to a foreign country—rather than within the 20 day period from date of service specified in Rule 12.

Paragraph (4) clarifies the effective date of service when service is waived; the provision is needed to resolve an issue arising when applicable law requires service of process to toll the statute of limitations. E.g., Morse v. Elmira Country Club, 752 F.2d 35 (2d Cir.1984). Cf. Walker v. Armco Steel Corp., 446 U.S. 740 (1980).

The provisions in former subdivision (c)(2)(C)(ii) of this rule may have been misleading to some parties. Some plaintiffs, not reading the rule carefully, supposed that receipt by the defendant of the mailed complaint had the effect both of establishing the jurisdiction of the court over the defendant's person and of tolling the statute of limitations in actions in which service of the summons is required to toll the limitations period. The revised rule is clear that, if the waiver is not returned and filed, the limitations period under such a law is not tolled and the action will not otherwise proceed until formal service of process is effected.

Some state limitations laws may toll an otherwise applicable statute at the time when the defendant receives notice of the action. Nevertheless, the device of requested waiver of service is not suitable if a limitations period which is about to expire is not tolled by filing the action. Unless there is ample time, the plaintiff should proceed directly to the formal methods for service identified in subdivisions (e), (f), or (h).

The procedure of requesting waiver of service should also not be used if the time for service under subdivision (m) will expire before the date on which the waiver must be returned. While a plaintiff has been allowed additional time for service in that situation, e.g., Prather v. Raymond Constr. Co., 570 F.Supp. 278 (N.D.Ga.1983), the court could refuse a request for additional time unless the defendant appears to have evaded service pursuant to subdivision (e) or (h). It may be noted that the presumptive time limit for service under subdivision (m) does not apply to service in a foreign country.

Paragraph (5) is a cost-shifting provision retained from the former rule. The costs that may be imposed on the defendant could include, for example, the cost of the time of a process server required to make contact with a defendant residing in a guarded apartment house or residential development. The paragraph is explicit that the costs of enforcing the cost-shifting provision are themselves recoverable from a defendant who fails to return the waiver. In the absence of such a provision, the purpose of the rule would be frustrated by the cost of its enforcement, which is likely to be high in relation to the small benefit secured by the plaintiff.

Some plaintiffs may send a notice and request for waiver and, without waiting for return of the waiver, also proceed with efforts to effect formal service on the defendant. To discourage this practice, the cost-shifting provisions in paragraphs (2) and (5) are limited to costs of effecting service incurred after the time expires for the defendant to return the waiver. Moreover, by returning the waiver within the time allowed and before being served with process, a defendant receives the benefit of the longer period for responding to the complaint afforded for waivers under paragraph (3).

Subdivision (e). This subdivision replaces former subdivisions (c)(2)(C)(i) and (d)(1). It provides a means for service of summons on individuals within a judicial district of the United States. Together with subdivision (f), it provides for service on persons anywhere, subject to constitutional and statutory constraints.

Service of the summons under this subdivision does not conclusively establish the jurisdiction of the court over the person of the defendant. A defendant may assert the territorial limits of the court's reach set forth in subdivision (k), including the constitutional limitations that may be imposed by the Due Process Clause of the Fifth Amendment.

Paragraph (1) authorizes service in any judicial district in conformity with state law. This paragraph sets forth the language of former subdivision (c)(2)(C)(i), which authorized the use of the law of the state in which the district court sits, but adds as an alternative the use of the law of the state in which the service is effected.

Paragraph (2) retains the text of the former subdivision (d)(1) and authorizes the use of the familiar methods of personal or abode service or service on an authorized agent in any judicial district.

To conform to these provisions, the former subdivision (e) bearing on proceedings against parties not found within the state is stricken. Likewise stricken is the first sentence of the former subdivision (f), which had restricted the authority of the federal process server to the state in which the district court sits.

Subdivision (f). This subdivision provides for service on individuals who are in a foreign country, replacing the former subdivision (i) that was added to Rule 4 in 1963. Reflecting the pattern of Rule 4 in incorporating state law limitations on the exercise of jurisdiction over persons, the former subdivision (i) limited service outside the United States to cases in which extraterritorial service was authorized by state or federal law. The new rule eliminates the requirement of explicit authorization. On occasion, service in a foreign country was held to be improper for lack of statutory authority. E.g., Martens v. Winder, 341 F.2d 197 (9th Cir.), cert. denied, 382 U.S. 937 (1965). This authority, however, was found to exist by implication. E.g., SEC v. VTR, Inc., 39 F.R.D. 19 (S.D.N.Y.1966). Given the substantial increase in the number of international transactions and events that are the subject of litigation in federal courts, it is appropriate to infer a general legislative authority to effect service on defendants in a foreign country.

A secondary effect of this provision for foreign service of a federal summons is to facilitate the use of federal long-arm law in actions brought to enforce the federal law against defendants who cannot be served under any state law but who can be constitutionally subjected to the jurisdiction of the federal court. Such a provision is set forth in paragraph (2) of subdivision (k) of this rule, applicable only to persons not subject to the territorial jurisdiction of any particular state.

Paragraph (1) gives effect to the Hague Convention on the Service Abroad of Judicial and Extrajudicial Documents, which entered into force for the United States on February 10, 1969. See 28 U.S.C.A., Fed.R.Civ.P. 4 (Supp.1986). This Convention is an important means of dealing with problems of service in a foreign country. See generally 1 B. Ristau, International Judicial Assistance §§ 4–1–1 to 4–5–2 (1990). Use of the Convention procedures, when available, is mandatory if documents must be transmitted abroad to effect service. See Volkswagenwerk Aktiengesellschaft v. Schlunk, 486 U.S. 694 (1988) (noting that voluntary use of these procedures may be desirable even when service could constitutionally be effected in another manner); J. Weis, The Federal Rules and the Hague Conventions: Concerns of Conformity and Comity, 50 U.Pitt.L.Rev. 903 (1989). Therefore, this paragraph provides that, when service is to be effected outside a judicial district of the United States, the methods of service appropriate under an applicable treaty shall be employed if available and if the treaty so requires.

The Hague Convention furnishes safeguards against the abridgment of rights of parties through inadequate notice. Article 15 provides for verification of actual notice or a demonstration that process was served by a method prescribed by the internal laws of the foreign state before a default judgment may be entered. Article 16 of the Convention also enables the judge to extend the time for appeal after judgment if the defendant shows a lack of adequate notice either to defend or to appeal the judgment, or has disclosed a prima facie case on the merits.

The Hague Convention does not specify a time within which a foreign country's Central Authority must effect service, but Article 15 does provide that alternate methods may be used if a Central Authority does not respond within six months. Generally, a Central Authority can be expected to respond much more quickly than that limit might permit, but there have been occasions when the signatory state was dilatory or refused to cooperate for substantive reasons. In such cases, resort may be had to the provision set forth in subdivision (f)(3).

Two minor changes in the text reflect the Hague Convention. First, the term "letter of request" has been added. Although these words are synonymous with "letter rogatory," "letter of request" is preferred in modern usage. The provision should not be interpreted to authorize use of a letter of request when there is in fact no treaty obligation on the receiving country to honor such a request from this country or when the United States does not extend diplomatic recognition to the foreign nation. Second, the passage formerly found in subdivision (i)(1)(B), "when service in either case is reasonably calculated to give actual notice," has been relocated.

Paragraph (2) provides alternative methods for use when internationally agreed methods are not intended to be exclusive, or where there is no international agreement applicable. It contains most of the language formerly set forth in subdivision (i) of the rule. Service by methods that would violate foreign law is not generally authorized. Subparagraphs (A) and (B) prescribe the more appropriate methods for conforming to local practice or using a local authority. Subparagraph (C) prescribes other methods authorized by the former rule.

Paragraph (3) authorizes the court to approve other methods of service not prohibited by international agreements. The Hague Convention, for example, authorizes special forms of service in cases of urgency if convention methods will not permit service within the time required by the circumstances. Other circumstances that might justify the use of additional methods include the failure of the foreign country's Central Authority to effect service within the six-month period provided by the Convention, or the refusal of the Central Authority to serve a complaint seeking punitive damages or to enforce the antitrust laws of the United States. In such cases, the court may direct a special method of service not explicitly authorized by international agreement if not prohibited by the agreement. Inasmuch as our Constitution requires that reasonable notice be given, an earnest effort should be made to devise a method of communication that is consistent with due process and minimizes offense to foreign law. A court may in some instances specially authorize use of ordinary mail. Cf. Levin v. Ruby Trading Corp., 248 F.Supp. 537 (S.D.N.Y.1965).

Subdivision (g). This subdivision retains the text of former subdivision (d)(2). Provision is made for service upon an infant or incompetent person in a foreign country.

Subdivision (h). This subdivision retains the text of former subdivision (d)(3), with changes reflecting those made in subdivision (e). It also contains the provisions for service on a corporation or association in a foreign country, as formerly found in subdivision (i).

Frequent use should be made of the Notice and Request procedure set forth in subdivision (d) in actions against corporations. Care must be taken, however, to address the request to an individual officer or authorized agent of the corporation. It is not effective use of the Notice and Request procedure if the mail is sent undirected to the mail room of the organization.

Subdivision (i). This subdivision retains much of the text of former subdivisions (d)(4) and (d)(5). Paragraph (1) provides for service of a summons on the United States; it amends former subdivision (d)(4) to permit the United States attorney to be served by registered or certified mail. The rule does not authorize the use of the Notice and Request procedure of revised subdivision (d) when the United States is the defendant. To assure proper handling of mail in the United States attorney's office, the authorized mail service must be specifically addressed to the civil process clerk of the office of the United States attorney.

Paragraph (2) replaces former subdivision (d)(5). Paragraph (3) saves the plaintiff from the hazard of losing a substantive right because of failure to comply with the complex requirements of multiple service under this subdivision. That risk has proved to be more than nominal. E.g., Whale v. United States, 792 F.2d 951 (9th Cir.1986). This provision should be read in connection with the provisions of subdivision (c) of Rule 15 to preclude the loss of substantive rights against the United States or its agencies, corporations, or officers resulting from a plaintiff's failure to correctly identify and serve all the persons who should be named or served.

Subdivision (j). This subdivision retains the text of former subdivision (d)(6) without material change. The waiver-of-service provision is also inapplicable to actions against governments subject to service pursuant to this subdivision.

The revision adds a new paragraph (1) referring to the statute governing service of a summons on a foreign state and its political subdivisions, agencies, and instrumentalities, the Foreign Sovereign Immunities Act of 1976, 28 U.S.C. § 1608. The caption of the subdivision reflects that change.

Subdivision (k). This subdivision replaces the former subdivision (f), with no change in the title. Paragraph (1) retains the substance of the former rule in explicitly authorizing the exercise of personal jurisdiction over persons who can be reached under state long-arm law, the "100-mile bulge" provision added in 1963, or the federal interpleader act. Paragraph (1)(D) is new, but merely calls attention to federal legislation that may provide for nationwide or even world-wide service of process in cases arising under particular federal laws. Congress has provided for nationwide service of process and full exercise of territorial jurisdiction by all district courts with respect to specified federal actions. See 1 R. Casad, Jurisdiction in Civil Actions (2d Ed.) chap. 5 (1991).

Paragraph (2) is new. It authorizes the exercise of territorial jurisdiction over the person of any defendant against whom is made a claim arising under any federal law if that person is subject to personal jurisdiction in no state. This addition is a companion to the amendments made in revised subdivisions (e) and (f).

This paragraph corrects a gap in the enforcement of federal law. Under the former rule, a problem was presented when the defendant was a non-resident of the United

States having contacts with the United States sufficient to justify the application of United States law and to satisfy federal standards of forum selection, but having insufficient contact with any single state to support jurisdiction under state long-arm legislation or meet the requirements of the Fourteenth Amendment limitation on state court territorial jurisdiction. In such cases, the defendant was shielded from the enforcement of federal law by the fortuity of a favorable limitation on the power of state courts, which was incorporated into the federal practice by the former rule. In this respect, the revision responds to the suggestion of the Supreme Court made in Omni Capital Int'l. v. Rudolf Wolff & Co., Ltd., 484 U.S. 97, 111 (1987).

There remain constitutional limitations on the exercise of territorial jurisdiction by federal courts over persons outside the United States. These restrictions arise from the Fifth Amendment rather than from the Fourteenth Amendment, which limits state-court reach and which was incorporated into federal practice by the reference to state law in the text of the former subdivision (e) that is deleted by this revision. The Fifth Amendment requires that any defendant have affiliating contacts with the United States sufficient to justify the exercise of personal jurisdiction over that party. Cf. Wells Fargo & Co. v. Wells Fargo Express Co., 556 F.2d 406, 418 (9th Cir.1977). There also may be a further Fifth Amendment constraint in that a plaintiff's forum selection might be so inconvenient to a defendant that it would be a denial of "fair play and substantial justice" required by the due process clause, even though the defendant had significant affiliating contacts with the United States. See DeJames v. Magnificent Carriers, 654 F.2d 280, 286 n. 3 (3rd Cir.), cert. denied, 454 U.S. 1085 (1981). Compare World–Wide Volkswagen Corp. v. Woodson, 444 U.S. 286, 293–294 (1980); Insurance Corp. of Ireland v. Compagnie des Bauxites de Guinee, 456 U.S. 694, 702–03 (1982); Burger King Corp. v. Rudzewicz, 471 U.S. 462, 476–78 (1985); Asahi Metal Indus. v. Superior Court of Cal., Solano County, 480 U.S. 102, 108–13 (1987). See generally R. Lusardi, Nationwide Service of Process: Due Process Limitations on the Power of the Sovereign, 33 Vill.L.Rev. 1 (1988).

This provision does not affect the operation of federal venue legislation. See generally 28 U.S.C. § 1391. Nor does it affect the operation of federal law providing for the change of venue. 28 U.S.C. §§ 1404, 1406. The availability of transfer for fairness and convenience under § 1404 should preclude most conflicts between the full exercise of territorial jurisdiction permitted by this rule and the Fifth Amendment requirement of "fair play and substantial justice."

The district court should be especially scrupulous to protect aliens who reside in a foreign country from forum selections so onerous that injustice could result. "[G]reat care and reserve should be exercised when extending our notions of personal jurisdiction into the international field." Asahi Metal Indus. v. Superior Court of Cal., Solano County, 480 U.S. 102, 115 (1987), quoting United States v. First Nat'l City Bank, 379 U.S. 378, 404 (1965) (Harlan, J., dissenting).

This narrow extension of the federal reach applies only if a claim is made against the defendant under federal law. It does not establish personal jurisdiction if the only claims are those arising under state law or the law of another country, even though there might be diversity or alienage subject matter jurisdiction as to such claims. If, however, personal jurisdiction is established under this paragraph with respect to a federal claim, then 28 U.S.C. § 1367(a) provides supplemental jurisdiction over related claims against that defendant, subject to the court's discretion to decline exercise of that jurisdiction under 28 U.S.C. § 1367(c).

Subdivision (*l*). This subdivision assembles in one place all the provisions of the present rule bearing on proof of service. No material change in the rule is effected. The provision that proof of service can be amended by leave of court is retained from the former subdivision (h). See generally 4A Wright & Miller, Federal Practice and Procedure § 1132 (2d ed. 1987).

Subdivision (m). This subdivision retains much of the language of the present subdivision (j).

The new subdivision explicitly provides that the court shall allow additional time if there is good cause for the plaintiff's failure to effect service in the prescribed 120 days, and authorizes the court to relieve a plaintiff of the consequences of an application of this subdivision even if there is no good cause shown. Such relief formerly was afforded in some cases, partly in reliance on Rule 6(b). Relief may be justified, for example, if the applicable statute of limitations would bar the refiled action, or if the defendant is evading service or conceals a defect in attempted service. E.g., Ditkof v. Owens–Illinois, Inc., 114 F.R.D. 104 (E.D.Mich. 1987). A specific instance of good cause is set forth in paragraph (3) of this rule, which provides for extensions if necessary to correct oversights in compliance with the requirements of multiple service in actions against the United States or its officers, agencies, and corporations. The district court should also take care to protect pro se plaintiffs from consequences of confusion or delay attending the resolution of an in forma pauperis petition. Robinson v. America's Best Contacts & Eyeglasses, 876 F.2d 596 (7th Cir. 1989).

The 1983 revision of this subdivision referred to the "party on whose behalf such service was required," rather than to the "plaintiff," a term used generically elsewhere in this rule to refer to any party initiating a claim against a person who is not a party to the action. To simplify the text, the revision returns to the usual practice in the rule of referring simply to the plaintiff even though its principles apply with equal force to defendants who may assert claims against nonparties under Rules 13(h), 14, 19, 20, or 21.

Subdivision (n). This subdivision provides for in rem and quasi-in-rem jurisdiction. Paragraph (1) incorporates any requirements of 28 U.S.C. § 1655 or similar provisions bearing on seizures or liens.

Paragraph (2) provides for other uses of quasi-in-rem jurisdiction but limits its use to exigent circumstances. Provisional remedies may be employed as a means to secure jurisdiction over the property of a defendant whose person is not within reach of the court, but occasions for the use of this provision should be rare, as where the defendant is a fugitive or assets are in imminent danger of disappearing. Until 1963, it was not possible under Rule 4 to assert jurisdiction in a federal court over the property of a defendant not personally served. The 1963 amendment to subdivision (e) authorized the use of state law procedures authorizing seizures of assets as a basis for jurisdiction. Given the liberal availability of long-arm jurisdiction, the exercise of power quasi-in-rem has become almost an anachronism. Circumstances too spare to affiliate the defendant to the forum state sufficiently to support long-arm jurisdiction over the defendant's person are also inadequate to support seizure of the defendant's assets fortuitously found within the state. Shaffer v. Heitner, 433 U.S. 186 (1977).

2000 Amendment

Paragraph (2)(B) is added to Rule 4(i) to require service on the United States when a United States officer or employee is sued in an individual capacity for acts or omissions occurring in connection with duties performed on behalf of the United States. Decided cases provide uncertain guidance on the question whether the United States must be served in such actions. *See Vaccaro v. Dobre*, 81 F.3d 854, 856–857 (9th Cir.1996); *Armstrong v. Sears*, 33 F.3d 182, 185–187 (2d Cir.1994); *Ecclesiastical Order of the Ism of Am v. Chasin*, 845 F.2d 113, 116 (6th Cir.1988); *Light v. Wolf*, 816 F.2d 746 (D.C.Cir.1987); *see also Simpkins v. District of Columbia*, 108 F.3d 366, 368–369 (D.C.Cir.1997). Service on the United States will help to protect the interest of the individual defendant in securing representation by the United States, and will expedite the process of determining whether the United States will provide representation. It has been understood that the individual defendant must be served as an individual defendant, a requirement that is made explicit. Invocation of the individual service provisions of subdivisions (e), (f), and (g) invokes also the waiver-of-service provisions of subdivision (d).

Paragraph 2(B) reaches service when an officer or employee of the United States is sued in an individual capacity "for acts or omissions occurring in connection with the performance of duties on behalf of the United States." This phrase has been chosen as a functional phrase that can be applied without the occasionally distracting associations of such phrases as "scope of employment," "color of office," or "arising out of the employment." Many actions are brought against individual federal officers or employees of the United States for acts or omissions that have no connection whatever to their governmental roles. There is no reason to require service on the United States in these actions. The connection to federal employment that requires service on the United States must be determined as a practical matter, considering whether the individual defendant has reasonable grounds to look to the United States for assistance and whether the United States has reasonable grounds for demanding formal notice of the action.

An action against a former officer or employee of the United States is covered by paragraph (2)(B) in the same way as an action against a present officer or employee. Termination of the relationship between the individual defendant and the United States does not reduce the need to serve the United States.

Paragraph (3) is amended to ensure that failure to serve the United States in an action governed by paragraph 2(B) does not defeat an action. This protection is adopted because there will be cases in which the plaintiff reasonably fails to appreciate the need to serve the United States . There is no requirement, however, that the plaintiff show that the failure to serve the United States was reasonable. A reasonable time to effect service on the United States must be allowed after the failure is pointed out. An additional change ensures that if the United States or United States attorney is served in an action governed by paragraph 2(A), additional time is to be allowed even though no officer, employee, agency, or corporation of the United States was served.

GAP Report

The most important changes were made to ensure that no one would read the seemingly independent provisions of paragraphs 2(A) and 2(B) to mean that service must be made twice both on the United States and on the United States employee when the employee is sued in both official and individual capacities. The word "only" was added in subparagraph (A) and the new phrase "whether or not the officer or employee is sued also in an individual capacity" was inserted in subparagraph (B).

Minor changes were made to include "Employees" in the catch-line for subdivision (i), and to add "or employee" in paragraph 2(A). Although it may seem awkward to think of suit against an employee in an official capacity, there is no clear definition that separates "officers" from "employees" for this purpose. The published proposal to amend Rule 12(a)(3) referred to actions against an employee sued in an official capacity, and it seemed better to make the rules parallel by adding "employee" to Rule 4(i)(2)(A) than by deleting it from Rule 12(a)(3)(A).

2007 Amendment

The language of Rule 4 has been amended as part of the general restyling of the Civil Rules to make them more easily understood and to make style and terminology consistent throughout the rules. These changes are intended to be stylistic only.

Rule 4(d)(1)(C) corrects an inadvertent error in former Rule 4(d)(2)(G). The defendant needs two copies of the waiver form, not an extra copy of the notice and request.

Rule 4(g) changes "infant" to "minor." "Infant" in the present rule means "minor." Modern word usage suggests that "minor" will better maintain the intended meaning. The same change from "infant" to "minor" is made throughout the rules. In addition, subdivision (f)(3) is added to the description of methods of service that the court may order; the addition ensures the evident intent that the court not order service by means prohibited by international agreement.

Rule 4(i)(4) corrects a misleading reference to "the plaintiff" in former Rule 4(i)(3). A party other than a plaintiff may need a reasonable time to effect service. Rule 4(i)(4) properly covers any party.

Former Rule 4(j)(2) refers to service upon an "other governmental organization subject to suit." This is changed to "any other state-created governmental organization that is subject to suit." The change entrenches the meaning indicated by the caption ("Serving a Foreign, State, or Local Government"), and the invocation of state law. It excludes any risk that this rule might be read to govern service on a federal agency, or other entities not created by state law.

The former provision describing service on interpleader claimants [former (k)(1)(C)] is deleted as redundant in light of the general provision in (k)(1)(C) recognizing personal jurisdiction authorized by a federal statute.

HISTORICAL NOTES

Revision Notes and Legislative Reports

1983 Acts. Statement by a Member of the House Committee on the Judiciary, see 1982 U.S.Code Cong. and Adm. News, p. 4434.

Effective and Applicability Provisions

1983 Acts. Amendment by Pub.L. 97–462 effective 45 days after Jan. 12, 1983, see section 4 of Pub.L. 97–462, set out as a note under section 2071 of this title.

CROSS REFERENCES

Actions on war risk insurance claims, see 46 USCA § 53912.

Civil monetary penalties and assessments for Federal old-age survivors and disability insurance benefits and social security, see 42 USCA § 1320a–8.

Executions in favor of United States, see 28 USCA § 2413.

Motion to quash return of service of summons, see Fed. Rules Civ.Proc. Form 19, 28 USCA.

Motions to dismiss or quash for lack of jurisdiction over person, insufficiency of process or service of process, see Fed.Rules Civ.Proc. Rule 12, 28 USCA.

Process generally, see 28 USCA § 1691 et seq.

Process in bankruptcy proceedings, see Fed.Rules Bankr. Proc. Rule 7004, 11 USCA.

Process to run outside State—

Actions under Security Act of 1933, see 15 USCA § 77v.

Actions under Security Act of 1934, see 15 USCA § 78aa.

Veteran's actions against United States on life insurance contracts, see 38 USCA § 1984.

Service of notice of application for leave to perpetuate testimony by taking deposition, see Fed.Rules Civ.Proc. Rule 27, 28 USCA.

Service on government under this rule in civil action for false claims, see 31 USCA § 3730.

Summons, see Fed.Rules Civ.Proc. Form 1, 28 USCA.

Venue of civil actions, see 28 USCA § 1391 et seq.

Rule 4.1. Serving Other Process

(a) In General. Process—other than a summons under Rule 4 or a subpoena under Rule 45—must be served by a United States marshal or deputy marshal or by a person specially appointed for that purpose. It may be served anywhere within the territorial limits of the state where the district court is located and, if authorized by a federal statute, beyond those limits. Proof of service must be made under Rule 4(*l*).

(b) Enforcing Orders: Committing for Civil Contempt. An order committing a person for civil contempt of a decree or injunction issued to enforce federal law may be served and enforced in any district. Any other order in a civil-contempt proceeding may be served only in the state where the issuing court is located or elsewhere in the United States within 100 miles from where the order was issued.

(Adopted April 22, 1993, effective December 1, 1993; amended April 30, 2007, effective December 1, 2007.)

ADVISORY COMMITTEE NOTES

1993 Adoption

This is a new rule. Its purpose is to separate those few provisions of the former Rule 4 bearing on matters other than service of a summons to allow greater textual clarity in Rule 4. Subdivision (a) contains no new language.

Subdivision (b) replaces the final clause of the penultimate sentence of the former subdivision 4(f), a clause added to the rule in 1963. The new rule provides for nationwide service of orders of civil commitment enforcing decrees of injunctions issued to compel compliance with federal law. The rule makes no change in the practice with respect to the enforcement of injunctions or decrees not involving the enforcement of federally-created rights.

Service of process is not required to notify a party of a decree or injunction, or of an order that the party show cause why that party should not be held in contempt of such an order. With respect to a party who has once been served with a summons, the service of the decree or injunction itself or of an order to show cause can be made pursuant to Rule 5. Thus, for example, an injunction may be served on a party through that person's attorney. *Chagas v. United States,* 369 F.2d 643 (5th Cir.1966). The same is true for service of an order to show cause. *Waffenschmidt v. Mackay,* 763 F.2d 711 (5th Cir.1985).

The new rule does not affect the reach of the court to impose criminal contempt sanctions. Nationwide enforcement of federal decrees and injunctions is already available with respect to criminal contempt: a federal court may effect the arrest of a criminal contemnor anywhere in the United States, 28 U.S.C. § 3041, and a contemnor when arrested may be subject to removal to the district in which punishment may be imposed. Fed.R.Crim.P. 40. Thus, the present law permits criminal contempt enforcement against a contemnor wherever that person may be found.

The effect of the revision is to provide a choice of civil or criminal contempt sanctions in those situations to which it applies. Contempt proceedings, whether civil or criminal, must be brought in the court that was allegedly defied by a contumacious act. *Ex parte Bradley,* 74 U.S. 366 (1869). This is so even if the offensive conduct or inaction occurred outside the district of the court in which the enforcement proceeding must be conducted. *E.g., McCourtney v. United States,* 291 Fed. 497 (8th Cir.), *cert. denied,* 263 U.S. 714 (1923). For this purpose, the rule as before does not distinguish between parties and other persons subject to contempt sanctions by reason of their relation or connection to parties.

2007 Amendment

The language of Rule 4.1 has been amended as part of the general restyling of the Civil Rules to make them more easily understood and to make style and terminology consistent throughout the rules. These changes are intended to be stylistic only.

Rule 5. Serving and Filing Pleadings and Other Papers

(a) Service: When Required.

(1) ***In General.*** Unless these rules provide otherwise, each of the following papers must be served on every party:

(A) an order stating that service is required;

(B) a pleading filed after the original complaint, unless the court orders otherwise under Rule 5(c) because there are numerous defendants;

(C) a discovery paper required to be served on a party, unless the court orders otherwise;

(D) a written motion, except one that may be heard ex parte; and

(E) a written notice, appearance, demand, or offer of judgment, or any similar paper.

(2) ***If a Party Fails to Appear.*** No service is required on a party who is in default for failing to appear. But a pleading that asserts a new claim for relief against such a party must be served on that party under Rule 4.

(3) ***Seizing Property.*** If an action is begun by seizing property and no person is or need be named as a defendant, any service required before the filing of an appearance, answer, or claim must be made on the person who had custody or possession of the property when it was seized.

(b) Service: How Made.

(1) ***Serving an Attorney.*** If a party is represented by an attorney, service under this rule must be made on the attorney unless the court orders service on the party.

(2) ***Service in General.*** A paper is served under this rule by:

(A) handing it to the person;

(B) leaving it:

(i) at the person's office with a clerk or other person in charge or, if no one is in charge, in a conspicuous place in the office; or

(ii) if the person has no office or the office is closed, at the person's dwelling or usual place of abode with someone of suitable age and discretion who resides there;

(C) mailing it to the person's last known address—in which event service is complete upon mailing;

(D) leaving it with the court clerk if the person has no known address;

(E) sending it by electronic means if the person consented in writing—in which event service is complete upon transmission, but is not effective if the serving party learns that it did not reach the person to be served; or

(F) delivering it by any other means that the person consented to in writing—in which event service is complete when the person making service delivers it to the agency designated to make delivery.

(3) ***Using Court Facilities.*** If a local rule so authorizes, a party may use the court's transmission facilities to make service under Rule 5(b)(2)(E).

(c) Serving Numerous Defendants.

(1) ***In General.*** If an action involves an unusually large number of defendants, the court may, on motion or on its own, order that:

(A) defendants' pleadings and replies to them need not be served on other defendants;

(B) any crossclaim, counterclaim, avoidance, or affirmative defense in those pleadings and replies to them will be treated as denied or avoided by all other parties; and

(C) filing any such pleading and serving it on the plaintiff constitutes notice of the pleading to all parties.

(2) ***Notifying Parties.*** A copy of every such order must be served on the parties as the court directs.

(d) Filing.

(1) ***Required Filings; Certificate of Service.*** Any paper after the complaint that is required to be served—together with a certificate of service—must be filed within a reasonable time after service. But disclosures under Rule 26(a)(1) or (2) and the following discovery requests and responses must not be filed until they are used in the proceeding or the court orders filing: depositions, interrogatories, requests for documents or tangible things or to permit entry onto land, and requests for admission.

(2) ***How Filing Is Made—In General.*** A paper is filed by delivering it:

(A) to the clerk; or

(B) to a judge who agrees to accept it for filing, and who must then note the filing date on the paper and promptly send it to the clerk.

(3) ***Electronic Filing, Signing, or Verification.*** A court may, by local rule, allow papers to be filed, signed, or verified by electronic means that are consistent with any technical standards established by the Judicial Conference of the United States. A local rule may require electronic filing only if reasonable exceptions are allowed. A paper filed electronically in

compliance with a local rule is a written paper for purposes of these rules.

(4) ***Acceptance by the Clerk.*** The clerk must not refuse to file a paper solely because it is not in the form prescribed by these rules or by a local rule or practice.

(Amended January 21, 1963, effective July 1, 1963; March 30, 1970, effective July 1, 1970; April 29, 1980, effective August 1, 1980; March 2, 1987, effective August 1, 1987; April 30, 1991, effective December 1, 1991; April 22, 1993, effective December 1, 1993; April 23, 1996, effective December 1, 1996; April 17, 2000, effective December 1, 2000; April 23, 2001, effective December 1, 2001; April 12, 2006, effective December 1, 2006; April 30, 2007, effective December 1, 2007.)

ADVISORY COMMITTEE NOTES

1937 Adoption

Note to Subdivisions (a) and (b). Compare 2 Minn.Stat. (1927) §§ 9240, 9241, 9242; N.Y.C.P.A. (1937) §§ 163, 164 and N.Y.R.C.P. (1937) Rules 20, 21; 2 Wash.Rev.Stat.Ann. (Remington, 1932) §§ 244 to 249.

Note to Subdivision (d). Compare the present practice under former Equity Rule 12 (Issue of Subpoena—Time for Answer).

1963 Amendment

The words "affected thereby," stricken out by the amendment, introduced a problem of interpretation. See 1 Barron & Holtzoff, *Federal Practice & Procedure* 760–61 (Wright ed. 1960). The amendment eliminates this difficulty and promotes full exchange of information among the parties by requiring service of papers on all the parties to the action, except as otherwise provided in the rules. See also subdivision (c) of Rule 5. So, for example, a third-party defendant is required to serve his answer to the third-party complaint not only upon the defendant but also upon the plaintiff. See amended Form 22–A and the Advisory Committee's Note thereto.

As to the method of serving papers upon a party whose address is unknown, see Rule 5(b).

1970 Amendment

The amendment makes clear that all papers relating to discovery which are required to be served on any party must be served on all parties, unless the court orders otherwise. The present language expressly includes notices and demands, but it is not explicit as to answers or responses as provided in Rules 33, 34, and 36. Discovery papers may be voluminous or the parties numerous, and the court is empowered to vary the requirement if in a given case it proves needlessly onerous.

In actions begun by seizure of property, service will at times have to be made before the absent owner of the property has filed an appearance. For example, a prompt deposition may be needed in a maritime action in rem. See Rules 30(a) and 30(b)(2) and the related notes. A provision is added authorizing service on the person having custody or possession of the property at the time of its seizure.

1980 Amendment

Subdivision (d). By the terms of this rule and Rule 30(f)(1) discovery materials must be promptly filed, although it often happens that no use is made of the materials after they are filed. Because the copies required for filing are an added expense and the large volume of discovery filings presents serious problems of storage in some districts, the Committee in 1978 first proposed that discovery materials not be filed unless on order of the court or for use in the proceedings. But such materials are sometimes of interest to those who may have no access to them except by a requirement of filing, such as members of a class, litigants similarly situated, or the public generally. Accordingly, this amendment and a change in Rule 30(f)(1) continue the requirement of filing but make it subject to an order of the court that discovery materials not be filed unless filing is requested by the court or is effected by parties who wish to use the materials in the proceeding.

1987 Amendment

The amendments are technical. No substantive change is intended.

1991 Amendment

Subdivision (d). This subdivision is amended to require that the person making service under the rule certify that service has been effected. Such a requirement has generally been imposed by local rule.

Having such information on file may be useful for many purposes, including proof of service if an issue arises concerning the effectiveness of the service. The certificate will generally specify the date as well as the manner of service, but parties employing private delivery services may sometimes be unable to specify the date of delivery. In the latter circumstance, a specification of the date of transmission of the paper to the delivery service may be sufficient for the purposes of this rule.

Subdivision (e). The words "*pleading and other*" are stricken as unnecessary. Pleadings are papers within the meaning of the rule. The revision also accommodates the development of the use of facsimile transmission for filing.

Several local district rules have directed the office of the clerk to refuse to accept for filing papers not conforming to certain requirements of form imposed by local rules or practice. This is not a suitable role for the office of the clerk, and the practice exposes litigants to the hazards of time bars; for these reasons, such rules are proscribed by this revision. The enforcement of these rules and of the local rules is a role for a judicial officer. A clerk may of course advise a party or counsel that a particular instrument is not in proper form, and may be directed to so inform the court.

1993 Amendments

This is a technical amendment, using the broader language of Rule 25 of the Federal Rules of Appellate Procedure. The district court—and the bankruptcy court by virtue of a cross-reference in Bankruptcy Rule 7005—can, by local rule, permit filing not only by facsimile transmissions but also by other electronic means, subject to standards approved by the Judicial Conference.

1996 Amendments

The present Rule 5(e) has authorized filing by facsimile or other electronic means on two conditions. The filing must be authorized by local rule. Use of this means of filing must be authorized by the Judicial Conference of the United States and must be consistent with standards established by the Judicial Conference. Attempts to develop Judicial Conference standards have demonstrated the value of several adjustments in the rule.

The most significant change discards the requirement that the Judicial Conference authorize local electronic filing rules. As before, each district may decide for itself whether it has the equipment and personnel required to establish electronic filing, but a district that wishes to establish electronic filing need no longer await Judicial Conference action.

The role of Judicial Conference standards is clarified by specifying that the standards are to govern technical matters. Technical standards can provide nationwide uniformity, enabling ready use of electronic filing without pausing to adjust for the otherwise inevitable variations among local rules. Judicial Conference adoption of technical standards should prove superior to specification in these rules. Electronic technology has advanced with great speed. The process of adopting Judicial Conference standards should prove speedier and more flexible in determining the time for the first uniform standards, in adjusting standards at appropriate intervals, and in sparing the Supreme Court and Congress the need to consider technological details. Until Judicial Conference standards are adopted, however, uniformity will occur only to the extent that local rules deliberately seek to copy other local rules.

It is anticipated that Judicial Conference standards will govern such technical specifications as data formatting, speed of transmission, means to transmit copies of supporting documents, and security of communication. Perhaps more important, standards must be established to assure proper maintenance and integrity of the record and to provide appropriate access and retrieval mechanisms. Local rules must address these issues until Judicial Conference standards are adopted.

The amended rule also makes clear the equality of filing by electronic means with written filings. An electronic filing that complies with the local rule satisfies all requirements for filing on paper, signature, or verification. An electronic filing that otherwise satisfies the requirements of 28 U.S.C. § 1746 need not be separately made in writing. Public access to electronic filings is governed by the same rules as govern written filings.

The separate reference to filing by facsimile transmission is deleted. Facsimile transmission continues to be included as an electronic means.

2000 Amendment

Subdivision (d). Rule 5(d) is amended to provide that disclosures under Rule 26(a)(1) and (2), and discovery requests and responses under Rules 30, 31, 33, 34, and 36 must not be filed until they are used in the action. "Discovery requests" includes deposition notices and "discovery responses" includes objections. The rule supersedes and invalidates local rules that forbid, permit, or require filing of these materials before they are used in the action. The former Rule 26(a)(4) requirement that disclosures under Rule 26(a)(1) and (2) be filed has been removed. Disclosures under Rule 26(a)(3), however, must be promptly filed as provided in Rule 26(a)(3). Filings in connection with Rule 35 examinations, which involve a motion proceeding when the parties do not agree, are unaffected by these amendments.

Recognizing the costs imposed on parties and courts by required filing of discovery materials that are never used in an action, Rule 5(d) was amended in 1980 to authorize court orders that excuse filing. Since then, many districts have adopted local rules that excuse or forbid filing. In 1989 the Judicial Conference Local Rules Project concluded that these local rules were inconsistent with Rule 5(d), but urged the Advisory Committee to consider amending the rule. *Local Rules Project* at 92 (1989). The Judicial Conference of the Ninth Circuit gave the Committee similar advice in 1997. The reality of nonfiling reflected in these local rules has even been assumed in drafting the national rules. In 1993, Rule 30(f)(1) was amended to direct that the officer presiding at a deposition file it with the court or send it to the attorney who arranged for the transcript or recording. The Committee Note explained that this alternative to filing was designed for "courts which direct that depositions not be automatically filed." Rule 30(f)(1) has been amended to conform to this change in Rule 5(d).

Although this amendment is based on widespread experience with local rules, and confirms the results directed by these local rules, it is designed to supersede and invalidate local rules. There is no apparent reason to have different filing rules in different districts. Even if districts vary in present capacities to store filed materials that are not used in an action, there is little reason to continue expending court resources for this purpose. These costs and burdens would likely change as parties make increased use of audio- and videotaped depositions. Equipment to facilitate review and reproduction of such discovery materials may prove costly to acquire, maintain, and operate.

The amended rule provides that discovery materials and disclosures under Rule 26(a)(1) and (a)(2) must not be filed until they are "used in the proceeding." This phrase is meant to refer to proceedings in court. This filing requirement is not triggered by "use" of discovery materials in other discovery activities, such as depositions. In connection with proceedings in court, however, the rule is to be interpreted broadly; any use of discovery materials in court in connection with a motion, a pretrial conference under Rule 16, or otherwise, should be interpreted as use in the proceeding.

Once discovery or disclosure materials are used in the proceeding, the filing requirements of Rule 5(d) should apply to them. But because the filing requirement applies only with regard to materials that are used, only those parts of voluminous materials that are actually used need be filed. Any party would be free to file other pertinent portions of materials that are so used. *See* Fed. R. Evid. 106; *cf.* Rule 32(a)(4). If the parties are unduly sparing in their submissions, the court may order further filings. By local rule, a court could provide appropriate direction regarding the filing of discovery materials, such as depositions, that are used in proceedings.

"Shall" is replaced by "must" under the program to conform amended rules to current style conventions when there is no ambiguity.

GAP Report

The Advisory Committee recommends no changes to either the amendments to Rule 5(d) or the Committee Note as published.

2001 Amendments

Rule 5(b) is restyled.

Rule 5(b)(1) makes it clear that the provision for service on a party's attorney applies only to service made under Rules 5(a) and 77(d). Service under Rules 4, 4.1, 45(b), and 71A(d)(3)—as well as rules that invoke those rules—must be made as provided in those rules.

Subparagraphs (A), (B), and (C) of Rule 5(b)(2) carry forward the method-of-service provisions of former Rule 5(b).

Subparagraph (D) of Rule 5(b)(2) is new. It authorizes service by electronic means or any other means, but only if consent is obtained from the person served. The consent must be express, and cannot be implied from conduct. Early experience with electronic filing as authorized by Rule 5(d) is positive, supporting service by electronic means as well. Consent is required, however, because it is not yet possible to assume universal entry into the world of electronic communication. Subparagraph (D) also authorizes service by nonelectronic means. The Rule 5(b)(2)(B) provision making mail service complete on mailing is extended in subparagraph (D) to make service by electronic means complete on transmission; transmission is effected when the sender does the last act that must be performed by the sender. Service by other agencies is complete on delivery to the designated agency.

Finally, subparagraph (D) authorizes adoption of local rules providing for service through the court. Electronic case filing systems will come to include the capacity to make service by using the court's facilities to transmit all documents filed in the case. It may prove most efficient to establish an environment in which a party can file with the court, making use of the court's transmission facilities to serve the filed paper on all other parties. Transmission might be by such means as direct transmission of the paper, or by transmission of a notice of filing that includes an electronic link for direct access to the paper. Because service is under subparagraph (D), consent must be obtained from the persons served.

Consent to service under Rule 5(b)(2)(D) must be in writing, which can be provided by electronic means. Parties are encouraged to specify the scope and duration of the consent. The specification should include at least the persons to whom service should be made, the appropriate address or location for such service—such as the e-mail address or facsimile machine number, and the format to be used for attachments. A district court may establish a registry or other facility that allows advance consent to service by specified means for future actions.

Rule 6(e) is amended to allow additional time to respond when service is made under Rule 5(b)(2)(D). The additional time does not relieve a party who consents to service under Rule 5(b)(2)(D) of the responsibilities to monitor the facility designated for receiving service and to provide prompt notice of any address change.

Paragraph (3) addresses a question that may arise from a literal reading of the provision that service by electronic means is complete on transmission. Electronic communication is rapidly improving, but lawyers report continuing failures of transmission, particularly with respect to attachments. Ordinarily the risk of non-receipt falls on the person being served, who has consented to this form of service. But the risk should not extend to situations in which the person attempting service learns that the attempted service in fact did not reach the person to be served. Given actual knowledge that the attempt failed, service is not effected. The person attempting service must either try again or show circumstances that justify dispensing with service.

Paragraph (3) does not address the similar questions that may arise when a person attempting service learns that service by means other than electronic means in fact did not reach the person to be served. Case law provides few illustrations of circumstances in which a person attempting service actually knows that the attempt failed but seeks to act as if service had been made. This negative history suggests there is no need to address these problems in Rule 5(b)(3). This silence does not imply any view on these issues, nor on the circumstances that justify various forms of judicial action even though service has not been made.

Changes Made After Publication and Comments

Rule 5(b)(2)(D) was changed to require that consent be "in writing."

Rule 5(b)(3) is new. The published proposal did not address the question of failed service in the text of the rule. Instead, the Committee Note included this statement: "As with other modes of service, however, actual notice that the transmission was not received defeats the presumption of receipt that arises from the provision that service is complete on transmission. The sender must take additional steps to effect service. Service by other agencies is complete on delivery to the designated agency." The addition of paragraph (3) was prompted by consideration of the draft Appellate Rule 25(c) that was prepared for the meeting of the Appellate Rules Advisory Committee. This draft provided: "Service by electronic means is complete on transmission, unless the party making service is notified that the paper was not received." Although Appellate Rule 25(c) is being prepared for publication and comment, while Civil Rule 5(b) has been published and otherwise is ready to recommend for adoption, it seemed desirable to achieve some parallel between the two rules.

The draft Rule 5(b)(3) submitted for consideration by the Advisory Committee covered all means of service except for leaving a copy with the clerk of the court when the person to be served has no known address. It was not limited to electronic service for fear that a provision limited to electronic service might generate unintended negative implications as to service by other means, particularly mail. This concern was strengthened by a small number of opinions that say that service by mail is effective, because complete on mailing, even when the person making service has prompt actual notice that the mail was not delivered. The Advisory Committee voted to limit Rule 5(b)(3) to service by electronic means because this means of service is relatively new, and seems likely to miscarry more frequently than service by post. It was suggested during the Advisory Committee meeting that the question of negative implication could be addressed in the Committee Note. There was little discussion of this possibility. The Committee Note submitted above includes a "no negative implications" paragraph prepared by the Reporter for consideration by the Standing Committee.

Complete Annotation Materials, see Title 28 U.S.C.A.

The Advisory Committee did not consider at all a question that was framed during the later meeting of the Appellate Rules Advisory Committee. As approved by the Advisory Committee, Rule 5(b)(3) defeats service by electronic means "if the party making service learns that the attempted service did not reach the person to be served." It says nothing about the time relevant to learning of the failure. The omission may seem glaring. Curing the omission, however, requires selection of a time. As revised, proposed Appellate Rule 25(c) requires that the party making service learn of the failure within three calendar days. The Appellate Rules Advisory Committee will have the luxury of public comment and another year to consider the desirability of this short period. If Civil Rule 5(b) is to be recommended for adoption now, no such luxury is available. This issue deserves careful consideration by the Standing Committee.

Several changes are made in the Committee Note. (1) It requires that consent "be express, and cannot be implied from conduct." This addition reflects a more general concern stimulated by a reported ruling that an e-mail address on a firm's letterhead implied consent to e-mail service. (2) The paragraph discussing service through the court's facilities is expanded by describing alternative methods, including an "electronic link." (3) There is a new paragraph that states that the requirement of written consent can be satisfied by electronic means, and that suggests matters that should be addressed by the consent. (4) A paragraph is added to note the additional response time provided by amended Rule 6(e). (5) The final two paragraphs address newly added Rule 5(b)(3). The first explains the rule that electronic service is not effective if the person making service learns that it did not reach the person to be served. The second paragraph seeks to defeat any negative implications that might arise from limiting Rule 5(b)(3) to electronic service, not mail, not other means consented to such as commercial express service, and not service on another person on behalf of the person to be served.

Rule 6(e)

The Advisory Committee recommended that no change be made in Civil Rule 6(e) to reflect the provisions of Civil Rule 5(b)(2)(D) that, with the consent of the person to be served, would allow service by electronic or other means. Absent change, service by these means would not affect the time for acting in response to the paper served. Comment was requested, however, on the alternative that would allow an additional 3 days to respond. The alternative Rule 6(e) amendments are cast in a form that permits ready incorporation in the Bankruptcy Rules. Several of the comments suggest that the added three days should be provided. Electronic transmission is not always instantaneous, and may fail for any of a number of reasons. It may take three days to arrange for transmission in readable form. Providing added time to respond will not discourage people from asking for consent to electronic transmission, and may encourage people to give consent. The more who consent, the quicker will come the improvements that will make electronic service ever more attractive. Consistency with the Bankruptcy Rules will be a good thing, and the Bankruptcy Rules Advisory Committee believes the additional three days should be allowed.

2006 Amendment

Amended Rule 5(e) acknowledges that many courts have required electronic filing by means of a standing order, procedures manual, or local rule. These local practices reflect the advantages that courts and most litigants realize from electronic filing. Courts that mandate electronic filing recognize the need to make exceptions when requiring electronic filing imposes a hardship on a party. Under amended Rule 5(e), a local rule that requires electronic filing must include reasonable exceptions, but Rule 5(e) does not define the scope of those exceptions. Experience with the local rules that have been adopted and that will emerge will aid in drafting new local rules and will facilitate gradual convergence on uniform exceptions, whether in local rules or in an amended Rule 5(e).

2007 Amendment

The language of Rule 5 has been amended as part of the general restyling of the Civil Rules to make them more easily understood and to make style and terminology consistent throughout the rules. These changes are intended to be stylistic only.

Rule 5(a)(1)(E) omits the former reference to a designation of record on appeal. Appellate Rule 10 is a self-contained provision for the record on appeal, and provides for service.

Former Rule 5(b)(2)(D) literally provided that a local rule may authorize use of the court's transmission facilities to make service by non-electronic means agreed to by the parties. That was not intended. Rule 5(b)(3) restores the intended meaning—court transmission facilities can be used only for service by electronic means.

Rule 5(d)(2)(B) provides that "a" judge may accept a paper for filing, replacing the reference in former Rule 5(e) to "the" judge. Some courts do not assign a designated judge to each case, and it may be important to have another judge accept a paper for filing even when a case is on the individual docket of a particular judge. The ministerial acts of accepting the paper, noting the time, and transmitting the paper to the court clerk do not interfere with the assigned judge's authority over the action.

CROSS REFERENCES

Additional time for service by mail, see Fed.Rules Civ. Proc. Rule 6, 28 USCA.

Jury trial, waiver by failing to file demand, see Fed.Rules Civ.Proc. Rule 38, 28 USCA.

Rule 5.1. Constitutional Challenge to A Statute—Notice, Certification, and Intervention

(a) Notice by a Party. A party that files a pleading, written motion, or other paper drawing into question the constitutionality of a federal or state statute must promptly:

(1) file a notice of constitutional question stating the question and identifying the paper that raises it, if:

(A) a federal statute is questioned and the parties do not include the United States, one of its agencies, or one of its officers or employees in an official capacity; or

(B) a state statute is questioned and the parties do not include the state, one of its agencies, or one of its officers or employees in an official capacity; and

(2) serve the notice and paper on the Attorney General of the United States if a federal statute is questioned—or on the state attorney general if a state statute is questioned—either by certified or registered mail or by sending it to an electronic address designated by the attorney general for this purpose.

(b) Certification by the Court. The court must, under 28 U.S.C. § 2403, certify to the appropriate attorney general that a statute has been questioned.

(c) Intervention; Final Decision on the Merits. Unless the court sets a later time, the attorney general may intervene within 60 days after the notice is filed or after the court certifies the challenge, whichever is earlier. Before the time to intervene expires, the court may reject the constitutional challenge, but may not enter a final judgment holding the statute unconstitutional.

(d) No Forfeiture. A party's failure to file and serve the notice, or the court's failure to certify, does not forfeit a constitutional claim or defense that is otherwise timely asserted.

(Effective December 1, 2006; amended April 30, 2007, effective December 1, 2007.)

ADVISORY COMMITTEE NOTES

2006 Adoption

Rule 5.1 implements 28 U.S.C. § 2403, replacing the final three sentences of Rule 24(c). New Rule 5.1 requires a party that files a pleading, written motion, or other paper drawing in question the constitutionality of a federal or state statute to file a notice of constitutional question and serve it on the United States Attorney General or state attorney general. The party must promptly file and serve the notice of constitutional question. This notice requirement supplements the court's duty to certify a constitutional challenge to the United States Attorney General or state attorney general. The notice of constitutional question will ensure that the attorney general is notified of constitutional challenges and has an opportunity to exercise the statutory right to intervene at the earliest possible point in the litigation. The court's certification obligation remains, and is the only notice when the constitutionality of a federal or state statute is drawn in question by means other than a party's pleading, written motion, or other paper.

Moving the notice and certification provisions from Rule 24(c) to a new rule is designed to attract the parties' attention to these provisions by locating them in the vicinity of the rules that require notice by service and pleading.

Rule 5.1 goes beyond the requirements of § 2403 and the former Rule 24(c) provisions by requiring notice and certification of a constitutional challenge to any federal or state statute, not only those "affecting the public interest." It is better to assure, through notice, that the attorney general is able to determine whether to seek intervention on the ground that the act or statute affects a public interest. Rule 5.1 refers to a "federal statute," rather than the § 2403 reference to an "Act of Congress," to maintain consistency in the Civil Rules vocabulary. In Rule 5.1 "statute" means any congressional enactment that would qualify as an "Act of Congress."

Unless the court sets a later time, the 60–day period for intervention runs from the time a party files a notice of constitutional question or from the time the court certifies a constitutional challenge, whichever is earlier. Rule 5.1(a) directs that a party promptly serve the notice of constitutional question. The court may extend the 60–period [So in original. Probably should read "60-day period".] on its own or on motion. One occasion for extension may arise if the court certifies a challenge under § 2403 after a party files a notice of constitutional question. Pretrial activities may continue without interruption during the intervention period, and the court retains authority to grant interlocutory relief. The court may reject a constitutional challenge to a statute at any time. But the court may not enter a final judgment holding a statute unconstitutional before the attorney general has responded or the intervention period has expired without response. This rule does not displace any of the statutory or rule procedures that permit dismissal of all or part of an action — including a constitutional challenge — at any time, even before service of process.

2007 Amendment

The language of Rule 5.1 has been amended as part of the general restyling of the Civil Rules to make them more easily understood and to make style and terminology consistent throughout the rules. These changes are intended to be stylistic only.

Rule 5.2. Privacy Protection For Filings Made with the Court

(a) Redacted Filings. Unless the court orders otherwise, in an electronic or paper filing with the court that contains an individual's social-security number, taxpayer-identification number, or birth date, the name of an individual known to be a minor, or a financial-account number, a party or nonparty making the filing may include only:

(1) the last four digits of the social-security number and taxpayer-identification number;

(2) the year of the individual's birth;

(3) the minor's initials; and

(4) the last four digits of the financial-account number.

(b) Exemptions from the Redaction Requirement. The redaction requirement does not apply to the following:

(1) a financial-account number that identifies the property allegedly subject to forfeiture in a forfeiture proceeding;
(2) the record of an administrative or agency proceeding;
(3) the official record of a state-court proceeding;
(4) the record of a court or tribunal, if that record was not subject to the redaction requirement when originally filed;
(5) a filing covered by Rule 5.2(c) or (d); and
(6) a pro se filing in an action brought under 28 U.S.C. §§ 2241, 2254, or 2255.

(c) **Limitations on Remote Access to Electronic Files; Social–Security Appeals and Immigration Cases.** Unless the court orders otherwise, in an action for benefits under the Social Security Act, and in an action or proceeding relating to an order of removal, to relief from removal, or to immigration benefits or detention, access to an electronic file is authorized as follows:
(1) the parties and their attorneys may have remote electronic access to any part of the case file, including the administrative record;
(2) any other person may have electronic access to the full record at the courthouse, but may have remote electronic access only to:
(A) the docket maintained by the court; and
(B) an opinion, order, judgment, or other disposition of the court, but not any other part of the case file or the administrative record.

(d) **Filings Made Under Seal.** The court may order that a filing be made under seal without redaction. The court may later unseal the filing or order the person who made the filing to file a redacted version for the public record.

(e) **Protective Orders.** For good cause, the court may by order in a case:
(1) require redaction of additional information; or
(2) limit or prohibit a nonparty's remote electronic access to a document filed with the court.

(f) **Option for Additional Unredacted Filing Under Seal.** A person making a redacted filing may also file an unredacted copy under seal. The court must retain the unredacted copy as part of the record.

(g) **Option for Filing a Reference List.** A filing that contains redacted information may be filed together with a reference list that identifies each item of redacted information and specifies an appropriate identifier that uniquely corresponds to each item listed. The list must be filed under seal and may be amended as of right. Any reference in the case to a listed identifier will be construed to refer to the corresponding item of information.

(h) **Waiver of Protection of Identifiers.** A person waives the protection of Rule 5.2(a) as to the person's own information by filing it without redaction and not under seal.

(Adopted April 30, 2007, effective December 1, 2007.)

ADVISORY COMMITTEE NOTES

2007 Adoption

The rule is adopted in compliance with section 205(c)(3) of the E–Government Act of 2002, Public Law 107–347. Section 205(c)(3) requires the Supreme Court to prescribe rules "to protect privacy and security concerns relating to electronic filing of documents and the public availability ... of documents filed electronically." The rule goes further than the E–Government Act in regulating paper filings even when they are not converted to electronic form. But the number of filings that remain in paper form is certain to diminish over time. Most districts scan paper filings into the electronic case file, where they become available to the public in the same way as documents initially filed in electronic form. It is electronic availability, not the form of the initial filing, that raises the privacy and security concerns addressed in the E–Government Act.

The rule is derived from and implements the policy adopted by the Judicial Conference in September 2001 to address the privacy concerns resulting from public access to electronic case files. See http://www.privacy.uscourts.gov/Policy.htm. The Judicial Conference policy is that documents in case files generally should be made available electronically to the same extent they are available at the courthouse, provided that certain "personal data identifiers" are not included in the public file.

While providing for the public filing of some information, such as the last four digits of an account number, the rule does not intend to establish a presumption that this information never could or should be protected. For example, it may well be necessary in individual cases to prevent remote access by nonparties to any part of an account number or social security number. It may also be necessary to protect information not covered by the redaction requirement—such as driver's license numbers and alien registration numbers—in a particular case. In such cases, protection may be sought under subdivision (d) or (e). Moreover, the Rule does not affect the protection available under other rules, such as Civil Rules 16 and 26(c), or under other sources of protective authority.

Parties must remember that any personal information not otherwise protected by sealing or redaction will be made available over the internet. Counsel should notify clients of this fact so that an informed decision may be made on what information is to be included in a document filed with the court.

The clerk is not required to review documents filed with the court for compliance with this rule. The responsibility to redact filings rests with counsel and the party or non-party making the filing.

Subdivision (c) provides for limited public access in Social Security cases and immigration cases. Those actions are entitled to special treatment due to the prevalence of sensitive information and the volume of filings. Remote electronic access by nonparties is limited to the docket and the written dispositions of the court unless the court orders otherwise. The rule contemplates, however, that nonparties can obtain full access to the case file at the courthouse, including access through the court's public computer terminal.

Subdivision (d) reflects the interplay between redaction and filing under seal. It does not limit or expand the judicially developed rules that govern sealing. But it does reflect the possibility that redaction may provide an alternative to sealing.

Subdivision (e) provides that the court can by order in a particular case for good cause require more extensive redaction than otherwise required by the Rule. Nothing in this subdivision is intended to affect the limitations on sealing that are otherwise applicable to the court.

Subdivision (f) allows a person who makes a redacted filing to file an unredacted document under seal. This provision is derived from section 205(c)(3)(iv) of the E-Government Act.

Subdivision (g) allows the option to file a register of redacted information. This provision is derived from section 205(c)(3)(v) of the E-Government Act, as amended in 2004. In accordance with the E-Government Act, subdivision (g) refers to "redacted" information. The term "redacted" is intended to govern a filing that is prepared with abbreviated identifiers in the first instance, as well as a filing in which a personal identifier is edited after its preparation.

Subdivision (h) allows a person to waive the protections of the rule as to that person's own personal information by filing it unsealed and in unredacted form. One may wish to waive the protection if it is determined that the costs of redaction outweigh the benefits to privacy. If a person files an unredacted identifier by mistake, that person may seek relief from the court.

Trial exhibits are subject to the redaction requirements of Rule 5.2 to the extent they are filed with the court. Trial exhibits that are not initially filed with the court must be redacted in accordance with the rule if and when they are filed as part of an appeal or for other reasons.

Rule 6. Computing and Extending Time; Time for Motion Papers

(a) Computing Time. The following rules apply in computing any time period specified in these rules or in any local rule, court order, or statute:

(1) ***Day of the Event Excluded.*** Exclude the day of the act, event, or default that begins the period.

(2) ***Exclusions from Brief Periods.*** Exclude intermediate Saturdays, Sundays, and legal holidays when the period is less than 11 days.

(3) ***Last Day.*** Include the last day of the period unless it is a Saturday, Sunday, legal holiday, or—if the act to be done is filing a paper in court—a day on which weather or other conditions make the clerk's office inaccessible. When the last day is excluded, the period runs until the end of the next day that is not a Saturday, Sunday, legal holiday, or day when the clerk's office is inaccessible.

(4) ***"Legal Holiday" Defined.*** As used in these rules, "legal holiday" means:

(A) the day set aside by statute for observing New Year's Day, Martin Luther King Jr.'s Birthday, Washington's Birthday, Memorial Day, Independence Day, Labor Day, Columbus Day, Veterans' Day, Thanksgiving Day, or Christmas Day; and

(B) any other day declared a holiday by the President, Congress, or the state where the district court is located.

(b) Extending Time.

(1) ***In General.*** When an act may or must be done within a specified time, the court may, for good cause, extend the time:

(A) with or without motion or notice if the court acts, or if a request is made, before the original time or its extension expires; or

(B) on motion made after the time has expired if the party failed to act because of excusable neglect.

(2) ***Exceptions.*** A court must not extend the time to act under Rules 50(b) and (d), 52(b), 59(b), (d), and (e), and 60(b), except as those rules allow.

(c) Motions, Notices of Hearing, and Affidavits.

(1) ***In General.*** A written motion and notice of the hearing must be served at least 5 days before the time specified for the hearing, with the following exceptions:

(A) when the motion may be heard ex parte;

(B) when these rules set a different time; or

(C) when a court order—which a party may, for good cause, apply for ex parte—sets a different time.

(2) ***Supporting Affidavit.*** Any affidavit supporting a motion must be served with the motion. Except as Rule 59(c) provides otherwise, any opposing affidavit must be served at least 1 day before the hearing, unless the court permits service at another time.

(d) Additional Time After Certain Kinds of Service. When a party may or must act within a specified time after service and service is made under Rule 5(b)(2)(C), (D), (E), or (F), 3 days are added after the period would otherwise expire under Rule 6(a).

(Amended December 27, 1946, effective March 19, 1948; January 21, 1963, effective July 1, 1963; February 28, 1966, effective July 1, 1966; December 4, 1967, effective July 1, 1968; March 1, 1971, effective July 1, 1971; April 28, 1983, effective August 1, 1983; April 29, 1985, effective August 1, 1985; March 2, 1987, effective August 1, 1987; April 29, 1999, effective December 1, 1999; April 23, 2001, effective December 1, 2001; April 25, 2005, effective December 1, 2005; April 30, 2007, effective December 1, 2007.)

ADVISORY COMMITTEE NOTES

1937 Adoption

Note to Subdivisions (a) and (b). These are amplifications along lines common in state practices, of [former] Equity Rule 80 (Computation of Time—Sundays and Holidays) and of the provisions for enlargement of time found in [former] Equity Rules 8 (Enforcement of Final Decrees) and 16 (Defendant to Answer—Default—Decree Pro Confesso). See also Rule XIII, Rules and Forms in Criminal Cases, 1934, 292 U.S. 661, 666. Compare Ala.Code Ann. (Michie, 1928) § 13 and former Law Rule 8 of the Rules of the Supreme Court of the District of Columbia (1924), superseded in 1929 by Law Rule 8, Rules of the District Court of the United States for the District of Columbia (1937).

Note to Subdivision (c). This eliminates the difficulties caused by the expiration of terms of court. Such statutes as U.S.C., Title 28, [former] § 12 (Trials not discontinued by new term) are not affected. Compare Rules of the United States District Court of Minnesota, Rule 25 (Minn.Stat. (Mason, Supp.1936), p. 1089).

Note to Subdivision (d). Compare 2 Minn.Stat. (Mason, 1927) § 9246; N.Y.R.C.P. (1937) Rules 60 and 64.

1946 Amendment

Note to Subdivision (b). The purpose of the amendment is to clarify the finality of judgments. Prior to the advent of the Federal Rules of Civil Procedure, the general rule that a court loses jurisdiction to disturb its judgments, upon the expiration of the term at which they were entered, had long been the classic device which (together with the statutory limits on the time for appeal) gave finality to judgments. See note to rule 73(a). Rule 6(c) abrogates that limit on judicial power. That limit was open to many objections, one of them being inequality of operation because, under it, the time for vacating a judgment rendered early in a term was much longer than for a judgment rendered near the end of the term.

The question to be met under rule 6(b) is: how far should the desire to allow correction of judgments be allowed to postpone their finality? The rules contain a number of provisions permitting the vacation or modification of judgments on various grounds. Each of these rules contains express time limits on the motions for granting of relief. Rule 6(b) is a rule of general application giving wide discretion to the court to enlarge these time limits or revive them after they have expired, the only exceptions stated in the original rule being a prohibition against enlarging the time specified in Rule 59(b) and (d) for making motions for or granting new trials, and a prohibition against enlarging the time fixed by law for taking an appeal. It should also be noted that Rule 6(b) itself contains no limitation of time within which the court may exercise its discretion, and since the expiration of the term does not end its power, there is now no time limit on the exercise of its discretion under Rule 6(b).

Decisions of lower federal courts suggest that some of the rules containing time limits which may be set aside under Rule 6(b) are Rules 25, 50(b), 52(b), 60(b), and 73(g).

In a number of cases the effect of Rule 6(b) on the time limitations of these rules has been considered. Certainly the rule is susceptible of the interpretation that the court is given the power in its discretion to relieve a party from failure to act within the times specified in any of these other rules, with only the exceptions stated in Rule 6(b), and in some cases the rule has been so construed.

With regard to Rule 25(a) for substitution, it was held in *Anderson v. Brady,* Ky.1941, 1 F.R.D. 589, 4 Fed.Rules Service 25a.1, Case 1, and in *Anderson v. Yungkau,* C.C.A.6, 1946, 153 F.2d 685, certiorari granted 66 S.Ct. 1025, 328 U.S. 829, 90 L.Ed. 1606, that under Rule 6(b) the court had no authority to allow substitution of parties after the expiration of the limit fixed in Rule 25(a).

As to Rules 50(b) for judgments notwithstanding the verdict and 52(b) for amendment of findings and vacation of judgment, it was recognized in *Leishman v. Associated Wholesale Electric Co.,* 1943, 63 S.Ct. 543, 318 U.S. 203, 87 L.Ed. 714, that Rule 6(b) allowed the district court to enlarge the time to make a motion for amended findings and judgment beyond the limit expressly fixed in Rule 52(b). See *Coca-Cola v. Busch,* E.D.Pa.1943, 7 Fed.Rules Service, 59b.2, Case 4. Obviously, if the time limit in Rule 52(b) could be set aside under Rule 6(b), the time limit in Rule 50(b) for granting judgment notwithstanding the verdict (and thus vacating the judgment entered "forthwith" on the verdict) likewise could be set aside.

As to Rule 59 on motions for a new trial, it has been settled that the time limits in Rule 59(b) and (d) for making motions for or granting new trial could not be set aside under Rule 6(b), because Rule 6(b) expressly refers to Rule 59, and forbids it. See *Safeway Stores, Inc. v. Coe,* App.D.C. 1943, 136 F.2d 771, 78 U.S.App.D.C. 19; *Jusino v. Morales & Tio,* C.C.A.1, 1944, 139 F.2d 946; *Coca-Cola Co. v. Busch,* E.D.Pa.1943, 7 Fed.Rules Service 59b.2, Case 4; *Peterson v. Chicago Great Western Ry. Co.,* D.Neb.1943, 3 F.R.D. 346, 7 Fed.Rules Service 59b.2, Case 1; *Leishman v. Associated Wholesale Electric Co.,* 1943, 63 S.Ct. 543, 318 U.S. 203, 87 L.Ed. 714.

As to Rule 60(b) for relief from a judgment, it was held in *Schram v. O'Connor,* Mich.1941, 5 Fed.Rules Serv. 6b.31, Case 1, 2 F.R.D. 192, s.c. 5 Fed.Rules Serv. 6b.31, Case 2, 2 F.R.D. 192, that the six-months time limit in original rule 60(b) for making a motion for relief from a judgment for surprise, mistake, or excusable neglect could be set aside under Rule 6(b). The contrary result was reached in *Wallace v. United States,* C.C.A.2, 1944, 142 F.2d 240, certiorari denied 65 S.Ct. 37, 323 U.S. 712, 89 L.Ed. 573; *Reed v. South Atlantic Steamship Co. of Del.,* Del.1942, 2 F.R.D. 475, 6 Fed.Rules Serv. 60b.31, Case 1.

As to Rule 73(g), fixing the time for docketing an appeal, it was held in *Ainsworth v. Gill Glass & Fixture Co.,* C.C.A.3, 1939, 104 F.2d 83, that under Rule 6(b) the district court, upon motion made after the expiration of the forty-day period, stated in Rule 73(g), but before the expiration of the ninety-day period therein specified, could permit the docketing of the appeal on a showing of excusable neglect. The contrary was held in *Mutual Benefit Health & Accident Ass'n v. Snyder,* C.C.A.6, 1940, 109 F.2d 469 and in *Burke v. Canfield,* 1940, 111 F.2d 526, 72 App.D.C. 127.

The amendment of Rule 6(b) now proposed is based on the view that there should be a definite point where it can be said a judgment is final; that the right method of dealing with the problem is to list in Rule 6(b) the various other rules whose time limits may not be set aside, and then, if the time limit in any of those other rules is too short, to amend that other rule to give a longer time. The further argument is that Rule 6(c) abolished the long standing device to produce finality in judgments through expiration of the term, and since that limitation on the jurisdiction of courts to set aside their own judgments has been removed by Rule 6(c), some other limitation must be substituted or judgments never can be said to be final.

In this connection reference is made to the established rule that if a motion for new trial is seasonably made, the mere making or pendency of the motion destroys the finality of the judgment, and even though the motion is ultimately denied, the full time for appeal starts anew from the date of denial. Also, a motion to amend the findings under Rule 52(b) has the same effect on the time for appeal. *Leishman v. Associated Wholesale Electric Co.,* 1943, 63 S.Ct. 543, 318 U.S. 203, 87 L.Ed. 714. By the same reasoning a motion for judgment under Rule 50(b), involving as it does the vacation of a judgment entered "forthwith" on the verdict (Rule 58), operates to postpone, until an order is made, the running of the time for appeal. The Committee believes that the abolition by Rule 6(c) of the old rule that a court's power over its judgments ends with the term, requires a substitute limitation, and that unless Rule 6(b) is amended to prevent enlargement of the times specified in Rules 50(b), 52(b) and 60(b), and the limitation as to Rule 59(b) and (d) is retained, no one can say when a judgment is final. This is also true with regard to proposed Rule 59(e), which authorizes a motion to alter or amend a judgment, hence that rule is also included in the enumeration in amended Rule 6(b). In consideration of the amendment, however, it should be noted that Rule 60(b) is also to be amended so as to lengthen the six-months period originally prescribed in that rule to one year.

As to Rule 25 on substitution, while finality is not involved, the limit there fixed should be controlling. That rule, as amended, gives the court power, upon showing of a reasonable excuse, to permit substitution after the expiration of the two-year period.

As to Rule 73(g), it is believed that the conflict in decisions should be resolved and not left to further litigation, and that the rule should be listed as one whose limitation may not be set aside under Rule 6(b).

As to Rule 59(c), fixing the time for serving affidavits on motion for new trial, it is believed that the court should have authority under Rule 6(b) to enlarge the time, because, once the motion for new trial is made, the judgment no longer has finality, and the extension of time for affidavits thus does not of itself disturb finality.

Other changes proposed in Rule 6(b) are merely clarifying and conforming. Thus "request" is substituted for "application" in clause (1) because an application is defined as a motion under Rule 7(b). The phrase "extend the time" is substituted for "enlarge the period" because the former is a more suitable expression and relates more clearly to both clauses (1) and (2). The final phrase in Rule 6(b), "or the period for taking an appeal as provided by law", is deleted and a reference to Rule 73(a) inserted, since it is proposed to state in that rule the time for appeal to a circuit court of appeals, which is the only appeal governed by the Federal Rules, and allows an extension of time. See Rule 72.

Subdivision (c). The purpose of this amendment is to prevent reliance upon the continued existence of a term as a source of power to disturb the finality of a judgment upon grounds other than those stated in these rules. See *Hill v. Hawes,* 1944, 64 S.Ct. 334, 320 U.S. 520, 88 L.Ed. 283; *Boaz v. Mutual Life Ins. Co. of New York,* C.C.A.8, 1944, 146 F.2d 321; *Bucy v. Nevada Construction Co.,* C.C.A.9, 1942, 125 F.2d 213.

1963 Amendment

Subdivision (a). This amendment is related to the amendment of Rule 77(c) changing the regulation of the days on which the clerk's office shall be open.

The wording of the first sentence of Rule 6(a) is clarified and the subdivision is made expressly applicable to computing periods of time set forth in local rules.

Saturday is to be treated in the same way as Sunday or a "legal holiday" in that it is not to be included when it falls on the last day of a computed period, nor counted as an intermediate day when the period is less than 7 days. "Legal holiday" is defined for purposes of this subdivision and amended Rule 77(c). Compare the definition of "holiday" in 11 U.S.C. § 1(18); also 5 U.S.C. § 86a; Executive Order No. 10358, *"Observance of Holidays,"* June 9, 1952, 17 Fed.Reg. 5269. In the light of these changes the last sentence of the present subdivision, dealing with half holidays, is eliminated.

With Saturdays and State holidays made "dies non" in certain cases by the amended subdivision, computation of the usual 5-day notice of motion or the 2-day notice to dissolve or modify a temporary restraining order may work out so as to cause embarrassing delay in urgent cases. The delay can be obviated by applying to the court to shorten the time, see Rules 6(d) and 65(b).

Subdivision (b). The prohibition against extending the time for taking action under Rule 25 (Substitution of parties) is eliminated. The only limitation of time provided for in amended Rule 25 is the 90-day period following a suggestion upon the record of the death of a party within which to make a motion to substitute the proper parties for the deceased party. See Rule 25(a)(1), as amended, and the Advisory Committee's Note thereto. It is intended that the court shall have discretion to enlarge that period.

1966 Amendment

P.L. 88–139, § 1, 77 Stat. 248, approved on October 16, 1963, amended 28 U.S.C. § 138 to read as follows: "The district court shall not hold formal terms." Thus Rule 6(c) is rendered unnecessary, and it is rescinded.

1967 Amendment

The amendment eliminates the references to Rule 73, which is to be abrogated.

1971 Amendment

The amendment adds Columbus Day to the list of legal holidays to conform the subdivision to the Act of June 28, 1968, 82 Stat. 250, which constituted Columbus Day a legal holiday effective after January 1, 1971.

The Act, which amended Title 5, U.S.C. § 6103(a), changes the day on which certain holidays are to be observed. Washington's Birthday, Memorial Day and Veterans Day are to be observed on the third Monday in February, the last Monday in May and the fourth Monday in October, respectively, rather than, as heretofore, on February 22, May 30, and November 11, respectively, Columbus Day is to be observed on the second Monday in October. New Year's Day, Independence Day, Thanksgiving Day and Christmas continue to be observed on the traditional days.

1983 Amendment

Subdivision (b). The amendment confers finality upon the judgments of magistrates by foreclosing enlargement of the time for appeal except as provided in new Rule 74(a) (20 day period for demonstration of excusable neglect).

1985 Amendment

Rule 6(a) is amended to acknowledge that weather conditions or other events may render the clerk's office inaccessible one or more days. Parties who are obliged to file something with the court during that period should not be penalized if they cannot do so. The amendment conforms to changes made in Federal Rule of Criminal Procedure 45(a), effective August 1, 1982.

The Rule also is amended to extend the exclusion of intermediate Saturdays, Sundays, and legal holidays to the computation of time periods less than 11 days. Under the current version of the Rule, parties bringing motions under rules with 10-day periods could have as few as 5 working days to prepare their motions. This hardship would be especially acute in the case of Rules 50(b) and (c)(2), 52(b), and 59(b), (d), and (e), which may not be enlarged at the discretion of the court. See Rule 6(b). If the exclusion of Saturdays, Sundays, and legal holidays will operate to cause excessive delay in urgent cases, the delay can be obviated by applying to the court to shorten the time. See Rule 6(b).

The Birthday of Martin Luther King, Jr., which becomes a legal holiday effective in 1986, has been added to the list of legal holidays enumerated in the Rule.

1987 Amendment

The amendments are technical. No substantive change is intended.

1999 Amendment

The reference to Rule 74(a) is stricken from the catalogue of time periods that cannot be extended by the district court. The change reflects the 1997 abrogation of Rule 74(a).

2001 Amendments

The additional three days provided by Rule 6(e) is extended to the means of service authorized by the new paragraph (D) added to Rule 5(b), including—with the consent of the person served—service by electronic or other means. The three-day addition is provided as well for service on a person with no known address by leaving a copy with the clerk of the court.

Changes Made After Publication and Comments

Proposed Rule 6(e) is the same as the "alternative proposal" that was published in August 1999.

2005 Amendments

Rule 6(e) is amended to remove any doubt as to the method for extending the time to respond after service by mail, leaving with the clerk of court, electronic means, or other means consented to by the party served. Three days are added after the prescribed period otherwise expires under Rule 6(a). Intermediate Saturdays, Sundays, and legal holidays are included in counting these added three days. If the third day is a Saturday, Sunday, or legal holiday, the last day to act is the next day that is not a Saturday, Sunday, or legal holiday. The effect of invoking the day when the prescribed period would otherwise expire under Rule 6(a) can be illustrated by assuming that the thirtieth day of a thirty-day period is a Saturday. Under Rule 6(a) the period expires on the next day that is not a Sunday or legal holiday. If the following Monday is a legal holiday, under Rule 6(a) the period expires on Tuesday. Three days are then added—Wednesday, Thursday, and Friday as the third and final day to act. If the period prescribed expires on a Friday, the three added days are Saturday, Sunday, and Monday, which is the third and final day to act unless it is a legal holiday. If Monday is a legal holiday, the next day that is not a legal holiday is the third and final day to act.

Application of Rule 6(e) to a period that is less than eleven days can be illustrated by a paper that is served by mailing on a Friday. If ten days are allowed to respond, intermediate Saturdays, Sundays, and legal holidays are excluded in determining when the period expires under Rule 6(a). If there is no legal holiday, the period expires on the Friday two weeks after the paper was mailed. The three added Rule 6(e) days are Saturday, Sunday, and Monday, which is the third and final day to act unless it is a legal holiday. If Monday is a legal holiday, the next day that is not a legal holiday is the final day to act.

2007 Amendment

The language of Rule 6 has been amended as part of the general restyling of the Civil Rules to make them more easily understood and to make style and terminology consistent throughout the rules. These changes are intended to be stylistic only.

HISTORICAL NOTES

Effective and Applicability Provisions

1946 Amendments. Effective date of amendment to this rule, see rule 86(b).

CROSS REFERENCES

Answer to—

Complaint, see Fed.Rules Civ.Proc. Rule 12, 28 USCA.

Cross-claim, see Fed.Rules Civ.Proc. Rule 12, 28 USCA.

Interrogatories, see Fed.Rules Civ.Proc. Rule 33, 28 USCA.

Answers and objections to admissions, see Fed.Rules Civ. Proc. Rule 36, 28 USCA.

Demand for jury trial, see Fed.Rules Civ.Proc. Rule 38, 28 USCA.

Motion for—

Amendment of findings, see Fed.Rules Civ.Proc. Rule 52, 28 USCA.

New trial, see Fed.Rules Civ.Proc. Rule 59, 28 USCA.
Relief from judgment or order, see Fed.Rules Civ.Proc. Rule 60, 28 USCA.
Motion to—
Alter or amend judgment, see Fed.Rules Civ.Proc. Rule 59, 28 USCA.
Set aside verdict and enter judgment, see Fed.Rules Civ.Proc. Rule 50, 28 USCA.
Notice of appeal, see 28 USCA § 2107.

Objections to interrogatories, see Fed.Rules Civ.Proc. Rule 33, 28 USCA.

Reply to counterclaim, see Fed.Rules Civ.Proc. Rule 12, 28 USCA.

Service by mail complete upon mailing, see Fed.Rules Civ.Proc. Rule 5, 28 USCA.

Substitution of parties, see Fed.Rules Civ.Proc. Rule 25, 28 USCA.

TITLE III. PLEADINGS AND MOTIONS

Rule 7. Pleadings Allowed; Form of Motions and Other Papers

(a) Pleadings. Only these pleadings are allowed:

(1) a complaint;

(2) an answer to a complaint;

(3) an answer to a counterclaim designated as a counterclaim;

(4) an answer to a crossclaim;

(5) a third-party complaint;

(6) an answer to a third-party complaint; and

(7) if the court orders one, a reply to an answer.

(b) Motions and Other Papers.

(1) ***In General.*** A request for a court order must be made by motion. The motion must:

(A) be in writing unless made during a hearing or trial;

(B) state with particularity the grounds for seeking the order; and

(C) state the relief sought.

(2) ***Form.*** The rules governing captions and other matters of form in pleadings apply to motions and other papers.

(Amended December 27, 1946, effective March 19, 1948; January 21, 1963, effective July 1, 1963; April 28, 1983, effective August 1, 1983; April 30, 2007, effective December 1, 2007.)

ADVISORY COMMITTEE NOTES

1937 Adoption

1. A provision designating pleadings and defining a motion is common in the state practice acts. See Smith-Hurd Ill.Stats. ch. 110, § 156 (Designation and order of pleadings); 2 Minn.Stat. (Mason, 1927) § 9246 (Definition of motion); and N.Y.C.P.A. (1937) § 113 (Definition of motion). Former Equity Rules 18 (Pleadings—Technical Forms Abrogated), 29 (Defenses—How Presented), and 33 (Testing Sufficiency of Defense) abolished technical forms of pleading, demurrers and pleas, and exceptions for insufficiency of an answer.

2. **Note to Subdivision (a).** This preserves the substance of [former] Equity Rule 31 (Reply—When Required—When Cause at Issue). Compare the English practice, *English Rules under the Judicature Act* (The Annual Practice, 1937) O. 23, r.r. 1, 2 (Reply to counterclaim; amended, 1933, to be subject to the rules applicable to defenses, O. 21). See O. 21, r.r. 1–14; O. 27, r. 13 (When pleadings deemed denied and put in issue). Under the codes the pleadings are generally limited. A reply is sometimes required to an affirmative defense in the answer. 1 Colo.Stat.Ann. (1935) § 66; Ore. Code Ann. (1930) §§ 1–614, 1–616. In other jurisdictions no reply is necessary to an affirmative defense in the answer, but a reply may be ordered by the court. N.C.Code Ann. (1935) § 525; 1 S.D.Comp.Laws (1929) § 2357. A reply to a counterclaim is usually required. Ark.Civ.Code (Crawford, 1934) §§ 123 to 125; Wis.Stat. (1935) §§ 263.20, 263.21. U.S.C. Title 28, [former] § 45 (District courts; practice and procedure in certain cases) is modified insofar as it may dispense with a reply to a counterclaim.

For amendment of pleadings, see Rule 15 dealing with amended and supplemental pleadings.

3. All statutes which use the words "petition", "bill of complaint", "plea", "demurrer", and other such terminology are modified in form by this rule.

1946 Amendment

Note. This amendment eliminates any question as to whether the compulsory reply, where a counterclaim is pleaded, is a reply only to the counterclaim or is a general reply to the answer containing the counterclaim. The Commentary, *Scope of Reply where Defendant Has Pleaded Counterclaim*, 1939, 1 Fed.Rules Serv. 672; *Fort Chartres and Ivy Landing Drainage and Levee District No. Five v. Thompson*, Ill.1945, 8 Fed.Rules Serv. 13.32, Case 1.

1963 Amendment

Certain redundant words are eliminated and the subdivision is modified to reflect the amendment of Rule 14(a) which in certain cases eliminates the requirement of obtaining leave to bring in a third-party defendant.

1983 Amendment

One of the reasons sanctions against improper motion practice have been employed infrequently is the lack of clarity of Rule 7. That rule has stated only generally that the pleading requirements relating to captions, signing, and other matters of form also apply to motions and other papers. The addition of Rule 7(b)(3) makes explicit the applicability of the signing requirement and the sanctions of Rule 11, which have been amplified.

2007 Amendment

The language of Rule 7 has been amended as part of the general restyling of the Civil Rules to make them more easily understood and to make style and terminology consistent throughout the rules. These changes are intended to be stylistic only.

Former Rule 7(a) stated that "there shall be * * * an answer to a cross-claim, if the answer contains a cross-claim * * *." Former Rule 12(a)(2) provided more generally that "[a] party served with a pleading stating a cross-claim against that party shall serve an answer thereto * * *." New Rule 7(a) corrects this inconsistency by providing for an answer to a crossclaim.

For the first time, Rule 7(a)(7) expressly authorizes the court to order a reply to a counterclaim answer. A reply may be as useful in this setting as a reply to an answer, a third-party answer, or a crossclaim answer.

Former Rule 7(b)(1) stated that the writing requirement is fulfilled if the motion is stated in a written notice of hearing. This statement was deleted as redundant because a single written document can satisfy the writing requirements both for a motion and for a Rule 6(c)(1) notice.

The cross-reference to Rule 11 in former Rule 7(b)(3) is deleted as redundant. Rule 11 applies by its own terms. The force and application of Rule 11 are not diminished by the deletion.

Former Rule 7(c) is deleted because it has done its work. If a motion or pleading is described as a demurrer, plea, or exception for insufficiency, the court will treat the paper as if properly captioned.

HISTORICAL NOTES

Effective and Applicability Provisions

1946 Amendments. Effective date of amendment to this rule, see rule 86(b).

CROSS REFERENCES

Procedure for motions in local practice, see Fed.Rules Civ.Proc. Rule 83, 28 USCA.

Service and filing of pleadings and other papers, see Fed.Rules Civ.Proc. Rule 5, 28 USCA.

Third party practice generally, see Fed.Rules Civ.Proc. Rule 14, 28 USCA.

Time for service of—

Answer or reply, see Fed.Rules Civ.Proc. Rule 12, 28 USCA.

Motions and affidavits, see Fed.Rules Civ.Proc. Rule 6, 28 USCA.

Treating defenses as counterclaims, see Fed.Rules Civ. Proc. Rule 8, 28 USCA.

Rule 7.1. Disclosure Statement

(a) Who Must File; Contents. A nongovernmental corporate party must file two copies of a disclosure statement that:

(1) identifies any parent corporation and any publicly held corporation owning 10% or more of its stock; or

(2) states that there is no such corporation.

(b) Time to File; Supplemental Filing. A party must:

(1) file the disclosure statement with its first appearance, pleading, petition, motion, response, or other request addressed to the court; and

(2) promptly file a supplemental statement if any required information changes.

(Adopted April 29, 2002, effective December 1, 2002; April 30, 2007, effective December 1, 2007.)

ADVISORY COMMITTEE NOTES

2002 Adoption

Rule 7.1 is drawn from Rule 26.1 of the Federal Rules of Appellate Procedure, with changes to adapt to the circumstances of district courts that dictate different provisions for the time of filing, number of copies, and the like. The information required by Rule 7.1(a) reflects the "financial interest" standard of Canon 3C(1)(c) of the Code of Conduct for United States Judges. This information will support properly informed disqualification decisions in situations that call for automatic disqualification under Canon 3C(1)(c). It does not cover all of the circumstances that may call for disqualification under the financial interest standard, and does not deal at all with other circumstances that may call for disqualification.

Although the disclosures required by Rule 7.1(a) may seem limited, they are calculated to reach a majority of the circumstances that are likely to call for disqualification on the basis of financial information that a judge may not know or recollect. Framing a rule that calls for more detailed disclosure will be difficult. Unnecessary disclosure requirements place a burden on the parties and on courts. Unnecessary disclosure of volumes of information may create a risk that a judge will overlook the one bit of information that might require disqualification, and also may create a risk that unnecessary disqualifications will be made rather than attempt to unravel a potentially difficult question. It has not been feasible to dictate more detailed disclosure requirements in Rule 7.1(a).

Rule 7.1 does not prohibit local rules that require disclosures in addition to those required by Rule 7.1. Developing experience with local disclosure practices and advances in electronic technology may provide a foundation for adopting more detailed disclosure requirements by future amendments of Rule 7.1.

Changes Made After Publication and Comment. The provisions that would require disclosure of additional information that may be required by the Judicial Conference have been deleted.

2007 Amendment

The language of Rule 7.1 has been amended as part of the general restyling of the Civil Rules to make them more easily understood and to make style and terminology consistent throughout the rules. These changes are intended to be stylistic only.

Rule 8. General Rules of Pleading

(a) Claim for Relief. A pleading that states a claim for relief must contain:

(1) a short and plain statement of the grounds for the court's jurisdiction, unless the court already has jurisdiction and the claim needs no new jurisdictional support;

(2) a short and plain statement of the claim showing that the pleader is entitled to relief; and

(3) a demand for the relief sought, which may include relief in the alternative or different types of relief.

(b) Defenses; Admissions and Denials.

(1) ***In General.*** In responding to a pleading, a party must:

(A) state in short and plain terms its defenses to each claim asserted against it; and

(B) admit or deny the allegations asserted against it by an opposing party.

(2) ***Denials—Responding to the Substance.*** A denial must fairly respond to the substance of the allegation.

(3) ***General and Specific Denials.*** A party that intends in good faith to deny all the allegations of a pleading—including the jurisdictional grounds—may do so by a general denial. A party that does not intend to deny all the allegations must either specifically deny designated allegations or generally deny all except those specifically admitted.

(4) ***Denying Part of an Allegation.*** A party that intends in good faith to deny only part of an allegation must admit the part that is true and deny the rest.

(5) ***Lacking Knowledge or Information.*** A party that lacks knowledge or information sufficient to form a belief about the truth of an allegation must so state, and the statement has the effect of a denial.

(6) ***Effect of Failing to Deny.*** An allegation—other than one relating to the amount of damages—is admitted if a responsive pleading is required and the allegation is not denied. If a responsive pleading is not required, an allegation is considered denied or avoided.

(c) Affirmative Defenses.

(1) ***In General.*** In responding to a pleading, a party must affirmatively state any avoidance or affirmative defense, including:

- accord and satisfaction;
- arbitration and award;
- assumption of risk;
- contributory negligence;
- discharge in bankruptcy;
- duress;
- estoppel;
- failure of consideration;
- fraud;
- illegality;
- injury by fellow servant;
- laches;
- license;
- payment;
- release;
- res judicata;
- statute of frauds;
- statute of limitations; and
- waiver.

(2) ***Mistaken Designation.*** If a party mistakenly designates a defense as a counterclaim, or a counterclaim as a defense, the court must, if justice requires, treat the pleading as though it were correctly designated, and may impose terms for doing so.

(d) Pleading to Be Concise and Direct; Alternative Statements; Inconsistency.

(1) ***In General.*** Each allegation must be simple, concise, and direct. No technical form is required.

(2) ***Alternative Statements of a Claim or Defense.*** A party may set out 2 or more statements of a claim or defense alternatively or hypothetically, either in a single count or defense or in separate ones. If a party makes alternative statements, the pleading is sufficient if any one of them is sufficient.

(3) ***Inconsistent Claims or Defenses.*** A party may state as many separate claims or defenses as it has, regardless of consistency.

(e) Construing Pleadings. Pleadings must be construed so as to do justice.

(Amended February 28, 1966, effective July 1, 1966; March 2, 1987, effective August 1, 1987; April 30, 2007, effective December 1, 2007.)

ADVISORY COMMITTEE NOTES

1937 Adoption

Note to Subdivision (a). See [former] Equity Rules 25 (Bill of Complaint—Contents), and 30 (Answer—Contents—Counterclaim). Compare 2 Ind.Stat.Ann. (Burns, 1933) §§ 2–1004, 2–1015; 2 Ohio Gen.Code Ann. (Page, 1926) §§ 11305, 11314; Utah Rev.Stat.Ann. (1933) §§ 104–7–2, 104–9–1.

See Rule 19(c) for the requirement of a statement in a claim for relief of the names of persons who ought to be parties and the reason for their omission.

See Rule 23(b) for particular requirements as to the complaint in a secondary action by shareholders.

Note to Subdivision (b). **1.** This rule supersedes the methods of pleading prescribed in U.S.C., Title 19, § 508 (Persons making seizures pleading general issue and proving special matter); U.S.C. Title 35, [former] §§ 40d (Proving under general issue, upon notice, that a statement in application for an extended patent is not true), 69 [now 282] (Pleading and proof in actions for infringement) and similar statutes.

2. This rule is, in part, [former] Equity Rule 30 (Answer—Contents—Counterclaim), with the matter on denials largely from the Connecticut practice. See Conn. Practice Book (1934) §§ 107, 108, and 122; Conn.Gen.Stat. (1930) §§ 5508 to 5514. Compare the English practice, *English Rules Under the Judicature Act* (The Annual Practice, 1937) O. 19, r.r. 17–20.

Note to Subdivision (c). This follows substantially *English Rules Under the Judicature Act* (The Annual Practice, 1937) O. 19, r. 15 and N.Y.C.P.A. (1937) § 242, with "surprise" omitted in this rule.

Note to Subdivision (d). The first sentence is similar to former Equity Rule 30 (Answer—Contents—Counterclaim). For the second sentence see former Equity Rule 31 (Reply—When Required—When Cause at Issue). This is similar to *English Rules Under the Judicature Act* (The Annual Practice, 1937) O. 19, r.r. 13, 18; and to the practice of the States.

Note to Subdivision (e). This rule is an elaboration upon [former] Equity Rule 30 (Answer—Contents—Counterclaim), plus a statement of the actual practice under some codes. Compare also [former] Equity Rule 18 (Pleadings—Technical Forms Abrogated). See Clark, *Code Pleading* (1928), pp. 171–4, 432–5; Hankin, *Alternative and Hypothetical Pleading* (1924), 33 Yale L.J. 365.

Note to Subdivision (f). A provision of like import is of frequent occurrence in the codes. Smith-Hurd Ill.Stats. ch. 110, § 157(3); 2 Minn.Stat. (Mason, 1927) § 9266; N.Y.C.P.A. (1937) § 275; 2 N.D.Comp.Laws Ann. (1913) § 7458.

1966 Amendment

The change here is consistent with the broad purposes of unification.

1987 Amendment

The amendments are technical. No substantive change is intended.

2007 Amendment

The language of Rule 8 has been amended as part of the general restyling of the Civil Rules to make them more easily understood and to make style and terminology consistent throughout the rules. These changes are intended to be stylistic only.

The former Rule 8(b) and 8(e) cross-references to Rule 11 are deleted as redundant. Rule 11 applies by its own terms. The force and application of Rule 11 are not diminished by the deletion.

Former Rule 8(b) required a pleader denying part of an averment to "specify so much of it as is true and material and * * * deny only the remainder." "[A]nd material" is deleted to avoid the implication that it is proper to deny something that the pleader believes to be true but not material.

Deletion of former Rule 8(e)(2)'s "whether based on legal, equitable, or maritime grounds" reflects the parallel deletions in Rule 1 and elsewhere. Merger is now successfully accomplished.

CROSS REFERENCES

Amendment of pleadings generally, see Fed.Rules Civ. Proc. Rule 15, 28 USCA.

Defenses in law or fact, how presented, see Fed.Rules Civ.Proc. Rule 12, 28 USCA.

Forms, see Fed.Rules Civ.Proc. Form 1 et seq., 28 USCA.

Joinder of claims, see Fed.Rules Civ.Proc. Rule 18, 28 USCA.

Relief granted in judgment even if not demanded, see Fed.Rules Civ.Proc. Rule 54, 28 USCA.

Reply to counterclaims denominated as such, see Fed.Rule Civ.Proc. Rule 7, 28 USCA.

Rule 9. Pleading Special Matters

(a) Capacity or Authority to Sue; Legal Existence.

(1) ***In General.*** Except when required to show that the court has jurisdiction, a pleading need not allege:

(A) a party's capacity to sue or be sued;

(B) a party's authority to sue or be sued in a representative capacity; or

(C) the legal existence of an organized association of persons that is made a party.

(2) ***Raising Those Issues.*** To raise any of those issues, a party must do so by a specific denial, which must state any supporting facts that are peculiarly within the party's knowledge.

(b) Fraud or Mistake; Conditions of Mind. In alleging fraud or mistake, a party must state with particularity the circumstances constituting fraud or mistake. Malice, intent, knowledge, and other conditions of a person's mind may be alleged generally.

(c) Conditions Precedent. In pleading conditions precedent, it suffices to allege generally that all conditions precedent have occurred or been performed. But when denying that a condition precedent has occurred or been performed, a party must do so with particularity.

(d) Official Document or Act. In pleading an official document or official act, it suffices to allege that the document was legally issued or the act legally done.

(e) Judgment. In pleading a judgment or decision of a domestic or foreign court, a judicial or quasi-judicial tribunal, or a board or officer, it suffices to plead the judgment or decision without showing jurisdiction to render it.

(f) Time and Place. An allegation of time or place is material when testing the sufficiency of a pleading.

(g) Special Damages. If an item of special damage is claimed, it must be specifically stated.

(h) Admiralty or Maritime Claim.

(1) ***How Designated.*** If a claim for relief is within the admiralty or maritime jurisdiction and also within the court's subject-matter jurisdiction on some other ground, the pleading may designate the claim as an admiralty or maritime claim for purposes of Rules 14(c), 38(e), and 82 and the Supplemental Rules for Admiralty or Maritime Claims and Asset Forfeiture Actions. A claim cognizable only in the admiralty or maritime jurisdiction is an admiralty or maritime claim for those purposes, whether or not so designated.

(2) ***Designation for Appeal.*** A case that includes an admiralty or maritime claim within this subdivision (h) is an admiralty case within 28 U.S.C. § 1292(a)(3).

(Amended February 28, 1966, effective July 1, 1966; December 4, 1967, effective July 1, 1968; March 30, 1970, effective July 1, 1970; March 2, 1987, effective August 1, 1987; April 11, 1997, effective December 1, 1997; April 12, 2006, effective December 1, 2006; April 30, 2007, effective December 1, 2007.)

ADVISORY COMMITTEE NOTES

1937 Adoption

Note to Subdivision (a). Compare [former] Equity Rule 25 (Bill of Complaint—Contents) requiring disability to be stated; Utah Rev.Stat.Ann. (1933) § 104–13–15, enumerating a number of situations where a general averment of capacity is sufficient. For provisions governing averment of incorporation, see 2 Minn.Stat. (Mason, 1927) § 9271; N.Y.R.C.P. (1937) Rule 93; 2 N.D.Comp.Laws Ann. (1913) § 7981 et seq.

Note to Subdivision (b). See *English Rules Under the Judicature Act* (The Annual Practice, 1937) O. 19, r. 22.

Note to Subdivision (c). The codes generally have this or a similar provision. See *English Rules Under the Judicature Act* (The Annual Practice, 1937) O. 19, r. 14; 2 Minn. Stat. (Mason, 1927) § 9273; N.Y.R.C.P. (1937) Rule 92; 2 N.D.Comp.Laws Ann. (1913) § 7461; 2 Wash.Rev.Stat.Ann. (Remington, 1932) § 288.

Note to Subdivision (e). The rule expands the usual code provisions on pleading a judgment by including judgments or decisions of administrative tribunals and foreign courts. Compare Ark.Civ.Code (Crawford, 1934) § 141; 2 Minn.Stat. (Mason, 1927) § 9269; N.Y.R.C.P. (1937) Rule 95; 2 Wash. Rev.Stat.Ann. (Remington, 1932) § 287.

1966 Amendment

Certain distinctive features of the admiralty practice must be preserved for what are now suits in admiralty. This raises the question: After unification, when a single form of action is established, how will the counterpart of the present suit in admiralty be identifiable? In part the question is easily answered. Some claims for relief can only be suits in admiralty, either because the admiralty jurisdiction is exclusive or because no nonmaritime ground of federal jurisdiction exists. Many claims, however, are cognizable by the district courts whether asserted in admiralty or in a civil action, assuming the existence of a nonmaritime ground of jurisdiction. Thus at present the pleader has power to determine procedural consequences by the way in which he exercises the classic privilege given by the saving-to-suitors clause (28 U.S.C. § 1333) or by equivalent statutory provisions. For example, a longshoreman's claim for personal injuries suffered by reason of the unseaworthiness of a vessel may be asserted in a suit in admiralty or, if diversity of citizenship exists, in a civil action. One of the important procedural consequences is that in the civil action either party may demand a jury trial, while in the suit in admiralty there is no right to jury trial except as provided by statute.

It is no part of the purpose of unification to inject a right to jury trial into those admiralty cases in which that right is not provided by statute. Similarly as will be more specifically noted below, there is no disposition to change the present law as to interlocutory appeals in admiralty, or as to the venue of suits in admiralty; and, of course, there is no disposition to inject into the civil practice as it now is the distinctively maritime remedies (maritime attachment and garnishment, actions in rem, possessory, petitory and partition actions and limitation of liability). The unified rules must therefore provide some device for preserving the present power of the pleader to determine whether these historically maritime procedures shall be applicable to his claim or not; the pleader must be afforded some means of designating his claim as the counterpart of the present suit in admiralty, where its character as such is not clear.

The problem is different from the similar one concerning the identification of claims that were formerly suits in equity. While that problem is not free from complexities, it is broadly true that the modern counterpart of the suit in equity is distinguishable from the former action at law by the character of the relief sought. This mode of identification is possible in only a limited category of admiralty cases. In large numbers of cases the relief sought in admiralty is simple money damages, indistinguishable from the remedy afforded by the common law. This is true, for example, in the case of the longshoreman's action for personal injuries stated above. After unification has abolished the distinction between civil actions and suits in admiralty, the complaint in such an action would be almost completely ambiguous as to the pleader's intentions regarding the procedure invoked. The allegation of diversity of citizenship might be regarded as a clue indicating an intention to proceed as at present under the saving-to-suitors clause; but this, too, would be ambiguous if there were also reference to the admiralty jurisdiction, and the pleader ought not be required to forego mention of all available jurisdictional grounds.

Other methods of solving the problem were carefully explored, but the Advisory Committee concluded that the preferable solution is to allow the pleader who now has power to determine procedural consequences by filing a suit in admiralty to exercise that power under unification, for the limited instances in which procedural differences will remain, by a simple statement in his pleading to the effect that the claim is an admiralty or maritime claim.

The choice made by the pleader in identifying or in failing to identify his claim as an admiralty or maritime claim is not an irrevocable election. The rule provides that the amendment of a pleading to add or withdraw an identifying statement is subject to the principles of Rule 15.

1968 Amendment

The amendment eliminates the reference to Rule 73 which is to be abrogated and transfers to Rule 9(h) the substance of Subsection (h) of Rule 73 which preserved the right to an interlocutory appeal in admiralty cases which is provided by 28 U.S.C. § 1292(a)(3).

1970 Amendment

The reference to Rule 26(a) is deleted, in light of the transfer of that subdivision to Rule 30(a) and the elimination of the de bene esse procedure therefrom. See the Advisory Committee's note to Rule 30(a).

1987 Amendment

The amendment is technical. No substantive change is intended.

1997 Amendment

Section 1292(a)(3) of the Judicial Code provides for appeal from "[i]nterlocutory decrees of * * * district courts * * * determining the rights and liabilities of the parties to admiralty cases in which appeals from final decrees are allowed."

Rule 9(h) was added in 1966 with the unification of civil and admiralty procedure. Civil Rule 73(h) was amended at the same time to provide that the § 1292(a)(3) reference "to admiralty cases shall be construed to mean admiralty and maritime claims within the meaning of Rule 9(h)." This provision was transferred to Rule 9(h) when the Appellate Rules were adopted.

A single case can include both admiralty or maritime claims and nonadmiralty claims or parties. This combination reveals an ambiguity in the statement in present Rule 9(h) that an admiralty "claim" is an admiralty "case." An order "determining the rights and liabilities of the parties" within the meaning of § 1292(a)(3) may resolve only a nonadmiralty claim, or may simultaneously resolve interdependent admiralty and non-admiralty claims. Can appeal be taken as to the nonadmiralty matter, because it is part of a case that includes an admiralty claim, or is appeal limited to the admiralty claim?

The courts of appeals have not achieved full uniformity in applying the § 1292(a)(3) requirement that an order "determin[e] the rights and liabilities of the parties." It is common to assert that the statute should be construed narrowly, under the general policy that exceptions to the final judgment rule should be construed narrowly. This policy would suggest that the ambiguity should be resolved by limiting the interlocutory appeal right to orders that determine the rights and liabilities of the parties to an admiralty claim.

A broader view is chosen by this amendment for two reasons. The statute applies to admiralty "cases," and may itself provide for appeal from an order that disposes of a nonadmiralty claim that is joined in a single case with an admiralty claim. Although a rule of court may help to clarify and implement a statutory grant of jurisdiction, the line is not always clear between permissible implementation and impermissible withdrawal of jurisdiction. In addition, so long as an order truly disposes of the rights and liabilities of the parties within the meaning of § 1292(a)(3), it may prove important to permit appeal as to the non-admiralty claim. Disposition of the non-admiralty claim, for example, may make it unnecessary to consider the admiralty claim and have the same effect on the case and parties as disposition of the admiralty claim. Or the admiralty and non-admiralty claims may be interdependent. An illustration is provided by Roco Carriers, Ltd. v. M/V Nurnberg Express, 899 F.2d 1292 (2d Cir.1990). Claims for losses of ocean shipments were made against two defendants, one subject to admiralty jurisdiction and the other not. Summary judgment was granted in favor of the admiralty defendant and against the nonadmiralty defendant. The nonadmiralty defendant's appeal was accepted, with the explanation that the determination of its liability was "integrally linked with the determination of non-liability" of the admiralty defendant, and that "section 1292(a)(3) is not limited to admiralty claims; instead, it refers to admiralty cases." 899 F.2d at 1297. The advantages of permitting appeal by the nonadmiralty defendant would be particularly clear if the plaintiff had appealed the summary judgment in favor of the admiralty defendant.

It must be emphasized that this amendment does not rest on any particular assumptions as to the meaning of the § 1292(a)(3) provision that limits interlocutory appeal to orders that determine the rights and liabilities of the parties. It simply reflects the conclusion that so long as the case involves an admiralty claim and an order otherwise meets statutory requirements, the opportunity to appeal should not turn on the circumstance that the order does—or does not—dispose of an admiralty claim. No attempt is made to invoke the authority conferred by 28 U.S.C. § 1292(e) to provide by rule for appeal of an interlocutory decision that is not otherwise provided for by other subsections of § 1292.

GAP Report on Rule 9(h). No changes have been made in the published proposal.

2006 Amendment

Rule 9(h) is amended to conform to the changed title of the Supplemental Rules.

2007 Amendment

The language of Rule 9 has been amended as part of the general restyling of the Civil Rules to make them more easily understood and to make style and terminology consistent throughout the rules. These changes are intended to be stylistic only.

Rule 15 governs pleading amendments of its own force. The former redundant statement that Rule 15 governs an amendment that adds or withdraws a Rule 9(h) designation as an admiralty or maritime claim is deleted. The elimination of paragraph (2) means that "(3)" will be redesignated as "(2)" in Style Rule 9(h).

CROSS REFERENCES

Capacity to sue or be sued, see Fed.Rules Civ.Proc. Rule 17, 28 USCA.

Pleading affirmative defenses, see Fed.Rules Civ.Proc. Rule 8, 28 USCA.

Proof of official record, see Fed.Rules Civ.Proc. Rule 44, 28 USCA.

Rule 10. Form of Pleadings

(a) Caption; Names of Parties. Every pleading must have a caption with the court's name, a title, a file number, and a Rule 7(a) designation. The title of the complaint must name all the parties; the title of other pleadings, after naming the first party on each side, may refer generally to other parties.

(b) Paragraphs; Separate Statements. A party must state its claims or defenses in numbered paragraphs, each limited as far as practicable to a single set of circumstances. A later pleading may refer by number to a paragraph in an earlier pleading. If doing so would promote clarity, each claim founded on a separate transaction or occurrence—and each defense other than a denial—must be stated in a separate count or defense.

(c) Adoption by Reference; Exhibits. A statement in a pleading may be adopted by reference elsewhere in the same pleading or in any other pleading or motion. A copy of a written instrument that is an exhibit to a pleading is a part of the pleading for all purposes.

(Amended April 30, 2007, effective December 1, 2007.)

ADVISORY COMMITTEE NOTES

1937 Adoption

The first sentence is derived in part from the opening statement of former Equity Rule 25 (Bill of Complaint—Contents). The remainder of the rule is an expansion in conformity with usual state provisions. For numbered paragraphs and separate statements, see Conn.Gen.Stat., 1930, § 5513; Smith-Hurd Ill.Stats. ch. 110, § 157(2); N.Y.R.C.P., (1937) Rule 90. For incorporation by reference, see N.Y.R.C.P., (1937) Rule 90. For written instruments as exhibits, see Smith-Hurd Ill.Stats. ch. 110, § 160.

2007 Amendment

The language of Rule 10 has been amended as part of the general restyling of the Civil Rules to make them more easily understood and to make style and terminology consistent throughout the rules. These changes are intended to be stylistic only.

CROSS REFERENCES

Captions in motions and other papers, see Fed.Rules Civ. Proc. Rule 7, 28 USCA.

Forms, see Fed.Rules Civ.Proc. Form 1 et seq., 28 USCA.

Rule 11. Signing Pleadings, Motions, and Other Papers; Representations to the Court; Sanctions

(a) Signature. Every pleading, written motion, and other paper must be signed by at least one attorney of record in the attorney's name—or by a party personally if the party is unrepresented. The paper must state the signer's address, e-mail address, and telephone number. Unless a rule or statute specifically states otherwise, a pleading need not be verified or accompanied by an affidavit. The court must strike an unsigned paper unless the omission is promptly corrected after being called to the attorney's or party's attention.

(b) Representations to the Court. By presenting to the court a pleading, written motion, or other paper—whether by signing, filing, submitting, or later advocating it—an attorney or unrepresented party certifies that to the best of the person's knowledge, information, and belief, formed after an inquiry reasonable under the circumstances:

(1) it is not being presented for any improper purpose, such as to harass, cause unnecessary delay, or needlessly increase the cost of litigation;

(2) the claims, defenses, and other legal contentions are warranted by existing law or by a nonfrivolous argument for extending, modifying, or reversing existing law or for establishing new law;

(3) the factual contentions have evidentiary support or, if specifically so identified, will likely have evidentiary support after a reasonable opportunity for further investigation or discovery; and

(4) the denials of factual contentions are warranted on the evidence or, if specifically so identified, are reasonably based on belief or a lack of information.

(c) Sanctions.

(1) ***In General.*** If, after notice and a reasonable opportunity to respond, the court determines that Rule 11(b) has been violated, the court may impose an appropriate sanction on any attorney, law firm, or party that violated the rule or is responsible for the violation. Absent exceptional circumstances, a law firm must be held jointly responsible for a violation committed by its partner, associate, or employee.

(2) ***Motion for Sanctions.*** A motion for sanctions must be made separately from any other motion and must describe the specific conduct that allegedly violates Rule 11(b). The motion must be served under Rule 5, but it must not

be filed or be presented to the court if the challenged paper, claim, defense, contention, or denial is withdrawn or appropriately corrected within 21 days after service or within another time the court sets. If warranted, the court may award to the prevailing party the reasonable expenses, including attorney's fees, incurred for the motion.

(3) ***On the Court's Initiative.*** On its own, the court may order an attorney, law firm, or party to show cause why conduct specifically described in the order has not violated Rule 11(b).

(4) ***Nature of a Sanction.*** A sanction imposed under this rule must be limited to what suffices to deter repetition of the conduct or comparable conduct by others similarly situated. The sanction may include nonmonetary directives; an order to pay a penalty into court; or, if imposed on motion and warranted for effective deterrence, an order directing payment to the movant of part or all of the reasonable attorney's fees and other expenses directly resulting from the violation.

(5) ***Limitations on Monetary Sanctions.*** The court must not impose a monetary sanction:

(A) against a represented party for violating Rule 11(b)(2); or

(B) on its own, unless it issued the show-cause order under Rule 11(c)(3) before voluntary dismissal or settlement of the claims made by or against the party that is, or whose attorneys are, to be sanctioned.

(6) ***Requirements for an Order.*** An order imposing a sanction must describe the sanctioned conduct and explain the basis for the sanction.

(d) Inapplicability to Discovery. This rule does not apply to disclosures and discovery requests, responses, objections, and motions under Rules 26 through 37.

(Amended April 28, 1983, effective August 1, 1983; March 2, 1987, effective August 1, 1987; April 22, 1993, effective December 1, 1993; April 30, 2007, effective December 1, 2007.)

ADVISORY COMMITTEE NOTES

1937 Adoption

This is substantially the content of [former] Equity Rules 24 (Signature of Counsel) and 21 (Scandal and Impertinence) consolidated and unified. Compare former Equity Rule 36 (Officers Before Whom Pleadings Verified). Compare to similar purposes, *English Rules Under the Judicature Act* (The Annual Practice, 1937) O. 19, r. 4, and *Great Australian Gold Mining Co. v. Martin*, L.R. 5 Ch.Div. 1, 10 (1877). Subscription of pleadings is required in many codes. 2 Minn.Stat. (Mason, 1927) § 9265; N.Y.R.C.P. (1937) Rule 91; 2 N.D.Comp.Laws Ann. (1913) § 7455.

This rule expressly continues any statute which requires a pleading to be verified or accompanied by an affidavit, such as: U.S.C., Title 28:

§ 381 [former] (Preliminary injunctions and temporary restraining orders)

§ 762 [now 1402] (Suit against the United States)

U.S.C., Title 28, § 829 [now 1927] (Costs; attorney liable for, when) is unaffected by this rule.

For complaints which must be verified under these rules, see Rules 23(b) (Secondary Action by Shareholders) and 65 (Injunctions).

For abolition of former rule in equity that the averments of an answer under oath must be overcome by the testimony of two witnesses or of one witness sustained by corroborating circumstances, see 12 P.S.Pa. § 1222; for the rule in equity itself, see *Greenfield v. Blumenthal*, C.C.A.3, 1934, 69 F.2d 294.

1983 Amendment

Since its original promulgation, Rule 11 has provided for the striking of pleadings and the imposition of disciplinary sanctions to check abuses in the signing of pleadings. Its provisions have always applied to motions and other papers by virtue of incorporation by reference in Rule 7(b)(2). The amendment and the addition of Rule 7(b)(3) expressly confirms this applicability.

Experience shows that in practice Rule 11 has not been effective in deterring abuses. See 6 Wright & Miller, *Federal Practice and Procedure: Civil* § 1334 (1971). There has been considerable confusion as to (1) the circumstances that should trigger striking a pleading or motion or taking disciplinary action, (2) the standard of conduct expected of attorneys who sign pleadings and motions, and (3) the range of available and appropriate sanctions. See Rodes, Ripple & Mooney, *Sanctions Imposable for Violations of the Federal Rules of Civil Procedure* 64–65, Federal Judicial Center (1981). The new language is intended to reduce the reluctance of courts to impose sanctions, see Moore, *Federal Practice* ¶ 7.05, at 1547, by emphasizing the responsibilities of the attorney and reenforcing those obligations by the imposition of sanctions.

The amended rule attempts to deal with the problem by building upon and expanding the equitable doctrine permitting the court to award expenses, including attorney's fees, to a litigant whose opponent acts in bad faith in instituting or conducting litigation. See, e.g., *Roadway Express, Inc. v. Piper*, 447 U.S. 752 (1980); *Hall v. Cole*, 412 U.S. 1, 5 (1973). Greater attention by the district courts to pleading and motion abuses and the imposition of sanctions when appropriate, should discourage dilatory or abusive tactics and help to streamline the litigation process by lessening frivolous claims or defenses.

The expanded nature of the lawyer's certification in the fifth sentence of amended Rule 11 recognizes that the litigation process may be abused for purposes other than delay. See, e.g., *Browning Debenture Holders' Committee v. DASA Corp.*, 560 F.2d 1078 (2d Cir.1977).

The words "good ground to support" the pleading in the original rule were interpreted to have both factual and legal elements. See, e.g., *Heart Disease Research Foundation v. General Motors Corp.*, 15 Fed.R.Serv.2d 1517, 1519 (S.D.N.Y.1972). They have been replaced by a standard of conduct that is more focused.

The new language stresses the need for some prefiling inquiry into both the facts and the law to satisfy the affirmative duty imposed by the rule. The standard is one of reasonableness under the circumstances. See *Kinee v. Abraham Lincoln Fed. Sav. & Loan Ass'n*, 365 F.Supp. 975 (E.D.Pa.1973). This standard is more stringent than the original good-faith formula and thus it is expected that a greater range of circumstances will trigger its violation. See *Nemeroff v. Abelson*, 620 F.2d 339 (2d Cir.1980).

The rule is not intended to chill an attorney's enthusiasm or creativity in pursuing factual or legal theories. The court is expected to avoid using the wisdom of hindsight and should test the signer's conduct by inquiring what was reasonable to believe at the time the pleading, motion, or other paper was submitted. Thus, what constitutes a reasonable inquiry may depend on such factors as how much time for investigation was available to the signer; whether he had to rely on a client for information as to the facts underlying the pleading, motion, or other paper; whether the pleading, motion, or other paper was based on a plausible view of the law; or whether he depended on forwarding counsel or another member of the bar.

The rule does not require a party or an attorney to disclose privileged communications or work product in order to show that the signing of the pleading, motion, or other paper is substantially justified. The provisions of Rule 26(c), including appropriate orders after *in camera* inspection by the court, remain available to protect a party claiming privilege or work product protection.

Amended Rule 11 continues to apply to anyone who signs a pleading, motion, or other paper. Although the standard is the same for unrepresented parties, who are obliged themselves to sign the pleadings, the court has sufficient discretion to take account of the special circumstances that often arise in *pro se* situations. See *Haines v. Kerner*, 404 U.S. 519 (1972).

The provision in the original rule for striking pleadings and motions as sham and false has been deleted. The passage has rarely been utilized, and decisions thereunder have tended to confuse the issue of attorney honesty with the merits of the action. See generally Risinger, *Honesty in Pleading and its Enforcement: Some "Striking" Problems with Fed.R.Civ.P. 11*, 61 Minn.L.Rev. 1 (1976). Motions under this provision generally present issues better dealt with under Rules 8, 12, or 56. See *Murchison v. Kirby*, 27 F.R.D. 14 (S.D.N.Y.1961); 5 Wright & Miller, *Federal Practice and Procedure: Civil* § 1334 (1969).

The former reference to the inclusion of scandalous or indecent matter, which is itself strong indication that an improper purpose underlies the pleading, motion, or other paper, also has been deleted as unnecessary. Such matter may be stricken under Rule 12(f) as well as dealt with under the more general language of amended Rule 11.

The text of the amended rule seeks to dispel apprehensions that efforts to obtain enforcement will be fruitless by insuring that the rule will be applied when properly invoked. The word "sanctions" in the caption, for example, stresses a deterrent orientation in dealing with improper pleadings, motions or other papers. This corresponds to the approach in imposing sanctions for discovery abuses. See *National Hockey League v. Metropolitan Hockey Club*, 427 U.S. 639 (1976) (per curiam). And the words "shall impose" in the last sentence focus the court's attention on the need to impose sanctions for pleading and motion abuses. The court, however, retains the necessary flexibility to deal appropriately with violations of the rule. It has discretion to tailor sanctions to the particular facts of the case, with which it should be well acquainted.

The references in the former text to wilfulness as a prerequisite to disciplinary action has been deleted. However, in considering the nature and severity of the sanctions to be imposed, the court should take account of the state of the attorney's or party's actual or presumed knowledge when the pleading or other paper was signed. Thus, for example, when a party is not represented by counsel, the absence of legal advice is an appropriate factor to be considered.

Courts currently appear to believe they may impose sanctions on their own motion. See *North American Trading Corp. v. Zale Corp.*, 73 F.R.D. 293 (S.D.N.Y.1979). Authority to do so has been made explicit in order to overcome the traditional reluctance of courts to intervene unless requested by one of the parties. The detection and punishment of a violation of the signing requirement, encouraged by the amended rule, is part of the court's responsibility for securing the system's effective operation.

If the duty imposed by the rule is violated, the court should have the discretion to impose sanctions on either the attorney, the party the signing attorney represents, or both, or on an unrepresented party who signed the pleading, and the new rule so provides. Although Rule 11 has been silent on the point, courts have claimed the power to impose sanctions on an attorney personally, either by imposing costs or employing the contempt technique. See 5 Wright & Miller, *Federal Practice and Procedure: Civil* § 1334 (1969); 2A Moore, *Federal Practice* ¶ 11.02, at 2104 n. 8. This power has been used infrequently. The amended rule should eliminate any doubt as to the propriety of assessing sanctions against the attorney.

Even though it is the attorney whose signature violates the rule, it may be appropriate under the circumstances of the case to impose a sanction on the client. See *Browning Debenture Holders' Committee v. DASA Corp.*, supra. This modification brings Rule 11 in line with practice under Rule 37, which allows sanctions for abuses during discovery to be imposed upon the party, the attorney, or both.

A party seeking sanctions should give notice to the court and the offending party promptly upon discovering a basis for doing so. The time when sanctions are to be imposed rests in the discretion of the trial judge. However, it is anticipated that in the case of pleadings the sanctions issue under Rule 11 normally will be determined at the end of the litigation, and in the case of motions at the time when the motion is decided or shortly thereafter. The procedure obviously must comport with due process requirements. The particular format to be followed should depend on the circumstances of the situation and the severity of the sanction under consideration. In many situations the judge's participation in the proceedings provides him with full knowledge of the relevant facts and little further inquiry will be necessary.

To assure that the efficiencies achieved through more effective operation of the pleading regimen will not be offset by the cost of satellite litigation over the imposition of sanctions, the court must to the extent possible limit the scope of sanction proceedings to the record. Thus, discovery should be conducted only by leave of the court, and then only in extraordinary circumstances.

Although the encompassing reference to "other papers" in new Rule 11 literally includes discovery papers, the certification requirement in that context is governed by proposed new Rule 26(g). Discovery motions, however, fall within the ambit of Rule 11.

1987 Amendment

The amendments are technical. No substantive change is intended.

1993 Amendments

Purpose of revision. This revision is intended to remedy problems that have arisen in the interpretation and application of the 1983 revision of the rule. For empirical examination of experience under the 1983 rule, see, *e.g.,* New York State Bar Committee on Federal Courts, *Sanctions and Attorneys' Fees* (1987); T. Willging, *The Rule 11 Sanctioning Process* (1989); American Judicature Society, *Report of the Third Circuit Task Force on Federal Rule of Civil Procedure 11* (S. Burbank ed., 1989); E. Wiggins, T. Willging, and D. Stienstra, *Report on Rule 11* (Federal Judicial Center 1991). For book-length analyses of the case law, see G. Joseph, *Sanctions: The Federal Law of Litigation Abuse* (1989); J. Solovy, *The Federal Law of Sanctions* (1991); G. Vairo, *Rule 11 Sanctions: Case Law Perspectives and Preventive Measures* (1991).

The rule retains the principle that attorneys and pro se litigants have an obligation to the court to refrain from conduct that frustrates the aims of Rule 1. The revision broadens the scope of this obligation, but places greater constraints on the imposition of sanctions and should reduce the number of motions for sanctions presented to the court. New subdivision (d) removes from the ambit of this rule all discovery requests, responses, objections, and motions subject to the provisions of Rule 26 through 37.

Subdivision (a). Retained in this subdivision are the provisions requiring signatures on pleadings, written motions, and other papers. Unsigned papers are to be received by the Clerk, but then are to be stricken if the omission of the signature is not corrected promptly after being called to the attention of the attorney or pro se litigant. Correction can be made by signing the paper on file or by submitting a duplicate that contains the signature. A court may require by local rule that papers contain additional identifying information regarding the parties or attorneys, such as telephone numbers to facilitate facsimile transmissions, though, as for omission of a signature, the paper should not be rejected for failure to provide such information.

The sentence in the former rule relating to the effect of answers under oath is no longer needed and has been eliminated. The provision in the former rule that signing a paper constitutes a certificate that it has been read by the signer also has been eliminated as unnecessary. The obligations imposed under subdivision (b) obviously require that a pleading, written motion, or other paper be read before it is filed or submitted to the court.

Subdivisions (b) and (c). These subdivisions restate the provisions requiring attorneys and pro se litigants to conduct a reasonable inquiry into the law and facts before signing pleadings, written motions, and other documents, and prescribing sanctions for violation of these obligations. The revision in part expands the responsibilities of litigants to the court, while providing greater constraints and flexibility in dealing with infractions of the rule. The rule continues to require litigants to "stop-and-think" before initially making legal or factual contentions. It also, however, emphasizes the duty of candor by subjecting litigants to potential sanctions for insisting upon a position after it is no longer tenable and by generally providing protection against sanctions if they withdraw or correct contentions after a potential violation is called to their attention.

The rule applies only to assertions contained in papers filed with or submitted to the court. It does not cover matters arising for the first time during oral presentations to the court, when counsel may make statements that would not have been made if there had been more time for study and reflection. However, a litigant's obligations with respect to the contents of these papers are not measured solely as of the time they are filed with or submitted to the court, but include reaffirming to the court and advocating positions contained in those pleadings and motions after learning that they cease to have any merit. For example, an attorney who during a pretrial conference insists on a claim or defense should be viewed as "presenting to the court" that contention and would be subject to the obligations of subdivision (b) measured as of that time. Similarly, if after a notice of removal is filed, a party urges in federal court the allegations of a pleading filed in state court (whether as claims, defenses, or in disputes regarding removal or remand), it would be viewed as "presenting"—and hence certifying to the district court under Rule 11—those allegations.

The certification with respect to allegations and other factual contentions is revised in recognition that sometimes a litigant may have good reason to believe that a fact is true or false but may need discovery, formal or informal, from opposing parties or third persons to gather and confirm the evidentiary basis for the allegation. Tolerance of factual contentions in initial pleadings by plaintiffs or defendants when specifically identified as made on information and belief does not relieve litigants from the obligation to conduct an appropriate investigation into the facts that is reasonable under the circumstances; it is not a license to join parties, make claims, or present defenses without any factual basis or justification. Moreover, if evidentiary support is not obtained after a reasonable opportunity for further investigation or discovery, the party has a duty under the rule not to persist with that contention. Subdivision (b) does not require a formal amendment to pleadings for which evidentiary support is not obtained, but rather calls upon a litigant not thereafter to advocate such claims or defenses.

The certification is that there is (or likely will be) "evidentiary support" for the allegation, not that the party will prevail with respect to its contention regarding the fact. That summary judgment is rendered against a party does not necessarily mean, for purposes of this certification, that it had no evidentiary support for its position. On the other hand, if a party has evidence with respect to a contention that would suffice to defeat a motion for summary judgment based thereon, it would have sufficient "evidentiary support" for purposes of Rule 11.

Denials of factual contentions involve somewhat different considerations. Often, of course, a denial is premised upon the existence of evidence contradicting the alleged fact. At other times a denial is permissible because, after an appropriate investigation, a party has no information concerning the matter or, indeed, has a reasonable basis for doubting the credibility of the only evidence relevant to the matter. A party should not deny an allegation it knows to be true; but it is not required, simply because it lacks contradictory evidence, to admit an allegation that it believes is not true.

The changes in subdivisions (b)(3) and (b)(4) will serve to equalize the burden of the rule upon plaintiffs and defendants, who under Rule 8(b) are in effect allowed to deny allegations by stating that from their initial investigation they lack sufficient information to form a belief as to the truth of the allegation. If, after further investigation or discovery, a denial is no longer warranted, the defendant should not continue to insist on that denial. While sometimes helpful, formal amendment of the pleadings to withdraw an allegation or denial is not required by subdivision (b).

Arguments for extensions, modifications, or reversals of existing law or for creation of new law do not violate subdivision (b)(2) provided they are "nonfrivolous." This establishes an objective standard, intended to eliminate any "empty-head pure-heart" justification for patently frivolous arguments. However, the extent to which a litigant has researched the issues and found some support for its theories even in minority opinions, in law review articles, or through consultation with other attorneys should certainly be taken into account in determining whether paragraph (2) has been violated. Although arguments for a change of law are not required to be specifically so identified, a contention that is so identified should be viewed with greater tolerance under the rule.

The court has available a variety of possible sanctions to impose for violations, such as striking the offending paper; issuing an admonition, reprimand, or censure; requiring participation in seminars or other educational programs; ordering a fine payable to the court; referring the matter to disciplinary authorities (or, in the case of government attorneys, to the Attorney General, Inspector General, or agency head), etc. *See Manual for Complex Litigation, Second,* § 42.3. The rule does not attempt to enumerate the factors a court should consider in deciding whether to impose a sanction or what sanctions would be appropriate in the circumstances; but, for emphasis, it does specifically note that a sanction may be nonmonetary as well as monetary. Whether the improper conduct was willful, or negligent; whether it was part of a pattern of activity, or an isolated event; whether it infected the entire pleading, or only one particular count or defense; whether the person has engaged in similar conduct in other litigation; whether it was intended to injure; what effect it had on the litigation process in time or expense; whether the responsible person is trained in the law; what amount, given the financial resources of the responsible person, is needed to deter that person from repetition in the same case; what amount is needed to deter similar activity by other litigants: all of these may in a particular case be proper considerations. The court has significant discretion in determining what sanctions, if any, should be imposed for a violation, subject to the principle that the sanctions should not be more severe than reasonably necessary to deter repetition of the conduct by the offending person or comparable conduct by similarly situated persons.

Since the purpose of Rule 11 sanctions is to deter rather than to compensate, the rule provides that, if a monetary sanction is imposed, it should ordinarily be paid into court as a penalty. However, under unusual circumstances, particularly for (b)(1) violations, deterrence may be ineffective unless the sanction not only requires the person violating the rule to make a monetary payment, but also directs that some or all of this payment be made to those injured by the violation. Accordingly, the rule authorizes the court, if requested in a motion and if so warranted, to award attorney's fees to another party. Any such award to another party, however, should not exceed the expenses and attorneys' fees for the services directly and unavoidably caused by the violation of the certification requirement. If, for example, a wholly unsupportable count were included in a multi-count complaint or counterclaim for the purpose of needlessly increasing the cost of litigation to an impecunious adversary, any award of expenses should be limited to those directly caused by inclusion of the improper count, and not those resulting from the filing of the complaint or answer itself. The award should not provide compensation for services that could have been avoided by an earlier disclosure of evidence or an earlier challenge to the groundless claims or defenses. Moreover, partial reimbursement of fees may constitute a sufficient deterrent with respect to violations by persons having modest financial resources. In cases brought under statutes providing for fees to be awarded to prevailing parties, the court should not employ cost-shifting under this rule in a manner that would be inconsistent with the standards that govern the statutory award of fees, such as stated in *Christiansburg Garment Co. v. EEOC,* 434 U.S. 412 (1978).

The sanction should be imposed on the persons—whether attorneys, law firms, or parties—who have violated the rule or who may be determined to be responsible for the violation. The person signing, filing, submitting, or advocating a document has a nondelegable responsibility to the court, and in most situations is the person to be sanctioned for a violation. Absent exceptional circumstances, a law firm is to be held also responsible when, as a result of a motion under subdivision (c)(1)(A), one of its partners, associates, or employees is determined to have violated the rule. Since such a motion may be filed only if the offending paper is not withdrawn or corrected within 21 days after service of the motion, it is appropriate that the law firm ordinarily be viewed as jointly responsible under established principles of agency. This provision is designed to remove the restrictions of the former rule. *Cf. Pavelic & LeFlore v. Marvel Entertainment Group,* 493 U.S. 120 (1989) (1983 version of Rule 11 does not permit sanctions against law firm of attorney signing groundless complaint).

The revision permits the court to consider whether other attorneys in the firm, co-counsel, other law firms, or the party itself should be held accountable for their part in causing a violation. When appropriate, the court can make an additional inquiry in order to determine whether the sanction should be imposed on such persons, firms, or parties either in addition to or, in unusual circumstances, instead of the person actually making the presentation to the court. For example, such an inquiry may be appropriate in cases involving governmental agencies or other institutional parties that frequently impose substantial restrictions on the discretion of individual attorneys employed by it.

Sanctions that involve monetary awards (such as a fine or an award of attorney's fees) may not be imposed on a represented party for causing a violation of subdivision (b)(2), involving frivolous contentions of law. Monetary responsibility for such violations is more properly placed solely on the party's attorneys. With this limitation, the rule should not be subject to attack under the Rules Enabling Act. See *Willy v. Coastal Corp.*, 503 U.S. 131 (1992); *Business Guides, Inc. v. Chromatic Communications Enter. Inc.*, 498 U.S. 533 (1991). This restriction does not limit the court's power to impose sanctions or remedial orders that may have collateral financial consequences upon a party, such as dismissal of a claim, preclusion of a defense, or preparation of amended pleadings.

Explicit provision is made for litigants to be provided notice of the alleged violation and an opportunity to respond before sanctions are imposed. Whether the matter should be decided solely on the basis of written submissions or should be scheduled for oral argument (or, indeed, for evidentiary presentation) will depend on the circumstances. If the court imposes a sanction, it must, unless waived, indicate its reasons in a written order or on the record; the court should not ordinarily have to explain its denial of a motion for sanctions. Whether a violation has occurred and what sanctions, if any, to impose for a violation are matters committed to the discretion of the trial court; accordingly, as under current law, the standard for appellate review of these decisions will be for abuse of discretion. *See Cooter & Gell v. Hartmarx Corp.*, 496 U.S. 384 (1990) (noting, however, that an abuse would be established if the court based its ruling on an erroneous view of the law or on a clearly erroneous assessment of the evidence).

The revision leaves for resolution on a case-by-case basis, considering the particular circumstances involved, the question as to when a motion for violation of Rule 11 should be served and when, if filed, it should be decided. Ordinarily the motion should be served promptly after the inappropriate paper is filed, and, if delayed too long, may be viewed as untimely. In other circumstances, it should not be served until the other party has had a reasonable opportunity for discovery. Given the "safe harbor" provisions discussed below, a party cannot delay serving its Rule 11 motion until conclusion of the case (or judicial rejection of the offending contention).

Rule 11 motions should not be made or threatened for minor, inconsequential violations of the standards prescribed by subdivision (b). They should not be employed as a discovery device or to test the legal sufficiency or efficacy of allegations in the pleadings; other motions are available for those purposes. Nor should Rule 11 motions be prepared to emphasize the merits of a party's position, to exact an unjust settlement, to intimidate an adversary into withdrawing contentions that are fairly debatable, to increase the costs of litigation, to create a conflict of interest between attorney and client, or to seek disclosure of matters otherwise protected by the attorney-client privilege or the work-product doctrine. As under the prior rule, the court may defer its ruling (or its decision as to the identity of the persons to be sanctioned) until final resolution of the case in order to avoid immediate conflicts of interest and to reduce the disruption created if a disclosure of attorney-client communications is needed to determine whether a violation occurred or to identify the person responsible for the violation.

The rule provides that requests for sanctions must be made as a separate motion, *i.e.*, not simply included as an additional prayer for relief contained in another motion. The motion for sanctions is not, however, to be filed until at least 21 days (or such other period as the court may set) after being served. If, during this period, the alleged violation is corrected, as by withdrawing (whether formally or informally) some allegation or contention, the motion should not be filed with the court. These provisions are intended to provide a type of "safe harbor" against motions under Rule 11 in that a party will not be subject to sanctions on the basis of another party's motion unless, after receiving the motion, it refuses to withdraw that position or to acknowledge candidly that it does not currently have evidence to support a specified allegation. Under the former rule, parties were sometimes reluctant to abandon a questionable contention lest that be viewed as evidence of a violation of Rule 11; under the revision, the timely withdrawal of a contention will protect a party against a motion for sanctions.

To stress the seriousness of a motion for sanctions and to define precisely the conduct claimed to violate the rule, the revision provides that the "safe harbor" period begins to run only upon service of the motion. In most cases, however, counsel should be expected to give informal notice to the other party, whether in person or by a telephone call or letter, of a potential violation before proceeding to prepare and serve a Rule 11 motion.

As under former Rule 11, the filing of a motion for sanctions is itself subject to the requirements of the rule and can lead to sanctions. However, service of a cross motion under Rule 11 should rarely be needed since under the revision the court may award to the person who prevails on a motion under Rule 11—whether the movant or the target of the motion—reasonable expenses, including attorney's fees, incurred in presenting or opposing the motion.

The power of the court to act on its own initiative is retained, but with the condition that this be done through a show cause order. This procedure provides the person with notice and an opportunity to respond. The revision provides that a monetary sanction imposed after a court-initiated show cause order be limited to a penalty payable to the court and that it be imposed only if the show cause order is issued before any voluntary dismissal or an agreement of the parties to settle the claims made by or against the litigant. Parties settling a case should not be subsequently faced with an unexpected order from the court leading to monetary sanctions that might have affected their willingness to settle or voluntarily dismiss a case. Since show cause orders will ordinarily be issued only in situations that are akin to a contempt of court, the rule does not provide a "safe harbor" to a litigant for withdrawing a claim, defense, etc., after a show cause order has been issued on the court's own initiative. Such corrective action, however, should be taken into account in deciding what—if any—sanction to impose if, after consideration of the litigant's response, the court concludes that a violation has occurred.

Subdivision (d). Rules 26(g) and 37 establish certification standards and sanctions that apply to discovery disclosures, requests, responses, objections, and motions. It is appropriate that Rules 26 through 37, which are specially designed for the discovery process, govern such documents and conduct rather than the more general provisions of Rule 11. Subdivision (d) has been added to accomplish this result.

Rule 11 is not the exclusive source for control of improper presentations of claims, defenses, or contentions. It does not supplant statutes permitting awards of attorney's fees to prevailing parties or alter the principles governing such awards. It does not inhibit the court in punishing for contempt, in exercising its inherent powers, or in imposing sanctions, awarding expenses, or directing remedial action authorized under other rules or under 28 U.S.C. § 1927. *See Chambers v. NASCO,* 501 U.S. 32 (1991). Chambers cautions, however, against reliance upon inherent powers if appropriate sanctions can be imposed under provisions such as Rule 11, and the procedures specified in Rule 11—notice, opportunity to respond, and findings—should ordinarily be employed when imposing a sanction under the court's inherent powers. Finally, it should be noted that Rule 11 does not preclude a party from initiating an independent action for malicious prosecution or abuse of process.

2007 Amendment

The language of Rule 11 has been amended as part of the general restyling of the Civil Rules to make them more easily understood and to make style and terminology consistent throughout the rules. These changes are intended to be stylistic only.

Providing an e-mail address is useful, but does not of itself signify consent to filing or service by e-mail.

CROSS REFERENCES

Private securities litigation and sanctions for abusive litigation, see 15 USCA §§ 77z–1 and 78u–4.

Signing of motions and other papers, see Fed.Rules Civ. Proc. Rule 7, 28 USCA.

Rule 12. Defenses and Objections: When and How Presented; Motion for Judgment on the Pleadings; Consolidating Motions; Waiving Defenses; Pretrial Hearing

(a) Time to Serve a Responsive Pleading.

(1) ***In General.*** Unless another time is specified by this rule or a federal statute, the time for serving a responsive pleading is as follows:

(A) A defendant must serve an answer:

(i) within 20 days after being served with the summons and complaint; or

(ii) if it has timely waived service under Rule 4(d), within 60 days after the request for a waiver was sent, or within 90 days after it was sent to the defendant outside any judicial district of the United States.

(B) A party must serve an answer to a counterclaim or crossclaim within 20 days after being served with the pleading that states the counterclaim or crossclaim.

(C) A party must serve a reply to an answer within 20 days after being served with an order to reply, unless the order specifies a different time.

(2) ***United States and Its Agencies, Officers, or Employees Sued in an Official Capacity.*** The United States, a United States agency, or a United States officer or employee sued only in an official capacity must serve an answer to a complaint, counterclaim, or crossclaim within 60 days after service on the United States attorney.

(3) ***United States Officers or Employees Sued in an Individual Capacity.*** A United States officer or employee sued in an individual capacity for an act or omission occurring in connection with duties performed on the United States' behalf must serve an answer to a complaint, counterclaim, or crossclaim within 60 days after service on the officer or employee or service on the United States attorney, whichever is later.

(4) ***Effect of a Motion.*** Unless the court sets a different time, serving a motion under this rule alters these periods as follows:

(A) if the court denies the motion or postpones its disposition until trial, the responsive pleading must be served within 10 days after notice of the court's action; or

(B) if the court grants a motion for a more definite statement, the responsive pleading must be served within 10 days after the more definite statement is served.

(b) How to Present Defenses. Every defense to a claim for relief in any pleading must be asserted in the responsive pleading if one is required. But a party may assert the following defenses by motion:

(1) lack of subject-matter jurisdiction;

(2) lack of personal jurisdiction;

(3) improper venue;

(4) insufficient process;

(5) insufficient service of process;

(6) failure to state a claim upon which relief can be granted; and

(7) failure to join a party under Rule 19.

A motion asserting any of these defenses must be made before pleading if a responsive pleading is allowed. If a pleading sets out a claim for relief that does not require a responsive pleading, an opposing party may assert at trial any defense to that claim. No defense or objection is waived by joining it with one or more other defenses or objections in a responsive pleading or in a motion.

(c) Motion for Judgment on the Pleadings. After the pleadings are closed—but early enough not to delay trial—a party may move for judgment on the pleadings.

(d) Result of Presenting Matters Outside the Pleadings. If, on a motion under Rule 12(b)(6) or 12(c), matters outside the pleadings are presented to and not excluded by the court, the motion must be treated as one for summary judgment under Rule 56. All parties must be given a reasonable opportunity to present all the material that is pertinent to the motion.

(e) Motion for a More Definite Statement. A party may move for a more definite statement of a pleading to which a responsive pleading is allowed but which is so vague or ambiguous that the party cannot reasonably prepare a response. The motion must be made before filing a responsive pleading and must point out the defects complained of and the details desired. If the court orders a more definite statement and the order is not obeyed within 10 days after notice of the order or within the time the court sets, the court may strike the pleading or issue any other appropriate order.

(f) Motion to Strike. The court may strike from a pleading an insufficient defense or any redundant, immaterial, impertinent, or scandalous matter. The court may act:

(1) on its own; or

(2) on motion made by a party either before responding to the pleading or, if a response is not allowed, within 20 days after being served with the pleading.

(g) Joining Motions.

(1) ***Right to Join.*** A motion under this rule may be joined with any other motion allowed by this rule.

(2) ***Limitation on Further Motions.*** Except as provided in Rule 12(h)(2) or (3), a party that makes a motion under this rule must not make another motion under this rule raising a defense or objection that was available to the party but omitted from its earlier motion.

(h) Waiving and Preserving Certain Defenses.

(1) ***When Some Are Waived.*** A party waives any defense listed in Rule 12(b)(2)-(5) by:

(A) omitting it from a motion in the circumstances described in Rule 12(g)(2); or

(B) failing to either:

(i) make it by motion under this rule; or

(ii) include it in a responsive pleading or in an amendment allowed by Rule 15(a)(1) as a matter of course.

(2) ***When to Raise Others.*** Failure to state a claim upon which relief can be granted, to join a person required by Rule 19(b), or to state a legal defense to a claim may be raised:

(A) in any pleading allowed or ordered under Rule 7(a);

(B) by a motion under Rule 12(c); or

(C) at trial.

(3) ***Lack of Subject-Matter Jurisdiction.*** If the court determines at any time that it lacks subject-matter jurisdiction, the court must dismiss the action.

(i) Hearing Before Trial. If a party so moves, any defense listed in Rule 12(b)(1)-(7)—whether made in a pleading or by motion—and a motion under Rule 12(c) must be heard and decided before trial unless the court orders a deferral until trial.

(Amended December 27, 1946, effective March 19, 1948; January 21, 1963, effective July 1, 1963; February 28, 1966, effective July 1, 1966; March 2, 1987, effective August 1, 1987; April 22, 1993, effective December 1, 1993; April 17, 2000, effective December 1, 2000; April 30, 2007, effective December 1, 2007.)

ADVISORY COMMITTEE NOTES

1937 Adoption

Note to Subdivision (a). 1. Compare [former] Equity Rules 12 (Issue of Subpoena—Time for Answer) and 31 (Reply—When Required—When Cause at Issue); 4 Mont. Rev.Codes Ann. (1935) §§ 9107, 9158; N.Y.C. P.A. (1937) § 263; N.Y.R.C.P. (1937) Rules 109–111.

2. U.S.C., Title 28, § 763 (now § 547) (Petition in action against United States; service; appearance by district attorney) provides that the United States as a defendant shall have 60 days within which to answer or otherwise defend. This and other statutes which provide 60 days for the United States or an officer or agency thereof to answer or otherwise defend are continued by this rule. In so far as any statutes not excepted in rule 81 provide a different time for a defendant to defend, such statutes are modified. See U.S.C., Title 28, [former] § 45 (District courts; practice and procedure in certain cases under the interstate commerce laws) (30 days).

3. Compare the last sentence of [former] Equity Rule 29 (Defenses—How Presented) and N.Y.C.P.A. (1937) § 283. See Rule 15(a) for time within which to plead to an amended pleading.

Note to Subdivisions (b) and (d). 1. See generally [former] Equity Rules 29 (Defenses—How Presented), 33 (Testing Sufficiency of Defense), 43 (Defect of Parties—Resisting Objection), and 44 (Defect of Parties—Tardy Objection); N.Y.C.P.A. (1937) §§ 277–280; N.Y.R.C.P. (1937) Rules 106–112; *English Rules Under the Judicature Act*

(The Annual Practice, 1937) O. 25, r.r. 1–4; Clark, *Code Pleading,* 1928, pp. 371–381.

2. For provisions authorizing defenses to be made in the answer or reply see *English Rules Under the Judicature Act,* (The Annual Practice, 1937) O. 25, r.r. 1–4; 1 Miss.Code Ann. (1930) §§ 378, 379. Compare Equity Rule 29 (Defenses—How Presented); U.S.C.A., Title 28, [former] § 45 (District Courts; practice and procedure in certain cases under the interstate commerce laws). U.S.C., Title 28, [former] § 45, substantially continued by this rule, provides: "No replication need be filed to the answer, and objections to the sufficiency of the petition or answer as not setting forth a cause of action or defense must be taken at the final hearing or by motion to dismiss the petition based on said grounds, which motion may be made at any time before answer is filed." Compare Calif.Code Civ.Proc., (Deering, 1937) § 433; 4 Nev.Comp.Laws (Hillyer, 1929) § 8600. For provisions that the defendant may demur and answer at the same time, see Calif.Code Civ.Proc. (Deering, 1937) § 431; 4 Nev.Comp. Laws (Hillyer, 1929) § 8598.

3. [Former] Equity Rule 29 (Defenses—How Presented) abolished demurrers and provided that defenses in point of law arising on the face of the bill should be made by motion to dismiss or in the answer, with further provision that every such point of law going to the whole or material part of the cause or causes stated might be called up and disposed of before final hearing "at the discretion of the court." Likewise many state practices have abolished the demurrer, or retain it only to attack substantial and not formal defects. See 6 Tenn.Code Ann. (Williams, 1934) § 8784; Ala.Code Ann. (Michie, 1928) § 9479; 2 Mass.Gen.Laws (Ter.Ed., 1932) ch. 231, §§ 15–18; Kansas Gen.Stat.Ann. (1935) §§ 60–705, 60–706.

Note to Subdivision (c). Compare [former] Equity Rule 33 (Testing Sufficiency of Defense); N.Y.R.C.P. (1937) Rules 111 and 112.

Note to Subdivisions (e) and (f). Compare [former] Equity Rules 20 (Further and Particular Statement in Pleading May be Required) and 21 (Scandal and Impertinence); *English Rules Under the Judicature Act* (The Annual Practice, 1937) O. 19, r.r. 7, 7a, 7b, 8; 4 Mont.Rev.Codes Ann. (1935) §§ 9166, 9167; N.Y.C.P.A. (1937) § 247; N.Y.C.P.A. (1937) Rules 103, 115, 116, 117; Wyo.Rev.Stat.Ann. (Courtright, 1931) §§ 89–1033, 89–1034.

Note to Subdivision (g). Compare Rules of the District Court of the United States for the District of Columbia (1937) Equity Rule 11; N.M. Rules of Pleading, Practice and Procedure, 38 N.M.Rep. vii. [105–408] (1934); Wash.Gen. Rules of the Superior Courts, 1 Wash.Rev.Stat.Ann. (Remington, 1932) p. 160, Rule VI(e) and (f).

Note to Subdivision (h). Compare Calif.Code Civ.Proc. (Deering, 1937) § 434; 2 Minn.Stat. (Mason, 1927) § 9252; N.Y.C.P.A. (1937) §§ 278 and 279; Wash.Gen.Rules of the Superior Courts, 1 Wash.Rev.Stat.Ann. (Remington, 1932) p. 160, Rule VI(e). This rule continues U.S.C.A., Title 28, former § 80 [now 1359, 1447, 1919] (Dismissal or remand) (of action over which district court lacks jurisdiction), while U.S.C.A., Title 28, § 399 (Amendments to show diverse citizenship) is continued by Rule 15.

1946 Amendment

Note. Subdivision (a). Various minor alterations in language have been made to improve the statement of the rule. All references to bills of particulars have been stricken in accordance with changes made in subdivision (e).

Subdivision (b). The addition of defense (7), "failure to join an indispensable party", cures an omission in the rules which are silent as to the mode of raising such failure. See Commentary, *Manner of Raising Objection of Non-Joinder of Indispensable Party,* 1940, 2 Fed.Rules Serv. 658, and, 1942, 5 Fed.Rules Serv. 820. In one case, *United States v. Metropolitan Life Ins. Co.,* E.D.Pa.1941, 36 F.Supp. 399, the failure to join an indispensable party was raised under Rule 12(c).

Rule 12(b)(6), permitting a motion to dismiss for failure of the complaint to state a claim on which relief can be granted, is substantially the same as the old demurrer for failure of a pleading to state a cause of action. Some courts have held that as the rule by its terms refers to statements in the complaint, extraneous matter on affidavits, depositions or otherwise, may not be introduced in support of the motion, or to resist it. On the other hand, in many cases the district courts have permitted the introduction of such material. When these cases have reached circuit courts of appeals in situations where the extraneous material so received shows that there is no genuine issue as to any material question of fact and that on the undisputed facts as disclosed by the affidavits or depositions, one party or the other is entitled to judgment as a matter of law, the circuit courts, properly enough, have been reluctant to dispose of the case merely on the face of the pleading, and in the interest of prompt disposition of the action have made a final disposition of it. In dealing with such situations the Second Circuit has made the sound suggestion that whatever its label or original basis, the motion may be treated as a motion for summary judgment and disposed of as such. *Samara v. United States,* C.C.A.2, 1942, 129 F.2d 594, certiorari denied 63 S.Ct. 258, 317 U.S. 686, 87 L.Ed. 549; *Boro Hall Corp. v. General Motors Corp.,* C.C.A.2, 1942, 124 F.2d 822, certiorari denied 63 S.Ct. 436, 317 U.S. 695, 87 L.Ed. 556. See, also, *Kithcart v. Metropolitan Life Ins. Co.,* C.C.A.8, 1945, 150 F.2d 997.

It has also been suggested that this practice could be justified on the ground that the federal rules permit "speaking" motions. The Committee entertains the view that on motion under Rule 12(b)(6) to dismiss for failure of the complaint to state a good claim, the trial court should have authority to permit the introduction of extraneous matter, such as may be offered on a motion for summary judgment, and if it does not exclude such matter the motion should then be treated as a motion for summary judgment and disposed of in the manner and on the conditions stated in Rule 56 relating to summary judgments, and, of course, in such a situation, when the case reaches the circuit court of appeals, that court should treat the motion in the same way. The Committee believes that such practice, however, should be tied to the summary judgment rule. The term "speaking motion" is not mentioned in the rules, and if there is such a thing its limitations are undefined. Where extraneous matter is received, by tying further proceedings to the summary judgment rule the courts have a definite basis in the rules for disposing of the motion.

The Committee emphasizes particularly the fact that the summary judgment rule does not permit a case to be disposed of by judgment on the merits on affidavits, which disclose a conflict on a material issue of fact, and unless this practice is tied to the summary judgment, rule, the extent to which a court, on the introduction of such extraneous matter, may resolve questions of fact on conflicting proof would be left uncertain.

The decisions dealing with this general situation may be generally grouped as follows: (1) cases dealing with the use of affidavits and other extraneous material on motions; (2) cases reversing judgments to prevent final determination on mere pleading allegations alone.

Under group (1) are: *Boro Hall Corp. v. General Motors Corp.*, C.C.A.2, 1942, 124 F.2d 822, certiorari denied 1943, 63 S.Ct. 436, 317 U.S. 695, 87 L.Ed. 556; *Gallup v. Caldwell*, C.C.A.3, 1941, 120 F.2d 90; *Central Mexico Light & Power Co. v. Munch*, C.C.A.2, 1940, 116 F.2d 85; *National Labor Relations Board v. Montgomery Ward & Co.*, 1944, 144 F.2d 528, 79 U.S.App.D.C. 200, certiorari denied 1944, 65 S.Ct. 134, 323 U.S. 774, 89 L.Ed. 619; *Urquhart v. American-La France Foamite Corp.*, 1944, 144 F.2d 542, 79 U.S.App.D.C. 219; *Samara v. United States*, C.C.A.2, 1942, 129 F.2d 594; *Cohen v. American Window Glass Co.*, C.C.A.2, 1942, 126 F.2d 111; *Sperry Products Inc. v. Association of American Railroads*, C.C.A.2, 1942, 132 F.2d 408; *Joint Council Dining Car Employees Local 370 v. Delaware, Lackawanna and Western R. Co.*, C.C.A.2, 1946, 157 F.2d 417; *Weeks v. Bareco Oil Co.*, C.C.A.7, 1941, 125 F.2d 84; *Carroll v. Morrison Hotel Corp.*, C.C.A.7, 1945, 149 F.2d 404; *Victory v. Manning*, C.C.A.3, 1942, 128 F.2d 415; *Locals No. 1470, No. 1469, and No. 1512 of International Longshoremen's Association v. Southern Pacific Co.*, C.C.A.5, 1942, 131 F.2d 605; *Lucking v. Delano*, C.C.A.6, 1942, 129 F.2d 283; *San Francisco Lodge No. 68 of International Association of Machinists v. Forrestal*, Cal.1944, 58 F.Supp. 466; *Benson v. Export Equipment Corp.*, 1945, 164 P.2d 380, 49 N.M. 356, construing New Mexico rule identical with Rule 12(b)(6); *F. E. Myers & Bros. Co. v. Gould Pumps, Inc.*, W.D.N.Y.1946, 9 Fed.Rules Serv. 12b.33, Case 2, 5 F.R.D. 132. Cf. *Kohler v. Jacobs*, C.C.A.5, 1943, 138 F.2d 440; *Cohen v. United States*, C.C.A.8, 1942, 129 F.2d 733.

Under group (2) are: *Sparks v. England*, C.C.A.8, 1940, 113 F.2d 579; *Continental Collieries, Inc. v. Shober*, C.C.A.3, 1942, 130 F.2d 631; *Downey v. Palmer*, C.C.A.2, 1940, 114 F.2d 116; *DeLoach v. Crowley's Inc.*, C.C.A.5, 1942, 128 F.2d 378; *Leimer v. State Mutual Life Assurance Co. of Worcester, Mass.*, C.C.A.8, 1940, 108 F.2d 302; *Rossiter v. Vogel*, C.C.A.2, 1943, 134 F.2d 908, compare s.c., C.C.A.2, 1945, 148 F.2d 292; *Karl Kiefer Machine Co. v. United States Bottlers Machinery Co.*, C.C.A.7, 1940, 113 F.2d 356; *Chicago Metallic Mfg. Co. v. Edward Katzinger Co.*, C.C.A.7, 1941, 123 F.2d 518; *Louisiana Farmers' Protective Union, Inc. v. Great Atlantic & Pacific Tea Co. of America, Inc.*, C.C.A.8, 1942, 131 F.2d 419; *Publicity Bldg. Realty Corp. v. Hannegan*, C.C.A.8, 1943, 139 F.2d 583; *Dioguardi v. Durning*, C.C.A.2, 1944, 139 F.2d 774; *Package Closure Corp. v. Sealright Co., Inc.*, C.C.A.2, 1944, 141 F.2d 972; *Tahir Erk v. Glenn L. Martin Co.*, C.C.A.4, 1941, 116 F.2d 865; *Bell v. Preferred Life Assurance Society of Montgomery, Ala.*, 1943, 64 S.Ct. 5, 320 U.S. 238, 88 L.Ed. 15.

The addition at the end of subdivision (b) makes it clear that on a motion under Rule 12(b)(6) extraneous material may not be considered if the court excludes it, but that if the court does not exclude such material the motion shall be treated as a motion for summary judgment and disposed of as provided in Rule 56. It will also be observed that if a motion under Rule 12(b)(6) is thus converted into a summary judgment motion, the amendment insures that both parties shall be given a reasonable opportunity to submit affidavits and extraneous proofs to avoid taking a party by surprise through the conversion of the motion into a motion for summary judgment. In this manner and to this extent the amendment regularizes the practice above described. As the courts are already dealing with cases in this way, the effect of this amendment is really only to define the practice carefully and apply the requirements of the summary judgment rule in the disposition of the motion.

Subdivision (c). The sentence appended to subdivision (c) performs the same function and is grounded on the same reasons as the corresponding sentence added in subdivision (b).

Subdivision (d). The change here was made necessary because of the addition of defense (7) in subdivision (b).

Subdivision (e). References in this subdivision to a bill of particulars have been deleted, and the motion provided for is confined to one for more definite statement to be obtained only in cases where the movant cannot reasonably be required to frame an answer or other responsive pleading to the pleading in question. With respect to preparations for trial, the party is properly relegated to the various methods of examination and discovery provided in the rules for that purpose. *Slusher v. Jones*, E.D.Ky.1943, 7 Fed.Rules Serv. 12e.231, Case 5, 3 F.R.D. 168; *Best Foods, Inc. v. General Mills, Inc.*, D.Del.1943, 7 Fed.Rules Serv. 12e.231, Case 7, 3 F.R.D. 275; *Braden v. Callaway*, E.D.Tenn.1943, 8 Fed. Rules Serv. 12e.231, Case 1 (". . . most courts . . . conclude that the definiteness required is only such as will be sufficient for the party to prepare responsive pleadings"). Accordingly, the reference to the 20 day time limit has also been eliminated, since the purpose of this present provision is to state a time period where the motion for a bill is made for the purpose of preparing for trial.

Rule 12(e) as originally drawn has been the subject of more judicial rulings than any other part of the rules, and has been much criticized by commentators, judges and members of the bar. See general discussion and cases cited in 1 Moore's *Federal Practice*, 1938, Cum.Supplement, § 12.07, under "Page 657"; also, Holtzoff, *New Federal Procedure and the Courts*, 1940, 35–41. And compare vote of Second Circuit Conference of Circuit and District Judges, June 1940, recommending the abolition of the bill of particulars; *Sun Valley Mfg. Co. v. Mylish*, E.D.Pa.1944, 8 Fed.Rules Serv. 12e.231, Case 6 ("Our experience . . . has demonstrated not only that 'the office of the bill of particulars is fast becoming obsolete' . . . but that in view of the adequate discovery procedure available under the Rules, motions for bills of particulars should be abolished altogether."); *Walling v. American Steamship Co.*, W.D.N.Y.1945, 4 F.R.D. 355, 8 Fed.Rules Serv. 12e.244, Case 8 (". . . the adoption of the rule was ill advised. It has led to confusion, duplication and delay.") The tendency of some courts freely to grant extended bills of particulars has served to neutralize any helpful benefits derived from rule 8, and has overlooked the intended use of the rules on depositions and discovery. The words "or to prepare for trial"—eliminated by the proposed amendment—have sometimes been seized upon as grounds for compulsory statement in the opposing pleading of all the details which the movant would have to meet at the trial. On the other hand, many courts have in effect read these words out of the rule. See *Walling v. Alabama Pipe Co.*, W.D.Mo. 1942, 3 F.R.D. 159, 6 Fed.Rules Serv. 12e.244, Case 7; *Fleming v. Mason & Dixon Lines, Inc.*, E.D.Tenn.1941, 42 F.Supp. 230; *Kellogg Co. v. National Biscuit Co.*, D.N.J. 1941, 38 F.Supp. 643; *Brown v. H. L. Green Co.*, S.D.N.Y. 1943, 7 Fed.Rules Serv. 12e.231, Case 6; *Pedersen v. Standard Accident Ins. Co.*, W.D.Mo.1945, 8 Fed.Rules Serv. 12e.231, Case 8; *Bowles v. Ohse*, D.Neb.1945, 4 F.R.D. 403, 9 Fed.Rules Serv. 12e.231, Case 1; *Klages v. Cohen*, E.D.N.Y. 1945, 9 Fed.Rules Serv. 8a.25, Case 4; *Bowles v. Lawrence*, D.Mass.1945, 8 Fed.Rules Serv. 12e.231, Case 19; *McKinney Tool & Mfg. Co. v. Hoyt*, N.D.Ohio 1945, 9 Fed.Rules Serv. 12e.235, Case 1; *Bowles v. Jack*, D.Minn.1945, 5 F.R.D. 1, 9 Fed.Rules Serv. 12e.244, Case 9. And it has been urged from the bench that the phrase be stricken, *Poole v. White*, N.D.W.Va.1941, 5 Fed.Rules Serv. 12e.231, Case 4, 2 F.R.D. 40. See also *Bowles v. Gabel*, W.D.Mo.1946, 9 Fed.Rules Serv. 12e.244, Case 10. ("The courts have never favored that portion of the rules which undertook to justify a motion of this kind for the purpose of aiding counsel in preparing his case for trial.").

Subdivision (f). This amendment affords a specific method of raising the insufficiency of a defense, a matter which has troubled some courts, although attack has been permitted in one way or another. See *Dysart v. Remington-Rand, Inc.*, D.Conn.1939, 31 F.Supp. 296; *Eastman Kodak Co. v. McAuley*, S.D.N.Y.1941, 4 Fed.Rules Serv., 12f.21, Case 8, 2 F.R.D. 21; *Schenley Distillers Corp. v. Renken*, E.D.S.C. 1940, 34 F.Supp. 678; *Yale Transport Corp. v. Yellow Truck & Coach Mfg. Co.*, S.D.N.Y.1944, 3 F.R.D. 440; *United States v. Turner Milk Co.*, N.D.Ill.1941, 4 Fed.Rules Serv. 12b.51, Case 3, 1 F.R.D. 643; *Teiger v. Stephan Oderwald, Inc.*, S.D.N.Y.1940, 31 F.Supp. 626; *Teplitsky v. Pennsylvania R. Co.*, N.D.Ill.1941, 38 F.Supp. 535; *Callagher v. Carroll*, E.D.N.Y.1939, 27 F.Supp. 568; *United States v. Palmer*, S.D.N.Y.1939, 28 F.Supp. 936. And see *Indemnity Ins. Co. of North America v. Pan American Airways, Inc.*, S.D.N.Y. 1944, 58 F.Supp. 338; Commentary, *Modes of Attacking Insufficient Defenses in the Answer*, 901, 1939, 1 Fed.Rules Serv. 669, 1940, 2 Fed.Rules Serv. 640.

Subdivision (g). The change in title conforms with the companion provision in subdivision (h).

The alteration of the "except" clause requires that other than provided in subdivision (h) a party who resorts to a motion to raise defenses specified in the rule, must include in one motion all that are then available to him. Under the original rule defenses which could be raised by motion were divided into two groups which could be the subjects of two successive motions.

Subdivision (h). The addition of the phrase relating to indispensable parties is one of necessity.

1963 Amendment

This amendment conforms to the amendment of Rule 4(e). See also the Advisory Committee's Note to amended Rule 4(b).

1966 Amendment

Subdivision (b)(7). The terminology of this subdivision is changed to accord with the amendment of Rule 19. See the Advisory Committee's Note to Rule 19, as amended, especially the third paragraph therein before the caption "Subdivision (c)."

Subdivision (g). Subdivision (g) has forbidden a defendant who makes a preanswer motion under this rule from making a further motion presenting any defense or objection which was available to him at the time he made the first motion and which he could have included, but did not in fact include therein. Thus if the defendant moves before answer to dismiss the complaint for failure to state a claim, he is barred from making a further motion presenting the defense of improper venue, if that defense was available to him when he made his original motion. Amended subdivision (g) is to the same effect. This required consolidation of defenses and objections in a Rule 12 motion is salutary in that it works against piecemeal consideration of a case. For exceptions to the requirement of consolidation, see the last clause of subdivision (g), referring to new subdivision (h)(2).

Subdivision (h). The question has arisen whether an omitted defense which cannot be made the basis of a second motion may nevertheless be pleaded in the answer. Subdivision (h) called for waiver of "* * * defenses and objections which he [defendant] does not present * * * by motion * * * or, if he has made no motion, in his answer * * *." If the clause "if he has made no motion," was read literally, it seemed that the omitted defense was waived and could not be pleaded in the answer. On the other hand, the clause might be read as adding nothing of substance to the preceding words; in that event it appeared that a defense was not waived by reason of being omitted from the motion and might be set up in the answer. The decisions were divided. Favoring waiver, see *Keef v. Derounian*, 6 F.R.D. 11 (N.D.Ill.1946); *Elbinger v. Precision Metal Workers Corp.*, 18 F.R.D. 467 (E.D.Wis.1956); see also *Rensing v. Turner Aviation Corp.*, 166 F.Supp. 790 (N.D.Ill.1958); *P. Beiersdorf & Co. v. Duke Laboratories, Inc.*, 10 F.R.D. 282 (S.D.N.Y. 1950); *Neset v. Christensen*, 92 F.Supp. 78 (E.D.N.Y.1950). Opposing waiver, see *Phillips v. Baker*, 121 F.2d 752 (9th Cir.1941); *Crum v. Graham*, 32 F.R.D. 173 (D.Mont.1963) (regretfully following the Phillips case); see also *Birnbaum v. Birrell*, 9 F.R.D. 72 (S.D.N.Y.1948); *Johnson v. Joseph Schlitz Brewing Co.*, 33 F.Supp. 176 (E.D.Tenn.1940); cf. *Carter v. American Bus Lines, Inc.*, 22 F.R.D. 323 (D.Neb. 1958).

Amended subdivision (h)(1)(A) eliminates the ambiguity and states that certain specified defenses which were available to a party when he made a preanswer motion, but which he omitted from the motion, are waived. The specified defenses are lack of jurisdiction over the person, improper venue, insufficiency of process, and insufficiency of service of process (see Rule 12(b)(2)–(5)). A party who by motion invites the court to pass upon a threshold defense should bring forward all the specified defenses he then has and thus allow the court to do a reasonably complete job. The waiver reinforces the policy of subdivision (g) forbidding successive motions.

By amended subdivision (h)(1)(B), the specified defenses, even if not waived by the operation of (A), are waived by the failure to raise them by a motion under Rule 12 or in the responsive pleading or any amendment thereof to which the party is entitled as a matter of course. The specified defenses are of such a character that they should not be delayed and brought up for the first time by means of an application to the court to amend the responsive pleading.

Since the language of the subdivisions is made clear, the party is put on fair notice of the effect of his actions and omissions and can guard himself against unintended waiver. It is to be noted that while the defenses specified in subdivision (h)(1) are subject to waiver as there provided, the more substantial defenses of failure to state a claim upon which relief can be granted, failure to join a party indispensable under Rule 19, and failure to state a legal defense to a claim (see Rule 12(b)(6), (7), (f)), as well as the defense of lack of jurisdiction over the subject matter (see Rule 12(b)(1)), are expressly preserved against waiver by amended subdivision (h)(2) and (3).

1987 Amendment

The amendments are technical. No substantive change is intended.

1993 Amendment

Subdivision (a) is divided into paragraphs for greater clarity, and paragraph (1)(B) is added to reflect amendments to Rule 4. Consistent with Rule 4(d)(3), a defendant that timely waives service is allowed 60 days from the date the request was mailed in which to respond to the complaint, with an additional 30 days afforded if the request was sent out of the country. Service is timely waived if the waiver is returned within the time specified in the request (30 days after the request was mailed, or 60 days if mailed out of the country) and before being formally served with process. Sometimes a plaintiff may attempt to serve a defendant with process while also sending the defendant a request for waiver of service; if the defendant executes the waiver of service within the time specified and before being served with process, it should have the longer time to respond afforded by waiving service.

The date of sending the request is to be inserted by the plaintiff on the face of the request for waiver and on the waiver itself. This date is used to measure the return day for the waiver form, so that the plaintiff can know on a day certain whether formal service of process will be necessary; it is also a useful date to measure the time for answer when service is waived. The defendant who returns the waiver is given additional time for answer in order to assure that it loses nothing by waiving service of process.

2000 Amendment

Rule 12(a)(3)(B) is added to complement the addition of Rule 4(i)(2)(B). The purposes that underlie the requirement that service be made on the United States in an action that asserts individual liability of a United States officer or employee for acts occurring in connection with the performance of duties on behalf of the United States also require that the time to answer be extended to 60 days. Time is needed for the United States to determine whether to provide representation to the defendant officer or employee. If the United States provides representation, the need for an extended answer period is the same as in actions against the United States, a United States agency, or a United States officer sued in an official capacity.

An action against a former officer or employee of the United States is covered by subparagraph (3)(B) in the same way as an action against a present officer or employee. Termination of the relationship between the individual defendant and the United States does not reduce the need for additional time to answer.

GAP Report

No changes are recommended for Rule 12 as published.

2007 Amendment

The language of Rule 12 has been amended as part of the general restyling of the Civil Rules to make them more easily understood and to make style and terminology consistent throughout the rules. These changes are intended to be stylistic only.

Former Rule 12(a)(4)(A) referred to an order that postpones disposition of a motion "until the trial on the merits." Rule 12(a)(4) now refers to postponing disposition "until trial." The new expression avoids the ambiguity that inheres in "trial on the merits," which may become confusing when there is a separate trial of a single issue or another event different from a single all-encompassing trial.

CROSS REFERENCES

Answer presenting defenses under subd. (b) of this rule, see Fed.Rules Civ.Proc. Form 20, 28 USCA.

Bill of particulars, see Fed.Rules Cr.Proc. Rule 7, 18 USCA.

Demurrers abolished, see Fed.Rules Civ.Proc. Rule 7, 28 USCA.

Demurrers abolished, see Fed.Rules Cr.Proc. Rule 12, 18 USCA.

Dismissal of actions—

- Claims of opposing party, judgment on counterclaim or cross-claim, see Fed.Rules Civ.Proc. Rule 13, 28 USCA.
- Class actions, see Fed.Rules Civ.Proc. Rule 23, 28 USCA.
- Costs of previously-dismissed action, see Fed.Rules Civ. Proc. Rule 41, 28 USCA.
- Depositions, right to use in former action, see Fed.Rules Civ.Proc. Rule 26, 28 USCA.
- Failure to serve answers to interrogatories, see Fed. Rules Civ.Proc. Rule 37, 28 USCA.
- Findings of fact and conclusions of law, necessity, see Fed.Rules Civ.Proc. Rule 52, 28 USCA.
- Voluntary and involuntary dismissal, see Fed.Rules Civ. Proc. Rule 41, 28 USCA.

Districts courts—

- Jurisdiction, see 28 USCA § 1331 et seq.
- Trials, hearings, and orders in chambers, see Fed.Rules Civ.Proc. Rule 77, 28 USCA.
- Venue, see 28 USCA § 1391 et seq.

Evidence on motions, see Fed.Rules Civ.Proc. Rule 43, 28 USCA.

Findings of fact and conclusions of law unnecessary, see Fed.Rules Civ.Proc. Rule 52, 28 USCA.

Indication of simplicity and brevity of statement, see Fed. Rules Civ.Proc. Rule 84, 28 USCA.

Judgment, definition of, see Fed.Rules Civ.Proc. Rule 54, 28 USCA.

Motion to dismiss, presenting defenses of failure to state claim, of lack of service of process, of improper venue, and of lack of jurisdiction under subd. (b) of this rule, see Fed.Rules Civ.Proc. Form 19, 28 USCA.

Motions—

Adoption of statement by reference, see Fed.Rules Civ. Proc. Rule 10, 28 USCA.

Courts always open for making, see 28 USCA § 452.

Evidence on, see Fed.Rules Civ.Proc. Rule 43, 28 USCA.

Extension of time, see Fed.Rules Civ.Proc. Rule 6, 28 USCA.

Form of, see Fed.Rules Civ.Proc. Rule 7, 28 USCA.

Motion day and oral hearings, see Fed.Rules Civ.Proc. Rule 78, 28 USCA.

Technical forms not required, see Fed.Rules Civ.Proc. Rule 8, 28 USCA.

Time for motions generally, see Fed.Rules Civ.Proc. Rule 6, 28 USCA.

Parties—

Necessary joinder, see Fed.Rules Civ.Proc. Rule 19, 28 USCA.

Third-party defendant, defenses to third-party plaintiff and plaintiff's claims, see Fed.Rules Civ.Proc. Rule 14, 28 USCA.

Pleadings—

Affirmative defenses, see Fed.Rules Civ.Proc. Rule 8, 28 USCA.

Form of, see Fed.Rules Civ.Proc. Rule 10, 28 USCA.

Pleadings allowed, see Fed.Rules Civ.Proc. Rule 7, 28 USCA.

Striking for failure to serve answer to interrogatory, see Fed.Rules Civ.Proc. Rule 37, 28 USCA.

Waiver of objections to venue, see 28 USCA § 1406.

Rule 13. Counterclaim and Crossclaim

(a) Compulsory Counterclaim.

(1) ***In General.*** A pleading must state as a counterclaim any claim that—at the time of its service—the pleader has against an opposing party if the claim:

(A) arises out of the transaction or occurrence that is the subject matter of the opposing party's claim; and

(B) does not require adding another party over whom the court cannot acquire jurisdiction.

(2) ***Exceptions.*** The pleader need not state the claim if:

(A) when the action was commenced, the claim was the subject of another pending action; or

(B) the opposing party sued on its claim by attachment or other process that did not establish personal jurisdiction over the pleader on that claim, and the pleader does not assert any counterclaim under this rule.

(b) Permissive Counterclaim. A pleading may state as a counterclaim against an opposing party any claim that is not compulsory.

(c) Relief Sought in a Counterclaim. A counterclaim need not diminish or defeat the recovery sought by the opposing party. It may request relief that exceeds in amount or differs in kind from the relief sought by the opposing party.

(d) Counterclaim Against the United States. These rules do not expand the right to assert a counterclaim—or to claim a credit—against the United States or a United States officer or agency.

(e) Counterclaim Maturing or Acquired After Pleading. The court may permit a party to file a supplemental pleading asserting a counterclaim that matured or was acquired by the party after serving an earlier pleading.

(f) Omitted Counterclaim. The court may permit a party to amend a pleading to add a counterclaim if it was omitted through oversight, inadvertence, or excusable neglect or if justice so requires.

(g) Crossclaim Against a Coparty. A pleading may state as a crossclaim any claim by one party against a coparty if the claim arises out of the transaction or occurrence that is the subject matter of the original action or of a counterclaim, or if the claim relates to any property that is the subject matter of the original action. The crossclaim may include a claim that the coparty is or may be liable to the cross-claimant for all or part of a claim asserted in the action against the cross-claimant.

(h) Joining Additional Parties. Rules 19 and 20 govern the addition of a person as a party to a counterclaim or crossclaim.

(i) Separate Trials; Separate Judgments. If the court orders separate trials under Rule 42(b), it may enter judgment on a counterclaim or crossclaim under Rule 54(b) when it has jurisdiction to do so, even if the opposing party's claims have been dismissed or otherwise resolved.

(Amended December 27, 1946, effective March 19, 1948; January 21, 1963, effective July 1, 1963; February 28, 1966, effective July 1, 1966; March 2, 1987, effective August 1, 1987; April 30, 2007, effective December 1, 2007.)

ADVISORY COMMITTEE NOTES

1937 Adoption

1. This is substantially [former] Equity Rule 30 (Answer—Contents—Counterclaim), broadened to include legal as well as equitable counterclaims.

2. Compare the English practice, *English Rules Under the Judicature Act* (The Annual Practice, 1937) O. 19, r.r. 2 and 3, and O. 21, r.r. 10–17; *Beddall v. Maitland,* L.R. 17 Ch.Div. 174, 181, 182 (1881).

3. Certain States have also adopted almost unrestricted provisions concerning both the subject matter of and the parties to a counterclaim. This seems to be the modern tendency. Ark.Civ.Code (Crawford, 1934) §§ 117 (as amended) and 118; N.J.Comp.Stat. (2 Cum.Supp. 1911–1924); N.Y.C.P.A. (1937) §§ 262, 266, 267 (all as amended, Laws of 1936, ch. 324), 268, 269, and 271; Wis.Stat. (1935) § 263.14(1)(c).

4. Most codes do not expressly provide for a counterclaim in the reply. Clark, *Code Pleading* (1928), p. 486. Ky.Codes (Carroll, 1932) Civ.Pract. § 98 does provide, however, for such counterclaim.

5. The provisions of this rule respecting counterclaims are subject to Rule 82 (Jurisdiction and Venue Unaffected). For a discussion of Federal jurisdiction and venue in regard to counterclaims and cross-claims, see Shulman and Jaegerman, *Some Jurisdictional Limitations in Federal Procedure* (1936), 45 Yale L.J. 393, 410 et seq.

6. This rule does not affect such statutes of the United States as U.S.C., Title 28, § 41(1) (now §§ 1332, 1345, 1359) (United States as plaintiff; civil suits at common law and in equity), relating to assigned claims in actions based on diversity of citizenship.

7. If the action proceeds to judgment without the interposition of a counterclaim as required by subdivision (a) of this rule, the counterclaim is barred. See *American Mills Co. v. American Surety Co.*, 260 U.S. 360, 43 S.Ct. 149, 67 L.Ed. 306 (1922); *Marconi Wireless Telegraph Co. v. National Electric Signalling Co.*, 206 Fed. 295 (E.D.N.Y., 1913); Hopkins, *Federal Equity Rules* (8th ed., 1933), p. 213; Simkins, *Federal Practice* (1934), p. 663.

8. For allowance of credits against the United States see U.S.C., Title 26, §§ 1672–1673 [sec. 7442] (Suits for refunds of internal revenue taxes—limitations); U.S.C., Title 28, § 774 (now § 2406) (Suits by United States against individuals; credits), [former] § 775 (Suits under postal laws; credits); U.S.C., Title 31, § 227 [now 3728] (Offsets against judgments and claims against United States).

1946 Amendment

Note. Subdivision (a). The use of the word "filing" was inadvertent. The word "serving" conforms with subdivision (e) and with usage generally throughout the rules.

The removal of the phrase "not the subject of a pending action" and the addition of the new clause at the end of the subdivision is designed to eliminate the ambiguity noted in *Prudential Insurance Co. of America v. Saxe,* App.D.C.1943, 77 U.S.App.D.C. 144, 134 F.2d 16, 33–34, cert. den., 1943, 319 U.S. 745, 63 S.Ct. 1033. The rewording of the subdivision in this respect insures against an undesirable possibility presented under the original rule whereby a party having a claim which would be the subject of a compulsory counterclaim could avoid stating it as such by bringing an independent action in another court after the commencement of the federal action but before serving his pleading in the federal action.

Subdivision (g). The amendment is to care for a situation such as where a second mortgagee is made defendant in a foreclosure proceeding and wishes to file a cross-complaint against the mortgagor in order to secure a personal judgment for the indebtedness and foreclose his lien. A claim of this sort by the second mortgagee may not necessarily arise out of the transaction or occurrence that is the subject matter of the original action under the terms of Rule 13(g).

Subdivision (h). The change clarifies the interdependence of Rules 13(i) and 54(b).

1963 Amendment

When a defendant, if he desires to defend his interest in property, is obliged to come in and litigate in a court to whose jurisdiction he could not ordinarily be subjected, fairness suggests that he should not be required to assert counterclaims, but should rather be permitted to do so at his election. If, however, he does elect to assert a counterclaim, it seems fair to require him to assert any other which is compulsory within the meaning of Rule 13(a). Clause (2), added by amendment to Rule 13(a), carries out this idea. It will apply to various cases described in Rule 4(e), as amended, where service is effected through attachment or other process by which the court does not acquire jurisdiction to render a personal judgment against the defendant. Clause (2) will also apply to actions commenced in State courts jurisdictionally grounded on attachment or the like, and removed to the Federal courts.

1966 Amendment

Rule 13(h), dealing with the joinder of additional parties to a counterclaim or cross-claim, has partaken of some of the textual difficulties of Rule 19 on necessary joinder of parties. See Advisory Committee's Note to Rule 19, as amended; cf. 3 *Moore's Federal Practice,* par. 13.39 (2d ed. 1963), and Supp. thereto; 1A Barron & Holtzoff, *Federal Practice and Procedure* § 399 (Wright ed. 1960). Rule 13(h) has also been inadequate in failing to call attention to the fact that a party pleading a counterclaim or cross-claim may join additional persons when the conditions for permissive joinder of parties under Rule 20 are satisfied.

The amendment of Rule 13(h) supplies the latter omission by expressly referring to Rule 20, as amended, and also incorporates by direct reference the revised criteria and procedures of Rule 19, as amended. Hereafter, for the purpose of determining who must or may be joined as additional parties to a counterclaim or cross-claim, the party pleading the claim is to be regarded as a plaintiff and the additional parties as plaintiffs or defendants as the case may be, and amended Rules 19 and 20 are to be applied in the usual fashion. See also Rules 13(a) (compulsory counterclaims) and 22 (interpleader).

The amendment of Rule 13(h), like the amendment of Rule 19, does not attempt to regulate Federal jurisdiction or venue. See Rule 82. It should be noted, however, that in some situations the decisional law has recognized "ancillary" Federal jurisdiction over counterclaims and cross-claims and "ancillary" venue as to parties to these claims.

1987 Amendment

The amendments are technical. No substantive change is intended.

2007 Amendment

The language of Rule 13 has been amended as part of the general restyling of the Civil Rules to make them more easily understood and to make style and terminology consistent throughout the rules. These changes are intended to be stylistic only.

The meaning of former Rule 13(b) is better expressed by deleting "not arising out of the transaction or occurrence that is the subject matter of the opposing party's claim." Both as a matter of intended meaning and current practice, a party may state as a permissive counterclaim a claim that does grow out of the same transaction or occurrence as an opposing party's claim even though one of the exceptions in Rule 13(a) means the claim is not a compulsory counterclaim.

CROSS REFERENCES

Counterclaim, see Fed.Rules Civ.Proc. Forms 20 and 21, 28 USCA.

Counterclaim—

- Generally, see West's Federal Forms § 2581.
- Default judgment against counter-claimants, see Fed. Rules Civ.Proc. Rule 55, 28 USCA.
- Dismissal, see Fed.Rules Civ.Proc. Rule 41, 28 USCA.
- Mistake in designation of defense, see Fed.Rules Civ. Proc. Rule 8, 28 USCA.
- Reply, see Fed.Rules Civ.Proc. Rule 7, 28 USCA.
- Requisites of pleading, see Fed.Rules Civ.Proc. Rule 8, 28 USCA.
- Service of pleadings, numerous defendants, see Fed. Rules Civ.Proc. Rule 5, 28 USCA.
- Summary judgment, see Fed.Rules Civ.Proc. Rule 56, 28 USCA.
- Third-party practice, see Fed.Rules Civ.Proc. Rule 14, 28 USCA.
- Time for reply by United States, see Fed.Rules Civ. Proc. Rule 12, 28 USCA.

Cross-claim, see Fed.Rules Civ.Proc. Form 20, 28 USCA.

Cross-claim—

- Answer to, if answer contains a cross-claim, see Fed. Rules Civ.Proc. Rule 7, 28 USCA.
- Default judgment, see Fed.Rules Civ.Proc. Rule 55, 28 USCA.
- Dismissal, see Fed.Rules Civ.Proc. Rule 41, 28 USCA.
- Joinder, see Fed.Rules Civ.Proc. Rule 18, 28 USCA.
- Requisites of pleading, see Fed.Rules Civ.Proc. Rule 8, 28 USCA.
- Service of pleadings, numerous defendants, see Fed. Rules Civ.Proc. Rule 5, 28 USCA.
- Summary judgment, see Fed.Rules Civ.Proc. Rule 56, 28 USCA.
- Third-party practice, see Fed.Rules Civ.Proc. Rule 14, 28 USCA.
- Time for answer by United States, see Fed.Rules Civ. Proc. Rule 12, 28 USCA.
- Time of service of reply, see Fed.Rules Civ.Proc. Rule 12, 28 USCA.
- Voluntary dismissal, see Fed.Rules Civ.Proc. Rule 41, 28 USCA.

Rule 14. Third–Party Practice

(a) When a Defending Party May Bring in a Third Party.

(1) ***Timing of the Summons and Complaint.*** A defending party may, as third-party plaintiff, serve a summons and complaint on a nonparty who is or may be liable to it for all or part of the claim against it. But the third-party plaintiff must, by motion, obtain the court's leave if it files the third-party complaint more than 10 days after serving its original answer.

(2) ***Third–Party Defendant's Claims and Defenses.*** The person served with the summons and third-party complaint—the "third-party defendant":

(A) must assert any defense against the third-party plaintiff's claim under Rule 12;

(B) must assert any counterclaim against the third-party plaintiff under Rule 13(a), and may assert any counterclaim against the third-party plaintiff under Rule 13(b) or any crossclaim against another third-party defendant under Rule 13(g);

(C) may assert against the plaintiff any defense that the third-party plaintiff has to the plaintiff's claim; and

(D) may also assert against the plaintiff any claim arising out of the transaction or occurrence that is the subject matter of the plaintiff's claim against the third-party plaintiff.

(3) ***Plaintiff's Claims Against a Third–Party Defendant.*** The plaintiff may assert against the third-party defendant any claim arising out of the transaction or occurrence that is the subject matter of the plaintiff's claim against the third-party plaintiff. The third-party defendant must then assert any defense under Rule 12 and any counterclaim under Rule 13(a), and may assert any counterclaim under Rule 13(b) or any crossclaim under Rule 13(g).

(4) ***Motion to Strike, Sever, or Try Separately.*** Any party may move to strike the third-party claim, to sever it, or to try it separately.

(5) ***Third–Party Defendant's Claim Against a Nonparty.*** A third-party defendant may proceed under this rule against a nonparty who is or may be liable to the third-party defendant for all or part of any claim against it.

(6) ***Third–Party Complaint In Rem.*** If it is within the admiralty or maritime jurisdiction, a third-party complaint may be in rem. In that event, a reference in this rule to the "summons" includes the warrant of arrest,

and a reference to the defendant or third-party plaintiff includes, when appropriate, a person who asserts a right under Supplemental Rule C(6)(a)(i) in the property arrested.

(b) When a Plaintiff May Bring in a Third Party. When a claim is asserted against a plaintiff, the plaintiff may bring in a third party if this rule would allow a defendant to do so.

(c) Admiralty or Maritime Claim.

(1) ***Scope of Impleader.*** If a plaintiff asserts an admiralty or maritime claim under Rule 9(h), the defendant or a person who asserts a right under Supplemental Rule C(6)(a)(i) may, as a third-party plaintiff, bring in a third-party defendant who may be wholly or partly liable—either to the plaintiff or to the third-party plaintiff—for remedy over, contribution, or otherwise on account of the same transaction, occurrence, or series of transactions or occurrences.

(2) ***Defending Against a Demand for Judgment for the Plaintiff.*** The third-party plaintiff may demand judgment in the plaintiff's favor against the third-party defendant. In that event, the third-party defendant must defend under Rule 12 against the plaintiff's claim as well as the third-party plaintiff's claim; and the action proceeds as if the plaintiff had sued both the third-party defendant and the third-party plaintiff.

(Amended December 27, 1946, effective March 19, 1948; January 21, 1963, effective July 1, 1963; February 28, 1966, effective July 1, 1966; March 2, 1987, effective August 1, 1987; April 17, 2000, effective December 1, 2000; April 12, 2006, effective December 1, 2006; April 30, 2007, effective December 1, 2007.)

ADVISORY COMMITTEE NOTES

1937 Adoption

Third-party impleader is in some aspects a modern innovation in law and equity although well known in admiralty. Because of its many advantages a liberal procedure with respect to it has developed in England, in the federal admiralty courts, and in some American state jurisdictions. See *English Rules Under the Judicature Act* (The Annual Practice, 1937) O. 16A, r.r. 1–13; United States Supreme Court Admiralty Rules (1920), Rule 56 (Right to Bring in Party Jointly Liable); 12 P.S.Pa. § 141; Wis.Stat. (1935) §§ 260.19, 260.20; N.Y.C.P.A. (1937) §§ 193(2), 211(a). Compare La. Code Pract. (Dart, 1932) §§ 378–388. For the practice in Texas as developed by judicial decision, see *Lottman v. Cuilla*, Tex.1926, 288 S.W. 123, 126. For a treatment of this subject see Gregory, *Legislative Loss Distribution in Negligence Actions* (1936); *Shulman and Jaegerman, Some Jurisdictional Limitations on Federal Procedure (1936)*, 45 Yale L.J. 393, 417 et seq.

Third-party impleader under the conformity act has been applied in actions at law in the Federal courts. *Lowry and Co., Inc. v. National City Bank of New York*, N.Y.1928, 28 F.2d 895; *Yellow Cab Co. of Philadelphia v. Rodgers*, C.C.A.3, 1932, 61 F.2d 729.

1946 Amendment

Note. The provisions in Rule 14(a) which relate to the impleading of a third party who is or may be liable to the plaintiff have been deleted by the proposed amendment. It has been held that under Rule 14(a) the plaintiff need not amend his complaint to state a claim against such third party if he does not wish to do so. *Satink v. Holland Township*, D.N.J.1940, 31 F.Supp. 229, noted, 1940, 88 U.Pa.L.Rev. 751; *Connelly v. Bender*, E.D.Mich.1941, 36 F.Supp. 368; *Whitmire v. Partin (Milton)*, E.D.Tenn.1941, 2 F.R.D. 83, 5 Fed.Rules Serv. 14a.513, Case 2; *Crim v. Lumbermen's Mutual Casualty Co.*, D.D.C.1939, 26 F.Supp. 715; *Carbola Chemical Co., Inc. v. Trundle*, S.D.N.Y.1943, 3 F.R.D. 502, 7 Fed.Rules Serv. 14a.224, Case 1; *Roadway Express, Inc. v. Automobile Ins. Co. of Hartford, Conn., (Providence Washington Ins. Co.)* N.D.Ohio 1945, 8 Fed.Rules Serv. 14a.513, Case 3. In *Delano v. Ives*, E.D.Pa.1941, 40 F.Supp. 672, the court said: ". . . the weight of authority is to the effect that a defendant cannot compel the plaintiff, who has sued him, to sue also a third party whom he does not wish to sue, by tendering in a third party complaint the third party as an additional defendant directly liable to the plaintiff." Thus impleader here amounts to no more than a mere offer of a party to the plaintiff, and if he rejects it, the attempt is a time-consuming futility. See *Satink v. Holland Township, supra; Malkin v. Arundel Corp.*, D.Md.1941, 36 F.Supp. 948; also Koenigsberger, *Suggestions for Changes in the Federal Rules of Civil Procedure*, 1941, 4 Fed.Rules Serv. 1010. But cf. *Atlantic Coast Line R. Co. v. United States Fidelity & Guaranty Co.*, Ga.1943, 52 F.Supp. 177. Moreover, in any case where the plaintiff could not have joined the third party originally because of jurisdictional limitations such as lack of diversity of citizenship, the majority view is that any attempt by the plaintiff to amend his complaint and assert a claim against the impleaded third party would be unavailing. *Hoskie v. Prudential Ins. Co. of America, (Lorrac Real Estate Corp.)*, E.D.N.Y.1941, 39 F.Supp. 305; *Johnson v. G. J. Sherrard Co., (New England Telephone & Telegraph Co.)*, D.Mass.1941, 5 Fed.Rules Serv. 14a.511, Case 1, 2 F.R.D. 164; *Thompson v. Cranston*, W.D.N.Y.1942, 6 Fed.Rules Serv. 14a.511, Case 1, 2 F.R.D. 270, affirmed CCA2d, 1942, 132 F.2d 631, certiorari denied 1945, 63 S.Ct. 1028, 319 U.S. 741, 87 L.Ed. 1698; *Friend v. Middle Atlantic Transportation Co.*, C.C.A.2, 1946, 153 F.2d 778, certiorari denied 1946, 66 S.Ct. 1370, 328 U.S. 865, 90 L.Ed. 1635; *Herrington v. Jones*, E.D.La.1941, 5 Fed.Rules Serv. 14a.511, Case 2, 2 F.R.D. 108; *Banks v. Employers' Liability Assurance Corp., (Central Surety & Ins. Corp.)* W.D.Mo.1943, 7 Fed.Rules Serv. 14a.11, Case 2; *Saunders v. Baltimore & Ohio R. Co.*, S.D.W.Va.1945, 9 Fed.Rules Serv. 14a.62, Case 2; *Hull v. United States Rubber Co. (Johnson Larsen and Co.)*, E.D.Mich.1945, 9 Fed.Rules Serv. 14a.62, Case 3. See also concurring opinion of Circuit Judge Minton in *People of State of Illinois for Use of Trust Co. of Chicago v. Maryland Casualty Co.*, C.C.A.7, 1942, 132 F.2d 850, 853. Contra: *Sklar v. Hayes (Singer)*, E.D.Pa.1941, 4 Fed.Rules Serv. 14a.511, Case 2, 1 F.R.D. 594. Discussion of the problem will be found in Commentary, *Amendment of Plaintiff's Pleading to Assert Claim Against Third-Party Defendant*, 1942, 5

Fed.Rules Serv. 811; Commentary, *Federal Jurisdiction in Third-Party Practice,* 1943, 6 Fed.Rules Serv. 766; Holtzoff, *Some Problems Under Federal Third-Party Practice,* 1941, 3 La.L.Rev. 408, 419–420; 1 Moore's *Federal Practice,* 1938, Cum.Supplement § 14.08. For these reasons therefore, the words "or to the plaintiff" in the first sentence of subdivision (a) have been removed by the amendment; and in conformance therewith the words "the plaintiff" in the second sentence of the subdivision, and the words "or to the third-party plaintiff" in the concluding sentence thereof have likewise been eliminated.

The third sentence of rule 14(a) has been expanded to clarify the right of the third-party defendant to assert any defenses which the third-party plaintiff may have to the plaintiff's claim. This protects the impleaded third-party defendant where the third-party plaintiff fails or neglects to assert a proper defense to the plaintiff's action. A new sentence has also been inserted giving the third-party defendant the right to assert directly against the original plaintiff any claim arising out of the transaction or occurrence that is the subject matter of the plaintiff's claim against the third-party plaintiff. This permits all claims arising out of the same transaction or occurrence to be heard and determined in the same action. See *Atlantic Coast Line R. Co. v. United States Fidelity & Guaranty Co.,* Ga.1943, 52 F.Supp. 177. Accordingly, the next to the last sentence of subdivision (a) has also been revised to make clear that the plaintiff may, if he desires, assert directly against the third-party defendant either by amendment or by a new pleading any claim he may have against him arising out of the transaction or occurrence that is the subject matter of the plaintiff's claim against the third-party plaintiff. In such a case, the third-party defendant then is entitled to assert the defenses, counter-claims and cross-claims provided in Rules 12 and 13.

The sentence reading "The third-party defendant is bound by the adjudication of the third-party plaintiff's liability to the plaintiff, as well as of his own to the plaintiff, or to the third-party plaintiff" has been stricken from Rule 14(a), not to change the law, but because the sentence states a rule of substantive law which is not within the scope of a procedural rule. It is not the purpose of the rules to state the effect of a judgment.

The elimination of the words "the third-party plaintiff, or any other party" from the second sentence of rule 14(a), together with the insertion of the new phrases therein, are not changes of substance but are merely for the purpose of clarification.

1963 Amendment

Under the amendment of the initial sentences of the subdivision, a defendant as a third-party plaintiff may freely and without leave of court bring in a third-party defendant if he files the third-party complaint not later than 10 days after he serves his original answer. When the impleader comes so early in the case, there is little value in requiring a preliminary ruling by the court on the propriety of the impleader.

After the third-party defendant is brought in, the court has discretion to strike the third-party claim if it is obviously unmeritorious and can only delay or prejudice the disposition of the plaintiff's claim, or to sever the third-party claim or accord it separate trial if confusion or prejudice would otherwise result. This discretion, applicable not merely to the cases covered by the amendment where the third-party defendant is brought in without leave, but to all impleaders under the rule, is emphasized in the next-to-last sentence of the subdivision, added by amendment.

In dispensing with leave of court for an impleader filed not later than 10 days after serving the answer, but retaining the leave requirement for impleaders sought to be effected thereafter, the amended subdivision takes a moderate position on the lines urged by some commentators, see Note, 43 Minn.L.Rev. 115 (1958); cf. Pa.R.Civ.P. 2252–53 (60 days after service on the defendant; Minn.R.Civ.P. 14.01 (45 days). Other commentators would dispense with the requirement of leave regardless of the time when impleader is effected, and would rely on subsequent action by the court to dismiss the impleader if it would unduly delay or complicate the litigation or would be otherwise objectionable. See 1A Barron & Holtzoff, *Federal Practice & Procedure* 649–50 (Wright ed. 1960); Comment, 58 Colum.L.Rev. 532, 546 (1958); cf. N.Y.Civ.Prac.Act § 193–a; Me.R.Civ.P. 14. The amended subdivision preserves the value of a preliminary screening, through the leave procedure, of impleaders attempted after the 10-day period.

The amendment applies also when an impleader is initiated by a third-party defendant against a person who may be liable to him, as provided in the last sentence of the subdivision.

1966 Amendment

Rule 14 was modeled on Admiralty Rule 56. An important feature of Admiralty Rule 56 was that it allowed impleader not only of a person who might be liable to the defendant by way of remedy over, but also of any person who might be liable to the plaintiff. The importance of this provision was that the defendant was entitled to insist that the plaintiff proceed to judgment against the third-party defendant. In certain cases this was a valuable implementation of a substantive right. For example, in a case of ship collision where a finding of mutual fault is possible, one shipowner, if sued alone, faces the prospect of an absolute judgment for the full amount of the damage suffered by an innocent third party; but if he can implead the owner of the other vessel, and if mutual fault is found, the judgment against the original defendant will be in the first instance only for a moiety of the damages; liability for the remainder will be conditioned on the plaintiff's inability to collect from the third-party defendant.

This feature was originally incorporated in Rule 14, but was eliminated by the amendment of 1946, so that under the amended rule a third party could not be impleaded on the basis that he might be liable to the plaintiff. One of the reasons for the amendment was that the Civil Rule, unlike the Admiralty Rule, did not require the plaintiff to go to judgment against the third-party defendant. Another reason was that where jurisdiction depended on diversity of citizenship the impleader of an adversary having the same citizenship as the plaintiff was not considered possible.

Retention of the admiralty practice in those cases that will be counterparts of a suit in admiralty is clearly desirable.

1987 Amendment

The amendments are technical. No substantive change is intended.

2000 Amendment

Subdivisions (a) and (c) are amended to reflect revisions in Supplemental Rule C(6).

GAP Report

Rule B(1)(a) was modified by moving "in an in personam action" out of paragraph (a) and into the first line of subdivision (1). This change makes it clear that all paragraphs of subdivision (1) apply when attachment is sought in an in personam action. Rule B(1)(d) was modified by changing the requirement that the clerk deliver the summons and process to the person or organization authorized to serve it. The new form requires only that the summons and process be delivered, not that the clerk effect the delivery. This change conforms to present practice in some districts and will facilitate rapid service. It matches the spirit of Civil Rule 4(b), which directs the clerk to issue the summons "to the plaintiff for service on the defendant." A parallel change is made in Rule C(3)(b).

2006 Amendment

Rule 14 is amended to conform to changes in designating the paragraphs of Supplemental Rule C(6).

2007 Amendment

The language of Rule 14 has been amended as part of the general restyling of the Civil Rules to make them more easily understood and to make style and terminology consistent throughout the rules. These changes are intended to be stylistic only.

Former Rule 14 twice refers to counterclaims under Rule 13. In each case, the operation of Rule 13(a) depends on the state of the action at the time the pleading is filed. If plaintiff and third-party defendant have become opposing parties because one has made a claim for relief against the other, Rule 13(a) requires assertion of any counterclaim that grows out of the transaction or occurrence that is the subject matter of that claim. Rules 14(a)(2)(B) and (a)(3) reflect the distinction between compulsory and permissive counterclaims.

A plaintiff should be on equal footing with the defendant in making third-party claims, whether the claim against the plaintiff is asserted as a counterclaim or as another form of claim. The limit imposed by the former reference to "counterclaim" is deleted.

CROSS REFERENCES

Third-party answer, service of third-party complaint, see Fed.Rules Civ.Proc. Rule 7, 28 USCA.

Third-party claim—

Dismissal of, see Fed.Rules Civ.Proc. Rule 41, 28 USCA.

Joinder, see Fed.Rules Civ.Proc. Rule 18, 28 USCA.

Judgment on less than all claims, see Fed.Rules Civ. Proc. Rule 54, 28 USCA.

Requisites, see Fed.Rules Civ.Proc. Rule 8, 28 USCA.

Separate trial, see Fed.Rules Civ.Proc. Rule 42, 28 USCA.

Third-party complaint, leave to summon person not an original party, see Fed.Rules Civ.Proc. Rule 7, 28 USCA.

Third-party plaintiff, default judgment against, see Fed. Rules Civ.Proc. Rule 55, 28 USCA.

Third-party tort liability to United States for hospital and medical care, see 42 USCA § 2651 et seq.

Rule 15. Amended and Supplemental Pleadings

(a) Amendments Before Trial.

(1) ***Amending as a Matter of Course.*** A party may amend its pleading once as a matter of course:

(A) before being served with a responsive pleading; or

(B) within 20 days after serving the pleading if a responsive pleading is not allowed and the action is not yet on the trial calendar.

(2) ***Other Amendments.*** In all other cases, a party may amend its pleading only with the opposing party's written consent or the court's leave. The court should freely give leave when justice so requires.

(3) ***Time to Respond.*** Unless the court orders otherwise, any required response to an amended pleading must be made within the time remaining to respond to the original pleading or within 10 days after service of the amended pleading, whichever is later.

(b) Amendments During and After Trial.

(1) ***Based on an Objection at Trial.*** If, at trial, a party objects that evidence is not within the issues raised in the pleadings, the court may permit the pleadings to be amended. The court should freely permit an amendment when doing so will aid in presenting the merits and the objecting party fails to satisfy the court that the evidence would prejudice that party's action or defense on the merits. The court may grant a continuance to enable the objecting party to meet the evidence.

(2) ***For Issues Tried by Consent.*** When an issue not raised by the pleadings is tried by the parties' express or implied consent, it must be treated in all respects as if raised in the pleadings. A party may move—at any time, even after judgment—to amend the pleadings to conform them to the evidence and to raise an unpleaded issue. But failure to amend does not affect the result of the trial of that issue.

(c) Relation Back of Amendments.

(1) ***When an Amendment Relates Back.*** An amendment to a pleading relates back to the date of the original pleading when:

(A) the law that provides the applicable statute of limitations allows relation back;

(B) the amendment asserts a claim or defense that arose out of the conduct, transaction, or occurrence set out—or attempted to be set out—in the original pleading; or

(C) the amendment changes the party or the naming of the party against whom a claim is asserted, if Rule 15(c)(1)(B) is satisfied and if, within the period provided by Rule 4(m) for serving the summons and complaint, the party to be brought in by amendment:

(i) received such notice of the action that it will not be prejudiced in defending on the merits; and

(ii) knew or should have known that the action would have been brought against it, but for a mistake concerning the proper party's identity.

(2) ***Notice to the United States.*** When the United States or a United States officer or agency is added as a defendant by amendment, the notice requirements of Rule 15(c)(1)(C)(i) and (ii) are satisfied if, during the stated period, process was delivered or mailed to the United States attorney or the United States attorney's designee, to the Attorney General of the United States, or to the officer or agency.

(d) Supplemental Pleadings. On motion and reasonable notice, the court may, on just terms, permit a party to serve a supplemental pleading setting out any transaction, occurrence, or event that happened after the date of the pleading to be supplemented. The court may permit supplementation even though the original pleading is defective in stating a claim or defense. The court may order that the opposing party plead to the supplemental pleading within a specified time.

(Amended January 21, 1963, effective July 1, 1963; February 28, 1966, effective July 1, 1966; March 2, 1987, effective August 1, 1987; April 30, 1991, effective December 1, 1991; amended by Pub.L. 102–198, § 11, December 9, 1991, 105 Stat. 1626; amended April 22, 1993, effective December 1, 1993; April 30, 2007, effective December 1, 2007.)

ADVISORY COMMITTEE NOTES

1937 Adoption

See generally for the present federal practice, [former] Equity Rules 19 (Amendments Generally), 28 (Amendment of Bill as of Course), 32 (Answer to Amended Bill), 34 (Supplemental Pleading), and 35 (Bills of Revivor and Supplemental Bills—Form); U.S.C. Title 28, § 399 [now 1653] (Amendments to show diverse citizenship) and [former] 777 (Defects of form; amendments). See *English Rules Under the Judicature Act* (The Annual Practice, 1937) O. 28, r. r. 1–13; O. 20, r. 4; O. 24, r. r. 1–3.

Note to Subdivision (a). The right to serve an amended pleading once as of course is common. 4 Mont.Rev.Codes Ann. (1935) § 9186; 1 Ore.Code Ann. (1930) § 1–904; 1 S.C.Code (Michie, 1932) § 493; *English Rules Under the Judicature Act* (The Annual Practice, 1937) O. 28, r. 2. Provision for amendment of pleading before trial, by leave of court, is in almost every code. If there is no statute the power of the court to grant leave is said to be inherent. Clark, *Code Pleading* (1928), pp. 498, 509.

Note to Subdivision (b). Compare [former] Equity Rule 19 (Amendments Generally) and code provisions which allow an amendment "at any time in furtherance of justice," (e.g., Ark.Civ.Code (Crawford, 1934) § 155) and which allow an amendment of pleadings to conform to the evidence, where the adverse party has not been misled and prejudiced (e.g., N.M.Stat.Ann. (Courtright, 1929) §§ 105–601, 105–602).

Note to Subdivision (c). "Relation back" is a well recognized doctrine of recent and now more frequent application. Compare Ala.Code Ann. (Michie, 1928) § 9513; Smith-Hurd Ill.Stats. ch. 110, § 170(2); 2 Wash.Rev.Stat.Ann. (Remington, 1932) § 308–3(4). See U.S.C., Title 28, § 399 [now 1653] (Amendments to show diverse citizenship) for a provision for "relation back".

Note to Subdivision (d). This is an adaptation of former Equity Rule 34 (Supplemental Pleading).

1963 Amendment

Rule 15(d) is intended to give the court broad discretion in allowing a supplemental pleading. However, some cases, opposed by other cases and criticized by the commentators, have taken the rigid and formalistic view that where the original complaint fails to state a claim upon which relief can be granted, leave to serve a supplemental complaint must be denied. See *Bonner v. Elizabeth Arden, Inc.*, 177 F.2d 703 (2d Cir. 1949); *Bowles v. Senderowitz,* 65 F.Supp. 548 (E.D.Pa.), rev'd on other grounds, 158 F.2d 435 (3d Cir. 1946), cert. denied, *Senderowitz v. Fleming,* 330 U.S. 848, 67 S.Ct. 1091, 91 L.Ed. 1292 (1947); cf. *LaSalle Nat. Bank v. 222 East Chestnut St. Corp.*, 267 F.2d 247 (7th Cir.), cert. denied, 361 U.S. 836, 80 S.Ct. 88, 4 L.Ed.2d 77 (1959). But see *Camilla Cotton Oil Co. v. Spencer Kellogg & Sons,* 257 F.2d 162 (5th Cir. 1958); *Genuth v. National Biscuit Co.,* 81 F.Supp. 213 (S.D.N.Y.1948), app. dism., 177 F.2d 962 (2d Cir. 1949); 3 Moore's *Federal Practice* ¶15.01[5] (Supp.1960); 1A Barron & Holtzoff, *Federal Practice & Procedure* 820–21 (Wright ed. 1960). Thus plaintiffs have sometimes been needlessly remitted to the difficulties of commencing a new action even though events occurring after the commencement of the original action have made clear the right to relief.

Under the amendment the court has discretion to permit a supplemental pleading despite the fact that the original pleading is defective. As in other situations where a supplemental pleading is offered, the court is to determine in the light of the particular circumstances whether filing should be permitted, and if so, upon what terms. The amendment does not attempt to deal with such questions as the relation of the statute of limitations to supplemental pleadings, the operation of the doctrine of laches, or the availability of other defenses. All these questions are for decision in accordance with the principles applicable to supplemental pleadings generally. Cf. *Blau v. Lamb,* 191 F.Supp. 906 (S.D.N.Y.1961); *Lendonsol Amusement Corp. v. B. & Q. Assoc., Inc.*, 23 F.R.Serv. 15d.3, Case 1 (D.Mass.1957).

1966 Amendment

Rule 15(c) is amplified to state more clearly when an amendment of a pleading changing the party against whom a claim is asserted (including an amendment to correct a misnomer or misdescription of a defendant) shall "relate back" to the date of the original pleading.

The problem has arisen most acutely in certain actions by private parties against officers or agencies of the United States. Thus an individual denied social security benefits by the Secretary of Health, Education, and Welfare may secure review of the decision by bringing a civil action against that officer within sixty days. 42 U.S.C. § 405(g) (Supp. III, 1962). In several recent cases the claimants instituted timely action but mistakenly named as defendant the United States, the Department of HEW, the "Federal Security Administration" (a nonexistent agency), and a Secretary who had retired from the office nineteen days before. Discovering their mistakes, the claimants moved to amend their complaints to name the proper defendant; by this time the statutory sixty-day period had expired. The motions were denied on the ground that the amendment "would amount to the commencement of a new proceeding and would not relate back in time so as to avoid the statutory provision * * * that suit be brought within sixty days * * *" *Cohn v. Federal Security Adm.*, 199 F.Supp. 884, 885 (W.D.N.Y.1961); see also *Cunningham v. United States,* 199 F.Supp. 541 (W.D.Mo.1958); *Hall v. Department of HEW,* 199 F.Supp. 833 (S.D.Tex.1960); *Sandridge v. Folsom, Secretary of HEW,* 200 F.Supp. 25 (M.D.Tenn.1959). [The Secretary of Health, Education, and Welfare has approved certain ameliorative regulations under 42 U.S.C. § 405(g). See 29 Fed. Reg. 8209 (June 30, 1964); Jacoby, *The Effect of Recent Changes in the Law of "Nonstatutory" Judicial Review,* 53 Geo.L.J. 19, 42–43 (1964); see also *Simmons v. United States Dept. HEW,* 328 F.2d 86 (3d Cir. 1964).]

Analysis in terms of "new proceeding" is traceable to *Davis v. L. L. Cohen & Co.,* 268 U.S. 638 (1925), and *Mellon v. Arkansas Land & Lumber Co.,* 275 U.S. 460 (1928), but those cases antedate the adoption of the Rules which import different criteria for determining when an amendment is to "relate back". As lower courts have continued to rely on the *Davis* and *Mellon* cases despite the contrary intent of the Rules, clarification of Rule 15(c) is considered advisable.

Relation back is intimately connected with the policy of the statute of limitations. The policy of the statute limiting the time for suit against the Secretary of HEW would not have been offended by allowing relation back in the situations described above. For the government was put on notice of the claim within the stated period—in the particular instances, by means of the initial delivery of process to a responsible government official (see Rule 4(d)(4) and (5)). In these circumstances, characterization of the amendment as a new proceeding is not responsive to the realty [sic], but is merely question-begging; and to deny relation back is to defeat unjustly the claimant's opportunity to prove his case. See the full discussion by Byse, *Suing the "Wrong" Defendant in Judicial Review of Federal Administrative Action: Proposals for Reform,* 77 Harv.L.Rev. 40 (1963); see also Ill.Civ.P. Act § 46(4).

Much the same question arises in other types of actions against the government (see *Byse,* supra, at 45 n. 15). In actions between private parties, the problem of relation back of amendments changing defendants has generally been better handled by the courts, but incorrect criteria have sometimes been applied, leading sporadically to doubtful results. See 1A Barron & Holtzoff, *Federal Practice & Procedure* § 451 (Wright ed. 1960); 1 id. § 186 (1960); 2 id. § 543 (1961); 3 *Moore's Federal Practice,* par. 15.15 (Cum.Supp. 1962); Annot., *Change in Party After Statute of Limitations Has Run,* 8 A.L.R.2d 6 (1949). Rule 15(c) has been amplified to provide a general solution. An amendment changing the party against whom a claim is asserted relates back if the amendment satisfies the usual condition of Rule 15(c) of "arising out of the conduct * * * set forth * * * in the original pleading," and if, within the applicable limitations period, the party brought in by amendment, first, received such notice of the institution of the action—the notice need not be formal—that he would not be prejudiced in defending the action, and, second, knew or should have known that the action would have been brought against him initially had there not been a mistake concerning the identity of the proper party. Revised Rule 15(c) goes on to provide specifically in the government cases that the first and second requirements are satisfied when the government has been notified in the manner there described (see Rule 4(d)(4) and (5)). As applied to the government cases, revised Rule 15(c) further advances the objectives of the 1961 amendment of Rule 25(d) (substitution of public officers).

The relation back of amendments changing plaintiffs is not expressly treated in revised Rule 15(c) since the problem is generally easier. Again the chief consideration of policy is that of the statute of limitations, and the attitude taken in revised Rule 15(c) toward change of defendants extends by analogy to amendments changing plaintiffs. Also relevant is the amendment of Rule 17(a) (real party in interest). To avoid forfeitures of just claims, revised Rule 17(a) would provide that no action shall be dismissed on the ground that it is not prosecuted in the name of the real party in interest until a reasonable time has been allowed for correction of the defect in the manner there stated.

1987 Amendment

The amendments are technical. No substantive change is intended.

1991 Amendment

The rule has been revised to prevent parties against whom claims are made from taking unjust advantage of otherwise inconsequential pleading errors to sustain a limitations defense.

Paragraph (c)(1). This provision is new. It is intended to make it clear that the rule does not apply to preclude any relation back that may be permitted under the applicable limitations law. Generally, the applicable limitations law will be state law. If federal jurisdiction is based on the citizenship of the parties, the primary reference is the law of the state in which the district court sits. *Walker v. Armco Steel Corp.,* 446 U.S. 740 (1980). If federal jurisdiction is based on a federal question, the reference may be to the law of the state governing relations between the parties. *E.g., Board of Regents v. Tomanio,* 446 U.S. 478 (1980). In some circumstances, the controlling limitations law may be federal law. *E.g., West v. Conrail, Inc.,* 107 S.Ct. 1538 (1987). Cf. *Burlington Northern R. Co. v. Woods,* 480 U.S. 1 (1987); *Stewart Organization v. Ricoh,* 108 S.Ct. 2239 (1988). Whatever may be the controlling body of limitations law, if that law affords a more forgiving principle of relation back than the one provided in this rule, it should be available to save the claim. Accord, *Marshall v. Mulrenin,* 508 F.2d 39 (1st cir.1974). If *Schiavone v. Fortune,* 106 S.Ct. 2379 (1986) implies the contrary, this paragraph is intended to make a material change in the rule.

Paragraph (c)(3). This paragraph has been revised to change the result in *Schiavone v. Fortune, supra,* with respect to the problem of a misnamed defendant. An intended defendant who is notified of an action within the period allowed by Rule 4(m) [subdivision (m) in Rule 4 was a proposed subdivision which was withdrawn by the Supreme Court] for service of a summons and complaint may not under the revised rule defeat the action on account of a defect in the pleading with respect to the defendant's name, provided that the requirements of clauses (A) and (B) have been met. If the notice requirement is met within the Rule 4(m) [subdivision (m) in Rule 4 was a proposed subdivision which was withdrawn by the Supreme Court] period, a complaint may be amended at any time to correct a formal defect such as a misnomer or misidentification. On the basis of the text of the former rule, the Court reached a result in *Schiavone v. Fortune* that was inconsistent with the liberal pleading practices secured by Rule 8. See Bauer, Schiavone: *An Un-Fortune-ate Illustration of the Supreme Court's Role as Interpreter of the Federal Rules of Civil Procedure,* 63 Notre Dame L.Rev. 720 (1988); Brussack, *Outrageous Fortune: The Case for Amending Rule 15(c) Again,* 61 S.Cal. L.Rev. 671 (1988); Lewis, *The Excessive History of Federal Rule 15(c) and Its Lessons for Civil Rules Revision,* 86 Mich.L.Rev. 1507 (1987).

In allowing a name-correcting amendment within the time allowed by Rule 4(m), this rule allows not only the 120 days specified in that rule, but also any additional time resulting from any extension ordered by the court pursuant to that rule, as may be granted, for example, if the defendant is a fugitive from service of the summons.

This revision, together with the revision of Rule 4(i) with respect to the failure of a plaintiff in an action against the United States to effect timely service on all the appropriate officials, is intended to produce results contrary to those reached in *Gardner v. Gartman,* 880 F.2d 797 (4th Cir. 1989), *Rys v. U.S. Postal Service,* 886 F.2d 443 (1st Cir. 1989), *Martin's Food & Liquor, Inc. v. U.S. Dept. of Agriculture,* 14 F.R.D.3d 86 (N.D.Ill.1988). *But cf. Montgomery v. United States Postal Service,* 867 F.2d 900 (5th Cir. 1989), *Warren v. Department of the Army,* 867 F.2d 1156 (8th Cir. 1989); *Miles v. Department of the Army,* 881 F.2d 777 (9th Cir. 1989), *Barsten v. Department of the Interior,* 896 F.2d 422 (9th Cir. 1990); *Brown v. Georgia Dept. of Revenue,* 881 F.2d 1018 (11th Cir. 1989).

1993 Amendments

The amendment conforms the cross reference to Rule 4 to the revision of that rule.

2007 Amendment

The language of Rule 15 has been amended as part of the general restyling of the Civil Rules to make them more easily understood and to make style and terminology consistent throughout the rules. These changes are intended to be stylistic only.

Former Rule 15(c)(3)(A) called for notice of the "institution" of the action. Rule 15(c)(1)(C)(i) omits the reference to "institution" as potentially confusing. What counts is that the party to be brought in have notice of the existence of the action, whether or not the notice includes details as to its "institution."

HISTORICAL NOTES

Effective and Applicability Provisions

1991 Acts. Section 11(a) of Pub.L. 102–198 amended subd. (c)(3) of this rule, as transmitted to the Congress by the Supreme Court pursuant to section 2074 of title 28, United States Code, to become effective on December 1, 1991.

CROSS REFERENCES

Jurisdiction, amendment to show, see 28 USCA § 1653.

Recasting of pleadings on removal of cause, see 28 USCA § 1447.

Substitution of successor to public officer by supplemental pleading, see Fed.Rules Civ.Proc. Rule 25, 28 USCA.

Time for service of pleadings, see Fed.Rules Civ.Proc. Rule 12, 28 USCA.

Rule 16. Pretrial Conferences; Scheduling; Management

(a) Purposes of a Pretrial Conference. In any action, the court may order the attorneys and any unrepresented parties to appear for one or more pretrial conferences for such purposes as:

(1) expediting disposition of the action;

(2) establishing early and continuing control so that the case will not be protracted because of lack of management;

(3) discouraging wasteful pretrial activities;

(4) improving the quality of the trial through more thorough preparation; and

(5) facilitating settlement.

(b) Scheduling.

(1) ***Scheduling Order.*** Except in categories of actions exempted by local rule, the district judge—or a magistrate judge when authorized by local rule—must issue a scheduling order:

(A) after receiving the parties' report under Rule 26(f); or

(B) after consulting with the parties' attorneys and any unrepresented parties at a scheduling conference or by telephone, mail, or other means.

(2) ***Time to Issue.*** The judge must issue the scheduling order as soon as practicable, but in any event within the earlier of 120 days after any defendant has been served with the

complaint or 90 days after any defendant has appeared.

(3) ***Contents of the Order.***

(A) *Required Contents.* The scheduling order must limit the time to join other parties, amend the pleadings, complete discovery, and file motions.

(B) *Permitted Contents.* The scheduling order may:

(i) modify the timing of disclosures under Rules 26(a) and 26(e)(1);

(ii) modify the extent of discovery;

(iii) provide for disclosure or discovery of electronically stored information;

(iv) include any agreements the parties reach for asserting claims of privilege or of protection as trial-preparation material after information is produced;

(v) set dates for pretrial conferences and for trial; and

(vi) include other appropriate matters.

(4) ***Modifying a Schedule.*** A schedule may be modified only for good cause and with the judge's consent.

(c) Attendance and Matters for Consideration at a Pretrial Conference.

(1) ***Attendance.*** A represented party must authorize at least one of its attorneys to make stipulations and admissions about all matters that can reasonably be anticipated for discussion at a pretrial conference. If appropriate, the court may require that a party or its representative be present or reasonably available by other means to consider possible settlement.

(2) ***Matters for Consideration.*** At any pretrial conference, the court may consider and take appropriate action on the following matters:

(A) formulating and simplifying the issues, and eliminating frivolous claims or defenses;

(B) amending the pleadings if necessary or desirable;

(C) obtaining admissions and stipulations about facts and documents to avoid unnecessary proof, and ruling in advance on the admissibility of evidence;

(D) avoiding unnecessary proof and cumulative evidence, and limiting the use of testimony under Federal Rule of Evidence 702;

(E) determining the appropriateness and timing of summary adjudication under Rule 56;

(F) controlling and scheduling discovery, including orders affecting disclosures and discovery under Rule 26 and Rules 29 through 37;

(G) identifying witnesses and documents, scheduling the filing and exchange of any pretrial briefs, and setting dates for further conferences and for trial;

(H) referring matters to a magistrate judge or a master;

(I) settling the case and using special procedures to assist in resolving the dispute when authorized by statute or local rule;

(J) determining the form and content of the pretrial order;

(K) disposing of pending motions;

(L) adopting special procedures for managing potentially difficult or protracted actions that may involve complex issues, multiple parties, difficult legal questions, or unusual proof problems;

(M) ordering a separate trial under Rule 42(b) of a claim, counterclaim, crossclaim, third-party claim, or particular issue;

(N) ordering the presentation of evidence early in the trial on a manageable issue that might, on the evidence, be the basis for a judgment as a matter of law under Rule 50(a) or a judgment on partial findings under Rule 52(c);

(O) establishing a reasonable limit on the time allowed to present evidence; and

(P) facilitating in other ways the just, speedy, and inexpensive disposition of the action.

(d) Pretrial Orders. After any conference under this rule, the court should issue an order reciting the action taken. This order controls the course of the action unless the court modifies it.

(e) Final Pretrial Conference and Orders. The court may hold a final pretrial conference to formulate a trial plan, including a plan to facilitate the admission of evidence. The conference must be held as close to the start of trial as is reasonable, and must be attended by at least one attorney who will conduct the trial for each party and by any unrepresented party. The court may modify the order issued after a final pretrial conference only to prevent manifest injustice.

(f) Sanctions.

(1) ***In General.*** On motion or on its own, the court may issue any just orders, including those authorized by Rule 37(b)(2)(A)(ii)-(vii), if a party or its attorney:

(A) fails to appear at a scheduling or other pretrial conference;

(B) is substantially unprepared to participate—or does not participate in good faith—in the conference; or

(C) fails to obey a scheduling or other pretrial order.

(2) ***Imposing Fees and Costs.*** Instead of or in addition to any other sanction, the court must order the party, its attorney, or both to pay the reasonable expenses—including attorney's fees—incurred because of any noncompliance with this rule, unless the noncompliance was substantially justified or other circumstances make an award of expenses unjust.

(Amended April 28, 1983, effective August 1, 1983; March 2, 1987, effective August 1, 1987; April 22, 1993, effective December 1, 1993; April 12, 2006, effective December 1, 2006; April 30, 2007, effective December 1, 2007.)

ADVISORY COMMITTEE NOTES

1937 Adoption

1. Similar rules of pre-trial procedure are now in force in Boston, Cleveland, Detroit, and Los Angeles, and a rule substantially like this one has been proposed for the urban centers of New York state. For a discussion of the successful operation of pre-trial procedure in relieving the congested condition of trial calendars of the courts in such cities and for the proposed New York plan, see *A Proposal for Minimizing Calendar Delay in Jury Cases* (Dec. 1936—published by the New York Law Society); *Pre-Trial Procedure and Administration,* Third Annual Report of the Judicial Council of the State of New York (1937), pages 207–243; *Report of the Commission on the Administration of Justice in New York State* (1934), pp. (288) to (290). See also *Pre-Trial Procedure in the Wayne Circuit Court,* Detroit, Michigan, Sixth Annual Report of the Judicial Council of Michigan (1936), pp. 63 to 75; and Sunderland, *The Theory and Practice of Pre-trial Procedure* (Dec. 1937) 36 Mich.L.Rev. 215–226, 21 J.Am.Jud. Soc. 125. Compare the English procedure known as the "summons for directions", *English Rules Under the Judicature Act* (The Annual Practice, 1937) O. 38a; and a similar procedure in New Jersey, N.J.S.A. 2:27–135, 2:27–136, 2:27–160; N.J. Supreme Court Rules, 2 N.J.Misc.Rep. (1924) 1230, Rules 94, 92, 93, 95 (the last three as amended 1933, 11 N.J.Misc.Rep. (1933) 955).

2. Compare the similar procedure under Rule 56(d) (Summary Judgment—Case Not Fully Adjudicated on Motion). Rule 12(g) (Consolidation of Motions), by requiring to some extent the consolidation of motions dealing with matters preliminary to trial, is a step in the same direction. In connection with clause (5) of this rule, see Rules 53(b) (Masters; Reference) and 53(e)(3) (Master's Report; In Jury Actions).

1983 Amendment

Introduction

Rule 16 has not been amended since the Federal Rules were promulgated in 1938. In many respects, the rule has been a success. For example, there is evidence that pretrial conferences may improve the quality of justice rendered in the federal courts by sharpening the preparation and presentation of cases, tending to eliminate trial surprise, and improving, as well as facilitating, the settlement process. See 6 Wright & Miller, *Federal Practice and Procedure:* Civil § 1522 (1971). However, in other respects particularly with regard to case management, the rule has not always been as helpful as it might have been. Thus there has been a widespread feeling that amendment is necessary to encourage pretrial management that meets the needs of modern litigation. See *Report of the National Commission for the Review of Antitrust Laws and Procedures* (1979).

Major criticism of Rule 16 has centered on the fact that its application can result in over-regulation of some cases and under-regulation of others. In simple, run-of-the-mill cases, attorneys have found pretrial requirements burdensome. It is claimed that over-administration leads to a series of mini-trials that result in a waste of an attorney's time and needless expense to a client. Pollack, *Pretrial Procedures More Effectively Handled,* 65 F.R.D. 475 (1974). This is especially likely to be true when pretrial proceedings occur long before trial. At the other end of the spectrum, the discretionary character of Rule 16 and its orientation toward a single conference late in the pretrial process has led to under-administration of complex or protracted cases. Without judicial guidance beginning shortly after institution, these cases often become mired in discovery.

Four sources of criticism of pretrial have been identified. First, conferences often are seen as a mere exchange of legalistic contentions without any real analysis of the particular case. Second, the result frequently is nothing but a formal agreement on minutiae. Third, the conferences are seen as unnecessary and time-consuming in cases that will be settled before trial. Fourth, the meetings can be ceremonial and ritualistic, having little effect on the trial and being of minimal value, particularly when the attorneys attending the sessions are not the ones who will try the case or lack authority to enter into binding stipulations. See generally *McCargo v. Hedrick,* 545 F.2d 393 (4th Cir.1976); Pollack, *Pretrial Procedures More Effectively Handled,* 65 F.R.D. 475 (1974); Rosenberg, *The Pretrial Conference and Effective Justice* 45 (1964).

There also have been difficulties with the pretrial orders that issue following Rule 16 conferences. When an order is entered far in advance of trial, some issues may not be properly formulated. Counsel naturally are cautious and often try to preserve as many options as possible. If the judge who tries the case did not conduct the conference, he could find it difficult to determine exactly what was agreed to at the conference. But any insistence on a detailed order may be too burdensome, depending on the nature or posture of the case.

Given the significant changes in federal civil litigation since 1938 that are not reflected in Rule 16, it has been extensively rewritten and expanded to meet the challenges of modern litigation. Empirical studies reveal that when a trial judge intervenes personally at an early stage to assume judicial control over a case and to schedule dates for completion by the parties of the principal pretrial steps, the case is disposed of by settlement or trial more efficiently and with less cost and delay than when the parties are left to their own devices. Flanders, *Case Management and Court Management in*

United States District Courts 17, Federal Judicial Center (1977). Thus, the rule mandates a pretrial scheduling order. However, although scheduling and pretrial conferences are encouraged in appropriate cases, they are not mandated.

Discussion

Subdivision (a); Pretrial Conferences; Objectives. The amended rule makes scheduling and case management an express goal of pretrial procedure. This is done in Rule 16(a) by shifting the emphasis away from a conference focused solely on the trial and toward a process of judicial management that embraces the entire pretrial phase, especially motions and discovery. In addition, the amendment explicitly recognizes some of the objectives of pretrial conferences and the powers that many courts already have assumed. Rule 16 thus will be a more accurate reflection of actual practice.

Subdivision (b); Scheduling and Planning. The most significant change in Rule 16 is the mandatory scheduling order described in Rule 16(b), which is based in part on Wisconsin Civil Procedure Rule 802.10. The idea of scheduling orders is not new. It has been used by many federal courts. See, *e.g.*, Southern District of Indiana, Local Rule 19.

Although a mandatory scheduling order encourages the court to become involved in case management early in the litigation, it represents a degree of judicial involvement that is not warranted in many cases. Thus, subdivision (b) permits each district court to promulgate a local rule under Rule 83 exempting certain categories of cases in which the burdens of scheduling orders exceed the administrative efficiencies that would be gained. See Eastern District of Virginia, Local Rule 12(1). Logical candidates for this treatment include social security disability matters, habeas corpus petitions, forfeitures, and reviews of certain administrative actions.

A scheduling conference may be requested either by the judge, a magistrate when authorized by district court rule, or a party within 120 days after the summons and complaint are filed. If a scheduling conference is not arranged within that time and the case is not exempted by local rule, a scheduling order must be issued under Rule 16(b), after some communication with the parties, which may be by telephone or mail rather than in person. The use of the term "judge" in subdivision (b) reflects the Advisory Committee's judgment that it is preferable that this task should be handled by a district judge rather than a magistrate, except when the magistrate is acting under 28 U.S.C. § 636(c). While personal supervision by the trial judge is preferred, the rule, in recognition of the impracticality or difficulty of complying with such a requirement in some districts, authorizes a district by local rule to delegate the duties to a magistrate. In order to formulate a practicable scheduling order, the judge, or a magistrate when authorized by district court rule, and attorneys are required to develop a timetable for the matters listed in Rule 16(b)(1)–(3). As indicated in Rule 16(b)(4)–(5), the order may also deal with a wide range of other matters. The rule is phrased permissively as to clauses (4) and (5), however, because scheduling these items at an early point may not be feasible or appropriate. Even though subdivision (b) relates only to scheduling, there is no reason why some of the procedural matters listed in Rule 16(c) cannot be addressed at the same time, at least when a scheduling conference is held.

Item (1) assures that at some point both the parties and the pleadings will be fixed, by setting a time within which joinder of parties shall be completed and the pleadings amended.

Item (2) requires setting time limits for interposing various motions that otherwise might be used as stalling techniques.

Item (3) deals with the problem of procrastination and delay by attorneys in a context in which scheduling is especially important-discovery. Scheduling the completion of discovery can serve some of the same functions as the conference described in Rule 26(f).

Item (4) refers to setting dates for conferences and for trial. Scheduling multiple pretrial conferences may well be desirable if the case is complex and the court believes that a more elaborate pretrial structure, such as that described in the *Manual for Complex Litigation*, should be employed. On the other hand, only one pretrial conference may be necessary in an uncomplicated case.

As long as the case is not exempted by local rule, the court must issue a written scheduling order even if no scheduling conference is called. The order, like pretrial orders under the former rule and those under new Rule 16(c), normally will "control the subsequent course of the action." See Rule 16(e). After consultation with the attorneys for the parties and any unrepresented parties-a formal motion is not necessary-the court may modify the schedule on a showing of good cause if it cannot reasonably be met despite the diligence of the party seeking the extension. Since the scheduling order is entered early in the litigation, this standard seems more appropriate than a "manifest injustice" or "substantial hardship" test. Otherwise, a fear that extensions will not be granted may encourage counsel to request the longest possible periods for completing pleading, joinder, and discovery. Moreover, changes in the court's calendar sometimes will oblige the judge or magistrate when authorized by district court rule to modify the scheduling order.

The district courts undoubtedly will develop several prototype scheduling orders for different types of cases. In addition, when no formal conference is held, the court may obtain scheduling information by telephone, mail, or otherwise. In many instances this will result in a scheduling order better suited to the individual case than a standard order, without taking the time that would be required by a formal conference.

Rule 16(b) assures that the judge will take some early control over the litigation, even when its character does not warrant holding a scheduling conference. Despite the fact that the process of preparing a scheduling order does not always bring the attorneys and judge together, the fixing of time limits serves

> to stimulate litigants to narrow the areas of inquiry and advocacy to those they believe are truly relevant and material. Time limits not only compress the amount of time for litigation, they should also reduce the amount of resources invested in litigation. Litigants are forced to establish discovery priorities and thus to do the most important work first.

Report of the National Commission for the Review of Antitrust Laws and Procedures 28 (1979).

Thus, except in exempted cases, the judge or a magistrate when authorized by district court rule will have taken some action in every case within 120 days after the complaint is filed that notifies the attorneys that the case will be moving toward trial. Subdivision (b) is reenforced by subdivision (f), which makes it clear that the sanctions for violating a scheduling order are the same as those for violating a pretrial order.

Subdivision (c); Subjects to be Discussed at Pretrial Conferences. This subdivision expands upon the list of things that may be discussed at a pretrial conference that appeared in original Rule 16. The intention is to encourage better planning and management of litigation. Increased judicial control during the pretrial process accelerates the processing and termination of cases. Flanders, *Case Management and Court Management in United States District Courts,* 39 Federal Judicial Center (1977). See also *Report of the National Commission for the Review of Antitrust Laws and Procedures* (1979).

The reference in Rule 16(c)(1) to "formulation" is intended to clarify and confirm the court's power to identify the litigable issues. It has been added in the hope of promoting efficiency and conserving judicial resources by identifying the real issues prior to trial, thereby saving time and expense for everyone. See generally *Meadow Gold Prods. Co. v. Wright,* 278 F.2d 867 (D.C.Cir.1960). The notion is emphasized by expressly authorizing the elimination of frivolous claims or defenses at a pretrial conference. There is no reason to require that this await a formal motion for summary judgment. Nor is there any reason for the court to wait for the parties to initiate the process called for in Rule 16(c)(1).

The timing of any attempt at issue formulation is a matter of judicial discretion. In relatively simple cases it may not be necessary or may take the form of a stipulation between counsel or a request by the court that counsel work together to draft a proposed order.

Counsel bear a substantial responsibility for assisting the court in identifying the factual issues worthy of trial. If counsel fail to identify an issue for the court, the right to have the issue tried is waived. Although an order specifying the issues is intended to be binding, it may be amended at trial to avoid manifest injustice. See Rule 16(e). However, the rule's effectiveness depends on the court employing its discretion sparingly.

Clause (6) acknowledges the widespread availability and use of magistrates. The corresponding provision in the original rule referred only to masters and limited the function of the reference to the making of "findings to be used as evidence" in a case to be tried to a jury. The new text is not limited and broadens the potential use of a magistrate to that permitted by the Magistrate's Act.

Clause (7) explicitly recognizes that it has become commonplace to discuss settlement at pretrial conferences. Since it obviously eases crowded court dockets and results in savings to the litigants and the judicial system, settlement should be facilitated at as early a stage of the litigation as possible. Although it is not the purpose of Rule 16(b)(7) to impose settlement negotiations on unwilling litigants, it is believed that providing a neutral forum for discussing the subject might foster it. See Moore's *Federal Practice* ¶ 16.17; 6 Wright & Miller, *Federal Practice and Procedure: Civil* § 1522 (1971). For instance, a judge to whom a case has been assigned may arrange, on his own motion or at a party's request, to have settlement conferences handled by another member of the court or by a magistrate. The rule does not make settlement conferences mandatory because they would be a waste of time in many cases. See Flanders, *Case Management and Court Management in the United States District Courts,* 39 Federal Judicial Center (1977). Requests for a conference from a party indicating a willingness to talk settlement normally should be honored, unless thought to be frivolous or dilatory.

A settlement conference is appropriate at any time. It may be held in conjunction with a pretrial or discovery conference, although various objectives of pretrial management, such as moving the case toward trial, may not always be compatible with settlement negotiations, and thus a separate settlement conference may be desirable. See 6 Wright & Miller, *Federal Practice and Procedure: Civil* § 1522, at p. 571 (1971).

In addition to settlement, Rule 16(c)(7) refers to exploring the use of procedures other than litigation to resolve the dispute. This includes urging the litigants to employ adjudicatory techniques outside the courthouse. See, for example, the experiment described in *Green, Marks & Olson, Settling Large Case Litigation: An Alternative Approach,* 11 Loyola of L.A.L.Rev. 493 (1978).

Rule 16(c)(10) authorizes the use of special pretrial procedures to expedite the adjudication of potentially difficult or protracted cases. Some district courts obviously have done so for many years. See Rubin, *The Managed Calendar: Some Pragmatic Suggestions About Achieving the Just, Speedy and Inexpensive Determination of Civil Cases in Federal Courts,* 4 Just.Sys.J. 135 (1976). Clause 10 provides an explicit authorization for such procedures and encourages their use. No particular techniques have been described; the Committee felt that flexibility and experience are the keys to efficient management of complex cases. Extensive guidance is offered in such documents as the *Manual for Complex Litigation.*

The rule simply identifies characteristics that make a case a strong candidate for special treatment. The four mentioned are illustrative, not exhaustive, and overlap to some degree. But experience has shown that one or more of them will be present in every protracted or difficult case and it seems desirable to set them out. See Kendig, *Procedures for Management of Non-Routine Cases,* 3 Hofstra L.Rev. 701 (1975).

The last sentence of subdivision (c) is new. See Wisconsin Civil Procedure Rule 802.11(2). It has been added to meet one of the criticisms of the present practice described earlier and insure proper preconference preparation so that the meeting is more than a ceremonial or ritualistic event. The reference to "authority" is not intended to insist upon the ability to settle the litigation. Nor should the rule be read to encourage the judge conducting the conference to compel attorneys to enter into stipulations or to make admissions that they consider to be unreasonable, that touch on matters that could not normally have been anticipated to arise at the conference, or on subjects of a dimension that normally require prior consultation with and approval from the client.

Subdivision (d); Final Pretrial Conference. This provision has been added to make it clear that the time between any final pretrial conference (which in a simple case may be the **only** pretrial conference) and trial should be as short as possible to be certain that the litigants make substantial progress with the case and avoid the inefficiency of having that preparation repeated when there is a delay between the last pretrial conference and trial. An optimum time of 10 days to two weeks has been suggested by one federal judge. Rubin, *The Managed Calendar: Some Pragmatic Suggestions About Achieving the Just, Speedy and Inexpensive Determination of Civil Cases in Federal Courts,* 4 Just. Sys.J. 135, 141 (1976). The Committee, however, concluded that it would be inappropriate to fix a precise time in the rule, given the numerous variables that could bear on the matter. Thus the timing has been left to the court's discretion.

At least one of the attorneys who will conduct the trial for each party must be present at the final pretrial conference. At this late date there should be no doubt as to which attorney or attorneys this will be. Since the agreements and stipulations made at this final conference will control the trial, the presence of lawyers who will be involved in it is especially useful to assist the judge in structuring the case, and to lead to a more effective trial.

Subdivision (e); Pretrial Orders. Rule 16(e) does not substantially change the portion of the original rule dealing with pretrial orders. The purpose of an order is to guide the course of the litigation and the language of the original rule making that clear has been retained. No compelling reason has been found for major revision, especially since this portion of the rule has been interpreted and clarified by over forty years of judicial decisions with comparatively little difficulty. See 6 Wright & Miller, *Federal Practice and Procedure: Civil* §§ 1521–30 (1971). Changes in language therefore have been kept to a minimum to avoid confusion.

Since the amended rule encourages more extensive pretrial management than did the original, two or more conferences may be held in many cases. The language of Rule 16(e) recognizes this possibility and the corresponding need to issue more than one pretrial order in a single case.

Once formulated, pretrial orders should not be changed lightly; but total inflexibility is undesirable. See, *e.g., Clark v. Pennsylvania R.R. Co.,* 328 F.2d 591 (2d Cir.1964). The exact words used to describe the standard for amending the pretrial order probably are less important than the meaning given them in practice. By not imposing any limitation on the ability to modify a pretrial order, the rule reflects the reality that in any process of continuous management, what is done at one conference may have to be altered at the next. In the case of the final pretrial order, however, a more stringent standard is called for and the words "to prevent manifest injustice," which appeared in the original rule, have been retained. They have the virtue of familiarity and adequately describe the restraint the trial judge should exercise.

Many local rules make the plaintiff's attorney responsible for drafting a proposed pretrial order, either before or after the conference. Others allow the court to appoint any of the attorneys to perform the task, and others leave it to the court. See Note, *Pretrial Conference: A Critical Examination of Local Rules Adopted by Federal District Courts,* 64 Va.L.Rev. 467 (1978). Rule 16 has never addressed this matter. Since there is no consensus about which method of drafting the order works best and there is no reason to believe that nationwide uniformity is needed, the rule has been left silent on the point. See *Handbook for Effective Pretrial Procedure,* 37 F.R.D. 225 (1964).

Subdivision (f); Sanctions. Original Rule 16 did not mention the sanctions that might be imposed for failing to comply with the rule. However, courts have not hesitated to enforce it by appropriate measures. See, e.g., *Link v. Wabash R. Co.,* 370 U.S. 628 (1962) (district court's dismissal under Rule 41(b) after plaintiff's attorney failed to appear at a pretrial conference upheld); *Admiral Theatre Corp. v. Douglas Theatre,* 585 F.2d 877 (8th Cir.1978) (district court has discretion to exclude exhibits or refuse to permit the testimony of a witness not listed prior to trial in contravention of its pretrial order).

To reflect that existing practice, and to obviate dependence upon Rule 41(b) or the court's inherent power to regulate litigation, *cf. Societe Internationale Pour Participations Industrielles et Commerciales, S.A. v. Rogers,* 357 U.S. 197 (1958), Rule 16(f) expressly provides for imposing sanctions on disobedient or recalcitrant parties, their attorneys, or both in four types of situations. Rodes, Ripple & Mooney, *Sanctions Imposable for Violations of the Federal Rules of Civil Procedure* 65–67, 80–84, Federal Judicial Center (1981). Furthermore, explicit reference to sanctions reenforces the rule's intention to encourage forceful judicial management.

Rule 16(f) incorporates portions of Rule 37(b)(2), which prescribes sanctions for failing to make discovery. This should facilitate application of Rule 16(f), since courts and lawyers already are familiar with the Rule 37 standards. Among the sanctions authorized by the new subdivision are: preclusion order, striking a pleading, staying the proceeding, default judgment, contempt, and charging a party, his attorney, or both with the expenses, including attorney's fees, caused by noncompliance. The contempt sanction, however, is only available for a violation of a court order. The references in Rule 16(f) are not exhaustive.

As is true under Rule 37(b)(2), the imposition of sanctions may be sought by either the court or a party. In addition, the court has discretion to impose whichever sanction it feels is appropriate under the circumstances. Its action is reviewable under the abuse-of-discretion standard. See *National Hockey League v. Metropolitan Hockey Club, Inc.,* 427 U.S. 639 (1976).

1987 Amendment

The amendments are technical. No substantive change is intended.

1993 Amendments

Subdivision (b). One purpose of this amendment is to provide a more appropriate deadline for the initial scheduling order required by the rule. The former rule directed that the order be entered within 120 days from the filing of the complaint. This requirement has created problems because Rule 4(m) allows 120 days for service and ordinarily at least one defendant should be available to participate in the process of formulating the scheduling order. The revision provides that the order is to be entered within 90 days after the date a defendant first appears (whether by answer or by a motion under Rule 12) or, if earlier (as may occur in some actions against the United States or if service is waived under Rule 4), within 120 days after service of the complaint on a defendant. The longer time provided by the revision is not intended to encourage unnecessary delays in entering the scheduling order. Indeed, in most cases the order can and should be entered at a much earlier date. Rather, the additional time is intended to alleviate problems in multi-defendant cases and should ordinarily be adequate to enable participation by all defendants initially named in the action.

In many cases the scheduling order can and should be entered before this deadline. However, when setting a scheduling conference, the court should take into account the effect this setting will have in establishing deadlines for the parties to meet under revised Rule 26(f) and to exchange information under revised Rule 26(a)(1). While the parties are expected to stipulate to additional time for making their disclosures when warranted by the circumstances, a scheduling conference held before defendants have had time to learn much about the case may result in diminishing the value of the Rule 26(f) meeting, the parties' proposed discovery plan, and indeed the conference itself.

New paragraph (4) has been added to highlight that it will frequently be desirable for the scheduling order to include provisions relating to the timing of disclosures under Rule 26(a). While the initial disclosures required by Rule 26(a)(1) will ordinarily have been made before entry of the scheduling order, the timing and sequence for disclosure of expert testimony and of the witnesses and exhibits to be used at trial should be tailored to the circumstances of the case and is a matter that should be considered at the initial scheduling conference. Similarly, the scheduling order might contain provisions modifying the extent of discovery (*e.g.,* number and length of depositions) otherwise permitted under these rules or by a local rule.

The report from the attorneys concerning their meeting and proposed discovery plan, as required by revised Rule 26(f), should be submitted to the court before the scheduling order is entered. Their proposals, particularly regarding matters on which they agree, should be of substantial value to the court in setting the timing and limitations on discovery and should reduce the time of the court needed to conduct a meaningful conference under Rule 16(b). As under the prior rule, while a scheduling order is mandated, a scheduling conference is not. However, in view of the benefits to be derived from the litigants and a judicial officer meeting in person, a Rule 16(b) conference should, to the extent practicable, be held in all cases that will involve discovery.

This subdivision, as well as subdivision (c)(8), also is revised to reflect the new title of United States Magistrate Judges pursuant to the Judicial Improvements Act of 1990.

Subdivision (c). The primary purposes of the changes in subdivision (c) are to call attention to the opportunities for structuring of trial under Rules 42, 50, and 52 and to eliminate questions that have occasionally been raised regarding the authority of the court to make appropriate orders designed either to facilitate settlement or to provide for an efficient and economical trial. The prefatory language of this subdivision is revised to clarify the court's power to enter appropriate orders at a conference notwithstanding the objection of a party. Of course settlement is dependent upon agreement by the parties and, indeed, a conference is most effective and productive when the parties participate in a spirit of cooperation and mindful of their responsibilities under Rule 1.

Paragraph (4) is revised to clarify that in advance of trial the court may address the need for, and possible limitations on, the use of expert testimony under Rule 702 of the Federal Rules of Evidence. Even when proposed expert testimony might be admissible under the standards of Rules 403 and 702 of the evidence rules, the court may preclude or limit such testimony if the cost to the litigants—which may include the cost to adversaries of securing testimony on the same subjects by other experts—would be unduly expensive given the needs of the case and the other evidence available at trial.

Paragraph (5) is added (and the remaining paragraphs renumbered) in recognition that use of Rule 56 to avoid or reduce the scope of trial is a topic that can, and often should, be considered at a pretrial conference. Renumbered paragraph (11) enables the court to rule on pending motions for summary adjudication that are ripe for decision at the time of the conference. Often, however, the potential use of Rule 56 is a matter that arises from discussions during a conference. The court may then call for motions to be filed.

Paragraph (6) is added to emphasize that a major objective of pretrial conferences should be to consider appropriate controls on the extent and timing of discovery. In many cases the court should also specify the times and sequence for disclosure of written reports from experts under revised Rule 26(a)(2)(B) and perhaps direct changes in the types of experts from whom written reports are required. Consideration should also be given to possible changes in the timing or form of the disclosure of trial witnesses and documents under Rule 26(a)(3).

Paragraph (9) is revised to describe more accurately the various procedures that, in addition to traditional settlement conferences, may be helpful in settling litigation. Even if a case cannot immediately be settled, the judge and attorneys can explore possible use of alternative procedures such as mini-trials, summary jury trials, mediation, neutral evaluation, and nonbinding arbitration that can lead to consensual resolution of the dispute without a full trial on the merits. The rule acknowledges the presence of statutes and local rules or plans that may authorize use of some of these procedures even when not agreed to by the parties. See 28 U.S.C. §§ 473(a)(6), 473(b)(4), 651–58; Section 104(b)(2), Pub.L. 101–650. The rule does not attempt to resolve questions as to the extent a court would be authorized to require such proceedings as an exercise of its inherent powers.

The amendment of paragraph (9) should be read in conjunction with the sentence added to the end of subdivision (c), authorizing the court to direct that, in appropriate cases, a responsible representative of the parties be present or available by telephone during a conference in order to discuss possible settlement of the case. The sentence refers to participation by a party or its representative. Whether this would be the individual party, an officer of a corporate party, a representative from an insurance carrier, or someone else would depend on the circumstances. Particularly in litigation in which governmental agencies or large amounts of money are involved, there may be no one with on-the-spot settlement authority, and the most that should be expected is access to a person who would have a major role in submitting a recommendation to the body or board with ultimate decision-making responsibility. The selection of the appropriate representative should ordinarily be left to the party and its counsel. Finally, it should be noted that the unwillingness of a party to be available, even by telephone, for a settlement conference may be a clear signal that the time and expense involved in pursuing settlement is likely to be unproductive and that personal participation by the parties should not be required.

The explicit authorization in the rule to require personal participation in the manner stated is not intended to limit the reasonable exercise of the court's inherent powers, *e.g., G. Heileman Brewing Co. v. Joseph Oat Corp.*, 871 F.2d 648 (7th Cir.1989), or its power to require party participation under the Civil Justice Reform Act of 1990. See 28 U.S.C. § 473(b)(5) (civil justice expense and delay reduction plans adopted by district courts may include requirement that representatives "with authority to bind [parties] in settlement discussions" be available during settlement conferences).

New paragraphs (13) and (14) are added to call attention to the opportunities for structuring of trial under Rule 42 and under revised Rules 50 and 52.

Paragraph (15) is also new. It supplements the power of the court to limit the extent of evidence under Rules 403 and 611(a) of the Federal Rules of Evidence, which typically would be invoked as a result of developments during trial. Limits on the length of trial established at a conference in advance of trial can provide the parties with a better opportunity to determine priorities and exercise selectivity in presenting evidence than when limits are imposed during trial. Any such limits must be reasonable under the circumstances, and ordinarily the court should impose them only after receiving appropriate submissions from the parties outlining the nature of the testimony expected to be presented through various witnesses, and the expected duration of direct and cross-examination.

2006 Amendment

The amendment to Rule 16(b) is designed to alert the court to the possible need to address the handling of discovery of electronically stored information early in the litigation if such discovery is expected to occur. Rule 26(f) is amended to direct the parties to discuss discovery of electronically stored information if such discovery is contemplated in the action. Form 35 is amended to call for a report to the court about the results of this discussion. In many instances, the court's involvement early in the litigation will help avoid difficulties that might otherwise arise.

Rule 16(b) is also amended to include among the topics that may be addressed in the scheduling order any agreements that the parties reach to facilitate discovery by minimizing the risk of waiver of privilege or work-product protection. Rule 26(f) is amended to add to the discovery plan the parties' proposal for the court to enter a case-management or other order adopting such an agreement. The parties may agree to various arrangements. For example, they may agree to initial provision of requested materials without waiver of privilege or protection to enable the party seeking production to designate the materials desired or protection for actual production, with the privilege review of only those materials to follow. Alternatively, they may agree that if privileged or protected information is inadvertently produced, the producing party may by timely notice assert the privilege or protection and obtain return of the materials without waiver. Other arrangements are possible. In most circumstances, a party who receives information under such an arrangement cannot assert that production of the information waived a claim of privilege or of protection as trial-preparation material.

An order that includes the parties' agreement may be helpful in avoiding delay and excessive cost in discovery. *See Manual for Complex Litigation* (4th) § 11.446. Rule 16(b)(6) recognizes the propriety of including such agreements in the court's order. The rule does not provide the court with authority to enter such a case-management or other order without party agreement, or limit the court's authority to act on motion.

2007 Amendment

The language of Rule 16 has been amended as part of the general restyling of the Civil Rules to make them more easily understood and to make style and terminology consistent throughout the rules. These changes are intended to be stylistic only.

When a party or its representative is not present, it is enough to be reasonably available by any suitable means, whether telephone or other communication device.

HISTORICAL NOTES

Change of Name

Reference to United States magistrate or to magistrate deemed to refer to United States magistrate judge pursuant to section 321 of Pub.L. 101–650, set out as a note under section 631 of this title.

TITLE IV. PARTIES

Rule 17. Plaintiff and Defendant; Capacity; Public Officers

(a) Real Party in Interest.

(1) ***Designation in General.*** An action must be prosecuted in the name of the real party in interest. The following may sue in their own names without joining the person for whose benefit the action is brought:

(A) an executor;

(B) an administrator;

(C) a guardian;

(D) a bailee;

(E) a trustee of an express trust;

(F) a party with whom or in whose name a contract has been made for another's benefit; and

(G) a party authorized by statute.

(2) ***Action in the Name of the United States for Another's Use or Benefit.*** When a federal statute so provides, an action for another's use or benefit must be brought in the name of the United States.

(3) ***Joinder of the Real Party in Interest.*** The court may not dismiss an action for failure to prosecute in the name of the real party in interest until, after an objection, a reasonable time has been allowed for the real party in interest to ratify, join, or be substituted into the action. After ratification, joinder, or substitution, the action proceeds as if it had been originally commenced by the real party in interest.

(b) **Capacity to Sue or Be Sued.** Capacity to sue or be sued is determined as follows:

(1) for an individual who is not acting in a representative capacity, by the law of the individual's domicile;

(2) for a corporation, by the law under which it was organized; and

(3) for all other parties, by the law of the state where the court is located, except that:

(A) a partnership or other unincorporated association with no such capacity under that state's law may sue or be sued in its common name to enforce a substantive right existing under the United States Constitution or laws; and

(B) *28 U.S.C.* §§ 754 and 959(a) govern the capacity of a receiver appointed by a United States court to sue or be sued in a United States court.

(c) **Minor or Incompetent Person.**

(1) ***With a Representative.*** The following representatives may sue or defend on behalf of a minor or an incompetent person:

(A) a general guardian;

(B) a committee;

(C) a conservator; or

(D) a like fiduciary.

(2) ***Without a Representative.*** A minor or an incompetent person who does not have a duly appointed representative may sue by a next friend or by a guardian ad litem. The court must appoint a guardian ad litem—or issue another appropriate order—to protect a minor or incompetent person who is unrepresented in an action.

(d) **Public Officer's Title and Name.** A public officer who sues or is sued in an official capacity may be designated by official title rather than by name, but the court may order that the officer's name be added.

(Amended December 27, 1946, effective March 19, 1948; December 29, 1948, effective October 20, 1949; February 28, 1966, effective July 1, 1966; March 2, 1987, effective August 1, 1987; April 25, 1988, effective August 1, 1988; amended by Pub.L. 100–690, Title VII, § 7049, November 18, 1988, 102 Stat. 4401 (although amendment by Pub.L. 100–690 could not be executed due to prior amendment by Court order which made the same change effective August 1, 1988); April 30, 2007, effective December 1, 2007.)

ADVISORY COMMITTEE NOTES

1937 Adoption

Note to Subdivision (a). The real party in interest provision, except for the last clause which is new, is taken verbatim from [former] Equity Rule 37 (Parties Generally—Intervention), except that the word "expressly" has been omitted. For similar provisions see N.Y.C.P.A., (1937) § 210; Wyo.Rev.Stat.Ann. (1931) §§ 89–501, 89–502, 89–503; *English Rules Under the Judicature Act* (The Annual Practice, 1937) O. 16, r. 8. See, also Equity Rule 41 (Suit to Execute Trusts of Will—Heir as Party). For examples of statutes of the United States providing particularly for an action for the use or benefit of another in the name of the United States, see U.S.C., Title 40, § 270b [see now 40 U.S.C.A. § 3133(b)] (Suit by persons furnishing labor and material for work on public building contracts * * * may sue on a payment bond, "in the name of the United States for the use of the person suing"); and U.S.C., Title 25, § 201 (Penalties under laws relating to Indians—how recovered). Compare U.S.C., Title 26, Int.Rev.Code [1939], § 3745(c) [former § 1645(c)] (Suits for penalties, fines, and forfeitures, under this title, where not otherwise provided for, to be in name of United States).

Note to Subdivision (b). For capacity see generally Clark and Moore, *New Federal Civil Procedure*—II. Pleadings and Parties, 44 Yale L.J. 1291, 1312–1317 (1935) and specifically *Coppedge v. Clinton,* 72 F.2d 531 (C.C.A.10th, 1934) (natural person); *David Lupton's Sons Co. v. Automobile Club of America,* 225 U.S. 489, 32 S.Ct. 711, 56 L.Ed. 1177, Ann.Cas.1914A, 699 (1912) (corporation); *Puerto Rico v. Russell & Co.,* 288 U.S. 476, 53 S.Ct. 447, 77 L.Ed. 903 (1933) (unincorporated assn.); *United Mine Workers of America v. Coronado Coal Co.,* 259 U.S. 344, 42 S.Ct. 570, 66 L.Ed. 975, 27 A.L.R. 762 (1922) (federal substantive right enforced against unincorporated association by suit against the association in its common name without naming all its members as parties). This rule follows the existing law as to such associations, as declared in the case last cited above. Compare *Moffat Tunnel League v. United States,* 289 U.S. 113, 53 S.Ct. 543, 77 L.Ed. 1069 (1933). See note to Rule 23, clause (1).

Note to Subdivision (c). The provision for infants and incompetent persons is substantially former Equity Rule 70 (Suits by or Against Incompetents) with slight additions. Compare the more detailed English provisions, *English Rules Under the Judicature Act* (The Annual Practice, 1937) O. 16, r.r. 16–21.

1946 Amendment

Note. The new matter [in subdivision (b)] makes clear the controlling character of Rule 66 regarding suits by or against a federal receiver in a federal court.

1948 Amendment

The amendment effective October 20, 1949, deleted the words "Rule 66" at the end of subdivision (b) and substituted the words "Title 28, U.S.C., §§ 754 and 959(a)".

1966 Amendment

The minor change in the text of the rule is designed to make it clear that the specific instances enumerated are not exceptions to, but illustrations of, the rule. These illustrations, of course, carry no negative implication to the effect that there are not other instances of recognition as the real party in interest of one whose standing as such may be in doubt. The enumeration is simply of cases in which there might be substantial doubt as to the issue but for the specific enumeration. There are other potentially arguable cases that are not excluded by the enumeration. For example, the enumeration states that the promisee in a contract for the benefit of a third party may sue as real party in interest; it does not say, because it is obvious, that the third-party beneficiary may sue (when the applicable law gives him that right.)

The rule adds to the illustrative list of real parties in interest a bailee—meaning, of course, a bailee suing on behalf of the bailor with respect to the property bailed. (When the possessor of property other than the owner sues for an invasion of the possessory interest he is the real party in interest.) The word "bailee" is added primarily to preserve the admiralty practice whereby the owner of a vessel as bailee of the cargo, or the master of the vessel as bailee of both vessel and cargo, sues for damage to either property interest or both. But there is no reason to limit such a provision to maritime situations. The owner of a warehouse in which household furniture is stored is equally entitled to sue on behalf of the numerous owners of the furniture stored. Cf. *Gulf Oil Corp. v. Gilbert*, 330 U.S. 501 (1947).

The provision that no action shall be dismissed on the ground that it is not prosecuted in the name of the real party in interest until a reasonable time has been allowed, after the objection has been raised, for ratification, substitution, etc., is added simply in the interests of justice. In its origin the rule concerning the real party in interest was permissive in purpose: it was designed to allow an assignee to sue in his own name. That having been accomplished, the modern function of the rule in its negative aspect is simply to protect the defendant against a subsequent action by the party actually entitled to recover, and to insure generally that the judgment will have its proper effect as res judicata.

This provision keeps pace with the law as it is actually developing. Modern decisions are inclined to be lenient when an honest mistake has been made in choosing the party in whose name the action is to be filed—in both maritime and nonmaritime cases. See *Levinson v. Deupree*, 345 U.S. 648 (1953); *Link Aviation, Inc. v. Downs*, 325 F.2d 613 (D.C.Cir. 1963). The provision should not be misunderstood or distorted. It is intended to prevent forfeiture when determination of the proper party to sue is difficult or when an understandable mistake has been made. It does not mean, for example, that, following an airplane crash in which all aboard were killed, an action may be filed in the name of John Doe (a fictitious person), as personal representative of Richard Roe (another fictitious person), in the hope that at a later time the attorney filing the action may substitute the real name of the real personal representative of a real victim, and have the benefit of suspension of the limitation period. It does not even mean, when an action is filed by the personal representative of John Smith, of Buffalo, in the good faith belief that he was aboard the flight, that upon discovery that Smith is alive and well, having missed the fatal flight, the representative of James Brown, of San Francisco, an actual victim, can be substituted to take advantage of the suspension of the limitation period. It is, in cases of this sort, intended to insure against forfeiture and injustice—in short, to codify in broad terms the salutary principle of *Levinson v. Deupree*, 345 U.S. 648 (1953), and *Link Aviation, Inc. v. Downs*, 325 F.2d 613 (D.C.Cir. 1963).

1987 Amendment

The amendments are technical. No substantive change is intended.

1988 Amendment

The amendment is technical. No substantive change is intended.

2007 Amendment

The language of Rule 17 has been amended as part of the general restyling of the Civil Rules to make them more easily understood and to make style and terminology consistent throughout the rules. These changes are intended to be stylistic only.

Rule 17(d) incorporates the provisions of former Rule 25(d)(2), which fit better with Rule 17.

HISTORICAL NOTES

Revision Notes and Legislative Reports

1988 Acts. For Related Reports, see 1988 U.S. Code Cong. and Adm.News, p. 5937.

CROSS REFERENCES

Action by—

One or more on behalf of class, see Fed.Rules Civ.Proc. Rule 23, 28 USCA.

United States for use of materialmen on public building contracts, see 40 USCA § 3133(b).

Perpetuation of testimony of minor or incompetent, see Fed.Rules Civ.Proc. Rule 27, 28 USCA.

Rule 18. Joinder of Claims

(a) In General. A party asserting a claim, counterclaim, crossclaim, or third-party claim may join, as independent or alternative claims, as many claims as it has against an opposing party.

(b) Joinder of Contingent Claims. A party may join two claims even though one of them is contingent on the disposition of the other; but the court may grant relief only in accordance with the parties' relative substantive rights. In particular, a plaintiff may state a claim for money and a claim to set aside a conveyance that is fraudulent as to that plaintiff, without first obtaining a judgment for the money.

(Amended February 28, 1966, effective July 1, 1966; March 2, 1987, effective August 1, 1987; April 30, 2007, effective December 1, 2007.)

ADVISORY COMMITTEE NOTES

1937 Adoption

Note to Subdivision (a). 1. Recent development, both in code and common law states, has been toward unlimited joinder of actions. See Ill.Rev.Stat. (1937) ch. 110, § 168; N.J.S.A. 2:27–37, as modified by N.J.Sup.Ct.Rules, Rule 21, 2 N.J.Misc. 1208 (1924); N.Y.C.P.A. (1937) § 258 as amended by Laws of 1935, ch. 339.

2. This provision for joinder of actions has been patterned upon [former] Equity Rule 26 (Joinder of Causes of Action) and broadened to include multiple parties. Compare the English practice, *English Rules Under the Judicature Act* (The Annual Practice, 1937) O. 18, r.r. 1–9 (noting rules 1 and 6). The earlier American codes set forth classes of joinder, following the now abandoned New York rule. See N.Y.C.P.A. § 258 before amended in 1935; Compare Kan. Gen.Stat.Ann. (1935) § 60–601; Wis.Stat.(1935) § 263.04 for the more liberal practice.

3. The provisions of this rule for the joinder of claims are subject to Rule 82 (Jurisdiction and Venue Unaffected). For the jurisdictional aspects of joinder of claims, see Shulman and Jaegerman, *Some Jurisdictional Limitations on Federal Procedure* (1936), 45 Yale L.J. 393, 397–410. For separate trials of joined claims, see Rule 42(b).

Note to Subdivision (b). This rule is inserted to make it clear that in a single action a party should be accorded all the relief to which he is entitled regardless of whether it is legal or equitable or both. This necessarily includes a deficiency judgment in foreclosure actions formerly provided for in [former] Equity Rule 10 (Decree for Deficiency in Foreclosures, Etc.). In respect to fraudulent conveyances the rule changes the former rule requiring a prior judgment against the owner (*Braun v. American Laundry Mach. Co.*, 56 F.2d 197 (S.D.N.Y. 1932)) to conform to the provisions of the Uniform Fraudulent Conveyance Act, §§ 9 and 10. See McLaughlin, *Application of the Uniform Fraudulent Conveyance Act*, 46 Harv.L.Rev. 404, 444 (1933).

1966 Amendment

The Rules "proceed upon the theory that no inconvenience can result from the joinder of any two or more matters in the pleadings, but only from trying two or more matters together which have little or nothing in common." Sunderland, *The New Federal Rules*, 45 W.Va.L.Q. 5, 13 (1938); see Clark, Code Pleading 58 (2d ed. 1947). Accordingly, Rule 18(a) has permitted a party to plead multiple claims of all types against an opposing party, subject to the court's power to direct an appropriate procedure for trying the claims. See Rules 42(b), 20(b), 21.

The liberal policy regarding joinder of claims in the pleadings extends to cases with multiple parties. However, the language used in the second sentence of Rule 18(a)—"if the requirements of Rules 19 [necessary joinder of parties], 20 [permissive joinder of parties], and 22 [interpleader] are satisfied"—has led some courts to infer that the rules regulating joinder of parties are intended to carry back to Rule 18(a) and to impose some special limits on joinder of claims in multiparty cases. In particular, Rule 20(a) has been read as restricting the operation of Rule 18(a) in certain situations in which a number of parties have been permissively joined in an action. In *Federal Housing Admr. v. Christianson*, 26 F.Supp. 419 (D.Conn.1939), the indorsee of two notes sued the three comakers of one note, and sought to join in the action a count on a second note which had been made by two of the three defendants. There was no doubt about the propriety of the joinder of the three parties defendant, for a right to relief was being asserted against all three defendants which arose out of a single "transaction" (the first note) and a question of fact or law "common" to all three defendants would arise in the action. See the text of Rule 20(a). The court, however, refused to allow the joinder of the count on the second note, on the ground that this right to relief, assumed to arise from a distinct transaction, did not involve a question common to all the defendants but only two of them. For analysis of the *Christianson* case and other authorities, see 2 Barron & Holtzoff, *Federal Practice & Procedure*, § 533.1 (Wright ed. 1961); 3 Moore's *Federal Practice*, par. 18.04[3] (2d ed. 1963).

If the court's view is followed, it becomes necessary to enter at the pleading stage into speculations about the exact relation between the claim sought to be joined against fewer than all the defendants properly joined in the action, and the claims asserted against all the defendants. Cf. Wright, *Joinder of Claims and Parties Under Modern Pleading Rules*, 36 Minn.L.Rev. 580, 605–06 (1952). Thus if it could be found in the Christianson situation that the claim on the second note arose out of the same transaction as the claim on the first or out of a transaction forming part of a "series," and that any question of fact or law with respect to the second note also arose with regard to the first, it would be held that the claim on the second note could be joined in the complaint. See 2 Barron & Holtzoff, supra, at 109; see also id. at 198 n. 60.4; cf. 3 Moore's *Federal Practice*, supra, at 1811. Such pleading niceties provide a basis for delaying and wasteful maneuver. It is more compatible with the design of the Rules to allow the claim to be joined in the pleading, leaving the question of possible separate trial of that claim to be later decided. See 2 Barron & Holtzoff, supra, § 533.1; Wright, supra, 36 Minn.L.Rev. at 604–11; *Developments in the Law—Multiparty Litigation in the Federal Courts*, 71 Harv. 874, 970–71 (1958); Commentary, *Relation Between Joinder of Parties and Joinder of Claims*, 5 F.R.Serv. 822 (1942). It is instructive to note that the court in the *Christianson* case, while holding that the claim on the second note could not be joined as a matter of pleading, held open the possibility that both claims would later be consolidated for trial under Rule 42(a). See 26 F.Supp. 419.

Rule 18(a) is now amended not only to overcome the *Christianson* decision and similar authority, but also to state clearly as a comprehensive proposition, that a party asserting a claim (an original claim, counterclaim, cross-claim, or third-party claim) may join as many claims as he has against an opposing party. See *Noland Co., Inc. v. Graver Tank & Mfg. Co.*, 301 F.2d 43, 49–51 (4th Cir.1962); but cf. *C. W. Humphrey Co. v. Security Alum. Co.*, 31 F.R.D. 41 (E.D.Mich.1962). This permitted joinder of claims is not affected by the fact that there are multiple parties in the action. The joinder of parties is governed by other rules operating independently.

It is emphasized that amended Rule 18(a) deals only with pleading. As already indicated, a claim properly joined as a matter of pleading need not be proceeded with together with the other claims if fairness or convenience justifies separate treatment.

Amended Rule 18(a), like the rule prior to amendment, does not purport to deal with questions of jurisdiction or venue which may arise with respect to claims properly joined as a matter of pleading. See Rule 82.

See also the amendment of Rule 20(a) and the Advisory Committee's Note thereto.

Free joinder of claims and remedies is one of the basic purposes of unification of the admiralty and civil procedure. The amendment accordingly provides for the inclusion in the rule of maritime claims as well as those which are legal and equitable in character.

1987 Amendment

The amendments are technical. No substantive change is intended.

2007 Amendment

The language of Rule 18 has been amended as part of the general restyling of the Civil Rules to make them more easily understood and to make style and terminology consistent throughout the rules. These changes are intended to be stylistic only.

Modification of the obscure former reference to a claim "heretofore cognizable only after another claim has been prosecuted to a conclusion" avoids any uncertainty whether Rule 18(b)'s meaning is fixed by retrospective inquiry from some particular date.

CROSS REFERENCES

Claim for debt and to set aside fraudulent conveyance, see Fed.Rules Civ.Proc. Form 13, 28 USCA.

Counterclaims and cross-claims, see Fed.Rules Civ.Proc. Rule 13, 28 USCA.

General rules of pleading, see Fed.Rules Civ.Proc. Rule 8, 28 USCA.

One form of action, see Fed.Rules Civ.Proc. Rule 2, 28 USCA.

Separate trials of claims, see Fed.Rules Civ.Proc. Rules 20 and 42, 28 USCA.

Severance of claim against party, see Fed.Rules Civ.Proc. Rule 20, 28 USCA.

Rule 19. Required Joinder of Parties

(a) Persons Required to Be Joined if Feasible.

(1) ***Required Party.*** A person who is subject to service of process and whose joinder will not deprive the court of subject-matter jurisdiction must be joined as a party if:

(A) in that person's absence, the court cannot accord complete relief among existing parties; or

(B) that person claims an interest relating to the subject of the action and is so situated that disposing of the action in the person's absence may:

(i) as a practical matter impair or impede the person's ability to protect the interest; or

(ii) leave an existing party subject to a substantial risk of incurring double, multiple, or otherwise inconsistent obligations because of the interest.

(2) ***Joinder by Court Order.*** If a person has not been joined as required, the court must order that the person be made a party. A person who refuses to join as a plaintiff may be made either a defendant or, in a proper case, an involuntary plaintiff.

(3) ***Venue.*** If a joined party objects to venue and the joinder would make venue improper, the court must dismiss that party.

(b) When Joinder Is Not Feasible. If a person who is required to be joined if feasible cannot be joined, the court must determine whether, in equity and good conscience, the action should proceed among the existing parties or should be dismissed. The factors for the court to consider include:

(1) the extent to which a judgment rendered in the person's absence might prejudice that person or the existing parties;

(2) the extent to which any prejudice could be lessened or avoided by:

(A) protective provisions in the judgment;

(B) shaping the relief; or

(C) other measures;

(3) whether a judgment rendered in the person's absence would be adequate; and

(4) whether the plaintiff would have an adequate remedy if the action were dismissed for nonjoinder.

(c) Pleading the Reasons for Nonjoinder. When asserting a claim for relief, a party must state:

(1) the name, if known, of any person who is required to be joined if feasible but is not joined; and

(2) the reasons for not joining that person.

(d) Exception for Class Actions. This rule is subject to Rule 23.

(Amended February 28, 1966, effective July 1, 1966; March 2, 1987, effective August 1, 1987; April 30, 2007, effective December 1, 2007.)

ADVISORY COMMITTEE NOTES

1937 Adoption

Note to Subdivision (a). The first sentence with verbal differences (e.g., "united" interest for "joint" interest) is to be found in [former] Equity Rule 37 (Parties Generally—Intervention). Such compulsory joinder provisions are common. Compare Alaska Comp.Laws (1933) § 3392 (containing in same sentence a "class suit" provision); Wyo.Rev.Stat. Ann. (Courtright, 1931) § 89–515 (immediately followed by "class suit" provisions, § 89–516). See also former Equity Rule 42 (Joint and Several Demands). For example of a proper case for involuntary plaintiff, see *Independent Wireless Telegraph Co. v. Radio Corp. of America*, 269 U.S. 459, 46 S.Ct. 166, 70 L.Ed. 357 (1926).

The joinder provisions of this rule are subject to Rule 82 (Jurisdiction and Venue Unaffected).

Note to Subdivision (b). For the substance of this rule see [former] Equity Rule 39 (Absence of Persons Who Would be Proper Parties) and U.S.C., Title 28, § 111 [now § 1391] (When part of several defendants cannot be served); *Camp v. Gress*, 250 U.S. 308, 39 S.Ct. 478, 63 L.Ed. 997 (1919). See also the second and third sentences of [former] Equity Rule 37 (Parties Generally—Intervention).

Note to Subdivision (c). For the substance of this rule see the fourth subdivision of [former] Equity Rule 25 (Bill of Complaint—Contents).

1966 Amendment

General Considerations

Whenever feasible, the persons materially interested in the subject of an action—see the more detailed description of these persons in the discussion of new subdivision (a) below—should be joined as parties so that they may be heard and a complete disposition made. When this comprehensive joinder cannot be accomplished—a situation which may be encountered in Federal courts because of limitations on service of process, subject matter jurisdiction, and venue—the case should be examined pragmatically and a choice made between the alternatives of proceeding with the action in the absence of particular interested persons, and dismissing the action.

Even if the court is mistaken in its decision to proceed in the absence of an interested person, it does not by that token deprive itself of the power to adjudicate as between the parties already before it through proper service of process. But the court can make a legally binding adjudication only between the parties actually joined in the action. It is true that an adjudication between the parties before the court may on occasion adversely affect the absent person as a practical matter, or leave a party exposed to a later inconsistent recovery by the absent person. These are factors which should be considered in deciding whether the action should proceed, or should rather be dismissed; but they do not themselves negate the court's power to adjudicate as between the parties who have been joined.

Defects in the Original Rule

The foregoing propositions were well understood in the older equity practice, see Hazard, *Indispensable Party: The Historical Origin of a Procedural Phantom*, 61 Colum.L.Rev. 1254 (1961), and Rule 19 could be and often was applied in consonance with them. But experience showed that the rule was defective in its phrasing and did not point clearly to the proper basis of decision.

Textual defects.—(1) The expression "persons * * * who ought to be parties if complete relief is to be accorded between those already parties," appearing in original subdivision (b), was apparently intended as a description of the persons whom it would be desirable to join in the action, all questions of feasibility of joinder being put to one side; but it was not adequately descriptive of those persons.

(2) The word "indispensable," appearing in original subdivision (b), was apparently intended as an inclusive reference to the interested persons in whose absence it would be advisable, all factors having been considered, to dismiss the action. Yet the sentence implied that there might be interested persons, not "indispensable," in whose absence the action ought also to be dismissed. Further, it seemed at least superficially plausible to equate the word "indispensable" with the expression "having a joint interest," appearing in subdivision (a). See *United States v. Washington Inst. of Tech., Inc.*, 138 F.2d 25, 26 (3d Cir. 1943); cf. *Chidester v. City of Newark*, 162 F.2d 598 (3d Cir. 1947). But persons holding an interest technically "joint" are not always so related to an action that it would be unwise to proceed without joining all of them, whereas persons holding an interest not technically "joint" may have this relation to an action. See Reed, *Compulsory Joinder of Parties in Civil Actions*, 55 Mich.L.Rev. 327, 356 ff., 483 (1957).

(3) The use of "indispensable" and "joint interest" in the context of original Rule 19 directed attention to the technical or abstract character of the rights or obligations of the persons whose joinder was in question, and correspondingly distracted attention from the pragmatic considerations which should be controlling.

(4) The original rule, in dealing with the feasibility of joining a person as a party to the action, besides referring to whether the person was "subject to the jurisdiction of the court as to both service of process and venue," spoke of whether the person could be made a party "without depriving the court of jurisdiction of the parties before it." The second quoted expression used "jurisdiction" in the sense of the competence of the court over the subject matter of the action, and in this sense the expression was apt. However, by a familiar confusion, the expression seems to have suggested to some that the absence from the lawsuit of a person who was "indispensable" or "who ought to be [a] part[y]" itself deprived the court of the power to adjudicate as between the parties already joined. See *Samuel Goldwyn, Inc. v. United Artists Corp.*, 113 F.2d 703, 707 (3d Cir. 1940); *McArthur v. Rosenbaum Co. of Pittsburgh*, 180 F.2d 617, 621 (3d Cir. 1949); cf. *Calcote v. Texas Pac. Coal & Oil Co.*, 157 F.2d 216 (5th Cir. 1946), cert. denied, 329 U.S. 782 (1946), noted in 56 Yale L.J. 1088 (1947); Reed, supra, 55 Mich. L.Rev. at 332–34.

Failure to point to correct basis of decision. The original rule did not state affirmatively what factors were relevant in deciding whether the action should proceed or be dismissed when joinder of interested persons was infeasible. In some instances courts did not undertake the relevant inquiry or were misled by the "jurisdiction" fallacy. In other instances there was undue preoccupation with abstract classifications of rights or obligations, as against consideration of the particular consequences of proceeding with the action and the ways by which these consequences might be ameliorated by the shaping of final relief or other precautions.

Although these difficulties cannot be said to have been general analysis of the cases showed that there was good reason for attempting to strengthen the rule. The literature also indicated how the rule should be reformed. See Reed, supra (discussion of the important case of *Shields v. Barrow,* 17 How. (58 U.S.) 130 (1854), appears at 55 Mich.L.Rev., p. 340 ff.); Hazard, supra; N.Y. Temporary Comm. on Courts, First Preliminary Report, Legis.Doc.1957, No. 6(b), pp. 28, 233; N.Y. Judicial Council, Twelfth Ann.Rep., Legis.Doc.1946, No. 17, p. 163; Joint Comm. on Michigan Procedural Revision, Final Report, Pt. III, p. 69 (1960); Note, *Indispensable Parties in the Federal Courts,* 65 Harv.L.Rev. 1050 (1952); *Developments in the Law—Multiparty Litigation in the Federal Courts,* 71 Harv.L.Rev. 874, 879 (1958); Mich.Gen.Court Rules, R. 205 (effective Jan. 1, 1963); N.Y.Civ.Prac.Law & Rules, § 1001 (effective Sept. 1, 1963).

The Amended Rule

New subdivision (a) defines the persons whose joinder in the action is desirable. Clause (1) stresses the desirability of joining those persons in whose absence the court would be obliged to grant partial or "hollow" rather than complete relief to the parties before the court. The interests that are being furthered here are not only those of the parties, but also that of the public in avoiding repeated lawsuits on the same essential subject matter. Clause (2)(i) recognizes the importance of protecting the person whose joinder is in question against the practical prejudice to him which may arise through a disposition of the action in his absence. Clause (2)(ii) recognizes the need for considering whether a party may be left, after the adjudication, in a position where a person not joined can subject him to a double or otherwise inconsistent liability. See Reed, supra, 55 Mich.L.Rev. at 330, 338; Note, supra, 65 Harv.L.Rev. at 1052–57; *Developments in the Law,* supra, 71 Harv.L.Rev. at 881–85.

The subdivision (a) definition of persons to be joined is not couched in terms of the abstract nature of their interests—"joint," "united," "separable," or the like. See N.Y. Temporary Comm. on Courts, First Preliminary Report, supra; Developments in the Law, supra, at 880. It should be noted particularly, however, that the description is not at variance with the settled authorities holding that a tortfeasor with the usual "joint-and-several" liability is merely a permissive party to an action against another with like liability. See 3 Moore's *Federal Practice* 2153 (2d ed. 1963); 2 Barron & Holtzoff, *Federal Practice & Procedure* § 513.8 (Wright ed. 1961). Joinder of these tortfeasors continues to be regulated by Rule 20; compare Rule 14 on third-party practice.

If a person as described in subdivision (a)(1)(2) is amenable to service of process and his joinder would not deprive the court of jurisdiction in the sense of competence over the action, he should be joined as a party; and if he has not been joined, the court should order him to be brought into the action. If a party joined has a valid objection to the venue and chooses to assert it, he will be dismissed from the action.

Subdivision (b).—When a person as described in subdivision (a)(1)–(2) cannot be made a party, the court is to determine whether in equity and good conscience the action should proceed among the parties already before it, or should be dismissed. That this decision is to be made in the light of pragmatic considerations has often been acknowledged by the courts. See *Roos v. Texas Co.,* 23 F.2d 171 (2d Cir. 1927), cert. denied 277 U.S. 587 (1928); *Niles-Bement-Pond Co. v. Iron Moulders' Union,* 254 U.S. 77, 80 (1920). The subdivision sets out four relevant considerations drawn from the experience revealed in the decided cases. The factors are to a certain extent overlapping, and they are not intended to exclude other considerations which may be applicable in particular situations.

The first factor brings in a consideration of what a judgment in the action would mean to the absentee. Would the absentee be adversely affected in a practical sense, and if so, would the prejudice be immediate and serious, or remote and minor? The possible collateral consequences of the judgment upon the parties already joined are also to be appraised. Would any party be exposed to a fresh action by the absentee, and if so, how serious is the threat? See the elaborate discussion in Reed, supra; cf. *A. L. Smith Iron Co. v. Dickson,* 141 F.2d 3 (2d Cir. 1944); *Caldwell Mfg. Co. v. Unique Balance Co.,* 18 F.R.D. 258 (S.D.N.Y.1955).

The second factor calls attention to the measures by which prejudice may be averted or lessened. The "shaping of relief" is a familiar expedient to this end. See, e.g., the award of money damages in lieu of specific relief where the latter might affect an absentee adversely. *Ward v. Deavers,* 203 F.2d 72 (D.C.Cir.1953); *Miller & Lux, Inc. v. Nickel,* 141 F.Supp. 41 (N.D.Calif.1956). On the use of "protective provisions," see *Roos v. Texas Co.,* supra; *Atwood v. Rhode Island Hosp. Trust Co.,* 275 Fed. 513, 519 (1st Cir. 1921), cert. denied, 257 U.S. 661 (1922); cf. *Stumpf v. Fidelity Gas Co.,* 294 F.2d 886 (9th Cir. 1961); and the general statement in *National Licorice Co. v. Labor Board,* 309 U.S. 350, 363 (1940).

Sometimes the party is himself able to take measures to avoid prejudice. Thus a defendant faced with a prospect of a second suit by an absentee may be in a position to bring the latter into the action by defensive interpleader. See *Hudson v. Newell,* 172 F.2d 848, 852 mod., 176 F.2d 546 (5th Cir. 1949); *Gauss v. Kirk,* 198 F.2d 83, 86 (D.C.Cir. 1952); *Abel v. Brayton Flying Service, Inc.,* 248 F.2d 713, 716 (5th Cir. 1957) (suggestion of possibility of counter-claim under Rule 13(h)); cf. *Parker Rust-Proof Co. v. Western Union Tel. Co.,* 105 F.2d 976 (2d Cir. 1939), cert. denied, 308 U.S. 597 (1939). So also the absentee may sometimes be able to avert prejudice to himself by voluntarily appearing in the action or intervening on an ancillary basis. See *Developments in the Law,* supra, 71 Harv.L.Rev. at 882; Annot., *Intervention or Subsequent Joinder of Parties as Affecting Jurisdiction of Federal Court Based on Diversity of Citizenship,* 134 A.L.R. 335 (1941); *Johnson v. Middleton,* 175 F.2d 535 (7th Cir. 1949); *Kentucky Nat. Gas Corp. v. Duggins,* 165 F.2d 1011 (6th Cir. 1948); *McComb v. McCormack,* 159 F.2d 219 (5th Cir. 1947). The court should consider whether this, in turn, would impose undue hardship on the absentee. (For the possibility of the court's informing an absentee of the pendency of the action, see comment under subdivision (c) below.)

The third factor—whether an "adequate" judgment can be rendered in the absence of a given person—calls attention to the extent of the relief that can be accorded among the parties joined. It meshes with the other factors, especially the "shaping of relief" mentioned under the second factor. Cf. *Kroese v. General Steel Castings Corp.,* 179 F.2d 760 (3d Cir. 1949), cert. denied, 339 U.S. 983 (1950).

The fourth factor, looking to the practical effects of a dismissal, indicates that the court should consider whether there is any assurance that the plaintiff, if dismissed, could sue effectively in another forum where better joinder would be possible. See *Fitzgerald v. Haynes,* 241 F.2d 417, 420 (3d Cir. 1957); *Fouke v. Schenewerk,* 197 F.2d 234, 236 (5th Cir. 1952); cf. *Warfield v. Marks,* 190 F.2d 178 (5th Cir. 1951).

The subdivision uses the word "indispensable" only in a conclusory sense, that is, a person is "regarded as indispensable" when he cannot be made a party and, upon consideration of the factors above mentioned, it is determined that in his absence it would be preferable to dismiss the action, rather than to retain it.

A person may be added as a party at any stage of the action on motion or on the court's initiative (see Rule 21); and a motion to dismiss, on the ground that a person has not been joined and justice requires that the action should not proceed in his absence, may be made as late as the trial on the merits (see Rule 12(h)(2), as amended; cf. Rule 12(b)(7), as amended). However, when the moving party is seeking dismissal in order to protect himself against a later suit by the absent person (subdivision (a)(2)(ii)), and is not seeking vicariously to protect the absent person against a prejudicial judgment (subdivision (a)(2)(i)), his undue delay in making the motion can properly be counted against him as a reason for denying the motion. A joinder question should be decided with reasonable promptness, but decision may properly be deferred if adequate information is not available at the time. Thus the relationship of an absent person to the action, and the practical effects of an adjudication upon him and others, may not be sufficiently revealed at the pleading stage; in such a case it would be appropriate to defer decision until the action was further advanced. Cf. Rule 12(d).

The amended rule makes no special provision for the problem arising in suits against subordinate Federal officials where it has often been set up as a defense that some superior officer must be joined. Frequently this defense has been accompanied by or intermingled with defenses of sovereign community or lack of consent of the United States to suit. So far as the issue of joinder can be isolated from the rest, the new subdivision seems better adapted to handle it than the predecessor provision. See the discussion in *Johnson v. Kirkland,* 290 F.2d 440, 446–47 (5th Cir. 1961) (stressing the practical orientation of the decisions); *Shaughnessy v. Pedreiro,* 349 U.S. 48, 54 (1955). Recent legislation, P.L. 87–748, 76 Stat. 744, approved October 5, 1962, adding §§ 1361, 1391(e) to Title 28, U.S.C., vests original jurisdiction in the District Courts over actions in the nature of mandamus to compel officials of the United States to perform their legal duties, and extends the range of service of process and liberalizes venue in these actions. If, then, it is found that a particular official should be joined in the action, the legislation will make it easy to bring him in.

Subdivision (c) parallels the predecessor subdivision (c) of Rule 19. In some situations it may be desirable to advise a person who has not been joined of the fact that the action is pending, and in particular cases the court in its discretion may itself convey this information by directing a letter or other informal notice to the absentee.

Subdivision (d) repeats the exception contained in the first clause of the predecessor subdivision (a).

1987 Amendment

The amendments are technical. No substantive change is intended.

2007 Amendment

The language of Rule 19 has been amended as part of the general restyling of the Civil Rules to make them more easily understood and to make style and terminology consistent throughout the rules. These changes are intended to be stylistic only.

Former Rule 19(b) described the conclusion that an action should be dismissed for inability to join a Rule 19(a) party by carrying forward traditional terminology: "the absent person being thus regarded as indispensable." "Indispensable" was used only to express a conclusion reached by applying the tests of Rule 19(b). It has been discarded as redundant.

CROSS REFERENCES

Class actions, see Fed.Rules Civ.Proc. Rule 23, 28 USCA.

Indispensable party, defense of failure to join, see Fed. Rules Civ.Proc. Rule 12, 28 USCA.

Interpleader, see Fed.Rules Civ.Proc. Rule 22, 28 USCA.

Intervention, see Fed.Rules Civ.Proc. Rule 24, 28 USCA.

Jurisdiction and venue unaffected by these rules, see Fed. Rules Civ.Proc. Rule 82, 28 USCA.

Lien enforcement, ordering absent defendant to appear or plead, see 28 USCA § 1655.

Misjoinder and non-joinder of parties, see Fed.Rules Civ. Proc. Rule 21, 28 USCA.

Permissive joinder of parties, see Fed.Rules Civ.Proc. Rule 20, 28 USCA.

Substitution of parties, see Fed.Rules Civ.Proc. Rule 25, 28 USCA.

Rule 20. Permissive Joinder of Parties

(a) Persons Who May Join or Be Joined.

(1) ***Plaintiffs.*** Persons may join in one action as plaintiffs if:

(A) they assert any right to relief jointly, severally, or in the alternative with respect to or arising out of the same transaction, occurrence, or series of transactions or occurrences; and

(B) any question of law or fact common to all plaintiffs will arise in the action.

(2) ***Defendants.*** Persons—as well as a vessel, cargo, or other property subject to admiralty process in rem—may be joined in one action as defendants if:

(A) any right to relief is asserted against them jointly, severally, or in the alternative with respect to or arising out of the same transaction, occurrence, or series of transactions or occurrences; and

(B) any question of law or fact common to all defendants will arise in the action.

(3) ***Extent of Relief.*** Neither a plaintiff nor a defendant need be interested in obtaining or defending against all the relief demanded. The court may grant judgment to one or more plaintiffs according to their rights, and against one or more defendants according to their liabilities.

(b) Protective Measures. The court may issue orders—including an order for separate trials—to protect a party against embarrassment, delay, expense, or other prejudice that arises from including a person against whom the party asserts no claim and who asserts no claim against the party.

(Amended February 28, 1966, effective July 1, 1966; March 2, 1987, effective August 1, 1987; April 30, 2007, effective December 1, 2007.)

ADVISORY COMMITTEE NOTES

1937 Adoption

The provisions for joinder here stated are in substance the provisions found in England, California, Illinois, New Jersey, and New York. They represent only a moderate expansion of the present federal equity practice to cover both law and equity actions.

With this rule compare also [former] Equity Rules 26 (Joinder of Causes of Action), 37 (Parties Generally—Intervention), 40 (Nominal Parties), and 42 (Joint and Several Demands).

The provisions of this rule for the joinder of parties are subject to Rule 82 (Jurisdiction and Venue Unaffected).

Note to Subdivision (a). The first sentence is derived from *English Rules Under the Judicature Act* (The Annual Practice, 1937) O. 16, r. 1. Compare Calif.Code Civ.Proc. (Deering, 1937) §§ 378, 379a; Ill.Rev.Stat. (1937) ch. 110, § 147–148; N.J.Comp.Stat. (2 Cum.Supp., 1911–1924), N.Y.C.P.A. (1937) §§ 209, 211. The second sentence is derived from *English Rules Under the Judicature Act* (The Annual Practice, 1937) O. 16, r. 4. The third sentence is derived from O. 16, r. 5, and the fourth from O. 16, r.r. 1 and 4.

Note to Subdivision (b). This is derived from *English Rules Under the Judicature Act* (The Annual Practice, 1937) O. 16, r.r. 1 and 5.

1966 Amendment

See the amendment of Rule 18(a) and the Advisory Committee's Note thereto. It has been thought that a lack of clarity in the antecedent of the word "them," as it appeared in two places in Rule 20(a), contributed to the view, taken by some courts, that this rule limited the joinder of claims in certain situations of permissive party joinder. Although the amendment of Rule 18(a) should make clear that this view is untenable, it has been considered advisable to amend Rule 20(a) to eliminate any ambiguity. See 2 Barron & Holtzoff, *Federal Practice & Procedure* 202 (Wright Ed. 1961).

A basic purpose of unification of admiralty and civil procedure is to reduce barriers to joinder; hence the reference to "any vessel," etc.

1987 Amendment

The amendments are technical. No substantive change is intended.

2007 Amendment

The language of Rule 20 has been amended as part of the general restyling of the Civil Rules to make them more easily understood and to make style and terminology consistent throughout the rules. These changes are intended to be stylistic only.

CROSS REFERENCES

Collusive or improper joinder of parties, jurisdiction of district courts, see 28 USCA § 1359.

Interpleader, see Fed.Rules Civ.Proc. Rule 22, 28 USCA.

Intervention, see Fed.Rules Civ.Proc. Rule 24, 28 USCA.

Joinder of persons needed for just adjudication, see Fed. Rules Civ.Proc. Rule 19, 28 USCA.

Misjoinder and non-joinder of parties, see Fed.Rules Civ. Proc. Rule 21, 28 USCA.

Substitution of parties, see Fed.Rules Civ.Proc. Rule 25, 28 USCA.

Rule 21. Misjoinder and Nonjoinder of Parties

Misjoinder of parties is not a ground for dismissing an action. On motion or on its own, the court may at any time, on just terms, add or drop a party. The court may also sever any claim against a party.

(Amended April 30, 2007, effective December 1, 2007.)

ADVISORY COMMITTEE NOTES

1937 Adoption

See *English Rules Under the Judicature Act* (The Annual Practice, 1937) O. 16, r. 11. See also [former] Equity Rules 43 (Defect of Parties—Resisting Objection) and 44 (Defect of Parties—Tardy Objection).

For separate trials see Rules 13(i) (Counterclaims and Cross-Claims: Separate Trials; Separate Judgments), 20(b) (Permissive Joinder of Parties: Separate Trials), and 42(b) (Separate Trials, generally) and the note to the latter rule.

2007 Amendment

The language of Rule 21 has been amended as part of the general restyling of the Civil Rules to make them more easily understood and to make style and terminology consistent throughout the rules. These changes are intended to be stylistic only.

CROSS REFERENCES

Collusive or improper joinder of parties, jurisdiction of district courts, see 28 USCA § 1359.

Intervention of parties, see Fed.Rules Civ.Proc. Rule 24, 28 USCA.

Joinder of persons needed for just adjudication, see Fed. Rules Civ.Proc. Rule 19, 28 USCA.

Permissive joinder of parties, see Fed.Rules Civ.Proc. Rule 20, 28 USCA.

Procedure after removal generally, see 28 USCA § 1447.

Rule 22. Interpleader

(a) Grounds.

(1) ***By a Plaintiff.*** Persons with claims that may expose a plaintiff to double or multiple liability may be joined as defendants and required to interplead. Joinder for interpleader is proper even though:

(A) the claims of the several claimants, or the titles on which their claims depend, lack a common origin or are adverse and independent rather than identical; or

(B) the plaintiff denies liability in whole or in part to any or all of the claimants.

(2) ***By a Defendant.*** A defendant exposed to similar liability may seek interpleader through a crossclaim or counterclaim.

(b) Relation to Other Rules and Statutes. This rule supplements—and does not limit—the joinder of parties allowed by Rule 20. The remedy this rule provides is in addition to—and does not supersede or limit—the remedy provided by 28 U.S.C. §§ 1335, 1397, and 2361. An action under those statutes must be conducted under these rules.

(Amended December 29, 1948, effective October 20, 1949; March 2, 1987, effective August 1, 1987; April 30, 2007, effective December 1, 2007.)

ADVISORY COMMITTEE NOTES

1937 Adoption

The first paragraph provides for interpleader relief along the newer and more liberal lines of joinder in the alternative. It avoids the confusion and restrictions that developed around actions of strict interpleader and actions in the nature of interpleader. Compare *John Hancock Mutual Life Insurance Co. v. Kegan et al.*, 22 F.Supp. 326 (D.C.Md.1938). It does not change the rules on service of process, jurisdiction, and venue, as established by judicial decision.

The second paragraph allows an action to be brought under the recent interpleader statute when applicable. By this paragraph all remedies under the statute are continued, but the manner of obtaining them is in accordance with these rules. For temporary restraining orders and preliminary injunctions under this statute, see Rule 65(e).

This rule substantially continues such statutory provisions as U.S.C., Title 38, § 445 [now 784] (Actions on claims; jurisdiction; parties; procedure; limitation; witnesses; definitions) (actions upon veterans' contracts of insurance with the United States), providing for interpleader by the United States where it acknowledges indebtedness under a contract of insurance with the United States; U.S.C., Title 49, § 97 (Interpleader of conflicting claimants) (by carrier which has issued bill of lading). See Chaffee, *The Federal Interpleader Act of 1936: I and II* (1936), 45 Yale L.J. 963, 1161.

1948 Amendment

The amendment effective October 20, 1949, substituted the reference to "Title 28, U.S.C., §§ 1335, 1397, and 2361," at the end of the first sentence of paragraph (2), for the reference to "Section 24(26) of the Judicial Code, as amended, U.S.C., Title 28, § 41(26)." The amendment also substituted the words "those provisions" in the second sentence of paragraph (2) for the words "that section."

1987 Amendment

The amendment is technical. No substantive change is intended.

2007 Amendment

The language of Rule 22 has been amended as part of the general restyling of the Civil Rules to make them more easily understood and to make style and terminology consistent throughout the rules. These changes are intended to be stylistic only.

CROSS REFERENCES

Jurisdiction of district courts of interpleader action, see 28 USCA § 1335.

Permissive joinder of parties, see Fed.Rules Civ.Proc. Rule 20, 28 USCA.

Process and procedure in interpleader action, see 28 USCA § 2361.

Venue of interpleader action, see 28 USCA § 1397.

Rule 23. Class Actions

(a) Prerequisites. One or more members of a class may sue or be sued as representative parties on behalf of all members only if:

(1) the class is so numerous that joinder of all members is impracticable;

(2) there are questions of law or fact common to the class;

(3) the claims or defenses of the representative parties are typical of the claims or defenses of the class; and

(4) the representative parties will fairly and adequately protect the interests of the class.

(b) Types of Class Actions. A class action may be maintained if Rule 23(a) is satisfied and if:

(1) prosecuting separate actions by or against individual class members would create a risk of:

(A) inconsistent or varying adjudications with respect to individual class members that would establish incompatible standards of conduct for the party opposing the class; or

(B) adjudications with respect to individual class members that, as a practical matter, would be dispositive of the interests of the other members not parties to the individual adjudications or would substantially impair or impede their ability to protect their interests;

(2) the party opposing the class has acted or refused to act on grounds that apply generally to the class, so that final injunctive relief or corresponding declaratory relief is appropriate respecting the class as a whole; or

(3) the court finds that the questions of law or fact common to class members predominate over any questions affecting only individual members, and that a class action is superior to other available methods for fairly and efficiently adjudicating the controversy. The matters pertinent to these findings include:

(A) the class members' interests in individually controlling the prosecution or defense of separate actions;

(B) the extent and nature of any litigation concerning the controversy already begun by or against class members;

(C) the desirability or undesirability of concentrating the litigation of the claims in the particular forum; and

(D) the likely difficulties in managing a class action.

(c) Certification Order; Notice to Class Members; Judgment; Issues Classes; Subclasses.

(1) ***Certification Order.***

(A) *Time to Issue.* At an early practicable time after a person sues or is sued as a class representative, the court must determine by order whether to certify the action as a class action.

(B) *Defining the Class; Appointing Class Counsel.* An order that certifies a class action must define the class and the class claims, issues, or defenses, and must appoint class counsel under Rule 23(g).

(C) *Altering or Amending the Order.* An order that grants or denies class certification may be altered or amended before final judgment.

(2) ***Notice.***

(A) *For (b)(1) or (b)(2) Classes.* For any class certified under Rule 23(b)(1) or (b)(2), the court may direct appropriate notice to the class.

(B) *For (b)(3) Classes.* For any class certified under Rule 23(b)(3), the court must direct to class members the best notice that is practicable under the circumstances, including individual notice to all members who can be identified through reasonable effort. The notice must clearly and concisely state in plain, easily understood language:

(i) the nature of the action;

(ii) the definition of the class certified;

(iii) the class claims, issues, or defenses;

(iv) that a class member may enter an appearance through an attorney if the member so desires;

(v) that the court will exclude from the class any member who requests exclusion;

(vi) the time and manner for requesting exclusion; and

(vii) the binding effect of a class judgment on members under Rule 23(c)(3).

(3) ***Judgment.*** Whether or not favorable to the class, the judgment in a class action must:

(A) for any class certified under Rule 23(b)(1) or (b)(2), include and describe those whom the court finds to be class members; and

(B) for any class certified under Rule 23(b)(3), include and specify or describe those to whom the Rule 23(c)(2) notice was directed, who have not requested exclusion, and whom the court finds to be class members.

(4) ***Particular Issues.*** When appropriate, an action may be brought or maintained as a class action with respect to particular issues.

(5) ***Subclasses.*** When appropriate, a class may be divided into subclasses that are each treated as a class under this rule.

(d) Conducting the Action.

(1) ***In General.*** In conducting an action under this rule, the court may issue orders that:

(A) determine the course of proceedings or prescribe measures to prevent undue repetition or complication in presenting evidence or argument;

(B) require—to protect class members and fairly conduct the action—giving appropriate notice to some or all class members of:

(i) any step in the action;

(ii) the proposed extent of the judgment; or

(iii) the members' opportunity to signify whether they consider the representation fair and adequate, to intervene and present claims or defenses, or to otherwise come into the action;

(C) impose conditions on the representative parties or on intervenors;

(D) require that the pleadings be amended to eliminate allegations about representation of absent persons and that the action proceed accordingly; or

(E) deal with similar procedural matters.

(2) ***Combining and Amending Orders.*** An order under Rule 23(d)(1) may be altered or amended from time to time and may be combined with an order under Rule 16.

(e) Settlement, Voluntary Dismissal, or Compromise. The claims, issues, or defenses of a certified class may be settled, voluntarily dismissed, or compromised only with the court's approval. The following procedures apply to a proposed settlement, voluntary dismissal, or compromise:

(1) The court must direct notice in a reasonable manner to all class members who would be bound by the proposal.

(2) If the proposal would bind class members, the court may approve it only after a hearing and on finding that it is fair, reasonable, and adequate.

(3) The parties seeking approval must file a statement identifying any agreement made in connection with the proposal.

(4) If the class action was previously certified under Rule 23(b)(3), the court may refuse to approve a settlement unless it affords a new opportunity to request exclusion to individual class members who had an earlier opportunity to request exclusion but did not do so.

(5) Any class member may object to the proposal if it requires court approval under this subdivision (e); the objection may be withdrawn only with the court's approval.

(f) Appeals. A court of appeals may permit an appeal from an order granting or denying class-action certification under this rule if a petition for permission to appeal is filed with the circuit clerk within 10 days after the order is entered. An appeal does not stay proceedings in the district court unless the district judge or the court of appeals so orders.

(g) Class Counsel.

(1) ***Appointing Class Counsel.*** Unless a statute provides otherwise, a court that certifies a class must appoint class counsel. In appointing class counsel, the court:

(A) must consider:

(i) the work counsel has done in identifying or investigating potential claims in the action;

(ii) counsel's experience in handling class actions, other complex litigation, and the types of claims asserted in the action;

(iii) counsel's knowledge of the applicable law; and

(iv) the resources that counsel will commit to representing the class;

(B) may consider any other matter pertinent to counsel's ability to fairly and adequately represent the interests of the class;

(C) may order potential class counsel to provide information on any subject pertinent to the appointment and to propose terms for attorney's fees and nontaxable costs;

(D) may include in the appointing order provisions about the award of attorney's fees or nontaxable costs under Rule 23(h); and

(E) may make further orders in connection with the appointment.

(2) ***Standard for Appointing Class Counsel.*** When one applicant seeks appointment as class counsel, the court may appoint that applicant only if the applicant is adequate under Rule 23(g)(1) and (4). If more than one adequate applicant seeks appointment, the court must appoint the applicant best able to represent the interests of the class.

(3) ***Interim Counsel.*** The court may designate interim counsel to act on behalf of a putative class before determining whether to certify the action as a class action.

(4) ***Duty of Class Counsel.*** Class counsel must fairly and adequately represent the interests of the class.

(h) Attorney's Fees and Nontaxable Costs. In a certified class action, the court may award reasonable attorney's fees and nontaxable costs that are authorized by law or by the parties' agreement. The following procedures apply:

(1) A claim for an award must be made by motion under Rule 54(d)(2), subject to the provisions of this subdivision (h), at a time the court sets. Notice of the motion must be served on all parties and, for motions by class counsel, directed to class members in a reasonable manner.

(2) A class member, or a party from whom payment is sought, may object to the motion.

(3) The court may hold a hearing and must find the facts and state its legal conclusions under Rule 52(a).

(4) The court may refer issues related to the amount of the award to a special master or a magistrate judge, as provided in Rule 54(d)(2)(D).

(Amended February 28, 1966, effective July 1, 1966; March 2, 1987, effective August 1, 1987; April 24, 1998, effective December 1, 1998; March 27, 2003, effective December 1, 2003; April 30, 2007, effective December 1, 2007.)

ADVISORY COMMITTEE NOTES

1937 Adoption

Note to Subdivision (a). This is a substantial restatement of [former] Equity Rule 38 (Representatives of Class) as that rule has been construed. It applies to all actions, whether formerly denominated legal or equitable. For a general analysis of class actions, effect of judgment, and requisites of jurisdiction see Moore, *Federal Rules of Civil Procedure: Some Problems Raised by the Preliminary Draft*, 25 Georgetown L.J. 551, 570 et seq. (1937); Moore and Cohn, *Federal Class Actions*, 32 Ill.L.Rev. 307 (1937); Moore and Cohn, *Federal Class Actions—Jurisdiction and Effect of Judgment*, 32 Ill.L.Rev. 555–567 (1938); Lesar, *Class Suits and the Federal Rules*, 22 Minn.L.Rev. 34 (1937); cf. Arnold and James, *Cases on Trials, Judgments and Appeals* (1936) 175; and see Blume, *Jurisdictional Amount in Representative Suits*, 15 Minn.L.Rev. 501 (1931).

The general test of [former] Equity Rule 38 (Representatives of Class) that the question should be "one of common or general interest to many persons constituting a class so numerous as to make it impracticable to bring them all before the court," is a common test. For states which require the two elements of a common or general interest and numerous persons, as provided for in [former] Equity Rule 38, see Del.Ch. Rule 113; Fla.Comp.Gen.Laws Ann. (Supp., 1936) § 4918(7); Georgia Code (1933) § 37–1002, and see *English Rules Under the Judicature Act* (The Annual Practice, 1937) O. 16, r. 9. For statutory provisions providing for class actions when the question is one of common or general interest or when the parties are numerous, see Ala.Code Ann. (Michie, 1928) § 5701; 2 Ind.Stat.Ann. (Burns, 1933) § 2–220; N.Y.C.P.A. (1937) 195; Wis.Stat. (1935) § 260.12. These statutes have, however, been uniformly construed as though phrased in the conjunctive. See *Garfein v. Stiglitz*, 260 Ky. 430, 86 S.W.2d 155 (1935). The rule adopts the test of [former] Equity Rule 38, but defines what constitutes a "common or general interest". Compare with code provisions which make the action dependent upon the propriety of joinder of the parties. See Blume, *The "Common Questions" Principle in the Code Provision for Representative Suits*, 30 Mich.L.Rev. 878 (1932). For discussion of what constitutes "numerous persons" see Wheaton, *Representative Suits Involving Numerous Litigants*, 19 Corn.L.Q. 399 (1934); Note, 36 Harv.L.Rev. 89 (1922).

Clause (1), Joint, Common, or Secondary Right. This clause is illustrated in actions brought by or against representatives of an unincorporated association. See *Oster v. Brotherhood of Locomotive Firemen and Enginemen*, 271 Pa. 419, 114 Atl. 377 (1921); *Pickett v. Walsh*, 192 Mass. 572, 78 N.E. 753, 6 L.R.A., N.S., 1067 (1906); *Colt v. Hicks*, 97 Ind.App. 177, 179 N.E. 335 (1932). Compare Rule 17(b) as to when an unincorporated association has capacity to sue or be sued in its common name; *United Mine Workers of America v. Coronado Coal Co.*, 42 S.Ct. 570, 259 U.S. 344, 66 L.Ed. 975, 27 A.L.R. 762 (1922) (an unincorporated association was sued as an entity for the purpose of enforcing against it a federal substantive right); Moore, *Federal Rules of Civil Procedure: Some Problems Raised by the Preliminary Draft*, 25 Georgetown L.J. 551, 566 (for discussion of jurisdictional requisites when an unincorporated association sues or is sued in its common name and jurisdiction is founded upon diversity of citizenship). For an action brought by representatives of one group against representatives of another group for distribution of a fund held by an unincorporated association, see *Smith v. Swormstedt*, 16 How. 288, 14 L.Ed. 942 (U.S. 1853). Compare *Christopher, et al. v. Brusselback*, 1938, 58 S.Ct. 350, 302 U.S. 500, 82 L.Ed. 388.

For an action to enforce rights held in common by policyholders against the corporate issuer of the policies, see *Supreme Tribe of Ben Hur v. Cauble*, 255 U.S. 356, 41 S.Ct. 338, 65 L.Ed. 673 (1921). See also *Terry v. Little*, 101 U.S. 216, 25 L.Ed. 864 (1880); *John A. Roebling's Sons Co. v. Kinnicutt*, 248 Fed. 596 (D.C.N.Y., 1917) dealing with the right held in common by creditors to enforce the statutory liability of stockholders.

Typical of a secondary action is a suit by stockholders to enforce a corporate right. For discussion of the general nature of these actions see *Ashwander v. Tennessee Valley Authority*, 297 U.S. 288, 56 S.Ct. 466, 80 L.Ed. 688 (1936); Glenn, *The Stockholder's Suit—Corporate and Individual Grievances*, 33 Yale L.J. 580 (1924); McLaughlin, *Capacity of Plaintiff-Stockholder to Terminate a Stockholder's Suit*, 46 Yale L.J. 421 (1937). See also Subdivision (b) of this rule which deals with Shareholder's Action; Note, 15 Minn.L.Rev. 453 (1931).

Clause (2). A creditor's action for liquidation or reorganization of a corporation is illustrative of this clause. An action by a stockholder against certain named defendants as representatives of numerous claimants presents a situation converse to the creditor's action.

Clause (3). See *Everglades Drainage League v. Napoleon Broward Drainage Dist.*, 253 Fed. 246 (D.C.Fla., 1918); *Gramling v. Maxwell*, 52 F.2d 256 (D.C.N.C., 1931), approved in 30 Mich.L.Rev. 624 (1932); *Skinner v. Mitchell*, 108 Kan. 861, 197 Pac. 569 (1921); *Duke of Bedford v. Ellis* (1901) A.C. 1, for class actions when there were numerous persons and there was only a question of law or fact common to them; and see Blume, *The "Common Questions" Principle in the Code Provision for Representative Suits*, 30 Mich. L.Rev. 878 (1932).

Note to Subdivision (b). This is [former] Equity Rule 27 (Stockholder's Bill) with verbal changes. See also *Hawes v. Oakland*, 104 U.S. 450, 26 L.Ed. 827 (1882) and former Equity Rule 94, promulgated January 23, 1882, 104 U.S. IX.

Note to Subdivision (c). See McLaughlin, Capacity of Plaintiff-Stockholder to Terminate a Stockholder's Suit, 46 Yale L.J. 421 (1937).

Supplementary Note

Note. Subdivision (b), relating to secondary actions by shareholders, provides among other things, that in such an action the complainant "shall aver (1) that the plaintiff was a shareholder at the time of the transaction of which he complains or that his share thereafter devolved on him by operation of law * * *".

As a result of the decision in *Erie R. Co. v. Tompkins*, 1938, 304 U.S. 64, 58 S.Ct. 817 (decided April 25, 1938, after this rule was promulgated by the Supreme Court, though before it took effect) a question has arisen as to whether the provision above quoted deals with a matter of substantive right or is a matter of procedure. If it is a matter of substantive law or right, then under *Erie R. Co. v. Tompkins* clause (1) may not be validly applied in cases pending in states whose local law permits a shareholder to maintain such actions, although not a shareholder at the time of the transactions complained of. The Advisory Committee, believing the question should be settled in the courts, proposes no change in Rule 23 but thinks rather that the situation should be explained in an appropriate note.

The rule has a long history. In *Hawes v. Oakland*, 1882, 104 U.S. 450, the Court held that a shareholder could not maintain such an action unless he owned shares at the time of the transactions complained of, or unless they devolved on him by operation of law. At that time the decision in *Swift v. Tyson*, 1842, 16 Peters 1, was the law, and the federal courts considered themselves free to establish their own principles of equity jurisprudence, so the Court was not in 1882 and has not been, until *Erie R. Co. v. Tompkins* in 1938, concerned with the question whether *Hawes v. Oakland* dealt with substantive right or procedure.

Following the decision in *Hawes v. Oakland*, and at the same term, the Court, to implement its decision, adopted [former] Equity Rule 94, which contained the same provision above quoted from Rule 23 F.R.C.P. The provision in [former] Equity Rule 94 was later embodied in [former] Equity Rule 27, of which the present Rule 23 is substantially a copy.

In *City of Quincy v. Steel*, 1887, 120 U.S. 241, 245, 7 S.Ct. 520, the Court referring to *Hawes v. Oakland* said: "In order to give effect to the principles there laid down, this Court at that term adopted Rule 94 of the rules of practice for courts of equity of the United States."

Some other cases dealing with [former] Equity Rules 94 or 27 prior to the decision in *Erie R. Co. v. Tompkins* are *Dimpfel v. Ohio & Miss. R.R.*, 1884, 3 S.Ct. 573, 110 U.S. 209, 28 L.Ed. 121; *Illinois Central R. Co. v. Adams*, 1901, 21 S.Ct. 251, 180 U.S. 28, 34, 45L.Ed. 410; *Venner v. Great Northern Ry.*, 1908, 28 S.Ct. 328, 209 U.S. 24, 30, 52 L.Ed. 666; *Jacobson v. General Motors Corp.*, S.D.N.Y.1938, 22 F.Supp. 255, 257. These cases generally treat *Hawes v. Oakland* as establishing a "principle" of equity, or as dealing not with jurisdiction but with the "right" to maintain an action, or have said that the defense under the equity rule is analogous to the defense that the plaintiff has no "title" and results in a dismissal "for want of equity."

Those state decisions which held that a shareholder acquiring stock after the event may maintain a derivative action are founded on the view that it is a right belonging to the shareholder at the time of the transaction and which passes as a right to the subsequent purchaser. See *Pollitz v. Gould*, 1911, 202 N.Y. 11, 94 N.E. 1088.

The first case arising after the decision in *Erie R. Co. v. Tompkins*, in which this problem was involved, was *Summers v. Hearst*, S.D.N.Y.1938, 23 F.Supp. 986. It concerned [former] Equity Rule 27, as Federal Rule 23 was not then in effect. In a well considered opinion Judge Leibell reviewed the decisions and said: "The federal cases that discuss this section of [former] Rule 27 support the view that it states a principle of substantive law." He quoted *Pollitz v. Gould*, 1911, 202 N.Y. 11, 94 N.E. 1088, as saying that the United States Supreme Court "seems to have been more concerned with establishing this rule as one of practice than of substantive law" but that "whether it be regarded as establishing a principle of law or a rule of practice, this authority has been subsequently followed in the United States courts."

He then concluded that, although the federal decisions treat the equity rule as "stating a principle of substantive law", if "[former] Equity Rule 27 is to be modified or revoked in view of *Erie R. Co. v. Tompkins*, it is not the province of this Court to suggest it, much less impliedly to follow that course by disregarding the mandatory provisions of the Rule."

In *Piccard v. Sperry Corporation*, S.D.N.Y.1941, 36 F.Supp. 1006, 1009–10, affirmed without opinion, C.C.A.2d 1941, 120 F.2d 328, a shareholder, not such at the time of the transactions complained of, sought to intervene. The court held an intervenor was as much subject to Rule 23 as an original plaintiff; and that the requirement of Rule 23(b) was "a matter of practice," not substance, and applied in New York where the state law was otherwise, despite *Erie R. Co. v. Tompkins*. In *New York v. Guaranty Trust Co. of New York*, C.C.A.2, 1944, 143 F.2d 503, rev'd on other grounds, 1945, 65 S.Ct. 1464, the court said: "Restrictions on the bringing of stockholders' actions, such as those imposed by F.R.C.P. 23(b) or other state statutes are procedural," citing the *Piccard* and other cases.

Some other federal decisions since 1938 touch the question.

In *Gallup v. Caldwell*, C.C.A.3, 1941, 120 F.2d 90, 95 arising in New Jersey, the point was raised but not decided, the court saying that it was not satisfied that the then New Jersey rule differed from Rule 23(b), and that "under the circumstances the proper course was to follow Rule 23(b)."

In *Mullins v. DeSoto Securities Co.*, W.D.La.1942, 45 F.Supp. 871, 878, the point was not decided, because the court found the Louisiana rule to be the same as that stated in Rule 23(b).

In *Toebelman v. Missouri-Kansas Pipe Line Co.*, D.Del. 1941, 41 F.Supp. 334, 340, the court dealt only with another part of Rule 23(b), relating to prior demands on the stockholders and did not discuss *Erie R. Co. v. Tompkins*, or its effect on the rule.

In *Perrott v. United States Banking Corp.*, D.Del.1944, 53 F.Supp. 953, it appeared that the Delaware law does not require the plaintiff to have owned shares at the time of the transaction complained of. The court sustained Rule 23(b), after discussion of the authorities, saying:

"It seems to me the rule does not go beyond procedure. * * * Simply because a particular plaintiff cannot qualify as a proper party to maintain such an action does not destroy or even whittle at the cause of action. The cause of action exists until a qualified plaintiff can get it started in a federal court."

In *Bankers Nat. Corp. v. Barr*, S.D.N.Y.1945, 9 Fed.Rules Serv. 23b.11, Case 1, the court held Rule 23(b) to be one of procedure, but that whether the plaintiff was a stockholder was a substantive question to be settled by state law.

The New York rule, as stated in *Pollitz v. Gould*, supra, has been altered by an act of the New York Legislature, Chapter 667, Laws of 1944, effective April 9, 1944, General Corporation Law, § 61, which provides that "in any action brought by a shareholder in the right of a * * * corporation, it must appear that the plaintiff was a stockholder at the time of the transaction of which he complains, or that his stock thereafter devolved upon him by operation of law." At the same time a further and separate provision was enacted, requiring under certain circumstances the giving of security for reasonable expenses and attorney's fees, to which security the corporation in whose right the action is brought and the defendants therein may have recourse. (Chapter 668, Laws of 1944, effective April 9, 1944, General Corporation

Law, § 61–b.) These provisions are aimed at so-called "strike" stockholders' suits and their attendant abuses. *Shielcrawt v. Moffett,* Ct.App.1945, 294 N.Y. 180, 61 N.E.2d 435, rev'g 51 N.Y.S.2d 188, aff'g 49 N.Y.S.2d 64; *Noel Associates, Inc. v. Merrill,* Sup.Ct.1944, 184 Misc. 646, 63 N.Y.S.2d 143.

Insofar as § 61 is concerned, it has been held that the section is procedural in nature. *Klum v. Clinton Trust Co.,* Sup.Ct.1944, 183 Misc. 340, 48 N.Y.S.2d 267; *Noel Associates, Inc. v. Merrill,* supra. In the latter case the court pointed out that "The 1944 amendment to Section 61 rejected the rule laid down in the Pollitz case and substituted, in place thereof, in its precise language, the rule which has long prevailed in the Federal Courts and which is now Rule 23(b) * * *". There is, nevertheless, a difference of opinion regarding the application of the statute to pending actions. See *Klum v. Clinton Trust Co.,* supra (applicable); *Noel Associates, Inc. v. Merrill,* supra (inapplicable).

With respect to § 61–b, which may be regarded as a separate problem, *Noel Associates, Inc. v. Merrill,* supra, it has been held that even though the statute is procedural in nature—a matter not definitely decided—the Legislature evinced no intent that the provisions should apply to actions pending when it became effective. *Shielcrawt v. Moffett,* supra. As to actions instituted after the effective date of the legislation, the constitutionality of § 61–b is in dispute. See *Wolf v. Atkinson,* Sup.Ct.1944, 182 Misc. 675, 49 N.Y.S.2d 703 (constitutional); *Citron v. Mangel Stores Corp.,* Sup.Ct. 1944, 50 N.Y.S.2d 416 (unconstitutional); Zlinkoff, *The American Investor and the Constitutionality of § 61–b of the New York General Corporation Law,* 1945, 54 Yale L.J. 352.

New Jersey also enacted a statute, similar to Chapters 667 and 668 of the New York law. See P.L.1945, Ch. 131, R.S.Cum.Supp. 14:3–15. The New Jersey provision similar to Chapter 668, § 61–b, differs, however, in that it specifically applies retroactively. It has been held that this provision is procedural and hence will not govern a pending action brought against a New Jersey corporation in the New York courts. *Shielcrawt v. Moffett,* Sup.Ct.N.Y.1945, 184 Misc. 1074, 56 N.Y.S.2d 134.

See, also generally, 2 Moore's *Federal Practice,* 1938, 2250–2253, and Cum.Supplement § 23.05.

The decisions here discussed show that the question is a debatable one, and that there is respectable authority for either view, with a recent trend towards the view that Rule 23(b)(1) is procedural. There is reason to say that the question is one which should not be decided by the Supreme Court ex parte, but left to await a judicial decision in a litigated case, and that in the light of the material in this note, the only inference to be drawn from a failure to amend Rule 23(b) would be that the question is postponed to await a litigated case.

The Advisory Committee is unanimously of the opinion that this course should be followed.

If, however, the final conclusion is that the rule deals with a matter of substantive right, then the rule should be amended by adding a provision that Rule 23(b)(1) does not apply in jurisdictions where state law permits a shareholder to maintain a secondary action, although he was not a shareholder at the time of the transactions of which he complains.

1966 Amendment

Difficulties with the original rule. The categories of class actions in the original rule were defined in terms of the abstract nature of the rights involved: the so-called "true" category was defined as involving "joint, common, or secondary rights"; the "hybrid" category, as involving "several" rights related to "specific property"; the "spurious" category, as involving "several" rights affected by a common question and related to common relief. It was thought that the definitions accurately described the situations amenable to the class-suit device, and also would indicate the proper extent of the judgment in each category, which would in turn help to determine the res judicata effect of the judgment if questioned in a later action. Thus the judgments in "true" and "hybrid" class actions would extend to the class (although in somewhat different ways); the judgment in a "spurious" class action would extend only to the parties including intervenors. See Moore, *Federal Rules of Civil Procedure: Some Problems Raised by the Preliminary Draft,* 25 Geo.L.J. 551, 570–76 (1937).

In practice the terms "joint," "common," etc., which were used as the basis of the Rule 23 classification proved obscure and uncertain. See Chafee, *Some Problems of Equity* 245–46, 256–57 (1950); Kalven & Rosenfield, *The Contemporary Function of the Class Suit,* 8 U. of Chi.L.Rev. 684, 707 & n. 73 (1941); Keeffe, Levy & Donovan, *Lee Defeats Ben Hur,* 33 Corn.L.Q. 327, 329–36 (1948); *Developments in the Law: Multiparty Litigation in the Federal Courts,* 71 Harv. L.Rev. 874, 931 (1958); Advisory Committee's Note to Rule 19, as amended. The courts had considerable difficulty with these terms. See, e.g., *Gullo v. Veterans' Coop. H. Assn.,* 13 F.R.D. 11 (D.D.C.1952); *Shipley v. Pittsburgh & L.E.R. Co.,* 70 F.Supp. 870 (W.D.Pa.1947); *Deckert v. Independence Shares Corp.,* 27 F.Supp. 763 (E.D.Pa.1939), rev'd 108 F.2d 51 (3d Cir. 1939), rev'd, 311 U.S. 282 (1940), on remand, 39 F.Supp. 592 (E.D.Pa.1941), rev'd sub nom. *Pennsylvania Co. for Ins. on Lives v. Deckert,* 123 F.2d 979 (3d Cir.1941) (see Chafee, supra, at 264–65).

Nor did the rule provide an adequate guide to the proper extent of the judgments in class actions. First, we find instances of the courts classifying actions as "true" or intimating that the judgments would be decisive for the class where these results seemed appropriate but were reached by dint of depriving the word "several" of coherent meaning. See, e.g., *System Federation No. 91 v. Reed,* 180 F.2d 991 (6th Cir.1950); *Wilson v. City of Paducah,* 100 F.Supp. 116 (W.D.Ky.1951); *Citizens Banking Co. v. Monticello State Bank,* 143 F.2d 261 (8th Cir.1944); *Redmond v. Commerce Trust Co.,* 144 F.2d 140 (8th Cir.1944), cert. denied, 323 U.S. 776 (1944); *United States v. American Optical Co.,* 97 F.Supp. 66 (N.D.Ill.1951); *National Hairdressers' & C. Assn. v. Philad Co.,* 34 F.Supp. 264 (D.Del.1940); 41 F.Supp. 701 (D.Del.1940), aff'd mem., 129 F.2d 1020 (3d Cir.1942). Second, we find cases classified by the courts as "spurious" in which, on a realistic view, it would seem fitting for the judgments to extend to the class. See, e.g., *Knapp v. Bankers Sec. Corp.,* 17 F.R.D. 245 (E.D.Pa.1954), aff'd 230 F.2d 717 (3d Cir.1956); *Giesecke v. Denver Tramway Corp.,* 81 F.Supp. 957 (D.Del.1949); *York v. Guaranty Trust Co.,* 143 F.2d 503 (2d Cir.1944), rev'd on grounds not here relevant, 326 U.S. 99 (1945) (see Chafee, supra, at 208); cf. *Webster Eisenlohr, Inc. v. Kalodner,* 145 F.2d 316, 320 (3d Cir.1944), cert. denied, 325 U.S. 867 (1945). But cf. the early decisions, *Duke of Bedford v. Ellis,* [1901] A.C. 1; *Sheffield Waterworks v. Yeomans,* L.R. 2 Ch.App. 8 (1866); *Brown v. Vermuden,* 1 Ch.Cas. 272, 22 Eng.Rep. 796 (1676).

The "spurious" action envisaged by original Rule 23 was in any event an anomaly because, although denominated a "class" action and pleaded as such, it was supposed not to adjudicate the rights or liabilities of any person not a party. It was believed to be an advantage of the "spurious" category that it would invite decisions that a member of the "class" could, like a member of the class in a "true" or "hybrid" action, intervene on an ancillary basis without being required to show an independent basis of Federal jurisdiction, and have the benefit of the date of the commencement of the action for purposes of the statute of limitations. See 3 Moore's *Federal Practice,* pars. 23.10[1], 23.12 (2d ed.1963). These results were attained in some instances but not in others. On the statute of limitations, see *Union Carbide & Carbon Corp. v. Nisley,* 300 F.2d 561 (10th Cir.1961), pet. cert. dism., 371 U.S. 801 (1963); but cf. *P. W. Husserl, Inc. v. Newman,* 25 F.R.D. 264 (S.D.N.Y.1960); *Athas v. Day,* 161 F.Supp. 916 (D.Colo.1958). On ancillary intervention, see *Amen v. Black,* 234 F.2d 12 (10th Cir.1956), cert. granted, 352 U.S. 888 (1956), dism. on stip., 355 U.S. 600 (1958); but cf. *Wagner v. Kemper,* 13 F.R.D. 128 (W.D.Mo.1952). The results, however, can hardly depend upon the mere appearance of a "spurious" category in the rule; they should turn on more basic considerations. See discussion of subdivision (c)(1) below.

Finally, the original rule did not squarely address itself to the question of the measures that might be taken during the course of the action to assure procedural fairness, particularly giving notice to members of the class, which may in turn be related in some instances to the extension of the judgment to the class. See Chafee, supra, at 230–31; Keeffe, Levy & Donovan, supra; *Developments in the law,* supra, 71 Harv. L.Rev. at 937–38; Note, *Binding Effect of Class Actions,* 67 Harv.L.Rev. 1059, 1062–65 (1954); Note, *Federal Class Actions: A Suggested Revision of Rule 23,* 46 Colum.L.Rev. 818, 833–36 (1946); Mich.Gen.Court R. 208.4 (effective Jan. 1, 1963); Idaho R.Civ.P. 23(d); Minn.R.Civ.P. 23.04; N.Dak.R.Civ.P. 23(d).

The amended rule describes in more practical terms the occasions for maintaining class actions; provides that all class actions maintained to the end as such will result in judgments including those whom the court finds to be members of the class, whether or not the judgment is favorable to the class; and refers to the measures which can be taken to assure the fair conduct of these actions.

Subdivision (a) states the prerequisites for maintaining any class action in terms of the numerousness of the class making joinder of the members impracticable, the existence of questions common to the class, and the desired qualifications of the representative parties. See Weinstein, *Revision of Procedure: Some Problems in Class Actions,* 9 Buffalo L.Rev. 433, 458–59 (1960); 2 Barron & Holtzoff, *Federal Practice & Procedure* § 562, at 265, § 572, at 351–52 (Wright ed. 1961). These are necessary but not sufficient conditions for a class action. See, e.g., *Giordano v. Radio Corp. of Am.,* 183 F.2d 558, 560 (3d Cir.1950); *Zachman v. Erwin,* 186 F.Supp. 681 (S.D.Tex.1959); *Baim & Blank, Inc. v. Warren-Connelly Co., Inc.,* 19 F.R.D. 108 (S.D.N.Y.1956). Subdivision (b) describes the additional elements which in varying situations justify the use of a class action.

Subdivision (b)(1). The difficulties which would be likely to arise if resort were had to separate actions by or against the individual members of the class here furnish the reasons for, and the principal key to, the propriety and value of utilizing the class-action device. The considerations stated under clauses (A) and (B) are comparable to certain of the elements which define the persons whose joinder in an action is desirable as stated in Rule 19(a), as amended. See amended Rule 19(a)(2)(i) and (ii), and the Advisory Committee's Note thereto; Hazard, *Indispensable Party: The Historical Origin of a Procedural Phantom,* 61 Colum.L.Rev. 1254, 1259–60 (1961); cf. 3 Moore, supra, par. 23.08, at 3435.

Clause (A): One person may have rights against, or be under duties toward, numerous persons constituting a class, and be so positioned that conflicting or varying adjudications in lawsuits with individual members of the class might establish incompatible standards to govern his conduct. The class action device can be used effectively to obviate the actual or virtual dilemma which would thus confront the party opposing the class. The matter has been stated thus: "The felt necessity for a class action is greatest when the courts are called upon to order or sanction the alteration of the status quo in circumstances such that a large number of persons are in a position to call on a single person to alter the status quo, or to complain if it is altered, and the possibility exists that [the] actor might be called upon to act in inconsistent ways." Louisell & Hazard, *Pleading and Procedure: State and Federal* 719 (1962); see *Supreme Tribe of Ben-Hur v. Cauble,* 255 U.S. 356, 366–67 (1921). To illustrate: Separate actions by individuals against a municipality to declare a bond issue invalid or condition or limit it, to prevent or limit the making of a particular appropriation or to compel or invalidate an assessment, might create a risk of inconsistent or varying determinations. In the same way, individual litigations of the rights and duties of riparian owners, or of landowners' rights and duties respecting a claimed nuisance, could create a possibility of incompatible adjudications. Actions by or against a class provide a ready and fair means of achieving unitary adjudication. See *Maricopa County Mun. Water Con. Dist. v. Looney,* 219 F.2d 529 (9th Cir.1955); *Rank v. Krug,* 142 F.Supp. 1, 154–59 (S.D.Calif.1956), on app., *State of California v. Rank,* 293 F.2d 340, 348 (9th Cir.1961); *Gart v. Cole,* 263 F.2d 244 (2d Cir.1959), cert. denied 359 U.S. 978 (1959); cf. *Martinez v. Maverick Cty. Water Con. & Imp. Dist.,* 219 F.2d 666 (5th Cir.1955); 3 Moore, supra, par. 23.11[2], at 3458–59.

Clause (B): This clause takes in situations where the judgment in a nonclass action by or against an individual member of the class, while not technically concluding the other members, might do so as a practical matter. The vice of an individual action would lie in the fact that the other members of the class, thus practically concluded, would have had no representation in the lawsuit. In an action by policy holders against a fraternal benefit association attacking a financial reorganization of the society, it would hardly have been practical, if indeed it would have been possible, to confine the effects of a validation of the reorganization to the individual plaintiffs. Consequently a class action was called for with adequate representation of all members of the class. See *Supreme Tribe of Ben-Hur v. Cauble,* 255 U.S. 356 (1921); *Waybright v. Columbian Mut. Life Ins. Co.,* 30 F.Supp. 885 (W.D.Tenn.1939); cf. *Smith v. Swormstedt,* 16 How. (57 U.S.) 288 (1853). For much the same reason actions by shareholders to compel the declaration of a dividend[,] the proper recognition and handling of redemption or pre-emption rights, or the like (or actions by the corporation for corresponding declarations of rights), should ordinarily be conducted as class actions, although the matter has been much obscured by the insistence that each shareholder has an individual claim. See *Knapp v. Bankers Securities Corp.*, 17 F.R.D. 245 (E.D.Pa.1954), aff'd, 230 F.2d 717 (3d Cir. 1956); *Giesecke v. Denver Tramway Corp.*, 81 F.Supp. 957 (D.Del.1949); *Zahn v. Transamerica Corp.*, 162 F.2d 36 (3d Cir.1947); *Speed v. Transamerica Corp.*, 100 F.Supp. 461 (D.Del.1951); *Sobel v. Whittier Corp.*, 95 F.Supp. 643 (E.D.Mich.1951), app. dism., 195 F.2d 361 (6th Cir.1952); *Goldberg v. Whittier Corp.*, 111 F.Supp. 382 (E.D.Mich.1953); *Dann v. Studebaker-Packard Corp.*, 288 F.2d 201 (6th Cir. 1961); *Edgerton v. Armour & Co.*, 94 F.Supp. 549 (S.D.Calif.1950); *Ames v. Mengel Co.*, 190 F.2d 344 (2d Cir.1951). (These shareholders' actions are to be distinguished from derivative actions by shareholders dealt with in new Rule 23.1). The same reasoning applies to an action which charges a breach of trust by an indenture trustee or other fiduciary similarly affecting the members of a large class of security holders or other beneficiaries, and which requires an accounting or like measures to restore the subject of the trust. See *Boesenberg v. Chicago T. & T. Co.*, 128 F.2d 245 (7th Cir.1942); *Citizens Banking Co. v. Monticello State Bank*, 143 F.2d 261 (8th Cir.1944); *Redmond v. Commerce Trust Co.*, 144 F.2d 140 (8th Cir.1944), cert. denied, 323 U.S. 776 (1944); cf. *York v. Guaranty Trust Co.*, 143 F.2d 503 (2d Cir.1944), rev'd on grounds not here relevant, 326 U.S. 99 (1945).

In various situations an adjudication as to one or more members of the class will necessarily or probably have an adverse practical effect on the interests of other members who should therefore be represented in the lawsuit. This is plainly the case when claims are made by numerous persons against a fund insufficient to satisfy all claims. A class action by or against representative members to settle the validity of the claims as a whole, or in groups, followed by separate proof of the amount of each valid claim and proportionate distribution of the fund, meets the problem. Cf. *Dickinson v. Burnham*, 197 F.2d 973 (2d Cir.1952), cert. denied, 344 U.S. 875 (1952); 3 Moore, supra, at par. 23.09. The same reasoning applies to an action by a creditor to set aside a fraudulent conveyance by the debtor and to appropriate the property to his claim, when the debtor's assets are insufficient to pay all creditors' claims. See *Heffernan v. Bennett & Armour*, 110 Cal.App.2d 564, 243 P.2d 846 (1952); cf. *City & County of San Francisco v. Market Street Ry.*, 95 Cal.App.2d 648, 213 P.2d 780 (1950). Similar problems, however, can arise in the absence of a fund either present or potential. A negative or mandatory injunction secured by one of a numerous class may disable the opposing party from performing claimed duties toward the other members of the class or materially affect his ability to do so. An adjudication as to movie "clearances and runs" nominally affecting only one exhibitor would often have practical effects on all the exhibitors in the same territorial area. Cf. *United States v. Paramount Pictures, Inc.*, 66 F.Supp. 323, 341–46 (S.D.N.Y. 1946); 334 U.S. 131, 144–48 (1948). Assuming a sufficiently numerous class of exhibitors, a class action would be advisable. (Here representation of subclasses of exhibitors could become necessary; see subdivision (c)(3)(B).)

Subdivision (b)(2). This subdivision is intended to reach situations where a party has taken action or refused to take action with respect to a class, and final relief of an injunctive nature or of a corresponding declaratory nature, settling the legality of the behavior with respect to the class as a whole, is appropriate. Declaratory relief "corresponds" to injunctive relief when as a practical matter it affords injunctive relief or serves as a basis for later injunctive relief. The subdivision does not extend to cases in which the appropriate final relief relates exclusively or predominantly to money damages. Action or inaction is directed to a class within the meaning of this subdivision even if it has taken effect or is threatened only as to one or a few members of the class, provided it is based on grounds which have general application to the class.

Illustrative are various actions in the civil-rights field where a party is charged with discriminating unlawfully against a class, usually one whose members are incapable of specific enumeration. See *Potts v. Flax*, 313 F.2d 284 (5th Cir. 1963); *Bailey v. Patterson*, 323 F.2d 201 (5th Cir. 1963), cert. denied, 376 U.S. 910, (1964); *Brunson v. Board of Trustees of School District No. 1, Clarendon Cty., S.C.*, 311 F.2d 107 (4th Cir. 1962), cert. denied, 373 U.S. 933 (1963); *Green v. School Bd. of Roanoke, Va.*, 304 F.2d 118 (4th Cir. 1962); *Orleans Parish School Bd. v. Bush*, 242 F.2d 156 (5th Cir. 1957), cert. denied, 354 U.S. 921 (1957); *Mannings v. Board of Public Inst. of Hillsborough County, Fla.*, 277 F.2d 370 (5th Cir. 1960); *Northcross v. Board of Ed. of City of Memphis*, 302 F.2d 818 (6th Cir. 1962), cert. denied, 370 U.S. 944 (1962); *Frasier v. Board of Trustees of Univ. of N.C.*, 134 F.Supp. 589 (M.D.N.C.1955, 3-judge court), aff'd 350 U.S. 979 (1956). Subdivision (b)(2) is not limited to civil-rights cases. Thus an action looking to specific or declaratory relief could be brought by a numerous class of purchasers, say retailers of a given description, against a seller alleged to have undertaken to sell to that class at prices higher than those set for other purchasers, say retailers of another description, when the applicable law forbids such a pricing differential. So also a patentee of a machine, charged with selling or licensing the machine on condition that purchasers or licensees also purchase or obtain licenses to use an ancillary unpatented machine, could be sued on a class basis by a numerous group of purchasers or licensees, or by a numerous group of competing sellers or licensors of the unpatented machine, to test the legality of the "tying" condition.

Subdivision (b)(3). In the situations to which this subdivision relates, class-action treatment is not as clearly called for as in those described above, but it may nevertheless be convenient and desirable depending upon the particular facts. Subdivision (b)(3) encompasses those cases in which a class action would achieve economies of time, effort, and expense, and promote uniformity of decision as to persons similarly situated, without sacrificing procedural fairness or bringing about other undesirable results. Cf. Chafee, supra, at 201.

The court is required to find, as a condition of holding that a class action may be maintained under this subdivision, that the questions common to the class predominate over the questions affecting individual members. It is only where this predominance exists that economies can be achieved by means of the class-action device. In this view, a fraud perpetrated on numerous persons by the use of similar misrepresentations may be an appealing situation for a class action, and it may remain so despite the need, if liability is found, for separate determination of the damages suffered by individuals within the class. On the other hand, although having some common core, a fraud case may be unsuited for treatment as a class action if there was material variation in the representations made or in the kinds or degrees of reliance by the persons to whom they were addressed. See *Oppenheimer v. F. J. Young & Co., Inc.*, 144 F.2d 387 (2d Cir. 1944); *Miller v. National City Bank of N.Y.*, 166 F.2d 723 (2d Cir. 1948); and for like problems in other contexts, see *Hughes v. Encyclopaedia Britannica*, 199 F.2d 295 (7th Cir. 1952); *Sturgeon v. Great Lakes Steel Corp.*, 143 F.2d 819 (6th Cir. 1944). A "mass accident" resulting in injuries to numerous persons is ordinarily not appropriate for a class action because of the likelihood that significant questions, not only of damages but of liability and defenses of liability, would be present, affecting the individuals in different ways. In these circumstances an action conducted nominally as a class action would degenerate in practice into multiple lawsuits separately tried. See *Pennsylvania R.R. v. United States*, 111 F.Supp. 80 (D.N.J.1953); cf. Weinstein, supra, 9 Buffalo L.Rev. at 469. Private damage claims by numerous individuals arising out of concerted antitrust violations may or may not involve predominating common questions. See *Union Carbide & Carbon Corp. v. Nisley*, 300 F.2d 561 (10th Cir. 1961), pet. cert. dism., 371 U.S. 801 (1963); cf. *Weeks v. Bareco Oil Co.*, 125 F.2d 84 (7th Cir. 1941); *Kainz v. Anheuser-Busch, Inc.*, 194 F.2d 737 (7th Cir. 1952); *Hess v. Anderson, Clayton & Co.*, 20 F.R.D. 466 (S.D.Calif.1957).

That common questions predominate is not itself sufficient to justify a class action under subdivision (b)(3), for another method of handling the litigious situation may be available which has greater practical advantages. Thus one or more actions agreed to by the parties as test or model actions may be preferable to a class action; or it may prove feasible and preferable to consolidate actions. Cf. Weinstein, supra, 9 Buffalo L.Rev. at 438–54. Even when a number of separate actions are proceeding simultaneously, experience shows that the burdens on the parties and the courts can sometimes be reduced by arrangements for avoiding repetitious discovery or the like. Currently the Coordinating Committee on Multiple Litigation in the United States District Courts (a subcommittee of the Committee on Trial Practice and Technique of the Judicial Conference of the United States) is charged with developing methods for expediting such massive litigation. To reinforce the point that the court with the aid of the parties ought to assess the relative advantages of alternative procedures for handling the total controversy, subdivision (b)(3) requires, as a further condition of maintaining the class action, that the court shall find that that procedure is "superior" to the others in the particular circumstances.

Factors (A)–(D) are listed, non-exhaustively, as pertinent to the findings. The court is to consider the interests of individual members of the class in controlling their own litigations and carrying them on as they see fit. See *Weeks v. Bareco Oil Co.*, 125 F.2d 84, 88–90, 93–94 (7th Cir. 1941) (anti-trust action); see also *Pentland v. Dravo Corp.*, 152 F.2d 851 (3d Cir. 1945), and Chafee, supra, at 273–75, regarding policy of Fair Labor Standards Act of 1938, § 16(b), 29 U.S.C. § 216(b), prior to amendment by Portal-to-Portal Act of 1947, § 5(a). [The present provisions of 29 U.S.C. § 216(b) are not intended to be affected by Rule 23, as amended.]

In this connection the court should inform itself of any litigation actually pending by or against the individuals. The interests of individuals in conducting separate lawsuits may be so strong as to call for denial of a class action. On the other hand, these interests may be theoretic rather than practical; the class may have a high degree of cohesion and prosecution of the action through representatives would be quite unobjectionable, or the amounts at stake for individuals may be so small that separate suits would be impracticable. The burden that separate suits would impose on the party opposing the class, or upon the court calendars, may also fairly be considered. (See the discussion, under subdivision (c)(2) below, of the right of members to be excluded from the class upon their request.)

Also pertinent is the question of the desirability of concentrating the trial of the claims in the particular forum by means of a class action, in contrast to allowing the claims to be litigated separately in forums to which they would ordinarily be brought. Finally, the court should consider the problems of management which are likely to arise in the conduct of a class action.

Subdivision (c)(1). In order to give clear definition to the action, this provision requires the court to determine, as early in the proceedings as may be practicable, whether an action brought as a class action is to be so maintained. The determination depends in each case on satisfaction of the terms of subdivision (a) and the relevant provisions of subdivision (b).

An order embodying a determination can be conditional; the court may rule, for example, that a class action may be maintained only if the representation is improved through intervention of additional parties of a stated type. A determination once made can be altered or amended before the decision on the merits if, upon fuller development of the facts, the original determination appears unsound. A negative determination means that the action should be stripped of its character as a class action. See subdivision (d)(4). Although an action thus becomes a nonclass action, the court may still be receptive to interventions before the decision on the merits so that the litigation may cover as many interests as can be conveniently handled; the questions whether the intervenors in the nonclass action shall be permitted to claim "ancillary" jurisdiction or the benefit of the date of the commencement of the action for purposes of the statute of limitations are to be decided by reference to the laws governing jurisdiction and limitations as they apply in particular contexts.

Whether the court should require notice to be given to members of the class of its intention to make a determination, or of the order embodying it, is left to the court's discretion under subdivision (d)(2).

Subdivision (c)(2) makes special provision for class actions maintained under subdivision (b)(3). As noted in the discussion of the latter subdivision, the interests of the individuals in pursing their own litigations may be so strong here as to warrant denial of a class action altogether. Even when a class action is maintained under subdivision (b)(3), this individual interest is respected. Thus the court is required to direct notice to the members of the class of the right of each member to be excluded from the class upon his request. A member who does not request exclusion may, if he wishes, enter an appearance in the action through his counsel; whether or not he does so, the judgment in the action will embrace him.

The notice[,] setting forth the alternatives open to the members of the class, is to be the best practicable under the circumstances, and shall include individual notice to the members who can be identified through reasonable effort. (For further discussion of this notice, see the statement under subdivision (d)(2) below.)

Subdivision (c)(3). The judgment in a class action maintained as such to the end will embrace the class, that is, in a class action under subdivision (b)(1) or (b)(2), those found by the court to be class members; in a class action under subdivision (b)(3), those to whom the notice prescribed by subdivision (c)(2) was directed, excepting those who requested exclusion or who are ultimately found by the court not to be members of the class. The judgment has this scope whether it is favorable or unfavorable to the class. In a (b)(1) or (b)(2) action the judgment "describes" the members of the class, but need not specify the individual members; in a (b)(3) action the judgment "specifies" the individual members who have been identified and described the others.

Compare subdivision (c)(4) as to actions conducted as class actions only with respect to particular issues. Where the class-action character of the lawsuit is based solely on the existence of a "limited fund," the judgment, while extending to all claims of class members against the fund, has ordinarily left unaffected the personal claims of nonappearing members against the debtor. See 3 Moore, supra, par. 23.11[4].

Hitherto, in a few actions conducted as "spurious" class actions and thus nominally designed to extend only to parties and others intervening before the determination of liability, courts have held or intimated that class members might be permitted to intervene after a decision on the merits favorable to their interests, in order to secure the benefits of the decision for themselves, although they would presumably be unaffected by an unfavorable decision. See, as to the propriety of this so-called "one-way" intervention in "spurious" actions, the conflicting views expressed in *Union Carbide & Carbon Corp. v. Nisley*, 300 F.2d 561 (10th Cir. 1961), pet. cert. dism., 371 U.S. 801 (1963); *York v. Guaranty Trust Co.*, 143 F.2d 503, 529 (2d Cir. 1944), rev'd on grounds not here relevant, 326 U.S. 99 (1945); *Pentland v. Dravo Corp.*, 152 F.2d 851, 856 (3d Cir. 1945); *Speed v. Transamerica Corp.*, 100 F.Supp. 461, 463 (D.Del.1951); *State Wholesale Grocers v. Great Atl. & Pac. Tea Co.*, 24 F.R.D. 510 (N.D.Ill.1959); *Alabama Ind. Serv. Stat. Assn. v. Shell Pet. Corp.*, 28 F.Supp. 386, 390 (N.D.Ala.1939); *Tolliver v. Cudahy Packing Co.*, 39 F.Supp. 337, 339 (E.D.Tenn.1941); Kalven & Rosenfield, supra, 8 U. of Chi.L.Rev. 684 (1941); Comment, 53 Nw.U.L.Rev. 627, 632–33 (1958); *Developments in the Law*, supra, 71 Harv.L.Rev. at 935; 2 Barron & Holtzoff, supra, § 568; but cf. *Lockwood v. Hercules Powder Co.*, 7 F.R.D. 24, 28–29 (W.D.Mo.1947); *Abram v. San Joaquin Cotton Oil Co.*, 46 F.Supp. 969, 976–77 (S.D.Calif.1942); Chafee, supra, at 280, 285; 3 Moore, supra, par. 23.12, at 3476. Under proposed subdivision (c)(3), one-way intervention is excluded; the action will have been early determined to be a class or nonclass action, and in the former case the judgment, whether or not favorable, will include the class, as above stated.

Although thus declaring that the judgment in a class action includes the class, as defined, subdivision (c)(3) does not disturb the recognized principle that the court conducting the action cannot predetermine the *res judicata* effect of the judgment; this can be tested only in a subsequent action. See Restatement, Judgments § 86, comment (h), § 116 (1942). The court, however, in framing the judgment in any suit brought as a class action, must decide what its extent or coverage shall be, and if the matter is carefully considered, questions of *res judicata* are less likely to be raised at a later time and if raised will be more satisfactorily answered. See Chafee, supra, at 294; Weinstein, supra, 9 Buffalo L.Rev. at 460.

Subdivision (c)(4). This provision recognizes that an action may be maintained as a class action as to particular issues only. For example, in a fraud or similar case the action may retain its "class" character only through the adjudication of liability to the class; the members of the class may thereafter be required to come in individually and prove the amounts of their respective claims.

Two or more classes may be represented in a single action. Where a class is found to include subclasses divergent in interest, the class may be divided correspondingly, and each subclass treated as a class.

Subdivision (d) is concerned with the fair and efficient conduct of the action and lists some types of orders which may be appropriate.

The court should consider how the proceedings are to be arranged in sequence, and what measures should be taken to simplify the proof and argument. See subdivision (d)(1). The orders resulting from this consideration, like the others referred to in subdivision (d), may be combined with a pretrial order under Rule 16, and are subject to modification as the case proceeds.

Subdivision (d)(2) sets out a non-exhaustive list of possible occasions for orders requiring notice to the class. Such notice is not a novel conception. For example, in "limited fund" cases, members of the class have been notified to present individual claims after the basic class decision. Notice has gone to members of a class so that they might express any opposition to the representation, see *United States v. American Optical Co.*, 97 F.Supp. 66 (N.D.Ill.1951), and 1950–51 CCH Trade Cases 64573–74 (par. 62869); cf. *Weeks v. Bareco Oil Co.*, 125 F.2d 84, 94 (7th Cir. 1941), and notice may encourage interventions to improve the representation of the class. Cf. *Oppenheimer v. F. J. Young & Co.*, 144 F.2d 387 (2d Cir. 1944). Notice has been used to poll members on a proposed modification of a consent decree. See record in *Sam Fox Publishing Co. v. United States*, 366 U.S. 683 (1961).

Subdivision (d)(2) does not require notice at any stage, but rather calls attention to its availability and invokes the court's discretion. In the degree that there is cohesiveness or unity in the class and the representation is effective, the need for notice to the class will tend toward a minimum. These indicators suggest that notice under subdivision (d)(2) may be particularly useful and advisable in certain class actions maintained under subdivision (b)(3), for example, to permit members of the class to object to the representation. Indeed, under subdivision (c)(2), notice must be ordered, and is not merely discretionary, to give the members in a subdivision (b)(3) class action an opportunity to secure exclusion from the class. This mandatory notice pursuant to subdivision (c)(2), together with any discretionary notice which the court may find it advisable to give under subdivision (d)(2), is designed to fulfill requirements of due process to which the class action procedure is of course subject. See *Hansberry v. Lee*, 311 U.S. 32 (1940); *Mullane v. Central Hanover Bank & Trust Co.*, 339 U.S. 306 (1950); cf. *Dickinson v.*

Burnham, 197 F.2d 973, 979 (2d Cir. 1952), and studies cited at 979 in 4; see also *All American Airways, Inc. v. Elderd*, 209 F.2d 247, 249 (2d Cir. 1954); *Gart v. Cole*, 263 F.2d 244, 248–49 (2d Cir. 1959), cert. denied, 359 U.S. 978 (1959).

Notice to members of the class, whenever employed under amended Rule 23, should be accommodated to the particular purpose but need not comply with the formalities for service of process. See Chafee, supra, at 230–31; *Brendle v. Smith*, 7 F.R.D. 119 (S.D.N.Y.1946). The fact that notice is given at one stage of the action does not mean that it must be given at subsequent stages. Notice is available fundamentally "for the protection of the members of the class or otherwise for the fair conduct of the action" and should not be used merely as a device for the undesirable solicitation of claims. See the discussion in *Cherner v. Transitron Electronic Corp.*, 201 F.Supp. 934 (D.Mass.1962); *Hormel v. United States*, 17 F.R.D. 303 (S.D.N.Y.1955).

In appropriate cases the court should notify interested government agencies of the pendency of the action or of particular steps therein.

Subdivision (d)(3) reflects the possibility of conditioning the maintenance of a class action, e.g., on the strengthening of the representation, see subdivision (c)(1) above; and recognizes that the imposition of conditions on intervenors may be required for the proper and efficient conduct of the action.

As to orders under subdivision (d)(4), see subdivision (c)(1) above.

Subdivision (e) requires approval of the court, after notice, for the dismissal or compromise of any class action.

1987 Amendment

The amendments are technical. No substantive change is intended.

1998 Amendments

Subdivision (f). This permissive interlocutory appeal provision is adopted under the power conferred by 28 U.S.C. § 1292(e). Appeal from an order granting or denying class certification is permitted in the sole discretion of the court of appeals. No other type of Rule 23 order is covered by this provision. The court of appeals is given unfettered discretion whether to permit the appeal, akin to the discretion exercised by the Supreme Court in acting on a petition for certiorari. This discretion suggests an analogy to the provision in 28 U.S.C. § 1292(b) for permissive appeal on certification by a district court. Subdivision (f), however, departs from the § 1291(b) model in two significant ways. It does not require that the district court certify the certification ruling for appeal, although the district court often can assist the parties and court of appeals by offering advice on the desirability of appeal. And it does not include the potentially limiting requirements of § 1292(b) that the district court order "involve[] a controlling question of law as to which there is substantial ground for difference of opinion and that an immediate appeal from the order may materially advance the ultimate termination of the litigation.

The courts of appeals will develop standards for granting review that reflect the changing areas of uncertainty in class litigation. The Federal Judicial Center study supports the view that many suits with class-action allegations present familiar and almost routine issues that are no more worthy of immediate appeal than many other interlocutory rulings. Yet several concerns justify expansion of present opportunities to appeal. An order denying certification may confront the plaintiff with a situation in which the only sure path to appellate review is by proceeding to final judgment on the merits of an individual claim that, standing alone, is far smaller than the costs of litigation. An order granting certification, on the other hand, may force a defendant to settle rather than incur the costs of defending a class action and run the risk of potentially ruinous liability. These concerns can be met at low cost by establishing in the court of appeals a discretionary power to grant interlocutory review in cases that show appeal-worthy certification issues.

Permission to appeal may be granted or denied on the basis of any consideration that the court of appeals finds persuasive. Permission is most likely to be granted when the certification decision turns on a novel or unsettled question of law, or when, as a practical matter, the decision on certification is likely dispositive of the litigation.

The district court, having worked through the certification decision, often will be able to provide cogent advice on the factors that bear on the decision whether to permit appeal. This advice can be particularly valuable if the certification decision is tentative. Even as to a firm certification decision, a statement of reasons bearing on the probably benefits and costs of immediate appeal can help focus the court of appeals decision, and may persuade the disappointed party that an attempt to appeal would be fruitless.

The 10–day period for seeking permission to appeal is designed to reduce the risk that attempted appeals will disrupt continuing proceedings. It is expected that the courts of appeals will act quickly in making the preliminary determination whether to permit appeal. Permission to appeal does not stay trial court proceedings. A stay should be sought first from the trial court. If the trial court refuses a stay, its action and any explanation of its views should weigh heavily with the court of appeals.

Appellate Rule 5 has been modified to establish the procedure for petitioning for leave to appeal under subdivision (f).

2003 Amendments

Subdivision (c). Subdivision (c) is amended in several respects. The requirement that the court determine whether to certify a class "as soon as practicable after commencement of an action" is replaced by requiring determination "at an early practicable time." The notice provisions are substantially revised.

Paragraph (1). Subdivision (c)(1)(A) is changed to require that the determination whether to certify a class be made "at an early practicable time." The "as soon as practicable" exaction neither reflects prevailing practice nor captures the many valid reasons that may justify deferring the initial certification decision. See Willging, Hooper & Niemic, *Empirical Study of Class Actions in Four Federal District Courts: Final Report to the Advisory Committee on Civil Rules 26–36* (Federal Judicial Center 1996).

Time may be needed to gather information necessary to make the certification decision. Although an evaluation of the probable outcome on the merits is not properly part of the certification decision, discovery in aid of the certification decision often includes information required to identify the nature of the issues that actually will be presented at trial. In this sense it is appropriate to conduct controlled discovery into the "merits," limited to those aspects relevant to making the certification decision on an informed basis. Active judicial supervision may be required to achieve the most effective balance that expedites an informed certification determination without forcing an artificial and ultimately wasteful division between "certification discovery" and "merits discovery." A critical need is to determine how the case will be tried. An increasing number of courts require a party requesting class certification to present a "trial plan" that describes the issues likely to be presented at trial and tests whether they are susceptible of class-wide proof. See Manual For Complex Litigation Third, § 21.213, p. 44; § 30.11, p. 214; § 30.12, p. 215.

Other considerations may affect the timing of the certification decision. The party opposing the class may prefer to win dismissal or summary judgment as to the individual plaintiffs without certification and without binding the class that might have been certified. Time may be needed to explore designation of class counsel under Rule 23(g), recognizing that in many cases the need to progress toward the certification determination may require designation of interim counsel under Rule 23(g)(2)(A).

Although many circumstances may justify deferring the certification decision, active management may be necessary to ensure that the certification decision is not unjustifiably delayed.

Subdivision (c)(1)(C) reflects two amendments. The provision that a class certification "may be conditional" is deleted. A court that is not satisfied that the requirements of Rule 23 have been met should refuse certification until they have been met. The provision that permits alteration or amendment of an order granting or denying class certification is amended to set the cut-off point at final judgment rather than "the decision on the merits." This change avoids the possible ambiguity in referring to "the decision on the merits." Following a determination of liability, for example, proceedings to define the remedy may demonstrate the need to amend the class definition or subdivide the class. In this setting the final judgment concept is pragmatic. It is not the same as the concept used for appeal purposes, but it should be flexible, particularly in protracted litigation.

The authority to amend an order under Rule 23(c)(1) before final judgment does not restore the practice of "one-way intervention" that was rejected by the 1966 revision of Rule 23. A determination of liability after certification, however, may show a need to amend the class definition. Decertification may be warranted after further proceedings.

If the definition of a class certified under Rule 23(b)(3) is altered to include members who have not been afforded notice and an opportunity to request exclusion, notice—including an opportunity to request exclusion—must be directed to the new class members under Rule 23(c)(2)(B).

Paragraph (2). The first change made in Rule 23(c)(2) is to call attention to the court's authority—already established in part by Rule 23(d)(2)—to direct notice of certification to a Rule 23(b)(1) or (b)(2) class. The present rule expressly requires notice only in actions certified under Rule 23(b)(3). Members of classes certified under Rules 23(b)(1) or (b)(2) have interests that may deserve protection by notice.

The authority to direct notice to class members in a (b)(1) or (b)(2) class action should be exercised with care. For several reasons, there may be less need for notice than in a (b)(3) class action. There is no right to request exclusion from a (b)(1) or (b)(2) class. The characteristics of the class may reduce the need for formal notice. The cost of providing notice, moreover, could easily cripple actions that do not seek damages. The court may decide not to direct notice after balancing the risk that notice costs may deter the pursuit of class relief against the benefits of notice.

When the court does direct certification notice in a (b)(1) or (b)(2) class action, the discretion and flexibility established by subdivision (c)(2)(A) extend to the method of giving notice. Notice facilitates the opportunity to participate. Notice calculated to reach a significant number of class members often will protect the interests of all. Informal methods may prove effective. A simple posting in a place visited by many class members, directing attention to a source of more detailed information, may suffice. The court should consider the costs of notice in relation to the probable reach of inexpensive methods.

If a Rule 23(b)(3) class is certified in conjunction with a (b)(2) class, the (c)(2)(B) notice requirements must be satisfied as to the (b)(3) class.

The direction that class-certification notice be couched in plain, easily understood language is a reminder of the need to work unremittingly at the difficult task of communicating with class members. It is difficult to provide information about most class actions that is both accurate and easily understood by class members who are not themselves lawyers. Factual uncertainty, legal complexity, and the complication of class-action procedure raise the barriers high. The Federal Judicial Center has created illustrative clear-notice forms that provide a helpful starting point for actions similar to those described in the forms.

Subdivision (e). Subdivision (e) is amended to strengthen the process of reviewing proposed class-action settlements. Settlement may be a desirable means of resolving a class action. But court review and approval are essential to assure adequate representation of class members who have not participated in shaping the settlement.

Paragraph (1). Subdivision (e)(1)(A) expressly recognizes the power of a class representative to settle class claims, issues, or defenses.

Rule 23(e)(1)(A) resolves the ambiguity in former Rule 23(e)'s reference to dismissal or compromise of "a class action." That language could be—and at times was—read to require court approval of settlements with putative class representatives that resolved only individual claims. See Manual for Complex Litigation Third, § 30.41. The new rule requires approval only if the claims, issues, or defenses of a certified class are resolved by a settlement, voluntary dismissal, or compromise.

Subdivision (e)(1)(B) carries forward the notice requirement of present Rule 23(e) when the settlement binds the class through claim or issue preclusion; notice is not required when the settlement binds only the individual class representatives. Notice of a settlement binding on the class is required either when the settlement follows class certification or when the decisions on certification and settlement proceed simultaneously.

Reasonable settlement notice may require individual notice in the manner required by Rule 23(c)(2)(B) for certification notice to a Rule 23(b)(3) class. Individual notice is appropriate, for example, if class members are required to take action—such as filing claims—to participate in the judgment, or if the court orders a settlement opt-out opportunity under Rule 23(e)(3).

Subdivision (e)(1)(C) confirms and mandates the already common practice of holding hearings as part of the process of approving settlement, voluntary dismissal, or compromise that would bind members of a class.

Subdivision (e)(1)(C) states the standard for approving a proposed settlement that would bind class members. The settlement must be fair, reasonable, and adequate. A helpful review of many factors that may deserve consideration is provided by *In re: Prudential Ins. Co. America Sales Practice Litigation Agent Actions,* 148 F.3d 283, 316–324 (3d Cir. 1998). Further guidance can be found in the Manual for Complex Litigation.

The court must make findings that support the conclusion that the settlement is fair, reasonable, and adequate. The findings must be set out in sufficient detail to explain to class members and the appellate court the factors that bear on applying the standard.

Settlement review also may provide an occasion to review the cogency of the initial class definition. The terms of the settlement themselves, or objections, may reveal divergent interests of class members and demonstrate the need to redefine the class or to designate subclasses. Redefinition of a class certified under Rule 23(b)(3) may require notice to new class members under Rule 23(c)(2)(B). See Rule 23(c)(1)(C).

Paragraph (2). Subdivision (e)(2) requires parties seeking approval of a settlement, voluntary dismissal, or compromise under Rule 23(e)(1) to file a statement identifying any agreement made in connection with the settlement. This provision does not change the basic requirement that the parties disclose all terms of the settlement or compromise that the court must approve under Rule 23(e)(1). It aims instead at related undertakings that, although seemingly separate, may have influenced the terms of the settlement by trading away possible advantages for the class in return for advantages for others. Doubts should be resolved in favor of identification.

Further inquiry into the agreements identified by the parties should not become the occasion for discovery by the parties or objectors. The court may direct the parties to provide to the court or other parties a summary or copy of the full terms of any agreement identified by the parties. The court also may direct the parties to provide a summary or copy of any agreement not identified by the parties that the court considers relevant to its review of a proposed settlement. In exercising discretion under this rule, the court may act in steps, calling first for a summary of any agreement that may have affected the settlement and then for a complete version if the summary does not provide an adequate basis for review. A direction to disclose a summary or copy of an agreement may raise concerns of confidentiality. Some agreements may include information that merits protection against general disclosure. And the court must provide an opportunity to claim work-product or other protections.

Paragraph (3). Subdivision (e)(3) authorizes the court to refuse to approve a settlement unless the settlement affords class members a new opportunity to request exclusion from a class certified under Rule 23(b)(3) after settlement terms are known. An agreement by the parties themselves to permit class members to elect exclusion at this point by the settlement agreement may be one factor supporting approval of the settlement. Often there is an opportunity to opt out at this point because the class is certified and settlement is reached in circumstances that lead to simultaneous notice of certification and notice of settlement. In these cases, the basic opportunity to elect exclusion applies without further complication. In some cases, particularly if settlement appears imminent at the time of certification, it may be possible to achieve equivalent protection by deferring notice and the opportunity to elect exclusion until actual settlement terms are known. This approach avoids the cost and potential confusion of providing two notices and makes the single notice more meaningful. But notice should not be delayed unduly after certification in the hope of settlement.

Rule 23(e)(3) authorizes the court to refuse to approve a settlement unless the settlement affords a new opportunity to elect exclusion in a case that settles after a certification decision if the earlier opportunity to elect exclusion provided with the certification notice has expired by the time of the settlement notice. A decision to remain in the class is likely to be more carefully considered and is better informed when settlement terms are known.

The opportunity to request exclusion from a proposed settlement is limited to members of a (b)(3) class. Exclusion may be requested only by individual class members; no class member may purport to opt out other class members by way of another class action.

The decision whether to approve a settlement that does not allow a new opportunity to elect exclusion is confided to the court's discretion. The court may make this decision before directing notice to the class under Rule 23(e)(1)(B) or after the Rule 23(e)(1)(C) hearing. Many factors may influence the court's decision. Among these are changes in the information available to class members since expiration of the first opportunity to request exclusion, and the nature of the individual class members' claims.

The terms set for permitting a new opportunity to elect exclusion from the proposed settlement of a Rule 23(b)(3) class action may address concerns of potential misuse. The court might direct, for example, that class members who elect exclusion are bound by rulings on the merits made before the settlement was proposed for approval. Still other terms or conditions may be appropriate.

Paragraph (4). Subdivision (e)(4) confirms the right of class members to object to a proposed settlement, voluntary dismissal, or compromise. The right is defined in relation to a disposition that, because it would bind the class, requires court approval under subdivision (e)(1)(C).

Subdivision (e)(4)(B) requires court approval for withdrawal of objections made under subdivision (e)(4)(A). Review follows automatically if the objections are withdrawn on terms that lead to modification of the settlement with the class. Review also is required if the objector formally withdraws the objections. If the objector simply abandons pursuit of the objection, the court may inquire into the circumstances.

Approval under paragraph (4)(B) may be given or denied with little need for further inquiry if the objection and the disposition go only to a protest that the individual treatment afforded the objector under the proposed settlement is unfair because of factors that distinguish the objector from other class members. Different considerations may apply if the objector has protested that the proposed settlement is not fair, reasonable, or adequate on grounds that apply generally to a class or subclass. Such objections, which purport to represent class-wide interests, may augment the opportunity for obstruction or delay. If such objections are surrendered on terms that do not affect the class settlement or the objector's participation in the class settlement, the court often can approve withdrawal of the objections without elaborate inquiry.

Once an objector appeals, control of the proceeding lies in the court of appeals. The court of appeals may undertake review and approval of a settlement with the objector, perhaps as part of appeal settlement procedures, or may remand to the district court to take advantage of the district court's familiarity with the action and settlement.

Subdivision (g). Subdivision (g) is new. It responds to the reality that the selection and activity of class counsel are often critically important to the successful handling of a class action. Until now, courts have scrutinized proposed class counsel as well as the class representative under Rule 23(a)(4). This experience has recognized the importance of judicial evaluation of the proposed lawyer for the class, and this new subdivision builds on that experience rather than introducing an entirely new element into the class certification process. Rule 23(a)(4) will continue to call for scrutiny of the proposed class representative, while this subdivision will guide the court in assessing proposed class counsel as part of the certification decision. This subdivision recognizes the importance of class counsel, states the obligation to represent the interests of the class, and provides a framework for selection of class counsel. The procedure and standards for appointment vary depending on whether there are multiple applicants to be class counsel. The new subdivision also provides a method by which the court may make directions from the outset about the potential fee award to class counsel in the event the action is successful.

Paragraph (1) sets out the basic requirement that class counsel be appointed if a class is certified and articulates the obligation of class counsel to represent the interests of the class, as opposed to the potentially conflicting interests of individual class members. It also sets out the factors the court should consider in assessing proposed class counsel.

Paragraph (1)(A) requires that the court appoint class counsel to represent the class. Class counsel must be appointed for all classes, including each subclass that the court certifies to represent divergent interests.

Paragraph (1)(A) does not apply if "a statute provides otherwise." This recognizes that provisions of the Private Securities Litigation Reform Act of 1995, Pub. L. No. 104–67, 109 Stat. 737 (1995) (codified in various sections of 15 U.S.C.), contain directives that bear on selection of a lead plaintiff and the retention of counsel. This subdivision does not purport to supersede or to affect the interpretation of those provisions, or any similar provisions of other legislation.

Paragraph 1(B) recognizes that the primary responsibility of class counsel, resulting from appointment as class counsel, is to represent the best interests of the class. The rule thus establishes the obligation of class counsel, an obligation that may be different from the customary obligations of counsel to individual clients. Appointment as class counsel means that the primary obligation of counsel is to the class rather than to any individual members of it. The class representatives do not have an unfettered right to "fire" class counsel. In the same vein, the class representatives cannot command class counsel to accept or reject a settlement proposal. To the contrary, class counsel must determine whether seeking the court's approval of a settlement would be in the best interests of the class as a whole.

Paragraph (1)(C) articulates the basic responsibility of the court to appoint class counsel who will provide the adequate representation called for by paragraph (1)(B). It identifies criteria that must be considered and invites the court to consider any other pertinent matters. Although couched in terms of the court's duty, the listing also informs counsel seeking appointment about the topics that should be addressed in an application for appointment or in the motion for class certification.

The court may direct potential class counsel to provide additional information about the topics mentioned in paragraph (1)(C) or about any other relevant topic. For example, the court may direct applicants to inform the court concerning any agreements about a prospective award of attorney fees or nontaxable costs, as such agreements may sometimes be significant in the selection of class counsel. The court might also direct that potential class counsel indicate how parallel litigation might be coordinated or consolidated with the action before the court.

The court may also direct counsel to propose terms for a potential award of attorney fees and nontaxable costs. Attorney fee awards are an important feature of class action practice, and attention to this subject from the outset may often be a productive technique. Paragraph (2)(C) therefore authorizes the court to provide directions about attorney fees and costs when appointing class counsel. Because there will be numerous class actions in which this information is not likely to be useful, the court need not consider it in all class actions.

Some information relevant to class counsel appointment may involve matters that include adversary preparation in a way that should be shielded from disclosure to other parties. An appropriate protective order may be necessary to preserve confidentiality.

In evaluating prospective class counsel, the court should weigh all pertinent factors. No single factor should necessarily be determinative in a given case. For example, the resources counsel will commit to the case must be appropriate to its needs, but the court should be careful not to limit consideration to lawyers with the greatest resources.

If, after review of all applicants, the court concludes that none would be satisfactory class counsel, it may deny class certification, reject all applications, recommend that an application be modified, invite new applications, or make any other appropriate order regarding selection and appointment of class counsel.

Paragraph (2). This paragraph sets out the procedure that should be followed in appointing class counsel. Although it affords substantial flexibility, it provides the framework for appointment of class counsel in all class actions. For counsel who filed the action, the materials submitted in support of the motion for class certification may suffice to justify appointment so long as the information described in paragraph (g)(1)(C) is included. If there are other applicants, they ordinarily would file a formal application detailing their suitability for the position.

In a plaintiff class action the court usually would appoint as class counsel only an attorney or attorneys who have sought appointment. Different considerations may apply in defendant class actions.

The rule states that the court should appoint "class counsel." In many instances, the applicant will be an individual attorney. In other cases, however, an entire firm, or perhaps numerous attorneys who are not otherwise affiliated but are collaborating on the action will apply. No rule of thumb exists to determine when such arrangements are appropriate; the court should be alert to the need for adequate staffing of the case, but also to the risk of overstaffing or an ungainly counsel structure.

Paragraph (2)(A) authorizes the court to designate interim counsel during the pre-certification period if necessary to protect the interests of the putative class. Rule 23(c)(1)(B) directs that the order certifying the class include appointment of class counsel. Before class certification, however, it will usually be important for an attorney to take action to prepare for the certification decision. The amendment to Rule 23(c)(1) recognizes that some discovery is often necessary for that determination. It also may be important to make or respond to motions before certification. Settlement may be discussed before certification. Ordinarily, such work is handled by the lawyer who filed the action. In some cases, however, there may be rivalry or uncertainty that makes formal designation of interim counsel appropriate. Rule 23(g)(2)(A) authorizes the court to designate interim counsel to act on behalf of the putative class before the certification decision is made. Failure to make the formal designation does not prevent the attorney who filed the action from proceeding in it. Whether or not formally designated interim counsel, an attorney who acts on behalf of the class before certification must act in the best interests of the class as a whole. For example, an attorney who negotiates a pre-certification settlement must seek a settlement that is fair, reasonable, and adequate for the class.

Rule 23(c)(1) provides that the court should decide whether to certify the class "at an early practicable time," and directs that class counsel should be appointed in the order certifying the class. In some cases, it may be appropriate for the court to allow a reasonable period after commencement of the action for filing applications to serve as class counsel. The primary ground for deferring appointment would be that there is reason to anticipate competing applications to serve as class counsel. Examples might include instances in which more than one class action has been filed, or in which other attorneys have filed individual actions on behalf of putative class members. The purpose of facilitating competing applications in such a case is to afford the best possible representation for the class. Another possible reason for deferring appointment would be that the initial applicant was found inadequate, but it seems appropriate to permit additional applications rather than deny class certification.

Paragraph (2)(B) states the basic standard the court should use in deciding whether to certify the class and appoint class counsel in the single applicant situation—that the applicant be able to provide the representation called for by paragraph (1)(B) in light of the factors identified in paragraph (1)(C).

If there are multiple adequate applicants, paragraph (2)(B) directs the court to select the class counsel best able to represent the interests of the class. This decision should also be made using the factors outlined in paragraph (1)(C), but in the multiple applicant situation the court is to go beyond scrutinizing the adequacy of counsel and make a comparison of the strengths of the various applicants. As with the decision whether to appoint the sole applicant for the posit ion, no single factor should be dispositive in selecting class counsel in cases in which there are multiple applicants. The fact that a given attorney filed the instant action, for example, might not weigh heavily in the decision if that lawyer had not done significant work identifying or investigating claims. Depending on the nature of the case, one important consideration might be the applicant's existing attorney-client relationship with the proposed class representative.

Paragraph (2)(C) builds on the appointment process by authorizing the court to include provisions regarding attorney fees in the order appointing class counsel. Courts may find it desirable to adopt guidelines for fees or nontaxable costs, or to direct class counsel to report to the court at regular intervals on the efforts undertaken in the action, to facilitate the court's later determination of a reasonable attorney fee.

Subdivision (h). Subdivision (h) is new. Fee awards are a powerful influence on the way attorneys initiate, develop, and conclude class actions. Class action attorney fee awards have heretofore been handled, along with all other attorney fee awards, under Rule 54(d)(2), but that rule is not addressed to the particular concerns of class actions. This subdivision is designed to work in tandem with new subdivision (g) on appointment of class counsel, which may afford an opportunity for the court to provide an early framework for an eventual fee award, or for monitoring the work of class counsel during the pendency of the action.

Subdivision (h) applies to "an action certified as a class action." This includes cases in which there is a simultaneous proposal for class certification and settlement even though technically the class may not be certified unless the court approves the settlement pursuant to review under Rule 23(e). When a settlement is proposed for Rule 23(e) approval, either after certification or with a request for certification, notice to class members about class counsel's fee motion would ordinarily accompany the notice to the class about the settlement proposal itself.

This subdivision does not undertake to create new grounds for an award of attorney fees or nontaxable costs. Instead, it applies when such awards are authorized by law or by agreement of the parties. Against that background, it provides a format for all awards of attorney fees and nontaxable costs in connection with a class action, not only the award to class counsel. In some situations, there may be a basis for making an award to other counsel whose work produced a beneficial result for the class, such as attorneys who acted for the class before certification but were not appointed class counsel, or attorneys who represented objectors to a proposed settlement under Rule 23(e) or to the fee motion of class counsel. Other situations in which fee awards are authorized by law or by agreement of the parties may exist.

This subdivision authorizes an award of "reasonable" attorney fees and nontaxable costs. This is the customary term for measurement of fee awards in cases in which counsel may obtain an award of fees under the "common fund" theory that applies in many class actions, and is used in many fee-shifting statutes. Depending on the circumstances, courts have approached the determination of what is reasonable in different ways. In particular, there is some variation among courts about whether in "common fund" cases the court should use the lodestar or a percentage method of determining what fee is reasonable. The rule does not attempt to resolve the question whether the lodestar or percentage approach should be viewed as preferable.

Active judicial involvement in measuring fee awards is singularly important to the proper operation of the class-action process. Continued reliance on caselaw development of fee-award measures does not diminish the court's responsibility. In a class action, the district court must ensure that the amount and mode of payment of attorney fees are fair and proper whether the fees come from a common fund or are otherwise paid. Even in the absence of objections, the court bears this responsibility.

Courts discharging this responsibility have looked to a variety of factors. One fundamental focus is the result actually achieved for class members, a basic consideration in any case in which fees are sought on the basis of a benefit achieved for class members. The Private Securities Litigation Reform Act of 1995 explicitly makes this factor a cap for a fee award in actions to which it applies. See 15 U.S.C. §§ 77z–1(a)(6); 78u–4(a)(6) (fee award should not exceed a "reasonable percentage of the amount of any damages and prejudgment interest actually paid to the class"). For a percentage approach to fee measurement, results achieved is the basic starting point.

In many instances, the court may need to proceed with care in assessing the value conferred on class members. Settlement regimes that provide for future payments, for example, may not result in significant actual payments to class members. In this connection, the court may need to scrutinize the manner and operation of any applicable claims procedure. In some cases, it may be appropriate to defer some portion of the fee award until actual payouts to class members are known. Settlements involving nonmonetary provisions for class members also deserve careful scrutiny to ensure that these provisions have actual value to the class. On occasion the court's Rule 23(e) review will provide a solid basis for this sort of evaluation, but in any event it is also important to assessing the fee award for the class.

At the same time, it is important to recognize that in some class actions the monetary relief obtained is not the sole determinant of an appropriate attorney fees award. Cf. *Blanchard v. Bergeron*, 489 U.S. 87, 95 (1989) (cautioning in an individual case against an "undesirable emphasis" on "the importance of the recovery of damages in civil rights litigation" that might "shortchange efforts to seek effective injunctive or declaratory relief").

Any directions or orders made by the court in connection with appointing class counsel under Rule 23(g) should weigh heavily in making a fee award under this subdivision.

Courts have also given weight to agreements among the parties regarding the fee motion, and to agreements between class counsel and others about the fees claimed by the motion. Rule 54(d)(2)(B) provides: "If directed by the court, the motion shall also disclose the terms of any agreement with respect to fees to be paid for the services for which claim is made." The agreement by a settling party not to oppose a fee application up to a certain amount, for example, is worthy of consideration, but the court remains responsible to determine a reasonable fee. "Side agreements" regarding fees provide at least perspective pertinent to an appropriate fee award.

In addition, courts may take account of the fees charged by class counsel or other attorneys for representing individual claimants or objectors in the case. In determining a fee for class counsel, the court's objective is to ensure an overall fee that is fair for counsel and equitable within the class. In some circumstances individual fee agreements between class counsel and class members might have provisions inconsistent with those goals, and the court might determine that adjustments in the class fee award were necessary as a result.

Finally, it is important to scrutinize separately the application for an award covering nontaxable costs. If costs were addressed in the order appointing class counsel, those directives should be a presumptive starting point in determining what is an appropriate award.

Paragraph (1). Any claim for an award of attorney fees must be sought by motion under Rule 54(d)(2), which invokes the provisions for timing of appeal in Rule 58 and Appellate Rule 4. Owing to the distinctive features of class action fee motions, however, the provisions of this subdivision control disposition of fee motions in class actions, while Rule 54(d)(2) applies to matters not addressed in this subdivision.

The court should direct when the fee motion must be filed. For motions by class counsel in cases subject to court review of a proposed settlement under Rule 23(e), it would be important to require the filing of at least the initial motion in time for inclusion of information about the motion in the notice to the class about the proposed settlement that is required by Rule 23(e). In cases litigated to judgment, the court might also order class counsel's motion to be filed promptly so that notice to the class under this subdivision (h) can be given.

Besides service of the motion on all parties, notice of class counsel's motion for attorney fees must be "directed to the class in a reasonable manner." Because members of the class have an interest in the arrangements for payment of class counsel whether that payment comes from the class fund or is made directly by another party, notice is required in all instances. In cases in which settlement approval is contemplated under Rule 23(e), notice of class counsel's fee motion should be combined with notice of the proposed settlement, and the provision regarding notice to the class is parallel to the requirements for notice under Rule 23(e). In adjudicated class actions, the court may calibrate the notice to avoid undue expense.

Paragraph (2). A class member and any party from whom payment is sought may object to the fee motion. Other parties—for example, nonsettling defendants—may not object because they lack a sufficient interest in the amount the court awards. The rule does not specify a time limit for making an objection. In setting the date objections are due, the court should provide sufficient time after the full fee motion is on file to enable potential objectors to examine the motion.

The court may allow an objector discovery relevant to the objections. In determining whether to allow discovery, the court should weigh the need for the information against the cost and delay that would attend discovery. See Rule 26(b)(2). One factor in determining whether to authorize discovery is the completeness of the material submitted in support of the fee motion, which depends in part on the fee measurement standard applicable to the case. If the motion provides thorough information, the burden should be on the objector to justify discovery to obtain further information.

Paragraph (3). Whether or not there are formal objections, the court must determine whether a fee award is justified and, if so, set a reasonable fee. The rule does not require a formal hearing in all cases. The form and extent of a hearing depend on the circumstances of the case. The rule does require findings and conclusions under Rule 52(a).

Paragraph (4). By incorporating Rule 54(d)(2), this provision gives the court broad authority to obtain assistance in determining the appropriate amount to award. In deciding whether to direct submission of such questions to a special master or magistrate judge, the court should give appropriate consideration to the cost and delay that such a process might entail.

2007 Amendment

The language of Rule 23 has been amended as part of the general restyling of the Civil Rules to make them more easily understood and to make style and terminology consistent throughout the rules. These changes are intended to be stylistic only.

Amended Rule 23(d)(2) carries forward the provisions of former Rule 23(d) that recognize two separate propositions. First, a Rule 23(d) order may be combined with a pretrial order under Rule 16. Second, the standard for amending the Rule 23(d) order continues to be the more open-ended standard for amending Rule 23(d) orders, not the more exacting standard for amending Rule 16 orders.

As part of the general restyling, intensifiers that provide emphasis but add no meaning are consistently deleted. Amended Rule 23(f) omits as redundant the explicit reference to court of appeals discretion in deciding whether to permit an interlocutory appeal. The omission does not in any way limit the unfettered discretion established by the original rule.

CROSS REFERENCES

Actions relating to unincorporated associations, see Fed. Rules Civ.Proc. Rule 23.2, 28 USCA.

Capacity of unincorporated association to sue or be sued, see Fed.Rules Civ.Proc. Rule 17, 28 USCA.

Coupon settlements, class actions, attorney fees, see 28 USCA § 1712.

Derivative actions by shareholders, see Fed.Rules Civ. Proc. Rule 23.1, 28 USCA.

Private securities litigation rebuttable presumption, see 15 USCA § 78u–4.

Procedure for class action settlements, protections and notice, generally, see 28 USCA § 1711 et seq.

Reduction of abusive litigation and rebuttable presumption, see 15 USCA § 77z–1.

Removal of interstate class actions to federal district court, review of remand orders, exceptions, see 28 USCA § 1453.

Service of process on corporations in stockholder's derivative action, see 28 USCA § 1695.

Venue in stockholder's derivative action, see 28 USCA § 1401.

Rule 23.1. Derivative Actions

(a) Prerequisites. This rule applies when one or more shareholders or members of a corporation or an unincorporated association bring a derivative action to enforce a right that the corporation or association may properly assert but has failed to enforce. The derivative action may not be maintained if it appears that the plaintiff does not fairly and adequately represent the interests of shareholders or members who are similarly situated in enforcing the right of the corporation or association.

(b) Pleading Requirements. The complaint must be verified and must:

(1) allege that the plaintiff was a shareholder or member at the time of the transaction complained of, or that the plaintiff's share or membership later devolved on it by operation of law;

(2) allege that the action is not a collusive one to confer jurisdiction that the court would otherwise lack; and

(3) state with particularity:

(A) any effort by the plaintiff to obtain the desired action from the directors or comparable authority and, if necessary, from the shareholders or members; and

(B) the reasons for not obtaining the action or not making the effort.

(c) Settlement, Dismissal, and Compromise. A derivative action may be settled, voluntarily dismissed, or compromised only with the court's approval. Notice of a proposed settlement, voluntary dismissal, or compromise must be given to shareholders or members in the manner that the court orders.

(Adopted February 28, 1966, effective July 1, 1966; amended March 2, 1987, effective August 1, 1987; April 30, 2007, effective December 1, 2007.)

ADVISORY COMMITTEE NOTES

1966 Addition

A derivative action by a shareholder of a corporation or by a member of an unincorporated association has distinctive aspects which require the special provisions set forth in the new rule. The next-to-the-last sentence recognizes that the question of adequacy of representation may arise when the plaintiff is one of a group of shareholders or members. Cf. 3 Moore's *Federal Practice*, par. 23.08 (2d ed. 1963).

The court has inherent power to provide for the conduct of the proceedings in a derivative action, including the power to determine the course of the proceedings and require that any appropriate notice be given to shareholders or members.

1987 Amendment

The amendments are technical. No substantive change is intended.

2007 Amendment

The language of Rule 23.1 has been amended as part of the general restyling of the Civil Rules to make them more easily understood and to make style and terminology consistent throughout the rules. These changes are intended to be stylistic only.

CROSS REFERENCES

Actions relating to unincorporated associations, see Fed. Rules Civ.Proc. Rule 23.2, 28 USCA.

Capacity of unincorporated association to sue or to be sued, see Fed.Rules Civ.Proc. Rule 17, 28 USCA.

Class actions, see Fed.Rules Civ.Proc. Rule 23, 28 USCA.

Service of process on corporations in stockholder's derivative action, see 28 USCA § 1695.

Venue in stockholder's derivative action, see 28 USCA § 1401.

Rule 23.2. Actions Relating to Unincorporated Associations

This rule applies to an action brought by or against the members of an unincorporated association as a class by naming certain members as representative parties. The action may be maintained only if it appears that those parties will fairly and adequately protect the interests of the association and its members. In conducting the action, the court may issue any appropriate orders corresponding with those in Rule 23(d), and the procedure for settlement, voluntary dismissal, or compromise must correspond with the procedure in Rule 23(e).

(Adopted February 28, 1966, effective July 1, 1966; amended April 30, 2007, effective December 1, 2007.)

ADVISORY COMMITTEE NOTES

1966 Addition

Although an action by or against representatives of the membership of an unincorporated association has often been viewed as a class action, the real or main purpose of this characterization has been to give "entity treatment" to the association when for formal reasons it cannot sue or be sued as a jural person under Rule 17(b). See Louisell & Hazard, *Pleading and Procedure: State and Federal* 718 (1962); 3 Moore's *Federal Practice*, par. 23.08 (2d ed. 1963); Story, J. in *West v. Randall*, 29 Fed.Cas. 718, 722–23, No. 17,424 (C.C.D.R.I.1820); and, for examples, *Gibbs v. Buck*, 307 U.S. 66 (1939); *Tunstall v. Brotherhood of Locomotive F. & E.*, 148 F.2d 403 (4th Cir. 1945); *Oskoian v. Canuel*, 269 F.2d 311 (1st Cir. 1959). Rule 23.2 deals separately with these actions, referring where appropriate to Rule 23.

2007 Amendment

The language of Rule 23.2 has been amended as part of the general restyling of the Civil Rules to make them more easily understood and to make style and terminology consistent throughout the rules. These changes are intended to be stylistic only.

CROSS REFERENCES

Capacity of unincorporated association to sue or be sued, see Fed.Rules Civ.Proc. Rule 17, 28 USCA.

Class actions, see Fed.Rules Civ.Proc. Rule 23, 28 USCA.

Derivative actions by shareholders, see Fed.Rules Civ. Proc. Rule 23.1, 28 USCA.

Rule 24. Intervention

(a) Intervention of Right. On timely motion, the court must permit anyone to intervene who:

(1) is given an unconditional right to intervene by a federal statute; or

(2) claims an interest relating to the property or transaction that is the subject of the action, and is so situated that disposing of the action may as a practical matter impair or impede the movant's ability to protect its interest, unless existing parties adequately represent that interest.

(b) Permissive Intervention.

(1) ***In General.*** On timely motion, the court may permit anyone to intervene who:

(A) is given a conditional right to intervene by a federal statute; or

(B) has a claim or defense that shares with the main action a common question of law or fact.

(2) ***By a Government Officer or Agency.*** On timely motion, the court may permit a federal or state governmental officer or agency to intervene if a party's claim or defense is based on:

(A) a statute or executive order administered by the officer or agency; or

(B) any regulation, order, requirement, or agreement issued or made under the statute or executive order.

(3) ***Delay or Prejudice.*** In exercising its discretion, the court must consider whether the intervention will unduly delay or prejudice the adjudication of the original parties' rights.

(c) Notice and Pleading Required. A motion to intervene must be served on the parties as provided in Rule 5. The motion must state the grounds for intervention and be accompanied by a pleading that sets out the claim or defense for which intervention is sought.

(Amended December 27, 1946, effective March 19, 1948; December 29, 1948, effective October 20, 1949; January 21, 1963, effective July 1, 1963; February 28, 1966, effective July 1, 1966; March 2, 1987, effective August 1, 1987; April 30,

1991, effective December 1, 1991; April 12, 2006, effective December 1, 2006; April 30, 2007, effective December 1, 2007.)

ADVISORY COMMITTEE NOTES

1937 Adoption

The right to intervene given by the following and similar statutes is preserved, but the procedure for its assertion is governed by this rule:

U.S.C., Title 28 former sections:

45a [now 2323] (Special attorneys; participation by Interstate Commerce Commission; intervention) (in certain cases under interstate commerce laws)

48 [now 2322] (Suits to be against United States; intervention by United States)

401 [now 2403] (Intervention by United States; constitutionality of Federal statute)

U.S.C., Title 40:

276a–2(b) [now 3162(a)(2)] (Bonds of contractors for public buildings or works; rights of persons furnishing labor and materials).

Compare with the last sentence of [former] Equity Rule 37 (Parties Generally—Intervention). This rule amplifies and restates the present federal practice at law and in equity. For the practice in admiralty see Admiralty Rules 34 (How Third Party May Intervene) and 42 (Claims Against Proceeds in Registry). See generally Moore and Levi, *Federal Intervention: I The Right to Intervene and Reorganization* (1936), 45 Yale L.J. 565. Under the codes two types of intervention are provided, one for the recovery of specific real or personal property (2 Ohio Gen.Code Ann. (Page, 1926) § 11263; Wyo.Rev.Stat.Ann. (Courtright, 1931) § 89–522), and the other allowing intervention generally when the applicant has an interest in the matter in litigation (1 Colo.Stat.Ann. (1935) Code Civ.Proc. § 22; La.Code Pract. (Dart, 1932) Arts. 389–394; Utah Rev.Stat.Ann. (1933) § 104–3–24). The English intervention practice is based upon various rules and decisions and falls into the two categories of absolute right and discretionary right. For the absolute right see *English Rules Under the Judicature Act* (The Annual Practice, 1937) O. 12, r. 24 (admiralty), r. 25 (land), r. 23 (probate); O. 57, r. 12 (execution); J.A. (1925) §§ 181, 182, 183(2) (divorce); *In re Metropolitan Amalgamated Estates, Ltd.,* (1912) 2 Ch. 497 (receivership); *Wilson v. Church,* 9 Ch.D. 552 (1878) (representative action). For the discretionary right see O. 16, r. 11 (non-joinder) and *Re Fowler,* 142 L.T.Jo. 94 (Ch.1916), *Vavasseur v. Krupp,* 9 Ch.D. 351 (1878) (persons out of the jurisdiction).

1946 Amendment

Note. Subdivision (a). The addition to subdivision (a)(3) covers the situation where property may be in the actual custody of some other officer or agency—such as the Secretary of the Treasury—but the control and disposition of the property is lodged in the court wherein the action is pending.

Subdivision (b). The addition in subdivision (b) permits the intervention of governmental officers or agencies in proper cases and thus avoids exclusionary constructions of the rule. For an example of the latter, see *Matter of Bender Body Co.,* Ref. Ohio 1941, 47 F.Supp. 224, holding that the Administrator of the Office of Price Administration, then acting under the authority of an Executive Order of the President, could not intervene in a bankruptcy proceeding to protest the sale of assets above ceiling prices. Compare, however, *Securities and Exchange Commission v. United States Realty & Improvement Co.,* 1940, 310 U.S. 434, 60 S.Ct. 1044, where permissive intervention of the Commission to protect the public interest in an arrangement proceeding under Chapter XI of the Bankruptcy Act was upheld. See also dissenting opinion in *Securities and Exchange Commission v. Long Island Lighting Co.,* C.C.A.2d 1945, 148 F.2d 252, judgment vacated as moot and case remanded with direction to dismiss complaint, 1945, 325 U.S. 833, 65 S.Ct. 1085. For discussion see Commentary, *Nature of Permissive Intervention Under Rule 24b,* 1940, 3 Fed.Rules Serv. 704; Berger, *Intervention by Public Agencies in Private Litigation in the Federal Courts,* 1940, 50 Yale L.J. 65.

Regarding the construction of subdivision (b)(2), see *Allen Calculators, Inc. v. National Cash Register Co.,* 1944, 64 S.Ct. 905, 322 U.S. 137, 88 L.Ed. 1188.

1948 Amendment

The amendment effective Oct. 20, 1949, substituted the reference to "Title 28, U.S.C.A. § 2403" at the end of subdivision (c) for the reference to "the Act of August 24, 1937, c. 754, § 1."

1963 Amendment

This amendment conforms to the amendment of Rule 5(a). See the Advisory Committee's Note to that amendment.

1966 Amendment

In attempting to overcome certain difficulties which have arisen in the application of present Rule 24(a)(2) and (3), this amendment draws upon the revision of the related Rules 19 (joinder of persons needed for just adjudication) and 23 (class actions), and the reasoning underlying that revision.

Rule 24(a)(3) as amended in 1948 provided for intervention of right where the applicant established that he would be adversely affected by the distribution or disposition of property involved in an action to which he had not been made a party. Significantly, some decided cases virtually disregarded the language of this provision. Thus Professor Moore states: "The concept of a fund has been applied so loosely that it is possible for a court to find a fund in almost any in personam action." 4 Moore's *Federal Practice,* par. 24.09[3], at 55 (2d ed. 1962), and see, e.g., *Formulabs, Inc. v. Hartley Pen Co.,* 275 F.2d 52 (9th Cir.1960). This development was quite natural, for Rule 24(a)(3) was unduly restricted. If an absentee would be substantially affected in a practical sense by the determination made in an action, he should, as a general rule, be entitled to intervene, and his right to do so should not depend on whether there is a fund to be distributed or otherwise disposed of. Intervention of right is here seen to be a kind of counterpart to Rule 19(a)(2)(i) on joinder of persons needed for a just adjudication: where, upon motion of a party in an action, an absentee should be joined so that he may protect his interest which as a practical matter may be substantially impaired by the disposition of the action, he ought to have a right to intervene in the action on his own motion. See Louisell & Hazard, *Pleading and Procedure: State and Federal* 749–50 (1962).

The general purpose of original Rule 24(a)(2) was to entitle an absentee, purportedly represented by a party, to intervene in the action if he could establish with fair probability that the representation was inadequate. Thus, where an action is being prosecuted or defended by a trustee, a beneficiary of the trust should have a right to intervene if he can show that the trustee's representation of his interest probably is inadequate; similarly a member of a class should have the right to intervene in a class action if he can show the inadequacy of the representation of his interest by the representative parties before the court.

Original Rule 24(a)(2), however, made it a condition of intervention that "the applicant is or may be bound by a judgment in the action," and this created difficulties with intervention in class actions. If the "bound" language was read literally in the sense of res judicata, it could defeat intervention in some meritorious cases. A member of a class to whom a judgment in a class action extended by its terms (see Rule 23(c)(3), as amended) might be entitled to show in a later action, when the judgment in the class action was claimed to operate as res judicata against him, that the "representative" in the class action had not in fact adequately represented him. If he could make this showing, the class-action judgment might be held not to bind him. See *Hansberry v. Lee,* 311 U.S. 32 (1940). If a class member sought to intervene in the class action proper, while it was still pending, on grounds of inadequacy of representation, he could be met with the argument: if the representation was in fact inadequate, he would not be "bound" by the judgment when it was subsequently asserted against him as res judicata, hence he was not entitled to intervene; if the representation was in fact adequate, there was no occasion or ground for intervention. See *Sam Fox Publishing Co. v. United States,* 366 U.S. 683 (1961); cf. *Sutphen Estates, Inc. v. United States,* 342 U.S. 19 (1951). This reasoning might be linguistically justified by original Rule 24(a)(2); but it could lead to poor results. Compare the discussion in *International M. & I. Corp. v. Von Clemm,* 301 F.2d 857 (2d Cir.1962); *Atlantic Refining Co. v. Standard Oil Co.,* 304 F.2d 387 (D.C.Cir. 1962). A class member who claims that his "representative" does not adequately represent him, and is able to establish that proposition with sufficient probability, should not be put to the risk of having a judgment entered in the action which by its terms extends to him, and be obliged to test the validity of the judgment as applied to his interest by a later collateral attack. Rather he should, as a general rule, be entitled to intervene in the action.

The amendment provides that an applicant is entitled to intervene in an action when his position is comparable to that of a person under Rule 19(a)(2)(i), as amended, unless his interest is already adequately represented in the action by existing parties. The Rule 19(a)(2)(i) criterion imports practical considerations, and the deletion of the "bound" language similarly frees the rule from undue preoccupation with strict considerations of res judicata.

The representation whose adequacy comes into question under the amended rule is not confined to formal representation like that provided by a trustee for his beneficiary or a representative party in a class action for a member of the class. A party to an action may provide practical representation to the absentee seeking intervention although no such formal relationship exists between them, and the adequacy of this practical representation will then have to be weighed. See *International M. & I. Crop. v. Von Clemm,* and *Atlantic Refining Co. v. Standard Oil Co.,* both supra; *Wolpe v. Poretsky,* 144 F.2d 505 (D.C.Cir.1944), cert. denied, 323 U.S. 777 (1944); cf. *Ford Motor Co. v. Bisanz Bros.,* 249 F.2d 22 (8th Cir.1957); and generally, Annot., 84 A.L.R.2d 1412 (1961).

An intervention of right under the amended rule may be subject to appropriate conditions or restrictions responsive among other things to the requirements of efficient conduct of the proceedings.

1987 Amendment

The amendments are technical. No substantive change is intended.

1991 Amendment

Language is added to bring Rule 24(c) into conformity with the statute cited, resolving some confusion reflected in district court rules. As the text provides, counsel challenging the constitutionality of legislation in an action in which the appropriate government is not a party should call the attention of the court to its duty to notify the appropriate governmental officers. The statute imposes the burden of notification on the court, not the party making the constitutional challenge, partly in order to protect against any possible waiver of constitutional rights by parties inattentive to the need for notice. For this reason, the failure of a party to call the court's attention to the matter cannot be treated as a waiver.

2006 Amendment

New Rule 5.1 replaces the final three sentences of Rule 24(c), implementing the provisions of 28 U.S.C. § 2403. Section 2403 requires notification to the Attorney General of the United States when the constitutionality of an Act of Congress is called in question, and to the state attorney general when the constitutionality of a state statute is drawn into question.

2007 Amendment

The language of Rule 24 has been amended as part of the general restyling of the Civil Rules to make them more easily understood and to make style and terminology consistent throughout the rules. These changes are intended to be stylistic only.

The former rule stated that the same procedure is followed when a United States statute gives a right to intervene. This statement is deleted because it added nothing.

CROSS REFERENCES

Intervention of—

Parties interested in action to enforce, suspend or annul orders of the Surface Transportation Board, see 28 USCA § 2323.

United States where constitutionality of federal statute is questioned, see 28 USCA § 2403.

Rule 25. Substitution of Parties

(a) Death.

(1) ***Substitution if the Claim Is Not Extinguished.*** If a party dies and the claim is not extinguished, the court may order substitution of the proper party. A motion for substitution may be made by any party or by the decedent's successor or representative. If the motion is not made within 90 days after service of a statement noting the death, the action by or against the decedent must be dismissed.

(2) ***Continuation Among the Remaining Parties.*** After a party's death, if the right sought to be enforced survives only to or against the remaining parties, the action does not abate, but proceeds in favor of or against the remaining parties. The death should be noted on the record.

(3) ***Service.*** A motion to substitute, together with a notice of hearing, must be served on the parties as provided in Rule 5 and on nonparties as provided in Rule 4. A statement noting death must be served in the same manner. Service may be made in any judicial district.

(b) Incompetency. If a party becomes incompetent, the court may, on motion, permit the action to be continued by or against the party's representative. The motion must be served as provided in Rule 25(a)(3).

(c) Transfer of Interest. If an interest is transferred, the action may be continued by or against the original party unless the court, on motion, orders the transferee to be substituted in the action or joined with the original party. The motion must be served as provided in Rule 25(a)(3).

(d) Public Officers; Death or Separation from Office. An action does not abate when a public officer who is a party in an official capacity dies, resigns, or otherwise ceases to hold office while the action is pending. The officer's successor is automatically substituted as a party. Later proceedings should be in the substituted party's name, but any misnomer not affecting the parties' substantial rights must be disregarded. The court may order substitution at any time, but the absence of such an order does not affect the substitution.

(Amended December 29, 1948, effective October 20, 1949; April 17, 1961, effective July 19, 1961; January 21, 1963, effective July 1, 1963; March 2, 1987, effective August 1, 1987; April 30, 2007, effective December 1, 2007.)

ADVISORY COMMITTEE NOTES

1937 Adoption

Note to Subdivision (a). 1. The first paragraph of this rule is based upon [former] Equity Rule 45 (Death of Party—Revivor) and U.S.C., Title 28, former § 778 (Death of parties; substitution of executor or administrator). The *scire facias* procedure provided for in the statute cited is superseded and the writ is abolished by Rule 81(b). Paragraph two states the content of U.S.C., Title 28, former § 779 (Death of one of several plaintiffs or defendants). With these two paragraphs compare generally *English Rules Under the Judicature Act* (The Annual Practice, 1937) O. 17, r.r. 1–10.

2. This rule modifies U.S.C., Title 28, [former] §§ 778 (Death of parties; substitution of executor or administrator), 779 (Death of one of several plaintiffs or defendants), and 780 (Survival of actions, suits, or proceedings, etc.), in so far as they differ from it.

Note to Subdivisions (b) and (c). These are a combination and adaptation of N.Y.C.P.A. (1937) § 83 and Calif.Code Civ.Proc. (1937) § 385; see also 4 Nev.Comp.Laws (Hillyer, 1929) § 8561.

Note to Subdivision (d). With the first and last sentences compare U.S.C.A., Title 28, former § 780 (Survival of actions, suits, or proceedings, etc.). With the second sentence of this subdivision compare *Ex parte La Prade*, 1933, 53 S.Ct. 682, 289 U.S. 444, 77 L.Ed. 1311.

1948 Amendment

The amendment effective October 19, 1949, inserted the words, "the Canal Zone, a territory, an insular possession," in the first sentence of subdivision (d), and, in the same sentence, after the phrase "or other governmental agency," deleted the words, "or any other officer specified in the Act of February 13, 1925, c. 229, § 11 (43 Stat. 941), formerly section 780 of this title."

1961 Amendment

Subdivision (d)(1). Present Rule 25(d) is generally considered to be unsatisfactory. 4 Moore's *Federal Practice* ¶25.01[7] (2d ed. 1950); Wright, *Amendments to the Federal Rules: The Function of a Continuing Rules Committee*, 7 Vand.L.Rev. 521, 529 (1954); *Developments in the Law—Remedies Against the United States and Its Officials*, 70 Harv.L.Rev. 827, 931–34 (1957). To require, as a condition of substituting a successor public officer as a party to a pending action, that an application be made with a showing that there is substantial need for continuing the litigation, can rarely serve any useful purpose and fosters a burdensome formality. And to prescribe a short, fixed time period for substitution which cannot be extended even by agreement, see *Snyder v. Buck*, 340 U.S. 15, 19 (1950), with the penalty of dismissal of the action, "makes a trap for unsuspecting litigants which seems unworthy of a great government." *Vibra Brush Corp. v. Schaffer*, 256 F.2d 681, 684 (2d Cir. 1958). Although courts have on occasion found means of undercutting the rule, e.g. *Acheson v. Furusho*, 212 F.2d 284 (9th Cir.1954) (substitution of defendant officer unnecessary on theory that only a declaration of status was sought), it has operated harshly in many instances, e.g. *Snyder v. Buck*, supra; *Poindexter v. Folsom*, 242 F.2d 516 (3d Cir.1957).

Under the amendment, the successor is automatically substituted as a party without an application or showing of need to continue the action. An order of substitution is not required, but may be entered at any time if a party desires or the court thinks fit.

The general term "public officer" is used in preference to the enumeration which appears in the present rule. It comprises Federal, State, and local officers.

The expression "in his official capacity" is to be interpreted in its context as part of a simple procedural rule for substitution; care should be taken not to distort its meaning by mistaken analogies to the doctrine of sovereign immunity from suit or the Eleventh Amendment. The amended rule will apply to all actions brought by public officers for the government, and to any action brought in form against a named officer, but intrinsically against the government or the office or the incumbent thereof whoever he may be from time to time during the action. Thus the amended rule will apply to actions against officers to compel performance of official duties or to obtain judicial review of their orders. It will also apply to actions to prevent officers from acting in excess of their authority or under authority not validly conferred, cf. *Philadelphia Co. v. Stimson,* 223 U.S. 605 (1912), or from enforcing unconstitutional enactments, cf. *Ex parte Young,* 209 U.S. 123 (1908); *Ex parte La Prade,* 289 U.S. 444 (1933). In general it will apply whenever effective relief would call for corrective behavior by the one then having official status and power, rather than one who has lost that status and power through ceasing to hold office. Cf. *Land v. Dollar,* 330 U.S. 731 (1947); *Larson v. Domestic & Foreign Commerce Corp.,* 337 U.S. 682 (1949). Excluded from the operation of the amended rule will be the relatively infrequent actions which are directed to securing money judgments against the named officers enforceable against their personal assets; in these cases Rule 25(a)(1), not Rule 25(d), applies to the question of substitution. Examples are actions against officers seeking to make them pay damages out of their own pockets for defamatory utterances or other misconduct in some way related to the office, see *Barr v. Matteo,* 360 U.S. 564 (1959); *Howard v. Lyons,* 360 U.S. 593 (1959); *Gregoire v. Biddle,* 177 F.2d 579 (2d Cir.1949), cert. denied, 339 U.S. 949 (1950). Another example is the anomalous action for a tax refund against a collector of internal revenue, see *Ignelzi v. Granger,* 16 F.R.D. 517 (W.D.Pa.1955), 28 U.S.C. § 2006, 4 Moore, supra, ¶25.05, p. 531; but see 28 U.S.C. § 1346(a)(1), authorizing the bringing of such suits against the United States rather than the officer.

Automatic substitution under the amended rule, being merely a procedural device for substituting a successor for a past officeholder as a party, is distinct from and does not affect any substantive issues which may be involved in the action. Thus a defense of immunity from suit will remain in the case despite a substitution.

Where the successor does not intend to pursue the policy of his predecessor which gave rise to the lawsuit, it will be open to him, after substitution, as plaintiff to seek voluntary dismissal of the action, or as defendant to seek to have the action dismissed as moot or to take other appropriate steps to avert a judgment or decree. Contrast *Ex parte La Prade,* supra; *Allen v. Regents of the University System,* 304 U.S. 439 (1938); *McGrath v. National Assn. of Mfgrs.,* 344 U.S. 804 (1952); *Danenberg v. Cohen,* 213 F.2d 944 (7th Cir.1954).

As the present amendment of Rule 25(d)(1) eliminates a specified time period to secure substitution of public officers, the reference in Rule 6(b) (regarding enlargement of time) to Rule 25 will no longer apply to these public-officer substitutions.

As to substitution on appeal, the rules of the appellate courts should be consulted.

Subdivision (d)(2). This provision, applicable in "official capacity" cases as described above, will encourage the use of the official title without any mention of the officer individually, thereby recognizing the intrinsic character of the action and helping to eliminate concern with the problem of substitution. If for any reason it seems desirable to add the individual's name, this may be done upon motion or on the court's initiative; thereafter the procedure of amended Rule 25(d)(1) will apply if the individual named ceases to hold office.

For examples of naming the officer or title rather than the officeholder, see *Annot.,* 102 A.L.R. 943, 948–52; *Comment,* 50 Mich.L.Rev. 443, 450 (1952); cf. 26 U.S.C. § 7484. Where an action is brought by or against a board or agency with continuity of existence, it has been often decided that there is no need to name the individual members and substitution is unnecessary when the personnel changes. 4 Moore, supra, ¶25.09, p. 536. The practice encouraged by amended Rule 25(d)(2) is similar.

1963 Amendment

Present Rule 25(a)(1), together with present Rule 6(b), results in an inflexible requirement that an action be dismissed as to a deceased party if substitution is not carried out within a fixed period measured from the time of the death. The hardships and inequities of this unyielding requirement plainly appear from the cases. See, e.g., *Anderson v. Yungkau,* 329 U.S. 482, 67 S.Ct. 428, 91 L.Ed. 436 (1947); *Iovino v. Waterson,* 274 F.2d 41 (1959), cert. denied, *Carlin v. Sovino,* 362 U.S. 949, 80 S.Ct. 860, 4 L.Ed.2d 867 (1960); *Perry v. Allen,* 239 F.2d 107 (5th Cir.1956); *Starnes v. Pennsylvania R.R.,* 26 F.R.D. 625 (E.D.N.Y.), aff'd per curiam, 295 F.2d 704 (2d Cir.1961), cert. denied, 369 U.S. 813, 82 S.Ct. 688, 7 L.Ed.2d 612 (1962); *Zdanok v. Glidden Co.,* 28 F.R.D. 346 (S.D.N.Y.1961). See also 4 Moore's *Federal Practice* ¶25.01[9] (Supp.1960); 2 Barron & Holtzoff, *Federal Practice & Procedure* § 621, at 420–21 (Wright ed.1961).

The amended rule establishes a time limit for the motion to substitute based not upon the time of the death, but rather upon the time information of the death is provided by means of a suggestion of death upon the record, i.e. service of a statement of the fact of the death. Cf. Ill.Ann.Stat., c. 110, § 54(2) (Smith-Hurd 1956). The motion may not be made later than 90 days after the service of the statement unless the period is extended pursuant to Rule 6(b), as amended. See the Advisory Committee's Note to amended Rule 6(b). See also the new Official Form 30.

A motion to substitute may be made by any party or by the representative of the deceased party without awaiting the suggestion of death. Indeed, the motion will usually be so made. If a party or the representative of the deceased party desires to limit the time within which another may make the motion, he may do so by suggesting the death upon the record.

A motion to substitute made within the prescribed time will ordinarily be granted, but under the permissive language of the first sentence of the amended rule ("the court may order") it may be denied by the court in the exercise of a sound discretion if made long after the death—as can occur if the suggestion of death is not made or is delayed—and circumstances have arisen rendering it unfair to allow substitution. Cf. *Anderson v. Yungkau,* supra, 329 U.S. at 485, 486, 67 S.Ct. at 430, 431, 91 L.Ed. 436, where it was noted under the present rule that settlement and distribution of the estate of a deceased defendant might be so far advanced as to warrant denial of a motion for substitution even though made within the time limit prescribed by that rule. Accordingly, a party interested in securing substitution under the amended rule should not assume that he can rest indefinitely awaiting the suggestion of death before he makes his motion to substitute.

1987 Amendment

The amendments are technical. No substantive change is intended.

2007 Amendment

The language of Rule 25 has been amended as part of the general restyling of the Civil Rules to make them more easily understood and to make style and terminology consistent throughout the rules. These changes are intended to be stylistic only.

Former Rule 25(d)(2) is transferred to become Rule 17(d) because it deals with designation of a public officer, not substitution.

HISTORICAL NOTES

Effective and Applicability Provisions

1961 Amendments. Amendment adopted on Apr. 17, 1961, effective July 19, 1961, see rule 86(d).

CROSS REFERENCES

Depositions, right to use after substitution, see Fed.Rules Civ.Proc. Rule 32, 28 USCA.

Extensions of time, see Fed.Rules Civ.Proc. Rule 6, 28 USCA.

TITLE V. DISCLOSURES AND DISCOVERY

ADVISORY COMMITTEE'S EXPLANATORY STATEMENT CONCERNING 1970 AMENDMENTS TO DISCOVERY RULES

This statement is intended to serve as a general introduction to the amendments of Rules 26–37, concerning discovery, as well as related amendments of other rules. A separate note of customary scope is appended to amendments proposed for each rule. This statement provides a framework for the consideration of individual rule changes.

Changes in the Discovery Rules

The discovery rules, as adopted in 1938, were a striking and imaginative departure from tradition. It was expected from the outset that they would be important, but experience has shown them to play an even larger role than was initially foreseen. Although the discovery rules have been amended since 1938, the changes were relatively few and narrowly focused, made in order to remedy specific defects. The amendments now proposed reflect the first comprehensive review of the discovery rules undertaken since 1938. These amendments make substantial changes in the discovery rules. Those summarized here are among the more important changes.

Scope of Discovery. New provisions are made and existing provisions changed affecting the scope of discovery: (1) The contents of insurance policies are made discoverable (Rule 26(b)(2)). (2) A showing of good cause is no longer required for discovery of documents and things and entry upon land (Rule 34). However, a showing of need is required for discovery of "trial preparation" materials other than a party's discovery of his own statement and a witness' discovery of his own statement; and protection is afforded against disclosure in such documents of mental impressions, conclusions, opinions, or legal theories concerning the litigation. (Rule 26(b)(3)). (3) Provision is made for discovery with respect to experts retained for trial preparation, and particularly those experts who will be called to testify at trial (Rule 26(b)(4)). (4) It is provided that interrogatories and requests for admission are not objectionable simply because they relate to matters of opinion or contention, subject of course to the supervisory power of the court (Rules 33(b), 36(a)). (5) Medical examination is made available as to certain nonparties. (Rule 35(a)).

Mechanics of Discovery. A variety of changes are made in the mechanics of the discovery process, affecting the sequence and timing of discovery, the respective obligations of the parties with respect to requests, responses, and motions for court orders, and the related powers of the court to enforce discovery requests and to protect against their abusive use. A new provision eliminates the automatic grant of priority in discovery to one side (Rule 26(d)). Another provides that a party is not under a duty to supplement his responses to requests for discovery, except as specified (Rule 26(e)).

Other changes in the mechanics of discovery are designed to encourage extrajudicial discovery with a minimum of court intervention. Among these are the following: (1) The requirement that a plaintiff seek leave of court for early discovery requests is eliminated or reduced, and motions for a court order under Rule 34 are made unnecessary. Motions under Rule 35 are continued. (2) Answers and objections are to be served together and an enlargement of the time for response is provided. (3) The party seeking discovery, rather than the objecting party, is made responsible for invoking judicial determination of discovery disputes not resolved by the parties. (4) Judicial sanctions are tightened with respect to unjustified insistence upon or objection to discovery. These changes bring Rules 33, 34, and 36 substantially into line with the procedure now provided for depositions.

Failure to amend Rule 35 in the same way is based upon two considerations. First, the Columbia Survey (described below) finds that only about 5 percent of medical examinations require court motions, of which about half result in court orders. Second and of greater importance, the interest of the person to be examined in the privacy of his person was recently stressed by the Supreme Court in *Schlagenhauf v. Holder*, 379 U.S. 104 (1964). The court emphasized the trial judge's responsibility to assure that the medical examination was justified, particularly as to its scope.

Rearrangement of Rules. A limited rearrangement of the discovery rules has been made, whereby certain provisions are transferred from one rule to another. The reasons for this rearrangement are discussed below in a separate section of this statement and the details are set out in a table at the end of this statement.

Optional Procedures. In two instances, new optional procedures have been made available. A new procedure is provided to a party seeking to take the deposition of a corporation or other organization (Rule 30(b)(6)). A party on whom interrogatories have been served requesting information derivable from his business records may under specified circumstances produce the records rather than give answers (Rule 33(c)).

Other Changes. This summary of changes is by no means exhaustive. Various changes have been made in order to improve, tighten, or clarify particular provisions, to resolve conflicts in the case law, and to improve language. All changes, whether mentioned here or not, are discussed in the appropriate note for each rule.

A Field Survey of Discovery Practice

Despite widespread acceptance of discovery as an essential part of litigation, disputes have inevitably arisen concerning the values claimed for discovery and abuses alleged to exist. Many disputes about discovery relate to particular rule provisions or court decisions and can be studied in traditional fashion with a view to specific amendment. Since discovery is in large measure extra-judicial, however, even these disputes may be enlightened by a study of discovery "in the field." And some of the larger questions concerning discovery can be pursued only by a study of its operation at the law office level and in unreported cases.

The Committee, therefore, invited the Project for Effective Justice of Columbia Law School to conduct a field survey of discovery. Funds were obtained from the Ford Foundation and the Walter E. Meyer Research Institute of Law, Inc. The survey was carried on under the direction of Prof. Maurice Rosenberg of Columbia Law School. The Project for Effective Justice has submitted a report to the Committee entitled "Field Survey of Federal Pretrial Discovery" (hereafter referred to as the Columbia Survey). The Committee is deeply grateful for the benefit of this extensive undertaking and is most appreciative of the cooperation of the Project and the funding organizations. The Committee is particularly grateful to Professor Rosenberg who not only directed the survey but has given much time in order to assist the Committee in assessing the results.

The Columbia Survey concludes, in general, that there is no empirical evidence to warrant a fundamental change in the philosophy of the discovery rules. No widespread or profound failings are disclosed in the scope or availability of discovery. The costs of discovery do not appear to be oppressive, as a general matter, either in relation to ability to pay or to the stakes of the litigation. Discovery frequently provides evidence that would not otherwise be available to the parties and thereby makes for a fairer trial or settlement. On the other hand, no positive evidence is found that discovery promotes settlement.

More specific findings of the Columbia Survey are described in other Committee notes, in relation to particular rule provisions and amendments. Those interested in more detailed information may obtain it from the Project for Effective Justice.

Rearrangement of the Discovery Rules

The present discovery rules are structured entirely in terms of individual discovery devices, except for Rule 27 which deals with perpetuation of testimony, and Rule 37 which provides sanctions to enforce discovery. Thus, Rules 26 and 28 to 32 are in terms addressed only to the taking of a deposition of a party or third person. Rules 33 to 36 then deal in succession with four additional discovery devices: Written interrogatories to parties, production for inspection of documents and things, physical or mental examination and requests for admission.

Under the rules as promulgated in 1938, therefore, each of the discovery devices was separate and self-contained. A defect of this arrangement is that there is no natural location in the discovery rules for provisions generally applicable to all discovery or to several discovery devices. From 1938 until the present, a few amendments have applied a discovery provision to several rules. For example, in 1948, the scope of deposition discovery in Rule 26(b) and the provision for protective orders in Rule 30(b) were incorporated by reference in Rules 33 and 34. The arrangement was adequate so long as there were few provisions governing discovery generally and these provisions were relatively simple.

As will be seen, however, a series of amendments are now proposed which govern most or all of the discovery devices. Proposals of a similar nature will probably be made in the future. Under these circumstances, it is very desirable, even necessary, that the discovery rules contain one rule addressing itself to discovery generally.

Rule 26 is obviously the most appropriate rule for this purpose. One of its subdivisions, Rule 26(b), in terms governs only scope of deposition discovery, but it has been expressly incorporated by reference in Rules 33 and 34 and is treated by courts as setting a general standard. By means of a transfer to Rule 26 of the provisions for protective orders now contained in Rule 30(b), and a transfer from Rule 26 of provisions addressed exclusively to depositions, Rule 26 is converted into a rule concerned with discovery generally. It becomes a convenient vehicle for the inclusion of new provisions dealing with the scope, timing, and regulation of discovery. Few additional transfers are needed. See table showing rearrangement of rules, set out following this statement.

There are, to be sure, disadvantages in transferring any provision from one rule to another. Familiarity with the present pattern, reinforced by the references made by prior court decisions and the various secondary writings about the rules, is not lightly to be sacrificed. Revision of treatises and other reference works is burdensome and costly. Moreover, many States have adopted the existing pattern as a model for their rules.

On the other hand, the amendments now proposed will in any event require revision of texts and reference works as well as reconsideration by States following the Federal model. If these amendments are to be incorporated in an understandable way, a rule with general discovery provisions is needed. As will be seen, the proposed rearrangement produces a more coherent and intelligible pattern for the discovery rules taken as a whole. The difficulties described are those encountered whenever statutes are reexamined and revised. Failure to rearrange the discovery rules now would freeze the present scheme, making future change even more difficult.

Table Showing Rearrangement of Rules

Existing Rule No.	New Rule No.
26(a)	30(a), 31(a)
26(c)	30(c)
26(d)	32(a)
26(e)	32(b)
26(f)	32(c)
30(a)	30(b)
30(b)	26(c)
32	32(d)

Rule 26. Duty to Disclose; General Provisions Governing Discovery

(a) Required Disclosures.

(1) ***Initial Disclosure.***

(A) *In General.* Except as exempted by Rule 26(a)(1)(B) or as otherwise stipulated or ordered by the court, a party must, without awaiting a discovery request, provide to the other parties:

(i) the name and, if known, the address and telephone number of each individual likely to have discoverable information—along with the subjects of that information—that the disclosing party may use to support its claims or defenses, unless the use would be solely for impeachment;

(ii) a copy—or a description by category and location—of all documents, electronically stored information, and tangible things that the disclosing party has in its possession, custody, or control and may use to support its claims or defenses, unless the use would be solely for impeachment;

(iii) a computation of each category of damages claimed by the disclosing party—who must also make available for inspection and copying as under Rule 34 the documents or other evidentiary material, unless privileged or protected from disclosure, on which each computation is based, including materials bearing on the nature and extent of injuries suffered; and

(iv) for inspection and copying as under Rule 34, any insurance agreement under which an insurance business may be liable to satisfy all or part of a possible judgment in the action or to indemnify or reimburse for payments made to satisfy the judgment.

(B) *Proceedings Exempt from Initial Disclosure.* The following proceedings are exempt from initial disclosure:

(i) an action for review on an administrative record;

(ii) a forfeiture action in rem arising from a federal statute;

(iii) a petition for habeas corpus or any other proceeding to challenge a criminal conviction or sentence;

(iv) an action brought without an attorney by a person in the custody of the United States, a state, or a state subdivision;

(v) an action to enforce or quash an administrative summons or subpoena;

(vi) an action by the United States to recover benefit payments;

(vii) an action by the United States to collect on a student loan guaranteed by the United States;

(viii) a proceeding ancillary to a proceeding in another court; and

(ix) an action to enforce an arbitration award.

(C) *Time for Initial Disclosures—In General.* A party must make the initial disclosures at or within 14 days after the parties' Rule 26(f) conference unless a different time is set by stipulation or court order, or unless a party objects during the conference that initial disclosures are not appropriate in this action and states the objection in the proposed discovery plan. In ruling on the objection, the court must determine what disclosures, if any, are to be made and must set the time for disclosure.

(D) *Time for Initial Disclosures—For Parties Served or Joined Later.* A party that is first served or otherwise joined after the Rule 26(f) conference must make the initial disclosures within 30 days after being served or joined, unless a different time is set by stipulation or court order.

(E) *Basis for Initial Disclosure; Unacceptable Excuses.* A party must make its initial disclosures based on the information then reasonably available to it. A party is not excused from making its disclosures because it has not fully investigated the case or because it challenges the sufficiency of another party's disclosures or because another party has not made its disclosures.

(2) ***Disclosure of Expert Testimony.***

(A) *In General.* In addition to the disclosures required by Rule 26(a)(1), a party must disclose to the other parties the identity of any witness it may use at trial to present evidence under Federal Rule of Evidence 702, 703, or 705.

(B) *Written Report.* Unless otherwise stipulated or ordered by the court, this disclosure must be accompanied by a written report—prepared and signed by the witness—if the witness is one retained or specially employed to provide expert testimony in the case or one whose duties as the party's employee regularly involve giving expert testimony. The report must contain:

(i) a complete statement of all opinions the witness will express and the basis and reasons for them;

(ii) the data or other information considered by the witness in forming them;

(iii) any exhibits that will be used to summarize or support them;

(iv) the witness's qualifications, including a list of all publications authored in the previous 10 years;

(v) a list of all other cases in which, during the previous four years, the witness testified as an expert at trial or by deposition; and

(vi) a statement of the compensation to be paid for the study and testimony in the case.

(C) *Time to Disclose Expert Testimony.* A party must make these disclosures at the times and in the sequence that the court orders. Absent a stipulation or a court order, the disclosures must be made:

(i) at least 90 days before the date set for trial or for the case to be ready for trial; or

(ii) if the evidence is intended solely to contradict or rebut evidence on the same subject matter identified by another party under Rule 26(a)(2)(B), within 30 days after the other party's disclosure.

(D) *Supplementing the Disclosure.* The parties must supplement these disclosures when required under Rule 26(e).

(3) ***Pretrial Disclosures.***

(A) *In General.* In addition to the disclosures required by Rule 26(a)(1) and (2), a party must provide to the other parties and promptly file the following information about the evidence that it may present at trial other than solely for impeachment:

(i) the name and, if not previously provided, the address and telephone number of each witness—separately identifying those the party expects to present and those it may call if the need arises;

(ii) the designation of those witnesses whose testimony the party expects to present by deposition and, if not taken stenographically, a transcript of the pertinent parts of the deposition; and

(iii) an identification of each document or other exhibit, including summaries of other evidence—separately identifying those items the party expects to offer and those it may offer if the need arises.

(B) *Time for Pretrial Disclosures; Objections.* Unless the court orders otherwise, these disclosures must be made at least 30 days before trial. Within 14 days after they are made, unless the court sets a different time, a party may serve and promptly file a list of the following objections: any objections to the use under Rule 32(a) of a deposition designated by another party under Rule 26(a)(3)(A)(ii); and any objection, together with the grounds for it, that may be made to the admissibility of materials identified under Rule 26(a)(3)(A)(iii). An objection not so made—except for one under Federal Rule of Evidence 402 or 403—is waived unless excused by the court for good cause.

(4) ***Form of Disclosures.*** Unless the court orders otherwise, all disclosures under Rule 26(a) must be in writing, signed, and served.

(b) Discovery Scope and Limits.

(1) ***Scope in General.*** Unless otherwise limited by court order, the scope of discovery is as follows: Parties may obtain discovery regarding any nonprivileged matter that is relevant to any party's claim or defense—including the existence, description, nature, custody, condition, and location of any documents or other tangible things and the identity and location of persons who know of any discoverable matter. For good cause, the court may order discovery of any matter relevant to the subject matter involved in the action. Relevant information need not be admissible at the

trial if the discovery appears reasonably calculated to lead to the discovery of admissible evidence. All discovery is subject to the limitations imposed by Rule 26(b)(2)(C).

(2) ***Limitations on Frequency and Extent.***

(A) *When Permitted.* By order, the court may alter the limits in these rules on the number of depositions and interrogatories or on the length of depositions under Rule 30. By order or local rule, the court may also limit the number of requests under Rule 36.

(B) *Specific Limitations on Electronically Stored Information.* A party need not provide discovery of electronically stored information from sources that the party identifies as not reasonably accessible because of undue burden or cost. On motion to compel discovery or for a protective order, the party from whom discovery is sought must show that the information is not reasonably accessible because of undue burden or cost. If that showing is made, the court may nonetheless order discovery from such sources if the requesting party shows good cause, considering the limitations of Rule 26(b)(2)(C). The court may specify conditions for the discovery.

(C) *When Required.* On motion or on its own, the court must limit the frequency or extent of discovery otherwise allowed by these rules or by local rule if it determines that:

(i) the discovery sought is unreasonably cumulative or duplicative, or can be obtained from some other source that is more convenient, less burdensome, or less expensive;

(ii) the party seeking discovery has had ample opportunity to obtain the information by discovery in the action; or

(iii) the burden or expense of the proposed discovery outweighs its likely benefit, considering the needs of the case, the amount in controversy, the parties' resources, the importance of the issues at stake in the action, and the importance of the discovery in resolving the issues.

(3) ***Trial Preparation: Materials.***

(A) *Documents and Tangible Things.* Ordinarily, a party may not discover documents and tangible things that are prepared in anticipation of litigation or for trial by or for another party or its representative (including the other party's attorney, consultant, surety, indemnitor, insurer, or agent). But, subject to Rule 26(b)(4), those materials may be discovered if:

(i) they are otherwise discoverable under Rule 26(b)(1); and

(ii) the party shows that it has substantial need for the materials to prepare its case and cannot, without undue hardship, obtain their substantial equivalent by other means.

(B) *Protection Against Disclosure.* If the court orders discovery of those materials, it must protect against disclosure of the mental impressions, conclusions, opinions, or legal theories of a party's attorney or other representative concerning the litigation.

(C) *Previous Statement.* Any party or other person may, on request and without the required showing, obtain the person's own previous statement about the action or its subject matter. If the request is refused, the person may move for a court order, and Rule 37(a)(5) applies to the award of expenses. A previous statement is either:

(i) a written statement that the person has signed or otherwise adopted or approved; or

(ii) a contemporaneous stenographic, mechanical, electrical, or other recording—or a transcription of it—that recites substantially verbatim the person's oral statement.

(4) ***Trial Preparation: Experts.***

(A) *Expert Who May Testify.* A party may depose any person who has been identified as an expert whose opinions may be presented at trial. If Rule 26(a)(2)(B) requires a report from the expert, the deposition may be conducted only after the report is provided.

(B) *Expert Employed Only for Trial Preparation.* Ordinarily, a party may not, by interrogatories or deposition, discover facts known or opinions held by an expert who has been retained or specially employed by another party in anticipation of litigation or to prepare for trial and who is not expected to be called as a witness at trial. But a party may do so only:

(i) as provided in Rule 35(b); or

(ii) on showing exceptional circumstances under which it is impracticable for the party to obtain facts or opinions on the same subject by other means.

(C) *Payment.* Unless manifest injustice would result, the court must require that the party seeking discovery:

(i) pay the expert a reasonable fee for time spent in responding to discovery under Rule 26(b)(4)(A) or (B); and

(ii) for discovery under (B), also pay the other party a fair portion of the fees and expenses it reasonably incurred in obtaining the expert's facts and opinions.

(5) ***Claiming Privilege or Protecting Trial-Preparation Materials.***

(A) *Information Withheld.* When a party withholds information otherwise discoverable by claiming that the information is privileged or subject to protection as trial-preparation material, the party must:

(i) expressly make the claim; and

(ii) describe the nature of the documents, communications, or tangible things not produced or disclosed—and do so in a manner that, without revealing information itself privileged or protected, will enable other parties to assess the claim.

(B) *Information Produced.* If information produced in discovery is subject to a claim of privilege or of protection as trial-preparation material, the party making the claim may notify any party that received the information of the claim and the basis for it. After being notified, a party must promptly return, sequester, or destroy the specified information and any copies it has; must not use or disclose the information until the claim is resolved; must take reasonable steps to retrieve the information if the party disclosed it before being notified; and may promptly present the information to the court under seal for a determination of the claim. The producing party must preserve the information until the claim is resolved.

(c) Protective Orders.

(1) ***In General.*** A party or any person from whom discovery is sought may move for a protective order in the court where the action is pending—or as an alternative on matters relating to a deposition, in the court for the district where the deposition will be taken. The motion must include a certification that the movant has in good faith conferred or attempted to confer with other affected parties in an effort to resolve the dispute without court action. The court may, for good cause, issue an order to protect a party or person from annoyance, embarrassment, oppression, or undue burden or expense, including one or more of the following:

(A) forbidding the disclosure or discovery;

(B) specifying terms, including time and place, for the disclosure or discovery;

(C) prescribing a discovery method other than the one selected by the party seeking discovery;

(D) forbidding inquiry into certain matters, or limiting the scope of disclosure or discovery to certain matters;

(E) designating the persons who may be present while the discovery is conducted;

(F) requiring that a deposition be sealed and opened only on court order;

(G) requiring that a trade secret or other confidential research, development, or commercial information not be revealed or be revealed only in a specified way; and

(H) requiring that the parties simultaneously file specified documents or information in sealed envelopes, to be opened as the court directs.

(2) ***Ordering Discovery.*** If a motion for a protective order is wholly or partly denied, the court may, on just terms, order that any party or person provide or permit discovery.

(3) ***Awarding Expenses.*** Rule 37(a)(5) applies to the award of expenses.

(d) Timing and Sequence of Discovery.

(1) ***Timing.*** A party may not seek discovery from any source before the parties have conferred as required by Rule 26(f), except in a proceeding exempted from initial disclosure under Rule 26(a)(1)(B), or when authorized by these rules, by stipulation, or by court order.

(2) ***Sequence.*** Unless, on motion, the court orders otherwise for the parties' and witnesses' convenience and in the interests of justice:

(A) methods of discovery may be used in any sequence; and

(B) discovery by one party does not require any other party to delay its discovery.

(e) Supplementing Disclosures and Responses.

(1) ***In General.*** A party who has made a disclosure under Rule 26(a)—or who has responded to an interrogatory, request for production, or request for admission—must supplement or correct its disclosure or response:

(A) in a timely manner if the party learns that in some material respect the disclosure or response is incomplete or incorrect, and if the additional or corrective information has not otherwise been made known to the other parties during the discovery process or in writing; or

(B) as ordered by the court.

(2) ***Expert Witness.*** For an expert whose report must be disclosed under Rule 26(a)(2)(B), the party's duty to supplement extends both to information included in the report and to information given during the expert's deposition. Any additions or changes to this information must be disclosed by the time the party's pretrial disclosures under Rule 26(a)(3) are due.

(f) Conference of the Parties; Planning for Discovery.

(1) ***Conference Timing.*** Except in a proceeding exempted from initial disclosure under Rule 26(a)(1)(B) or when the court orders otherwise, the parties must confer as soon as practicable—and in any event at least 21 days before a scheduling conference is to be held or a scheduling order is due under Rule 16(b).

(2) ***Conference Content; Parties' Responsibilities.*** In conferring, the parties must consider the nature and basis of their claims and defenses and the possibilities for promptly settling or resolving the case; make or arrange for the disclosures required by Rule 26(a)(1); discuss any issues about preserving discoverable information; and develop a proposed discovery plan. The attorneys of record and all unrepresented parties that have appeared in the case are jointly responsible for arranging the conference, for attempting in good faith to agree on the proposed discovery plan, and for submitting to the court within 14 days after the conference a written report outlining the plan. The court may order the parties or attorneys to attend the conference in person.

(3) ***Discovery Plan.*** A discovery plan must state the parties' views and proposals on:

(A) what changes should be made in the timing, form, or requirement for disclosures under Rule 26(a), including a statement of when initial disclosures were made or will be made;

(B) the subjects on which discovery may be needed, when discovery should be completed, and whether discovery should be conducted in phases or be limited to or focused on particular issues;

(C) any issues about disclosure or discovery of electronically stored information, including the form or forms in which it should be produced;

(D) any issues about claims of privilege or of protection as trial-preparation materials, including—if the parties agree on a procedure to assert these claims after production—whether to ask the court to include their agreement in an order;

(E) what changes should be made in the limitations on discovery imposed under these rules or by local rule, and what other limitations should be imposed; and

(F) any other orders that the court should issue under Rule 26(c) or under Rule 16(b) and (c).

(4) ***Expedited Schedule.*** If necessary to comply with its expedited schedule for Rule 16(b) conferences, a court may by local rule:

(A) require the parties' conference to occur less than 21 days before the scheduling conference is held or a scheduling order is due under Rule 16(b); and

(B) require the written report outlining the discovery plan to be filed less than 14 days after the parties' conference, or excuse the parties from submitting a written report and permit them to report orally on their discovery plan at the Rule 16(b) conference.

(g) Signing Disclosures and Discovery Requests, Responses, and Objections.

(1) ***Signature Required; Effect of Signature.*** Every disclosure under Rule 26(a)(1) or (a)(3) and every discovery request, response, or objection must be signed by at least one attorney of record in the attorney's own name—or by the party personally, if unrepresented—and must state the signer's address, e-mail address, and telephone number. By signing, an attorney or party certifies that to the best of the person's knowledge, information, and belief formed after a reasonable inquiry:

(A) with respect to a disclosure, it is complete and correct as of the time it is made; and

(B) with respect to a discovery request, response, or objection, it is:

(i) consistent with these rules and warranted by existing law or by a nonfrivolous argument for extending, modifying, or reversing existing law, or for establishing new law;

(ii) not interposed for any improper purpose, such as to harass, cause unnecessary delay, or needlessly increase the cost of litigation; and

(iii) neither unreasonable nor unduly burdensome or expensive, considering the needs of the case, prior discovery in the case, the amount in controversy, and the importance of the issues at stake in the action.

(2) ***Failure to Sign.*** Other parties have no duty to act on an unsigned disclosure, request, response, or objection until it is signed, and the court must strike it unless a signature is promptly supplied after the omission is called to the attorney's or party's attention.

(3) ***Sanction for Improper Certification.*** If a certification violates this rule without substantial justification, the court, on motion or on its own, must impose an appropriate sanction on the signer, the party on whose behalf the signer was acting, or both. The sanction may include an order to pay the reasonable expenses, including attorney's fees, caused by the violation.

(Amended December 27, 1946, effective March 19, 1948; January 21, 1963, effective July 1, 1963; February 28, 1966, effective July 1, 1966; March 30, 1970, effective July 1, 1970; April 29, 1980, effective August 1, 1980; April 28, 1983, effective August 1, 1983; March 2, 1987, effective August 1, 1987; April 22, 1993, effective December 1, 1993; April 17, 2000, effective December 1, 2000; April 12, 2006, effective December 1, 2006; April 30, 2007, effective December 1, 2007.)

ADVISORY COMMITTEE NOTES

1937 Adoption

Note to Subdivision (a). This rule freely authorizes the taking of depositions under the same circumstances and by the same methods whether for the purpose of discovery or for the purpose of obtaining evidence. Many states have adopted this practice on account of its simplicity and effectiveness, safeguarding it by imposing such restrictions upon the subsequent use of the deposition at the trial or hearing as are deemed advisable. See Ark.Civ.Code (Crawford, 1934) §§ 606 to 607; Calif.Code Civ.Proc. (Deering, 1937) § 2021; 1 Colo.Stat.Ann. (1935) Code Civ.Proc. § 376; Idaho Code Ann. (1932) § 16–906; Ill.Rules of Pract.Rule 19 (Smith-Hurd Ill.Stats. c. 110, § 259.19); Smith-Hurd Ill.Stats. c. 51, § 24; 2 Ind.Stat.Ann. (Burns, 1933) §§ 2–1501, 2–1506; Ky. Codes (Carroll, 1932) Civ.Pract. § 557; 1 Mo.Rev.Stat. (1929) § 1753; 4 Mont.Rev.Codes Ann. (1935) § 10645; Neb.Comp. Stat. (1929) ch. 20, §§ 1246–7; 4 Nev.Comp.Laws (Hillyer, 1929) § 9001; 2 N.H.Pub.Laws (1926) ch. 337, § 1; N.C.Code Ann. (1935) § 1809; 2 N.D.Comp.Laws Ann. (1913) §§ 7889 to 7897; 2 Ohio Gen.Code Ann. (Page, 1926) §§ 11525–6; 1 Ore.Code Ann. (1930) Tit. 9, § 1503; 1 S.D.Comp.Laws (1929) §§ 2713–16; Vernon's Ann.Civ.Stats. Tex. arts. 3738, 3752, 3769; Utah Rev.Stat.Ann. (1933) § 104–51–7; Wash.Rules of Practice adopted by the Supreme Ct., Rule 8, 2 Wash.Rev.Stat.Ann. (Remington, 1932) § 308–8; W.Va.Code (1931) ch. 57, art. 4, § 1. Compare [former] Equity Rules 47 (Depositions—To be Taken in Exceptional Instances); 54 (Depositions Under Revised Statutes, §§ 863, 865, 866, 867—Cross Examination); 58 (Discovery—Interrogatories—Inspection and Production of Documents—Admission of Execution or Genuineness).

This and subsequent rules incorporate, modify, and broaden the provisions for depositions under U.S.C., Title 28, [former] §§ 639 (Depositions *de bene esse;* when and where taken; notice), 640 (Same; mode of taking), 641 (Same; transmission to court), 644 (Depositions under *dedimus potestatem* and *in perpetuam*), 646 (Deposition under *dedimus potestatem;* how taken). These statutes are superseded in so far as they differ from this and subsequent rules. U.S.C. Title 28, [former] § 643 (Depositions; taken in mode prescribed by State laws) is superseded by the third sentence of Subdivision (a).

While a number of states permit discovery only from parties or their agents, others either make no distinction between parties or agents of parties and ordinary witnesses, or authorize the taking of ordinary depositions, without restriction, from any persons who have knowledge of relevant facts. See Ark.Civ.Code (Crawford, 1934) §§ 606 to 607; 1 Idaho Code Ann. (1932) § 16–906; Ill.Rules of Pract., Rule 19 (Smith-Hurd Ill.Stats. c. 110, § 259.19); Smith-Hurd Ill.Stats. c. 51, § 24; 2 Ind.Stat.Ann. (Burns, 1933) § 2–1501; Ky.Codes (Carroll, 1932) Civ.Pract. §§ 554 to 558; 2 Md. Ann.Code (Bagby, 1924) Art. 35, § 21; 2 Minn.Stat. (Mason, 1927) § 9820; Mo.St.Ann. §§ 1753, 1759, pp. 4023, 4026; Neb.Comp.Stat. (1929) ch. 20, §§ 1246–7; 2 N.H.Pub.Laws (1926) ch. 337, § 1; 2 N.D.Comp.Laws Ann. (1913) § 7897; 2 Ohio Gen.Code Ann. (Page, 1926) §§ 11525–6; 1 S.D.Comp. Laws (1929) §§ 2713–16; Vernon's Ann.Civil Stats.Tex. arts. 3738, 3752, 3769; Utah Rev.Stat.Ann. (1933) § 104–51–7; Wash.Rules of Practice adopted by Supreme Ct., Rule 8, 2 Wash.Rev.Stat.Ann. (Remington, 1932) § 308–8; W.Va.Code (1931) ch. 57, art. 4, § 1.

The more common practice in the United States is to take depositions on notice by the party desiring them, without any order from the court, and this has been followed in these rules. See Calif.Code Civ.Proc. (Deering, 1937) § 2031; 2 Fla.Comp.Gen.Laws Ann. (1927) §§ 4405–7; 1 Idaho Code Ann. (1932) § 16–902; Ill.Rules of Pract., Rule 19 (Smith-Hurd Ill.Stats. c. 110, § 259.19); Smith-Hurd Ill.Stats. c. 51, § 24; 2 Ind.Stat.Ann. (Burns, 1933) § 2–1502; Kan.Gen.Stat. Ann. (1935) § 60–2827; Ky.Codes (Carroll, 1932) Civ.Pract. § 565; 2 Minn.Stat. (Mason, 1927) § 9820; Mo.St.Ann. § 1761, p. 4029; 4 Mont.Rev.Codes Ann. (1935) § 10651; Nev.Comp.Laws (Hillyer, 1929) § 9002; N.C.Code Ann. (1935) § 1809; 2 N.D.Comp.Laws Ann. (1913) § 7895; Utah Rev.Stat.Ann. (1933) § 104–51–8.

Note to Subdivision (b). While the old chancery practice limited discovery to facts supporting the case of the party seeking it, this limitation has been largely abandoned by modern legislation. See Ala.Code Ann. (Michie, 1928) §§ 7764 to 7773; 2 Ind.Stat.Ann. (Burns, 1933) §§ 2–1028, 2–1506, 2–1728–2–1732; Iowa Code (1935) § 11185; Ky. Codes (Carroll, 1932) Civ.Pract. §§ 557, 606(8); La.Code Pract. (Dart, 1932) arts. 347–356; 2 Mass.Gen.Laws (Ter.Ed., 1932) ch. 231, §§ 61 to 67; Mo.St.Ann. §§ 1753, 1759, pp. 4023, 4026; Neb.Comp.Stat. (1929) §§ 20–1246, 20–1247; 2 N.H.Pub.Laws (1926) ch. 337, § 1; 2 Ohio Gen.Code Ann. (Page, 1926) §§ 11497, 11526; Vernon's Ann.Civ.Stats.Tex. arts. 3738, 3753, 3769; Wis.Stat. (1935) § 326.12; Ontario Consol.Rules of Pract. (1928) Rules 237–347; Quebec Code of Civ.Proc. (Curran, 1922) §§ 286 to 290.

Note to Subdivisions (d), (e), and (f). The restrictions here placed upon the use of depositions at the trial or hearing are substantially the same as those provided in U.S.C., Title 28, [former] § 641, for depositions taken, *de bene esse*, with the additional provision that any deposition may be used when the court finds the existence of exceptional circumstances. Compare English Rules Under the Judicature Act (The Annual Practice, 1937) O. 37, r. 18 (with additional provision permitting use of deposition by consent of the parties). See also [former] Equity Rule 64 (Former Depositions, Etc. May be Used Before Master); and 2 Minn. Stat. (Mason, 1927) § 9835 (Use in a subsequent action of a deposition filed in a previously dismissed action between the same parties and involving the same subject matter).

1946 Amendment

Note. Subdivision (a). The amendment eliminates the requirement of leave of court for the taking of a deposition except where a plaintiff seeks to take a deposition within 20 days after the commencement of the action. The retention of the requirement where a deposition is sought by a plaintiff within 20 days of the commencement of the action protects a defendant who has not had an opportunity to retain counsel and inform himself as to the nature of the suit; the plaintiff, of course, needs no such protection. The present rule forbids the plaintiff to take a deposition, without leave of court, before the answer is served. Sometimes the defendant delays the serving of an answer for more than 20 days, but as 20 days are sufficient time for him to obtain a lawyer, there is no reason to forbid the plaintiff to take a deposition without leave merely because the answer has not been served. In all cases, Rule 30(a) empowers the court, for cause shown, to alter the time of the taking of a deposition, and Rule 30(b) contains provisions giving ample protection to persons who are unreasonably pressed. The modified practice here adopted is along the line of that followed in various states. See e.g., 8 Mo.Rev.Stat.Ann.1939, § 1917; 2 Burns' Ind.Stat.Ann.1933, § 2–1506.

Subdivision (b). The amendments to subdivision (b) make clear the broad scope of examination and that it may cover not only evidence for use at the trial but also inquiry into matters in themselves inadmissible as evidence but which will lead to the discovery of such evidence. The purpose of discovery is to allow a broad search for facts, the names of witnesses, or any other matters which may aid a party in the preparation or presentation of his case. *Engl v. Aetna Life Ins. Co.*, C.C.A.2, 1943, 139 F.2d 469; *Mahler v. Pennsylvania R. Co.*, E.D.N.Y.1945, 8 Fed.Rules Serv. 33.351, Case 1. In such a preliminary inquiry admissibility at trial should not be the test as to whether the information sought is within the scope of proper examination. Such a standard unnecessarily curtails the utility of discovery practice. Of course, matters entirely without bearing either as direct evidence or as leads to evidence are not within the scope of inquiry, but to the extent that the examination develops useful information, it functions successfully as an instrument of discovery, even if it produces no testimony directly admissible. *Lewis v. United Air Lines Transportation Corp.*, D.Conn.1939, 27 F.Supp. 946; *Engl v. Aetna Life Ins. Co.*, supra; *Mahler v. Pennsylvania R. Co.*, supra; *Bloomer v. Sirian Lamp Co.*, D.Del.1944, 8 Fed.Rules Serv. 26b.31, Case 3; *Rosseau v. Langley*, N.Y.1945, 9 Fed.Rules Serv. 34.41, Case 1 (Rule 26 contemplates "examinations not merely for the narrow purpose of adducing testimony which may be offered in evidence but also for the broad discovery of information which may be useful in preparation for trial."); *Olson Transportation Co. v. Socony-Vacuum Co.*, E.D.Wis. 1944, 8 Fed.Rules Serv. 34.41, Case 2 (". . . the Rules . . . permit 'fishing' for evidence as they should."); Note, 1945, 45 Col.L.Rev. 482. Thus hearsay, while inadmissible itself, may suggest testimony which properly may be proved. Under Rule 26(b) several cases, however, have erroneously limited discovery on the basis of admissibility, holding that the word "relevant" in effect meant "material and competent under the rules of evidence". *Poppino v. Jones Store Co.*, W.D.Mo.1940, 1 F.R.D. 215, 3 Fed.Rules Serv. 26b.5, Case 1; *Benevento v. A. & P. Food Stores, Inc.*, E.D.N.Y.1939, 26 F.Supp. 424. Thus it has been said that inquiry might not be made into statements or other matters which, when disclosed, amounted only to hearsay. *See Maryland for use of Montvila v. Pan-American Bus Lines, Inc.*, D.Md.1940, 1 F.R.D. 213, 3 Fed.Rules Serv. 26b.211, Case 3; *Gitto v. "Italia," Societa Anonima Di Navigazione*, E.D.N.Y.1940, 31 F.Supp. 567; *Rose Silk Mills, Inc. v. Insurance Co. of North America*, S.D.N.Y.1939, 29 F.Supp. 504; *Colpak v. Hetterick*, E.D.N.Y.1941, 40 F.Supp. 350; *Matthies v. Peter F. Connolly Co.*, E.D.N.Y.1941, 6 Fed.Rules Serv. 30a.22, Case 1, 2 F.R.D. 277; *Matter of Examination of Citizens Casualty Co. of New York*, S.D.N.Y.1942, 3 F.R.D. 171, 7 Fed.Rules Serv. 26b.211, Case 1; *United States v. Silliman*, D.C.N.J.1944, 8 Fed.Rules Serv. 26b.52, Case 1. The contrary and better view, however, has often been stated. See, e.g., *Engl v. Aetna Life Ins. Co.*, supra; *Stevenson v. Melady*, S.D.N.Y. 1940, 3 Fed.Rules Serv. 26b.31, Case 1, 1 F.R.D. 329; *Lewis v. United Air Lines Transport Corp.*, supra; *Application of Zenith Radio Corp.*, E.D.Pa.1941, 4 Fed.Rules Serv. 30b.21, Case 1, 1 F.R.D. 627; *Steingut v. Guaranty Trust Co. of New York*, S.D.N.Y.1941, 1 F.R.D. 723, 4 Fed.Rules Serv. 26b.5, Case 2; *DeSeversky v. Republic Aviation Corp.*, E.D.N.Y.1941, 2 F.R.D. 183, 5 Fed.Rules Serv. 26b.31, Case 5; *Moore v. George A. Hormel & Co.*, S.D.N.Y.1942, 6 Fed.Rules Serv. 30b.41, Case 1, 2 F.R.D. 340; *Hercules Powder Co. v. Rohm & Haas Co.*, D.Del.1943, 7 Fed.Rules Serv. 45b.311, Case 2, 3 F.R.D. 302; *Bloomer v. Sirian Lamp Co.*, supra; *Crosby Steam Gage & Valve Co. v. Manning, Maxwell & Moore, Inc.*, D.Mass.1944, 8 Fed.Rules Serv. 26b.31, Case 1; *Patterson Oil Terminals, Inc. v. Charles Kurz & Co., Inc.*, E.D.Pa.1945, 9 Fed.Rules Serv. 33.321, Case 2; *Pueblo Trading Co. v. Reclamation Dist. No. 1500*, N.D.Cal.1945, 9 Fed.Rules Serv. 33.321, Case 4, 4 F.R.D. 471. See also discussion as to the broad scope of discovery in *Hoffman v. Palmer*, C.C.A.2, 1942, 129 F.2d 976, 995–997, affirmed 63 S.Ct. 477, 318 U.S. 109, 87 L.Ed. 645; Note, 1945, 45 Col.L.Rev. 482.

1963 Amendment

This amendment conforms to the amendment of Rule 28(b). See the next-to-last paragraph of the Advisory Committee's Note to that amendment.

1966 Amendment

The requirement that the plaintiff obtain leave of court in order to serve notice of taking of a deposition within 20 days after commencement of the action gives rise to difficulties when the prospective deponent is about to become unavailable for examination. The problem is not confined to admiralty, but has been of special concern in that context because of the mobility of vessels and their personnel. When Rule 26 was adopted as Admiralty Rule 30A in 1961, the problem was alleviated by permitting depositions *de bene esse,* for which leave of court is not required. See Advisory Committee's Note to Admiralty Rule 30A (1961).

A continuing study is being made in the effort to devise a modification of the 20-day rule appropriate to both the civil and admiralty practice to the end that Rule 26(a) shall state a uniform rule applicable alike to what are now civil actions and suits in admiralty. Meanwhile, the exigencies of maritime litigation require preservation, for the time being at least, of the traditional *de bene esse* procedure for the post-unification counterpart of the present suit in admiralty. Accordingly, the amendment provides for continued availability of that procedure in admiralty and maritime claims within the meaning of Rule 9(h).

1970 Amendment

A limited rearrangement of the discovery rules is made, whereby certain rule provisions are transferred, as follows: Existing Rule 26(a) is transferred to Rules 30(a) and 31(a). Existing Rule 26(c) is transferred to Rule 30(c). Existing Rules 26(d), (e), and (f) are transferred to Rule 32. Revisions of the transferred provisions, if any, are discussed in the notes appended to Rules 30, 31, and 32. In addition, Rule 30(b) is transferred to Rule 26(c). The purpose of this rearrangement is to establish Rule 26 as a rule governing discovery in general. (The reasons are set out in the Advisory Committee's explanatory statement.)

Subdivision (a)—Discovery Devices. This is a new subdivision listing all of the discovery devices provided in the discovery rules and establishing the relationship between the general provisions of Rule 26 and the specific rules for particular discovery devices. The provision that the frequency of use of these methods is not limited confirms existing law. It incorporates in general form a provision now found in Rule 33.

Subdivision (b)—Scope of Discovery. This subdivision is recast to cover the scope of discovery generally. It regulates the discovery obtainable through any of the discovery devices listed in Rule 26(a).

All provisions as to scope of discovery are subject to the initial qualification that the court may limit discovery in accordance with these rules. Rule 26(c) (transferred from 30(b)) confers broad powers on the courts to regulate or prevent discovery even though the materials sought are within the scope of 26(b), and these powers have always been freely exercised. For example, a party's income tax return is generally held not privileged, 2A Barron & Holtzoff, *Federal Practice and Procedure,* § 651.2 (Wright ed. 1961), and yet courts have recognized that interests in privacy may call for a measure of extra protection. E.g., *Wiesenberger v. W. E. Hutton & Co.,* 35 F.R.D. 556 (S.D.N.Y.1964). Similarly, the courts have in appropriate circumstances protected materials that are primarily of an impeaching character. These two types of materials merely illustrate the many situations, not capable of governance by precise rule, in which courts must exercise judgment. The new subsections in Rule 26(b) do not change existing law with respect to such situations.

Subdivision (b)(1)—In General. The language is changed to provide for the scope of discovery in general terms. The existing subdivision, although in terms applicable only to depositions, is incorporated by reference in existing Rules 33 and 34. Since decisions as to relevance to the subject matter of the action are made for discovery purposes well in advance of trial, a flexible treatment of relevance is required and the making of discovery, whether voluntary or under court order, is not a concession or determination of relevance for purposes of trial. *Cf.* 4 *Moore's Federal Practice* ¶26–16[1] (2d ed. 1966).

Subdivision (b)(2)—Insurance Policies. Both the cases and commentators are sharply in conflict on the question whether defendant's liability insurance coverage is subject to discovery in the usual situation when the insurance coverage is not itself admissible and does not bear on another issue in the case. Examples of Federal cases requiring disclosure and supporting comments: *Cook v. Welty,* 253 F.Supp. 875 (D.D.C.1966) (cases cited); *Johanek v. Aberle,* 27 F.R.D. 272 (D.Mont.1961); Williams, *Discovery of Dollar Limits in Liability Policies in Automobile Tort Cases,* 10 Ala.L.Rev. 355 (1958); Thode, *Some Reflections on the 1957 Amendments to the Texas Rules,* 37 Tex.L.Rev. 33, 40–42 (1958). Examples of Federal cases refusing disclosure and supporting comments: *Bisserier v. Manning,* 207 F.Supp. 476 (D.N.J.1962); *Cooper v. Stender,* 30 F.R.D. 389 (E.D.Tenn.1962); Frank, *Discovery and Insurance, Coverage,* 1959 Ins.L.J. 281; Fournier, *Pre-trial Discovery of Insurance Coverage and Limits,* 28 Ford.L.Rev. 215 (1959).

The division in reported cases is close. State decisions based on provisions similar to the federal rules are similarly divided. See cases collected in 2A Barron & Holtzoff, *Federal Practice and Procedure* § 647.1, nn. 45.5, 45.6 (Wright ed. 1961). It appears to be difficult if not impossible to obtain appellate review of the issue. Resolution by rule amendment is indicated. The question is essentially procedural in that it bears upon preparation for trial and settlement before trial, and courts confronting the question, however they have decided it, have generally treated it as procedural and governed by the rules.

The amendment resolves this issue in favor of disclosure. Most of the decisions denying discovery, some explicitly, reason from the text of Rule 26(b) that it permits discovery only of matters which will be admissible in evidence or appear reasonably calculated to lead to such evidence; they avoid considerations of policy, regarding them as foreclosed. See *Bisserier v. Manning, supra.* Some note also that facts about a defendant's financial status are not discoverable as such, prior to judgment with execution unsatisfied, and fear that, if courts hold insurance coverage discoverable, they must extend the principle to other aspects of the defendant's financial status. The cases favoring disclosure rely heavily on the practical significance of insurance in the decisions lawyers make about settlement and trial preparation. In *Clauss v. Danker,* 264 F.Supp. 246 (S.D.N.Y.1967), the court held that the rules forbid disclosure but called for an amendment to permit it.

Disclosure of insurance coverage will enable counsel for both sides to make the same realistic appraisal of the case, so that settlement and litigation strategy are based on knowledge and not speculation. It will conduce to settlement and avoid protracted litigation in some cases, though in others it may have an opposite effect. The amendment is limited to insurance coverage, which should be distinguished from any other facts concerning defendant's financial status (1) because insurance is an asset created specifically to satisfy the claim; (2) because the insurance company ordinarily controls the litigation; (3) because information about coverage is available only from defendant or his insurer; and (4) because disclosure does not involve a significant invasion of privacy.

Disclosure is required when the insurer "may be liable" on part or all of the judgment. Thus, an insurance company must disclose even when it contests liability under the policy, and such disclosure does not constitute a waiver of its claim. It is immaterial whether the liability is to satisfy the judgment directly or merely to indemnify or reimburse another after he pays the judgment.

The provision applies only to persons "carrying on an insurance business" and thus covers insurance companies and not the ordinary business concern that enters into a contract of indemnification. *Cf.* N.Y.Ins.Law § 41. Thus, the provision makes no change in existing law on discovery of indemnity agreements other than insurance agreements by persons carrying on an insurance business. Similarly, the provision does not cover the business concern that creates a reserve fund for purposes of self-insurance.

For some purposes other than discovery, an application for insurance is treated as a part of the insurance agreement. The provision makes clear that, for discovery purposes, the application is not to be so treated. The insurance application may contain personal and financial information concerning the insured, discovery of which is beyond the purpose of this provision.

In no instance does disclosure make the facts concerning insurance coverage admissible in evidence.

Subdivision (b)(3)—Trial Preparation: Materials. Some of the most controversial and vexing problems to emerge from the discovery rules have arisen out of requests for the production of documents or things prepared in anticipation of litigation or for trial. The existing rules make no explicit provision for such materials. Yet, two verbally distinct doctrines have developed, each conferring a qualified immunity on these materials—the "good cause" requirement in Rule 34 (now generally held applicable to discovery of documents via deposition under Rule 45 and interrogatories under Rule 33) and the work-product doctrine of *Hickman v. Taylor,* 329 U.S. 495 (1947). Both demand a showing of justification before production can be had, the one of "good cause" and the other variously described in the *Hickman* case: "necessity or justification," "denial * * * would unduly prejudice the preparation of petitioner's case," or "cause hardship or injustice" 329 U.S. at 509–510.

In deciding the *Hickman* case, the Supreme Court appears to have expressed a preference in 1947 for an approach to the problem of trial preparation materials by judicial decision rather than by rule. Sufficient experience has accumulated, however, with lower court applications of the *Hickman* decision to warrant a reappraisal.

The major difficulties visible in the existing case law are (1) confusion and disagreement as to whether "good cause" is made out by a showing of relevance and lack of privilege, or requires an additional showing of necessity, (2) confusion and disagreement as to the scope of the *Hickman* work-product doctrine, particularly whether it extends beyond work actually performed by lawyers, and (3) the resulting difficulty of relating the "good cause" required by Rule 34 and the "necessity or justification" of the work-product doctrine, so that their respective roles and the distinctions between them are understood.

Basic Standard.—Since Rule 34 in terms requires a showing of "good cause" for the production of all documents and things, whether or not trial preparation is involved, courts have felt that a single formula is called for and have differed over whether a showing of relevance and lack of privilege is enough or whether more must be shown. When the facts of the cases are studied, however, a distinction emerges based upon the type of materials. With respect to documents not obtained or prepared with an eye to litigation, the decisions, while not uniform, reflect a strong and increasing tendency to relate "good cause" to a showing that the documents are relevant to the subject matter of the action. *E.g., Connecticut Mutual Life Ins. Co. v. Shields,* 17 F.R.D. 273 (S.D.N.Y. 1959), with cases cited; *Houdry Process Corp. v. Commonwealth Oil Refining Co.,* 24 F.R.D. 58 (S.D.N.Y.1955); see *Bell v. Commercial Ins. Co.,* 280 F.2d 514, 517 (3d Cir. 1960). When the party whose documents are sought shows that the request for production is unduly burdensome or oppressive, courts have denied discovery for lack of "good cause", although they might just as easily have based their decision on the protective provisions of existing Rule 30(b) (new Rule 26(c)). *E.g., Lauer v. Tankrederi,* 39 F.R.D. 334 (E.D.Pa. 1966).

As to trial-preparation materials, however, the courts are increasingly interpreting "good cause" as requiring more than relevance. When lawyers have prepared or obtained the materials for trial, all courts require more than relevance; so much is clearly commanded by *Hickman.* But even as to the preparatory work of nonlawyers, while some courts ignore work-product and equate "good cause" with relevance, *e.g., Brown v. New York, N.H. & H.R.R.,* 17 F.R.D. 324 (S.D.N.Y.1955), the more recent trend is to read "good cause" as requiring inquiry into the importance of and need for the materials as well as into alternative sources for securing the same information. In *Guilford Nat'l Bank v. Southern Ry.,* 297 F.2d 921 (4th Cir. 1962), statements of witnesses obtained by claim agents were held not discoverable because both parties had had equal access to the witnesses at about the same time, shortly after the collision in question. The decision was based solely on Rule 34 and "good cause"; the court declined to rule on whether the statements were work-products. The court's treatment of "good cause" is quoted at length and with approval in *Schlagenhauf v. Holder,* 379 U.S. 104, 117–118 (1964). See also *Mitchell v. Bass,* 252 F.2d 513 (8th Cir. 1958); *Hauger v. Chicago, R.I. & Pac. R.R.,* 216 F.2d 501 (7th Cir. 1954); *Burke v. United States,* 32 F.R.D. 213 (E.D.N.Y.1963). While the opinions dealing with "good cause" do not often draw an explicit distinction between trial preparation materials and other materials, in fact an overwhelming proportion of the cases in which a special showing is required are cases involving trial preparation materials.

The rules are amended by eliminating the general requirement of "good cause" from Rule 34 but retaining a requirement of a special showing for trial preparation materials in this subdivision. The required showing is expressed, not in terms of "good cause" whose generality has tended to encourage confusion and controversy, but in terms of the elements of the special showing to be made: substantial need of the materials in the preparation of the case and inability without undue hardship to obtain the substantial equivalent of the materials by other means.

These changes conform to the holdings of the cases, when viewed in light of their facts. Apart from trial preparation, the fact that the materials sought are documentary does not in and of itself require a special showing beyond relevance and absence of privilege. The protective provisions are of course available, and if the party from whom production is sought raises a special issue of privacy (as with respect to income tax returns or grand jury minutes) or points to evidence primarily impeaching, or can show serious burden or expense, the court will exercise its traditional power to decide whether to issue a protective order. On the other hand, the requirement of a special showing for discovery of trial preparation materials reflects the view that each side's informal evaluation of its case should be protected, that each side should be encouraged to prepare independently, and that one side should not automatically have the benefit of the detailed preparatory work of the other side. See Field and McKusick, *Maine Civil Practice* 264 (1959).

Elimination of a "good cause" requirement from Rule 34 and the establishment of a requirement of a special showing in this subdivision will eliminate the confusion caused by having two verbally distinct requirements of justification that the courts have been unable to distinguish clearly. Moreover, the language of the subdivision suggests the factors which the courts should consider in determining whether the requisite showing has been made. The importance of the materials sought to the party seeking them in preparation of his case and the difficulty he will have obtaining them by other means are factors noted in the *Hickman* case. The courts should also consider the likelihood that the party, even if he obtains the information by independent means, will not have the substantial equivalent of the documents the production of which he seeks.

Consideration of these factors may well lead the court to distinguish between witness statements taken by an investigator, on the one hand, and other parts of the investigative file, on the other. The court in *Southern Ry. v. Lanham,* 403 F.2d 119 (5th Cir. 1968), while it naturally addressed itself to the "good cause" requirements of Rule 34, set forth as controlling considerations the factors contained in the language of this subdivision. The analysis of the court suggests circumstances under which witness statements will be discoverable. The witness may have given a fresh and contemporaneous account in a written statement while he is available to the party seeking discovery only a substantial time thereafter. *Lanham, supra* at 127–128; *Guilford, supra* at 926. Or he may be reluctant or hostile. *Lanham, supra* at 128–129; *Brookshire v. Pennsylvania RR,* 14 F.R.D. 154 (N.D.Ohio 1953); *Diamond v. Mohawk Rubber Co.,* 33 F.R.D. 264 (D.Colo.1963). Or he may have a lapse of memory. *Tannenbaum v. Walker,* 16 F.R.D. 570 (E.D.Pa. 1954). Or he may probably be deviating from his prior statement. *Cf. Hauger v. Chicago, R.I. & Pac. RR,* 216 F.2d 501 (7th Cir. 1954). On the other hand, a much stronger showing is needed to obtain evaluative materials in an investigator's reports. *Lanham, supra* at 131–133; *Pickett v. L. R. Ryan, Inc.,* 237 F.Supp. 198 (E.D.S.C.1965).

Materials assembled in the ordinary course of business, or pursuant to public requirements unrelated to litigation, or for other nonlitigation purposes are not under the qualified immunity provided by this subdivision. *Goosman v. A. Duie Pyle, Inc.,* 320 F.2d 45 (4th Cir. 1963); cf. *United States v. New York Foreign Trade Zone Operators, Inc.,* 304 F.2d 792 (2d Cir. 1962). No change is made in the existing doctrine, noted in the *Hickman* case, that one party may discover relevant facts known or available to the other party, even though such facts are contained in a document which is not itself discoverable.

Treatment of Lawyers; Special Protection of Mental Impressions, Conclusions, Opinions, and Legal Theories Concerning the Litigation.—The courts are divided as to whether the work-product doctrine extends to the preparatory work only of lawyers. The *Hickman* case left this issue open since the statements in that case were taken by a lawyer. As to courts of appeals compare *Alltmont v. United States,* 177 F.2d 971, 976 (3d Cir. 1949), cert. denied, 339 U.S. 967 (1950) (*Hickman* applied to statements obtained by FBI agents on theory it should apply to "all statements of prospective witnesses which a party has obtained for his trial counsel's use"), with *Southern Ry. v. Campbell,* 309 F.2d 569 (5th Cir. 1962) (Statements taken by claim agents not work-product), and *Guilford Nat'l Bank v. Southern Ry.,* 297 F.2d 921 (4th Cir. 1962) (avoiding issue of work-product as to claim agents, deciding case instead under Rule 34 "good cause"). Similarly, the district courts are divided on statements obtained by claim agents, compare, e.g., *Brown v. New York, N.H. & H.R.R.,* 17 F.R.D. 324 (S.D.N.Y.1955) with *Hanke v. Milwaukee Electric Ry. & Transp. Co.,* 7 F.R.D. 540 (E.D.Wis.1947); investigators, compare *Burke v. United States,* 32 F.R.D. 213 (E.D.N.Y.1963) with *Snyder v. United States,* 20 F.R.D. 7 (E.D.N.Y.1956); and insurers, compare *Gottlieb v. Bresler,* 24 F.R.D. 371 (D.D.C.1959) with *Burns v. Mulder,* 20 F.R.D. 605 (E.D.Pa.1957). See 4 Moore's *Federal Practice* ¶26.23[8.1] (2d ed. 1966); 2A Barron & Holtzoff, *Federal Practice and Procedure* § 652.2 (Wright ed. 1961).

A complication is introduced by the use made by courts of the "good cause" requirement of Rule 34, as described above. A court may conclude that trial preparation materials are not work-product because not the result of lawyer's work and yet hold that they are not producible because "good cause" has not been shown. *Cf. Guilford Nat'l Bank v. Southern Ry.,* 297 F.2d 921 (4th Cir. 1962), cited and described above. When the decisions on "good cause" are taken into account, the weight of authority affords protection of the preparatory work of both lawyers and nonlawyers (though not necessarily to the same extent) by requiring more than a showing of relevance to secure production.

Subdivision (b)(3) reflects the trend of the cases by requiring a special showing, not merely as to materials prepared by an attorney, but also as to materials prepared in anticipation of litigation or preparation for trial by or for a party or any representative acting on his behalf. The subdivision then goes on to protect against disclosure the mental impressions, conclusions, opinions, or legal theories concerning the litigation of an attorney or other representative of a party. The *Hickman* opinion drew special attention to the need for protecting an attorney against discovery of memoranda prepared from recollection of oral interviews. The courts have steadfastly safeguarded against disclosure of lawyers' mental impressions and legal theories, as well as mental impressions and subjective evaluations of investigators and claim-agents. In enforcing this provision of the subdivision, the courts will sometimes find it necessary to order disclosure of a document but with portions deleted.

Rules 33 and 36 have been revised in order to permit discovery calling for opinions, contentions, and admissions relating not only to fact but also to the application of law to fact. Under those rules, a party and his attorney or other representative may be required to disclose, to some extent, mental impressions, opinions, or conclusions. But documents or parts of documents containing these matters are protected against discovery by this subdivision. Even though a party may ultimately have to disclose in response to interrogatories or requests to admit, he is entitled to keep confidential documents containing such matters prepared for internal use.

Party's Right to Own Statement—An exception to the requirement of this subdivision enables a party to secure production of his own statement without any special showing. The cases are divided. Compare, *e.g., Safeway Stores, Inc. v. Reynolds*, 176 F.2d 476 (D.C. Cir.1949); *Shupe v. Pennsylvania R.R.*, 19 F.R.D. 144 (W.D.Pa.1956); with *e.g., New York Central R.R. v. Carr*, 251 F.2d 433 (4th Cir. 1957); *Belback v. Wilson Freight Forwarding Co.*, 40 F.R.D. 16 (W.D.Pa.1966).

Courts which treat a party's statement as though it were that of any witness overlook the fact that the party's statement is, without more, admissible in evidence. Ordinarily, a party gives a statement without insisting on a copy because he does not yet have a lawyer and does not understand the legal consequences of his actions. Thus, the statement is given at a time when he functions at a disadvantage. Discrepancies between his trial testimony and earlier statement may result from lapse of memory or ordinary inaccuracy; a written statement produced for the first time at trial may give such discrepancies a prominence which they do not deserve. In appropriate cases the court may order a party to be deposed before his statement is produced. *E.g., Smith v. Central Linen Service Co.*, 39 F.R.D. 15 (D.Md.1966); *McCoy v. General Motors Corp.*, 33 F.R.D. 354 (W.D.Pa. 1963).

Commentators strongly support the view that a party be able to secure his statement without a showing. 4 *Moore's Federal Practice* ¶26.23[8.4] (2d ed. 1966); 2A Barron & Holtzoff, *Federal Practice and Procedure* § 652.3 (Wright ed. 1961); see also Note, *Developments in the Law—Discovery*, 74 Harv.L.Rev. 940, 1039 (1961). The following states have by statute or rule taken the same position: *Statutes:* Fla.Stat.Ann. § 92.33; Ga.Code Ann. § 38–2109(b); La.Stat. Ann.R.S. 13:3732; Mass.Gen.Laws Ann. c. 271, § 44; Minn. Stat.Ann. § 602.01; N.Y.C.P.L.R. § 3101(e); *Rules:* Mo. R.C.P. 56.01(a); N.Dak.R.C.P. 34(b); Wyo.R.C.P. 34(b); *cf.* Mich.G.C.R. 306.2.

In order to clarify and tighten the provision on statements by a party, the term "statement" is defined. The definition is adapted from 18 U.S.C. § 3500(e) (Jencks Act). The statement of a party may of course be that of plaintiff or defendant, and it may be that of an individual or of a corporation or other organization.

Witness' Right to Own Statement.—A second exception to the requirement of this subdivision permits a non-party witness to obtain a copy of his own statement without any special showing. Many, though not all, of the considerations supporting a party's right to obtain his statement apply also to the non-party witness. Insurance companies are increasingly recognizing that a witness is entitled to a copy of his statement and are modifying their regular practice accordingly.

Subdivision (b)(4)—Trial Preparation: Experts. This is a new provision dealing with discovery of information (including facts and opinions) obtained by a party from an expert retained by that party in relation to litigation or obtained by the expert and not yet transmitted to the party. The subdivision deals separately with those experts whom the party expects to call as trial witnesses and with those experts who have been retained or specially employed by the party but who are not expected to be witnesses. It should be noted that the subdivision does not address itself to the expert whose information was not acquired in preparation for trial but rather because he was an actor or viewer with respect to transactions or occurrences that are part of the subject matter of the lawsuit. Such an expert should be treated as an ordinary witness.

Subsection (b)(4)(A) deals with discovery of information obtained by or through experts who will be called as witnesses at trial. The provision is responsive to problems suggested by a relatively recent line of authorities. Many of these cases present intricate and difficult issues as to which expert testimony is likely to be determinative. Prominent among them are food and drug, patent, and condemnation cases. See, *e.g., United States v. Nysco Laboratories, Inc.*, 26 F.R.D. 159, 162 (E.D.N.Y.1960) (food and drug); *E. I. du Pont de Nemours & Co. v. Phillips Petroleum Co.*, 24 F.R.D. 416, 421 (D.Del.1959) (patent); *Cold Metal Process Co. v. Aluminum Co. of America*, 7 F.R.D. 425 (N.D.Ohio 1947), aff'd, *Sachs v. Aluminum Co. of America*, 167 F.2d 570 (6th Cir. 1948) (same); *United States v. 50.34 Acres of Land*, 13 F.R.D. 19 (E.D.N.Y.1952) (condemnation).

In cases of this character, a prohibition against discovery of information held by expert witnesses produces in acute form the very evils that discovery has been created to prevent. Effective cross-examination of an expert witness requires advance preparation. The lawyer even with the help of his own experts frequently cannot anticipate the particular approach his adversary's expert will take or the data on which he will base his judgment on the stand. McGlothlin, *Some Practical Problems in Proof of Economic, Scientific, and Technical Facts*, 23 F.R.D. 467, 478 (1958). A California study of discovery and pretrial in condemnation cases notes that the only substitute for discovery of experts' valuation materials is "lengthy—and often fruitless—cross-examination during trial," and recommends pretrial exchange of such material. Calif.Law Rev.Comm'n, Discovery in Eminent Domain Proceedings 707–710 (Jan. 1963). Similarly, effective rebuttal requires advance knowledge of the line of testimony of the other side. If the latter is foreclosed by a rule against discovery, then the narrowing of issues and elimination of surprise which discovery normally produces are frustrated.

These considerations appear to account for the broadening of discovery against experts in the cases cited where expert testimony was central to the case. In some instances, the opinions are explicit in relating expanded discovery to improved cross-examination and rebuttal at trial. *Franks v. National Dairy Products Corp.*, 41 F.R.D. 234 (W.D.Tex. 1966); *United States v. 23.76 Acres*, 32 F.R.D. 593 (D.Md. 1963); see also an unpublished opinion of Judge Hincks, quoted in *United States v. 48 Jars, etc.*, 23 F.R.D. 192, 198

(D.D.C.1958). On the other hand, the need for a new provision is shown by the many cases in which discovery of expert trial witnesses is needed for effective cross-examination and rebuttal, and yet courts apply the traditional doctrine and refuse disclosure. *E.g., United States v. Certain Parcels of Land,* 25 F.R.D. 192 (N.D.Cal.1959); *United States v. Certain Acres,* 18 F.R.D. 98 (M.D.Ga.1955).

Although the trial problems flowing from lack of discovery of expert witnesses are most acute and noteworthy when the case turns largely on experts, the same problems are encountered when a single expert testifies. Thus, subdivision (b)(4)(A) draws no line between complex and simple cases, or between cases with many experts and those with but one. It establishes by rule substantially the procedure adopted by decision of the court in *Knighton v. Villian & Fassio,* 39 F.R.D. 11 (D.Md.1965). For a full analysis of the problem and strong recommendations to the same effect, see Friedenthal, *Discovery and Use of an Adverse Party's Expert Information,* 14 Stan.L.Rev. 455, 485–488 (1962); Long, *Discovery and Experts under the Federal Rules of Civil Procedure,* 38 F.R.D. 111 (1965).

Past judicial restrictions on discovery of an adversary's expert, particularly as to his opinions, reflect the fear that one side will benefit unduly from the other's better preparation. The procedure established in subsection (b)(4)(A) holds the risk to a minimum. Discovery is limited to trial witnesses, and may be obtained only at a time when the parties know who their expert witnesses will be. A party must as a practical matter prepare his own case in advance of that time, for he can hardly hope to build his case out of his opponent's experts.

Subdivision (b)(4)(A) provides for discovery of an expert who is to testify at the trial. A party can require one who intends to use the expert to state the substance of the testimony that the expert is expected to give. The court may order further discovery, and it has ample power to regulate its timing and scope and to prevent abuse. Ordinarily, the order for further discovery shall compensate the expert for his time, and may compensate the party who intends to use the expert for past expenses reasonably incurred in obtaining facts or opinions from the expert. Those provisions are likely to discourage abusive practices.

Subdivision (b)(4)(B) deals with an expert who has been retained or specially employed by the party in anticipation of litigation or preparation for trial (thus excluding an expert who is simply a general employee of the party not specially employed on the case), but who is not expected to be called as a witness. Under its provisions, a party may discover facts known or opinions held by such an expert only on a showing of exceptional circumstances under which it is impracticable for the party seeking discovery to obtain facts or opinions on the same subject by other means.

Subdivision (b)(4)(B) is concerned only with experts retained or specially consulted in relation to trial preparation. Thus the subdivision precludes discovery against experts who were informally consulted in preparation for trial, but not retained or specially employed. As an ancillary procedure, a party may on a proper showing require the other party to name experts retained or specially employed, but not those informally consulted.

These new provisions of subdivision (b)(4) repudiate the few decisions that have held an expert's information privileged simply because of his status as an expert, *e.g., American Oil Co. v. Pennsylvania Petroleum Products Co.,* 23 F.R.D. 680, 685–686 (D.R.I.1959). See *Louisell, Modern California Discovery* 315–316 (1963). They also reject as ill-considered the decisions which have sought to bring expert information within the work-product doctrine. See *United States v. McKay,* 372 F.2d 174, 176–177 (5th Cir. 1967). The provisions adopt a form of the more recently developed doctrine of "unfairness". See *e.g., United States v. 23.76 Acres of Land,* 32 F.R.D. 593, 597 (D.Md.1963); Louisell, *supra,* at 317–318; 4 *Moore's Federal Practice* 26.24 (2d ed. 1966).

Under subdivision (b)(4)(C), the court is directed or authorized to issue protective orders, including an order that the expert be paid a reasonable fee for time spent in responding to discovery, and that the party whose expert is made subject to discovery be paid a fair portion of the fees and expenses that the party incurred in obtaining information from the expert. The court may issue the latter order as a condition of discovery, or it may delay the order until after discovery is completed. These provisions for fees and expenses meet the objection that it is unfair to permit one side to obtain without cost the benefit of an expert's work for which the other side has paid, often a substantial sum. E.g., *Lewis v. United Air Lines Transp. Corp.,* 32 F.Supp. 21 (W.D.Pa.1940); *Walsh v. Reynolds Metal Co.,* 15 F.R.D. 376 (D.N.J.1954). On the other hand, a party may not obtain discovery simply by offering to pay fees and expenses. Cf. *Boynton v. R. J. Reynolds Tobacco Co.,* 36 F.Supp. 593 (D.Mass.1941).

In instances of discovery under subdivision (b)(4)(B), the court is directed to award fees and expenses to the other party, since the information is of direct value to the discovering party's preparation of his case. In ordering discovery under (b)(4)(A)(ii), the court has discretion whether to award fees and expenses to the other party; its decision should depend upon whether the discovering party is simply learning about the other party's case or is going beyond this to develop his own case. Even in cases where the court is directed to issue a protective order, it may decline to do so if it finds that manifest injustice would result. Thus, the court can protect, when necessary and appropriate, the interests of an indigent party.

Subdivision (c)—Protective Orders. The provisions of existing Rule 30(b) are transferred to this subdivision (c), as part of the rearrangement of Rule 26. The language has been changed to give it application to discovery generally. The subdivision recognizes the power of the court in the district where a deposition is being taken to make protective orders. Such power is needed when the deposition is being taken far from the court where the action is pending. The court in the district where the deposition is being taken may, and frequently will, remit the deponent or party to the court where the action is pending.

In addition, drafting changes are made to carry out and clarify the sense of the rule. Insertions are made to avoid any possible implication that a protective order does not extend to "time" as well as to "place" or may not safeguard against "undue burden or expense."

The new reference to trade secrets and other confidential commercial information reflects existing law. The courts have not given trade secrets automatic and complete immunity against disclosure, but have in each case weighed their claim to privacy against the need for disclosure. Frequently, they have been afforded a limited protection. See, *e.g.*, *Covey Oil Co. v. Continental Oil Co.*, 340 F.2d 993 (10th Cir. 1965); *Julius M. Ames Co. v. Bostitch, Inc.*, 235 F.Supp. 856 (S.D.N.Y.1964).

The subdivision contains new matter relating to sanctions. When a motion for a protective order is made and the court is disposed to deny it, the court may go a step further and issue an order to provide or permit discovery. This will bring the sanctions of Rule 37(b) directly into play. Since the court has heard the contentions of all interested persons, an affirmative order is justified. See *Rosenberg, Sanctions to Effectuate Pretrial Discovery,* 58 Col.L.Rev. 480, 492–493 (1958). In addition, the court may require the payment of expenses incurred in relation to the motion.

Subdivision (d)—Sequence and Priority. This new provision is concerned with the sequence in which parties may proceed with discovery and with related problems of timing. The principal effects of the new provision are first, to eliminate any fixed priority in the sequence of discovery, and second, to make clear and explicit the court's power to establish priority by an order issued in a particular case.

A priority rule developed by some courts, which confers priority on the party who first serves notice of taking a deposition, is unsatisfactory in several important respects:

First, this priority rule permits a party to establish a priority running to all depositions as to which he has given earlier notice. Since he can on a given day serve notice of taking many depositions he is in a position to delay his adversary's taking of depositions for an inordinate time. Some courts have ruled that deposition priority also permits a party to delay his answers to interrogatories and production of documents. *E.g., E. I. du Pont de Nemours & Co. v. Phillips Petroleum Co.,* 23 F.R.D. 237 (D.Del.1959); *but cf. Sturdevant v. Sears, Roebuck & Co.,* 32 F.R.D. 426 (W.D.Mo. 1963).

Second, since notice is the key to priority, if both parties wish to take depositions first a race results. See *Caldwell-Clements, Inc. v. McGraw-Hill Pub. Co.,* 11 F.R.D. 156 (S.D.N.Y.1951) (description of tactics used by parties). But the existing rules on notice of deposition create a race with runners starting from different positions. The plaintiff may not give notice without leave of court until 20 days after commencement of the action, whereas the defendant may serve notice at any time after commencement. Thus, a careful and prompt defendant can almost always secure priority. This advantage of defendants is fortuitous, because the purpose of requiring plaintiff to wait 20 days is to afford defendant an opportunity to obtain counsel, not to confer priority.

Third, although courts have ordered a change in the normal sequence of discovery on a number of occasions, *e.g., Kaeppler v. James H. Matthews & Co.,* 200 F.Supp. 229 (E.D.Pa.1961); *Park & Tilford Distillers Corp. v. Distillers Co.,* 19 F.R.D. 169 (S.D.N.Y.1956), and have at all times avowed discretion to vary the usual priority, most commentators are agreed that courts in fact grant relief only for "the most obviously compelling reasons." 2A Barron & Holtzoff, *Federal Practice and Procedure* 44–47 (Wright ed. 1961); see also Younger, *Priority of Pretrial Examination in the Federal Courts—A Comment,* 34 N.Y.U.L.Rev. 1271 (1959); Freund, *The Pleading and Pretrial of an Antitrust Claim,* 46 Corn.L.Q. 555, 564 (1964). Discontent with the fairness of actual practice has been evinced by other observers. Comments, 59 Yale L.J. 117, 134–136 (1949); Yudkin, *Some Refinements in Federal Discovery Procedure,* 11 Fed.B.J. 289, 296–297 (1951); *Developments in the Law-Discovery,* 74 Harv.L.Rev. 940, 954–958 (1961).

Despite these difficulties, some courts have adhered to the priority rule, presumably because it provides a test which is easily understood and applied by the parties without much court intervention. It thus permits deposition discovery to function extrajudicially, which the rules provide for and the courts desire. For these same reasons, courts are reluctant to make numerous exceptions to the rule.

The Columbia Survey makes clear that the problem of priority does not affect litigants generally. It found that most litigants do not move quickly to obtain discovery. In over half of the cases, both parties waited at least 50 days. During the first 20 days after commencement of the action—the period when defendant might assure his priority by noticing depositions—16 percent of the defendants acted to obtain discovery. A race could not have occurred in more than 16 percent of the cases and it undoubtedly occurred in fewer. On the other hand, five times as many defendants as plaintiffs served notice of deposition during the first 19 days. To the same effect, see Comment, *Tactical Use and Abuse of Depositions Under the Federal Rules,* 59 Yale L.J. 117, 134 (1949).

These findings do not mean, however, that the priority rule is satisfactory or that a problem of priority does not exist. The court decisions show that parties do battle on this issue and carry their disputes to court. The statistics show that these court cases are not typical. By the same token, they reveal that more extensive exercise of judicial discretion to vary the priority will not bring a flood of litigation, and that a change in the priority rule will in fact affect only a small fraction of the cases.

It is contended by some that there is no need to alter the existing priority practice. In support, it is urged that there is no evidence that injustices in fact result from present practice and that, in any event, the courts can and do promulgate local rules, as in New York, to deal with local situations and issue orders to avoid possible injustice in particular cases.

Subdivision (d) is based on the contrary view that the rule of priority based on notice is unsatisfactory and unfair in its operation. Subdivision (d) follows an approach adapted from Civil Rule 4 of the District Court for the Southern District of New York. That rule provides that starting 40 days after commencement of the action, unless otherwise ordered by the court, the fact that one party is taking a deposition shall not prevent another party from doing so "concurrently." In practice, the depositions are not usually taken simultaneously; rather, the parties work out arrangements for alternation in the taking of depositions. One party may take a complete deposition and then the other, or, if the depositions are extensive, one party deposes for a set time, and then the other. See *Caldwell-Clements, Inc. v. McCraw-Hill Pub. Co.,* 11 F.R.D. 156 (S.D.N.Y.1951).

In principle, one party's initiation of discovery should not wait upon the other's completion, unless delay is dictated by special considerations. Clearly the principle is feasible with respect to all methods of discovery other than depositions. And the experience of the Southern District of New York shows that the principle can be applied to depositions as well. The courts have not had an increase in motion business on this matter. Once it is clear to lawyers that they bargain on an equal footing, they are usually able to arrange for an orderly succession of depositions without judicial intervention. Professor Moore has called attention to Civil Rule 4 and suggested that it may usefully be extended to other areas. 4 *Moore's Federal Practice* 1154 (2d ed. 1966).

The court may upon motion and by order grant priority in a particular case. But a local court rule purporting to confer priority in certain classes of cases would be inconsistent with this subdivision and thus void.

Subdivision (e)—Supplementation of Responses. The rules do not now state whether interrogatories (and questions at deposition as well as requests for inspection and admissions) impose a "continuing burden" on the responding party to supplement his answers if he obtains new information. The issue is acute when new information renders substantially incomplete or inaccurate an answer which was complete and accurate when made. It is essential that the rules provide an answer to this question. The parties can adjust to a rule either way, once they know what it is. See 4 *Moore's Federal Practice* ¶33.25[4] (2d ed. 1966).

Arguments can be made both ways. Imposition of a continuing burden reduces the proliferation of additional sets of interrogatories. Some courts have adopted local rules establishing such a burden. *E.g.*, E.D.Pa.R. 20(f), quoted in *Taggart v. Vermont Transp. Co.*, 32 F.R.D. 587 (E.D.Pa. 1963); D.Me.R. 15(c). Others have imposed the burden by decision. *E.g.*, *Chenault v. Nebraska Farm Products, Inc.*, 9 F.R.D. 529, 533 (D.Nebr.1949). On the other hand, there are serious objections to the burden, especially in protracted cases. Although the party signs the answers, it is his lawyer who understands their significance and bears the responsibility to bring answers up to date. In a complex case all sorts of information reaches the party, who little understands its bearing on answers previously given to interrogatories. In practice, therefore, the lawyer under a continuing burden must periodically recheck all interrogatories and canvass all new information. But a full set of new answers may no longer be needed by the interrogating party. Some issues will have been dropped from the case, some questions are now seen as unimportant, and other questions must in any event be reformulated. See *Novick v. Pennsylvania R.R.*, 18 F.R.D. 296, 298 (W.D.Pa.1955).

Subdivision (e) provides that a party is not under a continuing burden except as expressly provided. Cf. Note, 68 Harv.L.Rev. 673, 677 (1955). An exception is made as to the identity of persons having knowledge of discoverable matters, because of the obvious importance to each side of knowing all witnesses and because information about witnesses routinely comes to each lawyer's attention. Many of the decisions on the issue of a continuing burden have in fact concerned the identity of witnesses. An exception is also made as to expert trial witnesses in order to carry out the provisions of Rule 26(b)(4). See *Diversified Products Corp. v. Sports Center Co.*, 42 F.R.D. 3 (D.Md.1967).

Another exception is made for the situation in which a party, or more frequently his lawyer, obtains actual knowledge that a prior response is incorrect. This exception does not impose a duty to check the accuracy of prior responses, but it prevents knowing concealment by a party or attorney. Finally, a duty to supplement may be imposed by order of the court in a particular case (including an order resulting from a pretrial conference) or by agreement of the parties. A party may of course make a new discovery request which requires supplementation of prior responses.

The duty will normally be enforced, in those limited instances where it is imposed, through sanctions imposed by the trial court, including exclusion of evidence, continuance, or other action, as the court may deem appropriate.

1980 Amendment

Subdivision (f). This subdivision is new. There has been widespread criticism of abuse of discovery. The Committee has considered a number of proposals to eliminate abuse, including a change in Rule 26(b)(1) with respect to the scope of discovery and a change in Rule 33(a) to limit the number of questions that can be asked by interrogatories to parties.

The Committee believes that abuse of discovery, while very serious in certain cases, is not so general as to require such basic changes in the rules that govern discovery in all cases. A very recent study of discovery in selected metropolitan districts tends to support its belief. P. Connolly, E. Holleman, & M. Kuhlman, *Judicial Controls and the Civil Litigative Process: Discovery* (Federal Judicial Center, 1978). In the judgment of the Committee abuse can best be prevented by intervention by the court as soon as abuse is threatened.

To this end this subdivision provides that counsel who has attempted without success to effect with opposing counsel a reasonable program or plan for discovery is entitled to the assistance of the court.

It is not contemplated that requests for discovery conferences will be made routinely. A relatively narrow discovery dispute should be resolved by resort to Rules 26(c) or 37(a), and if it appears that a request for a conference is in fact grounded in such a dispute, the court may refer counsel to those rules. If the court is persuaded that a request is frivolous or vexatious, it can strike it. See Rules 11 and 7(b)(2).

A number of courts routinely consider discovery matters in preliminary pretrial conferences held shortly after the pleadings are closed. This subdivision does not interfere with such a practice. It authorizes the court to combine a discovery conference with a pretrial conference under Rule 16 if a pretrial conference is held sufficiently early to prevent or curb abuse.

1983 Amendment

Excessive discovery and evasion or resistance to reasonable discovery requests pose significant problems. Recent studies have made some attempt to determine the sources and extent of the difficulties. See Brazil, *Civil Discovery: Lawyers' Views of its Effectiveness, Principal Problems and Abuses,* American Bar Foundation (1980); Connolly, Holleman & Kuhlman, *Judicial Controls and the Civil Litigative Process: Discovery,* Federal Judicial Center (1978); Ellington, *A Study of Sanctions for Discovery Abuse,* Department of Justice (1979); Schroeder & Frank, *The Proposed Changes in the Discovery Rules,* 1978 Ariz.St.L.J. 475.

The purpose of discovery is to provide a mechanism for making relevant information available to the litigants. "Mutual knowledge of all the relevant facts gathered by both parties is essential to proper litigation." *Hickman v. Taylor,* 329 U.S. 495, 507 (1947). Thus the spirit of the rules is violated when advocates attempt to use discovery tools as tactical weapons rather than to expose the facts and illuminate the issues by overuse of discovery or unnecessary use of defensive weapons or evasive responses. All of this results in excessively costly and time-consuming activities that are disproportionate to the nature of the case, the amount involved, or the issues or values at stake.

Given our adversary tradition and the current discovery rules, it is not surprising that there are many opportunities, if not incentives, for attorneys to engage in discovery that, although authorized by the broad, permissive terms of the rules, nevertheless results in delay. See Brazil, *The Adversary Character of Civil Discovery: A Critique and Proposals for Change,* 31 Vand.L.Rev. 1259 (1978). As a result, it has been said that the rules have "not infrequently [been] exploited to the disadvantage of justice." *Herbert v. Lando,* 441 U.S. 153, 179 (1979) (Powell, J., concurring). These practices impose costs on an already overburdened system and impede the fundamental goal of the "just, speedy, and inexpensive determination of every action." Fed.R.Civ.P. 1.

Subdivision (a); Discovery Methods. The deletion of the last sentence of Rule 26(a)(1), which provided that unless the court ordered otherwise under Rule 26(c) "the frequency of use" of the various discovery methods was not to be limited, is an attempt to address the problem of duplicative, redundant, and excessive discovery and to reduce it. The amendment, in conjunction with the changes in Rule 26(b)(1), is designed to encourage district judges to identify instances of needless discovery and to limit the use of the various discovery devices accordingly. The question may be raised by one of the parties, typically on a motion for a protective order, or by the court on its own initiative. It is entirely appropriate to consider a limitation on the frequency of use of discovery at a discovery conference under Rule 26(f) or at any other pretrial conference authorized by these rules. In considering the discovery needs of a particular case, the court should consider the factors described in Rule 26(b)(1).

Subdivision (b); Discovery Scope and Limits. Rule 26(b)(1) has been amended to add a sentence to deal with the problem of over-discovery. The objective is to guard against redundant or disproportionate discovery by giving the court authority to reduce the amount of discovery that may be directed to matters that are otherwise proper subjects of inquiry. The new sentence is intended to encourage judges to be more aggressive in identifying and discouraging discovery overuse. The grounds mentioned in the amended rule for limiting discovery reflect the existing practice of many courts in issuing protective orders under Rule 26(c). See, e.g., *Carlson Cos. v. Sperry & Hutchinson Co.,* 374 F.Supp. 1080 (D.Minn.1974); *Dolgow v. Anderson,* 53 F.R.D. 661 (E.D.N.Y.1971); *Mitchell v. American Tobacco Co.,* 33 F.R.D. 262 (M.D.Pa.1963); *Welty v. Clute,* 1 F.R.D. 446 (W.D.N.Y.1941). On the whole, however, district judges have been reluctant to limit the use of the discovery devices. See, *e.g., Apco Oil Co. v. Certified Transp., Inc.,* 46 F.R.D. 428 (W.D.Mo.1969). See generally 8 Wright & Miller, *Federal Practice and Procedure: Civil* §§ 2036, 2037, 2039, 2040 (1970).

The first element of the standard, Rule 26(b)(1)(i), is designed to minimize redundancy in discovery and encourage attorneys to be sensitive to the comparative costs of different methods of securing information. Subdivision (b)(1)(ii) also seeks to reduce repetitiveness and to oblige lawyers to think through their discovery activities in advance so that full utilization is made of each deposition, document request, or set of interrogatories. The elements of Rule 26(b)(1)(iii) address the problem of discovery that is disproportionate to the individual lawsuit as measured by such matters as its nature and complexity, the importance of the issues at stake in a case seeking damages, the limitations on a financially weak litigant to withstand extensive opposition to a discovery program or to respond to discovery requests, and the significance of the substantive issues, as measured in philosophic, social, or institutional terms. Thus the rule recognizes that many cases in public policy spheres, such as employment practices, free speech, and other matters, may have importance far beyond the monetary amount involved. The court must apply the standards in an even-handed manner that will prevent use of discovery to wage a war of attrition or as a device to coerce a party, whether financially weak or affluent.

The rule contemplates greater judicial involvement in the discovery process and thus acknowledges the reality that it cannot always operate on a self-regulating basis. See Connolly, Holleman & Kuhlman, *Judicial Controls and the Civil Litigative Process: Discovery* 77, Federal Judicial Center (1978). In an appropriate case the court could restrict the number of depositions, interrogatories, or the scope of a production request. But the court must be careful not to deprive a party of discovery that is reasonably necessary to afford a fair opportunity to develop and prepare the case.

The court may act on motion, or its own initiative. It is entirely appropriate to resort to the amended rule in conjunction with a discovery conference under Rule 26(f) or one of the other pretrial conferences authorized by the rules.

Subdivision (g); Signing of Discovery Requests, Responses, and Objections. Rule 26(g) imposes an affirmative duty to engage in pretrial discovery in a responsible manner that is consistent with the spirit and purposes of Rules 26 through 37. In addition, Rule 26(g) is designed to curb discovery abuse by explicitly encouraging the imposition of sanctions. The subdivision provides a deterrent to both excessive discovery and evasion by imposing a certification requirement that obliges each attorney to stop and think about the legitimacy of a discovery request, a response thereto, or an objection. The term "response" includes answers to interrogatories and to requests to admit as well as responses to production requests.

If primary responsibility for conducting discovery is to continue to rest with the litigants, they must be obliged to act responsibly and avoid abuse. With this in mind, Rule 26(g), which parallels the amendments to Rule 11, requires an attorney or unrepresented party to sign each discovery request, response, or objection. Motions relating to discovery are governed by Rule 11. However, since a discovery request, response, or objection usually deals with more specific subject matter than motions or papers, the elements that must be certified in connection with the former are spelled out more completely. The signature is a certification of the elements set forth in Rule 26(g).

Although the certification duty requires the lawyer to pause and consider the reasonableness of his request, response, or objection, it is not meant to discourage or restrict necessary and legitimate discovery. The rule simply requires that the attorney make a reasonable inquiry into the factual basis of his response, request, or objection.

The duty to make a "reasonable inquiry" is satisfied if the investigation undertaken by the attorney and the conclusions drawn therefrom are reasonable under the circumstances. It is an objective standard similar to the one imposed by Rule 11. See the Advisory Committee Note to Rule 11. See also *Kinee v. Abraham Lincoln Fed. Sav. & Loan Ass'n,* 365 F.Supp. 975 (E.D.Pa.1973). In making the inquiry, the attorney may rely on assertions by the client and on communications with other counsel in the case as long as that reliance is appropriate under the circumstances. Ultimately, what is reasonable is a matter for the court to decide on the totality of the circumstances.

Rule 26(g) does not require the signing attorney to certify the truthfulness of the client's factual responses to a discovery request. Rather, the signature certifies that the lawyer has made a reasonable effort to assure that the client has provided all the information and documents available to him that are responsive to the discovery demand. Thus, the lawyer's certification under Rule 26(g) should be distinguished from other signature requirements in the rules, such as those in Rules 30(e) and 33.

Nor does the rule require a party or an attorney to disclose privileged communications or work product in order to show that a discovery request, response, or objection is substantially justified. The provisions of Rule 26(c), including appropriate orders after *in camera* inspection by the court, remain available to protect a party claiming privilege or work product protection.

The signing requirement means that every discovery request, response, or objection should be grounded on a theory that is reasonable under the precedents or a good faith belief as to what should be the law. This standard is heavily dependent on the circumstances of each case. The certification speaks as of the time it is made. The duty to supplement discovery responses continues to be governed by Rule 26(e).

Concern about discovery abuse has led to widespread recognition that there is a need for more aggressive judicial control and supervision. *ACF Industries, Inc. v. EEOC,* 439 U.S. 1081 (1979) (certiorari denied) (Powell, J., dissenting). Sanctions to deter discovery abuse would be more effective if they were diligently applied "not merely to penalize those whose conduct may be deemed to warrant such a sanction, but to deter those who might be tempted to such conduct in the absence of such a deterrent." *National Hockey League v. Metropolitan Hockey Club,* 427 U.S. 639, 643 (1976). See also Note, *The Emerging Deterrence Orientation in the Imposition of Discovery Sanctions,* 91 Harv.L.Rev. 1033 (1978). Thus the premise of Rule 26(g) is that imposing sanctions on attorneys who fail to meet the rule's standards will significantly reduce abuse by imposing disadvantages therefor.

Because of the asserted reluctance to impose sanctions on attorneys who abuse the discovery rules, see Brazil, *Civil Discovery: Lawyers' Views of its Effectiveness, Principal Problems and Abuses,* American Bar Foundation (1980); Ellington, *A Study of Sanctions for Discovery Abuse,* Department of Justice (1979), Rule 26(g) makes explicit the authority judges now have to impose appropriate sanctions and requires them to use it. This authority derives from Rule 37, 28 U.S.C. § 1927, and the court's inherent power. See *Roadway Express, Inc. v. Piper,* 447 U.S. 752 (1980); *Martin v. Bell Helicopter Co.,* 85 F.R.D. 654, 661–62 (D.Col. 1980); Note, *Sanctions Imposed by Courts on Attorneys Who Abuse the Judicial Process,* 44 U.Chi.L.Rev. 619 (1977). The new rule mandates that sanctions be imposed on attorneys who fail to meet the standards established in the first portion of Rule 26(g). The nature of the sanction is a matter of judicial discretion to be exercised in light of the particular circumstances. The court may take into account any failure by the party seeking sanctions to invoke protection under Rule 26(c) at an early stage in the litigation.

The sanctioning process must comport with due process requirements. The kind of notice and hearing required will depend on the facts of the case and the severity of the sanction being considered. To prevent the proliferation of the sanction procedure and to avoid multiple hearings, discovery in any sanction proceeding normally should be permitted only when it is clearly required by the interests of justice. In most cases the court will be aware of the circumstances and only a brief hearing should be necessary.

1987 Amendment

The amendments are technical. No substantive change is intended.

1993 Amendments

Subdivision (a). Through the addition of paragraphs (1)–(4), this subdivision imposes on parties a duty to disclose, without awaiting formal discovery requests, certain basic information that is needed in most cases to prepare for trial or make an informed decision about settlement. The rule requires all parties (1) early in the case to exchange information regarding potential witnesses, documentary evidence, damages, and insurance, (2) at an appropriate time during the discovery period to identify expert witnesses and provide a detailed written statement of the testimony that may be offered at trial through specially retained experts, and (3) as the trial date approaches to identify the particular evidence that may be offered at trial. The enumeration in Rule 26(a) of items to be disclosed does not prevent a court from requiring by order or local rule that the parties disclose additional information without a discovery request. Nor are parties precluded from using traditional discovery methods to obtain further information regarding these matters, as for example asking an expert during a deposition about testimony given in other litigation beyond the four-year period specified in Rule 26(a)(2)(B).

A major purpose of the revision is to accelerate the exchange of basic information about the case and to eliminate the paper work involved in requesting such information, and the rule should be applied in a manner to achieve those objectives. The concepts of imposing a duty of disclosure were set forth in Brazil, *The Adversary Character of Civil Discovery: A Critique and Proposals for Change,* 31 *Vand. L.Rev.* 1348 (1978), and Schwarzer, *The Federal Rules, the Adversary Process, and Discovery Reform,* 50 *U.Pitt.L.Rev. 703, 721–23 (1989).*

The rule is based upon the experience of district courts that have required disclosure of some of this information through local rules, court-approved standard interrogatories, and standing orders. Most have required pretrial disclosure of the kind of information described in Rule 26(a)(3). Many have required written reports from experts containing information like that specified in Rule 26(a)(2)(B). While far more limited, the experience of the few state and federal courts that have required pre-discovery exchange of core information such as is contemplated in Rule 26(a)(1) indicates that savings in time and expense can be achieved, particularly if the litigants meet and discuss the issues in the case as a predicate for this exchange and if a judge supports the process, as by using the results to guide further proceedings in the case. Courts in Canada and the United Kingdom have for many years required disclosure of certain information without awaiting a request from an adversary.

Paragraph (1). As the functional equivalent of court-ordered interrogatories, this paragraph requires early disclosure, without need for any request, of four types of information that have been customarily secured early in litigation through formal discovery. The introductory clause permits the court, by local rule, to exempt all or particular types of cases from these disclosure requirement *[sic]* or to modify the nature of the information to be disclosed. It is expected that courts would, for example, exempt cases like Social Security reviews and government collection cases in which discovery would not be appropriate or would be unlikely. By order the court may eliminate or modify the disclosure requirements in a particular case, and similarly the parties, unless precluded by order or local rule, can stipulate to elimination or modification of the requirements for that case. The disclosure obligations specified in paragraph (1) will not be appropriate for all cases, and it is expected that changes in these obligations will be made by the court or parties when the circumstances warrant.

Authorization of these local variations is, in large measure, included in order to accommodate the Civil Justice Reform Act of 1990, which implicitly directs districts to experiment during the study period with differing procedures to reduce the time and expense of civil litigation. The civil justice delay and expense reduction plans adopted by the courts under the Act differ as to the type, form, and timing of disclosures required. Section 105(c)(1) of the Act calls for a report by the Judicial Conference to Congress by December 31, 1995, comparing experience in twenty of these courts; and section 105(c)(2)(B) contemplates that some changes in the Rules may then be needed. While these studies may indicate the desirability of further changes in Rule 26(a)(1), these changes probably could not become effective before December 1998 at the earliest. In the meantime, the present revision puts in place a series of disclosure obligations that, unless a court acts affirmatively to impose other requirements or indeed to reject all such requirements for the present, are designed to eliminate certain discovery, help focus the discovery that is needed, and facilitate preparation for trial or settlement.

Subparagraph (A) requires identification of all persons who, based on the investigation conducted thus far, are likely to have discoverable information relevant to the factual disputes between the parties. All persons with such information should be disclosed, whether or not their testimony will be supportive of the position of the disclosing party. As officers of the court, counsel are expected to disclose the identity of those persons who may be used by them as witnesses or who, if their potential testimony were known, might reasonably be expected to be deposed or called as a witness by any of the other parties. Indicating briefly the general topics on which such persons have information should not be burdensome, and will assist other parties in deciding which depositions will actually be needed.

Subparagraph (B) is included as a substitute for the inquiries routinely made about the existence and location of documents and other tangible things in the possession, custody, or control of the disclosing party. Although, unlike subdivision (a)(3)(C), an itemized listing of each exhibit is not required, the disclosure should describe and categorize, to the extent identified during the initial investigation, the nature and location of potentially relevant documents and records, including computerized data and other electronically-recorded information, sufficiently to enable opposing parties (1) to make an informed decision concerning which documents might need to be examined, at least initially, and (2) to frame their document requests in a manner likely to avoid squabbles resulting from the wording of the requests. As with potential witnesses, the requirement for disclosure of documents applies to all potentially relevant items then known to the party, whether or not supportive of its contentions in the case.

Unlike subparagraphs (C) and (D), subparagraph (B) does not require production of any documents. Of course, in cases involving few documents a disclosing party may prefer to provide copies of the documents rather than describe them, and the rule is written to afford this option to the disclosing party. If, as will be more typical, only the description is provided, the other parties are expected to obtain the documents desired by proceeding under Rule 34 or through informal requests. The disclosing party does not, by describing documents under subparagraph (B), waive its right to object to production on the basis of privilege or work product protection, or to assert that the documents are not sufficiently relevant to justify the burden or expense of production.

The initial disclosure requirements of subparagraphs (A) and (B) are limited to identification of potential evidence "relevant to disputed facts alleged with particularity in the pleadings." There is no need for a party to identify potential evidence with respect to allegations that are admitted. Broad, vague, and conclusory allegations sometimes tolerated in notice pleading—for example, the assertion that a product with many component parts is defective in some unspecified manner—should not impose upon responding parties the obligation at that point to search for and identify all persons possibly involved in, or all documents affecting, the design, manufacture, and assembly of the product. The greater the specificity and clarity of the allegations in the pleadings, the more complete should be the listing of potential witnesses and types of documentary evidence. Although paragraphs (1)(A) and (1)(B) by their terms refer to the factual disputes defined in the pleadings, the rule contemplates that these issues would be informally refined and clarified during the meeting of the parties under subdivision (f) and that the disclosure obligations would be adjusted in the light of these discussions. The disclosure requirements should, in short, be applied with common sense in light of the principles of Rule 1, keeping in mind the salutary purposes that the rule is intended to accomplish. The litigants should not indulge in gamesmanship with respect to the disclosure obligations.

Subparagraph (C) imposes a burden of disclosure that includes the functional equivalent of a standing Request for Production under Rule 34. A party claiming damages or other monetary relief must, in addition to disclosing the calculation of such damages, make available the supporting documents for inspection and copying as if a request for such materials had been made under Rule 34. This obligation applies only with respect to documents then reasonably available to it and not privileged or protected as work product. Likewise, a party would not be expected to provide a calculation of damages which, as in many patent infringement actions, depends on information in the possession of another party or person.

Subparagraph (D) replaces subdivision (b)(2) of Rule 26, and provides that liability insurance policies be made available for inspection and copying. The last two sentences of that subdivision have been omitted as unnecessary, not to signify any change of law. The disclosure of insurance information does not thereby render such information admissible in evidence. See Rule 411, Federal Rules of Evidence. Nor does subparagraph (D) require disclosure of applications for insurance, though in particular cases such information may be discoverable in accordance with revised subdivision (a)(5).

Unless the court directs a different time, the disclosures required by subdivision (a)(1) are to be made at or within 10 days after the meeting of the parties under subdivision (f). One of the purposes of this meeting is to refine the factual disputes with respect to which disclosures should be made under paragraphs (1)(A) and (1)(B), particularly if an answer has not been filed by a defendant, or, indeed, to afford the parties an opportunity to modify by stipulation the timing or scope of these obligations. The time of this meeting is generally left to the parties provided it is held at least 14 days before a scheduling conference is held or before a scheduling order is due under Rule 16(b). In cases in which no scheduling conference is held, this will mean that the meeting must ordinarily be held within 75 days after a defendant has first appeared in the case and hence that the initial disclosures would be due no later than 85 days after the first appearance of a defendant.

Before making its disclosures, a party has the obligation under subdivision (g)(1) to make a reasonable inquiry into the facts of the case. The rule does not demand an exhaustive investigation at this stage of the case, but one that is reasonable under the circumstances, focusing on the facts that are alleged with particularity in the pleadings. The type of investigation that can be expected at this point will vary based upon such factors as the number and complexity of the issues; the location, nature, number, and availability of potentially relevant witnesses and documents; the extent of past working relationships between the attorney and the client, particularly in handling related or similar litigation; and of course how long the party has to conduct an investigation, either before or after filing of the case. As provided in the last sentence of subdivision (a)(1), a party is not excused from the duty of disclosure merely because its investigation is incomplete. The party should make its initial disclosures based on the pleadings and the information then reasonably available to it. As its investigation continues and as the issues in the pleadings are clarified, it should supplement its disclosures as required by subdivision (e)(1). A party is not relieved from its obligation of disclosure merely because another party has not made its disclosures or has made an inadequate disclosure.

It will often be desirable, particularly if the claims made in the complaint are broadly stated, for the parties to have their Rule 26(f) meeting early in the case, perhaps before a defendant has answered the complaint or had time to conduct other than a cursory investigation. In such circumstances, in order to facilitate more meaningful and useful initial disclosures, they can and should stipulate to a period of more than 10 days after the meeting in which to make these disclosures, at least for defendants who had no advance notice of the potential litigation. A stipulation at an early meeting affording such a defendant at least 60 days after receiving the complaint in which to make its disclosures under subdivision (a)(1)—a period that is two weeks longer than the time formerly specified for responding to interrogatories served with a complaint—should be adequate and appropriate in most cases.

Paragraph (2). This paragraph imposes an additional duty to disclose information regarding expert testimony sufficiently in advance of trial that opposing parties have a reasonable opportunity to prepare for effective cross examination and perhaps arrange for expert testimony from other witnesses. Normally the court should prescribe a time for these disclosures in a scheduling order under Rule 16(b), and in most cases the party with the burden of proof on an issue should disclose its expert testimony on that issue before other parties are required to make their disclosures with respect to that issue. In the absence of such a direction, the disclosures are to be made by all parties at least 90 days before the trial date or the date by which the case is to be ready for trial, except that an additional 30 days is allowed (unless the court specifies another time) for disclosure of expert testimony to be used solely to contradict or rebut the testimony that may be presented by another party's expert. For a discussion of procedures that have been used to enhance the reliability of expert testimony, see M. Graham, *Expert Witness Testimony and the Federal Rules of Evidence: Insuring Adequate Assurance of Trustworthiness,* 1986 U.Ill.L.Rev. 90.

Paragraph (2)(B) requires that persons retained or specially employed to provide expert testimony, or whose duties as an employee of the party regularly involve the giving of expert testimony, must prepare a detailed and complete written report, stating the testimony the witness is expected to present during direct examination, together with the reasons therefor. The information disclosed under the former rule in answering interrogatories about the "substance" of expert testimony was frequently so sketchy and vague that it rarely dispensed with the need to depose the expert and often was even of little help in preparing for a deposition of the witness. Revised Rule 37(c)(1) provides an incentive for full disclosure; namely, that a party will not ordinarily be permitted to use on direct examination any expert testimony not so disclosed. Rule 26(a)(2)(B) does not preclude counsel from providing assistance to experts in preparing the reports, and indeed, with experts such as automobile mechanics, this assistance may be needed. Nevertheless, the report, which is intended to set forth the substance of the direct examination, should be written in a manner that reflects the testimony to be given by the witness and it must be signed by the witness.

The report is to disclose the data and other information considered by the expert and any exhibits or charts that summarize or support the expert's opinions. Given this obligation of disclosure, litigants should no longer be able to argue that materials furnished to their experts to be used in forming their opinions—whether or not ultimately relied upon by the expert—are privileged or otherwise protected from disclosure when such persons are testifying or being deposed.

Revised subdivision (b)(4)(A) authorizes the deposition of expert witnesses. Since depositions of experts required to prepare a written report may be taken only after the report has been served, the length of the deposition of such experts should be reduced, and in many cases the report may eliminate the need for a deposition. Revised subdivision (e)(1) requires disclosure of any material changes made in the opinions of an expert from whom a report is required, whether the changes are in the written report or in testimony given at a deposition.

For convenience, this rule and revised Rule 30 continue to use the term "expert" to refer to those persons who will testify under Rule 702 of the Federal Rules of Evidence with respect to scientific, technical, and other specialized matters. The requirement of a written report in paragraph (2)(B), however, applies only to those experts who are retained or specially employed to provide such testimony in the case or whose duties as an employee of a party regularly involve the giving of such testimony. A treating physician, for example, can be deposed or called to testify at trial without any requirement for a written report. By local rule, order, or written stipulation, the requirement of a written report may be waived for particular experts or imposed upon additional persons who will provide opinions under Rule 702.

Paragraph (3). This paragraph imposes an additional duty to disclose, without any request, information customarily needed in final preparation for trial. These disclosures are to be made in accordance with schedules adopted by the court under Rule 16(b) or by special order. If no such schedule is directed by the court, the disclosures are to be made at least 30 days before commencement of the trial. By its terms, rule 26(a)(3) does not require disclosure of evidence to be used solely for impeachment purposes; however, disclosure of such evidence—as well as other items relating to conduct of trial—may be required by local rule or a pretrial order.

Subparagraph (A) requires the parties to designate the persons whose testimony they may present as substantive evidence at trial, whether in person or by deposition. Those who will probably be called as witnesses should be listed separately from those who are not likely to be called but who are being listed in order to preserve the right to do so if needed because of developments during trial. Revised Rule 37(c)(1) provides that only persons so listed may be used at trial to present substantive evidence. This restriction does not apply unless the omission was "without substantial justification" and hence would not bar an unlisted witness if the need for such testimony is based upon developments during trial that could not reasonably have been anticipated—*e.g.*, a change of testimony.

Listing a witness does not obligate the party to secure the attendance of the person at trial, but should preclude the party from objecting if the person is called to testify by another party who did not list the person as a witness.

Subparagraph (B) requires the party to indicate which of these potential witnesses will be presented by deposition at trial. A party expecting to use at trial a deposition not recorded by stenographic means is required by revised Rule 32 to provide the court with a transcript of the pertinent portions of such depositions. This rule requires that copies of the transcript of a nonstenographic deposition be provided to other parties in advance of trial for verification, an obvious concern since counsel often utilize their own personnel to prepare transcripts from audio or video tapes. By order or local rule, the court may require that parties designate the particular portions of stenographic depositions to be used at trial.

Subparagraph (C) requires disclosure of exhibits, including summaries (whether to be offered in lieu of other documentary evidence or to be used as an aid in understanding such evidence), that may be offered as substantive evidence. The rule requires a separate listing of each such exhibit, though it should permit voluminous items of a similar or standardized character to be described by meaningful categories. For example, unless the court has otherwise directed, a series of vouchers might be shown collectively as a single exhibit with their starting and ending dates. As with witnesses, the exhibits that will probably be offered are to be listed separately from those which are unlikely to be offered but which are listed in order to preserve the right to do so if needed because of developments during trial. Under revised Rule 37(c)(1) the court can permit use of unlisted documents the need for which could not reasonably have been anticipated in advance of trial.

Upon receipt of these final pretrial disclosures, other parties have 14 days (unless a different time is specified by the court) to disclose any objections they wish to preserve to the usability of the deposition testimony or to the admissibility of the documentary evidence (other than under Rules 402 and 403 of the Federal Rules of Evidence). Similar provisions have become commonplace either in pretrial orders or by local rules, and significantly expedite the presentation of evidence at trial, as well as eliminate the need to have available witnesses to provide "foundation" testimony for most items of documentary evidence. The listing of a potential objection does not constitute the making of that objection or require the court to rule on the objection; rather, it preserves the right of the party to make the objection when and as appropriate during trial. The court may, however, elect to treat the listing as a motion "in limine" and rule upon the objections in advance of trial to the extent appropriate.

The time specified in the rule for the final pretrial disclosures is relatively close to the trial date. The objective is to eliminate the time and expense in making these disclosures of evidence and objections in those cases that settle shortly before trial, while affording a reasonable time for final preparation for trial in those cases that do not settle. In many cases, it will be desirable for the court in a scheduling or pretrial order to set an earlier time for disclosures of evidence and provide more time for disclosing potential objections.

Paragraph (4). This paragraph prescribes the form of disclosures. A signed written statement is required, reminding the parties and counsel of the solemnity of the obligations imposed; and the signature on the initial or pretrial disclosure is a certification under subdivision (g)(1) that it is complete and correct as of the time when made. Consistent with Rule 5(d), these disclosures are to be filed with the court unless otherwise directed. It is anticipated that many courts will direct that expert reports required under paragraph (2)(B) not be filed until needed in connection with a motion or for trial.

Paragraph (5). This paragraph is revised to take note of the availability of revised Rule 45 for inspection from nonparties of documents and premises without the need for a deposition.

Subdivision (b). This subdivision is revised in several respects. First, former paragraph (1) is subdivided into two paragraphs for ease of reference and to avoid renumbering of paragraphs (3) and (4). Textual changes are then made in new paragraph (2) to enable the court to keep tighter rein on the extent of discovery. The information explosion of recent decades has greatly increased both the potential cost of wide-ranging discovery and the potential for discovery to be used as an instrument for delay or oppression. Amendments to Rules 30, 31, and 33 place presumptive limits on the number of depositions and interrogatories, subject to leave of court to pursue additional discovery. The revisions in Rule 26(b)(2) are intended to provide the court with broader discretion to impose additional restrictions on the scope and extent of discovery and to authorize courts that develop case tracking systems based on the complexity of cases to increase or decrease by local rule the presumptive number of depositions and interrogatories allowed in particular types or classifications of cases. The revision also dispels any doubt as to the power of the court to impose limitations on the length of depositions under Rule 30 or on the number of requests for admission under Rule 36.

Second, former paragraph (2), relating to insurance, has been relocated as part of the required initial disclosures under subdivision (a)(1)(D), and revised to provide for disclosure of the policy itself.

Third, paragraph (4)(A) is revised to provide that experts who are expected to be witnesses will be subject to deposition prior to trial, conforming the norm stated in the rule to the actual practice followed in most courts, in which depositions of experts have become standard. Concerns regarding the expense of such depositions should be mitigated by the fact that the expert's fees for the deposition will ordinarily be borne by the party taking the deposition. The requirement under subdivision (a)(2)(B) of a complete and detailed report of the expected testimony of certain forensic experts may, moreover, eliminate the need for some such depositions or at least reduce the length of the depositions. Accordingly, the deposition of an expert required by subdivision (a)(2)(B) to provide a written report may be taken only after the report has been served.

Paragraph (4)(C), bearing on compensation of experts, is revised to take account of the changes in paragraph (4)(A).

Paragraph (5) is a new provision. A party must notify other parties if it is withholding materials otherwise subject to disclosure under the rule or pursuant to a discovery request because it is asserting a claim of privilege or work product protection. To withhold materials without such notice is contrary to the rule, subjects the party to sanctions under Rule 37(b)(2), and may be viewed as a waiver of the privilege or protection.

The party must also provide sufficient information to enable other parties to evaluate the applicability of the claimed privilege or protection. Although the person from whom the discovery is sought decides whether to claim a privilege or protection, the court ultimately decides whether, if this claim is challenged, the privilege or protection applies. Providing information pertinent to the applicability of the privilege or protection should reduce the need for in camera examination of the documents.

The rule does not attempt to define for each case what information must be provided when a party asserts a claim of privilege or work product protection. Details concerning time, persons, general subject matter, etc., may be appropriate if only a few items are withheld, but may be unduly burdensome when voluminous documents are claimed to be privileged or protected, particularly if the items can be described by categories. A party can seek relief through a protective order under subdivision (c) if compliance with the requirement for providing this information would be an unreasonable burden. In rare circumstances some of the pertinent information affecting applicability of the claim, such as the identity of the client, may itself be privileged; the rule provides that such information need not be disclosed.

The obligation to provide pertinent information concerning withheld privileged materials applies only to items "otherwise discoverable." If a broad discovery request is made—for example, for all documents of a particular type during a twenty year period—and the responding party believes in good faith that production of documents for more than the past three years would be unduly burdensome, it should make its objection to the breadth of the request and, with respect to the documents generated in that three year period, produce the unprivileged documents and describe those withheld under the claim of privilege. If the court later rules that documents for a seven year period are properly discoverable, the documents for the additional four years should then be either produced (if not privileged) or described (if claimed to be privileged).

Subdivision (c). The revision requires that before filing a motion for a protective order the movant must confer—either in person or by telephone—with the other affected parties in a good faith effort to resolve the discovery dispute without the need for court intervention. If the movant is unable to get opposing parties even to discuss the matter, the efforts in attempting to arrange such a conference should be indicated in the certificate.

Subdivision (d). This subdivision is revised to provide that formal discovery—as distinguished from interviews of potential witnesses and other informal discovery—not commence until the parties have met and conferred as required by subdivision (f). Discovery can begin earlier if authorized under Rule 30(a)(2)(C) (deposition of person about to leave the country) or by local rule, order, or stipulation. This will be appropriate in some cases, such as those involving requests for a preliminary injunction or motions challenging personal jurisdiction. If a local rule exempts any types of cases in which discovery may be needed from the requirement of a meeting under Rule 26(f), it should specify when discovery may commence in those cases.

The meeting of counsel is to take place as soon as practicable and in any event at least 14 days before the date of the scheduling conference under Rule 16(b) or the date a scheduling order is due under Rule 16(b). The court can assure that discovery is not unduly delayed either by entering a special order or by setting the case for a scheduling conference.

Subdivision (e). This subdivision is revised to provide that the requirement for supplementation applies to all disclosures required by subdivisions (a)(1)–(3). Like the former rule, the duty, while imposed on a "party," applies whether the corrective information is learned by the client or by the attorney. Supplementations need not be made as each new item of information is learned but should be made at appropriate intervals during the discovery period, and with special promptness as the trial date approaches. It may be useful for the scheduling order to specify the time or times when supplementations should be made.

The revision also clarifies that the obligation to supplement responses to formal discovery requests applies to interrogatories, requests for production, and requests for admissions, but not ordinarily to deposition testimony. However, with respect to experts from whom a written report is required under subdivision (a)(2)(B), changes in the opinions expressed by the expert whether in the report or at a subsequent deposition are subject to a duty of supplemental disclosure under subdivision (e)(1).

The obligation to supplement disclosures and discovery responses applies whenever a party learns that its prior disclosures or responses are in some material respect incomplete or incorrect. There is, however, no obligation to provide supplemental or corrective information that has been otherwise made known to the parties in writing or during the discovery process, as when a witness not previously disclosed is identified during the taking of a deposition or when an expert during a deposition corrects information contained in an earlier report.

Subdivision (f). This subdivision was added in 1980 to provide a party threatened with abusive discovery with a special means for obtaining judicial intervention other than through discrete motions under Rules 26(c) and 37(a). The amendment envisioned a two-step process: first, the parties would attempt to frame a mutually agreeable plan; second, the court would hold a "discovery conference" and then enter an order establishing a schedule and limitations for the conduct of discovery. It was contemplated that the procedure, an elective one triggered on request of a party, would be used in special cases rather than as a routine matter. As expected, the device has been used only sparingly in most courts, and judicial controls over the discovery process have ordinarily been imposed through scheduling orders under Rule 16(b) or through rulings on discovery motions.

The provisions relating to a conference with the court are removed from subdivision (f). This change does not signal any lessening of the importance of judicial supervision. Indeed, there is a greater need for early judicial involvement to consider the scope and timing of the disclosure requirements of Rule 26(a) and the presumptive limits on discovery imposed under these rules or by local rules. Rather, the change is made because the provisions addressing the use of conferences with the court to control discovery are more properly included in Rule 16, which is being revised to highlight the court's powers regarding the discovery process.

The desirability of some judicial control of discovery can hardly be doubted. Rule 16, as revised, requires that the court set a time for completion of discovery and authorizes various other orders affecting the scope, timing, and extent of discovery and disclosures. Before entering such orders, the court should consider the views of the parties, preferably by means of a conference, but at the least through written submissions. Moreover, it is desirable that the parties' proposals regarding discovery be developed through a process where they meet in person, informally explore the nature and basis of the issues, and discuss how discovery can be conducted most efficiently and economically.

As noted above, former subdivision (f) envisioned the development of proposed discovery plans as an optional procedure to be used in relatively few cases. The revised rule directs that in all cases not exempted by local rule or special order the litigants must meet in person and plan for discovery. Following this meeting, the parties submit to the court their proposals for a discovery plan and can begin formal discovery. Their report will assist the court in seeing that the timing and scope of disclosures under revised Rule 26(a) and the limitations on the extent of discovery under these rules and local rules are tailored to the circumstances of the particular case.

To assure that the court has the litigants' proposals before deciding on a scheduling order and that the commencement of discovery is not delayed unduly, the rule provides that the meeting of the parties take place as soon as practicable and in any event at least 14 days before a scheduling conference is held or before a scheduling order is due under Rule 16(b). (Rule 16(b) requires that a scheduling order be entered within 90 days after the first appearance of a defendant or, if earlier, within 120 days after the complaint has been served on any defendant.) The obligation to participate in the planning process is imposed on all parties that have appeared in the case, including defendants who, because of a pending Rule 12 motion, may not have yet filed an answer in the case. Each such party should attend the meeting, either through one of its attorneys or in person if unrepresented. If more parties are joined or appear after the initial meeting, an additional meeting may be desirable.

Subdivision (f) describes certain matters that should be accomplished at the meeting and included in the proposed discovery plan. This listing does not exclude consideration of other subjects, such as the time when any dispositive motions should be filed and when the case should be ready for trial.

The parties are directed under subdivision (a)(1) to make the disclosures required by that subdivision at or within 10 days after this meeting. In many cases the parties should use the meeting to exchange, discuss, and clarify their respective disclosures. In other cases, it may be more useful if the disclosures are delayed until after the parties have discussed at the meeting the claims and defenses in order to define the issues with respect to which the initial disclosures should be made. As discussed in the Notes to subdivision (a)(1), the parties may also need to consider whether a stipulation extending this 10–day period would be appropriate, as when a defendant would otherwise have less than 60 days after being served in which to make its initial disclosure. The parties should also discuss at the meeting what additional information, although not subject to the disclosure requirements, can be made available informally without the necessity for formal discovery requests.

The report is to be submitted to the court within 10 days after the meeting and should not be difficult to prepare. In most cases counsel should be able to agree that one of them will be responsible for its preparation and submission to the court. Form 35 has been added in the Appendix to the Rules, both to illustrate the type of report that is contemplated and to serve as a checklist for the meeting.

The litigants are expected to attempt in good faith to agree on the contents of the proposed discovery plan. If they cannot agree on all aspects of the plan, their report to the court should indicate the competing proposals of the parties on those items, as well as the matters on which they agree. Unfortunately, there may be cases in which, because of disagreements about time or place or for other reasons, the meeting is not attended by all parties or, indeed, no meeting takes place. In such situations, the report—or reports—should describe the circumstances and the court may need to consider sanctions under Rule 37(g).

By local rule or special order, the court can exempt particular cases or types of cases from the meet-and-confer requirement of subdivision (f). In general this should include any types of cases which are exempted by local rule from the requirement for a scheduling order under Rule 16(b), such as cases in which there will be no discovery (*e.g.*, bankruptcy appeals and reviews of social security determinations). In addition, the court may want to exempt cases in which discovery is rarely needed (*e.g.*, government collection cases and proceedings to enforce administrative summonses) or in which a meeting of the parties might be impracticable (*e.g.*, actions by unrepresented prisoners). Note that if a court exempts from the requirements for a meeting any types of cases in which discovery may be needed, it should indicate when discovery may commence in those cases.

Subdivision (g). Paragraph (1) is added to require signatures on disclosures, a requirement that parallels the provisions of paragraph (2) with respect to discovery requests, responses, and objections. The provisions of paragraph (3) have been modified to be consistent with Rules 37(a)(4) and 37(c)(1); in combination, these rules establish sanctions for violation of the rules regarding disclosures and discovery matters. Amended Rule 11 no longer applies to such violations.

2000 Amendment

Purposes of amendments. The Rule 26(a)(1) initial disclosure provisions are amended to establish a nationally uniform practice. The scope of the disclosure obligation is narrowed to cover only information that the disclosing party may use to support its position. In addition, the rule exempts specified categories of proceedings from initial disclosure, and permits a party who contends that disclosure is not appropriate in the circumstances of the case to present its objections to the court, which must then determine whether disclosure should be made. Related changes are made in Rules 26(d) and (f).

The initial disclosure requirements added by the 1993 amendments permitted local rules directing that disclosure would not be required or altering its operation. The inclusion of the "opt out" provision reflected the strong opposition to initial disclosure felt in some districts, and permitted experimentation with differing disclosure rules in those districts that were favorable to disclosure. The local option also recognized that—partly in response to the first publication in 1991 of a proposed disclosure rule—many districts had adopted a variety of disclosure programs under the aegis of the Civil Justice Reform Act. It was hoped that developing experience under a variety of disclosure systems would support eventual refinement of a uniform national disclosure practice. In addition, there was hope that local experience could identify categories of actions in which disclosure is not useful.

A striking array of local regimes in fact emerged for disclosure and related features introduced in 1993. *See* D. Stienstra, *Implementation of Disclosure in United States District Courts, With Specific Attention to Courts' Responses to Selected Amendments to Federal Rule of Civil Procedure 26* (Federal Judicial Center, March 30, 1998) (describing and categorizing local regimes). In its final report to Congress on the CJRA experience, the Judicial Conference recommended reexamination of the need for national uniformity, particularly in regard to initial disclosure. Judicial Conference, *Alternative Proposals for Reduction of Cost and Delay: Assessment of Principles, Guidelines and Techniques,* 175 F.R.D. 62, 98 (1997).

At the Committee's request, the Federal Judicial Center undertook a survey in 1997 to develop information on current disclosure and discovery practices. *See* T. Willging, J. Shapard, D. Stienstra & D. Miletich, *Discovery and Disclosure Practice, Problems, and Proposals for Change* (Federal Judicial Center, 1997). In addition, the Committee convened two conferences on discovery involving lawyers from around the country and received reports and recommendations on possible discovery amendments from a number of bar groups. Papers and other proceedings from the second conference are published in 39 Boston Col. L. Rev. 517–840 (1998).

The Committee has discerned widespread support for national uniformity. Many lawyers have experienced difficulty in coping with divergent disclosure and other practices as they move from one district to another. Lawyers surveyed by the Federal Judicial Center ranked adoption of a uniform national disclosure rule second among proposed rule changes (behind increased availability of judges to resolve discovery disputes) as a means to reduce litigation expenses without interfering with fair outcomes. *Discovery and Disclosure Practice, supra,* at 44–45. National uniformity is also a central purpose of the Rules Enabling Act of 1934, as amended, 28 U.S.C. §§ 2072–2077.

These amendments restore national uniformity to disclosure practice. Uniformity is also restored to other aspects of discovery by deleting most of the provisions authorizing local rules that vary the number of permitted discovery events or the length of depositions. Local rule options are also deleted from Rules 26(d) and (f).

Subdivision (a)(1). The amendments remove the authority to alter or opt out of the national disclosure requirements by local rule, invalidating not only formal local rules but also informal "standing" orders of an individual judge or court that purport to create exemptions from—or limit or expand—the disclosure provided under the national rule. *See* Rule 83. Case-specific orders remain proper, however, and are expressly required if a party objects that initial disclosure is not appropriate in the circumstances of the action. Specified categories of proceedings are excluded from initial disclosure under subdivision (a)(1)(E). In addition, the parties can stipulate to forgo disclosure, as was true before. But even in a case excluded by subdivision (a)(1)(E) or in which the parties stipulate to bypass disclosure, the court can order exchange of similar information in managing the action under Rule 16.

The initial disclosure obligation of subdivisions (a)(1)(A) and (B) has been narrowed to identification of witnesses and documents that the disclosing party may use to support its claims or defenses. "Use" includes any use at a pretrial conference, to support a motion, or at trial. The disclosure obligation is also triggered by intended use in discovery, apart from use to respond to a discovery request; use of a document to question a witness during a deposition is a common example. The disclosure obligation attaches both to witnesses and documents a party intends to use and also to witnesses and to documents the party intends to use if—in the language of Rule 26(a)(3)—"the need arises."

A party is no longer obligated to disclose witnesses or documents, whether favorable or unfavorable, that it does not intend to use. The obligation to disclose information the party may use connects directly to the exclusion sanction of Rule 37(c)(1). Because the disclosure obligation is limited to material that the party may use, it is no longer tied to particularized allegations in the pleadings. Subdivision (e)(1), which is unchanged, requires supplementation if information later acquired would have been subject to the disclosure requirement. As case preparation continues, a party must supplement its disclosures when it determines that it may use a witness or document that it did not previously intend to use.

The disclosure obligation applies to "claims and defenses," and therefore requires a party to disclose information it may use to support its denial or rebuttal of the allegations, claim, or defense of another party. It thereby bolsters the requirements of Rule 11(b)(4), which authorizes denials "warranted on the evidence," and disclosure should include the identity of any witness or document that the disclosing party may use to support such denials.

Subdivision (a)(3) presently excuses pretrial disclosure of information solely for impeachment. Impeachment information is similarly excluded from the initial disclosure requirement.

Subdivisions (a)(1)(C) and (D) are not changed. Should a case be exempted from initial disclosure by Rule 26(a)(1)(E) or by agreement or order, the insurance information described by subparagraph (D) should be subject to discovery, as it would have been under the principles of former Rule 26(b)(2), which was added in 1970 and deleted in 1993 as redundant in light of the new initial disclosure obligation.

New subdivision (a)(1)(E) excludes eight specified categories of proceedings from initial disclosure. The objective of this listing is to identify cases in which there is likely to be little or no discovery, or in which initial disclosure appears unlikely to contribute to the effective development of the case. The list was developed after a review of the categories excluded by local rules in various districts from the operation of Rule 16(b) and the conference requirements of subdivision (f). Subdivision (a)(1)(E) refers to categories of "proceedings" rather than categories of "actions" because some might not properly be labeled " actions." Case designations made by the parties or the clerk's office at the time of filing do not control application of the exemptions. The descriptions in the rule are generic and are intended to be administered by the parties—and, when needed, the courts—with the flexibility needed to adapt to gradual evolution in the types of proceedings that fall within these general categories. The exclusion of an action for review on an administrative record, for example, is intended to reach a proceeding that is framed as an " appeal" based solely on an administrative record. The exclusion should not apply to a proceeding in a form that commonly permits admission of new evidence to supplement the record. Item (vii), excluding a proceeding ancillary to proceedings in other courts, does not refer to bankruptcy proceedings; application of the Civil Rules to bankruptcy proceedings is determined by the Bankruptcy Rules.

Subdivision (a)(1)(E) is likely to exempt a substantial proportion of the cases in most districts from the initial disclosure requirement. Based on 1996 and 1997 case filing statistics, Federal Judicial Center staff estimate that, nationwide, these categories total approximately one-third of all civil filings.

The categories of proceedings listed in subdivision (a)(1)(E) are also exempted from the subdivision (f) conference requirement and from the subdivision (d) moratorium on discovery. Although there is no restriction on commencement of discovery in these cases, it is not expected that this opportunity will often lead to abuse since there is likely to be little or no discovery in most such cases. Should a defendant need more time to respond to discovery requests filed at the beginning of an exempted action, it can seek relief by motion under Rule 26(c) if the plaintiff is unwilling to defer the due date by agreement.

Subdivision (a)(1)(E)'s enumeration of exempt categories is exclusive. Although a case-specific order can alter or excuse initial disclosure, local rules or "standing" orders that purport to create general exemptions are invalid. *See* Rule 83.

The time for initial disclosure is extended to 14 days after the subdivision (f) conference unless the court orders otherwise. This change is integrated with corresponding changes requiring that the subdivision (f) conference be held 21 days before the Rule 16(b) scheduling conference or scheduling order, and that the report on the subdivision (f) conference be submitted to the court 14 days after the meeting. These changes provide a more orderly opportunity for the parties to review the disclosures, and for the court to consider the report. In many instances, the subdivision (f) conference and the effective preparation of the case would benefit from disclosure before the conference, and earlier disclosure is encouraged.

The presumptive disclosure date does not apply if a party objects to initial disclosure during the subdivision (f) conference and states its objection in the subdivision (f) discovery plan. The right to object to initial disclosure is not intended to afford parties an opportunity to "opt out" of disclosure unilaterally. It does provide an opportunity for an objecting party to present to the court its position that disclosure would be "inappropriate in the circumstances of the action." Making the objection permits the objecting party to present the question to the judge before any party is required to make disclosure. The court must then rule on the objection and determine what disclosures—if any—should be made. Ordinarily, this determination would be included in the Rule 16(b) scheduling order, but the court could handle the matter in a different fashion. Even when circumstances warrant suspending some disclosure obligations, others—such as the damages and insurance information called for by subdivisions (a)(1)(C) and (D)—may continue to be appropriate.

The presumptive disclosure date is also inapplicable to a party who is "first served or otherwise joined" after the subdivision (f) conference. This phrase refers to the date of service of a claim on a party in a defensive posture (such as a defendant or third-party defendant), and the date of joinder of a party added as a claimant or an intervenor. Absent court order or stipulation, a new party has 30 days in which to make its initial disclosures. But it is expected that later-added parties will ordinarily be treated the same as the original parties when the original parties have stipulated to forgo initial disclosure, or the court has ordered disclosure in a modified form.

Subdivision (a)(3). The amendment to Rule 5(d) forbids filing disclosures under subdivisions (a)(1) and (a)(2) until they are used in the proceeding, and this change is reflected in an amendment to subdivision (a)(4) . Disclosures under subdivision (a)(3), however, may be important to the court in connection with the final pretrial conference or otherwise in preparing for trial. The requirement that objections to certain matters be filed points up the court's need to be provided with these materials. Accordingly, the requirement that subdivision (a)(3) materials be filed has been moved from subdivision (a)(4) to subdivision (a)(3), and it has also been made clear that they—and any objections—should be filed "promptly."

Subdivision (a)(4). The filing requirement has been removed from this subdivision. Rule 5(d) has been amended to provide that disclosures under subdivisions (a)(1) and (a)(2) must not be filed until used in the proceeding. Subdivision (a)(3) has been amended to require that the disclosures it directs, and objections to them, be filed promptly. Subdivision (a)(4) continues to require that all disclosures under subdivisions (a)(1), (a)(2), and (a)(3) be in writing, signed, and served.

"Shall" is replaced by "must" under the program to conform amended rules to current style conventions when there is no ambiguity.

GAP Report

The Advisory Committee recommends that the amendments to Rules 26(a)(1)(A) and (B) be changed so that initial disclosure applies to information the disclosing party "may use to support" its claims or defenses. It also recommends changes in the Committee Note to explain that disclosure requirement. In addition, it recommends inclusion in the Note of further explanatory matter regarding the exclusion from initial disclosure provided in new Rule 26(a)(1)(E) for actions for review on an administrative record and the impact of these exclusions on bankruptcy proceedings. Minor wording improvements in the Note are also proposed.

Subdivision (b)(1). In 1978, the Committee published for comment a proposed amendment, suggested by the Section of Litigation of the American Bar Association, to refine the scope of discovery by deleting the "subject matter" language. This proposal was withdrawn, and the Committee has since then made other changes in the discovery rules to address concerns about overbroad discovery. Concerns about costs and delay of discovery have persisted nonetheless, and other bar groups have repeatedly renewed similar proposals for amendment to this subdivision to delete the "subject matter" language. Nearly one-third of the lawyers surveyed in 1997 by the Federal Judicial Center endorsed narrowing the scope of discovery as a means of reducing litigation expense without interfering with fair case resolutions. *Discovery and Disclosure Practice, supra*, at 44–45 (1997). The Committee has heard that in some instances, particularly cases involving large quantities of discovery, parties seek to justify discovery requests that sweep far beyond the claims and defenses of the parties on the ground that they nevertheless have a bearing on the "subject matter" involved in the action.

The amendments proposed for subdivision (b)(1) include one element of these earlier proposals but also differ from these proposals in significant ways. The similarity is that the amendments describe the scope of party-controlled discovery in terms of matter relevant to the claim or defense of any party. The court, however, retains authority to order discovery of any matter relevant to the subject matter involved in the action for good cause. The amendment is designed to involve the court more actively in regulating the breadth of sweeping or contentious discovery. The Committee has been informed repeatedly by lawyers that involvement of the court in managing discovery is an important method of controlling problems of inappropriately broad discovery. Increasing the availability of judicial officers to resolve discovery disputes and increasing court management of discovery were both strongly endorsed by the attorneys surveyed by the Federal Judicial Center. *See Discovery and Disclosure Practice, supra*, at 44. Under the amended provisions, if there is an objection that discovery goes beyond material relevant to the parties' claims or defenses, the court would become involved to determine whether the discovery is relevant to the claims or defenses and, if not, whether good cause exists for authorizing it so long as it is relevant to the subject matter of the action. The good-cause standard warranting broader discovery is meant to be flexible.

The Committee intends that the parties and the court focus on the actual claims and defenses involved in the action. The dividing line between information relevant to the claims and defenses and that relevant only to the subject matter of the action cannot be defined with precision. A variety of types of information not directly pertinent to the incident in suit could be relevant to the claims or defenses raised in a given action. For example, other incidents of the same type, or involving the same product, could be properly discoverable under the revised standard. Information about organizational arrangements or filing systems of a party could be discoverable if likely to yield or lead to the discovery of admissible information. Similarly, information that could be used to impeach a likely witness, although not otherwise relevant to the claims or defenses, might be properly discoverable. In each instance, the determination whether such information is discoverable because it is relevant to the claims or defenses depends on the circumstances of the pending action.

The rule change signals to the court that it has the authority to confine discovery to the claims and defenses asserted in the pleadings, and signals to the parties that they have no entitlement to discovery to develop new claims or defenses that are not already identified in the pleadings. In general, it is hoped that reasonable lawyers can cooperate to manage discovery without the need for judicial intervention. When judicial intervention is invoked, the actual scope of discovery should be determined according to the reasonable needs of the action. The court may permit broader discovery in a particular case depending on the circumstances of the case, the nature of the claims and defenses, and the scope of the discovery requested.

The amendments also modify the provision regarding discovery of information not admissible in evidence. As added in 1946, this sentence was designed to make clear that otherwise relevant material could not be withheld because it was hearsay or otherwise inadmissible. The Committee was concerned that the "reasonably calculated to lead to the discovery of admissible evidence" standard set forth in this sentence might swallow any other limitation on the scope of discovery. Accordingly, this sentence has been amended to clarify that information must be relevant to be discoverable, even though inadmissible, and that discovery of such material is permitted if reasonably calculated to lead to the discovery of admissible evidence. As used here, "relevant" means within the scope of discovery as defined in this subdivision, and it would include information relevant to the subject matter involved in the action if the court has ordered discovery to that limit based on a showing of good cause.

Finally, a sentence has been added calling attention to the limitations of subdivision (b)(2)(i), (ii), and (iii). These limitations apply to discovery that is otherwise within the scope of subdivision (b)(1). The Committee has been told repeatedly that courts have not implemented these limitations with the vigor that was contemplated. *See 8 Federal Practice & Procedure* § 2008.1 at 121. This otherwise redundant cross-reference has been added to emphasize the need for active judicial use of subdivision (b)(2) to control excessive discovery. *Cf. Crawford-El v. Britton*, 118 S. Ct. 1584, 1597 (1998) (quoting Rule 26(b)(2)(iii) and stating that "Rule 26 vests the trial judge with broad discretion to tailor discovery narrowly").

GAP Report

The Advisory Committee recommends changing the rule to authorize the court to expand discovery to any "matter"—not "information"—relevant to the subject matter involved in the action. In addition, it recommends additional clarifying material in the Committee Note about the impact of the change on some commonly disputed discovery topics, the relationship between cost-bearing under Rule 26(b)(2) and expansion of the scope of discovery on a showing of good cause, and the meaning of "relevant" in the revision to the last sentence of current subdivision (b)(1). In addition, some minor clarifications of language changes have been proposed for the Committee Note .

Subdivision (b)(2). Rules 30, 31, and 33 establish presumptive national limits on the numbers of depositions and interrogatories. New Rule 30(d)(2) establishes a presumptive limit on the length of depositions. Subdivision (b)(2) is amended to remove the previous permission for local rules that establish different presumptive limits on these discovery activities. There is no reason to believe that unique circumstances justify varying these nationally-applicable presumptive limits in certain districts. The limits can be modified by court order or agreement in an individual action, but "standing" orders imposing different presumptive limits are not authorized. Because there is no national rule limiting the number of Rule 36 requests for admissions, the rule continues to authorize local rules that impose numerical limits on them. This change is not intended to interfere with differentiated case management in districts that use this technique by case-specific order as part of their Rule 16 process.

Subdivision (d). The amendments remove the prior authority to exempt cases by local rule from the moratorium on discovery before the subdivision (f) conference, but the categories of proceedings exempted from initial disclosure under subdivision (a)(1)(E) are excluded from subdivision (d). The parties may agree to disregard the moratorium where it applies, and the court may so order in a case, but "standing" orders altering the moratorium are not authorized.

Subdivision (f). As in subdivision (d), the amendments remove the prior authority to exempt cases by local rule from the conference requirement. The Committee has been informed that the addition of the conference was one of the most successful changes made in the 1993 amendments, and it therefore has determined to apply the conference requirement nationwide. The categories of proceedings exempted from initial disclosure under subdivision (a)(1)(E) are exempted from the conference requirement for the reasons that warrant exclusion from initial disclosure. The court may order that the conference need not occur in a case where otherwise required, or that it occur in a case otherwise exempted by subdivision (a)(1)(E). "Standing" orders altering the conference requirement for categories of cases are not authorized.

The rule is amended to require only a "conference" of the parties, rather than a "meeting." There are important benefits to face-to-face discussion of the topics to be covered in the conference, and those benefits may be lost if other means of conferring were routinely used when face-to-face meetings would not impose burdens. Nevertheless, geographic conditions in some districts may exact costs far out of proportion to these benefits. The amendment allows the court by case-specific order to require a face-to-face meeting, but "standing" orders so requiring are not authorized.

As noted concerning the amendments to subdivision (a)(1), the time for the conference has been changed to at least 21 days before the Rule 16 scheduling conference, and the time for the report is changed to no more than 14 days after the Rule 26(f) conference. This should ensure that the court will have the report well in advance of the scheduling conference or the entry of the scheduling order.

Since Rule 16 was amended in 1983 to mandate some case management activities in all courts, it has included deadlines for Completing these tasks to ensure that all courts do so within a reasonable time. Rule 26(f) was fit into this scheme when it was adopted in 1993. It was never intended, however, that the national requirements that certain activities be completed by a certain time should delay case management in districts that move much faster than the national rules direct, and the rule is therefore amended to permit such a court to adopt a local rule that shortens the period specified for the completion of these tasks.

"Shall" is replaced by "must," "does," or an active verb under the program to conform amended rules to current style conventions when there is no ambiguity.

GAP Report

The Advisory Committee recommends adding a sentence to the published amendments to Rule 26(f) authorizing local rules shortening the time between the attorney conference and the court's action under Rule 16(b), and addition to the Committee Note of explanatory material about this change to the rule. This addition can be made without republication in response to public comments.

2006 Amendment

Subdivision (a). Rule 26(a)(1)(B) is amended to parallel Rule 34(a) by recognizing that a party must disclose electronically stored information as well as documents that it may use to support its claims or defenses. The term "electronically stored information" has the same broad meaning in Rule 26(a)(1) as in Rule 34(a). This amendment is consistent with the 1993 addition of Rule 26(a)(1)(B). The term "data compilations" is deleted as unnecessary because it is a subset of both documents and electronically stored information.

[Subdivision (a)(1)(E).] Civil forfeiture actions are added to the list of exemptions from Rule 26(a)(1) disclosure requirements. These actions are governed by new Supplemental Rule G. Disclosure is not likely to be useful.

Subdivision (b)(2). The amendment to Rule 26(b)(2) is designed to address issues raised by difficulties in locating, retrieving, and providing discovery of some electronically stored information. Electronic storage systems often make it easier to locate and retrieve information. These advantages are properly taken into account in determining the reasonable scope of discovery in a particular case. But some sources of electronically stored information can be accessed only with substantial burden and cost. In a particular case, these burdens and costs may make the information on such sources not reasonably accessible.

It is not possible to define in a rule the different types of technological features that may affect the burdens and costs of accessing electronically stored information. Information systems are designed to provide ready access to information used in regular ongoing activities. They also may be designed so as to provide ready access to information that is not regularly used. But a system may retain information on sources that are accessible only by incurring substantial burdens or costs. Subparagraph (B) is added to regulate discovery from such sources.

Under this rule, a responding party should produce electronically stored information that is relevant, not privileged, and reasonably accessible, subject to the (b)(2)(C) limitations that apply to all discovery. The responding party must also identify, by category or type, the sources containing potentially responsive information that it is neither searching nor producing. The identification should, to the extent possible, provide enough detail to enable the requesting party to evaluate the burdens and costs of providing the discovery and the likelihood of finding responsive information on the identified sources.

A party's identification of sources of electronically stored information as not reasonably accessible does not relieve the party of its common-law or statutory duties to preserve evidence. Whether a responding party is required to preserve unsearched sources of potentially responsive information that it believes are not reasonably accessible depends on the circumstances of each case. It is often useful for the parties to discuss this issue early in discovery.

The volume of — and the ability to search — much electronically stored information means that in many cases the responding party will be able to produce information from reasonably accessible sources that will fully satisfy the parties' discovery needs. In many circumstances the requesting party should obtain and evaluate the information from such sources before insisting that the responding party search and produce information contained on sources that are not reasonably accessible. If the requesting party continues to seek discovery of information from sources identified as not reasonably accessible, the parties should discuss the burdens and costs of accessing and retrieving the information, the needs that may establish good cause for requiring all or part of the requested discovery even if the information sought is not reasonably accessible, and conditions on obtaining and producing the information that may be appropriate.

If the parties cannot agree whether, or on what terms, sources identified as not reasonably accessible should be searched and discoverable information produced, the issue may be raised either by a motion to compel discovery or by a motion for a protective order. The parties must confer before bringing either motion. If the parties do not resolve the issue and the court must decide, the responding party must show that the identified sources of information are not reasonably accessible because of undue burden or cost. The requesting party may need discovery to test this assertion. Such discovery might take the form of requiring the responding party to conduct a sampling of information contained on the sources identified as not reasonably accessible; allowing some form of inspection of such sources; or taking depositions of witnesses knowledgeable about the responding party's information systems.

Once it is shown that a source of electronically stored information is not reasonably accessible, the requesting party may still obtain discovery by showing good cause, considering the limitations of Rule 26(b)(2)(C) that balance the costs and potential benefits of discovery. The decision whether to require a responding party to search for and produce information that is not reasonably accessible depends not only on the burdens and costs of doing so, but also on whether those burdens and costs can be justified in the circumstances of the case. Appropriate considerations may include: (1) the specificity of the discovery request; (2) the quantity of information available from other and more easily accessed sources; (3) the failure to produce relevant information that seems likely to have existed but is no longer available on more easily accessed sources; (4) the likelihood of finding relevant, responsive information that cannot be obtained from other, more easily accessed sources; (5) predictions as to the importance and usefulness of the further information; (6) the importance of the issues at stake in the litigation; and (7) the parties' resources.

The responding party has the burden as to one aspect of the inquiry — whether the identified sources are not reasonably accessible in light of the burdens and costs required to search for, retrieve, and produce whatever responsive information may be found. The requesting party has the burden of showing that its need for the discovery outweighs the burdens and costs of locating, retrieving, and producing the information. In some cases, the court will be able to determine whether the identified sources are not reasonably accessible and whether the requesting party has shown good cause for some or all of the discovery, consistent with the limitations of Rule 26(b)(2)(C), through a single proceeding or presentation. The good-cause determination, however, may be complicated because the court and parties may know little about what information the sources identified as not reasonably accessible might contain, whether it is relevant, or how valuable it may be to the litigation. In such cases, the parties may need some focused discovery, which may include sampling of the sources, to learn more about what burdens and costs are involved in accessing the information, what the information consists of, and how valuable it is for the litigation in light of information that can be obtained by exhausting other opportunities for discovery.

The good-cause inquiry and consideration of the Rule 26(b)(2)(C) limitations are coupled with the authority to set conditions for discovery. The conditions may take the form of limits on the amount, type, or sources of information required to be accessed and produced. The conditions may also include payment by the requesting party of part or all of the reasonable costs of obtaining information from sources that are not reasonably accessible. A requesting party's willingness to share or bear the access costs may be weighed by the court in determining whether there is good cause. But the producing party's burdens in reviewing the information for relevance and privilege may weigh against permitting the requested discovery.

The limitations of Rule 26(b)(2)(C) continue to apply to all discovery of electronically stored information, including that stored on reasonably accessible electronic sources.

Subdivision (b)(5). The Committee has repeatedly been advised that the risk of privilege waiver, and the work necessary to avoid it, add to the costs and delay of discovery. When the review is of electronically stored information, the risk of waiver, and the time and effort required to avoid it, can increase substantially because of the volume of electronically stored information and the difficulty in ensuring that all information to be produced has in fact been reviewed. Rule 26(b)(5)(A) provides a procedure for a party that has withheld information on the basis of privilege or protection as trial-preparation material to make the claim so that the requesting party can decide whether to contest the claim and the court can resolve the dispute. Rule 26(b)(5)(B) is added to provide a procedure for a party to assert a claim of privilege or trial-preparation material protection after information is produced in discovery in the action and, if the claim is contested, permit any party that received the information to present the matter to the court for resolution.

Rule 26(b)(5)(B) does not address whether the privilege or protection that is asserted after production was waived by the production. The courts have developed principles to determine whether, and under what circumstances, waiver results from inadvertent production of privileged or protected information. Rule 26(b)(5)(B) provides a procedure for presenting and addressing these issues. Rule 26(b)(5)(B) works in tandem with Rule 26(f), which is amended to direct the parties to discuss privilege issues in preparing their discovery plan, and which, with amended Rule 16(b), allows the parties to ask the court to include in an order any agreements the parties reach regarding issues of privilege or trial-preparation material protection. Agreements reached under Rule 26(f)(4) and orders including such agreements entered under Rule 16(b)(6) may be considered when a court determines whether a waiver has occurred. Such agreements and orders ordinarily control if they adopt procedures different from those in Rule 26(b)(5)(B).

A party asserting a claim of privilege or protection after production must give notice to the receiving party. That notice should be in writing unless the circumstances preclude it. Such circumstances could include the assertion of the claim during a deposition. The notice should be as specific as possible in identifying the information and stating the basis for the claim. Because the receiving party must decide whether to challenge the claim and may sequester the information and submit it to the court for a ruling on whether the claimed privilege or protection applies and whether it has been waived, the notice should be sufficiently detailed so as to enable the receiving party and the court to understand the basis for the claim and to determine whether waiver has occurred. Courts will continue to examine whether a claim of privilege or protection was made at a reasonable time when delay is part of the waiver determination under the governing law.

After receiving notice, each party that received the information must promptly return, sequester, or destroy the information and any copies it has. The option of sequestering or destroying the information is included in part because the receiving party may have incorporated the information in protected trial-preparation materials. No receiving party may use or disclose the information pending resolution of the privilege claim. The receiving party may present to the court the questions whether the information is privileged or protected as trial-preparation material, and whether the privilege or protection has been waived. If it does so, it must provide the court with the grounds for the privilege or protection specified in the producing party's notice, and serve all parties. In presenting the question, the party may use the content of the information only to the extent permitted by the applicable law of privilege, protection for trial-preparation material, and professional responsibility.

If a party disclosed the information to nonparties before receiving notice of a claim of privilege or protection as trial-preparation material, it must take reasonable steps to retrieve the information and to return it, sequester it until the claim is resolved, or destroy it.

Whether the information is returned or not, the producing party must preserve the information pending the court's ruling on whether the claim of privilege or of protection is properly asserted and whether it was waived. As with claims made under Rule 26(b)(5)(A), there may be no ruling if the other parties do not contest the claim.

Subdivision (f). Rule 26(f) is amended to direct the parties to discuss discovery of electronically stored information during their discovery-planning conference. The rule focuses on "issues relating to disclosure or discovery of electronically stored information"; the discussion is not required in cases not involving electronic discovery, and the amendment imposes no additional requirements in those cases. When the parties do anticipate disclosure or discovery of electronically stored information, discussion at the outset may avoid later difficulties or ease their resolution.

When a case involves discovery of electronically stored information, the issues to be addressed during the Rule 26(f) conference depend on the nature and extent of the contemplated discovery and of the parties' information systems. It may be important for the parties to discuss those systems, and accordingly important for counsel to become familiar with those systems before the conference. With that information, the parties can develop a discovery plan that takes into account the capabilities of their computer systems. In appropriate cases identification of, and early discovery from, individuals with special knowledge of a party's computer systems may be helpful.

The particular issues regarding electronically stored information that deserve attention during the discovery planning stage depend on the specifics of the given case. *See Manual for Complex Litigation* (4th) § 40.25(2) (listing topics for discussion in a proposed order regarding meet-and-confer sessions). For example, the parties may specify the topics for such discovery and the time period for which discovery will be sought. They may identify the various sources of such information within a party's control that should be searched for electronically stored information. They may discuss whether the information is reasonably accessible to the party that has it, including the burden or cost of retrieving and reviewing the information. *See* Rule 26(b)(2)(B). Rule 26(f)(3) explicitly directs the parties to discuss the form or forms in which electronically stored information might be produced. The parties may be able to reach agreement on the forms of production, making discovery more efficient. Rule 34(b) is amended to permit a requesting party to specify the form or forms in which it wants electronically stored information produced. If the requesting party does not specify a form, Rule 34(b) directs the responding party to state the forms it intends to use in the production. Early discussion of the forms of production may facilitate the application of Rule 34(b) by allowing the parties to determine what forms of production will meet both parties' needs. Early identification of disputes over the forms of production may help avoid the expense and delay of searches or productions using inappropriate forms.

Rule 26(f) is also amended to direct the parties to discuss any issues regarding preservation of discoverable information during their conference as they develop a discovery plan. This provision applies to all sorts of discoverable information, but can be particularly important with regard to electronically stored information. The volume and dynamic nature of electronically stored information may complicate preservation obligations. The ordinary operation of computers involves both the automatic creation and the automatic deletion or overwriting of certain information. Failure to address preservation issues early in the litigation increases uncertainty and raises a risk of disputes.

The parties' discussion should pay particular attention to the balance between the competing needs to preserve relevant evidence and to continue routine operations critical to ongoing activities. Complete or broad cessation of a party's routine computer operations could paralyze the party's activities. *Cf. Manual for Complex Litigation* (4th) § 11.422 ("A blanket preservation order may be prohibitively expensive and unduly burdensome for parties dependent on computer systems for their day-to-day operations.") The parties should take account of these considerations in their discussions, with the goal of agreeing on reasonable preservation steps.

The requirement that the parties discuss preservation does not imply that courts should routinely enter preservation orders. A preservation order entered over objections should be narrowly tailored. Ex parte preservation orders should issue only in exceptional circumstances.

Rule 26(f) is also amended to provide that the parties should discuss any issues relating to assertions of privilege or of protection as trial-preparation materials, including whether the parties can facilitate discovery by agreeing on procedures for asserting claims of privilege or protection after production and whether to ask the court to enter an order that includes any agreement the parties reach. The Committee has repeatedly been advised about the discovery difficulties that can result from efforts to guard against waiver of privilege and work-product protection. Frequently parties find it necessary to spend large amounts of time reviewing materials requested through discovery to avoid waiving privilege. These efforts are necessary because materials subject to a claim of privilege or protection are often difficult to identify. A failure to withhold even one such item may result in an argument that there has been a waiver of privilege as to all other privileged materials on that subject matter. Efforts to avoid the risk of waiver can impose substantial costs on the party producing the material and the time required for the privilege review can substantially delay access for the party seeking discovery.

These problems often become more acute when discovery of electronically stored information is sought. The volume of such data, and the informality that attends use of e-mail and some other types of electronically stored information, may make privilege determinations more difficult, and privilege review correspondingly more expensive and time consuming. Other aspects of electronically stored information pose particular difficulties for privilege review. For example, production may be sought of information automatically included in electronic files but not apparent to the creator or to readers. Computer programs may retain draft language, editorial comments, and other deleted matter (sometimes referred to as "embedded data" or "embedded edits") in an electronic file but not make them apparent to the reader. Information describing the history, tracking, or management of an electronic file (sometimes called "metadata") is usually not apparent to the reader viewing a hard copy or a screen image. Whether this information should be produced may be among the topics discussed in the Rule 26(f) conference. If it is, it may need to be reviewed to ensure that no privileged information is included, further complicating the task of privilege review.

Parties may attempt to minimize these costs and delays by agreeing to protocols that minimize the risk of waiver. They may agree that the responding party will provide certain requested materials for initial examination without waiving any privilege or protection — sometimes known as a "quick peek." The requesting party then designates the documents it wishes to have actually produced. This designation is the Rule 34 request. The responding party then responds in the usual course, screening only those documents actually requested for formal production and asserting privilege claims as provided in Rule 26(b)(5)(A). On other occasions, parties enter agreements — sometimes called "clawback agreements"— that production without intent to waive privilege or protection should not be a waiver so long as the responding party identifies the documents mistakenly produced, and that the documents should be returned under those circumstances. Other voluntary arrangements may be appropriate depending on the circumstances of each litigation. In most circumstances, a party who receives information under such an arrangement cannot assert that production of the information waived a claim of privilege or of protection as trial-preparation material.

Although these agreements may not be appropriate for all cases, in certain cases they can facilitate prompt and economical discovery by reducing delay before the discovering party obtains access to documents, and by reducing the cost and burden of review by the producing party. A case-management or other order including such agreements may further facilitate the discovery process. Form 35 is amended to include a report to the court about any agreement regarding protections against inadvertent forfeiture or waiver of privilege or protection that the parties have reached, and Rule 16(b) is amended to recognize that the court may include such an agreement in a case-management or other order. If the parties agree to entry of such an order, their proposal should be included in the report to the court.

Rule 26(b)(5)(B) is added to establish a parallel procedure to assert privilege or protection as trial-preparation material after production, leaving the question of waiver to later determination by the court.

2007 Amendment

The language of Rule 26 has been amended as part of the general restyling of the Civil Rules to make them more easily understood and to make style and terminology consistent throughout the rules. These changes are intended to be stylistic only.

Former Rule 26(a)(5) served as an index of the discovery methods provided by later rules. It was deleted as redundant. Deletion does not affect the right to pursue discovery in addition to disclosure.

Former Rule 26(b)(1) began with a general statement of the scope of discovery that appeared to function as a preface to each of the five numbered paragraphs that followed. This preface has been shifted to the text of paragraph (1) because it does not accurately reflect the limits embodied in paragraphs (2), (3), or (4), and because paragraph (5) does not address the scope of discovery.

The reference to discovery of "books" in former Rule 26(b)(1) was deleted to achieve consistent expression throughout the discovery rules. Books remain a proper subject of discovery.

Amended Rule 26(b)(3) states that a party may obtain a copy of the party's own previous statement "on request." Former Rule 26(b)(3) expressly made the request procedure available to a nonparty witness, but did not describe the procedure to be used by a party. This apparent gap is closed by adopting the request procedure, which ensures that a party need not invoke Rule 34 to obtain a copy of the party's own statement.

Rule 26(e) stated the duty to supplement or correct a disclosure or discovery response "to include information thereafter acquired." This apparent limit is not reflected in practice; parties recognize the duty to supplement or correct by providing information that was not originally provided although it was available at the time of the initial disclosure or response. These words are deleted to reflect the actual meaning of the present rule.

Former Rule 26(e) used different phrases to describe the time to supplement or correct a disclosure or discovery response. Disclosures were to be supplemented "at appropriate intervals." A prior discovery response must be "seasonably * * * amend[ed]." The fine distinction between these phrases has not been observed in practice. Amended Rule 26(e)(1)(A) uses the same phrase for disclosures and discovery responses. The party must supplement or correct "in a timely manner."

Former Rule 26(g)(1) did not call for striking an unsigned disclosure. The omission was an obvious drafting oversight. Amended Rule 26(g)(2) includes disclosures in the list of matters that the court must strike unless a signature is provided "promptly * * * after being called to the attorney's or party's attention."

Former Rule 26(b)(2)(A) referred to a "good faith" argument to extend existing law. Amended Rule 26(b)(1)(B)(i) changes this reference to a "nonfrivolous" argument to achieve consistency with Rule 11(b)(2).

As with the Rule 11 signature on a pleading, written motion, or other paper, disclosure and discovery signatures should include not only a postal address but also a telephone number and electronic-mail address. A signer who lacks one or more of those addresses need not supply a nonexistent item.

Rule 11(b)(2) recognizes that it is legitimate to argue for establishing new law. An argument to establish new law is equally legitimate in conducting discovery.

CROSS REFERENCES

Depositions—

Before action or pending appeal, see Fed.Rules Civ. Proc. Rule 27, 28 USCA.

Of witnesses upon written questions, see Fed.Rules Civ. Proc. Rule 31, 28 USCA.

Depositions upon oral examination, requirements of, see Fed.Rules Civ.Proc. Rule 30, 28 USCA.

Persons before whom depositions may be taken, see Fed. Rules Civ.Proc. Rule 28, 28 USCA.

Sanctions for failure to make or cooperate in discovery, see Fed.Rules Civ.Proc. Rule 37, 28 USCA.

Stipulations regarding taking depositions, see Fed.Rules Civ.Proc. Rule 29, 28 USCA.

Subpoena for taking depositions; time and place of examination, see Fed.Rules Civ.Proc. Rule 45, 28 USCA.

Summary judgment, opposing motion, see Fed.Rules Civ. Proc. Rule 56, 28 USCA.

Use of deposition in court proceedings, effect of errors, irregularities; objections to admissibility, see Fed.Rules Civ. Proc. Rule 32, 28 USCA.

Written interrogatories of party, see Fed.Rules Civ.Proc. Rule 33, 28 USCA.

Rule 27. Depositions to Perpetuate Testimony

(a) Before an Action Is Filed.

(1) ***Petition.*** A person who wants to perpetuate testimony about any matter cognizable in a United States court may file a verified petition in the district court for the district where any expected adverse party resides. The petition must ask for an order authorizing the petitioner to depose the named persons in order to perpetuate their testimony. The petition must be titled in the petitioner's name and must show:

(A) that the petitioner expects to be a party to an action cognizable in a United States court but cannot presently bring it or cause it to be brought;

(B) the subject matter of the expected action and the petitioner's interest;

(C) the facts that the petitioner wants to establish by the proposed testimony and the reasons to perpetuate it;

(D) the names or a description of the persons whom the petitioner expects to be adverse parties and their addresses, so far as known; and

(E) the name, address, and expected substance of the testimony of each deponent.

(2) ***Notice and Service.*** At least 20 days before the hearing date, the petitioner must serve each expected adverse party with a copy of the petition and a notice stating the time and place of the hearing. The notice may be served either inside or outside the district or state in the manner provided in Rule 4. If that service cannot be made with reasonable diligence on an expected adverse party, the court may order service by publication or otherwise. The court must appoint an attorney to represent persons not served in the manner provided in Rule 4 and to cross-examine the deponent if an unserved person is not otherwise represented. If any expected adverse party is a minor or is incompetent, Rule 17(c) applies.

(3) ***Order and Examination.*** If satisfied that perpetuating the testimony may prevent a failure or delay of justice, the court must issue an order that designates or describes the persons whose depositions may be taken, specifies the subject matter of the examinations, and states whether the depositions will be taken orally or by written interrogatories. The depositions may then be taken under these rules, and the court may issue orders like those authorized by Rules 34 and 35. A reference in these rules to the court where an action is pending means, for purposes of this rule, the court where the petition for the deposition was filed.

(4) ***Using the Deposition.*** A deposition to perpetuate testimony may be used under Rule 32(a) in any later-filed district-court action involving the same subject matter if the deposition either was taken under these rules or, although not so taken, would be admissible in evidence in the courts of the state where it was taken.

(b) Pending Appeal.

(1) ***In General.*** The court where a judgment has been rendered may, if an appeal has been taken or may still be taken, permit a party to depose witnesses to perpetuate their testimony for use in the event of further proceedings in that court.

(2) ***Motion.*** The party who wants to perpetuate testimony may move for leave to take the depositions, on the same notice and service as if the action were pending in the district court. The motion must show:

(A) the name, address, and expected substance of the testimony of each deponent; and

(B) the reasons for perpetuating the testimony.

(3) ***Court Order.*** If the court finds that perpetuating the testimony may prevent a failure or delay of justice, the court may permit the depositions to be taken and may issue orders like those authorized by Rules 34 and 35. The depositions may be taken and used as any other deposition taken in a pending district-court action.

(c) Perpetuation by an Action. This rule does not limit a court's power to entertain an action to perpetuate testimony.

(Amended December 27, 1946, effective March 19, 1948; December 29, 1948, effective October 20, 1949; March 1, 1971, effective July 1, 1971; March 2, 1987, effective August 1, 1987; April 25, 2005, effective December 1, 2005; April 30, 2007, effective December 1, 2007.)

ADVISORY COMMITTEE NOTES

1937 Adoption

Note to Subdivision (a). This rule offers a simple method of perpetuating testimony in cases where it is usually allowed under equity practice or under modern statutes. See *Arizona v. California,* 1934, 54 S.Ct. 735, 292 U.S. 341, 78 L.Ed. 1298; *Todd Engineering Dry Dock and Repair Co. v. United States,* C.C.A.5, 1929, 32 F.2d 734; *Hall v. Stout,* 4 Del.Ch. 269 (1871). For comparable state statutes see Ark.Civ.Code (Crawford, 1934) §§ 666 to 670; Calif.Code Civ.Proc. (Deering, 1937) 2083–2089; Smith-Hurd Ill.Stats. c. 51, §§ 39 to 46; Iowa Code (1935) §§ 11400 to 11407; 2 Mass.Gen.Laws (Ter.Ed., 1932) ch. 233, §§ 46 to 63; N.Y.C.P.A. (1937) § 295; Ohio Gen.Code Ann. (Throckmorton, 1936) §§ 12216 to 12222; Va.Code Ann. (Michie, 1936) § 6235; Wis.Stat. (1935) §§ 326.27 to 326.29. The appointment of an attorney to represent absent parties or parties not personally notified, or a guardian ad litem to represent minors and incompetents, is provided for in several of the above statutes.

Note to Subdivision (b). This follows the practice approved in *Richter v. Union Trust Co.,* 1885, 5 S.Ct. 1162, 115 U.S. 55, 29 L.Ed. 345, by extending the right to perpetuate testimony to cases pending an appeal.

Note to Subdivision (c). This preserves the right to employ a separate action to perpetuate testimony under U.S.C., Title 28, [former] § 644 (Depositions under *dedimus potestatem* and *in perpetuam*) as an alternate method.

1946 Amendment

Note. Since the second sentence in subdivision (a)(3) refers only to depositions, it is arguable that Rules 34 and 35 are inapplicable in proceedings to perpetuate testimony. The new matter [in subdivisions (a)(3) and (b)] clarifies. A conforming change is also made in subdivision (b).

1948 Amendment

The amendment effective October 1949, substituted the words "United States district court" in subdivision (a)(1) and (4) for "district court of the United States."

1971 Amendment

The reference intended in this subdivision is to the rule governing the use of depositions in court proceedings. Formerly Rule 26(d), that rule is now Rule 32(a). The subdivision is amended accordingly.

1987 Amendment

The amendments are technical. No substantive change is intended.

2005 Amendment

The outdated cross-reference to former Rule 4(d) is corrected to incorporate all Rule 4 methods of service. Former Rule 4(d) has been allocated to many different subdivisions of Rule 4. Former Rule 4(d) did not cover all categories of defendants or modes of service, and present Rule 4 reaches further than all of former Rule 4. But there is no reason to distinguish between the different categories of defendants and modes of service encompassed by Rule 4. Rule 4 service provides effective notice. Notice by such means should be provided to any expected adverse party that comes within Rule 4.

Other changes are made to conform Rule 27(a)(2) to current style conventions.

2007 Amendment

The language of Rule 27 has been amended as part of the general restyling of the Civil Rules to make them more easily understood and to make style and terminology consistent throughout the rules. These changes are intended to be stylistic only.

CROSS REFERENCES

Persons before whom depositions may be taken, see Fed. Rules Civ.Proc. Rule 28, 28 USCA.

Rule 28. Persons Before Whom Depositions May Be Taken

(a) Within the United States.

(1) ***In General.*** Within the United States or a territory or insular possession subject to United States jurisdiction, a deposition must be taken before:

(A) an officer authorized to administer oaths either by federal law or by the law in the place of examination; or

(B) a person appointed by the court where the action is pending to administer oaths and take testimony.

(2) ***Definition of "Officer".*** The term "officer" in Rules 30, 31, and 32 includes a person appointed by the court under this rule or designated by the parties under Rule 29(a).

(b) In a Foreign Country.

(1) ***In General.*** A deposition may be taken in a foreign country:

(A) under an applicable treaty or convention;

(B) under a letter of request, whether or not captioned a "letter rogatory";

(C) on notice, before a person authorized to administer oaths either by federal law or by the law in the place of examination; or

(D) before a person commissioned by the court to administer any necessary oath and take testimony.

(2) ***Issuing a Letter of Request or a Commission.*** A letter of request, a commission, or both may be issued:

(A) on appropriate terms after an application and notice of it; and

(B) without a showing that taking the deposition in another manner is impracticable or inconvenient.

(3) ***Form of a Request, Notice, or Commission.*** When a letter of request or any other device is used according to a treaty or convention, it must be captioned in the form prescribed by that treaty or convention. A letter of request may be addressed "To the Appropriate Authority in [name of country]." A deposition notice or a commission must designate by name or descriptive title the person before whom the deposition is to be taken.

(4) ***Letter of Request—Admitting Evidence.*** Evidence obtained in response to a letter of request need not be excluded merely because it is not a verbatim transcript, because the testimony was not taken under oath, or because of any similar departure from the requirements for depositions taken within the United States.

(c) Disqualification. A deposition must not be taken before a person who is any party's relative, employee, or attorney; who is related to or employed by any party's attorney; or who is financially interested in the action.

(Amended December 27, 1946, effective March 19, 1948; January 21, 1963, effective July 1, 1963; April 29, 1980, effective August 1, 1980; March 2, 1987, effective August 1, 1987; April 22, 1993, effective December 1, 1993; April 30, 2007, effective December 1, 2007.)

ADVISORY COMMITTEE NOTES

1937 Adoption

In effect this rule is substantially the same as U.S.C., Title 28, [former] § 639 (Depositions *de bene esse*; when and where taken; notice). U.S.C., Title 28, [former] § 642 (Depositions, acknowledgments, and affidavits taken by notaries public) does not conflict with subdivision (a).

1946 Amendments

Note. The added language [in subdivision (a)] provides for the situation, occasionally arising, when depositions must be taken in an isolated place where there is no one readily available who has the power to administer oaths and take testimony according to the terms of the rule as originally stated. In addition, the amendment affords a more convenient method of securing depositions in the case where state lines intervene between the location of various witnesses otherwise rather closely grouped. The amendment insures that the person appointed shall have adequate power to perform his duties. It has been held that a person authorized to act in the premises, as, for example, a master, may take testimony outside the district of his appointment. *Consolidated Fastener Co. v. Columbian Button & Fastener Co.*, C.C.N.D.N.Y.1898, 85 Fed. 54; *Mathieson Alkali Works v. Arnold, Hoffman & Co.*, C.C.A.1, 1929, 31 F.2d 1.

1963 Amendments

The amendment of clause (1) is designed to facilitate depositions in foreign countries by enlarging the class of persons before whom the depositions may be taken on notice. The class is no longer confined, as at present, to a secretary of embassy or legation, consul general, consul, vice consul, or consular agent of the United States. In a country that regards the taking of testimony by a foreign official in aid of litigation pending in a court of another country as an infringement upon its sovereignty, it will be expedient to notice depositions before officers of the country in which the examination is taken. See generally *Symposium, Letters Rogatory* (Grossman ed. 1956); Doyle, *Taking Evidence by Deposition and Letters Rogatory and Obtaining Documents in Foreign Territory*, Proc.A.B.A., Sec.Int'l & Comp.L. 37 (1959); Heilpern, *Procuring Evidence Abroad*, 14 Tul.L.Rev. 29 (1939); Jones, *International Judicial Assistance: Procedural Chaos and a Program for Reform*, 62 Yale L.J. 515, 526–29 (1953); Smit, *International Aspects of Federal Civil Procedure*, 61 Colum.L.Rev. 1031, 1056–58 (1961).

Clause (2) of amended subdivision (b), like the corresponding provision of subdivision (a) dealing with depositions taken in the United States, makes it clear that the appointment of a person by commission in itself confers power upon him to administer any necessary oath.

It has been held that a letter rogatory will not be issued unless the use of a notice or commission is shown to be impossible or impractical. See, e.g., *United States v. Matles*, 154 F.Supp. 574 (E.D.N.Y.1957); *The Edmund Fanning*, 89 F.Supp. 282 (E.D.N.Y.1950); *Branyan v. Koninklijke Luchtvaart Maatschappij*, 13 F.R.D. 425 (S.D.N.Y.1953). See also *Ali Akber Kiachif v. Philco International Corp.*, 10 F.R.D. 277 (S.D.N.Y.1950). The intent of the fourth sentence of the amended subdivision is to overcome this judicial antipathy and to permit a sound choice between depositions under a letter rogatory and on notice or by commission in the light of all the circumstances. In a case in which the foreign country will compel a witness to attend or testify in aid of a letter rogatory but not in aid of a commission, a letter rogatory may be preferred on the ground that it is less expensive to execute, even if there is plainly no need for compulsive process. A letter rogatory may also be preferred when it cannot be demonstrated that a witness will be recalcitrant or when the witness states that he is willing to testify voluntarily, but the contingency exists that he will change his mind at the last moment. In the latter case, it may be advisable to issue both a commission and a letter rogatory, the latter to be executed if the former fails. The choice between a letter rogatory and a commission may be conditioned by other factors, including the nature and extent of the assistance that the foreign country will give to the execution of either.

In executing a letter rogatory the courts of other countries may be expected to follow their customary procedure for taking testimony. See *United States v. Paraffin Wax*, 2255 Bags, 23 F.R.D. 289 (E.D.N.Y.1959). In many noncommon-law countries the judge questions the witness, sometimes without first administering an oath, the attorneys put any supplemental questions either to the witness or through the judge, and the judge dictates a summary of the testimony, which the witness acknowledges as correct. See *Jones, supra*, at 530–32; *Doyle, supra*, at 39–41. The last sentence of the amended subdivision provides, contrary to the implications of some authority, that evidence recorded in such a fashion need not be excluded on that account. See *The Mandu*, 11 F.Supp. 845 (E.D.N.Y.1935). But *cf. Nelson v. United States*, 17 Fed.Cas. 1340 (No. 10,116) (C.C.D.Pa. 1816); *Winthrop v. Union Ins. Co.*, 30 Fed.Cas. 376 (No. 17901) (C.C.D.Pa.1807). The specific reference to the lack of an oath or a verbatim transcript is intended to be illustrative. Whether or to what degree the value or weight of the evidence may be affected by the method of taking or recording the testimony is left for determination according to the circumstances of the particular case, *cf. Uebersee Finanz-Korporation, A.G. v. Brownell*, 121 F.Supp. 420 (D.D.C. 1954); *Danisch v. Guardian Life Ins. Co.*, 19 F.R.D. 235 (S.D.N.Y.1956); the testimony may indeed be so devoid of substance or probative value as to warrant its exclusion altogether.

Some foreign countries are hostile to allowing a deposition to be taken in their country, especially by notice or commission, or to lending assistance in the taking of a deposition. Thus compliance with the terms of amended subdivision (b) may not in all cases ensure completion of a deposition abroad. Examination of the law and policy of the particular foreign country in advance of attempting a deposition is therefore advisable. See 4 *Moore's Federal Practice* ¶¶28.05–28.08 (2d ed. 1950).

1980 Amendments

The amendments are clarifying.

1987 Amendments

The amendment is technical. No substantive change is intended.

1993 Amendments

This revision is intended to make effective use of the Hague Convention on the Taking of Evidence Abroad in Civil or Commercial Matters, and of any similar treaties that the United States may enter into in the future which provide procedures for taking depositions abroad. The party taking the deposition is ordinarily obliged to conform to an applicable treaty or convention if an effective deposition can be taken by such internationally approved means, even though a verbatim transcript is not available or testimony cannot be taken under oath. For a discussion of the impact of such treaties upon the discovery process, and of the application of principles of comity upon discovery in countries not signatories to a convention, see *Société Nationale Industrielle Aé-*

rospatiale v. United States District Court, 482 U.S. 522 (1987).

The term "letter of request" has been substituted in the rule for the term "letter rogatory" because it is the primary method provided by the Hague Convention. A letter rogatory is essentially a form of letter of request. There are several other minor changes that are designed merely to carry out the intent of the other alterations.

2007 Amendment

The language of Rule 28 has been amended as part of the general restyling of the Civil Rules to make them more easily understood and to make style and terminology consistent throughout the rules. These changes are intended to be stylistic only.

HISTORICAL NOTES

Treaties and Conventions; Taking of Evidence Abroad in Civil or Commercial Matters; Observance On and After Oct. 7, 1972, by United States and Citizens and Persons Subject to Jurisdiction of United States

For text of Convention, see provisions set out as a note under section 1781 of this title.

CROSS REFERENCES

Certification and filing of depositions by officer, see Fed. Rules Civ.Proc. Rule 30, 28 USCA.

Objections to admissibility of depositions, see Fed.Rules Civ.Proc. Rule 32, 28 USCA.

Procedures for taking of depositions, evidence abroad in civil or commercial matters, see 28 USCA § 1781.

Taking responses to written interrogatories and preparation of record, see Fed.Rules Civ.Proc. Rule 31, 28 USCA.

Rule 29. Stipulations About Discovery Procedure

Unless the court orders otherwise, the parties may stipulate that:

(a) a deposition may be taken before any person, at any time or place, on any notice, and in the manner specified—in which event it may be used in the same way as any other deposition; and

(b) other procedures governing or limiting discovery be modified—but a stipulation extending the time for any form of discovery must have court approval if it would interfere with the time set for completing discovery, for hearing a motion, or for trial.

(Amended March 30, 1970, effective July 1, 1970; April 22, 1993, effective December 1, 1993; April 30, 2007, effective December 1, 2007.)

ADVISORY COMMITTEE NOTES

1970 Amendment

There is no provision for stipulations varying the procedures by which methods of discovery other than depositions are governed. It is common practice for parties to agree on such variations, and the amendment recognizes such agreements and provides a formal mechanism in the rules for giving them effect. Any stipulation varying the procedures may be superseded by court order, and stipulations extending the time for response to discovery under Rules 33, 34, and 36 require court approval.

1993 Amendments

This rule is revised to give greater opportunity for litigants to agree upon modifications to the procedures governing discovery or to limitations upon discovery. Counsel are encouraged to agree on less expensive and time-consuming methods to obtain information, as through voluntary exchange of documents, use of interviews in lieu of depositions, etc. Likewise, when more depositions or interrogatories are needed than allowed under these rules or when more time is needed to complete a deposition than allowed under a local rule, they can, by agreeing to the additional discovery, eliminate the need for a special motion addressed to the court.

Under the revised rule, the litigants ordinarily are not required to obtain the court's approval of these stipulations. By order or local rule, the court can, however, direct that its approval be obtained for particular types of stipulations; and, in any event, approval must be obtained if a stipulation to extend the 30–day period for responding to interrogatories, requests for production, or requests for admissions would interfere with dates set by the court for completing discovery, for hearing of a motion, or for trial.

2007 Amendment

The language of Rule 29 has been amended as part of the general restyling of the Civil Rules to make them more easily understood and to make style and terminology consistent throughout the rules. These changes are intended to be stylistic only.

Rule 30. Depositions by Oral Examination

(a) When a Deposition May Be Taken.

(1) ***Without Leave.*** A party may, by oral questions, depose any person, including a party, without leave of court except as provided in Rule 30(a)(2). The deponent's attendance may be compelled by subpoena under Rule 45.

(2) ***With Leave.*** A party must obtain leave of court, and the court must grant leave to the extent consistent with Rule 26(b)(2):

(A) if the parties have not stipulated to the deposition and:

(i) the deposition would result in more than 10 depositions being taken under this rule or Rule 31 by the plaintiffs, or by the defendants, or by the third-party defendants;

(ii) the deponent has already been deposed in the case; or

(iii) the party seeks to take the deposition before the time specified in Rule

26(d), unless the party certifies in the notice, with supporting facts, that the deponent is expected to leave the United States and be unavailable for examination in this country after that time; or

(B) if the deponent is confined in prison.

(b) Notice of the Deposition; Other Formal Requirements.

(1) ***Notice in General.*** A party who wants to depose a person by oral questions must give reasonable written notice to every other party. The notice must state the time and place of the deposition and, if known, the deponent's name and address. If the name is unknown, the notice must provide a general description sufficient to identify the person or the particular class or group to which the person belongs.

(2) ***Producing Documents.*** If a subpoena duces tecum is to be served on the deponent, the materials designated for production, as set out in the subpoena, must be listed in the notice or in an attachment. The notice to a party deponent may be accompanied by a request under Rule 34 to produce documents and tangible things at the deposition.

(3) ***Method of Recording.***

(A) *Method Stated in the Notice.* The party who notices the deposition must state in the notice the method for recording the testimony. Unless the court orders otherwise, testimony may be recorded by audio, audiovisual, or stenographic means. The noticing party bears the recording costs. Any party may arrange to transcribe a deposition.

(B) *Additional Method.* With prior notice to the deponent and other parties, any party may designate another method for recording the testimony in addition to that specified in the original notice. That party bears the expense of the additional record or transcript unless the court orders otherwise.

(4) ***By Remote Means.*** The parties may stipulate—or the court may on motion order—that a deposition be taken by telephone or other remote means. For the purpose of this rule and Rules 28(a), 37(a)(2), and 37(b)(1), the deposition takes place where the deponent answers the questions.

(5) ***Officer's Duties.***

(A) *Before the Deposition.* Unless the parties stipulate otherwise, a deposition must be conducted before an officer appointed or designated under Rule 28. The officer must begin the deposition with an on-the-record statement that includes:

(i) the officer's name and business address;

(ii) the date, time, and place of the deposition;

(iii) the deponent's name;

(iv) the officer's administration of the oath or affirmation to the deponent; and

(v) the identity of all persons present.

(B) *Conducting the Deposition; Avoiding Distortion.* If the deposition is recorded nonstenographically, the officer must repeat the items in Rule 30(b)(5)(A)(i)-(iii) at the beginning of each unit of the recording medium. The deponent's and attorneys' appearance or demeanor must not be distorted through recording techniques.

(C) *After the Deposition.* At the end of a deposition, the officer must state on the record that the deposition is complete and must set out any stipulations made by the attorneys about custody of the transcript or recording and of the exhibits, or about any other pertinent matters.

(6) ***Notice or Subpoena Directed to an Organization.*** In its notice or subpoena, a party may name as the deponent a public or private corporation, a partnership, an association, a governmental agency, or other entity and must describe with reasonable particularity the matters for examination. The named organization must then designate one or more officers, directors, or managing agents, or designate other persons who consent to testify on its behalf; and it may set out the matters on which each person designated will testify. A subpoena must advise a nonparty organization of its duty to make this designation. The persons designated must testify about information known or reasonably available to the organization. This paragraph (6) does not preclude a deposition by any other procedure allowed by these rules.

(c) Examination and Cross–Examination; Record of the Examination; Objections; Written Questions.

(1) ***Examination and Cross–Examination.*** The examination and cross-examination of a deponent proceed as they would at trial under the Federal Rules of Evidence, except Rules 103 and 615. After putting the deponent under oath or affirmation, the officer must record

the testimony by the method designated under Rule 30(b)(3)(A). The testimony must be recorded by the officer personally or by a person acting in the presence and under the direction of the officer.

(2) ***Objections.*** An objection at the time of the examination—whether to evidence, to a party's conduct, to the officer's qualifications, to the manner of taking the deposition, or to any other aspect of the deposition—must be noted on the record, but the examination still proceeds; the testimony is taken subject to any objection. An objection must be stated concisely in a nonargumentative and nonsuggestive manner. A person may instruct a deponent not to answer only when necessary to preserve a privilege, to enforce a limitation ordered by the court, or to present a motion under Rule 30(d)(3).

(3) ***Participating Through Written Questions.*** Instead of participating in the oral examination, a party may serve written questions in a sealed envelope on the party noticing the deposition, who must deliver them to the officer. The officer must ask the deponent those questions and record the answers verbatim.

(d) Duration; Sanction; Motion to Terminate or Limit.

(1) ***Duration.*** Unless otherwise stipulated or ordered by the court, a deposition is limited to 1 day of 7 hours. The court must allow additional time consistent with Rule 26(b)(2) if needed to fairly examine the deponent or if the deponent, another person, or any other circumstance impedes or delays the examination.

(2) ***Sanction.*** The court may impose an appropriate sanction—including the reasonable expenses and attorney's fees incurred by any party—on a person who impedes, delays, or frustrates the fair examination of the deponent.

(3) ***Motion to Terminate or Limit.***

(A) *Grounds.* At any time during a deposition, the deponent or a party may move to terminate or limit it on the ground that it is being conducted in bad faith or in a manner that unreasonably annoys, embarrasses, or oppresses the deponent or party. The motion may be filed in the court where the action is pending or the deposition is being taken. If the objecting deponent or party so demands, the deposition must be suspended for the time necessary to obtain an order.

(B) *Order.* The court may order that the deposition be terminated or may limit its scope and manner as provided in Rule 26(c). If terminated, the deposition may be resumed only by order of the court where the action is pending.

(C) *Award of Expenses.* Rule 37(a)(5) applies to the award of expenses.

(e) Review by the Witness; Changes.

(1) ***Review; Statement of Changes.*** On request by the deponent or a party before the deposition is completed, the deponent must be allowed 30 days after being notified by the officer that the transcript or recording is available in which:

(A) to review the transcript or recording; and

(B) if there are changes in form or substance, to sign a statement listing the changes and the reasons for making them.

(2) ***Changes Indicated in the Officer's Certificate.*** The officer must note in the certificate prescribed by Rule 30(f)(1) whether a review was requested and, if so, must attach any changes the deponent makes during the 30–day period.

(f) Certification and Delivery; Exhibits; Copies of the Transcript or Recording; Filing.

(1) ***Certification and Delivery.*** The officer must certify in writing that the witness was duly sworn and that the deposition accurately records the witness's testimony. The certificate must accompany the record of the deposition. Unless the court orders otherwise, the officer must seal the deposition in an envelope or package bearing the title of the action and marked "Deposition of [witness's name]" and must promptly send it to the attorney who arranged for the transcript or recording. The attorney must store it under conditions that will protect it against loss, destruction, tampering, or deterioration.

(2) ***Documents and Tangible Things.***

(A) *Originals and Copies.* Documents and tangible things produced for inspection during a deposition must, on a party's request, be marked for identification and attached to the deposition. Any party may inspect and copy them. But if the person who produced them wants to keep the originals, the person may:

(i) offer copies to be marked, attached to the deposition, and then used as originals—after giving all parties a fair opportunity to verify the copies by comparing them with the originals; or

(ii) give all parties a fair opportunity to inspect and copy the originals after they are marked—in which event the originals may be used as if attached to the deposition.

(B) *Order Regarding the Originals.* Any party may move for an order that the originals be attached to the deposition pending final disposition of the case.

(3) ***Copies of the Transcript or Recording.*** Unless otherwise stipulated or ordered by the court, the officer must retain the stenographic notes of a deposition taken stenographically or a copy of the recording of a deposition taken by another method. When paid reasonable charges, the officer must furnish a copy of the transcript or recording to any party or the deponent.

(4) ***Notice of Filing.*** A party who files the deposition must promptly notify all other parties of the filing.

(g) Failure to Attend a Deposition or Serve a Subpoena; Expenses. A party who, expecting a deposition to be taken, attends in person or by an attorney may recover reasonable expenses for attending, including attorney's fees, if the noticing party failed to:

(1) attend and proceed with the deposition; or

(2) serve a subpoena on a nonparty deponent, who consequently did not attend.

(Amended January 21, 1963, effective July 1, 1963; March 30, 1970, effective July 1, 1970; March 1, 1971, effective July 1, 1971; November 20, 1972, effective July 1, 1975; April 29, 1980, effective August 1, 1980; March 2, 1987, effective August 1, 1987; April 22, 1993, effective December 1, 1993; April 17, 2000, effective December 1, 2000; April 30, 2007, effective December 1, 2007.)

ADVISORY COMMITTEE NOTES

1937 Adoption

Note to Subdivision (a). This is in accordance with common practice. See U.S.C., Title 28, [former] § 639 (Depositions *de bene esse*; when and where taken; notice), the relevant provisions of which are incorporated in this rule; West's Ann.Code Civ.Proc. § 2031; and statutes cited in respect to notice in the Note to Rule 26(a). The provision for enlarging or shortening the time of notice has been added to give flexibility to the rule.

Note to Subdivisions (b) and (d). These are introduced as a safeguard for the protection of parties and deponents on account of the unlimited right of discovery given by Rule 26.

Note to Subdivisions (c) and (e). These follow the general plan of [former] Equity Rule 51 (Evidence Taken Before Examiners, Etc.) and U.S.C., Title 28, [former] §§ 640 (Depositions *de bene esse*; mode of taking), and [former] 641 (Same; transmission to court), but are more specific. They also permit the deponent to require the officer to make changes in the deposition if the deponent is not satisfied with it. See also [former] Equity Rule 50 (Stenographer—Appointment—Fees.)

Note to Subdivision (f). Compare [former] Equity Rule 55 (Depositions Deemed Published When Filed.)

Note to Subdivision (g). This is similar to 2 Minn.Stat. (Mason, 1927) § 9833, but is more extensive.

1963 Amendments

This amendment corresponds to the change in Rule 4(d)(4). See Advisory Committee's Note to that amendment.

1970 Amendments

Subdivision (a). This subdivision contains the provisions of existing Rule 26(a), transferred here as part of the rearrangement relating to Rule 26. Existing Rule 30(a) is transferred to 30(b). Changes in language have been made to conform to the new arrangement.

This subdivision is further revised in regard to the requirement of leave of court for taking a deposition. The present procedure, requiring a plaintiff to obtain leave of court if he serves notice of taking a deposition within 20 days after commencement of the action, is changed in several respects. First, leave is required by reference to the time the deposition is to be taken rather than the date of serving notice of taking. Second, the 20-day period is extended to 30 days and runs from the service of summons and complaint on any defendant, rather than the commencement of the action. *Cf.* Ill.S.Ct.R. 19–1 S-H Ill.Ann.Stat. § 101.19–1. Third, leave is not required beyond the time that defendant initiates discovery, thus showing that he has retained counsel. As under the present practice, a party not afforded a reasonable opportunity to appear at a deposition, because he has not yet been served with process, is protected against use of the deposition at trial against him. See Rule 32(a), transferred from 26(d). Moreover, he can later redepose the witness if he so desires.

The purpose of requiring the plaintiff to obtain leave of court is, as stated by the Advisory Committee that proposed the present language of Rule 26(a), to protect "a defendant who has not had an opportunity to retain counsel and inform himself as to the nature of the suit." Note to 1948 amendment of Rule 26(a), quoted in 3A Barron & Holtzoff, *Federal Practice and Procedure* 455–456 (Wright ed. 1958). In order to assure defendant of this opportunity, the period is lengthened to 30 days. This protection, however, is relevant to the time of taking the deposition, not to the time that notice is served. Similarly, the protective period should run from the service of process rather than the filing of the complaint with the court. As stated in the note to Rule 26(d), the courts have used the service of notice as a convenient reference point for assigning priority in taking depositions, but with the elimination of priority in new Rule 26(d) the reference point is no longer needed. The new procedure is consistent in principle with the provisions of Rules 33, 34, and 36 as revised.

Plaintiff is excused from obtaining leave even during the initial 30-day period if he gives the special notice provided in subdivision (b)(2). The required notice must state that the person to be examined is about to go out of the district where the action is pending and more than 100 miles from the place of trial, or out of the United States, or on a voyage to sea, and will be unavailable for examination unless deposed within the 30-day period. These events occur most often in maritime litigation, when seamen are transferred from one port to another or are about to go to sea. Yet, there are analogous situations in nonmaritime litigation, and although the maritime problems are more common, a rule limited to claims in the admiralty and maritime jurisdiction is not justified.

In the recent unification of the civil and admiralty rules, this problem was temporarily met through addition in Rule 26(a) of a provision that depositions *de bene esse* may continue to be taken as to admiralty and maritime claims within the meaning of Rule 9(h). It was recognized at the time that "a uniform rule applicable alike to what are now civil actions and suits in admiralty" was clearly preferable, but the de bene esse procedure was adopted "for the time being at least." See Advisory Committee's Note in Report of the Judicial Conference: Proposed Amendments to Rules of Civil Procedure 43–44 (1966).

The changes in Rule 30(a) and the new Rule 30(b)(2) provide a formula applicable to ordinary civil as well as maritime claims. They replace the provision for depositions *de bene esse*. They authorize an early deposition without leave of court where the witness is about to depart and, unless his deposition is promptly taken, (1) it will be impossible or very difficult to depose him before trial or (2) his deposition can later be taken but only with substantially increased effort and expense. *Cf. S.S. Hai Chang,* 1966 A.M.C. 2239 (S.D.N.Y.1966), in which the deposing party is required to prepay expenses and counsel fees of the other party's lawyer when the action is pending in New York and depositions are to be taken on the West Coast. Defendant is protected by a provision that the deposition cannot be used against him if he was unable through exercise of diligence to obtain counsel to represent him.

The distance of 100 miles from place of trial is derived from the *de bene esse* provision and also conforms to the reach of a subpoena of the trial court, as provided in Rule 45(e). See also S.D.N.Y. Civ.R. 5(a). Some parts of the *de bene esse* provision are omitted from Rule 30(b)(2). Modern deposition practice adequately covers the witness who lives more than 100 miles away from place of trial. If a witness is aged or infirm, leave of court can be obtained.

Subdivision (b). Existing Rule 30(b) on protective orders has been transferred to Rule 26(c), and existing Rule 30(a) relating to the notice of taking deposition has been transferred to this subdivision. Because new material has been added, subsection numbers have been inserted.

Subdivision (b)(1). If a subpoena duces tecum is to be served, a copy thereof or a designation of the materials to be produced must accompany the notice. Each party is thereby enabled to prepare for the deposition more effectively.

Subdivision (b)(2). This subdivision is discussed in the note to subdivision (a), to which it relates.

Subdivision (b)(3). This provision is derived from existing Rule 30(a), with a minor change of language.

Subdivision (b)(4). In order to facilitate less expensive procedures, provision is made for the recording of testimony by other than stenographic means—*e.g.*, by mechanical, electronic, or photographic means. Because these methods give rise to problems of accuracy and trustworthiness, the party taking the deposition is required to apply for a court order. The order is to specify how the testimony is to be recorded, preserved, and filed, and it may contain whatever additional safeguards the court deems necessary.

Subdivision (b)(5). A provision is added to enable a party, through service of notice, to require another party to produce documents or things at the taking of his deposition. This may now be done as to a nonparty deponent through use of a subpoena duces tecum as authorized by Rule 45, but some courts have held that documents may be secured from a party only under Rule 34. See 2A Barron & Holtzoff, *Federal Practice and Procedure* § 644.1 n. 83.2, § 792 n. 16 (Wright ed. 1961). With the elimination of "good cause" from Rule 34, the reason for this restrictive doctrine has disappeared. *Cf.* N.Y.C.P.L.R. § 3111.

Whether production of documents or things should be obtained directly under Rule 34 or at the deposition under this rule will depend on the nature and volume of the documents or things. Both methods are made available. When the documents are few and simple, and closely related to the oral examination, ability to proceed via this rule will facilitate discovery. If the discovering party insists on examining many and complex documents at the taking of the deposition, thereby causing undue burdens on others, the latter may, under Rules 26(c) or 30(d), apply for a court order that the examining party proceed via Rule 34 alone.

Subdivision (b)(6). A new provision is added, whereby a party may name a corporation, partnership, association, or governmental agency as the deponent and designate the matters on which he requests examination, and the organization shall then name one or more of its officers, directors, or managing agents, or other persons consenting to appear and testify on its behalf with respect to matters known or reasonably available to the organization. *Cf.* Alberta Sup.Ct.R. 255. The organization may designate persons other than officers, directors, and managing agents, but only with their consent. Thus, an employee or agent who has an independent or conflicting interest in the litigation—for example, in a personal injury case—can refuse to testify on behalf of the organization.

This procedure supplements the existing practice whereby the examining party designates the corporate official to be deposed. Thus, if the examining party believes that certain officials who have not testified pursuant to this subdivision have added information, he may depose them. On the other hand, a court's decision whether to issue a protective order may take account of the availability and use made of the procedures provided in this subdivision.

The new procedure should be viewed as an added facility for discovery, one which may be advantageous to both sides as well as an improvement in the deposition process. It will reduce the difficulties now encountered in determining, prior to the taking of a deposition, whether a particular employee or agent is a "managing agent." See Note, *Discovery Against Corporations Under the Federal Rules*, 47 Iowa L.Rev. 1006–1016 (1962). It will curb the "bandying" by which officers or managing agents of a corporation are deposed in turn but each disclaims knowledge of facts that are clearly known to persons in the organization and thereby to it. *Cf. Haney v. Woodward & Lothrop, Inc.*, 330 F.2d 940, 944 (4th Cir. 1964). The provision should also assist organizations which find that an unnecessarily large number of their officers and agents are being deposed by a party uncertain of who in the organization has knowledge. Some courts have held that under the existing rules a corporation should not be burdened with choosing which person is to appear for it. E.g., *United States v. Gahagan Dredging Corp.*, 24 F.R.D. 328, 329 (S.D.N.Y.1958). This burden is not essentially different from that of answering interrogatories under Rule 33, and is in any case lighter than that of an examining party ignorant of who in the corporation has knowledge.

Subdivision (c). A new sentence is inserted at the beginning, representing the transfer of existing Rule 26(c) to this subdivision. Another addition conforms to the new provision in subdivision (b)(4).

The present rule provides that transcription shall be carried out unless all parties waive it. In view of the many depositions taken from which nothing useful is discovered, the revised language provides that transcription is to be performed if any party requests it. The fact of the request is relevant to the exercise of the court's discretion in determining who shall pay for transcription.

Parties choosing to serve written questions rather than participate personally in an oral deposition are directed to serve their questions on the party taking the deposition, since the officer is often not identified in advance. Confidentiality is preserved, since the questions may be served in a sealed envelope.

Subdivision (d). The assessment of expenses incurred in relation to motions made under this subdivision (d) is made subject to the provisions of Rule 37(a). The standards for assessment of expenses are more fully set out in Rule 37(a), and these standards should apply to the essentially similar motions of this subdivision.

Subdivision (e). The provision relating to the refusal of a witness to sign his deposition is tightened through insertion of a 30-day time period.

Subdivision (f)(1). A provision is added which codifies in a flexible way the procedure for handling exhibits related to the deposition and at the same time assures each party that he may inspect and copy documents and things produced by a nonparty witness in response to a subpoena duces tecum. As a general rule and in the absence of agreement to the contrary or order of the court, exhibits produced without objection are to be annexed to and returned with the deposition, but a witness may substitute copies for purposes of marking and he may obtain return of the exhibits. The right of the parties to inspect exhibits for identification and to make copies is assured. *Cf.* N.Y.C.P.L.R. § 3116(c).

1971 Amendments

The subdivision permits a party to name a corporation or other form of organization as a deponent in the notice of examination and to describe in the notice the matters about which discovery is desired. The organization is then obliged to designate natural persons to testify on its behalf. The amendment clarifies the procedure to be followed if a party desires to examine a non-party organization through persons designated by the organization. Under the rules, a subpoena rather than a notice of examination is served on a non-party to compel attendance at the taking of a deposition. The amendment provides that a subpoena may name a non-party organization as the deponent and may indicate the matters about which discovery is desired. In that event, the non-party organization must respond by designating natural persons, who are then obliged to testify as to matters known or reasonably available to the organization. To insure that a non-party organization that is not represented by counsel has knowledge of its duty to designate, the amendment directs the party seeking discovery to advise of the duty in the body of the subpoena.

1972 Amendments

Subdivision (c). Existing Rule 43(b), which is to be abrogated, deals with the use of leading questions, the calling, interrogation, impeachment, and scope of cross-examination of adverse parties, officers, etc. These topics are dealt with in many places in the Rules of Evidence. Moreover, many pertinent topics included in the Rules of Evidence are not mentioned in Rule 43(b), e.g. privilege. A reference to the Rules of Evidence generally is therefore made in subdivision (c) of Rule 30.

1980 Amendments

Subdivision (b)(4). It has been proposed that electronic recording of depositions be authorized as a matter of course, subject to the right of a party to seek an order that a deposition be recorded by stenographic means. The Committee is not satisfied that a case has been made for a reversal of present practice. The amendment is made to encourage parties to agree to the use of electronic recording of depositions so that conflicting claims with respect to the potential of electronic recording for reducing costs of depositions can be appraised in the light of greater experience. The provision that the parties may stipulate that depositions may be recorded by other than stenographic means seems implicit in Rule 29. The amendment makes it explicit. The provision that the stipulation or order shall designate the person before whom the deposition is to be taken is added to encourage the naming of the recording technician as that person, eliminating the necessity of the presence of one whose only function is to administer the oath. See Rules 28(a) and 29.

Subdivision (b)(7). Depositions by telephone are now authorized by Rule 29 upon stipulation of the parties. The amendment authorizes that method by order of the court. The final sentence is added to make it clear that when a deposition is taken by telephone it is taken in the district and at the place where the witness is to answer the questions rather than that where the questions are propounded.

Subdivision (f)(1). For the reasons set out in the Note following the amendment of Rule 5(d), the court may wish to permit the parties to retain depositions unless they are to be used in the action. The amendment of the first paragraph permits the court to so order.

The amendment of the second paragraph is clarifying. The purpose of the paragraph is to permit a person who produces materials at a deposition to offer copies for marking and annexation to the deposition. Such copies are a "substitute" for the originals, which are not to be marked and which can thereafter be used or even disposed of by the person who produces them. In the light of that purpose, the former language of the paragraph had been justly termed "opaque." Wright & Miller, *Federal Practice and Procedure: Civil* § 2114.

1987 Amendments

The amendments are technical. No substantive change is intended.

1993 Amendments

Subdivision (a). Paragraph (1) retains the first and third sentences from the former subdivision (a) without significant modification. The second and fourth sentences are relocated.

Paragraph (2) collects all provisions bearing on requirements of leave of court to take a deposition.

Paragraph (2)(A) is new. It provides a limit on the number of depositions the parties may take, absent leave of court or stipulation with the other parties. One aim of this revision is to assure judicial review under the standards stated in Rule 26(b)(2) before any side will be allowed to take more than ten depositions in a case without agreement of the other parties. A second objective is to emphasize that counsel have a professional obligation to develop a mutual cost-effective plan for discovery in the case. Leave to take additional depositions should be granted when consistent with the principles of Rule 26(b)(2), and in some cases the ten-per-side limit should be reduced in accordance with those same principles. Consideration should ordinarily be given at the planning meeting of the parties under Rule 26(f) and at the time of a scheduling conference under Rule 16(b) as to enlargements or reductions in the number of depositions, eliminating the need for special motions.

A deposition under Rule 30(b)(6) should, for purposes of this limit, be treated as a single deposition even though more than one person may be designated to testify.

In multi-party cases, the parties on any side are expected to confer and agree as to which depositions are most needed, given the presumptive limit on the number of depositions they can take without leave of court. If these disputes cannot be amicably resolved, the court can be requested to resolve the dispute or permit additional depositions.

Paragraph (2)(B) is new. It requires leave of court if any witness is to be deposed in the action more than once. This requirement does not apply when a deposition is temporarily recessed for convenience of counsel or the deponent or to enable additional materials to be gathered before resuming the deposition. If significant travel costs would be incurred to resume the deposition, the parties should consider the feasibility of conducting the balance of the examination by telephonic means.

Paragraph (2)(C) revises the second sentence of the former subdivision (a) as to when depositions may be taken. Consistent with the changes made in Rule 26(d), providing that formal discovery ordinarily not commence until after the litigants have met and conferred as directed in revised Rule 26(f), the rule requires leave of court or agreement of the parties if a deposition is to be taken before that time (except when a witness is about to leave the country).

Subdivision (b). The primary change in subdivision (b) is that parties will be authorized to record deposition testimony by nonstenographic means without first having to obtain permission of the court or agreement from other counsel.

Former subdivision (b)(2) is partly relocated in subdivision (a)(2)(C) of this rule. The latter two sentences of the first paragraph are deleted, in part because they are redundant to Rule 26(g) and in part because Rule 11 no longer applies to discovery requests. The second paragraph of the former subdivision (b)(2), relating to use of depositions at trial where a party was unable to obtain counsel in time for an accelerated deposition, is relocated in Rule 32.

New paragraph (2) confers on the party taking the deposition the choice of the method of recording, without the need to obtain prior court approval for one taken other than stenographically. A party choosing to record a deposition only by videotape or audiotape should understand that a transcript will be required by Rule 26(a)(3)(B) and Rule 32(c) if the deposition is later to be offered as evidence at trial or on a dispositive motion under Rule 56. Objections to the nonstenographic recording of a deposition, when warranted by the circumstances, can be presented to the court under Rule 26(c).

Paragraph (3) provides that other parties may arrange, at their own expense, for the recording of a deposition by a means (stenographic, visual, or sound) in addition to the method designated by the person noticing the deposition. The former provisions of this paragraph, relating to the court's power to change the date of a deposition, have been eliminated as redundant in view of Rule 26(c)(2).

Revised paragraph (4) requires that all depositions be recorded by an officer designated or appointed under Rule 28 and contains special provisions designed to provide basic safeguards to assure the utility and integrity of recordings taken other than stenographically.

Paragraph (7) is revised to authorize the taking of a deposition not only by telephone but also by other remote electronic means, such as satellite television, when agreed to by the parties or authorized by the court.

Subdivision (c). Minor changes are made in this subdivision to reflect those made in subdivision (b) and to complement the new provisions of subdivision (d)(1), aimed at reducing the number of interruptions during depositions.

In addition, the revision addresses a recurring problem as to whether other potential deponents can attend a deposition. Courts have disagreed, some holding that witnesses should be excluded through invocation of Rule 615 of the evidence rules, and others holding that witnesses may attend unless excluded by an order under Rule 26(c)(5). The revision provides that other witnesses are not automatically excluded from a deposition simply by the request of a party. Exclusion, however, can be ordered under Rule 26(c)(5) when appropriate; and, if exclusion is ordered, consideration should be given as to whether the excluded witnesses likewise should be precluded from reading, or being otherwise informed about, the testimony given in the earlier depositions. The revision addresses only the matter of attendance by potential deponents, and does not attempt to resolve issues concerning attendance by others, such as members of the public or press.

Subdivision (d). The first sentence of new paragraph (1) provides that any objections during a deposition must be made concisely and in a non-argumentative and non-suggestive manner. Depositions frequently have been unduly prolonged, if not unfairly frustrated, by lengthy objections and colloquy, often suggesting how the deponent should respond. While objections may, under the revised rule, be made during a deposition, they ordinarily should be limited to those that under Rule 32(d)(3) might be waived if not made at that time, *i.e.*, objections on grounds that might be immediately obviated, removed, or cured, such as to the form of a question or the responsiveness of an answer. Under Rule 32(b), other objections can, even without the so-called "usual stipulation" preserving objections, be raised for the first time at trial and therefore should be kept to a minimum during a deposition.

Directions to a deponent not to answer a question can be even more disruptive than objections. The second sentence of new paragraph (1) prohibits such directions except in the three circumstances indicated: to claim a privilege or protection against disclosure (*e.g.*, as work product), to enforce a court directive limiting the scope or length of permissible discovery, or to suspend a deposition to enable presentation of a motion under paragraph (3).

Paragraph (2) is added to this subdivision to dispel any doubts regarding the power of the court by order or local rule to establish limits on the length of depositions. The rule also explicitly authorizes the court to impose the cost resulting from obstructive tactics that unreasonably prolong a deposition on the person engaged in such obstruction. This sanction may be imposed on a non-party witness as well as a party or attorney, but is otherwise congruent with Rule 26(g).

It is anticipated that limits on the length of depositions prescribed by local rules would be presumptive only, subject to modification by the court or by agreement of the parties. Such modifications typically should be discussed by the parties in their meeting under Rule 26(f) and included in the scheduling order required by Rule 16(b). Additional time, moreover, should be allowed under the revised rule when justified under the principles stated in Rule 26(b)(2). To reduce the number of special motions, local rules should ordinarily permit—and indeed encourage—the parties to agree to additional time, as when, during the taking of a deposition, it becomes clear that some additional examination is needed.

Paragraph (3) authorizes appropriate sanctions not only when a deposition is unreasonably prolonged, but also when an attorney engages in other practices that improperly frustrate the fair examination of the deponent, such as making improper objections or giving directions not to answer prohibited by paragraph (1). In general, counsel should not engage in any conduct during a deposition that would not be allowed in the presence of a judicial officer. The making of an excessive number of unnecessary objections may itself constitute sanctionable conduct, as may the refusal of an attorney to agree with other counsel on a fair apportionment of the time allowed for examination of a deponent or a refusal to agree to a reasonable request for some additional time to complete a deposition, when that is permitted by the local rule or order.

Subdivision (e). Various changes are made in this subdivision to reduce problems sometimes encountered when depositions are taken stenographically. Reporters frequently have difficulties obtaining signatures—and the return of depositions—from deponents. Under the revision pre-filing review by the deponent is required only if requested before the deposition is completed. If review is requested, the deponent will be allowed 30 days to review the transcript or recording and to indicate any changes in form or substance. Signature of the deponent will be required only if review is requested and changes are made.

Subdivision (f). Minor changes are made in this subdivision to reflect those made in subdivision (b). In courts which direct that depositions not be automatically filed, the reporter can transmit the transcript or recording to the attorney taking the deposition (or ordering the transcript or record), who then becomes custodian for the court of the original record of the deposition. Pursuant to subdivision (f)(2), as under the prior rule, any other party is entitled to secure a copy of the deposition from the officer designated to take the deposition; accordingly, unless ordered or agreed, the officer must retain a copy of the recording or the stenographic notes.

2000 Amendment

Subdivision (d). Paragraph (1) has been amended to clarify the terms regarding behavior during depositions. The references to objections " to evidence" and limitations "on evidence" have been removed to avoid disputes about what is "evidence" and whether an objection is to, or a limitation is on, discovery instead. It is intended that the rule apply to any objection to a question or other issue arising during a deposition, and to any limitation imposed by the court in connection with a deposition, which might relate to duration or other matters.

The current rule places limitations on instructions that a witness not answer only when the instruction is made by a "party." Similar limitations should apply with regard to anyone who might purport to instruct a witness not to answer a question. Accordingly, the rule is amended to apply the limitation to instructions by any person. The amendment is not intended to confer new authority on nonparties to instruct witnesses to refuse to answer deposition questions. The amendment makes it clear that, whatever the legitimacy of giving such instructions, the nonparty is subject to the same limitations as parties.

Paragraph (2) imposes a presumptive durational limitation of one day of seven hours for any deposition. The Committee has been informed that overlong depositions can result in undue costs and delays in some circumstances. This limitation contemplates that there will be reasonable breaks during the day for lunch and other reasons, and that the only time to be counted is the time occupied by the actual deposition. For purposes of this durational limit, the deposition of each person designated under Rule 30(b)(6) should be considered a separate deposition. The presumptive duration may be extended, or otherwise altered, by agreement. Absent agreement, a court order is needed. The party seeking a court order to extend the examination, or otherwise alter the limitations, is expected to show good cause to justify such an order.

Parties considering extending the time for a deposition—and courts asked to order an extension—might consider a variety of factors. For example, if the witness needs an interpreter, that may prolong the examination. If the examination will cover events occurring over a long period of time, that may justify allowing additional time. In cases in which the witness will be questioned about numerous or lengthy documents, it is often desirable for the interrogating party to send copies of the documents to the witness sufficiently in advance of the deposition so that the witness can become familiar with them. Should the witness nevertheless not read the documents in advance, thereby prolonging the deposition, a court could consider that a reason for extending the time limit. If the examination reveals that documents have been requested but not produced, that may justify further examination once production has occurred. In multi-party cases, the need for each party to examine the witness may warrant additional time, although duplicative questioning should be avoided and parties with similar interests should strive to designate one lawyer to question about areas of common interest. Similarly, should the lawyer for the witness want to examine the witness, that may require additional time. Finally, with regard to expert witnesses, there may more often be a need for additional time—even after the submission of the report required by Rule 26(a)(2)—for full exploration of the theories upon which the witness relies.

It is expected that in most instances the parties and the witness will make reasonable accommodations to avoid the need for resort to the court. The limitation is phrased in terms of a single day on the assumption that ordinarily a single day would be preferable to a deposition extending over multiple days; if alternative arrangements would better suit the parties, they may agree to them. It is also assumed that there will be reasonable breaks during the day. Preoccupation with timing is to be avoided.

The rule directs the court to allow additional time where consistent with Rule 26(b)(2) if needed for a fair examination of the deponent. In addition, if the deponent or another person impedes or delays the examination, the court must authorize extra time. The amendment makes clear that additional time should also be allowed where the examination is impeded by an "other circumstance," which might include a power outage, a health emergency, or other event.

In keeping with the amendment to Rule 26(b)(2), the provision added in 1993 granting authority to adopt a local rule limiting the time permitted for depositions has been removed. The court may enter a case-specific order directing shorter depositions for all depositions in a case or with regard to a specific witness. The court may also order that a deposition be taken for limited periods on several days.

Paragraph (3) includes sanctions provisions formerly included in paragraph (2). It authorizes the court to impose an appropriate sanction on any person responsible for an impediment that frustrated the fair examination of the deponent. This could include the deponent, any party, or any other person involved in the deposition. If the impediment or delay results from an "other circumstance" under paragraph (2), ordinarily no sanction would be appropriate.

Former paragraph (3) has been renumbered (4) but is otherwise unchanged .

Subdivision (f)(1): This subdivision is amended because Rule 5(d) has been amended to direct that discovery materials, including depositions, ordinarily should not be filed. The rule already has provisions directing that the lawyer who arranged for the transcript or recording preserve the deposition. Rule 5(d) provides that, once the deposition is used in the proceeding, the attorney must file it with the court.

"Shall" is replaced by "must" or "may" under the program to conform amended rules to current style conventions when there is no ambiguity.

GAP Report

The Advisory Committee recommends deleting the requirement in the published proposed amendments that the deponent consent to extending a deposition beyond one day, and adding an amendment to Rule 30(f)(1) to conform to the published amendment to Rule 5(d) regarding filing of depositions. It also recommends conforming the Committee Note with regard to the deponent veto, and adding material to the Note to provide direction on computation of the durational limitation on depositions, to provide examples of situations in which the parties might agree—or the court order—that a deposition be extended, and to make clear that no new authority to instruct a witness is conferred by the amendment. One minor wording improvement in the Note is also suggested.

2007 Amendment

The language of Rule 30 has been amended as part of the general restyling of the Civil Rules to make them more easily understood and to make style and terminology consistent throughout the rules. These changes are intended to be stylistic only.

The right to arrange a deposition transcription should be open to any party, regardless of the means of recording and regardless of who noticed the deposition.

"[O]ther entity" is added to the list of organizations that may be named as deponent. The purpose is to ensure that the deposition process can be used to reach information known or reasonably available to an organization no matter what abstract fictive concept is used to describe the organization. Nothing is gained by wrangling over the place to fit into current rule language such entities as limited liability companies, limited partnerships, business trusts, more exotic common-law creations, or forms developed in other countries.

HISTORICAL NOTES

Effective Date of Amendment Proposed November 20, 1972

Amendment of this rule embraced by the order entered by the Supreme Court of the United States on November 20, 1972, effective on the 180th day beginning after January 2, 1975, see section 3 of Pub.L. 93–595, Jan. 2, 1975, 88 Stat. 1959, set out as a note under section 2071 of Title 28.

CROSS REFERENCES

Discovery and production of documents and things for inspection, copying, or photographing, see Fed.Rules Civ. Proc. Rule 34, 28 USCA.

Interrogatories to parties; scope and use at trial, see Fed.Rules Civ.Proc. Rule 33, 28 USCA.

Persons before whom deposition may be taken, see Fed. Rules Civ.Proc. Rule 28, 28 USCA.

Stipulations regarding discovery procedure, see Fed.Rules Civ.Proc. Rule 29, 28 USCA.

Subpoena for taking depositions; place of examination, see Fed.Rules Civ.Proc. Rule 45, 28 USCA.

United States magistrate judges, power to administer oaths and take depositions, see 28 USCA § 636.

Use of depositions in court proceedings; motion to suppress, effect of errors or irregularities, objections to admissibility, waiver of objections, see Fed.Rules Civ.Proc. Rule 32, 28 USCA.

Rule 31. Depositions by Written Questions

(a) When a Deposition May Be Taken.

(1) ***Without Leave.*** A party may, by written questions, depose any person, including a party, without leave of court except as provided in Rule 31(a)(2). The deponent's attendance may be compelled by subpoena under Rule 45.

(2) ***With Leave.*** A party must obtain leave of court, and the court must grant leave to the extent consistent with Rule 26(b)(2):

(A) if the parties have not stipulated to the deposition and:

(i) the deposition would result in more than 10 depositions being taken under this rule or Rule 30 by the plaintiffs, or by the defendants, or by the third-party defendants;

(ii) the deponent has already been deposed in the case; or

(iii) the party seeks to take a deposition before the time specified in Rule 26(d); or

(B) if the deponent is confined in prison.

(3) ***Service; Required Notice.*** A party who wants to depose a person by written questions must serve them on every other party, with a notice stating, if known, the deponent's name and address. If the name is unknown, the notice must provide a general description sufficient to identify the person or the particular class or group to which the person belongs. The notice must also state the name or descriptive title and the address of the officer before whom the deposition will be taken.

(4) ***Questions Directed to an Organization.*** A public or private corporation, a partnership, an association, or a governmental agency may be deposed by written questions in accordance with Rule 30(b)(6).

(5) ***Questions from Other Parties.*** Any questions to the deponent from other parties must be served on all parties as follows: cross-questions, within 14 days after being served with the notice and direct questions; redirect questions, within 7 days after being served with cross-questions; and recross-questions, within 7 days after being served with redirect questions. The court may, for good cause, extend or shorten these times.

(b) Delivery to the Officer; Officer's Duties. The party who noticed the deposition must deliver to the officer a copy of all the questions served and of the notice. The officer must promptly proceed in the manner provided in Rule 30(c), (e), and (f) to:

(1) take the deponent's testimony in response to the questions;

(2) prepare and certify the deposition; and

(3) send it to the party, attaching a copy of the questions and of the notice.

(c) Notice of Completion or Filing.

(1) ***Completion.*** The party who noticed the deposition must notify all other parties when it is completed.

(2) ***Filing.*** A party who files the deposition must promptly notify all other parties of the filing.

(Amended March 30, 1970, effective July 1, 1970; March 2, 1987, effective August 1, 1987; April 22, 1993, effective December 1, 1993; April 30, 2007, effective December 1, 2007.)

ADVISORY COMMITTEE NOTES

1937 Adoption

This rule is in accordance with common practice. In most of the states listed in the Note to Rule 26(a), provisions similar to this rule will be found in the statutes which in their respective statutory compilations follow those cited in the Note to Rule 26(a).

1970 Amendment

Confusion is created by the use of the same terminology to describe both the taking of a deposition upon "written interrogatories" pursuant to this rule and the serving of "written interrogatories" upon parties pursuant to Rule 33. The distinction between these two modes of discovery will be more readily and clearly grasped through substitution of the word "questions" for "interrogatories" throughout this rule.

Subdivision (a). A new paragraph is inserted at the beginning of this subdivision to conform to the rearrangement of provisions in Rules 26(a), 30(a), and 30(b).

The revised subdivision permits designation of the deponent by general description or by class or group. This conforms to the practice for depositions on oral examination.

The new procedure provided in Rule 30(b)(6) for taking the deposition of a corporation or other organization through persons designated by the organization is incorporated by reference.

The service of all questions, including cross, redirect, and recross, is to be made on all parties. This will inform the parties and enable them to participate fully in the procedure.

The time allowed for service of cross, redirect, and recross questions has been extended. Experience with the existing time limits shows them to be unrealistically short. No special restriction is placed on the time for serving the notice of taking the deposition and the first set of questions. Since no party is required to serve cross questions less than 30 days after the notice and questions are served, the defendant has sufficient time to obtain counsel. The court may for cause shown enlarge or shorten the time.

Subdivision (d). Since new Rule 26(c) provides for protective orders with respect to all discovery, and expressly provides that the court may order that one discovery device be used in place of another, subdivision (d) is eliminated as unnecessary.

1987 Amendment

The amendments are technical. No substantive change is intended.

1993 Amendments

Subdivision (a). The first paragraph of subdivision (a) is divided into two subparagraphs, with provisions comparable to those made in the revision of Rule 30. Changes are made in the former third paragraph, numbered in the revision as paragraph (4), to reduce the total time for developing cross-examination, redirect, and recross questions from 50 days to 28 days.

2007 Amendment

The language of Rule 31 has been amended as part of the general restyling of the Civil Rules to make them more easily understood and to make style and terminology consistent throughout the rules. These changes are intended to be stylistic only.

The party who noticed a deposition on written questions must notify all other parties when the deposition is completed, so that they may make use of the deposition. A deposition is completed when it is recorded and the deponent has either waived or exercised the right of review under Rule 30(e)(1).

CROSS REFERENCES

Written interrogatories of a party, see Fed.Rules Civ.Proc. Rule 33, 28 USCA.

Rule 32. Using Depositions in Court Proceedings

(a) Using Depositions.

(1) ***In General.*** At a hearing or trial, all or part of a deposition may be used against a party on these conditions:

(A) the party was present or represented at the taking of the deposition or had reasonable notice of it;

(B) it is used to the extent it would be admissible under the Federal Rules of Evidence if the deponent were present and testifying; and

(C) the use is allowed by Rule 32(a)(2) through (8).

(2) ***Impeachment and Other Uses.*** Any party may use a deposition to contradict or impeach the testimony given by the deponent as a witness, or for any other purpose allowed by the Federal Rules of Evidence.

(3) ***Deposition of Party, Agent, or Designee.*** An adverse party may use for any purpose the deposition of a party or anyone who, when deposed, was the party's officer, director, managing agent, or designee under Rule 30(b)(6) or 31(a)(4).

(4) ***Unavailable Witness.*** A party may use for any purpose the deposition of a witness, whether or not a party, if the court finds:

(A) that the witness is dead;

(B) that the witness is more than 100 miles from the place of hearing or trial or is outside the United States, unless it appears that the witness's absence was procured by the party offering the deposition;

(C) that the witness cannot attend or testify because of age, illness, infirmity, or imprisonment;

(D) that the party offering the deposition could not procure the witness's attendance by subpoena; or

(E) on motion and notice, that exceptional circumstances make it desirable—in the interest of justice and with due regard to the importance of live testimony in open court—to permit the deposition to be used.

(5) ***Limitations on Use.***

(A) *Deposition Taken on Short Notice.* A deposition must not be used against a party who, having received less than 11 days' notice of the deposition, promptly moved for a protective order under Rule 26(c)(1)(B) requesting that it not be taken or be taken at a different time or place—and this motion was still pending when the deposition was taken.

(B) *Unavailable Deponent; Party Could Not Obtain an Attorney.* A deposition taken without leave of court under the unavailability provision of Rule 30(a)(2)(A)(iii) must not be used against a party who shows that, when served with the notice, it could not, despite diligent efforts, obtain an attorney to represent it at the deposition.

(6) ***Using Part of a Deposition.*** If a party offers in evidence only part of a deposition, an adverse party may require the offeror to introduce other parts that in fairness should be considered with the part introduced, and any party may itself introduce any other parts.

(7) ***Substituting a Party.*** Substituting a party under Rule 25 does not affect the right to use a deposition previously taken.

(8) ***Deposition Taken in an Earlier Action.*** A deposition lawfully taken and, if required, filed in any federal- or state-court action may be used in a later action involving the same subject matter between the same parties, or their representatives or successors in interest, to the same extent as if taken in the later action. A deposition previously taken may

also be used as allowed by the Federal Rules of Evidence.

(b) Objections to Admissibility. Subject to Rules 28(b) and 32(d)(3), an objection may be made at a hearing or trial to the admission of any deposition testimony that would be inadmissible if the witness were present and testifying.

(c) Form of Presentation. Unless the court orders otherwise, a party must provide a transcript of any deposition testimony the party offers, but may provide the court with the testimony in nontranscript form as well. On any party's request, deposition testimony offered in a jury trial for any purpose other than impeachment must be presented in nontranscript form, if available, unless the court for good cause orders otherwise.

(d) Waiver of Objections.

(1) ***To the Notice.*** An objection to an error or irregularity in a deposition notice is waived unless promptly served in writing on the party giving the notice.

(2) ***To the Officer's Qualification.*** An objection based on disqualification of the officer before whom a deposition is to be taken is waived if not made:

(A) before the deposition begins; or

(B) promptly after the basis for disqualification becomes known or, with reasonable diligence, could have been known.

(3) ***To the Taking of the Deposition.***

(A) *Objection to Competence, Relevance, or Materiality.* An objection to a deponent's competence—or to the competence, relevance, or materiality of testimony—is not waived by a failure to make the objection before or during the deposition, unless the ground for it might have been corrected at that time.

(B) *Objection to an Error or Irregularity.* An objection to an error or irregularity at an oral examination is waived if:

(i) it relates to the manner of taking the deposition, the form of a question or answer, the oath or affirmation, a party's conduct, or other matters that might have been corrected at that time; and

(ii) it is not timely made during the deposition.

(C) *Objection to a Written Question.* An objection to the form of a written question under Rule 31 is waived if not served in writing on the party submitting the question within the time for serving responsive questions or, if the question is a recross-question, within 5 days after being served with it.

(4) ***To Completing and Returning the Deposition.*** An objection to how the officer transcribed the testimony—or prepared, signed, certified, sealed, endorsed, sent, or otherwise dealt with the deposition—is waived unless a motion to suppress is made promptly after the error or irregularity becomes known or, with reasonable diligence, could have been known.

(Amended March 30, 1970, effective July 1, 1970; November 20, 1972, effective July 1, 1975; April 29, 1980, effective August 1, 1980; March 2, 1987, effective August 1, 1987; April 22, 1993, effective December 1, 1993; April 30, 2007, effective December 1, 2007.)

ADVISORY COMMITTEE NOTES

1937 Adoption

This rule is in accordance with common practice. In most of the states listed in the note to rule 26, provisions similar to this rule will be found in the statutes which in their respective statutory compilations follow those cited in the Note to Rule 26.

1970 Amendment

As part of the rearrangement of the discovery rules, existing subdivisions (d), (e), and (f) of Rule 26 are transferred to Rule 32 as new subdivisions (a), (b), and (c). The provisions of Rule 32 are retained as subdivision (d) of Rule 32 with appropriate changes in the lettering and numbering of subheadings. The new rule is given a suitable new title. A beneficial byproduct of the rearrangement is that provisions which are naturally related to one another are placed in one rule.

A change is made in new Rule 32(a), whereby it is made clear that the rules of evidence are to be applied to depositions offered at trial as though the deponent were then present and testifying at trial. This eliminates the possibility of certain technical hearsay objections which are based, not on the contents of deponent's testimony, but on his absence from court. The language of present Rule 26(d) does not appear to authorize these technical objections, but it is not entirely clear. Note present Rule 26(e), transferred to Rule 32(b); see 2A Barron & Holtzoff, *Federal Practice and Procedure* 164–166 (Wright ed. 1961).

An addition in Rule 32(a)(2) provides for use of a deposition of a person designated by a corporation or other organization, which is a party, to testify on its behalf. This complements the new procedure for taking the deposition of a corporation or other organization provided in Rules 30(b)(6) and 31(a). The addition is appropriate, since the deposition is in substance and effect that of the corporation or other organization which is a party.

A change is made in the standard under which a party offering part of a deposition in evidence may be required to introduce additional parts of the deposition. The new standard is contained in a proposal made by the Advisory Committee on Rules of Evidence. See Rule 1–07 and accompanying Note, *Preliminary Draft of Proposed Rules of Evidence for the United States District Courts and Magistrates* 21–22 (March, 1969).

References to other rules are changed to conform to the rearrangement, and minor verbal changes have been made for clarification. The time for objecting to written questions served under Rule 31 is slightly extended.

1972 Amendment

Subdivision (c). The concept of "making a person one's own witness" appears to have had significance principally in two respects: impeachment and waiver of incompetency. Neither retains any vitality under the Rules of Evidence. The old prohibition against impeaching one's own witness is eliminated by Evidence Rule 607. The lack of recognition in the Rules of Evidence of state rules of incompetency in the Dead Man's area renders it unnecessary to consider aspects of waiver arising from calling the incompetent party-witness. Subdivision (c) is deleted because it appears to be no longer necessary in the light of the Rules of Evidence.

1980 Amendment

Subdivision (a)(1). Rule 801(d) of the Federal Rules of Evidence permits a prior inconsistent statement of a witness in a deposition to be used as substantive evidence. And Rule 801(d)(2) makes the statement of an agent or servant admissible against the principal under the circumstances described in the Rule. The language of the present subdivision is, therefore, too narrow.

Subdivision (a)(4). The requirement that a prior action must have been dismissed before depositions taken for use in it can be used in a subsequent action was doubtless an oversight, and the courts have ignored it. See Wright & Miller, *Federal Practice and Procedure: Civil* § 2150. The final sentence is added to reflect the fact that the Federal Rules of Evidence permit a broader use of depositions previously taken under certain circumstances. For example, Rule 804(b)(1) of the Federal Rules of Evidence provides that if a witness is unavailable, as that term is defined by the rule, his deposition in any earlier proceeding can be used against a party to the prior proceeding who had an opportunity and similar motive to develop the testimony of the witness.

1987 Amendment

The amendment is technical. No substantive change is intended.

1993 Amendments

Subdivision (a). The last sentence of revised subdivision (a) not only includes the substance of the provisions formerly contained in the second paragraph of Rule 30(b)(2), but adds a provision to deal with the situation when a party, receiving minimal notice of a proposed deposition, is unable to obtain a court ruling on its motion for a protective order seeking to delay or change the place of the deposition. Ordinarily a party does not obtain protection merely by the filing of a motion for a protective order under Rule 26(c); any protection is dependent upon the court's ruling. Under the revision, a party receiving less than 11 days notice of a deposition can, provided its motion for a protective order is filed promptly, be spared the risks resulting from nonattendance at the deposition held before its motion is ruled upon. Although the revision of Rule 32(a) covers only the risk that the deposition could be used against the non-appearing movant, it should also follow that, when the proposed deponent is the movant, the deponent would have "just cause" for failing to appear for purposes of Rule 37(d)(1). Inclusion of this provision is not intended to signify that 11 days' notice is the minimum advance notice for all depositions or that greater than 10 days should necessarily be deemed sufficient in all situations.

Subdivision (c). This new subdivision, inserted at the location of a subdivision previously abrogated, is included in view of the increased opportunities for video-recording and audio-recording of depositions under revised Rule 30(b). Under this rule a party may offer deposition testimony in any of the forms authorized under Rule 30(b) but, if offering it in a nonstenographic form, must provide the court with a transcript of the portions so offered. On request of any party in a jury trial, deposition testimony offered other than for impeachment purposes is to be presented in a nonstenographic form if available, unless the court directs otherwise. Note that under Rule 26(a)(3)(B) a party expecting to use nonstenographic deposition testimony as substantive evidence is required to provide other parties with a transcript in advance of trial.

2007 Amendment

The language of Rule 32 has been amended as part of the general restyling of the Civil Rules to make them more easily understood and to make style and terminology consistent throughout the rules. These changes are intended to be stylistic only.

Former Rule 32(a) applied "[a]t the trial or upon the hearing of a motion or an interlocutory proceeding." The amended rule describes the same events as "a hearing or trial."

The final paragraph of former Rule 32(a) allowed use in a later action of a deposition "lawfully taken and duly filed in the former action." Because of the 2000 amendment of Rule 5(d), many depositions are not filed. Amended Rule 32(a)(8) reflects this change by excluding use of an unfiled deposition only if filing was required in the former action.

HISTORICAL NOTES

References in Text

The Federal Rules of Evidence, referred to in subd. (a)(1), (2) and (8), are set out in this title.

Effective Date of Amendment Proposed November 20, 1972

Amendment of this rule embraced by the order entered by the Supreme Court of the United States on November 20, 1972, effective on the 180th day beginning after January 2, 1975, see section 3 of Pub.L. 93–595, Jan. 2, 1975, 88 Stat. 1959, set out as a note under section 2071 of Title 28.

CROSS REFERENCES

Presentence reports for guilty defendant of offense punishable by death notwithstanding this section, see 18 USCA § 3593.

Rejection of deposition by court after refusal to sign, see Fed.Rules Civ.Proc. Rule 30, 28 USCA.

Rule 33. Interrogatories to Parties

(a) In General.

(1) ***Number.*** Unless otherwise stipulated or ordered by the court, a party may serve on any other party no more than 25 written interrogatories, including all discrete subparts. Leave to serve additional interrogatories may be granted to the extent consistent with Rule 26(b)(2).

(2) ***Scope.*** An interrogatory may relate to any matter that may be inquired into under Rule 26(b). An interrogatory is not objectionable merely because it asks for an opinion or contention that relates to fact or the application of law to fact, but the court may order that the interrogatory need not be answered until designated discovery is complete, or until a pretrial conference or some other time.

(b) Answers and Objections.

(1) ***Responding Party.*** **The interrogatories must be answered:**

(A) by the party to whom they are directed; or

(B) if that party is a public or private corporation, a partnership, an association, or a governmental agency, by any officer or agent, who must furnish the information available to the party.

(2) ***Time to Respond.*** The responding party must serve its answers and any objections within 30 days after being served with the interrogatories. A shorter or longer time may be stipulated to under Rule 29 or be ordered by the court.

(3) ***Answering Each Interrogatory.*** Each interrogatory must, to the extent it is not objected to, be answered separately and fully in writing under oath.

(4) ***Objections.*** The grounds for objecting to an interrogatory must be stated with specificity. Any ground not stated in a timely objection is waived unless the court, for good cause, excuses the failure.

(5) ***Signature.*** The person who makes the answers must sign them, and the attorney who objects must sign any objections.

(c) Use. An answer to an interrogatory may be used to the extent allowed by the Federal Rules of Evidence.

(d) Option to Produce Business Records. If the answer to an interrogatory may be determined by examining, auditing, compiling, abstracting, or summarizing a party's business records (including electronically stored information), and if the burden of deriving or ascertaining the answer will be substantially the same for either party, the responding party may answer by:

(1) specifying the records that must be reviewed, in sufficient detail to enable the interrogating party to locate and identify them as readily as the responding party could; and

(2) giving the interrogating party a reasonable opportunity to examine and audit the records and to make copies, compilations, abstracts, or summaries.

(Amended December 27, 1946, effective March 19, 1948; March 30, 1970, effective July 1, 1970; April 29, 1980, effective August 1, 1980; April 22, 1993, effective December 1, 1993; April 12, 2006, effective December 1, 2006; April 30, 2007, effective December 1, 2007.)

ADVISORY COMMITTEE NOTES

1937 Adoption

This rule restates the substance of [former] Equity Rule 58 (Discovery—Interrogatories—Inspection and Production of Documents—Admission of Execution or Genuineness), with modifications to conform to these rules.

1946 Amendment

Note. The added second sentence in the first paragraph of Rule 33 conforms with a similar change in Rule 26(a) and will avoid litigation as to when the interrogatories may be served. Original Rule 33 does not state the times at which parties may serve written interrogatories upon each other. It has been the accepted view, however, that the times were the same in Rule 33 as those stated in Rule 26(a). *United States v. American Solvents & Chemical Corp. of California*, D.Del.1939, 30 F.Supp. 107; *Sheldon v. Great Lakes Transit Corp.*, W.D.N.Y.1942, 2 F.R.D. 272, 5 Fed.Rules Serv. 33.11, Case 3; *Musher Foundation, Inc., v. Alba Trading Co.*, S.D.N.Y.1941, 42 F.Supp. 281; 2 *Moore's Federal Practice*, 1938, 2621. The time within which leave of court must be secured by a plaintiff has been fixed at 10 days, in view of the fact that a defendant has 10 days within which to make objections in any case, which should give him ample time to engage counsel and prepare.

Further in the first paragraph of Rule 33, the word "service" is substituted for "delivery" in conformance with the use of the word "serve" elsewhere in the rule and generally throughout the rules. See also Note to Rule 13(a) herein. The portion of the rule dealing with practice on objections has been revised so as to afford a clearer statement of the procedure. The addition of the words "to interrogatories to which objection is made" insures that only the answers to the objectionable interrogatories may be deferred, and that the answers to interrogatories not objectionable shall be forthcoming within the time prescribed in the rule. Under the original wording, answers to all interrogatories may be withheld until objections, sometimes to but a few interrogatories, are determined. The amendment expedites the procedure of the rule and serves to eliminate the strike value of objections to minor interrogatories. The elimination of the last sentence of the original rule is in line with the policy stated subsequently in this note.

The added second paragraph in Rule 33 contributes clarity and specificity as to the use and scope of interrogatories to the parties. The field of inquiry will be as broad as the scope of examination under Rule 26(b). There is no reason why interrogatories should be more limited than depositions, particularly when the former represent an inexpensive means of securing useful information. See *Hoffman v. Wilson Line, Inc.*, E.D.Pa.1946, 9 Fed.Rules Serv. 33.514, Case 2; *Brewster v. Technicolor, Inc.*, N.Y.1941, 2 F.R.D. 186, 5 Fed.Rules Serv. 33.319, Case 3; *Kingsway Press, Inc. v. Farrell Publishing Corp.*, S.D.N.Y.1939, 30 F.Supp. 775. Under present Rule 33 some courts have unnecessarily restricted the breadth of inquiry on various grounds. See *Auer v. Hershey Creamery Co.*, D.N.J.1939, 2 Fed.Rules Serv. 33.31, Case 2, 1 F.R.D. 14; *Tudor v. Leslie*, D.Mass.1940, 1 F.R.D. 448, 4 Fed.Rules Serv. 33.324, Case 1. Other courts have read into the rule the requirement that interrogation should be directed only towards "important facts", and have tended to fix a more or less arbitrary limit as to the number of interrogatories which could be asked in any case. See *Knox v. Alter*, W.D.Pa.1942, 2 F.R.D. 337, 6 Fed.Rules Serv. 33.352, Case 1; *Byers Theaters, Inc. v. Murphy*, W.D.Va.1940, 3 Fed.Rules Serv. 33.31, Case 3, 1 F.R.D. 286; *Coca-Cola Co. v. Dixi-Cola Laboratories, Inc.*, D.Md.1939, 30 F.Supp. 275. See also comment on these restrictions in Holtzoff, *Instruments of Discovery under Federal Rules of Civil Procedure*, 1942, 41 Mich.L.Rev. 205, 216–217. Under amended Rule 33, the party interrogated is given the right to invoke such protective orders under Rule 30(b) as are appropriate to the situation. At the same time, it is provided that the number of or number of sets of interrogatories to be served may not be limited arbitrarily or as a general policy to any particular number, but that a limit may be fixed only as justice requires to avoid annoyance, expense, embarrassment or oppression in individual cases. The party interrogated, therefore, must show the necessity for limitation on that basis. It will be noted that in accord with this change the last sentence of the present rule, restricting the sets of interrogatories to be served, has been stricken. In *J. Schoeneman, Inc. v. Brauer*, W.D.Mo.1940, 1 F.R.D. 292, 3 Fed.Rules Serv. 33.31, Case 2, the court said: "Rule 33 * * * has been interpreted * * * as being just as broad in its implications as in the case of depositions * * * It makes no difference therefore, how many interrogatories are propounded. If the inquiries are pertinent the opposing party cannot complain." To the same effect, see *Canuso v. City of Niagara Falls*, W.D.N.Y.1945, 8 Fed.Rules Serv. 33.352, Case 1; *Hoffman v. Wilson Line, Inc.*, supra.

By virtue of express language in the added second paragraph of Rule 33, as amended, any uncertainty as to the use of the answers to interrogatories is removed. The omission of a provision on this score in the original rule has caused some difficulty. See, e.g., *Bailey v. New England Mutual Life Ins. Co.*, S.D.Cal.1940, 1 F.R.D. 494, 4 Fed.Rules Serv. 33.46, Case 1.

The second sentence of the second paragraph in Rule 33, as amended, concerns the situation where a party wishes to serve interrogatories on a party after having taken his deposition, or vice versa. It has been held that an oral examination of a party, after the submission to him and answer of interrogatories, would be permitted. *Howard v. State Marine Corp.*, S.D.N.Y.1940, 4 Fed.Rules Serv. 33.62, Case 1, 1 F.R.D. 499; *Stevens v. Minder Construction Co.*, S.D.N.Y.1943, 3 F.R.D. 498, 7 Fed.Rules Serv. 30b.31, Case 2. But objections have been sustained to interrogatories served after the oral deposition of a party had been taken. *McNally v. Simons*, S.D.N.Y.1940, 3 Fed.Rules Serv. 33.61, Case 1, 1 F.R.D. 254; *Currier v. Currier*, S.D.N.Y.1942, 3 F.R.D. 21, 6 Fed.Rules Serv. 33.61, Case 1. Rule 33, as amended, permits either interrogatories after a deposition or a deposition after interrogatories. It may be quite desirable or necessary to elicit additional information by the inexpensive method of interrogatories where a deposition has already been taken. The party to be interrogated, however, may seek a protective order from the court under Rule 30(b) where the additional deposition or interrogation works a hardship or injustice on the party from whom it is sought.

1970 Amendment

Subdivision (a). The mechanics of the operation of Rule 33 are substantially revised by the proposed amendment, with a view to reducing court intervention. There is general agreement that interrogatories spawn a greater percentage of objections and motions than any other discovery device. The Columbia Survey shows that, although half of the litigants resorted to depositions and about one-third used interrogatories, about 65 percent of the objections were made with respect to interrogatories and 26 percent related to depositions. See also Speck, *The Use of Discovery in United States District Courts*, 60 Yale L.J. 1132, 1144, 1151 (1951); Note, 36 Minn.L.Rev. 364, 379 (1952).

The procedures now provided in Rule 33 seem calculated to encourage objections and court motions. The time periods now allowed for responding to interrogatories—15 days for answers and 10 days for objections—are too short. The Columbia Survey shows that tardy response to interrogatories is common, virtually expected. The same was reported in Speck, *supra*, 60 Yale L.J. 1132, 1144. The time pressures tend to encourage objections as a means of gaining time to answer.

The time for objections is even shorter than for answers, and the party runs the risk that if he fails to object in time he may have waived his objections. *E.g., Cleminshaw v. Beech Aircraft Corp.*, 21 F.R.D. 300 (D.Del.1957); See 4 *Moore's Federal Practice*, ¶33.27 (2d ed. 1966); 2A Barron & Holtzoff, *Federal Practice and Procedure* 372–373 (Wright ed. 1961). It often seems easier to object than to seek an extension of time. Unlike Rules 30(d) and 37(a), Rule 33 imposes no sanction of expenses on a party whose objections are clearly unjustified.

Rule 33 assures that the objections will lead directly to court, through its requirement that they be served with a notice of hearing. Although this procedure does not preclude an out-of-court resolution of the dispute, the procedure tends to discourage informal negotiations. If answers are served and they are thought inadequate, the interrogating party may move under Rule 37(a) for an order compelling adequate answers. There is no assurance that the hearing on objections and that on inadequate answers will be heard together.

The amendment improves the procedure of Rule 33 in the following respects:

(1) The time allowed for response is increased to 30 days and this time period applies to both answers and objections, but a defendant need not respond in less than 45 days after service of the summons and complaint upon him. As is true under existing law, the responding party who believes that some parts or all of the interrogatories are objectionable may choose to seek a protective order under new Rule 26(c) or may serve objections under this rule. Unless he applies for a protective order, he is required to serve answers or objections in response to the interrogatories, subject to the sanctions provided in Rule 37(d). Answers and objections are served together, so that a response to each interrogatory is encouraged, and any failure to respond is easily noted.

(2) In view of the enlarged time permitted for response, it is no longer necessary to require leave of court for service of interrogatories. The purpose of this requirement—that defendant have time to obtain counsel before a response must be made—is adequately fulfilled by the requirement that interrogatories be served upon a party with or after service of the summons and complaint upon him.

Some would urge that the plaintiff nevertheless not be permitted to serve interrogatories with the complaint. They fear that a routine practice might be invited, whereby form interrogatories would accompany most complaints. More fundamentally, they feel that, since very general complaints are permitted in present-day pleading, it is fair that the defendant have a right to take the lead in serving interrogatories. (These views apply also to Rule 36.) The amendment of Rule 33 rejects these views, in favor of allowing both parties to go forward with discovery, each free to obtain the information he needs respecting the case.

(3) If objections are made, the burden is on the interrogating party to move under Rule 37(a) for a court order compelling answers, in the course of which the court will pass on the objections. The change in the burden of going forward does not alter the existing obligation of an objecting party to justify his objections. *E.g., Pressley v. Bochlke*, 33 F.R.D. 316 (W.D.N.C. 1963). If the discovering party asserts that an answer is incomplete or evasive, again he may look to Rule 37(a) for relief, and he should add this assertion to his motion to overrule objections. There is no requirement that the parties consult informally concerning their differences, but the new procedure should encourage consultation, and the court may by local rule require it.

The proposed changes are similar in approach to those adopted by California in 1961. See Calif.Code Civ.Proc. § 2030(a). The experience of the Los Angeles Superior Court is informally reported as showing that the California amendment resulted in a significant reduction in court motions concerning interrogatories. Rhode Island takes a similar approach. See R. 33, *R.I.R. Civ.Proc. Official Draft*, p. 74 (Boston Law Book Co.).

A change is made in subdivision (a) which is not related to the sequence of procedures. The restriction to "adverse" parties is eliminated. The courts have generally construed this restriction as precluding interrogatories unless an issue between the parties is disclosed by the pleadings—even though the parties may have conflicting interests. E.g., *Mozeika v. Kaufman Construction Co.*, 25 F.R.D. 233 (E.D.Pa.1960) (plaintiff and third-party defendant); *Biddle v. Hutchinson*, 24 F.R.D. 256 (M.D.Pa.1959) (codefendants). The resulting distinctions have often been highly technical. In *Schlagenhauf v. Holder*, 379 U.S. 104 (1964), the Supreme Court rejected a contention that examination under Rule 35 could be had only against an "opposing" party, as not in keeping "with the aims of a liberal, nontechnical application of the Federal Rules." 379 U.S. at 116. Eliminating the requirement of "adverse" parties from Rule 33 brings it into line with all other discovery rules.

A second change in subdivision (a) is the addition of the term "governmental agency" to the listing of organizations whose answers are to be made by any officer or agent of the organization. This does not involve any change in existing law. Compare the similar listing in Rule 30(b)(6).

The duty of a party to supplement his answers to interrogatories is governed by a new provision in Rule 26(e).

Subdivision (b). There are numerous and conflicting decisions on the question whether and to what extent interrogatories are limited to matters "of fact," or may elicit opinions, contentions, and legal conclusions. Compare, e.g., *Payer, Hewitt & Co. v. Bellanca Corp.*, 26 F.R.D. 219 (D.Del.1960) (opinions bad); *Zinsky v. New York Central R.R.*, 36 F.R.D. 680 (N.D.Ohio 1964) (factual opinion or contention good, but legal theory bad); *United States v. Carter Products, Inc.*, 28 F.R.D. 373 (S.D.N.Y.1961) (factual contentions and legal theories bad) with *Taylor v. Sound Steamship Lines, Inc.*, 100 F.Supp. 388 (D.Conn.1951) (opinions good); *Bynum v. United States*, 36 F.R.D. 14 (E.D.La.1964) (contentions as to facts constituting negligence good). For lists of the many conflicting authorities, see 4 *Moore's Federal Practice* ¶33.17 (2d ed. 1966); 2A Barron & Holtzoff, *Federal Practice and Procedure* § 768 (Wright ed. 1961).

Rule 33 is amended to provide that an interrogatory is not objectionable merely because it calls for an opinion or contention that relates to fact or the application of law to fact. Efforts to draw sharp lines between facts and opinions have invariably been unsuccessful, and the clear trend of the cases is to permit "factual" opinions. As to requests for opinions or contentions that call for the application of law to fact, they can be most useful in narrowing and sharpening the issues, which is a major purpose of discovery. See *Diversified Products Corp. v. Sports Center Co.*, 42 F.R.D. 3 (D.Md. 1967); Moore, *supra*; Field & McKusick, *Maine Civil Practice* § 26.18 (1959). On the other hand, under the new language interrogatories may not extend to issues of "pure law," *i.e.*, legal issues unrelated to the facts of the case. *Cf. United States v. Maryland & Va. Milk Producers Assn., Inc.*, 22 F.R.D. 300 (D.D.C.1958).

Since interrogatories involving mixed questions of law and fact may create disputes between the parties which are best resolved after much or all of the other discovery has been completed, the court is expressly authorized to defer an answer. Likewise, the court may delay determination until pretrial conference, if it believes that the dispute is best resolved in the presence of the judge.

The principal question raised with respect to the cases permitting such interrogatories is whether they reintroduce undesirable aspects of the prior pleading practice, whereby parties were chained to misconceived contentions or theories, and ultimate determination on the merits was frustrated. See James, *The Revival of Bills of Particulars under the Federal Rules*, 71 Harv.L.Rev. 1473 (1958). But there are few if any instances in the recorded cases demonstrating that such frustration has occurred. The general rule governing the use of answers to interrogatories is that under ordinary circumstances they do not limit proof. See, *e.g., McElroy v.*

United Air Lines, Inc., 21 F.R.D. 100 (W.D.Mo.1967); *Pressley v. Boehlke*, 33 F.R.D. 316, 317 (W.D.N.C.1963). Although in exceptional circumstances reliance on an answer may cause such prejudice that the court will hold the answering party bound to his answer, *e.g., Zielinski v. Philadelphia Piers, Inc.*, 139 F.Supp. 408 (E.D.Pa.1956), the interrogating party will ordinarily not be entitled to rely on the unchanging character of the answers he receives and cannot base prejudice on such reliance. The rule does not affect the power of a court to permit withdrawal or amendment of answers to interrogatories.

The use of answers to interrogatories at trial is made subject to the rules of evidence. The provisions governing use of depositions, to which Rule 33 presently refers, are not entirely apposite to answers to interrogatories, since deposition practice contemplates that all parties will ordinarily participate through cross-examination. See 4 *Moore's Federal Practice* ¶33.29[1] (2d ed. 1966).

Certain provisions are deleted from subdivision (b) because they are fully covered by new Rule 26(c) providing for protective orders and Rules 26(a) and 26(d). The language of the subdivision is thus simplified without any change of substance.

Subdivision (c). This is a new subdivision, adapted from Calif.Code Civ.Proc. § 2030(c), relating especially to interrogatories which require a party to engage in burdensome or expensive research into his own business records in order to give an answer. The subdivision gives the party an option to make the records available and place the burden of research of the party who seeks the information. "This provision, without undermining the liberal scope of interrogatory discovery, places the burden of discovery upon its potential benefittee," Louisell, *Modern California Discovery*, 124–125 (1963), and alleviates a problem which in the past has troubled Federal courts. See Speck, *The Use of Discovery in United States District Courts*, 60 Yale L.J. 1132, 1142–1144 (1951). The interrogating party is protected against abusive use of this provision through the requirement that the burden of ascertaining the answer be substantially the same for both sides. A respondent may not impose on an interrogating party a mass of records as to which research is feasible only for one familiar with the records. At the same time, the respondent unable to invoke this subdivision does not on that account lose the protection available to him under new Rule 26(c) against oppressive or unduly burdensome or expensive interrogatories. And even when the respondent successfully invokes the subdivision, the court is not deprived of its usual power, in appropriate cases, to require that the interrogating party reimburse the respondent for the expense of assembling his records and making them intelligible.

1980 Amendment

Subdivision (c). The Committee is advised that parties upon whom interrogatories are served have occasionally responded by directing the interrogating party to a mass of business records or by offering to make all of their records available, justifying the response by the option provided by this subdivision. Such practices are an abuse of the option. A party who is permitted by the terms of this subdivision to offer records for inspection in lieu of answering an interrogatory should offer them in a manner than permits the same direct and economical access that is available to the party. If the information sought exists in the form of compilations, abstracts or summaries then available to the responding party, those should be made available to the interrogating party. The final sentence is added to make it clear that a responding party has the duty to specify, by category and location, the records from which answers to interrogatories can be derived.

1993 Amendments

Purpose of Revision. The purpose of this revision is to reduce the frequency and increase the efficiency of interrogatory practice. The revision is based on experience with local rules. For ease of reference, subdivision (a) is divided into two subdivisions and the remaining subdivisions renumbered.

Subdivision (a). Revision of this subdivision limits interrogatory practice. Because Rule 26(a)(1)–(3) requires disclosure of much of the information previously obtained by this form of discovery, there should be less occasion to use it. Experience in over half of the district courts has confirmed that limitations on the number of interrogatories are useful and manageable. Moreover, because the device can be costly and may be used as a means of harassment, it is desirable to subject its use to the control of the court consistent with the principles stated in Rule 26(b)(2), particularly in multi-party cases where it has not been unusual for the same interrogatory to be propounded to a party by more than one of its adversaries.

Each party is allowed to serve 25 interrogatories upon any other party, but must secure leave of court (or a stipulation from the opposing party) to serve a larger number. Parties cannot evade this presumptive limitation through the device of joining as "subparts" questions that seek information about discrete separate subjects. However, a question asking about communications of a particular type should be treated as a single interrogatory even though it requests that the time, place, persons present, and contents be stated separately for each such communication.

As with the number of depositions authorized by Rule 30, leave to serve additional interrogatories is to be allowed when consistent with Rule 26(b)(2). The aim is not to prevent needed discovery, but to provide judicial scrutiny before parties make potentially excessive use of this discovery device. In many cases it will be appropriate for the court to permit a larger number of interrogatories in the scheduling order entered under Rule 16(b).

Unless leave of court is obtained, interrogatories may not be served prior to the meeting of the parties under Rule 26(f).

When a case with outstanding interrogatories exceeding the number permitted by this rule is removed to federal court, the interrogating party must seek leave allowing the additional interrogatories, specify which twenty-five are to be answered, or resubmit interrogatories that comply with the rule. Moreover, under Rule 26(d), the time for response would be measured from the date of the parties' meeting under Rule 26(f). See Rule 81(c), providing that these rules govern procedures after removal.

Subdivision (b). A separate subdivision is made of the former second paragraph of subdivision (a). Language is added to paragraph (1) of this subdivision to emphasize the duty of the responding party to provide full answers to the extent not objectionable. If, for example, an interrogatory seeking information about numerous facilities or products is deemed objectionable, but an interrogatory seeking information about a lesser number of facilities or products would not have been objectionable, the interrogatory should be answered with respect to the latter even though an objection is raised as to the balance of the facilities or products. Similarly, the fact that additional time may be needed to respond to some questions (or to some aspects of questions) should not justify a delay in responding to those questions (or other aspects of questions) that can be answered within the prescribed time.

Paragraph (4) is added to make clear that objections must be specifically justified, and that unstated or untimely grounds for objection ordinarily are waived. Note also the provisions of revised Rule 26(b)(5), which require a responding party to indicate when it is withholding information under a claim of privilege or as trial preparation materials.

These provisions should be read in light of Rule 26(g), authorizing the court to impose sanctions on a party and attorney making an unfounded objection to an interrogatory.

Subdivisions (c) and (d). The provisions of former subdivisions (b) and (c) are renumbered.

2006 Amendment

Rule 33(d) is amended to parallel Rule 34(a) by recognizing the importance of electronically stored information. The term "electronically stored information" has the same broad meaning in Rule 33(d) as in Rule 34(a). Much business information is stored only in electronic form; the Rule 33(d) option should be available with respect to such records as well.

Special difficulties may arise in using electronically stored information, either due to its form or because it is dependent on a particular computer system. Rule 33(d) allows a responding party to substitute access to documents or electronically stored information for an answer only if the burden of deriving the answer will be substantially the same for either party. Rule 33(d) states that a party electing to respond to an interrogatory by providing electronically stored information must ensure that the interrogating party can locate and identify it "as readily as can the party served," and that the responding party must give the interrogating party a "reasonable opportunity to examine, audit, or inspect" the information. Depending on the circumstances, satisfying these provisions with regard to electronically stored information may require the responding party to provide some combination of technical support, information on application software, or other assistance. The key question is whether such support enables the interrogating party to derive or ascertain the answer from the electronically stored information as readily as the responding party. A party that wishes to invoke Rule 33(d) by specifying electronically stored information may be required to provide direct access to its electronic information system, but only if that is necessary to afford the requesting party an adequate opportunity to derive or ascertain the answer to the interrogatory. In that situation, the responding party's need to protect sensitive interests of confidentiality or privacy may mean that it must derive or ascertain and provide the answer itself rather than invoke Rule 33(d).

2007 Amendment

The language of Rule 33 has been amended as part of the general restyling of the Civil Rules to make them more easily understood and to make style and terminology consistent throughout the rules. These changes are intended to be stylistic only.

The final sentence of former Rule 33(a) was a redundant cross-reference to the discovery moratorium provisions of Rule 26(d). Rule 26(d) is now familiar, obviating any need to carry forward the redundant cross-reference.

Former Rule 33(b)(5) was a redundant reminder of Rule 37(a) procedure and is omitted as no longer useful.

Former Rule 33(c) stated that an interrogatory "is not necessarily objectionable merely because an answer * * * involves an opinion or contention * * *." "[I]s not necessarily" seemed to imply that the interrogatory might be objectionable merely for this reason. This implication has been ignored in practice. Opinion and contention interrogatories are used routinely. Amended Rule 33(a)(2) embodies the current meaning of Rule 33 by omitting "necessarily."

Rule 34. Producing Documents, Electronically Stored Information, and Tangible Things, or Entering onto Land, for Inspection and Other Purposes

(a) In General. A party may serve on any other party a request within the scope of Rule 26(b):

(1) to produce and permit the requesting party or its representative to inspect, copy, test, or sample the following items in the responding party's possession, custody, or control:

(A) any designated documents or electronically stored information—including writings, drawings, graphs, charts, photographs, sound recordings, images, and other data or data compilations—stored in any medium from which information can be obtained either directly or, if necessary, after translation by the responding party into a reasonably usable form; or

(B) any designated tangible things; or

(2) to permit entry onto designated land or other property possessed or controlled by the responding party, so that the requesting party may inspect, measure, survey, photograph, test, or sample the property or any designated object or operation on it.

(b) Procedure.

(1) ***Contents of the Request.*** The request:

(A) must describe with reasonable particularity each item or category of items to be inspected;

(B) must specify a reasonable time, place, and manner for the inspection and for performing the related acts; and

(C) may specify the form or forms in which electronically stored information is to be produced.

(2) ***Responses and Objections.***

(A) *Time to Respond.* The party to whom the request is directed must respond in writing within 30 days after being served. A shorter or longer time may be stipulated to under Rule 29 or be ordered by the court.

(B) *Responding to Each Item.* For each item or category, the response must either state that inspection and related activities will be permitted as requested or state an objection to the request, including the reasons.

(C) *Objections.* An objection to part of a request must specify the part and permit inspection of the rest.

(D) *Responding to a Request for Production of Electronically Stored Information.* The response may state an objection to a requested form for producing electronically stored information. If the responding party objects to a requested form—or if no form was specified in the request—the party must state the form or forms it intends to use.

(E) *Producing the Documents or Electronically Stored Information.* Unless otherwise stipulated or ordered by the court, these procedures apply to producing documents or electronically stored information:

(i) A party must produce documents as they are kept in the usual course of business or must organize and label them to correspond to the categories in the request;

(ii) If a request does not specify a form for producing electronically stored information, a party must produce it in a form or forms in which it is ordinarily maintained or in a reasonably usable form or forms; and

(iii) A party need not produce the same electronically stored information in more than one form.

(c) **Nonparties.** As provided in Rule 45, a nonparty may be compelled to produce documents and tangible things or to permit an inspection.

(Amended December 27, 1946, effective March 19, 1948; March 30, 1970, effective July 1, 1970; April 29, 1980, effective August 1, 1980; March 2, 1987, effective August 1, 1987; April 30, 1991, effective December 1, 1991; April 22, 1993, effective December 1, 1993; April 12, 2006, effective December 1, 2006; April 30, 2007, effective December 1, 2007.)

ADVISORY COMMITTEE NOTES

1937 Adoption

In England orders are made for the inspection of documents, *English Rules Under the Judicature Act (The Annual Practice,* 1937) O. 31, r.r. 14, et seq., or for the inspection of tangible property or for entry upon land, O. 50, r. 3. Michigan provides for inspection of damaged property when such damage is the ground of the action. Mich.Court Rules Ann. (Searl, 1933) Rule 41, § 2.

Practically all states have statutes authorizing the court to order parties in possession or control of documents to permit other parties to inspect and copy them before trial. See Ragland, *Discovery Before Trial* (1932) Appendix, p. 267, setting out the statutes.

Compare [former] Equity Rule 58 (Discovery—Interrogatories—Inspection and Production of Documents—Admission of Execution or Genuineness) (fifth paragraph).

1946 Amendment

Note. The changes in clauses (1) and (2) correlate the scope of inquiry permitted under Rule 34 with that provided in Rule 26(b), and thus remove any ambiguity created by the former differences in language. As stated in *Olson Transportation Co. v. Socony-Vacuum Oil Co.,* E.D.Wis.1944, 8 Fed.Rules Serv. 34.41, Case 2, "* * * Rule 34 is a direct and simple method of discovery." At the same time the addition of the words following the term "parties" makes certain that the person in whose custody, possession, or control the evidence reposes may have the benefit of the applicable protective orders stated in Rule 30(b). This change should be considered in the light of the proposed expansion of Rule 30(b).

An objection has been made that the word "designated" in Rule 34 has been construed with undue strictness in some district court cases so as to require great and impracticable specificity in the description of documents, papers, books, etc., sought to be inspected. The Committee, however, believes that no amendment is needed, and that the proper meaning of "designated" as requiring specificity has already been delineated by the Supreme Court. *See Brown v. United States,* 1928, 48 S.Ct. 288, 276 U.S. 134, 143, 72 L.Ed. 500 ("The subpoena * * * specifies * * * with reasonable particularity the subjects to which the documents called for related."); *Consolidated Rendering Co. v. Vermont,* 1908, 28 S.Ct. 178, 207 U.S. 541, 543–544, 52 L.Ed. 327 ("We see no reason why all such books, papers and correspondence which related to the subject of inquiry, and were described with reasonable detail, should not be called for and the company directed to produce them. Otherwise, the State would be compelled to designate each particular paper which it desired, which presupposes an accurate knowledge of such papers, which the tribunal desiring the papers would probably rarely, if ever, have.").

1970 Amendment

Rule 34 is revised to accomplish the following major changes in the existing rule: (1) to eliminate the requirement of good cause; (2) to have the rule operate extrajudicially; (3) to include testing and sampling as well as inspecting or photographing tangible things; and (4) to make clear that the rule does not preclude an independent action for analogous discovery against persons not parties.

Subdivision (a). Good cause is eliminated because it has furnished an uncertain and erratic protection to the parties from whom production is sought and is now rendered unnecessary by virtue of the more specific provisions added to Rule 26(b) relating to materials assembled in preparation for trial and to experts retained or consulted by parties.

The good cause requirement was originally inserted in Rule 34 as a general protective provision in the absence of experience with the specific problems that would arise thereunder. As the note to Rule 26(b)(3) on trial preparation materials makes clear, good cause has been applied differently to varying classes of documents, though not without confusion. It has often been said in court opinions that good cause requires a consideration of need for the materials and of alternative means of obtaining them, i.e., something more than relevance and lack of privilege. But the overwhelming proportion of the cases in which the formula of good cause has been applied to require a special showing are those involving trial preparation. In practice, the courts have not treated documents as having a special immunity to discovery simply because of their being documents. Protection may be afforded to claims of privacy or secrecy or of undue burden or expense under what is now Rule 26(c) (previously Rule 30(b)). To be sure, an appraisal of "undue" burden inevitably entails consideration of the needs of the party seeking discovery. With special provisions added to govern trial preparation materials and experts, there is no longer any occasion to retain the requirement of good cause.

The revision of Rule 34 to have it operate extrajudicially, rather than by court order, is to a large extent a reflection of existing law office practice. The Columbia Survey shows that of the litigants seeking inspection of documents or things, only about 25 percent filed motions for court orders. This minor fraction nevertheless accounted for a significant number of motions. About half of these motions were uncontested and in almost all instances the party seeking production ultimately prevailed. Although an extrajudicial procedure will not drastically alter existing practice under Rule 34—it will conform to it in most cases—it has the potential of saving court time in a substantial though proportionately small number of cases tried annually.

The inclusion of testing and sampling of tangible things and objects or operations on land reflects a need frequently encountered by parties in preparation for trial. If the operation of a particular machine is the basis of a claim for negligent injury, it will often be necessary to test its operating parts or to sample and test the products it is producing. *Cf.* Mich.Gen.Ct.R. 310.1(1) (1963) (testing authorized).

The inclusive description of "documents" is revised to accord with changing technology. It makes clear that Rule 34 applies to electronics data compilations from which information can be obtained only with the use of detection devices, and that when the data can as a practical matter be made usable by the discovering party only through respondent's devices, respondent may be required to use his devices to translate the data into usable form. In many instances, this means that respondent will have to supply a print-out of computer data. The burden thus placed on respondent will vary from case to case, and the courts have ample power under Rule 26(c) to protect respondent against undue burden or expense, either by restricting discovery or requiring that the discovering party pay costs. Similarly, if the discovering party needs to check the electronic source itself, the court may protect respondent with respect to preservation of his records, confidentiality of nondiscoverable matters, and costs.

Subdivision (b). The procedure provided in Rule 34 is essentially the same as that in Rule 33, as amended, and the discussion in the note appended to that rule is relevant to Rule 34 as well. Problems peculiar to Rule 34 relate to the specific arrangements that must be worked out for inspection and related acts of copying, photographing, testing, or sampling. The rule provides that a request for inspection shall set forth the items to be inspected either by item or category, describing each with reasonable particularity, and shall specify a reasonable time, place, and manner of making the inspection.

Subdivision (c). Rule 34 as revised continues to apply only to parties. Comments from the bar make clear that in the preparation of cases for trial it is occasionally necessary to enter land or inspect large tangible things in the possession of a person not a party, and that some courts have dismissed independent actions in the nature of bills in equity for such discovery on the ground that Rule 34 is preemptive. While an ideal solution to this problem is to provide for discovery against persons not parties in Rule 34, both the jurisdictional and procedural problems are very complex. For the present, this subdivision makes clear that Rule 34 does not preclude independent actions for discovery against persons not parties.

1980 Amendment

Subdivision (b). The Committee is advised that, "It is apparently not rare for parties deliberately to mix critical documents with others in the hope of obscuring significance." *Report of the Special Committee for the Study of Discovery Abuse, Section of Litigation of the American Bar Association* (1977) 22. The sentence added by this subdivision follows the recommendation of the *Report.*

1987 Amendment

The amendment is technical. No substantive change is intended.

1991 Amendment

This amendment reflects the change effected by revision of Rule 45 to provide for subpoenas to compel non-parties to produce documents and things and to submit to inspections of premises. The deletion of the text of the former paragraph is not intended to preclude an independent action for production of documents or things or for permission to enter upon land, but such actions may no longer be necessary in light of this revision.

1993 Amendments

The rule is revised to reflect the change made by Rule 26(d), preventing a party from seeking formal discovery prior to the meeting of the parties required by Rule 26(f). Also, like a change made in Rule 33, the rule is modified to make clear that, if a request for production is objectionable only in part, production should be afforded with respect to the unobjectionable portions.

When a case with outstanding requests for production is removed to federal court, the time for response would be measured from the date of the parties' meeting. See Rule 81(c), providing that these rules govern procedures after removal.

2006 Amendment

Subdivision (a). As originally adopted, Rule 34 focused on discovery of "documents" and "things." In 1970, Rule 34(a) was amended to include discovery of data compilations, anticipating that the use of computerized information would increase. Since then, the growth in electronically stored information and in the variety of systems for creating and storing such information has been dramatic. Lawyers and judges interpreted the term "documents" to include electronically stored information because it was obviously improper to allow a party to evade discovery obligations on the basis that the label had not kept pace with changes in information technology. But it has become increasingly difficult to say that all forms of electronically stored information, many dynamic in nature, fit within the traditional concept of a "document." Electronically stored information may exist in dynamic databases and other forms far different from fixed expression on paper. Rule 34(a) is amended to confirm that discovery of electronically stored information stands on equal footing with discovery of paper documents. The change clarifies that Rule 34 applies to information that is fixed in a tangible form and to information that is stored in a medium from which it can be retrieved and examined. At the same time, a Rule 34 request for production of "documents" should be understood to encompass, and the response should include, electronically stored information unless discovery in the action has clearly distinguished between electronically stored information and "documents."

Discoverable information often exists in both paper and electronic form, and the same or similar information might exist in both. The items listed in Rule 34(a) show different ways in which information may be recorded or stored. Images, for example, might be hard-copy documents or electronically stored information. The wide variety of computer systems currently in use, and the rapidity of technological change, counsel against a limiting or precise definition of electronically stored information. Rule 34(a)(1) is expansive and includes any type of information that is stored electronically. A common example often sought in discovery is electronic communications, such as e-mail. The rule covers — either as documents or as electronically stored information — information "stored in any medium," to encompass future developments in computer technology. Rule 34(a)(1) is intended to be broad enough to cover all current types of computer-based information, and flexible enough to encompass future changes and developments.

References elsewhere in the rules to "electronically stored information" should be understood to invoke this expansive approach. A companion change is made to Rule 33(d), making it explicit that parties choosing to respond to an interrogatory by permitting access to responsive records may do so by providing access to electronically stored information. More generally, the term used in Rule 34(a)(1) appears in a number of other amendments, such as those to Rules 26(a)(1), 26(b)(2), 26(b)(5)(B), 26(f), 34(b), 37(f), and 45. In each of these rules, electronically stored information has the same broad meaning it has under Rule 34(a)(1). References to "documents" appear in discovery rules that are not amended, including Rules 30(f), 36(a), and 37(c)(2). These references should be interpreted to include electronically stored information as circumstances warrant.

The term "electronically stored information" is broad, but whether material that falls within this term should be produced, and in what form, are separate questions that must be addressed under Rules 26(b), 26(c), and 34(b).

The Rule 34(a) requirement that, if necessary, a party producing electronically stored information translate it into reasonably usable form does not address the issue of translating from one human language to another. *See In re Puerto Rico Elect. Power Auth.*, 687 F.2d 501, 504–510 (1st Cir. 1989).

Rule 34(a)(1) is also amended to make clear that parties may request an opportunity to test or sample materials sought under the rule in addition to inspecting and copying them. That opportunity may be important for both electronically stored information and hard-copy materials. The current rule is not clear that such testing or sampling is authorized; the amendment expressly permits it. As with any other form of discovery, issues of burden and intrusiveness raised by requests to test or sample can be addressed under Rules 26(b)(2) and 26(c). Inspection or testing of certain types of electronically stored information or of a responding party's electronic information system may raise issues of confidentiality or privacy. The addition of testing and sampling to Rule 34(a) with regard to documents and electronically stored information is not meant to create a routine right of direct access to a party's electronic information system, although such access might be justified in some circumstances. Courts should guard against undue intrusiveness resulting from inspecting or testing such systems.

Rule 34(a)(1) is further amended to make clear that tangible things must — like documents and land sought to be examined — be designated in the request.

Subdivision (b). Rule 34(b) provides that a party must produce documents as they are kept in the usual course of business or must organize and label them to correspond with the categories in the discovery request. The production of electronically stored information should be subject to comparable requirements to protect against deliberate or inadvertent production in ways that raise unnecessary obstacles for the requesting party. Rule 34(b) is amended to ensure similar protection for electronically stored information.

The amendment to Rule 34(b) permits the requesting party to designate the form or forms in which it wants electronically stored information produced. The form of production is more important to the exchange of electronically stored information than of hard-copy materials, although a party might specify hard copy as the requested form. Specification of the desired form or forms may facilitate the orderly, efficient, and cost-effective discovery of electronically stored information. The rule recognizes that different forms of production may be appropriate for different types of electronically stored information. Using current technology, for example, a party might be called upon to produce word processing documents, e-mail messages, electronic spreadsheets, different image or sound files, and material from databases. Requiring that such diverse types of electronically stored information all be produced in the same form could prove impossible, and even if possible could increase the cost and burdens of producing and using the information. The rule therefore provides that the requesting party may ask for different forms of production for different types of electronically stored information.

The rule does not require that the requesting party choose a form or forms of production. The requesting party may not have a preference. In some cases, the requesting party may not know what form the producing party uses to maintain its electronically stored information, although Rule 26(f)(3) is amended to call for discussion of the form of production in the parties' prediscovery conference.

The responding party also is involved in determining the form of production. In the written response to the production request that Rule 34 requires, the responding party must state the form it intends to use for producing electronically stored information if the requesting party does not specify a form or if the responding party objects to a form that the requesting party specifies. Stating the intended form before the production occurs may permit the parties to identify and seek to resolve disputes before the expense and work of the production occurs. A party that responds to a discovery request by simply producing electronically stored information in a form of its choice, without identifying that form in advance of the production in the response required by Rule 34(b), runs a risk that the requesting party can show that the produced form is not reasonably usable and that it is entitled to production of some or all of the information in an additional form. Additional time might be required to permit a responding party to assess the appropriate form or forms of production.

If the requesting party is not satisfied with the form stated by the responding party, or if the responding party has objected to the form specified by the requesting party, the parties must meet and confer under Rule 37(a)(2)(B) in an effort to resolve the matter before the requesting party can file a motion to compel. If they cannot agree and the court resolves the dispute, the court is not limited to the forms initially chosen by the requesting party, stated by the responding party, or specified in this rule for situations in which there is no court order or party agreement.

If the form of production is not specified by party agreement or court order, the responding party must produce electronically stored information either in a form or forms in which it is ordinarily maintained or in a form or forms that are reasonably usable. Rule 34(a) requires that, if necessary, a responding party "translate" information it produces into a "reasonably usable" form. Under some circumstances, the responding party may need to provide some reasonable amount of technical support, information on application software, or other reasonable assistance to enable the requesting party to use the information. The rule does not require a party to produce electronically stored information in the form it which it is ordinarily maintained, as long as it is produced in a reasonably usable form. But the option to produce in a reasonably usable form does not mean that a responding party is free to convert electronically stored information from the form in which it is ordinarily maintained to a different form that makes it more difficult or burdensome for the requesting party to use the information efficiently in the litigation. If the responding party ordinarily maintains the information it is producing in a way that makes it searchable by electronic means, the information should not be produced in a form that removes or significantly degrades this feature.

Some electronically stored information may be ordinarily maintained in a form that is not reasonably usable by any party. One example is "legacy" data that can be used only by superseded systems. The questions whether a producing party should be required to convert such information to a more usable form, or should be required to produce it at all, should be addressed under Rule 26(b)(2)(B).

Whether or not the requesting party specified the form of production, Rule 34(b) provides that the same electronically stored information ordinarily need be produced in only one form.

2007 Amendment

The language of Rule 34 has been amended as part of the general restyling of the Civil Rules to make them more easily understood and to make style and terminology consistent throughout the rules. These changes are intended to be stylistic only.

The final sentence in the first paragraph of former Rule 34(b) was a redundant cross-reference to the discovery moratorium provisions of Rule 26(d). Rule 26(d) is now familiar, obviating any need to carry forward the redundant cross-reference.

The redundant reminder of Rule 37(a) procedure in the second paragraph of former Rule 34(b) is omitted as no longer useful.

CROSS REFERENCES

Consequences of failure to comply with discovery order, see Fed.Rules Civ.Proc. Rule 37, 28 USCA.

Perpetuation of testimony, order and examination, see Fed.Rules Civ.Proc. Rule 27, 28 USCA.

Subpoena for production of documentary evidence, see Fed.Rules Civ.Proc. Rule 45, 28 USCA.

Summary judgment, continuance to procure discovery opposing, see Fed.Rules Civ.Proc. Rule 56, 28 USCA.

Rule 35. Physical and Mental Examinations

(a) Order for an Examination.

(1) ***In General.*** The court where the action is pending may order a party whose mental or physical condition—including blood group—is in controversy to submit to a physical or mental examination by a suitably licensed or certified examiner. The court has the same authority to order a party to produce for examination a person who is in its custody or under its legal control.

(2) ***Motion and Notice; Contents of the Order.*** The order:

(A) may be made only on motion for good cause and on notice to all parties and the person to be examined; and

(B) must specify the time, place, manner, conditions, and scope of the examination, as well as the person or persons who will perform it.

(b) Examiner's Report.

(1) ***Request by the Party or Person Examined.*** The party who moved for the examination must, on request, deliver to the requester a copy of the examiner's report, together with like reports of all earlier examinations of the same condition. The request may be made by the party against whom the examination order was issued or by the person examined.

(2) ***Contents.*** The examiner's report must be in writing and must set out in detail the examiner's findings, including diagnoses, conclusions, and the results of any tests.

(3) ***Request by the Moving Party.*** After delivering the reports, the party who moved for the examination may request—and is entitled to receive—from the party against whom the examination order was issued like reports of all earlier or later examinations of the same condition. But those reports need not be delivered by the party with custody or control of the person examined if the party shows that it could not obtain them.

(4) ***Waiver of Privilege.*** By requesting and obtaining the examiner's report, or by deposing the examiner, the party examined waives any privilege it may have—in that action or any other action involving the same controversy—concerning testimony about all examinations of the same condition.

(5) ***Failure to Deliver a Report.*** The court on motion may order—on just terms—that a party deliver the report of an examination. If the report is not provided, the court may exclude the examiner's testimony at trial.

(6) ***Scope.*** This subdivision (b) applies also to an examination made by the parties' agreement, unless the agreement states otherwise. This subdivision does not preclude obtaining an examiner's report or deposing an examiner under other rules.

(Amended March 30, 1970, effective July 1, 1970; March 2, 1987, effective August 1, 1987; amended by Pub.L. 100–690, Title VII, § 7047(b), November 18, 1988, 102 Stat. 4401; amended April 30, 1991, effective December 1, 1991; April 30, 2007, effective December 1, 2007.)

ADVISORY COMMITTEE NOTES

1937 Adoption

Physical examination of parties before trial is authorized by statute or rule in a number of states. See Ariz.Rev. Code Ann. (Struckmeyer, 1928) § 4468; Mich. Court Rules Ann. (Searl, 1933) Rule 41, § 2; 2 N.J.Comp.Stat. (1910); N.Y.C.P.A. (1937) § 306; 1 S.D.Comp.Laws (1929) § 2716A; 3 Wash.Rev.Stat.Ann. (Remington, 1932) § 1230–1.

Mental examination of parties is authorized in Iowa. Iowa Code (1935) ch. 491–F1. See McCash, *The Evolution of the Doctrine of Discovery and Its Present Status in Iowa,* 20 Ia.L.Rev. 68 (1934).

The constitutionality of legislation providing for physical examination of parties was sustained in *Lyon v. Manhattan Railway Co.,* 1894, 37 N.E. 113, 142 N.Y. 298, and *McGovern v. Hope,* 1899, 42 A. 830, 63 N.J.L. 76. In *Union Pacific Ry. Co. v. Botsford,* 1891, 11 S.Ct. 1000, 141 U.S. 250, 35 L.Ed. 734, it was held that the court could not order the physical examination of a party in the absence of statutory authority. But in *Camden and Suburban Ry. Co. v. Stetson,* 1900, 20 S.Ct. 617, 177 U.S. 172, 44 L.Ed. 721 where there was statutory authority for such examination, derived from a state statute made operative by the conformity act, the practice was sustained. Such authority is now found in the present rule made operative by the Act of June 19, 1934, c. 651, U.S.C., Title 28, § 2072, formerly §§ 723b (Rules in actions at law; Supreme Court authorized to make) and 723c (Union of equity and action at law rules; power of Supreme Court).

1970 Amendment

Subdivision (a). Rule 35(a) has hitherto provided only for an order requiring a party to submit to an examination. It is desirable to extend the rule to provide for an order against the party for examination of a person in his custody or under his legal control. As appears from the provisions of amended Rule 37(b)(2) and the comment under that rule, an order to "produce" the third person imposes only an obligation to use good faith efforts to produce the person.

The amendment will settle beyond doubt that a parent or guardian suing to recover for injuries to a minor may be ordered to produce the minor for examination. Further, the amendment expressly includes blood examination within the kinds of examinations that can be ordered under the rule. See *Beach v. Beach,* 114 F.2d 479 (D.C. Cir. 1940). Provisions similar to the amendment have been adopted in at least 10 States: Calif. Code Civ.Proc. § 2032; Ida.R.Civ.P. 35; Ill. S–H Ann. c. 110A, § 215; Md.R.P. 420; Mich.Gen.Ct.R. 311; Minn.R.Civ.P. 35; Mo.Vern.Ann.R.Civ.p. 60.01; N.Dak.R.Civ.P. 35; N.Y.C.P.L. § 3121; Wyo.R.Civ.P. 35.

The amendment makes no change in the requirements of Rule 35 that, before a court order may issue, the relevant physical or mental condition must be shown to be "in controversy" and "good cause" must be shown for the examination. Thus, the amendment has no effect on the recent decision of the Supreme Court in *Schlagenhauf v. Holder,* 379 U.S. 104 (1964), stressing the importance of these requirements and applying them to the facts of the case. The amendment makes no reference to employees of a party. Provisions relating to employees in the State statutes and rules cited above appear to have been virtually unused.

Subdivision (b)(1). This subdivision is amended to correct an imbalance in Rule 35(b)(1) as heretofore written. Under that text, a party causing a Rule 35(a) examination to be made is required to furnish to the party examined, on request, a copy of the examining physician's report. If he delivers this copy, he is in turn entitled to receive from the party examined reports of all examinations of the same condition previously or later made. But the rule has not in terms entitled the examined party to receive from the party causing the Rule 35(a) examination any reports of earlier examinations of the same condition to which the latter may have access. The amendment cures this defect. See La. Stat.Ann., Civ.Proc. art 1495 (1960); Utah R.Civ.P. 35(c).

The amendment specifies that the written report of the examining physician includes results of all tests made, such as results of X-rays and cardiograms. It also embodies changes required by the broadening of Rule 35(a) to take in persons who are not parties.

Subdivision (b)(3). This new subdivision removes any possible doubt that reports of examination may be obtained although no order for examination has been made under Rule 35(a). Examinations are very frequently made by agreement, and sometimes before the party examined has an attorney. The courts have uniformly ordered that reports be supplied, see 4 *Moore's Federal Practice* ¶35.06, n. 1 (2d ed. 1966); 2A Barron & Holtzoff, *Federal Practice and Procedure* § 823, n. 22 (Wright ed. 1961), and it appears best to fill the technical gap in the present rule.

The subdivision also makes clear that reports of examining physicians are discoverable not only under Rule 35(b), but under other rules as well. To be sure, if the report is privileged, then discovery is not permissible under any rule other than Rule 35(b) and it is permissible under Rule 35(b) only if the party requests a copy of the report of examination made by the other party's doctor. *Sher v. De Haven*, 199 F.2d 777 (D.C. Cir. 1952), *cert. denied* 345 U.S. 936 (1953). But if the report is unprivileged and is subject to discovery under the provisions of rules other than Rule 35(b)—such as Rules 34 or 26(b)(3) or (4)—discovery should not depend upon whether the person examined demands a copy of the report. Although a few cases have suggested the contrary, *e.g., Galloway v. National Dairy Products Corp.*, 24 F.R.D. 362 (E.D.Pa.1959), the better considered district court decisions hold that Rule 35(b) is not preemptive. *E.g., Leszynski v. Russ*, 29 F.R.D. 10, 12 (D.Md.1961) and cases cited. The question was recently given full consideration in *Buffington v. Wood*, 351 F.2d 292 (3d Cir. 1965), holding that Rule 35(b) is not preemptive.

1987 Amendment

The amendments are technical. No substantive change is intended.

1991 Amendment

The revision authorizes the court to require physical or mental examinations conducted by any person who is suitably licensed or certified.

The rule was revised in 1988 by Congressional enactment to authorize mental examinations by licensed clinical psychologists. This revision extends that amendment to include other certified or licensed professionals, such as dentists or occupational therapists, who are not physicians or clinical psychologists, but who may be well-qualified to give valuable testimony about the physical or mental condition that is the subject of dispute.

The requirement that the examiner be *suitably* licensed or certified is a new requirement. The court is thus expressly authorized to assess the credentials of the examiner to assure that no person is subjected to a court-ordered examination by an examiner whose testimony would be of such limited value that it would be unjust to require the person to undergo the invasion of privacy associated with the examination. This authority is not wholly new, for under the former rule, the court retained discretion to refuse to order an examination, or to restrict an examination. 8 WRIGHT & MILLER, FEDERAL PRACTICE & PROCEDURE § 2234 (1986 Supp.). The revision is intended to encourage the exercise of this discretion, especially with respect to examinations by persons having narrow qualifications.

The court's responsibility to determine the suitability of the examiner's qualifications applies even to a proposed examination by a physician. If the proposed examination and testimony calls for an expertise that the proposed examiner does not have, it should not be ordered, even if the proposed examiner is a physician. The rule does not, however, require that the license or certificate be conferred by the jurisdiction in which the examination is conducted.

2007 Amendment

The language of Rule 35 has been amended as part of the general restyling of the Civil Rules to make them more easily understood and to make style and terminology consistent throughout the rules. These changes are intended to be stylistic only.

HISTORICAL NOTES

Revision Notes and Legislative Reports

1988 Acts. For Related Reports, see 1988 U.S.Code Cong. and Adm.News, p. 5937.

CROSS REFERENCES

Consequences of failure to submit to examination, see Fed.Rules Civ.Proc. Rule 37, 28 USCA.

Perpetuation of testimony, order and examination, see Fed.Rules Civ.Proc. Rule 27, 28 USCA.

Rule 36. Requests for Admission

(a) Scope and Procedure.

(1) ***Scope.*** A party may serve on any other party a written request to admit, for purposes of the pending action only, the truth of any matters within the scope of Rule 26(b)(1) relating to:

(A) facts, the application of law to fact, or opinions about either; and

(B) the genuineness of any described documents.

(2) ***Form; Copy of a Document.*** Each matter must be separately stated. A request to admit the genuineness of a document must be accompanied by a copy of the document unless it is, or has been, otherwise furnished or made available for inspection and copying.

(3) ***Time to Respond; Effect of Not Responding.*** A matter is admitted unless, within 30 days after being served, the party to whom the request is directed serves on the requesting party a written answer or objection addressed to the matter and signed by the party or its attorney. A shorter or longer time for responding may be stipulated to under Rule 29 or be ordered by the court.

(4) ***Answer.*** If a matter is not admitted, the answer must specifically deny it or state in detail why the answering party cannot truthfully admit or deny it. A denial must fairly respond to the substance of the matter; and when good faith requires that a party qualify an answer or deny only a part of a matter, the answer must specify the part admitted and qualify or deny the rest. The answering party may assert lack of knowledge or information as a reason for failing to admit or deny only if the party states that it has made reasonable inquiry and that the information it knows or can readily obtain is insufficient to enable it to admit or deny.

(5) ***Objections.*** The grounds for objecting to a request must be stated. A party must not object solely on the ground that the request presents a genuine issue for trial.

(6) ***Motion Regarding the Sufficiency of an Answer or Objection.*** The requesting party may move to determine the sufficiency of an answer or objection. Unless the court finds an objection justified, it must order that an answer be served. On finding that an answer does not comply with this rule, the court may order either that the matter is admitted or that an amended answer be served. The court may defer its final decision until a pretrial conference or a specified time before trial. Rule 37(a)(5) applies to an award of expenses.

(b) Effect of an Admission; Withdrawing or Amending It. A matter admitted under this rule is conclusively established unless the court, on motion, permits the admission to be withdrawn or amended. Subject to Rule 16(e), the court may permit withdrawal or amendment if it would promote the presentation of the merits of the action and if the court is not persuaded that it would prejudice the requesting party in maintaining or defending the action on the merits. An admission under this rule is not an admission for any other purpose and cannot be used against the party in any other proceeding.

(Amended December 27, 1946, effective March 19, 1948; March 30, 1970, effective July 1, 1970; March 2, 1987, effective August 1, 1987; April 22, 1993, effective December 1, 1993; April 30, 2007, effective December 1, 2007.)

ADVISORY COMMITTEE NOTES

1937 Adoption

Compare similar rules: [Former] Equity Rule 58 (last paragraph, which provides for the admission of the execution and genuineness of documents); *English Rules Under the Judicature Act* (The Annual Practice, 1937) O. 32; Ill.Rev. Stat. (1937) ch. 110, § 182 and Rule 18 (Ill.Rev.Stat. (1937) ch. 110, § 259.18); 2 Mass.Gen.Laws (Ter.Ed., 1932) ch. 231, § 69; Mich. Court Rules Ann. (Searl, 1933) Rule 42; N.J. Comp.Stat. (2 Cum.Supp. 1911–1924); N.Y.C.P.A. (1937) §§ 322, 323; Wis.Stat. (1935) § 327.22.

1946 Amendment

Note. The first change in the first sentence of Rule 36(a) and the addition of the new second sentence, specifying when requests for admissions may be served, bring Rule 36 in line with amended Rules 26(a) and 33. There is no reason why these rules should not be treated alike. Other provisions of Rule 36(a) give the party whose admissions are requested adequate protection.

The second change in the first sentence of the rule [subdivision (a)] removes any uncertainty as to whether a party can be called upon to admit matters of fact other than those set forth in relevant documents described in and exhibited with the request. In *Smyth v. Kaufman*, C.C.A.2, 1940, 114 F.2d 40, it was held that the word "therein", now stricken from the rule [said subdivision] referred to the request and that a matter of fact not related to any document could be presented to the other party for admission or denial. The rule of this case is now clearly stated.

The substitution of the word "served" for "delivered" in the third sentence of the amended rule [said subdivision] is in conformance with the use of the word "serve" elsewhere in the rule and generally throughout the rules. See also Notes to Rules 13(a) and 33 herein. The substitution [in said subdivision] of "shorter or longer" for "further" will enable a court to designate a lesser period than 10 days for answer. This conforms with a similar provision already contained in Rule 33.

The addition of clause (1) [in said subdivision] specifies the method by which a party may challenge the propriety of a request to admit. There has been considerable difference of judicial opinion as to the correct method, if any, available to secure relief from an allegedly improper request. See Commentary, *Methods of Objecting to Notice to Admit,* 1942, 5 Fed.Rules Serv. 835; *International Carbonic Engineering Co. v. Natural Carbonic Products, Inc.*, S.D.Cal.1944, 57 F.Supp. 248. The changes in clause (1) are merely of a clarifying and conforming nature.

The first of the added last two sentences [in said subdivision] prevents an objection to a part of a request from holding up the answer, if any, to the remainder. See similar proposed change in Rule 33. The last sentence strengthens the rule by making the denial accurately reflect the party's position. It is taken, with necessary changes, from Rule 8(b).

1970 Amendment

Rule 36 serves two vital purposes, both of which are designed to reduce trial time. Admissions are sought, first to facilitate proof with respect to issues that cannot be eliminated from the case, and secondly, to narrow the issues by eliminating those that can be. The changes made in the rule are designed to serve these purposes more effectively. Certain disagreements in the courts about the proper scope of the rule are resolved. In addition, the procedural operation of the rule is brought into line with other discovery procedures, and the binding effect of an admission is clarified. See generally Finman, *The Request for Admissions in Federal Civil Procedure,* 71 Yale L.J. 371 (1962).

Subdivision (a). As revised, the subdivision provides that a request may be made to admit any matters within the scope of Rule 26(b) that relate to statements or opinions of fact or of the application of law to fact. It thereby eliminates the requirement that the matters be "of fact." This change resolves conflicts in the court decisions as to whether a request to admit matters of "opinion" and matters involving "mixed law and fact" is proper under the rule. As to "opinion," compare, *e.g., Jackson Buff Corp. v. Marcelle,* 20 F.R.D. 139 (E.D.N.Y.1957); *California v. The S. S. Jules Fribourg,* 19 F.R.D. 432 (N.D.Calif.1955), with *e.g., Photon, Inc. v. Harris Intertype, Inc.,* 28 F.R.D. 327 (D.Mass.1961); *Hise v. Lockwood Grader Corp.,* 153 F.Supp. 276 (D.Nebr.1957). As to "mixed law and fact" the majority of courts sustain objections, *e.g., Minnesota Mining and Mfg. Co. v. Norton Co.,* 36 F.R.D. 1 (N.D.Ohio 1964), but *McSparran v. Hanigan,* 225 F.Supp. 628 (E.D.Pa.1963) is to the contrary.

Not only is it difficult as a practical matter to separate "fact" from "opinion," see 4 *Moore's Federal Practice* ¶36.04 (2d ed. 1966); cf. 2A Barron & Holtzoff, *Federal Practice and Procedure* 317 (Wright ed. 1961), but an admission on a matter of opinion may facilitate proof or narrow the issues or both. An admission of a matter involving the application of law to fact may, in a given case, even more clearly narrow the issues. For example, an admission that an employee acted in the scope of his employment may remove a major issue from the trial. In *McSparran v. Hanigan, supra,* plaintiff admitted that "the premises on which said accident occurred, were occupied or under the control" of one of the defendants, 225 F.Supp. at 636. This admission, involving law as well as fact, removed one of the issues from the lawsuit and thereby reduced the proof required at trial. The amended provision does not authorize requests for admissions of law unrelated to the facts of the case.

Requests for admission involving the application of law to fact may create disputes between the parties which are best resolved in the presence of the judge after much or all of the other discovery has been completed. Power is therefore expressly conferred upon the court to defer decision until a pretrial conference is held or until a designated time prior to trial. On the other hand, the court should not automatically defer decision; in many instances, the importance of the admission lies in enabling the requesting party to avoid the burdensome accumulation of proof prior to the pretrial conference.

Courts have also divided on whether an answering party may properly object to request for admission as to matters which that party regards as "in dispute." Compare, *e.g., Syracuse Broadcasting Corp. v. Newhouse,* 271 F.2d 910, 917 (2d Cir. 1959); *Driver v. Gindy Mfg. Corp.,* 24 F.R.D. 473 (E.D.Pa.1959); with, *e.g., McGonigle v. Baxter,* 27 F.R.D. 504 (E.D.Pa.1961); *United States v. Ehbauer,* 13 F.R.D. 462 (W.D.Mo.1952). The proper response in such cases is an answer. The very purpose of the request is to ascertain whether the answering party is prepared to admit or regards the matter as presenting a genuine issue for trial. In his answer, the party may deny, or he may give as his reason for inability to admit or deny the existence of a genuine issue. The party runs no risk of sanctions if the matter is genuinely in issue, since Rule 37(c) provides a sanction of costs only when there are no good reasons for a failure to admit.

On the other hand, requests to admit may be so voluminous and so framed that the answering party finds the task of identifying what is in dispute and what is not unduly burdensome. If so, the responding party may obtain a protective order under Rule 26(c). Some of the decisions sustaining objections on "disputability" grounds could have been justified by the burdensome character of the requests. See, *e.g., Syracuse Broadcasting Corp. v. Newhouse, supra.*

Another sharp split of authority exists on the question whether a party may base his answer on lack of information or knowledge without seeking out additional information. One line of cases has held that a party may answer on the basis of such knowledge as he has at the time he answers. *E.g., Jackson Buff Corp. v. Marcelle,* 20 F.R.D. 139 (E.D.N.Y.1957); *Sladek v. General Motors Corp.,* 16 F.R.D. 104 (S.D.Iowa 1954). A larger group of cases, supported by commentators, has taken the view that if the responding party lacks knowledge, he must inform himself in reasonable fashion. *E.g., Hise v. Lockwood Grader Corp.,* 153 F.Supp. 276 (D.Nebr. 1957); *E. H. Tate Co. v. Jiffy Enterprises, Inc.,* 16 F.R.D. 571 (E.D.Pa.1954); Finman, *supra,* 71 Yale L.J. 371, 404–409; 4 *Moore's Federal Practice* ¶36.04 (2d ed. 1966); 2A Barron & Holtzoff, *Federal Practice and Procedure* 509 (Wright ed. 1961).

The rule as revised adopts the majority view, as in keeping with a basic principle of the discovery rules that a reasonable burden may be imposed on the parties when its discharge will facilitate preparation for trial and ease the trial process. It has been argued against this view that one side should not have the burden of "proving" the other side's case. The revised rule requires only that the answering party make reasonable inquiry and secure such knowledge and information as are readily obtainable by him. In most instances, the investigation will be necessary either to his own case or to preparation for rebuttal. Even when it is not, the information may be close enough at hand to be "readily obtainable." Rule 36 requires only that the party state that he has taken these steps. The sanction for failure of a party to inform himself before he answers lies in the award of costs after trial, as provided in Rule 37(c).

The requirement that the answer to a request for admission be sworn is deleted, in favor of a provision that the answer be signed by the party or by his attorney. The provisions of Rule 36 make it clear that admissions function very much as pleadings do. Thus, when a party admits in part and denies in part, his admission is for purposes of the pending action only and may not be used against him in any other proceeding. The broadening of the rule to encompass mixed questions of law and fact reinforces this feature. Rule 36 does not lack a sanction for false answers; Rule 37(c) furnishes an appropriate deterrent.

The existing language describing the available grounds for objection to a request for admission is eliminated as neither necessary nor helpful. The statement that objection may be made to any request which is "improper" adds nothing to the provisions that the party serve an answer or objection addressed to each matter and that he state his reasons for any objection. None of the other discovery rules sets forth grounds for objection, except so far as all are subject to the general provisions of Rule 26.

Changes are made in the sequence of procedures in Rule 36 so that they conform to the new procedures in Rules 33 and 34. The major changes are as follows:

(1) The normal time for response to a request for admissions is lengthened from 10 to 30 days, conforming more closely to prevailing practice. A defendant need not respond, however, in less than 45 days after service of the summons and complaint upon him. The court may lengthen or shorten the time when special situations require it.

(2) The present requirement that the plaintiff wait 10 days to serve requests without leave of court is eliminated. The revised provision accords with those in Rules 33 and 34.

(3) The requirement that the objecting party move automatically for a hearing on his objection is eliminated, and the burden is on the requesting party to move for an order. The change in the burden of going forward does not modify present law on burden of persuasion. The award of expenses incurred in relation to the motion is made subject to the comprehensive provisions of Rule 37(a)(4).

(4) A problem peculiar to Rule 36 arises if the responding party serves answers that are not in conformity with the requirements of the rule—for example, a denial is not "specific," or the explanation of inability to admit or deny is not "in detail." Rule 36 now makes no provision for court scrutiny of such answers before trial, and it seems to contemplate that defective answers bring about admissions just as effectively as if no answer had been served. Some cases have so held. *E.g., Southern Ry. Co. v. Crosby,* 201 F.2d 878 (4th Cir. 1953); *United States v. Laney,* 96 F.Supp. 482 (E.D.S.C.1951).

Giving a defective answer the automatic effect of an admission may cause unfair surprise. A responding party who purported to deny or to be unable to admit or deny will for the first time at trial confront the contention that he has made a binding admission. Since it is not always easy to know whether a denial is "specific" or an explanation is "in detail," neither party can know how the court will rule at trial and whether proof must be prepared. Some courts, therefore, have entertained motions to rule on defective answers. They have at times ordered that amended answers be served, when the defects were technical, and at other times have declared that the matter was admitted. *E.g., Woods v. Stewart,* 171 F.2d 544 (5th Cir. 1948); *SEC v. Kaye, Real & Co.,* 122 F.Supp. 639 (S.D.N.Y.1954); *Sieb's Hatcheries, Inc. v. Lindley,* 13 F.R.D. 113 (W.D.Ark.1952). The rule as revised conforms to the latter practice.

Subdivision (b). The rule does not how indicate the extent to which a party is bound by his admission. Some courts view admissions as the equivalent of sworn testimony. *E.g., Ark–Tenn Distributing Corp. v. Breidt,* 209 F.2d 359 (3d Cir. 1954); *United States v. Lemons,* 125 F.Supp. 686 (W.D.Ark.1954); 4 *Moore's Federal Practice* ¶36.08 (2d ed. 1966 Supp.). At least in some jurisdictions a party may rebut his own testimony, *e.g., Alamo v. Del Rosario,* 98 F.2d 328 (D.C.Cir.1938), and by analogy an admission made pursuant to Rule 36 may likewise be thought rebuttable. The courts in *Ark–Tenn* and *Lemons, supra,* reasoned in this way, although the results reached may be supported on different grounds. In *McSparran v. Hanigan,* 225 F.Supp. 628, 636–637 (E.D.Pa.1963), the court held that an admission is conclusively binding, though noting the confusion created by prior decisions.

The new provisions give an admission a conclusively binding effect, for purposes only of the pending action, unless the admission is withdrawn or amended. In form and substance a Rule 36 admission is comparable to an admission in pleadings or a stipulation drafted by counsel for use at trial, rather than to an evidentiary admission of a party. Louisell, *Modern California Discovery* § 8.07 (1963); 2A Barron & Holtzoff, *Federal Practice and Procedure* § 838 (Wright ed. 1961). Unless the party securing an admission can depend on its binding effect, he cannot safely avoid the expense of preparing to prove the very matters on which he has secured the admission, and the purpose of the rule is defeated. Field v. McKusick, *Maine Civil Practice* § 36.4 (1959); Finman, *supra,* 71 Yale L.J. 371, 418–426; Comment, 56 Nw.U.L.Rev. 679, 682–683 (1961).

Provision is made for withdrawal or amendment of an admission. This provision emphasizes the importance of having the action resolved on the merits, while at the same time assuring each party that justified reliance on an admission in preparation for trial will not operate to his prejudice. *Cf. Moosman v. Joseph P. Blitz, Inc.,* 358 F.2d 686 (2d Cir. 1966).

1987 Amendment

The amendments are technical. No substantive change is intended.

1993 Amendments

The rule is revised to reflect the change made by Rule 26(d), preventing a party from seeking formal discovery until after the meeting of the parties required by Rule 26(f).

2007 Amendment

The language of Rule 36 has been amended as part of the general restyling of the Civil Rules to make them more easily understood and to make style and terminology consistent throughout the rules. These changes are intended to be stylistic only.

The final sentence of the first paragraph of former Rule 36(a) was a redundant cross-reference to the discovery moratorium provisions of Rule 26(d). Rule 26(d) is now familiar, obviating any need to carry forward the redundant cross-reference. The redundant reminder of Rule 37(c) in the second paragraph was likewise omitted.

CROSS REFERENCES

Expenses on refusal to admit, see Fed.Rules Civ.Proc. Rule 37, 28 USCA.

Pretrial conferences, sanctions for failure to obey scheduling or order, see Fed.Rules Civ.Proc. Rule 16, 28 USCA.

Use of admissions on motions for summary judgment, see Fed.Rules Civ.Proc. Rule 56, 28 USCA.

Rule 37. Failure to Make Disclosures or to Cooperate in Discovery; Sanctions

(a) Motion for an Order Compelling Disclosure or Discovery.

(1) ***In General.*** On notice to other parties and all affected persons, a party may move for an order compelling disclosure or discovery. The motion must include a certification that the movant has in good faith conferred or attempted to confer with the person or party failing to make disclosure or discovery in an effort to obtain it without court action.

(2) ***Appropriate Court.*** A motion for an order to a party must be made in the court where the action is pending. A motion for an order to a nonparty must be made in the court where the discovery is or will be taken.

(3) ***Specific Motions.***

(A) *To Compel Disclosure.* If a party fails to make a disclosure required by Rule 26(a), any other party may move to compel disclosure and for appropriate sanctions.

(B) *To Compel a Discovery Response.* A party seeking discovery may move for an order compelling an answer, designation, production, or inspection. This motion may be made if:

(i) a deponent fails to answer a question asked under Rule 30 or 31;

(ii) a corporation or other entity fails to make a designation under Rule 30(b)(6) or 31(a)(4);

(iii) a party fails to answer an interrogatory submitted under Rule 33; or

(iv) a party fails to respond that inspection will be permitted—or fails to permit inspection—as requested under Rule 34.

(C) *Related to a Deposition.* When taking an oral deposition, the party asking a question may complete or adjourn the examination before moving for an order.

(4) ***Evasive or Incomplete Disclosure, Answer, or Response.*** For purposes of this subdivision (a), an evasive or incomplete disclosure, answer, or response must be treated as a failure to disclose, answer, or respond.

(5) ***Payment of Expenses; Protective Orders.***

(A) *If the Motion Is Granted (or Disclosure or Discovery Is Provided After Filing).* If the motion is granted—or if the disclosure or requested discovery is provided after the motion was filed—the court must, after giving an opportunity to be heard, require the party or deponent whose conduct necessitated the motion, the party or attorney advising that conduct, or both to pay the movant's reasonable expenses incurred in making the motion, including attorney's fees. But the court must not order this payment if:

(i) the movant filed the motion before attempting in good faith to obtain the disclosure or discovery without court action;

(ii) the opposing party's nondisclosure, response, or objection was substantially justified; or

(iii) other circumstances make an award of expenses unjust.

(B) *If the Motion Is Denied.* If the motion is denied, the court may issue any protective order authorized under Rule 26(c) and must, after giving an opportunity to be heard, require the movant, the attorney filing the motion, or both to pay the party or deponent who opposed the motion its reasonable expenses incurred in opposing the motion, including attorney's fees. But the court must not order this payment if the motion was substantially justified or other circumstances make an award of expenses unjust.

(C) *If the Motion Is Granted in Part and Denied in Part.* If the motion is granted in part and denied in part, the court may issue any protective order authorized under Rule 26(c) and may, after giving an opportunity to be heard, apportion the reasonable expenses for the motion.

(b) **Failure to Comply with a Court Order.**

(1) ***Sanctions in the District Where the Deposition Is Taken.*** If the court where the discovery is taken orders a deponent to be sworn or to answer a question and the deponent fails to obey, the failure may be treated as contempt of court.

(2) ***Sanctions in the District Where the Action Is Pending.***

(A) *For Not Obeying a Discovery Order.* If a party or a party's officer, director, or managing agent—or a witness designated under Rule 30(b)(6) or 31(a)(4)—fails to obey an order to provide or permit discovery, including an order under Rule 26(f), 35, or 37(a), the court where the action is pending may issue further just orders. They may include the following:

(i) directing that the matters embraced in the order or other designated facts be taken as established for purposes of the action, as the prevailing party claims;

(ii) prohibiting the disobedient party from supporting or opposing designated

claims or defenses, or from introducing designated matters in evidence;
(iii) striking pleadings in whole or in part;
(iv) staying further proceedings until the order is obeyed;
(v) dismissing the action or proceeding in whole or in part;
(vi) rendering a default judgment against the disobedient party; or
(vii) treating as contempt of court the failure to obey any order except an order to submit to a physical or mental examination.

(B) *For Not Producing a Person for Examination.* If a party fails to comply with an order under Rule 35(a) requiring it to produce another person for examination, the court may issue any of the orders listed in Rule 37(b)(2)(A)(i)-(vi), unless the disobedient party shows that it cannot produce the other person.

(C) *Payment of Expenses.* Instead of or in addition to the orders above, the court must order the disobedient party, the attorney advising that party, or both to pay the reasonable expenses, including attorney's fees, caused by the failure, unless the failure was substantially justified or other circumstances make an award of expenses unjust.

(c) Failure to Disclose, to Supplement an Earlier Response, or to Admit.

(1) ***Failure to Disclose or Supplement.*** If a party fails to provide information or identify a witness as required by Rule 26(a) or (e), the party is not allowed to use that information or witness to supply evidence on a motion, at a hearing, or at a trial, unless the failure was substantially justified or is harmless. In addition to or instead of this sanction, the court, on motion and after giving an opportunity to be heard:

(A) may order payment of the reasonable expenses, including attorney's fees, caused by the failure;
(B) may inform the jury of the party's failure; and
(C) may impose other appropriate sanctions, including any of the orders listed in Rule 37(b)(2)(A)(i)-(vi).

(2) ***Failure to Admit.*** If a party fails to admit what is requested under Rule 36 and if the requesting party later proves a document to be genuine or the matter true, the requesting party may move that the party who failed to admit pay the reasonable expenses, including attorney's fees, incurred in making that proof. The court must so order unless:

(A) the request was held objectionable under Rule 36(a);
(B) the admission sought was of no substantial importance;
(C) the party failing to admit had a reasonable ground to believe that it might prevail on the matter; or
(D) there was other good reason for the failure to admit.

(d) Party's Failure to Attend Its Own Deposition, Serve Answers to Interrogatories, or Respond to a Request for Inspection.

(1) ***In General.***

(A) *Motion; Grounds for Sanctions.* The court where the action is pending may, on motion, order sanctions if:
(i) a party or a party's officer, director, or managing agent—or a person designated under Rule 30(b)(6) or 31(a)(4)—fails, after being served with proper notice, to appear for that person's deposition; or
(ii) a party, after being properly served with interrogatories under Rule 33 or a request for inspection under Rule 34, fails to serve its answers, objections, or written response.

(B) *Certification.* A motion for sanctions for failing to answer or respond must include a certification that the movant has in good faith conferred or attempted to confer with the party failing to act in an effort to obtain the answer or response without court action.

(2) ***Unacceptable Excuse for Failing to Act.*** A failure described in Rule 37(d)(1)(A) is not excused on the ground that the discovery sought was objectionable, unless the party failing to act has a pending motion for a protective order under Rule 26(c).

(3) ***Types of Sanctions.*** Sanctions may include any of the orders listed in Rule 37(b)(2)(A)(i)-(vi). Instead of or in addition to these sanctions, the court must require the party failing to act, the attorney advising that party, or both to pay the reasonable expenses, including attorney's fees, caused by the failure, unless the failure was substantially justified or other circumstances make an award of expenses unjust.

(e) Failure to Provide Electronically Stored Information. Absent exceptional circumstances, a court may not impose sanctions under these rules on a party for failing to provide electronically stored information lost as a result of the routine, good-faith operation of an electronic information system.

(f) Failure to Participate in Framing a Discovery Plan. If a party or its attorney fails to participate in good faith in developing and submitting a proposed discovery plan as required by Rule 26(f), the court may, after giving an opportunity to be heard, require that party or attorney to pay to any other party the reasonable expenses, including attorney's fees, caused by the failure.

(Amended December 29, 1948, effective October 20, 1949; March 30, 1970, effective July 1, 1970; April 29, 1980, effective August 1, 1980; amended by Pub.L. 96–481, Title II, § 205(a), October 21, 1980, 94 Stat. 2330, effective October 1, 1981; amended March 2, 1987, effective August 1, 1987; April 22, 1993, effective December 1, 1993; April 17, 2000, effective December 1, 2000; April 12, 2006, effective December 1, 2006; April 30, 2007, effective December 1, 2007.)

ADVISORY COMMITTEE NOTES

1937 Adoption

The provisions of this rule authorizing orders establishing facts or excluding evidence or striking pleadings, or authorizing judgments of dismissal or default, for refusal to answer questions or permit inspection or otherwise make discovery, are in accord with *Hammond Packing Co. v. Arkansas*, 1909, 29 S.Ct. 370, 212 U.S. 322, 53 L.Ed. 530, 15 Ann.Cas. 645, which distinguishes between the justifiable use of such measures as a means of compelling the production of evidence, and their unjustifiable use, as in *Hovey v. Elliott*, 1897, 17 S.Ct. 841, 167 U.S. 409, 42 L.Ed. 215, for the mere purpose of punishing for contempt.

1948 Amendment

The amendment effective October 1949, substituted the reference to "Title 28, U.S.C., § 1783" in subdivision (e) for the reference to "the Act of July 3, 1926, c. 762, § 1 (44 Stat. 835), U.S.C., Title 28, § 711."

1970 Amendment

Rule 37 provides generally for sanctions against parties or persons unjustifiably resisting discovery. Experience has brought to light a number of defects in the language of the rule as well as instances in which it is not serving the purposes for which it was designed. See Rosenberg, *Sanctions to Effectuate Pretrial Discovery*, 58 Col.L.Rev. 480 (1958). In addition, changes being made in other discovery rules require conforming amendments to Rule 37.

Rule 37 sometimes refers to a "failure" to afford discovery and at other times to a "refusal" to do so. Taking note of this dual terminology, courts have imported into "refusal" a requirement of "wilfullness." See *Roth v. Paramount Pictures Corp.*, 8 F.R.D. 31 (W.D.Pa.1948); *Campbell v. Johnson*, 101 F.Supp. 705, 707 (S.D.N.Y.1951). In *Societe Internationale v. Rogers*, 357 U.S. 197 (1958), the Supreme Court concluded that the rather random use of these two terms in Rule 37 showed no design to use them with consistently distinctive meanings, that "refused" in Rule 37(b)(2) meant simply a failure to comply, and that wilfullness was relevant only to the selection of sanctions, if any, to be imposed. Nevertheless, after the decision in *Societe*, the court in *Hinson v. Michigan Mutual Liability Co.*, 275 F.2d 537 (5th Cir. 1960) once again ruled that "refusal" required wilfullness. Substitution of "failure" for "refusal" throughout Rule 37 should eliminate this confusion and bring the rule into harmony with the *Societe Internationale* decision. See Rosenberg, *supra*, 58 Col.L.Rev. 480, 489–490 (1958).

Subdivision (a). Rule 37(a) provides relief to a party seeking discovery against one who, with or without stated objections, fails to afford the discovery sought. It has always fully served this function in relation to depositions, but the amendments being made to Rules 33 and 34 give Rule 37(a) added scope and importance. Under existing Rule 33, a party objecting to interrogatories must make a motion for court hearing on his objections. The changes now made in Rules 33 and 37(a) make it clear that the interrogating party must move to compel answers, and the motion is provided for in Rule 37(a). Existing Rule 34, since it requires a court order prior to production of documents or things or permission to enter on land, has no relation to Rule 37(a). Amendments of Rules 34 and 37(a) create a procedure similar to that provided for Rule 33.

Subdivision (a)(1). This is a new provision making clear to which court a party may apply for an order compelling discovery. Existing Rule 37(a) refers only to the court in which the deposition is being taken; nevertheless, it has been held that the court where the action is pending has "inherent power" to compel a party deponent to answer. *Lincoln Laboratories, Inc. v. Savage Laboratories, Inc.*, 27 F.R.D. 476 (D.Del.1961). In relation to Rule 33 interrogatories and Rule 34 requests for inspection, the court where the action is pending is the appropriate enforcing tribunal. The new provision eliminates the need to resort to inherent power by spelling out the respective roles of the court where the action is pending and the court where the deposition is taken. In some instances, two courts are available to a party seeking to compel answers from a party deponent. The party seeking discovery may choose the court to which he will apply, but the court has power to remit the party to the other court as a more appropriate forum.

Subdivision (a)(2). This subdivision contains the substance of existing provisions of Rule 37(a) authorizing motions to compel answers to questions put at depositions and to interrogatories. New provisions authorize motions for orders compelling designation under Rules 30(b)(6) and 31(a) and compelling inspection in accordance with a request made under Rule 34. If the court denies a motion, in whole or part, it may accompany the denial with issuance of a protective order. Compare the converse provision in Rule 26(c).

Subdivision (a)(3). This new provision makes clear that an evasive or incomplete answer is to be considered, for purposes of subdivision (a), a failure to answer. The courts have consistently held that they have the power to compel adequate answers. *E.g., Cone Mills Corp. v. Joseph Bancroft & Sons Co.*, 33 F.R.D. 318 (D.Del.1963). This power is recognized and incorporated into the rule.

Subdivision (a)(4). This subdivision amends the provisions for award of expenses, including reasonable attorney's fees, to the prevailing party or person when a motion is made for an order compelling discovery. At present, an award of expenses is made only if the losing party or person is found to have acted without substantial justification. The change requires that expenses be awarded unless the conduct of the losing party or person is found to have been substantially justified. The test of "substantial justification" remains, but the change in language is intended to encourage judges to be more alert to abuses occurring in the discovery process.

On many occasions, to be sure, the dispute over discovery between the parties is genuine, though ultimately resolved one way or the other by the court. In such cases, the losing party is substantially justified in carrying the matter to court. But the rules should deter the abuse implicit in carrying or forcing a discovery dispute to court when no genuine dispute exists. And the potential or actual imposition of expenses is virtually the sole formal sanction in the rules to deter a party from pressing to a court hearing frivolous requests for or objections to discovery.

The present provision of Rule 37(a) that the court shall require payment if it finds that the defeated party acted without "substantial justification" may appear adequate, but in fact it has been little used. Only a handful of reported cases include an award of expenses, and the Columbia Survey found that in only one instance out of about 50 motions decided under Rule 37(a) did the court award expenses. It appears that the courts do not utilize the most important available sanction to deter abusive resort to the judiciary.

The proposed change provides in effect that expenses should ordinarily be awarded unless a court finds that the losing party acted justifiably in carrying his point to court. At the same time, a necessary flexibility is maintained, since the court retains the power to find that other circumstances make an award of expenses unjust—as where the prevailing party also acted unjustifiably. The amendment does not significantly narrow the discretion of the court, but rather presses the court to address itself to abusive practices. The present provision that expenses may be imposed upon either the party or his attorney or both is unchanged. But it is not contemplated that expenses will be imposed upon the attorney merely because the party is indigent.

Subdivision (b). This subdivision deals with sanctions for failure to comply with a court order. The present captions for subsections (1) and (2) entitled, "Contempt" and "Other Consequences," respectively, are confusing. One of the consequences listed in (2) is the arrest of the party, representing the exercise of the contempt power. The contents of the subsections show that the first authorizes the sanction of contempt (and no other) by the court in which the deposition is taken, whereas the second subsection authorizes a variety of sanctions, including contempt, which may be imposed by the court in which the action is pending. The captions of the subsections are changed to reflect their contents.

The scope of Rule 37(b)(2) is broadened by extending it to include any order "to provide or permit discovery," including orders issued under Rules 37(a) and 35. Various rules authorize orders for discovery—*e.g.,* Rule 35(b)(1), Rule 26(c) as revised, Rule 37(d). See Rosenberg, *supra,* 58 Col.L.Rev. 480, 484–486. Rule 37(b)(2) should provide comprehensively for enforcement of all these orders. *Cf. Societe Internationale v. Rogers,* 357 U.S. 197, 207 (1958). On the other hand, the reference to Rule 34 is deleted to conform to the changed procedure in that rule.

A new subsection (E) provides that sanctions which have been available against a party for failure to comply with an order under Rule 35(a) to submit to examination will now be available against him for his failure to comply with a Rule 35(a) order to produce a third person for examination, unless he shows that he is unable to produce the person. In this context, "unable" means in effect "unable in good faith." See *Societe Internationale v. Rogers,* 357 U.S. 197 (1958).

Subdivision (b)(2) is amplified to provide for payment of reasonable expenses caused by the failure to obey the order. Although Rules 37(b)(2) and 37(d) have been silent as to award of expenses, courts have nevertheless ordered them on occasion. *E.g., United Sheeplined Clothing Co. v. Arctic Fur Cap Corp.,* 165 F.Supp. 193 (S.D.N.Y.1958); *Austin Theatre, Inc. v. Warner Bros. Pictures, Inc.,* 22 F.R.D. 302 (S.D.N.Y. 1958). The provision places the burden on the disobedient party to avoid expenses by showing that his failure is justified or that special circumstances make an award of expenses unjust. Allocating the burden in this way conforms to the changed provisions as to expenses in Rule 37(a), and is particularly appropriate when a court order is disobeyed.

An added reference to directors of a party is similar to a change made in subdivision (d) and is explained in the note to that subdivision. The added reference to persons designated by a party under Rules 30(b)(6) or 31(a) to testify on behalf of the party carries out the new procedure in those rules for taking a deposition of a corporation or other organization.

Subdivision (c). Rule 37(c) provides a sanction for the enforcement of Rule 36 dealing with requests for admission. Rule 36 provides the mechanism whereby a party may obtain from another party in appropriate instances either (1) an admission, or (2) a sworn and specific denial or (3) a sworn statement "setting forth in detail the reasons why he cannot truthfully admit or deny." If the party obtains the second or third of these responses, in proper form, Rule 36 does not provide for a pretrial hearing on whether the response is warranted by the evidence thus far accumulated. Instead, Rule 37(c) is intended to provide posttrial relief in the form of a requirement that the party improperly refusing the admission pay the expenses of the other side in making the necessary proof at trial.

Rule 37(c), as now written, addresses itself in terms only to the sworn denial and is silent with respect to the statement of reasons for an inability to admit or deny. There is no apparent basis for this distinction, since the sanction provided in Rule 37(c) should deter all unjustified failures to admit. This omission in the rule has caused confused and diverse treatment in the courts. One court has held that if a party give inadequate reasons, he should be treated before trial as having denied the request, so that Rule 37(c) may apply. *Bertha Bldg. Corp. v. National Theatres Corp.,* 15 F.R.D. 339 (E.D.N.Y.1954). Another has held that the party should be treated as having admitted the request. *Heng Hsin Co. v. Stern, Morgenthau & Co.,* 20 Fed.Rules Serv. 36a.52, Case 1 (S.D.N.Y. Dec. 10, 1954). Still another has ordered a new response, without indicating what the outcome should be if the new response were inadequate. *United States Plywood Corp. v. Hudson Lumber Co.,* 127 F.Supp. 489, 497–498 (S.D.N.Y.1954). See generally Finman, *The Request for Admissions in Federal Civil Procedure,* 71 Yale L.J. 371,

426–430 (1962). The amendment eliminates this defect in Rule 37(c) by bringing within its scope all failures to admit.

Additional provisions in Rule 37(c) protect a party from having to pay expenses if the request for admission was held objectionable under Rule 36(a) or if the party failing to admit had reasonable ground to believe that he might prevail on the matter. The latter provision emphasizes that the true test under Rule 37(c) is not whether a party prevailed at trial but whether he acted reasonably in believing that he might prevail.

Subdivision (d). The scope of subdivision (d) is broadened to include responses to requests for inspection under Rule 34, thereby conforming to the new procedures of Rule 34.

Two related changes are made in subdivision (d): the permissible sanctions are broadened to include such orders "as are just"; and the requirement that the failure to appear or respond be "wilful" is eliminated. Although Rule 37(d) in terms provides for only three sanctions, all rather severe, the courts have interpreted it as permitting softer sanctions than those which it sets forth. E.g., *Gill v. Stolow,* 240 F.2d 669 (2d Cir.1957); *Saltzman v. Birrell,* 156 F.Supp. 538 (S.D.N.Y.1957); 2A Barron & Holtzoff, *Federal Practice and Procedure* 554–557 (Wright ed. 1961). The rule is changed to provide the greater flexibility as to sanctions which the cases show is needed.

The resulting flexibility as to sanctions eliminates any need to retain the requirement that the failure to appear or respond be "wilful." The concept of "wilful failure" is at best subtle and difficult, and the cases do not supply a bright line. Many courts have imposed sanctions without referring to wilfullness. E.g., *Milewski v. Schneider Transportation Co.,* 238 F.2d 397 (6th Cir.1956); *Dictograph Products, Inc. v. Kentworth Corp.,* 7 F.R.D. 543 (W.D.Ky.1947). In addition, in view of the possibility of light sanctions, even a negligent failure should come within Rule 37(d). If default is caused by counsel's ignorance of Federal practice, cf. *Dunn v. Pa. R.R.,* 96 F.Supp. 597 (N.D.Ohio 1951), or by his preoccupation with another aspect of the case, *cf. Maurer–Neuer, Inc. v. United Packinghouse Workers,* 26 F.R.D. 139 (D.Kans.1960), dismissal of the action and default judgment are not justified, but the imposition of expenses and fees may well be. "Wilfullness" continues to play a role, along with various other factors, in the choice of sanctions. Thus, the scheme conforms to Rule 37(b) as construed by the Supreme Court in *Societe Internationale v. Rogers,* 357 U.S. 197, 208 (1958).

A provision is added to make clear that a party may not properly remain completely silent even when he regards a notice to take his deposition or a set of interrogatories or requests to inspect as improper and objectionable. If he desires not to appear or not to respond, he must apply for a protective order. The cases are divided on whether a protective order must be sought. Compare *Collins v. Wayland,* 139 F.2d 677 (9th Cir. 1944), *cert. den.* 322 U.S. 744; *Bourgeois v. El Paso Natural Gas Co.,* 20 F.R.D. 358 (S.D.N.Y. 1957); *Loosley v. Stone,* 15 F.R.D. 373 (S.D.Ill.1954), with *Scarlatos v. Kulukundis,* 21 F.R.D. 185 (S.D.N.Y.1957); *Ross v. True Temper Corp.,* 11 F.R.D. 307 (N.D.Ohio 1951). Compare also Rosenberg, *supra,* 58 Col.L.Rev. 480, 496 (1958) with 2A Barron & Holtzoff, *Federal Practice and Procedure* 530–531 (Wright ed. 1961). The party from whom discovery is sought is afforded, through Rule 26(c), a fair and effective procedure whereby he can challenge the request made. At the same time, the total noncompliance with which Rule 37(d) is concerned may impose severe inconvenience or hardship on the discovering party and substantially delay the discovery process. Cf. 2B Barron & Holtzoff, *Federal Practice and Procedure* 306–307 (Wright ed. 1961) (response to a subpoena).

The failure of an officer or managing agent of a party to make discovery as required by present Rule 37(d) is treated as the failure of the party. The rule as revised provides similar treatment for a director of a party. There is slight warrant for the present distinction between officers and managing agents on the one hand and directors on the other. Although the legal power over a director to compel his making discovery may not be as great as over officers or managing agents, *Campbell v. General Motors Corp.,* 13 F.R.D. 331 (S.D.N.Y.1952), the practical differences are negligible. That a director's interests are normally aligned with those of his corporation is shown by the provisions of old Rule 26(d)(2), transferred to 32(a)(2) (deposition of director of party may be used at trial by an adverse party for any purpose) and of Rule 43(b) (director of party may be treated at trial as a hostile witness on direct examination by any adverse party). Moreover, in those rare instances when a corporation is unable through good faith efforts to compel a director to make discovery, it is unlikely that the court will impose sanctions. Cf. *Societe Internationale v. Rogers,* 357 U.S. 197 (1958).

Subdivision (e). The change in the caption conforms to the language of 28 U.S.C. § 1783, as amended in 1964.

Subdivision (f). Until recently, costs of a civil action could be awarded against the United States only when expressly provided by Act of Congress, and such provision was rarely made. See H.R.Rep.No. 1535, 89th Cong., 2d Sess., 2–3 (1966). To avoid any conflict with this doctrine, Rule 37(f) has provided that expenses and attorney's fees may not be imposed upon the United States under Rule 37. See 2A Barron & Holtzoff, *Federal Practice and Procedure* 857 (Wright ed. 1961).

A major change in the law was made in 1966, 80 Stat. 308, 28 U.S.C. § 2412 (1966), whereby a judgment for costs may ordinarily be awarded to the prevailing party in any civil action brought by or against the United States. Costs are not to include the fees and expenses of attorneys. In light of this legislative development, Rule 37(f) is amended to permit the award of expenses and fees against the United States under Rule 37, but only to the extent permitted by statute. The amendment brings Rule 37(f) into line with present and future statutory provisions.

1980 Amendment

Subdivision (b)(2). New Rule 26(f) provides that if a discovery conference is held, at its close the court shall enter an order respecting the subsequent conduct of discovery. The amendment provides that the sanctions available for violation of other court orders respecting discovery are available for violation of the discovery conference order.

Subdivision (e). Subdivision (e) is stricken. Title 28, U.S.C. § 1783 no longer refers to sanctions. The subdivision otherwise duplicates Rule 45(e)(2).

Subdivision (g). New Rule 26(f) imposes a duty on parties to participate in good faith in the framing of a discovery plan by agreement upon the request of any party. This subdivision authorizes the court to award to parties who participate in good faith in an attempt to frame a discovery plan the expenses incurred in the attempt if any party or his attorney fails to participate in good faith and thereby causes additional expense.

Failure of United States to Participate in Good Faith in Discovery. Rule 37 authorizes the court to direct that parties or attorneys who fail to participate in good faith in the discovery process pay the expenses, including attorneys' fees, incurred by other parties as a result of that failure. Since attorneys' fees cannot ordinarily be awarded against the United States (28 U.S.C. § 2412), there is often no practical remedy for the misconduct of its officers and attorneys. However, in the case of a government attorney who fails to participate in good faith in discovery, nothing prevents a court in an appropriate case from giving written notification of that fact to the Attorney General of the United States and other appropriate heads of offices or agencies thereof.

1987 Amendment

The amendments are technical. No substantive change is intended.

1993 Amendments

Subdivision (a). This subdivision is revised to reflect the revision of Rule 26(a), requiring disclosure of matters without a discovery request.

Pursuant to new subdivision (a)(2)(A), a party dissatisfied with the disclosure made by an opposing party may under this rule move for an order to compel disclosure. In providing for such a motion, the revised rule parallels the provisions of the former rule dealing with failures to answer particular interrogatories. Such a motion may be needed when the information to be disclosed might be helpful to the party seeking the disclosure but not to the party required to make the disclosure. If the party required to make the disclosure would need the material to support its own contentions, the more effective enforcement of the disclosure requirement will be to exclude the evidence not disclosed, as provided in subdivision (c)(1) of this revised rule.

Language is included in the new paragraph and added to the subparagraph (B) that requires litigants to seek to resolve discovery disputes by informal means before filing a motion with the court. This requirement is based on successful experience with similar local rules of court promulgated pursuant to Rule 83.

The last sentence of paragraph (2) is moved into paragraph (4).

Under revised paragraph (3), evasive or incomplete disclosures and responses to interrogatories and production requests are treated as failures to disclose or respond. Interrogatories and requests for production should not be read or interpreted in an artificially restrictive or hypertechnical manner to avoid disclosure of information fairly covered by the discovery request, and to do so is subject to appropriate sanctions under subdivision (a).

Revised paragraph (4) is divided into three subparagraphs for ease of reference, and in each the phrase "after opportunity for hearing" is changed to "after affording an opportunity to be heard" to make clear that the court can consider such questions on written submissions as well as on oral hearings.

Subparagraph (A) is revised to cover the situation where information that should have been produced without a motion to compel is produced after the motion is filed but before it is brought on for hearing. The rule also is revised to provide that a party should not be awarded its expenses for filing a motion that could have been avoided by conferring with opposing counsel.

Subparagraph (C) is revised to include the provision that formerly was contained in subdivision (a)(2) and to include the same requirement of an opportunity to be heard that is specified in subparagraphs (A) and (B).

Subdivision (c). The revision provides a self-executing sanction for failure to make a disclosure required by Rule 26(a), without need for a motion under subdivision (a)(2)(A).

Paragraph (1) prevents a party from using as evidence any witnesses or information that, without substantial justification, has not been disclosed as required by Rules 26(a) and 26(e)(1). This automatic sanction provides a strong inducement for disclosure of material that the disclosing party would expect to use as evidence, whether at a trial, at a hearing, or on a motion, such as one under Rule 56. As disclosure of evidence offered solely for impeachment purposes is not required under those rules, this preclusion sanction likewise does not apply to that evidence.

Limiting the automatic sanction to violations "without substantial justification," coupled with the exception for violations that are "harmless," is needed to avoid unduly harsh penalties in a variety of situations: *e.g.,* the inadvertent omission from a Rule 26(a)(1)(A) disclosure of the name of a potential witness known to all parties; the failure to list as a trial witness a person so listed by another party; or the lack of knowledge of a pro se litigant of the requirement to make disclosures. In the latter situation, however, exclusion would be proper if the requirement for disclosure had been called to the litigant's attention by either the court or another party.

Preclusion of evidence is not an effective incentive to compel disclosure of information that, being supportive of the position of the opposing party, might advantageously be concealed by the disclosing party. However, the rule provides the court with a wide range of other sanctions—such as declaring specified facts to be established, preventing contradictory evidence, or, like spoliation of evidence, allowing the jury to be informed of the fact of nondisclosure—that, though not self-executing, can be imposed when found to be warranted after a hearing. The failure to identify a witness or document in a disclosure statement would be admissible under the Federal Rules of Evidence under the same principles that allow a party's interrogatory answers to be offered against it.

Subdivision (d). This subdivision is revised to require that, where a party fails to file any response to interrogatories or a Rule 34 request, the discovering party should informally seek to obtain such responses before filing a motion for sanctions.

The last sentence of this subdivision is revised to clarify that it is the pendency of a motion for protective order that may be urged as an excuse for a violation of subdivision (d). If a party's motion has been denied, the party cannot argue that its subsequent failure to comply would be justified. In this connection, it should be noted that the filing of a motion under Rule 26(c) is not self-executing—the relief authorized under that rule depends on obtaining the court's order to that effect.

Subdivision (g). This subdivision is modified to conform to the revision of Rule 26(f).

2000 Amendment

Subdivision (c)(1). When this subdivision was added in 1993 to direct exclusion of materials not disclosed as required, the duty to supplement discovery responses pursuant to Rule 26(e)(2) was omitted. In the face of this omission, courts may rely on inherent power to sanction for failure to supplement as required by Rule 26(e)(2), *see 8 Federal Practice & Procedure* § 2050 at 607–09, but that is an uncertain and unregulated ground for imposing sanctions. There is no obvious occasion for a Rule 37(a) motion in connection with failure to supplement, and ordinarily only Rule 37(c)(1) exists as rule-based authority for sanctions if this supplementation obligation is violated.

The amendment explicitly adds failure to comply with Rule 26(e)(2) as a ground for sanctions under Rule 37(c)(1), including exclusion of withheld materials. The rule provides that this sanction power only applies when the failure to supplement was "without substantial justification." Even if the failure was not substantially justified, a party should be allowed to use the material that was not disclosed if the lack of earlier notice was harmless.

"Shall" is replaced by "is" under the program to conform amended rules to current style conventions when there is no ambiguity.

GAP Report

The Advisory Committee recommends that the published amendment proposal be modified to state that the exclusion sanction can apply to failure "to amend a prior response to discovery as required by Rule 26(e)(2)." In addition, one minor phrasing change is recommended for the Committee Note.

2006 Amendment

Subdivision (f). Subdivision (f) is new. It focuses on a distinctive feature of computer operations, the routine alteration and deletion of information that attends ordinary use. Many steps essential to computer operation may alter or destroy information, for reasons that have nothing to do with how that information might relate to litigation. As a result, the ordinary operation of computer systems creates a risk that a party may lose potentially discoverable information without culpable conduct on its part. Under Rule 37(f), absent exceptional circumstances, sanctions cannot be imposed for loss of electronically stored information resulting from the routine, good-faith operation of an electronic information system.

Rule 37(f) applies only to information lost due to the "routine operation of an electronic information system" — the ways in which such systems are generally designed, programmed, and implemented to meet the party's technical and business needs. The "routine operation" of computer systems includes the alteration and overwriting of information, often without the operator's specific direction or awareness, a feature with no direct counterpart in hard-copy documents. Such features are essential to the operation of electronic information systems.

Rule 37(f) applies to information lost due to the routine operation of an information system only if the operation was in good faith. Good faith in the routine operation of an information system may involve a party's intervention to modify or suspend certain features of that routine operation to prevent the loss of information, if that information is subject to a preservation obligation. A preservation obligation may arise from many sources, including common law, statutes, regulations, or a court order in the case. The good faith requirement of Rule 37(f) means that a party is not permitted to exploit the routine operation of an information system to thwart discovery obligations by allowing that operation to continue in order to destroy specific stored information that it is required to preserve. When a party is under a duty to preserve information because of pending or reasonably anticipated litigation, intervention in the routine operation of an information system is one aspect of what is often called a "litigation hold." Among the factors that bear on a party's good faith in the routine operation of an information system are the steps the party took to comply with a court order in the case or party agreement requiring preservation of specific electronically stored information.

Whether good faith would call for steps to prevent the loss of information on sources that the party believes are not reasonably accessible under Rule 26(b)(2) depends on the circumstances of each case. One factor is whether the party reasonably believes that the information on such sources is likely to be discoverable and not available from reasonably accessible sources.

The protection provided by Rule 37(f) applies only to sanctions "under these rules." It does not affect other sources of authority to impose sanctions or rules of professional responsibility.

This rule restricts the imposition of "sanctions." It does not prevent a court from making the kinds of adjustments frequently used in managing discovery if a party is unable to provide relevant responsive information. For example, a court could order the responding party to produce an additional witness for deposition, respond to additional interrogatories, or make similar attempts to provide substitutes or alternatives for some or all of the lost information.

2007 Amendment

The language of Rule 37 has been amended as part of the general restyling of the Civil Rules to make them more easily understood and to make style and terminology consistent throughout the rules. These changes are intended to be stylistic only.

HISTORICAL NOTES

Revision Notes and Legislative Reports

1980 Acts. Senate Report No. 96–974, Related House Report, and House Conference Report No. 96–1434, see 1980 U.S.Code Cong. and Adm.News, p. 4953.

Effective and Applicability Provisions

1980 Acts. Amendment by Pub.L. 96–481 effective Oct. 1, 1981, and applicable to adversary adjudication defined in section 504(b)(1)(C) of Title 5, and to civil actions and adversary adjudications described in section 2412 of Title 28,

Judiciary and Judicial Procedure, which are pending on, or commenced on or after Oct. 1, 1981, see section 208 of Pub.L. 96–481, set out as an Effective Date note under section 504 of Title 5, Government Organization and Employees.

CROSS REFERENCES

Failure to attend taking of a deposition or to serve subpoena, payment of expenses, see Fed.Rules Civ.Proc. Rule 30, 28 USCA.

TITLE VI. TRIALS

Rule 38. Right to a Jury Trial; Demand

(a) Right Preserved. The right of trial by jury as declared by the Seventh Amendment to the Constitution—or as provided by a federal statute—is preserved to the parties inviolate.

(b) Demand. On any issue triable of right by a jury, a party may demand a jury trial by:

(1) serving the other parties with a written demand—which may be included in a pleading—no later than 10 days after the last pleading directed to the issue is served; and

(2) filing the demand in accordance with Rule 5(d).

(c) Specifying Issues. In its demand, a party may specify the issues that it wishes to have tried by a jury; otherwise, it is considered to have demanded a jury trial on all the issues so triable. If the party has demanded a jury trial on only some issues, any other party may—within 10 days after being served with the demand or within a shorter time ordered by the court—serve a demand for a jury trial on any other or all factual issues triable by jury.

(d) Waiver; Withdrawal. A party waives a jury trial unless its demand is properly served and filed. A proper demand may be withdrawn only if the parties consent.

(e) Admiralty and Maritime Claims. These rules do not create a right to a jury trial on issues in a claim that is an admiralty or maritime claim under Rule 9(h).

(Amended February 28, 1966, effective July 1, 1966; March 2, 1987, effective August 1, 1987; April 22, 1993, effective December 1, 1993; April 30, 2007, effective December 1, 2007.)

ADVISORY COMMITTEE NOTES

1937 Adoption

This rule provides for the preservation of the constitutional right of trial by jury as directed in the enabling act (act of June 19, 1934, 48 Stat. 1064, U.S.C., Title 28, § 723c [sec. 2072]), and it and the next rule make definite provision for claim and waiver of jury trial, following the method used in many American states and in England and the British Dominions. Thus the claim must be made at once on initial pleading or appearance under Ill.Rev.Stat. (1937) ch. 110, § 188; 6 Tenn.Code Ann. (Williams, 1934) § 8734; compare Wyo.Rev.Stat.Ann. (1931) § 89–1320 (with answer or reply); within 10 days after the pleadings are completed or the case is at issue under 2 Conn.Gen.Stat. (1930) § 5624; Hawaii Rev.Laws (1935) § 4101; 2 Mass.Gen.Laws (Ter.Ed.1932) ch. 231, § 60; 3 Mich.Comp.Laws (1929) § 14263; Mich. Court Rules Ann. (Searl, 1933) Rule 33 (15 days); England (until 1933) O. 36, r.r. 2 and 6; and Ontario Jud. Act (1927) § 57(1) (4 days, or, where prior notice of trial, 2 days from such notice); or at a definite time varying under different codes, from 10 days before notice of trial to 10 days after notice, or, as in many, when the case is called for assignment, Ariz.Rev. Code Ann. (Struckmeyer, 1928) § 3802; Calif. Code Civ.Proc. (Deering, 1937) § 631, par. 4; Iowa Code (1935) § 10724; 4 Nev.Comp.Laws (Hillyer, 1929) § 8782; N.M. Stat.Ann. (Courtright, 1929) § 105–814; N.Y.C.P.A. (1937) § 426, subdivision 5 (applying to New York, Bronx, Richmond, Kings, and Queens Counties); R.I. Pub. Laws (1929), ch. 1327, amending R.I. Gen.Laws (1923) ch. 337, § 6; Utah Rev.Stat. Ann. (1933) § 104–23–6; 2 Wash.Rev.Stat.Ann. (Remington, 1932) § 316; England (4 days after notice of trial), Administration of Justice Act (1933) § 6 and amended rule under the Judicature Act (The Annual Practice, 1937), O. 36, r. 1; Australia High Court Procedure Act (1921) § 12, Rules, O. 33, r. 2; Alberta Rules of Ct. (1914) 172, 183, 184; British Columbia Sup.Ct.Rules (1925) O. 36, r.r. 2, 6, 11, and 16; New Brunswick Jud. Act (1927) O. 36, r.r. 2 and 5. See James, Trial by Jury and the New Federal Rules of Procedure (1936), 45 Yale L.J. 1022.

Rule 81(c) provides for claim for jury trial in removed actions.

The right to trial by jury as declared in U.S.C., Title 28, § 770 (Trial of issues of fact; by jury; exceptions), and similar statutes, is unaffected by this rule. This rule modifies U.S.C., Title 28, [former] § 773 (Trial of issues of fact; by court).

1966 Amendments

See Note to Rule 9(h), supra.

1987 Amendments

The amendments are technical. No substantive change is intended.

1993 Amendments

Language requiring the filing of a jury demand as provided in subdivision (d) is added to subdivision (b) to eliminate an apparent ambiguity between the two subdivisions. For proper scheduling of cases, it is important that jury demands not only be served on other parties, but also be filed with the court.

2007 Amendment

The language of Rule 38 has been amended as part of the general restyling of the Civil Rules to make them more easily understood and to make style and terminology consistent throughout the rules. These changes are intended to be stylistic only.

CROSS REFERENCES

Admiralty and maritime case, trial of issues of fact by jury, see 28 USCA § 1873.

Calendar to designate cases as "jury actions", see Fed. Rules Civ.Proc. Rule 79, 28 USCA.

Declaratory judgment actions, right to jury trial, see Fed. Rules Civ.Proc. Rule 57, 28 USCA.

Default judgment, right of trial by jury, see Fed.Rules Civ.Proc. Rule 55, 28 USCA.

Directed verdict, motion for which is not granted, not a waiver of trial by jury, see Fed.Rules Civ.Proc. Rule 50, 28 USCA.

Juries generally, see 28 USCA § 1861 et seq.

Recovery of forfeitures in actions on bonds and specialties, jury assessment of amount due, see 28 USCA § 1874.

Removed actions, time for service of jury demand, see Fed.Rules Civ.Proc. Rule 81, 28 USCA.

Supreme Court, jury trial in original actions at law, see 28 USCA § 1872.

Trial by jury or by the court, see Fed.Rules Civ.Proc. Rule 39, 28 USCA.

Trustee and receivers, right to jury trial in actions against, see 28 USCA § 959.

United States, jury trial denied in actions against, see 28 USCA § 2402.

Rule 39. Trial by Jury or by the Court

(a) When a Demand Is Made. When a jury trial has been demanded under Rule 38, the action must be designated on the docket as a jury action. The trial on all issues so demanded must be by jury unless:

(1) the parties or their attorneys file a stipulation to a nonjury trial or so stipulate on the record; or

(2) the court, on motion or on its own, finds that on some or all of those issues there is no federal right to a jury trial.

(b) When No Demand Is Made. Issues on which a jury trial is not properly demanded are to be tried by the court. But the court may, on motion, order a jury trial on any issue for which a jury might have been demanded.

(c) Advisory Jury; Jury Trial by Consent. In an action not triable of right by a jury, the court, on motion or on its own:

(1) may try any issue with an advisory jury; or

(2) may, with the parties' consent, try any issue by a jury whose verdict has the same effect as if a jury trial had been a matter of right, unless the action is against the United States and a federal statute provides for a nonjury trial.

(Amended April 30, 2007, effective December 1, 2007.)

ADVISORY COMMITTEE NOTES

1937 Adoption

The provisions for express waiver of jury trial found in U.S.C., Title 28, [former] § 773 (Trial of issues of fact; by court) are incorporated in this rule. See Rule 38, however, which extends the provisions for waiver of jury. U.S.C., Title 28, [former] § 772 (Trial of issues of fact; in equity in patent causes) is unaffected by this rule. When certain of the issues are to be tried by jury and others by the court, the court may determine the sequence in which such issues shall be tried. *See Liberty Oil Co. v. Condon Nat. Bank,* 260 U.S. 235, 43 S.Ct. 118, 67 L.Ed. 232 (1922).

A discretionary power in the courts to send issues of fact to the jury is common in state procedure. Compare Calif. Code Civ.Proc. (Deering, 1937) § 592; 1 Colo.Stat.Ann. (1935) Code Civ.Proc., ch. 12, § 191; Conn.Gen.Stat. (1930) § 5625; 2 Minn.Stat. (Mason, 1927) § 9288; 4 Mont.Rev. Codes Ann. (1935) § 9327; N.Y.C.P.A. (1937) § 430; 2 Ohio Gen.Code Ann. (Page, 1926) § 11380; 1 Okla.Stat.Ann. (Harlow, 1931) § 351 [12 Okl.St.Ann. § 557]; Utah Rev.Stat.Ann. (1933) § 104–23–5; 2 Wash.Rev.Stat.Ann. (Remington, 1932) § 315; Wis.Stat. (1935) § 270.07. See [former] Equity Rule 23 (Matters Ordinarily Determinable at Law When Arising in Suit in Equity to be Disposed of Therein) and U.S.C., Title 28 [former] § 772 (Trial of issues of fact; in equity in patent causes); *Colleton Merc. Mfg. Co. v. Savannah River Lumber Co.,* C.C.A.4, 1922, 280 F. 358; *Fed. Res. Bk. of San Francisco v. Idaho Grimm Alfalfa Seed Growers' Ass'n,* C.C.A.9, 1925, 8 F.2d 922, certiorari denied 46 S.Ct. 347, 270 U.S. 646, 70 L.Ed. 778 (1926); *Watt v. Starke,* 1879, 101 U.S. 247, 25 L.Ed. 826.

2007 Amendment

The language of Rule 39 has been amended as part of the general restyling of the Civil Rules to make them more easily understood and to make style and terminology consistent throughout the rules. These changes are intended to be stylistic only.

CROSS REFERENCES

Demand for jury trial, see Fed.Rules Civ.Proc. Rule 38, 28 USCA.

Enlargement of time after expiration of period prescribed, see Fed.Rules Civ.Proc. Rule 6, 28 USCA.

Findings of fact required in actions tried with an advisory jury, see Fed.Rules Civ.Proc. Rule 52, 28 USCA.

Report of masters in jury actions, see Fed.Rules Civ.Proc. Rule 53, 28 USCA.

Rule 40. Scheduling Cases for Trial

Each court must provide by rule for scheduling trials. The court must give priority to actions entitled to priority by a federal statute.

(Amended April 30, 2007, effective December 1, 2007.)

ADVISORY COMMITTEE NOTES

1937 Adoption

U.S.C., Title 28, [former] § 769 (Notice of case for trial) is modified. See former Equity Rule 56 (On Expiration of Time for Depositions, Case Goes on Trial Calendar). See also [former] Equity Rule 57 (Continuances).

For examples of statutes giving precedence, see U.S.C., Title 28, § 47 (now §§ 1253, 2101, 2325) (Injunctions as to orders of Interstate Commerce Commission); § 380 (now §§ 1253, 2101, 2284) (Injunctions; alleged unconstitutionality of state statutes); § 380a (now §§ 1253, 2101, 2284) (Same; Constitutionality of federal statute); [former] § 768 (Priority of cases where a state is party); Title 15, § 28 (Antitrust laws; suits against monopolies expedited); Title 22, § 240 (Petition for restoration of property seized as munitions of war, etc.); and Title 49, [former] § 44 (Proceedings in equity under interstate commerce laws; expedition of suits).

2007 Amendment

The language of Rule 40 has been amended as part of the general restyling of the Civil Rules to make them more easily understood and to make style and terminology consistent throughout the rules. These changes are intended to be stylistic only.

The best methods for scheduling trials depend on local conditions. It is useful to ensure that each district adopts an explicit rule for scheduling trials. It is not useful to limit or dictate the provisions of local rules.

CROSS REFERENCES

Adaption of local rules not inconsistent with these rules, see Fed.Rules Civ.Proc. Rule 83, 28 USCA.

Rule 41. Dismissal of Actions

(a) Voluntary Dismissal.

(1) ***By the Plaintiff.***

(A) *Without a Court Order.* Subject to Rules 23(e), 23.1(c), 23.2, and 66 and any applicable federal statute, the plaintiff may dismiss an action without a court order by filing:

(i) a notice of dismissal before the opposing party serves either an answer or a motion for summary judgment; or

(ii) a stipulation of dismissal signed by all parties who have appeared.

(B) *Effect.* Unless the notice or stipulation states otherwise, the dismissal is without prejudice. But if the plaintiff previously dismissed any federal-or state-court action based on or including the same claim, a notice of dismissal operates as an adjudication on the merits.

(2) ***By Court Order; Effect.*** Except as provided in Rule 41(a)(1), an action may be dismissed at the plaintiff's request only by court order, on terms that the court considers proper. If a defendant has pleaded a counterclaim before being served with the plaintiff's motion to dismiss, the action may be dismissed over the defendant's objection only if the counterclaim can remain pending for independent adjudication. Unless the order states otherwise, a dismissal under this paragraph (2) is without prejudice.

(b) Involuntary Dismissal; Effect. If the plaintiff fails to prosecute or to comply with these rules or a court order, a defendant may move to dismiss the action or any claim against it. Unless the dismissal order states otherwise, a dismissal under this subdivision (b) and any dismissal not under this rule—except one for lack of jurisdiction, improper venue, or failure to join a party under Rule 19—operates as an adjudication on the merits.

(c) Dismissing a Counterclaim, Crossclaim, or Third–Party Claim. This rule applies to a dismissal of any counterclaim, crossclaim, or third-party claim. A claimant's voluntary dismissal under Rule 41(a)(1)(A)(i) must be made:

(1) before a responsive pleading is served; or

(2) if there is no responsive pleading, before evidence is introduced at a hearing or trial.

(d) Costs of a Previously Dismissed Action. If a plaintiff who previously dismissed an action in any court files an action based on or including the same claim against the same defendant, the court:

(1) may order the plaintiff to pay all or part of the costs of that previous action; and

(2) may stay the proceedings until the plaintiff has complied.

(Amended December 27, 1946, effective March 19, 1948; January 21, 1963, effective July 1, 1963; February 28, 1966, effective July 1, 1966; December 4, 1967, effective July 1, 1968; March 2, 1987, effective August 1, 1987; April 30, 1991, effective December 1, 1991; April 30, 2007, effective December 1, 2007.)

ADVISORY COMMITTEE NOTES

1937 Adoption

Note to Subdivision (a). Compare Ill.Rev.Stat. (1937) c. 110, § 176, and *English Rules Under the Judicature Act* (The Annual Practice, 1937) O. 26.

Provisions regarding dismissal in such statutes as U.S.C., Title 8, § 164 [see 1329] (Jurisdiction of district courts in immigration cases) and U.S.C., Title 31, § 232 [now 3730] (Liability of persons making false claims against United States; suits) are preserved by paragraph (1).

Note to Subdivision (b). This provides for the equivalent of a nonsuit on motion by the defendant after the completion of the presentation of evidence by the plaintiff. Also, for actions tried without a jury, it provides the equivalent of the directed verdict practice for jury actions which is regulated by Rule 50.

1946 Amendment

Note. Subdivision (a). The insertion of the reference to Rule 66 correlates Rule 41(a)(1) with the express provisions concerning dismissal set forth in amended Rule 66 on receivers.

The change in Rule 41(a)(1)(i) gives the service of a motion for summary judgment by the adverse party the same effect in preventing unlimited dismissal as was originally given only to the service of an answer. The omission of reference to a motion for summary judgment in the original rule was subject to criticism. 3 *Moore's Federal Practice,* 1938, 3037–3038, n. 12. A motion for summary judgment may be forthcoming prior to answer, and if well taken will eliminate the necessity for an answer. Since such a motion may require even more research and preparation than the answer itself, there is good reason why the service of the motion, like that of the answer, should prevent a voluntary dismissal by the adversary without court approval.

The word "generally" has been stricken from Rule 41(a)(1)(ii) in order to avoid confusion and to conform with the elimination of the necessity for special appearance by original Rule 12(b).

Subdivision (b). In some cases tried without a jury, where at the close of plaintiff's evidence the defendant moves for dismissal under Rule 41(b) on the ground that plaintiff's evidence is insufficient for recovery, the plaintiff's own evidence may be conflicting or present questions of credibility. In ruling on the defendant's motion, questions arise as to the function of the judge in evaluating the testimony and whether findings should be made if the motion is sustained. Three circuits hold that as the judge is the trier of the facts in such a situation his function is not the same as on a motion to direct a verdict, where the jury is the trier of the facts, and that the judge in deciding such a motion in a non-jury case may pass on conflicts of evidence and credibility, and if he performs that function of evaluating the testimony and grants the motion on the merits, findings are required. *Young v. United States,* C.C.A.9, 1940, 111 F.2d 823; *Gary Theatre Co. v. Columbia Pictures Corporation,* C.C.A.7, 1941, 120 F.2d 891; *Bach v. Friden Calculating Machine Co., Inc.,* C.C.A.6, 1945, 148 F.2d 407. Cf. *Mateas v. Fred Harvey, a Corporation,* C.C.A.9, 1945, 146 F.2d 989. The Third Circuit has held that on such a motion the function of the court is the same as on a motion to direct in a jury case, and that the court should only decide whether there is evidence which would support a judgment for the plaintiff, and therefore, findings are not required by Rule 52. *Federal Deposit Insurance Corp. v. Mason,* C.C.A.3, 1940, 115 F.2d 548; *Schad v. Twentieth Century-Fox Film Corp.,* C.C.A.3, 1943, 136 F.2d 991. The added sentence in Rule 41(b) incorporates the view of the Sixth, Seventh and Ninth Circuits. See also 3 *Moore's Federal Practice,* 1938, Cum.Supplement § 41.03, under "Page 3045"; Commentary, *The Motion to Dismiss in Non-Jury Cases,* 1946, 9 Fed.Rules Serv., Comm.Pg. 41b.14.

1963 Amendment

Under the present text of the second sentence of this subdivision, the motion for dismissal at the close of the plaintiff's evidence may be made in a case tried to a jury as well as in a case tried without a jury. But, when made in a jury-tried case, this motion overlaps the motion for a directed verdict under Rule 50(a), which is also available in the same situation. It has been held that the standard to be applied in deciding the Rule 41(b) motion at the close of the plaintiff's evidence in a jury-tried case is the same as that used upon a motion for a directed verdict made at the same stage; and, just as the court need not make findings pursuant to Rule 52(a) when it directs a verdict, so in a jury-tried case it may omit these findings in granting the Rule 41(b) motion. See generally *O'Brien v. Westinghouse Electric Corp.,* 293 F.2d 1, 5–10 (3d Cir. 1961).

As indicated by the discussion in the *O'Brien* case, the overlap has caused confusion. Accordingly, the second and third sentences of Rule 41(b) are amended to provide that the motion for dismissal at the close of the plaintiff's evidence shall apply only to nonjury cases (including cases tried with an advisory jury). Hereafter the correct motion in jury-tried cases will be the motion for a directed verdict. This involves no change of substance. It should be noted that the court upon a motion for a directed verdict may in appropriate circumstances deny that motion and grant instead a new trial, or a voluntary dismissal without prejudice under Rule 41(a)(2). See 6 *Moore's Federal Practice* ¶59.08[5] (2d ed. 1954); *cf. Cone v. West Virginia Pulp & Paper Co.,* 330 U.S. 212, 217, 67 S.Ct. 752, 91 L.Ed. 849 (1947).

The first sentence of Rule 41(b), providing for dismissal for failure to prosecute or to comply with the Rules or any order of court, and the general provisions of the last sentence remain applicable in jury as well as nonjury cases.

The amendment of the last sentence of Rule 41(b) indicates that a dismissal for lack of an indispensable party does not operate as an adjudication on the merits. Such a dismissal does not bar a new action, for it is based merely "on a plaintiff's failure to comply with a precondition requisite to the Court's going forward to determine the merits of his substantive claim." See *Costello v. United States,* 365 U.S. 265, 284–288, 81 S.Ct. 534, 5 L.Ed.2d 551 & n. 5 (1961); *Mallow v. Hinde,* 12 Wheat. (25 U.S.) 193, 6 L.Ed. 599 (1827); Clark, *Code Pleading* 602 (2d ed. 1947); *Restatement of Judgments* § 49, comm. a, b (1942). This amendment corrects an omission from the rule and is consistent with an earlier amendment, effective in 1948, adding "the defense of failure to join an indispensable party" to clause (1) of Rule 12(h).

1966 Amendment

The terminology is changed to accord with the amendment of Rule 19. See that amended rule and the Advisory Committee's Note thereto.

1968 Amendment

The amendment corrects an inadvertent error in the reference to amended Rule 23.

1987 Amendment

The amendment is technical. No substantive change is intended.

1991 Amendment

Language is deleted that authorized the use of this rule as a means of terminating a non-jury action on the merits when the plaintiff has failed to carry a burden of proof in presenting the plaintiff's case. The device is replaced by the new provisions of Rule 52(c), which authorize entry of judgment against the defendant as well as the plaintiff, and earlier than the close of the case of the party against whom judgment is rendered. A motion to dismiss under Rule 41 on the ground that a plaintiff's evidence is legally insufficient should now be treated as a motion for judgment on partial findings as provided in Rule 52(c).

2007 Amendment

The language of Rule 41 has been amended as part of the general restyling of the Civil Rules to make them more easily understood and to make style and terminology consistent throughout the rules. These changes are intended to be stylistic only.

When Rule 23 was amended in 1966, Rules 23.1 and 23.2 were separated from Rule 23. Rule 41(a)(1) was not then amended to reflect the Rule 23 changes. In 1968 Rule 41(a)(1) was amended to correct the cross-reference to what had become Rule 23(e), but Rules 23.1 and 23.2 were inadvertently overlooked. Rules 23.1 and 23.2 are now added to the list of exceptions in Rule 41(a)(1)(A). This change does not affect established meaning. Rule 23.2 explicitly incorporates Rule 23(e), and thus was already absorbed directly into the exceptions in Rule 41(a)(1). Rule 23.1 requires court approval of a compromise or dismissal in language parallel to Rule 23(e) and thus supersedes the apparent right to dismiss by notice of dismissal.

CROSS REFERENCES

Approval of court for dismissal of class action, see Fed. Rules Civ.Proc. Rule 23, 28 USCA.

Costs, see Fed.Rules Civ.Proc. Rule 54, 28 USCA.

Counterclaim, cross-claim or third party claim, see Fed. Rules Civ.Proc. Rules 13 and 14, 28 USCA.

Discontinuance of civil actions arising under immigration laws, see 8 USCA § 1329.

Findings of fact in non-jury action, see Fed.Rules Civ.Proc. Rule 52, 28 USCA.

Motion for directed verdict at close of evidence offered by an opponent, see Fed.Rules Civ.Proc. Rule 50, 28 USCA.

Motion to dismiss, generally, see Fed.Rules Civ.Proc. Rule 12, 28 USCA.

Order of court for dismissal of action wherein receiver has been appointed, see Fed.Rules Civ.Proc. Rule 66, 28 USCA.

Production of documents, dismissal for failure of, see Fed. Rules Civ.Proc. Rule 37, 28 USCA.

Taxation of costs, see 28 USCA § 1920.

Withdrawal or discontinuance of false claim actions against United States, see 31 USCA § 3730.

Rule 42. Consolidation; Separate Trials

(a) Consolidation. If actions before the court involve a common question of law or fact, the court may:

(1) join for hearing or trial any or all matters at issue in the actions;

(2) consolidate the actions; or

(3) issue any other orders to avoid unnecessary cost or delay.

(b) Separate Trials. For convenience, to avoid prejudice, or to expedite and economize, the court may order a separate trial of one or more separate issues, claims, crossclaims, counterclaims, or third-party claims. When ordering a separate trial, the court must preserve any federal right to a jury trial.

(Amended February 28, 1966, effective July 1, 1966; April 30, 2007, effective December 1, 2007.)

ADVISORY COMMITTEE NOTES

1937 Adoption

Subdivision (a) is based upon U.S.C., Title 28, [former] § 734 (Orders to save costs; consolidation of causes of like nature) but in so far as the statute differs from this rule, it is modified.

For comparable statutes dealing with consolidation see Ark.Dig.Stat. (Crawford & Moses, 1921) § 1081; Calif.Code Civ.Proc. (Deering, 1937) § 1048; N.M.Stat.Ann. (Courtright, 1929) § 105–828; N.Y.C.P.A. (1937) §§ 96, 96a, and 97; American Judicature Society, Bulletin XIV, (1919) Art. 26.

For severance or separate trials see Calif.Code Civ.Proc. (Deering, 1937) § 1048; N.Y.C.P.A. (1937) § 96; American Judicature Society, Bulletin XIV (1919) Art. 3, § 2 and Art. 10, § 10. See also the third sentence of Equity Rule 29 (Defenses—How Presented) providing for discretionary separate hearing and disposition before trial of pleas in bar or abatement, and see also Rule 12(d) of these rules for preliminary hearings of defenses and objections.

For the entry of separate judgments, see Rule 54(b) (Judgment at Various Stages).

1966 Amendment

In certain suits in admiralty separation for trial of the issues of liability and damages (or of the extent of liability other than damages, such as salvage and general average) has been conducive to expedition and economy, especially because of the statutory right to interlocutory appeal in admiralty cases (which is of course preserved by these Rules). While separation of issues for trial is not to be routinely ordered, it is important that it be encouraged where experience has demonstrated its worth. Cf. Weinstein, *Routine Bifurcation of Negligence Trials,* 14 Vand. L.Rev. 831 (1961).

In cases (including some cases within the admiralty and maritime jurisdiction) in which the parties have a constitutional or statutory right of trial by jury, separation of issues may give rise to problems. See *e.g., United Air Lines, Inc. v. Wiener,* 286 F.2d 302 (9th Cir.1961). Accordingly, the proposed change in Rule 42 reiterates the mandate of Rule 38 respecting preservation of the right to jury trial.

2007 Amendment

The language of Rule 42 has been amended as part of the general restyling of the Civil Rules to make them more easily understood and to make style and terminology consistent throughout the rules. These changes are intended to be stylistic only.

CROSS REFERENCES

Preliminary hearings of defenses and objections, see Fed. Rules Civ.Proc. Rule 12, 28 USCA.

Separate—

Judgments, see Fed.Rules Civ.Proc. Rule 54, 28 USCA.

Trial for parties, see Fed.Rules Civ.Proc. Rule 20, 28 USCA.

Trials of counterclaims or cross-claims, see Fed.Rules Civ.Proc. Rule 13, 28 USCA.

Third party claims, see Fed.Rules Civ.Proc. Rule 14, 28 USCA.

Rule 43. Taking Testimony

(a) In Open Court. At trial, the witnesses' testimony must be taken in open court unless a federal statute, the Federal Rules of Evidence, these rules, or other rules adopted by the Supreme Court provide otherwise. For good cause in compelling circumstances and with appropriate safeguards, the court may permit testimony in open court by contemporaneous transmission from a different location.

(b) Affirmation Instead of an Oath. When these rules require an oath, a solemn affirmation suffices.

(c) Evidence on a Motion. When a motion relies on facts outside the record, the court may hear the matter on affidavits or may hear it wholly or partly on oral testimony or on depositions.

(d) Interpreter. The court may appoint an interpreter of its choosing; fix reasonable compensation to be paid from funds provided by law or by one or more parties; and tax the compensation as costs.

(Amended February 28, 1966, effective July 1, 1966; November 20, 1972, and December 18, 1972, effective July 1, 1975; March 2, 1987, effective August 1, 1987; April 23, 1996, effective December 1, 1996; April 30, 2007, effective December 1, 2007.)

ADVISORY COMMITTEE NOTES

1937 Adoption

Note to Subdivision (a). The first sentence is a restatement of the substance of U.S.C., Title 28, § 635 (Proof in common-law actions), [former] § 637 (see §§ 2072, 2073) (Proof in equity and admiralty), and [former] Equity Rule 46 (Trial—Testimony Usually Taken in Open Court—Rulings on Objections to Evidence). This rule abolishes in patent and trademark actions, the practice under [former] Equity Rule 48 of setting forth in affidavits the testimony in chief of expert witnesses whose testimony is directed to matters of opinion. The second and third sentences on admissibility of evidence and Subdivision (b) on contradiction and cross-examination modify U.S.C., Title 28, § 725 (now 1652) (Laws of states as rules of decision) insofar as that statute has been construed to prescribe conformity to state rules of evidence. Compare Callahan and Ferguson, *Evidence and the New Federal Rules of Civil Procedure,* 45 Yale L.J. 622 (1936), and *Same: 2,* 47 Yale L.J. 195 (1937). The last sentence modifies to the extent indicated U.S.C., Title 28, [former] § 631 (Competency of witnesses governed by State laws).

Note to Subdivision (b). See 4 *Wigmore on Evidence* (2d ed., 1923) § 1885 et seq.

Note to Subdivision (c). See [former] Equity Rule 46 (Trial—Testimony Usually Taken in Open Court-Rulings on Objections to Evidence). With the last sentence compare *Dowagiac v. Lochren,* 143 Fed. 211 (C.C.A. 8th, 1906). See also *Blease v. Garlington,* 92 U.S. 1, 23 L.Ed. 521 (1876); *Nelson v. United States,* 201 U.S. 92, 114, 26 S.Ct. 358, 50 L.Ed. 673 (1906); *Unkle v. Wills,* 281 Fed. 29 (C.C.A. 8th, 1922).

See Rule 61 for harmless error in either the admission or exclusion of evidence.

Note to Subdivision (d). See [former] Equity Rule 78 (Affirmation in Lieu of Oath) and U.S.C., Title 1, § 1 (Words importing singular number, masculine gender, etc.; extended application), providing for affirmation in lieu of oath.

Supplementary Note on Advisory Committee Regarding Rules 43 and 44

Note. These rules have been criticized and suggested improvements offered by commentators. 1 *Wigmore on Evidence,* 3d ed. 1940, 200–204; Green, *The Admissibility of Evidence Under the Federal Rules,* 1941, 55 Harv.L.Rev. 197. Cases indicate, however, that the rule is working better than these commentators had expected. *Boerner v. United States,* C.C.A.2d, 1941, 117 F.2d 387, cert. den., 1941, 313 U.S. 587, 61 S.Ct. 1120; *Mosson v. Liberty Fast Freight Co.,* C.C.A.2d, 1942, 124 F.2d, 448; *Hartford Accident & Indemnity Co. v. Olivier,* C.C.A. 5th, 1941, 123 F.2d 709; *Anzano v. Metropolitan Life Ins. Co. of New York,* C.C.A.3d, 1941, 118 F.2d 430; *Franzen v. E. I. DuPont De Nemours & Co.,* C.C.A.3d, 1944, 146 F.2d 837; *Fakouri v. Cadais,* C.C.A. 5th, 1945, 147 F.2d 667; *In re C. & P. Co.,* S.D.Cal.1945, 63 F.Supp. 400, 408. But cf. *United States v. Aluminum Co. of America,* S.D.N.Y.1938, 1 Fed.Rules Serv. 43a.3, Case 1; Note, 1946, 46 Col.L.Rev. 267. While consideration of a comprehensive and detailed set of rules of evidence seems very desirable, it has not been feasible for the Committee so far to undertake this important task. Such consideration should include the adaptability to federal practice of all or parts of the proposed Code of Evidence of the American Law Institute. See Armstrong, *Proposed Amendments to Federal Rules of Civil Procedure,* 4 F.R.D. 124, 137–138.

1966 Amendment

Note to Subdivision (f). This new subdivision [subdivision (f)] authorizes the court to appoint interpreters (including interpreters for the deaf), to provide for their compensation, and to tax the compensation as costs. Compare proposed subdivision (b) of Rule 28 of the Federal Rules of Criminal Procedure.

1972 Amendment

Rule 43, entitled Evidence, has heretofore served as the basic rule of evidence for civil cases in federal courts. Its very general provisions are superseded by the detailed provisions of the new Rules of Evidence. The original title and many of the provisions of the rule are, therefore, no longer appropriate.

Subdivision (a). The provision for taking testimony in open court is not duplicated in the Rules of Evidence and is retained. Those dealing with admissibility of evidence and competency of witnesses, however, are no longer needed or appropriate since those topics are covered at large in the Rules of Evidence. They are accordingly deleted. The language is broadened, however, to take account of acts of Congress dealing with the taking of testimony, as well as of the Rules of Evidence and any other rules adopted by the Supreme Court.

Subdivision (b). The subdivision is no longer needed or appropriate since the matters with which it deals are treated in the Rules of Evidence. The use of leading questions, both generally and in the interrogation of an adverse party or witness identified with him, is the subject of Evidence Rule 611(c). Who may impeach is treated in Evidence Rule 601 [sic; probably means 607], and scope of cross-examination is covered in Evidence Rule 611(b). The subdivision is accordingly deleted.

Subdivision (c). Offers of proof and making a record of excluded evidence are treated in Evidence Rule 103. The subdivision is no longer needed or appropriate and is deleted.

1987 Amendment

The amendment is technical. No substantive change is intended.

1996 Amendment

Rule 43(a) is revised to conform to the style conventions adopted for simplifying the present Civil Rules. The only intended changes of meaning are described below.

The requirement that testimony be taken "orally" is deleted. The deletion makes it clear that testimony of a witness may be given in open court by other means if the witness is not able to communicate orally. Writing or sign language are common examples. The development of advanced technology may enable testimony to be given by other means. A witness unable to sign or write by hand may be able to communicate through a computer or similar device.

Contemporaneous transmission of testimony from a different location is permitted only on showing good cause in compelling circumstances. The importance of presenting live testimony in court cannot be forgotten. The very ceremony of trial and the presence of the factfinder may exert a powerful force for truthtelling. The opportunity to judge the demeanor of a witness face-to-face is accorded great value in our tradition. Transmission cannot be justified merely by showing that it is inconvenient for the witness to attend the trial.

The most persuasive showings of good cause and compelling circumstances are likely to arise when a witness is unable to attend trial for unexpected reasons, such as accident or illness, but remains able to testify from a different place. Contemporaneous transmission may be better than an attempt to reschedule the trial, particularly if there is a risk that other—and perhaps more important—witnesses might not be available at a later time.

Other possible justifications for remote transmission must be approached cautiously. Ordinarily depositions, including video depositions, provide a superior means of securing the testimony of a witness who is beyond the reach of a trial subpoena, or of resolving difficulties in scheduling a trial that can be attended by all witnesses. Deposition procedures ensure the opportunity of all parties to be represented while the witness is testifying. An unforeseen need for the testimony of a remote witness that arises during trial, however, may establish good cause and compelling circumstances. Justification is particularly likely if the need arises from the interjection of new issues during trial or from the unexpected inability to present testimony as planned from a different witness.

Good cause and compelling circumstances may be established with relative ease if all parties agree that testimony should be presented by transmission. The court is not bound by a stipulation, however, and can insist on live testimony. Rejection of the parties' agreement will be influenced, among other factors, by the apparent importance of the testimony in the full context of the trial.

A party who could reasonably foresee the circumstances offered to justify transmission of testimony will have special difficulty in showing good cause and the compelling nature of the circumstances. Notice of a desire to transmit testimony from a different location should be given as soon as the reasons are known, to enable other parties to arrange a deposition, or to secure an advance ruling on transmission so as to know whether to prepare to be present with the witness while testifying.

No attempt is made to specify the means of transmission that may be used. Audio transmission without video images may be sufficient in some circumstances, particularly as to less important testimony. Video transmission ordinarily should be preferred when the cost is reasonable in relation to the matters in dispute, the means of the parties, and the circumstances that justify transmission. Transmission that merely produces the equivalent of a written statement ordinarily should not be used.

Safeguards must be adopted that ensure accurate identification of the witness and that protect against influence by persons present with the witness. Accurate transmission likewise must be assured.

Other safeguards should be employed to ensure that advance notice is given to all parties of foreseeable circumstances that may lead the proponent to offer testimony by transmission. Advance notice is important to protect the opportunity to argue for attendance of the witness at trial. Advance notice also ensures an opportunity to depose the witness, perhaps by video record, as a means of supplementing transmitted testimony.

2007 Amendment

The language of Rule 43 has been amended as part of the general restyling of the Civil Rules to make them more easily understood and to make style and terminology consistent throughout the rules. These changes are intended to be stylistic only.

HISTORICAL NOTES

References in Text

The Federal Rules of Evidence, referred to in subd. (a), are set out in this title.

CROSS REFERENCES

Amendment of pleading to conform to evidence, see Fed. Rules Civ.Proc. Rule 15, 28 USCA.

Compelling giving of testimony, application of rules, see Fed.Rules Civ.Proc. Rule 81, 28 USCA.

Depositions of witnesses in foreign country, see 28 USCA § 1781.

Evidence—

Generally, see 28 USCA § 1731 et seq.

Hearing before master, see Fed.Rules Civ.Proc. Rule 53, 28 USCA.

Exceptions to rulings unnecessary, see Fed.Rules Civ. Proc. Rule 46, 28 USCA.

Foreign law, determination of, see Fed.Rules Civ.Proc. Rule 44.1, 28 USCA.

Harmless error in admitting or excluding evidence, see Fed.Rules Civ.Proc. Rule 61, 28 USCA.

Interested persons, competency, see 28 USCA § 1822.

Offer of judgment, see Fed.Rules Civ.Proc. Rule 68, 28 USCA.

Perpetuation of testimony by action, see Fed.Rules Civ. Proc. Rule 27, 28 USCA.

Pre-trial procedure, see Fed.Rules Civ.Proc. Rule 16, 28 USCA.

Proof of official record, see Fed.Rules Civ.Proc. Rule 44, 28 USCA.

Record made in regular course of business, see 28 USCA § 1732.

Record on appeal, form of testimony included in, see Federal Rules of Appellate Procedure Rule 10, 28 USCA.

Subpoena for attendance of witnesses and obtaining evidence, see Fed.Rules Civ.Proc. Rule 45, 28 USCA.

United States, evidence to establish claim on default, see Fed.Rules Civ.Proc. Rule 55, 28 USCA.

Witnesses generally, see 28 USCA § 1821 et seq.

Rule 44. Proving an Official Record

(a) Means of Proving.

(1) ***Domestic Record.*** Each of the following evidences an official record—or an entry in it—that is otherwise admissible and is kept within the United States, any state, district, or commonwealth, or any territory subject to the administrative or judicial jurisdiction of the United States:

(A) an official publication of the record; or

(B) a copy attested by the officer with legal custody of the record—or by the officer's deputy—and accompanied by a certificate that the officer has custody. The certificate must be made under seal:

(i) by a judge of a court of record in the district or political subdivision where the record is kept; or

(ii) by any public officer with a seal of office and with official duties in the district or political subdivision where the record is kept.

(2) ***Foreign Record.***

(A) *In General.* Each of the following evidences a foreign official record—or an entry in it—that is otherwise admissible:

(i) an official publication of the record; or

(ii) the record—or a copy—that is attested by an authorized person and is accompanied either by a final certification of genuineness or by a certification under a treaty or convention to which the United States and the country where the record is located are parties.

(B) *Final Certification of Genuineness.* A final certification must certify the genuineness of the signature and official position of the attester or of any foreign official whose certificate of genuineness relates to the attestation or is in a chain of certificates of genuineness relating to the attestation. A final certification may be made by a secretary of a United States embassy or legation; by a consul general, vice consul, or consular agent of the United States; or by a diplomatic or consular official of the foreign country assigned or accredited to the United States.

(C) *Other Means of Proof.* If all parties have had a reasonable opportunity to investigate a foreign record's authenticity and accuracy, the court may, for good cause, either:

(i) admit an attested copy without final certification; or

(ii) permit the record to be evidenced by an attested summary with or without a final certification.

(b) Lack of a Record. A written statement that a diligent search of designated records revealed no record or entry of a specified tenor is admissible as evidence that the records contain no such record or entry. For domestic records, the statement must be authenticated under Rule 44(a)(1). For foreign records, the statement must comply with (a)(2)(C)(ii).

(c) Other Proof. A party may prove an official record—or an entry or lack of an entry in it—by any other method authorized by law.

(Amended February 28, 1966, effective July 1, 1966; March 2, 1987, effective August 1, 1987; April 30, 1991, effective December 1, 1991; April 30, 2007, effective December 1, 2007.)

ADVISORY COMMITTEE NOTES

1937 Adoption

This rule provides a simple and uniform method of proving public records, and entry or lack of entry therein, in all cases including those specifically provided for by statutes of the United States. Such statutes are not superseded, however, and proof may also be made according to their provisions whenever they differ from this rule. Some of those statutes are:

U.S.C., Title 28 [former sections]:

§ 661[now 1733] (Copies of department or corporation records and papers; admissibility; seal)

§ 662[now 1733] (Same; in office of General Counsel of the Treasury)

§ 663[now 1733] (Instruments and papers of Comptroller of Currency; admissibility)

§ 664[now 1733] (Organization certificates of national banks; admissibility)

§ 665[now 1733] (Transcripts from books of Treasury in suits against delinquents; admissibility)

§ 666[now 1733] (Same; certificate by Secretary or Assistant Secretary)

§ 670[now 1743] (Admissibility of copies of statements of demands by Post Office Department)

§ 671[now 1733] (Admissibility of copies of post office records and statement of accounts)

§ 672[former] (Admissibility of copies of records in General Land Office)

§ 673[now 1744] (Admissibility of copies of records, and so forth, of Patent Office)

§ 674[now 1745] (Copies of foreign letters patent as prima facie evidence)

§ 675[former] (Copies of specifications and drawings of patents admissible)

§ 676[now 1736] (Extracts from Journals of Congress admissible when injunction of secrecy removed)

§ 677[now 1740] (Copies of records in offices of United States consuls admissible)

§ 678[former] (Books and papers in certain district courts)

§ 679[former] (Records in clerks' offices, Western District of North Carolina)

§ 680[former] (Records in clerks' offices of former district of California)

§ 681[now 1734] (Original records lost or destroyed; certified copy admissible)

§ 682[now 1734] (Same; when certified copy not obtainable)

§ 685[now 1735] (Same; certified copy of official papers)

§ 687[now 1738] (Authentication of legislative acts; proof of judicial proceedings of State)

§ 688[now 1739] (Proofs of records in offices not pertaining to courts)

§ 689[now 1742] (Copies of foreign records relating to land titles)

§ 695[now 1732] (Writings and records made in regular course of business; admissibility)

§ 695e[now 1741] (Foreign documents on record in public offices; certification)

U.S.C., Title 1:

§ 30[now 112] (Statutes at large; contents; admissibility in evidence)

§ 30a[now 113] ("Little and Brown's" edition of laws and treaties competent evidence of Acts of Congress)

§ 54[now 204] (Codes and supplements as establishing prima facie the laws of United States and District of Columbia, etc.)

§ 55[now 208] (Copies of supplements to Code of Laws of United States and of District of Columbia Code and supplements; conclusive evidence of original)

U.S.C., Title 5:

§ 490[former] (Records of Department of Interior; authenticated copies as evidence)

U.S.C., Title 6:

§ 7[now Title 31, § 9306] (Surety Companies as sureties; appointment of agents; service of process)

U.S.C., Title 8:

§ 9a[see 1435(c)] (Citizenship of children of persons naturalized under certain laws; repatriation of native-born women married to aliens prior to September 22, 1922; copies of proceedings)

§ 356[see 1443] (Regulations for execution of naturalization laws; certified copies of papers as evidence)

§ 399b(d)[see 1443] (Certifications of naturalization records; authorization; admissibility as evidence)

U.S.C., Title 11:

§ 44(d), (e), (f), (g)[former] (Bankruptcy court proceedings and orders as evidence)

§ 204[former] (Extensions extended, etc.; evidence of confirmation)

§ 207(j)[former] (Corporate reorganizations; certified copy of decree as evidence)

U.S.C., Title 15:

§ 127 (Trade-mark records in Patent Office; copies as evidence)

U.S.C., Title 20:

§ 52 (Smithsonian Institution; evidence of title to site and buildings)

U.S.C., Title 25:

§ 6 (Bureau of Indian Affairs; seal; authenticated and certified documents; evidence)

U.S.C., Title 31:

§ 46[now 704] (Laws governing General Accounting Office; copies of books, records, etc., thereof as evidence)

U.S.C., Title 38:

§ 11g[see 202] (Seal of Veterans' Administration; authentication of copies of records)

U.S.C., Title 40:

§ 238 [former 44 U.S.C.A. § 300h] (National Archives; seal; reproduction of archives; fee; admissibility in evidence of reproductions)

§ 270c [see now 40 U.S.C.A. § 3133(a)] (Bonds of contractors for public works; right of person furnishing labor or material to copy of bond)

U.S.C., Title 43:

§§ 57–59 (Copies of land surveys, etc., in certain states and districts admissible as evidence)

§ 83 (General Land Office registers and receivers; transcripts of records as evidence)

U.S.C., Title 46:

§ 823 (Records of Maritime Commission; copies; publication of reports; evidence)

U.S.C., Title 47:

§ 154(m) (Federal Communications Commission; copies of reports and decisions as evidence)

§ 412 (Documents filed with Federal Communications Commission as public records; prima facie evidence; confidential records)

U.S.C., Title 49:

§ 14(3)[now 10310] (Interstate Commerce Commission reports and decisions; printing and distribution of copies)

§ 16(13)[now 10303(b)] (Copies of schedules, tariffs, etc. filed with Interstate Commerce Commission as evidence)

§ 19a(i)[now 10785(c)] (Valuation of property of carriers by Interstate Commerce Commission; final published valuations as evidence)

Supplementary Note of Advisory Committee Regarding Rules 43 and 44.

For supplementary note of Advisory Committee on this rule, see note under Rule 43.

1966 Amendment

Note to Subdivision (a)(1). These provisions on proof of official records kept within the United States are similar in substance to those heretofore appearing in Rule 44. There is a more exact description of the geographical areas covered. An official record kept in one of the areas enumerated qualifies for proof under subdivision (a)(1) even though it is not a United States official record. For example, an official record kept in one of these areas by a government in exile falls within subdivision (a)(1). It also falls within subdivision (a)(2) which may be availed of alternatively. Cf. *Banco de Espana v. Federal Reserve Bank,* 114 F.2d 438 (2d Cir. 1940).

Note to Subdivision (a)(2). Foreign official records may be proved, as heretofore, by means of official publications thereof. See *United States v. Aluminum Co. of America,* 1 F.R.D. 71 (S.D.N.Y.1939). Under this rule, a document that, on its face, appears to be an official publication, is admissible, unless a party opposing its admission into evidence shows that it lacks that character.

The rest of subdivision (a)(2) aims to provide greater clarity, efficiency, and flexibility in the procedure for authenticating copies of foreign official records.

The reference to attestation by "the officer having the legal custody of the record," hitherto appearing in Rule 44, has been found inappropriate for official records kept in foreign countries where the assumed relation between custody and the authority to attest does not obtain. See 2B Barron & Holtzoff, Federal Practice & Procedure § 992 (Wright ed. 1961). Accordingly it is provided that an attested copy may be obtained from any person authorized by the law of the foreign country to make the attestation without regard to whether he is charged with responsibility for maintaining the record or keeping it in his custody.

Under Rule 44 a United States foreign service officer has been called on to certify to the authority of the foreign official attesting the copy as well as the genuineness of his signature and his official position. See Schlesinger, *Comparative Law 57* (2d ed. 1959); Smit, *International Aspects of Federal Civil Procedure,* 61 Colum.L.Rev. 1031, 1063 (1961); 22 C.F.R. § 92.41(a), (e) (1958). This has created practical difficulties. For example, the question of the authority of the foreign officer might raise issues of foreign law which were beyond the knowledge of the United States officer. The difficulties are met under the amended rule by eliminating the element of the authority of the attesting foreign official from the scope of the certifying process, and by specifically permitting use of the chain-certificate method. Under this method, it is sufficient if the original attestation purports to have been issued by an authorized person and is accompanied by a certificate of another foreign official whose certificate may in turn be followed by that of a foreign official of higher rank. The process continues until a foreign official is reached as to whom the United States foreign service official (or a diplomatic or consular officer of the foreign country assigned or accredited to the United States) has adequate information upon which to base a "final certification." See *New York Life Ins. Co. v. Aronson,* 38 F.Supp. 687 (W.D.Pa.1941); 22 C.F.R. § 92.37 (1958).

The final certification (a term used in contradistinction to the certificates prepared by the foreign officials in a chain) relates to the incumbency and genuineness of signature of the foreign official who attested the copy of the record or, where the chain-certificate method is used, of a foreign official whose certificate appears in the chain, whether that certificate is the last in the chain or not. A final certification may be prepared on the basis of material on file in the consulate or any other satisfactory information.

Although the amended rule will generally facilitate proof of foreign official records, it is recognized that in some situations it may be difficult or even impossible to satisfy the basic requirements of the rule. There may be no United States consul in a particular foreign country; the foreign officials may not cooperate, peculiarities may exist or arise hereafter in the law or practice of a foreign country. See *United States v. Grabina,* 119 F.2d 863 (2d Cir. 1941); and, generally, Jones, *International Judicial Assistance: Procedural Chaos and a Program for Reform,* 62 Yale L.J. 515, 548–49 (1953). Therefore the final sentence of subdivision (a)(2) provides the court with discretion to admit an attested copy of a record without a final certification, or an attested summary of a record with or without a final certification. See Rep. of Comm. on Comparative Civ.Proc. & Prac., Proc. A.B.A., Sec. Int'l & Comp.L. 123, 130–31 (1952); Model Code of Evidence §§ 517, 519 (1942). This relaxation should be permitted only when it is shown that the party has been unable to satisfy the basic requirements of the amended rule despite his reasonable efforts. Moreover it is specially provided that the parties must be given a reasonable opportunity in these cases to examine into the authenticity and accuracy of the copy or summary.

Note to Subdivision (b). This provision relating to proof of lack of record is accommodated to the changes made in subdivision (a).

Note to Subdivision (c). The amendment insures that international agreements of the United States are unaffected by the rule. Several consular conventions contain provisions for reception of copies or summaries of foreign official records. See, e.g., Consular Conv. with Italy, May 8, 1878, art. X, 20 Stat. 725, T.S. No. 178 (Dept. State 1878). See also 28 U.S.C. §§ 1740–42, 1745; *Fakouri v. Cadais,* 149 F.2d 321 (5th Cir.1945), cert. denied 326 U.S. 742 (1945); 5 *Moore's Federal Practice,* par. 44.05 (2d ed. 1951).

1987 Amendment

The amendments are technical. No substantive change is intended.

1991 Amendment

The amendment to paragraph (a)(1) strikes the references to specific territories, two of which are no longer subject to the jurisdiction of the United States, and adds a generic term to describe governments having a relationship with the United States such that their official records should be treated as domestic records.

The amendment to paragraph (a)(2) adds a sentence to dispense with the final certification by diplomatic officers when the United States and the foreign country where the record is located are parties to a treaty or convention that abolishes or displaces the requirement. In that event the treaty or convention is to be followed. This changes the former procedure for authenticating foreign official records only with respect to records from countries that are parties to the Hague Convention Abolishing the Requirement of Legalization for Foreign Public Documents. Moreover, it does not affect the former practice of attesting the records, but only changes the method of certifying the attestation.

The Hague Public Documents Convention provides that the requirement of a final certification is abolished and replaced with a model *apostille,* which is to be issued by officials of the country where the records are located. See Hague Public Documents Convention, Arts. 2–4. The *apostille* certifies the signature, official position, and seal of the attesting officer. The authority who issues the *apostille* must maintain a register or card index showing the serial number of the *apostille* and other relevant information recorded on it. A foreign court can then check the serial number and information on the *apostille* with the issuing authority in order to guard against the use of fraudulent *apostilles.* This system provides a reliable method for maintaining the integrity of the authentication process, and the *apostille* can be accorded greater weight than the normal authentication procedure because foreign officials are more likely to know the precise capacity under their law of the attesting officer than would an American official. See generally Comment, *The United States and the Hague Convention Abolishing the Requirement of Legalization for Foreign Public Documents,* 11 HARV. INT'L L.J. 476, 482, 488 (1970).

2007 Amendment

The language of Rule 44 has been amended as part of the general restyling of the Civil Rules to make them more easily understood and to make style and terminology consistent throughout the rules. These changes are intended to be stylistic only.

CROSS REFERENCES

Authenticated and certified copy of government record by archivist admissible on evidence, see 44 USCA § 2116.

Rule 44.1. Determining Foreign Law

A party who intends to raise an issue about a foreign country's law must give notice by a pleading or other writing. In determining foreign law, the court may consider any relevant material or source, including testimony, whether or not submitted by a party or admissible under the Federal Rules of Evidence. The court's determination must be treated as a ruling on a question of law.

(Adopted February 28, 1966, effective July 1, 1966; amended November 20, 1972, effective July 1, 1975; March 2, 1987, effective August 1, 1987; April 30, 2007, effective December 1, 2007.)

ADVISORY COMMITTEE NOTES

1966 Adoption

Rule 44.1 is added by amendment to furnish Federal courts with a uniform and effective procedure for raising and determining an issue concerning the law of a foreign country.

To avoid unfair surprise, the *first sentence* of the new rule requires that a party who intends to raise an issue of foreign law shall give notice thereof. The uncertainty under Rule 8(a) about whether foreign law must be pleaded—compare *Siegelman v. Cunard White Star, Ltd.,* 221 F.2d 189 (2d Cir.1955), and *Pedersen v. United States,* 191 F.Supp. 95 (D. Guam 1961), with *Harrison v. United Fruit Co.,* 143 F.Supp. 598 (S.D.N.Y.1956)—is eliminated by the provision that the notice shall be "written" and "reasonable." It may, but need not be, incorporated in the pleadings. In some situations the pertinence of foreign law is apparent from the outset; accordingly the necessary investigation of that law will have been accomplished by the party at the pleading stage, and the notice can be given conveniently in the pleadings. In other situations the pertinence of foreign law may remain doubtful until the case is further developed. A requirement that notice of foreign law be given only through the medium of the pleadings would tend in the latter instances to force the party to engage in a peculiarly burdensome type of investigation which might turn out to be unnecessary; and correspondingly the adversary would be forced into a possible wasteful investigation. The liberal provisions for amendment of the pleadings afford help if the pleadings are used as the medium of giving notice of the foreign law; but it seems best to permit a written notice to be given outside of and later than the pleadings, provided the notice is reasonable.

The new rule does not attempt to set any definite limit on the party's time for giving the notice of an issue of foreign law; in some cases the issue may not become apparent until the trial and notice then given may still be reasonable. The stage which the case had reached at the time of the notice, the reason proffered by the party for his failure to give earlier notice, and the importance to the case as a whole of the issue of foreign law sought to be raised, are among the factors which the court should consider in deciding a question of the reasonableness of a notice. If notice is given by one party it need not be repeated by any other and serves as a basis for presentation of material on the foreign law by all parties.

The *second sentence* of the new rule describes the materials to which the court may resort in determining an issue of foreign law. Heretofore the district courts, applying Rule 43(a), have looked in certain cases to State law to find the rules of evidence by which the content of foreign-country law is to be established. The State laws vary; some embody procedures which are inefficient, time consuming and expensive. See, generally, Nussbaum, *Proving the Law of Foreign Countries,* 3 Am. J. Comp. L. 60 (1954). In all events the ordinary rules of evidence are often inapposite to the problem of determining foreign law and have in the past prevented examination of material which could have provided a proper basis for the determination. The new rule permits consideration by the court of any relevant material, including testimony, without regard to its admissibility under Rule 43. Cf. N.Y. Civ. Prac. Law & Rules, R. 4511 (effective Sept. 1, 1963); 2 Va. Code Ann. tit. 8, § 8–273; 2 W. Va. Code Ann. § 5711.

In further recognition of the peculiar nature of the issue of foreign law, the new rule provides that in determining this law the court is not limited by material presented by the parties; it may engage in its own research and consider any relevant material thus found. The court may have at its disposal better foreign law materials than counsel have presented, or may wish to reexamine and amplify material that has been presented by counsel in partisan fashion or in insufficient detail. On the other hand, the court is free to insist on a complete presentation by counsel.

There is no requirement that the court give formal notice to the parties of its intention to engage in its own research on an issue of foreign law which has been raised by them, or of its intention to raise and determine independently an issue not raised by them. Ordinarily the court should inform the parties of material it has found diverging substantially from the material which they have presented; and in general the court should give the parties an opportunity to analyze and counter new points upon which it proposes to rely. See Schlesinger, *Comparative Law* 142 (2d ed. 1959); Wyzanski, *A Trial Judge's Freedom and Responsibility,* 65 Harv. L.Rev. 1281, 1296 (1952); cf. *Siegelman v. Cunard White Star, Ltd.*, supra, 221 F.2d at 197. To require, however, that the court give formal notice from time to time as it proceeds with its study of the foreign law would add an element of undesirable rigidity to the procedure for determining issues of foreign law.

The new rule refrains from imposing an obligation on the court to take "judicial notice" of foreign law because this would put an extreme burden on the court in many cases; and it avoids use of the concept of "judicial notice" in any form because of the uncertain meaning of that concept as applied to foreign law. See, e.g., Stern, *Foreign Law in the Courts: Judicial Notice and Proof,* 45 Calif.L.Rev. 23, 43 (1957). Rather the rule provides flexible procedures for presenting and utilizing material on issues of foreign law by which a sound result can be achieved with fairness to the parties.

Under the *third sentence,* the court's determination of an issue of foreign law is to be treated as a ruling on a question of "law," not "fact," so that appellate review will not be narrowly confined by the "clearly erroneous" standard of Rule 52(a). *Cf. Uniform Judicial Notice of Foreign Law Act* § 3; Note, 72 Harv.L.Rev. 318 (1958).

The new rule parallels Article IV of the Uniform Interstate and International Procedure Act, approved by the Commissioners on Uniform State Laws in 1962, except that § 4.03 of Article IV states that "[t]he court, not the jury" shall determine foreign law. The new rule does not address itself to this problem, since the Rules refrain from allocating functions as between the court and the jury. See Rule 38(a). It has long been thought, however, that the jury is not the appropriate body to determine issues of foreign law. See, e.g., Story, *Conflict of Laws,* § 638 (1st ed. 1834, 8th ed. 1883); 1 Greenleaf, *Evidence,* § 486 (1st ed. 1842, 16th ed. 1899); 4 Wigmore, *Evidence* § 2558 (1st ed. 1905); 9 id. § 2558 (3d ed. 1940). The majority of the States have committed such issues to determination by the court. See Article 5 of the Uniform Judicial Notice of Foreign Law Act, adopted by twenty-six states, 9A U.L.A. 318 (1957) (Suppl.1961, at 134); N.Y.Civ.Prac.Law & Rules, R. 4511 (effective Sept. 1, 1963); Wigmore, loc. cit. And Federal courts that have considered the problem in recent years have reached the same conclusion without reliance on statute. See *Jansson v. Swedish American Line,* 185 F.2d 212, 216 (1st Cir.1950); *Bank of Nova Scotia v. San Miguel,* 196 F.2d 950, 957, n. 6 (1st Cir.1952); *Liechti v. Roche,* 198 F.2d 174 (5th Cir.1952); *Daniel Lumber Co. v. Empresas Hondureñas, S.A.*, 215 F.2d 465 (5th Cir.1954).

1972 Amendment

Since the purpose of the provision is to free the judge, in determining foreign law, from any restrictions imposed by evidence rules, a general reference to the Rules of Evidence is appropriate and is made.

1987 Amendment

The amendment is technical. No substantive change is intended.

2007 Amendment

The language of Rule 44.1 has been amended as part of the general restyling of the Civil Rules to make them more easily understood and to make style and terminology consistent throughout the rules. These changes are intended to be stylistic only.

HISTORICAL NOTES

References in Text

The Federal Rules of Evidence, referred to in text, are set out in this title.

Effective Date of Amendment Proposed November 20, 1972

Amendment of this rule embraced by the order entered by the Supreme Court of the United States on November 20, 1972, effective on the 180th day beginning after January 2,

1975, see section 3 of Pub.L. 93–595, Jan. 2, 1975, 88 Stat. 1959, set out as a note under section 2071 of Title 28.

Rule 45. Subpoena

(a) In General.

(1) ***Form and Contents.***

(A) *Requirements—In General.* Every subpoena must:

(i) state the court from which it issued;

(ii) state the title of the action, the court in which it is pending, and its civil-action number;

(iii) command each person to whom it is directed to do the following at a specified time and place: attend and testify; produce designated documents, electronically stored information, or tangible things in that person's possession, custody, or control; or permit the inspection of premises; and

(iv) set out the text of Rule 45(c) and (d).

(B) *Command to Attend a Deposition—Notice of the Recording Method.* A subpoena commanding attendance at a deposition must state the method for recording the testimony.

(C) *Combining or Separating a Command to Produce or to Permit Inspection; Specifying the Form for Electronically Stored Information.* A command to produce documents, electronically stored information, or tangible things or to permit the inspection of premises may be included in a subpoena commanding attendance at a deposition, hearing, or trial, or may be set out in a separate subpoena. A subpoena may specify the form or forms in which electronically stored information is to be produced.

(D) *Command to Produce; Included Obligations.* A command in a subpoena to produce documents, electronically stored information, or tangible things requires the responding party to permit inspection, copying, testing, or sampling of the materials.

(2) ***Issued from Which Court.* A subpoena must issue as follows:**

(A) for attendance at a hearing or trial, from the court for the district where the hearing or trial is to be held;

(B) for attendance at a deposition, from the court for the district where the deposition is to be taken; and

(C) for production or inspection, if separate from a subpoena commanding a person's attendance, from the court for the district where the production or inspection is to be made.

(3) ***Issued by Whom.*** The clerk must issue a subpoena, signed but otherwise in blank, to a party who requests it. That party must complete it before service. An attorney also may issue and sign a subpoena as an officer of:

(A) a court in which the attorney is authorized to practice; or

(B) a court for a district where a deposition is to be taken or production is to be made, if the attorney is authorized to practice in the court where the action is pending.

(b) Service.

(1) ***By Whom; Tendering Fees; Serving a Copy of Certain Subpoenas.*** Any person who is at least 18 years old and not a party may serve a subpoena. Serving a subpoena requires delivering a copy to the named person and, if the subpoena requires that person's attendance, tendering the fees for 1 day's attendance and the mileage allowed by law. Fees and mileage need not be tendered when the subpoena issues on behalf of the United States or any of its officers or agencies. If the subpoena commands the production of documents, electronically stored information, or tangible things or the inspection of premises before trial, then before it is served, a notice must be served on each party.

(2) ***Service in the United States.*** Subject to Rule 45(c)(3)(A)(ii), a subpoena may be served at any place:

(A) within the district of the issuing court;

(B) outside that district but within 100 miles of the place specified for the deposition, hearing, trial, production, or inspection;

(C) within the state of the issuing court if a state statute or court rule allows service at that place of a subpoena issued by a state court of general jurisdiction sitting in the place specified for the deposition, hearing, trial, production, or inspection; or

(D) that the court authorizes on motion and for good cause, if a federal statute so provides.

(3) ***Service in a Foreign Country.*** 28 U.S.C. § 1783 governs issuing and serving a subpoena directed to a United States national or resident who is in a foreign country.

(4) ***Proof of Service.*** Proving service, when necessary, requires filing with the issuing court a statement showing the date and manner of service and the names of the persons served.

The statement must be certified by the server.

(c) Protecting a Person Subject to a Subpoena.

(1) ***Avoiding Undue Burden or Expense; Sanctions.*** A party or attorney responsible for issuing and serving a subpoena must take reasonable steps to avoid imposing undue burden or expense on a person subject to the subpoena. The issuing court must enforce this duty and impose an appropriate sanction—which may include lost earnings and reasonable attorney's fees—on a party or attorney who fails to comply.

(2) ***Command to Produce Materials or Permit Inspection.***

(A) *Appearance Not Required.* A person commanded to produce documents, electronically stored information, or tangible things, or to permit the inspection of premises, need not appear in person at the place of production or inspection unless also commanded to appear for a deposition, hearing, or trial.

(B) *Objections.* A person commanded to produce documents or tangible things or to permit inspection may serve on the party or attorney designated in the subpoena a written objection to inspecting, copying, testing or sampling any or all of the materials or to inspecting the premises—or to producing electronically stored information in the form or forms requested. The objection must be served before the earlier of the time specified for compliance or 14 days after the subpoena is served. If an objection is made, the following rules apply:

(i) At any time, on notice to the commanded person, the serving party may move the issuing court for an order compelling production or inspection.

(ii) These acts may be required only as directed in the order, and the order must protect a person who is neither a party nor a party's officer from significant expense resulting from compliance.

(3) ***Quashing or Modifying a Subpoena.***

(A) *When Required.* On timely motion, the issuing court must quash or modify a subpoena that:

(i) fails to allow a reasonable time to comply;

(ii) requires a person who is neither a party nor a party's officer to travel more than 100 miles from where that person resides, is employed, or regularly transacts business in person—except that, subject to Rule 45(c)(3)(B)(iii), the person may be commanded to attend a trial by traveling from any such place within the state where the trial is held;

(iii) requires disclosure of privileged or other protected matter, if no exception or waiver applies; or

(iv) subjects a person to undue burden.

(B) *When Permitted.* To protect a person subject to or affected by a subpoena, the issuing court may, on motion, quash or modify the subpoena if it requires:

(i) disclosing a trade secret or other confidential research, development, or commercial information;

(ii) disclosing an unretained expert's opinion or information that does not describe specific occurrences in dispute and results from the expert's study that was not requested by a party; or

(iii) a person who is neither a party nor a party's officer to incur substantial expense to travel more than 100 miles to attend trial.

(C) *Specifying Conditions as an Alternative.* In the circumstances described in Rule 45(c)(3)(B), the court may, instead of quashing or modifying a subpoena, order appearance or production under specified conditions if the serving party:

(i) shows a substantial need for the testimony or material that cannot be otherwise met without undue hardship; and

(ii) ensures that the subpoenaed person will be reasonably compensated.

(d) Duties in Responding to a Subpoena.

(1) ***Producing Documents or Electronically Stored Information.*** These procedures apply to producing documents or electronically stored information:

(A) *Documents.* A person responding to a subpoena to produce documents must produce them as they are kept in the ordinary course of business or must organize and label them to correspond to the categories in the demand.

(B) *Form for Producing Electronically Stored Information Not Specified.* If a subpoena does not specify a form for producing electronically stored information, the person responding must produce it in a form or forms in which it is ordinarily maintained or in a reasonably usable form or forms.

(C) *Electronically Stored Information Produced in Only One Form.* The person responding need not produce the same electronically stored information in more than one form.

(D) *Inaccessible Electronically Stored Information.* The person responding need not provide discovery of electronically stored information from sources that the person identifies as not reasonably accessible because of undue burden or cost. On motion to compel discovery or for a protective order, the person responding must show that the information is not reasonably accessible because of undue burden or cost. If that showing is made, the court may nonetheless order discovery from such sources if the requesting party shows good cause, considering the limitations of Rule 26(b)(2)(C). The court may specify conditions for the discovery.

(2) ***Claiming Privilege or Protection.***

(A) *Information Withheld.* A person withholding subpoenaed information under a claim that it is privileged or subject to protection as trial-preparation material must:

(i) expressly make the claim; and

(ii) describe the nature of the withheld documents, communications, or tangible things in a manner that, without revealing information itself privileged or protected, will enable the parties to assess the claim.

(B) *Information Produced.* If information produced in response to a subpoena is subject to a claim of privilege or of protection as trial-preparation material, the person making the claim may notify any party that received the information of the claim and the basis for it. After being notified, a party must promptly return, sequester, or destroy the specified information and any copies it has; must not use or disclose the information until the claim is resolved; must take reasonable steps to retrieve the information if the party disclosed it before being notified; and may promptly present the information to the court under seal for a determination of the claim. The person who produced the information must preserve the information until the claim is resolved.

(e) Contempt. The issuing court may hold in contempt a person who, having been served, fails without adequate excuse to obey the subpoena. A nonparty's failure to obey must be excused if the subpoena purports to require the nonparty to attend or produce at a place outside the limits of Rule 45(c)(3)(A)(ii).

(Amended December 27, 1946, effective March 19, 1948; December 29, 1948, effective October 20, 1949; March 30, 1970, effective July 1, 1970; April 29, 1980, effective August 1, 1980; April 29, 1985, effective August 1, 1985; March 2, 1987, effective August 1, 1987; April 30, 1991, effective December 1, 1991; April 25, 2005, effective December 1, 2005; April 12, 2006, effective December 1, 2006; April 30, 2007, effective December 1, 2007.)

ADVISORY COMMITTEE NOTES

1937 Adoption

This rule applies to subpoenas ad testificandum and duces tecum issued by the district courts for attendance at a hearing or a trial, or to take depositions. It does not apply to the enforcement of subpoenas issued by administrative officers and commissions pursuant to statutory authority. The enforcement of such subpoenas by the district courts is regulated by appropriate statutes. Many of these statutes do not place any territorial limits on the validity of subpoenas so issued, but provide that they may be served anywhere within the United States. Among such statutes are the following:

U.S.C., Title 7, §§ 222 and 511n (Secretary of Agriculture)

U.S.C., Title 15, § 49 (Federal Trade Commission)

U.S.C., Title 15, §§ 77v(b), 78u(c), 79r(d) (Securities and Exchange Commission)

U.S.C., Title 16, §§ 797(g) and 825f (Federal Power Commission)

U.S.C., Title 19, § 1333(b) (Tariff Commission)

U.S.C., Title 22, §§ 268, 270d and 270e (International Commissions, etc.)

U.S.C., Title 26, §§ 614, 619(b) [see 7456] (Board of Tax Appeals)

U.S.C., Title 26, § 1523(a) [see 7608] (Internal Revenue Officers)

U.S.C., Title 29, § 161 (Labor Relations Board)

U.S.C., Title 33, § 506 (Secretary of Army)

U.S.C., Title 35, §§ 54 to 56 [now 24] (Patent Office proceedings)

U.S.C., Title 38, [former] § 133 (Veterans' Administration)

U.S.C., Title 41, § 39 (Secretary of Labor)

U.S.C., Title 45, § 157 Third. (h) (Board of Arbitration under Railway Labor Act)

U.S.C., Title 45, § 222(b) (Investigation Commission under Railroad Retirement Act of 1935)

U.S.C., Title 46, § 1124(b) (Maritime Commission)

U.S.C., Title 47, § 409(c) and (d) (Federal Communications Commission)

U.S.C., Title 49, § 12(2) and (3) [now 10321] (Interstate Commerce Commission)

U.S.C., Title 49, § 173a [see 1484] (Secretary of Commerce)

Note to Subdivisions (a) and (b). These simplify the form of subpoena as provided in U.S.C., Title 28, [former] § 655 (Witnesses; subpoena; form; attendance under); and broaden U.S.C, Title 28, [former] § 636 (Production for books and writings) to include all actions, and to extend to any person. With the provision for relief from an oppressive or unreasonable subpoena duces tecum, compare N.Y.C.P.A. (1937) § 411.

Note to Subdivision (c). This provides for the simple and convenient method of service permitted under many state codes; e.g., N.Y.C.P.A. (1937) §§ 220, 404, J.Ct.Act, § 191; 3 Wash.Rev.Stat.Ann. (Remington, 1932) § 1218. Compare former Equity Rule 15 (Process, by Whom Served).

For statutes governing fees and mileage of witnesses see:

U.S.C., Title 28 former sections:

600a[now 1871] (Per diem; mileage)

600c[now 1821, 1823] (Amount per diem and mileage for witnesses; subsistence)

600d[former] (Fees and mileage in certain states)

601[former] (Witnesses' fees; enumeration)

602[now 1824] (Fees and mileage of jurors and witnesses)

603[see Title 5, §§ 5515, 5537] (No officer of court to have witness fees)

Note to Subdivision (d). The method provided in paragraph (1) for the authorization of the issuance of subpoenas has been employed in some districts. See *Henning v. Boyle*, S.D.N.Y.1901, 112 F. 397. The requirement of an order for the issuance of a subpoena duces tecum is in accordance with U.S.C., Title 28, [former] § 647 (Deposition under dedimus potestatem; subpoena duces tecum). The provisions of paragraph (2) are in accordance with common practice. See U.S.C., Title 28, former § 648 (Deposition under dedimus potestatem; witnesses, when required to attend); N.Y.C.P.A. (1937) § 300; 1 N.J.Rev.Stat. (1937) 2:27–174.

Note to Subdivision (e). The first paragraph continues the substance of U.S.C., Title 28, [former] § 654 (Witnesses; subpoenas; may run into another district). Compare U.S.C., Title 11, [former] § 69 (Referees in bankruptcy; contempts before) (production of books and writings) which is not affected by this rule. For examples of statutes which allow the court, upon proper application and cause shown, to authorize the clerk of the court to issue a subpoena for a witness who lives in another district and at a greater distance than 100 miles from the place of the hearing or trial, see:

U.S.C., Title 15:

§ 23 (Suits by United States; subpoenas for witnesses) (under antitrust laws).

U.S.C., Title 38:

§ 445[now 784] (Actions on claims; jurisdiction; parties; procedure; limitation; witnesses; definitions) (Veterans' insurance contracts).

The second paragraph continues the present procedure applicable to certain witnesses who are in foreign countries. See U.S.C., Title 28, §§ 711 [now 1783] (Letters rogatory to take testimony of witness, addressed to court of foreign country; failure of witness to appear; subpoena) and 713 [now 1783] (Service of Subpoena on witness in foreign country).

Note to Subdivision (f). Compare [former] Equity Rule 52 (Attendance of Witnesses Before Commissioner, Master, or Examiner).

1946 Amendment

Note to Subdivision (b). The added words, "or tangible things" in subdivision (b) merely make the rule for the subpoena duces tecum at the trial conform to that of subdivision (d) for the subpoena at the taking of depositions. The insertion of the words "or modify" in clause (1) affords desirable flexibility.

Subdivision (d). The added last sentence of amended subdivision (d)(1) properly gives the subpoena for documents or tangible things the same scope as provided in Rule 26(b), thus promoting uniformity. The requirement in the last sentence of original Rule 45(d)(1)—to the effect that leave of court should be obtained for the issuance of such a subpoena—has been omitted. This requirement is unnecessary and oppressive on both counsel and court, and it had been criticized by district judges. There is no satisfactory reason for a differentiation between a subpoena for the production of documentary evidence by a witness at a trial (Rule 45(a)) and for the production of the same evidence at the taking of a deposition. Under this amendment, the person subpoenaed may obtain the protection afforded by any of the orders permitted under Rule 30(b) or Rule 45(b). See *Application of Zenith Radio Corp.*, E.D.Pa.1941, 4 F.Rules Serv. 30b.21. Case 1, 1 F.R.D. 627; *Fox v. House*, Okla.1939, 29 F.Supp. 673; *United States of America for the Use of Tilo Roofing Co., Inc. v. J. Slotnik Co.*, Conn.1944, 3 F.R.D. 408.

The changes in subdivisions (d)(2) give the court the same power in the case of residents of the district as is conferred in the case of non-residents, and permit the court to fix a place for attendance which may be more convenient and accessible for the parties than that specified in the rule.

1948 Amendment

The amendment effective October 1949, substituted the reference to "Title 28, U.S.C., § 1783" at the end of subdivision (e)(2) for the reference to "the Act of July 3, 1926, c. 762, §§ 1, 3 (44 Stat. 835), U.S.C., Title 28, § 713."

1970 Amendment

At present, when a subpoena duces tecum is issued to a deponent, he is required to produce the listed materials at the deposition, but is under no clear compulsion to permit their inspection and copying. This results in confusion and uncertainty before the time the deposition is taken, with no mechanism provided whereby the court can resolve the matter. Rule 45(d)(1), as revised, makes clear that the subpoena authorizes inspection and copying of the materials produced. The deponent is afforded full protection since he can object, thereby forcing the party serving the subpoena to obtain a court order if he wishes to inspect and copy. The procedure is thus analogous to that provided in Rule 34.

The changed references to other rules conform to changes made in those rules. The deletion of words in the clause describing the proper scope of the subpoena conforms to a change made in the language of Rule 34. The reference to Rule 26(b) is unchanged but encompasses new matter in that subdivision. The changes make it clear that the scope of discovery through a subpoena is the same as that applicable to Rule 34 and the other discovery rules.

1980 Amendment

Subdivision (d)(1). The amendment defines the term "proof of service" as used in the first sentence of the present subdivision. For want of a definition, the district court clerks have been obliged to fashion their own, with results that vary from district to district. All that seems required is a simple certification on a copy of the notice to take a deposition that the notice has been served on every other party to the action. That is the proof of service required by Rule 25(d) of both the Federal Rules of Appellate Procedure and the Supreme Court Rules.

Subdivision (e)(1). The amendment makes the reach of a subpoena of a district court at least as extensive as that of the state courts of general jurisdiction in the state in which the district court is held. Under the present rule the reach of a district court subpoena is often greater, since it extends throughout the district. No reason appears why it should be less, as it sometimes is because of the accident of district lines. Restrictions upon the reach of subpoenas are imposed to prevent undue inconvenience to witnesses. State statutes and rules of court are quite likely to reflect the varying degrees of difficulty and expense attendant upon local travel.

1985 Amendment

Present Rule 45(d)(2) has two sentences setting forth the territorial scope of deposition subpoenas. The first sentence is directed to depositions taken in the judicial district in which the deponent resides; the second sentence addresses situations in which the deponent is not a resident of the district in which the deposition is to take place. The Rule, as currently constituted, creates anomalous situations that often cause logistical problems in conducting litigation.

The first sentence of the present Rule states that a deponent may be required to attend only in the *county* wherein that person resides or is employed or transacts business in person, that is, where the person lives or works. Under this provision a deponent can be compelled, without court order, to travel from one end of that person's home county to the other, no matter how far that may be. The second sentence of the Rule is somewhat more flexible, stating that someone who does not reside in the district in which the deposition is to be taken can be required to attend in the county where the person is served with the subpoena, *or* within 40 miles from the place of service.

Under today's conditions there is no sound reason for distinguishing between residents of the district or county in which a deposition is to be taken and nonresidents, and the Rule is amended to provide that any person may be subpoenaed to attend a deposition within a specified radius from that person's residence, place of business, or where the person was served. The 40-mile radius has been increased to 100 miles.

1987 Amendment

The amendments are technical. No substantive change is intended.

1991 Amendment

Purposes of Revision. The purposes of this revision are (1) to clarify and enlarge the protections afforded persons who are required to assist the court by giving information or evidence; (2) to facilitate access outside the deposition procedure provided by Rule 30 to documents and other information in the possession of persons who are not parties; (3) to facilitate service of subpoenas for depositions or productions of evidence at places distant from the district in which an action is proceeding; (4) to enable the court to compel a witness found within the state in which the court sits to attend trial; (5) to clarify the organization of the text of the rule.

Subdivision (a). This subdivision is amended in seven significant respects.

First, Paragraph (a)(3) modifies the requirement that a subpoena be issued by the clerk of court. Provision is made for the issuance of subpoenas by attorneys as officers of the court. This revision perhaps culminates an evolution. Subpoenas were long issued by specific order of the court. As this became a burden to the court, general orders were made authorizing clerks to issue subpoenas on request. Since 1948, they have been issued in blank by the clerk of any federal court to any lawyer, the clerk serving as stationer to the bar. In allowing counsel to issue the subpoena, the rule is merely a recognition of present reality.

Although the subpoena is in a sense the command of the attorney who completes the form, defiance of a subpoena is nevertheless an act in defiance of a court order and exposes the defiant witness to contempt sanctions. In *ICC v. Brimson,* 154 U.S. 447 (1894), the Court upheld a statute directing federal courts to issue subpoenas to compel testimony before the ICC. In *CAB v. Hermann,* 353 U.S. 322 (1957), the Court approved as established practice the issuance of administrative subpoenas as a matter of absolute agency right. And in *NLRB v. Warren Co.,* 350 U.S. 107 (1955), the Court held that the lower court had no discretion to withhold sanctions against a contemnor who violated such subpoenas. The 1948 revision of Rule 45 put the attorney in a position similar to that of the administrative agency, as a public officer entitled to use the court's contempt power to investigate facts in dispute. Two courts of appeals have touched on the issue and have described lawyer-issued subpoenas as mandates of the court. *Waste Conversion, Inc. v. Rollins Environmental Services (NJ), Inc.,* 893 F.2d 605 (3d cir., 1990); *Fisher v. Marubent Cotton Corp.,* 526 F.2d 1338, 1340 (8th cir., 1975). Cf. *Young v. United States ex rel Vuitton et Fils S.A.,* 481 U.S. 787, 821 (1987) (Scalia, J., concurring). This revision makes the rule explicit that the attorney acts as an officer of the court in issuing and signing subpoenas.

Necessarily accompanying the evolution of this power of the lawyer as officer of the court is the development of increased responsibility and liability for the misuse of this power. The latter development is reflected in the provisions of subdivision (c) of this rule, and also in the requirement imposed by paragraph (3) of this subdivision that the attorney issuing a subpoena must sign it.

Second, Paragraph (a)(3) authorizes attorneys in distant districts to serve as officers authorized to issue commands in the name of the court. Any attorney permitted to represent a client in a federal court, even one admitted pro haec vice, has the same authority as a clerk to issue a subpoena from any federal court for the district in which the subpoena is served and enforced. In authorizing attorneys to issue subpoenas from distant courts, the amended rule effectively authorizes service of a subpoena anywhere in the United States by an attorney representing any party. This change is intended to ease the administrative burdens of inter-district law practice. The former rule resulted in delay and expense caused by the need to secure forms from clerks' offices some distance from the place at which the action proceeds. This change does not enlarge the burden on the witness.

Pursuant to Paragraph (a)(2), a subpoena for a deposition must still issue from the court in which the deposition or production would be compelled. Accordingly, a motion to quash such a subpoena if it overbears the limits of the subpoena power must, as under the previous rule, be presented to the court for the district in which the deposition would occur. Likewise, the court in whose name the subpoena is issued is responsible for its enforcement.

Third, in order to relieve attorneys of the need to secure an appropriate seal to affix to a subpoena issued as an officer of a distant court, the requirement that a subpoena be under seal is abolished by the provisions of Paragraph (a)(1).

Fourth, Paragraph (a)(1) authorizes the issuance of a subpoena to compel a non-party to produce evidence independent of any deposition. This revision spares the necessity of a deposition of the custodian of evidentiary material required to be produced. A party seeking additional production from a person subject to such a subpoena may serve an additional subpoena requiring additional production at the same time and place.

Fifth, Paragraph (a)(2) makes clear that the person subject to the subpoena is required to produce materials in that person's control whether or not the materials are located within the district or within the territory within which the subpoena can be served. The non-party witness is subject to the same scope of discovery under this rule as that person would be as a party to whom a request is addressed pursuant to Rule 34.

Sixth, Paragraph (a)(1) requires that the subpoena include a statement of the rights and duties of witnesses by setting forth in full the text of the new subdivisions (c) and (d).

Seventh, the revised rule authorizes the issuance of a subpoena to compel the inspection of premises in the possession of a non-party. Rule 34 has authorized such inspections of premises in the possession of a party as discovery compelled under Rule 37, but prior practice required an independent proceeding to secure such relief ancillary to the federal proceeding when the premises were not in the possession of a party. Practice in some states has long authorized such use of a subpoena for this purpose without apparent adverse consequence.

Subdivision (b). Paragraph (b)(1) retains the text of the former subdivision (c) with minor changes.

The reference to the United States marshal and deputy marshal is deleted because of the infrequency of the use of these officers for this purpose. Inasmuch as these officers meet the age requirement, they may still be used if available.

A provision requiring service of prior notice pursuant to Rule 5 of compulsory pretrial production or inspection has been added to paragraph (b)(1). The purpose of such notice is to afford other parties an opportunity to object to the production or inspection, or to serve a demand for additional documents or things. Such additional notice is not needed with respect to a deposition because of the requirement of notice imposed by Rule 30 or 31. But when production or inspection is sought independently of a deposition, other parties may need notice in order to monitor the discovery and in order to pursue access to any information that may or should be produced.

Paragraph (b)(2) retains language formerly set forth in subdivision (e) and extends its application to subpoenas for depositions or production.

Paragraph (b)(3) retains language formerly set forth in paragraph (d)(1) and extends its applications to subpoenas for trial or hearing or production.

Subdivision (c). This provision is new and states the rights of witnesses. It is not intended to diminish rights conferred by Rules 26–37 or any other authority.

Paragraph (c)(1) gives specific application to the principle stated in Rule 26(g) and specifies liability for earnings lost by a non-party witness as a result of a misuse of the subpoena. No change in existing law is thereby effected. Abuse of a subpoena is an actionable tort, *Board of Ed. v. Farmingdale Classroom Teach. Ass'n,* 38 N.Y.2d 397, 380 N.Y.S.2d 635, 343 N.E.2d 278 (1975), and the duty of the attorney to the non-party is also embodied in Model Rule of Professional Conduct 4.4. The liability of the attorney is correlative to the expanded power of the attorney to issue subpoenas. The liability may include the cost of fees to collect attorneys' fees owed as a result of a breach of this duty.

Paragraph (c)(2) retains language from the former subdivision (b) and paragraph (d)(1). The 10–day period for response to a subpoena is extended to 14 days to avoid the complex calculations associated with short time periods under Rule 6 and to allow a bit more time for such objections to be made.

A non-party required to produce documents or materials is protected against significant expense resulting from involuntary assistance to the court. This provision applies, for example, to a non-party required to provide a list of class members. The court is not required to fix the costs in advance of production, although this will often be the most satisfactory accommodation to protect the party seeking discovery from excessive costs. In some instances, it may be preferable to leave uncertain costs to be determined after the materials have been produced, provided that the risk of uncertainty is fully disclosed to the discovering party. See, *e.g., United States v. Columbia Broadcasting Systems, Inc.,* 666 F.2d 364 (9th Cir.1982).

Paragraph (c)(3) explicitly authorizes the quashing of a subpoena as a means of protecting a witness from misuse of the subpoena power. It replaces and enlarges on the former subdivision (b) of this rule and tracks the provisions of Rule 26(c). While largely repetitious, this rule is addressed to the witness who may read it on the subpoena, where it is required to be printed by the revised paragraph (a)(1) of this rule.

Subparagraph (c)(3)(A) identifies those circumstances in which a subpoena must be quashed or modified. It restates the former provisions with respect to the limits of mandatory travel that are set forth in the former paragraphs (d)(2) and (e)(1), with one important change. Under the revised rule, a federal court can compel a witness to come from any place in the state to attend trial, whether or not the local state law so provides. This extension is subject to the qualification provided in the next paragraph, which authorizes the court to condition enforcement of a subpoena compelling a non-party witness to bear substantial expense to attend trial. The traveling non-party witness may be entitled to reasonable compensation for the time and effort entailed.

Clause (c)(3)(A)(iv) requires the court to protect all persons from undue burden imposed by the use of the subpoena power. Illustratively, it might be unduly burdensome to compel an adversary to attend trial as a witness if the adversary is known to have no personal knowledge of matters in dispute, especially so if the adversary would be required to incur substantial travel burdens.

Subparagraph (c)(3)(B) identifies circumstances in which a subpoena should be quashed unless the party serving the subpoena shows a substantial need and the court can devise an appropriate accommodation to protect the interests of the witness. An additional circumstance in which such action is required is a request for costly production of documents; that situation is expressly governed by subparagraph (b)(2)(B)[1].

Clause (c)(3)(B)(i) authorizes the court to quash, modify, or condition a subpoena to protect the person subject to or affected by the subpoena from unnecessary or unduly harmful disclosures of confidential information. It corresponds to Rule 26(c)(7).

Clause (c)(3)(B)(ii) provides appropriate protection for the intellectual property of the non-party witness; it does not apply to the expert retained by a party, whose information is subject to the provisions of Rule 26(b)(4). A growing problem has been the use of subpoenas to compel the giving of evidence and information by unretained experts. Experts are not exempt from the duty to give evidence, even if they cannot be compelled to prepare themselves to give effective testimony, *e.g., Carter–Wallace, Inc. v. Otte,* 474 F.2d 529 (2d Cir.1972), but compulsion to give evidence may threaten the intellectual property of experts denied the opportunity to bargain for the value of their services. See generally Maurer, *Compelling the Expert Witness: Fairness and Utility Under the Federal Rules of Civil Procedure,* 19 GA.L.REV. 71 (1984); Note, *Discovery and Testimony of Unretained Experts,* 1987 DUKE L.J. 140. Arguably the compulsion to testify can be regarded as a "taking" of intellectual property. The rule establishes the right of such persons to withhold their expertise, at least unless the party seeking it makes the kind of showing required for a conditional denial of a motion to quash as provided in the final sentence of subparagraph (c)(3)(B); that requirement is the same as that necessary to secure work product under Rule 26(b)(3) and gives assurance of reasonable compensation. The Rule thus approves the accommodation of competing interests exemplified in *United States v. Columbia Broadcasting Systems Inc.,* 666 F.2d 364 (9th Cir.1982). See also *Wright v. Jeep Corporation,* 547 F.Supp. 871 (E.D.Mich.1982).

As stated in *Kaufman v. Edelstein,* 539 F.2d 811, 822 (2d Cir.1976), the district court's discretion in these matters should be informed by "the degree to which the expert is being called because of his knowledge of facts relevant to the case rather than in order to give opinion testimony; the difference between testifying to a previously formed or expressed opinion and forming a new one; the possibility that, for other reasons, the witness is a unique expert; the extent to which the calling party is able to show the unlikelihood that any comparable witness will willingly testify; and the degree to which the witness is able to show that he has been oppressed by having continually to testify. . . ."

Clause (c)(3)(B)(iii) protects non-party witnesses who may be burdened to perform the duty to travel in order to provide testimony at trial. The provision requires the court to condition a subpoena requiring travel of more than 100 miles on reasonable compensation.

Subdivision (d). This provision is new. Paragraph (d)(1) extends to non-parties the duty imposed on parties by the last paragraph of Rule 34(b), which was added in 1980.

Paragraph (d)(2) is new and corresponds to the new Rule 26(b)(5) [paragraph (5) in Rule 26(b) was a proposed paragraph which was withdrawn by the Supreme Court]. Its purpose is to provide a party whose discovery is constrained by a claim of privilege or work product protection with information sufficient to evaluate such a claim and to resist if it seems unjustified. The person claiming a privilege or protection cannot decide the limits of that party's own entitlement.

A party receiving a discovery request who asserts a privilege or protection but fails to disclose that claim is at risk of waiving the privilege or protection. A person claiming a privilege or protection who fails to provide adequate information about the privilege or protection claim to the party seeking the information is subject to an order to show cause why the person should not be held in contempt under subdivision (e). Motions for such orders and responses to motions are subject to the sanctions provisions of Rules 7 and 11.

A person served a subpoena that is too broad may be faced with a burdensome task to provide full information regarding all that person's claims to privilege or work product protection. Such a person is entitled to protection that may be secured through an objection made pursuant to paragraph (c)(2).

Subdivision (e). This provision retains most of the language of the former subdivision (f).

"Adequate cause" for a failure to obey a subpoena remains undefined. In at least some circumstances, a non-party might be guilty of contempt for refusing to obey a subpoena even though the subpoena manifestly overreaches the appropriate limits of the subpoena power. *E.g., Walker v. City of Birmingham,* 388 U.S. 307 (1967). But, because the command of the subpoena is not in fact one uttered by a judicial officer, contempt should be very sparingly applied when the non-party witness has been overborne by a party or attorney. The language added to subdivision (f) is intended to assure that result where a non-party has been commanded, on the signature of an attorney, to travel greater distances than can be compelled pursuant to this rule.

[1] So in original. Probably should be "subparagraph (c)(2)(B)".

2005 Amendments

This amendment closes a small gap in regard to notifying witnesses of the manner for recording a deposition. A deposition subpoena must state the method for recording the testimony.

Rule 30(b)(2) directs that the party noticing a deposition state in the notice the manner for recording the testimony, but the notice need not be served on the deponent. The deponent learns of the recording method only if the deponent is a party or is informed by a party. Rule 30(b)(3) permits another party to designate an additional method of recording with prior notice to the deponent and the other parties. The deponent thus has notice of the recording method when an additional method is designated. This amendment completes the notice provisions to ensure that a nonparty deponent has notice of the recording method when the recording method is described only in the deposition notice.

A subpoenaed witness does not have a right to refuse to proceed with a deposition due to objections to the manner of recording. But under rare circumstances, a nonparty witness might have a ground for seeking a protective order under Rule 26(c) with regard to the manner of recording or the use of the deposition if recorded in a certain manner. Should such a witness not learn of the manner of recording until the deposition begins, undesirable delay or complication might result. Advance notice of the recording method affords an opportunity to raise such protective issues.

Other changes are made to conform Rule 45(a)(2) to current style conventions.

2006 Amendments

Rule 45 is amended to conform the provisions for subpoenas to changes in other discovery rules, largely related to discovery of electronically stored information. Rule 34 is amended to provide in greater detail for the production of electronically stored information. Rule 45(a)(1)(C) is amended to recognize that electronically stored information, as defined in Rule 34(a), can also be sought by subpoena. Like Rule 34(b), Rule 45(a)(1) is amended to provide that the subpoena can designate a form or forms for production of electronic data. Rule 45(c)(2) is amended, like Rule 34(b), to authorize the person served with a subpoena to object to the requested form or forms. In addition, as under Rule 34(b), Rule 45(d)(1)(B) is amended to provide that if the subpoena does not specify the form or forms for electronically stored information, the person served with the subpoena must produce electronically stored information in a form or forms in which it is usually maintained or in a form or forms that are reasonably usable. Rule 45(d)(1)(C) is added to provide that the person producing electronically stored information should not have to produce the same information in more than one form unless so ordered by the court for good cause.

As with discovery of electronically stored information from parties, complying with a subpoena for such information may impose burdens on the responding person. Rule 45(c) provides protection against undue impositions on nonparties. For example, Rule 45(c)(1) directs that a party serving a subpoena "shall take reasonable steps to avoid imposing undue burden or expense on a person subject to the subpoena," and Rule 45(c)(2)(B) permits the person served with the subpoena to object to it and directs that an order requiring compliance "shall protect a person who is neither a party nor a party's officer from significant expense resulting from" compliance. Rule 45(d)(1)(D) is added to provide that the responding person need not provide discovery of electronically stored information from sources the party identifies as not reasonably accessible, unless the court orders such discovery for good cause, considering the limitations of Rule 26(b)(2)(C), on terms that protect a nonparty against significant expense. A parallel provision is added to Rule 26(b)(2).

Rule 45(a)(1)(B) is also amended, as is Rule 34(a), to provide that a subpoena is available to permit testing and sampling as well as inspection and copying. As in Rule 34, this change recognizes that on occasion the opportunity to perform testing or sampling may be important, both for documents and for electronically stored information. Because testing or sampling may present particular issues of burden or intrusion for the person served with the subpoena, however, the protective provisions of Rule 45(c) should be enforced with vigilance when such demands are made. Inspection or testing of certain types of electronically stored information or of a person's electronic information system may raise issues of confidentiality or privacy. The addition of sampling and testing to Rule 45(a) with regard to documents and electronically stored information is not meant to create a routine right of direct access to a person's electronic information system, although such access might be justified in some circumstances. Courts should guard against undue intrusiveness resulting from inspecting or testing such systems.

Rule 45(d)(2) is amended, as is Rule 26(b)(5), to add a procedure for assertion of privilege or of protection as trial-preparation materials after production. The receiving party may submit the information to the court for resolution of the privilege claim, as under Rule 26(b)(5)(B).

Other minor amendments are made to conform the rule to the changes described above.

2007 Amendment

The language of Rule 45 has been amended as part of the general restyling of the Civil Rules to make them more easily understood and to make style and terminology consistent throughout the rules. These changes are intended to be stylistic only.

The reference to discovery of "books" in former Rule 45(a)(1)(C) was deleted to achieve consistent expression throughout the discovery rules. Books remain a proper subject of discovery.

Former Rule 45(b)(1) required "prior notice" to each party of any commanded production of documents and things or inspection of premises. Courts have agreed that notice must be given "prior" to the return date, and have tended to converge on an interpretation that requires notice to the parties before the subpoena is served on the person commanded to produce or permit inspection. That interpretation is adopted in amended Rule 45(b)(1) to give clear notice of general present practice.

The language of former Rule 45(d)(2) addressing the manner of asserting privilege is replaced by adopting the wording of Rule 26(b)(5). The same meaning is better expressed in the same words.

HISTORICAL NOTES

Treaties and Conventions; Taking of Evidence Abroad in Civil or Commercial Matters; Observance On and After Oct. 7, 1972, by United States and Citizens and Persons Subject to Jurisdiction of United States

For text of Convention, see provisions set out as a note under section 1781 of this title.

CROSS REFERENCES

Motion for order for production of documents, see Fed. Rules Civ.Proc. Rule 34, 28 USCA.

Scope of deposition on oral examination, see Fed.Rules Civ.Proc. Rule 26, 28 USCA.

Subpoenas in civil cases brought by United States under antitrust laws, see 15 USCA § 23.

Rule 46. Objecting to a Ruling or Order

A formal exception to a ruling or order is unnecessary. When the ruling or order is requested or made, a party need only state the action that it wants the court to take or objects to, along with the grounds for the request or objection. Failing to object does not prejudice a party who had no opportunity to do so when the ruling or order was made.

(Amended March 2, 1987, effective August 1, 1987; April 30, 2007, effective December 1, 2007.)

ADVISORY COMMITTEE NOTES

1937 Adoption

Abolition of formal exceptions is often provided by statute. See Ill.Rev.Stat. (1937), ch. 110, § 204; Neb.Comp.Stat. (1929) § 20–1139; N.M.Stat.Ann. (Courtright, 1929) § 105–830; 2 N.D.Comp.Laws Ann. (1913) § 7653; Ohio Code Ann. (Throckmorton, 1936) § 11560; 1 S.D.Comp.Laws (1929) § 2542; Utah Rev.Stat.Ann. (1933) §§ 104–39–2, 104–24–18; Va.Rules of Court, Rule 22, 163 Va. v. xii (1935); Wis.Stat. (1935) § 270.39. Compare N.Y.C.P.A. (1937) §§ 583, 445, and 446, all as amended by L.1936, ch. 915. Rule 51 deals with objections to the court's instructions to the jury.

U.S.C., Title 28, [former] § 776 (Bill of exceptions; authentication; signing of by judge) and [former] § 875 (Review of findings in cases tried without a jury) are superseded insofar as they provide for formal exceptions, and a bill of exceptions.

1987 Amendment

The amendments are technical. No substantive change is intended.

2007 Amendments

The language of Rule 46 has been amended as part of the general restyling of the Civil Rules to make them more easily understood and to make style and terminology consistent throughout the rules. These changes are intended to be stylistic only.

CROSS REFERENCES

Exceptions unnecessary, see Fed.Rules Cr.Proc. Rule 51, 18 USCA.

Harmless error, see Fed.Rules Civ.Proc. Rule 61, 28 USCA.

Objections to instructions, see Fed.Rules Civ.Proc. Rule 51, 28 USCA.

Rule 47. Selecting Jurors

(a) **Examining Jurors.** The court may permit the parties or their attorneys to examine prospective jurors or may itself do so. If the court examines the jurors, it must permit the parties or their attorneys to make any further inquiry it considers proper, or must itself ask any of their additional questions it considers proper.

(b) **Peremptory Challenges.** The court must allow the number of peremptory challenges provided by 28 U.S.C. § 1870.

(c) **Excusing a Juror.** During trial or deliberation, the court may excuse a juror for good cause.

(Amended February 28, 1966, effective July 1, 1966; April 30, 1991, effective December 1, 1991; April 30, 2007, effective December 1, 2007.)

ADVISORY COMMITTEE NOTES

1937 Adoption

Note to Subdivision (a). This permits a practice found very useful by Federal trial judges. For an example of a state practice in which the examination by the court is supplemented by further inquiry by counsel, see Rule 27 of the Code of Rules for the District Courts of Minnesota, 186 Minn. xxxiii (1932), 3 Minn.Stat. (Mason, Supp.1936) Appendix 4, p. 1062.

Note to Subdivision (b). The provision for an alternate juror is one often found in modern state codes. See N.C.Code (1935) § 2330(a); Ohio Gen.Code Ann. (Page, Supp.1926–1935) § 11419–47; Pa.Stat.Ann. (Purdon, Supp. 1936) Title 17, § 1153; compare U.S.C., Title 28, [former] § 417a (Alternate jurors in criminal trials); 1 N.J.Rev.Stat. (1937) 2:91A–1, 2:91A–2, 2:91A–3.

Provisions for qualifying, drawing, and challenging of jurors are found in U.S.C., Title 28:

§ 411 [now 1861] (Qualifications and exemptions)

§ 412 [now 1864] (Manner of drawing)

§ 413 [now 1865] (Apportioned in district)

§ 415 [see 1862] (Not disqualified because of race or color)

§ 416 [now 1867] (Venire; service and return)

§ 417 [now 1866] (Talesmen for petit jurors)

§ 418 [now 1866] (Special juries)

§ 423 [now 1869] (Jurors not to serve more than once a year)

§ 424 [now 1870] (Challenges)

and D.C.Code (1930) Title 18, §§ 341 to 360 (Juries and Jury Commission) and Title 6, § 366 (Peremptory challenges).

1966 Amendment

The revision of this subdivision brings it into line with the amendment of Rule 24(c) of this Federal Rules of Criminal Procedure. That rule previously allowed four alternate jurors, as contrasted with the two allowed in civil cases, and the amendments increase the number to a maximum of six in all cases. The Advisory Committee's Note to amended Criminal Rule 24(c) points to experience demonstrating that four alternates may not be enough in some lengthy criminal trials; and the same may be said of civil trials. The Note adds:

"The words 'or are found to be' are added to the second sentence to make clear that an alternate juror may be called in the situation where it is first discovered during the trial that a juror was unable or disqualified to perform his duties at the time he was sworn."

1991 Amendment

Subdivision (b). The former provision for alternate jurors is stricken and the institution of the alternate juror abolished.

The former rule reflected the long-standing assumption that a jury would consist of exactly twelve members. It provided for additional jurors to be used as substitutes for jurors who are for any reason excused or disqualified from service after the commencement of the trial. Additional jurors were traditionally designated at the outset of the trial, and excused at the close of the evidence if they had not been promoted to full service on account of the elimination of one of the original jurors.

The use of alternate jurors has been a source of dissatisfaction with the jury system because of the burden it places on alternates who are required to listen to the evidence but denied the satisfaction of participating in its evaluation.

Subdivision (c). This provision makes it clear that the court may in appropriate circumstances excuse a juror during the jury deliberations without causing a mistrial. Sickness, family emergency or juror misconduct that might occasion a mistrial are examples of appropriate grounds for excusing a juror. It is not grounds for the dismissal of a juror that the juror refuses to join with fellow jurors in reaching a unanimous verdict.

2007 Amendments

The language of Rule 47 has been amended as part of the general restyling of the Civil Rules to make them more easily understood and to make style and terminology consistent throughout the rules. These changes are intended to be stylistic only.

CROSS REFERENCES

Challenges of jurors, see 28 USCA § 1870.

Jury trial of right, see Fed.Rules Civ.Proc. Rule 38, 28 USCA.

Manner of drawing trial jurors, see 28 USCA § 1864.

Qualifications of jurors, see 28 USCA § 1861.

Trial jurors, see Fed.Rules Cr.Proc. Rule 24, 18 USCA.

Rule 48. Number of Jurors; Verdict

A jury must initially have at least 6 and no more than 12 members, and each juror must participate in the verdict unless excused under Rule 47(c). Unless the parties stipulate otherwise, the verdict must be unanimous and be returned by a jury of at least 6 members.

(Amended April 30, 1991, effective December 1, 1991; April 30, 2007, effective December 1, 2007.)

ADVISORY COMMITTEE NOTES

1937 Adoption

For provisions in state codes, compare Utah Rev.Stat.Ann. (1933) § 48–0–5 (In civil cases parties may agree in open court on lesser number of jurors); 2 Wash.Rev.Stat.Ann. (Remington, 1932) § 323 (Parties may consent to any number of jurors not less than three).

1991 Amendment

The former rule was rendered obsolete by the adoption in many districts of local rules establishing six as the standard size for a civil jury.

It appears that the minimum size of a jury consistent with the Seventh Amendment is six. *Cf. Ballew v. Georgia*, 435 U.S. 223 (1978) (holding that a conviction based on a jury of less than six is a denial of due process of law). If the parties agree to trial before a smaller jury, a verdict can be taken, but the parties should not other than in exceptional circumstances be encouraged to waive the right to a jury of six, not only because of the constitutional stature of the right, but also because smaller juries are more erratic and less effective in serving to distribute responsibility for the exercise of judicial power.

Because the institution of the alternate juror has been abolished by the proposed revision of Rule 47, it will ordinarily be prudent and necessary, in order to provide for sickness or disability among jurors, to seat more than six jurors. The use of jurors in excess of six increases the representativeness of the jury and harms no interest of a party. *Ray v. Parkside Surgery Center*, 13 F.R.Serv. 585 (6th Cir.1989).

If the court takes the precaution of seating a jury larger than six, an illness occurring during the deliberation period will not result in a mistrial, as it did formerly, because all seated jurors will participate in the verdict and a sufficient number will remain to render a unanimous verdict of six or more.

In exceptional circumstances, as where a jury suffers depletions during trial and deliberation that are greater than can reasonably be expected, the parties may agree to be bound by a verdict rendered by fewer than six jurors. The court should not, however, rely upon the availability of such an agreement, for the use of juries smaller than six is problematic for reasons fully explained in *Ballew v. Georgia*, supra.

2007 Amendments

The language of Rule 48 has been amended as part of the general restyling of the Civil Rules to make them more easily understood and to make style and terminology consistent throughout the rules. These changes are intended to be stylistic only.

CROSS REFERENCES

Advisory jury, see Fed.Rules Civ.Proc. Rule 39, 28 USCA.

Jury trial of right, see Fed.Rules Civ.Proc. Rule 38, 28 USCA.

Right to jury trial, see USCA Const. Amend. VII.

Rule 49. Special Verdict; General Verdict and Questions

(a) Special Verdict.

(1) ***In General.*** The court may require a jury to return only a special verdict in the form of a special written finding on each issue of fact. The court may do so by:

(A) submitting written questions susceptible of a categorical or other brief answer;

(B) submitting written forms of the special findings that might properly be made under the pleadings and evidence; or

(C) using any other method that the court considers appropriate.

(2) ***Instructions.*** The court must give the instructions and explanations necessary to enable the jury to make its findings on each submitted issue.

(3) ***Issues Not Submitted.*** A party waives the right to a jury trial on any issue of fact raised by the pleadings or evidence but not submitted to the jury unless, before the jury retires, the party demands its submission to the jury. If the party does not demand submission, the court may make a finding on the issue. If the court makes no finding, it is considered to have made a finding consistent with its judgment on the special verdict.

(b) General Verdict with Answers to Written Questions.

(1) ***In General.*** The court may submit to the jury forms for a general verdict, together with written questions on one or more issues of fact that the jury must decide. The court must give the instructions and explanations necessary to enable the jury to render a general verdict and answer the questions in writing, and must direct the jury to do both.

(2) ***Verdict and Answers Consistent.*** When the general verdict and the answers are consistent, the court must approve, for entry under Rule 58, an appropriate judgment on the verdict and answers.

(3) ***Answers Inconsistent with the Verdict.*** When the answers are consistent with each other but one or more is inconsistent with the general verdict, the court may:

(A) approve, for entry under Rule 58, an appropriate judgment according to the answers, notwithstanding the general verdict;

(B) direct the jury to further consider its answers and verdict; or

(C) order a new trial.

(4) ***Answers Inconsistent with Each Other and the Verdict.*** When the answers are inconsistent with each other and one or more is also inconsistent with the general verdict, judgment must not be entered; instead, the court must direct the jury to further consider its answers and verdict, or must order a new trial.

(Amended January 21, 1963, effective July 1, 1963; March 2, 1987, effective August 1, 1987; April 30, 2007, effective December 1, 2007.)

ADVISORY COMMITTEE NOTES

1937 Adoption

The Federal courts are not bound to follow state statutes authorizing or requiring the court to ask a jury to find a special verdict or to answer interrogatories. *Victor American Fuel Co. v. Peccarich,* 209 Fed. 568 (C.C.A.8th, 1913), cert. den. 232 U.S. 727, 34 S.Ct. 603, 58 L.Ed. 817 (1914); *Spokane and I.E.R. Co. v. Campbell,* 217 Fed. 518 (C.C.A.9th, 1914), affd. 241 U.S. 497, 36 S.Ct. 683, 60 L.Ed. 1125 (1916); Simkins, *Federal Practice* (1934) § 186. The power of a territory to adopt by statute the practice under Subdivision (b) has been sustained. *Walker v. New Mexico and Southern Pacific R.R.,* 165 U.S. 593, 17 S.Ct. 421, 41 L.Ed. 837 (1897); *Southwestern Brewery and Ice Co. v. Schmidt,* 226 U.S. 162, 33 S.Ct. 68, 57 L.Ed. 170 (1912).

Compare Wis.Stat. (1935) §§ 270.27, 270.28 and 270.30; Green, *A New Development in Jury Trial* (1927), 13 A.B.A.J. 715; *Morgan, A Brief History of Special Verdicts and Special Interrogatories,* 1923, 32 Yale L.J. 575.

The provisions of U.S.C., Title 28, [former] § 400(3) (now §§ 2201, 2202) (Declaratory judgments authorized; procedure) permitting the submission of issues of fact to a jury are covered by this rule.

1963 Amendment

This amendment conforms to the amendment of Rule 58. See the Advisory Committee's Note to Rule 58, as amended.

1987 Amendment

The amendments are technical. No substantive change is intended.

2007 Amendments

The language of Rule 49 has been amended as part of the general restyling of the Civil Rules to make them more easily understood and to make style and terminology consistent throughout the rules. These changes are intended to be stylistic only.

CROSS REFERENCES

Advisory jury, see Fed.Rules Civ.Proc. Rule 39, 28 USCA.

New trial, see Fed.Rules Civ.Proc. Rule 59, 28 USCA.

Rule 50. Judgment as a Matter of Law in a Jury Trial; Related Motion for a New Trial; Conditional Ruling

(a) Judgment as a Matter of Law.

(1) ***In General.*** If a party has been fully heard on an issue during a jury trial and the court finds that a reasonable jury would not have a legally sufficient evidentiary basis to find for the party on that issue, the court may:

(A) resolve the issue against the party; and

(B) grant a motion for judgment as a matter of law against the party on a claim or defense that, under the controlling law, can be maintained or defeated only with a favorable finding on that issue.

(2) ***Motion.*** A motion for judgment as a matter of law may be made at any time before the case is submitted to the jury. The motion must specify the judgment sought and the law and facts that entitle the movant to the judgment.

(b) **Renewing the Motion After Trial; Alternative Motion for a New Trial.** If the court does not grant a motion for judgment as a matter of law made under Rule 50(a), the court is considered to have submitted the action to the jury subject to the court's later deciding the legal questions raised by the motion. No later than 10 days after the entry of judgment—or if the motion addresses a jury issue not decided by a verdict, no later than 10 days after the jury was discharged—the movant may file a renewed motion for judgment as a matter of law and may include an alternative or joint request for a new trial under Rule 59. In ruling on the renewed motion, the court may:

(1) allow judgment on the verdict, if the jury returned a verdict;

(2) order a new trial; or

(3) direct the entry of judgment as a matter of law.

(c) **Granting the Renewed Motion; Conditional Ruling on a Motion for a New Trial.**

(1) ***In General.*** If the court grants a renewed motion for judgment as a matter of law, it must also conditionally rule on any motion for a new trial by determining whether a new trial should be granted if the judgment is later vacated or reversed. The court must state the grounds for conditionally granting or denying the motion for a new trial.

(2) ***Effect of a Conditional Ruling.*** Conditionally granting the motion for a new trial does not affect the judgment's finality; if the judgment is reversed, the new trial must proceed unless the appellate court orders otherwise. If the motion for a new trial is conditionally denied, the appellee may assert error in that denial; if the judgment is reversed, the case must proceed as the appellate court orders.

(d) **Time for a Losing Party's New–Trial Motion.** Any motion for a new trial under Rule 59 by a party against whom judgment as a matter of law is rendered must be filed no later than 10 days after the entry of the judgment.

(e) **Denying the Motion for Judgment as a Matter of Law; Reversal on Appeal.** If the court denies the motion for judgment as a matter of law, the prevailing party may, as appellee, assert grounds entitling it to a new trial should the appellate court conclude that the trial court erred in denying the motion. If the appellate court reverses the judgment, it may order a new trial, direct the trial court to determine whether a new trial should be granted, or direct the entry of judgment.

(Amended January 21, 1963, effective July 1, 1963; March 2, 1987, effective August 1, 1987; April 30, 1991, effective December 1, 1991; April 22, 1993, effective December 1, 1993; April 27, 1995, effective December 1, 1995; April 12, 2006, effective December 1, 2006; April 30, 2007, effective December 1, 2007.)

ADVISORY COMMITTEE NOTES

1937 Adoption

Note to Subdivision (a). The present federal rule is changed to the extent that the formality of an express reservation of rights against waiver is no longer necessary. See *Sampliner v. Motion Picture Patents Co.,* 41 S.Ct. 79, 254 U.S. 233, 65 L.Ed. 240 (1920); *Union Indemnity Co. v. United States,* 74 F.2d 645 (C.C.A. 6th, 1935). The requirement that specific grounds for the motion for a directed verdict must be stated settles a conflict in the federal cases. See Simkins, *Federal Practice* (1934) § 189.

Note to Subdivision (b). For comparable state practice upheld under the conformity act, see *Baltimore and Carolina Line v. Redman,* 55 S.Ct. 890, 295 U.S. 654, 79 L.Ed. 1636 (1935); compare *Slocum v. New York Life Ins. Co.,* 33 S.Ct. 523, 228 U.S. 364, 57 L.Ed. 879, Ann.Cas.1914D, 1029 (1913).

See *Northern Ry. Co. v. Page,* 47 S.Ct. 491, 274 U.S. 65, 71 L.Ed. 929 (1927), following the Massachusetts practice of alternative verdicts, explained in Thorndike, *Trial by Jury in United States Courts,* 26 Harv.L.Rev. 732 (1913). See also Thayer, *Judicial Administration,* 63 U. of Pa.L.Rev. 585, 600–601, and note 32 (1915); Scott, *Trial by Jury and the Reform of Civil Procedure,* 31 Harv.L.Rev. 669, 685 (1918); Comment, 34 Mich.L.Rev. 93, 98 (1935).

1963 Amendment

Subdivision (a). The practice, after the court has granted a motion for a directed verdict, of requiring the jury to express assent to a verdict they did not reach by their own deliberations serves no useful purpose and may give offense to the members of the jury. See 2B Barron & Holtzoff, *Federal Practice & Procedure* § 1072, at 367 (Wright ed. 1961); Blume, *Origin and Development of the Directed Verdict,* 48 Mich.L.Rev. 555, 582–85, 589–90 (1950). The final sentence of the subdivision, added by amendment, provides that the court's order granting a motion for a directed verdict is effective in itself, and that no action need be taken by the foreman or other members of the jury. See Ariz. R.Civ.P. 50(c); cf. Fed.R.Crim.P. 29(a). No change is intended in the standard to be applied in deciding the motion. To assure this interpretation, and in the interest of simplicity, the traditional term, "directed verdict," is retained.

Subdivision (b). A motion for judgment notwithstanding the verdict will not lie unless it was preceded by a motion for a directed verdict made at the close of all the evidence.

The amendment of the second sentence of this subdivision sets the time limit for making the motion for judgment n.o.v. at 10 days after the entry of judgment, rather than 10 days after the reception of the verdict. Thus the time provision is made consistent with that contained in Rule 59(b) (time for motion for new trial) and Rule 52(b) (time for motion to amend findings by the court).

Subdivision (c) deals with the situation where a party joins a motion for a new trial with his motion for judgment n.o.v., or prays for a new trial in the alternative, and the motion for judgment n.o.v. is granted. The procedure to be followed in making rulings on the motion for the new trial, and the consequences of the rulings thereon, were partly set out in *Montgomery Ward & Co. v. Duncan,* 311 U.S. 243, 253, 61 S.Ct. 189, 85 L.Ed. 147 (1940), and have been further elaborated in later cases. See *Cone v. West Virginia Pulp & Paper Co.,* 330 U.S. 212, 67 S.Ct. 752, 91 L.Ed. 849 (1947); *Globe Liquor Co., Inc. v. San Roman,* 332 U.S. 571, 68 S.Ct. 246, 92 L.Ed. 177 (1948); *Fountain v. Filson,* 336 U.S. 681, 69 S.Ct. 754, 93 L.Ed. 971 (1949); *Johnson v. New York, N.H. & H.R.R. Co.,* 344 U.S. 48, 73 S.Ct. 125, 97 L.Ed. 77 (1952). However, courts as well as counsel have often misunderstood the procedure, and it will be helpful to summarize the proper practice in the text of the rule. The amendments do not alter the effects of a jury verdict or the scope of appellate review.

In the situation mentioned, subdivision (c)(1) requires that the court make a "conditional" ruling on the new-trial motion, i.e., a ruling which goes on the assumption that the motion for judgment n.o.v. was erroneously granted and will be reversed or vacated; and the court is required to state its grounds for the conditional ruling. Subdivision (c)(1) then spells out the consequences of a reversal of the judgment in the light of the conditional ruling on the new-trial motion.

If the motion for new trial has been conditionally granted, and the judgment is reversed, "the new trial shall proceed unless the appellate court has otherwise ordered." The party against whom the judgment n.o.v. was entered below may, as appellant, besides seeking to overthrow that judgment, also attack the conditional grant of the new trial. And the appellate court, if it reverses the judgment n.o.v., may in an appropriate case also reverse the conditional grant of the new trial and direct that judgment be entered on the verdict. See *Bailey v. Slentz,* 189 F.2d 406 (10th Cir. 1951); *Moist Cold Refrigerator Co. v. Lou Johnson Co.,* 249 F.2d 246 (9th Cir. 1957), cert. denied, 356 U.S. 968, 78 S.Ct. 1008, 2 L.Ed.2d 1074 (1958); *Peters v. Smith,* 221 F.2d 721 (3d Cir. 1955); *Dailey v. Timmer,* 292 F.2d 824 (3d Cir. 1961), explaining *Lind v. Schenley Industries, Inc.,* 278 F.2d 79 (3d Cir.), cert. denied, 364 U.S. 835, 81 S.Ct. 58, 5 L.Ed.2d 60 (1960); *Cox v. Pennsylvania R.R.,* 120 A.2d 214 (D.C.Mun. Ct.App.1956); 3 Barron & Holtzoff, *Federal Practice & Procedure* § 1302.1 at 346–47 (Wright ed. 1958); 6 *Moore's Federal Practice* ¶59.16 at 3915 n. 8a (2d ed. 1954).

If the motion for a new trial has been conditionally denied, and the judgment is reversed, "subsequent proceedings shall be in accordance with the order of the appellate court." The party in whose favor judgment n.o.v. was entered below may, as appellee, besides seeking to uphold that judgment, also urge on the appellate court that the trial court committed error in conditionally denying the new trial. The appellee may assert this error in his brief, without taking a cross-appeal. *Cf. Patterson v. Pennsylvania R.R.,* 238 F.2d 645, 650 (6th Cir. 1956); *Hughes v. St. Louis Nat. L. Baseball Club, Inc.,* 359 Mo. 993, 997, 224 S.W.2d 989, 992 (1949). If the appellate court concludes that the judgment cannot stand, but accepts the appellee's contention that there was error in the conditional denial of the new trial, it may order a new trial in lieu of directing the entry of judgment upon the verdict.

Subdivision (c)(2), which also deals with the situation where the trial court has granted the motion for judgment n.o.v., states that the verdict-winner may apply to the trial court for a new trial pursuant to Rule 59 after the judgment n.o.v. has been entered against him. In arguing to the trial court in opposition to the motion for judgment n.o.v., the verdict-winner may, and often will, contend that he is entitled, at the least, to a new trial, and the court has a range of discretion to grant a new trial or (where plaintiff won the verdict) to order a dismissal of the action without prejudice instead of granting judgment n.o.v. See *Cone v. West Virginia Pulp & Paper Co.,* supra, 330 U.S. at 217, 218, 67 S.Ct. at 755, 756, 91 L.Ed. 849. Subdivision (c)(2) is a reminder that the verdict-winner is entitled, even after entry of judgment n.o.v. against him, to move for a new trial in the usual course. If in these circumstances the motion is granted, the judgment is superseded.

In some unusual circumstances, however, the grant of the new-trial motion may be only conditional, and the judgment will not be superseded. See the situation in *Tribble v. Bruin,* 279 F.2d 424 (4th Cir. 1960) (upon a verdict for plaintiff, defendant moves for and obtains judgment n.o.v.; plaintiff moves for a new trial on the ground of inadequate damages; trial court might properly have granted plaintiff's motion, conditional upon reversal of the judgment n.o.v.).

Even if the verdict-winner makes no motion for a new trial, he is entitled upon his appeal from the judgment n.o.v. not only to urge that that judgment should be reversed and judgment entered upon the verdict, but that errors were committed during the trial which at the least entitle him to a new trial.

Subdivision (d) deals with the situation where judgment has been entered on the jury verdict, the motion for judgment n.o.v. and any motion for a new trial having been denied by the trial court. The verdict-winner, as appellee, besides seeking to uphold the judgment may urge upon the appellate court that in case the trial court is found to have erred in entering judgment on the verdict, there are grounds for granting him a new trial instead of directing the entry of judgment for his opponent. In appropriate cases the appellate court is not precluded from itself directing that a new trial be had. See *Weade v. Dichmann, Wright & Pugh, Inc.,* 337 U.S. 801, 69 S.Ct. 1326, 93 L.Ed. 1704 (1949). Nor is it precluded in proper cases from remanding the case for a determination by the trial court as to whether a new trial should be granted. The latter course is advisable where the grounds urged are suitable for the exercise of trial court discretion.

Subdivision (d) does not attempt a regulation of all aspects of the procedure where the motion for judgment n.o.v. and any accompanying motion for a new trial are denied, since the problems have not been fully canvassed in the decisions and the procedure is in some respects still in a formative stage. It is, however, designed to give guidance on certain important features of the practice.

1987 Amendment

The amendments are technical. No substantive change is intended.

1991 Amendment

Subdivision (a). The revision of this subdivision aims to facilitate the exercise by the court of its responsibility to assure the fidelity of its judgment to the controlling law, a responsibility imposed by the Due Process Clause of the Fifth Amendment. *Cf. Galloway v. United States,* 319 U.S. 372 (1943).

The revision abandons the familiar terminology of *direction of verdict* for several reasons. The term is misleading as a description of the relationship between judge and jury. It is also freighted with anachronisms some of which are the subject of the text of former subdivision (a) of this rule that is deleted in this revision. Thus, it should not be necessary to state in the text of this rule that a motion made pursuant to it is not a waiver of the right to jury trial, and only the antiquities of directed verdict practice suggest that it might have been. The term "judgment as a matter of law" is an almost equally familiar term and appears in the text of Rule 56; its use in Rule 50 calls attention to the relationship between the two rules. Finally, the change enables the rule to refer to preverdict and post-verdict motions with a terminology that does not conceal the common identity of two motions made at different times in the proceeding.

If a motion is denominated a motion for directed verdict or for judgment notwithstanding the verdict, the party's error is merely formal. Such a motion should be treated as a motion for judgment as a matter of law in accordance with this rule.

Paragraph (a)(1) articulates the standard for the granting of a motion for judgment as a matter of law. It effects no change in the existing standard. That existing standard was not expressed in the former rule, but was articulated in long-standing case law. *See generally* Cooper, *Directions for Directed Verdicts: A Compass for Federal Courts,* 55 MINN.L.REV. 903 (1971). The expressed standard makes clear that action taken under the rule is a performance of the court's duty to assure enforcement of the controlling law and is not an intrusion on any responsibility for factual determinations conferred on the jury by the Seventh Amendment or any other provision of federal law. Because this standard is also used as a reference point for entry of summary judgment under 56(a), it serves to link the two related provisions.

The revision authorizes the court to perform its duty to enter judgment as a matter of law at any time during the trial, as soon as it is apparent that either party is unable to carry a burden of proof that is essential to that party's case. Thus, the second sentence of paragraph (a)(1) authorizes the court to consider a motion for judgment as a matter of law as soon as a party has completed a presentation on a fact essential to that party's case. Such early action is appropriate when economy and expedition will be served. In no event, however, should the court enter judgment against a party who has not been apprised of the materiality of the dispositive fact and been afforded an opportunity to present any available evidence bearing on that fact. In order further to facilitate the exercise of the authority provided by this rule, Rule 16 is also revised to encourage the court to schedule an order of trial that proceeds first with a presentation on an issue that is likely to be dispositive, if such an issue is identified in the course of pretrial. Such scheduling can be appropriate where the court is uncertain whether favorable action should be taken under Rule 56. Thus, the revision affords the court the alternative of denying a motion for summary judgment while scheduling a separate trial of the issue under Rule 42(b) or scheduling the trial to begin with a presentation on that essential fact which the opposing party seems unlikely to be able to maintain.

Paragraph (a)(2) retains the requirement that a motion for judgment be made prior to the close of the trial, subject to renewal after a jury verdict has been rendered. The purpose of this requirement is to assure the responding party an opportunity to cure any deficiency in that party's proof that may have been overlooked until called to the party's attention by a late motion for judgment. Cf. *Farley Transp. Co. v. Santa Fe Trail Transp. Co.,* 786 F.2d 1342 (9th Cir.1986) ("If the moving party is then permitted to make a later attack on the evidence through a motion for judgment notwithstanding the verdict or an appeal, the opposing party may be prejudiced by having lost the opportunity to present additional evidence before the case was submitted to the jury"); *Benson v. Allphin,* 786 F.2d 268 (7th Cir.1986) ("the motion for directed verdict at the close of all the evidence provides the nonmovant an opportunity to do what he can to remedy the deficiencies in his case . . .); *McLaughlin v. The Fellows Gear Shaper Co.,* 4 F.R.Serv.3d 607 (3d Cir.1986) (per Adams, J., dissenting: "This Rule serves important practical purposes in ensuring that neither party is precluded from presenting the most persuasive case possible and in preventing unfair surprise after a matter has been submitted to the jury"). At one time, this requirement was held to be of constitutional stature, being compelled by the Seventh Amendment. Cf. *Slocum v. New York Insurance Co.,* 228 U.S. 364 (1913). But cf. *Baltimore & Carolina Line v. Redman,* 295 U.S. 654 (1935).

The second sentence of paragraph (a)(2) does impose a requirement that the moving party articulate the basis on which a judgment as a matter of law might be rendered. The articulation is necessary to achieve the purpose of the requirement that the motion be made before the case is submitted to the jury, so that the responding party may seek to correct any overlooked deficiencies in the proof. The revision thus alters the result in cases in which courts have used various techniques to avoid the requirement that a motion for a directed verdict be made as a predicate to a motion for judgment notwithstanding the verdict. E.g., *Benson v. Allphin,* 788 F.2d 268 (7th Cir.1986) ("this circuit has allowed something less than a formal motion for directed verdict to preserve a party's right to move for judgment notwithstanding the verdict"). *See generally* 9 WRIGHT & MILLER, FEDERAL PRACTICE AND PROCEDURE § 2537 (1971 and Supp.). The information required with the motion may be supplied by explicit reference to materials and argument previously supplied to the court.

This subdivision deals only with the entry of judgment and not with the resolution of particular factual issues as a matter of law. The court may, as before, properly refuse to instruct a jury to decide an issue if a reasonable jury could on the evidence presented decide that issue in only one way.

Subdivision (b). This provision retains the concept of the former rule that the post-verdict motion is a renewal of an earlier motion made at the close of the evidence. One purpose of this concept was to avoid any question arising under the Seventh Amendment. *Montgomery Ward & Co. v. Duncan*, 311 U.S. 243 (1940). It remains useful as a means of defining the appropriate issue posed by the post-verdict motion. A post-trial motion for judgment can be granted only on grounds advanced in the pre-verdict motion. *E.g., Kutner Buick, Inc. v. American Motors Corp.*, 848 F.2d 614 (3d Cir.1989).

Often it appears to the court or to the moving party that a motion for judgment as a matter of law made at the close of the evidence should be reserved for a post-verdict decision. This is so because a jury verdict for the moving party moots the issue and because a preverdict ruling gambles that a reversal may result in a new trial that might have been avoided. For these reasons, the court may often wisely decline to rule on a motion for judgment as a matter of law made at the close of the evidence, and it is not inappropriate for the moving party to suggest such a postponement of the ruling until after the verdict has been rendered.

In ruling on such a motion, the court should disregard any jury determination for which there is no legally sufficient evidentiary basis enabling a reasonable jury to make it. The court may then decide such issues as a matter of law and enter judgment if all other material issues have been decided by the jury on the basis of legally sufficient evidence, or by the court as a matter of law.

The revised rule is intended for use in this manner with Rule 49. Thus, the court may combine facts established as a matter of law either before trial under Rule 56 or at trial on the basis of the evidence presented with other facts determined by the jury under instructions provided under Rule 49 to support a proper judgment under this rule.

This provision also retains the former requirement that a post-trial motion under the rule must be made within 10 days after entry of a contrary judgment. The renewed motion must be served and filed as provided by Rule 5. A purpose of this requirement is to meet the requirements of F.R.App.P. 4(a)(4).

Subdivision (c). Revision of this subdivision conforms the language to the change in diction set forth in subdivision (a) of this revised rule.

Subdivision (d). Revision of this subdivision conforms the language to that of the previous subdivisions.

1993 Amendments

This technical amendment corrects an ambiguity in the text of the 1991 revision of the rule, which, as indicated in the Notes, was not intended to change the existing standards under which "directed verdicts" could be granted. This amendment makes clear that judgments as a matter of law in jury trials may be entered against both plaintiffs and defendants and with respect to issues or defenses that may not be wholly dispositive of a claim or defense.

1995 Amendments

The only change, other than stylistic, intended by this revision is to prescribe a uniform explicit time for filing of post-judgment motions under this rule—no later than 10 days after entry of the judgment. Previously, there was an inconsistency in the wording of Rules 50, 52, and 59 with respect to whether certain post-judgment motions had to be filed, or merely served, during that period. This inconsistency caused special problems when motions for a new trial were joined with other post-judgment motions. These motions affect the finality of the judgment, a matter often of importance to third persons as well as the parties and the court. The Committee believes that each of these rules should be revised to require filing before end of the 10–day period. Filing is an event that can be determined with certainty from court records. The phrase "no later than" is used—rather than "within"—to include post-judgment motions that sometimes are filed before actual entry of the judgment by the clerk. It should be noted that under Rule 6(a) Saturdays, Sundays, and legal holidays are excluded in measuring the 10–day period, and that under Rule 5 the motions when filed are to contain a certificate of service on other parties.

2006 Amendment

The language of Rule 50(a) has been amended as part of the general restyling of the Civil Rules to make them more easily understood and to make style and terminology consistent throughout the rules. These changes are intended to be stylistic only.

Rule 50(b) is amended to permit renewal of any Rule 50(a) motion for judgment as a matter of law, deleting the requirement that a motion be made at the close of all the evidence. Because the Rule 50(b) motion is only a renewal of the preverdict motion, it can be granted only on grounds advanced in the preverdict motion. The earlier motion informs the opposing party of the challenge to the sufficiency of the evidence and affords a clear opportunity to provide additional evidence that may be available. The earlier motion also alerts the court to the opportunity to simplify the trial by resolving some issues, or even all issues, without submission to the jury. This fulfillment of the functional needs that underlie present Rule 50(b) also satisfies the Seventh Amendment. Automatic reservation of the legal questions raised by the motion conforms to the decision in *Baltimore & Carolina Line v. Redman*, 297 U.S. 654 (1935).

This change responds to many decisions that have begun to move away from requiring a motion for judgment as a matter of law at the literal close of all the evidence. Although the requirement has been clearly established for several decades, lawyers continue to overlook it. The courts are slowly working away from the formal requirement. The amendment establishes the functional approach that courts have been unable to reach under the present rule and makes practice more consistent and predictable.

Many judges expressly invite motions at the close of all the evidence. The amendment is not intended to discourage this useful practice.

Finally, an explicit time limit is added for making a posttrial motion when the trial ends without a verdict or with a verdict that does not dispose of all issues suitable for resolution by verdict. The motion must be made no later than 10 days after the jury was discharged.

2007 Amendments

The language of Rule 50 has been amended as part of the general restyling of the Civil Rules to make them more easily understood and to make style and terminology consistent throughout the rules. These changes are intended to be stylistic only.

Former Rule 50(b) stated that the court reserves ruling on a motion for judgment as a matter of law made at the close of all the evidence "[i]f, for any reason, the court does not grant" the motion. The words "for any reason" reflected the proposition that the reservation is automatic and inescapable. The ruling is reserved even if the court explicitly denies the motion. The same result follows under the amended rule. If the motion is not granted, the ruling is reserved.

Amended Rule 50(e) identifies the appellate court's authority to direct the entry of judgment. This authority was not described in former Rule 50(d), but was recognized in *Weisgram v. Marley Co.*, 528 U.S. 440 (2000), and in *Neely v. Martin K. Eby Construction Company*, 386 U.S. 317 (1967). When Rule 50(d) was drafted in 1963, the Committee Note stated that "[s]ubdivision (d) does not attempt a regulation of all aspects of the procedure where the motion for judgment n.o.v. and any accompanying motion for a new trial are denied * * *." Express recognition of the authority to direct entry of judgment does not otherwise supersede this caution.

CROSS REFERENCES

Grounds for new trial, see Fed.Rules Civ.Proc. Rule 59, 28 USCA.

Involuntary dismissal at end of plaintiff's case, see Fed. Rules Civ.Proc. Rule 41, 28 USCA.

Motions for directed verdict abolished in criminal cases, see Fed.Rules Cr.Proc. Rule 29, 18 USCA.

Rule 51. Instructions to the Jury; Objections; Preserving a Claim of Error

(a) Requests.

(1) ***Before or at the Close of the Evidence.*** At the close of the evidence or at any earlier reasonable time that the court orders, a party may file and furnish to every other party written requests for the jury instructions it wants the court to give.

(2) ***After the Close of the Evidence.*** After the close of the evidence, a party may:

(A) file requests for instructions on issues that could not reasonably have been anticipated by an earlier time that the court set for requests; and

(B) with the court's permission, file untimely requests for instructions on any issue.

(b) Instructions. The court:

(1) must inform the parties of its proposed instructions and proposed action on the requests before instructing the jury and before final jury arguments;

(2) must give the parties an opportunity to object on the record and out of the jury's hearing before the instructions and arguments are delivered; and

(3) may instruct the jury at any time before the jury is discharged.

(c) Objections.

(1) ***How to Make.*** A party who objects to an instruction or the failure to give an instruction must do so on the record, stating distinctly the matter objected to and the grounds for the objection.

(2) ***When to Make.*** An objection is timely if:

(A) a party objects at the opportunity provided under Rule 51(b)(2); or

(B) a party was not informed of an instruction or action on a request before that opportunity to object, and the party objects promptly after learning that the instruction or request will be, or has been, given or refused.

(d) Assigning Error; Plain Error.

(1) ***Assigning Error.*** A party may assign as error:

(A) an error in an instruction actually given, if that party properly objected; or

(B) a failure to give an instruction, if that party properly requested it and—unless the court rejected the request in a definitive ruling on the record—also properly objected.

(2) ***Plain Error.*** A court may consider a plain error in the instructions that has not been preserved as required by Rule 51(d)(1) if the error affects substantial rights.

(Amended March 2, 1987, effective August 1, 1987; March 27, 2003, effective December 1, 2003; April 30, 2007, effective December 1, 2007.)

ADVISORY COMMITTEE NOTES

1937 Adoption

Supreme Court Rule 8 requires exceptions to the charge of the court to the jury which shall distinctly state the several matters of law in the charge to which exception is taken. Similar provisions appear in the rules of the various Circuit Courts of Appeals.

1987 Amendment

Although Rule 51 in its present form specifies that the court shall instruct the jury only after the arguments of the parties are completed, in some districts (typically those in states where the practice is otherwise) it is common for the parties to stipulate to instruction before the arguments. The purpose of the amendment is to give the court discretion to instruct the jury either before or after argument. Thus, the rule as revised will permit resort to the long-standing federal practice or to an alternative procedure, which has been praised because it gives counsel the opportunity to explain the instructions, argue their application to the facts and thereby give the jury the maximum assistance in determining the issues and arriving at a good verdict on the law and the evidence. As an ancillary benefit, this approach aids counsel by supplying a natural outline so that arguments may be directed to the essential fact issues which the jury must decide. See generally Raymond, *Merits and Demerits of the Missouri System of Instructing Juries,* 5 St. Louis U.L.J. 317 (1959). Moreover, if the court instructs before an argument, counsel then know the precise words the court has chosen and need not speculate as to the words the court will later use in its instructions. Finally, by instructing ahead of argument the court has the attention of the jurors when they are fresh and can give their full attention to the court's instructions. It is more difficult to hold the attention of jurors after lengthy arguments.

2003 Amendments

Rule 51 is revised to capture many of the interpretations that have emerged in practice. The revisions in text will make uniform the conclusions reached by a majority of decisions on each point. Additions also are made to cover some practices that cannot now be anchored in the text of Rule 51.

Scope. Rule 51 governs instructions to the trial jury on the law that governs the verdict. A variety of other instructions cannot practicably be brought within Rule 51. Among these instructions are preliminary instructions to a venire, and cautionary or limiting instructions delivered in immediate response to events at trial.

Requests. Subdivision (a) governs requests. Apart from the plain error doctrine recognized in subdivision (d)(2), a court is not obliged to instruct the jury on issues raised by the evidence unless a party requests an instruction. The revised rule recognizes the court's authority to direct that requests be submitted before trial.

The close-of-the-evidence deadline may come before trial is completed on all potential issues. Trial may be formally bifurcated or may be sequenced in some less formal manner. The close of the evidence is measured by the occurrence of two events: completion of all intended evidence on an identified phase of the trial and impending submission to the jury with instructions.

The risk in directing a pretrial request deadline is that trial evidence may raise new issues or reshape issues the parties thought they had understood. Courts need not insist on pretrial requests in all cases. Even if the request time is set before trial or early in the trial, subdivision (a)(2)(A) permits requests after the close of the evidence to address issues that could not reasonably have been anticipated at the earlier time for requests set by the court.

Subdivision (a)(2)(B) expressly recognizes the court's discretion to act on an untimely request. The most important consideration in exercising the discretion confirmed by subdivision (a)(2)(B) is the importance of the issue to the case—the closer the issue lies to the "plain error" that would be recognized under subdivision (d)(2), the better the reason to give an instruction. The cogency of the reason for failing to make a timely request also should be considered. To be considered under subdivision (a)(2)(B) a request should be made before final instructions and before final jury arguments. What is a "final" instruction and argument depends on the sequence of submitting the case to the jury. If separate portions of the case are submitted to the jury in sequence, the final arguments and final instructions are those made on submitting to the jury the portion of the case addressed by the arguments and instructions.

Instructions. Subdivision (b)(1) requires the court to inform the parties, before instructing the jury and before final jury arguments related to the instruction, of the proposed instructions as well as the proposed action on instruction requests. The time limit is addressed to final jury arguments to reflect the practice that allows interim argument s during trial in complex cases; it may not be feasible to develop final instructions before such interim arguments. It is enough that counsel know of the intended instructions before making final arguments addressed to the issue. If the trial is sequenced or bifurcated, the final arguments addressed to an issue may occur before the close of the entire trial.

Subdivision (b)(2) complements subdivision (b)(1) by carrying forward the opportunity to object established by present Rule 51. It makes explicit the opportunity to object on the record, ensuring a clear memorial of the objection.

Subdivision (b)(3) reflects common practice by authorizing instructions at any time after trial begins and before the jury is discharged.

Objections. Subdivision (c) states the right to object to an instruction or the failure to give an instruction. It carries forward the formula of present Rule 51 requiring that the objection state distinctly the matter objected to and the grounds of the objection, and makes explicit the requirement that the objection be made on the record. The provisions on the time to object make clear that it is timely to object promptly after learning of an instruction or action on a request when the court has not provided advance information as required by subdivision (b)(1). The need to repeat a request by way of objection is continued by new subdivision (d)(1)(B) except where the court made a definitive ruling on the record.

Preserving a claim of error and plain error. Many cases hold that a proper request for a jury instruction is not alone enough to preserve the right to appeal failure to give the instruction. The request must be renewed by objection. This doctrine is appropriate when the court may not have sufficiently focused on the request, or may believe that the request has been granted in substance although in different words. But this doctrine may also prove a trap for the unwary who fail to add an objection after the court has made it clear that the request has been considered and rejected on the merits. Subdivision (d)(1)(B) establishes authority to review the failure to grant a timely request, despite a failure to add an objection, when the court has made a definitive ruling on the record rejecting the request.

Many circuits have recognized that an error not preserved under Rule 51 may be reviewed in exceptional circumstances. The language adopted to capture these decisions in subdivision (d)(2) is borrowed from Criminal Rule 52. Although the language is the same, the context of civil litigation often differs from the context of criminal prosecution; actual application of the plain-error standard takes account of the differences. The Supreme Court has summarized application of Criminal Rule 52 as involving four elements: (1) there must be an error; (2) the error must be plain; (3) the error must affect substantial rights; and (4) the error must seriously affect the fairness, integrity, or public reputation of judicial proceedings. Johnson v. U.S., 520 U.S. 461, 466–467, 469–470 (1997). (The Johnson case quoted the fourth element from its decision in a civil action, U.S. v. Atkinson, 297 U.S. 157, 160 (1936): "In exceptional circumstances, especially in criminal cases, appellate courts, in the public interest, may, of their own motion, notice errors to which no exception has been taken, if the errors are obvious, or if they otherwise substantially affect the fairness, integrity, or public reputation of judicial proceedings.")

The court's duty to give correct jury instructions in a civil action is shaped by at least four factors.

The factor most directly implied by a "plain" error rule is the obviousness of the mistake. The importance of the error is a second major factor. The costs of correcting an error reflect a third factor that is affected by a variety of circumstances. In a case that seems close to the fundamental error line, account also may be taken of the impact a verdict may have on nonparties.

2007 Amendments

The language of Rule 51 has been amended as part of the general restyling of the Civil Rules to make them more easily understood and to make style and terminology consistent throughout the rules. These changes are intended to be stylistic only.

CROSS REFERENCES

Formal exceptions unnecessary, see Fed.Rules Civ.Proc. Rule 46, 28 USCA.

Motion for directed verdict, see Fed.Rules Civ.Proc. Rule 50, 28 USCA.

Rule 52. Findings and Conclusions by the Court; Judgment on Partial Findings

(a) Findings and Conclusions.

(1) ***In General.*** In an action tried on the facts without a jury or with an advisory jury, the court must find the facts specially and state its conclusions of law separately. The findings and conclusions may be stated on the record after the close of the evidence or may appear in an opinion or a memorandum of decision filed by the court. Judgment must be entered under Rule 58.

(2) ***For an Interlocutory Injunction.*** In granting or refusing an interlocutory injunction, the court must similarly state the findings and conclusions that support its action.

(3) ***For a Motion.*** The court is not required to state findings or conclusions when ruling on a motion under Rule 12 or 56 or, unless these rules provide otherwise, on any other motion.

(4) ***Effect of a Master's Findings.*** A master's findings, to the extent adopted by the court, must be considered the court's findings.

(5) ***Questioning the Evidentiary Support.*** A party may later question the sufficiency of the evidence supporting the findings, whether or not the party requested findings, objected to them, moved to amend them, or moved for partial findings.

(6) ***Setting Aside the Findings.*** Findings of fact, whether based on oral or other evidence, must not be set aside unless clearly erroneous, and the reviewing court must give due regard to the trial court's opportunity to judge the witnesses' credibility.

(b) Amended or Additional Findings. On a party's motion filed no later than 10 days after the entry of judgment, the court may amend its findings—or make additional findings—and may amend the judgment accordingly. The motion may accompany a motion for a new trial under Rule 59.

(c) Judgment on Partial Findings. If a party has been fully heard on an issue during a nonjury trial and the court finds against the party on that issue, the court may enter judgment against the party on a claim or defense that, under the controlling law, can be maintained or defeated only with a favorable finding on that issue. The court may, however, decline to render any judgment until the close of the evidence. A judgment on partial findings must be supported by findings of fact and conclusions of law as required by Rule 52(a).

(Amended December 27, 1946, effective March 19, 1948; January 21, 1963, effective July 1, 1963; April 28, 1983, effective August 1, 1983; April 29, 1985, effective August 1, 1985; April 30, 1991, effective December 1, 1991; April 22, 1993, effective December 1, 1993; April 27, 1995, effective December 1, 1995; April 30, 2007, effective December 1, 2007.)

ADVISORY COMMITTEE NOTES

1937 Adoption

See [former] Equity Rule 70½, as amended Nov. 25, 1935, (Findings of Fact and Conclusions of Law) and U.S.C., Title 28, [former] § 764 (Opinion, findings, and conclusions in action against United States) which are substantially continued in this rule. The provisions of U.S.C., Title 28, [former] §§ 773 (Trial of issues of fact; by court) and [former] 875 (Review in cases tried without a jury) are superseded in so far as they provide a different method of finding facts and a different method of appellate review. The rule stated in the third sentence of Subdivision (a) accords with the decisions on the scope of the review in modern federal equity practice. It is applicable to all classes of findings in cases tried without a jury whether the finding is of a fact concerning which there was conflict of testimony, or of a fact deduced or inferred from uncontradicted testimony. See *Silver King Coalition Mines Co. v. Silver King Consolidated Mining Co.*, C.C.A.8, 1913, 204 F. 166, certiorari denied 33 S.Ct. 1051, 229 U.S. 624, 57 L.Ed. 1356; *Warren v. Keep*, 1894, 15 S.Ct. 83, 155 U.S. 265, 39 L.Ed. 144; *Furrer v. Ferris*, 1892, 12 S.Ct. 821, 145 U.S. 132, 36 L.Ed. 649; *Tilghman v. Proctor*, 1888, 8 S.Ct. 894, 125 U.S. 136, 149, 31 L.Ed. 664; *Kimberly v. Arms*, 1889, 9 S.Ct. 355, 129 U.S. 512, 524, 32 L.Ed. 764. Compare *Kaeser & Blair Inc. v. Merchants' Ass'n*, C.C.A.6, 1933, 64 F.2d 575, 576; *Dunn v. Trefry*, C.C.A.1, 1919, 260 F. 147.

In the following states findings of fact are required in all cases tried without a jury (waiver by the parties being permitted as indicated at the end of the listing): Arkansas, Civ.Code (Crawford, 1934) § 364; California, Code Civ.Proc. (Deering, 1937) §§ 632, 634; Colorado, 1 Stat.Ann. (1935) Code Civ.Proc. §§ 232, 291 (in actions before referees or for possession of and damages to land); Connecticut, Gen.Stats. §§ 5660, 5664; Idaho, 1 Code Ann. (1932) §§ 7–302 through 7–305; Massachusetts (equity cases), 2 Gen.Laws (Ter.Ed., 1932) ch. 214, § 23; Minnesota, 2 Stat. (Mason, 1927) § 9311; Nevada, 4 Comp.Laws (Hillyer, 1929) §§ 8783–8784; New Jersey, Sup.Ct.Rule 113, 2 N.J.Misc. 1197, 1239 (1924); New Mexico, Stat.Ann. (Courtright, 1929) §§ 105–813; North Carolina, Code (1935) § 569; North Dakota, 2 Comp.Laws Ann. (1913) § 7641; Oregon, 2 Code Ann. (1930) §§ 2–502; South Carolina, Code (Michie, 1932) § 649; South Dakota, 1 Comp. Laws (1929) §§ 2525–2526; Utah, Rev.Stat.Ann. (1933) §§ 104–26–2, 104–26–3; Vermont (where jury trial waived), Pub.Laws (1933) § 2069; Washington, 2 Rev.Stat.Ann. (Remington, 1932) § 367; Wisconsin, Stat. (1935) § 270.33. The parties may waive this requirement for findings in California, Idaho, North Dakota, Nevada, New Mexico, Utah, and South Dakota.

In the following states the review of findings of fact in all non-jury cases, including jury waived cases, is assimilated to the equity review: Alabama, Code Ann. (Michie, 1928) §§ 9498, 8599; California, Code Civ.Proc. (Derring, 1937) § 956a; but see 20 Calif.Law Rev. 171 (1932); Colorado, *Johnson v. Kountze*, 1895, 43 P. 445, 21 Colo. 486, semble; Illinois, *Baker v. Hinricks*, 1934, 194 N.E. 284, 359 Ill. 138; *Weininger v. Metropolitan Fire Ins. Co.*, 1935, 195 N.E. 420, 359 Ill. 584, 98 A.L.R. 169; Minnesota, *State Bank of Gibbon v. Walter*, 1926, 208 N.W. 423, 167 Minn. 37; *Waldron v. Page*, 1934, 253 N.W. 894, 191 Minn. 302; New Jersey N.J.S.A. 2:27–241, 2:27–363, as interpreted in *Bussy v. Hatch*, 1920, 111 A. 546, 95 N.J.L. 56; New York, *York Mortgage Corporation v. Clotar Const. Corp.*, 1930, 172 N.E. 265, 254 N.Y. 128; North Dakota, Comp.Laws Ann. (1913) § 7846, as amended by N.D.Laws 1933, c. 208; *Milnor Holding Co. v. Holt*, 1933, 248 N.W. 315, 63 N.D. 362, 370; Oklahoma, *Wichita Mining and Improvement Co. v. Hale*, 1908, 94 P. 530, 20 Okl. 159; South Dakota, *Randall v. Burk Township*, 4 S.D. 337, 57 N.W. 4 (1893); Texas, *Custard v. Flowers*, 1929, 14 S.W.2d 109; Utah, Rev.Stat.Ann. (1933) § 104–41–5; Vermont, *Roberge v. Troy*, 1933, 163 A. 770, 105 Vt. 134; Washington, 2 Rev.Stat.Ann. (Remington, 1932) §§ 309–316; *McCullough v. Puget Sound Realty Associates*, 1913, 136 Pac. 1146, 76 Wash. 700, but see *Cornwall v. Anderson*, 1915, 148 P. 1, 85 Wash. 369; West Virginia, *Kinsey v. Carr*, 1906, 55 S.E. 1004, 60 W.Va. 449, semble; Wisconsin, Stat. (1935) § 251.09; *Campbell v. Sutliff*, 1927, 214 N.W. 374, 193 Wis. 370; *Gessler v. Erwin Co.*, 1924, 193 N.W. 303, 182 Wis. 315.

For examples of an assimilation of the review of findings of fact in cases tried without a jury to the review at law as made in several states, see Clark and Stone, *Review of Findings of Fact*, 4 U. of Chi.L.Rev. 190, 215 (1937).

1946 Amendment

Note to Subdivision (a). The amended rule makes clear that the requirement for findings of fact and conclusions of law thereon applies in a case with an advisory jury. This removes an ambiguity in the rule as originally stated, but carries into effect what has been considered its intent. 3 *Moore's Federal Practice*, 1938, 3119. *Hurwitz v. Hurwitz*, 1943, 136 F.2d 796, 78 U.S.App.D.C. 66.

The two sentences added at the end of Rule 52(a) eliminate certain difficulties which have arisen concerning findings and conclusions. The first of the two sentences permits findings of fact and conclusions of law to appear in an opinion or memorandum of decision. See, e.g., *United States v. One 1941 Ford Sedan*, S.D.Tex.1946, 65 F.Supp. 84. Under original Rule 52(a) some courts have expressed the view that findings and conclusions could not be incorporated in an opinion. *Detective Comics, Inc. v. Bruns Publications*, S.D.N.Y.1939, 28 F.Supp. 399; *Pennsylvania Co. for Insurance on Lives & Granting Annuities v. Cincinnati & L.E.R. Co.*, S.D.Ohio 1941, 43 F.Supp. 5; *United States v. Aluminum Co. of America*, S.D.N.Y.1941, 2 F.R.D. 224, 5 Fed. Rules Serv. 52a.11, Case 3; see also s.c., 44 F.Supp. 97. But, to the contrary, see *Wellman v. United States*, D.Mass.1938, 25 F.Supp. 868; *Cook v. United States*, D.Mass.1939, 26 F.Supp. 253; *Proctor v. White*, D.Mass.1939, 28 F.Supp. 161; *Green Valley Creamery, Inc. v. United States*, C.C.A.1, 1939, 108 F.2d 342. See also *Matton Oil Transfer Corp. v. The Dynamic*, C.C.A.2, 1941, 123 F.2d 999; *Carter Coal Co. v. Litz*, C.C.A.4, 1944, 140 F.2d 934; *Woodruff v. Heiser*, C.C.A.10, 1945, 150 F.2d 869; *Coca Cola Co. v. Busch*, Pa.1943, 7 Fed. Rules Serv. 59b.2, Case 4; Oglebay, *Some Developments in Bankruptcy Law*, 1944, 18 J. of Nat'l Ass'n of Ref. 68, 69. Findings of fact aid in the process of judgment and in defining for future cases the precise limitations of the issues and the determination thereon. Thus they not only aid the appellate court on review, *Hurwitz v. Hurwitz*, App.D.C.1943, 136 F.2d 796, 78 U.S.App.D.C. 66, but they are an important factor in the proper application of the doctrines of res judicata and estoppel by judgment. Nordbye, *Improvements in Statement of Findings of Fact and Conclusions of Law*, 1 F.R.D. 25, 26–27; *United States v. Forness*, C.C.A.2, 1942, 125 F.2d 928, certiorari denied 1942, 62 S.Ct. 1293, 316 U.S. 694, 86 L.Ed. 1764. These findings should represent the judge's own determination and not the long, often argumentative statements of successful counsel. *United States v. Forness*, supra; *United States v. Crescent Amusement Co.*, 1944, 1945, 65 S.Ct. 254, 323 U.S. 173, 89 L.Ed. 160. Consequently, they should be a part of the judge's opinion and decision, either stated therein or stated separately. *Matton Oil Transfer Corp. v. The Dynamic*, supra. But the judge need only make brief, definite, pertinent findings and conclusions upon the contested matters; there is no necessity for over-elaboration of detail or particularization of facts. *United States v. Forness*, supra; *United States v. Crescent Amusement Co.*, supra. See also *Petterson Lighterage & Towing Corp. v. New York Central*

R. Co., C.C.A.2, 1942, 126 F.2d 992; *Brown Paper Mill Co., Inc. v. Irwin*, C.C.A.8, 1943, 134 F.2d 337; *Allen Bradley Co. v. Local Union No. 3, I.B.E.W.*, C.C.A.2, 1944, 145 F.2d 215, reversed on other grounds 65 S.Ct. 1533, 325 U.S. 797; *Young v. Murphy, Ohio* 1946, 9 Fed.Rules Serv. 52a.11, Case 2.

The last sentence of Rule 52(a) as amended will remove any doubt that findings and conclusions are unnecessary upon decision of a motion, particularly one under Rule 12 or Rule 56, except as provided in amended Rule 41(b). As so holding, see *Thomas v. Peyser*, App.D.C.1941, 118 F.2d 369; *Schad v. Twentieth Century-Fox Corp.*, C.C.A.3, 1943, 136 F.2d 991; *Prudential Ins. Co. of America v. Goldstein*, N.Y.1942, 43 F.Supp. 767; *Somers Coal Co. v. United States*, N.D.Ohio 1942, 2 F.R.D. 532, 6 Fed.Rules Serv. 52a.1, Case 1; *Pen-Ken Oil & Gas Corp. v. Warfield Natural Gas Co.*, E.D.Ky.1942, 2 F.R.D. 355, 5 Fed. Rules Serv. 52a.1, Case 3; also Commentary, *Necessity of Findings of Fact*, 1941, 4 Fed. Rules Serv. 936.

1963 Amendment

This amendment conforms to the amendment of Rule 58. See the Advisory Committee's Note to Rule 58, as amended.

1983 Amendment

Rule 52(a) has been amended to revise its penultimate sentence to provide explicitly that the district judge may make the findings of fact and conclusions of law required in nonjury cases orally. Nothing in the prior text of the rule forbids this practice, which is widely utilized by district judges. See Christensen, *A Modest Proposal for Immeasurable Improvement*, 64 A.B.A.J. 693 (1978). The objective is to lighten the burden on the trial court in preparing findings in nonjury cases. In addition, the amendment should reduce the number of published district court opinions that embrace written findings.

1985 Amendment

Rule 52(a) has been amended (1) to avoid continued confusion and conflicts among the circuits as to the standard of appellate review of findings of fact by the court, (2) to eliminate the disparity between the standard of review as literally stated in Rule 52(a) and the practice of some courts of appeals, and (3) to promote nationwide uniformity. See Note, *Rule 52(a): Appellate Review of Findings of Fact Based on Documentary or Undisputed Evidence*, 49 Va. L.Rev. 506, 536 (1963).

Some courts of appeal have stated that when a trial court's findings do not rest on demeanor evidence and evaluation of a witness' credibility, there is no reason to defer to the trial court's findings and the appellate court more readily can find them to be clearly erroneous. See, e.g., *Marcum v. United States*, 621 F.2d 142, 144–45 (5th Cir.1980). Others go further, holding that appellate review may be had without application of the "clearly erroneous" test since the appellate court is in as good a position as the trial court to review a purely documentary record. See, *e.g., Atari, Inc. v. North American Philips Consumer Electronics Corp.*, 672 F.2d 607, 614 (7th Cir.), cert. denied, 459 U.S. 880 (1982); *Lydle v. United States*, 635 F.2d 763, 765 n. 1 (6th Cir.1981); *Swanson v. Baker Indus., Inc.*, 615 F.2d 479, 483 (8th Cir.1980); *Taylor v. Lombard*, 606 F.2d 371, 372 (2d Cir.1979), cert. denied, 445 U.S. 946 (1980); *Jack Kahn Music Co. v. Baldwin Piano & Organ Co.*, 604 F.2d 755, 758 (2d Cir.1979); *John R. Thompson Co. v. United States*, 477 F.2d 164, 167 (7th Cir.1973).

A third group has adopted the view that the "clearly erroneous" rule applies in all nonjury cases even when findings are based solely on documentary evidence or on inferences from undisputed facts. See, *e.g., Maxwell v. Sumner*, 673 F.2d 1031, 1036 (9th Cir.), *cert. denied*, 459 U.S. 976 (1982); *United States v. Texas Education Agency*, 647 F.2d 504, 506–07 (5th Cir.1981), *cert. denied*, 454 U.S. 1143 (1982); *Constructora Maza, Inc. v. Banco de Ponce*, 616 F.2d 573, 576 (1st Cir.1980); *In re Sierra Trading Corp.*, 482 F.2d 333, 337 (10th Cir.1973); *Case v. Morrisette*, 475 F.2d 1300, 1306–07 (D.C.Cir.1973).

The commentators also disagree as to the proper interpretation of the Rule. *Compare* Wright, *The Doubtful Omniscience of Appellate Courts*, 41 Minn.L.Rev. 751, 769–70 (1957) (language and intent of Rule support view that "clearly erroneous" test should apply to all forms of evidence), *and* 9 C. Wright & A. Miller, *Federal Practice and Procedure: Civil § 2587*, at 740 (1971) (language of the Rule is clear), *with* 5A J. Moore, *Federal Practice* ¶ 52.04, 2687–88 (2d ed. 1982) (Rule as written supports broader review of findings based on non-demeanor testimony).

The Supreme Court has not clearly resolved the issue. See, *Bose Corp. v. Consumers Union of United States, Inc.*, 466 U.S. 485, 104 S.Ct. 1949, 1958 (1984); *Pullman Standard v. Swint*, 456 U.S. 273, 293 (1982); *United States v. General Motors Corp.*, 384 U.S. 127, 141 n. 16 (1966); *United States v. United States Gypsum Co.*, 333 U.S. 364, 394–96 (1948).

The principal argument advanced in favor of a more searching appellate review of findings by the district court based solely on documentary evidence is that the rationale of Rule 52(a) does not apply when the findings do not rest on the trial court's assessment of credibility of the witnesses but on an evaluation of documentary proof and the drawing of inferences from it, thus eliminating the need for any special deference to the trial court's findings. These considerations are outweighed by the public interest in the stability and judicial economy that would be promoted by recognizing that the trial court, not the appellate tribunal, should be the finder of the facts. To permit courts of appeals to share more actively in the fact-finding function would tend to undermine the legitimacy of the district courts in the eyes of litigants, multiply appeals by encouraging appellate retrial of some factual issues, and needlessly reallocate judicial authority.

1991 Amendment

Subdivision (c) is added. It parallels the revised Rule 50(a), but is applicable to non-jury trials. It authorizes the court to enter judgment at any time that it can appropriately make a dispositive finding of fact on the evidence.

The new subdivision replaces part of Rule 41(b), which formerly authorized a dismissal at the close of the plaintiff's case if the plaintiff had failed to carry an essential burden of proof. Accordingly, the reference to Rule 41 formerly made in subdivision (a) of this rule is deleted.

As under the former Rule 41(b), the court retains discretion to enter no judgment prior to the close of the evidence.

Judgment entered under this rule differs from a summary judgment under Rule 56 in the nature of the evaluation made by the court. A judgment on partial findings is made after the court has heard all the evidence bearing on the crucial issue of fact, and the finding is reversible only if the appellate court finds it to be "clearly erroneous." A summary judgment, in contrast, is made on the basis of facts established on account of the absence of contrary evidence or presumptions; such establishments of fact are rulings on questions of law as provided in Rule 56(a) and are not shielded by the "clear error" standard of review.

1993 Amendments

This technical amendment corrects an ambiguity in the text of the 1991 revision of the rule, similar to the revision being made to Rule 50. This amendment makes clear that judgments as a matter of law in nonjury trials may be entered against both plaintiffs and defendants and with respect to issues or defenses that may not be wholly dispositive of a claim or defense.

1995 Amendments

The only change, other than stylistic, intended by this revision is to require that any motion to amend or add findings after a nonjury trial must be filed no later than 10 days after entry of the judgment. Previously, there was an inconsistency in the wording of Rules 50, 52, and 59 with respect to whether certain post-judgment motions had to be filed, or merely served, during that period. This inconsistency caused special problems when motions for a new trial were joined with other post-judgment motions. These motions affect the finality of the judgment, a matter often of importance to third persons as well as the parties and the court. The Committee believes that each of these rules should be revised to require filing before end of the 10–day period. Filing is an event that can be determined with certainty from court records. The phrase "no later than" is used—rather than "within"—to include post-judgment motions that sometimes are filed before actual entry of the judgment by the clerk. It should be noted that under Rule 6(a) Saturdays, Sundays, and legal holidays are excluded in measuring the 10–day period, and that under Rule 5 the motions when filed are to contain a certificate of service on other parties.

2007 Amendments

The language of Rule 52 has been amended as part of the general restyling of the Civil Rules to make them more easily understood and to make style and terminology consistent throughout the rules. These changes are intended to be stylistic only.

Former Rule 52(a) said that findings are unnecessary on decisions of motions "except as provided in subdivision (c) of this rule." Amended Rule 52(a)(3) says that findings are unnecessary "unless these rules provide otherwise." This change reflects provisions in other rules that require Rule 52 findings on deciding motions. Rules 23(e), 23(h), and 54(d)(2)(C) are examples.

Amended Rule 52(a)(5) includes provisions that appeared in former Rule 52(a) and 52(b). Rule 52(a) provided that requests for findings are not necessary for purposes of review. It applied both in an action tried on the facts without a jury and also in granting or refusing an interlocutory injunction. Rule 52(b), applicable to findings "made in actions tried without a jury," provided that the sufficiency of the evidence might be "later questioned whether or not in the district court the party raising the question objected to the findings, moved to amend them, or moved for partial findings." Former Rule 52(b) did not explicitly apply to decisions granting or refusing an interlocutory injunction. Amended Rule 52(a)(5) makes explicit the application of this part of former Rule 52(b) to interlocutory injunction decisions.

Former Rule 52(c) provided for judgment on partial findings, and referred to it as "judgment as a matter of law." Amended Rule 52(c) refers only to "judgment," to avoid any confusion with a Rule 50 judgment as a matter of law in a jury case. The standards that govern judgment as a matter of law in a jury case have no bearing on a decision under Rule 52(c).

CROSS REFERENCES

Advisory jury, see Fed.Rules Civ.Proc. Rule 39, 28 USCA.

Extension of time to apply for amendment of findings, limitation on, see Fed.Rules Civ.Proc. Rule 6, 28 USCA.

Master's report, inclusion of findings of fact and conclusions of law, see Fed.Rules Civ.Proc. Rule 53, 28 USCA.

Motion for additional findings, termination of running of time for appeal to court of appeals, see Federal Rules of Appellate Procedure Rule 4, 28 USCA.

Motion for new trial, amendment of findings on, see Fed. Rules Civ.Proc. Rule 59, 28 USCA.

Record on appeal to include findings, see Federal Rules of Appellate Procedure Rule 10, 28 USCA.

Special verdicts, making of findings on, see Fed.Rules Civ.Proc. Rule 49, 28 USCA.

Stay of proceedings to enforce judgment pending disposition of motion to amend, see Fed.Rules Civ.Proc. Rule 62, 28 USCA.

Rule 53. Masters

(a) Appointment.

- **(1)** ***Scope.*** Unless a statute provides otherwise, a court may appoint a master only to:
  - **(A)** perform duties consented to by the parties;
  - **(B)** hold trial proceedings and make or recommend findings of fact on issues to be decided without a jury if appointment is warranted by:
    - **(i)** some exceptional condition; or
    - **(ii)** the need to perform an accounting or resolve a difficult computation of damages; or
  - **(C)** address pretrial and posttrial matters that cannot be effectively and timely addressed by an available district judge or magistrate judge of the district.
- **(2)** ***Disqualification.*** A master must not have a relationship to the parties, attorneys, action, or court that would require disqualification of a judge under 28 U.S.C. § 455, unless the

parties, with the court's approval, consent to the appointment after the master discloses any potential grounds for disqualification.

(3) ***Possible Expense or Delay.*** In appointing a master, the court must consider the fairness of imposing the likely expenses on the parties and must protect against unreasonable expense or delay.

(b) Order Appointing a Master.

(1) ***Notice.*** Before appointing a master, the court must give the parties notice and an opportunity to be heard. Any party may suggest candidates for appointment.

(2) ***Contents.*** The appointing order must direct the master to proceed with all reasonable diligence and must state:

(A) the master's duties, including any investigation or enforcement duties, and any limits on the master's authority under Rule 53(c);

(B) the circumstances, if any, in which the master may communicate ex parte with the court or a party;

(C) the nature of the materials to be preserved and filed as the record of the master's activities;

(D) the time limits, method of filing the record, other procedures, and standards for reviewing the master's orders, findings, and recommendations; and

(E) the basis, terms, and procedure for fixing the master's compensation under Rule 53(g).

(3) ***Issuing.*** The court may issue the order only after:

(A) the master files an affidavit disclosing whether there is any ground for disqualification under 28 U.S.C. § 455; and

(B) if a ground is disclosed, the parties, with the court's approval, waive the disqualification.

(4) ***Amending.*** The order may be amended at any time after notice to the parties and an opportunity to be heard.

(c) Master's Authority.

(1) ***In General.*** Unless the appointing order directs otherwise, a master may:

(A) regulate all proceedings;

(B) take all appropriate measures to perform the assigned duties fairly and efficiently; and

(C) if conducting an evidentiary hearing, exercise the appointing court's power to compel, take, and record evidence.

(2) ***Sanctions.*** The master may by order impose on a party any noncontempt sanction provided by Rule 37 or 45, and may recommend a contempt sanction against a party and sanctions against a nonparty.

(d) Master's Orders. A master who issues an order must file it and promptly serve a copy on each party. The clerk must enter the order on the docket.

(e) Master's Reports. A master must report to the court as required by the appointing order. The master must file the report and promptly serve a copy on each party, unless the court orders otherwise.

(f) Action on the Master's Order, Report, or Recommendations.

(1) ***Opportunity for a Hearing; Action in General.*** In acting on a master's order, report, or recommendations, the court must give the parties notice and an opportunity to be heard; may receive evidence; and may adopt or affirm, modify, wholly or partly reject or reverse, or resubmit to the master with instructions.

(2) ***Time to Object or Move to Adopt or Modify.*** A party may file objections to—or a motion to adopt or modify—the master's order, report, or recommendations no later than 20 days after a copy is served, unless the court sets a different time.

(3) ***Reviewing Factual Findings.*** The court must decide de novo all objections to findings of fact made or recommended by a master, unless the parties, with the court's approval, stipulate that:

(A) the findings will be reviewed for clear error; or

(B) the findings of a master appointed under Rule 53(a)(1)(A) or (C) will be final.

(4) ***Reviewing Legal Conclusions.*** The court must decide de novo all objections to conclusions of law made or recommended by a master.

(5) ***Reviewing Procedural Matters.*** Unless the appointing order establishes a different standard of review, the court may set aside a master's ruling on a procedural matter only for an abuse of discretion.

(g) Compensation.

(1) ***Fixing Compensation.*** Before or after judgment, the court must fix the master's compensation on the basis and terms stated in the appointing order, but the court may set a new

basis and terms after giving notice and an opportunity to be heard.

(2) ***Payment.*** The compensation must be paid either:

(A) by a party or parties; or

(B) from a fund or subject matter of the action within the court's control.

(3) ***Allocating Payment.*** The court must allocate payment among the parties after considering the nature and amount of the controversy, the parties' means, and the extent to which any party is more responsible than other parties for the reference to a master. An interim allocation may be amended to reflect a decision on the merits.

(h) Appointing a Magistrate Judge. A magistrate judge is subject to this rule only when the order referring a matter to the magistrate judge states that the reference is made under this rule.

(Amended February 28, 1966, effective July 1, 1966; April 28, 1983, effective August 1, 1983; March 2, 1987, effective August 1, 1987; April 30, 1991, effective December 1, 1991; April 22, 1993, effective December 1, 1993; March 27, 2003, effective December 1, 2003; April 30, 2007, effective December 1, 2007.)

ADVISORY COMMITTEE NOTES

1937 Adoption

Note to Subdivision (a). This is a modification of former Equity Rule 68 (Appointment and Compensation of Masters).

Note to Subdivision (b). This is substantially the first sentence of [former] Equity Rule 59 (Reference to Master—Exceptional, Not Usual) extended to actions formerly legal. See *Ex parte Peterson,* 1920, 40 S.Ct. 543, 253 U.S. 300, 64 L.Ed. 919.

Note to Subdivision (c). This is [former] Equity Rules 62 (Powers of Master) and 65 (Claimants Before Master Examinable by Him) with slight modifications. Compare [former] Equity Rules 49 (Evidence Taken Before Examiners, Etc.) and 51 (Evidence Taken Before Examiners, Etc.).

Note to Subdivision (d). (1) This is substantially a combination of the second sentence of [former] Equity Rule 59 (Reference to Master—Exceptional, Not Usual) and [former] Equity Rule 60 (Proceedings Before Master). Compare [former] Equity Rule 53 (Notice of Taking Testimony Before Examiner, Etc.).

(2) This is substantially [former] Equity Rule 52 (Attendance of Witnesses Before Commissioner, Master, or Examiner).

(3) This is substantially [former] Equity Rule 63 (Form of Accounts Before Master).

Note to Subdivision (e). This contains the substance of [former] Equity Rules 61 (Master's Report—Documents Identified but not Set Forth), 61½ (Master's Report—Presumption as to Correctness—Review), and 66 (Return of Master's Report—Exceptions—Hearing), with modifications as to the form and effect of the report and for inclusion of reports by auditors, referees, and examiners, and references in actions formerly legal. Compare [former] Equity Rules 49 (Evidence Taken Before Examiners, Etc.) and 67 (Costs on Exceptions to Master's Report). See *Camden v. Stuart,* 144 U.S. 104, 12 S.Ct. 585, 36 L.Ed. 363 (1892); *Ex parte Peterson,* 253 U.S. 300, 40 S.Ct. 543, 64 L.Ed. 919 (1920).

1966 Amendment

These changes are designed to preserve the admiralty practice whereby difficult computations are referred to a commissioner or assessor, especially after an interlocutory judgment determining liability. As to separation of issues for trial see Rule 42(b).

1983 Amendment

Subdivision (a). The creation of full-time magistrates, who serve at government expense and have no nonjudicial duties competing for their time, eliminates the need to appoint standing masters. Thus the prior provision in Rule 53(a) authorizing the appointment of standing masters is deleted. Additionally, the definition of "master" in subdivision (a) now eliminates the superseded office of commissioner.

The term "special master" is retained in Rule 53 in order to maintain conformity with 28 U.S.C. § 636(b)(2), authorizing a judge to designate a magistrate "to serve as a special master pursuant to the applicable provisions of this title and the Federal Rules of Civil Procedure for the United States District Courts." Obviously, when a magistrate serves as a special master, the provisions for compensation of masters are inapplicable, and the amendment to subdivision (a) so provides.

Although the existence of magistrates may make the appointment of outside masters unnecessary in many instances, see, e.g., *Gautreaux v. Chicago Housing Authority,* 384 F.Supp. 37 (N.D.Ill.1974), mandamus denied *sub nom., Chicago Housing Authority v. Austin,* 511 F.2d 82 (7th Cir. 1975); *Avco Corp. v. American Tel. & Tel. Co.,* 68 F.R.D. 532 (S.D.Ohio 1975), such masters may prove useful when some special expertise is desired or when a magistrate is unavailable for lengthy and detailed supervision of a case.

Subdivision (b). The provisions of 28 U.S.C. § 636(b)(2) not only permit magistrates to serve as masters under Rule 53(b) but also eliminate the exceptional condition requirement of Rule 53(b) when the reference is made with the consent of the parties. The amendment to subdivision (b) brings Rule 53 into harmony with the statute by exempting magistrates, appointed with the consent of the parties, from the general requirement that some exceptional condition requires the reference. It should be noted that subdivision (b) does not address the question, raised in recent decisional law and commentary, as to whether the exceptional condition requirement is applicable when *private masters* who are not magistrates are appointed with the consent of the parties. See Silberman, *Masters and Magistrates Part II: The American Analogue,* 50 N.Y.U.L.Rev. 1297, 1354 (1975).

Subdivision (c). The amendment recognizes the abrogation of Federal Rule 43(c) by the Federal Rules of Evidence.

Subdivision (f). The new subdivision responds to confusion flowing from the dual authority for references of pretrial matters to magistrates. Such references can be made, with or without the consent of the parties, pursuant to Rule 53 or under 28 U.S.C. § 636(b)(1)(A) and (b)(1)(B). There are a number of distinctions between references made under the statute and under the rule. For example, under the statute nondispositive pretrial matters may be referred to a magistrate, without consent, for final determination with reconsideration by the district judge if the magistrate's order is clearly erroneous or contrary to law. Under the rule, however, the appointment of a master, without consent of the parties, to supervise discovery would require some exceptional condition (Rule 53(b)) and would subject the proceedings to the report procedures of Rule 53(e). If an order of reference does not clearly articulate the source of the court's authority the resulting proceedings could be subject to attack on grounds of the magistrate's noncompliance with the provisions of Rule 53. This subdivision therefore establishes a presumption that the limitations of Rule 53 are not applicable unless the reference is specifically made subject to Rule 53.

A magistrate serving as a special master under 28 U.S.C. § 636(b)(2) is governed by the provisions of Rule 53, with the exceptional condition requirement lifted in the case of a consensual reference.

1987 Amendment

The amendments are technical. No substantive change is intended.

1991 Amendment

The purpose of the revision is to expedite proceedings before a master. The former rule required only a filing of the master's report, with the clerk then notifying the parties of the filing. To receive a copy, a party would then be required to secure it from the clerk. By transmitting directly to the parties, the master can save some efforts of counsel. Some local rules have previously required such action by the master.

1993 Amendments

This revision is made to conform the rule to changes made by the Judicial Improvements Act of 1990.

2003 Amendments

Rule 53 is revised extensively to reflect changing practices in using masters. From the beginning in 1938, Rule 53 focused primarily on special masters who perform trial functions. Since then, however, courts have gained experience with masters appointed to perform a variety of pretrial and post-trial functions. See Willging, Hooper, Leary, Miletich, Reagan, & Shapard, *Special Masters' Incidence and Activity* (Federal Judicial Center 2000). This revised Rule 53 recognizes that in appropriate circumstances masters may properly be appointed to perform these functions and regulates such appointments. Rule 53 continues to address trial masters as well, but permits appointment of a trial master in an action to be tried to a jury only if the parties consent. The new rule clarifies the provisions that govern the appointment and function of masters for all purposes. Rule 53(g) also changes the standard of review for findings of fact made or recommended by a master. The core of the original Rule 53 remains, including its prescription that appointment of a master must be the exception and not the rule.

Special masters are appointed in many circumstances outside the Civil Rules. Rule 53 applies only to proceedings that Rule 1 brings within its reach.

Subdivision (a)(1)

District judges bear primary responsibility for the work of their courts. A master should be appointed only in limited circumstances. Subdivision (a)(1) describes three different standards, relating to appointments by consent of the parties, appointments for trial duties, and appointments for pretrial or post-trial duties.

Consent Masters. Subparagraph (a)(1)(A) authorizes appointment of a master with the parties' consent. Party consent does not require that the court make the appointment; the court retains unfettered discretion to refuse appointment.

Trial Masters. Use of masters for the core functions of trial has been progressively limited. These limits are reflected in the provisions of subparagraph (a)(1)(B) that restrict appointments to exercise trial functions. The Supreme Court gave clear direction to this trend in *La Buy v. Howes Leather Co.*, 352 U.S. 249 (1957); earlier roots are sketched in *Los Angeles Brush Mfg. Corp. v. James*, 272 U.S. 701 (1927). As to nonjury trials, this trend has developed through elaboration of the "exceptional condition" requirement in present Rule 53(b). This phrase is retained, and will continue to have the same force as it has developed. Although the provision that a reference "shall be the exception and not the rule" is deleted, its meaning is embraced for this setting by the exceptional condition requirement.

Subparagraph (a)(1)(B)(ii) carries forward the approach of present Rule 53(b), which exempts from the "exceptional condition" requirement "matters of account and of difficult computation of damages." This approach is justified only as to essentially ministerial determinations that require mastery of much detailed information but that do not require extensive determinations of credibility. Evaluations of witness credibility should only be assigned to a trial master when justified by an exceptional condition.

The use of a trial master without party consent is abolished as to matters to be decided by a jury unless a statute provides for this practice.

Abolition of the direct power to appoint a trial master as to issues to be decided by a jury leaves the way free to appoint a trial master with the consent of all parties. A trial master should be appointed in a jury case, with consent of the parties and concurrence of the court, only if the parties waive jury trial with respect to the issues submitted to the master or if the master's findings are to be submitted to the jury as evidence in the manner provided by former Rule 53(e)(3). In no circumstance may a master be appointed to preside at a jury trial.

The central function of a trial master is to preside over an evidentiary hearing on the merits of the claims or defenses in the action. This function distinguishes the trial master from most functions of pretrial and post-trial masters. If any master is to be used for such matters as a preliminary injunction hearing or a determination of complex damages issues, for example, the master should be a trial master. The line, however, is not distinct. A pretrial master might well conduct an evidentiary hearing on a discovery dispute, and a post-trial master might conduct evidentiary hearings on questions of compliance.

Rule 53 has long provided authority to report the evidence without recommendations in nonjury trials. This authority is omitted from Rule 53(a)(1)(B). In some circumstances a master may be appointed under Rule 53(a)(1)(A) or (C) to take evidence and report without recommendations.

For nonjury cases, a master also may be appointed to assist the court in discharging trial duties other than conducting an evidentiary hearing.

Pretrial and Post–Trial Masters. Subparagraph (a)(1)(C) authorizes appointment of a master to address pretrial or post-trial matters. Appointment is limited to matters that cannot be addressed effectively and in a timely fashion by an available district judge or magistrate judge of the district. A master's pretrial or post-trial duties may include matters that could be addressed by a judge, such as reviewing discovery documents for privilege, or duties that might not be suitable for a judge. Some forms of settlement negotiations, investigations, or administration of an organization are familiar examples of duties that a judge might not feel free to undertake.

Magistrate Judges. Particular attention should be paid to the prospect that a magistrate judge may be available for special assignments. United States magistrate judges are authorized by statute to perform many pretrial functions in civil actions. 28 U.S.C. § 636(b)(1). Ordinarily a district judge who delegates these functions should refer them to a magistrate judge acting as magistrate judge.

There is statutory authority to appoint a magistrate judge as special master. 28 U.S.C. § 636(b)(2). In special circumstances, or when expressly authorized by a statute other than § 636(b)(2), it may be appropriate to appoint a magistrate judge as a master when needed to perform functions outside those listed in § 636(b)(1). There is no apparent reason to appoint a magistrate judge to perform as master duties that could be performed in the role of magistrate judge. Party consent is required for trial before a magistrate judge, moreover, and this requirement should not be undercut by resort to Rule 53 unless specifically authorized by statute; see 42 U.S.C. § 2000e–5(f)(5).

Pretrial Masters. The appointment of masters to participate in pretrial proceedings has developed extensively over the last two decades as some district courts have felt the need for additional help in managing complex litigation. This practice is not well regulated by present Rule 53, which focuses on masters as trial participants. Rule 53 is amended to confirm the authority to appoint—and to regulate the use of—pretrial masters.

A pretrial master should be appointed only when the need is clear. Direct judicial performance of judicial functions may be particularly important in cases that involve important public issues or many parties. At the extreme, a broad delegation of pretrial responsibility as well as a delegation of trial responsibilities can run afoul of Article III.

A master also may be appointed to address matters that blur the divide between pretrial and trial functions. The court's responsibility to interpret patent claims as a matter of law, for example, may be greatly assisted by appointing a master who has expert knowledge of the field in which the patent operates. Review of the master's findings will be de novo under Rule 53(g)(4), but the advantages of initial determination by a master may make the process more effective and timely than disposition by the judge acting alone. Determination of foreign law may present comparable difficulties. The decision whether to appoint a master to address such matters is governed by subdivision (a)(1)(C), not the trial-master provisions of subdivision (a)(1)(B).

Post–Trial Masters. Courts have come to rely on masters to assist in framing and enforcing complex decrees. Present Rule 53 does not directly address this practice. Amended Rule 53 authorizes appointment of post-trial masters for these and similar purposes. The constraint of subdivision (a)(1)(C) limits this practice to cases in which the master's duties cannot be performed effectively and in a timely fashion by an available district judge or magistrate judge of the district.

Reliance on a master is appropriate when a complex decree requires complex policing, particularly when a party has proved resistant or intransigent. This practice has been recognized by the Supreme Court, see *Local 28, Sheet Metal Workers' Internat. Assn. v. EEOC*, 478 U.S. 421, 481–482 (1986). The master's role in enforcement may extend to investigation in ways that are quite unlike the traditional role of judicial officers in an adversary system.

Expert Witness Overlap. This rule does not address the difficulties that arise when a single person is appointed to perform overlapping roles as master and as court-appointed expert witness under Evidence Rule 706. Whatever combination of functions is involved, the Rule 53(a)(1)(B) limit that confines trial masters to issues to be decided by the court does not apply to a person who also is appointed as an expert witness under Evidence Rule 706.

Subdivision (a)(2) and (3)

Masters are subject to the Code of Conduct for United States Judges, with exceptions spelled out in the Code. Special care must be taken to ensure that there is no actual or apparent conflict of interest involving a master. The standard of disqualification is established by 28 U.S.C. § 455. The affidavit required by Rule 53(b)(3) provides an important source of information about possible grounds for disqualification, but careful inquiry should be made at the time of making the initial appointment. The disqualification standards established by § 455 are strict. Because a master is not a public judicial officer, it may be appropriate to permit the parties to consent to appointment of a particular person as master in circumstances that would require disqualification of a judge. The judge must be careful to ensure that no party feels any pressure to consent, but with such assurances—and with the judge's own determination that there is no troubling conflict of interests or disquieting appearance of impropriety—consent may justify an otherwise barred appointment.

One potential disqualification issue is peculiar to the master's role. It may happen that a master who is an attorney represents a client whose litigation is assigned to the judge who appointed the attorney as master. Other parties to the litigation may fear that the attorney-master will gain special respect from the judge. A flat prohibition on appearance before the appointing judge during the time of service as master, however, might in some circumstances unduly limit the opportunity to make a desirable appointment. These matters may be regulated to some extent by state rules of professional responsibility. The question of present conflicts, and the possibility of future conflicts, can be considered at the time of appointment. Depending on the circumstances, the judge may consider it appropriate to impose a non-appearance condition on the lawyer-master, and perhaps on the master's firm as well.

Subdivision (b)

The order appointing a pretrial master is vitally important in informing the master and the parties about the nature and extent of the master's duties and authority. Care must be taken to make the order as precise as possible. The parties must be given notice and opportunity to be heard on the question whether a master should be appointed and on the terms of the appointment. To the extent possible, the notice should describe the master's proposed duties, time to complete the duties, standards of review, and compensation. Often it will be useful to engage the parties in the process of identifying the master, inviting nominations, and reviewing potential candidates. Party involvement may be particularly useful if a pretrial master is expected to promote settlement.

The hearing requirement of Rule 53(b)(1) can be satisfied by an opportunity to make written submissions unless the circumstances require live testimony.

Rule 53(b)(2) requires precise designation of the master's duties and authority. Clear identification of any investigating or enforcement duties is particularly important. Clear delineation of topics for any reports or recommendations is also an important part of this process. And it is important to protect against delay by establishing a time schedule for performing the assigned duties. Early designation of the procedure for fixing the master's compensation also may provide useful guidance to the parties.

Ex parte communications between a master and the court present troubling questions. Ordinarily the order should prohibit such communications, assuring that the parties know where authority is lodged at each step of the proceedings. Prohibiting ex parte communications between master and court also can enhance the role of a settlement master by assuring the parties that settlement can be fostered by confidential revelations that will not be shared with the court. Yet there may be circumstances in which the master's role is enhanced by the opportunity for ex parte communications with the court. A master assigned to help coordinate multiple proceedings, for example, may benefit from off-the-record exchanges with the court about logistical matters. The rule does not directly regulate these matters. It requires only that the court exercise its discretion and address the topic in the order of appointment.

Similarly difficult questions surround ex part e communications between a master and the parties. Ex parte communications may be essential in seeking to advance settlement. Ex parte communications also may prove useful in other settings, as with in camera review of documents to resolve privilege questions. In most settings, however, ex parte communications with the parties should be discouraged or prohibited. The rule requires that the court address the topic in the order of appointment.

Subdivision (b)(2)(C) provides that the appointment order must state the nature of the materials to be preserved and filed as the record of the master's activities, and (b)(2)(D) requires that the order state the method of filing the record. It is not feasible to prescribe the nature of the record without regard to the nature of the master's duties. The records appropriate to discovery duties may be different from those appropriate to encouraging settlement, investigating possible violations of a complex decree, or making recommendations for trial findings. A basic requirement, however, is that the master must make and file a complete record of the evidence considered in making or recommending findings of fact on the basis of evidence. The order of appointment should routinely include this requirement unless the nature of the appointment precludes any prospect that the master will make or recommend evidence-based findings of fact. In some circumstances it may be appropriate for a party to file materials directly with the court as provided by Rule 5(e), but in many circumstances filing with the court may be inappropriate. Confidentiality is important with respect to many materials that may properly be considered by a master. Materials in the record can be transmitted to the court, and filed, in connection with review of a master's order, report, or recommendations under subdivisions (f) and (g). Independently of review proceedings, the court may direct filing of any materials that it wishes to make part of the public record.

The provision in subdivision (b)(2)(D) that the order must state the standards for reviewing the master's orders, findings, or recommendations is a reminder of the provisions of subdivision (g)(3) that recognize stipulations for review less searching than the presumptive requirement of de novo decision by the court. Subdivision (b)(2)(D) does not authorize the court to supersede the limits of subdivision (g)(3).

In setting the procedure for fixing the master's compensation, it is useful at the outset to establish specific guidelines to control total expense. The court has power under subdivision (h) to change the basis and terms for determining compensation after notice to the parties.

Subdivision (b)(3) permits entry of the order appointing a master only after the master has filed an affidavit disclosing whether there is any ground for disqualification under 28 U.S.C. § 455. If the affidavit discloses a possible ground for disqualification, the order can enter only if the court determines that there is no ground for disqualification or if the parties, knowing of the ground for disqualification, consent with the court's approval to waive the disqualification.

The provision in Rule 53(b)(4) for amending the order of appointment is as import ant as the provisions for the initial order. Anything that could be done in the initial order can be done by amendment. The hearing requirement can be satisfied by an opportunity to make written submissions unless the circumstances require live testimony.

Subdivision (c)

Subdivision (c) is a simplification of the provisions scattered throughout present Rule 53. It is intended to provide the broad and flexible authority necessary to discharge the master's responsibilities. The most important delineation of a master's authority and duties is provided by the Rule 53(b) appointing order.

Subdivision (d)

The subdivision (d) provisions for evidentiary hearings are reduced from the extensive provisions in current Rule 53. This simplification of the rule is not intended to diminish the authority that may be delegated to a master. Reliance is placed on the broad and general terms of subdivision (c).

Subdivision (e)

Subdivision (e) provides that a master's order must be filed and entered on the docket. It must be promptly served on the parties, a task ordinarily accomplished by mailing or other means as permitted by Rule 5(b). In some circumstances it may be appropriate to have the clerk's office assist the master in mailing the order to the parties.

Subdivision (f)

Subdivision (f) restates some of the provisions of present Rule 53(e)(1). The report is the master's primary means of communication with the court. The materials to be provided to support review of the report will depend on the nature of the report. The master should provide all portions of the record preserved under Rule 53(b)(2)(C) that the master deems relevant to the report. The parties may designate additional materials from the record, and may seek permission to supplement the record with evidence. The court may direct that additional materials from the record be provided and filed. Given the wide array of tasks that may be assigned to a pretrial master, there may be circumstances that justify sealing a report or review record against public access—a report on continuing or failed settlement efforts is the most likely example. A post-trial master may be assigned duties in formulating a decree that deserve similar protection. Such circumstances may even justify denying access to the report or review materials by the parties, although this step should be taken only for the most compelling reasons. Sealing is much less likely to be appropriate with respect to a trial master's report.

Before formally making an order, report, or recommendations, a master may find it helpful to circulate a draft to the parties for review and comment. The usefulness of this practice depends on the nature of the master's proposed action.

Subdivision (g)

The provisions of subdivision (g)(1), describing the court's powers to afford a hearing, take evidence, and act on a master's order, report, or recommendations are drawn from present Rule 53(e)(2), but are not limited, as present Rule 53(e)(2) is limited, to the report of a trial master in a nonjury action. The requirement that the court must afford an opportunity to be heard can be satisfied by taking written submissions when the court acts on the report without taking live testimony.

The subdivision (g)(2) time limits for objecting to—or seeking adoption or modification of—a master's order, report, or recommendations, are important. They are not jurisdictional. Although a court may properly refuse to entertain untimely review proceedings, the court may excuse the failure to seek timely review. The basic time period is lengthened to 20 days because the present 10–day period may be too short to permit thorough study and response to a complex report dealing with complex litigation. If no party asks the court to act on a master's report, the court is free to adopt the master's action or to disregard it at any relevant point in the proceedings.

Subdivision (g)(3) establishes the standards of review for a master's findings of fact or recommended findings of fact. The court must decide de novo all objections to findings of fact made or recommended by the master unless the parties stipulate, with the court's consent, that the findings will be reviewed for clear error or—with respect to a master appointed on the parties' consent or appointed to address pretrial or post-trial matters—that the findings will be final. Clear-error review is more likely to be appropriate with respect to findings that do not go to the merits of the underlying claims or defenses, such as findings of fact bearing on a privilege objection to a discovery request. Even if no objection is made, the court is free to decide the facts de novo; to review for clear error if an earlier approved stipulation provided clear-error review; or to withdraw its consent to a stipulation for clear-error review or finality, and then to decide de novo. If the court withdraws its consent to a stipulation for finality or clear-error review, it may reopen the opportunity to object.

Under Rule 53(g)(4), the court must decide de novo all objections to conclusions of law made or recommended by a master. As with findings of fact, the court also may decide conclusions of law de novo when no objection is made.

Apart from factual and legal questions, masters often make determinations that, when made by a trial court, would be treated as matters of procedural discretion. The court may set a standard for review of such matters in the order of appointment, and may amend the order to establish the standard. If no standard is set by the original or amended order appointing the master, review of procedural matters is for abuse of discretion. The subordinate role of the master means that the trial court's review for abuse of discretion may be more searching than the review that an appellate court makes of a trial court.

If a master makes a recommendation on any matter that does not fall within Rule 53(g)(3), (4), or (5), the court may act on the recommendation under Rule 53(g)(1).

Subdivision (h)

The need to pay compensation is a substantial reason for care in appointing private persons as masters.

Payment of the master's fees must be allocated among the parties and any property or subject-matter within the court's control. The amount in controversy and the means of the parties may provide some guidance in making the allocation. The nature of the dispute also may be important—parties pursuing matters of public interest, for example, may deserve special protection. A party whose unreasonable behavior has occasioned the need to appoint a master, on the other hand, may properly be charged all or a major portion of the master's fees. It may be proper to revise an interim allocation after decision on the merits. The revision need not await a decision that is final for purposes of appeal, but may be made to reflect disposition of a substantial portion of the case.

The basis and terms for fixing compensation should be stated in the order of appointment. The court retains power to alter the initial basis and terms, after notice and an opportunity to be heard, but should protect the parties against unfair surprise.

The provision of former Rule 53(a) that the "provision for compensation shall not apply when a United States Magistrate Judge is designated to serve as a master" is deleted as unnecessary. Other provisions of law preclude compensation.

Subdivision (i)

Rule 53(i) carries forward unchanged former Rule 53(f).

2007 Amendments

The language of Rule 53 has been amended as part of the general restyling of the Civil Rules to make them more easily understood and to make style and terminology consistent throughout the rules. These changes are intended to be stylistic only.

HISTORICAL NOTES

Change of Name

United States magistrate appointed under section 631 of Title 28, Judiciary and Judicial Procedure, to be known as United States magistrate judge after Dec. 1, 1990, with any reference to United States magistrate or magistrate in Title 28, in any other Federal statute, etc., deemed a reference to United States magistrate judge appointed under section 631 of Title 28, see section 321 of Pub.L. 101–650, set out as a note under section 631 of Title 28.

CROSS REFERENCES

Adoption of master's findings by court, see Fed.Rules Civ.Proc. Rule 52, 28 USCA.

Clerks of courts, ineligible to appointment as master, see 28 USCA § 957.

Default judgment, reference to determine account or amount of damages, see Fed.Rules Civ.Proc. Rule 55, 28 USCA.

Pre-trial determination as to preliminary reference, see Fed.Rules Civ.Proc. Rule 16, 28 USCA.

Report, judgment not required to recite, see Fed.Rules Civ.Proc. Rule 54, 28 USCA.

Three–Judge court, appointment of master by single judge, see 28 USCA § 2284.

United States magistrate judges, fees for attending to any reference, see 28 USCA § 633.

TITLE VII. JUDGMENT

Rule 54. Judgment; Costs

(a) Definition; Form. "Judgment" as used in these rules includes a decree and any order from which an appeal lies. A judgment should not include recitals of pleadings, a master's report, or a record of prior proceedings.

(b) Judgment on Multiple Claims or Involving Multiple Parties. When an action presents more than one claim for relief—whether as a claim, counterclaim, crossclaim, or third-party claim—or when multiple parties are involved, the court may direct entry of a final judgment as to one or more, but fewer than all, claims or parties only if the court expressly determines that there is no just reason for delay. Otherwise, any order or other decision, however designated, that adjudicates fewer than all the claims or the rights and liabilities of fewer than all the parties does not end the action as to any of the claims or parties and may be revised at any time before the entry of a judgment adjudicating all the claims and all the parties' rights and liabilities.

(c) Demand for Judgment; Relief to Be Granted. A default judgment must not differ in kind from, or exceed in amount, what is demanded in the pleadings. Every other final judgment should grant the relief to which each party is entitled, even if the party has not demanded that relief in its pleadings.

(d) Costs; Attorney's Fees.

(1) ***Costs Other Than Attorney's Fees.*** Unless a federal statute, these rules, or a court order provides otherwise, costs—other than attorney's fees—should be allowed to the prevailing party. But costs against the United States, its officers, and its agencies may be imposed only to the extent allowed by law. The clerk may tax costs on 1 day's notice. On motion served within the next 5 days, the court may review the clerk's action.

(2) ***Attorney's Fees.***

(A) *Claim to Be by Motion.* A claim for attorney's fees and related nontaxable expenses must be made by motion unless the substantive law requires those fees to be proved at trial as an element of damages.

(B) *Timing and Contents of the Motion.* Unless a statute or a court order provides otherwise, the motion must:

(i) be filed no later than 14 days after the entry of judgment;

(ii) specify the judgment and the statute, rule, or other grounds entitling the movant to the award;

(iii) state the amount sought or provide a fair estimate of it; and

(iv) disclose, if the court so orders, the terms of any agreement about fees for the services for which the claim is made.

(C) *Proceedings.* Subject to Rule 23(h), the court must, on a party's request, give an opportunity for adversary submissions on the motion in accordance with Rule 43(c) or 78. The court may decide issues of liability for fees before receiving submissions on the value of services. The court must find the facts and state its conclusions of law as provided in Rule 52(a).

(D) *Special Procedures by Local Rule; Reference to a Master or a Magistrate Judge.* By local rule, the court may establish special procedures to resolve fee-related issues without extensive evidentiary hearings. Also, the court may refer issues concerning the value of services to a special master under Rule 53 without regard to the limitations of Rule 53(a)(1), and may refer a motion for attorney's fees to a magistrate judge under Rule 72(b) as if it were a dispositive pretrial matter.

(E) *Exceptions.* Subparagraphs (A)-(D) do not apply to claims for fees and expenses as sanctions for violating these rules or as sanctions under 28 U.S.C. § 1927.

(Amended December 27, 1946, effective March 19, 1948; April 17, 1961, effective July 19, 1961; March 2, 1987, effective August 1, 1987; April 22, 1993, effective December 1, 1993; April 29, 2002, effective December 1, 2002; March 27, 2003, effective December 1, 2003; April 30, 2007, effective December 1, 2007.)

ADVISORY COMMITTEE NOTES

1937 Adoption

Note to Subdivision (a). The second sentence is derived substantially from [former] Equity Rule 71 (Form of Decree).

Note to Subdivision (b). This provides for the separate judgment of equity and code practice. See Wis.Stat. (1935) § 270.54; Compare N.Y.C.P.A. (1937) § 476.

Note to Subdivision (c). For the limitation on default contained in the first sentence, see 2 N.D.Comp.Laws Ann. (1913) § 7680; N.Y.C.P.A. (1937) § 479. Compare *English Rules Under the Judicature Act* (The Annual Practice, 1937) O. 13, r.r. 3–12. The remainder is a usual code provision. It makes clear that a judgment should give the relief to which a party is entitled, regardless of whether it is legal or equitable or both. This necessarily includes the deficiency judgment in foreclosure cases formerly provided for by Equity Rule 10 (Decree for Deficiency in Foreclosures, Etc.).

Note to Subdivision (d). For the present rule in common law actions, see *Ex parte Peterson,* 253 U.S. 300, 40 S.Ct. 543, 64 L.Ed. 919 (1920); Payne, *Costs in Common Law Actions in the Federal Courts* (1935), 21 Va.L.Rev. 397.

The provisions as to costs in actions in forma pauperis contained in U.S.C., Title 28, former §§ 832–836 [now 1915] are unaffected by this rule. Other sections of U.S.C., Title 28, which are unaffected by this rule are: [former] §§ 815 (Costs; plaintiff not entitled to, when), 821 [now 1928] (Costs; infringement of patent; disclaimer), 825 (Costs; several actions), 829 [now 1927] (Costs; attorney liable for, when), and 830 [now 1920] (Costs; bill of; taxation).

The provisions of the following and similar statutes as to costs against the United States and its officers and agencies are specifically continued:

U.S.C., Title 15, §§ 77v(a), 78aa, 79y (Securities and Exchange Commission)

U.S.C., Title 16, § 825p (Federal Power Commission)

U.S.C., Title 26, [former] §§ 3679(d) and 3745(d) (Internal revenue actions)

U.S.C., Title 26, [former] § 3770(b)(2) (Reimbursement of costs of recovery against revenue officers)

U.S.C., Title 28, [former] § 817 (Internal revenue actions)

U.S.C., Title 28, § 836 [now 1915] (United States—actions in *forma pauperis*)

U.S.C., Title 28, § 842 [now 2006] (Actions against revenue officers)

U.S.C., Title 28, § 870 [now 2408] (United States—in certain cases)

U.S.C., Title 28, [former] § 906 (United States—foreclosure actions)

U.S.C., Title 47, § 401 (Communications Commission)

The provisions of the following and similar statutes as to costs are unaffected:

U.S.C., Title 7, § 210(f) (Actions for damages based on an order of the Secretary of Agriculture under Stockyards Act)

U.S.C., Title 7, § 499g(c) (Appeals from reparations orders of Secretary of Agriculture under Perishable Commodities Act)

U.S.C., Title 8, [former] § 45 (Action against district attorneys in certain cases)

U.S.C., Title 15, § 15 (Actions for injuries due to violation of antitrust laws)

U.S.C., Title 15, § 72 (Actions for violation of law forbidding importation or sale of articles at less than market value or wholesale prices)

U.S.C., Title 15, § 77k (Actions by persons acquiring securities registered with untrue statements under Securities Act of 1933)

U.S.C., Title 15, § 78i(e) (Certain actions under the Securities Exchange Act of 1934)

U.S.C., Title 15, § 78r (Similar to 78i(e))

U.S.C., Title 15, § 96 (Infringement of trade-mark—damages)

U.S.C., Title 15, § 99 (Infringement of trade-mark—injunctions)

U.S.C., Title 15, § 124 (Infringement of trade-mark—damages)

U.S.C., Title 19, § 274 (Certain actions under customs law)

U.S.C., Title 30, § 32 (Action to determine right to possession of mineral lands in certain cases)

U.S.C., Title 31, §§ 232 [now 3730] and 234 [former] (Action for making false claims upon United States)

U.S.C., Title 33, § 926 (Actions under Harbor Workers' Compensation Act)

U.S.C., Title 35, § 67 [now 281, 284] (Infringement of patent—damages)

U.S.C., Title 35, § 69 [now 282] (Infringement of patent—pleading and proof)

U.S.C., Title 35, § 71 [now 288] (Infringement of patent—when specification too broad)

U.S.C., Title 45, § 153p (Actions for non-compliance with an order of National R.R. Adjustment Board for payment of money)

U.S.C., Title 46, [former] § 38 (Action for penalty for failure to register vessel)

U.S.C., Title 46, § 829 (Action based on non-compliance with an order of Maritime Commission for payment of money)

U.S.C., Title 46, § 941 (Certain actions under Ship Mortgage Act)

U.S.C., Title 46, § 1227 (Actions for damages for violation of certain provisions of the Merchant Marine Act, 1936)

U.S.C., Title 47, § 206 (Actions for certain violations of Communications Act of 1934)

U.S.C., Title 49, § 16(2) [now 11705] (Action based on non-compliance with an order of I.C.C. for payment of money)

1946 Amendment

Note. The historic rule in the federal courts has always prohibited piecemeal disposal of litigation and permitted appeals only from final judgments except in those special instances covered by statute. *Hohorst v. Hamburg—American Packet Co.*, 1893, 13 S.Ct. 590, 148 U.S. 262, 37 L.Ed. 443; *Rexford v. Brunswick-Balke-Collender Co.*, 1913, 33 S.Ct. 515, 228 U.S. 339, 57 L.Ed. 864; *Collins v. Miller*, 1920, 40 S.Ct. 347, 252 U.S. 364, 64 L.Ed. 616. Rule 54(b) was originally adopted in view of the wide scope and possible content of the newly created "civil action" in order to avoid the possible injustice of a delay in judgment of a distinctly separate claim to await adjudication of the entire case. It was not designed to overturn the settled federal rule stated above, which, indeed, has more recently been reiterated in *Catlin v. United States*, 1945, 65 S.Ct. 631, 324 U.S. 229, 89 L.Ed. 911. See also *United States v. Florian*, 1941, 61 S.Ct. 713, 312 U.S. 656, 85 L.Ed. 1105; *Reeves v. Beardall*, 1942, 62 S.Ct. 1085, 316 U.S. 283, 86 L.Ed. 1478.

Unfortunately, this was not always understood, and some confusion ensued. Hence situations arose where district courts made a piecemeal disposition of an action and entered what the parties thought amounted to a judgment, although a trial remained to be had on other claims similar or identical with those disposed of. In the interim the parties did not know their ultimate rights, and accordingly took an appeal, thus putting the finality of the partial judgment in question. While most appellate courts have reached a result generally in accord with the intent of the rule, yet there have been divergent precedents and division of views which have served to render the issues more clouded to the parties appellant. It hardly seems a case where multiplicity of precedents will tend to remove the problem from debate. The problem is presented and discussed in the following cases: *Atwater v. North American Coal Corp.*, C.C.A.2, 1940, 111 F.2d 125; *Rosenblum v. Dingfelder*, C.C.A.2, 1940, 111 F.2d 406; *Audi-Vision, Inc. v. RCA Mfg. Co., Inc.*, C.C.A.2, 1943, 136 F.2d 621; *Zalkind v. Scheinman*, C.C.A.2, 1943, 139 F.2d 895; *Oppenheimer v. F. J. Young & Co., Inc.*, C.C.A.2, 1944, 144 F.2d 387; *Libbey-Owens-Ford Glass Co. v. Sylvania Industrial Corp.*, C.C.A.2, 1946, 154 F.2d 814, certiorari denied 1946, 66 S.Ct. 1353, 328 U.S. 859, 90 L.Ed. 1630; *Zarati Steamship Co. v. Park Bridge Corp.*, C.C.A.2, 1946, 154 F.2d 377; *Baltimore and Ohio R. Co. v. United Fuel Gas Co.*, C.C.A.4, 1946, 154 F.2d 545; *Jefferson Electric Co. v. Sola Electric Co.*, C.C.A.7, 1941, 122 F.2d 124; *Leonard v. Socony-Vacuum Oil Co.*, C.C.A.7, 1942, 130 F.2d 535; *Markham v. Kasper*, C.C.A.7, 1945, 152 F.2d 270; *Hanney v. Franklin Fire Ins. Co. of Philadelphia*, C.C.A.9, 1944, 142 F.2d 864; *Toomey v. Toomey*, App.D.C.1945, 149 F.2d 19, 80 U.S.App. D.C. 77.

In view of the difficulty thus disclosed, the Advisory Committee in its two preliminary drafts of proposed amendments attempted to redefine the original rule with particular stress upon the interlocutory nature of partial judgments which did not adjudicate all claims arising out of a single transaction or occurrence. This attempt appeared to meet with almost universal approval from those of the profession commenting upon it, although there were, of course, helpful suggestions for additional changes in language or clarification of detail. But cf. Circuit Judge Frank's dissenting opinion in *Libbey-Owens-Ford Glass Co. v. Sylvania Industrial Corp.*, supra, n. 21 of the dissenting opinion. The Committee, however, became convinced on careful study of its own proposals that the seeds of ambiguity still remained, and that it had not completely solved the problem of piecemeal appeals. After extended consideration, it concluded that a retention of the older federal rule was desirable, and that this rule needed only the exercise of a discretionary power to afford a remedy in the infrequent harsh case to provide a simple, definite, workable rule. This is afforded by amended Rule 54(b). It re-establishes an ancient policy with clarity and precision. For the possibility of staying execution where not all claims are disposed of under Rule 54(b), see amended Rule 62(h).

1961 Amendment

This rule permitting appeal, upon the trial court's determination of "no just reason for delay," from a judgment upon one or more but less than all the claims in an action, has generally been given a sympathetic construction by the courts and its validity is settled. *Reeves v. Beardall*, 316 U.S. 283 (1942); *Sears, Roebuck & Co. v. Mackey*, 351 U.S. 427 (1956); *Cold Metal Process Co. v. United Engineering & Foundry Co.*, 351 U.S. 445 (1956).

A serious difficulty has, however, arisen because the rule speaks of claims but nowhere mentions parties. A line of cases has developed in the circuits consistently holding the rule to be inapplicable to the dismissal, even with the requisite trial court determination, of one or more but less than all defendants jointly charged in an action, i.e. charged with various forms of concerted or related wrongdoing or related liability. See *Mull v. Ackerman*, 279 F.2d 25 (2d Cir. 1960); *Richards v. Smith*, 276 F.2d 652 (5th Cir. 1960); *Hardy v. Bankers Life & Cas. Co.*, 222 F.2d 827 (7th Cir. 1955); *Steiner v. 20th Century-Fox Film Corp.*, 220 F.2d 105 (9th Cir. 1955). For purposes of Rule 54(b) it was arguable that there were as many "claims" as there were parties defendant and that the rule in its present text applied where less than all of the parties were dismissed, cf. *United Artists Corp. v. Masterpiece Productions, Inc.*, 221 F.2d 213, 215 (2d Cir. 1955); *Bowling Machines, Inc. v. First Nat. Bank*, 283 F.2d 39 (1st Cir. 1960); but the Courts of Appeals are now committed to an opposite view.

The danger of hardship through delay of appeal until the whole action is concluded may be at least as serious in the multiple-parties situations as in multiple-claims cases, see *Pabellon v. Grace Line, Inc.*, 191 F.2d 169, 179 (2d Cir. 1951), cert. denied, 342 U.S. 893 (1951), and courts and commentators have urged that Rule 54(b) be changed to take in the former. See *Reagan v. Traders & General Ins. Co.*, 255 F.2d 845 (5th Cir. 1958); *Meadows v. Greyhound Corp.*, 235 F.2d 233 (5th Cir. 1956); *Steiner v. 20th Century-Fox Film Corp.*, supra; 6 Moore's Federal Practice ¶54.34[2] (2d ed. 1953); 3 Barron & Holtzoff, *Federal Practice & Procedure* § 1193.2 (Wright ed. 1958); *Developments in the Law—Multiparty Litigation*, 71 Harv.L.Rev. 874, 981 (1958); Note, 62 Yale L.J. 263, 271 (1953); Ill.Ann.Stat. ch. 110, § 50(2) (Smith-Hurd 1956). The amendment accomplishes this purpose by referring explicitly to parties.

There has been some recent indication that interlocutory appeal under the provisions of 28 U.S.C. § 1292(b), added in 1958, may now be available for the multiple-parties cases here considered. See *Jaftex Corp. v. Randolph Mills, Inc.*, 282 F.2d 508 (2d Cir. 1960). The Rule 54(b) procedure seems preferable for those cases, and § 1292(b) should be held inapplicable to them when the rule is enlarged as here proposed. See *Luckenbach Steamship Co., Inc., v. H. Muehlstein & Co., Inc.*, 280 F.2d 755, 757 (2d Cir. 1960); 1 Barron & Holtzoff, supra, § 58.1, p. 321 (Wright ed. 1960).

1987 Amendment

The amendment is technical. No substantive change is intended.

1993 Amendments

Subdivision (d). This revision adds paragraph (2) to this subdivision to provide for a frequently recurring form of litigation not initially contemplated by the rules—disputes over the amount of attorneys' fees to be awarded in the large number of actions in which prevailing parties may be entitled to such awards or in which the court must determine the fees to be paid from a common fund. This revision seeks to harmonize and clarify procedures that have been developed through case law and local rules.

Paragraph (1). Former subdivision (d), providing for taxation of costs by the clerk, is renumbered as paragraph (1) and revised to exclude applications for attorneys' fees.

Paragraph (2). This new paragraph establishes a procedure for presenting claims for attorneys' fees, whether or not denominated as "costs." It applies also to requests for reimbursement of expenses, not taxable as costs, when recoverable under governing law incident to the award of fees. *Cf. West Virginia Univ. Hosp. v. Casey,* 499 U.S. 83 (1991), holding, prior to the Civil Rights Act of 1991, that expert witness fees were not recoverable under 42 U.S.C. § 1988. As noted in subparagraph (A), it does not, however, apply to fees recoverable as an element of damages, as when sought under the terms of a contract; such damages typically are to be claimed in a pleading and may involve issues to be resolved by a jury. Nor, as provided in subparagraph (E), does it apply to awards of fees as sanctions authorized or mandated under these rules or under 28 U.S.C. § 1927.

Subparagraph (B) provides a deadline for motions for attorneys' fees—14 days after final judgment unless the court or a statute specifies some other time. One purpose of this provision is to assure that the opposing party is informed of the claim before the time for appeal has elapsed. Prior law did not prescribe any specific time limit on claims for attorneys' fees. White v. New Hampshire Dep't of Employment Sec., 455 U.S. 445 (1982). In many nonjury cases the court will want to consider attorneys' fee issues immediately after rendering its judgment on the merits of the case. Note that the time for making claims is specifically stated in some legislation, such as the Equal Access to Justice Act, 28 U.S.C. § 2412(d)(1)(B) (30–day filing period).

Prompt filing affords an opportunity for the court to resolve fee disputes shortly after trial, while the services performed are freshly in mind. It also enables the court in appropriate circumstances to make its ruling on a fee request in time for any appellate review of a dispute over fees to proceed at the same time as review on the merits of the case.

Filing a motion for fees under this subdivision does not affect the finality or the appealability of a judgment, though revised Rule 58 provides a mechanism by which prior to appeal the court can suspend the finality to resolve a motion for fees. If an appeal on the merits of the case is taken, the court may rule on the claim for fees, may defer its ruling on the motion, or may deny the motion without prejudice, directing under subdivision (d)(2)(B) a new period for filing after the appeal has been resolved. A notice of appeal does not extend the time for filing a fee claim based on the initial judgment, but the court under subdivision (d)(2)(B) may effectively extend the period by permitting claims to be filed after resolution of the appeal. A new period for filing will automatically begin if a new judgment is entered following a reversal or remand by the appellate court or the granting of a motion under Rule 59.

The rule does not require that the motion be supported at the time of filing with the evidentiary material bearing on the fees. This material must of course be submitted in due course, according to such schedule as the court may direct in light of the circumstances of the case. What is required is the filing of a motion sufficient to alert the adversary and the court that there is a claim for fees, and the amount of such fees (or a fair estimate).

If directed by the court, the moving party is also required to disclose any fee agreement, including those between attorney and client, between attorneys sharing a fee to be awarded, and between adversaries made in partial settlement of a dispute where the settlement must be implemented by court action as may be required by Rules 23(e) and 23.1 or other like provisions. With respect to the fee arrangements requiring court approval, the court may also by local rule require disclosure immediately after such arrangements are agreed to. *E.g.*, Rule 5 of United States District Court for the Eastern District of New York; *cf. In re "Agent Orange" Product Liability Litigation (MDL 381),* 611 F.Supp. 1452, 1464 (E.D.N.Y.1985).

In the settlement of class actions resulting in a common fund from which fees will be sought, courts frequently have required that claims for fees be presented in advance of hearings to consider approval of the proposed settlement. The rule does not affect this practice, as it permits the court to require submissions of fee claims in advance of entry of judgment.

Subparagraph (C) assures the parties of an opportunity to make an appropriate presentation with respect to issues involving the evaluation of legal services. In some cases, an evidentiary hearing may be needed, but this is not required in every case. The amount of time to be allowed for the preparation of submissions both in support of and in opposition to awards should be tailored to the particular case.

The court is explicitly authorized to make a determination of the liability for fees before receiving submissions by the parties bearing on the amount of an award. This option may be appropriate in actions in which the liability issue is doubtful and the evaluation issues are numerous and complex.

The court may order disclosure of additional information, such as that bearing on prevailing local rates or on the appropriateness of particular services for which compensation is sought.

On rare occasion, the court may determine that discovery under Rules 26–37 would be useful to the parties. *Compare* Rules Governing Section 2254 Cases in the U.S. District Courts, Rule 6. *See* Note, *Determining the Reasonableness of Attorneys' Fees—the Discoverability of Billing Records,* 64 *B.U.L.Rev.* 241 (1984). In complex fee disputes, the court may use case management techniques to limit the scope of the dispute or to facilitate the settlement of fee award disputes.

Fee awards should be made in the form of a separate judgment under Rule 58 since such awards are subject to review in the court of appeals. To facilitate review, the paragraph provides that the court set forth its findings and conclusions as under Rule 52(a), though in most cases this explanation could be quite brief.

Subparagraph (D) explicitly authorizes the court to establish procedures facilitating the efficient and fair resolution of fee claims. A local rule, for example, might call for matters to be presented through affidavits, or might provide for issuance of proposed findings by the court, which would be treated as accepted by the parties unless objected to within a specified time. A court might also consider establishing a schedule reflecting customary fees or factors affecting fees within the community, as implicitly suggested by Justice O'Connor in *Pennsylvania v. Delaware Valley Citizens' Council,* 483 U.S. 711, 733 (1987) (O'Connor, J., concurring) (how particular markets compensate for contingency). *Cf. Thompson v. Kennickell,* 710 F.Supp. 1 (D.D.C.1989) (use of findings in other cases to promote consistency). The parties, of course, should be permitted to show that in the circumstances of the case such a schedule should not be applied or that different hourly rates would be appropriate.

The rule also explicitly permits, without need for a local rule, the court to refer issues regarding the amount of a fee award in a particular case to a master under Rule 53. The district judge may designate a magistrate judge to act as a master for this purpose or may refer a motion for attorneys' fees to a magistrate judge for proposed findings and recommendations under Rule 72(b). This authorization eliminates any controversy as to whether such references are permitted under Rule 53(b) as "matters of account and of difficult computation of damages" and whether motions for attorneys' fees can be treated as the equivalent of a dispositive pretrial matter that can be referred to a magistrate judge. For consistency and efficiency, all such matters might be referred to the same magistrate judge.

Subparagraph (E) excludes from this rule the award of fees as sanctions under these rules or under 28 U.S.C. § 1927.

2002 Amendments

Subdivision (d)(2)(C) is amended to delete the requirement that judgment on a motion for attorney fees be set forth in a separate document. This change complements the amendment of Rule 58(a)(1), which deletes the separate document requirement for an order disposing of a motion for attorney fees under Rule 54. These changes are made to support amendment of Rule 4 of the Federal Rules of Appellate Procedure. It continues to be important that a district court make clear its meaning when it intends an order to be the final disposition of a motion for attorney fees.

The requirement in subdivision (d)(2)(B) that a motion for attorney fees be not only filed but also served no later than 14 days after entry of judgment is changed to require filing only, to establish a parallel with Rules 50, 52, and 59. Service continues to be required under Rule 5(a).

2003 Amendments

Rule 54(d)(2)(D) is revised to reflect amendments to Rule 53.

2007 Amendments

The language of Rule 54 has been amended as part of the general restyling of the Civil Rules to make them more easily understood and to make style and terminology consistent throughout the rules. These changes are intended to be stylistic only.

The words "or class member" have been removed from Rule 54(d)(2)(C) because Rule 23(h)(2) now addresses objections by class members to attorney-fee motions. Rule 54(d)(2)(C) is amended to recognize that Rule 23(h) now controls those aspects of attorney-fee motions in class actions to which it is addressed.

HISTORICAL NOTES

Effective and Applicability Provisions

1961 Amendments. Amendment adopted on Apr. 17, 1961, effective July 19, 1961, see Rule 86(d).

CROSS REFERENCES

Appellate court directing entry of judgment, see 28 USCA § 2106.

Bond for costs on appeal, filing with notice of appeal, see Federal Rules of Appellate Procedure Rule 7, 28 USCA.

Books and records kept by the clerk; civil docket, index and correct copy of every final judgment, see Fed.Rules Civ.Proc. Rule 79, 28 USCA.

Claims Court judgment finding plaintiff indebted to United States as judgment of district court, see 28 USCA § 2508.

Costs—

- Absent defendant, setting aside judgment and pleading on payment of, see 28 USCA § 1655.
- Admissions on genuineness of documents or truth of factual matters, expenses on failure to make, see Fed.Rules Civ.Proc. Rule 37, 28 USCA.
- Claimant in proceedings to condemn or forfeit property seized, see 28 USCA § 2465.
- Clerk of court of appeals, payment into Treasury, see 28 USCA § 711.
- Contempt of witness in foreign country failing to respond to subpoena, see 28 USCA § 1784.
- Offer of judgment affecting, see Fed.Rules Civ.Proc. Rule 68, 28 USCA.
- Previously dismissed action, see Fed.Rules Civ.Proc. Rule 41, 28 USCA.
- Stay of execution and enforcement of judgment to obtain certiorari from Supreme Court, see 28 USCA § 2101.
- Summary judgment, affidavits presented in bad faith, see Fed.Rules Civ.Proc. Rule 56, 28 USCA.

Counterclaim or cross-claim, judgment on, see Fed.Rules Civ.Proc. Rule 13, 28 USCA.

Court record of judgment lost or destroyed, enforcement where United States is interested, see 28 USCA § 1735.

Declaratory judgment, see 28 USCA §§ 2201, 2202, Fed. Rules Civ.Proc. Rule 57, 28 USCA.

Default judgment; parties entitled to, see Fed.Rules Civ. Proc. Rule 55, 28 USCA.

District Courts; removal of cases from state courts, see 28 USCA § 1441 et seq.

Fees and costs, see 28 USCA § 1911 et seq.

Judgment as a matter of law in actions tried by jury; alternative motion for new trial, conditional ruling, see Fed. Rules Civ.Proc. Rule 50, 28 USCA.

Judgment for specific acts; vesting title, consequences of failure to comply, see Fed.Rules Civ.Proc. Rule 70, 28 USCA.

Jurisdiction of district court; diversity of citizenship, amount in controversy, see 28 USCA § 1332.

Modification or vacation of judgment, errors not affecting; substantial rights not ground for, see Fed.Rules Civ.Proc. Rule 61, 28 USCA.

Motion as termination of running of time for appeal, see Federal Rules of Appellate Procedure Rule 4, 28 USCA.

New trials; amendment of judgments, see Fed.Rules Civ. Proc. Rule 59, 28 USCA.

Pending actions and judgments, see 28 USCA § 1961 et seq.

Pleading judgment, see Fed.Rules Civ.Proc. Rule 9, 28 USCA.

Record on appeal, composition, see Federal Rules of Appellate Procedure Rule 10, 28 USCA.

Sales under judgment, see 28 USCA § 2001 et seq.

Single judge of Three-Judge court not to enter, see 28 USCA § 2284.

Stay of proceedings to enforce a judgment, generally, see Fed.Rules Civ.Proc. Rule 62, 28 USCA.

Stay or injunction pending appeal, proceedings against surety, see Federal Rules of Appellate Procedure Rule 8, 28 USCA.

Stipulation for stay of execution of process in rem issued in admiralty case, see 28 USCA § 2464.

Third party tort liability to United States for hospital and medical care, see 42 USCA § 2651 et seq.

Time—

Entry of judgment, generally, see Fed.Rules Civ.Proc. Rule 58, 28 USCA.

Extension of time for relief from judgment; motion to amend judgment, see Fed.Rules Civ.Proc. Rule 6, 28 USCA.

Motion for relief from judgment or order, grounds for; finality of judgment unaffected, see Fed.Rules Civ. Proc. Rule 60, 28 USCA.

Tort claims against, judgment as bar to action against employee, see 28 USCA § 2676.

United States as party; generally, see 28 USCA § 2401 et seq.

Verdict submitted on written interrogatories to jury, judgment on, see Fed.Rules Civ.Proc. Rule 49, 28 USCA.

Rule 55. Default; Default Judgment

(a) Entering a Default. When a party against whom a judgment for affirmative relief is sought has failed to plead or otherwise defend, and that failure is shown by affidavit or otherwise, the clerk must enter the party's default.

(b) Entering a Default Judgment.

(1) ***By the Clerk.*** If the plaintiff's claim is for a sum certain or a sum that can be made certain by computation, the clerk—on the plaintiff's request, with an affidavit showing the amount due—must enter judgment for that amount and costs against a defendant who has been defaulted for not appearing and who is neither a minor nor an incompetent person.

(2) ***By the Court.*** In all other cases, the party must apply to the court for a default judgment. A default judgment may be entered against a minor or incompetent person only if represented by a general guardian, conservator, or other like fiduciary who has appeared. If the party against whom a default judgment is sought has appeared personally or by a representative, that party or its representative must be served with written notice of the application at least 3 days before the hearing. The court may conduct hearings or make referrals—preserving any federal statutory right to a jury trial—when, to enter or effectuate judgment, it needs to:

(A) conduct an accounting;

(B) determine the amount of damages;

(C) establish the truth of any allegation by evidence; or

(D) investigate any other matter.

(c) Setting Aside a Default or a Default Judgment. The court may set aside an entry of default for good cause, and it may set aside a default judgment under Rule 60(b).

(d) Judgment Against the United States. A default judgment may be entered against the United States, its officers, or its agencies only if the claimant establishes a claim or right to relief by evidence that satisfies the court.

(Amended March 2, 1987, effective August 1, 1987; April 30, 2007, effective December 1, 2007.)

ADVISORY COMMITTEE NOTES

1937 Adoption

This represents the joining of the equity decree *pro confesso* (former Equity Rules 12 (Issue of Subpoena—Time for Answer), 16 (Defendant to Answer—Default—Decree *Pro Confesso*), 17 (Decree *Pro Confesso* to be Followed by Final

Decree—Setting Aside Default), 29 (Defenses—How Presented), 31 (Reply—When Required—When Cause at Issue)) and the judgment by default now governed by U.S.C., Title 28, [former] § 724 (Conformity act). For dismissal of an action for failure to comply with these rules or any order of the court, see Rule 41(b).

Note to Subdivision (a). The provision for the entry of default comes from the Massachusetts practice, 2 Mass.Gen. Laws (Ter.Ed., 1932) ch. 231, § 57. For affidavit of default, see 2 Minn.Stat. (Mason, 1927) § 9256.

Note to Subdivision (b). The provision in paragraph (1) for the entry of judgment by the clerk when plaintiff claims a sum certain is found in the N.Y.C.P.A. (1937) § 485, in Calif.Code Civ.Proc. (Deering, 1937) § 585(1), and in Conn.Practice Book (1934) § 47. For provisions similar to paragraph (2), compare Calif.Code, *supra,* § 585(2); N.Y.C.P.A. (1937) § 490; 2 Minn.Stat. (Mason, 1927) § 9256(3); 2 Wash.Rev.Stat.Ann. (Remington, 1932) § 411(2). U.S.C., Title 28, § 1874, formerly § 785 (Action to recover forfeiture in bond) and similar statutes are preserved by the last clause of paragraph (2).

Note to Subdivision (e). This restates substantially the last clause of U.S.C., Title 28, [former] § 763 (Action against the United States under the Tucker Act). As this rule governs in all actions against the United States, U.S.C., Title 28, [former] § 45 (Practice and procedure in certain cases under the interstate commerce laws) and similar statutes are modified insofar as they contain anything inconsistent therewith.

Supplementary Note

Note. The operation of Rule 55(b) (Judgment) is directly affected by the Soldiers' and Sailors' Civil Relief Act of 1940, 50 U.S.C. Appendix, § 501 et seq. Section 200 of the Act [50 U.S.C. Appendix, § 520] imposes specific requirements which must be fulfilled before a default judgment can be entered, e.g., *Ledwith v. Storkan,* D.Neb.1942, 6 Fed.Rules Serv. 60b.24, Case 2, 2 F.R.D. 539, and also provides for the vacation of a judgment in certain circumstances. See discussion in Commentary, Effect of Conscription Legislation on the Federal Rules, 1940, 3 Fed.Rules Serv. 725; 3 *Moore's Federal Practice,* 1938, Cum.Supplement § 55.02.

1987 Amendment

The amendments are technical. No substantive change is intended.

2007 Amendments

The language of Rule 55 has been amended as part of the general restyling of the Civil Rules to make them more easily understood and to make style and terminology consistent throughout the rules. These changes are intended to be stylistic only.

Former Rule 55(a) directed the clerk to enter a default when a party failed to plead or otherwise defend "as provided by these rules." The implication from the reference to defending "as provided by these rules" seemed to be that the clerk should enter a default even if a party did something showing an intent to defend, but that act was not specifically described by the rules. Courts in fact have rejected that implication. Acts that show an intent to defend have frequently prevented a default even though not connected to any particular rule. "[A]s provided by these rules" is deleted to reflect Rule 55(a)'s actual meaning.

Amended Rule 55 omits former Rule 55(d), which included two provisions. The first recognized that Rule 55 applies to described claimants. The list was incomplete and unnecessary. Rule 55(a) applies Rule 55 to any party against whom a judgment for affirmative relief is requested. The second provision was a redundant reminder that Rule 54(c) limits the relief available by default judgment.

CROSS REFERENCES

Failure to serve answers to interrogatories, entry of default judgment, see Fed.Rules Civ.Proc. Rule 37, 28 USCA.

Judgments; demand for, relief awarded on default, see Fed.Rules Civ.Proc. Rule 54, 28 USCA.

Summons as notice to defendant, judgment by default will be entered on failure to appear and defend, see Fed.Rules Civ.Proc. Rule 4, 28 USCA.

Rule 56. Summary Judgment

(a) By a Claiming Party. A party claiming relief may move, with or without supporting affidavits, for summary judgment on all or part of the claim. The motion may be filed at any time after:

(1) 20 days have passed from commencement of the action; or

(2) the opposing party serves a motion for summary judgment.

(b) By a Defending Party. A party against whom relief is sought may move at any time, with or without supporting affidavits, for summary judgment on all or part of the claim.

(c) Serving the Motion; Proceedings. The motion must be served at least 10 days before the day set for the hearing. An opposing party may serve opposing affidavits before the hearing day. The judgment sought should be rendered if the pleadings, the discovery and disclosure materials on file, and any affidavits show that there is no genuine issue as to any material fact and that the movant is entitled to judgment as a matter of law.

(d) Case Not Fully Adjudicated on the Motion.

(1) ***Establishing Facts.*** If summary judgment is not rendered on the whole action, the court should, to the extent practicable, determine what material facts are not genuinely at issue. The court should so determine by examining the pleadings and evidence before it and by interrogating the attorneys. It should then issue an order specifying what facts—including items of damages or other relief—are not genuinely at issue. The facts so specified must be treated as established in the action.

(2) ***Establishing Liability.*** An interlocutory summary judgment may be rendered on liability alone, even if there is a genuine issue on the amount of damages.

(e) Affidavits; Further Testimony.

(1) ***In General.*** A supporting or opposing affidavit must be made on personal knowledge, set out facts that would be admissible in evidence, and show that the affiant is competent to testify on the matters stated. If a paper or part of a paper is referred to in an affidavit, a sworn or certified copy must be attached to or served with the affidavit. The court may permit an affidavit to be supplemented or opposed by depositions, answers to interrogatories, or additional affidavits.

(2) ***Opposing Party's Obligation to Respond.*** When a motion for summary judgment is properly made and supported, an opposing party may not rely merely on allegations or denials in its own pleading; rather, its response must—by affidavits or as otherwise provided in this rule—set out specific facts showing a genuine issue for trial. If the opposing party does not so respond, summary judgment should, if appropriate, be entered against that party.

(f) When Affidavits Are Unavailable. If a party opposing the motion shows by affidavit that, for specified reasons, it cannot present facts essential to justify its opposition, the court may:

(1) deny the motion;

(2) order a continuance to enable affidavits to be obtained, depositions to be taken, or other discovery to be undertaken; or

(3) issue any other just order.

(g) Affidavit Submitted in Bad Faith. If satisfied that an affidavit under this rule is submitted in bad faith or solely for delay, the court must order the submitting party to pay the other party the reasonable expenses, including attorney's fees, it incurred as a result. An offending party or attorney may also be held in contempt.

(Amended December 27, 1946, effective March 19, 1948; January 21, 1963, effective July 1, 1963; March 2, 1987, effective August 1, 1987; April 30, 2007, effective December 1, 2007.)

ADVISORY COMMITTEE NOTES

1937 Adoption

This rule is applicable to all actions, including those against the United States or an officer or agency thereof.

Summary judgment procedure is a method for promptly disposing of actions in which there is no genuine issue as to any material fact. It has been extensively used in England for more than 50 years and has been adopted in a number of American states. New York, for example, has made great use of it. During the first nine years after its adoption there, the records of New York county alone show 5,600 applications for summary judgments. Report of the Commission on the Administration of Justice in New York State (1934), p. 383. See also *Third Annual Report of the Judicial Council of the State of New York* (1937), p. 30.

In England it was first employed only in cases of liquidated claims, but there has been a steady enlargement of the scope of the remedy until it is now used in actions to recover land or chattels and in all other actions at law, for liquidated or unliquidated claims, except for a few designated torts and breach of promise of marriage. *English Rules Under the Judicature Act* (The Annual Practice, 1937) O. 3, r. 6; Orders 14, 14A, and 15; see also O. 32, r. 6, authorizing an application for judgment at any time upon admissions. In Michigan (3 Comp.Laws (1929) § 14260) and Illinois (Smith-Hurd Ill.Stats. c. 110, §§ 181, 259.15, 259.16), it is not limited to liquidated demands. New York (N.Y.R.C.P. (1937) Rule 113; see also Rule 107) has brought so many classes of actions under the operation of the rule that the Commission on Administration of Justice in New York State (1934) recommend that all restrictions be removed and that the remedy be available "in any action" (p. 287). For the history and nature of the summary judgment procedure and citations of state statutes, see Clark and Samenow, *The Summary Judgment* (1929), 38 Yale L.J. 423.

Note to Subdivision (d). See Rule 16 (Pre-Trial Procedure; Formulating Issues) and the Note thereto.

Note to Subdivisions (e) and (f). These are similar to rules in Michigan. Mich.Court Rules Ann. (Searl, 1933) Rule 30.

1946 Amendment

Note to Subdivision (a). The amendment allows a claimant to move for a summary judgment at any time after the expiration of 20 days from the commencement of the action or after service of a motion for summary judgment by the adverse party. This will normally operate to permit an earlier motion by the claimant than under the original rule, where the phrase "at any time after the pleading in answer thereto has been served" operates to prevent a claimant from moving for summary judgment, even in a case clearly proper for its exercise, until a formal answer has been filed. Thus in *Peoples Bank v. Federal Reserve Bank of San Francisco*, N.D.Cal.1944, 58 F.Supp. 25, the plaintiff's countermotion for a summary judgment was stricken as premature, because the defendant had not filed an answer. Since Rule 12(a) allows at least 20 days for an answer, that time plus the 10 days required in Rule 56(c) means that under original Rule 56(a) a minimum period of 30 days necessarily has to elapse in every case before the claimant can be heard on his right to a summary judgment. An extension of time by the court or the service of preliminary motions of any kind will prolong that period even further. In many cases this merely represents unnecessary delay. See *United States v. Adler's Creamery, Inc.*, C.C.A.2, 1939, 107 F.2d 987. The changes are in the interest of more expeditious litigation. The 20-day period, as provided, gives the defendant an opportunity to secure counsel and determine a course of action. But in a case where the defendant himself makes a motion for summary judgment within that time, there is no reason to restrict the plaintiff and the amended rule so provides.

Subdivision (c). The amendment of Rule 56(c), by the addition of the final sentence, resolves a doubt expressed in *Sartor v. Arkansas Natural Gas Corp.*, 1944, 64 S.Ct. 724, 321 U.S. 620, 88 L.Ed. 967. See also Commentary, Summary Judgment as to Damages, 1944, 7 Fed.Rules Serv. 974; *Madeirense Do Brasil S/A v. Stulman-Emrick Lumber Co.*, C.C.A.2d, 1945, 147 F.2d 399, certiorari denied 1945, 65 S.Ct. 1201, 325 U.S. 861, 89 L.Ed. 1982. It makes clear that although the question of recovery depends on the amount of damages, the summary judgment rule is applicable and summary judgment may be granted in a proper case. If the case is not fully adjudicated it may be dealt with as provided in subdivision (d) of Rule 56, and the right to summary recovery determined by a preliminary order, interlocutory in character, and the precise amount of recovery left for trial.

Subdivision (d). Rule 54(a) defines "judgment" as including a decree and "any order from which an appeal lies." Subdivision (d) of Rule 56 indicates clearly, however, that a partial summary "judgment" is not a final judgment, and, therefore, that it is not appealable, unless in the particular case some statute allows an appeal from the interlocutory order involved. The partial summary judgment is merely a pretrial adjudication that certain issues shall be deemed established for the trial of the case. This adjudication is more nearly akin to the preliminary order under Rule 16, and likewise serves the purpose of speeding up litigation by eliminating before trial matters wherein there is no genuine issue of fact. See *Leonard v. Socony-Vacuum Oil Co.*, C.C.A.7, 1942, 130 F.2d 535; *Biggins v. Oltmer Iron Works*, C.C.A.7, 1946, 154 F.2d 214; 3 *Moore's Federal Practice*, 1938, 3190–3192. Since interlocutory appeals are not allowed, except where specifically provided by statute, see 3 Moore, op. cit. supra, 3155–3156, this interpretation is in line with that policy, *Leonard v. Socony-Vacuum Oil Co.*, supra. See also *Audi Vision Inc. v. RCA Mfg. Co.*, C.C.A.2, 1943, 136 F.2d 621; *Toomey v. Toomey*, 1945, 149 F.2d 19, 80 U.S.App.D.C. 77; *Biggins v. Oltmer Iron Works*, supra; *Catlin v. United States*, 1945, 65 S.Ct. 631, 324 U.S. 229, 89 L.Ed. 911.

1963 Amendment

Subdivision (c). By the amendment "answers to interrogatories" are included among the materials which may be considered on motion for summary judgment. The phrase was inadvertently omitted from the rule, see 3 Barron & Holtzoff, *Federal Practice & Procedure* 159–60 (Wright ed. 1958), and the courts have generally reached by interpretation the result which will hereafter be required by the text of the amended rule. See Annot., 74 A.L.R.2d 984 (1960).

Subdivision (e). The words "answers to interrogatories" are added in the third sentence of this subdivision to conform to the amendment of subdivision (c).

The last two sentences are added to overcome a line of cases, chiefly in the Third Circuit, which has impaired the utility of the summary judgment device. A typical case is as follows: A party supports his motion for summary judgment by affidavits or other evidentiary matter sufficient to show that there is no genuine issue as to a material fact. The adverse party, in opposing the motion, does not produce any evidentiary matter, or produces some but not enough to establish that there is a genuine issue for trial. Instead, the adverse party rests on averments of his pleadings which on their face present an issue. In this situation Third Circuit cases have taken the view that summary judgment must be denied, at least if the averments are "well-pleaded," and not suppositious, conclusory, or ultimate. See *Frederick Hart & Co., Inc. v. Recordgraph Corp.*, 169 F.2d 580 (3d Cir. 1948); *United States ex rel. Kolton v. Halpern*, 260 F.2d 590 (3d Cir. 1958); *United States ex rel. Nobles v. Ivey Bros. Constr. Co., Inc.*, 191 F.Supp. 383 (D.Del.1961); *Jamison v. Pennsylvania Salt Mfg. Co.*, 22 F.R.D. 238 (W.D.Pa.1958); *Bunny Bear, Inc. v. Dennis Mitchell Industries*, 139 F.Supp. 542 (E.D.Pa.1956); *Levy v. Equitable Life Assur. Society*, 18 F.R.D. 164 (E.D.Pa.1955).

The very mission of the summary judgment procedure is to pierce the pleadings and to assess the proof in order to see whether there is a genuine need for trial. The Third Circuit doctrine, which permits the pleadings themselves to stand in the way of granting an otherwise justified summary judgment, is incompatible with the basic purpose of the rule. See 6 *Moore's Federal Practice* 2069 (2d ed. 1953); 3 Barron & Holtzoff, supra, § 1235.1.

It is hoped that the amendment will contribute to the more effective utilization of the salutary device of summary judgment.

The amendment is not intended to derogate from the solemnity of the pleadings. Rather it recognizes that, despite the best efforts of counsel to make his pleadings accurate, they may be overwhelmingly contradicted by the proof available to his adversary.

Nor is the amendment designed to affect the ordinary standards applicable to the summary judgment motion. So, for example: Where an issue as to a material fact cannot be resolved without observation of the demeanor of witnesses in order to evaluate their credibility, summary judgment is not appropriate. Where the evidentiary matter in support of the motion does not establish the absence of a genuine issue, summary judgment must be denied even if no opposing evidentiary matter is presented. And summary judgment may be inappropriate where the party opposing it shows under subdivision (f) that he cannot at the time present facts essential to justify his opposition.

1987 Amendment

The amendments are technical. No substantive change is intended.

2007 Amendments

The language of Rule 56 has been amended as part of the general restyling of the Civil Rules to make them more easily understood and to make style and terminology consistent throughout the rules. These changes are intended to be stylistic only.

Former Rule 56(a) and (b) referred to summary-judgment motions on or against a claim, counterclaim, or crossclaim, or to obtain a declaratory judgment. The list was incomplete. Rule 56 applies to third-party claimants, intervenors, claimants in interpleader, and others. Amended Rule 56(a) and (b) carry forward the present meaning by referring to a party claiming relief and a party against whom relief is sought.

Former Rule 56(c), (d), and (e) stated circumstances in which summary judgment "shall be rendered," the court "shall if practicable" ascertain facts existing without substantial controversy, and "if appropriate, shall" enter summary judgment. In each place "shall" is changed to "should." It is established that although there is no discretion to enter summary judgment when there is a genuine issue as to any material fact, there is discretion to deny summary judgment when it appears that there is no genuine issue as to any material fact. *Kennedy v. Silas Mason Co.*, 334 U.S. 249, 256–257 (1948). Many lower court decisions are gathered in 10A Wright, Miller & Kane, Federal Practice & Procedure: Civil 3d, § 2728. "Should" in amended Rule 56(c) recognizes that courts will seldom exercise the discretion to deny summary judgment when there is no genuine issue as to any material fact. Similarly sparing exercise of this discretion is appropriate under Rule 56(e)(2). Rule 56(d)(1), on the other hand, reflects the more open-ended discretion to decide whether it is practicable to determine what material facts are not genuinely at issue.

Former Rule 56(d) used a variety of different phrases to express the Rule 56(c) standard for summary judgment—that there is no genuine issue as to any material fact. Amended Rule 56(d) adopts terms directly parallel to Rule 56(c).

CROSS REFERENCES

Dismissal of action prior to service of motion for summary judgment, see Fed.Rules Civ.Proc. Rule 41, 28 USCA.

Findings of fact and conclusions of law unnecessary, see Fed.Rules Civ.Proc. Rule 52, 28 USCA.

Injunctions, single judge not to enter summary judgment, see 28 USCA § 2284.

Jurisdiction for lawsuits against terrorist states and bar on motions to dismiss, see 28 USCA § 1605.

Motion for judgment on pleadings, see Fed.Rules Civ.Proc. Rule 12, 28 USCA.

Rule 57. Declaratory Judgment

These rules govern the procedure for obtaining a declaratory judgment under 28 U.S.C. § 2201. Rules 38 and 39 govern a demand for a jury trial. The existence of another adequate remedy does not preclude a declaratory judgment that is otherwise appropriate. The court may order a speedy hearing of a declaratory-judgment action.

(Amended December 29, 1948, effective October 20, 1949; April 30, 2007, effective December 1, 2007.)

ADVISORY COMMITTEE NOTES

1937 Adoption

The fact that a declaratory judgment may be granted "whether or not further relief is or could be prayed" indicates that declaratory relief is alternative or cumulative and not exclusive or extraordinary. A declaratory judgment is appropriate when it will "terminate the controversy" giving rise on undisputed or relatively undisputed facts, it operates frequently as a summary proceeding, justifying docketing the case for early hearing as on a motion, as provided for in California (Code Civ.Proc. (Deering, 1937) § 1062a), Michigan (3 Comp.Laws (1929) § 13904), and Kentucky (Codes (Carroll, 1932) Civ.Pract. § 639a–3).

The "controversy" must necessarily be "of a justiciable nature, thus excluding an advisory decree upon a hypothetical state of facts." *Ashwander v. Tennessee Valley Authority*, 1936, 56 S.Ct. 466, 473, 297 U.S. 288, 80 L.Ed. 688. The existence or non-existence of any right, duty, power, liability, privilege, disability, or immunity or of any fact upon which such legal relations depend, or of a status, may be declared. The petitioner must have a practical interest in the declaration sought and all parties having an interest therein or adversely affected must be made parties or be cited. A declaration may not be rendered if a special statutory proceeding has been provided for the adjudication of some special type of case, but general ordinary or extraordinary legal remedies, whether regulated by statute or not, are not deemed special statutory proceedings.

When declaratory relief will not be effective in settling the controversy, the court may decline to grant it. But the fact that another remedy would be equally effective affords no ground for declining declaratory relief. The demand for relief shall state with precision the declaratory judgment relief, cumulatively or in the alternative; but when coercive relief only is sought but is deemed ungrantable, or inappropriate, the court may *sua sponte*, if it serves a useful purpose, grant instead a declaration of rights. *Hasselbring v. Koepke*, 1933, 248 N.W. 869, 263 Mich. 466, 93 A.L.R. 1170. Written instruments, including ordinances and statutes, may be construed before or after breach at the petition of a properly interested party, process being served on the private parties or public officials interested. In other respects the Uniform Declaratory Judgment Act affords a guide to the scope and function of the Federal act. Compare *Aetna Life Insurance Co. v. Haworth*, 1937, 57 S.Ct. 461, 300 U.S. 227, 81 L.Ed. 617, 108 A.L.R. 1000; *Nashville, Chattanooga & St. Louis Ry. v. Wallace*, 1933, 53 S.Ct. 345, 288 U.S. 249, 77 L.Ed. 730, 87 A.L.R. 1191; *Gully, Tax Collector v. Interstate Natural Gas Co.*, 82 F.2d 145 (C.C.A.5, 1936); *Ohio Casualty Ins. Co. v. Plummer*, Tex.1935, 13 F.Supp. 169; Borchard, Declaratory Judgments (1934), *passim*.

1948 Amendment

The amendment effective October 1949, substituted the reference to "Title 28, U.S.C., § 2201" in the first sentence for the reference to "Section 274(d) of the Judicial Code, as amended, U.S.C., Title 28, § 400".

2007 Amendments

The language of Rule 57 has been amended as part of the general restyling of the Civil Rules to make them more easily understood and to make style and terminology consistent throughout the rules. These changes are intended to be stylistic only.

CROSS REFERENCES

Answers to written interrogatories to jury, see Fed.Rules Civ.Proc. Rule 49, 28 USCA.

Assignment of cases for trial, see Fed.Rules Civ.Proc. Rule 40, 28 USCA.

Creation of remedy and further relief in declaratory judgment actions, see 28 USCA §§ 2201, 2202.

Jury trial and advisory jury, see Fed.Rules Civ.Proc. Rules 38 and 39, 28 USCA.

Rule 58. Entering Judgment

(a) Separate Document. Every judgment and amended judgment must be set out in a separate document, but a separate document is not required for an order disposing of a motion:

(1) for judgment under Rule 50(b);

(2) to amend or make additional findings under Rule 52(b);

(3) for attorney's fees under Rule 54;

(4) for a new trial, or to alter or amend the judgment, under Rule 59; or

(5) for relief under Rule 60.

(b) Entering Judgment.

(1) ***Without the Court's Direction.*** Subject to Rule 54(b) and unless the court orders otherwise, the clerk must, without awaiting the court's direction, promptly prepare, sign, and enter the judgment when:

(A) the jury returns a general verdict;

(B) the court awards only costs or a sum certain; or

(C) the court denies all relief.

(2) ***Court's Approval Required.*** Subject to Rule 54(b), the court must promptly approve the form of the judgment, which the clerk must promptly enter, when:

(A) the jury returns a special verdict or a general verdict with answers to written questions; or

(B) the court grants other relief not described in this subdivision (b).

(c) Time of Entry. For purposes of these rules, judgment is entered at the following times:

(1) if a separate document is not required, when the judgment is entered in the civil docket under Rule 79(a); or

(2) if a separate document is required, when the judgment is entered in the civil docket under Rule 79(a) and the earlier of these events occurs:

(A) it is set out in a separate document; or

(B) 150 days have run from the entry in the civil docket.

(d) Request for Entry. A party may request that judgment be set out in a separate document as required by Rule 58(a).

(e) Cost or Fee Awards. Ordinarily, the entry of judgment may not be delayed, nor the time for appeal extended, in order to tax costs or award fees. But if a timely motion for attorney's fees is made under Rule 54(d)(2), the court may act before a notice of appeal has been filed and become effective to order that the motion have the same effect under Federal Rule of Appellate Procedure 4(a)(4) as a timely motion under Rule 59.

(Amended December 27, 1946, effective March 19, 1948; January 21, 1963, effective July 1, 1963; April 22, 1993, effective December 1, 1993; April 29, 2002, effective December 1, 2002; April 30, 2007, effective December 1, 2007.)

ADVISORY COMMITTEE NOTES

1937 Adoption

See Wis.Stat. (1935) § 270.31 (judgment entered forthwith on verdict of jury unless otherwise ordered), § 270.65 (where trial is by the court, entered by direction of the court), § 270.63 (entered by clerk on judgment on admitted claim for money). Compare 1 Idaho Code Ann. (1932) § 7–1101, and 4 Mont.Rev.Codes Ann. (1935) § 9403, which provide that judgment in jury cases be entered by clerk within 24 hours after verdict unless court otherwise directs. Conn.Practice Book (1934), § 200, provides that all judgments shall be entered within one week after rendition. In some States such as Washington, 2 Rev.Stat.Ann. (Remington, 1932), § 431, in jury cases the judgment is entered two days after the return of verdict to give time for making motion for new trial; § 435 (*ibid.*), provides that all judgments shall be entered by the clerk, subject to the court's direction.

1946 Amendment

Note. The reference to Rule 54(b) is made necessary by the amendment of that rule.

Two changes have been made in Rule 58 in order to clarify the practice. The substitution of the more inclusive phrase "all relief be denied" for the words "there be no recovery", makes it clear that the clerk shall enter the judgment forthwith in the situations specified without awaiting the filing of a formal judgment approved by the court. The phrase "all relief be denied" covers cases such as the denial of a bankrupt's discharge and similar situations where the relief sought is refused but there is literally no denial of a "recovery".

The addition of the last sentence in the rule emphasizes that judgments are to be entered promptly by the clerk without waiting for the taxing of costs. Certain district court rules, for example, Civil Rule 22 of the Southern District of New York—until its annulment Oct. 1, 1945, for conflict with this rule—and the like rule of the Eastern District of New York, are expressly in conflict with this provision, although the federal law is of long standing and well settled. *Fowler v. Hamill,* 1891, 11 S.Ct. 663, 139 U.S. 549, 35 L.Ed. 266; *Craig v. The Hartford,* C.C.Cal.1856, Fed.Cas. No. 3,333; *Tuttle v. Claflin,* C.C.A.2, 1895, 60 F. 7, certiorari denied 1897; 17 S.Ct. 992, 166 U.S. 721, 41 L.Ed. 1188; *Prescott & A.C. Ry. Co. v. Atchison, T. & S.F.R. Co.,* C.C.A.2, 1897, 84 F. 213; *Stallo v. Wagner,* C.C.A.2, 1917, 245 F. 636, 639–40; *Brown v. Parker,* C.C.A.8, 1899, 97 F. 446; *Allis-Chalmers v. United States,* C.C.A.7, 1908, 162 F. 679. And this applies even though state law is to the contrary. *United States v. Nordbye,* C.C.A.8, 1935, 75 F.2d 744, certiorari denied 56 S.Ct. 103, 296 U.S. 572, 80 L.Ed. 404. Inasmuch as it has been held that failure of the clerk thus to enter judgment is a "misprision" "not to be excused", *The Washington,* C.C.A.2,

1926, 16 F.2d 206, such a district court rule may have serious consequences for a district court clerk. Rules of this sort also provide for delay in entry of the judgment contrary to Rule 58. See *Commissioner of Internal Revenue v. Bedford's Estate,* 1945, 65 S.Ct. 1157, 325 U.S. 283, 91 L.Ed. 1611.

1963 Amendment

Under the present rule a distinction has sometimes been made between judgments on general jury verdicts, on the one hand, and, on the other, judgments upon decisions of the court that a party shall recover only money or costs or that all relief shall be denied. In the first situation, it is clear that the clerk should enter the judgment without awaiting a direction by the court unless the court otherwise orders. In the second situation it was intended that the clerk should similarly enter the judgment forthwith upon the court's decision; but because of the separate listing in the rule, and the use of the phrase "upon receipt . . . of the direction," the rule has sometimes been interpreted as requiring the clerk to await a separate direction of the court. All these judgments are usually uncomplicated, and should be handled in the same way. The amended rule accordingly deals with them as a single group in clause (1) (substituting the expression "only a sum certain" for the present expression "only money"), and requires the clerk to prepare, sign and enter them forthwith, without awaiting court direction, unless the court makes a contrary order. (The clerk's duty is ministerial and may be performed by a deputy clerk in the name of the clerk. See 28 U.S.C. § 956; cf. *Gilbertson v. United States,* 168 Fed. 672 (7th Cir. 1909).) The more complicated judgments described in clause (2) must be approved by the court before they are entered.

Rule 58 is designed to encourage all reasonable speed in formulating and entering the judgment when the case has been decided. Participation by the attorneys through the submission of forms of judgment involves needless expenditure of time and effort and promotes delay, except in special cases where counsel's assistance can be of real value. See *Matteson v. United States,* 240 F.2d 517, 518–19 (2d Cir. 1956). Accordingly, the amended rule provides that attorneys shall not submit forms of judgment unless directed to do so by the court. This applies to the judgments mentioned in clause (2) as well as clause (1).

Hitherto some difficulty has arisen, chiefly where the court has written an opinion or memorandum containing some apparently directive or dispositive words, e.g., "the plaintiff's motion [for summary judgment] is granted," see *United States v. F. & M. Schaefer Brewing Co.,* 356 U.S. 227, 229, 78 S.Ct. 674, 2 L.Ed.2d 721 (1958). Clerks on occasion have viewed these opinions or memoranda as being in themselves a sufficient basis for entering judgment in the civil docket as provided by Rule 79(a). However, where the opinion or memorandum has not contained all the elements of a judgment, or where the judge has later signed a formal judgment, it has become a matter of doubt whether the purported entry of judgment was effective, starting the time running for post-verdict motions and for the purpose of appeal. See id.; and compare *Blanchard v. Commonwealth Oil Co.,* 294 F.2d 834 (5th Cir. 1961); *United States v. Higginson,* 238 F.2d 439 (1st Cir. 1956); *Danzig v. Virgin Isle Hotel, Inc.,* 278 F.2d 580 (3d Cir. 1960); *Sears v. Austin,* 282 F.2d 340 (9th Cir. 1960), with *Matteson v. United States,* supra; *Erstling v. Southern Bell Tel. & Tel. Co.,* 255 F.2d 93 (5th Cir. 1958); *Barta v. Oglala Sioux Tribe,* 259 F.2d 553 (8th Cir. 1958) cert. denied, 358 U.S. 932, 79 S.Ct. 320, 3 L.Ed.2d 304 (1959); *Beacon Fed. S. & L. Assn. v. Federal Home L. Bank Bd.,* 266 F.2d 246 (7th Cir.), cert. denied, 361 U.S. 823, 80 S.Ct. 70, 4 L.Ed.2d 67 (1959); *Ram v. Paramount Film D. Corp.,* 278 F.2d 191 (4th Cir. 1960).

The amended rule eliminates these uncertainties by requiring that there be a judgment set out on a separate document—distinct from any opinion or memorandum—which provides the basis for the entry of judgment. That judgment shall be on separate documents is also indicated in Rule 79(b); and see General Rule 10 of the U.S. District Courts for the Eastern and Southern Districts of New York; *Ram v. Paramount Film D. Corp.,* supra, at 194.

See the amendment of Rule 79(a) and the new specimen forms of judgment, Forms 31 and 32.

See also Rule 55(b)(1) and (2) covering the subject of judgments by default.

1993 Amendments

Ordinarily the pendency or post-judgment filing of a claim for attorney's fees will not affect the time for appeal from the underlying judgment. See Budinich v. Becton Dickinson & Co., 486 U.S. 196 (1988). Particularly if the claim for fees involves substantial issues or is likely to be affected by the appellate decision, the district court may prefer to defer consideration of the claim for fees until after the appeal is resolved. However, in many cases it may be more efficient to decide fee questions before an appeal is taken so that appeals relating to the fee award can be heard at the same time as appeals relating to the merits of the case. This revision permits, but does not require, the court to delay the finality of the judgment for appellate purposes under revised Fed.R.App.P. 4(a) until the fee dispute is decided. To accomplish this result requires entry of an order by the district court before the time a notice of appeal becomes effective for appellate purposes. If the order is entered, the motion for attorney's fees is treated in the same manner as a timely motion under Rule 59.

2002 Amendments

Rule 58 has provided that a judgment is effective only when set forth on a separate document and entered as provided in Rule 79(a). This simple separate document requirement has been ignored in many cases. The result of failure to enter judgment on a separate document is that the time for making motions under Rules 50, 52, 54(d)(2)(B), 59, and some motions under Rule 60, never begins to run. The time to appeal under Appellate Rule 4(a) also does not begin to run. There have been few visible problems with respect to Rule 50, 52, 54(d)(2)(B), 59, or 60 motions, but there have been many and horridly confused problems under Appellate Rule 4(a). These amendments are designed to work in conjunction with Appellate Rule 4(a) to ensure that appeal time does not linger on indefinitely, and to maintain the integration of the time periods set for Rules 50, 52, 54(d)(2)(B), 59, and 60 with Appellate Rule 4(a).

Rule 58(a) preserves the core of the present separate document requirement, both for the initial judgment and for any amended judgment. No attempt is made to sort through the confusion that some courts have found in addressing the elements of a separate document. It is easy to prepare a separate document that recites the terms of the judgment without offering additional explanation or citation of authority. Forms 31 and 32 provide examples.

Rule 58 is amended, however, to address a problem that arises under Appellate Rule 4(a). Some courts treat such orders as those that deny a motion for new trial as a "judgment," so that appeal time does not start to run until the order is entered on a separate document. Without attempting to address the question whether such orders are appealable, and thus judgments as defined by Rule 54(a), the amendment provides that entry on a separate document is not required for an order disposing of the motions listed in Appellate Rule 4(a). The enumeration of motions drawn from the Appellate Rule 4(a) list is generalized by omitting details that are important for appeal time purposes but that would unnecessarily complicate the separate document requirement. As one example, it is not required that any of the enumerated motions be timely. Many of the enumerated motions are frequently made before judgment is entered. The exemption of the order disposing of the motion does not excuse the obligation to set forth the judgment itself on a separate document. And if disposition of the motion results in an amended judgment, the amended judgment must be set forth on a separate document.

Rule 58(b) discards the attempt to define the time when a judgment becomes "effective." Taken in conjunction with the Rule 54(a) definition of a judgment to include "any order from which an appeal lies," the former Rule 58 definition of effectiveness could cause strange difficulties in implementing pretrial orders that are appealable under interlocutory appeal provisions or under expansive theories of finality. Rule 58(b) replaces the definition of effectiveness with a new provision that defines the time when judgment is entered. If judgment is promptly set forth on a separate document, as should be done when required by Rule 58(a)(1), the new provision will not change the effect of Rule 58. But in the cases in which court and clerk fail to comply with this simple requirement, the motion time periods set by Rules 50, 52, 54, 59, and 60 begin to run after expiration of 150 days from entry of the judgment in the civil docket as required by Rule 79(a).

A companion amendment of Appellate Rule 4(a)(7) integrates these changes with the time to appeal.

The new all-purpose definition of the entry of judgment must be applied with common sense to other questions that may turn on the time when judgment is entered. If the 150-day provision in Rule 58(b)(2)(B)—designed to integrate the time for post-judgment motions with appeal time—serves no purpose, or would defeat the purpose of another rule, it should be disregarded. In theory, for example, the separate document requirement continues to apply to an interlocutory order that is appealable as a final decision under collateral-order doctrine. Appealability under collateral-order doctrine should not be complicated by failure to enter the order as a judgment on a separate document—there is little reason to force trial judges to speculate about the potential appealability of every order, and there is no means to ensure that the trial judge will always reach the same conclusion as the court of appeals. Appeal time should start to run when the collateral order is entered without regard to creation of a separate document and without awaiting expiration of the 150 days provided by Rule 58(b)(2). Drastic surgery on Rules 54(a) and 58 would be required to address this and related issues, however, and it is better to leave this conundrum to the pragmatic disregard that seems its present fate. The present amendments do not seem to make matters worse, apart from one false appearance. If a pretrial order is set forth on a separate document that meets the requirements of Rule 58(b), the time to move for reconsideration seems to begin to run, perhaps years before final judgment. And even if there is no separate document, the time to move for reconsideration seems to begin 150 days after entry in the civil docket. This apparent problem is resolved by Rule 54(b), which expressly permits revision of all orders not made final under Rule 54(b) "at any time before the entry of judgment adjudicating all the claims and the rights and liabilities of all the parties."

New Rule 58(d) replaces the provision that attorneys shall not submit forms of judgment except on direction of the court. This provision was added to Rule 58 to avoid the delays that were frequently encountered by the former practice of directing the attorneys for the prevailing party to prepare a form of judgment, and also to avoid the occasionally inept drafting that resulted from attorney-prepared judgments. See *11 Wright, Miller & Kane, Federal Practice & Procedure: Civil 2d, § 2786*. The express direction in Rule 58(a)(2) for prompt action by the clerk, and by the court if court action is required, addresses this concern. The new provision allowing any party to move for entry of judgment on a separate document will protect all needs for prompt commencement of the periods for motions, appeals, and execution or other enforcement.

Changes Made After Publication and Comment Minor style changes were made. The definition of the time of entering judgment in Rule 58(b) was extended to reach all Civil Rules, not only the Rules described in the published version—Rules 50, 52, 54(d)(2)(B), 59, 60, and 62. And the time of entry was extended from 60 days to 150 days after entry in the civil docket without a required separate document.

2007 Amendments

The language of Rule 58 has been amended as part of the general restyling of the Civil Rules to make them more easily understood and to make style and terminology consistent throughout the rules. These changes are intended to be stylistic only.

CROSS REFERENCES

General verdict accompanied by answers to interrogatories by jury, see Fed.Rules Civ.Proc. Rule 49, 28 USCA.

Judgment for particular claim or counterclaim, see Fed. Rules Civ.Proc. Rule 54, 28 USCA.

Notation of entry of judgment, see Fed.Rules Civ.Proc. Rule 79, 28 USCA.

Notice of entry of judgment, see Fed.Rules Civ.Proc. Rule 77, 28 USCA.

Record on appeal, see Federal Rules of Appellate Procedure Rule 10, 28 USCA.

Time for new trial, see Fed.Rules Civ.Proc. Rule 59, 28 USCA.

Time to appeal, see Federal Rules of Appellate Procedure Rule 4, 28 USCA.

Rule 59. New Trial; Altering or Amending a Judgment

(a) In General.

(1) ***Grounds for New Trial.*** The court may, on motion, grant a new trial on all or some of the issues—and to any party—as follows:

(A) after a jury trial, for any reason for which a new trial has heretofore been granted in an action at law in federal court; or

(B) after a nonjury trial, for any reason for which a rehearing has heretofore been granted in a suit in equity in federal court.

(2) ***Further Action After a Nonjury Trial.*** After a nonjury trial, the court may, on motion for a new trial, open the judgment if one has been entered, take additional testimony, amend findings of fact and conclusions of law or make new ones, and direct the entry of a new judgment.

(b) Time to File a Motion for a New Trial. A motion for a new trial must be filed no later than 10 days after the entry of judgment.

(c) Time to Serve Affidavits. When a motion for a new trial is based on affidavits, they must be filed with the motion. The opposing party has 10 days after being served to file opposing affidavits; but that period may be extended for up to 20 days, either by the court for good cause or by the parties' stipulation. The court may permit reply affidavits.

(d) New Trial on the Court's Initiative or for Reasons Not in the Motion. No later than 10 days after the entry of judgment, the court, on its own, may order a new trial for any reason that would justify granting one on a party's motion. After giving the parties notice and an opportunity to be heard, the court may grant a timely motion for a new trial for a reason not stated in the motion. In either event, the court must specify the reasons in its order.

(e) Motion to Alter or Amend a Judgment. A motion to alter or amend a judgment must be filed no later than 10 days after the entry of the judgment.

(Amended December 27, 1946, effective March 19, 1948; February 28, 1966, effective July 1, 1966; April 27, 1995, effective December 1, 1995; April 30, 2007, effective December 1, 2007.)

ADVISORY COMMITTEE NOTES

1937 Adoption

This rule represents an amalgamation of the petition for rehearing of [former] Equity Rule 69 (Petition for Rehearing) and the motion for new trial of 28 U.S.C., § 2111, formerly § 391 (New trials; harmless error), made in the light of the experience and provision of the code States. Compare Calif.Code Civ.Proc., Deering, 1937, §§ 656 to 663a, 28 U.S.C., § 2111, formerly § 391 (New trials; harmless error) is thus substantially continued in this rule. U.S.C., Title 28, [former] § 840 (Executions; stay on conditions) is modified insofar as it contains time provisions inconsistent with Subdivision (b). For the effect of the motion for new trial upon the time for taking an appeal see *Morse v. United States*, 1926, 46 S.Ct. 241, 270 U.S. 151, 70 L.Ed. 518; *Aspen Mining and Smelting Co. v. Billings*, 1893, 14 S.Ct. 4, 150 U.S. 31, 37 L.Ed. 986.

For partial new trials which are permissible under Subdivision (a), see *Gasoline Products Co., Inc. v. Champlin Refining Co.*, 1931, 51 S.Ct. 513, 283 U.S. 494, 75 L.Ed. 1188; *Schuerholz v. Roach*, C.C.A.4, 1932, 58 F.2d 32; *Simmons v. Fish*, 1912, 97 N.E. 102, 210 Mass. 563, Ann.Cas.1912D, 588 (sustaining and recommending the practice and citing federal cases and cases in accord from about sixteen States and contra from three States). The procedure in several States provides specifically for partial new trials. Ariz.Rev.Code Ann., Struckmeyer, 1928, § 3852; Calif.Code Civ.Proc., Deering, 1937, §§ 657, 662; Smith-Hurd Ill.Stats., 1937, c. 110, § 216 (Par. (f)); Md.Ann.Code, Bagby, 1924, Art. 5, §§ 25, 26; Mich.Court Rules Ann., Searl, 1933, Rule 47, § 2; Miss.Sup.Ct.Rule 12, 161 Miss. 903, 905, 1931; N.J.Sup.Ct. Rules 131, 132, 147, 2 N.J.Misc. 1197, 1246–1251, 1255, 1924; 2 N.D.Comp.Laws Ann., 1913, § 7844, as amended by N.D.Laws 1927, ch. 214.

1946 Amendment

Note. Subdivision (b). With the time for appeal to a circuit court of appeals reduced in general to 30 days by the proposed amendment of Rule 73(a), the utility of the original "except" clause, which permits a motion for a new trial on the ground of newly discovered evidence to be made before the expiration of the time for appeal, would have been seriously restricted. It was thought advisable, therefore, to take care of this matter in another way. By amendment of Rule 60(b), newly discovered evidence is made the basis for relief from a judgment, and the maximum time limit has been extended to one year. Accordingly the amendment of Rule 59(b) eliminates the "except" clause and its specific treatment of newly discovered evidence as a ground for a motion for new trial. This ground remains, however, as a basis for a motion for new trial served not later than 10 days after the entry of judgment. See also Rule 60(b).

As to the effect of a motion under subdivision (b) upon the running of appeal time, see amended Rule 73(a) and Note.

Note to Subdivision (e). This subdivision has been added to care for a situation such as that arising in *Boaz v. Mutual Life Ins. Co. of New York*, C.C.A.8, 1944, 146 F.2d 321, and makes clear that the district court possesses the power asserted in that case to alter or amend a judgment after its entry. The subdivision deals only with alteration or amendment of the original judgment in a case and does not relate to a judgment upon motion as provided in Rule 50(b). As to the effect of a motion under subdivision (e) upon the running of appeal time, see amended Rule 73(a) and Note.

The title of Rule 59 has been expanded to indicate the inclusion of this subdivision.

1966 Amendment

By narrow interpretation of Rule 59(b) and (d), it has been held that the trial court is without power to grant a motion for a new trial, timely served, by an order made more than 10 days after the entry of judgment, based upon a ground not stated in the motion but perceived and relied on by the trial court sua sponte. *Freid v. McGrath,* 133 F.2d 350 (D.C.Cir. 1942); *National Farmers Union Auto. & Cas. Co. v. Wood,* 207 F.2d 659 (10th Cir. 1953); *Bailey v. Slentz,* 189 F.2d 406 (10th Cir. 1951); *Marshall's U.S. Auto Supply, Inc. v. Cashman,* 111 F.2d 140 (10th Cir. 1940), cert. denied, 311 U.S. 667 (1940); but see *Steinberg v. Indemnity Ins. Co.,* 36 F.R.D. 253 (E.D.La.1964).

The result is undesirable. Just as the court has power under Rule 59(d) to grant a new trial of its own initiative within the 10 days, so it should have power, when an effective new trial motion has been made and is pending, to decide it on grounds thought meritorious by the court although not advanced in the motion. The second sentence added by amendment to Rule 59(d) confirms the court's power in the latter situation, with provision that the parties be afforded a hearing before the power is exercised. See 6 *Moore's Federal Practice,* par. 59.09[2] (2d ed. 1953).

In considering whether a given ground has or has not been advanced in the motion made by the party, it should be borne in mind that the particularity called for in stating the grounds for a new trial motion is the same as that required for all motions by Rule 7(b)(1). The latter rule does not require ritualistic detail but rather a fair indication to court and counsel of the substance of the grounds relied on. See *Lebeck v. William A. Jarvis Co.,* 250 F.2d 285 (3d Cir. 1957); *Tsai v. Rosenthal,* 297 F.2d 614 (8th Cir. 1961); *General Motors Corp. v. Perry,* 303 F.2d 544 (7th Cir. 1962); cf. *Grimm v. California Spray-Chemical Corp.,* 264 F.2d 145 (9th Cir. 1959); *Cooper v. Midwest Feed Products Co.,* 271 F.2d 177 (8th Cir. 1959).

1995 Amendments

The only change, other than stylistic, intended by this revision is to add explicit time limits for filing motions for a new trial, motions to alter or amend a judgment, and affidavits opposing a new trial motion. Previously, there was an inconsistency in the wording of Rules 50, 52, and 59 with respect to whether certain post-judgment motions had to be filed, or merely served, during the prescribed period. This inconsistency caused special problems when motions for a new trial were joined with other post-judgment motions. These motions affect the finality of the judgment, a matter often of importance to third persons as well as the parties and the court. The Committee believes that each of these rules should be revised to require filing before end of the 10–day period. Filing is an event that can be determined with certainty from court records. The phrase "no later than" is used—rather than "within"—to include post-judgment motions that sometimes are filed before actual entry of the judgment by the clerk. It should be noted that under Rule 5 the motions when filed are to contain a certificate of service on other parties. It also should be noted that under Rule 6(a) Saturdays, Sundays, and legal holidays are excluded in measuring the 10–day period, but that Bankruptcy Rule 9006(a) excludes intermediate Saturdays, Sundays, and legal holidays only in computing periods less than 8 days.

2007 Amendments

The language of Rule 59 has been amended as part of the general restyling of the Civil Rules to make them more easily understood and to make style and terminology consistent throughout the rules. These changes are intended to be stylistic only.

CROSS REFERENCES

Answers to written interrogatories inconsistent with general verdict as ground for ordering new trial, see Fed.Rules Civ.Proc. Rule 49, 28 USCA.

Claims Court, grounds for new trial, see 28 USCA § 2515.

Extension of time for motion, see Fed.Rules Civ.Proc. Rule 6, 28 USCA.

Harmless error not ground for new trial, see Fed.Rules Civ.Proc. Rule 61, 28 USCA.

Joinder of motion for new trial with renewal motion for judgment as a matter of law, see Fed.Rules Civ.Proc. Rule 50, 28 USCA.

Motion to amend findings or make additional findings, see Fed.Rules Civ.Proc. Rule 52, 28 USCA.

Stay of execution or proceedings to enforce judgment on motion for new trial, see Fed.Rules Civ.Proc. Rule 62, 28 USCA.

Termination of running of time for appeal to court of appeals, see Federal Rules of Appellate Procedure Rule 4, 28 USCA.

Rule 60. Relief from a Judgment or Order

(a) Corrections Based on Clerical Mistakes; Oversights and Omissions. The court may correct a clerical mistake or a mistake arising from oversight or omission whenever one is found in a judgment, order, or other part of the record. The court may do so on motion or on its own, with or without notice. But after an appeal has been docketed in the appellate court and while it is pending, such a mistake may be corrected only with the appellate court's leave.

(b) Grounds for Relief from a Final Judgment, Order, or Proceeding. On motion and just terms, the court may relieve a party or its legal representative from a final judgment, order, or proceeding for the following reasons:

(1) mistake, inadvertence, surprise, or excusable neglect;

(2) newly discovered evidence that, with reasonable diligence, could not have been discovered in time to move for a new trial under Rule 59(b);

(3) fraud (whether previously called intrinsic or extrinsic), misrepresentation, or misconduct by an opposing party;

(4) the judgment is void;

(5) the judgment has been satisfied, released or discharged; it is based on an earlier judgment that has been reversed or vacated; or applying it prospectively is no longer equitable; or

(6) any other reason that justifies relief.

(c) Timing and Effect of the Motion.

(1) ***Timing.*** A motion under Rule 60(b) must be made within a reasonable time—and for reasons (1), (2), and (3) no more than a year after the entry of the judgment or order or the date of the proceeding.

(2) ***Effect on Finality.*** The motion does not affect the judgment's finality or suspend its operation.

(d) Other Powers to Grant Relief. This rule does not limit a court's power to:

(1) entertain an independent action to relieve a party from a judgment, order, or proceeding;

(2) grant relief under 28 U.S.C. § 1655 to a defendant who was not personally notified of the action; or

(3) set aside a judgment for fraud on the court.

(e) Bills and Writs Abolished. The following are abolished: bills of review, bills in the nature of bills of review, and writs of coram nobis, coram vobis, and audita querela.

(Amended December 27, 1946, effective March 19, 1948; December 29, 1948, effective October 20, 1949; March 2, 1987, effective August 1, 1987; April 30, 2007, effective December 1, 2007.)

ADVISORY COMMITTEE NOTES

1937 Adoption

Note to Subdivision (a). See [former] Equity Rule 72 (Correction of Clerical Mistakes in Orders and Decrees); Mich.Court Rules Ann. (Searl, 1933) Rule 48, § 3; 2 Wash. Rev.Stat.Ann. (Remington, 1932) § 464(3); Wyo.Rev.Stat. Ann. (Courtright, 1931) § 89–2301(3). For an example of a very liberal provision for the correction of clerical errors and for amendment after judgment, see Va.Code Ann. (Michie, 1936) §§ 6329, 6333.

Note to Subdivision (b). Application to the court under this subdivision does not extend the time for taking an appeal, as distinguished from the motion for new trial. This section is based upon Calif.Code Civ.Proc. (Deering, 1937) § 473. See also N.Y.C.P.A. (1937) § 108; 2 Minn.Stat. (Mason, 1927) § 9283.

For the independent action to relieve against mistake, etc., see Dobie, *Federal Procedure,* pages 760 to 765, compare 639; and Simkins, *Federal Practice,* ch. CXXI (pp. 820 to 830) and ch. CXXII (pp. 831 to 834), compare § 214.

1946 Amendment

Note. Subdivision (a). The amendment incorporates the view expressed in *Perlman v. 322 West Seventy-Second Street, Co., Inc.,* C.C.A.2d, 1942, 127 F.2d 716; 3 *Moore's Federal Practice,* 1938, 3276, and further permits correction after docketing, with leave of the appellate court. Some courts have thought that upon the taking of an appeal the district court lost its power to act. See *Schram v. Safety Investment Co.,* E.D.Mich.1942, 45 F.Supp. 636; also *Miller v. United States,* C.C.A.7th, 1940, 114 F.2d 267.

Subdivision (b). When promulgated, the rules contained a number of provisions, including those found in Rule 60(b), describing the practice by a motion to obtain relief from judgments, and these rules, coupled with the reservation in Rule 60(b) of the right to entertain a new action to relieve a party from a judgment, were generally supposed to cover the field. Since the rules have been in force, decisions have been rendered that the use of bills of review, coram nobis, or audita querela, to obtain relief from final judgments is still proper, and that various remedies of this kind still exist although they are not mentioned in the rules and the practice is not prescribed in the rules. It is obvious that the rules should be complete in this respect and define the practice with respect to any existing rights or remedies to obtain relief from final judgments. For extended discussion of the old common law writs and equitable remedies, the interpretation of Rule 60, and proposals for change, see Moore and Rogers, *Federal Relief from Civil Judgments,* 1946, 55 Yale L.J. 623. See also 3 *Moore's Federal Practice,* 1938, 3254 et seq.; Commentary, *Effect of Rule 60b on Other Methods of Relief From Judgment,* 1941, 4 Fed.Rules Serv. 942, 945; *Wallace v. United States,* C.C.A.2d, 1944, 142 F.2d 240, certiorari denied 65 S.Ct. 37, 323 U.S. 712, 89 L.Ed. 573.

The reconstruction of Rule 60(b) has for one of its purposes a clarification of this situation. Two types of procedure to obtain relief from judgments are specified in the rules as it is proposed to amend them. One procedure is by motion in the court and in the action in which the judgment was rendered. The other procedure is by a new or independent action to obtain relief from a judgment, which action may or may not be begun in the court which rendered the judgment. Various rules, such as the one dealing with a motion for new trial and for amendment of judgments, Rule 59, one for amended findings, Rule 52, and one for judgment notwithstanding the verdict, Rule 50(b), and including the provisions of Rule 60(b) as amended, prescribe the various types of cases in which the practice by motion is permitted. In each case there is a limit upon the time within which resort to a motion is permitted, and this time limit may not be enlarged under Rule 6(b). If the right to make a motion is lost by the expiration of the time limits fixed in these rules, the only other procedural remedy is by a new or independent action to set aside a judgment upon those principles which have heretofore been applied in such an action. Where the independent action is resorted to, the limitations of time are those of laches or statutes of limitations. The Committee has endeavored to ascertain all the remedies and types of relief heretofore available by coram nobis, coram vobis, audita querela, bill of review, or bill in the nature of a bill of review. See Moore and Rogers, *Federal Relief from Civil Judgments,* 1946, 55 Yale L.J. 623, 659 to 682. It endeavored then to amend the rules to permit, either by motion or by independent action, the granting of various kinds of relief from judgments which were permitted in the federal courts prior to the adoption of these rules, and the amendment concludes with a provision abolishing the use of bills of review and the other common law writs referred to, and requiring the practice to be by motion or by independent action.

To illustrate the operation of the amendment, it will be noted that under Rule 59(b) as it now stands, without amendment, a motion for new trial on the ground of newly discovered evidence is permitted within ten days after the entry of the judgment, or after that time upon leave of the court. It is proposed to amend Rule 59(b) by providing that under that rule a motion for new trial shall be served not later than ten days after the entry of the judgment, whatever the ground be for the motion, whether error by the court or newly discovered evidence. On the other hand, one of the purposes of the bill of review in equity was to afford relief on the ground of newly discovered evidence long after the entry of the judgment. Therefore, to permit relief by a motion similar to that heretofore obtained on bill of review, Rule 60(b) as amended permits an application for relief to be made by motion, on the ground of newly discovered evidence, within one year after judgment. Such a motion under Rule 60(b) does not affect the finality of the judgment, but a motion under Rule 59, made within 10 days, does affect finality and the running of the time for appeal.

If these various amendments, including principally those to Rule 60(b), accomplish the purpose for which they are intended, the federal rules will deal with the practice in every sort of case in which relief from final judgments is asked, and prescribe the practice. With reference to the question whether, as the rules now exist, relief by coram nobis, bills of review, and so forth, is permissible, the generally accepted view is that the remedies are still available, although the precise relief obtained in a particular case by use of these ancillary remedies is shrouded in ancient lore and mystery. See *Wallace v. United States,* C.C.A.2d, 1944, 142 F.2d 240, certiorari denied 65 S.Ct. 37, 323 U.S. 712, 89 L.Ed. 573; *Fraser v. Doing,* App.D.C.1942, 130 F.2d 617; *Jones v. Watts,* C.C.A.5th, 1944, 142 F.2d 575; *Preveden v. Hahn,* S.D.N.Y.1941, 36 F.Supp. 952; *Cavallo v. Agwilines, Inc.,* S.D.N.Y.1942, 6 Fed.Rules Serv. 60b.31, Case 2, 2 F.R.D. 526; *McGinn v. United States,* D.C.Mass.1942, 6 Fed.Rules Serv. 60b.51, Case 3, 2 F.R.D. 562; *City of Shattuck, Oklahoma ex rel. Versluis v. Oliver,* W.D.Okl.1945, 8 Fed.Rules Serv. 60b.31, Case 3; Moore and Rogers, *Federal Relief from Civil Judgments,* 1946, 55 Yale L.J. 623, 631 to 653; 3 *Moore's Federal Practice,* 1938, 3254 et seq.; Commentary, *Effect of Rule 60b on Other Methods of Relief From Judgment,* op. cit. supra. Cf. *Norris v. Camp,* C.C.A.10th, 1944, 144 F.2d 1; Reed v. South Atlantic Steamship Co. of Delaware, *D.Del.1942, 2 F.R.D. 475, 6 Fed.Rules Serv. 60b.31, Case 1;* Laughlin v. Berens, *D.D.C.1945, 8 Fed.Rules Serv. 60b.51, Case 1, 73 W.L.R. 209.*

The transposition of the words "the court" and the addition of the word "and" at the beginning of the first sentence are merely verbal changes. The addition of the qualifying word "final" emphasizes the character of the judgments, orders or proceedings from which Rule 60(b) affords relief; and hence interlocutory judgments are not brought within the restrictions of the rule, but rather they are left subject to the complete power of the court rendering them to afford such relief from them as justice requires.

The qualifying pronoun "his" has been eliminated on the basis that it is too restrictive, and that the subdivision should include the mistake or neglect of others which may be just as material and call just as much for supervisory jurisdiction as where the judgment is taken against the party through *his* mistake, inadvertence, etc.

Fraud, whether intrinsic or extrinsic, misrepresentation, or other misconduct of an adverse party are express grounds for relief by motion under amended subdivision (b). There is no sound reason for their exclusion. The incorporation of fraud and the like within the scope of the rule also removes confusion as to the proper procedure. It has been held that relief from a judgment obtained by extrinsic fraud could be secured by motion within a "reasonable time," which might be after the time stated in the rule had run. *Fiske v. Buder,* C.C.A.8th, 1942, 125 F.2d 841; see also inferentially *Bucy v. Nevada Construction Co.,* C.C.A.9th, 1942, 125 F.2d 213. On the other hand, it has been suggested that in view of the fact that fraud was omitted from original Rule 60(b) as a ground for relief, an independent action was the only proper remedy. Commentary, *Effect of Rule 60b on Other Methods of Relief From Judgment,* 1941, 4 Fed.Rules Serv. 942, 945. The amendment settles this problem by making fraud an express ground for relief by motion; and under the saving clause, fraud may be urged as a basis for relief by independent action insofar as established doctrine permits. See Moore and Rogers, *Federal Relief from Civil Judgments,* 1946, 55 Yale L.J. 623, 653 to 659; 3 Moore's Federal Practice, 1938, 3267 et seq. And the rule expressly does not limit the power of the court, when fraud has been perpetrated upon it, to give relief under the saving clause. As an illustration of this situation, see *Hazel-Atlas Glass Co. v. Hartford Empire Co.,* 1944, 64 S.Ct. 997, 322 U.S. 238, 88 L.Ed. 1250.

The time limit for relief by motion in the court and in the action in which the judgment was rendered has been enlarged from six months to one year.

It should be noted that Rule 60(b) does not assume to define the substantive law as to the grounds for vacating judgments, but merely prescribes the practice in proceedings to obtain relief. It should also be noted that under § 200(4) of the Soldiers' and Sailors' Civil Relief Act of 1940, § 501 et seq. [§ 520(4)] of the Appendix to Title 50, a judgment rendered in any action or proceeding governed by the section may be vacated under certain specified circumstances upon proper application to the court.

1948 Amendment

The amendment effective October, 1949 substituted the reference to "Title 28, U.S.C. § 1655," in the next to the last sentence of subdivision (b), for the reference to "Section 57 of the Judicial Code, U.S.C., Title 28, § 118".

1987 Amendment

The amendment is technical. No substantive change is intended.

2007 Amendments

The language of Rule 60 has been amended as part of the general restyling of the Civil Rules to make them more easily understood and to make style and terminology consistent throughout the rules. These changes are intended to be stylistic only.

The final sentence of former Rule 60(b) said that the procedure for obtaining any relief from a judgment was by motion as prescribed in the Civil Rules or by an independent action. That provision is deleted as unnecessary. Relief continues to be available only as provided in the Civil Rules or by independent action.

CROSS REFERENCES

Enlargement of time under this rule prohibited, see Fed. Rules Civ.Proc. Rule 6, 28 USCA.

Formal terms of district court abolished, see 28 USCA § 138.

Stay of proceedings pending disposition of motion under this rule, see Fed.Rules Civ.Proc. Rule 62, 28 USCA.

Time for appeal, see 28 USCA § 2107.

Time for motion for new trial, see Fed.Rules Civ.Proc. Rule 59, 28 USCA.

Rule 61. Harmless Error

Unless justice requires otherwise, no error in admitting or excluding evidence—or any other error by the court or a party—is ground for granting a new trial, for setting aside a verdict, or for vacating, modifying, or otherwise disturbing a judgment or order. At every stage of the proceeding, the court must disregard all errors and defects that do not affect any party's substantial rights.

(Amended April 30, 2007, effective December 1, 2007.)

ADVISORY COMMITTEE NOTES

1937 Adoption

A combination of U.S.C., Title 28, § 2111, [former] § 391 (New trials; harmless error) and [former] § 777 (Defects of form; amendments) with modifications. See *McCandless v. United States*, 1936, 56 S.Ct. 764, 298 U.S. 342, 80 L.Ed. 1205. Compare [former] Equity Rule 72 (Correction of Clerical Mistakes in Orders and Decrees); and last sentence of [former] Equity Rule 46 (Trial—Testimony Usually Taken in Open Court—Rulings on Objections to Evidence). For the last sentence see the last sentence of [former] Equity Rule 19 (Amendments Generally).

2007 Amendments

The language of Rule 61 has been amended as part of the general restyling of the Civil Rules to make them more easily understood and to make style and terminology consistent throughout the rules. These changes are intended to be stylistic only.

CROSS REFERENCES

Admissibility of evidence generally, see Fed.Rules Civ. Proc. Rule 43, 28 USCA.

Formal exceptions unnecessary, see Fed.Rules Civ.Proc. Rule 46, 28 USCA.

Grounds for new trial, see Fed.Rules Civ.Proc. Rules 33 and 59, 28 USCA.

Harmless and plain error, see Fed.Rules Civ.Proc. Rule 52, 18 USCA.

Harmless error on appeal or certiorari, see 28 USCA § 2111.

Instructions to jury, see Fed.Rules Civ.Proc. Rule 51, 28 USCA.

Judgment as a matter of law in actions tried by jury; alternative motion for new trial, see Fed.Rules Civ.Proc. Rule 50, 28 USCA.

Motion to vacate judgment or order, see Fed.Rules Civ. Proc. Rule 60, 28 USCA.

Power of appellate court to affirm, modify, reverse, and remand case, see 28 USCA § 2106.

Rule 62. Stay of Proceedings to Enforce a Judgment

(a) Automatic Stay; Exceptions for Injunctions, Receiverships, and Patent Accountings. Except as stated in this rule, no execution may issue on a judgment, nor may proceedings be taken to enforce it, until 10 days have passed after its entry. But unless the court orders otherwise, the following are not stayed after being entered, even if an appeal is taken:

(1) an interlocutory or final judgment in an action for an injunction or a receivership; or

(2) a judgment or order that directs an accounting in an action for patent infringement.

(b) Stay Pending the Disposition of a Motion. On appropriate terms for the opposing party's security, the court may stay the execution of a judgment—or any proceedings to enforce it—pending disposition of any of the following motions:

(1) under Rule 50, for judgment as a matter of law;

(2) under Rule 52(b), to amend the findings or for additional findings;

(3) under Rule 59, for a new trial or to alter or amend a judgment; or

(4) under Rule 60, for relief from a judgment or order.

(c) Injunction Pending an Appeal. While an appeal is pending from an interlocutory order or final judgment that grants, dissolves, or denies an injunction, the court may suspend, modify, restore, or grant an injunction on terms for bond or other terms that secure the opposing party's rights. If the judgment appealed from is rendered by a statutory three-judge district court, the order must be made either:

(1) by that court sitting in open session; or

(2) by the assent of all its judges, as evidenced by their signatures.

(d) Stay with Bond on Appeal. If an appeal is taken, the appellant may obtain a stay by supersedeas bond, except in an action described in Rule 62(a)(1) or (2). The bond may be given upon or after filing the notice of appeal or after obtaining the order allowing the appeal. The stay takes effect when the court approves the bond.

(e) Stay Without Bond on an Appeal by the United States, Its Officers, or Its Agencies. The court must not require a bond, obligation, or other security from the appellant when granting a stay on an appeal by the United States, its officers, or its agencies or on an appeal directed by a department of the federal government.

(f) Stay in Favor of a Judgment Debtor Under State Law. If a judgment is a lien on the judgment debtor's property under the law of the state where the court is located, the judgment debtor is entitled to the same stay of execution the state court would give.

(g) Appellate Court's Power Not Limited. This rule does not limit the power of the appellate court or one of its judges or justices:

(1) to stay proceedings—or suspend, modify, restore, or grant an injunction—while an appeal is pending; or

(2) to issue an order to preserve the status quo or the effectiveness of the judgment to be entered.

(h) Stay with Multiple Claims or Parties. A court may stay the enforcement of a final judgment entered under Rule 54(b) until it enters a later judgment or judgments, and may prescribe terms necessary to secure the benefit of the stayed judgment for the party in whose favor it was entered.

(Amended December 27, 1946, effective March 19, 1948; December 29, 1948, effective October 20, 1949; April 17, 1961, effective July 19, 1961; March 2, 1987, effective August 1, 1987; April 30, 2007, effective December 1, 2007.)

ADVISORY COMMITTEE NOTES

1937 Adoption

Note to Subdivision (a). The first sentence states the substance of the last sentence of U.S.C., Title 28, [former] § 874 (Supersedeas). The remainder of the subdivision states the substance of the last clause of U.S.C., Title 28, § 1292, [formerly] § 227 (Appeals in proceedings for injunctions; receivers; and admiralty), and of §§ 1292, 2107, [formerly] § 227a (Appeals in suits in equity for infringement of letters patent for inventions; stay of proceedings for accounting), but extended to include final as well as interlocutory judgments.

Note to Subdivision (b). This modifies U.S.C., Title 28, [former] § 840 (Executions; stay on conditions).

Note to Subdivision (c). Compare [former] Equity Rule 74 (Injunction Pending Appeal); and *Cumberland Telephone and Telegraph Co. v. Louisiana Public Service Commission*, 1922, 43 S.Ct. 75, 260 U.S. 212, 67 L.Ed. 217. See Simkins, Federal Practice (1934), § 916, in regard to the effect of appeal on injunctions and the giving of bonds. See U.S.C., [former] Title 6 (Official and Penal Bonds) for bonds by surety companies. For statutes providing for a specially constituted district court of three judges, see:

U.S.C., Title 7:

§ 217 (Proceedings for suspension of orders of Secretary of Agriculture under Stockyards Act)—by reference.

§ 499k (Injunctions; application of injunction laws governing orders of Interstate Commerce Commission to orders of Secretary of Agriculture under Perishable Commodities Act)—by reference.

U.S.C., Title 15:

§ 28 (Antitrust laws; suits against monopolies expedited)

U.S.C., Title 28, former:

§ 47 [now 2325 (repealed)] (Injunctions as to orders of Interstate Commerce Commission, etc.)

§ 380 [now 2284] (Injunctions; alleged unconstitutionality of State statutes)

§ 380a [now 2284] (Same; constitutionality of federal statute)

U.S.C., Title 49:

§ 44 [former] (Suits in equity under interstate commerce laws; expedition of suits)

Note to Subdivision (d). This modifies U.S.C., Title 28, [former] § 874 (Supersedeas). See Rule 36(2), Rules of the Supreme Court of the United States, which governs supersedeas bonds on direct appeals to the Supreme Court, and Rule 73(d), of these rules, which governs supersedeas bonds on appeals to a circuit court of appeals. The provisions governing supersedeas bonds in both kinds of appeals are substantially the same.

Note to Subdivision (e). This states the substance of U.S.C., Title 28, § 2408, formerly § 870 (Bond; not required of the United States).

Note to Subdivision (f). This states the substance of U.S.C., Title 28, [former] § 841 (Executions; stay of one term) with appropriate modification to conform to the provisions of Rule 6(c) as to terms of court.

1946 Amendment

Note. Subdivision (a). [This subdivision not amended]. Sections 203 and 204 of the Soldiers' and Sailors' Civil Relief Act of 1940, 50 U.S.C., Appendix, § 501 et seq. [§§ 523, 524], provide under certain circumstances for the issuance and continuance of a stay of execution of any judgment or order entered against a person in military service. See *Bowsman v. Peterson*, D.Neb.1942, 45 F.Supp. 741. Section 201 of the Act [50 U.S.C. App. § 521] permits under certain circumstances the issuance of a stay of any action or proceeding at any stage thereof, where either the plaintiff or defendant is a person in military service. See also note to Rule 64 herein.

Subdivision (b). This change was necessary because of the proposed addition to Rule 59 of subdivision (e).

Subdivision (h). In proposing to revise Rule 54(b), the Committee thought it advisable to include a separate provision in Rule 62 for stay of enforcement of a final judgment in cases involving multiple claims.

1948 Amendment

The amendment effective October 1949 deleted at the end of subdivision (g) the following language which originally appeared after the word "entered": "and these rules do not supersede the provisions of Section 210 of the Judicial Code, as amended, U.S.C., Title 28, [former] § 47a, or of other statutes of the United States to the effect that stays pending appeals to the Supreme Court may be granted only by that court or a justice thereof."

1961 Amendment

The amendment adopted Apr. 17, 1961, effective July 19, 1961, eliminated words "on some but not all of the claims presented in the action" which followed "final judgment".

1987 Amendment

The amendment is technical. No substantive change is intended.

2007 Amendments

The language of Rule 62 has been amended as part of the general restyling of the Civil Rules to make them more easily understood and to make style and terminology consistent throughout the rules. These changes are intended to be stylistic only.

The final sentence of former Rule 62(a) referred to Rule 62(c). It is deleted as an unnecessary. Rule 62(c) governs of its own force.

CROSS REFERENCES

Deposit of bonds or notes of United States in lieu of surety, see 31 USCA § 9303.

Execution, see Fed.Rules Civ.Proc. Rule 69, 28 USCA.

Security not required of United States, see 28 USCA § 2408.

Stay of execution of judgment against person in military service, see 50 App. USCA § 524.

Supersedeas bond for stay on appeal to court of appeals, see Federal Rules of Appellate Procedure Rule 8, 28 USCA.

Rule 63. Judge's Inability to Proceed

If a judge conducting a hearing or trial is unable to proceed, any other judge may proceed upon certifying familiarity with the record and determining that the case may be completed without prejudice to the parties. In a hearing or a nonjury trial, the successor judge must, at a party's request, recall any witness whose testimony is material and disputed and who is available to testify again without undue burden. The successor judge may also recall any other witness.

(Amended March 2, 1987, effective August 1, 1987; April 30, 1991, effective December 1, 1991; April 30, 2007, effective December 1, 2007.)

ADVISORY COMMITTEE NOTES

1937 Adoption

This rule adapts and extends the provisions of U.S.C., Title 28, [former] § 776 (Bill of exceptions; authentication; signing of by judge) to include all duties to be performed by the judge after verdict or judgment. The statute is therefore superseded.

1987 Amendment

The amendments are technical. No substantive change is intended.

1991 Amendment

The revision substantially displaces the former rule. The former rule was limited to the disability of the judge, and made no provision for disqualification or possible other reasons for the withdrawal of the judge during proceedings. In making provision for other circumstances, the revision is not intended to encourage judges to discontinue participation in a trial for any but compelling reasons. Cf. *United States v. Lane*, 708 F.2d 1394, 1395–1397 (9th Cir.1983). Manifestly, a substitution should not be made for the personal convenience of the court, and the reasons for a substitution should be stated on the record.

The former rule made no provision for the withdrawal of the judge during the trial, but was limited to disqualification after trial. Several courts concluded that the text of the former rule prohibited substitution of a new judge prior to the points described in the rule, thus requiring a new trial, whether or not a fair disposition was within reach of a substitute judge. *E.g., Whalen v. Ford Motor Credit Co.*, 684 F.2d 272 (4th Cir.1982, en banc) *cert. denied*, 459 U.S. 910 (1982) (jury trial); *Arrow–Hart, Inc. v. Philip Carey Co.*, 552 F.2d 711 (6th Cir.1977) (non-jury trial). *See generally* Comment, *The Case of the Dead Judge: Fed.R.Civ.P. 63: Whalen v. Ford Motor Credit Co.*, 67 MINN.L.REV. 827 (1983).

The increasing length of federal trials has made it likely that the number of trials interrupted by the disability of the judge will increase. An efficient mechanism for completing these cases without unfairness is needed to prevent unnecessary expense and delay. To avoid the injustice that may result if the substitute judge proceeds despite unfamiliarity with the action, the new Rule provides, in language similar to Federal Rule of Criminal Procedure 25(a), that the successor judge must certify familiarity with the record and determine that the case may be completed before that judge without prejudice to the parties. This will necessarily require that there be available a transcript or a videotape of the proceedings prior to substitution. If there has been a long but incomplete jury trial, the prompt availability of the transcript or videotape is crucial to the effective use of this rule, for the jury cannot long be held while an extensive transcript is prepared without prejudice to one or all parties.

The revised text authorizes the substitute judge to make a finding of fact at a bench trial based on evidence heard by a different judge. This may be appropriate in limited circumstances. First, if a witness has become unavailable, the testimony recorded at trial can be considered by the successor judge pursuant to F.R.Ev. 804, being equivalent to a recorded deposition available for use at trial pursuant to Rule 32. For this purpose, a witness who is no longer subject to a subpoena to compel testimony at trial is unavailable. Secondly, the successor judge may determine that particular testimony is not material or is not disputed, and so need not be reheard. The propriety of proceeding in this manner may be marginally affected by the availability of a videotape record; a judge who has reviewed a trial on videotape may be entitled to greater confidence in his or her ability to proceed.

The court would, however, risk error to determine the credibility of a witness not seen or heard who is available to be recalled. Cf. *Anderson v. City of Bessemer City NC*, 470 U.S. 564, 575 (1985); *Marshall v. Jerrico Inc.*, 446 U.S. 238, 242 (1980). See also *United States v. Radatz*, 447 U.S. 667 (1980).

2007 Amendments

The language of Rule 63 has been amended as part of the general restyling of the Civil Rules to make them more easily understood and to make style and terminology consistent throughout the rules. These changes are intended to be stylistic only.

CROSS REFERENCES

Disability of judge; successor judge; certification of familiarity with record in order to proceed, see Fed.Rules Cr. Proc. Rule 25, 18 USCA.

Findings of fact and conclusions of law, see Fed.Rules Civ.Proc. Rule 52, 28 USCA.

New trial, see Fed.Rules Civ.Proc. Rule 59, 28 USCA.

TITLE VIII. PROVISIONAL AND FINAL REMEDIES

ADVISORY COMMITTEE NOTES

1991 Amendment

The purpose of the revision is to divide this chapter of the Rules into two. No substantive change is effected.

Rule 64. Seizing a Person or Property

(a) Remedies Under State Law—In General. At the commencement of and throughout an action, every remedy is available that, under the law of the state where the court is located, provides for seizing a person or property to secure satisfaction of the potential judgment. But a federal statute governs to the extent it applies.

(b) Specific Kinds of Remedies. The remedies available under this rule include the following—however designated and regardless of whether state procedure requires an independent action:

- arrest;
- attachment;
- garnishment;
- replevin;
- sequestration; and
- other corresponding or equivalent remedies.

(Amended April 30, 2007, effective December 1, 2007.)

ADVISORY COMMITTEE NOTES

1937 Adoption

This rule adopts the existing Federal law, except that it specifies the applicable State law to be that of the time when the remedy is sought. Under U.S.C., Title 28, [former] § 726 (Attachments as provided by State laws) the plaintiff was entitled to remedies by attachment or other process which were on June 1, 1872, provided by the applicable State law, and the district courts might, from time to time, by general rules, adopt such State laws as might be in force. This statute is superseded as are district court rules which are rendered unnecessary by the rule.

Lis pendens. No rule concerning lis pendens is stated, for this would appear to be a matter of substantive law affecting State laws of property. It has been held that in the absence of a State statute expressly providing for the recordation of notice of the pendency of Federal actions, the commencement of a Federal action is notice to all persons affected. *King v. Davis*, 137 F. 198 (W.D.Va., 1903). It has been held, however, that when a state statute does so provide expressly, its provisions are binding. *United States v. Calcasieu Timber Co.*, 236 F. 196 (C.C.A.5th, 1916).

For statutes of the United States on attachment, see, e.g.:

U.S.C., Title 28 former:

§ 737 [now 2710] (Attachment in postal suits)

§ 738 [now 2711] (Attachment; application for warrant)

§ 739 [now 2712] (Attachment; issue of warrant)

§ 740 [now 2713] (Attachment; trial of ownership of property)

§ 741 [now 2714] (Attachment; investment of proceeds of attached property)

§ 742 [now 2715] (Attachment; publication of attachment)

§ 743 [now 2716] (Attachment; personal notice of attachment)

§ 744 [now 2717] (Attachment; discharge; bond)

§ 745 [former] (Attachment; accrued rights not affected)

§ 746 (Attachments dissolved in conformity with State laws)

For statutes of the United States on garnishment, see, e.g.:

U.S.C., Title 28, former:

§ 748 [now 2405] (Garnishees in suits by United States against a corporation)

§ 749 [now 2405] (Same; issue tendered on denial of indebtedness)

§ 750 [now 2405] (Same; garnishee failing to appear)

For statutes of the United States on arrest, see, e.g.:

U.S.C., Title 28 former:

§ 376 [now 1651] (Writs of ne exeat)

§ 755 [former] (Special bail in suits for duties and penalties)

§ 756 [former] (Defendant giving bail in one district and committed in another)

§ 757 [former] (Defendant giving bail in one district and committed in another; defendant held until judgment in first suit)

§ 758 [former] (Bail and affidavits; taking by commissioners)
§ 759 [former] (Calling of bail in Kentucky)
§ 760 [former] (Clerks may take bail de bene esse)
§ 843 [now 2007] (Imprisonment for debt)
§ 844 [now 2007] (Imprisonment for debt; discharge according to State laws)
§ 845 [now 2007] (Imprisonment for debt; jail limits)

For statutes of the United States on replevin, see, e.g.:
U.S.C., Title 28:
§ 2463, formerly § 747 (Replevy of property taken under revenue laws).

Supplementary Note

Note. Sections 203 and 204 of the Soldiers' and Sailors' Civil Relief Act of 1940, 50 U.S.C.Appendix, § 501 et seq. [§§ 523 and 524], provide under certain circumstances for the issuance and continuance of a stay of the execution of any judgment entered against a person in military service, or the vacation or stay of any attachment or garnishment directed against such person's property, money, or debts in the hands of another. See also Note to Rule 62 herein.

2007 Amendments

The language of Rule 64 has been amended as part of the general restyling of the Civil Rules to make them more easily understood and to make style and terminology consistent throughout the rules. These changes are intended to be stylistic only.

Former Rule 64 stated that the Civil Rules govern an action in which any remedy available under Rule 64(a) is used. The Rules were said to govern from the time the action is commenced if filed in federal court, and from the time of removal if removed from state court. These provisions are deleted as redundant. Rule 1 establishes that the Civil Rules apply to all actions in a district court, and Rule 81(c)(1) adds reassurance that the Civil Rules apply to a removed action "after it is removed."

CROSS REFERENCES

Execution, see Fed.Rules Civ.Proc. Rule 69, 28 USCA.

Rule 65. Injunctions and Restraining Orders

(a) Preliminary Injunction.

(1) ***Notice.*** The court may issue a preliminary injunction only on notice to the adverse party.

(2) ***Consolidating the Hearing with the Trial on the Merits.*** Before or after beginning the hearing on a motion for a preliminary injunction, the court may advance the trial on the merits and consolidate it with the hearing. Even when consolidation is not ordered, evidence that is received on the motion and that would be admissible at trial becomes part of the trial record and need not be repeated at trial. But the court must preserve any party's right to a jury trial.

(b) Temporary Restraining Order.

(1) ***Issuing Without Notice.*** The court may issue a temporary restraining order without written or oral notice to the adverse party or its attorney only if:

(A) specific facts in an affidavit or a verified complaint clearly show that immediate and irreparable injury, loss, or damage will result to the movant before the adverse party can be heard in opposition; and

(B) the movant's attorney certifies in writing any efforts made to give notice and the reasons why it should not be required.

(2) ***Contents; Expiration.*** Every temporary restraining order issued without notice must state the date and hour it was issued; describe the injury and state why it is irreparable; state why the order was issued without notice; and be promptly filed in the clerk's office and entered in the record. The order expires at the time after entry—not to exceed 10 days—that the court sets, unless before that time the court, for good cause, extends it for a like period or the adverse party consents to a longer extension. The reasons for an extension must be entered in the record.

(3) ***Expediting the Preliminary–Injunction Hearing.*** If the order is issued without notice, the motion for a preliminary injunction must be set for hearing at the earliest possible time, taking precedence over all other matters except hearings on older matters of the same character. At the hearing, the party who obtained the order must proceed with the motion; if the party does not, the court must dissolve the order.

(4) ***Motion to Dissolve.*** On 2 days' notice to the party who obtained the order without notice—or on shorter notice set by the court—the adverse party may appear and move to dissolve or modify the order. The court must then hear and decide the motion as promptly as justice requires.

(c) Security. The court may issue a preliminary injunction or a temporary restraining order only if the movant gives security in an amount that the court considers proper to pay the costs and damages sustained by any party found to have been wrongfully enjoined or restrained. The United States, its officers, and its agencies are not required to give security.

(d) Contents and Scope of Every Injunction and Restraining Order.

(1) ***Contents.*** Every order granting an injunction and every restraining order must:

(A) state the reasons why it issued;

(B) state its terms specifically; and

(C) describe in reasonable detail—and not by referring to the complaint or other document—the act or acts restrained or required.

(2) ***Persons Bound.*** The order binds only the following who receive actual notice of it by personal service or otherwise:

(A) the parties;

(B) the parties' officers, agents, servants, employees, and attorneys; and

(C) other persons who are in active concert or participation with anyone described in Rule 65(d)(2)(A) or (B).

(e) Other Laws Not Modified. These rules do not modify the following:

(1) any federal statute relating to temporary restraining orders or preliminary injunctions in actions affecting employer and employee;

(2) 28 U.S.C. § 2361, which relates to preliminary injunctions in actions of interpleader or in the nature of interpleader; or

(3) 28 U.S.C. § 2284, which relates to actions that must be heard and decided by a three-judge district court.

(f) Copyright Impoundment. This rule applies to copyright-impoundment proceedings.

(Amended December 27, 1946, effective March 19, 1948; December 29, 1948, effective October 20, 1949; February 28, 1966, effective July 1, 1966; March 2, 1987, effective August 1, 1987; April 23, 2001, effective December 1, 2001; April 30, 2007, effective December 1, 2007.)

ADVISORY COMMITTEE NOTES

1937 Adoption

Note to Subdivisions (a) and (b). These are taken from U.S.C., Title 28, [former] § 381 (Injunctions; preliminary injunctions and temporary restraining orders).

Note to Subdivision (c). Except for the last sentence, this is substantially U.S.C., Title 28, [former] § 382 (Injunctions; security on issuance of). The last sentence continues the following and similar statutes which expressly except the United States or an officer or agency thereof from such security requirements: U.S.C. Title 15, §§ 77t(b), 78u(e), and 79r(f) (Securities and Exchange Commission). It also excepts the United States or an officer or agency thereof from such security requirements in any action in which a restraining order or interlocutory judgment of injunction issues in its favor whether there is an express statutory exception from such security requirements or not.

See U.S.C., [former] Title 6 (Official and Penal Bonds) for bonds by surety companies.

Note to Subdivision (d). This is substantially U.S.C., Title 28, [former] § 383 (Injunctions; requisites of order; binding effect).

Note to Subdivision (e). The words "relating to temporary restraining orders and preliminary injunctions in actions affecting employer and employee" are words of description and not of limitation.

Compare [former] Equity Rule 73 (Preliminary Injunctions and Temporary Restraining Orders) which is substantially equivalent to the statutes.

For other statutes dealing with injunctions which are continued, see e.g.:

U.S.C., Title 28 former:

§ 46 [now 2324] (Suits to enjoin orders of Interstate Commerce Commission to be against United States)

§ 47 [now 2325] (Injunctions as to orders of Interstate Commerce Commission; appeal to Supreme Court; time for taking)

§ 378 [former] (Injunctions; when granted)

§ 379 [now 2283] (Injunctions; stay in State courts)

§ 380 [now 1253, 2101, 2281, 2284] (Injunctions; alleged unconstitutionality of State statutes; appeal to Supreme Court)

§ 380a [now 1253, 2101, 2281, 2284] (Injunctions; constitutionality of Federal statute; application for hearing; appeal to Supreme Court)

U.S.C., Title 7:

§ 216 (Court proceedings to enforce orders; injunction)

§ 217 (Proceedings for suspension of orders)

U.S.C., Title 15:

§ 4 (Jurisdiction of courts; duty of district attorney; procedure)

§ 25 (Restraining violations; procedure)

§ 26 (Injunctive relief for private parties; exceptions)

§ 77t(b) (Injunctions and prosecution of offenses)

1946 Amendment

Note. It has been held that in actions on preliminary injunction bonds the district court has discretion to grant relief in the same proceeding or to require the institution of a new action on the bond. *Russell v. Farley,* 1881, 105 U.S. 433, 466. It is believed, however, that in all cases the litigant should have a right to proceed on the bond in the same proceeding, in the manner provided in Rule 73(f) for a similar situation. The paragraph added to Rule 65(c) insures this result and is in the interest of efficiency. There is no reason why Rules 65(c) and 73(f) should operate differently. Compare § 50, sub. n of the Bankruptcy Act, 11 U.S.C. § 78, sub. n, under which actions on all bonds furnished pursuant to the Act may be proceeded upon summarily in the bankruptcy court. See 2 *Collier on Bankruptcy,* 14th ed. by Moore and Oglebay, 1853–1854.

1948 Amendment

The amendment effective October 1949, changed subdivision (e) in the following respects: in the first clause the amendment substituted the words "any statute of the United States" for the words "the Act of October 15, 1914, c. 323, §§ 1 and 20 (38 Stat. 730), U.S.C., Title 29, §§ 52 and 53, or the Act of March 23, 1932, c. 90 (47 Stat. 70), U.S.C., Title 29, c. 6"; in the second clause of subdivision (e) the amendment substituted the reference to "Title 28, U.S.C., § 2361" for the reference to "Section 24(26) of the Judicial Code as amended, U.S.C., Title 28, § 41(26)"; and the third clause was amended to read "Title 28, U.S.C., § 2284," etc., as at present, instead of "the Act of August 24, 1937, c. 754, § 3, relating to actions to enjoin the enforcement of acts of Congress."

1966 Amendment

Subdivision (a)(2). This new subdivision provides express authority for consolidating the hearing of an application for a preliminary injunction with the trial on the merits. The authority can be exercised with particular profit when it appears that a substantial part of the evidence offered on the application will be relevant to the merits and will be presented in such form as to qualify for admission on the trial proper. Repetition of evidence is thereby avoided. The fact that the proceedings have been consolidated should cause no delay in the disposition of the application for the preliminary injunction, for the evidence will be directed in the first instance to that relief, and the preliminary injunction, if justified by the proof, may be issued in the course of the consolidated proceedings. Furthermore, to consolidate the proceedings will tend to expedite the final disposition of the action. It is believed that consolidation can be usefully availed of in many cases.

The subdivision further provides that even when consolidation is not ordered, evidence received in connection with an application for a preliminary injunction which would be admissible on the trial on the merits forms part of the trial record. This evidence need not be repeated on the trial. On the other hand, repetition is not altogether prohibited. That would be impractical and unwise. For example, a witness testifying comprehensively on the trial who has previously testified upon the application for a preliminary injunction might sometimes be hamstrung in telling his story if he could not go over some part of his prior testimony to connect it with his present testimony. So also, some repetition of testimony may be called for where the trial is conducted by a judge who did not hear the application for the preliminary injunction. In general, however, repetition can be avoided with an increase of efficiency in the conduct of the case and without any distortion of the presentation of evidence by the parties.

Since an application for a preliminary injunction may be made in an action in which, with respect to all or part of the merits, there is a right to trial by jury, it is appropriate to add the caution appearing in the last sentence of the subdivision. In such a case the jury will have to hear all the evidence bearing on its verdict, even if some part of the evidence has already been heard by the judge alone on the application for the preliminary injunction.

The subdivision is believed to reflect the substance of the best current practice and introduces no novel conception.

Subdivision (b). In view of the possibly drastic consequences of a temporary restraining order, the opposition should be heard, if feasible, before the order is granted. Many judges have properly insisted that, when time does not permit of formal notice of the application to the adverse party, some expedient, such as telephonic notice to the attorney for the adverse party, be resorted to if this can reasonably be done. On occasion, however, temporary restraining orders have been issued without any notice when it was feasible for some fair, although informal, notice to be given. See the emphatic criticisms in *Pennsylvania Rd. Co. v. Transport Workers Union,* 278 F.2d 693, 694 (3d Cir. 1960); *Arvida Corp. v. Sugarman,* 259 F.2d 428, 429 (2d Cir. 1958); *Lummus Co. v. Commonwealth Oil Ref. Co., Inc.,* 297 F.2d 80, 83 (2d Cir. 1961), cert. denied, 368 U.S. 986 (1962).

Heretofore the first sentence of subdivision (b), in referring to a notice "served" on the "adverse party" on which a "hearing" could be held, perhaps invited the interpretation that the order might be granted without notice if the circumstances did not permit of a formal hearing on the basis of a formal notice. The subdivision is amended to make it plain that informal notice, which may be communicated to the attorney rather than the adverse party, is to be preferred to no notice at all.

Before notice can be dispensed with, the applicant's counsel must give his certificate as to any efforts made to give notice and the reasons why notice should not be required. This certificate is in addition to the requirement of an affidavit or verified complaint setting forth the facts as to the irreparable injury which would result before the opposition could be heard.

The amended subdivision continues to recognize that a temporary restraining order may be issued without any notice when the circumstances warrant.

Subdivision (c). Original Rules 65 and 73 contained substantially identical provisions for summary proceedings against sureties on bonds required or permitted by the rules. There was fragmentary coverage of the same subject in the Admiralty Rules. Clearly, a single comprehensive rule is required, and is incorporated as Rule 65.1.

1987 Amendment

The amendments are technical. No substantive change is intended.

2001 Amendments

New subdivision (f) is added in conjunction with abrogation of the antiquated Copyright Rules of Practice adopted for proceedings under the 1909 Copyright Act. Courts have naturally turned to Rule 65 in response to the apparent inconsistency of the former Copyright Rules with the discretionary impoundment procedure adopted in 1976, 17 U.S.C. § 503(a). Rule 65 procedures also have assuaged well-founded doubts whether the Copyright Rules satisfy more contemporary requirements of due process. See, e.g., *Religious Technology Center v. Netcom On-Line Communications Servs., Inc.,* 923 F.Supp. 1231, 1260–1265 (N.D.Cal.1995); *Paramount Pictures Corp. v. Doe,* 821 F.Supp. 82 (E.D.N.Y. 1993); *WPOW, Inc. v. MRLJ Enterprises,* 584 F.Supp. 132 (D.D.C.1984).

A common question has arisen from the experience that notice of a proposed impoundment may enable an infringer to defeat the court's capacity to grant effective relief. Impoundment may be ordered on an ex parte basis under subdivision (b) if the applicant makes a strong showing of the reasons why notice is likely to defeat effective relief. Such no-notice procedures are authorized in trademark infringement proceedings, see 15 U.S.C. § 1116(d), and courts have provided clear illustrations of the kinds of showings that support ex parte relief. See *Matter of Vuitton et Fils S.A.,* 606 F.2d 1 (2d Cir.1979); *Vuitton v. White,* 945 F.2d 569 (3d Cir.1991). In applying the tests for no-notice relief, the court should ask whether impoundment is necessary, or whether adequate protection can be had by a less intrusive form of no-notice relief shaped as a temporary restraining order.

This new subdivision (f) does not limit use of trademark procedures in cases that combine trademark and copyright claims. Some observers believe that trademark procedures should be adopted for all copyright cases, a proposal better considered by Congressional processes than by rulemaking processes.

2007 Amendments

The language of Rule 65 has been amended as part of the general restyling of the Civil Rules to make them more easily understood and to make style and terminology consistent throughout the rules. These changes are intended to be stylistic only.

The final sentence of former Rule 65(c) referred to Rule 65.1. It is deleted as unnecessary. Rule 65.1 governs of its own force.

Rule 65(d)(2) clarifies two ambiguities in former Rule 65(d). The former rule was adapted from former 28 U.S.C. § 363, but omitted a comma that made clear the common doctrine that a party must have actual notice of an injunction in order to be bound by it. Amended Rule 65(d) restores the meaning of the earlier statute, and also makes clear the proposition that an injunction can be enforced against a person who acts in concert with a party's officer, agent, servant, employee, or attorney.

CROSS REFERENCES

Antitrust laws, restraining violation, see 15 USCA § 4.

Appeals—

Appellate court's power to suspend, modify or grant pending appeal; injunction pending, see Fed.Rules Civ.Proc. Rule 62, 28 USCA.

District courts to courts of appeals; interlocutory orders of district courts, see 28 USCA § 1292.

Atomic Energy Act, enjoining violation of Act or regulation, see 42 USCA § 2280.

Clayton Antitrust Act, violation of, see 15 USCA §§ 25 and 26.

Copyrights, injunction against infringement, see 17 USCA § 502.

Fair Labor Standards Act, restraint of violations of regulations, see 29 USCA § 217.

Federal Deposit Insurance Corporation termination of status as insured depository institution and applicability of rule, see 12 USCA § 1818.

Findings by the Court; judgment on partial findings, see Fed.Rules Civ.Proc. Rule 52, 28 USCA.

Internal revenue, prohibition of suits to restrain assessment or collection, see 26 USCA § 7421.

Labor-Management Relations Act—

Petition by Attorney General to enjoin strike or lockout, see 29 USCA § 178.

Restraining unfair labor practices, see 29 USCA §§ 160 and 161.

Patent infringement, see 35 USCA § 283.

Securities Act, actions to restrain violations, see 15 USCA § 77t.

Securities Exchange Act, restraint of violations, see 15 USCA § 78u.

Stay of state court proceedings, see 28 USCA § 2283.

Three-judge court, composition of, see 28 USCA § 2284.

Rule 65.1. Proceedings Against A Surety

Whenever these rules (including the Supplemental Rules for Admiralty or Maritime Claims and Asset Forfeiture Actions) require or allow a party to give security, and security is given through a bond or other undertaking with one or more sureties, each surety submits to the court's jurisdiction and irrevocably appoints the court clerk as its agent for receiving service of any papers that affect its liability on the bond or undertaking. The surety's liability may be enforced on motion without an independent action. The motion and any notice that the court orders may be served on the court clerk, who must promptly mail a copy of each to every surety whose address is known.

(Adopted February 28, 1966, effective July 1, 1966; amended March 2, 1987, effective August 1, 1987; April 12, 2006, effective December 1, 2006; April 30, 2007, effective December 1, 2007.)

ADVISORY COMMITTEE NOTES

1966 Addition

See Note to Rule 65.

1987 Amendment

The amendments are technical. No substantive change is intended.

2006 Amendment

Rule 65.1 is amended to conform to the changed title of the Supplemental Rules.

2007 Amendments

The language of Rule 65.1 has been amended as part of the general restyling of the Civil Rules to make them more easily understood and to make style and terminology consistent throughout the rules. These changes are intended to be stylistic only.

Rule 66. Receivers

These rules govern an action in which the appointment of a receiver is sought or a receiver sues or is sued. But the practice in administering an estate by a receiver or a similar court-appointed officer must accord with the historical practice in federal courts or with a local rule. An action in which a receiver has been appointed may be dismissed only by court order.

(Amended December 27, 1946, effective March 19, 1948; December 29, 1948, effective October 20, 1949; April 30, 2007, effective December 1, 2007.)

ADVISORY COMMITTEE NOTES

1946 Amendment

Note. The title of Rule 66 has been expanded to make clear the subject of the rule, i.e., federal equity receivers.

The first sentence added to Rule 66 prevents a dismissal by any party, after a federal equity receiver has been appointed, except upon leave of court. A party should not be permitted to oust the court and its officer without the consent of that court. See Civil Rule 31(e), Eastern District of Washington.

The second sentence added at the beginning of the rule deals with suits by or against a federal equity receiver. The first clause thereof eliminates the formal ceremony of an ancillary appointment before suit can be brought by a receiver, and is in accord with the more modern state practice, and with more expeditious and less expensive judicial administration. 2 *Moore's Federal Practice,* 1938, 2088–2091. For the rule necessitating ancillary appointment, see *Sterrett v. Second Nat. Bank,* 1918, 39 S.Ct. 27, 248 U.S. 73, 63 L.Ed. 135; *Kelley v. Queeney,* W.D.N.Y.1941, 41 F.Supp. 1015; see also *McCandless v. Furlaud,* 1934, 55 S.Ct. 42, 293 U.S. 67, 79 L.Ed. 202. This rule has been extensively criticized. First, *Extraterritorial Powers of Receivers,* 1932, 27 Ill.L.Rev. 271; Rose, *Extraterritorial Actions by Receivers,* 1933, 17 Minn. L.Rev. 704; Laughlin, *The Extraterritorial Powers of Receivers,* 1932, 45 Harv.L.Rev. 429; Clark and Moore, *A New Federal Civil Procedure—II, Pleadings and Parties,* 1935, 44 Yale L.J. 1291, 1312–1315; Note, 1932, 30 Mich.L.Rev. 1322. See also comment in *Bicknell v. Lloyd-Smith,* C.C.A.2d, 1940, 109 F.2d 527, certiorari denied 61 S.Ct. 15, 311 U.S. 650, 85 L.Ed. 416. The second clause of the sentence merely incorporates the well-known and general rule that, absent statutory authorization, a federal receiver cannot be sued without leave of the court which appointed him, applied in the federal courts since *Barton v. Barbour,* 1881, 104 U.S. 126. See also 1 *Clark on Receivers,* 2d ed., § 549. Under [§ 959 of this title, formerly] 28 U.S.C. § 125 leave of court is unnecessary when a receiver is sued "in respect of any act or transaction of his in carrying on the business" connected with the receivership property, but such suit is subject to the general equity jurisdiction of the court in which the receiver was appointed, so far as justice necessitates.

Capacity of a state court receiver to sue or be sued in Federal court is governed by Rule 17(b).

The last sentence added to Rule 66 assures the application of the rules in all matters except actual administration of the receivership estate itself. Since this implicitly carries with it the applicability of those rules relating to appellate procedure, the express reference thereto contained in Rule 66 has been stricken as superfluous. Under Rule 81(a)(1) the rules do not apply to bankruptcy proceedings except as they may be made applicable by order of the Supreme Court. Rule 66 is applicable to what is commonly known as a federal "chancery" or "equity" receiver, or similar type of court officer. It is not designed to regulate or affect receivers in bankruptcy, which are governed by the Bankruptcy Act and the General Orders. Since the Federal Rules are applicable in bankruptcy by virtue of General Orders in Bankruptcy 36 and 37 [see Appendix II following Rules of Bankruptcy Procedure, Title 11] only to the extent that they are not inconsistent with the Bankruptcy Act or the General Orders, Rule 66 is not applicable to bankruptcy receivers. See 1 *Collier on Bankruptcy,* 14th ed. by Moore and Oglebay, ¶¶2.23–2.36.

1948 Amendment

The amendment effective October 1949 deleted a sentence which formerly appeared immediately following the first sentence and which read as follows: "A receiver shall have the capacity to sue in any district court without ancillary appointment; but actions against a receiver may not be commenced without leave of the court appointing him except when authorized by a statute of the United States."

2007 Amendments

The language of Rule 66 has been amended as part of the general restyling of the Civil Rules to make them more easily understood and to make style and terminology consistent throughout the rules. These changes are intended to be stylistic only.

CROSS REFERENCES

Receiver suable without leave of court, see 28 USCA § 959.

Rule 67. Deposit into Court

(a) Depositing Property. If any part of the relief sought is a money judgment or the disposition of a sum of money or some other deliverable thing, a party—on notice to every other party and by leave of court—may deposit with the court all or part of the money or thing, whether or not that party claims any of it. The depositing party must deliver to the clerk a copy of the order permitting deposit.

(b) Investing and Withdrawing Funds. Money paid into court under this rule must be deposited and withdrawn in accordance with 28 U.S.C. §§ 2041 and 2042 and any like statute. The money must be deposited in an interest-bearing account or invested in a court-approved, interest-bearing instrument.

(Amended December 29, 1948, effective October 20, 1949; April 28, 1983, effective August 1, 1983; April 30, 2007, effective December 1, 2007.)

ADVISORY COMMITTEE NOTES

1937 Adoption

This rule provides for deposit in court generally, continuing similar special provisions contained in such statutes as U.S.C., Title 28, [§§ 1335, 1397, 2361, formerly] § 41(26) (Original jurisdiction of bills of interpleader, and of bills in the nature of interpleader). See generally *Howard v. United States,* 1902, 22 S.Ct. 543, 184 U.S. 676, 46 L.Ed. 754; United States Supreme Court Admiralty Rules (1920), Rules 37 (Bringing Funds into Court), 41 (Funds in Court Registry), and 42 (Claims Against Proceeds in Registry). With the first sentence, compare *English Rules Under the Judicature Act* (The Annual Practice, 1937) O. 22, r. 1(1).

1948 Amendment

The amendment effective October 1949 substituted the reference to "Title 28, U.S.C.A., §§ 2041, and 2042" for the reference to "Sections 995 and 996, Revised Statutes, as amended, U.S.C.A., Title 28, §§ 851, 852." The amendment also added the words "as amended" following the citation of the Act of June 26, 1934, c. 756, § 23, and, in the parenthetical citation immediately following, added the reference to "58 Stat. 845".

1983 Amendment

Rule 67 has been amended in three ways. The first change is the addition of the clause in the first sentence. Some courts have construed the present rule to permit deposit only when the party making it claims no interest in the fund or thing deposited. E.g., *Blasin-Stern v. Beech-Nut Life Savers Corp.*, 429 F.Supp. 533 (D. Puerto Rico 1975); *Dinkins v. General Aniline & Film Corp.*, 214 F.Supp. 281 (S.D.N.Y.1963). However, there are situations in which a litigant may wish to be relieved of responsibility for a sum or thing, but continue to claim an interest in all or part of it. In these cases the deposit-in-court procedure should be available; in addition to the advantages to the party making the deposit, the procedure gives other litigants assurance that any judgment will be collectable. The amendment is intended to accomplish that.

The second change is the addition of a requirement that the order of deposit be served on the clerk of the court in which the sum or thing is to be deposited. This is simply to assure that the clerk knows what is being deposited and what his responsibilities are with respect to the deposit. The latter point is particularly important since the rule as amended contemplates that deposits will be placed in interest-bearing accounts; the clerk must know what treatment has been ordered for the particular deposit.

The third change is to require that any money be deposited in an interest-bearing account or instrument approved by the court.

2007 Amendments

The language of Rule 67 has been amended as part of the general restyling of the Civil Rules to make them more easily understood and to make style and terminology consistent throughout the rules. These changes are intended to be stylistic only.

Rule 68. Offer of Judgment

(a) Making an Offer; Judgment on an Accepted Offer. More than 10 days before the trial begins, a party defending against a claim may serve on an opposing party an offer to allow judgment on specified terms, with the costs then accrued. If, within 10 days after being served, the opposing party serves written notice accepting the offer, either party may then file the offer and notice of acceptance, plus proof of service. The clerk must then enter judgment.

(b) Unaccepted Offer. An unaccepted offer is considered withdrawn, but it does not preclude a later offer. Evidence of an unaccepted offer is not admissible except in a proceeding to determine costs.

(c) Offer After Liability Is Determined. When one party's liability to another has been determined but the extent of liability remains to be determined by further proceedings, the party held liable may make an offer of judgment. It must be served within a reasonable time—but at least 10 days—before a hearing to determine the extent of liability.

(d) Paying Costs After an Unaccepted Offer. If the judgment that the offeree finally obtains is not more favorable than the unaccepted offer, the offeree must pay the costs incurred after the offer was made.

(Amended December 27, 1946, effective March 19, 1948; February 28, 1966, effective July 1, 1966; March 2, 1987, effective August 1, 1987; April 30, 2007, effective December 1, 2007.)

ADVISORY COMMITTEE NOTES

1937 Adoption

See 2 Minn.Stat. (Mason, 1927) § 9323; 4 Mont.Rev.Codes Ann. (1935) § 9770; N.Y.C.P.A. (1937) § 177.

For the recovery of costs against the United States, see Rule 54(d).

1946 Amendment

Note. The third sentence of Rule 68 has been altered to make clear that evidence of an unaccepted offer is admissible in a proceeding to determine the costs of the action but is not otherwise admissible.

The two sentences substituted for the deleted last sentence of the rule assure a party the right to make a second offer where the situation permits—as, for example, where a prior offer was not accepted but the plaintiff's judgment is nullified and a new trial ordered, whereupon the defendant desires to make a second offer. It is implicit, however, that as long as the case continues—whether there be a first, second or third trial—and the defendant makes no further offer, his first and only offer will operate to save him the costs from the time of that offer if the plaintiff ultimately obtains a judgment less than the sum offered. In the case of successive offers not accepted, the offeror is saved the costs incurred after the making of the offer which was equal to or greater than the judgment ultimately obtained. These provisions should serve to encourage settlements and avoid protracted litigation.

The phrase "before the trial begins", in the first sentence of the rule, has been construed in *Cover v. Chicago Eye Shield Co.*, C.C.A.7th, 1943, 136 F.2d 374, certiorari denied 64 S.Ct. 53, 320 U.S. 749, 88 L.Ed. 445.

1966 Amendment

This logical extension of the concept of offer of judgment is suggested by the common admiralty practice of determining liability before the amount of liability is determined.

1987 Amendment

The amendments are technical. No substantive change is intended.

2007 Amendments

The language of Rule 68 has been amended as part of the general restyling of the Civil Rules to make them more easily understood and to make style and terminology consistent throughout the rules. These changes are intended to be stylistic only.

Rule 69. Execution

(a) In General.

(1) ***Money Judgment; Applicable Procedure.*** A money judgment is enforced by a writ of execution, unless the court directs otherwise. The procedure on execution—and in proceedings supplementary to and in aid of judgment or execution—must accord with the procedure of the state where the court is located, but a federal statute governs to the extent it applies.

(2) ***Obtaining Discovery.*** In aid of the judgment or execution, the judgment creditor or a successor in interest whose interest appears of record may obtain discovery from any person—including the judgment debtor—as provided in these rules or by the procedure of the state where the court is located.

(b) Against Certain Public Officers. When a judgment has been entered against a revenue officer in the circumstances stated in 28 U.S.C. § 2006, or against an officer of Congress in the circumstances stated in 2 U.S.C. § 118, the judgment must be satisfied as those statutes provide.

(Amended December 29, 1948, effective October 20, 1949; March 30, 1970, effective July 1, 1970; March 2, 1987 effective August 1, 1987; April 30, 2007, effective December 1, 2007.)

ADVISORY COMMITTEE NOTES

1937 Adoption

Note to Subdivision (a). This follows in substance U.S.C. Title 28, [former] §§ 727 (Executions as provided by State laws) and [former 729] [now Title 42, § 1988] (Proceedings in vindication of civil rights), except that, as in the similar case of attachments (see note to Rule 64), the rule specifies the applicable state law to be that of the time when the remedy is sought, and thus renders unnecessary, as well as supersedeas, local district court rules.

Statutes of the United States on execution, when applicable, govern under this rule. Among these are:

U.S.C., Title 12:

§ 91 (Transfers by bank and other acts in contemplation of insolvency)

§ 632 (Jurisdiction of United States district courts in cases arising out of foreign banking jurisdiction where Federal reserve bank a party)

U.S.C., Title 19:

§ 199 (Judgments for customs duties, how payable)

U.S.C., Title 26 [I.R.C.1939]:

§ 1610(a) [former] (Surrender of property subject to distraint)

U.S.C., Title 28 former:

§ 122 [now 1656] (Creation of new district or transfer of territory; lien)

§ 350 [now 2101] (Time for making application for appeal or certiorari; stay pending application for certiorari)

§ 489 [now 547] (District Attorneys; reports to Department of Justice)

§ 574 [now 1921] (Marshals, fees enumerated)

§ 786 [former] (Judgments for duties; collected in coin)

§ 811 [now 1961] (Interest on judgments)

§ 838 [former] (Executions; run in all districts of State)

§ 839 [now 2413] (Executions; run in every State and Territory)

§ 840 [former] (Executions; stay on conditions), as modified by Rule 62(b)

§ 841 [former] (Executions; stay of one term), as modified by Rule 62(f)

§ 842 [now 2006] (Executions; against officers of revenue in cases of probable cause), as incorporated in Subdivision (b) of this rule

§ 843 [now 2007] (Imprisonment for debt)

§ 844 [now 2007] (Imprisonment for debt; discharge according to State laws)

§ 845 [now 2007] (Imprisonment for debt; jail limits)

§ 846 [now 2005] (Fieri Facias; appraisal of goods; appraisers)

§ 847 [now 2001] (Sales; real property under order or decree)

§ 848 [now 2004] (Sales; personal property under order or decree)

§ 849 [now 2002] (Sales; necessity of notice)

§ 850 [now 2003] (Sales; death of marshall after levy or after sale)

§ 869 [former] (Bond in former error and on appeal), as incorporated in Rule 73(c)

§ 874 [former] (Supersedeas), as modified by Rules 62(d) and 73(d)

U.S.C., Title 31:

§ 195 [now 3715] (Purchase on execution)

U.S.C., Title 33:

§ 918 (Collection of defaulted payments)

U.S.C., Title 49:

§ 74(g) [former] (Causes of action arising out of Federal control of railroads; execution and other process)

Special statutes of the United States on exemption from execution are also continued. Among these are:

U.S.C., Title 2:

§ 118 (Actions against officers of Congress for official acts)

U.S.C., Title 5 former:

§ 729 [see 8346, 8470] (Federal employees retirement annuities not subject to assignment, execution, levy or other legal process)

U.S.C., Title 10 former:

§ 610 [now 3690, 8690] (Exemption of enlisted men from arrest on civil process)

U.S.C., Title 22 former:

§ 21(h) [see 4060] (Foreign service retirement and disability system; establishment; rules and regulations; annuities; nonassignable; exemption from legal process)

U.S.C., Title 33:

§ 916 (Assignment and exemption from claims of creditors) (Longshoremen's and Harborworkers' Compensation Act)

U.S.C., Title 38 former:

§ 54 [see 3101] (Attachment, levy or seizure of moneys due pensioners prohibited)

§ 393 [former] (Army and Navy Medal of Honor Roll; pensions additional to other pensions; liability to attachment, etc.) Compare [former] Title 34, § 365(c) (Medal of Honor Roll; special pension to persons enrolled)

§ 618 [see 3101] (Benefits exempt from seizure under process and taxation; no deductions for indebtedness to United States)

U.S.C., Title 43:

§ 175 (Exemption from execution of homestead land)

U.S.C., Title 48 former:

§ 1371*o* (Panama canal and railroad retirement annuities, exemption from execution and so forth.)

Supplementary Note

Note. With respect to the provisions of the Soldiers' and Sailors' Civil Relief Act of 1940, 50 U.S.C. Appendix, § 501 et seq., see notes to Rules 62 and 64 herein.

1948 Amendment

The amendment effective October 1949, substituted the citation of "Title 28, U.S.C., § 2006" in subdivision (b) in place of the citation to "Section 989, Revised Statutes, U.S.C., Title 28, § 842".

1970 Amendment

The amendment assures that, in aid of execution on a judgment, all discovery procedures provided in the rules are available and not just discovery via the taking of a deposition. Under the present language, one court had held that Rule 34 discovery is unavailable to the judgment creditor. *M. Lowenstein & Sons, Inc. v. American Underwear Mfg. Co.*, 11 F.R.D. 172 (E.D.Pa.1951). Notwithstanding the language, and relying heavily on legislative history referring to Rule 33, the Fifth Circuit has held that a judgment creditor may invoke Rule 33 interrogatories. *United States v. McWhirter*, 376 F.2d 102 (5th Cir. 1967). But the court's reasoning does not extend to discovery except as provided in Rules 26–33. One commentator suggests that the existing language might properly be stretched to all discovery, 7 *Moore's Federal Practice* ¶69.05[1] (2d ed. 1966), but another believes that a rules amendment is needed. 3 Barron & Holtzoff, *Federal Practice and Procedure* 1484 (Wright ed. 1958). Both commentators and the court in *McWhirter* are clear that, as a matter of policy, Rule 69 should authorize the use of all discovery devices provided in the rules.

1987 Amendment

The amendments are technical. No substantive change is intended.

2007 Amendments

The language of Rule 69 has been amended as part of the general restyling of the Civil Rules to make them more easily understood and to make style and terminology consistent throughout the rules. These changes are intended to be stylistic only.

Amended Rule 69(b) incorporates directly the provisions of 2 U.S.C. § 118 and 28 U.S.C. § 2006, deleting the incomplete statement in former Rule 69(b) of the circumstances in which execution does not issue against an officer.

CROSS REFERENCES

Executions and judicial sales, see 28 USCA § 2001 et seq.

Executions in favor of United States, see 28 USCA § 2413.

Power to issue writ of execution, see 28 USCA § 1651.

Seizure of person or property for satisfaction of judgment, see Fed.Rules Civ.Proc. Rule 64, 28 USCA.

Stay of execution of judgment, see Fed.Rules Civ.Proc. Rule 62, 28 USCA.

Writ of execution for delivery of possession, see Fed.Rules Civ.Proc. Rule 70, 28 USCA.

Rule 70. Enforcing a Judgment for a Specific Act

(a) Party's Failure to Act; Ordering Another to Act. If a judgment requires a party to convey land, to deliver a deed or other document, or to perform any other specific act and the party fails to comply within the time specified, the court may order the act to be done—at the disobedient party's expense—by another person appointed by the court. When done, the act has the same effect as if done by the party.

(b) Vesting Title. If the real or personal property is within the district, the court—instead of ordering a conveyance—may enter a judgment divesting any party's title and vesting it in others. That judgment has the effect of a legally executed conveyance.

(c) Obtaining a Writ of Attachment or Sequestration. On application by a party entitled to performance of an act, the clerk must issue a writ of attachment or sequestration against the disobedient party's property to compel obedience.

(d) Obtaining a Writ of Execution or Assistance. On application by a party who obtains a judgment or order for possession, the clerk must issue a writ of execution or assistance.

(e) Holding in Contempt. The court may also hold the disobedient party in contempt.

(Amended April 30, 2007, effective December 1, 2007.)

ADVISORY COMMITTEE NOTES

1937 Adoption

Compare [former] Equity Rules 7 (Process, Mesne and Final), 8 (Enforcement of Final Decrees), and 9 (Writ of Assistance). To avoid possible confusion, both old and new denominations for attachment (sequestration) and execution (assistance) are used in this rule. Compare with the provision in this rule that the judgment may itself vest title, 6 Tenn.Ann.Code (Williams, 1934), § 10594; 2 Conn.Gen.Stat. (1930), § 5455; N.M.Stat.Ann. (Courtright, 1929), § 117–117; 2 Ohio Gen.Code Ann. (Page, 1926), § 11590; and England, Supreme Court of Judicature Act (1925), § 47.

2007 Amendments

The language of Rule 70 has been amended as part of the general restyling of the Civil Rules to make them more easily understood and to make style and terminology consistent throughout the rules. These changes are intended to be stylistic only.

CROSS REFERENCES

Contempts, power of court, see 18 USCA § 401.

Execution, see Fed.Rules Civ.Proc. Rule 69, 28 USCA.

Power to issue writs, see 28 USCA § 1651.

Remedies of attachment and sequestration, see Fed.Rules Civ.Proc. Rule 64, 28 USCA.

Rule 71. Enforcing Relief for or Against a Nonparty

When an order grants relief for a nonparty or may be enforced against a nonparty, the procedure for enforcing the order is the same as for a party.

(Amended March 2, 1987, effective August 1, 1987; April 30, 2007, effective December 1, 2007.)

ADVISORY COMMITTEE NOTES

1937 Adoption

Compare [former] Equity Rule 11 (Process in Behalf of and Against Persons Not Parties). Compare also *Terrell v. Allison*, 1875, 21 Wall. 289, 22 L.Ed. 634; *Farmers' Loan and Trust Co. v. Chicago and A. Ry. Co.*, C.C.Ind.1890, 44 F. 653; *Robert Findlay Mfg. Co. v. Hygrade Lighting Fixture Corp.*, E.D.N.Y.1923, 288 F. 80; *Thompson v. Smith*, C.C.Minn.1870, Fed.Cas. No. 13,977.

1987 Amendment

The amendments are technical. No substantive change is intended.

2007 Amendments

The language of Rule 71 has been amended as part of the general restyling of the Civil Rules to make them more easily understood and to make style and terminology consistent throughout the rules. These changes are intended to be stylistic only.

CROSS REFERENCES

Execution, see Fed.Rules Civ.Proc. Rule 69, 28 USCA.

Parties generally, see Fed.Rules Civ.Proc. Rule 17 et seq., 28 USCA.

Power to issue writs, see 28 USCA § 1651.

Process generally, see Fed.Rules Civ.Proc. Rule 4, 28 USCA.

Writs of attachment, sequestration and equivalent remedies, see Fed.Rules Civ.Proc. Rule 64, 28 USCA.

TITLE IX. SPECIAL PROCEEDINGS

Rule 71.1. Condemning Real or Personal Property

(a) Applicability of Other Rules. These rules govern proceedings to condemn real and personal property by eminent domain, except as this rule provides otherwise.

(b) Joinder of Properties. The plaintiff may join separate pieces of property in a single action, no matter whether they are owned by the same persons or sought for the same use.

(c) Complaint.

(1) *Caption.* The complaint must contain a caption as provided in Rule 10(a). The plaintiff must, however, name as defendants both the property—designated generally by kind, quantity, and location—and at least one owner of some part of or interest in the property.

(2) *Contents.* The complaint must contain a short and plain statement of the following:

(A) the authority for the taking;

(B) the uses for which the property is to be taken;

(C) a description sufficient to identify the property;

(D) the interests to be acquired; and

(E) for each piece of property, a designation of each defendant who has been joined as an owner or owner of an interest in it.

(3) *Parties.* When the action commences, the plaintiff need join as defendants only those persons who have or claim an interest in the property and whose names are then known. But before any hearing on compensation, the plaintiff must add as defendants all those persons who have or claim an interest and whose names have become known or can be found by a reasonably diligent search of the records, considering both the property's character and value and the interests to be acquired. All others may be made defendants under the designation "Unknown Owners."

(4) ***Procedure.*** Notice must be served on all defendants as provided in Rule 71.1(d), whether they were named as defendants when the action commenced or were added later. A defendant may answer as provided in Rule 71.1(e). The court, meanwhile, may order any distribution of a deposit that the facts warrant.

(5) ***Filing; Additional Copies.*** In addition to filing the complaint, the plaintiff must give the clerk at least one copy for the defendants' use and additional copies at the request of the clerk or a defendant.

(d) Process.

(1) ***Delivering Notice to the Clerk.*** On filing a complaint, the plaintiff must promptly deliver to the clerk joint or several notices directed to the named defendants. When adding defendants, the plaintiff must deliver to the clerk additional notices directed to the new defendants.

(2) ***Contents of the Notice.***

(A) *Main Contents.* Each notice must name the court, the title of the action, and the defendant to whom it is directed. It must describe the property sufficiently to identify it, but need not describe any property other than that to be taken from the named defendant. The notice must also state:

(i) that the action is to condemn property;

(ii) the interest to be taken;

(iii) the authority for the taking;

(iv) the uses for which the property is to be taken;

(v) that the defendant may serve an answer on the plaintiff's attorney within 20 days after being served with the notice;

(vi) that the failure to so serve an answer constitutes consent to the taking and to the court's authority to proceed with the action and fix the compensation; and

(vii) that a defendant who does not serve an answer may file a notice of appearance.

(B) *Conclusion.* The notice must conclude with the name, telephone number, and e-mail address of the plaintiff's attorney and an address within the district in which the action is brought where the attorney may be served.

(3) ***Serving the Notice.***

(A) *Personal Service.* When a defendant whose address is known resides within the United States or a territory subject to the administrative or judicial jurisdiction of the United States, personal service of the notice (without a copy of the complaint) must be made in accordance with Rule 4.

(B) Service by Publication.

(i) A defendant may be served by publication only when the plaintiff's attorney files a certificate stating that the attorney believes the defendant cannot be personally served, because after diligent inquiry within the state where the complaint is filed, the defendant's place of residence is still unknown or, if known, that it is beyond the territorial limits of personal service. Service is then made by publishing the notice—once a week for at least 3 successive weeks—in a newspaper published in the county where the property is located or, if there is no such newspaper, in a newspaper with general circulation where the property is located. Before the last publication, a copy of the notice must also be mailed to every defendant who cannot be personally served but whose place of residence is then known. Unknown owners may be served by publication in the same manner by a notice addressed to "Unknown Owners."

(ii) Service by publication is complete on the date of the last publication. The plaintiff's attorney must prove publication and mailing by a certificate, attach a printed copy of the published notice, and mark on the copy the newspaper's name and the dates of publication.

(4) ***Effect of Delivery and Service.*** Delivering the notice to the clerk and serving it have the same effect as serving a summons under Rule 4.

(5) ***Amending the Notice; Proof of Service and Amending the Proof.*** Rule 4(a)(2) governs amending the notice. Rule 4(*l*) governs proof of service and amending it.

(e) Appearance or Answer.

(1) ***Notice of Appearance.*** A defendant that has no objection or defense to the taking of its property may serve a notice of appearance designating the property in which it claims an interest. The defendant must then be given notice of all later proceedings affecting the defendant.

(2) ***Answer.*** A defendant that has an objection or defense to the taking must serve an answer within 20 days after being served with the notice. The answer must:

(A) identify the property in which the defendant claims an interest;

(B) state the nature and extent of the interest; and

(C) state all the defendant's objections and defenses to the taking.

(3) ***Waiver of Other Objections and Defenses; Evidence on Compensation.*** A defendant waives all objections and defenses not stated in its answer. No other pleading or motion asserting an additional objection or defense is allowed. But at the trial on compensation, a defendant—whether or not it has previously appeared or answered—may present evidence on the amount of compensation to be paid and may share in the award.

(f) Amending Pleadings. Without leave of court, the plaintiff may—as often as it wants—amend the complaint at any time before the trial on compensation. But no amendment may be made if it would result in a dismissal inconsistent with Rule 71.1(i)(1) or (2). The plaintiff need not serve a copy of an amendment, but must serve notice of the filing, as provided in Rule 5(b), on every affected party who has appeared and, as provided in Rule 71.1(d), on every affected party who has not appeared. In addition, the plaintiff must give the clerk at least one copy of each amendment for the defendants' use, and additional copies at the request of the clerk or a defendant. A defendant may appear or answer in the time and manner and with the same effect as provided in Rule 71.1(e).

(g) Substituting Parties. If a defendant dies, becomes incompetent, or transfers an interest after being joined, the court may, on motion and notice of hearing, order that the proper party be substituted. Service of the motion and notice on a nonparty must be made as provided in Rule 71.1(d)(3).

(h) Trial of the Issues.

(1) ***Issues Other Than Compensation; Compensation.*** In an action involving eminent domain under federal law, the court tries all issues, including compensation, except when compensation must be determined:

(A) by any tribunal specially constituted by a federal statute to determine compensation; or

(B) if there is no such tribunal, by a jury when a party demands one within the time to answer or within any additional time the court sets, unless the court appoints a commission.

(2) ***Appointing a Commission; Commission's Powers and Report.***

(A) *Reasons for Appointing.* If a party has demanded a jury, the court may instead appoint a three-person commission to determine compensation because of the character, location, or quantity of the property to be condemned or for other just reasons.

(B) *Alternate Commissioners.* The court may appoint up to two additional persons to serve as alternate commissioners to hear the case and replace commissioners who, before a decision is filed, the court finds unable or disqualified to perform their duties. Once the commission renders its final decision, the court must discharge any alternate who has not replaced a commissioner.

(C) *Examining the Prospective Commissioners.* Before making its appointments, the court must advise the parties of the identity and qualifications of each prospective commissioner and alternate, and may permit the parties to examine them. The parties may not suggest appointees, but for good cause may object to a prospective commissioner or alternate.

(D) *Commission's Powers and Report.* A commission has the powers of a master under Rule 53(c). Its action and report are determined by a majority. Rule 53(d), (e), and (f) apply to its action and report.

(i) Dismissal of the Action or a Defendant.

(1) ***Dismissing the Action.***

(A) *By the Plaintiff.* If no compensation hearing on a piece of property has begun, and if the plaintiff has not acquired title or a lesser interest or taken possession, the plaintiff may, without a court order, dismiss the action as to that property by filing a notice of dismissal briefly describing the property.

(B) *By Stipulation.* Before a judgment is entered vesting the plaintiff with title or a lesser interest in or possession of property, the plaintiff and affected defendants may, without a court order, dismiss the action in whole or in part by filing a stipulation of dismissal. And if the parties so stipulate, the court may vacate a judgment already entered.

(C) *By Court Order.* At any time before compensation has been determined and paid, the court may, after a motion and hearing, dismiss the action as to a piece of property. But if the plaintiff has already taken title, a lesser interest, or possession as to any part of it, the court must award compensation for the title, lesser interest, or possession taken.

(2) ***Dismissing a Defendant.*** The court may at any time dismiss a defendant who was unnecessarily or improperly joined.

(3) ***Effect.*** A dismissal is without prejudice unless otherwise stated in the notice, stipulation, or court order.

(j) **Deposit and Its Distribution.**

(1) ***Deposit.*** The plaintiff must deposit with the court any money required by law as a condition to the exercise of eminent domain and may make a deposit when allowed by statute.

(2) ***Distribution; Adjusting Distribution.*** After a deposit, the court and attorneys must expedite the proceedings so as to distribute the deposit and to determine and pay compensation. If the compensation finally awarded to a defendant exceeds the amount distributed to that defendant, the court must enter judgment against the plaintiff for the deficiency. If the compensation awarded to a defendant is less than the amount distributed to that defendant, the court must enter judgment against that defendant for the overpayment.

(k) **Condemnation Under a State's Power of Eminent Domain.** This rule governs an action involving eminent domain under state law. But if state law provides for trying an issue by jury—or for trying the issue of compensation by jury or commission or both—that law governs.

(*l*) **Costs.** Costs are not subject to Rule 54(d).

(Adopted April 30, 1951, effective August 1, 1951; amended January 21, 1963, effective July 1, 1963; April 29, 1985, effective August 1, 1985; March 2, 1987, effective August 1, 1987; April 25, 1988, effective August 1, 1988; amended by Pub.L. 100–690, Title VII, § 7050, November 18, 1988, 102 Stat. 4401 (although amendment by Pub.L. 100–690 could not be executed due to prior amendment by Court order which made the same change effective August 1, 1988); amended April 22, 1993, effective December 1, 1993; March 27, 2003, effective December 1, 2003; April 30, 2007, effective December 1, 2007.)

ADVISORY COMMITTEE NOTES

1951 Addition

Supplementary Report

The Court will remember that at its conference on December 2, 1948, the discussion was confined to subdivision (h) of the rule (* * *), the particular question being whether the tribunal to award compensation should be a commission or a jury in cases where the Congress has not made specific provision on the subject. The Advisory Committee was agreed from the outset that a rule should not be promulgated which would overturn the decision of the Congress as to the kind of tribunal to fix compensation, provided that the system established by Congress was found to be working well. We found two instances where the Congress had specified the kind of tribunal to fix compensation. One case was the District of Columbia ([former] §§ 361 to 386 of Title 40 [now D.C. Code, Title 16, § 1301 et seq.]) where a rather unique system exists under which the court is required in all cases to order the selection of a "jury" of five from among not less than twenty names drawn from "the special box provided by law." They must have the usual qualifications of jurors and in addition must be freeholders of the District and not in the service of the United States or the District. That system has been in effect for many years, and our inquiry revealed that it works well under the conditions prevailing in the District, and is satisfactory to the courts of the District, the legal profession and to property owners.

The other instance is that of the Tennessee Valley Authority, where the act of Congress (section 831x of Title 16) provides that compensation is fixed by three disinterested commissioners appointed by the court, whose award goes before the District Court for confirmation or modification. The Advisory Committee made a thorough inquiry into the practical operation of the TVA commission system. We obtained from counsel for the TVA the results of their experience, which afforded convincing proof that the commission system is preferable under the conditions affecting TVA and that the jury system would not work satisfactorily. We then, under date of February 6, 1947, wrote every Federal judge who had ever sat in a TVA condemnation case, asking his views as to whether the commission system is satisfactory and whether a jury system should be preferred. Of 21 responses from the judges 17 approved the commission system and opposed the substitution of a jury system for the TVA. Many of the judges went further and opposed the use of juries in any condemnation cases. Three of the judges preferred the jury system, and one dealt only with the TVA provision for a three judge district court. The Advisory Committee has not considered abolition of the three judge requirement of the TVA Act, because it seemed to raise a question of jurisdiction, which cannot be altered by rule. Nevertheless the Department of Justice continued its advocacy of the jury system for its asserted expedition and economy; and others favored a uniform procedure. In consequence of these divided counsels the Advisory Committee was itself divided, but in its May 1948 Report to the Court recommended the following rule as approved by a majority (* * *):

(h) Trial. If the action involves the exercise of the power of eminent domain under the law of the United States, any tribunal especially constituted by an Act of Congress governing the case for the trial of the issue of just compensation shall be the tribunal for the determination of that issue; but if there is no such specially constituted tribunal any party may have a trial by jury of the issue of just compensation by filing a demand therefor within the time allowed for answer or within such further time as the court may fix. Trial of all issues shall otherwise be by the court.

The effect of this was to preserve the existing systems in the District of Columbia and in TVA cases, but to provide for a jury to fix compensation in all other cases.

Before the Court's conference of December 2, 1948, the Chief Justice informed the Committee that the Court was particularly interested in the views expressed by Judge John Paul, Judge of the United States District Court for the Western District of Virginia, in a letter from him to the chairman of the Advisory Committee, dated February 13, 1947. Copies of all the letters from judges who had sat in TVA cases had been made available to the Court, and this letter from Judge Paul is one of them. Judge Paul strongly opposed jury trials and recommended the commission system in large projects like the TVA, and his views seemed to have impressed the Court and to have been the occasion for the conference.

The reasons which convinced the Advisory Committee that the use of commissioners instead of juries is desirable in TVA cases were these:

1. The TVA condemns large areas of land of similar kind, involving many owners. Uniformity in awards is essential. The commission system tends to prevent discrimination and provide for uniformity in compensation. The jury system tends to lack of uniformity. Once a reasonable and uniform standard of values for the area has been settled by a commission, litigation ends and settlements result.

2. Where large areas are involved many small landowners reside at great distances from the place where a court sits. It is a great hardship on humble people to have to travel long distances to attend a jury trial. A commission may travel around and receive the evidence of the owner near his home.

3. It is impracticable to take juries long distances to view the premises.

4. If the cases are tried by juries the burden on the time of the courts is excessive.

These considerations are the very ones Judge Paul stressed in his letter. He pointed out that they applied not only to the TVA but to other large governmental projects, such as flood control, hydroelectric power, reclamation, national forests, and others. So when the representatives of the Advisory Committee appeared at the Court's conference December 2, 1948, they found it difficult to justify the proposed provision in subdivision (h) of the rule that a jury should be used to fix compensation in all cases where Congress had not specified the tribunal. If our reasons for preserving the TVA system were sound, provision for a jury in similar projects of like magnitude seemed unsound.

Aware of the apparent inconsistency between the acceptance of the TVA system and the provision for a jury in all other cases, the members of the Committee attending the conference of December 2, 1948, then suggested that in the other cases the choice of jury or commission be left to the discretion of the District Court, going back to a suggestion previously made by Committee members and reported at page 15 of the Preliminary Draft of June 1947. They called the attention of the Court to the fact that the entire Advisory Committee had not been consulted about this suggestion and proposed that the draft be returned to the Committee for further consideration, and that was done.

The proposal we now make for subdivision (h) is as follows:

(h) Trial. If the action involves the exercise of the power of eminent domain under the law of the United States, any tribunal specially constituted by an Act of Congress governing the case for the trial of the issue of just compensation shall be the tribunal for the determination of that issue; but if there is no such specially constituted tribunal any party may have a trial by jury of the issue of just compensation by filing a demand therefor within the time allowed for answer or within such further time as the court may fix, unless the court in its discretion orders that, because of the character, location, or quantity of the property to be condemned, or for other reasons in the interest of justice, the issue of compensation shall be determined by a commission of three persons appointed by it. If a commission is appointed it shall have the powers of a master provided in subdivision (c) of Rule 53 and proceedings before it shall be governed by the provisions of paragraphs (1) and (2) of subdivision (d) of Rule 53. Its action and report shall be determined by a majority and its findings and report shall have the effect, and be dealt with by the court in accordance with the practice, prescribed in paragraph (2) of subdivision (e) of Rule 53. Trial of all issues shall otherwise be by the court.

In the 1948 draft the Committee had been almost evenly divided as between jury or commission and that made it easy for us to agree on the present draft. It would be difficult to state in a rule the various conditions to control the District Court in its choice and we have merely stated generally the matters which should be considered by the District Court.

The rule as now drafted seems to meet Judge Paul's objection. In large projects like the TVA the court may decide to use a commission. In a great number of cases involving only sites for buildings or other small areas, where use of a jury is appropriate, a jury may be chosen. The District Court's discretion may also be influenced by local preference or habit, and the preference of the Department of Justice and the reasons for its preference will doubtless be given weight. The Committee is convinced that there are some types of cases in which use of a commission is preferable and others in which a jury may be appropriately used, and that it would be a mistake to provide that the same kind of tribunal should be used in all cases. We think the available evidence clearly leads to that conclusion.

When this suggestion was made at the conference of December 2, 1948, representatives of the Department of Justice opposed it, expressing opposition to the use of a commission in any case. Their principal ground for opposition to commissions was then based on the assertion that the commission system is too expensive because courts allow commissioners too large compensation. The obvious answer to that is that the compensation of commissioners ought to be fixed or limited by law, as was done in the TVA Act, and the agency dealing with appropriations—either the Administrative Office or some other interested department of the government—should correct that evil, if evil there be, by obtaining such legislation. Authority to promulgate rules of procedure does not include power to fix compensation of government employees. The Advisory Committee is not convinced that even without such legislation the commission system is more expensive than the jury system. The expense of jury trials includes not only the per diem and mileage of the jurors impaneled for a case but like items for the entire venire. In computing cost of jury trials, the salaries of court officials, judges, clerks, marshals and deputies must be considered. No figures have been given to the Committee to establish that the cost of the commission system is the greater.

We earnestly recommend the rule as now drafted for promulgation by the Court, in the public interest.

The Advisory Committee have given more time to this rule, including time required for conferences with the Department of Justice to hear statements of its representatives, than has been required by any other rule. The rule may not be perfect but if faults develop in practice they may be promptly cured. Certainly the present conformity system is atrocious.

Under state practices, just compensation is normally determined by one of three methods: by commissioners; by commissioners with a right of appeal to and trial de novo before a jury; and by a jury, without a commission. A trial to the court or to the court including a master are, however, other methods that are occasionally used. Approximately 5 states use only commissioners; 23 states use commissioners with a trial de novo before a jury; and 18 states use only the jury. This classification is advisedly stated in approximate terms, since the same state may utilize diverse methods, depending upon different types of condemnations or upon the locality of the property, and since the methods used in a few states do not permit of a categorical classification. To reject the proposed rule and leave the situation as it is would not satisfy the views of the Department of Justice. The Department and the Advisory Committee agree that the use of a commission, with appeal to a jury, is a wasteful system.

The Department of Justice has a voluminous "Manual on Federal Eminent Domain," the 1940 edition of which has 948 pages with an appendix of 73 more pages. The title page informs us the preparation of the manual was begun during the incumbency of Attorney General Cummings, was continued under Attorney General Murphy, and completed during the incumbency of Attorney General Jackson. The preface contains the following statement:

> It should also be mentioned that the research incorporated in the manual would be of invaluable assistance in the drafting of a new uniform code, or rules of court, for federal condemnation proceedings, which are now greatly confused, not only by the existence of over seventy federal statutes governing condemnations for different purposes—statutes which sometimes conflict with one another—but also by the countless problems occasioned by the requirements of conformity to state law. Progress of the work has already demonstrated that the need for such reform exists.

It is not surprising that more than once Attorneys General have asked the Advisory Committee to prepare a federal rule and rescue the government from this morass.

The Department of Justice has twice tried and failed to persuade the Congress to provide that juries shall be used in all condemnation cases. The debates in Congress show that part of the opposition to the Department of Justice's bills came from representatives opposed to jury trials in all cases, and in part from a preference for the conformity system. Our present proposal opens the door for district judges to yield to local preferences on the subject. It does much for the Department's points of view. It is a great improvement over the present so-called conformity system. It does away with the wasteful "double" system prevailing in 23 states where awards by commissions are followed by jury trials.

Aside from the question as to the choice of a tribunal to award compensation, the proposed rule would afford a simple and improved procedure.

We turn now to an itemized explanation of the other changes we have made in the 1948 draft. Some of these result from recent amendments to the Judicial Code. Others result from a reconsideration by the Advisory Committee of provisions which we thought could be improved.

1. In the amended Judicial Code, the district courts are designated as "United States District Courts" instead of "District Courts of the United States," and a corresponding change has been made in the rule.

2. After the 1948 draft was referred back to the committee, the provision in subdivision (c)(2), relating to naming defendants, * * * which provided that the plaintiff shall add as defendants all persons having or claiming an interest in that property whose names can be ascertained by a search of the records to the extent commonly made by competent searchers of title in the vicinity "in light of the type and value of the property involved," the phrase in quotation marks was changed to read "in the light of the character and value of the property involved and the interests to be acquired."

The Department of Justice made a counter proposal * * * that there be substituted the words "reasonably diligent search of the records, considering the type." When the American Bar Association thereafter considered the draft, it approved the Advisory Committee's draft of this subdivision, but said that it had no objection to the Department's suggestion. Thereafter, in an effort to eliminate controversy, the Advisory Committee accepted the Department's suggestion as to (c)(2), using the word "character" instead of the word "type."

The Department of Justice also suggested that in subdivision (d)(3)(ii) relating to service by publication, the search for a defendant's residence as a preliminary to publication be limited to the state in which the complaint is filed. Here again the American Bar Association's report expressed the view that the Department's suggestion was unobjectionable and the Advisory Committee thereupon adopted it.

3. Subdivision (k) of the 1948 draft is as follows:

(k) Condemnation Under a State's Power of Eminent Domain. If the action involves the exercise of the power of eminent domain under the law of a state, the practice herein prescribed may be altered to the extent necessary to observe and enforce any condition affecting the substantial rights of a litigant attached by the state law to the exercise of the state's power of eminent domain.

Occasionally condemnation cases under a state's power of eminent domain reach a United States District Court because of diversity of citizenship. Such cases are rare, but provision should be made for them.

The 1948 draft of (k) required a district court to decide whether a provision of state law specifying the tribunal to award compensation is or is not a "condition" attached to the exercise of the state's power. On reconsideration we concluded that it would be wise to redraft (k) so as to avoid that troublesome question. As to conditions in state laws which affect the substantial rights of a litigant, the district courts would be bound to give them effect without any rule on the subject. Accordingly we present two alternative revisions. One suggestion supported by a majority of the Advisory Committee is as follows:

(k) Condemnation Under a State's Power of Eminent Domain. The practice herein prescribed governs in actions involving the exercise of the power of eminent domain under the law of a state, provided that if the state law makes provision for trial of any issue by jury, or for trial of the issue of compensation by jury or commission or both, that provision shall be followed.

The other is as follows:

(k) Condemnation Under a State's Power of Eminent Domain. The practice herein prescribed governs in actions involving the exercise of the power of eminent domain under the law of a state, provided that if the state law gives a right to a trial by jury such a trial shall in any case be allowed to the party demanding it within the time permitted by these rules, and in that event no hearing before a commission shall be had.

The first proposal accepts the state law as to the tribunals to fix compensation, and in that respect leaves the parties in precisely the same situation as if the case were pending in a state court, including the use of a commission with appeal to a jury, if the state law so provides. It has the effect of avoiding any question as to whether the decisions in *Erie R. Co. v. Tompkins* and later cases have application to a situation of this kind.

The second proposal gives the parties a right to a jury trial if that is provided for by state law, but prevents the use of both commission and jury. Those members of the Committee who favor the second proposal do so because of the obvious objections to the double trial, with a commission and appeal to a jury. As the decisions in *Erie R. Co. v. Tompkins* and later cases may have a bearing on this point, and the Committee is divided, we think both proposals should be placed before the Court.

4. The provision * * * of the 1948 draft * * * prescribing the effective date of the rule was drafted before the recent amendment of the Judicial Code on that subject. On May 10, 1950, the President approved an act which amended section 2072 of Title 28, United States Code, to read as follows:

> Such rules shall not take effect until they have been reported to Congress by the Chief Justice at or after the beginning of a regular session thereof but not later than the first day of May, and until the expiration of ninety days after they have been thus reported.

To conform to the statute now in force, we suggest a provision as follows:

Effective Date. This Rule 71A and the amendment to Rule 81(a) will take effect on August 1, 1951. Rule 71A governs all proceedings in actions brought after it takes effect and also all further proceedings in actions then pending, except to the extent that in the opinion of the court its application in a particular action pending when the rule takes effect would not be feasible or would work injustice, in which event the former procedure applies.

If the rule is not reported to Congress by May 1, 1951, this provision must be altered.

[Par. 3 of Supreme Court Order adopted Apr. 30, 1951, setting out this rule and providing for the abrogation of par. (7) of Rule 81(a), and providing for the Effective Date, as stated herein, was transmitted to Congress on May 1, 1951 by the Chief Justice of the United States (House Document No. 121, May 1, 1951, 82nd Cong., 1st Sess.), in conformity with § 2072 of this title. As no action was taken by Congress within the 90-day period required by that section, this rule and the abrogation of par. (7) of Rule 81(a) took effect on Aug. 1, 1951, as provided in said order.]

5. We call attention to the fact that the proposed rule does not contain a provision for the procedure to be followed in order to exercise the right of the United States to take immediate possession or title, when the condemnation proceeding is begun. There are several statutes conferring such a right which are cited in the original notes to the May 1948 draft * * *. The existence of this right is taken into account in the rule. In subdivision (c)(2), * * * it is stated: "Upon the commencement of the action, the plaintiff need join as defendants only the persons having or claiming an interest in the property whose names are then known." That is to enable the United States to exercise the right to immediate title or possession without the delay involved in ascertaining the names of all interested parties. The right is also taken into account in the provision relating to dismissal (paragraph (i), subdivisions (1), (2), and (3), * * *); also in paragraph (j) relating to deposits and their distribution.

The Advisory Committee considered whether the procedure for exercising the right should be specified in the rule and decided against it, as the procedure now being followed seems to be giving no trouble, and to draft a rule to fit all the statutes on the subject might create confusion.

The American Bar Association has taken an active interest in a rule for condemnation cases. In 1944 its House of Delegates adopted a resolution which among other things resolved:

> That before adoption by the Supreme Court of the United States of any redraft of the proposed rule, time and opportunity should be afforded to the bar to consider and make recommendations concerning any such redraft.

Accordingly, in 1950 the revised draft was submitted to the American Bar Association and its section of real property, probate and trust law appointed a committee to consider it. That committee was supplied with copies of the written statement from the Department of Justice giving the reasons relied on by the Department for preferring a rule to use juries in all cases. The Advisory Committee's report was approved at a meeting of the section of real property law, and by the House of Delegates at the annual meeting of

September 1950. The American Bar Association report gave particular attention to the question whether juries or commissions should be used to fix compensation, approved the Advisory Committee's solution appearing in their latest draft designed to allow use of commissions in projects comparable to the TVA, and rejected the proposal for use of juries in all cases.

In November 1950 a committee of the Federal Bar Association, the chairman of which was a Special Assistant to the Attorney General, made a report which reflected the attitude of the Department of Justice on the condemnation rule.

Aside from subdivision (h) about the tribunal to award compensation the final draft of the condemnation rule here presented has the approval of the American Bar Association and, we understand, the Department of Justice, and we do not know of any opposition to it. Subdivision (h) has the unanimous approval of the Advisory Committee and has been approved by the American Bar Association. The use of commissions in TVA cases, and, by fair inference, in cases comparable to the TVA, is supported by 17 out of 20 judges who up to 1947 had sat in TVA cases. The legal staff of the TVA has vigorously objected to the substitution of juries for commissions in TVA cases. We regret to report that the Department of Justice still asks that subdivision (h) be altered to provide for jury trials in an cases where Congress has not specified the tribunal. We understand that the Department approves the proposal that the system prevailing in 23 states for the "double" trial, by commission with appeal to and trial de novo before a jury, should be abolished, and also asks that on demand a jury should be substituted for a commission, in those states where use of a commission alone is now required. The Advisory Committee has no evidence that commissions do not operate satisfactorily in the case of projects comparable to the TVA.

Original Report

General Statement. 1. Background. When the Advisory Committee was formulating its recommendations to the Court concerning rules of procedure, which subsequently became the Federal Rules of 1938, the Committee concluded at an early stage not to fix the procedure in condemnation cases. This is a matter principally involving the exercise of the federal power of eminent domain, as very few condemnation cases involving the state's power reach the United States District Courts. The Committee's reasons at that time were that inasmuch as condemnation proceedings by the United States are governed by statutes of the United States, prescribing different procedure for various agencies and departments of the government, or, in the absence of such statutes, by local state practice under the Conformity Act (former § 258 of Title 40), it would be extremely difficult to draft a uniform rule satisfactory to the various agencies and departments of the government and to private parties; and that there was no general demand for a uniform rule. The Committee continued in that belief until shortly before the preparation of the April 1937 Draft of the Rules, when the officials of the Department of Justice having to do with condemnation cases urgently requested the Committee to propose rules on this subject. The Committee undertook the task and drafted a Condemnation Rule which appeared for the first time as Rule 74 of the April 1937 Draft. After the publication and distribution of this initial draft many objections were urged against it by counsel for various governmental agencies, whose procedure in condemnation cases was prescribed by federal statutes. Some of these agencies wanted to be excepted in whole or in part from the operation of the uniform rule proposed in April 1937. And the Department of Justice changed its position and stated that it preferred to have government condemnations conducted by local attorneys familiar with the state practice, which was applied under the Conformity Act where the Acts of Congress do not prescribe the practice; that it preferred to work under the Conformity Act without a uniform rule of procedure. The profession generally showed little interest in the proposed uniform rule. For these reasons the Advisory Committee in its Final Report to the Court in November 1937 proposed that all of Rule 74 be stricken and that the Federal Rules be made applicable only to appeals in condemnation cases. See note to Rule 74 of the Final Report.

Some of six or seven years later when the Advisory Committee was considering the subject of amendments to the Federal Rules both government officials and the profession generally urged the adoption of some uniform procedure. This demand grew out of the volume of condemnation proceedings instituted during the war, and the general feeling of dissatisfaction with the diverse condemnation procedures that were applicable in the federal courts. A strongly held belief was that both the sovereign's power to condemn and the property owner's right to compensation could be promoted by a simplified rule. As a consequence the Committee proposed a Rule 71A on the subject of condemnation in its Preliminary Draft of May 1944. In the Second Preliminary Draft of May 1945 this earlier proposed Rule 71A was, however, omitted. The Committee did not then feel that it had sufficient time to prepare a revised draft satisfactorily to it which would meet legitimate objections made to the draft of May 1944. To avoid unduly delaying the proposed amendments to existing rules the Committee concluded to proceed in the regular way with the preparation of the amendments to these rules and deal with the question of a condemnation rule as an independent matter. As a consequence it made no recommendations to the Court on condemnation in its Final Report of Proposed Amendments of June 1946; and the amendments which the Court adopted in December 1946 did not deal with condemnation. After concluding its task relative to amendments, the Committee returned to a consideration of eminent domain, its proposed Rule 71A of May 1944, the suggestions and criticisms that had been presented in the interim, and in June 1947 prepared and distributed to the profession another draft of a proposed condemnation rule. This draft contained several alternative provisions, specifically called attention to and asked for opinion relative to these matters, and in particular as to the constitution of the tribunal to award compensation. The present draft was based on the June 1947 formulation, in light of the advice of the profession on both matters of substance and form.

2. Statutory Provisions. The need for a uniform condemnation rule in the federal courts arises from the fact that by various statutes Congress has prescribed diverse procedures for certain condemnation proceedings, and, in the absence of such statutes, has prescribed conformity to local state practice under former § 258 of Title 40. This general conformity adds to the diversity of procedure since in the United States there are multifarious methods of procedure in existence. Thus in 1931 it was said that there were 269 different methods of judicial procedure in different classes of condemnation cases and 56 methods of nonjudicial or administrative procedure. First Report of Judicial Council of Michigan, 1931, § 46, pp. 55 to 56. These numbers have not decreased. Consequently, the general requirement of conformity to state practice and procedure, particularly where the condemnor is the United States, leads to expense, delay and uncertainty. In advocacy of a uniform federal rule, see Armstrong, *Proposed Amendments to Federal Rules for Civil Procedure,* 1944, 4 F.R.D. 124, 134; id., *Report of the Advisory Committee on Federal Rules of Civil Procedure Recommending Amendments,* 1946, 5 F.R.D. 339, 357.

There are a great variety of Acts of Congress authorizing the exercise of the power of eminent domain by the United States and its officers and agencies. These statutes for the most part do not specify the exact procedure to be followed, but where procedure is prescribed, it is by no means uniform.

The following are instances of Acts which merely authorize the exercise of the power without specific declaration as to the procedure:

U.S.C., Title 16:

§ 404c–11 (Mammoth Cave National Park; acquisition of lands, interests in lands or other property for park by the Secretary of the Interior).

§ 426d (Stones River National Park; acquisition of land for parks by the Secretary of the Army).

§ 450aa (George Washington Carver National Monument; acquisition of land by the Secretary of the Interior).

§ 517 (National forest reservation; title to lands to be acquired by the Secretary of Agriculture).

U.S.C., Title 42:

§§ 1805(b)(5), 1813(b) [now §§ 2061 and 2112, and §§ 2221 to 2224, respectively, of Title 42] (Atomic Energy Act).

The following are instances of Acts which authorized condemnation and declare that the procedure is to conform what that of similar actions in state courts:

U.S.C., Title 16:

§ 423k (Richmond National Battlefield Park; acquisition of lands by the Secretary of the Interior).

§ 814 (Exercise by water power licensee of power of eminent domain).

U.S.C., Title 24:

§ 78 [Repealed] (Condemnation of land for the former National Home for Disabled Volunteer Soldiers).

U.S.C., Title 33:

§ 591 (Condemnation of lands and materials for river and harbor improvement by the Secretary of the Army).

U.S.C., Title 40:

§ 257 [now § 3113] (Condemnation of realty for sites for public building and for other public uses by the Secretary of the Treasury authorized).

§ 258 [Omitted as superseded by this rule] (Same procedure).

U.S.C., Title 50:

§ 171 [Repealed and is now covered by § 2663 of Title 10] (Acquisition of land by the Secretary of the Army for national defense).

§ 172 [Repealed and is now covered by §§ 2664 and 2665 of Title 10] (Acquisition of property by the Secretary of the Army, etc., for production of lumber).

§ 632 App. [Omitted as terminated by § 645 of the Appendix to Title 50] (Second War Powers Act, 1942; acquisition of real property for war purposes by the Secretary of Army, the Secretary of the Navy and others).

The following are Acts in which a more or less complete code of procedure is set forth in connection with the taking:

U.S.C., Title 16:

§ 831x (Condemnation by Tennessee Valley Authority).

U.S.C., Title 40:

§ 361–386 [Repealed] [now D.C.Code, Title 16, § 1301 et seq.] (Acquisition of lands in District of Columbia for use of United States; condemnation).

3. Adjustment of Rule to Statutory Provisions. While it was apparent that the principle of uniformity should be the basis for a rule to replace the multiple diverse procedures set out above, there remained a serious question as to whether an exception could properly be made relative to the method of determining compensation. Where Congress had provided for conformity to state law the following were the general methods in use: an initial determination by commissioners, with appeal to a judge; an initial award, likewise made by commissioners, but with the appeal to a jury; and determination by a jury without a previous award by commissioners. In two situations Congress had specified the tribunal to determine the issue of compensation: condemnation by the Tennessee Valley Authority; and condemnation in the District of Columbia. Under the TVA procedure the initial determination of value is by three disinterested commissioners, appointed by the court, from a locality other than the one in which the land lies. Either party may except to the award of the commission; in that case the exceptions are to be heard by three district judges (unless the parties stipulate for a lesser number), with a right of appeal to the circuit court of appeals. The TVA is a regional agency. It is faced with the necessity of acquiring a very substantial acreage within a relatively small area, and charged with the task of carrying on within the Tennessee Valley and in cooperation with the local people a permanent program involving navigation and flood control, electric power, soil conservation, and general regional development. The success of this program is partially dependent upon the good will and cooperation of the people of the Tennessee Valley, and this in turn partially depends upon the land acquisition program. Disproportionate awards among landowners would create dissatisfaction and ill will. To secure uniformity in treatment Congress provided the rather unique procedure of the three-judge court to review de novo the initial award of the commissioners. This procedure has worked to the satisfaction of the property owners and the TVA. A full statement of the TVA position and experience is set forth in Preliminary Draft of Proposed Rule to Govern Condemnation Cases (June, 1947) 15–19. A large majority of the district judges with experience under this procedure approve it, subject to some objection to the requirement for a three-judge district court to review commissioners' awards. A statutory three-judge requirement is, however, jurisdictional and must be strictly followed. *Stratton v. St. Louis, Southwestern Ry. Co.,* 1930, 51 S.Ct. 8, 282 U.S. 10, 75 L.Ed. 135; *Ayrshire Collieries Corp. v. United States,* 1947, 67 S.Ct. 1168, 331 U.S. 132, 91 L.Ed. 1391. Hence except insofar as the TVA statute itself authorizes the parties to stipulate for a court of less than three judges, the requirement must be followed, and would seem to be beyond alteration by court rule even if change were thought desirable. Accordingly the TVA procedure is retained for the determination of compensation in TVA condemnation cases. It was also thought desirable to retain the specific method Congress had prescribed for the District of Columbia, which is a so-called jury of five appointed by the court. This is a local matter and the specific treatment accorded by Congress has given local satisfaction.

Aside from the foregoing limited exceptions dealing with the TVA and the District of Columbia, the question was whether a uniform method for determining compensation should be a commission with appeal to a district judge, or a commission with appeal to a jury, or a jury without a commission. Experience with the commission on a nationwide basis, and in particular with the utilization of a commission followed by an appeal to a jury, has been that the commission is time consuming and expensive. Furthermore, it is largely a futile procedure where it is preparatory to jury trial. Since in the bulk of states a land owner is entitled eventually to a jury trial, since the jury is a traditional tribunal for the determination of questions of value, and since experience with juries has proved satisfactory to both government and land owner, the right to jury trial is adopted as the general rule. Condemnation involving the TVA and the District of Columbia are the two exceptions. See Note to Subdivision (h), infra.

Note to Subdivision (a). As originally promulgated the Federal Rules governed appeals in condemnation proceedings but were not otherwise applicable. Rule 81(a)(7). Preappeal procedure, in the main, conformed to state procedure. See statutes and discussion, supra. The purpose of Rule 71A is to provide a uniform procedure for condemnation in the federal district courts, including the District of Columbia. To achieve this purpose Rule 71A prescribes such specialized procedure as is required by condemnation proceedings, otherwise it utilizes the general framework of the Federal Rules where specific detail is unnecessary. The adoption of Rule 71A, of course, renders paragraph (7) of Rule 81(a) unnecessary.

The promulgation of a rule for condemnation procedure is within the rulemaking power. The Enabling Act [Act of June 19, 1934, c. 651, §§ 1, 2 (48 Stat. 1064), former §§ 723b, 723c, now § 2072, of this title] gives the Supreme Court "the power to prescribe, by general rules * * * the forms of process, writs, pleadings, and motions, and the practice and procedure in civil actions at law." Such rules, however, must not abridge, enlarge, or modify substantive rights. In *Kohl v. United States*, 1875, 91 U.S. 367, 23 L.Ed. 449, a proceeding instituted by the United States to appropriate land for a postoffice site under a statute enacted for such purpose, the Supreme Court held that "a proceeding to take land in virtue of the government's eminent domain, and determining the compensation to be made for it, is * * * a suit at common law, when initiated in a court." See, also, *Madisonville Traction Co. v. Saint Bernard Mining Co.*, 1905, 25 S.Ct. 251, 196 U.S. 239, 49 L.Ed. 462, infra, under subdivision (k). And the Conformity Act [former § 258 of Title 40], which is superseded by Rule 71A, deals only with "practice, pleadings, forms and proceedings and not with matters of substantive laws." *United States v. 243.22 Acres of Land in Village of Farmingdale, Town of Babylon, Suffolk County, N.Y.*, D.C.N.Y.1942, 43 F.Supp. 561, affirmed 129 F.2d 678, certiorari denied 63 S.Ct. 441, 317 U.S. 698, 87 L.Ed. 558.

Rule 71A affords a uniform procedure for all cases of condemnation invoking the national power of eminent domain, and, to the extent stated in subdivision (k), for cases invoking a state's power of eminent domain; and supplants all statutes prescribing a different procedure. While the almost exclusive utility of the rule is for the condemnation of real property, it also applies to the condemnation of personal property, either as an incident to real property or as the sole object of the proceeding, when permitted or required by statute. See former § 438j [now § 5001] of Title 38 (World War Veterans' Relief Act); former §§ 1805, 1811, and 1813 of Title 42 (Atomic Energy Act); former § 79 [now § 100] of Title 50 (Nitrates Act); former §§ 161 to 165 and § 166, of Title 50 (Helium Gas Act). Requisitioning of personal property with the right in the owner to sue the United States, where the compensation cannot be agreed upon (see former § 1813 [now §§ 2221 to 2224] of Title 42, for example) will continue to be the normal method of acquiring personal property and Rule 71A in no way interferes with or restricts any such right. Only where the law requires or permits the formal procedure of condemnation to be utilized will the rule have any applicability to the acquisition of personal property.

Rule 71A is not intended to and does not supersede the Act of February 26, 1931, c. 307, §§ 1 to 5 (46 Stat. 1421), §§ 258a to 258e of Title 40, which is a supplementary condemnation statute, permissive in its nature and designed to permit the prompt acquisition of title by the United States, pending the condemnation proceeding, upon a deposit in court. See *United States v. 76,800 Acres, More or Less, of Land, in Bryan and Liberty Counties, Ga.*, D.C.Ga.1942, 44 F.Supp. 653; *United States v. 17,280 Acres of Land, More or Less, Situated in Saunders County, Neb.*, D.C.Neb.1942, 47 F.Supp. 267. The same is true insofar as the following or any other statutes authorize the acquisition of title or the taking of immediate possession:

U.S.C., Title 33:

§ 594 (When immediate possession of land may be taken; for a work of river and harbor improvements.)

U.S.C., Title 42:

§ 1813(b) [now §§ 2221 to 2224 of Title 42] (When immediate possession may be taken under Atomic Energy Act).

U.S.C., Title 50:

§ 171 [Repealed and is now covered by § 2663 of Title 10] (Acquisition of land by the Secretary of the Army for national defense).

§ 632 App. [Omitted as terminated by § 645 of the Appendix to Title 50] (Second War Powers Act, 1942; acquisition of real property for war purposes by the Secretary of the Army, the Secretary of the Navy, and others).

Note to Subdivision (b). This subdivision provides for broad joinder in accordance with the tenor of other rules such as Rule 18. To require separate condemnation proceedings for each piece of property separately owned would be unduly burdensome and would serve no useful purpose. And a restriction that only properties may be joined which are to be acquired for the same public use would also cause difficulty. For example, a unified project to widen a street, construct a bridge across a navigable river, and for the construction of approaches to the level of the bridge on both sides of the river might involve acquiring property for different public uses. Yet it is eminently desirable that the plaintiff may in one proceeding condemn all the property interests and rights necessary to carry out this project. Rule 21 which allows the court to sever and proceed separately with any claim against a party, and Rule 42(b) giving the court broad discretion to order separate trials give adequate protection to all defendants in condemnation proceedings.

Note to Subdivision (c). Since a condemnation proceeding is in rem and since a great many property owners are often involved, paragraph (1) requires the property to be named and only one of the owners. In other respects and caption will contain the name of the court, the title of the action, file number, and a designation of the pleading as a complaint in accordance with Rule 10(a).

Since the general standards of pleading are stated in other rules, paragraph (2) prescribes only the necessary detail for condemnation proceedings. Certain statutes allow the United States to acquire title or possession immediately upon commencement of an action. See the Act of February 26, 1931, c. 307, §§ 1 to 5 (46 Stat. 1421), §§ 258a to 258e of Title 40; and § 594 of Title 33, former § 1813(b) of Title 42, former § 171 of Title 50, former § 632 of the Appendix to Title 50, supra. To carry out the purpose of such statutes and to aid the condemnor in instituting the action even where title is not acquired at the outset, the plaintiff is initially required to join as defendants only the persons having or claiming an interest in the property whose names are then known. This is no way prejudices the property owner, who must eventually be joined as a defendant, served with process, and allowed to answer before there can be any hearing involving the compensation to be paid for his piece of property. The rule requires the plaintiff to name all persons having or claiming an interest in the property of whom the plaintiff has learned and, more importantly, those appearing of record. By charging the plaintiff with the necessity to make "a search of the records of the extent commonly made by competent searches of title in the vicinity in light of the type and value of the property involved" both the plaintiff and property owner are protected. Where a short term interest in property of little value is involved, as a two or three year easement over a vacant land for purposes of ingress and egress to other property, a search of the records covering a long period of time is not required. Where on the other hand fee simple title in valuable property is being condemned the search must necessarily cover a much longer period of time and be commensurate with the interests involved. But even here the search is related to the type made by competent title searchers in the vicinity. A search that extends back to the original patent may be feasible in some midwestern and western states and be proper under certain circumstances. In the Atlantic seaboard states such a search is normally not feasible nor desirable. There is a common sense business accommodation of what title searchers can and should do. For state statutes requiring persons appearing as owners or otherwise interested in the property to be named as defendants, see 3 Colo.Stat.Ann., 1935, c. 61, § 2; Ill.Ann.Stat. (Smith-Hurd) c. 47, § 2; 1 Iowa Code, 1946, § 472.3; Kans.Stat.Ann., 1935, § 26–101; 2 Mass.Laws Ann., 1932, c. 80A, § 4; 7 Mich.Stat.Ann., 1936, § 8.2; 2 Minn.Stat., Mason 1927, § 6541; 20 N.J.Stat.Ann., 1939, § 1–2; 3 Wash.Revised Stat., Remington, 1932, Title 6, § 891. For state provisions allowing persons whose names are not known to be designated under the descriptive term of "unknown owner", see Hawaii Revised Laws, 1945, c. 8, § 310 ("such [unknown] defendant may be joined in the petition under a fictitious name."); Ill.Ann.Stat. (Smith-Hurd) c. 47, § 2 ("Persons interested, whose names are unknown, may be made parties defendant by the description of the unknown owners; * * *"); Maryland Code Ann., 1939, Art. 33A, § 1 ("In case any owner or owners is or are not known, he or they may be described in such petition as the unknown owner or owners, or the unknown heir or heirs of a deceased owner."); 2 Mass.Laws Ann., 1932, c. 80A, § 4 ("Persons not in being, unascertained or unknown who may have an interest in any of such land shall be made parties respondent by such description as seems appropriate, * * *"); New Mex.Stat.Ann., 1941, § 25–901 ("the owners * * * shall be parties defendant, by name, if the names are known, and by description of the unknown owners of the land therein described, if their names are unknown."); Utah Code Ann., 1943, § 104–61–7 ("The names of all owners and claimants of the property, if known, or a statement that they are unknown, who must be styled defendants").

The last sentence of paragraph (2) enables the court to expedite the distribution of a deposit, in whole or in part, as soon as pertinent facts of ownership, value and the like are established. See also subdivision (j).

The signing of the complaint is governed by Rule 11.

Note to Subdivision (d). In lieu of a summons, which is the initial process in other civil actions under Rule 4(a), subdivision (d) provides for a notice which is to contain sufficient information so that the defendant in effect obtains the plaintiff's statement of his claim against the defendant to whom the notice is directed. Since the plaintiff's attorney is an officer of the court and to prevent unduly burdening the clerk of the court, paragraph (1) of subdivision (d) provides that plaintiff's attorney shall prepare and deliver a notice or notices to the clerk. Flexibility is provided by the provision for joint or several notices, and for additional notices. Where there are only a few defendants it may be convenient to prepare but one notice directed to all the defendants. In other cases where there are many defendants it will be more convenient to prepare two or more notices; but in any event a notice must be directed to each named defendant. Paragraph (2) provides that the notice is to be signed by the plaintiff's attorney. Since the notice is to be delivered to the clerk, the issuance of the notice will appear of record in the court. The clerk should forthwith deliver the notice or notices for service to the marshal or to a person specially appointed to serve the notice. Rule 4(a). The form of the notice is such that, in addition to informing the defendant of the plaintiff's statement of claim, it tells the defendant precisely what his rights are. Failure on the part of the defendant to serve an answer constitutes a consent to the taking and to the authority of the court to proceed to fix compensation therefor, but it does not preclude the defendant from presenting evidence as to the amount of compensation due him or in sharing the award of distribution. See subdivision (e); Form 28.

While under Rule 4(f) the territorial limits of a summons are normally the territorial limits of the state in which the district court is held, the territorial limits for personal service of a notice under Rule 71A(d)(3) are those of the nation. This extension of process is here proper since the aim of the condemnation proceeding is not to enforce any personal liability and the property owner is helped, not imposed upon, by the best type of service possible. If personal service cannot be made either because the defendant's whereabouts cannot be ascertained, or, if ascertained, the defendant cannot be personally served, as where he resides in a foreign country such as Canada or Mexico, then service by publication is proper. The provisions for this type of service are set forth in the rule and are in no way governed by § 118 [now § 1655] of this title.

Note to Subdivision (e). Departing from the scheme of Rule 12, subdivision (e) requires all defenses and objections to be presented in an answer and does not authorize a preliminary motion. There is little need for the latter in condemnation proceedings. The general standard of pleading is governed by other rules, particularly Rule 8, and this subdivision (e) merely prescribes what matters the answer should set forth. Merely by appearing in the action a defendant can receive notice of all proceedings affecting him. And without the necessity of answering a defendant may present evidence as to the amount of compensation due him, and he may share in the distribution of the award. See also subdivision (d)(2); Form 28.

Note to Subdivision (f). Due to the number of persons who may be interested in the property to be condemned, there is a likelihood that the plaintiff will need to amend his complaint, perhaps many times, to add new parties or state new issues. This subdivision recognizes that fact and does not burden the court with applications by the plaintiff for leave to amend. At the same time all defendants are adequately protected; and their need to amend the answer is adequately protected by Rule 15, which is applicable by virtue of subdivision (a) of this Rule 71A.

Note to Subdivision (g). A condemnation action is a proceeding in rem. Commencement of the action as against a defendant by virtue of his joinder pursuant to subdivision (c)(2) is the point of cut-off and there is no mandatory requirement for substitution because of a subsequent change of interest, although the court is given ample power to require substitution. Rule 25 is inconsistent with subdivision (g) and hence inapplicable. Accordingly, the time periods of Rule 25 do not govern to require dismissal nor to prevent substitution.

Note to Subdivision (h). This subdivision prescribes the method for determining the issue of just compensation in cases involving the federal power of eminent domain. The method of jury trial provided by subdivision (h) will normally apply in cases involving the state power by virtue of subdivision (k).

Congress has specially constituted a tribunal for the trial of the issue of just compensation in two instances: condemnation under the Tennessee Valley Authority Act; and condemnation in the District of Columbia. These tribunals are retained for reasons set forth in the General Statement: 3. Adjustment of Rule to Statutory Provisions, supra. Subdivision (h) also has prospective application so that if Congress should create another special tribunal, that tribunal will determine the issue of just compensation. Subject to these exceptions the general method of trial of that issue is to be by jury if any party demands it, otherwise that issue, as well as all other issues, are to be tried by the court.

As to the TVA procedure that is continued, § 831x of Title 16 requires that three commissioners be appointed to fix the compensation; that exceptions to their award are to be heard by three district judges (unless the parties stipulate for a lesser number) and that the district judges try the question de novo; that an appeal to the circuit court of appeals may be taken within 30 days from the filing of the decision of the district judges; and that the circuit court of appeals shall on the record fix compensation "without regard to the awards of findings theretofore made by the commissioners or the district judges." The mode of fixing compensation in the District of Columbia, which is also continued, is prescribed in former §§ 361 to 386 of Title 40. Under former § 371 the court is required in all cases to order the selection of a jury of five from among not less than 20 names, drawn "from the special box provided by law." They must have the usual qualifications of jurors and in addition must be freeholders of the District, and not in the service of the United States or the District. A special oath is administered to the chosen jurors. The trial proceeds in the ordinary way, except that the jury is allowed to separate after they have begun to consider their verdict.

There is no constitutional right to jury trial in a condemnation proceeding. *Bauman v. Ross,* 1897, 17 S.Ct. 966, 167 U.S. 548, 42 L.Ed. 270. See, also, Hines, *Does the Seventh Amendment to the Constitution of the United States Require Jury Trials in all Condemnation Proceedings?,* 1925, 11 Va.L.Rev. 505; Blair, *Federal Condemnation Proceedings and the Seventh Amendment,* 1927, 41 Harv.L.Rev. 29; 3 *Moore's Federal Practice,* 1938, 3007. Prior to Rule 71A, jury trial in federal condemnation proceedings was, however, enjoyed under the general conformity statute, former § 258 of Title 40, in states which provided for jury trial. See generally, 2 Lewis, *Eminent Domain,* 3d ed. 1909, §§ 509, 510; 3 Moore, op. cit. supra. Since the general conformity statute is superseded by Rule 71A, see supra under subdivision (a), and since it was believed that the rule to be substituted should likewise give a right to jury trial, subdivision (h) establishes that method as the general one for determining the issue of just compensation.

Note to Subdivision (i). Both the right of the plaintiff to dismiss by filing a notice of dismissal and the right of the court to permit a dismissal are circumscribed to the extent that where the plaintiff has acquired the title or a lesser interest or possession, viz., any property interest for which just compensation should be paid, the action may not be dismissed, without the defendant's consent, and the property owner remitted to another court, such as the Court of Claims, to recover just compensation for the property right taken. Circuity of action is thus prevented without increasing the liability of the plaintiff to pay just compensation for any interest that is taken. Freedom of dismissal is accorded, where both the condemnor and condemnee agree, up to the time of the entry of judgment vesting plaintiff with title. And power is given to the court, where the parties agree, to vacate the judgment and thus revest title in the property owner. In line with Rule 21, the court may at any time drop a defendant who has been unnecessarily or improperly joined as where it develops that he has no interest.

Note to Subdivision (j). Whatever the substantive law is concerning the necessity of making a deposit will continue to govern. For statutory provisions concerning deposit in court in condemnation proceedings by the United States, see § 258a of [former] Title 40; § 594 of Title 33; acquisition of title and possession statutes referred to in note to subdivision (a), supra. If the plaintiff is invoking the state's power of eminent domain the necessity of deposit will be governed by the state law. For discussion of such law, see 1 Nichols, Eminent Domain, 2d ed. 1917, §§ 209 to 216. For discussion of the function of deposit and the power of the court to enter judgment in cases both of deficiency and overpayment, see *United States v. Miller,* 1943, 63 S.Ct. 276, 317 U.S. 369, 87 L.Ed. 336, 147 A.L.R. 55, rehearing denied 63 S.Ct. 557, 318 U.S. 798, 87 L.Ed. 1162 (judgment in favor of plaintiff for overpayment ordered).

The court is to make distribution of the deposit as promptly as the facts of the case warrant. See also subdivision (c)(2).

Note to Subdivision (k). While the overwhelming number of cases that will be brought in the federal courts under this rule will be actions involving the federal power of eminent domain, a small percentage of cases may be instituted in the federal court or removed thereto on the basis of diversity or alienage which will involve the power of eminent domain under the law of a state. See *Boom Co. v. Patterson,* 1878, 98 U.S. 403, 25 L.Ed. 206; *Searl v. School District No. 2,* 1888, 8 S.Ct. 460, 124 U.S. 197, 31 L.Ed. 415; *Madisonville Traction Co. v. Saint Bernard Mining Co.,* 1905, 25 S.Ct. 251, 196 U.S. 239, 49 L.Ed. 462. In the Madisonville case, and in cases cited therein, it has been held that condemnation actions brought by state corporations in the exercise of a power delegated by the state might be governed by procedure prescribed by the laws of the United States, whether the cases were begun in or removed to the federal court. See, also, *Franzen v. Chicago, M. & St. P. Ry. Co.,* C.C.A.7th, 1921, 278 F. 370, 372.

Any condition affecting the substantial right of a litigant attached by state law is to be observed and enforced, such as making a deposit in court where the power of eminent domain is conditioned upon so doing. (See also subdivision (j). Subject to this qualification, subdivision (k) provides that in cases involving the state power of eminent domain, the practice prescribed by other subdivisions of Rule 71A shall govern.

Note to Subdivision (*l*). Since the condemnor will normally be the prevailing party and since he should not recover his costs against the property owner, Rule 54(d), which provides generally that costs shall go to the prevailing party, is made inapplicable. Without attempting to state what the rule on costs is, the effect of subdivision (*l*) is that costs shall be awarded in accordance with the law that has developed in condemnation cases. This has been summarized as follows: "Costs of condemnation proceedings are not assessable against the condemnee, unless by stipulation he agrees to assume some or all of them. Such normal expenses of the proceeding as bills for publication of notice, commissioners' fees, the cost of transporting commissioners and jurors to take a view, fees for attorneys to represent defendants who have failed to answer, and witness' fees, are properly charged to the government, though not taxed as costs. Similarly, if it is necessary that a conveyance be executed by a commissioner, the United States pay his fees and those for recording the deed. However, the distribution of the award is a matter in which the United States has no legal interest. Expenses incurred in ascertaining the identity of distributees and deciding between conflicting claimants are properly chargeable against the award, not against the United States, although United States attorneys are expected to aid the court in such matters as amici curiae." Lands Division Manual 861. For other discussion and citation, see *Grand River Dam Authority v. Jarvis,* C.C.A.10th, 1942, 124 F.2d 914. Costs may not be taxed against the United States except to the extent permitted by law. *United States v. 125.71 Acres of Land in Loyalhanna Tp., Westmoreland County, Pa.,* D.C.Pa.1944, 54 F.Supp. 193; Lands Division Manual 859. Even if it were thought desirable to allow the property owner's costs to be taxed against the United States, this is a matter for legislation and not court rule.

1963 Amendment

This amendment conforms to the amendment of Rule 4(f).

1985 Amendment

Rule 71A(h) provides that except when Congress has provided otherwise, the issue of just compensation in a condemnation case may be tried by a jury if one of the parties so demands, unless the court in its discretion orders the issue determined by a commission of three persons. In 1980, the Comptroller General of the United States in a Report to Congress recommended that use of the commission procedure should be encouraged in order to improve and expedite the trial of condemnation cases. The Report noted that long delays were being caused in many districts by such factors as crowded dockets, the precedence given criminal cases, the low priority accorded condemnation matters, and the high turnover of Assistant United States Attorneys. The Report concluded that revising Rule 71A to make the use of the commission procedure more attractive might alleviate the situation.

Accordingly, Rule 71A(h) is being amended in a number of respects designed to assure the quality and utility of a Rule 71A commission. First, the amended Rule will give the court discretion to appoint, in addition to the three members of a commission, up to two additional persons as alternate commissioners who would hear the case and be available, at any time up to the filing of the decision by the three-member commission, to replace any commissioner who becomes unable or disqualified to continue. The discretion to appoint alternate commissioners can be particularly useful in protracted cases, avoiding expensive retrials that have been required in some cases because of the death or disability of a commissioner. Prior to replacing a commissioner an alternate would not be present at, or participate in, the commission's deliberations.

Second, the amended Rule requires the court, before appointment, to advise the parties of the identity and qualifications of each prospective commissioner and alternate. The court then may authorize the examination of prospective appointees by the parties and each party has the right to challenge for cause. The objective is to insure that unbiased and competent commissioners are appointed.

The amended Rule does not prescribe a qualification standard for appointment to a commission, although it is understood that only persons possessing background and ability to appraise real estate valuation testimony and to award fair and just compensation on the basis thereof would be appointed. In most situations the chairperson should be a lawyer and all members should have some background qualifying them to weigh proof of value in the real estate field and, when possible, in the particular real estate market embracing the land in question.

The amended Rule should give litigants greater confidence in the commission procedure by affording them certain rights to participate in the appointment of commission members that are roughly comparable to the practice with regard to jury selection. This is accomplished by giving the court permission to allow the parties to examine prospective commissioners and by recognizing the right of each party to object to the appointment of any person for cause.

1987 Amendment

The amendments are technical. No substantive change is intended.

1988 Amendment

The amendment is technical. No substantive change is intended.

1993 Amendments

The references to the subdivisions of Rule 4 are deleted in light of the revision of that rule.

2003 Amendments

The references to specific subdivisions of Rule 53 are deleted or revised to reflect amendments of Rule 53.

2007 Amendments

The language of Rule 71A has been amended as part of the general restyling of the Civil Rules to make them more easily understood and to make style and terminology consistent throughout the rules. These changes are intended to be stylistic only.

Former Rule 71A has been redesignated as Rule 71.1 to conform to the designations used for all other rules added with the original numbering system.

Rule 71.1(e) allows a defendant to appear without answering. Former form 28 (now form 60) includes information about this right in the Rule 71.1(d)(2) notice. It is useful to confirm this practice in the rule.

The information that identifies the attorney is changed to include telephone number and electronic-mail address, in line with similar amendments to Rules 11(a) and 26(g)(1).

CROSS REFERENCES

Jurisdiction and venue in condemnation proceedings, see 28 USCA §§ 1358 and 1403.

Reclamation projects, compensation for rights-of-way, see 43 USCA § 945b.

Tennessee Valley Authority, procedure in condemnation proceedings, see 16 USCA § 831x.

Rule 72. Magistrate Judges: Pretrial Order

(a) Nondispositive Matters. When a pretrial matter not dispositive of a party's claim or defense is referred to a magistrate judge to hear and decide, the magistrate judge must promptly conduct the required proceedings and, when appropriate, issue a written order stating the decision. A party may serve and file objections to the order within 10 days after being served with a copy. A party may not assign as error a defect in the order not timely objected to. The district judge in the case must consider timely objections and modify or set aside any part of the order that is clearly erroneous or is contrary to law.

(b) Dispositive Motions and Prisoner Petitions.

(1) ***Findings and Recommendations.*** A magistrate judge must promptly conduct the required proceedings when assigned, without the parties' consent, to hear a pretrial matter dispositive of a claim or defense or a prisoner petition challenging the conditions of confinement. A record must be made of all evidentiary proceedings and may, at the magistrate judge's discretion, be made of any other proceedings. The magistrate judge must enter a recommended disposition, including, if appropriate, proposed findings of fact. The clerk must promptly mail a copy to each party.

(2) ***Objections.*** Within 10 days after being served with a copy of the recommended disposition, a party may serve and file specific written objections to the proposed findings and recommendations. A party may respond to another party's objections within 10 days after being served with a copy. Unless the district judge orders otherwise, the objecting party must promptly arrange for transcribing the record, or whatever portions of it the parties agree to or the magistrate judge considers sufficient.

(3) ***Resolving Objections.*** The district judge must determine de novo any part of the magistrate judge's disposition that has been properly objected to. The district judge may accept, reject, or modify the recommended disposition; receive further evidence; or return the matter to the magistrate judge with instructions.

(Former Rule 72 abrogated December 4, 1967, effective July 1, 1968; new Rule 72 adopted April 28, 1983, effective August 1, 1983; amended April 30, 1991, effective December 1, 1991; April 22, 1993, effective December 1, 1993; April 30, 2007, effective December 1, 2007.)

ADVISORY COMMITTEE NOTES

1983 Addition

Subdivision (a). This subdivision addresses court-ordered referrals of nondispositive matters under 28 U.S.C. § 636(b)(1)(A). The rule calls for a written order of the magistrate's disposition to preserve the record and facilitate review. An oral order read into the record by the magistrate will satisfy this requirement.

No specific procedures or timetables for raising objections to the magistrate's rulings on nondispositive matters are set forth in the Magistrates Act. The rule fixes a 10-day period in order to avoid uncertainty and provide uniformity that will eliminate the confusion that might arise if different periods were prescribed by local rule in different districts. It also is contemplated that a party who is successful before the magistrate will be afforded an opportunity to respond to objections raised to the magistrate's ruling.

The last sentence of subdivision (a) specifies that reconsideration of a magistrate's order, as provided for in the Magistrates Act, shall be by the district judge to whom the case is assigned. This rule does not restrict experimentation by the district courts under 28 U.S.C. § 636(b)(3) involving references of matters other than pretrial matters, such as appointment of counsel, taking of default judgments, and acceptance of jury verdicts when the judge is unavailable.

Subdivision (b). This subdivision governs court-ordered referrals of dispositive pretrial matters and prisoner petitions challenging conditions of confinement, pursuant to statutory authorization in 28 U.S.C. § 636(b)(1)(B). This rule does not extend to habeas corpus petitions, which are covered by the specific rules relating to proceedings under Sections 2254 and 2255 of Title 28.

This rule implements the statutory procedures for making objections to the magistrate's proposed findings and recommendations. The 10–day period, as specified in the statute, is subject to Rule 6(e) which provides for an additional 3–day period when service is made by mail. Although no specific provision appears in the Magistrates Act, the rule specifies a 10–day period for a party to respond to objections to the magistrate's recommendation.

Implementing the statutory requirements, the rule requires the district judge to whom the case is assigned to make a de novo determination of those portions of the report, findings, or recommendations to which timely objection is made. The term "de novo" signifies that the magistrate's findings are not protected by the clearly erroneous doctrine, but does not indicate that a second evidentiary hearing is required. See *United States v. Raddatz,* 417 [447] U.S. 667 (1980). See also Silberman, *Masters and Magistrates Part II: The American Analogue,* 50 N.Y.U. L.Rev. 1297, 1367 (1975). When no timely objection is filed, the court need only satisfy itself that there is no clear error on the face of the record in order to accept the recommendation. See *Campbell v. United States Dist. Court,* 501 F.2d 196, 206 (9th Cir.1974), cert. denied, 419 U.S. 879, quoted in House Report No. 94–1609, 94th Cong.2d Sess. (1976) at 3. Compare *Park Motor Mart, Inc. v. Ford Motor Co.,* 616 F.2d 603 (1st Cir.1980). Failure to make timely objection to the magistrate's report prior to its adoption by the district judge may constitute a waiver of appellate review of the district judge's order. *See United States v. Walters,* 638 F.2d 947 (6th Cir.1981).

1991 Amendment

This amendment is intended to eliminate a discrepancy in measuring the 10 days for serving and filing objections to a magistrate's action under subdivisions (a) and (b) of this Rule. The rule as promulgated in 1983 required objections to the magistrate's handling of nondispositive matters to be served and filed within 10 days of entry of the order, but required objections to dispositive motions to be made within 10 days of being served with a copy of the recommended disposition. Subdivision (a) is here amended to conform to subdivision (b) to avoid any confusion or technical defaults, particularly in connection with magistrate orders that rule on both dispositive and nondispositive matters.

The amendment is also intended to assure that objections to magistrate's orders that are not timely made shall not be considered. *Compare* Rule 51.

1993 Amendments

This revision is made to conform the rule to changes made by the Judicial Improvements Act of 1990.

2007 Amendments

The language of Rule 72 has been amended as part of the general restyling of the Civil Rules to make them more easily understood and to make style and terminology consistent throughout the rules. These changes are intended to be stylistic only.

HISTORICAL NOTES

Change of Name

Reference to United States magistrate or to magistrate deemed to refer to United States magistrate judge pursuant to section 321 of Pub.L. 101–650, set out as a note under section 631 of this title.

Rule 73. Magistrate Judges: Trial by Consent; Appeal

(a) Trial by Consent. When authorized under 28 U.S.C. § 636(c), a magistrate judge may, if all parties consent, conduct a civil action or proceeding, including a jury or nonjury trial. A record must be made in accordance with 28 U.S.C. § 636(c)(5).

(b) Consent Procedure.

(1) ***In General.*** When a magistrate judge has been designated to conduct civil actions or proceedings, the clerk must give the parties written notice of their opportunity to consent under 28 U.S.C. § 636(c). To signify their consent, the parties must jointly or separately file a statement consenting to the referral. A district judge or magistrate judge may be informed of a party's response to the clerk's notice only if all parties have consented to the referral.

(2) ***Reminding the Parties About Consenting.*** A district judge, magistrate judge, or other court official may remind the parties of the magistrate judge's availability, but must also advise them that they are free to withhold consent without adverse substantive consequences.

(3) ***Vacating a Referral.*** On its own for good cause—or when a party shows extraordinary circumstances—the district judge may vacate a referral to a magistrate judge under this rule.

(c) Appealing a Judgment. In accordance with 28 U.S.C. § 636(c)(3), an appeal from a judgment entered at a magistrate judge's direction may be taken to the court of appeals as would any other appeal from a district-court judgment.

(Former Rule 73 abrogated December 4, 1967, effective July 1, 1968; new Rule 73 adopted April 28, 1983, effective August 1, 1983; amended March 2, 1987, effective August 1, 1987; April 22, 1993, effective December 1, 1993; April 11, 1997, effective December 1, 1997; April 30, 2007, effective December 1, 2007.)

ADVISORY COMMITTEE NOTES

1983 Addition

Subdivision (a). This subdivision implements the broad authority of the 1979 amendments to the Magistrates Act, 28 U.S.C. § 636(c), which permit a magistrate to sit in lieu of a district judge and exercise civil jurisdiction over a case, when the parties consent. See McCabe, *The Federal Magistrate Act of 1979,* 16 Harv.J.Legis. 343, 364–79 (1979). In order to exercise this jurisdiction, a magistrate must be specially designated under 28 U.S.C. § 636(c)(1) by the district court or courts he serves. The only exception to a magistrate's exercise of civil jurisdiction, which includes the power to conduct jury and nonjury trials and decide dispositive motions, is the contempt power. A hearing on contempt is to be conducted by the district judge upon certification of the facts and an order to show cause by the magistrate. See 28 U.S.C. § 639(e). In view of 28 U.S.C. § 636(c)(1) and this rule, it is unnecessary to amend Rule 58 to provide that the decision of a magistrate is a "decision by the court" for the purposes of that rule and a "final decision of the district court" for purposes of 28 U.S.C. § 1291 governing appeals.

Subdivision (b). This subdivision implements the blind consent provision of 28 U.S.C. § 636(c)(2) and is designed to ensure that neither the judge nor the magistrate attempts to induce a party to consent to reference of a civil matter under this rule to a magistrate. See House Rep. No. 96–444, 96th Cong. 1st Sess. 8 (1979).

The rule opts for a uniform approach in implementing the consent provision by directing the clerk to notify the parties of their opportunity to elect to proceed before a magistrate and by requiring the execution and filing of a consent form or forms setting forth the election. However, flexibility at the local level is preserved in that local rules will determine how notice shall be communicated to the parties, and local rules will specify the time period within which an election must be made.

The last paragraph of subdivision (b) reiterates the provision in 28 U.S.C. § 636(c)(6) for vacating a reference to the magistrate.

Subdivision (c). Under 28 U.S.C. § 636(c)(3), the normal route of appeal from the judgment of a magistrate—the only route that will be available unless the parties otherwise agree in advance—is an appeal by the aggrieved party "directly to the appropriate United States court of appeals from the judgment of the magistrate in the same manner as an appeal from any other judgment of a district court." The quoted statutory language indicates Congress' intent that the same procedures and standards of appealability that govern appeals from district court judgments govern appeals from magistrates' judgments.

Subdivision (d). 28 U.S.C. § 636(c)(4) offers parties who consent to the exercise of civil jurisdiction by a magistrate an alternative appeal route to that provided in subdivision (c) of this rule. This optional appellate route was provided by Congress in recognition of the fact that not all civil cases warrant the same appellate treatment. In cases where the amount in controversy is not great and there are no difficult questions of law to be resolved, the parties may desire to avoid the expense and delay of appeal to the court of appeals by electing an appeal to the district judge. See McCabe, *The Federal Magistrate Act of 1979,* 16 Harv.J.Legis, 343, 388 (1979). This subdivision provides that the parties may elect the optional appeal route at the time of reference to a magistrate. To this end, the notice by the clerk under subdivision (b) of this rule shall explain the appeal option and the corollary restriction on review by the court of appeals. This approach will avoid later claims of lack of consent to the avenue of appeal. The choice of the alternative appeal route to the judge of the district court should be made by the parties in their forms of consent. Special appellate rules to govern appeals from a magistrate to a district judge appear in new Rules 74 through 76.

1987 Amendment

The amendment is technical. No substantive change is intended.

1993 Amendments

This revision is made to conform the rule to changes made by the Judicial Improvements Act of 1990. The Act requires that, when being reminded of the availability of a magistrate judge, the parties be advised that withholding of consent will have no "adverse substantive consequences." They may, however, be advised if the withholding of consent will have the adverse procedural consequence of a potential delay in trial.

1997 Amendments

The Federal Courts Improvement Act of 1996 repealed the former provisions of 28 U.S.C. § 636(c)(4) and (5) that enabled parties that had agreed to trial before a magistrate judge to agree also that appeal should be taken to the district court. Rule 73 is amended to conform to this change. Rules 74, 75, and 76 are abrogated for the same reason. The portions of Form 33 and Form 34 that referred to appeals to the district court also are deleted.

2007 Amendments

The language of Rule 73 has been amended as part of the general restyling of the Civil Rules to make them more easily understood and to make style and terminology consistent throughout the rules. These changes are intended to be stylistic only.

HISTORICAL NOTES

Change of Name

Reference to United States magistrate or to magistrate deemed to refer to United States magistrate judge pursuant to section 321 of Pub.L. 101–650, set out as a note under section 631 of this title.

Rule 74. Method of Appeal From Magistrate Judge to District Judge Under Title 28, U.S.C. § 636(c)(4) and Rule 73(d) [Abrogated]

(Former Rule 74 abrogated December 4, 1967, effective July 1, 1968; new Rule 74 adopted April 28, 1983, effective August 1, 1983; amended April 22, 1993, effective December 1, 1993; abrogated April 11, 1997, effective December 1, 1997; April 30, 2007, effective December 1, 2007.)

ADVISORY COMMITTEE NOTES

1997 Amendment

Rule 74 is abrogated for the reasons described in the Note to Rule 73.

2007 Amendment

Rule 74 was abrogated in 1997 to reflect repeal of the statute providing for appeal from a magistrate judge's judgment to the district court. The rule number is reserved for possible future use.

Rule 75. Proceedings On Appeal From Magistrate Judge to District Judge under Rule 73(d) [Abrogated]

(Former Rule 75 abrogated December 4, 1967, effective July 1, 1968; new Rule 75 adopted April 28, 1983, effective August 1, 1983; amended March 2, 1987, effective August 1, 1987; April 22, 1993, effective December 1, 1993; abrogated April 11, 1997, effective December 1, 1997; April 30, 2007, effective December 1, 2007.)

ADVISORY COMMITTEE NOTES

1997 Amendment

Rule 75 is abrogated for the reasons described in the Note to Rule 73.

2007 Amendment

Rule 75 was abrogated in 1997 to reflect repeal of the statute providing for appeal from a magistrate judge's judgment to the district court. The rule number is reserved for possible future use.

Rule 76. Judgment of the District Judge On The Appeal under Rule 73(d) and Costs [Abrogated]

(Former Rule 76 abrogated December 4, 1967, effective July 1, 1968; new Rule 76 adopted April 28, 1983, effective August 1, 1983; amended April 22, 1993, effective December 1, 1993; abrogated April 11, 1997, effective December 1, 1997; April 30, 2007, effective December 1, 2007.)

ADVISORY COMMITTEE NOTES

1997 Amendment

Rule 76 is abrogated for the reasons described in the Note to Rule 73.

2007 Amendment

Rule 76 was abrogated in 1997 to reflect repeal of the statute providing for appeal from a magistrate judge's judgment to the district court. The rule number is reserved for possible future use.

TITLE X. DISTRICT COURTS AND CLERKS: CONDUCTING BUSINESS; ISSUING ORDERS

Rule 77. Conducting Business; Clerk's Authority; Notice of an Order or Judgment

(a) When Court Is Open. Every district court is considered always open for filing any paper, issuing and returning process, making a motion, or entering an order.

(b) Place for Trial and Other Proceedings. Every trial on the merits must be conducted in open court and, so far as convenient, in a regular courtroom. Any other act or proceeding may be done or conducted by a judge in chambers, without the attendance of the clerk or other court official, and anywhere inside or outside the district. But no hearing—other than one ex parte—may be conducted outside the district unless all the affected parties consent.

(c) Clerk's Office Hours; Clerk's Orders.

(1) ***Hours.*** The clerk's office—with a clerk or deputy on duty—must be open during business hours every day except Saturdays, Sundays, and legal holidays. But a court may, by local rule or order, require that the office be open for specified hours on Saturday or a particular legal holiday other than one listed in Rule 6(a)(4)(A).

(2) ***Orders.*** Subject to the court's power to suspend, alter, or rescind the clerk's action for good cause, the clerk may:

(A) issue process;

(B) enter a default;

(C) enter a default judgment under Rule 55(b)(1); and

(D) act on any other matter that does not require the court's action.

(d) Serving Notice of an Order or Judgment.

(1) ***Service.*** Immediately after entering an order or judgment, the clerk must serve notice of the entry, as provided in Rule 5(b), on each party who is not in default for failing to appear. The clerk must record the service on

the docket. A party also may serve notice of the entry as provided in Rule 5(b).

(2) ***Time to Appeal Not Affected by Lack of Notice.*** Lack of notice of the entry does not affect the time for appeal or relieve—or authorize the court to relieve—a party for failing to appeal within the time allowed, except as allowed by Federal Rule of Appellate Procedure (4)(a).

(Amended December 27, 1946, effective March 19, 1948; January 21, 1963, effective July 1, 1963; December 4, 1967, effective July 1, 1968; March 1, 1971, effective July 1, 1971; March 2, 1987, effective August 1, 1987; April 30, 1991, effective December 1, 1991; April 23, 2001, effective December 1, 2001; April 30, 2007, effective December 1, 2007.)

ADVISORY COMMITTEE NOTES

1937 Adoption

This rule states the substance of U.S.C., Title 28, § 452, formerly § 13 (Courts open as courts of admiralty and equity). Compare [former] Equity Rules 1 (District Court Always Open For Certain Purposes—Orders at Chambers), 2 (Clerk's Office Always Open, Except, Etc.), 4 (Notice of Orders), and 5 (Motions Grantable of Course by Clerk).

1946 Amendment

Note. Rule 77(d) has been amended to avoid such situations as the one arising in *Hill v. Hawes*, 1944, 64 S.Ct. 334, 320 U.S. 520, 88 L.Ed. 283. In that case, an action instituted in the District Court for the District of Columbia, the clerk failed to give notice of the entry of a judgment for defendant as required by Rule 77(d). The time for taking an appeal then was 20 days under Rule 10 of the Court of Appeals (later enlarged by amendment to thirty days), and due to lack of notice of the entry of judgment the plaintiff failed to file his notice of appeal within the prescribed time. On this basis the trial court vacated the original judgment and then re-entered it, whereupon notice of appeal was filed. The Court of Appeals dismissed the appeal as taken too late. The Supreme Court, however, held that although rule 77(d) did not purport to attach any consequence to the clerk's failure to give notice as specified, the terms of the rule were such that the appellant was entitled to rely on it, and the trial court in such a case, in the exercise of a sound discretion, could vacate the former judgment and enter a new one, so that the appeal would be within the allowed time.

Because of Rule 6(c), which abolished the old rule that the expiration of the term ends a court's power over its judgment, the effect of the decision in *Hill v. Hawes* is to give the district court power, in its discretion and without time limit, and long after the term may have expired, to vacate a judgment and reenter it for the purpose of reviving the right of appeal. This seriously affects the finality of judgments. See also proposed Rule 6(c) and Note; proposed Rule 60(b) and Note; and proposed Rule 73(a) and Note.

Rule 77(d) as amended makes it clear that notification by the clerk of the entry of a judgment has nothing to do with the starting of the time for appeal; that time starts to run from the date of entry of judgment and not from the date of notice of the entry. Notification by the clerk is merely for the convenience of litigants. And lack of such notification in itself has no effect upon the time for appeal; but in considering an application for extension of time for appeal as provided in Rule 73(a), the court may take into account, as one of the factors affecting its decision, whether the clerk failed to give notice as provided in Rule 77(d) or the party failed to receive the clerk's notice. It need not, however, extend the time for appeal merely because the clerk's notice was not sent or received. It would, therefore, be entirely unsafe for a party to rely on absence of notice from the clerk of the entry of a judgment, or to rely on the adverse party's failure to serve notice of the entry of a judgment. Any party may, of course, serve timely notice of the entry of a judgment upon the adverse party and thus preclude a successful application, under Rule 73(a), for the extension of the time for appeal.

1963 Amendment

Subdivision (c). The amendment authorizes closing of the clerk's office on Saturday as far as civil business is concerned. However, a district court may require its clerk's office to remain open for specified hours on Saturdays or "legal holidays" other than those enumerated ("Legal holiday" is defined in Rule 6(a), as amended.) The clerk's offices of many district courts have customarily remained open on some of the days appointed as holidays by State law. This practice could be continued by local rule or order.

Subdivision (d). This amendment conforms to the amendment of Rule 5(a). See the Advisory Committee's Note to that amendment.

1968 Amendment

The provisions of Rule 73(a) are incorporated in Rule 4(a) of the Federal Rules of Appellate Procedure.

1971 Amendment

The amendment adds Columbus Day to the list of legal holidays. See the Note accompanying the amendment of Rule 6(a).

1987 Amendment

The amendments are technical. No substantive change is intended. The Birthday of Martin Luther King, Jr. is added to the list of national holidays in Rule 77.

1991 Amendment

This revision is a companion to the concurrent amendment to Rule 4 of the Federal Rules of Appellate Procedure. The purpose of the revisions is to permit district courts to ease strict sanctions now imposed on appellants whose notices of appeal are filed late because of their failure to receive notice of entry of a judgment. See, e.g. *Tucker v. Commonwealth Land Title Ins. Co.*, 800 F.2d 1054 (11th Cir.1986); *Ashby Enterprises, Ltd. v. Weitzman, Dym & Associates*, 780 F.2d 1043 (D.C.Cir.1986); *In re OPM Leasing Services, Inc.*, 769 F.2d 911 (2d Cir.1985); *Spika v. Village of Lombard, Ill.*, 763 F.2d 282 (7th Cir.1985); *Hall v. Community Mental Health Center of Beaver County*, 772 F.2d 42 (3d Cir.1985); *Wilson v. Atwood v. Stark*, 725 F.2d 255 (5th Cir. en banc), cert. dismissed, 105 S.Ct. 17 (1984); *Case v. BASF Wyandotte*, 727 F.2d 1034 (Fed.Cir.1984), cert. denied, 105 S.Ct. 386 (1984); *Hensley v. Chesapeake & Ohio R.R. Co.*, 651 F.2d 226 (4th

Cir.1981); *Buckeye Cellulose Corp. v. Electric Construction Co.*, 569 F.2d 1036 (8th Cir.1978).

Failure to receive notice may have increased in frequency with the growth in the caseload in the clerks' offices. The present strict rule imposes a duty on counsel to maintain contact with the court while a case is under submission. Such contact is more difficult to maintain if counsel is outside the district, as is increasingly common, and can be a burden to the court as well as counsel.

The effect of the revisions is to place a burden on prevailing parties who desire certainty that the time for appeal is running. Such parties can take the initiative to assure that their adversaries receive effective notice. An appropriate procedure for such notice is provided in Rule 5.

The revised rule lightens the responsibility but not the workload of the clerk's offices, for the duty of that office to give notice of entry of judgment must be maintained.

2001 Amendments

Rule 77(d) is amended to reflect changes in Rule 5(b). A few courts have experimented with serving Rule 77(d) notices by electronic means on parties who consent to this procedure. The success of these experiments warrants express authorization. Because service is made in the manner provided in Rule 5(b), party consent is required for service by electronic or other means described in Rule 5(b)(2)(D). The same provision is made for a party who wishes to ensure actual communication of the Rule 77(d) notice by also serving notice.

Changes Made After Publication and Comments

Rule 77(d) was amended to correct an oversight in the published version. The clerk is to note "service," not "mailing," on the docket.

2007 Amendments

The language of Rule 77 has been amended as part of the general restyling of the Civil Rules to make them more easily understood and to make style and terminology consistent throughout the rules. These changes are intended to be stylistic only.

HISTORICAL NOTES

References in Text

The Federal Rules of Appellate Procedure, referred to in subd. (d), are set out in Title 28, U.S.C.A., Federal Rules of Appellate Procedure.

CROSS REFERENCES

Books and records kept by clerk and entries therein, see Fed.Rules Civ.Proc. Rule 79, 28 USCA.

Courts always open, see Fed.Rules Cr.Proc. Rule 56, 18 USCA and 28 USCA § 452.

Entry of default judgment by clerk, see Fed.Rules Civ. Proc. Rule 55, 28 USCA.

Execution, see Fed.Rules Civ.Proc. Rule 69, 28 USCA.

Service of papers on attorney or party, see Fed.Rules Civ.Proc. Rule 5, 28 USCA.

Rule 78. Hearing Motions; Submission on Briefs

(a) Providing a Regular Schedule for Oral Hearings. A court may establish regular times and places for oral hearings on motions.

(b) Providing for Submission on Briefs. By rule or order, the court may provide for submitting and determining motions on briefs, without oral hearings.

(Amended March 2, 1987, effective August 1, 1987; April 30, 2007, effective December 1, 2007.)

ADVISORY COMMITTEE NOTES

1937 Adoption

Compare [former] Equity Rule 6 (Motion Day) with the first paragraph of this rule. The second paragraph authorizes a procedure found helpful for the expedition of business in some of the Federal and State courts. See Rule 43(e) of these rules dealing with evidence on motions. Compare *Civil Practice Rules of the Municipal Court of Chicago* (1935), Rules 269, 270, 271.

1987 Amendment

The amendment is technical. No substantive change is intended.

2007 Amendments

The language of Rule 78 has been amended as part of the general restyling of the Civil Rules to make them more easily understood and to make style and terminology consistent throughout the rules. These changes are intended to be stylistic only.

Rule 16 has superseded any need for the provision in former Rule 78 for orders for the advancement, conduct, and hearing of actions.

CROSS REFERENCES

Local rules not to be inconsistent with these rules, see Fed.Rules Civ.Proc. Rule 83, 28 USCA.

Motions, see Fed.Rules Civ.Proc. Rule 45, 28 USCA.

Motions and other papers, see Fed.Rules Civ.Proc. Rule 7, 28 USCA.

Service of affidavits in support of and in opposition to motions; timing, see Fed.Rules Civ.Proc. Rule 6, 28 USCA.

Use of affidavits on motions, see Fed.Rules Civ.Proc. Rule 43, 28 USCA.

Rule 79. Records Kept by the Clerk

(a) Civil Docket.

(1) ***In General.*** The clerk must keep a record known as the "civil docket" in the form and manner prescribed by the Director of the Administrative Office of the United States Courts with the approval of the Judicial Conference of the United States. The clerk must enter each civil action in the docket. Actions

must be assigned consecutive file numbers, which must be noted in the docket where the first entry of the action is made.

(2) ***Items to be Entered.*** The following items must be marked with the file number and entered chronologically in the docket:

(A) papers filed with the clerk;

(B) process issued, and proofs of service or other returns showing execution; and

(C) appearances, orders, verdicts, and judgments.

(3) ***Contents of Entries; Jury Trial Demanded.*** Each entry must briefly show the nature of the paper filed or writ issued, the substance of each proof of service or other return, and the substance and date of entry of each order and judgment. When a jury trial has been properly demanded or ordered, the clerk must enter the word "jury" in the docket.

(b) Civil Judgments and Orders. The clerk must keep a copy of every final judgment and appealable order; of every order affecting title to or a lien on real or personal property; and of any other order that the court directs to be kept. The clerk must keep these in the form and manner prescribed by the Director of the Administrative Office of the United States Courts with the approval of the Judicial Conference of the United States.

(c) Indexes; Calendars. Under the court's direction, the clerk must:

(1) keep indexes of the docket and of the judgments and orders described in Rule 79(b); and

(2) prepare calendars of all actions ready for trial, distinguishing jury trials from nonjury trials.

(d) Other Records. The clerk must keep any other records required by the Director of the Administrative Office of the United States Courts with the approval of the Judicial Conference of the United States.

(Amended December 27, 1946, effective March 19, 1948; December 29, 1948, effective October 20, 1949; January 21, 1963, effective July 1, 1963; April 30, 2007, effective December 1, 2007.)

ADVISORY COMMITTEE NOTES

1937 Adoption

Compare [former] Equity Rule 3 (Books Kept by Clerk and Entries Therein). In connection with this rule, see also the following statutes of the United States:

U.S.C., Title 5 former:

§ 301 [See Title 28, § 526] (Officials for investigation of official acts, records and accounts of marshals, attorneys, clerks of courts, United States commissioners, referees and trustees)

§ 318 [former] (Accounts of district attorneys)

U.S.C., Title 28 former:

§ 556 [former] (Clerks of district courts; books open to inspection)

§ 567 [now 751] (Same; accounts)

§ 568 [now 751] (Same; reports and accounts of moneys received; dockets)

§ 813 [former] (Indices of judgment debtors to be kept by clerks)

And see "Instructions to United States Attorneys, Marshals, Clerks and Commissioners" issued by the Attorney General of the United States.

1946 Amendment

Note. Subdivision (a). The amendment substitutes the Director of the Administrative Office of the United States Courts, acting subject to the approval of the Judicial Conference of Senior Circuit Judges, in the place of the Attorney General as a consequence of and in accordance with the provisions of the act establishing the Administrative Office and transferring functions thereto. Act of August 7, 1939, c. 501, §§ 1 to 7, 53 Stat. 1223, 28 U.S.C.A. §§ 601 to 610, formerly §§ 444 to 450.

Subdivision (b). The change in this subdivision does not alter the nature of the judgments and orders to be recorded in permanent form but it does away with the express requirement that they be recorded in a book. This merely gives latitude for the preservation of court records in other than book form, if that shall seem advisable, and permits with the approval of the Judicial Conference the adoption of such modern, space-saving methods as microphotography. See *Proposed Improvements in the Administration of the Offices of Clerks of United States District Courts,* prepared by the Bureau of the Budget, 1941, 38–42. See also Rule 55, Federal Rules of Criminal Procedure.

Subdivision (c). The words "Separate and" have been deleted as unduly rigid. There is no sufficient reason for requiring that the indices in all cases be separate; on the contrary, the requirement frequently increases the labor of persons searching the records as well as the labor of the clerk's force preparing them. The matter should be left to administrative discretion.

The other changes in the subdivision merely conform with those made in subdivision (b) of the rule.

Subdivision (d). Subdivision (d) is a new provision enabling the Administrative Office, with the approval of the Judicial Conference, to carry out any improvements in clerical procedure with respect to books and records which may be deemed advisable. See report cited in Note to subdivision (b), supra.

1948 Amendment

The amendment effective October 1949, substituted the name, "Judicial Conference of the United States," for "Judicial Conference of Senior Circuit Judges," in the first sentence of subdivision (a), and in subdivisions (b) and (d).

1963 Amendment

The terminology is clarified without any change of the prescribed practice. See amended Rule 58, and the Advisory Committee's Note thereto.

2007 Amendments

The language of Rule 79 has been amended as part of the general restyling of the Civil Rules to make them more easily understood and to make style and terminology consistent throughout the rules. These changes are intended to be stylistic only.

CROSS REFERENCES

Entry of judgment, see Fed.Rules Civ.Proc. Rule 58, 28 USCA.

Examination of court dockets by Director of Administrative Office of the United States Court, see 28 USCA § 604.

Filing of pleading and other papers with clerk or judge, see Fed.Rules Civ.Proc. Rule 5, 28 USCA.

Lien of judgment, see 28 USCA § 1962.

Notice of entry of judgment or order, see Fed.Rules Civ.Proc. Rule 77, 28 USCA.

Notice of entry of orders by clerk, see Fed.Rules Cr.Proc. Rule 49, 18 USCA.

Obsolete papers disposed of in accordance with rules of Judicial Conference of the United States, see 28 USCA § 457.

Records, see Fed.Rules Cr.Proc. Rule 55, 18 USCA.

Registration of judgments for money or property in other districts, see 28 USCA § 1963.

Return of execution of process, see Fed.Rules Civ.Proc. Rule 4, 28 USCA.

Survey and recommendation of Judicial Conference of the United States, see 28 USCA § 331.

Time for serving demand for jury trial, see Fed.Rules Civ.Proc. Rule 38, 28 USCA.

Rule 80. Stenographic Transcript as Evidence

If stenographically reported testimony at a hearing or trial is admissible in evidence at a later trial, the testimony may be proved by a transcript certified by the person who reported it.

(Amended December 27, 1946, effective March 19, 1948; April 30, 2007, effective December 1, 2007.)

ADVISORY COMMITTEE NOTES

1937 Adoption

Note to Subdivision (a). This follows substantially [former] Equity Rule 50 (Stenographer— Appointment— Fees). [This subdivision was abrogated. See amendment note of Advisory Committee below.]

Note to Subdivision (b). See *Reports of Conferences of Senior Circuit Judges with the Chief Justice of the United States* (1936), 22 A.B.A.J. 818, 819; (1937), 24 A.B.A.J. 75, 77. [This subdivision was abrogated. See amendment note of Advisory Committee below.]

Note to Subdivision (c). Compare Iowa Code (1935) § 11353.

1946 Amendment

Note. Subdivisions (a) and (b) of Rule 80 have been abrogated because of Public Law 222, 78th Cong., c. 3, 2d Sess., approved Jan. 20, 1944, 28 U.S.C. §§ 550, 604, 753, 1915, 1920, formerly § 9a, providing for the appointment of official stenographers for each district court, prescribing their duties, providing for the furnishing of transcripts, the taxation of the fees therefor as costs, and other related matters. This statute has now been implemented by Congressional appropriation available for the fiscal year beginning July 1, 1945.

Subdivision (c) of Rule 80 (Stenographic Report or Transcript as Evidence) has been retained unchanged.

2007 Amendments

The language of Rule 80 has been amended as part of the general restyling of the Civil Rules to make them more easily understood and to make style and terminology consistent throughout the rules. These changes are intended to be stylistic only.

CROSS REFERENCES

Appointment and compensation of court reporters; fees for transcripts, see 28 USCA § 753.

Fees of court reporter for stenographic transcript taxable as costs, see 28 USCA § 1920.

Payment by United States for fees for transcripts and printing record on appeal furnished persons proceeding in forma pauperis, see 28 USCA § 1915.

Proof of official record, see Fed.Rules Civ.Proc. Rule 44, 28 USCA.

TITLE XI. GENERAL PROVISIONS

Rule 81. Applicability of the Rules in General; Removed Actions

(a) Applicability to Particular Proceedings.

(1) ***Prize Proceedings.*** These rules do not apply to prize proceedings in admiralty governed by 10 U.S.C. §§ 7651–7681.

(2) ***Bankruptcy.*** These rules apply to bankruptcy proceedings to the extent provided by the Federal Rules of Bankruptcy Procedure.

(3) ***Citizenship.*** These rules apply to proceedings for admission to citizenship to the extent that the practice in those proceedings is not specified in federal statutes and has previously conformed to the practice in civil actions. The provisions of 8 U.S.C. § 1451 for service by publication and for answer apply in proceedings to cancel citizenship certificates.

(4) ***Special Writs.*** These rules apply to proceedings for habeas corpus and for quo warranto to the extent that the practice in those proceedings:

(A) is not specified in a federal statute, the Rules Governing Section 2254 Cases, or the Rules Governing Section 2255 Cases; and

(B) has previously conformed to the practice in civil actions.

(5) ***Proceedings Involving a Subpoena.*** These rules apply to proceedings to compel testimony or the production of documents through a subpoena issued by a United States officer or agency under a federal statute, except as otherwise provided by statute, by local rule, or by court order in the proceedings.

(6) ***Other Proceedings.*** These rules, to the extent applicable, govern proceedings under the following laws, except as these laws provide other procedures:

(A) 7 U.S.C. §§ 292, 499g(c), for reviewing an order of the Secretary of Agriculture;

(B) 9 U.S.C., relating to arbitration;

(C) 15 U.S.C. § 522, for reviewing an order of the Secretary of the Interior;

(D) 15 U.S.C. § 715d(c), for reviewing an order denying a certificate of clearance;

(E) 29 U.S.C. §§ 159, 160, for enforcing an order of the National Labor Relations Board;

(F) 33 U.S.C. §§ 918, 921, for enforcing or reviewing a compensation order under the Longshore and Harbor Workers' Compensation Act; and

(G) 45 U.S.C. § 159, for reviewing an arbitration award in a railway-labor dispute.

(b) Scire Facias and Mandamus. The writs of scire facias and mandamus are abolished. Relief previously available through them may be obtained by appropriate action or motion under these rules.

(c) Removed Actions.

(1) ***Applicability.*** These rules apply to a civil action after it is removed from a state court.

(2) ***Further Pleading.*** After removal, repleading is unnecessary unless the court orders it. A defendant who did not answer before removal must answer or present other defenses or objections under these rules within the longest of these periods:

(A) 20 days after receiving—through service or otherwise—a copy of the initial pleading stating the claim for relief;

(B) 20 days after being served with the summons for an initial pleading on file at the time of service; or

(C) 5 days after the notice of removal is filed.

(3) ***Demand for a Jury Trial.***

(A) *As Affected by State Law.* A party who, before removal, expressly demanded a jury trial in accordance with state law need not renew the demand after removal. If the state law did not require an express demand for a jury trial, a party need not make one after removal unless the court orders the parties to do so within a specified time. The court must so order at a party's request and may so order on its own. A party who fails to make a demand when so ordered waives a jury trial.

(B) *Under Rule 38.* If all necessary pleadings have been served at the time of removal, a party entitled to a jury trial under Rule 38 must be given one if the party serves a demand within 10 days after:

(i) it files a notice of removal; or

(ii) it is served with a notice of removal filed by another party.

(d) Law Applicable.

(1) ***State Law.*** When these rules refer to state law, the term "law" includes the state's statutes and the state's judicial decisions.

(2) ***District of Columbia.*** The term "state" includes, where appropriate, the District of Columbia. When these rules provide for state law to apply, in the District Court for the District of Columbia:

(A) the law applied in the District governs; and

(B) the term "federal statute" includes any Act of Congress that applies locally to the District.

(Amended December 28, 1939, effective April 3, 1941; December 27, 1946, effective March 19, 1948; December 29, 1948, effective October 20, 1949; April 30, 1951, effective August 1, 1951; January 21, 1963, effective July 1, 1963; February 28, 1966, effective July 1, 1966; December 4, 1967, effective July 1, 1968; March 1, 1971, effective July 1, 1971; March 2, 1987, effective August 1, 1987; April 23, 2001, effective December 1, 2001; April 29, 2002, effective December 1, 2002; April 30, 2007, effective December 1, 2007.)

ADVISORY COMMITTEE NOTES

1937 Adoption

Note to Subdivision (a). Paragraph (1): Compare the enabling act, Act of June 19, 1934, U.S.C., Title 28, § 2072, formerly § 723b (Rules in actions at law; Supreme Court authorized to make) and § 2072, formerly § 723c (Union of equity and action at law rules; power of Supreme Court). For the application of these rules in bankruptcy and copyright proceedings, see Orders xxxvi and xxxvii in Bankruptcy and Rule 1 of Rules of Practice and Procedure under § 25 of the copyright act, Act of March 4, 1909, U.S.C., Title 17, former § 25 [see 412, 501 et seq.] (Infringement and rules of procedure).

For examples of statutes which are preserved by paragraph (2) see: U.S.C., Title 8, [former] ch. 9 (Naturalization); Title 28, former ch. 14 [now 153] (Habeas corpus); Title 28, former §§ 377a to 377c [now D.C.Code, Title 16 § 3501 et seq.] (Quo warranto); and such forfeiture statutes as U.S.C., Title 7, former § 116 (Misbranded seeds, confiscation), and Title 21, § 334(b), formerly § 14 (Pure Food and Drug Act—condemnation of adulterated or misbranded Food; procedure). See also *443 Cans of Frozen Eggs Product v. U.S.*, 1912, 33 S.Ct. 50, 226 U.S. 172, 57 L.Ed. 174.

For examples of statutes which under paragraph (7) will continue to govern procedure in condemnation cases, see U.S.C. [former] Title 40, [former] § 258 (Condemnation of realty for sites for public building, etc., procedure); U.S.C., Title 16, § 831x (Condemnation by Tennessee Valley Authority); U.S.C., [former] Title 40, § 120 (Acquisition of lands for public use in District of Columbia); [former] Title 40, ch. 7 [now D.C.Code, Title 16, § 1301 et seq.] (Acquisition of lands in District of Columbia for use of United States; condemnation).

Note to Subdivision (b). Some statutes which will be affected by this subdivision are;

U.S.C., Title 7:
- § 222 (Federal Trade Commission powers adopted for enforcement of Stockyards Act) (By reference to Title 15, § 49)

U.S.C., Title 15:
- § 49 (Enforcement of Federal Trade Commission orders and antitrust laws)
- § 77t(c) (Enforcement of Securities and Exchange Commission orders and Securities Act of 1933)
- § 78u(f) (Same; Securities Exchange Act of 1934)
- § 79r(g) (Same; Public Utility Holding Company Act of 1935)

U.S.C., Title 16:
- § 820 (Proceedings in equity for revocation or to prevent violations of license of Federal Power Commission licensee)
- § 825m(b) (Mandamus to compel compliance with Federal Water Power Act, etc.)

U.S.C., Title 19:
- § 1333(c) (Mandamus to compel compliance with orders of Tariff Commission, etc.)

U.S.C., Title 28, former:
- § 377 [now 1651] (Power to issue writs)
- § 572 [now 1923] (Fees, attorneys, solicitors and proctors)
- § 778 [former] (Death of parties; substitution of executor or administrator). Compare Rule 25(a) (Substitution of parties; death), and the note thereto.

U.S.C., Title 33:
- § 495 (Removal of bridges over navigable waters)

U.S.C., Title 45:
- § 88 (Mandamus against Union Pacific Railroad Company)
- § 153(p) (Mandamus to enforce orders of Adjustment Board under Railway Labor Act)
- § 185 (Same; National Air Transport Adjustment Board) (By reference to § 153)

U.S.C., Title 47:
- § 11 (Powers of Federal Communications Commission)
- § 401(a) (Enforcement of Federal Communications Act and orders of Commission)
- § 406 (Same; Compelling furnishing of facilities; mandamus)

U.S.C., Title 49:
- § 19a(*l*) [now 11703] (Mandamus to compel compliance with Interstate Commerce Act)
- § 20(9) [now 11703] (Jurisdiction to compel compliance with interstate commerce laws by mandamus)

For comparable provisions in state practice see Smith-Hurd Ill.Stats.c. 110, § 179 (1937); Calif.Code Civ.Proc. (Deering, 1937) § 802.

Note to Subdivision (c). Such statutes as the following dealing with the removal of actions are substantially continued and made subject to these rules:

U.S.C., Title 28 former:
- § 71 [now 1441, 1445, 1447] (Removal of suits from state courts)
- § 72 [now 1446, 1447] (Same; procedure)
- § 73 [former] (Same; suits under grants of land from different states)
- § 74 [now 1443, 1446, 1447] (Same; causes against persons denied civil rights)
- § 75 [now 1446] (Same; petitioner in actual custody of state court)
- § 76 [now 1442, 1446, 1447] (Same; suits and prosecutions against revenue officers)
- § 77 [now 1442] (Same; suits by aliens)
- § 78 [now 1449] (Same; copies of records refused by clerk of state court)
- § 79 [now 1450] (Same; previous attachment bonds or orders)
- § 80 [now 1359, 1447, 1919] (Same; dismissal or remand)
- § 81 [now 1447] (Same; proceedings in suits removed)
- § 82 [former] (Same; record; filing and return)
- § 83 [now 1447, 1448] (Service of process after removal)

U.S.C., Title 28, §§ 1446, 1447, formerly § 72, supra, however, is modified by shortening the time for pleading in removed actions.

Note to Subdivision (e). The last sentence of this subdivision modifies U.S.C., Title 28, § 1652, formerly § 725 (Laws of States as rules of decision) in so far as that statute has been construed to govern matters of procedure and to exclude state judicial decisions relative thereto.

1946 Amendment

Note to Subdivision (a). Despite certain dicta to the contrary, *Lynn v. United States*, C.C.A.5th, 1940, 110 F.2d 586; *Mount Tivy Winery, Inc. v. Lewis*, N.D.Cal.1942, 42 F.Supp. 636, it is manifest that the rules apply to actions against the United States under the Tucker Act [28 U.S.C., §§ 41(20), 250, 251, 254, 257, 258, 287, 289, 292, 761–765 [now 791, 1346, 1401, 1402, 1491, 1493, 1496, 1501, 1503, 2071, 2072, 2411, 2412, 2501, 2506, 2509, 2510]]. See United States to use of *Foster Wheeler Corp. v. American Surety Co. of New York,* E.D.N.Y.1939, 25 F.Supp. 700; *Boerner v. United States,* E.D.N.Y.1939, 26 F.Supp. 769; *United States v. Gallagher,* C.C.A.9th, 1945, 151 F.2d 556. Rules 1 and 81 provide that the rules shall apply to all suits of a civil nature, whether cognizable as cases at law or in equity except those specifically excepted; and the character of the various proceedings excepted by express statement in Rule 81, as well as the language of the rules generally, shows that the term "civil action" [Rule 2] includes actions against the United States. Moreover, the rules in many places expressly make provision for the situation wherein the United States is a party as either plaintiff or defendant. See Rules 4(d)(4), 12(a), 13(d), 25(d), 37(f), 39(c), 45(c), 54(d), 55(e), 62(e), and 65(c). In *United States v. Sherwood,* 1941, 61 S.Ct. 767, 312 U.S. 584, 85 L.Ed. 1058, the Solicitor General expressly conceded in his brief for the United States that the rules apply to Tucker Act cases. The Solicitor General stated: "The Government, of course, recognizes that the Federal Rules of Civil Procedure apply to cases brought under the Tucker Act." (Brief for the United States, p. 31). Regarding *Lynn v. United States,* supra, the Solicitor General said: "In *Lynn v. United States* . . . the Circuit Court of Appeals for the Fifth Circuit went beyond the Government's contention there, and held that an action under the Tucker Act is neither an action at law nor a suit in equity and, seemingly, that the Federal Rules of Civil Procedure are, therefore, inapplicable. We think the suggestion is erroneous. Rules 4(d), 12(a), 39(c), and 55(e) expressly contemplate suits against the United States, and nothing in the enabling Act (48 Stat. 1064, 28 U.S.C. §§ 723b, 723c [see 2072]) suggests that the Rules are inapplicable to Tucker Act proceedings, which in terms are to accord with court rules and their subsequent modifications (Sec. 4, Act of March 3, 1887, 24 Stat. 505, 28 U.S.C. § 761 [see 2071, 2072])." (Brief for the United States, p. 31, n. 17.)

United States v. Sherwood, supra, emphasizes, however, that the application of the rules in Tucker Act cases affects only matters of procedure and does not operate to extend jurisdiction. See also Rule 82. In the Sherwood case, the New York Supreme Court, acting under § 795 of the New York Civil Practice Act, made an order, authorizing Sherwood, as a judgment creditor, to maintain a suit under the Tucker Act to recover damages from the United States for breach of its contract with the judgment debtor, Kaiser, for construction of a post office building. Sherwood brought suit against the United States and Kaiser in the District Court for the Eastern District of New York. The question before the United States Supreme Court was whether a United States District Court had jurisdiction to entertain a suit against the United States wherein private parties were joined as parties defendant. It was contended that either the Federal Rules of Civil Procedure or the Tucker Act, or both, embodied the consent of the United States to be sued in litigations in which issues between the plaintiff and third persons were to be adjudicated. Regarding the effect of the Federal Rules, the Court declared that nothing in the rules, so far as they may be applicable in Tucker Act cases, authorized the maintenance of any suit against the United States to which it had not otherwise consented. The matter involved was not one of procedure but of jurisdiction, the limits of which were marked by the consent of the United States to be sued. The jurisdiction thus limited is unaffected by the Federal Rules of Civil Procedure.

Subdivision (a)(2). The added sentence makes it clear that the rules have not superseded the requirements of U.S.C., Title 28, § 2253, formerly § 466. *Schenk v. Plummer,* C.C.A.9, 1940, 113 F.2d 726.

For correct application of the rules in proceedings for forfeiture of property for violation of a statute of the United States, such as under U.S.C., Title 22, § 405 (seizure of war materials intended for unlawful export) or U.S.C., Title 21, § 334(b) (Federal Food, Drug, and Cosmetic Act; formerly Title 21, U.S.C. § 14, Pure Food and Drug Act), see *Reynal v. United States,* C.C.A.5, 1945, 153 F.2d 929; *United States v. 108 Boxes of Cheddar Cheese,* S.D.Iowa 1943, 3 F.R.D. 40.

Subdivision (a)(3). The added sentence makes it clear that the rules apply to appeals from proceedings to enforce administrative subpoenas. See *Perkins v. Endicott Johnson Corp.,* C.C.A.2d 1942, 128 F.2d 208, affirmed on other grounds 63 S.Ct. 339, 317 U.S. 501, 87 L.Ed. 424; *Walling v. News Printing Inc.,* C.C.A.3, 1945, 148 F.2d 57; *McCrone v. United States,* 1939, 59 S.Ct. 685, 307 U.S. 61, 83 L.Ed. 1108. And, although the provision allows full recognition of the fact that the rigid application of the rules in the proceedings themselves may conflict with the summary determination desired, *Goodyear Tire & Rubber Co. v. National Relations Board,* C.C.A.6, 1941, 122 F.2d 450; *Cudahy Packing Co. v. National Labor Relations Board,* C.C.A.10, 1941, 117 F.2d 692, it is drawn so as to permit application of any of the rules in the proceedings whenever the district court deems them helpful. See, e.g., *Peoples Natural Gas Co. v. Federal Power Commission,* App.D.C.1942, 127 F.2d 153, certiorari denied 62 S.Ct. 1298, 316 U.S. 700, 86 L.Ed. 1769; *Martin v. Chandis Securities Co.,* C.C.A.9th, 1942, 128 F.2d 731. Compare the application of the rules in summary proceedings in bankruptcy under General Order 37. See 1 *Collier on Bankruptcy,* 14th ed. by Moore and Oglebay, 326–327; 2 Collier, op.cit.supra, 1401–1402; 3 Collier, op.cit.supra, 228–231; 4 Collier, op.cit.supra, 1199–1202.

Subdivision (a)(6). Section 405 of U.S.C., Title 8 originally referred to in the last sentence of paragraph (6), has been repealed and § 738 [now 1451], U.S.C., Title 8, has been enacted in its stead. The last sentence of paragraph (6) has, therefore, been amended in accordance with this change. The sentence has also been amended so as to refer directly to the statute regarding the provision of time for answer, thus avoiding any confusion attendant upon a change in the statute.

That portion of subdivision (a)(6) making the rules applicable to proceedings for enforcement or review of compensation orders under the Longshoremen's and Harbor Workers' Compensation Act [33 U.S.C. § 901 et seq.] was added by an amendment made pursuant to order of the Court, December 28, 1939, effective three months subsequent to the adjournment of the 76th Congress, January 3, 1941.

Subdivision (c). The change in subdivision (c) effects more speedy trials in removed actions. In some states many of the courts have only two terms a year. A case, if filed 20 days before a term, is returnable to that term, but if filed less than 20 days before a term, is returnable to the following term, which convenes six months later. Hence, under the original wording of Rule 81(c), where a case is filed less than 20 days before the term and is removed within a few days but before answer, it is possible for the defendant to delay interposing his answer or presenting his defenses by motion for six months or more. The rule as amended prevents this result.

Subdivision (f). The use of the phrase "the United States or an officer or agency thereof" in the rules (as e.g., in Rule 12(a) and amended Rule 73(a)) could raise the question of whether "officer" includes a collector of internal revenue, a former collector, or the personal representative of a deceased collector, against whom suits for tax refunds are frequently instituted. Difficulty might ensue for the reason that a suit against a collector or his representative has been held to be a personal action. *Sage v. United States,* 1919, 39 S.Ct. 415, 250 U.S. 33, 63 L.Ed. 828; *Smietanka v. Indiana Steel Co.,* 1921, 42 S.Ct. 1, 257 U.S. 1, 66 L.Ed. 99; *United States v. Nunnally Investment Co.,* 1942, 62 S.Ct. 1064, 316 U.S. 258, 86 L.Ed. 1455. The addition of subdivision (f) to Rule 81 dispels any doubts on the matter and avoids further litigation.

1948 Amendment

The amendment effective October 1949, substituted the words "United States District Court" for the words "District Court of the United States" in the last sentence of subdivision (a)(1) and in the first and third sentences of subdivision (e). The amendment substituted the words "United States district courts" in lieu of "district courts of the United States" in subdivision (a)(4) and (5) and in the first sentence of subdivision (c).

The amendment effective October 20, 1949, also made the following changes:

In subdivision (a)(1), the reference to "Title 17, U.S.C." was substituted for the reference to "the Act of March 4, 1909, c. 320, § 25 (35 Stat. 1081), as amended, U.S.C., Title 17, § 25."

In subdivision (a)(2), the reference to "Title 28, U.S.C., § 2253" was substituted for "U.S.C., Title 28, § 466."

In subdivision (a)(3), the reference in the first sentence to "Title 9, U.S.C.," was substituted for "the Act of February 12, 1925, c. 213 (43 Stat. 883), U.S.C., Title 9".

In subdivision (a)(5), the words "as amended" were inserted after the parenthetical citation of "(49 Stat. 453)," and after the citations of "Title 29, §§ 159 and 160," former references to subdivisions "(e), (g), and (i)" were deleted.

In subdivision (a)(6), after the words "These rules" at the beginning of the first sentence, the following words were deleted: "do not apply to proceedings under the Act of September 13, 1888, c. 1015, § 13 (25 Stat. 479), as amended, U.S.C., Title 8, [former] § 282, relating to deportation of Chinese; they". Also in the first sentence, after the parenthetical citation of "(44 Stat. 1434, 1436)," the words "as amended" were added. In the last sentence, the words "October 14, 1940, c. 876, § 338 (54 Stat. 1158)" were inserted in lieu of the words "June 29, 1906, c. 3592, § 15 (34 Stat. 601), as amended."

In subdivision (c), the word "all" originally appearing in the first sentence between the words "govern" and "procedure" was deleted. In the third sentence, the portion beginning with the words "20 days after the receipt" and including all the remainder of that sentence was substituted for the following language: "the time allowed for answer by the law of the state or within 5 days after the filing of the transcript of the record in the district court of the United States, whichever period is longer, but in any event within 20 days after the filing of the transcript". In the fourth or last sentence, after the words at the beginning of the sentence, "If at the time of removal all necessary pleadings have been," the word "served" was inserted in lieu of the word "filed," and the concluding words of the sentence, "petition for removal is filed if he is the petitioner," together with the final clause immediately following, were substituted for the words "record of the action is filed in the district court of the United States."

1963 Amendment

Subdivision (a)(4). This change reflects the transfer of functions from the Secretary of Commerce to the Secretary of the Interior made by 1939 Reorganization Plan No. II, § 4(e), 53 Stat. 1433.

Subdivision (a)(6). The proper current reference is to the 1952 statute superseding the 1940 statute.

Subdivision (c). Most of the cases have held that a party who has made a proper express demand for jury trial in the State court is not required to renew the demand after removal of the action. *Zakoscielny v. Waterman Steamship Corp.,* 16 F.R.D. 314 (D.Md.1954); *Talley v. American Bakeries Co.,* 15 F.R.D. 391 (E.D.Tenn.1954); *Rehrer v. Service Trucking Co.,* 15 F.R.D. 113 (D.Del.1953); 5 *Moore's Federal Practice* ¶38.39[3] (2d ed. 1951); 1 Barron & Holtzoff, *Federal Practice & Procedure* § 132 (Wright ed. 1960). But there is some authority to the contrary. *Petsel v. Chicago, B. & Q.R. Co.,* 101 F.Supp. 1006 (S.D.Iowa 1951); *Nelson v. American Nat. Bank & Trust Co.,* 9 F.R.D. 680 (E.D.Tenn. 1950). The amendment adopts the preponderant view.

In order still further to avoid unintended waivers of jury trial, the amendment provides that where by State law applicable in the court from which the case is removed a party is entitled to jury trial without making an express demand, he need not make a demand after removal. However, the district court for calendar or other purposes may on its own motion direct the parties to state whether they demand a jury, and the court must make such a direction upon the request of any party. Under the amendment a district court may find it convenient to establish a routine practice of giving these directions to the parties in appropriate cases.

Subdivision (f). The amendment recognizes the change of nomenclature made by Treasury Dept. Order 150–26(2), 18 Fed.Reg. 3499 (1953).

As to a special problem arising under Rule 25 (Substitution of parties) in actions for refund of taxes, see the Advisory Committee's Note to the amendment of Rule 25(d), effective July 19, 1961; and 4 *Moore's Federal Practice* ¶25.09 at 531 (2d ed. 1950).

1966 Amendment

See Note to Rule 1, supra.

Statutory proceedings to forfeit property for violation of the laws of the United States, formerly governed by the admiralty rules, will be governed by the unified and supplemental rules. See Supplemental Rule A.

Upon the recommendation of the judges of the United States District Court for the District of Columbia, the Federal Rules of Civil Procedure are made applicable to probate proceedings in that court. The exception with regard to adoption proceedings is removed because the court no longer has jurisdiction of those matters; and the words "mental health" are substituted for "lunacy" to conform to the current characterization in the District.

The purpose of the amendment to paragraph (3) is to permit the deletion from Rule 73(a) of the clause "unless a shorter time is provided by law." The 10 day period fixed for an appeal under 45 U.S.C. § 159 is the only instance of a shorter time provided for appeals in civil cases. Apart from the unsettling effect of the clause, it is eliminated because its retention would preserve the 15 day period heretofore allowed by 28 U.S.C. § 2107 for appeals from interlocutory decrees in admiralty, it being one of the purposes of the amendment to make the time for appeals in civil and admiralty cases uniform under the unified rules. See Advisory Committee's Note to subdivision (a) of Rule 73.

1968 Amendment

The amendments eliminate inappropriate references to appellate procedure.

1971 Amendment

Title 28, U.S.C., § 2243 now requires that the custodian of a person detained must respond to an application for a writ of habeas corpus "within three days unless for good cause additional time, not exceeding twenty days, is allowed." The amendment increases to forty days the additional time that the district court may allow in habeas corpus proceedings involving persons in custody pursuant to a judgment of a state court. The substantial increase in the number of such proceedings in recent years has placed a considerable burden on state authorities. Twenty days has proved in practice too short a time in which to prepare and file the return in many such cases. Allowance of additional time should, of course, be granted only for good cause.

While the time allowed in such a case for the return of the writ may not exceed forty days, this does not mean that the state must necessarily be limited to that period of time to provide for the federal court the transcript of the proceedings of a state trial or plenary hearing if the transcript must be prepared after the habeas corpus proceeding has begun in the federal court.

1987 Amendment

The amendments are technical. No substantive change is intended.

2001 Amendments

Former Copyright Rule 1 made the Civil Rules applicable to copyright proceedings except to the extent the Civil Rules were inconsistent with Copyright Rules. Abrogation of the Copyright Rules leaves the Civil Rules fully applicable to copyright proceedings. Rule 81(a)(1) is amended to reflect this change.

The District of Columbia Court Reform and Criminal Procedure Act of 1970, Pub.L. 91–358, 84 Stat. 473, transferred mental health proceedings formerly held in the United States District Court for the District of Columbia to local District of Columbia courts. The provision that the Civil Rules do not apply to these proceedings is deleted as superfluous.

The reference to incorporation of the Civil Rules in the Federal Rules of Bankruptcy Procedure has been restyled.

Changes Made After Publication and Comments

The Committee Note was amended to correct the inadvertent omission of a negative. As revised, it correctly reflects the language that is stricken from the rule.

2002 Amendments

This amendment brings Rule 81(a)(2) into accord with the Rules Governing § 2254 and § 2255 proceedings. In its present form, Rule 81(a)(2) includes return-time provisions that are inconsistent with the provisions in the Rules Governing §§ 2254 and 2255. The inconsistency should be eliminated, and it is better that the time provisions continue to be set out in the other rules without duplication in Rule 81. Rule 81 also directs that the writ be directed to the person having custody of the person detained. Similar directions exist in the § 2254 and § 2255 rules, providing additional detail for applicants subject to future custody. There is no need for partial duplication in Rule 81.

The provision that the civil rules apply to the extent that practice is not set forth in the § 2254 and § 2255 rules dovetails with the provisions in Rule 11 of the § 2254 rules and Rule 12 of the § 2255 rules.

Changes Made After Publication and Comment The only change since publication is deletion of an inadvertent reference to § 2241 proceedings.

2007 Amendments

The language of Rule 81 has been amended as part of the general restyling of the Civil Rules to make them more easily understood and to make style and terminology consistent throughout the rules. These changes are intended to be stylistic only.

Rule 81(c) has been revised to reflect the amendment of 28 U.S.C. § 1446(a) that changed the procedure for removal from a petition for removal to a notice of removal.

Former Rule 81(e), drafted before the decision in *Erie R.R. v. Tompkins*, 304 U.S. 64 (1938), defined state law to include "the statutes of that state and the state judicial decisions construing them." The *Erie* decision reinterpreted the Rules of Decision Act, now 28 U.S.C. § 1652, recognizing that the "laws" of the states include the common law established by judicial decisions. Long-established practice reflects this understanding, looking to state common law as well as statutes and court rules when a Civil Rule directs use of state law. Amended Rule 81(d)(1) adheres to this practice, including all state judicial decisions, not only those that construe state statutes.

Former Rule 81(f) is deleted. The office of district director of internal revenue was abolished by restructuring under the Internal Revenue Service Restructuring and Reform Act of 1998, Pub.L. 105–206, July 22, 1998, 26 U.S.C. § 1 Note.

HISTORICAL NOTES

Effective Date of Abrogation

Abrogation of par. (7) of subdivision (a) of this rule as effective Aug. 1, 1951, see Effective Date note incorporated within the Supplementary Report set out under the heading 1951 Addition in the Advisory Committee Notes appearing under Rule 71.1 of these rules.

Pending Actions

For applicability of Supreme Court amendments to pending cases, see Orders of the Supreme Court of the United States Adopting and Amending Rules set out preceding Rule 1 of these rules.

CROSS REFERENCES

Antitrust Civil Process Act petitions, application of rules, see 15 USCA § 1314.

Demand for jury trial, see Fed.Rules Civ.Proc. Rule 38, 28 USCA.

Habeas corpus, see 28 USCA § 2241 et seq.

Power of court to issue writs, see 28 USCA § 1651.

Procedure before and after removal generally, see 28 USCA §§ 1446, 1447.

Scope of rules, see Fed.Rules Civ.Proc. Rule 1, 28 USCA.

Rule 82. Jurisdiction and Venue Unaffected

These rules do not extend or limit the jurisdiction of the district courts or the venue of actions in those courts. An admiralty or maritime claim under Rule 9(h) is not a civil action for purposes of 28 U.S.C. §§ 1391–1392.

(Amended December 29, 1948, effective October 20, 1949; February 28, 1966, effective July 1, 1966; April 23, 2001, effective December 1, 2001; April 30, 2007, effective December 1, 2007.)

ADVISORY COMMITTEE NOTES

1937 Adoption

These rules grant extensive power of joining claims and counterclaims in one action, but, as this rule states, such grant does not extend federal jurisdiction. The rule is declaratory of existing practice under the [former] Federal Equity Rules with regard to such provisions as [former] Equity Rule 26 on Joinder of Causes of Action and [former] Equity Rule 30 on Counterclaims. Compare Shulman and Jaegerman, *Some Jurisdictional Limitations on Federal Procedure,* 45 Yale L.J. 393 (1936).

1948 Amendment

The amendment effective October 1949, substituted the words "United States district courts" for "district courts of the United States."

1966 Amendment

Title 28, U.S.C., § 1391(b) provides: "A civil action wherein jurisdiction is not founded solely on diversity of citizenship may be brought only in the judicial district where all defendants reside, except as otherwise provided by law." This provision cannot appropriately be applied to what were formerly suits in admiralty. The rationale of decisions holding it inapplicable rests largely on the use of the term "civil action": i.e., a suit in admiralty is not a "civil action" within the statute. By virtue of the amendment to Rule 1, the provisions of Rule 2 convert suits in admiralty into civil actions. The added sentence is necessary to avoid an undesirable change in existing law with respect to venue.

2001 Amendments

The final sentence of Rule 82 is amended to delete the reference to 28 U.S.C. § 1393, which has been repealed.

Style Comment

The recommendation that the change be made without publication carries with it a recommendation that style changes not be made. Styling would carry considerable risks. The first sentence of Rule 82, for example, states that the Civil Rules do not "extend or limit the jurisdiction of the United States district courts." That sentence is a flat lie if "jurisdiction" includes personal or quasi-in rem jurisdiction. The styling project on this rule requires publication and comment.

2007 Amendments

The language of Rule 82 has been amended as part of the general restyling of the Civil Rules to make them more easily understood and to make style and terminology consistent throughout the rules. These changes are intended to be stylistic only.

Rule 83. Rules by District Courts; Judge's Directives

(a) Local Rules.

(1) ***In General.*** After giving public notice and an opportunity for comment, a district court, acting by a majority of its district judges, may adopt and amend rules governing its practice. A local rule must be consistent with—but not duplicate—federal statutes and rules adopted under 28 U.S.C. §§ 2072 and 2075, and must conform to any uniform numbering system prescribed by the Judicial Conference of the United States. A local rule takes effect on the date specified by the district court and remains in effect unless amended by the court or abrogated by the judicial council of the circuit. Copies of rules and amendments must, on their adoption, be furnished to the judicial council and the Administrative Office of the United States Courts and be made available to the public.

(2) ***Requirement of Form.*** A local rule imposing a requirement of form must not be enforced in a way that causes a party to lose any right because of a nonwillful failure to comply.

(b) Procedure When There Is No Controlling Law. A judge may regulate practice in any manner consistent with federal law, rules adopted under 28 U.S.C. §§ 2072 and 2075, and the district's local rules. No sanction or other disadvantage may be imposed for noncompliance with any requirement not in federal law, federal rules, or the local rules unless the alleged violator has been furnished in the particular case with actual notice of the requirement.

(Amended April 29, 1985, effective August 1, 1985; April 27, 1995, effective December 1, 1995; April 30, 2007, effective December 1, 2007.)

ADVISORY COMMITTEE NOTES

1937 Adoption

This rule substantially continues U.S.C., Title 28, § 2071, formerly § 731 (Rules of practice in district courts) with the additional requirement that copies of such rules and amendments be furnished to the Supreme Court of the United States. See [former] Equity Rule 79 (Additional Rules by District Court). With the last sentence compare United States Supreme Court Admiralty Rules, 1920, Rule 44 (Right of Trial Courts to Make Rules of Practice) (originally promulgated in 1842).

1985 Amendment

Rule 83, which has not been amended since the Federal Rules were promulgated in 1938, permits each district to adopt local rules not inconsistent with the Federal Rules by a majority of the judges. The only other requirement is that copies be furnished to the Supreme Court.

The widespread adoption of local rules and the modest procedural prerequisites for their promulgation have led many commentators to question the soundness of the process as well as the validity of some rules. See 12 C. Wright & A. Miller, *Federal Practice and Procedure: Civil* § 3152, at 217 (1973); Caballero, *Is There an Over-Exercise of Local Rule-Making Powers by the United States District Courts?*, 24 Fed.Bar News 325 (1977). Although the desirability of local rules for promoting uniform practice within a district is widely accepted, several commentators also have suggested reforms to increase the quality, simplicity, and uniformity of the local rules. See Note, *Rule 83 and the Local Federal Rules*, 67 Colum.L.Rev. 1251 (1967), and Comment, *The Local Rules of Civil Procedure in the Federal District Courts—A Survey*, 1966 Duke L.J. 1011.

The amended Rule attempts, without impairing the procedural validity of existing local rules, to enhance the local rulemaking process by requiring appropriate public notice of proposed rules and an opportunity to comment on them. Although some district courts apparently consult the local bar before promulgating rules, many do not, which has led to criticism of a process that has district judges consulting only with each other. See 12 C. Wright & A. Miller, *supra*, § 3152, at 217; Blair, *The New Local Rules for Federal Practice in Iowa*, 23 Drake L.Rev. 517 (1974). The new language subjects local rulemaking to scrutiny similar to that accompanying the Federal Rules, administrative rulemaking, and legislation. It attempts to assure that the expert advice of practitioners and scholars is made available to the district court before local rules are promulgated. See Weinstein, *Reform of Court Rule-Making Procedures* 84–87, 127–37, 151 (1977).

The amended Rule does not detail the procedure for giving notice and an opportunity to be heard since conditions vary from district to district. Thus, there is no explicit requirement for a public hearing, although a district may consider that procedure appropriate in all or some rulemaking situations. See generally, Weinstein, *supra*, at 117–37, 151. The new Rule does not foreclose any other form of consultation. For example, it can be accomplished through the mechanism of an "Advisory Committee" similar to that employed by the Supreme Court in connection with the Federal Rules themselves.

The amended Rule provides that a local rule will take effect upon the date specified by the district court and will remain in effect unless amended by the district court or abrogated by the judicial council. The effectiveness of a local rule should not be deferred until approved by the judicial council because that might unduly delay promulgation of a local rule that should become effective immediately, especially since some councils do not meet frequently. Similarly, it was thought that to delay a local rule's effectiveness for a fixed period of time would be arbitrary and that to require the judicial council to abrogate a local rule within a specified time would be inconsistent with its power under 28 U.S.C. § 332 (1976) to nullify a local rule at any time. The expectation is that the judicial council will examine all local rules, including those currently in effect, with an eye toward determining whether they are valid and consistent with the Federal Rules, promote inter-district uniformity and efficiency, and do not undermine the basic objectives of the Federal Rules.

The amended Rule requires copies of local rules to be sent upon their promulgation to the judicial council and the Administrative Office of the United States Courts rather than to the Supreme Court. The Supreme Court was the appropriate filing place in 1938, when Rule 83 originally was promulgated, but the establishment of the Administrative Office makes it a more logical place to develop a centralized file of local rules. This procedure is consistent with both the Criminal and the Appellate Rules. See Fed.R.Crim.P. 57(a); Fed.R.App.P. 47. The Administrative Office also will be able to provide improved utilization of the file because of its recent development of a Local Rules Index.

The practice pursued by some judges of issuing standing orders has been controversial, particularly among members of the practicing bar. The last sentence in Rule 83 has been amended to make certain that standing orders are not inconsistent with the Federal Rules or any local district court rules. Beyond that, it is hoped that each district will adopt procedures, perhaps by local rule, for promulgating and reviewing single-judge standing orders.

1995 Amendments

Subdivision (a). This rule is amended to reflect the requirement that local rules be consistent not only with the national rules but also with Acts of Congress. The amendment also states that local rules should not repeat Acts of Congress or national rules.

The amendment also requires that the numbering of local rules conform with any uniform numbering system that may be prescribed by the Judicial Conference. Lack of uniform numbering might create unnecessary traps for counsel and litigants. A uniform numbering system would make it easier for an increasingly national bar and for litigants to locate a local rule that applies to a particular procedural issue.

Paragraph (2) is new. Its aim is to protect against loss of rights in the enforcement of local rules relating to matters of form. For example, a party should not be deprived of a right to a jury trial because its attorney, unaware of—or forgetting—a local rule directing that jury demands be noted in the caption of the case, includes a jury demand only in the body of the pleading. The proscription of paragraph (2) is narrowly drawn—covering only violations attributable to nonwillful failure to comply and only those involving local rules directed to matters of form. It does not limit the court's power to impose substantive penalties upon a party if it or its attorney contumaciously or willfully violates a local rule, even one involving merely a matter of form. Nor does it affect the court's power to enforce local rules that involve more than mere matters of form—for example, a local rule requiring parties to identify evidentiary matters relied upon to support or oppose motions for summary judgment.

Subdivision (b). This rule provides flexibility to the court in regulating practice when there is no controlling law. Specifically, it permits the court to regulate practice in any manner consistent with Acts of Congress, with rules adopted under 28 U.S.C. §§ 2072 and 2075, and with the district local rules.

This rule recognizes that courts rely on multiple directives to control practice. Some courts regulate practice through the published Federal Rules and the local rules of the court. Some courts also have used internal operating procedures, standing orders, and other internal directives. Although such directives continue to be authorized, they can lead to problems. Counsel or litigants may be unaware of various directives. In addition, the sheer volume of directives may impose an unreasonable barrier. For example, it may be difficult to obtain copies of the directives. Finally, counsel or litigants may be unfairly sanctioned for failing to comply with a directive. For these reasons, the amendment to this rule disapproves imposing any sanction or other disadvantage on a person for noncompliance with such an internal directive, unless the alleged violator has been furnished actual notice of the requirement in a particular case.

There should be no adverse consequence to a party or attorney for violating special requirements relating to practice before a particular court unless the party or attorney has actual notice of those requirements. Furnishing litigants with a copy outlining the judge's practices—or attaching instructions to a notice setting a case for conference or trial—would suffice to give actual notice, as would an order in a case specifically adopting by reference a judge's standing order and indicating how copies can be obtained.

2007 Amendments

The language of Rule 83 has been amended as part of the general restyling of the Civil Rules to make them more easily understood and to make style and terminology consistent throughout the rules. These changes are intended to be stylistic only.

HISTORICAL NOTES

Change of Name

Reference to United States magistrate or to magistrate deemed to refer to United States magistrate judge pursuant to section 321 of Pub.L. 101–650, set out as a note under section 631 of this title.

CROSS REFERENCES

Local rules, see Fed.Rules Cr.Proc. Rule 57, 18 USCA.

Rule-making power generally, see 28 USCA § 2071.

Rule 84. Forms

The forms in the Appendix suffice under these rules and illustrate the simplicity and brevity that these rules contemplate.

(Amended December 27, 1946, effective March 19, 1948; April 30, 2007, effective December 1, 2007.)

ADVISORY COMMITTEE NOTES

1937 Adoption

In accordance with the practice found useful in many codes, provision is here made for a limited number of official forms which may serve as guides in pleading. Compare 2 Mass.Gen.Laws (Ter.Ed., 1932) ch. 231, § 147, Forms 1–47; *English Annual Practice* (1937) Appendix A to M, inclusive; *Conn.Practice Book* (1934) Rules, 47–68, pp. 123 to 427.

1946 Amendment

Note. The amendment serves to emphasize that the forms contained in the Appendix of Forms are sufficient to withstand attack under the rules under which they are drawn, and that the practitioner using them may rely on them to that extent. The circuit courts of appeals generally have upheld the use of the forms as promoting desirable simplicity and brevity of statement. *Sierocinski v. E. I. DuPont DeNemours & Co.,* C.C.A.3, 1939, 103 F.2d 843; *Swift & Co. v. Young,* C.C.A.4, 1939, 107 F.2d 170; *Sparks v. England,* C.C.A.8, 1940, 113 F.2d 579; *Ramsouer v. Midland Valley R. Co.,* C.C.A.8, 1943, 135 F.2d 101. And the forms as a whole have met with widespread approval in the courts. See cases cited in 1 Moore's Federal Practice, 1938, Cum. Supplement § 8.07, under "Page 554"; see also Commentary, The Official Forms, 1941, 4 Fed.Rules Serv. 954. In Cook, "Facts" and "Statements of Fact", 1937, 4 U.Chi.L.Rev. 233, 245–246, it is said with reference to what is now Rule 84: ". . . pleaders in the federal courts are not to be left to guess as to the meaning of [the] language" in Rule 8(a) regarding the form of the complaint. "All of which is as it should be. In no other way can useless litigation be avoided." Ibid. The amended rule will operate to discourage isolated results such as those found in *Washburn v. Moorman Mfg. Co.,* S.D.Cal. 1938, 25 F.Supp. 546; *Employers Mutual Liability Ins. Co. of Wisconsin v. Blue Line Transfer Co.,* W.D.Mo.1941, 2 F.R.D. 121, 5 Fed.Rules Serv. 12e.235, Case 2.

2007 Amendments

The language of Rule 84 has been amended as part of the general restyling of the Civil Rules to make them more easily understood and to make style and terminology consistent throughout the rules. These changes are intended to be stylistic only.

Rule 85. Title

These rules may be cited as the Federal Rules of Civil Procedure.

(Amended April 30, 2007, effective December 1, 2007.)

ADVISORY COMMITTEE NOTES

2007 Amendments

The language of Rule 85 has been amended as part of the general restyling of the Civil Rules to make them more easily understood and to make style and terminology consistent throughout the rules. These changes are intended to be stylistic only.

Rule 86. Effective Dates

(a) In General. These rules and any amendments take effect at the time specified by the Supreme Court, subject to 28 U.S.C. § 2074. They govern:

(1) proceedings in an action commenced after their effective date; and

(2) proceedings after that date in an action then pending unless:

(A) the Supreme Court specifies otherwise; or

(B) the court determines that applying them in a particular action would be infeasible or work an injustice.

(b) December 1, 2007 Amendments. If any provision in Rules 1–5.1, 6–73, or 77–86 conflicts with another law, priority in time for the purpose of 28 U.S.C. § 2072(b) is not affected by the amendments taking effect on December 1, 2007.

(Amended December 27, 1946, effective March 19, 1948; December 29, 1948, effective October 20, 1949; April 17, 1961, effective July 19, 1961; January 21, 1963, and March 18, 1963, effective July 1, 1963; April 30, 2007, effective December 1, 2007.)

ADVISORY COMMITTEE NOTES

1937 Adoption

See former Equity Rule 81 (These Rules Effective February 1, 1913—Old Rules Abrogated).

2007 Amendments

The language of Rule 86 has been amended as part of the general restyling of the Civil Rules to make them more easily understood and to make style and terminology consistent throughout the rules. These changes are intended to be stylistic only.

The subdivisions that provided a list of the effective dates of the original Civil Rules and amendments made up to 1963 are deleted as no longer useful.

Rule 86(b) is added to clarify the relationship of amendments taking effect on December 1, 2007, to other laws for the purpose of applying the "supersession" clause in 28 U.S.C. § 2072(b). Section 2072(b) provides that a law in conflict with an Enabling Act Rule "shall be of no further force or effect after such rule[] ha[s] taken effect." The amendments that take effect on December 1, 2007, result from the general restyling of the Civil Rules and from a small number of technical revisions adopted on a parallel track. None of these amendments is intended to affect resolution of any conflict that might arise between a rule and another law. Rule 86(b) makes this intent explicit. Any conflict that arises should be resolved by looking to the date the specific conflicting rule provision first became effective.

HISTORICAL NOTES

Effective and Applicability Provisions

1948 Amendments. The first regular session of the 81st Congress adjourned sine die on Oct. 19, 1949, therefore the amendments to Rules 1, 17, 22, 24, 25, 27, 37, 45, 57, 60, 65, 66, 67, 69, 72–76, 79, 81, 82, and 86 and to forms 1, 19, 22, 23, and 27 became effective on Oct. 20, 1949, following the adjournment as provided for in subsection (c) of this rule.

1946 Amendments. The first regular session of the 80th Congress adjourned sine die on Friday, Dec. 19, 1947, therefore the amendments to Rules 6, 7, 12, 13, 14, 17, 24, 26, 27, 28, 33, 34, 36, 41, 45, 52, 54, 56, 58, 59, 60, 62, 65, 66, 68, 73, 75, 77, 79, 80, 81, 84, and 86, became effective Mar. 19, 1948 as provided for in subsection (b) of this rule.

Effective Date of 1966 Amendment; Transmission to Congress; Rescission

Sections 2 to 4 of the Order of the Supreme Court, dated Feb. 28, 1966, 383 U.S. 1031, provided:

"2. That the foregoing amendments and additions to the Rules of Civil Procedure shall take effect on July 1, 1966, and shall govern all proceedings in actions brought thereafter and also in all further proceedings in actions then pending, except to the extent that in the opinion of the court their application in a particular action then pending would not be feasible or would work injustice, in which event the former procedure applies.

"3. That the Chief Justice be, and he hereby is, authorized to transmit to the Congress the foregoing amendments and additions to the Rules of Civil Procedure in accordance with the provisions of Title 28, U.S.C., §§ 2072 and 2073.

"4. That: (a) subdivision (c) of Rule 6 of the Rules of Civil Procedure for the United States District Courts promulgated by this court on December 20, 1937, effective September 16, 1938; (b) Rule 2 of the Rules for Practice and Procedure under section 25 of An Act To amend and consolidate the Acts respecting copyright, approved March 4, 1909, promulgated by this court on June 1, 1909, effective July 1, 1909; and (c) the Rules of Practice in Admiralty and Maritime Cases, promulgated by this court on December 6, 1920, effective March 7, 1921, as revised, amended and supplemented, be, and they hereby are, rescinded, effective July 1, 1966."

CROSS REFERENCES

All laws in conflict with these rules to be of no further force and effect, see 28 USCA § 2072.

Effective date, see Fed.Rules Cr.Proc. Rule 59, 18 USCA.

APPENDIX OF FORMS

(See Rule 84)

Form 1. Caption

(Use on every summons, complaint, answer, motion, or other document.)

United States District Court
for the
______ District of ______

A B, Plaintiff	)	
	)	
v.	)	
	)	Civil Action No. ______
C D, Defendant	)	
	)	
v.	)	
	)	
E F, Third–Party Defendant	)	
(Use if needed.)	)	

(Name of Document)

(Added Apr. 30, 2007, eff. Dec. 1, 2007.)

Form 2. Date, Signature, Address, E–Mail Address, and Telephone Number

(Use at the conclusion of pleadings and other papers that require a signature.)

Date ______

______
(Signature of the attorney or unrepresented party)

______
(Printed name)

______
(Address)

______
(E-mail address)

______
(Telephone number)

(Added Apr. 30, 2007, eff. Dec. 1, 2007.)

Form 3. Summons

(Caption—See Form 1.)

To *name the defendant*:

A lawsuit has been filed against you.

Within 20 days after service of this summons on you (not counting the day you received it), you must serve on the plaintiff an answer to the attached complaint or a motion under Rule 12 of the Federal Rules of Civil Procedure. The answer or motion must be served on the plaintiff's attorney, ______, whose address is ______. If you fail to do so, judgment by default will be entered against you for the relief demanded in the complaint. You also must file your answer or motion with the court.

Date ______

______
Clerk of Court

(Court Seal)

(Use 60 days if the defendant is the United States or a United States agency, or is an officer or employee of the United States allowed 60 days by Rule 12(a)(3).)

(Added Apr. 30, 2007, eff. Dec. 1, 2007.)

Form 4. Summons on a Third–Party Complaint

(Caption—See Form 1.)

To *name the third-party defendant*:

A lawsuit has been filed against defendant ______, who as third-party plaintiff is making this claim against you to pay part or all of what [he] may owe to the plaintiff ______.

Within 20 days after service of this summons on you (not counting the day you received it), you must serve on the plaintiff and on the defendant an answer to the attached third-party complaint or a motion under Rule 12 of the Federal Rules of Civil Procedure. The answer or motion must be served on the defendant's attorney, ______ , whose address is, ______, and also on the plaintiff's attorney,

__________, whose address is, __________. If you fail to do so, judgment by default will be entered against you for the relief demanded in the third-party complaint. You also must file the answer or motion with the court and serve it on any other parties.

A copy of the plaintiff's complaint is also attached. You may—but are not required to—respond to it.

Date ______

____

Clerk of Court

(Court Seal)

(Added Apr. 30, 2007, eff. Dec. 1, 2007.)

Form 5. Notice of a Lawsuit and Request to Waive Service of a Summons

(Caption—See Form 1.)

To *(name the defendant—or if the defendant is a corporation, partnership, or association name an officer or agent authorized to receive service)*:

Why are you getting this?

A lawsuit has been filed against you, or the entity you represent, in this court under the number shown above. A copy of the complaint is attached.

This is not a summons, or an official notice from the court. It is a request that, to avoid expenses, you waive formal service of a summons by signing and returning the enclosed waiver. To avoid these expenses, you must return the signed waiver within (*give at least 30 days or at least 60 days if the defendant is outside any judicial district of the United States*) from the date shown below, which is the date this notice was sent. Two copies of the waiver form are enclosed, along with a stamped, self-addressed envelope or other prepaid means for returning one copy. You may keep the other copy.

What happens next?

If you return the signed waiver, I will file it with the court. The action will then proceed as if you had been served on the date the waiver is filed, but no summons will be served on you and you will have 60 days from the date this notice is sent (see the date below) to answer the complaint (or 90 days if this notice is sent to you outside any judicial district of the United States).

If you do not return the signed waiver within the time indicated, I will arrange to have the summons and complaint served on you. And I will ask the court to require you, or the entity you represent, to pay the expenses of making service.

Please read the enclosed statement about the duty to avoid unnecessary expenses.

I certify that this request is being sent to you on the date below.

(Date and sign—See Form 2.)

(Added Apr. 30, 2007, eff. Dec. 1, 2007.)

Form 6. Waiver of the Service of Summons

(Caption—See Form 1.)

To *name the plaintiff's attorney or the unrepresented plaintiff*:

I have received your request to waive service of a summons in this action along with a copy of the complaint, two copies of this waiver form, and a prepaid means of returning one signed copy of the form to you.

I, or the entity I represent, agree to save the expense of serving a summons and complaint in this case.

I understand that I, or the entity I represent, will keep all defenses or objections to the lawsuit, the court's jurisdiction, and the venue of the action, but that I waive any objections to the absence of a summons or of service.

I also understand that I, or the entity I represent, must file and serve an answer or a motion under Rule 12 within 60 days from ______, the date when this request was sent (or 90 days if it was sent outside the United States). If I fail to do so, a default judgment will be entered against me or the entity I represent.

(Date and sign—See Form 2.)

(Attach the following to Form 6.)

Duty to Avoid Unnecessary Expenses of Serving a Summons

Rule 4 of the Federal Rules of Civil Procedure requires certain defendants to cooperate in saving unnecessary expenses of serving a summons and complaint. A defendant who is located in the United States and who fails to return a signed waiver of service requested by a plaintiff located in the United States will be required to pay the expenses of service, unless the defendant shows good cause for the failure.

"Good cause" does *not* include a belief that the lawsuit is groundless, or that it has been brought in an improper venue, or that the court has no jurisdiction over this matter or over the defendant or the defendant's property.

If the waiver is signed and returned, you can still make these and all other defenses and objections, but you cannot object to the absence of a summons or of service.

If you waive service, then you must, within the time specified on the waiver form, serve an answer or a motion under Rule 12 on the plaintiff and file a copy with the court. By signing and returning the waiver form, you are allowed more time to respond than if a summons had been served.

(Added Apr. 30, 2007, eff. Dec. 1, 2007.)

Form 7. Statement of Jurisdiction

a. (*For diversity-of-citizenship jurisdiction.*) The plaintiff is [a citizen of *Michigan*] [a corporation incorporated under the laws of *Michigan* with its principal place of business in *Michigan*]. The defendant is [a citizen of *New York*] [a corporation incorporated under the laws of *New York* with its principal place of business in *New York*]. The amount in controversy, without interest and costs, exceeds the sum or value specified by 28 U.S.C. § 1332.

b. (*For federal-question jurisdiction.*) This action arises under [the United States Constitution, *specify the article or amendment and the section*] [a United States treaty *specify*] [a federal statute, ___ U.S.C. § ___].

c. (*For a claim in the admiralty or maritime jurisdiction.*) This is a case of admiralty or maritime jurisdiction. (*To invoke admiralty status under Rule 9(h) use the following:* This is an admiralty or maritime claim within the meaning of Rule 9(h).)

(Added Apr. 30, 2007, eff. Dec. 1, 2007.)

Form 8. Statement of Reasons for Omitting a Party

(*If a person who ought to be made a party under Rule 19(a) is not named, include this statement in accordance with Rule 19(c).*)

This complaint does not join as a party *name* who [is not subject to this court's personal jurisdiction] [cannot be made a party without depriving this court of subject-matter jurisdiction] because *state the reason.*

(Added Apr. 30, 2007, eff. Dec. 1, 2007.)

Form 9. Statement Noting a Party's Death

(Caption—See Form 1.)

In accordance with Rule 25(a) *name the person,* who is [a party to this action] [a representative of or successor to the deceased party] notes the death during the pendency of this action of *name,* [*describe as party* in this action].

(Date and sign—See Form 2.)

(Added Apr. 30, 2007, eff. Dec. 1, 2007.)

Form 10. Complaint to Recover a Sum Certain

(Caption—See Form 1.)

1. (Statement of Jurisdiction—See Form 7.)

(*Use one or more of the following as appropriate and include a demand for judgment.*)

(a) On a Promissory Note

2. On *date,* the defendant executed and delivered a note promising to pay the plaintiff on *date* the sum of $______ with interest at the rate of ___ percent. A copy of the note [is attached as Exhibit A] [is summarized as follows: ______.]

3. The defendant has not paid the amount owed.

(b) On an Account

2. The defendant owes the plaintiff $______ according to the account set out in Exhibit A.

(c) For Goods Sold and Delivered

2. The defendant owes the plaintiff $______ for goods sold and delivered by the plaintiff to the defendant from *date* to *date.*

(d) For Money Lent

2. The defendant owes the plaintiff $______ for money lent by the plaintiff to the defendant on *date.*

(e) For Money Paid by Mistake

2. The defendant owes the plaintiff $______ for money paid by mistake to the defendant on *date* under these circumstances: *describe with particularity in accordance with Rule 9(b).*

(f) For Money Had and Received

2. The defendant owes the plaintiff $______ for money that was received from *name* on *date* to be paid by the defendant to the plaintiff.

Demand for Judgment

Therefore, the plaintiff demands judgment against the defendant for $______, plus interest and costs.

(Date and sign—See Form 2.)

(Added Apr. 30, 2007, eff. Dec. 1, 2007.)

Form 11. Complaint for Negligence

(Caption—See Form 1.)

1. (Statement of Jurisdiction—See Form 7.)
2. On *date,* at *place,* the defendant negligently drove a motor vehicle against the plaintiff.
3. As a result, the plaintiff was physically injured, lost wages or income, suffered physical and mental pain, and incurred medical expenses of $______.

Therefore, the plaintiff demands judgment against the defendant for $______, plus costs.

(Date and sign—See Form 2).

(Added Apr. 30, 2007, eff. Dec. 1, 2007.)

Form 12. Complaint for Negligence when the Plaintiff Does Not Know Who is Responsible

(Caption—See Form 1.)

1. (Statement of Jurisdiction—See Form 7.)
2. On *date*, at *place*, defendant *name* or defendant *name* or both of them willfully or recklessly or negligently drove, or caused to be driven, a motor vehicle against the plaintiff.
3. As a result, the plaintiff was physically injured, lost wages or income, suffered mental and physical pain, and incurred medical expenses of $______.

Therefore, the plaintiff demands judgment against one or both defendants for $______, plus costs.

(Date and sign—See Form 2.)

(Added Apr. 30, 2007, eff. Dec. 1, 2007.)

Form 13. Complaint for Negligence Under the Federal Employers' Liability Act

(Caption—See Form 1.)

1. (Statement of Jurisdiction—See Form 7.)
2. At the times below, the defendant owned and operated in interstate commerce a railroad line that passed through a tunnel located at ______.
3. On *date*, the plaintiff was working to repair and enlarge the tunnel to make it convenient and safe for use in interstate commerce.
4. During this work, the defendant, as the employer, negligently put the plaintiff to work in a section of the tunnel that the defendant had left unprotected and unsupported.
5. The defendant's negligence caused the plaintiff to be injured by a rock that fell from an unsupported portion of the tunnel.
6. As a result, the plaintiff was physically injured, lost wages or income, suffered mental and physical pain, and incurred medical expenses of $______.

Therefore, the plaintiff demands judgment against the defendant for $______, and costs.

(Date and sign—See Form 2.)

(Added Apr. 30, 2007, eff. Dec. 1, 2007.)

Form 14. Complaint for Damages Under the Merchant Marine Act

(Caption—See Form 1.)

1. (Statement of Jurisdiction—See Form 7.)
2. At the times below, the defendant owned and operated the vessel *name* and used it to transport cargo for hire by water in interstate and foreign commerce.
3. On *date*, at *place*, the defendant hired the plaintiff under seamen's articles of customary form for a voyage from ______ to ______ and return at a wage of $______ a month and found, which is equal to a shore worker's wage of $______ a month.
4. On *date*, the vessel was at sea on the return voyage. (*Describe the weather and the condition of the vessel.*)
5. (*Describe as in Form 11 the defendant's negligent conduct.*)
6. As a result of the defendant's negligent conduct and the unseaworthiness of the vessel, the plaintiff was physically injured, has been incapable of any gainful activity, suffered mental and physical pain, and has incurred medical expenses of $______.

Therefore, the plaintiff demands judgment against the defendant for $______, plus costs.

(Date and sign—See Form 2.)

(Added Apr. 30, 2007, eff. Dec. 1, 2007.)

Form 15. Complaint for the Conversion of Property

(Caption—See Form 1.)

1. (Statement of Jurisdiction—See Form 7.)
2. On *date*, at *place*, the defendant converted to the defendant's own use property owned by the plaintiff. The property converted consists of *describe*.
3. The property is worth $______.

Therefore, the plaintiff demands judgment against the defendant for $______, plus costs.

(Date and sign—See Form 2.)

(Added Apr. 30, 2007, eff. Dec. 1, 2007.)

Form 16. Third-Party Complaint

(Caption—See Form 1.)

1. Plaintiff *name* has filed against defendant *name* a complaint, a copy of which is attached.
2. (*State grounds entitling defendant's name to recover from third-party defendant's name for (all or an identified share) of any judgment for plaintiff's name against defendant's name.*)

Therefore, the defendant demands judgment against *third-party defendant's name* for *all or an identified share* of sums that may be adjudged against the defendant in the plaintiff's favor.

(Date and sign—See Form 2.)

(Added Apr. 30, 2007, eff. Dec. 1, 2007.)

Form 17. Complaint for Specific Performance of a Contract to Convey Land

(Caption—See Form 1.)

1. (Statement of Jurisdiction—See Form 7.)
2. On *date*, the parties agreed to the contract [attached as Exhibit A][summarize the contract].
3. As agreed, the plaintiff tendered the purchase price and requested a conveyance of the land, but the defendant refused to accept the money or make a conveyance.
4. The plaintiff now offers to pay the purchase price.

Therefore, the plaintiff demands that:

(a) the defendant be required to specifically perform the agreement and pay damages of $______, plus interest and costs, or

(b) if specific performance is not ordered, the defendant be required to pay damages of $______, plus interest and costs.

(Date and sign—See Form 2.)

(Added Apr. 30, 2007, eff. Dec. 1, 2007.)

Form 18. Complaint for Patent Infringement

(Caption—See Form 1.)

1. (Statement of Jurisdiction—See Form 7.)
2. On *date*, United States Letters Patent No. ______ were issued to the plaintiff for an invention in an *electric motor*. The plaintiff owned the patent throughout the period of the defendant's infringing acts and still owns the patent.
3. The defendant has infringed and is still infringing the Letters Patent by making, selling, and using *electric motors* that embody the patented invention, and the defendant will continue to do so unless enjoined by this court.
4. The plaintiff has complied with the statutory requirement of placing a notice of the Letters Patent on all *electric motors* it manufactures and sells and has given the defendant written notice of the infringement.

Therefore, the plaintiff demands:

(a) a preliminary and final injunction against the continuing infringement;

(b) an accounting for damages; and

(c) interest and costs.

(Date and sign—See Form 2.)

(Added Apr. 30, 2007, eff. Dec. 1, 2007.)

Form 19. Complaint for Copyright Infringement and Unfair Competition

(Caption—See Form 1.)

1. (Statement of Jurisdiction—See Form 7.)
2. Before *date*, the plaintiff, a United States citizen, wrote a book entitled ______.
3. The book is an original work that may be copyrighted under United States law. A copy of the book is attached as Exhibit A.
4. Between *date* and *date*, the plaintiff applied to the copyright office and received a certificate of registration dated ______ and identified as *date, class, number*.
5. Since *date*, the plaintiff has either published or licensed for publication all copies of the book in compliance with the copyright laws and has remained the sole owner of the copyright.
6. After the copyright was issued, the defendant infringed the copyright by publishing and selling a book entitled ______, which was copied largely from the plaintiff's book. A copy of the defendant's book is attached as Exhibit B.
7. The plaintiff has notified the defendant in writing of the infringement.
8. The defendant continues to infringe the copyright by continuing to publish and sell the infringing book in violation of the copyright, and further has engaged in unfair trade practices and unfair competition in connection with its publication and sale of the infringing book, thus causing irreparable damage.

Therefore, the plaintiff demands that:

(a) until this case is decided the defendant and the defendant's agents be enjoined from disposing of any copies of the defendant's book by sale or otherwise;

(b) the defendant account for and pay as damages to the plaintiff all profits and advantages gained from unfair trade practices and unfair competition in selling the defendant's book, and all profits and advantages gained from infringing the plaintiff's copyright (but no less than the statutory minimum);

(c) the defendant deliver for impoundment all copies of the book in the defendant's possession or control and deliver for destruction all infringing copies and all plates, molds, and other materials for making infringing copies;

(d) the defendant pay the plaintiff interest, costs, and reasonable attorney's fees; and

(e) the plaintiff be awarded any other just relief.

(Date and sign—See Form 2.)

(Added Apr. 30, 2007, eff. Dec. 1, 2007.)

Form 20. Complaint for Interpleader and Declaratory Relief

(Caption—See Form 1.)

1. (Statement of Jurisdiction—See Form 7.)
2. On *date*, the plaintiff issued a life insurance policy on the life of *name* with *name* as the named beneficiary.
3. As a condition for keeping the policy in force, the policy required payment of a premium during the first year and then annually.
4. The premium due on *date* was never paid, and the policy lapsed after that date.
5. On *date* , after the policy had lapsed, both the insured and the named beneficiary died in an automobile collision.
6. Defendant *name* claims to be the beneficiary in place of *name* and has filed a claim to be paid the policy's full amount.
7. The other two defendants are representatives of the deceased persons' estates. Each defendant has filed a claim on behalf of each estate to receive payment of the policy's full amount.
8. If the policy was in force at the time of death, the plaintiff is in doubt about who should be paid.

Therefore, the plaintiff demands that:

(a) each defendant be restrained from commencing any action against the plaintiff on the policy;

(b) a judgment be entered that no defendant is entitled to the proceeds of the policy or any part of it, but if the court determines that the policy was in effect at the time of the insured's death, that the defendants be required to interplead and settle among themselves their rights to the proceeds, and that the plaintiff be discharged from all liability except to the defendant determined to be entitled to the proceeds; and

(c) the plaintiff recover its costs.

(Date and sign—See Form 2.)

(Added Apr. 30, 2007, eff. Dec. 1, 2007.)

Form 21. Complaint on a Claim for a Debt and to Set Aside a Fraudulent Conveyance Under Rule 18(b)

(Caption—See Form 1.)

1. (Statement of Jurisdiction—See Form 7.)
2. On *date*, defendant *name* signed a note promising to pay to the plaintiff on *date* the sum of $______ with interest at the rate of ___ percent. [The pleader may, but need not, attach a copy or plead the note verbatim.]
3. Defendant *name* owes the plaintiff the amount of the note and interest.
4. On *date*, defendant *name* conveyed all defendant's real and personal property *if less than all, describe it fully* to defendant *name* for the purpose of defrauding the plaintiff and hindering or delaying the collection of the debt.

Therefore, the plaintiff demands that:

(a) judgment for $______, plus costs, be entered against defendant(s) *name(s)*; and

(b) the conveyance to defendant *name* be declared void and any judgment granted be made a lien on the property.

(Date and sign—See Form 2.)

(Added Apr. 30, 2007, eff. Dec. 1, 2007.)

Form 30. Answer Presenting Defenses Under Rule 12(b)

(Caption—See Form 1.)

Responding to Allegations in the Complaint

1. Defendant admits the allegations in paragraphs ______.
2. Defendant lacks knowledge or information sufficient to form a belief about the truth of the allegations in paragraphs ______.
3. Defendant admits *identify part of the allegation* in paragraph ______ and denies or lacks knowledge or information sufficient to form a belief about the truth of the rest of the paragraph.

Failure to State a Claim

4. The complaint fails to state a claim upon which relief can be granted.

Failure to Join a Required Party

5. If there is a debt, it is owed jointly by the defendant and *name* who is a citizen of ______. This person can be made a party without depriving this court of jurisdiction over the existing parties.

Affirmative Defense–Statute of Limitations

6. The plaintiff's claim is barred by the statute of limitations because it arose more than ______ years before this action was commenced.

Counterclaim

7. (*Set forth any counterclaim in the same way a claim is pleaded in a complaint. Include a further statement of jurisdiction if needed.*)

Crossclaim

8. (*Set forth a crossclaim against a coparty in the same way a claim is pleaded in a complaint. Include a further statement of jurisdiction if needed.*)

(Date and sign—See Form 2.)

(Added Apr. 30, 2007, eff. Dec. 1, 2007.)

Form 31. Answer to a Complaint for Money Had and Received With a Counterclaim for Interpleader

(Caption—See Form 1.)

Response to the Allegations in the Complaint

(See Form 30.)

Counterclaim for Interpleader

1. The defendant received from name a deposit of $______.
2. The plaintiff demands payment of the deposit because of a purported assignment from name, who has notified the defendant that the assignment is not valid and who continues to hold the defendant responsible for the deposit.

Therefore, the defendant demands that:

(a) name be made a party to this action;

(b) the plaintiff and name be required to interplead their respective claims;

(c) the court decide whether the plaintiff or name or either of them is entitled to the deposit and discharge the defendant of any liability except to the person entitled to the deposit; and

(d) the defendant recover costs and attorney's fees.

(Date and sign—See Form 2.)

(Added Apr. 30, 2007, eff. Dec. 1, 2007.)

Form 40. Motion to Dismiss Under Rule 12(b) for Lack of Jurisdiction, Improper Venue, Insufficient Service of Process, or Failure to State a Claim

(Caption—See Form 1.)

The defendant moves to dismiss the action because:

1. the amount in controversy is less than the sum or value specified by 28 U.S.C. § 1332;
2. the defendant is not subject to the personal jurisdiction of this court;
3. venue is improper (this defendant does not reside in this district and no part of the events or omissions giving rise to the claim occurred in the district);
4. the defendant has not been properly served, as shown by the attached affidavits of ______; or
5. the complaint fails to state a claim upon which relief can be granted.

(Date and sign—See Form 2.)

(Added Apr. 30, 2007, eff. Dec. 1, 2007.)

Form 41. Motion to Bring in a Third–Party Defendant

(Caption—See Form 1.)

The defendant, as third-party plaintiff, moves for leave to serve on name a summons and third-party complaint, copies of which are attached.

(Date and sign—See Form 2.)

(Added Apr. 30, 2007, eff. Dec. 1, 2007.)

Form 42. Motion to Intervene as a Defendant Under Rule 24

(Caption—See Form 1.)

1. name moves for leave to intervene as a defendant in this action and to file the attached answer.

(*State grounds under Rule 24(a) or (b).*)

2. The plaintiff alleges patent infringement. We manufacture and sell to the defendant the articles involved, and we have a defense to the plaintiff's claim.
3. Our defense presents questions of law and fact that are common to this action.

(Date and sign—See Form 2.)

[An Intervener's Answer must be attached. See Form 30.]

(Added Apr. 30, 2007, eff. Dec. 1, 2007.)

Form 50. Request to Produce Documents and Tangible Things, or to Enter onto Land Under Rule 34

(Caption—See Form 1.)

The plaintiff name requests that the defendant name respond within ____ days to the following requests:

1. To produce and permit the plaintiff to inspect and copy and to test or sample the following documents, including electronically stored information:

(*Describe each document and the electronically stored information, either individually or by category.*)

(*State the time, place, and manner of the inspection and any related acts.*)

2. To produce and permit the plaintiff to inspect and copy—and to test or sample—the following tangible things:

(*Describe each thing, either individually or by category.*)

(*State the time, place, and manner of the inspection and any related acts.*)

3. To permit the plaintiff to enter onto the following land to inspect, photograph, test, or sample the property or an object or operation on the property.

(*Describe the property and each object or operation.*)

(*State the time and manner of the inspection and any related acts.*)

(Date and sign—See Form 2.)

(Added Apr. 30, 2007, eff. Dec. 1, 2007.)

Form 51. Request for Admissions Under Rule 36

(Caption—See Form 1.)

The plaintiff *name* asks the defendant *name* to respond within 30 days to these requests by admitting, for purposes of this action only and subject to objections to admissibility at trial:

1. The genuineness of the following documents, copies of which [are attached] [are or have been furnished or made available for inspection and copying].

(*List each document.*)

2. The truth of each of the following statements:

(*List each statement.*)

(Date and sign—See Form 2.)

(Added Apr. 30, 2007, eff. Dec. 1, 2007.)

Form 52. Report of the Parties' Planning Meeting

(Caption—See Form 1.)

1. The following persons participated in a Rule 26(f) conference on *date* by *state the method of conferring*:

(*e.g., name* representing the plaintiff.)

2. Initial Disclosures. The parties [have completed] [will complete by *date*] the initial disclosures required by Rule 26(a)(1).

3. Discovery Plan. The parties propose this discovery plan:

(*Use separate paragraphs or subparagraphs if the parties disagree.*)

(a) Discovery will be needed on these subjects: (*describe.*)

(b) (Dates for commencing and completing discovery, including discovery to be commenced or completed before other discovery.)

(c) (Maximum number of interrogatories by each party to another party, along with the dates the answers are due.)

(d) (Maximum number of requests for admission, along with the dates responses are due.)

(e) (Maximum number of depositions by each party.)

(f) (Limits on the length of depositions, in hours.)

(g) (Dates for exchanging reports of expert witnesses.)

(h) (Dates for supplementations under Rule 26(e).)

4. Other Items:

(a) (A date if the parties ask to meet with the court before a scheduling order.)

(b) (Requested dates for pretrial conferences.)

(c) (Final dates for the plaintiff to amend pleadings or to join parties.)

(d) (Final dates for the defendant to amend pleadings or to join parties.)

(e) (Final dates to file dispositive motions.)

(f) (State the prospects for settlement.)

(g) (Identify any alternative dispute resolution procedure that may enhance settlement prospects.)

(h) (Final dates for submitting Rule 26(a)(3) witness lists, designations of witnesses whose testimony will be presented by deposition, and exhibit lists.)

(i) (Final dates to file objections under Rule 26(a)(3).)

(j) (Suggested trial date and estimate of trial length.)

(k) (Other matters.)

(Date and sign—see Form 2.)

(Added Apr. 30, 2007, eff. Dec. 1, 2007.)

Form 60. Notice of Condemnation

(Caption—See Form 1.)

To *name the defendant.*

1. A complaint in condemnation has been filed in the United States District Court for the ______District of ______, to take property to use for *purpose*. The interest to be taken is *describe*. The court is located in the United States courthouse at this address: ______.
2. The property to be taken is described below. You have or claim an interest in it.

   (*Describe the property.*)
3. The authority for taking this property is *cite*.
4. If you want to object or present any defense to the taking you must serve an answer on the plaintiff's attorney within 20 days [after being served with this notice][from *(insert the date of the last publication of notice)*]. Send your answer to this address: ______.
5. Your answer must identify the property in which you claim an interest, state the nature and extent of that interest, and state all your objections and defenses to the taking. Objections and defenses not presented are waived.
6. If you fail to answer you consent to the taking and the court will enter a judgment that takes your described property interest.
7. Instead of answering, you may serve on the plaintiff's attorney a notice of appearance that designates the property in which you claim an interest. After you do that, you will receive a notice of any proceedings that affect you. Whether or not you have previously appeared or answered, you may present evidence at a trial to determine compensation for the property and share in the overall award.

(Date and sign—See Form 2.)

(Added Apr. 30, 2007, eff. Dec. 1, 2007.)

Form 61. Complaint for Condemnation

(Caption—See Form 1; name as defendants the property and at least one owner.)

1. (Statement of Jurisdiction—See Form 7.)
2. This is an action to take property under the power of eminent domain and to determine just compensation to be paid to the owners and parties in interest.
3. The authority for the taking is ______.
4. The property is to be used for ______.
5. The property to be taken is (*describe in enough detail for identification—or attach the description and state "is described in Exhibit A, attached."*)
6. The interest to be acquired is ______.
7. The persons known to the plaintiff to have or claim an interest in the property are: ______. (*For each person include the interest claimed.*)
8. There may be other persons who have or claim an interest in the property and whose names could not be found after a reasonably diligent search. They are made parties under the designation "Unknown Owners."

Therefore, the plaintiff demands judgment:

(a) condemning the property;

(b) determining and awarding just compensation; and

(c) granting any other lawful and proper relief.

(Date and sign—See Form 2.)

(Added Apr. 30, 2007, eff. Dec. 1, 2007.)

Form 70. Judgment on a Jury Verdict

(Caption—See Form 1.)

This action was tried by a jury with Judge ______ presiding, and the jury has rendered a verdict.

It is ordered that:

[the plaintiff *name* recover from the defendant *name* the amount of $______ with interest at the rate of ___%, along with costs.]

[the plaintiff recover nothing, the action be dismissed on the merits, and the defendant *name* recover costs from the plaintiff *name.*]

Date ______

____

Clerk of Court

(Added Apr. 30, 2007, eff. Dec. 1, 2007.)

Form 71. Judgment by the Court Without a Jury

(Caption—See Form 1.)

This action was tried by Judge ______ without a jury and the following decision was reached:

It is ordered that [the plaintiff *name* recover from the defendant *name* the amount of $______, with prejudgment interest at the rate of ___%, postjudgment interest at the rate of ___%, along with costs.] [the plaintiff recover nothing, the action be dismissed on the merits, and the defendant *name* recover costs from the plaintiff *name.*]

Date______________

____

Clerk of Court

(Added Apr. 30, 2007, eff. Dec. 1, 2007.)

Form 80. Notice of a Magistrate Judge's Availability

1. A magistrate judge is available under title 28 U.S.C. § 636(c) to conduct the proceedings in this case, including a jury or nonjury trial and the entry of final judgment. But a magistrate judge can be assigned only if all parties voluntarily consent.
2. You may withhold your consent without adverse substantive consequences. The identity of any party consenting or withholding consent will not be disclosed to the judge to whom the case is assigned or to any magistrate judge.
3. If a magistrate judge does hear your case, you may appeal directly to a United States court of appeals as you would if a district judge heard it.

A form called *Consent to an Assignment to a United States Magistrate Judge* is available from the court clerk's office.

(Added Apr. 30, 2007, eff. Dec. 1, 2007.)

Form 81. Consent to an Assignment to a Magistrate Judge

(Caption—See Form 1.)

I voluntarily consent to have a United States magistrate judge conduct all further proceedings in this case, including a trial, and order the entry of final judgment. (Return this form to the court clerk—not to a judge or magistrate judge.)

Date________________

____

Signature of the Party

(Added Apr. 30, 2007, eff. Dec. 1, 2007.)

Form 82. Order of Assignment to a Magistrate Judge

(Caption—See Form 1.)

With the parties' consent it is ordered that this case be assigned to United States Magistrate Judge ______ of this district to conduct all proceedings and enter final judgment in accordance with 28 U.S.C. § 636(c).

Date ________________

____

United States District Judge

(Added Apr. 30, 2007, eff. Dec. 1, 2007.)

SUPPLEMENTAL RULES FOR ADMIRALTY OR MARITIME CLAIMS AND ASSET FORFEITURE ACTIONS

Amendments received to December 1, 2008

ADVISORY COMMITTEE NOTES

1966 Adoption

The amendments to the Federal Rules of Civil Procedure to unify the civil and admiralty procedure, together with the Supplemental Rules for Certain Admiralty and Maritime Claims, completely superseded the Admiralty Rules, effective July 1, 1966. Accordingly, the latter were rescinded.

1985 Amendment

Since their promulgation in 1966, the Supplemental Rules for Certain Admiralty and Maritime Claims have preserved the special procedures of arrest and attachment unique to admiralty law. In recent years, however, these Rules have been challenged as violating the principles of procedural due process enunciated in the United States Supreme Court's decision in *Sniadach v. Family Finance Corp.*, 395 U.S. 337 (1969), and later developed in *Fuentes v. Shevin*, 407 U.S. 67 (1972); *Mitchell v. W.T. Grant Co.*, 416 U.S. 600 (1974); and *North Georgia Finishing, Inc. v. Di–Chem, Inc.*, 419 U.S. 601 (1975). These Supreme Court decisions provide five basic criteria for a constitutional seizure of property: (1) effective notice to persons having interests in the property seized, (2) judicial review prior to attachment, (3) avoidance of conclusory allegations in the complaint, (4) security posted by the plaintiff to protect the owner of the property under attachment, and (5) a meaningful and timely hearing after attachment.

Several commentators have found the Supplemental Rules lacking on some or all five grounds. *E.g.*, Batiza & Partridge, *The Constitutional Challenge to Maritime Seizures*, 26 Loy.L.Rev. 203 (1980); Morse, *The Conflict Between the Supreme Court Admiralty Rules and Sniadach–Fuentes: A Collision Course?*, 3 Fla.St.U.L.Rev. 1 (1975). The federal courts have varied in their disposition of challenges to the Supplemental Rules. The Fourth and Fifth Circuits have affirmed the constitutionality of Rule C. *Amstar Corp. v. S/S Alexandros T.*, 664 F.2d 904 (4th Cir.1981); *Merchants National Bank of Mobile v. The Dredge General G.L. Gillespie*, 663 F.2d 1338 (5th Cir.1981), *cert. dismissed*, 456 U.S. 966 (1982). However, a district court in the Ninth Circuit found Rule C unconstitutional. *Alyeska Pipeline Service Co. v. The Vessel Bay Ridge*, 509 F.Supp. 1115 (D. Alaska 1981), *appeal dismissed*, 703 F.2d 381 (9th Cir.1983). Rule B(1) has received similar inconsistent treatment. The Ninth and Eleventh Circuits have upheld its constitutionality. *Polar Shipping, Ltd. v. Oriental Shipping Corp.*, 680 F.2d 627 (9th Cir.1982); *Schiffahartsgesellschaft Leonhardt & Co. v. A. Bottacchi S.A. de Navegacion*, 732 F.2d 1543 (11th Cir.1984). On the other hand, a Washington district court has found it to be constitutionally deficient. *Grand Bahama Petroleum Co. v. Canadian Transportation Agencies, Ltd.*, 450 F.Supp. 447 (W.D. Wash. 1978). The constitutionality of both rules was questioned in *Techem Chem Co. v. M/T Choyo Maru*, 416 F.Supp. 960 (D. Md. 1976). Thus, there is uncertainty as to whether the current rules prescribe constitutionally sound procedures for guidance of courts and counsel. See generally Note, *Due Process in Admiralty Arrest and Attachment*, 56 Tex.L.Rev. 1091 (1978).

Due to the controversy and uncertainty that have surrounded the Supplemental Rules, local admiralty bars and the Maritime Law Association of the United States have sought to strengthen the constitutionality of maritime arrest and attachment by encouraging promulgation of local admiralty rules providing for prompt post-seizure hearings. Some districts also adopted rules calling for judicial scrutiny of applications for arrest or attachment. Nonetheless, the result has been a lack of uniformity and continued concern over the constitutionality of the existing practice. The amendments that follow are intended to provide rules that meet the requirements prescribed by the Supreme Court and to develop uniformity in the admiralty practice.

Rule A. Scope of Rules

(1) These Supplemental Rules apply to:

(A) the procedure in admiralty and maritime claims within the meaning of Rule 9(h) with respect to the following remedies:

(i) maritime attachment and garnishment,

(ii) actions in rem,

(iii) possessory, petitory, and partition actions, and

(iv) actions for exoneration from or limitation of liability;

(B) forfeiture actions in rem arising from a federal statute; and

(C) the procedure in statutory condemnation proceedings analogous to maritime actions in rem, whether within the admiralty and maritime jurisdiction or not. Except as otherwise provided, references in these Supplemental Rules to actions in rem include such analogous statutory condemnation proceedings.

(2) The Federal Rules of Civil Procedure also apply to the foregoing proceedings except to the extent that they are inconsistent with these Supplemental Rules.

(Added Feb. 28, 1966, eff. July 1, 1966, and amended Apr. 12, 2006, eff. Dec. 1, 2006)

ADVISORY COMMITTEE NOTES

1966 Adoption

Certain distinctively maritime remedies must be preserved in unified rules. The commencement of an action by attachment or garnishment has heretofore been practically unknown in federal jurisprudence except in admiralty, although the amendment of Rule 4(e) effective July 1, 1963, makes available that procedure in accordance with state law. The maritime proceeding in rem is unique, except as it has been emulated by statute, and is closely related to the substantive maritime law relating to liens. Arrest of the vessel or other maritime property is an historic remedy in controversies over title or right to possession, and in disputes among co-owners over the vessel's employment. The statutory right to limit liability is limited to owners of vessels, and has its own complexities. While the unified federal rules are generally applicable to these distinctive proceedings, certain special rules dealing with them are needed.

Arrest of the person and imprisonment for debt are not included because there remedies are not peculiarly maritime. The practice is not uniform but conforms to state law. See 2 Benedict § 286 [Note: reference is to the 6th Edition of Benedict on Admiralty and not to the current 7th Edition]; 28 U.S.C., § 2007; FRCP 64, 69. The relevant provisions of Admiralty Rules 2, 3, and 4 are unnecessary or obsolete.

No attempt is here made to compile a complete and self-contained code governing these distinctively maritime remedies. The more limited objective is to carry forward the relevant provisions of the former Rules of Practice for Admiralty and Maritime Cases, modernized and revised to some extent but still in the context of history and precedent. Accordingly, these Rules are not to be construed as limiting or impairing the traditional power of a district court, exercising the admiralty and maritime jurisdiction, to adapt its procedures and its remedies in the individual case, consistently with these rules, to secure the just, speedy, and inexpensive determination of every action. (See *Swift & Co., Packers v. Compania Columbiana Del Caribe, S/A*, 339 U.S. 684, (1950); Rule 1). In addition, of course, the district courts retain the power to make local rules not inconsistent with these rules. See Rule 83; cf. Admiralty Rule 44.

2006 Amendment

Rule A is amended to reflect the adoption of Rule G to govern procedure in civil forfeiture actions. Rule G(1) contemplates application of other Supplemental Rules to the extent that Rule G does not address an issue. One example is the Rule E(4)(c) provision for arresting intangible property.

Rule B. In Personam Actions: Attachment and Garnishment

(1) When Available; Complaint, Affidavit, Judicial Authorization, and Process. In an in personam action:

(a) If a defendant is not found within the district when a verified complaint praying for attachment and the affidavit required by Rule B(1)(b) are filed, a verified complaint may contain a prayer for process to attach the defendant's tangible or intangible personal property—up to the amount sued for—in the hands of garnishees named in the process.

(b) The plaintiff or the plaintiff's attorney must sign and file with the complaint an affidavit stating that, to the affiant's knowledge, or on information and belief, the defendant cannot be found within the district. The court must review the complaint and affidavit and, if the conditions of this Rule B appear to exist, enter an order so stating and authorizing process of attachment and garnishment. The clerk may issue supplemental process enforcing the court's order upon application without further court order.

(c) If the plaintiff or the plaintiff's attorney certifies that exigent circumstances make court review impracticable, the clerk must issue the summons and process of attachment and garnishment. The plaintiff has the burden in any post-attachment hearing under Rule E(4)(f) to show that exigent circumstances existed.

(d)(i) If the property is a vessel or tangible property on board a vessel, the summons, process, and any supplemental process must be delivered to the marshal for service.

(ii) If the property is other tangible or intangible property, the summons, process, and any supplemental process must be delivered to a person or organization authorized to serve it, who may be (A) a marshal; (B) someone under contract with the United States; (C) someone specially appointed by the court for that purpose; or, (D) in an action brought by the United States, any officer or employee of the United States.

(e) The plaintiff may invoke state-law remedies under Rule 64 for seizure of person or property for the purpose of securing satisfaction of the judgment.

(2) Notice to Defendant. No default judgment may be entered except upon proof—which may be by affidavit—that:

(a) the complaint, summons, and process of attachment or garnishment have been served on the defendant in a manner authorized by Rule 4;

(b) the plaintiff or the garnishee has mailed to the defendant the complaint, summons, and process of attachment or garnishment, using any form of mail requiring a return receipt; or

(c) the plaintiff or the garnishee has tried diligently to give notice of the action to the defendant but could not do so.

(3) Answer.

(a) By Garnishee. The garnishee shall serve an answer, together with answers to any interrogatories served with the complaint, within 20 days after service of process upon the garnishee. Interrogatories to the garnishee may be served with the complaint without leave of court. If the garnishee refuses or neglects to answer on oath as to the debts, credits, or effects of the defendant in the garnishee's hands, or any interrogatories concerning such debts, credits, and effects that may be propounded by the plaintiff, the court may award compulsory process against the garnishee. If the garnishee admits any debts, credits, or effects, they shall be held in the garnishee's hands or paid into the registry of the court, and shall be held in either case subject to the further order of the court.

(b) By Defendant. The defendant shall serve an answer within 30 days after process has been executed, whether by attachment of property or service on the garnishee.

(Added Feb. 28, 1966, eff. July 1, 1966, and amended Apr. 29, 1985, eff. Aug. 1, 1985; Mar. 2, 1987, eff. Aug. 1, 1987; Apr. 17, 2000, eff. Dec. 1, 2000; Apr. 25, 2005, eff. Dec. 1, 2005.)

ADVISORY COMMITTEE NOTES

1966 Adoption

Subdivision (1)

This preserves the traditional maritime remedy of attachment and garnishment, and carries forward the relevant substance of Admiralty Rule 2. In addition, or in the alternative, provision is made for the use of similar state remedies made available by the amendment of Rule 4(e) effective July 1, 1963. On the effect of appearance to defend against attachment see Rule E(8).

The rule follows closely the language of Admiralty Rule 2. No change is made with respect to the property subject to attachment. No change is made in the condition that makes the remedy available. The rules have never defined the clause, "if the defendant shall not be found within the district," and no definition is attempted here. The subject seems one best left for the time being to development on a case-by-case basis. The proposal does shift from the marshal (on whom it now rests in theory) to the plaintiff the burden of establishing that the defendant cannot be found in the district.

A change in the context of the practice is brought about by Rule 4(f), which will enable summons to be served throughout the state instead of, as heretofore, only within the district. The Advisory Committee considered whether the rule on attachment and garnishment should be correspondingly changed to permit those remedies only when the defendant cannot be found within the state and concluded that the remedy should not be so limited.

The effect is to enlarge the class of cases in which the plaintiff may proceed by attachment or garnishment although jurisdiction of the person of the defendant may be independently obtained. This is possible at the present time where, for example, a corporate defendant has appointed an agent within the district to accept service of process but is not carrying on activities there sufficient to subject it to jurisdiction. (*Seawind Compania, S.A. v. Crescent Line, Inc.*, 320 F.2d 580 (2d Cir.1963)), or where, though the foreign corporation's activities in the district are sufficient to subject it personally to the jurisdiction, there is in the district no officer on whom process can be served (*United States v. Cia. Naviera Continental, S.A.*, 178 F.Supp. 561, (S.D.N.Y.1959)).

Process of attachment or garnishment will be limited to the district. See Rule E(3)(a).

Subdivision (2)

The former Admiralty Rules did not provide for notice to the defendant in attachment and garnishment proceedings. None is required by the principles of due process, since it is assumed that the garnishee or custodian of the property attached will either notify the defendant or be deprived of the right to plead the judgment as a defense in an action against him by the defendant. *Harris v. Balk*, 198 U.S. 215 (1905); *Pennoyer v. Neff*, 95 U.S. 714 (1878). Modern conceptions of fairness, however, dictate that actual notice be given to persons known to claim an interest in the property that is the subject of the action where that is reasonably practicable. In attachment and garnishment proceedings the persons whose interests will be affected by the judgment are identified by the complaint. No substantial burden is imposed on the plaintiff by a simple requirement that he notify the defendant of the action by mail.

In the usual case the defendant is notified of the pendency of the proceedings by the garnishee or otherwise, and appears to claim the property and to make his answer. Hence notice by mail is not routinely required in all cases, but only in those in which the defendant has not appeared prior to the time when a default judgment is demanded. The rule therefore provides only that no default judgment shall be entered except upon proof of notice, or of inability to give notice despite diligent efforts to do so. Thus the burden of giving notice is further minimized.

In some cases the plaintiff may prefer to give notice by serving process in the usual way instead of simply by mail. (Rule 4(d).) In particular, if the defendant is in a foreign country the plaintiff may wish to utilize the modes of notice recently provided to facilitate compliance with foreign laws and procedures (Rule 4(i)). The rule provides for these alternatives.

The rule does not provide for notice by publication because there is no problem concerning unknown claimants, and publication has little utility in proportion to its expense where the identity of the defendant is known.

Subdivision (3)

Subdivision (a) incorporates the substance of Admiralty Rule 36.

The Admiralty Rules were silent as to when the garnishee and the defendant were to answer. See also 2 Benedict ch. XXIV [Reference is to the 6th Edition of Benedict on Admiralty and not to the current 7th Edition].

The rule proceeds on the assumption that uniform and definite periods of time for responsive pleadings should be substituted for return days (see the discussion under Rule C(6), below). Twenty days seems sufficient time for the garnishee to answer (cf. FRCP 12(a)), and an additional 10 days should suffice for the defendant. When allowance is made for the time required for notice to reach the defendant this gives the defendant in attachment and garnishment approximately the same time that defendants have to answer when personally served.

1985 Amendment

Rule B(1) has been amended to provide for judicial scrutiny before the issuance of any attachment or garnishment process. Its purpose is to eliminate doubts as to whether the Rule is consistent with the principles of procedural due process enunciated by the Supreme Court in *Sniadach v. Family Finance Corp.*, 395 U.S. 337 (1969); and later developed in *Fuentes v. Shevin*, 407 U.S. 67 (1972); *Mitchell v. W.T. Grant Co.*, 416 U.S. 600 (1974); and *North Georgia Finishing, Inc. v. Di-Chem, Inc.*, 419 U.S. 601 (1975). Such doubts were raised in *Grand Bahama Petroleum Co. v. Canadian Transportation Agencies, Ltd.*, 450 F.Supp. 447 (W.D.Wash.1978); and *Schiffahartsgesellschaft Leonhardt & Co. v. A. Bottacchi S.A. de Navegacion*, 552 F.Supp. 771 (S.D.Ga.1982), which was reversed, 732 F.2d 1543 (11th Cir. 1984). But compare *Polar Shipping Ltd. v. Oriental Shipping Corp.*, 680 F.2d 627 (9th Cir.1982), in which a majority of the panel upheld the constitutionality of Rule B because of the unique commercial context in which it is invoked. The practice described in Rule B(1) has been adopted in some districts by local rule. E.g., N.D. Calif. Local Rule 603.3; W.D.Wash. Local Admiralty Rule 15(d).

The rule envisions that the order will issue when the plaintiff makes a prima facie showing that he has a maritime claim against the defendant in the amount sued for and the defendant is not present in the district. A simple order with conclusory findings is contemplated. The reference to review by the "court" is broad enough to embrace review by a magistrate as well as by a district judge.

The new provision recognizes that in some situations, such as when the judge is unavailable and the ship is about to depart from the jurisdiction, it will be impracticable, if not impossible, to secure the judicial review contemplated by Rule B(1). When "exigent circumstances" exist, the rule enables the plaintiff to secure the issuance of the summons and process of attachment and garnishment, subject to a later showing that the necessary circumstances actually existed. This provision is intended to provide a safety valve without undermining the requirement of preattachment scrutiny. Thus, every effort to secure judicial review, including conducting a hearing by telephone, should be pursued before resorting to the exigent-circumstances procedure.

Rule B(1) also has been amended so that the garnishee shall be named in the "process" rather than in the "complaint." This should solve the problem presented in *Filia Compania Naviera, S.A. v. Petroship, S.A.*, 1983 A.M.C. 1 (S.D.N.Y.1982), and eliminate any need for an additional judicial review of the complaint and affidavit when a garnishee is added.

1987 Amendment

The amendments are technical. No substantive change is intended.

2000 Amendment

Rule B(1) is amended in two ways, and style changes have been made.

The service provisions of Rule C(3) are adopted in paragraph (d), providing alternatives to service by a marshal if the property to be seized is not a vessel or tangible property on board a vessel.

The provision that allows the plaintiff to invoke state attachment and garnishment remedies is amended to reflect the 1993 amendments of Civil Rule 4. Former Civil Rule 4(e), incorporated in Rule B(1), allowed general use of state quasi-in-rem jurisdiction if the defendant was not an inhabitant of, or found within, the state. Rule 4(e) was replaced in 1993 by Rule 4(n)(2), which permits use of state law to seize a defendant's assets only if personal jurisdiction over the defendant cannot be obtained in the district where the action is brought. Little purpose would be served by incorporating Rule 4(n)(2) in Rule B, since maritime attachment and garnishment are available whenever the defendant is not found within the district, a concept that allows attachment or garnishment even in some circumstances in which personal jurisdiction also can be asserted. In order to protect against any possibility that elimination of the reference to state quasi-in-rem jurisdiction remedies might seem to defeat continued use of state security devices, paragraph (e) expressly incorporates Civil Rule 64. Because Rule 64 looks only to security, not jurisdiction, the former reference to Rule E(8) is deleted as no longer relevant.

Rule B(2)(a) is amended to reflect the 1993 redistribution of the service provisions once found in Civil Rule 4(d) and (i). These provisions are now found in many different subdivisions of Rule 4. The new reference simply incorporates Rule 4, without designating the new subdivisions, because the function of Rule B(2) is simply to describe the methods of notice that suffice to support a default judgment. Style changes also have been made.

2005 Amendments

Rule B(1) is amended to incorporate the decisions in *Heidmar, Inc. v. Anomina Ravennate Di Armamento Sp.A. of Ravenna*, 132 F.3d 264, 267–268 (5th Cir. 1998), and *Navieros InterAmericanos, S.A. v. M/V Vasilia Express*, 120 F.3d 304, 314–315 (1st Cir. 1997). The time for determining whether a defendant is "found" in the district is set at the time of filing the verified complaint that prays for attachment and the affidavit required by Rule B(1)(b). As provided by Rule B(1)(b), the affidavit must be filed with the complaint. A defendant cannot defeat the security purpose of attachment by appointing an agent for service of process after the complaint and affidavit are filed. The complaint praying for attachment need not be the initial complaint. So long as the defendant is not found in the district, the prayer for attachment may be made in an amended complaint; the affidavit that the defendant cannot be found must be filed with the amended complaint.

Rule C. In Rem Actions: Special Provisions

(1) When Available. An action in rem may be brought:

(a) To enforce any maritime lien;

(b) Whenever a statute of the United States provides for a maritime action in rem or a proceeding analogous thereto.

Except as otherwise provided by law a party who may proceed in rem may also, or in the alternative, proceed in personam against any person who may be liable.

Statutory provisions exempting vessels or other property owned or possessed by or operated by or for the United States from arrest or seizure are not affected by this rule. When a statute so provides, an action against the United States or an instrumentality thereof may proceed on in rem principles.

(2) Complaint. In an action in rem the complaint must:

(a) be verified;

(b) describe with reasonable particularity the property that is the subject of the action; and

(c) state that the property is within the district or will be within the district while the action is pending.

(3) Judicial Authorization and Process.

(a) Arrest Warrant.

(i) The court must review the complaint and any supporting papers. If the conditions for an in rem action appear to exist, the court must issue an order directing the clerk to issue a warrant for the arrest of the vessel or other property that is the subject of the action.

(ii) If the plaintiff or the plaintiff's attorney certifies that exigent circumstances make court review impracticable, the clerk must promptly issue a summons and a warrant for the arrest of the vessel or other property that is the subject of the action. The plaintiff has the burden in any post-arrest hearing under Rule E(4)(f) to show that exigent circumstances existed.

(b) Service.

(i) If the property that is the subject of the action is a vessel or tangible property on board a vessel, the warrant and any supplemental process must be delivered to the marshal for service.

(ii) If the property that is the subject of the action is other property, tangible or intangible, the warrant and any supplemental process must be delivered to a person or organization authorized to enforce it, who may be: (A) a marshal; (B) someone under contract with the United States; (C) someone specially appointed by the court for that purpose; or, (D) in an action brought by the United States, any officer or employee of the United States.

(c) Deposit in Court. If the property that is the subject of the action consists in whole or in part of freight, the proceeds of property sold, or other intangible property, the clerk must issue—in addition to the warrant—a summons directing any person controlling the property to show cause why it should not be deposited in court to abide the judgment.

(d) Supplemental Process. The clerk may upon application issue supplemental process to enforce the court's order without further court order.

(4) Notice. No notice other than execution of process is required when the property that is the subject of the action has been released under Rule E(5). If the property is not released within 10 days after execution, the plaintiff must promptly—or within the time that the court allows—give public notice of the action and arrest in a newspaper designated by court order and having general circulation in the district, but publication may be terminated if the property is released before publication is completed. The notice must specify the time under Rule C(6) to file a statement of interest in or right against the seized property and to answer. This rule does not affect the notice requirements in an action to foreclose a preferred ship mortgage under 46 U.S.C. §§ 31301 et seq., as amended.

(5) Ancillary Process. In any action in rem in which process has been served as provided by this rule, if any part of the property that is the subject of the action has not been brought within the control of the court because it has been removed or sold, or because it is intangible property in the hands of a person who has not been served with process, the court may, on motion, order any person having possession or control of such property or its proceeds to show cause why it should not be delivered into the custody of the marshal or other person or organization having a warrant for the arrest of the property, or paid into court to abide the judgment; and, after hearing, the court may enter such judgment as law and justice may require.

(6) Responsive Pleading; Interrogatories.

(a) Statement of Interest; Answer. In an action in rem:

(i) a [1] person who asserts a right of possession or any ownership interest in the property that is the subject of the action must file a verified statement of right or interest:

(A) within 10 days after the execution of process, or

(B) within the time that the court allows;

(ii) the statement of right or interest must describe the interest in the property that supports the person's demand for its restitution or right to defend the action;

(iii) an agent, bailee, or attorney must state the authority to file a statement of right or interest on behalf of another; and

(iv) a person who asserts a right of possession or any ownership interest must serve an answer within 20 days after filing the statement of interest or right.

(b) Interrogatories. Interrogatories may be served with the complaint in an in rem action without leave of court. Answers to the interrogatories must be served with the answer to the complaint.

(Added Feb. 28, 1966, eff. July 1, 1966, and amended Apr. 29, 1985, eff. Aug. 1, 1985; Mar. 2, 1987, eff. Aug. 1, 1987; Apr. 30, 1991, eff. Dec. 1, 1991; Apr. 17, 2000, eff. Dec. 1, 2000; Apr. 29, 2002, eff. Dec. 1, 2002; Apr. 25, 2005, eff. Dec. 1, 2005; Apr. 12, 2006, eff. Dec. 1, 2006; Apr. 23, 2008, eff. Dec. 1, 2008.)

1 Text begins so in original.

ADVISORY COMMITTEE NOTES

1966 Adoption

Subdivision (1).

This rule is designed not only to preserve the proceeding in rem as it now exists in admiralty cases, but to preserve the substance of Admiralty Rules 13–18. The general reference to enforcement of any maritime lien is believed to state the existing law, and is an improvement over the enumeration in the former Admiralty Rules, which is repetitious and incomplete (e.g., there was no reference to general average). The reference to any maritime lien is intended to include liens created by state law which are enforceable in admiralty.

The main concern of Admiralty Rules 13–18 was with the question whether certain actions might be brought in rem or also, or in the alternative, in personam. Essentially, therefore, these rules deal with questions of substantive law, for in general an action in rem may be brought to enforce any maritime lien, and no action in personam may be brought when the substantive law imposes no personal liability.

These rules may be summarized as follows:

1. Cases in which the plaintiff may proceed in rem and/or in personam:

a. Suits for seamen's wages;

b. Suits by materialmen for supplies, repairs, etc.;

c. Suits for pilotage;

d. Suits for collision damages;

e. Suits founded on mere maritime hypothecation;

f. Suits for salvage.

2. Cases in which the plaintiff may proceed only in personam:

a. Suits for assault and beating.

3. Cases in which the plaintiff may proceed only in rem:

a. Suits on bottomry bonds.

The coverage is incomplete, since the rules omit mention of many cases in which the plaintiff may proceed in rem or in personam. This revision proceeds on the principle that it is preferable to make a general statement as to the availability of the remedies, leaving out conclusions on matters of substantive law. Clearly it is not necessary to enumerate the cases listed under Item 1, above, nor to try to complete the list.

The rule eliminates the provision of Admiralty Rule 15 that actions for assault and beating may be brought only in personam. A preliminary study fails to disclose any reason for the rule. It is subject to so many exceptions that it is calculated to deceive rather than to inform. A seaman may sue in rem when he has been beaten by a fellow member of the crew so vicious as to render the vessel unseaworthy, *The Rolph,* 293 Fed. 269, aff'd 299 Fed. 52 (9th Cir. 1923), or where the theory of the action is that a beating by the master is a breach of the obligation under the shipping articles to treat the seaman with proper kindness, *The David Evans,* 187 Fed. 775 (D.Hawaii 1911); and a passenger may sue in rem on the theory that the assault is a breach of the contract of passage, *The Western States,* 159 Fed. 354 (2d Cir. 1908). To say that an action for money damages may be brought only in personam seems equivalent to saying that a maritime lien shall not exist; and that, in turn, seems equivalent to announcing a rule of substantive law rather than a rule of procedure. Dropping the rule will leave it to the courts to determine whether a lien exists as a matter of substantive law.

The specific reference to bottomry bonds is omitted because, as a matter of hornbook substantive law, there is no personal liability on such bonds.

Subdivision (2).

This incorporates the substance of Admiralty Rules 21 and 22.

Subdivision (3).

Derived from Admiralty Rules 10 and 37. The provision that the warrant is to be issued by the clerk is new, but is assumed to state existing law.

There is remarkably little authority bearing on Rule 37, although the subject would seem to be an important one. The rule appears on its face to have provided for a sort of ancillary process, and this may well be the case when tangible property, such as a vessel, is arrested, and intangible property such as freight is incidentally involved. It can easily happen, however, that the only property against which the action may be brought is intangible, as where the owner of a vessel under charter has a lien on subfreights. See 2 Benedict § 299 and cases cited. [Reference is to the 6th Edition of Benedict on Admiralty and not to the current 7th Edition]. In such cases it would seem that the order to the person holding the fund is equivalent to original process, taking the place of the warrant for arrest. That being so, it would also seem that (1) there should be some provision for notice, comparable to that given when tangible property is arrested, and (2) it should not be necessary, as Rule 37 provided, to petition the court for issuance of the process, but that it should issue as of course. Accordingly the substance of Rule 37 is included in the rule covering ordinary process, and notice will be required by Rule C(4). Presumably the rules omit any requirement of notice in these cases because the holder of the funds (e.g., the cargo owner) would be required on general principles (cf. *Harris v. Balk,* 198 U.S. 215 (1905)) to notify his obligee (e.g., the charterer); but in actions in rem such notice seems plainly inadequate because there may be adverse claims to the fund (e.g., there may be liens against the subfreights for seamen's wages, etc.). Compare Admiralty Rule 9.

Subdivision (4).

This carries forward the notice provision of Admiralty Rule 10, with one modification. Notice by publication is too expensive and ineffective a formality to be routinely required. When, as usually happens, the vessel or other property is released on bond or otherwise there is no point in publishing notice; the vessel is freed from the claim of the plaintiff and no other interest in the vessel can be affected by the proceedings. If, however, the vessel is not released, general notice is required in order that all persons, including unknown claimants, may appear and be heard, and in order that the judgment in rem shall be binding on all the world.

Subdivision (5).

This incorporates the substance of Admiralty Rule 9.

There are remarkably few cases dealing directly with the rule. In The *George Prescott,* 10 Fed.Cas. 222 (No. 5,339) (E.D.N.Y.1865), the master and crew of a vessel libeled her for wages, and other lienors also filed libels. One of the lienors suggested to the court that prior to the arrest of the vessel the master had removed the sails, and asked that he be ordered to produce them. He admitted removing the sails and selling them, justifying on the ground that he held a mortgage on the vessel. He was ordered to pay the proceeds into court. Cf. *United States v. The Zarko,* 187 F.Supp. 371 (S.D.Cal.1960), where an armature belonging to a vessel subject to a preferred ship mortgage was in possession of a repairman claiming a lien.

It is evident that, though the rule has had a limited career in the reported cases, it is a potentially important one. It is also evident that the rule is framed in terms narrower than the principle that supports it. There is no apparent reason for limiting it to ships and their appurtenances (2 Benedict § 299) [Reference is to the 6th Edition of Benedict on Admiralty and not to the current 7th Edition]. Also, the reference to "third parties" in the existing rule seems unfortunate. In *The George Prescott,* the person who removed and sold the sails was a plaintiff in the action, and relief against him was just as necessary as if he had been a stranger.

Another situation in which process of this kind would seem to be useful is that in which the principal property that is the subject of the action is a vessel, but her pending freight is incidentally involved. The warrant of arrest, and notice of its service, should be all that is required by way of original process and notice; ancillary process without notice should suffice as to the incidental intangibles.

The distinction between Admiralty Rules 9 and 37 is not at once apparent, but seems to be this: Where the action was against property that could not be seized by the marshal because it was intangible, the original process was required to be similar to that issued against a garnishee, and general notice was required (though not provided for by the present rule; cf. Advisory Committee's Note to Rule C(3)). Under Admiralty Rule 9 property had been arrested and general notice had been given, but some of the property had been removed or for some other reason could not be arrested. Here no further notice was necessary.

The rule also makes provision for this kind of situation: The proceeding is against a vessel's pending freight only; summons has been served on the person supposedly holding the funds, and general notice has been given; it develops that another person holds all or part of the funds. Ancillary process should be available here without further notice. Subdivision (6).

Adherence to the practice of return days seems unsatisfactory. The practice varies significantly from district to district. A uniform rule should be provided so that any claimant or defendant can readily determine when he is required to file or serve a claim or answer.

A virtue of the return-day practice is that it requires claimants to come forward and identify themselves at an early stage of the proceedings—before they could fairly be required to answer. The draft is designed to preserve this feature of the present practice by requiring early filing of the claim. The time schedule contemplated in the draft is closely comparable to the present practice in the Southern District of New York, where the claimant has a minimum of 8 days to claim and three weeks thereafter to answer.

This rule also incorporates the substance of Admiralty Rule 25. The present rule's emphasis on "the true and bona fide owner" is omitted, since anyone having the right to possession can claim (2 Benedict § 324) [Reference is to the 6th Edition of Benedict on Admiralty and not to the current 7th Edition].

1985 Amendment

Rule C(3) has been amended to provide for judicial scrutiny before the issuance of any warrant of arrest. Its purpose is to eliminate any doubt as to the rule's constitutionality under the *Sniadach* line of cases. *Sniadach v. Family Finance Corp.,* 395 U.S. 337 (1969); *Fuentes v. Shevin,* 407 U.S. 67 (1972); *Mitchell v. W.T. Grant Co.,* 416 U.S. 600 (1974); and *North Georgia Finishing, Inc. v. Di-Chem, Inc.,* 419 U.S. 601 (1975). This was thought desirable even though both the Fourth and the Fifth Circuits have upheld the existing rule. *Amstar Corp. v. S/S Alexandros T.,* 664 F.2d 904 (4th Cir.1981); *Merchants National Bank of Mobile v. The Dredge General G.L. Gillespie,* 663 F.2d 1338 (5th Cir.1981), *cert. dismissed,* 456 U.S. 966 (1982). A contrary view was taken by Judge Tate in the *Merchants National Bank* case and by the district court in *Alyeska Pipeline Service Co. v. The Vessel Bay Ridge,* 509 F.Supp. 1115 (D.Alaska 1981), *appeal dismissed,* 703 F.2d 381 (9th Cir. 1983).

The rule envisions that the order will issue upon a prima facie showing that the plaintiff has an action in rem against the defendant in the amount sued for and that the property is within the district. A simple order with conclusory findings is contemplated. The reference to review by the "court" is broad enough to embrace a magistrate as well as a district judge.

The new provision recognizes that in some situations, such as when a judge is unavailable and the vessel is about to depart from the jurisdiction, it will be impracticable, if not impossible, to secure the judicial review contemplated by Rule C(3). When "exigent circumstances" exist, the rule enables the plaintiff to secure the issuance of the summons and warrant of arrest, subject to a later showing that the necessary circumstances actually existed. This provision is intended to provide a safety valve without undermining the requirement of pre-arrest scrutiny. Thus, every effort to secure judicial review, including conducting a hearing by telephone, should be pursued before invoking the exigent-circumstances procedure.

The foregoing requirements for prior court review or proof of exigent circumstances do not apply to actions by the United States for forfeitures for federal statutory violations. In such actions a prompt hearing is not constitutionally required, *United States v. Eight Thousand Eight Hundred and Fifty Dollars,* 103 S.Ct. 2005 (1983); *Calero-Toledo v. Pearson Yacht Leasing Co.,* 416 U.S. 663 (1974), and could prejudice the government in its prosecution of the claimants as defendants in parallel criminal proceedings since the forfeiture hearing could be misused by the defendants to obtain by way of civil discovery information to which they would not otherwise be entitled and subject the government and the courts to the unnecessary burden and expense of two hearings rather than one.

1987 Amendment

The amendments are technical. No substantive change is intended.

1991 Amendment

These amendments are designed to conform the rule to Fed.R.Civ.P. 4, as amended. As with recent amendments to Rule 4, it is intended to relieve the Marshals Service of the burden of using its limited personnel and facilities for execution of process in routine circumstances. Doing so may involve a contractual arrangement with a person or organization retained by the government to perform these services, or the use of other government officers and employees, or the special appointment by the court of persons available to perform suitably.

The seizure of a vessel, with or without cargo, remains a task assigned to the Marshal. Successful arrest of a vessel frequently requires the enforcement presence of an armed government official and the cooperation of the United States Coast Guard and other governmental authorities. If the marshal is called upon to seize the vessel, it is expected that the same officer will also be responsible for the seizure of any property on board the vessel at the time of seizure that is to be the object of arrest or attachment.

2000 Amendment

Style changes have been made throughout the revised portions of Rule C. Several changes of meaning have been made as well.

Subdivision 2. In rem jurisdiction originally extended only to property within the judicial district. Since 1986, Congress has enacted a number of jurisdictional and venue statutes for forfeiture and criminal matters that in some circumstances permit a court to exercise authority over property outside the district. 28 U.S.C. § 1355(b)(1) allows a forfeiture action in the district where an act or omission giving rise to forfeiture occurred, or in any other district where venue is established by § 1395 or by any other statute. Section 1355(b)(2) allows an action to be brought as provided in (b)(1) or in the United States District Court for the District of Columbia when the forfeiture property is located in a foreign country or has been seized by authority of a foreign government. Section 1355(d) allows a court with jurisdiction under § 1355(b) to cause service in any other district of process required to bring the forfeiture property before the court. Section 1395 establishes venue of a civil proceeding for forfeiture in the district where the forfeiture accrues or the defendant is found; in any district where the property is found; in any district into which the property is brought, if the property initially is outside any judicial district; or in any district where the vessel is arrested if the proceeding is an admiralty proceeding to forfeit a vessel. Section 1395(e) deals with a vessel or cargo entering a port of entry closed by the President, and transportation to or from a state or section declared to be in insurrection. 18 U.S.C. § 981(h) creates expanded jurisdiction and venue over property located elsewhere that is related to a criminal prosecution pending in the district. These amendments, and related amendments of Rule E(3), bring these Rules into step with the new statutes. No change is made as to admiralty and maritime proceedings that do not involve a forfeiture governed by one of the new statutes.

Subdivision (2) has been separated into lettered paragraphs to facilitate understanding.

Subdivision (3). Subdivision (3) has been rearranged and divided into lettered paragraphs to facilitate understanding.

Paragraph (b)(i) is amended to make it clear that any supplemental process addressed to a vessel or tangible property on board a vessel, as well as the original warrant, is to be served by the marshal.

Subdivision (4). Subdivision (4) has required that public notice state the time for filing an answer, but has not required that the notice set out the earlier time for filing a statement of interest or claim. The amendment requires that both times be stated.

A new provision is added, allowing termination of publication if the property is released more than 10 days after execution but before publication is completed. Termination will save money, and also will reduce the risk of confusion as to the status of the property.

Subdivision (6). Subdivision (6) has applied a single set of undifferentiated provisions to civil forfeiture proceedings and to in rem admiralty proceedings. Because some differences in procedure are desirable, these proceedings are separated by adopting a new paragraph (a) for civil forfeiture proceedings and recasting the present rule as paragraph (b) for in rem admiralty proceedings. The provision for interrogatories and answers is carried forward as paragraph (c). Although this established procedure for serving interrogatories with the complaint departs from the general provisions of Civil Rule 26(d), the special needs of expedition that often arise in admiralty justify continuing the practice.

Both paragraphs (a) and (b) require a statement of interest or right rather than the "claim" formerly required. The new wording permits parallel drafting, and facilitates cross-references in other rules. The substantive nature of the statement remains the same as the former claim. The requirements of (a) and (b) are, however, different in some respects.

In a forfeiture proceeding governed by paragraph (a), a statement must be filed by a person who asserts an interest in or a right against the property involved. This category includes every right against the property, such as a lien, whether or not it establishes ownership or a right to possession. In determining who has an interest in or a right against property, courts may continue to rely on precedents that have developed the meaning of "claims" or "claimants" for the purpose of civil forfeiture proceedings.

In an admiralty and maritime proceeding governed by paragraph (b), a statement is filed only by a person claiming a right of possession or ownership. Other claims against the property are advanced by intervention under Civil Rule 24, as it may be supplemented by local admiralty rules. The reference to ownership includes every interest that qualifies as ownership under domestic or foreign law. If an ownership interest is asserted, it makes no difference whether its character is legal, equitable, or something else.

Paragraph (a) provides more time than paragraph (b) for filing a statement. Admiralty and maritime in rem proceedings often present special needs for prompt action that do not commonly arise in forfeiture proceedings .

Paragraphs (a) and (b) do not limit the right to make a restricted appearance under Rule E(8).

2002 Amendments

Rule C(3) is amended to reflect the provisions of 18 U.S.C. § 985, enacted by the Civil Asset Forfeiture Reform Act of 2000, 114 Stat. 202, 214–215. Section 985 provides, subject to enumerated exceptions, that real property that is the subject of a civil forfeiture action is not to be seized until an order of forfeiture is entered. A civil forfeiture action is initiated by filing a complaint, posting notice, and serving notice on the property owner. The summons and arrest procedure is no longer appropriate.

Rule C(6)(a)(i)(A) is amended to adopt the provision enacted by 18 U.S.C. § 983(a)(4)(A), shortly before Rule C(6)(a)(i)(A) took effect, that sets the time for filing a verified statement as 30 days rather than 20 days, and that sets the first alternative event for measuring the 30 days as the date of service of the Government's complaint.

Rule C(6)(a)(iii) is amended to give notice of the provision enacted by 18 U.S.C. § 983(a)(4)(B) that requires that the answer in a forfeiture proceeding be filed within 20 days. Without this notice, unwary litigants might rely on the provision of Rule 5(d) that allows a reasonable time for filing after service.

Rule C(6)(b)(iv) is amended to change the requirement that an answer be filed within 20 days to a requirement that it be served within 20 days. Service is the ordinary requirement, as in Rule 12(a). Rule 5(d) requires filing within a reasonable time after service.

Changes Made After Publication and Comment No changes have been made since publication.

2005 Amendments

Rule C(6)(b)(i)(A) is amended to delete the reference to a time 10 days after completed publication under Rule C(4). This change corrects an oversight in the amendments made in 2000. Rule C(4) requires publication of notice only if the property that is the subject of the action is not released within 10 days after execution of process. Execution of process will always be earlier than publication.

2006 Amendment

Rule C is amended to reflect the adoption of Rule G to govern procedure in civil forfeiture actions.

2008 Amendments

Supplemental Rule C(6)(a)(i) is amended to correct an inadvertent omission in the 2006 amendment to Rule C. The amendment is technical and stylistic in nature. No substantive change is intended.

Rule D. Possessory, Petitory, and Partition Actions

In all actions for possession, partition, and to try title maintainable according to the course of the admiralty practice with respect to a vessel, in all actions so maintainable with respect to the possession of cargo or other maritime property, and in all actions by one or more part owners against the others to obtain security for the return of the vessel from any voyage undertaken without their consent, or by one or more part owners against the others to obtain possession of the vessel for any voyage on giving security for its safe return, the process shall be by a warrant of arrest of the vessel, cargo, or other property, and by notice in the manner provided by Rule B(2) to the adverse party or parties.

(Added Feb. 28, 1966, eff. July 1, 1966.)

ADVISORY COMMITTEE NOTES

1966 Adoption

This carries forward the substance of Admiralty Rule 19.

Rule 19 provided the remedy of arrest in controversies involving title and possession in general. See *The Tilton*, 23 Fed.Cas.1277 (No. 14,054) (C.C.D.Mass.1830). In addition it provided that remedy in controversies between co-owners respecting the employment of a vessel. It did not deal comprehensively with controversies between co-owners, omitting the remedy of partition. Presumably the omission is traceable to the fact that, when the rules were originally promulgated, concepts of substantive law (sometimes stated as concepts of jurisdiction) denied the remedy of partition except where the parties in disagreement were the owners of equal shares. See *The Steamboat Orleans*, 36 U.S. (11 Pet.) 175 (1837). The Supreme Court has now removed any doubt as to the jurisdiction of the district courts to partition a vessel, and has held in addition that no fixed principle of federal admiralty law limits the remedy to the case of equal shares. *Madruga v. Superior Court*, 346 U.S. 556 (1954). It is therefore appropriate to include a reference to partition in the rule.

Rule E. Actions in Rem and Quasi in Rem: General Provisions

(1) Applicability. Except as otherwise provided, this rule applies to actions in personam with process of maritime attachment and garnishment, actions in rem, and petitory, possessory, and partition actions, supplementing Rules B, C, and D.

(2) Complaint; Security.

(a) *Complaint.* In actions to which this rule is applicable the complaint shall state the circumstances from which the claim arises with such particularity that the defendant or claimant will be able, without moving for a more definite statement, to commence an investigation of the facts and to frame a responsive pleading.

(b) *Security for Costs.* Subject to the provisions of Rule 54(d) and of relevant statutes, the court may, on the filing of the complaint or on the appearance of any defendant, claimant, or any other party, or at any later time, require the plaintiff, defendant, claimant, or other party to give security, or additional security, in such sum as the court shall direct to pay all costs and expenses that shall be awarded against the party by any interlocutory order or by the final judgment, or on appeal by any appellate court.

(3) Process.

(a) In admiralty and maritime proceedings process in rem or of maritime attachment and garnishment may be served only within the district.

(b) Issuance and Delivery. Issuance and delivery of process in rem, or of maritime attachment and garnishment, shall be held in abeyance if the plaintiff so requests.

(4) Execution of Process; Marshal's Return; Custody of Property; Procedures for Release.

(a) *In General.* Upon issuance and delivery of the process, or, in the case of summons with process of attachment and garnishment, when it appears that the defendant cannot be found within the district, the marshal or other person or organization having a warrant shall forthwith execute the process in accordance with this subdivision (4), making due and prompt return.

(b) *Tangible Property.* If tangible property is to be attached or arrested, the marshal or other person or organization having the warrant shall take it into the marshal's possession for safe custody. If the character or situation of the property is such that the taking of actual possession is impracticable, the marshal or other person executing the process shall affix a copy thereof to the property in a conspicuous place and leave a copy of the complaint and process with the person having possession or the person's agent. In furtherance of the marshal's custody of any vessel the marshal is authorized to make a written request to the collector of customs not to grant clearance to such vessel until notified by the marshal or deputy marshal or by the clerk that the vessel has been released in accordance with these rules.

(c) *Intangible Property.* If intangible property is to be attached or arrested the marshal or other person or organization having the warrant shall execute the process by leaving with the garnishee or other obligor a copy of the complaint and process requiring the garnishee or other obligor to answer as provided in Rules B(3)(a) and C(6); or the marshal may accept for payment into the registry of the court the amount owed to the extent of the amount claimed by the plaintiff with interest and costs, in which event the garnishee or other obligor shall not be required to answer unless alias process shall be served.

(d) *Directions With Respect to Property in Custody.* The marshal or other person or organization having the warrant may at any time apply to the court for directions with respect to property that has been attached or arrested, and shall give notice of such application to any or all of the parties as the court may direct.

(e) *Expenses of Seizing and Keeping Property; Deposit.* These rules do not alter the provisions of Title 28, U.S.C., § 1921, as amended, relative to the expenses of seizing and keeping property attached or arrested and to the requirement of deposits to cover such expenses.

(f) *Procedure for Release From Arrest or Attachment.* Whenever property is arrested or attached, any person claiming an interest in it shall be entitled to a prompt hearing at which the plaintiff shall be required to show why the arrest or attachment should not be vacated or other relief granted consistent with these rules. This subdivision shall have no application to suits for seamen's wages when process is issued upon a certification of sufficient cause filed pursuant to Title 46, U.S.C. §§ 603 and 604 or to actions by the United States for forfeitures for violation of any statute of the United States.

(5) Release of Property.

(a) *Special Bond.* Whenever process of maritime attachment and garnishment or process in rem is issued the execution of such process shall be stayed, or the property released, on the giving of security, to be approved by the court or clerk, or by stipulation of the parties, conditioned to answer the judgment of the court or of any appellate court. The parties may stipulate the amount and nature of such security. In the event of the inability or refusal of the parties so to stipulate the court shall fix the principal sum of the bond or stipulation at an amount sufficient to cover the amount of the plaintiff's claim fairly stated with accrued interest and costs; but the principal sum shall in no event exceed (i) twice the amount of the plaintiff's claim or (ii) the value of the property on due appraisement, whichever is smaller. The bond or stipulation shall be conditioned for the payment of the principal sum and interest thereon at 6 per cent per annum.

(b) *General Bond.* The owner of any vessel may file a general bond or stipulation, with sufficient surety, to be approved by the court, conditioned to answer the judgment of such court in all or any actions that may be brought thereafter in such court in which the vessel is attached or arrested. Thereupon the execution of all such process against such vessel shall be stayed so long as the amount secured by such bond or stipulation is at least double the aggregate amount claimed by plaintiffs in all actions begun and pending in which such vessel has been attached or arrested. Judgments and remedies may be had on such bond or stipulation as if a special bond or stipulation had been filed in each of such actions. The district court may make necessary orders to carry this rule into effect, particularly as to the giving of proper notice of any action against or attachment of a vessel for which a general bond has been filed. Such bond or stipulation shall be indorsed by the clerk with a minute of the actions wherein process is so stayed. Further security may be required by the court at any time.

If a special bond or stipulation is given in a particular case, the liability on the general bond or stipulation shall cease as to that case.

(c) *Release by Consent or Stipulation; Order of Court or Clerk; Costs.* Any vessel, cargo, or other property in the custody of the marshal or other person or organization having the warrant may be released forthwith upon the marshal's acceptance and approval of a stipulation, bond, or other security, signed by the party on whose behalf the property is detained or the party's attorney and expressly authorizing such release, if all costs and charges of the court and its officers shall have first been paid. Otherwise no property in the custody of the marshal, other person or organization having the warrant, or other officer of the court shall be released without an order of the court; but such order may be entered as of course by the clerk, upon the giving of approved security as provided by law and these rules, or upon the dismissal or discontinuance of the action; but the marshal or other person or organization having the warrant shall not deliver any property so released until the costs and charges of the officers of the court shall first have been paid.

(d) *Possessory, Petitory, and Partition Actions.* The foregoing provisions of this subdivision (5) do not apply to petitory, possessory, and partition actions. In such cases the property arrested shall be released only by order of the court, on such terms and conditions and on the giving of such security as the court may require.

(6) Reduction or Impairment of Security. Whenever security is taken the court may, on motion and hearing, for good cause shown, reduce the amount of security given; and if the surety shall be or become insufficient, new or additional sureties may be required on motion and hearing.

(7) Security on Counterclaim.

(a) When a person who has given security for damages in the original action asserts a counterclaim that arises from the transaction or occurrence that is the subject of the original action, a plaintiff for whose benefit the security has been given must give security for damages demanded in the counterclaim unless the court for cause shown, directs otherwise. Proceedings on the original claim must be stayed until this security is given unless the court directs otherwise.

(b) The plaintiff is required to give security under Rule E(7)(a) when the United States or its corporate instrumentality counterclaims and would have been required to give security to respond in damages if a private party but is relieved by law from giving security.

(8) Restricted Appearance. An appearance to defend against an admiralty and maritime claim with respect to which there has issued process in rem, or process of attachment and garnishment, may be expressly restricted to the defense of such claim, and in that event is not an appearance for the purposes of any other claim with respect to which such process is not available or has not been served.

(9) Disposition of Property; Sales.

(a) Interlocutory Sales; Delivery.

(i) On application of a party, the marshal, or other person having custody of the property, the court may order all or part of the property sold—with the sales proceeds, or as much of them as will satisfy the judgment, paid into court to await further orders of the court—if:

(A) the attached or arrested property is perishable, or liable to deterioration, decay, or injury by being detained in custody pending the action;

(B) the expense of keeping the property is excessive or disproportionate; or

(C) there is an unreasonable delay in securing release of the property.

(ii) In the circumstances described in Rule E(9)(a)(i), the court, on motion by a defendant or a person filing a statement of interest or right under Rule C(6), may order that the property, rather than being sold, be delivered to the movant upon giving security under these rules.

(b) Sales; Proceeds. All sales of property shall be made by the marshal or a deputy marshal, or by other person or organization having the warrant, or by any other person assigned by the court where the marshal or other person or organization having the warrant is a party in interest; and the proceeds of sale shall be forthwith paid into the registry of the court to be disposed of according to law.

(10) Preservation of Property. When the owner or another person remains in possession of property attached or arrested under the provisions of Rule E(4)(b) that permit execution of process without taking actual possession, the court, on a party's motion or on its own, may enter any order necessary to preserve the property and to prevent its removal.

(Added Feb. 28, 1966, eff. July 1, 1966, and amended Apr. 29, 1985, eff. Aug. 1, 1985; Mar. 2, 1987, eff. Aug. 1, 1987; Apr. 30, 1991, eff. Dec. 1, 1991; Apr. 17, 2000, eff. Dec. 1, 2000; Apr. 12, 2006, eff. Dec. 1, 2006.)

ADVISORY COMMITTEE NOTES

1966 Adoption

Subdivisions (1), (2).

Adapted from Admiralty Rule 24. The rule is based on the assumption that there is no more need for security for costs in maritime personal actions than in civil cases generally, but that there is reason to retain the requirement for actions in which property is seized. As to proceedings for limitation of liability see Rule F(1).

Subdivision (3).

The Advisory Committee has concluded for practical reasons that process requiring seizure of property should continue to be served only within the geographical limits of the district. Compare Rule B(1), continuing the condition that process of attachment and garnishment may be served only if the defendant is not found within the district.

The provisions of Admiralty Rule 1 concerning the persons by whom process is to be served will be superseded by FRCP 4(c).

Subdivision (4).

This rule is intended to preserve the provisions of Admiralty Rules 10 and 36 relating to execution of process, custody of property seized by the marshal, and the marshal's return. It is also designed to make express provision for matters not heretofore covered.

The provision relating to clearance in subdivision (b) is suggested by Admiralty Rule 44 of the District of Maryland.

Subdivision (d) is suggested by English Rule 12, Order 75.

28 U.S.C., § 1921 as amended in 1962 contains detailed provisions relating to the expenses of seizing and preserving property attached or arrested.

Subdivision (5).

In addition to Admiralty Rule 11 (see Rule E(9)), the release of property seized on process of attachment or in rem was dealt with by Admiralty Rules 5, 6, 12, and 57, and 28 U.S.C., § 2464 (formerly Rev.Stat. § 941). The rule consolidates these provisions and makes them uniformly applicable to attachment and garnishment and actions in rem.

The rule restates the substance of Admiralty Rule 5. Admiralty Rule 12 dealt only with ships arrested on in rem process. Since the same ground appears to be covered more generally by 28 U.S.C., § 2464, the subject matter of Rule 12 is omitted. The substance of Admiralty Rule 57 is retained. 28 U.S.C., § 2464 is incorporated with changes of terminology, and with a substantial change as to the amount of the bond. See 2 Benedict 395 n. 1a [Reference is to the 6th Edition of Benedict on Admiralty and not to the current 7th Edition.] *The Lotosland,* 2 F.Supp. 42 (S.D.N.Y.1933). The provision for general bond is enlarged to include the contingency of attachment as well as arrest of the vessel.

Subdivision (6).

Adapted from Admiralty Rule 8.

Subdivision (7).

Derived from Admiralty Rule 50.

Title 46, U.S.C., § 783 extends the principle of Rule 50 to the Government when sued under the Public Vessels Act, presumably on the theory that the credit of the Government is the equivalent of the best security. The rule adopts this principle and extends it to all cases in which the Government is defendant although the Suits in Admiralty Act contains no parallel provisions.

Subdivision (8).

Under the liberal joinder provisions of unified rules the plaintiff will be enabled to join with maritime actions in rem, or maritime actions in personam with process of attachment and garnishment, claims with respect to which such process is not available, including nonmaritime claims. Unification should not, however, have the result that, in order to defend against an admiralty and maritime claim with respect to which process in rem or quasi in rem has been served, the claimant or defendant must subject himself personally to the jurisdiction of the court with reference to other claims with respect to which such process is not available or has not been served, especially when such other claims are nonmaritime. So far as attachment and garnishment are concerned this principle holds true whether process is issued according to admiralty tradition and the Supplemental Rules or according to Rule 4(e) as incorporated by Rule B(1).

A similar problem may arise with respect to civil actions other than admiralty and maritime claims within the meaning of Rule 9(h). That is to say, in an ordinary civil action, whether maritime or not, there may be joined in one action claims with respect to which process of attachment and garnishment is available under state law and Rule 4(e) and claims with respect to which such process is not available or has not been served. The general Rules of Civil Procedure do not specify whether an appearance in such cases to defend the claim with respect to which process of attachment and garnishment has issued is an appearance for the purposes of the other claims. In that context the question has been considered best left to case-by-case development. Where admiralty and maritime claims within the meaning of Rule 9(h) are concerned, however, it seems important to include a specific provision to avoid an unfortunate and unintended effect of unification. No inferences whatever as to the effect of such an appearance in an ordinary civil action should be drawn from the specific provision here and the absence of such a provision in the general Rules.

Subdivision (9).

Adapted from Admiralty Rules 11, 12, and 40. Subdivision (a) is necessary because of various provisions as to disposition of property in forfeiture proceedings. In addition to particular statutes, note the provisions of 28 U.S.C., §§ 2461–65.

The provision of Admiralty Rule 12 relating to unreasonable delay was limited to ships but should have broader application. See 2 Benedict 404 [Reference is to the 6th Edition of Benedict on Admiralty and not to the current 7th Edition]. Similarly, both Rules 11 and 12 were limited to actions in rem, but should equally apply to attached property.

1985 Amendment

Rule E(4)(f) makes available the type of prompt post-seizure hearing in proceedings under Supplemental Rules B and C that the Supreme Court has called for in a number of cases arising in other contexts. See *North Georgia Finishing, Inc. v. Di-Chem, Inc.,* 419 U.S. 601 (1975); *Mitchell v. W.T. Grant Co.,* 416 U.S. 600 (1974). Although post-attachment and post-arrest hearings always have been available on motion, an explicit statement emphasizing promptness and elaborating the procedure has been lacking in the Supplemental Rules. Rule E(4)(f) is designed to satisfy the constitutional requirement of due process by guaranteeing to the shipowner a prompt post-seizure hearing at which he can attack the complaint, the arrest, the security demanded, or any other alleged deficiency in the proceedings. The amendment also is intended to eliminate the previously disparate treatment under local rules of defendants whose property has been seized pursuant to Supplemental Rules B and C.

The new Rule E(4)(f) is based on a proposal by the Maritime Law Association of the United States and on local admiralty rules in the Eastern, Northern, and Southern Districts of New York. E.D.N.Y. Local Rule 13; N.D.N.Y. Local Rule 13; S.D.N.Y. Local Rule 12. Similar provisions have been adopted by other maritime districts. E.g., N.D.Calif. Local Rule 603.4; W.D.La. Local Admiralty Rule 21. Rule E(4)(f) will provide uniformity in practice and reduce constitutional uncertainties.

Rule E(4)(f) is triggered by the defendant or any other person with an interest in the property seized. Upon an oral or written application similar to that used in seeking a temporary restraining order, see Rule 65(b), the court is required to hold a hearing as promptly as possible to determine whether to allow the arrest or attachment to stand. The plaintiff has the burden of showing why the seizure should not be vacated. The hearing also may determine the amount of security to be granted or the propriety of imposing counter-security to protect the defendant from an improper seizure.

The foregoing requirements for prior court review or proof of exigent circumstances do not apply to actions by the United States for forfeitures for federal statutory violations. In such actions a prompt hearing is not constitutionally required, *United States v. Eight Thousand Eight Hundred and Fifty Dollars*, 103 S.Ct. 2005 (1983); *Calero-Toledo v. Pearson Yacht Leasing Co.*, 416 U.S. 663 (1974), and could prejudice the government in its prosecution of the claimants as defendants in parallel criminal proceedings since the forfeiture hearing could be misused by the defendants to obtain by way of civil discovery information to which they would not otherwise be entitled and subject the government and the courts to the unnecessary burden and expense of two hearings rather than one.

1987 Amendment

The amendments are technical. No substantive change is intended.

1991 Amendment

These amendments are designed to conform this rule to Fed.R.Civ.P. 4, as amended. They are intended to relieve the Marshals Service of the burden of using its limited personnel and facilities for execution of process in routine circumstances. Doing so may involve a contractual arrangement with a person or organization retained by the government to perform these services, or the use of other government officers and employees, or the special appointment by the court of persons available to perform suitably.

2000 Amendment

Style changes have been made throughout the revised portions of Rule E. Several changes of meaning have been made as well.

Subdivision (3). Subdivision (3) is amended to reflect the distinction drawn in Rule C(2)(c) and (d). Service in an admiralty or maritime proceeding still must be made within the district, as reflected in Rule C(2)(c), while service in forfeiture proceedings may be made outside the district when authorized by statute, as reflected in Rule C(2)(d).

Subdivision (7). Subdivision (7)(a) is amended to make it clear that a plaintiff need give security to meet a counterclaim only when the counterclaim is asserted by a person who has given security to respond in damages in the original action.

Subdivision (8). Subdivision (8) is amended to reflect the change in Rule B(1)(e) that deletes the former provision incorporating state quasi-in-rem jurisdiction. A restricted appearance is not appropriate when state law is invoked only for security under Civil Rule 64, not as a basis of quasi-in-rem jurisdiction. But if state law allows a special, limited, or restricted appearance as an incident of the remedy adopted from state law, the state practice applies through Rule 64 "in the manner provided by" state law.

Subdivision (9). Subdivision 9(b)(ii) is amended to reflect the change in Rule C(6) that substitutes a statement of interest or right for a claim.

Subdivision (10). Subdivision 10 is new. It makes clear the authority of the court to preserve and to prevent removal of attached or arrested property that remains in the possession of the owner or other person under Rule E(4)(b).

2006 Amendment

Rule E is amended to reflect the adoption of Rule G to govern procedure in civil forfeiture actions.

HISTORICAL NOTES

References in Text

Sections 603 and 604 of Title 46, referred to in subd. (4)(f), were repealed by Pub.L. 98–89, § 4(b), Aug. 26, 1983, 97 Stat. 600, section 1 of which enacted Title 46, Shipping.

Rule F. Limitation of Liability

(1) Time for Filing Complaint; Security. Not later than six months after receipt of a claim in writing, any vessel owner may file a complaint in the appropriate district court, as provided in subdivision (9) of this rule, for limitation of liability pursuant to statute. The owner (a) shall deposit with the court, for the benefit of claimants, a sum equal to the amount or value of the owner's interest in the vessel and pending freight, or approved security therefor, and in addition such sums, or approved security therefor, as the court may from time to time fix as necessary to carry out the provisions of the statutes as amended; or (b) at the owner's option shall transfer to a trustee to be appointed by the court, for the benefit of claimants, the owner's interest in the vessel and pending freight, together with such sums, or approved security therefor, as the court may from time to time fix as necessary to carry out the provisions of the statutes as amended. The plaintiff shall also give security for costs and, if the plaintiff elects to give security, for interest at the rate of 6 percent per annum from the date of the security.

(2) Complaint. The complaint shall set forth the facts on the basis of which the right to limit liability is asserted and all facts necessary to enable the court to determine the amount to which the owner's liability shall be limited. The complaint may demand exoneration from as well as limitation of liability. It shall state the voyage if any, on which the demands sought to be limited arose, with the date and place of its termination; the amount of all demands including all unsatisfied liens or claims of lien, in contract or in tort or otherwise, arising on that voyage, so far as known to the plaintiff, and what actions and proceedings, if any, are pending thereon; whether the vessel was damaged, lost, or abandoned, and, if so, when and where; the value of the vessel at the close of the voyage or, in case of wreck, the value of her wreckage, strippings, or proceeds, if any, and where and in whose possession they are; and the amount of any pending freight recovered or recoverable. If the plaintiff elects to transfer the plaintiff's interest in the vessel to a trustee, the complaint must further show any prior paramount liens thereon, and what voyages or trips, if any, she has made since the voyage or trip on which the claims sought to be limited arose, and any existing liens arising upon any such subsequent voyage or trip, with the amounts and causes thereof, and the names and addresses of the lienors, so far as known; and whether the vessel sustained any injury upon or by reason of such subsequent voyage or trip.

(3) Claims Against Owner; Injunction. Upon compliance by the owner with the requirements of subdivision (1) of this rule all claims and proceedings against the owner or the owner's property with respect to the matter in question shall cease. On application of the plaintiff the court shall enjoin the further prosecution of any action or proceeding against the plaintiff or the plaintiff's property with respect to any claim subject to limitation in the action.

(4) Notice to Claimants. Upon the owner's compliance with subdivision (1) of this rule the court shall issue a notice to all persons asserting claims with respect to which the complaint seeks limitation, admonishing them to file their respective claims with the clerk of the court and to serve on the attorneys for the plaintiff a copy thereof on or before a date to be named in the notice. The date so fixed shall not be less than 30 days after issuance of the notice. For cause shown, the court may enlarge the time within which claims may be filed. The notice shall be published in such newspaper or newspapers as the court may direct once a week for four successive weeks prior to the date fixed for the filing of claims. The plaintiff not later than the day of second publication shall also mail a copy of the notice to every person known to have made any claim against the vessel or the plaintiff arising out of the voyage or trip on which the claims sought to be limited arose. In cases involving death a copy of such notice shall be mailed to the decedent at the decedent's last known address, and also to any person who shall be known to have made any claim on account of such death.

(5) Claims and Answer. Claims shall be filed and served on or before the date specified in the notice provided for in subdivision (4) of this rule. Each claim shall specify the facts upon which the claimant relies in support of the claim, the items thereof, and the dates on which the same accrued. If a claimant desires to contest either the right to exoneration from or the right to limitation of liability the claimant shall file and serve an answer to the complaint unless the claim has included an answer.

(6) Information to be Given Claimants. Within 30 days after the date specified in the notice for filing claims, or within such time as the court thereafter may allow, the plaintiff shall mail to the attorney for each claimant (or if the claimant has no attorney to the claimant) a list setting forth (a) the name of each claimant, (b) the name and address of the claimant's attorney (if the claimant is known to have one), (c) the nature of the claim, i.e., whether property loss, property damage, death, personal injury etc., and (d) the amount thereof.

(7) Insufficiency of Fund or Security. Any claimant may by motion demand that the funds deposited in court or the security given by the plaintiff be increased on the ground that they are less than the value of the plaintiff's interest in the vessel and pending freight. Thereupon the court shall cause due appraisement to be made of the value of the plaintiff's interest in the vessel and pending freight; and if the court finds that the deposit or security is either insufficient or excessive it shall order its increase or reduction. In like manner any claimant may demand that the deposit or security be increased on the ground that it is insufficient to carry out the provisions of the statutes relating to claims in respect of loss of life or bodily injury; and, after notice and hearing, the court may similarly order that the deposit or security be increased or reduced.

(8) Objections to Claims: Distribution of Fund. Any interested party may question or controvert any claim without filing an objection thereto. Upon determination of liability the fund deposited or secured, or the proceeds of the vessel and pending freight, shall be divided pro rata, subject to all relevant provisions of law, among the several claimants in proportion to the amounts of their respective claims, duly proved, saving, however, to all parties any priority to which they may be legally entitled.

(9) Venue; Transfer. The complaint shall be filed in any district in which the vessel has been attached or arrested to answer for any claim with respect to which the plaintiff seeks to limit liability; or, if the vessel has not been attached or arrested, then in any district in which the owner has been sued with respect to any such claim. When the vessel has not been attached or arrested to answer the matters aforesaid, and suit has not been commenced against the owner, the proceedings may be had in the district in which the vessel may be, but if the vessel is not within any district and no suit has been commenced in any district, then the complaint may be filed in any district. For the convenience of parties and witnesses, in the interest of justice, the court may transfer the action to any district; if venue is wrongly laid the court shall dismiss or, if it be in the interest of justice, transfer the action to any district in which it could have been brought. If the vessel shall have been sold, the proceeds shall represent the vessel for the purposes of these rules.

(Added Feb. 28, 1966, eff. July 1, 1966, and amended Mar. 2, 1987, eff. Aug. 1, 1987.)

ADVISORY COMMITTEE NOTES

1966 Adoption

Subdivision (1).

The amendments of 1936 to the Limitation Act superseded to some extent the provisions of Admiralty Rule 51, especially with respect to the time of filing the complaint and with respect to security. The rule here incorporates in substance the 1936 amendment of the Act (46 U.S.C., § 185) with a slight modification to make it clear that the complaint may be filed at any time not later than six months after a claim has been lodged with the owner.

Subdivision (2).

Derived from Admiralty Rules 51 and 53.

Subdivision (3).

This is derived from the last sentence of 46 U.S.C. § 185 and the last paragraph of Admiralty Rule 51.

Subdivision (4).

Derived from Admiralty Rule 51.

Subdivision (5).

Derived from Admiralty Rules 52 and 53.

Subdivision (6).

Derived from Admiralty Rule 52.

Subdivision (7).

Derived from Admiralty Rule 52 and 46 U.S.C., § 185.

Subdivision (8).

Derived from Admiralty Rule 52.

Subdivision (9).

Derived from Admiralty Rule 54. The provision for transfer is revised to conform closely to the language of 28 U.S.C. §§ 1404(a) and 1406(a), though it retains the existing rule's provision for transfer to any district for convenience. The revision also makes clear what has been doubted: that the court may transfer if venue is wrongly laid.

1987 Amendment

The amendments are technical. No substantive change is intended.

Rule G. Forfeiture Actions In Rem

(1) Scope. This rule governs a forfeiture action in rem arising from a federal statute. To the extent that this rule does not address an issue, Supplemental Rules C and E and the Federal Rules of Civil Procedure also apply.

(2) Complaint. The complaint must:

(a) be verified;

(b) state the grounds for subject-matter jurisdiction, in rem jurisdiction over the defendant property, and venue;

(c) describe the property with reasonable particularity;

(d) if the property is tangible, state its location when any seizure occurred and — if different — its location when the action is filed;

(e) identify the statute under which the forfeiture action is brought; and

(f) state sufficiently detailed facts to support a reasonable belief that the government will be able to meet its burden of proof at trial.

(3) Judicial Authorization and Process.

(a) Real Property. If the defendant is real property, the government must proceed under 18 U.S.C. § 985.

(b) Other Property; Arrest Warrant. If the defendant is not real property:

(i) the clerk must issue a warrant to arrest the property if it is in the government's possession, custody, or control;

(ii) the court—on finding probable cause—must issue a warrant to arrest the property if it is not in the government's possession, custody, or control and is not subject to a judicial restraining order; and

(iii) a warrant is not necessary if the property is subject to a judicial restraining order.

(c) Execution of Process.

(i) The warrant and any supplemental process must be delivered to a person or organization authorized to execute it, who may be: (A) a marshal or any other United States officer or employee; (B) someone under contract with the United States; or (C) someone specially appointed by the court for that purpose.

(ii) The authorized person or organization must execute the warrant and any supplemental process on property in the United States as soon as practicable unless:

(A) the property is in the government's possession, custody, or control; or

(B) the court orders a different time when the complaint is under seal, the action is stayed before the warrant and supplemental process are executed, or the court finds other good cause.

(iii) The warrant and any supplemental process may be executed within the district or, when authorized by statute, outside the district.

(iv) If executing a warrant on property outside the United States is required, the warrant may be transmitted to an appropriate authority for serving process where the property is located.

(4) Notice.

(a) Notice by Publication.

(i) When Publication Is Required. A judgment of forfeiture may be entered only if the government has published notice of the action within a reasonable time after filing the complaint or at a time the court orders. But notice need not be published if:

(A) the defendant property is worth less than $1,000 and direct notice is sent under Rule G(4)(b) to every person the government can reasonably identify as a potential claimant; or

(B) the court finds that the cost of publication exceeds the property's value and that other means of notice would satisfy due process.

(ii) Content of the Notice. Unless the court orders otherwise, the notice must:

(A) describe the property with reasonable particularity;

(B) state the times under Rule G(5) to file a claim and to answer; and

(C) name the government attorney to be served with the claim and answer.

(iii) Frequency of Publication. Published notice must appear:

(A) once a week for three consecutive weeks; or

(B) only once if, before the action was filed, notice of nonjudicial forfeiture of the same property was published on an official internet government forfeiture site for at least 30 consecutive days, or in a newspaper of general circulation for three consecutive weeks in a district where publication is authorized under Rule G(4)(a)(iv).

(iv) Means of Publication. The government should select from the following options a means of publication reasonably calculated to notify potential claimants of the action:

(A) if the property is in the United States, publication in a newspaper generally circulated in the district where the action is filed, where the property was seized, or where property that was not seized is located;

(B) if the property is outside the United States, publication in a newspaper generally circulated in a district where the action is filed, in a newspaper generally circulated in the country where the property is located, or in legal notices published and generally circulated in the country where the property is located; or

(C) instead of (A) or (B), posting a notice on an official internet government forfeiture site for at least 30 consecutive days.

(b) Notice to Known Potential Claimants.

(i) Direct Notice Required. The government must send notice of the action and a copy of the complaint to any person who reasonably appears to be a potential claimant on the facts known to the government before the end of the time for filing a claim under Rule G(5)(a)(ii)(B).

(ii) Content of the Notice. The notice must state:

(A) the date when the notice is sent;

(B) a deadline for filing a claim, at least 35 days after the notice is sent;

(C) that an answer or a motion under Rule 12 must be filed no later than 20 days after filing the claim; and

(D) the name of the government attorney to be served with the claim and answer.

(iii) Sending Notice.

(A) The notice must be sent by means reasonably calculated to reach the potential claimant.

(B) Notice may be sent to the potential claimant or to the attorney representing the potential claimant with respect to the seizure of the property or in a related investigation, administrative forfeiture proceeding, or criminal case.

(C) Notice sent to a potential claimant who is incarcerated must be sent to the place of incarceration.

(D) Notice to a person arrested in connection with an offense giving rise to the forfeiture who is not incarcerated when notice is sent may be sent to the address that person last gave to the agency that arrested or released the person.

(E) Notice to a person from whom the property was seized who is not incarcerated when notice is sent may be sent to the last address that person gave to the agency that seized the property.

(iv) When Notice Is Sent. Notice by the following means is sent on the date when it is placed in the mail, delivered to a commercial carrier, or sent by electronic mail.

(v) Actual Notice. A potential claimant who had actual notice of a forfeiture action may not oppose or seek relief from forfeiture because of the government's failure to send the required notice.

(5) Responsive Pleadings.

(a) Filing a Claim.

(i) A person who asserts an interest in the defendant property may contest the forfeiture by filing a claim in the court where the action is pending. The claim must:

(A) identify the specific property claimed;

(B) identify the claimant and state the claimant's interest in the property;

(C) be signed by the claimant under penalty of perjury; and

(D) be served on the government attorney designated under Rule G(4)(a)(ii)(C) or (b)(ii)(D).

(ii) Unless the court for good cause sets a different time, the claim must be filed:

(A) by the time stated in a direct notice sent under Rule G(4)(b);

(B) if notice was published but direct notice was not sent to the claimant or the claimant's attorney, no later than 30 days after final publication of newspaper notice or legal notice under Rule G(4)(a) or no later than 60 days after the first day of publication on an official internet government forfeiture site; or

(C) if notice was not published and direct notice was not sent to the claimant or the claimant's attorney:

(1) if the property was in the government's possession, custody, or control when the complaint was filed, no later than 60 days after the filing, not counting any time when the complaint was under seal or when the action was stayed before execution of a warrant issued under Rule G(3)(b); or

(2) if the property was not in the government's possession, custody, or control when the complaint was filed, no later than 60 days after the government complied with 18 U.S.C. § 985(c) as to real property, or 60 days after process was executed on the property under Rule G(3).

(iii) A claim filed by a person asserting an interest as a bailee must identify the bailor, and if filed on the bailor's behalf must state the authority to do so.

(b) Answer. A claimant must serve and file an answer to the complaint or a motion under Rule 12 within 20 days after filing the claim. A claimant waives an objection to in rem jurisdiction or to venue if the objection is not made by motion or stated in the answer.

(6) Special Interrogatories.

(a) Time and Scope. The government may serve special interrogatories limited to the claimant's identity and relationship to the defendant property without the court's leave at any time after the claim is filed and before discovery is closed. But if the claimant serves a motion to dismiss the action, the government must serve the interrogatories within 20 days after the motion is served.

(b) Answers or Objections. Answers or objections to these interrogatories must be served within 20 days after the interrogatories are served.

(c) Government's Response Deferred. The government need not respond to a claimant's motion to dismiss the action under Rule G(8)(b) until 20 days after the claimant has answered these interrogatories.

(7) Preserving, Preventing Criminal Use, and Disposing of Property; Sales.

(a) Preserving and Preventing Criminal Use of Property. When the government does not have actual possession of the defendant property the court, on motion or on its own, may enter any order necessary to preserve the property, to prevent its removal or encumbrance, or to prevent its use in a criminal offense.

(b) Interlocutory Sale or Delivery.

(i) Order to Sell. On motion by a party or a person having custody of the property, the court may order all or part of the property sold if:

(A) the property is perishable or at risk of deterioration, decay, or injury by being detained in custody pending the action;

(B) the expense of keeping the property is excessive or is disproportionate to its fair market value;

(C) the property is subject to a mortgage or to taxes on which the owner is in default; or

(D) the court finds other good cause.

(ii) Who Makes the Sale. A sale must be made by a United States agency that has authority to sell the property, by the agency's contractor, or by any person the court designates.

(iii) Sale Procedures. The sale is governed by 28 U.S.C. §§ 2001, 2002, and 2004, unless all parties, with the court's approval, agree to the sale, aspects of the sale, or different procedures.

(iv) Sale Proceeds. Sale proceeds are a substitute res subject to forfeiture in place of the property that was sold. The proceeds must be held in an interest-bearing account maintained by the United States pending the conclusion of the forfeiture action.

(v) Delivery on a Claimant's Motion. The court may order that the property be delivered to the claimant pending the conclusion of the action if the claimant shows circumstances that would permit sale under Rule G(7)(b)(i) and gives security under these rules.

(c) Disposing of Forfeited Property. Upon entry of a forfeiture judgment, the property or proceeds from selling the property must be disposed of as provided by law.

(8) Motions.

(a) Motion To Suppress Use of the Property as Evidence. If the defendant property was seized, a party with standing to contest the lawfulness of the seizure may move to suppress use of the property as evidence. Suppression does not affect forfeiture of the property based on independently derived evidence.

(b) Motion To Dismiss the Action.

(i) A claimant who establishes standing to contest forfeiture may move to dismiss the action under Rule 12(b).

(ii) In an action governed by 18 U.S.C. § 983(a)(3)(D) the complaint may not be dismissed on the ground that the government did not have adequate evidence at the time the complaint was filed to establish the forfeitability of the property. The sufficiency of the complaint is governed by Rule G(2).

(c) Motion To Strike a Claim or Answer.

(i) At any time before trial, the government may move to strike a claim or answer:

(A) for failing to comply with Rule G(5) or (6), or

(B) because the claimant lacks standing.

(ii) The motion:

(A) must be decided before any motion by the claimant to dismiss the action; and

(B) may be presented as a motion for judgment on the pleadings or as a motion to determine after a hearing or by summary judgment whether the claimant can carry the burden of establishing standing by a preponderance of the evidence.

(d) Petition To Release Property.

(i) If a United States agency or an agency's contractor holds property for judicial or nonjudicial forfeiture under a statute governed by 18 U.S.C. § 983(f), a person who has filed a claim to the property may petition for its release under § 983(f).

(ii) If a petition for release is filed before a judicial forfeiture action is filed against the property, the petition may be filed either in the district where the property was seized or in the district where a warrant to seize the property issued. If a judicial forfeiture action against the property is later filed in another district — or if the government shows that the action will be filed in another district — the petition may be transferred to that district under 28 U.S.C. § 1404.

(e) Excessive Fines. A claimant may seek to mitigate a forfeiture under the Excessive Fines Clause of the Eighth Amendment by motion for summary judgment or by motion made after entry of a forfeiture judgment if:

(i) the claimant has pleaded the defense under Rule 8; and

(ii) the parties have had the opportunity to conduct civil discovery on the defense.

(9) Trial. Trial is to the court unless any party demands trial by jury under Rule 38.

(Added Apr. 12, 2006, eff. Dec. 1, 2006.)

ADVISORY COMMITTEE NOTES

2006 Adoption

Rule G is added to bring together the central procedures that govern civil forfeiture actions. Civil forfeiture actions are in rem proceedings, as are many admiralty proceedings. As the number of civil forfeiture actions has increased, however, reasons have appeared to create sharper distinctions within the framework of the Supplemental Rules. Civil forfeiture practice will benefit from distinctive provisions that express and focus developments in statutory, constitutional, and decisional law. Admiralty practice will be freed from the pressures that arise when the needs of civil forfeiture proceedings counsel interpretations of common rules that may not be suitable for admiralty proceedings.

Rule G generally applies to actions governed by the Civil Asset Forfeiture Reform Act of 2000 (CAFRA) and also to actions excluded from it. The rule refers to some specific CAFRA provisions; if these statutes are amended, the rule should be adapted to the new provisions during the period required to amend the rule.

Rule G is not completely self-contained. Subdivision (1) recognizes the need to rely at times on other Supplemental Rules and the place of the Supplemental Rules within the basic framework of the Civil Rules.

Supplemental Rules A, C, and E are amended to reflect the adoption of Rule G.

Subdivision (1).

Rule G is designed to include the distinctive procedures that govern a civil forfeiture action. Some details, however, are better supplied by relying on Rules C and E. Subdivision (1) incorporates those rules for issues not addressed by Rule G. This general incorporation is at times made explicit — subdivision (7)(b)(v), for example, invokes the security provisions of Rule E. But Rules C and E are not to be invoked to create conflicts with Rule G. They are to be used only when Rule G, fairly construed, does not address the issue.

The Civil Rules continue to provide the procedural framework within which Rule G and the other Supplemental Rules operate. Both Rule G(1) and Rule A state this basic proposition. Rule G, for example, does not address pleadings amendments. Civil Rule 15 applies, in light of the circumstances of a forfeiture action.

Subdivision (2).

Rule E(2)(a) requires that the complaint in an admiralty action "state the circumstances from which the claim arises with such particularity that the defendant or claimant will be able, without moving for a more definite statement, to commence an investigation of the facts and to frame a responsive pleading." Application of this standard to civil forfeiture actions has evolved to the standard stated in subdivision

(2)(f). The complaint must state sufficiently detailed facts to support a reasonable belief that the government will be able to meet its burden of proof at trial. *See U. S. v. Mondragon*, 313 F.3d 862 (4th Cir. 2002). Subdivision (2)(f) carries this forfeiture case law forward without change.

Subdivision (3).

Subdivision (3) governs in rem process in a civil forfeiture action.

Paragraph (a). Paragraph (a) reflects the provisions of 18 U.S.C. § 985.

Paragraph (b). Paragraph (b) addresses arrest warrants when the defendant is not real property. Subparagraph (i) directs the clerk to issue a warrant if the property is in the government's possession, custody, or control. If the property is not in the government's possession, custody, or control and is not subject to a restraining order, subparagraph (ii) provides that a warrant issues only if the court finds probable cause to arrest the property. This provision departs from former Rule C(3)(a)(i), which authorized issuance of summons and warrant by the clerk without a probable-cause finding. The probable-cause finding better protects the interests of persons interested in the property. Subparagraph (iii) recognizes that a warrant is not necessary if the property is subject to a judicial restraining order. The government remains free, however, to seek a warrant if it anticipates that the restraining order may be modified or vacated.

Paragraph (c). Subparagraph (ii) requires that the warrant and any supplemental process be served as soon as practicable unless the property is already in the government's possession, custody, or control. But it authorizes the court to order a different time. The authority to order a different time recognizes that the government may have secured orders sealing the complaint in a civil forfeiture action or have won a stay after filing. The seal or stay may be ordered for reasons, such as protection of an ongoing criminal investigation, that would be defeated by prompt service of the warrant. Subparagraph (ii) does not reflect any independent ground for ordering a seal or stay, but merely reflects the consequences for execution when sealing or a stay is ordered. A court also may order a different time for service if good cause is shown for reasons unrelated to a seal or stay. Subparagraph (iv) reflects the uncertainty surrounding service of an arrest warrant on property not in the United States. It is not possible to identify in the rule the appropriate authority for serving process in all other countries. Transmission of the warrant to an appropriate authority, moreover, does not ensure that the warrant will be executed. The rule requires only that the warrant be transmitted to an appropriate authority.

Subdivision (4).

Paragraph (a). Paragraph (a) reflects the traditional practice of publishing notice of an in rem action.

Subparagraph (i) recognizes two exceptions to the general publication requirement. Publication is not required if the defendant property is worth less than $1,000 and direct notice is sent to all reasonably identifiable potential claimants as required by subdivision (4)(b). Publication also is not required if the cost would exceed the property's value and the court finds that other means of notice would satisfy due process. Publication on a government-established internet forfeiture site, as contemplated by subparagraph (iv), would be at a low marginal publication cost, which would likely be the cost to compare to the property value.

Subparagraph (iv) states the basic criterion for selecting the means and method of publication. The purpose is to adopt a means reasonably calculated to reach potential claimants. The government should choose from among these means a method that is reasonably likely to reach potential claimants at a cost reasonable in the circumstances.

If the property is in the United States and newspaper notice is chosen, publication may be where the action is filed, where the property was seized, or — if the property was not seized — where the property is located. Choice among these places is influenced by the probable location of potential claimants.

If the property is not in the United States, account must be taken of the sensitivities that surround publication of legal notices in other countries. A foreign country may forbid local publication. If potential claimants are likely to be in the United States, publication in the district where the action is filed may be the best choice. If potential claimants are likely to be located abroad, the better choice may be publication by means generally circulated in the country where the property is located.

Newspaper publication is not a particularly effective means of notice for most potential claimants. Its traditional use is best defended by want of affordable alternatives. Paragraph (iv)(C) contemplates a government-created internet forfeiture site that would provide a single easily identified means of notice. Such a site could allow much more direct access to notice as to any specific property than publication provides.

Paragraph (b). Paragraph (b) is entirely new. For the first time, Rule G expressly recognizes the due process obligation to send notice to any person who reasonably appears to be a potential claimant.

Subparagraph (i) states the obligation to send notice. Many potential claimants will be known to the government because they have filed claims during the administrative forfeiture stage. Notice must be sent, however, no matter what source of information makes it reasonably appear that a person is a potential claimant. The duty to send notice terminates when the time for filing a claim expires.

Notice of the action does not require formal service of summons in the manner required by Rule 4 to initiate a personal action. The process that begins an in rem forfeiture action is addressed by subdivision (3). This process commonly gives notice to potential claimants. Publication of notice is required in addition to this process. Due process requirements have moved beyond these traditional means of notice, but are satisfied by practical means that are reasonably calculated to accomplish actual notice.

Subparagraph (ii)(B) directs that the notice state a deadline for filing a claim that is at least 35 days after the notice is sent. This provision applies both in actions that fall within 18 U.S.C. § 983(a)(4)(A) and in other actions. Section 983(a)(4)(A) states that a claim should be filed no later than 30 days after service of the complaint. The variation introduced by subparagraph (ii)(B) reflects the procedure of § 983(a)(2)(B) for nonjudicial forfeiture proceedings. The nonjudicial procedure requires that a claim be filed "not later than the deadline set forth in a personal notice letter (which may be not earlier than 35 days after the date the letter is sent) * * *." This procedure is as suitable in a civil forfeiture action as in a nonjudicial forfeiture proceeding. Thirty-five days after notice is sent ordinarily will extend the claim time by no more than a brief period; a claimant anxious to expedite proceedings can file the claim before the deadline; and the government has flexibility to set a still longer period when circumstances make that desirable.

Subparagraph (iii) begins by stating the basic requirement that notice must be sent by means reasonably calculated to reach the potential claimant. No attempt is made to list the various means that may be reasonable in different circumstances. It may be reasonable, for example, to rely on means that have already been established for communication with a particular potential claimant. The government's interest in choosing a means likely to accomplish actual notice is bolstered by its desire to avoid post-forfeiture challenges based on arguments that a different method would have been more likely to accomplish actual notice. Flexible rule language accommodates the rapid evolution of communications technology.

Notice may be directed to a potential claimant through counsel, but only to counsel already representing the claimant with respect to the seizure of the property, or in a related investigation, administrative forfeiture proceeding, or criminal case.

Subparagraph (iii)(C) reflects the basic proposition that notice to a potential claimant who is incarcerated must be sent to the place of incarceration. Notice directed to some other place, such as a pre-incarceration residence, is less likely to reach the potential claimant. This provision does not address due process questions that may arise if a particular prison has deficient procedures for delivering notice to prisoners. *See Dusenbery v. U.S.*, 534 U.S. 161 (2002).

Items (D) and (E) of subparagraph (iii) authorize the government to rely on an address given by a person who is not incarcerated. The address may have been given to the agency that arrested or released the person, or to the agency that seized the property. The government is not obliged to undertake an independent investigation to verify the address.

Subparagraph (iv) identifies the date on which notice is considered to be sent for some common means, without addressing the circumstances for choosing among the identified means or other means. The date of sending should be determined by analogy for means not listed. Facsimile transmission, for example, is sent upon transmission. Notice by personal delivery is sent on delivery.

Subparagraph (v), finally, reflects the purpose to effect actual notice by providing that a potential claimant who had actual notice of a forfeiture proceeding cannot oppose or seek relief from forfeiture because the government failed to comply with subdivision (4)(b).

Subdivision (5).

Paragraph (a). Paragraph (a) establishes that the first step of contesting a civil forfeiture action is to file a claim. A claim is required by 18 U.S.C. § 983(a)(4)(A) for actions covered by § 983. Paragraph (a) applies this procedure as well to actions not covered by § 983. "Claim" is used to describe this first pleading because of the statutory references to claim and claimant. It functions in the same way as the statement of interest prescribed for an admiralty proceeding by Rule C(6), and is not related to the distinctive meaning of "claim" in admiralty practice.

If the claimant states its interest in the property to be as bailee, the bailor must be identified. A bailee who files a claim on behalf of a bailor must state the bailee's authority to do so.

The claim must be signed under penalty of perjury by the person making it. An artificial body that can act only through an agent may authorize an agent to sign for it. Excusable inability of counsel to obtain an appropriate signature may be grounds for an extension of time to file the claim.

Paragraph (a)(ii) sets the time for filing a claim. Item (C) applies in the relatively rare circumstance in which notice is not published and the government did not send direct notice to the claimant because it did not know of the claimant or did not have an address for the claimant.

Paragraph (b). Under 18 U.S.C. § 983(a)(4)(B), which governs many forfeiture proceedings, a person who asserts an interest by filing a claim "shall file an answer to the Government's complaint for forfeiture not later than 20 days after the date of the filing of the claim." Paragraph (b) recognizes that this statute works within the general procedures established by Civil Rule 12. Rule 12(a)(4) suspends the time to answer when a Rule 12 motion is served within the time allowed to answer. Continued application of this rule to proceedings governed by § 983(a)(4)(B) serves all of the purposes advanced by Rule 12(a)(4), *see U. S. v. $8,221,877.16*, 330 F.3d 141 (3d Cir. 2003); permits a uniform procedure for all civil forfeiture actions; and recognizes that a motion under Rule 12 can be made only after a claim is filed that provides background for the motion.

Failure to present an objection to in rem jurisdiction or to venue by timely motion or answer waives the objection. Waiver of such objections is familiar. An answer may be amended to assert an objection initially omitted. But Civil Rule 15 should be applied to an amendment that for the first time raises an objection to in rem jurisdiction by analogy to the personal jurisdiction objection provision in Civil Rule 12(h)(1)(B). The amendment should be permitted only if it is permitted as a matter of course under Rule 15(a).

A claimant's motion to dismiss the action is further governed by subdivisions (6)(c), (8)(b), and (8)(c).

Subdivision (6).

Subdivision (6) illustrates the adaptation of an admiralty procedure to the different needs of civil forfeiture. Rule C(6) permits interrogatories to be served with the complaint in an in rem action without limiting the subjects of inquiry. Civil forfeiture practice does not require such an extensive departure from ordinary civil practice. It remains useful, however, to permit the government to file limited interrogatories at any time after a claim is filed to gather information that bears on the claimant's standing. Subdivisions (8)(b) and (c) allow a claimant to move to dismiss only if the claimant has standing, and recognize the government's right to move to dismiss a claim for lack of standing. Subdivision (6) interrogatories are integrated with these provisions in that the interrogatories are limited to the claimant's identity and relationship to the defendant property. If the claimant asserts a relationship to the property as bailee, the interrogatories can inquire into the bailor's interest in the property and the bailee's relationship to the bailor. The claimant can accelerate the time to serve subdivision (6) interrogatories by serving a motion to dismiss — the interrogatories must be served within 20 days after the motion is served. Integration is further accomplished by deferring the government's obligation to respond to a motion to dismiss until 20 days after the claimant moving to dismiss has answered the interrogatories.

Special interrogatories served under Rule G(6) do not count against the presumptive 25-interrogatory limit established by Rule 33(a). Rule 33 procedure otherwise applies to these interrogatories.

Subdivision (6) supersedes the discovery "moratorium" of Rule 26(d) and the broader interrogatories permitted for admiralty proceedings by Rule C(6).

Subdivision (7).

Paragraph (a). Paragraph (a) is adapted from Rule E(9)(b). It provides for preservation orders when the government does not have actual possession of the defendant property. It also goes beyond Rule E(9) by recognizing the need to prevent use of the defendant property in ongoing criminal offenses.

Paragraph (b). Paragraph (b)(i)(C) recognizes the authority, already exercised in some cases, to order sale of property subject to a defaulted mortgage or to defaulted taxes. The authority is narrowly confined to mortgages and tax liens; other lien interests may be addressed, if at all, only through the general good-cause provision. The court must carefully weigh the competing interests in each case.

Paragraph (b)(i)(D) establishes authority to order sale for good cause. Good cause may be shown when the property is subject to diminution in value. Care should be taken before ordering sale to avoid diminished value.

Paragraph (b)(iii) recognizes that if the court approves, the interests of all parties may be served by their agreement to sale, aspects of the sale, or sale procedures that depart from governing statutory procedures.

Paragraph (c) draws from Rule E(9)(a), (b), and (c). Disposition of the proceeds as provided by law may require resolution of disputed issues. A mortgagee's claim to the property or sale proceeds, for example, may be disputed on the ground that the mortgage is not genuine. An undisputed lien claim, on the other hand, may be recognized by payment after an interlocutory sale.

Subdivision (8).

Subdivision (8) addresses a number of issues that are unique to civil forfeiture actions.

Paragraph (a). Standing to suppress use of seized property as evidence is governed by principles distinct from the principles that govern claim standing. A claimant with standing to contest forfeiture may not have standing to seek suppression. Rule G does not of itself create a basis of suppression standing that does not otherwise exist.

Paragraph (b). Paragraph (b)(i) is one element of the system that integrates the procedures for determining a claimant's standing to claim and for deciding a claimant's motion to dismiss the action. Under paragraph (c)(ii), a motion to dismiss the action cannot be addressed until the court has decided any government motion to strike the claim or answer. This procedure is reflected in the (b)(i) reminder that a motion to dismiss the forfeiture action may be made only by a claimant who establishes claim standing. The government, moreover, need not respond to a claimant's motion to dismiss until 20 days after the claimant has answered any subdivision (6) interrogatories.

Paragraph (b)(ii) mirrors 18 U.S.C. § 983(a)(3)(D). It applies only to an action independently governed by § 983(a)(3)(D), implying nothing as to actions outside § 983(a)(3)(D). The adequacy of the complaint is measured against the pleading requirements of subdivision (2), not against the quality of the evidence available to the government when the complaint was filed.

Paragraph (c). As noted with paragraph (b), paragraph (c) governs the procedure for determining whether a claimant has standing. It does not address the principles that govern claim standing.

Paragraph (c)(i)(A) provides that the government may move to strike a claim or answer for failure to comply with the pleading requirements of subdivision (5) or to answer subdivision (6) interrogatories. As with other pleadings, the court should strike a claim or answer only if satisfied that an opportunity should not be afforded to cure the defects under Rule 15. Not every failure to respond to subdivision (6) interrogatories warrants an order striking the claim. But the special role that subdivision (6) plays in the scheme for determining claim standing may justify a somewhat more demanding approach than the general approach to discovery sanctions under Rule 37.

Paragraph (c)(ii) directs that a motion to strike a claim or answer be decided before any motion by the claimant to dismiss the action. A claimant who lacks standing is not entitled to challenge the forfeiture on the merits.

Paragraph (c)(ii) further identifies three procedures for addressing claim standing. If a claim fails on its face to show facts that support claim standing, the claim can be dismissed by judgment on the pleadings. If the claim shows facts that would support claim standing, those facts can be tested by a motion for summary judgment. If material facts are disputed, precluding a grant of summary judgment, the court may hold an evidentiary hearing. The evidentiary hearing is held by the court without a jury. The claimant has the burden to establish claim standing at a hearing; procedure on a government summary judgment motion reflects this allocation of the burden.

Paragraph (d). The hardship release provisions of 18 U.S.C. § 983(f) do not apply to a civil forfeiture action exempted from § 983 by § 983(i).

Paragraph (d)(ii) reflects the venue provisions of 18 U.S.C. § 983(f)(3)(A) as a guide to practitioners. In addition, it makes clear the status of a civil forfeiture action as a "civil action" eligible for transfer under 28 U.S.C. § 1404. A transfer decision must be made on the circumstances of the particular proceeding. The district where the forfeiture action is filed has the advantage of bringing all related proceedings together, avoiding the waste that flows from consideration of different parts of the same forfeiture proceeding in the court where the warrant issued or the court where the property was seized. Transfer to that court would serve consolidation, the purpose that underlies nationwide enforcement of a seizure warrant. But there may be offsetting advantages in retaining the petition where it was filed. The claimant may not be able to litigate, effectively or at all, in a distant court. Issues relevant to the petition may be better litigated where the property was seized or where the warrant issued. One element, for example, is whether the claimant has sufficient ties to the community to provide assurance that the property will be available at the time of trial. Another is whether continued government possession would prevent the claimant from working. Determining whether seizure of the claimant's automobile prevents work may turn on assessing the realities of local public transit facilities.

Paragraph (e). The Excessive Fines Clause of the Eighth Amendment forbids an excessive forfeiture. *U.S. v. Bajakajian*, 524 U.S. 321 (1998). 18 U.S.C. § 983(g) provides a "petition" "to determine whether the forfeiture was constitutionally excessive" based on finding "that the forfeiture is grossly disproportional to the offense." Paragraph (e) describes the procedure for § 983(g) mitigation petitions and adopts the same procedure for forfeiture actions that fall outside § 983(g). The procedure is by motion, either for summary judgment or for mitigation after a forfeiture judgment is entered. The claimant must give notice of this defense by pleading, but failure to raise the defense in the initial answer may be cured by amendment under Rule 15. The issues that bear on mitigation often are separate from the issues that determine forfeiture. For that reason it may be convenient to resolve the issue by summary judgment before trial on the forfeiture issues. Often, however, it will be more convenient to determine first whether the property is to be forfeited. Whichever time is chosen to address mitigation, the parties must have had the opportunity to conduct civil discovery on the defense. The extent and timing of discovery are governed by the ordinary rules.

Subdivision (9).

Subdivision (9) serves as a reminder of the need to demand jury trial under Rule 38. It does not expand the right to jury trial. *See U.S. v. One Parcel of Property Located at 32 Medley Lane*, 2005 WL 465421 (D.Conn.2005), ruling that the court, not the jury, determines whether a forfeiture is constitutionally excessive.

RULES OF EVIDENCE FOR UNITED STATES COURTS AND MAGISTRATES

Pub.L. 93–595, § 1, January 2, 1975, 88 Stat. 1926
Amendments received to December 1, 2008

ORDERS OF THE SUPREME COURT OF THE UNITED STATES ADOPTING AND AMENDING RULES

ORDER OF NOVEMBER 20, 1972

1. That the rules hereinafter set forth, to be known as the Federal Rules of Evidence, be, and they hereby are, prescribed pursuant to Sections 3402, 3771, and 3772, Title 18, United States Code, and Sections 2072 and 2075, Title 28, United States Code, to govern procedure, in the proceedings and to the extent set forth therein, in the United States courts of appeals, the United States district courts, the District Court for the District of the Canal Zone and the district courts of Guam and the Virgin Islands, and before United States magistrates.

2. That the aforementioned Federal Rules of Evidence shall take effect on July 1, 1973, and shall be applicable to actions and proceedings brought thereafter and also to further procedure in actions and proceedings then pending, except to the extent that in the opinion of the court their application in a particular action or proceeding then pending would not be feasible or would work injustice in which event the former procedure applies.

3. That subdivision (c) of Rule 30 and Rules 43 and 44.1 of the Federal Rules of Civil Procedure be, and they hereby are, amended, effective July 1, 1973, to read as hereinafter set forth:

[See amendments made thereby under the respective Rules of Civil Procedure.]

4. That subdivision (c) of Rule 32 of the Federal Rules of Civil Procedure be, and it hereby is, abrogated, effective July 1, 1973.

5. That Rules 26, 26.1 and 28 of the Federal Rules of Criminal Procedure be, and they hereby are, amended effective July 1, 1973, to read as hereinafter set forth.

[See amendments made thereby under the respective Rules of Criminal Procedure.]

6. That the Chief Justice be, and he hereby is, authorized to transmit the foregoing new rules and amendments to and abrogation of existing rules to the Congress at the beginning of its next regular session, in accordance with the provisions of Title 18 U.S.C. § 3771 and Title 28 U.S.C. §§ 2072 and 2075.

CONGRESSIONAL ACTION ON PROPOSED RULES OF EVIDENCE AND 1972 AMENDMENTS TO FEDERAL RULES OF CIVIL PROCEDURE AND FEDERAL RULES OF CRIMINAL PROCEDURE

Pub.L. 93–12, Mar. 30, 1973, 87 Stat. 9, provided: "That notwithstanding any other provisions of law, the Rules of Evidence for United States Courts and Magistrates, the Amendments to the Federal Rules of Civil Procedure, and the Amendments to the Federal Rules of Criminal Procedure, which are embraced by the orders entered by the Supreme Court of the United States on Monday, November 20, 1972, and Monday, December 18, 1972, shall have no force or effect except to the extent, and with such amendments, as they may be expressly approved by Act of Congress."

Pub.L. 93–595, § 3, Jan. 2, 1975, 88 Stat. 1959, provided that: "The Congress expressly approves the amendments to the Federal Rules of Civil Procedure, and the amendments to the Federal Rules of Criminal Procedure, which are embraced by the orders entered by the Supreme Court of the United States on November 20, 1972, and December 18, 1972, and such amendments shall take effect on the one hundred and eightieth day beginning after the date of the enactment of this Act [Jan. 2, 1975]."

ORDER OF APRIL 30, 1979

1. That Rule 410 of the Federal Rules of Evidence be, and it hereby is, amended to read as follows:

[See amendment made thereby following Rule 410, post.]

2. That the foregoing amendment to the Federal Rules of Evidence shall take effect on November 1, 1979, and shall be applicable to all proceedings then pending except to the extent that in the opinion of the court the application of the amended rule in a particular proceeding would not be feasible or would work injustice.

3. That THE CHIEF JUSTICE be, and he hereby is, authorized to transmit to the Congress the foregoing amendment to the Federal Rules of Evidence in accordance with the provisions of 28 U.S.C. § 2076.

CONGRESSIONAL ACTION ON AMENDMENT PROPOSED APRIL 30, 1979

Pub.L. 96–42, July 31, 1979, 93 Stat. 326, provided that the amendment proposed and transmitted to the Federal Rules of Evidence affecting rule 410, shall not take effect until Dec. 1, 1980, or until and then only to the extent approved by Act of Congress, whichever is earlier.

ORDER OF MARCH 2, 1987

1. That the Federal Rules of Evidence be, and they hereby are, amended by including therein amendments to Rules 101, 104, 106, 404, 405, 411, 602, 603, 604, 606, 607, 608, 609, 610, 611, 612, 613, 615, 701, 703, 705, 706, 801, 803, 804, 806, 902, 1004, 1007 and 1101, as hereinafter set forth:

[See amendments made thereby under respective rules, post.]

2. That the foregoing changes in the Federal Rules of Evidence shall take effect on October 1, 1987.

3. That THE CHIEF JUSTICE be, and he hereby is, authorized to transmit to the Congress the foregoing changes in the rules of evidence in accordance with the provisions of Section 2076 of Title 28, United States Code.

ORDER OF APRIL 25, 1988

1. That the Federal Rules of Evidence be, and they hereby are, amended by including therein amendments to Rules 101, 602, 608, 613, 615, 902, and 1101, as hereinafter set forth:

[See amendments made thereby under respective rules, post.]

2. That the foregoing changes in the Federal Rules of Evidence shall take effect on November 1, 1988.

3. That THE CHIEF JUSTICE be, and he hereby is, authorized to transmit to the Congress the foregoing changes in the rules of evidence in accordance with the provisions of Section 2076 of Title 28, United States Code.

ORDER OF JANUARY 26, 1990

1. That the Federal Rules of Evidence be, and they hereby are, amended by including therein amendments to Rule 609(a)(1) and (2), as hereinafter set forth:

[See amendment made thereby, post].

2. That the foregoing changes in the Federal Rules of Evidence shall take effect on December 1, 1990.

3. That THE CHIEF JUSTICE be, and he hereby is, authorized to transmit to the Congress the foregoing changes in the rules of evidence in accordance with the provisions of Section 2074 of Title 28, United States Code.

ORDER OF APRIL 30, 1991

1. That the Federal Rules of Evidence for the United States District Courts be, and they hereby are, amended by including therein amendments to Evidence Rules 404(b) and 1102.

[See amendments made thereby under respective rules, post.]

2. That the foregoing amendments to the Federal Rules of Evidence shall take effect on December 1, 1991, and shall govern in all proceedings thereafter commenced and, insofar as just and practicable, all proceedings then pending.

3. That THE CHIEF JUSTICE be, and he hereby is, authorized to transmit to the Congress the foregoing amendments to the Federal Rules of Evidence in accordance with the provisions of Section 2072 of Title 28, United States Code.

ORDER OF APRIL 22, 1993

1. That the Federal Rules of Evidence for the United States District Courts be, and they hereby are, amended by including therein amendments to Evidence Rules 101, 705, and 1101.

[See amendments made thereby under respective rules, post.]

2. That the foregoing amendments to the Federal Rules of Evidence shall take effect on December 1, 1993, and shall govern in all proceedings thereafter commenced and, insofar as just and practicable, all proceedings then pending.

3. That THE CHIEF JUSTICE be, and he hereby is, authorized to transmit to the Congress the foregoing amendments to the Federal Rules of Evidence in accordance with the provisions of Section 2072 of Title 28, United States Code.

ORDER OF APRIL 29, 1994

ORDERED:

1. That the Federal Rules of Evidence for the United States District Courts be, and they hereby are, amended by including therein an amendment to Evidence Rule 412.

[See amendment made hereby under Rule 412, post.]

2. That the foregoing amendment to the Federal Rules of Evidence shall take effect on December 1, 1994, and shall govern in all proceedings thereafter commenced and, insofar as just and practicable, all proceedings then pending.

3. That THE CHIEF JUSTICE be, and he hereby is, authorized to transmit to the Congress the foregoing amendment to the Federal Rules of Evidence in accordance with the provisions of Section 2072 of Title 28, United States Code.

ORDER OF APRIL 11, 1997

ORDERED:

1. That the Federal Rules of Evidence be, and they hereby are, amended by including therein amendments to Evidence Rules 407, 801, 803(24), 804(b)(5), and 806, and new Rules 804(b)(6) and 807.

[See amendments made thereby under respective rules, post.]

2. That the foregoing amendments to the Federal Rules of Evidence shall take effect on December 1, 1997, and shall govern in all proceedings thereafter commenced and, insofar as just and practicable, all proceedings then pending.

3. That THE CHIEF JUSTICE be, and hereby is, authorized to transmit to the Congress the foregoing amendments to the Federal Rules of Evidence in accordance with the provisions of Section 2072 of Title 28, United States Code.

ORDER OF APRIL 24, 1998

ORDERED:

1. That the Federal Rules of Evidence be, and they hereby are, amended by including therein amendments to Evidence Rule 615.

[See amendments made thereby under respective rules, post.]

2. That the foregoing amendments to the Federal Rules of Evidence shall take effect on December 1, 1998, and shall govern in all proceedings thereafter commenced and, insofar as just and practicable, all proceedings then pending.

3. That THE CHIEF JUSTICE be, and hereby is, authorized to transmit to the Congress the foregoing amendments to the Federal Rules of Evidence in accordance with the provisions of Section 2072 of Title 28, United States Code.

ORDER OF APRIL 17, 2000

ORDERED:

1. That the Federal Rules of Evidence for the United States District Courts be, and they hereby are, amended by including therein amendments to Evidence Rules 103, 404, 701, 702, 703, 803(6), and 902.

[See amendments made thereby under respective rules, post.]

2. That the foregoing amendments to the Federal Rules of Evidence shall take effect on December 1, 2000, and shall govern all proceedings thereafter commenced and, insofar as just and practicable, all proceedings then pending .

3. That THE CHIEF JUSTICE be, and hereby is, authorized to transmit to the Congress the foregoing amendments to the Federal Rules of Evidence in accordance with the provisions of Section 2072 of Title 28, United States Code.

ORDER OF MARCH 27, 2003

ORDERED:

1. That the Federal Rules of Evidence be, and they hereby are, amended by including therein the amendments to Evidence Rule 608(b).

[See amendments made thereby under respective rules, post.]

2. That the foregoing amendments to the Federal Rules of Evidence shall take effect on December 1, 2003, and shall govern in all proceedings thereafter commenced and, insofar as just and practicable, all proceedings then pending.

3. That THE CHIEF JUSTICE be, and hereby is, authorized to transmit to the Congress the foregoing amendments to the Federal Rules of Evidence in accordance with the provisions of Section 2072 of Title 28, United States Code.

ORDER OF APRIL 12, 2006

1. That the Federal Rules of Evidence be, and they hereby are, amended by including therein the amendments to Evidence Rules 404, 408, 606, and 609.

[See amendments made thereby under respective rules, post.]

2. That the foregoing amendments to the Federal Rules of Evidence shall take effect on December 1, 2006, and shall govern in all proceedings thereafter commenced and, insofar as just and practicable, all proceedings then pending.

3. That THE CHIEF JUSTICE be, and hereby is, authorized to transmit to the Congress the foregoing amendments to the Federal Rules of Evidence in accordance with the provisions of Section 2072 of Title 28, United States Code.

HISTORICAL NOTES

Revision Notes and Legislative Reports

For legislative history and purpose of Pub.L. 93–595, see House, Senate and Conference Reports, set out following the text of these rules.

Effective Date and Application of Rules

The Federal Rules of Evidence were adopted by order of the Supreme Court on Nov. 20, 1972, transmitted to Congress by the Chief Justice on Feb. 5, 1973, and to have become effective on July 1, 1973. Pub.L. 93–12, Mar. 30, 1973, 87 Stat. 9, provided that the proposed rules "shall have no force or effect except to the extent, and with such amendments, as they may be expressly approved by Act of Congress". Pub.L. 93–595, Jan. 2, 1975, 88 Stat. 1926, enacted the Federal Rules of Evidence proposed by the Supreme Court, with amendments made by Congress, to take effect on July 1, 1975.

The Rules have been amended Oct. 16, 1975, Pub.L. 94–113, § 1, 89 Stat. 576, eff. Oct. 31, 1975; Dec. 12, 1975, Pub.L. 94–149, § 1, 89 Stat. 805; Oct. 28, 1978, Pub.L. 95–540, § 2, 92 Stat. 2046; Nov. 6, 1978, Pub.L. 95–598, Title II, § 251, 92 Stat. 2673, eff. Oct. 1, 1979; Apr. 30, 1979, eff. Dec. 1, 1980; Apr. 2, 1982, Pub.L. 97–164, Title I, § 142, Title IV, § 402, 96 Stat. 45, 57, eff. Oct. 1, 1982; Oct. 12, 1984, Pub.L. 98–473, Title IV, § 406, 98 Stat. 2067; Mar. 2, 1987, eff. Oct. 1, 1987; Apr. 25, 1988, eff. Nov. 1, 1988; Nov. 18, 1988, Pub.L. 100–690, Title VII, §§ 7046, 7075, 102 Stat. 4400, 4405; Jan. 26, 1990, eff. Dec. 1, 1990; Apr. 30, 1991, eff. Dec. 1, 1991; Apr. 22, 1993, eff. Dec. 1, 1993; Apr. 29, 1994, eff. Dec. 1, 1994; Apr. 11, 1997, eff. Dec. 1, 1997; Apr. 24, 1998, eff. Dec. 1, 1998; Apr. 17, 2000, eff. Dec. 1, 2000; Mar. 27, 2003, eff. Dec. 1, 2003; Apr. 12, 2006, eff. Dec. 1, 2006.

ARTICLE I. GENERAL PROVISIONS

Rule

HISTORICAL NOTES

Change of Name

United States magistrate appointed under section 631 of Title 28, Judiciary and Judicial Procedure, to be known as United States magistrate judge after Dec. 1, 1990, with any reference to United States magistrate or magistrate in Title 28, in any other Federal statute, etc., deemed a reference to United States magistrate judge appointed under section 631 of Title 28, see section 321 of Pub.L. 101–650, set out as a note under section 631 of Title 28.

Rule 101. Scope

These rules govern proceedings in the courts of the United States and before the United States bankruptcy judges and United States magistrate judges, to the extent and with the exceptions stated in rule 1101.

(Pub.L. 93–595, § 1, Jan. 2, 1975, 88 Stat. 1929; Mar. 2, 1987, eff. Oct. 1, 1987; Apr. 25, 1988, eff. Nov. 1, 1988; Apr. 22, 1993, eff. Dec. 1, 1993.)

ADVISORY COMMITTEE NOTES

1972 Proposed Rules

Rule 1101 specifies in detail the courts, proceedings, questions, and stages of proceedings to which the rules apply in whole or in part.

1987 Amendments

United States bankruptcy judges are added to conform this rule with Rule 1101(b) and Bankruptcy Rule 9017.

1988 Amendments

The amendment is technical. No substantive change is intended.

1993 Amendments

This revision is made to conform the rule to changes made by the Judicial Improvements Act of 1990.

HISTORICAL NOTES

Change of Name

United States magistrate appointed under section 631 of Title 28, Judiciary and Judicial Procedure, to be known as United States magistrate judge after Dec. 1, 1990, with any reference to United States magistrate or magistrate in Title 28, in any other Federal statute, etc., deemed a reference to United States magistrate judge appointed under section 631 of Title 28, see section 321 of Pub.L. 101–650, set out as a note under section 631 of Title 28.

CROSS REFERENCES

Scope, see Fed.Rules Civ.Proc. Rule 1, 28 USCA.

Scope, see Fed.Rules Cr.Proc. Rule 1, 18 USCA.

Rule 102. Purpose and Construction

These rules shall be construed to secure fairness in administration, elimination of unjustifiable expense and delay, and promotion of growth and development of the law of evidence to the end that the truth may be ascertained and proceedings justly determined.

(Pub.L. 93–595, § 1, Jan. 2, 1975, 88 Stat.1929.)

ADVISORY COMMITTEE NOTES

1972 Proposed Rules

For similar provisions see Rule 2 of the Federal Rules of Criminal Procedure, Rule 1 of the Federal Rules of Civil Procedure, California Evidence Code § 2, and New Jersey Evidence Rule 5.

CROSS REFERENCES

Construction, see Fed.Rules Civ.Proc. Rule 1, 28 USCA.

Purpose and construction, see Fed.Rules Cr.Proc. Rule 2, 18 USCA.

Rule 103. Rulings on Evidence

(a) Effect of Erroneous Ruling.—Error may not be predicated upon a ruling which admits or excludes evidence unless a substantial right of the party is affected, and

(1) Objection.—In case the ruling is one admitting evidence, a timely objection or motion to strike appears of record, stating the specific ground of objection, if the specific ground was not apparent from the context; or

(2) Offer of Proof.—In case the ruling is one excluding evidence, the substance of the evidence was made known to the court by offer or was apparent from the context within which questions were asked.

Once the court makes a definitive ruling on the record admitting or excluding evidence, either at or before trial, a party need not renew an objection or offer of proof to preserve a claim of error for appeal.

(b) Record of Offer and Ruling.—The court may add any other or further statement which shows the character of the evidence, the form in which it was offered, the objection made, and the ruling thereon. It may direct the making of an offer in question and answer form.

(c) Hearing of Jury.—In jury cases, proceedings shall be conducted, to the extent practicable, so as to prevent inadmissible evidence from being suggested to the jury by any means, such as making statements or offers of proof or asking questions in the hearing of the jury.

(d) Plain Error.—Nothing in this rule precludes taking notice of plain errors affecting substantial rights although they were not brought to the attention of the court.

(Pub.L. 93–595, § 1, Jan. 2, 1975, 88 Stat. 1929; Apr. 17, 2000, eff. Dec. 1, 2000.)

ADVISORY COMMITTEE NOTES

1972 Proposed Rules

Note to Subdivision (a). Subdivision (a) states the law as generally accepted today. Rulings on evidence cannot be assigned as error unless (1) a substantial right is affected, and (2) the nature of the error was called to the attention of the judge, so as to alert him to the proper course of action and enable opposing counsel to take proper corrective measures. The objection and the offer of proof are the techniques for accomplishing these objectives. For similar provisions see Uniform Rules 4 and 5; California Evidence Code §§ 353 and 354; Kansas Code of Civil Procedure §§ 60–404 and 60–405. The rule does not purport to change the law with respect to harmless error. See 28 USC § 2111, F.R.Civ.P. 61, F.R.Crim.P. 52, and decisions construing them. The status of constitutional error as harmless or not is treated in Chapman v. California, 386 U.S. 18, 87 S.Ct. 824, 17 L.Ed.2d 705 (1967), reh. denied id. 987, 87 S.Ct. 1283, 18 L.Ed.2d 241.

Note to Subdivision (b). The first sentence is the third sentence of Rule 43(c) of the Federal Rules of Civil Procedure virtually verbatim. Its purpose is to reproduce for an appellate court, insofar as possible, a true reflection of what occurred in the trial court. The second sentence is in part derived from the final sentence of Rule 43(c). It is designed to resolve doubts as to what testimony the witness would have in fact given, and, in nonjury cases, to provide the appellate court with material for a possible final disposition of the case in the event of reversal of a ruling which excluded evidence. See 5 Moore's Federal Practice § 43.11 (2d ed. 1968). Application is made discretionary in view of the practical impossibility of formulating a satisfactory rule in mandatory terms.

Note to Subdivision (c). This subdivision proceeds on the supposition that a ruling which excludes evidence in a jury case is likely to be a pointless procedure if the excluded evidence nevertheless comes to the attention of the jury. *Bruton v. United States,* 389 U.S. 818, 88 S.Ct. 126, 19 L.Ed.2d 70 (1968). Rule 43(c) of the Federal Rules of Civil Procedure provides: "The court may require the offer to be made out of the hearing of the jury." *In re McConnell,* 370 U.S. 230, 82 S.Ct. 1288, 8 L.Ed.2d 434 (1962), left some doubt whether questions on which an offer is based must first be asked in the presence of the jury. The subdivision answers in the negative. The judge can foreclose a particular line of testimony and counsel can protect his record without a series of questions before the jury, designed at best to waste time and at worst "to waft into the jury box" the very matter sought to be excluded.

Note to Subdivision (d). This wording of the plain error principle is from Rule 52(b) of the Federal Rules of Criminal Procedure. While judicial unwillingness to be constructed by mechanical breakdowns of the adversary system has been more pronounced in criminal cases, there is no scarcity of decisions to the same effect in civil cases. In general, see Campbell, Extent to Which Courts of Review Will Consider Questions Not Properly Raised and Preserved, 7 Wis.L.Rev. 91, 160 (1932); Vestal, Sua Sponte Consideration in Appellate Review, 27 Fordham L.Rev. 477 (1958–59); 64 Harv.L.Rev. 652 (1951). In the nature of things the application of the plain error rule will be more likely with respect to the admission of evidence than to exclusion, since failure to comply with normal requirements of offers of proof is likely to produce a record which simply does not disclose the error.

2000 Amendment

The amendment applies to all rulings on evidence whether they occur at or before trial, including so-called "*in limine*" rulings. One of the most difficult questions arising from *in limine* and other evidentiary rulings is whether a losing party must renew an objection or offer of proof when the evidence is or would be offered at trial, in order to preserve a claim of error on appeal. Courts have taken differing approaches to this question. Some courts have held that a renewal at the time the evidence is to be offered at trial is always required. *See, e.g., Collins v. Wayne Corp.,* 621 F.2d 777 (5th Cir. 1980). Some courts have taken a more flexible approach, holding that renewal is not required if the issue decided is one that (1) was fairly presented to the trial court for an initial ruling, (2) may be decided as a final matter before the evidence is actually offered, and (3) was ruled on definitively by the trial judge, *See, e.g., Rosenfeld v. Basquiat,* 78 F.3d 84 (2d Cir. 1996) (admissibility of former testimony under the Dead Man's Statute; renewal not required). Other courts have distinguished between objections to evidence, which must be renewed when evidence is offered, and offers of proof, which need not be renewed after a definitive determination is made that the evidence is inadmissible. *See, e.g., Fusco v. General Motors Corp.,* 11 F.3d 259 (1st Cir. 1993). Another court, aware of this Committee's proposed amendment, has adopted its approach. *Wilson v. Williams,* 182 F. 3d 562 (7th Cir.1999) (en banc). Differing views on this question create uncertainty for litigants and unnecessary work for the appellate courts.

The amendment provides that a claim of error with respect to a definitive ruling is preserved for review when the party has otherwise satisfied the objection or offer of proof requirements of Rule 103(a). When the ruling is definitive, a renewed objection or offer of proof at the time the evidence is to be offered is more a formalism than a necessity. *See* Fed.R.Civ.P. 46 (formal exceptions unnecessary); Fed. R.Cr.P. 51 (same); *United States v. Mejia–Alarcon,* 995 F.2d 982, 986 (10th Cir. 1993) ("Requiring a party to renew an objection when the district court has issued a definitive ruling on a matter that can be fairly decided before trial would be in the nature of a formal exception and therefore unnecessary."). On the other hand, when the trial court appears to have reserved its ruling or to have indicated that the ruling is provisional, it makes sense to require the party to bring the issue to the court's attention subsequently. *See, e.g., United States v. Vest,* 116 F.3d 1179, 1188 (7th Cir. 1997) (where the trial court ruled *n limine* that testimony from defense witnesses could not be admitted, but allowed the defendant to seek leave at trial to call the witnesses should their testimony turn out to be relevant, the defendant's failure to seek such leave at trial meant that it was "too late to reopen the issue now on appeal"); *United States v. Valenti,* 60 F.3d 941 (2d Cir. 1995) (failure to proffer evidence at trial waives any claim of error where the trial judge had stated that he would reserve judgment on the *in limine* motion until he had heard the trial evidence).

The amendment imposes the obligation on counsel to clarify whether an *in limine* or other evidentiary ruling is definitive when there is doubt on that point. *See, e.g., Walden v. Georgia–Pacific Corp.,* 126 F.3d 506, 520 (3d Cir. 1997) (although "the district court told plaintiffs' counsel not to reargue every ruling, it did not countermand its clear opening statement that all of its rulings were tentative, and counsel never requested clarification, as he might have done.").

Even where the court's ruling is definitive, nothing in the amendment prohibits the court from revisiting its decision when the evidence is to be offered. If the court changes its initial ruling, or if the opposing party violates the terms of the initial ruling, objection must be made when the evidence is offered to preserve the claim of error for appeal. The error, if any, in such a situation occurs only when the evidence is offered and admitted. *United States Aviation Underwriters, Inc. v. Olympia Wings, Inc.,* 896 F.2d 949, 956 (5th Cir. 1990) ("objection is required to preserve error when an opponent, or the court itself, violates a motion *in limine* that was granted"); *United States v. Roenigk*, 810 F.2d 809 (8th Cir. 1987) (claim of error was not preserved where the defendant failed to object at trial to secure the benefit of a favorable advance ruling).

A definitive advance ruling is reviewed in light of the facts and circumstances before the trial court at the time of the ruling. If the relevant facts and circumstances change materially after the advance ruling has been made, those facts and circumstances cannot be relied upon on appeal unless they have been brought to the attention of the trial court by way of a renewed, and timely, objection, offer of proof, or motion to strike. *See Old Chief v. United States*, 519 U.S. 172, 182, n.6 (1997) ("It is important that a reviewing court evaluate the trial court's decision from its perspective when it had to rule and not indulge in review by hindsight."). Similarly, if the court decides in an advance ruling that proffered evidence is admissible subject to the eventual introduction by the proponent of a foundation for the evidence, and that foundation is never provided, the opponent cannot claim error based on the failure to establish the foundation unless the opponent calls that failure to the court's attention by a timely motion to strike or other suitable motion. *See Huddleston v. United States*, 485 U.S. 681, 690, n.7 (1988) ("It is, of course, not the responsibility of the judge *sua sponte* to ensure that the foundation evidence is offered; the objector must move to strike the evidence if at the close of the trial the offeror has failed to satisfy the condition.").

Nothing in the amendment is intended to affect the provisions of Fed.R.Civ.P. 72(a) or 28 U.S.C. § 636(b)(1) pertaining to nondispositive pretrial rulings by magistrate judges in proceedings that are not before a magistrate judge by consent of the parties. Fed.R.Civ.P. 72(a) provides that a party who fails to file a written objection to a magistrate judge's nondispositive order within ten days of receiving a copy "may not thereafter assign as error a defect" in the order. 28 U.S.C. § 636(b)(1) provides that any party "may serve and file written objections to such proposed findings and recommendations as provided by rules of court" within ten days of receiving a copy of the order. Several courts have held that a party must comply with this statutory provision in order to preserve a claim of error. *See, e.g., Wells v. Shriners Hospital*, 109 F.3d 198, 200 (4th Cir. 1997)("[i]n this circuit, as in others, a party 'may' file objections within ten days or he may not, as he chooses, but he 'shall' do so if he wishes further consideration."). When Fed.R.Civ.P. 72(a) or 28 U.S.C. § 636(b)(1) is operative, its requirement must be satisfied in order for a party to preserve a claim of error on appeal, even where Evidence Rule 103(a) would not require a subsequent objection or offer of proof.

Nothing in the amendment is intended to affect the rule set forth in *Luce v. United States*, 469 U.S. 38 (1984), and its progeny. The amendment provides that an objection or offer of proof need not be renewed to preserve a claim of error with respect to a definitive pretrial ruling. *Luce* answers affirmatively a separate question: whether a criminal defendant must testify at trial in order to preserve a claim of error predicated upon a trial court's decision to admit the defendant's prior convictions for impeachment. The *Luce* principle has been extended by many lower courts to other situations. *See United States v. DiMatteo*, 759 F.2d 831 (11th Cir. 1985) (applying *Luce* where the defendant's witness would be impeached with evidence offered under Rule 608). *See also United States v. Goldman*, 41 F.3d 785, 788 (1st Cir. 1994) ("Although *Luce* involved impeachment by conviction under Rule 609, the reasons given by the Supreme Court for requiring the defendant to testify apply with full force to the kind of Rule 403 and 404 objections that are advanced by Goldman in this case."); *Palmieri v. DeFaria*, 88 F.3d 136 (2d Cir. 1996) (where the plaintiff decided to take an adverse judgment rather than challenge an advance ruling by putting on evidence at trial, the *in limine* ruling would not be reviewed on appeal); *United States v. Ortiz*, 857 F.2d 900 (2d Cir. 1988) (where uncharged misconduct is ruled admissible if the defendant pursues a certain defense, the defendant must actually pursue that defense at trial in order to preserve a claim of error on appeal); *United States v. Bond*, 87 F.3d 695 (5th Cir. 1996) (where the trial court rules *in limine* that the defendant would waive his fifth amendment privilege were he to testify, the defendant must take the stand and testify in order to challenge that ruling on appeal).

The amendment does not purport to answer whether a party who objects to evidence that the court finds admissible in a definitive ruling, and who then offers the evidence to "remove the sting" of its anticipated prejudicial effect, thereby waives the right to appeal the trial court's ruling. *See, e.g., United States v. Fisher*, 106 F.3d 622 (5th Cir. 1997) (where the trial judge ruled *in limine* that the government could use a prior conviction to impeach the defendant if he testified, the defendant did not waive his right to appeal by introducing the conviction on direct examination); *Judd v. Rodman*, 105 F.3d 1339 (11th Cir. 1997) (an objection made *in limine* is sufficient to preserve a claim of error when the movant, as a matter of trial strategy, presents the objectionable evidence herself on direct examination to minimize its prejudicial effect); *Gill v. Thomas*, 83 F.3d 537, 540 (1st Cir. 1996) ("by offering the misdemeanor evidence himself, Gill waived his opportunity to object and thus did not preserve the issue for appeal"); *United States v. Williams*, 939 F.2d 721 (9th Cir. 1991) (objection to impeachment evidence was waived where the defendant was impeached on direct examination).

GAP Report—Proposed Amendment to Rule 103(a)

The Committee made the following changes to the published draft of the proposed amendment to Evidence Rule 103(a):

1. A minor stylistic change was made in the text, in accordance with the suggestion of the Style Subcommittee of the Standing Committee on Rules of Practice and Procedure.

2. The second sentence of the amended portion of the published draft was deleted, and the Committee Note was amended to reflect the fact that nothing in the amendment is intended to affect the rule of *Luce v. United States*.

3. The Committee Note was updated to include cases decided after the proposed amendment was issued for public comment.

4. The Committee Note was amended to include a reference to a Civil Rule and a statute requiring objections to certain Magistrate Judge rulings to be made to the District Court.

5. The Committee Note was revised to clarify that an advance ruling does not encompass subsequent developments at trial that might be the subject of an appeal.

HISTORICAL NOTES

Conference Committee Notes, House Report No. 93–1597

The House bill contains the word "judge". The Senate amendment substitutes the word "court" in order to conform with usage elsewhere in the House bill.

The Conference adopts the Senate amendment.

CROSS REFERENCES

Fair and impartial trial and jury, right to, see USCA Const. Amend. VI.

Harmless error, see 28 USCA § 2111.

Harmless error, see Fed.Rules Civ.Proc. Rule 61, 28 USCA.

Harmless error and plain error, see Fed.Rules Cr.Proc. Rule 52, 18 USCA.

Objections—

Absence of not prejudicial, see Fed.Rules Cr.Proc. Rule 51, 18 USCA.

Admissibility of depositions, see Fed.Rules Cr.Proc. Rule 15, 18 USCA.

Suppression of evidence—

Motion for return of property involved in seizure, see Fed.Rules Cr.Proc. Rule 41, 18 USCA.

Motion to suppress evidence, see Fed.Rules Cr.Proc. Rule 12, 18 USCA.

Objections, absence of on rulings not prejudicial, see Fed. Rules Civ.Proc. Rule 46, 28 USCA.

Rule 104. Preliminary Questions

(a) Questions of admissibility generally. Preliminary questions concerning the qualification of a person to be a witness, the existence of a privilege, or the admissibility of evidence shall be determined by the court, subject to the provisions of subdivision (b). In making its determination it is not bound by the rules of evidence except those with respect to privileges.

(b) Relevancy conditioned on fact. When the relevancy of evidence depends upon the fulfillment of a condition of fact, the court shall admit it upon, or subject to, the introduction of evidence sufficient to support a finding of the fulfillment of the condition.

(c) Hearing of jury. Hearings on the admissibility of confessions shall in all cases be conducted out of the hearing of the jury. Hearings on other preliminary matters shall be so conducted when the interests of justice require, or when an accused is a witness and so requests.

(d) Testimony by accused. The accused does not, by testifying upon a preliminary matter, become subject to cross-examination as to other issues in the case.

(e) Weight and credibility. This rule does not limit the right of a party to introduce before the jury evidence relevant to weight or credibility.

(Pub.L. 93–595, § 1, Jan. 2, 1975, 88 Stat.1930; Mar. 2, 1987, eff. Oct. 1, 1987.)

ADVISORY COMMITTEE NOTES

1972 Proposed Rule

Note to Subdivision (a). The applicability of a particular rule of evidence often depends upon the existence of a condition. Is the alleged expert a qualified physician? Is a witness whose former testimony is offered unavailable? Was a stranger present during a conversation between attorney and client? In each instance the admissibility of evidence will turn upon the answer to the question of the existence of the condition. Accepted practice, incorporated in the rule, places on the judge the responsibility for these determinations. McCormick § 53; Morgan, Basic Problems of Evidence 45–50 (1962).

To the extent that these inquiries are factual, the judge acts as a trier of fact. Often, however, rulings on evidence call for an evaluation in terms of a legally set standard. Thus when a hearsay statement is offered as a declaration against interest, a decision must be made whether it possesses the required against-interest characteristics. These decisions, too, are made by the judge.

In view of these considerations, this subdivision refers to preliminary requirements generally by the broad term "questions," without attempt at specification.

This subdivision is of general application. It must, however, be read as subject to the special provisions for "conditional relevancy" in subdivision (b) and those for confessions in subdivision (d).

If the question is factual in nature, the judge will of necessity receive evidence pro and con on the issue. The rule provides that the rules of evidence in general do not apply to this process. McCormick § 53, p. 123, n. 8, points out that the authorities are "scattered and inconclusive," and observes:

"Should the exclusionary law of evidence, 'the child of the jury system' in Thayer's phrase, be applied to this hearing before the judge? Sound sense backs the view that it should not, and that the judge should be empowered to hear any relevant evidence, such as affidavits or other reliable hearsay."

This view is reinforced by practical necessity in certain situations. An item, offered and objected to, may itself be considered in ruling on admissibility, though not yet admitted in evidence. Thus, the content of an asserted declaration against interest must be considered in ruling whether it is against interest. Again, common practice calls for considering the testimony of a witness, particularly a child, in determining competency. Another example is the requirement of Rule 602 dealing with personal knowledge. In the case of hearsay, it is enough, if the declarant "so far as appears [has] had an opportunity to observe the fact declared." McCormick, § 10, p. 19.

If concern is felt over the use of affidavits by the judge in preliminary hearings on admissibility, attention is directed to the many important judicial determinations made on the basis of affidavits. Rule 47 of the Federal Rules of Criminal Procedure provides:

"An application to the court for an order shall be by motion. * * * It may be supported by affidavit."

The Rules of Civil Procedure are more detailed. Rule 43(e), dealing with motions generally, provides:

"When a motion is based on facts not appearing of record the court may hear the matter on affidavits presented by the respective parties, but the court may direct that the matter be heard wholly or partly on oral testimony or depositions." Rule 4(g) provides for proof of service by affidavit. Rule 56 provides in detail for the entry of summary judgment based on affidavits. Affidavits may supply the foundation for temporary restraining orders under Rule 65(b).

The study made for the California Law Revision Commission recommended an amendment to Uniform Rule 2 as follows:

"In the determination of the issue aforesaid [preliminary determination], exclusionary rules shall not apply, subject, however, to Rule 45 and any valid claim of privilege." Tentative Recommendation and a Study Relating to the Uniform Rules of Evidence (Article VIII, Hearsay), Cal.Law Revision Comm'n, Rep., Rec. & Studies, 470 (1962). The proposal was not adopted in the California Evidence Code. The Uniform Rules are likewise silent on the subject. However, New Jersey Evidence Rule 8(1), dealing with preliminary inquiry by the judge, provides:

"In his determination the rules of evidence shall not apply except for Rule 4 [exclusion on grounds of confusion, etc.] or a valid claim of privilege."

Note to Subdivision (b). In some situations, the relevancy of an item of evidence, in the large sense, depends upon the existence of a particular preliminary fact. Thus when a spoken statement is relied upon to prove notice to X, it is without probative value unless X heard it. Or if a letter purporting to be from Y is relied upon to establish an admission by him, it has no probative value unless Y wrote or authorized it. Relevance in this sense has been labelled "conditional relevancy." Morgan, Basic Problems of Evidence 45–46 (1962). Problems arising in connection with it are to be distinguished from problems of logical relevancy, e.g., evidence in a murder case that accused on the day before purchased a weapon of the kind used in the killing, treated in Rule 401.

If preliminary questions of conditional relevancy were determined solely by the judge, as provided in subdivision (a), the functioning of the jury as a trier of fact would be greatly restricted and in some cases virtually destroyed. These are appropriate questions for juries. Accepted treatment, as provided in the rule, is consistent with that given fact questions generally. The judge makes a preliminary determination whether the foundation evidence is sufficient to support a finding of fulfillment of the condition. If so, the item is admitted. If after all the evidence on the issue is in, pro and con, the jury could reasonably conclude that fulfillment of the condition is not established, the issue is for them. If the evidence is not such as to allow a finding, the judge withdraws the matter from their consideration. Morgan, *supra;* California Evidence Code § 403; New Jersey Rule 8(2). See also Uniform Rules 19 and 67.

The order of proof here, as generally, is subject to the control of the judge.

Note to Subdivision (c). Preliminary hearings on the admissibility of confessions must be conducted outside the hearing of the jury. See *Jackson v. Denno,* 378 U.S. 368, 84 S.Ct. 1774, 12 L.Ed.2d 908 (1964). Otherwise, detailed treatment of when preliminary matters should be heard outside the hearing of the jury is not feasible. The procedure is time consuming. Not infrequently the same evidence which is relevant to the issue of establishment of fulfillment of a condition precedent to admissibility is also relevant to weight or credibility, and time is saved by taking foundation proof in the presence of the jury. Much evidence on preliminary questions, though not relevant to jury issues, may be heard by the jury with no adverse effect. A great deal must be left to the discretion of the judge who will act as the interests of justice require.

Note to Subdivision (d). The limitation upon cross-examination is designed to encourage participation by the accused in the determination of preliminary matters. He may testify concerning them without exposing himself to cross-examination generally. The provision is necessary because of the breadth of cross-examination under Rule 611(b).

The rule does not address itself to questions of the subsequent use of testimony given by an accused at a hearing on a preliminary matter. See *Walder v. United States,* 347 U.S. 62 (1954); *Simmons v. United States,* 390 U.S. 377 (1968); *Harris v. New York,* 401 U.S. 222 (1971).

Note to Subdivision (e). For similar provisions see Uniform Rule 8; California Evidence Code § 406; Kansas Code of Civil Procedure § 60–408; New Jersey Evidence Rule 8(1).

1974 Enactment

Rule 104(c) as submitted to the Congress provided that hearings on the admissibility of confessions shall be conducted outside the presence of the jury and hearings on all other preliminary matters should be so conducted when the interests of justice require. The Committee amended the Rule to provide that where an accused is a witness as to a preliminary matter, he has the right, upon his request, to be heard outside the jury's presence. Although recognizing that in some cases duplication of evidence would occur and that the procedure could be subject to abuse, the Committee believed that a proper regard for the right of an accused not to testify generally in the case dictates that he be given an option to testify out of the presence of the jury on preliminary matters.

The Committee construes the second sentence of subdivision (c) as applying to civil actions and proceedings as well as to criminal cases, and on this assumption has left the sentence unamended. House Report No. 93–650.

Under rule 104(c) the hearing on a preliminary matter may at times be conducted in front of the jury. Should an accused testify in such a hearing, waiving his privilege against self-incrimination as to the preliminary issue, rule 104(d) provides that he will not generally be subject to cross-examination as to any other issue. This rule is not, however, intended to immunize the accused from cross-examination where, in testifying about a preliminary issue, he injects other issues into the hearing. If he could not be cross-examined about any issues gratuitously raised by him beyond the scope of the preliminary matters, injustice might result. Accordingly, in order to prevent any such unjust result, the committee intends the rule to be construed to provide that the accused may subject himself to cross-examination as to issues raised by his own testimony upon a preliminary matter before a jury. Senate Report No. 93–1277.

1987 Amendments

The amendments are technical. No substantive change is intended.

CROSS REFERENCES

Cross-examination, scope of, see Fed.Rules Evid. Rule 611, 28 USCA.

Functions of court and jury, determination of admissibility, see Fed.Rules Evid. Rule 1008, 28 USCA.

Preliminary questions of fact, inapplicability of these rules to, see Fed.Rules Evid. Rule 1101, 28 USCA.

Privileges, see Fed.Rules Evid. Rule 501, 28 USCA.

Rape, relevancy of evidence conditioned upon fulfillment of fact, see Fed.Rules Evid. Rule 412, 28 USCA.

Relevancy and its limits, see Fed.Rules Evid. Rule 401 et seq., 28 USCA.

Self-incrimination, freedom from, see USCA Const. Amend. V.

Witnesses, see Fed.Rules Evid. Rule 601 et seq., 28 USCA.

Rule 105. Limited Admissibility

When evidence which is admissible as to one party or for one purpose but not admissible as to another party or for another purpose is admitted, the court, upon request, shall restrict the evidence to its proper scope and instruct the jury accordingly.

(Pub.L. 93–595, § 1, Jan. 2, 1975, 88 Stat. 1930.)

ADVISORY COMMITTEE NOTES

1972 Proposed Rules

A close relationship exists between this rule and Rule 403 which requires exclusion when "probative value is substantially outweighed by the danger of unfair prejudice, confusion of the issues, or misleading the jury." The present rule recognizes the practice of admitting evidence for a limited purpose and instructing the jury accordingly. The availability and effectiveness of this practice must be taken into consideration in reaching a decision whether to exclude for unfair prejudice under Rule 403. In *Bruton v. United States,* 389 U.S. 818, 88 S.Ct. 126, 19 L.Ed.2d 70 (1968), the Court ruled that a limiting instruction did not effectively protect the accused against the prejudicial effect of admitting in evidence the confession of a codefendant which implicated him. The decision does not, however, bar the use of limited admissibility with an instruction where the risk of prejudice is less serious.

Similar provisions are found in Uniform Rule 6; California Evidence Code § 355; Kansas Code of Civil Procedure § 60–406; New Jersey Evidence Rule 6. The wording of the present rule differs, however, in repelling any implication that limiting or curative instructions are sufficient in all situations.

1974 Enactment

Rule 106 as submitted by the Supreme Court (now Rule 105 in the bill) dealt with the subject of evidence which is admissible as to one party or for one purpose but is not admissible against another party or for another purpose. The Committee adopted this Rule without change on the understanding that it does not affect the authority of a court to order a severance in a multi-defendant case. House Report No. 93–650.

CROSS REFERENCES

Exclusion of evidence for prejudice, confusion, or waste of time, see Fed.Rules Evid. Rule 403, 28 USCA.

Rule 106. Remainder of or Related Writings or Recorded Statements

When a writing or recorded statement or part thereof is introduced by a party, an adverse party may require the introduction at that time of any other part or any other writing or recorded statement which ought in fairness to be considered contemporaneously with it.

(Pub.L. 93–595, § 1, Jan. 2, 1975, 88 Stat. 1930; Mar. 2, 1987, eff. Oct. 1, 1987.)

ADVISORY COMMITTEE NOTES

1972 Proposed Rules

The rule is an expression of the rule of completeness. McCormick § 56. It is manifested as to depositions in Rule 32(a)(4) of the Federal Rules of Civil Procedure, of which the proposed rule is substantially a restatement.

The rule is based on two considerations. The first is the misleading impression created by taking matters out of context. The second is the inadequacy of repair work when delayed to a point later in the trial. See McCormick § 56; California Evidence Code § 356. The rule does not in any way circumscribe the right of the adversary to develop the matter on cross-examination or as part of his own case.

For practical reasons, the rule is limited to writings and recorded statements and does not apply to conversations.

1987 Amendments

The amendments are technical. No substantive change is intended.

CROSS REFERENCES

Writings and recordings, admissibility of duplicates and other evidence of contents, see Fed.Rules.Evid. Rules 1003 and 1004, 28 USCA.

Depositions, admission of remainder of, see Fed.Rules Civ.Proc. Rule 32, 28 USCA.

ARTICLE II. JUDICIAL NOTICE

Rule 201. Judicial Notice of Adjudicative Facts

(a) Scope of rule. This rule governs only judicial notice of adjudicative facts.

(b) Kinds of facts. A judicially noticed fact must be one not subject to reasonable dispute in that it is either (1) generally known within the territorial jurisdiction of the trial court or (2) capable of accurate and ready determination by resort to sources whose accuracy cannot reasonably be questioned.

(c) When discretionary. A court may take judicial notice, whether requested or not.

(d) When mandatory. A court shall take judicial notice if requested by a party and supplied with the necessary information.

(e) Opportunity to be heard. A party is entitled upon timely request to an opportunity to be heard as to the propriety of taking judicial notice and the tenor of the matter noticed. In the absence of prior notification, the request may be made after judicial notice has been taken.

(f) Time of taking notice. Judicial notice may be taken at any stage of the proceeding.

(g) Instructing jury. In a civil action or proceeding, the court shall instruct the jury to accept as conclusive any fact judicially noticed. In a criminal case, the court shall instruct the jury that it may, but is not required to, accept as conclusive any fact judicially noticed.

(Pub.L. 93–595, § 1, Jan. 2, 1975, 88 Stat. 1930.)

ADVISORY COMMITTEE NOTES

1972 Proposed Rules

Note to Subdivision (a). This is the only evidence rule on the subject of judicial notice. It deals only with judicial notice of "adjudicative" facts. No rule deals with judicial notice of "legislative" facts. Judicial notice of matters of foreign law is treated in Rule 44.1 of the Federal Rules of Civil Procedure and Rule 26.1 of the Federal Rules of Criminal Procedure.

The omission of any treatment of legislative facts results from fundamental differences between adjudicative facts and legislative facts. Adjudicative facts are simply the facts of the particular case. Legislative facts, on the other hand, are those which have relevance to legal reasoning and the lawmaking process, whether in the formulation of a legal principle or ruling by a judge or court or in the enactment of a legislative body. The terminology was coined by Professor Kenneth Davis in his article An Approach to Problems of Evidence in the Administrative Process, 55 Harv.L.Rev. 364, 404–407 (1942). The following discussion draws extensively upon his writings. In addition, see the same author's Judicial Notice, 55 Colum.L.Rev. 945 (1955); Administrative Law Treatise, ch. 15 (1958); A System of Judicial Notice Based on Fairness and Convenience, in Perspectives of Law 69 (1964).

The usual method of establishing adjudicative facts is through the introduction of evidence, ordinarily consisting of the testimony of witnesses. If particular facts are outside the area of reasonable controversy, this process is dispensed with as unnecessary. A high degree of indisputability is the essential prerequisite.

Legislative facts are quite different. As Professor Davis says:

"My opinion is that judge-made law would stop growing if judges, in thinking about questions of law and policy, were forbidden to take into account the facts they believe, as distinguished from facts which are 'clearly * * * within the domain of the indisputable.' Facts most needed in thinking about difficult problems of law and policy have a way of being outside the domain of the clearly indisputable." A System of Judicial Notice Based on Fairness and Convenience, *supra*, at 82.

An illustration is *Hawkins v. United States,* 358 U.S. 74, 79 S.Ct. 136, 3 L.Ed.2d 125 (1958), in which the Court refused to discard the common law rule that one spouse could not testify against the other, saying, "Adverse testimony given in criminal proceedings would, we think, be likely to destroy almost any marriage." This conclusion has a large intermixture of fact, but the factual aspect is scarcely "indisputable." See Hutchins and Slesinger, Some Observations on the Law of Evidence—Family Relations, 13 Minn.L.Rev. 675 (1929). If the destructive effect of the giving of adverse testimony by a spouse is not indisputable, should the Court have refrained from considering it in the absence of supporting evidence?

"If the Model Code or the Uniform Rules had been applicable, the Court would have been barred from thinking about the essential factual ingredient of the problems before it, and such a result would be obviously intolerable. What the law needs at its growing points is more, not less, judicial thinking about the factual ingredients of problems of what the law ought to be, and the needed facts are seldom 'clearly' indisputable." Davis, *supra*, at 83.

Professor Morgan gave the following description of the methodology of determining domestic law:

"In determining the content or applicability of a rule of domestic law, the judge is unrestricted in his investigation and conclusion. He may reject the propositions of either party or of both parties. He may consult the sources of pertinent data to which they refer, or he may refuse to do so. He may make an independent search for persuasive data or rest content with what he has or what the parties present. * * * [T]he parties do no more than to assist; they control no part of the process." Morgan, Judicial Notice, 57 Harv. L.Rev. 269, 270–271 (1944).

This is the view which should govern judicial access to legislative facts. It renders inappropriate any limitation in the form of indisputability, any formal requirements of notice other than those already inherent in affording opportunity to hear and be heard and exchanging briefs, and any requirement of formal findings at any level. It should, however leave open the possibility of introducing evidence through regular channels in appropriate situations. See *Borden's*

Farm Products Co. v. Baldwin, 293 U.S. 194, 55 S.Ct. 187, 79 L.Ed. 281 (1934), where the cause was remanded for the taking of evidence as to the economic conditions and trade practices underlying the New York Milk Control Law.

Similar considerations govern the judicial use of non-adjudicative facts in ways other than formulating laws and rules. Thayer described them as a part of the judicial reasoning process.

"In conducting a process of judicial reasoning, as of other reasoning, not a step can be taken without assuming something which has not been proved; and the capacity to do this with competent judgment and efficiency, is imputed to judges and juries as part of their necessary mental outfit." Thayer, Preliminary Treatise on Evidence 279–280 (1898).

As Professor Davis points out, A System of Judicial Notice Based on Fairness and Convenience, in Perspectives of Law 69, 73 (1964), every case involves the use of hundreds or thousands of non-evidence facts. When a witness in an automobile accident case says "car," everyone, judge and jury included, furnishes, from non-evidence sources within himself, the supplementing information that the "car" is an automobile, not a railroad car, that it is self-propelled, probably by an internal combustion engine, that it may be assumed to have four wheels with pneumatic rubber tires, and so on. The judicial process cannot construct every case from scratch, like Descartes creating a world based on the postulate *Cogito, ergo sum.* These items could not possibly be introduced into evidence, and no one suggests that they be. Nor are they appropriate subjects for any formalized treatment of judicial notice of facts. See Levin and Levy, Persuading the Jury with Facts Not in Evidence: The Fiction–Science Spectrum, 105 U.Pa.L.Rev. 139 (1956).

Another aspect of what Thayer had in mind is the use of non-evidence facts to appraise or assess the adjudicative facts of the case. Pairs of cases from two jurisdictions illustrate this use and also the difference between non-evidence facts thus used and adjudicative facts. In People v. Strook, 347 Ill. 460, 179 N.E. 821 (1932), venue in Cook County had been held not established by testimony that the crime was committed at 7956 South Chicago Avenue, since judicial notice would not be taken that the address was in Chicago. However, the same court subsequently ruled that venue in Cook County was established by testimony that a crime occurred at 8900 South Anthony Avenue, since notice would be taken of the common practice of omitting the name of the city when speaking of local addresses, and the witness was testifying in Chicago. *People v. Pride,* 16 Ill.2d 82, 156 N.E.2d 551 (1951). And in *Hughes v. Vestal,* 264 N.C. 500, 142 S.E.2d 361 (1965), the Supreme Court of North Carolina disapproved the trial judge's admission in evidence of a state-published table of automobile stopping distances on the basis of judicial notice, though the court itself had referred to the same table in an earlier case in a "rhetorical and illustrative" way in determining that the defendant could not have stopped her car in time to avoid striking a child who suddenly appeared in the highway and that a nonsuit was properly granted. *Ennis v. Dupree,* 262 N.C. 224, 136 S.E.2d 702 (1964). See also *Brown v. Hale,* 263 N.C. 176, 139 S.E.2d 210 (1964); *Clayton v. Rimmer,* 262 N.C. 302, 136 S.E.2d 562 (1964). It is apparent that this use of non-evidence facts in evaluating the adjudicative facts of the case is not an appropriate subject for a formalized judicial notice treatment.

In view of these considerations, the regulation of judicial notice of facts by the present rule extends only to adjudicative facts.

What, then, are "adjudicative" facts? Davis refers to them as those "which relate to the parties," or more fully:

"When a court or an agency finds facts concerning the immediate parties—who did what, where, when, how, and with what motive or intent—the court or agency is performing an adjudicative function, and the facts are conveniently called adjudicative facts. * * *

"Stated in other terms, the adjudicative facts are those to which the law is applied in the process of adjudication. They are the facts that normally go to the jury in a jury case. They relate to the parties, their activities, their properties, their businesses." 2 Administrative Law Treatise 353.

Note to Subdivision (b). With respect to judicial notice of adjudicative facts, the tradition has been one of caution in requiring that the matter be beyond reasonable controversy. This tradition of circumspection appears to be soundly based, and no reason to depart from it is apparent. As Professor Davis says:

"The reason we use trial-type procedure, I think, is that we make the practical judgment, on the basis of experience, that taking evidence, subject to cross-examination and rebuttal, is the best way to resolve controversies involving disputes of adjudicative facts, that is, facts pertaining to the parties. The reason we require a determination on the record is that we think fair procedure in resolving disputes of adjudicative facts calls for giving each party a chance to meet in the appropriate fashion the facts that come to the tribunal's attention, and the appropriate fashion for meeting disputed adjudicative facts includes rebuttal evidence, cross-examination, usually confrontation, and argument (either written or oral or both). The key to a fair trial is opportunity to use the appropriate weapons (rebuttal evidence, cross-examination, and argument) to meet adverse materials that come to the tribunal's attention." A System of Judicial Notice Based on Fairness and Convenience, in Perspectives of Law 69, 93 (1964).

The rule proceeds upon the theory that these considerations call for dispensing with traditional methods of proof only in clear cases. Compare Professor Davis' conclusion that judicial notice should be a matter of convenience, subject to requirements of procedural fairness. *Id.,* 94.

This rule is consistent with Uniform Rule 9(1) and (2) which limit judicial notice of facts to those "so universally known that they cannot reasonably be the subject of dispute," those "so generally known or of such common notoriety within the territorial jurisdiction of the court that they cannot reasonably be the subject of dispute," and those "capable of immediate and accurate determination by resort to easily accessible sources of indisputable accuracy." The traditional textbook treatment has included these general categories (matters of common knowledge, facts capable of verification), McCormick §§ 324, 325, and then has passed on into detailed treatment of such specific topics as facts relating to the personnel and records of the court, *Id.* § 327, and other governmental facts, *Id.* § 328. The California draftsmen, with a background of detailed statutory regulation of judicial notice, followed a somewhat similar pattern. California Evidence Code §§ 451, 452. The Uniform Rules, however, were drafted on the theory that these particular matters are included within the general categories and need no specific mention. This approach is followed in the present rule.

The phrase "propositions of generalized knowledge," found in Uniform Rule 9(1) and (2) is not included in the present rule. It was, it is believed, originally included in Model Code Rules 801 and 802 primarily in order to afford some minimum recognition to the right of the judge in his "legislative" capacity (not acting as the trier of fact) to take judicial notice of very limited categories of generalized knowledge. The limitations thus imposed have been discarded herein as undesirable, unworkable, and contrary to existing practice. What is left, then, to be considered, is the status of a "proposition of generalized knowledge" as an "adjudicative" fact to be noticed judicially and communicated by the judge to the jury. Thus viewed, it is considered to be lacking practical significance. While judges use judicial notice of "propositions of generalized knowledge" in a variety of situations: determining the validity and meaning of statutes, formulating common law rules, deciding whether evidence should be admitted, assessing the sufficiency and effect of evidence, all are essentially nonadjudicative in nature. When judicial notice is seen as a significant vehicle for progress in the law, these are the areas involved, particularly in developing fields of scientific knowledge. See McCormick 712. It is not believed that judges now instruct juries as to "propositions of generalized knowledge" derived from encyclopedias or other sources, or that they are likely to do so, or, indeed, that it is desirable that they do so. There is a vast difference between ruling on the basis of judicial notice that radar evidence of speed is admissible and explaining to the jury its principles and degree of accuracy, or between using a table of stopping distances of automobiles at various speeds in a judicial evaluation of testimony and telling the jury its precise application in the case. For cases raising doubt as to the propriety of the use of medical texts by lay triers of fact in passing on disability claims in administrative proceedings, see *Sayers v. Gardner,* 380 F.2d 940 (6th Cir.1967); *Ross v. Gardner,* 365 F.2d 554 (6th Cir.1966); *Sosna v. Celebrezze,* 234 F.Supp. 289 (E.D.Pa.1964); *Glendenning v. Ribicoff,* 213 F.Supp. 301 (W.D.Mo.1962).

Notes to Subdivisions (c) and (d). Under subdivision (c) the judge has a discretionary authority to take judicial notice, regardless of whether he is so requested by a party. The taking of judicial notice is mandatory, under subdivision (d), only when a party requests it and the necessary information is supplied. This scheme is believed to reflect existing practice. It is simple and workable. It avoids troublesome distinctions in the many situations in which the process of taking judicial notice is not recognized as such.

Compare Uniform Rule 9 making judicial notice of facts universally known mandatory without request, and making judicial notice of facts generally known in the jurisdiction or capable of determination by resort to accurate sources discretionary in the absence of request but mandatory if request is made and the information furnished. But see Uniform Rule 10(3), which directs the judge to decline to take judicial notice if available information fails to convince him that the matter falls clearly within Uniform Rule 9 or is insufficient to enable him to notice it judicially. Substantially the same approach is found in California Evidence Code §§ 451–453 and in New Jersey Evidence Rule 9. In contrast, the present rule treats alike all adjudicative facts which are subject to judicial notice.

Note to Subdivision (e). Basic considerations of procedural fairness demand an opportunity to be heard on the propriety of taking judicial notice and the tenor of the matter noticed. The rule requires the granting of that opportunity upon request. No formal scheme of giving notice is provided. An adversely affected party may learn in advance that judicial notice is in contemplation, either by virtue of being served with a copy of a request by another party under subdivision (d) that judicial notice be taken, or through an advance indication by the judge. Or he may have no advance notice at all. The likelihood of the latter is enhanced by the frequent failure to recognize judicial notice as such. And in the absence of advance notice, a request made after the fact could not in fairness be considered untimely. See the provision for hearing on timely request in the Administrative Procedure Act, 5 U.S.C. § 556(e). See also Revised Model State Administrative Procedure Act (1961), 9C U.L.A. § 10(4) (Supp.1967).

Note to Subdivision (f). In accord with the usual view, judicial notice may be taken at any stage of the proceedings, whether in the trial court or on appeal. Uniform Rule 12; California Evidence Code § 459; Kansas Rules of Evidence § 60–412; New Jersey Evidence Rule 12; McCormick § 330, p. 712.

Note to Subdivision (g). Much of the controversy about judicial notice has centered upon the question whether evidence should be admitted in disproof of facts of which judicial notice is taken.

The writers have been divided. Favoring admissibility are Thayer, Preliminary Treatise on Evidence 308 (1898); 9 Wigmore § 2567; Davis, A System of Judicial Notice Based on Fairness and Convenience, in Perspectives of Law, 69, 76–77 (1964). Opposing admissibility are Keeffe, Landis and Shaad, Sense and Nonsense about Judicial Notice, 2 Stan. L.Rev. 664, 668 (1950); McNaughton, Judicial Notice—Excerpts Relating to the Morgan–Whitmore Controversy, 14 Vand.L.Rev. 779 (1961); Morgan, Judicial Notice, 57 Harv. L.Rev. 269, 279 (1944); McCormick 710–711. The Model Code and the Uniform Rules are predicated upon indisputability of judicially noticed facts.

The proponents of admitting evidence in disproof have concentrated largely upon legislative facts. Since the present rule deals only with judicial notice of adjudicative facts, arguments directed to legislative facts lose their relevancy.

Within its relatively narrow area of adjudicative facts, the rule contemplates there is to be no evidence before the jury in disproof. The judge instructs the jury to take judicially noticed facts as established. This position is justified by the undesirable effects of the opposite rule in limiting the rebutting party, though not his opponent, to admissible evidence, in defeating the reasons for judicial notice, and in affecting the substantive law to an extent and in ways largely unforeseeable. Ample protection and flexibility are afforded by the broad provision for opportunity to be heard on request, set forth in subdivision (e).

Authority upon the propriety of taking judicial notice against an accused in a criminal case with respect to matters other than venue is relatively meager. Proceeding upon the theory that the right of jury trial does not extend to matters which are beyond reasonable dispute, the rule does not distinguish between criminal and civil cases. *People v. Mayes,* 113 Cal. 618, 45 P. 860 (1896); *Ross v. United States,* 374 F.2d 97 (8th Cir.1967). Cf. *State v. Main,* 94 R.I. 338,

180 A.2d 814 (1962); *State v. Lawrence,* 120 Utah 323, 234 P.2d 600 (1951).

Note on Judicial Notice of Law. By rules effective July 1, 1966, the method of invoking the law of a foreign country is covered elsewhere. Rule 44.1 of the Federal Rules of Civil Procedure; Rule 26.1 of the Federal Rules of Criminal Procedure. These two new admirably designed rules are founded upon the assumption that the manner in which law is fed into the judicial process is never a proper concern of the rules of evidence but rather of the rules of procedure. The Advisory Committee on Evidence, believing that this assumption is entirely correct, proposes no evidence rule with respect to judicial notice of law, and suggests that those matters of law which, in addition to foreign-country law, have traditionally been treated as requiring pleading and proof and more recently as the subject of judicial notice be left to the Rules of Civil and Criminal Procedure.

1974 Enactment

Rule 201(g) as received from the Supreme Court provided that when judicial notice of a fact is taken, the court shall instruct the jury to accept that fact as established. Being of the view that mandatory instruction to a jury in a criminal case to accept as conclusive any fact judicially noticed is inappropriate because contrary to the spirit of the Sixth Amendment right to a jury trial, the Committee adopted the 1969 Advisory Committee draft of this subsection, allowing a mandatory instruction in civil actions and proceedings and a discretionary instruction in criminal cases. House Report No. 93–650.

CROSS REFERENCES

Determination of foreign law, see Fed.Rules Civ.Proc. Rule 44.1, 28 USCA.

Determination of foreign law, see Fed.Rules Cr.Proc. Rule 26.1, 18 USCA.

Due process right to notice and hearing, see USCA Const. Amend. XIV.

Instructions, see Fed.Rules Civ.Proc. Rule 51, 28 USCA.

Instructions, see Fed.Rules Cr.Proc. Rule 30, 18 USCA.

ARTICLE III. PRESUMPTIONS IN CIVIL ACTIONS AND PROCEEDINGS

Rule 301. Presumptions in General in Civil Actions and Proceedings

In all civil actions and proceedings not otherwise provided for by Act of Congress or by these rules, a presumption imposes on the party against whom it is directed the burden of going forward with evidence to rebut or meet the presumption, but does not shift to such party the burden of proof in the sense of the risk of nonpersuasion, which remains throughout the trial upon the party on whom it was originally cast.

(Pub.L. 93–595, § 1, Jan. 2, 1975, 88 Stat. 1931.)

ADVISORY COMMITTEE NOTES

1972 Proposed Rules

This rule governs presumptions generally. See Rule 302 for presumptions controlled by state law and Rule 303 [deleted] for those against an accused in a criminal case.

Presumptions governed by this rule are given the effect of placing upon the opposing party the burden of establishing the nonexistence of the presumed fact, once the party invoking the presumption establishes the basic facts giving rise to it. The same considerations of fairness, policy, and probability which dictate the allocation of the burden of the various elements of a case as between the prima facie case of a plaintiff and affirmative defenses also underlie the creation of presumptions. These considerations are not satisfied by giving a lesser effect to presumptions. Morgan and Maguire, Looking Backward and Forward at Evidence, 50 Harv. L.Rev. 909, 913 (1937); Morgan, Instructing the Jury upon Presumptions and Burden of Proof, 47 Harv.L.Rev. 59, 82 (1933); Cleary, Presuming and Pleading: An Essay on Juristic Immaturity, 12 Stan.L.Rev. 5 (1959).

The so-called "bursting bubble" theory, under which a presumption vanishes upon the introduction of evidence which would support a finding of the nonexistence of the presumed fact, even though not believed, is rejected as according presumptions too "slight and evanescent" an effect. Morgan and Maguire, *supra,* at p. 913.

In the opinion of the Advisory Committee, no constitutional infirmity attends this view of presumptions. In *Mobile, J. & K. C. R. Co. v. Turnipseed,* 219 U.S. 35, 31 S.Ct. 136, 55 L.Ed. 78 (1910), the Court upheld a Mississippi statute which provided that in actions against railroads proof of injury inflicted by the running of trains should be prima facie evidence of negligence by the railroad. The injury in the case had resulted from a derailment. The opinion made the points (1) that the only effect of the statute was to impose on the railroad the duty of producing some evidence to the contrary, (2) that an inference may be supplied by law if there is a rational connection between the fact proved and the fact presumed, as long as the opposite party is not precluded from presenting his evidence to the contrary, and (3) that considerations of public policy arising from the character of the business justified the application in question. Nineteen years later, in *Western & Atlantic R. Co. v. Henderson,* 279 U.S. 639, 49 S.Ct. 445, 73 L.Ed. 884 (1929), the Court overturned a Georgia statute making railroads liable for damages done by trains, unless the railroad made it appear that reasonable care had been used, the presumption being against the railroad. The declaration alleged the death of plaintiff's husband from a grade crossing collision, due to specified acts of negligence by defendant. The jury were instructed that proof of the injury raised a presumption of negligence; the burden shifted to the railroad to prove ordinary care; and unless it did so, they should find for plaintiff. The instruction was held erroneous in an opinion stating (1) that there was no rational connection between the mere fact of collision and negligence on the part of anyone, and (2) that the statute was different from that in *Turnipseed* in imposing a burden upon the railroad. The reader is left in a state of some confusion. Is the difference between a derailment and a grade crossing collision of no significance? Would the *Turnipseed* presumption have been bad if it had imposed a burden of persuasion on defendant, although that would in nowise have impaired its "rational connection"? If *Henderson* forbids imposing a burden of persuasion on defendants, what happens to affirmative defenses?

Two factors serve to explain *Henderson.* The first was that it was common ground that negligence was indispensable to liability. Plaintiff thought so, drafted her complaint accordingly, and relied upon the presumption. But how in logic could the same presumption establish her alternative grounds of negligence that the engineer was so blind he could not see decedent's truck and that he failed to stop after he saw it? Second, take away the basic assumption of no liability without fault, as *Turnipseed* intimated might be done ("considerations of public policy arising out of the character of the business"), and the structure of the decision in *Henderson* fails. No question of logic would have arisen if the statute had simply said: a prima facie case of liability is made by proof of injury by a train; lack of negligence is an affirmative defense, to be pleaded and proved as other affirmative defenses. The problem would be one of economic due process only. While it seems likely that the Supreme Court of 1929 would have voted that due process was denied, that result today would be unlikely. See, for example, the shift in the direction of absolute liability in the consumer cases. Prosser, The Assault upon the Citadel (Strict Liability to the Consumer), 69 Yale L.J. 1099 (1960).

Any doubt as to the constitutional permissibility of a presumption imposing a burden of persuasion of the nonexistence of the presumed fact in civil cases is laid at rest by *Dick v. New York Life Ins. Co.,* 359 U.S. 437, 79 S.Ct. 921, 3 L.Ed.2d 935 (1959). The Court unhesitatingly applied the North Dakota rule that the presumption against suicide imposed on defendant the burden of proving that the death of insured, under an accidental death clause, was due to suicide.

"Proof of coverage and of death by gunshot wound shifts the burden to the insurer to establish that the death of the insured was due to his suicide." 359 U.S. at 443, 79 S.Ct. at 925.

"In a case like this one, North Dakota presumes that death was accidental and places on the insurer the burden of proving that death resulted from suicide." *Id.* at 446, 79 S.Ct. at 927.

The rational connection requirement survives in criminal cases, *Tot v. United States,* 319 U.S. 463, 63 S.Ct. 1241, 87 L.Ed. 1519 (1943), because the Court has been unwilling to extend into that area the greater-includes-the-lesser theory of *Ferry v. Ramsey,* 277 U.S. 88, 48 S.Ct. 443, 72 L.Ed. 796 (1928). In that case the Court sustained a Kansas statute under which bank directors were personally liable for deposits made with their assent and with knowledge of insolvency, and the fact of insolvency was prima facie evidence of assent and knowledge of insolvency. Mr. Justice Holmes pointed out that the state legislature could have made the directors personally liable to depositors in every case. Since the statute imposed a less stringent liability, "the thing to be considered is the result reached, not the possibly inartificial or clumsy way of reaching it." *Id.* at 94, 48 S.Ct. at 444. Mr. Justice Sutherland dissented: though the state could have created an absolute liability, it did not purport to do so; a rational connection was necessary, but lacking, between the liability created and the prima facie evidence of it; the result might be different if the basis of the presumption were being open for business.

The Sutherland view has prevailed in criminal cases by virtue of the higher standard of notice there required. The fiction that everyone is presumed to know the law is applied to the substantive law of crimes as an alternative to complete unenforceability. But the need does not extend to criminal evidence and procedure, and the fiction does not encompass them. "Rational connection" is not fictional or artificial, and so it is reasonable to suppose that Gainey should have known that his presence at the site of an illicit still could convict him of being connected with (carrying on) the business, *United States v. Gainey,* 380 U.S. 63, 85 S.Ct. 754, 13 L.Ed.2d 658 (1965), but not that Romano should have known that his presence at a still could convict him of possessing it, *United States v. Romano,* 382 U.S. 136, 86 S.Ct. 279, 15 L.Ed.2d 210 (1965).

In his dissent in Gainey, Mr. Justice Black put it more artistically:

"It might be argued, although the Court does not so argue or hold, that Congress if it wished could make presence at a still a crime in itself, and so Congress should be free to create crimes which are called 'possession' and 'carrying on an illegal distillery business' but which are defined in such a way that unexplained presence is sufficient and indisputable evidence in all cases to support conviction for those offenses. See *Ferry v. Ramsey,* 277 U.S. 88, 48 S.Ct. 443, 72 L.Ed. 796. Assuming for the sake of argument that Congress could make unexplained presence a criminal act, and ignoring also the refusal of this Court in other cases to uphold a statutory presumption on such a theory, see *Heiner v. Donnan,* 285 U.S. 312, 52 S.Ct. 358, 76 L.Ed. 772, there is no indication here that Congress intended to adopt such a misleading method of draftsmanship, nor in my judgment could the statutory provisions if so construed escape condemnation for vagueness, under the principles applied in *Lanzetta v. New Jersey,* 306 U.S. 451, 59 S.Ct. 618, 83 L.Ed. 888, and many other cases." 380 U.S. at 84, n. 12, 85 S.Ct. at 766.

And the majority opinion in *Romano* agreed with him:

"It may be, of course, that Congress has the power to make presence at an illegal still a punishable crime, but we find no clear indication that it intended to so exercise this power. The crime remains possession, not presence, and with all due deference to the judgment of Congress, the former may not constitutionally be inferred from the latter." 382 U.S. at 144, 86 S.Ct. at 284.

The rule does not spell out the procedural aspects of its application. Questions as to when the evidence warrants submission of a presumption and what instructions are proper under varying states of fact are believed to present no particular difficulties.

1974 Enactment

Rule 301 as submitted by the Supreme Court provided that in all cases a presumption imposes on the party against whom it is directed the burden of proving that the nonexistence of the presumed fact is more probable than its existence. The Committee limited the scope of Rule 301 to "civil actions and proceedings" to effectuate its decision not to deal with the question of presumptions in criminal cases. (See note on [proposed] Rule 303 in discussion of Rules deleted). With respect to the weight to be given a presumption in a civil case, the Committee agreed with the judgment implicit in the Court's version that the so-called "bursting bubble" theory of presumptions, whereby a presumption vanishes upon the appearance of any contradicting evidence by the other party, gives to presumptions too slight an effect. On the other hand, the Committee believed that the Rule proposed by the Court, whereby a presumption permanently alters the burden of persuasion, no matter how much contradicting evidence is introduced—a view shared by only a few courts—lends too great a force to presumptions. Accordingly, the Committee amended the Rule to adopt an intermediate position under which a presumption does not vanish upon the introduction of contradicting evidence, and does not change the burden of persuasion; instead it is merely deemed sufficient evidence of the fact presumed, to be considered by the jury or other finder of fact. House Report No. 93–650.

The rule governs presumptions in civil cases generally. Rule 302 provides for presumptions in cases controlled by State law.

As submitted by the Supreme Court, presumptions governed by this rule were given the effect of placing upon the opposing party the burden of establishing the nonexistence of the presumed fact, once the party invoking the presumption established the basic facts giving rise to it.

Instead of imposing a burden of persuasion on the party against whom the presumption is directed, the House adopted a provision which shifted the burden of going forward with the evidence. They further provided that "even though met with contradicting evidence, a presumption is sufficient evidence of the fact presumed, to be considered by the trier of fact." The effect of the amendment is that presumptions are to be treated as evidence.

The committee feels the House amendment is ill-advised. As the joint committees (the Standing Committee on Practice and Procedure of the Judicial Conference and the Advisory Committee on the Rules of Evidence) stated: "Presumptions are not evidence, but ways of dealing with evidence." This treatment requires juries to perform the task of considering "as evidence" facts upon which they have no direct evidence and which may confuse them in performance of their duties. California had a rule much like that contained in the House amendment. It was sharply criticized by Justice Traynor in *Speck v. Sarver* [20 Cal.2d 585, 128 P.2d 16, 21 (1942)] and was repealed after 93 troublesome years [Cal.Ev.Code 1965 § 600].

Professor McCormick gives a concise and compelling critique of the presumption as evidence rule:

"Another solution, formerly more popular than now, is to instruct the jury that the presumption is 'evidence', to be weighed and considered with the testimony in the case. This avoids the danger that the jury may infer that the presumption is conclusive, but it probably means little to the jury, and certainly runs counter to accepted theories of the nature of evidence." [McCormick, Evidence, 669 (1954); *Id.* 825 (2d ed. 1972)].

For these reasons the committee has deleted that provision of the House-passed rule that treats presumptions as evidence. The effect of the rule as adopted by the committee is to make clear that while evidence of facts giving rise to a presumption shifts the burden of coming forward with evidence to rebut or meet the presumption, it does not shift the burden of persuasion on the existence of the presumed facts. The burden of persuasion remains on the party to whom it is allocated under the rules governing the allocation in the first instance.

The court may instruct the jury that they may infer the existence of the presumed fact from proof of the basic facts giving rise to the presumption. However, it would be inappropriate under this rule to instruct the jury that the inference they are to draw is conclusive. Senate Report 93–1277.

The House bill provides that a presumption in civil actions and proceedings shifts to the party against whom it is directed the burden of going forward with evidence to meet or rebut it. Even though evidence contradicting the presumption is offered, a presumption is considered sufficient evidence of the presumed fact to be considered by the jury. The Senate amendment provides that a presumption shifts to the party against whom it is directed the burden of going forward with evidence to meet or rebut the presumption, but it does not shift to that party the burden of persuasion on the existence of the presumed fact.

Under the Senate amendment, a presumption is sufficient to get a party past an adverse party's motion to dismiss made at the end of his case-in-chief. If the adverse party offers no evidence contradicting the presumed fact, the court will instruct the jury that if it finds the basic facts, it may presume the existence of the presumed fact. If the adverse party does offer evidence contradicting the presumed fact, the court cannot instruct the jury that it may *presume* the existence of the presumed fact from proof of the basic facts. The court may, however, instruct the jury that it may infer the existence of the presumed fact from proof of the basic facts.

The conference adopts the Senate amendment. House Conference Report No. 93–1597.

CROSS REFERENCES

Self-authentication—

Foreign public documents, see Fed.Rules Evid. Rule 902, 28 USCA.

Presumptions under Acts of Congress, see Fed.Rules Evid. Rule 902, 28 USCA.

Rule 302. Applicability of State Law in Civil Actions and Proceedings

In civil actions and proceedings, the effect of a presumption respecting a fact which is an element of a claim or defense as to which State law supplies the rule of decision is determined in accordance with State law.

(Pub.L. 93–595, § 1, Jan. 2, 1975, 88 Stat. 1931.)

ADVISORY COMMITTEE NOTES

1972 Proposed Rules

A series of Supreme Court decisions in diversity cases leaves no doubt of the relevance of *Erie Railroad Co. v. Tompkins,* 304 U.S. 64, 58 S.Ct. 817, 82 L.Ed. 1188 (1938), to questions of burden of proof. These decisions are *Cities*

Service Oil Co. v. Dunlap, 308 U.S. 208, 60 S.Ct. 201, 84 L.Ed. 196 (1939), *Palmer v. Hoffman,* 318 U.S. 109, 63 S.Ct. 477, 87 L.Ed. 645 (1943), and *Dick v. New York Life Ins. Co.,* 359 U.S. 437, 79 S.Ct. 921, 3 L.Ed.2d 935 (1959). They involved burden of proof, respectively, as to status as bona fide purchaser, contributory negligence, and nonaccidental death (suicide) of an insured. In each instance the state rule was held to be applicable. It does not follow, however, that all presumptions in diversity cases are governed by state law. In each case cited, the burden of proof question had to do with a substantive element of the claim or defense. Application of the state law is called for only when the presumption operates upon such an element. Accordingly the rule does not apply state law when the presumption operates upon a lesser aspect of the case, i.e. "tactical" presumptions.

The situations in which the state law is applied have been tagged for convenience in the preceding discussion as "diversity cases." The designation is not a completely accurate one since *Erie* applies to any claim or issue having its source in state law, regardless of the basis of federal jurisdiction, and does not apply to a federal claim or issue, even though jurisdiction is based on diversity. *Vestal, Erie R.R. v. Tompkins:* A Projection, 48 Iowa L.Rev. 248, 257 (1963); Hart and Wechsler, The Federal Courts and the Federal System, 697 (1953); 1A Moore, Federal Practice ¶ 0.305[3] (2d ed. 1965); Wright, Federal Courts, 217–218 (1963). Hence the rule employs, as appropriately descriptive, the phrase "as to which state law supplies the rule of decision." See A.L.I. Study of the Division of Jurisdiction Between State and Federal Courts, § 2344(c), p. 40, P.F.D. No. 1 (1965).

CROSS REFERENCES

State laws as rules of decision, see 28 USCA § 1652.

ARTICLE IV. RELEVANCY AND ITS LIMITS

Rule 401. Definition of "Relevant Evidence"

"Relevant evidence" means evidence having any tendency to make the existence of any fact that is of consequence to the determination of the action more probable or less probable than it would be without the evidence.

(Pub.L. 93–595, § 1, Jan. 2, 1975, 88 Stat.1931.)

ADVISORY COMMITTEE NOTES

1972 Proposed Rules

Problems of relevancy call for an answer to the question whether an item of evidence, when tested by the processes of legal reasoning, possesses sufficient probative value to justify receiving it in evidence. Thus, assessment of the probative value of evidence that a person purchased a revolver shortly prior to a fatal shooting with which he is charged is a matter of analysis and reasoning.

The variety of relevancy problems is coextensive with the ingenuity of counsel in using circumstantial evidence as a means of proof. An enormous number of cases fall in no set pattern, and this rule is designed as a guide for handling them. On the other hand, some situations recur with sufficient frequency to create patterns susceptible of treatment by specific rules. Rule 404 and those following it are of that variety; they also serve as illustrations of the application of the present rule as limited by the exclusionary principles of Rule 403.

Passing mention should be made of so-called "conditional" relevancy. Morgan, Basic Problems of Evidence 45–46 (1962). In this situation, probative value depends not only upon satisfying the basic requirement of relevancy as described above but also upon the existence of some matter of fact. For example, if evidence of a spoken statement is relied upon to prove notice, probative value is lacking unless the person sought to be charged heard the statement. The problem is one of fact, and the only rules needed are for the purpose of determining the respective functions of judge and jury. See Rules 104(b) and 901. The discussion which follows in the present note is concerned with relevancy generally, not with any particular problem of conditional relevancy.

Relevancy is not an inherent characteristic of any item of evidence but exists only as a relation between an item of evidence and a matter properly provable in the case. Does the item of evidence tend to prove the matter sought to be proved? Whether the relationship exists depends upon principles evolved by experience or science, applied logically to the situation at hand. James, Relevancy, Probability and the Law, 29 Calif.L.Rev. 689, 696, n. 15 (1941), in Selected Writings on Evidence and Trial 610, 615, n. 15 (Fryer ed. 1957). The rule summarizes this relationship as a "tendency to make the existence" of the fact to be proved "more probable or less probable." Compare Uniform Rule 1(2) which states the crux of relevancy as "a tendency in reason," thus perhaps emphasizing unduly the logical process and ignoring the need to draw upon experience or science to validate the general principle upon which relevancy in a particular situation depends.

The standard of probability under the rule is "more * * * probable than it would be without the evidence." Any more stringent requirement is unworkable and unrealistic. As McCormick § 152, p. 317, says, "A brick is not a wall," or, as Falknor, Extrinsic Policies Affecting Admissibility, 10 Rutgers L.Rev. 574, 576 (1956), quotes Professor McBaine, "* * * [I]t is not to be supposed that every witness can make a home run." Dealing with probability in the language of the rule has the added virtue of avoiding confusion between questions of admissibility and questions of the sufficiency of the evidence.

The rule uses the phrase "fact that is of consequence to the determination of the action" to describe the kind of fact to which proof may properly be directed. The language is that of California Evidence Code § 210; it has the advantage of avoiding the loosely used and ambiguous word "material." Tentative Recommendation and a Study Relating to the Uniform Rules of Evidence (Art. I. General Provisions), Cal.Law Revision Comm'n, Rep., Rec. & Studies, 10–11 (1964). The fact to be proved may be ultimate, intermediate, or evidentiary; it matters not, so long as it is of consequence in the determination of the action. Cf. Uniform Rule 1(2) which requires that the evidence relate to a "material" fact.

The fact to which the evidence is directed need not be in dispute. While situations will arise which call for the exclusion of evidence offered to prove a point conceded by the opponent, the ruling should be made on the basis of such considerations as waste of time and undue prejudice (see Rule 403), rather than under any general requirement that evidence is admissible only if directed to matters in dispute. Evidence which is essentially background in nature can scarcely be said to involve disputed matter, yet it is universally offered and admitted as an aid to understanding. Charts, photographs, views of real estate, murder weapons, and many other items of evidence fall in this category. A rule limiting admissibility to evidence directed to a controversial point would invite the exclusion of this helpful evidence, or at least the raising of endless questions over its admission. Cf. California Evidence Code § 210, defining relevant evidence in terms of tendency to prove a disputed fact.

CROSS REFERENCES

Eye witness testimony, see 18 USCA § 3502.

Relevancy conditioned on fact, admissibility of evidence, see Fed.Rules Evid. Rule 104, 28 USCA.

Rule 402. Relevant Evidence Generally Admissible; Irrelevant Evidence Inadmissible

All relevant evidence is admissible, except as otherwise provided by the Constitution of the United States, by Act of Congress, by these rules, or by other rules prescribed by the Supreme Court pursuant to statutory authority. Evidence which is not relevant is not admissible.

(Pub.L. 93–595, § 1, Jan. 2, 1975, 88 Stat. 1931.)

ADVISORY COMMITTEE NOTES

1972 Proposed Rules

The provisions that all relevant evidence is admissible, with certain exceptions, and that evidence which is not relevant is not admissible are "a presupposition involved in the very conception of a rational system of evidence." Thayer, Preliminary Treatise on Evidence 264 (1898). They constitute the foundation upon which the structure of admission and exclusion rests. For similar provisions see California Evidence Code §§ 350, 351. Provisions that all relevant evidence is admissible are found in Uniform Rule 7(f); Kansas Code of Civil Procedure § 60–407(f); and New Jersey Evidence Rule 7(f); but the exclusion of evidence which is not relevant is left to implication.

Not all relevant evidence is admissible. The exclusion of relevant evidence occurs in a variety of situations and may be called for by these rules, by the Rules of Civil and Criminal Procedure, by Bankruptcy Rules, by Act of Congress, or by constitutional considerations.

Succeeding rules in the present article, in response to the demands of particular policies, require the exclusion of evidence despite its relevancy. In addition, Article V recognizes a number of privileges; Article VI imposes limitations upon witnesses and the manner of dealing with them; Article VII specifies requirements with respect to opinions and expert testimony; Article VIII excludes hearsay not falling within an exception; Article IX spells out the handling of authentication and identification; and Article X restricts the manner of proving the contents of writings and recordings.

The Rules of Civil and Criminal Procedure in some instances require the exclusion of relevant evidence. For example, Rules 30(b) and 32(a)(3) of the Rules of Civil Procedure, by imposing requirements of notice and unavailability of the deponent, place limits on the use of relevant depositions. Similarly, Rule 15 of the Rules of Criminal Procedure restricts the use of depositions in criminal cases, even though relevant. And the effective enforcement of the command, originally statutory and now found in Rule 5(a) of the Rules of Criminal Procedure, that an arrested person be taken without unnecessary delay before a commissioner or other similar officer is held to require the exclusion of statements elicited during detention in violation thereof. *Mallory v. United States,* 354 U.S. 449, 77 S.Ct. 1356, 1 L.Ed.2d 1479 (1957); 18 U.S.C. § 3501(c).

While congressional enactments in the field of evidence have generally tended to expand admissibility beyond the scope of the common law rules, in some particular situations they have restricted the admissibility of relevant evidence. Most of this legislation has consisted of the formulation of a privilege or of a prohibition against disclosure. 8 U.S.C. § 1202(f), records of refusal of visas or permits to enter United States confidential, subject to discretion of Secretary of State to make available to court upon certification of need; 10 U.S.C. § 3693, replacement certificate of honorable discharge from Army not admissible in evidence; 10 U.S.C. § 8693, same as to Air Force; 11 U.S.C. § 25(a)(10), testimony given by bankrupt on his examination not admissible in criminal proceedings against him, except that given in hearing upon objection to discharge; 11 U.S.C. § 205(a), railroad reorganization petition, if dismissed, not admissible in evidence; 11 U.S.C. § 403(a), list of creditors filed with municipal composition plan not an admission; 13 U.S.C. § 9(a), census information confidential, retained copies of reports privileged; 47 U.S.C. § 605, interception and divulgence of wire or radio communications prohibited unless authorized by sender. These statutory provisions would remain undisturbed by the rules.

The rule recognizes but makes no attempt to spell out the constitutional considerations which impose basic limitations upon the admissibility of relevant evidence. Examples are evidence obtained by unlawful search and seizure. *Weeks v. United States,* 232 U.S. 383, 34 S.Ct. 341, 58 L.Ed. 652 (1914); *Katz v. United States,* 389 U.S. 347, 88 S.Ct. 507, 19 L.Ed.2d 576 (1967); incriminating statement elicited from an accused in violation of right to counsel. *Massiah v. United States,* 377 U.S. 201, 84 S.Ct. 1199, 12 L.Ed.2d 246 (1964).

1974 Enactment

Rule 402 as submitted to the Congress contained the phrase "or by other rules adopted by the Supreme Court". To accommodate the view that the Congress should not appear to acquiesce in the Court's judgment that it has authority under the existing Rules Enabling Acts to promulgate Rules of Evidence, the Committee amended the above phrase to read "or by other rules prescribed by the Supreme Court pursuant to statutory authority" in this and other Rules where the reference appears. House Report No. 93–650.

CROSS REFERENCES

Aliens, confidentiality of Department of State records of issuance or refusal of visas, see 8 USCA § 1202.

Census information, confidential nature of, see 13 USCA § 9.

Certificates of discharge, replacements as evidence, see 10 USCA § 1041.

Confession, delay in bringing detainee before magistrate affecting admissibility of, see 18 USCA § 3501.

Eye witness testimony, see 18 USCA § 3502.

Relevancy conditioned on fact, see Fed.Rules Evid. Rule 104, 28 USCA.

Notice to and availability of deponent as determining admissibility of depositions, see Fed.Rules Civ.Proc. Rules 30, 32, 28 USCA.

Notice to and availability of deponent as determining admissibility of depositions, see Fed.Rules Cr.Proc. Rule 15, 18 USCA.

Proceedings before magistrate, exclusion of evidence obtained in violation of rights, see Fed.Rules Cr.Proc. Rule 5, 18 USCA.

Testimony of debtor and of persons examined—

Immunity from self-incrimination, see 11 USCA § 344.

Immunity of witnesses, see 18 USCA § 6001 et seq.

Wire or radio communications, unauthorized use or publication prohibited, see 47 USCA § 605.

Rule 403. Exclusion of Relevant Evidence on Grounds of Prejudice, Confusion, or Waste of Time

Although relevant, evidence may be excluded if its probative value is substantially outweighed by the danger of unfair prejudice, confusion of the issues, or misleading the jury, or by considerations of undue delay, waste of time, or needless presentation of cumulative evidence.

(Pub.L. 93–595, § 1, Jan. 2, 1975, 88 Stat. 1932.)

ADVISORY COMMITTEE NOTES

1972 Proposed Rules

The case law recognizes that certain circumstances call for the exclusion of evidence which is of unquestioned relevance. These circumstances entail risks which range all the way from inducing decision on a purely emotional basis, at one extreme, to nothing more harmful than merely wasting time, at the other extreme. Situations in this area call for balancing the probative value of and need for the evidence against the harm likely to result from its admission. Slough, Relevancy Unraveled, 5 Kan.L.Rev. 1, 12–15 (1956); Trautman, Logical or Legal Relevancy—A Conflict in Theory, 5 Van. L.Rev. 385, 392 (1952); McCormick § 152, pp. 319–321. The rules which follow in this Article are concrete applications evolved for particular situations. However, they reflect the policies underlying the present rule, which is designed as a guide for the handling of situations for which no specific rules have been formulated.

Exclusion for risk of unfair prejudice, confusion of issues, misleading the jury, or waste of time, all find ample support in the authorities. "Unfair prejudice" within its context means an undue tendency to suggest decision on an improper basis, commonly, though not necessarily, an emotional one.

The rule does not enumerate surprise as a ground for exclusion, in this respect following Wigmore's view of the common law. 6 Wigmore § 1849. Cf. McCormick § 152, p. 320, n. 29, listing unfair surprise as a ground for exclusion but stating that it is usually "coupled with the danger of prejudice and confusion of issues." While Uniform Rule 45 incorporates surprise as a ground and is followed in Kansas Code of Civil Procedure § 60–445, surprise is not included in California Evidence Code § 352 or New Jersey Rule 4, though both the latter otherwise substantially embody Uniform Rule 45. While it can scarcely be doubted that claims of unfair surprise may still be justified despite procedural requirements of notice and instrumentalities of discovery, the granting of a continuance is a more appropriate remedy than exclusion of the evidence. Tentative Recommendation and a Study Relating to the Uniform Rules of Evidence (Art. VI. Extrinsic Policies Affecting Admissibility), Cal.Law Revision Comm'n, Rep., Rec. & Studies, 612 (1964). Moreover, the impact of a rule excluding evidence on the ground of surprise would be difficult to estimate.

In reaching a decision whether to exclude on grounds of unfair prejudice, consideration should be given to the probable effectiveness or lack of effectiveness of a limiting instruction. See Rule 106 [now 105] and Advisory Committee's Note thereunder. The availability of other means of proof may also be an appropriate factor.

CROSS REFERENCES

Eye witness testimony, see 18 USCA § 3502.

Limiting admissibility of evidence to proper scope and parties, see Fed.Rules Evid. Rule 105, 28 USCA.

Rule 404. Character Evidence Not Admissible To Prove Conduct; Exceptions; Other Crimes

(a) Character evidence generally.—Evidence of a person's character or a trait of character is not admissible for the purpose of proving action in conformity therewith on a particular occasion, except:

(1) Character of accused.—In a criminal case, evidence of a pertinent trait of character offered by an accused, or by the prosecution to rebut the same, or if evidence of a trait of character of the alleged victim of the crime is offered by an accused and admitted under Rule 404(a)(2), evidence of the same trait of character of the accused offered by the prosecution;

(2) Character of alleged victim.—In a criminal case, and subject to the limitations imposed by Rule 412, evidence of a pertinent trait of character of the alleged victim of the crime offered by an accused, or by the prosecution to rebut the same, or evidence of a character trait of peacefulness of the alleged victim offered by the prosecution in a homicide case to rebut evidence that the alleged victim was the first aggressor;

(3) Character of witness.—Evidence of the character of a witness, as provided in Rules 607, 608, and 609.

(b) Other Crimes, Wrongs, or Acts.—Evidence of other crimes, wrongs, or acts is not admissible to prove the character of a person in order to show action in conformity therewith. It may, however, be admissible for other purposes, such as proof of motive, opportunity, intent, preparation, plan, knowledge, identity, or absence of mistake or accident, provided that upon request by the accused, the prosecution in a criminal case shall provide reasonable notice in advance of trial, or during trial if the court excuses pretrial notice on good cause shown, of the general nature of any such evidence it intends to introduce at trial.

(Pub.L. 93–595, § 1, Jan. 2, 1975, 88 Stat.1932; Mar. 2, 1987, eff. Oct. 1, 1987; Apr. 30, 1991, eff. Dec. 1, 1991; Apr. 17, 2000, eff. Dec. 1, 2000; Apr. 12, 2006, eff. Dec. 1, 2006.)

ADVISORY COMMITTEE NOTES

1972 Proposed Rules

Note to Subdivision (a). This subdivision deals with the basic question whether character evidence should be admitted. Once the admissibility of character evidence in some form is established under this rule, reference must then be made to Rule 405, which follows, in order to determine the appropriate method of proof. If the character is that of a witness, see Rules 608 and 610 for methods of proof.

Character questions arise in two fundamentally different ways. (1) Character may itself be an element of a crime, claim, or defense. A situation of this kind is commonly referred to as "character in issue." Illustrations are: the chastity of the victim under a statute specifying her chastity as an element of the crime of seduction, or the competency of the driver in an action for negligently entrusting a motor vehicle to an incompetent driver. No problem of the general relevancy of character evidence is involved, and the present rule therefore has no provision on the subject. The only question relates to allowable methods of proof, as to which see Rule 405, immediately following. (2) Character evidence is susceptible of being used for the purpose of suggesting an inference that the person acted on the occasion in question consistently with his character. This use of character is often described as "circumstantial." Illustrations are: evidence of a violent disposition to prove that the person was the aggressor in an affray, or evidence of honesty in disproof of a charge of theft. This circumstantial use of character evidence raises questions of relevancy as well as questions of allowable methods of proof.

In most jurisdictions today, the circumstantial use of character is rejected but with important exceptions: (1) an accused may introduce pertinent evidence of good character (often misleadingly described as "putting his character in issue"), in which event the prosecution may rebut with evidence of bad character; (2) an accused may introduce pertinent evidence of the character of the victim, as in support of a claim of self-defense to a charge of homicide or consent in a case of rape, and the prosecution may introduce similar evidence in rebuttal of the character evidence, or, in a homicide case, to rebut a claim that deceased was the first aggressor, however proved; and (3) the character of a witness may be gone into as bearing on his credibility. McCormick §§ 155–161. This pattern is incorporated in the rule. While its basis lies more in history and experience than in logic an underlying justification can fairly be found in terms of the relative presence and absence of prejudice in the various situations. Falknor, Extrinsic Policies Affecting Admissibility, 10 Rutgers L.Rev. 574, 584 (1956); McCormick § 157. In any event, the criminal rule is so deeply imbedded in our jurisprudence as to assume almost constitutional proportions and to override doubts of the basic relevancy of the evidence.

The limitation to pertinent traits of character, rather than character generally, in paragraphs (1) and (2) is in accordance with the prevailing view. McCormick § 158, p. 334. A similar provision in Rule 608, to which reference is made in paragraph (3), limits character evidence respecting witnesses to the trait of truthfulness or untruthfulness.

The argument is made that circumstantial use of character ought to be allowed in civil cases to the same extent as in criminal cases, i.e. evidence of good (nonprejudicial) character would be admissible in the first instance, subject to rebuttal by evidence of bad character. Falknor, Extrinsic Policies Affecting Admissibility, 10 Rutgers L.Rev. 574, 581–583 (1956); Tentative Recommendation and a Study Relating to the Uniform Rules of Evidence (Art. VI. Extrinsic Policies Affecting Admissibility), Cal.Law Revision Comm'n, Rep., Rec. & Studies, 657–658 (1964). Uniform Rule 47 goes farther, in that it assumes that character evidence in general satisfies the conditions of relevancy, except as provided in Uniform Rule 48. The difficulty with expanding the use of character evidence in civil cases is set forth by the California Law Revision Commission in its ultimate rejection of Uniform Rule 47, *id.*, 615:

"Character evidence is of slight probative value and may be very prejudicial. It tends to distract the trier of fact from the main question of what actually happened on the particular occasion. It subtly permits the trier of fact to reward the good man and to punish the bad man because of their respective characters despite what the evidence in the case shows actually happened."

Much of the force of the position of those favoring greater use of character evidence in civil cases is dissipated by their support of Uniform Rule 48 which excludes the evidence in negligence cases, where it could be expected to achieve its maximum usefulness. Moreover, expanding concepts of "character," which seem of necessity to extend into such areas as psychiatric evaluation and psychological testing, coupled with expanded admissibility, would open up such vistas of mental examinations as caused the Court concern in *Schlagenhauf v. Holder,* 379 U.S. 104, 85 S.Ct. 234, 13 L.Ed.2d 152 (1964). It is believed that those espousing change have not met the burden of persuasion.

Note to Subdivision (b). Subdivision (b) deals with a specialized but important application of the general rule excluding circumstantial use of character evidence. Consistently with that rule, evidence of other crimes, wrongs, or acts is not admissible to prove character as a basis for suggesting the inference that conduct on a particular occasion was in conformity with it. However, the evidence may be offered for another purpose, such as proof of motive, opportunity, and so on, which does not fall within the prohibition. In this situation the rule does not require that the evidence be excluded. No mechanical solution is offered. The determination must be made whether the danger of undue prejudice outweighs the probative value of the evidence in view of the availability of other means of proof and other facts appropriate for making decision of this kind under Rule 403. Slough and Knightly, Other Vices, Other Crimes, 41 Iowa L.Rev. 325 (1956).

1974 Enactment

Note to Subdivision (b). The second sentence of Rule 404(b) as submitted to the Congress began with the words "This subdivision does not exclude the evidence when offered". The Committee amended this language to read "It may, however, be admissible", the words used in the 1971 Advisory Committee draft, on the ground that this formulation properly placed greater emphasis on admissibility than did the final Court version. House Report No. 93–650.

Note to Subdivision (b). This rule provides that evidence of other crimes, wrongs, or acts is not admissible to prove character but may be admissible for other specified purposes such as proof of motive.

Although your committee sees no necessity in amending the rule itself, it anticipates that the use of the discretionary word "may" with respect to the admissibility of evidence of crimes, wrongs, or acts is not intended to confer any arbitrary discretion on the trial judge. Rather, it is anticipated that with respect to permissible uses for such evidence, the trial judge may exclude it only on the basis of those considerations set forth in Rule 403, i.e., prejudice, confusion or waste of time. Senate Report No. 93–1277.

1987 Amendments

The amendments are technical. No substantive change is intended.

1991 Amendments

Rule 404(b) has emerged as one of the most cited Rules in the Rules of Evidence. And in many criminal cases evidence of an accused's extrinsic acts is viewed as an important asset in the prosecution's case against an accused. Although there are a few reported decisions on use of such evidence by the defense, *see, e.g., United States v. McClure,* 546 F.2d 670 (5th Cir.1990) (acts of informant offered in entrapment defense), the overwhelming number of cases involve introduction of that evidence by the prosecution.

The amendment to Rule 404(b) adds a pretrial notice requirement in criminal cases and is intended to reduce surprise and promote early resolution on the issue of admissibility. The notice requirement thus places Rule 404(b) in the mainstream with notice and disclosure provisions in other rules of evidence. *See, e.g.,* Rule 412 (written motion of intent to offer evidence under rule), Rule 609 (written notice of intent to offer conviction older than 10 years), Rule 803(24) and 804(b)(5) (notice of intent to use residual hearsay exceptions).

The Rule expects that counsel for both the defense and the prosecution will submit the necessary request and information in a reasonable and timely fashion. Other than requiring pretrial notice, no specific time limits are stated in recognition that what constitutes a reasonable request or disclosure will depend largely on the circumstances of each case. *Compare* Fla.Stat.Ann. § 90.404(2)(b) (notice must be given at least 10 days before trial) *with* Tex.R.Evid. 404(b) (no time limit).

Likewise, no specific form of notice is required. The Committee considered and rejected a requirement that the notice satisfy the particularity requirements normally required of language used in a charging instrument. *Cf.* Fla.Stat.Ann. § 90.404(2)(b) (written disclosure must describe uncharged misconduct with particularity required of an indictment or information). Instead, the Committee opted for a generalized notice provision which requires the prosecution to apprise the defense of the general nature of the evidence of extrinsic acts. The Committee does not intend that the amendment will supercede other rules of admissibility or disclosure, such as the Jencks Act, 18 U.S.C. § 3500, et. seq. nor require the prosecution to disclose directly or indirectly the names and addresses of its witnesses, something it is currently not required to do under Federal Rule of Criminal Procedure 16.

The amendment requires the prosecution to provide notice, regardless of how it intends to use the extrinsic act evidence at trial, i.e., during its case-in-chief, for impeachment, or for possible rebuttal. The court in its discretion may, under the facts, decide that the particular request or notice was not reasonable, either because of the lack of timeliness or completeness. Because the notice requirement serves as condition precedent to admissibility of 404(b) evidence, the offered evidence is inadmissible if the court decides that the notice requirement has not been met.

Nothing in the amendment precludes the court from requiring the government to provide it with an opportunity to rule *in limine* on 404(b) evidence before it is offered or even mentioned during trial. When ruling *in limine*, the court may require the government to disclose to it the specifics of such evidence which the court must consider in determining admissibility.

The amendment does not extend to evidence of acts which are "intrinsic" to the charged offense, *see United States v. Williams*, 900 F.2d 823 (5th Cir.1990) (noting distinction between 404(b) evidence and intrinsic offense evidence). Nor is the amendment intended to redefine what evidence would otherwise be admissible under Rule 404(b). Finally, the Committee does not intend through the amendment to affect the role of the court and the jury in considering such evidence. *See United States v. Huddleston*, 485 U.S. 681, 108 S.Ct. 1496 (1988).

2000 Amendments

Rule 404(a)(1) has been amended to provide that when the accused attacks the character of an alleged victim under subdivision (a)(2) of this Rule, the door is opened to an attack on the same character trait of the accused. Current law does not allow the government to introduce negative character evidence as to the accused unless the accused introduces evidence of good character. *See, e.g., United States v. Fountain*, 768 F.2d 790 (7th Cir. 1985) (when the accused offers proof of self-defense, this permits proof of the alleged victim's character trait for peacefulness, but it does not permit proof of the accused's character trait for violence).

The amendment makes clear that the accused cannot attack the alleged victim's character and yet remain shielded from the disclosure of equally relevant evidence concerning the same character trait of the accused. For example, in a murder case with a claim of self-defense, the accused, to bolster this defense, might offer evidence of the alleged victim's violent disposition. If the government has evidence that the accused has a violent character, but is not allowed to offer this evidence as part of its rebuttal, the jury has only part of the information it needs for an informed assessment of the probabilities as to who was the initial aggressor. This may be the case even if evidence of the accused's prior violent acts is admitted under Rule 404(b), because such evidence can be admitted only for limited purposes and not to show action in conformity with the accused's character on a specific occasion. Thus, the amendment is designed to permit a more balanced presentation of character evidence when an accused chooses to attack the character of the alleged victim.

The amendment does not affect the admissibility of evidence of specific acts of uncharged misconduct offered for a purpose other than proving character under Rule 404(b). Nor does it affect the standards for proof of character by evidence of other sexual behavior or sexual offenses under Rules 412–415. By its placement in Rule 404(a)(1), the amendment covers only proof of character by way of reputation or opinion.

The amendment does not permit proof of the accused's character if the accused merely uses character evidence for a purpose other than to prove the alleged victim's propensity to act in a certain way. *See United States v. Burks*, 470 F.2d 432, 434–5 (D.C.Cir. 1972) (evidence of the alleged victim's violent character, when known by the accused, was admissible "on the issue of whether or not the defendant reasonably feared he was in danger of imminent great bodily harm"). Finally, the amendment does not permit proof of the accused's character when the accused attacks the alleged victim's character as a witness under Rule 608 or 609.

The term "alleged" is inserted before each reference to "victim" in the Rule, in order to provide consistency with Evidence Rule 412.

GAP Report—Proposed Amendment to Rule 404(a)

The Committee made the following changes to the published draft of the proposed amendment to Evidence Rule 404(a):

1. The term "a pertinent trait of character" was changed to "the same trait of character," in order to limit the scope of the government's rebuttal. The Committee Note was revised to accord with this change in the text.

2. The word "alleged" was added before each reference in the Rule to a "victim" in order to provide consistency with Evidence Rule 412. The Committee Note was amended to accord with this change in the text.

3. The Committee Note was amended to clarify that rebuttal is not permitted under this Rule if the accused proffers evidence of the alleged victim's character for a purpose other than to prove the alleged victim's propensity to act in a certain manner.

2006 Amendments

The Rule has been amended to clarify that in a civil case evidence of a person's character is never admissible to prove that the person acted in conformity with the character trait. The amendment resolves the dispute in the case law over whether the exceptions in subdivisions (a)(1) and (2) permit the circumstantial use of character evidence in civil cases. *Compare Carson v. Polley*, 689 F.2d 562, 576 (5th Cir. 1982) ("when a central issue in a case is close to one of a criminal nature, the exceptions to the Rule 404(a) ban on character evidence may be invoked"), *with SEC v. Towers Financial Corp.*, 966 F.Supp. 203 (S.D.N.Y. 1997) (relying on the terms "accused" and "prosecution" in Rule 404(a) to conclude that the exceptions in subdivisions (a)(1) and (2) are inapplicable in civil cases). The amendment is consistent with the original intent of the Rule, which was to prohibit the circumstantial use of character evidence in civil cases, even where closely related to criminal charges. *See Ginter v. Northwestern Mut. Life Ins. Co.*, 576 F.Supp. 627, 629–30 (D. Ky.1984) ("It seems beyond peradventure of doubt that the drafters of F.R.Evi. 404(a) explicitly intended that all character evidence, except where 'character is at issue' was to be excluded" in civil cases).

The circumstantial use of character evidence is generally discouraged because it carries serious risks of prejudice, confusion and delay. *See Michelson v. United States*, 335 U.S. 469, 476 (1948) ("The overriding policy of excluding such evidence, despite its admitted probative value, is the practical experience that its disallowance tends to prevent confusion of issues, unfair surprise and undue prejudice."). In criminal cases, the so-called "mercy rule" permits a criminal defendant to introduce evidence of pertinent character traits of the defendant and the victim. But that is because the accused, whose liberty is at stake, may need "a counterweight against the strong investigative and prosecutorial resources of the government." C. Mueller & L. Kirkpatrick, *Evidence: Practice Under the Rules*, pp. 264–5 (2d ed. 1999). See also Richard Uviller, *Evidence of Character to Prove Conduct: Illusion, Illogic, and Injustice in the Courtroom*, 130 U.Pa.

L.Rev. 845, 855 (1982) (the rule prohibiting circumstantial use of character evidence "was relaxed to allow the criminal defendant with so much at stake and so little available in the way of conventional proof to have special dispensation to tell the factfinder just what sort of person he really is"). Those concerns do not apply to parties in civil cases.

The amendment also clarifies that evidence otherwise admissible under Rule 404(a)(2) may nonetheless be excluded in a criminal case involving sexual misconduct. In such a case, the admissibility of evidence of the victim's sexual behavior and predisposition is governed by the more stringent provisions of Rule 412.

Nothing in the amendment is intended to affect the scope of Rule 404(b). While Rule 404(b) refers to the "accused," the "prosecution," and a "criminal case," it does so only in the context of a notice requirement. The admissibility standards of Rule 404(b) remain fully applicable to both civil and criminal cases.

CROSS REFERENCES

Civil commitment for narcotic addiction not conviction; use of test results on cross-examination, see 28 USCA § 2904.

Extortionate credit transactions, admissibility of evidence to show—

Reputation as to collection practices, see 18 USCA § 892.

Reputation of defendant within community, see 18 USCA § 894.

Threat as means of collection, see 18 USCA § 894.

Witnesses, evidence of religious beliefs or opinions, see Fed.Rules Evid. Rule 610, 28 USCA.

Rule 405. Methods of Proving Character

(a) Reputation or opinion. In all cases in which evidence of character or a trait of character of a person is admissible, proof may be made by testimony as to reputation or by testimony in the form of an opinion. On cross-examination, inquiry is allowable into relevant specific instances of conduct.

(b) Specific instances of conduct. In cases in which character or a trait of character of a person is an essential element of a charge, claim, or defense, proof may also be made of specific instances of that person's conduct.

(Pub.L. 93–595, § 1, Jan. 2, 1975, 88 Stat. 1932; Mar. 2, 1987, eff. Oct. 1, 1987.)

ADVISORY COMMITTEE NOTES

1972 Proposed Rules

The rule deals only with allowable methods of proving character, not with the admissibility of character evidence, which is covered in Rule 404.

Of the three methods of proving character provided by the rule, evidence of specific instances of conduct is the most convincing. At the same time it possesses the greatest capacity to arouse prejudice, to confuse, to surprise, and to consume time. Consequently the rule confines the use of evidence of this kind to cases in which character is, in the strict sense, in issue and hence deserving of a searching inquiry. When character is used circumstantially and hence occupies a lesser status in the case, proof may be only by reputation and opinion. These latter methods are also available when character is in issue. This treatment is, with respect to specific instances of conduct and reputation, conventional contemporary common law doctrine. McCormick § 153.

In recognizing opinion as a means of proving character, the rule departs from usual contemporary practice in favor of that of an earlier day. See 7 Wigmore § 1986, pointing out that the earlier practice permitted opinion and arguing strongly for evidence based on personal knowledge and belief as contrasted with "the secondhand, irresponsible product of multiplied guesses and gossip which we term 'reputation'." It seems likely that the persistence of reputation evidence is due to its largely being opinion in disguise. Traditionally character has been regarded primarily in moral overtones of good and bad: chaste, peaceable, truthful, honest. Nevertheless, on occasion nonmoral considerations crop up, as in the case of the incompetent driver, and this seems bound to happen increasingly. If character is defined as the kind of person one is, then account must be taken of varying ways of arriving at the estimate. These may range from the opinion of the employer who has found the man honest to the opinion of the psychiatrist based upon examination and testing. No effective dividing line exists between character and mental capacity, and the latter traditionally has been provable by opinion.

According to the great majority of cases, on cross-examination inquiry is allowable as to whether the reputation witness has heard of particular instances of conduct pertinent to the trait in question. *Michelson v. United States,* 335 U.S. 469, 69 S.Ct. 213, 93 L.Ed. 168 (1948); Annot., 47 A.L.R.2d 1258. The theory is that, since the reputation witness relates what he has heard, the inquiry tends to shed light on the accuracy of his hearing and reporting. Accordingly, the opinion witness would be asked whether he knew, as well as whether he had heard. The fact is, of course, that these distinctions are of slight if any practical significance, and the second sentence of subdivision (a) eliminates them as a factor in formulating questions. This recognition of the propriety of inquiring into specific instances of conduct does not circumscribe inquiry otherwise into the bases of opinion and reputation testimony.

The express allowance of inquiry into specific instances of conduct on cross-examination in subdivision (a) and the express allowance of it as part of a case in chief when character is actually in issue in subdivision (b) contemplate that testimony of specific instances is not generally permissible on the direct examination of an ordinary opinion witness to character. Similarly as to witnesses to the character of witnesses under Rule 608(b). Opinion testimony on direct in these situations ought in general to correspond to reputation testimony as now given, *i.e.,* be confined to the nature and extent of observation and acquaintance upon which the opinion is based. See Rule 701.

1974 Enactment

Note to Subdivision (a). Rule 405(a) as submitted proposed to change existing law by allowing evidence of character in the form of opinion as well as reputation testimony. Fearing, among other reasons, that wholesale allowance of opinion testimony might tend to turn a trial into a swearing contest between conflicting character witnesses, the Committee decided to delete from this Rule, as well as from Rule 608(a) which involves a related problem, reference to opinion testimony. House Report No. 93–650.

The Senate makes two language changes in the nature of conforming amendments. The Conference adopts the Senate amendments. House Report No. 93–1597.

1987 Amendments

The amendment is technical. No substantive change is intended.

CROSS REFERENCES

Civil commitment for narcotic addiction not conviction; use of test results on cross-examination, see 28 USCA § 2904.

Extortionate credit transactions, admissibility of evidence to show—

Reputation as to collection practices, see 18 USCA § 892.

Reputation of defendant within community, see 18 USCA § 894.

Threat as means of collection, see 18 USCA § 894.

Witnesses—

Character and conduct, see Fed.Rules Evid. Rule 608, 28 USCA.

Impeachment by conviction of crime, see Fed.Rules Evid. Rule 609, 28 USCA.

Opinion testimony, see Fed.Rules Evid. Rule 701, 28 USCA.

Religious opinions or beliefs, see Fed.Rules Evid. Rule 610, 28 USCA.

Rule 406. Habit; Routine Practice

Evidence of the habit of a person or of the routine practice of an organization, whether corroborated or not and regardless of the presence of eyewitnesses, is relevant to prove that the conduct of the person or organization on a particular occasion was in conformity with the habit or routine practice.

(Pub.L. 93–595, § 1, Jan. 2, 1975, 88 Stat. 1932.)

ADVISORY COMMITTEE NOTES

1972 Proposed Rules

An oft-quoted paragraph, McCormick, § 162, p. 340, describes habit in terms effectively contrasting it with character:

"Character and habit are close akin. Character is a generalized description of one's disposition, or of one's disposition in respect to a general trait, such as honesty, temperance, or peacefulness. 'Habit,' in modern usage, both lay and psychological, is more specific. It describes one's regular response to a repeated specific situation. If we speak of character for care, we think of the person's tendency to act prudently in all the varying situations of life, in business, family life, in handling automobiles and in walking across the street. A habit, on the other hand, is the person's regular practice of meeting a particular kind of situation with a specific type of conduct, such as the habit of going down a particular stairway two stairs at a time, or of giving the hand-signal for a left turn, or of alighting from railway cars while they are moving. The doing of the habitual acts may become semi-automatic."

Equivalent behavior on the part of a group is designated "routine practice of an organization" in the rule.

Agreement is general that habit evidence is highly persuasive as proof of conduct on a particular occasion. Again quoting McCormick § 162, p. 341:

"Character may be thought of as the sum of one's habits though doubtless it is more than this. But unquestionably the uniformity of one's response to habit is far greater than the consistency with which one's conduct conforms to character or disposition. Even though character comes in only exceptionally as evidence of an act, surely any sensible man in investigating whether X did a particular act would be greatly helped in his inquiry by evidence as to whether he was in the habit of doing it."

When disagreement has appeared, its focus has been upon the question what constitutes habit, and the reason for this is readily apparent. The extent to which instances must be multiplied and consistency of behavior maintained in order to rise to the status of habit inevitably gives rise to differences of opinion. Lewan, Rationale of Habit Evidence, 16 Syracuse L.Rev. 39, 49 (1964). While adequacy of sampling and uniformity of response are key factors, precise standards for measuring their sufficiency for evidence purposes cannot be formulated.

The rule is consistent with prevailing views. Much evidence is excluded simply because of failure to achieve the status of habit. Thus, evidence of intemperate "habits" is generally excluded when offered as proof of drunkenness in accident cases, Annot., 46 A.L.R.2d 103, and evidence of other assaults is inadmissible to prove the instant one in a civil assault action, Annot., 66 A.L.R.2d 806. In *Levin v. United States,* 119 U.S.App.D.C. 156, 338 F.2d 265 (1964), testimony as to the religious "habits" of the accused, offered as tending to prove that he was at home observing the Sabbath rather than out obtaining money through larceny by trick, was held properly excluded:

"It seems apparent to us that an individual's religious practices would not be the type of activities which would lend themselves to the characterization of 'invariable regularity.' [1 Wigmore 520.] Certainly the very volitional basis of the activity raises serious questions as to its invariable nature, and hence its probative value." *Id.* at 272.

These rulings are not inconsistent with the trend towards admitting evidence of business transactions between one of the parties and a third person as tending to prove that he made the same bargain or proposal in the litigated situation. Slough, Relevancy Unraveled, 6 Kan.L.Rev. 38–41 (1957). Nor are they inconsistent with such cases as *Whittemore v. Lockheed Aircraft Corp.,* 65 Cal.App.2d 737, 151 P.2d 670 (1944), upholding the admission of evidence that plaintiff's intestate had on four other occasions flown planes from defendant's factory for delivery to his employer airline, offered to prove that he was piloting rather than a guest on a plane which crashed and killed all on board while en route for delivery.

A considerable body of authority has required that evidence of the routine practice of an organization be corroborated as a condition precedent to its admission in evidence. Slough, Relevancy Unraveled, 5 Kan.L.Rev. 404, 449 (1957).

This requirement is specifically rejected by the rule on the ground that it relates to the sufficiency of the evidence rather than admissibility. A similar position is taken in New Jersey Rule 49. The rule also rejects the requirement of the absence of eyewitnesses, sometimes encountered with respect to admitting habit evidence to prove freedom from contributory negligence in wrongful death cases. For comment critical of the requirements see Frank, J., in *Cereste v. New York*, N.H. & H.R. Co., 231 F.2d 50 (2d Cir.1956), cert. denied 351 U.S. 951, 76 S.Ct. 848, 100 L.Ed. 1475, 10 Vand.L.Rev. 447 (1957); McCormick § 162, p. 342. The omission of the requirement from the California Evidence Code is said to have effected its elimination. Comment, Cal.Ev.Code § 1105.

CROSS REFERENCES

Opinion testimony by lay witnesses, see Fed.Rules Evid. Rule 701, 28 USCA.

Rule 407. Subsequent Remedial Measures

When, after an injury or harm allegedly caused by an event, measures are taken that, if taken previously, would have made the injury or harm less likely to occur, evidence of the subsequent measures is not admissible to prove negligence, culpable conduct, a defect in a product, a defect in a product's design, or a need for a warning or instruction. This rule does not require the exclusion of evidence of subsequent measures when offered for another purpose, such as proving ownership, control, or feasibility of precautionary measures, if controverted, or impeachment.

(Pub.L. 93–595, § 1, Jan. 2, 1975, 88 Stat. 1932; Apr. 11, 1997, eff. Dec. 1, 1997.)

ADVISORY COMMITTEE NOTES

1972 Proposed Rules

The rule incorporates conventional doctrine which excludes evidence of subsequent remedial measures as proof of an admission of fault. The rule rests on two grounds. (1) The conduct is not in fact an admission, since the conduct is equally consistent with injury by mere accident or through contributory negligence. Or, as Baron Bramwell put it, the rule rejects the notion that "because the world gets wiser as it gets older, therefore it was foolish before." *Hart v. Lancashire & Yorkshire Ry. Co.*, 21 L.T.R. N.S. 261, 263 (1869). Under a liberal theory of relevancy this ground alone would not support exclusion as the inference is still a possible one. (2) The other, and more impressive, ground for exclusion rests on a social policy of encouraging people to take, or at least not discouraging them from taking, steps in furtherance of added safety. The courts have applied this principle to exclude evidence of subsequent repairs, installation of safety devices, changes in company rules, and discharge of employees, and the language of the present rule is broad enough to encompass all of them. See Falknor, Extrinsic Policies Affecting Admissibility, 10 Rutgers L.Rev. 574, 590 (1956).

The second sentence of the rule directs attention to the limitations of the rule. Exclusion is called for only when the evidence of subsequent remedial measures is offered as proof of negligence or culpable conduct. In effect it rejects the suggested inference that fault is admitted. Other purposes are, however, allowable, including ownership or control, existence of duty, and feasibility of precautionary measures, if controverted, and impeachment. 2 Wigmore § 283; Annot., 64 A.L.R.2d 1296. Two recent federal cases are illustrative. *Boeing Airplane Co. v. Brown*, 291 F.2d 310 (9th Cir.1961), an action against an airplane manufacturer for using an allegedly defectively designed alternator shaft which caused a plane crash, upheld the admission of evidence of subsequent design modification for the purpose of showing that design changes and safeguards were feasible. And *Powers v. J.B. Michael & Co.*, 329 F.2d 674 (6th Cir.1964), an action against a road contractor for negligent failure to put out warning signs, sustained the admission of evidence that defendant subsequently put out signs to show that the portion of the road in question was under defendant's control. The requirement that the other purpose be controverted calls for automatic exclusion unless a genuine issue be present and allows the opposing party to lay the groundwork for exclusion by making an admission. Otherwise the factors of undue prejudice, confusion of issues, misleading the jury, and waste of time remain for consideration under Rule 403.

For comparable rules, see Uniform Rule 51; California Evidence Code § 1151; Kansas Code of Civil Procedure § 60–451; New Jersey Evidence Rule 51.

1997 Amendments

The amendment to Rule 407 makes two changes in the rule. First, the words "an injury or harm allegedly caused by" were added to clarify that the rule applies only to changes made after the occurrence that produced the damages giving rise to the action. Evidence of measures taken by the defendant prior to the "event" causing "injury or harm" do not fall within the exclusionary scope of Rule 407 even if they occurred after the manufacture or design of the product. See *Chase v. General Motors Corp.*, 856 F.2d 17, 21–22 (4th Cir. 1988).

Second, Rule 407 has been amended to provide that evidence of subsequent remedial measures may not be used to prove "a defect in a product or its design, or that a warning or instruction should have accompanied a product." This amendment adopts the view of a majority of the circuits that have interpreted Rule 407 to apply to products liability actions. See *Raymond v. Raymond Corp., 938 F.2d 1518, 1522 (1st Cir. 1991); In re Joint Eastern District and Southern District Asbestos Litigation v. Armstrong World industries, Inc.*, 995 F.2d 343 (2d Cir. 1993); *Cann v. Ford Motor Co.*, 658 F.2d 54, 60 (2d Cir. 1981), *cert. denied*, 456 U.S. 960 (1982); *Kelly v. Crown Equipment Co.*, 970 F.2d 1273, 1275 (3d Cir. 1992); *Werner v. Upjohn, Inc.*, 628 F.2d 848 (4th Cir. 1980); *cert. denied*, 449 U.S. 1080 (1981); *Grenada Steel Industries, Inc. v. Alabama Oxygen Co., Inc.*, 695 F.2d 883 (5th Cir. 1983); *Bauman v. Volkswagenwerk Aktiengesellschaft*, 621 F.2d 230, 232 (6th Cir. 1980); *Flaminio v. Honda Motor Company, Ltd.*, 733 F.2d 463, 469 (7th Cir. 1984); *Gauthier v. AMF, Inc.*, 788 F.2d 634, 636–37 (9th Cir. 1986).

Although this amendment adopts a uniform federal rule, it should be noted that evidence of subsequent remedial measures may be admissible pursuant to the second sentence of Rule 407. Evidence of subsequent measures that is not barred by Rule 407 may still be subject to exclusion on Rule

403 grounds when the dangers of prejudice or confusion substantially outweigh the probative value of the evidence.

Rule 408. Compromise and Offers to Compromise

(a) Prohibited uses.—Evidence of the following is not admissible on behalf of any party, when offered to prove liability for, invalidity of, or amount of a claim that was disputed as to validity or amount, or to impeach through a prior inconsistent statement or contradiction:

(1) furnishing or offering or promising to furnish—or accepting or offering or promising to accept—a valuable consideration in compromising or attempting to compromise the claim; and

(2) conduct or statements made in compromise negotiations regarding the claim, except when offered in a criminal case and the negotiations related to a claim by a public office or agency in the exercise of regulatory, investigative, or enforcement authority.

(b) Permitted uses.—This rule does not require exclusion if the evidence is offered for purposes not prohibited by subdivision (a). Examples of permissible purposes include proving a witness's bias or prejudice; negating a contention of undue delay; and proving an effort to obstruct a criminal investigation or prosecution.

(Pub.L. 93–595, § 1, Jan. 2, 1975, 88 Stat. 1933; Apr. 12, 2006, eff. Dec. 1, 2006.)

ADVISORY COMMITTEE NOTES

1972 Proposed Rules

As a matter of general agreement, evidence of an offer to compromise a claim is not receivable in evidence as an admission of, as the case may be, the validity or invalidity of the claim. As with evidence of subsequent remedial measures, dealt with in Rule 407, exclusion may be based on two grounds. (1) The evidence is irrelevant, since the offer may be motivated by a desire for peace rather than from any concession of weakness of position. The validity of this position will vary as the amount of the offer varies in relation to the size of the claim and may also be influenced by other circumstances. (2) A more consistently impressive ground is promotion of the public policy favoring the compromise and settlement of disputes. McCormick §§ 76, 251. While the rule is ordinarily phrased in terms of offers of compromise, it is apparent that a similar attitude must be taken with respect to completed compromises when offered against a party thereto. This latter situation will not, of course, ordinarily occur except when a party to the present litigation has compromised with a third person.

The same policy underlies the provision of Rule 68 of the Federal Rules of Civil Procedure that evidence of an unaccepted offer of judgment is not admissible except in a proceeding to determine costs.

The practical value of the common law rule has been greatly diminished by its inapplicability to admissions of fact, even though made in the course of compromise negotiations, unless hypothetical, stated to be "without prejudice," or so connected with the offer as to be inseparable from it. McCormick § 251, pp. 540–541. An inevitable effect is to inhibit freedom of communication with respect to compromise, even among lawyers. Another effect is the generation of controversy over whether a given statement falls within or without the protected area. These considerations account for the expansion of the rule herewith to include evidence of conduct or statements made in compromise negotiations, as well as the offer or completed compromise itself. For similar provisions see California Evidence Code §§ 1152, 1154.

The policy considerations which underlie the rule do not come into play when the effort is to induce a creditor to settle an admittedly due amount for a lesser sum. McCormick § 251, p. 540. Hence the rule requires that the claim be disputed as to either validity or amount.

The final sentence of the rule serves to point out some limitations upon its applicability. Since the rule excludes only when the purpose is proving the validity or invalidity of the claim or its amount, an offer for another purpose is not within the rule. The illustrative situations mentioned in the rule are supported by the authorities. As to proving bias or prejudice of a witness, see Annot., 161 A.L.R. 395, *contra, Fenberg v. Rosenthal,* 348 Ill.App. 510, 109 N.E.2d 402 (1952), and negativing a contention of lack of due diligence in presenting a claim, 4 Wigmore § 1061. An effort to "buy off" the prosecution or a prosecuting witness in a criminal case is not within the policy of the rule of exclusion. McCormick § 251, p. 542.

For other rules of similar import, see Uniform Rules 52 and 53; California Evidence Code §§ 1152, 1154; Kansas Code of Civil Procedure §§ 60–452, 60–453; New Jersey Evidence Rules 52 and 53.

1974 Enactment

Under existing federal law evidence of conduct and statements made in compromise negotiations is admissible in subsequent litigation between the parties. The second sentence of Rule 408 as submitted by the Supreme Court proposed to reverse that doctrine in the interest of further promoting non-judicial settlement of disputes. Some agencies of government expressed the view that the Court formulation was likely to impede rather than assist efforts to achieve settlement of disputes. For one thing, it is not always easy to tell when compromise negotiations begin, and informal dealings end. Also, parties dealing with government agencies would be reluctant to furnish factual information at preliminary meetings; they would wait until "compromise negotiations" began and thus hopefully effect an immunity for themselves with respect to the evidence supplied. In light of these considerations, the Committee recast the Rule so that admissions of liability or opinions given during compromise negotiations continue inadmissible, but evidence of unqualified factual assertions is admissible. The latter aspect of the Rule is drafted, however, so as to preserve other possible objections to the introduction of such evidence. The Committee intends no modification of current law whereby a party may protect himself from future use of his statements by couching them in hypothetical conditional form. House Report No. 93–650.

This rule as reported makes evidence of settlement or attempted settlement of a disputed claim inadmissible when offered as an admission of liability or the amount of liability. The purpose of this rule is to encourage settlements which would be discouraged if such evidence were admissible.

Under present law, in most jurisdictions, statements of fact made during settlement negotiations, however, are excepted from this ban and are admissible. The only escape from admissibility of statements of fact made in a settlement negotiation is if the declarant or his representative expressly states that the statement is hypothetical in nature or is made without prejudice. Rule 408 as submitted by the Court reversed the traditional rule. It would have brought statements of fact within the ban and made them, as well as an offer of settlement, inadmissible.

The House amended the rule and would continue to make evidence of facts disclosed during compromise negotiations admissible. It thus reverted to the traditional rule. The House committee report states that the committee intends to preserve current law under which a party may protect himself by couching his statements in hypothetical form [See House Report No. 93–650 above]. The real impact of this amendment, however, is to deprive the rule of much of its salutary effect. The exception for factual admissions was believed by the Advisory Committee to hamper free communication between parties and thus to constitute an unjustifiable restraint upon efforts to negotiate settlements—the encouragement of which is the purpose of the rule. Further, by protecting hypothetically phrased statements, it constituted a preference for the sophisticated, and a trap for the unwary.

Three States which had adopted rules of evidence patterned after the proposed rules prescribed by the Supreme Court opted for versions of rule 408 identical with the Supreme Court draft with respect to the inadmissibility of conduct or statements made in compromise negotiations [Nev.Rev.Stats. § 48.105; N.Mex.Stats.Anno. (1973 Supp.) § 20–4–408; West's Wis.Stats.Anno. (1973 Supp.) § 904.08].

For these reasons, the committee has deleted the House amendment and restored the rule to the version submitted by the Supreme Court with one additional amendment. This amendment adds a sentence to insure that evidence, such as documents, is not rendered inadmissible merely because it is presented in the course of compromise negotiations if the evidence is otherwise discoverable. A party should not be able to immunize from admissibility documents otherwise discoverable merely by offering them in a compromise negotiation. Senate Report No. 93–1277.

The House bill provides that evidence of admissions of liability or opinions given during compromise negotiations is not admissible, but that evidence of facts disclosed during compromise negotiations is not inadmissible by virtue of having been first disclosed in the compromise negotiations. The Senate amendment provides that evidence of conduct or statements made in compromise negotiations is not admissible. The Senate amendment also provides that the rule does not require the exclusion of any evidence otherwise discoverable merely because it is presented in the course of compromise negotiations.

The House bill was drafted to meet the objection of executive agencies that under the rule as proposed by the Supreme Court, a party could present a fact during compromise negotiations and thereby prevent an opposing party from offering evidence of that fact at trial even though such evidence was obtained from independent sources. The Senate amendment expressly precludes this result.

The Conference adopts the Senate amendment. House Report No. 93–1597.

2006 Amendment

Rule 408 has been amended to settle some questions in the courts about the scope of the Rule, and to make it easier to read. First, the amendment provides that Rule 408 does not prohibit the introduction in a criminal case of statements or conduct during compromise negotiations regarding a civil dispute by a government regulatory, investigative, or enforcement agency. *See, e.g., United States v. Prewitt*, 34 F.3d 436, 439 (7th Cir. 1994) (admissions of fault made in compromise of a civil securities enforcement action were admissible against the accused in a subsequent criminal action for mail fraud). Where an individual makes a statement in the presence of government agents, its subsequent admission in a criminal case should not be unexpected. The individual can seek to protect against subsequent disclosure through negotiation and agreement with the civil regulator or an attorney for the government.

Statements made in compromise negotiations of a claim by a government agency may be excluded in criminal cases where the circumstances so warrant under Rule 403. For example, if an individual was unrepresented at the time the statement was made in a civil enforcement proceeding, its probative value in a subsequent criminal case may be minimal. But there is no absolute exclusion imposed by Rule 408.

In contrast, statements made during compromise negotiations of other disputed claims are not admissible in subsequent criminal litigation, when offered to prove liability for, invalidity of, or amount of those claims. When private parties enter into compromise negotiations they cannot protect against the subsequent use of statements in criminal cases by way of private ordering. The inability to guarantee protection against subsequent use could lead to parties refusing to admit fault, even if by doing so they could favorably settle the private matter. Such a chill on settlement negotiations would be contrary to the policy of Rule 408.

The amendment distinguishes statements and conduct (such as a direct admission of fault) made in compromise negotiations of a civil claim by a government agency from an offer or acceptance of a compromise of such a claim. An offer or acceptance of a compromise of any civil claim is excluded under the Rule if offered against the defendant as an admission of fault. In that case, the predicate for the evidence would be that the defendant, by compromising with the government agency, has admitted the validity and amount of the civil claim, and that this admission has sufficient probative value to be considered as evidence of guilt. But unlike a direct statement of fault, an offer or acceptance of a compromise is not very probative of the defendant's guilt. Moreover, admitting such an offer or acceptance could deter a defendant from settling a civil regulatory action, for fear of evidentiary use in a subsequent criminal action. *See, e.g.*, Fishman, *Jones on Evidence, Civil and Criminal*, § 22:16 at 199, n.83 (7th ed. 2000) ("A target of a potential criminal investigation may be unwilling to settle civil claims against him if by doing so he increases the risk of prosecution and conviction.").

The amendment retains the language of the original rule that bars compromise evidence only when offered as evidence of the "validity," "invalidity," or "amount" of the disputed claim. The intent is to retain the extensive case law finding Rule 408 inapplicable when compromise evidence is offered for a purpose other than to prove the validity, invalidity, or amount of a disputed claim. *See, e.g., Athey v. Farmers Ins. Exchange*, 234 F.3d 357 (8th Cir. 2000) (evidence of settlement offer by insurer was properly admitted to prove insurer's bad faith); *Coakley & Williams v. Structural Concrete Equip.*, 973 F.2d 349 (4th Cir. 1992) (evidence of settlement is not precluded by Rule 408 where offered to prove a party's intent with respect to the scope of a release); *Cates v. Morgan Portable Bldg. Corp.*, 708 F.2d 683 (7th Cir. 1985) (Rule 408 does not bar evidence of a settlement when offered to prove a breach of the settlement agreement, as the purpose of the evidence is to prove the fact of settlement as opposed to the validity or amount of the underlying claim); *Uforma/Shelby Bus. Forms, Inc. v. NLRB*, 111 F.3d 1284 (6th Cir. 1997) (threats made in settlement negotiations were admissible; Rule 408 is inapplicable when the claim is based upon a wrong that is committed during the course of settlement negotiations). So for example, Rule 408 is inapplicable if offered to show that a party made fraudulent statements in order to settle a litigation.

The amendment does not affect the case law providing that Rule 408 is inapplicable when evidence of the compromise is offered to prove notice. *See, e.g., United States v. Austin*, 54 F.3d 394 (7th Cir. 1995) (no error to admit evidence of the defendant's settlement with the FTC, because it was offered to prove that the defendant was on notice that subsequent similar conduct was wrongful); *Spell v. McDaniel*, 824 F.2d 1380 (4th Cir. 1987) (in a civil rights action alleging that an officer used excessive force, a prior settlement by the City of another brutality claim was properly admitted to prove that the City was on notice of aggressive behavior by police officers).

The amendment prohibits the use of statements made in settlement negotiations when offered to impeach by prior inconsistent statement or through contradiction. Such broad impeachment would tend to swallow the exclusionary rule and would impair the public policy of promoting settlements. *See McCormick on Evidence* at 186 (5th ed. 1999) ("Use of statements made in compromise negotiations to impeach the testimony of a party, which is not specifically treated in Rule 408, is fraught with danger of misuse of the statements to prove liability, threatens frank interchange of information during negotiations, and generally should not be permitted."). *See also EEOC v. Gear Petroleum, Inc.*, 948 F.2d 1542 (10th Cir.1991) (letter sent as part of settlement negotiation cannot be used to impeach defense witnesses by way of contradiction or prior inconsistent statement; such broad impeachment would undermine the policy of encouraging uninhibited settlement negotiations).

The amendment makes clear that Rule 408 excludes compromise evidence even when a party seeks to admit its own settlement offer or statements made in settlement negotiations. If a party were to reveal its own statement or offer, this could itself reveal the fact that the adversary entered into settlement negotiations. The protections of Rule 408 cannot be waived unilaterally because the Rule, by definition, protects both parties from having the fact of negotiation disclosed to the jury. Moreover, proof of statements and offers made in settlement would often have to be made through the testimony of attorneys, leading to the risks and costs of disqualification. *See generally Pierce v. F.R. Tripler & Co.*, 955 F.2d 820, 828 (2d Cir. 1992) (settlement offers are excluded under Rule 408 even if it is the offeror who seeks to admit them; noting that the "widespread admissibility of the substance of settlement offers could bring with it a rash of motions for disqualification of a party's chosen counsel who would likely become a witness at trial").

The sentence of the Rule referring to evidence "otherwise discoverable" has been deleted as superfluous. *See, e.g.*, Advisory Committee Note to Maine Rule of Evidence 408 (refusing to include the sentence in the Maine version of Rule 408 and noting that the sentence "seems to state what the law would be if it were omitted"); Advisory Committee Note to Wyoming Rule of Evidence 408 (refusing to include the sentence in Wyoming Rule 408 on the ground that it was "superfluous"). The intent of the sentence was to prevent a party from trying to immunize admissible information, such as a pre-existing document, through the pretense of disclosing it during compromise negotiations. *See Ramada Development Co. v. Rauch*, 644 F.2d 1097 (5th Cir. 1981). But even without the sentence, the Rule cannot be read to protect pre-existing information simply because it was presented to the adversary in compromise negotiations.

CROSS REFERENCES

Offer of judgment inadmissible as evidence, exception, see Fed.Rules Civ.Proc. Rule 68, 28 USCA.

Rule 409. Payment of Medical and Similar Expenses

Evidence of furnishing or offering or promising to pay medical, hospital, or similar expenses occasioned by an injury is not admissible to prove liability for the injury.

(Pub.L. 93–595, § 1, Jan. 2, 1975, 88 Stat.1933.)

ADVISORY COMMITTEE NOTES

1972 Proposed Rules

The considerations underlying this rule parallel those underlying Rules 407 and 408, which deal respectively with subsequent remedial measures and offers of compromise. As stated in Annot., 20 A.L.R.2d 291, 293:

"[G]enerally, evidence of payment of medical, hospital, or similar expenses of an injured party by the opposing party, is not admissible, the reason often given being that such payment or offer is usually made from humane impulses and not from an admission of liability, and that to hold otherwise would tend to discourage assistance to the injured person."

Contrary to Rule 408, dealing with offers of compromise, the present rule does not extend to conduct or statements not a part of the act of furnishing or offering or promising to pay. This difference in treatment arises from fundamental differences in nature. Communication is essential if compromises are to be effected, and consequently broad protection of statements is needed. This is not so in cases of payments or offers or promises to pay medical expenses, where factual statements may be expected to be incidental in nature.

For rules on the same subject, but phrased in terms of "humanitarian motives," see Uniform Rule 52; California

Evidence Code § 1152; Kansas Code of Civil Procedure § 60–452; New Jersey Evidence Rule 52.

Rule 410. Inadmissibility of Pleas, Plea Discussions, and Related Statements

Except as otherwise provided in this rule, evidence of the following is not, in any civil or criminal proceeding, admissible against the defendant who made the plea or was a participant in the plea discussions:

(1) a plea of guilty which was later withdrawn;

(2) a plea of nolo contendere;

(3) any statement made in the course of any proceedings under Rule 11 of the Federal Rules of Criminal Procedure or comparable state procedure regarding either of the foregoing pleas; or

(4) any statement made in the course of plea discussions with an attorney for the prosecuting authority which do not result in a plea of guilty or which result in a plea of guilty later withdrawn.

However, such a statement is admissible (i) in any proceeding wherein another statement made in the course of the same plea or plea discussions has been introduced and the statement ought in fairness be considered contemporaneously with it, or (ii) in a criminal proceeding for perjury or false statement if the statement was made by the defendant under oath, on the record and in the presence of counsel.

(Pub.L. 93–595, § 1, Jan. 2, 1975, 88 Stat. 1933; Pub.L. 94–149, § 1(9), Dec. 12, 1975, 89 Stat. 805; Apr. 30, 1979, eff. Dec. 1, 1980.)

ADVISORY COMMITTEE NOTES

1972 Proposed Rules

Withdrawn pleas of guilty were held inadmissible in federal prosecutions in *Kercheval v. United States,* 274 U.S. 220, 47 S.Ct. 582, 71 L.Ed. 1009 (1927). The Court pointed out that to admit the withdrawn plea would effectively set at naught the allowance of withdrawal and place the accused in a dilemma utterly inconsistent with the decision to award him a trial. The New York Court of Appeals, in *People v. Spitaleri,* 9 N.Y.2d 168, 212 N.Y.S.2d 53, 173 N.E.2d 35 (1961), reexamined and overturned its earlier decisions which had allowed admission. In addition to the reasons set forth in Kercheval, which was quoted at length, the court pointed out that the effect of admitting the plea was to compel defendant to take the stand by way of explanation and to open the way for the prosecution to call the lawyer who had represented him at the time of entering the plea. State court decisions for and against admissibility are collected in Annot., 86 A.L.R.2d 326.

Pleas of *nolo contendere* are recognized by Rule 11 of the Rules of Criminal Procedure, although the law of numerous States is to the contrary. The present rule gives effect to the principal traditional characteristic of the *nolo* plea, i.e. avoiding the admission of guilt which is inherent in pleas of guilty. This position is consistent with the construction of Section 5 of the Clayton Act, 15 U.S.C. § 16(a), recognizing the inconclusive and compromise nature of judgments based on *nolo* pleas. *General Electric Co. v. City of San Antonio,* 334 F.2d 480 (5th Cir.1964); *Commonwealth Edison Co. v. Allis–Chalmers Mfg. Co.,* 323 F.2d 412 (7th Cir.1963), cert. denied 376 U.S. 939, 84 S.Ct. 794, 11 L.Ed.2d 659; *Armco Steel Corp. v. North Dakota,* 376 F.2d 206 (8th Cir.1967); *City of Burbank v. General Electric Co.,* 329 F.2d 825 (9th Cir.1964). See also state court decisions in Annot., 18 A.L.R.2d 1287, 1314.

Exclusion of offers to plead guilty or *nolo* has as its purpose the promotion of disposition of criminal cases by compromise. As pointed out in McCormick § 251, p. 543.

"Effective criminal law administration in many localities would hardly be possible if a large proportion of the charges were not disposed of by such compromises."

See also *People v. Hamilton,* 60 Cal.2d 105, 32 Cal.Rptr. 4, 383 P.2d 412 (1963), discussing legislation designed to achieve this result. As with compromise offers generally, Rule 408, free communication is needed, and security against having an offer of compromise or related statement admitted in evidence effectively encourages it.

Limiting the exclusionary rule to use against the accused is consistent with the purpose of the rule, since the possibility of use for or against other persons will not impair the effectiveness of withdrawing pleas or the freedom of discussion which the rule is designed to foster. See A.B.A. Standards Relating to Pleas of Guilty § 2.2 (1968). See also the narrower provisions of New Jersey Evidence Rule 52(2) and the unlimited exclusion provided in California Evidence Code § 1153.

1974 Enactment

The Committee added the phrase "Except as otherwise provided by Act of Congress" to Rule 410 as submitted by the Court in order to preserve particular congressional policy judgments as to the effect of a plea of guilty or of nolo contendere. See 15 U.S.C. 16(a). The Committee intends that its amendment refers to both present statutes and statutes subsequently enacted. House Report No. 93–650.

As adopted by the House, rule 410 would make inadmissible pleas of guilty or nolo contendere subsequently withdrawn as well as offers to make such pleas. Such a rule is clearly justified as a means of encouraging pleading. However, the House rule would then go on to render inadmissible for any purpose statements made in connection with these pleas or offers as well.

The committee finds this aspect of the House rule unjustified. Of course, in certain circumstances such statements should be excluded. If, for example, a plea is vitiated because of coercion, statements made in connection with the plea may also have been coerced and should be inadmissible on that basis. In other cases, however, voluntary statements of an accused made in court on the record, in connection with a plea, and determined by a court to be reliable should be admissible even though the plea is subsequently withdrawn. This is particularly true in those cases where, if the House rule were in effect, a defendant would be able to contradict his previous statements and thereby lie with impunity [See *Harris v. New York,* 401 U.S. 222 (1971)]. To prevent such an injustice, the rule has been modified to permit the use of such statements for the limited purposes of impeachment and in subsequent perjury or false statement prosecutions. Senate Report No. 93–1277.

The House bill provides that evidence of a guilty or nolo contendere plea, of an offer of either plea, or of statements made in connection with such pleas or offers of such pleas, is inadmissible in any civil or criminal action, case or proceeding against the person making such plea or offer. The Senate amendment makes the rule inapplicable to a voluntary and reliable statement made in court on the record where the statement is offered in a subsequent prosecution of the declarant for perjury or false statement.

The issues raised by Rule 410 are also raised by proposed Rule 11(e)(6) of the Federal Rules of Criminal Procedure presently pending before Congress. This proposed rule, which deals with the admissibility of pleas of guilty or nolo contendere, offers to make such pleas, and statements made in connection with such pleas, was promulgated by the Supreme Court on April 22, 1974, and in the absence of congressional action will become effective on August 1, 1975. The conferees intend to make no change in the presently-existing case law until that date, leaving the courts free to develop rules in this area on a case-by-case basis.

The Conferees further determined that the issues presented by the use of guilty and nolo contendere pleas, offers of such pleas, and statements made in connection with such pleas or offers, can be explored in greater detail during Congressional consideration of Rule 11(e)(6) of the Federal Rules of Criminal Procedure. The Conferees believe, therefore, that it is best to defer its effective date until August 1, 1975. The Conferees intend that Rule 410 would be superseded by any subsequent Federal Rule of Criminal Procedure or act of Congress with which it is inconsistent, if the Federal Rule of Criminal Procedure or Act of Congress takes effect or becomes law after the date of the enactment of the act establishing the rules of evidence.

The conference adopts the Senate amendment with an amendment that expresses the above intentions. House Report No. 93–1597.

1979 Amendments

Present rule 410 conforms to rule 11(e)(6) of the Federal Rules of Criminal Procedure. A proposed amendment to rule 11(e)(6) would clarify the circumstances in which pleas, plea discussions and related statements are inadmissible in evidence: see Advisory Committee Note thereto. The amendment proposed above would make comparable changes in rule 410.

HISTORICAL NOTES

Revision Notes and Legislative Reports

1975 Acts. House Report No. 94–599, see 1975 U.S. Code Cong. and Adm. News, p. 1585.

References in Text

Rule 11 of the Federal Rules of Criminal Procedure, referred to in par. (3), is classified to Title 18, Federal Rules of Criminal Procedure.

CROSS REFERENCES

Antitrust actions, final judgments or decrees in favor of government as prima facie evidence, see 15 USCA § 16.

Arrest of judgment motion, time, see Fed.Rules Cr.Proc. Rule 34, 18 USCA.

Motion attacking sentence, see 28 USCA § 2255.

Withdrawal of plea of guilty or nolo contendere, see Fed. Rules Cr.Proc. Rule 32, 18 USCA.

Admissibility of statements made in plea negotiations. Daniel J. Capra, 211 N.Y.L.J. 3 (May 13, 1994).

Evidentiary admissions of defense counsel in federal criminal cases. Gary S. Humble, 24 Am.Crim.L.Rev. 93 (1986).

Federal Rules of Evidence and the political process. David P. Leonard, 22 Fordham Urb.L.J. 305 (1995).

Making form follow function: Considerations in creating and applying a statutory parent-child privilege. J. Tyson Covey, 1990 U.Ill.L.Rev. 879 (1990).

Plea for nolo. Joel Cohen, 215 N.Y.L.J. 1 (Jan. 16, 1996).

Preview of the 1994–95 Supreme Court term. Elkan Abramowitz, 212 N.Y.L.J. 3 (Nov. 1, 1994).

Proffer and informal immunity agreements. Elkan Abramowitz, 213 N.Y.L.J. 3 (March 7, 1995).

Will plea bargaining survive United States v. Mezzanatto? 74 Or.L.Rev. 1365 (1995).

Rule 411. Liability Insurance

Evidence that a person was or was not insured against liability is not admissible upon the issue whether the person acted negligently or otherwise wrongfully. This rule does not require the exclusion of evidence of insurance against liability when offered for another purpose, such as proof of agency, ownership, or control, or bias or prejudice of a witness.

(Pub.L. 93–595, § 1, Jan. 2, 1975, 88 Stat.1933; Mar. 2, 1987, eff. Oct. 1, 1987.)

ADVISORY COMMITTEE NOTES

1972 Proposed Rules

The courts have with substantial unanimity rejected evidence of liability insurance for the purpose of proving fault, and absence of liability insurance as proof of lack of fault. At best the inference of fault from the fact of insurance coverage is a tenuous one, as is its converse. More important, no doubt, has been the feeling that knowledge of the presence or absence of liability insurance would induce juries to decide cases on improper grounds. McCormick § 168; Annot., 4 A.L.R.2d 761. The rule is drafted in broad terms so as to include contributory negligence or other fault of a plaintiff as well as fault of a defendant.

The second sentence points out the limits of the rule, using well established illustrations. *Id.*

For similar rules see Uniform Rule 54; California Evidence Code § 1155; Kansas Code of Civil Procedure § 60–454; New Jersey Evidence Rule 54.

1987 Amendments

The amendment is technical. No substantive change is intended.

CROSS REFERENCES

Discovery of insurance agreements, see Fed.Rules Civ. Proc. Rule 26, 28 USCA.

Rule 412. Sex Offense Cases; Relevance of Alleged Victim's Past Sexual Behavior or Alleged Sexual Predisposition

(a) Evidence generally inadmissible.—The following evidence is not admissible in any civil or criminal proceeding involving alleged sexual misconduct except as provided in subdivisions (b) and (c):

(1) Evidence offered to prove that any alleged victim engaged in other sexual behavior.

(2) Evidence offered to prove any alleged victim's sexual predisposition.

(b) Exceptions.—

(1) In a criminal case, the following evidence is admissible, if otherwise admissible under these rules:

(A) evidence of specific instances of sexual behavior by the alleged victim offered to prove that a person other than the accused was the source of semen, injury or other physical evidence;

(B) evidence of specific instances of sexual behavior by the alleged victim with respect to the person accused of the sexual misconduct offered by the accused to prove consent or by the prosecution; and

(C) evidence the exclusion of which would violate the constitutional rights of the defendant.

(2) In a civil case, evidence offered to prove the sexual behavior or sexual predisposition of any alleged victim is admissible if it is otherwise admissible under these rules and its probative value substantially outweighs the danger of harm to any victim and of unfair prejudice to any party. Evidence of an alleged victim's reputation is admissible only if it has been placed in controversy by the alleged victim.

(c) Procedure to determine admissibility.—

(1) A party intending to offer evidence under subdivision (b) must—

(A) file a written motion at least 14 days before trial specifically describing the evidence and stating the purpose for which it is offered unless the court, for good cause requires a different time for filing or permits filing during trial; and

(B) serve the motion on all parties and notify the alleged victim or, when appropriate, the alleged victim's guardian or representative.

(2) Before admitting evidence under this rule the court must conduct a hearing in camera and afford the victim and parties a right to attend and be heard. The motion, related papers, and the record of the hearing must be sealed and remain under seal unless the court orders otherwise.

(Added Pub.L. 95–540, § 2(a), Oct. 28, 1978, 92 Stat. 2046, and amended Pub.L. 100–690, Title VII, § 7046(a), Nov. 18, 1988, 102 Stat. 4400; Apr. 29, 1994, eff. Dec. 1, 1994; Pub.L. 103–322, Title IV, § 40141(b), Sept. 13, 1994, 108 Stat. 1919.)

ADVISORY COMMITTEE NOTES

1994 Amendments

Rule 412 has been revised to diminish some of the confusion engendered by the original rule and to expand the protection afforded alleged victims of sexual misconduct. Rule 412 applies to both civil and criminal proceedings. The rule aims to safeguard the alleged victim against the invasion of privacy, potential embarrassment and sexual stereotyping that is associated with public disclosure of intimate sexual details and the infusion of sexual innuendo into the factfinding process. By affording victims protection in most instances, the rule also encourages victims of sexual misconduct to institute and to participate in legal proceedings against alleged offenders

Rule 412 seeks to achieve these objectives by barring evidence relating to the alleged victim's sexual behavior or alleged sexual predisposition, whether offered as substantive evidence of for impeachment, except in designated circumstances in which the probative value of the evidence significantly outweighs possible harm to the victim.

The revised rule applies in all cases involving sexual misconduct without regard to whether the alleged victim or person accused is a party to the litigation. Rule 412 extends to "pattern" witnesses in both criminal and civil cases whose testimony about other instances of sexual misconduct by the person accused is otherwise admissible. When the case does not involve alleged sexual misconduct, evidence relating to a third-party witness' alleged sexual activities is not within the ambit of Rule 412. The witness will, however, be protected by other rules such as Rules 404 and 608, as well as Rule 403.

The terminology "alleged victim" is used because there will frequently be a factual dispute as to whether sexual misconduct occurred. It does not connote any requirement that the misconduct be alleged in the pleadings. Rule 412 does not, however, apply unless the person against whom the evidence is offered can reasonably be characterized as a "victim of alleged sexual misconduct." When this is not the case, as for instance in a defamation action involving statements concerning sexual misconduct in which the evidence is offered to show that the alleged defamatory statements were true or did not damage the plaintiff's reputation, neither Rule 404 nor this rule will operate to bar the evidence; Rule 401 and 403 will continue to control. Rule 412 will, however, apply in a Title VII action in which the plaintiff has alleged sexual harassment.

The reference to a person "accused" is also used in a non-technical sense. There is no requirement that there be a criminal charge pending against the person or even that the misconduct would constitute a criminal offense. Evidence offered to prove allegedly false prior claims by the victim is not barred by Rule 412. However, the evidence is subject to the requirements of Rule 404.

Subdivision (a). As amended, Rule 412 bars evidence offered to prove the victim's sexual behavior and alleged sexual predisposition. Evidence, which might otherwise be admissible under Rules 402, 404(b), 405, 607, 608, 609 of some other evidence rule, must be excluded if Rule 412 so requires. The word "other" is used to suggest some flexibility in admitting evidence "intrinsic" to the alleged sexual misconduct. *Cf.* Committee Note to 1991 amendment to Rule 404(b)

Past sexual behavior connotes all activities that involve actual physical conduct, i.e. sexual intercourse or sexual contact. *See, e.g., United States v. Galloway*, 937 F.2d 542 (10th Cir. 1991), *cert. denied*, 113 S.Ct. 418 (1992) (use of contraceptives inadmissible since use implies sexual activity); *United States v. One Feather*, 702 F.2d 736 (8th Cir. 1983) (birth of an illegitimate child inadmissible); *State v. Carmichael*, 727 P.2d 918, 925 (Kan. 1986) (evidence of venereal disease inadmissible). In addition, the word "behavior" should be construed to include activities of the mind, such as fantasies of dreams. *See* 23 C. Wright and K. Graham, Jr., *Federal Practice and Procedure*, § 5384 at p. 548 (1980) ("While there may be some doubt under statutes that require 'conduct,' it would seem that the language of Rule 412 is broad enough to encompass the behavior of the mind.").

The rule has been amended to also exclude all other evidence relating to an alleged victim of sexual misconduct that is offered to prove a sexual predisposition. This amendment is designed to exclude evidence that does not directly refer to sexual activities or thoughts but that the proponent believes may have a sexual connotation for the factfinder. Admission of such evidence would contravene Rule 412's objectives of shielding the alleged victim from potential embarrassment and safeguarding the victim against stereotypical thinking. Consequently, unless the (b)(2) exception is satisfied, evidence such as that relating to the alleged victim's mode of dress, speech, or life-style will not be admissible.

The introductory phrase in subdivision (a) was deleted because it lacked clarity and contained no explicit reference to the other provisions of the law that were intended to be overridden. The conditional clause, "except as provided in subdivisions (b) and (c)" is intended to make clear that evidence of the types described in subdivision (a) is admissible only under the strictures of those sections.

The reason for extending the rule to all criminal cases is obvious. The strong social policy of protecting a victim's privacy and encouraging victims to come forward to report criminal acts is not confined to cases that involve a charge of sexual assault. The need to protect the victim is equally great when a defendant is charged with kidnapping, and evidence is offered, either to prove motive or as background, that the defendant sexually assaulted the victim.

The reason for extending Rule 412 to civil cases is equally obvious. The need to protect alleged victims against invasions of privacy, potential embarrassment, and unwarranted sexual stereotyping, and the wish to encourage victims to come forward when they have been sexually molested do not disappear because the context has shifted from a criminal prosecution to a claim for damages or injunctive relief. There is a strong social policy in not only punishing those who engage in sexual misconduct, but in also providing relief to the victim. Thus, Rule 412 applies in any civil case in which a person claims to be the victim of sexual misconduct, such as actions for sexual battery or sexual harassment.

Subdivision (b). Subdivision (b) spells out the specific circumstances in which some evidence may be admissible that would otherwise be barred by the general rule expressed in subdivision (a). As amended, Rule 412 will be virtually unchanged in criminal cases, but will provide protection to any person alleged to be a victim of sexual misconduct regardless of the charge actually brought against an accused. A new exception has been added for civil cases.

In a criminal case, evidence may be admitted under subdivision (b)(1) pursuant to three possible exceptions, provided the evidence also satisfies other requirements for admissibility specified in the Federal Rules of Evidence, including Rule 403. Subdivisions (b)(1)(A) and (b)(1)(B) require proof in the form of specific instances of sexual behavior in recognition of the limited probative value and dubious reliability of evidence of reputation or evidence in the form of an opinion.

Under subdivision (b)(1)(A), evidence of specific instances of sexual behavior with persons other than the person whose sexual misconduct is alleged may be admissible if it is offered to prove that another person was the source of semen, injury or other physical evidence. Where the prosecution has directly or indirectly asserted that the physical evidence originated with the accused, the defendant must be afforded an opportunity to prove that another person was responsible. See *United States v. Begay*, 937 F.2d 515, 523 n. 10 (10th Cir. 1991). Evidence offered for the specific purpose identified in this subdivision may still be excluded if it does not satisfy Rules 401 or 403. *See, e.g., United States v. Azure*, 845 F.2d 1503, 1505-06 (8th Cir. 1988) (10 year old victim's injuries indicated recent use of force; court excluded evidence of consensual sexual activities with witness who testified at in camera hearing that he had never hurt victim and failed to establish recent activities).

Under the exception in subdivision (b)(1)(B), evidence of specific instances of sexual behavior with respect to the person whose sexual misconduct is alleged is admissible if offered to prove consent, or offered by the prosecution. Admissible pursuant to this exception might be evidence of prior instances of sexual activities between the alleged victim and the accused, as well as statements in which the alleged victim expresses an intent to engage in sexual intercourse with the accused, or voiced sexual fantasies involving that specific accused. In a prosecution for child sexual abuse, for example, evidence of uncharged sexual activity between the accused and the alleged victim offered by the prosecution may be admissible pursuant to Rule 404(b) to show a pattern of behavior. Evidence relating to the victim's alleged sexual predisposition is not admissible pursuant to this exception.

Under subdivision (b)(1)(C), evidence of specific instances of conduct may not be excluded if the result would be to deny a criminal defendant the protections afforded by the Constitution. For example, statements in which the victim has expressed an intent to have sex with the first person encountered on a particular occasion might not be excluded without violating the due process right of a rape defendant seeking to prove consent. Recognition of this basic principle was expressed on subdivision (b)(1) of the original rule. The United States Supreme Court has recognized that in various circumstances a defendant may have a right to introduce evidence otherwise precluded by an evidence rule under the Confrontation Clause. *See, e.g., Olden v. Kentucky*, 488 U.S. 227 (1988) (defendant in rape cases had right to inquire into alleged victim's cohabitation with another man to show bias).

Subdivision (b)(2) governs the admissibility of otherwise proscribed evidence in civil cases. It employs a balancing test rather than the specific exceptions stated in subdivision (b)(1) in recognition of the difficulty of foreseeing future developments in the law. Greater flexibility is needed to accommodate evolving causes of action such as claims for sexual harassment.

The balancing test requires the proponent of the evidence, whether plaintiff or defendant, to convince the court that the probative value of the proffered evidence "substantially outweighs the danger of harm to any victim and of unfair prejudice of any party." This test for admitting evidence offered to prove sexual behavior or sexual propensity in civil cases differs in three respects from the general rule governing admissibility set forth in Rule 403. First, it Reverses that usual procedure spelled out in Rule 403 by shifting the burden to the proponent to demonstrate admissibility rather than making the opponent justify exclusion of the evidence. Second, the standard expressed in subdivision (b)(2) is more stringent than in the original rule; it raises the threshold for admission by requiring that the probative value of the evidence *substantially* outweigh the specified dangers. Finally, the Rule 412 test puts "harm to the victim" on the scale in addition to prejudice to the parties.

Evidence of reputation may be received in a civil case only if the alleged victim has put his or her reputation into controversy. The victim may do so without making a specific allegation in a pleading. *Cf.* Fed.R.Civ.P. 35(a).

Subdivision (c). Amended subdivision (c) is more concise and understandable than the subdivision it replaces. The requirement of a motion before trial is continued in the amended rule, as is the provision that a late motion may be permitted for good cause shown. In deciding whether to permit late filing, the court may take into account the conditions previously included in the rule: namely whether the evidence is newly discovered and could not have been obtained earlier through the existence of due diligence, and whether the issue to which such evidence relates has newly arisen in the case. The rule recognizes that in some instances the circumstances that justify an application to introduce evidence otherwise barred by Rule 412 will not become apparent until trial.

The amended rule provides that before admitting evidence that falls within that prohibition of Rule 412(a), the court must hold a hearing in camera at which the alleged victim and any party must be afforded the right to be present and an opportunity to be heard. All papers connected with the motion must be kept and remain under seal during the course of trial and appellate proceedings unless otherwise ordered. This is to assure that the privacy of the alleged victim is preserved in all cases in which the court rules that proffered evidence is not admissible, and in which the hearing refers to matters that are not received, or are received in another form.

The procedures set forth in subdivision (c) do not apply to discovery of a victim's past sexual conduct or predisposition in civil cases, which will be continued to be governed by Fed. R. Civ. P. 26. In order not to undermine the rationale of Rule 412, however, courts should enter appropriate orders pursuant to Fed. R. Civ. P. 26 (c) to protect the victim against unwarranted inquiries and to ensure confidentiality. Courts should presumptively issue protective orders barring discovery unless the party seeking discovery makes a showing that the evidence sought to be discovered would be relevant under the facts and theories of the particular case, and cannot be obtained except through discovery. In an action for sexual harassment, for instance, while some evidence of the alleged victim's sexual behavior and/or predisposition in the workplace may perhaps be relevant, non-work place conduct will usually be irrelevant. *Cf. Burns v. McGregor Electronic Industries, Inc.*, 989 F.2d 959, 962-63 (8th Cir. 1993) (posing for a nude magazine outside work hours is irrelevant to issue of unwelcomeness of sexual advances at work). Confidentiality orders should be presumptively granted as well.

One substantive change made in subdivision (c) is the elimination of the following sentence: "Notwithstanding subdivision (b) of Rule 104, if the relevancy of the evidence which the accused seeks to offer in trial depends upon the fulfillment of a condition of fact, the court, at the hearing in chambers or at a subsequent hearing in chambers scheduled for such purpose, shall accept evidence on the issue of whether such condition of fact is fulfilled and shall determine such issue." On its face, this language would appear to authorize a trial judge to exclude evidence of past sexual conduct between alleged victim and an accused or a defendant in a civil case based upon the judge's belief that such past acts did not occur. Such an authorization raises questions of invasion of the right to a jury trial under the Sixth and Seventh Amendments. *See* 1 S. Saltzburg & M. Martin, *Federal Rules of Evidence Manual*, 396-97 (5th ed. 1990).

The Advisory Committee concluded that the amended rule provided adequate protection for all persons claiming to be the victims of sexual misconduct, and that it was inadvisable to continue to include a provision in the rule that has been confusing and that raises substantial constitutional issues. [Advisory Committee Note adopted by Congressional Conference Report accompanying Pub.L. 103–322. See H.R. Conf. Rep. No. 103–711, 103rd Cong., 2nd Sess., 383 (1994).]

Congressional Discussion

The following discussion in the House of Representatives of October 10, 1978, preceded passage of H.R. 4727, which enacted Rule 412. The discussion appears in 124 Cong.Record, at page H. 11944.

Mr. MANN. Mr. Speaker, I yield myself such time as I may consume.

Mr. Speaker, for many years in this country, evidentiary rules have permitted the introduction of evidence about a rape victim's prior sexual conduct. Defense lawyers were permitted great latitude in bringing out intimate details about a rape victim's life. Such evidence quite often serves no real purpose and only results in embarrassment to the rape victim and unwarranted public intrusion into her private life.

The evidentiary rules that permit such inquiry have in recent years come under question; and the States have taken the lead to change and modernize their evidentiary rules about evidence of a rape victim's prior sexual behavior. The bill before us similarly seeks to modernize the Federal Evidentiary rules.

The present Federal Rules of Evidence reflect the traditional approach. If a defendant in a rape case raises the defense of consent, that defendant may then offer evidence about the victim's prior sexual behavior. Such evidence may be in the form of opinion evidence, evidence of reputation, or evidence of specific instances of behavior. Rule 404(a)(2) of the Federal Rules of Evidence permits the introduction of evidence of a "pertinent character trait." The advisory committee note to that rule cites, as an example of what the rule covers, the character of a rape victim when the issue is consent. Rule 405 of the Federal Rules of Evidence permits the use of opinion or reputation evidence or the use of evidence of specific behavior to show a character trait.

Thus, Federal evidentiary rules permit a wide ranging inquiry into the private conduct of a rape victim, even though that conduct may have at best a tenuous connection to the offense for which the defendant is being tried.

H.R. 4727 amends the Federal Rules of Evidence to add a new rule, applicable only in criminal cases, to spell out when, and under what conditions, evidence of a rape victim's prior sexual behavior can be admitted. The new rule provides that reputation or opinion evidence about a rape victim's prior sexual behavior is not admissible. The new rule also provides that a court cannot admit evidence of specific instances of a rape victim's prior sexual conduct except in three circumstances.

The first circumstance is where the Constitution requires that the evidence be admitted. This exception is intended to cover those infrequent instances where, because of an unusual chain of circumstances, the general rule of inadmissibility, if followed, would result in denying the defendant a constitutional right.

The second circumstance in which the defendant can offer evidence of specific instances of a rape victim's prior sexual behavior is where the defendant raises the issue of consent and the evidence is of sexual behavior with the defendant. To admit such evidence, however, the court must find that the evidence is relevant and that its probative value outweighs the danger of unfair prejudice.

The third circumstance in which a court can admit evidence of specific instances of a rape victim's prior sexual behavior is where the evidence is of behavior with someone other than the defendant and is offered by the defendant on the issue of whether or not he was the source of semen or injury. Again, such evidence will be admitted only if the court finds that the evidence is relevant and that its probative value outweighs the danger of unfair prejudice.

The new rule further provides that before evidence is admitted under any of these exceptions, there must be an in camera hearing—that is, a proceeding that takes place in the judge's chambers out of the presence of the jury and the general public. At this hearing, the defendant will present the evidence he intends to offer and be able to argue why it should be admitted. The prosecution, of course, will be able to argue against that evidence being admitted.

The purpose of the in camera hearing is twofold. It gives the defendant an opportunity to demonstrate to the court why certain evidence is admissible and ought to be presented to the jury. At the same time, it protects the privacy of the rape victim in those instances when the court finds that evidence is inadmissible. Of course, if the court finds the evidence to be admissible, the evidence will be presented to the jury in open court.

The effect of this legislation, therefore, is to preclude the routine use of evidence of specific instances of a rape victim's prior sexual behavior. Such evidence will be admitted only in clearly and narrowly defined circumstances and only after an in camera hearing. In determining the admissibility of such evidence, the court will consider all of the facts and circumstances surrounding the evidence, such as the amount of time that lapsed between the alleged prior act and the rape charged in the prosecution. The greater the lapse of time, of course, the less likely it is that such evidence will be admitted.

Mr. Speaker, the principal purpose of this legislation is to protect rape victims from the degrading and embarrassing disclosure of intimate details about their private lives. It does so by narrowly circumscribing when such evidence may be admitted. It does not do so, however, by sacrificing any constitutional right possessed by the defendant. The bill before us fairly balances the interests involved—the rape victim's interest in protecting her private life from unwarranted public exposure; the defendant's interest in being able adequately to present a defense by offering relevant and probative evidence; and society's interest in a fair trial, one where unduly prejudicial evidence is not permitted to becloud the issues before the jury.

I urge support of the bill.

Mr. WIGGINS. Mr. Speaker, I yield myself such time as I may consume.

(Mr. WIGGINS asked and was given permission to revise and extend his remarks.)

Mr. WIGGINS. Mr. Speaker, this legislation addresses itself to a subject that is certainly a proper one for our consideration. Many of us have been troubled for years about the indiscriminate and prejudicial use of testimony with respect to a victim's prior sexual behavior in rape and similar cases. This bill deals with that problem. It is not, in my opinion, Mr. Speaker, a perfect bill in the manner in which it deals with the problem, but my objections are not so fundamental as would lead me to oppose the bill.

I think, Mr. Speaker, that it is unwise to adopt a per se rule absolutely excluding evidence of reputation and opinion with respect to the victim—and this bill does that—but it is difficult for me to foresee the specific case in which such evidence might be admissible. The trouble is this, Mr. Speaker: None of us can foresee perfectly all of the various circumstances under which the propriety of evidence might be before the court. If this bill has a defect, in my view it is because it adopts a per se rule with respect to opinion and reputation evidence.

Alternatively we might have permitted that evidence to be considered in camera as we do other evidence under the bill.

I should note, however, in fairness, having expressed minor reservations, that the bill before the House at this time does improve significantly upon the bill which was presented to our committee.

I will not detail all of those improvements but simply observe that the bill upon which we shall soon vote is a superior product to that which was initially considered by our subcommittee.

Mr. Speaker, I ask my colleagues to vote for this legislation as being, on balance, worthy of their support, and urge its adoption.

I reserve the balance of my time.

Mr. MANN. Mr. Speaker, this legislation has more than 100 cosponsors, but its principal sponsor, as well as its architect is the gentlewoman from New York (Ms. Holtzman). As the drafter of the legislation she will be able to provide additional information about the probable scope and effect of the legislation.

I yield such time as she may consume to the gentlewoman from New York (Ms. Holtzman).

(Ms. HOLTZMAN asked and was given permission to revise and extend her remarks.)

Ms. HOLTZMAN. Mr. Speaker, I would like to begin first by complimenting the distinguished gentleman from South Carolina (Mr. Mann), the chairman of the subcommittee, for his understanding of the need for corrective legislation in this area and for the fairness with which he has conducted the subcommittee hearings. I would like also to compliment the other members of the subcommittee, including the gentleman from California (Mr. Wiggins).

Too often in this country victims of rape are humiliated and harassed when they report and prosecute the rape. Bullied and cross-examined about their prior sexual experiences, many find the trial almost as degrading as the rape itself. Since rape trials become inquisitions into the victim's morality, not trials of the defendant's innocence or guilt, it is not surprising that it is the least reported crime. It is estimated that as few as one in ten rapes is ever reported.

Mr. Speaker, over 30 States have taken some action to limit the vulnerability of rape victims to such humiliating cross-examination of their past sexual experiences and intimate personal histories. In federal courts, however, it is permissible still to subject rape victims to brutal cross-examination about their past sexual histories. H.R. 4727 would rectify this problem in Federal courts and I hope, also serve as a model to suggest to the remaining states that reform of existing rape laws is important to the equity of our criminal justice system.

H.R. 4727 applies only to criminal rape cases in Federal courts. The bill provides that neither the prosecution nor the defense can introduce any reputation or opinion evidence about the victim's past sexual conduct. It does permit, however, the introduction of specific evidence about the victim's past sexual conduct in three very limited circumstances.

First, this evidence can be introduced if it deals with the victim's past sexual relations with the defendant and is relevant to the issue of whether she consented. Second, when the defendant claims he had no relations with the victim, he can use evidence of the victim's past sexual relations with others if the evidence rebuts the victim's claim that the rape caused certain physical consequences, such as semen or injury. Finally, the evidence can be introduced if it is constitutionally required. This last exception, added in subcommittee, will insure that the defendant's constitutional rights are protected.

Before any such evidence can be introduced, however, the court must determine at a hearing in chambers that the evidence falls within one of the exceptions.

Furthermore, unless constitutionally required, the evidence of specific instances of prior sexual conduct cannot be introduced at all it if would be more prejudicial and inflammatory that probative.

Mr. Speaker, I urge adoption of this bill. It will protect women from both injustice and indignity.

Mr. MANN. Mr. Speaker, I have no further requests for time, and I yield back the balance of my time.

Mr. WIGGINS. Mr. Speaker, I have no further requests for time, and yield back the balance of my time.

The SPEAKER pro tempore. The question is on the motion offered by the gentleman from South Carolina (Mr. Mann) that the House suspend the rules and pass the bill H.R. 4727, as amended.

The question was taken; and (two-thirds having voted in favor thereof) the rules were suspended and the bill, as amended, was passed.

A motion to reconsider was laid on the table.

HISTORICAL NOTES

Revision Notes and Legislative Reports

1988 Acts. For Related Reports, see 1988 U.S. Code Cong. and Adm. News, p. 5937.

Effective and Applicability Provisions

1978 Acts. Section 3 of Pub.L. 95–540 provided that: "The amendments made by this Act [enacting this rule] shall apply to trials which begin more than thirty days after the date of the enactment of this Act [Oct. 28, 1978]."

Rule 413. Evidence of Similar Crimes in Sexual Assault Cases

(a) In a criminal case in which the defendant is accused of an offense of sexual assault, evidence of the defendant's commission of another offense or offenses of sexual assault is admissible, and may be considered for its bearing on any matter to which it is relevant.

(b) In a case in which the Government intends to offer evidence under this rule, the attorney for the Government shall disclose the evidence to the defendant, including statements of witnesses or a summary of the substance of any testimony that is expected to be offered, at least fifteen days before the scheduled date of trial or at such later time as the court may allow for good cause.

(c) This rule shall not be construed to limit the admission or consideration of evidence under any other rule.

(d) For purposes of this rule and Rule 415, "offense of sexual assault" means a crime under Federal law or the law of a State (as defined in section 513 of title 18, United States Code) that involved—

(1) any conduct proscribed by chapter 109A of title 18, United States Code;

(2) contact, without consent, between any part of the defendant's body or an object and the genitals or anus of another person;

(3) contact, without consent, between the genitals or anus of the defendant and any part of another person's body;

(4) deriving sexual pleasure or gratification from the infliction of death, bodily injury, or physical pain on another person; or

(5) an attempt or conspiracy to engage in conduct described in paragraphs (1)–(4).

(Added Pub.L. 103–322, Title XXXII, § 320935(a), Sept. 13, 1994, 108 Stat. 2136.)

HISTORICAL NOTES

Effective and Applicability Provisions

Section 320935(b) to (e) of Pub.L. 103–322, as amended Pub.L. 104–208, Div. A, Title I, § 101(a), [Title I, § 120], Sept. 30, 1996, 110 Stat. 3009–25, provided that:

"**(b) Implementation.**—The amendments made by subsection (a) [enacting Federal Rules of Evidence 413, 414, and 415] shall become effective pursuant to subsection (d).

"**(c) Recommendations by Judicial Conference.**—Not later than 150 days after the date of enactment of this Act [Sept. 13, 1994], the Judicial Conference of the United States shall transmit to Congress a report containing recommendations for amending the Federal Rules of Evidence as they affect the admission of evidence of a defendant's prior sexual assault or child molestation crimes in cases involving sexual assault and child molestation. The Rules Enabling Act [28 U.S.C.A. § 2072] shall not apply to the recommendations made by the Judicial Conference pursuant to this section.

"**(d) Congressional action.**—

"(1) If the recommendations described in subsection (c) are the same as the amendment made by subsection (a) [enacting Federal Rules of Evidence 413, 414, and 415], then the amendments made by subsection (a) shall become effective 30 days after the transmittal of the recommendations.

"(2) If the recommendations described in subsection (c) are different than the amendments made by subsection (a) [enacting Federal Rules of Evidence 413, 414, and 415], the amendments made by subsection (a) shall become effective 150 days after the transmittal of the recommendations unless otherwise provided by law.

"(3) If the Judicial Conference fails to comply with subsection (c), the amendments made by subsection (a) [enacting Federal of Evidence 413, 414, and 415] shall become effective 150 days after the date the recommendations were due under subsection (c) unless otherwise provided by law.

"**(e) Application.**—The amendments made by subsection (a) [enacting Federal Rules of Evidence 413, 414, and 415] shall apply to proceedings commenced on or after the effective date of such amendments, including all trials commenced on or after the effective date of such amendments."

[The Judicial Conference transmitted a report to Congress on Feb. 9, 1995, containing recommendations described in subsec. (c) different than the amendments made by section 320935(a) of Pub.L. 103–322. Congress did not follow the recommendations submitted or provide otherwise by law. Accordingly, Rules 413, 414, and 415, as added by section 320935(a) of Pub.L. 103–322, became effective on July 9, 1995.]

Submitted to the Congress in accordance with section 320935 of the Violent Crime Control and Law Enforcement Act of 1994 (Pub.L. No. 103–322)

I. INTRODUCTION

This report is transmitted to Congress in accordance with the Violent Crime Control and Law Enforcement Act of 1994, Pub.L. No. 103–322 (September 13, 1994). Section 320935 of the Act invited the Judicial Conference of the United States within 150 days (February 10, 1995) to submit "a report containing recommendations for amending the Federal Rules of Evidence as they affect the admission of evidence of a defendant's prior sexual assault or child molestation crimes in cases involving sexual assault or child molestation."

Under the Act, new Rules 413, 414, and 415 would be added to the Federal Rules of Evidence. These Rules would admit evidence of a defendant's past similar acts in criminal and civil cases involving a sexual assault or child molestation offense for its bearing on any matter to which it is relevant. The effective date of new Rules 413–415 is contingent in part upon the nature of the recommendations submitted by the Judicial Conference.

After careful study, the Judicial Conference urges Congress to reconsider its decision on the policy questions underlying the new rules for reasons set out in Part III below.

If Congress does not reconsider its decision on the underlying policy questions, the Judicial Conference recommends incorporation of the provisions of new Rules 413–415 as amendments to Rules 404 and 405 of the Federal Rules of Evidence. The amendments would not change the substance of the congressional enactment but would clarify drafting ambiguities and eliminate possible constitutional infirmities.

II. BACKGROUND

Under the Act, the Judicial Conference was provided 150 days within which to make and submit to Congress alternative recommendations to new Evidence Rules 413–415. Consideration of Rules 413–415 by the Judicial Conference was specifically excepted from the exacting review procedures set forth in the Rules Enabling Act (codified at 28 U.S.C. §§ 2071–2077). Although the Conference acted on these new rules on an expedited basis to meet the Act's deadlines, the review process was thorough.

The new rules would apply to both civil and criminal cases. Accordingly, the Judicial Conference's Advisory Committee on Criminal Rules and the Advisory Committee on Civil Rules reviewed the rules at separate meetings in October 1994. At the same time and in preparation for its consideration of the new rules, the Advisory Committee on Evidence Rules sent out a notice soliciting comment on new Evidence Rules 413, 414, and 415. The notice was sent to the courts, including all federal judges, about 900 evidence law professors, 40 women's rights organizations, and 1,000 other individuals and interested organizations.

III. DISCUSSION

On October 17–18, 1994, the Advisory Committee on Evidence Rules met in Washington, D.C. It considered the public responses, which included 84 written comments, representing 112 individuals, 8 local and 8 national legal organizations. The overwhelming majority of judges, lawyers, law professors, and legal organizations who responded opposed new Evidence Rules 413, 414, and 415. The principal objections expressed were that the rules would permit the admission of unfairly prejudicial evidence and contained numerous drafting problems not intended by their authors.

The Advisory Committee on Evidence Rules submitted its report to the Judicial Conference Committee on Rules of Practice and Procedure (Standing Committee) for review at its January 11–13, 1995 meeting. The committee's report was unanimous except for a dissenting vote by the representative of the Department of Justice. The advisory committee believed that the concerns expressed by Congress and embodied in new Evidence Rules 413, 414, and 415 are already adequately addressed in the existing Federal Rules of Evidence. In particular, Evidence Rule 404(b) now allows the admission of evidence against a criminal defendant of the commission of prior crimes, wrongs, or acts for specified purposes, including to show intent, plan, motive, preparation, identity, knowledge, or absence of mistake or accident.

Furthermore, the new rules, which are not supported by empirical evidence, could diminish significantly the protections that have safeguarded persons accused in criminal cases and parties in civil cases against undue prejudice. These protections form a fundamental part of American jurisprudence and have evolved under long-standing rules and case law. A significant concern identified by the committee was the danger of convicting a criminal defendant for past, as opposed to charged, behavior or for being a bad person.

In addition, the advisory committee concluded that, because prior bad acts would be admissible even though not the subject of a conviction, mini-trials within trials concerning those acts would result when a defendant seeks to rebut such evidence. The committee also noticed that many of the comments received had concluded that the Rules, as drafted, were mandatory—that is, such evidence had to be admitted regardless of other rules of evidence such as the hearsay rule or the Rule 403 balancing test. The committee believed that this position was arguable because Rules 413–415 declare without qualification that such evidence "is admissible." In contrast, the new Rule 412, passed as part of the same legislation, provided that certain evidence "is admissible if it is otherwise admissible under these Rules." Fed.R.Evid. 412(b)(2). If the critics are right, Rules 413–415 free the prosecution from rules that apply to the defendant—including the hearsay rule and Rule 403. If so, serious constitutional questions would arise.

The Advisory Committees on Criminal and Civil Rules unanimously, except for representatives of the Department of Justice, also opposed the new rules. Those committees also concluded that the new rules would permit the introduction of unreliable but highly prejudicial evidence and would complicate trials by causing mini-trials of other alleged wrongs. After the advisory committees reported, the Standing Committee unanimously, again except for the representative of the Department of Justice, agreed with the view of the advisory committees.

It is important to note the highly unusual unanimity of the members of the Standing and Advisory Committees, composed of over 40 judges, practicing lawyers, and academicians, in taking the view that Rules 413–415 are undesirable. Indeed, the only supporters of the Rules were representatives of the Department of Justice.

For these reasons, the Standing Committee recommended that Congress reconsider its decision on the policy questions embodied in new Evidence Rules 413, 414, and 415.

However, if Congress will not reconsider its decision on the policy questions, the Standing Committee recommended that Congress consider an alternative draft recommended by the Advisory Committee on Evidence Rules. That Committee drafted proposed amendments to existing Evidence Rules 404 and 405 that would both correct ambiguities and possible constitutional infirmities identified in new Evidence Rules 413, 414, and 415 yet still effectuate Congressional intent. In particular, the proposed amendments:

(1) expressly apply the other rules of evidence to evidence offered under the new rules;

(2) expressly allow the party against whom such evidence is offered to use similar evidence in rebuttal;

(3) expressly enumerate the factors to be weighed by a court in making its Rule 403 determination;

(4) render the notice provisions consistent with the provisions in existing Rule 404 regarding criminal cases;

(5) eliminate the special notice provisions of Rules 413–415 in civil cases so that notice will be required as provided in the Federal Rules of Civil Procedure; and

(6) permit reputation or opinion evidence after such evidence is offered by the accused or defendant.

The Standing Committee reviewed the new rules and the alternative recommendations. It concurred with the views of the Evidence Rules Committee and recommended that the Judicial Conference adopt them.

IV. RECOMMENDATIONS

The Judicial Conference concurs with the views of the Standing Committee and urges that Congress reconsider its policy determinations underlying Evidence Rules 413–415. In the alternative, the attached amendments to Evidence Rules 404 and 405 are recommended, in lieu of new Evidence Rules 413, 414, and 415. The alternative amendments to Evidence Rules 404 and 405 are accompanied by the Advisory Committee Notes, which explain them in detail.

RULE 404. CHARACTER EVIDENCE NOT ADMISSIBLE TO PROVE CONDUCT; EXCEPTIONS; OTHER CRIMES

* * * * * *

(4) Character in sexual misconduct cases. Evidence of another act of sexual assault or child molestation, or evidence to rebut such proof or an inference therefrom, if that evidence is otherwise admissible under these rules, in a criminal case in which the accused is charged with sexual assault or child molestation, or in a civil case in which a claim is predicated on a party's alleged commission of sexual assault or child molestation.

(A) In weighing the probative value of such evidence, the court may, as part of its rule 403 determination, consider:

(i) proximity in time to the charged or predicate misconduct;

(ii) similarity to the charged or predicate misconduct;

(iii) frequency of the other acts;

(iv) surrounding circumstances;

(v) relevant intervening events; and

(vi) other relevant similarities or differences.

(B) In a criminal case in which the prosecution intends to offer evidence under this subdivision, it must disclose the evidence, including statements of witnesses or a summary of the substance of any testimony, at a reasonable time in advance of trial, or during trial if the court excuses pretrial notice on good cause shown.

(C) For purposes of this subdivision.

(i) "sexual assault" means conduct—or an attempt or conspiracy to engage in conduct—of the type proscribed by chapter 109A of title 18, United States Code, or conduct that involved deriving sexual pleasure or gratification from inflicting death, bodily injury, or physical pain on another person irrespective of the age of the victim—regardless of whether that conduct would have subjected the actor to federal jurisdiction.

(ii) "child molestation" means conduct—or an attempt or conspiracy to engage in conduct—of the type proscribed by chapter 110 of title 18, United States Code, or conduct, committed in relation to a child below the age of 14 years, either of the type proscribed by chapter 109A of title 18, United States Code, or that involved deriving sexual pleasure or gratification from inflicting death, bodily injury, or physical pain on another person—regardless of whether that conduct would have subjected the actor to federal jurisdiction.

(b) Other crimes, wrongs, or acts. Evidence of other crimes, wrongs, or acts is not admissible to prove the character of a person in order to show action in conformity therewith except as provided in subdivision (a)....

Note to Rule 404(a)(4)

The Committee has redrafted Rules 413, 414 and 415 which the Violent Crime Control and Law Enforcement Act of 1994 conditionally added to the Federal Rules of Evidence.[1] These modifications do not change the substance of the congressional enactment. The changes were made in order to integrate the provisions both substantively and stylistically with the existing Rules of Evidence; to illuminate the intent expressed by the principal drafters of the measure; to clarify drafting ambiguities that might necessitate considerable judicial attention if they remained unresolved; and to eliminate possible constitutional infirmities.

The Committee placed the new provisions in Rule 404 because this rule governs the admissibility of character evidence. The congressional enactment constitutes a new exception to the general rule stated in subdivision (a). The Committee also combined the three separate rules proposed by Congress into one subdivision (a)(4) in accordance with the rules' customary practice of treating criminal and civil issues jointly. An amendment to Rule 405 has been added because the authorization of a new form of character evidence in this rule has an impact on methods of proving character that were not explicitly addressed by Congress. The stylistic changes are self-evident. They are particularly noticeable in the definition section in subdivision (a)(4)(C) in which the Committee eliminated, without any change in meaning, graphic details of sexual acts.

The Committee added language that explicitly provides that evidence under this subdivision must satisfy other rules of evidence such as the hearsay rules in Article VIII and the expert testimony rules in Article VII. Although principal sponsors of the legislation had stated that they intended other evidentiary rules to apply, the Committee believes that the opening phrase of the new subdivision 'if otherwise admissible under these rules' is needed to clarify the relationship between subdivision (a)(4) and other evidentiary provisions.

The Committee also expressly made subdivision (a)(4) subject to Rule 403 balancing in accordance with the repeatedly stated objectives of the legislation's sponsors with which representatives of the Justice Department expressed agreement. Many commentators on Rules 413–415 had objected that Rule 403's applicability was obscured by the actual language employed.

In addition to clarifying the drafters' intent, an explicit reference to Rule 403 may be essential to insulate the rule against constitutional challenge. Constitutional concerns also led the Committee to acknowledge specifically the opposing party's right to offer in rebuttal character evidence that the rules would otherwise bar, including evidence of a third person's prior acts of sexual misconduct offered to prove that the third person rather than the party committed the acts in issue.

In order to minimize the need for extensive and time-consuming judicial interpretation, the Committee listed factors that a court may consider in discharging Rule 403 balancing. Proximity in time is taken into account in a related rule. See Rule 609(b). Similarity, frequency and surrounding circumstances have long been considered by courts in handling other crimes evidence pursuant to Rule 404(b). Relevant intervening events, such as extensive medical treatment of the accused between the time of the prior proffered act and the charged act, may affect the strength of the propensity inference for which the evidence is offered. The final factor—'other relevant similarities or differences'—is added in recognition of the endless variety of circumstances that confront a trial court in rulings on admissibility. Although subdivision (4)(A) explicitly refers to factors that bear on probative value, this enumeration does not eliminate a judge's responsibility to take into account the other factors mentioned in Rule 403 itself—'the danger of unfair prejudice, confusion of the issues, ... misleading the jury, ... undue delay, waste of time, or needless presentation of cumulative evidence.' In addition, the Advisory Committee Note to Rule 403 reminds judges that 'The availability of other means of proof may also be an appropriate factor.'

The Committee altered slightly the notice provision in criminal cases. Providing the trial court with some discretion to excuse pretrial notice was thought preferable to the inflexible 15–day rule provided in Rules 414 and 415. Furthermore, the formulation is identical to that contained in the 1991 amendment to Rule 404(b) so that no confusion will result from having two somewhat different notice provisions in the same rule. The Committee eliminated the notice provision for civil cases stated in Rule 415 because it did not believe that Congress intended to alter the usual time table for disclosure and discovery provided by the Federal Rules of Civil Procedure.

The definition section was simplified with no change in meaning. The reference to 'the law of a State' was eliminated as unnecessarily confusing and restrictive. Conduct committed outside the United States ought equally to be eligible for admission. Evidence offered pursuant to subdivision (a)(4) must relate to a form of conduct proscribed by either chapter 109A or 110 of title 18, United States Code, regardless of whether the actor was subject to federal jurisdiction.

RULE 405. METHODS OF PROVING CHARACTER

(a) Reputation or opinion. In all cases in which evidence of character or a trait of character of a person is admissible, proof may be made by testimony as to reputation or by testimony in the form of an opinion except as provided in subdivision (c) of this rule. On cross-examination, inquiry is allowable into relevant specific instances of conduct.

* * * * * * *

(c) Proof in sexual misconduct cases. In a case in which evidence is offered under rule 404(a)(4), proof may be made by specific instances of conduct, testimony as to reputation, or testimony in the form of an opinion, except that the prosecution or claimant may offer reputation or opinion testimony only after the opposing party has offered such testimony.

Note to Rule 405(c)

The addition of a new subdivision (a)(4) to Rule 404 necessitates adding a new subdivision (c) to Rule 405 to govern methods of proof. Congress clearly intended no change in the preexisting law that precludes the prosecution or a claimant from offering reputation or opinion testimony in its case in chief to prove that the opposing party acted in conformity with character. When evidence is admissible pursuant to Rule 404(a)(4), the proponents proof must consist of specific instances of conduct. The opposing party, however, is free to respond with reputation or opinion testimony (including expert testimony if otherwise admissible) as well as evidence of specific instances. In a criminal case, the admissibility of reputation or opinion testimony would, in any event, be authorized by Rule 404(a)(1). The extension to civil cases is essential in order to provide the opponent with an adequate opportunity to refute allegations about a character for sexual misconduct. Once the opposing party offers reputation or opinion testimony, however, the prosecution or claimant may counter using such methods of proof.

[1] Congress provided that the rules would take effect unless within a specified time period the Judicial Conference made recommendations to amend the rules that Congress enacted.

Congressional Discussion

Floor Statement of the Principal House Sponsor, Representative Susan Molinari, Concerning the Prior Crimes Evidence Rules for Sexual Assault and Child Molestation Cases (Cong.Rec. H8991–92, Aug. 21, 1994):

Mr. Speaker, the revised conference bill contains a critical reform that I have long sought to protect the public from crimes of sexual violence—general rules of admissibility in sexual assault and child molestation cases for evidence that the defendant has committed offenses of the same type on other occasions. The enactment of this reform is first and foremost a triumph for the public—for the women who will not be raped and the children who will not be molested because we have strengthened the legal system's tools for bringing the perpetrators of these atrocious crimes to justice.

Senator Dole and I initially proposed this reform in February of 1991 in the Women's Equal Opportunity Act bill, and we later re-introduced it in the Sexual Assault Prevention Act bills of the 102d and 103d Congresses. The proposal also enjoyed the strong support of the Administration in the 102d Congress, and was included in President Bush's violent crime bill of that Congress, S. 635. The Senate passed the proposed rules on Nov. 5, 1993, by a vote of 75 to 19, in a crime bill amendment offered by Senate Dole. This Chamber endorsed the same rules on June 29, 1994, by a vote of 348 to 62, through a motion to instruct conferees that I offered.

The rules in the revised conference bill are substantially identical to our earlier proposals. We have agreed to a temporary deferral of the effective date of the new rules, pending a report by the Judicial Conference, in order to accommodate procedural objections raised by opponents of the reform. However, regardless of what the Judicial Conference may recommend, the new rules will take effect within at most 300 days of the enactment of this legislation, unless repealed or modified by subsequent legislation.

The need for these rules, their precedential support, their interpretation, and the issues and policy questions they raise have been analyzed at length in the legislative history of this proposal. I would direct the Members' attention particularly to two earlier statements:

The first is the portion of the section-by-section analysis accompanying these rules in section 801 of S. 635, which President Bush transmitted to Congress in 1991. That statement appears on pages S 3238 [to] S 3242 of the daily edition of the Congressional Record for March 13, 1991.

The second is the prepared text of an address—entitled "Evidence of Propensity and Probability in Sex Offense Cases and Other Cases"—by Senior Counsel David J. Karp of the Office of Policy Development of the U.S. Department of Justice. Mr. Karp, who is the author of the new evidence rules, presented this statement on behalf of the Justice Department to the Evidence Section of the Association of American Law Schools on January 9, 1993. The statement provided a detailed account of the views of the legislative sponsors and the Administration concerning the proposed reform, and should also be considered an authoritative part of its legislative history.

These earlier statements address the issues raised by this reform in considerable detail. In my present remarks, I will simply emphasize the following essential points:

The new rules will supersede in sex offense cases the restrictive aspects of Federal Rule of Evidence 404(b). In contrast to Rule 404(b)'s general prohibition of evidence of character or propensity, the new rules for sex offense cases authorize admission and consideration of evidence of an uncharged offense for its bearing "on any matter to which it is relevant." This includes the defendant's propensity to commit sexual assault or child molestation offenses, and assessment of the probability or improbability that the defendant has been falsely or mistakenly accused of such an offense.

In other respects, the general standards of the rules of evidence will continue to apply, including the restrictions on hearsay evidence and the court's authority under Evidence Rule 403 to exclude evidence whose probative value is substantially outweighed by its prejudicial effect. Also, the government (or the plaintiff in a civil case) will generally have to disclose to the defendant any evidence that is to be offered under the new rules at least 15 days before trial.

The proposed reform is critical to the protection of the public from rapists and child molesters, and is justified by the distinctive characteristics of the cases it will affect. In child molestation cases, for example, a history of similar acts tends to be exceptionally probative because it shows an unusual disposition of the defendant—a sexual or sadosexual interest in children—that simply does not exist in ordinary people. Moreover, such cases require reliance on child victims whose credibility can readily be attacked in the absence of substantial corroboration. In such cases, there is a compelling public interest in admitting all significant evidence that will illumine the credibility of the charge and any denial by the defense.

Similarly, adult-victim sexual assault cases are distinctive, and often turn on difficult credibility determinations. Alleged consent by the victim is rarely an issue in prosecutions for other violent crimes—the accused mugger does not claim that the victim freely handed over [his] wallet as a gift—but the defendant in a rape case often contends that the victim engaged in consensual sex and then falsely accused him. Knowledge that the defendant has committed rapes on other occasions is frequently critical in assessing the relative plausibility of these claims and accurately deciding cases that would otherwise become unresolvable swearing matches.

The practical effect of the new rules is to put evidence of uncharged offenses in sexual assault and child molestation cases on the same footing as other types of relevant evidence that are not subject to a special exclusionary rule. The presumption is in favor of admission. The underlying legislative judgment is that the evidence admissible pursuant to the proposed rules is typically relevant and probative, and that its probative value is normally not outweighed by any risk of prejudice or other adverse effects.

In line with this judgment, the rules do not impose arbitrary or artificial restrictions on the admissibility of evidence. Evidence of offenses for which the defendant has not previously been prosecuted or convicted will be admissible, as well as evidence of prior convictions. No time limit is imposed on the uncharged offenses for which evidence may be admitted; as a practical matter, evidence of other sex offenses by the defendant is often probative and properly admitted, notwithstanding very substantial lapses of time in relation to the charged offense or offenses. *See, e.g., United States v. Hadley*, 918 F.2d 848, 850–51 (9th Cir. 1990), *cert. dismissed*, 113 S.Ct. 486 (1992) (evidence of offenses occurring up to 15 years earlier admitted); *State v. Plymate*, 345 N.W.2d 327 (Neb.1984) (evidence of defendant's commission of other child molestations more than 20 years earlier admitted).

Finally, the practical efficacy of these rules will depend on faithful execution by judges of the will of Congress in adopting this critical reform. To implement the legislative intent, the courts must liberally construe these rules to provide the basis for a fully informed decision of sexual assault and child molestation cases, including assessment of the defendant's propensities and questions of probability in light of the defendant's past conduct.

Rule 414. Evidence of Similar Crimes in Child Molestation Cases

(a) In a criminal case in which the defendant is accused of an offense of child molestation, evidence of the defendant's commission of another offense or offenses of child molestation is admissible, and may be considered for its bearing on any matter to which it is relevant.

(b) In a case in which the Government intends to offer evidence under this rule, the attorney for the Government shall disclose the evidence to the defendant, including statements of witnesses or a summary of the substance of any testimony that is expected to be offered, at least fifteen days before the scheduled date of trial or at such later time as the court may allow for good cause.

(c) This rule shall not be construed to limit the admission or consideration of evidence under any other rule.

(d) For purposes of this rule and Rule 415, "child" means a person below the age of fourteen, and "offense of child molestation" means a crime under Federal law or the law of a State (as defined in section 513 of title 18, United States Code) that involved—

(1) any conduct proscribed by chapter 109A of title 18, United States Code, that was committed in relation to a child;

(2) any conduct proscribed by chapter 110 of title 18, United States Code;

(3) contact between any part of the defendant's body or an object and the genitals or anus of a child;

(4) contact between the genitals or anus of the defendant and any part of the body of a child;

(5) deriving sexual pleasure or gratification from the infliction of death, bodily injury, or physical pain on a child; or

(6) an attempt or conspiracy to engage in conduct described in paragraphs (1)–(5).

(Added Pub.L. 103–322, Title XXXII, § 320935(a), Sept. 13, 1994, 108 Stat. 2135.)

HISTORICAL NOTES

Effective and Applicability Provisions

1995 Acts. Rule effective July 9, 1995, see section 320935(b) to (e) of Pub.L. 103–322, set out as a note under rule 413 of these rules.

Congressional Discussion

See Floor Statement following Rule 413.

Rule 415. Evidence of Similar Acts in Civil Cases Concerning Sexual Assault or Child Molestation

(a) In a civil case in which a claim for damages or other relief is predicated on a party's alleged commission of conduct constituting an offense of sexual assault or child molestation, evidence of that party's commission of another offense or offenses of sexual assault or child molestation is admissible and may be considered as provided in Rule 413 and Rule 414 of these rules.

(b) A party who intends to offer evidence under this Rule shall disclose the evidence to the party against whom it will be offered, including statements of witnesses or a summary of the substance of any testimony that is expected to be offered, at least fifteen days before the scheduled date of trial or at such later time as the court may allow for good cause.

(c) This rule shall not be construed to limit the admission or consideration of evidence under any other rule.

(Added Pub.L. 103–322, Title XXXII, § 320935(a), Sept. 13, 1994, 108 Stat. 2137.)

HISTORICAL NOTES

Effective and Applicability Provisions

1995 Acts. Rule effective July 9, 1995, see section 320935(b) to (e) of Pub.L. 103–322, set out as a note under rule 413 of these rules.

Congressional Discussion

See Floor Statement following Rule 413.

ARTICLE V. PRIVILEGES

Rule 501. General Rule

Except as otherwise required by the Constitution of the United States or provided by Act of Congress or in rules prescribed by the Supreme Court pursuant to statutory authority, the privilege of a witness, person, government, State, or political subdivision thereof shall be governed by the principles of the common law as they may be interpreted by the courts of the United States in the light of reason and experience. However, in civil actions and proceedings, with respect to an element of a claim or defense as to which State law supplies the rule of decision, the privilege of a witness, person, government, State, or political subdivision thereof shall be determined in accordance with State law.

(Pub.L. 93–595, § 1, Jan. 2, 1975, 88 Stat. 1933.)

ADVISORY COMMITTEE NOTES

1974 Enactment

Article V as submitted to Congress contained thirteen Rules. Nine of those Rules defined specific non-constitutional privileges which the federal courts must recognize (i.e. required reports, lawyer-client, psychotherapist-patient, husband-wife, communications to clergymen, political vote, trade secrets, secrets of state and other official information, and identity of informer.) Another Rule provided that only those privileges set forth in Article V or in some other Act of Congress could be recognized by the federal courts. The three remaining Rules addressed collateral problems as to waiver of privilege by voluntary disclosure, privileged matter disclosed under compulsion or without opportunity to claim privilege, comment upon or inference from a claim of privilege, and jury instruction with regard thereto.

The Committee amended Article V to eliminate all of the Court's specific Rules on privileges. Instead, the Committee, through a single Rule, 501, left the law of privileges in its present state and further provided that privileges shall continue to be developed by the courts of the United States under a uniform standard applicable both in civil and criminal cases. That standard, derived from Rule 26 of the Federal Rules of Criminal Procedure, mandates the application of the principles of the common law as interpreted by the courts of the United States in the light of reason and experience. The words "person, government, State, or political subdivision thereof" were added by the Committee to the lone term "witnesses" used in Rule 26 to make clear that, as under present law, not only witnesses may have privileges. The Committee also included in its amendment a proviso modeled after Rule 302 and similar to language added by the Committee to Rule 601 relating to the competency of witnesses. The proviso is designed to require the application of State privilege law in civil actions and proceedings governed by *Erie R. Co. v. Tompkins,* 304 U.S. 64 (1938), a result in accord with current federal court decisions. See *Republic Gear Co. v. Borg–Warner Corp.,* 381 F.2d 551, 555–556 n. 2 (2nd Cir.1967). The Committee deemed the proviso to be necessary in the light of the Advisory Committee's view (see its note to Court [proposed] Rule 501) that this result is not mandated under *Erie.*

The rationale underlying the proviso is that federal law should not supersede that of the States in substantive areas such as privilege absent a compelling reason. The Committee believes that in civil cases in the federal courts where an element of a claim or defense is not grounded upon a federal question, there is no federal interest strong enough to justify departure from State policy. In addition, the Committee considered that the Court's proposed Article V would have promoted forum shopping in some civil actions, depending upon differences in the privilege law applied as among the State and federal courts. The Committee's proviso, on the other hand, under which the federal courts are bound to apply the State's privilege law in actions founded upon a State-created right or defense, removes the incentive to "shop". House Report No. 93–650.

Article V as submitted to Congress contained 13 rules. Nine of those rules defined specific nonconstitutional privileges which the Federal courts must recognize (i.e., required reports, lawyer-client, psychotherapist-patient, husband-wife, communications to clergymen, political vote, trade secrets, secrets of state and other official information, and identity of informer). Many of these rules contained controversial modifications or restrictions upon common law privileges. As noted supra, the House amended article V to eliminate all of the Court's specific rules on privileges. Through a single rule, 501, the House provided that privileges shall be governed by the principles of the common law as interpreted by the courts of the United States in the light of reason and experience (a standard derived from rule 26 of the Federal Rules of Criminal Procedure) except in the case of an element of a civil claim or defense as to which State law supplies the rule of decision, in which event state privilege law was to govern.

The committee agrees with the main thrust of the House amendment: that a federally developed common law based on modern reason and experience shall apply except where the State nature of the issues renders deference to State privilege law the wiser course, as in the usual diversity case. The committee understands that thrust of the House amendment to require that State privilege law be applied in "diversity" cases (actions on questions of State law between citizens of different States arising under 28 U.S.C. § 1332). The language of the House amendment, however, goes beyond this in some respects, and falls short of it in others: State privilege law applies even in nondiversity, Federal question civil cases, where an issue governed by State substantive law is the object of the evidence (such issues do sometimes arise in such cases); and, in all instances where State privilege law is to be applied, e.g., on proof of a State issue in a diversity case, a close reading reveals that State privilege law is not to be applied unless the matter to be proved is an element of that state claim or defense, as distinguished from a step along the way in the proof of it.

The committee is concerned that the language used in the House amendment could be difficult to apply. It provides that "in civil actions * * * with respect to an element of a claim or defense as to which State law supplies the rule of decision," State law on privilege applies. The question of what is an element of a claim or defense is likely to engender considerable litigation. If the matter in question constitutes an element of a claim, State law supplies the privilege rule; whereas if it is a mere item of proof with respect to a claim, then, even though State law might supply the rule of decision, Federal law on the privilege would apply. Further, disputes will arise as to how the rule should be applied in an antitrust action or in a tax case where the Federal statute is silent as to a particular aspect of the substantive law in question, but Federal cases had incorporated State law by reference to State law. [For a discussion of reference to State substantive law, see note on Federal Incorporation by Reference of State Law, Hart & Wechsler, The Federal Courts and the Federal System, pp. 491–494 (2d ed. 1973).] Is a claim (or defense) based on such a reference a claim or defense as to which federal or State law supplies the rule of decision?

Another problem not entirely avoidable is the complexity or difficulty the rule introduces into the trial of a Federal case containing a combination of Federal and State claims and defenses, e.g. an action involving Federal antitrust and State unfair competition claims. Two different bodies of privilege law would need to be consulted. It may even develop that the same witness-testimony might be relevant on both counts and privileged as to one but not the other. [The problems with the House formulation are discussed in Rothstein, The Proposed Amendments to the Federal Rules of Evidence, 62 Georgetown University Law Journal 125 (1973) at notes 25, 26 and 70–74 and accompanying text.]

The formulation adopted by the House is pregnant with litigious mischief. The committee has, therefore, adopted what we believe will be a clearer and more practical guideline for determining when courts should respect State rules of privilege. Basically, it provides that in criminal and Federal question civil cases, federally evolved rules on privilege should apply since it is Federal policy which is being enforced. [It is also intended that the Federal law of privileges should be applied with respect to pendent State law claims when they arise in a Federal question case.] Conversely, in diversity cases where the litigation in question turns on a substantive question of State law, and is brought in the Federal courts because the parties reside in different States, the committee believes it is clear that State rules of privilege should apply unless the proof is directed at a claim or defense for which Federal law supplies the rule of decision (a situation which would not commonly arise.) [While such a situation might require use of two bodies of privilege law, federal and state, in the same case, nevertheless the occasions on which this would be required are considerably reduced as compared with the House version, and confined to situations where the Federal and State interests are such as to justify application of neither privilege law to the case as a whole. If the rule proposed here results in two conflicting bodies of privilege law applying to the same piece of evidence in the same case, it is contemplated that the rule favoring reception of the evidence should be applied. This policy is based on the present rule 43(a) of the Federal Rules of Civil Procedure which provides: In any case, the statute or rule which favors the reception of the evidence governs and the evidence shall be presented according to the most convenient method prescribed in any of the statutes or rules to which reference is herein made.] It is intended that the State rules of privilege should apply equally in original diversity actions and diversity actions removed under 28 U.S.C. § 1441(b).

Two other comments on the privilege rule should be made. The committee has received a considerable volume of correspondence from psychiatric organizations and psychiatrists concerning the deletion of rule 504 of the rule submitted by the Supreme Court. It should be clearly understood that, in approving this general rule as to privileges, the action of Congress should not be understood as disapproving any recognition of a psychiatrist-patient, or husband-wife, or any other of the enumerated privileges contained in the Supreme Court rules. Rather, our action should be understood as reflecting the view that the recognition of a privilege based on a confidential relationship and other privileges should be determined on a case-by-case basis.

Further, we would understand that the prohibition against spouses testifying against each other is considered a rule of privilege and covered by this rule and not by rule 601 of the competency of witnesses. Senate Report No. 93–1277.

Rule 501 deals with the privilege of a witness not to testify. Both the House and Senate bills provide that federal privilege law applies in criminal cases. In civil actions and proceedings, the House bill provides that state privilege law applies "to an element of a claim or defense as to which State law supplies the rule of decision." The Senate bill provides that "in civil actions and proceedings arising under 28 U.S.C. § 1332 or 28 U.S.C. § 1335, or between citizens of different States and removed under 28 U.S.C. § 1441(b) the privilege of a witness, person, government, State or political subdivision thereof is determined in accordance with State law, unless with respect to the particular claim or defense, Federal law supplies the rule of decision."

The wording of the House and Senate bills differs in the treatment of civil actions and proceedings. The rule in the House bill applies to evidence that relates to "an element of a claim or defense." If an item of proof tends to support or defeat a claim or defense, or an element of a claim or defense, and if state law supplies the rule of decision for that claim or defense, then state privilege law applies to that item of proof.

Under the provision in the House bill, therefore, state privilege law will usually apply in diversity cases. There may be diversity cases, however, where a claim or defense is based upon federal law. In such instances, federal privilege law will apply to evidence relevant to the federal claim or defense. See *Sola Electric Co. v. Jefferson Electric Co.*, 317 U.S. 173 (1942).

In nondiversity jurisdiction civil cases, federal privilege law will generally apply. In those situations where a federal court adopts or incorporates state law to fill interstices or gaps in federal statutory phrases, the court generally will apply federal privilege law. As Justice Jackson has said:

> A federal court sitting in a non-diversity case such as this does not sit as a local tribunal. In some cases it may see fit for special reasons to give the law of a particular state highly persuasive or even controlling effect, but in the last analysis its decision turns upon the law of the United States, not that of any state.

D'Oench, Duhme & Co. v. Federal Deposit Insurance Corp., 315 U.S. 447, 471 (1942) (Jackson, J., concurring). When a federal court chooses to absorb state law, it is applying the state law as a matter of federal common law. Thus, state law does not supply the rule of decision (even though the federal court may apply a rule derived from state decisions), and state privilege law would not apply. See C.A. Wright, Federal Courts 251–252 (2d ed. 1970); *Holmberg v. Armbrecht*, 327 U.S. 392 (1946); *DeSylva v. Ballentine*, 351 U.S. 570, 581 (1956); 9 Wright & Miller, Federal Rules and Procedure § 2408.

In civil actions and proceedings, where the rule of decision as to a claim or defense or as to an element of a claim or defense is supplied by state law, the House provision requires that state privilege law apply.

The Conference adopts the House provision. House Report No. 93–1597.

CROSS REFERENCES

Aliens, confidentiality of Department of State records of issuance or refusal of visas, see 8 USCA § 1202.

Atomic energy, development and control of, licensee incident reports as evidence, see 42 USCA § 2240.

Census information as confidential, see 13 USCA § 9.

Certificates of discharge, replacements as evidence, see 10 USCA § 1041.

Competency of accused as witness on own request, see 18 USCA § 3481.

Depositions upon written questions, see Fed.Rules Civ. Proc. Rule 31, 28 USCA.

Discovery, general provisions concerning, see Fed.Rules Civ.Proc. Rule 26, 28 USCA.

Discovery and inspection of statements, confessions, etc., in possession of government, see Fed.Rules Cr.Proc. Rule 16, 18 USCA.

Drug addiction and rehabilitation—

Hearing, examination, etc., to determine addiction inadmissible in criminal proceedings, see 42 USCA § 3419.

Hospitalization, treatment or voluntary commitment, evidence of inadmissible and confidential, see 42 USCA § 260.

Physician-patient privilege inapplicable in hearings or other proceedings or rehabilitation, see 42 USCA § 3420.

Equal employment opportunity conciliation proceedings, inadmissibility as evidence in subsequent proceedings, see 42 USCA § 2000e–5.

Government agencies, publication of public information, see 5 USCA § 552.

Government witnesses, statements and report of not subject to subpoena, discovery, or inspection, see 18 USCA § 3500.

Grand jury proceedings, secrecy of, see Fed.Rules Cr. Proc. Rule 6, 18 USCA.

Importation of alien for immoral purpose, testimony of spouse admissible, see 8 USCA § 1328.

Liability insurance, discovery proceedings, see Fed.Rules Civ.Proc. Rule 26, 28 USCA.

Physician-patient privilege, waiver of, see Fed.Rules Civ. Proc. Rule 35, 28 USCA.

Presentence investigation report, disclosure of contents, see Fed.Rules Cr.Proc. Rule 32, 18 USCA.

Public availability of information filed with Securities and Exchange Commission, see 15 USCA § 78x.

Safety appliances and railroad equipment, reports of and investigation of accidents, see 49 USCA §§ 20703 and 20903.

Self-incrimination, protection against, see USCA Const. Amend. V.

State laws as rules of decision, see 28 USCA § 1652.

Subpoena for taking depositions, see Fed.Rules Civ.Proc. Rule 45, 28 USCA.

Testimony of debtor and of persons examined—

Immunity from self-incrimination, see 11 USCA § 344.

Immunity of witnesses, see 18 USCA § 6001 et seq.

Wire or radio communications, unauthorized use or publication prohibited, see 47 USCA § 605.

Rule 502. Attorney–Client Privilege and Work Product; Limitations on Waiver

The following provisions apply, in the circumstances set out, to disclosure of a communication or information covered by the attorney-client privilege or work-product protection.

(a) Disclosure made in a Federal proceeding or to a Federal office or agency; scope of a waiver.—When the disclosure is made in a Federal proceeding or to a Federal office or agency and waives the attorney-client privilege or work-product protection, the waiver extends to an undisclosed communication or information in a Federal or State proceeding only if:

(1) the waiver is intentional;

(2) the disclosed and undisclosed communications or information concern the same subject matter; and

(3) they ought in fairness to be considered together.

(b) Inadvertent disclosure.—When made in a Federal proceeding or to a Federal office or agency, the disclosure does not operate as a waiver in a Federal or State proceeding if:

(1) the disclosure is inadvertent;

(2) the holder of the privilege or protection took reasonable steps to prevent disclosure; and

(3) the holder promptly took reasonable steps to rectify the error, including (if applicable) following Federal Rule of Civil Procedure 26(b)(5)(B).

(c) Disclosure made in a State proceeding.—When the disclosure is made in a State proceeding and is not the subject of a State-court order concerning waiver, the disclosure does not operate as a waiver in a Federal proceeding if the disclosure:

(1) would not be a waiver under this rule if it had been made in a Federal proceeding; or

(2) is not a waiver under the law of the State where the disclosure occurred.

(d) Controlling effect of a court order.—A Federal court may order that the privilege or protection is not waived by disclosure connected with the litigation pending before the court—in which event the disclosure is also not a waiver in any other Federal or State proceeding.

(e) Controlling effect of a party agreement.—An agreement on the effect of disclosure in a Federal proceeding is binding only on the parties to the agreement, unless it is incorporated into a court order.

(f) Controlling effect of this rule.—Notwithstanding Rules 101 and 1101, this rule applies to State proceedings and to Federal court-annexed and Federal court-mandated arbitration proceedings, in the circumstances set out in the rule. And notwithstanding Rule 501, this rule applies even if State law provides the rule of decision.

(g) Definitions.—In this rule:

(1) 'attorney-client privilege" means the protection that applicable law provides for confidential attorney-client communications; and

(2) 'work-product protection" means the protection that applicable law provides for tangible material (or its intangible equivalent) prepared in anticipation of litigation or for trial.

(Pub.L. 110–322, § 1(a), Sept. 19, 2008, 122 Stat. 3537.)

HISTORICAL NOTES

Revision Notes and Legislative Reports

2008 Acts. Senate Report No. 110–264, see 2008 U.S. Code Cong. and Adm. News, p. 1305.

Effective and Applicability Provisions

2008 Acts. Pub.L. 110–322, § 1(c), Sept. 19, 2008, 122 Stat. 3538, provided that: "The amendments made by this Act [enacting this rule] shall apply in all proceedings commenced after the date of enactment of this Act [Sept. 19, 2008] and, insofar as is just and practicable, in all proceedings pending on such date of enactment [Sept. 19, 2008]."

ARTICLE VI. WITNESSES

Rule

Rule 601. General Rule of Competency

Every person is competent to be a witness except as otherwise provided in these rules. However, in civil actions and proceedings, with respect to an element of a claim or defense as to which State law supplies the rule of decision, the competency of a witness shall be determined in accordance with State law.

(Pub.L. 93–595, § 1, Jan. 2, 1975, 88 Stat.1934.)

ADVISORY COMMITTEE NOTES

1972 Proposed Rules

This general ground-clearing eliminates all grounds of incompetency not specifically recognized in the succeeding rules of this Article. Included among the grounds thus abolished are religious belief, conviction of crime, and connection with the litigation as a party or interested person or spouse of a party or interested person. With the exception of the so-called Dead Man's Acts, American jurisdictions generally have ceased to recognize these grounds.

The Dead Man's Acts are surviving traces of the common law disqualification of parties and interested persons. They exist in variety too great to convey conviction of their wisdom and effectiveness. These rules contain no provision of this kind. For the reasoning underlying the decision not to give effect to state statutes in diversity cases, see the Advisory Committee's Note to Rule 501.

No mental or moral qualifications for testifying as a witness are specified. Standards of mental capacity have proved elusive in actual application. A leading commentator observes that few witnesses are disqualified on that ground. Weihofen, Testimonial Competence and Credibility, 34 Geo.

Wash.L.Rev. 53 (1965). Discretion is regularly exercised in favor of allowing the testimony. A witness wholly without capacity is difficult to imagine. The question is one particularly suited to the jury as one of weight and credibility, subject to judicial authority to review the sufficiency of the evidence. 2 Wigmore §§ 501, 509. Standards of moral qualification in practice consist essentially of evaluating a person's truthfulness in terms of his own answers about it. Their principal utility is in affording an opportunity on voir dire examination to impress upon the witness his moral duty. This result may, however, be accomplished more directly, and without haggling in terms of legal standards, by the manner of administering the oath or affirmation under Rule 603.

Admissibility of religious belief as a ground of impeachment is treated in Rule 610. Conviction of crime as a ground of impeachment is the subject of Rule 609. Marital relationship is the basis for privilege under Rule 505. Interest in the outcome of litigation and mental capacity are, of course, highly relevant to credibility and require no special treatment to render them admissible along with other matters bearing upon the perception, memory, and narration of witnesses.

1974 Enactment

Rule 601 as submitted to the Congress provided that "Every person is competent to be a witness except as otherwise provided in these rules." One effect of the Rule as proposed would have been to abolish age, mental capacity, and other grounds recognized in some State jurisdictions as making a person incompetent as a witness. The greatest controversy centered around the Rule's rendering inapplicable in the federal courts the so-called Dead Man's Statutes which exist in some States. Acknowledging that there is substantial disagreement as to the merit of Dead Man's Statutes, the Committee nevertheless believed that where such statutes have been enacted they represent State policy which should not be overturned in the absence of a compelling federal interest. The Committee therefore amended the Rule to make competency in civil actions determinable in accordance with State law with respect to elements of claims or defenses as to which State law supplies the rule of decision. Cf. *Courtland v. Walston & Co., Inc.*, 340 F.Supp. 1076, 1087–1092 (S.D.N.Y.1972). House Report No. 93–650.

The amendment to rule 601 parallels the treatment accorded Rule 501 discussed immediately above. Senate Report No. 93–1277.

Rule 601 deals with competency of witnesses. Both the House and Senate bills provide that federal competency law applies in criminal cases. In civil actions and proceedings, the House bill provides that state competency law applies "to an element of a claim or defense as to which State law supplies the rule of decision." The Senate bill provides that "in civil actions and proceedings arising under 28 U.S.C. § 1332 or 28 U.S.C. § 1335, or between citizens of different States and removed under 28 U.S.C. § 1441(b) the competency of a witness, person, government, State or political subdivision thereof is determined in accordance with State law, unless with respect to the particular claim or defense, Federal law supplies the rule of decision."

The wording of the House and Senate bills differs in the treatment of civil actions and proceedings. The rule in the House bill applies to evidence that relates to "an element of a claim or defense." If an item of proof tends to support or defeat a claim or defense, or an element of a claim or defense, and if state law supplies the rule of decision for that claim or defense, then state competency law applies to that item of proof.

For reasons similar to those underlying its action on Rule 501, the Conference adopts the House provision. House Report No. 93–1597.

CROSS REFERENCES

Accused at own request as competent witness, see 18 USCA § 3481.

Competency of interested persons; share of penalties payable, see 28 USCA § 1822.

Oral testimony in open court, see Fed.Rules Civ.Proc. Rule 43, 28 USCA.

Oral testimony in open court, see Fed.Rules Cr.Proc. Rule 26, 18 USCA.

Privileges of witnesses, general rule, see Fed.Rules Evid. Rule 501, 28 USCA.

State laws as rules of decision, see 28 USCA § 1652.

Rule 602. Lack of Personal Knowledge

A witness may not testify to a matter unless evidence is introduced sufficient to support a finding that the witness has personal knowledge of the matter. Evidence to prove personal knowledge may, but need not, consist of the witness' own testimony. This rule is subject to the provisions of rule 703, relating to opinion testimony by expert witnesses.

(Pub.L. 93–595, § 1, Jan. 2, 1975, 88 Stat. 1934; Mar. 2, 1987, eff. Oct. 1, 1987; Apr. 25, 1988, eff. Nov. 1, 1988.)

ADVISORY COMMITTEE NOTES

1972 Proposed Rules

"* * * [T]he rule requiring that a witness who testifies to a fact which can be perceived by the senses must have had an opportunity to observe, and must have actually observed the fact" is a "most pervasive manifestation" of the common law insistence upon "the most reliable sources of information." McCormick § 10, p. 19. These foundation requirements may, of course, be furnished by the testimony of the witness himself; hence personal knowledge is not an absolute but may consist of what the witness thinks he knows from personal perception. 2 Wigmore § 650. It will be observed that the rule is in fact a specialized application of the provisions of Rule 104(b) on conditional relevancy.

This rule does not govern the situation of a witness who testifies to a hearsay statement as such, if he has personal knowledge of the making of the statement. Rules 801 and 805 would be applicable. This rule would, however, prevent him from testifying to the subject matter of the hearsay statement, as he has no personal knowledge of it.

The reference to Rule 703 is designed to avoid any question of conflict between the present rule and the provisions of that rule allowing an expert to express opinions based on facts of which he does not have personal knowledge.

1987 Amendments

The amendments are technical. No substantive change is intended.

1988 Amendments

The amendment is technical. No substantive change is intended.

CROSS REFERENCES

Hearsay evidence, generally, see Fed.Rules Evid. Rule 801 et seq., 28 USCA.

Relevancy of evidence as conditional, see Fed.Rules Evid. Rule 104, 28 USCA.

Rule 603. Oath or Affirmation

Before testifying, every witness shall be required to declare that the witness will testify truthfully, by oath or affirmation administered in a form calculated to awaken the witness' conscience and impress the witness' mind with the duty to do so.

(Pub.L. 93–595, § 1, Jan. 2, 1975, 88 Stat. 1934; Mar. 2, 1987, eff. Oct. 1, 1987.)

ADVISORY COMMITTEE NOTES

1972 Proposed Rules

The rule is designed to afford the flexibility required in dealing with religious adults, atheists, conscientious objectors, mental defectives, and children. Affirmation is simply a solemn undertaking to tell the truth; no special verbal formula is required. As is true generally, affirmation is recognized by federal law. "Oath" includes affirmation, 1 U.S.C. § 1; judges and clerks may administer oaths and affirmations, 28 U.S.C. §§ 459, 953; and affirmations are acceptable in lieu of oaths under Rule 43(d) of the Federal Rules of Civil Procedure. Perjury by a witness is a crime, 18 U.S.C. § 1621.

1987 Amendments

The amendments are technical. No substantive change is intended.

CROSS REFERENCES

Administration of oaths and affirmations—

Clerk of court and deputies, see 28 USCA § 953.

Justice or judge of United States, see 28 USCA § 459.

Affirmation in lieu of oath, see Fed.Rules Civ.Proc. Rule 43, 28 USCA.

Examination of debtor under oath, see 11 USCA § 343.

False declarations before grand jury or court, see 18 USCA § 1623.

Oath as including affirmation, see Fed.Rules Cr.Proc. Rule 54, 18 USCA.

"Oath" as including affirmation, see 1 USCA § 1.

Perjury, generally, see 18 USCA § 1621.

Rule 604. Interpreters

An interpreter is subject to the provisions of these rules relating to qualification as an expert and the administration of an oath or affirmation to make a true translation.

(Pub.L. 93–595, § 1, Jan. 2, 1975, 88 Stat. 1934; Mar. 2, 1987, eff. Oct. 1, 1987.)

ADVISORY COMMITTEE NOTES

1972 Proposed Rules

The rule implements Rule 43(f) of the Federal Rules of Civil Procedure and Rule 28(b) of the Federal Rules of Criminal Procedure, both of which contain provisions for the appointment and compensation of interpreters.

1987 Amendments

The amendment is technical. No substantive change is intended.

CROSS REFERENCES

Appointment and compensation of interpreters, see Fed. Rules Civ.Proc. Rule 43, 28 USCA.

Appointment and compensation of interpreters, see Fed. Rules Cr.Proc. Rule 28, 18 USCA.

Foreign documents, depositions to authenticate, see 18 USCA § 3493.

Opinions and expert testimony, see Fed.Rules Evid. Rule 701 et seq., 28 USCA.

Rule 605. Competency of Judge as Witness

The judge presiding at the trial may not testify in that trial as a witness. No objection need be made in order to preserve the point.

(Pub.L. 93–595, § 1, Jan. 2, 1975, 88 Stat. 1934.)

ADVISORY COMMITTEE NOTES

1972 Proposed Rules

In view of the mandate of 28 U.S.C. § 455 that a judge disqualify himself in "any case in which he * * * is or has been a material witness," the likelihood that the presiding judge in a federal court might be called to testify in the trial over which he is presiding is slight. Nevertheless the possibility is not totally eliminated.

The solution here presented is a broad rule of incompetency, rather than such alternatives as incompetency only as to material matters, leaving the matter to the discretion of the judge, or recognizing no incompetency. The choice is the result of inability to evolve satisfactory answers to questions which arise when the judge abandons the bench for the witness stand. Who rules on objections? Who compels him to answer? Can he rule impartially on the weight and admissibility of his own testimony? Can he be impeached or cross-examined effectively? Can he, in a jury trial, avoid conferring his seal of approval on one side in the eyes of the jury? Can he, in a bench trial, avoid an involvement destructive of impartiality? The rule of general incompetency has substantial support. See Report of the Special Committee on the Propriety of Judges Appearing as Witnesses, 36 A.B.A.J. 630 (1950); cases collected in Annot. 157 A.L.R. 311;

McCormick § 68, p. 147; Uniform Rule 42; California Evidence Code § 703; Kansas Code of Civil Procedure § 60–442; New Jersey Evidence Rule 42. Cf. 6 Wigmore § 1909, which advocates leaving the matter to the discretion of the judge, and statutes to that effect collected in Annot. 157 A.L.R. 311.

The rule provides an "automatic" objection. To require an actual objection would confront the opponent with a choice between not objecting, with the result of allowing the testimony, and objecting, with the probable result of excluding the testimony but at the price of continuing the trial before a judge likely to feel that his integrity had been attacked by the objector.

CROSS REFERENCES

Disqualification of judge to dispose of criminal contempt, see Fed.Rules Cr.Proc. Rule 42, 18 USCA.

Disqualification of justice, judge, or magistrate, see 28 USCA § 455.

Rule 606. Competency of Juror as Witness

(a) At the trial. A member of the jury may not testify as a witness before that jury in the trial of the case in which the juror is sitting. If the juror is called so to testify, the opposing party shall be afforded an opportunity to object out of the presence of the jury.

(b) Inquiry into validity of verdict or indictment. Upon an inquiry into the validity of a verdict or indictment, a juror may not testify as to any matter or statement occurring during the course of the jury's deliberations or to the effect of anything upon that or any other juror's mind or emotions as influencing the juror to assent to or dissent from the verdict or indictment or concerning the juror's mental processes in connection therewith. But a juror may testify about (1) whether extraneous prejudicial information was improperly brought to the jury's attention, (2) whether any outside influence was improperly brought to bear upon any juror, or (3) whether there was a mistake in entering the verdict onto the verdict form. A juror's affidavit or evidence of any statement by the juror may not be received on a matter about which the juror would be precluded from testifying.

(Pub.L. 93–595, § 1, Jan. 2, 1975, 88 Stat. 1934; Pub.L. 94–149, § 1(10), Dec. 12, 1975, 89 Stat. 805; Mar. 2, 1987, eff. Oct. 1, 1987; Apr. 12, 2006, eff. Dec. 1, 2006.)

ADVISORY COMMITTEE NOTES

1972 Proposed Rules

Note to Subdivision (a). The considerations which bear upon the permissibility of testimony by a juror in the trial in which he is sitting as juror bear an obvious similarity to those evoked when the judge is called as a witness. See Advisory Committee's Note to Rule 605. The judge is not, however in this instance so involved as to call for departure from usual principles requiring objection to be made; hence the only provision on objection is that opportunity be afforded for its making out of the presence of the jury. Compare Rule 605.

Note to Subdivision (b). Whether testimony, affidavits, or statements of jurors should be received for the purpose of invalidating or supporting a verdict or indictment, and if so, under what circumstances, has given rise to substantial differences of opinion. The familiar rubric that a juror may not impeach his own verdict, dating from Lord Mansfield's time, is a gross oversimplification. The values sought to be promoted by excluding the evidence include freedom of deliberation, stability and finality of verdicts, and protection of jurors against annoyance and embarrassment. *McDonald v. Pless,* 238 U.S. 264, 35 S.Ct. 783, 59 L.Ed. 1300 (1915). On the other hand, simply putting verdicts beyond effective reach can only promote irregularity and injustice. The rule offers an accommodation between these competing considerations.

The mental operations and emotional reactions of jurors in arriving at a given result would, if allowed as a subject of inquiry, place every verdict at the mercy of jurors and invite tampering and harassment. See *Grenz v. Werre,* 129 N.W.2d 681 (N.D.1964). The authorities are in virtually complete accord in excluding the evidence. Fryer, Note on Disqualification of Witnesses, Selected Writings on Evidence and Trial 345, 347 (Fryer ed. 1957); Maguire, Weinstein, et al., Cases on Evidence 887 (5th ed. 1965); 8 Wigmore § 2349 (McNaughton Rev.1961). As to matters other than mental operations and emotional reactions of jurors, substantial authority refuses to allow a juror to disclose irregularities which occur in the jury room, but allows his testimony as to irregularities occurring outside and allows outsiders to testify as to occurrences both inside and out. 8 Wigmore § 2354 (McNaughton Rev.1961). However, the door of the jury room is not necessarily a satisfactory dividing point, and the Supreme Court has refused to accept it for every situation. *Mattox v. United States,* 146 U.S. 140, 13 S.Ct. 50, 36 L.Ed. 917 (1892).

Under the federal decisions the central focus has been upon insulation of the manner in which the jury reached its verdict, and this protection extends to each of the components of deliberation, including arguments, statements, discussions, mental and emotional reactions, votes, and any other feature of the process. Thus testimony or affidavits of jurors have been held incompetent to show a compromise verdict. *Hyde v. United States,* 225 U.S. 347, 382 (1912); a quotient verdict, *McDonald v. Pless,* 238 U.S. 264 (1915); speculation as to insurance coverage. *Holden v. Porter,* 405 F.2d 878 (10th Cir.1969); *Farmers Coop. Elev. Ass'n v. Strand,* 382 F.2d 224, 230 (8th Cir.1967), cert. denied 389 U.S. 1014; misinterpretation of instructions, *Farmers Coop. Elev. Ass'n v. Strand,* supra; mistake in returning verdict, *United States v. Chereton,* 309 F.2d 197 (6th Cir.1962); interpretation of guilty plea by one defendant as implicating others, *United States v. Crosby,* 294 F.2d 928, 949 (2d Cir.1961). The policy does not, however, foreclose testimony by jurors as to prejudicial extraneous information or influences injected into or brought to bear upon the deliberative process. Thus a juror is recognized as competent to testify to statements by the bailiff or the introduction of a prejudicial newspaper account into the jury room, *Mattox v. United States,* 146 U.S. 140 (1892). See also *Parker v. Gladden,* 385 U.S. 363 (1966).

This rule does not purport to specify the substantive grounds for setting aside verdicts for irregularity; it deals only with the competency of jurors to testify concerning those grounds. Allowing them to testify as to matters other than their own inner reactions involves no particular hazard to the values sought to be protected. The rule is based upon this conclusion. It makes no attempt to specify the substantive grounds for setting aside verdicts for irregularity.

See also Rule 6(e) of the Federal Rules of Criminal Procedure and 18 U.S.C. § 3500, governing the secrecy of grand jury proceedings. The present rule does not relate to secrecy and disclosure but to the competency of certain witnesses and evidence.

1974 Enactment

Note to Subdivision (b). As proposed by the Court, Rule 606(b) limited testimony by a juror in the course of an inquiry into the validity of a verdict or indictment. He could testify as to the influence of extraneous prejudicial information brought to the jury's attention (e.g. a radio newscast or a newspaper account) or an outside influence which improperly had been brought to bear upon a juror (e.g. a threat to the safety of a member of his family), but he could not testify as to other irregularities which occurred in the jury room. Under this formulation a quotient verdict could not be attacked through the testimony of a juror, nor could a juror testify to the drunken condition of a fellow juror which so disabled him that he could not participate in the jury's deliberations.

The 1969 and 1971 Advisory Committee drafts would have permitted a member of the jury to testify concerning these kinds of irregularities in the jury room. The Advisory Committee note in the 1971 draft stated that "* * * the door of the jury room is not a satisfactory dividing point, and the Supreme Court has refused to accept it." The Advisory Committee further commented that—

> The trend has been to draw the dividing line between testimony as to mental processes, on the one hand, and as to the existence of conditions or occurrences of events calculated improperly to influence the verdict on the other hand, without regard to whether the happening is within or without the jury room. * * * The jurors are the persons who know what really happened. Allowing them to testify as to matters other than their own reactions involves no particular hazard to the values sought to be protected. The rule is based upon this conclusion. It makes no attempt to specify the substantive grounds for setting aside verdicts for irregularity.

Objective jury misconduct may be testified to in California, Florida, Iowa, Kansas, Nebraska, New Jersey, North Dakota, Ohio, Oregon, Tennessee, Texas, and Washington.

Persuaded that the better practice is that provided for in the earlier drafts, the Committee amended subdivision (b) to read in the text of those drafts. House Report No. 93–650.

Note to Subdivision (b). As adopted by the House, this rule would permit the impeachment of verdicts by inquiry into, not the mental processes of the jurors, but what happened in terms of conduct in the jury room. This extension of the ability to impeach a verdict is felt to be unwarranted and ill-advised.

The rule passed by the House embodies a suggestion by the Advisory Committee of the Judicial Conference that is considerably broader than the final version adopted by the Supreme Court, which embodied long-accepted Federal law. Although forbidding the impeachment of verdicts by inquiry into the jurors' mental processes, it deletes from the Supreme Court version the proscription against testimony "as to any matter or statement occurring during the course of the jury's deliberations." This deletion would have the effect of opening verdicts up to challenge on the basis of what happened during the jury's internal deliberations, for example, where a juror alleged that the jury refused to follow the trial judge's instructions or that some of the jurors did not take part in deliberations.

Permitting an individual to attack a jury verdict based upon the jury's internal deliberations has long been recognized as unwise by the Supreme Court. In *McDonald v. Pless,* the Court stated:

* * * * * * *

> [L]et it once be established that verdicts solemnly made and publicly returned into court can be attacked and set aside on the testimony of those who took part in their publication and all verdicts could be, and many would be, followed by an inquiry in the hope of discovering something which might invalidate the finding. Jurors would be harassed and beset by the defeated party in an effort to secure from them evidence of facts which might establish misconduct sufficient to set aside a verdict. If evidence thus secured could be thus used, the result would be to make what was intended to be a private deliberation, the constant subject of public investigation—to the destruction of all frankness and freedom of discussion and conference [238 U.S. 264, at 267 (1914)].

* * * * * * *

As it stands then, the rule would permit the harassment of former jurors by losing parties as well as the possible exploitation of disgruntled or otherwise badly-motivated ex-jurors.

Public policy requires a finality to litigation. And common fairness requires that absolute privacy be preserved for jurors to engage in the full and free debate necessary to the attainment of just verdicts. Jurors will not be able to function effectively if their deliberations are to be scrutinized in post-trial litigation. In the interest of protecting the jury system and the citizens who make it work, rule 606 should not permit any inquiry into the internal deliberations of the jurors. Senate Report No. 93–1277.

Note to Subdivision (b). Rule 606(b) deals with juror testimony in an inquiry into the validity of a verdict or indictment. The House bill provides that a juror cannot testify about his mental processes or about the effect of anything upon his or another juror's mind as influencing him to assent to or dissent from a verdict or indictment. Thus, the House bill allows a juror to testify about objective matters occurring during the jury's deliberation, such as the misconduct of another juror or the reaching of a quotient verdict. The Senate bill does not permit juror testimony about any matter or statement occurring during the course of the jury's deliberations. The Senate bill does provide, however, that a juror may testify on the question whether extraneous prejudicial information was improperly brought to the jury's attention and on the question whether any outside influence was improperly brought to bear on any juror.

The Conference adopts the Senate amendment. The Conferees believe that jurors should be encouraged to be conscientious in promptly reporting to the court misconduct that occurs during jury deliberations. House Report No. 93–1597.

1987 Amendments

The amendments are technical. No substantive change is intended.

2006 Amendments

Rule 606(b) has been amended to provide that juror testimony may be used to prove that the verdict reported was the result of a mistake in entering the verdict on the verdict form. The amendment responds to a divergence between the text of the Rule and the case law that has established an exception for proof of clerical errors. *See, e.g., Plummer v. Springfield Term. Ry.*, 5 F.3d 1, 3 (1st Cir. 1993) ("A number of circuits hold, and we agree, that juror testimony regarding an alleged clerical error, such as announcing a verdict different than that agreed upon, does not challenge the validity of the verdict or the deliberation of mental processes, and therefore is not subject to Rule 606(b)."); *Teevee Toons, Inc., v. MP3.Com, Inc.*, 148 F.Supp.2d 276, 278 (S.D.N.Y. 2001) (noting that Rule 606(b) has been silent regarding inquiries designed to confirm the accuracy of a verdict).

In adopting the exception for proof of mistakes in entering the verdict on the verdict form, the amendment specifically rejects the broader exception, adopted by some courts, permitting the use of juror testimony to prove that the jurors were operating under a misunderstanding about the consequences of the result that they agreed upon. *See, e.g., Attridge v. Cencorp Div. of Dover Techs. Int'l, Inc.*, 836 F.2d 113, 116 (2d Cir. 1987); *Eastridge Development Co., v. Halpert Associates, Inc.*, 853 F.2d 772 (10th Cir. 1988). The broader exception is rejected because an inquiry into whether the jury misunderstood or misapplied an instruction goes to the jurors' mental processes underlying the verdict, rather than the verdict's accuracy in capturing what the jurors had agreed upon. *See, e.g.* , *Karl v. Burlington Northern R.R.*, 880 F.2d 68, 74 (8th Cir. 1989) (error to receive juror testimony on whether verdict was the result of jurors' misunderstanding of instructions: "The jurors did not state that the figure written by the foreman was different from that which they agreed upon, but indicated that the figure the foreman wrote down was intended to be a net figure, not a gross figure. Receiving such statements violates Rule 606(b) because the testimony relates to how the jury interpreted the court's instructions, and concerns the jurors' 'mental processes,' which is forbidden by the rule."); *Robles v. Exxon Corp.*, 862 F.2d 1201, 1208 (5th Cir. 1989) ("the alleged error here goes to the substance of what the jury was asked to decide, necessarily implicating the jury's mental processes insofar as it questions the jury's understanding of the court's instructions and application of those instructions to the facts of the case"). Thus, the exception established by the amendment is limited to cases such as "where the jury foreperson wrote down, in response to an interrogatory, a number different from that agreed upon by the jury, or mistakenly stated that the defendant was 'guilty' when the jury had actually agreed that the defendant was not guilty." *Id.*

It should be noted that the possibility of errors in the verdict form will be reduced substantially by polling the jury. Rule 606(b) does not, of course, prevent this precaution. *See* 8 C. Wigmore, *Evidence*, § 2350 at 691 (McNaughten ed. 1961) (noting that the reasons for the rule barring juror testimony, "namely, the dangers of uncertainty and of tampering with the jurors to procure testimony, disappear in large part if such investigation as may be desired is *made by the judge* and takes place *before the jurors' discharge* and separation") (emphasis in original). Errors that come to light after polling the jury "may be corrected on the spot, or the jury may be sent out to continue deliberations, or, if necessary, a new trial may be ordered." C. Mueller & L. Kirkpatrick, *Evidence Under the Rules* at 671 (2d ed. 1999) (citing *Sincox v. United States*, 571 F.2d 876, 878–79 (5th Cir. 1978)).

HISTORICAL NOTES

Revision Notes and Legislative Reports

1975 Acts. House Report No. 94–599, see 1975 U.S. Code Cong. and Adm. News, p. 1585.

CROSS REFERENCES

Grand jury, secrecy of proceedings and disclosure, see Fed.Rules Cr.Proc. Rule 6, 18 USCA.

Statements and reports of witnesses, demands for, see 18 USCA § 3500.

Rule 607. Who May Impeach

The credibility of a witness may be attacked by any party, including the party calling the witness.

(Pub.L. 93–595, § 1, Jan. 2, 1975, 88 Stat.1934; Mar. 2, 1987, eff. Oct. 1, 1987.)

ADVISORY COMMITTEE NOTES

1972 Proposed Rules

The traditional rule against impeaching one's own witness is abandoned as based on false premises. A party does not hold out his witnesses as worthy of belief, since he rarely has a free choice in selecting them. Denial of the right leaves the party at the mercy of the witness and the adversary. If the impeachment is by a prior statement, it is free from hearsay dangers and is excluded from the category of hearsay under Rule 801(d)(1). Ladd, Impeachment of One's Own Witness—New Developments, 4 U.Chi.L.Rev. 69 (1936); McCormick § 38; 3 Wigmore §§ 896–918. The substantial inroads into the old rule made over the years by decisions, rules, and statutes are evidence of doubts as to its basic soundness and workability. Cases are collected in 3 Wigmore § 905. Revised Rule 32(a)(1) of the Federal Rules of Civil Procedure allows any party to impeach a witness by means of his deposition, and Rule 43(b) has allowed the calling and impeachment of an adverse party or person identified with him. Illustrative statutes allowing a party to impeach his own witness under varying circumstances are Ill.Rev.Stats.1967, c. 110, § 60; Mass.Laws Annot. 1959, c. 233, § 23; 20 N.M.Stats.Annot. 1953, § 20–2–4; N.Y. CPLR § 4514 (McKinney 1963); 12 Vt.Stats.Annot.1959, §§ 1641a, 1642. Complete judicial rejection of the old rule is found in *United States v. Freeman*, 302 F.2d 347 (2d Cir.1962). The same result is reached in Uniform Rule 20; California Evidence Code § 785; Kansas Code of Civil Procedure § 60–420. See also New Jersey Evidence Rule 20.

1987 Amendments

The amendment is technical. No substantive change is intended.

CROSS REFERENCES

Character evidence, inadmissibility to prove conduct, see Fed.Rules Evid. Rule 404, 28 USCA.

Cross-examination, right of, see USCA Const. Amend. VI.

Depositions, use for impeachment of deponent, see Fed. Rules Civ.Proc. Rule 32, 28 USCA.

Depositions, use for impeachment of deponent, see Fed. Rules Cr.Proc. Rule 15, 18 USCA.

Prior statements of witnesses not hearsay where witness cross-examined, see Fed.Rules Evid. Rule 801, 28 USCA.

Relevant evidence excluded on grounds of prejudice, confusion, or cumulation, see Fed.Rules Evid. Rule 403, 28 USCA.

Rule 608. Evidence of Character and Conduct of Witness

(a) Opinion and reputation evidence of character. The credibility of a witness may be attacked or supported by evidence in the form of opinion or reputation, but subject to these limitations: (1) the evidence may refer only to character for truthfulness or untruthfulness, and (2) evidence of truthful character is admissible only after the character of the witness for truthfulness has been attacked by opinion or reputation evidence or otherwise.

(b) Specific instances of conduct. Specific instances of the conduct of a witness, for the purpose of attacking or supporting the witness' character for truthfulness, other than conviction of crime as provided in rule 609, may not be proved by extrinsic evidence. They may, however, in the discretion of the court, if probative of truthfulness or untruthfulness, be inquired into on cross-examination of the witness (1) concerning the witness' character for truthfulness or untruthfulness, or (2) concerning the character for truthfulness or untruthfulness of another witness as to which character the witness being cross-examined has testified.

The giving of testimony, whether by an accused or by any other witness, does not operate as a waiver of the accused's or the witness' privilege against self-incrimination when examined with respect to matters that relate only to character for truthfulness.

(Pub.L. 93–595, § 1, Jan. 2, 1975, 88 Stat.1935; Mar. 2, 1987, eff. Oct. 1, 1987; Apr. 25, 1988, eff. Nov. 1, 1988; Mar. 27, 2003, eff. Dec. 1, 2003.)

ADVISORY COMMITTEE NOTES

1972 Proposed Rules

Note to Subdivision (a). In Rule 404(a) the general position is taken that character evidence is not admissible for the purpose of proving that the person acted in conformity therewith, subject, however, to several exceptions, one of which is character evidence of a witness as bearing upon his credibility. The present rule develops that exception.

In accordance with the bulk of judicial authority, the inquiry is strictly limited to character for veracity, rather than allowing evidence as to character generally. The result is to sharpen relevancy, to reduce surprise, waste of time, and confusion, and to make the lot of the witness somewhat less unattractive. McCormick § 44.

The use of opinion and reputation evidence as means of proving the character of witnesses is consistent with Rule 405(a). While the modern practice has purported to exclude opinion, witnesses who testify to reputation seem in fact often to be giving their opinions, disguised somewhat misleadingly as reputation. See McCormick § 44. And even under the modern practice, a common relaxation has allowed inquiry as to whether the witnesses would believe the principal witness under oath. *United States v. Walker,* 313 F.2d 236 (6th Cir.1963), and cases cited therein; McCormick § 44, pp. 94–95, n. 3.

Character evidence in support of credibility is admissible under the rule only after the witness' character has first been attacked, as has been the case at common law. Maguire, Weinstein, et al., Cases on Evidence 295 (5th ed. 1965); McCormick § 49, p. 105; 4 Wigmore § 1104. The enormous needless consumption of time which a contrary practice would entail justifies the limitation. Opinion or reputation that the witness is untruthful specifically qualifies as an attack under the rule, and evidence of misconduct, including conviction of crime, and of corruption also fall within this category. Evidence of bias or interest does not. McCormick § 49; 4 Wigmore §§ 1106, 1107. Whether evidence in the form of contradiction is an attack upon the character of the witness must depend upon the circumstances. McCormick § 49. Cf. 4 Wigmore §§ 1108, 1109.

As to the use of specific instances on direct by an opinion witness, see the Advisory Committee's Note to Rule 405, *supra.*

Note to Subdivision (b). In conformity with Rule 405, which forecloses use of evidence of specific incidents as proof in chief of character unless character is an issue in the case, the present rule generally bars evidence of specific instances of conduct of a witness for the purpose of attacking or supporting his credibility. There are, however, two exceptions: (1) specific instances are provable when they have been the subject of criminal conviction, and (2) specific instances may be inquired into on cross-examination of the principal witness or of a witness giving an opinion of his character for truthfulness.

(1) Conviction of crime as a technique of impeachment is treated in detail in Rule 609, and here is merely recognized as an exception to the general rule excluding evidence of specific incidents for impeachment purposes.

(2) Particular instances of conduct, though not the subject of criminal conviction, may be inquired into on cross-examination of the principal witness himself or of a witness who testifies concerning his character for truthfulness. Effective cross-examination demands that some allowance be made for going into matters of this kind, but the possibilities of abuse are substantial. Consequently safeguards are erected in the form of specific requirements that the instances inquired into

be probative of truthfulness or its opposite and not remote in time. Also, the overriding protection of Rule 403 requires that probative value not be outweighed by danger of unfair prejudice, confusion of issues, or misleading the jury, and that of Rule 611 bars harassment and undue embarrassment.

The final sentence constitutes a rejection of the doctrine of such cases as *People v. Sorge,* 301 N.Y. 198, 93 N.E.2d 637 (1950), that any past criminal act relevant to credibility may be inquired into on cross-examination, in apparent disregard of the privilege against self-incrimination. While it is clear that an ordinary witness cannot make a partial disclosure of incriminating matter and then invoke the privilege on cross-examination, no tenable contention can be made that merely by testifying he waives his right to foreclose inquiry on cross-examination into criminal activities for the purpose of attacking his credibility. So to hold would reduce the privilege to a nullity. While it is true that an accused, unlike an ordinary witness, has an option whether to testify, if the option can be exercised only at the price of opening up inquiry as to any and all criminal acts committed during his lifetime, the right to testify could scarcely be said to possess much vitality. In *Griffin v. California,* 380 U.S. 609, 85 S.Ct. 1229, 14 L.Ed.2d 106 (1965), the Court held that allowing comment on the election of an accused not to testify exacted a constitutionally impermissible price, and so here. While no specific provision in terms confers constitutional status on the right of an accused to take the stand in his own defense, the existence of the right is so completely recognized that a denial of it or substantial infringement upon it would surely be of due process dimensions. See *Ferguson v. Georgia,* 365 U.S. 570, 81 S.Ct. 756, 5 L.Ed.2d 783 (1961); McCormick § 131; 8 Wigmore § 2276 (McNaughton Rev.1961). In any event, wholly aside from constitutional considerations, the provision represents a sound policy.

1974 Enactment

Note to Subdivision (a). Rule 608(a) as submitted by the Court permitted attack to be made upon the character for truthfulness or untruthfulness of a witness either by reputation or opinion testimony. For the same reason underlying its decision to eliminate the admissibility of opinion testimony in Rule 405(a), the Committee amended Rule 608(a) to delete the reference to opinion testimony.

Note to Subdivision (b). The second sentence of Rule 608(b) as submitted by the Court permitted specific instances of misconduct of a witness to be inquired into on cross-examination for the purpose of attacking his credibility, if probative of truthfulness or untruthfulness, "and not remote in time". Such cross-examination could be of the witness himself or of another witness who testifies as to "his" character for truthfulness or untruthfulness.

The Committee amended the Rule to emphasize the discretionary power of the court in permitting such testimony and deleted the reference to remoteness in time as being unnecessary and confusing (remoteness from time of trial or remoteness from the incident involved?). As recast, the Committee amendment also makes clear the antecedent of "his" in the original Court proposal. House Report No. 93–650.

The Senate amendment adds the words "opinion or" to conform the first sentence of the rule with the remainder of the rule.

The Conference adopts the Senate amendment. House Report No. 93–1597.

1987 Amendments

The amendments are technical. No substantive change is intended.

1988 Amendments

The amendment is technical. No substantive change is intended.

2003 Amendments

The Rule has been amended to clarify that the absolute prohibition on extrinsic evidence applies only when the sole reason for proffering that evidence is to attack or support the witness' character for truthfulness. *See United States v. Abel,* 469 U.S. 45 (1984); *United States v. Fusco,* 748 F.2d 996 (5th Cir. 1984) (Rule 608(b) limits the use of evidence "designed to show that the witness has done things, unrelated to the suit being tried, that make him more or less believable per se"); Ohio R.Evid. 608(b). On occasion the Rule's use of the overbroad term "credibility" has been read "to bar extrinsic evidence for bias, competency and contradiction impeachment since they too deal with credibility." American Bar Association Section of Litigation, *Emerging Problems Under the Federal Rules of Evidence* at 161 (3d ed. 1998). The amendment conforms the language of the Rule to its original intent, which was to impose an absolute bar on extrinsic evidence only if the sole purpose for offering the evidence was to prove the witness' character for veracity. *See* Advisory Committee Note to Rule 608(b) (stating that the Rule is "[i]n conformity with Rule 405, which forecloses use of evidence of specific incidents as proof in chief of character unless character is in issue in the case . . . ").

By limiting the application of the Rule to proof of a witness' character for truthfulness, the amendment leaves the admissibility of extrinsic evidence offered for other grounds of impeachment (such as contradiction, prior inconsistent statement, bias and mental capacity) to Rules 402 and 403. *See, e.g., United States v. Winchenbach,* 197 F.3d 548 (1st Cir. 1999) (admissibility of a prior inconsistent statement offered for impeachment is governed by Rules 402 and 403, not Rule 608(b)); *United States v. Tarantino,* 846 F.2d 1384 (D.C. Cir. 1988) (admissibility of extrinsic evidence offered to contradict a witness is governed by Rules 402 and 403); *United States v. Lindemann,* 85 F.3d 1232 (7th Cir. 1996) (admissibility of extrinsic evidence of bias is governed by Rules 402 and 403).

It should be noted that the extrinsic evidence prohibition of Rule 608(b) bars any reference to the consequences that a witness might have suffered as a result of an alleged bad act. For example, Rule 608(b) prohibits counsel from mentioning that a witness was suspended or disciplined for the conduct that is the subject of impeachment, when that conduct is offered only to prove the character of the witness. *See United States v. Davis,* 183 F.3d 231, 257 n.12 (3d Cir. 1999) (emphasizing that in attacking the defendant's character for truthfulness "the government cannot make reference to Davis's forty-four day suspension or that Internal Affairs found that he lied about" an incident because "[s]uch evidence would not only be hearsay to the extent it contains assertion of fact, it would be inadmissible extrinsic evidence under Rule 608(b)"). *See also* Stephen A. Saltzburg, *Impeaching the Witness: Prior Bad Acts and Extrinsic Evidence*, 7 Crim. Just. 28, 31 (Winter 1993) ("counsel should not be permitted to circumvent the no-extrinsic-evidence provision by tucking a third person's opinion about prior acts into a question asked of the witness who has denied the act").

For purposes of consistency the term "credibility" has been replaced by the term "character for truthfulness" in the last sentence of subdivision (b). The term "credibility" is also used in subdivision (a). But the Committee found it unnecessary to substitute "character for truthfulness" for "credibility" in Rule 608(a), because subdivision (a)(1) already serves to limit impeachment to proof of such character.

Rules 609(a) and 610 also use the term "credibility" when the intent of those Rules is to regulate impeachment of a witness' character for truthfulness. No inference should be derived from the fact that the Committee proposed an amendment to Rule 608(b) but not to Rules 609 and 610.

CROSS REFERENCES

Character evidence—

Inadmissible to prove conduct; exceptions, see Fed. Rules Evid. Rule 404, 28 USCA.

Methods of proving character, see Fed.Rules Evid. Rule 405, 28 USCA.

Civil commitment for narcotic addiction not conviction; use of test results on cross-examination, see 28 USCA § 2904.

Extortionate credit transactions, admissibility of evidence to show—

Reputation as to collection practices, see 18 USCA § 892.

Reputation of defendant within community, see 18 USCA § 894.

Threat as means of collection, see 18 USCA § 894.

Immunity of witnesses, order compelling testimony, see 18 USCA §§ 6002 and 6003.

Opinion evidence, see Fed.Rules Evid. Rule 701 et seq., 28 USCA.

Prejudice, confusion, or waste of time, exclusion of evidence for, see Fed.Rules Evid. Rule 403, 28 USCA.

Self-incrimination, see USCA Const. Amend. V.

Rule 609. Impeachment by Evidence of Conviction of Crime

(a) General rule.—For the purpose of attacking the character for truthfulness of a witness,

(1) evidence that a witness other than an accused has been convicted of a crime shall be admitted, subject to Rule 403, if the crime was punishable by death or imprisonment in excess of one year under the law under which the witness was convicted, and evidence that an accused has been convicted of such a crime shall be admitted if the court determines that the probative value of admitting this evidence outweighs its prejudicial effect to the accused; and

(2) evidence that any witness has been convicted of a crime shall be admitted regardless of the punishment, if it readily can be determined that establishing the elements of the crime required proof or admission of an act of dishonesty or false statement by the witness.

(b) Time limit. Evidence of a conviction under this rule is not admissible if a period of more than ten years has elapsed since the date of the conviction or of the release of the witness from the confinement imposed for that conviction, whichever is the later date, unless the court determines, in the interests of justice, that the probative value of the conviction supported by specific facts and circumstances substantially outweighs its prejudicial effect. However, evidence of a conviction more than 10 years old as calculated herein, is not admissible unless the proponent gives to the adverse party sufficient advance written notice of intent to use such evidence to provide the adverse party with a fair opportunity to contest the use of such evidence.

(c) Effect of pardon, annulment, or certificate of rehabilitation.—Evidence of a conviction is not admissible under this rule if (1) the conviction has been the subject of a pardon, annulment, certificate of rehabilitation, or other equivalent procedure based on a finding of the rehabilitation of the person convicted, and that person has not been convicted of a subsequent crime that was punishable by death or imprisonment in excess of one year, or (2) the conviction has been the subject of a pardon, annulment, or other equivalent procedure based on a finding of innocence.

(d) Juvenile adjudications. Evidence of juvenile adjudications is generally not admissible under this rule. The court may, however, in a criminal case allow evidence of a juvenile adjudication of a witness other than the accused if conviction of the offense would be admissible to attack the credibility of an adult and the court is satisfied that admission in evidence is necessary for a fair determination of the issue of guilt or innocence.

(e) Pendency of appeal. The pendency of an appeal therefrom does not render evidence of a conviction inadmissible. Evidence of the pendency of an appeal is admissible.

(Pub.L. 93–595, § 1, Jan. 2, 1975, 88 Stat.1935; Mar. 2, 1987, eff. Oct. 1, 1987; Jan. 26, 1990, eff. Dec. 1, 1990; Apr. 12, 2006, eff. Dec. 1, 2006.)

ADVISORY COMMITTEE NOTES

1972 Proposed Rules

As a means of impeachment, evidence of conviction of crime is significant only because it stands as proof of the commission of the underlying criminal act. There is little dissent from the general proposition that at least some crimes are relevant to credibility but much disagreement among the cases and commentators about which crimes are usable for this purpose. See McCormick § 43; 2 Wright, Federal Practice and Procedure: Criminal § 416 (1969). The weight of traditional authority has been to allow use of felonies generally, without regard to the nature of the particular offense, and of *crimen falsi* without regard to the grade of the offense. This is the view accepted by Congress in the 1970 amendment of § 14–305 of the District of Columbia Code, P.L. 91–358, 84 Stat. 473. Uniform Rule 21 and Model Code Rule 106 permit only crimes involving "dishonesty or false statement." Others have thought that the trial judge should have discretion to exclude convictions if the probative value of the evidence of the crime is substantially outweighed by the danger of unfair prejudice. *Luck v. United States,* 121 U.S.App.D.C. 151, 348 F.2d 763 (1965); McGowan, Impeachment of Criminal Defendants by Prior Convictions, 1970 Law & Soc.Order 1. Whatever may be the merits of those views, this rule is drafted to accord with the Congressional policy manifested in the 1970 legislation.

The proposed rule incorporates certain basic safeguards, in terms applicable to all witnesses but of particular significance to an accused who elects to testify. These protections include the imposition of definite time limitations, giving effect to demonstrated rehabilitation, and generally excluding juvenile adjudications.

Note to Subdivision (a). For purposes of impeachment, crimes are divided into two categories by the rule: (1) those of what is generally regarded as felony grade, without particular regard to the nature of the offense, and (2) those involving dishonesty or false statement, without regard to the grade of the offense. Probable convictions are not limited to violations of federal law. By reason of our constitutional structure, the federal catalog of crimes is far from being a complete one, and resort must be had to the laws of the states for the specification of many crimes. For example, simple theft as compared with theft from interstate commerce. Other instances of borrowing are the Assimilative Crimes Act, making the state law of crimes applicable to the special territorial and maritime jurisdiction of the United States, 18 U.S.C. § 13, and the provision of the Judicial Code disqualifying persons as jurors on the grounds of state as well as federal convictions, 28 U.S.C. § 1865. For evaluation of the crime in terms of seriousness, reference is made to the congressional measurement of felony (subject to imprisonment in excess of one year) rather than adopting state definitions which vary considerably. See 28 U.S.C. § 1865, *supra,* disqualifying jurors for conviction in state or federal court of crime punishable by imprisonment for more than one year.

Note to Subdivision (b). Few statutes recognize a time limit on impeachment by evidence of conviction. However, practical considerations of fairness and relevancy demand that some boundary be recognized. See Ladd, Credibility Tests—Current Trends, 89 U.Pa.L.Rev. 166, 176–177 (1940). This portion of the rule is derived from the proposal advanced in Recommendation Proposing in Evidence Code, § 788(5), p. 142, Cal.Law Rev.Comm'n (1965), though not adopted. See California Evidence Code § 788.

Note to Subdivision (c). A pardon or its equivalent granted solely for the purpose of restoring civil rights lost by virtue of a conviction has no relevance to an inquiry into character. If, however, the pardon or other proceeding is hinged upon a showing of rehabilitation the situation is otherwise. The result under the rule is to render the conviction inadmissible. The alternative of allowing in evidence both the conviction and the rehabilitation has not been adopted for reasons of policy, economy of time, and difficulties of evaluation.

A similar provision is contained in California Evidence Code § 788. Cf. A.L.I. Model Penal Code, Proposed Official Draft § 306.6(3)(e) (1962), and discussion in A.L.I. Proceedings 310 (1961).

Pardons based on innocence have the effect, of course, of nullifying the conviction *ab initio.*

Note to Subdivision (d). The prevailing view has been that a juvenile adjudication is not usable for impeachment. *Thomas v. United States,* 74 App.D.C. 167, 121 F.2d 905 (1941); *Cotton v. United States,* 355 F.2d 480 (10th Cir.1966). This conclusion was based upon a variety of circumstances. By virtue of its informality, frequently diminished quantum of required proof, and other departures from accepted standards for criminal trials under the theory of *parens patriae,* the juvenile adjudication was considered to lack the precision and general probative value of the criminal conviction. While *In re Gault,* 387 U.S. 1, 87 S.Ct. 1428, 18 L.Ed.2d 527 (1967), no doubt eliminates these characteristics insofar as objectionable, other obstacles remain. Practical problems of administration are raised by the common provisions in juvenile legislation that records be kept confidential and that they be destroyed after a short time. While *Gault* was skeptical as to the realities of confidentiality of juvenile records, it also saw no constitutional obstacles to improvement. 387 U.S. at 25, 87 S.Ct. 1428. See also Note, Rights and Rehabilitation in the Juvenile Courts, 67 Colum.L.Rev. 281, 289 (1967). In addition, policy considerations much akin to those which dictate exclusion of adult convictions after rehabilitation has been established strongly suggest a rule of excluding juvenile adjudications. Admittedly, however, the rehabilitative process may in a given case be a demonstrated failure, or the strategic importance of a given witness may be so great as to require the overriding of general policy in the interests of particular justice. See *Giles v. Maryland,* 386 U.S. 66, 87 S.Ct. 793, 17 L.Ed.2d 737 (1967). Wigmore was outspoken in his condemnation of the disallowance of juvenile adjudications to impeach, especially when the witness is the complainant in a case of molesting a minor. 1 Wigmore § 196; 3 *Id.* §§ 924a, 980. The rule recognizes discretion in the judge to effect an accommodation among these various factors by departing from the general principle of exclusion. In deference to the general pattern and policy of juvenile statutes, however, no discretion is accorded when the witness is the accused in a criminal case.

Note to Subdivision (e). The presumption of correctness which ought to attend judicial proceedings supports the position that pendency of an appeal does not preclude use of a conviction for impeachment. *United States v. Empire Packing Co.,* 174 F.2d 16 (7th Cir.1949), cert. denied 337 U.S. 959, 69 S.Ct. 1534, 93 L.Ed. 1758; *Bloch v. United States,* 226 F.2d 185 (9th Cir.1955), cert. denied 350 U.S. 948, 76 S.Ct. 323, 100 L.Ed. 826 and 353 U.S. 959, 77 S.Ct. 868, 1 L.Ed.2d 910; and see *Newman v. United States,* 331 F.2d 968 (8th Cir.1964). *Contra, Campbell v. United States,* 85 U.S.App.D.C. 133, 176 F.2d 45 (1949). The pendency of an appeal is, however, a qualifying circumstance properly considerable.

1974 Enactment

Note to Subdivision (a). Rule 609(a) as submitted by the Court was modeled after Section 133(a) of Public Law

91–358, 14 D.C.Code 305(b)(1), enacted in 1970. The Rule provided that:

> For the purpose of attacking the credibility of a witness, evidence that he has been convicted of a crime is admissible but only if the crime (1) was punishable by death or imprisonment in excess of one year under the law under which he was convicted or (2) involved dishonesty or false statement regardless of the punishment.

As reported to the Committee by the Subcommittee, Rule 609(a) was amended to read as follows:

> For the purpose of attacking the credibility of a witness, evidence that he has been convicted of a crime is admissible only if the crime (1) was punishable by death or imprisonment in excess of one year, unless the court determines that the danger of unfair prejudice outweighs the probative value of the evidence of the conviction, or (2) involved dishonesty or false statement.

In full committee, the provision was amended to permit attack upon the credibility of a witness by prior conviction only if the prior crime involved dishonesty or false statement. While recognizing that the prevailing doctrine in the federal courts and in most States allows a witness to be impeached by evidence of prior felony convictions without restriction as to type, the Committee was of the view that, because of the danger of unfair prejudice in such practice and the deterrent effect upon an accused who might wish to testify, and even upon a witness who was not the accused, cross-examination by evidence of prior conviction should be limited to those kinds of convictions bearing directly on credibility, *i.e.,* crimes involving dishonesty or false statement.

Note to Subdivision (b). Rule 609(b) as submitted by the Court was modeled after Section 133(a) of Public Law 91–358, 14 D.C.Code 305(b)(2)(B), enacted in 1970. The Rule provided:

> Evidence of a conviction under this rule is not admissible if a period of more than ten years has elapsed since the date of the release of the witness from confinement imposed for his most recent conviction, or the expiration of the period of his parole, probation, or sentence granted or imposed with respect to his most recent conviction, whichever is the later date.

Under this formulation, a witness' entire past record of criminal convictions could be used for impeachment (provided the conviction met the standard of subdivision (a)), if the witness had been most recently released from confinement, or the period of his parole or probation had expired, within ten years of the conviction.

The Committee amended the Rule to read in the text of the 1971 Advisory Committee version to provide that upon the expiration of ten years from the date of a conviction of a witness, or of his release from confinement for that offense, that conviction may no longer be used for impeachment. The Committee was of the view that after ten years following a person's release from confinement (or from the date of his conviction) the probative value of the conviction with respect to that person's credibility diminished to a point where it should no longer be admissible.

Note to Subdivision (c). Rule 609(c) as submitted by the Court provided in part that evidence of a witness' prior conviction is not admissible to attack his credibility if the conviction was the subject of a pardon, annulment, or other equivalent procedure, based on a showing of rehabilitation, and the witness has not been convicted of a subsequent crime. The Committee amended the Rule to provide that the "subsequent crime" must have been "punishable by death or imprisonment in excess of one year", on the ground that a subsequent conviction of an offense not a felony is insufficient to rebut the finding that the witness has been rehabilitated. The Committee also intends that the words "based on a finding of the rehabilitation of the person convicted" apply not only to "certificate of rehabilitation, or other equivalent procedure", but also to "pardon" and "annulment.". House Report No. 93–650.

Note to Subdivision (a). As proposed by the Supreme Court, the rule would allow the use of prior convictions to impeach if the crime was a felony or a misdemeanor if the misdemeanor involved dishonesty or false statement. As modified by the House, the rule would admit prior convictions for impeachment purposes only if the offense, whether felony or misdemeanor, involved dishonesty or false statement.

The committee has adopted a modified version of the House-passed rule. In your committee's view, the danger of unfair prejudice is far greater when the accused, as opposed to other witnesses, testifies, because the jury may be prejudiced not merely on the question of credibility but also on the ultimate question of guilt or innocence. Therefore, with respect to defendants, the committee agreed with the House limitation that only offenses involved false statement or dishonesty may be used. By that phrase, the committee means crimes such as perjury or subornation of perjury, false statement, criminal fraud, embezzlement or false pretense, or any other offense, in the nature of *crimen falsi* the commission of which involves some element of untruthfulness, deceit or falsification bearing on the accused's propensity to testify truthfully.

With respect to other witnesses, in addition to any prior conviction involving false statement or dishonesty, any other felony may be used to impeach if, and only if, the court finds that the probative value of such evidence outweighs its prejudicial effect against the party offering that witness.

Notwithstanding this provision, proof of any prior offense otherwise admissible under Rule 404 could still be offered for the purposes sanctioned by that rule. Furthermore, the committee intends that notwithstanding this rule, a defendant's misrepresentation regarding the existence or nature of prior convictions may be met by rebuttal evidence, including the record of such prior convictions. Similarly, such records may be offered to rebut representations made by the defendant regarding his attitude toward or willingness to commit a general category of offense, although denials or other representations by the defendant regarding the specific conduct which forms the basis of the charge against him shall not make prior convictions admissible to rebut such statement.

In regard to either type of representation, of course, prior convictions may be offered in rebuttal only if the defendant's statement is made in response to defense counsel's questions or is made gratuitously in the course of cross-examination. Prior convictions may not be offered as rebuttal evidence if the prosecution has sought to circumvent the purpose of this rule by asking questions which elicit such representations from the defendant.

One other clarifying amendment has been added to this subsection, that is, to provide that the admissibility of evidence of a prior conviction is permitted only upon cross-examination of a witness. It is not admissible if a person does not testify. It is to be understood, however, that a court record of a prior conviction is admissible to prove that conviction if the witness has forgotten or denies its existence.

Note to Subdivision (b). Although convictions over ten years old generally do not have much probative value, there may be exceptional circumstances under which the conviction substantially bears on the credibility of the witness. Rather than exclude all convictions over 10 years old, the committee adopted an amendment in the form of a final clause to the section granting the court discretion to admit convictions over 10 years old, but only upon a determination by the court that the probative value of the conviction supported by specific facts and circumstances, substantially outweighs its prejudicial effect.

It is intended that convictions over 10 years old will be admitted very rarely and only in exceptional circumstances. The rules provide that the decision be supported by specific facts and circumstances thus requiring the court to make specific findings on the record as to the particular facts and circumstances it has considered in determining that the probative value of the conviction substantially outweighs its prejudicial impact. It is expected that, in fairness, the court will give the party against whom the conviction is introduced a full and adequate opportunity to contest its admission. Senate Report No. 93–1277.

Rule 609 defines when a party may use evidence of a prior conviction in order to impeach a witness. The Senate amendments make changes in two subsections of Rule 609.

Note to Subdivision (a). The House bill provides that the credibility of a witness can be attacked by proof of prior conviction of a crime only if the crime involves dishonesty or false statement. The Senate amendment provides that a witness' credibility may be attacked if the crime (1) was punishable by death or imprisonment in excess of one year under the law under which he was convicted or (2) involves dishonesty or false statement, regardless of the punishment.

The Conference adopts the Senate amendment with an amendment. The Conference amendment provides that the credibility of a witness, whether a defendant or someone else, may be attacked by proof of a prior conviction but only if the crime: (1) was punishable by death or imprisonment in excess of one year under the law under which he was convicted and the court determines that the probative value of the conviction outweighs its prejudicial effect to the defendant; or (2) involved dishonesty or false statement regardless of the punishment.

By the phrase "dishonesty and false statement" the Conference means crimes such as perjury or subornation of perjury, false statement, criminal fraud, embezzlement, or false pretense, or any other offense in the nature of *crimen falsi,* the commission of which involves some element of deceit, untruthfulness, or falsification bearing on the accused's propensity to testify truthfully.

The admission of prior convictions involving dishonesty and false statement is not within the discretion of the Court. Such convictions are peculiarly probative of credibility and, under this rule, are always to be admitted. Thus, judicial discretion granted with respect to the admissibility of other prior convictions is not applicable to those involving dishonesty or false statement.

With regard to the discretionary standard established by paragraph (1) of Rule 609(a), the Conference determined that the prejudicial effect to be weighed against the probative value of the conviction is specifically the prejudicial effect *to the defendant.* The danger of prejudice to a witness other than the defendant (such as injury to the witness' reputation in his community) was considered and rejected by the Conference as an element to be weighed in determining admissibility. It was the judgment of the Conference that the danger of prejudice to a nondefendant witness is outweighed by the need for the trier of fact to have as much relevant evidence on the issue of credibility as possible. Such evidence should only be excluded where it presents a danger of improperly influencing the outcome of the trial by persuading the trier of fact to convict the defendant on the basis of his prior criminal record.

Note to Subdivision (b). The House bill provides in subsection (b) that evidence of conviction of a crime may not be used for impeachment purposes under subsection (a) if more than ten years have elapsed since the date of the conviction or the date the witness was released from confinement imposed for the conviction, whichever is later. The Senate amendment permits the use of convictions older than ten years, if the court determines, in the interests of justice, that the probative value of the conviction, supported by specific facts and circumstances, substantially outweighs its prejudicial effect.

The Conference adopts the Senate amendment with an amendment requiring notice by a party that he intends to request that the court allow him to use a conviction older than ten years. The Conferees anticipate that a written notice, in order to give the adversary a fair opportunity to contest the use of the evidence, will ordinarily include such information as the date of the conviction, the jurisdiction, and the offense or statute involved. In order to eliminate the possibility that the flexibility of this provision may impair the ability of a party-opponent to prepare for trial, the Conferees intend that the notice provision operate to avoid surprise. House Report No. 93–1597.

1987 Amendments

The amendments are technical. No substantive change is intended.

1990 Amendments

The amendment to Rule 609(a) makes two changes in the rule. The first change removes from the rule the limitation that the conviction may only be elicited during cross-examination, a limitation that virtually every circuit has found to be inapplicable. It is common for witnesses to reveal on direct examination their convictions to "remove the sting" of the impeachment. *See e.g., United States v. Bad Cob,* 560 F.2d 877 (8th Cir.1977). The amendment does not contemplate that a court will necessarily permit proof of prior convictions through testimony, which might be time-consuming and more prejudicial than proof through a written record. Rules 403 and 611(a) provide sufficient authority for the court to protect against unfair or disruptive methods of proof.

The second change effected by the amendment resolves an ambiguity as to the relationship of Rules 609 and 403 with respect to impeachment of witnesses other than the criminal defendant. *See, Green v. Bock Laundry Machine Co.,* 109 S.Ct. 1981, 490 U.S. 504 (1989). The amendment does not disturb the special balancing test for the criminal defendant who chooses to testify. Thus, the rule recognizes that, in virtually every case in which prior convictions are used to impeach the testifying defendant, the defendant faces a unique risk of prejudice—*i.e.*, the danger that convictions that would be excluded under Fed.R.Evid. 404 will be misused by a jury as propensity evidence despite their introduction solely for impeachment purposes. Although the rule does not forbid all use of convictions to impeach a defendant, it requires that the government show that the probative value of convictions as impeachment evidence outweighs their prejudicial effect.

Prior to the amendment, the rule appeared to give the defendant the benefit of the special balancing test when defense witnesses other than the defendant were called to testify. In practice, however, the concern about unfairness to the defendant is most acute when the defendant's own convictions are offered as evidence. Almost all of the decided cases concern this type of impeachment, and the amendment does not deprive the defendant of any meaningful protection, since Rule 403 now clearly protects against unfair impeachment of any defense witness other than the defendant. There are cases in which a defendant might be prejudiced when a defense witness is impeached. Such cases may arise, for example, when the witness bears a special relationship to the defendant such that the defendant is likely to suffer some spill-over effect from impeachment of the witness.

The amendment also protects other litigants from unfair impeachment of their witnesses. The danger of prejudice from the use of prior convictions is not confined to criminal defendants. Although the danger that prior convictions will be misused as character evidence is particularly acute when the defendant is impeached, the danger exists in other situations as well. The amendment reflects the view that it is desirable to protect all litigants from the unfair use of prior convictions, and that the ordinary balancing test of Rule 403, which provides that evidence shall not be excluded unless its prejudicial effect substantially outweighs its probative value, is appropriate for assessing the admissibility of prior convictions for impeachment of any witness other than a criminal defendant.

The amendment reflects a judgment that decisions interpreting Rule 609(a) as requiring a trial court to admit convictions in civil cases that have little, if anything, to do with credibility reach undesirable results. *See, e.g., Diggs v. Lyons,* 741 F.2d 577 (3d Cir.1984), *cert. denied,* 105 S.Ct. 2157 (1985). The amendment provides the same protection against unfair prejudice arising from prior convictions used for impeachment purposes as the rules provide for other evidence. The amendment finds support in decided cases. *See, e.g., Petty v. Ideco,* 761 F.2d 1146 (5th Cir.1985); *Czaka v. Hickman,* 703 F.2d 317 (8th Cir.1983).

Fewer decided cases address the question whether Rule 609(a) provides any protection against unduly prejudicial prior convictions used to impeach government witnesses. Some courts have read Rule 609(a) as giving the government no protection for its witnesses. *See, e.g., United States v. Thorne,* 547 F.2d 56 (8th Cir.1976); *United States v. Nevitt,* 563 F.2d 406 (9th Cir.1977), *cert. denied,* 444 U.S. 847 (1979). This approach also is rejected by the amendment. There are cases in which impeachment of government witnesses with prior convictions that have little, if anything, to do with credibility may result in unfair prejudice to the government's interest in a fair trial and unnecessary embarrassment to a witness. Fed.R.Evid. 412 already recognizes this and excluded certain evidence of past sexual behavior in the context of prosecutions for sexual assaults.

The amendment applies the general balancing test of Rule 403 to protect all litigants against unfair impeachment of witnesses. The balancing test protects civil litigants, the government in criminal cases, and the defendant in a criminal case who calls other witnesses. The amendment addresses prior convictions offered under Rule 609, not for other purposes, and does not run afoul, therefore, of *Davis v. Alaska,* 415 U.S. 308 (1974). *Davis* involved the use of a prior juvenile adjudication not to prove a past law violation, but to prove bias. The defendant in a criminal case has the right to demonstrate the bias of a witness and to be assured a fair trial, but not to unduly prejudice a trier of fact. *See generally* Rule 412. In any case in which the trial court believes that confrontation rights require admission of impeachment evidence, obviously the Constitution would take precedence over the rule.

The probability that prior convictions of an ordinary government witness will be unduly prejudicial is low in most criminal cases. Since the behavior of the witness is not the issue in dispute in most cases, there is little chance that the trier of fact will misuse the convictions offered as impeachment evidence as propensity evidence. Thus, trial courts will be skeptical when the government objects to impeachment of its witnesses with prior convictions. Only when the government is able to point to a real danger of prejudice that is sufficient to outweigh substantially the probative value of the conviction for impeachment purposes will the conviction be excluded.

The amendment continues to divide subdivision (a) into subsections (1) and (2) thus facilitating retrieval under current computerized research programs which distinguish the two provisions. The Committee recommended no substantive change in subdivision (a)(2), even though some cases raise a concern about the proper interpretation of the words "dishonesty or false statement." These words were used but not explained in the original Advisory Committee Note accompanying Rule 609. Congress extensively debated the rule, and the Report of the House and Senate Conference Committee states that "[b]y the phrase 'dishonesty and false statement,' the Conference means crimes such as perjury, subornation of perjury, false statement, criminal fraud, embezzlement, or false pretense, or any other offense in the nature of *crimen falsi,* commission of which involves some element of deceit, untruthfulness, or falsification bearing on the accused's propensity to testify truthfully." The Advisory Committee concluded that the Conference Report provides sufficient guidance to trial courts and that no amendment is necessary, notwithstanding some decisions that take an unduly broad view of "dishonesty," admitting convictions such as for bank robbery or bank larceny. Subsection (a)(2) continues to apply to any witness, including a criminal defendant.

Finally, the Committee determined that it was unnecessary to add to the rule language stating that, when a prior conviction is offered under Rule 609, the trial court is to consider the probative value of the prior conviction *for impeachment,* not for other purposes. The Committee concluded that the title of the rule, its first sentence, and its placement among the impeachment rules clearly establish that evidence offered under Rule 609 is offered only for purposes of impeachment.

2006 Amendments

The amendment provides that Rule 609(a)(2) mandates the admission of evidence of a conviction only when the conviction required the proof of (or in the case of a guilty plea, the admission of) an act of dishonesty or false statement. Evidence of all other convictions is inadmissible under this subsection, irrespective of whether the witness exhibited dishonesty or made a false statement in the process of the commission of the crime of conviction. Thus, evidence that a witness was convicted for a crime of violence, such as murder, is not admissible under Rule 609(a)(2), even if the witness acted deceitfully in the course of committing the crime.

The amendment is meant to give effect to the legislative intent to limit the convictions that are to be automatically admitted under subdivision (a)(2). The Conference Committee provided that by "dishonesty and false statement" it meant "crimes such as perjury, subornation of perjury, false statement, criminal fraud, embezzlement, or false pretense, or any other offense in the nature of *crimen falsi*, the commission of which involves some element of deceit, untruthfulness, or falsification bearing on the [witness's] propensity to testify truthfully." Historically, offenses classified as *crimina falsi* have included only those crimes in which the ultimate criminal act was itself an act of deceit. *See* Green, *Deceit and the Classification of Crimes: Federal Rule of Evidence 609(a)(2) and the Origins of* Crimen Falsi, 90 J. Crim. L. & Criminology 1087 (2000).

Evidence of crimes in the nature of *crimina falsi* must be admitted under Rule 609(a)(2), regardless of how such crimes are specifically charged. For example, evidence that a witness was convicted of making a false claim to a federal agent is admissible under this subdivision regardless of whether the crime was charged under a section that expressly references deceit (e.g., 18 U.S.C. § 1001, Material Misrepresentation to the Federal Government) or a section that does not (*e.g.*, 18 U.S.C. § 1503, Obstruction of Justice).

The amendment requires that the proponent have ready proof that the conviction required the factfinder to find, or the defendant to admit, an act of dishonesty or false statement. Ordinarily, the statutory elements of the crime will indicate whether it is one of dishonesty or false statement. Where the deceitful nature of the crime is not apparent from the statute and the face of the judgment — as, for example, where the conviction simply records a finding of guilt for a statutory offense that does not reference deceit expressly — a proponent may offer information such as an indictment, a statement of admitted facts, or jury instructions to show that the factfinder had to find, or the defendant had to admit, an act of dishonesty or false statement in order for the witness to have been convicted. *Cf. Taylor v. United States*, 495 U.S. 575, 602 (1990) (providing that a trial court may look to a charging instrument or jury instructions to ascertain the nature of a prior offense where the statute is insufficiently clear on its face); *Shepard v. United States,* 125 S.Ct. 1254 (2005) (the inquiry to determine whether a guilty plea to a crime defined by a nongeneric statute necessarily admitted elements of the generic offense was limited to the charging document's terms, the terms of a plea agreement or transcript of colloquy between judge and defendant in which the factual basis for the plea was confirmed by the defendant, or a comparable judicial record). But the amendment does not contemplate a "mini-trial" in which the court plumbs the record of the previous proceeding to determine whether the crime was in the nature of *crimen falsi.*

The amendment also substitutes the term "character for truthfulness" for the term "credibility" in the first sentence of the Rule. The limitations of Rule 609 are not applicable if a conviction is admitted for a purpose other than to prove the witness's character for untruthfulness. *See, e.g., United States v. Lopez,* 979 F.2d 1024 (5th Cir. 1992) (Rule 609 was not applicable where the conviction was offered for purposes of contradiction). The use of the term "credibility" in subdivision (d) is retained, however, as that subdivision is intended to govern the use of a juvenile adjudication for any type of impeachment.

CROSS REFERENCES

Character evidence, inadmissibility to prove conduct, see Fed.Rules Evid. Rule 404, 28 USCA.

Civil commitment for narcotic addiction not conviction; use of test results on cross-examination, see 28 USCA § 2904.

Laws of states adopted for areas within federal jurisdiction, see 18 USCA § 13.

Rule 610. Religious Beliefs or Opinions

Evidence of the beliefs or opinions of a witness on matters of religion is not admissible for the purpose of showing that by reason of their nature the witness' credibility is impaired or enhanced.

(Pub.L. 93–595, § 1, Jan. 2, 1975, 88 Stat.1936; Mar. 2, 1987, eff. Oct. 1, 1987.)

ADVISORY COMMITTEE NOTES

1972 Proposed Rules

While the rule forecloses inquiry into the religious beliefs or opinions of a witness for the purpose of showing that his character for truthfulness is affected by their nature, an inquiry for the purpose of showing interest or bias because of them is not within the prohibition. Thus disclosure of affiliation with a church which is a party to the litigation would be allowable under the rule. Cf. Tucker v. Reil, 51 Ariz. 357, 77 P.2d 203 (1938). To the same effect, though less specifically worded, is California Evidence Code § 789. See 3 Wigmore § 936.

1987 Amendments

The amendment is technical. No substantive change is intended.

Rule 611. Mode and Order of Interrogation and Presentation

(a) Control by court. The court shall exercise reasonable control over the mode and order of interrogating witnesses and presenting evidence so as to (1) make the interrogation and presentation effective for the ascertainment of the truth, (2) avoid needless consumption of time, and (3) protect witnesses from harassment or undue embarrassment.

(b) Scope of cross-examination. Cross-examination should be limited to the subject matter of the direct examination and matters affecting the credibility of the witness. The court may, in the exercise of discretion, permit inquiry into additional matters as if on direct examination.

(c) Leading questions. Leading questions should not be used on the direct examination of a witness except as may be necessary to develop the witness' testimony. Ordinarily leading questions should be permitted on cross-examination. When a party calls a hostile witness, an adverse party, or a witness identified with an adverse party, interrogation may be by leading questions.

(Pub.L. 93–595, § 1, Jan. 2, 1975, 88 Stat. 1936; Mar. 2, 1987, eff. Oct. 1, 1987.)

ADVISORY COMMITTEE NOTES

1972 Proposed Rules

Note to Subdivision (a). Spelling out detailed rules to govern the mode and order of interrogating witnesses and presenting evidence is neither desirable nor feasible. The ultimate responsibility for the effective working of the adversary system rests with the judge. The rule sets forth the objectives which he should seek to attain.

Item (1) restates in broad terms the power and obligation of the judge as developed under common law principles. It covers such concerns as whether testimony shall be in the form of a free narrative or responses to specific questions, McCormick § 5, the order of calling witnesses and presenting evidence, 6 Wigmore § 1867, the use of demonstrative evidence, McCormick § 179, and the many other questions arising during the course of a trial which can be solved only by the judge's common sense and fairness in view of the particular circumstances.

Item (2) is addressed to avoidance of needless consumption of time, a matter of daily concern in the disposition of cases. A companion piece is found in the discretion vested in the judge to exclude evidence as a waste of time in Rule 403(b).

Item (3) calls for a judgment under the particular circumstances whether interrogation tactics entail harassment or undue embarrassment. Pertinent circumstances include the importance of the testimony, the nature of the inquiry, its relevance to credibility, waste of time, and confusion. McCormick § 42. In *Alford v. United States,* 282 U.S. 687, 694, 51 S.Ct. 218, 75 L.Ed. 624 (1931), the Court pointed out that, while the trial judge should protect the witness from questions which "go beyond the bounds of proper cross-examination merely to harass, annoy or humiliate," this protection by no means forecloses efforts to discredit the witness. Reference to the transcript of the prosecutor's cross-examination in *Berger v. United States,* 295 U.S. 78, 55 S.Ct. 629, 79 L.Ed. 1314 (1935), serves to lay at rest any doubts as to the need for judicial control in this area.

The inquiry into specific instances of conduct of a witness allowed under Rule 608(b) is, of course, subject to this rule.

Note to Subdivision (b). The tradition in the federal courts and in numerous state courts has been to limit the scope of cross-examination to matters testified to on direct, plus matters bearing upon the credibility of the witness. Various reasons have been advanced to justify the rule of limited cross-examination. (1) A party vouches for his own witness but only to the extent of matters elicited on direct. *Resurrection Gold Mining Co. v. Fortune Gold Mining Co.,* 129 F. 668, 675 (8th Cir.1904), quoted in Maguire, Weinstein, et al., Cases on Evidence 277, n. 38 (5th ed. 1965). But the concept of vouching is discredited, and Rule 607 rejects it. (2) A party cannot ask his own witness leading questions. This is a problem properly solved in terms of what is necessary for a proper development of the testimony rather than by a mechanistic formula similar to the vouching concept. See discussion under subdivision (c). (3) A practice of limited cross-examination promotes orderly presentation of the case. *Finch v. Weiner,* 109 Conn. 616, 145 A. 31 (1929). While this latter reason has merit, the matter is essentially one of the order of presentation and not one in which involvement at the appellate level is likely to prove fruitful. See, for example, *Moyer v. Aetna Life Ins. Co.,* 126 F.2d 141 (3rd Cir.1942); *Butler v. New York Central R. Co.,* 253 F.2d 281 (7th Cir.1958); *United States v. Johnson,* 285 F.2d 35 (9th Cir.1960); *Union Automobile Indemnity Ass'n v. Capitol Indemnity Ins. Co.,* 310 F.2d 318 (7th Cir.1962). In evaluating these considerations, McCormick says:

"The foregoing considerations favoring the wide-open or restrictive rules may well be thought to be fairly evenly balanced. There is another factor, however, which seems to swing the balance overwhelmingly in favor of the wide-open rule. This is the consideration of economy of time and energy. Obviously, the wide-open rule presents little or no opportunity for dispute in its application. The restrictive practice in all its forms, on the other hand, is productive in many court rooms, of continual bickering over the choice of the numerous variations of the 'scope of the direct' criterion, and of their application to particular cross-questions. These controversies are often reventilated on appeal, and reversals for error in their determination are frequent. Observance of these vague and ambiguous restrictions is a matter of constant and hampering concern to the cross-examiner. If these efforts, delays and misprisions were the necessary incidents to the guarding of substantive rights or the fundamentals of fair trial, they might be worth the cost. As the price of the choice of an obviously debatable regulation of the order of evidence, the sacrifice seems misguided. The American Bar Association's Committee for the Improvement of the Law of Evidence for the year 1937–38 said this:

'The rule limiting cross-examination to the precise subject of the direct examination is probably the most frequent rule (except the Opinion rule) leading in the trial practice today to refined and technical quibbles which obstruct the progress of the trial, confuse the jury, and give rise to appeal on technical grounds only. Some of the instances in which Supreme Courts have ordered new trials for the mere transgression of this rule about the order of evidence have been astounding.

'We recommend that the rule allowing questions upon any part of the issue known to the witness * * * be adopted. * * *' " McCormick, § 27, p. 51. See also 5 Moore's Federal Practice ¶ 43.10 (2nd ed. 1964).

The provision of the second sentence, that the judge may in the interests of justice limit inquiry into new matters on cross-examination, is designed for those situations in which the result otherwise would be confusion, complication, or protraction of the case, not as a matter of rule but as demonstrable in the actual development of the particular case.

The rule does not purport to determine the extent to which an accused who elects to testify thereby waives his privilege against self-incrimination. The question is a constitutional one, rather than a mere matter of administering the trial. Under *Simmons v. United States,* 390 U.S. 377, 88 S.Ct. 967, 19 L.Ed.2d 1247 (1968), no general waiver occurs when the accused testifies on such preliminary matters as the validity of a search and seizure or the admissibility of a confession. Rule 104(d), *supra.* When he testifies on the merits, however, can he foreclose inquiry into an aspect or element of the crime by avoiding it on direct? The affirmative answer given in *Tucker v. United States,* 5 F.2d 818 (8th Cir.1925), is inconsistent with the description of the waiver as extending to "all other relevant facts" in *Johnson v. United States,* 318 U.S. 189, 195, 63 S.Ct. 549, 87 L.Ed. 704 (1943). See also *Brown v. United States,* 356 U.S. 148, 78 S.Ct. 622, 2 L.Ed.2d 589 (1958). The situation of an accused who desires to testify on some but not all counts of a multiple-count indictment is one to be approached, in the first instance at least, as a problem of severance under Rule 14 of the Federal Rules of Criminal Procedure. *Cross v. United States,* 118 U.S.App. D.C. 324, 335 F.2d 987 (1964). Cf. *United States v. Baker,* 262 F.Supp. 657, 686 (D.D.C.1966). In all events, the extent of the waiver of the privilege against self-incrimination ought not to be determined as a by-product of a rule on scope of cross-examination.

Note to Subdivision (c). The rule continues the traditional view that the suggestive powers of the leading question are as a general proposition undesirable. Within this tradition, however, numerous exceptions have achieved recognition: The witness who is hostile, unwilling, or biased; the child witness or the adult with communication problems; the witness whose recollection is exhausted; and undisputed preliminary matters. 3 Wigmore §§ 774–778. An almost total unwillingness to reverse for infractions has been manifested by appellate courts. See cases cited in 3 Wigmore § 770. The matter clearly falls within the area of control by the judge over the mode and order of interrogation and presentation and accordingly is phrased in words of suggestion rather than command.

The rule also conforms to tradition in making the use of leading questions on cross-examination a matter of right. The purpose of the qualification "ordinarily" is to furnish a basis for denying the use of leading questions when the cross-examination is cross-examination in form only and not in fact, as for example the "cross-examination" of a party by his own counsel after being called by the opponent (savoring more of re-direct) or of an insured defendant who proves to be friendly to the plaintiff.

The final sentence deals with categories of witnesses automatically regarded and treated as hostile. Rule 43(b) of the Federal Rules of Civil Procedure has included only "an adverse party or an officer, director, or managing agent of a public or private corporation or of a partnership or association which is an adverse party." This limitation virtually to persons whose statements would stand as admissions is believed to be an unduly narrow concept of those who may safely be regarded as hostile without further demonstration. See, for example, *Maryland Casualty Co. v. Kador,* 225 F.2d 120 (5th Cir.1955), and *Degelos v. Fidelity and Casualty Co.,* 313 F.2d 809 (5th Cir.1963), holding despite the language of Rule 43(b) that an insured fell within it, though not a party in an action under the Louisiana direct action statute. The phrase of the rule, "witness identified with" an adverse party, is designed to enlarge the category of persons thus callable.

1974 Enactment

Note to Subdivision (b). As submitted by the Court, Rule 611(b) provided:

> A witness may be cross-examined on any matter relevant to any issue in the case, including credibility. In the interests of justice, the judge may limit cross-examination with respect to matters not testified to on direct examination.

The Committee amended this provision to return to the rule which prevails in the federal courts and thirty-nine State jurisdictions. As amended, the Rule is in the text of the 1969 Advisory Committee draft. It limits cross-examination to credibility and to matters testified to on direct examination, unless the judge permits more, in which event the cross-examiner must proceed as if on direct examination. This traditional rule facilitates orderly presentation by each party at trial. Further, in light of existing discovery procedures, there appears to be no need to abandon the traditional rule.

Note to Subdivision (c). The third sentence of Rule 611(c) as submitted by the Court provided that:

> In civil cases, a party is entitled to call an adverse party or witness identified with him and interrogate by leading questions.

The Committee amended this Rule to permit leading questions to be used with respect to any hostile witness, not only an adverse party or person identified with such adverse party. The Committee also substituted the word "When" for the phrase "In civil cases" to reflect the possibility that in criminal cases a defendant may be entitled to call witnesses identified with the government, in which event the Committee believed the defendant should be permitted to inquire with leading questions. House Report No. 93–650.

Note to Subdivision (b). Rule 611(b) as submitted by the Supreme Court permitted a broad scope of cross-examination: "cross-examination on any matter relevant to any issue in the case" unless the judge, in the interests of justice, limited the scope of cross-examination.

The House narrowed the Rule to the more traditional practice of limiting cross-examination to the subject matter of direct examination (and credibility), but with discretion in the judge to permit inquiry into additional matters in situations where that would aid in the development of the evidence or otherwise facilitate the conduct of the trial.

The committee agrees with the House amendment. Although there are good arguments in support of broad cross-examination from perspectives of developing all relevant evidence, we believe the factors of insuring an orderly and predictable development of the evidence weigh in favor of the narrower rule, especially when discretion is given to the trial judge to permit inquiry into additional matters. The committee expressly approves this discretion and believes it will permit sufficient flexibility allowing a broader scope of cross-examination whenever appropriate.

The House amendment providing broader discretionary cross-examination permitted inquiry into additional matters only as if on direct examination. As a general rule, we concur with this limitation, however, we would understand that this limitation would not preclude the utilization of leading questions if the conditions of subsection (c) of this rule were met, bearing in mind the judge's discretion in any case to limit the scope of cross-examination [see McCormick on Evidence, §§ 24–26 (especially 24) (2d ed. 1972)].

Further, the committee has received correspondence from Federal judges commenting on the applicability of this rule to section 1407 of title 28. It is the committee's judgment that this rule as reported by the House is flexible enough to provide sufficiently broad cross-examination in appropriate situations in multidistrict litigation.

Note to Subdivision (c). As submitted by the Supreme Court, the rule provided: "In civil cases, a party is entitled to call an adverse party or witness identified with him and interrogate by leading questions."

The final sentence of subsection (c) was amended by the House for the purpose of clarifying the fact that a "hostile witness"—that is a witness who is hostile in fact—could be subject to interrogation by leading questions. The rule as submitted by the Supreme Court declared certain witnesses hostile as a matter of law and thus subject to interrogation by leading questions without any showing of hostility in fact. These were adverse parties or witnesses identified with adverse parties. However, the wording of the first sentence of subsection (c) while generally prohibiting the use of leading questions on direct examination, also provides "except as may be necessary to develop his testimony." Further, the first paragraph of the Advisory Committee note explaining the subsection makes clear that they intended that leading questions could be asked of a hostile witness or a witness who was unwilling or biased and even though that witness was not associated with an adverse party. Thus, we question whether the House amendment was necessary.

However, concluding that it was not intended to affect the meaning of the first sentence of the subsection and was intended solely to clarify the fact that leading questions are permissible in the interrogation of a witness, who is hostile in fact, the committee accepts that House amendment.

The final sentence of this subsection was also amended by the House to cover criminal as well as civil cases. The committee accepts this amendment, but notes that it may be difficult in criminal cases to determine when a witness is "identified with an adverse party," and thus the rule should be applied with caution. Senate Report No. 93–1277.

1987 Amendments

The amendment is technical. No substantive change is intended.

CROSS REFERENCES

Civil commitment for narcotic addiction not conviction; use of test results on cross-examination, see 28 USCA § 2904.

Cross-examination, right of, see USCA Const. Amend. VI.

Indictment, jury list, and list of witnesses furnished prisoner in capital cases, see 18 USCA § 3432.

Prejudice, confusion, or waste of time, exclusion of evidence for, see Fed.Rules Evid. Rule 403, 28 USCA.

Self-incrimination, protection against, see USCA Const. Amend. V.

Testimony by accused on preliminary matter, scope of cross-examination, see Fed.Rules. Evid. Rule 104, 28 USCA.

Rule 612. Writing Used to Refresh Memory

Except as otherwise provided in criminal proceedings by section 3500 of title 18, United States Code, if a witness uses a writing to refresh memory for the purpose of testifying, either—

(1) while testifying, or

(2) before testifying, if the court in its discretion determines it is necessary in the interests of justice,

an adverse party is entitled to have the writing produced at the hearing, to inspect it, to cross-examine the witness thereon, and to introduce in evidence those portions which relate to the testimony of the witness. If it is claimed that the writing contains matters not related to the subject matter of the testimony the court shall examine the writing in camera, excise any portions not so related, and order delivery of the remainder to the party entitled thereto. Any portion withheld over objections shall be preserved and made available to the appellate court in the event of an appeal. If a writing is not produced or delivered pursuant to order under this rule, the court shall make any order justice requires, except that in criminal cases when the prosecution elects not to comply, the order shall be one striking the testimony or, if the court in its discretion determines that the interests of justice so require, declaring a mistrial.

(Pub.L. 93–595, § 1, Jan. 2, 1975, 88 Stat. 1936; Mar. 2, 1987, eff. Oct. 1, 1987.)

ADVISORY COMMITTEE NOTES

1972 Proposed Rules

The treatment of writings used to refresh recollection while on the stand is in accord with settled doctrine. McCormick § 9, p. 15. The bulk of the case law has, however, denied the existence of any right to access by the opponent when the writing is used prior to taking the stand, though the judge may have discretion in the matter. *Goldman v. United States,* 316 U.S. 129, 62 S.Ct. 993, 86 L.Ed. 1322 (1942); *Needelman v. United States,* 261 F.2d 802 (5th Cir.1958), cert. dismissed 362 U.S. 600, 80 S.Ct. 960, 4 L.Ed.2d 980, rehearing denied 363 U.S. 858, 80 S.Ct. 1606, 4 L.Ed.2d 1739, Annot., 82 A.L.R.2d 473, 562 and 7 A.L.R.3d 181, 247. An increasing group of cases has repudiated the distinction. *People v. Scott,* 29 Ill.2d 97, 193 N.E.2d 814 (1963); *State v. Mucci,* 25 N.J. 423, 136 A.2d 761 (1957); *State v. Hunt,* 25 N.J. 514, 138 A.2d 1 (1958); *State v. Deslovers,* 40 R.I. 89, 100 A. 64 (1917), and this position is believed to be correct. As Wigmore put it, "the risk of imposition and the need of safeguard is just as great" in both situations. 3 Wigmore § 762, p. 111. To the same effect is McCormick, § 9, p. 17.

The purpose of the phrase "for the purpose of testifying" is to safeguard against using the rule as a pretext for wholesale exploration of an opposing party's files and to insure that access is limited only to those writings which may fairly be said in fact to have an impact upon the testimony of the witness.

The purpose of the rule is the same as that of the *Jencks* statute, 18 U.S.C. § 3500: to promote the search of credibility and memory. The same sensitivity to disclosure of government files may be involved; hence the rule is expressly made subject to the statute, subdivision (a) of which provides: "In any criminal prosecution brought by the United States, no statement or report in the possession of the United States which was made by a Government witness or prospective Government witness (other than the defendant) shall be the subject of subpena, discovery, or inspection until said witness has testified on direct examination in the trial of the case." Items falling within the purview of the statute are producible only as provided by its terms, *Palermo v. United States,* 360 U.S. 343, 351 (1959), and disclosure under the rule is limited similarly by the statutory conditions. With this limitation in mind, some differences of application may be noted. The *Jencks* statute applies only to statements of witnesses; the rule is not so limited. The statute applies only to criminal cases; the rule applies to all cases. The statute applies only to government witnesses; the rule applies to all witnesses. The statute contains no requirement that the statement be consulted for purposes of refreshment before or while testifying; the rule so requires. Since many writings would qualify under either statute or rule, a substantial overlap exists, but the identity of procedures makes this of no importance.

The consequences of nonproduction by the government in a criminal case are those of the *Jencks* statute, striking the testimony or in exceptional cases a mistrial. 18 U.S.C. § 3500(d). In other cases these alternatives are unduly limited, and such possibilities as contempt, dismissal, finding issues against the offender, and the like are available. See Rule 16(g) of the Federal Rules of Criminal Procedure and Rule 37(b) of the Federal Rules of Civil Procedure for appropriate sanctions.

1974 Enactment

As submitted to Congress, Rule 612 provided that except as set forth in 18 U.S.C. 3500, if a witness uses a writing to refresh his memory for the purpose of testifying, "either before or while testifying," an adverse party is entitled to have the writing produced at the hearing, to inspect it, to cross-examine the witness on it, and to introduce in evidence those portions relating to the witness' testimony. The Committee amended the Rule so as still to require the production of writings used by a witness while testifying, but to render the production of writings used by a witness to refresh his memory before testifying discretionary with the court in the interests of justice, as is the case under existing federal law. See Goldman v. United States, 316 U.S. 129 (1942). The Committee considered that permitting an adverse party to require the production of writings used before testifying could result in fishing expeditions among a multitude of papers which a witness may have used in preparing for trial.

The Committee intends that nothing in the Rule be construed as barring the assertion of a privilege with respect to writings used by a witness to refresh his memory. House Report No. 93–650.

1987 Amendments

The amendment is technical. No substantive change is intended.

CROSS REFERENCES

Confrontation with, and cross-examination of, witnesses, see USCA Const. Amend. VI.

Discovery and inspection of statements and reports, failure to comply with order, see Fed.Rules Cr.Proc. Rule 16, 18 USCA.

Refusal to make discovery or comply with order, see Fed.Rules Civ.Proc. Rule 37, 28 USCA.

Rule 613. Prior Statements of Witnesses

(a) Examining witness concerning prior statement. In examining a witness concerning a prior statement made by the witness, whether written or not, the statement need not be shown nor its contents disclosed to the witness at that time, but on request the same shall be shown or disclosed to opposing counsel.

(b) Extrinsic evidence of prior inconsistent statement of witness. Extrinsic evidence of a prior inconsistent statement by a witness is not admissible unless the witness is afforded an opportunity to explain or deny the same and the opposite party is afforded an opportunity to interrogate the witness thereon, or the interests of justice otherwise require. This provision does not apply to admissions of a party-opponent as defined in rule 801(d)(2).

(Pub.L. 93–595, § 1, Jan. 2, 1975, 88 Stat.1936; Mar. 2, 1987, eff. Oct. 1, 1987; Apr. 25, 1988, eff. Nov. 1, 1988.)

ADVISORY COMMITTEE NOTES

1972 Proposed Rules

Note to Subdivision (a). The Queen's Case, 2 Br. & B. 284, 129 Eng.Rep. 976 (1820), laid down the requirement that a cross-examiner, prior to questioning the witness about his own prior statement in writing, must first show it to the witness. Abolished by statute in the country of its origin, the requirement nevertheless gained currency in the United States. The rule abolishes this useless impediment, to cross-examination. Ladd, Some Observations on Credibility: Impeachment of Witnesses, 52 Cornell L.Q. 239, 246–247 (1967); McCormick § 28; 4 Wigmore §§ 1259–1260. Both oral and written statements are included.

The provision for disclosure to counsel is designed to protect against unwarranted insinuations that a statement has been made when the fact is to the contrary.

The rule does not defeat the application of Rule 1002 relating to production of the original when the contents of a writing are sought to be proved. Nor does it defeat the application of Rule 26(b)(3) of the Rules of Civil Procedure, as revised, entitling a person on request to a copy of his own statement, though the operation of the latter may be suspended temporarily.

Note to Subdivision (b). The familiar foundation requirement that an impeaching statement first be shown to the witness before it can be proved by extrinsic evidence is preserved but with some modifications. See Ladd, Some Observations on Credibility: Impeachment of Witnesses, 52 Cornell L.Q. 239, 247 (1967). The traditional insistence that the attendance of the witness be directed to the statement on cross-examination is relaxed in favor of simply providing the witness an opportunity to explain and the opposite party an opportunity to examine on the statement, with no specification of any particular time or sequence. Under this procedure, several collusive witnesses can be examined before disclosure of a joint prior inconsistent statement. See Comment to California Evidence Code § 770. Also, dangers of oversight are reduced. See McCormick § 37, p. 68.

In order to allow for such eventualities as the witness becoming unavailable by the time the statement is discovered, a measure of discretion is conferred upon the judge. Similar provisions are found in California Evidence Code § 770 and New Jersey Evidence Rule 22(b).

Under principles of *expression unius* the rule does not apply to impeachment by evidence of prior inconsistent conduct. The use of inconsistent statements to impeach a hearsay declaration is treated in Rule 806.

1987 Amendments

The amendments are technical. No substantive change is intended.

1988 Amendments

The amendment is technical. No substantive change is intended.

CROSS REFERENCES

Attacking and supporting credibility of declarant, see Fed. Rules Evid. Rule 806, 28 USCA.

Contents of writings, recordings, and photographs, original required to prove, see Fed.Rules Evid. Rule 1004, 28 USCA.

Depositions and discovery, trial preparation, see Fed.Rules Civ.Proc. Rule 26, 28 USCA.

Rule 614. Calling and Interrogation of Witnesses by Court

(a) Calling by court. The court may, on its own motion or at the suggestion of a party, call witnesses, and all parties are entitled to cross-examine witnesses thus called.

(b) Interrogation by court. The court may interrogate witnesses, whether called by itself or by a party.

(c) Objections. Objections to the calling of witnesses by the court or to interrogation by it may be made at the time or at the next available opportunity when the jury is not present.

(Pub.L. 93–595, § 1, Jan. 2, 1975, 88 Stat.1937.)

ADVISORY COMMITTEE NOTES

1972 Proposed Rules

Note to Subdivision (a). While exercised more frequently in criminal than in civil cases, the authority of the judge to call witnesses is well established. McCormick § 8, p. 14; Maguire, Weinstein, et al., Cases on Evidence 303–304 (5th ed. 1965); 9 Wigmore § 2484. One reason for the practice, the old rule against impeaching one's own witness, no longer exists by virtue of Rule 607, *supra*. Other reasons remain, however, to justify the continuation of the practice of calling court's witnesses. The right to cross-examine, with all it implies, is assured. The tendency of juries to associate a witness with the party calling him, regardless of technical aspects of vouching, is avoided. And the judge is not imprisoned within the case as made by the parties.

Note to Subdivision (b). The authority of the judge to question witnesses is also well established. McCormick § 8, pp. 12–13; Maguire, Weinstein, et al., Cases on Evidence 737–739 (5th ed. 1965); 3 Wigmore § 784. The authority is, of course, abused when the judge abandons his proper role and assumes that of advocate, but the manner in which interrogation should be conducted and the proper extent of its exercise are not susceptible of formulation in a rule. The omission in no sense precludes courts of review from continuing to reverse for abuse.

Note to Subdivision (c). The provision relating to objections is designed to relieve counsel of the embarrassment attendant upon objecting to questions by the judge in the presence of the jury, while at the same time assuring that objections are made in apt time to afford the opportunity to take possible corrective measures. Compare the "automatic" objection feature of Rule 605 when the judge is called as a witness.

CROSS REFERENCES

Confrontation with, and cross-examination of, witnesses, see USCA Const. Amend. VI.

Contempt for failure of subpoenaed foreigner to appear, see 28 USCA § 1784.

Subpoena of foreigners or foreign documents, see 28 USCA § 1783.

Rule 615. Exclusion of Witnesses

At the request of a party the court shall order witnesses excluded so that they cannot hear the testimony of other witnesses, and it may make the order of its own motion. This rule does not authorize exclusion of (1) a party who is a natural person, or (2) an officer or employee of a party which is not a natural person designated as its representative by its attorney, or (3) a person whose presence is shown by a party to be essential to the presentation of the party's cause, or (4) a person authorized by statute to be present.

(Pub.L. 93–595, § 1, Jan. 2, 1975, 88 Stat.1937; Mar. 2, 1987, eff. Oct. 1, 1987; Apr. 25, 1988, eff. Nov. 1, 1988; Pub.L. 100–690, Nov. 18, 1988, Title VII, § 7075(a), 102 Stat. 4405; Apr. 24, 1998, eff. Dec. 1, 1998.)

ADVISORY COMMITTEE NOTES

1972 Proposed Rules

The efficacy of excluding or sequestering witnesses has long been recognized as a means of discouraging and exposing fabrication, inaccuracy, and collusion. 6 Wigmore §§ 1837–1838. The authority of the judge is admitted, the only question being whether the matter is committed to his discretion or one of right. The rule takes the latter position. No time is specified for making the request.

Several categories of persons are excepted. (1) Exclusion of persons who are parties would raise serious problems of confrontation and due process. Under accepted practice they are not subject to exclusion. 6 Wigmore § 1841. (2) As the equivalent of the right of a natural-person party to be present, a party which is not a natural person is entitled to have a representative present. Most of the cases have involved allowing a police officer who has been in charge of an investigation to remain in court despite the fact that he will be a witness. United States v. Infanzon, 235 F.2d 318, (2d Cir.1956); *Portomene v. United States,* 221 F.2d 582 (5th Cir.1955); *Powell v. United States,* 208 F.2d 618 (6th Cir. 1953); *Jones v. United States,* 252 F.Supp. 781 (W.D.Okl. 1966). Designation of the representative by the attorney rather than by the client may at first glance appear to be an inversion of the attorney-client relationship, but it may be assumed that the attorney will follow the wishes of the client, and the solution is simple and workable. See California Evidence Code § 777. (3) The category contemplates such persons as an agent who handled the transaction being litigated or an expert needed to advise counsel in the management of the litigation. See 6 Wigmore § 1841, n. 4.

1974 Enactment

Many district courts permit government counsel to have an investigative agent at counsel table throughout the trial although the agent is or may be a witness. The practice is permitted as an exception to the rule of exclusion and compares with the situation defense counsel finds himself in—he always has the client with him to consult during the trial. The investigative agent's presence may be extremely important to government counsel, especially when the case is complex or involves some specialized subject matter. The agent, too, having lived with the case for a long time, may be able to assist in meeting trial surprises where the best-prepared counsel would otherwise have difficulty. Yet, it would not seem the Government could often meet the burden under rule 615 of showing that the agent's presence is essential. Furthermore, it could be dangerous to use the agent as a witness as early in the case as possible, so that he might then help counsel as a nonwitness, since the agent's testimony could be needed in rebuttal. Using another, nonwitness agent from the same investigative agency would not generally meet government counsel's needs.

This problem is solved if it is clear that investigative agents are within the group specified under the second exception made in the rule, for "an officer or employee of a party which is not a natural person designated as its representative by its attorney." It is our understanding that this was the intention of the House committee. It is certainly this committee's construction of the rule. Senate Report No. 93–1277.

1987 Amendments

The amendment is technical. No substantive change is intended.

1988 Amendments

The amendment is technical. No substantive change is intended.

1998 Amendments

The amendment is in response to: (1) the Victim's Rights and Restitution Act of 1990, 42 U.S.C. § 10606, which guarantees, within certain limits, the right of a crime victim to attend the trial; and (2) the Victim Rights Clarification Act of 1997 (18 U.S.C. § 3510).

HISTORICAL NOTES

Revision Notes and Legislative Reports

1988 Acts. For Related Reports, see 1988 U.S. Code Cong. and Adm. News, p. 5937.

1988 Amendments. Pub.L. 100–690 inserted "a" before "party which is not a natural person".

Rules 616 to 700. Reserved for future legislation

ARTICLE VII. OPINIONS AND EXPERT TESTIMONY

Rule

Rule 701. Opinion Testimony by Lay Witnesses

If the witness is not testifying as an expert, the witness' testimony in the form of opinions or inferences is limited to those opinions or inferences which are (a) rationally based on the perception of the witness, (b) helpful to a clear understanding of the witness' testimony or the determination of a fact in issue, and (c) not based on scientific, technical, or other specialized knowledge within the scope of Rule 702.

(Pub.L. 93–595, § 1, Jan. 2, 1975, 88 Stat.1937; Mar. 2, 1987, eff. Oct. 1, 1987; Apr. 17, 2000, eff. Dec. 1, 2000.)

ADVISORY COMMITTEE NOTES

1972 Proposed Rules

The rule retains the traditional objective of putting the trier of fact in possession of an accurate reproduction of the event.

Limitation (a) is the familiar requirement of first-hand knowledge or observation.

Limitation (b) is phrased in terms of requiring testimony to be helpful in resolving issues. Witnesses often find difficulty in expressing themselves in language which is not that of an opinion or conclusion. While the courts have made concessions in certain recurring situations, necessity as a standard for permitting opinions and conclusions has proved too elusive and too unadaptable to particular situations for purposes of satisfactory judicial administration. McCormick § 11. Moreover, the practical impossibility of determining by rule what is a "fact," demonstrated by a century of litigation of the question of what is a fact for purposes of pleading under the Field Code, extends into evidence also. 7 Wigmore § 1919. The rule assumes that the natural characteristics of the adversary system will generally lead to an acceptable result, since the detailed account carries more conviction than the broad assertion, and a lawyer can be expected to display his witness to the best advantage. If he fails to do so, cross-examination and argument will point up the weakness. See Ladd, Expert Testimony, 5 Vand.L.Rev. 414, 415–417 (1952). If, despite these considerations, attempts are made to introduce meaningless assertions which amount to little more than choosing up sides, exclusion for lack of helpfulness is called for by the rule.

The language of the rule is substantially that of Uniform Rule 56(1). Similar provisions are California Evidence Code § 800; Kansas Code of Civil Procedure § 60–456(a); New Jersey Evidence Rule 56(1).

1987 Amendments

The amendments are technical. No substantive change is intended.

2000 Amendments

Rule 701 has been amended to eliminate the risk that the reliability requirements set forth in Rule 702 will be evaded through the simple expedient of proffering an expert in lay witness clothing. Under the amendment, a witness' testimony must be scrutinized under the rules regulating expert opinion to the extent that the witness is providing testimony based on scientific, technical, or other specialized knowledge within the scope of Rule 702. *See generally Asplundh Mfg. Div. v. Benton Harbor Eng'g*, 57 F.3d 1190 (3d Cir. 1995). By channeling testimony that is actually expert testimony to Rule 702, the amendment also ensures that a party will not evade the expert witness disclosure requirements set forth in Fed.R.Civ.P. 26 and Fed.R.Crim.P. 16 by simply calling an expert witness in the guise of a layperson. *See* Joseph, *Emerging Expert Issues Under the 1993 Disclosure Amendments to the Federal Rules of Civil Procedure*, 164 F.R.D. 97, 108 (1996) (noting that "there is no good reason to allow what is essentially surprise expert testimony." and that "the Court should be vigilant to preclude manipulative conduct designed to thwart the expert disclosure and discovery process") *See also United States v. Figueroa–Lopez*, 125 F.3d 1241, 1246 (9th Cir. 1997) (law enforcement agents testifying that the defendant's conduct was consistent with that of a drug trafficker could not testify as lay witnesses; to permit such testimony under Rule 701 "subverts the requirements of Federal Rule of Criminal Procedure 16(a)(1)(E)").

The amendment does not distinguish between expert and lay *witnesses*, but rather between expert and lay *testimony*. Certainly it is possible for the same witness to provide both lay and expert testimony in a single case. *See, e.g, United States v. Figueroa–Lopez*, 125 F.3d 1241, 1246 (9th Cir. 1997) (law enforcement agents could testify that the defendant was acting suspiciously, without being qualified as experts; however, the rules on experts were applicable where the agents testified on the basis of extensive experience that the defendant was using code words to refer to drug quantities and prices). The amendment makes clear that any part of a witness' testimony that is based upon scientific, technical, or other specialized knowledge within the scope of Rule 702 is governed by the standards of Rule 702 and the corresponding disclosure requirements of the Civil and Criminal Rules.

The amendment is not intended to affect the "prototypical example[s] of the type of evidence contemplated by the adoption of Rule 701 relat[ing] to the appearance of persons or things, identity, the manner of conduct, competency of a person, degrees of light or darkness, sound, size, weight, distance, and an endless number of items that cannot be described factually in words apart from inferences." *Asplundh Mfg. Div. v. Benton Harbor Eng' g*, 57 F.3d 1190, 1196 (3d Cir. 1995).

For example, most courts have permitted the owner or officer of a business to testify to the value or projected profits of the business, without the necessity of qualifying the witness as an accountant, appraiser, or similar expert. *See, e.g., Lightning Lube, Inc. v. Witco Corp.* 4 F.3d 1153 (3d Cir. 1993) (no abuse of discretion in permitting the plaintiff's owner to give lay opinion testimony as to damages, as it was based on his knowledge and participation in the day-to-day affairs of the business). Such opinion testimony is admitted not because of experience, training or specialized knowledge within the realm of an expert, but because of the particularized knowledge that the witness has by virtue of his or her position in the business. The amendment does not purport to change this analysis. Similarly, courts have permitted lay witnesses to testify that a substance appeared to be a narcotic, so long as a foundation of familiarity with the substance is established. *See, e.g., United States v. Westbrook*, 896 F.2d 330 (8th Cir. 1990) (two lay witnesses who were heavy amphetamine users were properly permitted to testify that a substance was amphetamine; but it was error to permit another witness to make such an identification where she had no experience with amphetamines). Such testimony is not based on specialized knowledge within the scope of Rule 702, but rather is based upon a layperson's personal knowledge. If, however, that witness were to describe how a narcotic was manufactured, or to describe the intricate workings of a narcotic distribution network, then the witness would have to qualify as an expert under Rule 702. *United States v . Figueroa–Lopez, supra.*

The amendment incorporates the distinctions set forth in *State v. Brown*, 836 S.W.2d 530, 549 (1992), a case involving former Tennessee Rule of Evidence 701, a rule that precluded lay witness testimony based on "special knowledge." In *Brown*, the court declared that the distinction between lay and expert witness testimony is that lay testimony "results from a process of reasoning familiar in everyday life," while expert testimony "results from a process of reasoning which can be mastered only by specialists in the field." The court in *Brown* noted that a lay witness with experience could testify that a substance appeared to be blood, but that a witness would have to qualify as an expert before he could testify that bruising around the eyes is indicative of skull trauma. That is the kind of distinction made by the amendment to this Rule.

GAP Report—Proposed Amendment to Rule 701

The Committee made the following changes to the published draft of the proposed amendment to Evidence Rule 701:

1. The words "within the scope of Rule 702" were added at the end of the proposed amendment, to emphasize that the Rule does not require witnesses to qualify as experts unless their testimony is of the type traditionally considered within the purview of Rule 702. The Committee Note was amended to accord with this textual change.

2. The Committee Note was revised to provide further examples of the kind of testimony that could and could not be proffered under the limitation imposed by the proposed amendment.

Rule 702. Testimony by Experts

If scientific, technical, or other specialized knowledge will assist the trier of fact to understand the evidence or to determine a fact in issue, a witness qualified as an expert by knowledge, skill, experience, training, or education, may testify thereto in the form of an opinion or otherwise, if (1) the testimony is based upon sufficient facts or data, (2) the testimony is the product of reliable principles and methods, and (3) the witness has applied the principles and methods reliably to the facts of the case.

(Pub.L. 93–595, § 1, Jan. 2, 1975, 88 Stat. 1937; Apr. 17, 2000, eff. Dec. 1, 2000.)

ADVISORY COMMITTEE NOTES

1972 Proposed Rules

An intelligent evaluation of facts is often difficult or impossible without the application of some scientific, technical, or other specialized knowledge. The most common source of this knowledge is the expert witness, although there are other techniques for supplying it.

Most of the literature assumes that experts testify only in the form of opinions. The assumption is logically unfounded. The rule accordingly recognizes that an expert on the stand may give a dissertation or exposition of scientific or other principles relevant to the case, leaving the trier of fact to apply them to the facts. Since much of the criticism of expert testimony has centered upon the hypothetical question, it seems wise to recognize that opinions are not indispensable and to encourage the use of expert testimony in non-opinion form when counsel believes the trier can itself draw the requisite inference. The use of opinions is not abolished by the rule, however. It will continue to be permissible for the experts to take the further step of suggesting the inference which should be drawn from applying the specialized knowledge to the facts. See Rules 703 to 705.

Whether the situation is a proper one for the use of expert testimony is to be determined on the basis of assisting the trier. "There is no more certain test for determining when experts may be used than the common sense inquiry whether the untrained layman would be qualified to determine intelligently and to the best possible degree the particular issue without enlightenment from those having a specialized understanding of the subject involved in the dispute." Ladd, Expert Testimony, 5 Vand.L.Rev. 414, 418 (1952). When opinions are excluded, it is because they are unhelpful and therefore superfluous and a waste of time. 7 Wigmore § 1918.

The rule is broadly phrased. The fields of knowledge which may be drawn upon are not limited merely to the "scientific" and "technical" but extend to all "specialized" knowledge. Similarly, the expert is viewed, not in a narrow sense, but as a person qualified by "knowledge, skill, experience, training or education." Thus within the scope of the rule are not only experts in the strictest sense of the word, e.g., physicians, physicists, and architects, but also the large group sometimes called "skilled" witnesses, such as bankers or landowners testifying to land values.

2000 Amendments

Rule 702 has been amended in response to *Daubert v. Merrell Dow Pharmaceuticals, Inc.*, 509 U.S. 579 (1993), and to the many cases applying *Daubert*, including *Kumho Tire Co. v. Carmichael*, 119 S.Ct. 1167 (1999). In *Daubert* the Court charged trial judges with the responsibility of acting as gatekeepers to exclude unreliable expert testimony, and the Court in *Kumho* clarified that this gatekeeper function applies to all expert testimony, not just testimony based in science. *See also Kumho*, 119 S.Ct. at 1178 (citing the Committee Note to the proposed amendment to Rule 702, which had been released for public comment before the date of the *Kumho* decision). The amendment affirms the trial court's role as gatekeeper and provides some general standards that the trial court must use to assess the reliability and helpfulness of proffered expert testimony. Consistently with *Kumho*, the Rule as amended provides that all types of expert testimony present questions of admissibility for the trial court in deciding whether the evidence is reliable and helpful. Consequently, the admissibility of all expert testimony is governed by the principles of Rule 104(a). Under that Rule, the proponent has the burden of establishing that the pertinent admissibility requirements are met by a preponderance of the evidence. *See Bourjaily v. United States*, 483 U.S. 171 (1987).

Daubert set forth a non-exclusive checklist for trial courts to use in assessing the reliability of scientific expert testimony. The specific factors explicated by the *Daubert* Court are (1) whether the expert's technique or theory can be or has been tested—that is, whether the expert's theory can be challenged in some objective sense, or whether it is instead simply a subjective, conclusory approach that cannot reasonably be assessed for reliability; (2) whether the technique or theory has been subject to peer review and publication; (3) the known or potential rate of error of the technique or theory when applied; (4) the existence and maintenance of standards and controls; and (5) whether the technique or theory has been generally accepted in the scientific community. The Court in *Kumho* held that these factors might also be applicable in assessing the reliability of non-scientific expert testimony, depending upon "the particular circumstances of the particular case at issue." 119 S.Ct. at 1175.

No attempt has been made to "codify" these specific factors. *Daubert* itself emphasized that the factors were neither exclusive nor dispositive. Other cases have recognized that not all of the specific *Daubert* factors can apply to every type of expert testimony. In addition to *Kumho*, 119 S.Ct. at 1175, *see Tyus v. Urban Search Management*, 102 F.3d 256 (7th Cir. 1996) (noting that the factors mentioned by the Court in *Daubert* do not neatly apply to expert testimony from a sociologist). *See also Kannankeril v. Terminix Int'l, Inc.*, 128 F.3d 802, 809 (3d Cir. 1997) (holding that lack of peer review or publication was not dispositive where the expert's opinion was supported by "widely accepted scientific knowledge"). The standards set forth in the amendment are broad enough to require consideration of any or all of the specific *Daubert* factors where appropriate.

Courts both before and after *Daubert* have found other factors relevant in determining whether expert testimony is sufficiently reliable to be considered by the trier of fact. These factors include:

(1) Whether experts are "proposing to testify about matters growing naturally and directly out of research they have conducted independent of the litigation, or whether they have developed their opinions expressly for purposes of testifying." *Daubert v. Merrell Dow Pharmaceuticals, Inc.*, 43 F.3d 1311, 1317 (9th Cir. 1995).

(2) Whether the expert has unjustifiably extrapolated from an accepted premise to an unfounded conclusion. *See General Elec. Co. v. Joiner*, 522 U.S. 136, 146 (1997) (noting that in some cases a trial court "may conclude that there is simply too great an analytical gap between the data and the opinion proffered").

(3) Whether the expert has adequately accounted for obvious alternative explanations. *See Claar v. Burlington N.R.R.*, 29 F.3d 499 (9th Cir. 1994) (testimony excluded where the expert failed to consider other obvious causes for the plaintiff's condition). *Compare Ambrosini v. Labarraque*, 101 F.3d 129 (D.C. Cir. 1996) (the possibility of some uneliminated causes presents a question of weight, so long as the most obvious causes have been considered and reasonably ruled out by the expert).

(4) Whether the expert "is being as careful as he would be in his regular professional work outside his paid litigation consulting." *Sheehan v. Daily Racing Form, Inc.*, 104 F.3d 940, 942 (7th Cir. 1997). *See Kumho Tire Co. v. Carmichael*, 119 S.Ct. 1167, 1176 (1999) (*Daubert* requires the trial court to assure itself that the expert "employs in the courtroom the same level of intellectual rigor that characterizes the practice of an expert in the relevant field").

(5) Whether the field of expertise claimed by the expert is known to reach reliable results for the type of opinion the expert would give. *See Kumho Tire Co. v. Carmichael*, 119 S.Ct.1167, 1175 (1999) (*Daubert's* general acceptance factor does not "help show that an expert's testimony is reliable where the discipline itself lacks reliability, as for example, do theories grounded in any so-called generally accepted principles of astrology or necromancy."), *Moore v. Ashland Chemical, Inc.*, 151 F.3d 269 (5th Cir. 1998) (en banc) (clinical doctor was properly precluded from testifying to the toxicological cause of the plaintiff's respiratory problem, where the opinion was not sufficiently grounded in scientific methodology); *Sterling v. Velsicol Chem. Corp.*, 855 F.2d 1188 (6th Cir. 1988) (rejecting testimony based on "clinical ecology" as unfounded and unreliable).

All of these factors remain relevant to the determination of the reliability of expert testimony under the Rule as amended. Other factors may also be relevant. *See Kumho*, 119 S.Ct. 1167, 1176 ("[W]e conclude that the trial judge must have considerable leeway in deciding in a particular case how to go about determining whether particular expert testimony is reliable."). Yet no single factor is necessarily dispositive of the reliability of a particular expert's testimony. *See, e.g., Heller v. Shaw Industries, Inc.*, 167 F.3d 146, 155 (3d Cir. 1999) ("not only must each stage of the expert's testimony be reliable, but each stage must be evaluated practically and flexibly without bright-line exclusionary (or inclusionary) rules."); *Daubert v. Merrell Dow Pharmaceuticals, Inc.*, 43 F.3d 1311, 1317, n.5 (9th Cir. 1995) (noting that some expert disciplines "have the courtroom as a principal theatre of operations" and as to these disciplines "the fact that the expert has developed an expertise principally for purposes of litigation will obviously not be a substantial consideration.").

A review of the caselaw after *Daubert* shows that the rejection of expert testimony is the exception rather than the rule. *Daubert* did not work a "seachange over federal evidence law," and "the trial court's role as gatekeeper is not intended to serve as a replacement for the adversary system." *United States v. 14.38 Acres of Land Situated in Leflore County, Mississippi*, 80 F.3d 1074, 1078 (5th Cir. 1996). As the Court in *Daubert* stated: "Vigorous cross-examination, presentation of contrary evidence, and careful instruction on the burden of proof are the traditional and appropriate means of attacking shaky but admissible evidence." 509 U.S. at 595. Likewise, this amendment is not intended to provide an excuse for an automatic challenge to the testimony of every expert. *See Kumho Tire Co. v . Carmichael*, 119 S.Ct.1167, 1176 (1999) (noting that the trial judge has the discretion "both to avoid unnecessary 'reliability' proceedings in ordinary cases where the reliability of an expert's methods is properly taken for granted, and to require appropriate proceedings in the less usual or more complex cases where cause for questioning the expert's reliability arises.").

When a trial court, applying this amendment, rules that an expert's testimony is reliable, this does not necessarily mean that contradictory expert testimony is unreliable. The amendment is broad enough to permit testimony that is the product of competing principles or methods in the same field of expertise. *See, e.g., Heller v. Shaw Industries, Inc.*, 167 F.3d 146, 160 (3d Cir. 1999) (expert testimony cannot be excluded simply because the expert uses one test rather than another, when both tests are accepted in the field and both reach reliable results). As the court stated in *In re Paoli R.R. Yard PCB Litigation*, 35 F.3d 717, 744 (3d Cir. 1994), proponents "do not have to demonstrate to the judge by a preponderance of the evidence that the assessments of their experts are correct, they only have to demonstrate by a preponderance of evidence that their opinions are reliable.... The evidentiary requirement of reliability is lower than the merits standard of correctness." *See also Daubert v. Merrell Dow Pharmaceuticals, Inc.*, 43 F.3d 1311, 1318 (9th Cir. 1995) (scientific experts might be permitted to testify if they could show that the methods they used were also employed by "a recognized minority of scientists in their field."); *Ruiz-Troche v. Pepsi Cola*, 161 F.3d 77, 85 (1st Cir. 1998) ("*Daubert* neither requires nor empowers trial courts to determine which of several competing scientific theories has the best provenance.").

The Court in *Daubert* declared that the "focus, of course, must be solely on principles and methodology, not on the conclusions they generate." 509 U.S. at 595. Yet as the Court later recognized, "conclusions and methodology are not entirely distinct from one another." *General Elec. Co. v. Joiner*, 522 U.S. 136, 146 (1997). Under the amendment, as under

Daubert, when an expert purports to apply principles and methods in accordance with professional standards, and yet reaches a conclusion that other experts in the field would not reach, the trial court may fairly suspect that the principles and methods have not been faithfully applied. *See Lust v. Merrell Dow Pharmaceuticals, Inc.*, 89 F.3d 594, 598 (9th Cir. 1996). The amendment specifically provides that the trial court must scrutinize not only the principles and methods used by the expert, but also whether those principles and methods have been properly applied to the facts of the case. As the court noted in *In re Paoli R.R. Yard PCB Litig.*, 35 F.3d 717, 745 (3d Cir. 1994), "*any* step that renders the analysis unreliable ... renders the expert's testimony inadmissible. *This is true whether the step completely changes a reliable methodology or merely misapplies that methodology.*"

If the expert purports to apply principles and methods to the facts of the case, it is important that this application be conducted reliably. Yet it might also be important in some cases for an expert to educate the factfinder about general principles, without ever attempting to apply these principles to the specific facts of the case. For example, experts might instruct the factfinder on the principles of thermodynamics, or bloodclotting, or on how financial markets respond to corporate reports, without ever knowing about or trying to tie their testimony into the facts of the case. The amendment does not alter the venerable practice of using expert testimony to educate the factfinder on general principles. For this kind of generalized testimony, Rule 702 simply requires that: (1) the expert be qualified; (2) the testimony address a subject matter on which the factfinder can be assisted by an expert; (3) the testimony be reliable; and (4) the testimony "fit" the facts of the case.

As stated earlier, the amendment does not distinguish between scientific and other forms of expert testimony. The trial court's gatekeeping function applies to testimony by any expert. *See Kumho Tire Co. v. Carmichael*, 119 S.Ct. 1167, 1171 (1999) ("We conclude that *Daubert's* general holding—setting forth the trial judge's general 'gatekeeping' obligation—applies not only to testimony based on 'scientific' knowledge, but also to testimony based on 'technical' and 'other specialized' knowledge."). While the relevant factors for determining reliability will vary from expertise to expertise, the amendment rejects the premise that an expert's testimony should be treated more permissively simply because it is outside the realm of science. An opinion from an expert who is not a scientist should receive the same degree of scrutiny for reliability as an opinion from an expert who purports to be a scientist. *See Watkins v. Telsmith, Inc.*, 121 F.3d 984, 991 (5th Cir. 1997) ("[I]t seems exactly backwards that experts who purport to rely on general engineering principles and practical experience might escape screening by the district court simply by stating that their conclusions were not reached by any particular method or technique."). Some types of expert testimony will be more objectively verifiable, and subject to the expectations of falsifiability, peer review, and publication, than others. Some types of expert testimony will not rely on anything like a scientific method, and so will have to be evaluated by reference to other standard principles attendant to the particular area of expertise. The trial judge in all cases of proffered expert testimony must find that it is properly grounded, well-reasoned, and not speculative before it can be admitted. The expert's testimony must be grounded in an accepted body of learning or experience in the expert's field, and the expert must explain how the conclusion is so grounded. *See, e.g.*, American College of Trial Lawyers, *Standards and Procedures for Determining the Admissibility of Expert Testimony after* Daubert, *157 F.R.D. 571, 579 (1994) ("[W] hether the testimony concerns economic principles, accounting standards, property valuation or other non-scientific subjects, it should be evaluated by reference to the 'knowledge and experience' of that particular field.").*

The amendment requires that the testimony must be the product of reliable principles and methods that are reliably applied to the facts of the case. While the terms "principles" and "methods" may convey a certain impression when applied to scientific knowledge, they remain relevant when applied to testimony based on technical or other specialized knowledge. For example, when a law enforcement agent testifies regarding the use of code words in a drug transaction, the principle used by the agent is that participants in such transactions regularly use code words to conceal the nature of their activities. The method used by the agent is the application of extensive experience to analyze the meaning of the conversations. So long as the principles and methods are reliable and applied reliably to the facts of the case, this type of testimony should be admitted.

Nothing in this amendment is intended to suggest that experience alone—or experience in conjunction with other knowledge, skill, training or education—may not provide a sufficient foundation for expert testimony. To the contrary, the text of Rule 702 expressly contemplates that an expert may be qualified on the basis of experience. In certain fields, experience is the predominant, if not sole, basis for a great deal of reliable expert testimony. *See, e.g., United States v. Jones*, 107 F.3d 1147 (6th Cir. 1997) (no abuse of discretion in admitting the testimony of a handwriting examiner who had years of practical experience and extensive training, and who explained his methodology in detail); *Tassin v. Sears Roebuck*, 946 F.Supp. 1241, 1248 (M.D.La. 1996) (design engineer's testimony can be admissible when the expert's opinions "are based on facts, a reasonable investigation, and traditional technical/mechanical expertise, and he provides a reasonable link between the information and procedures he uses and the conclusions he reaches"). *See also Kumho Tire Co. v. Carmichael*, 119 S.Ct. 1167, 1178 (1999) (stating that "no one denies that an expert might draw a conclusion from a set of observations based on extensive and specialized experience.").

If the witness is relying solely or primarily on experience, then the witness must explain how that experience leads to the conclusion reached, why that experience is a sufficient basis for the opinion, and how that experience is reliably applied to the facts. The trial court's gatekeeping function requires more than simply "taking the expert's word for it." *See Daubert v. Merrell Dow Pharmaceuticals, Inc.*, 43 F.3d 1311, 1319 (9th Cir. 1995) ("We've been presented with only the experts' qualifications, their conclusions and their assurances of reliability. Under *Daubert*, that's not enough."). The more subjective and controversial the expert's inquiry, the more likely the testimony should be excluded as unreliable. *See O'Conner v. Commonwealth Edison Co.*, 13 F.3d 1090 (7th Cir. 1994) (expert testimony based on a completely subjective methodology held properly excluded). *See also Kumho Tire Co. v. Carmichael*, 119 S.Ct . 1167, 1176 (1999) ("[I]t will at times be useful to ask even of a witness whose expertise is based purely on experience, say, a perfume tester able to distinguish among 140 odors at a sniff, whether his preparation is of a kind that others in the field would recognize as acceptable.").

Subpart (1) of Rule 702 calls for a quantitative rather than qualitative analysis. The amendment requires that expert testimony be based on sufficient underlying "facts or data." The term "data" is intended to encompass the reliable opinions of other experts. See the original Advisory Committee Note to Rule 703. The language "facts or data" is broad enough to allow an expert to rely on hypothetical facts that are supported by the evidence. *Id.*

When facts are in dispute, experts sometimes reach different conclusions based on competing versions of the facts. The emphasis in the amendment on " sufficient facts or data" is not intended to authorize a trial court to exclude an expert's testimony on the ground that the court believes one version of the facts and not the other.

There has been some confusion over the relationship between Rules 702 and 703. The amendment makes clear that the sufficiency of the basis of an expert' s testimony is to be decided under Rule 702. Rule 702 sets forth the overarching requirement of reliability, and an analysis of the sufficiency of the expert's basis cannot be divorced from the ultimate reliability of the expert's opinion. In contrast, the "reasonable reliance" requirement of Rule 703 is a relatively narrow inquiry. When an expert relies on inadmissible information, Rule 703 requires the trial court to determine whether that information is of a type reasonably relied on by other experts in the field. If so, the expert can rely on the information in reaching an opinion. However, the question whether the expert is relying on a *sufficient* basis of information—whether admissible information or not—is governed by the requirements of Rule 702.

The amendment makes no attempt to set forth procedural requirements for exercising the trial court's gatekeeping function over expert testimony. *See* Daniel J. Capra, *The Daubert Puzzle*, 38 Ga.L.Rev. 699, 766 (1998) ("Trial courts should be allowed substantial discretion in dealing with *Daubert* questions; any attempt to codify procedures will likely give rise to unnecessary changes in practice and create difficult questions for appellate review."). Courts have shown considerable ingenuity and flexibility in considering challenges to expert testimony under *Daubert*, and it is contemplated that this will continue under the amended Rule. *See, e.g., Cortes-Irizarry v. Corporacion Insular*, 111 F.3d 184 (1st Cir. 1997) (discussing the application of *Daubert* in ruling on a motion for summary judgment); *In re Paoli R.R. Yard PCB Litig.*, 35 F.3d 717, 736, 739 (3d Cir. 1994) (discussing the use of *in limine* hearings); *Claar v. Burlington N.R.R.*, 29 F.3d 499, 502–05 (9th Cir. 1994) (discussing the trial court's technique of ordering experts to submit serial affidavits explaining the reasoning and methods underlying their conclusions).

The amendment continues the practice of the original Rule in referring to a qualified witness as an "expert." This was done to provide continuity and to minimize change. The use of the term "expert" in the Rule does not, however, mean that a jury should actually be informed that a qualified witness is testifying as an "expert." Indeed, there is much to be said for a practice that prohibits the use of the term "expert" by both the parties and the court at trial. Such a practice "ensures that trial courts do not inadvertently put their stamp of authority" on a witness's opinion, and protects against the jury's being "overwhelmed by the so-called 'experts'." Hon. Charles Richey, *Proposals to Eliminate the Prejudicial Effect of the Use of the Word "Expert" Under the Federal Rules of Evidence in Criminal and Civil Jury Trials*, 154 F.R.D. 537, 559 (1994) (setting forth limiting instructions and a standing order employed to prohibit the use of the term " expert" injury trials).

GAP Report—Proposed Amendment to Rule 702

The Committee made the following changes to the published draft of the proposed amendment to Evidence Rule 702:

1. The word "reliable" was deleted from Subpart (1) of the proposed amendment, in order to avoid an overlap with Evidence Rule 703, and to clarify that an expert opinion need not be excluded simply because it is based on hypothetical facts. The Committee Note was amended to accord with this textual change.

2. The Committee Note was amended throughout to include pertinent references to the Supreme Court's decision in *Kumho Tire Co. v. Carmichael*, which was rendered after the proposed amendment was released for public comment. Other citations were updated as well.

3. The Committee Note was revised to emphasize that the amendment is not intended to limit the right to jury trial, nor to permit a challenge to the testimony of every expert, nor to preclude the testimony of experience-based experts, nor to prohibit testimony based on competing methodologies within a field of expertise.

4. Language was added to the Committee Note to clarify that no single factor is necessarily dispositive of the reliability inquiry mandated by Evidence Rule 702.

Rule 703. Bases of Opinion Testimony by Experts

The facts or data in the particular case upon which an expert bases an opinion or inference may be those perceived by or made known to the expert at or before the hearing. If of a type reasonably relied upon by experts in the particular field in forming opinions or inferences upon the subject, the facts or data need not be admissible in evidence in order for the opinion or inference to be admitted. Facts or data that are otherwise inadmissible shall not be disclosed to the jury by the proponent of the opinion or inference unless the court determines that their probative value in assisting the jury to evaluate the expert's opinion substantially outweighs their prejudicial effect.

(Pub.L. 93–595, § 1, Jan. 2, 1975, 88 Stat.1937; Mar. 2, 1987, eff. Oct. 1, 1987; Apr. 17, 2000, eff. Dec. 1, 2000.)

ADVISORY COMMITTEE NOTES

1972 Proposed Rules

Facts or data upon which expert opinions are based may, under the rule, be derived from three possible sources. The first is the firsthand observation of the witness with opinions based thereon traditionally allowed. A treating physician affords an example. Rheingold, The Basis of Medical Testimony, 15 Vand.L.Rev. 473, 489 (1962). Whether he must first relate his observations is treated in Rule 705. The second source, presentation at the trial, also reflects existing practice. The technique may be the familiar hypothetical question or having the expert attend the trial and hear the testimony establishing the facts. Problems of determining what testimony the expert relied upon, when the latter technique is employed and the testimony is in conflict, may be resolved by resort to Rule 705. The third source contemplated by the rule consists of presentation of data to the expert outside of court and other than by his own perception. In this respect the rule is designed to broaden the basis for expert opinions beyond that current in many jurisdictions and to bring the judicial practice into line with the practice of the experts themselves when not in court. Thus a physician in his own practice bases his diagnosis on information from numerous sources and of considerable variety, including statements by patients and relatives, reports and opinions from nurses, technicians and other doctors, hospital records, and X rays. Most of them are admissible in evidence, but only with the expenditure of substantial time in producing and examining various authenticating witnesses. The physician makes life-and-death decisions in reliance upon them. His validation, expertly performed and subject to cross-examination, ought to suffice for judicial purposes. Rheingold, *supra*, at 531; McCormick § 15. A similar provision is California Evidence Code § 801(b).

The rule also offers a more satisfactory basis for ruling upon the admissibility of public opinion poll evidence. Attention is directed to the validity of the techniques employed rather than to relatively fruitless inquiries whether hearsay is involved. See Judge Feinberg's careful analysis in Zippo Mfg. Co. v. Rogers Imports, Inc., 216 F.Supp. 670 (S.D.N.Y. 1963). See also Blum et al., The Art of Opinion Research: A Lawyer's Appraisal of an Emerging Service, 24 U.Chi.L.Rev. 1 (1956); Bonynge Trademark Surveys and Techniques and Their Use in Litigation, 48 A.B.A.J. 329 (1962); Zeisel, The Uniqueness of Survey Evidence, 45 Cornell L.Q. 322 (1960); Annot., 76 A.L.R.2d 919.

If it be feared that enlargement of permissible data may tend to break down the rules of exclusion unduly, notice should be taken that the rule requires that the facts or data "be of a type reasonably relied upon by experts in the particular field." The language would not warrant admitting in evidence the opinion of an "accidentologist" as to the point of impact in an automobile collision based on statements of bystanders since this requirement is not satisfied. See Comment, Cal.Law Rev.Comm'n, Recommendation Proposing an Evidence Code 148–150 (1965).

1987 Amendments

The amendment is technical. No substantive change is intended.

2000 Amendments

Rule 703 has been amended to emphasize that when an expert reasonably relies on inadmissible information to form an opinion or inference, the underlying information is not admissible simply because the opinion or inference is admitted. Courts have reached different results on how to treat inadmissible information when it is reasonably relied upon by an expert in forming an opinion or drawing an inference. *Compare United States v. Rollins*, 862 F.2d 1282 (7th Cir. 1988) (admitting, as part of the basis of an FBI agent's expert opinion on the meaning of code language, the hearsay statements of an informant), *with United States v. 0.59 Acres of Land*, 109 F.3d 1493 (9th Cir. 1997) (error to admit hearsay offered as the basis of an expert opinion, without a limiting instruction). Commentators have also taken differing views. *See e.g.*, Ronald Carlson, *Policing the Bases of Modern Expert Testimony*, 39 Vand.L.Rev. 577 (1986) (advocating limits on the jury's consideration of otherwise inadmissible evidence used as the basis for an expert opinion); Paul Rice, *Inadmissible Evidence as a Basis for Expert Testimony: A Response to Professor Carlson*, 40 Vand.L.Rev. 583 (1987) (advocating unrestricted use of information reasonably relied upon by an expert).

When information is reasonably relied upon by an expert and yet is admissible only for the purpose of assisting the jury in evaluating an expert's opinion, a trial court applying this Rule must consider the information's probative value in assisting the jury to weigh the expert's opinion on the one hand, and the risk of prejudice resulting from the jury's potential misuse of the information for substantive purposes on the other. The information may be disclosed to the jury, upon objection, only if the trial court finds that the probative value of the information in assisting the jury to evaluate the expert's opinion substantially outweighs its prejudicial effect. If the otherwise inadmissible information is admitted under this balancing test, the trial judge must give a limiting instruction upon request, informing the jury that the underlying information must not be used for substantive purposes. *See* Rule 105. In determining the appropriate course, the trial court should consider the probable effectiveness or lack of effectiveness of a limiting instruction under the particular circumstances.

The amendment governs only the disclosure to the jury of information that is reasonably relied on by an expert, when that information is not admissible for substantive purposes. It is not intended to affect the admissibility of an expert's testimony. Nor does the amendment prevent an expert from relying on information that is inadmissible for substantive purposes.

Nothing in this Rule restricts the presentation of underlying expert facts or data when offered by an adverse party. *See* Rule 705. Of course, an adversary's attack on an expert's basis will often open the door to a proponent's rebuttal with information that was reasonably relied upon by the expert, even if that information would not have been discloseable initially under the balancing test provided by this amendment. Moreover, in some circumstances the proponent might wish to disclose information that is relied upon by the expert in order to "remove the sting" from the opponent's anticipated attack, and thereby prevent the jury from drawing an unfair negative inference. The trial court should take this consideration into account in applying the balancing test provided by this amendment.

This amendment covers facts or data that cannot be admitted for any purpose other than to assist the jury to evaluate the expert's opinion. The balancing test provided in this amendment is not applicable to facts or data that are admissible for any other purpose but have not yet been offered for such a purpose at the time the expert testifies.

The amendment provides a presumption against disclosure to the jury of information used as the basis of an expert's opinion and not admissible for any substantive purpose, when that information is offered by the proponent of the expert. In a multi-party case, where one party proffers an expert whose testimony is also beneficial to other parties, each such party should be deemed a "proponent" within the meaning of the amendment.

GAP Report—Proposed Amendment to Rule 703

The Committee made the following changes to the published draft of the proposed amendment to Evidence Rule 703:

1. A minor stylistic change was made in the text, in accordance with the suggestion of the Style Subcommittee of the Standing Committee on Rules of Practice and Procedure.

2. The words "in assisting the jury to evaluate the expert's opinion" were added to the text, to specify the proper purpose for offering the otherwise inadmissible information relied on by an expert. The Committee Note was revised to accord with this change in the text.

3. Stylistic changes were made to the Committee Note.

4. The Committee Note was revised to emphasize that the balancing test set forth in the proposal should be used to determine whether an expert's basis may be disclosed to the jury either (1) in rebuttal or (2) on direct examination to "remove the sting" of an opponent's anticipated attack on an expert's basis.

CROSS REFERENCES

Personal knowledge evidence of as prerequisite to testimony by witness, see Fed.Rules Evid. Rule 602, 28 USCA.

Rule 704. Opinion on Ultimate Issue

(a) Except as provided in subdivision (b), testimony in the form of an opinion or inference otherwise admissible is not objectionable because it embraces an ultimate issue to be decided by the trier of fact.

(b) No expert witness testifying with respect to the mental state or condition of a defendant in a criminal case may state an opinion or inference as to whether the defendant did or did not have the mental state or condition constituting an element of the crime charged or of a defense thereto. Such ultimate issues are matters for the trier of fact alone.

(Pub.L. 93–595, § 1, Jan. 2, 1975, 88 Stat. 1937; Pub.L. 98–473, Title IV, § 406, Oct. 12, 1984, 98 Stat. 2067.)

ADVISORY COMMITTEE NOTES

1972 Proposed Rules

The basic approach to opinions, lay and expert, in these rules is to admit them when helpful to the trier of fact. In order to render this approach fully effective and to allay any doubt on the subject, the so-called "ultimate issue" rule is specifically abolished by the instant rule.

The older cases often contained strictures against allowing witnesses to express opinions upon ultimate issues, as a particular aspect of the rule against opinions. The rule was unduly restrictive, difficult of application, and generally served only to deprive the trier of fact of useful information. 7 Wigmore §§ 1920, 1921; McCormick § 12. The basis usually assigned for the rule, to prevent the witness from "usurping the province of the jury," is aptly characterized as "empty rhetoric." 7 Wigmore § 1920, p. 17. Efforts to meet the felt needs of particular situations led to odd verbal circumlocutions which were said not to violate the rule. Thus a witness could express his estimate of the criminal responsibility of an accused in terms of sanity or insanity, but not in terms of ability to tell right from wrong or other more modern standard. And in cases of medical causation, witnesses were sometimes required to couch their opinions in cautious phrases of "might or could," rather than "did," though the result was to deprive many opinions of the positiveness to which they were entitled, accompanied by the hazard of a ruling of insufficiency to support a verdict. In other instances the rule was simply disregarded, and, as concessions to need, opinions were allowed upon such matters as intoxication, speed, handwriting, and value, although more precise coincidence with an ultimate issue would scarcely be possible.

Many modern decisions illustrate the trend to abandon the rule completely. People v. Wilson, 25 Cal.2d 341, 153 P.2d 720 (1944), whether abortion necessary to save life of patient; *Clifford–Jacobs Forging Co. v. Industrial Comm.*, 19 Ill.2d 236, 166 N.E.2d 582 (1960), medical causation; *Dowling v. L. H. Shattuck*, Inc., 91 N.H. 234, 17 A.2d 529 (1941), proper method of shoring ditch; *Schweiger v. Solbeck*, 191 Or. 454, 230 P.2d 195 (1951), cause of landslide. In each instance the opinion was allowed.

The abolition of the ultimate issue rule does not lower the bars so as to admit all opinions. Under Rules 701 and 702, opinions must be helpful to the trier of fact, and Rule 403 provides for exclusion of evidence which wastes time. These provisions afford ample assurances against the admission of opinions which would merely tell the jury what result to reach, somewhat in the manner of the oath-helpers of an earlier day. They also stand ready to exclude opinions phrased in terms of inadequately explored legal criteria. Thus the question, "Did T have capacity to make a will?" would be excluded, while the question, "Did T have sufficient mental capacity to know the nature and extent of his property and the natural objects of his bounty and to formulate a rational scheme of distribution?" would be allowed. McCormick § 12.

For similar provisions see Uniform Rule 56(4); California Evidence Code § 805; Kansas Code of Civil Procedure § 60–456(d); New Jersey Evidence Rule 56(3).

CROSS REFERENCES

Relevancy of evidence and its limits, see Fed.Rules Evid. Rule 401 et seq., 28 USCA.

Rule 705. Disclosure of Facts or Data Underlying Expert Opinion

The expert may testify in terms of opinion or inference and give reasons therefor without first testifying to the underlying facts or data, unless the court requires otherwise. The expert may in any event be required to disclose the underlying facts or data on cross-examination.

(Pub.L. 93–595, § 1, Jan. 2, 1975, 88 Stat. 1938; Mar. 2, 1987, eff. Oct. 1, 1987; Apr. 22, 1993, eff. Dec. 1, 1993.)

ADVISORY COMMITTEE NOTES

1972 Proposed Rules

The hypothetical question has been the target of a great deal of criticism as encouraging partisan bias, affording an opportunity for summing up in the middle of the case, and as complex and time consuming. Ladd, Expert Testimony, 5 Vand.L.Rev. 414, 426–427 (1952). While the rule allows counsel to make disclosure of the underlying facts or data as a preliminary to the giving of an expert opinion, if he chooses, the instances in which he is required to do so are reduced. This is true whether the expert bases his opinion on data furnished him at secondhand or observed by him at firsthand.

The elimination of the requirement of preliminary disclosure at the trial of underlying facts or data has a long background of support. In 1937 the Commissioners on Uniform State Laws incorporated a provision to this effect in their Model Expert Testimony Act, which furnished the basis for Uniform Rules 57 and 58. Rule 4515, N.Y. CPLR (McKinney 1963), provides:

"Unless the court orders otherwise, questions calling for the opinion of an expert witness need not be hypothetical in form, and the witness may state his opinion and reasons without first specifying the data upon which it is based. Upon cross-examination, he may be required to specify the data * * *."

See also California Evidence Code § 802; Kansas Code of Civil Procedure §§ 60–456, 60–457; New Jersey Evidence Rules 57, 58.

If the objection is made that leaving it to the cross-examiner to bring out the supporting data is essentially unfair, the answer is that he is under no compulsion to bring out any facts or data except those unfavorable to the opinion. The answer assumes that the cross-examiner has the advance knowledge which is essential for effective cross-examination. This advance knowledge has been afforded, though imperfectly, by the traditional foundation requirement. Rule 26(b)(4) of the Rules of Civil Procedure, as revised, provides for substantial discovery in this area, obviating in large measure the obstacles which have been raised in some instances to discovery of findings, underlying data, and even the identity of the experts. Friedenthal Discovery and Use of an Adverse Party's Expert Information, 14 Stan.L.Rev. 455 (1962).

These safeguards are reinforced by the discretionary power of the judge to require preliminary disclosure in any event.

1987 Amendment

The amendment is technical. No substantive change is intended.

1993 Amendment

This rule, which relates to the manner of presenting testimony at trial, is revised to avoid an arguable conflict with revised Rules 26(a)(2)(B) and 26(e)(1) of the Federal Rules of Civil Procedure or with revised Rule 16 of the Federal Rules of Criminal Procedure, which require disclosure in advance of trial of the basis and reasons for an expert's opinions.

If a serious question is raised under Rule 702 or 703 as to the admissibility of expert testimony, disclosure of the underlying facts or data on which opinions are based may, of course, be needed by the court before deciding whether, and to what extent, the person should be allowed to testify. This rule does not preclude such an inquiry.

CROSS REFERENCES

Scope of discovery, see Fed.Rules Civ.Proc. Rule 26, 28 USCA.

Rule 706. Court Appointed Experts

(a) Appointment. The court may on its own motion or on the motion of any party enter an order to show cause why expert witnesses should not be appointed, and may request the parties to submit nominations. The court may appoint any expert witnesses agreed upon by the parties, and may appoint expert witnesses of its own selection. An expert witness shall not be appointed by the court unless the witness consents to act. A witness so appointed shall be informed of the witness' duties by the court in writing, a copy of which shall be filed with the clerk, or at a conference in which the parties shall have opportunity to participate. A witness so appointed shall advise the parties of the witness' findings, if any; the witness' deposition may be taken by any party; and the witness may be called to testify by the court or any party. The witness shall be subject to cross-examination by each party, including a party calling the witness.

(b) Compensation. Expert witnesses so appointed are entitled to reasonable compensation in whatever sum the court may allow. The compensation thus fixed is payable from funds which may be provided by law in criminal cases and civil actions and proceedings involving just compensation under the fifth amendment. In other civil actions and proceedings the compensation shall be paid by the parties in such proportion and at such time as the court directs, and thereafter charged in like manner as other costs.

(c) Disclosure of appointment. In the exercise of its discretion, the court may authorize disclosure to the jury of the fact that the court appointed the expert witness.

(d) Parties' experts of own selection. Nothing in this rule limits the parties in calling expert witnesses of their own selection.

(Pub.L. 93–595, § 1, Jan. 2, 1975, 88 Stat.1938; Mar. 2, 1987, eff. Oct. 1, 1987.)

ADVISORY COMMITTEE NOTES

1972 Proposed Rules

The practice of shopping for experts, the venality of some experts, and the reluctance of many reputable experts to involve themselves in litigation, have been matters of deep concern. Though the contention is made that court appointed experts acquire an aura of infallibility to which they are not entitled, Levy, Impartial Medical Testimony—Revisited, 34 Temple L.Q. 416 (1961), the trend is increasingly to provide for their use. While experience indicates that actual appointment is a relatively infrequent occurrence, the assumption may be made that the availability of the procedure in itself decreases the need for resorting to it. The ever-present possibility that the judge may appoint an expert in a given case must inevitably exert a sobering effect on the expert witness of a party and upon the person utilizing his services.

The inherent power of a trial judge to appoint an expert of his own choosing is virtually unquestioned. *Scott v. Spanjer Bros., Inc.,* 298 F.2d 928 (2d Cir.1962); *Danville Tobacco Assn. v. Bryant–Buckner Associates,* Inc., 333 F.2d 202 (4th Cir.1964); Sink, The Unused Power of a Federal Judge to Call His Own Expert Witnesses, 29 S.Cal.L.Rev. 195 (1956); 2 Wigmore § 563, 9 *id.* § 2484; Annot., 95 A.L.R.2d 383. Hence the problem becomes largely one of detail.

The New York plan is well known and is described in Report by Special Committee of the Association of the Bar of the City of New York: Impartial Medical Testimony (1956). On recommendation of the Section of Judicial Administration, local adoption of an impartial medical plan was endorsed by the American Bar Association. 82 A.B.A.Rep. 184–185 (1957). Descriptions and analyses of plans in effect in various parts of the country are found in Van Dusen, A United States District Judge's View of the Impartial Medical Expert System, 32 F.R.D. 498 (1963); Wick and Kightlinger, Impartial Medical Testimony Under the Federal Civil Rules: A Tale of Three Doctors, 34 Ins. Counsel J. 115 (1967); and numerous articles collected in Klein, Judicial Administration and the Legal Profession 393 (1963). Statutes and rules include California Evidence Code §§ 730–733; Illinois Supreme Court Rule 215(d), Ill.Rev.Stat.1969, c. 110A, § 215(d); Burns Indiana Stats.1956, § 9–1702; Wisconsin Stats.Annot.1958, § 957.27.

In the federal practice, a comprehensive scheme for court appointed experts was initiated with the adoption of Rule 28 of the Federal Rules of Criminal Procedure in 1946. The Judicial Conference of the United States in 1953 considered court appointed experts in civil cases, but only with respect to whether they should be compensated from public funds, a proposal which was rejected. Report of the Judicial Conference of the United States 23 (1953). The present rule expands the practice to include civil cases.

Note to Subdivision (a). Subdivision (a) is based on Rule 28 of the Federal Rules of Criminal Procedure, with a few changes, mainly in the interest of clarity. Language has been added to provide specifically for the appointment either on motion of a party or on the judge's own motion. A provision subjecting the court appointed expert to deposition procedures has been incorporated. The rule has been revised to make definite the right of any party, including the party calling him, to cross-examine.

Note to Subdivision (b). Subdivision (b) combines the present provision for compensation in criminal cases with what seems to be a fair and feasible handling of civil cases, originally found in the Model Act and carried from there into Uniform Rule 60. See also California Evidence Code §§ 730–731. The special provision for Fifth Amendment compensation cases is designed to guard against reducing constitutionally guaranteed just compensation by requiring the recipient to pay costs. See Rule 71A(*l*) of the Rules of Civil Procedure.

Note to Subdivision (c). Subdivision (c) seems to be essential if the use of court appointed experts is to be fully effective. Uniform Rule 61 so provides.

Note to Subdivision (d). Subdivision (d) is in essence the last sentence of Rule 28(a) of the Federal Rules of Criminal Procedure.

1987 Amendment

The amendments are technical. No substantive change is intended.

CROSS REFERENCES

Appointment of interpreters, see Fed.Rules Cr.Proc. Rule 28, 18 USCA.

ARTICLE VIII. HEARSAY

Rule

ADVISORY COMMITTEE NOTES

1972 Proposed Rules

Introductory Note; The Hearsay Problem. The factors to be considered in evaluating the testimony of a witness are perception, memory, and narration. Morgan, Hearsay Dangers and the Application of the Hearsay Concept, 62 Harv. L.Rev. 177 (1948), Selected Writings on Evidence and Trial 764, 765 (Fryer ed. 1957); Shientag, Cross–Examination—A Judge's Viewpoint, 3 Record 12 (1948); Strahorn, A Reconsideration of the Hearsay Rule and Admissions, 85 U.Pa. L.Rev. 484, 485 (1937), Selected Writings, *supra,* 756, 757; Weinstein, Probative Force of Hearsay, 46 Iowa L.Rev. 331 (1961). Sometimes a fourth is added, sincerity, but in fact it seems merely to be an aspect of the three already mentioned.

In order to encourage the witness to do his best with respect to each of these factors, and to expose any inaccuracies which may enter in, the Anglo–American tradition has evolved three conditions under which witnesses will ideally be required to testify: (1) under oath, (2) in the personal presence of the trier of fact, (3) subject to cross-examination.

(1) Standard procedure calls for the swearing of witnesses. While the practice is perhaps less effective than in an earlier time, no disposition to relax the requirement is apparent, other than to allow affirmation by persons with scruples against taking oaths.

(2) The demeanor of the witness traditionally has been believed to furnish trier and opponent with valuable clues. *Universal Camera Corp. v. N.L.R.B.,* 340 U.S. 474, 495–496, 71 S.Ct. 456, 95 L.Ed. 456 (1951); Sahm, Demeanor Evidence: Elusive and Intangible Imponderables, 47 A.B.A.J. 580 (1961), quoting numerous authorities. The witness himself will probably be impressed with the solemnity of the

occasion and the possibility of public disgrace. Willingness to falsify may reasonably become more difficult in the presence of the person against whom directed. Rules 26 and 43(a) of the Federal Rules of Criminal and Civil Procedure, respectively, include the general requirement that testimony be taken orally in open court. The Sixth Amendment right of confrontation is a manifestation of these beliefs and attitudes.

(3) Emphasis on the basis of the hearsay rule today tends to center upon the condition of cross-examination. All may not agree with Wigmore that cross-examination is "beyond doubt the greatest legal engine ever invented for the discovery of truth," but all will agree with his statement that it has become a "vital feature" of the Anglo-American system. 5 Wigmore § 1367, p. 29. The belief, or perhaps hope, that cross-examination is effective in exposing imperfections of perception, memory, and narration is fundamental. Morgan, Foreword to Model Code of Evidence 37 (1942).

The logic of the preceding discussion might suggest that no testimony be received unless in full compliance with the three ideal conditions. No one advocates this position. Common sense tells that much evidence which is not given under the three conditions may be inherently superior to much that is. Moreover, when the choice is between evidence which is less than best and no evidence at all, only clear folly would dictate an across-the-board policy of doing without. The problem thus resolves itself into effecting a sensible accommodation between these considerations and the desirability of giving testimony under the ideal conditions.

The solution evolved by the common law has been a general rule excluding hearsay but subject to numerous exceptions under circumstances supposed to furnish guarantees of trustworthiness. Criticisms of this scheme are that it is bulky and complex, fails to screen good from bad hearsay realistically, and inhibits the growth of the law of evidence.

Since no one advocates excluding all hearsay, three possible solutions may be considered: (1) abolish the rule against hearsay and admit all hearsay; (2) admit hearsay possessing sufficient probative force, but with procedural safeguards; (3) revise the present system of class exceptions.

(1) Abolition of the hearsay rule would be the simplest solution. The effect would not be automatically to abolish the giving of testimony under ideal conditions. If the declarant were available, compliance with the ideal conditions would be optional with either party. Thus the proponent could call the declarant as a witness as a form of presentation more impressive than his hearsay statement. Or the opponent could call the declarant to be cross-examined upon his statement. This is the tenor of Uniform Rule 63(1), admitting the hearsay declaration of a person "who is present at the hearing and available for cross-examination." Compare the treatment of declarations of available declarants in Rule 801(d)(1) of the instant rules. If the declarant were unavailable, a rule of free admissibility would make no distinctions in terms of degrees of noncompliance with the ideal conditions and would exact no quid pro quo in the form of assurances of trustworthiness. Rule 503 of the Model Code did exactly that, providing for the admissibility of any hearsay declaration by an unavailable declarant, finding support in the Massachusetts act of 1898, enacted at the instance of Thayer, Mass.Gen.L.1932, c. 233, § 65, and in the English act of 1938, St.1938, c. 28, Evidence. Both are limited to civil cases. The draftsmen of the Uniform Rules chose a less advanced and more conventional position. Comment, Uniform Rule 63. The present Advisory Committee has been unconvinced of the wisdom of abandoning the traditional requirement of some particular assurance of credibility as a condition precedent to admitting the hearsay declaration of an unavailable declarant.

In criminal cases, the Sixth Amendment requirement of confrontation would no doubt move into a large part of the area presently occupied by the hearsay rule in the event of the abolition of the latter. The resultant split between civil and criminal evidence is regarded as an undesirable development.

(2) Abandonment of the system of class exceptions in favor of individual treatment in the setting of the particular case, accompanied by procedural safeguards, has been impressively advocated. Weinstein, The Probative Force of Hearsay, 46 Iowa L.Rev. 331 (1961). Admissibility would be determined by weighing the probative force of the evidence against the possibility of prejudice, waste of time, and the availability of more satisfactory evidence. The bases of the traditional hearsay exceptions would be helpful in assessing probative force. Ladd, The Relationship of the Principles of Exclusionary Rules of Evidence to the Problem of Proof, 18 Minn.L.Rev. 506 (1934). Procedural safeguards would consist of notice of intention to use hearsay, free comment by the judge on the weight of the evidence, and a greater measure of authority in both trial and appellate judges to deal with evidence on the basis of weight. The Advisory Committee has rejected this approach to hearsay as involving too great a measure of judicial discretion, minimizing the predictability of rulings, enhancing the difficulties of preparation for trial, adding a further element to the already overcomplicated congeries of pretrial procedures, and requiring substantially different rules for civil and criminal cases. The only way in which the probative force of hearsay differs from the probative force of other testimony is in the absence of oath, demeanor, and cross-examination as aids in determining credibility. For a judge to exclude evidence because he does not believe it has been described as "altogether atypical, extraordinary. * * *" Chadbourn, Bentham and the Hearsay Rule—A Benthamic View of Rule 63(4)(c) of the Uniform Rules of Evidence, 75 Harv.L.Rev. 932, 947 (1962).

(3) The approach to hearsay in these rules is that of the common law, i.e., a general rule excluding hearsay, with exceptions under which evidence is not required to be excluded even though hearsay. The traditional hearsay exceptions are drawn upon for the exceptions, collected under two rules, one dealing with situations where availability of the declarant is regarded as immaterial and the other with those where unavailability is made a condition to the admission of the hearsay statement. Each of the two rules concludes with a provision for hearsay statements not within one of the specified exceptions "but having comparable circumstantial guarantees of trustworthiness." Rules 803(24) and 804(b)(6). This plan is submitted as calculated to encourage growth and development in this area of the law, while conserving the values and experience of the past as a guide to the future.

Confrontation and Due Process. Until very recently, decisions invoking the confrontation clause of the Sixth Amendment were surprisingly few, a fact probably explainable by the former inapplicability of the clause to the states and by the hearsay rule's occupancy of much the same ground. The pattern which emerges from the earlier cases invoking the clause is substantially that of the hearsay rule, applied to criminal cases: an accused is entitled to have the witnesses against him testify under oath, in the presence of himself and trier, subject to cross-examination; yet considerations of public policy and necessity require the recognition of such exceptions as dying declarations and former testimony of unavailable witnesses. *Mattox v. United States,* 156 U.S. 237, 15 S.Ct. 337, 39 L.Ed. 409 (1895); *Motes v. United States,* 178 U.S. 458, 20 S.Ct. 993, 44 L.Ed. 1150 (1900); *Delaney v. United States,* 263 U.S. 586, 44 S.Ct. 206, 68 L.Ed. 462 (1924). Beginning with *Snyder v. Massachusetts,* 291 U.S. 97, 54 S.Ct. 330, 78 L.Ed. 674 (1934), the Court began to speak of confrontation as an aspect of procedural due process, thus extending its applicability to state cases and to federal cases other than criminal. The language of *Snyder* was that of an elastic concept of hearsay. The deportation case of *Bridges v. Wixon,* 326 U.S. 135, 65 S.Ct. 1443, 89 L.Ed. 2103 (1945), may be read broadly as imposing a strictly construed right of confrontation in all kinds of cases or narrowly as the product of a failure of the Immigration and Naturalization Service to follow its own rules. *In re Oliver,* 333 U.S. 257, 68 S.Ct. 499, 92 L.Ed. 682 (1948), ruled that cross-examination was essential to due process in a state contempt proceeding, but in *United States v. Nugent,* 346 U.S. 1, 73 S.Ct. 991, 97 L.Ed. 1417 (1953), the court held that it was not an essential aspect of a "hearing" for a conscientious objector under the Selective Service Act. *Stein v. New York,* 346 U.S. 156, 196, 73 S.Ct. 1077, 97 L.Ed. 1522 (1953), disclaimed any purpose to read the hearsay rule into the Fourteenth Amendment, but in *Greene v. McElroy,* 360 U.S. 474, 79 S.Ct. 1400, 3 L.Ed.2d 1377 (1959), revocation of security clearance without confrontation and cross-examination was held unauthorized, and a similar result was reached in *Willner v. Committee on Character,* 373 U.S. 96, 83 S.Ct. 1175, 10 L.Ed.2d 224 (1963). Ascertaining the constitutional dimensions of the confrontation-hearsay aggregate against the background of these cases is a matter of some difficulty, yet the general pattern is at least not inconsistent with that of the hearsay rule.

In 1965 the confrontation clause was held applicable to the states. *Pointer v. Texas,* 380 U.S. 400, 85 S.Ct. 1065, 13 L.Ed.2d 923 (1965). Prosecution use of former testimony given at a preliminary hearing where petitioner was not represented by counsel was a violation of the clause. The same result would have followed under conventional hearsay doctrine read in the light of a constitutional right to counsel, and nothing in the opinion suggests any difference in essential outline between the hearsay rule and the right of confrontation. In the companion case of *Douglas v. Alabama,* 380 U.S. 415, 85 S.Ct. 1074, 13 L.Ed.2d 934 (1965), however, the result reached by applying the confrontation clause is one reached less readily via the hearsay rule. A confession implicating petitioner was put before the jury by reading it to the witness in portions and asking if he made that statement. The witness refused to answer on grounds of self-incrimination. The result, said the Court, was to deny cross-examination, and hence confrontation. True, it could broadly be said that the confession was a hearsay statement which for all practical purposes was put in evidence. Yet a more easily accepted explanation of the opinion is that its real thrust was in the direction of curbing undesirable prosecutorial behavior, rather than merely applying rules of exclusion, and that the confrontation clause was the means selected to achieve this end. Comparable facts and a like result appeared in *Brookhart v. Janis,* 384 U.S. 1, 86 S.Ct. 1245, 16 L.Ed.2d 314 (1966).

The pattern suggested in *Douglas* was developed further and more distinctly in a pair of cases at the end of the 1966 term. *United States v. Wade,* 388 U.S. 218, 87 S.Ct. 1926, 18 L.Ed.2d 1149 (1967), and *Gilbert v. California,* 388 U.S. 263, 87 S.Ct. 1951, 18 L.Ed.2d 1178 (1967), hinged upon practices followed in identifying accused persons before trial. This pretrial identification was said to be so decisive an aspect of the case that accused was entitled to have counsel present; a pretrial identification made in the absence of counsel was not itself receivable in evidence and, in addition, might fatally infect a courtroom identification. The presence of counsel at the earlier identification was described as a necessary prerequisite for "a meaningful confrontation at trial." *United States v. Wade, supra,* 388 U.S. at p. 236, 87 S.Ct. at p. 1937. *Wade* involved no evidence of the fact of a prior identification and hence was not susceptible of being decided on hearsay grounds. In *Gilbert,* witnesses did testify to an earlier identification, readily classifiable as hearsay under a fairly strict view of what constitutes hearsay. The Court, however, carefully avoided basing the decision on the hearsay ground, choosing confrontation instead. 388 U.S. 263, 272, n. 3, 87 S.Ct. 1951. See also *Parker v. Gladden,* 385 U.S. 363, 87 S.Ct. 468, 17 L.Ed.2d 420 (1966), holding that the right of confrontation was violated when the bailiff made prejudicial statements to jurors, and Note, 75 Yale L.J. 1434 (1966).

Under the earlier cases, the confrontation clause may have been little more than a constitutional embodiment of the hearsay rule, even including traditional exceptions but with some room for expanding them along similar lines. But under the recent cases the impact of the clause clearly extends beyond the confines of the hearsay rule. These considerations have led the Advisory Committee to conclude that a hearsay rule can function usefully as an adjunct to the confrontation right in constitutional areas and independently in nonconstitutional areas. In recognition of the separateness of the confrontation clause and the hearsay rule, and to avoid inviting collisions between them or between the hearsay rule and other exclusionary principles, the exceptions set forth in Rules 803 and 804 are stated in terms of exemption from the general exclusionary mandate of the hearsay rule, rather than in positive terms of admissibility. See Uniform Rule 63(1) to (31) and California Evidence Code §§ 1200–1340.

Rule 801. Definitions

The following definitions apply under this article:

(a) Statement. A "statement" is (1) an oral or written assertion or (2) nonverbal conduct of a person, if it is intended by the person as an assertion.

(b) Declarant. A "declarant" is a person who makes a statement.

(c) Hearsay. "Hearsay" is a statement, other than one made by the declarant while testifying at the trial or hearing, offered in evidence to prove the truth of the matter asserted.

(d) Statements which are not hearsay. A statement is not hearsay if—

(1) Prior statement by witness. The declarant testifies at the trial or hearing and is subject to cross-examination concerning the statement, and the statement is (A) inconsistent with the declarant's testimony, and was given under oath subject to the penalty of perjury at a trial, hearing, or other proceeding, or in a deposition, or (B) consistent with the declarant's testimony and is offered to rebut an express or implied charge against the declarant of recent fabrication or improper influence or motive, or (C) one of identification of a person made after perceiving the person; or

(2) Admission by party-opponent. The statement is offered against a party and is (A) the party's own statement, in either an individual or a representative capacity or (B) a statement of which the party has manifested an adoption or belief in its truth, or (C) a statement by a person authorized by the party to make a statement concerning the subject, or (D) a statement by the party's agent or servant concerning a matter within the scope of the agency or employment, made during the existence of the relationship, or (E) a statement by a coconspirator of a party during the course and in furtherance of the conspiracy. The contents of the statement shall be considered but are not alone sufficient to establish the declarant's authority under subdivision (C), the agency or employment relationship and scope thereof under subdivision (D), or the existence of the conspiracy and the participation therein of the declarant and the party against whom the statement is offered under subdivision (E).

(Pub.L. 93–595, § 1, Jan. 2, 1975, 88 Stat.1938; Pub.L. 94–113, § 1, Oct. 16, 1975, 89 Stat. 576; Mar. 2, 1987, eff. Oct. 1, 1987; Apr. 11, 1997, eff. Dec. 1, 1997.)

ADVISORY COMMITTEE NOTES

1972 Proposed Rules

Note to Subdivision (a). The definition of "statement" assumes importance because the term is used in the definition of hearsay in subdivision (c). The effect of the definition of "statement" is to exclude from the operation of the hearsay rule all evidence of conduct, verbal or nonverbal, not intended as an assertion. The key to the definition is that nothing is an assertion unless intended to be one.

It can scarcely be doubted that an assertion made in words is intended by the declarant to be an assertion. Hence verbal assertions readily fall into the category of "statement." Whether nonverbal conduct should be regarded as a statement for purposes of defining hearsay requires further consideration. Some nonverbal conduct, such as the act of pointing to identify a suspect in a lineup, is clearly the equivalent of words, assertive in nature, and to be regarded as a statement. Other nonverbal conduct, however, may be offered as evidence that the person acted as he did because of his belief in the existence of the condition sought to be proved, from which belief the existence of the condition may be inferred. This sequence is, arguably, in effect an assertion of the existence of the condition and hence properly includable within the hearsay concept. See Morgan, Hearsay Dangers and the Application of the Hearsay Concept, 62 Harv.L.Rev. 177, 214, 217 (1948), and the elaboration in Finman, Implied Assertions as Hearsay: Some Criticisms of the Uniform Rules of Evidence, 14 Stan.L.Rev. 682 (1962). Admittedly evidence of this character is untested with respect to the perception, memory, and narration (or their equivalents) of the actor, but the Advisory Committee is of the view that these dangers are minimal in the absence of an intent to assert and do not justify the loss of the evidence on hearsay grounds. No class of evidence is free of the possibility of fabrication, but the likelihood is less with nonverbal than with assertive verbal conduct. The situations giving rise to the nonverbal conduct are such as virtually to eliminate questions of sincerity. Motivation, the nature of the conduct, and the presence or absence of reliance will bear heavily upon the weight to be given the evidence. Falknor, The "Hear-Say" Rule as a "See-Do" Rule: Evidence of Conduct, 33 Rocky Mt.L.Rev. 133 (1961). Similar considerations govern nonassertive verbal conduct and verbal conduct which is assertive but offered as a basis for inferring something other than the matter asserted, also excluded from the definition of hearsay by the language of subdivision (c).

When evidence of conduct is offered on the theory that it is not a statement, and hence not hearsay, a preliminary determination will be required to determine whether an assertion is intended. The rule is so worded as to place the burden upon the party claiming that the intention existed; ambiguous and doubtful cases will be resolved against him and in favor of admissibility. The determination involves no greater difficulty than many other preliminary questions of fact. Maguire, The Hearsay System: Around and Through the Thicket, 14 Vand.L.Rev. 741, 765–767 (1961).

For similar approaches, see Uniform Rule 62(1); California Evidence Code §§ 225, 1200; Kansas Code of Civil Procedure § 60–459(a); New Jersey Evidence Rule 62(1).

Note to Subdivision (c). The definition follows along familiar lines in including only statements offered to prove the truth of the matter asserted. McCormick § 225; 5 Wigmore § 1361, 6 *id.* § 1766. If the significance of an offered statement lies solely in the fact that it was made, no issue is raised as to the truth of anything asserted, and the statement is not hearsay. *Emich Motors Corp. v. General Motors Corp.*, 181 F.2d 70 (7th Cir.1950), rev'd on other grounds 340 U.S. 558, 71 S.Ct. 408, 95 L.Ed. 534, letters of complaint from customers offered as a reason for cancellation of dealer's franchise, to rebut contention that franchise was revoked for refusal to finance sales through affiliated finance company. The effect is to exclude from hearsay the entire category of "verbal acts" and "verbal parts of an act," in which the statement itself affects the legal rights of the parties or is a circumstance bearing on conduct affecting their rights.

The definition of hearsay must, of course, be read with reference to the definition of statement set forth in subdivision (a).

Testimony given by a witness in the course of court proceedings is excluded since there is compliance with all the ideal conditions for testifying.

Note to Subdivision (d). Several types of statements which would otherwise literally fall within the definition are expressly excluded from it:

(1) *Prior statement by witness.* Considerable controversy has attended the question whether a prior out-of-court statement by a person now available for cross-examination concerning it, under oath and in the presence of the trier of fact, should be classed as hearsay. If the witness admits on the stand that he made the statement and that it was true, he adopts the statement and there is no hearsay problem. The hearsay problem arises when the witness on the stand denies having made the statement or admits having made it but denies its truth. The argument in favor of treating these latter statements as hearsay is based upon the ground that the conditions of oath, cross-examination, and demeanor observation did not prevail at the time the statement was made and cannot adequately be supplied by the later examination. The logic of the situation is troublesome. So far as concerns the oath, its mere presence has never been regarded as sufficient to remove a statement from the hearsay category, and it receives much less emphasis than cross-examination as a truth-compelling device. While strong expressions are found to the effect that no conviction can be had or important right taken away on the basis of statements not made under fear of prosecution for perjury, *Bridges v. Wixon,* 326 U.S. 135, 65 S.Ct. 1443, 89 L.Ed. 2103 (1945), the fact is that, of the many common law exceptions to the hearsay rule, only that for reported testimony has required the statement to have been made under oath. Nor is it satisfactorily explained why cross-examination cannot be conducted subsequently with success. The decisions contending most vigorously for its inadequacy in fact demonstrate quite thorough exploration of the weaknesses and doubts attending the earlier statement. *State v. Saporen,* 205 Minn. 358, 285 N.W. 898 (1939); *Ruhala v. Roby,* 379 Mich. 102, 150 N.W.2d 146 (1967); *People v. Johnson,* 68 Cal.2d 646, 68 Cal.Rptr. 599, 441 P.2d 111 (1968). In respect to demeanor, as Judge Learned Hand observed in *Di Carlo v. United States,* 6 F.2d 364 (2d Cir.1925), when the jury decides that the truth is not what the witness says now, but what he said before, they are still deciding from what they see and hear in court. The bulk of the case law nevertheless has been against allowing prior statements of witnesses to be used generally as substantive evidence. Most of the writers and Uniform Rule 63(1) have taken the opposite position.

The position taken by the Advisory Committee in formulating this part of the rule is funded upon an unwillingness to countenance the general use of prior prepared statements as substantive evidence, but with a recognition that particular circumstances call for a contrary result. The judgment is one more of experience than of logic. The rule requires in each instance, as a general safeguard, that the declarant actually testify as a witness, and it then enumerates three situations in which the statement is excepted from the category of hearsay. Compare Uniform Rule 63(1) which allows any out-of-court statement of a declarant who is present at the trial and available for cross-examination.

(A) Prior inconsistent statements traditionally have been admissible to impeach but not as substantive evidence. Under the rule they are substantive evidence. As has been said by the California Law Revision Commission with respect to a similar provision:

"Section 1235 admits inconsistent statements of witnesses because the dangers against which the hearsay rule is designed to protect are largely nonexistent. The declarant is in court and may be examined and cross-examined in regard to his statements and their subject matter. In many cases, the inconsistent statement is more likely to be true than the testimony of the witness at the trial because it was made nearer in time to the matter to which it relates and is less likely to be influenced by the controversy that gave rise to the litigation. The trier of fact has the declarant before it and can observe his demeanor and the nature of his testimony as he denies or tries to explain away the inconsistency. Hence, it is in as good a position to determine the truth or falsity of the prior statement as it is to determine the truth or falsity of the inconsistent testimony given in court. Moreover, Section 1235 will provide a party with desirable protection against the 'turncoat' witness who changes his story on the stand and deprives the party calling him of evidence essential to his case." Comment, California Evidence Code § 1235. See also McCormick § 39. The Advisory Committee finds these views more convincing than those expressed in *People v. Johnson,* 68 Cal.2d 646, 68 Cal.Rptr. 599, 441 P.2d 111 (1968). The constitutionality of the Advisory Committee's view was upheld in *California v. Green,* 399 U.S. 149, 90 S.Ct. 1930, 26 L.Ed.2d 489 (1970). Moreover, the requirement that the statement be inconsistent with the testimony given assures a thorough exploration of both versions while the witness is on the stand and bars any general and indiscriminate use of previously prepared statements.

(B) Prior consistent statements traditionally have been admissible to rebut charges of recent fabrication or improper influence or motive but not as substantive evidence. Under the rule they are substantive evidence. The prior statement is consistent with the testimony given on the stand, and, if the opposite party wishes to open the door for its admission in evidence, no sound reason is apparent why it should not be received generally.

(C) The admission of evidence of identification finds substantial support, although it falls beyond a doubt in the category of prior out-of-court statements. Illustrative are *People v. Gould,* 54 Cal.2d 621, 7 Cal.Rptr. 273, 354 P.2d 865 (1960); *Judy v. State,* 218 Md. 168, 146 A.2d 29 (1958); *State v. Simmons,* 63 Wash.2d 17, 385 P.2d 389 (1963); California Evidence Code § 1238; New Jersey Evidence Rule 63(1)(c); N.Y.Code of Criminal Procedure § 393–b. Further cases are found in 4 Wigmore § 1130. The basis is the generally unsatisfactory and inconclusive nature of courtroom identifications as compared with those made at an earlier time under less suggestive conditions. The Supreme Court considered the admissibility of evidence of prior identification in *Gilbert v. California,* 388 U.S. 263, 87 S.Ct. 1951, 18 L.Ed.2d 1178 (1967). Exclusion of lineup identification was held to be required because the accused did not then have the assistance of counsel. Significantly, the Court carefully refrained from placing its decision on the ground that testimony as to the making of a prior out-of-court identification ("That's the man") violated either the hearsay rule or the right of confrontation because not made under oath, subject to immediate cross-examination, in the presence of the trier. Instead the Court observed:

"There is a split among the States concerning the admissibility of prior extra-judicial identifications, as independent evidence of identity, both by the witness and third parties present at the prior identification. See 71 ALR2d 449. It has been held that the prior identification is hearsay, and, when admitted through the testimony of the identifier, is merely a prior consistent statement. The recent trend, however, is to admit the prior identification under the exception that admits as substantive evidence a prior communication by a witness who is available for cross-examination at the trial. See 5 ALR2d Later Case Service 1225–1228. * * * " 388 U.S. at 272, n. 3, 87 S.Ct. at 1956.

(2) *Admissions.* Admissions by a party-opponent are excluded from the category of hearsay on the theory that their admissibility in evidence is the result of the adversary system rather than satisfaction of the conditions of the hearsay rule. Strahorn, A Reconsideration of the Hearsay Rule and Admissions, 85 U.Pa.L.Rev. 484, 564 (1937); Morgan, Basic Problems of Evidence 265 (1962); 4 Wigmore § 1048. No guarantee of trustworthiness is required in the case of an admission. The freedom which admissions have enjoyed from technical demands of searching for an assurance of truthworthiness in some against-interest circumstance, and from the restrictive influences of the opinion rule and the rule requiring firsthand knowledge, when taken with the apparently prevalent satisfaction with the results, calls for generous treatment of this avenue to admissibility.

The rule specifies five categories of statements for which the responsibility of a party is considered sufficient to justify reception in evidence against him:

(A) A party's own statement is the classic example of an admission. If he has a representative capacity and the statement is offered against him in that capacity, no inquiry whether he was acting in the representative capacity in making the statement is required; the statement need only be relevant to represent affairs. To the same effect in California Evidence Code § 1220. Compare Uniform Rule 63(7), requiring a statement to be made in a representative capacity to be admissible against a party in a representative capacity.

(B) Under established principles an admission may be made by adopting or acquiescing in the statement of another. While knowledge of contents would ordinarily be essential, this is not inevitably so: "X is a reliable person and knows what he is talking about." See McCormick § 246, p. 527, n. 15. Adoption or acquiescence may be manifested in any appropriate manner. When silence is relied upon, the theory is that the person would, under the circumstances, protest the statement made in his presence, if untrue. The decision in each case calls for an evaluation in terms of probable human behavior. In civil cases, the results have generally been satisfactory. In criminal cases, however, troublesome questions have been raised by decisions holding that failure to deny is an admission: the inference is a fairly weak one, to begin with; silence may be motivated by advice of counsel or realization that "anything you say may be used against you"; unusual opportunity is afforded to manufacture evidence; and encroachment upon the privilege against self-incrimination seems inescapably to be involved. However, recent decisions of the Supreme Court relating to custodial interrogation and the right to counsel appear to resolve these difficulties. Hence the rule contains no special provisions concerning failure to deny in criminal cases.

(C) No authority is required for the general proposition that a statement authorized by a party to be made should have the status of an admission by the party. However, the question arises whether only statements to third persons should be so regarded, to the exclusion of statements by the agent to the principal. The rule is phrased broadly so as to encompass both. While it may be argued that the agent authorized to make statements to his principal does not speak for him, Morgan, Basic Problems of Evidence 273 (1962), communication to an outsider has not generally been thought to be an essential characteristic of an admission. Thus a party's books or records are usable against him, without regard to any intent to disclose to third persons. 5 Wigmore § 1557. See also McCormick § 78, pp. 159–161. In accord is New Jersey Evidence Rule 63(8)(a). Cf. Uniform Rule 63(8)(a) and California Evidence Code § 1222 which limit status as an admission in this regard to statements authorized by the party to be made "for" him, which is perhaps an ambiguous limitation to statements to third persons. Falknor, Vicarious Admissions and the Uniform Rules, 14 Vand.L.Rev. 855, 860–861 (1961).

(D) The tradition has been to test the admissibility of statements by agents, as admissions, by applying the usual test of agency. Was the admission made by the agent acting in the scope of his employment? Since few principals employ agents for the purpose of making damaging statements, the usual result was exclusion of the statement. Dissatisfaction with this loss of valuable and helpful evidence has been increasing. A substantial trend favors admitting statements related to a matter within the scope of the agency or employment. *Grayson v. Williams,* 256 F.2d 61 (10th Cir. 1958); *Koninklijke Luchtvaart Maatschappij N.V. KLM Royal Dutch Airlines v. Tuller,* 110 U.S.App.D.C. 282, 292 F.2d 775, 784 (1961); *Martin v. Savage Truck Lines,* Inc., 121 F.Supp. 417 (D.D.C.1954), and numerous state court decisions collected in 4 Wigmore, 1964 Supp. pp. 66–73, with comments by the editor that the statements should have been excluded as not within scope of agency. For the traditional view see *Northern Oil Co. v. Socony Mobil Oil Co.,* 347 F.2d 81, 85 (2d Cir.1965) and cases cited therein. Similar provisions are found in Uniform Rule 63(9)(a), Kansas Code of Civil Procedure § 60–460(i)(1), and New Jersey Evidence Rule 63(9)(a).

(E) The limitation upon the admissibility of statements of co-conspirators to those made "during the course and in furtherance of the conspiracy" is in the accepted pattern. While the broadened view of agency taken in item (iv) might suggest wider admissibility of statements of co-conspirators, the agency theory of conspiracy is at best a fiction and ought not to serve as a basis for admissibility beyond that already established. See Levie, Hearsay and Conspiracy, 52 Mich. L.Rev. 1159 (1954); Comment, 25 U.Chi.L.Rev. 530 (1958). The rule is consistent with the position of the Supreme Court in denying admissibility to statements made after the objectives of the conspiracy have either failed or been achieved. *Krulewitch v. United States,* 336 U.S. 440, 69 S.Ct. 716, 93 L.Ed. 790 (1949); *Wong Sun v. United States,* 371 U.S. 471, 490, 83 S.Ct. 407, 9 L.Ed.2d 441 (1963). For similarly limited provisions see California Evidence Code § 1223 and New Jersey Rule 63(9)(b). Cf. Uniform Rule 63(9)(b).

1974 Enactment

Note to Subdivision (d)(1). Present federal law, except in the Second Circuit, permits the use of prior inconsistent statements of a witness for impeachment only. Rule 801(d)(1) as proposed by the Court would have permitted all such statements to be admissible as substantive evidence, an approach followed by a small but growing number of State jurisdictions and recently held constitutional in California v. Green, 399 U.S. 149 (1970). Although there was some support expressed for the Court Rule, based largely on the need to counteract the effect of witness intimidation in criminal cases, the Committee decided to adopt a compromise version of the Rule similar to the position of the Second Circuit. The Rule as amended draws a distinction between types of prior inconsistent statements (other than statements of identification of a person made after perceiving him which are currently admissible, see United States v. Anderson, 406 F.2d 719, 720 (4th Cir.), cert. denied, 395 U.S. 967 (1969)) and allows only those made while the declarant was subject to cross-examination at a trial or hearing or in a deposition, to be admissible for their truth. Compare United States v. DeSisto, 329 F.2d 929 (2nd Cir.), cert. denied, 377 U.S. 979 (1964); United States v. Cunningham, 446 F.2d 194 (2nd Cir.1971) (restricting the admissibility of prior inconsistent statements as substantive evidence to those made under oath in a formal proceeding, but not requiring that there have been an opportunity for cross-examination). The rationale for the Committee's decision is that (1) unlike in most other situations involving unsworn or oral statements, there can be no dispute as to whether the prior statement was made; and (2) the context of a formal proceeding, an oath, and the opportunity for cross-examination provide firm additional assurances of the reliability of the prior statement. House Report No. 93–650.

Note to Subdivision (d)(1)(A). Rule 801 defines what is and what is not hearsay for the purpose of admitting a prior statement as substantive evidence. A prior statement of a witness at a trial or hearing which is inconsistent with his testimony is, of course, always admissible for the purpose of impeaching the witness' credibility.

As submitted by the Supreme Court, subdivision (d)(1)(A) made admissible as substantive evidence the prior statement of a witness inconsistent with his present testimony.

The House severely limited the admissibility of prior inconsistent statements by adding a requirement that the prior statement must have been subject to cross-examination, thus precluding even the use of grand jury statements. The requirement that the prior statement must have been subject to cross-examination appears unnecessary since this rule comes into play only when the witness testifies in the present trial. At that time, he is on the stand and can explain an earlier position and be cross-examined as to both.

The requirement that the statement be under oath also appears unnecessary. Notwithstanding the absence of an oath contemporaneous with the statement, the witness, when on the stand, qualifying or denying the prior statement, is under oath. In any event, of all the many recognized exceptions to the hearsay rule, only one (former testimony) requires that the out-of-court statement have been made under oath. With respect to the lack of evidence of the demeanor of the witness at the time of the prior statement, it would be difficult to improve upon Judge Learned Hand's observation that when the jury decides that the truth is not what the witness says now but what he said before, they are still deciding from what they see and hear in court. [*Di Carlo v. U.S.*, 6 F.2d 364 (2d Cir.1925)].

The rule as submitted by the Court has positive advantages. The prior statement was made nearer in time to the events, when memory was fresher and intervening influences had not been brought into play. A realistic method is provided for dealing with the turncoat witness who changes his story on the stand [see Comment, California Evidence Code § 1235; McCormick, Evidence, § 38 (2nd ed. 1972)].

New Jersey, California, and Utah have adopted a rule similar to this one; and Nevada, New Mexico, and Wisconsin have adopted the identical Federal rule.

For all of these reasons, we think the House amendment should be rejected and the rule as submitted by the Supreme Court reinstated. [It would appear that some of the opposition to this Rule is based on a concern that a person could be convicted solely upon evidence admissible under this Rule. The Rule, however, is not addressed to the question of the sufficiency of evidence to send a case to the jury, but merely as to its admissibility. Factual circumstances could well arise where, if this were the sole evidence, dismissal would be appropriate.]

Note to Subdivision (d)(1)(C). As submitted by the Supreme Court and as passed by the House, subdivision (d)(1)(C) of rule 801 made admissible the prior statement identifying a person made after perceiving him. The committee decided to delete this provision because of the concern that a person could be convicted solely upon evidence admissible under this subdivision.

Note to Subdivision 801(d)(2)(E). The House approved the long-accepted rule that "a statement by a coconspirator of a party during the course and in furtherance of the conspiracy" is not hearsay as it was submitted by the Supreme Court. While the rule refers to a coconspirator, it is this committee's understanding that the rule is meant to carry forward the universally accepted doctrine that a joint venturer is considered as a coconspirator for the purposes of this rule even though no conspiracy has been charged. *United States v. Rinaldi*, 393 F.2d 97, 99 (2d Cir.), cert. denied 393 U.S. 913 (1968); *United States v. Spencer*, 415 F.2d 1301, 1304 (7th Cir., 1969). Senate Report No. 93–1277.

Rule 801 supplies some basic definitions for the rules of evidence that deal with hearsay. Rule 801(d)(1) defines certain statements as not hearsay. The Senate amendments make two changes in it.

Note to Subdivision (d)(1)(A). The House bill provides that a statement is not hearsay if the declarant testifies and is subject to cross-examination concerning the statement and if the statement is inconsistent with his testimony and was given under oath subject to cross-examination and subject to the penalty of perjury at a trial or hearing or in a deposition. The Senate amendment drops the requirement that the prior statement be given under oath subject to cross-examination and subject to the penalty of perjury at a trial or hearing or in a deposition.

The Conference adopts the Senate amendment with an amendment, so that the rule now requires that the prior inconsistent statement be given under oath subject to the penalty of perjury at a trial, hearing, or other proceeding, or in a deposition. The rule as adopted covers statements before a grand jury. Prior inconsistent statements may, of course, be used for impeaching the credibility of a witness. When the prior inconsistent statement is one made by a defendant in a criminal case, it is covered by Rule 801(d)(2).

Note to Subdivision (d)(1)(C). The House bill provides that a statement is not hearsay if the declarant testifies and is subject to cross-examination concerning the statement and the statement is one of identification of a person made after perceiving him. The Senate amendment eliminated this provision.

The Conference adopts the Senate amendment. House Report No. 93–1597.

1987 Amendment

The amendments are technical. No substantive change is intended.

1997 Amendment

Rule 801(d)(2) has been amended in order to respond to three issues raised by *Bourjaily v. United States*, 483 U.S. 171 (1987). First, the amendment codifies the holding in *Bourjaily* by stating expressly that a court shall consider the contents of a coconspirator's statement in determining "the existence of the conspiracy and the participation therein of the declarant and the party against whom the statement is offered." According to *Bourjaily*, Rule 104(a) requires these preliminary questions to be established by a preponderance of the evidence.

Second, the amendment resolves an issue on which the Court had reserved decision. It provides that the contents of the declarant's statement do not alone suffice to establish a conspiracy in which the declarant and the defendant participated. The court must consider in addition the circumstances surrounding the statement, such as the identity of the speaker, the context in which the statement was made, or evidence corroborating the contents of the statement in making its determination as to each preliminary question. This amendment is in accordance with existing practice. Every court of appeals that has resolved this issue requires some evidence in addition to the contents of the statement. *See, e.g.*, *United States v. Beckham*, 968 F.2d 47, 51 (D.C.Cir. 1992); *United States v. Sepulveda*, 15 F.3d 1161, 1181–82 (1st Cir.1993), *cert. denied*, 114 S.Ct. 2714 (1994); *United States v. Daly*, 842 F.2d 1380, 1386 (2d Cir.), *cert. denied*, 488 U.S. 821 (1988); *United States v. Clark*, 18 F.3d 1337, 1341–42 (6th Cir.), *cert. denied*, 115 S.Ct. 152 (1994); *United States v. Zambrana*, 841 F.2d 1320, 1344–45 (7th Cir.1988); *United States v. Silverman*, 861 F.2d 571, 577 (9th Cir.1988); *United States v. Gordon*, 844 F.2d 1397, 1402 (9th Cir.1988); *United States v. Hernandez*, 829 F.2d 988, 993 (10th Cir. 1987), *cert. denied*, 485 U.S. 1013 (1988); *United States v. Byrom*, 910 F.2d 725, 736 (11th Cir.1990).

Third, the amendment extends the reasoning of Bourjaily to statements offered under subdivisions (C) and (D) of Rule 801(d)(2). In Bourjaily, the Court rejected treating foundational facts pursuant to the law of agency in favor of an evidentiary approach governed by Rule 104(a). The Advisory Committee believes it appropriate to treat analogously preliminary questions relating to the declarant's authority under subdivision (C), and the agency or employment relationship and scope thereof under subdivision (D).

GAP Report on Rule 801. The word "shall" was substituted for the word "may" in line 19. The second sentence of the committee note was changed accordingly.

HISTORICAL NOTES

For legislative history and purpose of Pub.L. 94–113, see 1975 U.S.Code Cong. and Adm.News, p. 1092.

Effective and Applicability Provisions

1975 Acts. Section 2 of Pub.L. 94–113 provided that: "This Act [enacting cl. (c) of subd. (d)] shall become effective on the fifteenth day after the date of the enactment of this Act [Oct. 16, 1975]."

CROSS REFERENCES

Attacking and supporting credibility of party-opponent, see Fed.Rules Evid. Rule 806, 28 USCA.

Confrontation with, and cross-examination of, witnesses, see USCA Const. Amend. VI.

Oral testimony in open court, see Fed.Rules Cr.Proc. Rule 26, 18 USCA.

Oral testimony in open court, see Fed.Rules Civ.Proc. Rule 43, 28 USCA.

Prior statements of witnesses, see Fed.Rules Evid. Rule 613, 28 USCA.

Statements, admission of remainder of, see Fed.Rules Evid. Rule 106, 28 USCA.

Rule 802. Hearsay Rule

Hearsay is not admissible except as provided by these rules or by other rules prescribed by the Supreme Court pursuant to statutory authority or by Act of Congress.

(Pub.L. 93–595, § 1, Jan. 2, 1975, 88 Stat. 1939.)

ADVISORY COMMITTEE NOTES

1972 Proposed Rules

The provision excepting from the operation of the rule hearsay which is made admissible by other rules adopted by the Supreme Court or by Act of Congress continues the admissibility thereunder of hearsay which would not qualify under these Evidence Rules. The following examples illustrate the working of the exception:

Federal Rules of Civil Procedure

Rule 4(g): proof of service by affidavit.

Rule 32: admissibility of depositions.

Rule 43(e): affidavits when motion based on facts not appearing of record.

Rule 56: affidavits in summary judgment proceedings.

Rule 65(b): showing by affidavit for temporary restraining order.

Federal Rules of Criminal Procedure

Rule 4(a): affidavits to show grounds for issuing warrants.

Rule 12(b)(4): affidavits to determine issues of fact in connection with motions.

Acts of Congress

10 U.S.C. § 7730: affidavits of unavailable witnesses in actions for damages caused by vessel in naval service, or towage or salvage of same, when taking of testimony or bringing of action delayed or stayed on security grounds.

29 U.S.C. § 161(4): affidavit as proof of service in NLRB proceedings.

38 U.S.C. § 5206: affidavit as proof of posting notice of sale of unclaimed property by Veterans Administration.

CROSS REFERENCES

Affidavits—

Motion on facts not appearing of record, see Fed.Rules Civ.Proc. Rule 43, 28 USCA.

Motions, determination of issues of fact on, see Fed. Rules Cr.Proc. Rule 12, 18 USCA.

Process, proof of service, see Fed.Rules Civ.proc. Rule 4, 28 USCA.

Proof of posting notice of sale of unclaimed property by Veterans' Administration, see 38 USCA § 8506.

Proof of service in National Labor Relations Board proceedings, see 29 USCA § 161.

Summary judgment proceedings, see Fed.Rules Civ. Proc. Rule 56, 28 USCA.

Temporary restraining order, see Fed.Rules Civ.Proc. Rule 65, 28 USCA.

Unavailable witnesses in actions for damages caused by vessel in naval service, or towage or salvage of same, when taking of testimony or bringing of action delayed or stayed on security grounds, see 10 USCA § 7730.

Warrants, issuance upon showing grounds, see Fed. Rules Cr.Proc. Rule 4, 18 USCA.

Depositions, admissibility of in court proceedings, see Fed. Rules Civ.Proc. Rule 32, 28 USCA.

Rule 803. Hearsay Exceptions; Availability of Declarant Immaterial

The following are not excluded by the hearsay rule, even though the declarant is available as a witness:

(1) Present sense impression. A statement describing or explaining an event or condition made while the declarant was perceiving the event or condition, or immediately thereafter.

(2) Excited utterance. A statement relating to a startling event or condition made while the declarant was under the stress of excitement caused by the event or condition.

(3) Then existing mental, emotional, or physical condition. A statement of the declarant's then existing state of mind, emotion, sensation, or physical condition (such as intent, plan, motive, design, mental feeling, pain, and bodily health), but not including a statement of memory or belief to prove the fact remembered or believed unless it relates to the execution, revocation, identification, or terms of declarant's will.

(4) Statements for purposes of medical diagnosis or treatment. Statements made for purposes of medical diagnosis or treatment and describing medical history, or past or present symptoms, pain, or sensations, or the inception or general character of the cause or external source thereof insofar as reasonably pertinent to diagnosis or treatment.

(5) Recorded recollection. A memorandum or record concerning a matter about which a witness once had knowledge but now has insufficient recollection to enable the witness to testify fully and accurately, shown to have been made or adopted by the witness when the matter was fresh in the witness' memory and to reflect that knowledge correctly. If admitted, the memorandum or record may be read into evidence but may not itself be received as an exhibit unless offered by an adverse party.

(6) Records of Regularly Conducted Activity.—A memorandum, report, record, or data compilation, in any form, of acts, events, conditions, opinions, or diagnoses, made at or near the time by, or from information transmitted by, a person with knowledge, if kept in the course of a regularly conducted business activity, and if it was the regular practice of that business activity to make the memorandum, report, record or data compilation, all as shown by the testimony of the custodian or other qualified witness, or by certification that complies with Rule 902(11), Rule 902(12), or a statute permitting certification, unless the source of information or the method or circumstances of preparation indicate lack of trustworthiness. The term "business" as used in this paragraph includes business, institution, association, profession, occupation, and calling of every kind, whether or not conducted for profit.

(7) Absence of entry in records kept in accordance with the provisions of paragraph (6). Evidence that a matter is not included in the memoranda reports, records, or data compilations, in any form, kept in accordance with the provisions of paragraph (6), to prove the nonoccurrence or nonexistence of the matter, if the matter was of a kind of which a memorandum, report, record, or data compilation was regularly made and preserved, unless the sources of information or other circumstances indicate lack of trustworthiness.

(8) Public records and reports. Records, reports, statements, or data compilations, in any form, of public offices or agencies, setting forth (A) the activities of the office or agency, or (B) matters observed pursuant to duty imposed by law as to which matters there was a duty to report, excluding, however, in criminal cases matters observed by police officers and other law enforcement personnel, or (C) in civil actions and proceedings and against the Government in criminal cases, factual findings resulting from an investigation made pursuant to authority granted by law, unless the sources of information or other circumstances indicate lack of trustworthiness.

(9) Records of vital statistics. Records or data compilations, in any form, of births, fetal deaths, deaths, or marriages, if the report thereof was made to a public office pursuant to requirements of law.

(10) Absence of public record or entry. To prove the absence of a record, report, statement, or data compilation, in any form, or the nonoccurrence or nonexistence of a matter of which a record, report, statement, or data compilation, in any form, was regularly made and preserved by a public office or agency, evidence in the form of a certification in accordance with rule 902, or testimony, that diligent search failed to disclose the record, report, statement, or data compilation, or entry.

(11) Records of religious organizations. Statements of births, marriages, divorces, deaths, legitimacy, ancestry, relationship by blood or marriage, or other similar facts of personal or family history, contained in a regularly kept record of a religious organization.

(12) Marriage, baptismal, and similar certificates. Statements of fact contained in a certificate that the maker performed a marriage or other ceremony or administered a sacrament, made by a clergyman, public official, or other person authorized by the rules or practices of a religious organization or by law to perform the act certified, and purporting to have been issued at the time of the act or within a reasonable time thereafter.

(13) Family records. Statements of fact concerning personal or family history contained in family Bibles, genealogies, charts, engravings on rings, inscriptions on family portraits, engravings on urns, crypts, or tombstones, or the like.

(14) Records of documents affecting an interest in property. The record of a document purporting to establish or affect an interest in property, as proof of the content of the original recorded document and its execution and delivery by each person by whom it purports to have been executed, if the record is a record of a public office and an applicable statute authorizes the recording of documents of that kind in that office.

(15) Statements in documents affecting an interest in property. A statement contained in a document purporting to establish or affect an interest in property if the matter stated was relevant to the purpose of the document, unless dealings with the property since the document was made have been inconsistent with the truth of the statement or the purport of the document.

(16) Statements in ancient documents. Statements in a document in existence twenty years or more the authenticity of which is established.

(17) Market reports, commercial publications. Market quotations, tabulations, lists, directories, or other published compilations, generally used and relied upon by the public or by persons in particular occupations.

(18) Learned treatises. To the extent called to the attention of an expert witness upon cross-examination or relied upon by the expert witness in direct examination, statements contained in published treatises, periodicals, or pamphlets on a subject of history, medicine, or other science or art, established as a reliable authority by the testimony or admission of the witness or by other expert testimony or by judicial notice. If admitted, the statements may be read into evidence but may not be received as exhibits.

(19) Reputation concerning personal or family history. Reputation among members of a person's family by blood, adoption, or marriage, or among a person's associates, or in the community, concerning a person's birth, adoption, marriage, divorce, death, legitimacy, relationship by blood, adoption, or marriage, ancestry, or other similar fact of personal or family history.

(20) Reputation concerning boundaries or general history. Reputation in a community, arising before the controversy, as to boundaries of or customs affecting lands in the community, and reputation as to events of general history important to the community or State or nation in which located.

(21) Reputation as to character. Reputation of a person's character among associates or in the community.

(22) Judgment of previous conviction. Evidence of a final judgment, entered after a trial or upon a plea of guilty (but not upon a plea of nolo contendere), adjudging a person guilty of a crime punishable by death or imprisonment in excess of one year, to prove any fact essential to sustain the judgment, but not including, when offered by the Government in a criminal prosecution for purposes other than impeachment, judgments against persons other than the accused. The pendency of an appeal may be shown but does not affect admissibility.

(23) Judgment as to personal, family, or general history, or boundaries. Judgments as proof of matters of personal, family or general history, or boundaries, essential to the judgment, if the same would be provable by evidence of reputation.

(24) [Transferred to Rule 807]

(Pub.L. 93–595, § 1, Jan. 2, 1975, 88 Stat. 1939; Pub.L. 94–149, § 1(11), Dec. 12, 1975, 89 Stat. 805; Mar. 2, 1987, eff. Oct. 1, 1987; Apr. 11, 1997, eff. Dec. 1, 1997; Apr. 17, 2000, eff. Dec. 1, 2000.)

ADVISORY COMMITTEE NOTES

1972 Proposed Rules

The exceptions are phrased in terms of nonapplication of the hearsay rule, rather than in positive terms of admissibility, in order to repel any implication that other possible grounds for exclusion are eliminated from consideration.

The present rule proceeds upon the theory that under appropriate circumstances a hearsay statement may possess circumstantial guarantees of trustworthiness sufficient to justify nonproduction of the declarant in person at the trial even though he may be available. The theory finds vast support in the many exceptions to the hearsay rule developed by the common law in which unavailability of the declarant is not a relevant factor. The present rule is a synthesis of them, with revision where modern developments and conditions are believed to make that course appropriate.

In a hearsay situation, the declarant is, of course, a witness, and neither this rule nor Rule 804 dispenses with the requirement of firsthand knowledge. It may appear from his statement or be inferable from circumstances. See Rule 602.

Note to Paragraphs (1) and (2). In considerable measure these two examples overlap, though based on somewhat different theories. The most significant practical difference will lie in the time lapse allowable between event and statement.

The underlying theory of Exception [paragraph] (1) is that substantial contemporaneity of event and statement negate the likelihood of deliberate or conscious misrepresentation. Moreover, if the witness is the declarant, he may be examined on the statement. If the witness is not the declarant, he may be examined as to the circumstances as an aid in evaluating the statement. Morgan, Basic Problems of Evidence 340–341 (1962).

The theory of Exception [paragraph] (2) is simply that circumstances may produce a condition of excitement which temporarily stills the capacity of reflection and produces utterances free of conscious fabrication. 6 Wigmore § 1747, p. 135. Spontaneity is the key factor in each instance, though arrived at by somewhat different routes. Both are needed in order to avoid needless niggling.

While the theory of Exception [paragraph] (2) has been criticized on the ground that excitement impairs accuracy of observation as well as eliminating conscious fabrication, Hutchins and Slesinger, Some Observations on the Law of Evidence: Spontaneous Exclamations, 28 Colum.L.Rev. 432 (1928), it finds support in cases without number. See cases in 6 Wigmore § 1750; Annot. 53 A.L.R.2d 1245 (statements as to cause of or responsibility for motor vehicle accident); Annot., 4 A.L.R.3d 149 (accusatory statements by homicide victims). Since unexciting events are less likely to evoke comment, decisions involving Exception [paragraph] (1) are far less numerous. Illustrative are *Tampa Elec. Co. v. Getrost,* 151 Fla. 558, 10 So.2d 83 (1942); *Houston Oxygen Co. v. Davis,* 139 Tex. 1, 161 S.W.2d 474 (1942); and cases cited in McCormick § 273, p. 585, n. 4.

With respect to the *time element,* Exception [paragraph] (1) recognizes that in many, if not most, instances precise contemporaneity is not possible and hence a slight lapse is allowable. Under Exception [paragraph] (2) the standard of measurement is the duration of the state of excitement. "How long can excitement prevail? Obviously there are no pat answers and the character of the transaction or event will largely determine the significance of the time factor." Slough, Spontaneous Statements and State of Mind, 46 Iowa L.Rev. 224, 243 (1961); McCormick § 272, p. 580.

Participation by the declarant is not required: a nonparticipant may be moved to describe what he perceives, and one may be startled by an event in which he is not an actor. Slough, *supra;* McCormick, *supra;* 6 Wigmore § 1755; Annot. 78 A.L.R.2d 300.

Whether *proof of the startling event* may be made by the statement itself is largely an academic question, since in most cases there is present at least circumstantial evidence that something of a startling nature must have occurred. For cases in which the evidence consists of the condition of the declarant (injuries, state of shock), see *Insurance Co. v. Mosely,* 75 U.S. (8 Wall.) 397, 19 L.Ed. 437 (1869); *Wheeler v. United States,* 93 U.S. App.D.C. 159, 211 F.2d 19 (1953), cert. denied 347 U.S. 1019, 74 S.Ct. 876, 98 L.Ed. 1140; *Wetherbee v. Safety Casualty Co.,* 219 F.2d 274 (5th Cir. 1955); *Lampe v. United States,* 97 U.S.App.D.C. 160, 229 F.2d 43 (1956). Nevertheless, on occasion the only evidence may be the content of the statement itself, and rulings that it may be sufficient are described as "increasing," Slough, *supra* at 246, and as the "prevailing practice," McCormick § 272, p. 579. Illustrative are *Armour & Co. v. Industrial Commission,* 78 Colo. 569, 243 P. 546 (1926); *Young v. Stewart,* 191 N.C. 297, 131 S.E. 735 (1926). Moreover, under Rule 104(a) the judge is not limited by the hearsay rule in passing upon preliminary questions of fact.

Proof of declarant's perception by his statement presents similar considerations when declarant is identified. *People v. Poland,* 22 Ill.2d 175, 174 N.E.2d 804 (1961). However, when declarant is an unidentified bystander, the cases indicate hesitancy in upholding the statement alone as sufficient, *Garrett v. Howden,* 73 N.M. 307, 387 P.2d 874 (1963); *Beck v. Dye,* 200 Wash. 1, 92 P.2d 1113 (1939), a result which would under appropriate circumstances be consistent with the rule.

Permissible *subject matter* of the statement is limited under Exception [paragraph] (1) to description or explanation of the event or condition, the assumption being that spontaneity, in the absence of a startling event, may extend no farther. In Exception [paragraph] (2), however, the statement need only "relate" to the startling event or condition, thus affording a broader scope of subject matter coverage. 6 Wigmore §§ 1750, 1754. See *Sanitary Grocery Co. v. Snead,* 67 App.D.C. 129, 90 F.2d 374 (1937), slip-and-fall case sustaining admissibility of clerk's statement. "That has been on the floor for a couple of hours," and *Murphy Auto Parts Co., Inc. v. Ball,* 101 U.S.App.D.C. 416, 249 F.2d 508 (1957), upholding admission, on issue of driver's agency, of his statement that he had to call on a customer and was in a hurry to get home. Quick, Hearsay, Excitement, Necessity and the Uniform Rules: A Reappraisal of Rule 63(4), 6 Wayne L.Rev. 204, 206–209 (1960).

Similar provisions are found in Uniform Rule 63(4)(a) and (b); California Evidence Code § 1240 (as to Exception (2) only); Kansas Code of Civil Procedure § 60–460(d)(1) and (2); New Jersey Evidence Rule 63(4).

Note to Paragraph (3). Exception [paragraph] (3) is essentially a specialized application of Exception [paragraph] (1), presented separately to enhance its usefulness and accessibility. See McCormick §§ 265, 268.

The exclusion of "statements of memory or belief to prove the fact remembered or believed" is necessary to avoid the virtual destruction of the hearsay rule which would otherwise result from allowing state of mind, provable by a hearsay statement, to serve as the basis for an inference of the happening of the event which produced the state of mind. *Shepard v. United States,* 290 U.S. 96, 54 S.Ct. 22, 78 L.Ed.

196 (1933); Maguire, The Hillmon Case—Thirty-three Years After, 38 Harv.L.Rev. 709, 719–731 (1925); Hinton, States of Mind and the Hearsay Rule, 1 U.Chi.L.Rev. 394, 421–423 (1934). The rule of *Mutual Life Ins. Co. v. Hillmon,* 145 U.S. 285, 12 S.Ct. 909, 36 L.Ed. 706 (1892), allowing evidence of intention as tending to prove the doing of the act intended, is, of course, left undisturbed.

The carving out, from the exclusion mentioned in the preceding paragraph, of declarations relating to the execution, revocation, identification, or terms of declarant's will represents and *ad hoc* judgment which finds ample reinforcement in the decisions, resting on practical grounds of necessity and expediency rather than logic. McCormick § 271, pp. 577–578; Annot. 34 A.L.R.2d 588, 62 A.L.R.2d 855. A similar recognition of the need for and practical value of this kind of evidence is found in California Evidence Code § 1260.

Note to Paragraph (4). Even those few jurisdictions which have shied away from generally admitting statements of present condition have allowed them if made to a physician for purposes of diagnosis and treatment in view of the patient's strong motivation to be truthful. McCormick § 266, p. 563. The same guarantee of trustworthiness extends to statements of past conditions and medical history, made for purposes of diagnosis or treatment. It also extends to statements as to causation, reasonably pertinent to the same purposes, in accord with the current trend. *Shell Oil Co. v. Industrial Commission,* 2 Ill.2d 590, 119 N.E.2d 224 (1954); McCormick § 266, p. 564; New Jersey Evidence Rule 63(12)(c). Statements as to fault would not ordinarily qualify under this latter language. Thus a patient's statement that he was struck by an automobile would qualify but not his statement that the car was driven through a red light. Under the exception the statement need not have been made to a physician. Statements to hospital attendants, ambulance drivers, or even members of the family might be included.

Conventional doctrine has excluded from the hearsay exception, as not within its guarantee of truthfulness, statements to a physician consulted only for the purpose of enabling him to testify. While these statements were not admissible as substantive evidence, the expert was allowed to state the basis of his opinion, including statements of this kind. The distinction thus called for was one most unlikely to be made by juries. The rule accordingly rejects the limitation. This position is consistent with the provision of Rule 703 that the facts on which expert testimony is based need not be admissible in evidence if of a kind ordinarily relied upon by experts in the field.

Note to Paragraph (5). A hearsay exception for recorded recollection is generally recognized and has been described as having "long been favored by the federal and practically all the state courts that have had occasion to decide the question." *United States v. Kelly,* 349 F.2d 720, 770 (2d Cir.1965), citing numerous cases and sustaining the exception against a claimed denial of the right of confrontation. Many additional cases are cited in Annot., 82 A.L.R.2d 473, 520. The guarantee of trustworthiness is found in the reliability inherent in a record made while events were still fresh in mind and accurately reflecting them. *Owens v. State,* 67 Md. 307, 316, 10 A. 210, 212 (1887).

The principal controversy attending the exception has centered, not upon the propriety of the exception itself, but upon the question whether a preliminary requirement of impaired memory on the part of the witness should be imposed. The authorities are divided. If regard be had only to the accuracy of the evidence, admittedly impairment of the memory of the witness adds nothing to it and should not be required. McCormick § 277, p. 593; 3 Wigmore § 738, p. 76; *Jordan v. People,* 151 Colo. 133, 376 P.2d 699 (1962), cert. denied 373 U.S. 944, 83 S.Ct. 1553, 10 L.Ed.2d 699; *Hall v. State,* 223 Md. 158, 162 A.2d 751 (1960); *State v. Bindhammer,* 44 N.J. 372, 209 A.2d 124 (1965). Nevertheless, the absence of the requirement, it is believed, would encourage the use of statements carefully prepared for purposes of litigation under the supervision of attorneys, investigators, or claim adjusters. Hence the example includes a requirement that the witness not have "sufficient recollection to enable him to testify fully and accurately." To the same effect are California Evidence Code § 1237 and New Jersey Rule 63(1)(b), and this has been the position of the federal courts. *Vicksburg & Meridian R.R. v. O'Brien,* 119 U.S. 99, 7 S.Ct. 118, 30 L.Ed. 299 (1886); Ahern v. Webb, 268 F.2d 45 (10th Cir.1959); and see *N.L.R.B. v. Hudson Pulp and Paper Corp.,* 273 F.2d 660, 665 (5th Cir.1960); *N.L.R.B. v. Federal Dairy Co.,* 297 F.2d 487 (1st Cir.1962). But cf. *United States v. Adams,* 385 F.2d 548 (2d Cir.1967).

No attempt is made in the exception to spell out the method of establishing the initial knowledge or the contemporaneity and accuracy of the record, leaving them to be dealt with as the circumstances of the particular case might indicate. Multiple person involvement in the process of observing and recording, as in *Rathbun v. Brancatella,* 93 N.J.L. 222, 107 A. 279 (1919), is entirely consistent with the exception.

Locating the exception at this place in the scheme of the rules is a matter of choice. There were two other possibilities. The first was to regard the statement as one of the group of prior statements of a testifying witness which are excluded entirely from the category of hearsay by Rule 801(d)(1). That category, however, requires that declarant be "subject to cross-examination," as to which the impaired memory aspect of the exception raises doubts. The other possibility was to include the exception among those covered by Rule 804. Since unavailability is required by that rule and lack of memory is listed as a species of unavailability by the definition of the term in Rule 804(a)(3), that treatment at first impression would seem appropriate. The fact is, however, that the unavailability requirement of the exception is of a limited and peculiar nature. Accordingly, the exception is located at this point rather than in the context of a rule where unavailability is conceived of more broadly.

Note to Paragraph (6). Exception [paragraph] (6) represents an area which has received much attention from those seeking to improve the law of evidence. The Commonwealth Fund Act was the result of a study completed in 1927 by a distinguished committee under the chairmanship of Professor Morgan. Morgan et al., The Law of Evidence: Some Proposals for its Reform 63 (1927). With changes too minor to mention, it was adopted by Congress in 1936 as the rule for federal courts. 28 U.S.C. § 1732. A number of states took similar action. The Commissioners on Uniform State Laws in 1936 promulgated the Uniform Business Records as Evidence Act, 9A U.L.A. 506, which has acquired a substantial following in the states. Model Code Rule 514 and Uniform Rule 63(13) also deal with the subject. Difference of varying degrees of importance exist among these various treatments.

These reform efforts were largely within the context of business and commercial records, as the kind usually encountered, and concentrated considerable attention upon relaxing the requirement of producing as witnesses, or accounting for the nonproduction of, all participants in the process of gathering, transmitting, and recording information which the common law had evolved as a burdensome and crippling aspect of using records of this type. In their areas of primary emphasis on witnesses to be called and the general admissibility of ordinary business and commercial records, the Commonwealth Fund Act and the Uniform Act appear to have worked well. The exception seeks to preserve their advantages.

On the subject of what witnesses must be called, the Commonwealth Fund Act eliminated the common law requirement of calling or accounting for all participants by failing to mention it. *United States v. Mortimer,* 118 F.2d 266 (2d Cir.1941); *La Porte v. United States,* 300 F.2d 878 (9th Cir.1962); McCormick § 290, p. 608. Model Code Rule 514 and Uniform Rule 63(13) did likewise. The Uniform Act, however, abolished the common law requirement in express terms, providing that the requisite foundation testimony might be furnished by "the custodian or other qualified witness." Uniform Business Records as Evidence Act, § 2; 9A U.L.A. 506. The exception follows the Uniform Act in this respect.

The element of unusual reliability of business records is said variously to be supplied by systematic checking, by regularity and continuity which produce habits of precision, by actual experience of business in relying upon them, or by a duty to make an accurate record as part of a continuing job or occupation. McCormick §§ 281, 286, 287; Laughlin, Business Entries and the Like, 46 Iowa L.Rev. 276 (1961). The model statutes and rules have sought to capture these factors and to extend their impact by employing the phrase "regular course of business," in conjunction with a definition of "business" far broader than its ordinarily accepted meaning. The result is a tendency unduly to emphasize a requirement of routineness and repetitiveness and an insistence that other types of records be squeezed into the fact patterns which give rise to traditional business records. The rule therefore adopts the phrase "the course of a regularly conducted activity" as capturing the essential basis of the hearsay exception as it has evolved and the essential element which can be abstracted from the various specifications of what is a "business."

Amplification of the kinds of activities producing admissible records has given rise to problems which conventional business records by their nature avoid. They are problems of the source of the recorded information, of entries in opinion form, of motivation, and of involvement as participant in the matters recorded.

Sources of information presented no substantial problem with ordinary business records. All participants, including the observer or participant furnishing the information to be recorded, were acting routinely, under a duty of accuracy, with employer reliance on the result, or in short "in the regular course of business." If, however, the supplier of the information does not act in the regular course, an essential link is broken; the assurance of accuracy does not extend to the information itself, and the fact that it may be recorded with scrupulous accuracy is of no avail. An illustration is the police report incorporating information obtained from a bystander: the officer qualifies as acting in the regular course but the informant does not. The leading case, *Johnson v. Lutz,* 253 N.Y. 124, 170 N.E. 517 (1930), held that a report thus prepared was inadmissible. Most of the authorities have agreed with the decision. Gencarella v. Fyfe, 171 F.2d 419 (1st Cir.1948); *Gordon v. Robinson,* 210 F.2d 192 (3d Cir.1954); *Standard Oil Co. of California v. Moore,* 251 F.2d 188, 214 (9th Cir.1957), cert. denied 356 U.S. 975, 78 S.Ct. 1139, 2 L.Ed.2d 1148; *Yates v. Bair Transport,* Inc., 249 F.Supp. 681 (S.D.N.Y.1965); Annot., 69 A.L.R.2d 1148. Cf. *Hawkins v. Gorea Motor Express, Inc.,* 360 F.2d 933 (2d Cir.1966); *Contra,* 5 Wigmore § 1530a, n. 1, pp. 391–392. The point is not dealt with specifically in the Commonwealth Fund Act, the Uniform Act, or Uniform Rule 63(13). However, Model Code Rule 514 contains the requirement "that it was the regular course of that business for one with personal knowledge * * * to make such a memorandum or record or to transmit information thereof to be included in such a memorandum or record * * *." The rule follows this lead in requiring an informant with knowledge acting in the course of the regularly conducted activity.

Entries in the form of opinions were not encountered in traditional business records in view of the purely factual nature of the items recorded, but they are now commonly encountered with respect to medical diagnoses, prognoses, and test results, as well as occasionally in other areas. The Commonwealth Fund Act provided only for records of an "act, transaction, occurrence, or event," while the Uniform Act, Model Code Rule 514, and Uniform Rule 63(13) merely added the ambiguous term "condition." The limited phrasing of the Commonwealth Fund Act, 28 U.S.C. § 1732, may account for the reluctance of some federal decisions to admit diagnostic entries. *New York Life Ins. Co. v. Taylor,* 79 U.S.App.D.C. 66, 147 F.2d 297 (1945); *Lyles v. United States,* 103 U.S.App.D.C. 22, 254 F.2d 725 (1957), cert. denied 356 U.S. 961, 78 S.Ct. 997, 2 L.Ed.2d 1067; *England v. United States,* 174 F.2d 466 (5th Cir.1949); *Skogen v. Dow Chemical Co.,* 375 F.2d 692 (8th Cir.1967). Other federal decisions, however, experienced no difficulty in freely admitting diagnostic entries. *Reed v. Order of United Commercial Travelers,* 123 F.2d 252 (2d Cir.1941); *Buckminster's Estate v. Commissioner of Internal Revenue,* 147 F.2d 331 (2d Cir.1944); *Medina v. Erickson,* 226 F.2d 475 (9th Cir. 1955); *Thomas v. Hogan,* 308 F.2d 355 (4th Cir.1962); *Glawe v. Rulon,* 284 F.2d 495 (8th Cir.1960). In the state courts, the trend favors admissibility. Borucki v. MacKenzie Bros. Co., 125 Conn. 92, 3 A.2d 224 (1938); *Allen v. St. Louis Public Service Co.,* 365 Mo. 677, 285 S.W.2d 663, 55 A.L.R.2d 1022 (1956); *People v. Kohlmeyer,* 284 N.Y. 366, 31 N.E.2d 490 (1940); *Weis v. Weis,* 147 Ohio St. 416, 72 N.E.2d 245 (1947). In order to make clear its adherence to the latter position, the rule specifically includes both diagnoses and opinions, in addition to acts, events, and conditions, as proper subjects of admissible entries.

Problems of the motivation of the informant have been a source of difficulty and disagreement. In *Palmer v. Hoffman,* 318 U.S. 109, 63 S.Ct. 477, 87 L.Ed. 645 (1943), exclusion of an accident report made by the since deceased engineer, offered by defendant railroad trustees in a grade crossing collision case, was upheld. The report was not "in the regular course of business," not a record of the systematic conduct of the business as a business, said the Court. The report was prepared for use in litigating, not railroading. While the opinion mentions the motivation of the engineer only obliquely, the emphasis on records of routine operations is significant only by virtue of impact on motivation to be accurate. Absence of routineness raises lack of motivation to be accurate. The opinion of the Court of Appeals had gone beyond mere lack of motive to be accurate: the engineer's statement was "dripping with motivations to misrepresent." *Hoffman v. Palmer,* 129 F.2d 976, 991 (2d Cir.1942). The direct introduction of motivation is a disturbing factor, since absence of motive to misrepresent has not traditionally been a requirement of the rule; that records might be self-serving has not been a ground for exclusion. Laughlin, Business Records and the Like, 46 Iowa L.Rev. 276, 285 (1961). As Judge Clark said in his dissent, "I submit that there is hardly a grocer's account book which could not be excluded on that basis." 129 F.2d at 1002. A physician's evaluation report of a personal injury litigant would appear to be in the routine of his business. If the report is offered by the party at whose instance it was made, however, it has been held inadmissible, *Yates v. Bair Transport, Inc.,* 249 F.Supp. 681 (S.D.N.Y.1965), otherwise if offered by the opposite party, *Korte v. New York, N.H. & H.R. Co.,* 191 F.2d 86 (2d Cir.1951), cert. denied 342 U.S. 868, 72 S.Ct. 108, 96 L.Ed. 652.

The decisions hinge on motivation and which party is entitled to be concerned about it. Professor McCormick believed that the doctor's report or the accident report were sufficiently routine to justify admissibility. McCormick § 287, p. 604. Yet hesitation must be experienced in admitting everything which is observed and recorded in the course of a regularly conducted activity. Efforts to set a limit are illustrated by *Hartzog v. United States,* 217 F.2d 706 (4th Cir.1954), error to admit worksheets made by since deceased deputy collector in preparation for the instant income tax evasion prosecution, and *United States v. Ware,* 247 F.2d 698 (7th Cir.1957), error to admit narcotics agents' records of purchases. See also Exception [paragraph] (8), *infra,* as to the public record aspects of records of this nature. Some decisions have been satisfied as to motivation of an accident report if made pursuant to statutory duty, United States v. New York Foreign Trade Zone Operators, 304 F.2d 792 (2d Cir.1962); Taylor v. Baltimore & O.R. Co., 344 F.2d 281 (2d Cir.1965), since the report was oriented in a direction other than the litigation which ensued. Cf. Matthews v. United States, 217 F.2d 409 (5th Cir.1954). The formulation of specific terms which would assure satisfactory results in all cases is not possible. Consequently the rule proceeds from the base that records made in the course of a regularly conducted activity will be taken as admissible but subject to authority to exclude if "the sources of information or other circumstances indicate lack of trustworthiness."

Occasional decisions have reached for enhanced accuracy by requiring involvement as a participant in matters reported. *Clainos v. United States,* 82 U.S.App.D.C. 278, 163 F.2d 593 (1947), error to admit police records of convictions; *Standard Oil Co. of California v. Moore,* 251 F.2d 188 (9th Cir.1957), cert. denied 356 U.S. 975, 78 S.Ct. 1139, 2 L.Ed.2d 1148, error to admit employees' records of observed business practices of others. The rule includes no requirement of this nature. Wholly acceptable records may involve matters merely observed, e.g. the weather.

The form which the "record" may assume under the rule is described broadly as a "memorandum, report, record, or data compilation, in any form." The expression "data compilation" is used as broadly descriptive of any means of storing information other than the conventional words and figures in written or documentary form. It includes, but is by no means limited to, electronic computer storage. The term is borrowed from revised Rule 34(a) of the Rules of Civil Procedure.

Note to Paragraph (7). Failure of a record to mention a matter which would ordinarily be mentioned is satisfactory evidence of its nonexistence. Uniform Rule 63(14), Comment. While probably not hearsay as defined in Rule 801, *supra,* decisions may be found which class the evidence not only as hearsay but also as not within any exception. In order to set the question at rest in favor of admissibility, it is specifically treated here. McCormick § 289, p. 609; Morgan, Basic Problems of Evidence 314 (1962); 5 Wigmore § 1531; Uniform Rule 63(14); California Evidence Code § 1272; Kansas Code of Civil Procedure § 60–460(n); New Jersey Evidence Rule 63(14).

Note to Paragraph (8). Public records are a recognized hearsay exception at common law and have been the subject of statutes without number. McCormick § 291. See, for example, 28 U.S.C. § 1733, the relative narrowness of which is illustrated by its nonapplicability to nonfederal public agencies, thus necessitating resort to the less appropriate business record exception to the hearsay rule. *Kay v. United States,* 255 F.2d 476 (4th Cir.1958). The rule makes no distinction between federal and nonfederal offices and agencies.

Justification for the exception is the assumption that a public official will perform his duty properly and the unlikelihood that he will remember details independently of the record. *Wong Wing Foo v. McGrath,* 196 F.2d 120 (9th Cir.1952), and see *Chesapeake & Delaware Canal Co. v. United States,* 250 U.S. 123, 39 S.Ct. 407, 63 L.Ed. 889 (1919). As to items (a) and (b), further support is found in the reliability factors underlying records of regularly conducted activities generally. See Exception [paragraph] (6), supra.

(a) Cases illustrating the admissibility of records of the office's or agency's own activities are numerous. *Chesapeake & Delaware Canal Co. v. United States,* 250 U.S. 123, 39 S.Ct. 407, 63 L.Ed. 889 (1919), Treasury records of miscellaneous receipts and disbursements; *Howard v. Perrin,* 200 U.S. 71, 26 S.Ct. 195, 50 L.Ed. 374 (1906), General Land Office records; *Ballew v. United States,* 160 U.S. 187, 16 S.Ct. 263, 40 L.Ed. 388 (1895). Pension Office records.

(b) Cases sustaining admissibility of records of matters observed are also numerous. *United States v. Van Hook,* 284 F.2d 489 (7th Cir.1960), remanded for resentencing 365 U.S. 609, 81 S.Ct. 823, 5 L.Ed.2d 821, letter from induction officer to District Attorney, pursuant to army regulations, stating fact and circumstances of refusal to be inducted; *T'Kach v. United States,* 242 F.2d 937 (5th Cir.1957), affidavit of White House personnel officer that search of records showed no employment of accused, charged with fraudulently representing himself as an envoy of the President; *Minnehaha County v. Kelley,* 150 F.2d 356 (8th Cir.1945); Weather Bureau records of rainfall; *United States v. Meyer,* 113 F.2d 387 (7th Cir.1940), cert. denied 311 U.S. 706, 61 S.Ct. 174, 85 L.Ed. 459, map prepared by government engineer from information furnished by men working under his supervision.

(c) The more controversial area of public records is that of the so-called "evaluative" report. The disagreement among the decisions has been due in part, no doubt, to the variety of situations encountered, as well as to differences in principle. Sustaining admissibility are such cases as *United States v. Dumas,* 149 U.S. 278, 13 S.Ct. 872, 37 L.Ed. 734 (1893), statement of account certified by Postmaster General in action against postmaster; *McCarty v. United States,* 185 F.2d 520 (5th Cir.1950), reh. denied 187 F.2d 234, Certificate of Settlement of General Accounting Office showing indebtedness and letter from Army official stating Government had performed, in action on contract to purchase and remove waste food from Army camp; *Moran v. Pittsburgh–Des Moines Steel Co.,* 183 F.2d 467 (3d Cir.1950), report of Bureau of Mines as to cause of gas tank explosion; Petition of W___, 164 F.Supp. 659 (E.D.Pa.1958), report by Immigration and Naturalization Service investigator that petitioner was known in community as wife of man to whom she was not married. To the opposite effect and denying admissibility are *Franklin v. Skelly Oil Co.,* 141 F.2d 568 (10th Cir. 1944), State Fire Marshal's report of cause of gas explosion; *Lomax Transp. Co. v. United States,* 183 F.2d 331 (9th Cir.1950), Certificate of Settlement from General Accounting Office in action for naval supplies lost in warehouse fire; *Yung Jin Teung v. Dulles,* 229 F.2d 244 (2d Cir.1956), "Status Reports" offered to justify delay in processing passport applications. Police reports have generally been excluded except to the extent to which they incorporate firsthand observations of the officer. Annot., 69 A.L.R.2d 1148. Various kinds of evaluative reports are admissible under federal statutes: 7 U.S.C. § 78, findings of Secretary of Agriculture prima facie evidence of true grade of grain; 7 U.S.C. § 210(f), findings of Secretary of Agriculture prima facie evidence in action for damages against stockyard owner; 7 U.S.C. § 292, order by Secretary of Agriculture prima facie evidence in judicial enforcement proceedings against producers association monopoly; 7 U.S.C. § 1622(h), Department of Agriculture inspection certificates of products shipped in interstate commerce prima facie evidence; 8 U.S.C. § 1440(c), separation of alien from military service on conditions other than honorable provable by certificate from department in proceedings to revoke citizenship; 18 U.S.C. § 4245, certificate of Director of Prisons that convicted person has been examined and found probably incompetent at time of trial prima facie evidence in court hearing on competency; 42 U.S.C. § 269(b), bill of health by appropriate official prima facie evidence of vessel's sanitary history and condition and compliance with regulations; 46 U.S.C. § 679, certificate of consul presumptive evidence of refusal of master to transport destitute seamen to United States. While these statutory exceptions to the hearsay rule are left undisturbed, Rule 802, the willingness of Congress to recognize a substantial measure of admissibility for evaluative reports is a helpful guide.

Factors which may be of assistance in passing upon the admissibility of evaluative reports include: (1) the timeliness of the investigation, McCormick, Can the Courts Make Wider Use of Reports of Official Investigations? 42 Iowa L.Rev. 363 (1957); (2) the special skill or experience of the official, *id.,* (3) whether a hearing was held and the level at which conducted, Franklin v. Skelly Oil Co., 141 F.2d 568 (10th Cir.1944); (4) possible motivation problems suggested by Palmer v. Hoffman, 318 U.S. 109, 63 S.Ct. 477, 87 L.Ed. 645 (1943). Others no doubt could be added.

The formulation of an approach which would give appropriate weight to all possible factors in every situation is an obvious impossibility. Hence the rule, as in Exception [paragraph] (6), assumes admissibility in the first instance but with ample provision for escape if sufficient negative factors are present. In one respect, however, the rule with respect to evaluative reports under item (c) is very specific: they are admissible only in civil cases and against the government in criminal cases in view of the almost certain collision with confrontation rights which would result from their use against the accused in a criminal case.

Note to Paragraph (9). Records of vital statistics are commonly the subject of particular statutes making them admissible in evidence, Uniform Vital Statistics Act, 9C U.L.A. 350 (1957). The rule is in principle narrower than Uniform Rule 63(16) which includes reports required of persons performing functions authorized by statute, yet in practical effect the two are substantially the same. Comment Uniform Rule 63(16). The exception as drafted is in the pattern of California Evidence Code § 1281.

Note to Paragraph (10). The principle of proving nonoccurrence of an event by evidence of the absence of a record which would regularly be made of its occurrence, developed in Exception [paragraph] (7) with respect to regularly conducted activities, is here extended to public records of the kind mentioned in Exceptions [paragraphs] (8) and (9). 5 Wigmore § 1633(6), p. 519. Some harmless duplication no doubt exists with Exception [paragraph] (7). For instances of federal statutes recognizing this method of proof, see 8 U.S.C. § 1284(b), proof of absence of alien crewman's name from outgoing manifest prima facie evidence of failure to detain or deport, and 42 U.S.C. § 405(c)(3), (4)(B), (4)(C), absence of HEW [Department of Health, Education, and Welfare] record prima facie evidence of no wages or self-employment income.

The rule includes situations in which absence of a record may itself be the ultimate focal point of inquiry, e.g. People v. Love, 310 Ill. 558, 142 N.E. 204 (1923), certificate of Secretary of State admitted to show failure to file documents required by Securities Law, as well as cases where the absence of a record is offered as proof of the nonoccurrence of an event ordinarily recorded.

The refusal of the common law to allow proof by certificate of the lack of a record or entry has no apparent justification, 5 Wigmore § 1678(7), p. 752. The rule takes the opposite position, as to Uniform Rule 63(17); California Evidence Code § 1284; Kansas Code of Civil Procedure § 60–460(c); New Jersey Evidence Rule 63(17). Congress has recognized certification as evidence of the lack of a record. 8 U.S.C. § 1360(d), certificate of Attorney General or other designated officer that no record of Immigration and Naturalization Service of specified nature or entry therein is found, admissible in alien cases.

Note to Paragraph (11). Records of activities of religious organizations are currently recognized as admissible at least to the extent of the business records exception to the hearsay rule, 5 Wigmore § 1523, p. 371, and Exception [paragraph] (6) would be applicable. However, both the business record doctrine and Exception [paragraph] (6) require that the person furnishing the information be one in the business or activity. The result is such decisions as Daily v. Grand Lodge, 311 Ill. 184, 142 N.E. 478 (1924), holding a church record admissible to prove fact, date, and place of baptism, but not age of child except that he had at least been born at the time. In view of the unlikelihood that false information would be furnished on occasions of this kind, the rule contains no requirement that the informant be in the course of the activity. See California Evidence Code § 1315 and Comment.

Note to Paragraph (12). The principle of proof by certification is recognized as to public officials in Exceptions [paragraphs] (8) and (10), and with respect to authentication in Rule 902. The present exception is a duplication to the extent that it deals with a certificate by a public official, as in the case of a judge who performs a marriage ceremony. The area covered by the rule is, however, substantially larger and extends the certification procedure to clergymen and the like who perform marriages and other ceremonies or administer sacraments. Thus certificates of such matters as baptism or confirmation, as well as marriage, are included. In principle they are as acceptable evidence as certificates of public officers. See 5 Wigmore § 1645, as to marriage certificates. When the person executing the certificate is not a public official, the self-authenticating character of documents purporting to emanate from public officials, see Rule 902, is lacking and proof is required that the person was authorized and did make the certificate. The time element, however, may safely be taken as supplied by the certificate, once authority and authenticity are established, particularly in view of the presumption that a document was executed on the date it bears.

For similar rules, some limited to certificates of marriage, with variations in foundation requirements, see Uniform Rule 63(18); California Evidence Code § 1316; Kansas Code of Civil Procedure § 60–460(p); New Jersey Evidence Rule 63(18).

Note to Paragraph (13). Records of family history kept in family Bibles have by long tradition been received in evidence. 5 Wigmore §§ 1495, 1496, citing numerous statutes and decisions. See also Regulations, Social Security Administration, 20 C.F.R. § 404.703(c), recognizing family Bible entries as proof of age in the absence of public or church records. Opinions in the area also include inscriptions on tombstones, publicly displayed pedigrees, and engravings on rings. Wigmore, *supra.* The rule is substantially identical in coverage with California Evidence Code § 1312.

Note to Paragraph (14). The recording of title documents is a purely statutory development. Under any theory of the admissibility of public records, the records would be receivable as evidence of the contents of the recorded document, else the recording process would be reduced to a nullity. When, however, the record is offered for the further purpose of proving execution and delivery, a problem of lack of firsthand knowledge by the recorder, not present as to contents, is presented. This problem is solved, seemingly in all jurisdictions, by qualifying for recording only those documents shown by a specified procedure, either acknowledgement or a form of probate, to have been executed and delivered. 5 Wigmore §§ 1647–1651. Thus what may appear in the rule, at first glance, as endowing the record with an effect independently of local law and inviting difficulties of an *Erie* nature under *Cities Service Oil Co. v. Dunlap,* 308 U.S. 208, 60 S.Ct. 201, 84 L.Ed. 196 (1939), is not present, since the local law in fact governs under the example.

Note to Paragraph (15). Dispositive documents often contain recitals of fact. Thus a deed purporting to have been executed by an attorney in fact may recite the existence of the power of attorney, or a deed may recite that the grantors are all the heirs of the last record owner. Under the rule, these recitals are exempted from the hearsay rule. The circumstances under which dispositive documents are executed and the requirement that the recital be germane to the purpose of the document are believed to be adequate guarantees of trustworthiness, particularly in view of the nonapplicability of the rule if dealings with the property have been inconsistent with the document. The age of the document is of no significance, though in practical application the document will most often be an ancient one. See Uniform Rule 63(29), Comment.

Similar provisions are contained in Uniform Rule 63(29); California Evidence Code § 1330; Kansas Code of Civil Procedure § 60–460(aa); New Jersey Evidence Rule 63(29).

Note to Paragraph (16). Authenticating a document as ancient, essentially in the pattern of the common law, as provided in Rule 901(b)(8), leaves open as a separate question the admissibility of assertive statements contained therein as against a hearsay objection. 7 Wigmore § 2145a. Wigmore further states that the ancient document technique of authentication is universally conceded to apply to all sorts of documents, including letters, records, contracts, maps, and certificates, in addition to title documents, citing numerous decisions. *Id.* § 2145. Since most of these items are significant evidentially only insofar as they are assertive, their admission in evidence must be as a hearsay exception. But see 5 *id.* § 1573, p. 429, referring to recitals in ancient deeds as a "limited" hearsay exception. The former position is believed to be the correct one in reason and authority. As pointed out in McCormick § 298, danger of mistake is minimized by authentication requirements, and age affords assurance that the writing antedates the present controversy. See *Dallas County v. Commercial Union Assurance Co.,* 286 F.2d 388 (5th Cir.1961), upholding admissibility of 58–year–old newspaper story. Cf. Morgan, Basic Problems of Evidence 364 (1962), but see *id.* 254.

For a similar provision, but with the added requirement that "the statement has since generally been acted upon as true by persons having an interest in the matter," see California Evidence Code § 1331.

Note to Paragraph (17). Ample authority at common law supported the admission in evidence of items falling in this category. While Wigmore's text is narrowly oriented to lists, etc., prepared for the use of a trade or profession, 6 Wigmore § 1702, authorities are cited which include other kinds of publications, for example, newspaper market reports, telephone directories, and city directories. *Id.* §§ 1702–1706. The basis of trustworthiness is general reliance by the public or by a particular segment of it, and the motivation of the compiler to foster reliance by being accurate.

For similar provisions, see Uniform Rule 63(30); California Evidence Code § 1340; Kansas Code of Civil Procedure § 60–460(bb); New Jersey Evidence Rule 63(30). Uniform Commercial Code § 2–724 provides for admissibility in evidence of "reports in official publications or trade journals or in newspapers or periodicals of general circulation published as the reports of such [established commodity] market."

Note to Paragraph (18). The writers have generally favored the admissibility of learned treatises, McCormick § 296, p. 621; Morgan, Basic Problems of Evidence 366 (1962); 6 Wigmore § 1692, with the support of occasional decisions and rules, *City of Dothan v. Hardy,* 237 Ala. 603,

188 So. 264 (1939); *Lewandowski v. Preferred Risk Mut. Ins. Co.*, 33 Wis.2d 69, 146 N.W.2d 505 (1966), 66 Mich.L.Rev. 183 (1967); Uniform Rule 63(31); Kansas Code of Civil Procedure § 60–460(cc), but the great weight of authority has been that learned treatises are not admissible as substantive evidence though usable in the cross-examination of experts. The foundation of the minority view is that the hearsay objection must be regarded as unimpressive when directed against treatises since a high standard of accuracy is engendered by various factors: the treatise is written primarily and impartially for professionals, subject to scrutiny and exposure for inaccuracy, with the reputation of the writer at stake. 6 Wigmore § 1692. Sound as this position may be with respect to trustworthiness, there is, nevertheless, an additional difficulty in the likelihood that the treatise will be misunderstood and misapplied without expert assistance and supervision. This difficulty is recognized in the cases demonstrating unwillingness to sustain findings relative to disability on the basis of judicially noticed medical texts. *Ross v. Gardner*, 365 F.2d 554 (6th Cir.1966); *Sayers v. Gardner*, 380 F.2d 940 (6th Cir.1967); *Colwell v. Gardner*, 386 F.2d 56 (6th Cir.1967); *Glendenning v. Ribicoff*, 213 F.Supp. 301 (W.D.Mo.1962); *Cook v. Celebrezze*, 217 F.Supp. 366 (W.D.Mo.1963); *Sosna v. Celebrezze*, 234 F.Supp. 289 (E.D.Pa.1964); and see *McDaniel v. Celebrezze*, 331 F.2d 426 (4th Cir.1964). The rule avoids the danger of misunderstanding and misapplication by limiting the use of treatises as substantive evidence to situations in which an expert is on the stand and available to explain and assist in the application of the treatise if desired. The limitation upon receiving the publication itself physically in evidence, contained in the last sentence, is designed, to further this policy.

The relevance of the use of treatises on cross-examination is evident. This use of treatises has been the subject of varied views. The most restrictive position is that the witness must have stated expressly on direct his reliance upon the treatise. A slightly more liberal approach still insists upon reliance but allows it to be developed on cross-examination. Further relaxation dispenses with reliance but requires recognition as an authority by the witness, developable on cross-examination. The greatest liberality is found in decisions allowing use of the treatise on cross-examination when its status as an authority is established by any means. Annot., 60 A.L.R.2d 77. The exception is hinged upon this last position, which is that of the Supreme Court, *Reilly v. Pinkus*, 338 U.S. 269, 70 S.Ct. 110, 94 L.Ed. 63 (1949), and of recent well considered state court decisions, *City of St. Petersburg v. Ferguson*, 193 So.2d 648 (Fla.App.1967), cert. denied Fla., 201 So.2d 556; *Darling v. Charleston Memorial Community Hospital*, 33 Ill.2d 326, 211 N.E.2d 253 (1965); *Dabroe v. Rhodes Co.*, 64 Wash.2d 431, 392 P.2d 317 (1964).

In Reilly v. Pinkus, *supra*, the Court pointed out that testing of professional knowledge was incomplete without exploration of the witness' knowledge of and attitude toward established treatises in the field. The process works equally well in reverse and furnishes the basis of the rule.

The rule does not require that the witness rely upon or recognize the treatise as authoritative, thus avoiding the possibility that the expert may at the outset block cross-examination by refusing to concede reliance or authoritativeness. Dabroe v. Rhodes Co., *supra*. Moreover, the rule avoids the unreality of admitting evidence for the purpose of impeachment only, with an instruction to the jury not to consider it otherwise. The parallel to the treatment of prior inconsistent statements will be apparent. See Rules 613(b) and 801(d)(1).

Note to Paragraphs (19), (20) and (21). Trustworthiness in reputation evidence is found "when the topic is such that the facts are likely to have been inquired about and that persons having personal knowledge have disclosed facts which have thus been discussed in the community; and thus the community's conclusion, if any has been formed, is likely to be a trustworthy one." 5 Wigmore § 1580, p. 444, and see also § 1583. On this common foundation, reputation as to land boundaries, customs, general history, character, and marriage have come to be regarded as admissible. The breadth of the underlying principle suggests the formulation of an equally broad exception, but tradition has in fact been much narrower and more particularized, and this is the pattern of these exceptions in the rule.

Exception [paragraph] (19) is concerned with matters of personal and family history. Marriage is universally conceded to be a proper subject of proof by evidence of reputation in the community. 5 Wigmore § 1602. As to such items as legitimacy, relationship, adoption, birth, and death, the decisions are divided. *Id.* § 1605. All seem to be susceptible to being the subject of well founded repute. The "world" in which the reputation may exist may be family, associates, or community. This world has proved capable of expanding with changing times from the single uncomplicated neighborhood, in which all activities take place, to the multiple and unrelated worlds of work, religious affiliation, and social activity, in each of which a reputation may be generated. *People v. Reeves*, 360 Ill. 55, 195 N.E. 443 (1935); *State v. Axilrod*, 248 Minn. 204, 79 N.W.2d 677 (1956); Mass.Stat. 1947, c. 410, M.G.L.A. c. 233 § 21A; 5 Wigmore § 1616. The family has often served as the point of beginning for allowing community reputation. 5 Wigmore § 1488. For comparable provisions see Uniform Rule 63(26), (27)(c); California Evidence Code §§ 1313, 1314; Kansas Code of Civil Procedure § 60–460(x), (y)(3); New Jersey Evidence Rule 63(26), (27)(c).

The first portion of Exception [paragraph] (20) is based upon the general admissibility of evidence of reputation as to land boundaries and land customs, expanded in this country to include private as well as public boundaries. McCormick § 299, p. 625. The reputation is required to antedate the controversy, though not to be ancient. The second portion is likewise supported by authority, *id.*, and is designed to facilitate proof of events when judicial notice is not available. The historical character of the subject matter dispenses with any need that the reputation antedate the controversy with respect to which it is offered. For similar provisions see Uniform Rule 63(27)(a), (b); California Evidence Code §§ 1320–1322; Kansas Code of Civil Procedure § 60–460(y), (1), (2); New Jersey Evidence Rule 63(27)(a), (b).

Exception [paragraph] (21) recognizes the traditional acceptance of reputation evidence as a means of proving human character. McCormick §§ 44, 158. The exception deals only with the hearsay aspect of this kind of evidence. Limitations upon admissibility based on other grounds will be found in Rules 404, relevancy of character evidence generally, and 608, character of witness. The exception is in effect a reiteration, in the context of hearsay, of Rule 405(a). Similar provisions are contained in Uniform Rule 63(28); California

Evidence Code § 1324; Kansas Code of Civil Procedure § 60–460(z); New Jersey Evidence Rule 63(28).

Note to Paragraph (22). When the status of a former judgment is under consideration in subsequent litigation, three possibilities must be noted: (1) the former judgment is conclusive under the doctrine of res judicata, either as a bar or a collateral estoppel; or (2) it is admissible in evidence for what it is worth; or (3) it may be of no effect at all. The first situation does not involve any problem of evidence except in the way that principles of substantive law generally bear upon the relevancy and materiality of evidence. The rule does not deal with the substantive effect of the judgment as a bar or collateral estoppel. When, however, the doctrine of res judicata does not apply to make the judgment either a bar or a collateral estoppel, a choice is presented between the second and third alternatives. The rule adopts the second for judgments of criminal conviction of felony grade. This is the direction of the decisions, Annot., 18 A.L.R.2d 1287, 1299, which manifest an increasing reluctance to reject *in toto* the validity of the law's factfinding processes outside the confines of res judicata and collateral estoppel. While this may leave a jury with the evidence of conviction but without means to evaluate it, as suggested by Judge Hinton, Note 27 Ill.L.Rev. 195 (1932), it seems safe to assume that the jury will give it substantial effect unless defendant offers a satisfactory explanation, a possibility not foreclosed by the provision. But see *North River Ins. Co. v. Militello,* 104 Colo. 28, 88 P.2d 567 (1939), in which the jury found for plaintiff on a fire policy despite the introduction of his conviction for arson. For supporting federal decisions see Clark, J., in *New York & Cuba Mail S.S. Co. v. Continental Cas. Co.,* 117 F.2d 404, 411 (2d Cir.1941); *Connecticut Fire Ins. Co. v. Farrara,* 277 F.2d 388 (8th Cir.1960).

Practical considerations require exclusion of convictions of minor offenses, not because the administration of justice in its lower echelons must be inferior, but because motivation to defend at this level is often minimal or nonexistent. *Cope v. Goble,* 39 Cal.App.2d 448, 103 P.2d 598 (1940); *Jones v. Talbot,* 87 Idaho 498, 394 P.2d 316 (1964); *Warren v. Marsh,* 215 Minn. 615, 11 N.W.2d 528 (1943); Annot., 18 A.L.R.2d 1287, 1295–1297; 16 Brooklyn L.Rev. 286 (1950); 50 Colum.L.Rev. 529 (1950); 35 Cornell L.Q. 872 (1950). Hence the rule includes only convictions of felony grade, measured by federal standards.

Judgments of conviction based upon pleas of *nolo contendere* are not included. This position is consistent with the treatment of *nolo* pleas in Rule 410 and the authorities cited in the Advisory Committee's Note in support thereof.

While these rules do not in general purport to resolve constitutional issues, they have in general been drafted with a view to avoiding collision with constitutional principles. Consequently the exception does not include evidence of the conviction of a third person, offered against the accused in a criminal prosecution to prove any fact essential to sustain the judgment of conviction. A contrary position would seem clearly to violate the right of confrontation. *Kirby v. United States,* 174 U.S. 47, 19 S.Ct. 574, 43 L.Ed. 890 (1899), error to convict of possessing stolen postage stamps with the only evidence of theft being the record of conviction of the thieves. The situation is to be distinguished from cases in which conviction of another person is an element of the crime, e.g. 15 U.S.C. § 902(d), interstate shipment of firearms to a known convicted felon, and, as specifically provided, from impeachment.

For comparable provisions see Uniform Rule 63(20); California Evidence Code § 1300; Kansas Code of Civil Procedure § 60–460(r); New Jersey Evidence Rule 63(20).

Note to Paragraph (23). A hearsay exception in this area was originally justified on the ground that verdicts were evidence of reputation. As trial by jury graduated from the category of neighborhood inquests, this theory lost its validity. It was never valid as to chancery decrees. Nevertheless the rule persisted, though the judges and writers shifted ground and began saying that the judgment or decree was as good evidence as reputation. See *City of London v. Clerke,* Carth. 181, 90 Eng.Rep. 710 (K.B. 1691); *Neill v. Duke of Devonshire,* 8 App.Cas. 135 (1882). The shift appears to be correct, since the process of inquiry, sifting, and scrutiny which is relied upon to render reputation reliable is present in perhaps greater measure in the process of litigation. While this might suggest a broader area of application, the affinity to reputation is strong, and paragraph [paragraph] (23) goes no further, not even including character.

The leading case in the *United States, Patterson v. Gaines,* 47 U.S. (6 How.) 550, 599, 12 L.Ed. 553 (1847), follows in the pattern of the English decisions, mentioning as illustrative matters thus provable: manorial rights, public rights of way, immemorial custom, disputed boundary, and pedigree. More recent recognition of the principle is found in *Grant Bros. Construction Co. v. United States,* 232 U.S. 647, 34 S.Ct. 452, 58 L.Ed. 776 (1914), in action for penalties under Alien Contract Labor Law, decision of board of inquiry of Immigration Service admissible to prove alienage of laborers, as a matter of pedigree; *United States v. Mid-Continent Petroleum Corp.,* 67 F.2d 37 (10th Cir.1933), records of commission enrolling Indians admissible on pedigree; *Jung Yen Loy v. Cahill,* 81 F.2d 809 (9th Cir.1936), board decisions as to citizenship of plaintiff's father admissible in proceeding for declaration of citizenship. *Contra,* In re Estate of Cunha, 49 Haw. 273, 414 P.2d 925 (1966).

1974 Enactment

Note to Paragraph (3). Rule 803(3) was approved in the form submitted by the Court to Congress. However, the Committee intends that the Rule be construed to limit the doctrine of *Mutual Life Insurance Co. v. Hillmon,* 145 U.S. 285, 295–300 (1892), so as to render statements of intent by a declarant admissible only to prove his future conduct, not the future conduct of another person.

Note to Paragraph (4). After giving particular attention to the question of physical examination made solely to enable a physician to testify, the Committee approved Rule 803(4) as submitted to Congress, with the understanding that it is not intended in any way to adversely affect present privilege rules or those subsequently adopted.

Note to Paragraph (5). Rule 803(5) as submitted by the Court permitted the reading into evidence of a memorandum or record concerning a matter about which a witness once had knowledge but now has insufficient recollection to enable him to testify accurately and fully, "shown to have been made when the matter was fresh in his memory and to reflect that knowledge correctly." The Committee amended this Rule to add the words "or adopted by the witness" after the phrase "shown to have been made", a treatment consistent with the definition of "statement" in the Jencks Act, 18 U.S.C. 3500. Moreover, it is the Committee's understanding that a memorandum or report, although barred under this Rule, would nonetheless be admissible if it came within another hearsay exception. This last stated principle is deemed applicable to all the hearsay rules.

Note to Paragraph (6). Rule 803(6) as submitted by the Court permitted a record made "in the course of a regularly conducted activity" to be admissible in certain circumstances. The Committee believed there were insufficient guarantees of reliability in records made in the course of activities falling outside the scope of "business" activities as that term is broadly defined in 28 U.S.C. 1732. Moreover, the Committee concluded that the additional requirement of Section 1732 that it must have been the regular practice of a business to make the record is a necessary further assurance of its trustworthiness. The Committee accordingly amended the Rule to incorporate these limitations.

Note to Paragraph (7). Rule 803(7) as submitted by the Court concerned the *absence* of entry in the records of a "regularly conducted activity." The Committee amended this Rule to conform with its action with respect to Rule 803(6).

Note to Paragraph (8). The Committee approved Rule 803(8) without substantive change from the form in which it was submitted by the Court. The Committee intends that the phrase "factual findings" be strictly construed and that evaluations or opinions contained in public reports shall not be admissible under this Rule.

Note to Paragraph (13). The Committee approved this Rule in the form submitted by the Court, intending that the phrase "Statements of fact concerning personal or family history" be read to include the specific types of such statements enumerated in Rule 803(11). House Report No. 93–650.

Note to Paragraph (4). The House approved this rule as it was submitted by the Supreme Court "with the understanding that it is not intended in any way to adversely affect present privilege rules." We also approve this rule, and we would point out with respect to the question of its relation to privileges, it must be read in conjunction with rule 35 of the Federal Rules of Civil Procedure which provides that whenever the physical or mental condition of a party (plaintiff or defendant) is in controversy, the court may require him to submit to an examination by a physician. It is these examinations which will normally be admitted under this exception.

Note to Paragraph (5). Rule 803(5) as submitted by the Court permitted the reading into evidence of a memorandum or record concerning a matter about which a witness once had knowledge but now has insufficient recollection to enable him to testify accurately and fully, "shown to have been made when the matter was fresh in his memory and to reflect that knowledge correctly." The House amended the rule to add the words "or adopted by the witness" after the phrase "shown to have been made," language parallel to the Jencks Act [18 U.S.C. § 3500].

The committee accepts the House amendment with the understanding and belief that it was not intended to narrow the scope of applicability of the rule. In fact, we understand it to clarify the rule's applicability to a memorandum adopted by the witness as well as one made by him. While the rule as submitted by the Court was silent on the question of who made the memorandum, we view the House amendment as a helpful clarification, noting, however, that the Advisory Committee's note to this rule suggests that the important thing is the accuracy of the memorandum rather than who made it.

The committee does not view the House amendment as precluding admissibility in situations in which multiple participants were involved.

When the verifying witness has not prepared the report, but merely examined it and found it accurate, he has adopted the report, and it is therefore admissible. The rule should also be interpreted to cover other situations involving multiple participants, e.g., employer dictating to secretary, secretary making memorandum at direction of employer, or information being passed along a chain of persons, as in *Curtis v. Bradley* [65 Conn. 99, 31 Atl. 591 (1894); see, also, *Rathbun v. Brancatella,* 93 N.J.L. 222, 107 Atl. 279 (1919); see, also, McCormick on Evidence, § 303 (2d ed. 1972)].

The committee also accepts the understanding of the House that a memorandum or report, although barred under this rule, would nonetheless be admissible if it came within another hearsay exception. We consider this principle to be applicable to all the hearsay rules.

Note to Paragraph (6). Rule 803(6) as submitted by the Supreme Court permitted a record made in the course of a regularly conducted activity to be admissible in certain circumstances. This rule constituted a broadening of the traditional business records hearsay exception which has been long advocated by scholars and judges active in the law of evidence.

The House felt there were insufficient guarantees of reliability of records not within a broadly defined business records exception. We disagree. Even under the House definition of "business" including profession, occupation, and "calling of every kind," the records of many regularly conducted activities will, or may be, excluded from evidence. Under the principle of ejusdem generis, the intent of "calling of every kind" would seem to be related to work-related endeavors—e.g., butcher, baker, artist, etc.

Thus, it appears that the records of many institutions or groups might not be admissible under the House amendments. For example, schools, churches, and hospitals will not normally be considered businesses within the definition. Yet, these are groups which keep financial and other records on a regular basis in a manner similar to business enterprises. We believe these records are of equivalent trustworthiness and should be admitted into evidence.

Three states, which have recently codified their evidence rules, have adopted the Supreme Court version of rule 803(6), providing for admission of memoranda of a "regularly conducted activity." None adopted the words "business activity" used in the House amendment. [See Nev.Rev.Stats. § 15.135; N.Mex.Stats. (1973 Supp.) § 20–4–803(6); West's Wis.Stats.Anno. (1973 Supp.) § 908.03(6).]

Therefore, the committee deleted the word "business" as it appears before the word "activity". The last sentence then is unnecessary and was also deleted.

It is the understanding of the committee that the use of the phrase "person with knowledge" is not intended to imply that the party seeking to introduce the memorandum, report, record, or data compilation must be able to produce, or even identify, the specific individual upon whose first-hand knowledge the memorandum, report, record or data compilation was based. A sufficient foundation for the introduction of such evidence will be laid if the party seeking to introduce the evidence is able to show that it was the regular practice of the activity to base such memorandums, reports, records, or data compilations upon a transmission from a person with knowledge, e.g., in the case of the content of a shipment of goods, upon a report from the company's receiving agent or in the case of a computer printout, upon a report from the company's computer programmer or one who has knowledge of the particular record system. In short, the scope of the phrase "person with knowledge" is meant to be coterminous with the custodian of the evidence or other qualified witness. The committee believes this represents the desired rule in light of the complex nature of modern business organizations.

Note to Paragraph (8). The House approved rule 803(8), as submitted by the Supreme Court, with one substantive change. It excluded from the hearsay exception reports containing matters observed by police officers and other law enforcement personnel in criminal cases. Ostensibly, the reason for this exclusion is that observations by police officers at the scene of the crime or the apprehension of the defendant are not as reliable as observations by public officials in other cases because of the adversarial nature of the confrontation between the police and the defendant in criminal cases.

The committee accepts the House's decision to exclude such recorded observations where the police officer is available to testify in court about his observation. However, where he is unavailable as unavailability is defined in rule 804(a)(4) and (a)(5), the report should be admitted as the best available evidence. Accordingly, the committee has amended rule 803(8) to refer to the provision of [proposed] rule 804(b)(5) [deleted], which allows the admission of such reports, records or other statements where the police officer or other law enforcement officer is unavailable because of death, then existing physical or mental illness or infirmity, or not being successfully subject to legal process.

The House Judiciary Committee report contained a statement of intent that "the phrase 'factual findings' in subdivision (c) be strictly construed and that evaluations or opinions contained in public reports shall not be admissible under this rule." The committee takes strong exception to this limiting understanding of the application of the rule. We do not think it reflects an understanding of the intended operation of the rule as explained in the Advisory Committee notes to this subsection. The Advisory Committee notes on subsection (c) of this subdivision point out that various kinds of evaluative reports are now admissible under Federal statutes. 7 U.S.C. § 78, findings of Secretary of Agriculture prima facie evidence of true grade of grain; 42 U.S.C. § 269(b), bill of health by appropriate official prima facie evidence of vessel's sanitary history and condition and compliance with regulations. These statutory exceptions to the hearsay rule are preserved. Rule 802. The willingness of Congress to recognize these and other such evaluative reports provides a helpful guide in determining the kind of reports which are intended to be admissible under this rule. We think the restrictive interpretation of the House overlooks the fact that while the Advisory Committee assumes admissibility in the first instance of evaluative reports, they are not admissible if, as the rule states, "the sources of information or other circumstances indicate lack of trustworthiness."

The Advisory Committee explains the factors to be considered:

* * * * * * *

Factors which may be assistance in passing upon the admissibility of evaluative reports include: (1) the timeliness of the investigation, McCormick, Can the Courts Make Wider Use of Reports of Official Investigations? 42 Iowa L.Rev. 363 (1957); (2) the special skill or experience of the official, id.; (3) whether a hearing was held and the level at which conducted, *Franklin v. Skelly Oil Co.*, 141 F.2d 568 (19th Cir.1944); (4) possible motivation problems suggested by *Palmer v. Hoffman*, 318 U.S. 109, 63 S.Ct. 477, 87 L.Ed. 645 (1943). Others no doubt could be added.

* * * * * * *

The committee concludes that the language of the rule together with the explanation provided by the Advisory Committee furnish sufficient guidance on the admissibility of evaluative reports.

Note to Paragraph (24). The proposed Rules of Evidence submitted to Congress contained identical provisions in rules 803 and 804 (which set forth the various hearsay exceptions), admitting any hearsay statement not specifically covered by any of the stated exceptions, if the hearsay statement was found to have "comparable circumstantial guarantees of trustworthiness." The House deleted these provisions (proposed rules 803(24) and 804(b)(6)[(5)]) as injecting "too much uncertainty" into the law of evidence and impairing the ability of practitioners to prepare for trial. The House felt that rule 102, which directs the courts to construe the Rules of Evidence so as to promote growth and development, would permit sufficient flexibility to admit hearsay evidence in appropriate cases under various factual situations that might arise.

We disagree with the total rejection of a residual hearsay exception. While we view rule 102 as being intended to provide for a broader construction and interpretation of these rules, we feel that, without a separate residual provision, the specifically enumerated exceptions could become tortured beyond any reasonable circumstances which they were intended to include (even if broadly construed). Moreover, these exceptions, while they reflect the most typical and well recognized exceptions to the hearsay rule, may not encompass every situation in which the reliability and appropriateness of a particular piece of hearsay evidence make clear that it should be heard and considered by the trier of fact.

The committee believes that there are certain exceptional circumstances where evidence which is found by a court to have guarantees of trustworthiness equivalent to or exceeding the guarantees reflected by the presently listed exceptions, and to have a high degree of prolativeness [sic] and necessity could properly be admissible.

The case of *Dallas County v. Commercial Union Assoc. Co., Ltd.*, 286 F.2d 388 (5th Cir.1961) illustrates the point. The issue in that case was whether the tower of the county courthouse collapsed because it was struck by lightning (covered by insurance) or because of structural weakness and deterioration of the structure (not covered). Investigation of the structure revealed the presence of charcoal and charred timbers. In order to show that lightning may not have been the cause of the charring, the insurer offered a copy of a local newspaper published over 50 years earlier containing an unsigned article describing a fire in the courthouse while it was under construction. The court found that the newspaper did not qualify for admission as a business record or an ancient document and did not fit within any other recognized hearsay exception. The court concluded, however, that the article was trustworthy because it was inconceivable that a newspaper reporter in a small town would report a fire in the courthouse if none had occurred. See also *United States v. Barbati*, 284 F.Supp. 409 (E.D.N.Y.1968).

Because exceptional cases like the *Dallas County* case may arise in the future, the committee has decided to reinstate a residual exception for rules 803 and 804(b).

The committee, however, also agrees with those supporters of the House version who felt that an overly broad residual hearsay exception could emasculate the hearsay rule and the recognized exceptions or vitiate the rationale behind codification of the rules.

Therefore, the committee has adopted a residual exception for rules 803 and 804(b) of much narrower scope and applicability than the Supreme Court version. In order to qualify for admission, a hearsay statement not falling within one of the recognized exceptions would have to satisfy at least four conditions. First, it must have "equivalent circumstantial guarantees of trustworthiness." Second, it must be offered as evidence of a material fact. Third, the court must determine that the statement "is more probative on the point for which it is offered than any other evidence which the proponent can procure through reasonable efforts." This requirement is intended to insure that only statements which have high probative value and necessity may qualify for admission under the residual exceptions. Fourth, the court must determine that "the general purposes of these rules and the interests of justice will best be served by admission of the statement into evidence."

It is intended that the residual hearsay exceptions will be used very rarely, and only in exceptional circumstances. The committee does not intend to establish a broad license for trial judges to admit hearsay statements that do not fall within one of the other exceptions contained in rules 803 and 804(b). The residual exceptions are not meant to authorize major judicial revisions of the hearsay rule, including its present exceptions. Such major revisions are best accomplished by legislative action. It is intended that in any case in which evidence is sought to be admitted under these subsections, the trial judge will exercise no less care, reflection and caution than the courts did under the common law in establishing the now-recognized exceptions to the hearsay rule.

In order to establish a well-defined jurisprudence, the special facts and circumstances which, in the court's judgment, indicates that the statement has a sufficiently high degree of trustworthiness and necessity to justify its admission should be stated on the record. It is expected that the court will give the opposing party a full and adequate opportunity to contest the admission of any statement sought to be introduced under these subsections. Senate Report No. 93–1277.

Rule 803 defines when hearsay statements are admissible in evidence even though the declarant is available as a witness. The Senate amendments make three changes in this rule.

Note to Paragraph (6). The House bill provides in subsection (6) that records of a regularly conducted "business" activity qualify for admission into evidence as an exception to the hearsay rule. "Business" is defined as including "business, profession, occupation and calling of every kind." The Senate amendment drops the requirement that the records be those of a "business" activity and eliminates the definition of "business." The Senate amendment provides that records are admissible if they are records of a regularly conducted "activity."

The Conference adopts the House provision that the records must be those of a regularly conducted "business" activity. The Conferees changed the definition of "business" contained in the House provision in order to make it clear that the records of institutions and associations like schools, churches and hospitals are admissible under this provision. The records of public schools and hospitals are also covered by Rule 803(8), which deals with public records and reports.

Note to Paragraph (8). The Senate amendment adds language, not contained in the House bill, that refers to another rule that was added by the Senate in another amendment ([proposed] Rule 804(b)(5)—Criminal law enforcement records and reports [deleted]).

In view of its action on [proposed] Rule 804(b)(5) (Criminal law enforcement records and reports) [deleted], the Conference does not adopt the Senate amendment and restores the bill to the House version.

Note to Paragraph (24). The Senate amendment adds a new subsection, (24), which makes admissible a hearsay statement not specifically covered by any of the previous twenty-three subsections, if the statement has equivalent circumstantial guarantees of trustworthiness and if the court determines that (A) the statement is offered as evidence of a material fact; (B) the statement is more probative on the point for which it is offered than any other evidence the proponent can procure through reasonable efforts; and (C) the general purposes of these rules and the interests of justice will best be served by admission of the statement into evidence.

The House bill eliminated a similar, but broader, provision because of the conviction that such a provision injected too much uncertainty into the law of evidence regarding hearsay and impaired the ability of a litigant to prepare adequately for trial.

The Conference adopts the Senate amendment with an amendment that provides that a party intending to request the court to use a statement under this provision must notify any adverse party of this intention as well as of the particulars of the statement, including the name and address of the declarant. This notice must be given sufficiently in advance of the trial or hearing to provide any adverse party with a fair opportunity to prepare to contest the use of the statement. House Report No. 93–1597.

1987 Amendment

The amendments are technical. No substantive change is intended.

1997 Amendment

The contents of Rule 803(24) and Rule 804(b)(5) have been combined and transferred to a new Rule 807. This was done to facilitate additions to Rules 803 and 804. No change in meaning is intended.

GAP Report on Rule 803. The words "Transferred to Rule 807" were substituted for "Abrogated."

2000 Amendment

The amendment provides that the foundation requirements of Rule 803(6) can be satisfied under certain circumstances without the expense and inconvenience of producing time-consuming foundation witnesses. Under current law, courts have generally required foundation witnesses to testify. *See, e.g., Tongil Co., Ltd. v. Hyundai Merchant Marine Corp.*, 968 F.2d 999 (9th Cir. 1992) (reversing a judgment based on business records where a qualified person filed an affidavit but did not testify). Protections are provided by the authentication requirements of Rule 902(11) for domestic records, Rule 902(12) for foreign records in civil cases, and 18 U.S.C. § 3505 for foreign records in criminal cases.

GAP Report—Proposed Amendment to Rule 803(6)

The Committee made no changes to the published draft of the proposed amendment to Evidence Rule 803(6).

HISTORICAL NOTES

Revision Notes and Legislative Reports

1975 Acts. House Report No. 94–599, see 1975 U.S. Code Cong. and Adm. News, p. 1585.

CROSS REFERENCES

Alien crewman, prima facie evidence of failure to deport, see 8 USCA § 1284.

Certification written by Attorney General of no record entries as admissible evidence, see 8 USCA § 1360.

Character evidence—

Methods of proving character, see Fed.Rules Evid. Rule 405, 28 USCA.

Opinion and reputation evidence and specific conduct, see Fed.Rules Evid. Rule 608, 28 USCA.

Proof of character, see Fed.Rules Evid. Rule 404, 28 USCA.

Confrontation with, and cross-examination of, witnesses, see USCA Const. Amend. VI.

Construction of these rules to secure fairness and development of law of evidence, see Fed.Rules Evid. Rule 102, 28 USCA.

Distribution and marketing of agricultural products, certificates of inspection of products as prima facie evidence, see 7 USCA § 1622.

Findings and orders of Secretary of Agriculture as prima facie evidence—

Associations of agricultural products producers, see 7 USCA § 292.

Official grade designation of grain, see 7 USCA § 78.

Packers and stockyards, see 7 USCA § 210.

Government records and papers, admissibility of, see 28 USCA § 1733.

Naturalization of aliens through active-duty service in armed forces, revocation, see 8 USCA § 1440.

Personal knowledge of witness, necessity of, see Fed.Rules Evid. Rule 602, 28 USCA.

Plea of guilty or nolo contendere, admissibility of pleas, discussions, and related statements, see Fed.Rules Evid. Rule 410, 28 USCA.

Preliminary questions as to admissibility, privileges, etc., see Fed.Rules Evid. Rule 104, 28 USCA.

Prior statements of witnesses, extrinsic evidence, see Fed. Rules Evid. Rule 613, 28 USCA.

Production of documents and things and entry upon land for inspection, see Fed.Rules Civ.Proc. Rule 34, 28 USCA.

Quarantine and inspection of ports of entry, bills of health as evidence of statements therein, see 42 USCA § 269.

Records in regular course of business, see 28 USCA § 1732.

Report of examining physician on person's physical or mental condition, discovery of, see Fed.Rules Civ.Proc. Rule 35, 28 USCA.

Self-authentication of public records, documents, etc., see Fed.Rules Evid. Rule 902, 28 USCA.

Social Security, etc., benefits, records of Commissioner of Social Security as evidence, see 42 USCA § 405.

Rule 804. Hearsay Exceptions; Declarant Unavailable

(a) Definition of unavailability. "Unavailability as a witness" includes situations in which the declarant—

(1) is exempted by ruling of the court on the ground of privilege from testifying concerning the subject matter of the declarant's statement; or

(2) persists in refusing to testify concerning the subject matter of the declarant's statement despite an order of the court to do so; or

(3) testifies to a lack of memory of the subject matter of the declarant's statement; or

(4) is unable to be present or to testify at the hearing because of death or then existing physical or mental illness or infirmity; or

(5) is absent from the hearing and the proponent of a statement has been unable to procure the declarant's attendance (or in the case of a hearsay exception under subdivision (b)(2), (3), or (4), the declarant's attendance or testimony) by process or other reasonable means.

A declarant is not unavailable as a witness if exemption, refusal, claim of lack of memory, inability, or absence is due to the procurement or wrongdoing of the proponent of a statement for the purpose of preventing the witness from attending or testifying.

(b) Hearsay exceptions. The following are not excluded by the hearsay rule if the declarant is unavailable as a witness:

(1) Former testimony. Testimony given as a witness at another hearing of the same or a different proceeding, or in a deposition taken in compliance with law in the course of the same or another proceeding, if the party against whom the testimony is now offered, or, in a civil action or proceeding, a predecessor in interest, had an opportunity and similar motive to develop the testimony by direct, cross, or redirect examination.

(2) Statement under belief of impending death. In a prosecution for homicide or in a civil action or proceeding, a statement made by a declarant while believing that the declarant's death was imminent, concerning the cause or circumstances of what the declarant believed to be impending death.

(3) Statement against interest. A statement which was at the time of its making so far contrary to the declarant's pecuniary or proprietary interest, or so far tended to subject the declarant to civil or criminal liability, or to render invalid a claim by the declarant against another, that a reasonable person in the declarant's position would not have made the statement unless believing it to be true. A statement tending to expose the declarant to criminal liability and offered to exculpate the accused is not admissible unless corroborating circumstances clearly indicate the trustworthiness of the statement.

(4) Statement of personal or family history. (A) A statement concerning the declarant's own birth, adoption, marriage, divorce, legitimacy, relationship by blood, adoption, or marriage, ancestry, or other similar fact of personal or family history, even though declarant had no means of acquiring personal knowledge of the matter stated; or (B) a statement concerning the foregoing matters, and death also, of another person, if the declarant was related to the other by blood, adoption, or marriage or was so intimately associated with the other's family as to be likely to have accurate information concerning the matter declared.

(5) [Transferred to Rule 807]

(6) Forfeiture by wrongdoing. A statement offered against a party that has engaged or acquiesced in wrongdoing that was intended to, and did, procure the unavailability of the declarant as a witness.

(Pub.L. 93–595, § 1, Jan. 2, 1975, 88 Stat. 1942; Pub.L. 94–149, § 1(12), (13), Dec. 12, 1975, 89 Stat. 806; Mar. 2, 1987, eff. Oct. 1, 1987; Pub.L. 100–690, Title VII, § 7075(b), Nov. 18, 1988, 102 Stat. 4405; Apr. 11, 1997, eff. Dec. 1, 1997.)

ADVISORY COMMITTEE NOTES

1972 Proposed Rules

As to firsthand knowledge on the part of hearsay declarants, see the introductory portion of the Advisory Committee's Note to Rule 803.

Note to Subdivision (a). The definition of unavailability implements the division of hearsay exceptions into two categories by Rules 803 and 804(b).

At common law the unavailability requirement was evolved in connection with particular hearsay exceptions rather than along general lines. For example, see the separate explications of unavailability in relation to former testimony, declarations against interest, and statements of pedigree, separately developed in McCormick §§ 234, 257, and 297. However, no reason is apparent for making distinctions as to what satisfies unavailability for the different exceptions. The treatment in the rule is therefore uniform although differences in the range of process for witnesses between civil and criminal cases will lead to a less exacting requirement under item (5). See Rule 45(e) of the Federal Rules of Civil Procedure and Rule 17(e) of the Federal Rules of Criminal Procedure.

Five instances of unavailability are specified:

(1) Substantial authority supports the position that exercise of a claim of privilege by the declarant satisfies the requirement of unavailability (usually in connection with former testimony). *Wyatt v. State,* 35 Ala.App. 147, 46 So.2d 837 (1950); *State v. Stewart,* 85 Kan. 404, 116 P. 489 (1911); Annot., 45 A.L.R.2d 1354; Uniform Rule 62(7)(a); California Evidence Code § 240(a)(1); Kansas Code of Civil Procedure § 60–459(g)(1). A ruling by the judge is required, which clearly implies that an actual claim of privilege must be made.

(2) A witness is rendered unavailable if he simply refuses to testify concerning the subject matter of his statement despite judicial pressures to do so, a position supported by similar considerations of practicality. *Johnson v. People,* 152 Colo. 586, 384 P.2d 454 (1963); *People v. Pickett,* 339 Mich. 294, 63 N.W.2d 681, 45 A.L.R.2d 1341 (1954). *Contra, Pleau v. State,* 255 Wis. 362, 38 N.W.2d 496 (1949).

(3) The position that a claimed lack of memory by the witness of the subject matter of his statement constitutes unavailability likewise finds support in the cases, though not without dissent. McCormick § 234, p. 494. If the claim is successful, the practical effect is to put the testimony beyond reach, as in the other instances. In this instance, however, it will be noted that the lack of memory must be established by the testimony of the witness himself, which clearly contemplates his production and subjection to cross-examination.

(4) Death and infirmity find general recognition as grounds. McCormick §§ 234, 257, 297; Uniform Rule 62(7)(c); California Evidence Code § 240(a)(3); Kansas Code of Civil Procedure § 60–459(g)(3); New Jersey Evidence Rule 62(6)(c). See also the provisions on use of depositions in Rule 32(a)(3) of the Federal Rules of Civil Procedure and Rule 15(e) of the Federal Rules of Criminal Procedure.

(5) Absence from the hearing coupled with inability to compel attendance by process or other reasonable means also satisfies the requirement. McCormick § 234; Uniform Rule 62(7)(d) and (e); California Evidence Code § 240(a)(4) and (5); Kansas Code of Civil Procedure § 60–459(g)(4) and (5); New Jersey Rule 62(6)(b) and (d). See the discussion of procuring attendance of witnesses who are nonresidents or in custody in *Barber v. Page,* 390 U.S. 719, 88 S.Ct. 1318, 20 L.Ed.2d 255 (1968).

If the conditions otherwise constituting unavailability result from the procurement or wrongdoing of the proponent of the statement, the requirement is not satisfied. The rule contains no requirement that an attempt be made to take the deposition of a declarant.

Note to Subdivision (b). Rule 803, *supra*, is based upon the assumption that a hearsay statement falling within one of its exceptions possesses qualities which justify the conclusion that whether the declarant is available or unavailable is not a relevant factor in determining admissibility. The instant rule proceeds upon a different theory: hearsay which admittedly is not equal in quality to testimony of the declarant on the stand may nevertheless be admitted if the declarant is unavailable and if his statement meets a specified standard. The rule expresses preferences: testimony given on the stand in person is preferred over hearsay, and hearsay, if of the specified quality, is preferred over complete loss of the evidence of the declarant. The exceptions evolved at common law with respect to declarations of unavailable declarants furnish the basis for the exceptions enumerated in the proposal. The term "unavailable" is defined in subdivision (a).

Exception (1). Former testimony does not rely upon some set of circumstances to substitute for oath and cross-examination, since both oath and opportunity to cross-examine were present in fact. The only missing one of the ideal conditions for the giving of testimony is the presence of trier and opponent ("demeanor evidence"). This is lacking with all hearsay exceptions. Hence it may be argued that former testimony is the strongest hearsay and should be included under Rule 803, supra. However, opportunity to observe demeanor is what in a large measure confers depth and meaning upon oath and cross-examination. Thus in cases under Rule 803 demeanor lacks the significance which it possesses with respect to testimony. In any event, the tradition, founded in experience, uniformly favors production of the witness if he is available. The exception indicates continuation of the policy. This preference for the presence of the witness is apparent also in rules and statutes on the use of depositions, which deal with substantially the same problem.

Under the exception, the testimony may be offered (1) against the party *against* whom it was previously offered or (2) against the party *by* whom it was previously offered. In each instance the question resolves itself into whether fairness allows imposing, upon the party against whom now offered, the handling of the witness of the earlier occasion. (1) If the party against whom now offered is the one against whom the testimony was offered previously, no unfairness is apparent in requiring him to accept his own prior conduct of cross-examination or decision not to cross-examine. Only demeanor has been lost, and that is inherent in the situation. (2) If the party against whom now offered is the one *by* whom the testimony was offered previously, a satisfactory answer becomes somewhat more difficult. One possibility is to proceed somewhat along the line of an adoptive admission, i.e. by offering the testimony proponent in effect adopts it. However, this theory savors of discarded concepts of witnesses' belonging to a party, of litigants' ability to pick and choose witnesses, and of vouching for one's own witnesses. Cf. McCormick § 246, pp. 526–527; 4 Wigmore § 1075. A more direct and acceptable approach is simply to recognize direct and redirect examination of one's own witness as the equivalent of cross-examining an opponent's witness. Falknor, Former Testimony and the Uniform Rules: A Comment, 38 N.Y.U.L.Rev. 651, n. 1 (1963); McCormick § 231, p. 483. See also 5 Wigmore § 1389. Allowable techniques for dealing with hostile, double-crossing, forgetful, and mentally deficient witnesses leave no substance to a claim that one could not adequately develop his own witness at the former hearing. An even less appealing argument is presented when failure to develop fully was the result of a deliberate choice.

The common law did not limit the admissibility of former testimony to that given in an earlier trial of the same case, although it did require identity of issues as a means of insuring that the former handling of the witness was the equivalent of what would now be done if the opportunity were presented. Modern decisions reduce the requirement to "substantial" identity. McCormick § 233. Since identity of issues is significant only in that it bears on motive and interest in developing fully the testimony of the witness, expressing the matter in the latter terms is preferable. *Id.* Testimony given at a preliminary hearing was held in *California v. Green,* 399 U.S. 149, 90 S.Ct. 1930, 26 L.Ed.2d 489 (1970), to satisfy confrontation requirements in this respect.

As a further assurance of fairness in thrusting upon a party the prior handling of the witness, the common law also insisted upon identity of parties, deviating only to the extent of allowing substitution of successors in a narrowly construed privity. Mutuality as an aspect of identity is now generally discredited, and the requirement of identity of the offering party disappears except as it might affect motive to develop the testimony. Falknor, *supra,* at 652; McCormick § 232, pp. 487–488. The question remains whether strict identity, or privity, should continue as a requirement with respect to the party against whom offered. The rule departs to the extent of allowing substitution of one with the right and opportunity to develop the testimony with similar motive and interest. This position is supported by modern decisions. McCormick § 232, pp. 489–490; 5 Wigmore § 1388.

Provisions of the same tenor will be found in Uniform Rule 63(3)(b); California Evidence Code §§ 1290–1292; Kansas Code of Civil Procedure § 60–460(c)(2); New Jersey Evidence Rule 63(3). Unlike the rule, the latter three provide either that former testimony is not admissible if the right of confrontation is denied or that it is not admissible if the accused was not a party to the prior hearing. The genesis of these limitations is a caveat in Uniform Rule 63(3) Comment that use of former testimony against an accused may violate his right of confrontation. *Mattox v. United States,* 156 U.S. 237, 15 S.Ct. 337, 39 L.Ed. 409 (1895), held that the right was not violated by the Government's use, on a retrial of the same case, of testimony given at the first trial by two witnesses since deceased. The decision leaves open the questions (1) whether direct and redirect are equivalent to cross-examination for purposes of confrontation, (2) whether testimony given in a different proceeding is acceptable, and (3) whether the accused must himself have been a party to the earlier proceeding or whether a similarly situated person will serve the purpose. Professor Falknor concluded that, if a dying declaration untested by cross-examination is constitutionally admissible, former testimony tested by the cross-examination of one similarly situated does not offend against confrontation. Falknor, *supra,* at 659–660. The constitutional acceptability of dying declarations has often been conceded. *Mattox v. United States,* 156 U.S. 237, 243, 15 S.Ct. 337, 39 L.Ed. 409 (1895); *Kirby v. United States,* 174

U.S. 47, 61, 19 S.Ct. 574, 43 L.Ed. 890 (1899); *Pointer v. Texas*, 380 U.S. 400, 407, 85 S.Ct. 1065, 13 L.Ed.2d 923 (1965).

Exception (2). The exception is the familiar dying declaration of the common law, expanded somewhat beyond its traditionally narrow limits. While the original religious justification for the exception may have lost its conviction for some persons over the years, it can scarcely be doubted that powerful psychological pressures are present. See 5 Wigmore § 1443 and the classic statement of Chief Baron Eyre in Rex v. Woodcock, 1 Leach 500, 502, 168 Eng.Rep. 352, 353 (K.B.1789).

The common law required that the statement be that of the victim, offered in a prosecution for criminal homicide. Thus declarations by victims in prosecutions for other crimes, e.g. a declaration by a rape victim who dies in childbirth, and all declarations in civil cases were outside the scope of the exception. An occasional statute has removed these restrictions, as in Colo.R.S. § 52–1–20, or has expanded the area of offenses to include abortions, 5 Wigmore § 1432, p. 224, n. 4. Kansas by decision extended the exception to civil cases. *Thurston v. Fritz*, 91 Kan. 468, 138 P. 625 (1914). While the common law exception no doubt originated as a result of the exceptional need for the evidence in homicide cases, the theory of admissibility applies equally in civil cases and in prosecutions for crimes other than homicide. The same considerations suggest abandonment of the limitation to circumstances attending the event in question, yet when the statement deals with matters other than the supposed death, its influence is believed to be sufficiently attenuated to justify the limitation. Unavailability is not limited to death. See subdivision (a) of this rule. Any problem as to declarations phrased in terms of opinion is laid at rest by Rule 701, and continuation of a requirement of firsthand knowledge is assured by Rule 602.

Comparable provisions are found in Uniform Rule 63(5); California Evidence Code § 1242; Kansas Code of Civil Procedure § 60–460(e); New Jersey Evidence Rule 63(5).

Exception (3). The circumstantial guaranty of reliability for declarations against interest is the assumption that persons do not make statements which are damaging to themselves unless satisfied for good reason that they are true. *Hileman v. Northwest Engineering Co.*, 346 F.2d 668 (6th Cir.1965). If the statement is that of a party, offered by his opponent, it comes in as an admission, Rule 803(d)(2) [sic; probably should be "Rule 801(d)(2)"], and there is no occasion to inquire whether it is against interest, this not being a condition precedent to admissibility of admissions by opponents.

The common law required that the interest declared against be pecuniary or proprietary but within this limitation demonstrated striking ingenuity in discovering an against-interest aspect. Higham v. Ridgway, 10 East 109, 103 Eng.Rep. 717 (K.B.1808); Reg. v. Overseers of Birmingham, 1 B. & S. 763, 121 Eng.Rep. 897 (Q.B.1861); McCormick, § 256, p. 551, nn. 2 and 3.

The exception discards the common law limitation and expands to the full logical limit. One result is to remove doubt as to the admissibility of declarations tending to establish a tort liability against the declarant or to extinguish one which might be asserted by him, in accordance with the trend of the decisions in this country. McCormick § 254, pp. 548–549. Another is to allow statements tending to expose declarant to hatred, ridicule, or disgrace, the motivation here being considered to be as strong as when financial interests are at stake. McCormick § 255, p. 551. And finally, exposure to criminal liability satisfies the against-interest requirement. The refusal of the common law to concede the adequacy of a penal interest was no doubt indefensible in logic, see the dissent of Mr. Justice Holmes in *Donnelly v. United States*, 228 U.S. 243, 33 S.Ct. 449, 57 L.Ed. 820 (1913), but one senses in the decisions a distrust of evidence of confessions by third persons offered to exculpate the accused arising from suspicions of fabrication either of the fact of the making of the confession or in its contents, enhanced in either instance by the required unavailability of the declarant. Nevertheless, an increasing amount of decisional law recognizes exposure to punishment for crime as a sufficient stake. *People v. Spriggs*, 60 Cal.2d 868, 36 Cal.Rptr. 841, 389 P.2d 377 (1964); *Sutter v. Easterly*, 354 Mo. 282, 189 S.W.2d 284 (1945); Band's Refuse Removal, Inc. v. Fairlawn Borough, 62 N.J.Super. 522, 163 A.2d 465 (1960); *Newberry v. Commonwealth*, 191 Va. 445, 61 S.E.2d 318 (1950); Annot., 162 A.L.R. 446. The requirement of corroboration is included in the rule in order to effect an accommodation between these competing considerations. When the statement is offered by the accused by way of exculpation, the resulting situation is not adapted to control by rulings as to the weight of the evidence, and hence the provision is cast in terms of a requirement preliminary to admissibility. Cf. Rule 406(a). The requirement of corroboration should be construed in such a manner as to effectuate its purpose of circumventing fabrication.

Ordinarily the third-party confession is thought of in terms of exculpating the accused, but this is by no means always or necessarily the case: it may include statements implicating him, and under the general theory of declarations against interest they would be admissible as related statements. Douglas v. Alabama, 380 U.S. 415, 85 S.Ct. 1074, 13 L.Ed.2d 934 (1965), and Bruton v. United States, 389 U.S. 818, 88 S.Ct. 126, 19 L.Ed.2d 70 (1968), both involved confessions by codefendants which implicated the accused. While the confession was not actually offered in evidence in *Douglas*, the procedure followed effectively put it before the jury, which the Court ruled to be error. Whether the confession might have been admissible as a declaration against penal interest was not considered or discussed. *Bruton* assumed the inadmissibility, as against the accused, of the implicating confession of his codefendant, and centered upon the question of the effectiveness of a limiting instruction. These decisions, however, by no means require that all statements implicating another person be excluded from the category of declarations against interest. Whether a statement is in fact against interest must be determined from the circumstances of each case. Thus a statement admitting guilt and implicating another person, made while in custody, may well be motivated by a desire to curry favor with the authorities and hence fail to qualify as against interest. See the dissenting opinion of Mr. Justice White in *Bruton*. On the other hand, the same words spoken under different circumstances, e.g., to an acquaintance, would have no difficulty in qualifying. The rule does not purport to deal with questions of the right of confrontation.

The balancing of self-serving against dissenting aspects of a declaration is discussed in McCormick § 256.

For comparable provisions, see Uniform Rule 63(10); California Evidence Code § 1230; Kansas Code of Civil Procedure § 60–460(j); New Jersey Evidence Rule 63(10).

Exception (4). The general common law requirement that a declaration in this area must have been made *ante litem motam* has been dropped, as bearing more appropriately on weight than admissibility. See 5 Wigmore § 1483. Item (i)[(A)] specifically disclaims any need of firsthand knowledge respecting declarant's own personal history. In some instances it is self-evident (marriage) and in others impossible and traditionally not required (date of birth). Item (ii)[(B)] deals with declarations concerning the history of another person. As at common law, declarant is qualified if related by blood or marriage. 5 Wigmore § 1489. In addition, and contrary to the common law, declarant qualifies by virtue of intimate association with the family. *Id.*, § 1487. The requirement sometimes encountered that when the subject of the statement is the relationship between two other persons the declarant must qualify as to both is omitted. Relationship is reciprocal. *Id.*, § 1491.

For comparable provisions, see Uniform Rule 63(23), (24), (25); California Evidence Code §§ 1310, 1311; Kansas Code of Civil Procedure § 60–460(u), (v), (w); New Jersey Evidence Rules 63–23), 63(24), 63(25).

1974 Enactment

Note to Subdivision (a)(3). Rule 804(a)(3) was approved in the form submitted by the Court. However, the Committee intends no change in existing federal law under which the court may choose to disbelieve the declarant's testimony as to his lack of memory. See *United States v. Insana*, 423 F.2d 1165, 1169–1170 (2nd Cir.), cert. denied, 400 U.S. 841 (1970).

Note to Subdivision (a)(5). Rule 804(a)(5) as submitted to the Congress provided, as one type of situation in which a declarant would be deemed "unavailable", that he be "absent from the hearing and the proponent of his statement has been unable to procure his attendance by process or other reasonable means." The Committee amended the Rule to insert after the word "attendance" the parenthetical expression "(or, in the case of a hearsay exception under subdivision (b)(2), (3), or (4), his attendance or testimony)". The amendment is designed primarily to require that an attempt be made to depose a witness (as well as to seek his attendance) as a precondition to the witness being deemed unavailable. The Committee, however, recognized the propriety of an exception to this additional requirement when it is the declarant's former testimony that is sought to be admitted under subdivision (b)(1).

Note to Subdivision (b)(1). Rule 804(b)(1) as submitted by the Court allowed prior testimony of an unavailable witness to be admissible if the party against whom it is offered or a person "with motive and interest similar" to his had an opportunity to examine the witness. The Committee considered that it is generally unfair to impose upon the party against whom the hearsay evidence is being offered responsibility for the manner in which the witness was previously handled by another party. The sole exception to this, in the Committee's view, is when a party's predecessor in interest in a civil action or proceeding had an opportunity and similar motive to examine the witness. The Committee amended the Rule to reflect these policy determinations.

Note to Subdivision (b)(2). Rule 804(b)(3) as submitted by the Court (now Rule 804(b)(2) in the bill) proposed to expand the traditional scope of the dying declaration exception (i.e. a statement of the victim in a homicide case as to the cause or circumstances of his believed imminent death) to allow such statements in all criminal and civil cases. The Committee did not consider dying declarations as among the most reliable forms of hearsay. Consequently, it amended the provision to limit their admissibility in criminal cases to homicide prosecutions, where exceptional need for the evidence is present. This is existing law. At the same time, the Committee approved the expansion to civil actions and proceedings where the stakes do not involve possible imprisonment, although noting that this could lead to forum shopping in some instances.

Note to Subdivision (b)(3). Rule 804(b)(4) as submitted by the Court (now Rule 804(b)(3) in the bill) provided as follows:

Statement against interest.—A statement which was at the time of its making so far contrary to the declarant's pecuniary or proprietary interest or so far tended to subject him to civil or criminal liability or to render invalid a claim by him against another or to make him an object of hatred, ridicule, or disgrace, that a reasonable man in his position would not have made the statement unless he believed it to be true. A statement tending to exculpate the accused is not admissible unless corroborated.

The Committee determined to retain the traditional hearsay exception for statements against pecuniary or proprietary interest. However, it deemed the Court's additional references to statements tending to subject a declarant to civil liability or to render invalid a claim by him against another to be redundant as included within the scope of the reference to statements against pecuniary or proprietary interest. See *Gichner v. Antonio Triano Tile and Marble Co.*, 410 F.2d 238 (D.C.Cir.1968). Those additional references were accordingly deleted.

The Court's Rule also proposed to expand the hearsay limitation from its present federal limitation to include statements subjecting the declarant to criminal liability and statements tending to make him an object of hatred, ridicule, or disgrace. The Committee eliminated the latter category from the subdivision as lacking sufficient guarantees of reliability. See *United States v. Dovico*, 380 F.2d 325, 327 nn. 2, 4 (2nd Cir.), cert. denied, 389 U.S. 944 (1967). As for statements against penal interest, the Committee shared the view of the Court that some such statements do possess adequate assurances of reliability and should be admissible. It believed, however, as did the Court, that statements of this type tending to exculpate the accused are more suspect and so should have their admissibility conditioned upon some further provision insuring trustworthiness. The proposal in the Court Rule to add a requirement of simple corroboration was, however, deemed ineffective to accomplish this purpose since the accused's own testimony might suffice while not necessarily increasing the reliability of the hearsay statement. The Committee settled upon the language "unless corroborating circumstances clearly indicate the trustworthiness of the statement" as affording a proper standard and degree of discretion. It was contemplated that the result in such cases as *Donnelly v. United States*, 228 U.S. 243 (1912), where the circumstances plainly indicated reliability, would be changed. The Committee also added to the Rule the final sentence from the 1971 Advisory Committee draft, designed to codify the doctrine of *Bruton v. United States,* 391 U.S. 123 (1968). The Committee does not intend to affect the existing exception to the *Bruton* principle where the codefendant takes the stand and is subject to cross-examination, but believed there was no need to make specific provision for this situation in the Rule, since in that event the declarant would not be "unavailable". House Report No. 93–650.

Note to Subdivision (a)(5). Subdivision (a) of rule 804 as submitted by the Supreme Court defined the conditions under which a witness was considered to be unavailable. It was amended in the House.

The purpose of the amendment, according to the report of the House Committee on the Judiciary, is "primarily to require that an attempt be made to depose a witness (as well as to seek his attendance) as a precondition to the witness being unavailable."

Under the House amendment, before a witness is declared unavailable, a party must try to depose a witness (declarant) with respect to dying declarations, declarations against interest, and declarations of pedigree. None of these situations would seem to warrant this needless, impractical and highly restrictive complication. A good case can be made for eliminating the unavailability requirement entirely for declarations against interest cases. [Uniform rule 63(10); Kan. Stat.Anno. 60–460(j); 2A N.J.Stats.Anno. 84–63(10).]

In dying declaration cases, the declarant will usually, though not necessarily, be deceased at the time of trial. Pedigree statements which are admittedly and necessarily based largely on word of mouth are not greatly fortified by a deposition requirement.

Depositions are expensive and time-consuming. In any event, deposition procedures are available to those who wish to resort to them. Moreover, the deposition procedures of the Civil Rules and Criminal Rules are only imperfectly adapted to implementing the amendment. No purpose is served unless the deposition, if taken, may be used in evidence. Under Civil Rule (a)(3) the Criminal Rule 15(e), a deposition, though taken, may not be admissible, and under Criminal Rule 15(a) substantial obstacles exist in the way of even taking a deposition.

For these reasons, the committee deleted the House amendment.

The committee understands that the rule as to unavailability, as explained by the Advisory Committee "contains no requirement that an attempt be made to take the deposition of a declarant." In reflecting the committee's judgment, the statement is accurate insofar as it goes. Where, however, the proponent of the statement, with knowledge of the existence of the statement, fails to confront the declarant with the statement at the taking of the deposition, then the proponent should not, in fairness, be permitted to treat the declarant as "unavailable" simply because the declarant was not amenable to process compelling his attendance at trial. The committee does not consider it necessary to amend the rule to this effect because such a situation abuses, not conforms to, the rule. Fairness would preclude a person from introducing a hearsay statement on a particular issue if the person taking the deposition was aware of the issue at the time of the deposition but failed to depose the unavailable witness on that issue.

Note to Subdivision (b)(1). Former testimony.—Rule 804(b)(1) as submitted by the Court allowed prior testimony of an unavailable witness to be admissible if the party against whom it is offered or a person "with motive and interest similar" to his had an opportunity to examine the witness.

The House amended the rule to apply only to a party's predecessor in interest. Although the committee recognizes considerable merit to the rule submitted by the Supreme Court, a position which has been advocated by many scholars and judges, we have concluded that the difference between the two versions is not great and we accept the House amendment.

Note to Subdivision (b)(3). The rule defines those statements which are considered to be against interest and thus of sufficient trustworthiness to be admissible even though hearsay. With regard to the type of interest declared against, the version submitted by the Supreme Court included inter alia, statements tending to subject a declarant to civil liability or to invalidate a claim by him against another. The House struck these provisions as redundant. In view of the conflicting case law construing pecuniary or proprietary interests narrowly so as to exclude, e.g., tort cases, this deletion could be misconstrued.

Three States which have recently codified their rules of evidence have followed the Supreme Court's version of this rule, i.e., that a statement is against interest if it tends to subject a declarant to civil liability. [Nev.Rev.Stats. § 51.345; N.Mex.Stats. (1973 Supp.) § 20–4–804(4); West's Wis.Stats.Anno. (1973 Supp.) § 908.045(4).]

The committee believes that the reference to statements tending to subject a person to civil liability constitutes a desirable clarification of the scope of the rule. Therefore, we have reinstated the Supreme Court language on this matter.

The Court rule also proposed to expand the hearsay limitation from its present federal limitation to include statements subjecting the declarant to statements tending to make him an object of hatred, ridicule, or disgrace. The House eliminated the latter category from the subdivision as lacking sufficient guarantees of reliability. Although there is considerable support for the admissibility of such statements (all three of the State rules referred to supra, would admit such statements), we accept the deletion by the House.

The House amended this exception to add a sentence making inadmissible a statement or confession offered against the accused in a criminal case, made by a codefendant or other person implicating both himself and the accused. The sentence was added to codify the constitutional principle announced in *Bruton v. United States,* 391 U.S. 123 (1968). Bruton held that the admission of the extrajudicial hearsay statement of one codefendant inculpating a second codefendant violated the confrontation clause of the sixth amendment.

The committee decided to delete this provision because the basic approach of the rules is to avoid codifying, or attempting to codify, constitutional evidentiary principles, such as the fifth amendment's right against self-incrimination and, here, the sixth amendment's right of confrontation. Codification of a constitutional principle is unnecessary and, where the principle is under development, often unwise. Furthermore, the House provision does not appear to recognize the exceptions to the *Bruton* rule, e.g. where the codefendant takes the stand and is subject to cross examination; where the accused confessed, see *United States v. Mancusi*, 404 F.2d 296 (2d Cir.1968), cert. denied 397 U.S. 942 (1907); where the accused was placed at the scene of the crime, see *United States v. Zelker*, 452 F.2d 1009 (2d Cir.1971). For these reasons, the committee decided to delete this provision.

Note to Subdivision (b)(5). See Note to Paragraph (24), Notes of Committee on the Judiciary, Senate Report No. 93–1277, set out as a note under rule 803 of these rules. Senate Report No. 93–1277.

Rule 804 defines what hearsay statements are admissible in evidence if the declarant is unavailable as a witness. The Senate amendments make four changes in the rule.

Note to Subdivision (a)(5). Subsection (a) defines the term "unavailability as a witness". The House bill provides in subsection (a)(5) that the party who desires to use the statement must be unable to procure the declarant's attendance by process or other reasonable means. In the case of dying declarations, statements against interest and statements of personal or family history, the House bill requires that the proponent must also be unable to procure the declarant's *testimony* (such as by deposition or interrogatories) by process or other reasonable means. The Senate amendment eliminates this latter provision.

The Conference adopts the provision contained in the House bill.

Note to Subdivision (b)(3). The Senate amendment to subsection (b)(3) provides that a statement is against interest and not excluded by the hearsay rule when the declarant is unavailable as a witness, if the statement tends to subject a person to civil or criminal liability or renders invalid a claim by him against another. The House bill did not refer specifically to civil liability and to rendering invalid a claim against another. The Senate amendment also deletes from the House bill the provision that subsection (b)(3) does not apply to a statement or confession, made by a codefendant or another, which implicates the accused and the person who made the statement, when that statement or confession is offered against the accused in a criminal case.

The Conference adopts the Senate amendment. The Conferees intend to include within the purview of this rule, statements subjecting a person to civil liability and statements rendering claims invalid. The Conferees agree to delete the provision regarding statements by a codefendant, thereby reflecting the general approach in the Rules of Evidence to avoid attempting to codify constitutional evidentiary principles.

Note to Subdivision (b)(5). The Senate amendment adds a new subsection, (b)(6) [now (b)(5)], which makes admissible a hearsay statement not specifically covered by any of the five previous subsections, if the statement has equivalent circumstantial guarantees of trustworthiness and if the court determines that (A) the statement is offered as evidence of a material fact; (B) the statement is more probative on the point for which it is offered than any other evidence the proponent can procure through reasonable efforts; and (C) the general purposes of these rules and the interests of justice will best be served by admission of the statement into evidence.

The House bill eliminated a similar, but broader, provision because of the conviction that such a provision injected too much uncertainty into the law of evidence regarding hearsay and impaired the ability of a litigant to prepare adequately for trial.

The Conference adopts the Senate amendment with an amendment that renumbers this subsection and provides that a party intending to request the court to use a statement under this provision must notify any adverse party of this intention as well as of the particulars of the statement, including the name and address of the declarant. This notice must be given sufficiently in advance of the trial or hearing to provide any adverse party with a fair opportunity to prepare to contest the use of the statement. House Report No. 93–1597.

1987 Amendments

The amendments are technical. No substantive change is intended.

1997 Amendments

Subdivision (b)(5). The contents of Rule 803(24) and Rule 804(b)(5) have been combined and transferred to a new Rule 807. This was done to facilitate additions to Rules 803 and 804. No change in meaning is intended.

Subdivision (b)(6). Rule 804(b)(6) has been added to provide that a party forfeits the right to object on hearsay grounds to the admission of a declarant's prior statement when the party's deliberate wrongdoing or acquiescence therein procured the unavailability of the declarant as a witness. This recognizes the need for a prophylactic rule to deal with abhorrent behavior "which strikes at the heart of the system of justice itself." *United States v. Mastrangelo*, 693 F.2d 269, 273 (2d Cir.1982), *cert. denied*, 467 U.S. 1204 (1984). The wrongdoing need not consist of a criminal act. The rule applies to all parties, including the government.

Every circuit that has resolved the question has recognized the principle of forfeiture by misconduct, although the tests for determining whether there is a forfeiture have varied. *See, e.g., United States v. Aguiar*, 975 F.2d 45, 47 (2d Cir.1992); *United States v. Potamitis*, 739 F.2d 784, 789 (2d Cir.), *cert. denied*, 469 U.S. 918 (1984); *Steele v. Taylor*, 684 F.2d 1193, 1199 (6th Cir.1982), *cert. denied*, 460 U.S. 1053 (1983); United States v. Balano, 618 F.2d 624, 629 (10th Cir.1979), *cert. denied*, 449 U.S. 840 (1980); *United States v. Carlson*, 547 F.2d 1346, 1358–59 (8th Cir.), *cert. denied*, 431 U.S. 914 (1977). The foregoing cases apply a preponderance of the evidence standard. *Contra United States v. Thevis*, 665 F.2d 616, 631 (5th Cir.) (clear and convincing standard), *cert. denied*, 459 U.S. 825 (1982). The usual Rule 104(a) preponderance of the evidence standard has been adopted in light of the behavior the new Rule 804(b)(6) seeks to discourage.

GAP Report on Rule 804(b)(5). The words "Transferred to Rule 807" were substituted for "Abrogated".

GAP Report on Rule 804(b)(6). The title of the rule was changed to "Forfeiture by wrongdoing." The word "who" in line 24 was changed to "that" to indicate that the rule is potentially applicable against the government. Two sentences were added to the first paragraph of the committee note to clarify that the wrongdoing need not be criminal in nature, and to indicate the rule's potential applicability to the government. The word "forfeiture" was substituted for "waiver" in the note.

HISTORICAL NOTES

Revision Notes and Legislative Reports

1975 Acts. House Report No. 94–599, see 1975 U.S. Code Cong. and Adm. News, p. 1585.

CROSS REFERENCES

Confrontation with, and cross-examination of, witnesses, see USCA Const. Amend. VI.

Depositions, use of at trials, see Fed.Rules Civ.Proc. Rule 32, 28 USCA.

Depositions, use of at trial, see Fed.Rules Cr.Proc. Rule 15, 18 USCA.

Subpoena of witnesses for a hearing or trial, see Fed.Rules Civ.Proc. Rule 45, 28 USCA.

Rule 805. Hearsay Within Hearsay

Hearsay included within hearsay is not excluded under the hearsay rule if each part of the combined statements conforms with an exception to the hearsay rule provided in these rules.

(Pub.L. 93–595, § 1, Jan. 2, 1975, 88 Stat. 1943.)

ADVISORY COMMITTEE NOTES

1972 Proposed Rules

On principle it scarcely seems open to doubt that the hearsay rule should not call for exclusion of a hearsay statement which includes a further hearsay statement when both conform to the requirements of a hearsay exception. Thus a hospital record might contain an entry of the patient's age based on information furnished by his wife. The hospital record would qualify as a regular entry except that the person who furnished the information was not acting in the routine of the business. However, her statement independently qualifies as a statement of pedigree (if she is unavailable) or as a statement made for purposes of diagnosis or treatment, and hence each link in the chain falls under sufficient assurances. Or, further to illustrate, a dying declaration may incorporate a declaration against interest by another declarant. See McCormick § 290, p. 611.

CROSS REFERENCES

Character and conduct of witness, opinion and reputation evidence, see Fed.Rules Evid. Rule 608, 28 USCA.

Extrinsic evidence of prior statements of witnesses, see Fed.Rules Evid. Rule 613, 28 USCA.

Impeachment by evidence of conviction and crime, see Fed.Rules Evid. Rule 609, 28 USCA.

Rule 806. Attacking and Supporting Credibility of Declarant

When a hearsay statement, or a statement defined in Rule 801(d)(2)(C), (D), or (E), has been admitted in evidence, the credibility of the declarant may be attacked, and if attacked may be supported, by any evidence which would be admissible for those purposes if declarant had testified as a witness. Evidence of a statement or conduct by the declarant at any time, inconsistent with the declarant's hearsay statement, is not subject to any requirement that the declarant may have been afforded an opportunity to deny or explain. If the party against whom a hearsay statement has been admitted calls the declarant as a witness, the party is entitled to examine the declarant on the statement as if under cross-examination.

(Pub.L. 93–595, § 1, Jan. 2, 1975, 88 Stat. 1943; Mar. 2, 1987, eff. Oct. 1, 1987; Apr. 11, 1997, eff. Dec. 1, 1997.)

ADVISORY COMMITTEE NOTES

1972 Proposed Rules

The declarant of a hearsay statement which is admitted in evidence is in effect a witness. His credibility should in fairness be subject to impeachment and support as though he had in fact testified. See Rules 608 and 609. There are however, some special aspects of the impeaching of a hearsay declarant which require consideration. These special aspects center upon impeachment by inconsistent statement, arise from factual differences which exist between the use of hearsay and an actual witness and also between various kinds of hearsay, and involve the question of applying to declarants the general rule disallowing evidence of an inconsistent statement to impeach a witness unless he is afforded an opportunity to deny or explain. See Rule 613(b).

The principal difference between using hearsay and an actual witness is that the inconsistent statement will in the case of the witness almost inevitably of necessity in the nature of things be a *prior* statement, which it is entirely possible and feasible to call to his attention, while in the case of hearsay the inconsistent statement may well be a *subsequent* one, which practically precludes calling it to the attention of the declarant. The result of insisting upon observation of this impossible requirement in the hearsay situation is to deny the opponent, already barred from cross-examination, any benefit of this important technique of impeachment. The writers favor allowing the subsequent statement. McCormick § 37, p. 69; 3 Wigmore § 1033. The cases, however, are divided. Cases allowing the impeachment include *People v. Collup,* 27 Cal.2d 829, 167 P.2d 714 (1946); *People v. Rosoto,* 58 Cal.2d 304, 23 Cal.Rptr. 779, 373 P.2d 867 (1962); *Carver v. United States,* 164 U.S. 694, 17 S.Ct. 228, 41 L.Ed. 602 (1897). *Contra, Mattox v. United States,* 156 U.S. 237, 15 S.Ct. 337, 39 L.Ed. 409 (1895); *People v. Hines,* 284 N.Y. 93, 29 N.E.2d 483 (1940). The force of *Mattox,* where the hearsay was the former testimony of a deceased witness and the denial of use of a subsequent inconsistent statement was upheld, is much diminished by *Carver,* where the hearsay was a dying declaration and denial of use of a subsequent inconsistent statement resulted in reversal. The difference in the particular brand of hearsay seems unimportant when the inconsistent statement is a *subsequent* one. True, the opponent is not totally deprived of cross-examination when the hearsay is former testimony or a deposition but he is deprived of cross-examining on the statement or along lines suggested by it. Mr. Justice Shiras, with two justices joining him, dissented vigorously in *Mattox.*

When the impeaching statement was made prior to the hearsay statement, differences in the kinds of hearsay appear which arguably may justify differences in treatment. If the hearsay consisted of a simple statement by the witness, e.g. a dying declaration or a declaration against interest, the feasibility of affording him an opportunity to deny or explain encounters the same practical impossibility as where the statement is a subsequent one, just discussed, although here the impossibility arises from the total absence of anything resembling a hearing at which the matter could be put to him. The courts by a large majority have ruled in favor of allowing the statement to be used under these circumstances. McCormick § 37, p. 69; 3 Wigmore § 1033. If, however, the hearsay consists of former testimony or a deposition, the possibility of calling the prior statement to the attention of the witness or deponent is not ruled out, since the opportunity to cross-examine was available. It might thus be concluded that with former testimony or depositions the conventional foundation should be insisted upon. Most of the cases involve depositions, and Wigmore describes them as divided. 3 Wigmore § 1031. Deposition procedures at best are cumbersome and expensive, and to require the laying of the foundation may impose an undue burden. Under the federal practice, there is no way of knowing with certainty at the time of taking a deposition whether it is merely for discovery or will ultimately end up in evidence. With respect to both former testimony and depositions the possibility exists that knowledge of the statement might not be acquired until after the time of the cross-examination. Moreover, the expanded admissibility of former testimony and depositions under Rule 804(b)(1) calls for a correspondingly expanded approach to impeachment. The rule dispenses with the requirement in all hearsay situations, which is readily administered and best calculated to lead to fair results.

Notice should be taken that Rule 26(f) of the Federal Rules of Civil Procedure, as originally submitted by the Advisory Committee, ended with the following:

"* * * and, without having first called them to the deponent's attention, may show statements contradictory thereto made at any time by the deponent."

This language did not appear in the rule as promulgated in December, 1937. See 4 Moore's Federal Practice ¶¶ 26.01[9], 26.35 (2d ed.1967). In 1951, Nebraska adopted a provision strongly resembling the one stricken from the federal rule:

"Any party may impeach any adverse deponent by self-contradiction without having laid foundation for such impeachment at the time such deposition was taken." R.S.Neb. § 25–1267.07.

For similar provisions, see Uniform Rule 65; California Evidence Code § 1202; Kansas Code of Civil Procedure § 60–462; New Jersey Evidence Rule 65.

The provision for cross-examination of a declarant upon his hearsay statement is a corollary of general principles of cross-examination. A similar provision is found in California Evidence Code § 1203.

1974 Enactment

Rule 906, as passed by the House and as proposed by the Supreme Court provides that whenever a hearsay statement is admitted, the credibility of the declarant of the statement may be attacked, and if attacked may be supported, by any evidence which would be admissible for those purposes if the declarant had testified as a witness. Rule 801 defines what is a hearsay statement. While statements by a person authorized by a party-opponent to make a statement concerning the subject, by the party-opponent's agent or by a coconspirator of a party—see rule 801(d)(2)(c), (d) and (e)—are traditionally defined as exceptions to the hearsay rule, rule 801 defines such admission by a party-opponent as statements which are not hearsay. Consequently, rule 806 by referring exclusively to the admission of hearsay statements, does not appear to allow the credibility of the declarant to be attacked when the declarant is a coconspirator, agent or authorized spokesman. The committee is of the view that such statements should open the declarant to attacks on his credibility. Indeed, the reason such statements are excluded from the operation of rule 806 is likely attributable to the drafting technique used to codify the hearsay rule, viz. some statements, instead of being referred to as exceptions to the hearsay rule, are defined as statements which are not hearsay. The phrase "or a statement defined in rule 801(d)(2)(c), (d) and (e)" is added to the rule in order to subject the declarant of such statements, like the declarant of hearsay statements, to attacks on his credibility. [The committee considered it unnecessary to include statements contained in rule 801(d)(2)(A) and (B)—the statement by the party-opponent himself or the statement of which he has manifested his adoption—because the credibility of the party-opponent is always subject to an attack on his credibility]. Senate Report No. 93–1277.

The Senate amendment permits an attack upon the credibility of the declarant of a statement if the statement is one by a person authorized by a party-opponent to make a statement concerning the subject, one by an agent of a party-opponent, or one by a coconspirator of the party-opponent, as these statements are defined in Rules 801(d)(2)(C), (D) and (E). The House bill has no such provision.

The Conference adopts the Senate amendment. The Senate amendment conforms the rule to present practice. House Report No. 93–1597.

1987 Amendments

The amendments are technical. No substantive change is intended.

1997 Amendments

The amendment is technical. No substantive change is intended.

GAP Report. Restylization changes in the rule were eliminated.

Rule 807. Residual Exception

A statement not specifically covered by Rule 803 or 804 but having equivalent circumstantial guarantees of trustworthiness, is not excluded by the hearsay rule, if the court determines that (A) the statement is offered as evidence of a material fact; (B) the statement is more probative on the point for which it is offered than any other evidence which the proponent can procure through reasonable efforts; and (C) the general purposes of these rules and the interests of justice will best be served by admission of the statement into evidence. However, a statement may not be admitted under this exception unless the proponent of it makes known to the adverse party sufficiently in advance of the trial or hearing to provide the adverse party with a fair opportunity to prepare to meet it, the proponent's intention to offer the statement and the particulars of it, including the name and address of the declarant.

(Added Apr. 11, 1997, eff. Dec. 1, 1997.)

ADVISORY COMMITTEE NOTES

1997 Amendments

The contents of Rule 803(24) and Rule 804(b)(5) have been combined and transferred to a new Rule 807. This was done to facilitate additions to Rules 803 and 804. No change in meaning is intended.

GAP Report on Rule 807. Restylization changes in the rule were eliminated.

ARTICLE IX. AUTHENTICATION AND IDENTIFICATION

Rule 901. Requirement of Authentication or Identification

(a) General provision. The requirement of authentication or identification as a condition precedent to admissibility is satisfied by evidence sufficient to support a finding that the matter in question is what its proponent claims.

(b) Illustrations. By way of illustration only, and not by way of limitation, the following are examples of authentication or identification conforming with the requirements of this rule:

(1) Testimony of witness with knowledge. Testimony that a matter is what it is claimed to be.

(2) Nonexpert opinion on handwriting. Nonexpert opinion as to the genuineness of handwriting, based upon familiarity not acquired for purposes of the litigation.

(3) Comparison by trier or expert witness. Comparison by the trier of fact or by expert witnesses with specimens which have been authenticated.

(4) Distinctive characteristics and the like. Appearance, contents, substance, internal patterns, or other distinctive characteristics, taken in conjunction with circumstances.

(5) Voice identification. Identification of a voice, whether heard firsthand or through mechanical or electronic transmission or recording, by opinion based upon hearing the voice at any time under circumstances connecting it with the alleged speaker.

(6) Telephone conversations. Telephone conversations, by evidence that a call was made to the number assigned at the time by the telephone company to a particular person or business, if (A) in the case of a person, circumstances, including self-identification, show the person answering to be the one called, or (B) in the case of a business, the call was made to a place of business and the conversation related to business reasonably transacted over the telephone.

(7) Public records or reports. Evidence that a writing authorized by law to be recorded or filed and in fact recorded or filed in a public office, or a purported public record, report, statement, or data compilation, in any form, is from the public office where items of this nature are kept.

(8) Ancient documents or data compilation. Evidence that a document or data compilation, in any form, (A) is in such condition as to create no suspicion concerning its authenticity, (B) was in a place where it, if authentic, would likely be, and (C) has been in existence 20 years or more at the time it is offered.

(9) Process or system. Evidence describing a process or system used to produce a result and showing that the process or system produces an accurate result.

(10) Methods provided by statute or rule. Any method of authentication or identification provided by Act of Congress or by other rules prescribed by the Supreme Court pursuant to statutory authority.

(Pub.L. 93–595, § 1, Jan. 2, 1975, 88 Stat.1943.)

ADVISORY COMMITTEE NOTES

1972 Proposed Rules

Note to Subdivision (a). Authentication and identification represent a special aspect of relevancy. Michael and Adler, Real Proof, 5 Vand.L.Rev. 344, 362 (1952); McCormick §§ 179, 185; Morgan, Basic Problems of Evidence 378 (1962). Thus a telephone conversation may be irrelevant because on an unrelated topic or because the speaker is not identified. The latter aspect is the one here involved. Wigmore describes the need for authentication as "an inherent logical necessity." 7 Wigmore § 2129, p. 564.

This requirement of showing authenticity or identity falls in the category of relevancy dependent upon fulfillment of a condition of fact and is governed by the procedure set forth in Rule 104(b).

The common law approach to authentication of documents has been criticized as an "attitude of agnosticism," McCormick, Cases on Evidence 388, n. 4 (3rd ed. 1956), as one which "departs sharply from men's customs in ordinary affairs," and as presenting only a slight obstacle to the introduction of forgeries in comparison to the time and expense devoted to proving genuine writings which correctly show their origin on their face, McCormick § 185, pp. 395, 396. Today, such available procedures as requests to admit and pretrial conference afford the means of eliminating much of the need for authentication or identification. Also, significant inroads upon the traditional insistence on authentication and identification have been made by accepting as at least prima facie genuine items of the kind treated in Rule 902, *infra*. However, the need for suitable methods of proof still remains, since criminal cases pose their own obstacles to the use of preliminary procedures, unforeseen contingencies may arise, and cases of genuine controversy will still occur.

Note to Subdivision (b). The treatment of authentication and identification draws largely upon the experience embodied in the common law and in statutes to furnish illustrative applications of the general principle set forth in subdivision (a). The examples are not intended as an exclusive enumeration of allowable methods but are meant to guide and suggest, leaving room for growth and development in this area of the law.

The examples relate for the most part to documents, with some attention given to voice communications and computer printouts. As Wigmore noted, no special rules have been developed for authenticating chattels. Wigmore, Code of Evidence § 2086 (3rd ed. 1942).

It should be observed that compliance with requirements of authentication or identification by no means assures admission of an item into evidence, as other bars, hearsay for example, may remain.

Example (1). Example (1) contemplates a broad spectrum ranging from testimony of a witness who was present at the signing of a document to testimony establishing narcotics as taken from an accused and accounting for custody through the period until trial, including laboratory analysis. See California Evidence Code § 1413, eyewitness to signing.

Example (2). Example (2) states conventional doctrine as to lay identification of handwriting, which recognizes that a sufficient familiarity with the handwriting of another person may be acquired by seeing him write, by exchanging correspondence, or by other means, to afford a basis for identifying it on subsequent occasions. McCormick § 189. See also California Evidence Code § 1416. Testimony based upon familiarity acquired for purposes of the litigation is reserved to the expert under the example which follows.

Example (3). The history of common law restrictions upon the technique of proving or disproving the genuineness of a disputed specimen of handwriting through comparison with a genuine specimen, by either the testimony of expert witnesses or direct viewing by the triers themselves, is detailed in 7 Wigmore §§ 1991–1994. In breaking away, the English Common Law Procedure Act of 1854, 17 and 18 Vict., c. 125, § 27, cautiously allowed expert or trier to use exemplars "proved to the satisfaction of the judge to be genuine" for purposes of comparison. The language found its way into numerous statutes in this country, e.g., California Evidence Code §§ 1417, 1418. While explainable as a measure of prudence in the process of breaking with precedent in the handwriting situation, the reservation to the judge of the question of the genuineness of exemplars and the imposition of an unusually high standard of persuasion are at variance with the general treatment of relevancy which depends upon fulfillment of a condition of fact. Rule 104(b). No similar attitude is found in other comparison situations, e.g., ballistics comparison by jury, as in *Evans v. Commonwealth,* 230 Ky. 411, 19 S.W.2d 1091 (1929), or by experts, Annot., 26 A.L.R.2d 892, and no reason appears for its continued existence in handwriting cases. Consequently Example (3) sets no higher standard for handwriting specimens and treats all comparison situations alike, to be governed by Rule 104(b). This approach is consistent with 28 U.S.C. § 1731: "The admitted or proved handwriting of any person shall be admissible, for purposes of comparison, to determine genuineness of other handwriting attributed to such person."

Precedent supports the acceptance of visual comparison as sufficiently satisfying preliminary authentication requirements for admission in evidence. *Brandon v. Collins,* 267 F.2d 731 (2d Cir.1959); *Wausau Sulphate Fibre Co. v. Commissioner of Internal Revenue,* 61 F.2d 879 (7th Cir. 1932); *Desimone v. United States,* 227 F.2d 864 (9th Cir. 1955).

Example (4). The characteristics of the offered item itself, considered in the light of circumstances, afford authentication techniques in great variety. Thus a document or telephone conversation may be shown to have emanated from a particular person by virtue of its disclosing knowledge of facts known peculiarly to him; *Globe Automatic Sprinkler Co. v. Braniff,* 89 Okl. 105, 214 P. 127 (1923); California Evidence Code § 1421; similarly, a letter may be authenticated by content and circumstances indicating it was in reply to a duly authenticated one. McCormick § 192; California Evidence Code § 1420. Language patterns may indicate authenticity or its opposite. *Magnuson v. State,* 187 Wis. 122, 203 N.W. 749 (1925); Arens and Meadow, Psycholinguistics and the Confession Dilemma, 56 Colum.L.Rev. 19 (1956).

Example (5). Since aural voice identification is not a subject of expert testimony, the requisite familiarity may be acquired either before or after the particular speaking which is the subject of the identification, in this respect resembling visual identification of a person rather than identification of handwriting. Cf. Example (2), *supra, People v. Nichols,* 378 Ill. 487, 38 N.E.2d 766 (1942); *McGuire v. State,* 200 Md. 601, 92 A.2d 582 (1952); *State v. McGee,* 336 Mo. 1082, 83 S.W.2d 98 (1935).

Example (6). The cases are in agreement that a mere assertion of his identity by a person talking on the telephone is not sufficient evidence of the authenticity of the conversation and that additional evidence of his identity is required. The additional evidence need not fall in any set pattern. Thus the content of his statements or the reply technique, under Example (4), *supra*, or voice identification under Example (5), may furnish the necessary foundation. Outgoing calls made by the witness involve additional factors bearing upon authenticity. The calling of a number assigned by the telephone company reasonably supports the assumption that the listing is correct and that the number is the one reached. If the number is that of a place of business, the mass of authority allows an ensuing conversation if it relates to business reasonably transacted over the telephone, on the theory that the maintenance of the telephone connection is an invitation to do business without further identification. *Matton v. Hoover Co.,* 350 Mo. 506, 166 S.W.2d 557 (1942); *City of Pawhuska v. Crutchfield,* 147 Okl. 4, 293 P. 1095 (1930); *Zurich General Acc. & Liability Ins. Co. v. Baum,* 159 Va. 404, 165 S.E. 518 (1932). Otherwise, some additional circumstance of identification of the speaker is required. The authorities divide on the question whether the self-identifying statement of the person answering suffices. Example (6) answers in the affirmative on the assumption that usual conduct respecting telephone calls furnish adequate assurances of regularity, bearing in mind that the entire matter is open to exploration before the trier of fact. In general, see McCormick § 193; 7 Wigmore § 2155; Annot., 71 A.L.R. 5, 105 id. 326.

Example (7). Public records are regularly authenticated by proof of custody, without more. McCormick § 191; 7 Wigmore §§ 2158, 2159. The example extends the principle to include data stored in computers and similar methods, of which increasing use in the public records area may be expected. See California Evidence Code §§ 1532, 1600.

Example (8). The familiar ancient document rule of the common law is extended to include data stored electronically or by other similar means. Since the importance of appearance diminishes in this situation, the importance of custody or place where found increases correspondingly. This expansion is necessary in view of the widespread use of methods of storing data in forms other than conventional written records.

Any time period selected is bound to be arbitrary. The common law period of 30 years is here reduced to 20 years, with some shift of emphasis from the probable unavailability of witnesses to the unlikeliness of a still viable fraud after the lapse of time. The shorter period is specified in the English Evidence Act of 1938, 1 & 2 Geo. 6, c. 28, and in Oregon R.S.1963, § 41.360(34). See also the numerous statutes prescribing periods of less than 30 years in the case of recorded documents. 7 Wigmore § 2143.

The application of Example (8) is not subject to any limitation to title documents or to any requirement that possession, in the case of a title document, has been consistent with the document. See McCormick § 190.

Example (9). Example (9) is designed for situations in which the accuracy of a result is dependent upon a process or system which produces it. X rays afford a familiar instance. Among more recent developments is the computer, as to which see Transport Indemnity Co. v. Seib, 178 Neb. 253, 132 N.W.2d 871 (1965); *State v. Veres,* 7 Ariz.App. 117, 436 P.2d 629 (1968); *Merrick v. United States Rubber Co.,* 7 Ariz.App. 433, 440 P.2d 314 (1968); Freed, Computer Print–Outs as Evidence, 16 Am.Jur.Proof of Facts 273; Symposium, Law and Computers in the Mid–Sixties, ALI–ABA (1966); 37 Albany L.Rev. 61 (1967). Example (9) does not, of course, foreclose taking judicial notice of the accuracy of the process or system.

Example (10). The example makes clear that methods of authentication provided by Act of Congress and by the Rules of Civil and Criminal Procedure or by Bankruptcy Rules are not intended to be superseded. Illustrative are the provisions for authentication of official records in Civil Procedure Rule 44 and Criminal Procedure Rule 27, for authentication of records of proceedings by court reporters in 28 U.S.C. § 753(b) and Civil Procedure Rule 80(c), and for authentication of depositions in Civil Procedure Rule 30(f).

CROSS REFERENCES

Authentication—

Acts of legislature of state, territory, or possession for evidence, see 28 USCA § 1738.

Consul, documents and papers in office for evidence, see 28 USCA § 1740.

Extradition proceedings, evidence, see 18 USCA § 3190.

Foreign documents, commission to consular officers to authenticate, see 18 USCA §§ 3492 to 3496.

Foreign documents, evidence, see 18 USCA §§ 3491 and 3492.

Foreign patent documents, etc., copies, evidence, see 28 USCA § 1745.

Foreign records, etc., copies, etc., as evidence, see 28 USCA § 1741.

Patent Office documents, evidence, see 28 USCA § 1744.

Plant Variety Protection Office, documents and certificates evidencing protection authenticated with seal of, see 7 USCA § 2322.

Postal Service, records of, seal used for, see 39 USCA § 207.

Records or books of state, territory, or possession for use as evidence, see 28 USCA § 1739.

Vice consul, documents and papers in office for evidence, see 28 USCA § 1740.

Court reporters, shorthand or mechanical recording, see 28 USCA § 753.

Depositions, certification and filing by officer, see Fed. Rules Civ.Proc. Rule 30, 28 USCA.

Handwriting, admitted or proved, see 28 USCA § 1731.

Official record, proof of, see Fed.Rules Cr.Proc. Rule 27, 18 USCA.

Proof of official record, authentication, see Fed.Rules Civ. Proc. Rule 44, 28 USCA.

Relevancy conditional on fact, see Fed.Rules Evid. Rule 104, 28 USCA.

Stenographic report or transcript as evidence, see Fed. Rules Civ.Proc. Rule 80, 28 USCA.

Rule 902. Self-authentication

Extrinsic evidence of authenticity as a condition precedent to admissibility is not required with respect to the following:

(1) Domestic public documents under seal. A document bearing a seal purporting to be that of the United States, or of any State, district, Commonwealth, territory, or insular possession thereof, or the Panama Canal Zone, or the Trust Territory of the Pacific Islands, or of a political subdivision, department, officer, or agency thereof, and a signature purporting to be an attestation or execution.

(2) Domestic public documents not under seal. A document purporting to bear the signature in the official capacity of an officer or employee of any entity included in paragraph (1) hereof, having no seal, if a public officer having a seal and having official duties in the district or political subdivision of the officer or employee certifies under seal that the signer has the official capacity and that the signature is genuine.

(3) Foreign public documents. A document purporting to be executed or attested in an official capacity by a person authorized by the laws of a foreign country to make the execution or attestation, and accompanied by a final certification as to the genuineness of the signature and official position (A) of the executing or attesting person, or (B) of any foreign official whose certificate of genuineness of signature and official position relates to the execution or attestation or is in a chain of certificates of genuineness of signature and official position relating to the execution or attestation. A final certification may be made by a secretary of an embassy or legation, consul general, consul, vice consul, or consular agent of the United States, or a diplomatic or consular official of the foreign country assigned or accredited to the United States. If reasonable opportunity has been given to all parties to investigate the authenticity and accuracy of official documents, the court may, for good cause shown, order that they be treated as presumptively authentic without final certification or permit them to be evidenced by an attested summary with or without final certification.

(4) Certified copies of public records. A copy of an official record or report or entry therein, or of a document authorized by law to be recorded or filed and actually recorded or filed in a public office, including data compilations in any form, certified as correct by the custodian or other person authorized to make the certification, by certificate complying with paragraph (1), (2), or (3) of this rule or complying with any Act of Congress or rule prescribed by the Supreme Court pursuant to statutory authority.

(5) Official publications. Books, pamphlets, or other publications purporting to be issued by public authority.

(6) Newspapers and periodicals. Printed materials purporting to be newspapers or periodicals.

(7) Trade inscriptions and the like. Inscriptions, signs, tags, or labels purporting to have been affixed in the course of business and indicating ownership, control, or origin.

(8) Acknowledged documents. Documents accompanied by a certificate of acknowledgment executed in the manner provided by law by a notary public or other officer authorized by law to take acknowledgments.

(9) Commercial paper and related documents. Commercial paper, signatures thereon, and documents relating thereto to the extent provided by general commercial law.

(10) Presumptions under Acts of Congress. Any signature, document, or other matter declared by Act of Congress to be presumptively or prima facie genuine or authentic.

(11) Certified Domestic Records of Regularly Conducted Activity.—The original or a duplicate of a domestic record of regularly conducted activity that would be admissible under Rule 803(6) if accompanied by a written declaration of its custodian or other qualified person, in a manner complying with any Act of Congress or rule prescribed by the Supreme Court pursuant to statutory authority, certifying that the record—

(A) was made at or near the time of the occurrence of the matters set forth by, or from information transmitted by, a person with knowledge of those matters;

(B) was kept in the course of the regularly conducted activity; and

(C) was made by the regularly conducted activity as a regular practice.

A party intending to offer a record into evidence under this paragraph must provide written notice of that intention to all adverse parties, and must make the record and declaration available for inspection sufficiently in advance of their offer into evidence to provide an adverse party with a fair opportunity to challenge them.

(12) Certified Foreign Records of Regularly Conducted Activity.—In a civil case, the original or a duplicate of a foreign record of regularly conducted activity that would be admissible under Rule 803(6) if accompanied by a written declaration by its custodian or other qualified person certifying that the record—

(A) was made at or near the time of the occurrence of the matters set forth by, or from information transmitted by, a person with knowledge of those matters;

(B) was kept in the course of the regularly conducted activity; and

(C) was made by the regularly conducted activity as a regular practice.

The declaration must be signed in a manner that, if falsely made, would subject the maker to criminal penalty under the laws of the country where the declaration is signed. A party intending to offer a record into evidence under this paragraph must provide written notice of that intention to all adverse parties, and must make the record and declaration available for inspection sufficiently in advance of their offer into evidence to provide an adverse party with a fair opportunity to challenge them.

(Pub.L. 93–595, § 1, Jan. 2, 1975, 88 Stat. 1944; Mar. 2, 1987, eff. Oct. 1, 1987; Apr. 25, 1988, eff. Nov. 1, 1988; Apr. 17, 2000, eff. Dec. 1, 2000.)

ADVISORY COMMITTEE NOTES

1972 Proposed Rules

Case law and statutes have, over the years, developed a substantial body of instances in which authenticity is taken as sufficiently established for purposes of admissibility without extrinsic evidence to that effect, sometimes for reasons of policy but perhaps more often because practical considerations reduce the possibility of unauthenticity to a very small dimension. The present rule collects and incorporates these situations, in some instances expanding them to occupy a larger area which their underlying considerations justify. In no instance is the opposite party foreclosed from disputing authenticity.

Note to Paragraph (1). The acceptance of documents bearing a public seal and signature, most often encountered in practice in the form of acknowledgments or certificates authenticating copies of public records, is actually of broad application. Whether theoretically based in whole or in part upon judicial notice, the practical underlying considerations are that forgery is a crime and detection is fairly easy and certain. 7 Wigmore § 2161, p. 638; California Evidence Code § 1452. More than 50 provisions for judicial notice of official seals are contained in the United States Code.

Note to Paragraph (2). While statutes are found which raise a presumption of genuineness of purported official signatures in the absence of an official seal, 7 Wigmore § 2167; California Evidence Code § 1453, the greater ease of effecting a forgery under these circumstances is apparent. Hence this paragraph of the rule calls for authentication by an officer who has a seal. Notarial acts by members of the armed forces and other special situations are covered in paragraph (10).

Note to Paragraph (3). Paragraph (3) provides a method for extending the presumption of authenticity to foreign official documents by a procedure of certification. It is derived from Rule 44(a)(2) of the Rules of Civil Procedure but is broader in applying to public documents rather than being limited to public records.

Note to Paragraph (4). The common law and innumerable statutes have recognized the procedure of authenticating copies of public records by certificate. The certificate qualifies as a public document, receivable as authentic when in conformity with paragraph (1), (2), or (3). Rule 44(a) of the Rules of Civil Procedure and Rule 27 of the Rules of Criminal Procedure have provided authentication procedures of this nature for both domestic and foreign public records. It will be observed that the certification procedure here provided extends only to public records, reports, and recorded documents, all including data compilations, and does not apply to public documents generally. Hence documents provable when presented in original form under paragraphs (1), (2), or (3) may not be provable by certified copy under paragraph (4).

Note to Paragraph (5). Dispensing with preliminary proof of the genuineness of purportedly official publications, most commonly encountered in connection with statutes, court reports, rules, and regulations, has been greatly enlarged by statutes and decisions. 5 Wigmore § 1684. Paragraph (5), it will be noted, does not confer admissibility upon all official publications; it merely provides a means whereby their authenticity may be taken as established for purposes of admissibility. Rule 44(a) of the Rules of Civil Procedure has been to the same effect.

Note to Paragraph (6). The likelihood of forgery of newspapers or periodicals is slight indeed. Hence no danger is apparent in receiving them. Establishing the authenticity of the publication may, of course, leave still open questions of authority and responsibility for items therein contained. See 7 Wigmore § 2150. Cf. 39 U.S.C. § 4005(b), public advertisement prima facie evidence of agency of person named, in postal fraud order proceeding; Canadian Uniform Evidence Act, Draft of 1936, printed copy of newspaper prima facie evidence that notices or advertisements were authorized.

Note to Paragraph (7). Several factors justify dispensing with preliminary proof of genuineness of commercial and mercantile labels and the like. The risk of forgery is minimal. Trademark infringement involves serious penalties. Great efforts are devoted to inducing the public to buy in reliance on brand names, and substantial protection is given them. Hence the fairness of this treatment finds recognition in the cases. *Curtiss Candy Co. v. Johnson,* 163 Miss. 426, 141 So. 762 (1932), Baby Ruth candy bar; *Doyle v. Continental Baking Co.,* 262 Mass. 516, 160 N.E. 325 (1928), loaf of bread; *Weiner v. Mager & Throne, Inc.,* 167 Misc. 338, 3 N.Y.S.2d 918 (1938), same. And see W.Va.Code 1966, § 47–3–5, trademark on bottle prima facie evidence of ownership. *Contra, Keegan v. Green Giant Co.,* 150 Me. 283, 110 A.2d 599 (1954); *Murphy v. Campbell Soup Co.,* 62 F.2d 564 (1st Cir.1933). Cattle brands have received similar acceptance in the western states. Rev.Code Mont.1947, § 46–606, *State v. Wolfley,* 75 Kan. 406, 89 P. 1046 (1907); Annot., 11 L.R.A.(N.S.) 87. Inscriptions on trains and vehicles are held to be prima facie evidence of ownership or control. *Pittsburgh, Ft. W. & C. Ry. v. Callaghan,* 157 Ill. 406, 41 N.E. 909 (1895); 9 Wigmore § 2510a. See also the provision of 19 U.S.C. § 1615(2) that marks, labels, brands, or stamps indicating foreign origin are prima facie evidence of foreign origin of merchandise.

Note to Paragraph (8). In virtually every state, acknowledged title documents are receivable in evidence without further proof. Statutes are collected in 5 Wigmore § 1676. If this authentication suffices for documents of the importance of those affecting titles, logic scarcely permits denying this method when other kinds of documents are involved. Instances of broadly inclusive statutes are California Evidence Code § 1451 and N.Y.CPLR 4538, McKinney's Consol.Laws 1963.

Note to Paragraph (9). Issues of the authenticity of commercial paper in federal courts will usually arise in diversity cases, will involve an element of a cause of action or defense, and with respect to presumptions and burden of proof will be controlled by *Erie Railroad Co. v. Tompkins,* 304 U.S. 64, 58 S.Ct. 817, 82 L.Ed. 1188 (1938). Rule 302, *supra.* There may, however, be questions of authenticity involving lesser segments of a case or the case may be one governed by federal common law. *Clearfield Trust Co. v. United States,* 318 U.S. 363, 63 S.Ct. 573, 87 L.Ed. 838 (1943). Cf. *United States v. Yazell,* 382 U.S. 341, 86 S.Ct. 500, 15 L.Ed.2d 404 (1966). In these situations, resort to the useful authentication provisions of the Uniform Commercial Code is provided for. While the phrasing is in terms of "general commercial law," in order to avoid the potential complications inherent in borrowing local statutes, today one would have difficulty in determining the general commercial law without referring to the Code. See *Williams v. Walker–Thomas Furniture Co.,* 121 U.S.App.D.C. 315, 350 F.2d 445 (1965). Pertinent Code provisions are sections 1–202, 3–307, and 3–510, dealing with third-party documents, signatures on negotiable instruments, protests, and statements of dishonor.

Note to Paragraph (10). The paragraph continues in effect dispensations with preliminary proof of genuineness provided in various Acts of Congress. See, for example, 10 U.S.C. § 936, signature, without seal, together with title, prima facie evidence of authenticity of acts of certain military personnel who are given notarial powers; 15 U.S.C. § 77f(a), signature on SEC registration presumed genuine; 26 U.S.C. § 6064, signature to tax return prima facie genuine.

1974 Enactment

Note to Paragraph (8). Rule 902(8) as submitted by the Court referred to certificates of acknowledgment "under the hand and seal of" a notary public or other officer authorized by law to take acknowledgments. The Committee amended the Rule to eliminate the requirement, believed to be inconsistent with the law in some States, that a notary public must affix a seal to a document acknowledged before him. As amended the Rule merely requires that the document be executed in the manner prescribed by State law.

Note to Paragraph (9). The Committee approved Rule 902(9) as submitted by the Court. With respect to the meaning of the phrase "general commercial law", the Committee intends that the Uniform Commercial Code, which has been adopted in virtually every State, will be followed generally, but that federal commercial law will apply where federal commercial paper is involved. See Clearfield Trust Co. v. United States, 318 U.S. 363 (1943). Further, in those instances in which the issues are governed by Erie R. Co. v. Tompkins, 304 U.S. 64 (1938), State law will apply irrespective of whether it is the Uniform Commercial Code. House Report No. 93–650.

1987 Amendments

The amendments are technical. No substantive change is intended.

1988 Amendments

These two sentences were inadvertently eliminated from the 1987 amendments. The amendment is technical. No substantive change is intended.

2000 Amendments

The amendment adds two new paragraphs to the rule on self-authentication. It sets forth a procedure by which parties can authenticate certain records of regularly conducted activity, other than through the testimony of a foundation witness. See the amendment to Rule 803(6). 18 U.S.C. § 3505 currently provides a means for certifying foreign records of regularly conducted activity in criminal cases, and this amendment is intended to establish a similar procedure for domestic records, and for foreign records offered in civil cases.

A declaration that satisfies 28 U.S.C. § 1746 would satisfy the declaration requirement of Rule 902(11), as would any comparable certification under oath.

The notice requirement in Rules 902(11) and (12) is intended to give the opponent of the evidence a full opportunity to test the adequacy of the foundation set forth in the declaration.

GAP Report—Proposed Amendment to Rule 902

The Committee made the following changes to the published draft of the proposed amendment to Evidence Rule 902:

1. Minor stylistic changes were made in the text, in accordance with suggestions of the Style Subcommittee of the Standing Committee on Rules of Practice and Procedure.

2. The phrase "in a manner complying with any Act of Congress or rule prescribed by the Supreme Court pursuant to statutory authority" was added to proposed Rule 902(11), to provide consistency with Evidence Rule 902(4). The Committee Note was amended to accord with this textual change.

3. Minor stylistic changes were made in the text to provide a uniform construction of the terms "declaration" and "certifying."

4. The notice provisions in the text were revised to clarify that the proponent must make both the declaration and the underlying record available for inspection.

CROSS REFERENCES

Acts of legislature of state, territory, or possession, see 28 USCA § 1738.

Armed forces, authority to administer oaths and to act as notary, see 10 USCA § 936.

Documents of Patent and Trademark Office, copies of, see 28 USCA §§ 1744 and 1745.

Forfeiture proceedings in custom actions, marks, labels, brands, stamps, as evidence, see 19 USCA § 1615.

Fraudulent and lottery matter, public advertisement that remittances may be made by mail as prima facie evidence, see 39 USCA § 3005.

Government records and papers, see 28 USCA § 1733.

Proof of official foreign record, see Fed.Rules Civ.Proc. Rule 44, 28 USCA.

Proof of official record, see Fed.Rules Cr.Proc. Rule 27, 18 USCA.

Public records, proof of, see Fed.Rules Evid. Rule 1005, 28 USCA.

Securities, signing of registration statements, see 15 USCA § 77f.

State law, applicability of in civil actions and proceedings, see Fed.Rules Evid. Rule 302, 28 USCA.

Tax returns, signature presumed authentic, see 26 USCA § 6064.

Rule 903. Subscribing Witness' Testimony Unnecessary

The testimony of a subscribing witness is not necessary to authenticate a writing unless required by the laws of the jurisdiction whose laws govern the validity of the writing.

(Pub.L. 93–595, § 1, Jan. 2, 1975, 88 Stat.1945.)

ADVISORY COMMITTEE NOTES

1972 Proposed Rules

The common law required that attesting witnesses be produced or accounted for. Today the requirement has generally been abolished except with respect to documents which must be attested to be valid, e.g. wills in some states. McCormick § 188. Uniform Rule 71; California Evidence Code § 1411; Kansas Code of Civil Procedure § 60–468; New Jersey Evidence Rule 71; New York CPLR Rule 4537.

ARTICLE X. CONTENTS OF WRITINGS, RECORDINGS AND PHOTOGRAPHS

Rule 1001. Definitions

For purposes of this article the following definitions are applicable:

(1) Writings and recordings. "Writings" and "recordings" consist of letters, words, or numbers, or their equivalent, set down by handwriting, typewriting, printing, photostating, photographing, magnetic impulse, mechanical or electronic recording, or other form of data compilation.

(2) Photographs. "Photographs" include still photographs, X-ray films, video tapes, and motion pictures.

(3) Original. An "original" of a writing or recording is the writing or recording itself or any counterpart intended to have the same effect by a person executing or issuing it. An "original" of a photograph includes the negative or any print therefrom. If data are stored in a computer or similar device, any printout or other output readable by sight, shown to reflect the data accurately, is an "original".

(4) Duplicate. A "duplicate" is a counterpart produced by the same impression as the original, or from the same matrix, or by means of photography, including enlargements and miniatures, or by mechanical or electronic re-recording, or by chemical reproduction, or by other equivalent techniques which accurately reproduces the original.

(Pub.L. 93–595, § 1, Jan. 2, 1975, 88 Stat. 1945.)

ADVISORY COMMITTEE NOTES

1972 Proposed Rules

In an earlier day, when discovery and other related procedures were strictly limited, the misleading named "best evidence rule" afforded substantial guarantees against inaccuracies and fraud by its insistence upon production or original documents. The great enlargement of the scope of discovery and related procedures in recent times has measurably reduced the need for the rule. Nevertheless important areas of usefulness persist: discovery of documents outside the jurisdiction may require substantial outlay of time and money; the unanticipated document may not practically be discoverable; criminal cases have built-in limitations on discovery. Cleary and Strong, The Best Evidence Rule: An Evaluation in Context, 51 Iowa L.Rev. 825 (1966).

Note to Paragraph (1). Traditionally the rule requiring the original centered upon accumulations of data and expressions affecting legal relations set forth in words and figures. this meant that the rule was one essentially related to writings. Present day techniques have expanded methods of storing data, yet the essential form which the information ultimately assumes for usable purposes is words and figures. Hence the considerations underlying the rule dictate its expansion to include computers, photographic systems, and other modern developments.

Note to Paragraph (3). In most instances, what is an original will be self-evident and further refinement will be unnecessary. However, in some instances particularized definition is required. A carbon copy of a contract executed in duplicate becomes an original, as does a sales ticket carbon copy given to a customer. While strictly speaking the original of a photograph might be thought to be only the negative, practicality and common usage require that any print from the negative be regarded as an original. Similarly, practicality and usage confer the status of original upon any computer printout. *Transport Indemnity Co. v. Seib*, 178 Neb. 253, 132 N.W.2d 871 (1965).

Note to Paragraph (4). The definition describes "copies" produced by methods possessing an accuracy which virtually eliminates the possibility of error. Copies thus produced are given the status of originals in large measure by Rule 1003, *infra.* Copies subsequently produced manually, whether handwritten or typed, are not within the definition. It should be noted that what is an original for some purposes may be a duplicate for others. Thus a bank's microfilm record of checks cleared is the original as a record. However, a print offered as a copy of a check whose contents are in controversy is a duplicate. This result is substantially consistent with 28 U.S.C. § 1732(b). Compare 26 U.S.C. § 7513(c), giving full status as originals to photographic reproductions of tax returns and other documents, made by authority of the Secretary of the Treasury, and 44 U.S.C. § 399(a), giving original status to photographic copies in the National Archives.

1974 Enactment

Note to Paragraph (2). The Committee amended this Rule expressly to include "video tapes" in the definition of "photographs." House Report No. 93–650.

CROSS REFERENCES

Copies of government records and papers, admissibility, see 28 USCA § 1733.

National archives, legal status of photographic copies as originals, see 44 USCA § 2116.

Records made in regular course of business, admissibility, see 28 USCA § 1732.

Rule 1002. Requirement of Original

To prove the content of a writing, recording, or photograph, the original writing, recording, or photograph is required, except as otherwise provided in these rules or by Act of Congress.

(Pub.L. 93–595, § 1, Jan. 2, 1975, 88 Stat. 1946.)

ADVISORY COMMITTEE NOTES

1972 Proposed Rules

The rule is the familiar one requiring production of the original of a document to prove its contents, expanded to include writings, recordings, and photographs, as defined in Rule 1001(1) and (2), *supra*.

Application of the rule requires a resolution of the question whether contents are sought to be proved. Thus an event may be proved by nondocumentary evidence, even though a written record of it was made. If, however, the event is sought to be proved by the written record, the rule applies. For example, payment may be proved without producing the written receipt which was given. Earnings may be proved without producing books of account in which they are entered. McCormick § 198; 4 Wigmore § 1245. Nor does the rule apply to testimony that books or records have been examined and found not to contain any reference to a designated matter.

The assumption should not be made that the rule will come into operation on every occasion when use is made of a photograph in evidence. On the contrary, the rule will seldom apply to ordinary photographs. In most instances a party *wishes* to introduce the item and the question raised is the propriety of receiving it in evidence. Cases in which an offer is made of the testimony of a witness as to what he saw in a photograph or motion picture, without producing the same, are most unusual. The usual course is for a witness on the stand to identify the photograph or motion picture as a correct representation of events which he saw or of a scene with which he is familiar. In fact he adopts the picture as his testimony, or, in common parlance, uses the picture to illustrate his testimony. Under these circumstances, no effort is made to prove the contents of the picture, and the rule is inapplicable. Paradis, The Celluloid Witness, 37 U.Colo. L.Rev. 235, 249–251 (1965).

On occasion, however, situations arise in which contents are sought to be proved. Copyright, defamation, and invasion of privacy by photograph or motion picture falls in this category. Similarly as to situations in which the picture is offered as having independent probative value, e.g. automatic photograph of bank robber. See *People v. Doggett,* 83 Cal.App.2d 405, 188 P.2d 792 (1948), photograph of defendants engaged in indecent act; Mouser and Philbin, Photographic Evidence—Is There a Recognized Basis for Admissibility? 8 Hastings L.J. 310 (1957). the most commonly encountered of this latter group is of course, the X ray, with substantial authority calling for production of the original. *Daniels v. Iowa City,* 191 Iowa 811, 183 N.W. 415 (1921); *Cellamare v. Third Acc. Transit Corp.*, 273 App.Div. 260, 77 N.Y.S.2d 91 (1948); *Patrick & Tilman v. Matkin,* 154 Okl. 232, 7 P.2d 414 (1932); *Mendoza v. Rivera,* 78 P.R.R. 569 (1955).

It should be noted, however, that Rule 703, *supra,* allows an expert to give an opinion based on matters not in evidence, and the present rule must be read as being limited accordingly in its application. Hospital records which may be admitted as business records under Rule 803(6) commonly contain reports interpreting X-rays by the staff radiologist, who qualifies as an expert, and these reports need not be excluded from the records by the instant rule.

The reference to Acts of Congress is made in view of such statutory provisions as 26 U.S.C. § 7513, photographic reproductions of tax returns and documents, made by authority of the Secretary of the Treasury, treated as originals, and 44 U.S.C. § 399(a), photographic copies in National Archives treated as originals.

CROSS REFERENCES

National archives, legal status of photographic copies as originals, see 44 USCA § 2116.

Rule 1003. Admissibility of Duplicates

A duplicate is admissible to the same extent as an original unless (1) a genuine question is raised as to the authenticity of the original or (2) in the circumstances it would be unfair to admit the duplicate in lieu of the original.

(Pub.L. 93–595, § 1, Jan. 2, 1975, 88 Stat. 1946.)

ADVISORY COMMITTEE NOTES

1972 Proposed Rules

When the only concern is with getting the words or other contents before the court with accuracy and precision, then a counterpart serves equally as well as the original, if the counterpart is the product of a method which insures accuracy and genuineness. By definition in Rule 1001(4), *supra,* a "duplicate" possesses this character.

Therefore, if no genuine issue exists as to authenticity and no other reason exists for requiring the original, a duplicate is admissible under the rule. This position finds support in the decisions, *Myrick v. United States,* 332 F.2d 279 (5th Cir.1964), no error in admitting photostatic copies of checks instead of original microfilm in absence of suggestion to trial judge that photostats were incorrect; *Johns v. United States,* 323 F.2d 421 (5th Cir.1963), not error to admit concededly accurate tape recording made from original wire recording; *Sauget v. Johnston,* 315 F.2d 816 (9th Cir.1963), not error to admit copy of agreement when opponent had original and did not on appeal claim any discrepancy. Other reasons for acquiring the original may be present when only a part of the original is reproduced and the remainder is needed for cross-examination or may disclose matters qualifying the part offered or otherwise useful to the opposing party. *United States v. Alexander,* 326 F.2d 736 (4th Cir. 1964). And see *Toho Bussan Kaisha, Ltd. v. American President Lines, Ltd.*, 265 F.2d 418, 76 A.L.R.2d 1344 (2d Cir.1959).

1974 Enactment

The Committee approved this Rule in the form submitted by the Court, with the expectation that the courts would be liberal in deciding that a "genuine question is raised as to the authenticity of the original." House Report No. 93–650.

Rule 1004. Admissibility of Other Evidence of Contents

The original is not required, and other evidence of the contents of a writing, recording, or photograph is admissible if—

(1) **Originals lost or destroyed.** All originals are lost or have been destroyed, unless the proponent lost or destroyed them in bad faith; or

(2) **Original not obtainable.** No original can be obtained by any available judicial process or procedure; or

(3) **Original in possession of opponent.** At a time when an original was under the control of the party against whom offered, that party was put on notice, by the pleadings or otherwise, that the contents would be a subject of proof at the hearing, and that party does not produce the original at the hearing; or

(4) **Collateral matters.** The writing, recording, or photograph is not closely related to a controlling issue.

(Pub.L. 93–595, § 1, Jan. 2, 1975, 88 Stat. 1946; Mar. 2, 1987, eff. Oct. 1, 1987.)

ADVISORY COMMITTEE NOTES

1972 Proposed Rules

Basically the rule requiring the production of the original as proof of contents has developed as a rule of preference: if failure to produce the original is satisfactorily explained, secondary evidence is admissible. The instant rule specifies the circumstances under which production of the original is excused.

The rule recognizes no "degrees" of secondary evidence. While strict logic might call for extending the principle of preference beyond simply preferring the original, the formulation of a hierarchy of preferences and a procedure for making it effective is believed to involve unwarranted complexities. Most, if not all, that would be accomplished by an extended scheme of preferences will, in any event, be achieved through the normal motivation of a party to present the most convincing evidence possible and the arguments and procedures available to his opponent if he does not. Compare McCormick § 207.

Note to Paragraph (1). Loss or destruction of the original, unless due to bad faith of the proponent, is a satisfactory explanation of nonproduction. McCormick § 201.

Note to Paragraph (2). When the original is in the possession of a third person, inability to procure it from him by resort to process or other judicial procedure is a sufficient explanation of nonproduction. Judicial procedure includes subpoena duces tecum as an incident to the taking of a deposition in another jurisdiction. No further showing is required. See McCormick § 202.

Note to Paragraph (3). A party who has an original in his control has no need for the protection of the rule if put on notice that proof of contents will be made. He can ward off secondary evidence by offering the original. The notice procedure here provided is not to be confused with orders to produce or other discovery procedures, as the purpose of the procedure under this rule is to afford the opposite party an opportunity to produce the original, not to compel him to do so. McCormick § 203.

Note to Paragraph (4). While difficult to define with precision, situations arise in which no good purpose is served by production of the original. Examples are the newspaper in an action for the price of publishing defendant's advertisement, *Foster–Holcomb Investment Co. v. Little Rock Publishing Co.*, 151 Ark. 449, 236 S.W. 597 (1922), and the streetcar transfer of plaintiff claiming status as a passenger, *Chicago City Ry. Co. v. Carroll*, 206 Ill. 318, 68 N.E. 1087 (1903). Numerous cases are collected in McCormick § 200, p. 412, n. 1.

1974 Enactment

Note to Paragraph (1). The Committee approved Rule 1004(1) in the form submitted to Congress. However, the Committee intends that loss or destruction of an original by another person at the instigation of the proponent should be considered as tantamount to loss or destruction in bad faith by the proponent himself. House Report No. 93–650.

1987 Amendments

The amendments are technical. No substantive change is intended.

Rule 1005. Public Records

The contents of an official record, or of a document authorized to be recorded or filed and actually recorded or filed, including data compilations in any form, if otherwise admissible, may be proved by copy, certified as correct in accordance with rule 902 or testified to be correct by a witness who has compared it with the original. If a copy which complies with the foregoing cannot be obtained by the exercise of reasonable diligence, then other evidence of the contents may be given.

(Pub.L. 93–595, § 1, Jan. 2, 1975, 88 Stat. 1946.)

ADVISORY COMMITTEE NOTES

1972 Proposed Rules

Public records call for somewhat different treatment. Removing them from their usual place of keeping would be attended by serious inconvenience to the public and to the custodian. As a consequence judicial decisions and statutes commonly hold that no explanation need be given for failure to produce the original of a public record. McCormick § 204; 4 Wigmore §§ 1215–1228. This blanket dispensation from producing or accounting for the original would open the door to the introduction of every kind of secondary evidence of contents of public records were it not for the preference given certified or compared copies. Recognition of degrees of secondary evidence in this situation is an appropriate *quid pro quo* for not applying the requirement of producing the original.

The provisions of 28 U.S.C. § 1733(b) apply only to departments or agencies of the United States. The rule, however, applies to public records generally and is comparable in scope in this respect to Rule 44(a) of the Rules of Civil Procedure.

CROSS REFERENCES

Code and supplements to Code of Laws of United States, and District of Columbia, prima facie evidence of original, see 1 USCA § 204.

Government records and papers, admissibility of authenticated copies or transcripts, see 28 USCA § 1733.

Proof of official domestic records, see Fed.Rules Civ.Proc. Rule 44, 28 USCA.

Statutes at large, admissibility in evidence, see 1 USCA § 112.

Treaties, public acts, etc., admissibility in evidence, see 1 USCA § 113.

Rule 1006. Summaries

The contents of voluminous writings, recordings, or photographs which cannot conveniently be examined in court may be presented in the form of a chart, summary, or calculation. The originals, or duplicates, shall be made available for examination or copying, or both, by other parties at reasonable time and place. The court may order that they be produced in court.

(Pub.L. 93–595, § 1, Jan. 2, 1975, 88 Stat. 1946.)

ADVISORY COMMITTEE NOTES

1972 Proposed Rules

The admission of summaries of voluminous books, records, or documents offers the only practicable means of making their contents available to judge and jury. The rule recognizes this practice, with appropriate safeguards. 4 Wigmore § 1230.

Rule 1007. Testimony or Written Admission of Party

Contents of writings, recordings, or photographs may be proved by the testimony or deposition of the party against whom offered or by that party's written admission, without accounting for the nonproduction of the original.

(Pub.L. 93–595, § 1, Jan. 2, 1975, 88 Stat. 1947; Mar. 2, 1987, eff. Oct. 1, 1987.)

ADVISORY COMMITTEE NOTES

1972 Proposed Rules

While the parent case, *Slatterie v. Pooley,* 6 M. & W. 664, 151 Eng.Rep. 579 (Exch.1840), allows proof of contents by evidence of an oral admission by the party against whom offered, without accounting for nonproduction of the original, the risk of inaccuracy is substantial and the decision is at odds with the purpose of the rule giving preference to the original. See 4 Wigmore § 1255. The instant rule follows Professor McCormick's suggestion of limiting this use of admissions to those made in the course of giving testimony or in writing. McCormick § 208, p. 424. The limitation, of course, does not call for excluding evidence of an oral admission when nonproduction of the original has been accounted for and secondary evidence generally has become admissible. Rule 1004, supra.

A similar provision is contained in New Jersey Evidence Rule 70(1)(h).

1987 Amendments

The amendment is technical. No substantive change is intended.

CROSS REFERENCES

Depositions, see Fed.Rules Cr.Proc. Rule 15, 18 USCA.

Depositions and discovery, see Fed.Rules Civ.Proc. Rule 26 et seq., 28 USCA.

Rule 1008. Functions of Court and Jury

When the admissibility of other evidence of contents of writings, recordings, or photographs under these rules depends upon the fulfillment of a condition of fact, the question whether the condition has been fulfilled is ordinarily for the court to determine in accordance with the provisions of rule 104. However, when an issue is raised (a) whether the asserted writing ever existed, or (b) whether another writing, recording, or photograph produced at the trial is the original, or (c) whether other evidence of contents correctly reflects the contents, the issue is for the trier of fact to determine as in the case of other issues of fact.

(Pub.L. 93–595, § 1, Jan. 2, 1975, 88 Stat. 1947.)

ADVISORY COMMITTEE NOTES

1972 Proposed Rules

Most preliminary questions of fact in connection with applying the rule preferring the original as evidence of contents are for the judge, under the general principles announced in Rule 104, *supra.* Thus, the question whether the loss of the originals has been established, or of the fulfillment of other conditions specified in Rule 1004, supra, is for the judge. However, questions may arise which go beyond the mere administration of the rule preferring the original and into the merits of the controversy. For example, plaintiff offers secondary evidence of the contents of an alleged contract, after first introducing evidence of loss of the original, and defendant counters with evidence that no such contract was ever executed. If the judge decides that the contract was never executed and excludes the secondary evidence, the case is at an end without ever going to the jury on a central issue. Levin, Authentication and Content of Writings, 10 Rutgers L.Rev. 632, 644 (1956). The latter portion of the instant rule is designed to insure treatment of these situations as raising jury questions. The decision is not one for uncontrolled discretion of the jury but is subject to the control exercised generally by the judge over jury determinations. See Rule 104(b), *supra.*

For similar provisions, see Uniform Rule 70(2); Kansas Code of Civil Procedure § 60–467(b); New Jersey Evidence Rule 70(2), (3).

ARTICLE XI. MISCELLANEOUS RULES

Rule 1101. Applicability of Rules

(a) Courts and judges. These rules apply to the United States district courts, the District Court of Guam, the District Court of the Virgin Islands, the District Court for the Northern Mariana Islands, the United States courts of appeals, the United States Claims Court, and to United States bankruptcy judges and United States magistrate judges, in the actions, cases, and proceedings and to the extent hereinafter set forth. The terms "judge" and "court" in these rules include United States bankruptcy judges and United States magistrate judges.

(b) Proceedings generally. These rules apply generally to civil actions and proceedings, including admiralty and maritime cases, to criminal cases and proceedings, to contempt proceedings except those in which the court may act summarily, and to proceedings and cases under title 11, United States Code.

(c) Rule of privilege. The rule with respect to privileges applies at all stages of all actions, cases, and proceedings.

(d) Rules inapplicable. The rules (other than with respect to privileges) do not apply in the following situations:

(1) Preliminary questions of fact. The determination of questions of fact preliminary to admissibility of evidence when the issue is to be determined by the court under rule 104.

(2) Grand jury. Proceedings before grand juries.

(3) Miscellaneous proceedings. Proceedings for extradition or rendition; preliminary examinations in criminal cases; sentencing, or granting or revoking probation; issuance of warrants for arrest, criminal summonses, and search warrants; and proceedings with respect to release on bail or otherwise.

(e) Rules applicable in part. In the following proceedings these rules apply to the extent that matters of evidence are not provided for in the statutes which govern procedure therein or in other rules prescribed by the Supreme Court pursuant to statutory authority: the trial of misdemeanors and other petty offenses before United States magistrate judges; review of agency actions when the facts are subject to trial de novo under section 706(2)(F) of title 5, United States Code; review of orders of the Secretary of Agriculture under section 2 of the Act entitled "An Act to authorize association of producers of agricultural products" approved February 18, 1922 (7 U.S.C. 292), and under sections 6 and 7(c) of the Perishable Agricultural Commodities Act, 1930 (7 U.S.C. 499f, 499g(c)); naturalization and revocation of naturalization under sections 310–318 of the Immigration and Nationality Act (8 U.S.C. 1421–1429); prize proceedings in admiralty under sections 7651–7681 of title 10, United States Code; review of orders of the Secretary of the Interior under section 2 of the Act entitled "An Act authorizing associations of producers of aquatic products" approved June 25, 1934 (15 U.S.C. 522); review of orders of petroleum control boards under section 5 of the Act entitled "An Act to regulate interstate and foreign commerce in petroleum and its products by prohibiting the shipment in such commerce of petroleum and its products produced in violation of State law, and for other purposes", approved February 22, 1935 (15 U.S.C. 715d); actions for fines, penalties, or forfeitures under part V of title IV of the Tariff Act of 1930 (19 U.S.C. 1581–1624), or under the Anti–Smuggling Act (19 U.S.C. 1701–1711); criminal libel for condemnation, exclusion of imports, or other proceedings under the Federal Food, Drug, and Cosmetic Act (21 U.S.C. 301–392); disputes between seamen under sections 4079, 4080, and 4081 of the Revised Statutes (22 U.S.C. 256–258); habeas corpus under sections 2241–2254 of title 28, United States Code; motions to vacate, set aside or correct sentence under section 2255 of title 28, United States Code; actions for penalties for refusal to transport destitute seamen under section 4578 of the Revised Statutes (46 U.S.C. 679); actions against the United States under the Act entitled "An Act authorizing suits against the United States in admiralty for damage caused by and salvage service rendered to public vessels belonging to the United States, and for other purposes", approved March 3, 1925 (46 U.S.C. 781–790), as implemented by section 7730 of title 10, United States Code.

(Pub.L. 93–595, § 1, Jan. 2, 1975, 88 Stat. 1947; Pub.L. 94–149, § 1(14), Dec. 12, 1975, 89 Stat. 806; Pub.L. 95–598, Title II, § 251, Nov. 6, 1978, 92 Stat. 2673; Pub.L. 97–164, Title I, § 142, Apr. 2, 1982, 96 Stat. 45; Mar. 2, 1987, eff. Oct. 1, 1987; Apr. 25, 1988, eff. Nov. 1, 1988; Pub.L. 100–690, Title VII, § 7075(c), Nov. 18, 1988, 102 Stat. 4405; Apr. 22, 1993, eff. Dec. 1, 1993.)

ADVISORY COMMITTEE NOTES

1972 Proposed Rules

Note to Subdivision (a). The various enabling acts contain differences in phraseology in their descriptions of the courts over which the Supreme Court's power to make rules of practice and procedure extends. The act concerning civil actions, as amended in 1966, refers to "the district courts * * * of the United States in civil actions, including admiralty and maritime cases. * * *" 28 U.S.C. § 2072, Pub.L. 89–773, § 1, 80 Stat. 1323. The bankruptcy authorization is for rules of practice and procedure "under the Bankruptcy Act." 28 U.S.C. § 2075, Pub.L. 88–623, § 1, 78 Stat. 1001. The Bankruptcy Act in turn creates bankruptcy courts of "the United States district courts and the district courts of the Territories and possessions to which this title is or may hereafter be applicable." 11 U.S.C. §§ 1(10), 11(a). The provision as to criminal rules up to and including verdicts applies to "criminal cases and proceedings to punish for criminal contempt of court in the United States district courts, in the district courts for the districts of the Canal Zone and Virgin Islands, in the Supreme Court of Puerto Rico, and in proceedings before United States magistrates." 18 U.S.C. § 3771.

These various provisions do not in terms describe the same courts. In congressional usage the phrase "district courts of the United States," without further qualification, traditionally has included the district courts established by Congress in the states under Article III of the Constitution, which are "constitutional" courts, and has not included the territorial courts created under Article IV, Section 3, clause 2, which are "legislative" courts. *Hornbuckle v. Toombs*, 85 U.S. 648, 21 L.Ed. 966 (1873). However, any doubt as to the inclusion of the District Court for the District of Columbia in the phrase is laid at rest by the provisions of the Judicial Code constituting the judicial districts, 28 U.S.C. § 81 et seq., creating district courts therein, id. § 132, and specifically providing that the term "district court of the United States" means the court so constituted. *Id.* § 451. The District of Columbia is included. *Id.* § 88. Moreover, when these provisions were enacted, reference to the District of Columbia was deleted from the original civil rules enabling act. 28 U.S.C. § 2072. Likewise Puerto Rico is made a district, with a district court, and included in the term. *Id.* § 119. The question is simply one of the extent of the authority conferred by Congress. With respect to civil rules it seems clearly to include the district courts in the states, the District Court for the District of Columbia, and the District Court for the District of Puerto Rico.

The bankruptcy coverage is broader. The bankruptcy courts include "the United States district courts," which includes those enumerated above. Bankruptcy courts also include "the district courts of the Territories and possessions to which this title is or may hereafter be applicable." 11 U.S.C. §§ 1(10), 11(a). These courts include the district courts of Guam and the Virgin Islands. 48 U.S.C. §§ 1424(b), 1615. Professor Moore points out that whether the District Court for the District of the Canal Zone is a court of bankruptcy "is not free from doubt in view of the fact that no other statute expressly or inferentially provides for the applicability of the Bankruptcy Act in the Zone." He further observes that while there seems to be little doubt that the Zone is a territory or possession within the meaning of the Bankruptcy Act, 11 U.S.C. § 1(10), it must be noted that the appendix to the Canal Zone Code of 1934 did not list the Act among the laws of the United States applicable to the Zone. 1 Moore's Collier on Bankruptcy ¶ 1.10, pp. 67, 72, n. 25 (14th ed. 1967). The Code of 1962 confers on the district court jurisdiction of:

"(4) actions and proceedings involving laws of the United States applicable to the Canal Zone; and

"(5) other matters and proceedings wherein jurisdiction is conferred by this Code or any other law." Canal Zone Code, 1962, Title 3, § 141.

Admiralty jurisdiction is expressly conferred. *Id.* § 142. General powers are conferred on the district court, "if the course of proceeding is not specifically prescribed by this Code, by the statute, or by applicable rule of the Supreme Court of the United States * * *" *Id.* § 279. Neither these provisions nor § 1(10) of the Bankruptcy Act ("district courts of the Territories and possessions to which this title is or may hereafter be applicable") furnishes a satisfactory answer as to the status of the District Court for the District of the Canal Zone as a court of bankruptcy. However, the fact is that this court exercises no bankruptcy jurisdiction in practice.

The criminal rules enabling act specified United States district courts, district courts for the districts of the Canal Zone and the Virgin Islands, the Supreme Court of the Commonwealth of Puerto Rico, and proceedings before United States commissioners. Aside from the addition of commissioners, now magistrates, this scheme differs from the bankruptcy pattern in that it makes no mention of the District Court of Guam but by specific mention removes the Canal Zone from the doubtful list.

The further difference in including the Supreme Court of the Commonwealth of Puerto Rico seems not to be significant for present purposes, since the Supreme Court of the Commonwealth of Puerto Rico is an appellate court. The Rules of Criminal Procedure have not been made applicable to it, as being unneeded and inappropriate, Rule 54(a) of the Federal Rules of Criminal Procedure, and the same approach is indicated with respect to rules of evidence.

If one were to stop at this point and frame a rule governing the applicability of the proposed rules of evidence in terms of the authority conferred by the three enabling acts, an irregular pattern would emerge as follows:

Civil actions, including admiralty and maritime cases—district courts in the states, District of Columbia, and Puerto Rico.

Bankruptcy—same as civil actions, plus Guam and Virgin Islands.

Criminal cases—same as civil actions, plus Canal Zone and Virgin Islands (but not Guam).

This irregular pattern need not, however, be accepted. Originally the Advisory Committee on the Rules of Civil Procedure took the position that, although the phrase "district courts of the United States" did not include territorial courts, provisions in the organic laws of Puerto Rico and Hawaii would make the rules applicable to the district courts thereof, though this would not be so as to Alaska, the Virgin Islands, or the Canal Zone, whose organic acts contained no corresponding provisions. At the suggestion of the Court, however, the Advisory Committee struck from its notes a statement to the above effect. 2 Moore's Federal Practice ¶ 1.07 (2nd ed. 1967); 1 Barron and Holtzoff, Federal Practice and Procedure § 121 (Wright ed. 1960). Congress thereafter by various enactments provided that the rules and future amendments thereto should apply to the district courts of Hawaii, 53 Stat. 841 (1939), Puerto Rico, 54 Stat. 22 (1940), Alaska, 63 Stat. 445 (1949), Guam, 64 Stat. 384–390 (1950), and the Virgin Islands, 68 Stat. 497, 507 (1954). The original enabling act for rules of criminal procedure specifically mentioned the district courts of the Canal Zone and the Virgin Islands. The Commonwealth of Puerto Rico was blanketed in by creating its court a "district court of the United States" as previously described. Although Guam is not mentioned in either the enabling act or in the expanded definition of "district court of the United States," the Supreme Court in 1956 amended Rule 54(a) to state that the Rules of Criminal Procedure are applicable in Guam. The Court took this step following the enactment of legislation by Congress in 1950 that rules theretofore or thereafter promulgated by the Court in civil cases, admiralty, criminal cases and bankruptcy should apply to the District Court of Guam, 48 U.S.C. § 1424(b), and two Ninth Circuit decisions upholding the applicability of the Rules of Criminal Procedure to Guam. *Pugh v. United States*, 212 F.2d 761 (9th Cir.1954); *Hatchett v. Guam*, 212 F.2d 767 (9th Cir.1954); Orfield, The Scope of the Federal Rules of Criminal Procedure, 38 U. of Det.L.J. 173, 187 (1960).

From this history, the reasonable conclusion is that Congressional enactment of a provision that rules and future amendments shall apply in the courts of a territory or possession is the equivalent of mention in an enabling act and that a rule on scope and applicability may properly be drafted accordingly. Therefore the pattern set by Rule 54 of the Federal Rules of Criminal Procedure is here followed.

The substitution of magistrates in lieu of commissioners is made in pursuance of the Federal Magistrates Act, P.L. 90–578, approved October 17, 1968, 82 Stat. 1107.

Note to Subdivision (b). Subdivision (b) is a combination of the language of the enabling acts, supra, with respect to the kinds of proceedings in which the making of rules is authorized. It is subject to the qualifications expressed in the subdivisions which follow.

Note to Subdivision (c). Subdivision (c) singling out the rules of privilege for special treatment, is made necessary by the limited applicability of the remaining rules.

Note to Subdivision (d). The rule is not intended as an expression as to when due process or other constitutional provisions may require an evidentiary hearing. Paragraph (1) restates, for convenience, the provisions of the second sentence of Rule 104(a), *supra*. See Advisory Committee's Note to that rule.

(2) While some states have statutory requirements that indictments be based on "legal evidence," and there is some case law to the effect that the rules of evidence apply to grand jury proceedings, 1 Wigmore § 4(5), the Supreme Court has not accepted this view. In *Costello v. United States*, 350 U.S. 359, 76 S.Ct. 406, 100 L.Ed. 397 (1965), the Court refused to allow an indictment to be attacked, for either constitutional or policy reasons, on the ground that only hearsay evidence was presented.

"It would run counter to the whole history of the grand jury institution, in which laymen conduct their inquiries unfettered by technical rules. Neither justice nor the concept of a fair trial requires such a change." *Id.* at 364. The rule as drafted does not deal with the evidence required to support an indictment.

(3) The rule exempts preliminary examinations in criminal cases. Authority as to the applicability of the rules of evidence to preliminary examinations has been meagre and conflicting. Goldstein, The State and the Accused: Balance of Advantage in Criminal Procedure, 69 Yale L.J. 1149, 1168, n. 53 (1960); Comment, Preliminary Hearings on Indictable Offenses in Philadelphia, 106 U. of Pa.L.Rev. 589, 592–593 (1958). Hearsay testimony is, however, customarily received in such examinations. Thus in a Dyer Act case, for example, an affidavit may properly be used in a preliminary examination to prove ownership of the stolen vehicle, thus saving the victim of the crime the hardship of having to travel twice to a distant district for the sole purpose of testifying as to ownership. It is believed that the extent of the applicability of the Rules of Evidence to preliminary examinations should be appropriately dealt with by the Federal Rules of Criminal Procedure which regulate those proceedings.

Extradition and rendition proceedings are governed in detail by statute. 18 U.S.C. §§ 3181–3195. They are essentially administrative in character. Traditionally the rules of evidence have not applied. 1 Wigmore § 4(6). Extradition proceedings are accepted from the operation of the Rules of Criminal Procedure. Rule 54(b)(5) of Federal Rules of Criminal Procedure.

The rules of evidence have not been regarded as applicable to sentencing or probation proceedings, where great reliance is placed upon the presentence investigation and report. Rule 32(c) of the Federal Rules of Criminal Procedure requires a presentence investigation and report in every case unless the court otherwise directs. In *Williams v. New York*, 337 U.S. 241, 69 S.Ct. 1079, 93 L.Ed. 1337 (1949), in which the judge overruled a jury recommendation of life imprisonment and imposed a death sentence, the Court said that due process does not require confrontation or cross-examination in sentencing or passing on probation, and that the judge has broad discretion as to the sources and types of information relied upon. Compare the recommendation that the substance of all derogatory information be disclosed to the defendant, in A.B.A. Project on Minimum Standards for Criminal Justice, Sentencing Alternatives and Procedures § 4.4, Tentative Draft (1967, Sobeloff, Chm.). Williams was adhered to in *Specht v. Patterson*, 386 U.S. 605, 87 S.Ct. 1209, 18 L.Ed.2d 326 (1967), but not extended to a proceeding under the Colorado Sex Offenders Act, which was said to be a new charge leading in effect to punishment, more like the recidivist statutes where opportunity must be given to be heard on the habitual criminal issue.

Warrants for arrest, criminal summonses, and search warrants are issued upon complaint or affidavit showing probable cause. Rules 4(a) and 41(c) of the Federal Rules of Criminal Procedure. The nature of the proceedings makes application of the formal rules of evidence inappropriate and impracticable.

Criminal contempts are punishable summarily if the judge certifies that he saw or heard the contempt and that it was committed in the presence of the court. Rule 42(a) of the Federal Rules of Criminal Procedure. The circumstances which preclude application of the rules of evidence in this situation are not present, however, in other cases of criminal contempt.

Proceedings with respect to release on bail or otherwise do not call for application of the rules of evidence. The governing statute specifically provides:

"Information stated in, or offered in connection with, any order entered pursuant to this section need not conform to the rules pertaining to the admissibility of evidence in a court of law." 18 U.S.C.A. § 3146(f). This provision is consistent with the type of inquiry contemplated in A.B.A. Project on

Minimum Standards for Criminal Justice, Standards Relating to Pretrial Release, § 4.5(b), (c), p. 16 (1968). The references to the weight of the evidence against the accused, in Rule 46(a)(1), (c) of the Federal Rules of Criminal Procedure and in 18 U.S.C.A. § 3146(b), as a factor to be considered, clearly do not have in view evidence introduced at a hearing under the rules of evidence.

The rule does not exempt habeas corpus proceedings. The Supreme Court held in *Walker v. Johnston,* 312 U.S. 275, 61 S.Ct. 574, 85 L.Ed. 830 (1941), that the practice of disposing of matters of fact on affidavit, which prevailed in some circuits, did not "satisfy the command of the statute that the judge shall proceed 'to determine the facts of the case, by hearing the testimony and arguments.' " This view accords with the emphasis in *Townsend v. Sain,* 372 U.S. 293, 83 S.Ct. 745, 9 L.Ed.2d 770 (1963), upon trial-type proceedings, *id.* 311, 83 S.Ct. 745, with demeanor evidence as a significant factor, *id.* 322, 83 S.Ct. 745, in applications by state prisoners aggrieved by unconstitutional detentions. Hence subdivision (3) applies the rules to habeas corpus proceedings to the extent not inconsistent with the statute.

Note to Subdivision (e). In a substantial number of special proceedings, *ad hoc* evaluation has resulted in the promulgation of particularized evidentiary provisions, by Act of Congress or by rule adopted by the Supreme Court. Well adapted to the particular proceedings, though not apt candidates for inclusion in a set of general rules, they are left undisturbed. Otherwise, however, the rules of evidence are applicable to the proceedings enumerated in the subdivision.

1974 Enactment

Note to Subdivision (a). Subdivision (a) as submitted to the Congress, in stating the courts and judges to which the Rules of Evidence apply, omitted the Court of Claims and commissioners of that Court. At the request of the Court of Claims, the Committee amended the Rule to include the Court and its commissioners within the purview of the Rules.

Note to Subdivision (b). Subdivision (b) was amended merely to substitute positive law citations for those which were not. House Report No. 93–650.

1987 Amendments

Subdivision (a) is amended to delete the reference to the District Court for the District of the Canal Zone, which no longer exists, and to add the District Court for the Northern Mariana Islands. The United States bankruptcy judges are added to conform the subdivision with Rule 1101(b) and Bankruptcy Rule 9017.

1988 Amendments

The amendments are technical. No substantive change is intended.

1993 Amendments

This revision is made to conform the rule to changes in terminology made by Rule 58 of the Federal Rules of Criminal Procedure and to the changes in the title of United States magistrates made by the Judicial Improvements Act of 1990.

HISTORICAL NOTES

Revision Notes and Legislative Reports

1975 Acts. House Report No. 94–599, see 1975 U.S. Code Cong. and Adm. News, p. 1585.

1982 Acts. Senate Report No. 97–275, see 1982 U.S. Code Cong. and Adm. News, p. 11.

References in Text

The Tariff Act of 1930, referred to in subsec. (e), is Act June 17, 1930, c. 497, 46 Stat. 590, as amended, which is classified principally to chapter 4 (section 1202 et seq.) of Title 19, Customs Duties. Part V of Title IV of the Tariff Act of 1930 enacted part V (section 1581 et seq.) of subtitle III of chapter 4 of Title 19. For complete classification of this Act to the Code, see section 1654 of Title 19 and Tables.

The Anti–Smuggling Act (19 U.S.C. 1701–1711), referred to in subsec. (e), is Act Aug. 5, 1935, c. 438, 49 Stat. 517, as amended, which is classified principally to chapter 5 (section 1701 et seq.) of Title 19, Customs Duties. For complete classification of this Act to the Code, see section 1711 of Title 19 and Tables.

The Federal Food, Drug, and Cosmetic Act (21 U.S.C. 301–392), referred to in subsec. (e), is Act June 25, 1938, c. 675, 52 Stat. 1040, as amended, which is classified generally to chapter 9 (section 301 et seq.) of Title 21, Food and Drugs. For complete classification of this Act to the Code, see section 301 of Title 21 and Tables.

"An Act authorizing suits against the United States in admiralty for damage caused by and salvage service rendered to public vessels belonging to the United States, and for other purposes," approved Mar. 3, 1925 (46 U.S.C. 781–790), referred to in subsec. (e), is Act Mar. 3, 1925, c. 428, 43 Stat. 1112, as amended, known as the "Public Vessels Act", which is classified generally to chapter 22 (section 781 et seq.) of Title 46, Shipping. For complete classification of this Act to the Code, see Short Title note set out under section 781 of Title 46 and Tables.

Effective and Applicability Provisions

1982 Acts. Amendment by Pub.L. 97–164 effective Oct. 1, 1982, see section 402 of Pub.L. 97–164, set out as a note under section 171 of this title.

1978 Acts. Amendment of subds. (a) and (b) of this rule by section 251 of Pub.L. 95–598 effective Oct. 1, 1979, see section 402(c) of Pub.L. 95–598, set out as a note preceding section 101 of Title 11, Bankruptcy.

Change of Name

United States magistrate appointed under section 631 of Title 28, Judiciary and Judicial Procedure, to be known as United States magistrate judge after Dec. 1, 1990, with any reference to United States magistrate or magistrate in Title 28, in any other Federal statute, etc., deemed a reference to United States magistrate judge appointed under section 631 of Title 28, see section 321 of Pub.L. 101–650, set out as a note under section 631 of Title 28.

Pending Actions

Amendments of Supreme Court to the Federal Rules of Evidence effective December 1, 1993, applicable, insofar as just and practicable, in all proceedings then pending, pursuant to the Order of April 22, 1993.

CROSS REFERENCES

Applicability of rules to all criminal proceedings in United States district courts, see Fed.Rules Cr.Proc. Rule 54, 18 USCA.

Bankruptcy—

Rules, power of Supreme Court to prescribe, see 28 USCA § 2075.

District courts—

Creation and composition of, see 28 USCA § 132.

Guam, applicability of rules to, see 48 USCA § 1424.

Northern Mariana Islands, applicability of rules to, see 48 USCA § 1821.

Supreme court, power to prescribe rules of procedure, see 28 USCA § 2072.

Territorial composition, see 28 USCA § 81 et seq.

Virgin Islands, applicability of rules to, see 48 USCA § 1614.

Extradition, see 18 USCA § 3181 et seq.

General provisions applicable to courts and judges, see 28 USCA § 451 et seq.

Judicial power, tenure, and compensation, generally, see USCA Const. Art. III, § 1.

Scope of rules, see Fed.Rules Evid. Rule 101, 28 USCA.

Rule 1102. Amendments

Amendments to the Federal Rules of Evidence may be made as provided in section 2072 of title 28 of the United States Code.

(Pub.L. 93–595, § 1, Jan. 2, 1975, 88 Stat.1948); Apr. 30, 1991, eff. Dec. 1, 1991.)

ADVISORY COMMITTEE NOTES

1991 Amendments

The amendment is technical. No substantive change is intended.

Rule 1103. Title

These rules may be known and cited as the Federal Rules of Evidence.

(Pub.L. 93–595, § 1, Jan. 2, 1975, 88 Stat.1948.)

HISTORICAL NOTES

Short Title

1978 Amendments. Pub.L. 95–540, § 1, Oct. 28, 1978, 92 Stat. 2046, provided: "That this Act [enacting rule 412 of these rules and a provision set out as a note under rule 412 of these rules] may be cited as the 'Privacy Protection for Rape Victims Act of 1978'."

SELECTED FEDERAL RULES OF APPELLATE PROCEDURE

Amendments received to December 1, 2008

Rule 1. Scope of Rules; Title

(a) Scope of Rules.

(1) These rules govern procedure in the United States courts of appeals.

(2) When these rules provide for filing a motion or other document in the district court, the procedure must comply with the practice of the district court.

(b) [Abrogated]

(c) Title. These rules are to be known as the Federal Rules of Appellate Procedure.

(As amended Apr. 30, 1979, eff. Aug. 1, 1979; Apr. 25, 1989, eff. Dec. 1, 1989; Apr. 29, 1994, eff. Dec. 1, 1994; Apr. 24, 1998, eff. Dec. 1, 1998; Apr. 29, 2002, eff. Dec. 1, 2002.)

ADVISORY COMMITTEE NOTES

1967 Adoption

These rules are drawn under the authority of 28 U.S.C. § 2072 as amended by the Act of November 6, 1966, 80 Stat. 1323 (1 U.S.Code Cong. & Ad.News, p. 1546 (1966)) (Rules of Civil Procedure); 28 U.S.C. § 2075 (Bankruptcy Rules); and 18 U.S.C. §§ 3771 [§ 3771 of Title 18, Crimes and Criminal Procedure] (Procedure to and including verdict) and 3772 [§ 3772 of Title 18] (Procedure after verdict). Those statutes combine to give to the Supreme Court power to make rules of practice and procedure for all cases within the jurisdiction of the courts of appeals. By the terms of the statutes, after the rules have taken effect all laws in conflict with them are of no further force or effect. Practice and procedure in the eleven courts of appeals are now regulated by rules promulgated by each court under the authority of 28 U.S.C. § 2071. Rule 47 expressly authorizes the courts of appeals to make rules of practice not inconsistent with these rules.

As indicated by the titles under which they are found, the following rules are of special application: Rules 3 through 12 apply to appeals from judgments and orders of the district courts; Rules 13 and 14 apply to appeals from decisions of the Tax Court (Rule 13 establishes an appeal as the mode of review of decisions of the Tax Court in place of the present petition for review); Rules 15 through 20 apply to proceedings for review or enforcement of orders of administrative agencies, boards, commissions and officers. Rules 22 through 24 regulate habeas corpus proceedings and appeals in forma pauperis. All other rules apply to all proceedings in the courts of appeals.

1979 Amendment

The Federal Rules of Appellate Procedure were designed as an integrated set of rules to be followed in appeals to the courts of appeals, covering all steps in the appellate process, whether they take place in the district court or in the court of appeals, and with their adoption Rules 72 to 76 of the F.R.C.P. [rules 72 to 76, Federal Rules of Civil Procedure] were abrogated. In some instances, however, the F.R.A.P. provide that a motion or application for relief may, or must, be made in the district court. See Rules 4(a), 10(b) and 24. The proposed amendment would make it clear that when this is so the motion or application is to be made in the form and manner prescribed by the F.R.C.P. or F.R.Cr.P. [Federal Rules Criminal Procedure] and local rules relating to the form and presentation of motions and is not governed by Rule 27 of the F.R.A.P. See Rule 7(b) of the F.R.C.P. [rule 7(b), Federal Rules of Civil Procedure] and Rule 47 of the F.R.Cr.P. [rule 47, Federal Rules of Criminal Procedure].

1989 Amendment

The amendment is technical. No substantive change is intended.

1994 Amendment

Subdivision (c). A new subdivision is added to the rule. The text of new subdivision (c) has been moved from Rule 48 to Rule 1 to allow the addition of new rules at the end of the existing set of appellate rules without burying the title provision among other rules. In a similar fashion the Bankruptcy Rules combine the provisions governing the scope of the rules and the title in the first rule.

1998 Amendments

The language and organization of the rule are amended to make the rule more easily understood. In addition to changes made to improve the understanding, the Advisory Committee has changed language to make style and terminology consistent throughout the appellate rules. These changes are intended to be stylistic only. The Advisory Committee recommends deleting the language in subdivision (a) that describes the different types of proceedings that may be brought in a court of appeals. The Advisory Committee believes that the language is unnecessary and that it s omission does not work any substantive change.

2002 Amendments

Subdivision (b). Two recent enactments make it likely that, in the future, one or more of the Federal Rules of Appellate Procedure ("FRAP") will extend or limit the jurisdiction of the courts of appeals. In 1990, Congress amended the Rules Enabling Act to give the Supreme Court authority to use the federal rules of practice and procedure to define when a ruling of a district court is final for purposes of 28 U.S.C. § 1291. *See* 28 U.S.C. § 2072(c). In 1992, Congress amended 28 U.S.C. § 1292 to give the Supreme Court authority to use the federal rules of practice and procedure to provide for appeals of interlocutory decisions that are not already authorized by 28 U.S.C. § 1292. *See* 28 U.S.C. § 1292(e). Both § 1291 and § 1292 are unquestionably jurisdictional statutes, and thus, as soon as FRAP is amended to define finality for purposes of the former or to authorize interlocutory appeals not provided for by the latter, FRAP will "extend or limit the jurisdiction of the courts of appeals," and subdivision (b) will become obsolete. For that reason, subdivision (b) has been abrogated.

Changes Made After Publication and Comments No changes were made to the text of the proposed amendment or to the Committee Note.

HISTORICAL NOTES

Pending Actions

Amendments of Supreme Court to Federal Rules of Appellate Procedure effective December 1, 1993, applicable, insofar as just and practicable, in all proceedings then pending, pursuant to the Order of April 22, 1993.

CROSS REFERENCES

Authority to create courts inferior to Supreme Court, see USCA Const. Art. III § 1.

"Court of the United States" as including courts of appeals, see 28 USCA § 451.

Creation and composition of courts, see 28 USCA § 43.

Forging or counterfeiting seals of courts, penalties, see 18 USCA § 505.

Number and composition of circuits, see 28 USCA § 41.

Writs and process issued by court to be under seal, see 28 USCA § 1691.

Rule 6. Appeal in a Bankruptcy Case From a Final Judgment, Order, or Decree of a District Court or Bankruptcy Appellate Panel

(a) Appeal From a Judgment, Order, or Decree of a District Court Exercising Original Jurisdiction in a Bankruptcy Case. An appeal to a court of appeals from a final judgment, order, or decree of a district court exercising jurisdiction under 28 U.S.C. § 1334 is taken as any other civil appeal under these rules.

(b) Appeal From a Judgment, Order, or Decree of a District Court or Bankruptcy Appellate Panel Exercising Appellate Jurisdiction in a Bankruptcy Case.

(1) Applicability of Other Rules. These rules apply to an appeal to a court of appeals under 28 U.S.C. § 158(d) from a final judgment, order, or decree of a district court or bankruptcy appellate panel exercising appellate jurisdiction under 28 U.S.C. § 158(a) or (b). But there are 3 exceptions:

(A) Rules 4(a)(4), 4(b), 9, 10, 11, 12(b), 13–20, 22–23, and 24(b) do not apply;

(B) the reference in Rule 3(c) to 'Form 1 in the Appendix of Forms' must be read as a reference to Form 5; and

(C) when the appeal is from a bankruptcy appellate panel, the term 'district court,' as used in any applicable rule, means 'appellate panel.'

(2) Additional Rules. In addition to the rules made applicable by Rule 6(b)(1), the following rules apply:

(A) Motion for rehearing.

(i) If a timely motion for rehearing under Bankruptcy Rule 8015 is filed, the time to appeal for all parties runs from the entry of the order disposing of the motion. A notice of appeal filed after the district court or bankruptcy appellate panel announces or enters a judgment, order, or decree—but before disposition of the motion for rehearing—becomes effective when the order disposing of the motion for rehearing is entered.

(ii) Appellate review of the order disposing of the motion requires the party, in compliance with Rules 3(c) and 6(b)(1)(B), to amend a previously filed notice of appeal. A party intending to challenge an altered or amended judgment, order, or decree must file a notice of appeal or amended notice of appeal within the time prescribed by Rule 4—excluding Rules 4(a)(4) and 4(b)—measured from the entry of the order disposing of the motion.

(iii) No additional fee is required to file an amended notice.

(B) The record on appeal.

(i) Within 10 days after filing the notice of appeal, the appellant must file with the clerk possessing the record assembled in accordance with Bankruptcy Rule 8006—and serve on the appellee—a statement of the issues to be presented on appeal and a designation of the record to be certified and sent to the circuit clerk.

(ii) An appellee who believes that other parts of the record are necessary must, within 10 days after being served with the appellant's designation, file with the clerk and serve on the appellant a designation of additional parts to be included.

(iii) The record on appeal consists of:

- the redesignated record as provided above;
- the proceedings in the district court or bankruptcy appellate panel; and
- a certified copy of the docket entries prepared by the clerk under Rule 3(d).

(C) Forwarding the record.

(i) When the record is complete, the district clerk or bankruptcy appellate panel clerk must number the documents constituting the record and send them promptly to the circuit clerk together with a list of the documents correspondingly numbered and reasonably identified. Unless directed to do so by a party or the circuit clerk, the clerk will not send to the court of appeals documents of unusual bulk or weight, physical exhibits other than documents, or other parts of the record designated for omission by local rule of the court of appeals. If the exhibits are unusually bulky or heavy, a party must arrange with the clerks in advance for their transportation and receipt.

(ii) All parties must do whatever else is necessary to enable the clerk to assemble and forward the record. The court of appeals may provide by rule or order that a certified copy of the docket entries be sent in place of the redesignated record, but any party may request at any time during the pendency of the appeal that the redesignated record be sent.

(D) Filing the record. Upon receiving the record—or a certified copy of the docket entries sent in place of the redesignated record—the circuit clerk must file it and immediately notify all parties of the filing date.

(Added Apr. 25, 1989, eff. Dec. 1, 1989, and amended Apr. 30, 1991, eff. Dec. 1, 1991; Apr. 22, 1993, eff. Dec. 1, 1993; Apr. 24, 1998, eff. Dec. 1, 1998.)

ADVISORY COMMITTEE NOTES

1989 Addition

A new Rule 6 is proposed. The Bankruptcy Reform Act of 1978, Pub.L. No. 95–598, 92 Stat. 2549, the Supreme Court decision in *Northern Pipeline Construction Co. v. Marathon Pipe Line Co.,* 458 U.S. 50 (1982), and the Bankruptcy Amendments and Federal Judgeship Act of 1984, Pub.L. No. 98–353, 98 Stat. 333, have made the existing Rule 6 obsolete.

Subdivision (a). Subdivision (a) provides that when a district court exercises original jurisdiction in a bankruptcy matter, rather than referring it to a bankruptcy judge for a final determination, the appeal should be taken in identical fashion as appeals from district court decisions in other civil actions. A district court exercises original jurisdiction and this subdivision applies when the district court enters a final order or judgment upon consideration of a bankruptcy judge's proposed findings of fact and conclusions of law in a non-core proceeding pursuant to 28 U.S.C. § 157(c)(1) or when a district court withdraws a proceeding pursuant to 28 U.S.C. § 157(d). This subdivision is included to avoid uncertainty arising from the question of whether a bankruptcy case is a civil case. The rules refer at various points to the procedure "in a civil case", *see,* e.g. Rule 4(a)(1). Subdivision (a) makes it clear that such rules apply to an appeal from a district court bankruptcy decision.

Subdivision (b). Subdivision (b) governs appeals that follow intermediate review of a bankruptcy judge's decision by a district court or a bankruptcy appellate panel.

Subdivision (b)(1). Subdivision (b)(1) provides for the general applicability of the Federal Rules of Appellate Procedure, with specified exceptions, to appeals covered by subdivision (b) and makes necessary word adjustments.

Subdivision (b)(2). Paragraph (i) provides that the time for filing a notice of appeal shall begin to run anew from the entry of an order denying a rehearing or from the entry of a subsequent judgment. The Committee deliberately omitted from the rule any provision governing the validity of a notice of appeal filed prior to the entry of an order denying a rehearing; the Committee intended to leave undisturbed the current state of the law on that issue. Paragraph (ii) calls for a redesignation of the appellate record assembled in the bankruptcy court pursuant to Rule 8006 of the Rules of Bankruptcy Procedure. After an intermediate appeal, a party may well narrow the focus of its efforts on the second appeal and a redesignation of the record may eliminate unnecessary material. The proceedings during the first appeal are included to cover the possibility that independent error in the intermediate appeal, for example failure to follow appropriate procedures, may be assigned in the court of appeals. Paragraph (iii) provides for the transmission of the record and tracks the appropriate subsections of Rule 11. Paragraph (iv) provides for the filing of the record and notices to the parties. Paragraph (ii) and Paragraph (iv) both refer to "a certified copy of the docket entries". The "docket entries" referred to are the docket entries in the district court or the bankruptcy appellate panel, not the entire docket in the bankruptcy court.

1993 Amendments

Note to Subparagraph (b)(2)(i). The amendment accompanies concurrent changes to Rule 4(a)(4). Although Rule 6 never included language such as that being changed in Rule 4(a)(4), language that made a notice of appeal void if it was filed before, or during the pendency of, certain posttrial motions, courts have found that a notice of appeal is premature if it is filed before the court disposes of a motion for rehearing. See, e.g., *In re X-Cel, Inc.*, 823 F.2d 192 (7th Cir.1987); *In re Shah,* 859 F.2d 1463 (10th Cir.1988). The Committee wants to achieve the same result here as in Rule 4, the elimination of a procedural trap.

1998 Amendments

The language and organization of the rule are amended to make the rule more easily understood. In addition to changes made to improve the understanding, the Advisory Committee has changed language to make style and terminology consistent throughout the appellate rules. These changes are intended to be stylistic only.

Subdivision (b). Language is added to Rule 6(b)(2)(A)(ii) to conform with the corresponding provision in Rule 4(a)(4). The new language is clarifying rather than substantive. The existing rule states that a party intending to challenge an alteration or amendment of a judgment must file an amended notice of appeal. Of course, if a party has not previously filed a notice of appeal, the party would simply file a notice of appeal not an amended one. The new language states that the party must file "a notice of appeal or amended notice of appeal."

Complete Annotation Materials, see Title 28 U.S.C.A.

Form 5. Notice of Appeal to a Court of Appeals from a Judgment or Order of a District Court or a Bankruptcy Appellate Panel

United States District Court for the ....
District of ....

In re)
)
....,)
Debtor)
) File No..........
....,)
Plaintiff)
)
v.)
)
....,)
Defendant)

Notice of Appeal to
United States Court of Appeals
for the .... Circuit

.........................., the plaintiff [or defendant or other party] appeals to the United States Court of Appeals for the .... Circuit from the final judgment [or order or decree] of the district court for the district of .... [or bankruptcy appellate panel of the .... circuit], entered in this case on ...., 20.... [here describe the judgment, order, or decree] ....

The parties to the judgment [or order or decree] appealed from and the names and addresses of their respective attorneys are as follows:

Dated ....
Signed ....
Attorney for Appellant

Address: ....
....

(Added Apr. 25, 1989, eff. Dec. 1, 1989; Mar. 27, 2003, eff. Dec. 1, 2003.)

court in the judicial district in which the trustee has been appointed.

(iii)(A) Paragraphs (d)(1)(i) and (ii) of this section shall not apply to a spouse of a standing trustee who was employed by the standing trustee as of August 1, 1995.

(B) For all other relatives employed by a standing trustee as of August 1, 1995, paragraphs (d)(1)(i) and (ii) of this section shall be fully implemented by October 1, 1998, unless specifically provided below:

(1) The United States Trustee shall have the discretion to grant a written waiver for a period of time not to exceed 2 years upon a written showing by the standing trustee of compelling circumstances that make the continued employment of a relative necessary for a standing trustee's performance of his or her duties and written evidence that the salary to be paid is at or below market rate.

(2) Additional waivers, not to exceed a period of two years each, may be granted under paragraph (d)(1)(iii)(B)(1) of this section provided the standing trustee makes a similar written showing within 90 days prior to the expiration of a present waiver and the United States Trustee determines that the circumstances for waiver are met.

(3) No waivers will be granted for a relative of the United States Trustee or of an Assistant United States Trustee.

(2) Related Party Transactions.

(i) A standing trustee shall not direct debtors or creditors of a bankruptcy case administered by the standing trustee to an individual or entity that provides products or services, such as insurance or financial counseling, if a standing trustee is a relative of that individual or if the standing trustee or relative has a financial or ownership interest in the entity.

(ii) A standing trustee shall not, on behalf of the trust, contract or allocate expenses with himself or herself, with a relative, or with any entity in which the standing trustee or a relative of the standing trustee has a financial or ownership interest if the costs are to be paid as an expense out of the fiduciary expense fund.

(iii)(A) The United States Trustee may grant a waiver from compliance with paragraph (d)(2)(ii) of this section for up to three years following the appointment of a standing trustee if the newly-appointed standing trustee can demonstrate in writing that a waiver is necessary and the cost is at or below market.

(B) The United States Trustee may grant a provisional waiver from compliance with the allocation prohibition contained in paragraph (d)(2)(ii) of this section if one of the following conditions is present:

(1) A standing trustee has insufficient receipts to earn maximum annual compensation as determined by the Director during any one of the last three fiscal years and provides the United States Trustee with an appraisal or other written evidence that the allocation is necessary and the allocated cost is at or below market rate for that good or service, or

(2) A Chapter 13 standing trustee also serves as a trustee in Chapter 12 cases and provides the United States Trustee with an appraisal or other written evidence that the allocation is necessary and the allocated cost is at or below market rate for that good or service.

(C) Except as otherwise provided in this paragraph, a standing trustee may seek a reasonable extension of time from the United States Trustee to comply with paragraph (d)(2)(ii) of this section. To obtain an extension, a standing trustee must demonstrate by an appraisal or other written evidence, satisfactory to the United States Trustee, that the expense is necessary and at or below market rate. In no event shall an extension be granted for the use and occupation of real estate beyond October 1, 2005. For personal property and personal service contracts, no extension shall be granted beyond October 1, 1998.

(3) Employment of Other Standing Trustees. A standing trustee shall not employ or contract with another standing trustee to provide personal services for compensation payable from the fiduciary expense fund. This section does not prohibit the standing trustee from reimbursing the actual, necessary expenses incurred by another standing trustee who provides necessary assistance to the standing trustee provided that the reimbursement has been pre-approved by the United States Trustee.

(e) Paragraph (d) of this section is effective July 2, 1997. As to those standing trustees who are appointed as of July 2, 1997, paragraph (d) will be applicable on the first day of their next fiscal year (i.e., October 1, 1997, for chapter 13 trustees and January 1, 1998, for chapter 12 trustees).

[62 FR 30183, June 2, 1997]

§ 58.5 Non-discrimination in appointment.

The U.S. Trustees shall not discriminate on the basis of race, color, religion, sex, national origin or age in appointments to the private panel of trustees or of standing trustees and in this regard shall assure equal opportunity for all appointees and applicants for appointment to the private panel of trustees or as standing trustee. Each U.S. Trustee shall be guided by the policies and requirements of Executive Order 11478 of August 8, 1969, relating to equal employment opportunity in the Federal Government, section 717 of the Civil Rights Act of 1964, as amended (42 U.S.C. 2000e–16), section 15 of the Age Discrimination in

Employment Act of 1967, as amended (29 U.S.C. 633a), and the regulations of the Office of Personnel Management relating to equal employment opportunity (5 CFR Part 713).

[Order No. 921–80, 45 FR 82631, Dec. 16, 1980, as amended by Order No. 960–81, 46 FR 52360, Oct. 27, 1981]

§ 58.6 Procedures for suspension and removal of panel trustees and standing trustees.

(a) A United States Trustee shall notify a panel trustee or a standing trustee in writing of any decision to suspend or terminate the assignment of cases to the trustee including, where applicable, any decision not to renew the trustee's term appointment. The notice shall state the reason(s) for the decision and should refer to, or be accompanied by copies of, pertinent materials upon which the United States Trustee has relied and any prior communications in which the United States Trustee has advised the trustee of the potential action. The notice shall be sent to the office of the trustee by overnight courier, for delivery the next business day. The reasons may include, but are in no way limited to:

(1) Failure to safeguard or to account for estate funds and assets;

(2) Failure to perform duties in a timely and consistently satisfactory manner;

(3) Failure to comply with the provisions of the Code, the Bankruptcy Rules, and local rules of court;

(4) Failure to cooperate and to comply with orders, instructions and policies of the court, the bankruptcy clerk or the United States Trustee;

(5) Substandard performance of general duties and case management in comparison to other members of the chapter 7 panel or other standing trustees;

(6) Failure to display proper temperament in dealing with judges, clerks, attorneys, creditors, debtors, the United States Trustee and the general public;

(7) Failure to adequately monitor the work of professionals or others employed by the trustee to assist in the administration of cases;

(8) Failure to file timely, accurate reports, including interim reports, final reports, and final accounts;

(9) Failure to meet the eligibility requirements of 11 U.S.C. 321 or the qualifications set forth in 28 CFR 58.3 and 58.4 and in 11 U.S.C. 322;

(10) Failure to attend in person or appropriately conduct the 11 U.S.C. 341(a) meeting of creditors;

(11) Action by or pending before a court or state licensing agency which calls the trustee's competence, financial responsibility or trustworthiness into question;

(12) Routine inability to accept assigned cases due to conflicts of interest or to the trustee's unwillingness or incapacity to serve;

(13) Change in the composition of the chapter 7 panel pursuant to a system established by the United States Trustee under 28 CFR 58.1;

(14) A determination by the United States Trustee that the interests of efficient case administration or a decline in the number of cases warrant a reduction in the number of panel trustees or standing trustees.

(b) The notice shall advise the trustee that the decision is final and unreviewable unless the trustee requests in writing a review by the Director, Executive Office for United States Trustees, no later than 20 calendar days from the date of issuance of the United States Trustee's notice ("request for review"). In order to be timely, a request for review must be received by the Office of the Director no later than 20 calendar days from the date of the United States Trustee's notice to the trustee.

(c) A decision by a United States Trustee to suspend or terminate the assignment of cases to a trustee shall take effect upon the expiration of a trustee's time to seek review from the Director or, if the trustee timely seeks such review, upon the issuance of a final written decision by the Director.

(d) Notwithstanding paragraph (c) of this section, a United States Trustee's decision to suspend or terminate the assignment of cases to a trustee may include, or may later be supplemented by an interim directive, by which the United States trustee may immediately discontinue assigning cases to a trustee during the review period. A United States Trustee may issue such an interim directive if the United States Trustee specifically finds that:

(1) A continued assignment of cases to the trustee places the safety of estate assets at risk;

(2) The trustee appears to be ineligible to serve under applicable law, rule, or regulation;

(3) The trustee has engaged in conduct that appears to be dishonest, deceitful, fraudulent, or criminal in nature; or

(4) The trustee appears to have engaged in other gross misconduct that is unbefitting his or her position as trustee or violates the trustee's duties.

(e) If the United States Trustee issues an interim directive, the trustee may seek a stay of the interim directive from the Director if the trustee has timely filed a request for review under paragraph (b) of this section.

(f) The trustee's written request for review shall fully describe why the trustee disagrees with the United States Trustee's decision, and shall be accompanied by all documents and materials that the trustee wants the Director to consider in reviewing the decision. The trustee shall send a copy of the request for review, and the accompanying documents and materials, to the United States Trustee by overnight courier, for delivery the next business day. The trustee may request that specific documents in the possession of the United States Trustee be transmitted to the Director for inclusion in the record.

(g) The United States Trustee shall have 15 calendar days from the date of the trustee's request for review to submit to the Director a written response regarding the matters raised in the trustee's request for review. The United States Trustee shall provide a copy of this response to the trustee. Both copies shall be sent by overnight courier, for delivery the next business day.

(h) The Director may seek additional information from any party in the manner and to the extent the Director deems appropriate.

(i) Unless the trustee and the United States Trustee agree to a longer period of time, the Director shall issue a written decision no later than 30 calendar days from the receipt of the United States Trustee's response to the trustee's request for review. That decision shall determine whether the United States Trustee's decision is supported by the record and the action is an appropriate exercise of the United States Trustee's discretion, and shall adopt, modify or reject the United States Trustee's decision to suspend or terminate the assignment of future cases to the trustee. The Director's decision shall constitute final agency action.

(j) In reaching a determination, the Director may specify a person to act as a reviewing official. The reviewing official shall not be a person who was involved in the United States Trustee's decision or a Program employee who is located within the region of the United States Trustee who made the decision. The reviewing official's duties shall be specified by the Director on a case by case basis, and may include reviewing the record, obtaining additional information from the participants, providing the Director with written recommendations, or such other duties as the Director shall prescribe in a particular case.

(k) This rule does not authorize a trustee to seek review of any decision to increase the size of the chapter 7 panel or to appoint additional standing trustees in the district or region.

(*l*) A trustee who files a request for review shall bear his or her own costs and expenses, including counsel fees.

[62 FR 51750, Oct. 2, 1997]

§ 58.7 Procedures for Completing Uniform Forms of Trustee Final Reports in Cases Filed Under Chapters 7, 12, and 13 of the Bankruptcy Code.

Text of section added by 73 FR 58444, effective April 1, 2009.

(a) UST Form 101–7–TFR, Chapter 7 Trustee's Final Report. A chapter 7 trustee must complete UST Form 101–7–TFR final report (TFR) in preparation for closing an asset case. This report must be submitted to the United States Trustee after liquidating the estate's assets, but before making distribution to creditors, and before filing it with the United States Bankruptcy Court. The TFR must contain the trustee's certification, under penalty of perjury, that all assets have been liquidated or properly accounted for and that funds of the estate are available for distribution. Pursuant to 28 U.S.C. 589b(d), the TFR must also contain the following:

(1) Summary of the trustee's case administration;

(2) Copies of the estate's financial records;

(3) List of allowed claims;

(4) Fees and administrative expenses; and

(5) Proposed dividend distribution to creditors.

(b) UST Form 101–7–NFR Chapter 7 Trustee's Notice of Trustee's Final Report. After the TFR has been reviewed by the United States Trustee and filed with the United States Bankruptcy Court, if the net proceeds realized in an estate exceed the amounts specified in Fed. R. Bankr. P. 2002(f)(8), UST Form 101–7–NFR (NFR) must be sent to all creditors as the notice required under Fed. R. Bankr. P. 2002(f). The NFR must show the receipts, approved disbursements, and any balance identified on the TFR, as well as the information required in the TFR's Exhibit D. In addition, the NFR must identify the procedures for objecting to any fee application or to the TFR.

(c) UST Form 101–7–TDR Chapter 7 Trustee's Final Account, Certification The Estate Has Been Fully Administered and Application of Trustee To Be Discharged. After distributing all estate funds, a trustee must submit to the United States Trustee and file with the United States Bankruptcy Court the trustee's final account, UST Form 101–7–TDR (TDR). The TDR must contain the trustee's certification, under penalty of perjury, that the estate has been fully administered and the trustee's request to be discharged as trustee. Pursuant to 28 U.S.C. 589b(d), the TDR must also include the following:

(1) The length of time the case was pending;

(2) Assets abandoned;

(3) Assets exempted;

(4) Receipts and disbursements of the estate;

(5) Claims asserted;

(6) Claims allowed; and,

(7) Distributions to claimants and claims discharged without payment, in each case by appropriate category.

(d) UST Form 101–7–NDR Chapter 7 Trustee's Report of No Distribution. In cases where there is no distribution of funds the case trustee must submit to the United States Trustee and file with the United States Bankruptcy Court UST Form 101–7–NDR (NDR). The NDR must contain the trustee's certification that the estate has been fully administered, that the trustee has neither received nor disbursed any property or money on account of the estate, and that there is no property available for distribution over and above that exempted by law. In addition, the NDR must set forth the trustee's request to be discharged as trustee. Pursuant to 28 U.S.C. 589b(d), the NDR must also include the following information:

(1) The length of time the case was pending;

(2) Assets abandoned;

(3) Assets exempted;

(4) Claims asserted;

(5) Claims scheduled; and,

(6) claims scheduled to be discharged without payment.

(e) UST Form 101–12–FR–S, Chapter 12 Standing Trustee's Final Report and Account and UST Form 101–13–FR–S, Chapter 13 Standing Trustee's Final Report and Account. After the final distribution to creditors in a chapter 12 or 13 case in which a standing trustee has been appointed, a trustee must submit to the United States Trustee and file with the United States Bankruptcy Court either UST Form 101–12–FR–S for chapter 12 cases or UST Form 101–13–FR–S for chapter 13 cases, which are the trustee's final report and account. In these forms, a trustee must include a certification that the estate has been fully administered if not converted to another chapter and a request to be discharged as trustee. Pursuant to 28 U.S.C. 589b(d), these forms must also include the following information:

(1) The length of time the case was pending;

(2) Assets abandoned;

(3) Assets exempted;

(4) Receipts and disbursements of the estate;

(5) Expenses of administration, including for use under section 707(b), actual costs of administering cases under chapter 12 or 13 (as applicable) of title 11;

(6) Claims asserted;

(7) Claims allowed;

(8) Distributions to claimants and claims discharged without payment, in each case by appropriate category;

(9) Date of confirmation of the plan;

(10) Date of each modification thereto; and,

(11) Defaults by the debtor in performance under the plan.

(f) UST Form 101–12–FR–C, Chapter 12 Case Trustee's Final Report and Account, and UST Form 101–13–FR–C, Chapter 13 Case Trustee's Final Report and Account. After the final distribution to creditors in a chapter 12 or 13 case in which a case trustee has been appointed, the trustee must submit to the United States Trustee and file with the United States Bankruptcy Court either UST Form 101–12–FR–C for chapter 12 cases, or UST Form 101–13–FR–C for chapter 13 cases, which are the trustee's final report and account. In these forms, a trustee must include a certification, submitted under penalty of perjury, that the estate has been fully administered if not converted to another chapter and the trustee's request to be discharged from further duties as trustee. Pursuant to 28 U.S.C. 589b(d), these forms must also include the following information:

(1) The length of time the case was pending;

(2) Assets abandoned;

(3) Assets exempted;

(4) Receipts and disbursements of the estate;

(5) Expenses of administration, including for use under section 707(b), actual costs of administering cases under chapter 12 or 13 (as applicable) of title 11;

(6) Claims asserted;

(7) Claims allowed;

(8) Distributions to claimants and claims discharged without payment, in each case by appropriate category;

(9) Date of confirmation of the plan;

(10) Date of each modification thereto; and,

(11) defaults by the debtor in performance under the plan.

(g) Mandatory Usage of Uniform Forms. The Uniform Forms associated with this rule must be utilized by trustees when completing their final reports and final accounts. All trustees serving in districts where a United States Trustee is serving must use the Uniform Forms in the administration of their cases, in the same manner, and with the same content, as set forth in this rule:

(1) All Uniform Forms may be electronically or mechanically reproduced so long as all the content and the form remain consistent with the Uniform Forms as they are posted on EOUST's Web site;

(2) The Uniform Forms shall be filed via the United States Bankruptcy Courts Case Management/Electronic Case Filing System (CM/ECF) as a "smart form" meaning the forms are data enabled, unless the court offers an automated process that has been ap-

proved by EOUST, such as the virtual NDR event through CM/ECF.

[73 FR 58444, Oct. 7, 2008]

§ 58.15 Qualifications for approval as a nonprofit budget and credit counseling agency.

(a) Definition of agency. As used in this section the term "agency" means nonprofit budget and credit counseling agency.

(b) Qualifications. To be included on the list of approved nonprofit budget and credit counseling agencies under 11 U.S.C. 111 an agency shall meet the qualifications set forth in paragraphs (d) through (i) of this section. An agency shall continuously meet these qualifications in order to remain included on this list when the list is updated thereafter.

(c) Preemption. Nothing contained in these regulations or the related application, appendices or instructions is intended to preempt any applicable law or regulation governing the conduct or operations of an agency.

(d) Structure and organization. A nonprofit budget and credit counseling agency must:

(1) Be organized and operated as a nonprofit entity;

(2) Be in compliance with all applicable laws and regulations of the United States and each state, commonwealth, district, or territory of the United States in which the agency conducts credit counseling services;

(3) Have an independent board of directors the majority of which:

(i) Are not employed by such agency; and

(ii) Will not directly or indirectly benefit financially from the outcome of the counseling services provided by such agency;

(4) Ensure that no member of the board of directors or trustees, officer, manager, employee, counselor, or agent is a United States Trustee Program employee, a panel or standing trustee, a Federal judge, a Federal court employee, a certified public accountant that performs audits of the agency's trust accounts, or a person with a financial or familial connection to the United States Trustee Program.

(5) Avoid any conduct or transactions that generate or create the appearance of generating a private benefit for any individual or group related or connected to the Agency.

(e) Fees. If a fee is charged for counseling services, charge a reasonable fee, and provide services without regard to ability to pay the fee; the agency's criteria for providing services without a fee or at a reduced rate must be provided to the United States Trustee. In addition, an agency shall:

(1) Have sufficient computer capabilities or secure access to issue certificates of completion of credit counseling in conformance with the directives established by the EOUST;

(2) Not withhold a certificate of counseling completion because of a client's inability to pay;

(3) Advise the client of the fee schedule before services are provided and inform the client that services are available for free or at a reduced rate based on a client's ability to pay;

(4) Issue a certificate to any client who completes credit counseling and a budget analysis, regardless of whether a client agrees to participate in a debt management plan and without regard to the client's ability to pay;

(5) Issue the certificate within one business day to a client after completion of the required counseling or upon the earlier of the following:

(i) A request by a client for the issuance of a certificate; or

(ii) The completion or termination of a counseling session, which may include the administration of a debt management plan;

(6) Not charge a separate fee for the issuance of a certificate of counseling unless the agency has clearly disclosed such fee before the initial credit counseling session;

(7) Issue a certificate to each spouse whether counseling was provided individually or in a joint session;

(8) Maintain adequate records to issue replacement certificates and to verify the authenticity of certificates filed by bankruptcy debtors;

(9) Provide full disclosures to a client, including funding sources, counselor qualifications, possible impact on credit reports, the cost of services to be paid by the client and how such costs will be paid, before services are rendered and regardless of whether the client enters into a debt management plan.

(f) Standards for counseling and counselors. Agencies and credit counselors shall not, unless otherwise authorized by law, provide legal advice on any matter. Agencies and credit counselors shall:

(1) Provide adequate briefings, budget analysis, and credit counseling services to clients lasting an average of 60 to 90 minutes in length that include an outline of available counseling opportunities to resolve a client's credit problems, an analysis of the client's current financial condition, discussion of the factors that caused such financial condition, and assistance in developing a plan to respond to the client's problems without incurring negative amortization of debt;

(2) Provide trained counselors who receive no commissions or bonuses based on the outcome of the counseling services provided by such agency, and who

have adequate experience, and have been adequately trained to provide counseling services to individuals in financial difficulty, including the matters described in sub-paragraph (1) of this paragraph. A counselor shall be deemed to have adequate training and experience to provide credit counseling and budget analysis if the counselor is accredited or certified by a recognized independent organization, or has successfully completed a course of study acceptable to the United States Trustee and has worked a minimum of six months in a related area, including personal finance, budgeting, and debt management. The United States Trustee Program does not endorse any specific course or certification program;

(3) Demonstrate adequate experience and background in providing credit counseling, which means, at a minimum, that an agency must:

(i) Have experience in providing credit counseling for the previous two years. Alternatively, if an agency fails to meet the two-year requirement, the agency must currently employ in each office location that serves clients at least one office supervisor with experience and background in providing credit counseling for no less than two of the five years preceding the relevant application date, including only experience obtained on or after January 1, 2003; and

(ii) If an agency offers telephone or Internet credit counseling services, the agency must, in addition to all other requirements, demonstrate sufficient experience and proficiency in designing and providing such services over the telephone and/or Internet, including verification procedures to identify the person receiving the counseling services and to ensure that the counseling services are properly completed.

(g) Activity report. Upon application for annual approval, the agency must furnish an estimate of the information requested in Appendix E, "Activity Report for Approved Agencies," of the application projected to the end of either the probationary period or annual period. Within thirty (30) days after the completion of either the probationary period or annual period, the agency must furnish an amended Appendix E which includes the actual information.

(h) Agency declarations and acknowledgments.

(1) The agency's president, chairman, trustee, or other authorized official is required to declare, by signing the application, that such individual is authorized to complete the application on behalf of the agency; that such individual has read and knows the contents of the application and all enclosures and attachments submitted; and that such individual affirms under penalty of perjury that all of the representations and statements contained therein are true and correct to the best of such individual's knowledge, information, and belief;

(2) By executing and submitting the "Application for Approval as a Nonprofit Budget and Credit Counseling Agency," the agency acknowledges and agrees to abide by the prohibitions, limitations, and obligations set forth in Appendix A, "Acknowledgments, Agreements, and Declarations in Support of Application for Approval as a Nonprofit Budget and Credit Counseling Agency," of the application which include, but are not limited to, the following:

(i) Making all records relating to the agency's compliance with 11 U.S.C. 111 available to the United States Trustee and EOUST upon request and cooperating with the United States Trustee and EOUST for any scheduled or unscheduled on-site visits and customer service audits;

(ii) Cooperating with the United States Trustee and the EOUST in timely responding to any questions or inquiries concerning the agency's operations and services;

(iii) Not excluding a creditor from a debt management plan because the creditor declines to make a "fair share" contribution to the agency;

(iv) Agreeing that any forms, agreements, contracts, or other materials provided to a client will not limit the client's right to seek damages against an agency as provided for in 11 U.S.C. 111(g)(2);

(v) Conducting a state and Federal criminal background check at least every five years for each person providing credit counseling services, if such criminal background check is authorized under state law, and not employing as a counselor anyone who has been convicted of any felony, or a crime involving fraud, dishonesty, or false statements, unless the United States Trustee determines, upon review and in his or her discretion, circumstances warrant a waiver of this employment requirement. The state criminal background check shall be conducted in the state where the counselor resides. If a criminal background check is not authorized by state law, the agency shall obtain a sworn statement from each counselor, at least every five years, which attests to whether the counselor has been convicted of any felony or a crime involving fraud, dishonesty, or false statements;

(vi) Referring clients for counseling services only to agencies that are approved by the United States Trustee;

(vii) Complying with the EOUST's directions on approved advertising, which is located in Appendix A to the application;

(viii) Not disclosing or providing to a credit reporting agency information concerning whether a client has received or sought instruction concerning credit counseling or personal financial management from an agency, and not selling information about a client to any third party without the client's written permission, regardless of whether the counseling is presented in a classroom, on the telephone, on the Internet, or any other venue;

(3) Upon request of the United States Trustee or EOUST, an agency shall submit a completed and signed tax waiver, which authorizes the United States Trustee or EOUST to seek confidential information regarding the agency from the Internal Revenue Service.

(i) Agency financial requirements and surety bonds.

(1) If an agency offers debt management plans, the agency must have adequate financial resources to provide continuing support services for budgeting plans over the life of any repayment plan, and provide for the safekeeping and payment of client funds, including an annual audit of the trust accounts in accordance with generally accepted auditing standards by an independent certified public accountant, and appropriate employee bonding; which includes:

(i) Depositing all client funds into a trust account insured by a Federal institution with respect to each client. The records creating the trust account must demonstrate that the trust account was established in a fiduciary capacity and must comply with the Federal institution's regulations so that each client's funds are insured up to the maximum amount allowable by the Federal institution;

(ii) Keeping and maintaining books, accounts, and records to provide a clear and readily understandable record of all business conducted by the agency; and

(iii) Obtaining a surety bond payable to the United States in an amount which is the lesser of:

(A) Two percent of the agency's prior year disbursements made from trust accounts; or

(B) Equal to the average daily balance maintained in all trust accounts for the six months prior to submission of the application. At a minimum, the bond must be $5,000;

(2) An agency may receive an offset or credit for the surety bond amount as follows:

(i) The agency has obtained a surety bond, or similar cash, securities, insurance (other than employee fidelity insurance), or letter of credit, in compliance with the requirements of the state, commonwealth, district, or territory ("state") in which the agency seeks approval from the United States Trustee;

(ii) The surety bond, or similar cash, securities, insurance (other than employee fidelity insurance), or letter of credit provides protection for the clients of the agency;

(iii) The surety bond, or similar cash, securities, insurance, or letter of credit, must be written in favor of the state or the appropriate state agency; and

(iv) The offset or credit is based on the annual disbursements or average daily bank balance directly related to the clients in the particular state;

(3) An agency must have adequate employee bonding or fidelity insurance. The amount of such bonding or fidelity shall be 50 percent of the surety bond amount calculated prior to any offset/credit that the agency may receive for state bonds. At a minimum, the employee bond or fidelity insurance must be $5,000;

(4) An agency may receive an offset or credit in the employee bond/fidelity insurance amount as follows:

(i) The agency has obtained an employee bond or fidelity insurance in compliance with the requirements of a state, commonwealth, district, or territory in which the agency seeks approval from the United States Trustee;

(ii) The deductible cannot exceed a reasonable amount considering the financial resources of the agency; and

(iii) The offset/credit is based on the annual disbursements or average daily bank balance directly related to the clients in the particular state;

(5) If the agency has contracted with another entity ("service provider") to administer any part of its debt management plan, the service provider is approved by the United States Trustee as a nonprofit budget and credit counseling agency, or the service provider is specifically covered under the agency's surety bond or has a surety bond in a sufficient amount to provide for the safekeeping of the agency's client funds, and the service provider agrees in writing to allow the United States Trustee or EOUST to audit the trust accounts maintained by the service provider and to review the service provider's internal controls and administrative procedures.

[71 FR 38078, July 5, 2006]

§ 58.16 Procedures for inclusion on the approved list.

(a) As used in this section the term "agency" means nonprofit budget and credit counseling agency.

(b) Each nonprofit budget and credit counseling agency seeking to be included on the list of approved agencies must complete in its entirety the application form EOUST–CC1, "Application for Approval as a Nonprofit Budget and Credit Counseling Agency" (application), including all appendices, and submit it at the address indicated on the application.

(c) The application must be executed under penalty of perjury in a manner specified in 28 U.S.C. 1746.

(d) An application may not be accepted by the EOUST unless it is complete and has been signed by an agency representative who is authorized to sign on behalf of the agency. An application that is incomplete or has been altered, amended, or changed in any respect from the application at the United States Trustee Program's Web site may not be accepted by the EOUST. Such an application will be denied, and no further action will be taken on the request for inclusion on the approved list until a new application is submitted that corrects the defects.

(e) The EOUST will not accept an application submitted by an agency on behalf of another individual or group of individuals. Each agency that desires to be included on the approved list must submit its own application.

(f) Each agency must submit a new application 45 to 60 days before expiration of its six month probationary period or annual period to be considered for annual approval. After the application is completed and signed, the originals must be mailed to the EOUST, Credit Counseling Application Processing, at the address indicated on the application. The EOUST will not accept a photocopy or facsimile of the application.

(g) An agency whose name appears on the list incorrectly may submit a written request that the name be corrected. An agency whose name appears on the list may submit a written request that its name be removed from the list.

(h) By submitting an application, the agency expressly consents to the release and disclosure of the agency's name on the approved list and the publication of the agency's contact information.

(i) Obligation to Update Information:

(1) The agency has a continuing duty to promptly notify the EOUST of any circumstances that would materially alter or change a response to any section of the application, including but not limited to, changes in the location of primary or satellite business office(s); the principal contact person; name or fictitious name under which the agency does business; management, including the board of directors; a merger or consolidation with another entity; and the banks or financial institutions used by the agency;

(2) The agency shall request approval by amendment to its application, and prior to occurrence of the following changes:

(i) Cancellation or change in amount of the surety bond or employee fidelity bond or insurance;

(ii) The engagement of a service provider to provide counseling services to administer debt management plans, or to otherwise control or account for client funds;

(iii) An increase in the fees, contributions, or payments received from clients for counseling services or a change in the agency's policy for the reduction or waiver of fees;

(iv) Expansion into additional judicial districts or withdrawal from judicial districts where the agency is approved; and

(v) Method of delivery or type of counseling services;

(3) The agency must include with any amendment to its application, a newly executed "certification and signature;"

(4) The agency will notify the EOUST immediately upon the occurrence of any of the below noted events:

(i) Cancellation or termination of tax exempt status of the agency by the Internal Revenue Service;

(ii) Cessation of business of the agency or of any office of the agency;

(iii) Termination or cancellation of any surety bond or fidelity insurance;

(iv) Any action brought against the agency by a Federal or state agency, including, but not limited to, the Federal Trade Commission, or any action against the surety bond or fidelity insurance;

(v) Any action by a state agency to suspend the license or cancel other authorization to do business;

(vi) A suspension by an accreditation organization or denial of accreditation;

(vii) Withdrawal as an approved agency; and

(viii) Change in the agency's nonprofit status;

(j) An approved agency may not transfer or assign its United States Trustee approval under section 111 as a nonprofit budget and credit counseling agency to any party.

[71 FR 38078, 38080, July 5, 2006]

§ 58.17 Procedures for denying an application or removing an agency from the approved list, and the administrative review rights granted to denied or removed agencies.

(a) As used in this section the term "agency" means nonprofit budget and credit counseling agency.

(b) No administrative review will be granted to any applicant that submitted an incomplete application and had its application denied due to incompleteness and failed to subsequently submit a completed application.

(c) The agency shall be notified in writing of any decision to deny the agency's application or to remove the agency from the approved list ("notice"). The notice shall state the reason(s) for the decision and shall reference any documents or communications with the agency, which were relied upon in making the denial or removal decision. If such documents or communications were not provided to the United States Trustee or the EOUST by the agency, copies of the documents or communications shall be provided with the notice. The notice shall be sent to the agency by overnight courier, for delivery the next business day.

(d) The notice shall advise the agency that the decision is final unless the agency requests in writing a review ("request for review") by the Director, Executive Office for United States Trustees ("Director"), no later than 20 calendar days from the date of issuance of the denial or removal notice. In order to be timely, a request for review must be received at the Office of the Director no later than 20 calendar days from the date of the denial or removal notice to the agency.

(e) A decision to remove an agency from the approved list shall take effect upon the expiration of an agency's time to seek review from the Director or, if the agency timely seeks such review, upon the issuance of a final written decision by the Director.

(f) Notwithstanding sub-paragraph (e) of this section, a decision to remove an agency from the approved list may include, or may later be supplemented by, an interim directive, which may immediately remove an agency from the approved list. Such an interim directive may be issued if one or more of the following are specifically found:

(1) The agency is not providing for the safekeeping and payment of client funds;

(2) The agency's surety bond has been canceled;

(3) The agency made a material false statement on the application;

(4) The agency (board of directors, officer, manager, employee, counselor, or agent) has engaged in conduct that is dishonest, deceitful, fraudulent, or criminal in nature;

(5) The agency (board of directors, officer, manager, employee, counselor, or agent) has engaged in other gross misconduct that is unbefitting the agency's position as an approved agency;

(6) The agency's nonprofit status has been revoked by the entity that issued the agency its nonprofit status;

(7) Revocation of the agency's license to do business in a particular state, provided the immediate removal shall apply only to the federal judicial districts within the particular state; or

(8) The Internal Revenue Service revokes the agency's tax exempt status.

(g) The agency's request for review shall fully describe why the agency disagrees with the denial or removal decision, and shall be accompanied by all documents and materials that the agency wants the Director to consider in reviewing the decision. The agency shall send a copy of the request for review, and the accompanying documents and materials, to the Director by overnight courier, for delivery the next business day, and must be received by the Director within 20 calendar days of the denial or removal notice.

(h) The Director may seek additional information from any party, in the manner and to the extent the Director deems appropriate.

(i) The Director shall issue a written decision no later than 45 calendar days from the receipt of the agency's request for review, unless the agency agrees to a longer period of time or the Director extends the period. That decision shall determine whether the denial or removal decision is supported by the record and the action is an appropriate exercise of discretion, and shall adopt, modify, or reject the denial or removal decision. The Director's decision shall constitute final government agency action.

(j) In reaching a determination, the Director may specify a person to act as a reviewing official. The reviewing official shall not be a person who was involved in the denial or removal decision. The reviewing official's duties shall be specified by the Director on a case by case basis, and may include reviewing the record, obtaining additional information from the participants, providing the Director with written recommendations, or such other duties as the Director shall prescribe in a particular case.

(k) An agency that files a request for review shall bear its own costs and expenses, including counsel fees.

[71 FR 38078, 38081, July 5, 2006]

§§ 58.18 to 58.24 [Reserved]

[71 FR 38082, July 5, 2006]

§ 58.25 Qualifications for approval as providers of a personal financial management instructional course:

(a) Definition of provider. As used in this section the term "provider" means a provider of a personal financial management instructional course.

(b) Qualifications. To be included on the list of approved providers under 11 U.S.C. 111, a provider shall meet the qualifications set forth in paragraphs (d) through (k) of this section. A provider shall continuously meet these qualifications in order to remain included on this list when the list is updated thereafter.

(c) Preemption. Nothing contained in these regulations or the related application, appendices or instructions is intended to preempt any applicable law or regulation governing the conduct or operations of a provider.

(d) Structure and organization. A provider of a personal financial management instructional course must be in compliance with all applicable laws and regulations of the United States and each state, commonwealth, district, or territory of the United States in which the provider conducts courses. Nothing contained in these instructions, the application, or the appendices thereto, is intended to preempt any applicable law or regulation governing the conduct or operations of the provider.

(e) Standards for teachers. A provider shall employ trained personnel with adequate experience and training in providing effective instruction and services, which means the provider shall employ, at a minimum, an individual who holds at least one of the following current certifications and/or accreditations, or who has equivalent training or experience, to supervise instructors:

(1) A state teacher's certificate in any subject;

(2) Certification as a Certified Financial Planner (CFP);

(3) Certification or accreditation as a credit counselor or a financial counselor by a recognized independent organization;

(4) Certification by the American Association of Family and Consumer Sciences;

(5) Registered as a Registered Financial Consultant (RFC); or

(6) Certified as a Certified Public Accountant (CPA).

(f) Learning materials and methodologies. A provider shall provide learning materials and teaching methodologies designed to assist debtors in understanding personal financial management and that are consistent with stated objectives directly related to the goals of such instructional course, which include written information and instruction on all of the following topics:

(1) Budget development, which consists of the following:

(i) Setting short-term and long-term financial goals, as well as developing skills to assist in achieving these goals;

(ii) Calculating gross monthly income and net monthly income;

(iii) Identifying and classifying monthly expenses as fixed, variable, or periodic;

(2) Money management, which consists of the following:

(i) Keeping adequate financial records;

(ii) Developing decision-making skills required to distinguish between wants and needs, and to comparison shop for goods and services;

(iii) Maintaining appropriate levels of insurance coverage, taking into account the types and costs of insurance;

(iv) Saving for emergencies, for periodic payments, and for financial goals;

(3) Wise use of credit, which consists of the following:

(i) The types, sources, and costs of credit and loans;

(ii) Identifying debt warning signs;

(iii) Appropriate use of credit and alternatives to credit use;

(iv) Checking a credit rating;

(4) Consumer information, which consists of the following:

(i) Public and non-profit resources for consumer assistance;

(ii) Applicable consumer protection laws and regulations, such as those governing correction of a credit record and protection against consumer fraud.

(g) Course procedures. A provider shall ensure the following procedures are followed:

(1) Generally, the provider shall:

(i) Require each debtor student to provide proof of identification, to provide his/her bankruptcy case number, and to sign in and sign out of the course;

(ii) Conduct the course for a minimum of two hours in length. Courses offered via the Internet or telephone should be designed for completion with a minimum of two hours;

(iii) At the end of the course, collect from each debtor student a completed course evaluation. The evaluation shall be in a form acceptable to the EOUST;

(2) For classroom instruction, the provider shall ensure:

(i) A teacher is present for purposes of instruction and interaction with debtor students;

(ii) Class size is reasonably limited to ensure an effective presentation of the course materials;

(3) For telephone instruction, the provider shall:

(i) Provide a toll-free telephone number;

(ii) Comply with the Americans with Disabilities Act and also include a toll-free number for deaf or hearing-impaired debtor students, e.g. TTY, TDD, or Text Telephone;

(iii) Employ adequate procedures to ensure that the debtor student is the individual who completed the course;

(iv) Ensure that a teacher is present telephonically for purposes of instruction and interaction with debtor students;

(v) Provide copies of the learning materials to debtor students before the telephone instruction session;

(4) For Internet instruction, the provider shall:

(i) Comply with the Americans with Disabilities Act and its application to the Internet;

(ii) Employ adequate procedures to ensure that the debtor student is the individual who completed the course and that the individual received two hours of instruction;

(iii) Ensure that a teacher will respond within one business day to a debtor student's questions or comments;

(5) In addition to meeting all other requirements, the provider who conducts telephone or Internet courses must demonstrate sufficient experience and proficiency in designing and providing services over the telephone or Internet.

(h) Facilities. A provider shall provide adequate facilities situated in a reasonably convenient location at which such instructional course is offered, except that such facilities may include the provisions of such instructional course by telephone or through the Internet, if such instructional course is effective;

(1) The provider shall ensure that any facility used by debtor students complies with all applicable laws and regulations including, but not limited to, the Americans with Disabilities Act Accessibility Guidelines, and all federal, state, and local fire, health, safety, and occupancy laws, codes, rules, or regulations.

(i) Activity report and records. A provider shall prepare and retain reasonable records (which shall include the debtor's bankruptcy case number) to permit evaluation of the effectiveness of such instructional course, including any evaluation of satisfaction of instructional course requirements for each debtor attending such instructional course, which shall be available for inspection and evaluation by the EOUST or the United States Trustee for the district in which such instructional course is offered;

(1) Upon application for annual approval, the provider must furnish an estimate of the information requested in Appendix F to the application, projected to the end of either the probationary period or annual period. Within 30 days after the completion of either the probationary period or annual period, the provider must furnish an amended Appendix F which includes the actual information;

(2) Make all records related to the provider's compliance with 11 U.S.C. 111 available to the United States Trustee or EOUST upon request and cooperate with the United States Trustee or EOUST for any scheduled or unscheduled on-site visit or customer service audit.

(j) Fees and certificates. If a fee is charged for counseling services, a provider shall charge a reasonable fee, and provide services without regard to ability to pay the fee; the provider's criteria for providing services without a fee or at a reduced rate must be provided to the United States Trustee. In addition, a provider shall:

(1) Have sufficient computer capabilities to issue certificates of completion of an instructional course in conformance with the directives established by the EOUST;

(2) Advise the debtor student of the fee schedule before the instructional course is provided and inform the debtor student that services are available for free or at a reduced rate based on the debtor student's ability to pay;

(3) Issue certificates to any debtor student who completes an instructional course without regard to the debtor student's ability to pay;

(4) Issue the certificate within three business days to a debtor student after completion of the required instructional course;

(5) Not withhold the issuance of a certificate because of a debtor student's failure to obtain a passing grade on a quiz, examination, or test. Although a test may be incorporated into the curriculum to evaluate the effectiveness of the course and to ensure that the course has been completed, the provider cannot deny a certificate to a debtor student if the debtor student has completed the course as designed;

(6) Not charge a separate fee for the issuance of a certificate unless the provider has clearly disclosed such fee before the beginning of the instructional course;

(7) Issue a certificate to each spouse in a joint case whether the course is completed independently or jointly;

(8) Maintain adequate records to issue replacement certificates and to verify the authenticity of certificates filed by bankruptcy debtors.

(k) Provider declarations and acknowledgments.

(1) The provider's owner, president, chairman, trustee, or other authorized official is required to declare, by signing the application, that such individual is authorized to complete the application on behalf of the provider; that such individual has read and knows the contents of the application and all enclosures and attachments submitted; and to affirm under penalty of perjury that all of the representations and statements contained therein are true and correct to the best of such individual's knowledge, information, and belief;

(2) The provider shall disclose the following information to each debtor student before the commencement of the instructional course:

(i) The provider's fee schedule, including any cost to the debtor student in addition to the course fee;

(ii) A statement that the course is offered to debtor students without regard to a debtor student's ability to pay;

(iii) The qualifications, including educational and training background, of the provider's teachers;

(iv) A schedule of course dates, times, and locations;

(v) A statement that the provider does not pay or receive fees or other consideration for the referral of debtor students to or by the provider;

(vi) A statement that, upon completion of the course, the provider will provide a certificate of course completion to the debtor student;

(3) By executing and submitting the "Application for Approval as a Provider of a Personal Financial Management Instructional Course," the provider acknowledges and agrees to abide by the prohibitions, limitations, and obligations set forth in Appendix A, "Acknowledgments, Agreements, and Declarations in Support of Application for Approval as a Provider of a Personal Financial Management Instructional Course," which include, but are not limited to, the following:

(i) Ensuring that no member of the board of directors or trustees, owner, officer, manager, employee, or agent is a United States Trustee Program employee, panel trustee, or person with a financial or familial connection to a panel trustee or an employee of the United States Trustee Program. For purposes of this paragraph, a person is not deemed to have a financial relationship to a panel trustee solely because the person is an employee of the panel trustee;

(ii) Not paying or receiving referral fees or other consideration for the referral of debtor students;

(iii) Ensuring that the course will not contain any commercial advertising, and that the provider shall not promote, market, or sell financial products; solicit business of any type; or sell information about the debtor to any third party without the debtor's permission, whether the course is presented in a classroom, on the telephone, or on the Internet;

(iv) Complying with the EOUST's directions on approved advertising, which is located in Appendix A to the application;

(v) Cooperating with the EOUST and the United States Trustee in timely responding to any questions or inquiries concerning the provider's operations and/or instructional course;

(vi) Consenting that any forms, agreements, contracts, or other materials furnished to a debtor student will not limit the debtor student's ability to bring an action or claim under the provision of the United States Bankruptcy Code. 11 U.S.C. 101 et. seq.

(*l*) Universities. Accredited universities and community colleges ("universities") are eligible to apply to become providers using a streamlined version of the application. Universities need to complete only the following portions of the application:

(1) In section 1—General Information Concerning the Provider—complete sections: 1.1, 1.2, 1.3, 1.4, 1.5, 1.6, 1.8, and 1.10;

(2) In section 4—Learning Materials and Methodologies—complete sections: 4.1, 4.2, 4.4, 4.5, 4.6, 4.7, and 4.8;

(3) In section 6—Fees and Issuance of Certificates—complete section 6.1;

(4) In section 7—Activity Report for Approved Providers—complete section 7.1;

(5) In section 8—Acknowledgments, Agreements, and Declarations—complete sections 8.1 and 8.2;

(6) In section 9—Certification and Signature—execute the application as indicated in the instructions;

(7) Completed applications should be submitted to the EOUST in accordance with the procedures in section 58.19.

[71 FR 38082, July 5, 2006]

§ 58.26 Procedures for inclusion on the approved provider list.

(a) As used in this section the term "provider" means a provider of a personal financial management instructional course.

(b) Each provider seeking to be included on the list of approved providers must complete in its entirety the application form EOUST–DE1, "Application for Approval as a Provider of a Personal Financial Management Course" (application), including all appendices, and submit it at the address indicated on the application. Accredited universities may complete only the portions of the application as indicated in section 58.25(*l*).

(c) The application must be executed under penalty of perjury in a manner specified in 28 U.S.C. 1746.

(d) An application will not be accepted by the EOUST unless it is complete and has been signed by a provider representative who is authorized to sign on behalf of the provider. An application that is incomplete or has been altered, amended, or changed in any respect from the application at the United States Trustee Program's Web site will not be accepted by the EOUST. Such an application will be denied, and no further action on the request for inclusion on the approved list will be taken until a new application is submitted that corrects the defects.

(e) The EOUST will not accept an application submitted by a provider on behalf of another individual or group of individuals. Each provider that desires to be included on the approved list must submit its own application.

(f) Each provider must submit a new application 45 to 60 days before expiration of its six month probationary period or annual period to be considered for annual approval. After the application is completed and signed, the originals and a copy must be mailed to the EOUST, Debtor Education Provider Application Processing, at the address indicated on the application. The EOUST will not accept a photocopy or facsimile of the application in lieu of the original.

(g) A provider whose name appears on the list incorrectly may submit a written request that the name be corrected. A provider whose name appears on the list may submit a written request that its name be removed from the list.

(h) By submitting an application, the provider expressly consents to the release and disclosure of the provider's name on the approved list, and the publication of the provider's contact information.

(i) Obligation to Update Information:

(1) The provider has a continuing duty to promptly notify the EOUST of any circumstances that would materially alter or change a response to any section of the application, including but not limited to, changes in the location of primary or satellite business office(s); the principal contact person; name or fictitious name under which the provider does business; management, including the board of directors; and a merger or consolidation with another entity;

(2) The provider shall request approval by amendment to its application, and prior to occurrence of the following changes:

(i) An increase in the fees, contributions, or payments received from debtor students for the instructional course or a change in the provider's policy for the reduction or waiver of fees;

(ii) Expansion into additional judicial districts or withdrawal from judicial districts where the provider is approved; and

(iii) Method of delivery type of instructional services or course curriculum;

(3) The provider must include with any amendment to its application, a newly executed "certification and signature;"

(4) The provider will notify the EOUST immediately upon the occurrence of any of the below noted events:

(i) Cessation of business of the provider or of any office of the provider;

(ii) Any action by a state agency to suspend the license or cancel other authorization to do business;

(iii) A suspension by an accreditation organization or denial of accreditation; and

(iv) Withdrawal as an approved provider;

(j) An approved provider may not transfer or assign its United States Trustee approval under section 111 as a provider of a personal financial management instructional course.

[71 FR 38082, 38084, July 5, 2006]

§ 58.27 Procedures for denying an application or removing a provider from the approved list, and the administrative review rights granted to denied or removed providers.

(a) As used in this section the term "provider" means a provider of a personal financial management instructional course.

(b) No administrative review will be granted to any applicant that submitted an incomplete application and had its application denied due to incompleteness and failed to subsequently submit a completed application.

(c) The provider shall be notified in writing of any decision denying the provider's application or to remove the provider from the approved list ("notice"). The notice shall state the reason(s) for the decision and shall reference any documents or communications with the provider, which were relied upon in making the denial or removal decision. If such documents or communications were not provided to the United States Trustee or the EOUST by the provider, copies of the documents or communications shall be provided with the notice. The notice shall be sent to the provider by overnight courier, for delivery the next business day.

(d) The notice shall advise the provider that the decision is final unless the provider requests in writing a review ("request for review") by the Director, Executive Office for United States Trustees ("Director"), no later than 20 calendar days from the date of issuance of the denial or removal notice. In order to be timely, a request for review must be received at the Office of the Director no later than 20 calendar days from the date of the removal notice to the provider.

(e) A decision to remove a provider from the approved list shall take effect upon the expiration of a provider's time to seek review from the Director or, if the provider timely seeks such review, upon the issuance of a final written decision by the Director.

(f) Notwithstanding sub-paragraph (e) of this section, a decision to remove a provider from the approved list may include, or may later be supplemented by, an interim directive, which may immediately remove a provider from the approved list. Such an interim directive may be issued if one or more of the following are specifically found:

(1) The provider made a material false statement on the application;

(2) The provider (board of directors, officer, manager, employee, counselor, or agent) has engaged in conduct that is dishonest, deceitful, fraudulent, or criminal in nature;

(3) The provider (board of directors, officer, manager, employee, counselor, or agent) has engaged in other gross misconduct that is unbefitting the provider's position as an approved provider;

(4) Revocation of the provider's license to do business in a particular state, provided the immediate removal shall apply only to the federal judicial districts within the particular state.

(g) The provider's request for review shall fully describe why the provider disagrees with the denial or removal decision, and shall be accompanied by all documents and materials that the provider wants the Director to consider in reviewing the decision. The provider shall send a copy of the request for review, and the accompanying documents and materials, to the Director by overnight courier, for delivery the next business day, and must be received by the Director within 20 calendar days of the denial or removal notice.

(h) The Director may seek additional information from any party, in the manner and to the extent the Director deems appropriate.

(i) The Director shall issue a written decision no later than 45 calendar days from the receipt of the provider's request for review, unless the provider agrees to a longer period of time or the Director extends the period. That decision shall determine whether the denial or removal decision is supported by the record and the action is an appropriate exercise of discretion, and shall adopt, modify, or reject the denial or removal decision. The Director's decision shall constitute final government agency action.

(j) In reaching a determination, the Director may specify a person to act as a reviewing official. The reviewing official shall not be a person who was involved in the denial or removal decision. The reviewing official's duties shall be specified by the Director on a case by case basis, and may include reviewing the record, obtaining additional information from the participants, providing the Director with written recommendations, or such other duties as the Director shall prescribe in a particular case.

(k) A provider that files a request for review shall bear its own costs and expenses, including counsel fees.

[71 FR 38082, 38084, July 5, 2006]

Appendix A to Part 58—Guidelines for Reviewing Applications for Compensation and Reimbursement of Expenses Filed Under 11 U.S.C. 330

(a) General Information. (1) The Bankruptcy Reform Act of 1994 amended the responsibilities of the United States Trustees under 28 U.S.C. 586(a)(3)(A) to provide that, whenever they deem appropriate, United States Trustees will review applications for compensation and reimbursement of expenses under section 330 of the Bankruptcy Code, 11 U.S.C. 101, et seq. ("Code"), in accordance with procedural guidelines ("Guidelines") adopted by the Executive Office for United States Trustees ("Executive Office"). The following Guidelines have been adopted by the Executive Office and are to be uniformly applied by the United States Trustees except when circumstances warrant different treatment.

(2) The United States Trustees shall use these Guidelines in all cases commenced on or after October 22, 1994.

(3) The Guidelines are not intended to supersede local rules of court, but should be read as complementing the procedures set forth in local rules.

(4) Nothing in the Guidelines should be construed:

(i) To limit the United States Trustee's discretion to request additional information necessary for the review of a particular application or type of application or to refer any information provided to the United States Trustee to any investigatory or prosecutorial authority of the United States or a state;

(ii) To limit the United States Trustee's discretion to determine whether to file comments or objections to applications; or

(iii) To create any private right of action on the part of any person enforceable in litigation with the United States Trustee or the United States.

(5) Recognizing that the final authority to award compensation and reimbursement under section 330 of the Code is vested in the Court, the Guidelines focus on the disclosure of information relevant to a proper award under the law. In evaluating fees for professional services, it is relevant to consider various factors including the following: the time spent; the rates charged; whether the services were necessary to the administration of, or beneficial towards the completion of, the case at the time they were rendered; whether services were performed within a reasonable time commensurate with the complexity, importance, and nature of the problem, issue, or task addressed; and whether compensation is reasonable based on the customary compensation charged by comparably skilled practitioners in non-bankruptcy cases. The Guidelines thus reflect standards and procedures articulated in section 330 of the Code and Rule 2016 of

the Federal Rules of Bankruptcy Procedure for awarding compensation to trustees and to professionals employed under section 327 or 1103. Applications that contain the information requested in these Guidelines will facilitate review by the Court, the parties, and the United States Trustee.

(6) Fee applications submitted by trustees are subject to the same standard of review as are applications of other professionals and will be evaluated according to the principles articulated in these Guidelines. Each United States Trustee should establish whether and to what extent trustees can deviate from the format specified in these Guidelines without substantially affecting the ability of the United States Trustee to review and comment on their fee applications in a manner consistent with the requirements of the law.

(b) Contents of Applications for Compensation and Reimbursement of Expenses. All applications should include sufficient detail to demonstrate compliance with the standards set forth in 11 U.S.C. § 330. The fee application should also contain sufficient information about the case and the applicant so that the Court, the creditors, and the United States Trustee can review it without searching for relevant information in other documents. The following will facilitate review of the application.

(1) Information about the Applicant and the Application. The following information should be provided in every fee application:

(i) Date the bankruptcy petition was filed, date of the order approving employment, identity of the party represented, date services commenced, and whether the applicant is seeking compensation under a provision of the Bankruptcy Code other than section 330.

(ii) Terms and conditions of employment and compensation, source of compensation, existence and terms controlling use of a retainer, and any budgetary or other limitations on fees.

(iii) Names and hourly rates of all applicant's professionals and paraprofessionals who billed time, explanation of any changes in hourly rates from those previously charged, and statement of whether the compensation is based on the customary compensation charged by comparably skilled practitioners in cases other than cases under title 11.

(iv) Whether the application is interim or final, and the dates of previous orders on interim compensation or reimbursement of expenses along with the amounts requested and the amounts allowed or disallowed, amounts of all previous payments, and amount of any allowed fees and expenses remaining unpaid.

(v) Whether the person on whose behalf the applicant is employed has been given the opportunity to review the application and whether that person has approved the requested amount.

(vi) When an application is filed less than 120 days after the order for relief or after a prior application to the Court, the date and terms of the order allowing leave to file at shortened intervals.

(vii) Time period of the services or expenses covered by the application.

(2) Case Status. The following information should be provided to the extent that it is known to or can be reasonably ascertained by the applicant:

(i) In a chapter 7 case, a summary of the administration of the case including all moneys received and disbursed in the case, when the case is expected to close, and, if applicant is seeking an interim award, whether it is feasible to make an interim distribution to creditors without prejudicing the rights of any creditor holding a claim of equal or higher priority.

(ii) In a chapter 11 case, whether a plan and disclosure statement have been filed and, if not yet filed, when the plan and disclosure statement are expected to be filed; whether all quarterly fees have been paid to the United States Trustee; and whether all monthly operating reports have been filed.

(iii) In every case, the amount of cash on hand or on deposit, the amount and nature of accrued unpaid administrative expenses, and the amount of unencumbered funds in the estate.

(iv) Any material changes in the status of the case that occur after the filing of the fee application should be raised, orally or in writing, at the hearing on the application or, if a hearing is not required, prior to the expiration of the time period for objection.

(3) Summary Sheet. All applications should contain a summary or cover sheet that provides a synopsis of the following information:

(i) Total compensation and expenses requested and any amount(s) previously requested;

(ii) Total compensation and expenses previously awarded by the court;

(iii) Name and applicable billing rate for each person who billed time during the period, and date of bar admission for each attorney;

(iv) Total hours billed and total amount of billing for each person who billed time during billing period; and

(v) Computation of blended hourly rate for persons who billed time during period, excluding paralegal or other paraprofessional time.

(4) Project Billing Format. (i) To facilitate effective review of the application, all time and service entries should be arranged by project categories. The project categories set forth in Exhibit A should be used to the extent applicable. A separate project category should be used for administrative matters

and, if payment is requested, for fee application preparation.

(ii) The United States Trustee has discretion to determine that the project billing format is not necessary in a particular case or in a particular class of cases. Applicants should be encouraged to consult with the United States Trustee if there is a question as to the need for project billing in any particular case.

(iii) Each project category should contain a narrative summary of the following information:

(A) a description of the project, its necessity and benefit to the estate, and the status of the project including all pending litigation for which compensation and reimbursement are requested;

(B) identification of each person providing services on the project; and

(C) a statement of the number of hours spent and the amount of compensation requested for each professional and paraprofessional on the project.

(iv) Time and service entries are to be reported in chronological order under the appropriate project category.

(v) Time entries should be kept contemporaneously with the services rendered in time periods of tenths of an hour. Services should be noted in detail and not combined or "lumped" together, with each service showing a separate time entry; however, tasks performed in a project which total a de minimis amount of time can be combined or lumped together if they do not exceed .5 hours on a daily aggregate. Time entries for telephone calls, letters, and other communications should give sufficient detail to identify the parties to and the nature of the communication. Time entries for court hearings and conferences should identify the subject of the hearing or conference. If more than one professional from the applicant firm attends a hearing or conference, the applicant should explain the need for multiple attendees.

(5) Reimbursement for Actual, Necessary Expenses. Any expense for which reimbursement is sought must be actual and necessary and supported by documentation as appropriate. Factors relevant to a determination that the expense is proper include the following:

(i) Whether the expense is reasonable and economical. For example, first class and other luxurious travel mode or accommodations will normally be objectionable.

(ii) Whether the requested expenses are customarily charged to non-bankruptcy clients of the applicant.

(iii) Whether applicant has provided a detailed itemization of all expenses including the date incurred, description of expense (e.g., type of travel, type of fare, rate, destination), method of computation, and, where relevant, name of the person incurring the expense and purpose of the expense. Itemized expenses should be identified by their nature (e.g., long distance telephone, copy costs, messengers, computer research, airline travel, etc.) and by the month incurred. Unusual items require more detailed explanations and should be allocated, where practicable, to specific projects.

(iv) Whether applicant has prorated expenses where appropriate between the estate and other cases (e.g., travel expenses applicable to more than one case) and has adequately explained the basis for any such proration.

(v) Whether expenses incurred by the applicant to third parties are limited to the actual amounts billed to, or paid by, the applicant on behalf of the estate.

(vi) Whether applicant can demonstrate that the amount requested for expenses incurred in-house reflect the actual cost of such expenses to the applicant. The United States Trustee may establish an objection ceiling for any in-house expenses that are routinely incurred and for which the actual cost cannot easily be determined by most professionals (e.g., photocopies, facsimile charges, and mileage).

(vii) Whether the expenses appear to be in the nature nonreimbursable overhead. Overhead consists of all continuous administrative or general costs incident to the operation of the applicant's office and not particularly attributable to an individual client or case. Overhead includes, but is not limited to, word processing, proofreading, secretarial and other clerical services, rent, utilities, office equipment and furnishings, insurance, taxes, local telephones and monthly car phone charges, lighting, heating and cooling, and library and publication charges.

(viii) Whether applicant has adhered to allowable rates for expenses as fixed by local rule or order of the Court.

Exhibit A—Project Categories

Here is a list of suggested project categories for use in most bankruptcy cases. Only one category should be used for a given activity. Professionals should make their best effort to be consistent in their use of categories, whether within a particular firm or by different firms working on the same case. It would be appropriate for all professionals to discuss the categories in advance and agree generally on how activities will be categorized. This list is not exclusive. The application may contain additional categories as the case requires. They are generally more applicable to attorneys in chapter 7 and chapter 11, but may be used by all professionals as appropriate.

Asset Analysis and Recovery: Identification and review of potential assets including causes of action and non-litigation recoveries.

Asset Disposition: Sales, leases (§ 365 matters), abandonment and related transaction work.

Business Operations: Issues related to debtor-in-possession operating in chapter 11 such as employee, vendor, tenant issues and other similar problems.

Case Administration: Coordination and compliance activities, including preparation of statement of financial affairs; schedules; list of contracts; United States Trustee interim statements and operating reports; contacts with the United States Trustee; general creditor inquiries.

Claims Administration and Objections: Specific claim inquiries; bar date motions; analyses, objections and allowances of claims.

Employee Benefits/Pensions: Review issues such as severance, retention, 401K coverage and continuance of pension plan.

Fee/Employment Applicants: Preparation of employment and fee applications for self or others; motions to establish interim procedures.

Fee/Employment Objections: Review of and objections to the employment and fee applications of others.

Financing: Matters under §§ 361, 363 and 364 including cash collateral and secured claims; loan document analysis.

Litigation: There should be a separate category established for each matter (e.g., XYZ Litigation).

Meetings of Creditors: Preparing for and attending the conference of creditors, the § 341(a) meeting and other creditors' committee meetings.

Plan and Disclosure Statement: Formulation, presentation and confirmation; compliance with the plan confirmation order, related orders and rules; disbursement and case closing activities, except those related to the allowance and objections to allowance of claims.

Relief From Stay Proceedings: Matters relating to termination or continuation of automatic stay under § 362.

The following categories are generally more applicable to accountants and financial advisors, but may be used by all professionals as appropriate.

Accounting/Auditing: Activities related to maintaining and auditing books of account, preparation of financial statements and account analysis.

Business Analysis: Preparation and review of company business plan; development and review of strategies; preparation and review of cash flow forecasts and feasibility studies.

Corporate Finance: Review financial aspects of potential mergers, acquisitions and disposition of company or subsidiaries.

Data Analysis: Management information systems review, installation and analysis, construction, maintenance and reporting of significant case financial data, lease rejection, claims, etc.

Litigation Consulting: Providing consulting and expert witness services relating to various bankruptcy matters such as insolvency, feasibility, avoiding actions, forensic accounting, etc.

Reconstruction Accounting: Reconstructing books and records from past transactions and bringing accounting current.

Tax Issues: Analysis of tax issues and preparation of state and federal tax returns.

Valuation: Appraise or review appraisals of assets.

[61 FR 24890, May 17, 1996]

*

INDEX TO BANKRUPTCY CODE, RULES AND FORMS

References are to U.S. Code sections unless otherwise indicated.

CITATIONS

BKR	**Bankruptcy Rule**
BKR Form	**Bankruptcy Form**
FRCVP	**Federal Rules of Civil Procedure**
FRE	**Federal Rules of Evidence**
FRAP	**Federal Rules of Appellate Procedure**

†